INTERNATIONAL INTELLECTUAL PROPERTY LAW AND POLICY

By

Graeme B. Dinwoodie

Professor of Law
Chicago-Kent College of Law

William O. Hennessey

Professor of Law
Franklin Pierce Law Center

Shira Perlmutter

Vice President and Associate General Counsel,
Intellectual Property Policy, AOL Time Warner, Inc.

Former Associate Register for Policy and International Affairs,
U.S. Copyright Office

Former Consultant on Copyright and Electronic Commerce,
World Intellectual Property Organization

CASEBOOK SERIES

LexisNexis™

Library of Congress Cataloging-in-Publication Data

Dinwoodie, Graeme B.
International intellectual property law and policy/by Graeme B. Dinwoodie, William O.
Hennessey, Shira Perlmutter

    p. cm.
Includes index.
ISBN 0-8205-4525-2 (hbk.)
    1. Intellectual Property (International Law) I. Hennessey, William O. II. Perlmutter,
Shira. III. Title.
K1401 .D56 2001
341.7'58—dc21

2001038041
CIP

Editorial Offices
744 Broad Street, Newark, NJ 07102 (973) 820-2000
201 Mission St., San Francisco, CA 94105-1831 (415) 908-3200
701 East Water Street, Charlottesville, VA 22902-7587 (804) 972-7600
www.lexis.com

(Pub.3068)

For our parents,

David and Isa

Graeme

Bill and Molly

Bill

Dan and Felice

Shira

Preface

We have each been teaching courses in international intellectual property law for several years. This book builds upon the materials that we have used in those courses, albeit with considerable expansion and refinement. The evolution of our materials reflects not only the experience of teaching but also the transformation of the subject. From a "niche" course taught at only a few law schools in the early to mid-1990s, international intellectual property law is fast becoming a staple of the intellectual property curriculum.

Perhaps this should not be surprising. The social, economic and technological changes of the late twentieth century have highlighted the importance of international intellectual property law and policy. One no longer can think or write about, or understand, intellectual property law without considering its international dimension; international developments often drive the content and direction of domestic intellectual property law. Nor, increasingly, can the development of international law and international relations be studied without attention to intellectual property law and policy.

The last couple of years, in particular, have witnessed an explosion of interest in the subject. That interest is the product of several forces, including the incorporation of intellectual property commitments within the primary international trade regime, the development of digital communication technologies which inevitably transcend national borders, the increasing exploitation of products in global markets, and greater public awareness of the role of intellectual property in shaping the conditions in which we live.

Heightened interest in the subject mirrors the frenetic pace of international lawmaking activity in many different fora. Our casebook reflects the causes and consequences of this activity. The very creation of the book embodies the internationalized flavor of modern life. The most substantial work on the project has been undertaken during the last three years, during which time the authors were variously based in Cincinnati, Philadelphia, Chicago, Beijing, Concord, Washington, Geneva and New York. The casebook also reflects the variety of ways in which one can now conceive of a course in international intellectual property law: as a traditional public international law course, as a specialty focus in modern international economic regulation, or as an important case study in international civil litigation.

A word about our approach to selection and editing of materials. We each teach somewhat different courses in international intellectual property law and policy. The book is consciously designed to permit variation (or concentration) tailored to the interests of the particular instructor and students. Thus, we generally group together materials pertaining separately to each of copyright, patent and trademark. But it is important to recognize and discuss the themes that transcend particular intellectual property regimes. Similarly, we largely discuss mechanisms for the acquisition and enforcement of intellectual property rights by private rightholders separately from the development of principles of public international intellectual property law among states. But it is our common preference to expose students to both the public and private aspects of the discipline. An understanding of the interaction between state-to-state relations and private enforcement of rights is crucial to appreciate fully the dynamic underlying the development of this body of law. Our approach to the materials has thus been infused by constant revisiting of integrated and core questions of international intellectual property policy that pervade the subject.

The casebook includes many materials that a student of U.S. intellectual property law might not have encountered. Reading foreign cases and reports of international dispute settlement tribunals is not the equivalent of reading U.S. case reports; and treaty provisions differ in style and structure from statutory text. While we have edited foreign and international materials to improve their use as teaching instruments, we believe that some part of the learning experience involves exposure to these primary materials. We have thus endeavored to retain the style of the original whenever possible. We have also included more articles than typically found in a casebook, especially in discussing the negotiation of treaty provisions. Again, we made a conscious decision that an understanding of this subject requires an appreciation of the more varied sources of thought that distinguish this discipline.

The book, in sum, reflects our collective vision of the system of international intellectual property law. Principal responsibility for the subject matter was, however, divided as follows: Graeme authored the materials on trademark and unfair competition law, geographical indications, and designs; Bill authored the materials on patent and trade secrets; and Shira authored the materials on copyright and related rights. Graeme also was primarily responsible for the materials on private enforcement of rights and state-to-state dispute resolution. Although we did not attempt to compromise our individual styles, we have sought to present a unified book that is both versatile and integrated.

The materials in the book are drawn from a wide variety of sources, and we are grateful to every one of the authors and publishers who graciously permitted our reproduction of their work. Several sources are, however, essential to any study of this subject, and we acknowledge them here both to express our gratitude and as a pointer to students pursuing research. The World Intellectual Property Organization makes available a wealth of information; we visit the WIPO web site (www.wipo.int) on a daily basis. The Max Planck Institute for Foreign and International Patent, Copyright and Competition Law (based in Munich, Germany) publishes many important works, most notably (for our purposes) the International Review of Industrial Property and Copyright Law (which contains English translations of many foreign materials, particularly case law). The annual Fordham Conference on International Intellectual Property Law and Policy, organized by Hugh Hansen, is a place of pilgrimage for anyone interested in this subject, and the published conference proceedings are a rich source of topical information. More recently, the Journal of World Intellectual Property, and the European Trade Mark Reports and the European Copyright and Design Reports, the latter two of which are edited by Jeremy Phillips, have emerged as indispensable reading. The European Intellectual Property Review offers perspectives on world intellectual property law that belie the geographic limitations of its title. To make the volume of materials manageable, we have of course edited the work of others. This is indicated by ellipses. Deletions of citations are indicated by the bracketed word [cit.] Most footnotes have been omitted without indication; those that remain retain their original numbering.

This book would not have been possible without the support and assistance of many people. Foremost among these is Richard Wilder, with whom we conceived the book before he assumed responsibilities at WIPO that precluded his further involvement in achieving our common conception. Nonetheless, his intellectual fingerprints are manifest through the final product and we are indebted to Richard for his continuing generous assistance. We also benefitted greatly from comments received from the fifteen intellectual property professors who used the materials at different stages between conception and final product, as well as those colleagues and policymakers who offered comments or suggestions on draft sections. In particular, we thank Winifried Arnold, Homer Blair, Chris Blank, Francois Curçhod, Christine Farley, Tom Field, Christine Galbraith, Jane Ginsburg, Hans Goldrian, Hugh Hansen, Larry Helfer, Craig Jepson, Karl Jorda, Lydia Loren, Dean Marks, Maria Martin-Prat, Mike Meller, Victor Nabhan, Joseph Straus, Michael Van Alstine and David Welkowitz. Brian Havel not only offered comments based upon his teaching of the materials, but also reviewed the entire manuscript in almost final form. We are immensely grateful.

Students in our classes at several schools offered helpful comments, and various deans supported our project in different but always important ways, including Jim Duggan, Dick Hesse, John Hutson, Chuck Mooney, Eric Neisser, Hank Perritt, Ralph Rohner, Joe Tomain and Robert Viles. We were fortunate to have splendid research assistance from Kevin Bowman, Marc Browning, Michelle Escola, Megan Gervase, J. Mike Hurst, David Lafkas, Eric Moran, Brad McPeek, Jason Otto, Abhijat Parikh, Susan Street, and Sheng Wu.

We are very grateful for the secretarial and publishing support provided by Silvana Burgese, Teresa Burgin, Betty Burks, Ellen Bosman, Julie Colleluori, Olga Lizunova and Connie Miller. Finally, thanks to our publishers, particularly Heather Dean, Adriana Sciortino, and Lee Freudberg, for validating and encouraging our conception of how to present materials in international intellectual property law and policy. We hope and trust that the final product justifies their faith.

During the course of writing this book, we have been associated with a variety of institutions. Our colleagues in each institution have contributed immeasurably to the development of our views on international intellectual property law and policy. The views expressed in this book are, however, solely those of the authors and do not necessarily reflect the views of any of the institutions, whether academic, governmental, intergovernmental, or business, with which we have been, or currently are, affiliated.

GRAEME B. DINWOODIE
WILLIAM O. HENNESSEY
SHIRA PERLMUTTER

July 1, 2001

SUMMARY OF CONTENTS

Page

PART I. OVERVIEW AND INTRODUCTION

Chapter 1. Overview and Introduction

PART II. PRINCIPLES OF INTERNATIONAL PROTECTION

Chapter 2. International Law and Institutions

Chapter 3. Industrial Property Law

Chapter 4. Copyright and Related Rights

Page

Page

PART IV. ISSUES IN INTERNATIONAL INTELLECTUAL PROPERTY LAW AND POLICY LOOKING FORWARD

Chapter 8. Issues in International Intellectual Property Law and Policy Looking Forward

TABLE OF CONTENTS

Page

Chapter 3. Industrial Property Law

Page

Page

Page

Page

Page

Page

Page

PART III: ACQUISITION AND ENFORCEMENT OF RIGHTS INTERNATIONALLY

Chapter 6. Mechanisms for the Acquisition of Industrial Property Rights

Page

Page

Page

Chapter 7. International Enforcement of Intellectual Property Rights by Rights Holders

Page

Page

Page

PART IV. ISSUES IN INTERNATIONAL INTELLECTUAL PROPERTY LAW AND POLICY LOOKING FORWARD

Chapter 8. Issues in International Intellectual Property Law and Policy Looking Forward

PART I

OVERVIEW AND INTRODUCTION

Chapter 1

OVERVIEW AND INTRODUCTION

§ 1.01   Overview

Increasingly, intellectual property is becoming the subject of significant public international law, that is, part of the web of rights and obligations that exist among sovereign countries. We devote Part II of the book (consisting of Chapters 2-5) to this topic. After introducing (in Chapter 2) some of the basic principles and institutions of public international law upon which public international intellectual property law is founded, we address the development and substantive content of public international intellectual property law in Chapters 3-4. Chapter 3 focuses on industrial property law (trademarks, patents, trade secrets, designs, and geographical indications), and Chapter 4 addresses literary and artistic property (copyright and neighboring rights). This division of the body of intellectual property law reflects an historical division that is under increasing pressure from new kinds of rights. But we largely adhere to it throughout the book. The subject matter of several important treaties corresponds to the distinction; the registration of patents and (some) trademarks raises common issues not found in copyright, such as securing registrations on a multinational basis; and, it is consistent with our efforts to structure the materials in a modular fashion and thus permit their use by instructors teaching any number of subdivisions of the broad topic of international intellectual property law. In Chapter 5, we conclude our analysis of public international intellectual property law proper by considering the means and institutions through which states resolve disputes regarding compliance with their international obligations.

Intellectual property rights are, however, territorial in nature. Classically, and still typically, this means that those rights are national in scope. There is, as yet, no such thing as a global patent, copyright or trademark. Public international intellectual property laws necessarily build and are dependent upon *national* laws and *private* rights. Countries have a responsibility to implement their international obligations in national intellectual property laws. Thus, whether countries are complying with their international obligations in the field of intellectual property law is largely determined by analysis of their national laws. Countries are motivated to engage in public international lawmaking by the demands of national concerns and by the limitations of national solutions to multinational problems. And although countries construct and administer systems of intellectual property (through administrative agencies and court systems), intellectual property laws are to a great extent used and enforced by private actors. The acquisition, transfer and exploitation of rights is also largely a matter of private arrangement.

This is not to say that international intellectual property law is devoid of public interests. To the contrary, public concerns do (and should) permeate the development of this field. Intellectual property law implements and furthers significant social, cultural and economic values; and those values are placed front and center in the international context. But it does mean that an understanding of the international intellectual property system requires an appreciation of the means of private enforcement of rights (largely at a national level). Thus, Part III of the book addresses matters of private international intellectual property law. Chapter 6 focuses on the mechanisms established by international agreement to facilitate multinational acquisition of industrial property rights. And Chapter 7 looks at private enforcement of rights in an international setting. We conclude in Part IV by considering the future directions of international intellectual property law.

Although the cases included in this book are primarily drawn from the United States, we have also included materials from elsewhere. U.S. intellectual property laws often differ from those found in other countries, although the basic principles of most national laws are similar (and becoming more so with every passing year). We hew to the view that comparative analysis—an examination of how others deal with similar problems—is instructive in and of itself. Such analysis offers an additional perspective from which to evaluate the content of domestic law. But the reasons are even more practical in the study of international intellectual property law. First, the national laws of many countries (or regional groupings of countries, such as the European Union) will be relevant to any transaction involving a foreign or multinational component. And transactions that involve foreign or multinational aspects—whether the persons involved or the conduct at issue—are increasing daily. The subject matter of intellectual property, as well as its role in the development of electronic commerce, places it at the vortex of globalization. Second, the national laws of individual countries throughout the world comprise the raw material for any consideration of public international intellectual property laws. The differences among, and limits and effects of, national laws dictate the priorities of international intellectual property institutions and laws.

Throughout, we have provided explanations of relevant national laws in so far as they affect the developments in international intellectual property law and policy that we discuss. In this book, however, we have not included an exhaustive comparative survey of national laws. For those seeking to pursue a more detailed comparative study, we have developed materials that will soon separately be published as part of three additional books: International and Comparative Copyright Law, International and Comparative Trademark and Unfair Competition Law, and International and Comparative Patent Law. These books contain the relevant international materials from this book as well as more extensive comparative national materials.

§ 1.02 Introductory Themes

This introductory chapter contains materials that raise some of the basic themes that we will encounter throughout our study of international intellectual property law. As you read these materials, consider how recent social, economic and political changes have altered the importance of intellectual property, the nature of intellectual property lawmaking, the character of scholarly and public policy debates, and the role and practice of lawyers.

GEORGE KOUMANTOS, REFLECTIONS ON THE CONCEPT OF INTELLECTUAL PROPERTY*

Intellectual Property and Information Law: Essays in Honor of Herman Cohen Jehoram 39-45 (1998)

Terminology

Historical research gives us an indication of when the term "intellectual property" first appeared in the sense in which it is used today. Its first official use goes back to the 1950s, when the two International Bureaux set up under the Paris Convention for the Protection of Industrial Property (1883) and the Berne Convention for the Protection of Literary and Artistic Works (1886) to administer the two Conventions—the two bureaux were amalgamated in 1893—were named "Bureaux Internationaux Réunis pour la Propriété Intellectuelle" (BIRPI). These were the forerunners of the "Organisation Mondiale de la Propriété Intellectuelle" [in English, the World Intellectual Property Organization, or "WIPO"] founded in 1967 in Stockholm.

This first official use of the term determines its purport, which coincides with that of the two jointly administered Conventions . . . To begin with, the concept of intellectual property covered literary and artistic property (subsequently more commonly known as "droit d'auteur" ("author's rights") or "copyright" in common law countries—dealt with by the Berne Convention), patents (. . . dealt with by the Paris Convention) and trademarks (. . . also dealt with by the Paris Convention). Another matter dealt with by the [Paris] Convention, the law of unfair competition, could also be regarded as an aspect of intellectual property, but there are some doubts on this point . . . Intellectual property, like most concepts, has with time experienced several shifts in its meaning. . . .

. . . .

Meaning of the Concept

As already indicated, the concept of intellectual property was originally designed to cover ownership of literary and artistic works, inventions (patents) and trademarks. What these three objects of intellectual property have in common is their intangibility. . . . The object of the rights constituting intellectual property is not the tangible support incorporating a literary or artistic work, invention or trademark, but rather the form of the work, the invention, the relationship between a symbol and a business, as such.

This shared characteristic allows for the subsequent enlargement of the concept of intellectual property. This enlargement extends the concept to (a) rights which already existed but were not systematically categorized and (b) rights newly recognized as a result of technological development—where the object of a right transcends tangible support, that right is (or should be) included in the concept of intellectual property.

Thus the concept now covers the following, in addition to patents, trademarks and literary and artistic works:

a. designs and models, which are regulated in part both by the two Conventions cited—Paris and Berne—and the domestic laws of many countries;

b. commercial names, mentioned in the Paris Convention as an object of industrial property and recognized as such . . . by the domestic laws of several countries . . .

c. neighbouring rights, regulated internationally by the Rome Convention of 1961 on the protection of performing artists, producers of gramophone records and broadcasting organizations, and nationally by special provisions, often included in the laws on copyright, and often extending the protection to other categories;

d. plant production rights, which are the subject of an international Convention signed in Paris (in 1961 "for the protection of plant production rights") and revised at Geneva (1978 and 1991), and the domestic laws of the 32 countries that ratified the Convention;

e. the topographies of semiconductor products, which are protected by a Treaty signed at Washington (1989, "on intellectual property regarding integrated circuits," not in force) and European Union Directive 87/54 "on the legal protection of topographies of semiconductor products", which has been incorporated in the domestic law of the EU countries;

f. databases, when protected by a sui generis right—but this new area of intellectual property requires more detailed explanation.

The system adopted by the European Union for databases, [cit], provides two types of protection for this modern form of collection, which is both a work of the mind and a product of investment: copyright protection . . . and protection by a sui generis right (provided the database involves a major investment). This right . . . is in the nature of a neighbouring right and should therefore fall under the heading of intellectual property. But even leaving aside its resemblance to neighbouring rights, the sui generis right over databases should be considered as falling under the heading of intellectual property because of the intangible nature of its object.

. . . .

It remains to be seen whether the list should end here or whether it should be extended to include other objects. The Paris Convention already includes rules on unfair competition in the concept of industrial property. The TRIPS Agreement includes in its list of objects of intellectual property (Article 1 paragraph 2) geographical indications (Articles 22-24) and trade secrets (industrial and commercial, Article 39), in addition to those already mentioned . . . What can we say about this position adopted by two major international agreements?

It should be noted, first of all, that the two additional objects included in the TRIPS Agreement lists merely constitute specific cases of protection against unfair competition. This is stated explicitly in the case of secrets ("to provide effective protection against unfair competition", Article 39 paragraph 1), but the same holds true of [laws permitting the use of] geographical indications [of origin by only producers from the geographical area in question]: it would not be possible to conceive of a subjective right of ownership to a connection between a product and a territorial area, since a right of this kind would belong to all the producers acting in the territorial area and could not be transferred, inherited etc.

The question, then, is whether the rules on unfair competition give rise to objects of intellectual property. From the historical point of view, it should be easy to answer in the affirmative: given that unfair competition is one of the matters regulated by the Paris Convention and the administration of this Convention was one of the factors that led to the first official use of the term "intellectual property" . . . it would seem that this term obviously includes unfair competition. But things are more complicated . . .

Intellectual property, like any other kind of property, is a subjective right relating to an object—in the case of intellectual property a work, invention, trademark etc. At first sight the rules on unfair competition do not give rise to a subjective right and consequently do not relate to an object; they merely forbid certain acts, and interested parties can cite them when applying for the prohibition to be enforced. At the heart of the rules on unfair competition is not an object to be protected but an act to be prevented. This cannot therefore be referred to as property nor, in consequence, as intellectual property.

There is an objection that could be made to this conclusion, however. We have seen that the rules on unfair competition, by forbidding certain acts, aim to protect a specific object, a business as a structured entity consisting of goods, legal relationships and market status (goodwill); the rules on unfair competition would thus give rise to a subjective right and would protect an object. If we accept this principle, the right over the business, created indirectly by the rules on unfair competition, should partake of the nature of intellectual property, since its object, the actual structure of the business, is of the intangible nature required.

. . . .

Different Rules

[T]here are . . . differences in the legal regulation of each of the rights that constitute intellectual property. Thus the rules concerning the object and the extent of the right, as well as the extent of the protection, differ.

First, the object: copyright protects the form or other original aspects of personal intellectual creation in science or art; trademark law protects the connection between a word (or several words) or a picture and the business from which a product or service emanates; and patent law protects invention, i.e., a new solution to a technical problem which can be applied industrially. Here we have three different objects, the first of which is a creation of the mind, the second of commerce and the third of industry or craft.

Then we have the manner of acquisition: copyright is acquired by the mere fact of intellectual creation, without any formalities, in every country in the world (except the United States, to some extent); a trademark on the other hand, is acquired by recording it in the register of trademarks once it has been checked as complying with the conditions—although the mere fact of using it can give rise to certain restricted rights; and the right to use an invention is acquired by the issue of a patent once the formal conditions and basic conditions have been checked (this latter check is cursory in some countries).

Lastly, we have the extent of the protection: first the duration, which, in the case of copyright, varies depending on the domestic laws, with a minimum of fifty years laid down by the Berne Convention, which has now become seventy years in the European Union; in the case of trademarks it lasts ten years and can be renewed indefinitely; patents last twenty years and are non-renewable. Then [sanctions and remedies for infringement] differ as between the three types of right . . .

Monopolies?

The list of differences in the legal regime governing the various rights which constitute intellectual property is a long one. To this we need to add the major differences based on the economic, social and cultural functions of each of them. It is sometimes argued that the rights that constitute intellectual property create monopoly situations . . .

The idea that monopolies are the consequence of exclusive rights that constitute intellectual property is based on the hypothesis that all the objects of these rights are unique. But we need to remember that, in very many cases, the objects of intellectual property are interchangeable: if the right holder of the right to an object lays down exorbitant terms for a licence the user may substitute a different object—such competition breaks the monopoly.

But that is not all: it would be wrong to equate the different categories of rights covered by the concept of intellectual property with regard to the economic, social or cultural weight any monopoly situations created by them could have. After all, there is a big difference between preventing the use of a medicine by virtue of a monopoly and preventing the use of a song or novel. This is why the introduction of non-voluntary licences is often advocated in some areas. Given that the needs differ in intensity, non-voluntary licences (or any other restriction of intellectual property) should be a last resort, and their acceptability and terms and conditions should be examined on a case-by-case basis. To give the same treatment to the different objects of intellectual property goes against a sense of justice.

Is the Concept Justified?

[There are, therefore,] a large number of differences between the various rights covered by the concept of intellectual property—differences relating to the legal basis (national and international) for their protection, the solutions to certain problems which are common to all of them, their legal regulation, and their economic, social and cultural functions. We have even seen that including these rights in a single concept could result in their being given the same or similar treatment (notably in relation to non-voluntary licences and restrictions), failing to appreciate the need to differentiate. Are there enough common factors to justify the mere existence of the concept of intellectual property?

The need for a common administration for the various international Conventions on the specific rights covered by intellectual property cannot be regarded as an adequate raison d'être—albeit this may lie at the root of the concept. What would seem to justify its existence is the fact, already mentioned, that all the rights it covers have an essential common feature: the intangible nature of their respective objects and the consequences of this.

But this is not all: the objects of the rights covered by the concept of intellectual property are manifestations of human creativity. The purpose of regulating these rights is to protect this creativity and the creations emanating from it: literary, artistic and scientific works in the case of copyright, technical innovations in the case of patents, and business enterprise in the case of trademarks. It is this idea of protecting creativity that is the most important common factor in all these rights and the main justification for the concept of intellectual property.

————

Professor Koumantos references several landmark intellectual property treaties, which we will examine in detail at different parts of the book. The Paris Convention for the Protection of Industrial Property is a multinational agreement to which 160 countries are now party. The Berne Convention for the Protection of Literary and Artistic Works was concluded three years after the Paris Convention and now has 144 signatory parties. These two agreements were the principal international intellectual property agreements for over 100 years, and were revised at successive diplomatic conferences throughout the twentieth century (the most recent being the revision of the Berne Convention in Paris in 1971). The last decade of the twentieth century saw a flurry of activity on other fronts. Professor Koumantos mentions two intellectual property laws of the European Union (EU). The EU has become a powerful influence on the direction and content of international intellectual property laws, in part through its promulgation of "regional" intellectual property laws applicable throughout the territories of its increasingly numerous member states (now fifteen). And, in 1994, when the Uruguay Round of the General Agreement on Tariffs and Trade (GATT) was successfully completed, this hugely significant trade agreement included within it the Agreement on Trade Related Aspects of Intellectual Property (TRIPS). The content and revision of these and other leading agreements, as well as the role of the World Intellectual Property Organization (which administers the Paris and Berne Conventions), the EU, and the World Trade Organization (under whose auspices the TRIPS Agreement is monitored and enforced), are dealt with in detail in Part II *infra*.

ANDREW SULLIVAN, DOT-COMMUNIST MANIFESTO[*]
New York Times Magazine, June 11, 2000 at 30

A sharp, unexpected twang of conscience hit me the other day. It occurred to me as I was merrily downloading the umpteenth Pet Shop Boys B side from another Napster user's hard drive. Was this theft? Nobody, I rationalized, was going to be without the Extended Rollo Mix of "New York City Boy" because of my actions. All Napster is, after all, is a huge database of MP3 files, a musical commune dreamed up by a college-freshman geek. And sharing a database isn't theft. If you agree to join the Napster "community," you agree to share every MP3 you have with any other Napsterite who is online at the same time you are. . . . .

So whom was I hurting by copying one lousy song? Sure, I'd avoided paying a record company a royalty—but it was rich enough already. Likewise the Pet Shop Boys. And it wasn't as if I'd smuggled a disc out of Tower Records in a knapsack. It wasn't even in any meaningful sense "mine," since other Napster users could now download it from me without my even noticing. Neither had it been in any meaningful sense "theirs"—once they agreed to pool their own MP3 collection with those of other Napsterites.

What exactly was going on here? The only workable definition is communism. . . . By turning physical property into endlessly duplicable e-property, the ancient human problem of "mine-thine" has been essentially solved. . . .

J. THOMAS McCARTHY, INTELLECTUAL PROPERTY—AMERICA'S OVERLOOKED EXPORT[**]
20 U. DAYTON L. REV. 809, 809-819 (1995)

I. INTRODUCTION: THE CHANGING FACE OF AMERICAN INDUSTRY

As we rush through each busy day, we often have to take no more than a hurried glance at the newspaper or at the news on television to see what's going on in the world. Sometimes we see an item that seems trivial on its face, but we subliminally recognize: "That's an amazing development! Things are changing faster than I thought."

A few years ago I saw one of those seemingly trivial facts noted in the business page and realized: "This is an important signal that the America I grew up with had irrevocably changed." What I saw in the newspaper was that the people who run the Dow Jones Index—a list of thirty industrial stocks representing a cross section of American commerce—dropped U.S. Steel from the list and replaced it with the Walt Disney Company. While the announcement may sound inconsequential, the fact that a steel giant was replaced by an entertainment empire is a symbol which keynotes the subject of this Essay.

Chicago Tribune columnist Bob Greene headlined his column on the subject: "A Mouse Replaces Men of Steel." Greene noted that the Dow Jones Index has always been the paramount financial symbol of U.S. business and industry. The Dow Jones industrial average was what American business was all about. It symbolized the source of America's strength and prosperity—or at least a dream of prosperity. A dream that has driven millions of people around the world to get to America at all costs—no matter what the odds—from countries as diverse as China, Russia, and Cuba.

Growing up in the 1940s and 1950s, I lived in what was then America's biggest factory town—Detroit, Michigan. I was taught that America was a great place to live and a robust and strong nation because it made millions of things that people all around the world wanted. Documentaries boosting American industry always seemed to include a shot of the Ford River Rouge plant (complete with smokestacks belching smoke) or a shot of white hot steel being rolled in a Pittsburgh foundry. Needless to say, U.S. Steel was a major part of that view of industrial America.

U.S. Steel stood shoulder to shoulder on the Dow Jones Index with manufacturing companies like Caterpillar, Chevron Oil, General Electric, Goodyear, and Union Carbide. What is a company whose major asset is Mickey Mouse doing with these brawny types?

The face of American business is changing, and changing fast. What America makes and what the rest of the world wants to buy is also changing. In ten years, Disney has grown "from an ailing $2 billion Hollywood also-ran into a $22 billion empire." . . .

Disney sells entertainment through movies, videos, television programs, theme parks, books and records. But what exactly is the basis of the Disney empire? We knew that the heart of U.S. Steel was property—those huge mills spewing sparks, belching smoke and turning out rolled steel twenty-four hours a day. But what is the property that is at the heart of a company like Disney? It is a new kind of property. We call it intellectual property. Intellectual, only because it is a property right in the products of the intellect—a product of the human mind, as opposed to real estate or tangible objects.

I know that I am oversimplifying to make my point. Of course, U.S. Steel had intellectual property in know how and engineering innovations. Disney, of course, owns a substantial amount of highly valuable real estate. But I want to focus on the heart of the fundamental differences between these two companies in order to illustrate how this simple substitution of one company for the other on the Dow Jones Index symbolizes the new era we are entering. Some call it the information age.

II. WHAT IS INTELLECTUAL PROPERTY?

Basically, the subject of all kinds of intellectual property is information. The job of intellectual property law is to create property rights in newly created information. We are continually told that we are entering a post-industrial information age. An age in which by far the most valuable thing to own and control is information—technological information, business information, political information and information about people. . . .

One of the wealthiest and most influential people in America today is Bill Gates, founder of Microsoft. Gates does not get the media coverage of a politician, but I think he is just as influential. And what product does Microsoft make? Nothing tangible, really. . . .   .

    . . . .

III. INTELLECTUAL PROPERTY AND EXPORTS

Intellectual property has become one of the few bright spots in the otherwise dreary U.S. balance-of-trade picture. The rest of the world does not want to buy American cars or steel in the quantities purchased in years past. The world does want, however, to buy our computer programs, our movie and television entertainment and our high-tech information.

The United States enjoys a remarkable seventy-five percent of the international market for prepackaged computer software and a whopping sixty percent of the world market for software-related services. With the exception of agriculture, intellectual property producers make a larger positive contribution to the U.S. trade balance than any other U.S. industry. Although the statistics are largely guesses, U.S. exports of intellectual property have purportedly doubled in recent years and have been estimated to constitute as much as twenty-five percent of U.S. exports. Foreign sales in the copyright industry—publishing, computer programs, film making and the like—are larger than those of paper, plastics, rubber, lumber, pharmaceuticals, textiles and telephone equipment combined.

IV. PRESSURE ON OTHER NATIONS

A great deal of media coverage recently has been devoted to international economic agreements like the North American Free Trade Agreement (NAFTA) and the General Agreement on Tariffs and Trade (GATT). Each have significant intellectual property components built into them. The U.S. government is also conducting bilateral negotiations with several nations, including Japan and the People's Republic of China, seeking changes in their intellectual property laws. Why all this effort by our government, especially in the GATT negotiations, to include intellectual property as a key element of international trade agreements and treaty organizations?

Periodically, on the business page, we read that the U.S. Trade Representative threatens trade sanctions against a foreign nation under so-called "Special 301" or "Super 301" powers. In 1988, Congress created "Special 301," a power given to the U.S. Trade Representative to investigate and identify foreign nations that unjustifiably restrict U.S. commerce. For example, Special 301 gives the U.S. Trade Representative the power to ensure that foreign nations are adequately protecting U.S. intellectual property.

The Trade Representative can start a long, involved process that could eventually result in the imposition of trade sanctions by the President. These sanctions might include placing confiscatory duties on certain goods imported into the United States from the offending nation. Such sanctions are almost like a nuclear deterrent in the world trade war. To my knowledge, the United States has never actually imposed sanctions for failure to give adequate protection for intellectual property, although it has threatened to do so against the People's Republic of China on more than one occasion.

. . . .

Our government seeks to put pressure on other governments, especially those in Asia, to raise the level of their intellectual property protection and enforcement. But why should Americans care whether the People's Republic of China winks at piracy of computer programs and compact discs?

We care because if no intellectual property protection exists regarding technical and entertainment information, then we have little to sell to the rest of the world. In the old days of selling cars, steel, and aluminum to the rest of the world, the kind of patent, trademark and copyright laws implemented by other nations did not make a lot of difference. Their intellectual property laws were their business. Now it is our business.

American businesses suffer the most when an Asian government tolerates the widespread pirating of computer programs and CDs and the Asian market becomes flooded with pirated products. This occurs because America supplies the bulk of the world's software and music, as well as video tapes. While the Asian nations produce most of the hardware used in the entertainment and computer industries, such as televisions, CD players, and PC clones, America supplies the content for that hardware—the shows, songs, and software that makes the hardware valuable. If foreign nations do not recognize or enforce intellectual property laws, then America has nothing to sell. . .

If an American company sells only a few copies of a computer program or video because social customs permit widespread reproduction, then much less incentive exists to produce the product in the first place. Fewer copies will be produced and fewer Americans will be hired to produce those copies. In the information age, ineffective intellectual property protection and enforcement results in less protectable material produced. This phenomenon bodes poorly for the future of the United States, because we cannot compete in a world market for producing steel or clothes or VCRs when manufacturers in developing nations can pay what we would regard as a less than living wage. That leads to cries for protectionist legislation like trade barriers and tariffs.

. . . .

VI. DEMANDS OF FOREIGN TRADE DRIVE CHANGES IN UNITED STATES LAW

A new phenomenon in U.S. intellectual property law is that changes in our domestic law are being driven by the needs of world trade. For the first 200 years of our nation's history, we very loosely based our intellectual property laws on those of Great Britain. As the years went by, however, our laws became more and more idiosyncratic. Our intellectual property laws developed so differently from those of the rest of the world that they became a real impediment to free trade.

For example, we are still the only nation in the world to have a "first to invent" rule in our patent system to resolve situations in which more than one person claims to have created the same patentable invention. In the United States, the inventor who was first to invent the invention—not the first to file a patent application—is the owner of the patent. This rule requires an elaborate procedure called an "interference." The purpose of interference proceedings is to reveal who was first to conceive of and reduce the invention to practice. Interference proceedings will become even more elaborate now that GATT has been implemented in U.S. law. Among other changes, GATT expands the range of possible locations in which inventive activity counts towards priority to include activity that occurs within any of the World Trade Organization member countries.

In 1989, the United States changed to an intent to use trademark application system because we were the only nation in the world clinging to the notion that you had to use your trademark before you could apply to register it. We changed to a trademark registration system in which the merchant had an option and could choose to file the old way or the new way—via an "intent to use statement" prior to any use whatsoever of the designation intended to be used in the future as a trademark. Today, nearly half of all trademark applications are filed under the new intent to use system.

Similarly, until 1989, the United States was almost the only nation in the world to require that all distributed copies of software be marked with a copyright notice—the name, date and an encircled "c." If this technicality was not observed, the author or computer programmer lost the copyright. This highly technical requirement was not removed until 1989 when the United States became the last developed nation to join the Berne Union, the premier international copyright treaty organization.

Several recent changes in U.S. law were also required by the NAFTA and GATT agreements. All of these changes were driven by the need for harmonizing the United States' laws with those of our trading partners. No major trading nation in today's world can enjoy the indulgence of having intellectual property laws significantly different from those of the world community. In one sense, unusual intellectual property laws are a tariff and an unnatural barrier to world trade.

VII. Intellectual Property Laws Try to Keep Up to Date

Our present intellectual property laws are having trouble keeping up with the accelerating pace of innovation. . . . .

In the trademark area, technology makes counterfeiting easier than ever, making the war on trademark counterfeiting harder than ever. It is estimated that world-wide losses to U.S. firms from counterfeiting are approaching $75 billion. Counterfeiting of status marks for luxury items, like fake Rolex watches, is not the real problem. The real counterfeiting problem is fake drugs and defective industrial parts.[20] Almost nine out of every ten fasteners, such as bolts and screws, used in the United States are imported, and it is estimated that more than six of every ten fasteners are counterfeit. Even more threatening are the counterfeit and ineffective drugs and pharmaceuticals that have caused hundreds of deaths in developing nations.

Looming on the horizon in the copyright field is the impact of the much discussed information superhighway. What will be its effect on the ability to charge for reproduction and display of copyrighted works? Millions of people are plugging into electronic networks such as the Internet, which connects your personal computer with any other computer in the world. This means that you can send any computer program, anything in print, or any picture, on the "net." The item can be put on an electronic bulletin board, where anyone, anywhere in the world, can download it. How can you charge for the use of such copying and how can you even know copying has taken place? This puts copyright law right in the middle of cyberspace.

As computers plug into the global net and so-called cyberspace, the physical containers in which we are used to seeing information bottled up—like floppy disks and CD-ROMs—may become obsolete. Once that happens, all products of the information age, from books to films to computer programs, will exist as speeding electrons dancing around the world on the computer net. Where do we put the copyright turnstile on the global computer network in order to charge users and copiers?

. . .

VIII. Conclusion

Now the United States prepares to enter the information age and the twenty-first century, where intellectual property will be more important than property in land, buildings or objects. This will be an age in which the most important exports of the United States will be information and the means to control it, store it, and access it.

This will be an age in which all information will be broken into digital bits and sent back and forth around the world to be read on computer screens from Singapore to Chicago to Moscow. But who will thrive and prosper from this

---

[20] See Boeing Probes "Bogus" Parts Claims, S.F. Chron., Aug. 27, 1988, at A4 ("Some Boeing 737, 747, and 757 jet airliners manufactured since mid-1986 were fitted with more than 2000 allegedly counterfeit ball bearings that an engineer said could 'pose serious hazards'. . . .").

torrent of information zipping around the world? Like every other age throughout history, this will be an age of "haves" and "have nots." There will be those who have the knowledge and ability to control and access data and those who do not. There will still be plenty of piecework and manufacturing jobs, but they may be low-paying and located mainly in whatever nation is just emerging from its feudal, pre-industrial state of development.

As we read in the newspapers every day, it seems that while half the world is rushing to embrace the post-industrial information age, the other half seems to be sliding back into a medieval horror of cruel despotic governments, bloody ethnic civil war, widespread famine and killer epidemics. In part, it is a result of the information age that we are made so much aware of what happened this morning in Somalia or Rwanda or Bosnia. With hand-held videocameras, ubiquitous satellite disks and CNN, visual images appear almost instantaneously. Will the information age help or hurt efforts to solve age-old problems such as war and famine? . . .

As we enter the information age, both we and the world intellectual property system will have to change and adjust to new realities. Paradoxically, the world is getting bigger and smaller at the same time. The world is getting bigger because its population, now almost 5.7 billion, is growing at a record pace of more than ninety million persons a year.

At the same time, the world is getting smaller as global communications via computer networks make it easier to communicate and swap huge amounts of information. There is no doubt that in this new world, intellectual property must, and will, grow in importance. Intellectual property is the law's recognition that information is property—and we all know that property is power.

INTELLECTUAL PROPERTY AND THE NATIONAL INFORMATION INFRASTRUCTURE
Report of the Working Group on Intellectual Property Rights 117-119
(U.S. Dept. of Commerce 1995)

At the February 1995 G-7 Ministerial Meeting on the Global Information Infrastructure (GII), the Ministers noted that unless rules for the effective protection of intellectual property are taken into account from the outset, the development of the international information superhighway will be severely hindered. How disparate domestic information infrastructures will evolve into a GII will depend on the rules of the road, and one of the most important sets of rules will be those ensuring protection for the works of intellectual property that move through international channels and into the emerging national information infrastructures. As a result, Ministers endorsed the need to work in international fora, including the World Intellectual Property Organization (WIPO), to achieve standards for the adequate and effective protection of intellectual property in international electronic commerce.

Development of the GII will make copyright laws and international copyright rules a concern for every user. When the globe is blanketed with digital information dissemination systems, a user in one country will be able to manipulate information resources in another country in ways that may violate that country's copyright laws. Indeed, it may be difficult to determine where and when possible infringements may take place because, under the present level of development, a user in France can access a database in the United States and have a copy downloaded to a computer in Sweden. Whose copyright law would apply to such a transaction? Because copyright laws are territorial, and the standards of protection embodied in the international conventions leave room for national legislative determinations, acts that may constitute infringement in one country may not be an infringement in another country. The complexity that such a system creates will make "electronic commerce" over the information superhighways difficult unless the United States moves promptly to identify needs for protection and initiates efforts to work toward a new level of international copyright harmonization.

U.S. copyright industries are significant contributors to the United States' current trade accounts, reducing our balance of payments deficit by some $45.8 billion in 1993. Inadequacies in the present system of intellectual property protection for copyrights and neighboring or related rights, and the consequent losses to these industries from piracy and from trade barriers arising from differences in forms of protection, have been estimated by industry to cost them $15 to 17 billion annually. Improved protection for copyrights and neighboring rights would contribute to reducing these losses and improving the balance of payments.

An important aspect of the participation of foreign entities through a GII in the U.S. domestic information infrastructure is the provision of adequate and effective intellectual property protection in the country wishing to participate. To the extent that participation in the NII (National Information Infrastructure) can be linked to the provision of intellectual property protection, it will promote the ability of U.S. businesses to use the NII and the GII to disseminate works to foreign consumers via other countries' information infrastructures. If commercial enterprises are to make full use of the capabilities of the NII to communicate and deliver information and entertainment products, there must be assurances that their intellectual property rights will be protected effectively under strong copyright laws in all countries participating in a GII.

In considering linkages, careful consideration will have to be given to obligations under international intellectual property treaties and other international agreements, such as the North American Free Trade Agreement (NAFTA) and the World Trade Organization (WTO) Agreement on the Trade-Related Aspects of Intellectual Property (TRIPS Agreement), especially in view of the various intellectual property and market access provisions in those agreements.

GRAEME B. DINWOODIE, THE INTEGRATION OF DOMESTIC AND INTERNATIONAL INTELLECTUAL PROPERTY LAWMAKING[*]
23 COLUM.-V.L.A. J.L. & ARTS 307, 307-08 (1999)

It is increasingly impossible to analyze intellectual property law and policy without reference to international lawmaking. That is not, however, merely because several recent domestic reforms have been prompted by international developments.[1] Indeed, because of significant U.S. influence in the formation of contemporary intellectual property treaties, U.S. law has undergone less change than most in order to comply with newly-assumed international obligations. Nor is it merely because, in an era of global trade and technological advances, a state is unable effectively to regulate economic activity on its own. Rather, the need for a broader awareness flows most directly from the integration of the international and domestic lawmaking processes.

Consider this historical example. As nations met in Berlin in 1908 to revise the Berne Convention, the United States received an invitation to attend "with full freedom of action." Instead, however, the Register of Copyrights attended only as an observer. The reason might now seem unduly quaint.

> [T]he Register of Copyrights explained to the Conference that the United States found it impractical to send a delegate authorized to commit it to actual adhesion to the Berne Convention since some of the questions to be discussed there were pending before the Congress and premature action at the Convention might embarrass the legislative branch of the Government.[2]

Today, in contrast, there is a conscious blending of domestic and international lawmaking. International lawmaking demands attention to Washington; and domestic lawmaking cannot be conducted without regard for what is going on in Brussels, Geneva, Tokyo and elsewhere. Indeed, in some areas of intellectual property, we may be moving toward a single lawmaking process that embodies a series of complex relations among national, regional and global institutions and laws.

Within the United States, this biplay between national and international fora—in particular, between executive branch activity at the international level, and legislative activity in Congress—has been treated by some with a certain suspicion. This interaction is, however, essential in a global age. And it should not be disconcerting. The Constitution sets out a process for concluding and

---

[*]Copyright 1999, Graeme B. Dinwoodie

[1]*See, e.g.*, Sonny Bono Copyright Term Extension Act, Pub. L. No. 105-298, tit. I, 112 Stat. 2827 (1998) (extending term of copyright partly in response to EU Term Directive); Digital Millennium Copyright Act, Pub. L. No. 105-304, 112 Stat. 2860 (1998) Tit. I (implementing WIPO Copyright Treaty); Uruguay Round Agreements Act, Pub. L. No. 103-465, 108 Stat. 4809 (1994), Tit. V (implementing TRIPS Agreement); Trademark Law Treaty Implementation Act, Pub. L. No. 105-330, 112 Stat. 3064 (1998), Tit. I (implementing Trademark Law Treaty).

[2]Barbara Ringer, *The Role of the United States in International Copyright—Past, Present and Future*, 56 GEO. L.J. 1050, 1057 (1968).

ratifying treaties, and a separate process for enacting legislation. Each mechanism has its own limits. It would be somewhat surprising if each branch of government did not use the leverage with which it is endowed by the constitutional scheme. In any event, this blending or integration of lawmaking is a political reality of which we must take account in our assessment of how intellectual property law is made.

RUTH L. GANA, HAS CREATIVITY DIED IN THE THIRD WORLD? SOME IMPLICATIONS OF THE INTERNATIONALIZATION OF INTELLECTUAL PROPERTY*
24 DENV. J. INT'L L. & POL. 109, 112-16 & 141-42 (1995)

[A]ll forms of creative expression—mechanical, literary, or artistic—are value driven. The nature and variety of goods produced in any society is, initially, a function of needs as the popular adage "necessity is the mother of invention" attests. More important, however, the laws which protect these inventions—laws which define what is to be protected and how that protection is to be effected—reflect the underlying values of a society. Intellectual property law, like other law "is more than just another opinion; not because it embodies all right values, or because the values it does embody tend from time to time to reflect those of a majority or plurality, but because it is the value of values. Law is the principle institution through which a society can assert its values."

Further, the selection of what goods to protect and the nature of such protection is shaped by values and needs in accordance with a society's perceptions of what constitutes "the good life." Nowhere is this more reflected than in the Anglo-American philosophy of copyright protection which seeks to balance private reward and encouragement of creative activity with public benefit of access to a goodly supply of literary works. In Macauley's celebrated 1841 speech in the English House of Commons, the need for copyright was expressed as a matter of value and perceptions of what is needed for a good life. . . . .In the United States, Thomas Jefferson's famed letter to Isaac McPherson on the protection of intellectual property reveals a similar understanding of the incidents of the good life and society. . . .

The idea that copyright, as well as other forms of exclusive privileges, was a necessary part of the good society reflects values such as liberty, property, private enterprise, accumulation of capital and rapid consumption; in a word, values that nurture capitalism. . . .

. . . .

The modern debate over intellectual property protection in developing countries has failed to take account of cultural differences which affect the understanding of what constitutes property or what may rightfully be the subject of private ownership. . . . [I]t is important for the modern debate to link intellectual property laws to the social realities of societies in developing countries. Not only may this yield more effective approaches to securing

---

enforcement of intellectual property rights in developing countries, it also presents the possibility that western based intellectual property laws may have some real impact on industrial innovative activity in these countries, thus contributing to the economic welfare of the Third World. However, . . . culture may influence what is created but it is those values, rooted in a conception of a good society, that determine how and what kind of intellectual property laws societies enact.

. . . .

SOME IMPLICATIONS

It is quite clear that one of the central motivations behind the TRIPS agreement was to target enforceability of foreign intellectual property rights in developing countries. As such, the global model of intellectual property protection imposed by the agreement is not a reflection of the need to encourage creativity or to promote the public welfare. Rather, the chief aim of the agreement is to secure from these countries and societies the full monopoly benefits that western intellectual property laws offer. The implications of these strategic moves are many . . .

. . . .

The need to maintain incentives to encourage creative activity is limited, in many respects, to western market democracies. These democracies revolve, in large part, around individual autonomy and liberty, notwithstanding the greater social loss of nonmaterial value that individualism tends to breed. The successful commodification of intellectual goods can only be achieved in a society which embraces this sort of rugged individualism. Until indigenous societies reach this point, the international community may have to come to terms with a persistent level of piracy in international trade. Piracy, however, cannot simply be explained mechanically in economic terms based on the reasoning that poverty necessitates the availability of cheap products. For many of these societies, the difficulty in introducing western copyright principles is that these principles attempt to overturn social values which are centuries old. The laws protecting intellectual goods in these societies simply reflect fundamental notions of what the society considers to be the appropriate subject of exclusive ownership. The duplication of literary work is thus, for example, not perceived as stealing but as making a good thing accessible to the general public. Knowledge in many indigenous societies is not perceived as something that can be commodified or objectified through law. It is impossible to ignore such fundamental conceptions in these communities.

In addition to responding to a persistent level of piracy, the internationalization of intellectual property also suggests that there is some way to objectively measure protection of intellectual property. By not taking into account the possibility of alternative forms of protection, the TRIPS agreement, as did its predecessor treaties, presupposes that "all civilized nations" will and must recognize this global model of intellectual property protection. By mandating this model, governments in developing countries are faced with the difficult job of destroying, or at least attempting to destroy, native conceptions about life and living and about what constitutes an ordered society. The allocation of material value to goods, and the way in which this value is expressed, is grounded firmly in the history of the evolution of a people. The internationalization of intellectual property threatens to undermine, if not totally destroy, the values that indigenous systems ascribe to intellectual property and the manner in which they allocate rights to intellectual goods.

What the internationalization of intellectual property implies, ultimately, is that there is only one way to participate in the international economy and that is by playing in accordance with prescribed rules, regardless of its impact on a group of peoples. It is a message that is not unfamiliar in the history of world affairs, and yet it is a message which, so history informs us, has caused devastation of unimagined proportions to human society. The next few years will reveal just how far native peoples, indigenous groups, and developing countries will fare in the preservation of their cultural patrimony and in their ability to determine the identity of their group in an increasingly hostile international economic environment.

P. JOHN KOZYRIS, COMPARATIVE LAW FOR THE TWENTY-FIRST CENTURY: NEW HORIZONS AND NEW TECHNOLOGIES*
69 TUL. L. REV. 165, 167-178 (1994)

COMPARATIVE LAW HERE AND NOW

Before gazing at the crystal ball, I will articulate three noncontroversial propositions about the here and now of comparative law; and before investigating the new horizons of comparative law, I will review the impact of new technologies.

My first proposition is that the utility of the comparative method is beyond dispute. Comparative law not only provides alternative solutions to be used in legal reform but also gives us a better understanding of our existing law. In short, it is an indispensable tool of legal science. In addition, the internationalization of transactions and the increasing applicability of foreign law make comparative law an indispensable tool of the legal practitioner.

In 1951, Professor Ferdinand Stone told a story which rings true now more than ever. The story was about a man who traveled "from place to place upon the earth."

> [W]herever he went he would pick up bricks and compare them carefully one with another. His conduct excited comment. One man said, "he must be seeking the most perfect of all bricks." Another said, "he must be seeking to describe the qualities inherent in all bricks." Still another of a practical turn of mind said, "he is probably seeking a brick of just the right shape and color to fit into his wall." And still another said, "it is possible that he is not interested in the

---

bricks as such but in their composition. Perhaps, he would set up a kiln of his own for making bricks."[15]

My comment is that these are all valid descriptions of the use of the comparative method today.

Any science, theoretical or applied, that would limit itself to one nation would be laughable.[16] Nevertheless, confused by the historical school and cowed by legal positivism, we have developed too parochial a view of legal science. We have lost sight of the fact that law is a universal phenomenon, and not just the temporal product of the lawmaker in a particular society. Common denominators in the human social condition demand a unified legal science. To be sure, a lawyer normally practices within one country and thus must acquire specialized, practical knowledge of local laws.[17] But a lawyer, even in the most mundane practice, will be impoverished if he wears the blinders of his own jurisdiction.

The great reliance on the comparative method in the world today testifies to its validity. In both the contexts of the conglomeration of states, such as the European Economic Community, now the European Union, which has become a vibrant comparative law lab, and of the disintegration of empires, as in the East where massive law reform is taking place, comparative law has proved vital.

In the United States, the best evidence of our recognition of the value of comparative law is that we teach even domestic law by the comparative method. No self-respecting law school teaches merely the laws of its own state. The Brandeisian idea of the states as law labs is deeply ingrained. Why do we teach in this manner even when many of the students are likely to practice in-state? The comparative method is a natural in America because we typically teach through fact patterns and cases, not statutes. We reward students not so much for right answers as for seeing as many angles as possible and for arguing in every plausible policy direction, which necessitates transcending the boundaries of any one jurisdiction.

The main reason why we do not use much truly foreign law rather than sister-state law in our teaching is logistical, not conceptual. We face serious linguistic and cultural obstacles. Besides, there already exists too much material to cover from the United States materials alone. Yet, we are missing an important dimension by just keeping to one nation, however big and diverse it may be.

My second, and rather obvious point, is that you cannot truly pursue the comparative method through the study of formal legal texts alone. It is necessary to get to know what is behind the texts and also, even more important, how they function. This requires understanding the legal culture that produced the laws, and more broadly, the social and economic structures

---

[15]Ferdinand F. Stone, *The End to Be Served by Comparative Law*, 25 TUL. L. REV. 325 (1951).

[16]For example, imagine the sciences of medicine or horticulture confining themselves only to American medicine or American horticulture.

[17]Similarly, an American horticulturist may not typically specialize in jungle flora, or an American doctor may not become an expert on amoebiasis or yellow fever.

and the ethical and political values that support them. Laws cannot be grasped in an idealized form outside the context of the society that created them. Before a legal model can be transplanted, the conditions in the two societies—the one from which it comes and the one to which it goes—must be taken into account. To be sure, the more similar the societies, the less the need to engage in elaborate socio-legal studies. Eventually, the global village created under industrialization, urbanization, and the homogenizing influence of the global mass media may reduce such need even further. But we still have a long way to go before we can assume compatibility.

My third and final point on the here and now of comparative law is that, in the last half century or so, comparative law has exhibited remarkable stability within the United States and abroad. . . . [W]ith one apparent and one real exception, . . . the fundamentals of comparative law have not changed much in our times.

The apparent change relates to the growing literature from outside the United States and Western Europe, especially from Asia and Africa, as well as from some formerly communist nations. It would thus appear that comparative law is moving from eurocentric to global. There is some truth to this perception, but it is important to see it in the proper light. For example, close to half of the space in the first two issues of this year's American Journal of Comparative Law is devoted to judicial review in Korea and Poland, the Korean press law, the notion of legal personality in China, and legal thinking in Micronesia. Yet, with the exception of the last piece, the discourse is conducted with the traditional tools of the western legal tradition. Even the Micronesian article represents an exercise in western legal realism. What has happened, I believe, and this is starkly evident in Eastern Europe, is that the western legal tradition has spread all over the developed and developing world under the rubric of modernization. In the process, the western tradition has undoubtedly been enriched by other legal cultures. However, it remains dominant and, if anything, is becoming universal.

The real change relates to the shift of the center of gravity from private law and formal criminal law to public and regulatory law. The reasons why modern comparative law originally focused on private themes are rather clear. The great Roman law tradition, systematized and refined by legal science over the centuries, exploded into an array of comprehensive private law codes. These codes were not only detailed and stable but also traced their pedigree to reason, making them ideally suited to textual comparison and to the pursuit of erudite distinctions and penumbral nuances. By contrast, public and regulatory law was seen not only as more rough, raw, and untidy, but also as more positive, expressing the will of the sovereign, and more temporal, connected to the volksgeist of particular places and periods.

The centrality of public and regulatory law, however, has never been questioned. As the nations of the world, especially after World War II, were seeking their way in constitutionalism and liberal democracy, comparative constitutional law, starting with judicial review and expanding into political, civil, and human rights, attracted a lot of attention. With both the formation and disintegration of composite states, such as the European Union and the Soviet Union, comparative federalism has become a hot, complex, and fascinating topic. In the economic sphere, antitrust and, more recently, environmental law have also claimed their place under the sun of comparison.

In fact, comparative work in public law is more difficult because it requires not only technical expertise but also the ability to delve into policy issues in diverse social contexts. But the more that the conditions in the world become homogenized, the more the organization of power within societies falls into typical patterns, and the easier it becomes to control the variables necessary to use the comparative method fruitfully.

. . . .

NEW TECHNOLOGIES

In switching the discussion from the here and now of comparative law to new horizons for the twenty-first century, let me say a few words about the implications of new technologies. Printed materials on foreign law, especially in the English language, have become available at a fast pace. . . .

The most remarkable revolution in technology, however, has occurred in electronics. We all know how Lexis and Westlaw have dramatically changed the modes and speed of domestic legal research. In the comparative field, together with the Internet, Lexis and Westlaw are also doing quite a lot. First, they provide instant access to foreign materials in English, which are otherwise difficult, if not impossible to find, especially in updated form. Second, Lexis has crossed the language barrier, giving us numerous materials in French. Other languages, at least those using the Latin alphabet, could easily be added. Third, the Internet not only provides access to specialized library catalogues but also enables faculty and other law professionals to communicate, form discussion groups, and share their ideas all over the world. And this is only the beginning. Before the end of the twentieth century, let alone the next century, these services will grow exponentially and their cost will decline. Foreign law information will be at every lawyer's fingertips, and most of it will be in the new lingua franca, English.

It is also very important to note that Lexis and Westlaw are not merely opening doors to information. As they become dominant worldwide, they set the standards for law retrieval along the patterns of the common law system, especially the American one, which relies heavily on key words and factual similarities rather than on statutory texts or conceptual analysis. As lawyers in other nations learn to use these services, they are bound to be influenced by the subtle shift in legal method from civilian deduction to common law induction.

NEW HORIZONS

. . . .

Let me conclude by briefly outlining my main points. Comparative law is now technologically easier, has crossed over from the private into the public domain, and is needed now more than ever because of the expansion of international transactions; the globalization of legal culture; and the movements for unification, federation, and law reform around the world. . . . In the twenty-first century, the United States would be well served if it were to make a public commitment to promote the scientific study of law, not only for the sake of study, but also to insulate our laws from the influence of special interests and to make them more systematic, consistent, and technically expert. . . .

WILLIAM L. KEEFAUVER, THE NEED FOR INTERNATIONAL THINKING IN INTELLECTUAL PROPERTY LAW*
37 IDEA 181 (1996)

In the late 1930s, Senator Arthur Vandenberg of Michigan was one of the leading isolationists in the U.S. Senate. But toward the end of the decade, as events in Europe were beginning to overtake us, he made a sudden conversion and became an internationalist. Because Senator Vandenberg was highly respected in foreign policy, I naively thought that this marked the end of isolationism. I was obviously a little premature, however, because even today we continue to hear proponents of isolationism, including a recent candidate for President of the United States.

My focus here, however, is intellectual property, not politics. Intellectual property specialists from long before Senator Vandenberg have had to practice in the international field, making it essential for them to understand the laws and practices of many countries. But in those days, intellectual property specialists were what I would call "multinational" lawyers rather than international lawyers due to the lack of congruency between the laws of the different countries.

In the 1970s, a strong trend toward globalization of markets began. This trend was stimulated not only by advances in telecommunications, but also by the desires of suppliers to seek additional sources of revenue beyond their borders. Others found it necessary to counterattack by entering the home markets of these new foreign competitors. Simultaneously, the sometimes significant differences around the world in intellectual property protection began colliding with each other as companies formed business ventures across national lines. It then became important to see whether these friction points could be reduced.

. . . .

[I]t is market forces, not intellectual property lawyers, which have globalized the practice, and it is up to us as practitioners to make globalization work for our clients. With a focus on our clients, we must work to reduce some of the friction points by working for beneficial changes in conflicting laws and by becoming sufficiently knowledgeable of the laws and practices of other countries.

. . . .

Like many U.S. companies, my company, AT&T, had a domestic patent attorney group which focused on the United States and a foreign group to deal with other countries. However, it was during the period since the 1970s that I became aware of the globalization trend. I was also convinced that in order to represent client interests adequately, it was no longer sufficient for lawyers working in the United States to think of themselves solely as U.S. practitioners. So I announced a new paradigm for AT&T: henceforth, there would be no such dichotomy; every lawyer would be a global lawyer and have to become sufficiently knowledgeable to deal with the patent laws of all countries in which the corporation was interested.

This new paradigm meant worldwide patent prosecution responsibility. Also, when helping clients develop intellectual property strategies, the new global lawyer would do so from a worldwide perspective. Although I felt I was announcing a "sea of change," it met with little resistance. It had become obvious that we could no longer live on our own little island of U.S. law and claim to be providing adequate client representation. We simply had to know what was happening throughout the world.

Much of AT&T's globalization was driven by joint venture activity. Like many other companies, AT&T found that the only way to enter certain foreign markets was through joint ventures with local firms. If you have ever negotiated or looked at a joint venture agreement, you know that a major component is often the intellectual property piece which usually covers patents, trademarks, copyrights, software, and technical information. Quite often, a joint venture agreement has rights flowing to and from many countries. It takes a lot of creativity to reach agreement and usually involves negotiations by lawyers and businesspeople from several countries.

The intellectual property lawyers almost inevitably get involved in the business aspects of the deal since the allocation of rights often depends on the structuring of the work agreement and vice versa. Significantly, these negotiations are truly negotiations and are quite different from those of previous decades when a U.S. company could simply dictate the terms. All of this has not only been instructive, but also very helpful in broadening the perspectives of practitioners accustomed to thinking only of U.S. law.

Some of our U.S. colleagues continue to feel that to think internationally or to talk about compromise and change in U.S. law is to somehow put the United States in second place. My view is very clearly the opposite. Thinking internationally does not put the U.S. in second place. Rather, you have to think internationally to put the United States and your company or client in first place.

Certainly, all aspects of intellectual property now have a global dimension. Fortunately, we have been able to harmonize some of the more serious differences in copyright law as well as trademark law, and to some extent, patent law. These harmonization efforts, taken with the TRIPS agreement, should make it even more natural to think of intellectual property in international terms. Lawyers who do not think in these terms simply are not fulfilling their duties to their clients.

In a global market place there is little room for isolationism, and it is clear that our clients are thinking in international terms. We, as intellectual property lawyers, must have the same frame of reference as our clients to adequately and ethically support them.

NOTES AND QUESTIONS

(1) **The Changing U.S. Economy.** The development that begins Professor McCarthy's essay has since been repeated. On October 26, 1999, the editors of the *Wall Street Journal* (who select the stocks that comprise the Dow Jones Index) announced that in order to make the Dow Jones Index "even more representative of the evolving U.S. economy," the Index would no longer include the oil company Chevron, the retail chain Sears Roebuck, the chemical company Union Carbide, and Goodyear Tire and Rubber Co., but instead would include Intel, Microsoft, Home Depot (the specialty retailer), and SBC Communications, one of the regional Bell phone companies. *See* Floyd Norris, *Dow Takes On a New, High-Technology Look*, Oct. 27, 1999, N.Y. TIMES at C1 (noting that "until 1997, the Dow had just one large computer technology company, IBM. Then it added Hewlett-Packard, and now it is adding Microsoft, the dominant personal computer software company, and Intel, the leading maker of semiconductor chips for such computers.").

(2) **Globalization**. The term "globalization" is frequently used to describe some of the contemporary phenomena discussed in the preceding excerpts. What does this (probably over-used) term mean? What is causing these changes in legal practice, economic priorities, lawmaking, and scholarly inquiry? Do the descriptions of social, political and economic change offered in these excerpts capture all the causes of globalization? Do they consider all the effects? To what extent should we critique the reasons for these changes, or should we simply address their consequences? What is the role of intellectual property law, or intellectual property lawyers or policymakers, in the midst of these changes? Are you persuaded by Keefauver's distinction between intellectual property law and politics? Is it the role of lawyers "to make globalization work for our clients"?

(3) **The Significance of Intellectual Property in a Global Economy**. What characteristics of intellectual property explain its social, economic and political significance? Professor McCarthy suggests that Microsoft founder Bill Gates may be "one of the most influential people in America today." Why might that be the case? To what extent does ownership of intellectual property confer more influence or power in modern society than ownership of tangible property? Which of its characteristics have forced policymakers to address intellectual property law on the international stage? Are there considerations other than the inherent characteristics of intellectual property that have driven efforts to address intellectual property internationally? What might those external forces be? Do you agree with Professor McCarthy's assessment that "if foreign nations

do not recognize or enforce intellectual property laws, then America has nothing to sell"?

(4) **The Costs and Benefits of Different National Laws.** What are the costs and benefits of intellectual property laws differing from country to country? Does this depend upon the nature of the differences? Which differences are likely to produce net gains, and which ones are likely to produce net costs? Are there circumstances in which possibly divergent national approaches might be necessary, or even desirable? In which circumstances is internationalization most warranted or most necessary? Who benefits from international standards of intellectual property law?

(5) **The Values Underlying Intellectual Property Laws.** What are the consequences of calling products of creativity "property?" How universal are the concerns articulated by McCarthy and Keefauver? What are the premises upon which these writers found their vision of intellectual property? A noted economist who is a wholesale critic of the intellectual property system argues that:

> [T]he idea that people should be paid to be creative is a point of view that stems from the Judeo-Christian and Muslim belief in a God who created humankind in His image. It has no analogue in Hindu, Buddhist, or Confucian societies. There are real differences in beliefs about what should be freely available in the public domain and what should be for sale in the private marketplace.

Lester Thurow, *Needed: A New System of Intellectual Property Rights*, HARV. BUS. REV., Sept. 1997, at 95, 100; *see also* DAVID F. NOBLE, THE RELIGION OF TECHNOLOGY (1999). Is establishment of a strong intellectual property system in a country which has a non-Western cultural and religious heritage necessarily an indication that it is becoming Westernized, or becoming "modernized"? Are there any differences between modernization and Westernization? Is the Western paradigm becoming universal, as Professor Kozyris suggests?

(6) **Thinking Internationally.** What does Keefauver mean by "thinking internationally"? Is that what Professors McCarthy, Dinwoodie, Kozyris and Gana are doing? What would be the consequences of American "isolationism" in the field of intellectual property law? Political commentators have noted that there are two different forms of isolationism: one "rests partly on a fearful assessment of America's ability to compete in a global economy. The other derives not from . . . insecurities . . . but, conversely, from a supreme self-confidence that America can go it alone, that its wealth and military power make international treaties unnecessary." *Isolationism's Return*, N.Y. TIMES, Oct. 31, 1999, at WK14. To what extent does either of these isolationist philosophies carry weight in determining the policy that the United States should adopt toward international intellectual property relations? Are there dangers in too effusive an embrace of international lawmaking? Two prominent scholars have noted that:

[H]ow radically the world intellectual property policymaking arena has changed in the last several years. In this climate, it is literally possible for an as yet unimplemented legislative initiative of one government to become an international minimum standard for other governments before most people affected by it . . . even know that proposals for new intellectual property rights have been put on the table.

J.H. Reichman & Pamela Samuelson, *Intellectual Property Rights in Data?*, 50 VAND. L. REV. 51, 76 (1997).

Several U.S. academic commentators have bemoaned the extent to which national legislatures in developed countries have been captured by industries seeking higher levels of intellectual property protection. Even before we consider these international lawmaking institutions in detail, would you expect special interests to have more or less influence in an enlarged and more multifaceted lawmaking process (involving, as we will see, foreign legislatures, international intellectual property institutions such as the World Intellectual Property Organization, treaty negotiators, trade representatives, and dispute panels convened under the aegis of the World Trade Organization) than before the U.S. Congress? What information would you want to know to answer this question?

(7) **Civil Law Systems.** Civil law systems are generally founded on extensive statutory statements (normally, codifications) of the law, and these form the basis for judicial analysis. Civil law systems thus do not generally use a system of case law precedent where courts are *bound* to follow rules announced in certain earlier decisions. Courts in civil law countries are, however, generally influenced by prior decisions. Although earlier cases are not formally a "source of law," they naturally form part of the legal debate regarding the appropriate resolution of similar disputes. Courts in civil law countries aim to decide like cases alike, and they recognize the reality of the parties' appealing to higher courts that may have rendered the earlier decisions. Moreover, some civil law systems adhere to a philosophy of *jurisprudence constante*, under which a pattern of similar like decisions justifies the application of a constant rule. This philosophy requires a series of decisions before the reasoning underlying those decisions holds sway with later courts; a common law system of binding precedent gives greater weight to single decisions of courts of a particular level. But opinions in civilian systems are framed less formally by the need to consider prior decisions. This should be borne in mind in reading certain non-U.S. cases. (Decisions of courts in common law countries other than the United States may also be structured differently, for other reasons.) The concept of binding precedent develops most easily in legal systems where significant case law develops, and where there is routinized and accessible reporting of that case law. What other requirements are essential in order to employ a system of binding precedent? In what ways, other than contributing toward a system of binding precedent, might decided case law be used to further important public policy objectives?

A leading twentieth century Scottish judge, Lord Cooper, whose position on the highest Scottish court exposed him to a traditionally civilian system with a modern (English) common law influence, described the methodological differences between the civilian and common law systems thus:

> A civilian system differs from a common law system much as rationalism differs from empiricism or deduction from induction. The civilian naturally reasons from principles to instances, the common lawyer from instances to principles. The civilian puts faith in syllogisms, the common lawyer in precedents; the first silently asking himself as each new problem arises, "What should we do this time" and the second asking aloud in the same situation, "What did we do last time?" . . .The instinct of a civilian is to systematise. The working rule of the common lawyer is *solvitur ambulando.*

Thomas Mackay Cooper, *The Common Law and The Civil Law–A Scot's View,* 63 HARV. L. REV. 468, 470-71 (1950). Is one of these methodologies inherently more suited to the demands of an international environment? Do you agree with Professor Kozyris that technological developments will result in an international shift toward the common law methodology of induction? Do any of the developments described in these materials suggest countervailing tendencies?

§ 1.03   Territoriality of Intellectual Property Rights

As we will see, over the past century and a quarter a vast body of international intellectual property law has been developed. But it is a fundamental (if paradoxical) principle of international intellectual property law that, with very few exceptions, intellectual property rights are national in nature. And the nature of those national rights is determined largely by national laws (even if the national laws of a particular country are significantly shaped by the obligations of that country under international intellectual property law). We will periodically discuss the extent to which recent developments derogate from this principle of territoriality. The principle is, however, the starting point for any study of international intellectual property law: intellectual property laws operate territorially, and intellectual property rights are thus national in scope.

COMPUTER ASSOCIATES INT'L, INC. v. ALTAI, INC.
126 F.3d 365 (2d Cir. 1997)

JOHN M. WALKER, JR., CIRCUIT JUDGE:

Defendant-appellant, Altai, Inc. ("Altai"), appeals from the order of the United States District Court for the Eastern District of New York (Dennis R. Hurley, District Judge) denying its motion for an injunction against Computer

Associates International, Inc. ("Computer Associates"). The issue on appeal is whether, under a theory of either claim or issue preclusion, a federal court should enjoin Computer Associates from pursuing an action claiming copyright infringement of a computer program in a French forum where Computer Associates has previously brought and lost a United States copyright infringement action based on the same computer program in federal court. Because we agree with the district court that *res judicata* and collateral estoppel are inapplicable under the circumstances of this case, we affirm.

I. BACKGROUND

A. The United States Action

In August of 1988, Computer Associates brought a copyright infringement . . . action in the Eastern District of New York against Altai, alleging that Altai had copied substantial portions of Computer Associates's ADAPTER computer program into Altai's OSCAR 3.4 and OSCAR 3.5 computer programs in violation of Computer Associates's United States copyright (the "United States action"). On August 9, 1991, following a trial, the district court found that Altai's OSCAR 3.4 computer program infringed Computer Associates's copyright, but held that OSCAR 3.5 was not substantially similar to the ADAPTER portion of Computer Associates's SCHEDULER program and therefore did not infringe Computer Associates's copyright. Computer Assocs. Int'l, Inc. v. Altai, Inc., 775 F.Supp. 544, 560-62 (E.D.N.Y.1991) ("Altai I"). [On December 17, 1992, the Second Circuit affirmed the district court's findings and judgment with regards to Computer Associates's copyright claims. Computer Assocs. Int'l, Inc. v. Altai, Inc., 982 F.2d 693, 715, 720 (2d Cir.1992) ("Altai II")].

B. The French Action

On January 23, 1990, Computer Associates and L'Agence pour la Protection des Programmes ("L'Agence") secured an *ex parte* order from the President of the Tribunal de Grande Instance in Bobigny, France, authorizing seizure of computer programs and business records from the offices of Altai's French distributor, la Société FASTER, S.A.R.L. ("FASTER"), and enjoining FASTER from distributing or marketing its products. On February 2, 1990, a raid of FASTER's offices yielded five object code tapes of Altai software that contained OSCAR 3.5 code.

On February 15, 1990, one month before trial commenced in the United States, Computer Associates and L'Agence filed an action in the Tribunal de Commerce in Bobigny, France (the "Commercial Court"), against Altai and FASTER, charging violations of Computer Associates's French copyright (the "French action"). The French action centered on Computer Associates's allegations that Altai's importation and FASTER's distribution of OSCAR 3.5 in France violated Computer Associates's French copyright.

On October 1, 1991, Altai brought to the Commercial Court's attention the district court's holding in *Altai I* that its OSCAR 3.5 computer program did not violate Computer Associates's United States copyright and of the status of Computer Associates's appeal to the Second Circuit. Trial in the French action was postponed until September 10, 1992.

On September 16, 1992, Altai requested a stay of the French proceeding from the Tribunal de Grande Instance in Paris (the "Tribunal"), pending disposition of Altai's request for an *exequatur*, which would make the judgment in *Altai I* enforceable in France and allow Altai to introduce the judgment during the course of the French action in the Commercial Court. On October 22, 1992, the Commercial Court issued a stay. The *exequatur* was issued by the Tribunal in June 1993.

On May 14, 1994, Computer Associates moved to resume the French proceedings, and on November 25, 1994, trial in the Commercial Court began. On January 20, 1995, the Commercial Court found that Altai's OSCAR 3.5 program did not violate Computer Associates's rights under French copyright law. The Commercial Court specifically rejected Altai's argument that the United States decision in *Altai I* governed the disposition of the French action. The Commercial Court stated:

> [T]he United States decision was made with reference to United States law which, even if it is close to French law with regard to the protection of literary and artistic works, cannot be completely and immediately identified with French law without an analysis of the facts under French law. Jurisprudence on the matter of software protection is in flux, as the United States decision shows, with each case having to be considered individually . . .

On April 25, 1995, Computer Associates appealed the decision to the Paris Court of Appeals which scheduled briefing for May 13, 1998, and oral argument for June 18, 1998.

C.   Motion To Enjoin French Copyright Infringement Action

On November 16, 1994, Altai moved in the Eastern District of New York to enjoin Computer Associates from continuing to litigate the action in France. On February 22, 1995, in light of the January 20, 1995 decision of the Commercial Court in its favor, Altai voluntarily withdrew this motion.

On April 11, 1995, after learning of Computer Associates's plan to appeal the decision of the Commercial Court, Altai reactivated its motion to enjoin Computer Associates from continuing to proceed with its French action. On June 17, 1996, the district court denied Altai's motion to enjoin Computer Associates from pursuing its French action. This appeal followed.

II. DISCUSSION

On appeal, Altai contends: (i) that Computer Associates's United States action for violation of its United States copyright precludes, under the doctrine of *res judicata*, its French action for violation of its French copyright; (ii) that, alternatively, Computer Associates is collaterally estopped from claiming that OSCAR 3.5 violates its French copyright because, in the United States action, judgment was rendered to the effect that OSCAR 3.5 does not violate Computer Associates's United States copyright; and (iii) finally, an antisuit injunction is appropriate, because comity concerns which caution against enjoining parties to a parallel foreign proceeding are inapplicable when, as here, judgment has already been rendered in the United States action. We address each contention in turn.

. . .

A. Res Judicata

Altai argues that the doctrine of *res judicata* bars Computer Associates from litigating its French action because Computer Associates could have raised its French copyright claims during the course of its United States action on its United States copyright claims. We disagree.

Under the doctrine of *res judicata*, a final judgment on the merits in an action "precludes the parties or their privies from relitigating issues that were or could have been raised in that action." Federated Dep't Stores, Inc. v. Moitie, 452 U.S. 394, 398 (1981).

> Simply put, the doctrine of *res judicata* provides that when a final judgment has been entered on the merits of a case, [i]t is a finality as to the claim or demand in controversy, concluding parties and those in privity with them, not only as to every matter which was offered and received to sustain or defeat the claim or demand, but as to any other admissible matter which might have been offered for that purpose.

SEC v. First Jersey Sec., Inc., 101 F.3d 1450, 1463 (2d Cir.1996); [cit]. *Res judicata* therefore bars the subsequent litigation of any claims arising from the transaction or series of transactions which was the subject of the prior suit. [cit].

The burden is on the party seeking to invoke *res judicata* to prove that the doctrine bars the second action. [cit]. Without a demonstration that the conduct complained of in the French action occurred prior to the initiation of the United States action, *res judicata* is simply inapplicable. As we have noted previously:

> With respect to the determination of whether a second suit is barred by res judicata, the fact that both suits involved essentially the same course of wrongful conduct is not decisive; nor is it dispositive

that the two proceedings involved the same parties, similar or overlapping facts, and similar legal issues. A first judgment will generally have preclusive effect only where the transaction or connected series of transactions at issue in both suits is the same, that is where the same evidence is needed to support both claims, and where the facts essential to the second were present in the first.

Interoceanica Corp., 107 F.3d at 91 (quoting *SEC v. First Jersey Sec.*, 101 F.3d 1450, 1463-64 (2d Cir.1996)).

In this case, Altai has failed to meet its burden of showing that the conduct which forms the basis of the French action—the unauthorized importation into France of Computer Associates's copyrighted work, and the subsequent distribution of the work in that country—occurred prior to August 1988 when the action was filed in New York. Altai simply asserts that the actions giving rise to the French action "took place prior to February 15, 1990, the date [the French action] was filed" and that they "took place well before [Computer Associates's] United States claims went to trial on March 28, 1990." Absent evidence that the French action is based on conduct by Altai and by FASTER that occurred prior to August 1988, *res judicata* will not bar Computer Associates from pursuing its claims in France.

Altai argues that *res judicata* bars the French action nonetheless, because Computer Associates could have amended its complaint in the United States action to assert its French copyright claims of which it became aware prior to the beginning of trial in the United States. We disagree.

For the purposes of *res judicata*, "[t]he scope of litigation is framed by the complaint at the time it is filed." [cit]. The *res judicata* doctrine does not apply to new rights acquired during the action which might have been, but which were not, litigated. [cit]. Although a plaintiff may seek leave to file a supplemental pleading to assert a new claim based on actionable conduct which the defendant engaged in after a lawsuit is commenced, [cit], he is not required to do so. [cit]. [Computer Associates] was under no obligation to amend its complaint in the United States action, and *res judicata* does not bar litigation of claims arising from transactions which occurred after the United States action was brought.

Even if we were to assume that the French suit arose from transactions identical to those in the United States suit, there is a second reason why Altai may not invoke *res judicata* to bar the French action: the New York federal district court in the United States action could not have exercised personal jurisdiction over FASTER, a principal party to the French suit. *Res judicata* will not apply where "'the initial forum did not have the power to award the full measure of relief sought in the later litigation.'" [cit] . . .

    . . .

In conclusion, there are two reasons why *res judicata* does not prevent Computer Associates from maintaining its action based on French copyright claims in France: (i) the infringing conduct which formed the basis of the French action occurred after the filing of the United States action; and (ii) the New York federal district court lacked personal jurisdiction over FASTER. We therefore affirm the district court.

B. Collateral Estoppel

Altai argues, in the alternative, that Computer Associates is collaterally estopped from claiming that OSCAR 3.5 infringes its French copyright. We disagree.

The doctrine of collateral estoppel

> bars a party from relitigating in a second proceeding an issue of fact or law that was litigated and actually decided in a prior proceeding, if that party had a full and fair opportunity to litigate the issue in the prior proceeding and the decision of the issue was necessary to support a valid and final judgment on the merits.

Metromedia Co. v. Fugazy, 983 F.2d 350, 365 (2d Cir.1992). For collateral estoppel to apply, the issues in each action must be identical, and issues are not identical when the legal standards governing their resolution are significantly different. [cit].

On appeal, Altai asserts that the French standard for copyrightability of computer programs is not "significantly different" from the standard applied in the United States because, as under United States copyright law, French law protects expression and not ideas. Such a superficial comparison begs key questions: What constitutes expression or ideas in the context of computer software, to what extent may expression be copied with impunity when it is necessary to the communication of the idea, how much expression is not original with the plaintiff or is in the public domain? Altai's argument is far from sufficient to show that the two copyright standards in France and the United States are "identical" as required for application of collateral estoppel. The Commercial Court arrived at a similar conclusion, refusing Altai's request to give the decision in the United States action dispositive effect. We, therefore, affirm the district court's decision that collateral estoppel does not bar litigation of the French action.

C. Foreign Antisuit Injunction

It is well established that a federal court has the power to enjoin a foreign suit by persons subject to its jurisdiction; however, due regard for principles of international comity require that this power should be "used sparingly." China Trade & Dev. Corp. v. M.V. Choong Yong, 837 F.2d 33, 36 (2d Cir.1987); [cit]. Antisuit injunctions should be "granted only with care and great restraint." *China Trade*, 837 F.2d at 36 (internal quotation marks omitted). Ordinarily when the courts of two sovereigns have *in personam* jurisdiction, one court will not try to restrain proceedings before the other.

In determining whether to enjoin foreign litigation, a court must consider, as a threshold matter, whether (i) the parties to both suits are the same and (ii) resolution of the case before the enjoining court would be dispositive of the action to be enjoined. [cit].

Altai argues that the *China Trade* factors are inapplicable where a final judgment has been reached in the United States forum. We need not decide whether the *China Trade* factors are inapplicable when a final judgment issues in a United States action because we hold that, in this case, the injunction is not necessary to protect our jurisdiction or the integrity of our judgment. While Altai may experience as vexatious Computer Associates' decision to pursue its rights in France, the French action would in no way affect the decision rendered by a court of the United States. In short, the action in this country involved violations of Computer Associates's United States copyright, and the French action involves violations of Computer Associates's French copyright. We can discern no basis for enjoining Computer Associates from pursuing its French action; moreover, the interests of comity caution against such an injunction.

III. CONCLUSION

Based on the foregoing, we affirm the decision of the district court denying Altai's motion to enjoin Computer Associates from continuing to litigate its French copyright infringement action against Altai and FASTER in France, based on actions that occurred in France.

NOTES AND QUESTIONS

(1) **The Principle of Territoriality.** Define precisely the causes of action being pursued by Computer Associates in the United States and France, respectively. How are they different? What intellectual property rights does Computer Associates hold in the ADAPTER computer program?

(2) **Serial National Litigation.** The need for an intellectual property owner in a multinational dispute to pursue separate national litigation for separate violations of separate national intellectual property rights is not restricted to copyright. *See, e.g.,* Euromarket Designs, Inc. v. Crate and Barrel Limited and Miriam Peters, 96 F. Supp.2d 824 (N. D. Ill. 2000) (claim for infringement of U.S. trademark rights in mark CRATE & BARREL); Euromarket Designs Inc. v. Peters, [2000] E.T.M.R. 1025 (Ch. D. 2000) (Eng.) (claim for infringement of U.K. trademark rights in mark CRATE & BARREL). Some of the devices currently used, and being proposed, to mitigate the inefficiencies of serial national litigation are discussed in detail in Part III *infra*.

PART II

PRINCIPLES OF INTERNATIONAL PROTECTION

Chapter 2

INTERNATIONAL LAW AND INSTITUTIONS

§ 2.01 The Nature and Sources of International Law

The system of nation states as we know it grew slowly over a period of centuries, crystallizing in Western Europe in the mid-seventeenth century with the Peace of Westphalia of 1648, then spread to North and South America first, and to Africa and Asia only later. The term "international law" was coined by Jeremy Bentham in 1789 in his *Introduction to the Principles of Morals and Legislation*. An older term, the "law of nations," from Roman times had referred to a universal law (*jus gentium*), an ethically determined "law of peoples" or even "law of tribes." Bentham's international law, by contrast, refers to the rules of engagement among nation states, distinguishable from the internal law of any of those states. In common parlance, the internal law of a nation-state is referred to as "municipal" or "local" law. Although the term "law of nations" is used less frequently today, the basic concept remains embodied in part in the term "customary international law."

Few nation states had significantly developed intellectual property laws in place at the beginning of the nineteenth century. The history of international intellectual property cooperation is much more recent, beginning in earnest only during the last three decades of the nineteenth century in the form of written international agreements. By that era, the modern view of international law espoused by Bentham had become the predominant one. In the milieu of the nineteenth century international system, positive international law gained its readiest expression in the form of treaties between nation states; and the expository jurisprudence of the period placed the explicit agreements between nation states in a hierarchy above empirical observations as to customary law between them or logically or ethically derived principles by which nation states should behave. Consequently, at least until very recently, few would have argued that intellectual property rights were determined by principles of customary international law. It is doubtful that most states today would accept any assertion that they were obliged to protect intellectual property rights of citizens of other states other than by express agreement in the form of a treaty or statute. But an understanding of the broader structure of international law is essential to an appreciation of the ways in which contemporary international intellectual property law and policy may be breaking new ground.

RESTATEMENT OF THE LAW (THIRD), FOREIGN RELATIONS LAW OF THE UNITED STATES, § 102[*]

Sources of International Law

(1) A rule of international law is one that has been accepted as such by the international community of states

  (a) in the form of customary law;

  (b) by international agreement; or

  (c) by derivation from general principles common to the major legal systems of the world.

(2) Customary international law results from a general and consistent practice of states followed by them from a sense of legal obligation.

(3) International agreements create law for the states parties thereto and may lead to the creation of customary international law when such agreements are intended for adherence by states generally and are in fact widely accepted.

(4) General principles common to the major legal systems, even if not incorporated or reflected in customary law or international agreement, may be invoked as supplementary rules of international law where appropriate.

Comments and Illustrations

. . . .

b. *Practice as customary law.* "Practice of states," Subsection (2), includes diplomatic acts and instructions as well as public measures and other governmental acts and official statements of policy, whether they are unilateral or undertaken in cooperation with other states, for example in organizations such as the Organization for Economic Cooperation and Development (OECD). Inaction may constitute state practice, as when a state acquiesces in acts of another state that affect its legal rights. The practice necessary to create customary law may be of comparatively short duration, but under Subsection (2) it must be "general and consistent." A practice can be general even if it is not universally followed; there is no precise formula to indicate how widespread a practice must be, but it should reflect wide acceptance among the states particularly involved in the relevant activity. Failure of a significant number of important states to adopt a practice can prevent a principle from becoming general customary law though it might become "particular customary law" for the participating states. [cit]. A principle of customary law is not binding on a state that declares its dissent from the principle during its development. [cit].

c. *Opinio juris.* For a practice of states to become a rule of customary international law it must appear that the states follow the practice from a sense of legal obligation (*opinio juris sive necessitatis*); a practice that is generally followed but which states feel legally free to disregard does not contribute to customary law. A practice initially followed by states as a matter of courtesy or habit may become law when states generally come to believe that they are under a legal obligation to comply with it. It is often difficult to determine when that transformation into law has taken place. Explicit evidence of a sense of legal obligation (e.g., by official statements) is not necessary; *opinio juris* may be inferred from acts or omissions.

d. *Dissenting views and new states.* Although customary law may be built by the acquiescence as well as by the actions of states (Comment b) and become generally binding on all states, in principle a state that indicates its dissent from a practice while the law is still in the process of development is not bound by that rule even after it matures. . . . As to the possibility of dissent from peremptory norms (*jus cogens*), a state that enters the international system after a practice has ripened into a rule of international law is bound by that rule.

e. *General and special custom.* The practice of states in a regional or other special grouping may create "regional," "special," or "particular" customary law for those states inter se. . . .

f. *International agreement as source of law.* An international agreement creates obligations binding between the parties under international law. [cit]. Ordinarily, an agreement between states is a source of law only in the sense that a private contract may be said to make law for the parties under the domestic law of contracts. Multilateral agreements open to all states, however, are increasingly used for general legislation, whether to make new law, as in human rights . . . or for codifying and developing customary law, as in the Vienna Convention on the Law of Treaties. . . . International agreements may contribute to customary law.

g. *Binding resolutions of international organizations.* Some international agreements that are constitutions or charters of international organizations confer power on those organizations to impose binding obligations on their members by resolution, usually by qualified majorities. Such obligations derive their authority from the international agreement constituting the organization, and resolutions so adopted by the organization can be seen as "secondary sources" of international law for its members.

. . . .

i. *International agreements codifying or contributing to customary law.* International agreements constitute practice of states and as such can contribute to the growth of customary law under Subsection (2). [cit]. Some multilateral agreements may come to be law for non-parties that do not actively dissent. That may be the effect where a multilateral agreement is designed for adherence by states generally, is widely accepted, and is not rejected by a significant number of important states. A wide network of similar bilateral arrangements on a subject may constitute practice and also result in customary law. . . .

j. *Conflict between international agreement and customary law.* Customary law and law made by international agreement have equal authority as international law. Unless the parties evince a contrary intention, a rule established by agreement supersedes for them a prior inconsistent rule of customary international law. However, an agreement will not supersede a prior rule of customary law that is a peremptory norm of international law; and an agreement will not supersede customary law if the agreement is invalid because it violates such a peremptory norm. *See* Comment k. A new rule of customary law will supersede inconsistent obligations created by earlier agreement if the parties so intend and the intention is clearly manifested. . . .

k. *Peremptory norms of international law (jus cogens).* Some rules of international law are recognized by the international community of states as peremptory, permitting no derogation. These rules prevail over and invalidate international agreements and other rules of international law in conflict with them. Such a peremptory norm is subject to modification only by a subsequent norm of international law having the same character. It is generally accepted that the principles of the United Nations Charter prohibiting the use of force [cit] have the character of *jus cogens.* . .

l. *General principles as secondary source of law.* Much of international law, whether customary or constituted by agreement, reflects principles analogous to those found in the major legal systems of the world, and historically may derive from them or from a more remote common origin. [cit]. General principles common to systems of national law may be resorted to as an independent source of law. That source of law may be important when there has not been practice by states sufficient to give the particular principle status as customary law and the principle has not been legislated by general international agreement. . . .

Reporters' Notes

. . . .

2. *Customary law.* No definition of customary law has received universal agreement, but the essence of Subsection (2) has wide acceptance. [cit]. Each element in attempted definitions has raised difficulties. There have been philosophical debates about the very basis of the definition: how can practice build law? Most troublesome conceptually has been the circularity in the suggestion that law is built by practice based on a sense of legal obligation: how, it is asked, can there be a sense of legal obligation before the law from which the legal obligation derives has matured? Such conceptual difficulties, however, have not prevented acceptance of customary law essentially as here defined. . . .

Earlier definitions implied that establishment of custom required that the practice of states continue over an extended period of time. That requirement began to lose its force after the Second World War, perhaps because improved communication made the practice of states widely and quickly known, at least where there is broad acceptance and no or little objection. . . . .

The practice of states that builds customary law takes many forms and includes what states do in or through international organizations. [cit]. The United Nations General Assembly in particular has adopted resolutions, declarations, and other statements of principles that in some circumstances contribute to the process of making customary law, insofar as statements and votes of governments are kinds of state practice, [cit], and may be expressions of *opinio juris.* [cit]. The contributions of such resolutions and of the statements and votes supporting them to the lawmaking process will differ widely, depending on factors such as the subject of the resolution, whether it purports to reflect legal principles, how large a majority it commands and how numerous and important are the dissenting states, whether it is widely supported (including in particular the states principally affected), and whether it is later confirmed by other practice.

. . . .

Resolutions that may contribute to customary law are to be distinguished from resolutions that are legally binding on members [cit]. The latter, too, may reflect state practice or *opinio juris,* but they derive their authority from the charter of the organization, an international agreement in which states parties agreed to be bound by some of its acts. International conferences, especially those engaged in codifying customary law, provide occasions for expressions by states as to the law on particular questions. General consensus as to the law at such a conference confirms customary law or contributes to its creation.

The development of customary law has been described as part of a "process of continuous interaction, of continuous demand and response," among decision-makers of different states. These "create expectations that effective power will be restrained and exercised in certain uniformities of pattern. . . . The reciprocal tolerances . . . create the expectations of patterns and uniformity in decision, of practice in accord with rule, commonly regarded as law." [cit].

That a rule of customary law is not binding on any state indicating its dissent during the development of the rule (Comment d) is an accepted application of the traditional principle that international law essentially depends on the consent of states. [cit]. Refusal of states to adopt or acquiesce in a practice has often prevented its development into a principle of customary law, but instances of dissent and exemption from practice that developed into principles of general customary law have been few. . . .

———

Interpretation of treaties is central to an understanding of international intellectual property law. An intellectual property treaty creates obligations that bind the signatory states notwithstanding that the internal law of the signatory differs from that state's international obligations. The customary law of treaties is now codified in the Vienna Convention on the Law of Treaties of 1969. Although the United States has not yet ratified the Vienna Convention, it takes the position that the interpretive provisions of the Convention are largely consistent with the interpretive principles of customary international law.

VIENNA CONVENTION ON THE LAW OF TREATIES
May 23, 1969, 1155 U.N.T.S. 331

Article 26

Every treaty in force is binding upon the parties to it and must be performed by them in good faith.

Article 27

A party may not invoke the provisions of its internal law as justification for its failure to perform a treaty. . . .

Article 31

(1) A treaty shall be interpreted in good faith in accordance with the ordinary meaning to be given to the terms of the treaty in their context and in the light of its object and purpose.

(2) The context for the purpose of the interpretation of a treaty shall comprise, in addition to the text, including its preamble and annexes:

  (a) any agreement relating to the treaty which was made between all the parties in connexion with the conclusion of the treaty;

  (b) any instrument which was made by one or more parties in connexion with the conclusion of the treaty and accepted by the other parties as an instrument related to the treaty.

(3) There shall be taken into account, together with the context:

  (a) any subsequent agreement between the parties regarding the interpretation of the treaty or the application of its provisions;

  (b) any subsequent practice in the application of the treaty which establishes the agreement of the parties regarding its interpretation;

  (c) any relevant rules of international law applicable in the relations between the parties.

. . . .

Article 32

Recourse may be had to supplementary means of interpretation, including the preparatory work of the treaty and the circumstances of its conclusion, in order to confirm the meaning resulting from the application of article 31, or to determine the meaning when the interpretation according to article 31:

(a) leaves the meaning ambiguous or obscure; or

(b) leads to a result which is manifestly absurd or unreasonable.

———

NOTES AND QUESTIONS

(1) **The Objects of Rights and Obligations Under International Law.** Who should be bound by international law in the sense used by Bentham? What premises underlie the Benthamite notion of international law as merely a set of rules agreed among states to regulate their relations inter se? What are the consequences of a philosophy of international law that treats states as the only legitimate actors? Who has rights under such a vision of international law? Who should be bound by an "ethically-derived" set of laws, by the "law of nations" or "customary international law"? Are there circumstances where private actors should be bound by norms of international law? *See* Kadic v. Karadzic, 70 F.3d 232, 239 (2d Cir. 1995).

(2) **State Practice and International Law.** How would you answer the question posed by the Reporters to the Restatement: how and why can practice build law? Is there a reason why practice may play a larger role in the identification of international, as opposed to internal national, law? How should the normative force of such "law" differ, if at all, from provisions of international treaties?

(3) **International Obligations and National Sovereignty.** Why would it be in a state's best interest voluntarily to enter into agreements and assume international legal obligations? To what extent is the acceptance of obligations under international law a derogation from national sovereignty?

§ 2.02 International Intellectual Property Instruments

The earliest efforts to move beyond purely national protection of intellectual property involved bilateral agreements between two countries. In response to some of the deficiencies of bilateral agreements, the late nineteenth century saw the development of multilateral agreements. These multilateral intellectual property treaties established unions of member countries that reached agreement on a number of common principles. They did not supplant national legislation; rather, they imposed upon member countries certain obligations as to how they will treat each other's products. As noted in Chapter 1, the two most important of these treaties were originally negotiated in the late nineteenth century. They have been updated periodically, and are still in force.*

———

* To complicate matters further, the different revisions are known as Acts, for example the 1971 Paris Act of the Berne Convention. Each new Act requires a new accession in order for a country to be bound by the new standards it contains. This means that different countries that are all party to Berne or Paris may be bound by different requirements. As a practical matter, however, because the TRIPS Agreement requires the application of the most recent Act of Berne and Paris, this latest version will be applied by virtually all Berne and Paris members.

They are the Berne Convention for the Protection of Literary and Artistic Works and the Paris Convention for the Protection of Industrial Property. A number of other multilateral intellectual property treaties, narrower in coverage and in membership than the Berne and Paris Conventions, have been concluded since then.

In the late twentieth century, different types of multilateral instruments governing intellectual property began to emerge. They were the outgrowth of a recognition that intellectual property had become important not only in itself but as a major component of global commerce. As a result, countries negotiating agreements on general commercial issues, such as trade and investment, began to incorporate provisions dealing with intellectual property. Some of these agreements are open to any country to join; others are regional agreements concluded among closed groups of countries with geographical ties. Similarly, when the European Union ("EU") was created in order to achieve a common market, intellectual property laws were identified as a potential barrier to trade. As a result, the EU has taken a number of initiatives intended to facilitate the acquisition and exploitation of intellectual property community-wide.

The most important trade agreement incorporating intellectual property provisions is the Agreement on Trade-Related Aspects of Intellectual Property Rights, known as the TRIPS Agreement. The TRIPS Agreement is an annex to the agreement creating the World Trade Organization, which itself was an outgrowth of the Uruguay Round of the General Agreement on Tariffs and Trade. TRIPS was negotiated over the course of five years, and concluded as part of the Uruguay Round in 1994. It contains provisions relating to copyrights (and related rights, in the terminology of many countries), patents, trademarks, trade secrets, and semiconductor chips. It incorporates most of the substantive obligations of the Berne and Paris Conventions.

All of these types of instruments co-exist today. Accordingly, an entity that seeks to exploit intellectual property outside the borders of its own country, or a lawyer advising such an entity, should be aware of the existence and coverage of a range of treaties: those relating to intellectual property specifically, to trade, and to investment; bilateral and multilateral agreements; and directives that harmonize the laws of the EU member states. All are described in this book, and many are reproduced in the Documentary Supplement.

Each of these multilateral treaties is administered by one or more international intergovernmental body. These organizations arrange and host meetings of their member countries to discuss, apply or update the relevant treaty, may assist in interpreting the treaty's provisions, and in the case of treaties which establish some sort of procedural mechanism like a filing system, actually operate the system. *See infra* Chapter 6. Their budgets are overseen by the governments of their member states. Depending on the organization, operating funds are provided by a combination of government contributions and/or by private sector fees for services. Each organization has an administrative staff, known as the International Bureau or Secretariat, which includes professionals from a variety of different member states.

The multilateral intellectual property treaties, including the Berne Convention and the Paris Convention, are administered by the World

Intellectual Property Organization ("WIPO") (known in French as the *Organisation Mondiale de la Propriété Intellectuelle* ("OMPI")). Some are administered in conjunction with other organizations, such as UNESCO and the International Labor Organization ("ILO"). The TRIPS Agreement, as an annex to the World Trade Organization Agreement, is administered by the TRIPS Council of the World Trade Organization ("WTO"). These institutions are described in more detail below. *See infra* § 2.03.

Eligibility to join a treaty depends on the terms of the treaty itself. The TRIPS Agreement requires membership in the WTO; admission to the WTO requires agreement by the member states, upon satisfaction of a number of criteria relating to all of the trade issues covered by the WTO Agreement itself, not simply intellectual property. Regional agreements are limited to countries within the defined region. As a general matter, countries are expected or required to bring their laws into compliance with treaty obligations before joining.

As a practical matter, willingness to adhere to the multilateral intellectual property treaties has often been determined by balance of trade considerations: the country's status as primarily an exporter or an importer of the relevant form of intellectual property. The first signatories to the Berne Convention were primarily European countries, and the convention's rules were modeled on European *droit d'auteur* systems. Historically, developing countries have been reluctant to accede, at various times demanding special rules and concessions before they would do so. It was not until the late nineteenth century, for example, that the United States was ready to protect any foreign works within its borders, and not until nearly 100 years later that it joined the Berne Convention. Today, as the leading exporter of intellectual property in the world, the United States is a strong advocate for treaty membership and implementation.

The specific inclusion of intellectual property on the trade agenda in the 1980s, however, tipped the balance further toward widespread treaty membership. The advantages of various trade partnerships gave countries additional incentives, apart from an interest in protecting their own intellectual property exports. Joining the WTO, for example, provides many trade benefits, such as most favored nation status, that have been viewed by many countries as outweighing any detriment from providing protection to foreign intellectual property. Today, membership in the major multilateral conventions is quite high. Few countries that are substantial exporters or importers of intellectual property have not yet been brought into the international intellectual property community. Full compliance, of course, is another story, which will be discussed in Chapters 3-5.

§ 2.03   Leading International Institutions and Actors

As suggested above, the development of international intellectual property is undertaken by an increasingly broad range of institutions. These institutions include intergovernmental organizations, regional groupings of nation-states, international trade bodies, and private international law reform bodies. As intellectual property assumes a place of greater significance in social and economic policy, the number of relevant institutions multiplies. What follows is a description of the primary institutional "players" involved in the process of developing international intellectual property law and policy.

[A]   The World Intellectual Property Organization

The World Intellectual Property Organization ("WIPO") was established in 1967, succeeding to the role of the Bureaux for the Protection of Intellectual Property (which was best known by its French acronym "BIRPI"), and is charged with "promoting the protection of intellectual property throughout the world through cooperation among states and, where appropriate, in collaboration with any other international organization." Convention Establishing the World Intellectual Property Organization signed at Stockholm, July 14, 1967 and as amended on September 28, 1979, art. 3(i). WIPO is an intergovernmental organization of 175 member nations with an International Bureau based in Geneva, and is a specialized agency of the United Nations. Prior to the TRIPS Agreement, WIPO was the dominant multilateral forum in which international intellectual property law was developed, and it remains one of the two leading fora along with the WTO (the latter including both the TRIPS Council and WTO Dispute Settlement Body).

Most of the major multinational intellectual property agreements establish unions consisting of all states that have adhered to the treaty in question. (Thus, for example, the international body responsible for the Paris Convention is referred to as the Paris Union.) The union in question is governed by an Assembly, consisting of the adherent countries, and by an Executive Committee. Since 1967, the WIPO has, as noted above, been the administrator of most major unions and treaties, with the principal exception of the TRIPS Agreement. (And, as we will see below, the WTO and the WIPO have concluded an agreement, envisaged by Article 68 of TRIPS, that gives WIPO an important role in the TRIPS system.)

WIPO thus remains a forum (arguably still the primary forum) for the drafting, discussion, revision and conclusion of new intellectual property treaties, as well as the development of intellectual property norms through less formal lawmaking processes (such as the adoption of resolutions or the promulgation of model laws). In addition, WIPO offers significant specialized expertise to countries seeking to develop or improve their intellectual property laws. Indeed, this "technical" or "education" function is becoming a bigger part of WIPO's role. In recent years, WIPO has also established an Arbitration Center for administration of private (i.e., involving individuals rather than states) international intellectual property disputes. Although this center was underused at first, the adjudication of disputes between trademark owners and domain name holders has since late 1999 been a boon to the center. The domain name-related activities of the center are discussed in detail in Chapter 7.

[B]   The World Trade Organization

One of the most significant developments in modern international intellectual property law has been the conclusion of the TRIPS Agreement. The TRIPS Agreement augmented the minimum standards of intellectual property protection found in previous international agreements, which is notable in and of itself. But perhaps more importantly, the TRIPS Agreement, which is an Annex to the Agreement Establishing the World Trade Organization (the WTO), brought intellectual property within the institutional infrastructure of the world's multilateral trading system. This was important not only because it provided certain countries non-intellectual property related incentives to join the community of intellectual property respecting nations, but also because disputes regarding compliance with TRIPS were subsumed within the dispute settlement system of the WTO. We will study the WTO dispute settlement system (involving both dispute settlement panels and a standing Appellate Body) in detail in Chapter 5. For present purposes, it should be noted only that decisions rendered under the WTO dispute settlement system are backed up by effective enforcement mechanisms; member states found to be in violation of TRIPS provisions must revise their laws under pain of penalties that include the imposition of trade sanctions.

Pre-TRIPS, the position was quite different. Proposals to amend the Paris Convention to submit disputes to the Permanent Court of International Justice, the predecessor to the International Court of Justice, were made as far back as 1925. But the United States vehemently opposed the proposal, and it was not until the 1967 revision that the Paris Convention contained the possibility of referring disputes between states to the International Court of Justice. *See* Paris Convention art. 28. Article 28 has, however, never been invoked; neither has Article 33 of the Berne Convention, which contains a similar provision. Of itself, the incorporation of international intellectual property obligations within an effective dispute settlement mechanism thus makes the WTO an important part of the modern international intellectual property system. The dispute settlement system is, however, only part of the WTO apparatus that contributes to the ongoing development of international intellectual property law: another important body is the TRIPS Council.

THE TRIPS COUNCIL[*]

The Council for TRIPS is the body, open to all Members of the WTO, that has responsibility for the administration of the [TRIPS] Agreement, in particular monitoring the operation of the agreement. The council also constitutes a forum for consultations on any problems relating to TRIPS arising between countries as well as for clarifying and interpreting provisions of the agreement. The aim

---

[*] This discussion of the TRIPS Council is excerpted from Matthijs Geuze & Hannu Wager, *WTO Dispute Settlement Practice Relating to the TRIPS Agreement*, J. INT'L ECON. L. 347, 382-84 (1999). Copyright 1999, Oxford University Press. Reprinted with permission.

is, whenever possible, to resolve differences between countries without the need for formal recourse to dispute settlement. The council meets in Geneva formally some five times a year as well as informally as necessary.

One of the characteristics of the former GATT and now of the WTO is the detailed and continuous follow-up of the implementation of obligations and the monitoring of compliance with them. The underlying belief is that unless there is detailed monitoring of compliance with international commitments, those commitments will be worth much less. Monitoring of compliance in the council is done in two main ways.

First, the TRIPS Council is a body in which any member can raise any issue relating to compliance by other parties. This has happened on a number of occasions, either in relation to the practices of a specific country or the application of a specific provision.

The second approach to monitoring compliance is a systematic examination of each member's national implementing legislation by the other members, involving the notification and review of the legislation of members.

Article 63.2 of the TRIPS Agreement requires members to notify the laws and regulations made effective by that member pertaining to the subject matter of the agreement to the Council for TRIPS in order to assist the Council in its review of the operation of the agreement. Laws and regulations should be notified promptly as of the time that the corresponding substantive obligation starts to apply. Given the difficulty of examining legislation relevant to many of the enforcement obligations in the agreement, members have undertaken, in addition to notifying legislative texts, to provide information on how they are meeting these obligations by responding to a checklist of twenty-five questions.

These notifications are the basis for reviews of implementing legislation carried out by the council. The council completed in the year 1997 its first review exercise that focused on those WTO members who no longer benefitted from a transition period, i.e. the developed countries. The council continued in the first part of 1998 [with] the review of six members whose legislation had already been subject to the 1996/97 review exercise but for whom the review had not been completed by the end of 1997. Including the questions of the Checklist of Issues on Enforcement, the review of the legislation of the thirty-three members taken up in the period between 1996 and the first part of 1998 generated responses to some 5,000 questions recorded in some 3,000 pages of documentation. Furthermore, the council reviewed in the autumn of 1998 the legislation of three members who had negotiated their accession to the WTO and, while applying a TRIPS transition period, had not yet been subject to the review.

One of the benefits of the review mechanism is that it is seen as an important vehicle for resolving issues that might otherwise become the subject of formal dispute settlement proceedings. Some of the more specific benefits include the *ex ante* effect of greater care in drafting legislation from the knowledge that new legislation will be reviewed, and the clearing up of misunderstandings about a country's legislation.

The review process also provides an opportunity to identify deficiencies in notified laws and regulations, as well as differences in interpretation. In a significant number of instances, the country whose legislation was under review has been willing to accept that it still has further work to do in order to make its laws conform fully with the WTO's rules. Some of the differences in interpretation will be discussed bilaterally. If they are not resolved in that way, they could eventually turn into formal disputes under the WTO dispute settlement proceedings.

A number of issues that have been subject to the invocation of the dispute settlement procedure have also been the focus of attention in the review process. For example, in the review of legislation on copyright and related rights, all members that were reviewed were asked to explain how they provide protection to pre-existing works, performances and phonograms. Similarly, in the review of legislation on enforcement, most members were asked to provide additional information on the way provisional measures could be ordered *inaudita altera parte*. Certain issues that were initially raised in the review of a given country were subsequently taken up in the dispute settlement proceedings.[98]

Consequently, in addition to panel and Appellate Body reports and notified mutually agreed solutions, useful information relevant to questions of interpretation of TRIPS provisions may also be obtained from the questions raised on the floor of the TRIPS Council and the answers given by members.

[C]   The European Union

[1]   Background to the European Union

The European Union ("EU") is presently comprised of fifteen member states: Austria, Belgium, Denmark, Finland, France, Germany, Greece, Ireland, Italy, Luxembourg, The Netherlands, Portugal, Spain, Sweden and the United Kingdom. The EU, and the intellectual property law that it develops, has over the past decade become a significant variable in the intellectual property lawmaking process internationally. The imprint of EU legislation can be found not only on the intellectual property laws in the member states of the union; EU legislation has also influenced the shape of national intellectual property laws outside the EU, as well as multinational intellectual property agreements. This influence arises in various ways. Non-EU countries that are within the European Economic Area ("EEA")—which is comprised of the EU countries plus Iceland, Norway and Lichtenstein—must also comply with various laws of the EU including its intellectual property laws. The proposed enlargement of the EU to accept new members, principally from Central and Eastern Europe, is not too distant, and other countries in the area have thus felt a need to align their laws with those of the EU. *See* Thomas Helbling, *Shapes as Trade Marks?—The*

---

[98]It should be noted that the review does not, either explicitly or implicitly, lead to the granting of a "clean bill of health" to a member's legislation. The fact that a matter was not raised or, if raised, not pursued in the follow-up to the review does not in any way prejudice other members' right to raise the matter subsequently and, ultimately, have recourse to dispute settlement.

Struggle to Register Three-Dimensional Signs: A Comparative Study of United Kingdom and Swiss Law, 1997 INTELL. PROP. Q. 413, 417 (discussing reform of Swiss trademark law). Finally, the intensive legislative activity of the EU in recent years means that the EU has developed a series of laws which serve as useful models for countries seeking to introduce or modernize their own intellectual property laws.

Recent legislative developments involving intellectual property law in the EU have also found an echo in the United States. To cite only a couple of recent examples, the EU Database Directive adopted in 1996, *see infra* Chapter 4, has framed the discussion of database protection both on the multinational level and within the United States. Similarly, the Term Directive, which extended the term of copyright protection within Europe to life of the author plus seventy years, is in large part what motivated the parallel Sonny Bono Copyright Term Extension Act in the United States. *See infra* Chapter 4. Indeed, the extent of this influence led one scholar to write that there was a need for independent congressional investigation of the limits of cultural policy so as "to free U.S. innovation law from the grip of unelected foreign bureaucrats who have surrendered to sectoral protectionist demands." J. H. Reichman, *The Duration of Copyright and the Limits of Cultural Policy,* 14 CARD. ARTS & ENT. L.J. 625, 653 (1996).

Although the European Economic Community (and with it the collective grouping called the European Communities) was established in 1957 by the Treaty of Rome, an international agreement concluded among six countries, the entity that we now call the EU was only established in 1991 by the Treaty on European Union (the Maastricht Treaty). The union rests on three so-called "pillars":

(1) the European Communities (i.e., the former European Economic Community now renamed the "European Community" or "EC", the European Coal and Steel Community and the European Atomic Energy Community);

(2) the process of formal intergovernmental cooperation in the fields of foreign and security policy; and

(3) the process of formal intergovernmental cooperation in justice and home affairs (such as asylum policy, police co-operation).

Strictly speaking, intellectual property legislation is pursued through the legislative workings of the EC. The articles of the Treaty of Rome, the foundational document of the European Communities in 1957, have undergone successive revision over the course of the last forty-two years and are now codified in the EC Treaty. In 1998, these revisions were systematically consolidated, causing extensive renumbering of the treaty's articles. If we have edited pre-1998 EU materials (such as pre-98 court opinions) to reflect the new numbering, this editing is indicated through the customary use of square brackets; references to "ex-Article __" are references to the number of the relevant article in the older text.

[2]   The Institutions of the European Union

The European Commission is central to the European project, and is essentially the administrative branch of the EU. The Council and the European Parliament require a proposal from the Commission before adopting legislation. The Commission is also central to the enforcement of EU law, by ensuring that member states are complying with their obligations under that law. Finally, the Commission has responsibility for negotiating and monitoring the union's international trade relationships. The Commission is based in Brussels, has twenty members, two each from the big five countries (France, Germany, Italy, Spain and the United Kingdom) and one from each of the other ten member states. Each commissioner serves a five year term. The appointed nature of the Commission has led to claims of a "democracy deficit" in the EU. Recent institutional reforms have attempted to remedy that by ensuring greater oversight by the elected body, the Parliament. The full Commission has to be approved by Parliament before its members can take office, and they can (as seen by the political maneuvering in 1999) be required to resign en bloc by a parliamentary vote of censure. Until recently, the Commission was divided into twenty-six numbered directorates-general ("DG"s). As of October 1, 1999, under a new organizational structure implemented by Commission President Romano Prodi, the DGs are now referred to by title rather than by number. Each DG is headed by a director-general, reporting to a commissioner who has the political and administrative responsibility for the work of the DG. Responsibility for intellectual property law is assigned to the DG with primary responsibility for the internal market (formerly called DG XV) and additional relevant activity can be found in the Information Society DG.

The Council of the European Communities is comprised of fifteen members, one from each member state government. The precise membership of the Council depends upon the subject matter before it. If the matter relates to finance, the fifteen governments will send their finance ministers; if the matter relates to transport, the fifteen governments will send their transport ministers. There are twenty-five of these different "subject-matters," with intellectual property being dealt with at the Internal Market Council meetings. The Presidency of the Council rotates among the fifteen member states, changing every six months. Voting in the Council is weighted, with the big four countries (Germany, France, the U.K. and Italy) receiving ten votes, Spain eight votes and the smaller countries receiving lesser numbers reflecting their different sizes.

The European Parliament sits in Strasbourg, France, but its committees also meet frequently in Brussels for ease of access to the Commission. The role of the European Parliament in the lawmaking process has increased as the EU has matured, partly because of the Parliament's status as the only directly elected body involved in the legislative process. The numbers of MEPs from each country corresponds approximately with that country's population, although the MEPs sit and act by political grouping rather than by nationality.

The European Court of Justice is discussed separately below.

[3]   Legislative Instruments

The legislation of the EU may take two primary forms. A *Regulation* has general application, is binding in its entirety and is directly applicable in all member states. It does not require national implementing legislation to become effective in member states. It is essentially a federal law of Europe. A *Directive*, in contrast, is not directly applicable in the member states. Its provisions normally require positive implementation (called "transposition") in the domestic laws of the member states.* Article 249 (ex-Article 189) provides that "A Directive shall be binding as to the result to be achieved . . . but shall leave to the national authorities the choice of form and methods". A directive is not unlike a model state law, but one that states are obliged to enact (with some minor room for tailoring to the specialities of their own system). Directives must be given effect by a stated date by each of the member states. If the member state fails to transpose the directive by that date, the Commission may bring an action against the member state before the Court of Justice.

[4]   Legislative Process

The European Commission initiates all legislation of the EC. Without the Commission, there is no legislation. The degree of involvement of the Council and the Parliament varies depending upon which provision of the Treaty of Rome the Commission rests its authority to propose the legislation. Different provisions implicate different legislative procedures. The precise legislative procedure involved is set out in great detail in the relevant authorizing provision, but there are two basic paradigms.

Under *the consultation procedure,* the opinion of Parliament must be obtained by the Council before acting on and adopting a legislative proposal of the Commission. But that is the sum of the Parliament's formal involvement. The Parliament thus has little ability to affect legislation that is pursued under this procedure; unanimous approval by the Council is, however, required. This procedure is followed, for example, where legislation rests upon the authority of Article 308 (ex-Article 235) of the EC Treaty, which might be viewed as the "Necessary and Proper" clause of the Treaty of Rome. Article 308 authorizes appropriate Community measures if necessary to attain the objectives of the Community even if the Treaty has not provided the necessary powers. This authority has been used to enact Community-level intellectual property regulations creating unitary EU-wide rights. *See infra* Chapter 6.

However, the bulk of the intellectual property legislation enacted or considered by the EU has taken the form of harmonization directives. Harmonization of the laws of member states is essential if the territorial nature of intellectual property rights is not to frustrate the free movement of goods, an

---

*The European Court of Justice has held that certain provisions of directives may be treated as directly creating rights in member states, notwithstanding lack of adequate transposition by the member state in question, under the doctrine of "direct effect". This doctrine should not be confused with the question of direct applicability.

objective which lies at the heart of the EU. The harmonization of intellectual property laws among the member states has typically been attempted by the Commission pursuant to Article 95 (ex-Article 100a) of the EC Treaty, which provides authority to enact legislation necessary to complete the internal market. Legislation proposed under that Article involves the *codecision* (or *joint legislative*) procedure. This procedure, which enhanced the role of the Parliament in the making of legislation, was introduced by the Maastricht Treaty in 1992. With respect to legislation proposed under this procedure, Parliament has a veto: if it rejects the so-called "common position" of the Council, the Council cannot adopt the legislation. Although Parliament has a greater ability to influence and halt legislation under this procedure, the Council is able to act by a qualified majority (i.e., with the support of states possessing a defined number of votes in the Council). Although Parliament has the power, by an absolute majority of votes cast, to veto legislation considered under the codecision procedure, it has exercised that prerogative only rarely. It *has* used the power, however. In 1995, Parliament used its power under the codecision procedure to block enactment of the first effort at a Biotechnology Patent Directive. *See infra* Chapter 3.

[5]   The Judicial Process

The European Court of Justice ("ECJ"), which sits in Luxembourg, is comprised of fifteen judges (one from each state), appointed for six year terms. The president of the court is selected by the members of the court themselves, and he or she will serve in that capacity for a renewable term of three years. In 1989, *the Court of First Instance* ("CFI") was created to help the ECJ deal with an increasingly busy workload, but there is no established system of inferior EU "federal" courts. The composition of the Court of First Instance is likewise fifteen judges appointed for six year terms, and again the president is chosen by the judges themselves. The court (and the Court of First Instance) sits in chambers of three or five, but can sit in plenary session when a member state or community institution (i.e., the Commission, Council or Parliament) that is party to the case requests that, or if the case is particularly complex. It was announced in December 1999 that the European Parliament is to consider interim measures to lessen the workload of the ECJ by increasing the responsibility of the Court of First Instance. Proposals are being considered to increase the number of CFI judges from fifteen to twenty-one, to assist mainly with intellectual property cases.

In the early stages of the case, the president assigns one judge as rapporteur, and an advocate-general is assigned to the case. There are nine advocates-general. The advocates-general listen to the argument along with the judges, and then deliver their opinions on the case in advance of the court issuing a decision. The opinion of the advocate-general is often extremely influential (and typically more lengthy than the judgement issued by the Court). The decisions of the Court are reached by majority vote, but no dissenting opinions are issued and judgments are signed by all the judges who participated in the case. The judgments of the Court tend to be more cryptic and more sparsely reasoned than U.S. opinions. The court does not adhere to stare decisis, but it does follow the continental European philosophy of *jurisprudence constante* in seeking to have some uniformity in the application of the law.

The Court of Justice has jurisdiction to hear a variety of types of cases, the most important of which are:

(1) *Enforcement Actions.* An action may be brought under Article 226 (ex-Article 169) against a member state for failure to fulfil an obligation under Community law. *See, e.g.,* Case C-213/98, Commission v. Ireland, Eur. Cur. L. 36, Nov. 1999 (E.C.J. Oct. 12, 1999) (upholding Commission action against Ireland under Article 169 for failure to implement Rental Rights Directive and rejecting Irish defense that implementation was awaiting full-scale review of Irish copyright legislation.) This will normally be brought by the Commission, but may also be brought (under ex-Article 170) by another member state. The remedy is to require compliance or, if that does not occur, to impose fines.

(2) *Preliminary Reference Procedure.* Perhaps the most important jurisdiction of the Court of Justice for the purpose of intellectual property law has been its "preliminary reference" jurisdiction under Article 234 (ex-Article 177).[*] Issues of EU law arise with increasing frequency in litigation in EU member states. In order to prevent divergent national court decisions from leading to conflicting interpretations of Community law, if an issue of Community law arises before a national court that national court may, and in some cases must, seek a preliminary ruling from the Court of Justice on the relevant question. Although the reference is made by the national court, the private litigants in the national proceedings may appear before the Court of Justice when it hears the reference. Article 234 does not establish the Court of Justice as a court of final appeal above the national court systems (at least not conceptually); this is a reference procedure common in many jurisdictions. The national court will frame a question to be answered by the Court of Justice; the Court of Justice will apply the law and provide a ruling in the form of an answer to that question; and the national court will then apply the relevant law to the case at hand taking into account the answer of the Court.

[6]   The Relationship Between National and Union Law

One of the most important early decisions of the Court of Justice was to declare the supremacy of Community law. If there is a conflict between applicable Community law and a provision of national law, the national law will be subordinated to Community law. These decisions, in the formative years of the Community, essentially wove a Supremacy Clause into the constitutional fabric of the Union. And it is through this principle that the European Court of Justice developed case law on intellectual property law. The Court strictly has no jurisdiction to interpret or rule on matters of national law absent harmonization of those laws by Community legislation or a conflict between those national laws and the laws of the EC. In the early years, before EU

---

[*]The jurisdiction of the Court of First Instance is more limited; most importantly it does not include the preliminary reference procedure.

harmonization of national intellectual property laws, the Court reached intellectual property issues primarily in the context of analyzing their consonance with the competition law principles found in Articles 81-82 (ex-Articles 85-86) of the EC Treaty or with the free movement principles found in Articles 28 & 30 (ex-Articles 30 & 36). The latter relation—with free trade principles—took the Court on variety of detours before developing its current exhaustion jurisprudence. Perhaps because this was the context in which the early case law arose—whether intellectual property rights interfered with higher Community objectives—the Court was seen as suspicious of broad intellectual property rights. The Court's case load tended to place it in the role of preventing the assertion of national intellectual property rights in such a way as to partition the EU market. The Court still considers intellectual property issues in that context,[*] but in the last few years, an increasingly large part of the Court's intellectual property caseload has been generated by the need to assist national courts in interpreting the various intellectual property harmonization directives as they are given effect in national law.

[7]   The Evolution of EU Attitudes to Intellectual Property Rights

The foundations of the EU are built on principles of free trade and a common market. As noted above, the initial attention to intellectual property law by the EU was thus prompted by a concern that the territorially-founded intellectual property laws of the different member states did not operate to restrict or impede the free flow of goods or the functioning of an efficient market. From that early perspective, reform of intellectual property law has assumed a more affirmative place on the EU agenda. As the political objectives of the Union have widened to include (more explicitly) such matters as industry competitiveness, the ability of intellectual property protection to encourage innovative activity in Europe has received a greater prominence, particularly on the legislative side of the ledger. In the late 1980s and the 1990s, therefore, the activity in the EU in connection with intellectual property reform was quite hectic. And the legislative developments since 1988 have all, for the most part, resulted in greater and more consistent protection of intellectual property rights in the EU.

As noted above, the largest part of the legislative agenda in the field of intellectual property law has been harmonization directives. These directives were brought forward by the Commission as part of efforts to complete the "internal market" by 1992. The harmonization that has been effected by these instruments has tended to be partial or fragmentary in nature. Thus, for example, the Trademark Directive harmonized registered trademark laws, but left untouched unregistered trademark or unfair competition laws. Similarly,

---

[*] The Court has also considered the concordance of national intellectual property laws with other provisions of the EC Treaty. See, *e.g.*, Phil Collins v. Imtrat, 1994 F.S.R. 166 (E.C.J. 1993) (holding that because discrimination on grounds of nationality is prohibited under the EC Treaty, the application of reciprocity requirements to deny protection to citizens of other EU states under multinational intellectual property treaties was a violation of EU law). *See infra* Chapter 4.

the early reforms of copyright law were sector-specific, targeted harmonization; the Commission only rarely included so-called "horizontal provisions," which would apply to all copyrighted works, in harmonization directives. For example, the software directive establishes levels of copyright protection for software; the database directive does the same for databases.

In the case of industrial property rights, which are largely based upon registration, the Commission has sought to go further and enact unitary Community-wide rights. The alternative of harmonizing member states' laws (which had been used in eradicating differences in national protection accorded computer software, databases and semiconductor topographies) would be inadequate in this context. Harmonization in itself would not preclude the partitioning of markets that territorial protection creates; and where registered rights are involved, unlike the rights by which databases or software were protected, harmonization would not substantially reduce the costs involved in applying for rights separately in each country. The introduction of a single, autonomous law obviates the problems wrought by territorial protection. The first of these "unitary Community-wide laws" was created in 1994, when the EU enacted the Trademark Regulation, which created the Community Trade Mark. Applications for a Community Trademark registration are determined by the Office for Harmonization in the Internal Market ("OHIM") which was set up in Alicante, Spain. Also now pending is a Regulation that would create unitary EU-wide design rights. And in June 1997, the Commission issued a Green Paper on reform of the patent system that asked whether it was time to introduce a unitary Community patent. *See infra* § 6.04[A][4].

[8]   The Status of the EU in International Intellectual Property Law

The EU may sign international agreements along with the member states. The Commission has responsibility for negotiating and monitoring the Union's international trade relationships. In *Opinion 1/94 on the Agreement Establishing the World Trade Organization*, [1995] 1 C.M.L.R. 205 (E.C.J. 1995), the European Court of Justice was asked to determine who had the competence to conclude and sign various agreements incorporated into or annexed to the World Trade Organization Agreement, including TRIPS. The Commission argued that the negotiation and ratification of TRIPS fell exclusively within the competence of the Community because of internal Community harmonization in the services sector, and that consequently the individual member states should not have co-signed the TRIPS agreement. The Court concluded that because there had only been partial harmonization achieved in the field of intellectual property, the Community and the member states were jointly competent to conclude TRIPS. Accordingly, the Commission (on behalf of the EU) and the member states each signed the agreements.

The incomplete federal status of the EU has raised problems in determining whether it has a right to a separate vote in international intellectual property assemblies. The newly formed Standing Committee on the Law of Trademarks, Industrial Designs and Geographical Indications decided at its first session in

Geneva in July 1998 that membership in the Standing Committee would also be extended to the EU, provided that it shall not have the right to vote. Different solutions have been adopted in different contexts, such as in the negotiation of the Madrid Protocol and the WIPO Copyright Treaty. *See infra* Chapters 4 & 6.

[D]   UNESCO

The United Nations Educational, Scientific and Cultural Organization ("UNESCO") came into being at the conclusion of the Second World War and currently has 188 member states. The principal goal of UNESCO is to contribute to peace and security in the world by promoting collaboration among nations through education, science, culture and communication. The founding documents of the Organization declare that:

> Since wars begin in the minds of men, it is in the minds of men that the defences of peace must be constructed. . . A peace based exclusively upon the political and economic arrangements of governments would not be a peace which could secure the unanimous, lasting and sincere support of the peoples of the world, and the peace must therefore be founded, if it is not to fail, upon the intellectual and moral solidarity of mankind.

In addition to acting as a forum for discussion of these issues, which inevitably impinge upon matters of intellectual property law and policy, UNESCO provides technical assistance to member states and prepares the way for the adoption of international instruments pertaining to matters within its remit.   The Organization also serves as administrator of the Universal Copyright Convention.

UNESCO is served by a Secretariat based in Paris and in sixty different offices scattered throughout the world; the Secretariat implements decisions taken by the member states in setting the Organization's agenda. UNESCO serves as an important link to a large number of non-governmental organizations with which it has official relations (and other NGOs with which it has informal relations).

[E]   OECD

The Organisation for Economic Co-operation and Development ("OECD") consists of twenty-nine member countries, largely from the developed world. The OECD provides a forum for member governments to discuss economic and social policy, including issues relating to intellectual property protection and ecommerce. Its role is as much to provide the opportunity for policy discussion as to produce formal international agreements. Although member states tend to be wealthier nations, membership in the OECD is conditioned only upon a country's commitment to a market economy and a pluralistic democracy. The original membership has expanded from Europe and North America, and now includes Japan, Australia, New Zealand, Finland, Mexico, the Czech Republic, Hungary, Poland and Korea.

The work of the organization and its constituent governments is supported by a Secretariat based in Paris. The work of the OECD Secretariat is financed by the member countries, with contributions calculated according to the weight of the member state's economy. (The United States is the biggest contributor followed by Japan.) The Secretariat, which is comprised of economists, scientists, lawyers and other professional staff, produces a wide range of data and research reports for use by the governments in the formulation of economic policies. Member countries meet and exchange information in committees; countries are represented either by government ministers or by personnel from the member's permanent delegation to the OECD. The principal (and decision-making) organ of the OECD is the Council, which meets at ministerial level annually. (A representative of the European Commission now attends these meetings along with a representative from each member state.)

As intellectual property becomes a more significant part of economic policy, the OECD has afforded the topic greater attention. At present, the question of ecommerce in particular is the subject of OECD study and thus the policies and decisions of the Organization, consisting as it does of extremely influential and powerful countries, will help to shape the principles of intellectual property law at the heart of the digital revolution.

[F]   The Hague Conference on Private International Law

The first session of the Hague Conference on private international law was convened in 1893 by the Netherlands government. The Conference entered into a new era in 1955 with the entry into force of a statute which made the Conference a permanent intergovernmental organization. Since 1956, regular plenary sessions have been held every four years, the nineteenth of which met in 2000. The purpose of the Hague Conference is "to work for the progressive unification of the rules of private international law", primarily by the negotiation and drafting of multilateral treaties in various aspects of private international law. Thus, the Conference has addressed matters of international judicial and administrative co-operation (such as service of process or taking of evidence abroad), conflict of laws, and jurisdiction and enforcement of foreign judgments. This last topic is currently under heated discussion, and a draft convention under consideration contains provisions targeted particularly at international intellectual property litigation. *See infra* Chapter 7.

The initial research work of the Conference is undertaken by a permanent Secretariat based in the Hague, with the early drafts of proposed conventions prepared by special commissions made up of governmental experts. The drafts are then discussed and adopted at a plenary session of the Hague Conference, which is a diplomatic conference. The texts adopted are brought together in a Final Act that is signed by the delegations. Under the rules of procedure of the plenary sessions each member state has one vote. Decisions are taken by a majority of the votes cast by the delegations of member states which are present at the vote.

Formally, the Netherlands standing government committee on private international law sets the agenda for the plenary sessions, but in practice the special commissions of governmental experts meeting between sessions make recommendations to the plenary sessions which are considered and acted on by the plenary sessions.

The Hague Conference maintains continuing contacts with a number of international organizations involved in private international lawmaking, including the United Nations Commission on International Trade Law ("UNCITRAL") and the International Institute for the Unification of Private Law ("UNIDROIT").

§ 2.04   The Negotiation of Intellectual Property Treaties

The treaty negotiation process itself is an interesting and important part of the landscape of international intellectual property law. Bilateral negotiations are relatively simple, involving two countries working together each to gain certain benefits. As might be expected, the multilateral version becomes more complex both procedurally and substantively, as a greater number of diverse approaches and viewpoints must be heard and accommodated.

Bilateral agreements come about when two countries each sees something to be gained from making mutual promises. Some bilateral agreements relate specifically to one or more forms of intellectual property, such as the copyright agreement recently concluded between the United States and Vietnam. Others are agreements on trade or investment issues, which include aspects of intellectual property rights. Some developed countries prepare model agreements covering particular subjects, which are then adapted to the circumstances of the negotiating partner. With any of these bilateral agreements, representatives from the two countries' governments work together informally over an undefined period of time until they reach agreement.

Regional agreements almost by definition are trade agreements. Typically, contiguous or neighboring countries in a particular geographic region decide to work out the terms and conditions to remove market barriers between them. Often these terms include agreements on how to treat each other's intellectual property. The negotiation process is similar to the process for bilateral agreements, with representatives of several countries' governments working together in a closed, informal process.

Multilateral agreements, in contrast, are more institutionalized. They take place on the premises, and with the technical and administrative support, of intergovernmental organizations. Such agreements in essence establish an international framework or system that the negotiating countries agree is appropriate, and then those and other countries have the option of choosing whether to be bound by the obligations set out in the agreement.

The negotiating process for a multilateral agreement varies, depending primarily on which intergovernmental organization is involved. In any such negotiation, there are certain constants: formal negotiations take place with the help of simultaneous interpreters, translating statements into all of the official languages recognized by that intergovernmental organization. Informal but official negotiations also take place, sometimes with interpreters and sometimes without. Interspersed throughout are constant unofficial bilateral and smaller group discussions, in hallways, offices, meeting rooms and even coffee bars or restaurants. Many politically or theoretically difficult points may be resolved in these private talks, to be adopted by the larger group.

It is important to the dynamic of negotiations that each country, no matter what its size or the level of its economic interest in the issue under discussion, has only one vote. Accordingly, no single country can unilaterally determine a result. Nevertheless, a country or group of countries whose participation is critical to the success of the treaty may have great influence in the process, either by persuading others to follow its lead, or by threatening to withdraw from negotiations. Moreover, votes are rarely taken. Decisions are generally made by consensus, with voting only as a last resort on particularly controversial issues. Indeed, arguments have been made that treaty provisions or agreed statements adopted by less than consensus should be deemed less authoritative.

One of the hallmarks of multilateral negotiations is the formation of groups of countries with some type of common interest, that work together to develop a unified strategic position. Such groups may be comprised of highly industrialized countries, sharing an economic stake in strong protection for the intellectual property that they export. Or they may be developing countries from a particular region of the world, perhaps sharing a legal system or cultural concerns. These groups range from formally recognized U.N. groupings to informal and ad hoc alliances. In recent years, for example, the developing country members of WIPO have formed regional groups, respectively covering Latin America and the Caribbean, Africa, and Asia. The Arab countries and countries in Central and Eastern Europe also work cooperatively to make their collective voices heard. At meetings and conferences discussing or negotiating potential treaty language, a significant amount of time is spent determining the geographic and economic distribution of positions as officers presiding over the proceedings—the chair and vice-chairs of various committees.

While there are a number of international bodies that have sponsored treaty negotiations of various types, the major multilateral treaties today that deal with intellectual property have been sponsored by the WIPO and WTO. The WIPO process is markedly different from the WTO process in a number of respects. First, and most notably, the private sector plays a significant role at WIPO negotiations. Nongovernmental organizations ("NGOs") that have been accredited by the Secretariat are permitted to attend most preparatory meetings as well as the formal negotiating sessions. Such NGOs may be trade associations of commercial entities, or groups representing consumers, environmentalists, or other nonprofit interests. Not only do they observe, they also participate, making "interventions" to explain to governments their positions on the issues. The WTO process is less open. Not only is the private sector excluded from meetings and negotiating sessions, but WTO documents submitted or drafted by governments or the Secretariat are restricted in their distribution, and may only be made available to member governments unless and until they are specifically de-restricted.

Second, the process in the two organizations proceeds at a different rhythm and pace. The typical WIPO process is as follows: the Secretariat will identify a subject area that merits attention, organize one or more symposia and conferences in different locations to bring interested parties, academics and government policy-makers together to discuss it, and then place the subject on the organization's agenda. From then on, it will be a topic of discussion in ongoing meetings of a Committee of Experts, composed of government delegations representing WIPO member countries, usually taking place a few months apart over a period of several years.* Once the relevant Committee determines that the subject is ripe for consideration and negotiation of a treaty, it will recommend to the Governing Bodies (officials from member countries) that a Diplomatic Conference be convened, along with a schedule for preparatory work for the Conference. A Diplomatic Conference may take place in Geneva or in a member state that extends an invitation and typically continues for a set time period lasting several weeks. The treaty must be concluded within that time period; negotiations will normally not continue if they are not successful at that point. (It is theoretically possible to extend a diplomatic conference over several sessions, although this is rarely done and even more rarely successful.)

In the WTO, the negotiation of intellectual property provisions is part of a bigger and more extended series of negotiations, known as a "round." A new round is scheduled whenever member countries decide that there are sufficient outstanding trade issues on which further agreement would be useful. In the past, this has generally occurred at intervals of approximately four years. Preparatory work for a round is done through a combination of informal contacts and ministerial summit meetings, in which issues and concerns are identified and parameters established. Negotiations themselves take place over a lengthy period of time, with delegations convening to negotiate for a week every month or so over a period of years. Different members of the delegation will negotiate the details of particular issues within their competence, proceeding simultaneously. Final negotiations are concluded at a high political level, where trade-offs may be made among unrelated legal subjects. Deadlines are imposed at various stages, but are often extended.

———

*In the past, separate Committees of Experts have been convened to deal with separate topics—for example, a Committee of Experts on the issue of database protection, and a separate Committee of Experts on the issue of audiovisual performers' rights. In reality, however, the membership of the committees was almost identical. As of the fall of 1998, WIPO has instead convened Standing Committees, each addressing a broad area of intellectual property. Thus, one standing committee deals with copyright and related rights, one with patents, and a third with trademark and unfair competition. The work of the standing committees, and the new forms of international intellectual property lawmaking that they represent, is discussed below in the context of specific proposals.

NOTES AND QUESTIONS

(1) **Bilateral Agreements.** What are the deficiencies of bilateral agreements between two countries under which each agrees to offer intellectual property protection to the nationals of the other? What advantages do multilateral agreements offer? Are there any advantages to bilateral negotiation?

(2) **The Effect of Treaties on the Content of International Intellectual Property Law.** From the discussion of the recent history of international intellectual property treaties, what (possible) changes can you identify in the nature and sources of contemporary international intellectual property law?

(3) **Institutional Comparisons.** Compare the structures and objectives of the various institutions of international intellectual property lawmaking discussed in Sections 2.02-04. How are they different? In light of those differences, how would you expect the international lawmaking process (broadly construed) within each institution to differ, and how would you expect the outcomes of those processes to vary? What are the strengths and weaknesses of each institution as an instrument of international intellectual property lawmaking?

(4) **The EU as a Model for Global Unions.** The EU has become a hugely significant force in international intellectual property lawmaking. It is often claimed that the EU is a microcosm of the global economy and should thus be a model for a broader global union of states. What would it take to replicate the EU at a global level? In what ways would the operating premises of international law require modification? What hurdles would such a project face? Why were the EU member states able to overcome them? In April 2001, leaders from thirty-four countries agreed to establish a Free Trade Area of the Americas by 2005. Will the development of regional institutions that address intellectual property issues make it easier or harder to achieve broader global solutions?

(5) **The Role of National Law.** Note that national intellectual property laws are not automatically (or even typically) supplanted by international agreements. A review of national laws—as is conducted by the TRIPS Council and by the European Commission, to name but two institutions—is thus a crucial measure of the success of international law. In what ways is the review of the TRIPS Council different from that of the European Commission? In what ways does the TRIPS Council activities contribute to the development of international intellectual property law? International agreements clearly shape the content of national intellectual property laws. To what extent and in what ways might national law shape international intellectual property laws?

(6) **Inter-National Alliances.** Which groupings of countries would you expect to coalesce in the negotiation of intellectual property treaties? Is the fault line between developed and developing countries the only one that matters? Can you see others that might be relevant in the future?

§ 2.05 Treaties Under United States Law

The term "treaty" means something different in U.S. law than it does in international law. As used in the Vienna Convention on the Law of Treaties, a "treaty" means any "international agreement concluded between two States in written form and governed by international law." Vienna Convention art. 2(1)(a). Note that the Restatement uses the term "international agreements" to describe the compacts that are a source of international law. As used in the U.S. Constitution, Art. II, § 2, the word "treaty" has a special meaning related to how one kind of international agreement becomes law within the United States: it is an agreement that is made "by and with the advice and consent of the Senate."

TREATIES AND OTHER INTERNATIONAL AGREEMENTS: THE ROLE OF THE UNITED STATES SENATE
S-Prt. 103-53, Study Prepared for the Committee On Foreign Relations, U.S. Senate (1993)

TREATIES UNDER INTERNATIONAL LAW

Under international law an international agreement is generally considered to be a treaty and binding on the parties if it meets four criteria:

(1) The parties intend the agreement to be legally binding and the agreement is subject to international law;

(2) The agreement deals with significant matters;

(3) The agreement clearly and specifically describes the legal obligations of the parties;

(4) The form indicates an intention to conclude a treaty, although the substance of the agreement rather than the form is the governing factor.

International law makes no distinction between treaties and executive agreements. Executive agreements, especially if significant enough to be reported to Congress under the Case-Zablocki Act, are to all intents and purposes binding treaties under international law.

On the other hand, many international undertakings and foreign policy statements, such as unilateral statements of intent, joint communiqués, and final acts of conferences, are not intended to be legally binding and are not considered treaties.

TREATIES UNDER UNITED STATES LAW

Under the Constitution, a treaty, like a Federal statute, is part of the "supreme Law of the Land." Self-executing treaties, . . . which do not require implementing legislation, automatically become effective as domestic law immediately upon entry into force. Other treaties do not become effective as domestic law until implementing legislation is enacted, and then technically it is the legislation, not the treaty unless incorporated into the legislation, that is the law of the land.

Sometimes it is not clear on the face of a treaty whether it is self-executing or requires implementing legislation. Some treaties expressly call for implementing legislation or deal with subjects clearly requiring congressional action, such as the appropriation of funds or enactment of domestic penal provisions. The question of whether or not a treaty requires implementing legislation or is self-executing is a matter of interpretation largely by the executive branch or, less frequently, by the courts. On occasion, the Senate includes an understanding in the resolution of ratification that certain provisions are not self-executing or that the President is to exchange or deposit the instrument of ratification only after implementation legislation has been enacted.

When a treaty is deemed self-executing, it overrides any conflicting provision of the law of an individual state. If a treaty is in irreconcilable conflict with a Federal law, the one later in time prevails, although courts generally try to harmonize domestic and international obligations whenever possible.

EXECUTIVE AGREEMENTS UNDER U.S. LAW

The status in domestic law of executive agreements, that is, international agreements made by the executive branch but not submitted to the Senate for its advice and consent, is less clear. Executive agreements may validly coexist with treaties, but it is not clear that all subjects dealt with by treaty may also be dealt with by executive agreement, especially if the agreement is concluded on the sole authority of the President. Three types of executive agreements and their domestic legal status are discussed below.

(1) Congressional-Executive Agreements

Most executive agreements are either explicitly or implicitly authorized in advance by Congress or submitted to Congress for approval. Some areas in which Congress has authorized the conclusion of international agreements are postal conventions, foreign trade, foreign military assistance, foreign economic assistance, atomic energy cooperation, and international fishery rights. Sometimes Congress has authorized conclusion of agreements but required the executive branch to submit the agreements to Congress for approval by legislation or for a specified waiting period before taking effect. Congress has also sometimes approved by joint resolution international agreements involving matters that are frequently handled by treaty, including such subjects as participation in international organizations, arms control measures, and acquisition of territory. The constitutionality of this type of agreement seems well established and Congress has authorized or approved them frequently.

(2) Agreements Pursuant to Treaties

Some executive agreements are expressly authorized by treaty or an authorization for them may be reasonably inferred from the provisions of a prior treaty. Examples include arrangements and understandings under the North Atlantic Treaty and other security treaties. The President's authority to conclude agreements pursuant to treaties seems well established, although controversy occasionally arises over whether particular agreements were within the purview of an existing treaty.

(3) Presidential or Sole Executive Agreements

Some executive agreements are concluded solely on the basis of the President's independent constitutional authority and do not have an underlying explicit or implied authorization by treaty or statute. Authorities which Presidents claim as a basis for such agreements include:

— The President's general executive authority in Article II, section 1, of the Constitution;

— His power as Commander in Chief of the Army and Navy in Article II, section 2, clause 1;

— The treaty clause itself for agreements which might be part of the process of negotiating a treaty, Article II, section 2, clause 2;

— His authority to receive Ambassadors and other public Ministers, Article II, section 3;

— His duty to "take care that the laws be faithfully executed," Article II, section 3.

Courts have indicated that executive agreements based solely on the President's independent constitutional authority can supersede conflicting provisions of State law, but opinions differ regarding the extent to which they can supersede a prior act of Congress. What judicial authority exists seems to indicate that they cannot.

. . . .

THE HOUSE ROLE IN TREATIES

Because treaties become part of the law of the land, concern is sometimes expressed that the House of Representatives does not share in the treaty power. The Framers confined the treaty-making power to the President and the Senate in the belief that the latter's smaller size would enable it to be a confidential partner in the negotiations. The need for maintaining secrecy during negotiations and acting with speed were also cited as justifications for not including the House. In addition, by making the treaty power a national power and requiring the advice and consent of the Senate, the Framers gave expression to their desire to form a strong central government while affording the States ample safeguards.

The Supreme Court, in *INS v. Chadha*, cited the Senate's power to advise and consent to treaties negotiated by the President "as one of only four provisions in the Constitution, explicit and unambiguous, by which one House may act alone with the unreviewable force of law, not subject to the President's veto." In 1945 the House adopted a resolution to amend the Constitution to require the advice and consent of both Houses for treaties, but the Senate did not act on the measure.

The House from the beginning has played a role in treaties that require implementing legislation. On occasion, as in 1796 with the Jay Treaty, problems have arisen when Presidents have completed ratification of treaties and then called upon Congress to pass implementing legislation to prevent the United States from defaulting on its international obligations. Or treaties approved by the Senate have remained unfulfilled for long periods because implementing legislation was not passed.

The increasing use of statutory agreements has also equalized to some extent the role of the House vis-à-vis the Senate in the making of international agreements. Executive agreements authorized or approved by legislation give a majority in the House and Senate the power analogous to the Senate's advice and consent by a two-thirds majority.

. . . .

INCREASING USE OF EXECUTIVE AGREEMENTS

As the United States became more involved in world affairs, international agreements multiplied. Most of the growth was in executive agreements. . . . In the 1980s, the United States entered into three or four hundred executive agreements per year, compared to 8 to 26 treaties per year.

The executive branch found it was much easier to conclude an executive agreement than a treaty because it was not submitted to the Senate. . . . The Senate, too, accepted executive agreements as an alternate method of making many international agreements, since submitting all agreements to the Senate as treaties would either overwhelm the Senate with work or force approval to become perfunctory.

Of most concern to the Senate were executive agreements concluded solely on the President's own authority, without any authority from Congress. In other executive agreements, the Senate played a role anyway. In the case of executive agreements concluded under the authority of a treaty, the Senate consented to the original treaty. In the case of congressional-executive agreements, both Houses passed the legislation that authorized, required scrutiny of, or approved the agreements.

NOTES AND QUESTIONS

(1) **Trade Agreements as Executive or Congressional-Executive Agreements**. The Constitution grants the President the power "by and with the Advice and Consent of the Senate to make Treaties," U.S. CONST. ART II, §2, but grants Congress the power "to lay and collect Taxes, Duties, Imposts and Excises. . ." U.S. CONST. ART I, §8, CL.1. Thus, all agreements that affect import duties (tariffs) must be in the form of legislation passed by both houses of Congress rather than in the form of a treaty submitted to the Senate for its "Advice and Consent." Both the North American Free Trade Agreement Implementation Act of 1993, Pub. L. 103-182, and the Uruguay Agreements Act of 1994, Pub. L. 103-465, originated as bills in the House of Representatives.

(2) **The Increase in Executive Agreements**. Why might the use of executive agreements be increasing as of late? What are the advantages of using such agreements? *See* Sol Picciotto, *Networks in International Economic Integration: Fragmented States and the Dilemmas of Neo-Liberalism*, 17 NW. J. INT'L L. & BUS. 1014, 1050 (1997). Are there any dangers in Presidents making extensive use of executive agreements? For an example of a pure executive agreement negotiated by the U.S. Trade Representative not involving Congress in any direct way, see China-United States: Agreement Regarding Intellectual Property Rights, 34 I.L.M. 881 (1995) (a so-called "Memorandum of Understanding"). Are such administrative arrangements, which do not involve Congress in any way, subject to any constitutional limits? Does the fact that the China-U.S. agreement concerns obligations imposed only on China affect your analysis?

(3) **Fast-Track Authority**. Both the NAFTA Implementation Act and Uruguay Round Agreements Act were passed under the so-called "fast track" procedure. Section 151 of the Trade Act of 1974 (19 U.S.C.§ 2191) set forth specific procedures giving the President the ability to negotiate trade agreements with the understanding that Congress will either pass or reject the agreement without modification within ninety days. Section 161 (19 U.S.C. § 2211) required the U.S. Trade Representative to keep members of Congress informed on the status of trade agreement negotiations and to consult on a continuing basis with the House Ways and Means Committee and the Senate Finance Committee. Although the President's fast-track authority has since expired, President Bush has recently requested that Congress grant him something similar (albeit under the different name of "trade promotion authority"). Why would the legislative branch continue to give the President this type of deference? One critic of the system of trade agreement approval has said:

> The international trade system operates contrary to every principle of democracy and government accountability embedded in U.S. domestic policymaking. Secrecy pervades the entire system. Trade officials operate behind closed doors with no public record of their activities when they negotiate or implement trade agreements or when they resolve disputes arising under them. As a result, there are

no mechanisms for the public to monitor the development or implementation of international trade policy. To compound matters, trade decision-makers owe their allegiances to the trade regime and make no attempt to invite or incorporate other views. There are no avenues for public participation to ensure that other perspectives are taken into account. Thus, in the coming era of "government by trade agreements," domestic prerogatives will be foreclosed or made more costly by trade bureaucrats secretly negotiating agreements and adjudicating disputes thousands of miles away.

Patti Goldman, *Symposium: The Democratization of the Development of United States Trade Policy*, 27 CORNELL INT'L L.J. 631, 633 (1994).

Assuming such criticism is valid, does the opaqueness of the process of negotiation of trade agreements provide any benefits to the political branches of government? Do these benefits justify fast track treatment? Is legislation enacted pursuant to fast-track authority constitutional? Can it be argued that the procedure circumvents Article II, Section 2's treaty power, and that that provision represents the sole constitutional means of making an international agreement? *See* Made in the USA Foundation v. United States, 56 F. Supp.2d 1226 (N.D. Ala. 1999) (holding that the Treaty Clause did not constitute the exclusive means of enacting international commercial agreements, given Congress's plenary powers to regulate foreign commerce and the President's inherent authority under Article II to manage the nation's affairs), *aff'd*, 242 F.2d 1300 (11th Cir. 2001) (affirming because whether NAFTA was a treaty requiring Senate ratification pursuant to the Treaty Clause was a nonjusticiable political question).

————

ROBERTSON v. GENERAL ELECTRIC CO.
32 F.2d 495 (4th Cir. 1929)

PARKER, CIRCUIT JUDGE:

[The Paris Convention requires signatory states to recognize so-called "rights of priority," under which a patent applicant in one country is afforded twelve months in which to apply for a patent on the invention in another signatory country without the first patent acting to bar the grant of the patent in the second country. Both the United States and Germany had implemented such rights of priority in their national laws. Stoffregen, a German, filed a German patent application on October 11, 1915. Because of World War I, however, it was impossible for nationals of the combatants to file patent applications in enemy countries. Accordingly, Section 308 of the Treaty of Peace of Versailles provided that rights of priority available under international conventions shall be extended until "six months after the coming into force" of the Versailles Treaty. Before the Versailles Treaty came into force, the U.S. Congress enacted the Nolan Act of March 3, 1921, which specifically extended the time for filing patent applications for six months, until September 3, 1921. On November 2, 1921, the treaty of peace between the United States and Germany, known as the Treaty of Berlin, was ratified; and on November 11, 1921, it took effect upon the exchange of ratifications. Without specifically mentioning Section 308, the Treaty of Berlin stated that "the periods of time . . . of the Treaty of Versailles shall run, with respect to any act or election on the part of the United States, from the date of the coming into force of the present treaty." Stoffregen delayed filing an application for a patent with the U.S. Patent Office until May 10, 1922. It was rejected by the Patent Office Examiner on the ground that it had been filed more than twelve months after the filing of the foreign application, which decision was affirmed by the Court of Appeals for the District of Columbia. Appellees then filed a bill in the district court under R.S. 4915 (current 35 U.S.C. § 145) arguing that the Treaty of Berlin extended the effect of Section 308 for six months from the entry into force of the Treaty of Berlin. The district court agreed. The Fourth Circuit here reverses that decision.]

Th[is] bring[s] us to the second ground upon which we think that the prayer of complainants must be denied, viz.: That, even if the Treaty of Berlin is to be construed as incorporating Section 308 of the Versailles Treaty. . . complainants are not entitled to the patent applied for, because the section is not self-executing and no legislation has been enacted to carry it into effect. Assuming that a treaty provision affecting patents may be made self-executing, so that no supporting legislation is necessary under the Constitution to give rise to individual rights thereunder, we are satisfied that section 308 was not intended to be, and is not, such a self-executing provision.

The rule as to whether a treaty is self-executing or not is clearly stated by Chief Justice Marshall in Foster & Elam v. Neilson, 2 Pet. 253, 313 as follows:

> A treaty is, in its nature, a contract between two nations, not a legislative act. It does not generally effect, of itself, the object to be accomplished, especially so far as its operation is infraterritorial, but is carried into execution by the sovereign power of the respective parties to the instrument. In the United States, a different principle is established. Our Constitution declares a treaty to be the law of the land. It is, consequently, to be regarded in courts of justice as equivalent to an act of the Legislature, whenever it operates of itself, without the aid of any legislative provision. *But when the terms of the stipulation import a contract—when either of the parties engages to perform a particular act, the treaty addresses itself to the political, not the judicial department; and the Legislature must execute the contract, before it can become a rule for the court.* (Italics ours.)

The language of section 308 is that "the rights of priority . . . shall be extended by each of the high contracting parties," etc. This not only uses language of futurity, "shall be extended," as to a matter operating as to each nation infraterritorially, and not between nations, but it also provides that the extension shall be made, not by the instrument itself, but "by each of the high contracting parties." In other words, to use the language of Chief Justice Marshall, each of the parties "engages to perform a particular act," and therefore "the treaty addresses itself to the political, not the judicial, department, and the Legislature must execute the contract before it can become a rule for the court."

It was the opinion of Attorney General Miller (19 Op. Attys. Gen. 273) that, as Congress alone was given by the Constitution the power "to promote the progress of science and useful arts by securing for limited times to authors and inventors the exclusive right to their respective writings and discoveries," treaty provisions relating to patent rights must be deemed dependent upon legislation in aid thereof. And this seems to have been the view also of Judge Lowell in United Shoe Machinery Co. v. Duplessis Shoe Machinery Co. (C.C.) 148 F. 31, and there is much to be said in its favor. Patent rights differ from many other rights which are the subject of treaties, in that they are created by and dependent upon statutes which only Congress has power to enact. Furthermore, the right under a patent is not one which extends across national boundaries, and is therefore necessarily a matter for regulation by treaty, but is one which must be enjoyed within the territory of the nation. We think, however, that the better view is that a treaty affecting patent rights may be so drawn as to be self-executing. See United Shoe Machinery Co. v. Duplessis Shoe Mach. Co. (C.C.A. 1st) 155 F. 842. [cit]. But the reasons which led to the doubt as to whether a treaty could be so drawn as to effect patent rights, without supporting legislation by Congress, are matters which must be considered in the interpretation of treaties affecting patents; and they require that such treaties be held not self-executing, unless their language compels a different interpretation.

Patent rights are valid, of course, only within the country granting the patent. They are created by statute, and complicated administrative machinery is provided for the application of the statutory provisions. Treaties are drafted ordinarily to accomplish certain general results, and in the nature of things cannot regulate details and ought not to interfere with the domestic machinery which the several countries have provided for the regulation of patents. For these reasons, unless a contrary intention is clearly indicated, they should be construed, not as of themselves making changes in the patent laws, but as contemplating that the various parties signatory will enact appropriate legislation and promulgate proper rules to effectuate the ends which they are designed to accomplish.

This rule of construction has been uniformly followed in this country, and treaties affecting patent rights have been held to be not self-effectuating, where the purpose that they should be carried out by supporting legislation was not by any means so clearly indicated as in the section of the treaty under consideration. Thus article II of the [Paris] Convention of March 20, 1883, provided:

> The subjects or citizens of each of the contracting States shall enjoy, in all the other states of the Union, so far as concerns patents for inventions, trade or commercial marks, and the commercial name, the advantages that the respective laws thereof at present accord, or

shall afterwards accord to subjects or citizens. In consequence they shall have the same protection as these latter, and the same legal recourse against all infringements of their rights, under reserve of complying with the formalities and conditions imposed upon subjects or citizens by the domestic legislation of each state.

In the opinion of Attorney General Miller, referred to above, this article was held not to be self-executing, but to require the support of legislation before it became a rule for the courts to follow. While the constitutional question to which we have adverted was discussed, the opinion was finally based upon the proposition that the treaty was a contract operating in the future intraterritorially. The Attorney General said:

> It is not necessary to the decision of the question submitted to me in the matter under consideration to determine whether all the provisions of treaties, whose execution requires the exercise of powers submitted to Congress, must be so submitted before they become law to the courts and executive departments, for the treaty under consideration is a reciprocal one; each party to it covenants to grant in the future to the subjects and citizens of the other parties certain special rights in consideration of the granting of like special rights to its subjects or citizens. It is a contract operative in the future infraterritorially. It is therefore not self-executing, but requires legislation to render it effective for the modification of existing laws.

In *Rousseau v. Brown*, 21 App.D.C. 73, a citizen of France based his claim upon the provisions of the Convention of March 20, 1883. In denying his claim, the court said:

> The convention is in the nature of a contract between the parties thereto, and is not self-executing. It requires the action of Congress to give it full force and effect. *This is the construction that has been placed upon it by most of the parties to it*, and they have adopted legislation giving effect to it. . . . But without regard to the action of other states, *the uniform construction of that convention by the Patent Office officials, and by the courts of this country, has been that the convention is not self-executing*, but requires the aid of an act of Congress. (Italics ours.) . . .

The Convention of Brussels of December 14, 1900, changed the priority period for patents to twelve months and inserted in the prior convention a section known as article "4*bis*," as follows:

Patents applied for in the different contracting States by persons admitted to the benefit of the convention under the terms of articles 2 and 3 shall be independent of the patents obtained for the same invention in the other states adherents or nonadherents to the Union.

There was some controversy in the lower courts as to whether this was a self-executing provision or not, but the Supreme Court, in Cameron Septic Tank Co. v. Knoxville, 227 U.S. 39, set these controversies at rest by showing that it was the sense of Congress that the treaty required legislation to become effective, that this was the understanding of other nations also, and that the act of 1903 was passed to carry it into effect. The court said:

> The act of 1903 was then enacted, and if there could be any doubt that it expressed the sense of Congress and those concerned with the treaty that it required legislation to become effective, such doubt would be entirely removed by the legislative action of other states. It appears from the report of the committee on patents of the Senate and of the House of Representatives on the proposed legislation that 13 countries had adopted legislation giving full force and effect to the provisions of the additional act either in the form of a general law or by specific amendment to other laws providing for carrying into force the provisions of the additional act as regards the extension of the 'delay and priority' to twelve months. Other countries were mentioned as being expected to do so. In explaining the object of the bill the member in charge of it in the House of Representatives said that it was to carry into effect the additional act of the convention held at Brussels in December, 1900.... If it [the treaty] be not self-executing, as it is certainly the sense of Congress that it was not and seems also to be the sense of some of the other contracting nations, and as the act of 1903 did not make effective article 4bis, the provisions of section 4887 apply to the Cameron patent and caused it to expire with the British patent for the same invention.

In the light of these decisions, relating to treaties the language of which does not negative the idea of self-execution near so plainly as does that of section 308 of the Treaty of Versailles, it is clear that that section cannot reasonably be construed as self-executing. As no legislation has been passed in aid of it, except the Nolan Act, the time limit of which had expired before complainants filed their application, it follows that there is nothing upon which they can base the extension of priority rights for which they contend.

. . . .

Reversed.

GENERAL MOTORS CORP. v. IGNACIO LOPEZ DE ARRIORTUA
948 F. Supp. 684 (E.D.Mich. 1996)

EDMUNDS, DISTRICT JUDGE.

Plaintiffs, General Motors Corporation ("GM") and Adam Opel AG ("Opel"), brought suit against Defendants alleging theft of trade secrets and conspiracy. GM is an American corporation and Opel is a German corporation wholly owned by GM. Defendants include:

1. Volkswagen AG, a German corporation ("VW")
2. Volkswagen of America, Inc., wholly owned by Volkswagen AG ("VWOA")
3. The "Lopez Group," including . . . Jose Ignacio Lopez, a former executive at GM Espana, Opel, and GM (Europe) AG. On February 1, 1993 he became group vice president of GM. Subsequently, on March 10, 1993, he resigned from GM and moved to Germany. On March 16, he joined VW and was appointed to its management board. . . .

Plaintiffs allege that while Lopez was a high level GM executive, he secretly communicated with VW representatives and agreed to leave GM and join VW. He agreed to bring confidential business plans and trade secret information with him. Lopez worked with the other Lopez Group Defendants to secretly collect confidential information. In March of 1993, the Lopez Group Defendants left GM and Opel to join VW where they were paid significantly higher salaries. They allegedly took over 20 cartons of stolen documents with them. Plaintiffs allege that Defendants copied the documents and entered them into VW computers, and then proceeded to shred the documents and cover up the theft.

On March 7, 1996, Plaintiffs filed this suit. Counts 3 and 4 of their complaint allege that Defendants violated the Lanham Act, 15 U.S.C. § 1126, and that Defendants violated the Copyright Act. [cit]. The complaint further alleges that VW has used and continues to use the trade secret information to reduce its costs and to increase its market share. Defendants moved to dismiss count 3 (Lanham Act) and count 4 (Copyright Act). For the reasons set forth below, Defendants' motions are denied.

. . .

All Defendants (except those who have not been served) have moved to dismiss count 3 of the complaint. Count 3 alleges that Defendants violated the substantive terms of the Paris Convention, an international agreement incorporated into section 44 of the Lanham Act. [cit]. Defendants contend that the Lanham Act does not incorporate any substantive provisions of the Paris Convention, and thus that Plaintiffs have failed to state a viable claim for relief. They argue that the Paris Convention only required that signatory nations provide the same trademark protection to foreign citizens that they provide to their own citizens. Courts are split on the issue of whether section 44(b) of the Lanham Act incorporates substantive rights set forth in the Paris Convention.

Generally, the Lanham Act prohibits two types of unfair competition: trademark infringement (15 U.S.C. § 1114) and false designation of origin or "passing off" (15 U.S.C. § 1125). In addition, the Lanham Act provides rights stipulated by international conventions respecting unfair competition. Section 1127 provides:

> The intent of this chapter is . . . to provide rights and remedies stipulated by treaties and conventions respecting trade-marks, trade names, and unfair competition entered into between the United States and foreign nations.

This purpose is implemented in sections 44(b), (h), and (i). Section 44(b) provides:

> Any person whose country of origin is a party to any convention or treaty relating to trademarks . . . to which the United States is also a party . . . shall be entitled to the benefits of this section under the conditions expressed herein *to the extent necessary to give effect to any provision of such convention [or] treaty . . . in addition to the rights to which any owner of a mark is otherwise entitled* by this chapter.

15 U.S.C. § 1126(b) (emphasis added). Under section 44(h), foreign citizens are entitled to protection against unfair competition as follows:

> Any person designated in subsection (b) of this section as entitled to the benefits and subject to the provisions of this chapter shall be entitled to effective protection against unfair competition, and the remedies provided in this chapter for infringement of marks shall be available so far as they may be appropriate in repressing acts of unfair competition.

15 U.S.C. § 1126(h). The Act specifically provides under section 44(i) that United States citizens shall have the same rights as foreigners. "Citizens or residents of the United States shall have the same benefits as are granted by this section to persons described in subsection (b) of this section." 15 U.S.C. 1126(i).

One treaty incorporated by this section is the International Convention for the Protection of Industrial Property, the Paris Convention. 24 U.S.T. 2140 (July 14, 1967). The Paris Convention requires signatory nations to prohibit unfair competition.

> (1) The countries of the Union are bound to assure to nationals of

such countries effective protection against unfair competition.[3]

(2) Any act of competition contrary to honest practices in industrial or commercial matters constitutes an act of unfair competition.

Paris Convention, article 10*bis*. The broad concept of unfair competition set forth in the Paris Convention has been described as follows:

> Article 10*bis* is not premised upon the narrow meaning of "unfair competition" as it was understood in American common law, but adopts the more liberal construction of the European countries such as France, Germany and Switzerland . . . The statement that unfair competition is competition "contrary to honest practice" is not a definition; it merely expresses the concept that a particular act of competition is to be condemned as unfair because it is inconsistent with currently accepted standards of honest practice. It impliedly affirms that unfair competition is too broad a concept to be limited to any narrow definition such as for instance, passing off.

4A Rudolf Callmann, *The Law of Unfair Competition, Trademarks and Monopolies*, § 2610 (4th ed. 1994). The United States and Germany are both signatories to the Paris Convention.

Defendants concede that the Lanham Act incorporates the Paris Convention. However, they contend that the Paris Convention does not provide substantive rights, and that it only requires "national treatment." One authority on trademark law explained this interpretation of the Convention:

> The Paris Convention is essentially a compact between the various member countries to accord in their own countries to citizens of the other contracting parties' trademark and other rights comparable to those accorded their own citizens by their domestic law. *The underlying principle is that foreign nationals should be given the same treatment in each of the member countries as that country makes available to its own citizens ["national treatment"].* The Convention is not premised upon the idea that the trademark laws of each member nation shall be given extraterritorial application, but on exactly the converse principle that each nation's law shall have only territorial application.

In re Compagnie Generale Maritime, 993 F.2d 841, 850 (Fed. Cir.1993) (Nies, J., dissenting) (quoting 1 McCarthy, *Trademarks and Unfair Competition*, § 19:24, at 927 (2d ed. 1984) (emphasis added)).

Agreeing with the "national treatment" analysis, in *Vanity Fair Mills, Inc. v. T. Eaton Co.* 234 F.2d 633, 644 (2d Cir. 1956), the Second Circuit interpreted

---

[3]Article 10*ter* of the Paris Convention also requires signatory nations to provide for legal remedies to enforce Article 10*bis*. . . .

the Paris Convention and the Lanham Act as providing only limited protection from acts of unfair competition. In that case, plaintiff was an American company who brought suit against a Canadian company, alleging that the defendant violated plaintiff's trademark when it sold goods in Canada using plaintiff's "Vanity Fair" label. The court held that the Paris Convention was premised on the concept of national treatment and that the laws of the signatory nations should not have extraterritorial application. Thus, plaintiff could not hold the defendant Canadian corporation liable under American law for a trademark violation that occurred in Canada. *See also Majorica S.A. v. Majorca International, Ltd.*, 687 F.Supp. 92 (S.D.N.Y.1988) (following *Vanity Fair*, court held that where Spanish Company sued American Company, Spanish law was not entitled to application in U.S. under Paris Convention). . . .

Contrary to *Vanity Fair*, other courts have held that the Lanham Act incorporates international agreements. In *Toho Co. v. Sears, Roebuck & Co.*, 645 F.2d 788, 792 (9th Cir.1981), a Japanese company brought suit against Sears, an American company, alleging unfair competition. The court explained that sections 44(b) and (h) incorporated the provisions of a treaty between the United States and Japan. "The federal right created by subsection 44(h) is coextensive with the substantive provisions of the treaty involved. . . . [S]ubsections (b) and (h) work together to provide federal rights and remedies implementing federal unfair competition treaties." *Toho*, 645 F.2d at 792. The U.S.-Japan treaty only required national treatment. Thus, the court reasoned that the Japanese company was entitled to bring the same claims as an American company would be entitled to bring: both claims for trademark infringement and false designation of origin under the Lanham Act as well as a claim for unfair competition under state law.

. . . .

Still other courts have taken *Toho* one step further and have held that the Lanham Act incorporates the substantive provisions of the Paris Convention and thus creates a federal law of unfair competition applicable in international disputes. In *Maison Lazard et Compagnie v. Manfra, Tordella & Brooks, Inc.*, 585 F.Supp. 1286, 1289 (S.D.N.Y.1984), a French company brought suit against an American company, alleging that the American company sold commemorative Olympic coins overseas in violation of the plaintiff's exclusive right to make such sales. In essence, the French company claimed that the defendant misappropriated an exclusive right and that this constituted unfair competition under the Paris Convention. The court followed *Toho*, holding that the Lanham Act incorporated the Convention. Because the Paris Convention provides broad protection from unfair competition, the court held that the plaintiff had a valid federal claim for misappropriation of an exclusive right. [cit].

The court is persuaded that *Toho* and *Maison Lazard* properly interpret the Lanham Act as incorporating the substantive provisions of the Paris Convention. The express purpose of the Lanham Act dictates this result. "The intent of this chapter is . . . to provide rights and remedies stipulated by treaties and conventions. . . ." 15 U.S.C. § 1127. The Paris Convention provides that signatory countries must protect individuals from unfair competition. Article 10*bis*. Subsection (b) of the Lanham Act implements this concept by providing that foreigners are entitled to benefits "to the extent necessary to give effect to any provision" of a convention. Subsection (h) specifies that foreigners are entitled "to protection against unfair competition."

The intent of Congress to incorporate substantive rights is further manifested in subsection (i), which provides that United States citizens shall be entitled to the same rights as foreign citizens. It was necessary to enact subsection (i) to make it clear that United States citizens were entitled to *additional* rights provided by the treaties incorporated. If the incorporation of the treaty did not incorporate additional rights, it would have been unnecessary to enact section 44(i). Interpreting section 44(b) as merely requiring "national treatment" renders section 44(i) superfluous. Courts must interpret statutes so as to give effect to every word and to avoid rendering certain language superfluous. . . .

The legislative history also reveals Congressional intent to incorporate additional rights and to provide such rights both to foreigners and to citizens. Congress expressed its concern that Americans be given the same protection from unfair competition as foreigners.

> We have the curious anomaly of this Government giving by treaty and by law with respect to trade-marks and unfair competition to nationals of foreign governments greater rights than it gives its own citizens. . . . This [subsection 44(i) in the final draft] is an attempt to put the citizen on an equality with the foreigner. . . .

Hearings on H.R. 4744 Before the Subcomm. on Trademarks of the House Comm. on Patents, 76th Cong., 1st Sess. (1939), p. 164. Congress also explained that the Paris Convention prohibited unfair competition more broadly than did the Lanham Act. "The European Convention [meaning the Paris Convention] however, goes much farther than that and prohibits commercial bribery among other things. . . ." *Id.* at 168.[4]

The legislative history also reveals that Congress specifically considered whether it should broadly prohibit unfair competition. A prior draft of section 44 included the following as subsection (g):

> All acts of unfair competition in commerce are declared to be unlawful and the provisions of section 32 to 35 inclusive shall be applicable thereto.

Id. at 163. One Congressman pointed out that the term "unfair competition" included all types of artificial interference with trade, including disparagement, trade bribery, and the like. [cit]. This draft of the statute provided the rights

---

[4] Defendants also contend that if the Paris Convention provides substantive rights it is not clear what those rights are. While the precise nature of these rights is not clear at this juncture, it is clear that the rights provided by the Paris Convention include protection from commercial bribery. It also should be noted that because Plaintiffs seek the enforcement of foreign law, it is their obligation to inform the court of the content of that law. *Rolnick v. El Al Israel Airlines, Ltd.*, 551 F.Supp. 261 (E.D.N.Y.1982).

that the United States was obligated to provide by the Paris Convention. [cit]. At the subcommittee hearing, the legislators decided that the term "unfair competition" as used in subsection (g) was "dangerously broad," *id.* at 167, and that subsection (g) should be deleted. [cit]. The legislators did not acknowledge that by deleting subsection (g), the statute failed to fully incorporate the Paris Convention.

However, the legislators reversed this position. The final version of the statute contains language substantially similar to the deleted subsection (g). As discussed above, section 44(h) provides foreigners with "effective protection against unfair competition." The inclusion of this language is consistent with Congress' concern that it fully implement the Paris Convention, including the Convention's broad prohibition of unfair competition.

Opel seeks the right to sue for unfair competition pursuant to 44(h), and GM seeks to enforce the same rights pursuant to section 44(i). Because the Lanham Act incorporates the Paris Convention's broad prohibition against unfair competition, Plaintiffs have stated a claim.[5]

Defendants also claim that the Lanham Act does not reach extraterritorial acts. This is incorrect. Congress has the power to regulate even entirely foreign commerce where it has a substantial effect on commerce between the states or between the United States and foreign countries. *Vanity Fair*, 234 F.2d at 641. *Accord Consolidated Gold Fields PLC v. Minorco, S.A.*, 871 F.2d 252, 261-62 (2d Cir.1989) (federal statutes apply if underlying conduct occurred within U.S. or if conduct which occurred abroad has substantial effects within U.S.). "Particularly is this true when a conspiracy is alleged with acts in furtherance of that conspiracy taking place in both the United States and foreign countries." *Id.* *See also Steele v. Bulova Watch Co.*, 344 U.S. 280 (1952) (holding U.S. citizen who sold infringing watches only in foreign countries liable under Lanham Act).

. . .

Defendants' joint motion to dismiss counts 3 and 4 is DENIED

NOTES AND QUESTIONS

(1) **Self-Execution Generally.** The *Robertson* court proceeds on the assumption that patent treaties may be self-executing. Are there any reasons why we should be cautious before treating intellectual property treaties (or treaties affecting certain types of intellectual property) as self-executing? What are the advantages of treating a treaty as self-executing? What difficulties are

---

[5]Defendants also argue that interpreting section 44 as incorporating the Paris Convention would eliminate diversity jurisdiction in all actions involving unfair competition. This is overstated. The court's holding is limited to the circumstances of this case. The Lanham Act incorporates the substantive provisions of the Paris Convention and thus creates a federal law of unfair competition applicable in international disputes. Diversity jurisdiction would still apply in a domestic dispute. It should also be noted that this issue is not before the court. The court has proper federal question jurisdiction in this case.

caused national courts or administrative officials if the United States relies on treaty self-execution rather than implementing legislation as a means of fulfilling its treaty obligations?

(2) **Alternatives to Self-Execution**. In what ways, if any, is the holding of the *Lopez* court different from treating Article 10*bis* of the Paris Convention as self-executing? How would you describe what Congress has done in the provisions of Section 44 of the Lanham Act quoted in *Lopez*? In what other ways could U.S. compliance with Article 10*bis* have been achieved? (We will discuss Article 10*bis* in greater detail in Chapter 3.) In certain circumstances, principles of EU directives may be treated as directly effective in member state law notwithstanding the lack of legislative transposition into national law. *See supra* § 2.03[C]. In what ways is giving direct effect to directives different from treating a treaty as self-executing?

(3) **The Paris Convention and Self-Execution.** It has never been clear whether the leading multilateral trademark treaties (including the Paris Convention) were self-executing in the United States. The U.S. Supreme Court held that the Inter-American Trademark Convention was self-executing, *see* Bacardi Corp. of Am. v. Domenech, 311 U.S. 150, 159 (1940), but (as the *Robertson* court noted) the U.S. Attorney-General issued an opinion in 1889 declaring that the Paris Convention of 1883 was not self-executing. *See* 19 Op. Att'y Gen. 273 (1889). Courts have been split on the latter question. *See generally* John B. Pegram, *Trademark Law Revision: Section 44*, 78 Trademark Rep. 141, 158-162 (1988). Although most courts have rejected claims that the Paris Convention is self-executing, *see, e.g.,* French Republic v. Saratoga Vichy Spring Co., 191 U.S. 427, 438 (1903), lower courts appear to be more receptive to the argument of late. *See, e.g.,* Laboratories Roldan C. v. Tex Int'l, 902 F. Supp. 1555, 1568 (S.D. Fla. 1995) (recognizing claim under Article 10*bis* of the Paris Convention); Benard Indus. v. Bayer, 38 U.S.P.Q.2d 1422, 1426 (S.D. Fla. 1996) (permitting claim under Paris Convention to proceed). The arguments in favor of self-execution are probably stronger with respect to some texts of the Convention than others. *See* Pegram, *supra*, at 161-162 (noting arguments that "whatever the effect of the London text, the likelihood that the Lisbon text is not self-executing has been recognized"). Compare the following provisions:

> The carrying out of the reciprocal obligations contained in the present Convention is subject, as far as necessary, to the observance of the formalities and rules established by the constitutional laws of those of the countries of the Union which are bound to procure the application, which they undertake to do with as little delay as possible.

London Text (1934), art. 17

It is understood that at the time an instrument of ratification or accession is deposited on behalf of a country, such country will be in a position under its domestic law to give effect to the provisions of this Convention.

Lisbon Text (1958), art. 17

(1) Any country party to this Convention undertakes to adopt, in accordance with its constitution, the measures necessary to ensure the application of this Convention.

(2) It is understood that, at the time a country deposits its instrument of ratification or accession, it will be in a position under its domestic law to give effect to the provisions of this Convention.

Stockholm text (1967), art. 25.

(4) **The Berne Convention and Self-Execution.** Congress has made clear that the principal copyright treaty is not self-executing in the United States. Section 104(c) of the Copyright Act of 1976, as amended by the Berne Convention Implementation Act of 1988, Pub. L. No. 100-568, 102 Stat. 2853 (1988), provides that:

No right or interest in a work eligible for protection under this title may be claimed by virtue of, or in reliance upon, the provisions of the Berne Convention, or the adherence of the United States thereto. Any rights in a work eligible for protection under this title that derive from this title, other Federal or State statutes, or the common law, shall not be expanded or reduced by virtue of, or in reliance upon, the provisions of the Berne Convention, or the adherence of the United States thereto.

The declarations of Congress in Section 2 of the Berne Implementation Act similarly expressly prohibit any direct incorporation of the Berne Convention standards into U.S. copyright law:

The Congress makes the following declarations:

(1) The Convention for the Protection of Literary and Artistic Works, Signed at Berne, Switzerland, on September 9, 1886, and all acts, protocols, and revisions thereto (hereafter referred to as the "Berne Convention") are not self-executing under the Constitution and laws of the United States.

(2) The obligations of the United States under the Berne Convention may be performed only pursuant to appropriate domestic law.

(3) The amendments made by this Act, together with the law as it

exists on the date of the enactment of this Act, satisfy the obligations of the United States in adhering to the Berne Convention and no further rights or interests shall be recognized or created for that purpose.

No similar provision has been enacted into either the Lanham Act of 1946 or the Patent Act of 1952. Why is Congress apparently more sensitive about self-execution of the Berne copyright convention than of the Paris industrial property convention?

§ 2.06   National Treatment and Unconditional Most-Favored Nation [MFN] Treatment

Bilateral intellectual property agreements were generally based on the principle of *reciprocity*. In essence, each country would agree to protect intellectual property from the other country under its own legal system, but only to the same extent that the other country extended protection to the first country's intellectual property. But by the late nineteenth century, it became clear that reciprocity had certain negative aspects: it was burdensome to apply, since it required determining the contents of the other country's laws; it discriminated against foreign right holders relative to national right holders; and the scope of protection for the same type of intellectual property could be quite different within the same country, depending on which country was its source.

In contrast, the general approach of the leading multilateral treaties concluded at the end of the nineteenth century was to replace the principle of reciprocity of protection with that of *national treatment*: member countries were required to give nationals of other member countries the same protection that they give their own nationals. National treatment has been the cornerstone of both the Paris Convention (Article 2) and the Berne Convention (Article 5), for over a century. It is also found in the intellectual property provisions of recent trade agreements: Article 1703 of the NAFTA and Article 3 of TRIPS require the states party to those agreements to observe the principle of national treatment. National treatment thus substitutes a rule of non-discrimination for the principle of reciprocity. To accept the principle of national treatment is implicitly to accept the proposition that states may differ in their substantive laws, but that international cooperation between states on important matters is itself valuable consideration, over and above any special benefits that may accrue in exchange for reciprocal benefits from that state.* In order to avoid substantial discrepancies in levels of protection in different countries, these national treatment-based treaties typically also require certain minimum rights to be granted to nationals of other member countries.

---

*Some states (and international agreements) go even further. The European Patent Convention, for example, goes beyond national treatment and provides access to all applicants without consideration of nationality, residence, membership in a treaty system, or other status.

International trade agreements embody two concepts that can be grouped under the general heading of a principle of non-discrimination: national treatment, as discussed above, and *most favored nation* ("MFN") treatment. MFN requires that, if a state that is a party to the trade system grants benefits or bounties to other states, then such benefits will be accorded all states within the multilateral system. Unconditional MFN treatment is the cornerstone of the modern multilateral trading system which began with the establishment of the GATT in 1948. Article I of the GATT requires member states to accord "any advantage, favour, privilege, or immunity [granted to the products of one state] immediately and unconditionally" to all other contracting parties.

In the early development of the world trading system prior to 1986, intellectual property rights were not directly included in GATT's unconditional MFN obligations. GATT Article XX(d) states:

> Subject to the requirement that such measures are not applied in a manner which would constitute a means of arbitrary or unjustifiable discrimination between countries where the same conditions prevail, or a disguised restriction on international trade, nothing in this Agreement shall be construed to prevent the adoption or enforcement by any contracting party of measures:
>
> . . . .
>
> (d) necessary to secure compliance with laws or regulations which are not inconsistent with the provisions of this Agreement, including those relating to the protection of patents, trade marks and copyrights, and the prevention of deceptive practices.

The MFN principles of GATT were, however, incorporated into the international intellectual property system in the TRIPS Agreement in 1994. *See* TRIPS Agreement art. 4.

J.H. REICHMAN, UNIVERSAL MINIMUM STANDARDS OF INTELLECTUAL PROPERTY PROTECTION UNDER THE TRIPS COMPONENT OF THE WTO AGREEMENT*
29 INT. LAW. 345, 347-51 (1995)

Perhaps the most important "basic principle" that applies virtually across the board is that of national treatment of (that is, nondiscrimination against) foreign rights holders.[15] This principle of equal treatment under the domestic laws is then carried over to relations between states in the most-favored-nation (MFN) provisions of article 4. The latter article ostensibly prevents one member country from offering a better intellectual property deal than is required by

---

*Copyright 1995, American Bar Association; J.H. Reichman. Reprinted with permission.

[15]*See* TRIPS, art. 3(1). . . However, the requirement of national treatment is expressly subject to exceptions already provided in the Paris and Berne Conventions, and to exceptions recognized in both the [Rome Convention and in the IPIC Treaty]. *See* TRIPS Agreement, arts. 1(3) n.1, 3(1).

international law[17] to nationals of a second member country and then denying similar advantages to the nationals of other member countries.

Taken together, the national treatment and MFN provisions attempt to rectify the damage that some states recently inflicted on the international intellectual property system by unilaterally asserting claims of material reciprocity with respect to hybrid legal regimes falling in the penumbra between the Paris and Berne Conventions. In practice, however, certain express limitations could diminish the effectiveness of these basic requirements. For example, while the national treatment and MFN clauses both apply "with regard to the protection of intellectual property," it turns out that, for purposes of the TRIPS Agreement, the term "intellectual property" refers only to seven of the eight subject-matter categories enumerated in sections 1 through 7 of Part II. These include (1) copyrights and related rights; (2) trademarks and (3) geographical indications; (4) industrial designs; (5) patents; (6) integrated circuit designs; and (7) trade secrets or confidential information. As regards neighboring rights covered by the International Convention for the Protection of Performers, Producers of Phonograms and Broadcasting Organizations (Rome Convention), national treatment and the MFN clause apply only to those rights that the TRIPS Agreement selectively provides, but not to rights generally flowing from that Convention.

The precise mesh of these provisions remains to be seen, but the following overall framework seems plausible. First, international intellectual property treaties existing at the time that the TRIPS Agreement takes effect are generally immunized from the MFN clause (but not the national treatment clause except as expressly provided) under a grandfather provision within the TRIPS Agreement, which only this Agreement can override.[24] Second, existing and future agreements establishing "customs unions and free-trade areas" of a regional character may, to varying degrees, be immunized from applying MFN treatment, and possibly national treatment, to some non-TRIPS-mandated intellectual property measures affecting intra-regional adherents, at least insofar as past practice under article XXIV of the [GATT] is carried over to the WTO Agreement and applied to intellectual property rights. Third, states otherwise contemplating unilateral measures to protect intellectual property rights in the future must generally weigh the costs and benefits of nonreciprocity with respect to other WTO member countries, unless the measures contemplated fall outside the seven categories of "intellectual property" recognized by the TRIPS Agreement[27] and outside the residual

---

[17]*Cf. id.* art. 1(1) (allowing member states to "implement in their [domestic] law more extensive protection than is required by this Agreement").

[24]*See* TRIPS Agreement, art. 4(d) (with the proviso that immunized measures "not constitute an arbitrary or unjustifiable discrimination against nationals of other members"); *see also id.* art. 4(b) (exempting inconsistent provisions of Berne Convention and Rome Convention).

[27]On this reading, the TRIPS Agreement would appear to override unilateral claims to material reciprocity like those incorporated into the United Kingdom's unregistered design right of 1988 . . . and into the United States' Semiconductor Chip Protection Act of 1984. . . This follows because industrial designs and integrated circuit designs fall within the operative definition of intellectual property. In practice, the need for reciprocity under the SCPA was obviated by TRIPS Agreement arts. 35-38, which harmonize the protection of integrated circuit designs.

national treatment clauses of the Paris and Berne Conventions.[28]

Whether any specific measures that were arguably not cognizable under existing conventions, such as the European Union's . . . regime to protect electronic data bases or certain levies for private copying of audio and visual recordings like those implemented in France, may escape the MFN and national treatment clauses of the TRIPS Agreement will thus depend on a variety of factors. These include evolving state practice with respect to regional trade agreements and the extent to which decision makers interpret "intellectual property" as narrowly defining the seven categories of subject matter to be protected or as broadly defining certain modalities of protection. It may also depend on who interprets these clauses, given the uncertain jurisdictional and substantive powers of the WTO panels to be established under binding dispute-resolution procedures set out in the TRIPS Agreement. In any event, the drafters seem to have built in some incentives for states contemplating new protectionist measures to seek to address their needs within the framework of ongoing multilateral discussions affecting barriers to trade in general.

Beyond these equal-treatment obligations, states must accord to the nationals of other member states those international minimum standards of intellectual property protection that are comprised within "the treatment provided for in this [TRIPS] Agreement." One component of this "TRIPS treatment" consists of the basic substantive provisions of the Paris Convention . . ., of the Berne Convention . . ., and of the Treaty on Intellectual Property in Respect of Integrated Circuits (IPIC Treaty). The other component consists of minimum standards that the TRIPS Agreement applies irrespective of preexisting international norms and sometimes at the expense of those norms.[37] In either case, the relevant standards "are integral parts of this WTO Agreement, binding on all members."[38]

MURRAY v. BRITISH BROADCASTING CORP.
81 F.3d 287 (2d Cir. 1996)

WINTER, CIRCUIT JUDGE:

Dominic Murray, a British national, appeals from Judge Stanton's dismissal of his complaint based on the doctrine of *forum non conveniens*. The action was brought against the British Broadcasting Corporation ("the BBC"), a corporation organized under the laws of the United Kingdom, and BBC Lionheart Television International ("Lionheart"), a Delaware corporation and

---

[28]*See* TRIPS Agreement, arts. 2(1) and 9(1), respectively incorporating by reference Paris Convention, art. 2(1), and Berne Convention, art. 5(1).

[37]*See, e.g.*, TRIPS Agreement, arts. 1(3) (TRIPS treatment), 9(1) (mandating compliance with substantive provisions of Berne Convention, except for art. 6*bis* concerning moral rights).

[38]WTO Agreement, art. II(2) (distinguishing "Multilateral Trade Agreements," including TRIPS, that are binding on all members from "Plurilateral Trade Agreements," *see id.* art. II(3), which create obligations only for members that have accepted them).

wholly-owned subsidiary of the BBC. It asserted claims based on copyright infringement under both United States and English law, false designation of origin, and unfair competition. Murray's principal arguments on appeal are that *forum non conveniens* was misapplied either because the district court should have granted greater deference to his choice of forum or because a contingent fee arrangement is not available in the United Kingdom for this kind of litigation. Alternatively, Murray contends that the district court abused its discretion in weighing the various factors applicable under *forum non conveniens* doctrine. We affirm.

BACKGROUND

Murray is a self-employed designer and manufacturer of costumes and props in London, England. In July 1992, the BBC engaged Murray to produce a disguise costume for Noel Edmonds, the host of a BBC television program styled "Noel's House Party." The costume, named Mr. Blobby, was to be worn by Edmonds in order to surprise celebrity guests on the program. The British public began identifying Mr. Blobby as a character rather than a costume. As a consequence, the Mr. Blobby costume, now worn by an actor instead of Mr. Edmonds, has become an unexpected success and has been put to a wider use. In 1993, the BBC began authorizing and licensing products bearing the likeness of Mr. Blobby in the United Kingdom. According to Murray, he consulted with English counsel at that time concerning an action for infringement of his copyright in the Mr. Blobby costume. He allegedly declined to pursue his claim because he could neither pay the 100,000 to 200,000 pounds necessary to bring his case to trial nor post the security necessary to obtain a loan for that amount. In June 1994, the defendants brought Mr. Blobby to New York for his American debut at the International Licensing and Merchandising Conference and Exposition and began actively marketing Mr. Blobby in the United States. Shortly thereafter, Murray obtained American counsel under a contingent fee arrangement. This action ensued. Although it appears that no Mr. Blobby products have yet been produced for the American market, Murray has also filed suit against several alleged licensees, which is still pending in the Southern District. As noted, Judge Stanton dismissed the action against the BBC and Lionheart on the ground of *forum non conveniens,* [cit], and Murray brought this appeal.

DISCUSSION

1. Deference to Murray's Choice of Forum

The doctrine of *forum non conveniens* permits a court to "resist imposition upon its jurisdiction even when jurisdiction is authorized by the letter of a general venue statute," [cit], if dismissal would "best serve the convenience of the parties and the ends of justice." [cit]. There is ordinarily a strong presumption in favor of the plaintiff's choice of forum. [cit]. Where a foreign plaintiff is concerned, however, its choice of forum is entitled to less deference. [cit]. The Supreme Court has emphasized that this rule is not based on a desire to disadvantage foreign plaintiffs but rather on a realistic prediction concerning the ultimate convenience of the forum . . .

Murray quarrels with neither the rule concerning foreign plaintiffs nor the reason underlying it. Instead, he argues that his choice of an American forum must, as a matter of law, be accorded the deference given domestic plaintiffs because of the Berne Convention for the Protection of Literary and Artistic Works, to which both the United States and the United Kingdom are signatories. This is a matter of law that we review *de novo*.

The Convention provides in pertinent part that "the extent of protection, *as well as the means of redress afforded to the author to protect his rights*, shall be governed exclusively by the laws of the country where protection is claimed." Berne Convention for the Protection of Literary and Artistic Works, Paris Text, July 24, 1971, Art. 5(2), . . . Under the Berne Convention, Murray argues, he is deemed to be in the shoes of an American plaintiff and entitled to greater deference in his choice of forum than the district court believed. The principle set out in Article 5, paragraph 2 of the Berne Convention is one of "national treatment," [cit], a choice-of-law rule mandating that the applicable law be the copyright law of the country in which the infringement occurred, not that of the country of which the author is a citizen or in which the work was first published. [cit]. Murray argues, in essence, that the principle of national treatment contained in the Berne Convention mandates procedural opportunities identical to those accorded American plaintiffs alleging copyright infringement. We disagree.

Murray relies on Irish Nat'l Ins. Co. v. Aer Lingus Teoranta, 739 F.2d 90 (2d Cir. 1984), in which we held that the Treaty of Friendship, Commerce and Navigation between the United States and Ireland required the application of the same *forum non conveniens* standards to the Irish plaintiff as a court would have applied to a United States citizen. *Id.* at 91-92. However, we do not agree that *Aer Lingus* applies in the instant matter. The Treaty of Friendship, Commerce and Navigation between the United States and Ireland provided for "national treatment with respect to . . . having access to the courts of justice." *Id.* at 91 (internal quotation marks and citation omitted). In contrast, the national treatment provision of the Berne Convention contains no such language. We are confident that the inclusion of the quoted language in the Treaty with Ireland was not superfluous, and its omission in the Berne Convention was no oversight. When drafters of international agreements seek to provide equal access to national courts, the long-established practice is to do so explicitly. The United States first concluded a treaty with such a provision in 1775, [cit], and explicit "access to courts" clauses appear regularly in treaties to which the United States is a signatory. Indeed, over a dozen treaties have included such language since 1990.

History and practice thus teach that a principle of equal access must be explicitly adopted. In the absence of such an explicit provision in the Berne Convention, we cannot construe a simple declaration of "national treatment" to imply such a principle and to extend *Aer Lingus* and cases following it to this case. [cit].

. . . .

2. *Existence of an Alternative Forum*

When addressing a motion to dismiss for *forum non conveniens*, a court must determine whether an alternative forum is available, because application of the doctrine "presupposes at least two forums in which the defendant is amenable to process." [cit]. The requirement of an alternative forum is ordinarily satisfied if the defendant is amenable to process in another jurisdiction, except in "rare circumstances" when "the remedy offered by the other forum is clearly unsatisfactory." The BBC can obviously be sued in the United Kingdom. Murray argues, however, that he is financially unable to litigate this dispute in England because a contingent-fee arrangement is not permitted in this kind of case. In his view, this professed inability to bring suit renders the English forum unavailable as a matter of law. We review this legal issue *de novo* but disagree with Murray.

[The Court recognized a division of authority on whether financial hardships facing a plaintiff in an alternative forum as a result of the absence of contingent fee arrangements may cause a forum to be deemed unavailable, but followed the majority rule that treated this as one factor to be considered in the balancing of interests performed *after* the determination of whether an alternative forum is available.]

3. *The Balancing of Interests*

. . . .

Murray argues that two public interest factors weigh strongly in favor of permitting his American action to go forward. First, he argues that American copyright law will apply to his copyright infringement claims arising in the United States, militating in favor of an American forum. Murray argues second that the district court erroneously failed to acknowledge that the United States has localized interests in this controversy: the "obvious interest in securing compliance with this nation's laws by citizens of foreign nations who have dealings within this jurisdiction," London Film Productions Ltd. v. Intercontinental Communications, Inc., 580 F. Supp. 47, 49 (S.D.N.Y. 1984), and an interest in whether Mr. Blobby merchandise will be available for sale in the United States. Once again, we disagree.

We are, quite frankly, at a loss to see how this lawsuit has any but the most attenuated American connection. The central issue in dispute concerns the circumstances surrounding the creation of Mr. Blobby. Once that dispute is resolved, the right to exploit the character will be quickly resolved. The crux of the matter, therefore, involves a dispute between British citizens over events that took place exclusively in the United Kingdom. Moreover, it appears that much of the dispute over the creation of Mr. Blobby implicates contract law. British law governs those issues. The United States thus has virtually no interest in resolving the truly disputed issues.

The Berne Convention's national treatment principle insures that no matter where Murray brings his claim, United States copyright law would apply to exploitation of the character in this country. We therefore see little chance that the United States' interest in the application of its laws would be ill-served by a lawsuit in an English forum. Murray makes a great deal of the need to bring additional litigation in the United States to enforce his copyright if this matter is dismissed in favor of an English forum. However, he has offered no reason why his action against the American licensees of Mr. Blobby, currently pending in the Southern District of New York, may not be placed on the suspense calendar pending a resolution of the truly disputed issues in the English courts. Again, once those issues are resolved, everything else will fall into place.

Finally, we note that the forum in which actual infringement of Murray's putative copyright has occurred is not the United States but England. It appears that no Mr. Blobby products have yet been produced for the American market. In virtually all respects, the connection of this case to the United States is as tenuous as its connection to the United Kingdom is strong. We therefore hold that the district court did not abuse its discretion in finding that the public interest factors militated in favor of dismissal.

[The Court also concluded that the district court had properly balanced the private interest factors, and that the financial difficulties Murray may encounter in litigating in England are not sufficiently severe to tip the private interest inquiry in Murray's favor.] We note first that the unavailability of contingent fee arrangements in England is of little weight in the present matter. The availability of such arrangements in the United States is based on a policy decision regarding the assertion of rights in American courts where the parties or the claims have some tangible connection with this country. The decision to permit contingent fee arrangements was not designed to suck foreign parties disputing foreign claims over foreign events into American courts. There is, therefore, no American policy regarding contingent fees that weighs in favor of resolving the underlying dispute over the rights to Mr. Blobby in an American court.

. . . .

We affirm.

NOTES AND QUESTIONS

(1) **National Treatment and Territoriality.** The principle of national treatment is in many respects a corollary of the principle of territoriality: the legality of conduct occurring in the United States will be determined by U.S. law, and the legality of conduct occurring in the United Kingdom will be determined by U.K. law. National treatment simply mandates that U.K. authors bringing a copyright action in the United States will be entitled to the same treatment as would a U.S. author, and that a U.S. author suing for copyright infringement in the United Kingdom will receive the same protection as would a British author. Did Mr. Murray receive national treatment? Why should the ability to enforce a copyright not be an essential part of the national

treatment principle? (We will address particular claims regarding the scope of the national treatment obligation in Chapters 3-4.) Are there other grounds upon which the defendants in *Murray* might have repelled the plaintiff's arguments based upon Article 5 of the Berne Convention?

(2) **Reciprocity.** As Professor Reichman notes, in the few years before the conclusion of the TRIPS Agreement, several nations had enacted new rights that they claimed were not subject to the national treatment obligations of the Paris and Berne Conventions because the rights were of a kind not covered by those conventions. Instead, these countries, such as the United States with respect to semi-conductor chip protection, the United Kingdom as regards unregistered design protection, and the EU with respect to *sui generis* database protection, conditioned the protection of foreign authors, creators or designers on reciprocal protection being afforded their authors in the country from which the foreign national came. Why was there a flurry of reciprocity-based rights in the years preceding the conclusion of TRIPS? Are there advantages to conditioning new forms of intellectual property protection on reciprocal protection?

(3) **MFN in Intellectual Property Law.** What does the incorporation of MFN obligations, which previously had no place in intellectual property treaties, do to the dynamic of international intellectual property relations? What objectives are MFN obligations intended to achieve with respect to intellectual property law?

(4) **The Meaning of "Intellectual Property."** In determining the scope of the MFN and national treatment provisions of the TRIPS Agreement—which involves interpretation of the term "intellectual property," as defined in Article 1(2) of TRIPS—might the analysis suggested by Professor Koumantos, *supra* § 1.02, be of assistance? If the term was interpreted consistent with the notion discussed by Professor Koumantos, would the EU be able to condition database rights offered under its 1996 Database Directive, *see infra* Chapter 4, on reciprocity? In its 1993 Term Directive, *see infra* Chapter 4, the EU conditioned the extended term of copyright protection (life of the author plus seventy years) for non-EU authors on reciprocity, citing the so-called rule of the shorter term in Article 7(8) of the Berne Convention. Why could it do this even after TRIPS?

(5) **The Role of the Broader GATT Agreement and General International Economic Law.** The incorporation in the TRIPS Agreement of minimum standards for the protection of intellectual property was based in part upon the assertion that inadequate protection of intellectual property in some GATT member states had trade-distorting effects and there was a need for a "level playing field." Some scholars have argued that provisions such as Article XX(d) of the GATT provide a broader context for TRIPS and, rejecting the notion of "fair trade" as a new standard of international economic law, have suggested that "national welfare" (particularly in developing countries) continues to be a ground for legitimate discrimination which states may invoke in interpreting specific WTO agreements, such as TRIPS. *See* Edward A. Laing, *Equal Access/Non-discrimination and Legitimate Discrimination in International Economic Law*, 14 WIS. INT'L L.J. 246 (1996).

Chapter 3

INDUSTRIAL PROPERTY

§ 3.01 Trademark And Unfair Competition Law

[A]   Territoriality in Trademark Law

Trademark laws, like all intellectual property laws, are territorial in nature. As a general matter, ownership of trademark rights in one country affords no rights to use that mark (or to enjoin others from using the mark) in another country. A trademark has a separate existence in each independent legal system that accords and recognizes trademark rights; indeed, the same mark may be owned by different persons in different countries. International commerce has brought into sharp focus the problems and complexities of such geographic formalism. And as we will see below, efforts continue to reach international agreement on principles of trademark law that transcend national borders. Those international agreements are, however, premised upon underlying notions of territoriality.

Under U.S. trademark law, where two persons use the same inherently distinctive mark on the same goods, priority (and hence ownership) of rights depends upon which person was the first to use the mark in commerce. In the registration context, Section 2(d) of the Lanham Act provides that registration will be denied to a mark that, when used on the applicant's goods, is likely to be confused with a mark previously registered or used in the United States by another person. The following cases illustrate the operation of the principle of territoriality in applying those rules.

MOTHER'S RESTAURANTS v. MOTHER'S OTHER KITCHEN, INC.
218 U.S.P.Q. 1046 (TTAB 1983)

KRUGMAN, BOARD MEMBER:

An application has been filed by Mother's Other Kitchen, Inc. to register MOTHER'S OTHER KITCHEN for carry out restaurant services. The word KITCHEN has been disclaimed apart from the mark as shown.

Registration has been opposed by Mother's Restaurants, Incorporated. As grounds for opposition, opposer asserts that applicant's mark so resembles opposer's previously registered mark MOTHER'S PIZZA PARLOUR for restaurant services (the term PIZZA PARLOUR being disclaimed apart from the mark) and previously used marks MOTHER'S and MOTHER'S PIZZA PARLOUR & SPAGHETTI HOUSE both for restaurant services, as to be likely, when applied to applicant's services, to cause confusion, mistake or to deceive.

. . . .

With respect to the question of opposer's asserted priority in the pleaded marks MOTHER'S and MOTHER'S PIZZA PARLOUR & SPAGHETTI HOUSE, opposer has shown by way of testimony that its predecessor in interest opened a restaurant under the name MOTHER'S PIZZA PARLOUR in Hamilton, Ontario, Canada on December 1, 1970; that some 55 additional restaurants under the same name subsequently opened up in Canada and the United States; that the first restaurant opened in the United States was in November 1977 in Columbus, Ohio; that opposer since 1971 has used its marks MOTHER'S and MOTHER'S PIZZA PARLOUR & SPAGHETTI HOUSE in radio advertisements; that many of the radio advertisements used during the period 1971-1977 were broadcast on Canadian radio stations having radio signals reaching the United States, specifically, parts of New York and Michigan; that in 1975, opposer began a promotional campaign for its Canadian restaurants whereby promotional materials were distributed at tourist information booths in southern Ontario; that these promotional packages contained discount coupons and take-out menus using the term MOTHER'S; that some 50,000 promotional packages were distributed in the summer of 1975 and the promotional campaign has continued every summer to the present with over 100,000 promotional packages distributed in 1981; and that Americans have dined in opposer's Canadian restaurants as evidenced by a market survey as well as letters from Americans containing comments about their dining experiences at opposer's restaurants as well as business inquiries concerning franchise opportunities from interested Americans. It is opposer's position that applicant, not having taken any testimony or offered any evidence, is limited to its filing date as its date of first use (October 14, 1976); that the aforementioned promotional activities of opposer predated applicant's filing date; and that by virtue of opposer's radio spot advertising and promotional efforts directed to Americans entering Canada from the United States along tourist routes, opposer created good will in the United States market and established service mark rights in MOTHER'S and MOTHER'S PIZZA PARLOUR & SPAGHETTI HOUSE as of 1971. . . . [W]e decline to hold that opposer's promotional activities in Canada regarding MOTHER'S and MOTHER'S PIZZA PARLOUR & SPAGHETTI HOUSE prior to 1976 resulted in superior rights in said marks in the United States so as to preclude applicant from registering a confusingly similar mark. Rather, it is our view that prior use and advertising of a mark in connection with goods or services marketed in a foreign country (whether said advertising occurs inside or outside the United States) creates no priority rights in said mark in the United States as against one who, in good faith, has adopted the same or similar mark for the same or similar goods or services in the United States prior to the foreigner's first use of the mark on goods or services sold and/or offered in the United States . . . at least unless it can be shown that the foreign party's mark was, at the time of the adoption and first use of a similar mark by the first user in the United States, a "famous" mark within the meaning of Vaudable v. Montmartre, Inc., 193 N.Y.S.2d 332 (N.Y. Sup. Ct. 1959). Under the circumstances, we will limit our determination of the question of likelihood of confusion to an analysis of the mark covered by opposer's registration MOTHER'S PIZZA PARLOUR for restaurant services vis-a-vis the mark covered by applicant's application MOTHER'S OTHER KITCHEN for carry out restaurant services.

. . . .

. . . We conclude that purchasers familiar with MOTHER'S PIZZA PARLOUR restaurants would, upon coming into contact with MOTHER'S OTHER KITCHEN carry out restaurants, be likely to believe that they were somehow related as to ownership or that they otherwise shared a common sponsorship or origin. Accordingly, we hold that confusion as to source or origin would be likely for purposes of Section 2(d) of the Trademark Act.

The opposition is sustained and registration to applicant is refused.

ALLEN, BOARD MEMBER, concurring in part, dissenting in part:

I fully agree with the decision of the majority holding that opposer's pre-1976 promotional activities in Canada, including spillover advertising into the United States, on behalf of MOTHER'S and MOTHER'S PIZZA PARLOUR & SPAGHETTI HOUSE restaurants in Canada did not bestow upon opposer any superior rights in these service marks in the United States. . . .

. . . .

Determination of the issue should not be influenced by whether the case involves goods or services. Although the requirement of use is more easily satisfied in the case of services—use in advertising being sufficient—the definition of commerce in the Trademark Act of 1946 is the same for either kind of mark. . . . [I]n the instant case, the only impact of the spillover advertising is on commerce within Canada. The rendering of the services is in Canada, by Canadian persons and entities. The profit, if any, emanating from the rendering of such services accrues to Canadian citizens. To avail oneself of the services one must be in Canada. Thus, there is no impact as a result of the spillover advertising on commerce between Canada and the United States. Accordingly, the prior spillover advertising of MOTHER'S and MOTHER'S PIZZA PARLOUR & SPAGHETTI HOUSE created no rights or priority for opposer in the United States.

It should be added that the contrary result urged by opposer herein would have enormous consequences, in terms of uncertainty, on our trademark system. Considering the rapid technological advances in telecommunications, especially satellite communications, a television signal transmitting advertising of a restaurant in a distant foreign land can be captured and viewed or retransmitted in the United States by the use of sophisticated disk antennae aimed at the communications satellite and associated equipment. Thus, if mere use of a mark in restaurant services advertising created rights in the United States, without a filing somewhere on a Register capable of being searched, the adoption of a restaurant mark in the United States would be extremely hazardous.

[Board Member Allen disagreed with the majority's conclusion on the question of likely confusion with the prior mark that remained for analysis, and would thus have dismissed the opposition.]

VAUDABLE v. MONTMARTRE, INC.
193 N.Y.S.2d 332 (Sup. Ct. 1959).

HENRY CLAY GREENBERG, JUSTICE.

Plaintiffs, owner and operator of the famous Maxim's restaurant in Paris, move for summary judgment in this action for a permanent injunction restraining defendants, owner and operator of a newly opened restaurant in the Gramercy Park section of this city, from using the name Maxim's. . . .

The French restaurant, Maxim's, was established in 1893 by an individual whose given name was Maxime. It was subsequently sold and all rights therein acquired by plaintiffs. It received wide publicity as the setting of a substantial portion of Lehar's operetta, The Merry Widow, has been the subject over a long period of years of numerous newspaper and magazine articles, and has been mentioned by name and filmed in movies and television. There is no doubt as to its unique and eminent position as a restaurant of international fame and prestige. It is, of course, well known in this country, particularly to the class of people residing in the cosmopolitan city of New York who dine out. Plaintiffs have registered the mark MAXIM'S with the United States Patent Office for catering services and wines, and have merchandised and sold food products under that name, or a variant thereof, in the United States.

The affidavits and exhibits establish not merely that defendants copied the name MAXIM'S but endeavored to create the illusion of identity with plaintiffs' restaurant. They took the name of Montmartre, a Parisian subdivision, as their corporate name. The decor of their restaurant is so similar in its red and gold color scheme to the French restaurant as to be described in a newspaper article as its 'replica'. The most significant evidence, however, is the imitation of plaintiffs' distinctive style of script printing of the name MAXIM'S. Defendants' form of denial is pregnant with admission of the charge. They deny the distinctive script printing in their use of the name MAXIM'S on the doormat, the match books and the menus, but do not deny such type of printing on the awning, over the door, on credit application cards and in their advertising. The exhibits annexed prove the truth of the charge.

Defendants contend that the name "Maxim" became popular after the invention by two gentlemen bearing that name of smokeless powder and the machine gun and that it has been used in many different types of business. But plaintiffs and their predecessors in title made this name famous in the high-class restaurant field. Whatever the source of the name, it is the origination and development of its use in a particular field which may entitle the user thereof to protection by virtue of the secondary meaning acquired therein.

It is obvious that defendants' purpose is to appropriate the good will plaintiffs have created in the name MAXIM'S as a restaurant establishment. The fact that they are not in present actual competition is immaterial (Maison Prunier v. Prunier's Restaurant & Cafe, Inc., 159 Misc. 551). A wrongful attempt to suggest an association or connection of some sort is sufficient to warrant relief to prevent confusion in the public mind as well as dilution of plaintiffs' trade name [cit]; and the more distinctive and unique the name, the greater the need for protection from dilution of its distinctive quality (Tiffany & Co. v. Tiffany Productions, Inc., 147 Misc. 679, aff'd, 237 App.Div. 801, aff'd, 262 N.Y. 482).

The trend of the law, both statutory and decisional, has been to extend the scope of the doctrine of unfair competition, whose basic principle is that commercial unfairness should be restrained whenever it appears that there has been a misappropriation, for the advantage of one person, of a property right belonging to another. [cit]. These plaintiffs are clearly entitled to relief in view of defendants' appropriation of their trade name and calculated imitation of features associated with plaintiffs' restaurant.

No evidence sufficient to create a triable issue of estoppel has been set forth by defendants. Mere failure to proceed against users of the name in other fields or areas is not such acquiescence as precludes the granting of injunctive relief against the present defendants in a field or area where plaintiffs' interests are involved. . . .

Nor is there any evidence of abandonment. The Parisian restaurant, closed during the war, was reopened in 1946 by plaintiffs and fully developed thereafter with expansion of certain activities into other fields and countries. "To constitute an abandonment there must not only be nonuser, but an intent to abandon." [cit]. The facts here shown establish the very reverse of an intent to abandon.

Plaintiffs are accordingly entitled to an injunction restraining defendants from use of the name MAXIM'S, and to an assessment to ascertain the amount of damages, if any, occasioned by defendants' wrongful acts of unfair competition, as demanded in the complaint.

PERSON'S CO., LTD. v. CHRISTMAN
900 F.2d 1565 (Fed. Cir. 1990)

SMITH, SENIOR CIRCUIT JUDGE

Person's Co., Ltd. appeals from the decision of the Patent and Trademark Office Trademark Trial and Appeal Board (Board) which granted summary judgment in favor of Larry Christman and ordered the cancellation of appellant's registration for the mark PERSON'S for various apparel items. Appellant Person's Co. seeks cancellation of Christman's registration for the mark PERSON'S for wearing apparel on the following grounds: likelihood of confusion based on its prior foreign use . . . and unfair competition within the meaning of the Paris Convention. We affirm the Board's decision.

Background

The facts pertinent to this appeal are as follows: In 1977, Takaya Iwasaki first applied a stylized logo bearing the name PERSON'S to clothing in his native Japan. Two years later Iwasaki formed Person's Co., Ltd., a Japanese corporation, to market and distribute the clothing items in retail stores located in Japan.

In 1981, Larry Christman, a U.S. citizen and employee of a sportswear wholesaler, visited a Person's Co. retail store while on a business trip to Japan. Christman purchased several clothing items bearing the PERSON'S logo and returned with them to the United States. After consulting with legal counsel and being advised that no one had yet established a claim to the logo in the United States, Christman developed designs for his own PERSON'S brand sportswear line based on appellant's products he had purchased in Japan. In February 1982, Christman contracted with a clothing manufacturer to produce clothing articles with the PERSON'S logo attached. These clothing items were sold, beginning in April 1982, to sportswear retailers in the northwestern United States. Christman formed Team Concepts, Ltd., a Washington corporation, in May 1983 to continue merchandising his sportswear line, which had expanded to include additional articles such as shoulder bags. All the sportswear marketed by Team Concepts bore either the mark PERSON'S or a copy of appellant's globe logo; many of the clothing styles were apparently copied directly from appellant's designs.

In April 1983, Christman filed an application for U.S. trademark registration in an effort to protect the PERSON'S mark. Christman believed himself to be the exclusive owner of the right to use and register the mark in the United States and apparently had no knowledge that appellant soon intended to introduce its similar sportswear line under the identical mark in the U.S. market. Christman's registration issued in September 1984 for use on wearing apparel.

In the interim between Christman's first sale and the issuance of his registration, Person's Co., Ltd. became a well known and highly respected force in the Japanese fashion industry. The company, which had previously sold garments under the PERSON'S mark only in Japan, began implementing its plan to sell goods under this mark in the United States. According to Mr. Iwasaki, purchases by buyers for resale in the United States occurred as early as November 1982. This was some seven months subsequent to Christman's first sales in the United States. Person's Co. filed an application for U.S. trademark registration in the following year, and, in 1985, engaged an export trading company to introduce its goods into the U.S. market. The registration for the mark PERSON'S issued in August 1985 for use on luggage, clothing and accessories. After recording U.S. sales near $4,000,000 in 1985, Person's Co. granted California distributor Zip Zone International a license to manufacture and sell goods under the PERSON'S mark in the United States.

In early 1986, appellant's advertising in the U.S. became known to Christman and both parties became aware of confusion in the marketplace. Person's Co. initiated an action to cancel Christman's registration on the following grounds: (1) likelihood of confusion; (2) abandonment; and (3) unfair competition within the meaning of the Paris Convention. Christman counterclaimed and asserted prior use and likelihood of confusion as grounds for cancellation of the Person's Co. registration.

After some discovery, Christman filed a motion with the Board for summary judgment on all counts. In a well reasoned decision, the Board held for Christman on the grounds that Person's use of the mark in Japan could not be used to establish priority against a "good faith" senior user in U.S. commerce. The Board found no evidence to suggest that the PERSON'S mark had acquired any notoriety in this country at the time of its adoption by Christman. Therefore, appellant had no reputation or goodwill upon which Christman could have intended to trade, rendering the unfair competition provisions of the Paris Convention inapplicable . . . . The Board granted summary judgment to Christman and ordered appellant's registration cancelled.

The Board held in its opinion on reconsideration that Christman had not adopted the mark in bad faith despite his appropriation of a mark in use by appellant in a foreign country. The Board adopted the view that copying a mark in use in a foreign country is not in bad faith unless the foreign mark is famous in the United States or the copying is undertaken for the purpose of interfering with the prior user's planned expansion into the United States. Person's Co. appeals and requests that this court direct the Board to enter summary judgment in its favor.

Issues

Does knowledge of a mark's use outside U.S. commerce preclude good faith adoption and use of the identical mark in the United States prior to the entry of the foreign user into the domestic market?

. . . .

Priority

The first ground asserted for cancellation in the present action is section 2(d) of the Lanham Act; each party claims prior use of registered marks which unquestionably are confusingly similar and affixed to similar goods.

Section 1 of the Lanham Act states that "the owner of a trademark *used in commerce* may register his trademark . . . ." The term "commerce" is defined in Section 45 of the Act as ". . . all commerce which may be lawfully regulated by Congress." No specific Constitutional language gives Congress power to regulate trademarks, so the power of the federal government to provide for trademark registration comes only under its commerce power. The term "used in commerce" in the Lanham Act refers to a sale or transportation of goods bearing the mark in or having an effect on: (1) United States interstate commerce; (2) United States commerce with foreign nations; or (3) United States commerce with the Indian Tribes.

In the present case, appellant Person's Co. relies on its use of the mark in Japan in an attempt to support its claim for priority in the United States. Such foreign use has no effect on U.S. commerce and cannot form the basis for a holding that appellant has priority here. The concept of territoriality is basic to trademark law; trademark rights exist in each country solely according to that country's statutory scheme. Christman was the first to use the mark in

United States commerce and the first to obtain a federal registration thereon. Appellant has no basis upon which to claim priority and is the junior user under these facts.[16]

Bad Faith

Appellant vigorously asserts that Christman's adoption and use of the mark in the United States subsequent to Person's Co.'s adoption in Japan is tainted with "bad faith" and that the priority in the United States obtained thereby is insufficient to establish rights superior to those arising from Person's Co.'s prior adoption in a foreign country. Relying on Woman's World Shops, Inc. v. Lane Bryant, Inc., [5 USPQ2d 1985 (TTAB 1985)] Person's Co. argues that a "remote junior user" of a mark obtains no right superior to the "senior user" if the "junior user" has adopted the mark with knowledge of the "senior user's" prior use.[18] In *Woman's World*, the senior user utilized the mark within a limited geographical area. A junior user from a different geographical area of the United States sought unrestricted federal registration for a nearly identical mark, with the exception to its virtually exclusive rights being those of the known senior user. The Board held that such an appropriation with knowledge failed to satisfy the good faith requirements of the Lanham Act and denied the concurrent use rights sought by the junior user. Person's Co. cites *Woman's World* for the proposition that a junior user's adoption and use of a mark with knowledge of another's prior use constitutes bad faith. It is urged that this principle is equitable in nature and should not be limited to knowledge of use within the territory of the United States.

While the facts of the present case are analogous to those in *Woman's World*, the case is distinguishable in one significant respect. In *Woman's World*, the first use of the mark by both the junior and senior users was in United States commerce. In the case at bar, appellant Person's Co., while first to adopt the mark, was not the first user in the United States. Christman is the senior user, and we are aware of no case where a senior user has been charged with bad faith. The concept of bad faith adoption applies to remote junior users seeking concurrent use registrations; in such cases, the likelihood of customer confusion in the remote area may be presumed from proof of the junior user's knowledge. In the present case, when Christman initiated use of the mark, Person's Co. had not yet entered U.S. commerce. The Person's Co. had no goodwill in the United States and the PERSON'S mark had no reputation here. Appellant's argument ignores the territorial nature of trademark rights.

---

[16] ... The statutory scheme set forth in § 44 [of the Lanham Act] is in place to lower barriers to entry and assist foreign applicants in establishing business goodwill in the United States. Person's Co. does not assert rights under § 44, which if properly applied, might have been used to secure priority over Christman.

[18] Appellant repeatedly makes reference to a "world economy" and considers Christman to be the remote junior user of the mark. Although Person's did adopt the mark in Japan prior to Christman's use in United States commerce, the use in Japan cannot be relied upon to acquire U.S. trademark rights. Christman is the senior user as that term is defined under U.S. trademark law.

Appellant next asserts that Christman's knowledge of its prior use of the mark in Japan should preclude his acquisition of superior trademark rights in the United States. The Board found that, at the time of registration, Christman was not aware of appellant's intention to enter the U.S. clothing and accessories market in the future. Christman obtained a trademark search on the PERSON'S mark and an opinion of competent counsel that the mark was "available" in the United States. Since appellant had taken no steps to secure registration of the mark in the United States, Christman was aware of no basis for Person's Co. to assert superior rights to use and registration here. Appellant would have us infer bad faith adoption because of Christman's awareness of its use of the mark in Japan, but an inference of bad faith requires something more than mere knowledge of prior use of a similar mark in a foreign country.

As the Board noted below, Christman's prior use in U.S. commerce cannot be discounted solely because he was aware of appellant's use of the mark in Japan. While adoption of a mark with knowledge of a prior actual user in U.S. commerce may give rise to cognizable equities as between the parties, no such equities may be based upon knowledge of a similar mark's existence or on a problematical intent to use such a similar mark in the future. Knowledge of a foreign use does not preclude good faith adoption and use in the United States. While there is some case law supporting a finding of bad faith where (1) the foreign mark is famous here[23] or (2) the use is a nominal one made solely to block the prior foreign user's planned expansion into the United States,[24] as the Board correctly found, neither of these circumstances is present in this case.

We agree with the Board's conclusion that Christman's adoption and use of the mark were in good faith. Christman's adoption of the mark occurred at a time when appellant had not yet entered U.S. commerce; therefore, no prior user was in place to give Christman notice of appellant's potential U.S. rights. Christman's conduct in appropriating and using appellant's mark in a market where he believed the Japanese manufacturer did not compete can hardly be considered unscrupulous commercial conduct.[25] Christman adopted the trademark being used by appellant in Japan, but appellant has not identified any aspect of U.S. trademark law violated by such action. Trademark rights under the Lanham Act arise solely out of use of the mark in U.S. commerce or from ownership of a foreign registration thereon; "the law pertaining to registration of trademarks does not regulate all aspects of business morality." [cit]. When the law has been crafted with the clarity of crystal, it also has the qualities of a glass slipper: it cannot be shoe-horned onto facts it does not fit, no matter how appealing they might appear.

---

[23]See, e.g., Vaudable v. Montmartre, Inc., 20 Misc. 2d 757 (N.Y. Sup. Ct. 1959); Mother's Restaurants, Inc. v. Mother's Other Kitchen, Inc., 218 U.S.P.Q. (BNA) 1046 (TTAB 1983).

[24]See Davidoff Extension, S.A. v. Davidoff Int'l., 221 U.S.P.Q. (BNA) 465 (S.D. Fla. 1983).

[25]See Bulk Mfg. Co. v. Schoenbach Prod. Co., 208 U.S.P.Q. (BNA) 664, 667-68 (S.D.N.Y. 1980).

The Paris Convention

Appellant next claims that Christman's adoption and use of the PERSON'S mark in the United States constitutes unfair competition under Articles 6*bis* and 10*bis* of the Paris Convention. It is well settled that the Trademark Trial and Appeal Board cannot adjudicate unfair competition issues in a cancellation or opposition proceeding. The Board's function is to determine whether there is a right to secure or to maintain a registration.

. . . .

Conclusion

In *United Drug Co. v. Rectanus Co.*, [248 U.S. 90(1918)], the Supreme Court of the United States determined that "there is no such thing as property in a trademark except as a right appurtenant to an established business or trade in connection with which the mark is employed. . . . Its function is simply to designate the goods as the product of a particular trader and to protect his goodwill against the sale of another's product as his; and it is not the subject of property except in connection with an existing business." In the present case, appellant failed to secure protection for its mark through use in U.S. commerce; therefore, no established business or product line was in place from which trademark rights could arise. Christman was the first to use the mark in U.S. commerce. This first use was not tainted with bad faith by Christman's mere knowledge of appellant's prior foreign use, so the Board's conclusion on the issue of priority was correct. . . . Accordingly, the grant of summary judgment was entirely in order, and the Board's decision is affirmed.

BUTI v. IMPRESSA PEROSA, S.R.L.
139 F.3d 98 (2d Cir. 1998)

COTE, DISTRICT JUDGE (sitting by designation):

[In June 1994, plaintiff Buti commenced plans to open a franchise of theme restaurants, similar to Hard Rock Cafe or Planet Hollywood, but focusing on the fashion model industry instead of rock and roll or film. Buti hired a law firm to perform a trademark search of the "Fashion Cafe" name. After the law firm reported that there was no use or registration of the "Fashion Cafe" mark in the United States, Buti filed an application with the U.S. Patent and Trademark Office for registration of the mark "Fashion Cafe." In early December 1994, Buti publicized the groundbreaking for the New York Fashion Cafe, which generated thousands of television, newspaper and magazine articles worldwide. Plaintiff's Fashion Cafe restaurant opened in New York on April 7, 1995, serving high quality American cuisine and marketing an extensive line of souvenirs bearing the Fashion Cafe Logo.

Giorgio Santambrogio is an officer and part owner of defendant Impressa Perosa, an Italian company. Santambrogio has ownership interests in a modeling agency located in Milan, Italy, and a restaurant cafe in Milan known as the Fashion Cafe, which opened in 1987. Impressa Perosa registered the Fashion Cafe trademark in Italy in April 1988. Santambrogio never opened a restaurant in the United States, nor did he ever sell any food or other merchandise in the United States. When Santambrogio visited the U.S., he promoted his Milan Fashion Cafe by giving models free T-shirts, small gift items with the Milan Fashion Cafe name, business cards and vouchers for free food and beverages. Santambrogio had a "fantasy in his brain" that he would approach American hotel chains such as Hilton or Sheraton and try to expand his Milan restaurant into a United States chain, but he admits that he never approached any of the hotel chains about his idea.

After receiving a cease and desist letter from Impressa Perosa, Buti filed an action seeking a declaratory judgment that he had superior rights to the name "Fashion Cafe" in the United States. The District Court accepted the recommendation of the magistrate and granted Buti summary judgment. The defendant appealed.]

DISCUSSION

... Both sides agree that the critical question in determining their respective rights in the Fashion Cafe name is which party first "used" the name "in commerce" as that phrase is defined by Section 45 of the Lanham Act.

"Use in Commerce"

The Lanham Act authorizes trademark registration only for marks that are "used in commerce." 15 U.S.C. § 1051. In the context of the restaurant "services" at issue in this case, "use in commerce" is defined by Section 45 of the Lanham Act as:

> bona fide use of a mark in the ordinary course of trade, and not made merely to reserve a right in a mark. . . .
>
> [A] mark shall be deemed to be in use in commerce . . . on services when it is *used or displayed in the sale or advertising of services and the services are rendered in commerce,* or the services are rendered in more than one State or in the United States and a foreign country and the person rendering the services is engaged in commerce in connection with the services.

15 U.S.C. § 1127 (emphasis added). Impressa asserts, and Buti accepts, that the italicized portion of the definition is the section applicable in this case.

[T]he parties' disagreement with respect to the meaning of Section 45 centers on Impressa's contention that Santambrogio's advertising and promotional activities in the United States constituted sufficient "use" of the Fashion Cafe name "in commerce" as to merit protection under the Lanham Act. Notwithstanding this disagreement over the statutory concept of "use," however, the parties are in complete accord as to the meaning under Section 45 of "commerce." That is, Impressa and Buti acknowledge, as they must, that "commerce," for purposes of delimiting "use in commerce" under the Lanham Act, is expressly defined by Section 45 to be "all commerce which may lawfully be regulated by Congress." 15 U.S.C. § 1127. We recently affirmed that the "history and text of the Lanham Act show that 'use in commerce' reflects Congress's intent to legislate to the limits of its authority under the Commerce Clause." United We Stand America, Inc. v. United We Stand, America New York, Inc., 128 F.3d 86, 92 (2d Cir.1997). [cit]. The Supreme Court, moreover, has made clear that Congress's authority under the Commerce Clause extends to activity that "substantially affects" interstate commerce. See United States v. Lopez, 514 U.S. 549, 559 (1995). In the trademark context, the limits of Congress's Commerce Clause authority are manifested by the cases that define the extraterritorial reach of the Lanham Act. . . .

This case, of course, involves the reverse, or perhaps the mirror image, of the issue presented in [that] line of cases; we are concerned here not with the extraterritorial force of our trademark laws to regulate or redress the conduct of a foreign citizen in a foreign land, but with the ability of that foreign citizen to gain the protection of our trademark laws, and the degree of interaction with our nation's commerce that is required of him to receive that protection. Impressa nevertheless has implicitly acknowledged, through several pivotal concessions, that the question whether it may derive the benefits of the Lanham Act is dictated by one of the same inquiries that guided the decision in [the extra-territoriality cases in this Circuit], namely, whether Impressa has conducted the affairs of its Milan Fashion Cafe in such a way as to "substantially affect" United States interstate or foreign commerce, and thereby fall within Congress's authority under the Commerce Clause. Thus Impressa conceded at oral argument that: (1) the food and drink services of the Milan Fashion Cafe form no part of the trade between Italy and the United States; and (2) Congress has no constitutional authority to regulate the operation of the Fashion Cafe in Milan. These admissions, even if only a recognition of the fact that Impressa's registration and use of the Fashion Cafe name in Italy has not, given the territorial nature of trademark rights, secured it any rights in the name under the Lanham Act, [cit], nonetheless have dramatically narrowed the issue to be decided in this appeal.

"Services Rendered in Commerce"

As indicated, the crux of the parties' dispute is whether Santambrogio's advertising and promotional activities in the United States on behalf of the Milan Fashion Cafe were sufficient to establish Impressa's "use in commerce" of the Fashion Cafe name, within the meaning of Section 45 of the Lanham Act, where it is undisputed that Impressa rendered no restaurant services, nor operated any other business, under that name in the United States. We believe the answer lies in first principles. The Supreme Court explained long ago that the right to a particular mark grows out of its use, not its mere adoption; its function is simply to designate the goods as the product of a particular trader and to protect his good will against the sale of another's product as his; and it is not the subject of property except in connection with an existing business.

United Drug Co. v. Theodore Rectanus Co., 248 U.S. 90, 97 (1918) . . . Accordingly, one who registers and owns a trademark thereby "acquires the right to prevent his goods from being confused with those of others and to prevent his own trade from being diverted to competitors through their use of misleading marks." [cit]. The right so acquired, however, exists only "as a right *appurtenant to an established business or trade* in connection with which the mark is employed." *United Drug*, 248 U.S. at 97 (emphasis added). Under this rule, therefore, Santambrogio's mere advertising of the Fashion Cafe mark, standing alone, did not constitute "use" of the mark within the meaning of the Lanham Act. . . .

The question thus remaining—apparently one of first impression in the federal courts—is whether Santambrogio's promotional activities in the United States merited Lanham Act protection for Impressa's mark based on the ongoing business of Impressa's Fashion Cafe in Milan. . . . [A]lthough courts may not have addressed the issue of whether U.S. advertising of a foreign business establishes United States trademark rights, the TTAB has, adversely to Impressa [in Mother's Restaurants Inc. v. Mother's Other Kitchen, Inc.].[2]

The principle articulated in *Mother's Restaurants* was not new, the TTAB having said as much several times previously. . . . Moreover, the TTAB continues to adhere to the *Mother's Restaurants* position today. . . .

We have noted on many occasions that the decisions of the TTAB, while not binding on courts within this circuit, are nonetheless to "be accorded great weight." [cit]. We take particular comfort in our reliance on the TTAB decisions . . . because the principles enunciated therein rest on a solid footing. As previously explained, the notion that trademark rights exist only as rights "appurtenant to an established business or trade in connection with which the mark is employed," *United Drug*, 248 U.S. at 97, has an enduring pedigree. Even with respect to the specific question in this case—whether the domestic advertising of an exclusively foreign company's trademark constitutes "use" of the mark under the Lanham Act—the TTAB's answer in the negative represents a well-founded application of basic trademark doctrine. Indeed, we believe the Supreme Court reached essentially the same determination, albeit in dicta, eighty years ago:

[T]he expression, sometimes met with, that a trade-mark right is not

---

[2]The TTAB indicated that the only exception to the rule in *Mother's Restaurants*, other than—implicitly—where the prior United States user failed to act in good faith, would be when "it can be shown that the foreign party's mark was . . . a 'famous' mark within the meaning of Vaudable v. Montmartre, Inc. . . . The "famous mark" exception has no application here given that Impressa has made no claim under that doctrine and that the record would not support such an argument in any event.

limited in its enjoyment by territorial bounds, is true only in the sense that *wherever the trade goes, attended by the use of the mark*, the right of the trader to be protected against the sale by others of their wares in the place of his wares will be sustained.

Id. at 98 (emphasis added). Thus, the TTAB's ruling in *Mother's Restaurants* and other cases properly reserves United States trademark protection to those foreign companies whose actual "trade goes, attended by the use of [its] mark," into United States interstate or foreign commerce. So that the issue is no longer in doubt, we hold, in keeping with the TTAB's longstanding view and the District Court's decision in this case, that the mere advertising or promotion of a mark in the United States is insufficient to constitute "use" of the mark "in commerce," within the meaning of the Lanham Act, where that advertising or promotion is unaccompanied by any actual rendering in the United States or in "commerce which may lawfully be regulated by Congress," of the services "in connection with which the mark is employed," *United Drug*, 248 U.S. at 97.

. . . .

McDONALD'S CORP. v. McDONALD'S CORP. LTD
[1997] FSR 200 (Supreme Court 1996) (Jamaica)

CHESTER ORR J.:

. . . .

The plaintiff is a corporation existing under the laws of the states of Delaware, United States of America. It develops, operates franchises and services a world-wide chain of restaurants which operate under the trade name and trade mark "McDonald's". It opened its first McDonald's restaurant in 1955 and as of March 1,1995, the plaintiff and its licensees were operating 15,963 restaurants in 79 countries including the Caribbean.

. . . .

The plaintiff contends that during the 1970s and 1980s it actively pursued the possibility of opening restaurants in Jamaica but that this proved not to be feasible due principally to the stringent foreign exchange regulations in force in Jamaica which were not relaxed until 1994. The defendants seek to rebut this contention by adverting to the fact that during this period a number of foreign restaurant chains, including Burger King, Shakey's and Kentucky Fried Chicken commenced business in Jamaica.

During the period the plaintiff received inquiries from more than 80 individuals, the majority of whom were Jamaican entrepreneurs including the first defendant, expressing an interest in obtaining a licence from the plaintiff to operate in Jamaica.

On July 3,1981, the attorneys for the first defendant wrote to the plaintiff offering to become the plaintiff's franchisee in Jamaica, . . . The plaintiff states that it rejected the offer. . . .

. . . .

In or about November 1992, the first defendant [which had operated a restaurant at 1 Cargill Avenue since 1971] decided to have the building at 1 Cargill Avenue completely refurbished and renovated in an effort to modernise and upgrade the facilities in accordance with the many fast-food outlets which had by then opened in Jamaica . . . . The renovation continued in 1993 but was not completed until the middle of 1995. . . .

In 1994, the plaintiff formalized plans to open restaurants in Jamaica. An announcement was made at a press conference in October 1994 and the opening of the restaurant at Ironshore, Montego Bay was extensively advertised.

. . . .

The re-opening of the restaurant at 1 Cargill Avenue was also advertised. Eventually both restaurants were opened. The first defendant's at Cargill Avenue on September 26, 1995 and the plaintiff's at Ironshire on September 28, 1995.

The menu boards and tray liners at Cargill Avenue contained items prefixed by "McD" which the plaintiff states is a colourable imitation of its items. The defendants removed these items and state that it was done in error.

The necessary elements to establish passing off were stated in *Erven Warnink BV and others v J Townend & Sons (Hull) Ltd and others* [1979] 2 All ER 927 (the Advocaat Case).

. . . .

Lord Fraser of Tullybelton at 943 formulated the test thus:

> It is essential for the plaintiff in a passing off action to show at least the following facts: (1) that his business consists of, or includes, selling in England a class of goods to which the particular trade name applies; (2) that the class of goods is clearly defined, and that in the minds of the public, or a section of the public, in England, the trade name distinguishes that class from other similar goods; (3) that because of the reputation of the goods, there is good will attached to the name; (4) that he, the plaintiff, as a member of the class of those who sell the goods, is the owner of goodwill in England which is of substantial value; (5) that he has suffered, or is really likely to suffer, substantial damage to his property in the goodwill by reason of the defendants selling goods which are falsely described by the trade name to which the goodwill is attached.

The question arises as to whether the plaintiff has goodwill in Jamaica. There is conflict between the authorities on this point. In *The Athletes Foot Marketing Associates Inc v Cobra Sports Ltd and Another* [1980] RPC 343 Walton J stated the position thus at 349:

> There appear, on the cases, to be two schools of thought about this. There is what was described in argument as a "hard line" school of thought, which maintains that it is essential for the plaintiff to have

carried on a trade in the country . . . and a much less demanding approach, which suggests that something less than that will do (well exemplified by *Maxim's Limited v Dye* [1977] 1 WLR 1155, the case concerning the famous restaurant).

In *Maxim's Limited v Dye* it was held that a plaintiff could establish that he had goodwill in England in respect of a foreign business which the courts would protect without it having to be shown that he carried on business in England.

. . . .

. . . Several cases were cited to me from countries in the Commonwealth . . . supporting both schools of thought. In some of the later cases it was held that it is not necessary for the plaintiff to have a place of business in the jurisdiction, it is sufficient if he has customers there.

In the *Athletes Foot* case, Walton J said at 357:

> . . . the position in law appears to be relatively clear. That is to say it does not matter that the plaintiffs are not at present actually carrying on business in this country, provided that they have customers here. Equally, it is of no moment, if they have no customers here, that they have a reputation in the general sense of the word in this country. It is also of no moment that that reputation may have been brought about by advertising; this can be of no moment, unless . . . it brings in customers, when, of course, once again there is no need to rely upon it.

In *Pete Waterman Limited and Others v CBS United Kingdom Limited* [1993] EMLR 27, Sir Nicholas Browne-Wilkinson V-C, as he then was, after reviewing the authorities said at 58:

> The presence of customers in this country is sufficient to constitute the carrying on of business here whether or not there is otherwise a place of business here and whether or not the services are provided here. Once it is found that there are customers, it is open to find that there is a business here to which the local goodwill is attached.

. . . .

In *Conagra Inc v McCain Foods Aust Pty Ltd* [1992] 23 IPR 193, a decision of the Full Court of the Federal Court of Australia, . . . it was held:

> It is not necessary that a plaintiff, to maintain a passing off action, have a place of business in Australia nor for his goods to be sold here. It is sufficient if his goods have a reputation in Australia among persons of a sufficient degree to establish there is a likelihood of deception among consumers and damage to his reputation. Reputation may be proved by a variety of means including

advertisements on various forms of media and exposure of people within the forum to the goods of the overseas owner.

[Walton J. in *Athletes Foot*] considered it inappropriate to make a final decision between these two schools of thought on interlocutory proceedings. I entirely agree. However, the plaintiff claims it can succeed on both schools of thought. On the one hand it had a reputation in Jamaica prior to the opening of its restaurant at Ironshore on September 28, 1995. This reputation was acquired, inter alia, by advertisements and visitors from Jamaica to its restaurants abroad. On the other hand, it has an established business and customers in Jamaica since September 28, 1995.

[The defendants argued that] the relevant date for determining whether the defendants have in fact damaged the goodwill of the plaintiff is the year 1971 when the first defendant company was formed. At this date the plaintiff had opened restaurants in only four countries, viz, the United States of America, Canada, Puerto Rico and Costa Rica.

[The court decided that these were issues best left for trial and decision based upon a full evidentiary airing. The court concluded that the balance of convenience lay in preserving the status quo until trial, which it achieved by refusing the application for an injunction by the plaintiff and the grant of the defendants' application for an injunction restraining the plaintiff from opening a restaurant in Kingston under the name McDonald's.]

Jian Tools for Sales Inc v. Roderick Manhattan Grp. Ltd., [1995] FSR 924 (Ch. D. 1995) (Eng.). The plaintiff (Jian) was a Californian company that owned U.S. trademark rights in the mark "BizPlan Builder" for a software product designed to assist in the production of a business plan. 250,000 copies of the software had been sold worldwide, in 20 countries including the United States and the U.K. BizPlan Builder was written for U.S. resident users. It used U.S. dollars as currency and the assumption was made that the organization for which a business plan is to be written is established on a U.S. pattern and operates in a U.S. environment, in particular in legal, fiscal and economic structures. Jian had no place of business in the U.K. and did not itself carry on business within it in the sense of having any of its employees active there in selling its product.

In early 1994, the predecessor of RMG was approached by Jian with a view to its undertaking the anglicization of Jian's BizPlan Builder software, which was necessary to market the product successfully in the U.K. RMG's principal business consisted of republishing for use in the United Kingdom computer software prepared abroad. Negotiations failed, however, and although Jian wrote to RMG on January 29, 1995 indicating that it intended to use its mark worldwide, RMG launched its own product (designed to perform in the U.K. essentially the same function as Jian's BizPlan Builder performed in the United States) under the mark "BusinessPlan Builder." Jian successfully sought an interim injunction based upon passing-off. The principal issue before the court was whether Jian had goodwill in the name "BizPlan Builder" which an English court should protect. To make out a passing off claim under English law, Jian was required to demonstrate goodwill in the U.K. in connection with the name BizPlan Builder as of the date when the defendants started to use the name BusinessPlan Builder.

The court noted that reputation by itself would not suffice; there must be goodwill which cannot exist as an item of property without a business to which the goodwill is annexed. The court quoted *Athletes Foot Marketing Associates Inc v Cobra Sports Ltd* [1980] RPC 343, where Walton J at page 350 said:

> ... it would appear to me that, as a matter of principle, no trader can complain of passing off as against him in any territory—and it will usually be defined by national boundaries, although it is well conceivable in the modern world that it will not—in which he has no customers, nobody who is in a trade relation with him. This will normally shortly be expressed by saying that he does not carry on any trade in that particular country ... but the inwardness of it will be that he has no customers in that country: no people who buy his goods or make use of his services (as the case may be) there.

The court read this to mean that if a plaintiff has no customers in this jurisdiction he will not succeed before the U.K. courts in an action for passing off. But it did not follow, the court concluded, that if one customer within the jurisdiction can be found there necessarily is goodwill in the U.K. which the court should protect, even in relation to a plaintiff who has substantial goodwill in other jurisdictions.

The defendants argued that U.K. sales of BizPlan Builder software were so few that they should be regarded as insufficient to support an action in passing off. Jian claimed since 1988 to have sold 193 products to 168 customers resident in the U.K. The defendant contested this number, arguing (among other things) that some of the customers in the U.K. should be disregarded as being customers of Jian's United States business rather than any business Jian had in the U.K. Most U.K. purchasers had a United States or Canadian factor of one sort or another. For example, some bought the product as a result of seeing magazines that were either published in the United States but circulating in the U.K. or bought by the purchaser in the United States. One of the purchases from the U.K. was a replacement by a satisfied U.K. customer of a previous version bought in the United States. Two U.K. purchases were as a result of a recommendation from a Canadian or United States acquaintance. Three customers who gave testimony had made the purchases while on visits in the United States. In assessing whether Jian had goodwill within the U.K. the court was unwilling to disregard all those who bought Jian's product for reasons having their origins outside the U.K. Although the court accepted that goodwill is local as between jurisdictions, it did not follow that a business should be regarded as divisible in the same way and have customers apportioned–for the purposes of determining where goodwill is situated–according to the historic reason for which they have become customers.

In determining whether the plaintiff had made out a triable case that goodwill existed, the court also suggested that the nature of the goods sold or services rendered is something which should be taken into account. It may be significant, the court suggested, that the eating, drinking and making merry involved in cases involving bars and restaurants is essentially a local activity as compared with other rather more durable activities. Applying this conclusion to the case before him, the judge found that the software product was not ephemeral but capable of continued use. He also took into account the fact that although the potential market for the software in question was quite substantial, the products were not saleable to more than a fraction of the population. They were not articles of everyday household utility. On balance, therefore, he concluded that the number of customers Jian had within the jurisdiction was not so small that it could be said on this ground alone that it is not seriously arguable that it has goodwill locally situated within the jurisdiction.

In so holding, the court also distinguished the *Budweiser* case, where the plaintiff American company, when the defendant entered the market, had no customers at all within the jurisdiction, if one ignored the special customers in American PXs and the embassy. According to the court, the principal issue there was whether these sales should be ignored. If they were not ignored but were relevant, as the Court of Appeal there held they were not, there would have been an amply sufficient customer base to support goodwill in the U.K. *Budweiser* was therefore not directly concerned with the problem of a very small customer base in the U.K. in connection with substantial foreign goodwill. Defendant argued that the sales of the software made to U.K. customers were analogous to the sales to PX customers in *Budweiser* because they were generated by foreign sources, such as foreign magazine inspired purchases and recommendations by foreign residents and purchases while in North America. The court rejected the analogy, finding that whereas the PX purchases in the Budweiser case were purchases which no member of the general public could make, however hard he tried, there was no such watertight compartment here and the sales which Jian has succeeded in making, though few in number and transatlantically inspired, were on the open market in the normal sense of the word.

Accordingly, the court found a triable issue on the question of goodwill and granted the interim injunction.

NOTES AND QUESTIONS

(1) **The Effect of Prior Registrations.** Would the outcome in *Mother's* have been different if the opposer had owned Canadian registrations on the previously used marks? Why did the *Mother's* panel treat the opposer's U.S.-registered marks differently from the previously used marks?

(2) **Advertising as Use.** The *Mother's* panel was unwilling to sustain an opposition based upon prior use or advertising of a mark in connection with

goods or services marketed in a foreign country regardless of whether such advertising occurred inside or outside the United States. Should the location of the advertising use be relevant? Do you agree with the analysis in *Buti*? If Mr. Santambrogio had met with U.S. hotel chains regarding expansion into the United States, should this have changed the court's conclusion? *See* Linville v. Rinard, 26 U.S.P.Q.2d 1046 (T.T.A.B. 1983) (finding lack of U.S. use of the mark ULTRACUTS by Canadian beauty salon notwithstanding meetings in the United States with possible franchisees).

(3) **Territoriality and the Goal of Certainty.** In his separate opinion in *Mother's*, Board Member Allen suggested that treating spillover advertising as akin to use in the United States would "have enormous consequences, in terms of uncertainty, on our trademark system." What are the dire consequences to which Allen is referring? In what way are the "certainty" consequences of treating spillover advertising as use any different from according protection to unregistered marks based on use in commerce?

(4) **The "Famous Mark" Exception.** The *Vaudable* court noted both Maxim's "unique and eminent position as a restaurant of international fame and prestige" and the fact that Maxim's was "well known in this country, particularly to the class of people residing in the cosmopolitan city of New York who dine out." Which of these observations was the predicate for the court's holding? Are these observations different? What other considerations might have provided the basis for the court's decision? The court concluded that plaintiffs were entitled to an injunction and to any "damages occasioned by the defendants' wrongful acts of unfair competition." What damages had been sustained by the plaintiffs? Why was an injunction necessary? Which rights of the plaintiff did the injunction protect? Why did the *Vaudable* court consider the question of abandonment? Was the continuity of use in France relevant to the matter before the New York court?

(5) **The "Bad Faith" Exception.** How does the doctrine developed by the U.S. courts to address the conflict between internationally-exploited marks compare with the doctrine of the "good faith remote junior user," by which the courts determine the rights of geographically distant users of the mark within the United States? *See* United Drug Co. v. Theodore Rectanus Co., 248 U.S. 90, 101 (1918) (recognizing junior user's rights because "no suggestion of a sinister purpose" in its adoption of the mark); *see also* Woman's World Shops, Inc. v. Lane Bryant, 5 U.S.P.Q.2d 1985, 1987 (T.T.A.B. 1988) (junior user's adoption of mark *with knowledge* of senior user's prior remote use on similar goods destroys junior user's claim to being a good faith remote junior user); RESTATEMENT (THIRD) OF UNFAIR COMPETITION § 19 cmt. d (1995) (recognizing split in courts as to whether knowledge is determinative of junior user's bad faith, and advocating evaluation of knowledge based upon totality of circumstances). Is there a basis for drawing a distinction between these two scenarios, depending upon whether the first user has used in a geographically distant country or a state on the other coast of the United States?

Should *knowledge* of the foreign use of a well-known mark be sufficient to prevent its subsequent adoption in the United States? *See Pan American Convention* (Feb. 11, 1929), ch. II., art. 7 (knowledge of use of the mark in any

Contracting State bars domestic registration); *see also* James A. Carney, *Setting Sights on Trademark Piracy: The Need for Greater Protection Against Imitation of Foreign Trademarks*, 81 TRADEMARK REP. 30 (1991) (arguing for knowledge standard); Beth Fulkerson, *Theft by Territorialism: A Case for Revising TRIPS to Protect Trademarks from National Market Foreclosure*, 17 MICH. J. INT'L L. 801 (1996) (supporting Carney's proposal); Thomas J. Hoffman & Susan E. Brownstone, *Protection of Rights Acquired by International Reputation Without Use or Registration*, 71 TRADEMARK REP. 1 (1981). If so, to what extent would the principle of territoriality have been attenuated? If not, to what extent have standards of fair play and principles of honest business practices been sacrificed?

Does the *Person's* decision rest primarily upon an examination of (1) Mr. Christman's conduct or knowledge, (2) the nature of the use of the mark made by the Person's Co., or (3) the public awareness of the mark in the United States? Are these considerations related? Do you agree that "Christman's conduct in appropriating and using appellant's mark in a market where he believed the Japanese manufacturer did not compete can hardly be considered unscrupulous commercial conduct"? Why is it different from the defendant's conduct in *Vaudable*? In *Bulk Manufacturing Co., Inc. v. Schoenbach Prods. Co.*, 208 U.S.P.Q. 664 (S.D.N.Y. 1980), the plaintiff claimed trade dress rights in the design of a vending machine. The plaintiff had modeled its machine after a similar machine which its president had purchased in England. The president testified that a survey revealed that the machine was not being sold in the United States at the time. The defendant produced an identical machine, and claimed unclean hands (the copying of the English product) on the part of the plaintiff when the plaintiff sought equitable relief. The court concluded that "plaintiff's conduct in copying and selling the English machine in a market where it believed that the English manufacturer did not compete can hardly be considered unscrupulous commercial conduct, and thus . . . the defense of unclean hands is inapplicable." Is this assessment of commercial morality still accurate today? Should that affect our analysis of trademark issues? How do the interests of consumers weigh in any analysis of bad faith?

(6) **Comparing the U.S. Cases.** Should the geographic proximity between Canada and the United States justify a different approach in *Mother's* than in *Buti* or *Person's*? Are there any other grounds upon which to treat Canadian use differently from Italian or Japanese use?

(7) **Relevance of the Goods or Services in Question.** In *Mother's*, Board Member Allen also commented that "determination of the issue should not be influenced by whether the case involves goods or services. Although the requirement of use is more easily satisfied in the case of services–use in advertising being sufficient–the definition of commerce in the Trademark Act of 1946 is the same for either kind of mark." The English court in *Jian Tools*, unrestrained by the Lanham Act's definition, appears to believe otherwise. Should the analysis of use be different when dealing with different goods or services?

(8) **A Constant Meaning for "Use"?** The concept of use arises in different areas of trademark analysis. In addition to priority (*Mother's*), the extent of

third party use of similar marks can affect assessment of a mark's distinctiveness, and use is central to the question of abandonment. Should our territorality-based concept of use be different in these different contexts?

(9) **Applying the U.S. Case Law.** You are counsel to Honest Hugh Inc. ("HHI"), a small New York company involved in the "import-export" business. The CEO of HHI is Mr. Hugh Heffer. While vacationing in Scotland, Mr. Heffer purchased several specially windproofed lambswool sweaters sold under the trademark "GALLUS," which is woven discreetly into the upper half of the sweater. (Unaware of the typical Scottish August climate, Mr. Heffer had packed only light clothing.) Mr. Heffer noticed that the GALLUS sweaters were selling very well, and indeed found them extremely comfortable and aesthetically pleasing. GALLUS sweaters are manufactured and sold by a Scottish company, Pride Sweaters, Inc. ("Pride"), and are aimed at the high quality end of the market. Despite being quite expensive, GALLUS sweaters have sold well throughout Europe, partly because various golfers have endorsed the products by wearing them during golfing events that are televised globally. Pride sells the sweaters mostly in northern European countries, where their windproof qualities are particularly appreciated. Thus far, Pride has not sold any GALLUS sweaters in the United States, but has sold a lighter cotton sweater under a different trademark in the golf products market in the United States. Upon returning to New York, Mr. Heffer made some inquiries and discovered that GALLUS sweaters were not sold in the United States, although he became aware of Pride's other U.S. activities. He would like to distribute sweaters under the GALLUS name in the United States. A trademark search reveals that no conflicting mark is registered or being used in the United States. Would you advise Mr. Heffer that he can manufacture and distribute sweaters in the United States under the GALLUS mark? What additional information, if any, would you find helpful? Should Mr. Heffer inquire of Pride whether they intend to expand into the United States? Should he contact Pride and seek to negotiate a U.S. distribution agreement?

(10) **Alternative Standards.** Identify the different standards to which the Jamaican Supreme Court in *McDonald's* considered holding the plaintiff in its attempt to establish rights in Jamaica. Which, if any, of these standards are more lenient than those found in U.S. law and which are stricter? How would *Buti* or *Mother's* be decided under the approach of the court in *Jian Tools*? If you were a Jamaican legislator seeking to further Jamaica's economic interests, which standard would you wish to establish? Would your answer be different if you were a French legislator seeking to further French economic interests?

(11) **International Treaty Provisions.** Although *Person's* was decided without reliance upon international treaties, the court does make reference to several rules derived from the Paris Convention which may in certain circumstances affect the analysis of similar factual scenarios. This explains the court's seemingly cryptic observation in footnote 16 that "Person's Co. does not assert rights under § 44, which if properly applied, might have been used to secure priority over Christman." Similarly, Article 6*bis* of the Paris Convention imposes obligations on signatory states to offer specific protection to marks that are "well-known," and Article 10*bis* of the same convention imposes an obligation to prevent unfair competition. These three provisions are discussed

below. We will reconsider the *Person's* case after reading the material on these treaty provisions.

(12) **Internet Use and Territoriality.** A Canadian court has declined to attach weight, in assessing distinctiveness, to extensive third party use of an identical mark on web sites located in other countries that were electronically accessible from Canada. *See* Tele-Direct (Pub.) v. Canadian Bus. Online, Federal Court of Canada (Sept. 17, 1997), reported at EIPR N-33 (Mar. 1998); *see also* Tele-Direct (Pub.) Inc. v. American Bus. Info., Inc., (1994) 58 C.P.R. (3d) 10. The defendant argued that the mark YELLOW PAGES for telephone directories had become generic in Canada, and in support of that argument cited extensive uncontrolled third party use of the mark in material circulated electronically but originating in the United States rather than Canada. The court refused to consider this international (internet) use in determining distinctiveness of the YELLOW PAGES mark, concluding that "spillover from usage in the U.S." did not constitute third party use in Canada. In what ways should our concept of use accommodate the reality of modern technology, which does not respect geographic borders as product marketing and distribution formerly did? Should the "rapid technological advances" to which Board Member Allen refers in *Mother's* cause us to rethink territoriality-based rules rather than retrench them? Should the ubiquity of the internet force us to reconsider approaches such as that followed in *Mother's*? Is internet use the same as the so-called "spillover" use at issue in *Mother's*? By holding to the traditional approach, are we attempting to establish territorial boundaries where none exist in fact? If the good faith remote junior user rules were extended to the international context, and the junior user has used the mark on the internet, what would be the geographic area to which the junior user should be restricted? Is internet use global use?

(13) **WIPO Standing Committee Proposals on "Use on the Internet."** Some of these internet-related questions have recently been considered by the WIPO Standing Committee on the Law of Trademarks, Industrial Designs and Geographical Indications ("SCT"). *See* Proposed Joint Recommendation Concerning the Protection of Marks, and Other Industrial Property Rights in Signs, on the Internet, WIPO Doc. No. SCT/6/7 (March 30, 2001). Over the past two years the committee has sought to harmonize national approaches to the question of "use" of marks on the internet, and has therefore developed a draft set of provisions on the concept of "use." In use-based systems, such as the United States, the concept is obviously central to the acquisition of rights. But even in registration-based systems (which are much more common), the maintenance and enforcement of rights may require use of the mark by the producer, and infringement depends upon use of the mark by the defendant. Use is central to trademark law, whether in a use-based or registration-based system. We will discuss the SCT draft provisions in greater detail in Chapter 7. But, distilled to their essence, under the draft provisions, use of a sign (such as a mark) on the internet would only be treated as use in any particular state if the use of the sign had a "commercial effect" in that state. The proposal further details the factors relevant to a determination whether a mark has a commercial effect in a state. The factors are non-exhaustive and include whether the user is doing or planning to do business in a particular state

(although use of the sign can have a commercial effect in a country without the user doing business there). The language and currency used on the web site where the sign is used, as well as any explicit disclaimer of the ability to delivery goods in a particular state, would be relevant. Actual restraints on the ability of the producer to deliver goods (for example, regulatory hurdles) would also provide guidance, as would whether the web site had actually been visited by persons from a particular state. The interactivity of the web site might also be an important factor. The draft was finalized by the SCT in March 2001, and a non-binding resolution approving the provisions will be voted on by the WIPO Assembly in September 2001. Based upon this short summary of the SCT proposals, if a similar concept of "commercial effect" were applied to the context of radio transmissions, would the opposer in *Mother's* have been treated as having "used" its mark in the United States?

[B]   Global Marketing And Trademark Law

Trademark law is a law of the marketplace, a *lex mercatoria*. As the most dominant branch of the law of unfair competition, it is a law that purports to regulate competitive conduct. Like all regulatory instruments, it must mirror, and be tailored to, the environment it regulates. The marketplace is changing. Determining what differentiates the current marketplace from historical models, whether viewed in purely commercial terms or with a broader perspective, will help us set the priorities for international trademark law and policy.

Therefore, what are the essential characteristics of the modern marketplace (and of contemporary society)? How is global marketing—the buzz phrase for the new millennium—different from international marketing? In what ways has the opportunity to market a product internationally affected corporate marketing strategies? In what ways has corporate reaction to that opportunity affected consumers and, more broadly, society? Are these changes desirable? Why do many companies view global marketing as a competitive imperative? In what ways has the internet affected the globalization of product manufacture and marketing? If a corporation decides to use the internet as part of a marketing strategy, what implications arise for its brand policies and management of its trademark portfolio? How will this new marketplace affect the type of trademarks that companies adopt? Consider the following excerpts.

BARBARA WICKENS, GETTING THE MESSAGE
Maclean's, February 1, 1993, at 54

. . . [U]ntil 1988, Gillette marketed its products country by country. But now . . . Gillette's top-level executives in Boston make all major strategic decisions, while company executives in each area execute that strategy. "As a multinational marketer, we constrained ourselves to the boundaries, cultures and traditions of the individual nations," said [Donald McDuff, President of Gillette Canada.] "As a global marketer, we strive to look for commonalities, versus looking for differences." Indeed, one TV ad that Gillette used in 17 countries simply showed a series of smiling, clean shaven men in a variety of everyday situations.

MIXED-UP MEDIA MESSAGES
U.S. News & World Rep., Dec. 9, 1991 at 61

The United States and the Soviet Union may be laying down their big guns for the 1990s. Not so the superpowers of soft drinks. Coca-Cola and PepsiCo are escalating the war for market supremacy both at home and abroad. In a shot that will soon be heard—and seen—around the world, Coke will air its first truly global ads next month, an effort that will beam the same message into living rooms from Milan to Milwaukee.

With the U.S. soft-drink market expanding a measly 2 to 3 percent annually—and some international markets growing five times as fast—it's not hard to see where the future lies. Coke saw it long ago and now garners 80 percent of its operating profits overseas. Although Pepsi is pouring $ 1 billion into foreign operations over the next two years, international soft-drink sales currently constitute just 5 percent of its annual earnings. Moreover, it stands little hope of catching Coke around the world because it is outsold by a 4-to-1 margin abroad.

. . . .

Coca-Cola was once on the cutting edge of advertising creativity. It taught the world to sing in perfect harmony, and it defined the real thing—often in unforgettable 30-second electronic sonnets. But in the 1980s the unthinkable happened, and the world's leading cola brand found itself grappling with Pepsi in the televised struggle for consumers' hearts, minds and money. . . .

The cola king is now poised to regain its creative crown. Last week, Coke aired two of its more than 20 new commercials for 1992 on network television. For the first time in its history, the company's ads have been conceived and executed with a global market in mind. And beginning next month, its commercials will be televised simultaneously in hundreds of countries around the world.

Instead of trying to be cool and hip like Pepsi, the new ads extol universal brotherhood and emphasize Coke's widespread global recognition. "'We might have erred [in trying to be trendy]," says Coca-Cola's director of global marketing Peter Sealy. "So we've returned to the brand's enduring values." One commercial called "Sasha" features a young Polish boy recently adopted by an American couple. Unnerved upon meeting his new relatives for the first time, the shy youngster nonetheless lights up when he spies a can of Classic Coke.

. . . .

By developing its ads for global consumption, Coca-Cola has acknowledged that it is targeting the world market, where it dominates Pepsi, rather than the United States, where it still heatedly competes with its rival. Over the past decade, Coke has made an aggressive push overseas, rapidly building up its foreign bottling network. Coke's four key brands now control 44 percent of the world soft-drink market, and strong international sales have helped the company's earnings grow at an annual rate of 19 percent over the last five years. Coke has set its sights in the right direction, according to most analysts. Despite a commanding overseas presence, the company's potential for international expansion remains enormous. In America, for example, each person over the age of 8 consumes 300 eight-ounce servings of soda a year; but outside the United States, the number drops precipitously, to just 43 eight-ounce servings annually.

The global risk? Coke's new communications strategy is not without risks. The company has long faced the dilemma of protecting its well-scrubbed all-American image while still appealing to trend conscious teens, a key cola-guzzling group. And, as in any global campaign, a broad-based advertising approach could miss where more-targeted, culture-specific commercials would hit. "Global advertising is often much too broad," says Jack Trout, president of Trout & Ries, a marketing-strategy firm in Greenwich, Conn. "In an effort to have one global idea, it's hard to focus on key problems that emerge country by country."

But Coke is confident that its message about brotherly love and brand loyalty will transcend local barriers. . . . Like so many global marketers, Coke is betting that what plays in America will play around the world as well.

JOHN QUELCH & LISA KLEIN,
THE INTERNET AND INTERNATIONAL MARKETING
Sloan Management Review, March 1, 1996, at 60

A major challenge for multinational corporations is the management of global brands and corporate name or logo identification. Consumers may be confused if a company and its subsidiaries have several Web sites, each communicating a different format, image, message and content. 3M, which has one site for its entire product line, has a focused corporate identity and firm control over the marketing actions of its divisions and subsidiaries. However, many multinationals with one brand name have allowed local entities to develop sites ad hoc and now have several sites around the globe that require tighter coordination. . . . On the other hand, developing one site for each brand—while costly and limiting to cross-selling—is preferable when the brands have distinct markets and images. . . . Recognizing the importance of brand names, many multinational corporations are establishing single Web sites for each brand.

. . . .

The Web promises to reinforce the trend toward English as the lingua franca of commerce. There are significant obstacles in translating Chinese and Japanese to the computer, especially the large number of local dialects. . . .

. . . .

[And] cultural barriers remain. When setting up a traditional business operation in a foreign country, managers usually have numerous conversations with local partners and visit the country several times. With a virtual business, the need for such contacts is minimized, and cultural differences may not be as apparent. . . .

LANGUAGE BARRIERS

Language differences can, occasionally, present impediments to global marketing. Consider the following well-known examples.

* The name Coca-Cola in China was first rendered as ke-kou-ke-la. Unfortunately, the Coke company did not discover until after thousands of signs had been printed that the phrase means "bite the wax tadpole" or "female horse stuffed with wax" depending on the dialect. Coke then researched 40,000 Chinese characters and found a phonetic equivalent, "ko-kou-ko-le," which can be loosely translated as "happiness in the mouth."

* In Taiwan, the translation of the Pepsi slogan "Come alive with the Pepsi generation" came out as "Pepsi will bring your ancestors back from the dead."

* Also in Chinese, the Kentucky Fried Chicken slogan "Finger-lickin' good" came out as "eat your fingers off."

* The American slogan for Salem cigarettes, "Salem—Feeling Free," got translated in the Japanese market into "When smoking Salem, you feel so refreshed that your mind seems to be free and empty."

* When General Motors introduced the Chevy Nova in South America, it was apparently unaware that "no va" means "it won't go." After the company figured out why it wasn't selling any cars, it renamed the car the Caribe in its Spanish markets.

* Ford had a similar problem in Brazil when the Pinto flopped. The company found out that Pinto was Brazilian slang for "tiny male genitals." Ford pried all the nameplates off and substituted Corcel.

* Chicken man Frank Perdue's slogan, "It takes a tough man to make a tender chicken," got terribly mangled in another Spanish translation. A photo of Perdue with one of his birds appeared on billboards all over Mexico with a caption that explained "It takes a hard man to make a chicken aroused."

QUESTIONS

What are (or should be) the consequences for legal systems and legal rules when cultural and commercial borders do not correspond to physical territories? *See* Richard Thompson Ford, *Beyond Borders: A Partial Response to Richard Briffault*, 48 STAN. L. REV. 1173, 1194 (1996) ("Borders are not inherently significant; they are significant because we attach significance to them."). If new borders are generated by product affinity, consumer attitudes and other socio-cultural phenomena, how should trademark law adapt? Should trademark law simply react to how these factors affect product development, distribution, and marketing, or should trademark law assume a more constitutive role? Should it seek to shape the new "borders"? If so, according to which values? Should it seek to facilitate others in establishing those borders and patterns of behavior? If so, who should it facilitate?

[C] Language and Territory

OTOKOYAMA CO. LTD. v. WINE OF JAPAN IMPORT, INC.
175 F.3d 266 (2d Cir. 1999)

LEVAL, CIRCUIT JUDGE:

This is a trademark dispute between two importers of Japanese sake. Otokoyama Co. Ltd., the registered owner of four U.S. trademarks for the word "otokoyama" and Japanese language pictograms signifying that word, filed suit against Wine of Japan Import, Inc., alleging, inter alia, that defendant infringed its trademark in violation of the Lanham Act, by importing a brand of sake labelled "Mutsu Otokoyama." Defendant counterclaimed, seeking to cancel plaintiff's trademarks under § 14 of the Lanham Act, 15 U.S.C. § 1064. Defendant contended that 1) otokoyama is a generic term signifying a type of sake and is therefore ineligible for trademark protection, and 2) plaintiff's trademarks were "obtained fraudulently" within the meaning of 15 U.S.C. § 1064(3).

After a hearing, the district court granted plaintiff's motion for a preliminary injunction. On appeal from that order, defendant argues that the district court erred when it refused to consider evidence of the meaning and usage of otokoyama in Japan and refused to consider a ruling of the Japanese trademark office denying plaintiff's application for trademark protection on the ground that otokoyama is generic. We agree that the district court erred in both respects. Applying the correct legal standard and crediting defendant with the improperly excluded evidence, we find that defendant raises sufficient doubt as to the validity of plaintiff's trademark to overcome plaintiff's showing of likelihood of success. We therefore vacate the preliminary injunction.

BACKGROUND

Plaintiff, a Japanese corporation, has been brewing sake—a Japanese wine made from fermented rice—on the northern island of Hokkaido since the 1930s. In Japan, its sake is sold under the name "Hokkai Otokoyama," Hokkai being a reference to the island of Hokkaido. Since 1984, plaintiff has imported its sake into the U.S., where it is marketed and sold as "Otokoyama" brand sake. Plaintiff registered the English transliteration of otokoyama and three trademarks of Japanese pictograms comprising otokoyama with the U.S. Trademark Office.

Defendant is a domestic corporation, which imports various brands of sake into the U.S. Defendant's importation and sale of sake under the designation "Mutsu Otokoyama," begun in or around 1997, is the subject of this suit. As noted, plaintiff claims the defendant's use of otokoyama infringes plaintiff's trademark, while defendant claims that because otokoyama is a generic word for a type of sake, it is not eligible for use as a trademark for sake.

In Japanese pictograms, the word otokoyama is comprised of the characters for "man" and "mountain." The parties dispute the meaning and history of the word in relation to sake, but they agree that its use in Japan in relation to sake dates back at least to the Edo period, which began in the seventeenth century. Paintings from the period show samurai warriors drinking from sake barrels displaying the characters for otokoyama. In Japan, between ten and twenty brewers in addition to plaintiff designate sake as "otokoyama," often (like plaintiff) adding a geographical modifier.

Plaintiff has been unsuccessful in its attempts to obtain trademark rights in Japan for otokoyama. In 1962 (then doing business under the name Yamazaki Shuzo K.K.) plaintiff sought to register the characters for "Hokkai Otokoyama" as a trademark in Japan. The application was rejected, and in 1966 the Japanese Patent Office ("JPO") affirmed the rejection. The JPO issued a written decision, whose exact translation is disputed,[1] but which apparently signified that the word otokoyama was not eligible for trademark protection because of its longstanding use as a designation for sake by other traders in the industry.

In 1984, plaintiff became the first company to market sake labelled otokoyama in the United States. Two years later, plaintiff petitioned the United States Patent and Trademark Office ("USPTO") to register the Kanji characters for otokoyama. In processing plaintiff's application, the USPTO asked plaintiff to provide an English translation of the characters. Plaintiff responded with a sworn statement that "to applicant's knowledge, the mark is an arbitrary, fanciful term. Accordingly, the mark cannot be translated." The USPTO granted plaintiff's request to register the mark in 1988.

Between 1992 and 1995, plaintiff sought and obtained U.S. registrations for

---

[1]The parties have advanced a variety of translations of the JPO's decision. Defendant's exhibits include three translations:

1) "It is self-explanatory that Japanese (kanji) letters comprising [otokoyama] have been treated as long years' customary written symbol of goods=SEISYU (Japanese equivalent to refined sake (liquor))."; and

2) "[I]t is clear that the characters forming the word Otokoyama have a long history of customary use in the industry for products designated as seishu ['refined liquor']."; and

3) "It is obvious that the character 'Otokoyama' is a trademark which has been used commonly by traders in this industry for 'sake' products from old times."

Plaintiff claimed that the correct translation is as follows: "It is clear that the characters of 'Otokoyama' is a trademark/brand which has been commonly used in this industry for the product 'seishu' from olden times."

three other otokoyama trademarks: one each for the Katakana and Hiragana[2] characters for otokoyama, and one for the English transliteration. Again the USPTO asked for English translations, to which plaintiff again responded in sworn declarations that otokoyama is "an arbitrary, fanciful" term that "has no meaning and cannot be translated."

In April, 1997, plaintiff wrote to defendant demanding that it cease importation, distribution, advertisement and sale of "Mutsu Otokoyama." Defendant replied that it believed plaintiff's trademarks were invalid, and refused.

Plaintiff filed suit, alleging trademark infringement, unfair competition, and false designation of origin under the Lanham Act, as well as state law violations, and moved for a preliminary injunction. As noted, defendant challenged the validity of plaintiff's trademarks on two grounds: first, that otokoyama is a generic term for a type of sake, and second, that plaintiff secured its U.S. registrations by fraudulent misrepresentations that concealed from the USPTO otokoyama's usage as a generic term in Japan.

At the preliminary injunction hearing, the court declined to consider any meaning the word otokoyama might have outside the United States, stating that "[t]he meaning of a term outside of the United States is irrelevant" to a determination of entitlement to the protection of the U.S. trademark laws. *Otokoyama Co. Ltd. v. Wine of Japan Import, Inc.*, 985 F. Supp. 372, 376 (S.D.N.Y.1997). The court also declined to consider defendant's proffer of the 1966 decision of the Japanese Patent Office which denied plaintiff's request to register otokoyama in Japan. [cit]. Concluding that plaintiff had shown both irreparable harm and likelihood of success on the merits, the court granted the preliminary injunction. [cit].

DISCUSSION

... [T]he plaintiff in a trademark infringement action establishes a likelihood of success by showing both 1) a legal, exclusive right to the mark, and 2) a likelihood that customers will be confused as to the source of the infringing product. [cit]. To prove likelihood of success below, plaintiff showed that since 1984 it had been importing and selling its sake in the United States under the label "otokoyama," that it had registered this trademark with the USPTO, and that it had successfully protected the mark against unauthorized use by others.

We review a district court's decision to grant or deny a preliminary injunction for abuse of discretion, which is shown if, inter alia, the district court applies the incorrect legal standard. [cit]. Because the court applied the wrong legal standard and excluded relevant evidence favorable to the defendant's claim, we vacate the injunction.

Defendant contends the district court erred in refusing to consider evidence that otokayama is a generic term for sake, or a type of sake, in the Japanese language as spoken in Japan, and that the district court erred in excluding the

---

[2]Katakana, Hiragana, and Kanji are apparently three different writing systems in the Japanese language.

decision of the Japanese Patent Office. We agree with defendant that the district court was mistaken in its understanding of the potential significance of the meaning of otokoyama in the Japanese language. We also agree with the defendant that the ruling of the Japanese Patent Office may have been admissible for certain relevant purposes.

I.

It is a bedrock principle of trademark law that no trader may acquire the exclusive right to the use of a term by which the covered goods or services are designated in the language. Such a term is "generic." Generic terms are not eligible for protection as trademarks; everyone may use them to refer to the goods they designate. [cit.] This rule protects the interest of the consuming public in understanding the nature of goods offered for sale, as well as a fair marketplace among competitors by insuring that every provider may refer to his goods as what they are. *See* CES Publ'g Corp. v. St. Regis Publications, Inc., 531 F.2d 11, 13 (2d Cir.1975) (Friendly, J.) ("To allow trademark protection for generic terms, *i.e.*, names which describe the genus of goods being sold, [is impermissible because] a competitor could not describe his goods as what they are.") (citations omitted); *see also* Restatement (Third) of Unfair Competition § 15 cmt. b ("A seller . . . cannot remove a generic term from the public domain and cast upon competitors the burden of using an alternative name.").

The same rule applies when the word designates the product in a language other than English. This extension rests on the assumption that there are (or someday will be) customers in the United States who speak that foreign language. Because of the diversity of the population of the United States, coupled with temporary visitors, all of whom are part of the United States marketplace, commerce in the United States utilizes innumerable foreign languages. No merchant may obtain the exclusive right over a trademark designation if that exclusivity would prevent competitors from designating a product as what it is in the foreign language their customers know best. Courts and the USPTO apply this policy, known as the doctrine of "foreign equivalents," [cit], to make generic foreign words ineligible for private ownership as trademarks. *See* Weiss Noodle [Co. v. Golden Cracknel & Speciality Co.], 290 F.2d 845, 84647 (C.C.P.A. 1961) (applying ban on trademarking generic names to foreign equivalents, and holding that "ha-lush-ka," phonetic spelling of Hungarian word for "egg noodles," is non-protectible); *see also In re Le Sorbet, Inc.*, 228 U.S.P.Q. 27, 28 (T.T.A.B.1985)("sorbet," French word for fruit ice, held non-protectible); *In re Hag Aktiengesellschaft*, 155 U.S.P.Q. 598, 599-600 (T.T.A.B.1967)("kaba," coffee in Serbian and Ukranian, held non-protectible).

This rule, furthermore, does not apply only to words that designate an entire species. Generic words for sub-classifications or varieties of a good are similarly ineligible for trademark protection. *See, e.g.*, Genesee Brewing Co., Inc. v. Stroh Brewing Co., 124 F.3d 137, 148-49 (2d Cir.1997) ("honey brown" held generic for type of ale); *In re Cooperativa Produttori Latte E Fontina Valle D'Acosta*, 230 U.S.P.Q. 131, 134 (T.T.A.B.1986) ("fontina" held generic for a type of cheese); *In re Northland Aluminum Prods.*, 221 U.S.P.Q. 1110, 1112 (T.T.A.B.1984), ("bundt" held generic for variety of ring-shaped coffee cake), aff'd, 777 F.2d 1556, 1561 (Fed.Cir.1985); Italian Swiss Colony v. Italian Vineyard Co., 158 Cal. 252, 257 (1910)("tipo" held generic Italian word for a chianti wine). A word may also be generic by virtue of its association with a particular region, cultural movement, or legend. *See* Holland v. C. & A. Import Corp., 8 F. Supp. 259, 260 (S.D.N.Y.1934) ("Est Est Est" held generic for wine from Italy's Montefiascone region); *In re Ricci-Italian Silversmiths, Inc.*, 16 U.S.P.Q.2d 1727, 1729 (T.T.A.B.1990) ("art deco" held generic for flatware made in design style introduced at L'Exposition Internationale des Arts Decoratifs et Industriels Modernes in Paris); *In re Bauhaus Designs Canada Ltd.*, 12 U.S.P.Q.2d 2001, 2003 (T.T.A.B.1989) ("bauhaus" held generic for style of furniture developed at Germany's Bauhaus school of design); [cit].

The defendant contended in the district court that the word "otokoyama" falls within the generic category. It claimed that in Japanese, otokoyama has long been understood as designating a variety of "dry, manly sake" that originated more than 300 years ago. The district court, however, declined to accord any significance to the Japanese meaning of the word. The court stated that the Japanese meaning of otokoyama is "irrelevant to the U.S. PTO's determination of [plaintiff's] trademark rights. . . . [T]he meaning of the term 'otokoyama' in Japan is not relevant to this action."

For the reasons explained above, this was error. If otokoyama in Japanese signifies a type of sake, and one United States merchant were given the exclusive right to use that word to designate its brand of sake, competing merchants would be prevented from calling their product by the word which designates that product in Japanese. Any Japanese-speaking customers and others who are familiar with the Japanese terminology would be misled to believe that there is only one brand of otokoyama available in the United States. *See* Restatement (Third) of Unfair Competition, § 15 cmt. a ("Competitors denied access to a [generic] term that denominates goods or services to prospective purchasers would be at a distinct disadvantage in communicating information regarding the nature or characteristics of their product. Consumers would be forced either to spend additional time and money investigating the characteristics of competing goods or to pay a premium price to the seller with trademark rights in the accepted generic term.").

The meaning of otokoyama in Japanese, and particularly whether it designates sake, or a type or category of sake, was therefore highly relevant to whether plaintiff may assert the exclusive right to use that word as a mark applied to sake. Defendant should have been allowed to introduce evidence of otokoyama's meaning and usage in Japan to support its claim that the mark is generic and therefore ineligible for protection as a trademark. In light of this error, the district court's finding that plaintiff is likely to succeed on the merits cannot be sustained.

II.

Defendant also challenges the district court's exclusion of the ruling of the

Japanese Patent Office denying plaintiff trademark rights in Japan. The district court, citing *Vanity Fair Mills, Inc. v. T. Eaton Co.*, 234 F.2d 633, 639 (2d Cir. 1956), ruled that the JPO decision was irrelevant. [cit]. We disagree.

We disagree first with the district court's understanding of the precedent it cited. It is true that a claimant's rights (or lack of rights) to a trademark in the United States cannot be established by the fact that the claimant was found by a foreign court to have (or not to have) rights over the same mark in a foreign country. That is what the *Vanity Fair* opinion meant by its broad statement to the effect that "the decisions of foreign courts concerning the respective trademark rights of the parties are irrelevant and inadmissible." [cit]. It does not follow, however, that foreign court decisions are never relevant or admissible for any purpose in a U.S. trademark dispute. Indeed, as authority for the quoted proposition, the *Vanity Fair* opinion cited our ruling in *George W. Luft Co. v. Zande Cosmetic Co.*, 142 F.2d 536, 539 (2d Cir. 1944), which ruled that foreign decisions were relevant and admissible. In *Luft*, the defendant offered various foreign registrations of the disputed mark to prove that the defendants might lawfully use the mark within the foreign country that granted the registration. The district court had excluded them in reliance on *City of Carlsbad v. Kutnow*, 68 F. 794 (S.D.N.Y.), *aff'd*, 71 F. 167 (2d Cir. 1895). The *Luft* Court pointed out that in Carlsbad, "the purpose of introducing the English registration was to prove that the defendants were privileged to use [the mark] on sales in the United States. *On this issue* a foreign trade-mark was rightly held irrelevant, for clearly the English law could not confer [a trademark right] which our courts were bound to recognize." 142 F.2d at 539 (emphasis added). The opinion goes on, however, to say "We do not think that the *Carlsbad* case controls the case at bar." *Id.* Because "the purpose of offering the foreign registrations was not to establish the privilege of using the [mark] in the United States but to prove that the defendants might lawfully use it within the foreign country which granted the registration," *id.*, the court found that the foreign decisions were relevant and admissible and the district court had erred in failing to consider them.

Whether a foreign decision is relevant in a trademark case in our courts depends on the purpose for which it is offered. The fact that a litigant has been awarded or denied rights over a mark in a foreign country ordinarily does not determine its entitlement to the mark in the United States. The foreign court decision is not admissible if that is the purpose of the offer. But if, as in *Luft*, the foreign decision is competent evidence of a relevant fact, it is relevant and admissible to prove that fact.

Defendant offered the decision of the JPO for two purposes. First, it was offered to prove the fact assertedly found by the JPO that the word otokoyama in Japanese refers to a type or class of sake. Second, it was offered as evidence supporting defendant's claim that plaintiff committed fraud on the trademark office in the prosecution of its application for registration. [cit]. The theory of this offer was to show plaintiff's awareness that the word otokoyama was not an "arbitrary, fanciful term . . . [that] cannot be translated," as plaintiff represented to the trademark examiner. Both purposes are relevant to defendant's claims. It was error to exclude the JPO decision on grounds of relevance.

* * *

. . . The evidence defendant sought unsuccessfully to introduce at the preliminary injunction hearing was sufficient to undermine plaintiff's likelihood of success on the merits, but was not necessarily sufficient to carry the defendant's burden of proving that otokoyama is generic.[4] Whether otokoyama is generic in Japanese as defendant contends remains to be seen based on the evidence that will be presented at trial. We hold only that the improperly excluded evidence casts sufficient doubt on the validity of plaintiff's trademark, and on plaintiff's likelihood of success, to require that we vacate the preliminary injunction.

CONCLUSION

The preliminary injunction in plaintiff's favor is hereby vacated. The case is remanded for trial.

Orto Conserviera Cameranese Di Giacchetti Marino v. Bioconserve, S.R.L., 49 U.S.P.Q.2d 2013 (S.D.N.Y. 1999).

[The defendant had registered BELLA DI CERIGNOLA as its trademark for olives. The plaintiff sought cancellation of the mark on the ground that BELLA DI CERIGNOLA is a generic term used to describe a particular type of olive. The court concluded that the term was generic in both Italy and the United States; this was sufficient to resolve the case. Judge Martin took his analysis further, however.] Even if the Court were to conclude that BELLA DI CERIGNOLA had not yet become generic in this country, it would be reluctant to permit defendants to use it as a trademark for olives because to do so would preclude producers of Italian olives from selling them using the generic designation by which they are known in the country of origin. There are cases that state that, in determining whether a term used as a trademark is generic, the courts should consider only its use in this country and the fact that the term may be generic in another country is of no consequence. Anheuser-Busch Inc. v. The Stroh Brewery Co., 750 F.2d 631, 642 (8th Cir. 1984); Abercrombie & Fitch v. Hunting World, 537 F.2d 4, 9 (2d Cir. 1976); Seiko Sporting Goods USA, Inc. v. Kabushiki Kaisha Hattori Tokeiten, 545 F. Supp. 221, 226 (S.D.N.Y. 1982). However, the facts of this case suggest that, as a general rule, such

---

[4]Defendant's evidence included the following: It cited the 1966 JPO decision denying plaintiff permission to register otokoyama as a trademark. It submitted an affidavit from its own president, an importer of Japanese sake since 1973, asserting that otokoyama signifies "a type of dry sake" in Japan. It offered entries from two sake "encyclopedias" and a suppliers list of Japanese brewers showing that a number of brewers of sake use the word otokoyama. Finally, it offered plaintiff's promotional pamphlet and website advertising, which refer to otokoyama's Edo-age origins and representation on sake barrels from the period. It offered neither Japanese dictionary definitions nor testimony of independent experts in the Japanese liquor industry on the meaning of otokoyama.

reasoning is too parochial for the modern world of international commerce. It does not strain the bounds of judicial notice to recognize that those who are interested in gourmet foods are often people who travel internationally or, at least, keep abreast of international developments in the food market. Thus an item of produce that is practically unknown in this country can become relatively popular within a brief period. To allow the first importer of such a product to use its generic designation in the country of origin as a trademark would give that importer a competitive advantage that the law of trademark should not allow. [cit].

In any event, even if the Court was persuaded that the term BELLA DI CERIGNOLA was not generic, it would at best be descriptive as applied to these olives. While the defendants contend that the mark is not descriptive, one need not be an Italian scholar to recognize that "Bella di Cerignola" means beauty of or from Cerignola. Thus, a consumer seeing a jar of BELLA DI CERIGNOLA olives would no doubt read the label as referring to the beautiful olives from Cerignola. Since BELLA DI CERIGNOLA is at best descriptive, defendants would only be entitled to preclude the plaintiffs from using it by showing that it had taken on a secondary meaning, so that consumers perceived it as identifying defendants' olives. While defendants have established that they use the words "Bella di Cerignola" in a stylized form as part of a label that serves as their trademark for a variety of products, they have not established that the typical consumer who sees the words "Bella di Cerignola" affixed to a tray of olives, or a competitor's jar, would assume that the olives originated with the defendants. To establish a valid trademark, defendants "must show that the primary significance of the term in the minds of the consuming public is not the product but the producer." *Kellogg Co. v. National Biscuit Co.*, 305 U.S. 111, 118 (1938). . . .

NOTES AND QUESTIONS

(1) **Purpose of the Doctrine of Foreign Equivalents.** Whose interests are being protected or furthered by considering the meaning of a foreign term when translated into English? *Cf. In re* Le Sorbet, Inc., 228 U.S.P.Q. 27, 30-31 (T.T.A.B. 1985) (discussing international trade implications). What benefit does the doctrine achieve? Who or what was the court protecting in *Otokoyama*?

(2) **Determining the Meaning of the Foreign Term.** Is Judge Martin's approach in *Orto Conserviera Cameranese Di Giachetti Marino* consistent with the Second Circuit's opinion in *Otokoyama*? (A panel of the Second Circuit affirmed Judge Martin's decision. *See* 205 F.3d 1324 (2d Cir. 2000)). Is the inquiry as to whether a term is generic in Japanese (or Italian) the same as whether the term is generic in Japan (or Italy)? *Cf.* V & V Food Prods., Inc. v. Cacique Cheese Co., Inc., 683 F. Supp. 662, 669-70 (N.D. Ill. 1988) (perception of term Chihuahua in Mexico irrelevant notwithstanding that Mexican-Americans were relevant purchasing public in the United States). How should a court determine whether a term is generic in a foreign language? *See* Enrique

Bernat v. Guadalajara, Inc., 210 F.3d 439 (5th Cir. 2000) (finding term "Chupa" for lollipops generic because it is a generic Spanish word for lollipop, but refusing to place dispositive weight upon literal dictionary definition). To what extent, in *Otokoyama* on remand, will the determination of the Japanese Patent Office assist the court in making a determination under U.S. law? *See* Otokoyama Co. v. Wine of Japan Import, Inc., N.Y.L.J. Aug. 8, 2000 (S.D.N.Y. 2000) (finding mark generic), *aff'd*, 2001 W.L. 345188 (2d Cir. 2001).

(3) **Contexts in which the Doctrine of Foreign Equivalents is Applied.** The doctrine of foreign equivalents is applied by U.S. courts not only in determining the distinctiveness of foreign terms used as marks, but also in assessing whether there is confusing similarity between two marks (one of which is a foreign term) under section 2(d) or in an infringement proceeding under sections 32 or 43(a) of the Lanham Act. *See, e.g.,* Horn's Inc. v. Sanofi Beaute, Inc., 963 F. Supp. 318, 322-23 (S.D.N.Y. 1997) (finding mark HERE AND THERE not infringed by DECI DELA, which can translate as "here and there"). Should the doctrine be given a more or less expansive application depending upon the context in which it is used?

(4) **Scope of the Doctrine Generally.** Some courts have declined to apply the doctrine and translate the foreign term where the foreign expression was one that even those knowledgeable in that language would not translate. *See, e.g.,* Continental Nut Co. v. Le Cordon Bleu, 494 F.2d 1395 (C.C.P.A. 1974) (CORDON BLEU not equivalent to BLUE RIBBON). The doctrine of foreign equivalents is, therefore, not an inflexible rule. Courts must make commonsense determinations as to whether the doctrine should be applied. For example, the term NIKE, a well-known mark for sports apparel, means "overcomers" in Greek. How should that affect your analysis of whether the sports apparel company can prevent a securities company from using the identical mark? *Cf.* Nike, Inc. v. Nike Sec., 50 U.S.P.Q.2d 1202 (N.D. Ill. 1999). What are the "commonsense" considerations that you would use in determining whether to apply the doctrine of foreign equivalents? If the plaintiff's claim rested on a dilution theory, how would the doctrine's application be affected?

(5) **Combination Marks.** Should the doctrine of foreign equivalents apply when the claimed mark is a combination of foreign and domestic terms? *See In re* Johanna Farms, Inc., 8 U.S.P.Q.2d 1408 (T.T.A.B. 1988) (not applying doctrine and protecting mark because the commercial impression of the phrase LA YOGURT was changed by use of a combination of French and English); French Transit, Ltd. v. Modern Coupon Sys., Inc., 818 F. Supp. 635 (S.D.N.Y. 1993).

(6) **Double Translations.** If there is alleged confusion between two marks in different foreign languages, but with the same English meaning, should the doctrine be applied? *See* Miguel Torres S.A. v. Casa Vinicola Gerardi Cesari S.R.L., 49 U.S.P.Q.2d 2018, 2020 (T.T.A.B. 1999) (opposition proceeding involving Spanish and Italian marks with similar English translations).

(7) **Linguistic Proficiency.** Should the doctrine be applied where consumers are generally unable to make the translation? That is to say, should the foreign language used be relevant to whether a court applies the doctrine? For example, while American consumers may understand French or Spanish, should we assume knowledge of languages less common in the U.S. (such as

Swahili, or a dead language such as Latin)? *Cf.* General Cigar Co. v. GDM, Inc., 988 F. Supp. 647, 660 (S.D.N.Y 1997) (... hether American cigar consu... COHIBA and the same word ... the indigenous population o... used in the mark, or the ease o... ntal Daily News, Inc., 230 U.S... why descriptive words repres... differently from descriptive w... er than assume American con... rm, might it be better to asse... case basis? *Cf.* Kundry S.A.'s ... marks Registry 1997) (refusi... n of term in determining s ... as no evidence showing a gen... Kingdom with the Spanish la... age proficiency be relevant? (... er in southern U.S. states tha...

(8) **Similarit**... *i Beaute, Inc.,* 963 F. Supp. 31... s mark HERE AND THERE ... _____ DELA, which can translate as "he... ___ .... The court noted that although it would use the translated term to assess similarity of meaning, it would use the foreign term in assessing similarity of sight and sound, and found the marks not to be confusingly similar. In comparing the similarity of how marks sound, should it be assumed that consumers know how to pronounce foreign languages correctly? *See* JouJou Designs Inc. v. JOJO Ligne Internationale, Inc., 821 F. Supp. 1347, 1354 (N.D. Cal. 1992) (pronunciation in French); Miguel Torres S.A. v. Casa Vinicola Gerardi Cesari S.R.L., 49 U.S.P.Q.2d 2018, 2020 (T.T.A.B. 1999) (noting, where one mark was in Spanish and the conflicting mark was in Italian, that the marks may be pronounced in very similar manner given that Italian and Spanish are both Romance languages with common roots).

(9) **Globalization.** In what ways might it be appropriate to reconfigure the doctrine of foreign equivalents given the changes in contemporary society? *See* John T. Cross, *Language and the Law: The Special Role of Trademarks, Trade Names, and Other Trade Emblems,* 76 NEB. L. REV. 95, 137-40 (1997) (arguing that current doctrine is too strict and suggesting presumption in favor of protecting foreign terms even where they are widely recognized translations of generic English terms). What effect will technological developments have on the analysis of foreign language terms? Does globalization suggest the need for a stronger or weaker application of the doctrine?

(10) **The Internet.** Whatshappenin.com is an online entertainment guide that provides information about clubs, music, and bars (among other things) in different U.S. cities. It wishes to enjoin the use of the mark quepasa.com as an internet domain name for a similar service offered by a rival company. *See* Victoria Colliver, *Tongues Tangle in Web Site War,* S.F. EXAM., Oct. 13, 1999, at B1. Quepasa.com was launched one year after whatshappenin.com. Quepasa.com's website is primarily, although not exclusively, in the Spanish

language. Should the rival's use of the Quepasa mark be enjoined? (The plaintiff alleges that "que pasa" translates from Spanish as "what's happening." Would it matter that the literal translation of "what's happening" in Spanish is "que estapando"?) Is there any additional information about the respective sites that would help you decide? If the rival's website was Spanish-based, and was found at http://www.quepasa.es rather than at http://www.quepasa.com, would your analysis change? *Cf.* Avery Dennison v. Sumpton, 189 F.3d 868, 880-81 (9th Cir. 1999) (discussing relevance of different top level domain name to dilution analysis). The relationship between domain names and trademarks is considered in more detail *infra* Chapter 7.

Many foreign countries apply doctrines not unlike the doctrine of foreign equivalents. *See, e.g.,* Judgment of Feb. 23, 1996, *Tribunal de Grande Instance de Paris*, noted at 86 TRADEMARK REP. 898, 900 (1996) (holding that a foreign term can be a trademark although court will consider whether the foreign term had become part of the language used in France and whether it would be understood, in translation, by the French public). Significant German case law has developed on the protectability of foreign (especially English) terms. Some excerpts from recent opinions follow.

"Partner With the Best" Trade Mark Application, Case 30 W (pat.) 202/95, Federal Supreme Court (Jan. 27, 1997), 1998 E.T.M.R. 679.

[Registration was sought in Germany of the mark PARTNER WITH THE BEST for use in connection with, inter alia "electronic and electrical appliances; components and parts; included in Class 9" and various specialized items of office and laboratory furniture. The German Patent Office initially rejected the application on the grounds of lack of distinctiveness as well as the need to keep the phrase freely available for general use (each of which were independent grounds for refusal of an application under German law). Ultimately, the Examiner based his decision solely on the lack of distinctiveness. The applicants filed an appeal. In the appeal, the applicants made particular reference to the fact that the applied-for mark had been registered in numerous territories—in particular English-speaking territories—which suggested, it was argued, that there was no need to keep the mark available for use by others. The applicants raised the following question on appeal: "can a string of words in a foreign language (in this instance English) be refused registration in Germany purely on the basis of lack of distinctiveness, when it is protected as a trade mark in the main economic territories of that foreign language (in this instance the United Kingdom and the United States) and is thereby monopolised by the applicants?" The appeal was unsuccessful; the Federal Supreme Court affirmed the Examiner's conclusion on distinctiveness.]

The public has no cause to see an adequately distinguishing indication of company in the English language statement. The use of English expressions in advertising has long been common . . . In fact, it may now almost be described as predominant.

This is in particular the case for the goods specified in this application, being either technical equipment itself or (specialist) furniture specifically intended for such equipment.

In the field of Class 9 goods, as for other electrical and electronic devices, the English language has become predominant. Certain expressions do not even have passable German equivalents (see *"Das Streiflicht"*, a column in the *Süddeutsche Zeitung* of January 7, 1997 called "Software"). Even in relation to goods which address a much wider portion of the public, such as textiles, the use of the English language is widespread. . . .

This trend has strengthened in recent years, in particular through access to the Internet which constantly opens up new sources. Specifically in this field, languages are being suppressed, since search commands may only be entered in English and one reaches many more people using English.

A search on the Internet for the complete text of the actual mark at issue here–that is "Partner with the best", produced the following results: in the newspaper *Die Welt* there were two instances; through the Alta Vista search engine there were approximately 800,000 documents; and the "Yahoo" search engine identified 833,500 documents–all of which contained the search words: "partner" "with" "the" and "best".

. . . .

Also, the indication from the applicants that the marks had been registered in other countries could not lead to a different result. In the decision *The Home Depot* (BIPMZ 1997, 26) the German Court considered that registrations overseas merely reduced the importance of keeping the mark available in the interest of the public, whose use of the mark overseas is already "blocked" by the registration. . . .

The application therefore lacks distinctiveness as it would be interpreted as a mere advertisement. . . . Whether, and to what extent, there exists a need to keep the mark available for general use over and above this therefore does not need to be decided. However, it appears from the searches that the string of words is in reality widely used in connection with products on the market, so that it certainly also falls within the definition of nonregistrability. . . .

Case 28 W (Pat.) 153/95 (Chinese Characters), Federal Patent Court, July 24, 1996 (Germany), reported at 29 I.I.C. 361 (1998)[*]

A sequence of Chinese characters . . . was filed as a trademark for the goods "meat, fish, poultry and game, and for preserved meat, fish, poultry and game," as well as for various class 42 services.

The . . . German Patent Office denied protection to the trademark for lack of distinctive character, holding that, as a recognizable sequence of oriental

---

[*]English Translation by the Max Planck Institute for Foreign and International Patent, Copyright and Competition Law (Munich, Germany).

characters, the mark merely had the effect for the German public [of an indication of geographical origin], without the uniqueness necessary to designate a particular business, particularly since its complex structures made it impossible to individualize the mark pictorially; hence the mark was not memorable for the public.

In its appeal against this decision, the applicant points out that, even according to the previous case law, oriental characters were not to be denied distinctive character as a general principle, which must apply all the more so under the new Trademark Act. Furthermore, the behavior of the public had changed in recent years as a result of China's involvement in the western business world, such that the dismissal of the present application, which moreover had a marked visual effect, amounted to a discrimination of the applicant, particularly in light of the German Patent Office's practice of registering trademarks in other scripts (*e.g.*, Cyrillic).

At the suggestion of this Court, the applicant submitted an expert opinion on the semantic content of the Chinese characters filed. According to the evidence of the court interpreter, the characters are pronounced "Quan Ju De" and are the name of a duck restaurant.

[The appeal is upheld.] This Court cannot find any obstacle to registration within the meaning of Secs. 37(l) and 8(2)(1) and (2) of the new Trademark Act . . . Neither is there a legitimate interest in free use of the Chinese characters for which registration is requested, nor do they lack distinctive character.

First of all, this Court finds that there is no doubt that the mark filed satisfies the (abstract) conditions required for registration as a trademark within the meaning of Sec. 3 of the new Trademark Act, since it presents a complete, unified entity which, while containing a number of visual design elements, is ultimately comparable to elaborate ornaments or extravagantly designed labels, etc., whose entitlement to registration as a trademark has never been called into question despite their complex structure. Nor do the contested decisions reveal any such obstacles.

This Court does not share the views of the Patent Office on the lack of distinctive character. It is true that the contested decisions clearly follow the previous case law of the Federal Patent Court, according to which oriental characters lack the distinctive character required for a trademark since they can only be retained through an unreasonable degree of attentiveness or because the public interprets them merely as an indication of the oriental origins of the goods in question.

However, this view fails to take account of the changed legal and factual conditions. In the opinion of this Court, in particular a specific memorability, in the sense that the public would unambiguously identify and reproduce the trademark, cannot be required either with respect to the capability of registration as a trademark referred to above, or in the context of the distinctive character required by trademark law, particularly since such distinctiveness varies considerably from case to case . . . This means, however, that in the present case the finding of distinctive character cannot be made dependent on whether the trademark embodies an immediately recognizable semantic content and can be specified unambiguously, or on whether the observer can for instance note all the component parts that comprise the characters in question. [cit]. On the contrary, the sole decisive factor must be whether, in conjunction with the products and services for which it is requested, it can be understood by the public as an indication of business origin. There is nothing in trademark law that imposes the conclusion reached by the German Patent Office that the case must be determined on the basis of the fact that most consumers, when confronted with the trademark in question in their daily transactions, can be expected only to perceive some oriental characters and hence to interpret them merely as an indication of geographical origin. Thus by virtue of Sec. 33(2) of the new Trademark Act, every application of a trademark for which a filing date exists is entitled to registration, and such entitlement cannot be negated by sweeping statements about the public's interpretation. In addition, according to Sec. 26(4) of the new Trademark Act, in the future the affixation of a trademark to goods intended exclusively for export will be sufficient for the trademark to be deemed to be used in Germany. The purpose of this provision, namely to protect goods destined exclusively for export, would not be met if characters used in such economic centers as Japan and China were excluded from registration in the German Trademark Register as a matter of principle. Such an approach would conflict not only with the fact that the People's Republic of China, for instance, has been a member of the Madrid Trademark Agreement since 1989, but also with the interests of the commercial circles in question in being able to use a German registration in order to obtain an [International Registration] trademark with validity for China for Chinese characters as part of their activities on this market. Nor, at least as far as concerns the intention of the Act, should the fact be ignored that Germany is bound by the Agreement on Trade-Related Aspects of Industrial Property (TRIPS Agreement), even though its provisions are not directly applicable in terms of creating rights for the individual.

Irrespective of these legal considerations, however, it can today no longer be assumed, given the developments in the world's economy and the continuous growth of cultural and touristic relationships with the countries of the Far East, that the German public, when it perceives Chinese characters in connection with products or services, only associates them with the concept of an indication of geographical origin. In trademark law terms, however, this means that without any additional substantiated findings, the application for a trademark for Chinese characters cannot be denied distinctive character, at least in cases where, as here, the mark consists of a small number of sufficiently characterizing features and hence appears thoroughly capable of influencing the memory of the public in question as the indicator of business origin.

Nor, finally is there any legitimate interest in the free use of the characters filed. According to the expert opinion submitted to the files, the characters have no coherent meaning in the sense of words, but simply transcribe as the sound of the applicant's company name. Thus with respect to the goods and services for which they are requested, these characters have no meaning whatsoever, and particularly not as descriptive terms.

Ergopanel Trade Mark Application, Federal Patent Court, May 21, 1997
(Germany), 1997 E.T.M.R. 495

There exists the necessity to keep the applied-for ERGOPANEL mark free for general use under section 8(2)(2) of the Trade Marks Act . . . for the goods for which the opposed application has been specified, [namely, various electronic items].

As the term ERGOPANEL is not to be found in the dictionary, nor is there evidence of its use in trade, it may thus be assumed that it is a newly created hybrid word. However, even new words may be subject to the necessity to be kept available for general use where the meaning of the word is derived from a statement about the goods and where the fitting term may therefore serve as a description of the goods. This is the case in the present application.

The applied-for mark is clearly composed of the word "ergo" and the English word "panel" (meaning a control panel or console). The specified goods include items which would have such control consoles. This is also true of the "graphic steering apparatus," for example a graphics board, and for the "speech producing apparatus" wherein text is audibly reproduced. Thus the term "panel" is apt to describe the nature of the named goods in the domestic language (German). This is not diminished by the fact that the word is English. The term "panel" may not be expected to be part of everyone's basic English vocabulary; however, it is to be found in numerous dictionaries–even those which are concise and cover a limited range of words.

In addition to this, the English language is widely the primary language in this field, used not only by the experts, but also in advertising, etc. In this technical field, it is to be assumed that the word "panel" would be understood as a description of the goods by a significant proportion of the trade (experts and consumers).

[The court reviewed various uses of the term "ergo" in advertising]. Taking this background into account, the applied-for term presents a descriptive reference which is commonly used in advertising and in language which conveys the sense of an "ergonomically shaped control panel" and/or "fitted with an ergonomically shaped control panel". The mark is therefore excluded from registration for the goods for the benefit of the applicants' competitors.

The alleged U.K. registration was not considered as no certified evidence of this registration was submitted. In general however, it can be noted that the partial harmonisation of the trade mark laws of the European Union Member States through the harmonisation directive of December 21, 1988 does not create any binding precedent between the decisions of the Patent and Trade Mark Offices or the courts of the Member States, even if it were only in the sense of an "indication". For, provided that the German trade mark laws incorporate the harmonisation guidelines, there can be a European convergence of national rules. These requirements were also met by the officials and courts responsible for the decision-making practices of the other E.U. Member States. The resulting effects of harmonisation cannot however themselves be synchronised by the partial harmonisation.

Just as the harmonisation directive may be utilised in order to ignore decisions in other E.U. States, so it can be raised against positive decisions to allow a registration.

In addition, a decision on the registrability of a mark in a national examination procedure depends not only upon the harmonised law but also to a considerable extent upon the non-harmonised law (in particular as to procedural matters and requirements) regarding the evidence and assessment of domestic trading conditions. The characteristics of the trade may differ between States, despite the aim of creating a common market.

For this reason too, it will also in future be impossible to avoid discrepancies between the decisions of different E.U. Member States. This is also the view of the European legislature.

According to Article 7(2) of the Community Trade Mark Regulation . . . an application is to be refused where there exist obstacles to its registration under Article 3(1) in any part of the E.U., according to Article 7(1). The position taken by the applicant would thus mean that an applicant could obtain–through the alleged harmonisation of decisions–a bundle of national rights which would be denied by the legislature at the Community Trade Mark level.

An extension of the effects of the harmonisation guidelines toward some precursory or indicatory decisions by the Patent or Trade Mark Offices and courts of other E.U. Member States not only ignores the boundary between a Community-wide right to protection and national rights based (at least partly) upon harmonised law; it is also contrary to the expressed laws of the Community Trade Mark.

Furthermore, it is also not clear as to the basis for the implicit assumption of the applicant, that the harmonised rules by the other Patent and Trade Mark Offices of the E.U. would be better put into practice than through the domestic offices and court. [cit].

NOTES AND QUESTIONS

(1) **The Effect of the Internet.** Is the incorporation of technological developments into trademark analysis (such as seen in the remarks of the German Federal Supreme Court in *Partner With the Best*) an appropriate one? In what ways does the court's reliance upon internet use alter traditional assumptions about trademark law? *See* Tele-Direct (Publications) v. Canadian Bus. Online, Federal Court of Canada (Sept. 17, 1997), reported at EIPR N-33 (Mar. 1998) (rejecting reliance); *cf.* General Cigar Co. v. GDM, Inc., 988 F. Supp. 647, 650 n.6 (S.D.N.Y. 1997) (rejecting reliance). A recent report published by the United Nations noted that 80% of web sites are written in English, although fewer than 10% of the world's population speaks English. *See* HUMAN DEVELOPMENT REPORT, 1999 at 6 (Oxford Univ. Press. 1999).

(2) **English as the New Lingua Franca.** Several German courts have (like the court in *Ergopanel*) been persuaded to translate the English term to

German, and thus to afford lesser protection, because the mark is used in a field where English is commonly used. *See, e.g.*, Case 26 W 90/95, Federal Patent Court, July 10, 1996 (Germany), noted at 19 EUR. INTELL. PROP. REV. D-209 (1997) (rejecting mark "FOR YOU" for tobacco products and noting use of English in tobacco advertising); Case 26 W (Pat.) 130/95, Federal Patent Court, Feb. 19, 1997 (Germany), 1998 E.T.M.R. 386, 388 (YES for tobacco products); *see also* Case 24 W (Pat.) 229/91, Federal Patent Court, Apr. 13, 1993 (Germany), noted at 84 TRADEMARK REP. 903, 904 (1994) (noting that because English is the technical language in the computer business English terms cannot be considered foreign terms and thus rejecting registration of COMPUTER ASSOCIATES for software).

(3) **Relevance of Foreign Registrations.** In *The Home Depot*, the German Federal Supreme Court had (as the *Partner With the Best* court suggests) appeared to offer broad protection to marks that were comprised of several foreign language terms. *See* Case I ZB 10/94, *The Home Depot*, Federal Supreme Court, June 7, 1996 (Germany), reported at 29 I.I.C. 459 (accepting registration of THE HOME DEPOT for home and garden products). There, the court rejected the lower court's dissection of applicant's mark into three separate terms, each of which was (when understood in German) descriptive. *See also* Case 28 W (Pat.) 272/96, Federal Patent Court (Germany), noted at, 11 WORLD INTELL. PROP. REP. 191 (1997) (following *Home Depot* and accepting registration of SELECTSHIFT for gears for motor vehicles). Six months later, in *Partner with the Best*, the court commented that it had taken the appeal because in recent decisions (such as *The Home Depot*) the court appeared to have endorsed the view that "foreign language expressions are in principle capable of distinguishing and are not required to be kept available for general use, at least when the trade mark protection has already been granted overseas." As the *Partner With the Best* court noted, "while such indications by foreign registrations have constantly been rejected by the Federal Supreme Court it appears that [we] wish to afford foreign registrations greater weight." Accordingly, the court sought to clarify the position. In so doing, it suggested that it was a "fantasy that the German Patent Office could take into account legal evaluation by other countries." Among the difficulties identified by the court were that the Lanham Act allows registration on the basis of acquired distinctiveness, but the German court could not tell whether registration followed application of section 2(f) of the Lanham Act. Thus, although *The Home Depot* represented some liberalization insofar as it recognized that a foreign registration indicates a lack of a legitimate interest in free use of the foreign term in Germany, it should not be taken as a wholesale invitation to register foreign term marks in Germany. *See* Case I ZB 7/95, Federal Supreme Court, June 19, 1997 (Germany), noted at 12 WORLD INTELL. PROP. REP. 80 (1998) (rejecting registration for ACTIVE LINE for leather goods). Why would the basis for the foreign registration (e.g., under the Lanham Act) be relevant to the German Trademark Office?

(4) **Intra-EU Deference.** As the *Ergopanel* court suggested, despite substantive harmonization, the registration of a mark in one member state of the EU will not compel another member state to grant a registration in its jurisdiction. *See* Warnaco Inc.'s Application, 1997 E.T.M.R. 505, 507 (UK

Trademarks Registry, July 14, 1997). The reluctance of examiners to consider registration in other jurisdictions extends also to the EU Community Trademark Office, which does not feel bound by national registrations granted by offices of countries within the EU. *See, e.g., SOS Arana Alimentacion's Application*, O.H.I.M., First Board of Appeal, R 54/1998-1 (June 16, 1998) (EU), *noted at* 1998 E.T.M.R. 708; *see also New Zealand Lotteries Commission's Application*, O.H.I.M., Third Board of Appeal, Case R 37/1998-3/0 (July 13, 1998) (EU), 1998 E.T.M.R. 569 (prior non-EU registrations may be taken into account by examiner but not binding). This issue is discussed more fully *infra* § 6.05[A][2].

[D]   The Trademark Lawmaking Dynamic

ROBERT DENICOLA, SOME THOUGHTS ON THE DYNAMICS OF FEDERAL TRADEMARK LEGISLATION AND THE TRADEMARK DILUTION ACT OF 1995[*]
59 LAW & CONTEMP. PROB. 75, 80-83 (1996)

To be successful, trademark law must respond effectively to complex and sometimes inconsistent interests. Protection against infringement reduces the cost to consumers of acquiring reliable information about the source of a product and, hence, about its anticipated characteristics and quality. Protection also encourages investment in good will by ensuring trademark owners the opportunity to capture the rewards of a favorable reputation. But trademark law must also be responsive to the public interest in competition. Excessive protection can inhibit the communication of useful information by other sellers in the marketplace, and rights in packaging and product features can deprive competitors of access to elements crucial to effective competition. As trade symbols enter the general vocabulary, the law must also take account of the constitutional protection afforded noncommercial speech. These latter interests–the interests weighing against protection–are more likely to be represented effectively in common law adjudication than in the legislative process.

In trademark litigation, one party or the other will typically find it expedient to cloak itself tightly in the public interest. However, an adversarial process forces attention on pros and cons of such interests. The judiciary may systematically err in one direction or another, but usually not for lack of exposure to the real or imagined interests at issue.

The legislative process is more problematic. Owners of well-known trademarks are generally well-off and well-organized. They are important constituents in every political district, and their lobbying capabilities are impressive. Their chief trade organization, the United States (now International) Trademark Association, was single-handedly responsible for the 1988 Trademark Revision Act. On the other hand, small market entrants looking for a leg up, manufacturers specializing in knock-offs, supermarket shoppers, and parodists (let alone t-shirt bootleggers) are not, as a general matter, well represented in the legislative process. At best, they are left in the unenviable position of relying on testimony by public-spirited academic economists, or even law professors. This imbalance is troubling, whether we view the legislative process as a rational balancing of interests in furtherance of the general welfare or as a market in legislation.[27] From this perspective, a legislative strategy built on the codification of common law trademark principles is appealing—an intuition that the Lanham Act has generally heeded for fifty years. Unfortunately, this welcome conservatism, overwhelmed by an increasing fixation on international markets, may be ending.

Attention to the international dimension of intellectual property law is altogether prudent, to a point. For trademarks, the Paris Convention has long been the principal international treaty. Members, including the United States, promise national treatment for citizens of other member states and also agree to maintain at least a specified minimum level of trademark protection. More recently, there have been moves to harmonize trademark registration procedures (the Trademark Law Treaty) and to create a central application system for foreign registrations (the Madrid Protocol). In addition, the recent NAFTA and GATT trade agreements both produced modest changes to the federal trademark statute. The difficulty lies, however, not so much in statutory amendments implementing formal treaty obligations, but in impassioned pleas for ever-increasing protection rationalized by assertions about foreign revenues and trade balances.

There are trade-based arguments for increased domestic intellectual property protection suitable for every occasion. When the level of intellectual property protection in a foreign country is higher than in the United States, American works marketed in that country are sometimes limited on a reciprocity rationale to the lower level of protection available here. Thus, the argument is straightforward: Raise the level of protection for works at home, and Americans will suddenly earn billions more through expanded rights abroad.

. . . .

Perhaps surprisingly, trade-based arguments are popular even when the domestic law of the United States provides the same or greater protection than foreign law. Enactment of increased domestic protection, it is said, shows our good faith and strengthens the hand of our negotiators pressing for greater protection of American works abroad. This holier-than-thou attitude seems nothing short of miraculous to those who remember the American position prior

---

[27] . . . Copyright revision may reflect yet another model of the legislative process. Unlike trademarks, both owners and users of copyrighted subject matter are well organized. Much of the 1976 Copyright Act and its subsequent amendments were drafted, not by legislators or their staffs, but by affected interest groups during protracted negotiations. Jessica D. Litman, *Copyright, Compromise, and Legislative History*, 72 CORNELL L. REV. 857 (1987). Groups not at the table were frequently shortchanged. *See* Jessica Litman, *Copyright Legislation and Technological Change*, 68 OR. L. REV. 275 (1989).

Consideration of deceptive advertising issues under the Lanham Act is not hobbled by the imbalance in representation that plagues trademark issues. Large companies can as easily find themselves on one side of advertising complaints as on the other, and here the media is also a consistent player in the legislative process.

to the 1980s. For decades, the United States showed little embarrassment in preaching the virtues of strong intellectual property protection abroad while lingering with the sinners outside the Berne Convention, which serves as the chief international agreement on copyright.

Regardless of the relative levels of domestic and foreign protection, the lure of increased revenues from abroad creates unremitting pressure to expand the scope of intellectual property protection at home. The Lanham Act is not immune to these arguments. They may well have tipped the balance in the case of the recent dilution amendment.

MARSHALL LEAFFER, PROTECTING UNITED STATES INTELLECTUAL PROPERTY ABROAD: TOWARD A NEW MULTILATERALISM*
76 IOWA L. REV. 273, 281-285 (1991)

The inadequate protection of intellectual property in developing countries can be viewed at two levels: the meager or nonexistent governmental enforcement of the law and the deficient coverage of intellectual property in the law itself. . .

A lax attitude in protecting intellectual property offers, at least in the short run, attractive benefits for pirates and consuming nations. Pirates of intellectual property enjoy lower production costs and are in a better position than legitimate producers to satisfy demands in developing countries. Pirates can do so because they merely copy products rather than develop their own and pay no royalties to the owner or creator. By copying only successful products, the pirate avoids the risk of market failure.

Barring effective regulation, the piracy of intellectual property pays off because it involves little risk and provides a healthy return on investment. Pirates enrich themselves and, in the short run, the countries in which they operate. Through piracy, developing countries can procure needed goods and services at little cost, while industries that specialize in producing counterfeit goods employ thousands of workers. When compared to these tangible gains, the threat that investment from Western countries might be withdrawn is secondary to immediate development needs.

In Third World countries, the piracy of intellectual property is justified by an ideology of development. Ready access to intellectual property is viewed as important to development, whereas the enforcement of intellectual property law is considered a burden on development. Thus, developing countries resist allocating scarce government resources to the enforcement of intellectual property rights.[43]   As with the importation of capital, the importation of

---

[43]The prime example of developing countries' attitudes toward intellectual property is represented by the United Nations Conference on Trade and Development, known as UNCTAD. Created in 1964, UNCTAD has been primarily involved in intellectual property. Its various position papers reflect the developing countries' concern about access to innovative and creative works originating in developed countries. For a discussion of UNCTAD, see Spitals, *The UNCTAD Report on the Role of Trademarks in Developing Countries: An Analysis*, 3 N.Y.L. SCH. J. INT'L COMP. L. 369 (1981).

intellectual property often is viewed as a tool to dominate and exploit the economic potential of the importing countries. Paying for imports or making royalty payments imposes economic burdens and fosters a negative balance of trade.

In addition to this ideology, developing countries provide weak or nonexistent protection for, perhaps, a more basic reason. Intellectual property is simply too new of a concept to have developed a tradition of legal protection. Unlike Western countries, developing countries have few strong lobbies of inventors, authors, or companies that benefit from strong intellectual property laws.

. . . .

Nonetheless, one can perceive a change in perspective. The origin of this change can be traced to both local firms and consumers, themselves victimized by unrestrained piracy in two ways. First, some local companies are owners of indigenously developed intellectual property and suffer along with Western companies from inadequate legal protection. Piracy deprives these local businesses of sales and the ability to provide employment, and it discourages local companies from engaging in their own research and development. Second, absent adequate protection, Western firms will less readily transfer technology to local companies. Such direct foreign investment is vital to development because it disseminates state-of-the-art technology into the economy.

Consumers in developing countries also are directly victimized by counterfeit goods that threaten the public health and welfare in these countries. These inferior and sometimes dangerous products are sold widely to Third World consumers, who are vulnerable because of lax government enforcement.

. . . .

Virtually every major producer of brand name clothing, shoes, jewelry, agricultural chemicals, and pharmaceuticals has been victimized by organized piracy and inadequate protection under trademark law in various Third World countries. In many of those markets, trademarked goods are counterfeited overtly. Many of these counterfeit goods make their way into the United States and other foreign markets.

Some developing countries have displayed hostility toward trademark protection in their substantive law. This attitude is nurtured by a fear that foreign licensors of trademarks exploit both local businesses and vulnerable consumers. Foreign licensors are perceived as having superior bargaining power, permitting them to impose terms unfavorable to the local licensee. In addition to potentially onerous terms in the licensing contract, local authorities believe that the increased use of trademarks will become an insurmountable obstacle to achieving economic self-sufficiency. According to this theory, the public's dependence on products identified by foreign trademarks makes it difficult for local producers to establish recognition for their own goods. This position is supported by the United Nations Conference on Trade and Development ("UNCTAD").[49]

---

[49]Established in 1964 as a permanent organ of the General Assembly of the United Nations, UNCTAD was given the responsibility of establishing principles concerning trade between industrialized nations and developing countries. *See* Ball, *Attitudes of Developing Countries to Trademarks*, 74 TRADEMARK REP. 160, 162 n.8 (1983).

Some claim that consumers in developing countries are exploited by entrenched brand names. They argue that the foreign trademarks encourage irrational preferences among vulnerable, largely illiterate consumers in the developing countries. The foreign trademark functions as an insidious vehicle for persuasive advertising, which modifies healthy consumption patterns.

A proposed Mexican law provides a good example of an attempt to curtail the effect of foreign trademarks. In 1976, Mexico passed a law that required the local linking of trademarks. The Mexican "linking law," which has never gone into effect (due in part to foreign outcry), would have forced the use of foreign trademarks in connection with domestic trademarks. It mandated that all foreign trademarks used in connection with goods produced in Mexico would have to be associated with a Mexican mark. The linking law constituted a form of trademark expropriation, allowing the local licensee to enjoy a free ride on the reputation and goodwill embodied in the foreign mark. By this means, the local licensee hoped that the public would come to associate the particular goods involved with the licensee's trademark.[54] Thus, if the license were terminated, the local licensee would enjoy an autonomous goodwill acquired during the period of dual use. Although this postlicense goodwill could result in a degree of public deception, Mexico was willing to pay this price to subsidize local industry and to accept the risk that foreign trademark owners would hesitate in licensing their products to Mexican firms.

Linking laws are not the only practice hostile to trademark licensors. Other examples of the antitrademark attitude are found in countries that prohibit the importation of certain categories of trademark goods such as pharmaceutical products. In addition, some countries have attempted confiscation of foreign trademarks. Other laws have forced the trademark owner to manufacture the product on which the mark is affixed in the local country.

NOTES AND QUESTIONS

(1) **Developing Countries.** The particular concerns of developing countries with respect to the enforcement of trademark rights has received significant attention in the scholarly literature. *See, e.g.,* William H. Ball, Jr., *Attitudes of Developing Countries to Trademarks,* 74 TRADEMARK REP. 160 (1984); W.R. Cornish & Jennifer Phillips, *The Economic Function of Trade Marks: An Analysis With Special Reference to Developing Countries,* 13 I.I.C. 41 (1982); Monique Gabay, *The Role of Trademarks in Consumer Protection and*

---

[54] *See* Gabay, *The Role of Trademarks in Consumer Protection and Development in the Developing Countries,* 3 INDUS. PROP. 102, 111 (1981). That trademarks may be used as a means of persuasive advertising is nothing new, and even if foreign marks were eliminated, local marks may serve the same purpose. It is hard to see how the public would gain by a virtual confiscation of foreign marks. Whatever gains may occur from less persuasive advertising could well be offset by a loss of foreign investment in the developing country. Trademark licensing encourages economic development in the Third World, as does licensing of all intellectual property. Only by licensing can the Third World gain the necessary technological know-how, marketing expertise, and international reputation of the licensor.

Development in Developing Countries, 3 INDUS. PROP. 102 (1981); Peter O'Brien, *The International Trademark System and the Developing Countries,* 19 IDEA 89 (1978).

(2) **Colonization by Trademark Law.** Keith Aoki has written that "the colonization of the Nation-state by the private corporate sovereigns is at hand. . . . Western media images are transforming the world and constructing a hegemonic world culture modeled on the rampant consumerism of the United States. 'Advertising and media images exert powerful psychological pressures to seek a better, more 'civilized' life, based on the urban, Western consumerist model. Individual and cultural self-esteem are eroded by the advertising stereotypes of happy, blond, blue-eyed, clean Western consumers.'" Keith Aoki, *How the World Dreams Itself to Be American: Reflections on the Relationship Between the Expanding Scope of Trademark Protection and Free Speech Norms,* 17 LOY. L.A. ENT. L.J. 523, 525 (1997). What role, if any, should trademark law play in resisting (or implementing) such cultural models? Can it have a significant effect in one direction or the other? Is broad-based adoption of the values of the developed world more likely to occur with effective trademark protection or without such protection?

(3) **Domestic/International Parallels.** Would you expect parallels between the positions being staked out in domestic debates regarding the content of trademark law and those reflected at the international bargaining table? How might the dialogue differ, and what consequences should that have for the way in which we make trademark law domestically and internationally?

[E]   An Overview of International Agreements Concerning Trademarks

[1] Types of Multilateral Trademark Agreements

In the following Sections, we will discuss a range of international trademark agreements. These agreements derogate in different ways from the model of discrete national, territorial forms of trademark protection; they contain provisions that represent varying degrees of internationalization. The principal mechanisms included within these agreements can be roughly grouped as follows:

1. *National Treatment.* National treatment obligations require that a state provide nationals of other countries the same trademark protection as it would its own citizens. As we have seen above, this principle was the foundation of the great conventions of the late nineteenth century, namely the Paris Convention and the Berne Convention.

2. *Multinational Protection Facilitators.* These represent different means by which, without moving significantly from the country-by-country approach to the acquisition of rights, member states facilitate the procurement of national trademark registrations in multiple countries. These provisions are intended to reduce the transaction costs and time-sensitive vulnerabilities engendered by serial (although ideally simultaneous) national trademark filings. They do

not minimize differences between different national trademarks laws; rather, they attempt to minimize the costs and consequences of those differences.

These facilitation mechanisms take many different forms that depart from the sovereign territorial model in more or less revolutionary respects; they rely to varying degrees upon new institutional or administrative constructs, as well as on reform of national trademark law. The primary such vehicles are as follows:

Mandatory Acceptance of Serial Applications. These provisions require member states to register certain marks previously registered in other member states of the relevant union, subject only to enumerated exceptions.

Priority Rights. Priority provisions require member states to accord priority of rights in one country based upon the date of registration in another.

Procedural Harmonization. Procedural harmonization takes the form of standardizing national registration procedures, classification procedures and maintenance formalities, all with the goal of reducing transaction costs incurred by virtue of adherence to a system of separate national filings.

Centralized Filing Systems. Centralized filing systems involve the establishment of international institutional structures and mechanisms that facilitate the acquisition of rights, again on a multinational basis, yet ultimately resulting in ownership of various national trademark registrations.

3. *Substantive Harmonization.* Substantive harmonization consists of multinational agreement on substantive standards and principles of trademark protection that are then implemented in domestic national laws. Harmonization is ostensibly an attempt to minimize the differences that exist among national trademark laws. This form of harmonization has (at the global level) thus far primarily involved agreement upon substantive *minimum* levels of protection. More tightly-defined harmonization is, however, occurring in regional contexts such as the EU. And there is now debate in international intellectual property circles regarding the scope and nature of the harmonization process.

4. *Unitary Supranational Protection.* The grant of unitary, supranational rights throughout an economic region comprised of several nations is in the vanguard of a movement beyond multinational protection and toward the substantial elimination of territorial rights (or the establishment of rights throughout larger territorial areas). This concept may potentially take many forms, depending upon the scope of the rights and the institutional structures—the nature of the registering authority, and the centralized or developed nature of the enforcement and judicial authorities—that grant, administer and interpret the substantive rights.

PRELIMINARY QUESTIONS

As you read the provisions of the main multilateral agreements contained in this Chapter, consider whether (and to what extent) the quickening pace of globalization requires further retreat from the principle of territoriality and national sovereignty. Before we review the primary agreements, however, consider the following preliminary questions—we will revisit these issues, and you may perhaps reconsider your initial responses, throughout this Chapter.

Is a universal or supranational trademark law a utopian dream? Is it workable? If so, would it be desirable? What institutional mechanisms must accompany any such effort? As an alternative to territoriality, on the one hand, and supranationality (or universality) on the other, is regionality a concept that is either feasible or attractive? What are its advantages and disadvantages in comparison with territoriality or universality? Is it more consistent with the current political and economic climate? Would it merely be a transitional phase to universality, or a long-term governing concept? Who should be developing the principles of international trademark law? Should each development await the convening of a diplomatic conference or should we invest particular specialized bodies with authority to reflect more dynamic changes? *Cf.* W.R. Cornish, *Genevan Bootstraps*, 19 EUR. INTELL. PROP. REV. 336 (1997) (commenting on role of WIPO).

[2] Surveying the Landscape

The advent of an international marketplace precipitated the first major multilateral international industrial property convention addressing trademarks and unfair competition, the Paris Convention of 1883. The Paris Convention did not, however, disrupt the prevailing notion of separate, sovereign national laws. Trademark rights and laws remained national in nature, even if those laws were influenced by relatively low-level international obligations. And, in this, trademark law corresponded with the marketplace. Products may have been sold in different national markets, but each was viewed as a new and separate trading area with new and separate issues of production and marketing.

A global marketplace is quite different from an international marketplace. Just as the international marketplace brought forth the Paris Convention, the demands of the late twentieth century mercantile environment delivered the TRIPS Agreement. In this Section, we devote principal attention to the provisions found in these two agreements. They represent the major chronological (and, as we shall see, perhaps conceptual) bookends of public international trademark law. But, in addition, because the TRIPS Agreement incorporates by reference the obligations of the Paris Convention, they have also become intertwined with each other; their blended corpus thus contains most of the substantive obligations of international trademark law.

Before turning to consider the Paris Convention and TRIPS in detail, however, we will first briefly introduce a series of other international agreements that both complete the landscape of international trademark law and help to frame and explain the development of TRIPS. Finally, in this Chapter, after an in-depth analysis of the Paris Convention and TRIPS, we will discuss regional multilateral agreements (principally, NAFTA and developments in the EU that increasingly influence the shape of international trademark law, as well as one significant treaty concluded since TRIPS (namely, the Trademark Law Treaty). We deal separately with those agreements that solely establish mechanisms for the multinational acquisition of trademark rights (principally, the Madrid Agreement, the Madrid Protocol, and the European Community Trademark Regulation) in Chapter 6.

HARRIET R. FREEMAN, RESHAPING PROTECTION IN TODAY'S GLOBAL VILLAGE: LOOKING BEYOND GATT'S URUGUAY ROUND TOWARD GLOBAL TRADEMARK HARMONIZATION AND CENTRALIZATION*
1 ILSA J. INT'L & COMP. L. 67, 72-95 (1995)

This section delineates, in historical order, the principal international agreements which contain trademark rights and obligations. . . .

A.   *Paris Convention for the Protection of Industrial Property of 1883, as revised and amended (Paris Convention)*

. . . The Paris Convention provides trademark protection based on national treatment, priority rights, and registration. . . . [It] prohibits any signatory from requiring domicile or establishment in its country to obtain trademark protection. National treatment for trademark protection existed prior to the Paris Convention and has continued as the basis for most international agreements offering trademark protection. The Paris Convention has been criticized because of its use of national treatment which allows a country to avoid providing trademark protection for foreigners if it does not provide trademark protection for its citizens.

. . . The domestic laws of each country determine the conditions for the filing and registration of a trademark. The Paris Convention does not provide for centralized filing or registration. Thus, a trademark owner must file and register in each country where protection is desired unless another agreement exists which provides for centralization of filing and registration. [The Paris Convention also sets some minimum standards for national trademark laws in Union countries. The Paris Convention is discussed in more detail below.]

B. *Madrid Agreement Concerning the International Registration of Marks of 1891, as revised and amended (Madrid Agreement)*

In 1891, some of the Paris Union countries established the Madrid Agreement to create a uniform system for the international filing and registration of trademarks. The Madrid Agreement allows its member countries to "secure protection [in all Madrid Union countries] for their [trademarks], registered in the country of origin, by filing the said [trademarks] at the International Bureau . . ., through the intermediary of the Office of the said country of origin.". . . Although general support existed in the United States for a centralized trademark filing and registration system, the United States did not join the Madrid Agreement. [The Madrid Agreement is considered separately in *infra* § 6.02].

. . . .

C. *Pan American Convention of 1929, as revised, including the General Inter-American Convention for the Protection of Trademarks (Pan American Convention)*

The Pan American Convention of 1929, as revised, consists of two separate parts: a [General] Convention for Trade Mark and Commercial Protection, and a Protocol on Inter-American Registration of Trade Marks. . . . Although the Convention provides for national treatment and a centralized filing and registration system, it does not strengthen the Paris Convention nor the Madrid Agreement. . . .

Fourteen nations of the Western Hemisphere, including the United States, but not Canada, are parties to at least one of the conventions. The United States is a member of the Pan American Convention, but it renounced the Protocol in the mid-1940s. The Bureau administering the Convention, the Inter-American Trade Mark Bureau, was located in Havana, Cuba, but it has closed.

Compared to the Paris Convention, this Convention never acquired any significance. Now, with GATT 94 and other recent regional developments, this Convention becomes irrelevant. [Certain aspects of the Inter-American Convention are considered separately below.]

D. *Nice Agreement Concerning the International Classification of Goods and Services for the Purposes of the Registration of Marks of 1957, as revised*

The Nice Agreement constitutes an international trademark classification agreement . . . When registering a trademark, most countries require the applicant to describe the goods and services to be protected. However, such description may be problematic because trademark classification systems in various countries differ in the particularity of their description requirements. Thus, the International Bureau [of WIPO] established the International Classification system, creating specific descriptive classes for filing an international application. If, at any time, the International Classification system needs to be changed or revised, the Committee of Experts may make such changes or revisions.

. . . .The Nice Agreement is procedural in nature; it does not address any substantive trademark issues. No rights or obligations flow from any classification designation in the Nice Agreement. However, it does facilitate trademark searching which may help to prevent trademark confusion and infringement.

E. Convention Establishing the World Intellectual Property Organization of 1967, as revised (WIPO)

. . . Currently, the WIPO administers seventeen multilateral and regional agreements, such as the Paris Convention, the Madrid Agreement, and the Nice Agreement. Within its committee structure [since replaced in 1998 by standing committees*], two groups focus[ed] on international trademark law: the Permanent Committee on Industrial Property Information ad hoc Working Group on Trademark Information (PCIPI/TI) and the Committee of Experts on the Harmonization of Laws for the Protection of Marks (CEHLPM). The PCIPI/TI explore[d] trademark information collection and storage including trademark search systems, examination methods, application numbering systems, and classifications. The CEHLPM examine[d] harmonization of the trademark laws and recently developed a trademark administration treaty to facilitate worldwide trademark filing called the TLT.

At its inception, some WIPO convention delegates thought "[the WIPO's] existence [would] affect trademark rights at least in the [sense] of affording a better structured and administrated vehicle through which our trademark interests [could] be identified and debated." However, by 1987, the United States General Accounting Office, Division of National Security and International Affairs (GAO) concluded that although the WIPO constitutes the foremost multilateral intellectual property forum, the government had made only limited progress towards strengthening international intellectual property rights and obligations through the WIPO. The GAO further concluded that this limited progress was due to the United States government actively opposing the efforts of developing countries to weaken existing international standards for trademark protection. . . .

. . . .

F. Vienna Trademark Registration Treaty, 1973 (TRT)

The TRT resulted from the WIPO's failure to negotiate a revision to the Madrid Agreement acceptable to the countries, including the United States, which refused to accede to the Madrid Agreement but wanted to participate in

---

*[Ed. Note: In March 1998, the Assemblies of Member States of WIPO approved the establishment of the Standing Committee of the Law of Trademarks, Industrial Designs and Geographical Indications. The standing committee format is designed to provide a more effective and streamlined mechanism for consideration of international trademark and design issues.]

an international filing and registration system. When the negotiations deadlocked, the WIPO asked the United States for a solution, and the United States responded by proposing the TRT.

The TRT created a compromise between those countries establishing ownership based on registration without priority of trademark use and those requiring priority of trademark use. It . . . eliminated the United States' priority of trademark use requirement in favor of a declaration of intention to use. In addition, it allowed a minimum of three years with a discretionary extension to five years or more before trademark use becomes mandatory. It also permitted national law to bar an infringement action until after actual trademark use occurred within its borders.

. . . Although over fifty countries participated in the Vienna diplomatic conference, the TRT was ratified only by the five Paris Union countries which brought the TRT into force: Burkina Faso, Congo, Gabon, the Soviet Union, and Togo. . . .

G. *Protocol Relating to the Madrid Agreement Concerning the International Regulation of Marks of 1989 (Madrid Protocol)*

After the TRT failed to attract sufficient signatories to make it viable, the Madrid Union requested the WIPO to continue considering changes to the Madrid Agreement which would allow Great Britain, Ireland, Denmark, Greece, and the United States to join. The WIPO responded with the Madrid Protocol. Initially, the international trademark community, including the United States, hailed the Madrid Protocol as acceptable to everyone. [The Madrid Protocol is considered separately *infra* § 6.02].

NOTES AND QUESTIONS

(1) **Bilateral Agreements.** In addition to these multilateral agreements, the United States has entered into several bilateral treaties that provide reciprocal protection under trademarks laws for parties of the signatory nations. For example, in April 1996, the United States and Taiwan entered into such an agreement. Taiwanese nationals thus receive the benefits of section 44 of the Lanham Act.

(2) **"National Treatment Plus."** What does Harriet Freeman mean by the statement that "The Paris Convention has been criticized because of its use of national treatment which allows a country to avoid providing trademark protection for foreigners if it does not provide trademark protection for its citizens"? The Berne Convention also provides for national treatment in the case of copyright, but that concept was largely heralded rather than "criticized." In what ways is the Paris Convention different from the Berne Convention so as to provoke this response from Freeman?

(3) **Accessions to International Trademark Treaties**. Up-to-date listings of countries that are party to the primary international conventions are available online at the WIPO home page (www.wipo.int).

[F]   The Paris Convention

[1] History and Basic Principles

A SHORT HISTORY OF THE PARIS CONVENTION[*]

Prior to the Paris Convention, at least sixty-nine bipartite treaties provided some form of protection for foreigners' trademarks. Practically all of these early treaties used the same general form for reciprocal protection of trademarks, namely, that the subjects of each of the contracting states shall enjoy respectively in the other state the same protection as nationals. A few bilateral treaties, some involving the United States, assured some form of protection in one country to trademarks affixed to goods in the other country, thus protecting marks on exports of those countries.

After conferences in 1873 and 1878 failed to reach agreement on a multilateral intellectual property treaty, the French government invited other states to the International Conference of 1880, which was attended by representatives of eighteen nations, including the United States. At the opening session, the French proposed creation of a union which would lay down a number of principles for protection of industrial property generally. The delegates from the United States were among those who declared that they lacked necessary instructions. Subsequently the United States delegation received instructions insisting upon a reservation that the conclusions of the conference on the subject of trademarks "must be considered as absolutely subordinate to such legislative provisions as may hereafter be made by this country."

In the end, a Draft Convention, together with a Final Protocol, was adopted and signed "procès-verbal" by the delegates of all the countries represented at the 1880 Conference. The French government called an International Convention at Paris in March 1883, at which time certain reservations and explanations were inserted into the Final Protocol, the main text of the Convention no longer being open to revision.

Eleven nations, but not the United States, signed the Convention and Final Protocol. The following year, representatives of those nations completed the final step of exchanging ratifications, and the acts of accession of four other nations were deposited. A month later, the Convention went into effect on July 7, 1884. The United States acceded to the Convention on May 30, 1887.

---

[*]Excerpted from John B. Pegram, *Trademark Law Revision: Section 44*, 78 TRADEMARK REP. 141, 153-54 (1988). Copyright 1986, 1988, John B. Pegram. Reprinted with permission.

JOANNA SCHMIDT-SZALEWSKI, THE INTERNATIONAL PROTECTION OF TRADEMARKS AFTER THE TRIPS AGREEMENT[*]
9 DUKE J. COMP. & INT'L L. 189, 193-201 (1998)

GENERAL PRINCIPLES

A. *Principles Relating to the Substance of Protection*

[T]he Paris Convention . . . contains two basic principles of international law that members must enforce in their reciprocal relations. The first is the national treatment principle, discussed generally in Article 2 and specifically as it relates to trademarks in Article 6, sections 1 and 2. The second is the principle of independence of rights, as embodied in Article 6, section 3.

a. *National Treatment Principle.* The principle of national treatment is applicable to all industrial property rights. The principle generally states that a member state may not subject foreigners benefitting from the Paris Convention to higher industrial property protection standards than those applicable to its own citizens.[37] In addition, it is not necessary to [show] that a trademark has been registered in the country of origin prior to registering it in another member state.[38] For example, if a citizen or corporation of Singapore wishes to obtain an industrial property right in France, where both countries are Paris Convention member states, the Singapore national will obtain the right under the same conditions as a French citizen or corporation. . . .

To understand fully the practical impact of the national treatment principle, it is necessary to understand that a member state may refuse industrial property rights protection to citizens or corporations of states that are not members of the Paris Convention. A member state may also subject non-member protections to stricter conditions than those applicable to its own nationals. For instance, because Thailand has not ratified the Paris Convention, a member state of the Convention could refuse to protect industrial property rights claimed by Thai citizens or corporations. A member state could also subject protection for these non-members to a condition of reciprocity, residence, the payment of a supplementary fee, or anything else.

. . . .

b. *The Principle of Independence of Rights.* Under the principle of independence of rights, a trademark granted in a member state is independent from those that already exist in other member states for the same object,

---

[37]*See* Paris Convention, art. 2. Article 2(1) of the Paris Convention provides the nationals of any member state with the same advantages that domestic laws grant to nationals of the states where the protection is sought; reciprocity is denied. *See id.* art. 6(2). . . .

[38]*See* Paris Convention, art. 6(2). Article 6(2) of the Paris Convention states: "However, an application for the registration of a mark filed by a national of a country of the Union in any other country of the Union may not be refused, nor may a registration be invalidated, on the ground that filing, registration, or renewal, has not been effected in the country of origin." *Id.*

including in the country where it was first protected. [Art. 6(3).] Consequently, trademarks consisting of the same sign designating the same goods and belonging to the same owner in several Paris Convention member states are independent from one another. This rule extends the national treatment principle to an extreme because the trademark owner is subject exclusively to the national law of each country. The nullification, refusal, or transfer, for example, of the trademark in one member state has no influence on the rights protected in another member state.

The exceptions to the principle of independence include the priority right and the protection of the trademark "as such." The priority right in Article 4 is designed to facilitate the international protection of industrial property rights. Within six months from the first application in a member state, the applicant may file for registration of the same trademark in other member states using the date of the first application. [Art. 4C.] As a result, disclosures or uses of the trademark within the priority period are not grounds for nullification of the mark. [Art. 4B.] This priority right exception does not apply to service marks under the Paris Convention.

The second exception is the protection of the trademark "as such" in Article 6*quinquies*. This exception aims to solve the difficulties that arise from the existence of different prerequisites for trademark protection in different countries. For instance, some national laws prohibit registration of numbers or letters, whereas others allow such trademarks. Under such a system it would be impossible for a trademark holder to use a mark in the same form in several countries. The Paris Convention resolves this problem by providing that a trademark that has been registered in its country of origin in compliance with local law is to be registered in other contracting states "as it is," or in French, "*telle quelle.*"

. . . .

B. *Principles Relating to the Procedure of Protection*

. . . Article 12 of the Paris Convention provides the relevant procedural provisions, stating that each member state must "establish a special industrial property service, and a central office for the communication to the public of patents, utility models, industrial designs, and trademarks." Furthermore, under Article 12, each member state's service must publish an official periodical sheet.

. . . .

TRADEMARK PROTECTION IN THE PARIS UNION

The "Paris Union" consists of the 1883 Paris Convention and a series of agreements subsequently signed within the Paris Convention's framework.

A. *The Paris Convention of 1883*

While the Paris Convention provides some rules specific to certain categories of industrial property rights, such as patents, trademarks, and industrial designs, in general, the Convention leaves further implementation of its directives to be applied through the member states' national laws. To this extent, it achieves a limited harmonization of international trademark law. The few trademark rules provided by the Paris Convention relate to the acquisition and content of a trademark right.

1. Rules on the Acquisition of Rights

a. *Prohibited Signs.* According to the Paris Convention, member states must prohibit trademark protection of certain official signs such as emblems of states, signs of control and guaranty, and emblems of international intergovernmental organizations. [Art. 16*ter*.]

b. *Protection of Well-Known Marks.* Even if they have not been registered, well-known marks benefit from an extended protection based on notoriety. [Art. 6*bis*]. Such marks are protected against all unauthorized use, even if they appear on goods different from those for which the mark was originally registered or used. Evidence of a well-known mark's notoriety must be found in the country where the protection of the mark is sought.

c. *Service Marks.* While they do not have to provide for the registration of such marks, member states have an obligation to protect service marks under Article 6*sexies*. However, the marks may be protected by other rules such as unfair competition.

d. *Collective Marks.* Member states have an obligation to protect collective marks under Article 7*bis*. These marks belong to a so-called association. However, such an association's existence cannot be contrary to the law of the country of origin.

e. *Nature of the Goods to which the Mark is Applied.* The nature of the product to which a trademark is applied may not impede the registration of the mark. [Art. 7.] For example, even if the marketing of certain goods is prohibited, the trademark applied to the goods may still be registered.

f. *Temporary Protection.* Member states have an obligation to grant temporary protection for trademarks during official international exhibitions. [Art. 11.]

g. *Specific Mention.* Member states may not require as a condition of protection that the product bear a specific mention of the trademark registration. [Art. 5D.]

2. Rules on the Content of Rights

a. *Use.* Member states may require that the rightsholder effectively uses the trademark. [Art. 5C(1).] When an owner fails to use the trademark within a reasonable period of time, and does not have a valid reason for the disuse, the owner may be deprived of the trademark right.

b. *Co-Owners.* Simultaneous use of the trademark by co-owners to designate identical or similar products will not limit the trademark's protection, so long as the use does not deceive the public and is not contrary to public interest. [Art. 5C(3).]

c. *Grace Periods.* A grace period of at least six months must be granted for payment of fees due for maintenance or renewal of the trademark right. [Art. 5*bis*(1).

. . . .

B. *Conventions Based on Paris*

Article 19 of the Paris Convention permits the conclusion of special agreements between member states. Presently, four such special agreements exist relating to trademarks: the Madrid Agreement, the Trademark Registration Treaty, the Madrid Protocol, and the Trademark Law Treaty.

. . . .

———

The Paris Convention was last revised at Stockholm in 1967; further revision efforts were undertaken throughout the early 1980s, but no agreement was reached. Despite this impasse, the Paris Convention clearly contributed toward the development of international trademark law in at least three ways mentioned by Professor Schmidt-Szalewski. First, it obliged signatory states to accord nationals of other member nations the same treatment as granted its own nationals (art. 2): this principle of "national treatment" is essentially an international equal protection clause for trademark applicants and owners. Second, it included certain minimal procedural mechanisms to facilitate the acquisition of trademark rights on a multinational basis: more particularly, it required that a mark registered in one country be accepted in other countries as it is, or "*telle quelle*" (art. 6 of original text, now art. 6*quinquies*), and created rights of priority (art. 4). Finally, it obliged member states to provide certain basic levels of trademark and unfair competition protection, so-called "substantive minima" (*e.g.*, arts. 6*bis*, 10*bis*). We will examine each of these contributions in turn, but first we briefly discuss the means by which the Paris Convention is implemented in national law. This discussion will also allow us to consider one of the substantive minima contained in the Convention, namely Article 10*bis*.

[2] Implementation in National Law

The United States acceded to the Paris Convention on May 30, 1887. The convention was revised successively at Washington (1911), the Hague (1925), London (1934), Lisbon (1958), and Stockholm (1967). The United States has acceded to the 1967 Stockholm text; this will soon be the almost universal Paris

Convention text in light of the requirement imposed upon WTO members by Article 2 of TRIPS to adhere to the Stockholm text.

As discussed in Chapter 2, not all treaties are self-executing. And different countries follow different mechanisms for making treaty provisions part of their respective laws. In the United Kingdom, for example, treaties are not self-executing and require affirmative implementation to be effective. In the United States, some (but not all) treaties are self-executing. U.S. courts have been split on the question of whether the trademark provisions of the Paris Convention are self-executing. In 1946, section 44 of the Lanham Act was enacted largely to ensure implementation of the treaty obligations of the United States. But the role of the convention in U.S. law remains unclear, as the following cases illustrate.

THE PARIS CONVENTION, ARTICLE 10*bis*

(1) The countries of the Union are bound to assure to nationals of such countries effective protection against unfair competition.

(2) Any act of competition contrary to honest practices in industrial or commercial matters constitutes an act of unfair competition.

(3) The following in particular shall be prohibited:

1. All acts of such a nature as to create confusion by any means whatever with the establishment, the goods, or the industrial or commercial activities, of a competitor;

2. False allegations in the course of trade of such a nature as to discredit the establishment, the goods, or the industrial or commercial activities, of a competitor;

3. Indications or allegations the use of which in the course of trade is liable to mislead the public as to the nature, the manufacturing process, the characteristics, the suitability for their purpose, or the quantity, of the goods.

VANITY FAIR MILLS v. T. EATON CO.
234 F.2d 633, 640-644 (2d Cir. 1956)

WATERMAN, C.J.

[The plaintiff, a Pennsylvania corporation, which owned rights to the mark VANITY FAIR in the United States, sought to apply the Lanham Act extraterritorially to acts of alleged trademark infringement by a Canadian defendant occurring both in the United States and in Canada. The court declined to apply the Lanham Act extraterritorially to the Canadian conduct. *See infra* Chapter 7. The plaintiff also alleged U.S. jurisdiction over the

Canadian conduct under the Paris Convention (1934 London text, which was the most recent text at the time), either directly or through the implementing provisions of section 44 of the Lanham Act.]

I. *The International Convention*

Plaintiff asserts that the International Convention for the Protection of Industrial Property (Paris Union) [cit.], to which both the United States and Canada are parties, is self-executing; that by virtue of Article VI of the Constitution it is a part of the law of this country which is to be enforced by its courts; and that the Convention has created rights available to plaintiff which protect it against trade-mark infringement and unfair competition in foreign countries. Plaintiff would appear to be correct in arguing that no special legislation in the United States was necessary to make the International Convention effective here,[9] but it erroneously maintains that the Convention created private rights *under American law* for acts of unfair competition occurring in foreign countries.

The International Convention is essentially a compact between the various member countries to accord in their own countries to citizens of the other contracting parties trade-mark and other rights comparable to those accorded their own citizens by their domestic law. The underlying principle is that foreign nationals should be given the same treatment in each of the member countries as that country makes available to its own citizens. In addition, the Convention sought to create uniformity in certain respects by obligating each member nation "to assure to nationals of countries of the Union an effective protection against unfair competition." [Art. 10*bis*].

The Convention is not premised upon the idea that the trade-mark and related laws of each member nation shall be given extraterritorial application, but on exactly the converse principle that each nation's law shall have only territorial application. Thus a foreign national of a member nation using his trade-mark in commerce in the United States is accorded extensive protection here against infringement and other types of unfair competition by virtue of United States membership in the Convention. But that protection has its source in, and is subject to the limitations of, American law, not the law of the foreign national's own country. Likewise, the International Convention provides protection to a United States trade-mark owner such as plaintiff against unfair competition and trade-mark infringement in Canada—but only to the extent that Canadian law recognizes the treaty obligation as creating private rights or has made the Convention operative by implementing legislation. Under Canadian law, unlike United States law, the International Convention was not effective to create any private rights in Canada without legislative implementation. However, the obligations undertaken by the Dominion of Canada under this treaty have been implemented by legislation, most recently by the Canadian Trade Marks Act of 1953. [cit.] If plaintiff has any rights under the International Convention (other than through section 44

---

[9]Bacardi Corp. of Am. v. Domenech, 311 U.S. 150 (1940); [cit].

of the Lanham Act, discussed below), they are derived from this Canadian law, and not from the fact that the International Convention may be a self executing treaty which is a part of the law of this country.

II.   *The Lanham Act*

[The court rejected plaintiff's request to apply the Lanham Act extraterritorially under the principles laid down by the Supreme Court in *Steele v. Bulova Watch, infra* Chapter 7.]

B. *Section 44 of the Lanham Act*

Plaintiff's alternative contention is that Section 44 of the Lanham Act, which is entitled "International Conventions," affords to United States citizens all possible remedies against unfair competition by foreigners who are nationals of convention countries, including the relief requested in this case. Subsection (b) of section 44 specifies that nationals of foreign countries signatory to certain named conventions (including the Paris Union signed by Canada) are "entitled to the benefits . . . (of the Act) to the extent . . . essential to give effect to (the conventions)." Subsection (g) then provides that the trade names of persons described in subsection (b), *i.e.*, nationals of foreign countries which have signed the conventions, "shall be protected without the obligation of filing or registration whether or not they form parts of marks", and subsection (h) provides that the same persons "shall be entitled to effective protection against unfair competition . . ." Finally, subsection (i) provides that "citizens or residents of the United States shall have the same benefits as are granted by this section to persons described in subsection (b) . . ." Thus section 44 first implements the international agreements by providing certain foreign nationals with the benefits contained in those agreements, then, in subsection (i), places American citizens on an equal footing by providing them with the same benefits. [cit]. Since American citizens are given only the same benefits granted to eligible foreign nationals, the benefits conferred on foreign nationals must be examined to see whether they have any extraterritorial application.

   The benefits provided by section 44 (without attempting to be exhaustive) may be summarized as follows: a foreign national may register his foreign mark upon the production of a certificate of registration issued by his country of origin, even though he has not used his mark in United States commerce, § 44(c), 15 U.S.C.A. § 1126(c); in determining priority of filing, if the foreign national has filed for registration in the United States within six months after filing abroad, he may make use of his foreign filing date but if his foreign registration antedates the six month period, he may use only his United States filing date, § 44(d), 15 U.S.C.A. § 1126(d); a foreign national may register his foreign marks on the Principal Register if they are eligible, and, if not, on the Supplemental Register, § 44(e), 15 U.S.C.A. § 1126(e); a foreign national may prevent the importation into the United States of goods bearing infringing marks or names, § 42, 15 U.S.C.A. § 1124; once a foreign mark has been registered under the Lanham Act, its status in the United States is independent of the continued validity of its registration abroad, and its duration, validity, and transfer in the United States are governed by "the provisions of this chapter", § 44(f), 15 U.S.C.A. § 1126(f). It will be noted that all of these benefits are internal to the United States in the sense that they confer on foreign nationals certain rights in the United States. None of them could have extraterritorial application, for all of them relate solely to the registration and protection of marks within the United States.

We now come to the two remaining benefits specified in section 44, and the ones upon which plaintiff relies: the provision in subsection (g) protecting trade-names without the obligation of filing or registration, and the provision in subsection (h) entitling eligible foreign nationals "to effective protection against unfair competition" and making available "the remedies provided in this chapter for infringement of marks . . . so far as they may be appropriate in repressing acts of unfair competition." Here again, we think that these benefits are limited in application to within the United States. It is true that they are not expressly so limited, but it seems inconceivable that Congress meant by this language to extend to all eligible foreign nationals a remedy *in the United States against unfair competition occurring in their own countries.* Moreover, if section 44 were so interpreted, it would apply to commerce which is beyond the Congressional power to regulate, and a serious constitutional question would be created. In the absence of any Congressional intent to provide remedies of such extensive application, we interpret section 44 in a manner which avoids constitutional questions and which carries out the underlying principle of the International Conventions sought to be implemented by section 44—the principle that each nation shall apply its national law equally to foreigners and citizens alike.

Since United States citizens are given by subsection (i) of section 44 only the same benefits which the Act extends to eligible foreign nationals, and since the benefits conferred on those foreign nationals have no extraterritorial application, the benefits accorded to citizens by this section can likewise have no extraterritorial application.[16]

. . . .

GENERAL MOTORS CORP. v. IGNACIO LOPEZ DE ARRIORTUA
948 F. Supp. 684 (E.D. Mich. 1996)

Please read the opinion reproduced *supra* page 71.

---

[16]The fact that United States citizens have already been given benefits by other provisions of the Lanham Act similar or identical to those contained in section 44 should not obscure the fact that subsection (i) added certain rights which United States citizens would not otherwise have had. For example, citizens or residents of the United States who have a "bona fide and effective business or commercial establishment" in a foreign country, within the meaning of subsection (b), may register any trade-marks which they have registered in that foreign country in the same manner as that provided for foreign nationals and with the same filing priorities. . . .

NOTES AND QUESTIONS

(1) **Section 44 and a Federal Law of Unfair Competition.** The meaning of section 44(i) of the Lanham Act has always been unclear. Textually, it extends to U.S. nationals the same rights that section 44 accords foreign nationals. The Ninth Circuit initially interpreted the provision broadly to create a federal right of unfair competition, but courts have largely retreated from that position (particularly in light of the robust development of section 43(a)). *See* J. Thomas McCarthy, *Lanham Act § 43(a): The Sleeping Giant Is Now Wide Awake,* 59 LAW & CONTEMP. PROB. 45, 49-50 (1996) (describing rise and fall of section 44(i)).

(2) **The Meaning of Section 44.** Which of the competing interpretations of the intersection between section 44 of the Lanham Act and the terms of the Paris Convention is most persuasive? What weight should be given to section 44(b), which explicitly but generally implements the Paris Convention together with other conventions or treaties relating to trademarks, trade names, or unfair competition? What effect will the different interpretations by the *Vanity Fair* and *Lopez* courts have on competitors' rights under the Lanham Act? How might the development of trademark and unfair competition law in the U.S. courts be affected by the different approaches of those courts? In light of the confusion surrounding the meaning of section 44, some prominent commentators have argued that Congress should provide a specific delineation of the rights provided foreign nationals. *See* John B. Pegram, *Trademark Law Revision: Section 44,* 78 TRADEMARK REP. 141, 142 (1988). Would that help?

(3) **Reconciling *Lopez* and *Vanity Fair*.** In *Scotch Whisky Ass'n v. Majestic Distilling Co.,* 958 F.2d 594 (4th Cir. 1992), an association of Scotch whisky distillers ("SWA") sought to restrain a Maryland-based liquor bottler and distributor (Majestic) from marketing gin and vodka under the name BLACK WATCH and a label containing images evocative of Scotland. SWA pursued its unfair competition claims against Majestic under section 43(a) of the Lanham Act, Articles 10 and 10*bis* of the Paris Union Convention (1883) via sections 44(b) and (h) of the Lanham Act, and Maryland state law. The court regarded the scope of each of these claims as coterminous and concluded that the SWA was required to show a likelihood of confusion as to the product's origin to make out any of these claims (which it failed to do). The court specifically rejected SWA's contention that the rights conferred by the Paris Union Convention exceed those conferred by the Lanham Act. The court's opinion also noted, however, that "subsections 44(b) and 44(h) work together to provide foreign nationals with rights under United States law which are coextensive with the substantive provisions of the treaty involved." In particular, the court noted that:

> the language of section 43(a) of the Lanham Act is . . . more specific than that used in the Paris Union Convention. By its use of generalities, the convention provisions relied on by SWA might well cover acts of unfair competition beyond those related to the unfair use of trademarks. However, it is the alleged unfair use of trademarks that is involved in

this litigation, specifically the deceptive use of a description of a product's origin. The broad language of the Paris Union Convention in its application here cannot apply to a spectrum of unfair competition that is broader than that covering the use of trademarks which deceptively indicate a product's origin. We think then, as apparently did the district court, that vis-á-vis trademark protection, the Paris Union Convention gives no greater protection than that already provided by section 43(a) of the Lanham Act.

Does this dictum suggest an interpretation that might (contrary to the assumption of the *Lopez* court) permit the reconciliation of *Vanity Fair* and *Lopez*? Is the *Scotch Whisky Association* interpretation of the interaction between section 44 and the Paris Convention a plausible one? Does it suggest that trademark-related actions under Article 10*bis* be treated as co-extensive with Lanham Act claims but non-trademark based claims beyond the reach of section 43 of the Lanham Act be permitted? Would there be a basis for such a distinction?

(4) **Cases Applying Section 44.** In *Laboratorios Roldan, C. Por A. v. Tex Int'l, Inc.* 902 F. Supp. 1555 (S.D. Fla. 1995), the plaintiff had owned the registered mark ROLDAN for soap in the Dominican Republic in 1959. Since 1990, the plaintiff has made a version of its soap for export to, and sale in, the United States, but did not itself sell its product directly into the United States. The defendants were among those who imported plaintiff's products from the Dominican Republic for sale in the United States, primarily to wholesalers and retailers in South Florida. In response to customers' requests for ROLDAN soap, the defendants sought to secure a distribution agreement with the plaintiff for the territories of the United States, Canada, the Caribbean and Africa. When negotiations failed, the defendants formed a corporation called Roldan Corporation to produce and market products under the name ROLDAN. The defendants were not licensed by the plaintiff to make or sell ROLDAN products, and the defendants' ROLDAN products were not made with the authority or consent of plaintiff, and were not made according to plaintiff's quality control or supervision.

Defendants sold the soap in packaging that used a trade dress that was nearly identical to the trade dress that plaintiff had used since 1970 or 1971 for its soap product. The packaging of this product stated in Spanish and French that it was made "for Roldan" in "the European Economic Community." Evidence before the court demonstrated that purchasers believed that the defendants' products were made by the plaintiff or someone affiliated or associated with plaintiff, such as a subsidiary. The plaintiff experienced displacement of the market for its products: sales decreased approximately eighteen percent (18%) as a result of the defendants' activity. Moreover, consumer complaints were being received by the plaintiff about soap that it did not produce. The plaintiff brought an action under section 43 of the Lanham Act and under section 44(h) of the Lanham Act/Paris Convention. The court found that the plaintiff was likely to prevail under both claims. As regards the section 43(a) claim, the court held that the plaintiff established first use of its trademark and trade dress in the United States and was thus entitled to restrain confusingly similar use by the defendants. The court also recognized likely success on the section 44(h) claim, taken in combination with Articles 6*bis* and 10*bis* of the Paris Convention. The court concluded that the defendant's "behavior constitutes unfair competition which article 10*bis* of the Paris Convention exists to protect against" and that because plaintiff's trade dress is well known, plaintiff was likely to prevail under Article 6*bis* as well.

Likewise, in *Benard Indus. Inc. v. Bayer Aktiengesellschaft*, 38 U.S.P.Q.2d 1422 (S.D.Fla. 1996), the court permitted a plaintiff to proceed on claims under each of Section 43, the unfair competition provisions of the Paris Convention, and the equivalent provisions under the Pan American Convention. The court concluded, citing *Scotch Whisky Association*, that the Paris Convention "may well cover acts of unfair competition beyond those related to the unfair use of trademarks" and "because Bayer alleges multiple factual bases for its claim of unfair competition, including infringement and false advertising and use of trade dress, the reasoning in *Scotch Whisky* does not persuade the Court that it is beyond a doubt that Bayer can prove no set of facts which would entitle it to relief under the Conventions." What did the section 44 claim add to the plaintiff's position in either of these cases? In what circumstances would a plaintiff prevail under section 44 but lose under section 43?

Similarly, in *Davidoff Extension S.A. v. Davidoff Int'l, Inc.*, 612 F. Supp. 4 (S.D.Fla. 1984), the plaintiff was a Swiss corporation that had registered its trademark DAVIDOFF for high quality cigars with the U.S. PTO. The principal of the plaintiff corporation, Zino Davidoff, was a worldwide known personality in the tobacco industry and had achieved extensive press media coverage and also published a book on cigars. The defendant (Hoffman) began producing generic cigars using the Davidoff name. The defendant defended the plaintiff's trademark infringement suit by arguing that the plaintiff had not used its name or its products in the United States. The court rejected this claim, but also noted that the plaintiff had registered the mark DAVIDOFF in Switzerland (a Paris Union country). Noting both that it viewed the Paris Convention as self-executing, and that section 44 of the Lanham Act explicitly implements the Paris Convention, the court listed "three benefits" that the convention conferred on plaintiff:

> (1) Plaintiff may obtain a U.S. registration of its trademark DAVIDOFF for tobacco products, smokers' articles, etc. without alleging use of its trademark in the United States because plaintiff has a Swiss trademark Registration for its trademark: Lanham Act § 44(c), (e); Paris Convention Article 6*quinquies* . . . ;
>
> (2) Plaintiff's trade name is to be protected without the obligation of any filing or registration: Lanham Act § 44(g); Paris Convention Article 8; and
>
> (3) Plaintiff is to be protected from unfair competition: Lanham Act § 44(h); Paris Convention Article 10*bis*. . . .

As a consequence, the court concluded that "defendants' argument that plaintiff is not using its trademark in the United States and that its U.S.

registrations of the trademark were fraudulent appears inconsequential." Does this reasoning suggest that a claim under Article 10*bis* might not require domestic U.S. use by a plaintiff? Assuming that the Swiss company in *Davidoff* had not used the DAVIDOFF mark in the United States (and the court appeared willing to decide in favor of the Swiss company even if such use had not been proved), what differentiates the conduct of Mr. Hoffman in *Davidoff* from that of Mr. Christman in *Person's*? *See supra* § 3.01[A].

(5) **The Content of Paris-Derived Rights.** The *Lopez* court decided that the plaintiffs stated a claim under the Paris Convention. But how should the court subsequently determine the content of the rights against unfair competition that the defendants have allegedly violated? In footnote 4, the court notes that "if the Paris Convention grants substantive rights it is not clear what those rights are." This suggests some type of international standard emanating from the text and history of the convention itself. The court continues, however, to warn that "because the plaintiff seeks enforcement of foreign law, it is their obligation to inform the court of the content of that law." What does the court mean by "foreign law"? German law? International law, as grounded in the text of the Paris Convention? International standards as evidenced by the evidence of persons engaged in international trade today? The leading authority on the Paris Convention has written that "what is to be understood by 'competition' will be determined in each country according to its own concepts" but that whether an act is contrary to honest practices in industrial or commercial matters is not limited to honest practices existing in the country where protection against unfair competition is sought but should also take into account "honest practices established in international trade." G.H.C. BODENHAUSEN, GUIDE TO THE APPLICATION OF THE PARIS CONVENTION FOR THE PROTECTION OF INDUSTRIAL PROPERTY 142-46 (1968). Similarly, the notes that accompany WIPO's Model Provisions on Protection Against Unfair Competition argue for account to be taken of conceptions of honest practices in international trade, rather than solely the country where the conduct occurs. *See* Model Provisions on Protection Against Unfair Competition, Notes 1.03, 1.04 (WIPO 1996). What sources or authorities should courts consult to determine those standards? Are there universal standards of honesty or fairness in commercial practice? From what sources do we fill those terms with meaning in the domestic context? Should those standards be different in the international context? In footnote 5, the *Lopez* court suggests that "the Lanham Act incorporates the substantive provisions of the Paris Convention and thus creates a federal law of unfair competition applicable in international disputes. Diversity jurisdiction would still apply in a domestic dispute." How would you determine whether a dispute was "international," thus warranting treatment under "a federal law of unfair competition applicable in international disputes"?

(6) **Article 10*bis*.** What precisely is the obligation imposed on member states by Article 10*bis*? Must protection be provided only against a competitor alleged to be dishonest, or is it sufficient to invoke the protection of Article 10*bis* that its conduct is regarded as unfair? What does Article 10*bis*(3) add to the first two provisions of Article 10*bis*? *Cf.* BODENHAUSEN, *supra*, at 142 (suggesting that paragraphs (2) and (3) "are so worded that they must be considered self-executing, in countries which admit this possibility, and must therefore be

directly applied by the judicial or administrative authorities of the country where protection against unfair competition is sought"). Does Article 10*bis*(3) assist in the interpretation of Article 10*bis* as a whole?

Protection against unfair competition is achieved by countries through a wide range of different means. It is clear that member states may base compliance with Article 10*bis* on common law principles, on specially enacted legislation, or a combination of both. The type of legislation varies significantly: it may proscribe acts of unfair competition generally or provide an exhaustive list of prohibited acts; it may impose civil or criminal or administrative sanctions; and, it may protect competitors and consumers under different provisions. Member states may achieve the result demanded by Article 10*bis* through a combination of some or all of these different elements. What are the advantages of these different approaches? To what extent should these questions be left to courts or addressed by legislatures? Which mix would you advocate? Which laws could be said to implement the obligations of the United States under Article 10*bis*?

(7) **WIPO Model Provisions on Protection Against Unfair Competition.** In 1996, the WIPO published Model Provisions on Protection Against Unfair Competition. These provisions built upon a study commissioned by WIPO from the Max Planck Institute and published in 1994. *See* PROTECTION AGAINST UNFAIR COMPETITION: ANALYSIS OF THE PRESENT WORLD SITUATION (1994). The report was seen as "a first step in a series of activities with respect to improved protection against unfair competition." Charles Gielen, *WIPO and Unfair Competition*, 19 EUR. INTELL. PROP. REV. 78 (1997). The notes that accompany the Model Provisions claim to "implement that obligation [under Article 10*bis*] by defining, in Articles 2-6, the principal acts or practices against which protection is to be granted and by providing a basis for protection against any other acts of unfair competition." Note 1.1. Are these stated objectives consistent with Professor Gielen's observation?

Article 1(b) of the Model Provisions expressly provides that any person "damaged or likely to be damaged by an act of unfair competition shall be entitled to remedies referred to in . . . ." But the Article has intentionally been unfinished, to be completed after a WIPO study on the enforcement of intellectual property rights. In this task, the notes suggest that provisions of Part III of the TRIPS Agreement will be of significance. *See infra* § 7.02. Professor Gielen notes that Article 2, which elaborates upon obligations in respect of acts causing confusion, contains "terminology [that] has been modernized in respect of the provisions from the [Paris] Convention." Gielen, *supra*. In the text of the article, this modernization takes the form of expressly recognizing forms of identifiers such as "product appearance" and "a celebrity or well-known fictional character" that have been in the vanguard of the expansion of trademark protection since the drafting of the Paris Convention. (Bodenhausen suggested in 1968 that Article 10*bis*(3) extends to confusingly similar uses of packages as well as words.) The notes to Article 2 also acknowledge modern trademark developments by recognizing that to be actionable, confusion need not be as to source or origin, but should also include "confusion with respect to affiliation." Article 3 goes even further and provides that "any act or practice, in the course of industrial or commercial activities, that damages, or is likely to damage, the goodwill or reputation of another's enterprise shall constitute an act of unfair competition, regardless of whether such act or practice causes confusion." This dilution protection, meaning protection against "the lessening of the distinctive character or advertising value of a trademark," is expressly made applicable by Article 3(2) to identifiers such as "product appearance" and "a celebrity or well-known fictional character."

To what extent do the Model Provisions expand obligations under international conventions? Do they simply recognize a modern interpretation of those obligations? What are the advantages and disadvantages of the use of mechanisms such as the Model Provisions to "modernize" or "interpret" or "implement" the obligations set forth in international treaties? *See* Gielen, *supra* ("The Model Provisions drawn up by WIPO are an extremely useful tool for countries wishing to adopt or improve legislation on unfair competition. They are certainly a modernisation of Article 10*bis* of the Paris Convention, the importance of which has now been reinforced by Article 2 of TRIPS."); *cf.* Lund Trading v. Kohler Co., 163 F.3d 27 (1st Cir. 1998) (noting genuine issues regarding the constitutionality of dilution protection for product designs under federal dilution legislation). Professor Cornish has criticized the Model Provisions as exceeding the scope of proper WIPO authority:

> Under [Article 15(5) of] the Paris Convention, the [International] Bureau [of WIPO] is required to conduct studies and provide services designed to facilitate the protection of industrial property. On the other hand, it has no power to pronounce on interpretation or application of the Convention and so may express no opinion on the merits of contested views between Member States.

William R. Cornish, *Genevan Bootstraps*, 19 EUR. INTELL. PROP. REV. 336 (1997) ("To claim that 'implementation' of the Paris Convention is not interpretation of it would be complete bosh."). Putting aside the question of proper WIPO conduct, what are the dangers of WIPO Model Laws such as these? WIPO has published several. What weight should be given to the Model Provisions and the accompanying notes prepared by WIPO should compliance with international trademark and unfair competition obligations come before the World Trade Organization? Should the "no-interpretation" rule imposed upon WIPO by Article 15(5) of Paris be repealed?

(8) **Unfair Competition Law as Intellectual Property.** Article 1(2) of the Paris Convention includes protection against unfair competition as one of the objects of industrial property protection. In the notes to the WIPO Model Provisions, reference is made to the obligation under Article 2 of the TRIPS Agreement to implement Article 10*bis*. Protection against unfair competition is not, however, expressly one of the "intellectual property rights" specified in Article 1(2) of TRIPS as subject to the full rigors of the TRIPS Agreement.

[3] National Treatment

Application of the national treatment obligations of Article 2 of the Paris Convention, implemented in section 44(b) of the Lanham Act, should be straightforward. *See e.g.,* Schweitzer Dict Co. v. P&K Trading Inc., 1998 WL 472505 (E.D.N.Y. 1998) (because South Korea is a signatory to the Paris Convention, its nationals may assert the protections of the Lanham Act). Indeed, the inclusion of a provision guaranteeing national treatment was largely uncontroversial in 1883, having even then formed part of several existing industrial property conventions. Nationality is not, however, the only connecting factor that generates national treatment. Others are assimilated to nationals of member states. *See* Article 3 ("Nationals of countries outside the Union who are domiciled or who have real and effective establishments in the territory of one of the countries of the Union shall be treated in the same manner as nationals of the countries of the Union"). What are the consequences of expanding the "connecting factors" that permit enjoyment of the benefits of the union? Are there any reasons why you would recommend contraction (or further expansion) of the connecting factors?

[4] Mechanisms Facilitating Multinational Rights

The principal mechanisms in the Paris Convention that facilitate the acquisition of trademark rights on a multinational basis are the right of priority (Article 4) and the so-called *telle quelle* provision (now Article 6*quinquies*). Before reading the following two cases, you should carefully read both of these provisions, which can be found in the documentary supplement, as well as Section 44 of the Lanham Act, which implements those obligations and which we reproduce in pertinent part below. Also read Article 6 of the Paris Convention, which affirms the general principles that the conditions for filing and registration of marks are to be determined in each country by the relevant domestic legislation, and that trademark registrations in one country are independent of registrations in other countries of the Paris Union. The right of priority and the *telle quelle* provision are, in different ways, exceptions to the general principle of independent registrations.

———

LANHAM ACT, SECTION 44

. . . .

(b) **Benefits of section to persons whose country of origin is party to convention or treaty.** Any person whose country of origin is a party to any convention or treaty relating to trademarks, trade or commercial names, or the repression of unfair competition, to which the United States is also a party, or extends reciprocal rights to nationals of the United States by law, shall be entitled to the benefits of this section under the conditions expressed herein to the extent necessary to give effect to any provision of such convention, treaty or reciprocal law, in addition to the rights to which any owner of a mark is otherwise entitled by this chapter.

(c) **Prior registration in country of origin; country of origin defined**. No registration of a mark in the United States by a person described in subsection (b) of this section shall be granted until such mark has been registered in the country of origin of the applicant, unless the applicant alleges use in commerce. For the purposes of this section, the country of origin of the applicant is the country in which he has a bona fide and effective industrial or commercial establishment, or if he has not such an establishment the country in which he is domiciled, or if he has not a domicile in any of the countries described in subsection (b) of this section, the country of which he is a national.

(d) **Right of priority**. An application for registration of a mark under section 1051, 1053, 1054, 1091 of this title, or subsection (e) of this section, filed by a person described in subsection (b) of this section who has previously duly filed an application for registration of the same mark in one of the countries described in subsection (b) of this section shall be accorded the same force and effect as would be accorded to the same application if filed in the United States on the same date on which the application was first filed in such foreign country: *Provided*, That:

(1) the application in the United States is filed within six months from the date on which the application was first filed in the foreign country;

(2) the application conforms as nearly as practicable to the requirements of this chapter, including a statement that the applicant has a bona fide intention to use the mark in commerce;

(3) the rights acquired by third parties before the date of the filing of the first application in the foreign country shall in no way be affected by a registration obtained on an application filed under this subsection;

(4) nothing in this subsection shall entitle the owner of a registration granted under this section to sue for acts committed prior to the date on which his mark was registered in this country unless the registration is based on use in commerce.

In like manner and subject to the same conditions and requirements, the right provided in this section may be based upon a subsequent regularly filed application in the same foreign country, instead of the first filed foreign application: *Provided*, That any foreign application filed prior to such subsequent application has been withdrawn, abandoned, or otherwise disposed of, without having been laid open to public inspection and without leaving any rights outstanding, and has not served, nor thereafter shall serve, as a basis for claiming a right of priority.

(e) **Registration on principal or supplemental register; copy of foreign registration**. A mark duly registered in the country of origin of the foreign applicant may be registered on the principal register if eligible, otherwise on the supplemental register in this chapter provided. Such applicant shall submit, within such time period as may be prescribed by the Director, a certification or a certified copy of the registration in the country of origin of the applicant. The application must state the applicant's bona fide intention to use the mark in commerce, but use in commerce shall not be required prior to registration.

(f) **Domestic registration independent of foreign registration.** The registration of a mark under the provisions of subsections (c), (d), and (e) of this section by a person described in subsection (b) of this section shall be independent of the registration in the country of origin and the duration, validity, or transfer in the United States of such registration shall be governed by the provisions of this chapter.

. . . .

(i) **Citizens or residents of the United States entitled to benefits of section.** Citizens or residents of the United States shall have the same benefits as are granted by this section to persons described in subsection (b).

SCM CORPORATION v. LANGIS FOODS LTD.
539 F.2d 196 (D.C. Cir. 1976)

OPINION FOR THE COURT BY CIRCUIT JUDGE McGOWAN.

This case presents the issue whether a corporate foreign national, which has applied for a trademark registration in its home country, has priority in registering that trademark in the United States over a domestic corporation when: (1) the foreign national filed a trademark application in its home country without prior use of the trademark in any country; (2) the foreign national subsequently filed a timely application to register the trademark in the United States based upon the earlier application in its home country; (3) the foreign national used the trademark in its home country, but not in the United States prior to filing its United States application; and (4) the domestic corporation used the trademark in the United States after the foreign national's home country application was filed but before the foreign national's United States application was filed. The District Court concluded that the domestic corporation was entitled to registration of the trademark. [cit]. For the reasons set forth below, we reverse.

I.

On March 28, 1969, appellant Langis Foods, a Canadian corporation, filed applications to register three trademarks in Canada APPLE TREE, ORANGE TREE, and LEMON TREE. Shortly thereafter, on May 15, 1969, Langis used these marks in Canada.[2] Appellee SCM Corporation, a domestic corporation,

---

[2]Canada, unlike the United States, authorizes an applicant to seek registration of a "proposed trademark" before the mark is actually used. Canadian registration is granted only if a declaration is filed alleging that use of the trademark in Canada has commenced. . . .

[Ed. Note: In 1988, the United States amended its trademark statute to permit "intent-to-use"

apparently started to use the LEMON TREE trademark [for a beverage product similar to that sold by Langis] in this country on the same day. Both Langis and SCM subsequently applied to the United States Patent Office to register these trademarks: SCM's application, filed on June 18, 1969, requested registration of the LEMON TREE trademark; Langis's application, filed on September 19, 1969, requested registration of three trademarks LEMON TREE, ORANGE TREE, and APPLE TREE. While these applications were pending in the Patent Office, SCM began using the marks ORANGE TREE and LIME TREE in the United States in June of 1970, and on July 22 of that year applied to the Patent Office to register those marks.

In August of 1971, the Patent Office published Langis's trademarks APPLE TREE and ORANGE TREE in its "Official Gazette" for purposes of opposition. Two months later, the Office issued a registration to Langis for the trademark LEMON TREE. SCM Corporation then instituted oppositions to the APPLE TREE and ORANGE TREE applications, and also filed a petition to cancel the LEMON TREE registration. On May 7, 1973, the Trademark Trial and Appeal Board denied the petition to cancel and dismissed the oppositions on the ground that, pursuant to section 44(d) of the Trademark Act of 1946," (Langis) is entitled herein as a matter of right to rely upon the filing dates of its Canadian applications, i.e., March 28, 1969, and hence that it possesses superior rights in its marks as against [SCM]." [cit].

SCM then filed a complaint in the District Court seeking to have the LEMON TREE registration canceled and the APPLE TREE and ORANGE TREE registrations denied. The District Court granted SCM's motion for summary judgment on the ground that "prior right in a trademark in the United States depends on priority of use in the United States and is not affected by priority of use in a foreign country." [cit]. Since Langis used the marks in Canada but not in the United States, the court canceled the LEMON TREE registration and remanded the proceedings opposing ORANGE TREE and APPLE TREE to the Board. This appeal is taken from that final order.

II.

Appellee SCM directs our attention to section 2(d) of the Trademark Act of 1946, which appears to preclude registration of the disputed trademarks by Langis. That section provides that "[n]o trade-mark . . . shall be refused registration on the principal register on account of its nature unless it (d) Consists of or comprises a mark which so resembles . . . a mark or trade name *previously used in the United States by another* and not abandoned, as to be likely, when applied to the goods of the applicant, to cause confusion, or to cause mistake, or to deceive . . . ." *Id.* (emphasis added). Langis has admitted that SCM was the first to use the marks in the United States, and nowhere suggests that SCM has abandoned them. Therefore, SCM argues, section 2(d) is "*in haec verba* a complete bar to Langis obtaining or maintaining registrations for its marks." [cit].

---

applications, modeled in large part upon the Canadian provisions.]

This argument must, however, be evaluated in light of legislative attempts to reconcile differences between the American and foreign systems of trademark registration. In the United States, federal registration under the Lanham Act is generally based upon first use. *E.g.,* §§ 1051(a)(1), 1127. Canada, however, employs a system which allows registration of a trademark without prior use. *See* note 2 *supra.* Certain provisions of the Lanham Act were designed to provide some protection to trademarks already registered elsewhere by foreign nationals, and Langis relies for protection specifically on section 44(d), which provides in relevant part that a trademark registration application filed by a foreign national "shall be accorded the same force and effect as would be accorded to the same application if filed in the United States on the same date on which the application was first filed in (the) foreign country. . . ." *Id.* § 1126(d).

Both SCM and Langis recognize that section 44(d) protects trademarks for which registration applications have first been filed in a foreign country. The dispute in this case goes only to the precise scope of that statutory protection. SCM contends that section 44(d) gives a foreign applicant a *constructive filing date* in the United States as of the date of the foreign filing; the filing date is important because the party with the later filing date bears the burden of proving that it possesses the prior right to the mark. [cit]. SCM would concede that it had the burden of proof in this proceeding with respect to the right to register LEMON TREE since its actual filing date was subsequent to Langis's "constructive filing date" of March 28, 1969. The District Court accepted this view of section 44(d), and since Langis admitted that it had not used the mark in the United States, granted summary judgment for SCM.

Appellant Langis offers a second and, in our view, more plausible interpretation of section 44(d). Langis suggests that section 44(d) grants a foreign applicant which has used the trademark in its home country *after* the foreign filing but *prior* to the actual United States filing a *constructive use date* as of the date of the foreign filing. Under this view, Langis would have priority since its constructive use date of March 28, 1969 preceded SCM's actual use date of May 15, 1969.

We think the structure of the Lanham Act reinforces Langis's interpretation of section 44(d). In the first place, section 1 of the Act requires an applicant for registration to indicate the date the trademark was first used in commerce in the United States; but foreign nationals applying pursuant to section 44(d) are exempted from that requirement, 15 U.S.C. § 1126(d)(2). Moreover, the 1946 Act deals specifically with the protection to be accorded to rights acquired by third parties, and it expressly protects only those "rights acquired by third parties before the date of the filing of the first application in the foreign country . . . ." *Id.* § 1126(d)(3). The Lanham Act also provides that nothing in section 44(d) "shall entitle the owner of a registration granted under . . . section (44) to sue for acts committed prior to the date on which his mark was registered in this country unless the registration is based on use in commerce." *Id.* § 1126(d)(4). The clear implication is that section 44 recognizes registration based on something other than "use in commerce," namely, a foreign registration. *See id.* § 1126(e).

Finally, there is section 44(b) of the Act, which provides:

> Any person whose country of origin is a party to any convention or treaty relating to trademarks, trade or commercial names, or the repression of unfair competition, to which the United States is also a party, or extends reciprocal rights to nationals of the United States by law, *shall be entitled to the benefits of this section under the conditions expressed herein to the extent necessary to give effect to any provision of such convention, treaty or reciprocal law, in addition to the rights to which any owner of a mark is otherwise entitled by this chapter.*

Id. § 1126(b) (1970) (emphasis added); *see id.* § 1126(c), (e). This intent to give effect to the provisions of applicable treaties and conventions concerning trademarks is further evidenced in section 45 of the Act, which declares that the intent of Congress in enacting the 1946 Act was "to provide rights and remedies stipulated by treaties and conventions respecting trade-marks...."[9] *Id.* § 1127. An examination of the relevant international treaty, the International Convention for the Protection of Industrial Property (the Paris Union Treaty), resolves whatever doubt we may have concerning the reach of section 44(d).

As revised in London in 1934, Article 4 of the Paris Union Treaty provides:

> A.(1) Any person who has duly applied for ... the registration of a ... trade mark in one of the countries of the Union ... shall enjoy for the purposes of registration in other countries a right of priority during the periods hereinafter stated [six months for trademarks].
>
> (2) Any filing having the value of a formal national filing by virtue of the internal law of each country of the Union or of international treaties

---

[9]*See* S.Rep.No.1333, 79th Cong., 2d Sess. 4-5 (1946):

The (1946) Act is substantially the act of February 20, 1905...

... (I)deas concerning trademark protection have changed in the last 40 years and the statutes have not kept pace with the commercial development. In addition the United States has become a party to a number of international conventions dealing with trade-marks, commercial names, and the repression of unfair competition. These conventions have been ratified, but it is a question whether they are self-executing, and whether they do not need to be implemented by appropriate legislation.

Industrialists in this country have been seriously handicapped in securing protection in foreign countries due to our failure to carry out, by statute, our international obligations. There has been no serious attempt fully to secure to nationals of countries signatory to the conventions their trade-mark rights in this country and to protect them against the wrongs for which protection has been guaranteed by the conventions. Naturally under such circumstances foreign governments do not always give to citizens of the United States their convention rights. To remedy this discreditable situation is merely an act of international good faith.

This bill attempts to accomplish these various things:

. . . .

2. To carry out by statute our international commitments to the end that American traders in foreign countries may secure the protection to their marks to which they are entitled.

concluded among several countries of the Union shall be recognized as giving rise to a right of priority.

B. Consequently, *subsequent filing in one of the other countries of the Union before the expiration of these periods shall not be invalidated through any acts accomplished in the interval, as, for instance, by another filing, . . . or by use of the trade mark, and these facts cannot give rise to any right of third parties or any personal possession. The rights acquired by third parties before the day of the first application on which priority is based shall be reserved by the internal legislation of each country of the Union.*

53 Stat. 1748, T.S. 941 (emphasis added). This revised version clearly provides that an intervening use during the priority period cannot give rise to rights on the part of third parties. The only rights of third parties specifically protected are "[those] rights acquired by third parties *before* the day of the first application on which priority is based."[11] Thus, to the extent that the property rights in this case depend on the Paris Union Treaty, Article 4 reinforces our conclusion that a foreign applicant's mark must be protected in this country from the date of the foreign application even as against an intervening first use by another in the United States. [cit].

III.

Our holding in this case is that section 44(d) of the Trademark Act of 1946, which implements Article 4 of the Paris Union Treaty, accorded appellant Langis a "right to priority" for the six months following the filing of its Canadian application for registration, that is to say, from March 28, 1969 to

---

[11]As first adopted in Paris on March 20, 1883, and as ratified by the United States on March 29, 1887, 25 Stat. 1372, T.S. 379, Article 4 of the treaty read as follows:

> Any one who shall have regularly deposited an application for . . . a trade or commercial mark, in one of the contracting States, shall enjoy for the purpose of making the deposit in the other States, and *under reserve of the rights of third parties*, a right of priority during the periods hereinafter determined [generally three months].

> In consequence, the deposit subsequently made in one of the other States of the Union, before the expiration of these periods cannot be invalidated by acts performed in the interval, especially by another deposit, [or] by the employment of the mark. (Emphasis added).

Although this version of Article 4 specifically provided that a subsequent filing could not be invalidated through any acts accomplished during the period of priority, including another filing or use of the mark, the fact that the Article also subjected the right of priority to the "rights of third parties" left some doubt as to whether that exception applied only to rights in a mark acquired prior to the foreign filing date or whether the exception in effect accorded protection to third party rights acquired after the foreign filing date. That ambiguity was clarified in the 1934 revision at London, which was ratified by the United States in 1938. 53 Stat. 1748, T.S. 941.

September 27, 1969; and that an intervening use in the United States during that period cannot invalidate Langis's right to registration in this country pursuant to an application filed on September 19, 1969.[12] We recognize that section 2(d) prohibits registration of a trademark "previously used in the United States by another," but we cannot read that section in isolation from the context of the rest of the statute. . . .Our task is to endeavor to harmonize and give full effect to both sections 2(d) and 44(d). . . .We need only interpret the word "previously" in section 2(d) to mean "before the filing date in the Convention country" in order to give meaning to both statutory provisions. As our earlier discussion indicates, both the structure of the Act and its legislative history support such an interpretation.

Since in our view Langis is entitled to a valid federal trademark registration, we reverse the decision of the District Court and remand the case with directions to dismiss the complaint.

---

[12]There are three possible positions that can be argued with respect to the use requirements applicable to section 44 filings by foreign nationals: (1) foreign nationals must allege use in commerce; (2) though use in commerce is not required, foreign nationals must nevertheless allege use somewhere; or (3) foreign nationals are not required to allege use at all. Section 44(d)(2) of the 1946 Act clearly exempts section 44(d) applications from the section 1 requirement that applications allege use in commerce. . . . As to the other two possible positions, the official policy of the Patent Office has shifted with some regularity. *See* British Insulated Callender's Cables, Ltd., 83 U.S.P.Q. 319 (Comm'r 1949) (there must be an allegation of use "somewhere"), *overruled* in Societe Fromageries Bel, 105 U.S.P.Q. 392 (Comm'r 1955) (the "*Merry Cow*" case) (there is no use requirement), *overruled* in Certain Incomplete Trademark Applications, 137 U.S.P.Q. 69 (Comm'r 1963) (there must be an allegation of use somewhere). And there has been considerable disagreement among commentators on that issue. [cit]. The Trademark Trial and Appeal Board opinion in the instant case erroneously states that appellant Langis "had made no use of the marks. . . prior to the filing of its applications in this country." 177 U.S.P.Q. at 718. Nevertheless, the Board, citing the *Merry Cow* case, upheld Langis's registration, thus overruling Certain Incomplete Trademark Applications, *supra*, and reinstating the policy that there is no use requirement.

In the de novo proceeding below, the District Court reviewed the Paris Union Treaty and the Trademark Act of 1946 and concluded that "(t)he decision of the Board . . . which reverts to the "*Merry Cow*" doctrine . . . is . . . in error." [cit]. In this respect, the opinion of the District Court is dictum. The record in the District Court clearly indicates that the applications filed by Langis with the Patent Office alleged use of the marks in Canada, during the applicable six month period, and there was thus no reason for the District Court to rule on the *Merry Cow* issue. The fact that the Trademark Trial and Appeal Board found it necessary to reach that question given its misstatement of the facts does not mean that, despite a record indicating to the contrary, the question was presented to the District Court. Appellee SCM contends that the "*Merry Cow*" issue is not presented by this case, and we agree.

CROCKER NAT'L BANK v. CANADIAN IMPERIAL BANK OF COMMERCE

223 U.S.P.Q. 909 (T.T.A.B. en banc 1984)*

ALLEN, BOARD MEMBER:

Before us is a motion for summary judgment brought by opposer Crocker National Bank (hereinafter, Crocker), [owner of the mark COMMUNICASH] in an opposition against registration of the mark "COMMCASH" for "banking services," subject of an application filed by Canadian Imperial Bank of Commerce (hereinafter, Canadian Imperial), pursuant to Section 44 of the Lanham Trademark Act. The sole ground of the [present] motion is that the application for registration is void ab initio in that no allegation of use somewhere on or before the filing date of the United States application has been made and no specimens demonstrating such use have been provided. We deny the motion on the basis that both of these requirements are inconsistent with the International Convention of Paris for the Protection of Industrial Property[3] as it has been implemented by Section 44 of the Trademark Act and need not, for that reason, be complied with. We also find that Canadian Imperial, the non-moving party, is entitled to partial summary judgment on the same issue and dismiss the part of Crocker's claim which is based on the above ground.

. . . .

The principal issue presented herein was previously the subject of a decision of this Board, widely known in the trademark literature as the LEMON TREE case. [SCM]. In LEMON TREE, the Board unanimously decided that there was nothing in the Trademark Act authorizing the Office to require "of a foreign applicant under Section 44(d) use of its mark prior to the filing of its application in [its] home country," and that to require a showing of such use was inconsistent with the Paris Convention by which Canada, the country of origin of the applicant in the case, and the United States are bound. We also held in that decision that the Canadian applicant was entitled to rely upon the filing dates of the corresponding Canadian applications which were filed less than six months before the United States application was filed, which finding determined the issue of priority in favor of the Canadian applicant. The Board's decision on the priority issue was eventually affirmed by the Court of Appeals, District of Columbia Circuit. However, the ruling concerning the requirement to demonstrate use somewhere was not decided. In that regard, both the

---

*[Ed. Note: Crocker Bank's opposition was eventually sustained on other grounds. *See* Crocker National Bank v. Canadian Imperial Bank of Commerce, 228 U.S.P.Q. 689 (T.T.A.B. 1986), *aff'd sub nom*, Canadian Imperial Bank of Commerce v. Wells Fargo Bank, 811 F.2d 1490 (Fed. Cir. 1987). The issue of whether Article 6 of the London text of the Paris Convention and section 44 permitted registration without use anywhere was not considered on appeal to the Federal Circuit.]

[3]Both Canada and the United States are bound by the revision of the cited convention (hereinafter, "Paris Convention"), done at London on June 3, 1934. 53 Stat. 1748. . . As of the filing date of Canadian Imperial's United States application, Canada had not ratified the substantive provisions (Articles 1-12), including the article herein involved, of any subsequent text. Consequently, to the extent that our decision relies upon the Paris Convention, it is the London text which must control.

Board's holding that the requirement was contrary to law and the reversal of that holding by the District Court for the District of Columbia in the de novo proceeding were held to be dicta because the records in both our and the District Court's proceeding clearly indicated that the Canadian applicant had, in fact, used the involved marks in Canada prior to the filing date of the United States applications therefor.

. . .[I]n order to reach the conclusion that the aforementioned filing date requirements for foreign applicants under Section 44 are contrary to the statute, we find it necessary to overrule *Certain Incomplete Trademark Applications,* 137 U.S.P.Q. 69 (Com'r Pats. 1963). . . . However, before reaching that point in our analysis, in view of the uncertain history of the Office position on this issue over many, many years, we set forth below the facts, established on this record, upon which our decision depends.

On November 10, 1980, Canadian Imperial filed in the Canadian Trade Marks Office an application for registration of the mark COMMCASH in respect of "banking services." This application was based on proposed use of the mark sought to be registered in Canada.[18] Within six months of the Canadian filing, namely, on May 7, 1981, Canadian Imperial filed an application in the United States Patent and Trademark Office seeking registration of the identical mark for identical services. The United States application was filed pursuant to Section 44(d) of the Trademark Act in view of the previously filed Canadian application. On the face of the United States application, it is unmistakably clear that Canadian Imperial had not used the mark sought to be registered on or prior to the U.S. filing date.

. . . There is no other evidence before us which is inconsistent with that conclusion. Accordingly, Canadian Imperial's opposition to the motion for summary judgment wholly depends on our decision herein that the requirement for an allegation of use somewhere on or prior to the U.S. filing date and the requirement of specimens demonstrating such use are contrary to law.

The starting point of our analysis is the decision of the D.C. Circuit Court of Appeals in *SCM Corporation v. Langis Foods, Ltd.* While . . . *SCM* does not specifically determine the issue before us, the unanimously supported opinion of Judge McGowan in that case announced or confirmed several principles in regard to section 44 and the Paris Convention which must be considered in our analysis and determination of the present case. These principles are set forth below in a form which relates the *SCM* principles (verbatim text) to the issue now before us.

(i) Recognizing that the Trademark Act requires an applicant who is the owner of a trademark used in commerce to specify "the mode or manner in which the mark is used in connection with [the] goods" (§ 1(a)(1)) and to submit "specimens or facsimiles of the mark as actually used" (§ 1(a)(3)), we cannot read these sections in isolation from the context of the rest of the statute. Our task is to harmonize and give effect to both sections 1 and 44(c), (d) and (e).

---

[18]Under Canadian law, an applicant may seek registration of a "proposed trademark" before the mark is actually used. After an application for registration of a proposed trade mark has been allowed, the applicant is notified accordingly and is required, within six months after the date of the notice, to file a declaration that use of the mark in Canada has commenced.

(ii) The argument that § 1 of the Act renders void any application filed by a foreign applicant under § 44 which does not contain an allegation of use somewhere of the mark sought to be registered or is not accompanied by the prescribed specimens or facsimiles must be evaluated in the light of legislative attempts to reconcile differences between the American and foreign systems of trademark registration. [cit.]

(iii) The clear implication [from §§ 44(d)(2), (d)(3) and (d)(4)] is that section 44 recognizes registration based on something other than "use in commerce", namely, a foreign registration. *See* [15 U.S.C.] § 1126(e); [cit.]

(iv) In that the clear intent of section 44 was to give effect to the provision of applicable treaties and conventions concerning trademarks . . . an [e]xamination of the relevant international treaty–the International Convention for the Protection of Industrial Property [as revised in London in 1934]–is necessary to resolve whatever doubt we may have concerning the reach of section 44(d).

(v) [T]o the extent that the property rights in this case depend on the Paris Union Treaty, Article 4 reinforces our conclusion that a foreign applicant's mark must be protected in this country from the date of the foreign application even as against an intervening first use by another in the United States. To this end section 44(d) grants a foreign applicant . . . a constructive use date as of the date of the foreign filing.

The viability of the above principles in interpreting Section 44 issues has been confirmed, without any known dissent, in commentaries on the decision by text writers and authors of subsequently published law review articles.

Statutory Construction

Guided by SCM principle (i), and by decisions of other federal courts concerning statutory construction of the Trademark Act, we conclude that the rationale applied in early Office decisions on the issue before us, and in *Certain Incomplete*, was seriously flawed. Under these decisions, the holding that use of a trademark somewhere and the submission of specimens evidencing such use continued to be required of § 44 applicants was based on the proposition that all trademarks registrable under the Act had to comply with each of the requirements of section 1, except those which were specifically exempted in section 44. According to this narrow construction, while exemptions were found in section 44(c) (*British Insulated*) and in section 44(d) (*Certain Incomplete*) for the allegation of use in commerce, no exemption was found for the requirement of specimens or facsimiles of the marks as actually used or for the statement of the mode, manner or method of applying or affixing or otherwise using the mark on or in connection with the goods. This analysis made no effort to harmonize the non-Convention sections with section 44 (SCM principle (i)) or to interpret the statute so as to reconcile differences between the American and foreign systems of trademark registration (SCM principle (ii)). To the contrary, the decisions tried to force everything in section 44(c), (d) and (e) into the framework of section 1 of the Act, apparently motivated by the desire to preserve in the registration system as much of our common law notion that a trademark is a creature of use and cannot exist without it as section 44 and the

Paris Convention would permit, and by a reluctance to give foreign proprietors of marks a status under that section more favorable than that given domestic owners under non-Convention provisions.

Even without any reference to the legislative history of the Trademark Act of 1946 or to the purposes of the Paris Convention which Section 44 was enacted to implement, these interpretations present inconsistencies which are apparent from the structure of the Act itself and an evaluation of its sections "to produce a harmonious whole."

Firstly, it should be noted that there are no references in Section 44 to "use somewhere," nor to the requirement of specimens, nor to mode of use. As to this point, the argument has been that the requirements of Section 1 apply to foreign nationals registering under Section 44 through incorporation by reference. Thus, section 44(d) refers to "an application for registration of a mark under sections 1 . . . etc. . . .," and Section 44(e) necessarily incorporates the same requirements by its use of the phrase "the Principal Register if eligible. . .". Implicit in this argument is that Section 44 does not provide an alternative means of acquiring trademark rights; hence, Section 1 applies equally to domestic applicants and foreign applicants filing under Section 44. However, to conclude that Section 1 is applicable to Section 44 applicants except for those requirements specifically exempted, is inconsistent with Section 1 which, by that section's very terms, is limited to an application filed by "the owner[s] of . . . trademark[s] used in commerce." Obviously, when a foreign applicant under Section 44 has elected to take advantage of the "use in commerce" exemption,[28] use of the trademark in commerce is not involved. For this reason, the notion that Section 1 must apply in its entirety to both foreign and domestic applicants is specious.

Secondly, because of the language of section 44(d)(2), the determination that only the use in commerce allegation is exempted does not give effect to the remaining words of this paragraph, i.e., the proviso "that the application conforms as nearly as practicable to the requirements of this Act," which . . . we must do even under ordinary rules of statutory construction. Thus, had the "use

---

[28]Although the Lanham Act is not a model of clarity, a surprisingly persistent misconception about Section 44(d) is that it is exclusively for the benefit of a foreign applicant which has not used its mark in commerce and has filed a first application within the preceding six months in its country of origin. This is wrong on both counts. In the first place, the plain meaning of subsection (d)(2) is that the waiver of use in commerce is optional with the applicant. Thus, a qualified foreign entity may file a first application in any one of the countries satisfying the § 44(b) definition on January 1; use the mark in United States commerce on April 1, and file a U.S. application on June 30, claiming both use in commerce and a right of priority as of the filing date of the foreign application. In such a case, since use in commerce, not the country of origin registration, is the basis for registration in the United States, the applicant need not submit a certified copy of the registration in its country of origin, or of any other foreign country, for that matter. See Trademark Manual of Examining Procedure (TMEP) P1003 (Rev. Dec., 1983). In fact, the contrary interpretation would violate the express terms of Article 4 of the Paris Convention, that the right of priority is not dependent upon the ultimate fate of the application on which it is based. [cit]. Secondly, it is clear that where a U.S. application claims both use in commerce and a right of priority the filing which gives rise to the right of priority need not be in the country of origin of the applicant but can be in any "one of the countries described in [§ 44(b)]." It may frequently be the case that the priority country and the country of origin are one and the same, but this is because many applicants choose to file first in their home countries, not because they are required to do so.

. . .

in commerce allegation" been the only exemption intended, there would have been no reason for the first phrase. Accordingly, giving effect to each part of the statute, it is presumed that Section 44(d)(2) was also intended to exempt other conditions which the Section 44 applicant could not, from a practicability standpoint, conform to. In *Certain Incomplete*, analysis of this part of the subsection is disposed of merely by the statement that compliance with the requirements for specimens and allegations relating to the manner in which the mark is used on the goods is not impracticable, without any further explanation. . . . [T]he *Certain Incomplete* conclusion is unsupportable in that neither of these requirements was practicable for a foreign applicant whose home country does not require use as a pre-requisite of filing, and who had not, for that reason, commenced commercial marketing of his product or service within the six months period between the filing date of the foreign application on which priority is based and the date of filing of a corresponding application in the United States. Hence, to conform to the requirements in most cases required the applicant to effect use of the mark solely for the purpose of the United States application. In this regard, SCM principle (ii) instructs us to evaluate the issue before us in light of the effort to reconcile differences between the American and foreign systems of trademark registration. In 1946, the laws of none of the other countries bound by the Paris Convention or by "The General Inter-American Convention for Trade-Mark and Commercial Protection" (hereinafter, Inter-American Convention), the two multilateral conventions deemed applicable to § 44(c), (d), and (e) cases, required that actual use of the mark be alleged or demonstrated prior to the filing of an application for registration.[31] Accordingly, the foreign entities located in the other countries with which we had treaty obligations were in no position to effect normal commercial use of their marks before filing applications in the United States with valid claims of priority, to which these applicants are also entitled.[32] From

---

[31]The approach of not requiring any use prior to the filing of a trademark application is followed in the entire world with the exception of the United States and the Philippines, whose law was patterned after our own. (Some would add Burma and other pure common law countries, but the only "registration" in such countries is merely an advertisement of one's common law rights.); [cit]. In 1934, when the London text of the Paris Convention was negotiated, the United States was the only signatory having such a requirement, and the same was true in 1946 when the Lanham Act implementing that text was enacted. (The Philippines became a member of the Paris Union in 1965 when it ratified the 1957 Lisbon Act.). . .

[32]Accordingly, unless the *Certain Incomplete* interpretation of the statute anticipates that a foreign applicant can lawfully satisfy the requirements as to use somewhere by effecting a token, non-commercial sale, it is apparent that the two conditions are from a practicable standpoint not possible to satisfy within the Paris Convention priority period. The very purpose of laws which permit the filing of trademark applications without use is to enable business entities to file applications as soon as possible after adoption, so that their right to use the selected mark is preserved pending development of their commercial marketing plans. Deferral of use requirements also makes it possible for the proprietor to ascertain through the registration procedure whether the selected mark is registrable before committing resources in marketing developments which depend upon the mark's availability (e.g., packaging, advertising, etc.). [cit]. The practicality of such laws is extolled by U.S. practitioners who specialize in international practice, see *e.g.*, Offner, *International Trademark Protection*, 30, *et seq.* (1965), and rightly so, in that without them, United States firms would be hard put to protect potential international expansion of their American trademarks. *See* Allen, "Protection of Product Identity Abroad: Some New Light on an Old Problem?" 55 TRADEMARK REP. 707 (1965). The position of other Paris Union countries as to the desirability of deferring initial use requirements in their laws was articulated during negotiation

this standpoint, it is a short step in statutory construction to conclude that the practicability exception referred to those formal requirements which were ancillary to the United States pre-filing use requirement, the same logic by which the statements as to dates of first use and first use in commerce were exempted by the Rules of Practice for such applicants. [cit].

For the above reasons, we reject the analysis in *Certain Incomplete, British Insulated* and other cases applying the narrow construction that the provisions of Section 1 must prevail except for the specifically named "use in commerce" requirement. This conclusion, of course, leaves for decision the question of what other interpretations are possible which are consistent with the *SCM* principles. There are, at least, two other possibilities: first, that the statute as a whole must be interpreted to exempt all requirements outside of section 44 relating to use prior to the filing of an application in the United States by a foreign applicant qualified under Section 44(b) because such requirements are not practicable for this class of applicants; or, second, that Section 44 is an independent provision, standing on its own feet with respect to applications for registration depending upon it and the conventions as the bases for United States registration, except for such formal requirements and conditions for registration as are consistent with the purposes of the conventions and the implementing statute.[33] While the first alternative follows logically from what we have already said, the second depends upon an analysis of the treaty and the legislative history of the statute.

Paris Convention

Our starting point is the Paris Convention, and in particular, for reasons already stated, the London text of that convention. SCM principle (iv). We are here concerned primarily with Article 6, the relevant parts of which (in English translation) are reproduced below.[*]

---

of the "Trademark Registration Treaty," signed but not yet ratified by the United States. [cit]. The impracticability of the requirements is also apparent from the facts of the instant case. It is clear that it was not feasible for Canadian Imperial to have supplied any specimens other than the prints of the mark COMMCASH as it was to be used.

[33] A third possibility, that the text of the Paris Convention which is controlling here, *i.e.,* the London Act of 1934, is self-executing, in which case, the question is determined by an evaluation of that treaty, unfettered by uncertainties of construction of the 1946 Trademark Act, is not considered. . . . [A] finding that the London text is self-executing is not critical to our analysis here. The Lanham Act's clear purpose was to carry out the provisions of the Paris Convention, and the London text was the version of that treaty which next preceded enactment of the Lanham Act with that clear purpose in mind. To hold otherwise might create doubt unnecessarily as to whether a different result would pertain in cases involving applicants whose countries of origin are bound by later texts in respect of which the Convention's self-executing character may have changed. . . .

[*][Ed. Note: Article 6 of the London text is Article 6*quinquies* of the current Act of the Paris Convention.]

Article 6

A. *Every trade-mark registered in the country of origin shall be admitted for registration and protected in the form originally registered in the other countries of the Union under the reservations indicated below.* . . .

B. (1) *Nevertheless, the following marks may be refused* or canceled:

1. Those which are of such a nature as to prejudice rights acquired by third parties in the country where protection is applied for.

2. Those which have no distinctive character, or which consist exclusively of signs or indications which serve in trade to designate the kind, quality, quantity, destination, value, place of origin, or time of production, or which have become customary in the current language, or in the bona fide and unquestioned usages of the trade in the country in which protection is sought. In arriving at a decision as to the distinctiveness of the character of a mark, all the circumstances of the case must be taken into account, and in particular the length of time that such a mark has been in use.

3. *Those which are contrary to morality or public order*, especially those which are of a nature to deceive the public. It is to be understood that a mark cannot be considered as contrary to public order for the sole reason that it does not conform to some legislative requirement concerning trade-marks, except in circumstances where this requirement itself relates to public order.

(2) Trade-marks cannot be refused in the other countries of the Union on the sole ground that they differ from the marks protected in the country of origin only by elements not altering the distinctive character and not affecting the identity of the marks in the form under which they have been registered in the aforesaid country of origin. (Emphasis supplied to show the original 1883 text.)

There is no question that an unvarnished reading of Article 6 cannot justify excluding the registration or protection of a mark registered in the country of origin based upon the failure of the foreign applicant to comply with the requirements pertaining to use of the mark either in the United States or elsewhere. A straightforward analysis of Article 6 is set forth in Mrs. Leeds' decision in *Fromageries Bel*, at 102 U.S.P.Q. 398:

Reduced to its simplest form, Article 6 merely means that when a registration of a mark has issued in an applicant's home country ("country of origin") in accordance with the law of that country, the United States Patent Office will, upon receipt of a properly executed application, a copy of the home registration, a drawing of the mark, and the filing fee, accept the foreign registration at face value and issue a registration in the United States, unless the mark infringes rights previously acquired by another, or it has no distinctive character, or is contrary to morality or public order.

In *Certain Incomplete*, the above analysis is challenged and, by that decision, overruled, based on an interpretation of Article 6 in a footnote which spans four pages of the opinion, 137 U.S.P.Q. 72-75, note 8. The primary argument in *Certain Incomplete* is that the intention of Article 6 of the Paris Convention was "to deal only with the form or nature of the mark itself." *Id.* This argument breaks down into three parts: first, that the only object of Article 6 is the so-called "telle quelle" principle, *i.e.*, having to do with the form or character of the mark rather than the conditions and requirements for registration; second, that Article 6 has no application whatsoever to a mark sought to be registered in a country (*i.e.*, the United States), under whose law a mark cannot be a trademark unless it has been used in trade in connection with particular goods; and third, that the requirements pertaining to use somewhere are formal requirements which are not intended to be excluded as grounds for refusal by Article 6. Based on our interpretation of the treaty and its history, we conclude that none of the above arguments justifies imposition of the filing requirements herein imposed.

"telle quelle"

An essential element of this part of the argument, which encompasses the greater part of *Certain Incomplete's* lengthy footnote 8, is that paragraph B of the Article is only concerned with the form or nature of the mark. . . . Several examples are given, *i.e.* words written in the particular alphabetic characters of the language of the country (*e.g.* the Slavic Cyrillic alphabet), containers for products or configurations of goods, word trademarks containing more than a certain number of letters, etc. The readily apparent problem with this argument is that some of the grounds have nothing whatsoever to do with the form or nature of the mark and others are only remotely related. This is best illustrated by the very first ground of refusal under paragraph B of Article 6 which is akin to section 2(d) of our Trademark Act. It goes without saying that the likelihood of confusion of purchasers due to a mark's similarity with the mark of another which is registered or has been previously used is an extrinsic ground having nothing to do with the mark's intrinsic form or nature.

An even more extreme view is that paragraph B in its entirety is applicable only to marks which are also questioned because of their form or nature. According to this position, a mark in the Cyrillic alphabet would have to be accepted unless it could also be refused because it would prejudice the rights of others, or was not distinctive, etc., but all other marks (*e.g.*, a transliteration of the Cyrillic term into Arabic characters) could also be refused on any other ground applicable to nationals of the concerned country.

It is conceded that some countries may have thought that Article 6 had such a limited scope when it was originally conceived and much of the argument in *Certain Incomplete* reverts back to this original text, the substance of which was restricted to the portion of Article 6 which we have emphasized in the above cited English language translation. Thus, in its inception, the first sentence of the Article was the same as it is now but the only reservation concerned refusal of registration of trademarks contrary to morality or public order. Even as to that text, the viewpoint expressed in *Certain Incomplete* is only one of the interpretations which were debated at length in international governmental and non-governmental circles in the decade which followed its promulgation. During these debates, there were two widely divergent interpretations of Article 6. On the one hand the position of France, also supported by countries whose trademark laws were influenced by civil law concepts, was that the article binds the countries to grant protection to a mark duly registered in the country of origin even if it did not properly constitute a trademark according to the domestic law of those countries. On the other hand, the position of Great Britain, shared also by Switzerland and others, was that the article only excluded refusal of protection of a mark registered in the country of origin on account of its external form except if registration would constitute an offense against public order within its own boundaries.

Nowhere was the matter of use involved in these discussions and there was little active participation on the part of the United States.[38] In fact, the focus of the debate centered on the very strict British prohibition against the registration or protection of non-distinctive signs. Interestingly, one of the cases in point concerned an American trademark SYRUP OF FIGS which had been sought to be registered by its United States owner in Great Britain under the Paris Convention based upon an 1885 registration of the mark in the United States. The High Court of Justice (Chancery) affirmed the refusal of registration, refusing to apply Article 6 of the Convention [because the British trademark statute did not fully implement Article 6. But the court conceded that under the Convention the mark ought to have been registered.].[39] This decision and others were used to illustrate the broad scope which had been contemplated by Article 6. On the other hand, opponents of this view were adamant in the opposite viewpoint, generally supported by the contention that Article 6 should not be applicable to terms like SYRUP OF FIGS which were not, in fact, trademarks at all, or, alternatively, that the registration of such terms would be contrary to morality or public order. Eventually, there emerged several schools of thought as to how this impasse should be overcome. One view was that there should be an internationally accepted definition of a trademark acceptable to all parties to the Paris Convention. This solution would have preserved the French view of Article 6, establishing a truly international system of trademark protection based on a country of origin registration.[40] The other more practical view was to expand the "morality or public order" reservation to encompass other grounds of national refusal. In the subsequent development

---

[38]Mac Georgii, an American lawyer, proposed at the 1897 AIPPI Congress that the Convention be amended to provide that adoption and use of a mark in any one of the member countries be treated as adoption and use in all of the others. . . . Apparently Georgii's idea never materialized, no doubt because the concept of trademark rights based solely on adoption and use was foreign to the civil law countries.

[39]40 Ch.D. 620 (1888); [cit]. The decision turned on the principle of English law that a treaty is part of the domestic law only to the extent that it has been implemented by an Act of Parliament.

[40]The idea of an internationally accepted definition of a trademark has been discussed from time to time by international trademark specialists but never with much success. [cit].

of the Convention through its revisions in 1911 at Washington, in 1925 at The Hague, and in 1934 at London, the latter solution became the basis of paragraph B of Article 6. Thus, whereas there may be some doubt as to the original intention of Article 6, its generally accepted meaning in 1946 when the Lanham Act was enacted by the Congress was that paragraph B of the article extended far beyond the "telle quelle" principle in paragraph A, establishing a minimum standard for all member countries as to what grounds for refusal of registration of any mark duly registered in the country of origin can be imposed by the other countries.[42] Had the United States entertained serious reservations as to such interpretation, it is reasonable to assume that that position would have been put forward by United States delegates at the several international conferences held between Paris in 1883 and London in 1934, or that limitations on the effects of Article 6 in our trademark legislation would have been proposed in connection with the ratification of those treaties. In fact, no such positions were put forward or legislative proposals advanced. We also find no reference in Article 6B to the possibility of refusal of registration or protection on the ground that the mark has not been used somewhere prior to the application for registration and at none of the conferences referred to was that possibility proposed by the United States or any other country.[43]

A Mark That Has Not Been Used In Trade Is Not A Trademark

There is nothing in the Convention history (and *Certain Incomplete* does not contend that there is) which supports this argument and it appears to rest solely on the statement in that decision as to the (common law) concept of trademark rights in the United States. [cit.] From the standpoint of the Convention, there is no question that acceptance of the thesis that a country can avoid the proscriptions of Article 6 merely by a definitional exclusion of the entire article destroys its effect altogether. This aspect of *Certain Incomplete* depends on an interpretation of Article 6 which contradicts its very essence. As in the case of Article 4, Article 6 is one of those provisions of the Paris Convention which guarantee rights to persons assimilated to its benefits beyond those accorded by the "national treatment" principle.[44] Accordingly, it is not

---

[42] . . . It may be added that the Paris Convention does not define the substantive law of its parties but rather sets out the broad principles under which the laws of the countries can operate. [cit]. Internationally, the development of Article 6B is very important. In fact, an entire system of international registration of trademarks, the so-called "Madrid Arrangement," is based upon the broadened scope of this article. . . . By its terms, an international registration of a trademark may not be refused protection in any member country of the arrangement except on a ground which is comprised by Article 6 B. . . .

[43] There was an effort in the Drafting Committee at the Lisbon Conference of 1958 to amend the preamble of paragraph B of Article 6*quinquies* (Article 6 in the London text herein involved) so that the grounds of refusal would no longer be interpreted as being restrictive (exhaustive), *i.e.* that refusal might be based on other grounds applicable under the domestic law. However, this effort failed and, in fact, the exhaustiveness of the grounds was made even more clear. . . .

[44] Article 2 expressly protects these benefits from being abrogated by providing that the application of national treatment is "without prejudice to the rights specially provided by the present Convention." There is no question that Article 6 provides one of those special benefits, as *SCM* held in the case of Article 4, and as its very placement in the separate provision of the Act relating to international obligations demonstrates.

possible to justify a refusal to accord such effects merely by carving out an exception (*i.e.*, the requirement that only a used trademark can be registered) which is applicable to one's nationals. The same position was asserted long ago by Great Britain to justify the refusal to accord any effect to the original text of Article 6 where the mark was non-distinctive or generic, since the French position did not consider such marks capable of refusal unless the terms comprising them were immoral or contrary to public order. In fact, the resulting impasse was one of the reasons which impelled broadening of the grounds of refusal in the second part of Article 6 during subsequent revision conferences. More significantly, such interpretation has been specifically condemned by the United States Supreme Court in *Bacardi*, construing the very similar language in Inter-American Convention;s Article 3.[46]

Formal Requirements

While no express reference to national formal requirements imposed on applicants relying upon their home country registrations appeared in Article 6 until the Lisbon text of 1958, to which the United States is bound, but Canada is not, there is little question that the article has always been understood as not excluding them.[47] On the other hand, formalities imposed by the countries as a means of avoiding the substantive effects of the article have long been condemned. The question of treaty interpretation then is whether the required allegation of use somewhere and of specimens demonstrating such use are in one category (acceptable formalities and conditions of domestic law) or the other (means of avoiding the substantive effects of Article 6B).

It is in the first instance clear that both requirements are creatures of Office decisions concerning applications filed by applicants claiming the benefits of the convention rather than statutory provisions or rules which relate to all applicants for registration. [The Board outlined the history of the requirements, noting slight differences in details from those rules applied to applicants under section 1: for example, the Section 44 applicant was required to show specimens used in "trade" somewhere rather than in commerce subject to the regulation by Congress.]

That these requirements are necessary to evidence ownership of the mark subject of the country of origin registration is also, from the standpoint of the Convention, not supportable. ... [F]rom the treaty viewpoint, ownership of the mark subject of the country of origin registration, which is the basis of the § 44(c) and (e) registration, is determined under the "telle quelle" principle

---

[46] Article 3 reads as follows:

> Every mark duly registered or legally protected in one of the Contracting States shall be admitted to registration or deposit and legally protected in the other Contracting States, upon compliance with the formal provisions of the domestic law of such States.

[47] The reason is clear from the provision in Article 2 that to be entitled to the same treatment as citizens of each other country of the Union, a foreign national had to comply with the formalities and conditions imposed upon those citizens. [cit]. Included were such matters as the form of the application, the effects of registration and the means of protection. [cit].

according to the law in the country of origin, not the country of subsequent filing based on that registration.[50] The best evidence of ownership of a trademark in most countries is a registration of the mark, not evidence of its use. It should also be noted notwithstanding the clear implication to the contrary in *Certain Incomplete*, at 137 U.S.P.Q. 74, note 8, that specimens of use of a mark sought to be registered are not among the conditions and requirements for obtaining a registration in any country in the world except the United States and the Philippines.

In consideration of the above points, we disagree with the conclusion that the two requirements imposed herein are justified under Article 6 of the Paris Convention (London text) on the ground that they are formalities generally applicable to all applicants under the statute.

[The Board's conclusion was not altered by analysis of the new Article 6 added at the Lisbon Conference. Article 6(1) provides that the conditions and requirements for registration in each of the countries have to be fulfilled even by Paris Convention applicants, these being matters for national legislation. First, the case was governed by the London text. Second, even if the Lisbon (or a subsequent) text had been applicable, because in subsequent Acts, the countries undertook to adopt measures necessary to ensure the application of the convention (Lisbon, Article 17; Stockholm, Article 25) and the United States had not made amendments related to the requirements and conditions for registration, the panel presumed that no amendment to § 44(d)(2) was believed necessary and that the then accepted practice of not requiring any allegations or specimens of use of foreign applicants filing under § 44 was not inconsistent with the Lisbon text.]

In view of the above, we find no support for the argument that the requirements imposed herein are justified as formalities. By definition, a formality involves compliance with formal or conventional rules. Here, as we have already indicated, requiring specimens of actual use somewhere excludes an entire class of applicants domiciled in countries wherein use is not required prior to the filing of a trademark application. To suggest that such applicants can simply wait until they are able to comply with the requirement of use somewhere ignores altogether the companion benefit, asserted in the instant case, under Article 4, implemented by § 44(d), *i.e.*, the right of priority based upon the foreign applicant's first filing in another country of the Union less than six months prior the United States filing date. Since the interest of the foreign entity in the new mark has already been disclosed to the public by the filing of a trademark application elsewhere, foregoing the right of priority benefit involves the risk of loss of rights in the United States due to the intervening use in this country of the same mark by another (perhaps a "pirate" who has learned about the foreign mark from the data base of a foreign country). Such loss of the right of priority benefit is even more ludicrous in light of the decision in *SCM*, since by that decision the foreign applicant was held entitled by its

---

[50]The situation is no different than is the case with the existence of the country of origin registration, the definition of the mark (*i.e.*, its form and nature), the goods and/or services, etc. These matters are necessarily governed by the law of the country under whose authority the registration (constitutive or declarative of the trademark right) was granted.

filing in the foreign country to a constructive use in the United States for purposes of priority of rights.[57]

The Lanham Act

We now turn to the question of whether the purposes of the Paris Convention (Article 6) have been implemented by the Trademark Act of 1946. We conclude that they have, and that the only proper construction of § 44(c), (d) and (e) is that a foreign national qualified under § 44(b) is entitled to an alternative basis for registration of a trademark registered in its country of origin without regard to whether such mark is in use prior to the application's filing date. Based on this interpretation, the two requirements imposed in the instant case, i.e., an allegation of use somewhere and specimens demonstrating such use, are contrary to the statute.

The most important reason for our conclusion is that this interpretation is the only one which is consistent with the Paris Convention (and the Inter-American Convention), which § 44 was intended to implement and we are bound, where there is any doubt, to apply that construction which gives full effect to provisions of this treaty. That Congress had the power to create an alternative method of acquiring trademark rights in the United States without use is also settled. Under the common law, the property interest in a trademark which provides an owner with its exclusive right to use the mark is based on the owner's use of the mark in connection with a trade or business, and the modification of this common law property right is a power vested in the states. However, it is also clear that the federal treaty power makes it possible for the United States to sign and ratify an international agreement which alters the local law of trademark ownership.[60]

The second reason is that the only other possible substantive reason for the two requirements, i.e., that use unrelated to United States commerce creates a right to register in the United States, would be an even more substantial departure from the common law in that it is totally inconsistent with the well established territoriality principle that use in a foreign country cannot create trademark rights in the United States. It is also almost preposterous to infer that merely by failing expressly to exclude two formalities generally related to use in commerce applications, Congress could have intended such a radical departure from established law. There have been no decisions since which come

---

[57]*SCM, supra*, 190 U.S.P.Q. at 291-292. Because of this "constructive" use effect, Zelnick also suggests that refusing filing dates to foreign entities who anticipate filing trademark applications in the United States within the six month priority period "would appear to be counter-productive" from the standpoint of American interests in that the delay resulting from having to comply with our use (somewhere) requirement defers the time (within that 6 months) in which these "constructively used" marks are available in our own data base of marks subject of pending applications. Zelnick, *Shaking the Lemon Tree*, 67 TRADEMARK REP. 329, 345-6 (1977).

[60]Montgomery and Reed, "*Constitutionality Report on Proposed Trademark Registration Treaty*," 63 TRADEMARK REP. 575, 580-582 (1972). Note also that in the *Trade-Mark Cases* the question of the "treaty making power over trade-marks, and of the duty of Congress to pass any laws necessary to carry treaties into effect was expressly reserved." 100 U.S. 82, 92, 96-97.

close to affirming the principle that use in a foreign country establishes ownership rights in the United States.[62]

Thirdly, as it has been construed in *SCM*, (SCM principle (iii)), the above interpretation is the only one which is consistent with § 44(d) in its entirety, particularly when § 44(d)(4) is taken into account. The latter paragraph limits the effect of a registration granted under § 44 in an infringement action to "acts committed prior to the date on which [the] mark was registered in [the United States] *unless the registration is based on use in commerce.*" (Emphasis added.) According to SCM, a clear implication from this paragraph is that § 44 recognizes registration based on something other than "use in commerce" namely, a foreign registration. Since a civil action based on a federal registration can, in no event, be based on acts prior to the date of its registration, it goes without saying that paragraph (d)(4) must have been added to § 44(d) in order to make clear that § 44 impinges on the common law rights of a trademark owner in the United States only to the extent that an infringement action can be based upon a federal registration secured under § 44. It necessarily follows (i.e. if (d)(4) is to have any meaning) that § 44 was intended to provide a basis for registration other than common law use.

The situation is different, of course, where the applicant merely claiming priority pursuant to § 44(d) seeks registration based on use in commerce. In that case, nothing in § 44(d)(4) precludes a common law infringement action based on the use in commerce which commenced on a date between the date of filing in the country on which the claim of priority was based and the United States filing date.

It is significant to note that the court in SCM made specific reference to § 44(e) in concluding that § 44 recognizes a basis for registration other than use in commerce. By this reference, the court recognizes that it is a provision outside § 44(d), *i.e.,* § 44(e), that provides the registration basis for a § 44(d) application which is not based on use in commerce. Thus, whereas the court did not decide in that case the issue now before us, it appears that in recognizing an alternative basis for registration all that it left undecided was whether evidence of foreign use is a necessary formality as to that basis. One commentator has even interpreted *SCM* as laying the groundwork for a holding that "constructive use" as of the filing date in a priority case be deemed to satisfy the use in commerce requirement in section 1 of the Act. [Zelnick, *Shaking The Lemon Tree, supra.*] Such a construction goes far beyond what is necessary for our purposes herein and we question whether this was intended, especially in view of § 44(d)(4).

The Legislative History

[The legislative history behind the enactment of Section 44 confirmed the Board's conclusion.] That the interpretation reaches beyond traditional common

---

[62] ... The famous marks doctrine of the Paris Convention is not an exception, of course, since that doctrine applies in the United States only where a mark has become so well-known through long use and extensive promotion in a foreign country that confusion is likely here even in the absence of use. [cit].

law concepts as to the basis for ownership rights in a trademark is consistent with the broad scope intended of other § 44 provisions, especially § 44(h) in respect of the protection of foreign nationals against unfair competition beyond that accorded under the common law of the states. Thus, in construing all of the section 44 provisions, the evidence is overwhelming from its legislative history that the intention of the Act was to implement the convention to the fullest extent possible.

. . . .

For the foregoing reasons, Crocker's motion for summary judgment on the ground that Canadian Imperial's application for registration is void *ab initio* is denied. We further hold that Canadian Imperial is entitled to partial summary judgment on the same issue although a cross-motion therefor has not been made. . . . To the extent that it is in conflict with our decision herein, the decision in *In re Certain Incomplete Trademark Applications* is expressly overruled.

———

Linville v. Rinard, 26 U.S.P.Q.2d 1508 (T.T.A.B. 1993). Meril Rivard obtained a registration for ULTRACUTS for hairdressing and beauty salons pursuant to section 44(e) on the basis of a Canadian registration. However, Rivard made no use of the mark in the U.S. for a period of five years and cancellation of the registration was sought by Mark Linville. The Board found that the mark had been abandoned.

> There is no genuine issue that respondent did not use his mark for services rendered in the United States between 1986, when his registration issued, and 1991, when the petition for cancellation was filed. This, as a matter of law, establishes prima facie abandonment of the mark, because once a registration issues on the basis of section 44, it stands on the same footing as any other registration, the registration date being the trigger of the two-year period for commencing use. *See* Oromeccanica, Inc. v. Ottmar Botzenhardt, 223 USPQ 59 (TTAB 1983), *rev'd on other grounds*, 226 USPQ 996 (CD Cal 1985). The terms "use" and "nonuse" in the statute mean use and nonuse in the United States. Imperial Tobacco Ltd. v. Philip Morris Inc., 899 F.2d 1575 (Fed. Cir. 1990). . . .

The Board noted further that:

> this case is . . . similar to *Imperial Tobacco Ltd. v. Philip Morris Inc.*, which involved a petition to cancel a registration obtained pursuant to Section 44(e) on the basis of the registrant's prior United Kingdom registration. The Court [there] stated that: "A foreign trademark may be known by reputation in this country and may even be protectable under concepts of unfair competition, but such mark is not entitled to either initial or continued registration where the statutory requirements for registration cannot be met." 14

U.S.P.Q.2d at 1393. The mere fact that residents of the United States have availed themselves of respondent's services while in Canada does not constitute technical trademark use of respondent's service mark which is sufficient to obtain or maintain a registration in the United States. The concept of territoriality is basic to trademark law, [cit], and it is a fundamental rule that activity outside of the United States is ineffective to create rights in marks within the United States. . . .

The Board's opinion was appealed and the litigation continued for several years. Ultimately, however, the Board's conclusion was affirmed by the Federal Circuit. *See* 133 F.3d 1446 (Fed. Cir. 1998).

NOTES AND QUESTIONS

(1) **The Different Texts of the Paris Convention**. Why did the *Crocker Bank* court discuss the London text of the Convention? The London text was revised at Lisbon in 1958 and in Stockholm in 1967. *See* Paris Convention art. 27; G.H.C. BODENHAUSEN, GUIDE TO THE APPLICATION OF THE PARIS CONVENTION FOR THE PROTECTION OF INDUSTRIAL PROPERTY 18-19, 212-15 (1968). Article 6 of the London text, discussed in *Crocker Bank*, is found in Article 6*quinquies* of the current (Stockholm 1967) text of the Paris Convention.

(2) **Opposition to the *Crocker Bank* Rule.** In 1977, after the *SCM* decision, the PTO proposed a rule change to adopt the view of the use requirement expressed there by the Board (but not reached by the D.C. Circuit) and later adopted in *Crocker Bank*. The proposal was withdrawn in the face of widespread criticism from the private trademark bar. Why did the proposal receive such a critical response? *See* John B. Pegram, *Section 44 Revision: After the 1988 Act*, 79 TRADEMARK REP. 220, 225-26 (1989); *see also* Alan Zelnick, *Shaking the Lemon Tree: Use and the Paris Union Treaty*, 67 TRADEMARK REP. 329, 345-46 (1977) (suggesting arguments why U.S. trademark applicants benefit from not requiring specimens of use from section 44(d) applicants). John Pegram suggested a compromise rule that required section 44 applicants to allege use somewhere, even if not use in commerce. *See id.* at 227. Would you support such a rule, either as a matter of policy or as an appropriate implementation of the Paris Convention?

(3) **Resistance to the *Crocker Bank* Rule**. Some commentators, critical of the *Crocker Bank* decision, have cautioned litigants not to rely upon its holding before courts. *See, e.g.*, John B. Pegram, *Trademark Law Revision: Section 44*, 78 TRADEMARK REP. 141, 155-56 (1988). Although the Board has confirmed the interpretation it announced in *Crocker Bank*, see *Lane Ltd. v. Jackson Int'l Trading Co.*, 33 U.S.P.Q.2d 1351, 1357 (T.T.A.B. 1994), there has been judicial criticism of that interpretation. The late Judge Helen Nies of the Federal Circuit sought unsuccessfully to raise the issue *sua sponte*, claiming that *Crocker Bank* was incorrectly decided. *See In re* Compagnie Generale Maritime,

993 F.2d 841, 855 (Fed. Cir. 1993) (Nies J., dissenting). The disagreement over this aspect of section 44 has been left largely unresolved by authoritative judicial interpretation because of the limited scope of appellate review of examiner decisions not to grant a filing date. *See id.* at 847 (Nies J., dissenting); John B. Pegram, *Trademark Law Revision: Section 44*, 78 TRADEMARK REP. 141, 151 n.59 (1988).

(4) **Basis for Application/Basis for Registration**. Section 44 provides two additional bases for application: section 44(e) applications rest upon a foreign registration, while section 44(d) applications are predicated upon a foreign application. But only section 44(e) establishes an additional basis for registration. Section 44(d) establishes a priority right, *see* Paris Convention art. 4, and permits application based upon a foreign *application*. But absent the foreign application becoming a foreign registration (or use in commerce occurring) in the applicant's country of origin, the U.S. application under section 44(d) will not mature into a registration. *See* 15 U.S.C. §1126(c).

(5) **The Relationship between Section 44(d) and Section 44(e)**. The *Crocker Bank* benefits are available to section 44 applicants regardless of whether they seek the benefits of priority under section 44(d). *See* Hawaiian Host, Inc. v. Rowntree Mackintosh PLC, 225 U.S.P.Q. 628 (T.T.A.B. 1985). And the benefits of a section 44(d) priority date can also be asserted by any qualified applicant filing both under section 44 and under a section 1 basis within six months of a foreign application. *See* Elexis Corp. v. Sunwatch, Inc., 27 U.S.P.Q.2d 1798 (T.T.A.B. 1993). Why might a foreign applicant who can take advantage of section 44(d) priority rest an application also upon a basis other than section 44, such as an intent to use under section 1(b)? *See* James Walsh, *Tips From the Trademark Examining Operation: The Impact of the TLRA of 1988 on the Filing of Applications Under Section 44 of the Trademark Act*, 80 TRADEMARK REP. 421, 426-27 (1990); *see also In re* Paperboard Indus. Corp., 41 U.S.P.Q.2d 1159 (Comm'r Pat. & Tm. 1996).

(6) **Beneficiaries of Section 44.** A U.S. company can obtain the benefit of section 44(e) if a foreign nation that is a member of a relevant convention is its "country of origin." *See In re* International Barrier Corp., 231 U.S.P.Q. 310 (T.T.A.B. 1986) (Delaware corporation with bona fide and effective industrial establishment in Canada); *cf. In re* De Luxe N.V., 990 F.2d 607 (Fed. Cir. 1993) (permitting U.S. assignee of section 44 application to continue with application notwithstanding non-assignment of predicate foreign application). This is possible if the company has a real and effective industrial or commercial establishment in such a nation. *See* 15 U.S.C. §1126(c). The predicate registration must be issued by the applicant's "country of origin," although such an applicant can rely on an application in another Convention country to ground a claim of priority under section 44(d). *See id.*

(7) **Intent-to-use Requirement.** In 1988, the Trademark Law Revision Act amended slightly the obligations imposed upon an applicant under section 44. Such an applicant is now, like an intent to use applicant under section 1(b), required to allege a bona fide intent to use the mark in commerce. *See* 15 U.S.C. § 1126(d)(2). These reforms were intended to reduce the preference that foreign section 44 applicants received over domestic section 1 applicants. Does this requirement violate the Paris Convention? *See In re* Unisearch Ltd., 21

U.S.P.Q.2d 1559 (Comm'r Pat. & Tm. 1991). Even with this additional requirement, section 44 applicants continue to receive the benefit under *Crocker Bank* of not being required to allege use prior to issuance of registration; domestic intent-to-use applicants must make such a showing. *See* 15 U.S.C. § 1051(d). What relief should a Section 44 registrant be able to obtain in the United States prior to U.S. use? *Cf.* Dawn Donut Co. v. Hart's Food Stores, Inc., 267 F.2d 358 (2d Cir. 1959); Warnervision Entm't v. Empire of Carolina, 101 F.3d 259 (2d Cir. 1996).

(8) **Principle of Independence of Rights.** Any registration obtained on the basis of section 44(e) is independent of the registration of the country of origin, and its continued validity and maintenance is a matter for U.S. law. *See* 15 U.S.C. §1126(f). If a rival company believes that the foreign registration upon which the section 44 application is based is invalid, how should it proceed? *See* Fioravanti v. Fioravanti Corrado S.R.L., 230 U.S.P.Q. 36 (T.T.A.B. 1986); Marie Claire Album S.A. v. Kruger GmbH & Co. KG, 29 U.S.P.Q.2d 1792 (T.T.A.B. 1993); *cf.* American Standard, Inc. v. Sanitary Wares Mfg. Corp., 3 U.S.P.Q.2d 1637 (D.D.C. 1987).

(9) **The Evolution of *Telle Quelle*.** The potential difficulties with Article 6*quinquies* were apparent from its first incarnation as Article 6 of the 1883 text. At its most internationalist, the original text of the clause could be read to require Union countries to recognize and enforce trademark rights acquired in other Union countries. Because this did not reflect the intention of the signatory states, additional, less absolute language was sought; this eventually became the phrase "*telle quelle.*" In addition, a Final Protocol accompanied (and was declared to be part of) the 1883 text and it included the following provision:

> Paragraph 1 of Article 6 should be understood in the sense that no trademark may be excluded from protection in one of the States of the Union for the sole reason that it does not comply, with regard to the signs of which it is composed, with the conditions of the laws of that State, provided it complies on this point with the laws of the country of origin and that it has been properly filed there. Subject to this exception, which only concerns the form of the mark, and subject to the provision of the other Articles of the Convention, each State shall apply its domestic law.

See BODENHAUSEN, *supra,* at 110.

The Protocol was omitted from the 1911 text, and Article 6 was revised to enumerate the limited cases in which a trademark granted by a fellow Union country may be refused recognition under Article 6. (Those grounds are now found in paragraph B of Article 6*quinquies*). The provision was further revised in the succeeding texts of the Convention and is now Article 6*quinquies*. What meaning or effect might attach to these textual revisions? *Compare* John B. Pegram, *Trademark Law Revision: Section 44,* 78 TRADEMARK REP. 141, 157-58 (1988); BODENHAUSEN, *supra,* at 110; Zelnick, *supra,* at 338 (1977).

(10) **Application of Telle Quelle in U.S. Law.** Despite the broad language in *Crocker Bank* and in some scholarly articles at the time of that decision, the

Lanham Act permits registration of marks for which application was made under section 44 only where the mark is otherwise eligible for registration. All the usual bars to registration may be invoked by the PTO, although (at least under *Crocker Bank*) use cannot be required. Moreover, the mark for which registration is sought under section 44 must be "a substantially exact representation" of the mark for which the predicate foreign registration was granted. *See In re* Hacot-Colombier, 105 F.3d 616 (Fed. Cir. 1997) (change sufficient to deny section 44 benefits.)

In light of the decision in *Crocker Bank*, in an application invoking the benefits of section 44, should the *telle quelle* principle require the U.S. Patent & Trademark Office to accept the (typically broader) specification of goods contained in the foreign application upon which the section 44 claim is based? *See In re* Société Générale des Eaux Minerales de Vittel S.A., 1 U.S.P.Q.2d 1296, 1298-99 (T.T.A.B. 1986) (permitting the PTO to require more particularized specification of goods in line with U.S. practice), *rev'd on other grounds*, 3 U.S.P.Q.2d 1450 (Fed. Cir. 1987).

Article 6(1) specifically reserves to each state the right to determine the conditions for the filing and registration of trademarks. How is this line to be drawn? Alan Zelnick argued after *SCM* that "while it is true that the language of [Article 6*quinquies*] appears to have been directed only to the form and nature of the mark or features internal or intrinsic to the mark itself, nevertheless it seems clear that there is an inherent limitation on the power of member states to promulgate 'conditions' which have the effect of limiting the right to register marks otherwise clearly registerable under Section [6*quinquies*(A)]." Zelnick, *supra* at 341. This highly internationalist argument is a minority viewpoint. Both the leading international commentator on the Paris Convention and the leading U.S. commentator of the time on international trademark law adopt a more restrictive view of the *telle quelle* obligation. *See* BODEHAUSEN, *supra,* at 110; Stephen P. Ladas, PATENTS, TRADEMARKS AND RELATED RIGHTS: NATIONAL AND INTERNATIONAL PROTECTION § 654, at 1221 (1975). Under Zelnick's argument, would the *telle quelle* principle require foreign countries to accept registration of olfactory marks registered in the United States even if such countries did not accept registration of such marks? *Cf.* Zelnick, *supra,* at 340 (discussing mandatory registration of marks comprised of numerals in countries that, formerly at least, did not accept such marks for registration). How is your answer affected by the adoption of a definition of "trademark" in the TRIPS Agreement that does not include such marks? *See* TRIPS art. 15. TRIPS was intended to enact a regime of "Paris plus" as regards trademarks; if the agreed-upon definition in Article 15 affects your analysis, does TRIPS represent a regime of "Paris minus" in some regards? *See generally* L. Ellwood, *The Industrial Property Convention and the Telle Quelle Clause,* 46 TRADEMARK REP. 36 (1956).

(11) **The Paris Article 6 Debate and International Trademark Philosophies**. The history of the Paris Convention recited in the *Crocker Bank* opinion reveals several different approaches to international trademark protection contemplated by negotiating parties and national legislators or advocates. Identify those different approaches. Can you tell which prevailed? Which is reflected in the Lanham Act? To what extent does the Paris

Convention embody an internationalist approach to trademark protection? On what issues has national trademark law been subordinated to international principles, and on which issues has national sovereignty been retained? As we discuss more recent international trademark agreements consider whether the issues that the international community has subjected to international regulation are the same issues upon which the Paris Convention (as interpreted by *Crocker Bank*) focused. Which aspects of national trademark law created the problems presented in *SCM* and *Crocker Bank*?

[5] Substantive Minima in the Paris Convention: Well-Known Marks

As indicated in the excerpt from Professor Schmidt-Szalewski above, the Paris Convention included various provisions requiring member states to provide minimum levels of protection. Two of these "substantive minima" are of particular importance. We discussed the first of these, Article 10*bis*, above in the context of the *Lopez* opinion. The second substantive minima warranting detailed attention is Article 6*bis*. In this Section we will consider Article 6*bis* and later treaty provisions, most notably Article 16 of TRIPS, that build upon Article 6*bis*. This will serve as a segue to, in our next section, a separate analysis of TRIPS provisions other than Article 16.

Article 6*bis* requires member states:

> *ex officio* if their legislation so permits, or at the request of an interested party, to refuse or to cancel the registration, and to prohibit the use, of a trade mark which constitutes a reproduction, an imitation, or a translation, liable to create confusion, of a mark considered by the competent authority of the country of registration or use to be well known in that country as being already the mark of a person entitled to the benefits of this Convention and used for identical or similar goods."

As Bodenhausen noted in 1968, "the purpose of [Article 6*bis*] is to avoid the registration and use of a trademark, liable to create confusion with another mark already well known in the country of such registration or use, although the latter well-known mark is not, or not yet, protected in that country by a registration which would normally prevent the registration or use of the conflicting mark." G.H.C. BODENHAUSEN, GUIDE TO THE APPLICATION OF THE PARIS CONVENTION FOR THE PROTECTION OF INDUSTRIAL PROPERTY 90 (1968). To some extent, the treatment of well-known marks in Article 6*bis* is a derogation from the principle of territoriality.

FREDERICK W. MOSTERT, WELL-KNOWN AND FAMOUS MARKS: IS HARMONY POSSIBLE IN THE GLOBAL VILLAGE?*
86 TRADEMARK REP. 103, 103-06, 114-17, 140 (1996)

Our global village provides increasing opportunities for us, as world citizens, to purchase internationally famous branded goods and services. In fact, brands are usually preceded by their reputations. Branded goods or services are often pre-advertised and pre-sold even though they are not yet physically present in the market of any particular country. Media dissemination and modern advertising are becoming less and less limited by national boundaries in view of sophisticated communication, technology and the frequency of travel.

Satellite traffic over our village has increased from one satellite in 1957 to an estimated 2,300 satellites today. Globalcasting via satellite has accordingly become the daily norm. In turn, this single development has facilitated brand exposure exponentially. For instance: universally attractive events (which are sponsored by brand owning companies) such as the OLYMPIC GAMES are estimated to be viewed by over one billion viewers (approximately 17 percent of the world's population) on a single day. The last WORLD SOCCER CUP was viewed by approximately half a billion viewers per match and FORMULA 1 RACING is watched by about 0.3 billion viewers per race during 16 Grand Prix races a year in 121 countries. More direct modern promotion through web-sites on the Internet has also assisted brand stimulus and exposure on a worldwide basis.

Not only satellite traffic but also jet travel has risen rapidly in the second half of the century. Estimates are, for example, that approximately 1,000 BOEING 747 Jumbo Jets (not to mention other models) are currently negotiating their way through the airways in order to transport passengers on a daily basis across the globe. Such frequent travel for reasons of business, study or pleasure allows people to become familiar with various brands in other countries.

In such a smaller but more intensely networked world, brand manufacturers are no longer confined to local markets. They function in an integrated global market place. Brand producers find themselves providing goods and services in bigger and bigger markets created by free trade pacts and the creation of single markets throughout the world. Brands such as COCA-COLA, McDONALD'S, CARTIER, SMIRNOFF, ROLLS-ROYCE, FERRARI, KODAK, SONY, CNN and DHL have virtually become household names to the global citizen. Against the reality of this background, there is certainly no doubt in the minds of businessmen that the reputation and good will attached to their famous brands have become detached from national and local borders.

The global village does, however, provide ever increasing temptations to local villagers to trade on the reputation of globally famous trademarks. Such "enterprising entrepreneurs" are equally assisted by modern technology. No longer will these "entrepreneurs" need to attend trade shows elsewhere only to run back to a local jurisdiction ahead of the original trademark owner in order to be the first to register the particular trademark. These days they are more likely to rely on a host of information retrieval resources made possible by

---

digital communication technology. It is not surprising therefore that the [WIPO] indicated in a recent memorandum that: "National Trademark Offices are often confronted with the problem that so-called 'trademark pirates' apply for the registration of marks ahead in time of the true owners." The reason is that the brand owning companies who own such well-known trademarks frequently find that they have not yet been in a position to expand their business activities under those marks nor have they obtained registrations for their marks in all jurisdictions. Even the most famous marks are not used everywhere, and it is not possible to register and maintain trademark registrations in all international classes in all jurisdictions. Similarly, there are often instances where the owner has filed an application to register the mark, but is caught by the lengthy official process that is involved before the mark can be registered. Meanwhile, a "trademark pirate" may have stolen a march on the owner by being the first to use a similar mark. In the event of such a preemption, the question is simply whether the company whose mark's reputation extends to the particular country should be afforded protection, or whether the local enterprise–who intercepted the owner and first used or registered the well-known trademark in the local jurisdiction–should be permitted to do so. For instance, if Pizza Hut had not yet commenced business activities under its well-known service mark in Cyprus, should a local imitator be allowed to open a PIZZA HUT restaurant and sell frozen pizza pies in Cyprus? When copiers attempt to register and use the WHIRLPOOL trademark in relation to washing machines in India, should they be permitted to do so? Should businessmen in Paraguay be permitted to register or use the McDONALD'S trademark with respect to hamburgers without authorization?

Brand owners are confronted with the need to protect their well-known trademarks on a global basis. Such a need for protection is particularly significant if one keeps in mind that the brands COCA-COLA, MARLBORO and IBM together have been estimated to be worth close to $100 billion (US) as intellectual property assets. It is, therefore, not surprising that the appropriate protection of well-known marks and intellectual property has become a significant factor in the trading relations between nations . . . . Not only are the equities and the economic concerns of trademark owners at stake but also the international standards of fair play and comity between nations. The protection of the global trading system through the prevention of piracy and unfair exploitation of well-known marks has become essential.

Consequently, for businesses who battle in the commercial trenches of the modern international market place, a strict adherence to the more traditional territorial concept of trademarks has become an economic concern of global proportions. In addition, it should be noted that the recognition and protection of well-known marks differ from country to country: the definitions and criteria in this area of trademark law remain elusive. . . .

It is apparent that clearer guidelines and a more universal approach based on common principles are urgently required to combat piracy throughout the world.

. . . .

PARAMETERS OF A WELL-KNOWN MARK

The establishment of a set of guidelines or criteria to determine whether a mark is well-known is of increasing importance in view of international trade and the need for effective recognition and protection of well-known marks. Almost as important, is the necessity to provide a clear content to the concept "well-known mark." . . .

Courts and commentators use a variety of terms to refer to well-known marks, including "notorious," "famous," "highly-renowned," "highly-reputed" and "exceptionally well-known" marks.[38] These terms have such a large degree of overlap and inter-connection that their multiple use has caused a fair amount of confusion. In fact, an illustrious panel of experts on well-known marks indicated that such "usage reflects no more than a linguistic muddle." The better view seems to be one that focuses on the universal term provided in Article 6bis of the Paris Convention of a well-known mark: "marque notoirement connue," "notorisch bekannte Marke," "marchio notoriamente conosciuto" or "marca notoriamente conocida." . . . In the context of trademark law, therefore, a well-known mark can be characterized as a mark which is known to a substantial segment of the relevant public in the sense of being associated with the particular goods or services.

It has often been suggested that a special category of well-known marks, i.e., "famous" marks be recognized. Famous marks are considered to have a higher degree of reputation than well-known marks and therefore deserve a broader scope of protection against unauthorized use on non-competing goods or services. The wider ambit of protection afforded to famous marks on non-competing goods or services to which their commercial magnetism extends, consequently constitutes an exception to the "principle of speciality." The "principle of speciality" stipulates that trademarks can only be protected in relation to the same or similar goods or services covered by their use or registration. The rigidity of this principle has hampered the extended protection required on non-competing goods in countries such as Italy. In sum, a famous mark can be viewed as a mark which is known to a large section of the public.[45]

---

[38] Andre R. Bertrand, *French Trade Mark Law: From the Well-Known Brand to the Famous Brand*, 4 EIPR 142, 142 (1993) states for example with respect to French law that distinctions between the various degrees of brand awareness may be drawn: "Maître Mathély distinguishes in ascending order, between major [grand] brands, well-known [notoire] brands and brands which could be described as illustrious [glorieux].' As for French judicial practice, it refers not only to 'well-known' (notoire or notoirement connue) brands, but also to those which are 'very well-known' (de très grande notoriété), or even 'exceptionally well-known' (d'une exceptionnelle notoriété), without–up to now–having drawn any legal inferences from these various qualifications. . . ."

[45] . . . Bertrand, at 142 refers to the following distinction between "well-known" and "famous" marks:

(1) The "well-known" brand proper, which is a "trade mark recognised by a large fraction of the circles concerned with the production, sale or use of the goods in question and which is clearly perceived as indicating a particular origin of these products," and

(2) The "famous" (renomme) brand, or "very famous" (de haute renomme) brand which would, so to speak, be a trade mark known internationally or worldwide.

The reverse seems to apply in Brazil, *see* Luiz Henrique do Amaral, *Famous Marks: The Brazilian*

It should be noted that a highly precise, strict differentiation between "famous" and "well-known" marks beyond the degree of reputation required is not possible as these concepts are relative. What is clear though, is that the higher the degree of reputation or commercial magnetism acquired by a mark, the broader its scope of protection. In fact, the more well-known or famous a mark is, the more inclined the courts will be to assume that injury is present.

. . . .

. . . "Good will" eloquently described by Lord MacNaghten as "the attractive force which brings in custom," still represents an accurate description of this concept in the market place. No longer can physical locality be considered as one of the most important and visible factors to establish good will. Contemporary consumers do not concern themselves with the site of the manufacturing plant or the actual location of the headquarters of the trademark owner. They are more interested in the continuous level of quality symbolized by internationally well-known or famous marks such as MONTBLANC, HEINZ, REEBOK, CHANEL and MARS. The speed and extent to which reputations can be established are almost limitless in view of the increasing sophistication of international communication, spillover advertising, the frequency of travel and the peripatetic behavior of the modern consumer. The force of such international advertising and travel exposes the consumer public to well-known and famous trademarks throughout the world. In today's business world good will generates a commercial magnetism whose power may be perceived far beyond its original intended scope. When the owner of a well-known or famous mark has established an exclusive association between the mark and its goods or services, the owner has acquired good will, "an attractive force which brings in custom." Merely because such an owner is unable to demonstrate the physical presence of its products or services within the jurisdiction, does not detract from the reality and importance of this intangible asset and the various forms of permanent damage which can be suffered beyond traditional diversion of custom. The realities of the modern market place dictate that the most sensible approach to measure the extent of good will is to recognize its manifest international character and to determine its geographical scope in a given case by regarding it as a question of fact.

_____

NOTES AND QUESTIONS

(1) **Beneficiaries of Well-Known Mark Protection**. Does Mostert's prescription favor particular social or economic institutions over others? Who stands to benefit from enhanced protection for well-known marks? What characteristics identify the group of persons with whose problems Mostert appears most concerned?

_____

Case, 83 TMR 394, 406 (1993) where there is a court ruling that defines "famous" marks as those marks which have been registered under domestic legislation while "well-known" marks are marks which have become internationally recognized and are not registered under national law.

(2) **Article 6*bis* and "New" Marks**. In *Philips Elec. BV v. Remington Consumer Prods.* [1998] RPC 283 (Ch. D. 1997) (UK), Philips sought to restrain the distribution of Remington shavers similar to its three headed rotary design. Among its claims (discussed more fully *infra*), Philips alleged infringement of section 56(2) of the 1994 U.K. Trademarks Act, which implements Article 6*bis* of the Paris Convention. The U.K. court rejected the claim for several reasons. The first has widespread support, namely that "the true purpose of this provision is to deal with people who use a mark which does cause confusion, even if the plaintiff has no business (and no goodwill, in the English law of passing off sense) here"; the court held that Remington's use would not cause confusion. *See also* McDonald's Corp. v Joburgers Drive-In Restaurant (Pty) Ltd. 1997 S.A.L.R. 1 (App. Div. 1997) (SA) (noting confusion foundation of Article 6*bis*). In effect, the court suggested, Article 6*bis* "puts the plaintiff who has a reputation but no business here in the same position as if he had a business here." The second reason tendered by the court is more questionable. The court concluded that a product shape in three dimensions was not a trademark for the purposes of section 56 and the Paris Convention. The court noted that "at the time of introduction of Article 6*bis* (1927) no-one would have dreamt that the provision covered engineering artefacts of this sort. And the meaning cannot widen with time. And even now that shapes can be trademarks for Europe, that is not so for many other countries." Is it relevant to the interpretation of section 56–or the U.K.'s obligations under Article 6*bis* of the Paris Convention–what the understanding of the drafters of Article 6*bis* was with respect to product design marks? If so, in what ways and to what extent? Should it be relevant that "even now that shapes can be trade marks for Europe, that is not so for many other countries"?

(3) **Article 6*bis* and U.S. Law**. Review *Mother's, Vaudable, Person's*, and *Buti, supra* § 3.01[A]. Are the principles articulated in those cases consistent with Article 6*bis*? Although the *Vaudable* court did not discuss rights that might have existed under the Paris Convention, could the plaintiff have asserted a claim under Article 6*bis* or Article 10*bis* of the Paris Convention? Is the *Vaudable* standard different from that required by Article 6*bis*? *See Mother's* (Allen, concurring) ("it seems to me that the Vaudable decision according protection to the famous Maxim's restaurant name in the United States . . . is inapplicable to this case since that decision was based on a theory of unfair competition, namely misappropriation, under the law of the State of New York. Under Federal law, it seems to me that application of the well-known marks doctrine depends upon whether the applicable text of the Paris Convention, in this case, the 1934 London text, and, in particular, Article 6*bis* of that Convention, is self-executing."). Should the Person's Company have had a claim under Article 6*bis*?

(4) **Protection Without Registration *or* Use**. At the 1958 Revision Conference, an attempt expressly to *require* member states to protect well-known trademarks where they have not been *used* (as opposed to not registered) in the country where protection was sought was defeated by 25 votes to 2. *See* G.H.C. BODENHAUSEN, GUIDE TO THE APPLICATION OF THE PARIS CONVENTION FOR THE PROTECTION OF INDUSTRIAL PROPERTY 91 (1968). Member States are free under the Paris Convention, however, to provide protection without regard

to use, and that approach commands increasing support as an internationally-mandated standard. *See* Report of the First Session of the Committee of Experts on Well-Known Marks in Geneva on November 13-16, 1995, WIPO Document No. WKM/CE/I/3, at ¶¶ 75-80 (Nov. 16, 1995) (majority of countries believed that protection of well-known marks should be available regardless of whether a mark was used in the territory in which protection was sought). Many countries offer relief based upon the international reputation of a mark without there being domestic use. *See, e.g,* Al Hayat Pub. Co. v. Ahmed Sokarno (Australia), *reported in* 10 WORLD INTELL. PROP. REP. 207 (1996); CW Communication Inc. v. KK Denpa (Tokyo High Court, 1992), *reported in* [1996] EUR. INTELL. PROP. REV. D-171 (June 1996); Orkin Exterminating Co. v. Pestco of Canada Ltd. (1985) 5 CPR (3d) 433 (granting U.S. plaintiff an injunction against the use of a mark in Canada notwithstanding plaintiff's non-use in Canada). For a discussion of English law, see David Rose, *Season of Goodwill: Passing Off and Overseas Traders*, 18 EUR. INTELL. PROP. REV. 356 (1996). Do U.S. courts follow the strict interpretation of article 6*bis* of the Paris Convention, or do they offer protection to well-known marks without use in the U.S.? Should the United States adopt this more liberal position in excess of the requirements of Article 6*bis* of the Paris Convention? (Consider the typical basis upon which the United States recognizes priority of rights.) What interests would—or does, in the case of countries following the more protective approach—this extension serve? What types of producers benefit most from protection without requiring use in the country in which protection is sought? The WIPO General Assemblies recently agreed to a non-binding resolution on well-known marks that stipulates that a well-known mark will be protected in a specific country on the ground that it is well-known, even if the mark is not registered or used in that country. *See infra.*

(5) **Rights of a Trademark Owner Under Article 6*bis*.** The "protection without use" question cannot be divorced from the rest of Article 6*bis*. The language of Article 6*bis* holds open the possibility that the owners of well-known marks may oppose (or obtain cancellation of) registrations for confusingly similar marks in countries without having first used or registered the mark in those countries. Since the Lisbon revision of the Convention in 1958, however, the provision also enables the mark owner to enjoin the *use* of such confusingly similar marks without having itself used or registered the mark in the relevant country. Is it appropriate that a mark owner can ensure that there is *no* use of a mark by any producer in a country? What adverse consequences flow from such a possibility?

(6) **Nature of Relief Under Article 6*bis*.** Even if the United States protects well-known marks without use in the United States, should an injunction issue to the owner of the well-known mark absent plans to expand into the United States? What does Article 6*bis* require? In the context of two domestic users, the majority of U.S. courts have been reluctant to grant the owner of a federal U.S. trademark registration an injunction to prevent use by a junior user in a geographic area into which the senior user has no current plans to expand. *See, e.g.,* Dawn Donut Co. v. Hart's Food Stores, Inc., 267 F.2d 358 (2d Cir. 1959) (because plaintiff registration owner and defendant junior user used the mark in separate markets and there was no present prospect that plaintiff would

expand into defendant's market, the court concluded that confusion was unlikely and denied an injunction); *see also* Comidas Exquisitos, Inc. v. O'Malley & McGee's Inc., 775 F.2d 260, 262 (8th Cir. 1985) (senior user and registrant is only entitled to an injunction when it proves a likelihood of expansion into the junior user's area). *But see* Sterling Brewing, Inc. v. Cold Spring Brewing Corp., 100 F. Supp. 412, 417-18 (D. Mass. 1951) (granting immediate injunction against defendant's use in an area in which plaintiff registrant did not use the mark and into which plaintiff could not reasonably be expected to expand).

(7) **Defining "Well-Known Marks."** Owners of foreign marks that seek protection for their marks in the U.S. based solely upon the reputation of these marks must prove that such marks have achieved well-known status. What are the means by which well-known status may be demonstrated? What criteria should be taken into account? Should a mark's status be determined by whether a fixed percentage of consumer recognition is revealed by survey evidence? Is such an objective standard desirable or workable? Would a flexible standard be more appropriate? What other objective definitions of reputation could be used? For example, should international agreements (or national laws implementing Article 6*bis*) provide that a mark will be well-known only after 10 years' continuous use? Only after a certain volume of sales? Should such levels of use or notoriety be necessary (but not dispositive) or sufficient?

(8) **Bad Faith Registration of Well-Known Marks**. Article 6*bis*(2) provides that "a period of at least five years from the date of registration shall be allowed for requesting the cancellation of such a mark. The countries of the Union may provide for a period within which the prohibition of use must be requested." But under Article 6*bis*(3), an action by the owner of the well-known mark to cancel its mark registered or used by another in bad faith is subject to no time limit. Under which provision of the Lanham Act would the owner of a well-known mark seek cancellation of the registration of such a mark? *See* 15 U.S.C. § 1064. What does Article 6*bis*(3) mean by "bad faith"? *See* BODENHAUSEN, *supra*, at 92 ("Bad faith will normally exist when the person who registers or uses the conflicting mark knew of the well-known mark and presumably intended to profit from the possible confusion between that mark and the one he has registered or used").

TRIPS AGREEMENT, ARTICLE 16

(1) The owner of a registered trade mark shall have the exclusive right to prevent all third parties not having the owner's consent from using in the course of trade identical or similar signs for goods or services which are identical or similar to those in respect of which the trademark is registered where such use would result in a likelihood of confusion. In case of the use of an identical sign for identical goods or services, a likelihood of confusion shall be presumed. The rights described above shall not prejudice any existing prior rights, nor shall they affect the possibility of members making rights available on the basis of use.

(2) Article 6*bis* of the Paris Convention (1967) shall apply, *mutatis mutandis*, to services. In determining whether a trade mark is well-known, members shall take account of the knowledge of the trade mark in the relevant sector of the public, including knowledge in the member concerned which has been obtained as a result of the promotion of the trademark.

(3) Article 6*bis* of the Paris Convention (1967) shall apply, *mutatis mutandis*, to goods or services which are not similar to those in respect of which a trade mark is registered, provided that use of that trade mark in relation to those goods or services would indicate a connection between those goods or services and the owner of the registered trade mark and provided that the interests of the owner of the registered trade mark are likely to be damaged by such use.

PAUL J. HEALD, TRADEMARKS AND GEOGRAPHICAL INDICATIONS: EXPLORING THE CONTOURS OF THE TRIPS AGREEMENT*
29 Vand. J. Transnat'l L. 635, 641-43, 654-55 (1996)

Rights of Registrants

Article 16 [of the TRIPS Agreement] grants the owner of a registered mark the right to prevent confusing uses of an identical or similar mark on identical or similar goods. As under U.S. law, a presumption of confusion arises when identical marks are used on identical goods. Unlike under the Paris Convention, however, TRIPS service marks receive protection equal to that of marks affixed to goods or trade names.

Owners of "well-known" marks obtain additional protection against certain uses of their marks on dissimilar goods. Unfortunately, "well-known" is defined in neither the TRIPS Agreement nor the Paris Convention. Although TRIPS provides that "the knowledge of the trademark in the relevant sector of the public, including knowledge in that member obtained as a result of the promotion of the trademark" shall be taken into account, no further guidance is given. Prior discussion and litigation of the definition of well-known merely emphasizes the uncertain protection of marks when used on unrelated goods. Under the Lanham Act, a trademark owner is protected from confusing uses of its mark on dissimilar goods irrespective of the relative fame of the mark.[48]

TRIPS protection of well-known marks against uses on dissimilar goods appears limited to situations involving what the Lanham Act describes as "confusion . . . as to . . . sponsorship." In a false sponsorship case, the trademark owner must prove that consumers are likely to believe that the infringing goods

---

[48] *See* McGregor-Doniger, Inc. v. Drizzle Inc., 599 F.2d 1126, 1130 (2d Cir. 1979) (setting out eight-factor test to determine infringement in cases involving non-competing goods). The fame of a mark, however, is a component in the test used to judge likelihood of confusion.

are authorized, licensed, or officially approved by the trademark owner. This differs from state law causes of action for trademark dilution, which do not require confusion or mistaken belief, but purport to provide a remedy for the "tarnishment" or "dilution" of the trademark's intrinsic value. Article 16 of TRIPS requires that a dissimilar use "indicate a connection between [the infringing] goods or services and the owner of the registered trademark." The requirement of a mistaken belief in a "connection between those goods" seems much closer to the traditional Lanham Act false sponsorship cause of action than to a cause of action for dilution.

. . . .

IMPLEMENTING LEGISLATION IN THE UNITED STATES

Although some recent commentary suggests TRIPS may require the passage of a federal dilution statute, Article 16 need not be read so broadly. At least two credible arguments can be made against the need to amend. First, Article 16 requires that consumers perceive a "connection" between the use of the owner's trademark and the dissimilar goods on which the offending use has been made. Traditional dilution doctrine in the United States does not require that consumers perceive any "connection." For example, a chestnut example of the dilution doctrine posits the prohibition of the use of "Rolls Royce" by a peanut vendor in the Bowery. No one believes Rolls Royce autos have any connection to peanuts; Rolls Royce merely wants to maintain control over what is a valuable part of its industrial property. The "connection" requirement is better understood to establish a cause of action for false sponsorship or association, remedies for which are already found in the Lanham Act.

Second, Article 16 incorporates Article 6bis of the Paris Convention, which prohibits reproductions, imitations, and translations of well-known marks from uses on identical or similar goods that are "liable to create confusion." After stating that Article 6bis shall apply mutatis mutandis to dissimilar goods and services, thereby expanding the existing level of protection, Article 16 of the TRIPS Agreement adds the "connection" qualifier. Article 16 might plausibly be read to retain fully the confusion element of Article 6bis,[139] thereby requiring that consumers be confused by the perceived connection between the infringer's use of another's trademark. So understood, no amendment to the Lanham Act is necessary to create a cause of action independent of confusion. No federal cause of action for dilution is necessary to harmonize domestic law with the TRIPS Agreement.[140]

---

[139]See G.H.C. BODENHAUSEN, GUIDE TO THE APPLICATION OF THE PARIS CONVENTION, at 90 (Article 6bis requires proof of confusion.)

[140]Ladas' discussion of failed attempts to amend the Paris Convention to provide international antidilution protection for "marks of great reputation" (not merely well-known marks) is quite illuminating. See 2 Stephen P. Ladas, Patents, Trademarks and Related Rights: National and International Protection 1258-63 (1975). Unadopted draft agreements exhibit language that is not found in the TRIPS Agreement. For example, one resolution adopted by the Berlin Congress provided disjunctively that marks of "higher reputation" be protected from uses that were likely "to mislead the public or be harmful to the proprietor of the mark." Id. at 1262. Article 16 of the TRIPS Agreement conjunctively prohibits uses that "indicate a connection between those goods or

NOTES AND QUESTIONS

(1) **Protection for Service Marks**. The Paris Convention does not extend the protection of Article 6*bis* to service marks (although signatory countries were free to do so). *See* TRIPS Agreement art. 6*bis*(1) (restricting provision to use of the mark on similar or identical *goods*). Article 16(2) of the TRIPS Agreement remedies that (intentional) omission from the Paris Convention by providing for the application of Article 6*bis* to service marks. *See also* Trademark Law Treaty art. 16 (requiring contracting parties to extend protections of Paris Convention to service marks).

(2) **Protection for Unregistered Marks**. The language of Article 16(3) of the TRIPS Agreement suggests that this provision only applies to well-known marks that are *registered*. Annette Kur has argued that the reference to registration is a drafting error. *See* Annette Kur, *TRIPS and Trademark Law*, *in* 18 STUDIES IN INDUSTRIAL PROPERTY AND COPYRIGHT LAW 93, 108 (Friedrich-Karl Beier & Gerhard Schricker eds. 1996). Dr. Kur notes that early drafts of the TRIPS Agreement contained a provision which required registration as a condition for protection but that this provision was not included in the final text. Therefore, the mention of registration in Article 16(3) was overlooked when the text was finalized. Moreover, that registration would be required under Article 16(3) is anomalous with the premise for extending protection to well-known marks under Article 6*bis*. *See* Frederick W. Mostert, *Well-Known And Famous Marks: Is Harmony Possible In The Global Village*, 86 TRADEMARK REP. 103, 117 n.49 (1996) (suggesting that the Benelux provision requiring registration as a precondition for protection is "strictly speaking" in conflict with Article 6*bis*). In any event, Article 16(3) establishes *minimum* standards of protection such that Members may extend protection to unregistered well-known marks. *See* 15 U.S.C. § 1125(c) (federal dilution provision).

(3) **International Fame**. The language of Article 16(2), when read in the context of Article 6*bis*, strongly suggests that a mark must be well-known in the country where protection is sought in order to claim the benefits of the provision. Why not consider the international popularity of a mark as a sufficient basis for extending protection notwithstanding the absence of notoriety in the country where protection is sought? Such arguments were advanced during the negotiations for the TRIPS Agreement but failed. *See* Kur, *supra*, at 106 n.59 (noting U.S. proposal and Indian opposition thereto). What are the arguments for and against such an approach? How would international popularity be determined? Is "international" popularity different from "foreign" popularity? In *Buti*, would the Italian defendant owner of the Fashion Cafe in Milan have had priority in the United States under an "international popularity" standard?

---

services and the owner of the registered trademark and provided that the interests of the owner . . . are likely to be damaged by such use." TRIPS, art. 16(3).

(4) **Well-Known to Whom?** Article 16(2) states that a mark must be well-known to the *relevant sector of the public*. Mostert argues that this language evinces the drafters' intention that the mark need not be well-known to the entire population of the country where protection is sought but only to the mark's target audience. *See* FREDERICK MOSTERT, FAMOUS AND WELL-KNOWN MARKS 26 (1997); *see also* NAFTA art. 1708(b) ("No party may require that the reputation of a trademark extend beyond the sector of the public that normally deals with the relevant goods or services"). In what circumstances might this interpretation have important practical consequences for the owner of a mark seeking to invoke the protection of Article 16(2)? *Cf.* Mead Data Central Inc. v. Toyota Motor Sales, 875 F.2d 1026, 1030-31 (2d Cir. 1989). Might the breadth of a mark's notoriety (*i.e.* whether it extends to a particular group of purchasers or to the public at large) be a criterion by which to determine "fame" and thus whether a mark should receive extended protection?

(5) **Terminology**. As Mostert notes, different countries use different terminology to describe the concept of a "well-known mark." Mostert argues, however, that:

> [a]s long as the focus remains on the outcome of the factual enquiry, the confusion which may result from over formalistic terminology or labeling could be avoided. Has the mark in question in fact acquired a sufficient reputation, fame or well-known status among the consuming public to warrant extended protection to the particular territory or in respect of non-competing goods or services?

MOSTERT, *supra*, at 21. Is this standard helpful? Should efforts be made to conform terminology internationally, or is that an elevation of form over substance as Mostert implies? *See World Trademark Symposium: Famous Marks*, 82 TRADEMARK REP. 987, 989 (1992) (noting that current multitude of terms reflects "no more than a linguistic muddle" and suggesting use only of the term "well-known" marks, meaning marks with a broader reputation than most marks, and "famous" marks that possess an even broader reputation).

(6) **EU Trademark Directive**. The EU harmonization directive, *see infra*, extends protection of marks which have a *reputation* to dissimilar goods or services where the defendant's use of the mark would have the effect of *taking an unfair advantage* of the plaintiff's reputed mark. *See* Trademark Directive art. 5(2). Do the provisions of the Harmonization Directive meet the requirements of Article 16(3)? *See* Kur, *supra*, at 108 n.66 (noting statement of European Commission representatives at the Meeting of Committee of Experts on Well-Known Marks that the EC was in compliance with TRIPS because "reputation" is a less demanding standard than "well-known" marks); Case C375/97, General Motors Corp. v. Yplon SA, 1999 E.T.M.R. 950 (E.C.J. 1999) (holding that the term "reputation" suggested that the mark must be "fairly well known" and identifying factors that the national court might consider).

(7) **Registry for Well-Known Marks**. The WIPO Committee of Experts on Well-Known Marks meeting in Geneva in 1995 and 1996 considered the merits of establishing, by treaty, an international registry for well-known marks. The

proposal encountered substantial opposition. Why? What advantages might an international registry provide? *See World Trademark Symposium: Famous Marks*, 82 TRADEMARK REP. 989, 991 (1992). What rights would flow from inclusion in an international registry? What requirements would be imposed upon trademark owners seeking entry on such a register? How would the register be administered?

(8) **Expanded Protection for Well-Known Marks.** In 1995, the WIPO Committee of Experts on Well-Known Marks addressed the need for establishing a framework for extending protection of well-known marks to dissimilar goods or services. The International Bureau's memorandum considered by the Committee described two bases for extending the protection accorded to well-known marks along these lines. First, a special category of well-known marks, *i.e.*, famous marks, could be recognized with a greater showing of notoriety meriting a greater degree of protection (*i.e.*, against uses on dissimilar goods). How would you distinguish between "well-known" marks and "famous" marks? What would be the criteria for determining whether a mark is famous? Consider the following proposed definition:

> A *famous* mark is a mark which is extremely widely-known in the country concerned to at least 80% of the potential purchasers of the goods or services for which it is known, and to at least 90% of the relevant trade circles. Furthermore a famous mark must be a registered mark at least in its owner's home territory, and have a value, calculated by an internationally acceptable method, of at least $4000 [sic] million.

David H. Tatham, *What is a Famous Brand?* 22 (1995) (paper delivered in connection with speech at MARQUES 1995 Annual Conference), *quoted in* Miles J. Alexander & Michael K. Heilbronner, *Dilution Under Section 43(c) of the Lanham Act*, 59 LAW & CONTEMP. PROBS. 93, 106 n.76 1996). What other forms of enhanced protection might be appropriate for those marks that are so well-known as to be considered famous?

The second approach calls for identifying *conditions* under which protection of a mark would be extended to uses on dissimilar goods or services. Article 16(3) of the TRIPS Agreement incorporates this latter idea by extending protection of well-known marks where the mark's use on noncompeting goods indicates "a connection between those goods or services and the owner of the registered trademark and [where] the interests of the owner of the registered trademark are likely to be damaged by such use." *See* TRIPS Agreement art. 16(3). Which of the two approaches do you prefer? How will the mark owner demonstrate the necessary damage where it has not used the mark in the U.S., or where the mark has been adopted by the defendant for use on noncompeting goods or services? Is the possible preclusion from the U.S. market or from expanding the range of products for which the mark may be used too speculative? If inhibition of likely market expansion were a means of showing "likely damage" under a national law implementing Article 16(3), to what extent would U.S. multinationals wishing to protect their marks abroad possess an advantage over smaller companies from lesser developed countries?

THE FEDERAL DILUTION ACT OF 1995:
H.R. REP. NO. 374, 104TH CONG., 1ST SESS. 4 (1995)

[T]he recently-concluded [TRIPS Agreement] . . . includes a provision designed to provide dilution protection to famous marks. Thus, enactment of this bill will be consistent with the terms of the agreement, as well as the Paris Convention, of which the U.S. is also a member. Passage of a federal dilution statute would also assist the executive branch in its bilateral and multilateral negotiations with other countries to secure greater protection for the famous marks owned by U.S. companies. Foreign countries are reluctant to change their laws to protect famous U.S. marks if the U.S. itself does not afford special protection for such marks.

It should be noted that as originally introduced, H.R. 1295 only applied to famous registered marks. However, based on testimony by the Patent & Trademark Office, Congresswoman Patricia Schroeder offered an amendment . . . to include all famous marks falling within the scope of the bill. The Patent & Trademark Office made a compelling case that limiting the federal remedy against dilution to those famous marks that are registered is not within the spirit of the United States' position as a leader setting the standards for strong worldwide protection of intellectual property. Such a limitation would undercut the United States' position with our trading partners, which is that famous marks should be protected regardless of whether the marks are registered in the country where protection is sought.

NOTES AND QUESTIONS

(1) **The Meaning of TRIPS Article 16(3)**. Congress apparently detected the presence of some international obligations when it enacted the Federal Trademark Dilution Act of 1995. Are you persuaded by Professor Heald's argument that TRIPS did not require the enactment of a federal dilution statute in the United States? *See* Robert C. Denicola, *Some Thoughts on the Dynamics of Federal Trademark Legislation and the Trademark Dilution Act of 1995*, 59 LAW & CONTEMP. PROBS. 75, 84 n.40 (1996) (suggesting that "it is not at all clear" that Article 16(3) requires the enactment of a dilution statute); *cf.* J.H. Reichman, *Universal Minimum Standards of Intellectual Property Protection Under the TRIPS Component of the WTO Agreement*, 29 INT. LAW. 345, 363 (1995). Mostert has suggested that:

[Article 16(3)] will probably serve as the basis for legal action founded on a likelihood of business connection or sponsorship, [but] it is also possible that this provision will form the grounds, where appropriate, of an action of trademark dilution in the absence of any confusion but where some association of the well-known mark with the goods or services of the registered owner is present.

Frederick W. Mostert, *Well-Known and Famous Marks: Is Harmony Possible in the Global Village*, 86 TRADEMARK REP. 103, 130 (1996). Does Mostert's interpretation differ in substance from Professor Heald's? *See* Paul J. Heald, *Trademarks and Geographical Indications: Exploring the Countours of the TRIPS Agreement*, 29 VAND. J. TRANSNAT'L L. 635 (1996) ("The 'connection' requirement is better understood to establish a cause of action for false sponsorship or association, remedies for which are already found in the Lanham Act."); *see also infra* § 3.01[I][3][a] (discussing EU Trademark Directive confusion/association debate).

(2) **Dilution in the PTO.** If the TRIPS Agreement does mandate protection against dilution, does the Federal Dilution Act of 1995 implement U.S. obligations fully? Congress recently amended the Lanham Act to permit trademark registrations to be opposed or canceled on the grounds of the dilution of the distinctiveness of a prior mark, but the PTO Examiners will not consider such grounds in their examination of an application.

(3) **International Influence in U.S. Dilution Law.** Noting the international impetus for the Federal Dilution Act of 1995, *see* Ringling Bros.-Barnum & Bailey Combined Shows v. B.E. Windows Corp., 40 U.S.P.Q.2d 1010, 1014 (S.D.N.Y. 1996), some U.S. courts have referred to non-U.S. dilution laws to support their interpretation of the scope of the U.S. statute. *See, e.g.,* Ringling Bros.-Barnum & Bailey Combined Shows v. Utah Division of Travel Development, 40 U.S.P.Q.2d 1303, 1305-06 (E.D. Va. 1996).

(4) **International Protection Against Dilution.** If you were the head of the U.S. delegation negotiating a further revision to international trademark obligations, what additional protections of famous marks would you argue for, and what arguments would you use to persuade other nations of the merit of your position? Would an international obligation (or, depending upon your interpretation of Article 16(3), a more explicit international obligation) to protect certain marks against non-confusing uses that dilute the distinctiveness of a mark be appropriate? What is the purpose of such protection?

FREDERICK W. MOSTERT, WELL-KNOWN AND FAMOUS MARKS: IS HARMONY POSSIBLE IN THE GLOBAL VILLAGE?*
86 TRADEMARK REP. 103, 133-36 (1996)

In keeping with the requirements of modern commerce, the selling power, advertising function and commercial magnetism of a mark are protected against unauthorized use on non-competing goods or services in some jurisdictions. Such commercial magnetism is protected through an action to restrain trademark dilution. A dilution action is usually available where there is no likelihood of confusion and in the absence of competition in circumstances where there is an erosion of the communication or advertising function of a trademark.[124]

The advertising function of a trademark is reflected in the ability of the mark to call to mind the specific product and to evoke associations of satisfaction and desirability with that product. For example, the COCA-COLA mark calls to mind the satisfaction and desirability associated with a pleasant-tasting, popular, dark-colored soft drink, while the ROLLS-ROYCE mark evokes notions of high quality in an automobile. The more exclusive such an association between the mark and the product in the public's mind, the stronger will be the attention of the public focused on the specific goods.

A claim of trademark dilution consequently provides trademark owners with a tool to prevent the parasitic use of the commercial magnetism of a trademark on non-competing goods. This form of legal action serves to forestall erosion of the exclusive association between a mark and the particular goods or services in relation to which it is used.[126] Trademark dilution usually occurs by way of either blurring or tarnishing. In cases of blurring an erosion or watering down of the singularity and exclusivity of the trademark to call to mind a specific product is at issue. Obviously, the more a trademark is used on a wide variety of goods, becoming saturated in the process, the less the particular mark will call to mind and focus the public's attention on the plaintiff's particular product. If, for example, the TIFFANY mark has become well-known in connection with jewelry, and it is used on a plethora of other goods such as chocolates, clothing,

---

[124]There is no reason why an action for dilution should not be available for protecting a famous mark on competing goods as well. *See* Jonathan E. Moskin, *Dilution or Delusion: The Rational Limits of Trademark Protection*, 83 TMR 122, 129 (1993).

Similarly, an action for trademark dilution should also cover the protection of well-known trade dress as opposed to word marks only. For instance, the well-known OSCAR trophy, *Academy of Motion Picture Arts & Sciences v. Creative House Promotion, Inc.*, 944 F2d 1446 (CA 9 1991), the distinctive COKE bottle shape, *Coca-Cola Co. v. Alma-Leo U.S.A., Inc*, 719 F Supp 725 (ND Ill 1989), and the AMERICAN EXPRESS green credit card, *American Express Co. v. Vibra Approved Laboratories Corp.*, 10 USPQ2d 2006 (SDNY 1989), have all been the subject of dilution protection (as referred to by Laura M. Slenzak, *Dilution Law in the United States and Canada: A Review of the State of the Law and a Proposal for United States Federal Dilution Protection*, 83 TMR 205, 217 (1993)).

A dilution action providing protection to trade dress against unauthorized use on competing goods is particularly needed in the United Kingdom where such an action is apparently not available. The "look-alikes" phenomenon demonstrates the lack of protection in this area. *See* in general Belinda Mills, *Own Label Products and the "Look-Alike" Phenomenon: A Lack of Trade Dress and Unfair Competition Protection?*, 3 EIPR 116 (1995).

[126]The German Federal Supreme Court (Quick case, GRUR 182, 186 (1959)) has eloquently described an action for trademark dilution in the following terms:

> The consideration underlying this special anti-dilution protection is that the owner of such a distinctive mark has a legitimate interest in continuing to maintain the position of exclusivity he acquired through large expenditures of time and money and that everything which could impair the originality and distinctive character of its distinctive mark, as well as the advertising effectiveness derived from its uniqueness, is to be avoided. Its basic purpose is not to prevent any form of confusion but to protect an acquired asset against impairment.

Translation by Gerhard Schricker, *Protection of Famous Trademarks Against Dilution in Germany*, 11 IIC 166, 171 (1980).

a motion picture house, and a restaurant, the likelihood that the TIFFANY mark will still exclusively call to mind its owner's jewelry products becomes increasingly diminished.

Equally, the unauthorized use of a trademark in an offensive or unsavory context could tarnish the ability of the trademark to call to mind the associations of satisfaction and desirability linked with the particular product. In the "4711" perfume case the "4711" mark had become well-known in respect of the plaintiff's perfume. The German Federal Supreme Court had no difficulty in prohibiting the defendant, a sewer company, from using "4711" on a malodorous tank truck despite the fact that the numbers "4711" comprised the defendant's telephone number.

In order to be successful in a claim for trademark dilution, the plaintiff will usually be required to prove (1) that its mark has become famous or possesses a distinctive quality capable of dilution, and (2) a likelihood that such mark will be diluted by "blurring" or "tarnishing."

NOTES AND QUESTIONS

(1) **The Subjects of Dilution Protection.** Should all marks be protected against "diluting" uses? Or should these enhanced quasi-property rights be restricted to a subset of marks? *See* 15 U.S.C. § 1125(c) (protecting "famous marks" against "dilution of the distinctive quality of the mark"). Might this be the context in which to draw a distinction between "famous" marks and "well-known marks"?

(2) **The Meaning of Dilution in International Law.** For which acts of a defendant should an international anti-dilution agreement provide mark-owners with relief? *See* WIPO Model Law on Unfair Competition art. 3 ("[D]ilution of goodwill or reputation" means the lessening of the distinctive character or advertising value of a trademark, trade name or other business identifier, the appearance of a product or the presentation of products or services, or of a celebrity or well-known fictional character."). Under state laws in the United States prior to the enactment of the Federal Dilution Act of 1995, dilution causes of action generally rested upon proof of "blurring" or "tarnishment." The federal statute, although not explicit, has been interpreted as targeting similar acts. *But see* Miles J. Alexander & Michael K. Heilbronner, *Dilution Under Section 43(c) of the Lanham Act*, 59 LAW & CONTEMP. PROBS. 93, 121-25 (1996) (noting that, despite legislative history reference to tarnishment claims, the language of the federal statute may not support tarnishment claims). Is tarnishment a concept that is peculiarly cultural or country specific and not susceptible to international harmonization? Does that matter? Should a harmonization effort accept culturally driven deviations from an international norm provided the general standard of protecting against "tarnishment" is upheld? *Cf.* G.H.C. BODENHAUSEN, GUIDE TO THE APPLICATION OF THE PARIS CONVENTION, 144 (1968) (suggesting that the concept of "unfair competition" under the Paris Convention must be determined by the standards of each

country in which protection is sought). Should such an effort provide only protection against blurring? *See* Robert C. Denicola, *Some Thoughts on the Dynamics of Federal Trademark Legislation and the Trademark Dilution Act of 1995*, 59 LAW & CONTEMP. PROB. 75, 90 (1996) ("Our obligations under the TRIPS Agreement . . . extend at most to protection against unauthorized use of a mark as a trademark. Tarnishment of American marks abroad unrelated to their use as another's trademark has never been a significant trade issue.").

(3) **Free Speech Concerns.** Efforts to enact federal dilution laws met opposition on the grounds that such laws might impose burdens on the exercise of free speech. Such concerns are particularly aroused by "tarnishment"-type claims. The U.S. federal dilution law attempted to accommodate free speech concerns in section 43(c)(4). *See* 15 U.S.C. § 1125(c)(4). It is not always clear, however, even within a single country, what uses are commercial and which implicate broader social or political concerns. *See* San Francisco Arts & Athletics, Inc. v. U. S. Olympic Comm., 483 U.S. 522 (1987) (upholding statutory rights of U.S. Olympic Committee in the word "Olympic" without regard to whether defendant's use was confusing) (enjoining use of term "Gay Olympics"). Given that many countries provide protection for freedom of speech that differs in nature and degree from that accorded in the United States, *see* Matusevich v. Telnikoff, 877 F. Supp. 1 (D.D.C. 1995) (declining to enforce British libel judgment because, if applied in the U.S., British libel law would violate the First Amendment), would it be possible to draft an international agreement on dilution that incorporated free speech limits acceptable to a broad group of countries?

(4) **New Categories of Dilution?** Should other uses of marks be considered actionable? What might they be? *Cf.* John Deere & Co. v. MTD Prods., Inc., 41 F.3d 39 (2d Cir. 1994) (apparently recognizing a third–albeit undefinable–category of dilution); Hormel Foods Corp. v. Jim Henson Prods., 73 F.3d 497, 507 (2d Cir. 1996) (interpreting *Deere* as a "recognition of a broad view of tarnishment"). Mostert suggests that the EU harmonization directive, which premises a cause of action on "taking unfair advantage of the distinctiveness" of a mark, evidences a proprietary rights approach that extends protection beyond blurring and tarnishment. *See* Mostert, *Well-Known and Famous Marks: Is Harmony Possible in the Global Village?, supra* at 136-37. In particular, Mostert mentions a decision of the German Federal Supreme Court enjoining a defendant from "taking an unfair advantage" of the Rolls Royce mark which the defendant wished to use for the promotion of whiskey products. *See Rolls Royce* case (German Federal Supreme Court, 9 Dec. 1982) [1983] GRUR 247, 15 I.I.C. 240 (1984). Is a showing of bad-faith determinative of whether a defendant has taken unfair advantage of another's well-known mark? If the Rolls Royce mark had not been blurred or tarnished (such that the dilution of the mark, as traditionally conceived, was not at issue), to what extent does this decision confer a monopoly status upon the Rolls Royce mark?

1999 WIPO RESOLUTION ON WELL-KNOWN MARKS

It is clear from the materials above that although member countries are now required to implement common obligations under both Article 6*bis* of the Paris Convention and Article 16 of TRIPS, there is no consistency of approach, terminology, or meaning in national laws. To remedy this divergence, in 1995 WIPO convened a Committee of Experts to consider all questions relevant to the correct application of Article 6*bis*. Upon the structural reorganization of WIPO, this work was taken on by the Standing Committee on the Law of Trademarks, Industrial Designs and Geographical Indications ("SCT"). The SCT submitted a draft resolution on well known marks for consideration at a joint meeting of the General Assembly of WIPO and the Assembly of the Paris Union, and in September 1999 the Member States adopted a final version of that resolution.

The resolution, among other things, provides specific criteria for the definition of well-known marks. In part because neither Article 6*bis* of the Paris Convention nor Article 16 of TRIPS defines in detail the concept of a well-known mark, different countries adopt quite disparate approaches to the protection of well-known marks. In some countries, a numerical threshold of recognition (*e.g.*, 80% among relevant members of the public) is required to establish that a mark is well-known; other countries apply less mathematical tests. And, as described above by Mostert, many countries have developed hierarchies of fame, distinguishing among marks that are "famous," "marks with a reputation," and "well-known marks," to mention but a few of the concepts; in these countries, a different scope of rights attaches to a mark depending upon where it falls in the hierarchy.

Under the resolution, regard should be had to various non-exclusive factors including: the degree of knowledge or recognition of the mark in the relevant sector of the public, including actual and potential consumers, persons involved in channels of distribution of the goods in question, and business circles dealing with such goods; duration, extent, and geographical area of use (or advertising or promotion) of the mark; duration and geographical area of any registrations for the mark; the record of enforcement of rights in the mark; and, any value associated with the mark. *Compare* 15 U.S.C. § 1125(c)(1) (listing factors to be considered in determining whether mark is "famous" for purpose of protection against dilution). Excerpts from the resolution, and from the debate in the Assembly that preceded its adoption, follow.

JOINT RESOLUTION CONCERNING
PROVISIONS ON THE PROTECTION OF WELL-KNOWN MARKS
General Report of the Assemblies of the Member States of WIPO,
34th Annual Meeting, Doc. A/34/16 ¶¶ 171-83 (Sept. 1999)

The Delegation of Paraguay, speaking on behalf of the Latin American and Caribbean Group, supported the text of the Joint Recommendation, as an additional element to the highest level of protection for well-known marks. It considered that the provisions adopted by the Standing Committee on Trademarks would be useful in assuring recognition and protection of well-known marks. As some delegations of its Group had expressed objections to the content of specific provisions, . . . the delegation requested that these be reflected in the Report of the General Assembly. The [twelve] countries which did not join the consensus in the Standing Committee on Trademarks with respect to particular provisions are enumerated in paragraph 8 of the [Memorandum by the Director-General Regarding Joint Resolution Concerning Provisions on the Protection of Well-Known Marks, Doc. A/34/13 (Aug. 4, 1999)].

The Delegation of Indonesia, speaking on behalf of the Asian Group, stated that its Group could support the amended Joint Recommendation. However, as many delegations still had reservations on specific provisions, it hoped that the Joint Recommendation could be reviewed at an appropriate time in the future to address these concerns.

The Delegation of Uganda, speaking on behalf of the African Group, stated that, while the proposed Joint Recommendation addressed some of its concerns, the Group supported the proposed text in the spirit of compromise.

The Delegation of Japan, speaking on behalf of Group B, stated that adoption of the Joint Recommendation was a significant step in the protection of well-known marks, and that its Group supported the text as suggested.

. . . .

The Delegation of Argentina stated that it could join the consensus on the basis of the proposed compromise. The delegation did not, [however], consider the work of the Standing Committee on the Law of Trademarks to have been satisfactory, as the provisions had been adopted with a large number of reservations. . . . The delegation considered that, from a legal point of view, no process whose purpose was to develop international provisions within the ambit of WIPO, or the provisions deriving therefrom, should establish links binding the Member States of the Organization to other conventions, agreements or treaties that were not under its jurisdiction, or with other intergovernmental organizations. Such links might seriously endanger the international legal responsibility of WIPO Member States, as well as create a legal insecurity generating the opposite results to those intended. The delegation of Argentina said that it subscribed to the concept expounded by another delegation in the course of the Assemblies' debates, to the effect that the creation of de facto norms should be avoided. . . . The delegation added that such approaches [as were being contemplated by the Organization regarding the "progressive development of the law"] require permanent transparency of the negotiation and decision-making processes, as well as a clear vision of the objectives. In this respect, the delegation reiterated the need for the WIPO General Assembly to define a mechanism, open to all Member States, within which the progressive development of law could be studied and discussed in order to reach solutions acceptable to all.

The Delegation of Spain recognized the importance of protection of well-known marks. Although it had difficulties with Article 4(1)(b) of the provisions, it could join the consensus concerning the Joint Recommendation.

The Delegation of Japan recalled that the provisions on well-known marks had been discussed for over five years by experts, and that industry circles needed to protect well-known marks. The delegation regretted that the original

Joint Resolution was not adopted, but joined the consensus to contribute to the protection of well-known marks.

. . . .

The International Bureau read out a statement submitted by the Delegation of Sweden, which welcomed the Joint Recommendation and considered it important. It noted that the provisions had the nature of a non-binding recommendation and, in general, supported its contents. . . .

The General Assembly and the Assembly of the Paris Union approved the following Joint Recommendation by consensus:

Joint Recommendation

The Assembly of the Paris Union for the Protection of Industrial Property and the General Assembly of the World Intellectual Property Organization (WIPO),

Taking into account the provisions of the Paris Convention for the Protection of Industrial Property relative to the protection of well-known marks;

Recommend that each Member State may consider the use of any of the provisions adopted by the Standing Committee on the Law of Trademarks, Industrial Designs and Geographical Indications (SCT) at its Second Session, Second Part, as guidelines for the protection for well-known marks;

It is further recommended to each Member State of the Paris Union or of WIPO which is also a member of a regional intergovernmental organization that has competence in the area of registration of trademarks, to bring to the attention of that organization the possibility of protecting well-known marks in accordance, *mutatis mutandis*, with the provisions contained herein.

. . . .

Article 2

Determination of Whether a Mark is a Well-Known Mark in a Member State

(1)(a) [Factors for Consideration] In determining whether a mark is a well-known mark, the competent authority shall take into account any circumstances from which it may be inferred that the mark is well known.

(b) In particular, the competent authority shall consider information submitted to it with respect to factors from which it may be inferred that the mark is, or is not, well known, including, but not limited to, information concerning the following:

1. the degree of knowledge or recognition of the mark in the relevant sector of the public;

2. the duration, extent and geographical area of any use of the mark;

3. the duration, extent and geographical area of any promotion of the mark, including advertising or publicity and the presentation, at fairs or exhibitions, of the goods and/or services to which the mark applies;

4. the duration and geographical area of any registrations, and/or any applications for registration, of the mark, to the extent that they reflect use or recognition of the mark;

5. the record of successful enforcement of rights in the mark, in particular, the extent to which the mark was recognized as well known by competent authorities;

6. the value associated with the mark.

(c) The above factors, which are guidelines to assist the competent authority to determine whether the mark is a well-known mark, are not pre-conditions for reaching that determination. Rather, the determination in each case will depend upon the particular circumstances of that case. In some cases all of the factors may be relevant. In other cases some of the factors may be relevant. In still other cases none of the factors may be relevant, and the decision may be based on additional factors that are not listed in subparagraph (b), above. Such additional factors may be relevant, alone, or in combination with one or more of the factors listed in subparagraph (b), above.

(2)(a) [Relevant Sector of the Public]. Relevant sectors of the public shall include, but shall not necessarily be limited to:

(i) actual and/or potential consumers of the type of goods and/or services to which the mark applies;

(ii) persons involved in channels of distribution of the type of goods and/or services to which the mark applies;

(iii) business circles dealing with the type of goods and/or services to which the mark applies.

(b) Where a mark is determined to be well known in at least one relevant sector of the public in a Member State, the mark shall be considered by the Member State to be a well-known mark.

(c) Where a mark is determined to be known in at least one relevant sector of the public in a Member State, the mark may be considered by the Member State to be a well-known mark.

(d) A Member State may determine that a mark is a well-known mark, even if the mark is not well known or, if the Member States applies subparagraph (c), known, in any relevant sector of the public of the Member State.

(3)(a) [Factors Which Shall Not Be Required] A Member State shall not require, as a condition for determining whether a mark is a well-known mark:

(i) that the mark has been used in, or that the mark has been registered or that an application for registration of the mark has been filed in or in respect of, the Member State;

(ii) that the mark is well known in, or that the mark has been registered or that an application for registration of the mark has been filed in or in respect of, any jurisdiction other than the Member State; or

(iii) that the mark is well known by the public at large in the Member State.

(b) Notwithstanding subparagraph (a)(ii), a Member State may, for the purpose of applying paragraph (2)(d), require that the mark be well known in one or more jurisdictions other than the Member State.

Article 3

Protection of Well-Known Marks; Bad Faith

(1) A Member State shall protect a well-known mark against conflicting marks, business identifiers and domain names, at least with effect from the time when the mark has become well known in the Member State.

(2) Bad faith may be considered as one factor among others in assessing competing interests in applying [Articles 3-6] of these Provisions.

Article 4

Conflicting Marks

(1)(a) A mark shall be deemed to be in conflict with a well-known mark where that mark, or an essential part thereof, constitutes a reproduction, an imitation, a translation, or a transliteration, liable to create confusion, of the well-known mark, if the mark, or an essential part thereof, is used, is the subject of an application for registration, or is registered, in respect of goods and/or services which are identical or similar to the goods and/or services to which the well-known mark applies.

(b) Irrespective of the goods and/or services for which a mark is used, is the subject of an application for registration, or is registered, that mark shall be deemed to be in conflict with a well-known mark where the mark, or an essential part thereof, constitutes a reproduction, an imitation, a translation, or a transliteration of the well-known mark, and where at least one of the following conditions is fulfilled:

(i) the use of that mark would indicate a connection between the goods and/or services for which the mark is used, is the subject of an application for registration, or is registered, and the owner of the well-known mark, and would be likely to damage his interests;

(ii) the use of that mark is likely to impair or dilute in an unfair manner the distinctive character of the well-known mark;

(iii) the use of that mark would take unfair advantage of the distinctive character of the well-known mark.

(c) Notwithstanding Article 2(3)(a)(iii), for the purpose of applying paragraph (1)(b)(ii) and (iii) [of this Article], a Member State may require that the well-known mark be well known by the public at large.

(d) Notwithstanding paragraphs (2) to (4), a Member State shall not be required to apply:

(i) paragraph (1)(a) to determine whether a mark is in conflict with a well-known mark, if the mark was used or registered, or an application for its registration was filed, in or in respect of the Member State, in respect of goods and/or services which are identical or similar to the goods and/or services to which the well-known mark applies, before the well-known mark became well known in the Member State;

(ii) paragraph (1)(b) to determine whether a mark is in conflict with a well-known mark, to the extent that the mark was used, was the subject of an application for registration, or was registered, in or in respect of the Member State for particular goods and/or services, before the well-known mark became well known in the Member State;

except where the mark has been used or registered, or the application for its registration has been filed, in bad faith.

(2) If the applicable law allows third parties to oppose the registration of a mark, a conflict with a well-known mark under paragraph (1)(a) shall constitute a ground for opposition.

(3)(a) The owner of a well-known mark shall be entitled to request, during a period which shall not be less than five years beginning from the date on which the fact of registration was made known to the public by the Office, the invalidation, by a decision of the competent authority, of the registration of a mark which is in conflict with the well-known mark.

(b) If the registration of a mark may be invalidated by a competent authority on its own initiative, a conflict with a well-known mark shall, during a period which shall not be less than five years beginning from the date on which the fact of registration was made known to the public by the Office, be a ground for such invalidation.

(4) [Prohibition of Use] The owner of a well-known mark shall be entitled to request the prohibition, by a decision of the competent authority, of the use of a mark which is in conflict with the well-known mark. Such request shall be admissible for a period which shall not be less than five years beginning from the time the owner of the well-known mark had knowledge of the use of the conflicting mark.

(5) [No Time Limit in Case of Registration or Use in Bad Faith] (a) Notwithstanding paragraph (3), a Member State may not prescribe any time limit for requesting the invalidation of the registration of a mark which is in conflict with a well-known mark if the conflicting mark was registered in bad faith.

(b) Notwithstanding paragraph (4), a Member State may not prescribe any time limit for requesting the prohibition of the use of a mark which is in conflict with a well-known mark if the conflicting mark was used in bad faith.

(c) In determining bad faith for the purposes of this paragraph, the competent authority shall take into consideration whether the person who obtained the registration of or used the mark which is in conflict with a well-known mark had, at the time when the mark was used or registered, or the application for its registration was filed, knowledge of, or reason to know of, the well-known mark.

(6) [No Time Limit in Case of Registration Without Use] Notwithstanding paragraph (3), a Member State may not prescribe any time limit for requesting

the invalidation of the registration of a mark which is in conflict with a well-known mark, if that mark was registered, but never used.

. . . .

Article 6
Conflicting Domain Names

(1) [Conflicting Domain Names] A domain name shall be deemed to be in conflict with a well-known mark at least where that domain name, or an essential part thereof, constitutes a reproduction, an imitation, a translation, or a transliteration of the well-known mark, and the domain name has been registered or used in bad faith.

(2) [Cancellation; Transfer] The owner of a well-known mark shall be entitled to request, by a decision of the competent authority, that the registrant of the conflicting domain name cancel the registration, or transfer it to the owner of the well-known mark.

NOTES AND QUESTIONS

(1) **Extensions of TRIPS?** In enacting the Federal Trademark Dilution Act of 1995, Congress suggested that TRIPS mandated protection against dilution for famous marks. The articles in the resolution explicitly require dilution protection for well known marks in language that goes beyond Article 16(3) of TRIPS. *See* Article 4(1)(b)(ii)-(iii). The Notes accompanying the draft provisions indicated that these provisions are intended to catch not only acts of blurring and tarnishment but also "free riding" on the goodwill of the well known mark. *See* Draft Provisions on the Protection of Well Known Marks 21 (Standing Committee on the Law of Trademarks, Industrial Designs and Geographical Indications, Second Session, Second Part, June 7-12, 1999) (May 10, 1999, WIPO Doc. SCT/2/8). Should the United States implement the changes suggested by the resolution? What changes in U.S. law would be required? Does the content of this resolution, and the debate before which it was adopted, provide clarity to doubts that you may have had regarding the interpretation of Article 6*bis* of Paris and Article 16 of TRIPS?

(2) **The Role of Soft Law**. Although the SCT believed it preferable in the long term that the provisions be incorporated in a treaty, the resolution procedure was used in order to permit WIPO to react more quickly to developments and to avoid what the Organization sees as the lengthier process of drafting treaties. While a resolution is non-binding on member states, WIPO officials have expressed the view that members will be "under a moral obligation" to comply with the recommendations contained in the resolution. Is this a good way to develop international trademark law? (Although this resolution takes the form of non binding "soft" law, its provisions have been given significant play by intellectual property holders seeking to obtain protection for well-known marks

in ICANN discussions.) How persuasive are the concerns expressed by the Argentinian delegation? What concerns underlie the intervention by that delegation?

[G] The TRIPS Agreement

PAUL J. HEALD, TRADEMARKS AND GEOGRAPHICAL INDICATIONS: EXPLORING THE CONTOURS OF THE TRIPS AGREEMENT*
29 VAND. J. TRANSNAT'L L. 635 (1996)

. . . In general, . . . the most substantial changes in trademark protection [required by TRIPS] will occur outside the United States, brought about by augmented substantive standards and vastly improved enforcement procedures. The TRIPS trademark sections could go further to ensure the free flow of goods and services, but, overall, U.S. businesses and consumers should be pleased.

. . . .

[Substantive Standards]

Part I of the TRIPS Agreement requires members of the World Trade Organization (WTO) to adopt the minimum standards of protection detailed in the Paris Convention [Art. 1] and Part II of the Agreement [Art. 2]. It also allows member states to implement trademark protection beyond the minimum standards, but requires that each member state must extend the same augmented rights to non-nationals of other member states as to its nationals.[9] [The Agreement] not only prevents a member from preferring its own citizens over non-nationals from other member states but also generally prohibits discrimination between nationals of different member states. Therefore, with some exceptions, any advantage granted "by a Member to the nationals of any other country shall be accorded immediately and unconditionally to the nationals of all other Members."

. . . .

1. Definition of "Trademark"

Unlike the Paris Convention, Article 15(1) of the TRIPS Agreement begins its trademark provisions with a broad definition of "protectable subject matter" that includes "[a]ny sign . . . capable of distinguishing . . . goods or services of one undertaking from those of other undertakings . . . ." The definition of "signs" includes not only word marks but also "personal names, letters, numerals,

---

*Copyright 1996, Paul J. Heald; Vanderbilt Journal of Transnational Law. Reprinted with permission.

[9]See TRIPS, art. 3 (subject to any exceptions contained in the Paris Convention). . . . The Lanham Act already provides this protection in the United States for foreign nationals. See 15 U.S.C. § 1126(b).

figurative elements, and combinations of colors." The requirement that a mark be "capable of distinguishing" goods clearly excludes generic "marks" from the definition. Unfortunately for those seeking protection for their trade dress, Article 15 does not include product shape or packaging in its definition, although some protection may be available through the incorporation of the unfair competition principles of the Paris Convention.

2. *Eligibility for Registration*

Article 15 also makes "signs," as therein defined, prima facie eligible for trademark registration. Member states may, however, condition registration of descriptive marks upon proof of secondary meaning, and they may require that a mark be "visually perceptible." Article 15 also requires other factors relevant under the Paris Convention to be considered in the decision to register. Therefore, registration of certain flags and emblems is prohibited, and member states may deny registration to deceptive marks, to those confusingly similar to marks already properly registered by another,[27] and to those that "designate the kind, quality, intended purpose, value, [and] place of origin of the goods." Paris Convention, art. 6*quinquies*(B)(2). . . .

. . . .

3. *Rights of Registrants*

[Article 16 sets out the rights that must be accorded a trademark owner, but other provisions permit member states to recognize important exceptions to those rights. For example, under Article 17], a member state may permit a fair use of a mark that consists of descriptive terms. . . .

. . . .

Other limitations apply through the incorporation of the Paris Convention. For example, a registered trademark can be subject to preexisting rights established by another entity in the country in which protection is claimed.[57] This is consistent with the Lanham Act provision that if a business has used a mark in good faith in the United States, then the rights acquired by a subsequent registration of the mark by another entity are subject to the prior use. This result is permitted by the TRIPS Agreement but not dictated by it—a member state may establish a strict first-to-file system. . . .

4. *Assignments and Licensing*

Unlike the Paris Convention and the Lanham Act, the TRIPS Agreement unequivocally grants trademark owners the right to assign their trademarks

---

[27] *See* Paris Convention, arts. 6*quinquies*(B)(3), 10*bis*(3).
[57] *See* Paris Convention, art. 6*quinquies*(B)(1).

"with or without the transfer of the business to which the trademark belongs."[60] In some cases, Article 21 could be interpreted to allow the assignment of a trademark without its attendant goodwill; under the Lanham Act and at common law, this transaction would result in the abandonment of the mark. For example, the owner of the mark "Mondo-Choc Cookies" might sell its mark without transferring the cookie recipe (a trade secret), the unique machines necessary to make the cookies, or any other of its assets (*i.e.*, all the things that constitute the owner's "business"). In this scenario, the goodwill attendant to the trademark has not been transferred by the owner; the assignment of the mark, therefore, is void as against public policy and the mark is abandoned. Article 21 of the TRIPS Agreement may suggest a different result.[63] Congress has not amended the Lanham Act to provide for such assignments.

Finally, [Article 21 of] the TRIPS Agreement prohibits compulsory licensing of trademarks, something that has never been allowed under U.S. domestic law, but which was permissible under the Paris Convention.[67] Members are also prohibited [by Article 20] from requiring a foreign trademark to be tied to a domestic mark in order to be registered.

. . . .

[Enforcement Provisions]

Several commentators have noted that the enforcement provisions of the TRIPS Agreement are the most promising sections in the Agreement. Under [Article 9(6) of] the Paris Convention, a country was under no obligation to enact legislation permitting seizure or prohibiting importation of infringing goods. [Article 41(1) of] the TRIPS Agreement mandates that "Members shall ensure that enforcement procedures . . . permit effective action against any act of infringement . . . covered by this Agreement," including injunctive relief, money damages, and strong border control measures. Members must also provide for criminal prosecution–including seizure, forfeiture, and destruction of infringing goods–in cases of willful trademark counterfeiting. The procedures and safeguards for stopping infringing goods at the border are spelled out in detail and should greatly improve a trademark owner's ability to stop the flow of infringing goods in international commerce.

. . . .

---

[60]TRIPS, art. 21. *But see* Paris Convention, art. *6quater*(1) (requiring "transfer of the business or goodwill to which the mark belongs").

[63]One could argue, however, that Article 21 of the TRIPS Agreement only negates the Paris Convention requirement of the transfer of "the business," leaving intact the disjunctive requirement of the transfer of "the goodwill." *See* Paris Convention, art. *6quater*(1). This interpretation would strongly reinforce the prior clear need to assign the goodwill along with the trademark.

[67]*See* Paris Convention, art. 5(c). . . .

II. A Normative Critique of the TRIPS Agreement

No international agreement can be perfect, and the TRIPS accord is no exception. While some portions of the Agreement deserve applause, others are less satisfying.

. . . .

The TRIPS Agreement is good news for trademark owners around the world. Under the Paris Convention, the substantive levels of protection were lower, enforcement procedures were not absolutely required, and no credible body existed to resolve inter-sovereign disputes. TRIPS establishes substantive levels of protection that are at least equal to those of the Lanham Act, and requires adequate enforcement mechanisms to be put in place in all member states. Best of all, the WTO monitors a dispute resolution process, providing a forum for the sanction and coercion of noncomplying nations.

One should not expect official noncompliance to be an overwhelming problem. The protection afforded trademarks under TRIPS does not merely benefit corporations in a few wealthy nations, but prevents marketplace confusion that is detrimental to the interests of consumers in every nation. People who buy jeans in Brazil, Thailand, and Poland, for example, should all benefit from increased honesty in labeling. Even a country that exports significant amounts of counterfeit goods has incentives to comply, given the benefit of increased protection for its own consumers. Unlike copyright and patent protection, which impose high, short-term costs on consumers, trademark law increases consumer wealth by improving consumer information. The myth that trademark protection under a confusion rationale results in higher prices (or other monopolistic practices to the detriment of consumers) was convincingly exploded long ago. Of course, corruption of officials by traders in counterfeit goods may be a problem, and locales that remain unreasonably dubious about the benefits of protection may resist. . . .

. . . .

One . . . disappointing aspect of the TRIPS Agreement, and one that is unlikely to be changed, is the movement toward registration of trademarks without use. Although a member state is not required to permit registration of trademarks that have never been, and may never be, used in commerce, neither is it required to make use a prerequisite for registration [Art. 15(3)]. The economic rationale for requiring use before registration is quite compelling. Without a use requirement, an incentive exists for entrepreneurs to register large numbers of trademarks and license them to others.[158] As Landes and Posner note, "The 'banking' of trademarks in countries such as Japan that have a pure registration system does occur and has made it more costly to enter markets in those countries." As noted above, GATT is supposed to make the penetration of new goods into markets easier, not more difficult. Furthermore, basing the

---

[158]"A firm allowed to register trademarks without using them might invest substantial resources in thinking up plausible new brand names. . . . The ownership of a vast number of them, and the aggregate licensing revenues that such ownership would command, would be a magnet drawing resources into the activity of creating brand names, probably beyond the optimal level of such investment." Landes & Posner, [*An Economic Analysis of Trademark Law*] at 281.

property right on use is consistent with the underlying social function of trademarks–identifying and distinguishing goods. When a good is not available for sale, the trademark cannot confer a benefit. "Thus, conditioning trademark rights on use is a way of limiting the use of scarce enforcement resources to situations in which the rights in question are likely to yield net social benefits."[160] Requiring use before registration would probably generate an efficiency gain that would benefit international markets.

III. Conclusion

The TRIPS Agreement is a significant improvement over prior ineffectual regimes governing the international protection of intellectual property. Although TRIPS' sections on geographical indications create uncertainty and TRIPS fails to endorse gray market goods or to require that trademark registration be predicated on actual use in commerce, the Agreement mandates high substantive standards and effective enforcement that should foster both the development and movement of goods and technology. Although U.S. trademark law is still not quite in compliance with all of the mandates of the TRIPS Agreement, its deviations from the mandated standards are relatively unimportant. The fact that Congress felt it had to make only two minor amendments to the Lanham Act indicates the great extent to which the TRIPS Agreement mirrors U.S. federal law. As a result, in the next ten years,[161] U.S. trademark owners doing business overseas will be encountering legal systems that look more and more like their own.

Please read Article 2(1) and Article 15-21 of the TRIPS Agreement, which are reproduced in the Documentary Supplement.

NOTES AND QUESTIONS

(1) **Restrictions on Use Requirements.** Article 15(3), while permitting registration (or renewal) to be conditioned on actual use of the mark in commerce, prohibits use as a prerequisite to an application. Member states must therefore adopt either a registration-based system or permit intent-to-use applications. Article 15 requires member states to afford applicants at least three years to make any required use of the mark before the application can be rejected for non-use. *Compare* Paris Convention art. 5(C)(1) (requiring

---

[160]*Id.* at 282. Landes and Posner note, however, that: "The solution is not ideal; it could lead to the premature development and marketing of goods by a firm eager to establish a right in a nifty trademark. But if the elasticity of supply of brand names is as high as we believe, very few individual trademarks will be so valuable apart from the products that they name that a firm will distort its marketing decisions in order to appropriate a particular name."

[161]*See* TRIPS, art. 66 (least developed country members have up to ten years to comply with substantive TRIPS standards).

"reasonable period"). Does the Lanham Act comply with this provision? *See* 15 U.S.C. § 1051(d). *Compare* Trademarks Act (Canada) § 40(3) (declarations of use to be filed by the later of six months after Notice of Allowance and three years after date of application). A former Deputy Commissioner has suggested that the trademark bar consider whether the period for which intent-to-use applicants might extend their obligation to file a statement of use should be shortened. *See* Phillip G. Hampton, *Remarks to All Ohio Annual Institute on Intellectual Property* (Cincinnati, Sept. 11, 1997). What alternatives might the U.S. PTO consider, short of reducing the period during which to file a statement of use, that would encourage earlier attention to Notices of Allowance while complying with obligations under TRIPS?

(2) **Abandonment**. Article 19 of the TRIPS Agreement requires that if "use is required to maintain a registration, the registration may be canceled only after an uninterrupted period of at least three years of non-use." As a consequence, the abandonment provision in the Lanham Act, under which a set period of nonuse gives rise to a presumption of abandonment was, amended from two to three years. This presumptive period does not , however, wholly define the approach of U.S. law to abandonment through nonuse. In particular, the definition provides that abandonment occurs when "use has been discontinued with intent not to resume such use." Intent may be presumed after three years, but it may be found to exist before that period. Does the Lanham Act violate Article 19 of TRIPS? *See* Heald, *supra*, at 653 (arguing that "given that most cancellations for abandonment proceed under the statutory presumption rather than after proof of intent to abandon, this incongruence between TRIPS and U.S. federal law may not prove particularly troublesome"). Article 19(1) requires non-use to be excused when it is the result of circumstances "arising independently of the will of the" trademark owner that are "obstacles to the use of the trademark," such as import restrictions or other government requirements for the goods upon which the trademark is used.

(3) **Trademark Subject Matter**. The expansion in protectable trademark subject matter that culminated in the U.S. in the *Qualitex v. Jacobsen*, 514 U.S. 159 (1995) decision has been reflected at the international level. Article 15 of the TRIPS Agreement provides that:

> Any sign, or any combination of signs, capable of distinguishing the goods or services of one undertaking from those of other undertakings, shall be capable of constituting a trademark. Such signs, in particular words including personal names, letters, numerals, figurative elements and combinations of colours as well as any combination of such signs, shall be eligible for registration as trademarks. . . . Members may require, as a condition of registration, that signs be visually perceptible.

See also EC Trademark Harmonisation Directive, Council Directive 89/104, [1989] O.J. L40/1, art. 2 ("A trademark may consist of any sign capable of being represented graphically, particularly words, including personal names, designs, letters, numerals, the shape of goods or their packaging, provided that such signs are capable of distinguishing the goods or services of one undertaking from those of other undertaking."); EC Trademark Regulation, Council Regulation 40/94, [1994] O.J. L11/1, art. 4. Should (or could) these definitions of trademark subject-matter be any broader? *Cf. In re* Clarke, 17 U.S.P.Q.2d 1238 (T.T.A.B. 1990) (olfactory marks may be registered); Sumitomo Rubber Indus., Trade Mark No. 6,106,1361 (U.K.) (registration of smell of roses applied to tires), *reported in* SWEET & MAXWELL'S EUROPEAN TRADE MARK LITIGATION HANDBOOK 565 (Isabel Davies ed., 1998). Over sixty countries now permit registration of three dimensional marks as trademarks. *See* Thomas Helbling, *Shapes as Trade Marks?–The Struggle to Register Three-Dimensional Signs: A Comparative Study of United Kingdom and Swiss Law*, 1997 INTELL. PROP. Q. 413, 413. Why do you think that the definition of trademark in TRIPS did not include product design, as both the United States and the European Union had proposed in their respective drafts of the provision?

(4) **Grounds for Refusal to Register**. Refusal of protection is permissible only to the extent that the grounds do not conflict with the provisions of the Paris Convention. *See* TRIPS Agreement art. 15(2). Thus, if registration in the country in question would infringe on the prior rights of third parties, if the mark lacks distinctiveness or consists exclusively of descriptive terms, or if the mark is contrary to accepted principles of morality or public order, or if it would deceive the public, registration may be denied. *See* Paris Convention art. 6*quinquies*(B)(1)-(3).

(5) **Trademark Registration Procedures**. Article 15 of TRIPS requires that Member States publish trademarks that are registered and provide an opportunity for cancellation proceedings; but it does not mandate the type of pre-issuance opposition proceedings available under section 13 of the Lanham Act. The procedural rules governing application, registration, and cancellation proceedings are largely left to member states, subject to compliance with the general principles stated in Article 62(1) to (5) and Article 41. Article 5 of TRIPS provides that national treatment and MFN status do not apply to procedures for the acquisition and maintenance of rights outlined in treaties concluded under the auspices of the WIPO (*i.e.*, the Madrid Agreement, the Madrid Protocol, or the Trademark Registration Treaty).

(6) **Licensing**. National approaches to licensing issues are left largely unregulated by TRIPS. Article 20 permits member states to require mark owners to indicate that the product has been manufactured by a licensee or other party. *See also* TRIPS Agreement art. 40(2) (members may specify in their national legislation appropriate measures to prevent or control licensing practices that restrict competition, have adverse effects on trade, or impede the transfer or dissemination of technology). Under Article 19(2), however, use of a trademark by another person shall be recognized as a valid use on condition it is done under the control of the trademark owner (*e.g.*, by a licensee or related company). Licensing rules are also subject to the national treatment provisions, such that foreign licensees cannot be subjected to more burdensome conditions than domestic licensees. Finally, Article 21 prohibits compulsory licensing.

The public official charged with enforcement of the Canadian Competition Act recently sought to compel a trademark owner to license use of its trademark as part of the remedies for an alleged violation of competition law. *See* Director of

Investigation and Research v. Tele-Direct (Publications) Inc., et al,. (1997) 73 CPR (3d) 1. Tele-Direct owned the marks YELLOW PAGES and WALKING FINGER for advertising services and telephone directories, and published telephone directories for telephone companies throughout Canada. The competition authorities asserted that by refusing to license use of the marks to selected competing suppliers of advertising services, Tele-Direct was abusing its trademark rights and engaging in anticompetitive acts. The competition authorities sought an order that the mark owner "license, at the request of independent advertising agencies, including consultants, and on commercially reasonable terms and conditions, the trademarks registered for [the mark owner's] own use in relation to telephone directories." These efforts were rejected by the Canadian Competition Tribunal. The Tribunal concluded that a refusal to license a trademark to certain persons was not an anticompetitive act; indeed, section 79(5) of the Canadian Competition Act explicitly provides that the mere assertion of an intellectual property right, even if exclusionary in effect, did not of itself amount to a misuse of trademark. The Tribunal accordingly did not need to consider whether, if it had found selective licensing to be a violation of the Competition Act, it had jurisdiction to grant the relief requested. It did note, however, that the selective licensing of trademarks was consistent with the statutory trademark scheme. For a discussion of the *Tele-Direct* decision, see Sheldon Burshtein, *Trademark Owners May Choose Licensees in Canada*, TRADEMARK WORLD, Mar. 1998, at 16. Would the grant of the relief requested by the Canadian competition authorities if ordered against a foreign trademark owner be a violation of TRIPS? *See* TRIPS Agreement art. 21. What if the relief were ordered against a Canadian trademark owner? How, without using compulsory licensing, might trademark law address the potentially anticompetitive effects of granting rights in the mark YELLOW PAGES for telephone directories? (You might consider whether YELLOW PAGES and the WALKING FINGERS logo for telephone directories are protected in the U.S. *See* BellSouth Corp. v. White Directory Pubs. Inc., 49 U.S.P.Q.2d 1801 (M.D.N.C. 1999).) Should the means by which the potentially anticompetitive effects of mark ownership is addressed affect analysis of TRIPS compliance?

Similar efforts by the U.S. competition authorities to order compulsory licensing of trademarks were rebuffed twenty years earlier. *See In re* Borden, 92 F.T.C. 669 (1976), *rev'd*, 92 F.T.C. 807 (1978). *See generally* F.M. Scherer, *The Posnerian Harvest: Separating Wheat from Chaff*, 86 YALE L.J. 974 (1977). Why has the U.S. Court of Appeals for the Seventh Circuit called the notion of compulsory licensing of trademarks "absurd"? *See* Jack Walters & Sons Corp. v. Morton Bldg., Inc., 737 F.2d 698, 704 (7th Cir. 1984). Copyrights and patents may, in certain circumstances, be subject to compulsory licensing; what makes trademark law different? The Canadian immunization of liability for mere assertion of intellectual property rights is largely replicated in the United States, *see* Professional Real Estate Investors v. Columbia Pictures, 508 U.S. 49 (1993), but this does not mean that anticompetitive provisions attached to a trademark license will be free from challenge under U.S. law. Moreover, the Lanham Act does enables defendants to resist an infringement action on the ground that the trademark owner is using the mark in such a way as to violate the antitrust laws. *See* 15 U.S.C. § 1083(b)(7). This defense has, however, rarely been invoked. *See* Daniel M. McClure, *Trademarks and Competition: The Recent History*, 59 LAW & CONTEMP. PROBS. 13, 25 n.80 (1996).

(7) **Encumbrances Upon Trademark Use**. Article 20 of TRIPS provides that "the use of a trademark in the course of trade shall not be unjustifiably encumbered by special requirements, such as use with another trademark, use in a special form, or use in a manner detrimental to its capability to distinguish the goods or services of one undertaking from those of other undertakings." If the European Commission, as part of its efforts to regulate health and safety, informed pharmaceutical companies that to market drugs in the European Union they must own a trademark common to all countries of the EU (and point to the Community Trademark Regulation when objection is made), would Article 20 of TRIPS be violated? Under Article 20, can member states require that any trademark used on tobacco be accompanied by a health warning? Can a member state prohibit the use of trademarks commonly associated with tobacco on goods sold to minors? If the Mexican drug law effectively declared pharmaceutical trademarks as generic (permitting or requiring pharmacists to fill the prescription for a branded drug with a generic equivalent), would this violate TRIPS?

(8) **Assignment**. Section 10 of the Lanham Act provides that "a registered mark or a mark for which application to register has been filed shall be assignable with the goodwill of the business in which the mark is used, or with that part of the goodwill of the business connected with the use of and symbolized by the mark." Does this provision comply with Article 21? *See* TRIPS Agreement art. 21 (providing that an owner must be free to assign its trademark, with or without transferring the business to which the trademark belongs). Might it violate Article 21 in certain circumstances but not others?

(9) **Permissible Third Party Use**. The provision in Article 17 that allows states to permit third parties use of a trademark in cases of fair use or for use as a descriptive term is conditioned upon such provisions taking into account the legitimate interests of the trademark owner and of third parties. What does this mean?

[H]   Regional Trademark Agreements (I): The Benelux Convention on Trade Marks

The Benelux Convention on Trade Marks, concluded on March 19, 1962 between the three Benelux Member States, Belgium, Luxembourg, and the Netherlands, established uniform trademark laws throughout those three countries. The process of harmonization went beyond an approximation of legislation, however, and the Benelux Court of Justice was established by a treaty signed in Brussels on March 13, 1965. It is composed of judges of the supreme courts of each of those three states. Under Article 6(3) of that treaty and Article 10 of the Trade Marks Convention, the national courts are bound to submit questions on the interpretation of the Uniform Benelux Law on Trademarks to the Benelux Court for a preliminary ruling. Article 7(2) of the same treaty provides that national courts which then give judgment in the case shall be bound by the interpretation given in the judgment delivered by the

Benelux Court. The provisions of the uniform Benelux trademark law have had significant influence on the development of EU trademark law, such as the EU Trademark Harmonization Directive. Taking this process further, since January 1, 1971, the Netherlands, Belgium, and Luxembourg have had a unitary trademark system. Again, this can be seen as a precursor to the CTM system of the EU described *infra* § 6.05[A].

[I]   Regional Trademark Agreements (II): The European Union

[1] An Introduction to Trademark Reform in the EU

From the earliest days of the European Communities, the Commission has sought to harmonize trademark law throughout the Community. Increases in intra-community trade suggested the need for a system that facilitated the EU-wide marketing and distribution of goods and services. Disparate national trademark laws often served instead to impede the free movement of goods throughout the Community by imposing additional costs, complexities, and uncertainties on trademark owners; and territorial rights threatened to partition the common market that was at the center of the European project. The ideal solution to these problems was the creation of a Community Trade Mark ("CTM"), granting a unitary right throughout the entire EU, which eventually was realized in 1996. But the Commission accepted that national trademark laws would (and should) continue to exist, and thus sought to minimize the differences that existed among those laws by adopting a harmonization directive. The Trademark Harmonization Directive was adopted in 1988, well in advance of the adoption of the Regulation on the Community Trademark creating the CTM. (The CTM system is separately considered in Chapter 6.) Member states were obliged to implement the provisions of the directive in their national laws by 1992.

The substantive principles underlying the directive mirror those in the later-adopted regulation establishing the CTM system; many provisions in the directive (e.g., those dealing with registrability of trademarks and the scope of rights) use precisely the same language as found in the regulation. But the regulation contains a more extensive set of trademark rules. The harmonization achieved by the 1988 directive was consciously a limited harmonization of national trademark laws. (The directive is portentously entitled the "First Trademark Harmonisation Directive.") These limits take two primary forms. First, various issues of national trademark law are not addressed in the directive. For example, the directive harmonizes only laws concerning registered trademarks; member states remain free to offer disparate protection (or no protection) to marks based upon use, and are entitled to leave in place whatever protections against unfair competition they each feel are appropriate. The directive also leaves questions of procedure concerning registration, nullity, and invalidity of trademarks to individual states. And member states may establish separate rules with respect to the transfer or assignment of trademarks. Second, even where an issue is exhaustively covered by the directive, only some of its provisions are mandatory; certain other provisions are regarded as optional, and may be excluded from the national legislation in the member state's discretion. That is, although on matters addressed in the directive, its provisions are exhaustive (i.e., member states cannot add any other provisions on the topic), the member state is not always obliged to implement every one of the list of exhaustive provisions. The nature of the provision can be detected in the language of the article in question: mandatory provisions state "the Member States *shall. . .*", while optional articles provide that "the Member States *may . . .*". This is seen most significantly in the grounds for refusal of a registration or invalidity, *see* Trademark Directive arts. 3-4, and in the scope of rights granted by a registration. *See* Baywatch Prod. Co., Inc. v. The Home Video Channel, [1997] FSR 22 (Ch. D.)(Eng.) *infra.*[*] For example, under Article 4(1) and (2) member states must refuse or declare invalid a registration that is identical with an earlier mark and registered or applied for in connection with identical goods or services, or is similar to an earlier mark for similar goods or services such as to cause a likelihood of confusion. For this purpose, earlier trademarks are those CTMs, national or international trademarks, which were applied for before the date of application of the trademark, or marks that before that date were well-known under Article *6bis* of the Paris Convention. Seven optional grounds for refusal or invalidation of later trademarks in conflicts with earlier rights are listed, and member states may include in their national laws as many or as few of these as they wish. Most importantly, Article 4(4)(a) contains a ground based upon dilution of the distinctive character or repute of an earlier mark, and Article 4(4)(b) allows member states to deny registration based upon prior unregistered rights.

Although most of the EU countries operate registration-based systems, it was thought important to limit the amount of deadwood on the registers in the EU and thus Article 10(1) requires that trademarks must be genuinely used in the member state in connection with the goods or services in respect of which they are registered within five years after the date of completion of the registration procedure and within an uninterrupted period of five years after any suspension of such use. Absent such use (or proper reasons for non-use), the registration may not be the basis for opposing or seeking to invalidate another registration, and may itself be subject to revocation. Article 12(1) introduces a liberalizing twist to the use requirement, which is borrowed from Germany. A registration will not be revoked for non-use where genuine use of the trademark has been started or resumed during the interval between expiry of the five-year period of non-use and filing of the application for revocation.

---

[*]Article 3 states the absolute grounds for denial or invalidation and Article 4 contains the relative grounds. This distinction assumes more fundamental significance in the CTM system, because member states remain free under the directive to apply these grounds either *ex officio* or in opposition or *inter partes* proceedings.

PETER JAFFEY, THE NEW EUROPEAN TRADE MARKS REGIME*
28 I.I.C. 153, 187-91 (1997)

Economic Integration, Priority and Exclusivity

The new European law allows the Member States discretion over matters of priority and exclusivity in their national registers. In different jurisdictions the law may traditionally have reflected different judgements over the objectives of a registered system, *i.e.* over the relative importance of notice, security, facilitation of enforcement, and economic integration within the jurisdiction–and correspondingly different judgements of the desirability of exclusivity and full priority. In England, the main objective seems to have been facilitation of enforcement, and in consequence the register did not confer full priority or exclusivity, and a limited range of marks were admissible. In other European countries, security or notice may have been given more weight, and consequently registration made available to a wider range of marks and rights to unregistered marks excluded or made vulnerable to a subsequent registration.

Under the new system, however, each country cannot be considered in isolation. The objective of harmonisation is economic integration. If this objective were the only consideration, one would expect national registers, in addition to admitting a suitable range of marks to a property regime, to admit the full range of marks capable of being distinctive under a system of full priority or maybe even exclusivity. Where a business is venturing into a new part of the Community it is more valuable to it to be able to rely exclusively on the register to give it protection against unregistered marks than is the case where it is operating only in its own home market since here it is much easier to establish what marks are in use by other means. However a system that encouraged or required registration would tend to favor large companies at the expense of small ones, and would impose particular difficulties of adjustment in jurisdictions like the United Kingdom in which there is a longstanding tradition of reliance on unregistered marks.[129] Furthermore, it should be borne in mind that the importance of enhancing the status of registration depends on the degree to which traders are in any case required for other reasons, *e.g.* because of the danger of infringing an unregistered design, to be familiar with the local market place.

---

[129]In allowing member states to determine for themselves the status of unregistered marks, the directive favors those countries that choose to offer a greater degree of protection for unregistered marks, since a trader from such a country venturing into a country with a lesser degree of protection for unregistered marks will be less likely having searched the registers and made his own application for registration to be faced with an unregistered mark having priority over his than his counterpart venturing in the opposite direction.

NOTES AND QUESTIONS

(1) **The Broader Effect of Implementation (Transposition) Exercises**. The provisions of the Trademark Directive require affirmative implementation in the national laws of the member states of the EU. The manner and source of implementation in each member state is documented by Dr. Kur in Annette Kur, *Harmonization of Trademark Laws in Europe*, 28 I.I.C. 1, 4-8 (1997). *See also* Barbara E. Cookson, *The Progress of European Harmonisation*, 19 EUR. INTELL. PROP. REV. 462 (1997). Harmonization implementation exercises often create reform opportunities that extend beyond effectuation of binding obligations to change laws. Several European countries (but by no means all) used the EU trademark harmonization exercise to undertake a wholesale review of existing trademark legislation. *See* Kur, *supra*, at 5 (discussing German response); *see also* Jaffey, *supra*, at 153 (discussing U.K. reforms); Marie Danielle Poisson-Schodermeier, *Changes in French Trade Mark Law: The 1991 Act*, 14 EUR. INTELL. PROP. REV. 104 (1992) (discussing new French statute). Similarly, although the directive did not seek to impose upon national laws all the rules ultimately contained in the Trademark Regulation, the negotiation of a complete CTM system provided a thorough airing of different views on all significant aspects of trademark law. Thus, many member states adopted substantive rules found in the regulation although not required to do so by the directive. What does this say about the potential of harmonization efforts to achieve substantively similar trademark laws on a broader basis? If you were a member of a national negotiating team, how would this observation affect your strategy in engineering a further trademark harmonization instrument? Does this alter your view of the efficacy of "limited harmonization" exercises? *Cf.* Kur, *supra*, at 7-8 ("In spite of the fact that the harmonization efforts as required by the directive have been completed . . ., it has to be acknowledged that we are still far from the goal of complete harmonization of law and practice in all the member states".).

(2) **The Relationship Between EU Harmonization Exercises and Broader Multilateral Initiatives**. The drafting of the harmonization directive took place against the backdrop of broader multilateral negotiations, and not long after the member states implemented the directive in their national laws, the TRIPS Agreement and the Trademark Law Treaty were concluded. In some respects these multilateral agreements went further than the directive (which had been adopted six years earlier). For example, Article 21 of the TRIPS Agreement provides that trademarks can be assigned with or without an accompanying business whereas the directive did not address that issue. (This caused the further amendment of the Greek Trademark Act, which had been revised in 1994 to implement the directive, to delete the requirement of a transfer of a business along with the assignment of trademark rights.) Is it surprising that the TRIPS Agreement, agreed upon by over one hundred countries, included provisions omitted from the Trademark Harmonization Directive? What might explain this? In what ways is the Trademark Harmonization Directive conceptually different from the TRIPS Agreement?

(3) **Assignment and Licensing**. One of the biggest issues left largely untouched by the directive was the assignment and licensing of rights.

Reflecting traditional concerns regarding the effect of trademark licensing upon the consuming public, at the time of the directive some member states (such as Greece, Finland, and Sweden) conditioned the validity of such grants upon review or registration by the relevant authority for possible consumer confusion. Yet, the directive arguably embraces a property-based notion of trademarks, which might over time have an effect on these traditional approaches to licensing notwithstanding the lack of an express provision.

(4) **Partial Harmonization.** Why did the Trademark Harmonization Directive not attempt to harmonize the laws of member states relating to unregistered trademarks or registration procedures? Will that omission affect the capacity of the directive to achieve the Commission's objectives? In what ways, if any, does harmonization of *part* of an area of law, but not the entire body of law, affect the balance that intellectual property laws are intended to strike?

(5) **Optional Provisions.** Why did the Directive include optional and mandatory provisions? What purpose does each type of provision serve? To what extent will "[d]ifferent national traditions and attitudes . . . still have a considerable impact on the manner in which the provisions are applied and assessed by the competent authorities," as Annette Kur has argued? If so, what is the realistic goal of harmonization?

(6) **Incorporating Use-Based Rights in Harmonization.** Not unlike U.S. trademark protection, U.K. trademark law is comprised both of unregistered protection under the common law tort of passing off, and protection for registered marks under the Trade Marks Act 1994. *See* RUTH E. ANNAND & HELEN E. NORMAN, BLACKSTONE'S GUIDE TO THE TRADE MARKS ACT 1994 (1994). Article 4(4)(b) of the directive, which permits (but does not require) a member state to deny registration on the ground of an unregistered mark previously used, reflects efforts by the United Kingdom to preserve its concept of unregistered common law rights. Without this provision, would the directive's decision not to harmonize unregistered rights have been of significance? How does the inclusion of Article 4(4)(b) affect the scope of the harmonization endeavor? How will it affect trademark owners seeking certainty of protection for their marks within Europe? *Cf.* Kur, *supra*, at 10-11 (discussing different approaches of member states to the existence of prior used but unregistered marks as a ground for denial or invalidation of registrations). Under the Community Trademark Regulation, the owner of a senior but unregistered mark (recognized under the law of a member state) may oppose a Community registration unless its mark "is of merely local significance." *See* Trademark Regulation art. 8(4). If the mark is merely of "local significance," the senior owner may enjoin use by the Community registrant in that local area if national law so permits. *See id.* art. 107.

(7) **Harmonization and Economic Integration.** Fair and free competition is a principal concern of the European Commission. Does harmonization of intellectual property laws inevitably and necessarily contribute to fairer competition? Between whom might it distort competition? Does it, as Peter Jaffey has argued, "in itself contribute to economic integration"?

(8) **Keep in Mind . . .** Reconsider each of these questions as you read the materials in this section. If your views change, what has caused them to

change? Which aspects of the following post-harmonization decisions do you find surprising?

[2] Trademark Subject Matter, Distinctiveness and Exclusions From Protection

TRADEMARK DIRECTIVE, ARTICLES 2-3

Article 2

A trade mark may consist of any sign capable of being represented graphically, particularly words, including personal names, designs, letters, numerals, the shape of goods or of their packaging, provided that such signs are capable of distinguishing the goods or services of one undertaking from those of other undertakings.

Article 3

1. The following shall not be registered or if registered shall be liable to be declared invalid:

(a) signs which cannot constitute a trade mark;

(b) trade marks which are devoid of any distinctive character;

(c) trade marks which consist exclusively of signs or indications which may serve, in trade, to designate the kind, quality, quantity, intended purpose, value, geographical origin, or the time of production of the goods or of rendering of the service, or other characteristics of the goods or service;

(d) trade marks which consist exclusively of signs or indications which have become customary in the current language or in the bona fide and established practices of the trade;

(e) signs which consist exclusively of:

– the shape which results from the nature of the goods themselves, or

– the shape of goods which is necessary to obtain a technical result, or

– the shape which gives substantial value to the goods;

(f) trade marks which are contrary to public policy or to accepted principles of morality;

(g) trade marks which are of such a nature as to deceive the public, for instance as to the nature, quality or geographical origin of the goods or service;

(h) trade marks which have not been authorized by the competent authorities and are to be refused or invalidated pursuant to Article 6*ter* of the Paris Convention

. . . .

3. A trade mark shall not be refused registration or be declared invalid in accordance with paragraph 1 (b), (c) or (d) if, before the date of application for

registration and following the use which has been made of it, it has acquired a distinctive character. Any Member State may in addition provide that this provision shall also apply where the distinctive character was acquired after the date of application for registration or after the date of registration.

PHILIPS ELEC. BV v. REMINGTON CONSUMER PRODS.
[1998] RPC 283 (Ch. D. 1997) (UK)

JACOB J: Philips and Remington are well-known names for electric shavers. This is one of a number of world-wide battles between them. The principal issue, world-wide, is whether Philips, by trade mark registration, or like right dependant on the appearance of working parts, can obtain a permanent monopoly of a desirable form of manufacture, namely three headed rotary shavers in which the three heads are arranged in an equilateral triangle.

The Philips Shaver

Philips have always made what are called the "rotary" sort of shaver [which] . . . works by the use of a circular slitted foil under which electric cutters rotate. The stubble pokes through the slits and is chopped off by the fast rotating cutters underneath. The early versions were "single-headed": there was just one circular set of slits with a single rotor underneath. . . . In 1951 Philips introduced the two headed shaver. This too was a success. It continues until this day, the two headed face remaining essentially unchanged in appearance.

In 1966 Philips added a third rotary head. This increased the speed of shaving, not by 50 per cent but by about 15 to 20 per cent: there is a law of diminishing returns with shavers as with other things. The three heads are arranged in an equilateral triangle and project slightly from a triangular "face plate"–an equilateral triangle with rounded corners. The three headed shaver was also a success. . . .

Remington Shavers

Remington's shavers have for many years always been of the reciprocating or "vibra" kind. A row or cutters moves from side to side underneath a thin perforated foil. Others (Braun, Panasonic and Sunbeam, for instance) also make this kind. The general appearance of reciprocating shavers is well known. The foil is generally rectangular, curved along its shorter side. No-one suggests that the appearance of such shavers is indicative of any particular manufacturer.

Remington have now started making a rotary shaver. Hitherto this was a type of shaver unique to Philips. The model the subject of the current dispute is the DT55, which can be used wet or dry. Philips have not yet made a wet/dry model. It has three heads arranged in an equilateral triangle within a plain face plate. It is this shaver which is said to infringe one or more of the Philips intellectual property rights referred to below. . . . It is not suggested that there is anything dishonest about the DT55–in particular it is not said that it deceives the public.

Philips Intellectual Property Rights

[Philips' patents on the shavers had expired. In addition to the trademark claim that comprised most of Mr. Justice Jacob's opinion, Philips unsuccessfully asserted registered design infringement.]

Philips have sought to register and have registered in a number of countries a picture of the face of their three headed shaver . . . It is registered in Class 8 for "electric shavers included in Class 8." . . .

It is the validity and, if valid, the scope of this registration which is the principal issue which I have to decide. Even though it is only a picture which is formally the subject of the registration, both sides, in my judgment rightly, treated it as a registration covering also a three-dimensional shape. It would be quite artificial to regard a straight picture of a thing, and the thing itself, as significantly different under a law of trade marks which permits shapes to be registered.

Philips also have the well known word trade mark "Philishave." No one doubts that the registration of this is valid, that it is very well known and that it is distinctive of Philips and none other. It has always been used for Philips shavers. The picture registered trade mark has never been used by Philips as the sole means of identification of trade source. It has never been trusted by Philips to do this job on its own, a matter plainly relevant in considering acquired distinctiveness. It is at best a "limping trade mark," needing the crutch of "Philishave" in use. . . .

. . . .

THE TRADE MARK CASE

This is the principal issue. It turns partly on the facts but mainly on the true construction of the [Trademark Directive]. . . This was implemented by the 1994 [Trade Marks] Act. I commented in *British Sugar plc v James Robertson & Sons Ltd* [1996] RPC 281 at page 291 on the complication caused by our Parliamentary draftsman by his failure simply to copy the language of the Directive. In this case the parties were agreed that the Act had the same meaning as the Directive and were prepared to argue the case directly from its language. . . .

The Attacks on Validity

It is common ground that although the mark was registered before the new Act its validity is to be judged as if it had been registered under the Act,

Schedule 3 paragraph 2. Remington say the registration is bad for the following reasons:

1. That the mark does not satisfy the requirements of § 1(1) [and thus is unregisterable under Section 3(1)(a). Section 1(1), implementing Article 2, provides that "a trade mark means any sign capable of being represented graphically which is capable of distinguishing goods or services of one undertaking from those of other undertakings. A trade mark may, in particular, consist of words (including personal names), designs, letters, numerals or the shape of goods or their packaging." Section 3(1)(a) provides that signs which do not satisfy the requirements of section 1(1) are not to be registered.];

2. That the mark is devoid of distinctive character, contrary to § 3(1)(b) [Art. 3.1(b)];

3. That the mark consists exclusively of a sign or indication which serves to designate, in trade, the kind . . . or intended purpose of the goods, contrary to § 3(1)(c) [Art. 3.1(c)];

4. That the mark consists exclusively of one or more of the matters identified in § 3(2)(a)-(c) [Art.3.1(e)];

5. That the mark is registered contrary to public policy contrary to § 3(3) [Art. 3.1(f)].

In relation to grounds (2) and (3) above Philips seek to justify the registration on the grounds that the mark has acquired a distinctive character as provided for by the proviso to section 3(1) [Art. 3.3]. . . .

The Facts

Distinctiveness–the public reaction to the face

Before turning to the law it is convenient to make my findings of fact. Philips say the mark is now distinctive of them. They relied upon their advertising to the trade and public over the years, and upon the public's reaction when shown the Remington shaver to establish distinctiveness of the three headed face shape. They also rely upon some trade witnesses. They say that the appearance of the face of their three headed shavers is now distinctive of them and none other: that it is an "icon", or more colourfully, the "face of Philips."

. . . .

The advertising all shows the Philips shavers with prominence being given to the head. Most of them have been three-headed though some have been two-headed. Philips have particularly been concerned to show the public how their rotary shaver works–and to emphasise the virtues of their rotary system. This is hardly surprising because their principal rivals in the United Kingdom have all made reciprocating razors. . . . It is clear that this advertising has worked–the interested public knows about rotary shavers and when they see one (including the Remington) they understand from its appearance how it works as [was established by] trade and public witnesses . . .

. . . .

[Witnesses were shown the Remington DT55.] The evidence established that the three-headed shape indicated how the shaver worked, namely just like the well-known Philishave, and that that shape was associated with Philips.

By "associated" (a word of potentially wide meaning) I mean this: that the general reaction of the public to the DT55 was that they thought of Philips. A substantial proportion would, if the product had not been marked "Remington" have assumed that the DT55 was made by Philips. A small proportion (not enough to matter) might have surmised that the product was made by Philips for Remington.

. . . .

Engineering considerations

Philips say that one does not have to use a shape like their face to make a rotary shaver. You do not have to use three heads, if you do you do not have to arrange them in an equilateral triangle, and even if you do, [you do] not have to have a flat face plate or indeed a face plate at all. Thus, they say, the particular shape of the head should be regarded as inessential–as akin to a fancy design. To prove their point, Philips provided evidence from [two industrial designers, each of whom] showed alternative possible designs, some of which plainly do not look like the registered mark. One alternative design was actually constructed by [one of the designers] for use in some Swedish proceedings to which I must refer later. It has three standard heads, but they are arranged in a flat isosceles triangle rather than an equilateral triangle. You could, say Philips, even arrange the heads in a straight line as one minor and unsuccessful manufacturer, Arno, did. The Arno product was not sold here.

There is some truth in this: it is possible to make an effective rotary shaver which would be outside the scope of the trade mark protection. Quite where the protection would stop is not clear. A number of the alternatives proposed by Philips in their evidence would, and some (including the Swedish mock-up) might, fall within the scope of the trade mark as being sufficiently similar to the trade mark as to create a likelihood of confusion on the part of the public. In the latter context it must be remembered that Philips have much emphasised the virtues of rotary shaving as such and themselves make a shaver with an alternative configuration, namely the two-header. Some members of the public might well speculate that Philips have just come up with a variant of the equilateral triangle, if they were to look at just the face of one of these alternatives.

However it is also the case that the engineering scope for variation outside the trade mark is very limited. Moreover the three headed shape of the present Philips design is one of the best possible ways of making a rotary shaver. . . . And in engineering terms, it is simpler, if you are making a three-headed device, to arrange the cutters at the corners of an equilateral triangle.

The Significance of This Case

So, if Philips are right, they will have obtained a permanent monopoly in respect of matters of significant engineering design by virtue of a trade mark registration. Mr Pumfrey [counsel for Philips] does not shrink from this. He says it is a consequence of the Directive. He further accepted that if Philips are right then many other manufacturers whose products are recognised from their appearance would be in the same position. He said that once a whole or a part of an article is recognised by the public as emanating from a particular manufacturer, then a picture of the article or a picture of part of the article, or indeed the shape of an article or part of it, can (a) be registered and (b) the registration can be used to stop a copy of that product for ever and ever. Moreover this is so even where the copy is a perfectly honest product marked clearly with the name of its manufacturer so no-one could be deceived by the product in commerce. The only derogation (apart from the express exceptions of Article 3(1)(e)) from this perpetual protection which Mr Pumfrey was prepared to accept was that the shape must be kept distinctive by use.

The Federal Court of Appeal of Canada in *Remington Rand v Philips*, took the same view of the importance of what is at stake in holding (of course under different legislation) that the corresponding Philips Canadian trade mark registration was invalid. MacGuigan JA, giving the judgment of the court [noted the danger that registration of functional elements might allow the applicants, in effect, to obtain patents under the guise of trade marks].

Incidentally the Canadian court also made much the same findings of fact as I have. It said:

> Shaver heads in general are utilitarian in nature, and . . . the equilateral triangular configuration is one of the better designs for a triple headed shaver. Here the shaver heads are functional and the three-headed equilateral triangular configuration is functional. The design mark, by depicting those functional elements, is primarily functional.

"Not a sign?"

Remington suggest, though this is not at the forefront of their argument, that the shape is not a "sign" at all. What is a "sign"? Can the thing itself also be a "sign"? If one is not careful one is likely here to end up discussing metaphysical points–hardly the sort of thing appropriate for a law designed for men of commerce. I think a "sign" is anything which can convey information. I appreciate that this is extremely wide, but I can see no reason to limit the meaning of the word. The only qualification expressed in the Directive is that it be capable of being represented graphically. I am not concerned with the meaning of this qualification.

What I conclude is confirmed by recital 7(b), which emphasises the necessity to list the examples of "sign"–note the contrast with recital 7(c) which sets out the need to list the grounds of invalidity "in an exhaustive manner". You need the examples of a sign to see just how wide the meaning is. What the examples have in common is the ability to convey information. At this point it does not matter what sort of information is conveyed. It is the proviso to Recital 7(b), "capable of distinguishing", which serves to limit the sort of sign which can be registered.[*]

Here, on my findings of fact, the picture does convey a message–as indeed even Remington contend, so it is a "sign".

"Capable of distinguishing/devoid of any distinctive character" [Arts 3.1(a) and (b)]

Under Article 3.1(a) a sign which cannot constitute a trade mark cannot be validly registered. A requirement for a sign to be a trade mark is that it be "capable of distinguishing." Under Article 3.1(b) a trade mark (note the change from "sign") which is devoid of any distinctive character cannot be validly registered, though if it has acquired a distinctive character it can be (Article 3.3). So, if you actually write the requirement for a sign to be a trade mark into Article 3(1)(b) it says a trade mark is invalid if it is: "A sign which is capable of distinguishing which is devoid of any distinctive character."

This seems (and indeed is) confusing. What is the distinction between the requirement that a sign be "capable of distinguishing" (as to which there is no provision saving signs having acquired distinctiveness) and a trade mark devoid of distinctive character (as to which there is such a saving provision)? Is there a kind of sign which is "incapable", even if it has acquired distinctiveness? If not, what does the requirement of "capability" add to the requirement of a "distinctiveness character"?

Under the old British law there were some kinds of mark which the law regarded as unregistrable even if they were completely distinctive of the mark owner for the goods concerned: "Yorkshire" for copper tubing (*Yorkshire Copper Works' Application* (1953) 71 RPC 150) and "York" for trailers (YORK Trade Mark [1984] RPC 231) are the paradigm cases. The names were unregistrable even though they denoted the goods of a particular manufacturer completely–when used as trade marks. The reason for the refusal was that

---

[*][Ed. Note: Older directives did not number recitals; more recent ones do. Mr. Justice Jacob assigned numbers to the recitals of the Trademark Directive. Recitals 7(a)-(c) read:

7(a) Whereas attainment of the objectives at which this approximation of laws is aiming requires that the conditions for obtaining and continuing to hold a registered trade mark are, in general, identical in all Member States;

(b) whereas, to this end, it is necessary to list examples of signs which may constitute a trade mark, provided that such signs are capable of distinguishing the goods or services of one undertaking from those of other undertakings;

(c) whereas the grounds for refusal or invalidity concerning the trade mark itself, for example, the absence of any distinctive character, or concerning conflicts between the trade mark and earlier rights, are to be listed in an exhaustive manner even if some of these grounds are listed as an option for the Member States which will therefore be able to maintain or introduce those grounds in their legislation; . . .]

registration might interfere with bona fide uses of the mark (*e.g.* as part of an address) which others might want to make. . . .

Mr. Pumfrey submits that all that old law has been swept away. He is, of course, right. We now have a new European law and one cannot get any help from the details of the old law of any particular European country. But it does not follow that the sort of concepts and safeguards provided for in the old laws (or indeed the laws of countries outside the European Union) have no place under the law. On the contrary one is bound to bump up against the same sort of problem under the new law as under other laws. For some matters are basic to any rational law of trade marks. I believe this case involves such a problem, involving as it does the question of the extent to which trade mark law, conferring a perpetual monopoly, can interfere with the freedom within the European Union of manufacturers to make an artefact of a desirable and good engineering design.

With that sort of consideration in mind I turn to the Directive. Recital 7(b) emphasises that capability of distinguishing is a fundamental requirement of the sort of sign which can be registered. I do not think one can disregard this. It is in my opinion important that a capacity to distinguish is put forward as a limitation, at this very early stage. I further think it significant to note that Recital 10(a) places particular importance on the purpose of a trade mark–to guarantee trade origin.* If that is what trade marks are for, then a sign which can never fully do that is not, in my judgment, to be regarded as capable of distinguishing.

I think that is the case here. Philips can never get away from the fact that the sign primarily denotes function. More use could not make a difference. The sign can never only denote shavers made by Philips and no-one else because it primarily says "here is a three headed rotary shaver." It is not "capable"of denoting only Philips goods. That is why the public's reaction to the DT55 was essentially there is a three headed shaver "put out by Remington" The reaction would have been different if the shaver had been marked "Philishave"as well as "Remington." This shows the "sign"is not distinctive in the sense of a true trade mark such as Philishave.

I do not think in so holding I am resurrecting the old British law. On the contrary I think there is a difference between this sort of case and the Yorkshire sort. In the latter the word had truly come to denote the goods of one undertaking. True it also meant a county, but not when used for copper tubing. For copper tubing it had come to say "here is tubing made by the Yorkshire Copper Works" and nothing else. "Yorkshire" would be registrable now. It is the sort of trade mark "devoid of distinctive character" which can be saved by proof of factual distinctiveness. The same goes for the shape of the Coca-Cola bottle (unregistrable under the old law *COCA-COLA Trade Marks* [1986] RPC 421). This says "my contents are from the Coca-Cola company" and really conveys no other message.

---

*[Ed. Note: Recital 10(a) reads: "Whereas the protection afforded by the registered trade mark, the function of which is in particular to guarantee the trade mark as an indication of origin, is absolute in the case of identity between the mark and the sign and goods or services; . . . ."]

In *British Sugar plc v James Robertson & Sons Ltd* [1996] RPC 281 I said at page 305:

> Section 1(1) has two parts, sign, and capable of distinguishing. Sign is not in issue: a word is plainly included within the meaning of sign as the remainder of section 1 indicates. But what about capable of distinguishing? Does this add any requirement beyond that found in section 3(1)? Section 3(1)(b) bars the registration of a mark which is devoid of distinctive character unless it has in fact acquired a distinctive character. I cannot see that the closing words of the first sentence of section 1(1) add anything to this. If a mark on its face is non-distinctive (and ordinary descriptive and laudatory words fall into this class) but is shown to have a distinctive character in fact then it must be capable of distinguishing. Under [the old U.K. law, to be registrable, a mark] had to be capable of distinguishing. But the Pickwickian position was that some marks, even though 100% distinctive in fact, were not regarded as capable of distinguishing within the meaning of that provision. I do not think the Directive and the 1994 Act take this more limited meaning over.
>
> . . . .
>
> That is not to say that there are some signs which cannot in practice be registered. But the reason is simply that the applicant will be unable to prove the mark has become a trade mark in practice–"Soap" for "soap" is an example. The bar (no pun intended) will be factual not legal.

Thus I think the real question here is whether there is a factual bar preventing the sign from really being distinctive. I think the test for this is to ask whether, no matter how much the sign may be used and recognised, it can really serve to convey in substance only the message: "here are a particular trader's goods." The point is important because the sign conveys the primary message "here is a three headed rotary shaver–from what you see you know how this device works."

Mr. Pumfrey said that there was a fallacy in the supposition that a mark could not be both descriptive and distinctive. . . . Now it is of course the case that a mark (particularly a word mark) may be both distinctive of a particular manufacturer and yet also convey something by way of a description of the goods–Mr. Pumfrey gave "Weldmesh" for welded mesh as an example. The word denotes the welded mesh of a particular manufacturer (*See WELDMESH Trade Mark* [1966] RPC 220). But you can take this argument too far. There are words which are so descriptive that they cannot be trade marks–"soap" for "soap." The difference is one of degree, but important nonetheless. There are degrees of descriptiveness ranging from skillful but covert allusion to the common word for the goods. On the scale of distinctiveness you come to a point when a word is so descriptive that it is incapable of distinguishing properly, even if it does so partially. If that is the position then it is "incapable of distinguishing" within the meaning of Article 2 of the Directive. And likewise the mark is then devoid of distinctive character. Other, less descriptive, words may not be in that class: they may, given use and recognition as a trade mark, come in substance to say: here are the goods of a particular trader. Such words become trade marks "by nurture, not nature" to use the happy conjunction of words borrowed from other fields of learning by Mr Hobbs QC in *AD 2000 Trade Mark* [1997] RPC 168. It is this sort of word which is contemplated by Article 3.1(b). I put it this way in *British Sugar plc v James Robertson & Sons Ltd* [1996] RPC 281 at page 306:

> What does 'devoid of any distinctive character' mean? I think the phrase requires consideration of the mark on its own, assuming no use. Is it the sort of word (or other sign) which cannot do the job of distinguishing without first educating the public that it is a trade mark?

What I have said about word marks is true also of picture marks. They too may be more or less descriptive. A picture of an article is equivalent to a description of it–both convey information. If the picture is simply of an artefact which traders might legitimately wish to manufacture then to my mind it is just like the common word for it and, like the word for it, incapable of distinguishing.

Mr. Pumfrey also argued that it was not right to import the sort of considerations contained in Article 3.1(e) (*i.e.* shape "resulting from nature", necessary to obtain a technical result, or giving "substantial value") into the requirements of capability of distinguishing and not being devoid of distinctive character. They are separate objections he said. I do not think necessarily so. I can see nothing in the Directive which suggests that the various grounds of objection to validity may not overlap. On the contrary it seems to me to be inherent that they will–a sign which is incapable of distinguishing must also be devoid of distinctive character, for example. Or a shape which gives substantial value may do so because it obtains a technical result.

[Mr. Justice Jacob also rejected the argument that a word (or other sign) is to be treated as a trademark when it had come to denote the goods of a particular trader even without displacing the ordinary meaning of the word. He concluded that "unless the word, when used for the goods concerned, has in practice displaced its ordinary meaning, it will not properly denote the trader's" goods and none other. Here the sign of a three headed shaver denotes such a shaver. To some if no word trade mark is used, it also suggests manufacture by Philips.]

I conclude that the sign of a three headed shaver is incapable of distinguishing the goods of Philips from those of others and that it is devoid of distinctive character. In so holding I am conscious that I depart from the conclusion of the Swedish Court of Appeal in *Ide Line AG v Philips Electronics* [1997] ETMR 377. In that case a Swedish company sought cancellation of a trade mark registration of Philips. The mark consisted of a picture of a three-headed shaver, similar, but not quite the same, as the registered mark in suit. The Swedish company apparently wishes to import three headed rotary razors from Japan (where such shavers are on the market). The court dealt with the question of distinctiveness very shortly, I suspect because the real emphasis of the argument was devoted to the function objection. The majority . . . simply said this at page 385:

> Section 13(1) of the Trade Marks Act 1960 provides that, when assessing whether a trade mark has distinctiveness, all circumstances shall be considered, in particular to what extent and how long the mark has been in use. Market surveys show that the shaving unit is strongly established on the market for Philips. Considering this, it is proved that the trade mark has distinctiveness.

And Judge Goran Nilsson simply agreed. It does not seem to have been submitted that the appearance of a three-headed rotary shaver, as embodied in the picture, was not capable of distinguishing because it denoted such a shaver and how it worked. I do not know to what extent the views of members of the public were tested by questioning in Sweden. Indeed I do not know what form the market research took. . . .

Trade mark which consists exclusively of a sign which may serve, in trade, to designate the kind . . . intended purpose, . . . or other characteristics of goods [Art. 3(1)(c), mark saveable upon proof of acquired distinctive character, Art. 3.3]

If I am wrong about my conclusions on the first two grounds of attack I go on to consider the other grounds, beginning with Article 3(1)(c).

Remington submit that the picture here is no more than a two-dimensional reproduction of a three dimensional working part. There is no capricious addition (e.g. in the way of a fancy embellishment). They further say that in trade the picture may serve to denote the kind of goods or intended purpose of the goods. It is enough that the picture "may" have this effect, though Remington go on to submit that it does. I think this is obviously right. The mark, if it is to be saved, must be saved by the proviso to section 3(1), *i.e.* Art. 3.3. This calls for proof of acquisition of a distinctive character. In my view that means proof that the public take the face shape as a trade mark of Philips and not as a picture of the goods. For all the reasons I have given I think that the evidence falls short of this requirement.

Sign which consists exclusively of one of the three specified matters [Art. 3.1(e)]

General observations

The language has gone back to the word "sign" and proof of factual distinctiveness does not save a registration. The parties were agreed that, if any feature of the shape which is not trivial does not fall within one of the exclusions, the exceptions do not apply. Thereafter they diverged. Philips submitted that all three specified matters are of very narrow scope. Indeed, as it seems to me, the submission really meant that these exceptions can hardly apply at all because one could hardly think of any examples which can fit. I hardly think that can be right. I think the provisions must be construed in a purposive manner, bearing in mind that the intention is to set up a law of trade marks and not some other law, particularly a patent or design law.

Sign which consists exclusively of the shape which results from the nature of' the goods themselves

Philips suggest that the exclusion is very narrow–something like the shape of an American football for a registration of a trade mark for American footballs. I doubt it can be that narrow, and even that suggestion has difficulties. Suppose the registration was for "balls" and not just American footballs?

This provision, considered purely academically, poses problems. What are "the goods themselves"? A shape will define part or the whole appearance of a given object. If that object is regarded as the goods then the shape will always result from the nature of the goods. Take this case. If you regard "the goods" as "rotary shavers having three equilateral heads and a face plate" then the shape results from the nature of the goods. If on the other hand you regard "the goods" as just rotary shavers, or more generally electric shavers or more generally as shavers, electric or otherwise, then the shape does not result from the nature of the goods.

How then does one define what "the goods" are? It was suggested at one point that one should take the specification of goods for which the mark is registered. But that specification will be partly adventitious. Philips' registration is for "electric shavers." It could have been wider, for "mechanical shavers" and possibly even for "shavers" as such. Or it could have been narrower, "three headed rotary shavers," for instance. So I do not think one can simply go by the specification of goods. I think the correct answer is partly one of degree. The nature of the goods is not an academic question. One is here considering the goods as articles of commerce, for this is a provision about trade marks. I think one must ask what the goods are as a practical business matter. The answer depends on how they are viewed in practice as articles of commerce. The answer here, I think, is as "electric shavers." By and large such shavers are seen as a single type of commercial article. True it is there are subsets (the various sorts of vibra and the two and three headed rotaries of Philips) but as a generality they are one sort of commercial article.

If I am right, then the picture concerned (regarded as in substance a shape mark) does not result from the nature of the goods themselves.

Shape of goods which is necessary to give a technical result

Of the three limbs of Article 3.1(e) it was this upon which the debate mainly concentrated. Mr Pumfrey submitted that because you can get an equally good shave from rotary shavers, even three headed rotary shavers, of shapes other than that shown in the picture, the shape was not one which consisted exclusively of a shape which is necessary to obtain a technical result. In short, provided the trade mark owner can show that some other shape will also do the job, his "sign" is not within this exclusion, no matter how functional it may be.

It was this argument which found favour with the majority of the Swedish Court of Appeal in *Ide Line*. They were particularly impressed by the flat isosceles triangle shaver made specially by Philips for those proceedings. They said at pages 386 and 387:

> According to the Swedish wording, a shape which is necessary to obtain a technical result is excluded from registration. Thus it is not enough that the shape is functional. The shape must also be necessary to obtain the result. In consequence of this, it is necessary to consider what other possible ways there are, if any, to reach results.
>
> The reasoning above leads to the conclusion that it should be considered whether a trade mark which provides a function gives an undue exclusive right to a technical solution. Objective standards should be used when this assessment is done. Considerable regard should be taken as to what is known regarding the possibility of solving the discussed problem with alternative methods. To the extent that the supply on the market is used as an aid, it must be considered whether the chosen solutions are dependent on technical implications or on the competition situation. The fact that one design dominates a market can depend entirely or to a certain extent on the fact that the shape is used by a company which is dominant in the market. Trade mark law is not intended to solve such possible problems in the market; on the contrary, the dominance could depend on the company having a strong trade mark which prevents others from using its design.
>
> . . . .

Judge Goran Nilsson dissented. He said at page 391:

> The European Community has as its task, inter alia, to promote a harmonised and well balanced development of industry within the Community as a whole. In order to achieve this goal, an order which ensures that competition within the internal market not be distorted is desired. In consequence, it is obvious that the directive should not be allowed to restrain competition by creating a production monopoly for technical solutions for which protection otherwise would not be granted through trade mark law.
>
> If the shape of a product is not exclusively motivated by its function and thus the existing non-functional design elements do have distinctiveness, section 13(2) of the Trade Marks Act [Article 3.1(e) of the Directive], according to its wording, would not be a hindrance for registration. According to one model of interpretation, this

provision relates only to such technical result which is expected to be reached with the shape to the extent that there is no obstacle for registration when an equal result can be obtained with another shape. Such an interpretation would mean that an exclusively functional shape would be covered by the hindrance when the shape cannot be varied in order to obtain a certain technical result. Another conceivable way to interpret the provision would be to make a total analysis of the elements of the shape of the product and consider whether these are caused by purely technical reasons in relation to the result which is desired. Only if that is the case would there be a hindrance against registration. Where there are several possibilities to obtain a technical result of equal value, but the right to manufacture a product that is advantageous from a manufacturing point of view, is exclusively granted to one manufacturer by way of a trade mark right, the first model of interpretation would grant an exclusive right under the protection of trade mark law for technical solutions which could not be obtained by other means. Moreover, that model would lead to arbitrary and complicated assessments in the registration procedure. For these reasons the provision should be interpreted to be a hindrance to registration of trade marks, the shape of which are solely motivated by the technical result. Then a product which has a shape, which is solely motivated by function will–even if there are alternative means to reach the same technical result–be excluded from protection as a trade mark. This interpretation does not open the possibility for obtaining trade mark protection for products which have a shape which is solely dictated by function.

. . . .

The configuration of three shaving heads in an equilateral triangle seems natural. The shape covers a large shaving area with the smallest possible area and it is of importance for the shaving result. Also, the shape results in a shaver which is easily handled. For the purposes of construction this shape also has the advantage that the driving of the rotating cutters can, when the cutters rotate in the same direction, be achieved with fewer cogwheels than with any other configuration of the shaving heads. It has not been disputed that the driving of the cutters in a prototype manufactured by Philips with three shaving heads placed in another configuration needed two more cogwheels than when the shaving heads are placed in an equilateral triangle. Fewer movable parts will probably have significance for the cost of manufacturing and for reliability. Considering this, the configuration of the shaving heads cannot be considered as arbitrary. Thus the shape is technically motivated.

To a large extent the shape of the face plate is determined by the configuration of the shaving heads. The face plate has been shaped dependant on the shaving heads in order to create a unit which can reach most parts of the face. The shape of the face plate with rounded corners and slightly convex sides undoubtedly contributes to a smooth and efficient shaving even where it is difficult to reach, such as under the nose. The hairs that have been cut off are kept under the face plate, which can be removed in order to clean it and to carry out maintenance. It is important that the face plate is designed in such a way that it is simple to remove and put back. The design chosen by Philips enables this. Therefore, also the shape of the face plate must be considered as functional.

I understand that Ide Line are appealing this decision to the Swedish Supreme Court. The Court of Appeal was tempted to refer the case to the European Court of Justice. So was I. It will get there in due course, I expect. If it is referred in Sweden and my judgment is pending on appeal it may well be sensible for our Court of Appeal also to refer the case. It would seem that more questions have been raised in this case than were raised in Sweden and so a reference from here may add to any questions posed by the Swedish Supreme Court. Besides, Remington are not parties to the Swedish case.

. . . .

For the present, I must form my own view of the provision. I think Judge Nilsson was broadly right, though I would qualify what he says a little. The difficulty with the majority view, which is in substance Philips' submission here, is that it gives the provision no or almost no scope at all. This is because one can hardly think of any object which must be of a particular shape to perform a function. Moreover it seems unlikely that the Council and Commission, in promulgating the Directive, intended to make it possible to obtain permanent monopolies in matters of significant engineering design.

Turning back to the question of scope, it happens English law has had to face this problem before, in the context of registered designs. The Registered Design Act 1949 barred registration as a design "features of shape or configuration which are dictated solely by the function which the article to be made in that shape or configuration has to perform." On one view the words meant, as is contended here, does the article have to have that shape to work? In *Amp Inc v Utilux Pty Ltd* [1972] RPC 103 at page 109 Lord Reid rejected that meaning [because it would reduce the scope of the provision almost to vanishing point. It would be difficult to imagine any actual case where one shape and one shape alone will work.] I likewise think that the framers of the Directive must have intended a more reasonable result.

I have some minor qualification of Judge Nilsson's interpretation—"shape which is solely motivated by the technical result." The difficulty is the word "motivated." That suggests the question is subjective, thus involving an inquiry into the designer's purpose. That cannot be right, and I do not think Judge Nilsson meant the test to be subjective. So I would pose the inquiry thus: in substance does the shape solely achieve a technical result? I add the qualification "in substance" because I do not believe that shapes with trivial embellishments or variants are outside the exclusion from registrability.

Applying that test I conclude that the shape registered as a trade mark consists exclusively of a shape which is necessary to obtain a technical result.

That is the substance of the Philips head–it is the "business end" of the shaver and has a shaving shape.

Shape which gives substantial value to the goods

Good trade marks add value to goods–that is one of the things they are for. So one must not take this exclusion too literally. I think what is meant is an exclusion of shapes which exclusively add some sort of value (design or functional appearance or perhaps something else though I cannot think of anything) to the goods disregarding any value attributable to a trade mark (*i.e.* source identification) function. A question of degree is obviously involved. For instance the Rolls-Royce grille adds value to a Rolls-Royce. But it does so primarily because it signifies Rolls-Royce and not because of its inherent shape.

Philips say the three-headed shape does not in itself add substantial value to the product, which they suggest is a shaver in the generic sense. "The choice of the three-headed shape does not have an effect on the essential value of the product," says their closing argument. I reject that argument. Philips in their advertising over the years have strained every nerve to educate the public that their rotary shaver and its three headed shape works well. The public believe that to be so and when they see that shape they recognise a shaver of the type which they know does work. Primarily the three-headed shape is recognised as having an engineering function and for that reason it adds substantial value to the product.

Philips also argue here, as they have argued elsewhere, that this exclusion should be not be regarded as overlapping with the other exclusions, particularly the "technical result" exclusion. I reject that. As I have already indicated I think the various exclusions in the Directive can and do overlap.

Mark registered contrary to public policy contrary to section 3(3) [Article 3.1(f)].

Remington rely upon this provision lightly. They say that if one of the other provisions (particularly those in Article 3(2)(a)-(c) do not apply then the registration should be regarded as contrary to public policy. They identify that policy in the language of the White Paper leading to the Act [which noted a concern that the trademark system not be used to obtain an automatic and indefinite extension of the monopoly conferred by a patent, design, or copyright]

. . . .

In this connection Remington rely upon the fact that the three-headed shape was included in various patent claims as recorded above. However, for the reasons I gave in *British Sugar* the White Paper cannot be used as an aid to construction of the Directive and hence our Act. Moreover the policy set out in the White Paper is said to be derived from Article 3(1)(e), not 3(1)(f).

. . . Article 3(1)(f) is not concerned with this sort of matter–it is, as Mr Pumfrey submitted, confined to matters such as are covered by the French legal term *ordre publique*, a matter involving some sort of question of morality. It is not concerned with economic grounds of objection.

I would only add this about the "it-was-once-patented, or expired right" point. In general there is no rule of law which prevents one type of intellectual property right from running parallel to another. . . . Unless there is a specific provision preventing rights from co-existing, then they just do. An example of a non-overlap provision is section 11(1) of the 1994 Act, specifically providing that one registered mark cannot be infringed by the use of another.

The notion that there may not be parallel rights seems to be based on two fallacies, or perhaps one expressed in two different ways. One is that by applying for one form of monopoly the applicant is abandoning all others (the "election theory" . . . . The other is that by obtaining such a monopoly for a fixed term the applicant is deemed to dedicate the subject of the monopoly to the public when the monopoly expires (the "dedication theory"). Both notions are self-evidently contrary to what a real right holder would want. Why should he give anything up? A social scientist might, I suppose, say that the "consideration" for the grant of, say a patent, is the public's right to use the invention after expiry (a theory used to justify the patent system in the past, *see e.g.* per Graham J in *American Cyanamid (Dann's Patent)* [1970] RPC 306 at pages 326-327). But that theory has no place in the modern statutory scheme of things as was held by the House of Lords to be so even under the 1949 Act in *Dann* itself [1971] RPC 425. Still less does it have any application to modern intellectual property legislation.

Thus I think the expired patent point in itself is of no assistance to Remington. The real point is that what one sees is essentially an engineering artefact which, because that is so, is not truly distinctive, and does not properly perform a trade mark function.

. . . .

Infringement: Specific Provisions

. . . Mr Pumfrey submitted on this basis that this was a case of identical marks and goods. Thus he said it was within section 10(1).* The argument involves the proposition that the face of the DT55 is identical with the registered mark. I think this is hopeless. I have said that in practice both sides treated the registered mark as covering a three-dimensional shape. But the actual mark registered is only a picture. I think a consumer would notice the difference between shaving with the DT55 and doing so with a picture.

---

*[Ed. Note: Section 10(1): A person infringes a registered trade mark if he uses in the course of trade a sign which is identical with the trade mark in relation to goods or services which are identical with those for which it is registered.

(2) A person infringes a registered trade mark if he uses in the course of trade a sign where because:

(a) the sign is identical with the trade mark and is used in relation to goods or services similar to those for which the trade mark is registered, or

(b) the sign is similar to the trade mark and is used in relation to goods or services identical with or similar to those for which the trade mark is registered, there exists a likelihood of confusion on the part of the public, which includes the likelihood of association with the trade mark.]

Moreover there are visual differences between the picture and the face of the DT55. Mr Pumfrey says they are slight–and so they are. But that means that the registered mark and the allegedly infringing sign are not identical and so this is not a section 10(1) case.

As to section 10(2) I think the "sign" of the DT55 face is plainly confusingly similar to the registered mark. The fact that this is so in a non-trade mark manner is the real point under section 10(2). . . . I prefer not to decide the point in this case.

Infringement–Defence under Section 11(2) [Article 6.1]?*

I have already noted that Remington's use is honest. It was suggested that it was otherwise than in accordance with honest practices in industrial and commercial matters. It was submitted that Remington "copied", and I suspect they did. After all Philips have shown over the years how to construct an efficient rotary shaver and the three headed sort is one of the best ways of making such a shaver. It is not contrary to law to copy, or even to come unnecessarily close to the product of a rival trader–unless of course the public are deceived or some other intellectual property right is infringed. If this were not so manufacturers would gain permanent monopolies.

Thus the real question is whether the DT55 face is an "indication as to the kind, quality etc" of section 11(2)(b) [Article 6.1(b)]. The language of the defence mirrors that of the objection to validity which I have already considered, namely section 3(1)(a) [Article 3.1]. For the reasons I have already given I think the sign does indeed fall within that language. Indeed if there is a difference it is that the defence is wider than the objection to validity. For Article 3.1 uses the words consist exclusively . . . whereas the defence is not so limited.

Now in *British Sugar* I said at pages [298-99]:

> First I think, unlike section 10, one must here look at the whole context of the use. You cannot tell whether the use is descriptive or not from the use of the sign alone.
>
> . . . .
>
> If the defendant's mark is descriptive to some but has trade mark significance to others, he will not be within the section.

---

*[Ed. Note: Section 11(2) provides that a registered trade mark is not infringed by . . . (b) the use of indications concerning the kind, quality, quantity, intended purpose, value, geographical origin, the time of production of goods or of rendering, of services, or other characteristics of goods or services, . . . provided the use is in accordance with honest practices in industrial or commercial matters. Article 6.1 provides that "The trade mark shall not entitle the proprietor to prohibit a third party from using, in the course of trade, . . . (b) indications concerning the kind, quality, quantity, intended purpose, value, geographical origin, the time of production of goods or of rendering of the service, or other characteristics of goods or services . . . provided he uses them in accordance with honest practices in industrial or commercial matters."]

I have concluded on the facts that Remington's use is, in substance, just descriptive. It denotes a three-headed shaver. In the context of its use the face does not denote trade origin and accordingly is within the section.

Ide Line Aktiebolag v. Philips Elec. NV, [1997] E.T.M.R. 377 (Stockholm District Court 1997). As Mr Justice Jacob noted in *Philips*, in this case, the plaintiff wished to import into Sweden a three headed rotary shaver and thus sought cancellation of Philips' Swedish trademark registrations on the product design for shavers and a declaration that the shavers that it sought to import did not infringe Philips' trademark rights. A majority of the court found Philips' trademark distinctive (on the basis of market surveys showing acquired distinctiveness) and that the design did not exclusively consist of a shape necessary to obtain a technical result because the same result could be obtained by a number of differently shaped shaving heads. Accordingly, the registration was valid, and the differences between the two products were too insignificant to warrant a declaration of noninfringement. Like Mr. Justice Jacob, the Swedish court commented on the genesis of the new Swedish law in the Trademark Directive. The approach of the dissenting Swedish judge to the fact that the new law was derived from the directive is quoted at length above by Mr. Justice Jacob. The Swedish majority commented that "in comparison with previous Swedish law, the directive came to signify a broadening of the possibility to protect a technically motivated shape." Moreover, the majority argued that in interpreting section 13(2) of the Swedish Act [Article 3.1(e) of the directive], which was intended to balance the protection of valuable trademarks and the desire to avoid competitive advantage through the grant of perpetual rights in a technical function, "the Court is to use the wording of the Directive and a general balancing of reasons." The majority also recognized that there were strong arguments to refer a question to the European Court of Justice under ex-Article 177 but refrained from doing so because the case was still at first instance and neither party had requested a reference. The approach of the majority in *Ide Line* is not atypical. The Swedish courts have offered quite extensive protection to product design trade dress in recent years. *See* Stokke Fabrikker v. Playmaster [1998] E.T.M.R. 395 (Ljungby District Court 1997) (protecting design of baby's high chair on basis of acquired distinctiveness notwithstanding expiry of patent on product and continued copyright protection).

Car Wheel Rim Trade Mark Application, IZB 1/95, [1998] E.T.M.R. 584 (Federal Supreme Court 1997) (Germany). The applicant sought to register as a trademark the design of its wheel rim for alloy wheel rims for private cars. The German Patent Office denied the application on the grounds that the mark was "merely an immediately recognizable, true-to-life reproduction of an alloy wheel rim from a top view, which lacks the requisite distinctiveness under section 4(2)(1) of the German Trademarks Act." The Bundespatentgericht denied the applicant's appeal, reasoning that, because the design for which registration was sought was a very simple design, it must be kept available for general use. The need to keep a limited variety of designs available for use meant that a strict standard of distinctiveness must be applied. While acknowledging that wheel designs could be configured so differently that a representation of their appearance could indicate their origin, that is not the case with the majority of wheel rim designs (including the one in question). Moreover, the Bundespatentgericht concluded, the vast majority of the public would not regard the design of a wheel rim as designating a specific manufacturer. The applicant's further appeal to the Federal Supreme Court failed on the grounds of lack of distinctiveness. In the course of its opinion, the Federal Supreme Court addressed the applicant's argument that regard should be had to the registration of other wheel rim designs (both of the applicant and others) with foreign offices:

> It is true that decisions of the Bundespatentgericht recognize that overseas registrations do have meaning in relation to domestic cases, when a mark is a foreign word mark (BGH, Decision of June 7, 1996–IZB 10/94, *The Home Depot*). This decision relates to countries of the language of the mark to be considered, as these are as a rule better able to decide upon the descriptive meaning of such mark, their ability to distinguish and the need to keep them available for general use than are the German authorities dealing with the German application.
>
> This principle cannot however simply be applied to device marks, as this special knowledge of the overseas registration authorities is not required in this consideration of device marks which bear no relation to language. . . .
>
> Therefore, the references to registrations for the countries Japan, Canada, Liechtenstein, and Switzerland are not taken into account in [this] decision . . . .
>
> As far as the appeal refers to registration in the Member States of the European Union (Austria, the Benelux states, Spain, France and Italy) again little may be drawn for the present case. Although these Member States are bound by the [Trademark Harmonization] Directive to adopt uniform requirements for registerability of marks, it does not automatically mean that marks registered overseas under the harmonised law are automatically of relevance to a domestic application.

Product designs have, however, been registered as trademarks in Germany since the implementation of the Directive, and the German law of unfair competition may also provide protection. The central issue in the early decisions under the new German statute appears to be distinctiveness, with the federal Patent Tribunal taking the view (not unlike the recent trend in U.S. federal courts) that a strict standard of distinctiveness is required to prevent restricting the production choices of competitors. *See* Jochen Engelhardt, *Protection of Three Dimensional Trademarks Under German Trademark Law of 1995: First Cases Try to Shape the Landscape*, 13 WIPO Rep. 70 (1998); *see also* Frauke Henning-Bodewig & Heijo E. Ruijsenaars, *Alternative Protection for Product Designs: A Comparative View on German and Benelux Law*, 83 TRADEMARK REP. 439 (1993). Indeed, the test being developed is not unlike that articulated by the Second Circuit in *Landscape Forms, Inc. v. Columbia Cascade Co.*, 113 F.3d 373 (2d Cir. 1997). *See* Engelhardt, *supra*, at 70 (reporting that a design trademark will be distinctive if "it is likely to serve the customer as a means of recognizing a particular firm's goods and thus allow him to distinguish the same or similar products made by different manufacturers").

NOTE: PASSING OFF CASES UNDER U.K. LAW

Prior to the 1994 Trademarks Act, the limited scope of trademark subject matter forced producers to seek protection using the tort of passing off, which largely operated as the U.K.'s unregistered trademark law. *See* Edge v. Nicolls & Sons, [1911] A.C. 693 (H.L.). The two leading cases are *Erven Warnink v. Townend & Sons*, [1979] A.C. 731 (H.L.) (Eng.) and *Reckitt & Coleman Prods. v. Borden*, [1990] R.P.C. 341 (H.L.) (Eng.). Although stated slightly differently by Lord Diplock in the *Warnink* case, the three basic elements of the tort of passing off do not (unsurprisingly) sound unlike a trademark claim: the plaintiff's mark must have reputation; the use by the defendant must amount to a misrepresentation; and there must be damage to the goodwill of the plaintiff. Using this tort, producers had obtained protection against confusingly similar versions of various containers such as the Haig Dimple whisky bottle, *see* John Haig & Co. v. Forth Blending, 1953 R.P.C. 259 (Court of Session, 1953) (Sco.), and a yellow, lemon-shaped plastic container for lemon juice. *See* Reckitt & Coleman Prods. v. Borden, [1990] R.P.C. 341 (H.L.) (Eng.). In certain circumstances, this may also protect the product design itself. *See* Hodgkinson & Corby Ltd. v. Wards Mobility Servs., Ltd., [1994] 1 W.L.R. 1564 (Ch. D. 1994). Indeed, in *Hodgkinson*, Mr. Justice Jacob suggested that a passing off action did not, unlike the new trademarks legislation, contain any functionality defense. In this context, therefore, passing off may offer more expansive protection than trademark registration. *But see Hodgkinson*, [1994] 1 W.L.R. at 1564 (finding for defendant based upon lack of confusion). Complaints about the adequacy of the tort in protecting producers against unauthorized imitation flow more from the strictness with which the courts have interpreted the elements of the cause of action than the tort itself. For example, U.K. courts have been skeptical of the value of survey evidence in proving confusion, even although they have been demanding in requiring proof of confusion. *See* Ruth E. Annand, *Lookalikes under the New United Kingdom Trade Marks Act 1994*, 86 TRADEMARK REP. 142, 160-67 (1996). Moreover, while continental European courts have used a broader tort of unfair competition to address and curtail what they see as free-riding on the efforts of others, the U.K. tort of passing off has been more cautiously applied. The philosophical difference is perhaps best expressed by a passage from the opinion of Mr. Justice Jacob in *Hodgkinson*: "There is no tort of copying. There is no tort of taking a man's market or customers. Neither the market nor the customers are the plaintiff's to own. There is no tort of making use of another's good will as such. There is no tort of competition." [1994] 1 W.L.R. at 1569.

NOTES AND QUESTIONS

(1) **Later Proceedings in *Philips*.** The decision of Mr. Justice Jacob in *Philips* was appealed to the court of appeal. Although the court appeared largely supportive of the lower court's reasoning and of the relatively narrow interpretation of product design protection offered by Mr. Justice Jacob, it agreed that a reference should be made to the European Court of Justice. *See* Philips Elec. v. Remington Consumer Prods., 1999 R.P.C. 809 (Ct. App. 1999) (U.K.). The advocate-general recently issued his opinion, and the Court's judgment is awaited. *See* note 3 below. Should the matter have been referred to the European Court of Justice by the trial court? Both the U.K. and Swedish courts mentioned the possibility but did not make a reference. Does this suggest some disadvantages with the reference procedure that the lower courts wished to avoid?

(2) **Distinctiveness of Product Design.** To be registered as a trademark, the design must both be distinctive and not be subject to the three (functionality-type) exclusions found in Article 3.1 of the directive. What precisely is the test for determining distinctiveness under the directive? What roles, respectively, do the concepts of "capable of distinguishing" and "devoid of distinctive character" play in that assessment? Can you draw parallels to any U.S. conceptual devices? How would Mr. Justice Jacob determine distinctiveness? Is his test/analysis helpful? Does it implement the goal of protecting source-identifying product designs?

The question of distinctiveness of designs is one upon which there is little agreement within national jurisdictions let alone internationally. For example, should courts assume that the public usually does not conceive the shape of a product as an indication of commercial source and thus require proof of secondary meaning? Would this be consistent with the Directive? Would it matter if different countries took different approaches to this issue or applied different tests to determine this question? If one country that offers generous copyright protection to designs adopts a stricter approach to trademark protection, should its copyright law be taken into account in assessing compliance with the directive? If not, why not?

Other U.K. courts have followed the lead of Mr. Justice Jacob in *Philips* and have interpreted the distinctiveness requirement strictly in trade dress cases. *See, e.g.*, Procter & Gamble v. Registrar of Trade Marks (Ct. App., 17 Feb. 1999) (U.K.) (affirming denial of registration of the shape of containers for household products because it was devoid of distinctive character). The *Car Wheel Rim* case suggests that German law is being interpreted like that of the United Kingdom. The EU Trademark Office, the "Office for Harmonisation of the Internal Market," recently accepted for the first time a three dimensional mark consisting of the product itself. The registration–of the shape of the Lego building block–was granted based upon acquired distinctiveness under Article 7(3) of the Trademark Regulation. *See* Application No. 107029, CTM Bulletin No. 90/1998, at 57 (Nov. 23, 1998).

(3) **Article 3.1(e) Exclusions.** Are you satisfied that Mr. Justice Jacob's interpretation of the three Article 3.1(e) exclusions implements the objectives of the directive? Are the tests he articulates to implement those exclusions workable? Do they produce results consistent with the objectives of the directive? Do you prefer the interpretation of the Swedish court in this regard? Although the U.K. court of appeal referred seven questions to the Court of Justice, the advocate-general recently issued his opinion suggesting that the case could be resolved through application of the exclusion of "signs which consist exclusively of the shape of goods which is necessary to obtain a technical result." *See* Case C-299/99, Philips Electronics v. Remington Consumer Prods. (Jan. 23, 2001) (Opinion of Advocate-General Ruiz-Jarabo Colomor). He concluded that the shape in question "appeared to be the perfect example of a merely functional shape," *id.* at ¶ 20, and endorsed Mr. Justice Jacob's approach to the question of alternative designs: "there is nothing in the wording of [Article 3(1)(e)] which makes it possible to conclude that a merely functional shape could be registered if another shape, capable of achieving a comparable result, exists." *Id.* at ¶ 28. He supported this literal interpretation by reference to what he saw as the purpose of the exclusion, namely to prevent trademark law from extending the life of other intellectual property rights that are limited in time. *See id.* at ¶¶ 30-31. Indeed, the advocate-general found further support in the slightly different scope of exclusion of functional designs in the EU design directive, *see infra* § 3.03[B], which, he maintained, would deny protection for design features that are "solely *dictated* by technical function." *See id.* at ¶¶ 32-34 (emphasis in original). The advocate-general read the trademark functionality exclusion as more easily triggered than the design directive exclusion: in the case of designs, "the feature concerned must not only be *necessary* but *essential* in order to achieve a particular technical result." *Id.* at ¶ 34. (In footnote 8, the advocate-general explained that the "semantic contrast which exists in the German version [of the directives] between the adjectives 'erforderlich' and 'bedingt' is particularly telling.") This reading made sense, the advocate-general suggested, because of the different scope of protection offered under trademark law (potentially perpetual) and under the design directive (limited in time). *See id.* at ¶¶ 36-38. To what extent should interpretation of the functionality exclusion be influenced by the interpretation of the parallel provisions in other regimes, such as copyright or design law? *See* Design Directive art. 7.

As in other areas, it has been suggested that because this exclusion echoes earlier Benelux case law, that case law should be given some weight in interpreting the exclusion. Annette Kur has cautioned against this, not only because "Article 3(1)(e) is a provision of genuine Community law and should be interpreted autonomously and on its own merits" but because "Benelux case law in itself is neither perfectly clear nor consistent in this respect." Annette Kur, *Harmonization of Trademark Laws in Europe*, 28 I.I.C. 1 (1997) (discussing different approaches to protection of the shape of the Lego building blocks in Belgium and Holland). Moreover, functionality exclusions could be found in most member states that accepted registration of product designs prior to the adoption of the directive. In his recent opinion in *Philips*, the advocate-general suggested that "explanations as to how the provision at issue came about–as a means of ascertaining the intention of the legislature–are not particularly helpful, nor, in any event, can they supplement the higher considerations on which I base my arguments." Case C-299/99, Philips Electronics v. Remington Consumer Prods. ¶ 41 (Jan. 23, 2001) (Opinion of Advocate-General Ruiz-Jarabo Colomor). This appears to endorse Dr. Kur's view: how do national courts interpret and apply "a provision of genuine Community law . . . autonomously and on its own merits"?

What is the meaning of the exclusion of features that provide "substantial value"? How might this provision be interpreted? Annette Kur has suggested that a broad interpretation of the clause would result in a violation of Article 15(2) of the TRIPS Agreement and thus member states should disregard the provision. *See* Annette Kur, *TRIPS and Trademark Law*, in FROM GATT TO TRIPS: THE AGREEMENT ON TRADE-RELATED ASPECTS OF INTELLECTUAL PROPERTY RIGHTS (Beier & Schricker eds. 1996). Do you agree, either with Dr. Kur's interpretation or her proposed solution?

The functionality rule contained in Article 3 does not apply to the protection of unregistered product design trademarks because the directive seeks only to harmonize the law of registered trademarks. Yet, if protection for unregistered marks was available under the law of passing off or unfair competition where forbidden by the mandatory exclusion of Article 3, the purposes underlying Article 3 would be severely compromised. *See* Peter Jaffey, *The New European Trademarks Regime*, 28 I.I.C. 153 (1997) (suggesting that "there is no generally recognized doctrine of functionality in the law of passing off, although there may be one or two cases in which the suggestion of such a doctrine may be discerned"). How should a national court faced with efforts to protect product designs under passing off approach such an issue?

Can these exclusions be analogized to any concepts used (either presently or historically) in U.S. law? *See* RESTATEMENT (THIRD) OF UNFAIR COMPETITION § 17 (1995); Traffix Devices, Inc. v. Marketing Displays, 69 U.S.L.W. 4172 (2001). If so, what from the U.S. experience might usefully inform the interpretation of these provisions by EU national courts? *See* RUTH E. ANNAND & HELEN NORMAN, BLACKSTONE'S GUIDE TO THE TRADE MARKS ACT 1994, at 84-87 (1994).

(4) **Alternative Solutions in *Philips?*** Mr. Justice Jacob appears to find that "the general reaction of the public to the DT55 was that they thought of Philips." Does this not suggest that the mark was distinctive? If not, why not? Mr. Justice Jacob goes on to explain that "a substantial portion [of the public] would, if the product had not been marked 'Remington', have assumed that the DT55 was made by Philips." Do these two excerpts from the opinion suggest a better resolution of the case more closely tied to the factual findings?

(5) **Post-Directive Interpretation by National Courts.** Has Mr. Justice Jacob given full recognition to the change in U.K. law that the directive (and the implementing legislation) was intended to effect? Does he recognize the possibility of product designs acting as trademarks? As a trademark applicant in the United Kingdom, how confident would you be that U.K. law would now

offer trademark registration to product shapes? *See* Registration No. 2000986 (Sept. 29, 1995) (U.K.) (registration granted for shape of Toblerone chocolate bar). Prior to the 1994 Act, U.K. law restricted trademark registrations to two-dimensional signs; the shapes of products were protected, if at all, under patent, copyright, or design laws. Are there any aspects of the *Philips* opinion that suggest that Mr. Justice Jacob is resisting the change? To what extent should reference be made to the principles formerly applicable under U.K. law? See Procter & Gamble v. Registrar of Trade Marks (Ct. App., Jan. 29, 1999) (noting need to treat pre-directive case law with caution). What type of use should be made of the directive? What is its relevance in interpreting national laws? Are Mr. Justice Jacob, the Swedish majority, and Judge Nilsson (the dissenting Swedish judge) using the EU genealogy of their respective laws in the same way? If their approaches are different, which is most appropriate? *See* Jennifer Davis, *How the Trade Marks Act Shapes Up to Perpetual Monopolies*, [1998] CAMB. L.J. 263, 266 (describing the *Philips* judgment as fitting "squarely within the traditional British approach, although it is presented with a contemporary, free market, European gloss").

(6) **Different Results in Different EU States**. How problematic is it that the Swedish court protected almost the same design—purportedly applying the same law? What might explain the different result? Why did Mr. Justice Jacob reach a different conclusion? To what extent did he disagree with the Swedish court's interpretation of the directive? Might there be good reason for the Swedish courts and the U.K. courts to reach different conclusions? Are these reasons more or less persuasive with different parts of trademark analysis (for example, in assessing each of inherent distinctiveness, secondary meaning, functionality, likelihood of confusion, or dilution)? What (non-mandatory) influence would you expect determinations (a) of other national courts of the EU, (b) of the European Court of Justice, and (c) of the Community Trademark Office (the OHIM), to have on national courts' interpretations of their own trademark laws? What effect should they have? What will (or should) affect the extent of that influence? *See* Jochen Pagenberg, *Opposition Proceedings for the Community Trademark—New Strategies in Trademark Law*, 29 I.I.C. 406, 418 (1998) (noting scholarly criticism of failure to consider decisions of other countries on harmonized trademark law). What weight should Mr. Justice Jacob have given the Swedish opinion, and why?

Should the German Patent Office take account of registrations issued abroad? Is the distinction drawn by the Court between the *Home Depot* case and the analysis of design marks a good one? Why should the language expertise of a foreign office be relevant to whether rights are granted in Germany, but their expertise on designs not relevant? Should the registrations in other EU countries be given more weight than registrations of non-EU countries? What weight should Mr. Justice Jacob have given the Canadian opinion to which he referred in *Philips*?

The OHIM does not have any automatic right to present written submissions to the Court of Justice when it hears a case on the meaning of the Trademark Directive, notwithstanding the use of the same language in the regulation that the office is required to apply. Accordingly, officials from the office have indicated that they would like to have input into the Commission pleadings in such cases.

(7) **Harmonization and the Judicial Task**. How should harmonization affect the way that judges decide cases under national trademark law? Peter Jaffey has argued that:

> [because] it seems likely that different traditions will guide judges in different jurisdictions towards different interpretations of the Directive, . . .successful harmonisation requires each Member State to understand and elucidate its own law even more fully than is necessary for the normal domestic process of application, development and even reform, for which a common tradition allows a certain amount to remain unstated.

Peter Jaffey, *The New European Trademarks Regime*, 28 I.I.C. 153, 191 (1997). Why might this be so? For what additional aspects of judicial analysis will transparency be more crucial than was formerly the case?

NOTE: PROTECTION OF COLOR PER SE AND OTHER NON-TRADITIONAL TRADEMARKS UNDER THE DIRECTIVE

Libertel v. Benelux Trademark Office (Ct. App., The Hague, June 4, 1998), *reported at* 21 EUR. INTELL. PROP. REV. N-8 (1999), *appeal pending*. Libertel sought to register the color orange per se as a mark for telecommunication services. The Benelux Trademark Office rejected the application for lack of distinctiveness, and this was affirmed by the Court of Appeal in The Hague. The court acknowledged that color could serve as a trademark, but suggested that colors were rarely appropriate as trademarks, pointing both to problems of color depletion and the use of colors by consumers for informational purposes other than brand identification (e.g., the colors red and blue to indicate pure and milk chocolate). The Court was particularly concerned about granting rights in the color orange, which is the Dutch national color. Libertel sought to rely on evidence that its mark had acquired distinctiveness, but because the Benelux Trademarks Act had not incorporated the optional Article 3.3 of the directive (which permits member states to consider distinctiveness acquired after the date of filing) the court considered only evidence of distinctiveness as of the date of filing. At that time, Libertel had used the color orange for only one year and normally in connection with the word LIBERTEL.

The EU Trademark Office (the OHIM) has recognized that color per se may be registered as a Community Trademark (CTM). *See* Case R/122/98-3, Wm. Wrigley/Light Green (Bd. of App., Dec. 18, 1998); Case R 7/1997-3, ORANGE ¶ 16 (OHIM, Feb. 12, 1998). In its *Wrigley* opinion, the OHIM Board of Appeal summarized the approaches taken by different member states under their national laws.

> On the one hand, it is true that the [Trademark Regulation], unlike the harmonised trade mark laws of certain Member states, does not expressly include a colour per se, without a delimitation in extent or by shape, amongst the possible forms of trade marks. In this respect, in France, Article L 711-1(2)(c) of the Intellectual Property Code includes *"combinaison ou nuances de couleurs"* ("combinations or shades of colours"). Similarly, in Italy, Article 16 of Decree No 929 of 21 June 1942 includes *"le combinazioni o le tonalità cromatiche"* ("colour combinations or tonalities"). Likewise, in Germany, Section 3(1) of the Trade Mark Act includes *"sonstige Aufmachungen einschließlich Farben und Farbzusammenstellungen"* ("other forms including colours and combination of colours").... On the other hand, it is also true that the wording of the [Regulation], unlike as in Spain and Portugal, does not expressly exclude a colour per se from being conferred protection. In Spain, Article 11(1) of Trade Mark Law No 32/88 provides in material part: *"No podrán registrarse como marcas . . . los siguientes: . . .* (g) *El color por sí solo. Sin embargo, podrá registrarse siempre que esté delimitado por una forma determinada"* ("The following may not be registered: . . . (g) colour in itself. It may, however, be registered provided it is delimited by a given form"). Similarly, in Portugal, Article 166(1)(d) of the Industrial Property Code (Decree Law No 16/95) provides that a trade mark may not consist of "colours, except when they are combined together or with graphics, wording or other elements in a particular and distinctive manner.

As these varied textual changes in the national laws of EU member states would suggest, a uniform approach to the protection of color has not yet evolved at the national level within the EU. *See* Vincenzo Jandoli, *Comment on* Aquatherm v. Tubiplast, 20 EUR. INTELL. PROP. REV. N-113 (1998) (noting that, despite Article 16 of the 1992 Italian Trademark Law's inclusion of "tones of color" within trademark subject matter, courts remain hesitant to recognize color per se as a trademark). At the CTM level, the OHIM concluded that color per se could be registered because a teleological interpretation of the Trademark Regulation suggested that it could fall within the meaning of the term "signs" in Article 4 of the regulation, was capable of performing the distinguishing function of a trademark, and could be represented graphically by means of a two-dimensional optical reproduction of the shade claimed. (Indeed, the board noted that "since data may nowadays be stored electronically, it is now no longer necessary to specify a colour code, which would otherwise be needed, in order to preserve the colour shade [in a specimen] indefinitely without deterioration over time."). Thus, although the board expressed the view that "consumers are not accustomed to making an assumption about the origin of goods on the basis of their color . . . in the absence of a graphic or textual element [and thus] a color per se is not normally used as a means of identification in practice," it concluded that "to restrict the protection of colour marks to a specific presentation would be contrary to the spirit of Community trade mark law." In *Wrigley*, the board upheld a denial of registration where the light green color for which registration was sought was not particularly unique. But the board observed that it might have reached a different conclusion had a claim been based upon acquired distinctiveness.

What limits on trademark subject-matter may be imposed by member states in light of the definition of trademark in the Directive—"any sign capable of being represented graphically"? Professor Gielen suggests that "even smells appear not to be excluded, although graphical representation might cause a problem." *Cf. In re* Clarke, 17 U.S.P.Q.2d 1238, 1240 n.6 (T.T.A.B. 1990) (noting the descriptive text that the registration certificate for olfactory mark would bear and commenting that "the era of scratch and sniff registrations is not yet upon us"). Can sound marks be "graphically represented"? *See* Annette Kur, *Harmonization of Trademark Laws in Europe*, 28 I.I.C. 1, 15 (1997) (reporting negative responses of the administrative authorities in Denmark and Sweden). Why should "graphic representation" confine the scope of trademark subject matter?

WINDSURFING CHIEMSEE PRODUKTIONS-UND VERTRIEBS GMBH (WSC) v. WALTER HUBER AND FRANZ ATTENBERGER
[1999] E.T.M.R. 585 (ECJ 1999)

JUDGMENT OF THE COURT

[T]he Landgericht München I (Regional Court, Munich I) referred to the Court for a preliminary ruling under Article 234 EC [formerly Article 177] a number of questions on the interpretation of Articles 3(1)(c) and 3(3) of [the Trademark Harmonisation Directive.]

Those questions were raised in two sets of proceedings between Windsurfing Chiemsee Produktions-und Vertriebs GmbH (hereinafter 'Windsurfing Chiemsee'), on the one hand, and Boots-und-Segelzubehör Walter Huber (hereinafter 'Huber') and Franz Attenberger, on the other, relating to the use by Huber and Mr Attenberger of the designation 'Chiemsee' for the sale of sportswear.

. . . .

National Law

The Markengesetz (Law on Trade Marks), which has been applicable since 1 January 1995, transposed the Directive into German law. Under Section 8(2)(2) of the Markengesetz, trade marks "which consist exclusively of . . . indications which may serve in trade to designate the . . . geographical origin . . . or other characteristics of the goods" are to be refused registration.

Pursuant to Section 8(3) of the Markengesetz, Section 8(2)(2) does not apply "if the mark, before the time of the decision on registration, as a result of its use for the goods . . . in respect of which registration has been applied for, has gained acceptance among the relevant class of persons."

The Main Proceedings and the Questions Referred

The Chiemsee is the largest lake in Bavaria, with an area of 80 km². It is a tourist destination and surfing is one of the activities carried on there. The surrounding area, called the 'Chiemgau,' is primarily agricultural.

Windsurfing Chiemsee, which is based near the shores of the Chiemsee, sells sports fashion clothing, shoes and other sports goods which are designed by a sister company based in the same place, but are manufactured elsewhere. The goods bear the designation 'Chiemsee.' Between 1992 and 1994, Windsurfing Chiemsee registered that designation in Germany as a picture trade mark in the form of various graphic designs, in some cases with additional features or words such as 'Chiemsee Jeans' and 'Windsurfing–Chiemsee–Active Wear.'

According to the orders for reference, there is no German trade mark by which the word 'Chiemsee' as such is protected. The German registration authorities have hitherto regarded the word 'Chiemsee' as an indication which may serve to designate geographical origin and which is consequently incapable of registration as a trade mark. However, they have allowed the various particular graphic representations of the word 'Chiemsee' and the additional accompanying features to be registered as picture marks.

Huber has been selling sports clothing such as T-shirts and sweat-shirts since 1995 in a town situated near the shores of the Chiemsee. The clothing bears the designation 'Chiemsee,' but this is depicted in a different graphic form from that of the trade marks which identify Windsurfing Chiemsee's products.

Mr Attenberger sells the same type of sports clothing in the Chiemsee area, also bearing the designation 'Chiemsee,' but using different graphic forms and, for certain products, additional features different from those of Windsurfing Chiemsee.

In the main proceedings, Windsurfing Chiemsee challenges the use by Huber and Mr Attenberger of the name 'Chiemsee,' claiming that, notwithstanding the differences in graphic representation of the marks on the products in question, there is a likelihood of confusion with its designation 'Chiemsee' with which, it claims, the public is familiar and which has in any case been in use since 1990.

The defendants in the main proceedings, on the other hand, contend that, since the word 'Chiemsee' is an indication which designates geographical origin and must consequently remain available, it is not capable of protection, and that using it in a different graphic form from that used by Windsurfing Chiemsee cannot create any likelihood of confusion.

The Landgericht München I makes the following observations in its orders for reference:

. . . .

— in order for the main proceedings to be decided, it must be determined whether and, if so, to what extent the interpretation of Article 3(1)(c) of the Directive is affected and restricted by a 'need to leave free' ('Freihaltebedürfnis'), which under German case-law must be a real, current or serious need. If it is unnecessary to have regard to or to evaluate a 'serious need to leave free', then the word 'Chiemsee' is automatically covered by Article 3(1)(c), because it may in any event serve to designate the geographical origin of clothing. If, however, consideration must be given to a 'serious need to leave free,' then the fact that there is no textile industry on the shores of the Chiemsee must also be taken into account. The plaintiff's products may be designed there, but they are manufactured abroad;

. . . .

— the question then arises whether Article 3(3) of the Directive implies that a sign is capable of registration when it has been used as a trade mark for a sufficient length of time and to a sufficient degree, such that a not inconsiderable proportion of the relevant circles view it as a trade mark or whether, as the German legislature has suggested by its use of the concept of 'trade acceptance' ('Verkehrsdurchsetzung') in Section 8(3) of the Markengesetz, the strict requirements which it has hitherto been German practice to impose continue to apply—which would suggest, inter alia, that the extent of 'trade acceptance' required varies according to how important it is for the designation to be left free ('Freihalteinteresse').

In those circumstances, the Landgericht München I, seeking guidance on the interpretation of the Directive, decided to stay proceedings and refer the following questions to the Court of Justice for a preliminary ruling:

1. Questions on Article 3(1)(c):

[The German court sought guidance inter alia on (i) whether the exclusion in Article 3(1)(c) applied only where other businesses already use the word in question to designate the geographical origin of their goods of similar type, or was the mere possibility of such use sufficient, and (ii) whether there must in addition be a need for the use of that indication of origin, for instance because goods of that kind, produced in that region, enjoy a special reputation.]

2. Questions on the first sentence of Article 3(3):

What requirements follow from this provision for the registrability of a descriptive designation under Article 3(1)(c)?

In particular, are the requirements the same in all cases, or are the requirements different according to the degree of the need to leave free?

Is in particular the view hitherto taken in the German case-law, namely that in the case of descriptive designations which need to be left free, trade acceptance in more than 50% of the trade circles concerned is required and is to be demonstrated, compatible with that provision?

Do requirements follow from this provision as to the manner in which descriptive character acquired by use is to be ascertained?

By order of the President of the Court of 8 July 1997, the two cases were joined for the purposes of the written and oral procedure and the judgment.

Questions on Article 3(1)(c) of the Directive

By those questions, which may conveniently be considered together, the national court is essentially asking in what circumstances Article 3(1)(c) of the Directive precludes registration of a trade mark which consists exclusively of a geographical name. In particular, it is asking:

– if the application of Article 3(1)(c) depends on whether there is a real, current or serious need to leave the sign or indication free; and

– what connection there must be between the geographical location and the goods in respect of which registration of the geographical name for that location as a trade mark is applied for.

Windsurfing Chiemsee claims that Article 3(1)(c) of the Directive precludes registration of an indication of geographical origin as a trade mark only where the indication in fact designates a specified place, several undertakings manufacture the goods in respect of which protection is applied for in that place, and the place name is habitually used to designate the geographical origin of those goods.

Huber and Mr Attenberger contend that the fact that there is a serious possibility that a name may in future be used to designate geographical origin in the sector of the goods in question is sufficient to preclude registration of that name as a trade mark under Article 3(1)(c) of the Directive. That provision is not, in their view, directed exclusively at indications of origin which relate to manufacture of the goods.

The Italian Government submits that it must be left open to each undertaking to avail itself of the possibility of using, whether for manufacture or for trade, an indication of geographical origin to designate goods which are connected in any way with a particular place. The mere fact that the indication can be used to designate geographical origin is sufficient for Article 3(1)(c) to come into play and there does not appear to be any need for the possibility to be of a particular kind in order for that provision to apply.

The Commission considers that Article 3(1)(c) should be interpreted as meaning that the question whether there are grounds for refusing registration does not depend on the existence or otherwise in a particular case of a real or serious need to leave a sign or indication free for the benefit of third parties. In the case of sports fashion goods, the place or area where those goods were designed and, if relevant, where the undertaking which placed the order for their manufacture is based, are covered by indications of geographical origin under Article 3(1)(c).

It should first of all be observed that Article 3(1)(c) of the Directive provides that registration is to be refused in respect of descriptive marks, that is to say marks composed exclusively of signs or indications which may serve to designate the characteristics of the categories of goods or services in respect of which registration is applied for.

However, Article 3(1)(c) of the Directive pursues an aim which is in the public interest, namely that descriptive signs or indications relating to the categories of goods or services in respect of which registration is applied for may be freely used by all, including as collective marks or as part of complex or graphic marks. Article 3(1)(c) therefore prevents such signs and indications from being reserved to one undertaking alone because they have been registered as trade marks.

As regards, more particularly, signs or indications which may serve to designate the geographical origin of the categories of goods in relation to which registration of the mark is applied for, especially geographical names, it is in the public interest that they remain available, not least because they may be an indication of the quality and other characteristics of the categories of goods concerned, and may also, in various ways, influence consumer tastes by, for instance, associating the goods with a place that may give rise to a favourable response.

The public interest underlying the provision which the national court has asked the Court to interpret is also evident in the fact that it is open to the Member States, under Article 15(2) of the Directive, to provide, by way of derogation from Article 3(1)(c), that signs or indications which may serve to designate the geographical origin of the goods may constitute collective marks.

In addition, Article 6(1)(b) of the Directive, to which the national court refers in its questions, does not run counter to what has been stated as to the objective of Article 3(1)(c), nor does it have a decisive bearing on the interpretation of that provision. Indeed, Article 6(1)(b), which aims, *inter alia*, to resolve the problems posed by registration of a mark consisting wholly or partly of a geographical name, does not confer on third parties the right to use the name as a trade mark but merely guarantees their right to use it descriptively, that is to say, as an indication of geographical origin, provided that it is used in accordance with honest practices in industrial and commercial matters.

Article 3(1)(c) of the Directive is not confined to prohibiting the registration of geographical names as trade marks solely where they designate specified geographical locations which are already famous, or are known for the category of goods concerned, and which are therefore associated with those goods in the mind of the relevant class of persons, that is to say in the trade and amongst average consumers of that category of goods in the territory in respect of which registration is applied for.

Indeed, it is clear from the actual wording of Article 3(1)(c), which refers to '. . . indications which may serve . . . to designate . . . geographical origin,' that geographical names which are liable to be used by undertakings must remain available to such undertakings as indications of the geographical origin of the category of goods concerned.

Thus, under Article 3(1)(c) of the Directive, the competent authority must assess whether a geographical name in respect of which application for registration as a trade mark is made designates a place which is currently associated in the mind of the relevant class of persons with the category of goods concerned, or whether it is reasonable to assume that such an association may be established in the future.

In the latter case, when assessing whether the geographical name is capable, in the mind of the relevant class of persons, of designating the origin of the category of goods in question, regard must be had more particularly to the degree of familiarity amongst such persons with that name, with the characteristics of the place designated by the name, and with the category of goods concerned.

In that connection, Article 3(1)(c) of the Directive does not in principle preclude the registration of geographical names which are unknown to the relevant class of persons–or at least unknown as the designation of a geographical location–or of names in respect of which, because of the type of place they designate (say, a mountain or lake), such persons are unlikely to believe that the category of goods concerned originates there.

However, it cannot be ruled out that the name of a lake may serve to designate geographical origin within the meaning of Article 3(1)(c), even for goods such as those in the main proceedings, provided that the name could be understood by the relevant class of persons to include the shores of the lake or the surrounding area.

It follows from the foregoing that the application of Article 3(1)(c) of the Directive does not depend on there being a real, current or serious need to leave a sign or indication free ('Freihaltebedürfnis') under German case-law . . . .

Finally, it is important to note that, whilst an indication of the geographical origin of goods to which Article 3(1)(c) of the Directive applies usually indicates the place where the goods were or could be manufactured, the connection between a category of goods and a geographical location might depend on other ties, such as the fact that the goods were conceived and designed in the geographical location concerned.

. . . .

Questions on the first sentence of Article 3(3) of the Directive

By those questions, the national court is essentially asking what requirements must be met, for the purposes of the first sentence of Article 3(3) of the Directive, in order for a mark to have acquired distinctive character through use. In particular, it is asking whether those requirements differ according to the extent of the need to keep the mark free ('Freihaltebedürfnis'), and whether that provision lays down any requirements as to how distinctive character acquired through use is to be assessed.

Windsurfing Chiemsee claims that the degree of distinctive character required under Article 3(3) is the same as that initially required on registration of a mark, and that the concept of the need to keep a mark free is consequently of no relevance. It argues that there need not be specific trade acceptance amongst the relevant class of persons. When assessing distinctive character acquired through use, all the evidence must be admitted and evaluated, including evidence relating to the turnover of the mark, advertising costs and press reports.

Huber contends that Article 3(3) of the Directive and Section 8(3) of the Markengesetz represent 'two sides of the same coin.' Where Article 3(3) refers to the result, that is to say the acquisition of distinctive character, Section 8(3) focuses on the way in which that result was achieved, namely trade acceptance of the mark amongst the relevant class of persons as a distinctive sign of the goods. Whether or not a descriptive name is registrable depends on the case in point and particularly on the importance of leaving the name free. The requirement that trade acceptance of descriptive names should extend to more than 50% of the relevant class of persons is compatible with Article 3(3) of the Directive. Huber further submits that the method to be used to assess trade acceptance of a mark is a matter for national law.

Mr. Attenberger contends that the requirements as to distinctive character under Article 3(3) of the Directive differ from those under Article 3(1)(b), and that the concept of distinctive character is akin to that of 'trade acceptance' under Section 8(3) of the Markengesetz. In his submission, a descriptive mark acquires distinctive character through use if at least 50% of the relevant class of persons throughout the Member State under consideration recognise the sign used as an identifying commercial sign. The required degree of trade acceptance depends on how important it is for the sign to be left free. It is for the national court to determine, under the procedural provisions of its national law, the method by which distinctive character acquired through use is to be assessed.

The Italian Government contends that, where a mark containing a geographical name has acquired a single distinctive character through use unconnected with its graphic representation, there is no reason to deny the proprietor of that mark the broadest possible protection, even to the detriment of third parties. It should be left to the national court to make that assessment, which warrants caution in the absence of precise guidance from the Directive.

The Commission submits that a mark acquires distinctive character through use under Article 3(3) of the Directive if consumers regard the indication in question as a trade mark before an application for registration is made, and that the need to keep it free is of relatively little consequence in this respect. In addition, it argues that distinctive character must be assessed by examining each case individually, but that it need not be established that trade acceptance extends to over 50% of the relevant class of persons. In the Commission's view, account should be taken not only of opinion polls but also, for instance, of statements from chambers of commerce and industry, trade and professional associations and experts.

The first point to note is that Article 3(3) of the Directive provides that a sign may, through use, acquire a distinctive character which it initially lacked and thus be registered as a trade mark. It is therefore through the use made of it that the sign acquires the distinctive character which is a prerequisite for its registration.

Article 3(3) therefore constitutes a major exception to the rule laid down in Articles 3(1)(b), (c) and (d), whereby registration is to be refused in relation to trade marks which are devoid of any distinctive character, descriptive marks, and marks which consist exclusively of indications which have become customary in the current language or in the bona fide and established practices of the trade.

Secondly, just as distinctive character is one of the general conditions for registering a trade mark under Article 3(1)(b), distinctive character acquired through use means that the mark must serve to identify the product in respect of which registration is applied for as originating from a particular undertaking, and thus to distinguish that product from goods of other undertakings.

It follows that a geographical name may be registered as a trade mark if, following the use which has been made of it, it has come to identify the product in respect of which registration is applied for as originating from a particular undertaking and thus to distinguish that product from goods of other undertakings. Where that is the case, the geographical designation has gained a new significance and its connotation, no longer purely descriptive, justifies its registration as a trade mark.

Windsurfing Chiemsee and the Commission are therefore right to assert that Article 3(3) does not permit any differentiation as regards distinctiveness by reference to the perceived importance of keeping the geographical name available for use by other undertakings.

In determining whether a mark has acquired distinctive character following the use made of it, the competent authority must make an overall assessment of the evidence that the mark has come to identify the product concerned as originating from a particular undertaking, and thus to distinguish that product from goods of other undertakings.

In that connection, regard must be had in particular to the specific nature of the geographical name in question. Indeed, where a geographical name is very well known, it can acquire distinctive character under Article 3(3) of the Directive only if there has been long-standing and intensive use of the mark by the undertaking applying for registration. A fortiori, where a name is already familiar as an indication of geographical origin in relation to a certain category of goods, an undertaking applying for registration of the name in respect of goods in that category must show that the use of the mark—both long-standing and intensive—is particularly well established.

In assessing the distinctive character of a mark in respect of which registration has been applied for, the following may also be taken into account: the market share held by the mark; how intensive, geographically widespread and long-standing use of the mark has been; the amount invested by the undertaking in promoting the mark; the proportion of the relevant class of persons who, because of the mark, identify goods as originating from a particular undertaking; and statements from chambers of commerce and industry or other trade and professional associations.

If, on the basis of those factors, the competent authority finds that the relevant class of persons, or at least a significant proportion thereof, identify goods as originating from a particular undertaking because of the trade mark, it must hold that the requirement for registering the mark laid down in Article 3(3) of the Directive is satisfied. However, the circumstances in which that requirement may be regarded as satisfied cannot be shown to exist solely by reference to general, abstract data such as predetermined percentages.

As regards the method to be used to assess the distinctive character of a mark in respect of which registration is applied for, Community law does not preclude the competent authority, where it has particular difficulty in that connection, from having recourse, under the conditions laid down by its own national law, to an opinion poll as guidance for its judgment (*see*, to that effect, Case C-210/96 Gut Springenheide and Tusky [1998] ECR I-4657, paragraph 37).

. . . .

NOTES AND QUESTIONS

(1) **Autonomous EU Law**. To what extent is the German national court being instructed to apply autonomous EU trademark law, and to what extent may it continue to rely on long-standing principles of German trademark law? What considerations should dictate the issues upon which national laws must give way to autonomous principles of EU trademark law? What weight should the German court give to a recent opinion by an advocate-general in a case before the European Court of Justice interpreting the parallel provision in the Trademark Regulation? In that case, Procter & Gamble v. Office for Harmonisation in the Internal Market, Case C-383/99 P (Advocate General Jacobs, E.C.J. April 5, 2001), the advocate-general suggested that it is "better to think of Article 7(1)(c) of the Trademark Regulation, [the parallel provision to Article 3(1)(c) of the directive], as not intended to prevent any monopolising of ordinary descriptive terms but rather to avoid the registration of descriptive brand names for which no protection could be available." The advocate-general acknowledged the inconsistency between his position and *Windsurfing Chiemsee*, which he attributed to the special context of the *Windsurfing* case (namely, geographic terms).

(2) **Survey Evidence**. National judicial attitudes may continue to intrude upon efforts to effect a convergence in trademark laws in the EU because of divergence in the use of survey evidence. For example, German and Scandinavian courts are more willing to rely on such evidence on the question of secondary meaning than in assessing likely confusion. The U.K. courts are generally less receptive to consumer survey evidence. And other countries will have regard to the evidence in either setting. *See* Annette Kur, *Harmonisation of Trademark Laws in Europe*, 28 I.I.C. 1 (1997) (discussing varied approaches).

[3] Scope of Trademark Rights Under the Directive

ARTICLE 5 OF THE TRADEMARK DIRECTIVE
Rights Conferred by a Trade Mark

(1) The registered trade mark shall confer on the proprietor exclusive rights therein. The proprietor shall be entitled to prevent all third parties not having his consent from using in the course of trade–

(a) any sign which is identical with the trade mark in relation to goods or services which are identical with those for which the trade mark is registered;

(b) any sign where, because of its identity with, or similarity to, the trade mark and the identity or similarity of the goods or services covered by the trade mark and the sign, there exists a likelihood of confusion on the part of the public, which includes the likelihood of association between the sign and the trade mark.

(2) Any Member State may also provide that the proprietor shall be entitled to prevent all third parties not having his consent from using in the course of trade any sign which is identical with, or similar to, the trade mark in relation to goods or services which are not similar to those for which the trade mark is registered, where the latter has a reputation in the Member State and where use of that sign without due cause takes unfair advantage of, or is detrimental to, the distinctive character or the repute of the trade mark.

TRADE MARKS ACT 1994 (U.K.)
Infringement of Registered Trade Mark

10(1) A person infringes a registered trade mark if he uses in the course of trade a sign which is identical with the trade mark in relation to goods or services which are identical with those for which it is registered.

(2) A person infringes a registered trade mark if he uses in the course of trade a sign where because–

(a) the sign is identical with the trade mark and is used in relation to goods or services similar to those for which the trade mark is registered, or

(b) the sign is similar to the trade mark and is used in relation to goods or services identical with or similar to those for which the trade mark is registered,

there exists a likelihood of confusion on the part of the public, which includes the likelihood of association with the trade mark.

(3) A person infringes a registered trade mark if he uses in the course of trade a sign which

(a) is identical with or similar to the trade mark, and

(b) is used in relation to goods or services which are not similar to those for which the trade mark is registered, where the trade mark has a reputation in the United Kingdom and the use of the sign, being without due cause, takes unfair advantage of, or is detrimental to, the distinctive character or the repute of the trade mark.

a. Likelihood of Association

WAGAMAMA LTD v. CITY CENTRE RESTAURANTS PLC
[1995] FSR 713 (Ch. D.) (Eng).

LADDIE J.

This is an action for registered trade mark infringement and passing off. The plaintiff company, Wagamama Limited, owns and operates a [Japanese-style] restaurant under the name WAGAMAMA. It is also the proprietor of three registered trade marks. Each mark consists of the word WAGAMAMA. These registrations are in classes 32, 33 and 42 and cover a range of services and goods including restaurant services, catering services, beer, alcoholic and non-alcoholic drinks and mineral water. In this action nothing turns on the precise goods covered by the registrations nor is the validity of any of the registrations in issue.

[The court noted that WAGAMAMA has been very successful and that it was not in dispute that the plaintiff owns a significant reputation in its mark WAGAMAMA, at least in relation to its business of running an inexpensive Japanese-style noodle bar.] The defendant is also in the restaurant business. It, or its wholly owned subsidiaries, run a number of restaurant chains. . . .

In late 1993 the defendant decided to develop another branded restaurant chain. In the words used by the defendant's witnesses, this was to be an American theme restaurant with Indian decor and food. Mr Fysh, who appeared for the plaintiff, described it as having a decor evoking the atmosphere of an up station Indian Civil Service club of the Raj which had been recently visited by a wealthy and benevolent American. The name eventually chosen for this new chain was RAJAMAMA. The first restaurant bearing this name was opened at the very end of April 1995.

. . . .

It is convenient to consider the issue of trade mark infringement first. This part of the case raises an important question of law: what acts now constitute an infringement of a registered trade mark?

TRADE MARK INFRINGEMENT

The Statutory Framework

Infringement in this action is to be determined in accordance with [Section 10 of] the Trade Marks Act 1994 (the 1994 Act). . . .

These provisions are new to our law. Prior to the 1994 Act, infringement of a registered trade mark was covered by the Trade Marks Act 1938 (the 1938 Act). . . .

Infringement under the 1938 Act

Under the 1938 Act, to find infringement the court compared the mark as registered with the mark as used by the alleged infringer. Whether there was infringement was determined by answering the question "is the mark of which complaint is made confusingly similar" to the one which is registered. The case law in which section 4(1) of the 1938 Act and its predecessors were considered, made it clear that what counted was confusion as to the source of the goods or services bearing the offensive mark. In essence the court would determine whether, as a result of similarities between the marks, goods or services bearing the alleged infringer's mark were likely to be thought to be derived from or connected with the proprietor of the registered mark. . . . If . . . . the marks were too similar, usually infringement would be found even if in the market place the infringer took steps to prevent confusion in fact occurring–for example by putting disclaimers on his goods. Indeed the proprietor might not have used his registered mark at all so confusion in the market place would be impossible, yet he could succeed in infringement proceedings at least until the mark was removed from the register for non-use. To this extent therefore, a registered trade mark created a monopoly which might sometimes go beyond what was strictly necessary to protect the proprietor's goods and his reputation. Nevertheless the confusion which was looked for was confusion as to source or origin of the goods. It was enough that the similarity of the marks would make a customer believe that the alleged infringer's goods were associated with the proprietor's goods or services, for example that they were an extension of the range of goods made by the proprietor; *see* Ravenhead Brick Co v Ruabon Brick Co (1937) 54 RPC 341 (the *"Rus"/"Sanrus"* case). However even in these cases, the association had to be an association as to source or origin. In this action this type of confusion as to source has been referred to by both parties as "classic infringement."

Infringement under the 1994 Act

There is no dispute between the parties that such classic infringement by confusion as to the source or origin of goods or services will also constitute an infringement under section 10 of the 1994 Act. The plaintiff alleges that there is such classic infringement in this case. That is a matter to which I will return later. However the plaintiff goes further. It says that section 10 of the 1994 Act, particularly section 10(2), covers confusion in a much broader sense. It is said that the registered proprietor can prevent mere association between the marks. It is argued that there will now be infringement if, on seeing the defendant's mark, the registered mark would be "called to mind" by a customer even if there is no possibility of the customer being under any misapprehension as to the origin of the goods. This is a new concept to those steeped in British trade mark law.

To illustrate his point, Mr Fysh referred to a number of witness statements. In these various members of the public said inter alia that on hearing the name RAJAMAMA their first thoughts were of WAGAMAMA because the names sound similar. Mr Fysh said that even if their evidence had stopped there that sort of association without any more indicates trade mark infringement. He said that this was so even if the customer would have no doubt when considering just the trade marks that they are similar but unconnected. This type of association in which there is no confusion as to origin but the infringing mark "brings to mind" the registered one, I shall refer to in this judgment as "non-origin association."

The arguments advanced in favour of this wide scope to infringement are based upon the existence of the words "a likelihood of confusion on the part of the public, which includes the likelihood of association with the trade mark" which are to be found at the end of section 10(2). Mr Fysh accepted that the reference to likelihood of confusion covered classic infringement as discussed above but he argued that there were only two possible constructions which could be put upon the final words "which includes the likelihood of association with the trade mark." Either these words added nothing to the requirement of confusion and merely performed the function of clarifying that association in the classic sense was included within the scope of infringement or it is a deeming provision which has the effect of extending trade mark protection so as to cover non-origin association. He says the latter is the proper construction and in support of this he deployed a number of arguments. First he says that by applying purely domestic principles of interpretation of statutes, his construction is correct. Secondly he advances a group of arguments based upon the European origins of the 1994 Act in support of the proposition that our trade mark law must be construed to be consistent with Benelux trade mark law where non-origin association has for some years been accepted as a form of trade mark infringement. I shall consider separately each of these routes.

The Domestic Interpretation Route

In *Hill v William Hill (Park Lane) Ltd* [1949] AC 530 at 546, Viscount Simon said:

> ... it is to be observed that though a Parliamentary enactment (like parliamentary eloquence) is capable of saying the same thing twice over without adding anything to what has already been said once, this repetition in the case of an Act of Parliament is not to be assumed. When the legislature enacts a particular phrase in a statute the presumption is that it is saying something which has not been said immediately before. The rule that a meaning should, if possible, be given to every word in the statute implies that, unless there is good reason to the contrary, the words add something which would not be there if the words were left out.

Based on this, Mr Fysh says that the words "which includes the likelihood of association with the trade mark" at the end of section 10(2) must do more than merely repeat what is already covered by the earlier words. It must cover something other than classical infringement.

I do not accept this argument. What Viscount Simon was doing was trying to work out, from the words used, what the legislative intent was. At that time it was no doubt believed, or at least hoped, that British legislation was drafted with precision and economy. It was therefore legitimate to start from the premise that each word used in a statute was necessary and there was no tautology. Even by 1949 this was recognised as an assumption which was not always to be trusted. In the *Hill* case Viscount Jowitt pointed out that the legislature sometimes indulged in tautology. . . .

When construing the 1994 Act it is necessary to bear in mind the legislative context. The Act was intended, amongst other things, to implement [the Trademark Harmonisation Directive]. In particular, the provisions of section 10 of the Act are intended to implement the provisions of Article 5 of that Directive. The court's task is to try to discover the intent behind the words used by the legislature. It would be wrong to apply rules of construction developed during a period when one philosophy of draftmanship was prevalent to a statute drafted when an entirely different philosophy applied. In particular it is quite artificial for the court to pretend that each word of a modern statute which has been lifted more or less verbatim from an EC directive was chosen with the economy which was believed to have been applied to the drafting of British statutes of purely domestic origin. There is no basis upon which the court can assume that the original Directive was drafted so as to avoid tautology. It follows that there is no reason to conclude that the last 10 words in section 10(2) must have been included for the purpose of expanding the scope of infringement.

Indeed, viewed solely linguistically, section 10(2) appears to point away from Mr Fysh's construction. If the words "likelihood of association with the trade mark" cover non-origin association, they cover classical infringement, that is to say likelihood of confusion, also. However, if this is so there would not be any point in including the reference in section 10(2) to "likelihood of confusion" since it is comprehended within "likelihood of association." Furthermore it is unconventional use of language to provide that the smaller (*i.e.* likelihood of confusion) includes the larger (*i.e.* likelihood of association) which would appear to be what the section says if Mr Fysh is correct.

It is therefore necessary to consider Mr Fysh's other arguments on construction.

The European Interpretation Route

Mr Fysh pointed to the fact that the words "the likelihood of association with the trade mark" in our Act are taken from Article 5(1) of the 1988 Directive. [Mr. Justice Laddie quoted the language of Article 5(1)].

The words "which includes the likelihood of association between the sign and the trade mark" in the Directive are said to be derived from Benelux trade mark law where they cover non-origin association. Therefore Mr Fysh says that the words must be treated as having the same meaning in the 1994 Act as they do in Benelux law. There are three arguments which he deploys in support of this. First he says that a document exists which indicates that the words in the Directive were intended to have the meaning for which he contends. Secondly he says that whether or not any document exists which so indicates, it is a matter of common knowledge that the words were inserted in the Directive for this purpose. Thirdly he says that the Directive was supposed to introduce a new era of trade mark law harmony in the European Union. Since the Benelux courts have construed their equivalent trade mark law derived from the Directive to cover non-origin association, the British courts should do likewise both as a matter of comity and to help deliver the harmony which the Directive hoped to secure.

In support of the arguments based on Benelux law, the plaintiff has adduced evidence from Professor Charles Gielen. . . . One of his principal areas of practice is trade mark law. In his witness statement he says as follows:

> Whether a guiding principle or not, what is certain is that in attempting to harmonise Member States' trade mark law, the Commission have imposed upon Member States a requirement to incorporate the likelihood of association concept as developed under Benelux law.

He explained the width of the Benelux concept of likelihood of association. For example he gave the following evidence:

Q. Can you just help me on this: if Company A has a registered trademark, and Company B comes on to the market with another trademark where the marks have similarities, but no member of the public would be confused as to origin, but some members of the public say: "Well that has a passing similarity. It brings to mind the company A's mark, but I know that they are nothing to do with each other." Would that be an infringement?

A. That is an infringement, yes.

Q. In that case, the infringement would have the effect of protecting Company A?

A. Yes.

Q. Well beyond what is necessary to safeguard his trade, his actual trade?

A. Well I think it protects his actual trade, because if the relevant part of the public thinks of trademark A when seeing trademark B, the effect of that is, in fact, loss of exclusivity and dilution. So, I think the Benelux concept of association includes that danger.

I will now consider each of Mr Fysh's arguments and the conclusions to which Professor Gielen has come.

Minutes of the Council Meeting

Professor Gielen exhibits to his witness statement a document (the "Gielen document") which, in so far as material, is in the following terms:

ANNEX

STATEMENTS

for entry in the minutes of the Council meeting
at which the Directive is adopted

5. Re Article 4(1)(b) and Article 5(1)(b)

(a) . . .

(b) "The Council and the Commission note that "likelihood of association" is a concept which in particular has been developed by Benelux case-law".

. . . Professor Gielen . . . said that he believed from a source of his that the statement as recorded above was in fact entered on the Council minutes. . . . The Council minutes are confidential. The Gielen document is not a copy of them. In my view it would be wrong for the court to draw any conclusions as to the meaning of a directive on the basis of suggestions as to what is said in the minutes when the minutes themselves are closed to inspection.

The provenance of the wording is notorious

Mr Fysh's second argument is that it is common knowledge that the wording in Article 5 of the Directive is derived from Benelux law and is intended to convey into the trade mark law of all Member States the same concepts. In other words it does not matter that the minutes of Council meeting are confidential because everyone knows what was intended. . . .

For the purpose of this case it is right to consider the issue from first principles. [I]t is permissible to refer to travaux préparatoires in construing European legislation. On the other hand, . . . it is not permissible to refer to confidential Council minutes. In my view it would be wrong and dangerous to rely on Chinese whispers as to the origin and meaning of such legislation, no matter how commonly believed. What if the popular belief in fact is wrong? How do you challenge it? . . . .

Comity

The purpose of the 1988 Directive was to ensure a measure of uniformity between the trade mark laws of Member States of the European Union. For that reason it is right that British courts should pay regard to decisions in the courts of other Member States on equivalent provisions in their law. However it is apparent from the expert evidence of Professor Gielen that the Benelux courts have simply assumed that the Directive made no alteration to their domestic law. [Certain other authors] suggest that this assumption may well have been wrong. In any event, the obligation of the English court is to decide what the proper construction is. If that construction differs from that adopted in the Benelux countries, one, at least, is wrong. It would not be right for an English court to follow the route adopted by the courts of another Member State if it is firmly of a different view simply because the other court expressed a view first. The scope of European legislation is too important to be decided on a first past the post basis.

The Court's approach to construction

Since none of the arguments on construction put forward by the plaintiff is acceptable, it is necessary to approach the Directive and the 1994 Act from first principles.

Monopolies are the antithesis of competition. Intellectual property rights such as patents, trade marks and copyright can create barriers to trade within a country. They can create barriers to trade between countries. Differences between the laws of Member States of the European Union may add further obstructions to inter-state trade because what is permissible under the law of one Member State may be prohibited under the law of its neighbour. However, both at the domestic level and at the international level monopolies can be tolerated or even encouraged if they assist the development of commerce in some other way. Patent monopolies are the classic example. A valid patent may prevent competitors from entering a given field of commerce for up to 20 years. But this is a price which society, through its legislators, has agreed to pay to secure the increased investment in research and development which it is hoped patent monopolies will encourage. The important factor to bear in mind is that what justifies the monopoly is not the monopoly itself but the extent to which it gives, or is hoped to give, a benefit to commerce which compensates for the temporary restraint on competition. The monopoly is an adjunct to, and is designed to promote, commerce. This is central to the western system of commerce. Monopolies are the exception, not the rule. *Marsden v Saville Street Co* (1878) LR 3 Ex D 203. They need to be justified. As long ago as 1615 in this country it was said that the effect of an unjustified monopoly was "to take away free trade, which is the birthright of every subject" (The Clothworkers of Ipswich (1615) Godbolt 252).

Trade marks have historically been used to protect the trade with which they are associated. . . .That the primary function of trade marks is to indicate origin of goods or services has . . . been accepted by the European Court of Justice. In [*SA CNL-Sucal NV v HAG* [1990] 3 CMLR 571 (*HAG II*)], the court said at 608:

> Consequently, as the Court has stated on many occasions, the specific subject-matter of a trade mark right is to grant the owner the right to use the mark for the first marketing of a product and, in this way, to protect him against competitors who would like to abuse the position and reputation of the mark by selling products to which the mark has been improperly affixed. To determine the exact effect of this exclusive right which is granted to the owner of the mark, it is necessary to take account of the essential function of the mark, which is to give the consumer or final user a guarantee of the identity of the origin of the marked product by enabling him to distinguish, without any possible confusion, that product from others of a different provenance. [cit].

Furthermore in *Deutsche Renault AG v Audi AG* [1995] 1 CMLR 461, the Court has also indicated that the essential function of a trade mark extends to protection from association as to origin. In that case the Court said at 483, 484:

> . . . According to German law, there is a risk of confusion between two trade marks not only when the trade concerned might mistakenly assume that the goods concerned come from one and the same undertaking (direct risk of confusion) but also when the mistaken assumption relates to the existence of an organisational or economic link between the undertakings concerned, such as a licensing agreement under which one undertaking is authorised to manufacture a product with the same properties as the product of the other (risk of confusion in the broader sense).
>
> No exception can be taken under community law to the protection granted by a national law against this last-mentioned risk of confusion since it corresponds to the specific subject-matter of the trade mark right which, as stated above, consists in protecting the proprietor against the risk of confusion.

As mentioned above, there are two possible constructions which may be placed on Article 5 of the 1988 Directive and section 10(2) of the 1994 Act. The rights of the proprietor against alleged infringers may be limited to classic infringement which includes association as to origin or, following the Benelux route, it could cover not only classic infringement but also non-origin association. In my view, the former construction is to be preferred. If the broader scope were to be adopted, the Directive and our Act would be creating a new type of monopoly not related to the proprietor's trade but in the trade mark itself. Such a monopoly could be likened to a quasi-copyright in the mark. However, unlike copyright, there would be no fixed duration for the right and it would be a true monopoly effective against copyist and non-copyist alike. I can see nothing in the terms of the Directive (or our Act), or in any secondary material which I could legitimately take into account, which would lead me to assume that this was its objective. On the contrary, the preamble to the Directive seems to point in the opposite direction since it states:

> Whereas the protection afforded by the registered trade mark, the function of which is in particular to guarantee the trade mark as an indication of origin, . . .

Furthermore there appears to be little commercial justification for any such extension of trade mark rights. If it had been the intention to make the directive identical with Benelux law on this important issue it could have said so. Indeed, in view of the fact that to have done so would have been significantly to expand trade mark rights and thereby significantly restrict the freedom of traders to compete, I would have expected any such expansion to have been stated in clear and unambiguous words so that traders throughout the European Union would be able to appreciate that their legislators had created a new broad monopoly. As it is, no such clear and unambiguous words have been used and the language of the Directive and the 1994 Act is consistent with the rights being restricted to classical infringement.

It follows that this Court cannot follow the route adopted by the Benelux courts on this issue. This is regrettable since one of the main objectives of the 1988 Directive was to avoid differences in scope of trade mark rights which could lead to barriers to inter-state trade. Nevertheless the natural inclination to come to a conclusion which would further harmony on this issue is not so strong that I am prepared to agree that a new millstone round the neck of traders has been created when that is not my view. If the plaintiff is to succeed in its case of trade mark infringement it must do so on the classic grounds.

Does the defendant infringe?

. . . .

I have come to the conclusion that the defendant's mark . . . is so similar to the plaintiff's registered mark that in use there exists a substantial likelihood of confusion on the part of the relevant public. That confusion is likely to take the form that some members of the public as a result of imperfect recollection will think that the marks are the same while others will think that they are associated in the sense that one is an extension of the other. . . . It follows that the plaintiff succeeds on the issue of trade mark infringement.

PASSING OFF

. . . .

If the plaintiff is to succeed on its claim for passing off, it is necessary for it to prove that there has been a misrepresentation giving rise to a real likelihood of damage. [The court concluded that the possibility of confusion and imperfect recollection are significant and thus that the allegation of passing off was also made out.]

— — —

NOTES AND QUESTIONS

(1) **Interpreting Harmonization-Inspired National Law**. Is Mr. Justice Laddie suggesting the need for a different interpretative philosophy when reading statutes implementing international obligations? If so, what differences would be appropriate? Does the *Wagamama* opinion pay sufficient regard to the decision of Benelux courts? What amount of deference is owed in the name of comity? Was the EU legislation intentionally vague in its reference to "likelihood of association"? Why might that be so?

(2) **Measuring the Success of Harmonization**. Do you agree with the contention of Paul Harris that the *Wagamama* decision "calls into question what function a trademark serves and whether the modernising legislation of both the Directive and the Trade Marks Act 1994 have really achieved all that was claimed in respect of them"? Paul Harris, *UK Trade Mark Law: Are You Confused?*, 17 EUR. INTELL. PROP. REV. 601, 603 (1995). Assuming that *Wagamama* was correctly decided, what has the directive and the 1994 legislation achieved? If it was incorrectly decided, what does that teach about the means by which harmonisation efforts should be approached in future? What are the advantages, if any, of continuing to permit national courts to offer interpretations of principles that are intended to be common throughout the European Union? *Cf.* Heidi Hurdle, *Jacob J. Treats Us All*, 18 EUR. INTELL. PROP. REV. 299, 304 (1996) (speed with which trademark disputes are being handled in the U.K. courts is good news for the U.K. legal system "which faces increasing competition from others in the EU, such as that of the Dutch system"). Would other alternatives, such as a single European law, enforced nationally, be preferable?

(3) **A Deceptiveness Standard**. Peter Jaffey concludes that:

> leaving aside the reference to association, the test [under Section 10(2) of the 1994 Act] is ostensibly a deceptiveness test, as is appropriate where registration is not limited to inherently distinctive marks. If this is the case, the test is distinct from that previously applicable to trade mark infringement in English law, where the similarity test applied, and instead corresponds to that applied in passing off (and possibly to the infringement of a trade mark registered under the Lanham Act).

If Jaffey is correct about the prior U.K. infringement test, what does this mean for Mr. Justice Laddie's reasoning?

(4) **Likelihood of Association**. How different are the "likelihood of association" and "likelihood of confusion as to association" standards? Section 32 of the Lanham Act, 15 U.S.C. § 1114, imposes liability upon "any person who,

without the consent of the registrant, uses . . . the registered mark in connection with the sale, offering for sale, distribution, or advertising of any goods or services in connection with which such use is likely to cause confusion," but no longer limits actionable confusion to source-confusion. In 1962, Congress amended section 32 of the Lanham Act, Pub. L. No. 87-772, 76 Stat. 769, evincing "a clear purpose to outlaw the use of trademarks which are likely to cause confusion, mistake or deception of any kind, not merely of purchasers nor simply as to source of origin." Syntex Labs. v. Norwich Pharmacal, Co., 437 F.2d 566, 568 (2d Cir. 1971); *see also* 15 U.S.C. § 1125(a)(1)(A).

(5) **Relationship of Section 10(2) and Section 10(3)**. It has been argued that insisting on likely confusion under section 10(2) creates the anomaly that a mark may receive greater protection through an action for dilution under section 10(3) against use on dissimilar goods than upon similar goods (under the allegedly more restrictive section 10(2)). *See, e.g.*, Ruth E. Annand, *Lookalikes under the New United Kingdom Trade Marks Act 1994*, 86 TRADEMARK REP. 142, 157 (1996). Which aspect of confusion-based actions does this argument miss? (Hint: why was protection against dilution thought necessary in the first place?)

(6) **The *Wagamama* Debate**. The merits of Mr. Justice Laddie's interpretation of section 10(2) has been the subject of a long-running (and extremely spirited) debate between Anselm Kamperman Sanders and Peter Prescott. *See* Anselm Kamperman Sanders, *The Wagamama Decision: Back to the Dark Ages of Trade Mark Law*, 18 EUR. INTELL. PROP. REV. 3 (1996); Peter Prescott, *Think Before You Waga Finger*, 18 EUR. INTELL. PROP. REV. 317 (1996); Anselm Kamperman Sanders, *The Return to Wagamama*, 18 EUR. INTELL. PROP. REV. 521 (1996); Peter Prescott, *Has the Benelux Trade Mark Law Been Written into the Directive*, 19 EUR. INTELL. PROP. REV. 99 (1997).

(7) **Article 4(1)(b)**. Article 4(1)(b) of the directive provides that

> a trade mark shall not be registered or, if registered, shall be liable to be declared invalid . . . if because of its identity with, or similarity to, the earlier trade mark and the identity or similarity of the goods or services covered by the trade marks, there exists a likelihood of confusion on the part of the public, which includes the likelihood of association with the earlier trade mark.

This is the same language as considered in the infringement context in *Wagamama*. In 1997, in *Sabel v. Puma*, the European Court of Justice issued an opinion holding that Article 4(1)(b) is to be interpreted as meaning that "the mere association which the public might make between two trade marks as a result of their analogous semantic content is not in itself a sufficient ground for concluding that there is a likelihood of confusion within the meaning of that provision." The Court was essentially asked to determine whether, as the Benelux government claimed, Article 4(1)(b) can apply where there is no likelihood of direct or indirect confusion, but only a likelihood of association in the strict sense. That interpretation of the directive, which was rejected in *Wagamama*, was contested by both the U.K. government and by the

Commission. Does the decision of the European Court of Justice in *Sabel* mandate a change in Benelux trademark law? The Benelux courts tried for some time to find room for ambiguity in the Court of Justice's *Sabel* decision, *see* Marca Mode v. Adidas AG, [1999] E.T.M.R. 791, 796-97 (Sup. Ct.) (Neth.), but the Court of Justice has rebuffed any efforts to limit *Sabel* in a recent decision. *See* Adidas AG v. Marca Mode CV, [2000] E.T.M.R. 723 (E.C.J. 2000) (confirming the *Wagamama* interpretation).

British Sugar Plc v. James Robertson & Sons Ltd, 1996 R.P.C. 281 (Chancery Division) (UK). The plaintiff owned the registration in the U.K. for the word TREAT for dessert sauces and syrup. The defendant produced a toffee flavored spread, and on the background of the label used the phrase "Robertson's Toffee Treat" coupled with a description "Irresistibly rich toffee spread." In his opinion, Mr. Justice Jacob canvassed various significant issues of substantive trademark law, as well as various issues pertinent to the question of harmonization. First, the court rejected the threshold argument by the defendant that, under Section 10 of the U.K. Act, infringement only occurs where the defendant uses the mark "as a trade mark." (A purely descriptive fair use by a defendant may, however, be protected by section 11(2), a provision noted in *Philips. See also Bravado Merchandising Services Ltd v Mainstream Publishing (Edinburgh Ltd)*, 1996 FSR 205.) The argument of the defendant rested upon Section 9 of the U.K. Act. Section 9(1) provides that:

> The proprietor of a registered trade mark has exclusive rights in the trade mark which are infringed by use of the trade mark in the United Kingdom without his consent. The acts amounting to infringement, if done without the consent of the proprietor, are specified in section 10.

The defendant argued that there was a gloss which must be read into all the infringement provisions, namely that the sign must be used as a trade mark. As a result, because the defendant (it was argued) did not use "Treat" as a trade mark, there could be no infringement within section 10. Mr. Justice Jacob noted that the words in section 9(1), "by the use of the trade mark," were not in the Directive. Thus, he concluded that the gloss suggested by the defendant, which depended on these words, "could not apply to the Directive." The judge noted in passing that "the infringement provisions are supposed to be implementing Article 5. For reasons which baffle me our Parliamentary draftsman did not simply copy this. He set about re-writing it."

Instead, the court concluded that Section 10 requires the court to see whether the sign registered as a trade mark is used in the course of trade and then to consider whether that use falls within one of the three defining subsections, namely:

Same goods/same mark: section 10(1);

Same mark/similar goods, and

similar mark/same or similar goods: section 10(2);

Same or similar mark/dissimilar goods: section 10(3).

The court concluded that the defendant's product did not fall within the specification of goods for which the mark is registered ("dessert sauce or syrup") and thus the case was dealt with under Section 10(2). TREAT was the very mark registered and was clearly used by Robertson's. The questions arising under section 10(2)(a) are:

(1) Is the mark used in the course of trade?

(2) Are the goods for which it is used similar to those covered by the registration?

(3) Is there a likelihood of confusion because of that similarity?

The plaintiff sought to elide the questions of confusion and similarity, arguing that there is "use in relation to a product so similar to a dessert sauce that there exists a likelihood of confusion because the product may or will be used for identical purposes." Mr. Justice Jacob rejected the attempt, arguing that "the sub-section does not merely ask will there be confusion?: it asks is there similarity of goods?, and, if so, is there a likelihood of confusion? The point is important. For if one elides the two questions then a "strong" mark would get protection for a greater range of goods than a "weak" mark. For instance Kodak for socks or bicycles might well cause confusion, yet these goods are plainly dissimilar from films or cameras. I think the question of similarity of goods is wholly independent of the particular mark the subject of registration or the defendant's sign." Mr. Justice Jacob continued:

> How then is the court to approach the question of similarity? Neither the Act nor Directive . . . provides assistance. Given [that] that is so I think I must consider the matter as a matter of principle. First it should be noted that the wider the scope of the concept, the wider the absolute scope of protection of a mark may be. In effect a registration covers the goods of the specification plus similar goods. No one may use the registered mark or a similar mark for any of those goods unless he has some other defense. This suggests caution. Otherwise, however narrow a specification, the actual protection will be wide. In particular this would be so in the important sort of case where a mark owner only got registration on the basis of actual distinctiveness for a narrow class of goods. It would surely be wrong that he should then in practice get protection for a wide range of goods. If a man wants wide protection he can always ask for it and will get it only if his claim is justified. The old rule that you could not infringe if your goods were even just outside a specification was too rigid. It meant (to use a classic example of Mr. TA Blanco White QC) that a registration of a mark for "3-holed razor blades imported from Venezuala" could not be infringed by use of the mark on a 2-holed razor blade so imported. But I do not think that the introduction of infringement for similar goods has vastly widened the scope of potential protection. . . .[T]he following factors must be relevant in considering whether there is or is not similarity:

(a) The respective uses of the respective goods or services;

(b) The respective users of the respective goods or services;

(c) The physical nature of the goods or acts of service;

(d) The respective trade channels through which the goods or services reach the market;

(e) In the case of self-serve consumer items, where in practice they are respectively found or likely to be found in supermarkets and in particular whether they are, or are likely to be, found on the same or different shelves;

(f) The extent to which the respective goods or services are competitive. This inquiry may take into account how those in trade classify goods, for instance whether market research companies, who of course act for industry, put the goods or services in the same or different sectors.

Applying this test, the court concluded that the spread is not to be regarded as similar to the dessert sauces and syrups of the registration and thus there is no infringement.

Throughout the opinion, Mr. Justice Jacob was also skeptical about counsel's reference to legislative history, in the form of parliamentary statements, for assistance. Such reference has only recently been endorsed by the U.K. courts. *See* Pepper v Hart [1993] AC 593 (House of Lords) (allowing reference to Hansard to find out the meaning of Parliament in certain limited cases where a statutory intention is ambiguous.) He suggested that:

> In the case of a provision intended to implement a Directive I cannot think that the *Pepper* principle can apply. The intention of Parliament is to implement whatever the Directive means. Views expressed in Parliament about the meaning, even by [a] Minister, cannot assist in resolving any ambiguity which stems from the Directive itself. Neither the courts of any other country whose trade marks laws are supposed to implement the Directive, or the European Court of Justice in interpreting it, would refer to what a British Minister said in Parliament in the course of implementation here. It would be irrelevant. What matters is the language of the Directive. That is why it is so important that those responsible for this kind of legislation make serious efforts to be clear. If they are not then the process of litigation imposed on industry will ensure an ultimate cost to the public of the Union.

NOTES AND QUESTIONS

(1) **Harmonization of Text**. As several cases clearly demonstrate, harmonization of the text of national trademark laws will not necessarily result

in uniformity of either approach or result throughout the EU. In any event, what does "harmonization of text" mean in a community with eleven official languages and where the directive is sometimes implemented through paraphrase rather than direct translation? Mr. Justice Jacob expressed bafflement at the decision of the legislative drafters to rewrite the language of the directive when drafting the implementing legislation (rather than merely copying the language). Why might this approach have been adopted by the legislative drafters? Would you advise national legislatures to enact the language of directives verbatim? What is to be gained from paraphrasing where a turnkey provision already exists?

(2) **Similarity and Confusion**. Mr. Justice Jacob refused to elide the elements of similarity and confusion in the infringement provision of the U.K. act because it would result in disparate treatment for strong and weak marks. Would that not be an appropriate result? *Cf. Polaroid Corp. v. Polarad Elec. Corp.*, 287 F.2d 492 (2d Cir. 1961) (including strength of the marks as a factor relevant to likelihood of confusion analysis).

(3) **"Use as a Mark"**. For further discussion of whether Article 5 requires that a defendant's use of the mark is, as a threshold matter, "to distinguish the goods in question," see *BMW v. Deenik* [1999] 1 C.M.L.R. 1099, ¶¶ 38-40 (E.C.J. 1999).

(4) **Invalidity Issues**. In his opinion, Mr. Justice Jacob also found the TREAT mark invalid. For a discussion of the question of distinctiveness upon which he based that decision, see Heidi Hurdle, *Jacob J. Treats Us All*, 18 EUR. INTELL. PROP. REV. 299, 302-304 (1996); Andrew Inglis, *Registrability and Enforcement of Inherently Non-Distinctive Trade Marks in the United Kingdom*, 19 EUR. INTELL. PROP. REV. 138 (1997). Compare Article 3 of the directive with section 2 of the Lanham Act. Inglis has suggested that *British Sugar* "should be regarded as sounding a note of warning to trade mark proprietors in relation to descriptive marks." Registerability and invalidity issues may ultimately benefit from even greater centralizing and harmonizing influence as a result of the involvement of the EC Trademark Office in interpreting the scope of rights under the EU Trademark Regulation.

b. Taking Unfair Advantage of, or Being Detrimental to, the Distinctive Character or the Repute of the Trade Mark

GENERAL MOTORS CORPORATION v. YPLON SA
1999 E.T.M.R. 950 (E.C.J. 1999)

JUDGMENT: By judgment of 30 October 1997, received at the Court on 3 November 1997, the Tribunal de Commerce (Commercial Court), Tournai, referred to the Court for a preliminary ruling under Article 177 of the EC Treaty (now Article 234 EC) a question on the interpretation of Article 5(2) of the First [Trademark Harmonisation Directive.]

The question has been raised in proceedings between General Motors Corporation established in Detroit, United States of America, and Yplon SA, established at Estaimpuis, Belgium, concerning the use of the mark CHEVY.

. . . .

The Benelux legislation

Article 13(A)(1)(c) of the Uniform Benelux Law on Trade Marks (hereinafter the Uniform Benelux Law), which transposed into Benelux law Article 5(2) of the Directive, provides:

> Without prejudice to any application of the ordinary law governing civil liability, the exclusive rights in a trade mark shall entitle the proprietor to oppose:
>
> . . . .
>
> (c) any use, in the course of trade and without due cause, of a trade mark which has a reputation in the Benelux countries or of a similar sign for goods which are not similar to those for which the trade mark is registered, where use of that sign would take unfair advantage of, or would be detrimental to, the distinctive character or the repute of the trade mark; . . .

That provision, which took effect on 1 January 1996, replaced, as from that date, the old Article 13(A)(2) of the Uniform Benelux Law . . . .

The dispute in the main proceedings

General Motors is the proprietor of the Benelux trade mark CHEVY, which was registered on 18 October 1971 at the Benelux Trade Mark Office for Class 4, 7, 9, 11 and 12 products, and in particular for motor vehicles. That registration asserts the rights acquired under an earlier Belgian registration on 1 September 1961 and earlier use in the Netherlands in 1961 and in Luxembourg in 1962. Nowadays, the mark CHEVY is used more specifically in Belgium to designate vans and similar vehicles.

Yplon is also the proprietor of the Benelux trade mark CHEVY, registered at the Benelux Trade Mark Office on 30 March 1988 for Class 3 products and then on 10 July 1991 for Class 1, 3 and 5 products. It uses those trade marks for detergents and various cleaning products. It is also the proprietor of the trade mark CHEVY in other countries, including several Member States.

On 28 December 1995 General Motors applied to the Tribunal de Commerce, Tournai, for an injunction restraining Yplon from using the sign CHEVY to designate detergents or cleaning products on the ground that such use entails dilution of its own trade mark and thus damages its advertising function. Its action is based, as regards the period prior to 1 January 1996, on the old Article 13(A)(2) of the Uniform Benelux Law and, as from 1 January 1996, on the new Article 13(A)(1)(c) of that Law. It maintains in this regard that its mark CHEVY is a trade mark of repute within the meaning of the latter provision.

Yplon is defending the action on the ground, in particular, that General Motors has not shown that its trade mark has a reputation in the Benelux countries within the meaning of the new Article 13(A)(1)(c) of the Uniform Benelux Law.

The Tribunal de Commerce took the view that determination of the case required clarification of the concept of a trade mark having a reputation and of the question whether the reputation must exist throughout the Benelux countries or whether it is sufficient for it to exist in part of that territory and decided to stay proceedings and refer the following question to the Court for a preliminary ruling:

> On reading Article 13(A)(1)(c) of the Uniform Benelux Law introduced pursuant to the amending protocol in force since 1 January 1996, what is the proper construction of the term "repute of the trade mark" and may it also be said that such "repute" applies throughout the Benelux countries or to part thereof?

The question referred for a preliminary ruling

By its question the national court is essentially asking the Court of Justice to explain the meaning of the expression "has a reputation" which is used, in Article 5(2) of the Directive, to specify the first of the two conditions which a registered trade mark must satisfy in order to enjoy protection extending to non-similar goods or services and to say whether that condition must be satisfied throughout the Benelux countries or whether it is sufficient for it to be satisfied in part of that territory.

General Motors contends that, in order to have a reputation within the meaning of Article 5(2) of the Directive, the earlier trade mark must be known by the public concerned, but not to the extent of being "well-known" within the meaning of Article 6*bis* of the Paris Convention . . . which is a term to which express reference is made, albeit in a different context, in Article 4(2)(d) of the Directive. General Motors further considers that it is sufficient for the trade mark concerned to have a reputation in a substantial part of the territory of a Member State, which may cover a community or a region of that State.

Yplon, on the other hand, contends that a trade mark registered in respect of a product or service intended for the public at large has a reputation within the meaning of Article 5(2) of the Directive when it is known by a wide section of that public. The principle of speciality can be departed from only for trade marks which can be associated spontaneously with a particular product or service. The reputation of the trade mark in question should exist throughout the territory of a Member State or, in the case of the Benelux countries, throughout one of those countries.

The Belgian Government argues that a trade mark "having a reputation" should be construed flexibly and that there is a difference of degree between a mark with a reputation and a well-known mark. The degree to which a trade mark is well known cannot be evaluated in the abstract by, for example, setting a percentage. A reputation in any single one of the three Benelux countries applies throughout the Benelux territory.

The French Government submits that the Court should reply that a trade mark's reputation within the meaning of Article 5(2) of the Directive cannot be defined precisely. It is a question of assessing case by case whether the earlier trade mark is known by a wide section of the public concerned by the products covered by the two marks and whether the earlier mark is of sufficient repute that the public associates it with the later contested mark. Once it is established that the earlier mark does have a reputation, the strength of that reputation then determines the extent of the protection afforded by Article 5(2) of the Directive. Territorially, a reputation in a single Benelux country is sufficient.

The Netherlands Government submits that it is sufficient for the trade mark to have a reputation with the public at which it is aimed. The degree of knowledge required cannot be indicated in abstract terms. It has to be ascertained whether, in view of all the circumstances, the earlier mark has a reputation which may be harmed if it is used for non-similar products. The mark does not have to be known throughout a Member State or, in the case of Benelux trade marks, throughout the Benelux territory.

The United Kingdom Government submits that the decisive question is whether use is made without due cause of the later mark and whether this allows unfair advantage to be taken of, or detriment to be caused to, the distinctive character or the repute of the earlier trade mark. The answer to that question depends on an overall assessment of all the relevant factors and, in particular, of the distinctive character inherent in the mark, the extent of the repute which it has gained, the degree of similarity between the two marks and the extent of the differences between the products or services covered. Protection should be afforded to all trade marks which have acquired a reputation and qualificative criteria should then be applied to limit the protection to marks whose reputation justifies it, protection being granted only where clear evidence of actual harm is adduced. In law, it is not necessary for the reputation to extend throughout the territory of a Member State. However, in practice, proof of actual damage could not be adduced in the case of a trade mark whose reputation is limited to a part of a Member State.

In the Commission's submission, a "trade mark with a reputation" should be understood as meaning a trade mark having a reputation with the public concerned. This is something which is clearly distinguished from a well-known mark referred to in Article 6bis of the Paris Convention. It is sufficient for the mark to have a reputation in a substantial part of the Benelux territory and marks having a reputation in a region merit as much protection as marks having a reputation throughout the Benelux territory.

The Court observes that the first condition for the wider protection provided for in Article 5(2) of the Directive is expressed by the words "er renommeret" in the Danish version of that provision; "bekannt ist" in the German version; "Ἔχει φήμη" in the Greek version; "goce de renombre" in the Spanish version; "jouit d'une renommee" in the French version; "gode di notorietà" in the Italian version; "bekend is" in the Dutch version; "goze de prestigio" in the Portuguese version; "laajalti tunnettu" in the Finnish version; "är känt" in the Swedish version; and by the words "has a reputation" in the English version.

The German, Dutch and Swedish versions use words signifying that the trade mark must "be known" without indicating the extent of knowledge required, whereas the other language versions use the term "reputation" or expressions implying, like that term, at a quantitative level a certain degree of knowledge amongst the public.

That nuance, which does not entail any real contradiction, is due to the greater neutrality of the terms used in the German, Dutch and Swedish versions. Despite that nuance, it cannot be denied that, in the context of a uniform interpretation of Community law, a knowledge threshold requirement emerges from a comparison of all the language versions of the Directive.

Such a requirement is also indicated by the general scheme and purpose of the Directive. In so far as Article 5(2) of the Directive, unlike Article 5(1), protects trade marks registered for non-similar products or services, its first condition implies a certain degree of knowledge of the earlier trade mark among the public. It is only where there is a sufficient degree of knowledge of that mark that the public, when confronted by the later trade mark, may possibly make an association between the two trade marks, even when used for non-similar products or services, and that the earlier trade mark may consequently be damaged.

The public amongst which the earlier trade mark must have acquired a reputation is that concerned by that trade mark, that is to say, depending on the product or service marketed, either the public at large or a more specialised public, for example traders in a specific sector.

It cannot be inferred from either the letter or the spirit of Article 5(2) of the Directive that the trade mark must be known by a given percentage of the public so defined.

The degree of knowledge required must be considered to be reached when the earlier mark is known by a significant part of the public concerned by the products or services covered by that trade mark.

In examining whether this condition is fulfilled, the national court must take into consideration all the relevant facts of the case, in particular the market share held by the trade mark, the intensity, geographical extent and duration of its use, and the size of the investment made by the undertaking in promoting it.

Territorially, the condition is fulfilled when, in the terms of Article 5(2) of the Directive, the trade mark "has a reputation in the Member State." In the absence of any definition of the Community provision in this respect, a trade mark cannot be required to have "a reputation throughout" the territory of the Member State. It is sufficient for it to exist in a substantial part of it.

As far as trade marks registered at the Benelux Trade Mark Office are concerned, the Benelux territory must be treated like the territory of a Member State, since Article 1 of the Directive regards Benelux trade marks as trade marks registered in a Member State. Article 5(2) must therefore be understood as meaning "a reputation acquired in" the Benelux territory. For the same reasons as those relating to the condition as to the existence of a reputation in a Member State, a Benelux trade mark cannot therefore be required to have a reputation throughout the Benelux territory. It is sufficient for a Benelux trade mark to have a reputation in a substantial part of the Benelux territory, which part may consist of a part of one of the Benelux countries.

If, at the end of its examination, the national court decides that the condition as to the existence of a reputation is fulfilled, as regards both the public concerned and the territory in question, it must then go on to examine the second condition laid down in Article 5(2) of the Directive, which is that the earlier trade mark must be detrimentally affected without due cause. Here it should be observed that the stronger the earlier mark's distinctive character and reputation the easier it will be to accept that detriment has been caused to it.

The answer to be given to the question referred must therefore be that Article 5(2) of the Directive is to be interpreted as meaning that, in order to enjoy protection extending to non-similar products or services, a registered trade mark must be known by a significant part of the public concerned by the products or services which it covers. In the Benelux territory, it is sufficient for the registered trade mark to be known by a significant part of the public concerned in a substantial part of that territory, which part may consist of a part of one of the countries composing that territory.

BAYWATCH PROD. CO., INC. v. THE HOME VIDEO CHANNEL
[1997] FSR 22 (Chancery Division) (Eng.)

CRYSTAL QC (DEPUTY JUDGE):

The Baywatch Series

The plaintiff is the producer of the weekly television series known as Baywatch or the Baywatch Series ("Baywatch"). Baywatch is set in California and features a team of lifeguards who patrol the Santa Monica beaches. The members of the team wear a distinctive uniform consisting of a red jacket and a red costume with a circular badge on the left-hand side. The badge includes a logo and the words "Baywatch" and "Lifeguard." The key female character in the series is played by the actress Pamela Anderson-Lee who has "an hour-glass" figure and long blond hair. Each programme in the series involves at least one rescue by the lifeguards which invariably involves the lifeguards running along the beach together and may also involve resuscitation of the victim.

The plaintiff's case is that the Baywatch series is a light entertainment family programme with a strong moral theme.

Trade Marks

The plaintiff is the registered proprietor of United Kingdom registered trade marks Nos. 2009012 and 2013330 "BAYWATCH, the trade marks." The trade marks are registered for a large range of goods in Classes 3, 5, 9, 14, 16, 24, 25, 28 and 30. Under Class 9 they are registered inter alia in respect of "video tapes and video discs" all featuring "music, action-adventure, comedy, animation, sports or exercise." The plaintiff has no registration for television programmes or anything relating to broadcasting.

Baywatch in the United Kingdom

Baywatch was first shown in the United Kingdom in 1992. The programme is shown weekly on Saturday or Sunday evenings at around 6.00 p.m. . . . The success of the television programme enables the plaintiff to license use of the trade marks to third parties in connection with the manufacture of a wide variety of merchandise. The merchandise has been on sale in the United Kingdom since mid-1994. Licensees in the United Kingdom are authorised to use the name Baywatch and a logo on goods ranging from sunglasses, swim suits, bed-linen, magazines, clothing, dolls, cakes, posters and games to chocolate Easter eggs. These items are available through a variety of high street stores, such as Debenhams, WH Smith, Woolworth, BHS and TOYS 'R' US. The retail value of merchandise sold in the United Kingdom since 1994 totals more than £12 million.

The Adult Channel

The defendant broadcasts the adult channel on television. This channel contains adult entertainment of an erotic nature. The channel is transmitted between midnight and 4.00 am United Kingdom time. It can be received only by those who choose to subscribe to it either by being connected to a cable television system, where available, or via their own satellite dish with a special viewing card. People cannot view the adult channel by chance. They have to subscribe after which they receive a separate viewing card which has to be inserted into their integrated receiver decoder every time they want to view. Furthermore, they have to wait until the early hours of the morning before the adult channel is broadcast. There are said to be approximately 150,000 homes subscribing to the adult channel of which 15,000 to 20,000 homes are outside the United Kingdom.

The Babewatch Series

. . . I was invited by both counsel to view in court, and did view, extracts from videos of the Babewatch programme broadcast on May 25, 1996 and from one episode of Baywatch. The Babewatch programme broadcast on May 25, 1996 begins with a beach scene not dissimilar to that in Baywatch with actresses wearing red swimming costumes, carrying red floats and running along the beach. The beach scenes are filmed on a beach which looks similar to that used as the setting in Baywatch. After a brief introduction reminiscent of the opening scenes of Baywatch, the Babewatch programme contains sexually explicit material, including scenes of oral and group sex. . . .

The Plaintiff's Case

The plaintiff contends that the defendant's use of BABEWATCH, a similar trade mark to the registered trade mark BAYWATCH in connection with a television programme, was clearly intended to take advantage of the reputation and distinctive character of the plaintiff's trade marks. Significantly, however, the plaintiff accepts for the purpose of this motion that it cannot point to any actual evidence of confusion on the part of the public between the Baywatch series and the Babewatch series.

The plaintiff also asserts that the Babewatch television programme tarnishes the reputation of the Baywatch series. There is a dispute between the parties as to the nature of that reputation. The defendant contends that the Baywatch series is not a clean-cut family show with a whiter-than-white reputation. It is accepted that I cannot resolve that issue on this motion.

By this motion, the plaintiff now seeks an interlocutory injunction to restrain the defendant from rebroadcasting the Babewatch series until there has been a speedy trial of these proceedings. . . .

The Causes of Action

The plaintiff seeks to rely on three causes of action. These are:

1. Trade mark infringement under section 10(2) of the Trade Marks Act 1994 ("the 1994 Act").

2. Trade mark infringement under section 10(3) of the 1994 Act; and

3. Passing off.

[Plaintiff] principally relies on the claim for trade mark infringement under section 10(3).

Section 10(2) of the 1994 Act

Section 10(2), so far as material for present purposes, only applies where, because a sign is similar to a registered trade mark and is used in relation to goods or services similar to those for which the trade mark is registered, there exists a likelihood of confusion on the part of the public which includes the likelihood of association with the trade mark.

[Noting the comment by Mr. Justice Jacob in *British Sugar* that confusion is a question separate from similarity, the court continued that in] this case, it is not in my judgment arguable that there is a similarity between the Baywatch series and the Babewatch series. The use by the defendant of the sign BABEWATCH in relation to its TV programme, broadcast in encrypted form in the early hours on the adult channel, is not use of a sign similar to the mark BAYWATCH such that there exists a likelihood of confusion on the part of the public. Nor do I think that it is arguable that television programmes with an adult content and video tapes and video discs all featuring music, action-adventure, comedy, animation, sports or exercise are similar goods or services within the meaning of section 10 of the 1994 Act. The plaintiff has led no evidence which suggests that they are similar.

If there is no similarity of goods or services in a particular case, then the question of whether there is a likelihood of confusion because of that similarity does not arise. The requisite confusion for the purposes of section 10(2) is confusion as to the origin of goods or services. (*See Wagamama Limited v City-Centre Restaurants Plc* [1995] FSR 713, particularly at 730 per Laddie J.) It is not sufficient if one mark merely leads to a likelihood of recall of the other mark.

However, as the issue of likelihood of confusion was fully argued, and as it is relevant for reasons given later in this judgment to the claim based on section 10(3) of the 1994 Act, it is convenient for me to discuss the question of confusion at this stage. . . . In my judgment the plaintiff cannot make out an arguable case [of there being a likelihood of confusion] under section 10(2) of the 1994 Act.

Section 10(3)

Section 10(3) is in the following terms:

(3) A person infringes a registered trade mark if he uses in the course of trade a sign which

(a)   is identical with or similar to the trade mark, and

(b)   is used in relation to goods or services which are not similar to those for which the trade mark is registered where the trade mark has a reputation in the United Kingdom and the use of the sign, being without due cause, takes unfair advantage of, or is detrimental to, the distinctive character or the repute of the trade mark.

[The] plaintiff submits that the subsection is there to provide relief where one trader takes unfair advantage of another through the appropriation of that other's goodwill or acts to the other's detriment by tarnishing the other's reputation through the detrimental association of the sign and the registered trade mark. He contends that the subsection applies irrespective of whether a plaintiff can point to the existence of a likelihood of confusion on the part of the public.

I do not think this submission is well founded. Section 10(3) can only apply where a sign is used which is similar to the trade mark and is used in relation to goods or services which are not similar to those for which the mark is registered. The use of the concept of similarity in section 10(3)(a) introduces in my judgment the ingredient of a likelihood of confusion on the part of the public into section 10(3). Section 10(2) protection is given in relation to similar goods or services where, because of the similarity, there exists a likelihood of confusion on the part of the public. It would, it seems to me, be illogical for section 10(3) to give a greater protection in relation to non-similar goods or services by dispensing with the ingredient of a likelihood of confusion than the protection afforded to similar goods under section 10(2). Neither the EU Directive nor the White Paper appear to me to give any real support to [plaintiff's] submission.

Mr Alexander . . . drew my attention to the unreported decision of Knox J in *BASF Plc v CEP (UK) Plc* October 26, 1995. Knox J's decision was given in the context of a motion for an interlocutory injunction. At page 14 of the transcript in the course of dealing with a claim based on section 10(3), he said this:

> So far as taking unfair advantage of the plaintiff's mark is concerned I see no evidence of it whatever since, in the absence of relevant confusion, I see no basis for finding that unfair advantage has been or is threatened to be taken.

And again at the bottom of page 14 and the top of page 15 of the transcript, Knox J observed:

> If the protection given by section 10(3) went that far, much of the effect of having classes of goods in relation to the registration of trade marks would disappear. Nor indeed did Miss McFarland's argument put the case under section 10(3) on any such wide basis. In my view neither the distinctive character nor the repute of the plaintiff's mark is adversely affected when there is no risk of relevant confusion.

The learned judge then went on to observe that it was neither necessary nor desirable for him to seek to express definitive views on the exact scope of section 10(3), but concluded that in the context of the evidence before him there was no arguable case of a relevant detriment, as I understand his judgment, because there was no evidence of relevant confusion.

It seems to me that the approach of Knox J to the construction of section 10(3) is consistent with the approach to the construction of that subsection which I have ventured to suggest above. Accordingly, in my judgment section 10(3) only applies where:

> 1. A sign which is similar to the trade mark, so that there is a likelihood of confusion on the part of the public, is used in relation to goods and services which are not similar to the mark.
> 2. The mark has a reputation in the United Kingdom.

3. The use of the sign, being without due cause, takes advantage of, or is detrimental to the distinctive character or the repute of the trade mark.

Having regard to my views on the question of a likelihood of confusion under section 10(2) mentioned above, in my judgment the plaintiff cannot make out an arguable case in respect of the first necessary ingredient required by section 10(3).

Passing Off

Passing off is a cause of action to protect reputation and goodwill from damage caused by a misrepresentation. . . . The absence of any substantial factor pointing towards confusion seems to me to be fatal to the existence of such a cause of action in the circumstances of this case. In my judgment the plaintiff cannot make out an arguable case on passing off either.

Oasis Stores Ltd.'s Trade Mark Application, [1998] R.P.C. 631 (Trade Marks Registry, 1998) (U.K.). The applicant sought to register the mark EVEREADY for contraceptives and condoms. Its application was opposed by a company that for many years had sold batteries, torches, smoke alarms and related products under the mark EVER READY and owned various registrations for such marks (both as words and device marks). Opposition was based both on section 5(4)(a) of the Trademarks Act (which prevents the registration of marks where the use of the mark sought to be registered would amount to passing off of the goods of another), and on section 5(3) (which prevents registration of a mark where the earlier mark has a reputation in the U.K. and the use of the later mark would, "without due cause, take unfair advantage of, or be detrimental to, the distinctive character or repute of the earlier trade mark"). The panel held that, because of the dissimilarity of goods, there would be no confusion between the marks and thus the opposition under section 5(4)(a) failed. And the opposition under section 5(3) failed because, even though the panel declined to follow *Baywatch*'s interpretation of the parallel language in section 10(3) and found instead that section 5(3) did not require a likelihood of confusion, the panel concluded that:

> simply being reminded of a similar trade mark with a reputation for dissimilar goods necessarily amounts to taking unfair advantage of the repute of that mark. The opponent's chances of success may have been better if they were able to point to some specific aspect of their reputation for batteries etc. sold under their mark which was likely, through (non-origin) association, to benefit the applicant's mark to some extent. However, . . . the opponents have not established any such conceptual connection between their reputation for batteries etc., and [condoms or contraceptives].

Nor had the opposer demonstrated that the applicant's use would be detrimental to the distinctive character of the opposer's mark. The panel noted that:

> Any use of the same or a similar mark for dissimilar goods or services is liable, to some extent, to dilute the distinctiveness of the earlier mark. The provision is clearly not intended to have the sweeping effect of preventing the registration of any mark which is the same as, or similar to, a trade mark with a reputation. It therefore appears to be a matter of degree.

The panel suggested that the type of detriment being addressed by the provision was "detriment to the reputation of the earlier mark in some material fashion." But that was not satisfied here.

> Not many years ago contraceptives in general, and condoms in particular, were the sort of goods generally regarded with some embarrassment. They were perhaps at the fringe of what might be considered acceptable for social discussion. However, for reasons which I need not go into here, the position today appears to me to be somewhat different. The use of condoms is now widely promoted and encouraged. The result of this appears to me to be that there is far more open discussion about the value of such goods and the stigma previously associated them is much reduced, if not entirely eliminated. . . . There are no doubt some people who still find the notion of condoms objectionable or embarrassing. However, I find it impossible to believe that any significant number of persons are going to be so embarrassed as to be less likely to choose EVER READY batteries, simply because EVEREADY is also a trade mark used by another proprietor for contraceptives. . . . The opponents have also expressed concern that use of such a similar mark on contraceptives will make the opponents' mark liable to become the butt of misplaced humour and even ridicule. If that were likely I would feel inclined to accept that the repute of the opponents' mark could be at risk. However, in my view, the difficulty that the opponents have had in coming up with any conceptual connection between the respective goods makes it unlikely that normal and fair use of the applicants' mark will produce that result.

NOTES AND QUESTIONS

(1) **Dilution and Confusion**. If *Baywatch* is correctly decided, what does section 10(3) add to the rights of a trademark owner? That is to say, if likelihood of confusion is an element of liability under section 10(3), or an element of the parallel ground for opposition under section 5(3), what do these

provisions add to the explicitly confusion-based provisions in section 10(2) and section 5(4)? *See* Marks & Spencer plc v. One in a Million, 1998 F.S.R. 265. Not all commentators and courts regard confusion as an element of liability under section 10(3). In addition to the decision of the panel in *Oasis Stores* interpreting the parallel opposition provision, see Ruth E. Annand, *Lookalikes Under the New United Kingdom Trade Marks Act 1994*, 86 TRADEMARK REP. 142, 157 n.87 (1996). What is meant by the phrase "takes unfair advantage of, or is detrimental to, the distinctive character or the repute of the trade mark"?

(2) **Effect of *Sabel* Ruling on Dilution Provision.** In *Sabel v. Puma*, the European Court of Justice supported its interpretation of Article 4 by noting that its interpretation, *see supra*, was "not inconsistent with Article 4(3) and 4(4)(a) and Article 5(2) of the directive, which permit the proprietor of a trade mark which has a reputation to prohibit the use without due cause of signs identical with or similar to his mark and do not require proof of likelihood of confusion, even where there is no similarity between the goods in question. . . . Unlike Article 4(1)(b), those provisions apply exclusively to marks which have a reputation and on condition that use of the third party's mark without due cause takes unfair advantage of, or is detrimental to, the distinctive character or the repute of the trade mark." Is the interpretation of the *Baywatch* court consistent with the reasoning of the European Court in *Sabel*? If it is, what consequence attaches to that, given that section 10(3) and section 5(3) were optional provisions in the directive? *See Oasis Stores*, 1998 R.P.C. at 631. The European Court has jurisdiction to interpret the meaning of secondary EU legislation. If the Court interpreted section 10(3) as not requiring confusion, could the U.K. courts ignore the interpretation of the European Court on such an optional provision? If not, why not? What options would the U.K. legislature have available to it? Should a member state be entitled to enact a level of protection between the lower mandatory level (confusion-based) and the higher optional level (with genuine dilution protection added)?

c. Post-Sale Confusion

The expansion in the purpose and function of trademarks–from source-identifiers to something approaching a full-blown property right–is reflected in much European trademark scholarship. (Of course, the same trend can be seen elsewhere, *see* Lisa H. Johnston, *Drifting Toward Trademark Rights in Gross*, 85 TRADEMARK REP. 19, 23-24 (1995), although resistance to trademarks as property appears less vocal in Europe.) Many of the disputes, such as that litigated in *Wagamama*, stem from a disagreement over the wisdom of such an expansion.

Another area in which expansion in the purpose and function of trademarks has been invoked to support broader trademark rights is in rendering actionable post-sale confusion. The U.S. courts have for some time recognized the relevance of post-sale confusion to trademark rights. Indeed, in 1962, section 32 of the Lanham Act was amended to make clear that use giving rise to a likelihood of confusion was actionable, irrespective of whether its was the purchaser who was likely to be confused. *See* Syntex Labs. v. Norwich Pharmacal, Co., 437 F.2d 566, 568 (2d Cir. 1971).

The German appellate courts have recently split on the relevance of post-sale confusion in two cases brought against the same defendant. *See* Ludwig Kouker, *Is the Purpose of the Trademark Law Limited Only to Protecting Purchasers?–Analysis Under United States and German Trademark Law*, 87 TRADEMARK REP. 151 (1997). The defendant was a supplier of humorous novelty items. In each case it offered a large quantity of individually packaged condoms for sale in a candy jar or display box, each individually wrapped and bearing a different label. The subject of the dispute in the Hamburg proceedings was a condom packaged in a transparent wrapper with a sticker indicating "NIVEAU milk" and another sticker stating "It's like NIVEA for the first time." (This was a play on words in German: NIVEA = nie weher = never sorer.) The Bremen case involved a condom packaged in a folded pack that looked like a book of matches, with an illustration of a MARS candy bar and the imprint "A MARS a day for Sex-Sport and Play."

> The Hamburg Court . . . rejected the trademark infringement claim in this context, holding that the protective purpose of the trademark was exhausted once the product was purchased by the consumer. Therefore, trademark rights were not relevant to the further use of the contraceptive. The Bremen Court . . . held that trademark infringement had been established because persons who acquired the Mars packages, but had not purchased them in a shop, may regard the products as some form of advertising which the plaintiffs had authorized. The Federal Supreme Court affirmed the decision of the Bremen Appeal Court and upheld the injunction based on trademark infringement, without discussing the subject [of post-sale confusion] in detail. . . .
>
> In the author's view, the legal recognition of the advertising function of a trademark . . . requires that the different market sectors be considered when evaluating the perceptions of those who do not take part in the distribution chain, but come into contact with potentially infringing products more or less by chance. . . Logically, this function of a mark may be subsequently jeopardized through the further use of products after acquisition by the end-consumer, as a result of which trademark law may quite certainly be affected, contrary to the opinion of the Hamburg Appeal Court. This applies even more so in cases where the products alleged to infringe the mark are not simply used by the end-consumer for their naturally intended purpose but can be seen or used by a different circle of persons. This would undoubtedly include so-called novelty items, such as those that were the subject of the Hamburg and Bremen decisions. After all, such novelty items fulfill their purpose only when they are delivered to third parties and the advertising or mark used in each case brings to mind the actual trademark.

Kouker, *supra*. For other discussions of the importance of recognizing the actionability of post-sale confusion, see Ian Karet, *Passing Off and Trade Marks: Confusing Times Ahead?*, 17 EUR. INTELL. PROP. REV. 3 (1995) (discussing English and New Zealand law and concluding that, unless a plaintiff is able to rely on post-sale confusion, the action for passing off will be used less and less); *see also* Ruth Annand, *Lookalikes Under the New United Kingdom Trade Marks Act 1994*, 86 TRADEMARK REP. 142, 147 n.36 (1996) (suggesting that the United Kingdom does not recognize post sale confusion as actionable under either trademark or passing off).

QUESTIONS

Reconsider the questions asked before we considered international trademark instruments. What are the characteristics of harmonized systems of trademark protection (effected by the directive), as opposed to the unified or unitary systems (created by the regulation) that we will consider in Chapter 6? What considerations support one legislative strategy over the other? What consequences flow from following one approach over the other? What are the different points on the continuum from harmonized to unified systems, and what variables define these points? How is the harmonization effected by the Trademark Directive different from that caused by the Paris Convention or TRIPS? Why is it different?

[J]   Regional Trademark Agreements (III):
Inter-American Agreements

THOMAS D. DRESCHER, NATURE AND SCOPE OF TRADEMARK PROVISIONS UNDER TRIPS AND THE PAN-AMERICAN CONVENTION[*]
87 TRADEMARK REP. 319 (1997)

The Inter-American Convention for Trademark and Commercial Protection, or the "Pan-American Convention" ("PAC"), signed at Washington in 1929, was the last of many efforts to provide a uniform standard of trademark protection throughout the Americas. The Convention was originally accompanied by a Protocol on Inter-American Registration of Trade Marks which has long since been renounced by the United States. The Convention itself, however, remains in effect. Its members include the United States, Colombia, Cuba, Guatemala, Haiti, Honduras, Nicaragua, Panama, Paraguay and Peru. . . .

---

[*]Copyright 1997, Thomas D. Drescher. Reprinted with permission.

II. THE PAN-AMERICAN CONVENTION, TRIPS, AND THE FREE TRADE AREA OF THE AMERICAS ("FTAA")

The purpose of this article is to review the trademark provisions of the Pan-American Convention and TRIPS in order to ascertain whether they are compatible and whether in some respects the Pan-American Convention might serve as a suitable model for the trademark provisions under the current FTAA initiative to achieve harmonization of trademark law through the Americas.

III. A COMPARISON OF THE TRADEMARK PROVISIONS OF THE PAN-AMERICAN CONVENTION AND TRIPS

A. Minimum Standards

TRIPS provides that "Members may, but shall not be obligated to, implement in their law more extensive protection than is required by this Agreement, provided that such protection does not contravene the provisions of this Agreement." [art. 1(1)]. Thus, the compatibility of the Pan-American Convention with TRIPS will depend on whether the Pan-American Convention (1) meets at least the minimum standards and (2) does not otherwise contravene TRIPS.

B. National Treatment

[In Article 1, the Pan-American Convention requires Contracting States to grant national treatment to nationals of other Contracting States with respect to trademarks, trade names, and the repression of unfair competition and false indications of geographical origin or source.]

C. Protectible Subject Matter

. . . .

The Pan-American Convention does not expressly define trademarks subject to its protection. Under the Pan-American Convention, marks lacking any distinctive character or otherwise generic are not registrable. In determining distinctiveness, "a significance distinctive of the applicant's goods" acquired through use is to be taken into account. Thus, the subject matter protectible as a mark under the Pan-American Convention appears to contemplate signs "capable of distinguishing" goods or services, and, as permitted by TRIPS, the Pan-American Convention recognizes distinctiveness acquired through use.

. . . .

The Pan-American Convention generally follows the Paris Convention (and, hence, TRIPS (Article 15(2)) in stating that registration "may be refused" of marks which (1) infringe the rights of third-parties in the nation where registration is claimed, (2) are devoid of distinctive character, and (3) offend public morals. Both Conventions provide for refusal of registration of marks containing, without authorization, various national symbols. In addition, the Pan-American Convention provides for the denial of registration to marks which (1) expose persons or institutions to ridicule or contempt, (2) contain "racial types" or scenes typical or characteristic of any of the Contracting States, other than that of the origin of the mark, or (3) have as a principal distinguishing element the trade name of a person engaged in any of the Contracting States in the manufacture, or trade of goods in the same class. These additional grounds for refusal would not appear to derogate from the provisions of the Paris Convention and, therefore, do not conflict with TRIPS, Article 15(2).

D. Registration

. . . .

The Pan-American Convention provides that a person can apply for protection of its mark either "directly to the proper office of the State in which he desires to obtain protection, or through the Inter-American Trade Mark Bureau referred to in the Protocol. . . ." Further, marks "registered or legally protected in one of the Contracting States shall be admitted to registration" in the other Contracting States, provided they comply with the domestic law of such states. Thus, under the Pan-American Convention, registration may be obtained in a Contracting State without the need for a supporting registration in the country of origin, and whether or not use is required to apply for or maintain a registration would be a matter of the domestic law of each State. The principle of territoriality is recognized at Article 10, which provides that each registration shall exist independently of registrations in any other Contracting State. The Pan-American Convention contains no mandate that use not be a requirement for filing an application, nor does it specify a period of time after which a mark may be canceled for nonuse, and, therefore, in these respects does not meet the minimum standards of TRIPS.

E. Term of Protection

The Pan-American Convention provides that the period of protection "shall be the period fixed by the laws of the State in which registration, deposit or renewal is made at the time when made." As a result, the period of protection would have to be raised to a uniform term of not less than seven (7) years to be compatible with Article 18 of TRIPS, and ten (10) years to comply with Article 1708, Section 7, of the North American Free Trade Agreement ("NAFTA").

F. Enforceability of Registrations

. . . .

1. Opposition

The Pan-American Convention sets forth in some detail a trademark owner's right to oppose or seek the cancellation of a mark Article 7, "Opposition," provides as follows:

> Any owner of a mark protected in one of the Contracting States in accordance with its domestic law, who may know that some other person is using or applying to register or deposit an interfering mark in any other of the Contracting States, shall have the right to oppose such use, registration or deposit and shall have the right to employ all legal means, procedure or recourse provided in the country in which such interfering mark is being used or where its registration or deposit is being sought, and upon proof that the person who is using such mark or applying to register or deposit it, had knowledge of the existence and continuous use in any of the Contracting States of the mark on which opposition is based upon goods of the same class, the opposer may claim for himself the preferential right to use such mark in the country where the opposition is made or priority to register or deposit it in such country, upon compliance with the requirements established by the domestic legislation in such country and by this Convention.

While Article 7 does not specify precisely what legal means, procedure or recourse a Contracting State must provide an opposer, the opposition rights conferred upon a trademark owner are noteworthy: (1) the right to oppose is granted to the owner of a mark "protected," not necessarily registered, in a Contracting State; (2) the right to oppose covers not only registration but also use by the offending party; (3) the trademark owner need not be registered or using its mark in the Contracting State where it is opposing the interfering mark; (4) the opposer succeeds to the rights of the user of the interfering mark upon proof that the person "had knowledge of the existence and continuous use in any of the Contracting States" of opposer's mark on the same class of goods; but, (5) the right to oppose does not appear to depend upon proof of such knowledge.

Arguably, this right of opposition encompasses the protection given well-known, or "famous," marks at Article 6*bis* of the Paris Convention, and incorporated at Article 16(2),(3) of TRIPS. TRIPS extends Articles 6*bis* protection to goods not similar to those on which the famous mark is registered. The Pan-American Convention may be similarly construed. Article 7 does not limit the trademark owner's right to oppose to marks being used on the same class of goods, but provides that where such is the case, the opposer may succeed to the infringer's preferential rights.

2. Cancellation

Article 8 of the Pan-American Convention provides for cancellation of an "interfering mark" as follows:

> When the owner of a mark seeks the registration or deposit of the mark in a Contracting State other than that of origin of the mark and such registration or deposit is refused because of the previous registration or deposit of an interfering mark, he shall have the right to apply for and obtain the cancellation or annulment of the interfering mark upon proving, in accordance with the legal procedure of the country in which cancellation is sought, the stipulations in Paragraph (a) and those of either Paragraph (b) or (c) below:

> (a) That he enjoyed legal protection for his mark in another of the Contracting States prior to the date of the application for the registration or deposit which he seeks to cancel; and

> (b) that the claimant of the interfering mark, the cancellation of which is sought, had knowledge of the use, employment, registration or deposit in any of the Contracting States of the mark for the specific goods to which said interfering mark is applied, prior to adoption and use thereof or prior to the filing of the application or deposit of the mark which is sought to be canceled; or

> (c) that the owner of the mark who seeks cancellation based on a prior right to the ownership and use of such mark, has traded or trades with or in the country in which cancellation is sought, and that goods designated by his mark have circulated and circulate in said country from a date prior to the filing of the application for registration or deposit for the mark, the cancellation which is claimed, or prior to the adoption and use of the same.

Article 8 thus provides alternative grounds for cancellation. Article 8(b) considers the nature of use of the interfering mark in conjunction with the interfering party's prior knowledge of the owner's rights, whether or not the owner's mark has actually been used in the country where cancellation is sought. Article 8(c), on the other hand, contemplates cancellation where the owner's mark has been used in the country where cancellation is sought. Significantly, Article 8(c) does not require that such use be on the specific goods on which the interfering mark is used.

The Pan-American Convention refers to opposition or cancellation of "interfering marks." Presumably, these may be either identical or similar marks.[27] The Pan-American Convention does not expressly apply a likelihood

---

[27] See TRIPS, Article 16(1).

of confusion standard or a presumption of likelihood of confusion, as does TRIPS at Article 16(1). It does, however, provide that the opposer or party seeking cancellation may use "all legal means" provided in the country where cancellation is sought.

The international protection provided under Articles 7 and 8 of the Pan-American Convention arguably goes beyond TRIPS and Article 6*bis* of the Paris Convention. While the Pan-American Convention opposition and cancellation procedures would encompass "famous" marks, it is not limited to such marks. In both Articles 7 and 8 it is not the public's knowledge of the mark, but, rather, the infringer's knowledge of the owner's mark (or, alternatively, prior trade in goods under the owner's mark)[28] that is significant, though not absolutely necessary, for enforcement of the trademark owner's rights. It may be that these provisions of the Pan-American Convention would, if properly implemented, provide a higher level of protection against infringement than the rights conferred under TRIPS.

G. Unauthorized Use By Agent

The Pan-American Convention gives the owner of a mark the right to demand cancellation of a registration by his agent in another Contracting State and to succeed to protection for himself as of the date of the agent's application.[29]

H. Transfer of Marks

"The transfer of the ownership of a registered or deposited mark in the country of its original registration shall be effective and shall be recognized in the other Contracting States. . . ." Transfers are recognized so long as they are executed and registered in accordance with the law of the country in which the transfer took place. TRIPS, in contrast, provides that the owner of a registered mark "shall have the right to assign the trade mark with or without the transfer of the business to which the trade mark belongs." Thus, there may be a conflict between the TRIPS mandate and the Pan-American Convention were any of its Contracting States not to permit assignment without the transfer of the relevant business.

IV. CONCLUSION

Under the Pan-American Convention, certain issues including (1) the basis for filing an application, (2) the term of registration, (3) the minimal period of nonuse which allows cancellation, and (4) the transfer of marks with or without the relevant business, are left to the domestic laws of the Contracting States, and may not meet minimum TRIPS standards. Significantly, however, there are a number of points where the Pan-American Convention appears to meet

---

[28]PAC, Article 8(c).
[29]PAC, Article 12; . . .

and perhaps, with regard to enforcement, even exceed minimum TRIPS standards. These include (1) national treatment, (2) protectible subject matter, (3) enforceability of registrations and of marks "protected" in any Contracting State, with or without use in the country in which protection is sought, and (4) unauthorized use by agents.

One of the more intriguing questions is whether the accompanying and long since defunct Protocol, which provided for a type of centralized registration among the Americas, might be worth reviewing, keeping in mind that the Pan-American Convention was never very popular among the nations within the Americas. For example, Argentina, Brazil, Chile, and Mexico failed to ratify it. Perhaps the next step, then, is to examine the Pan-American Convention in light of NAFTA to determine whether certain of its features, or its Protocol, might offer any insights into the process and requirements of hemispheric harmonization.

HAVANA CLUB HOLDING, S.A. v. GALLEON S.A.
203 F.3d 116 (2d Cir. 2000)

JON O. NEWMAN, CIRCUIT JUDGE

This appeal, raising issues concerning the Cuban embargo, arises from a dispute between two rum producers over the rights to the "Havana Club" trademark and trade name. Havana Club Holding, S.A. ("HCH") and Havana Club International, S.A. ("HCI") appeal from the June 28, 1999, judgment of the United States District Court for the Southern District of New York (Shira A. Scheindlin, District Judge), dismissing trademark, trade name, and false advertising claims against Defendants-Appellees Bacardi & Company Ltd. and Bacardi-Martini USA, Inc. We conclude that the Cuban embargo barred assignment to HCH of the "Havana Club" trademark registered in the United States, that we are precluded by statute from enforcing whatever rights HCI might have to trade name protection under the General Inter-American Convention for Trade Mark and Commercial Protection, and that HCI lacks standing to assert its false advertising and unfair competition claims under the Lanham Act. We therefore affirm.

Background

Plaintiff-Appellant HCI is a joint stock company organized under the laws of Cuba, with its domicile and principal place of business in Cuba. Plaintiff-Appellant HCH, a Luxembourg corporation, owns the "Havana Club" trademark in certain countries outside the United States. Defendant-Appellee Bacardi & Company is a corporation organized in Liechtenstein and headquartered in the Bahamas, and Defendant-Appellee Bacardi-Martini USA is a Delaware corporation (collectively "Bacardi"). Defendant Galleon S.A. has merged into Bacardi & Company.

Before the Cuban revolution, Jose Arechabala, S.A. ("JASA"), a Cuban corporation owned principally by members of the Arechabala family, produced "Havana Club" rum and owned the trademark "Havana Club" for use with its rum. JASA exported its rum to the United States until 1960, when the Cuban government, under the leadership of Fidel Castro, seized and expropriated JASA's assets. Neither JASA nor its owners ever received compensation for the seized assets from the Cuban government.

The Cuban embargo. In 1963, the United States imposed an embargo on Cuba, reflected in the Cuban Assets Control Regulations ("CACR"), as amended, 31 C.F.R. §§ 515.101-515.901 (1999), promulgated pursuant to section 5(b) of the Trading with the Enemy Act of 1917, as amended, 12 U.S.C. § 95a ("TWEA"). In 1996, Congress enacted the Cuban Liberty and Democratic Solidarity (LIBERTAD) Act ("LIBERTAD Act"), Pub. L. No. 104-114, 110 Stat. 785 (1996), which, among other things, codified the regulations implementing the Cuban embargo, *see* 22 U.S.C. § 6032(h). The Secretary of the Treasury has the authority to administer the Cuban embargo, which he has delegated to the Office of Foreign Assets Control ("OFAC"), *see* 31 C.F.R. § 515.802.

The trademarks and their assignment. From 1972 to 1993, Empresa Cubana Exportadora De Alimentos y Productos Varios ("Cubaexport"), a Cuban state enterprise, exclusively exported "Havana Club" rum, primarily to Eastern Europe and the Soviet Union. Cubaexport registered the "Havana Club" trademark with [the] Cuban authorities in 1974 under Registration No. 110,353, and with the United States Patent and Trademark Office ("USPTO") in 1976 under Registration No. 1,031,651. In 1993, Cubaexport sought to reorganize and find a foreign partner for its "Havana Club" rum business. Havana Rum & Liquors, S.A. ("HR & L"), a newly formed Cuban company, entered into a joint venture agreement with Pernod Ricard, S.A. ("Pernod"), a French company distributing liquor internationally. Under a November 1993 agreement between Pernod and HR & L, HCI and HCH were formed. In an agreement dated January 10, 1994, Cubaexport assigned trademark Registration No. 1,031,651, the United States registration for the "Havana Club" trademark, to HR & L, and in a subsequent agreement dated June 22, 1994, HR & L assigned this trademark to HCH. In 1996, HCH renewed the United States registration of the "Havana Club" mark for a term of ten years.

In April 1997, Bacardi & Co. purchased the Arechabala family's rights (if any) to the "Havana Club" trademark, the related goodwill of the business, and any rum business assets still owned by the Arechabala family.

OFAC's actions concerning the assignments. After an October 5, 1995, application to OFAC for a "specific" license authorizing the 1994 assignments of the "Havana Club" trademark from Cubaexport to HR & L, and from HR & L to HCH,[1] OFAC, on November 13, 1995, issued to Cubaexport License No. C-18147, which approved the two assignments and authorized all necessary transactions incident to the assignments of the mark.

---

[1]The CACR authorizes both "general" licenses, [cit], which permit classes or categories of transactions with Cuban nationals, *see, e.g., id.* § 515.542(a) (common carriers of mail), and "specific" licenses, *see id.* § 515.318, which require individualized determinations and approvals by OFAC, *see, e.g., id.* § 515.521 (authorizing specific licenses to unblock shares of qualifying United States permanent residents in "U.S.-located assets" of Cuban corporations).

However, on April 17, 1997, after the instant lawsuit was filed in the District Court, OFAC issued a Notice of Revocation, [retroactively] revoking License No. C-18147 [on the basis of "facts and circumstances that have come to the attention of this Office which were not included in the application of October 5, 1995" and declaring any actions taken pursuant to the license were "null and void as to matters under the jurisdiction of the Office of Foreign Assets Control."].

The parties' sales of rum. Since 1994, HCI has exported rum under the "Havana Club" trademark under an exclusive license to that mark from HCH. From 1994 to 1998, HCI sold over 38 million bottles of "Havana Club" rum, with approximately 30 percent of the sales in Cuba–including sales to Americans traveling in Cuba–and the remainder exported principally to Spain, France, Germany, Italy, Canada, Mexico, Bolivia, and Panama. Under travel regulations imposed by OFAC, the class of travelers permitted to visit Cuba may reenter the United States with up to $100 in Cuban-origin goods for personal use. Havana Club rum and cigars are the most popular items brought back.

Because of the Cuban embargo, however, HCI's "Havana Club" rum has never been sold in the United States. HCI intends to export its rum to the United States as soon as legally possible. HCI anticipates using its current marketing strategy of emphasizing the quality and character of its rum based primarily upon its Cuban origin. The label on HCI's "Havana Club" rum portrays the city of Havana and contains the phrase "El Ron de Cuba" ("The Rum of Cuba"). HCI's advertising also stresses the product's Cuban origin.

Beginning in 1995, Bacardi-Martini's predecessor-in-interest, Galleon S.A., produced rum in the Bahamas bearing the "Havana Club" name, and distributed sixteen cases of this rum in the United States. From May 1996 to August 1996, Bacardi distributed an additional 906 cases of "Havana Club" rum in the United States.

The pending lawsuit. In December 1996, HCH and HCI filed the instant action to enjoin Bacardi from using the "Havana Club" trademark, alleging violations of sections 32 and 43(a) of the Trademark Act of 1946 ("Lanham Act") . . . . Among Bacardi's defenses was a claim that OFAC's specific license to HCH, authorizing the assignments of the U.S. trademark, was invalid because HCH obtained the mark by fraud. . . .

In August 1997, the District Court ruled that HCH had no rights to the "Havana Club" trademark because the specific license to assign the mark to HCH had been nullified by OFAC's revocation of the specific license and because the CACR's general license authority under 31 C.F.R. § 515.527(a) did not authorize the assignment. *See* Havana Club Holding, S.A. v. Galleon, S.A., 974 F. Supp. 302, 306-07 (S.D.N.Y.1997) ("Havana Club II").[2] After rejecting the Appellants' claim of rights to the "Havana Club" mark, the Court granted the Appellants' motion to amend their Complaint to assert rights to the "Havana Club" trade name under sections 44(g) & 44(h) of the Lanham Act, and Chapter

---

[2]Although acknowledging that the nullification of the assignment caused the rights in the mark to revert to Cubaexport, the assignor, the District Court did not cancel the United States registration for "Havana Club" because Cubaexport was not a party to the litigation. [cit].

III of the General Inter-American Convention for Trade Mark and Commercial Protection, Feb. 20, 1929, 46 Stat. 2907, 2926-30 ("IAC"). Both Cuba and the United States are signatories to the IAC. [cit]. The District Court subsequently dismissed several counter claims. *See* Havana Club Holding, S.A. v. Galleon, S.A., No. 96 CIV. 9655(SAS), 1998 WL 150983 (S.D.N.Y. Mar.31, 1998) ("Havana Club III ").

During the bench trial, the District Court ruled that HCH, a Luxembourg corporation, could not claim rights to trade name protection under the IAC because Luxembourg was not a party to the IAC. *See* Havana Club Holding, S.A. v. Galleon, S.A., 62 F. Supp.2d 1085, 1089 (S.D.N.Y.1999) ("Havana Club IV "). After trial, the District Court ruled that it was prohibited from enforcing HCI's trade name rights under the IAC by section 211(b) of the Omnibus Consolidated and Emergency Supplemental Appropriations Act, 1999, Pub. L. No. 105-277, § 211(b), 112 Stat. 2681, 2681-88 (1998) ("Omnibus Act"), which Congress enacted on October 21, 1998. *See* Havana Club IV, 62 F. Supp. 2d at 1091-95.

The District Court also ruled that HCI lacked standing to assert its claim under section 43(a) of the Lanham Act. HCI had alleged that Bacardi's use of the mark "Havana Club" and its label–which features a sketch of Malecon, a seafront boulevard in Havana–falsely designated Cuba as the place of origin of Bacardi's rum, when in fact Bacardi produced it in the Bahamas. The District Court held that HCI had no standing to pursue this claim, because the Cuban embargo prevented HCI from selling its rum in the United States, and thereby from suffering commercial injury because of Bacardi's actions. The District Court added, "Any competitive injury plaintiffs will suffer based upon their intent to enter the U.S. market once the embargo is lifted is simply too remote and uncertain to provide them with standing." Havana Club IV, 62 F. Supp. 2d at 1099. . . .

Discussion

I. Trademark

HCH contends that Bacardi infringed its rights to the "Havana Club" trademark registered in the United States. The basic issue on the trademark claim is whether HCH has any rights to the mark. Although HCH purported to acquire rights by assignments from Cubaexport to HR & L and from HR & L to HCH, HCH recognizes that to have enforceable rights in the United States, it must find authority for the assignment somewhere in United States law, because in the absence of such authority, the Cuban embargo renders null and void the transfer of trademark registrations in which a Cuban national or entity has an interest.[3]

---

[3]Unless authorized, the Cuban embargo prohibits, with respect to property in which a Cuban national or entity has an interest, (1) "[a]ll dealings in, including, without limitation, transfers . . . of, any property . . . or evidences of ownership of property by any person subject to the jurisdiction of the United States"; (2) "[a]ll transfers outside the United States with regard to any property or property interest subject to the jurisdiction of the United States"; and (3) "[a]ny transaction for the

As authority for the assignments, HCH's Complaint in this litigation initially invoked the "specific" license issued by OFAC in November 1995, which "licensed" the assignments. However, after OFAC revoked the specific license in 1997, HCH has relied on the "general" licensing authority in 31 C.F.R. § 515.527.[4] Section 515.527(a) states:

> Transactions *related* to the registration and renewal in the United States Patent and Trademark Office . . . in which . . . a Cuban national has an interest are authorized.

31 C.F.R. § 515.527(a)(1) (emphasis added). This provision was added in 1995, more than a year after HCH became the assignee of the "Havana Club" trademark. *See* Certain Transactions With Respect To United States Intellectual Property, 60 Fed. Reg. 54,194, 54,196 (1995). HCH contends that, even though OFAC revoked the specific license to assign the "Havana Club" trademark, the assignments remain valid under the general authorization of section 515.527(a)(1) as transactions "related to" the registration and renewal of a trademark. HCH also contends that if section 515.527(a)(1) is not construed to authorize the assignments, HCH will be denied treaty rights protected by the IAC. We disagree with both arguments.

(a) *Whether the CACR prohibit the assignments.* Before considering the meaning of section 515.527(a)(1), we encounter an express prohibition against HCH's claim set forth earlier in Subpart E of Part 515, which contains section 515.527(a)(1). Section 515.502(a) provides:

> No . . . authorization contained in this part . . . shall be deemed to authorize or validate any transaction effected *prior* to the issuance thereof, unless such . . . authorization specifically so provides.

31 C.F.R. § 515.502(a) (emphasis added). The assignments for which HCH claims to find authorization in section 515.527 were "effected" in 1994, prior to the issuance of section 515.527 in 1995, [cit], and section 515.527(a)(1) does not "specifically so provide[ ]" for authorization of transactions that occurred prior

---

purpose or which has the effect of evading or avoiding any of the prohibitions" above. 31 C.F.R. § 515.201(b), (c).

These prohibitions apply where a Cuban national or entity has an interest of "any nature whatsoever, direct or indirect," in the property transferred. *Id.* § 515.312. The embargo defines "property" to include trademarks, *see id.* § 515.311, and specifically defines "transfer" to include "the making, execution, or delivery of any assignment," *id.* §515.310. Any transfer of property in violation of the Cuban embargo "is null and void and shall not be the basis for the assertion or recognition of any interest in or right, remedy, power or privilege with respect to such property." *Id.* § 515.203(a).

[4]The Appellants' initial brief in this Court implies some reliance on the special license by asserting that "cancellation of HCH's interest in the Registration" violates treaty rights under the IAC, see Brief for Appellants at 55, suggesting that the cancellation, if unlawful, leaves the special license in force. We consider the IAC issue below. However, the reply brief unequivocally asserts, "The core issue is whether the CACR general license covers the transfer. . . ." Reply Brief for Appellants at 26.

to its issuance. Therefore, whether or not section 515.527(a)(1) might be interpreted to authorize assignments occurring after its effective date, this provision cannot authorize the 1994 assignments of the "Havana Club" trademark to HCH.[6]

Even if section 515.502(a) were not an obstacle, we would not accept HCH's argument that section 515.527(a)(1) should be interpreted to authorize the 1994 assignments as transactions "related to" a trademark renewal. Although phrases like "related to" are properly given a broad meaning in some statutes and regulations, [cit], the context in which the phrase is used illuminates its meaning. . . .[T]he context here precludes a broad reading. Section 515.527(a)(1) creates an exception to the broad prohibitions of the Cuban embargo. If every assignment of a trademark, for which the registration was subsequently renewed, were considered a transaction "related to" trademark renewal, the exception created by section 515.527(a)(1) would swallow much of the general rule of the Cuban embargo prohibiting transfers of trademarks.

Even if the text of section 515.527(a)(1) arguably applied to the assignments at issue, OFAC, the agency that promulgated the provision and that administers the Cuban embargo, interprets section 515.527 not to authorize assignments. R. Richard Newcomb, Director of OFAC, stated in a 1996 letter to Appellee's counsel that section 515.527:

> allows only for the registration and renewal of intellectual property; § 515.527 does not convey to the registrant the authority to assign the registrant's interest in a patent, trademark, or copyright registered in the United States to another person. Such an assignment would require authorization by OFAC in the form of a specific license . . . .In the absence of OFAC authorization, the assignment of rights to the U.S.-registered trademark would be null and void.

Under this interpretation, only Cubaexport, the original registrant of the United States registration for the "Havana Club" trademark, has the authority to renew the "Havana Club" trademark, and a specific license is required in order to assign it.

(b) *Article 11 of the IAC.* HCH contends that failure to recognize its rights as assignee of the United States registration for the "Havana Club" trademark would nullify rights guaranteed by Article 11 of the IAC. Article 11 provides:

> The transfer of the ownership of a registered or deposited mark in the country of its original registration shall be effective and shall be recognized in the other Contracting States, provided that reliable

---

[6] If HCH were to meet the obstacle of section 515.502(a) by obtaining assignments of the "Havana Club" trademark from Cubaexport now (after issuance of section 515.527(a)(1)), it would encounter the further obstacle of section 211(a)(1) of the Omnibus Act, discussed below, which, without any issue as to retroactivity, would prohibit future assignments of confiscated trademarks without the consent of the original owner.

> proof be furnished that such transfer has been executed and registered in accordance with the internal law of the State in which such transfer took place. Such transfer shall be recorded in accordance with the legislation of the country in which it is to be effective.

46 Stat. at 2922-24. Since the "Havana Club" mark registered in the United States was originally registered in Cuba and was transferred in accordance with Cuban law, Article 11 purports to assure that the transfer to HCH will be recognized in the United States. The disputed issue is whether the Cuban embargo has abrogated the rights that Section 11 of the IAC would otherwise protect.

A "treaty will not be deemed to have been abrogated or modified by a later statute unless such purpose on the part of Congress has been clearly expressed." [cit]. Although neither the CACR nor the LIBERTAD Act refers expressly to the IAC, the question of abrogation does not turn on whether the IAC has been expressly identified for abrogation. Congress is not required to investigate the array of international agreements that arguably provide some protection that it wishes to annul and then assemble a check-list reciting each one. What is required is a clear expression by Congress of a purpose to override protection that a treaty would otherwise provide.

With respect to the Cuban embargo, the purpose of Congress could not be more clear. Congress wished to prevent any Cuban national or entity from attracting hard currency into Cuba by selling, assigning, or otherwise transferring rights subject to United States jurisdiction. The CACR make this clear, and the LIBERTAD Act, by codifying the CACR, provides unmistakable evidence of congressional purpose. We must therefore accord primacy to the prohibition of the CACR that bars a Cuban national or entity from transferring a United States trademark.

HCH contends that since the "related to" phrase of section 515.527(a)(1) could be interpreted to authorize the assignments at issue, the interpretation favoring HCH should be adopted in order to avoid a conflict with section 11 of the IAC. We disagree. First, that argument fails to reckon with the absolute prohibition of section 515.502(a), which prevents section 515.527(a)(1) from validating assignments that were made before the issuance of the latter provision. Second, wholly apart from section 515.502(a), section 515.527(a)(1) cannot be interpreted as HCH contends without substantially undermining the CACR's general prohibitions, as applied to United States trademarks. Thus, we would reject HCH's interpretation even if we did not have the benefit of OFAC's interpretation. Third, even if the interpretation of section 515.527(a)(1) were fairly debatable, the interpretation of the provision given by the agency charged with enforcing the embargo is normally controlling. [cit]. Whether or not deference to an administrative agency's interpretation of its own provisions would override treaty provisions in other contexts, we have no doubt that Congress, whose purpose we are ultimately obliged to follow on this issue, expects that OFAC's restrictive interpretation of section 515.527(a)(1) will override any conflicting treaty protection.

Moreover, in 1996, after OFAC promulgated section 515.527, Congress clearly expressed its intent to prohibit transfers of property, including intellectual property, confiscated by the Cuban government by enacting the LIBERTAD Act. Finding that the Castro government was "offering foreign investors the opportunity to purchase an equity interest in, manage, or enter into joint ventures" involving confiscated property in order to obtain "badly needed financial benefit, including hard currency, oil, and productive investment and expertise," 22 U.S.C. § 6081(5), (6), Congress established a civil remedy for any United States national owning a claim to "property" confiscated by the Cuban government after January 1, 1959, against "any person" who "traffics" in such property, *id.* § 6082(a)(1)(A), and broadly defined "property" specifically to include "trademarks," *id.* § 6023(12)(A). By doing so, Congress intended "to create a 'chilling effect' that will deny the current Cuban regime venture capital, discourage *third-country nationals* from seeking to profit from illegally confiscated property, and help preserve such property until such time as the rightful owners can successfully assert their claim," H. REP. NO. 104-202, at 25 (1996), *reprinted in* 1996 U.S.C.C.A.N. 527, 530 (emphasis added). In other words, Congress sought to discourage business arrangements like Cubaexport's joint venture with Pernod, the venture that led to both the creation of HCH and the assignments of a trademark confiscated by the Castro regime from JASA.[8]

By invoking the 1996 LIBERTAD Act as evidence of Congress's purpose to prohibit the assignments we do not retroactively apply that Act to prohibit the assignments in this case.[9] The 1994 assignments are unauthorized because OFAC revoked the specific license for them and the alleged source of a general licensing authority for them is unavailing. The LIBERTAD Act is simply evidence of congressional purpose that the result we reach should prevail over any contrary arguments, including those based on the IAC.

In the same vein, we note that Congress has recently explicitly spoken to restrict the scope of section 515.527. Section 211(a)(1) of the Omnibus Act provides:

> Notwithstanding any other provision of law, no transaction or payment shall be authorized or approved pursuant to section 515.527 of title 31, Code of Federal Regulations, as in effect on September 9, 1998, with respect to a mark, trade name, or commercial name that is the same as or substantially similar to a mark, trade name, or commercial name that was used in connection with a business or assets that were confiscated unless the original owner of the mark, trade name, or commercial name, or the bona fide

---

[8]We need not determine whether JASA abandoned the "Havana Club" mark by not renewing that mark with the USPTO after the United States imposed the Cuban embargo. We note, however, that in 1962, two years after Cuba expropriated JASA's assets, Congress amended the Lanham Act to allow applications for renewing registered trademarks to show that "any nonuse" of the mark "is due to special circumstances which excuse such nonuse and it is not due to any intention to abandon the mark." [cit].

[9]Although a statute could be prospectively applied to bar an injunctive remedy with respect to a previously acquired property, it would arguably encounter retroactivity objections if applied, of its own force, to invalidate a prior acquisition. [cit].

successor-in-interest has expressly consented.

112 Stat. at 2681-88. Section 515.527 has been amended to include this restriction. *See* 31 C.F.R. § 515.527(a)(2).

As with the LIBERTAD Act, we cite section 211(a)(1), not to apply its terms to invalidate the 1994 assignments (an arguably retroactive application), but only to indicate that interpreting section 515.527(a)(1) not to authorize the assignments fully vindicates Congress's purpose not to permit assignment of confiscated trademarks without the consent of the original owner. [cit].

For all of these reasons, HCH has no enforceable rights to the "Havana Club" trademark.

II. Trade Name Protection Under the Inter-American Convention

HCI contends that Bacardi infringed its rights under the IAC to protection of the "Havana Club" trade name. The IAC provides that any manufacturer "domiciled or established" in a signatory country that uses a particular trade name or commercial name may enjoin the use of that name in another signatory country that is "identical with or deceptively similar to" its trade name. IAC, art. 18, 46 Stat. at 2928-30. A trade or commercial name need not be registered to be protected. *See* IAC, art. 14.

Rights to trade names and commercial names arising under treaties may be asserted under section 44(b) of the Lanham Act . . . . Section 44(g) of the Lanham Act adds, "Trade names or commercial names of persons described in subsection (b) of this section shall be protected without the obligation of filing or registration whether or not they form parts of marks." *Id.* § 1126(g). The terms "trade name" and "commercial name" are defined as "any name used by a person to identify his or her business or vocation." *Id.* § 1127.

On October 21, 1998, before the bench trial in this case, Congress passed section 211 of the Omnibus Act, which provides in pertinent part:

> (b) No U.S. court shall recognize, enforce or otherwise validate any assertion of treaty rights by a designated national or its successor-in-interest under sections 44(b) or (e) of the Trademark Act of 1946 for a mark, trade name, or commercial name that is the same as or substantially similar to a mark, trade name, or commercial name that was used in connection with a business or assets that were confiscated unless the original owner of such mark, trade name, or commercial name, or the bona fide successor-in-interest has expressly consented.
>
> (c) The Secretary of the Treasury shall promulgate such rules and regulations as are necessary to carry out the provisions of this section.
>
> (d) [the statute defined "designated national" and "confiscated" by reference to terms used elsewhere in the CFR.]

112 Stat. at 2681-88.

Section 211(b) applies in this case. This Court is a "U.S. court" under section 211(b). HCI is a "designated national" under section 211(b) because HCI is organized under the laws of Cuba, is domiciled in Cuba, and has its principal place of business in Cuba. [cit].

Applying section 211(b), the District Court ruled that it precluded HCI's assertion of treaty rights under sections 44(b) or (e) of the Lanham Act and thereby precluded HCI's claims under the IAC. HCI disputes this ruling on several grounds. HCI first argues that it does not need sections 44(b) and (e) of the Lanham Act to assert its rights under the IAC because upon ratification, the IAC became law in the United States without the aid of additional legislation. *See* Bacardi Corp. of America v. Domenech, 311 U.S. 150, 161 (1940). This argument presumes that when Congress enacted section 44(b) of the Lanham Act, it intended to incorporate into law only those treaties that were not self-executing at the time.

The original text of section 44(b) and the legislative history, however, suggest otherwise. When enacted in 1946, section 44(b) of the Lanham Act specifically incorporated the treaty rights of:

> [p]ersons who are nationals of, domiciled in, or have a bona fide and effective business or commercial establishment in any foreign country, which is a party to (1) the International Convention for the Protection of Industrial Property... or (2) *the General Inter-American Convention for Trade Mark and Commercial Protection* ... *or* (3) any other convention or treaty relating to trade-marks, trade or commercial names, or the repression of unfair competition to which the United States is a party . . . .

Trademark Act of 1946, ch. 540, § 44(b) (emphasis added).[12] Although the Supreme Court had already ruled the IAC to be self-executing, *see* Bacardi Corp., 311 U.S. at 161, Congress specifically referred to the IAC in section 44(b) because Congress simply was not sure whether the trademark treaties had acquired the force of law. The Senate Report explained:

> These conventions have been ratified, but it is a question whether they are self-executing, and whether they do not need to be implemented by appropriate legislation. Industrialists in this country have been seriously handicapped in securing protection in foreign countries due to our failure to carry out, by statute, our international obligations.

S. REP. NO. 79-1333 (1946), *reprinted in* 1946 U.S. CODE & CONG. SERV. 1274, 1276. Accordingly, Congress intended the Lanham Act "[t]o carry out *by statute*

---

[12]In 1962, Congress amended section 44(b) to exclude the references to the two specific treaties, *see* § 20, 76 Stat. at 774, presumably in an effort to "revis[e] the language to a more understandable form," S. REP. NO. 87-2107 (1962)

our international commitments to the end that American traders in foreign countries may secure the protection to their marks to which they are entitled." *Id.* (emphasis added). Indeed, referring specifically to "inter-American conventions," Congress aimed to eliminate "these sources of friction with our Latin-American friends" and "facilitate mutual trade in this hemisphere" by ensuring the protection of their trademark rights in the United States. *Id.*[13] Therefore, HCI must assert its rights under the IAC pursuant to section 44(b) of the Lanham Act.

Second, HCI argues that, because HCI's rights to the "Havana Club" trade name existed before Congress enacted section 211(b), the District Court improperly applied section 211(b) retroactively. To determine whether section 211(b) may apply retroactively, we would normally first inquire "whether Congress has expressly prescribed the statute's proper reach." [cit]. Since section 211 does not clearly indicate that it should be applied retroactively, the traditional presumption against retroactivity would likely apply. [cit].

In this case, however, we can apply section 211(b) to bar relief on HCI's trade name claim because when an "intervening statute authorizes or affects the propriety of prospective relief, application of the new provision is not retroactive." [cit]. Because HCI seeks only injunctive relief, this Court can properly apply section 211(b).

Third, HCI argues that section 211(b) does not apply when the trade name at issue has been abandoned. Section 211(b) [refers to assets that were "confiscated"]. By "confiscated," section 211(b) refers to the nationalization, expropriation, or other seizure of property by the Cuban Government on or after January 1, 1959. [cit]. It is undisputed that JASA used the "Havana Club" name until the Cuban government expropriated the business in 1960 and has not expressly consented to HCI's use of the "Havana Club" name.

Nevertheless, HCI argues that JASA had abandoned its rights to the "Havana Club" trade name long before HCI started to use the name (as "Havana Club International") in 1994. Despite the lack of an explicit abandonment defense, HCI urges this Court to construe section 211(b) to include an abandonment exception because (1) interpreting section 211(b) otherwise would abrogate the IAC, and (2) abandonment, as a defense that arises out of common law, must not be presumed to be abrogated by section 211(b) absent express indication of Congress's intent to do so. However, we will not create an abandonment exception to section 211(b). Section 211(b) requires only that a trade name "was used" in connection with a confiscated business or asset, not that the trade name continues to be used. *See* United States v. Wilson, 503 U.S. 329, 333 (1992) ("Congress' use of a verb tense is significant in construing statutes."). Moreover, Congress knows how to enact an abandonment defense; it has already provided conditions under which any trademark, service mark, collective mark, or certification mark shall be deemed abandoned. *See* 15 U.S.C.

---

[13]*Cf.* Vanity Fair Mills, Inc. v. T. Eaton Co., 234 F.2d 633, 641 (2d Cir.1956) (noting that in trademark dispute involving sales of allegedly infringing goods in Canada, the only rights plaintiff could assert under the International Convention for the Protection of Industrial Property "*other than through* section 44 of the Lanham Act . . . are derived from . . . Canadian law, and not from the fact that the International Convention may be a self-executing treaty which is a part of the law of this country") (emphasis added).

§ 1127. It is not likely that Congress wished to disadvantage a company that understandably ceased to use its trade name after the confiscation of its business.

Fourth, [HCI argued that "Havana Club" trade name was never confiscated within the meaning of the statute because, even if no compensation were granted, the confiscated business allegedly had no positive net value at the time of expropriation. The court rejected that argument because the embargo's definition of confiscated property contemplates only three ways in which property expropriated by Cuba can avoid becoming classified as "confiscated" and neither existed here.]

III. False Advertising

HCI disputes the District Court's finding that it does not have standing to assert its "false advertising" claim [under section 43(a) of the Lanham Act]. To establish standing under section 43(a), the plaintiff must

> demonstrate a "reasonable interest to be protected" against the advertiser's false or misleading claims, and a "reasonable basis" for believing that this interest is likely to be damaged by the false or misleading advertising. The "reasonable basis" prong embodies a requirement that the plaintiff show both likely injury and a causal nexus to the false advertising.

[cit]. "Although a section 43 plaintiff need not be a direct competitor, it is apparent that, at a minimum, standing to bring a section 43 claim requires the potential for a commercial or competitive injury." Berni v. International Gourmet Restaurants of America, Inc., 838 F.2d 642, 648 (2d Cir. 1988) (citations omitted) . . . .

[The court rejected HCI's argument that it has standing under the current version of section 43(a), because HCI does business "in the locality falsely indicated as that of origin" by Bacardi, namely, Havana.]

Second, to establish the likelihood of commercial injury for the purposes of standing, HCI argues that Bacardi's use of the "Havana Club" name will adversely affect HCI's current and future sales of its rum to U.S. visitors to Cuba. The fact that HCI sells to Americans traveling in Cuba, however, does not necessarily demonstrate the likelihood that the distribution of Bacardi's "Havana Club" rum in the United States will hurt HCI sales to those persons in Cuba. Although HCI presented consumer surveys that reported that "33% of Americans think that it is legal to sell rum from Cuba in the United States and 9% do not know whether it is legal or illegal," the District Court noted that "it is intuitively doubtful that these finding[s] would apply to U.S. travelers authorized to visit Cuba." Havana Club Holding IV, 62 F. Supp. 2d at 1100 n. 11. We will not disturb this finding on appeal. . . .

    . . . .

Third, HCI argues that the District Court erred in finding HCI's ability to enter the U.S. market to be too remote at this point to confer standing. Although this Court has conferred standing for section 43(a) claims based on a showing of potential commercial injury, not all potential commercial injuries are sufficient to confer standing. [cit].

HCI characterizes its injuries as (1) the "lost ability to use the HAVANA CLUB name in the U.S. through Bacardi's accumulation of rights-by-use," (2) "loss of the key selling points in the U.S. of being the single source of both HAVANA CLUB rum and Cuban-origin rum," and (3) "damaged reputation of Cuban-origin rum," or more generally, "the imminent loss of their prime selling advantage." Even if HCI competes with Bacardi in markets elsewhere in the world, standing requires that HCI demonstrate at least potential commercial injury in the United States, because Bacardi sells "Havana Club" rum only in the United States. Because HCI's rum does not now compete with Bacardi's rum in the United States, HCI's alleged injury amounts to the present diminution in the speculative value of its sales of Cuban-origin rum in the United States market once the United States government removes the obstacle of the Cuban embargo.

That obstacle is formidable. The LIBERTAD Act not only codified the economic embargo of Cuba, [cit], and strengthened its measures, [cit], but also authorized the President to take steps to suspend the embargo only after determining that a "transition government in Cuba is in power," [cit], and authorized the President to take steps to terminate the embargo only after determining that "a democratically elected government in Cuba is in power," [cit]. At this time, the President has not determined that a "transition government," let alone a "democratically elected" government, exists in Cuba.

HCI points to recent efforts in Congress to pass legislation to lift portions of the Cuban embargo. However, by conferring standing to HCI based on its own prediction of Congress's actions, this Court would expand its authority well beyond any zone of twilight that might exist between legislative and judicial authority.

HCI also seeks to support standing by relying on *G.H. Mumm Champagne v. Eastern Wine Corp.*, 142 F.2d 499 (2d Cir.1944), and section 10(g) of the TWEA. Its arguments are unavailing. Mumm is a pre-Lanham Act action to enjoin trademark infringement and unfair competition, not a false advertising action, and its facts are readily distinguishable from those in this case. In *Mumm*, a French company had registered the trademarks at issue and had contracted with a Delaware company in 1938, prior to World War II, to sell only the French company's champagne.[15] *See id.* at 500. After upholding the Delaware

---

[15]In the contract, the French company agreed that it alone would protect and enforce its trademark rights in the United States. *See id.* at 502. Soon thereafter, as the district court in Mumm explained, France was "occupied by the armed forces of the German Reich. . . . Because of conditions due to the existing war, the [Delaware company] is, and has been, unable to communicate with the [French company]." G.H. Mumm Champagne v. Eastern Wine Corp., 52 F. Supp. 167, 169-70 (S.D.N.Y.1943). Observing that the war had made "impossible the performance of that promise" by the French company to protect its marks, we construed the contract to authorize the Delaware company, under those circumstances, to seek to enjoin trademark infringement on the French company's behalf. *Mumm*, 142 F.2d at 502. Although we referred to sections 10(g) and (h) of the TWEA, we did so only to note that the TWEA did not preclude the Delaware company's

company's entitlement to an injunction, the Court considered "the rather barren question" whether to uphold its right to obtain an injunction on behalf of the French company, "barren, because one injunction is as good as two." *Id.* at 502. Despite the lack of significance of an injunction on behalf of the French company, we affirmed it because the infringement risked lost sales in the United States by the Delaware company, which might have resulted in lost profits by the French company "provided sales lost by the Delaware company resulted in sales lost by it to that company."[16] In the pending case, however, unlike the French company in *Mumm*, HCI has no United States partner selling its product in the United States, and therefore no loss of profits derived indirectly from lost sales in the United States will occur.

Nor does section 10(g) itself aid HCI. Section 10(g) provides that "[a]ny enemy, or ally of enemy, may institute and prosecute suits in equity ... to enjoin infringement of letters patent, trade-mark, print, label, and copyrights in the United States owned or controlled by said enemy or ally of enemy, in the same manner and to the extent that he would be entitled so to do if the United States was not at war." 50 U.S.C. app. § 10(g). HCI does not contend that it may sue under section 10(g); in the absence of a state of war with Cuba, HCI is not an "enemy." Nevertheless, it argues that if its section 43(a) claim is rejected for lack of standing, then section 10(g) could not be used by those plaintiffs within the section's coverage. The argument does not help HCI.

In the first place, section 10(g) would not apply to a false designation of origin claim under section 43(a) of the Lanham Act. A plaintiff need not "own [ ] or control[ ]" a registered trademark to bring a section 43(a) action. Any rum producer selling its product in the United States can obtain standing to complain about Bacardi's allegedly false designation of origin as long as it can demonstrate the commercial injury required for an action under section 43(a).

Secondly, to the extent that HCI analogizes false designation claims to trademark infringement claims, section 10(g) provides no escape from traditional standing requirements. Section 10(g) permits a covered plaintiff to institute an infringement action "to the extent that he would be entitled so to do if the United States was not at war." . . .

IV. Unfair Competition

Finally, HCI argues that it has standing to sue under section 44(h) of the Lanham Act for unfair competition. . . . Rights under Section 44(h) are co-extensive with treaty rights under section 44(b), including treaty rights "relating to ... the repression of unfair competition."[18] . . . *See* Toho Co. v. Sears,

---

limited authority under the contract to seek to enjoin trademark infringement on the French company's behalf. *See Mumm*, 142 F.2d at 503.

[16]Whether the possibility of lost profits by the French company might have resulted from loss of an increase in its account with the Delaware company as the latter depleted its stock of pre-war imported champagne, or from some other arrangement is not indicated in the Court's opinion.

[18]If the unfair competition claim were viable, it would not encounter the obstacle of section 211(b) of the Omnibus Act, which does not expressly preclude a court from enforcing treaty rights under section 44(b) relating to the repression of unfair competition.

Roebuck & Co., 645 F.2d 788, 792 (9th Cir.1981) ("The grant in subsection (h) of effective protection against unfair competition is tailored to the provisions of the unfair competition treaties by subsection (b), which extends the benefits of section 44 only to the extent necessary to give effect to the treaties."); American Auto. Ass'n v. Spiegel, 205 F.2d 771, 774 (2d Cir.1953) ("Since [section 44(h)] is limited to 'persons designated in subsection (b)', we look to that subsection to learn its scope.").

HCI essentially argues that it must demonstrate less to obtain standing to assert its section 44(h) claim than is required for its section 43(a) claim. Article 21(c) of the IAC defines an act of "unfair competition" to include "[t]he use of false indications of geographical origin or source of goods, by words, symbols, or other means which tend in that respect to deceive the public in the country in which these acts occur." 46 Stat. at 2932. We note, however, that article 21 of the IAC authorizes the prohibition of its specified acts of unfair competition "unless otherwise effectively dealt with under the domestic laws of the Contracting States." *Id.* HCI's section 44(h) claim amounts to little more than the re-assertion of its section 43(a) claim because article 21(c) of the IAC prohibits a subset of the conduct already effectively prohibited under American law by section 43(a). We therefore conclude as a matter of law that HCI has failed to state a viable claim under section 44(h).

Notes and Questions

(1) **The Scope of Section 211**. Does section 211 explicitly abrogate rights to bring an unfair competition claim? *See* Paris Convention art. 10*bis*; Lanham Act, § 44(b). If it does not, what is the practical effect of section 211? At what point would the plaintiffs' likely entry into the U.S. market be insufficiently remote so that standing to pursue such a claim would be recognized by the court?

(2) **TRIPS Violation**. Cuba has argued that Section 211 violates several provisions of the TRIPS Agreement, and Cuba's position is supported not only by the EU (Pernod is a French company) but also by many other WTO members, including Brazil and India. At the TRIPS Council Meeting on April 21-22, 1999, Cuba complained that the United States had not responded to its request for an explanation of the TRIPS-compatibility of section 211. (The United States had taken the position that, under WTO Rules, it need provide Cuba only with details of the legislation and not any explanation of its compliance with TRIPS.) On July 3, 2000 the EU requested the establishment of a WTO dispute panel with the United States regarding section 211, and a panel was constituted in September 2000. The EU claims that section 211 violates Articles 2, 15, 16, 41-42, and 62 of TRIPS? Are the claims meritorious? *See EU and Cuba Attack U.S. Law Denying Trademark Holder Protections*, 57 Pat. Trad. & Copr. J. (BNA) 544 (Apr. 29, 1999). A report by the WTO panel was expected as this book went to press.

(3) **Cuba's Response.** In response to the decision in *Havana Club II*, President Fidel Castro declared that "I hope no-one complains if one day we begin to produce Coca-Cola. We might be able to make it better, and on the can we'll put: Cuban Coca-Cola." Ana Radelat, *Decision on Trademark Rights for a Rum Spurs a Global Dispute*, N.Y. TIMES, June 1, 1999, C1 at C6. President Castro also threatened to remove protection for hundreds of American trademarks registered in Cuba. Could Cuba legally respond in this fashion?

(4) **Bacardi's Response.** Bacardi purchased the rights from the Arechabala family after the lawsuit was filed in New York, and then sought further legislative support. Section 211 was sponsored by the two Florida senators in the U.S. Senate at the behest of Bacardi, which has a large Florida operation. (Indeed, the Madrid Protocol accession, *see infra* § 6.02[A], is being politically delayed pending resolution of the *Havana Rum* dispute.) Some U.S. business organizations have called for the repeal of section 211. Would you support a repeal? Bacardi has said that it will pursue registration of its mark with the U.S. Patent and Trademark Office. If you were an examining attorney at the PTO, how would you respond to the application?

NOTE: NAFTA AND FREE TRADE AREA OF THE AMERICAS

The first meeting of the Preparatory Committee ("PrepCom") of representatives from thirty-four countries seeking to develop the Free Trade Area of the Americas took place in 1997. A separate FTAA Intellectual Property Working Group is considering the intellectual property provisions that might be part of any such development. This would build upon the trademark provisions of NAFTA and TRIPS. NAFTA was signed one year prior to TRIPS, and its trademark provisions (like its copyright and patent provisions) are very similar to TRIPS. To the extent there are differences, NAFTA would appear slightly more protective of trademark rights. For example, whereas the definition of trademark in TRIPS does not expressly make reference to product design, the definition of trademark in Article 1708(1) of NAFTA includes "the shape of goods." *See generally* Daniel R. Bereskin, *A Comparison of the Trademark Provisions of NAFTA and TRIPS*, 83 TRADEMARK REP. 1 (1993).

[K] Trademark Law Treaty

While the TRIPS Agreement was being concluded, WIPO was completing the Trademark Law Treaty ("TLT"). At present, the provisions of the TLT are not incorporated into TRIPS. The goals are not unrelated, however. The TLT is intended to facilitate multinational registration, and TRIPS does (as regards all intellectual property rights) impose general standards of procedural fairness and openness.

The TLT was adopted at a diplomatic conference convened by WIPO in 1994. The objectives underlying the TLT are more limited than those behind the

Madrid Agreement or the Madrid Protocol. It is intended to simplify and harmonize trademark registration and renewal procedures by establishing maximum procedural requirements that a member country can impose as a condition to an application, a registration, or recording of an assignment. The TLT also provides a set of standardized forms which must be recognized by TLT member countries. (More substantively, it requires member countries to treat service marks equally with trademarks.)

The TLT came into force on August 1, 1996 and has been ratified by twenty-six countries. The U.S. Senate ratified the TLT on June 26, 1998, *see* Treaty Doc. 105-35, and Congress subsequently enacted legislation, the Trademark Law Treaty Implementation Act ("TLTIA"), Pub. L. No. 105-330, 112 Stat. 3064 (1998), in order to conform U.S. law to the treaty requirements. The legislation became effective on October 30, 1999. *See id.*, § 110. On May 12, 2000, the United States formally deposited its instrument of TLT ratification with WIPO.

U.S. law was already largely compatible with the TLT, and thus the changes that the TLTIA made to the Lanham Act are relatively minor and quite technical. Most of the amendments, which should facilitate the acquisition and maintenance of registrations, were intended to eliminate procedural requirements not permitted by the TLT. *See, e.g.*, TLT art. 3(1) (establishing comprehensive list of elements that may be required in a trademark application). Congress took the opportunity, however, to simplify procedural complexities surrounding registration even where this was not strictly required by the treaty. For example, it expanded the group of persons who may verify a declaration of use or intent to use for a corporate applicant. The previously strict requirement, which was particularly difficult to apply to foreign corporate structures, often caused applicants to lose filing dates on extremely technical grounds. *See* H.R. Rep. No. 194, 105th Cong. 1st Sess. 12 (1997). Likewise, motivated by the "goal of the TLT to simplify the registration process worldwide" rather than any particular treaty provision, the standard for revival of an application abandoned during the examination process for failure to respond to an Office Action was liberalized from an applicant's "unavoidable delay" to an "unintentional" failure to respond. *See* TLTIA § 104; 15 U.S.C. § 1062(b).

In direct response to treaty obligations, Section 1 of the amended Lanham Act now distinguishes between the written application and the declaration of use or intention to use; the latter must be verified by the applicant, but the written application need not. *See* TLTIA § 103. The PTO also revised its rules prescribing the elements necessary for a complete application and filing date. *See* 64 Fed. Reg. 48900 (Sept. 8, 1999). Applications filed prior to October 30, 1999 must meet the minimum filing requirements that were in effect on the date of the filing. Among other things, the revisions to the PTO Rules reduced the number of specimens of use that must be filed. *See* Rules 2.56(a), 2.76 (b)(2), 2.88(b)(2). The PTO anticipates publishing and issuing marks in color in the future. In the interim, the revised rules dispense with the need to comply with the PTO's "color lining system" (found in former Rule 2.52) on the drawing of the mark; instead, a written description of the use of any color contained in the mark will be required. The implementing legislation also eliminated the requirement–again, not permitted by the treaty–of a statement of the manner in which a mark is used or intended to be used in connection with the goods or services specified in the application.

The registration maintenance and renewal obligations found in Sections 8-9 of the Lanham Act did not fully comply with the TLT. *See* TLT art. 13(1) (establishing comprehensive list of elements that may be required in a trademark renewal application). Whether the implementing legislation effects the necessary changes is not entirely clear. *See* TLTIA §§ 105-106 (amending sections 8-9 of the Lanham Act). At the very least, Congress adopted a minimalist approach to compliance on this issue, in contrast to its embrace of the spirit of the treaty in other areas where it acted without the compulsion of international obligation. Article 13(4)(iii) expressly prohibits requiring a declaration and/or evidence of use as part of a registration renewal request. Section 8 of the Lanham Act previously required the filing of an affidavit of use necessary to maintain a registration between the fifth and sixth year after registration; section 9 required a similar filing during renewals of a registration. Although this latter requirement is proscribed by Article 13 of the TLT, and thus eliminated from section 9 renewal obligations, *see* TLTIA § 106, Congress effectively circumvented the prohibition by imposing the Section 8 obligation to file an affidavit of use not only between five-six years after registration, but also in the year preceding every ten-year anniversary of the registration. *See* TLTIA § 105. This essentially has the same effect as a Section 9 affidavit of use obligation, but Congress expressed the view that this approach is consistent with the TLT. Although the United States has been candid about its minimalist interpretation of these obligations, the sophistry behind this recasting of the section 9 affidavit of use obligation is merely emphasized by the otherwise commendable effort in sections 105-106 of the TLTIA to harmonize the filing requirements under section 8 and section 9 of the Lanham Act. (These harmonized provisions include a common "window" starting one year before the end of the sixth or tenth year after registration, respectively, and a common six-month grace period, available upon payment of a surcharge, after each filing "window" closes). The implementation strategy adopted by Congress was justified as part of a continuing commitment to ensuring the integrity of the Register by the removal of deadwood—in short, a commitment to the use-based philosophy of U.S. trademark law in the face of international pressures in the opposite direction. Ironically, if the minimum standards of the TLT are (as proposed by the United States in September 1998) included as minimum standards in a revised TRIPS Agreement, the question of U.S. compliance might be raised before a WTO Dispute Settlement Panel.

The implementing legislation also amended Section 10 of the Lanham Act to require the PTO to record a change of ownership without submission of a copy of the underlying assignment document. *See* TLTIA § 107. Again, the statute authorizes the PTO to determine what information it will record and maintain regarding assignments. Although the PTO may not require a statement of proof of the transfer of goodwill in order to record an assignment, *see* TLT art. 11(4)(iv), section 10 still requires that a mark may be assigned only with accompanying goodwill. Finally, where an application is based on a foreign registration under section 44(e), the applicant will no longer require to include a certificate or certified copy of the foreign registration in order to receive a filing date. *See* TLTIA § 108; TLT art. 5. The amendment allows the applicant to submit such documentation within such time limits as the Commissioner may prescribe. The revised rules require submission before the mark is published for opposition or approved for registration on the Supplemental Register.

The TLT will have greater significance for U.S. applicants filing abroad, because the treaty also prohibits an array of procedural (and costly) prerequisites formerly common in other countries. For example, the treaty does not allow a country to require notarization and legalization of signatures, except where a registration is being surrendered. *See* TLT art. 8(4). Because so much of the treaty relates to administrative procedures, however, the full effect of the TLT may not be seen until national trademark offices adopt revised administrative procedures. Moreover, Article 22 allows signatory states to delay compliance with some of the TLT obligations for six years (developed countries) or eight years (developing countries).

§ 3.02   Geographical Indications

Words or symbols with geographic significance are frequently used in the marketing of products: consider, for example, Waterford crystal, and Idaho potatoes. But each of these geographic terms—Waterford and Idaho—is used (and understood) in a different sense when applied to goods. "Waterford" identifies the world's leading manufacturer of high-quality cut lead crystal; "Idaho" indicates for consumers the geographic origin from which the potatoes in question come. The former ("Waterford") is a trademark; the latter ("Idaho") is a geographical indication. IDAHO is not a trademark because, unlike WATERFORD, it does not identify the goods of a single producer and distinguish them from others. *See* 15 U.S.C. § 1127 (definition of "trademark"). As these examples demonstrate, the interaction with trademark protection will be an important part of the discussion of geographical indications of origin.

Terminology in this area is somewhat confusing, and (because U.S. law historically has had no separate protection for geographical indications) largely derived from European usage. Generally speaking, the term "geographical indication" encompasses both "indications of source" and "appellations of origin." "Indications of source" is commonly understood to mean a word or other symbol that indicates that a product originates in a specific geographic region. "Appellation of Origin" refers to a word or symbol that indicates both that the product originates from a specific geographic region and that it possesses the qualities or characteristics for which that place is known. For example, the designation ROQUEFORT for cheese would be an appellation of origin because its use suggests certain qualities associated with cheese from this French municipality; in contrast use of that same geographic designation for clothing from Roquefort would merely be an indication of source because Roquefort is not particularly well-known for producing clothing of any particular, distinctive quality.

The protection afforded geographical indications varies widely from country to country, and typically focuses on addressing one or more of three issues: (i) protecting the right of regional producers to use (and control use of) geographic terms as appellations of origin; (ii) enjoining the use of geographic terms on goods that do not come from the geographic place in question; and (iii) the conflict that occurs between one person who uses a geographical term as part of her trademark and the group that seeks to use the same geographical term as an appellation of origin.

In the international context, the ultimate goal of negotiators may be to install a system addressing all geographical indications. The short-term priority, primarily driven by European nations, however, has been to regulate the use of such designations for wines and spirits. It is in this area that the European economic interest is at its greatest. And it is in this area that U.S. law has (arguably) been most deficient, finding several geographic terms used with wines–such as "champagne"–generic on the grounds that the term identifies for U.S. consumers a type of product; this status renders the term unprotectable and freely usable as a matter of U.S. trademark law, even if the wine does not come from the denominated region (such as the Champagne region of France). Accordingly, treaties on geographical indications frequently contain both generally applicable provisions and specific provisions targeted at the wine industry.

[A]   Current International Agreements in General

ALBRECHT CONRAD, THE PROTECTION OF GEOGRAPHICAL INDICATIONS IN THE TRIPS AGREEMENT*
86 TRADEMARK REP. 11 (1996)

INTERNATIONAL PROTECTION BEFORE TRIPS

A. Existing Multilateral Treaties

1. Historical Development

The beginning of international protection of geographical indications dates back to the conclusion of the Paris Convention . . . in 1883, which included as protectible subject matter "indications of source or appellations of origin," Article 1(2). However, Article 10 prohibited the use of false geographical indications only if they were accompanied by a false, fictitious, or deceptive trade name. With the scope of protection so narrowly defined, the provision lacked effectiveness, and soon a number of countries undertook to establish a new union for the protection of geographical indications: The Madrid Agreement [for the Prevention of False or Misleading Indications of Source on Goods] of 1891 ("Madrid Agreement"). In spite of the active participation of many countries in the drafting process, only a few decided to become members, and important countries such as the United States, Italy, Germany, Belgium, and

---

almost all the South American countries did not accede. Although several countries have since joined, the limited number of member states still remains a principal defect of the Madrid Agreement.

In 1958, the Revision Conference for the Paris Convention of Lisbon adopted a few changes regarding geographical indications, including the cancellation of the above-mentioned restriction of the scope of protection. However, a group of countries, dissatisfied with the amendments, made a new attempt to foster protection of geographical indications: the Lisbon Agreement for the Protection of Appellations of Origin and their International Registration ("Lisbon Agreement").[*] This agreement set a relatively high standard of protection and has now been taken as one of the models for the drafting of the TRIPS provisions. Despite its high standard (or perhaps because of it), even fewer countries have adhered to the Lisbon Agreement.

Today, the three main conventions result in three concentric groups of states:

(1) A small number of members of the Lisbon Agreement (17 members) with an international registration of geographic origins and strict protection.

(2) A larger number of member states of the Madrid Agreement (31 members), bound mainly to implement border measures and to prevent the dilution of geographical indications into generic terms.

(3) The large number of member states of the Paris Convention (117 members), agreeing mainly to border measures for false indications without defining the conditions for protection.

2. The Paris Convention

The protection of geographical indications under the Paris Convention is very limited. Indications of Source and Appellations of Origin are included among the objects of its protection, Article 1. Thus, nationals of member countries enjoy "National Treatment," Article 2. The provision concerning geographical indications alone, Article 10, as revised at the Revision Conference of Lisbon (1958), refers back to Article 9 and mainly provides for border measures against the importation of goods bearing false representations of origin, but only if such measures are available under the law of the member country. The agreement does not, however, define "indication of origin," nor does it state when a representation is false. The protection is left to the member countries. Therefore, Articles 10 and 9 in effect contain very little that is not already provided for by Article 2.

. . . .

Article 10bis (3) of the Convention, regarding unfair competition, prohibits indications as to the "characteristics" of the goods, if they are liable to mislead the public. This might suggest that in cases where a geographical name is understood in commerce not only as an indication of origin but also as a description of the product's quality or "characteristics," the indication is protected under Article 10bis. The indication "Champagne" on an American

---

[*][Ed. Note: This agreement is often referred to as the "Lisbon Arrangement."]

bottle of sparkling wine, e.g., could be misleading, if the public is likely to think that the product originated in France and the characteristics of French "Champagne" are noticeably different. Article 10*bis* would apply here because "Champagne" not only indicates French origin but also certain characteristics.[71]

The legislative history of Article 10*bis*(3) shows, however, that the provision is not applicable to representations of geographic origin. Article 10*bis* was introduced at the Lisbon Revision Conference in 1958; it is based on the Austrian proposal which read:

> Indications or allegations, the use of which in the course of trade is liable to mislead the public as to the nature, the origin, the manufacturing process, the characteristics, the suitability for their purpose or the quantity of the goods.

The words "the origin" were then struck out because of the veto by the United States delegation who declared that the inclusion of the reference to geographical origin would cause too many problems in United States law and therefore they could not consent to it. The rest of the proposal then became Article 10*bis*(3). Thus, the Paris Convention prevents only the importation of goods containing false geographical indications but it is not applicable to indications that are merely misleading.[73]

3. The Madrid Agreement*

The Madrid Agreement exceeds the Paris Convention on three points. First, [Art. 1(1)] extends the protection to misleading geographical indications [by requiring signatory states to seize "goods bearing a false or misleading indication" of origin in a signatory country]. Second, Article 3*bis*, which was adopted by the Revision Conference of London (1934), prohibits the use of false representations on the product itself and in advertising or other forms of public announcements. Third, and most important is Article 4, which prohibits member countries from treating geographical indications of wines as generic terms. However, divergent views in reference to the construction of the provision exist (for example, regarding the use of terms like "type" or "style" with the indication), and thus its practical use is very restricted. Moreover,

---

[71]This interpretation is suggested by Louis C. Lenzen, *Bacchus in the Hinterlands: A Study of Denominations of Origin in French and American Wine-Labeling Laws*, 58 TMR 145, 185 (1968).

. . . .

[73]Geographical indications can be misleading although not "false"; *see Bundesgerichtshof* GRUR 1958, 39 ("*Rosenheimer Gummimantel*"). Raincoats, advertised as "*Rosenheimer Gummimantel*" created the impression that they were made by a certain producer, which was misleading; however, they had been produced in Rosenheim, a German town ("*Rosenheimer Gummimantel*" apparently had acquired "secondary meaning"). Benson . . . gives the example of "California Chablis" for a term that is not false but could nevertheless be misleading.

*[Ed. Note: This Madrid Agreement of 1891, often referred to as the "Madrid Arrangement," should not be confused with the Madrid Agreement Concerning the International Registration of Marks, also of 1891, which is a far more significant treaty and is dealt with *infra* § 6.02[A].]

many nations have not acceded to the Agreement, which is another reason for its limited importance.

4. The Lisbon Agreement

The Lisbon Agreement was an attempt to secure effective and enforceable protection of geographical indications on a new basis. Its focus is not restricted to border measures, as in the Paris Convention or the Madrid Agreement, but also includes adoption of a registration system comparable to that of trademarks, drafted after the model of the "Madrid Agreement Concerning the International Registration of Marks" [discussed *infra* § 6.02[A]]. The object of the Lisbon Agreement concerns appellations of origin, as defined in Article 2(1). The definition employs the French interpretation of "appellations d'origine" by restricting the indications protected to cases in which the quality and characteristics are "exclusively or essentially due to the geographical environment, including natural and human factors." The main feature of the agreement is that these appellations of origin are "recognized and protected as such (*à ce titre*) in the country of origin and registered at the International Bureau of Intellectual Property," an agency of WIPO. Thus, the various countries are free to adopt any form of procedure to register geographical indications, be it by judicial or administrative determination. Once registered, a geographic indication is protected in other member countries "in accordance with this agreement" (Article 1). The countries have to ensure that any kind of usurpation or imitation is prohibited under their laws, including the use of terms like "type" or "style" along with the indication (Article 3); no geographical indication can be deemed generic in any other country as long as it is protected in its country of origin (Article 6).

The main problem with the Lisbon Agreement is that very few states have become members.[76] Two critical points have prevented important nations from joining. First, international protection is granted only if the geographical indication is protected in the country of origin "as such"; hence, the concept of protection through the law of unfair competition or the law of advertising is not recognized. A number of states are not willing to transform their system of protection in order to be compatible with the standards of the Lisbon Agreement. Second, the Agreement does not make exceptions for terms that have already become generic in some member countries.[77] The issue of genericness is one of the difficult problems on the international level which has hindered the negotiating process of TRIPS.

---

[76]Countries which have traditionally protected geographical indications such as Switzerland, Spain, or Germany have not become members. The United States also is not a member. A group of thirteen African states, however, has expressed their willingness to adhere to the treaty, *see* Agreement of Libreville, Ind. Prop. 394 (1970).

[77]On that point the Agreement is directly contrary to the United States trademark law and the Bureau of Alcohol, Tobacco and Firearms (BATF) regulations (*see* 27 CFR § 4.24(c)(1)) and was the main reason why the United States has not become a member; *see also* Lee Bendekgey & Caroline H. Mead, *International Protection of Appellations of Origin and Other Geographic Indications*, 82 TMR 765, 781 (1992).

B. Examples of Bilateral Treaties

Bilateral treaties have a long tradition in the field of the protection of geographical indications . . . [but have not] yielded effective protection because the parties failed to determine the scope of protection. An example . . . is the treaty [T.S. No. 514 1/2] between Portugal and the United States of 1910, in which the names "Porto" and "Madeira" were to be protected by the United States; in that case the United States decided to implement the protective provisions by means of the law of advertising. As a result, the discussion regarding whether or not the duty to "protect" these terms included a prohibition of "Porto" or "Madeira" accompanied by "kind" or "type," debated since the Madrid Agreement, was simply carried over into this agreement. . . .

After the failure of the Lisbon Agreement, a new type of treaty was developed. Lists of protected geographical names accompany the agreements, and the producers from each of these regions retain exclusive right to use the name. The scope of protection is then determined under the law of the country of origin. As a result, the country of origin controls the requirements for the legitimate use of certain geographical indications at home and abroad. No country has to alter its own laws in order to accomplish greater protection under the regime of a international treaty.[80] Rules of one country are "exported" together with its goods into another country. In this manner, a number of critical stumbling-blocks are avoided, but some problems have emerged as well. In each case of alleged violation, the court must apply the law of the country of origin instead of its own laws (which would be applicable under the Conflict of Laws rules of most countries).[81] Thus, the objection of the United States to the Lisbon Agreement, i.e., that American courts would be bound by the decisions of a foreign jurisdiction, would apply to these agreements as well. Finally, the countries which practice protection through the consumer-oriented approach of unfair competition are again at a disadvantage because it is very unlikely that a court in the forum state would conduct a survey of the perception of consumers in the country of origin of the product. Nevertheless, the model has spread rapidly in Europe. The main handicap to its adoption on a multilateral level is certainly its requirement that contracting states have a comparable standard of protection. The vast differences between the laws of the GATT/TRIPS members practically exclude such a possibility.

C. Conclusion: Problems of International Protection

A number of attempts to institute the international protection of geographical indications have been made, yet many interested producers and observers still

---

[80]Examples are the treaties between France and Germany (concluded August 3, 1960 . .), between France and Switzerland (concluded May 14, 1974 . . .) or between France and Italy (April 28, 1964, *reprinted in* 8 INDUSTRIAL PROPERTY 253 (1969)); recently the EC also has concluded a similar treaty with Australia, *see* 7 WIPR 87 (1993); Des Ryan, *The Protection of Geographical Indications in Australia under the EC/Australian Wine Agreement*, 12 EIPR 521 (1994).

[81] . . .For the United States, see EUGENE F. SCOLES & PETER HAY, CONFLICT OF LAWS, at 627, 630 (2d ed 1992). . . .

await a break-through. The Paris Convention has more than a hundred members, but does not contain substantial provisions for the protection of geographical indications. The Madrid Agreement offers only a little more than vague border measures to its thirty-one members. The Agreement of Lisbon, finally, embodies the choice for effective protection at the cost of having less than twenty members. The bilateral treaty models described above essentially incur the same difficulties: either the scope of protection remains undefined and effective protection depends upon the good will of each member country, or the agreement requires a standard of uniformity that is simply non-existent. . . .

PROTECTION UNDER TRIPS

A. Basic Concepts and Legislative History

. . . In the Spring of 1990, the EC presented a Draft Agreement which would serve as a model for the provisions on geographical indications. Subsequently, drafts were proffered by other countries, including the United States. Article 18 of the United States Draft reads in its pertinent part:

> Contracting Parties shall protect geographical indications that certify regional origin by providing for their registration as certification or collective marks.

The provision drew on the law of trademarks, a notion that in the United States had been the predominant approach towards protection of geographical indications. The proposal imposes a relatively narrow scope of possible implementations on the member countries. This seems rather unrealistic, especially in view of the fact that some of the countries which traditionally have protected geographical indications have long pursued other forms of protection. The failure of the Lisbon Agreement demonstrates the difficulties of an agreement that includes the obligation of the members to substantially alter their laws. The EC countries, some of them among the original proponents of international protection in the Lisbon Agreement, had learned their lesson; as long as effective protection was secured, they chose not to suggest a system of international registration (at least not for the moment). This approach gave the members an opportunity to keep their own laws. The proposal did not seek to introduce a distinction between special (statutory) protection for certain appellations of origin and a more general concept of indications of source. This has certainly made matters easier for the many nations whose legal tradition was not familiar with the protection of geographical indications.

The trouble spot, however, was the attempt to prevent geographical indications, particularly wines and spirits, from becoming generic terms. The protection of wines and spirits was probably the most important reason that the EC introduced the whole topic to the GATT and it proved to be a tough problem. In contrast to the other topics of the Intellectual Property package, this battle was not the typical line-up between the first and the third world, but between the United States and the EC. In essence, it was a fight over agricultural subsidies. The question of additional protection for wines and spirits, finally settled in Article 23, remained one of the principal obstacles to the conclusion of GATT/TRIPS.

. . . .

B. Substantive Standards: Articles 22-24 TRIPS

1. Definition of Geographical Indications: Article 22(1)

The TRIPS Agreement includes a definition of the term "geographical indications," [namely an indication that identifies goods that originate from a particular place in a Member State "where a given quality, reputation, or other characteristic of the good is essentially attributable to its geographical origin."]. Neither the Paris Convention nor the Madrid Agreement contains a similar provision and the failure of the Lisbon Agreement was to a large extent due to its restrictive definition. The United States proposal for TRIPS also lacked a description of what was to be protected.

Article 22(1) is derived from Article 2 of the Lisbon Agreement which reads:

> In this Agreement "appellation of origin" means the geographical name of a country, region or locality, which serves to designate a product originating therein, the quality and characteristics of which are due exclusively or essentially to the geographical environment, including natural and human factors.

The WIPO Model Law contains a definition of appellations of origin that is broader but essentially similar . . . .

Article 22 protects only products for which a relationship between their qualities or characteristics and their origin can be shown. However, as in the Lisbon Agreement, no test is offered to determine what is "essentially attributable." In the Lisbon Agreement, the lack of a standard is not as critical because protection is granted only to indications that are protected "as such" in their countries of origin and registered at the "International Bureau." . . .

The restrictive notion of the TRIPS Agreement, to require a link between the characteristics of the product and the place of origin, goes back to French law after the adoption of the law of 1919. This law did not contain a definition and thus required judges to develop a standard of their own.[93] The French courts have subsequently denied protection as appellations of origin to famous

---

[93] A definition was introduced in 1966 . . [and] followed the findings of the courts; it is now to be found in L. 115-1 and in the Code de la Propriété Intellectuelle, L.721-1 (*see* Law of July 26, 1993, Journal Officiel 37 (1993)).

products, such as Camembert or Moutarde de Dijon,[95] arguing that no characteristics or natural resources of the region accounted for their characteristics. Factors that have been considered in determining whether certain qualities are "attributable" to the geographical area include soil, climate, fauna, and flora.

When the definition was introduced through Article 19 of the EC Draft of 1990, it still contained an equivalent to the last part of the Lisbon definition: "including natural and human factors." In the Dunkel-Draft [prepared by GATT Director Arthur Dunkel in 1991] the definition was omitted and the point apparently was not discussed extensively. However, the omission may be significant. In view of the Lisbon and the WIPO Model Law, Article 22(1) could be construed to exclude human factors. For the protection of Sheffield Silver or Meissen Porcelain, for example, the origin of the raw materials in the area remains the only factor relevant to determine its protectability, not the tradition and craftsmanship that was handed down over generations. The scope of goods that can be protected by geographical indications is narrowed almost exclusively to agricultural products; manufacturers are not protected even if their product is "essentially" linked to the cultural heritage of the region.

Another restrictive and significant feature of the definition is that only "goods" are included. This appears to be contrary to the general concept of TRIPS. The US Draft, in accordance with the United States' law on certification marks, did not contain such a restriction. The Director General of WIPO had included "services" in his proposed amendment of Article 10*bis*(3) in 1977.[101]

2. Substantive Standard: Article 22(2)

Article 22(2) contains the basic concept for the substantive standards that the TRIPS Agreement was trying to accomplish throughout its member states. [It requires, in respect of geographical indications, the provision of legal means for "interested parties to prevent: (a) the use of any means in the designation or presentation of a good that indicates or suggests that the good in question originates in a geographical area other than the true place of origin in a manner which misleads the public as to the geographical origin of the good; and (b) any use which constitutes an act of unfair competition within the meaning of Article 10*bis* of the Paris Convention"]. . . .

a. Consumer Protection: Articles 22(2)(a) and (4)

The wording of Article 22(2)(a) is relatively broad and leaves ample space for different countries to apply their national concepts in order to comply with the provision. It is derived from Article 20(1) of the EC Draft, which was intended to protect geographical indications against any act that would mislead the

---

[95]Paris, March 19, 1929, Gazette du Palais 1929, 1, 831; the producers were, however, obliged to reveal the true place of origin–a parallel to the semi-generic geographical indications in the United States.

[101] . . . Geographic indications for services can be found in the field of tourism [cit].

public as to the product's true place of origin, prohibiting among other things "the use of any means in the designation or presentation of the product likely to suggest a link between the product and any other geographical area other than the true place of origin."

According to Article 22(2)(a), two requirements must be fulfilled in order to allege a violation. A representation on a certain good must suggest its origin (be geographically descriptive); and this suggestion must be false or misleading. Geographical descriptiveness seems easy to identify but two troubling cases should be noted. The first is the problem of generic terms; when a geographic designation is identified with a type of product rather than with a geographical area it no longer suggests that the product originated in the particular region. As this problem is treated as one of the exceptions in Article 24(6), it is addressed later. The other problem is the question of indirect indications of origin and the use of symbols instead of geographic names: the word "Bordeaux" on a bottle, for example, clearly indicates the origin of the wine. Other wineries, however, may have chosen a distinctive form of their bottle that suggests product origin to the consumer.[103] These forms of presentation can become as indicative for users as a name on the product. The wording of Article 22(2) is unclear as to whether or not it includes such indications. . . . [T]he wording "any means in the designation or presentation" suggests that any mark, sign, or design shall be included, as long as a goods-place-association can be shown. Hence, symbols representing a landmark or geographic location are prohibited, if they give rise to an erroneous association with a place.[106]

An additional safeguard has been included in Article 22(4) to prevent a true statement which is nevertheless misleading as to the origin of the goods from undermining the effectiveness of the provision. Accordingly, renaming the Napa Valley Champagne, Burgundy or Chablis would be of no avail to California wine-growers—a soothing prospect for the French producers.

b. The Incorporation of Article 10*bis* of the Paris Convention: Article 22(2)(b)

The provision was part of the Dunkel-Draft. The EC Draft was aimed at preventing any use which constitutes unfair competition, and thus the incorporation of Article 10*bis* seems a logical wording of the provision. However, in view of the legislative history of Article 10*bis*, i.e., the refusal of the Revision Conference of the Paris Convention in 1958 to include protection of

---

[103]One of the examples that was most fought-over in Europe is the German "Bocksbeutel," a wine that is sold only in a specific bottle. In Germany, that form of bottle is reserved for the region of Franconia and a few villages in Baden. When similar bottles were imported, the German courts granted an injunction because 47% of the consumers asked in a survey presumed that wine in such a bottle could only be of German origin (see Bundesgerichtshof, GRUR 1971, 313 "Bocksbeutel"). The European Court of Justice (ECJ) reversed on the grounds that the injunction was contrary to Articles 30, 36 of the EEC Treaty, as long as the Italian producers had used the bottle in good faith for a considerable amount of time, *see* ECJ 16/83, 1984 E.C.R. 1299.

[106]As long as the perception of the public in the country of use is the determinative criterion for an alleged violation, not all fantasy names or arbitrary uses of geographical names (such as "Atlantic" for magazines or "North Pole" for cigarettes) are prohibited. For a different opinion on that point with respect to the EC Draft, see Bendekgey and Mead, *supra* note 77 at 786.

geographic origin in Article 10*bis*, its application "with respect to geographical indications" within TRIPS is surprising and rather odd. It extends the purview of Article 10*bis* for the members of GATT/TRIPS without revealing that it is not simply the incorporation of a parallel treaty but an extension of its scope.

. . . Although most cases that constitute a violation of Article 10*bis* of the Paris Convention are covered also by Article 22(2)(a), the inclusion of the two sections is based upon the various interests protected by unfair competition law: Article 22(2)(b) protects the interests of producers and merchants, whereas Article 22(2)(a) is aimed at representations misleading the public, *i.e.*, consumers, Article 22(2)(b).

. . . .

3. Wines and Spirits: Articles 23 and 24(6)

The provision on wines and spirits is one of the most closely fought-over provisions in the whole GATT. The legal issue is the degeneration of geographical indications into generic terms and must be read together with the exception in Article 24(6) which, although applicable to the whole section, especially pertains to the problems of wines and spirits.

In the United States, under the regulations of BATF, the general rule is that a name of geographic significance may be used only to designate wines of the origin indicated by such name, unless the names have been found to be generic or semi-generic. [*See* 27 C.F.R § 4.24(c)(1) (1993)]. Only two names have been found to be generic, Vermouth and Sake. [*Id.* § 4.24(b)(2)]. Sixteen names, however, are deemed to be semi-generic, including Chianti, Burgundy, Champagne and Chablis. According to the regulations, they can be used as long as the real origin is used in direct conjunction with the name. Therefore "California Chablis" and "American Champagne" could become a problem in international trade.

Several techniques can be used to prevent geographical indications from becoming generic terms, and the EC has attempted to consider three. First, the conversion of geographical names into generic terms can be prohibited by law; such a provision is contained in the Madrid Agreement (Article 4) and was proposed by the EC Draft. It was not adopted by the Dunkel-Draft, however, and it is not part of the TRIPS now. The second technique is to prohibit strategies which on their face prevent deception of the public by adding "style" or "type" to the geographical name or indicating the true place of origin, but which nevertheless dilute the perception of the name. This approach has been accepted under Article 23(1), [which requires member states to provide means for interested parties to prevent use of a geographical indication identifying wines or spirits for those products not originating in the place identified, even when the true origin is indicated or the geographical indication is used in translation or accompanied by expressions such as "style" etc.] A sparkling wine "type Champagne" could have been dealt with under Article 22(2)(a) as long as the statement as a whole is still likely to mislead the public. For wines, Article 23(1) precludes the defense that the presentation of the goods is not deceptive or misleading. The third possible technique which has also been incorporated into the Agreement (Article 23(2)) relates to the law of trademarks: it prohibits registration when a trademark is primarily geographically descriptive. This technique is treated . . . below.

Articles 23(1) and (2) seem to implement a fairly effective standard of protection to prevent names from becoming "generic terms." However, important exceptions can be found in Article 24(6). The first part of (6) suspends the application of Articles 22-24 in a member state (Forum 2), if a geographical name of Forum 1 is a generic term in Forum 2. The second part specifically addresses the problem that wines are often named after the grapes used in them and that these names are often indirect indications of origin (e.g., "Riesling" for German or Alsatian wine). In that case, as long as the grape "existed" at the date of entry into force of the World Trade Organization (WTO), the use of its name is allowed.

In view of the intense discussion that took place before the provisions on wines and spirits were adopted, one may question whether they will effectively restrict the use of "Champagne," "Bordeaux," "Chablis" or the like for products originating outside of France. The United States delegation charged that the EC was trying to re-institute names as protected geographical indications which had lost their geographical descriptiveness in the United States and had become generic or semi-generic terms. If there was such an attempt to roll back years of common usage, the United States delegation prevented it from succeeding. . . . On the other hand, Articles 23(1) and (2) will not permit more geographical names to lose their geographical connotation and will therefore provide an effective standard for the future.

4. Relation to Trademarks

Since geographical names have much in common with trade names or marks, the determination of the relationship between trademarks and geographical names seems very important for any national or international regulatory concept. In fact, most countries have implemented provisions at the national level to the effect that it is generally not possible to register as a trademark a term which merely consists of a geographical name.[127] Therefore it is surprising that none of the international agreements have so far attempted to resolve the problem. TRIPS, for the first time implementing substantive standards of protection, now includes a resolution of the issue: the registrability of geographical names as trademarks in general (Article 22(3)), and of wines in particular (Article 23(2)). A grandfather clause is added in Article 24(5).

Article 21(2) of the EC Draft plainly barred the registration of a trademark which contained or consisted of a geographical indication. This would have included prohibiting a name regardless of its deceptiveness to the public, whether the name actually identified a single business source or merely consisted of a fantasy name. The EC Draft was not acceptable to the United

---

[127] See, e.g., France (Article L. 711-4 du Code de la Propriété Intellectuelle), United States (Lanham Act § 2(e)), Germany (Article 8(2) MarkenG), Italy (Article 18, 1(e) of the Trademark Law of June 6, 1942, last amended by decree of December 12, 1992). Exceptions in cases in which the name has acquired "secondary meaning" or is used merely as a fantasy name confirm this rule.

States where registration as a trademark is possible if the geographical name has acquired "secondary meaning," i.e., does not denote merely the origin of the product but also identifies a single business source. The TRIPS Agreement is a compromise between the two concepts: it generally adopts a view similar to the United States concept by making eligibility for registration as a trademark subject to the perception of the public (Article 22(3)). Thereby it systematically follows the approach that is taken by Article 22. However, for wines and spirits, economically the most important businesses, no trademark can be registered if it contains or consists of a geographical indication identifying wines or spirits [and the wines or spirits do not have that geographic origin], regardless of its level of perceived deceptiveness to the public. [Art. 23(2)].

Article 24(5) adds two exceptions to the [provisions on the] registrability of trademarks. Section (a) states that a mark that was registered in good faith before the TRIPS Agreement will continue to be a valid trademark. It remains to be decided what "in good faith" means here. Commonly, the term "in good faith" is construed to mean that the party did not (and was not required to) know of the rights of other parties. If "good faith" is construed to mean "not knowing of the existence of the other party," the scope of the exception is considerably smaller, because a geographical name is rarely used without knowledge of its origin. Another interpretation could stress the point that the owner of the trademark did not know about the "right" of the other party (under Articles 22 and 23 TRIPS), in which case the term "in good faith" adds nothing to the [other] requirements [of Article 24(5)]. The case of "Chablis With a Twist" may illustrate the problem, even though the United States law has changed since the decision. The case involved the attempt to register a trademark for "Chablis With a Twist" in the United States; the French [administrative agency responsible for use of the name] INAO took exception with the registration but its opposition was dismissed on the grounds that "Chablis" was a generic name for a certain wine and thus not "primarily geographically deceptively misdescriptive." Can the use of the trademark "Chablis With a Twist" be deemed to be "in good faith," although the owner certainly knew of the claims of the INAO? The question has to be answered in the affirmative for two reasons. The first is a consequence of Article 24(6) which allows the use of geographical indications if they have become generic terms. Accordingly, the members of TRIPS must be able to make regulations concerning the use of such generic terms which can include their eligibility for registration as a trademark. The second is that Article 24(5) is aimed at preserving the status quo where trademark owners have used the mark in accordance with their own laws and have acquired a reputation for their product that warrants protection just as much as the protection of a geographical name. As its main object is not to reverse past developments, more than the mere knowledge of another party's potential claim must be shown in order to allege that the trademark owner did not act "in good faith." The most adequate solution would be to interpret "in good faith" as meaning "without deceptive or misleading intent," thus excluding the protection of past deceptions while acknowledging legitimate uses of a name over considerable time.

The second exception, section (b), seems slightly more problematic under policy considerations: a trademark consisting of a geographical indication is valid as long as it was registered before the geographical name was protected in its country of origin. Accordingly, a country that does not yet have a system of protection for geographical indications, but decides to adopt one now, may find that its names have already been registered as trademarks in foreign countries. In such a case, the reciprocity TRIPS appears to offer exists only on paper. In 1977, a number of developing countries expressed fear that their geographical names may be registered in the developed nations before they become known in the world market. Although Article 24(5)(b) may serve to expedite the process of implementing these provisions in developing countries, it still gives an unwarranted advantage to the countries which have long recognized geographical indications.

On the whole, the provisions on trademarks show an important feature of the section: TRIPS protects future misappropriation and moderately restricts its scope of application where past developments cannot be reversed.

5. Exceptions: Articles 24(4)-(9)

Two of the most important exceptions, Articles 24(5) and (6), have been treated above. Two more are mentioned here. Article 24(4) addresses the question of parallel use of geographical names for wines and spirits; it is tantamount to an acknowledgment that TRIPS does not and cannot reverse past developments in the field. Thus, if a name has been used for at least ten years preceding the Ministerial Meeting concluding the Uruguay Round or "in good faith" for a shorter period of time preceding that date, the user can continue to do so. . . . The most famous example of continuous use is the case of Budweiser beer. Since the thirteenth century beer has been brewed in Budweis, Bohemia and named accordingly. Since the nineteenth century, "Budweiser" has, however, also been the name of an American beer, which, after much litigation in the United States, was deemed to have acquired "secondary meaning," so that it could be registered as a trademark. Although the name is still fought over, TRIPS does not attempt to settle the matter and allows use in each of its member countries.

An example of use "in good faith" is the case of "Bocksbeutel" that has been mentioned above. In that case the European Court of Justice (ECJ) decided that Germany could not limit the importation of Italian wine on the grounds that the wine was presented in distinctive "Bocksbeutel" bottles, even if the bottle was protected as an indirect indication of origin in Germany, as long as the Italian wine producers had used the bottles for a long time "in good faith." The court regarded as plain that the Italian producers had not chosen this distinctive bottle shape to make the wine look like "Bocksbeutel" but because it had been their way of presenting the product for more than a hundred years.

Article 24(9) is also noteworthy because it contains an exception from the National Treatment concept and a restriction of the protectible indications which is not part of the trademark section. Even if the public in one country (Forum 1) identifies a geographical name with its region of origin in another country (Forum 2) so that use of a false indication would mislead the public, TRIPS does not require Forum 1 to protect the indication as long as it is not protected in Forum 2. The notion here is that it would be unreasonable to restrict the use of "Moutarde de Dijon" in the whole world to products of Dijon while Moutarde de Dijon has become a generic term in France and can therefore be used for any French mustard.

6. Problems of National Treatment

The problems that will be incurred by the application of Articles 3 and 4 to geographical indications are the same problems that have caused existing international agreements to fail. One is the question of registration of geographical names. Under the Romanistic approach, the protectible names must be defined by a legislative, administrative, or judicial act. Names which are not addressed by special regulations are protected against unfair competition, but that protection may not be applied as strictly because all the national products are covered by another strict regime. TRIPS has, however, recognized this problem "officially" in Article 23, where the intent to undertake negotiations is made part of the provision on "Wines and Spirits." Another problem concerns the fact that knowledge of geography becomes important if public opinion is to determine whether or not a name is eligible for protection as a geographical indication. The public will presumably be more familiar with domestic geography than with foreign, and is thus much more likely to find domestic names geographically descriptive or misdescriptive than foreign names.

These are only two cases in which the application of the laws of the members could lead to discriminatory practices which could only be avoided by harmonizing the laws of the members–a task that would by far exceed the mandate of the Uruguay Round.

CONCLUSION

The TRIPS provisions are designed to protect geographical indications from three abuses: first, the use of false or misleading geographical indications; second, the registration of geographical indications as trademarks; and third, the dilution of geographical indications into generic terms. The first goal, to prevent false or misleading abuses, is resolved in a general fashion in Article 22, with stricter rules for wines and spirits in Article 23(1). The provision can be implemented in various ways, including the law of unfair competition, advertising, certification marks, or special provisions that enjoin others from using the name. It is easy to predict that it will not be the implementation of the general principle that will cause trouble, but its application. Every country will have different standards, as they had before, and in this area, dispute settlement and other enforcement measures will have little effect. The second goal, to prevent the registrability of geographical indications as trademarks, seems fairly easy to implement and control; accordingly, the United States included a provision in the Lanham Act that is based on the TRIPS provision. However, the grandfather clause will ensure that past registrations remain valid. Finally, as for the degeneration of geographical indications into generic terms, a fairly moderate approach has been taken, again with the exception of wines and spirits. For other products, protection is granted through Article 22 and, as noted above, different views and customs will prevail regarding the generic significance of certain terms.

In conclusion, it should be stressed that in TRIPS, more countries have agreed on substantive standards for the protection of geographical indications than ever before in an international agreement. The protection of geographical indications will undoubtedly grow—for better or for worse. The battle between the EC and the United States has led to a compromise that will prevent future abuses and the degeneration of geographical names into generic terms, but will preserve the status quo of today.

NOTE: THE LISBON ARRANGEMENT

The Lisbon Arrangement establishes a system for international registration of appellations of origin. After filing and obtaining protection of an appellation of origin in their home country, producers may deposit the application with WIPO and seek extension of that protection in all countries that are members of the Lisbon Arrangement. Countries in which extended protection is sought have one year in which to raise objections under Article 5(4), and are given some latitude to determine whether, under their own laws, protection should be granted. But once the one-year period has expired without objection, the appellation of origin will be protected in the additional countries. Article 6 requires that, once registered, members are prohibited from deeming the term generic provided that it remains protected in its country of origin. Any conflicting trademark usages of the protected geographical indication (even prior usages) must cease within two years. *See* art. 5(6). Is the Lisbon Arrangement over-ridden by TRIPS? *See* Lisbon Arrangement art. 5(6); TRIPS art. 24(5).

The dispute over the BUDWEISER mark for beer in Israel illustrates the operation of the Lisbon Arrangement. Budejovicky Budvar is a brewery based in the town of Budweis, Czech Republic (or, *Budejovice*, in Czech). In the late nineteenth century, the town had a substantial reputation for brewing beer, and the beer sold by Budejovicky Budvar came to be known as BUDWEISER, a term which the company has used on its beer since then. Anheuser-Busch is a U.S. producer of beer which it markets under the trademark BUDWEISER; American BUDWEISER beer does not come from the Czech town, although the inspiration for the name came from there. BUDWEISER is a Czech-originated appellation of origin registered in Israel under the Lisbon Arrangement, in the name of Budejovicky Budvar. In 1984, Anheuser-Busch brought an action in Israel against Budejovicky Budvar in which they contended that the Czech company had no rights to BUDWEISER. The Israeli Supreme Court held that, under the Israeli statute implementing the Lisbon Arrangement, as long as the appellation is protected in the country of origin, Anheuser-Busch cannot contest the validity of the appellation of origin. (In this regard, the Israeli law provides more protection against challenge than the Lisbon Agreement requires; the

Lisbon Agreement prohibits challenge on genericism grounds, whereas the Israeli statute forecloses any challenge to Lisbon-initiated registrations. *See* Howard Poliner, *Appellations of Origin in Israel Pursuant to the Lisbon Agreement*, 21 EUR. INTELL. PROP. REV. 149, 152 (1999).) The rights granted are absolute; the only question is whether the person that used the appellation was authorized to do so.

The Israeli Budweiser litigation is part of an ongoing worldwide dispute between the two companies. *See generally* Robert M. Kunstadt & Gregor Buhler, *Bud Battle Illustrates Perils of Geographic Marks*, NAT. L.J., May 18, 1998. Neither company has fully prevailed, and in many countries concurrent use has been permitted by the courts. *See, e.g., In re Budweiser Trade Mark Application*, 1998 R.P.C. 669 (Ch. D. 1998) (Eng.) (permitting concurrent trademark registrations); *see also* Andrew Inglis & Joel Barry, *"Budweiser": The Decision of Solomon*, 20 EUR. INTELL. PROP. REV. 320 (1998). In considering–as we will later–whether and how the United States might incorporate protection for geographical indications into its law, bear in mind that the term BUDWEISER is a registered appellation of origin and that Anheuser-Busch owns trademark rights in that term for beer in the United States.

NOTE: NAFTA AND TRIPS IMPLEMENTATION

Article 1712 of the NAFTA imposes obligations with respect to geographical indications not unlike those contained in the TRIPS Agreement. Thus, for example, Article 1712(2) of the NAFTA mirrors the prohibition (found in Article 22(3) of TRIPS) against the registration of trademarks consisting of geographical indications that mislead the public as to the origin of the product. TRIPS went beyond NAFTA, however, in making specific provisions for geographical indications used on wine, reflecting the relative economic importance of wine producers in Europe and North America. *See generally* Daniel R. Bereskin, *A Comparison of the Trademark Provisions of NAFTA and TRIPS*, 83 TRADEMARK REP. 1 (1993). The United States implemented its NAFTA obligations with respect to geographical indications primarily by amending the Lanham Act to make the bar on primarily geographically deceptively misdescriptive marks absolute (section 2(e)(3)), rather than conditional upon secondary meaning. As with TRIPS, the NAFTA sought to protect acquired rights, and thus section 2(e)(3) grandfathers trademark rights in such marks that have acquired distinctiveness before December 8, 1993 (the effective date of the NAFTA Implementation Act). Because of the NAFTA-necessitated amendments to the Lanham Act in 1993, the TRIPS Agreement (concluded the following year) required very little action on the part of the U.S. legislature. The sole additional change made to the Lanham Act was the addition of a wine and spirits-specific bar to registration in section 2(a). *See infra* Notes and Questions, note 13. Otherwise, the United States adopted the position that the protection afforded by the Lanham Act and the regulation of the sale of alcoholic beverages by the Bureau of Alcohol, Tobacco and Firearms

(BATF) satisfied its obligations with respect to geographical indications under TRIPS and the NAFTA.

NOTES AND QUESTIONS

(1) **Political Alliances.** The pressure to adopt provisions on geographical indications was seen by some countries as an attempt by the European countries to buttress sectors that are significant in the European economy by excluding upstart competitors. Is there anything in the nature and history of protection for geographic indications that suggests an inherent (and perhaps unchangeable) bias toward the European countries? What explains the diametrically opposed views of the EU and the United States–who were allied for most of the TRIPS negotiation–on the issue of geographical indications? The leading supporter of the EU efforts to include protection for geographical indications was Switzerland. Why was Switzerland interested in protecting geographical indications? *See* Thomas Helbling, *The Term 'Swiss' on Trade Goods: A Denomination of Origin and its Legal Protection in the United Kingdom*, 19 EUR. INTELL. PROP. REV. 51, 53 (1997).

(2) **Developing Countries.** In 1977, developing countries proposed a revision of the Paris Convention to prohibit registration and use of geographic terms by firms not located in the region in question out of a fear that "before their appellations of origin became known in the world market, the terms may be adopted as trademarks by producers in the developed world." J. Thomas McCarthy & Veronica Colby Devitt, *Protection of Geographic Denominations: Domestic and International*, 69 TRADEMARK REP. 199, 203-04 (1979). Professor Heald suggests that "the increased protection of geographic indications [in TRIPS] should provide incentives for underdeveloped member states to develop local industries and market agricultural products worldwide under an exclusive indication of source." Paul J. Heald, *Trademark and Geographical Indications: Exploring the Contours of the TRIPS Agreement*, 29 VAND. J. TRANS. L. 635, 656 (1996). Do the TRIPS provisions on geographical indications represent a victory for developing countries? Do any of the provisions of TRIPS present problems for developing countries? Would the 1977 proposal have been a more favorable approach for developing countries?

(3) **Different Conceptual Approaches**. The final text of Articles 22-24 of TRIPS is a heavily-worked compromise. What were the problems of adopting either an approach based wholly on unfair competition principles or an approach based wholly on registration? If an international system were constructed upon principles of unfair competition (public perception and public deception), what difficulties would that present? *Cf. In re* Société Générale Des Eaux Minérales De Vittel, 824 F.2d 957, 959 (Fed. Cir. 1987) (noting difficulties that arise where issue turns on the public's response to symbols more common in other countries). Alternatively, what problems would there be with an international system where lists of protected terms were drawn up and exchanged, and the terms on those lists provided with absolute protection? How

radical a shift would such an approach be for the United States? *Cf.* Paris Convention art. 6*ter* (requiring an absolute prohibition against the use or registration of certain national symbols such as the flag, coat of arms or other national insignia); Lanham Act § 2(b).

(4) **The Use of "Type" or "Style."** One of the important provisions of the Lisbon Arrangement is that under Article 3, signatory states must prevent unauthorized use of the appellation of origin even if it is accompanied by terms like "type" or "style." Why is that type of provision–seen also in Article 23(1) of TRIPS–important? Does this form of protection have analogies in modern mainstream trademark protection? Given the nature of appellations of origin, why might you expect analogies to modern notions of trademark protection?

(5) **Standing**. The issue of who is an "interested party" under Articles 22-24 of TRIPS is crucial because Articles 22(2) and 23(1) require that such persons be afforded the legal means to prevent uses that violate the applicable standards. Article 10 of the Paris Convention–the earliest provision addressing geographical indications, and applied to TRIPS by Article 2–defines "interested party" to include producers and merchants of the goods in question who are situated either in the place falsely indicated as the origin of the goods or in the country where such false indication is used. Under the philosophy of Article 10, competitors would thus clearly appear to be interested parties. Are governmental organizations such as the Institut National Des Appellations d'Origine (INAO), the French government agency that supervises French geographical indications, "interested parties"? What are the "interests" that INAO has in the private enforcement of these provisions? Should one government be compelled to permit the agency of another government to sue in their national courts for enforcement of TRIPS obligations? The U.S. courts have granted INAO representational standing, *see* Institut Nat. Des Appellations d'Origine v. Vintners Int'l Co., Inc., 958 F.2d 1574 (Fed. Cir. 1992), but is that mandated by TRIPS? Are consumers interested parties such that they must be accorded standing to protect geographical indications? In several countries–such as Germany, for example–consumers (or consumer protection agencies) have standing to bring actions grounded in unfair competition.

(6) **Definitional Questions**. Review the definition of "geographical indication" in Article 22(1) of TRIPS. Is the "California" look, used in the marketing of California wines, a geographical indication within the meaning of Article 22(1)? *See* Kendall-Jackson Winery Inc. v. Gallo Winery, 150 F.3d 1042 (9th Cir. 1998) (noting that the combination of an exposed cork, a rounded flange, and a neck label on a wine bottle creates the "California look," which consumers might have come to expect on a bottle of Californian wine). Does the use of that "look" by other than California wine producers fall within the scope of Article 22(2)(a)'s prohibition, assuming that its use will mislead consumers? If consumers would not be misled, is such a use covered by the stricter wine-specific provision in Article 23(1)? If so, how would that use be enjoined under U.S. law? (Answering these questions may require you to consider whether you are persuaded by Conrad's explanation of why indirect geographical indications are covered by Article 22(2).)

(7) **False or Misleading**. According to Conrad, "two requirements must be fulfilled in order to allege a violation [under Article 22(2)(a)]. A representation

on a certain good must suggest its origin (be geographically descriptive); and this suggestion must be false or misleading." Do you agree with this interpretation of Article 22(2)(a)? Article 22(4) extends the provisions of Article 22 to circumstances where the geographical indication used is literally true as to the product's origin but still falsely represents to the public that the goods originate in another territory. Thus, a couturier from Paris, Texas, may not use the mark PARIS on his clothes—notwithstanding geographical truth—if consumers would believe that those clothes came from Paris, France. Does this provision contain any inherent bias?

(8) **Protection of Existing Trademarks**. Geographical terms are currently used by producers, often as trademarks, on products throughout the world. Thus, the NAFTA Agreement recognized that in heightening protection for geographical indications of origin, there was a need to protect rights that had been acquired prior to the conclusion of the agreement. TRIPS is similarly premised. In the TRIPS Agreement, this recognition takes the form of the various exceptions found in Article 24(4)-(6), which prevent the new obligations to protect geographical indications from interfering with existing trademark rights in geographic terms or with existing uses of geographical designations. Article 24(5) is arguably different in kind from the other two provisions: in what way?

(9) **Grandfathering of Generic Terms**. Article 24(6) excepts members from complying with the new provisions with respect to geographic terms that have become generic in that country. Different countries have quite different tests, however, for when a term becomes generic. *See* Heald, *supra* at 648-49 (noting, for example, that in Switzerland, "a geographic name must have been used for decades to describe a material quality, and must still be understood as such by all interested persons in order to be deemed generic"). How should a WTO panel interpret the scope of the "generic" exception in Article 24(6)? *Cf.* Madrid Arrangement art. 4 (expressly reserving questions of which geographic terms were generic, and thus not covered by the agreement, to national tribunals, except for products of the vine).

(10) **Homonymous Indications**. Article 23(3) provides that in the case of homonymous geographical indications for wines protection shall be accorded to each indication. This provision—which leaves the conditions of concurrent use to national laws—is subject to Article 22(4), which would trump Article 23(3) if one literally true use would in fact falsely represent that the goods originated in the other territory. Thus, as Conrad explains, strategic renaming of Californian valleys after those of France would not be a means of circumventing the protection of the TRIPS Agreement.

(11) **Means of Enforcement**. Article 22(2)(a) of TRIPS and Article 1712(1)(a) of the NAFTA require signatory states to provide an interested party with the means of prohibiting the use of a geographical indication of origin that misleads the public as to the geographical origin of the goods upon which it is used. Does the availability of an action under section 43(a) of the Lanham Act ensure U.S. compliance? In what respects might the section 43(a) action be deficient? Compare section 43(a)(1)(A) of the Lanham Act and Article 22(2)(a) of TRIPS. Could any deficiency in implementing Article 22(2) be repaired by the

introduction of stricter administrative regulations by the FTC or the BATF? *Cf.* TRIPS art. 42(1).

(12) **U.S. Compliance**. Does the absolute bar on registration of primarily geographically deceptively misdescriptive marks under section 2(e)(3) fully implement the United States' obligations under Article 22(3) of TRIPS to deny registration to any mark consisting of a geographical indication that misleads the public as to the true origin of the product? *See* Peter M. Brody, *Protection of Geographical Indications in the Wake of TRIPS: Existing United States Laws and the Administration's Proposed Legislation*, 84 TRADEMARK REP. 520, 524-26 (1994).

(13) **Wines and Spirits**. Notwithstanding the inclusion of a separate (and more protective) set of provisions regarding wines and spirits, the United States adopted a minimalist approach to implementation of these obligations. Thus, section 2(a) of the Lanham Act now bars from registration a

> geographical indication which, when used on or in connection with wines or spirits, identifies a place other than the origin of the goods and is first used on or in connection with wines and spirits by the applicant on or after one year after the date [*i.e.*, January 1, 1996] upon which the WTO Agreement enters into force with respect to the United States.

Does the grandfather provision in section 2(a) comply with the scope of the exceptions in Articles 24(4)-(5)? *Cf.* Heald, *supra* at 651-52 (discussing Article 24(4) exception).

Although section 2(a) creates a non-confusion based basis for challenging an offending trademark registration and thus implements Article 23(2), Article 23(1) requires that means be available to stop nonconfusing uses of designations on wines and spirits. At the time that the TRIPS Agreement was concluded, section 43(a) provided an action to enjoin a confusing use of such an indication but it was doubtful whether U.S. law offered relief where the use was non-confusing and thus U.S. law appeared noncompliant. Has the enactment of section 43(c) of the Lanham Act, which provides dilution protection to famous marks, corrected the omission? Can the BATF regulations be relied upon to remedy any failings with respect to Article 23(1)? *See* TRIPS art. 23(1) n. 4. If the BATF regulations can be relied upon to justify compliance, do the current regulations meet the TRIPS standard? *See* 27 C.F.R. § 4.24 (wines); § 5.22(k) (spirits).

(14) **Treatment of Wines Under General Provisions**. Under what circumstances, if any, do the general provisions of Article 22 mandate broader protection for wine-related geographical indications than the wine-specific provisions in Article 23?

(15) **Using Definitions to Grandfather Generics**. One of the most important objectives for U.S. negotiators was to retain free use of terms–such as CHAMPAGNE or CHABLIS–previously held to be generic by the U.S. courts. This was achieved primarily by Article 24(6). Professor Heald has suggested

another means by which, without reliance upon the exceptions, the continued general use of such terms could be justified under TRIPS. Heald focuses on the definition of "geographical indications" in Article 22(1) as words that

> identify a good as originating in the territory of a Member . . . where a given quality, reputation or other characteristic of the good is essentially attributable to its geographic origin, and argues that because generic geographic wine marks (such as CHABLIS) no longer describe a product that originates there but rather a variety of wine, they do not come within the definition of geographical indication.

Heald, *supra*, at 646-47. Professor Heald notes also, however, that the amendment to section 2(a) of the Lanham Act did not define "geographical indications." Do any consequences attach to this?

(16) **Geographical Indications and Property Rights.** Professor Marshall Leaffer has commented that the changes to the Lanham Act implementing TRIPS and NAFTA "explicitly recognize for the first time the protection of appellations of origin." Marshall Leaffer, *Appellations of Origin and Geographic Indications in U.S. Law after NAFTA and GATT*, 2 INT'L INTELL. PROP. L. & POL. 45-1 (Hugh Hansen ed. 1998). Do you agree? If so, which amendments effected this result? Professor Leaffer also argues that these changes "reflect an ongoing drift away from the original basis of U.S. trademark law, consumer confusion, to a recognition of trademarks as an absolute property rights." *Id.* In what way, and to what extent, do these changes create absolute property rights?

[B]   European Union Regulations

The EU has enacted several separate and detailed regulations governing the use, among other things, of geographical designations for wines, sparkling wines, spirits, and agricultural products and foodstuffs.[*] Under the principal Wine Regulation, for example, the description and presentation of wines and grape musts should not be "incorrect or likely to cause confusion" regarding, among other things, their origin. *See* Council Regulation No. 2392/89 Laying Down General Rules for the Description and Presentation of Wines and Grape Musts art. 40(1). That regulation also provides that such confusion is not obviated by use of terms such as "type" or "method," etc. *See id.* In effect, geographical indications for wines are protected against misleading uses by unauthorized persons, and any conflicting registered trademark may be used

---

[*] *See* Council Regulation No. 823/87 (wine); Council Regulation No. 2392/89 Laying Down General Rules for the Description and Presentation of Wines and Grape Musts, 1989 O.J. (L 232) 13, as *amended by* Council Regulations No. 1601/91 & 3897/91; Council Regulation No. 2333/92 of 13 July 1992 Laying Down General Rules for the Description and Presentation of Sparkling Wines and Aerated Sparkling Wines, 1992 O.J. (L 213) 9; Council Regulation No. 1576/89 (spirits); Council Regulation No. 2081/92 on the Protection of Geographical Indications and Designations of Origin for Agricultural Products and Foodstuffs, 1992 O.J. (L 208) 1 (July 24, 1992).

at the latest until December 31, 2002. *See* art. 40(3) (listing conditions necessary to take advantage of this derogation). This prioritization of geographical indications over registered trademarks–one of the perennial issues in this area–was limited by a 1991 amendment that permits continued trademark use after 2002 if the mark was registered twenty-five years before recognition of the geographical indication. (This was prompted by concern that, under the initial legislation, the Spanish wine producer Miguel Torres would, in 2002, lose his long-standing registered trademark in the term TORRES for wine because the Portugese legislation recognized a new wine producing region called TORRES VEDRAS.)

The Foodstuffs Regulation, which establishes a community-wide registration system for designations of origin applied to agricultural products intended for human consumption (excluding wines and spirits, but including beers and spring waters), has proven more controversial both within the EU and internationally. In a recent decision, Denmark, Germany and France successfully brought an action against the Commission under ex-Article 173 of the EC Treaty (now Article 230) seeking annulment of the Foodstuffs Regulation in so far as it registers the designation FETA for cheese as a protected designation of origin. *See* Denmark, Germany and France v. The Commission, 1999 E.T.M.R. 478 (E.C.J. 1999). Article 17 of the initial 1992 regulation established a transitional procedure (the so-called "simplified procedure") by which member states could, within six months of the date of the 1992 regulation, submit names to be registered on the Community Register as protected geographical indications of origin or designations of origin. This procedure was intended to cover, and register expeditiously on the Community Register, those terms protected (by registration or usage) in member states prior to the regulation's enactment. Greece's application to register the name FETA was accepted by the Commission, and thus included in the list of protected designations of origin found in the annex to a 1996 regulation. *See* Council Regulation (EC) No. 1107/96 of 12 June 1996, O.J. 1996 (L 148) 1. (The Council of Ministers had potential input under Article 15, but was unable to reach agreement within the stated time, and thus the 1996 regulation was in effect a Commission product.) The effect of this determination was that FETA could only be used on salted white cheese made in accordance with the specification accompanying the application to register FETA (which required, most importantly, that FETA cheese be made with the milk of goats and sheep coming exclusively from certain regions of Greece).[*]

But FETA cheese had been produced outside Greece for some time (*e.g.*, in Denmark since 1963) with cow's milk from other than Greece. Although the simplified procedure did not allow formal opposition proceedings, *see* art. 17(2), various member states made clear their objection to the registration of FETA before the 1996 regulation was finalized on the ground that the term FETA was generic. *See* 1992 Regulation arts. 3(1) (excluding protection for generic terms), 17(2) (same). Indeed, a majority of member states asked the Commission to include FETA on an alternative list that the Commission was required to

---

[*]The symbol chosen for use with protected designations is a blue and yellow logo showing furrows in a ploughed field.

complete recording those foodstuff terms that were generic and thus unregisterable under the 1992 regulation. When the Commission, after having taken advice from its advisory Scientific Committee for Designations of Origin, rejected these arguments, the member states involved filed their annulment action under ex-Article 173 and renewed their argument that FETA is a generic mark that is unprotectable under the regulation.

The 1992 regulation provided an express standard for determining whether a term is generic. (Indeed, the Commission found that several terms–such as BRIE, CAMEMBERT, or CHEDDAR–were generic.) Under Article 3(1),

> to establish whether or not a name has become generic, account shall be taken of all factors, in particular: the existing situation in the Member State in which the name originates and in areas of consumption, the existing situation in other Member States, and the relevant national or Community laws.

Although FETA was protected in Greece and (by virtue of a bilateral Greece-Austria agreement) Austria, the term was used generically in several other EU countries. Consumer surveys conducted by the Commission were inconclusive, with reaction varying among different countries.

The Court of Justice annulled the registration of FETA because the Commission had failed to give proper weight to all the factors in Article 3(1)–in particular the widespread generic use of FETA throughout member states other than the country of origin (Greece)–and had failed to take into account the effect that registration would have on the continued marketing of products legally sold within the Community prior to the regulation. This latter consideration is an express ground for opposition proceedings, *see* art. 7(4), which are not available under the simplified procedure, but the Court held that the Commission should have, in any event, taken it into account in determining whether FETA satisfied the substantive requirements of the regulation.

The Commission may still, on the development of new evidence or further analysis of the question, register FETA as a protected designation of origin, but in the interim it has been removed from the list of protected terms. What values or objectives has the Court furthered or elevated in its conclusion? Has one of the objectives of the regulation–to offer consistent protection of geographical indications throughout Europe–been harmed or helped? May Danish FETA cheese now be distributed in Greece? *See* art. 17(3); *see also* Consorzio per La Tutela Del Formaggio Gorgonzola v. Kaserei Champignon Hofmeister Gmbh & Co. [1999] 1 C.M.L.R. 1203, 1223 (E.C.J. 1999) (rejecting argument that plaintiff can rely on national law that is broader than Community level law after a decision has been taken on the registration of the name at the Community level). With hindsight, would it have been better for Greece not to seek registration for FETA? What are Austria's obligations now under the bilateral agreement with Greece? In light of this decision, and in particular the positions taken by the dueling member states, is international harmonization of protection for geographical indications possible?

FETA was registered after application by Greece under the transitional simplified procedure, but under the "normal" registration procedure (arts. 5-7), applications for registration are to be sent by "groups" of producers working with the agricultural product in question to the member state in which the geographical area is located. (For example, if application for FETA had been made under this procedure, cheese producers in certain regions of Greece would have forwarded an application to the government of Greece.) Article 12 of the regulation makes the registration system available to groups from non-EU countries provided both (1) that the group can provide guarantees of product and indication control that mirror those required of EU groups, and (2) that the non-EU country provides equivalent protection to the name as that available in the EU. This latter reciprocity provision does, of course, present problems for U.S. groups seeking to participate in the EU system.

The application must include a product "specification." The specification includes such matters as: the name of the product; a description of the product including the raw materials, if appropriate, and the principal physical, chemical, microbiological and/or organoleptic characteristics of the product; the definition of the geographical area; evidence that the agricultural product or the foodstuff originates in the geographical area; a description of the method of obtaining the product and the details bearing out the link with the geographical environment or the geographical origin; and details of the inspection procedures required to ensure that foodstuffs bearing the designation comply with the specification. *See* art. 4(2) (listing minimum requirements of specification). As with terms registered under the simplified procedure, producers may only use a protected designation of origin or geographical indication with an agricultural product or foodstuff if their product complies with the applicable specification. *See* art. 4(1). And member states must make available, at the expense of the group of producers using the protected name, approved inspection authorities that will ensure compliance with the requirements laid down in the specification. *See* art. 10.

If the member state, after review of the application, believes that registration is justified, that member state forwards the application to the Commission. In addition to Commission scrutiny of the application, under the normal registration procedure the regulation provides for an opposition procedure if the Commission concludes that the name qualifies for protection (and publishes it in the Official Journal). The opposition can be grounded not only in failure to comply with the general requirements of Article 2 but also upon the term being generic or upon registration jeopardizing the existence of an entirely or partly identical name or trademark or the existence of products which are legally on the market for at least five years preceding the date of the publication of the term in the Official Journal. *See* art. 7(4); *see also* Council Regulation (EC) No. 535/97 of 7 March 1997, O.J. (1997 L 83) 3 (amending grounds for opposition). If an opposition is filed, the Commission will first request the member states involved to resolve the matter by agreement and, if that is not possible, will decide the matter "having regard to traditional fair practice and actual likelihood of confusion." Art. 7(5). The procedural rules governing the Commission's decision-making process are set out in Article 15. Opposition to an indication registered under the system can only be filed by an EU Member country, not by individuals. *See* art. 7(1). But individuals resident or established in member states are entitled to make representations to their respective countries regarding opposition. *See* art. 7(3).

Articles 13-14 set out the rights that attach to a protected term, and they address each of the issues typically found in geographical indications legislation. Article 13 (1)(a) provides a broad scope of protection against direct or indirect use of the indication by others on comparable products or where the use would "exploit the reputation" of the indication. Article 13(1)(b) extends the prohibition against any "misuse, imitation or evocation" even if the true origin of the product is indicated or the protected term is accompanied by an expression such as "style" or "type," although member countries were entitled to make the extended protection of paragraph (1)(b) subject to a five-year "phase-out" period (now expired) under national law for existing users in countries where the term has been used legally for at least five years preceding the enactment of the regulation. *See* art. 13(2). Article 13(3) provides that a protected term may not become generic. And Article 14 prohibits the grant of conflicting trademark registrations (after publication of the application for registration as a geographical indication) for products of the same type that would come within the prohibitions of Article 13.

In March 1999, the Court of Justice handed down an important decision providing guidance both on the scope of rights available under the regulation and on the relationship between geographical indications and trademark rights. *See* Consorzio per La Tutela Del Formaggio Gorgonzola v. Kaserei Champignon Hofmeister Gmbh & Co. [1999] 1 C.M.L.R. 1203 (E.C.J. 1999). The term GORGONZOLA, which derives its name from the former village (now a suburb of Milan) in the province of Milan, Italy, was registered on the Community register as a protected designation of origin for soft cheese marbled with blue mold. *See* Commission Regulation (EC) No. 1107/96 (11) on 21 June 1996, art. 1 (listing terms protected under the simplified procedure). A consortium of producers of Gorgonzola cheese that supervised use of the term GORGONZOLA brought an action in Austria to restrain a German cheese producer from marketing a soft blue mold cheese under the designation CAMBOZOLA and to obtain cancellation of the defendant's Austrian trademark registration for CAMBOZOLA. The defendant had marketed CAMBOZOLA in Germany since 1977 and in Austria since 1983, and CAMBOZOLA is sold in almost all other member states. In 1983, the defendant had registered the trademark CAMBOZOLA in Austria for milk and milk products, including cheese (notwithstanding that the term GORGONZOLA had, since 1954, been a protected geographical indication under an international agreement to which Austria was a party). Although the defendant did not use the term GORGONZOLA and the packaging for CAMBOZOLA indicated that it was produced in Germany, the members of the consortium were concerned about the defendant's usage because they typically add to the protected designation of origin GORGONZOLA specific trading names to identify their dairies, generally including the component "-zola."

In the Austrian courts, the defendant argued that, because the cheese was lawfully put on the market under the name CAMBOZOLA in its country of origin (Germany) and imported into Austria, any injunction granted by the

Austrian courts would restrict trade contrary to former Article 30 of the EC Treaty (now Article 28). The Austrian court sought guidance from the European Court of Justice as to whether an injunction was contrary to ex-Article 30 or justified by Article 36 (now Article 30); the Court instead took the opportunity to interpret the Foodstuffs Regulation because that interpretation might resolve the dispute before the national court. The plaintiff had claimed that the defendant's use came within Article 13(1)(b), which protects registered names against "any misuse, imitation or evocation, even if the true origin of the product is indicated or if the protected name is translated or accompanied by an expression such as 'style,' 'type,' 'method,' 'as produced in,' 'imitation.'" The defendant argued (1) that CAMBOZOLA is not an evocation of GORGONZOLA within the meaning of Article 13 of the regulation, because that concept must not be interpreted any more broadly than is absolutely necessary to protect industrial and commercial property, since a broad interpretation would run counter to the principle of the free movement of goods; (2) that part only of a protected name is not protected as such; and (3) that because the objective of the regulation is to prevent designations of origin from becoming generic names and the use of the mark CAMBOZOLA can never cause GORGONZOLA to become a generic name, the principle of proportionality prevents a broad interpretation of "evocation."

The Court of Justice rejected all three of the defendant's arguments. The Court held that "evocation . . . covers a situation where the term used to designate a product incorporates part of a protected designation, so that when the consumer is confronted with the name of the product, the image triggered in his mind is that of the product whose designation is protected." Moreover, the Court endorsed the view of the advocate-general that evocation does not require likelihood of confusion, and concluded that

> since the product at issue is a soft blue cheese which is not dissimilar in appearance to GORGONZOLA, it would seem reasonable to conclude that a protected name is indeed evoked where the term used to designate that product ends in the same two syllables and contains the same number of syllables, with the result that the phonetic and visual similarity between the two terms is obvious.

The Court continued with its analysis, however, because Article 14 permits the continued use of an earlier registered trademark in defined circumstances, namely where the mark was registered in good faith before the date when the application for registration of the designation of origin or geographical indication was lodged and there are no grounds for invalidation of the trademark under Articles 3(1)(c) and 3(1)(g) of the EU Trademark Directive. *See* art. 14(2). The advocate-general had suggested that good faith required an analysis of whether "the owner of the mark took all reasonable steps at the time of registration to satisfy himself that use of the mark was compatible with the national law (including any applicable international provisions) then in force." (¶ 50). The Court did not disagree with or endorse that formulation (other than to indicate that good faith must indeed be assessed in light of national and international legislation in place at the time) but stressed that it was for the national court to decide both the question of good faith and also whether there existed a sufficiently serious risk that consumers would be deceived by the use of CAMBOZOLA so as to prohibit registration of the mark under Article 3(1)(g) of the Trademark Directive. *See* Trademark Directive art. 3(1)(g) (prohibiting registration if the mark in question is of such a nature as to deceive the public as to the nature, quality or geographical origin of the product for which it is registered); art. 3(1)(c) (prohibiting in pertinent part registration of marks that consist exclusively of signs or indications that serve to designate the geographical origin of the product). With this guidance, the case was sent back to the Austrian courts. Does the scope of protection suggested by the European Court of Justice strike an appropriate balance between the different concerns discussed in this Section, such that it might be a model for international negotiation?

Should the defendant have prevailed before the Court of Justice based on other provisions of the regulation? What about Article 13(2)'s five-year phase-out period? *See* Opinion of Advocate General Jacobs, at ¶ 46. On remand, how would you decide the question of whether there is infringement under Article 13(1)(b)? *Cf.* Gorgonzola/Cambozola [1999] E.T.M.R. 135 (Upper County Court, Frankfurt, 1997) (Germany) (deciding same issue before Court of Justice opinion in *Consorzio per La Tutela Del Formaggio Gorgonzola*). Which group of consumers should be relevant in answering this question? *See id.* at 140 (using German consumers as relevant standard). What is the scope of Article 14(1)? Should defendant's Austrian trademark registration for CAMBOZOLA be canceled? Is it possible that a prior national trademark registration might be valid under Article 14(1) but prohibited from use under Article 14(2)? How would you decide the Article 14(2) case on remand to the Austrian court? After considering those questions, ask whether the Foodstuff Regulation provides priority to geographical indications or trademarks. *See* art. 14(3); *cf.* FREDERICK W. MOSTERT, FAMOUS AND WELL KNOWN MARKS 107 n.123 (1997) (describing Article 14 as embodying a "more equitable" treatment of the trademark/geographical indication conflict). Should we seek a system under which conflicting trademarks and geographical indications can co-exist in the same territory, adopt a preference for one form of intellectual property over the other (and which would be preferred), or follow a strict "first in time, first in right" rule without differentiation between the marks and geographical indications? Or are there legal devices by which the different philosophies can each be accommodated? *Cf.* TRIPS arts. 24(5), 24(7). And does focusing on the priority relationship between marks and geographical indications obscure other policy objectives underlying the protection of geographical indications (which can be pursued without significant impact on trademark law)?

The Foodstuffs Regulation has been subject to criticism from the United States. On June 1, 1999, the United States requested consultations with the EU pursuant to Article 4.4 of the Understanding on Rules and Procedures Governing the Settlement of Disputes ("DSU") and Article 64 of TRIPS regarding the regulation. The United States has argued that EU Regulation 2081/92 does not provide national treatment with respect to geographical indications, and does not provide sufficient protection to pre-existing trademarks that are similar or identical to a geographical indication. The U.S.

request stated that "this situation appears to be inconsistent with the European Communities' obligations under the TRIPS Agreement, including but not necessarily limited to Articles 3, 16, 24, 63 and 65 of the TRIPS Agreement." In what ways might the EU Regulation violate TRIPS, and which specific provisions of the articles referenced by the United States in its request are implicated? Are there any additional provisions that the U.S. request could have referenced? *See* Clark W. Lackert, *Geographical Indications: What Does the WTO TRIPS Agreement Require*, TRADEMARK WORLD Aug. 1998 at 22, 30; Florent Gevers, *Conflict Between Trademarks and Geographical Indications–The Point of View of the International Association for the Protection of Industrial Property*, WIPO Symposium on the International Protection of Geographical Indications, Melbourne 143, 152-53 (1995) (discussing Article 16 arguments). Consultations are still ongoing between the parties.

While international pressures threaten the validity of the regulation from without, developments within the member states of the EU (in particular, the United Kingdom) may have reduced its effectiveness and prompt some minor amendments. In *Consorzio Del Prosciutto di Parma v. Asda Food Stores Ltd.*, [1999] 1 C.M.L.R. 696 (Ct. App. 1998) (Eng.), the English Court of Appeal held that the Foodstuff Regulation did not have direct effect in the United Kingdom, and thus private parties could not sue to enforce the prohibitions of Articles 13-14. PROSCIUTTO DI PARMA for ham was registered on the Community register pursuant to the simplified procedure under Article 17. The association of Parma ham producers responsible under Italian law for enforcing compliance with regulations on the production and marketing of Parma ham brought an action against Asda Stores, an English retailer who sold Parma ham that had been produced in accordance with the specification accompanying the community registration but not sliced and packaged as required by that specification. Asda conceded that under the EC Treaty, a regulation was directly applicable in member states without the enactment of national legislation, but argued (successfully) that the Foodstuffs Regulation did not confer rights of enforcement upon individuals because it was not of direct effect. To be directly effective, a community provision must be "clear, precise, unconditional and complete" and must "provide a [Community] source of information to enable the relevant class of persons to be simply and cheaply informed of their rights." The court of appeal held that the regulation did not meet that standard for several reasons: First, there is no need for the regulation to have direct effect and allow private enforcement because it provides a detailed procedure for enforcement of rights by member states and the Commission under Article 11 where other states are not offering the requisite protection to registered indications. Second, because the Community register did not contain the full terms of the specifications (these were contained in the Italian government's application and in a referenced Italian government executive order), private parties could not cheaply apprize themselves of the relevant requirements, thus failing the test of transparency. Finally, it would be "unusual to have individuals asserting rights, akin to monopoly rights, granted in respect of specifications that had not been verified" or examined by the Commission (because the registration in this case had been granted under the simplified procedure without any opposition). Furthermore, the court held that because the regulation had been enacted pursuant to provisions of the EC

Treaty dealing with the EU's Common Agricultural Policy, it could not provide protection for steps such as the slicing of ham (which did not implicate questions of agricultural policy). *Cf.* Consorzio Per La Promozione Dello Speck v. Christianell (Tribunale Di Bolzano, April 21, 1998) (Italy), *noted at* 1998 E.T.M.R. 537 (enforcing specification requirements relating to packaging and slicing of ham); Matthew Gloag & Son v. Welsh Distillers Ltd., [1998] F.S.R. 718, 727 (Ch. D. 1998) (Eng.) (declining to dismiss private cause of action under Spirits Regulation). The consortium sought leave to appeal to the House of Lords. If that leave is not granted, what steps are available to the consortium to enforce its Community registration? *See* Foodstuffs Regulation art. 11. How might the regulation be amended to remedy the lack of transparency about which the *Parma* court complained?

Although the *Parma* decision limits private enforcement of regulation-derived rights in the United Kingdom, producers are not without any private means of redress in that country. The U.K. courts have on several occasions recognized the use of an "extended" (rather than the "classical") form of the tort of passing off to protect appellations of origin. *See, e.g.*, Chocosuisse v. Cadbury, 1998 E.T.M.R. 205 (Ch. D. 1997) (Eng.) (recognizing an action in tort to protect the goodwill in a shared reputation, and enjoining use of term SWISS and other Swiss indicia for chocolate bar not made of Swiss chocolate where Swiss chocolate was perceived to have a distinctive quality by U.K. consumers), *aff'd*, 1999 E.T.M.R. 1020 (Ct. App. 1999). Indeed, in *Chocosuisse*, Mr. Justice Laddie described this right as "a civilly enforceable right similar to an appellation contrôlée," 1998 E.T.M.R. at 216, and recognized the standing of Chocosuisse, a trade association of Swiss chocolate manufacturers, to bring such an action. The court of appeal affirmed the grant of an injunction against the use of the term SWISS and other Swiss indicia, but questioned whether the trade association (as opposed to individual Swiss chocolate producers) had standing to sue either in its own right or in a representative capacity under English rules of procedure. *See generally* Thomas Helbling, *The Term "Swiss" on Trade Goods: A Denomination of Origin and its Legal Protection in the United Kingdom*, 19 EUR. INTELL. PROP. REV. 51, 53-58 (1997) (discussing options available to protect geographical indications under U.K. law).

[C] Other Regional and Bilateral Agreements

Bilateral agreements with respect to geographical designations have in the past been common. For example, in 1971, France and the United States agreed that France would prohibit the sale in France of products bearing the mark BOURBON to designate whisky unless made in the United States, and that the United States would prevent the use of various terms, including COGNAC for brandy, by persons other than those entitled to make such use under the French law of appellations of origin. *See* J. Thomas McCarthy & Veronica Colby Devitt, *Protection of Geographic Denominations: Domestic and International*, 69 TRADEMARK REP. 199, 226 n.155 (1979); Institut National Des Appellations d'Origine v. Brown-Forman Corp., 47 U.S.P.Q.2d 1875, 1878 n.2 (T.T.A.B. 1998) (discussing treaty). Indeed, as recently as 1983, the EU and the United States entered into a non-intellectual property-specific wine agreement, embodied in an exchange of letters, in which the EU accepted the importation of American wines treated with various additives, and the United States agreed to act to prevent the genericization of various geographic terms. *See* Leigh Ann Lindquist, *Champagne or Champagne? An Examination of U.S. Failure to Comply with the Geographical Provisions of the TRIPS Agreement*, 27 GA. J. INT'L & COMP. L. 309 (1999). This agreement was to have expired in 1997, but has been twice extended (now until December 31, 2003) to enable negotiations between the two parties on all pending wine-related issues to occur.

The European Union has recently concluded bilateral agreements governing reciprocal protection of listed geographical indications on wine with seven countries, including most notably Australia. *See generally* Des Ryan, *The Protection of Geographical Indications in Australia under the EC/Australian Wine Agreement*, 16 EUR. INTELL. PROP. REV. 521 (1994). For a full listing of these agreements, *see* Lindquist, *supra* at n.104. The European Commission has also recently reached an agreement with the Republic of South Africa under which South Africa would (after a transition period of twelve years) prohibit use of the geographical indications "port" and "sherry" on the fortified wines exported from South Africa. The European Parliament has, however, asked the Commission to reconsider the agreement. *See* 13 WIPO REP. 115 (1999). Why did Australia enter into such an agreement with the EU? What are the benefits that will accrue to Australia? What are the benefits South Africa is seeking? Is this now a viable or permissible means of developing this area of international intellectual property? *See* TRIPS arts. 1(2), 4.

In addition to the EU legislation, other regional treaties, such as the Mercosur Protocol (art. 19), the Andean Community Decision 344, and the Central American Convention (arts. 74-75), also include provisions addressing the use of geographical indications. Article 23 of the Pan-American Convention did likewise. The Cartagena Agreement (arts. 1291-42) establishes a registration system for appellations of origin, and provides registered terms with protection against any unauthorized use. *See* art. 131.

[D]   Revision of TRIPS Pursuant to Articles 23-24

The provisions on geographical indications were some of the most contentious in the entire GATT Uruguay Round negotiation. The provisions that resulted represent a hard-fought compromise. But many issues remained unresolved, and to this end Articles 23-24 established a continuing obligation to negotiate further on these matters in the TRIPS Council. Article 23(4) requires member states to undertake negotiations regarding "the establishment of a multilateral system of notification and registration of geographical indications for wines." In Article 24, members agreed to enter into more generalized negotiations "aimed at increasing protection of individual geographical indication." Art. 24(1). Article 24(1) expressly commits countries to reconsider the exceptions to protection now found in Articles 24(4)-(8), and Article 24(3) contains a standstill-plus agreement that prevents member states from reducing the protection that the member state granted geographical indications immediately prior to the entry into force of the WTO Agreement.

Both the EU and the United States (with Japan) have offered proposals for a multilateral register of geographical indications for wines. The EU proposal, first submitted in 1998, and revised in 2000, would extend not only to wines but also to spirits (with the possibility of adding other products at a later stage). Members would not be required to submit names to be protected (according to the EU this made the system "voluntary") but indications accepted for registration (after one year in which countries could file an opposition based on the grounds set out in Article 24 of the TRIPS Agreement) would be protected in all WTO countries. Critics of the EU proposal suggested that its expansion beyond wines took it outside the scope of Article 23(4) and argued that the requirement that a registered term be protected in all WTO countries belied its description as "voluntary." The rival U.S.-Japanese proposal–which was supported by Canada, Australia, New Zealand and Chile, among others–was first discussed at the February 1999 TRIPS Council Meeting. Under this (minimalist) proposal, the WTO would publish a list (supplied by member countries) of designations being protected in each respective country, and WTO member countries would agree to refer to this list in making decisions about domestic protection. The proponents of the U.S.-Japan proposal argued that it reflected the wide divergence in countries' methods of protecting geographical indications, but the EU complained that this rival proposal amounted to "little more than the creation of a database." Progress on this question has been slow and no agreement appears imminent.

The lack of detail in the initial EU proposal concerning how any challenges to registration would be resolved troubled some countries. For example, would WTO panels be involved? At the April 2001 TRIPS Council meeting Hungary presented a new proposal that addressed this question. The Hungarian proposal would provide for arbitration among WTO members in the event of opposition to registration of a name. It also differs from the EU proposal in two other respects: first, it would permit challenge to a registration on grounds derived from Article 22 of the TRIPS Agreement (as well as Article 24); and, second, registration on the multilateral register would have effect only in countries that voluntarily participated in the system rather than in all WTO countries.

QUESTIONS

The United States–as revealed both by its WTO complaint against the EU and by the narrowness of its international register proposals in the TRIPS Council–is clearly unpersuaded of the case for offering broad protection to geographical indications (whether for wine or for other products). Is this a wise position for the United States to adopt? If you were a consumer advocate, for which position would you argue? If you were trying to persuade the U.S. Trade Representative to change its position, which arguments would you make? *See*

Leigh Ann Lindquist, *Champagne or Champagne? An Examination of U.S. Failure to Comply with the Geographical Provisions of the TRIPS Agreement*, 27 GA. J. INT'L & COMP. L. 309 (1999). What about wine–and about the marketing and sale of wines–might justify support for preferring geographical designations over trademarks in this one product sector? How might you use or deal with the following data: wine consumption among Europeans is declining, but the market is expanding in Asia; Californian wines are viewed by many as the premier wines of the new world; between one quarter and one third of wine sold in the United States is marketed under what the BATF Regulations call semi-generic names; and wine sales of higher-priced wines in the United States is increasing, suggesting (it is claimed) an increasingly sophisticated wine consumer in the United States. *See id.*

[E]   Developments in WIPO

WIPO has long been interested in developing an international approach to geographical indications. Draft treaties have been prepared, *see* Draft Treaty on the Protection of Geographical Indications, WIPO Doc. TAO/II/2 (1975), and model laws have been drafted, *see* Model Law for Developing Countries on Appellations of Origin and Indications of Source, WIPO Pub. No. 809(E) (1975). The Draft Treaty was largely based upon the Lisbon Arrangement, but would have extended protection beyond appellations of origin to all geographical indications. It would have absolutely prohibited trademark registration of indications of source, but given previous users of such terms five years to cease use. *See generally* J. Thomas McCarthy & Veronica Colby Devitt, *Protection of Geographic Denominations: Domestic and International*, 69 TRADEMARK REP. 199, 208-09 (1979); Lee Bendekgey & Caroline H. Mead, *International Protection of Appellations of Origin and Other Geographic Indications*, 82 TRADEMARK REP. 765, 783-84 (1992).

At the first session of the newly formed WIPO Standing Committee on the Law of Trademarks, Industrial Designs and Geographical Indications in Geneva in July 1998, delegations were split on whether to give priority to work on the protection of geographical indications. The debate centered on whether or not to duplicate the work being conducted in the TRIPS Council, and not whether this was an important issue. *See* Standing Committee on the Law of Trademarks, Industrial Designs and Geographical Indications, First Session (July 13-17, 1998), Report Prepared by the International Bureau ¶¶ 28-29. It was decided that the International Bureau of WIPO would continue monitoring developments in the field, and would continue preparations for a world-wide symposium to be held in the biennium. *See id.* ¶ 31; *see also WIPO Symposium on the International Protection of Geographical Indications*, Melbourne (1995); *WIPO Symposium on the Protection of Geographical Indications in the Worldwide Context*, Eger, Hungary (1997).

§ 3.03   Industrial Designs

Unlike patents, copyrights, or trademarks, the regulation of design protection at the international level is quite minimal. Because designs are potentially protectable in some countries not only under a design code proper, but also under other forms of intellectual property, provisions are scattered throughout a variety of intellectual property treaties without significant concentration in any one. In this Section, we review those provisions that do exist in multilateral treaties, including in the regional context (such as the EU) where greater and more substantial progress has occurred of late. Treaties establishing mechanisms for obtaining design rights on a multinational basis–principally the Hague Agreement–are dealt with separately *infra* §§ 6.03, 6.06.

[A]   Multilateral Agreements

ANNETTE KUR, TRIPS AND DESIGN PROTECTION*
in FROM GATT TO TRIPS: THE AGREEMENT ON TRADE-RELATED ASPECTS OF INTELLECTUAL PROPERTY RIGHTS 141, 144-56 (Beier & Schricker eds. 1996)

II. INTERNATIONAL DESIGN PROTECTION BEFORE TRIPS

1. Paris Convention

Industrial designs are included among the objects of industrial property protection covered by Art. 1(2) of the Paris Convention. Pursuant to Art. 5*quinquies* of this Convention all countries of the Union are obliged to grant protection to industrial designs and models. Yet this not interpreted so as to mean that protection must be granted on the basis of *sui generis* legislation; it is sufficient that it is accorded by other means–typically under copyright law or as protection against unfair competition.

[Article 5B] prohibits . . . rights in industrial designs or models [from being] declared forfeited as a result of either failure to work or importation of corresponding products.[18] In contrast, such a prohibition does not exist in relation to compulsory licenses. . . .

. . . .

2. Revised Berne Convention (RBC)

As a result of the hybrid nature of design protection, the relevant regulations cannot be found in the Paris Convention alone, rather, they are also anchored

---

*Copyright 1996, Annette Kur. Reprinted with permission.

[18]In contrast, such a possibility does exist regarding utility models and patents in accordance with Art. 5A of the Paris Convention.

in copyright conventions–here, however, not under the category of industrial designs and models, but under that of applied art. This category of works protected by copyright has been included in . . . Article 2(1) RBC since 1908 (Berlin). Furthermore, during the Brussels conference (1948) an attempt was made to establish as a matter of principle that works of applied art should not be excluded from copyright protection *per se*, even where they are used industrially; yet these efforts failed in the face of opposition inter alia from Italy and the United Kingdom. Instead, it was established that each national legislature was free to determine whether, and to what extent, utilitarian objects may obtain protection on the basis of copyright law. Where the national legislature grants protection to works of applied art, a minimum 25-year term of protection is obligatory by virtue of Art. 7(4) RBC.

The substantive reciprocity clause of Art. 2(7) RBC also stems from the absence of an internationally effective obligation to grant copyright protection to industrially utilized designs: where a member of the Berne Union grants copyright protection to works of its nationals in addition to specific design protection,[25] this protection must only be extended to the works of foreigners who are nationals of another Berne Union country if it would also be possible to claim copyright protection for the same work in such foreigners' country of origin. This clause was of practical significance, for example, in relations between Italy (which practically excludes copyright protection for products that are eligible for design protection) and France (where designs enjoy supplementary full copyright protection on the basis of the "unité de l'art" doctrine). . . .

3. Universal Copyright Convention (UCC)

In contrast to the RBC, the text of the Universal Copyright Convention does not contain an explicit reference to works of applied art within the context of its (non-exclusive) catalogue of protected works. However, it may be inferred from Art. IV(3) of the UCC that this Convention proceeds from the possibility of granting copyright protection to such works: according to this provision the term of protection for works of applied art must run for at least 10 years.

4. Agreement of The Hague Concerning Industrial Designs

Although the possibility of pure copyright protection for designs is not excluded by international law and is still practised in a number of countries, the large majority of countries grants design protection primarily on the basis of specific legislation that normally requires entry in the register or deposit of the design as a prerequisite of protection. For these states the Agreement of The Hague offers the possibility of a central deposit of the design at the WIPO in

---

[25]Where specific design protection does not exist in a certain country (*e.g.* in Greece), but where copyright law constitutes the only possibility of obtaining protection, foreign designs shall enjoy protection under copyright law even where this possibility is excluded under the law of the country of origin of the design at issue.

Geneva and thus–subject to the eligibility of the design for protection under national law–of obtaining protection in all or selected contracting states. [The Hague Agreement is discussed in detail *infra* § 6.03].

III. Provisions of the TRIPS Agreement Relevant to Design Law

1. Copyright

. . . .

Apart from [the obligation to comply with the provisions of the Paris and Berne Conventions], the copyright regulations in Part II, Section 1 of the TRIPS Agreement do not contain any statement on the protection of industrially utilized works of applied art. The TRIPS text therefore does not give rise to any new developments regarding the copyright protection of designs . . . The Members are not prevented from granting protection to such works on the exclusive basis of specific design protection legislation, excluding completely a cumulative claim to copyright protection. To an even lesser degree are they prevented from making copyright protection for works of applied art dependent upon extremely strict requirements, whether with regard to the artistic qualification of the work [e.g., in Germany], to its "separability" from the utilitarian object in which it is embodied [e.g., U.S. or Italian law], or to the number of permissible copies of the work, etc. [e.g., U.K. or Irish law].

2. Specific Design Protection

(a) Basis of the Right

Specific provisions on the protection of industrial designs and models are contained in Part II, Section 4 (Arts. 25 and 26) of the TRIPS Agreement. They represent a very brief regulation of the issue. The provisions leave open the question as to how the right to a design shall come into existence, in particular whether this can only take place by means of registration or also through use of the design.

Where the right is obtained by means of registration, the regulations of Article 62 must be respected. The necessary formalities must be kept at a reasonable level (Art. 62(1)); moreover, . . . the grant or registration of the right [must be] possible within a reasonable period of time (Art. 62(2)). The spirit of this provision conflicts to a certain extent with the procedures of registration of design rights in the US and Japan. [I]n these countries registration does not take place until after sometimes lengthy examinations, which, especially with regard to designs with a short life-span, can entail the risk of a total depreciation in the value of the rights granted.

. . . .

(c) Individual Provisions

* Art. 25(1), first/second sentences (subject-matter of protection, requirements for protection)

The text of Art. 25(1) obliges the Members to protect independently created designs, insofar as they fulfill the prerequisites of novelty or originality. This provision does not define the term design nor [the types of product whose design is covered by the provisions], thus leaving scope for individual national definitions.

As a matter of principle, the wording of Art. 25(1), first sentence, requires subjective novelty of the design (it must be 'independently created'); it is only in this case that the international obligation to protect industrial designs takes effect. In addition to the requirement of independent creation,[44] novelty and originality are mentioned as principal requirements for protection. It is argued that by listing these protection criteria in alternative form ("... that are new or original"), the negotiating parties intended to make clear that as a matter of principle [Members] should be prohibited [from imposing] cumulative requirements (i.e. "new *and* original"). This was intended to ensure that the threshold for protection is not raised to an exceedingly high level by TRIPS Members.[47] It seems doubtful however whether the manner in which this intent was expressed in Art. 25(1) will be sufficient to encompass the underlying objectives. According to Art. 25(1), second sentence, it is still possible for Members to deny protection if the design does not differ *significantly* from what was known previously; and the application of this criterion can in practice amount to a rather high threshold for protection. Moreover, the wording of the second sentence allows the Member countries to continue dividing the assessment of protectability into two "logical steps": namely to assess whether a given design is already known (assessment of novelty) and subsequently to ask whether a sufficient difference from the relevant comparative material can be established (assessment of originality/individual character). The only consequence of Art. 25(1), first sentence, if any, will therefore be that in future these two steps will have to be covered by a single term–be it "novelty" or "originality."

Other issues have been left undecided: for example whether an absolute or in any respect (timewise, geographical,[51] or with reference to the knowledge of the participating expert circles) relative meaning of the term novelty shall be applied. Finally, as mentioned above, it is left to the discretion of the national

---

[44]This means that in this case the criterion of "originality" is not automatically identical to that of "independently created," as is otherwise frequently the case in the Anglo-American use of language.

[47][This seems] to date back to an early Japanese contribution, [cit], dated November 23, 1987, where the proposal to stipulate both novelty and originality as cumulative criteria for protection was motivated by references to patent law, claiming that since design rights conferred principally the same protection as patents, equally restrictive criteria should apply in both fields.

[51]In that only publications within the domestic territory may be taken into account; *e.g.* in the UK, Australia, Canada, etc. . . .

legislature whether a strict or rather generous standard will apply as regards the threshold for acquiring protection: whilst by adding the word "significantly" it is clarified that a high threshold would also comply with Art. 25(1), the provision on the other hand does not contain anything that would prevent national legislatures from coming very close to a requirement of mere subjective novelty.

The wording of Art. 25(1) does pose a special problem for US law, in which the patent law criterion of non-obviousness is applied as the protection requirement for industrial designs. In this respect, in the literature reference is made to footnote 5 concerning Art. 27(1) of the TRIPS Agreement, where, with respect to patentability, it is stated explicitly that a Member country may interpret the term "inventive step" in the sense of "non-obvious." Owing to the fact that such a reference is missing in Art. 25, which regulates the protection requirements for designs, it is concluded that in future in US law only novelty or originality, yet not non-obviousness, may be required as protection criteria in design law.[54]

* Art. 25(1), third sentence (exclusion from protection of functionally dictated designs)

The principle that design protection, being restricted to the exterior appearance of products, necessarily meets its limits where it would lead to protection of technical ideas, . . . is generally accepted and applies to most design laws–whether in the form of explicit regulation or as a principle developed in case law. However, the practical interpretation of this principle is subject to considerable variations.

In its broadest form, this principle is applied in order to limit design protection to those utilitarian objects the "raison d'être" of which essentially lies in pleasing the observer's eye, e.g. to fabric designs, jewellery, decorative articles, etc. This means that articles where the functional purpose obviously prevails and which are not primarily purchased according to optical aspects, e.g. tools, kitchen appliances, office items, etc., are excluded from protection. A more flexible alternative to this point of view [excludes from protection] not whole product groups, but only such designs . . . that represent an improvement in functionality–e.g. that render a pair of scissors easier to manage or improve the user friendliness of office machines, etc. [But] this approach ignores the fact that good product design means combining form and function in an optimal manner, . . . and results in the exclusion from protection of particularly successful designs.

Having recognized this fundamental contradiction, some legislatures consequently limited the exclusion from protection to those rare cases in which the designer had no other option at his or her disposal in order to achieve a certain function–for only in these exceptional cases would protection of the design necessarily lead to protection of the technical idea, contradicting the inherent function of design protection.

---

[54]Reichman, 1993 FORDHAM INTELL. PROP., MEDIA & ENT. L. J. 171, 245 (1993); however, the US legislature has not adopted this argument.

Yet this narrow, modern way of viewing the matter is not laid down as an internationally valid standard in Art. 25(1), third sentence of the TRIPS Agreement. The possibility of excluding "designs dictated essentially by technical or functional considerations" means that the national legislatures may continue to restrict design protection to products or design elements that essentially serve a decorative purpose.[57]

It remains questionable whether Art. 25(1), third sentence, constitutes a final regulation of any possible exclusionary clauses, or whether the national legislatures will still have a broader scope for regulation in this respect. . . . The issue could . . . affect rules which, for systematic[58] or economic[59] reasons exclude certain product categories from protection,[60] or which establish other special requirements regarding the eligibility for design protection (for example the requirement that the design must be visible in the course of use in accordance with the purpose of the protected item,[61] or that products may not be protected as designs if they are not distributed separately . . .[62]).

A strictly literal interpretation of Art. 25(1), third sentence, could in fact lead to the conclusion that the TRIPS Members are not entitled to exclude designs for reasons other than their functionality. However, in view of the rather vague character of this provision, this conclusion appears somewhat questionable; in particular, it can hardly be assumed that there was a serious intention to declare unlawful the exclusion from protection of "immoral" designs, an exclusion that is anchored in most of the design laws throughout the world. The strict wording and the (presumable) intention of the rule thus do not tally.

. . . .

* Art. 25(2) (Special conditions for protection of textile designs)

Art. 25(2) obliges all members of the TRIPS Agreement to pay particular consideration to the special requirements of the textile industry. This rule was motivated by the specific, frequently lamented problems of this branch of industry: as a rule textile designs are developed in large numbers and are

---

[57] A so-called must-fit-exception is doubtlessly also permissible pursuant to art. 25(1), third sentence, as provided for in UK law [cit] and in art. 9 of the proposal for a Community Design Regulation. . . .

[58] E.g. the exclusion of computer programs and semi-conductor products contained in Art. 3(b) of the proposal for a Community Design Regulation, based on the assumption that otherwise undesirable overlaps with the EU Directives concerning this subject matter would arise. . .

[59] In particular in the case of rules directed towards excluding spare parts from design protection, such as the must-match rule in UK law. [cit]. The South African Design Act of 1993 is similar, excluding 'spare parts' from registration as functional designs (in contrast to which they may still claim protection as aesthetic designs subject to fulfillment of the prerequisites).

[60] E.g., the US proposal for a sui generis design law, presented in the House of Representatives concurrently to the GATT negotiations, in 1991, H.R. 1790: according to Sec. 1002 of this proposal designs for "motor vehicle glass, including windshields and side and rear vision glass" should be excluded from protection.

[61] Following a recommendation of the European Parliament, the amended texts for the proposals for a Community Design Regulation and Directive stipulate the visibility of the design during ordinary use. The same effect results from the US requirement of "ornamentality."

[62] See, e.g., In re Ford Motor Co. Ltd.'s Design Application, [1994] R.P.C. 545 (Ch. D. 1994).

subject to extremely rapid changes that often take place from one season to the next. The effectiveness of traditional design protection founded upon entry in the register and publication therefore seems questionable for reasons of time and costs. At the same time, however, the textile industry relies on effective protection, because in this branch of industry in particular, deliberate and mass copying of new designs poses a grave problem.

Specific regulations aimed at reducing the registration procedure and costs for short-lived designs that are developed in large numbers are already anchored in numerous national design laws. [F]or example, . . . rules allow the combination of a larger number of designs in one single registration (multiple applications) and the possibility of deferring publication, with the result that the costs of publication of the design can be saved [for] a . . . brief period (which in the ideal case corresponds to the life-span of a fashionable design). A further possibility, even more advantageous for the textile industry, is the possibility of acquiring informal protection, whether on the basis of design law provided for in the proposal for a Community Design Regulation or on the basis of other laws.

Article 25(2) obliges the Members of the TRIPS Agreement to make available (at least) one of the workable possibilities of obtaining simplified, less expensive protection. The members are free to choose between fulfilling this obligation within the framework of either design or copyright regulations.

German design law already complies with the obligation under Art. 25(2) of the TRIPS Agreement by offering both multiple application (Section 7(9) Design Act) and deferred publication (Section 8b Design Act); the same applies to most of the other European states. Moreover, a real improvement in the protection of short-lived textile designs will result from the proposed Community Design Regulation, which provides for three-year protection for non-registered designs.

In principle, the design laws of the US and Japan do not offer any possibility of providing inexpensive and (considerably) faster protection for textile designs. However, in the US the possibility exists of obtaining copyright protection for two-dimensional textile designs; the criterion of separability, otherwise applied strictly, is not [as severe] with regard to [protection of] two-dimensional designs.[63] In contrast, in Japan no alleviation is provided with respect to the copyright protection of two-dimensional designs. In practice, there is the possibility of claiming protection against slavish imitation on the basis of the amended law against unfair competition. As Art. 25(2) explicitly mentions design and copyright protection only, this hardly appears to meet the requirements of the TRIPS Agreement.

* Art. 26(1) (Contents of Protection)

Article 26(1) lists the rights . . . to which design right owners are entitled. According to this list the manufacture, sale or importation of articles "bearing or embodying a design" are [to be] prohibited, if the design "is a copy, or

---

[63]Problems regarding the compatibility of US law with art. 25(2), TRIPS Agreement, remain with respect to three-dimensional forms (shapes of clothing etc.) . . . .

substantially a copy" and "when such acts are undertaken for commercial purposes." In contrast to copyright law, for example, from the outset acts undertaken in the private sphere are not considered infringements. The [use] of the term "copy" means that . . . it will also be possible to restrict design protection to those cases in which the infringer was familiar with the previously existing design, in analogy to copyright law. On the other hand, Art. 26(1) does not preclude more far-reaching regulations with a true monopoly effect, such as are contained in most design laws throughout the world.

* Art. 26(2) (Exceptions from design protection)

According to Art. 26(2) the TRIPS Members are permitted to provide limited exceptions to the protection of industrial designs or models, inasfar as these do not unreasonably conflict with the normal exploitation of *the designs* and do not unreasonably prejudice the legitimate interests of the design owners, whereby the legitimate interests of third parties must also be taken into account.

The wording of this provision, corresponding to similar provisions in other parts of the TRIPS Agreement,[70] is basically consistent with Art. 9(2) of the Revised Berne Convention.[71] [T]he general permission of reproduction for private use of protected works is based upon this provision. In the case of design protection such an explicit exemption is not required, because infringement as referred to in Art. 26(1) only covers acts that are undertaken for commercial purposes.

Examples of exceptions that do not fall within the private sphere, but which must doubtlessly be deemed permissible according to Art. 26(2), are, for example, the display of the design for experimental or educational purposes; the. . . . . use of the design as equipment on a vehicle etc. that enters the territory of the country of protection temporarily; the importation of parts for the purpose of repairing such vehicles; and the carrying out of such a repair . . .

In addition, compulsory licenses or other rules allowing use of protected designs at reasonable conditions must also be considered to conform with TRIPS. Such regulations are not *per se* irreconcilable with the legitimate interests of the proprietor of the design, nor are they declared unlawful in either the Paris Convention or in the TRIPS Agreement itself, although proposals to this effect were submitted and discussed during the negotiations.[73]

---

[70] *E.g.* for patent law (Art. 30) and trademark law (Art. 17).

[71] However, Art. 9(2), Revised Berne Convention, is confined to reproduction; in addition, there is no reference to the "legitimate interests of third parties."

[73] Proposals to declare the compulsory licensing of industrial designs unlawful were submitted by the following delegations: Switzerland, Austria, Hong Kong. The US proposal suggested subjecting compulsory licenses for industrial designs to the same requirements as patents. . . .

NOTES AND QUESTIONS

(1) **Priority Rights**. Article 4(C)(1) of the Paris Convention establishes a six month priority period to facilitate the serial acquisition of design rights on a multinational basis. These are expressly implemented in U.S. design protection systems. *See* Patent Act, 35 U.S.C. § 172 (six month priority available for design patent applicant); Vessel Hull Design Protection Act, 17 U.S.C. § 1311 (same for vessel hull design right owner).

(2) **Notice Requirements**. Under Article 5(D) of the Paris Convention design protection may not be conditioned upon notice. If the United States were to implement its Paris Convention and TRIPS obligations by constructing a broad-based design regime based upon the Vessel Hull Design Protection Act, would the current notice provisions, *see* 17 U.S.C. §§ 1306-1307 (content of notice and effect of omission of notice), require amendment? *Cf* 17 U.S.C. § 405 (effect of omission of copyright notice); Berne Convention art. 5(2) (enjoyment and exercise of protected rights shall not be subject to any formality). *See* Pierre Maugué, *The International Protection of Industrial Designs under the International Conventions*, 19 U. BALT. L. REV. 393, 394 (1989) (discussing effect of Article 5(D)).

(3) **U.S. Compliance.** The United States adopted the position that the industrial design provisions of TRIPS did not require the amendment of U.S. law. Does the United States comply with TRIPS obligations with respect to industrial designs? If not, in what respects is U.S. law deficient? Does TRIPS require the enactment of a *sui generis* design law? *See* Uma Suthersanen, *Breaking Down the Intellectual Property Barriers*, 2 INTELL. PROP. Q 267, 275 (1998) (answering in the affirmative); Kur, *supra*, at 149 (expressing doubt about such an interpretation). If not (and if, therefore, the United States can rely on its design patent protection to comply with TRIPS), does the United States need to modify any of the particular provisions of the design patent statute? Do you agree with Dr. Kur's relatively minimalist interpretation of the obligations imposed by Article 25(1) of TRIPS? *See* J. H. Reichman, *Universal Minimum Standards of Intellectual Property Protection under the TRIPS Component of the WTO Agreement*, 29 INT. LAW. 345, 376 (1995).

(4) **Exclusions**. Dr. Kur suggests that the third sentence of Article 25(1), permitting members to exclude protection for designs that are "dictated essentially by technical or functional considerations," does not constitute what she calls "a final regulation of any possible exclusionary clauses," meaning that that provision does not constitute the only ground upon which a group of designs can be excluded from the universe of protected subject matter. How does that provision interact with Article 26(2), which sets out a standard that any exceptions to protection must meet?

(5) **Term**. Under Article 26(3) of TRIPS, protection must endure for at least ten years, which may have been of some influence in selecting the length of protection for protection under the U.S. Vessel Hull Design Protection Act. *See* 17 U.S.C. §§ 1300 et seq.

(6) **Cumulation**. During the TRIPS negotiations, the Swiss delegation proposed a clause in the design provisions that would have required design

protection to be offered independently of copyright or other forms of protection. Would there have been advantages to such an approach? What difficulties would this have engendered?

———————

CASE NO. 4 Ob 95/91
Austrian Supreme Court, Nov. 5, 1991
25 I.I.C. 126 (1994)

The architect Le Corbusier, who died in 1965, designed from 1928-1929 a series of models for furniture that are classed as being in the Bauhaus style. These models, designed in collaboration with the architect's assistants Charlotte Perriand and Pierre Jeanneret, include an infinitely adjustable lounge chair that was manufactured by the Atelier Thonet, Paris, in a number of variations . . . .

On November 26, 1987, the plaintiff, a joint stock company under Italian law, renewed the agreement it had concluded with the Le Corbusier Trust as heir and holder of Le Corbusier's copyright and as representative of Charlotte Perriand and of Pierre Jeanneret's heir, concerning the manufacture and sale of furniture by Le Corbusier, Charlotte Perriand and Pierre Jeanneret. This agreement granted the plaintiff the exclusive worldwide right to manufacture and sell Le Corbusier furniture, including the infinitely adjustable lounge chair (referred to in the agreement as "LC 4"). The plaintiff has manufactured and distributed a nickel-plated steel version of the LC 4 chair since 1974. . . .

The defendant is engaged in the furniture trade in Klagenfurt. In the period from 1988 to 1990 it took delivery from "Danish Rattan AS," Denmark, of a total of seven chairs . . . Some of these were then resold to retailers in Austria, whereby the defendant used a catalogue published by Danish Rattan AS, which contained [several] illustrations of . . . chairs [that were similar to the LC4 and the 1928 prototype of the infinitely adjustable lounge chair.]

 . . . .

[The] plaintiff requests an interlocutory injunction enjoining the defendant from offering and selling an imitation of the Le Corbusier lounge chair, claiming that it enjoyed the exclusive and worldwide right to exploit the models of Le Corbusier and his assistants, which rights thus included the Republic of Austria. The infinitely adjustable lounge chair was a work of applied art and thus entitled to copyright protection. This world-famous chair was not based upon the work of another artist. Its individuality was to be found above all in the three-part division in the line forming the sitting and reclining surface, the prominent neck-rest cylinder, and the semicircular support structure contrasting with the broken line of the reclining surface. By selling the imitations of these chairs, the defendant had infringed the plaintiff's exploitation rights. If the infinitely adjustable lounge chair did not enjoy copyright protection, the defendant's activity was in breach of Section 1, Act Against Unfair Competition.

 . . . .

FROM THE OPINION:

The [lower court] rightly applied Austrian law to the questions whether the infinitely adjustable lounge chair was a work to which copyright protection applied and whether the chairs distributed by the defendant and manufactured by Danish Rattan AS amounted to a plagiarism of these chairs. If the chair created abroad was (also) issued at the same time in Austria (although no findings were made on this point) within the meaning of Section 9(2) of the Copyright Act, then it is entitled to copyright protection by virtue of Section 95; if on the other hand it was created by a foreign author and issued abroad, then according to Section 96 of the Copyright Act its protection derives from international treaties or on the basis of reciprocity.

Since the architect Le Corbusier was a French national, and the chair he and his assistants designed was manufactured by the French Atelier Thonet in 1928, it can be assumed that the chair was issued in Union countries of the Berne Convention for the Protection of Literary and Artistic Works, of which Austria is also a member. Both countries are also contracting states of the Universal Copyright Convention, whereby the relationship between them is governed by the Paris version of the Berne Convention and of the Universal Copyright Convention. In countries that are Union countries of the Revised Berne Convention and contracting states of the Universal Copyright Convention, protection under the Revised Berne Convention takes priority (Art. XVII(1) of the Universal Copyright Convention (Paris)). "Convention works" of the Berne Convention–i.e., works originating in one of the Union countries (Art. 5(4) of the Berne Convention (Paris))–are entitled to exclusive protection under the Convention in the countries of the Union. Article 5(1) of the Berne Convention (Paris) grants the same protection to authors from a country of the Union as is granted to works by a national. Copyright protection, which in Austria is also granted to works of applied art [cit] also extends to the scope of application of the Berne Convention; Austria has not availed itself of the possibility of restricting the protection of works of applied art. Works of applied art have also enjoyed copyright protection in the country of origin, France, since the Law of 1902, and this irrespective of whether they are also protected by virtue of the Law on Designs and Models. [cit]. Hence works of applied art from France are also entitled to copyright protection in Austria (Art. 2(7) Berne Convention (Paris Act)).

As this Court held in its decision, *Markt-Stahl-Stuht* [cit], the intention of the work, *i.e.* the purpose for which it has been created, is irrelevant for the question of copyright protection. Artistic works that fulfill the requirements of creativity and creativity in a work (individuality) of Section 1(1) of the Copyright Act can claim copyright protection and design protection. The border between copyright protection (artistic protection) and model protection must not, however, be set too low. On the contrary, there must be a considerable "aesthetic excess" or a corresponding artistic creativity. Similarly one and the same utility object can enjoy both artistic protection and patent or utility model protection simultaneously.

According to the literature and case law, a product of the human intellect is an individual intellectual creation (a "work") within the meaning of Section 1 of the Copyright Act if it is the result of creative intellectual activity and if the uniqueness distinguishing it from other works is derived from the personality of its author. The latter should find expression in such a way that it imposes upon the work the mark of uniqueness and its provenance from the author. In other words the work should be given form by the innermost essence of intellectual creativity. In the field of works of art, [cit], this form must be conceptually linked with a certain degree of originality. Here, a certain creativity in a work is necessary, an idea that has been given a form that bears the mark of the author's personal individuality, or at least is distinguishable by virtue of a personal touch from other products of a similar kind. [cit]. Works belonging to an artistic style whose intention is to derive the aesthetic shapes of utility objects exclusively from their purpose, avoiding any decorative additions ("functional form"), could have an aesthetic effect, but are not necessarily protected as works of art as a result. If an artistic movement deliberately rejects all non-functionally determined elements of design, thus by its very nature having less scope for design at its disposal than other artistic styles, i.e. permitting less of the author's individuality to enter into the work, then the protection to which it is entitled is also correspondingly diminished. [cit].

In the same decision, this Court also held that novel technical solutions are not entitled to copyright protection. In the case of a combination of technology and art in one work, examination must be made of the extent to which the design elements used are determined by technical factors and to what extent they have been selected for reasons of form, taste, beauty, or aesthetics. Nor is the choice of a geometrical shape alone sufficient to justify recognition as a work of art, since the geometrical shape of itself is in the public domain. Nor, likewise, can an artistic style be eligible for copyright protection in its own right.

According to the decisions referred to above, this question must be answered on the basis of the conditions applying at the time the work was created. Subsequent developments, on the other hand, must be ignored, since otherwise creations whose remarkable artistic uniqueness provided the stimulus for a large number of similar products would lose their protection within a short time.

. . . .

Despite its functional purpose, the chair designed by Le Corbusier and his assistants in 1928 contains an abundance of details that impose upon it the mark of uniqueness. Mention should be made here above all of the particular contrast between the broken line formed by the sitting and reclining surface and the arc-shaped supporting structure that serves both as contact element to the base and to enable infinite adjustment. It is not apparent that the chair only makes use of known features, or that its form is the necessary result of the technical function of the individual elements. In addition, the design of the head and foot of the chair also reveals traits of individuality; these latter shapes are neither determined by the purpose of the chair, nor made up of elements of a particular artistic style. All of these individual characteristics can be seen in the illustration of the prototype submitted in evidence; it is not obvious why this should not amount to evidence of the required creativity in a work. There is no indication that the [1928] "prototype" . . . is only a reproduction of "some possibly" original model. Nor does the fact that a number of variations of the chair were created have any consequence upon its creativity in a work. Furthermore the defendant has failed to present any concrete argument why the chair should be the mere result of ergonomic principles and a technical idea. Nor has the defendant stated which work served as a model for the architect Le Corbusier: the lounge chair designed by Ludwig Mies van der Rohe merely incorporates the three-part division of the sitting and reclining surface; Le Corbusier's lounge chair, with its infinitely variable adjustment, is completely different in the execution of the details. Nor has the defendant claimed that the van der Rohe chair was created before that of Le Corbusier. Thus the defendant has failed to fulfil his burden of proof to establish the contrary. In the absence of sufficient concrete claims and suitable counter-evidence, it must therefore be assumed in the hearing on the interlocutory injunction that the lounge chair was created independently by Le Corbusier and his assistants and that its shape is neither determined by a technical principle or by the chair's function, nor is it part of the public domain.

. . . All the chairs illustrated in the catalog used by the defendant incorporate the characteristic features of the infinitely adjustable lounge chair. . . . Hence the plaintiff has sufficiently established that these chairs amount to an infringement of his exploitation rights. . . .

NOTES AND QUESTIONS

(1) **Article 2(7) of the Berne Convention**. Article 2(7) effectively enables countries offering designs protection under both copyright and *sui generis* design laws to condition copyright protection for foreign nationals' works of applied art on substantive reciprocity. But how is satisfaction of that condition to be assessed? It is quite clear that France–the leading adherent to the unity of art philosophy–offers copyright protection that meets the reciprocity standard. But what if an Austrian national seeks protection in French courts for a design first issued in Austria: would Article 2(7) oblige France to provide protection? *See* SAM RICKETSON, THE BERNE CONVENTION FOR THE PROTECTION OF LITERARY AND ARTISTIC WORKS 1886-1986, at 278-79 (1986) (discussing when copyright protection can be denied); *cf.* Kur, *supra*, at 146 (suggesting that the reciprocity provision is important between Italy and France because Italy "practically excludes" copyright protection for designs).

(2) **Reciprocity After TRIPS.** Does Article 2(7) of the Berne Convention–which derogates from the principle of national treatment–remain operative after TRIPS? *See* TRIPS art. 3(1). Should it? What does it now achieve? When negotiated at the Brussels Revision Conference in 1948, Article 2(7) embodied a compromise negotiated largely by European countries to accommodate their disparate approaches to copyright protection for designs; in particular, Italy and the United Kingdom held firm against the French position that works of applied art should be fully brought within the Berne Convention regardless of whether the works were industrially applied designs. *See*

RICKETSON, *supra*, at 276-78. Yet, although Article 2(7) now formally governs relations of most Berne members, the very countries of Europe who generated the provision have now been compelled to repeal the application of Article 2(7) because of the *Phil Collins* decision. *See infra* Chapter 4. The early Commission drafts of the design directive discussed below, prompted by the same policy objectives as the *Phil Collins* decision, would have reached the same result legislatively. *See* Proposed Design Regulation art. 100(3); Proposed Design Directive art. 18(2). Thus, even if TRIPS permits continued application of the substantive reciprocity requirement, should Article 2(7) be changed? If so, in what way?

(3) **Standard of Originality.** How does the standard applied by the Austrian court to determine originality measure against recent international articulations of copyright originality? Does that provide the basis for international agreement on protection of applied art? If not, what obstacles remain?

(4) **The Universal Copyright Convention.** Why were the provisions of the Universal Copyright Convention inapplicable in this case? *See* Universal Copyright Convention art. XVII; RICKETSON, *supra*, at 854-55. Why might the rules under Austrian law applicable to the protectability of the *Le Corbusier* chair be affected by whether the "chair was issued at the same time in Austria" as abroad?

[B]   Regional Agreements

THE EUROPEAN UNION*

In 1993, the European Commission proposed two new legislative instruments that would dramatically revise design protection within the EU. The wide divergence in the means by which EU member states currently protect designs generates additional expense and complications for the producer seeking to obtain protection for its design throughout those countries. The Commission was moved to act by the concern that this expense created significant barriers to the market entry of small or medium sized firms, and threatened the competitiveness of European industry. In addition, however, the Commission recognized–as it had before in proposing trademark reform–that territorial (national) intellectual property rights threaten to disrupt the workings of a common market and interfere with the free movement of goods. Accordingly, the Commission proposed a regulation that would create unitary EU-wide design rights, consisting of a three-year unregistered design right and a registered right that could, with appropriate filings, endure for twenty-five years. The regulation has not yet been adopted, but a revised proposal was published by the Commission in November 2000. *See* Amended Proposal for a

---

*This analysis is based upon a more lengthy (and earlier) consideration of the proposals in Graeme B. Dinwoodie, *Federalized Functionalism: The Future of Design Protection in the European Union*, 24 AM. INTELL. PROP. L. ASS'N Q.J. 611 (1996).

Council Regulation on Community Design, COM(2000)660 final/2 (Nov. 23, 2000). The proposed regulation is discussed in greater detail *infra* § 6.06.

Although the centrepiece of the proposals was the regulation creating EU-wide rights, the Commission concluded that there was no justification for wholly preempting national design protection. Indeed, even if the Commission wished to replace national forms of protection with the Community level regime, member states could not immediately dismantle their local systems because of pre-existing rights acquired under those systems. Thus the proposed regulation was supplemented by a harmonization directive, containing provisions substantially identical to the regulation, that would harmonize the registered design laws of the member states with each other and with the substantive provisions of the EU-wide system of protection. The co-existence of national and community level systems mirrors the approach the Commission adopted in addressing reform of trademark law. An amended version of the directive was enacted in 1998. *See* Directive 98/71/EC of the European Parliament and of the Council of 13 October 1998 on The Legal Protection of Design, O.J. L 289 (Oct. 28, 1998).

The legislative instruments in combination address three different rights: The Registered Community Design Right and the Unregistered Community Design Right proposed in the regulation, both of which would exist at the community level and provide unitary protection throughout the union; and the registered design rights that must exist under the laws of each member state once the member state implements the provisions of the directive. The basic principles underlying the regulation and the directive are the same and govern all three of these types of rights. *See generally* EUROPEAN DESIGN PROTECTION: COMMENTARY TO DIRECTIVE AND REGULATION PROPOSALS (Mario Franzosi ed., 1996).

The scope of the directive is less ambitious than the regulation: it seeks to harmonize national registered design laws, *see* Directive art. 2, but it neither requires member states to introduce unregistered design right protection at the national level, nor obliges the United Kingdom to make amendments to its existing unregistered design law. Moreover, whereas the regulation addresses the entire range of issues pertinent to a self-standing system of design protection, the directive harmonizes only the core elements of existing systems and leaves many issues to the member states. For example, article 14 of the proposed regulation provides that where a design has been developed by an employee in the execution of his duties or following instructions given by his employer the community rights in that design will vest in the employer. In contrast, the directive makes no provision on this question, leaving the allocation of national rights between employer and employee to national law.

For the purpose of the Design Directive, design is defined as "the appearance of the whole or a part of a product resulting from the features of, in particular, the lines, contours, colours, shape, texture and/or materials of the product itself and/or its ornamentation." Art. 1(a). The most important aspect of the definition of design, however, is what it does *not* include: it contains no reference to the aesthetic or functional nature of the design. This is arguably the most important contribution that these proposals make to the advancement of design protection laws. In repudiating the functional/aesthetic dichotomy, the

Commission boldly has grasped the nettle of functionalism, which must be done if the problem of design protection is to be resolved. The United Kingdom had addressed this issue in 1988 in the enactment of its unregistered design legislation–which protected aesthetic and functional designs alike–but U.K. law does still distinguish between aesthetic and functional designs in that functional designs cannot obtain registered protection because of that system's "eye-appeal" requirement. The directive goes further and requires the registered design laws of member states to protect the external appearance of a product whether that appearance is pure decoration, has no aesthetic content, or is a combination of functional and aesthetic elements. There is no intention to restrict these new protections to designs that appeal to the eye. Instead of confining protection by restricting the universe of protectable subject-matter, the directive instead requires the registered design laws of member states to circumscribe protection through application of prescribed thresholds and exclusions.

The thresholds to community design protection follow a common structural model: a two-step test that assesses (1) whether the design is different from other designs, and (2) whether the development of the design beyond prior designs involves more than minimal creativity on the part of the designer. More specifically, to obtain protection, a design must be new, and have individual character. *See* art. 3(2). Novelty consists of no identical design or immaterially different design having previously been made available to the public as of the date of the filing of the application. *See* art. 4. The novelty standard is universal, not local, and no time limit will restrict the designs that might be regarded as prior art. *See* art. 6. The Commission intends that novelty for design purposes be a much less difficult standard than the patent requirement of the same name, and one of the principal drafters of the proposals has characterized the novelty standard demanded under the design proposals as one of "false novelty."

To avoid providing protection to designs that differ only in small details from a prior design, a supplementary threshold is contemplated by the proposals. A design will be protected only if it possesses "individual character." This will be the concept that truly sets the outside parameters of prima facie protection. A design shall "be considered to have an individual character if the overall impression it produces on the informed user differs from the overall impression produced on such a user by any design which has [previously] been made available to the public." Art. 5. All explanations of the concept tendered by the Commission suggest the clear intent to bring within the scope of protection incremental improvements upon prior designs: such designs arguably possess individual character if they *are* different, even if that difference might have been an obvious one to develop. Individual character does not connote a flash of genius; it simply requires the noticeable and non-trivial development of designs beyond what has gone before. The Commission clearly wished to ensure that adaptations of existing designs are protected by the new design right.

Although the "individual character" standard is somewhat vague, the legislation explicitly mandates consideration of the degree of freedom that the designer enjoyed in developing the design. That is to say, in a crowded field a smaller advance from prior designs will more easily warrant the conclusion of individual character. *See* art. 5(2). Of course, the scope of protection that such designs receive will be correspondingly limited; if there is little room for exceptional creativity on the part of the first designer, he cannot be heard to complain if the same restrictions compel a later designer to create a design that bears a resemblance to his in some respect. *See* art. 9(2).

In a system that broadly envisages the protection of functional designs on conditions that intentionally do not approach those required of applicants for utility patents, the exclusions from protection assume paramount importance. Protecting the appearance of a functional design clearly raises the possibility of incidentally affecting the ability of others to practice that function. Without the caution that this should impel, and the exclusions it justifies, there exists the *potential* that this form of protection might be anticompetitive and offer overbroad protection to functional items. Thus, any designs that are "solely dictated by the technical function [of the product]" are excluded from protection by Article 7(1) of the directive. Similar exclusions are found in many design laws through the world. The Commission argued that if the design is dictated by the function of the product, the creative choices exercised by the designer are necessarily minimized (or even non-existent). Such an exclusion might also be justified, however, by recognition of the countervailing competitive concerns that are implicated by the protection of functional designs on standards less demanding than those imposed by patent law.

Courts that have considered this question have struggled with whether the term "dictated" is causative or mandatory (i.e., whether the term connotes that functional concerns explain the design or necessitate the design). Although this provision is an essential bulwark against design rights for functional designs circumventing the rigors of the utility patent system, it must not be construed too broadly (i.e., as merely causative). The mere fact that a design is influenced by functional considerations should not disqualify it from protection. Otherwise, the innovation of these proposals–the elimination of the threshold distinction between aesthetics and function–will prove illusory and functionalist design will remain excluded from protection.

Another interpretation of this provision, that flows from viewing the term "dictated" as meaning "mandated," would focus on whether any alternative designs exist: if they do, the design is not solely dictated by the technical function of the product. Such a test has analogues in many intellectual property regimes, including U.S. trade dress law, U.S. design patent law, U.S. copyright law and in the "multiplicity of forms" test found in French copyright and designs patent law. If the test calls simply for a determination of whether there are *any* other designs, however, there remains a danger that the *few* designs that will enable the product to function may be depleted by the successive grant of design rights in those respective possibilities to a small number of producers.

A more flexible interpretation might consider whether there are a sufficient number of designs to permit competition or, in the philosophy of the Commission, to require more than minimal creative choices on the part of the designer. This reading of Article 7(1) would avoid the problem of "design depletion," a concern implicitly recognized by Lord Morris when the House of Lords interpreted broadly the exclusion of designs "dictated solely by function" from U.K. registered design protection. *See* Amp v. Utilux, [1972] R.P.C. 103,

114 (noting that if provision required consideration only of whether alternative shapes existed "the designer could register a separate design in respect of each different shape"). A less mathematical approach has also been adopted by courts in other countries of the European Union already incorporating this exclusion in their design laws. And further parallels can be drawn to judicial interpretation of the idea/expression dichotomy in copyright law, to which the Commission expressly likens this exclusion. Where there is only one way of expressing the idea, that expression will be treated as having merged with the idea and will be unprotectable by copyright. Courts have, however, interpreted that concept broadly and have denied protection where the expression is one of only a limited number of ways of expressing the idea. The EU design legislation would benefit from a similar breadth of interpretation. Thus, although mere functional influences should not result in the denial of protection, nor should the mere availability of a single other alternative be sufficient to ensure protection. That might cause oligopolies rather than monopolies, but the competitive harm would be little different.

The EU proposals contain two additional exclusions from protection that bear confusingly similar popular labels (which were taken from the 1988 U.K. reforms): "must-fit" and "must-match." The must-fit exclusion deals with mechanical synchronicity, while the must-match provision deals with visual synchronicity. Article 7(2) of the Directive creates an exclusion for mechanical interconnections, that is:

> [F]eatures of appearance of a product which must necessarily be reproduced in their exact form and dimensions in order to permit the product in which the design is incorporated or to which it is applied to be mechanically connected or placed in, around or against another product so that either product may perform its function.

The exclusion of interconnections reveals the continuing conviction of the Commission that interoperability and standardization will enhance the competitive environment. As the Commission's *Green Paper* explained:

> Consumers should, for example, be able to replace a vacuum cleaner hose of a given make by another hose which fits into the vacuum cleaner. In principle, the design of the vacuum cleaner hoses qualifies for design protection just as does the design of the vacuum cleaner itself. To ensure interoperability and competition in the spare parts aftermarket in respect of a wide range of household articles, motor vehicles, consumer electronics etc., it appears advisable to exclude from protection those features of a design which would have to be reproduced necessarily in their exact form and dimensions in order for the component part to fit into the complex product for which it is intended.

GREEN PAPER ON THE LEGAL PROTECTION OF INDUSTRIAL DESIGN, WORKING DOCUMENT OF THE SERVICES OF THE COMMISSION, ¶ 5.4.10.1 (1991).

The most rancorous part of the EU design debate concerned what came to be known as the "repair clause." *See* art. 14. This clause addressed the scope of protection for the design of certain spare parts, so-called "must-match" designs, *i.e.,* designs where "the product incorporating the design or to which the design is applied is a component part of a complex product upon whose appearance the protected design is dependent." Amended Proposed Directive art. 14. Must-match designs involve visual, rather than mechanical, correlation. The most commonly cited example of a must-match design, which has also occasioned the greatest controversy, is the design of car body panels. The initial approach of the Commission was to place a limit of three years (from first marketing of the product) on the right of the design owner to stop third parties manufacturing and selling must-match parts for the purpose of repairing the complex product (e.g., the car) so as to restore its original appearance. Opposition to *any* period of exclusive rights was fierce, however, and the Commission accepted that a lesser scope of protection might be appropriate. In the first amended proposal, the Commission settled on a remuneration right for the design owner as against such third parties. That alternative did not, however, attract the support of the qualified majority of member states necessary to enact the directive.

The Council then adopted a common position in which it abandoned efforts at (apparently impossible-to-reach) compromise and mandated no special provision for spare parts. Instead, the limit of provision on spare parts was the imposition of an obligation upon the Commission, five years after implementation of the directive, to prepare an analysis of the effect of the directive on competition. Finally, after a conciliation procedure among Council, the Parliament and the Commission, the directive was passed with a compromise "standstill plus" provision. Article 14 of the enacted directive provides that:

> Until such time as amendments to this Directive are adopted on a proposal from the Commission [as contemplated within 4 years by Article 18], member states shall maintain in force their existing legal provisions relating to the use of the design of a component part used for the purpose of the repair of a complex product so as to restore its original appearance and shall introduce changes to those provisions only if the purpose is to liberalize the market for such parts [i.e., reduce protection].

In the interim, even before the directive is implemented (triggering the Commission's obligation to produce an analysis of the effect of the directive on the spare parts market) the Commission has initiated a consultation exercise among interested parties (car parts manufacturers and insurance companies) in the hope of reaching a voluntary resolution of the dispute.

Like most registered design laws, registration will confer upon the holder the exclusive right to use the design and to prevent the unauthorized third party use of the design or designs that do not produce "on the informed user a different overall impression." Arts. 9, 12. Registered designs may, by timely application, receive protection of this patent-like nature for up to twenty-five years. *See* art. 10. The concerns of industry regarding the costs and delay of design registration have largely been addressed in the regulation, where unregistered rights will be available and community-level registered rights will be granted after a relatively cursory examination. Accordingly, the directive does not compel member states (such as the United Kingdom) to dismantle any system of substantive examination used under their registered design laws.

The provisions in the initial draft of the directive *requiring* member states to provide full cumulation with copyright has undergone significant revision during the legislative process. Despite the Commission's reluctance to tackle broad-based copyright harmonization, the initial proposals provided that member states would not be permitted to deny copyright on the basis that the functional elements of the designs were not separable from the artistic elements or that the design had been applied industrially to a certain number of articles. *See* Proposed Directive art. 18. These provisions were aimed at Italy and the United Kingdom, both of which effectively exclude functional designs from copyright protection. Italy excludes designs from copyright by application of the rule of separability, and the United Kingdom now achieves the same by a combination of rules that focus on the industrial application of a design to articles of fifty or more. *See* Italian Copyright Law of April 22, 1941, *amended by* Decree No. 195, January 8, 1979, art. 2(4); Copyright, Designs & Patents Act, 1988, §§ 51-53, 236.

The Commission expressly and forcefully rejected the number of products to which the design is applied as of any relevance in determining the availability of protection. In the enacted directive, however, the Commission has agreed not to force Italy or the United Kingdom to surrender these exclusionary provisions. *See* Directive art. 17 ("The extent to which, and the conditions under which, [copyright] protection is conferred, including the level of originality required, shall be determined by each member state."). That is to say, while formally the Commission has insisted on mandatory cumulation of protection under copyright law, it has made no attempt to harmonize generally the conditions under which designs are accorded protection under the copyright code in each member state. Accordingly, the wide variances in copyright laws will continue to plague producers seeking protection throughout the European Union.

NOTES AND QUESTIONS

(1) **Definition of "design".** The definition of design in the Design Directive includes both two- and three-dimensional design. The U.K. statute, on which to some extent the EU legislation was patterned, makes some distinction between two- and three- dimensional designs. *See, e.g.,* Copyright, Designs & Patents Act, 1988 § 213(3)(c) (surface decoration can be protected only as *registered* design). Similarly, although not explicit, in the United States, two-dimensional designs are more apt to receive copyright protection than three-dimensional designs. Are there reasons to treat two- and three-dimensional designs differently?

(2) **Protection of Functional Designs.** Why is it important that the EU proposals make no distinction between aesthetic and functional designs? What dangers does the inclusion of functional designs generate? Are the benefits received from their inclusion in the directive worth the costs or risks? How might those costs or risks be controlled or minimized? One writer has suggested that the definition of "design" in the directive–and, in particular, the use of the term "appearance"–defeats the Commission's stated objective of protecting modern functionalist industrial design. *See* Uma Suthersanen, *Breaking Down the Intellectual Property Barriers*, 2 INTELL. PROP. Q 267, 274-75 (1998); *cf.* 2 STEPHEN P. LADAS, PATENTS, TRADEMARKS AND RELATED RIGHTS 869 (1975) (suggesting broader conception of "appearance"). Review the definition of "design" in Article 1(a): What types of designs are excluded by the limitations built into the definition? Does it by its terms offer protection to functionalist design?

(3) **Software and Hybrids.** The community design regime will not protect the design of computer software; the Commission is relying instead on the Software Directive to delineate the scope of protection available to those works. *See* Design Directive art. 1(b). Professor Reichman has argued that the problems that face industrial design and those that confront software possess sufficient similarities as to warrant treatment by a common regime of intellectual property protection rather than a set of separately tailored laws. *See* J.H. Reichman, *Legal Hybrids Between the Patent and Copyright Paradigms*, 94 COLUM. L. REV. 2432, 2511-19 (1994) (describing common problems of industrial designs and software in receiving appropriate protection under patent and copyright paradigms); *see also* Pamela Samuelson, et. al., *A Manifesto Concerning the Legal Protection of Computer Programs*, 94 COLUM. L. REV. 2308, 2356-57 (1994) (noting parallels). What are the merits and problems of such an approach?

(4) **The Threshold for Protection**. The Commission considered basing protection upon a threshold of originality (the subjective notion of the design being original to the designer, and not copied, regardless of objective similarity to other designs). What arguments might have supported adoption of such a threshold? Why you think that the Commission rejected that threshold? The Commission could also have adopted a modified copyright originality threshold, such as found in the Vessel Hull Design Protection Act, 17 U.S.C. §§ 1301(b), 1302(a)(2), the Semiconductor Chip Protection Act of 1984, 17 U.S.C. §§ 902(b) (1994) (protecting mask works that are original and that are not staple, commonplace, or familiar in the semiconductor industry), and in the U.K.'s unregistered design code. *See* Copyright, Designs & Patents Act, 1988, §§ 213(1), 213(4) (providing unregistered design protection to designs that are "original" and not "commonplace in the design field in question at the time of its creation"). What are the advantages of each respective approach? What difficulties might arise from adopting a new threshold falling between the relatively well-understood thresholds of patent and copyright? In light of the diverse approaches to protectability in member states prior to the enactment of the directive, what institutional forces might help establish common understanding of these terms in practice? The courts might embrace certain conceptual approaches that would help. *See* Dinwoodie, *supra*, at 662 (arguing

for affirmative endorsement of link between degree of differential required to escape infringement and that required to demonstrate individual character).

(5) **Prior Art.** The prior art to be considered in the analysis of individual character and novelty is determined universally. In its *Green Paper*, the Commission had suggested that "a test of universal objective novelty cannot be fulfilled and therefore should not be imposed." Why not? Why might a universal standard be inappropriate for designs? What dangers flow from the reversal of that policy? *See* Design Directive art. 6(1) (adding a "safeguard clause" introduced by the European Parliament that excludes from prior art disclosures that "could not reasonably have become known in the normal course of business to the circles specialized in the sector concerned operating within the Community" at the date of the application.).

(6) **Reliance on Competition Law.** One response to the threat of anticompetitive consequences flowing from the protection of functional designs is to fall back on principles of competition law to deal with any specific instances in which the grant or the enforcement of rights is anticompetitive. *See* Friedreich-Karl Beier, *Protection for Spare Parts in the Proposals for a European Design Law*, 25 I.I.C. 840, 842 (1994); Audrey Horton, *European Design Law and the Spare Parts Dilemma: The Proposed Regulation and Directive*, 16 EUR. INTELL. PROP. REV. 51, 54 (1994). Instead, the Commission sought to address the competitive concerns directly in the construction of the design regime through the use of carefully tailored exceptions. (The outcome of the spare parts debate suggests that they were not entirely successful). Which approach is preferable? Why? *See* Dinwoodie, *supra*, at 665-69.

(7) **Must-Match Exclusions.** Essential mechanical designs will, to a large extent, be caught by the must-fit exception or by the specific exclusion of so-called "under the hood" designs. *See* Directive art. 3(3). Why should the protection of must-match designs--designs where "the product incorporating the design or to which the design is applied is a component part of a complex product upon whose appearance the protected design is dependent"--be restricted? Consider the prototypical case of car body panels. *See* Bernhard Posner, *The Proposed EC Industrial Design Directive and Regulation: An Update and Analysis*, 2 INT'L INTELL. PROP. L. & POL. at 46-10 (1998); *see also* British Leyland Motor Corp. v. Armstrong Patents Co., [1986] 1 All E.R. 850, 864 (1986) (Lord Templeman) (noting that if copyright gives exclusive rights in spare parts for cars "the purchaser of a BL car sells his soul to the company store"). Are there any costs to allowing free copying of the design of spare parts? What does the term "complex product," with respect to which the must-match provision and its permission to copy in order to supply the repair market applies, mean? *See* Directive art. 1(c). What products other than cars might be encompassed by this term? And what makes a design "dependent upon the appearance" of the complex product? *See* Dietrich C. Ohlgart, *Commentary in* EUROPEAN DESIGN PROTECTION, *supra*, at 154-55 (rehearsing different interpretations of "dependent"); *see also* Jeremy J. Phillips, *Commentary, in* EUROPEAN DESIGN PROTECTION, *supra*, at 164 (suggesting that "[i]n respect of a motor vehicle, the door panels would be covered [by the spare parts provision] but not such non-integral or possibly ornamental accessories for cars as wing mirrors or steering wheels").

(8) **TRIPS Compliance.** Did the earlier versions of the Design Directive's must-match provision–otherwise called the "repair clause"–comply with TRIPS? Recall that the initial proposal would have required member states, after three years of protection, to permit third parties to manufacture and sell certain protected parts of complex products (so-called "must-match" parts) for repair purposes. The amended proposal made the repair clause right immediately exercisable, but only upon payment of fair and reasonable remuneration to the design owner. Would either of these approaches–which may yet be the basis of an amended directive when the Commission reports in four years, and which may be adopted in design legislation pending elsewhere, including the United States–be a violation of TRIPS? *See* TRIPS art. 26(2) (permissible exceptions); art. 26(3) (requiring minimum of ten years protection); *see also* Annette Kur, *TRIPS and Design Protection, in* FROM GATT TO TRIPS: THE AGREEMENT ON TRADE-RELATED ASPECTS OF INTELLECTUAL PROPERTY RIGHTS 141, 157-59 (Beier & Schricker eds., 1996) (arguing that repair clause proposals were consistent with TRIPS). If you believe that either of these approaches would violate TRIPS, what does that mean for the U.K. design law, which absolutely excludes protection for "must-match" parts and thus bars causes of action even against direct competitors of the original manufacturer?

(9) **Cumulation.** The directive does not regulate the cumulation of rights under member states' copyright, unfair competition, unregistered design, utility model and other laws. Article 16 permits member states to grant protection under any of these alternative regimes. (The only mandatory provision is Article 17, which purports to require cumulative copyright protection; but this provision is rendered meaningless because member states may determine the extent of such protection and the conditions upon which it is available.) What are the consequences of the Commission's reluctance to regulate (and, in particular, limit) cumulative protection? *See* Dinwoodie, *supra*, at 710-19.

To augment the plethora of possible (and different) protections, the Commission has also proposed a directive harmonizing the utility model laws in the EU. *See* Proposal for a European Parliament and Council Directive Approximating the Legal Arrangements for the Protection of Inventions By Utility Model, COM(97)691 final, O.J. C 36 (Mar. 2, 1998); Amended Proposal for a European Parliament and Council Directive Approximating the Legal Arrangements for the Protection of Inventions by Utility Model, [cite] (June 30, 1999). Utility model laws are a form of registered (but unexamined) industrial property that confer exclusive rights (normally for a shorter term than patent) on technical inventions that do not display the level of inventiveness required for patent protection. In addition to harmonizing existing national utility model provisions, the directive would require the enactment of utility model laws in countries (such as the United Kingdom, Sweden and Luxembourg) where such laws do not currently exist. The directive would require member states to accord ten years of utility model protection to subpatentable functional inventions, and its interaction with design protection for functional designs is not clear. *Cf.* Opinion of the Economic and Social Committee on the Green Paper: The Protection of Utility Models in the Single Market, O.J. C 174/6, ¶ 5.2.1 (June 17, 1996) (suggesting that the Commission had not in its initial *Green Paper* taken sufficient account of the relationship between utility model protection and the protection of functional designs under the unregistered design scheme); Green Paper on the Protection of Utility Models in the Single Market, COM(95)370 final at 2 n.7 (distinguishing subject matter of design rights from the technical invention, which can be protected by utility model laws, on basis that design rights accorded protection to "the outward form of an object. . ."). For a thorough and insightful analysis, both of the EU proposals and utility model protection generally, see Mark D. Janis, *Second Tier Patent Protection*, 40 HARV. INT'L L. J. 151 (1999).

§ 3.04 Patent Law

[A] Beginnings of International Patent Cooperation

VENETIAN PATENT LAW OF THE 19TH MARCH 1474

There are in this city, and also there come temporarily by reason of its greatness and goodness, men from different places and most clever minds, capable of devising and inventing all manner of ingenious contrivances. And should it be provided, that the works and contrivances invented by them, others having seen them could not make them and take their honour, men of such kind would exert their minds, invent and make things which would be of no small utility and benefit to our State.

Therefore, decision will be passed that, by authority of this Council, each person who will make in this city any new and ingenious contrivance, not made heretofore in our dominion, as soon as it is reduced to perfection, so that it can be used and exercised, shall give notice of the same to the office of our Provisioners of Common. It being forbidden to any other in any territory and place of ours to make any other contrivance in the form and resemblance thereof, without the consent and licence of the author up to ten years.

And, however, should anybody make it, the aforesaid author and inventor will have the liberty to cite him before any office of this city, by which office the aforesaid who shall infringe be forced to pay him the sum of one hundred ducates and the contrivance be immediately destroyed. Being then in liberty of our Government at his will to take and use in his need any of said contrivances and instruments, with this condition, however, that no others than the authors shall exercise them.

STATUTE OF MONOPOLIES, 21 JAMES I, CH. 3 (England, 1623)
quoted in 1 Robinson on Patents 13 (1890)

An Act concerning monopolies and dispensations of penal laws and the forfeiture thereof:

I. Whereas your majesty, in the year 1610, published a book declaring that all grants of monopolies, and of the benefit of penal laws, and of the power of dispensing with law, and of compounding penalties, are contrary to law; and whereas your majesty then expressly commanded that no suitor should ever apply for such grants; and whereas, nevertheless, such grants have been applied for and allowed; Therefore to make void all these, and to prevent the like in time to come, may it please your majesty that it be declared and enacted by authority of this present parliament "that all monopolies and all commissions, grants, licenses, charters, and letters-patent, heretofore made or granted, or hereafter to be made or granted, to any person or persons...whatsoever, of or for the sole buying, selling, making, working, or using of anything, within this realm or the dominions of Wales, or of any other monopolies" and all licenses to do anything contrary to law, or to confer authority on others so to do... "are altogether contrary to the laws of this realm, and so are and shall be utterly void, and of none effect, and in no wise to be put in use or execution."

. . . .

VI. Provided also, and be it declared and enacted: That any declaration before mentioned shall not extend to any letters-patent and grants of privilege, of the term of fourteen years or under, hereafter to be made, of the sole working or making of any manner of new manufactures, within this realm, to the true and first inventor and inventors of such manufactures, which others, at the time of making such letters-patent and grant, shall not use, so as also they be not contrary to the law, nor mischievous to the state, by raising prices of commodities at home, or hurt of trade, or generally inconvenient; The said fourteen years to be accounted from the date of the first letters-patent or grant of such privilege, hereafter to be made; but that the same shall be of such force as they should be, if this act had never been made and of none other.

ERICH KAUFER, THE ECONOMICS OF THE PATENT SYSTEM 2-10 (1989)[*]

The practice of granting property rights in what we now call inventions had its historical roots in mining law. During the Middle Ages, the term "invention" had a meaning much closer to what we would now call "discovery," *e.g.*, of new ore resources, than the meaning accepted under modern patent law. In medieval Latin, "invenire" meant (accidental) discovery, while "ars" was used to connote derived technological know-how. Medieval orders in the archives of Innsbruck Austria consistently refer to "Perkwerks Erfyndung," that is, to the "invention" of mining sites. The Alps were an ore mining area from at least the time of the Celtic settlement. In such mining areas, there was a long common laws tradition concerning the mining, timber use, and water use property rights of those who were first to "invent" an ore site. As new ore locations were found in Saxony, Silesia, and Bohemia, the miners brought their unwritten common law with them. The law then became incorporated into the decisions of specialized mining courts and into the "Constitutiones Juris Metallici" promulgated by King Wenceslaus II in the year 1300. . . .

In 1409, Venice granted the German Henricus von Heslingen a privilege to exploit an ore mine and use needed water and timber according to the common law prevailing in Germany. In the following decades, Venetian ore mining grew rapidly, necessitating a more formalized legal statute. In 1488 the Venetian Senate promulgated the *Statuto Mineraria*.

. . . .

Meanwhile, institutions were also evolving to deal with "inventions"—often called "edificium et ingenium" in the Latin texts—of a more specifically technological character. They took two rather different forms. One important example was the privilege granted by the Venetian Senate in 1460 to a young German, Jacobus de Valperga, who had devised a new type of water pump. The grant stated that as long as Jacobus lived, no one could make the pump without an express license from Jacobus. Violation carried a penalty of 1,000 ducats and destruction of the offending machinery. However, Jacobus was obliged to grant licenses if reasonable royalties were offered. Thus, the focus was on preventing imitation of Jacobus' machine *without his permission*, and the privilege was limited by what we would now call a compulsory licensing provision. In contrast, another privilege granted in the same year to master engineer Guilielmus Lombardus reserved to Guilielmus exclusive monopoly rights in making certain furnaces, with no provision for "compulsory" licenses. The Venetian administrative practice distinguished between an invention privilege and a trade privilege. Jacobus asked for protection guaranteeing him license revenues from all who used his invention. Guilielmus, on the other hand, received a guarantee that no one could compete with him in selling the product that incorporated his invention.

Monopoly privileges, with or without licensing provisions, were not the only way Venice sought to foster technical advance. Venice's large and important naval weapons factory, the Arsenale, is not known to have conferred them. As the precursor of today's nationalized enterprise, the Arsenale instead attracted technically skilled persons by offering high salaries and benefits such as free housing.

As the 15th century progressed, Venice experienced a period of severe financial difficulties, partly because of its wars to extend its claims on the Italian Terra Firma and partly because of threats from the Turks. It therefore placed increasing emphasis on monopoly privileges as a substitute for government subsidies. In 1474, only a year after the Senate decided to build the Arsenale Novissimo, a formal patent code was promulgated. . . .

The code specified that the subject invention had to be proven workable and useful, if only by means of a model. . . . Also, no imitation was permitted for ten years without express permission from the inventor. However, the Republic retained the right to use the invention for its own purposes. An otherwise unauthorized use carried a penalty of one hundred ducats and destruction of the offending device. But the administrative practice that followed also included provisions for compulsory licensing and the revocation of patents not used commercially. Thus, the patent code, based in large part upon the decision in the matter of Jacobus de Valperga, must be seen as an instrument designed to attract engineers to the Republic. It was not an instrument to stimulate artisan production by granting monopolistic trade privileges . . . like the one issued to Guilielmus Lombardus.

As the grant of patents spread northward, and with the emergence of absolutist governments, tension mounted between grants with licensing provisions and those that conferred unconditional monopoly privileges, with or without some element of invention or innovation. Under the reign of Queen Elizabeth I in England, patent grants were used increasingly to implement mercantilist policy, and especially to benefit royal favorites. Parliament and the Crown clashed over who had, or ought to have, the prerogative of granting monopoly privileges. In 1623, Parliament prevailed decisively, passing the *Statute of Monopolies*. Among other privileges, patents were declared illegal, except for grants to the true and first inventor or inventors of a new manufacture. Newness had no international meaning; it was sufficient if the manufacture was new to England. The duration was to be fourteen years. This term was chosen because it encompassed the time it took to train two successive generations of apprentices, each serving a term of seven years. Thus, Parliament expressed its desire to protect the know-how accumulated by masters in implementing an invention.

In France, systematic use of patents as an instrument of mercantilist policy began in the middle of the 16th century. For the most part, privileges were granted only after a careful review of the benefits from encouraging a new trade. The monopoly restrictions were usually limited to a geographic boundary of ten miles, but narrower or wider territorial boundaries were sometimes set. In the first decades of the 18th century, such restrictions came increasingly to be used to protect established trades and manufacturers. Even before the Revolution, public opinion gravitated toward rejecting patents as contrary to the freedom of trade. To underline the break with the past brought about by the Revolution, the patent law of 1791 spoke only of "brevets d'inventions" and declared that the inventor had a natural property right to his invention. In this, the previous view of patents as a grant of royal privilege was replaced by a justification rooted in the rights of the citizen.

In the "Constituante" debate over French patent law, the British patent system, as it had evolved from the Statute of Monopolies, was referred to as a model case. It also became a model for British colonies in North America. Massachusetts passed a similar law in 1641. Connecticut followed suit in 1672. South Carolina (1691) was the first to speak of patents not as sovereign grants, but as a fulfillment of the rights of the inventor.

More than one hundred years passed before there were significant new developments. Then, in 1789, the American Constitution gave Congress the power:

> . . . to promote the progress of science and useful arts, by securing for limited times to authors and inventors the exclusive right to their respective writings and discoveries.

In 1790 the first U.S. federal patent law was promulgated. Like its predecessor in South Carolina, it rested in the premise that the inventor had a right to claim a patent on what he had invented. Furthermore, in order to ensure that patents were granted only for "new and useful" inventions, an official examination prior to the patent's issuance was required. In 1793, this prior examination was replaced by mere notification to the Secretary of State (initially, Thomas Jefferson). But in 1836, it was reinstituted, and it has been a part of the U.S. patent system, like most modern patent systems, ever since.

. . . .

In the German-speaking parts of Europe, monopoly privileges had a varied history. Empress Maria Theresa of Austria was unsympathetic, refusing to grant privileges because she found them "hoechst schaedlich" (highly detrimental). Her adversary, Frederik of Prussia, adopted a more receptive policy, granting numerous monopoly privileges for the introduction of new arts. Yet in Austria as in Prussia, monopoly privileges had been established in many trades as the nineteenth century dawned. There, as in the western European lands, they were widely disliked as misuses of royal prerogative.

This association between patents and monopoly privileges gave birth to an energetic anti-patent movement. The seeds were sown by the Napoleonic reordering of the German territories. Some territories in the Rhine area adopted the French patent law of 1791. The territories of southern Germany gave up the practice of privileged grants. But soon "polytechnical associations" were founded, lobbying for the introduction of patent laws and, especially in Bavaria and Wuerttemberg, for tariff protection. By 1825, both kingdoms had laws granting patents on inventions that were new to the kingdom.

Tension rose as Prussia began to dominate policy among the German territories. In 1806, after its defeat by Napoleon, Prussia instituted reforms under which a new kind of civil servant, nourished inter alia on the ideas of Adam Smith, gained power. The Prussian government pushed for free trade among the German territories, and as remnants of mercantilist policy, patents were seen as a barrier to free trade. By 1862, all tariffs had been abolished inside Germany. In that same year, a free trade treaty with France marked the high point of the free trade movement's influence. The Prussian government argued concurrently that all patent laws in the German territories should be abolished

A similarly strong anti-patent movement led to the repeal of the Dutch patent law in 1869. In 1872, the British House of Lords accepted a substantial revision of existing patent law. Between 1849 and 1863, the Swiss parliament rejected four petitions to introduce a patent law.

However, strong counter-forces were also in motion. Prussia was an agrarian state at the beginning of the 19th century. Between 1850 and 1870, the German territories, especially the Prussian ones, were industrializing rapidly. Industrial leaders like the Siemens brothers, one working in Berlin and the other in London, organized pro-patent support groups. Second, world exhibitions emerged, and participation in them became a matter of national prestige. Germany received its first genuine recognition as an industrial nation at the Paris exhibition of 1867. Potential American participants refused to participate in the Vienna exhibition of 1873 unless the German-nations agreed to provide provisional patent protection on the American inventions put on display. Third, the free trade movement in Prussia proved to have shallow roots. Since Austria under the Habsburg monarchy had adopted a strongly protectionist development policy, the creation of a German free trade area was a political tactic used by Prussia for excluding Austria from the German union. Once this goal was achieved, the free trade movement was supported less vigorously. Fourth, at the 1873 Vienna exhibition, a patent congress proposed to introduce into national patent laws strict compulsory licensing principles. To the extent that the proposal was accepted, it undermined the objection that patents were mere mercantilist monopoly privileges. Fifth and finally, the year 1873 marked the onset of a worldwide depression, which in turn precipitated a movement away from free trade and toward protectionism. Tariffs and patents now appeared to be important protectionist instruments.

With these changes, the anti-patent tide ebbed. In 1874, the British government backed off from the drastic patent reform proposal already approved by the House of Lords. In 1877, the German Reich adopted a patent law.

Switzerland played a wavering but pivotal role in the new patent law developments. Patent laws were rejected by popular referenda in Switzerland in 1866 and 1882. Nevertheless, Switzerland participated actively in drafting the Paris Convention, signed in 1883 by Belgium, Brazil, France, Guatemala, Italy, the Netherlands, Portugal, Spain, El Salvador, and Serbia as well as Switzerland. The Convention created mechanisms for world-wide patent grant coordination. Although it had no patent system of its own, Switzerland was charged with administering and supervising the Paris Convention. In accepting this role, the Swiss government agreed to initiate a domestic patent system as soon as possible. Meanwhile, Swiss public opinion was changing, in part because one of the largest Swiss industries, the watch industry, was experiencing intense competition from imitators. In July 1887, a Swiss patent statute was overwhelmingly approved in a referendum. However, because the newly emerging Swiss chemical industry still found it advantageous to imitate the technology of its more advanced German rivals, the Swiss law limited patentability to mechanical inventions only. This prompted the German Reich to threaten Switzerland with retaliatory tariffs. In 1907 Switzerland backed off, extending coverage under its patent law to chemical process inventions (but not product inventions).

EMERSON STRINGHAM, PATENTS AND GEBRAUCHMUSTER IN INTERNATIONAL LAW 36 (1934)

A Union of German Engineers 6th meeting in Braunschweig, 1863 urged the adoption of a German patent law. However, there was serious opposition to patents in the trading states of the German Zollverein. The Zollverein Treaty of 1842 made this anti-patent stance explicit. Conformably with Article III of this treaty, the parties pledged themselves not to grant patents under which the inventor would obtain the exclusive right: to import the patented object; to sell; to distribute, or finally to utilize. The patentees were permitted to prohibit only the manufacture of the object in the country concerned or the industrial use of machines, tools, or manufacturing processes. The basic tendency of all these provisions is obvious. A patentee possessed the exclusive right of producing the object in his own country but he was not permitted to break through the domestic customs boundary either directly by prohibiting import, or indirectly by prosecuting those who carried on trade with imported patented goods. . . . [P]atent law reflects the economic polarity of nationalism seeking to exclude foreign competition and internationalism seeking to enter foreign markets.

QUESTIONS

Is the right to exclude foreigners from a national market more important than the right of nationals to sell in foreign markets? To what extent are national patents today seen as a barrier to free trade, in league with tariffs? (The question of exhaustion of rights will be discussed *infra* Chapter 7 in connection with parallel importation of patented goods.)

[B]   The Development of International Patent Treaties

The United States first extended patent protection to foreigners in 1800, *See* Pennock v. Dialogue, 27 U.S. 1 (1829). Under the French patent law of 1791 as revised in 1844, the printing of a patent in the United States or another country automatically destroyed novelty in France. So by seeking patent protection in one country, an inventor jeopardized his chances for gaining protection in other countries, such as France, upon publication of the first filing. European states other than Germany established patent laws in the middle years of the nineteenth century as a lure to attract foreign technologies: Spain (1826), Portugal (1837), Austria (1852), Belgium (1854), Italy (1859). Switzerland never had a patent law until 1907. Holland, a trading state, established a patent law by statute in 1817, but abolished it in 1869. Sweden's law of 1859 was limited to nationals. The 1854 Belgian patent act is still in force.

Historical events in the 1870s impelled the industrializing nations of Europe and the United States toward harmonization of patent laws. What emerged from the discussions during that decade became the foundation of the modern international patent system as we know it.

[1]   The Making of the Paris Convention: the Congress of Vienna of 1873

In view of the great diversity of existing laws on the subject of patents for inventions, and the changes in the present international commercial relations, it is urgently important that the government seek, at the earliest possible date, to achieve an international accord on the protection of industrial property (patents for invention).

From the voeux of the Washington Conference of 1873.

HEINRICH KRONSTEIN & IRENE TILL, A REEVALUATION OF THE INTERNATIONAL PATENT CONVENTION[*]
12 LAW AND CONTEMPORARY PROBLEMS, 765, 766-76 (1947)

The United States entered the [Paris] Union in 1887; Germany, the last industrial power to join, did so on May 10, 1901. As often happens in the history of treaties the actual decisions were reached before the first country signed. The creative period of the Union was between 1872 and 1881. During this period the negotiations on the international patent convention were the battlefield for three opposing philosophies: (1) the anti-patent movement, aimed at the destruction of the patent system; (2) recognition of patents as private property; (3) the recognition of patents as an instrument of public policy. Certainly the issue of patents versus no-patents had to be disposed of first. The fight on this point marked the first battle between the United States and the newly organized Germany of Bismarck.

The initial invitation for an international conference on patent rights came from the Austrian Government in 1872. The invitation specifically stated, however, that the suggestion came from the United States:

> [F]ollowing a suggestion of the Government of the United States of America, the General Direction of the Universal Exposition intends to unite with the Exposition an International Congress, which shall discuss the question of patent right; should this discussion, as may be foreseen, induce a vote in favor of Patent protection, it will then be the task of this Congress, on the basis of the experience of various countries and the materials collected, to proceed to a declaration of fundamental principles for an International Reform of Patent Legislation.

American leadership in the conference was eagerly anticipated by the United States Commissioner of Patents. He wrote to the Secretary of the Interior on May 29, 1873:

> I regard the patent congress to be held at Vienna of the very greatest importance and the world looks to this government for the presentation of matters for consideration and discussion. If the American system can be properly presented before that Congress, discreetly and cautiously sustained with facts and figures, I feel confident that the best results can be expected.

The very fact of American parentage elevated the prestige of the conference. The proposal for international patent protection did not come from the semi-feudal country of Austria, conspicuously lacking in industrial development; it came from the United States, already at the forefront industrially and with the strongest patent system in the world.

The invitation stated the issue between the patent and the anti-patent forces in forthright manner:

> There exists today an antipatent movement which since 1860 has extended too far and the causes of which movement bear, in part at least, too much upon views which are generally acknowledged by the economical progress of our age, to justify at this time as hitherto a partial solution of that problem. The complete abolition of all Patents for inventions, such is the motto of this movement; Patent protection, the maintenance and improvement of the existing Patent law, if possible in simple form, and by international agreement: such is the watchword of the other. The present condition of Patent legislation in the most enlightened and progressive countries shows on which side the majority stands; with the exception of Switzerland and with her, Holland, which recently abolished her Patent law, the legislation of all the other Industrial States today recognizes the protection of Patents as a necessity.

Germany, as the leader of the anti-patent movement, is not mentioned in the invitation, reference being made only to Holland and Switzerland. There is no doubt, however, that it was the larger country which the organizers of the conference really had in mind. As early as 1868 Bismarck, as Chancellor of the North German Federation, had gone on record as hostile to any form of patent protection. On May 10, 1872, the German Parliament discussed, for the first time in the history of the German Reich, the patent problem. There the position of Bismarck was made even clearer. His representative announced that it would not be undesirable "if the Parliament would use the opportunity of the discussion to express itself in favor of the full abolition of patent protection;" in Bismarck's opinion, the example of Holland deserved to be copied. However, it was pointed out to the Parliament that public opinion in Germany might be unprepared for the step:

> [S]ince only people who have a private interest in patent protection can express their views in public . . . The Society of German Engineers has repeatedly and actively come out in favor of patent protection. However, not all engineers share this opinion; only considerations for influential interests prevent them from expressing their opinion in public.

Thus, in the summer of 1872, the issue was joined. The organizers of the conference were fully aware that, in a competitive business economy, the world could not live half with patents and half without patents. The invitation to the conference sets forth the interdependence among national patent systems in the following classical statement:

> We live no longer in the day of Industrial action, which is strictly confined and is removed from foreign competition, and where slow communication prevents or delays the utilization of inventions. We live at a time of liberal Customs policy; Steam and Electricity have newly united once isolated seats of industry in a way undreamt of; and the mutual exchange of goods shows today a magnitude which a generation ago one could not have imagined. Under such altered relations the Patent granted for an invention in one country becomes in fact a restriction unprofitable and obstructive, if the same invention without limitation or increase in price, becomes in an adjoining country common property. The artisan who in the one country must work with the auxiliary material there patented and therefore dearer in price, will suffer an essential injury as soon as the same material is produced in the other country, not only without restriction, but with a damaging competition. Moreover a continuance of the hitherto antagonistic views and measures would scarcely conduce to the preservation of general harmony; and if, for example, Patent protection were maintained in one country, so as to attract thereby skilled operatives from another, then the danger of disturbance of the International industrial balance might readily be apprehended. Such and similar inconveniences can only be met by the common action of all civilized States, disposed to the maintenance of Patent protection.

The American delegation to the Vienna conference was an able one. The Assistant Commissioner of Patents, J. M. Thatcher, headed the group; his experience and knowledge of the United States patent system gave him a leading role in the negotiations. Unlike many American delegations to international conferences, it was also well prepared. M. D. Leggett, Commissioner of Patents, recommended that our representative should: . . . Present and explain the American Patent System, calling special attention to:

> 1. The justice and expedience of granting patents for new and useful inventions to *original inventors*, and to such only.
>
> 2. The importance of thorough preliminary Official examination to determine the questions of novelty.
>
> 3. The influence of our Patent System upon the industrial interests of the country.
>
> 4. The liberal spirit of our Patent Laws towards the citizens of other countries.
>
> In addition, he should press as a matter of justice between nations, that:
>
> 1. Mere importers should not receive patents.

2. That patents granted in one country to citizens of another, should not be subject to such restrictions as to time and place of manufacture, as to render such patents comparatively worthless.

He of course should be instructed to make no concessions that can be interpreted as abandoning any of the essential features of our system.

Thatcher's own report indicates the tenor of the conference. He said:

It was the general, I may say universally expressed, opinion in the congress at Vienna that in order to secure the advancement of the mechanic arts in their own countries and to prevent the emigration of their most skilled artisans, it was necessary to secure a reform in European patent legislation.

Count Andrassy, the premier of the Austrian Government, put it in a very few words during an interview with the permanent committee when he said:

I look to England and I look to America, and I find that they are the foremost countries of the world in manufactures. I find also, upon examining their laws, that they have the best patent systems in the world.

Putting these two facts together, I conclude that the one is dependent upon the other, and therefore I am in favor of a thorough reorganization and revision of the patent laws of Austria.

The Vienna conference made this general attitude manifest in its set of resolutions. It declared that the existence of a patent law was a requirement "of all civilized nations;" and foresaw "great injury . . . inflicted upon countries which have no rational patent laws by the native inventive talent emigrating to more congenial countries where their labor is legally protected." The conference endorsed the "English, American, and Belgian patent laws, and the draft of a patent law prepared for Germany by the society of German engineers" (Bismarck's opponents!). One small bone was thrown to the opponents of an air-tight patent system. A recommendation provided:

It is advisable to establish legal rules, according to which the patentee may be induced, in cases in which the public interest should require it, to allow the use of his invention to all suitable applicants, for an adequate compensation.

Later this resolution was described by one of its drafters as mere propaganda against the enemies of patents.

Thus the Vienna conference was an outstanding American victory, won by a purposeful policy. It is an anticlimax to read in the interdepartmental correspondence that at the last moment the State Department lacked sufficient funds to send an American representative unless he could personally assume a substantial share of the cost of the trip.

Bismarck immediately found himself confronted with a combined attack from within and without Germany. The Society of German Engineers was already hard at work; and now it had the added prestige of powerful support from abroad. Bismarck was forced to retreat. In 1876 he called a committee of experts to study the patent situation. In February, 1877, he submitted a patent bill to Parliament. The eminent Charles Lyon-Cacn made the following observations on this development:

> A complete understanding of this important bill depends on an understanding of the principles which motivate the government. The government has never admitted that the institution of patents has anything to do with its ideas of justice. The government does not even seem to be convinced that the patent system actually favors the progress of industry. It suggested the passing of the bill only because Germany cannot stand isolated in the middle of all great nations which have patent statutes. In fact, the government in its memorandum explaining the new step stated: "Germany, resolved to suppress the patent system, could effectively take steps to this end only if other countries were expected to follow. This is, however, more than doubtful; and such a step would certainly result in the complete isolation of Germany for many years".

III.

The American victory in the issue of patent *versus* no-patent, decisive as it was, merely transferred the battlefront to the next stage. This was the issue of patents as private property rights as against patents as instrument of public policy. The impending struggle was foreseen in the American-Austrian discussions of 1872. The American Government opened the dispute by complaining against the Austrian principle providing for forfeiture of patent rights if local manufacturing were not begun within one year from the grant of the patent. Here was a clear statement of the issue. John Jay, then American Ambassador in Vienna, pointed out to the Austrian Minister for Foreign Affairs on March 17, 1872:

> It has been suggested that the differences in the statutes of different countries, in regard to patents, may be generally traced to a difference in the general view taken of the character and position of the patentee; whether he is looked upon as a monopolist who owes all his rights to exceptional law, and who must be jealously watched and severely restricted; or whether he is regarded as a public benefactor, who is to be tenderly and kindly treated. The legislation of Congress

has inclined more and more to the latter view; and, while adopting, as the true principle, that the inventor and public are both to be treated rationally, justly, and impartially, its tendency has been to give more and more liberally encouragement and assistance to useful inventors.

John Jay frankly assured Count Andrassy that the President would "cordially embrace this opportunity of cementing the friendship of the two countries and of advancing their common interests by a generous and harmonious policy"–if only Austria would modify its patent law in conformity with the United States statute and would agree to full reciprocity in matters of patents between the two countries.

This American view toward patents was novel. It stemmed from an actual faith that, in a competitive economy, patents under the control of private owners would not be subjected to abuse.[2]

The files of the United States Patent Office contain a constant reiteration of this theme; they reveal an absolute faith in the beneficent effects of an uncontrolled patent system. It was precisely this freedom, it was believed, which accounted for the rapid technological advance in the United States.[3]

In consequence, the Patent Office violently opposed any kind of governmental interference–whether against foreign inventors in this country or American inventors abroad. At every opportunity in the correspondence of the patent commissioners with foreign patent offices–through State Department channels

---

[2]Here and there some doubts were raised in the faith. At a Senate patent hearing in 1877, Senator Wasleigh said bluntly, "While a man has a right to put his horse into his own barn, and not use it himself, he has no right to lock up his invention and let nobody use it. It is his duty to let his invention go out to the world." The reply of A.H.Walker, patent attorney, is a statement of the dominant American position:

"He has no such duty with reference to the period of his monopoly at all. The only duty he has is to spread the description of the invention on the records of the Patent Office, so that *after* the monopoly has expired, whether it be in fourteen, or seventeen, or twenty-one years, it will be free to the world. He has no duty publish that invention, or introduce it during the life of the monopoly; and if he chooses to let it die as useless, there is no law or reason why he shall not be permitted to do so. . . . As I understand the theory of the law, it is his *absolute* property during the life of the monopoly and is *not* qualified. Indeed, that is the language of the Constitution itself, viz., that the right is exclusive. . . ." Arguments before the Committee on Patents of the U.S. Senate and House of Representatives, Misc. Doc. No. 50, 45th Cong., 2d Sess. 36 (1878).

[3]At the 1877 patent hearing, J.J.Storrow, patent attorney, testified: "Sir William Thomson went home from our Centennial Exhibition, and just as he got home he appeared before the British Association, before the section of steam-engineering, of which he is the president, and, in giving them an account of what he had seen in this country, he called their attention very sharply to the effect of patent laws on the improvement of labor-saving machinery. He told them that unless the countries of Europe speedily amended their patent laws, and unless they amended them in a contrary direction to the bill pending in Parliament, they must understand that they would lose their manufacturing supremacy and that America would take it from them". . . . Storrow goes on to quote approvingly the remarks of Hulse, English judge of textile machinery at the Centennial: "As regards extent of invention and ingenuity, the United States was far ahead of other nations . . . The extraordinary extent of ingenuity and invention existing in the United States, and manifested throughout the exhibition, I attribute to the natural aptitude of the people, fostered and stimulated by an admirable patent law and system, and to the appreciation of inventions by the people generally." Arguments before the Committee on Patents, Misc. Doc. No. 50, 45th Cong., 2d Sess. 318 (1878).

or in direct negotiation–the view is developed that only international cooperation and mutual recognition of private property in patents can serve the final aim of the highest technological advance everywhere. The constant reiteration of this gospel by the most highly industrialized country in the world was bound to have an enormous effect.

But such an approach was in direct conflict with established tradition abroad. The American philosophy was genuinely new. True, the speeches of the French Revolution were aflame with this doctrine; Mirabeau exultantly speaks of inventions and patents as private property equal to any other form of private property. But, in fact, the French never drew the logical conclusion from these theories. The patent statute of France after the Revolution provided that patents should be forfeited in the event that patented goods were imported into France. Such a provision was a clear denial of the private property aspect of a patent, and made patents an instrument of public policy to bring manufacturing plants into France. This law still existed at the time of the Vienna conference.

The English patent statute of 1623 had the same purpose. . . . Obviously, the American view expressed in John Jay's letter had nothing in common with the traditional European approach. The question for the Germans–once they had abandoned their original hostility to the patent system–was which view they would adopt. Quite naturally they turned to the early English position. They were newcomers in the industrial hierarchy; they had all of the anti-monopolistic attitudes of the upstart competitor. They immediately adopted the position that patents should not be granted as a matter of right to every inventor, but should be permitted only in those fields in which the public interest justified the grant. Nor were they prepared to look upon patents as private property, to be granted to outsiders without limitation. Patents were a qualified right, subject to governmental interference in the interest of the nation.

Bismarck's committee of experts meeting in 1876 was fully dominated by this older view. One of its members was founder of the Siemens Combine. He was already concerned about the possibility that American Edison and British Thomson-Houston would take out many patents in Germany–before the German firms could develop their own research. He said bluntly:

> You might consider a rule that patentees are bound to grant licenses as an interference with the right of the inventor; but such a rule is absolutely necessary. The interests of [German] industries require that licenses be made available as a matter of right. Today industry is developing rapidly; and as a result monopolization of inventions and abuse of patent rights will inevitably expose large segments of industry to serious injury. The government must protect industry against these dangers. From abroad another danger may arise. Inventive work is far more developed in England, United States and France than in Germany. Up to the present the number of patents taken out in Germany by foreigners has been small because the scope of protection given to the inventor has been insufficient. New legislation will lead to a substantial increase of foreign patentees. We shall experience a wave of foreign–particularly American–patent

applications. These patents will not be taken out in order to protect industrial plants established or to be established in Germany; they will be taken out to monopolize production abroad. These articles will be imported into this country.

Such a danger must be met. It is not enough to provide that foreign patentees be required to submit "evidence" that they have established a plant in Germany. Such evidence may be mere "shadow"; they can merely keep a small domestic production going to maintain their patents. The French have an effective weapon–a rule that patents shall be forfeited if an inventor imports or permits others to import patented goods. However, the French method is inconvenient to trade interests, and would meet serious objection here. The requirement of actual manufacture under the patent would be excellent if the patentee were forced to show production in such quantities that domestic needs are actually met.

The same end can best be achieved by requiring that licenses be granted. The administration of this plan may be difficult. But the administrative agencies and the courts should be able to meet the difficulties and to come to a modus vivendi. Royalties should be based on the importance of the inventions. . . . Siemens ended with the proposal that licenses of right should be made available at the end of the fifth year of patent protection. He felt that any other arrangement would be inconsistent with the public interest.

This same meeting was attended by one of the founders of the Hoechst Farbwerke, predecessor of I. G. Farben. Bruening took the position that the entire chemical industry should lie outside of patent protection. He said:

In the chemical industry the most harmful effects of patents are made clearly evident. Patents in France and England prevented the development of new chemical branches such as the manufacturing of aniline and alizarin dyes. Invention in chemical technology consists largely in an idea, and the practical exploitation of this idea usually involves enormous difficulties. In England and France patents for the manufacturing of aniline and alizarin dyes have been issued to the inventors who have not succeeded in the effective exploitation of their invention. In those countries monopolistic organizations came into existence which could not themselves produce and their major function was to prevent the development of other plants. In Germany, however, the chemical industry was able to expand because no patent protection prevented the free play of competition.

In the meantime the American view of patents as private property came into popularity in other countries. Between 1873, the year of the Vienna conference, and 1878, the year of the Paris convention, the American view prevailed in all the following formula was submitted at the Paris meeting:

> The right of inventors and industrial creators in their own work or
> the right of the industrialists in their trademarks is a property right
> which has its basis in natural law. The law enacted by each nation
> does not create these rights but only regulates them.

The Swiss delegation joined issue by offering a counter motion:

> The rights of the inventor and creative worker are a creation of
> equitable and useful principles of the law of each nation which should
> reconcile this right of the inventor, based on the grant of a temporary
> monopoly, with the rights of society.

The Swiss motion was voted down and the "property" motion won, though the
clause "which has its basis in natural law" was eliminated.

Once an international convention declared inventions and patents a type of
private property, it was only logical to grant to the "owners" of such property
equal protection under the law, whatever their nationality might be. In the
philosophy prevailing at the end of the nineteenth century, no principle was
more sacred than the mutual protection of the vested interests of private
property. Once patents were recognized as a type of private property there was
no possible justification for the continuance of the forfeiture penalty for
importation of patented goods or for the harsh rules respecting working clauses.
The French system broke down almost immediately, and the working clauses
gradually fell into disuse. The priority rule made its obsequious entry as a
simple convenience for the property owner.

Germany continued to remain outside of the convention during the Eighties
and mid-Nineties. In that country the scope of the patent grant was limited in
the interest of encouraging further invention, and patents were subjected to
compulsory licensing. But in 1897, at the Brussels convention, Germany
appeared and prepared the way for her retreat. One of her major concerns was
the elimination of the working clause. To this end she won the ardent support
of the United States.

In 1901 Germany joined the Union. In a short time she became, along with
the United States, the most ardent defender of the Union. In the later
conferences the two countries worked together effectively to strengthen the
protections accorded the patentee. In fact, the International Patent Convention
can now almost be referred to as an American-German patent alliance.

NOTES AND QUESTIONS

(1) **The Forfeiture Principle**. The Congress of Vienna of 1873, at which the
French government was not represented, adopted the principle of preliminary
examination and the policy of no forfeiture for failure to work the invention
within a country. This was countered by the French at the Paris Congress of

1878 which adopted the principle of forfeiture for nonworking of the invention within and eliminated preliminary examination. This development led to a deadlock between the parties on most substantive provisions in the negotiations leading up to the eventual signing of the Paris Convention in 1883. What remained was virtually all procedural: the national treatment provision of Article 2 and the right of priority of Article 4, with the provisions on forfeiture, requirements to work the patent within any country where patent protection was sought forming the next stage of international negotiations. The history of Article 5 will be discussed below.

(2) **National Treatment or Reciprocity**. At the time of the Paris Convention, Switzerland participated actively although it did not have and had never had a patent law. Under the principles of national treatment enshrined in Article 1, Switzerland was not required to protect inventions by patents even though Swiss inventors would enjoy patent protection in other countries of the union which did provide patent protection. Is this fair? Efficient? Patent laws were rejected by popular referenda in Switzerland in 1866 and 1882. When Switzerland agreed to administer and supervise the Paris Convention, it also agreed to enact a patent law. Such a law passed overwhelmingly in 1887 (by referendum) with the support of the Swiss watch industry, but chemical processes were excluded until 1907, when the law was changed due to threats of tariff retaliation from Germany, where the chemical industry was strong. (The examination of inventions in the watch industry arts is still treated as a special case under Swiss law.) Does this example indicate the strength of national treatment or its opposite, reciprocity, as the basis for international recognition of rights?

(3) **International Public Policy?** Putting the question another way, to what extent is an international agreement providing patent protection for foreign nationals a question of reciprocal national self-interest and to what extent is it international public policy? Is it a "compact between the individual countries party to it with reciprocal rights and obligations, or an instrument seeking to regulate interests, claims, and demands pressing upon the national and international level?" 1 STEPHEN P. LADAS, PATENTS, TRADEMARKS AND RELATED RIGHTS: NATIONAL AND INTERNATIONAL PROTECTION 12 (1975).

(4) **The Inventor as Patent Applicant**. At the Washington Patent Conference of 1874, the U.S. position was that "only the inventor himself, or his legal representative, should be entitled to a patent." At the same time, "the applicant in German law was not required to be himself the inventor, patents were granted without any question of authorship to the first comer." STRINGHAM, *supra*, at 53, 144. Is this an ideological or a practical distinction? This will be discussed further below in the context of Article 4*ter* of the Paris Convention.

[2] The Paris Convention of 1883 and the Right of Priority

Notwithstanding false starts and setbacks during the decade-long course of deliberations leading to the signing of the Paris Convention in 1883, its legacy has been an unmitigated success. Article 1 created the Paris Union, the deliberative body of the convention. As noted above, although it had no patent system of its own, Switzerland was charged with administering and supervising the Paris Convention and agreed to initiate a domestic patent system as soon as possible. WIPO became a specialized agency within the United Nations Organization system in 1974. That event ushered in a new period in international intellectual property law, as the post-colonial states of Africa and Asia became participants in what had up until then been a club of developed nations.

Articles 2 (national treatment) and 4 (right of priority) of the Paris Convention form the bedrock of the international patent system. The right of priority includes priority of invention in the U.S. first-to-invent system and priority of application in the first-to-file system employed in the rest of the world. Friction between the first to invent system and the first to file system over the right of priority must be dealt with to explore how inventors from first to file countries are treated in a first to invent system and vice versa. The principles of national treatment and right of priority are inseparable.

The first to file system is simpler because it eliminates the need for costly interference proceedings. According to Article 4(3) of the Strasbourg Convention of 1963, and EPC Article 54(3), an unpublished patent application is viewed as part of the prior art for purposes of determining novelty of an invention in a later filed application. This is necessitated by the very logic of a first-to-file patent system. There are two main motivations behind the first-to-file systems both of which are based upon economic efficiency. First, there is the incentive of the "race to the Patent Office," which encourages inventors to disclose their inventions to the public earlier rather than later. In the first-to-file system, patent applications are generally published after eighteen months, and competitors are blessed with relatively inexpensive and timely access to patent information. A second motive is to increase certainty as to patent ownership and thereby decrease legal transaction costs, since interference proceedings are eliminated. The motives behind the U.S. first-to-invent system are more complex, and relate to what are genuinely perceived to be the venerable traditions and exceptionalism of the U.S. patent system.

A key development in the early establishment of international patent law was the adoption in 1883 of the principle of "convention priority" in Article 4 of the Paris Convention. Under this principle, the date of a patent application in one member state is accepted as the date for establishing priority of invention for that applicant in any of the other member states where a counterpart application is filed within a period of months (originally six, and now twelve) in the second country. A certain amount of friction has arisen between the United States, with its first-to-invent system, and countries which have a first-to-file system, because the fundamental differences between the two systems are difficult to reconcile.

35 U.S.C. §102. CONDITIONS FOR PATENTABILITY; NOVELTY

A person shall be entitled to a patent unless–

. . . .

(e) the invention was described in a patent granted on an application for patent by another filed in the United States before the invention thereof by the applicant for patent, or

. . . .

(g) before the applicant's invention thereof the invention was made in this country by another who had not abandoned, suppressed, or concealed it. In determining priority of invention there shall be considered not only the respective dates of conception and reduction to practice of the invention, but also the reasonable diligence of one who was first to conceive and last to reduce to practice, from a time prior to conception by the other.

PARIS CONVENTION, ARTICLE 4 (1883)

A. (1) Any person who has duly applied for a patent . . . in one of the countries of the Union, or his legal representative or assignee, shall enjoy *for the purposes of registration in other countries* a right of priority during the periods hereinafter stated.

(2) Any filing having the value of a formal national filing by virtue of the internal law of each country of the Union or of international treaties concluded among several countries of the Union shall be recognized as giving rise to a right of priority.

B. Consequently, subsequent filing in one of the other countries of the Union before the expiration of these Periods shall not be invalidated *through any acts accomplished in the interval, as, for instance, by another filing,* by publication of the invention or the working thereof, by the sale of copies of the design or model, or by use of the trade mark, and these facts cannot give rise to any right of third parties or any personal possession. The rights acquired by third parties before the day of the first application on which priority is based shad be reserved by the internal legislation of each country of the Union. [emphasis added]

. . . .

APPLICATION OF HANS HILMER
359 F.2d 859 (CCPA 1966)

[Habicht first won an interference over Hilmer in which he was held to have a right of priority on a single count (a "count" refers to subject matter corresponding to a claim) as of the date of his original Swiss application on January 24, 1957. Hilmer had filed his original application in Germany on July 31, 1957. Then Habicht filed his U.S. counterpart application on January 23, 1958. Finally, Hilmer filed his U.S. counterpart application on July 25, 1958. Habicht's disclosure included additional subject matter which Hilmer disclosed and claimed. The examiner rejected Hilmer's application as obvious by combining the Habicht disclosure with another reference. The Patent Office Board of Appeals affirmed, and held that Habicht's disclosure had effect as prior art as of his foreign filing date in Switzerland, under 35 U.S.C. § 119, which is entitled 'Benefit of Earlier Filing Date in Foreign Countries: Right of Priority'. The Court of Customs and Patent Appeals reversed, holding that Section 119 only deals with "right of priority" and does not confer status as "prior art", and so does not provide for the use of the entire contents of a U.S. patent application which matures into a patent as a reference effective as of its convention priority date for the purpose of defeating another U.S. patent under 35 USC Section 102(e).]

RICH, JUDGE. . . . A patent may be 'entitled' to a foreign filing date for some purposes and not for others, just as a patent may be 'used' in two ways. A patent owner uses his patent as a legal right to exclude others, granted to him under 35 U.S.C. § 154. Others, wholly unrelated to the patentee, use a patent, not as a legal right, but simply as evidence of prior invention or prior art, *i.e.*, as a 'reference.' This is not an exercise of the patent right. This is how the Patent Office is 'using' the Habicht patent. These are totally different things, governed by different law, founded on different theories, and developed through different histories. . . . [T]he board said:

> The Examiner insists, however, that the effective date of the Habicht patent is January 24, 1957, the date of an application filed in Switzerland which is claimed by Habicht under 35 USC § 119. Appellants have not overcome this earlier date of Habicht. The issue is hence presented of whether the foreign priority date of a United States patent can be used as the effective filing date of the patent when it is used as a reference (and this is the second statement of the issue by the board.) Our conclusion is that the priority date governs.
> . . . .

This is the decision alleged to be in error. We think it was error. . . . While it may be that the world is shrinking and the very concept of 'foreign' should be abolished for the good of mankind, this is not a constitution we are expounding but specific statutes enacted to accomplish specific purposes, the meaning of which should stay put, absent intervening Congressional modifications, for well-understood reasons. . . . The board's conclusion is that the foreign priority date of a U.S. patent is its effective date as a reference. . . . [T]he board's statement is:

> Our conclusion is arrived at simply by considering sections 102(e) and the first paragraph of section 119 of the statute together...
>
> Section 119 refers to two applications for the same invention stemming from the same inventor, one a first application filed in a foreign country and the other a later application filed in the United States. . . . Section 119 provides that under the specified circumstances, and subject to the requirements of the second paragraph which are not in question here, the second application, filed in the United States, 'shall have the same effect' as it would have if filed in the United States on the date on which the application was filed in the foreign country. This language is plain; it gives the application the status of an application filed in the United States on a particular date. Section 102(e) provides that a patent may not be obtained if the invention was described in a patent granted on an application for patent by another filed in the United States before the invention thereof by the applicant. This paragraph makes the filing date of a U.S. patent (note the omission of 'in the United States') the effective date as a reference. It refers to an application filed in the United States and since section 119 provides that the application shall have the same effect as if filed in this country on a particular date, these two provisions must be read together and the filing date of the foreign application becomes the effective date of the United States reference patent.

This is so plausible that one's impulse is to say "Q.E.D." We find the reasoning at fault, however, and the interpretation untenable. To discuss it we must have section 119 before us, insofar as applicable:

> § 119. Benefit of earlier filing date in foreign country; right of priority. An application for patent for an invention filed in this country by any person who has, or whose legal representatives or assigns have, previously regularly filed an application for a patent for the same invention in a foreign country which affords similar privileges in the case of applications filed in the United States or to citizens of the United States, *shall have the same effect* as the same application would have if filed in this country on the date on which the application for patent for the same invention was first filed in such foreign country, if the application in this country is filed within twelve months from the earliest date on which such foreign application was filed; *but* no patent shall be granted on any application for patent for an invention which had been patented or described in a printed publication in any country *more than one year before the date of the actual filing* of the application in this country,

or which had been in public use or on sale in this country more than
one year prior to such filing.

No application for patent shall be entitled *to his right of priority*
unless (here follows the requirement for filing certain papers in the
Patent Office and claiming priority not in question here, as the board
held) * * *.[Emphasis ours]

The board's construction is based on the idea that the language of the statute
is plain, that it means what it says, and that what it says is that the application
filed abroad is to have the *same effect* as though it were filed here-- *for all
purposes.* We can reverse the statement to say that the actual U.S. application
is to have the same effect as though it were filed in the U.S. on the day when the
foreign application was filed, the whole thing being a question of effective date.
We take it either way because it makes no difference here.

Before getting into history, we note first that there is in the very words of the
statute a refutation of this literalism. It says 'shall have the same effect' and
it then says 'but' for several situations it shall *not* have the same effect, namely,
it does not enjoy the foreign date with respect to any of the patent-defeating
provisions based on publication or patenting anywhere in the world or public
use or being on sale in this country *more than one year before the date of actual
filing in this country.*

As to the other statute involved, we point out that the words of section 102(e),
which the board 'simply' reads together with section 119, also seem plain.
Perhaps they mean precisely what *they* say in specifying, as an express
patent-defeating provision, an application by another describing the invention
but only as of the date it is *'filed in the United States.'*

The great logical flaw we see in the board's reasoning is in its premise (or is
it an a priori conclusion?) that 'these two provisions must be read together.'
Doing so, it says [Section] 119 in effect destroys the plain meaning of 102(e) but
the board will not indulge the reverse construction in which the plain words of
102(e) limit the apparent meaning of 119. We see no reason for reading these
two provisions together and the board has stated none. We believe, with the
dissenting board member, that [Sections] 119 and 102(e) deal with unrelated
concepts and further that the historical origins of the two sections show neither
was intended to affect the other, wherefore they should not be read together in
violation of the most basic rule of statutory construction, the 'master rule,' of
carrying out the legislative intent. . . .

SECTION 119

We shall now take up the history and purpose of section 119. The board
opinion devotes the equivalent of four pages in the printed record to a scholarly
and detailed review of the history of section 119 with all of which we agree,
except for the interwoven conclusions as to its meaning as it bears on the
effective date of a U.S. patent used as a reference.

The board shows that the predecessor statute (R.S. 4887), containing the words 'shall have the same force and effect,' was enacted March 3, 1903 (32 Stat. 1225). Theodore Roosevelt signed it into law. The bill was drafted and proposed by a Commission created by Act of Congress in 1898 (30 Stat. 431) to study the effect of the Convention of Paris for the Protection of Industrial Property of 20th March 1883, which was under revision at Brussels even as the Commission deliberated, the revision being adopted at Brussels on 14th December 1900. (It was last revised at Lisbon on 31st October 1958.) The Commission made a report November 27, 1900, printed in 1902, entitled 'Report of the Commissioners Appointed to Revise the Laws Relating to Patents, Trademarks, and Trade Names, with Reference to Existing Conventions and Treaties,' which is fairly descriptive of its purpose. The section entitled 'The Revision of the Patent Law,' which we have read, extends from page 6 to page 39. It begins by saying (p. 6):

> We have found it desirable in considering the question of revision of the patent law to first consider what changes in the law are needed to give full force and effect to the treaty obligations which the United States has undertaken touching the protection of inventions made by the subjects or citizens of certain foreign countries.

Under the heading 'Priority Under the Convention,' it says: The second provision of the Convention to be noticed, and one which may be of very great advantage to those of our citizens who desire to secure patents in foreign countries for their inventions, is that contained in article 4, and relates to the so called 'delay of priority,' or 'period of priority.'

It then explained that in most countries no valid patent can be obtained if before the application is filed, the invention has been described in a printed publication, either in the country of application or even, as in the case of France and six other countries, in any country; that the same was true as to public use of the invention; and that the convention gives applicants in member countries a period (then 7 months, soon extended to 12) in which they can file applications in other countries after the filing in their own country and obtain valid patents notwithstanding publication or use in the interval and before the filing of the foreign application. This, it explained, is the 'delay of priority.' In plain English, it was the right of an applicant to have the foreign application treated at law as prior to the intervening publication or public use, though in fact it was not, by giving a right to that applicant to delay filing in the foreign country, instead of filing simultaneously with the home application, yet have it treated as though filed on the date of the home application. This is what today we call simply 'Convention priority,' or just 'priority.' The foreign filing date is the 'convention date' or the 'priority date.' This priority right was a protection to one who was trying to obtain patents in foreign countries, the protection being against patent-defeating provisions of national laws based on events intervening between the time of filing at home and filing abroad. Under the heading 'Recapitulation of Advantages Secured by the Convention,' the Commission said, so far as relevant here:

The advantages to our citizens in the matter of patents directly afforded by the convention may be thus recapitulated.

First. The enjoyment in foreign countries of equal rights with subjects or citizens of those countries.

Second. The 'delay of priority' of seven months within which to file applications abroad after filing in this country.

Third. The privilege of introducing articles embodying the invention manufactured in this country into foreign countries to a certain extent without thereby causing the forfeiture of the patents taken out there.

Note the emphasis repeatedly placed in the Commission Report on advantages to United States citizens. It was felt we should do what was necessary to comply with the reciprocity provisions to enjoy the benefits of the convention for our own citizens. It was also believed that by reason of Opinions of Attorneys General, Vol. 19, 273, 'the International Convention, in so far as the agreements therein contained are not in accordance with the present laws of the United States, is without force and effect; that it is not self-executing, but requires legislation to render it effective ... and ... it is our opinion that such legislation should be adopted. . . .' (Report p.19.) Specific to the question here, the Commission Report says:

We are, therefore, of the opinion that an amendment to the law should be made, providing that the foreign application shall have, in case an application is filed in this country by the applicant abroad within the specified period, the same effect as if filed here on the day it was filed abroad.

The board thinks this 'shows the intention of the Commissioners' to create 'a status of (an application) having been filed in the U.S. for all purpose. . . .' In the context of this case, that means for the purpose of using a U.S. patent, obtained with a claim of priority, as a prior art patent to defeat the right of a third party to a patent on subject matter which does not patentably distinguish from anything that happens to be disclosed in such patent–or at least from anything disclosed 'relevant to the (there) claimed invention,' depending on which recent board opinion one looks at. We have read every word of the Commission Report looking for any suggestion of such a concept and have found none. All the board found was the above quotation. We deem it wholly inadequate as a basis for finding an intent to create a 'status' for an application–to say nothing of the patent granted thereon–'for all purposes.' There are other factors to consider which negative any such legislative intent.

There is another sentence in the Commission Report we should consider. . . . It called attention to the fact that in most foreign countries the patent is granted to the first to apply and said:

The Convention has created an exception to the rule and made an application in any State of the Union for the Protection of Industrial Property of the same effect as an application in the country where an application is subsequently made within the time specified as a period of priority.

This couples very nicely with the wording of the first recommendation for a change in U.S. laws on page 27 where it was said:

First. The application for a patent filed within seven [extended to 12] months of the filing of an application for a patent for the same invention in any foreign country which is a party to the International Convention should be given the same force as regards the question of priority that it would have if filed on the date on which the foreign application was filed.

The Commission, page 36, recommended proposed legislation, which is, in substance, the amendment to R.S. 4887 which was passed and is, with no change in substance, what we have today in section 119. The proposed bill in the Commission Report was entitled 'A Bill to give effect to treaty stipulations relating to letters patent for inventions.' The Act passed was entitled 'An Act To effectuate the provisions of the additional act of the international convention for the protection of industrial property.' Throughout, the same phrase has always appeared, 'shall have the same force and effect,' until it was simplified in the 1952 codification to 'shall have the same effect.' This change was mere modernization in legislative drafting. The Revisers Note to the section says: 'The first paragraph is the same as the present law with changes in language.' The Federico Commentary on the 1952 Act, 35 U.S.C.A., says (p. 29):

This so-called right of priority was provided for in the second paragraph of R.S. 4887 which is the basis for the first paragraph of section 119 of this title. . . . (he here states the 4 conditions for obtaining the right) . . . The new statute made no changes in these conditions of the corresponding part of the old statute except to revise the language slightly. . . .

We need not guess what Congress has since believed to be the meaning of the disputed words in section 119, for it has spoken clearly. World wars interfere with normal commerce in industrial property. The one-year period of priority being too short for people in 'enemy' countries, we had after World War I a Nolan Act (41 Stat. 1313, Mar. 3, 1921) and after World War II a Boykin Act. Foreign countries had reciprocal acts. One purpose was to extend the period of priority. House Report No. 1498, January 28, 1946, by Mr. Boykin, accompanied H.R. 5223 which became Public Law 690 of the 79th Cong., 2d Sess., Aug. 8, 1946, 60 Stat. 940. Section 1 of the bill, the report says, was to extend 'the so-called period of priority,' which then existed under R.S. 4887. On p. 3 the report says:

> In this connection, it may be observed that the portion of the statute which provides that the filing of a foreign application—shall have the same force and effect as the same application would have if filed in this country on the date on which the application for patent for the same invention, discovery, or design was first filed in such foreign country—is intended to mean 'shall have the same force and effect,' etc., insofar as applicant's right to a patent is concerned. This statutory provision has no bearing upon the right of another party to a patent except in the case of an interference where the two parties are claiming the same patentable invention.

U.S. Code Congressional Service 1946, p. 1493.

We emphasize none of those words because we wish to emphasize them all. We cannot readily imagine a clearer, more definitive statement as to the legislature's own view of the words 'same effect,' which now appear in section 119. This statement flatly contradicts the board's views. The board does not mention it. . . .

For the foregoing reasons, we are clearly of the opinion that section 119 is not to be read as anything more than it was originally intended to be by its drafters, the Commission appointed under the 1898 Act of Congress, namely, a revision of our statutes to provide for a right of priority in conformity with the International Convention, for the benefit of United States citizens, by creating the necessary reciprocity with foreign members of the then Paris Union.

The board has mentioned that it was not limited in its terms to that treaty, which is true, so that it also functions relative to other treaties and reciprocal laws. We are unable to deduce from this any intent to affect the date as of which U.S. reference patents are effective. Nor can we do so by reason of another 'deviation' from the Convention the board finds in section 4887 (now 119) as to the protection of third parties.

SECTION 102(e)

[The Court then discusses the rule established in *Alexander Milburn Co. v. Davis-Bournonville Co.*, 270 U.S. 390 (1926) and its enactment into 35 USC Section 102(e), concerning prior art which was not publicly known at the time of a patent application–so-called "secret prior art."]

We need not go into the reasoning of the *Milburn* case, which has its weaknesses, because all that matters is the rule of law it established: That a complete description of an invention in a U.S. patent application, filed before the date of invention of another, if it matures into a patent, may be used to show that that other was not the first inventor. This was a patent-defeating, judge-made rule and now is section 102(e). The rule has been expanded somewhat subsequent to 1926 so that the reference patent may be used as of its U.S. filing date as a general prior art reference. . . .

What has always been pointed out in attacks on the *Milburn* rule, or in attempts to limit it, is that it uses, as prior knowledge, information which was secret at the time as of which it is used–the contents of U.S. patent applications which are preserved in secrecy, generally speaking, 35 U.S.C. § 122. This is true, and we think there is some validity to the argument that that which is secret should be in a different category from knowledge which is public. Nevertheless we have the rule. However, we are not disposed to extend that rule, which applies to the date of filing applications in the United States, the actual filing date when the disclosure is on deposit in the U.S. Patent Office and on its way, in due course, to publication in an issued patent.

The board's new view, as expressed in this case . . . has the practical potential effect of pushing back the date of the unpublished, secret disclosures, which ultimately have effect as prior art references in the form of U.S. patents, by the full one-year priority period of section 119. We think the *Milburn* rule, as codified in section 102(e), goes far enough in that direction. We see no valid reason to go further, certainly no compelling reason.

We have seen that section 119 originated in 1903 and that its purpose was to grant protective priority rights so that the United States might be a participating member in the International Convention by giving reciprocal priority rights to foreign applicants with respect to the obtaining of patents. We have also seen that section 102(e) was the codification of a court-developed patent-defeating rule based on a statutory requirement that an applicant's invention must not have been previously known by others in this country. We see no such relation between these two rules of law as requires them to be read together and it is our view that section 119 should not be so read with 102(e) as to modify the express limitation of the latter to applications 'filed in the United States.' . . .

Section 102(e) was a codification of the *Milburn* doctrine. The *Milburn* case accorded a U.S. patent effect as a reference as of its U.S. filing date and stated that the policy of the statute on domestic inventions 'cannot be applied to foreign affairs.' No foreign date was involved in the case. The codifying statute specifies that the date as of which the patent has effect is the date of filing 'in the United States.'

R.S. 4887, predecessor of section 119, was in effect from 1903 to 1952 when it was incorporated unchanged in the present statutes. An examination of the legislative history of that statute fails to reveal a scintilla of evidence that it was ever intended to give 'status' to an application or to serve as a patent-defeating provision except insofar as the application, or patent issuing thereon, becomes involved in a priority contest. The *Milburn* rule, under which U.S. patents are used as prior art references for all matter disclosed in them as of their U.S. filing dates has been consistently and continuously applied since its inception in 1926, if not earlier under lower court decisions, by the United States Patent Office, the agency charged with the administration of the patent system, in accordance with the view . . . that R.S. 4887, and later section 119, does not make a U.S. patent effective as a reference as of a foreign priority date to which it may be entitled. . . . [S]ection 119 does not affect the express provision of 102(e) as to filing 'in the United States' and the decision of the board that the Swiss filing date of Habicht is the effective date of his U.S. patent as a reference must be reversed.

[The Court remanded the case for the Board to clarify its position on two remaining claims in the application, the validity of which had not been previously decided. The Board rejected them as obvious based on Habicht's foreign filing under 35 U.S.C. §§ 102(g), 119, and 104. The CCPA again reversed (*In re Hilmer*, 424 F.2d 1108 (CCPA 1970), "*Hilmer II*"), holding that the "subject matter" of Habicht's claim was prior art, if at all, as of the application's U.S. filing date, and could not be cited as prior art against Hilmer.]

PATENT COOPERATION TREATY, ARTICLE 64(4)

(a) Any State whose national law provides for prior art effect of its patents as from a date before publication, but does not equate for prior art purposes the priority date claimed under the Paris Convention for the Protection of Industrial Property to the actual filing date in that State, may declare that the filing outside that State of an international application designating that State is not equated to an actual filing in that State for prior art purposes.

(b) Any State making a declaration under subparagraph (a) shall to that extent not be bound by the provisions of Article 11(3).

(c) Any State making a declaration under subparagraph (a) shall, at the same time, state in writing the date from which, and the conditions under which, the prior art effect of any international application designating that State becomes effective in that State. This statement may be modified at any time by notification addressed to the Director General.

NOTES AND QUESTIONS

(1) **The Function of Patent Specification and Claims.** How different is the function of the specification from that of the claims of a patent application for determining novelty and obviousness? Article 54(3) EPC states that the content of prior filed European patent applications which are later published shall be considered as comprised in the state of the art. But Article 56 adds, "If the state of the art also includes documents within the meaning of Article 54, paragraph 3, these documents are not to be considered in deciding whether there has been an inventive step." Prior to 1977, only the claims of a British patent application were used to determine novelty of a later filed application. The European Patent Office (and the British Patent Act of 1977) uses the whole contents of an application for purposes of determining the novelty (but not obviousness) of a later filed application. According to the *Hilmer* rule, contents of a prior filed U.S. application affect determinations both of novelty and of

obviousness. Do differences between the first-to-file and the first-to-invent systems account for all the differences in approach and effect?

(2) **Must the "True" Inventor Be First?** Is the *Hilmer* case about novelty and nonobviousness or about priority? In most of the world, priority means priority of *application* by a *true* inventor or her assigns—not priority of *invention* by a true and *first* inventor. Is the question merely one of how to define the word "first"?

(3) **The "Last in Time" Rule.** The *Hilmer* court states that the *Milburn* rule "has its weaknesses." Is the *Hilmer* court primarily determined to limit the scope of section 119's treatment of foreign applicants or the scope of section 102(e)'s secret prior art effect? Does your answer affect whether the United States is in compliance with its treaty obligations? Should the court have reconciled its interpretation of section 119 in light of the Restatement's formula for treaty interpretation? Under section 115 of the Restatement, an act of Congress supersedes a provision of an international agreement as law of the United States "if the purpose of the act to supersede the earlier rule or provision is clear or if the act and the earlier rule or provision cannot be fairly reconciled." RESTATEMENT (THIRD) OF THE LAW, FOREIGN RELATIONS LAW OF THE UNITED STATES § 115 (1987). Is section 102(e) clearly irreconcilable with Article 4? Does the codification of the *Milburn* Rule in 35 U.S.C. § 102(e) in 1952 supercede the effect of Paris Convention Article 4 in U.S. law?

(4) **What Result?** G filed an application in Germany on January 3, 1998, disclosing W and X, and disclosing Y as known related technology. On February 3, 1998, A files an application in the U.S. disclosing and claiming X, Y, and Z. On March 3, 1998 G files in the U.S., claiming W and X. Assume that Z is obvious if, but only if, W, X, or Y constitute prior art and that W is obvious if, but only if, Z constitutes prior art. In an interference proceeding in the U.S. between G and A, what are their respective rights? *See* Donald W. Chisum, *Foreign Activity and Patentability under U.S. Law*, 11 I.I.C. 26, 39 (1980).

(5) **Whittling Down *Hilmer*.** A series of amendments to U.S. patent laws during the 1990s relate to the *Hilmer* doctrine. Until 1994, Section 104 of the Patent Act did not allow parties outside the United States located in what were to become WTO countries to prove dates of invention taking place outside the U.S. in U.S. Patent Office interference proceedings or in the courts. Under Section 104, so the reasoning went, U.S. law did not discriminate against foreign *inventors* (which would be a violation of national treatment under the Paris Convention), but against foreign *inventions* (i.e., foreign inventors could always prove their dates of invention if they desired to, simply by choosing to carry out their acts of invention and reduction to practice in the United States). Section 104 was amended in 1994 to allow proof of date of invention in any WTO country, with the intent of bringing the U.S. into compliance with its article 27.1 TRIPS obligation not to discriminate as to the place of invention. Another provision of the 1994 Uruguay Round Agreements Act established a domestic priority system allowing for the filing of a provisional patent application requiring neither a claim nor an oath or declaration. *See generally* Charles A. Eldering et al., *Comparative Analysis Of Provisional Patent Applications Under US And UK Law*, 79 J. PAT. OFF. SOC'Y 791 (1997). Further relevant amendments were made to the Patent Act in 1999, providing for publication of

most U.S. applications eighteen months from their first priority date and amending of Section 102(e) to recognize the prior art effect of a published U.S. national application, or a PCT application, in the English language and designating the United States, as of its filing date wherever in the PCT Member States. However, the 1999 amendment of Section 102(g) "preserves the *Hilmer* doctrine . . . by precluding Section 104 prior invention showings outside the US from constituting prior art, except in the context of an interference." Richard Neifeld, *Analysis of the New Patent Laws Enacted November 29, 1999*, 82 J. PAT. OFF. SOC'Y 181, 189 (2000).

(6) **Continuing *Hilmer* Controversy.** Scholarship on the controversy over the *Hilmer* doctrine could fill an entire book. For some interesting illustrative viewpoints, see Kate H. Murashige, *The Hilmer Doctrine, Self-Collision, Novelty and the Definition of Prior Art*, 26 J. MARSHALL. L. REV. 549 (1993); C. Douglas Thomas, *Secret Prior Art–Get Your Priorities Straight!*, HARV. J.L. & TECH. 147 (1996); Harold C. Wegner, *TRIPS Boomerang–Obligations For Domestic Reform*, 29 VAND. J. TRANSNAT'L L. 535 (1996); R.B. Brody, *U.S. Treaty Law, The Paris Convention*, 35 USC § 119; 53 J. PAT. OFF. SOC'Y 194 (1971). More recently, the question of U.S. compliance with the TRIPS Agreement has been questioned as a result, among other things, of the Hilmer doctrine. *See* Lauren A. Degnan, *Does U.S. Patent Law Comply with TRIPS Articles 3 and 27 With Respect to the Treatment of Inventive Activity?*, 78 J. PAT. OFF. SOC'Y 108 (1996); Todd R. Miller, *Inventions Made in U.S.A.: Foreign 'Equality' Under Applicable International Treaties*, 27 I.I.C. 587 (1996). New proposals in WIPO for changing the definitions of prior art and novelty in the context of substantive harmonization of patent law will be discussed below. *See infra* § 3.04[E].

[C] Substantive Principles in the Paris Convention: Exploitation of the Patented Invention and the Scope of the Right to Exclude

PARIS CONVENTION, ARTICLE 5 (1883)

The introduction by the patentee into countries where the patent has been granted, of articles manufactured in any other of the States of the Union shall not entail forfeiture. The patentee, however, shall be subject to the obligation of working his patent conformably to the laws of the country into which he has introduced the patented articles.

———

After the Paris Union was formed in 1883, much of the subsequent patent deliberations of its members revolved around the important issue of the scope of the patent right vis-a-vis the rights of third parties, touching again and again on the question of whether a patent is primarily a personal property right or an instrument of public policy. A Conference of Revision was held in Rome in 1886 to discuss Article 5, on the question of forfeiture of the patent right. France insisted that Article 5 should be amended to allow forfeiture of a patent for importing a patented product into a country where there was patent protection. Conversely, Belgium insisted that there be no forfeiture of a patent whatsoever—even where the patent had not been not worked within the country. Attempts to harmonize patent classification were rejected. Article 5 on exploitation of the patent was a prime source of contention for over a half-century, until the Lisbon Conference of 1958. Whether forfeiture of a patent constitutes expropriation, whether compulsory licensing or working requirements unduly hinder the rights of the patentee remain hotly debated questions even today. The history of Article 5 from its original articulation set out above to its final formulation just below is discussed in the next reading.

PARIS CONVENTION, ARTICLE 5 (LISBON ACT 1958)

A.–(1) The importation by the patentee into the country the patent has been granted of articles manufactured in any of the countries of the Union shall not entail forfeiture of the patent.

(2) Each country of the Union shall have the right to take legislative measures providing for the grant of compulsory licences to prevent the abuses which might result from the exclusive rights conferred by the patent, for example, failure to work.

(3) Forfeiture of the patent shall not be prescribed except in cases where the grant of compulsory licences would not have been sufficient to prevent such abuses. No proceeding for the forfeiture or revocation of a patent may be instituted before the expiration of two years from the grant of the first compulsory license.

(4) An application for a compulsory licence may not be made on the ground of failure to work or insufficient working before the expiration of a period of four years from the date of filing of the patent application or three years from the date of the grant of the patent, whichever period last expires; it shall be refused if the patentee justifies his inaction by legitimate reasons. Such a compulsory licence shall be non-exclusive and shall not be transferable, even in the form of the grant of a sub-licence, except with that part of the enterprise or goodwill using such licence.

(5) The foregoing provisions shall be applicable, *mutatis mutandis* to utility models.

B.–The protection of industrial designs shall not, under any circumstance, be liable to any forfeiture either by reason of failure to work or by reason of the importation of articles corresponding to those which are protected.

. . .

D.–No indication or mention of the patent, of the utility modes of the registration of the trademark, or of the deposit of the industrial design shall be required upon the product as a condition of recognition of the right to protection.

REVISION CONFERENCES*
excerpted from ULF ANDERFELT, INTERNATIONAL PATENT-LEGISLATION
AND DEVELOPING COUNTRIES 72-92 (1971)

[T]he following examination of the evolution of the Convention will deal exclusively with the rules concerning the exploitation of patents. Such rules are contained in Article 5 and prescribe the limits of the extent to which national laws may require patentees to exploit their inventions, and the types of sanctions allowed to enforce such requirements. Although certain other rules of the Convention, such as those that define the administrative measures that a country may impose on foreigners and rules concerning the right of third parties, may have a certain economic impact, the measures concerning the exploitation of patented inventions allowed under the Convention remain by far the most important features of the Convention in terms of their economic significance.

The texts of the first two revision conferences are of little interest since neither of them was ratified. The principal question at the first of these two, held in Rome in 1886, was the continuation of the efforts against compulsory working requirements. When discussion on this point was resumed at the second conference, held in Madrid in 1890, the suggestion was made that compulsory licensing be substituted for compulsory working as the most equitable method of conciliating the interests of individuals and those of society.

I. THE REVISION CONFERENCE OF BRUSSELS, 1897–1900

At this conference the Belgian proposal, made in 1880, for a total ban on revocation for non-working when a patent was being worked in one member country, was repeated, but it was again rejected, this time by a majority of the delegates. The Bureau, taking note of the difficulties created by the unanimity rule, which had led to the non-ratification of two previous revision texts, for the first time (as far as patents are concerned) introduced a proposal for the creation of a restricted union to which countries could adhere, which agreed to adopt a rule by which the sanction of revocation for non-working would be replaced by compulsory licensing. The general opinion, however, was not in favor of restricted unions in patent matters. As no agreement could be reached on any of the major proposals when the conference met in 1897, and in order not to have to close the conference without any tangible results, it was adjourned for the time being. Three years later, Belgium, having in the meantime conferred with the governments of some countries, which had opposed some amendments in 1897, recalled the conference and agreements were reached on several points.

The Bureau, having dropped its proposal for a restricted union, now suggested a clause prohibiting the revocation of a patent for non-working before the lapse of three years from the date of application, with the further qualification that

---

revocation would only be allowed in cases in which the patentee could not justify his inaction. Unsuccessful efforts to license was suggested as justification. Though agreement on this last point could not be reached, the clause as such was accepted, leaving it to each country to decide what constituted justification.

The insertion of this clause may raise two questions: could other sanctions be used before the end of the three-year period, and could revocation be used as a sanction at any time in cases in which the patentee misused his monopoly power other than by non-working? Akerman has answered the first question in the negative, which seems reasonable in view of the fact that forfeiture was the only sanction mentioned in the debates. The fact that causes for sanctions other than non-working were not mentioned may for the same reason be taken to indicate that revocation for whatever reason was prohibited for three years; such an extensive interpretation does not seem reasonable. The question is of some interest since a later revision conference (The Hague, 1925) introduced the concept of "abuse" of the patentee's monopoly power. Akerman, devoting much effort to show that the evolution of the Convention, and in particular Article 5, marks an increased awareness of the importance of society's interests, sees in the introduction of the wider concept of the abuse of monopoly power the major indication and support for his thesis. While a closer examination of this point will be made later, it is here merely suggested that the more plausible interpretation of the new clause must be that no limitation was imposed on sanctions that might apply, according to national laws, for other causes.

Despite the fact that the principle of unanimity in theory gives an equally important voice to each member, it is obvious that economically more powerful States can wield considerable influence at times. This was shown in a particular form at the Brussels conference. Both Germany and Austria, neither of which was yet a member, had made it clearly known that, while they were prepared to join the Union, their adherence depended on the adoption of certain amendments, of which the limitation of the sanction of revocation was the most important. From the deliberations it is evident that the decisions taken were strongly influenced by the desirability to accommodate these countries.

2. THE REVISION CONFERENCE OF WASHINGTON OF 1911

In view of the strong opposition of many countries to the abolition of revocation, the Bureau now proposed the following addition to Article 5: while the sanction of revocation should in principle be replaced by compulsory licensing, each country should retain the right to demand that consumers be adequately supplied, and that licenses be given on reasonable terms if asked for, at the risk of revocation; the use of this power should, however, be limited to cases in which parties immediately concerned, *i.e.*, consumers and producers, had complained of not being able to either buy goods or obtain licenses; and the three-year rule limiting the use of revocation should be retained in any case. The Bureau proposal also contained the suggestion that countries, not willing to accept the new proposal, should be able to continue applying the existing provisions.

This latter suggestion would have introduced what is known as the "reservation system," which had been adopted for instance by the Berne Union. As had been the case at Brussels when the suggestion of a restricted union was made, now also a strong opposition against splitting the unity of the rules of the Convention manifested itself.

In their counter-proposals, several countries rejected the Bureau's proposal, which largely substituted compulsory licensing for compulsory working, on the grounds that their national laws were not in agreement with such a provision. The British proposal is particularly interesting in view of the fact that Britain had been a co-sponsor in 1880 of the Belgian proposal to abolish the sanction of revocation for nonworking completely. The British change of mind on this point was due to the introduction of compulsory working in a Patent Act amendment in 1907.

The Bureau, in proposing the new Article 5, evidently had in mind the new English patent law. Referring to new circumstances which had appeared in some countries since the Brussels Conference, the Bureau said that, in order to avoid a regression from the progress already achieved, new provisions tending to conciliate the "legitimate rights" of inventors and the "requirements of public interest" might be desirable. Though reference to "public interest" has always been invoked, both to defend and reject proposed changes, the Bureau, for the abovementioned reason, seems to have gone further in stressing the public interest at Washington than at any other conference, even with due consideration for the second point mentioned below. The new proposal concerning Article 5 was based on the following ideas according to the Bureau: (1) is necessary to give the industry of every country the possibility of utilizing any invention on a footing of equality with all other countries protecting that invention; (2) any intentional bias must be prevented from operating either in favor of the inventor against the public interest or against the inventor in favor of any particular interest; and (3) certain countries apparently wish to retain the faculty to take the necessary measures assuring the introduction either of new industries likely to benefit their economies or of products demanded by their consumers. It must of course be recognized that, though in general the interests of society and of individual patentees, as far as working provisions are concerned, are supposed to be in opposition, this may not always be so. Besides the opinion that there are no differences between the two groups of interests, this seems to be the case particularly of large industrial countries with a large or major portion of their patent grants given to its own nationals, and whose nationals hold significant numbers of patents in other countries.

A German proposal to the Conference suggested the substitution of compulsory licensing for revocation as a sanction for non-working, to be used after the three-year period. A number of countries opposed the proposal—Austria, France, Great Britain, the Netherlands and Spain. The position of France is particularly interesting. Far from basing itself on the principles of "inherent rights of inventors," the French rejection of this proposal stated, in fact, that the working obligation had its rationale in the economic necessity of feeding the national industry of the patent-granting country with the discoveries and inventions there patented. Similar positions were taken by other countries in later conferences. This debate clearly indicates the existence of conflicting interests between inventors and society. The fact that only certain countries, and sometimes not the same ones, took such positions from conference to conference, further indicates the existence of differences of interest among countries in the matter of the international protection of patents.

After the German proposal was rejected, the general opinion was in favor of retaining the *status quo*. Thus, at the Washington Conference no change was made that affected the manner in which a patentee could be obliged to exploit his patent by national law. On the whole, only minor changes concerning patents were agreed upon.

3. THE REVISION CONFERENCE OF THE HAGUE 1925

At this conference the contents of Article 5 were changed in the following respects: in paragraph 2 the essential change was the substitution of the concept of "abuses which might result from the exclusive rights conferred by the patent" for that of "non-working;" a paragraph 3 was inserted, in which the idea of compulsory licenses was introduced for the first time. The paragraph stated that measures to prevent abuses "shall not entail forfeiture unless the grant of compulsory licenses is insufficient to prevent such abuses;" and finally a fourth paragraph was created essentially containing the second part of paragraph 2 of the Washington text, but with the following changes: the three-year period would start from the date of the patent grant rather than from the filing date of the patent application, and the patentee could exonerate himself by proving "the existence of legitimate excuses" rather than "by justifying his inaction."

This text gave rise to several, sometimes conflicting, interpretations. In order to suggest the most valid interpretation, the various propositions and opinions expressed at the conference will be examined as well as comments made on them afterwards.

The proposal of the Bureau suggested the deletion of compulsory working provisions, replacing them with provisions for compulsory licenses after the three-year period, in countries that wanted to prevent an invention from not being worked locally. The Bureau motivated this proposal with the fact that membership was now considerable and that the maintenance of compulsory working clauses in all but one of the Member States (the exception being the United States) was not rational, since if the patentee does not work his invention in a country it is generally because he can work it more profitably in another country, in which case the consumer will pay less.

Later the Bureau added the following particular argument (which has been echoed by several authors commenting on this conference):

> The obligation for the foreign patentee to manufacture in the country may lead to the establishment of a foreign industry towards which the local manufacturers would not be favorable.

Although this latter argument must be seen in the context of the climate of strong economic nationalism that reigned after the First World War, it is of interest today in the case of developing countries whose very objective it is to attract foreign investment in industrial manufacturing.

Several countries objected to the suggestion to abolish any working requirements completely, which was raised this time by the United States. Spain, opposing the proposal, observed that if the abolishment of any working requirement may be favorable to the large, industrialized countries, assuring them complete control of export markets, such a measure would prejudice the interests of less industrialized countries by transforming the patent monopoly into a trading monopoly inimical to the development of local industry.

Three countries (Japan, Poland and Yugoslavia) were also opposed to the abolition of the sanction of revocation for non-working and proposed the maintenance of the *status quo*. All three countries gave essentially the same arguments. The Polish declaration may be taken as an example. The refusal to abolish revocation was based on the fact that the Polish industry was far from being as developed as those of the great Western Powers and that the government had the duty to protect and assure the development of local industry. Therefore, it could not agree to let Polish industry be stifled by the importation of patent protected products. The most significant argument, considering that these countries were then comparable to the developing countries of today, and one that was made by all three, purported to indicate that compulsory licenses were not always a reliable remedy because of the difficulties of finding local licensees.

As it appeared impossible to reach agreement on the abolishment of revocation, the President of the second subcommittee on patents wondered if anyhow, it would not be possible to work out a compromise text, "taking into account the understandable apprehension, that the suggestion has created within certain delegations."

A compromise proposal, introduced by Great Britain and the United States, was adopted and became paragraphs two, three and four of Article 5. The sanction of revocation was maintained but was not to be used unless "the grant of compulsory licenses is insufficient to prevent such abuses" [Article 5 (3)]. Diverging opinions have been expressed on the problem of whether an actual grant of a compulsory license had to precede revocation, or whether direct revocation could take place (still only after three years), if a compulsory license was considered insufficient.

The drafting committee, in its comments on the new text of Article 5, observed that it laid down the principle of abolishing revocation and provided the means of compulsory licenses to oblige the patentee to work his patent or to sanction his inaction. It added, however, that the article even permitted the application of revocation if the compulsory license is not sufficient "in fact." The expression "in fact" would seem to indicate that actual proof of insufficiency was necessary before a patent could be revoked. Ladas apparently agrees with this point of view when he says that "only in case such a license does not prevent the abuse of the exclusive right granted to the patentee, his patent may be forfeited." The corollary to such an interpretation would imply that a country lacking a compulsory license system—it may have previously relied exclusively on revocation to sanction non-working—would suddenly be deprived of any sanction at all. This would neither be a logical result of the gradual evolution of the Convention nor take account of the adamant opposition of certain countries to the abolishment of revocation.

There is one interpretation that can be effectively defended, and which would agree with all the authors, who have maintained that the introduction of compulsory licenses in the Convention was merely a recognition of the *principle* of substituting compulsory licenses for revocation. It has been proposed by Ackerman. He observes that the Bureau's interpretation of the new rules permitted member countries to take any measures deemed necessary to assure local exploitation. Referring to the categoric refusal of some countries to abolish revocation, he therefore concludes that each country is free to decide, given their economic and social conditions, whether the granting of compulsory licenses will be insufficient, and whether therefore only a revocation will effectively eliminate abuses of the patent monopoly.

The important innovation at the Hague, in the text of Article 5, is the substitution of the concept of "the abuses which might result from the exclusive rights conferred by the patent" for that of "non-working." The concept of "abuse of monopoly power" was introduced by the Anglo-American compromise proposal and was clearly inspired by the British Patent Act. The phrase "for example, failure to work" was inserted at the request of one delegation, in order to make it clear that non-working might constitute such an abuse. As far as non-exploitation is concerned, the new text has been interpreted to mean that such inaction in itself is not liable to sanctions, and sanctions are allowed only if it is considered an abuse of the patentee's monopoly power.

Since until 1925 the Convention had only regulated the obligation to work and its sanctions, Akerman believes that the introduction of the wider concept of "abuse of monopoly power" into the Convention was a step increasing the powers of society in its efforts to prevent harmful practices due to patent monopolies and contrary to the public interest, by giving it wider powers of control than it had had before.

Although prior to 1925, the Convention text had only dealt with non-working, this did not mean that other actions by a patentee deemed harmful by society could not have been subject to sanctions by virtue of a national law. The only plausible explanation for the fact that the Convention text treated only sanctions against non-working is that it did not regulate other abuses, leaving the Union countries free to legislate on the matter. From what has been suggested above, with reference to the Brussels Conference, on the non-applicability of the three-year grace period to sanctions for causes other than non-working, and, moreover, taking into consideration the British proposal during the Washington Conference to expressly make non-working the only case in which the period was applicable, the obvious conclusion seems to be that the introduction of the concept of "abuse of monopoly power" was, in fact, a further curtailment of society's right to control the use made of the monopoly power that a patent gives its holder.

The third and final modification of Article 5 changed the starting date of the three-year period from that of the patent application to that of the patent grant. It appears that there was little opposition to this change. It meant a substantially greater protection for the patentee against sanctions especially in countries that used the examination system.

Of the three changes introduced in Article 5 at the Hague, the introduction of the concept of compulsory licenses would certainly have the most long term influence, even though initially it may have had less practical value. The appearance of the concept of "abuse of monopoly power," which now included among other causes the only previously, regulated cause for sanction—non-working—must be considered a gain for the patentee, as must also the third change prolonging the period during which sanctions could not be taken. Thus there seems little justification for the opinion that the new Article 5 as revised at the Hague, took account of any increased awareness of the interests of society (as opposed to those of the patentee).

4. THE REVISION CONFERENCE OF LONDON 1934

At this conference only paragraph 4 was amended, but the change was important. Whereas the text of paragraph 4 in its earlier version contained the expression "the patent may not be subjected to such measures before the expiration of three years," the new text provided that "an application for a compulsory license may not be made before the expiration of three years." A second sentence was added, reading: "No proceedings for the forfeiture or revocation of a patent may be instituted before the expiration of two years from the grant of the first compulsory license."

The Bureau suggested one change of Article 5. The proposed amendment, aimed at the abolition of the sanction of revocation for non-working, would mean a revision of paragraph 3. The draft amendment for a new paragraph 3 read: "These measures may foresee *the compulsory license as a sanction for non-working but not the revocation of the patent grant.*" The Bureau after affirming that according to the Hague text, the countries that had opposed the abolition of revocation, fearing that the importation of patented products would retard their industrial development, were still free to maintain that compulsory licenses were not sufficient to avert the disadvantages of non-working, nevertheless maintained that it was difficult to admit that an abuse of the monopoly power exists, when the patentee is prepared "to satisfy all needs of the local market." Although one may take issue with the assertion that the patentee is prepared to satisfy all needs of the local market—in a monopoly market the meaning of satisfaction of consumers is by definition far removed from the general significance of that term—as well as his professed readiness to license, there is another fundamental consideration that may invalidate the statement. As several countries observed at the Hague and would do again at this conference, the sanction of compulsory licenses may not be effective because of the difficulty to find licensees. It is possible that less industrialized countries are primarily concerned less with the abuse on the part of the foreign patentee than with the ability of the patent system to meet the particular requirements of industrialization of developing countries. On the other hand, to the extent that certain sanctions for non-working are in reality ineffective, this might encourage abuse.

Three counter-proposals submitted by Member States are of particular interest. A Mexican suggestion for a new paragraph 3 would keep compulsory licensing but not the sanction of revocation. Instead a country would be able to sanction non-working with a "reasonable reduction" of the duration of the patent. The Polish delegation proposed an amendment of the existing paragraph 3 containing the rule, that non-working should not be considered an abuse in the case where the demand of the local market did not justify local production. In motivating its standpoint, the Polish delegation referred to its declaration at the Hague, and stated that the Polish Government must support its industry, and that it could not accept importation of patented products in the cases in which it was proved that the costs of local production would be covered by national demand. It concluded that Poland, *in order to prevent abuses detrimental to its local industry, could not accept the abolition of revocation.* The significance of this approach is that it tries to solve the problem of the case in which the foreign patentee and the national authorities do not evaluate the possibilities for local production in the same way.

The Czechoslovakian delegation, in a general commentary on the Bureau proposals, declared, that the changes suggested were evidently based on" the desire to satisfy the multiple claims of modern international commerce," and that it was certain, "that the proposals of the Bureau were likely to considerably improve the position of patentee internationally." Nevertheless, it continued:

> One must not lose sight of the fact that this improvement entails a weakening of the economic position of nationals to the advantage of foreigners. Given the proportion that exists between the manufacturing and trade of small countries such as Czechoslovakia, on the one hand, and foreign competition, on the other hand, it is to be feared that the advantages will far from compensate for the disadvantages to the national economy, if the Bureau programme was adopted.

The Czech delegation then declared that already the changes brought about at the Hague had come to lie heavily on the Czechoslovakian manufacturers and merchants. Therefore their government had to examine the Bureau proposal with the utmost care and oppose any reform, which might bring further disadvantages to its nationals. For these economic reasons the Czechoslovakian delegation proposed some amendments to the Bureau proposal. The specific proposal concerning Article 5 submitted by Czechoslovakia did not go beyond amending the existing paragraph 3 in the manner suggested by the Polish delegation.

A compromise proposal was worked out that left paragraph 3 unchanged and introduced a revision of paragraph 4, according to which the sanction of revocation would be kept, but under the condition that it could be invoked only two years after a compulsory license had been granted. In committee this compromise was accepted by the majority, and during the session of the Conference sitting as a committee of the whole only Japan did not vote in favor of it. The new paragraph 4 of Article 5 was finally adopted in plenary session without discussion.

Even though the only textual change in Article 5 at the London Conference appeared in its fourth paragraph, it also had repercussions on the preceding paragraph. Whereas the third paragraph in its Hague version only constituted an affirmation of a theoretical principle, described as a "moral commitment," that revocation should not be resorted to unless a compulsory license was insufficient, the London version of paragraph 3, in virtue of the second sentence of paragraph 4, constituted a "unionist rule," *i.e.*, compulsory for all its members.

The greater awareness of the interests of society (in opposition to those of patentees) which, according to Akerman, was manifest at the Hague Conference, would logically also have to have been present at the London Conference. Just as no indication of such an influence could be found in the results of the first of these conferences, the same seems to be true for the second, unless one does not mean, that since the protection of patentees was not reinforced even further, the interests of society prevailed.

5. THE REVISION CONFERENCE OF LISBON 1958

The revision of Article 5 at Lisbon left only its first paragraph unchanged. Paragraph 2, which recognized the right of Member States to take the necessary legislative measures to prevent abuses, now stated that this right was limited to taking measures "providing for the grant of compulsory licenses." In the first part of paragraph 3, the words "is insufficient", indicating the cases in which revocation was allowed, were replaced by "would not have been sufficient." The former second sentence of the fourth paragraph was inserted as a new, second part of paragraph 3. In the new paragraph 4, the introductory words "In any case" were deleted. Furthermore, the application of "grace" periods, during which no compulsory licenses could be granted, was expressly limited to cases of non-working or insufficient working. A certain adjustment concerning the length of such periods was made. Finally a new phrase was added stating that compulsory licenses should be nonexclusive and non-transferable.

A Turkish proposal to the Conference may be significant, for it shows an increased awareness of the particular position of less industrialized countries. It is also important because it contains the first suggestion to reduce the period during which the patentee is protected against sanctions for non-working. Observing that during every revision conference, including Lisbon, the period of time mentioned in Article 5 (A) had been extended, and referring to what Poland and other countries had said on this question at London, the Turkish proposal said, in part, that the present proposal, in creating an effective monopoly, would fortify the position of the very advanced industrialized countries, which was the reason why countries with less satisfactory economic conditions would maintain their refusal to accept the proposed text. The Turkish proposal continues by arguing for a reduction of this period. Considering the present rhythm of growth of new technology if would be

Law Library

Due Date: 16/12/2003   21:30

Title: International intellectual
              property law and policy /
              by Graeme B. Dinwoodie,
              William O. Hennessey, Shira
              Perlmutter.
Author:
Classmark: 341.43 D

Item number: 1611407788

****
*   Please return this item on or   *
*   before the due date   *
****

advisable to decide on a very short period for many inventions or else the advantages of the compulsory license will be lost.

It further pointed out that although it is possible to limit the initial freedom of importation by means of restrictions, this cannot possibly help these countries during the specified period of time. The Turkish delegation therefore concludes that the proposed text would create conditions tending to widen the gap between the more and the less industrialized countries, and that unless the period during which sanctions cannot be applied, according to the existing rule, was reduced, Turkey would have to take internal measures to guarantee, such a reduction.

As at all previous revision conferences the proposal to abolish revocation as a sanction for non-working, raised by the Bureau, was opposed by several countries. Among these were Brazil, Iraq and Yugoslavia. According to their experience, the threat of compulsory licenses—especially in the case of developing countries—was insufficient as a remedy against non-working. The patentee often could not find a local manufacturer able to exploit the patent.

It is interesting to note that Austria and Italy also opposed the move to abolish revocation. The Austrian delegation declared that it could not support the proposal since "such a measure would risk to delay the working of patents in small countries," while the Italian delegation was of the opinion that one could not entirely abandon the system of revocation "without prejudicing the industrial development of the country."

In these two cases the stage of economic development was not mentioned. Instead a difference between larger and smaller countries was suggested; this idea stems from the fact that the percentage of nationals holding patents is generally lower in smaller countries.

When paragraph 4 was discussed, the question of whether or not the patentee should benefit from the "grace" period in all cases of abuse, or merely in the case of non-working and insufficient working, was definitely settled. According to the London text the benefit of this delay in pronouncing sanctions was applicable to all cases of abuse. At Lisbon, however, an almost unanimous opinion held that the patentee should benefit from this delay only in cases of non-working and insufficient working.

The drafting committee, set forth the motivations for proposing a text which with only one change, became the new paragraphs 2, 3 and 4 of Article 5A.

In paragraph 2 the expression "each contracting country shall have the right to take the necessary legislative measures" was replaced by "each country of the Union shall have the right to take legislative measures providing for the grant of compulsory licenses," in order to make it clear that the primary sanction should be compulsory licenses.

Paragraph 3 was to contain the existing text of paragraph 3 of the London text (saying that a patent cannot be revoked unless the grant of a compulsory license is insufficient), plus the second sentence of paragraph 4 of the London text (revocation can only take place two years after the first compulsory license). In its motivation for the proposed paragraph 3 the Report of the drafting committee said in part, that, in the unanimous opinion of the Committee, revocation could not constitute a primary sanction against non-working (defaut d'exploitation) [sic] but could only be applied once the granting of a compulsory license had proved itself ineffective. Though the drafting committee speaks of "non-working" there is no doubt that what is meant is abuse in general. It might seem that the unanimous opinion of the drafting committee, and the insertion of the second sentence of paragraph 4 of the London text in the new paragraph 3, would definitely settle the matter of the interpretation of that latter paragraph. But first of all the drafting committee consisted of only six countries, five of which had voted for the abolition of revocation in the case of non-working and all of which were highly industrialized countries. More important, however, is the fact that the one change which the text, submitted by the drafting committee, underwent before being adopted by the committee of the whole was that the words "would be insufficient" (ne suffirait pas) appearing in the sentence "Forfeiture of the patent shall not be prescribed except in cases in which the grant of compulsory licenses would be insufficient" were replaced by "would not have been sufficient" (n'aurait pas suffi). This change in wording would seem to leave open the possibility of interpreting paragraph 3 to the effect that revocation can also be resorted to in cases in which a compulsory license is supposed to be insufficient *if it were tried*.

As for paragraph 4, finally, the report of the drafting committee said that, despite the opinion expressed by certain delegations that the "grace" period should be provided for all cases of abuse, the committee, with the support of all members, limited the application of the period before which no compulsory license can be granted to the cases of non-working and insufficient working. Finally, the drafting committee suggested that this period should be either three years from the grant of the patent (the formula of the London text) or four years from the date of the patent application, as a compromise between *status quo* and the Bureau proposal. With the one change in paragraph 3, mentioned above, the text submitted by the drafting committee was adopted by the Committee of the whole and later by the Conference without discussion.

How is one to interpret Article 5A as it emerged from the Lisbon revision Conference? Paragraph 2 raises no problem. From the text itself it is clear that the sanction of compulsory license has been made the primary sanction. This is equally clear from the proposals submitted to the Conference and opinions expressed during it. Paragraph 3, however, as shown above, raises the question of whether and to what extent the principle of the previous paragraph is attenuated. The drafting committee evidently intended to limit the possibility of revoking patents to cases in which a compulsory license had, in fact, proved itself insufficient. But, for the reasons explained previously, the final wording of this paragraph appears to lead to the possible interpretation that, in fact, it constitutes a concession to the interests of those countries, that maintained steadfastly during the Conference that the threat of compulsory licenses was often insufficient to avoid abuses or to remedy them. As paragraph 4 expressly limits itself to cases of non-working and insufficient working, this interpretation of paragraph 3 would mean that a country, upon judging that a compulsory license would not be sufficient to prevent or rectify a certain abuse of the monopoly power of the patentee, could directly declare a patent forfeited in all cases save those regulated specifically by paragraph 4. No author commenting on the Lisbon text has, however, mentioned such an interpretation.

As for paragraph 4 two changes are evident. The first is that the only abuses now benefitting from a "grace" period before compulsory licenses may be imposed are non-working or insufficient working, whereas earlier all abuses, and, according to the interpretation of some countries, even grounds other than abuses by the patentee, such as cases involving particular public interests, were subject to the provisions of paragraph 4. Thus, there is one tangible change in favor of the interests of society. The second change amounted to a possible prolongation of the grace period. Though its effect was only to benefit patentees in countries that had pre-examination systems, it confirms the contention that the period of effective protection for the patentee might be not only the specified period but also the time between the application for and the granting of a patent.

NOTES AND QUESTIONS

(1) **Working Requirements and Economic Efficiency**. The United States has never had a working requirement in connection with its patent law. Germany had a working requirement until 1911 but did not use it other than for the purpose of making reciprocal agreements with other nations. A British authority has observed that "the U.S. has always, by geography and economic position, been able to remain aloof from this sort of requirement." WILLIAM CORNISH, INTELLECTUAL PROPERTY: PATENTS, COPYRIGHT, TRADE MARKS AND ALLIED RIGHTS 72 n.51 (2d ed. 1989). Is there anything more than geography and economy to the American position? With regard to the British addition of compulsory licensing in section 15 of the 1905 Patents Act, Cornish continues:

> As in seventeenth century England, any country which offers patents to foreigners will want the invention to be exploited to the advantage of its own economy. It may indeed take measures to make the patent more than a cover protecting the import of foreign-made goods. If it has a domestic industry that competes with the foreign patentee there may be a particular cause for jealousy. This certainly was the motiv[ating] force behind the introduction into the British system of provisions allowing the grant of compulsory licences on the ground that the invention was not being worked domestically: the success of the German and Swiss chemical industries in the late nineteenth century was built to a substantial degree on the holding of key patents. The French originally went even further, making revocation of the patent the penalty for importing patented articles from abroad; lifting this draconian sanction was made a precondition of membership in the Paris Convention. Article 5A(1). The majority of patenting countries now have some form of compulsory working requirement, which the Paris Convention allows to be sanctioned by compulsory licensing once three years have elapsed from grant; and by revocation if compulsory licensing fails after two years to produce

the required result. Provisions of this kind in national law are not only offensive to notions of international comity supposedly underlying the Convention; they are also economically unsound in any case where efficiencies of scale demand production in one place for international markets.

(2) **The Lever of Reciprocity.** In the face of threats from the United States to follow the British example of 1905, in 1909 Germany signed a reciprocal treaty with the United States exempting U.S. patent owners from the German patent law's working requirements. 36 Stat. L. 2178. The German working requirement (section 11) was itself repealed in 1911, and an amendment substituting compulsory licensing was added. By 1914, Germany supplied ninety percent of U.S. dyestuffs and the U.S. industry consisted largely of small assembly plants operating on German intermediates. The treaty has been called "one-sided" since the United States never had such requirements in its patent law. EMERSON STRINGHAM, PATENTS AND GEBRAUCHMUSTER in INTERNATIONAL LAW 110-11 (1934).

(3) **The Consensus Rule.** The successive Conferences of Revision mentioned by Anderfelt were held pursuant to Article 14 of the Paris Convention, which states that:

> The present convention shall be submitted to periodical revisions with a view to the introduction of amendments calculated to improve the system of the Union. . . . For this purpose, conferences shall be had successively in one of the contracting countries between the delegates of the said countries.

A consensus rule that requires unanimity of the parties for any amendments to the Convention was present from the very beginnings of the Paris Union. A modification of the unanimity requirement was proposed by Mexico at the London Conference in 1934, but it did not succeed. The consensus rule, which still exists in the Paris Assembly today, has been pivotal in shaping the character and tone of the International Bureau's efforts to introduce improvements into the Paris Convention throughout the various revisions and the nature of the changes which have been made in the treaty text. At the same time, as noted by Anderfelt, the economically more powerful states can wield considerable influence during deliberations. How do powerful states wield their influence in international fora, consistent with the principles of equality which underpin the international legal system?

(4) **Does Elimination of Local Working Requirements Favor Local Industry?** The International Bureau's discussion of the Hague Revision of 1925 notes the argument that "[t]he obligation for the foreign patentee to manufacture in the country may lead to the establishment of a foreign industry towards which the local manufacturers would not be favorable." Does the overtly protectionist argument against working requirements for foreign patentees in favor of local manufacturers comport with the realities of foreign investment practices? Stringham observed that prior to World War I, "as a

general rule Germans did not establish enterprises in the United States due to the absence of measures about compulsory licensing." STRINGHAM, *supra*, at 110-11, esp. 176ff. Compare the discussion of compulsory licensing in studies such as Robert M. Sherwood, *The TRIPS Agreement: Implications For Developing Countries*, 37 IDEA 491, 496 (1997), with reference to "non-robust systems," "trade-enhancing systems" such as TRIPS, and "investment-stimulating systems," described in Edwin Mansfield, *Intellectual Property, Technology, and Economic Growth*, 64 ECONOMIC IMPACT 12 (1988) (measuring private rates of investment) and Joseph Straus, *Implications of the TRIPS Agreement in the Field of Patent Law*, in FROM GATT TO TRIPS: THE AGREEMENT ON TRADE-RELATED ASPECTS of INTELLECTUAL PROPERTY RIGHTS 160, 202-08 (1996). Are there valid justifications for the views of opponents of foreign investment in developing countries?

(5) **Enforcement of the Paris Convention.** At the Hague Conference of 1925, the United States proposed to switch to a reciprocity system for non-compliance by other states. "Among the general principles, the American delegates proposed an amendment which would have permitted reprisals as between member countries, the objective of the American delegates being to force concessions in the matter of compulsory working and annual taxes." The proposal was withdrawn as being "contrary to the principles of the union." STRINGHAM, *supra*, at 85.

(6) **Inventors Rights.** Another provision added in London in 1934 was the right of the inventor to be named (Article 4*ter*), proposed by Italy and Holland. The right of the inventor to see his name figure in the patent, even when taken by a third party, was adopted, but another proposal regarding remuneration due to an employee or a salaried worker for his invention, which had first been urged by the International Bureau of Labor in 1929, was rejected. Although such rights are powerful, for example, in modern German patent law, in the United States, employee inventors generally have no rights in their inventions if they reasonably relate to the activities of the employer. Is the right of an inventor to be named in the patent a "moral right"? Should firms be required to compensate their employees for assigning their inventions?

(7) **Intervening Rights and Prior User Rights**. The question of intervening rights was also an important one in the period in question. As originally stated in 1883, Article 4 provided that: "Any one who shall have regularly deposited an application for a patent of invention . . . in one of the contracting States, shall enjoy for the purpose of making the deposit in the other States, and *under reserve of the rights of third parties* ["*sous reserve des droits de tiers*"], a right of priority during the periods hereinafter determined." A Dutch delegate thought the better expression would have been "*except for rights which had already been legitimately acquired by third parties*" ["*sauf les droits qui seraient deja acquis légitimement par les tiers.*"] *See* 1 STEPHEN P. LADAS, PATENTS, TRADEMARKS AND RELATED RIGHTS: NATIONAL AND INTERNATIONAL PROTECTION 499 (1975). The language was not fixed until the London Conference, where the reservation of right of personal possession of an invention [*Vorbenutzungsrecht*] after the priority date was suppressed by the addition of Article 4(B) of the convention. Thenceforward, no prior user rights could arise during the period of priority, while the rights acquired by third

parties before the first application, serving as the basis of the right of priority, continued to be regulated according to the internal legislation of each country.

(8) **Abuse of Patent Rights.** Is Anderfelt persuasive about the need for states to have some semblance of the power of revocation of a patent to make the sanction of a compulsory license effective? Is the specter of patent owners in large economically powerful countries abusing the patent monopoly to create a "trading monopoly" with all manufacturing in the home market a real one? We will pursue the topic further in the discussion of parallel imports and exhaustion of right in Chapter 7.

(9) **Ratchet Effect?** The United States was apparently very pleased with the outcome of the London Conference of 1934:

> Commissioner Coe stated categorically in 1935 that "while the international convention for the protection of industrial property was revised in a number of points, those revisions invariably approached the American law; and every other country in the world belonging to this convention, or practically every other one, yielded its own domestic law in favor of what is apparently regarded as the superior patent laws of the United States.

Hearings before the Committee on Patents on H.R. 4523 Pt. I, 74th Cong. 1st. Sess. 1067, 1068 (1935). The 1990s have sometimes been called the Golden Age of the patent system by American judges and scholars. To what extent can the trend in international patent negotiations over the past century be seen to have been one favoring stronger and stronger patent protection?

[D] Harmonization of Substantive Patent Law

The following readings cover the first real contemporary attempts at international harmonization of substantive patent law beginning in the mid-1980s with negotiations (1) in the WIPO on a "Treaty Supplementing the Paris Convention as Far as Patents are Concerned" and (2) in the GATT on minimum standards of substantive patent law, which were ultimately incorporated into the TRIPS Agreement. Following the failure to conclude a treaty on substantive patent harmonization within WIPO in June 1991, discussed in the readings, the focus of attention shifted to the WTO. Negotiations in WIPO continued on the much more modest task of harmonization of procedure. The TRIPS Agreement came into effect at the beginning of 1995, giving the industrialized countries much of what they had sought from developing nations. Harmonization of patent application procedure culminated in the signing of the WIPO Patent Law Treaty ("PLT") in June, 2000.

[1] The Failed Substantive Patent Law Treaty

LEE J. SCHROEDER, THE HARMONIZATION OF PATENT LAWS[*]
C567 ALI-ABA 473, 473-78 (1990)

INTRODUCTION

Several efforts to harmonize the patent laws of the various countries of the world, including the United States, are presently underway. The most comprehensive effort is taking place within [WIPO] . . . The focus of that effort is to develop a treaty which will harmonize the patent laws of the countries or groups of countries adhering to that treaty.

A second and related effort is the on-going attempt to internationally address the trade-related aspects of intellectual property and raise the levels of intellectual property protection including patent protection. This effort is taking place within the . . . Uruguay round of trade talks under the [GATT]. . . The two activities are interrelated in that some elements of patent law under discussion in the WIPO exercise are also under discussion in the GATT exercise.

THE WIPO EFFORT

The effort to develop a treaty to harmonize the patent laws of different countries began in 1984 with the convening of several meetings by WIPO to study the availability of a grace period for overcoming the public disclosure of an invention before the filing a patent application. If a publication disclosing an invention occurs within a grace period prior to the filing of a patent application, the applicant may still be awarded a patent for that invention. The matter of a grace period offering applicants up to 12 months before the filing of a patent application during which the applicant can overcome his own disclosure of the invention or the disclosure of a third party is well-known in the United States. But such a grace period is not a part of the patent laws of most other countries of the world. The U.S. participants at these first meetings sought to have the concept of a grace period accepted by the many countries that do not have a grace period or have a very limited grace period.

The grace period meetings were quite contentious and agreement was only obtained to further study the matter. The grace period topic was next considered along with two other topics in a 1985 WIPO meeting of a committee of experts to harmonize provisions in laws for the protection of inventions. The two additional topics were the requirements to be met in a patent application to obtain a filing date and the requirements for naming an inventor. Over the next five years, some eight additional meetings of the WIPO committee of experts were held and further new topics were introduced and discussed, so that by the time of a meeting this past June, the draft treaty which has evolved consists of some 37 articles and eight rules. . . .

. . . A diplomatic conference is now scheduled for June 3-28, 1991. As the draft treaty has many provisions which have the potential to require changes to U.S. law should the United States adhere to the treaty, I will briefly discuss some of those provisions. . . .

THE MORE CONTROVERSIAL PROVISIONS

Patent Awarded to First to File: Article 13

Probably the most controversial change to the U.S. patent law that would be required by the draft treaty is to award patents to the inventor that first files an application and not the first person that invents, as with our present system.

The first-to-file system is the system followed by the entire world other than for the United States and the Philippines which follow the first-to-invent approach. Canada had a first-to-invent system until the beginning of this year and legislation is now being considered by the Philippines to change to a first-to-file system.

Opponents in the U.S. of the first-to-file system argue that the first-to-file system would greatly increase the number of applications filed in the United States and the applications would be of a poor quality. The opponents of the first-to-file system also argue that the first-to-file system would be unconstitutional, lacks fairness in that a second inventor who has invented later in time might get the patent and that the first-to-file system favors the large corporation over the individual inventor or the small business.

On the other hand, those who advocate that our first-to-invent system should be replaced by a first-to-file system note that the first-to-file system brings with it a degree of certainty, and that the first-to-invent system advantage of being able to show that one person is the first to invent is a very costly procedure out of the reach of most but very large corporations. Furthermore, even the very large corporations often do not engage in first inventor or interference contests, but instead negotiate cross-licensing arrangements.

While our present system to show that one is a first inventor is costly in terms of money, those that advocate the first-to-file system point to the unfortunate loss of time that is built into the first-to-invent system, because inventors are not under the time pressure to move more quickly as under a first-to-file system. They argue that the first-to-invent system served the United States well when the United States had an isolated economy or had a wide-based technological lead, but unfortunately at present the United States has to worry about the technological advances of others, and those others are not moving slowly as they do not have the luxury of time and being able to rely on an earlier date of invention. First-to-invent is wonderful if all you have to worry about is others inventing in the United States, which is now the situation in fewer and fewer technological fields.

Another argument that those that advocate the first-to-file system for the United States is that the majority of filers in the United States are already operating with such a system. This includes the applicants of almost half of the applications that originate from abroad, and most of the applicants filing for U.S. corporations, as they also file the same applications abroad.

Both sides of the debate attempt to refute the arguments offered by the other side. The opponents of the first-to-file system point to the historical record of the United States having a first-to-invent system for over 150 years and the fact that the concept of a first-to-file system for the United States was thoroughly reviewed following the proposal in the 1966 report of the President's Commission to study the U.S. patent system. It is interesting to note that in Congressional hearings on bills before the Congress resulting from the 1966 President's Commission report, a change to first-to-file was opposed by the various patent bar groups and a number of industry groups but was supported by some inventor groups and small business groups.

Grace Period: Article 12

While the issue of first-to-file versus first-to-invent may be the most controversial, or at least the issue that is receiving the most attention, there are other issues that are equally, and quite possibly, more important that are part of the harmonization effort. Of particular interest is the grace period which was mentioned earlier. At present in the United States one has the opportunity to swear behind any publication that takes place in the year immediately before the filing of a patent application. If a researcher publishes his or her work and then six months later decides to file a patent application, his or her own publication would not be a bar to obtaining a patent in the United States.

Furthermore, the publications of others within a year of the filing date of the application also would not be a bar in the United States if the inventor can swear to a date of invention earlier than the date of the publication.

While a grace period is well-known in the United States, it is not found in the patent laws of many other countries. Researchers or inventors in the United States who publish before filing, give up their patent rights in much of the rest of the world as their own publications will be cited against them in their attempt to obtain foreign patents. What the draft treaty now contains is a provision which will provide a grace period for the persons who publish their works prior to filing patent applications.

The grace period provision now under consideration in the draft treaty gives persons who publish their inventions prior to the time a patent application is filed, rights only over the publication by the inventor or by another who obtained information regarding the invention either directly or indirectly from the inventor. It does not given an inventor any protection against the independent activity and publication by another prior to the filing of the inventor's application. The grace period which is provided in the draft treaty is a grace period on which the prudent inventor should not ordinarily rely. However, the provision will be available to excuse the uninformed individuals that unfortunately publish their inventions prior to the time their patent applications are filed from the adverse effect of their own publications.

Early Publication of a Patent Application: Article 15

A third provision that is often held by many of the other countries to the negotiations to be a necessary element to accompany first-to-file and the grace period is the provision calling for publication of the patent application 18 months after the application is filed. In recent negotiations, the United States has attempted, without much success, to have this provision be optional with any country. In the most recent meeting, the United States proposed that a country could optionally publish by 24 months. This would permit the United States to rely on its patents as a publication for most of the applications. The concept of publication optionally at 24 months was accepted by others at least to the extent that it will be included as an option in the text which will go forward to the diplomatic conference.

Advocates of a mandatory early publication of patent applications for the United States argue that this would give the U.S. public the information in foreign origin applications sooner and such information would be published in English. It is their belief that at present only large corporations with extensive information networks have the resources to obtain and translate all the 18-month publications from around the world. It would also give the U.S. public earlier information about the earlier notice of some U.S.-origin applications. Opponents of a mandatory early publication requirement argue that an inventor should not be faced with a publication of his application if patent protection is not obtainable. If an adverse indication regarding patentability was received early enough in the process, the applicant could withdraw the application before it is published and preserve any trade secrets. However, such an early and definite indication may not always be possible even with the 18-month average pendency of applications in the United States unless the optional 24-month publication regime would be available.

OTHER SIGNIFICANT PROVISIONS

Reversal of Burden of Proof for Patented Processes: Article 24

A draft treaty provision provides for the reversal of the burden of proof under certain circumstances in regard to the products of allegedly infringed patented processes. The criteria for the reversal of the burden is still under discussion. Some of the countries wish to limit the availability of the reversal to situations where the product is new whereas others including the United States are seeking to have other criteria. The developing countries prefer to have no provision on the matter.

RECENT LIMITATIONS BY THE DEVELOPING COUNTRIES

While most of the discussions that have taken place in earlier meetings involved North/North discussions, *i.e.*, discussions among the developed countries, this changed dramatically in the [June 1990] session. In that meeting some 25 developing countries introduced a series of proposals into the discussions. One of the proposals of the developing countries permits numerous exceptions to the patenting of all technologies as now called for by Article 10 Alternative A of the draft treaty. The developing countries proposal essentially permits any country to patent or not patent any technology, as it wishes. Other developing country proposals call for no patent term requirement, no obligation regarding the reversal of the burden of proof for certain infringement proceedings and a weak provision regarding rights conferred by a patent. Several new topics have also been proposed by the developing countries, but have not as yet been discussed. One proposal obliges the rights holder to make a "best mode" disclosure, to work the invention and "in respect of license contracts and contracts assigning patents, to refrain from engaging in abusive, restrictive or anticompetitive practices adversely affecting the transfer of technology." Another proposal ensures the compliance of the rights holder with these obligations by authorizing any country to take appropriate measures including the grant of non-voluntary licenses and the revocation or forfeiture of the patent.

THE GATT EFFORT

The new round of trade talks under the GATT began in 1986 and are scheduled to be concluded in December 1990. . . .

Among the patent topics proposed by the United States and others and under discussion in the GATT [TRIPS] talks, are patentable subject matter, a minimum patent term, minimum rights conferred by patents, and enforcement of those rights. An obligation to have a first-to-file patent system has also been called for by others. The developing countries have also introduced proposals in the GATT discussions similar to those they introduced in WIPO setting forth obligations of patent holders and authorizing countries to take remedial measures to ensure compliance with those obligations.

THE IMPACT OF GATT ON WIPO EFFORTS

While the various countries in the patent law harmonization discussions are each attempting to preserve as much of their [sic] existing patent law as possible, the final decisions which will be taken on some of the patent law harmonization topics may depend on the results of the discussion of like topics in the new round of [GATT] trade talks . . . A final determination by the GATT negotiations is expected by December 7, 1990. That determination will undoubtedly heavily influence the WIPO results for the overlapping patent topics. If the GATT successfully concludes the present round of talks and intellectual property and patents is part of the results, those results will dictate the nature of the related provisions in the WIPO draft treaty.

FUTURE WIPO EFFORTS

In a WIPO committee of experts meeting from October 29 to November 9, 1990, Articles 18 to 37 of the draft treaty will be discussed. These discussions will include most of the developing countries proposals. From these discussions and the discussions which took place in June on Articles 1 to 17, WIPO will develop a basic proposal for the diplomatic conference to consider. The basic proposal will contain alternatives for a number of the more contentious topics. The Government of the Netherlands has extended an invitation to host the diplomatic conference and the diplomatic conference will be held in The Hague from June 3 to 28, 1991. Fortunately, this is after the conclusion of the GATT talks.

OUTLOOK

What is the outlook for the United States? Conclusion of a GATT agreement which includes intellectual property and patents in particular is possible and it will dictate some of the patent provisions of a patent law harmonization treaty. The United States is being faced with an ever-increasingly more powerful and united Europe and a somewhat more strident and organized group of developing countries. The United States must carefully consider the value of patent law harmonization, now or in the very near future, not only for our rights holders but also for the future technological, economic and industrial well-being of this country. Clearly, harmonization of the patent laws of the world could serve the interests of the United States and clearly, some sort of patent law harmonization treaty is possible. What is not clear is what has to be in the final treaty in order to obtain sufficient support in the United States for adherence to the treaty and the passage of the necessary implementing legislation. What we hope to achieve in the treaty as concluded are provisions which on balance will be acceptable to most U.S. interests.

. . . .

INTERVENTION OF H.F. MANBECK
(HEAD, UNITED STATES DELEGATION)
Records of the First Part of the Diplomatic Conference for the Conclusion
of a Treaty Supplementing The Paris Convention as Far as Patents
Are Concerned, Nineteenth Meeting, Main Committee I
The Hague (June 19, 1991)

Mr. MANBECK (United States of America) . . . expressed the hope that all present understood and believed that the United States would like to see the development of a successful harmonization treaty which would simplify and expedite the obtaining of patent protection around the world and strengthen the protection once granted. During the series of meetings of the Committee of Experts that preceded the Diplomatic Conference, a draft treaty evolved that required changes in the laws of all countries in the interests of harmonization, yet allowed countries to optionally maintain certain aspects of their existing national or regional patent laws. The United States was being asked to make a number of changes in its laws. The changes included, apart from first-to-file, mandatory publication of applications, a patent term measured from the filing date, the right to prevent importation of patented products, elimination of the *Hilmer* rule concerning the effective date of foreign-origin United States patents, to mention a few. It was that draft treaty that had been considered by the various interest groups in the United States and supported by some and objected to by others. Some of the support had been conditioned on the inclusion of certain features, as had been heard from some United States interest groups, and some of the objections were limited to certain provisions, namely, of course, first-to-file.

What now faced the United States negotiators during the interval between the sessions of the Diplomatic Conference was the task of convincing its various interest groups and the United States Congress that the present package was still of overall benefit to the United States' interests. That would be difficult to do because the text that had evolved during the first session of the Diplomatic Conference represented a shift away from United States interests.

He stated that his Delegation understood the disappointment of many participants regarding its request to amend Article 9 in order to maximize its chances of participation in the final version of the treaty. It had heard them and understood that they wanted it to reconsider its position and to seek a consensus that would allow it to move to a first-to-file system. He hoped they would understand when he told them that, based on the direction of negotiations during those past three weeks, the interested circles in the United States might never get to the point of approving first-to-file because they might well lose interest and enthusiasm while evaluating the many changes the Treaty would presently require in the law of the United States of America, coupled with the loss of the strengthening improvements sought by the Delegation of the United States of America in the basic proposal. If the United States had to make major changes in its law, and obtain no improvements in the laws of others, it was not realistic to think that a treaty along such lines could be approved in the United States.

He turned then to some of the specific problems that had been created for the United States at the Conference. First, it would be particularly difficult for its various interest groups to understand and agree to a provision in the treaty which would require the United States to consider oral disclosures anywhere in the world as prior art. He did not believe his Delegation could explain satisfactorily to its Congress that it would be required to issue patents on inventions which differed only in obvious details from the disclosures contained in earlier-filed United States patent applications—imposing confusion on the U.S. public in the name of reducing so-called secret prior art. It would be precluded from its present practice of always including the inventor's name on patent documents. It would be required to accept changes in its claim practice regarding multiple dependent claims even though no one at the Conference could cite a compelling example of the need to have that type of practice.

Not only was the United States being asked to make those changes to its law, but it was now facing the possibility that a number of improvements it had sought in the protection of inventions in other countries would not be realized.

One of the major improvements it thought the Treaty would provide was an effective Article regarding the time limits for promptly completing examination. Although that Article had not been deleted, it noted that a majority of the government delegations present spoke against it. Without some discipline on time limits, there would be no guarantee in the Treaty of obtaining a meaningful term of patent protection. Likewise, the requirement to provide applicants with the ability to file by referring to earlier applications had been made optional. Its interested circles would not like that. The elimination of self-collision seemed not to be achievable based on the discussion on that topic. His Delegation simply did not understand why. Prior user rights were also a difficult subject, new to it, and as to which it trusted a suitable compromise would be achieved.

It was his hope that in the interval between the sessions careful consideration would be given to accommodating the interests of all countries, and particularly those of the United States, so that a significant number of countries, such as his, that would be required to make fundamental changes to their law. would have sufficient reasons to conclude that, overall, the Treaty would be beneficial and warranted adherence. His Delegation would work to satisfy the needs of other delegations and hoped that it could do so, but it would certainly not be successful unless others could likewise agree to satisfy its needs. . . .

NOTES AND QUESTIONS

(1) **The "Balanced Package": First-to-File and Grace Period**. Part of the "balanced package" sought by the United States in exchange for abandoning its first-to-invent system was a worldwide grace period. This initiative was vigorously supported by inventor communities in many countries, including Germany. Germany had a grace period in its patent law until the entry into force of the Strasbourg Unification Convention. *See* Heinz Bardehle, *The WIPO Harmonization Treaty and the Grace Period*, 30 IND. PROP. 372 (1991). In June, 1999, the Intergovernmental Conference of the members of the EPO began explorations of the possibility of instituting a grace period in Europe. A summary of those discussions and arguments (both pro and con) can be found at http://www.epo.co.at/news/headlns/2000_07_25_e.htm

(2) **Bilateral Measures.** In January 1994, the U.S. Secretary of Commerce announced that negotiations toward substantive harmonization of patent law had collapsed, and the U.S. Commissioner of Patents announced that the USPTO had reached an agreement with the Japanese Patent Office to support eighteen-month publication of patent applications in the United States in exchange for removal of post-grant opposition proceedings in Japan and permission to file applications in the JPO in English. Both announcements were made on the same day. Publication of most U.S. patent applications at eighteen months from filing became part of U.S. law in 1999. *See* 35 U.S.C. § 122(b).

(3) **Success for Developed Countries in TRIPS.** While the June 1990 revolt by twenty-five developing countries, referenced in Commissioner

Manbeck's intervention, triggered the U.S. response, the primary reason for the failure of the PLT negotiations in 1991 was the inability of the United States to abandon its first-to-invent system. Two years later, the United States got the real prize that it wanted from the developing countries in the form of Article 27 of the TRIPS Agreement which states that "patents shall be available for any inventions, whether products or processes, in all fields of technology, provided that they are new, involve an inventive step and are capable of industrial application. Subject to paragraph 4 of Article 65, paragraph 8 of Article 70 and paragraph 3 of this Article, patents shall be available and patent rights enjoyable without discrimination as to the place of invention, the field of technology and whether products are imported or locally produced." The history of TRIPS as set forth in the *Canada-Pharmaceuticals* decision excerpted in the following section refers to those negotiations.

[2] The TRIPS Agreement

J.H. REICHMAN, UNIVERSAL MINIMUM STANDARDS OF INTELLECTUAL PROPERTY PROTECTION UNDER THE TRIPS COMPONENT OF THE WTO AGREEMENT[*]
29 INT. LAWYER 345, 351-58 (1995)

In the course of multilateral negotiations to revise the Paris Convention that preceded the Uruguay Round, the developed countries sought to elevate its rudimentary standards concerning patentable inventions while the developing countries demanded preferential measures that would have weakened even the preexisting obligations that states owed foreign inventors under their domestic laws. The TRIPS Agreement breaks this impasse and fills many of the gaps in the international patent system with uniform minimum standards of protection that reflect the practices of the developed countries. The TRIPS Agreement also establishes new rules governing permissible limitations on the foreign patentee's scope of protection, and these rules reflect compromise efforts by both sides to balance private and public interests.

1. Normative Structure

The developed countries scored major achievements in elevating and harmonizing minimum standards of patent protection, especially with regard to basic criteria of eligibility and duration, which the Paris Convention had not addressed. The following provisions are noteworthy:

(1) Member states may not exclude any field of technology from patentability as a whole, and they may not discriminate as to the place of invention when rights are granted.

(2) The domestic patent laws (including that of the United States) must provide a uniform term of twenty years of protection from the filing date, such

---

protection must depend on uniform conditions of eligibility, and specified exclusive rights must be granted.

(3) The patentee's bundle of exclusive rights must include the right to supply the market with imports of the patented products.

(4) Logically, the obligation to work patents locally under article 5A of the Paris Convention appears overridden by the right to supply imports, at least in principle.

These achievements build on standards previously established by the Paris Convention, such as the rights of priority, which even WTO members who do not adhere to this Convention must now respect. Single countries may deviate from these universal patent-law standards only to the extent that they benefit from longer or shorter periods of transitional relief, which vary with the beneficiary's status as either a "developing country" or a "least-developed country (LDC)."

For example, developing countries may postpone implementing most of the required standards for a period of at least five years, and even ten years with respect to fields of technology previously excluded under their domestic patent laws. LDCs obtain a reprieve for ten years, while a showing of hardship may qualify them for further delays and other concessions. Nevertheless, a pipeline provision, clarified at the last minute, safeguards existing pharmaceutical and agrochemical patents, which, if otherwise eligible, must obtain at least five years of exclusive marketing rights even in those developing countries that did not previously grant patents in these fields.

Because inventors in developed countries are eventually entitled to obtain and enforce patents everywhere, competitive pressures in developing countries ought to shift from subject matter exclusions of patentability to scope of protection issues bearing on single patents, as occurs in developed countries. Firms in developing countries may thus exploit disclosed information in order to work around the claimed inventions as well as any unpatented know-how they fairly obtain, whether disclosed or not. The lack of international standards defining the doctrine of equivalents affords additional room in which to maneuver. Arguably, states may also apply a broad experimental use exception so long as the rights holders are notified.

The extent to which developing countries will themselves benefit from stronger patent systems—as distinct from compensatory market access—depends in part on the willingness of firms in developed countries either to increase direct investments in developing countries or to license more of their advanced technology to local firms. Moreover, familiarization with the benefits of the patent system could stimulate greater investment in domestic research and development and should encourage the private sector to develop its own intellectual property. Nevertheless, the value of a patent system to developing countries remains controversial, and single developing countries could suffer hardship because of a growing dependence on foreign patents with few countervailing benefits. In such a case, one must acknowledge the achievements of the developing-country negotiators, who have built numerous safeguards and escape hatches into the TRIPS Agreement.

2. Limits of the Patentee's Exclusive Rights.

Article 30 of the TRIPS Agreement declares that states should tolerate only "limited exceptions to the exclusive rights" that article 28 confers. But other articles permit exceptions to the exclusive rights when needed "to protect public health and nutrition, and to promote the public interest in sectors of vital importance" to economic development; to prevent "abuse of intellectual property rights," including the imposition of unreasonable commercial terms; and to counteract unreasonable trade restraints and practices that "adversely affect the international transfer of technology." Governments may also attempt to invoke language in article 7 that envisions the effective transfer and dissemination of technology among member countries and the maintenance of social and economic welfare as further grounds for regulatory action limiting grants of exclusive rights in appropriate circumstances. These and other articles thus preserve, and may even expand, preexisting grounds for limiting a patentee's exclusive rights under article 5A of the Paris Convention, which some developed-country delegations had hoped to abrogate.

a. Compulsory Licenses in General.

The standard form of remedial action remains compulsory licensing, as it was under article 5A of the Paris Convention, subject to important refinements and conditions that article 31 of the TRIPS Agreement attempts to introduce. In principle, both the public-interest exception and measures to prevent abuse, respectively stipulated in articles 8(1) and 8(2) of the TRIPS Agreement, could justify resort to compulsory licensing. In the past, however, arguments about the meaning of "abuse" engendered considerable controversy. A few developed countries, notably the United States, limited the concept to anticompetitive practices bordering on antitrust violations. Most other countries—and a leading commentator—considered the doctrine of abuse applicable if a patentee fails to work the patent locally in due course or "refuses to grant licenses on reasonable terms and thereby hampers industrial development, or does not supply the national market with sufficient quantities of the patented product, or demands excessive prices for such products."

The TRIPS Agreement merges this broader concept of abuse with the public-interest exception for purposes of compulsory licensing under article 31. However, considerable effort has been made to discredit the nonworking of foreign patents locally as a sufficient basis for triggering such licenses. The TRIPS Agreement then subjects all nonexclusive compulsory licenses sounding in any of the bases established by articles 8(1) and 8(2) to the conditions of article 31.

So long as the grounds for triggering a nonexclusive compulsory license are rooted in the broad notion of "abuse" under article 8(1), say, because of public-interest considerations or because the patentee refused to authorize the desired use "on reasonable commercial terms and conditions," article 31 requires the would-be licensee to seek a negotiated license from the right holder, and failing this, to pay equitable compensation. The victorious licensee could not normally export the products resulting from use of the patent under such a compulsory license. Nor could the licensee exclude the foreign patentee from subsequently working the patent locally—in direct competition with the former—once the latter had rectified any grievances that might have justified issuance of a compulsory license in the first place.

In contrast, a complainant who seeks a compulsory license under article 8(2) to rectify abuse of a patent in the narrow, technical sense familiar from United States law will remain exempt from both the duty to negotiate and restrictions on exports, provided that some judicial or administrative authority deems the patentee's conduct anticompetitive. In such a case, "the need to correct anticompetitive practices may be taken into account in determining the amount of remuneration" the patentee will receive.

The sole exception to the compulsory licensing scheme available under article 31 is for patented "semi-conductor technology." Article 31(c), as revised at the last minute, now limits the granting of compulsory licenses for "other use" of such technology to instances of "public non commercial use" or to situations in which the compulsory license obviates judicially determined "anticompetitive practices." Whether unpatented semiconductor layout designs subject to integrated circuit laws are also immunized from compulsory licenses for "other use" remains to be clarified, as discussed below. In any event, these provisions make it harder for interested parties in developing countries to start up local semiconductor industries by persuading their governments to seize foreign semiconductor technologies in the name of overriding public interest.

On balance, Article 31 helps to insulate foreign patentees from confiscatory practices that earlier proposals to reform Article 5A of the Paris Convention appeared to tolerate, while it affords the developing countries broad grounds for curbing conduct that seriously compromises their national development strategies. Apart from semiconductor technologies, the requirement that would-be compulsory licensees negotiate seriously with rights holders to obtain exclusive licenses on reasonable terms should increase the pressure on foreign patentees to accommodate pricing and other strategies to local market conditions. This, in turn, should lessen the need for governments to seek compulsory licensing in the first instance.

b. New Dimensions of the Public-Interest Exception.

Beyond traditional notions of "public interest" and "abuse," the TRIPS Agreement introduces new and more expansive concepts whose outer limits have yet to be delineated at the international level. In particular, article 7 stresses the "promotion of technological innovation and . . . the transfer and dissemination of technology . . . in a manner conducive to social and economic welfare." Article 8(1) expands potential public-interest exceptions to sectors other than public health and nutrition that are "of vital importance to . . . socio-economic and technological development," and article 8(2) seeks to ensure "the international transfer of technology." In addition, article 66 underscores the LDCs' "need for flexibility to create a viable technological base," and it must be read in conjunction with the other provisions favoring this group of countries.

All these provisions arm developing and least-developed countries with legal grounds for maintaining a considerable degree of domestic control over intellectual property policies in a post TRIPS environment, including the imposition of compulsory licenses within article 31 of the TRIPS Agreement and article 5A of the Paris Convention. While the meaning of any particular clause must emerge from evolving state practice, taken together they clearly sanction public-interest exceptions of importance to the developing countries while rejecting the more extreme measures these countries proposed during the Paris Revision process. Eventually, specific public-interest safeguards essential to national economic development will have to be worked out on a case-by case basis, in order to deal with particular complaints about the socially harmful effects of technological dependency that are not offset by enhanced market access, and the resulting compromises are likely to give both sides less than they want.

TRIPS AGREEMENT

Article 2

1. In respect of Parts II, III and IV of this Agreement, Members shall comply with Articles 1-12 and 19 of the Paris Convention (1967). . . .

Article 27(1)
Patentable Subject Matter

Patents shall be available and patent rights enjoyable without discrimination as to the field of technology.

Article 28
Rights Conferred

(1) A patent shall confer on its owner the following exclusive rights:

(a) where the subject matter of a patent is a product, to prevent third parties not having the owner's consent from the acts of: making, using, offering for sale, selling, or importing for these purposes that product;

(b) where the subject matter of a patent is a process, to prevent third parties not having the owner's consent from the act of using the process, and from the acts of: using, offering for sale, selling, or importing for these purposes at least the product obtained directly by that process.

Article 30
Exceptions to Rights Conferred

Members may provide limited exceptions to the exclusive rights conferred by a patent, provided that such exceptions do not unreasonably conflict with a normal exploitation of the patent and do not unreasonably prejudice the legitimate interests of the patent owner, taking account of the legitimate interests of third parties.

Article 31
Other Use Without Authorization of the Right Holder

Where the law of a Member allows for other use of the subject matter of a patent without the authorization of the right holder, including use by the government or third parties authorized by the government, the following provisions shall be respected:

(a) authorization of such use shall be considered on its individual merits;

(b) such use may only be permitted if, prior to such use, the proposed user has made efforts to obtain authorization from the right holder on reasonable commercial terms and conditions and that such efforts have not been successful within a reasonable period of time. This requirement may be waived by a Member in the case of a national emergency or other circumstances of extreme urgency or in cases of public non-commercial use. In situations of national emergency or other circumstances of extreme urgency, the right holder shall, nevertheless, be notified as soon as reasonably practicable. In the case of public non-commercial use, where the government or contractor, without making a patent search, knows or has demonstrable grounds to know that a valid patent is or will be used by or for the government, the right holder shall be informed promptly;

(c) the scope and duration of such use shall be limited to the purpose for which it was authorized, and in the case of semi-conductor technology shall only be for public non-commercial use or to remedy a practice determined after judicial or administrative process to be anti-competitive.

(d) such use shall be non-exclusive;

(e) such use shall be non-assignable, except with that part of the enterprise or goodwill which enjoys such use;

(f) any such use shall be authorized predominantly for the supply of the domestic market of the Member authorizing such use;

(g) authorization for such use shall be liable, subject to adequate protection of the legitimate interests of the persons so authorized, to be terminated if and when the circumstances which led to it cease to exist and are unlikely to recur. The competent authority shall have the authority to review, upon motivated request, the continued existence of these circumstances;

(h) the right holder shall be paid adequate remuneration in the circumstances of each case, taking into account the economic value of the authorization;

(i) the legal validity of any decision relating to the authorization of such use shall be subject to judicial review or other independent review by a distinct higher authority in that Member;

(j) any decision relating to the remuneration provided in respect of such use shall be subject to judicial review or other independent review by a distinct higher authority in that Member;

(k) Members are not obliged to apply the conditions set forth in subparagraphs (b) and (f) above where such use is permitted to remedy a practice determined after judicial or administrative process to be anti-competitive. The need to correct anti-competitive practices may be taken into account in determining the amount of remuneration in such cases. Competent authorities shall have the authority to refuse termination of authorization if and when the conditions which led to such authorization are likely to recur;

(l) where such use is authorized to permit the exploitation of a patent ("the second patent") which cannot be exploited without infringing another patent ("the first patent"), the following additional conditions shall apply:

(i) the invention claimed in the second patent shall involve an important technical advance of considerable economic significance in relation to the invention claimed in the first patent;

(ii) the owner of the first patent shall be entitled to a cross-licence on reasonable terms to use the invention claimed in the second patent; and

(iii) the use authorized in respect of the first patent shall be non- assignable except with the assignment of the second patent.

Article 32

Revocation/Forfeiture

An opportunity for judicial review of any decision to revoke or forfeit a patent shall be available.

Article 33

Term of Protection

The term of protection available shall not end before the expiration of a period of twenty years counted from the filing date.

NOTES AND QUESTIONS

(1) **Patent Policy in Developing Countries**. It is sometimes suggested that developing countries benefit directly by strengthening their patent systems. *See* Edmund W. Kitch, *The Patent Policy of Developing Countries*, 13 UCLA PAC. BASIN L.J. 166 (1995). There is considerable opposition to this view

from some writers in developing countries, such as Argentina, who assert that strong patents lead not to more investment or inventiveness in developing countries but rather to more wealth transfer from the developing to the developed countries. *See, e.g.,* Carlos Maria Correa, *Intellectual Property Rights and Foreign Direct Investment*, (ECOSOC ST/CTC/SER.A/24 1993). A more strident rhetoric, by an academic writer opining that the TRIPS Agreement is "amoral," is found in Michelle McGrath, *The Patent Provisions in TRIPS: Protecting Reasonable Remuneration for Services Rendered–or the Latest Development in Western Colonialism*, 18 EUR. INTELL. PROP. REV. 398 (1996). The terms of the North-South intellectual property debate as posed by the developing nations in the early days of the Uruguay Round were straightforward and simple: "How can the developing nations in the South get the best access to technological innovations made *elsewhere*–that is, in the developed countries of the North?" Intellectual property protection was deemed an issue for the developed world not the developing one. Submissions made by Brazil and India, among others, at the beginning of the Uruguay round reflected the following sentiments:

• rigid IP protection impedes access to latest technological innovations, and therefore restricts the participation of developing countries in international trade;

• "abusive use" of IPRs distorts international trade;

• what is "trade-related" about intellectual property rights is the restrictive and anticompetitive behavior of the owners of intellectual property and not the behavior of commercial interests in developing countries or that of their governments;

• patent systems can have adverse effects in critical sectors such as food production, poverty alleviation, health care and disease prevention, and have a dampening effect on the promotion of R&D in developing countries and in improving their technological capabilities;

• systems for the protection of IPRs are by nature monopolistic and sovereign nations should be free to attune their own systems of intellectual property protection to their own needs and conditions.

(2) **IP and IPRs.** What is the difference in usage between the terms "intellectual property" ("IP") and "intellectual property *rights*" ("IPRs")? In the context of international trade law, the latter term is common. The reverse is true in the international intellectual property community. According to one commentator:

> Characterizing patent protections as a kind of intellectual property "right" was a first step in setting the terms of debate. This characterization is of course not novel; patents, trademarks, and copyrights have long been viewed as intellectual property rights. This is evidenced, in part, by the common reference to intellectual property rights by the acronym "IPR." Nor is the characterization, from a legal standpoint, startling or at all surprising. Lawyers commonly understand that the holders of government-authorized powers have "rights," without attaching any particular moral force to

the term. In the debate over international patent policy, however, the use of the term "right" exercised an important influence. As a preliminary matter, it is important to recognize that while "rights" may be commonplace in legal discourse, the allocation or recognition of a right may nonetheless privilege certain actions or relations. Characterizing something as a right tends to immunize it from challenge both in practice and in the realm of ideas. To transgress a right is to "violate" it, to commit a wrong. To define something as a right is to remove it, more or less, from political challenge. Even if it is not considered a "natural" right; in moral terms, a right is supposed to be somewhat inviolate.

While rights talk may have the general effect in legal discourse of elevating the defined conduct or relationship above politics, that effect was particularly strong in the case of patent policy. The vociferous insistence of industry and the U.S. government assumed a moral character This was an especially notable accomplishment in light of the intangible nature of intellectual property. Additionally, intellectual property is more obviously a creation of the state than other sorts of property. Hence it intuitively enjoys less of a moral right than other property claims. At the practical level, one does not receive a patent until an invention is certified by the state as new, useful, and nonobvious. This makes it unusually clear that the state could choose not to grant the right at all. At the conceptual level, patent rights evaporate after a set period. Governments may grant patents for longer or shorter periods, on conditions, or not at all. The characterization of an inventor or producer's intellectual property interest as a "right" works to obscure the contingent nature of the patent.

Robert Weissman, *A Long, Strange TRIPS: The Pharmaceutical Industry Drive to Harmonize Global Intellectual Property Rules, and the Remaining WTO Legal Alternatives Available to Third World Countries*, 17 U. PA. J. INT'L ECON. L. 1069, 1086-87 (1996). Is the author correct that the nature of a patent is merely contingent? Does the term "IPRs" frame the debate in a way different than the term "IP" does–particularly with regard to the identity of the owner? Or is this a distinction without a difference? Are "rights" created by statutes? *See generally* R. NOZICK, ANARCHY, STATE AND UTOPIA (1974); Ned Miltenberg, *The Revolutionary Right to a Remedy*, TRIAL 48-52 (March 1988).

(3) **Refocusing TRIPS**. The U.S. position at the start of the Uruguay Round leading to the eventual adoption of the TRIPS Agreement is set forth in a 1987 General Accounting Office report entitled *International Trade: Strengthening Worldwide Protection of Intellectual Property Rights*, GAO/NSIAD-87-65; *see also* OTA, *Disseminating Information: Evolution of a Concept*, 64 ECON. IMPACT 18 (1988). The entire focus of the report is on foreign piracy of U.S. intellectual property. There is no mention of compulsory licensing allowed to member states under Article 5 of the Paris Convention as part of the U.S. agenda. For an interesting discussion of the history of the shift in the U.S. position, see generally MICHAEL P. RYAN, KNOWLEDGE DIPLOMACY (1998).

(4) **How Often are Compulsory Licenses Used?** An excellent survey of compulsory licensing policies and of compulsory licensing provisions worldwide just prior to the enactment of the TRIPS Agreement in 1995 may be found in Gianna Julian-Arnold, *International Compulsory Licensing: The Rationales and the Reality,* 33 IDEA: J.L. & TECH. 349 (1993). Rarely are such provisions exercised. It has been noted that, for example, in Australia, there have been only two applications ever for a compulsory license, and both were rejected. *See* THOMAS A. MANDEVILLE, UNDERSTANDING NOVELTY: INFORMATION, TECHNOLOGICAL CHANGE AND THE PATENT SYSTEM 24 (1996).

(5) **Limiting Exclusive Rights**. It has been asserted that Article 30 of TRIPS allows a state to establish working requirements. Would such a course of action be consistent with Article 5 of the Paris Convention as incorporated by Article 3 of TRIPS? What about price controls? Can a developing country use the lever of price controls to achieve what it cannot through compulsory licensing? *See* Weissman, *supra,* at 1111-23; *see also* Richard P. Rozek & Ruth Berkowitz, *The Effects of Patent Protection on the Prices of Pharmaceutical Products–Is Intellectual Property Protection Raising the Drug Bill in Developing Countries?,* 1 J. WORLD INTELL. PROP. 179 (1998); Thomas G. Field, Jr., *Pharmaceuticals and Intellectual Property: Meeting Needs Throughout the World,* 31 IDEA 3 (1990).

(6) **Have the Developing Countries Turned the TRIPS Table?** The recent AIDS epidemic has set the stage for a dramatic coda to a century of negotiations concerning the right of states to set working requirements for foreign patentees. After six months of failed consultations, on January 8, 2001, the USTR filed a request for a WTO panel to address Brazil's refusal to amend Article 68 of its industrial property law of 1996, contending that the law was inconsistent with Brazil's obligations under Articles 27.1 and 28 of TRIPS. *See* WT/DS199/3 (Jan. 9, 2001). The United States stated:

> The [TRIPS] Agreement prohibits discrimination regarding the availability of patents and the enjoyment of patent rights on the basis of whether products are imported or locally produced. This obligation prohibits Members of the [WTO] from requiring 'local working.' i.e., local production of the patented invention as a condition for enjoying exclusive patent rights. Article 68 of Brazil's 1996 industrial property law . . . , however, imposes a 'local working' requirement which stipulates that a patent shall be subject to compulsory licensing if the subject matter of the patent is not 'worked' in the territory of Brazil. Specifically, a compulsory license shall be granted on a patent if the patented product is not manufactured in Brazil or if the patent process is not used in Brazil. In addition, if a patent owner chooses to exploit the patent through importation rather than 'local working,' then Article 68 will allow others to import either the patented product or the product obtained from the patented process.

Brazil quickly countered with a request at the WTO for consultations with the U.S., charging that Chapter 18 of the U.S. patent law violates the TRIPS agreement. (That chapter requires certain firms with title to U.S. government-funded inventions to manufacture "substantially in the United States" unless the requirement is waived. *See* 35 U.S.C.§ 204; WT/DS224/1, Feb. 7, 2001. http://www.ipo.org/2001/IPcourts/Brazil.pdf. Shortly thereafter, the non-governmental organization "Doctors Without Borders" announced in Mumbai (Bombay) India that it intended to buy anti-AIDS drugs from the Indian company Cipla, Ltd. to distribute without charge in developing countries. On March 13, new U.S. Trade Representative Robert Zoellick was quoted as voicing concern over a potential backlash against the drug industry for aggressively asserting patent rights in the face of the HIV/AIDS crisis. While emphasizing his support for intellectual property, he said, "If [the pharmaceutical companies] don't get ahead of this issue [the HIV/AIDS issue], the hostility that generates could put at risk the whole intellectual property rights system." Paul Blustein, *Getting Out in Front on Trade: New U.S. Trade Representative Adds "Values" to His Globalization Plan*, WASH. POST, March 13, 2001, at E1. The next day, Bristol-Myers-Squibb said that it would not use patent rights to stop generic drug makers from selling low-cost versions of one of its HIV/AIDS drugs in Africa, and that it would sell the drug in Africa at below cost. Two weeks later, on March 29, 2001, Merck & Co. Inc. pledged to Brazil to cut the price of two AIDS-fighting drugs in a bid to prevent Brazil from producing its own versions of the patented drugs.

(7) **Compulsory Licensing and AIDS.** The history of how pharmaceutical companies holding patents on AIDS medicines have dealt with the AIDS crisis in Africa is interesting for what it reveals about the interface between international law and international politics. In 1997, South Africa amended its Medicines and Related Substances Control Act No. 101 of 1965, adding Section 15C as follows:

> The minister may prescribe conditions for the supply of more affordable medicines in certain circumstances so as to protect the health of the public, and in particular may–
>
> (a) notwithstanding anything to the contrary contained in the Patents Act, 1978 (Act No. 57 of 1978), determine that the rights with regard to any medicine under a patent granted in the Republic shall not extend to acts in respect of such medicine which has been put onto the market by the owner of the medicine, or with his or her consent;
>
> (b) prescribe the conditions on which any medicine which is identical in composition, meets the same quality standard and is intended to have the same proprietary name as that of another medicine already registered in the Republic, but which is imported by a person other than the person who is the holder of the registration certificate of the medicine already registered and which originates from any site of manufacture of the original manufacturer as approved by the council in the prescribed manner, may be imported:
>
> (c) prescribe the registration procedure for, as well as the use of, the medicine referred to in paragraph (b).

On October 21, 1998, the United States enacted Public Law 105-277, "An Act Making omnibus consolidated and emergency appropriations for the fiscal year ending September 30, 1999, and for other purposes." Included was the following provision:

> Provided further, That none of the funds appropriated under this heading may be made available or assistance for the central Government of the Republic of South Africa, until the Secretary of State reports in writing to the appropriate committees of the Congress on the steps being taken by the United States Government to work with the Government of the Republic of South Africa to negotiate the repeal, suspension, or termination of section 15(c) of South Africa's Medicines and Related Substances Control Amendment Act No. 90 of 1997.

Subsequently, thirty-nine pharmaceutical companies brought suit in a South African court to have Section 15(c) declared unconstitutional, and in late 2000, GlaxoWellcome sent cease and desist letters to generic drug manufacturers over imports of its patented retrovirals lamivudine and zidovudine into Africa. In January 2001, the Pharmaceutical Research and Manufacturers of America petitioned USTR for listing of South Africa on a Section 301 watch list. *See infra* § 5.02[A] (discussing Section 301).

In February, 2001, Joseph Papovich, the assistant U.S. Trade Representative for intellectual property rights, stated that President George Bush was "not considering a change in the present flexible policy" on compulsory licensing of drugs by AIDS-stricken countries. The February 22, 2001 *New York Times* reported that "the U.S. will not seek sanctions against poor countries overwhelmed by the AIDS epidemic that try to force down the price of patented anti-AIDS drugs by legalizing the importation or manufacture of generic versions. The administration, . . . will not try to punish such countries even if American drug makers complain or American patent laws are being broken— as long as the country adheres to the rules agreed under World Trade Organization treaties."

Six weeks later, in early April 2001, the drug companies withdrew their suit. (Stock prices plummeted the next day.) South Africa allegedly has represented to the companies (and to the U.S.) that it will comply with its TRIPS obligations. Does Section 15(c) refer only to AIDS drugs? If the law is not amended, is South Africa TRIPS-compliant? By settling the case, have the pharmaceutical companies agreed not to challenge compulsory licensing of other medications, should it occur? Prozac? Viagra? *See Settlement Does Little Harm To Drug Firms; Lawsuit: Dropping South Africa AIDS Case Has More Symbolic Than Practical Weight, But It Could Embolden Other Countries,* L.A. TIMES, Apr. 21, 2001. On April 5, 2001, the African countries of the WTO secured WTO approval to consider the relationship of intellectual property protection and access to medicine at the June 2001 meeting of the TRIPS Council. In response, the United States stated that it is "committed to fighting the HIV/AIDS epidemic, but expressed concern that intellectual property rights protection is seen as a barrier to that effort."

CANADA—PATENT PROTECTION OF PHARMACEUTICAL PRODUCTS
Doc. WT/DS114/R (WTO Dispute Settlement Panel, Mar. 17, 2000)

II. Factual Aspects

[Section 55.2 of Canada's Patent Act excluded from liability for infringement for making, using, or selling a patented product or using a patented process "solely for uses reasonably related to the development and submission of information required under any law of Canada, a province or a country other than Canada that regulates the manufacture, construction, use or sale of any product" or "during the applicable period provided for by the regulations, for the manufacture and storage of articles intended for sale after the date on which the term of the patent expires." It also provided that the Governor in Council "may make regulations for the purposes of subsection (2), but any period provided for by the regulations must terminate immediately preceding the date on which the term of the patent expires."]

The regulatory review procedure [for new drugs] is time consuming. It may take from one to two-and-a-half years to complete. However, prior to this period, a generic manufacturer will have spent from two to four years in the development of its regulatory submission. Thus, the overall time required for a generic manufacturer to develop its submission and to complete the regulatory review process ranges from three to six-and-a-half years. After the development of its regulatory submission, the generic manufacturer will file an Abbreviated New Drug Submission ("ANDS") with Health Canada. The generic manufacturer files an ANDS because, typically, it is relying on comparative studies to a drug product that has proven to be safe and effective. An innovator, on the other hand, would file a New Drug Submission, since it must provide full pre-clinical and clinical data to establish the safety and efficacy of the drug in question. For an innovator, it takes approximately eight to 12 years to develop a drug and receive regulatory approval, which takes place during the 20-year patent term. The resulting period of market exclusivity under the current Canadian Patent Act varies from drug to drug. Estimated averages, at the time that the Act came into force, range from eight to ten years, according to the Pharmaceutical Manufacturers Association of Canada (PMAC), or 12 to 14 years, according to the Canadian Drug Manufacturers Association (CDMA).

. . . .

III. Findings And Recommendations Requested By The Parties

The European Communities and their member States requested the Panel to make the following rulings, findings and recommendations: . . .

That Canada, by allowing manufacturing and stockpiling of pharmaceutical products without the consent of the patent holder during the six months immediately prior to the expiration of the

20-year patent term by virtue of the provisions of Section 55.2(2) and 55.2(3) of the Patent Act together with the Manufacturing and Storage of Patented Medicines Regulations, violated its obligations under Article 28.1 together with Article 33 of the TRIPS Agreement.

That Canada, by treating patent holders in the field of pharmaceutical inventions by virtue of these provisions less favourably than inventions in all other fields of technology, violated its obligations under Article 27.1 of the TRIPS Agreement requiring patents to be available and patent rights enjoyable without discrimination as to the field of technology.

That the provisions of Section 55.2(1) concerning activities related to the development and submission of information required to obtain marketing approval for pharmaceutical products carried out without the consent of the patent holder violated the provisions of Article 28.1 of the TRIPS Agreement.

That Canada, by treating patent holders in the field of pharmaceutical inventions by virtue of these provisions less favourably than inventions in all other fields of technology, violated its obligations under Article 27.1 of the TRIPS Agreement requiring patents to be available and patent rights enjoyable without discrimination as to the field of technology.

That the violations referred to above constituted prima facie nullification or impairment under Article 64.1 of the TRIPS Agreement, Article XXIII of GATT 1994 and Article 3.8 of the DSU.

That the DSB request Canada to bring its domestic legislation into conformity with its obligations under the TRIPS Agreement.

Canada requested the Panel to reject the complaints of the European Communities and their member States on the basis of the following findings:

Section 55.2(1) and 55.2(2) of the Patent Act conform with Canada's obligations under the TRIPS Agreement, because:

(a) Each of these provisions is a "limited exception" to the exclusive rights conferred by a patent within the meaning of Article 30 of the TRIPS Agreement;

(b) Neither of these provisions discriminates, within the meaning of Article 27 of the TRIPS Agreement, as to the field of technology in which any relevant invention occurs or has occurred, because: the prohibition in Article 27.1 against discrimination on the basis of field of technology does not apply to allowable limited exceptions, or, if the Panel were to find Article 27.1 applicable, because: the limited exceptions of Section 55.2(1) and 55.2(2) are not expressly related to any particular field of technology;

(c) Neither of these provisions reduces the minimum term of protection referred to in Article 33 of the TRIPS Agreement to a term that is less than that minimum.

IV. Arguments of the Parties

A. European Communities

. . . .

The European Communities and their member States argued that, by allowing manufacturing and stockpiling of pharmaceutical products under Sections 55.2(2) and (3) of the Patent Act together with the Manufacturing and Storage of Patented Medicines Regulations during the six months immediately prior to the expiration of the 20-year patent term, Canada breached its obligations under Articles 28.1 and 33 of the TRIPS Agreement. The following points were advanced in support of this argument:

* Canadian law allowed all the acts referred to in Article 28.1(a) of the TRIPS Agreement, if a product patent was concerned, and Article 28.1(b) of the Agreement, if a process patent was concerned, with the sole exception of the act of selling to a distributor or consumer without the consent of the patent owner from six months before the expiry of the 20-year patent term. In other words Canada only provided for 19 years and six months of the minimum patent protection as mandated by Articles 28.1 and 33 of the TRIPS Agreement.

* In practical terms this meant that anybody in Canada was allowed to perform the acts of making, constructing and using of the invention during the last six months of the patent term without the authorization of the patent holder. This possibility was automatic for anybody in Canada, i.e. no particular authorization had to be applied for and eventually granted by a Canadian authority. The faculty was entirely unqualified in terms of the extent and volume of the use and no royalty fees whatsoever had to be paid to the patent holder nor did the latter have any right to be informed of such unauthorized use of his invention. Both product and process patents were subject to this denial of protection.

* To the best of the knowledge of the European Communities and their member States, Canada was the only country in the world–industrialized or developing–which allowed manufacturing and stockpiling of products covered by a patent during the term of such a patent. Canada itself recognized that, at least in the United States and the member States of the European Communities, such a possibility did not exist.

The European Communities and their member States argued that, by treating patent holders in the field of pharmaceutical inventions less favourably than inventions in all other fields of technology, Canada infringed its obligations contained in Article 27.1 of the TRIPS Agreement. The following points were advanced in support of this argument:

* The Canadian patent legislation, which under Section 55.2(2) and 55.2(3) together with the Manufacturing and Storage of Patented Medicines Regulations practically speaking provided only for a 19-year term of patent protection, applied exclusively to product and process patents for inventions in the field of pharmaceutical products. During the legislative process, other fields of technology were not even considered and no draft legislation to extend the scope of these provisions to other or all fields of technology was, according to the information available to the European Communities and their Member States, presently pending in the Canadian legislature. In this context, it was also noteworthy that Section 55.2(2) of the Canadian Patent Act was, taken in isolation, an inoperative provision and created only legal effects through the promulgation of the Manufacturing and Storage of Patented Medicines Regulations. This Regulation was expressly limited to "patented medicines" and could not apply to any other product.

* Thus, the Canadian legislation discriminated against pharmaceutical inventions by treating them less favourably than inventions in all other fields of technology and therefore Canada violated its obligations under Article 27.1 of the TRIPS Agreement.

The European Communities and their member States argued that Section 55.2(1) of the Canadian Patent Act allowed all activities related to the development and submission of information required to obtain marketing approval for pharmaceutical products carried out by a third party without the consent of the patent holder at any time during the patent term, notwithstanding the exclusive rights stipulated in Article 28.1 of the TRIPS Agreement. These activities were completely unlimited in quantity and extent and included the acts of offering for sale and selling, at least insofar as any manufacturer of the patented product or process could invoke this right, if only the final purchaser of the product had the intention to use the product for "[] uses reasonably related to the development and submission of information required under the law of Canada, a province or a country other than Canada that regulates the manufacture, construction, use or sale of any product". Therefore, Section 55.2(1) of the Canadian Patent Act had to be considered to be incompatible with the provisions of Article 28.1(a) and (b) of the TRIPS Agreement. The following points were advanced in support of this argument:

* The permissible activities under Section 55.2(1) of the Canadian Patent Act were not limited in time. In other words, they might be performed without the consent of the right holder at any point in time during the 20-year patent term.

* Section 55.2(1) of the Patent Act took away all the rights a patent granted its owner, i.e. making, constructing, using (this included importing) and selling, and did not stipulate any quantitative limits for these activities. The only limitation set out by the law consisted in the objective of these activities, i.e. they must be "reasonably related to the development and submission of information" required for obtaining marketing approval anywhere in the world.

* The requirements for obtaining marketing approval for pharmaceutical products in industrialized countries were similar and broadly focused on three criteria: safety, quality and efficacy of the product. Thus, the documentation required by the national drug administrations contained information on the composition, manufacture, quality control and stability of the product. This included also in Canada proof that a full production line was viable and could involve full batch testing, which in turn required the production of significant quantities of the product protected by a patent. The non-clinical testing information that was required related to the pharmacological effects of the product in relation to the proposed use in humans and to the toxicological effects of the product on the organism and in different organs. The clinical test data which had to be compiled constituted by far the most important part of the marketing approval activities as far as time, resources and costs were concerned. It was typically subdivided into three phases starting out from tests in small doses administered to a small number of patients (phase I) to the use of the product in wide-ranging comparative studies involving large numbers of patients which could go into tens of thousands for some indications (phases II and III).

   *   It was also noteworthy that Section 55.2(1) of the Canadian Patent Act did not only allow all the activities mentioned in the text to be carried out by somebody who had himself the intention to use the substances for preparing his application for marketing approval, but allowed such activities as manufacturing, importing and selling for anybody, if only the results of these activities were eventually intended to be used by somebody else for his application to a marketing approval authority in any country of the world. Here it was important to understand that, while research-based pharmaceutical companies did generally produce the active pharmaceutical ingredients in-house, many—in particular small and medium-sized—copy (generic) producers sourced the active ingredients from independent manufacturers domestically or from abroad. The reason for this was linked to the fact that the production of the active ingredients was often highly capital intensive and once the equipment was in place and running, huge quantities could be manufactured by a very small staff in a short period of time.

   *   The interplay and cumulation of all these possibilities led to a situation that very significant quantities of the products protected by a patent could be manufactured, imported and sold without the consent of the patent holder at any time during the patent term.

   *   There existed no provisions under the laws of the EC member States which would allow a party to carry out the activities referred to in Section 55.2(1) of the Canadian Patent Act without the consent of the patent owner.

The European Communities and their member States argued that, by allowing all the activities referred to . . . above related to the development and submission of information required to obtain marketing approval for pharmaceutical products and carried out by a third party without the consent of the patent holder at any time during the patent term, Canada treated holders of pharmaceutical patents less favourably than holders of patents in all other fields of technology and thus violated its obligations under Article 27.1 of the TRIPS Agreement. The following points were advanced in support of this argument:

   *   It was true that Section 55.2(1) of the Canadian Patent Act did not mention expressly pharmaceuticals or medicines, but referred to cases where "Canada, a province or a country other than Canada [] regulates the manufacture, construction, use or sale of any product"; it was in effect only applied to pharmaceutical products. This was not astonishing because the considerations in relation to the formulation and adoption of Bill C-91, of which Section 55.2(1) of the Patent Act formed a pivotal part, were exclusively concerned with the treatment of pharmaceutical products.

   *   While the text of the law read as if this provision would apply to all fields of technology, it did in practice only apply to pharmaceuticals. This became apparent from the legislative history of this provision, where in the

discussions—to the extent that reports were available to the European Communities and their member States—other areas of technology were not even mentioned. The Canadian authorities had confirmed in the formal consultations under the DSU that this provision was applied only to pharmaceuticals. This was particularly interesting in a situation where for many other categories of products "the development and submission of information [is] required under any law of Canada, a province or a country other than Canada that regulates the manufacture, construction, use or sale of (such) products". The product categories meeting this condition included agricultural chemical products, certain foodstuffs, motor vehicles, aircraft, ships and many more.

*   While the manufacture, construction, use or sale of a great plethora of products were, under the laws of Canada, its provinces or any other country, subject to regulations, Section 55.2(1) of the Patent Act did not apply to these other fields of products; in none of these areas did Section 55.2(1) of the Patent Act apply. This was confirmed by Canada in the formal consultations under the DSU.

The European Communities and their member States advanced the following information about the historical developments in Canada as well as a comparison between the situation in Canada before and after the introduction of Bill C-91 and the Manufacturing and Storage of Patented Medicines Regulations in 1993, taking the view that the curtailment of patent rights for pharmaceuticals as pursued by Canada was incompatible with the patent provisions of the TRIPS Agreement independently of whether it was presented as a compulsory licence, as under the pre-C-91 system or as "exceptions" under the C-91 system itself:

*   Patent protection in Canada had been in place for many decades and also inventions in the field of pharmaceuticals had been patentable under the ordinary conditions. As early as 1923, Canada modified the patent protection for pharmaceuticals by introducing a regime of compulsory licences for pharmaceuticals. Compulsory licences allowed a third party without the authorization of the owner of the patent to make, use or sell patented pharmaceuticals. The compulsory licence could be granted at any time during the patent term. The patentee was entitled to the payment of royalties by the beneficiary of the compulsory licence.

*   Because the granting of the compulsory licences was subject to the requirement that the active ingredients used in the pharmaceutical product be produced in Canada, few compulsory licences were effectively granted at the time, since it was difficult to obtain Canadian-made active ingredients.

*   In 1969, the requirement to produce the active ingredient in Canada was dropped having as a consequence that numerous compulsory licences were granted thereafter. The licensing fee amounted generally to 4 per cent of the sales price of the products produced under the compulsory licence, which often covered several patents.

*   In 1987, the Canadian Patent Act was further amended by replacing the previous term of protection of 17 years from the time the patent was granted by one of 20 years from the time the patent application was filed. This amendment entered into force in 1989. Under this new regime, compulsory licences continued to be available but were limited in time. Such compulsory licences could be obtained after the patented product had been on the Canadian market for seven years, if the licensee intended to produce in Canada, or ten years if he intended to import the active ingredient. These amendments had as practical effect that the patent holder was guaranteed at least seven years (ten years if the holder of the compulsory licence did not intend to produce or source locally) of patent protection.

* Canada further modified its patent laws by the Patent Act Amendment Act, 1992 (Bill C-91), which entered into force in February 1993. While inventions in the area of pharmaceuticals were under the pre-C-91 patent regime only patentable as process patents (or so-called 'product-by-process patents'), product patents for pharmaceutical inventions were only introduced by C-91 in 1993. The major modification consisted of the elimination of the existing compulsory licensing system for pharmaceuticals and the introduction of exceptions to the patent rights of the holder of a patent in the area of pharmaceuticals which were at issue in the present case. In order to understand the motivation of the Canadian authorities one had to look at the historic situation in 1991 and 1992 as far as international rulemaking on intellectual property issues to which Canada was a party was concerned.

* In December 1991, the then Director-General of the General Agreement on Tariffs and Trade, Arthur Dunkel, had compiled a Draft Final Act for the conclusion of the Uruguay Round negotiations, which also contained a text of the draft Agreement on Trade-Related Aspects of Intellectual Property Rights (TRIPS).[27] The text of the TRIPS Agreement as contained in the so-called

---

[27]The EC provided the following short negotiating history of the TRIPS Agreement:

"At the Ministerial Conference which launched the Uruguay Round of Multilateral Trade Negotiations at Punta del Este, Uruguay in September 1986, TRIPS was included into the negotiation agenda as one of the so-called new topics. Multilateral rulemaking in the IPR area was so far dominated by the World Intellectual Property Organisation (WIPO) which administers or co-administers practically all important conventions in this area. There existed at the outset fundamental divergencies between industrialized countries, who wished to achieve a comprehensive coverage of all intellectual property rights and developing countries (LDCs) who wanted to limit work to a Code against trade in counterfeit goods. During the negotiating process the view of those who pursued a comprehensive approach prevailed. This had as a consequence that practically all existing IPRs were included in TRIPs. To start with the principles of national treatment and most favoured nation treatment (the latter being a novelty in the area of IPRs) were stipulated. The most important WIPO conventions (the Paris Convention covering industrial property rights and the Berne Convention covering copyright as well as the Washington Treaty for the protection of semiconductor topographies) were included by reference, also to make these conventions subject to an efficient dispute settlement system. Over and above the level provided for under the provisions of these conventions the substantive levels of protection were set at the level prevailing in the mid 1980s in the industrialized countries. Furthermore extensive rules for the enforcement of the substantive IPR standards were sought for, which constituted an absolute novelty for international IPR rulemaking. The Dunkel text on TRIPS of December 1991 to which reference was made under point 19 above, became almost verbatim part of the Final Act adopted at the Marrakech Ministerial Conference in April 1994 which successfully concluded the Uruguay Round Negotiations. The substantive provisions for the protection of patents are contained in Section 5 of Part II, i.e. Articles 27 to 34 of the TRIPS Agreement. Article 27.1 TRIPS sets out the principle that patents have to be available in all fields of technology if the general conditions for the grant of a patent are met. This is of fundamental importance because many countries, in particular developing countries, had not made—and some still today do not make—available patents for specific areas of technology, notably pharmaceuticals, agrochemicals or foodstuffs. Article 27.2 and 27.3 TRIPS give the option to exclude a number of well defined subject matter from patentability,

Dunkel text was informally agreed by all parties to the negotiations and became practically verbatim part of the Agreement finally adopted in 1994 in Marrakesh. The TRIPS Agreement contained in Article 31 detailed provisions on "Use Without the Authorization of the Right Holder". It was certain that the Canadian regime on compulsory licences for pharmaceutical products existing in the pre-C-91 system would have been incompatible with Article 31 of the TRIPS Agreement. This had been expressly admitted by the Canadian Government.

* While the Uruguay Round negotiations were somewhat in limbo in 1991/1992, the negotiations on a North American Free Trade Agreement (NAFTA) between Canada, Mexico and the United States of America were concluded in 1992 and the agreement was signed at the end of 1992. NAFTA contained in Chapter Seventeen extensive disciplines on the protection of intellectual property rights. The provisions of Chapter Seventeen were largely based on, and in many instances were a verbatim reproduction of, the provisions of the then draft TRIPS Agreement.[29] Article 31 of the TRIPS Agreement was reproduced almost identically in Article 1709(10) of NAFTA. Thus, the Canadian compulsory licensing system for pharmaceuticals in the pre-C-91 system would also have been incompatible with Canada's obligations under NAFTA, in particular its Article 1709(10). This conclusion had been expressly stated by the Canadian Government.

* In order to fully appreciate the Canadian 'philosophy' for patent protection in the area of pharmaceutical products, it was important to understand the interplay between pharmaceutical research, patenting of inventions and granting of marketing approval for medicinal products. From the moment an application for a pharmaceutical product or process patent was filed until the resulting pharmaceutical product could be effectively marketed it took on average between eight and 12 years. This period of eight to 12 years was necessary for product development which included important periods for

---

which is largely derived from modern pieces of IPR legislation as the European Patent Convention (EPC) (compare in particular Article 53 EPC). Article 28 TRIPS describes in detail the rights, which are conferred on a patent owner once the patent has been granted. Article 29 TRIPS stipulates the duties which a patent applicant has to meet and Article 30 TRIPS addresses exceptions to rights conferred which WTO members may provide. Article 31 TRIPS deals primarily with what is generally termed as compulsory licences and sets out detailed rules for the grant of such licences. Article 32 TRIPS addresses revocation and forfeiture and Article 33 TRIPS mandates a minimum term of protection for patents of 20 years from filing. Finally, Article 34 TRIPS establishes rules for process patents and provides in particular for a reversal of the burden of proof in an infringement procedure. While transitional periods for the benefit of LDCs (including—under certain conditions—so-called economies in transition) and least developed countries (LLDCs) are still running, all industrialized country members of the WTO had to comply fully with all the obligations flowing from the TRIPS Agreement as of 1 January 1996 (see Articles 65 and 66 TRIPS). Thus Canada's obligations vis-a-vis the EC and their Member States had to be met fully as of 1 January 1996." The EC also referred to Gervais, "The TRIPS Agreement: Drafting History and Analysis", London 1998, pages 3 to 28.

[29]Reference was made to Dr Herz, who was part of the Canadian TRIPS and NAFTA negotiating team, who had written: ". . .with respect to IPRs, NAFTA closely tracks the language of the 1991 Dunkel Draft of the TRIPS negotiating text. Therefore, NAFTA's chapter 17: Intellectual property and TRIPS generally are textually close enough to ensure that interpretations in the meaning of the one would be directly relevant to the elucidation of the other. IP related findings of eventual NAFTA panels may, therefore, powerfully influence TRIPS interpretation and vice-versa." (Canada-US L.J. Vol. 23, (1997), at p. 281).

pre-clinical and clinical testing. Subsequent to the testing activities, the submissions for the marketing approval authority had to be prepared and the latter had to process the submitted information. This meant in practical terms that, under the present patent law provisions of Canada, a holder of a pharmaceutical patent enjoyed an effective patent term of eight to 12 years in which he could claim exclusivity on the market and it was during this period that all R&D costs had to be depreciated on sales. Under the pre-C-91 system, compulsory licences were automatically granted to all Canadian operators who wanted to copy the invention after the patented pharmaceutical product had been on the Canadian market for at least seven years (or ten years if the active ingredients for the generic product were imported). Furthermore, a period of at least two-and-a-half years for obtaining marketing approval in Canada for the copy product had to be taken into consideration because, under the previous Canadian patent law, producers of copy products could only start to generate pre-marketing approval testing activities once the compulsory licence had been granted. For the holder of the patent for the original product this system provided for a period of effective market exclusivity from nine-and-a-half years to 12 years. This also had as a consequence that the effective market exclusivity for the patent holder went in certain cases beyond the end of the 20-year patent term. To put it in a nutshell, the economic situation in terms of effective market exclusivity for the holder of the patent under the old 1989 to 1993 system, which granted on average 11 years , was indeed very similar to the C-91 system from 1994, which granted on average a market exclusivity for the patent holder of ten years.

The European Communities and their member States, in support of their claims, also advanced information of the economic losses suffered by their pharmaceutical industry from the effects of Sections 55.2(1) and 55.2(2) of the Patent Act together with the Manufacturing and Storage of Patented Medicines Regulations. The European research-based pharmaceutical industry (EFPIA) had made an analysis of its alleged losses suffered in Canada, which exceeded the amount of C$ 100 million per year. This analysis was based on the conservative assumption that, while the operation of the provisions referred to above would allow copy manufacturers to market the product immediately upon patent expiry, in the absence of these provisions effective marketing would only be possible at the earliest two years after patent term expiry. The extrapolation was based on sales of the top 100 original pharmaceutical products sold in Canada between 1995 and 1997.

In respect of Article 30 of the TRIPS Agreement, the European Communities and their member States initially took the position that, while Canada, during the formal consultations under the DSU, had invoked Article 30 of the TRIPS Agreement to justify the measures at issue, it had done so in a rather summary and rudimentary manner. Therefore, the EC limited itself in its first written submission in this regard to stating that their view was that the Canadian measures could not be justified under Article 30, because the conditions set out in this provision were not met: the curtailment of patent rights under Canadian legislation did not constitute "limited exceptions to the exclusive rights conferred by a patent". Furthermore, the exceptions unreasonably conflicted with a normal exploitation of a patent and unreasonably prejudiced the legitimate interests of the patent owner, taking account of the legitimate interests of third parties. In any event, a violation of Article 27.1 of the TRIPS Agreement could not be justified under Article 30.

B. Canada

Canada, in response, requested the Panel to dismiss the complaint of the European Communities and their member States, submitting that:

(1) Canada's exceptions to the exclusive rights conferred by a patent were "limited exceptions" within the meaning of Article 30 of the TRIPS Agreement, because they: did not conflict in any mode or manner with the "normal exploitation" of a patent; they did not prejudice, or if they did, they did" not "unreasonably prejudice" the "legitimate interests" of a patentee taking account of the "legitimate interests" of third parties; and the third party interests that the exceptions took account of were "legitimate interests" of relevant third parties.

(2)(a) the prohibition in Article 27.1 of the TRIPS Agreement against discrimination on the basis of field of technology did not apply to allowable limited exceptions;

(2)(b) in any event, Canada's limited exceptions to the exclusive rights conferred by a patent did not discriminate as to the field of technology in which an invention occurred, because they related to products that were subject to laws regulating the manufacture, construction, use or sale of a product and were not expressly related to any particular field of technology; and

(3) as regards Article 33 of the TRIPS Agreement, Canada's limited exceptions to the exclusive rights conferred by a patent did not reduce the term of protection accorded to a patent, because they did nothing to impair a patentee's right to exploit its patent for the full term of protection by working the patent for its private commercial advantage.

Canada argued that the essential question in these proceedings was whether the provisions of Section 55.2(1) and 55.2(2) were "limited exceptions to the exclusive rights conferred by a patent", within the meaning of Article 30 of the TRIPS Agreement. According to Canada, these two measures:

(a) were "limited exceptions" within the meaning of Article 30, since they allowed patent owners complete freedom to exploit their rights throughout the full term of patent protection, leaving the monopoly of commercial exploitation and the exclusivity of economic benefits unimpaired for the life of the patent;

(b) did not conflict with a normal exploitation of a patent or prejudice the legitimate interests of the patent owner, since they only affected the patent owner's commercial exploitation after the patent had expired;

(c) in any event, took into account Canada's national interest in measures conducive to social welfare and the achievement of a balance between rights and obligations, both of which were recognized objectives in Article 7 of the TRIPS Agreement; and

(d) in particular, as required by Article 30, took account of the legitimate interests of third parties, in that:

* they allowed potential competitors to compete freely with the patentee after the patent expired, consistent with the policy of full competition underlying the requirement of Article 29 that, in return for the grant of patent protection, patentees must disclose their inventions to the public; the provision of Article 33 that the exclusive rights be conferred for a specified term only; and the authorization in Article 40 of national measures to prevent abuse of intellectual property rights having an adverse effect on competition; and

* they sought to protect public health—a value recognized in Article 8.1 of the TRIPS Agreement—through promoting access to cost-effective generic medicines following patent expiry and, in this connection, they took into account the legitimate interests of individuals, private insurers and public sector entities that financed health care in maintaining access to affordable medicines.

According to Canada, Article 30 allowed uses that did not unreasonably conflict with a normal exploitation of the patent or unreasonably prejudice the legitimate interests of the patent owner, taking account of the legitimate interests of third parties. Canada submitted that Article 30 therefore authorized measures that limited exclusive rights, provided that no commercial exploitation—i.e. sales—took place during the patent term. Any other interpretation would:

* ignore the existence of the word "unreasonably" in Article 30 and, thereby, the fact that conflicts with normal exploitation and prejudice to the patent owner's interests were allowed;

* disregard the public policy principles inherent in Articles 29 and 33, which encouraged free and open competition with the patent owner immediately upon expiry of the patent; and

* as a consequence, where regulatory review delayed the entry of competing products on the market, promote the practice of enforcing patent rights within the patent term so as to extend the monopoly of the patent owner beyond the term, a policy which the European Communities and their member States had sought to have included in the Agreement, but which had not been so included, i.e. as the European Communities and their member States made plain in their first written submission, they sought to win through litigation the windfall period of protection that they could not secure by negotiation.

Canada further referred to the interpretative rule set out in Article 31 of the Vienna Convention on the Law of Treaties and argued that the terms of any international treaty, including the TRIPS Agreement, were to be interpreted in good faith in accordance with their ordinary meaning in their context and in light of the object and purpose of the treaty. When the exception provisions in Part II of the TRIPS Agreement were interpreted in accordance with this rule, it became apparent that Article 30 provided a general and flexible authority for Members to adopt measures that balanced the interests of patent owners with the interests of others, as Article 7 of the Agreement expressly stated was an objective of the TRIPS Agreement.

* The language of Article 30 was markedly different from other provisions, which allowed exceptions to treaty rights. For example, GATT 1994, Article XX, required—as in paragraph(b)—that the exception measures be necessary to protect human health, and it contained additional restrictions in its chapeau portion. No similar restrictions were required under Article 30. Similarly, Article 13 of the TRIPS Agreement (and Article 9(2) of the Berne Convention for the Protection of Literary and Artistic Works (1971), upon which Article 13 was modelled), did not allow conflict with a normal exploitation of the work.

* Thus, the TRIPS Agreement contemplated that Members might, in implementing their obligations within their legal systems, adopt measures which, like those in issue here, introduced limited exceptions to the exclusive rights conferred by a patent and confined the patent monopoly to the specific term for which it was granted, in the interests of promoting full competition in regulated-product markets after the expiry of that term and of realizing the cost-saving benefits that competition in those markets (particularly the health care products market) conferred on society. The TRIPS Agreement did not contemplate that these important societal interests should be overridden by an alleged right of patentees to exploit time-consuming regulatory review system–which were neither designed nor intended to protect intellectual property rights–in order to extend the term of patent protection and to gain a windfall monopoly.

* Equally, the TRIPS Agreement did not contemplate that these important societal interests should be overridden by the anti-discrimination requirement of its Article 27.1. This provision was not intended to require "across-the-board" derogations from patent rights. That would only defeat the purpose of Article 30 of permitting exceptions that were "limited", and would compel the application of exceptions where they were not needed. Instead, since Article 27.1 did not purport to define the "patent rights" that it required to be made available and enjoyable without discrimination, those rights were the ones enumerated in Article 28.1 of the Agreement, subject to any exception that might be made under Article 30. This interpretation gave effect to the language of Article 27.1 in its context rather than in isolation, and achieved the balance contemplated by Article 7 as an objective of the TRIPS Agreement.

Object, Purpose and Meaning

In order to answer the essential question in these proceedings, i.e. whether the challenged measures were "limited exceptions" within the meaning of Article 30, Canada argued that the language of Article 30 must be interpreted according to the rules of interpretation contained in the Vienna Convention on the Law of Treaties. Article 31, paragraph 1, of that Convention set out the basic principle that "[a] treaty shall be interpreted in good faith in accordance with the ordinary meaning to be given to the terms of the treaty in their context and in the light of its object and purpose". Article 31, paragraph 2, of the Vienna Convention went on to specify that the context in which treaty terms were to be read included, among other things, the preamble to the treaty. Canada advanced the following points as being important to bear in mind in seeking to ascertain the scope of Article 30:

* The first recital in the Preamble of the TRIPS Agreement stated that Members were "[d]esiring to reduce distortions and impediments to international trade, and taking into account the need to promote effective and adequate protection of intellectual property rights, and *to ensure that measures and procedures to enforce intellectual property rights do not themselves become barriers to legitimate trade*" (emphasis added by Canada). The Preamble thus evidenced Members' understanding that protection for intellectual property rights should not go beyond what was "effective and adequate", since any greater level of security would imperil other important interests.

* That basic understanding was expanded upon in Article 7 of the Agreement, where its objectives were stated. Article 7 made it clear that intellectual property rights were not conferred in a vacuum, and that the TRIPS Agreement therefore did not aim to achieve a degree of protection for those rights which would unduly prejudice the vital public interest in social and economic welfare or the rights of others. Article 7 provided that "[t]he protection and enforcement of intellectual property rights should contribute to the promotion of technological innovation and to the transfer and dissemination of technology, to the mutual advantage of producers and users of technological knowledge and in a manner conducive to *social and economic welfare*, and to *a balance of rights and obligations*" (emphasis added by Canada).

* When Article 30 was read in context, it could be seen that it reflected the recognition and agreement of Members that the full application of all Article 28 rights at all times and in all circumstances would be inconsistent with the "balanced" objectives of the TRIPS Agreement. Unlike provisions such as Articles 31 and 40, which permitted measures that curtailed the rights of patent holders only where specified conditions were met, Article 30 granted Members the discretion to limit the full application of patent rights in light of the particular circumstances that prevailed in their respective jurisdictions, when balance was required and when social and economic welfare had to be considered. The existence of such a discretion was consistent with the provision of Article 1.1 that Members should be free to determine the appropriate method of implementing the provisions of the TRIPS Agreement, which provisions of course included Articles 7 and 30 as well as Articles 27, 28 and 33.

* The provision of this discretion, in the interests of achieving an appropriate balance in each of the national legal systems, reflected Members' desire to ensure that the limitations on the scope of patent rights that existed within–or were contemplated for–their own intellectual property laws at the time the Agreement was being negotiated would be taken into account.

* During the Uruguay Round, an adequate exception provision had been an integral part of the negotiations. Proposals, particularly for exceptions to patent rights, had been made by many Members.

* Although agreeing on the need for safeguard provisions, the negotiators could not agree on the specific circumstances that would merit protection, and had chosen the broad criteria-based text that now appeared as Article 30. Article 30 was not limited to any particular circumstance. It was not limited by reference to any particular purpose or policy objective. It was not limited to any particular type of exception. It was not limited by reference to an exhaustive list of eligible exceptions. Nor was it limited by reference to an illustrative, but non-exhaustive list of special cases justifying an exception.

* More particularly, Article 30 did not require a Member invoking its application to prove that its measure was not a disguised restriction on international trade, unlike the chapeau of GATT 1994, Article XX. Similarly, Article 30 did not require a Member to prove that its measure was the least trade-restrictive possible, unlike Article 2.2 of the Agreement on Technical Barriers to Trade and Article 5.6 of the Agreement on the Application of Sanitary and Phytosanitary Measures. Neither did it require a Member to prove that its measure was necessary for any particular purpose, such as "to protect human, animal or plant life or health", as in paragraph (b) of GATT 1994, Article XX. In addition, unlike Article 2.2 of the Agreement on Technical Barriers to Trade, there was nothing in Article 30 even requiring that a Member's measure fulfil a particular objective or take account of the risks that non-fulfilment would create.

   *   Article 30 also differed significantly from the other exceptions of the TRIPS Agreement itself. Article 13 (copyright) stipulated that "Members shall confine limitations or exceptions to exclusive rights to *certain special cases which do not conflict with a normal exploitation* of the work and do not unreasonably prejudice the legitimate interests of the right holder". Article 17 (trademarks) provided that "Members may provide limited exceptions to the rights conferred by a trademark, *such as fair use of descriptive terms*, provided that such exceptions take account of the legitimate interests of the owner of the trademark and of third parties" (emphases added).

   *   By way of contrast, Article 30 was not confined to certain special cases or fair use, and it did allow conflict with a normal exploitation of the patent, provided that the conflict was not unreasonable. In other words, unlike the other provisions referred to above, there was nothing in Article 30 indicating a limited or special application.

   *   The extent or scope of the exceptions authorized by Article 30 were only restricted by the requirements that:

      (a) they must be "limited";

      (b) they must not "unreasonably conflict with a normal exploitation of the patent [. . .] taking account of the legitimate interests of third parties"; and

      (c) they must not "[. . .] unreasonably prejudice the legitimate interests of the patent owner, taking account of the legitimate interests of third parties".

Canada argued that the exceptions created by subsections 55.2(1) and (2) of its Patent Act met each of the above requirements, for the following reasons.

(i) Section 55.2(1) and 55.2(2) created limited exceptions

   *   Canada's measures were "limited" within the ordinary meaning of that word. The early working exception was restricted to the narrow circumstance where a third party made, constructed, used or sold a patented invention solely for purposes reasonably related to regulatory review. The stockpiling exception could only be used by the person who had relied on the first exception, and was limited to the last six months of the relevant patent. Neither measure affected commercial sales by the patent holder during the term or any other economic benefit of a patent, such as the profit that could be earned through licensing royalties or the sale of the right.

* Subsection 55.2(1) permitted a third party to use a patented invention without infringement liability only where the third party made, constructed, used or sold a patented invention solely for uses of the invention that were reasonably related to the development and submission of information required under any law that regulated the manufacture, construction, use or sale of a product to which the invention related. (The reference to selling the invention was necessitated by the fact that a generic drug manufacturer had to usually purchase the active ingredient for its product from a fine chemical producer. Other technical "transfers" made in the course of a regulatory review submission would include administration of the drug to test subjects and use of an outside laboratory for priority testing.)

* The contention by the European Communities and their member States that the activities excepted from infringement liability were unlimited in time, quantity and extent, could not be reconciled with the unequivocal wording that Canada's Parliament had used. In particular, the allegations that "very significant quantities of the products protected by a patent" could be manufactured, imported and sold, and that "only the final purchaser of the product" need have the intention to use it for the purposes of a regulatory submission, were at complete variance with the clear requirement that "any person" who engaged in the activities must do so "solely" for uses connected with the development of a regulatory submission. Every other use of a patented invention would be exposed to infringement liability. Significantly, the EC did not explain how this plain language could be misconstrued in the manner for which it contended, and did not refer to any rule of statutory interpretation in support of its position.

* Subsection 55.2(2) permitted only the third party who made, constructed, used or sold a patented invention, in the manner contemplated by subsection 55.2(1), to make, construct or use the invention without infringement liability during the last six months of the patent term only for the purposes of the manufacture and storage of articles intended for sale after the date on which the term of the patent expired.

* The attack of the European Communities and their member States on this exception again adopted an interpretation of the language which was not supported by the plain meaning of the words used. The EU alleged that the stockpiling provision could be relied upon by "anybody in Canada." Manifestly, that was not so. Subsection 55.2(2) was expressly limited in its application to a person who had engaged in the activities specified in subsection 55.2(1), i.e. a person who had developed information for the purposes of a regulatory submission. Nothing in the language of subsection 55.2(2) lent any support to the allegation that it had a broader application, and the EC offered no explanation at all for interpreting it that way.

* While limiting the right to bring infringement proceedings in the narrow circumstances described in subsections 55.2(1) and 55.2(2), the excepting measures did not otherwise curtail any of the exclusive rights enjoyed by the patent owner. The right holder continued, throughout the full term of protection, to possess the right to bring infringement proceedings to restrain others from any acts of making, using, offering for sale, selling or importing the patented subject-matter outside the restricted scope of the exceptions under

Section 55.2. The unsubstantiated allegation that widespread infringing activities could occur during the patent term did not respect the ordinary meaning of the words actually used in the exceptions.

* In fact, all of the effects which the European Communities and their member States complained about occurred after the term of protection had expired. The extension of market exclusivity which was lost because generic manufacturers were permitted to make regulatory submissions during the term was of course a post-expiry phenomenon. So too were the lost profits that a patent owner would otherwise have realized during that extended period. These effects were simply the practical consequences of legislation designed to ensure that lower-cost competitive products, particularly drug products, reached the market as soon as possible after patent expiry. They were purely commercial concepts, not violations of intellectual property law rights which the TRIPS Agreement either recognized or sought to counteract. The attempt of the European Communities and their member States to equate Canada's present regime with its previous compulsory licensing system failed to acknowledge that all of the principal effects of compulsory licensing were felt during the term of patent protection. A compulsory licensee was permitted to work a patented invention in full competition with the patent owner. That was plainly not the case under the challenged measures, since they prohibited all commercial sales until after patent expiry.

* Additionally, the suggestion of the European Communities and their member States that the period of market exclusivity for the patent holder was about the same under the limited exceptions regime as it was under the former compulsory licensing system was based on a wrong assumption. The pre-Bill C-91 law permitted a compulsory licence to be issued at any time. However, that law went on to provide that such licences would only become effective to permit otherwise infringing activities linked to "sale for consumption in Canada" after the patented product had been on the Canadian market for seven to ten years. The EC was wrong in thinking that this law prevented holders of compulsory licences from undertaking the kinds of activities now envisaged by subsections 55.2(1) and 55.2(2) before the period of suspension had expired, and that the patentee's period of exclusivity was effectively extended. The Supreme Court of Canada had earlier held that such activities were covered by the experimental use defence.

* In any event, even if the respective periods of market exclusivity were about the same, that result would be of no significance in these proceedings. Compulsory licensing was an approach to cost containment adopted by Canada which was fully consistent with the then-existing international rules respecting intellectual property law. When it appeared that those rules would be adjusted by the TRIPS Agreement, Canada moved to amend its domestic legislation, in order to be consistent with the new obligations. Even if conformity with the new obligations resulted in about the same period of market exclusivity as was produced by conformity with the previous rules, that would simply be a coincidence, not a matter of any consequence under the TRIPS Agreement. Again, the effective period of market exclusivity cited by the EU was a purely commercial concept, not an intellectual property law right or concept which the TRIPS Agreement recognized.

(ii) Section 55.2(1) and 55.2(2) did not conflict with a normal exploitation of the patent

*   The exclusive rights conferred by a patent were normally exploited by "working" the patent for commercial gain. Typically, this would involve the patentee engaging in any combination of the following activities: using the patent to manufacture and sell the product as a monopolist; licensing the right to use the invention to others in return for the payment of royalty or other compensation; and selling either a part or the whole of its property right in the invention and its patent. None of these activities was impaired or prevented by the limited exceptions created by subsections 55.2(1) and 55.2(2). The patentee retained the full, unfettered and exclusive right to work the patent for commercial reward during the full term of protection whether by exercising: the unimpaired exclusive right to manufacture and sell the product; the unimpaired exclusive right to license the right to use the invention to others in return for the payment of valuable consideration; and the unimpaired exclusive right to sell, in whole or in part, its property right in the invention and patent. Therefore, at no time during the term of protection, did either exception conflict in any mode or manner with a normal exploitation of the patent.

*   Where there was no conflict, "unreasonableness" was not at issue.

(iii) Section 55.2(1) and 55.2(2) did not prejudice the legitimate interests of the patent owner

*   The legitimate interests of a patent owner must, by definition, be interests that related to the rights and duties that the patent laws conferred or imposed, as the case might be, on persons who had developed or subsequently acquired a patentable invention. In other words, legitimate interests arose from the status of being a patent holder, not from the more general status of being a business person or a manufacturer. Thus, in return for disclosing an invention to the public and obtaining the grant of a patent, a patent holder had a legitimate interest in exploiting and enforcing for the duration of the term of protection the exclusive right to "work" the patent as a monopolist and to earn the economic returns that rewarded inventive activity and investment. After the term of protection expired, however, the interest in exploiting the invention could no longer be that of a monopolist. Instead, the interest was reduced to: (a) the right to compete on the open market; (b) any trademark interest in the brand name, which subsisted after patent expiry; (c) any right to prevent "passing off" at common law; and (d) any copyright interest in materials describing the product. None of these interests pertained to patent protection and none was affected by Canada's limited exceptions.

*   Since the exceptions created by subsections 55.2(1) and 55.2(2) did not conflict with the normal exploitation of the patent during the term of protection, they did nothing to prejudice the legitimate interest of the patent owner in respect of the right to exploit the patent for the full duration of its term of protection. Similarly, since they did not impair a patentee's right to bring infringement proceedings at any time during the term of protection to restrain others from making any commercial sale of the patented invention, they did nothing to prejudice the patent owner's legitimate interest in prohibiting commercial exploitation during the term of protection.

*   The interest that a patentee could have in restraining, during the term of protection, the activities that were sheltered from infringement liability by subsections 55.2(1) and 55.2(2) involved exploiting regulatory review laws which delayed the market entry of competitor products subject to those laws, in order to extend the patentee's monopoly beyond the term of protection specified by the patent law. As was apparent from their submission, it was that windfall period of protection that the European Communities and their member States asserted here. Such gratuitous distortion of the competitive market could not be said to be a legitimate interest. That interest could not be said to be legitimate, because by treaty and domestic law prescription, patents only conferred exclusive rights for a specified term. When the prescribed term expired, so did the exclusive rights. Accordingly, and notwithstanding the private economic advantage that would be obtained by doing so, a patentee could have no legitimate interest deriving from patent law in exercising its exclusive use and enforcement rights within the term of protection to achieve, through exploitation of regulatory review laws, a de facto extension of that term of protection beyond the prescribed period, thereby unilaterally altering the bargain between the patentee and society. In this respect, the interests of a patentee of a pharmaceutical invention could be no different from those of patentees in other fields of technology.

(iv)   Section 55.2(1) and 55.2(2) took account of the legitimate interests of third parties

*   If, however, a patentee's "normal exploitation" involved more than working the patent for commercial gain, or if the patentee's "legitimate interest" included exercising its exclusive rights during the term so as to extend the term unilaterally beyond the period specified by statute, neither the exploitation nor the interest was affected unreasonably by the disputed measures, "taking "account of the legitimate interests of third parties".

*   In this context, "third parties" had to be a reference to those who were adverse in interest to the patent owner. Persons not adverse in interest, such as licensees, were already covered by the protection that was extended to the patent owner. Consequently, "third parties" had to mean all those who, not having a property interest in the patent, had an interest in the availability, consumption, cost or production of regulated products that were subject to the protection of a patent. Thus "third parties" included society at large, individual and institutional consumers of such regulated products and would-be competitor producers of those products. In the particular case of pharmaceutical products, the "third parties" included the individual users of Canada's health care system and the public and private sector entities that paid for it.

*   This reading of Article 30 was the one that gave proper effect to its terms in the context in which they were found. The TRIPS Agreement as a whole was framed so as to achieve balance between competing interests, and to ensure that the assertion of patent rights did not prevent the realization of other important societal objectives. As stated in the first recital of its Preamble and in the objectives endorsed by its Article 7, the TRIPS Agreement was not intended to promote patent rights at the expense of legitimate trade, social and economic welfare, and the rights of others. In order to achieve the desired balance, these latter interests had been recognized in the reference in Article 30 to "third parties".

*   The interests of these third parties were that the exclusive rights granted to patentees for a specified term of protection would be extinguished on the expiry of that term and that competitive conditions would thereafter govern the operation of the previously monopolized market for the regulated products at issue. The interest in the reinstatement of competition was not merely a "legitimate interest", it was a right which derived from the first principles of patent law. As stated in a report to Congress by the United States House of Representatives Committee on Energy and Commerce: "[T]he Constitution empowers Congress to grant exclusive rights to an inventor for a limited time. That limited time should be a definite time and, thereafter, immediate competition should be encouraged."

*   Third parties therefore had an undeniably legitimate interest in measures which ensured that patent rights were not exercisable in a manner that effectively extended the term of protection sanctioned by statute, thereby giving the former patentee a gratuitous monopoly and restraining trade unreasonably in the post-expiry market.

*   In this regard, it was significant that Articles 8.2 and 40 acknowledged that Members could invoke measures to control the abuse of patent rights by curtailing, whether by compulsory licence or revocation, the patent right for some or all of the remainder of its term of protection. Where such measures could be taken consistently with the Agreement to control the exercise of intellectual property rights that had an abusive or anti-competitive effect during the term specified for their protection, then a fortiori similar measures, which did not conflict with a normal exploitation of the patent, could also be taken consistently with the Agreement to prevent the anti-competitive effects of the patent after its term of protection had expired.

*   The legitimacy of the third party interest in the adoption of measures like those enacted by Section 55.2 to counteract the post-expiry monopoly for regulated products was particularly pronounced in the cases of both users and payers of health care products. Public health was a value whose importance was recognized as a matter of principle in Article 8.1 of the TRIPS Agreement. Accordingly, the exercise of exclusive rights in respect of regulated health care products during the term of protection to extend the patentee's monopoly into the post-expiry market was of particular concern in the pharmaceutical products sector: "It is generally accepted that the scope and duration of the patent monopoly must be limited, because monopolies are inherently economically inefficient. A monopolist profits by reducing output below competitive levels and correspondingly raising the price, causing a 'deadweight loss' to society. In the pharmaceutical context, outside the patent term, a monopoly would mean that the quantity of drugs available to society would be less than optimal, due to sales at prices considerably higher than marginal cost."

*   The cost of health care was a major concern for all WTO Member countries. A significant component of health care costs was the expense of drug therapies. Most Members, including both parties to this dispute, had taken positive measures to contain those costs, including direct price controls and incentives to encourage the use of generic drugs. The latter were particularly relevant here, since the creation of sophisticated and technical review requirements had meant that the only way to ensure a supply of generic drugs in the market as soon after patent expiry as possible was through an exception to the patent monopoly for purposes related solely to the development of information required to obtain marketing authorization for competitive versions of a patented product.

*   The use of generic medicines resulted in important economies for the public health care system, and so contributed to its viability and the protection of public health. In view of this, it was not surprising that Members had pursued a wide variety of measures to promote the use of generic drug products: "The actual level of growth of the generic market is becoming increasingly influenced by regulatory measures being introduced by governments and other payers for health care aimed either at forcing or encouraging the increased use of generic products. These measures have been introduced in response to the rising costs of health care in the major markets."

*   Measures that sought to control the costs of the health care system and to ensure access to needed drug therapies were obviously conducive to social welfare. As such, they could properly be adopted by Members pursuant to Article 30, as a means of achieving the balance contemplated by Article 7. In the post-expiry market, the interests of consumers and payers in ensuring access to less costly generic drugs were legitimate and important, while a patentee's interest in extending the period of monopoly was not one that was recognized in the TRIPS Agreement, let alone sanctioned as legitimate.

*   The legitimacy of measures to promote the use of generic drug products as means of protecting public health was endorsed by the World Health Organization (WHO). In its resolution scheduled for adoption in May 1999, in connection with its Revised Drug Strategy, the WHO encouraged its members "to explore and review their options under relevant international agreements, including trade agreements, to safeguard access to essential drugs". The WHO's Revised Drug Strategy also called for the use of generic drugs as a necessary means for ensuring a supply of essential drugs for individuals in all member states: "Drug supply is certainly one component of an essential drug policy whose economic advantages have been most studied. Generic drug programmes are today probably the most relevant economic strategy for drug supply. The most important economic feature of generic drugs is that, *unlike the situation with named brands, they allow for competition among producers of a given drug*." (emphasis added by Canada).

*   Thus, society at large and individual and institutional consumers of the health care system had an undeniably legitimate, indeed essential, interest in assuring the availability of competitively priced generic medicines as soon after patent expiry as possible. Canada's measures served that interest, and in doing so complied with the fundamental objectives, referred to in the TRIPS Agreement, of promoting social welfare and achieving balance between rights and obligations, while protecting the legitimate interests of intellectual property rights holders.

Canada argued that, firstly, Article 33, read in its context, was clearly limited to defining the longevity of a patent right and did not define the right itself, advancing the following points:

*   Patent rights were defined by Article 28, subject of course to any exceptions that might be authorized by Article 30. Thus, to the extent that Article 33 had any bearing on the existence or content of a right, it was subject to the provisions of Articles 28 and 30 of the Agreement.

*   Accordingly if, pursuant to the authority of Article 30, the scope of a right under Article 28 was restricted in a manner that could be said to reduce the minimum term of protection, Article 33 could not operate to negate the restriction and restore the right to its original or ordinary scope. It could not operate in that fashion, because the result produced would plainly be absurd.

*   If Article 33 could negate an exception under Article 30, then the national laws of all Members which contained exceptions that curtailed, in whole or in part, the scope of a right under Article 28 and thereby limited its enjoyment for the whole or a part of the term of protection, would reduce the term by the degree of curtailment and so contravene or not be consistent with the obligation imposed by Article 33.

Canada then argued that, in any event, neither subsection 55.2(1) nor subsection 55.2(2) of the Patent Act reduced the minimum term of protection referred to in Article 33 of the TRIPS Agreement to a term that was less than that minimum. According to Canada, subsections 55.2(1) and 55.2(2) created limited exceptions which did not conflict with the normal exploitation of a patent so as to reduce the term of protection accorded to the patent. Referring to its arguments as to why the provisions in question created "limited exceptions" within the meaning of Article 30 of the TRIPS Agreement, it drew attention to the following points:

*   A patentee whose rights might be affected by the application of the limited exceptions retained the full, unfettered and exclusive right to work the patent for commercial reward during the full term of protection, whether the "working" involved the monopolistic manufacture and sale of the product; the licensing of the right of use to others for valuable consideration; or the sale, in whole or part, of the property right in the patent.

*   Similarly, a patentee affected by the limited exceptions continued, throughout the full term of protection, to possess the right to bring infringement proceedings to restrain others from any commercial sale of the patented invention.

*   Furthermore, in addition to retaining the rights to work and to restrain, where a person who had used an invention in the manner contemplated by the exceptions sought marketing authorization for a pharmaceutical product during the term of protection on the basis of an allegation that the person would not infringe the product or product-by-process patent, the patentee could bring a summary proceeding under the Patented Medicines (Notice of Compliance) Regulations to challenge that allegation and, where successful, prohibit the issuance of the marketing authorization until the expiry of the patent.

*   Where a patentee could bring such proceedings to prevent the issuance of a marketing approval certificate until the expiry, at the conclusion of the full term of protection, of its patent, it could not be tenably argued that the limited exceptions created by subsections 55.2(1) and 55.2(2) of the Patent Act reduced the term of protection to a term shorter than the term prescribed by Article 33.

. . . .

VII. Findings

. . . .

C. Principles of Interpretation

The legal issues in this dispute primarily involve differences over interpretation of the key TRIPS provisions invoked by the parties, chiefly Articles 27.1, 30 and 33. The rules that govern the interpretation of WTO agreements are the rules of treaty interpretation stated in Articles 31 and 32 of the Vienna Convention. The starting point is the rule of Article 31(1) which states:

> A treaty is to be interpreted in good faith in accordance with the ordinary meaning to be given to the terms of the treaty in their context and in the light of its object and purpose.

The parties have submitted arguments on each of these elements, as well as further arguments based on subsequent practice by certain WTO Members, thus relying on Article 31(3)(b), which reads in relevant part as follows:

> There shall be taken into account, together with the context: (a) [];
> (b) any subsequent practice in the application of the treaty which establishes the agreement of the parties regarding its interpretation."

The parties have also advanced arguments based on the negotiating history of the TRIPS provisions in dispute. Negotiating history falls within the category of "Supplementary Means of Interpretation" and is governed by the rule of Article 32 of the Vienna Convention, which provides as follows:

> Recourse may be had to supplementary means of interpretation, including the preparatory work of the treaty and the circumstances of its conclusion, in order to confirm the meaning resulting from the application of Article 31, or to determine the meaning when the interpretation according to Article 31:
>
> (a) leaves the meaning ambiguous or obscure; or
>
> (b) leads to a result which is manifestly absurd or unreasonable.

. . . .

D. Burden of Proof

[I]n the present case, it was the Panel's view that the EC bears the burden to present evidence and argument sufficient to establish a prima facie case that Canada has violated Articles 27.1, 28.1 and 33 of the TRIPS Agreement. It would be up to Canada to advance sufficient argument and evidence to rebut such a prima facie case. Canada has, for all practical purposes, conceded the violation of Article 28, because it has resorted to the exception of Article 30 of the TRIPS Agreement in this case. Since Article 30 is an exception to the obligations of the TRIPS Agreement, it would be up to Canada to demonstrate that the provisions of Sections 55.2(1) and 55.2(2) comply with the criteria laid down in Article 30. It is on this basis that the Panel approached the analysis of the claims submitted to it.

E. Section 55.2(2) (The Stockpiling Exception)

The Panel began by considering the claims of violation concerning Section 55.2(2), the so-called stockpiling provision. It began by considering the EC claim that this measure was in violation of Article 28.1 of the TRIPS Agreement, and Canada's defence that the measure was an exception authorized by Article 30 of the Agreement.

. . . .

Both parties agreed upon the basic structure of Article 30. Article 30 establishes three criteria that must be met in order to qualify for an exception: (1) the exception must be "limited"; (2) the exception must not "unreasonably conflict with normal exploitation of the patent" ; (3) the exception must not "unreasonably prejudice the legitimate interests of the patent owner, taking account of the legitimate interests of third parties". The three conditions are cumulative, each being a separate and independent requirement that must be satisfied. Failure to comply with any one of the three conditions results in the Article 30 exception being disallowed.

The three conditions must, of course, be interpreted in relation to each other. Each of the three must be presumed to mean something different from the other two, or else there would be redundancy. Normally, the order of listing can be read to suggest that an exception that complies with the first condition can nevertheless violate the second or third, and that one which complies with the first and second can still violate the third. The syntax of Article 30 supports the conclusion that an exception may be "limited" and yet fail to satisfy one or both of the other two conditions. The ordering further suggests that an exception that does not "unreasonably conflict with normal exploitation" could nonetheless "unreasonably prejudice the legitimate interests of the patent owner".

. . . .

In the Panel's view, Article 30's very existence amounts to a recognition that the definition of patent rights contained in Article 28 would need certain adjustments. On the other hand, the three limiting conditions attached to Article 30 testify strongly that the negotiators of the Agreement did not intend

Article 30 to bring about what would be equivalent to a renegotiation of the basic balance of the Agreement. Obviously, the exact scope of Article 30's authority will depend on the specific meaning given to its limiting conditions. The words of those conditions must be examined with particular care on this point. Both the goals and the limitations stated in Articles 7 and 8.1 must obviously be borne in mind when doing so as well as those of other provisions of the TRIPS Agreement which indicate its object and purposes.

Canada asserted that the word "limited" should be interpreted according to the conventional dictionary definition, such as "confined within definite limits", or "restricted in scope, extent, amount". Canada argued that the stockpiling exception in Section 55.2(2) is restricted in scope because it has only a limited impact on a patent owner's rights. The stockpiling exception, Canada noted, does not affect the patent owner's right to an exclusive market for "commercial" sales during the patent term, since the product that is manufactured and stockpiled during the final six months of the term cannot be sold in competition with the patent owner until the patent expires. By "commercial sales", Canada clearly meant sales to the ultimate consumer, because it acknowledged that sales of patented ingredients to producers engaged in authorized stockpiling is permitted. Thus, Canada was arguing that an exception is "limited" as long as the exclusive right to sell to the ultimate consumer during the term of the patent is preserved. In addition, Canada also claimed that the exception is further limited by the six-month duration of the exception, and by the fact that it can be used only by persons that have made, constructed or used the invention under Section 55.2(1).

The EC interpreted the word "limited" to connote a narrow exception, one that could be described by words such as "narrow, small, minor, insignificant or restricted". The EC measured the "limited" quality of the proposed exception by reference to its impact on the exclusionary rights granted to the patent owner under Article 28.1. Applying that measure, the EC contended that the stockpiling exception is not "limited" because it takes away three of the five Article 28.1 rights - the rights to exclude "making", "using" and "importing". The EC argued that the impairment of three out of five basic rights is in itself extensive enough to be considered "not limited". The EC further contended that limitation of the exception to the last six months of the patent term does not constitute a limited impairment of rights when six months is taken as a percentage of the 20-year patent term, and especially not when taken as a percentage of the actual eight to 12-year period of effective market exclusivity enjoyed by most patented pharmaceuticals. In addition, the EC noted, there was no limitation on the quantities that could be produced during this period, nor any limitation on the markets in which such products could be sold. Finally, the EC pointed out that no royalty fees are due for such production, and that the patent holder does not even have a right to be informed of the use of the patent.

In considering how to approach the parties' conflicting positions regarding the meaning of the term "limited exceptions", the Panel was aware that the text of Article 30 has antecedents in the text of Article 9(2) of the Berne Convention. However, the words "limited exceptions" in Article 30 of the TRIPS Agreement are different from the corresponding words in Article 9(2) of the Berne Convention, which reads "in certain special cases". The Panel examined the documented negotiating history of TRIPS Article 30 with respect to the reasons why negotiators may have chosen to use the term "limited exceptions" in place of "in special circumstances". The negotiating records show only that the term "limited exceptions" was employed very early in the drafting process, well before the decision to adopt a text modelled on Berne Article 9(2), but do not indicate why it was retained in the later draft texts modelled on Berne Article 9(2).

The Panel agreed with the EC that, as used in this context, the word "limited" has a narrower connotation than the rather broad definitions cited by Canada. Although the word itself can have both broad and narrow definitions, the narrower being indicated by examples such as "a mail train taking only a limited number of passengers", the narrower definition is the more appropriate when the word "limited" is used as part of the phrase "limited exceptions". The word "exception" by itself connotes a limited derogation, one that does not undercut the body of rules from which it is made. When a treaty uses the term "limited exceptions", the word "limited" must be given a meaning separate from the limitation implicit in the word "exception" itself. The term "limited exceptions" must therefore be read to connote a narrow exception—one which makes only a small diminution of the rights in question.

The Panel agreed with the EC interpretation that "limited" is to be measured by the extent to which the exclusive rights of the patent owner have been curtailed. The full text of Article 30 refers to "limited exceptions to the exclusive rights conferred by a patent". In the absence of other indications, the Panel concluded that it would be justified in reading the text literally, focusing on the extent to which legal rights have been curtailed, rather than the size or extent of the economic impact. In support of this conclusion, the Panel noted that the following two conditions of Article 30 ask more particularly about the economic impact of the exception, and provide two sets of standards by which such impact may be judged. The term "limited exceptions" is the only one of the three conditions in Article 30 under which the extent of the curtailment of rights as such is dealt with.

In the Panel's view, the question of whether the stockpiling exception is a "limited" exception turns on the extent to which the patent owner's rights to exclude "making" and "using" the patented product have been curtailed. The right to exclude "making" and "using" provides protection, additional to that provided by the right to exclude sale, during the entire term of the patent by cutting off the supply of competing goods at the source and by preventing use of such products however obtained. With no limitations at all upon the quantity of production, the stockpiling exception removes that protection entirely during the last six months of the patent term, without regard to what other, subsequent, consequences it might have. By this effect alone, the stockpiling exception can be said to abrogate such rights entirely during the time it is in effect.

In view of Canada's emphasis on preserving commercial benefits before the expiration of the patent, the Panel also considered whether the market advantage gained by the patent owner in the months after expiration of the patent could also be considered a purpose of the patent owner's rights to exclude "making" and "using" during the term of the patent. In both theory and practice, the Panel concluded that such additional market benefits were within the purpose of these rights. In theory, the rights of the patent owner are generally viewed as a right to prevent competitive commercial activity by others, and manufacturing for commercial sale is a quintessential competitive commercial activity, whose character is not altered by a mere delay in the commercial reward. In practical terms, it must be recognized that enforcement of the right to exclude "making" and "using" during the patent term will necessarily give all patent owners, for all products, a short period of extended market exclusivity after the patent expires. The repeated enactment of such exclusionary rights with knowledge of their universal market effects can only be understood as an affirmation of the purpose to produce those market effects.

For both these reasons, the Panel concluded that the stockpiling exception of Section 55.2(2) constitutes a substantial curtailment of the exclusionary rights required to be granted to patent owners under Article 28.1 of the TRIPS Agreement. Without seeking to define exactly what level of curtailment would be disqualifying, it was clear to the Panel that an exception which results in a substantial curtailment of this dimension cannot be considered a "limited exceptions" within the meaning of Article 30 of the Agreement.

Neither of the two "limitations" upon the scope of the measure are sufficient to alter this conclusion. First, the fact that the exception can only be used by those persons who have utilized the regulatory review exception of Section 55.2(1) does limit the scope of the exception both to those persons and to products requiring regulatory approval. In regard to the limitation to such persons, the Panel considered this was not a real limitation since only persons who satisfy regulatory requirements would be entitled to market the product. In regard to the limitation to such products, the Panel considered that the fact that an exception does not apply at all to other products in no way changes its effect with regard to the criteria of Article 30. Each exception must be evaluated with regard to its impact on each affected patent, independently. Second, the fact that the exception applied only to the last six months of the patent term obviously does reduce its impact on all affected patented products, but the Panel agreed with the EC that six months was a commercially significant period of time, especially since there were no limits at all on the volume of production allowed, or the market destination of such production.

Having concluded that the exception in Section 55.2(2) of the Canadian Patent Act does not satisfy the first condition of Article 30 of the TRIPS Agreement, the Panel therefore concluded that Section 55.2(2) is inconsistent with Canada's obligations under Article 28.1 of the Agreement. This conclusion, in turn, made it unnecessary to consider any of the other claims of inconsistency raised by the European Communities. Accordingly, the Panel did not consider the claims of inconsistency under the second and third conditions of Article 30, the claim of inconsistency with TRIPS Article 27.1, and the claim of inconsistency with Article 33.

. . . .

F. Section 55.2(1) (The Regulatory Review Exception)

[The panel concluded that Canada's regulatory review exception is a "limited exceptions" within the meaning of TRIPS Article 30.]

The second condition of Article 30 prohibits exceptions that "unreasonably conflict with a normal exploitation of the patent". Canada took the position that "exploitation" of the patent involves the extraction of commercial value from the patent by "working" the patent, either by selling the product in a market from which competitors are excluded, or by licensing others to do so, or by selling the patent rights outright. The European Communities also defined "exploitation" by referring to the same three ways of "working" a patent. The parties differed primarily on their interpretation of the term "normal".

. . . .

The normal practice of exploitation by patent owners, as with owners of any other intellectual property right, is to exclude all forms of competition that could detract significantly from the economic returns anticipated from a patent's grant of market exclusivity. The specific forms of patent exploitation are not static, of course, for to be effective exploitation must adapt to changing forms of competition due to technological development and the evolution of marketing practices. Protection of all normal exploitation practices is a key element of the policy reflected in all patent laws. Patent laws establish a carefully defined period of market exclusivity as an inducement to innovation, and the policy of those laws cannot be achieved unless patent owners are permitted to take effective advantage of that inducement once it has been defined.

Canada has raised the argument that market exclusivity occurring after the 20-year patent term expires should not be regarded as "normal". The Panel was unable to accept that as a categorical proposition. Some of the basic rights granted to all patent owners, and routinely exercised by all patent owners, will typically produce a certain period of market exclusivity after the expiration of a patent. For example, the separate right to prevent "making" the patented product during the term of the patent often prevents competitors from building an inventory needed to enter the market immediately upon expiration of a patent. There is nothing abnormal about that more or less brief period of market exclusivity after the patent has expired.

The Panel considered that Canada was on firmer ground, however, in arguing that the additional period of de facto market exclusivity created by using patent rights to preclude submissions for regulatory authorization should not be considered "normal". The additional period of market exclusivity in this situation is not a natural or normal consequence of enforcing patent rights. It is an unintended consequence of the conjunction of the patent laws with product regulatory laws, where the combination of patent rights with the time demands of the regulatory process gives a greater than normal period of market exclusivity to the enforcement of certain patent rights. It is likewise a form of exploitation that most patent owners do not in fact employ. For the vast majority of patented products, there is no marketing regulation of the kind covered by Section 55.2(1), and thus there is no possibility to extend patent exclusivity by delaying the marketing approval process for competitors.

[The panel found that the regulatory review exception did not conflict with the "normal" exploitation of patents within the meaning of Article 30.]

The third condition of Article 30 is the requirement that the proposed exception must not"unreasonably prejudice the legitimate interests of the patent owner, taking into account the legitimate interests of third parties". Although Canada, as the party asserting the exception provided for in Article 30, bears the burden of proving compliance with the conditions of that exception, the order of proof is complicated by the fact that the condition involves proving a negative. One cannot demonstrate that no legitimate interest of the patent owner has been prejudiced until one knows what claims of legitimate interest can be made. Likewise, the weight of legitimate third party interests cannot be fully appraised until the legitimacy and weight of the patent owner's legitimate interests, if any, are defined. Accordingly, without disturbing the ultimate burden of proof, the Panel chose to analyse the issues presented by the third condition of Article 30 according to the logical sequence in which those issues became defined.

. . . .

To make sense of the term "legitimate interests" in this context, that term must be defined in the way that it is often used in legal discourse—as a normative claim calling for protection of interests that are "justifiable" in the sense that they are supported by relevant public policies or other social norms. This is the sense of the word that often appears in statements such as "X has no legitimate interest in being able to do Y". We may take as an illustration one of the most widely adopted Article 30-type exceptions in national patent laws—the exception under which use of the patented product for scientific experimentation, during the term of the patent and without consent, is not an infringement. It is often argued that this exception is based on the notion that a key public policy purpose underlying patent laws is to facilitate the dissemination and advancement of technical knowledge and that allowing the patent owner to prevent experimental use during the term of the patent would frustrate part of the purpose of the requirement that the nature of the invention be disclosed to the public. To the contrary, the argument concludes, under the policy of the patent laws, both society and the scientist have a "legitimate interest" in using the patent disclosure to support the advance of science and technology. While the Panel draws no conclusion about the correctness of any such national exceptions in terms of Article 30 of the TRIPS Agreement, it does adopt the general meaning of the term "legitimate interests" contained in legal analysis of this type.

. . . .

The negotiating history of the TRIPS Agreement itself casts no further illumination on the meaning of the term "legitimate interests", but the negotiating history of Article 9(2) of the Berne Convention, from which the text of the third condition was clearly drawn, does tend to affirm the Panel's interpretation of that term. With regard to the TRIPS negotiations themselves, the meaning of several important drafting changes turns out to be equivocal upon closer examination. The negotiating records of the TRIPS Agreement itself show that the first drafts of the provision that was to become Article 30 contemplated authorizing "limited exceptions" that would be defined by an illustrative list of exceptions—private use, scientific use, prior use, a traditional exception for pharmacists, and the like. Eventually, this illustrative list approach was abandoned in favour of a more general authorization following the outlines of the present Article 30. The negotiating records of the TRIPS Agreement give no explanation of the reason for this decision.

The text of the present, more general version of Article 30 of the TRIPS Agreement was obviously based on the text of Article 9(2) of the Berne Convention. Berne Article 9(2) deals with exceptions to the copyright holder's right to exclude reproduction of its copyrighted work without permission. The text of Article 9(2) is as follows:

> It shall be a matter for legislation in the countries of the Union to permit the reproduction of [literary and artistic] works in certain special cases, provided that such reproduction does not conflict with a normal exploitation of the work and does not unreasonably prejudice the legitimate interests of the author.

The text of Berne Article 9(2) was not adopted into Article 30 of the TRIPS Agreement without change. Whereas the final condition in Berne Article 9(2) ("legitimate interests") simply refers to the legitimate interests of the author, the TRIPS negotiators added in Article 30 the instruction that account must be taken of "the legitimate interests of third parties". Absent further explanation in the records of the TRIPS negotiations, however, the Panel was not able to attach a substantive meaning to this change other than what is already obvious in the text itself, namely that the reference to the "legitimate interests of third parties" makes sense only if the term "legitimate interests" is construed as a concept broader than legal interests.

. . . .

In sum, after consideration of the ordinary meaning of the term "legitimate interests", as it is used in Article 30, the Panel was unable to accept the EC's interpretation of that term as referring to legal interests pursuant to Article 28.1. Accordingly, the Panel was unable to accept the primary EC argument with regard to the third condition of Article 30. It found that the EC argument based solely on the patent owner's legal rights pursuant to Article 28.1, without reference to any more particular normative claims of interest, did not raise a relevant claim of non-compliance with the third condition of Article 30.

After reaching the previous conclusion concerning the EC's primary argument under the "legitimate interests" condition of Article 30, the Panel then directed its attention to another line of argument raised in statements made by the EC and by one third party. This second line of argument called attention to the fact that patent owners whose innovative products are subject to marketing approval requirements suffer a loss of economic benefits to the extent that delays in obtaining government approval prevent them from marketing their product during a substantial part of the patent term. According to information supplied by Canada, regulatory approval of new pharmaceuticals usually does not occur until approximately eight to 12 years after the patent application has been filed, due to the time needed to complete development of the product and the time needed to comply with the regulatory procedure itself. The result in the case of pharmaceuticals, therefore, is that the innovative producer is in fact able to market its patented product in only the remaining eight to 12 years of the 20-year patent term, thus receiving an effective period of market exclusivity that is only 40-60 per cent of the period of exclusivity normally envisaged in a 20-year patent term. The EC argued that patent owners who suffer a reduction of effective market exclusivity from such delays should be entitled to impose the same type of delay in connection with corresponding regulatory requirements upon the market entry of competing products. According to the EC,

> [T]here exists no reason why the research based pharmaceutical enterprise is obliged to accept the economic consequence of patent term erosion because of marketing approval requirements which reduce their effective term of protection to 12-8 years while the copy producer should be entirely compensated for the economic consequence of the need of marketing approval for his generic product, and at the expense of the inventor and patent holder.

. . . .

The type of normative claim put forward by the EC has been affirmed by a number of governments that have enacted de jure extensions of the patent term, primarily in the case of pharmaceutical products, to compensate for the de facto diminution of the normal period of market exclusivity due to delays in obtaining marketing approval. According to the information submitted to the Panel, such extensions have been enacted by the European Communities, Switzerland, the United States, Japan, Australia and Israel. The EC and Switzerland have done so while at the same time allowing patent owners to continue to use their exclusionary rights to gain an additional, de facto extension of market exclusivity by preventing competitors from applying for regulatory approval during the term of the patent. The other countries that have enacted de jure patent term extensions have also, either by legislation or by judicial decision, created a regulatory review exception similar to Section 55.2(1), thereby eliminating the possibility of an additional de facto extension of market exclusivity.

. . . .

This positive response to the claim for compensatory adjustment has not been universal, however. In addition to Canada, several countries have adopted, or are in the process of adopting, regulatory review exceptions similar to Section 55.2(1) of the Canadian Patent Act, thereby removing the de facto extension of market exclusivity, but these countries have not enacted, and are not planning to enact, any de jure extensions of the patent term for producers adversely affected by delayed marketing approval. When regulatory review exceptions are enacted in this manner, they represent a decision not to restore any of the period of market exclusivity due to lost delays in obtaining marketing approval. Taken as a whole, these government decisions may represent either disagreement with the normative claim made by the EC in this proceeding, or they may simply represent a conclusion that such claims are outweighed by other equally legitimate interests.

On balance, the Panel concluded that the interest claimed on behalf of patent owners whose effective period of market exclusivity had been reduced by delays in marketing approval was neither so compelling nor so widely recognized that it could be regarded as a "legitimate interest" within the meaning of Article 30 of the TRIPS Agreement. Notwithstanding the number of governments that had responded positively to that claimed interest by granting compensatory patent term extensions, the issue itself was of relatively recent standing, and the community of governments was obviously still divided over the merits of such claims. Moreover, the Panel believed that it was significant that concerns about regulatory review exceptions in general, although well known at the time of the TRIPS negotiations, were apparently not clear enough, or compelling enough, to make their way explicitly into the recorded agenda of the TRIPS negotiations. The Panel believed that Article 30's "legitimate interests" concept should not be used to decide, through adjudication, a normative policy issue that is still obviously a matter of unresolved political debate.

Consequently, having considered the two claims of "legitimate interest" put forward by the EC, and having found that neither of these claimed interests can be considered "legitimate interests" within the meaning of the third condition of Article 30 of the TRIPS Agreement, the Panel concluded that Canada had demonstrated to the Panel's satisfaction that Section 55.2(1) of Canada's Patent Act did not prejudice "legitimate interests" of affected patent owners within the meaning of Article 30.

Having reviewed the conformity of Section 55.2(1) with each of the three conditions for an exception under Article 30 of the TRIPS Agreement, the Panel concluded that Section 55.2(1) does satisfy all three conditions of Article 30, and thus is not inconsistent with Canada's obligations under Article 28.1 of the TRIPS Agreement.

[The Panel concluded that the anti-discrimination rule of Article 27.1 does apply to exceptions of the kind authorized by Article 30.]

We turn, accordingly, to the question of whether Section 55.2(1) of the Canadian Patent Act discriminates as to fields of technology.

. . . .

With regard to the issue of de jure discrimination, the Panel concluded that the European Communities had not presented sufficient evidence to raise the issue in the face of Canada's formal declaration that the exception of Section 55.2(1) was not limited to pharmaceutical products. Absent other evidence, the words of the statute compelled the Panel to accept Canada's assurance that the exception was legally available to every product that was subject to marketing approval requirements. In reaching this conclusion, the Panel took note that its legal finding of conformity on this point was based on a finding as to the meaning of the Canadian law that was in turn based on Canada's representations as to the meaning of that law, and that this finding of conformity would no longer be warranted if, and to the extent that, Canada's representations as to the meaning of that law were to prove wrong.

. . . .

In sum, the Panel found that the evidence in record before it did not raise a plausible claim of discrimination under Article 27.1 of the TRIPS Agreement.

It was not proved that the legal scope of Section 55.2(1) was limited to pharmaceutical products, as would normally be required to raise a claim of de jure discrimination. Likewise, it was not proved that the adverse effects of Section 55.2(1) were limited to the pharmaceutical industry, or that the objective indications of purpose demonstrated a purpose to impose disadvantages on pharmaceutical patents in particular, as is often required to raise a claim of de facto discrimination. Having found that the record did not raise any of these basic elements of a discrimination claim, the Panel was able to find that Section 55.2(1) is not inconsistent with Canada's obligations under Article 27.1 of the TRIPS Agreement. Because the record did not present issues requiring any more precise interpretation of the term "discrimination" in Article 27.1, none was made.

VIII. Conclusions

In light of the findings above, the Panel has concluded as follows:

(1) Section 55.2(1) of Canada's Patent Act is not inconsistent with Canada's obligations under Article 27.1 and Article 28.1 of the TRIPS Agreement.

(2) Section 55.2(2) of Canada's Patent Act is not consistent with the requirements of Article 28.1 of the TRIPS Agreement.

Accordingly, the Panel recommends that the Dispute Settlement Body request that Canada bring Section 55.2(2) into conformity with Canada's obligations under the TRIPS Agreement.

NOTES AND QUESTIONS

(1) **WTO Adjudication**. The Canada-Pharmaceuticals panel report holds that Article 30's "legitimate interests" concept "should not be used to decide, through adjudication, a normative policy issue that is still obviously a matter of unresolved political debate." What does this say about the nature of the WTO panel/Appellate Body system? We will return to this issue *infra* Chapter 5.

(2) **Scope of TRIPS Article 33**. On May 5, 2000, the WTO published another panel report on Canada's patent law, upon a request of the United States. *See* Canada-Term of Patent Protection, WT/DS170/R (WTO DSB Panel, May 5, 2000). The panel agreed with the United States that Canada's failure to grant a term of at least twenty years from filing on patent applications filed under the Canadian Patent Act prior to 1989 was a violation of its obligation under Article 33 to provide a term of not less than twenty years from filing and its obligation under Article 70.2 to provide protection to "all subject matter existing at the date of application of [TRIPS]." In the course of its decision, the panel stated:

Interpretation of Article 33 as a minimum standard for the expiry of the available term of protection ("minimum standard") is also borne out by Article 1.1 of the TRIPS Agreement which forms part of the context of Article 33. Article 1.1 provides: "Members shall give effect to the provisions of this Agreement. Members may, but shall not be obliged to, implement in their law more extensive protection than is required by this Agreement, provided that such protection does not contravene the provisions of this Agreement."

Article 1.1 confirms that the TRIPS Agreement is a minimum standards agreement in respect of intellectual property rights. The textual reading of Article 1.1 suggests that Members are to "give effect" to, inter alia, Article 33 which obligates Members to make available a term of protection for patents that does not end before 20 years from the date of filing.

By making available a term of protection that runs 17 years from the date of grant for those patents that were filed before 1 October 1989, Section 45 of Canada's Patent Act, on its face, does not meet the minimum standard of Article 33 in all cases. This is confirmed by the figures presented by Canada which show that there were still extant, as of 1 January 2000, approximately 66,936 Old Act patents, representing approximately 40 per cent of the total 169,966 Old Act patents, that would expire before 20 years from the date of filing.

¶¶ 6.86-87.

Canada appealed the panel's adverse decision to the Appellate Body in June, 2000, arguing that according to Article 70.1, the TRIPS Agreement did not give rise to obligations in respect of patents granted under the old law because such patent grants were "acts" which occurred before the date of application of the Agreement. The Appellate Body affirmed in a decision published on September 18, 2000 (WT/DS170/AB/R). Distinguishing between "'acts' and the 'rights' created by those 'acts'" (paras. 56-60), it stated that "[a] contrary interpretation would seriously erode the scope of the other provisions of Article 70, especially the explicit provisions of Article 70.2." The Appellate Body found that its interpretation of Article 70 did not amount to a retroactive application of the TRIPS Agreement, and was in conformity with the non-retroactivity principles codified in Article 28 of the Vienna Convention on the Law of Treaties. It went on to summarily affirm the panel's interpretation of Articles 33 and 70.2, and recommended that the DSB request Canada to bring Section 45 into conformity with its obligations under TRIPS.

(3) **Tactical Considerations.** Are industrialized states such as EC or the US likely to bring cases against developing nations for failures similar to Canada's? If so, are such states likely to comply with an unfavorable ruling? The predicted and actual alignment of parties in WTO proceedings is discussed *infra* § 5.03[A].

(4) **Viability of "TRIPS-plus" noncompliance sanctions.** Has "TRIPS-plus" become defunct as a basis for Special 301 proceedings concerning patent protection in developing countries? *See infra* § 5.02 (discussing Special 301). The U.S. at one time asserted that countries could still be subject to Special 301 proceedings even if they were in compliance with the compulsory licensing

provisions found in Article 31 of TRIPS. However, in January 2001, USTR Ambassador Barshevsky announced that, in engaging the other countries of the western hemisphere in FTAA negotiations, the U.S. would limit its response to circumstances in which FTAA countries use a patented product or process, or allow third parties to do so, without the patent holder's consent. Where FTAA countries provide for such use, it must adhere to the requirements applicable to compulsory licensing set out in Article 31 of the TRIPS Agreement and Article 5A(4) of the Paris Convention (and, impliedly, no higher.) The U.S. proposal also stated that it will no longer challenge generic pharmaceutical or agricultural chemical manufacturers for making, using or selling a patented product or process to obtain government marketing approval during the term of the patent so that they can compete with the patent owner soon after the patent expires. Under the U.S. proposal, FTAA countries would agree that so long as the patent remains valid the product or process may be made, used, or sold in their country by competitors only to meet marketing approval requirements. *See* http://www.ustr.gov/regions/whemisphere/intel.html. It makes no mention of the ongoing dispute in the WTO with Brazil over working requirement and compulsory licensing provisions set forth in the Brazilian patent law.

[E] Harmonization of Patent Law: The New Patent Law Treaty

Unwilling to admit failure, and after the successful conclusion of TRIPS, WIPO subsequently revived the Patent Law Treaty talks with scope limited to the harmonization of procedures and formalities of patent applications. Those negotiations led to the successful completion at a diplomatic conference on June 2, 2000, of a new Patent Law Treaty ("PLT") that was signed by forty-three states and regional patent offices, including the United States and the EPO. The PLT harmonization provisions agreed to at the Diplomatic Conference were concerned solely with the form of the application since the United States maintained that it was not in a position to discuss further substantive patent law in any form whatsoever. Recently, however, the U.S. has shifted its position on discussing substantive international harmonization of patent law—even to include ultimately discussing what is now called the "first-inventor-to-file" principle in exchange for the adoption of a grace period in Europe once again. The next reading indicates the current scope of those discussions. The PLT will be treated at greater length in Chapter 6 in the context of the multinational acquisition of industrial property rights.

**SUGGESTIONS FOR THE FURTHER DEVELOPMENT
OF INTERNATIONAL PATENT LAW**
WIPO Standing Committee on the Law of Patents
Fourth Session, Geneva, November 6-10, 2000
WIPO Document No. SCP/4/2 September 25, 2000

I. *Introduction*

During the 1998-1999 biennium, the Standing Committee on the Law of
Patents (SCP) devoted its time to the negotiation and finalization of the Patent
Law Treaty (PLT), which was adopted at the Diplomatic Conference for the
Adoption of the PLT, held in Geneva from May 11 to June 2, 2000. Concerning
the future work of the SCP, during its earlier sessions as well as at the PLT
Diplomatic Conference, a considerable number of delegations and
representatives have expressed their wish to consider issues related to further
harmonization of substantive requirements of patent law after the conclusion
of the PLT. The present document contains suggestions for issues related to
further harmonization of patent laws for consideration by the SCP at its fourth
session (the first time the SCP will meet during the 2000-2001 biennium), and
at its future sessions.

II. *Issues related to further harmonization for consideration by the SCP*

A number of delegations and representatives had expressed the position . . .
that discussions concerning further harmonization, in particular harmonization
of substantive issues of patent law, should be resumed as soon as possible after
the conclusion of the Diplomatic Conference. In this context, it may be noted
that, at its third meeting held on May 4 and 5, 2000, the Industry Advisory
Commission of WIPO adopted a Resolution calling for "work, in the medium
term, on a treaty on the harmonization of substantive patent law, with a view
to facilitating greater mutual recognition of search and examination results by
patent offices." In addition, the Policy Advisory Commission of WIPO made
several recommendations at its meeting of June 15, 2000, among which one
reads as follows: "that efforts should be made towards further substantive
harmonization in the field of industrial property law, in particular, patent law."

It should be noted that the Patent Cooperation Treaty (PCT), which has
established a system for the filing of international patent applications having
the same effect as national applications filed in each of the PCT Contracting
States designated in the international application, contains a number of
principles of substantive patent law applicable to the international phase
provided under the PCT. However, it may also be noted that PCT Article 27(5)
allows a Contracting State to apply any substantive conditions of patentability
as it desires during the national phase.

In response to international calls for harmonization of national and regional
patent laws, negotiations had started, as early as 1985, on a draft Treaty
Supplementing the Paris Convention as far as Patents are Concerned (hereafter
referred to as "draft Patent Harmonization Treaty 1991"), which was discussed

at the first part of a Diplomatic Conference in 1991, but never concluded. The draft Patent Harmonization Treaty of 1991 included substantive as well as formal aspects of patent law. Some of its provisions, for instance those on patentable subject matter, rights conferred, term of protection and reversal of burden of proof for process patents, were incorporated into the Agreement on Trade-Related Aspects of Intellectual Property Rights (TRIPS Agreement), concluded in 1994. Nevertheless, a number of issues in respect of national and regional patent law have neither been addressed by the TRIPS Agreement, nor by any other worldwide international treaty on patent law, in particular not by the recently adopted PLT, which covers only patent formalities. . . .

The need for further patent harmonization beyond the PLT arises mainly from the fact that the costs of obtaining broad patent protection on an international level have become extremely high. The objective of further harmonization should therefore be to lower costs. This goal can, however, only be envisaged if a number of basic legal principles underlying the grant of patents are harmonized.

In view of the present situation and the objective mentioned above, the International Bureau suggests that at least the following basic issues underlying the grant of patents, which are of particular importance to the further development of the international patent system, could be included in the discussions of the SCP: the definitions of prior art, novelty, inventive step (non-obviousness) and industrial applicability (utility); sufficiency of disclosure; and the structure and interpretation of claims.

In order to facilitate discussions of the SCP concerning the desirability and feasibility of further harmonizing patent law, each of the six mentioned issues are described below by (1) explaining the basic issue, [and] (2) giving examples of the present status of laws and practices between different systems showing the existence of, or need for further, harmonization, ...

A. Prior art

The basic issue. Prior art is generally understood to constitute the body of knowledge which was available to the public before the filing date or, if priority is claimed, before the priority date, of a patent application. Identifying the relevant prior art is one of the cornerstones of patent examination, since such prior art will be evaluated during examination to determine the patentability of the invention concerned. It is by comparing the invention for which protection is sought with the prior art that novelty and inventive step (non-obviousness) of the invention are established. Furthermore, prior art will, after the grant of a patent, be determining in order to evaluate the validity or invalidity of the patent.

Some of the issues to be considered in the context of prior art include, in particular, notions such as "availability to the public," "person skilled in the art," and "means of making available to the public." Further items to be considered are, in particular, issues such as non-prejudicial disclosures, the grace period, or the question of applications filed earlier than, but published after, the date of filing of the application concerned.

Status of harmonization.   The PCT states in Rules 33.1 and 64 what the relevant prior art for the purposes of the international search and international preliminary examination under PCT Articles 15(2) and 33(2) and (3) shall consist of. However, the definition of the term "prior art," as well as its use in patent practice, still varies widely in different patent laws. Such divergences do, obviously, have different consequences with regard to the examination of patent applications in different countries, which may, ultimately, lead to the grant of a patent in certain countries, while in others, for the same invention, no patent will be granted, or the patent may be invalidated after grant. The following examples may illustrate some of the existing differences:

(a) In certain countries, prior art is constituted by everything that has been made available to the public anywhere in the world by any means before the filing or priority date of the application. On the other hand, in other countries, non-written disclosures, such as oral disclosures, or use outside their jurisdiction, do not form part of the prior art, and thus do not constitute a bar to patentability.

(b) While certain patent systems require a concrete disclosure for complying with the standard of "availability to the public," others provide that the theoretical possibility of having access to the information is sufficient.

(c) The law of certain countries provides for a general grace period, during which the invention may be disclosed without its patentability being affected, while other countries provide only for a grace period limited to certain specific cases. Another category of countries provides only for non-prejudicial disclosures in the cases of certain international exhibitions and evident abuse in respect of the applicant. In this context, it may be mentioned that Article 11 of the Paris Convention for the Protection of Industrial Property (Paris Convention) requires the countries of the Paris Union to grant temporary protection to inventions shown at certain international exhibitions.

(d) Applications, which have been filed before, but were published only after, the filing of the application under consideration, are considered in a different way in different countries as far as prior art is concerned. . . .

B. *Novelty*

The basic issue.   The requirement of novelty is one of the essential and universally recognized conditions of patentability. According to this principle, an invention shall be considered to be new if it is not comprised in the prior art. Novelty therefore results from the comparison between the existing prior art at the date of filing (or the date of priority) and the claimed invention. The underlying reason for the requirement of novelty is that nothing should be withdrawn from public use that already belongs to the public domain.

Status of harmonization.   For the purposes of PCT international preliminary examination (but not necessarily of the national phase), the novelty requirement is contained in Article 33(2) of the PCT, which states that an invention shall be considered novel if it is not anticipated by the prior art as defined in the Regulations. For the purposes of novelty, the relevant description of prior art is contained in PCT Rule 64. This shows how closely the novelty requirement is linked to the notion of prior art, since anything which forms part of the prior art would, in principle, destroy the novelty of the invention. In light of the important divergences identified in the definition and application of the term "prior art" as described above, it is evident that the requirement of novelty is also defined and applied in different ways throughout the world.

Besides this close link to the prior art, there are further issues, which are closely related to the discussion on novelty: for instance, which kind of use should destroy the novelty of an invention. Such divergences may lead to the recognition of the novelty of the invention in certain countries, but not in others. The following examples may illustrate some of the existing differences:

(a) In principle, all of the differences mentioned above, in respect of the definition of prior art have a bearing on novelty, i.e., the definition of prior art itself, the requirements relating to the disclosure of the invention, the existence and nature of a grace period, if any, etc.

(b) Public use of the invention anywhere in the world destroys novelty in certain patent systems, while in others, this consequence depends on the place of use. According to certain laws, even non-public use may be prejudicial to novelty, while in others, non-public use could never lead to the destruction of novelty. . . .

C. *Inventive step (non-obviousness)*

The basic issue. The term inventive step (or inventive activity), called non-obviousness in some countries, is, like novelty, one of the fundamental requirements of patentability. It is, in principle, widely recognized throughout different patent systems. An invention is considered to involve an inventive step or to be non-obvious if, compared to the prior art, it is not obvious to a person skilled in the art. Thus, while the criteria of novelty is fulfilled as soon as there is any kind of difference between the claimed invention and the prior art, inventive step is only found if there is a certain qualitative difference between the prior art and the invention. This may not be the case if the claimed invention would, at the date of filing or of priority, have been obvious for a person skilled in the art.

In a similar way as it is the case with regard to novelty, inventive step or non-obviousness is examined in comparison to the existing prior art at the date of filing or of priority of the application in question. Therefore, any difference between patent systems with regard to the definition of prior art will influence the result of any examination of inventive step or non-obviousness. Beyond this rather obvious conclusion, however, there are further divergences in the application of that term, the most important of which are summarized below.

Status of harmonization. For the purposes of PCT international preliminary examination (but not necessarily of the national phase), the inventive step requirement is contained in Article 33(3) of the PCT, which states that an invention shall be considered to involve an inventive step if, having regard to the prior art as defined in the Regulations, it is not, at the prescribed relevant date, obvious to a person skilled in the art. The relevant description of prior art is contained in PCT Rule 64. Nevertheless, as stated above, the examination of inventive step varies considerably in different systems depending on how prior art is defined. Some specific differences are outlined below:

(a) Not only the definition of the term inventive step as such, but also its practical application vary considerably. For example, certain systems apply the so-called "problem and solution" approach, comprising (1) the determination of the closest prior art, (2) the establishment of the technical problem to be solved, and (3) establishing whether, considering the technical problem and the closest prior art, the invention would be obvious to the person skilled in the art. Other systems have developed different methods for the examination of inventive activity.

(b) The notion of a person skilled in the art is not defined in the same way in all patent systems: sometimes, that term means a person with thorough knowledge of the relevant technical field (without necessarily being a specialist), while in other cases, the person skilled in the art may be close to a layman.

(c) While certain systems consider the contents of previously filed applications to destroy novelty and inventive step of a later filed application, others consider these contents only in respect of novelty, but not when assessing the requirement of inventive step.

(d) In certain systems, for the determination of inventive step, different items of prior art may be combined together, if such combination would have been obvious to the person skilled in the art.

D. *Industrial applicability (utility)*

The basic issue. "Industrial applicability" or "utility" in certain countries is the third widely recognized requirement of patentability. Its objective is to exclude from patentability inventions, which have no utility in any field of industry, which do not achieve the objective, claimed by the invention (e.g., *perpetuum mobile*) or which may only be used for private purposes.

Status of harmonization. For the purposes of PCT international preliminary examination (but not necessarily of the national phase), the requirement of "industrial applicability" is contained in PCT Article 33(4), which states that an invention shall be considered industrially applicable if, according to its nature, it can be made or used in any kind of industry. The said provision further states that the term "industry" is to be understood in its broadest sense, as in the Paris Convention. In addition, it may be mentioned that certain systems use the term "utility" rather than "industrial applicability." However, these terms do not have exactly the same meaning:

(a) In those systems which use the term "industrial applicability," it means in general that the invention must be able to be used in any kind of industry, whereby the term "industry" has to be understood in a broad sense, including agriculture.

(b) The term "utility," on the other hand, is a somewhat more complex notion, according to which it may be examined, in particular, whether an invention is able to do something, whether it works to solve the problem it is supposed to solve, and whether it has some social benefit.

E. *Sufficiency of disclosure*

The basic issue. The disclosure of the invention to the public is considered to be the counterpart for receiving the exclusive right conferred by a patent. The disclosure allows the public to know the most recent technical developments and to freely use the technical teaching after the expiration of the patent (or if the patent is not granted). Adequate disclosure is therefore an important obligation of the applicant.

In principle, where the invention is not, or is not sufficiently, disclosed, no patent may be granted, or a granted patent may be invalidated. As a general principle, and notwithstanding the further explanations . . . below, an invention is disclosed if it can be carried out by a person skilled in the art as fully claimed based on the patent specification, without need for any additional inventiveness. Furthermore, the disclosure must be such that it shows the way to safely and repeatedly achieve the claimed result. Thus, a causal link between the claimed elements and the alleged technical result must exist.

The disclosure does not need to be in the description or in the claims only, but may result from the whole patent specification, and in some cases also from teachings in the prior art. But what needs to be disclosed is the invention, and the invention is defined by the claims. This leads, at least in many legal systems, to the conclusion that the claims must be supported by the description.

One particular case related to the disclosure of the invention is the issue of broad claims. in certain cases, the claims are drafted so broadly that the invention cannot, even by using other parts of the specification, such as the description or the drawings, be carried out by the person skilled in the art. This occurs more frequently in particular fields, for example, chemistry and biotechnology. Patents may be invalidated, or at least partly invalidated, if the breadth of the claims exceeds the disclosure in the specification.

Status of harmonization   Article 5 and Rule 5.1(a) of the PCT state the following:

Article 5: The Description

The description shall disclose the invention in a manner sufficiently clear and complete for the invention to be carried out by a person skilled in the art.

Rule 5: The Description

5.1 *Manner of the Description*

(a) The description shall first state the title of the invention as appearing in the request and shall:

(i) specify the technical field to which the invention relates;

(ii) indicate the background art which, as far as known to the applicant, can be regarded as useful for the understanding, searching and examination of the invention, and, preferably, cite the documents reflecting such art;

(iii) disclose the invention, as claimed, in such terms that the technical problem (even if not expressly stated as such) and its solution can be understood, and state the advantageous effects, if any, of the invention with reference to the background art;

(iv) briefly describe the figures in the drawings, if any;

(v) set forth at least the best mode contemplated by the applicant for carrying out the invention claimed; this shall be done in terms of examples, where appropriate, and with reference to the drawings, if any; where the national law of the designated State does not require the description of the best mode but is satisfied with the description of any mode (whether it is the best contemplated or not), failure to describe the best mode contemplated shall have no effect in that State;

(vi) indicate explicitly, when it is not obvious from the description or nature of the invention, the way in which the invention is capable of exploitation in industry and the way in which it can be made and used, or, if it can only be used, the way in which it can be used; the term "industry" is to be understood in its broadest sense as in the Paris Convention for the Protection of Industrial Property.

The main divergence in the definition and application of the disclosure requirement is that certain patent systems request a disclosure allowing a person skilled in the art to carry out the invention, while other systems require the application to disclose the best mode known to the inventor to carry out the invention.

F. *Drafting and interpretation of claims*

The basic issue. The claims define the invention, and thus the scope of protection of the patent. They are therefore the heart of the patent. This is true in particular after the grant of the patent, since others may not commercially use what is covered by the claims, but may use any other information contained in the specification. It is therefore particularly important that claims contain all the important features of the claimed invention. The claims form the basis for the examination as to the patentability of the invention. In addition, they may be affected by partial renunciation or invalidity of the patent, and they are relevant for the question of unity of invention. They also play a role when defining the contents of two inventions in the case of dependency or priority contests under the first to invent system, and when assessing the identity of inventions in the framework of the prohibition of double patenting.

When talking about claims, there are two different aspects to take into consideration: firstly, the drafting of the claims, and secondly the interpretation of the claims.

Status of harmonization. Article 6 of the PCT states the following:

Article 6: The Claims

The claim or claims shall define the matter for which protection is sought. Claims shall be clear and concise. They shall be fully supported by the description.

In addition, PCT Rule 6 contains, in particular, indications on the manner of claiming, on the numbering of claims, as well as further details. In the context of claims, it may be mentioned that PCT Rule 13 deals with the issue of unity of invention.

Nevertheless, both the drafting and the interpretation of claims diverge significantly in different legal systems, which may lead to different scopes of protection for the same invention, and to different results in the case of invalidity determinations. Some of these differences are described below.

Drafting of claims

(a) Certain systems require that only the *technical* features of the invention be contained in the claims, but not other features, such as economical or other elements. This is not the case for all patent systems. It has to be noted, however, that not all systems require an invention to have a technical character.

(b) While certain patent systems require a two-part form of the claims (the first part containing the designation of the subject matter belonging to the prior art, the second part being the characterizing part indicating the new technical features for which protection is claimed), other systems do not require this kind of structure, so that the prior art basis does not always appear in the claims.

(c) Certain patent laws allow for a plurality of closely related independent claims reflecting a single inventive concept to be contained in the same application ("unity of invention"), while according to other laws, the respective provisions are applied in a very narrow manner.

(d) While certain legal systems allow for different categories of claims, such as for instance product, process or apparatus claim, to be included in the same application, other patent systems have restrictions in this respect.

(e) Certain patent systems provide for restrictions on the dependency of sub-claims, which lead to a high number of dependent claims and, in certain offices, to high costs due to additional fees to be paid for each claim in excess of a certain number.

(f) Certain systems allow the lack of support of the claims by the description to be a ground for rejection or invalidation of the patent.

Interpretation of claims

(a) In most patent systems, the literal text of the claims forms the basis for the determination of the scope of protection of the patent. However, while certain systems do not allow an interpretation of the claims to go much beyond their wording, others have developed a broad way of interpreting the claims.

(b) In certain systems the claims have to be interpreted in an objective manner, while in others, what the inventor subjectively had intended to say is taken into consideration.

(c) In certain patent systems, only the description and the drawings may be used in order to interpret the claims. In other systems, further—or additional—means of interpreting the claims may be allowed.

(d) While certain legal systems provide that equivalents are covered by the claims, other legal systems do not provide for equivalents. In many systems, the doctrine of equivalents has been developed by case law, and is not to be found in statutory law. Systems vary widely as to the scope of equivalents applied.

(e) The possibilities to amend the claims during examination, as well as after the grant of the patent, vary considerably in different systems.

IV. *Conclusion*

In view of the above, the SCP is invited to note and consider the suggested issues related to the further development of international patent law. The SCP is invited, in particular, to express its guidance to the International Bureau as to whether and to what extent the mentioned issues should be included in the future work of the SCP.

[F]   Sui Generis Protection of Plants

FREE DISTRIBUTION VERSUS CONTROLLED CULTIVATION

As early as 1556, Spain's Council of the Indies (convened in Madrid) passed legislation making it illegal for foreigners to explore for plants in Spain's New World possessions. During the seventeenth and eighteenth centuries, botanical gardens were established in many European metropolitan states, the most famous being the British Empire collection of plants at Kew Gardens outside London. Such botanical gardens were established to develop systematic collections of plants for study, development, distribution, and commercialization throughout the colonial empires. Plant specimens were not distributed except in connection with the establishment of plantations within the British colonies controlled from London. A mere 100 plants were introduced to Great Britain during the sixteenth century. That figure rose to 1,000 in the seventeenth and 9,000 in the eighteenth centuries. A memorable example was Captain Bligh's mission on the Bounty to bring back breadfruit plants from Tahiti for plantations in the British West Indies.

Common staples from the Americas such as maize, potatoes, squash, tomatoes, peanuts, beans, and sunflowers were transferred to the eastern hemisphere. But equally, if not more, important were strategic plants requiring tropical empires such as spices, sugar, bananas, coffee, tea, rubber, and indigo. The Darjeeling tea industry was started in Calcutta with plants shipped on British ships from Shanghai. The rubber plantations of southeast Asia were built on propagations from disease-free rubber trees spirited out of northeast Brazil in 1876. Within a few years, Brazil's share of rubber exports plummeted from 100% to 5% while the British share rose from 0 to 75 %. Northeast Brazil became a depressed area and remains so to this day. Similarly, expensive cinchona exports from the Andes, used to extract quinine for malaria treatment, dropped 75% in a three-year period in the 1880s as production began on British colonial plantations in labor-rich Asia.

Control of plant production within the European empires emanated from control of the physical plants themselves. "The U.S. government made no effort to limit or control the dissemination of the plants it collected. In fact, the aim was to spread seeds widely and encourage the expansion and adaptation of American agriculture." CARY FOWLER, UNNATURAL SELECTION: TECHNOLOGY, POLITICS AND PLANT EVOLUTION xvii (1994). (Much of the following discussion is based on Fowler's account.)

Plant collection did not begin in earnest in the United States until Henry Ellsworth, a large landowner, became the first commissioner of patents in 1836. Ellsworth established a seed collection and distribution program at the Patent Office in 1839. The Shaker colonies of the northeast U.S. had been the first to develop seed packets for distribution. That function was taken over by the U.S. Patent Office in 1849 and later transferred to the Department of Agriculture.

In the late nineteenth century, over one-third of the budget of the U.S. Department of Agriculture was devoted to seed collection and distribution. The structure of American farming after the Civil War was quite different from that in the colonial empires and the ante-bellum South. American farms were small. Farmers were seed savers because of a lack of commercially reliable sources. That changed between 1860 and 1920. Commercial seed companies began to develop new seeds, and it became more economical for farmers to purchase new varieties produced by the commercial companies than to breed their own varieties.

LEGAL PROTECTION FOR NURSERIES PRODUCING ORNAMENTAL PLANTS AND FRUIT TREES

The United States Congress passed the Plant Patent Act of 1930 at the behest not of commercial seed companies but of commercial nurseries. In the United States, the plant patent statute (35 U.S.C. §§ 161-164) protects asexually reproduced plants commercially propagated through cuttings (clones) or grafts as opposed to seeds. Whereas plant breeders (seed companies) can be thought of as inventors, nurserymen are more properly described as discoverers. Practically all varieties of fruits are the result of chance discoveries and there is no "scientific" breeding of new varieties. In contrast to farmers, for whom the starting material is the same as the final product, the commercial nurseries do not compete with their customers because it is more cost effective for orchards and gardeners to buy stock than to raise it. The grant of the plant patent is the right to exclude others from asexually reproducing the plant or selling or using the plant so reproduced. 35 U.S.C. § 163.

The scope of protection for plant patents is very limited. Plant patent law covers fruits and flowers such as roses but specifically excepts potatoes and Jerusalem artichokes from coverage as well as all seed-propagated plants. Tuber-propagated plants alone among asexually reproduced plants are propagated by the same part of the plant that is sold as food. When the Plant Patent Act was passed, it was thought to have been politically inexpedient to include products which were staple foods such as corn, wheat, rice, and potatoes.

LEGAL PROTECTION FOR SEEDS (PLANT VARIETIES)

Plant breeding for uniformity was still rudimentary in the 1930s, so there was neither much pressure for patent protection nor ability to meet patent uniformity standards. The Netherlands adopted its Breeder's Ordinance in 1941, which provided a limited exclusive right for breeders of agriculturally important species to market the first generation of certified seed and a broader right to market propagating material. Corporate breeding programs began in earnest in the 1950s. Scientific plant breeding uses the principles of Mendelian genetics through sexual reproduction to produce consistent characteristics (desirable traits) which were not achieved by a blending of the characteristics of the parents as had been previously thought but by isolating them. When two closely related variations are crossed, there is produced a generation of inbreds which display what had been a recessive trait. The inbreds are then recrossed producing a hybrid which has the strength of the starting generation and displaying what had been a beneficial recessive trait in a ratio of 1:3. The breeder can place a "technological lock" (sometimes called "nature's patent") on the improved strain because only inbreds breed true, whereas hybrids do not. Therefore, breeding companies which sell the hybrid seeds but strictly control access to the inbreds thereby maintain the hybrid as a trade secret. Once the inbreds have been identified and preserved, the resultant hybrid is stable and will always have the same consistent traits. The customers of seed companies (the farmers) can own the seed they purchase, but the seed produced does not constitute breeding material.

THE UPOV CONVENTION

There developed a split between seed companies (particularly seed corn producers) which pursued research into hybrids and non-breeding seed companies which did not. Pressure from research-oriented seed companies investing in hybrid research grew toward recognition of "plant breeder's rights," protecting them from generic seed companies which did not. The Union for the Protection of New Varieties of Plants ("*Union pour la Protection des Obtentions*

Végétales" ["UPOV"]) was drafted at the international Convention of the same name and adopted by member nations on December 2, 1961 at a diplomatic conference in Paris. The treaty made the various breeder's rights laws of the signatories subject to the principle of national treatment and provided a definition of "variety" to apply "to any cultivar, clone, line, stock or hybrid which is capable of cultivation" (Article 2) as long as it is "clearly distinguishable by one or more important characteristics from any other variety whose existence is a matter of common knowledge at the time when protection is applied for." The variety also had to be capable of precise description and be given a denomination by which it would be known which was not proprietary. The position of secretary-general of the union is held by the director-general of WIPO.

Nine years after the first international convention of UPOV, in 1970, the United States adopted the Plant Variety Protection Act, ("PVPA"). (7 U.S.C. §§ 2321 *et. seq.*) Like the UPOV Convention, the PVPA does not provide patent-like protection. It is a registration system which issues a Certificate of Plant Variety Protection to the breeder of any novel variety of sexually reproduced plant. The certificate holder has the exclusive right to sell or reproduce the plant, or to use it to produce (as distinguished from develop) a hybrid or different variety, extending for a period of eighteen years from the date of issue. Both of these *sui generis* forms of protection prevented other companies from multiplying and reselling registered varieties. Protection is provided for the varieties themselves—not the genes which determine their traits, and under the 1978 Act, breeders are free to use protected varieties to produce new varieties. Six vegetables were omitted from coverage (carrots, celery, cucumbers, okra, peppers and tomatoes) due to opposition not from farmers but from large food processors, such as the Campbell Soup Company, which develop and consume their own varieties of those crops and traditionally benefit from publicly and privately available germplasm stocks.

The UPOV Convention was amended in 1972, 1978, and 1991. The U.S. joined the 1978 version of the convention in 1981. By 1973, U.S. farm exports came to exceed chemicals and consumer goods in value. Viewed biologically, both laws provided protection for varieties, that is, for certain combinations of genes. The genes themselves were not made patentable. Breeders are left free to use patented varieties (with unpatented genes) to produce new combinations of genes and new patentable varieties. Furthermore, farmers retained the "right" to save his or her protected seed for replanting (or for resale, if the farmer was not principally in the business of reselling protected varieties).

Under the 1978 Act, a breeder is entitled to protection even if the variety for which protection is sought is a naturally occurring plant. Under the 1991 Act, discovery of a naturally occurring plant is not sufficient. The breeder must have somehow developed the variety in order to secure protection. Article 5(3) of the 1978 Act allowed other breeders to use a protected variety for creating new varieties without authorization.

Conditions for grant were tightened and the scope of the breeder's rights were extended significantly under the 1991 UPOV Act. To receive protection, a variety must meet the requirements of novelty, distinctness, uniformity, and stability. Extension of the scope of the right includes requiring authorization for any multiplication for production. The "farmer's right" to store and plant seed was replaced by a "farmer's privilege" requiring authorization of the breeder. The exception for experimentation and creation of other varieties was narrowed to eliminate use to create a variety which is an essential derivation of the protected variety. (Article 15) It was thought that modern biotechnology allows such close manipulation of genes that there was increasing likelihood for minor variations to be exploited as loopholes to protection of the variety—so-called "cosmetic breeding." The accession of Bulgaria and the Russian Federation on March 24, 1998 triggered the entry into force of the 1991 Act on April 24, 1998. As of that date, there were thirty-seven members of the Union and seven signatories of the 1991 text. (Bulgaria, Denmark, Germany, Israel, Netherlands, Russian Federation, and Sweden.)

Critics of plant breeder's rights complain of the growing separation between the farmer and the tools of farming. Farmers dependent on commercial seed producers for ever more efficient and pesticide/herbicide compatible hybrids no longer retain their old seed varieties.

> The explosion of diversity which had been ignited by seed collection and distribution programs and by immigration was wiped out as farmers ceased saving their own seed. Irrespective of the quality of these varieties relative to purchased seed, the farmer lost a measure of self-reliance in the process. And some portion of the germplasm itself, with all of its adaptation to different American environments, pests, diseases, and cultures became extinct, never again to be seen or used by a farmer or professional plant breeder.

FOWLER, *supra* at 118. "Genetic erosion" is an unintended consequence of modern plant breeding. To the extent that a breeder produces a successful variety, it may displace genetic material needed for future breeding programs.

Advocates of UPOV's system of breeder's rights point out that by the year 2020, the world population may reach 8 billion with 83 % living in developing countries. As productive farmland shrinks in the wake of urbanization, there is no option but to produce more food on less land. It becomes clear that the relevance of the small farmer is fading and the world is moving toward food production by agribusiness. *See, e.g.*, http://www.upov.int/eng/newplant/need var.htm. The relevance of *sui generis* protection for plants where utility patent protection is allowed for the underlying genetic material is open to question in developed countries. However, American companies are supportive of the United States entering the 1991 Act for purposes of achieving national treatment in those countries which choose to use a *sui generis* system. Under the TRIPS Agreement, Article 27(3)(b), WTO members must provide either patent protection or sui generis protection for plants.

. . . .

CONVENTION FOR THE PROTECTION OF PLANTS

S. Treaty Doc. No. 104-17, Signed October 25, 1991
Read the first time in the Senate September 5, 1995

LETTER OF SUBMITTAL

DEPARTMENT OF STATE
Washington, May 10, 1995.

The PRESIDENT,
The White House.

I have the honor to submit to you [the 1991 Act of the UPOV Convention]. I recommend that the 1991 Act of the UPOV Convention be transmitted to the Senate for its advice and consent to ratification, subject to a reservation under Article 35(2) of the 1991 Act, which allows states party to the 1978 Act to retain their present patent systems for certain varieties of plants.

. . . .

Member States of the Convention constitute the International Union for the Protection of New Varieties of Plants (the UPOV Union), whose objective is to promote the protection of the rights of plant breeders in new plant varieties.

. . . .

Several considerations prompted the member States to revise the Convention at a Diplomatic Conference held in Geneva, Switzerland in March of 1991. Those considerations were: 1) recognition that the protection offered to breeders under previous Acts of the Convention was not adequate; 2) the need for the Convention to reflect technological changes in the breeding of new plant varieties; and 3) the need to clarify certain provisions of the 1978 Act.

Ten member States of UPOV signed the 1991 Act at the conclusion of the Conference. The 1991 Act remained open for signature by UPOV member States until March 31, 1991, by which time 16 States, including the United States, had signed the Convention.

... In the United States, implementing legislation was enacted as Public Law 103-349, on October 6, 1994.

The main aim of the Convention is to promote the protection of the rights of the breeder in new plant varieties. In that regard, the Convention not only requires member States to provide protection for new varieties of plants, but also contains explicit and detailed rules on the conditions and arrangements for granting protection. Further, it prescribes the scope of protection, including possible restrictions and exceptions thereto, establishes, with some limitations, the principle of national treatment for plant breeders from other member States, and provides for a right of priority.

The Convention, as revised by the 1991 Act, would afford additional protection to plant breeders, as follows:

First, the 1991 Act requires Contracting Parties, after certain transitional periods, to protect varieties of all genera and species of the plant kingdom.

Second, the 1991 Act redefines a breeder's right to cover, among other things, the production of a variety's propagating material by others for any purpose. The 1991 Act also expressly permits member States to exclude from the reach of the breeder's right, the practice of farmers to save seed.

Third, the 1991 Act extends breeders' rights to include harvested material of the protected variety.

Fourth, the 1991 Act puts an end to the common practice, permitted by the present Convention, of using protected varieties to derive and freely commercialize other varieties that, although differing to some degree, maintain the essential characteristics of the initial variety.

Finally, the 1991 Act is silent regarding the title of protection under which a breeder's right may be granted. This would afford member States the freedom to provide protection for plant varieties through patents and sui generis breeders' rights, thus affording them greater flexibility in determining how to protect new plant varieties most effectively.

These and other features of the 1991 Act would enhance the protection afforded to breeders of new plant varieties not only in the United States, but also in those future member States where patent protection for plant varieties is not now obtainable, and in present member States where protection of plant breeders' rights is either weak or unavailable for a significant number of plant species and genera.

. . . .

Prompt ratification of the 1991 Act of the UPOV Convention will demonstrate the United States commitment to effective protection for intellectual property in the area of new plant variety development. Ratification of this Convention is consistent, therefore, with United States foreign policy of encouraging other countries to provide adequate and effective protection for intellectual property generally, and for new plant varieties in particular.

I recommend, therefore, that the 1991 Act of the UPOV Convention be transmitted to the Senate as soon as possible for its advice and consent to ratification, subject to a reservation under Article 35(2), which allows parties to the 1978 Act to retain their present plant patent systems for certain varieties of plants.

Respectfully submitted,

PETER TARNOFF

TRIPS AGREEMENT, ARTICLE 27

1. Subject to the provisions of paragraphs 2 and 3 below, patents shall be available for any inventions, whether products or processes, in all fields of technology, provided that they are new, involve an inventive step and are capable of industrial application. Subject to paragraph 4 of Article 65, paragraph 8 of Article 70 and paragraph 3 of this Article, patents shall be available and patent rights enjoyable without discrimination as to the place of invention, the field of technology and whether products are imported or locally produced.

. . . .

3. Members may also exclude from patentability:

. . . .

(b) plants and animals other than microorganisms, and essentially biological processes for the production of plants or animals other than non-biological and microbiological processes. However, Members shall provide for the protection of plant varieties either by patents or by an effective sui generis system or by any combination thereof. The provisions of this sub-paragraph shall be reviewed four years after the entry into force of the Agreement Establishing the WTO.

NOTES AND QUESTIONS

(1) **Patent Rights and Breeders Rights**. The scope of patentable subject matter for biotechnology expands, what is the role of "breeder's rights?" The chief patent counsel of a multinational agribusiness company stated to your editor that his company rarely uses the PVPA registration system, but strongly supports U.S. entry into the 1991 UPOV Convention. Why?

(2) **Legal Protection and Financial Investment.** A 1988 report of the Office of Technology Assessment noted substantial increases in private investment in agricultural research following the *Chakrabarty* decision. The same study also notes that investment shifted toward research on major crops such as corn and soybeans, and away from research on minor crops at the same time that the USDA abandoned its role in seed and plant variety development and genetic erosion concerns grow. Is the policy trade-off worth the risks? *See* OFFICE OF TECHNOLOGY ASSESSMENT, NEW DEVELOPMENTS IN BIOTECHNOLOGY: PATENTING LIFE 75-81, Doc. No. Y3.T22/2:2B52/4/V.5/pt.3/agric.

(3) **1991 UPOV**. A good summary of the 1991 amendments to the UPOV Convention can be found in Barry Greengrass, *The 1991 Act of the UPOV Convention*, 12 EUR. INTELL. PROP REV. 466 (1991).

(4) **Plant Patents as Copyright-Like Protection.** The U.S. Plant Patent Act protects only against copying and not against independent discovery or invention. *See* David Bennett Bernstein, *Is a Plant Patent a Form of Copyright?*, 25 IDEA 31 (1985).

(5) **What Does The Term "Sui Generis" Mean in TRIPS Article 27(3)((b)?** Could a developing country adopt the text of the 1978 UPOV Convention, no longer open for accession, as a form of sui generis protection for plants. Changes are underway in developing countries regarding the protection of plant varieties, in compliance with Article 27 of the TRIPS Agreement. Not all parties are pleased at the prospect of India's decision to grant sui generis protection to plant varieties. *See* Biswajit Dhar & Sachin Chaturvedi, *Introducing Plant Breeders' Rights in India–A Critical Evaluation of the Proposed Legislation,* 1 J. WORLD INTEL. PROP. 245 (1998).

(6) **TRIPS and the CBD.** The OECD Committee for Scientific and Technological Policy released a report in 1996 summarizing the genetic resource issue and explaining how the new international context created by the Convention on Biological Diversity ("CBD") and the TRIPS agreement might influence the exploitation of genetic resources. *See Intellectual Property, Technology Transfer and Genetic Resources–An OECD Survey of Current Practices and Policies* (OECD, 1996), *available at* http://www.oecd.org/dsti/biotech/. The United States signed the CBD on June 3, 1993, but ratification by the Senate is unlikely in the near future.

(7) **Concerns in Developing Countries.** According to a *Statement from Peoples' Movements & NGOs in Southeast Asia to the World Trade Organization* dated May 1998 and published by the Filipino Farmer/Scientist Partnership for Development:

> Rice is life in Southeast and other parts of Asia. It has been the cornerstone of our food, our languages, our cultures–in short, our life for thousands of years. Over the centuries, farming communities throughout the region have developed, nurtured and conserved over a hundred thousand distinct varieties of rice to suit different tastes and needs.
>
> The Green Revolution spearheaded by the International Rice Research Institute ("IRRI") in the 1960s resulted the loss of this diversity from farmers' fields and the spread of wholly unsustainable farming systems which require high energy inputs such as pesticides, fertilizers, so-called 'high-yielding' seeds, irrigation systems and supervised credit schemes. In this process, farmers lost control of their own seeds, their own knowledge and their own self-confidence. Today, people are struggling throughout the region to rebuild more sustainable agriculture systems hinged on farmers' control of genetic resources and local knowledge.
>
> In the past, the whole cycle of the rice economy was under the control of farmers themselves, from production through distribution. Today, global corporations are taking over the rice sector. With the expansion of industrial farming, global corporations–and their local subsidiaries established their predominance in the rice sector through research programs, interference in policy-making, and their exports of farm machinery, pesticides and fertilizers. Now, through the use of genetic engineering, they are increasing their control over our rice cultures. The kinds of rice that we are promised through this

technology threaten the environment and public health. For example, herbicide tolerant rice will lead to increased pesticide use. Rice incorporating Bacillus thuringiensis genes will disrupt ecological balances. Both of these are unsafe for consumers and will lead to allergic reactions, increased antibiotic resistance and other health hazards. New hybrids–such as those based on the so-called "Terminator Technology"–will force farmers to buy rice seed every planting season from transnational corporations.

The extension of the patent system through the [TRIPS Agreement] gives global corporations the right to claim monopoly ownership over rice–and life itself. Companies in the industrialized world have already started to claim intellectual property rights on rice. A derivative of IR-8, IRRI's "miracle rice", was monopolised through IPR in the United States already in the 1980s. Recently, RiceTec, a company in Texas, has taken out a patent on basmati rice. This is biopiracy against India and Pakistan. The same company and many others in the US are now marketing what they label as Jasmine rice. This is not only intellectual and cultural theft, it also directly threatens farm communities in Southeast Asia. Jasmine rice comes from Thailand, where it is grown today by over five million resource-poor farmers who are trying to develop ecological alternatives for Jasmine ice production and marketing.

MASIPAG at *masipag@mozcom.com*. Are these claims legitimate? The issues will be explored further below in the discussion of the European Directive on Biotechnological Inventions. We will also return to these issues in Chapter 8.

[G] Regional Harmonization: the European Union

Regional harmonization of patent law and of exploitation of patent rights is most highly developed in the context of European integration. The following two readings discuss the 1996 European Regulation on Technology Licensing and the 1998 European Directive on the Legal Protection of Biotechnological Inventions. The European Patent System will be discussed at greater length in Chapter 6 in the context of the multinational acquisition of industrial property rights.

BRYAN HARRIS, TECHNOLOGY LICENSING IN THE EUROPEAN UNION[*]
38 IDEA 139 (1997)

I. THE PROHIBITION OF RESTRICTIVE AGREEMENTS

Intellectual property law creates monopolies; antitrust law condemns them. The reconciliation of these two bodies of law presents endless difficulties for both judges and lawmakers. This article examines the recent efforts of the legislators of the European Union to balance these opposing interests through the enactment of a coherent set of rules on certain categories of technology transfer agreements. These rules are known as the Commission Regulation on the Application of Article 85(3) of the Treaty establishing the European Community to Certain Categories of Technology Transfer Agreements.[1]

We begin by exploring how the antitrust or competition rules are applied in the European Union. Article 85(1) of the Treaty establishing the European Community (the EC Treaty)[2] prohibits agreements between undertakings which may affect trade between member states and which have as their object or effect the prevention, restriction, or distortion of trade. However, under Article 85(3) of the EC Treaty, the provisions of Article 85(1) may be declared inapplicable in the case of agreements or categories of agreements between undertakings when certain conditions are fulfilled. A declaration of inapplicability is made by the Commission of the European Communities and the arrangements for exempting categories of agreements, as distinct from individual or specific agreements, take the form of so-called "block exemption" regulations. In other words, an agreement such as a technology transfer license may or may not restrict competition, and if such an agreement does restrict competition, it may or may not qualify for exemption. These are matters on which the Commission rules,[3] and from which there is a right of appeal to the Court of Justice of the European Communities (or, since 1988, to the Court of First Instance). The establishment of a block exemption for patent licenses took many years to achieve and the establishment of such an exemption for know-how licenses took even longer. Patent licenses, know-how licenses, and licenses with mixed elements, including those that contain clauses on trademark and copyright licensing, are currently covered by the new block exemption regulation on Technology Transfer Agreements.

---

[*]Copyright 1997, Bryan Harris.

[1]The regulation of 31 January 1996, on the Application of Article 85(3) of the TREATY ESTABLISHING THE EUROPEAN COMMUNITY, to Certain Categories of Technology Transfer Agreements, 1996 O.J. (L 31) 2. [hereinafter "the Regulation"].

[2]TREATY ESTABLISHING THE EUROPEAN COMMUNITY, Feb. 7, 1992, 1 C.M.L.R. 573 (1992) *incorporating changes made by* TREATY ON EUROPEAN UNION, Feb. 7, 1992 O.J. (C 224) 1 (1992), [1992] 1 C.M.L.R. 719 (1992).

[3]EC Treaty art. 155.

II. EXEMPTION OF CATEGORIES OF AGREEMENTS ("BLOCK EXEMPTIONS")

Before discussing the content of Commission Regulation 240/96, it is helpful to explain how a block exemption regulation eases the burden on licensors, licensees, and their advisers. Without block exemptions, only individual exemptions can be granted by the Commission under Article 85(3) of the EC Treaty, and the process of obtaining an individual exemption can be slow and hazardous. The process tends to be slow because of the large backlog of individual cases being investigated at any given time by the Commission. The process tends to be hazardous because its quasi-judicial character allows for objections by third parties, hearings, and even the interjection of political considerations.[4] By contrast, a block exemption is essentially automatic. If a licensing agreement satisfies the terms of the block exemption regulation, no further formalities need be followed. The parties save time and trouble, and the Commission does not become bogged down in individual proceedings.

The New Technology Licensing Regulation

The Regulation seeks to: (1) combine the earlier regulations on patent licensing and know-how licensing into a single regulation, (2) allow for a certain amount of overlap between industrial property rights, and (3) simplify the previous law. Whether the third objective is being achieved remains to be seen. Although industrial interests have generally welcomed the Regulation, there is some skepticism.

In combining patent and know-how licensing in a single regulation, the Commission has created three categories of license agreements: "pure" patent licensing agreements, "pure" know-how licensing agreements, and "mixed" agreements that, according to the Commission, are playing an increasingly important role in the transfer of technology. Both pure and mixed agreements may contain provisions for licensing other intellectual property rights, such as trademarks, design rights, copyright, and software protection. These provisions are covered by the regulation to the extent that they contribute to the licensing of technology and are only ancillary provisions. However, the regulation does not cover what may be described in antitrust parlance as "horizontal" agreements.

Over the years, block exemption regulations have tended to conform to a fairly recognizable pattern. Essentially, the scheme of the Regulation is as follows: Article 1(1) declares that Article 85(1) of the EC Treaty—the prohibition on restrictive agreements—shall not apply to certain categories of agreements that include one or more of the obligations set out in the Article. In other words, Article 1 both defines the agreements in question and exempts them. Article 2(1) allows the exemption to apply to agreements notwithstanding the presence of certain clauses that are generally not restrictive of competition and which are set out in the Article. Article 2 is intended to clarify the status of certain

---

[4]Council Regulation 17/62/EEC, art. 19, 1962 O.J. (L 13), *see generally*, Commission Regulation 99/63/EEC, 1963 O.J. (L 127).

provisions that may appear restrictive but are regarded by the Commission as acceptable. Article 3 lists the circumstances, including the presence of certain clauses in an agreement, that will ensure that the licensing agreement does not qualify for exemption under the regulation. Finally, the Regulation contains Articles providing for exclusions, special cases, and the withdrawal of exemption in certain circumstances.[16]

Definition and Exemption: Article 1

Following the pattern noted above, Article 1 of the regulation defines the agreements and exempts them.[17] The definition has three parts: (1) the broad description of the types of agreements concerned, (2) the condition that only two undertakings are party to the agreement, and (3) the list of obligations, the inclusion of one or more of which brings the agreement within the scope of the regulation.

The types of agreements concerned are pure patent or know-how licensing agreements and mixed patent and know-how licensing agreements. These agreements include those that contain ancillary provisions relating to intellectual property rights other than patents or know-how. The limitation to agreements to which only two undertakings are a party has been mentioned. However, it should be noted that the case law of the Court of Justice of the European Communities has much to say on what constitutes an undertaking. It may be a person or a company (a natural or legal person, in continental law) and may include a variety of entities, including public bodies if, in this context, they are carrying out an economic function.

There are eight qualifying obligations:

1. an obligation on the licensor not to license other undertakings to exploit a licensed technology in a licensed territory;

2. an obligation on the licensor not to exploit a licensed technology in a licensed territory;

3. an obligation on the licensee not to exploit a licensed technology in a territory of the licensor within the common market [sole license];

4. an obligation on the licensee not to manufacture or use a licensed product, or use a licensed process in territories within the common market that are licensed to other licensees;

5. an obligation on the licensee not to pursue an active policy of putting a licensed product on the market in territories within the common market that are licensed to other licensees, and in particular not to engage in advertising specifically aimed at those territories or to establish any branch or maintain any distribution depot there;

---

[16]*See* Council Regulation 19/65/EEC, 1965-1966 O.J. Spec. Ed. 36 (block exemption regulations are made by the Commission under powers delegated by the Council).

[17]Article 1 is explained and justified by Recitals 10 and 12-16. Recitals are essential to the regulation, under Article 190 of the EC Treaty, and may be cited in proceedings.

6. an obligation on the licensee not to put a licensed product on the market in territories licensed to other licensees within the common market in response to unsolicited orders;

7. an obligation on the licensee to use only the licensor's trademark or trade dress to distinguish a licensed product during the term of the agreement, provided the licensee is not prevented from identifying itself as the manufacturer of the licensed products; and

8. an obligation on the licensee to limit production of a licensed product to the quantities required in manufacturing the licensee's products and to sell the licensed product only as an integral part of or a replacement part for the licensee's own products or otherwise in connection with the sale of these products, provided that such quantities are freely determined by the licensee.

The rules are concerned with the question of territoriality, not purely for reasons of competition. This is because one of the main objects of the EC Treaty was to create a single market without barriers to interstate trade. If intellectual property rights are given absolute territorial protection in the member states, the principle of free movement of goods throughout the Community would be jeopardized. In any event, the Court of Justice ruled in 1982 that absolute territorial protection could not be exempted, and the original block exemption regulation on patent licensing agreements was drafted with the Court's ruling in mind.[21]

Permitted Clauses: Article 2

Article 2 deals with permitted clauses in agreements covered by the regulation. There is an oddity in the wording of Article 2, which provides that the exemption applies to agreements "notwithstanding" the presence of the clauses listed in the Article. This gives the impression that the clauses are accepted on sufferance. But Article 2 goes on to describe the clauses as ones "which are not generally restrictive of competition." This suggests that the list is there simply *ex abundanti cautela* (from an abundance of caution), but the Article is clearly more important than a simple declaration of what is not regarded as objectionable.

As a guide to patentees and their legal advisers on the clauses that are permitted in technology transfer licensing agreements, the following list from Article 2 is invaluable:

1. an obligation on the licensee not to divulge the know-how communicated by the licensor (the licensee may be held to this obligation after the agreement has expired);

2. an obligation on the licensee not to grant sublicenses or to assign the license;

3. an obligation on the licensee not to exploit licensed know-how or patents after termination of an agreement as long as the know-how is still secret or the patents are still in force;

---

[21]Case 258/78, *Nungesser v. Commission*, 1982 E.C.R. 2015 (1983) (sometimes referred to as the *Maize Seed* case).

4. an obligation on the licensee to grant to the licensor a license in respect of improvements to or new applications of the licensed technology, provided that: (*a*) in the case of severable improvements, such a license is not exclusive, so that the licensee is free to use the improvements or to license them to third parties, insofar as such licensing does not involve disclosure of the know-how communicated by the licensor that is still secret; and (*b*) the licensor undertakes to grant an exclusive or non-exclusive license of improvements to the licensee;

5. an obligation on the licensee to observe minimum quality specifications, including technical specifications, for a licensed product or to procure goods or services from an undertaking designated by the licensor, insofar as these quality specifications, products or services are necessary for a technically proper exploitation of the licensed technology, or for ensuring that the product of the licensee conforms to the minimum quality specifications that are applicable to the licensor and other licensees, and to allow the licensor to carry out related checks;

6. an obligation to inform the licensor of misappropriation of know-how, infringement of licensed patents, or to take or assist the licensor in instituting legal action against such misappropriation or infringement;

7. an obligation on the licensee to continue paying royalties: (*a*) until the end of the agreement in the amounts, for the periods, and according to the methods freely determined by the parties, in the event of the know-how becoming publicly known other than by action of the licensor, without prejudice to the payment of any additional damages in the event of the know-how becoming publicly known by the action of the licensee in breach of the agreement; or (*b*) over a period going beyond the duration of the licensed patents, in order to facilitate payment;

8. an obligation on the licensee to restrict exploitation of the licensed technology to one or more technical fields of application covered by the licensed technology or to one or more product markets;

9. an obligation on the licensee to pay a minimum royalty, to produce a minimum quantity of a licensed product, or to carry out a minimum number of operations exploiting the licensed technology;

10. an obligation on the licensor to grant to the licensee any more favorable terms that the licensor may grant to another undertaking after the agreement is entered into;

11. an obligation on the licensee to mark a licensed product with an indication of the licensor's name or of the licensed patent;

12. an obligation on the licensee not to use the licensor's technology to construct facilities for third parties (this is without prejudice to the right of the licensee to increase the capacity of its own facilities or to set up additional facilities for use on normal commercial terms, including the payment of additional royalties);

13. an obligation on the licensee to supply only a limited quantity of a licensed product to a particular customer, where the license was granted so that the customer might have a second source of supply inside the licensed territory (this provision shall also apply where the customer is the licensee and the license that was granted in order to provide a second source of supply provides that the

customer is to manufacture the licensed products itself or have them manufactured by a subcontractor);

14. a reservation by the licensor of the right to exercise the rights conferred by a patent to oppose the exploitation of the technology by the licensee outside the licensed territory;

15. a reservation by the licensor of the right to terminate the agreement if the licensee contests the secret or substantial nature of licensed know-how or challenges the validity of licensed patents within the common market belonging to the licensor or undertakings connected with it;

16. a reservation by the licensor of the right to terminate a patent license agreement if the licensee raises the claim that such a patent is not necessary;[22]

17. an obligation on the licensee to use best efforts to manufacture and market a licensed product; and

18. a reservation by the licensor of the right to terminate the exclusivity granted to the licensee and to stop licensing improvements to licensee when the licensee enters into competition within the common market with the licensor, with undertakings connected with the licensor or with other undertakings in respect of research and development, production, use or distribution of competing products, and to require the licensee to prove that the licensed know-how is not being used for the production of products and the provision of services other than those licensed.

As the opening words of Article 2 suggest, there are occasions when the clauses listed above are restrictive of competition. In these circumstances, they are exempted, even if they are not accompanied by any of the obligations exempted by Article 1. The rationale is that when clauses are acceptable and not restrictive of competition, they fall squarely within Article 2. However, when clauses are restrictive of competition but are nevertheless acceptable, they are more in the nature of qualifying clauses typical of those listed in Article 1. Clauses similar to those listed in Article 2 but having a more limited scope are also exempted on the same terms.

Exemption Not Applied: Article 3

Article 2 is referred to by some lawyers as the "white list," while Article 3 is known as the "black list." Articles 1 and 2 pave the way for exemption, whereas Article 3 sets out the circumstances where no exemption applies. The circumstances covered by Article 3 are those in which:

1. one party is restricted in the determination of prices, components of prices, or discounts for the licensed products;

---

[22]If a licensee claims that a patent is not necessary, perhaps because the substantial part of the design or process is in the public domain, or covered by know-how, the licensor of that patent may terminate the licensing agreement. This right to terminate the licensing agreement is not considered to be restrictive of competition. If it turns out that the licensee is wrong in claiming that the patent is unnecessary, he may expose himself to patent infringement proceedings. Also in this case, the licensor or other party pursuing infringement proceedings, would not be in breach of the rules on competition.

2. one party is restricted from competing within the common market with the other party, with undertakings connected with the other party or with other undertakings in respect of research and development, production, use, or distribution of competing products;[23]

3. one or both of the parties are required, without any objectively justified reason, to: (a) refuse to meet orders from users or resellers in their respective territories who would market products in other territories within the common market, or (b) make it difficult for users or resellers to obtain the products from other resellers within the common market, and in particular to exercise intellectual property rights or take measures so as to prevent users or resellers from obtaining outside products, or from putting on the market, in the licensed territory, products which have been lawfully put on the market, within the common market, by the licensor or with the licensor's consent, or (c) do so as a result of a concerted practice between them;

4. the parties were already competing manufacturers before the grant of the license and one of them is restricted, within the same technical field of use or within the same product market, as to the customers it may serve, in particular by being prohibited from supplying certain classes of users, employing certain forms of distribution, or with the aim of sharing customers, using certain types of packaging for the products

5. the quality of the licensed products one party may manufacture or sell, or the number of operations exploiting a licensed technology the party may carry out, are subject to limitations;

6. the licensee is obliged to assign, in whole or in part, to the licensor, rights to improvements to or new applications of a licensed technology; or

7. the licensor is prohibited (whether in separate agreements or through automatic extension of an agreement's initial duration for a period exceeding the length in Article 1(2) and (3)) from licensing other undertakings to exploit a licensed technology in the licensed territory, or from exploiting a licensed technology in the other party's territory, or other licensees' territories.

Heading this list is the question of price-fixing, which is anathema to the Commission. There are few cases in which the Commission or Court has approved price restrictions. It is not surprising that the inclusion of a clause on price restriction rules out the chance that the agreement will be covered by the block exemption regulation. Nor is it surprising that the inclusion of a non-competition clause should have the same effect. A refusal-to-supply clause is subject to an objectively justified reason, but field-of-use restrictions are viewed more strictly. As for improvements in a licensed technology, the Commission has always tended to support the rights of the licensee as against those of the licensor.[31] Clauses favoring the licensor, by way of an obligation to assign rights to improvements, take the agreement out of the scope of the exemption.

---

[23]This is without prejudice to the last two clauses contained in the "white list."

[31]There is a certain amount of case law on pricing, non-competition clauses, refusal-to-supply, field-of-use restrictions, and improvements in technology, but for the most part this case law antedates the 1984 and 1989 regulations. In recent years the Commission has tended to apply somewhat different, and perhaps more pragmatic, principles to its handling of the cases in this field. For these reasons, the case law is not quoted extensively, and, indeed, readers are advised to cite them with considerable caution, given the changed circumstances.

The Opposition Procedure

It does not require a great feat of imagination to conceive of agreements which nearly comply with the terms of the Regulation, but fall just outside its scope because they contain obligations restrictive of competition that are not explicitly covered by Articles 1 and 2, and not expressly ruled out under Article 3. Under Article 4, these agreements are subject to an opposition procedure. The Commission must be notified of the agreements, but unless the Commission formally opposes exemption within a period of four months, the agreements will be "automatically" exempted. If an agreement is opposed, it is open to the parties either to show that the conditions of Article 85(3) of the EC Treaty are satisfied, or to amend the agreement in such a way as to persuade the Commission that the conditions of Article 85(3) are satisfied.

Exclusions

Article 5 of the Regulation specifies the types of agreements excluded from the scope of the regulation because of the circumstances in which these agreements are made. Broadly, these are horizontal agreements involving the pooling of technologies, the activities of joint ventures, reciprocal licensing and the like. There are provisions in this Article for *de minimis* principles to apply, so that some agreements of these types may be automatically exempted. For example, if the products and services covered by the agreement do not account for more than a given share of the market, the agreement is exempted from the regulation.

Circumstances Similar to Exclusive Licensing

Given the similarity between sales and exclusive licensing, and the danger that the requirements of the Regulation might be avoided by presenting exclusive licenses as assignments, Article 6 applies the exemption to agreements concerning the assignment and acquisition of patents or know-how where the risk associated with exploitation remains with the assignor. Article 6 also applies to licensing agreements where the licensor is not the holder of a patent or know-how but is authorized by the holder to grant the license (as in the case of sublicenses) and to licensing agreements in which the parties' rights or obligations are assumed by connected undertakings.

Withdrawal of the Benefit of the Regulation

Where the Commission finds that an agreement exempted by the Regulation nevertheless has certain effects which are incompatible with the conditions laid down in Article 85(3), the Commission may withdraw the benefit of the Regulation. These are factual, economic effects of actual circumstances which may vitiate an otherwise acceptable agreement. Article 6, which sets out these circumstances in general terms, also refers to four specific circumstances that are likely to persuade the Commission to withdraw the benefit of the Regulation. One refers to cases in which the effect of the agreement is to prevent a licensed product from being exposed, in a licensed territory, to effective competition from identical goods or services, or from goods or services considered by users as interchangeable in view of their characteristics, price, and intended use. This condition is especially apt to occur where the licensee's market share exceeds forty percent. Originally, the Commission wanted to make the forty percent market share a basic test of whether the Regulation should apply to certain agreements at all, but this was vigorously opposed, so the Commission had to make do with a reference to market share in subsidiary provisions of the regulation. Nevertheless, the inclusion of this provision in the withdrawal Article is a warning to parties to technology licensing agreements that the Commission, impressed by the ability of some powerful operators to manipulate the market by means of licensing agreements, will in certain cases pay close attention to market shares and the potential domination of the market.

Definitions

Most of the remaining provisions of the Regulation are concerned with definitions. Article 8, for example, includes a number of rights related to patents. Thus, patent applications, utility models, applications for registration of utility models, topographies of semi-conductor products, *certificats d'utilité* and *certificats d'addition* under French law, as well as applications for those certificates, supplementary protection certificates, and plant breeders' certificates, are all deemed to be patents for the purposes of the regulation.

Of the seventeen definitions set out in Article 10 of the Regulation, those concerned with the meaning of "know-how" are among the most important. Under the Article, "know-how" itself means a body of technical information that is secret, substantial and identified in any appropriate form. "Secret" means that a know-how package in the precise configuration and assembly of its components is not generally known or easily accessible. It is not limited to the narrow sense that each individual component of the know-how should be totally unknown or unobtainable outside the licensor's business. "Substantial" means that know-how includes information that must be useful, *i.e.*, can reasonably be expected at the date of conclusion of the agreement to be capable of improving the competitive position of the licensee. For example, know-how could enable the licensee to enter a new market or provide an advantage in competition. "Identified" is defined as the manner in which the know-how is described or recorded, to make it possible to verify that it satisfies the criteria of secrecy and substantiality, and to ensure that the licensee is not unduly restricted in exploiting the technology. To be identified, know-how can either be set out in the licensing agreement, in a separate document, or recorded in any other appropriate form, no later than shortly after the know-how is transferred, provided that the separate document or other record can be made available if the need arises.

Article 10 also defines the terms "necessary patents" and "parallel patents," which appear in paragraphs (2) and (3) of Article 1, that govern the periods to which an exemption applies. "Necessary patents" are those in which the patent is necessary for utilizing a licensed technology where, in the absence of such license, the realization of the licensed technology would not be possible, or would be possible only to a lesser extent, or in more difficult or costly conditions. Such patents must therefore be of technical, legal or economic interest to the licensee. "Parallel patents," on the other hand, are patents that, in spite of the absence of national rule unification concerning industrial property, protect the same invention in various Member States.

Miscellaneous Provisions

Article 9 provides for confidentiality.[41] Article 11 provides for the expiration of the earlier Commission Regulations 2349/84 on patents, and 556/89 on know-how. Article 12 provides for review of The Regulation. Article 13 provides that the Regulation is in force from April 1, 1996, to March 31, 2006.

Comment

Given the complexity of the subject, the hostility of industrial interests to earlier drafts of the regulation, the difficulty of reconciling the need to restrict licenses to the extent required to make investment worthwhile,[42] and the need to ensure that restrictions are consistent with competitive trade, the Commission has done an unenviable task well. Many more patent licensing and other technology licensing agreements will be covered by the automatic exemption implicit in the Regulation. This is largely due to the broadening of the base of the Regulation. Relatively few patent licenses have proven to be "pure" patent licenses. Many agreements in the past had failed to fit into a precise mold.

Industrial interests still have some reservations about the Regulation—specifically about the market share principle. A great deal depends on how far the Commission takes advantage of the opposition procedure, and of the right to withdraw the benefit of the Regulation. In other words, we shall have to wait and see how well The Regulation operates in practice. This may be hard to judge, since the very nature of automatic exemption under the block exemption regulation is that it is invisible.[43] The Commission may have to publicly assess the application of The Regulation, probably in its annual reports on competition policy. The first of these assessments will be awaited with interest.

---

[41]This provision adds to the general requirement of confidentiality contained in EC TREATY art. 214.

[42]The investment factor influenced the Court of Justice in *Nungesser*, 1982 E.C.R. at 2015.

[43]As the cases covered by the regulation do not have to be tracked, the Commission has no statistics of the numbers of agreements automatically exempted.

EUROPEAN UNION BIOTECHNOLOGY DIRECTIVE

Unlike the Commission Regulation discussed above, issued in accordance with ex-Article 235 (now Article 308) of the EC Treaty, European Community directives seeking approximation of national laws are intended to be more responsive to national cultural variations. *See supra* § 2.03[C][3] (discussing EU legislative instruments). An example is the directive on the legal protection of biotechnological inventions. Following a 1985 European Commission White Paper calling for approximation of intellectual property laws to complete the internal market, a draft directive containing guidelines for biotechnology inventions was proposed by the European Commission in 1988. The Commission noted that revolutionary changes in biotechnology, unforeseen when the European Patent Convention (with its exclusions from patentability) was drafted, had taken place. This 1988 draft directive was vehemently opposed by members of the Green parties in the European Parliament. A modified proposal incorporating provisions on ethics, farmers' "privilege," and compulsory licensing was issued in late 1992. After six years of political give-and-take between the Council, Commission, and Parliament, the revised Directive below was promulgated in early 1998. In the recitals of its preamble, the Directive makes findings concerning the increasingly important role biotechnological invention play in the Community's industrial development. It notes that research and development require a considerable amount of high-risk investment and therefore only adequate legal protection can make it profitable, but that concepts in national laws based upon the EPC and UPOV conventions had created uncertainty regarding the protection of biotechnological and certain microbiological inventions in Europe. As eventually adopted, the directive attempts at a political compromise between environmental and animal rights activists on the one hand, and proponents of a U.S.-style system with very narrow exceptions to the general rule that "anything under the sun made by man" is patentable. As of December 2000, the Biotechnology Directive had been implemented into the national law in Denmark, Finland, Ireland, and the United Kingdom. A draft law was adopted in October 2000 by the German cabinet, for presentation in the German Parliament in 2001.

CONVENTION ON THE GRANT OF EUROPEAN PATENTS (EUROPEAN PATENT CONVENTION)
13 I.L.M. 271 (1974), as revised November 2000

Article 53

European patents shall not be granted in respect of

(a) inventions the publication or exploitation of which would be contrary to "ordre public" or morality, provided that the exploitation shall not be deemed to be so contrary merely because it is prohibited by law or regulation in some or all of the Contracting States;

(b) plant or animal varieties or essentially biological processes for the production of plants or animals; this provision does not apply to microbiological processes or the products thereof.

(c) methods for treatment of the human or animal body by surgery or therapy and diagnostic methods practised on the human or animal body; these provisions shall not apply to products, in particular substances or compositions, for use in any of these methods.[*]

DIRECTIVE OF THE EUROPEAN PARLIAMENT AND OF THE COUNCIL ON THE LEGAL PROTECTION OF BIOTECHNOLOGICAL INVENTIONS
1998 OJ (L213) 13 (July 30, 1998)

The European Parliament and the Council of the European Union,

Having regard to the Treaty establishing the European Community, and in particular Article 100a thereof,

Having regard to the proposal from the Commission,

Having regard to the Opinion of the Economic and Social Committee,

Acting in accordance with the procedure laid down in Article 189b of the Treaty,

. . . .

(13) Whereas the Community's legal framework for the protection of biotechnological inventions can be limited to laying down certain principles as they apply to the patentability of biological material as such, such principles being intended in particular to determine the difference between inventions and discoveries with regard to the patentability of certain elements of human origin, to the scope of protection conferred by a patent on a biotechnological invention, to the right to use a deposit mechanism in addition to written descriptions and lastly to the option of obtaining non-exclusive compulsory licences in respect of interdependence between plant varieties and inventions, and conversely;

(14) Whereas a patent for invention does not authorize the holder to implement that invention, but merely entitles him to prohibit third parties from exploiting it for industrial and commercial purposes; whereas, consequently, substantive patent law cannot serve to replace or render superfluous national, European or international law which may impose restrictions or prohibitions or which concerns the monitoring of research and of the use or commercialization of its results, notably from the point of view of the requirements of public health, safety, environmental protection, animal welfare, the preservation of genetic diversity and compliance with certain ethical standards;

(15) Whereas no prohibition or exclusion exists in national or European patent law (Munich Convention) which precludes a priori the patentability of biological matter;

---

[*][Ed. Note: Article 53(c) EPC was formerly Article 52(4) EPC].

. . . .

(31) Whereas a plant grouping which is characterized by a particular gene (and not its whole genome) is not covered by the protection of new varieties and is therefore not excluded from patentability even if it comprises new varieties of plants;

. . . .

(36) Whereas the TRIPS Agreement provides for the possibility that members of the World Trade Organisation may exclude from patentability inventions, the prevention within their territory of the commercial exploitation of which is necessary to protect ordre public or morality, including to protect human, animal or plant life or health or to avoid serious prejudice to the environment, provided that such exclusion is not made merely because the exploitation is prohibited by their law;

(37) Whereas the principle whereby inventions must be excluded from patentability where their commercial exploitation offends against ordre public or morality must also be stressed in this Directive;

. . . .

(40) Whereas there is a consensus within the Community that interventions in the human germ line and the cloning of human beings offends against ordre public and morality; whereas it is therefore important to exclude unequivocally from patentability processes for modifying the germ line genetic identity of human beings and processes for cloning human beings;

. . . .

(43) Whereas pursuant to Article F(2) of the Treaty on European Union, the Union is to respect fundamental rights, as guaranteed by the European Convention for the Protection of Human Rights and Fundamental Freedoms signed in Rome on 4 November 1950 and as they result from the constitutional traditions common to the Member States, as general principles of Community law;

. . . .

(55) Whereas following Decision 93/626/EEC (7) the Community is party to the Convention on Biological Diversity of 5 June 1992; whereas, in this regard, Member States must give particular weight to Articles 3 and 8(j), the second sentence of Article 16(2) and Article 16(5) of the Convention when bringing into force the laws, regulations and administrative provisions necessary to comply with this Directive;

(56) Whereas the Third Conference of the Parties to the Biodiversity Convention, which took place in November 1996, noted in Decision III/17 that 'further work is required to help develop a common appreciation of the relationship between intellectual property rights and the relevant provisions of the TRIPS Agreement and the Convention on Biological Diversity, in particular on issues relating to technology transfer and conservation and sustainable use of biological diversity and the fair and equitable sharing of benefits arising out of the use of genetic resources, including the protection of knowledge, innovations and practices of indigenous and local communities embodying

traditional lifestyles relevant for the conservation and sustainable use of biological diversity,

HAVE ADOPTED THIS DIRECTIVE:

CHAPTER I. Patentability

Article 1

1. Member States shall protect biotechnological inventions under national patent law. They shall, if necessary, adjust their national patent law to take account of the provisions of this Directive. . . .

Article 2

1. For the purposes of this Directive,

(a) "biological material" means any material containing genetic information and capable of reproducing itself or being reproduced in a biological system;

(b) "microbiological process" means any process involving or performed upon or resulting in microbiological material.

2. A process for the production of plants or animals is essentially biological if it consists entirely of natural phenomena such as crossing or selection.

3. The concept of "plant variety" is defined by Article 5 of Regulation (EC) No 2100/94.

Article 3

1. For the purposes of this Directive, inventions which are new, which involve an inventive step and which are susceptible of industrial application shall be patentable even if they concern a product consisting of or containing biological material or a process by means of which biological material is produced, processed or used.

2. Biological material which is isolated from its natural environment or produced by means of a technical process may be the subject of an invention even if it previously occurred in nature.

Article 4

1. The following shall not be patentable;

(a) plant and animal varieties;

(b) essentially biological processes for the production of plants or animals.

2. Inventions which concern plants or animals shall be patentable if the technical feasibility of the invention is not confined to a particular plant or animal variety.

3. Paragraph 1(b) shall be without prejudice to the patentability of inventions which concern a microbiological or other technical process or a product obtained by means of such a process.

Article 5

1. The human body, at the various stages of its formation and development, and the simple discovery of one of its elements, including the sequence or partial sequence of a gene, cannot constitute patentable inventions.

2. An element isolated from the human body or otherwise produced by means of a technical process, including the sequence or partial sequence of a gene, may constitute a patentable invention, even if the structure of that element is identical to that of a natural element.

3. The industrial application of a sequenced or a partial sequence of a gene must be disclosed in the patent application.

Article 6

1. Inventions shall be considered unpatentable where their commercial exploitation would be contrary to ordre public or morality; however, exploitation shall not be deemed to be so contrary merely because it is prohibited by law or regulation.

2. On the basis of paragraph 1, the following, in particular, shall be considered unpatentable:

(a) processes for cloning human beings;

(b) processes for modifying the germ line genetic identity of human beings;

(c) uses of human embryos for industrial or commercial purposes;

(d) processes for modifying the genetic identity of animals which are likely to cause them suffering without any substantial medical benefit to man or animal, and also animals resulting from such processes.

Article 7

The Commission's European Group on Ethics in Science and New Technologies evaluates all ethical aspects of biotechnology.

NOTES AND QUESTIONS

(1) **Regulation or Directive**. Consider the purpose of the EU legislative instruments. *See supra* § 2.03[C][3]. Why do you think that the regulation process was chosen for technology transfer but not for biotechnological inventions?

(2) **EPC Article 53(c) and Directive Article 3**. "The new proposal draws a clear distinction between inventions and discoveries and does not include the famous word 'as such.'" Dominique Vandergheynst, *The New Proposal for a Directive on the Legal Protection of Biotechnological Inventions*, in BIOTECHNOLOGY, PATENTS AND MORALITY 175 (Sterckx ed., 1997). Does the directive simplify the issues for a future European national court attempting in a subsequent case to interpret those articles? Or must we (and they) wait for national legislation. Proposals to have the EU accede to the European Patent Convention and thereby give it a voice in EPO activities are under consideration. The European Commission issued its proposed Council Regulation on the Community Patent on August 1, 2000. The Community patent will be discussed in Chapter 6 in the context of regional mechanisms for the acquisition of industrial property rights.

(3) **Patenting Life forms and Food Security**. Opponents of patents on life forms in Europe state that as a consequence of legal recognition of patent rights, farmers will become dependent on multinational corporations, breeders will not be able to breed, consumers will pay higher prices for food and medicine, public research will be undermined, European producers will become further concentrated, genetic diversity will be eroded, private corporations will control the food supply, Third World farmers will lose the initiative to conserve old varieties, animals will be exposed to increased suffering, and respect for human rights, for nature, and for life itself will be eroded. *See* Luc Vankrunkelsven, *The Case For and Against the Patenting of Biotechnological Inventions*, in BIOTECHNOLOGY, PATENTS AND MORALITY 216-18 (Sterckx ed., 1997). Does the directive address any of these concerns? Or does it merely paper over them?

(4) **Cross-Sectoral Developments**. Recital 56 refers to the Third Conference of the Parties of the Convention on Biological Diversity, which was held in Buenos Aires in November 1996. The report of that conference in turn refers to discussions that are taking place in the Committee on Trade and Environment of the WTO regarding the relationship between the Convention on Biological Diversity and the TRIPS Agreement, a subject discussed *infra* § 8.03. *See* Provisional Agenda of the Third Meeting, UNEP/CBD/COP/3/22 22 (Sept. 1996) and the Advance Report entitled: *The Convention on Biological Diversity and the Agreement on Trade-Related Intellectual Property Rights (TRIPS): Relationships And Synergies*, UNEP/CBD/COP/3/23 (Oct. 5, 1996). Do references to international environmental, biodiversity, and trade agreements in recitals of European directives create direct obligations on the member states, regardless of whether they are signatories of the referenced treaties? The international economic issues surrounding the patenting of biotechnological inventions are discussed in William H. Lesser, *International Treaties and Other Legal and Economic Issues Relating to the Ownership and Use of Genetic*

Resources, in GLOBAL GENETIC RESOURCES: ACCESS, OWNERSHIP, AND INTELLECTUAL PROPERTY RIGHTS (K. Elaine Hoagland ed., 1997).

(5) **Potential Impact of the Biotechnology Directive**. For a preliminary assessment of the biotechnology directive, see *Patenting Biotech Inventions–The European Directive*, 1 J. OF BIOLAW & BUS. 24-27 (Summer 1998); Giuseppe Sena, *Directive on Biotechnological Inventions: Patentability of Discoveries*, 30 I.I.C. 731 (1999).

§ 3.05 Trade Secrets

[A] History

THE FIRST SUCCESSFUL FACTORY[*]
excerpted from Mitchell Wilson, AMERICAN SCIENCE AND INVENTION:
A PICTORIAL HISTORY 84-86 (New York 1954)

The first true factory in America was not a native product. Before Samuel Slater opened his mill in Pawtucket, there were many shops which employed a number of hands; but a factory is more than many people working together under the same roof. The American factory, as Eli Whitney designed it, was the third step taken in a changing attitude towards the manufacture of goods.

Until the late eighteenth century, the form of the factory, or manufactory, was simply an enlargement of the way in which a single artisan made every part himself. When he received more orders than he himself could fill, he took in a helper who learned first by doing the simplest tasks, and then in turn reached the stage where he too was able to make the entire article by himself. In some cases, where very many men were employed, it was natural that certain workers would be given only those tasks at which they excelled, and the finished product would then be the result of several men's handiwork.

This was the method of work in shops from the times of antiquity, and it was not changed until late in the eighteenth century, when the division of labor became a conscious process. There could be no machinery developed to make the separate parts of a product until the artisan himself was aware that there *were* separate steps to be performed. Whitney's "American System of Manufacture" therefore could not be applied until this division of labor had taken place.

The English factory system, popularly identified with the cotton mills, was based on this rationalization of labor. The separate steps of carding, roving. spinning. and weaving were assigned to different groups of individuals all working under the same roof, and [Sir Richard] Arkwright was the first man to drive the primitive spinning wheels and looms by drive belts from a water wheel. Even this simple step was so revolutionary that the "water loom"–and a powered loom–became a magical phrase.

---

[*]Copyright 1954, Simon & Schuster, Inc. Reprinted with permission.

After the Revolution, many attempts were made to introduce factory methods in the new republic. The first cotton mill in Massachusetts was built in Beverly in 1787, but in three years it was ready to close. The factories generally failed because the machinery was inadequate, and because Americans preferred English importations. Various states offered bounties and rewards to encourage manufacture, but every effort failed. To import machinery from England was impossible because the British government refused to allow any of its new inventions to leave the country. The American states advertised their bounties in English newspapers to entice English workmen to emigrate; but that too was against the law. England was determined to keep its technological knowledge to itself.

One such advertisement by the Pennsylvania Legislature appeared in Derbyshire. It was read by young Samuel Slater, just finishing his apprenticeship. He had worked for Jedediah Strutt, a partner of Arkwright, and Slater had learned how to use and repair every machine in the factory. He asked Strutt to tell him what his future might be if he remained where he was. Strutt told him to work hard and save his money and he would get his just rewards.

He knew exactly what risks he was running by trying to leave the country. He was careful to avoid taking any sketches of machinery and he did not even tell his mother and brothers of his plans. He went to London, got his passage, and just as the vessel was preparing to leave, he wrote to his family, telling them where he was going.

In 1789 he landed in Philadelphia where he made inquiries about the true situation in the republic. He was told that a mill had recently been completed in Providence by Moses Brown, the famous Quaker merchant [and patron of Brown University], and that Brown was desperately looking for a manager. Slater wrote to Brown, telling him his background and applying for the position.

Moses Brown replied at once and made this handsome offer to Slater: if he could work the machinery they had on hand, all the profits of the business less the cost and interest on the machinery were to go to Slater along with the credit as well as the advantages of perfecting the first water mill in America. In other words' Brown was willing to give the factory to Slater. There is no other record of a man applying for a job by letter and getting the entire plant by return mail.

2. British Know-how In Pawtucket

When Slater went to Pawtucket with Brown to inspect the machines, his rosy dreams wilted. "These will not do," he protested." They are good for nothing in their present condition. Nor could they be made to answer."

He proposed to make a clean start and build the series of machines which were known as the "Arkwright Patent." He had brought no drawings but he had memorized the designs of the machines invented by Crompton and Hargreaves as well as Arkwright.

Most American machinists were inadequate; the only metal articles being made were scythes, anchors, horse-shoes, nails, and cannon shot. Fortunately, a Nantucket Quaker named Oziel Wilkinson then lived with his family in

Pawtucket. Wilkinson was a blacksmith who had made spades and shovels in quantity for turnpike building. He had been the first to make cold-rolled nails. Slater boarded with them, and Wilkinson was willing to help. Without him, Slater would have been helpless. . . .

On December 21, 1790, the little factory began to produce, but business was feeble. When seventy-two spindles were working and the plant had been operating for twenty months, the preference for English yarn left them with several thousand pounds that could not be moved at any price. Not until a loom was added did American cotton begin to find a market. Ten years after Slater landed in America, Almy, Brown and Slater were doing sufficiently well to open a second factory. Scores of imitators followed, but Slater kept well in the lead, and eventually the firm established mills in New Hampshire and Massachusetts, despite the growing competition from innovators.

Drawing on his English training, Slater staffed his factory with children from four to ten years old. The machines were simple, and the parents were delighted to have their children doing something useful in pleasant surroundings. He measured his break with the English tradition by the good food and humane treatment given his hands. In England, the working children were ill-fed, beaten, driven to early drunkenness and degradation. In a time when American children were put to work around the term as soon as they could walk, the Slater factory system was very highly rated.

Slater neither invented anything, nor improved what he brought here; but he was the first in this country to set up a system of manufacture in which the successive steps of the skilled artisan were broken down into such simple components that a group of children could outproduce the finest craftsman. It was the one system ideally suited to a country that was to be plagued by a shortage of skilled manpower for another seventy-five years. No one saw any discrepancy between such a system and the American goal of enhancing the dignity and human value of the individual. The American factory fed, clothed, and equipped men for the fight against the hostile universe; and the factory system was actually considered to be a victory for the American creed of freedom.

    . . . .

[B] Modern International Agreements for the Protection of Trade Secrets

The first international agreement containing any explicit provisions for the protection of trade secrets was the North American Free Trade Agreement, signed by the United States on December 8, 1993. The following year (to the day) the legislation implementing the TRIPS Agreement, which contained similar provisions on the protection of "undisclosed information, *see* art. 39, was passed by the U.S. Congress.

ADRIAN OTTEN & HANNU WAGER, COMPLIANCE WITH TRIPS: THE EMERGING WORLD VIEW*
29 VAND. J. TRANS'L L. 391 (1996)

The TRIPS Agreement contains a section that, for the first time in international public law, explicitly requires undisclosed information (trade secrets or know-how) to benefit from protection. The protection must apply to information that is secret, that has commercial value because it is secret, and that has been subject to reasonable steps to keep it secret. The Agreement does not require undisclosed information to be treated as a form of property, but it does require that a person lawfully in control of such information have the ability to prevent it from being disclosed to, acquired by, or used by others without his or her consent in a manner contrary to honest commercial practices. The Agreement also contains provisions on undisclosed test data and other data whose submission is required by governments as a condition of approving the marketing of pharmaceutical or agricultural chemical products that use new chemical entities. In such a situation, the member state concerned must protect the data against unfair commercial use.

NORTH AMERICAN FREE TRADE AGREEMENT
Article 1711: Trade Secrets

1. Each Party shall provide the legal means for any person to prevent trade secrets from being disclosed to, acquired by, or used by others without the consent of the person lawfully in control of the information in a manner contrary to honest commercial practices, in so far as:

(a) the information is secret in the sense that it is not, as a body or in the precise configuration and assembly of its components, generally known among or readily accessible to persons that normally deal with the kind of information in question;

(b) the information has actual or potential commercial value because it is secret; and

(c) the person lawfully in control of the information has taken reasonable steps under the circumstances to keep it secret.

2. A Party may require that to qualify for protection a trade secret must be evidenced in documents, electronic or magnetic means, optical discs, microfilms, films or other similar instruments.

3. No Party may limit the duration of protection for trade secrets, so long as the conditions in paragraph 1 exist.

4. No Party may discourage or impede the voluntary licensing of trade secrets by imposing excessive or discriminatory conditions on such licenses, or conditions that dilute the value of the trade secrets.

5. If a Party requires, as a condition for approving the marketing of pharmaceutical or agricultural chemical products that utilize new chemical entities, the submission of undisclosed test or other data necessary to determine

---

whether the use of such products is safe and effective, the Party shall protect against disclosure of the data of persons making such submissions, where the origination of such data involves considerable effort, except where the disclosure is necessary to protect the public or unless steps are taken to ensure that the data is protected against unfair commercial use.

6. Each Party shall provide that for data subject to paragraph 5 that are submitted to the Party after the date of entry into force of this Agreement, no person other than the person that submitted them may, without the latter's permission, rely on such data in support of an application for product approval during a reasonable period of time after their submission. For this purpose, a reasonable period shall normally mean not less than five years from the date on which the Party granted approval to the person that produced the data for approval to market its product, taking account of the nature of the data and the person's efforts and expenditures in producing them. Subject to this provision, there shall be no limitation on any Party to implement abbreviated approval procedures for such products on the basis of bioequivalence and bioavailability studies.

7. Where a Party relies upon a marketing approval granted by another Party, the reasonable period of exclusive use of the data submitted in connection with obtaining the approval relied upon shall commence with the date of the first marketing approval relied upon.

. . . .

[C]   Regional Agreements: Europe

BLOCK EXEMPTION ON TECHNOLOGY TRANSFER AGREEMENTS: TRADE SECRETS AND KNOW-HOW
EU Competition Bulletin, OJ L 31, 9.2.1996

. . . .

1.3.40. Commission Regulation (EC) No 240/96 on the application of Article 85(3) of the Treaty to certain categories of technology transfer agreements.

Adopted by the Commission on 31 January. The Regulation, which enters into force on 1 April, simplifies and makes more flexible the rules applicable to licensing agreements, thus helping to promote the spread of new technologies within the European Union.

Article 10

For purposes of this Regulation:

(1) 'know-how' means a body of technical information that is secret, substantial and identified in any appropriate form;

(2) 'secret' means that the know-how package as a body or in the precise configuration and assembly of its components is not generally known or easily accessible, so that part of its value consists in the lead which the licensee gains

when it is communicated to him; it is not limited to the narrow sense that each individual component of the know-how should be totally unknown or unobtainable outside the licensor's business;

(3) 'substantial' means that the know-how includes information which must be useful, *i.e.* can reasonably be expected at the date of conclusion of the agreement to be capable of improving the competitive position of the licensee, for example by helping him to enter a new market or giving him an advantage in competition with other manufacturers or providers of services who do not have access to the licensed secret know-how or other comparable secret know-how;

(4) 'identified' means that the know-how is described or recorded in such a manner as to make it possible to verify that it satisfies the criteria of secrecy and substantiality and to ensure that the licensee is not unduly restricted in his exploitation of how own technology, to be identified the know-how can either be set out in the licence agreement or in a separate document or recorded in any other appropriate form at the latest when the know-how is transferred or shortly thereafter, provided that the separate document or other record can be made available if the need arises;

. . . .

NOTES AND QUESTIONS

(1) **Trade Secrets in NAFTA and TRIPS.** The NAFTA was the first international agreement to include the protection of trade secrets. The TRIPS Agreement, although negotiated before, was finalized after the NAFTA. *See* Laurinda L. Hicks & James R. Holbein, *Convergence of National Intellectual Property Norms in International Trading Agreements*, 12 AM. U. J. INT'L L. & POL'Y 769, 796 (1997).

(2) **Article 1711 as "TRIPS Plus."** A significant benefit for pharmaceutical and agrochemical patent owners under NAFTA is preventing generic companies from having access to expensively-produced test data submitted to governments in abbreviated new drug applications.

> [I]n terms of substantive obligations, NAFTA adds a number of significant TRIPS-plus features. For trade secrets, both TRIPS and NAFTA require confidentiality for undisclosed test data submitted to governments for approving the marketing of pharmaceutical or agricultural-chemical products that utilize new chemical entities. However, NAFTA goes further by also requiring non-reliance. For normally at least five years, NAFTA Parties are not to rely on the first applicant's confidential test data to approve a second applicant's request for approval to market a generic copy of the first applicant's product.

Allen Z. Hertz, *NAFTA Revisited: Shaping the Trident: Intellectual Property Under NAFTA, Investment Protection Agreements and the World Trade Organization*, 23 CAN.- U.S. L.J. 261, 282 (1996).

(3) **Article 10*bis* of the Paris Convention.** Are the undisclosed information provisions of TRIPS and NAFTA different from the unfair competition principles of Article 10*bis* of the Paris Convention? Or are they, as a recent article asserts, fundamentally identical. *See* Carlos Correa, *Intellectual Property Rights in Latin America: Is There Still Room for Differentiation?*, 29 N.Y.U. J. INT'L L. & POL. 109, 132 (1997). In this regard, recall the *Lopez* case discussed in Chapter 2.

(4) **Criminalization of Trade Secret Misappropriation.** Article 61 of TRIPS mandates criminal procedures only for willful trademark counterfeiting or copyright piracy on a commercial scale but not for deliberate trade secret misappropriation or "economic espionage." Trade secret misappropriation amounting to economic espionage was criminalized in the United States by the Economic Espionage Act of 1996. *See* 18 U.S.C. § 1831. The Act provides for prison sentences of up to fifteen years. In January 2001, the Computer Crimes and Intellectual Property Section (CCIPS) of the U.S. Department of Justice published a manual on prosecuting intellectual property crimes (also on the DOJ website at http://www.cybercrime.gov) reporting recent economic espionage cases, indictments, arrests, prosecutions, convictions, fines and sentences. The number of such cases seems to be growing. What is the likelihood that criminal sanctions for trade secret misappropriation (or economic espionage) will become more widespread, and perhaps become part of an international agreement in the near future?

(5) **"Do as We Say, Not as We Did."** The beginnings of the American industrial revolution were built on the uncompensated transfer of Arkwright's trade secrets and patented technology from England to the United States. What should be the response of the United States to contemporary "developing countries" who accuse the United States of preaching what it did not practice? *See* Dru Brenner-Beck, *Do As I Say, Not As I Did*, 11 UCLA PAC. BASIN L. J. 84 (1992).

Chapter 4

COPYRIGHT AND RELATED RIGHTS

§ 4.01 General Concepts and Background

We have entitled this chapter "Copyright and Related Rights." This all-encompassing nomenclature conceals a division that has great significance in international copyright, namely, the distinction between *droit d'auteur* (or author's right) systems and copyright systems.

> Copyright and author's right are the two great legal traditions for protecting literary and artistic works. The copyright tradition is associated with the common law world—England, where the tradition began, the former British colonies, and the countries of the British Commonwealth. The tradition of author's right is rooted in the civil law system and prevails in the countries of the European continent and their former colonies in Latin America, Africa and Asia.

PAUL GOLDSTEIN, INTERNATIONAL COPYRIGHT 3 (2001). These two different traditions reflect different philosophical justifications. The *droit d'auteur* system is largely premised upon notions of natural rights and the inherent right of an author to the fruits of her intellectual and creative endeavors. The copyright system accords protection to authors for more instrumentalist reasons: the grant of rights is intended as an incentive to creativity and hence to the production of a wide variety of works, to the betterment of society. The Copyright Clause of the United States Constitution, which authorizes the enactment of copyright legislation by the U.S. Congress, embodies this instrumentalist philosophy. *See* U.S. CONST. art. I, § 8 cl. 8 (authorizing Congress to "promote the progress of science and the useful arts, by securing for limited times to authors and inventors the exclusive right to their respective writings and discoveries").

Scholars have noted that traces of natural rights thought can be found in U.S. copyright policymaking, and that French copyright law—the paradigmatic *droit d'auteur* system—contains a flavor of instrumentalism. *See, e.g.,* Jane C. Ginsburg, *A Tale of Two Copyrights: Literary Property in Revolutionary France and America in* OF AUTHORS AND ORIGINS: ESSAYS IN COPYRIGHT LAW 131 (Sherman and Strowel eds., 1994) (suggesting greater congruity between early U.S. and French literary property regimes than conventionally understood). But the predominant theoretical grounding of the two systems affects such important issues as the moral rights (*droit moral*) of authors and the ownership of copyright in works prepared for others for hire. And differences between the two systems, sometimes reflecting their different philosophical emphases and sometimes reflecting mere historical accident, do frame and color much of the debate in international copyright law. As you consider these debates, ask which of these factors (or any other) is the principal cause of disagreement.

Our title for this chapter highlights another important distinction. Different philosophies exist as to the nature of protection accorded new forms of subject matter. Under *droit d'auteur* systems, producers of phonograms, broadcasters and performers are not considered authors, but are granted rights under a different rubric, known as "neighboring rights" or "related rights" (the latter is the more traditional term and the former the more modern). These rights are generally narrower than authors' rights in both scope and duration. In some countries, related rights are also provided to "videograms" and "printed editions"—material that requires investment to produce but does not qualify for copyright because it is not considered original authorship. The concept of neighboring or related rights does not exist in U.S. law; subject matter either qualifies for copyright protection or it does not (in which case it may be protected by other laws, such as other provisions of Title 17 or unfair competition law, but these are not known as "related rights"). Phonograms ("sound recordings" in U.S. terminology) are within the subject matter of copyright, as are performances in some circumstances; broadcasts may qualify for copyright protection (as audiovisual works or compilations) but are also protected under the Federal Communications Act.

SHIRA PERLMUTTER, FUTURE DIRECTIONS IN INTERNATIONAL COPYRIGHT[*]
16 CARDOZO ARTS & ENT. L.J. 369 (1998)

. . . Links are forged between [national copyright] laws by international relationships, including formal treaties, regional commitments, and the ongoing give and take of trade interactions. . . .

A. *National Laws*

[Some] harmonization [of national laws] has also been accomplished on a regional level. The major initiatives to date have taken place within the common market of the European Union ("EU"). The EU has engaged in a process of harmonizing the copyright laws of the member states in areas that affect their common market, by issuing several directives requiring them to implement detailed provisions relating to specific rights or subject matter. While there have been some difficulties with adequate and timely implementation, the eventual result will be greater homogeneity within the EU, beyond the level of harmonization that has been achieved elsewhere. At the same time, by conditioning rights for non-Europeans on reciprocity, these directives apply real economic pressure on other countries to harmonize their

---

systems to the same extent.

B. Copyright Treaties

One major set of links among national systems is supplied by international treaties on the subject of copyright and neighboring rights. Chief among these treaties is the Berne Convention for the Protection of Literary and Artistic Works ("Berne Convention"). Dating back to 1886, the Berne Convention today enjoys a membership of more than 120 countries. . . .

Another multilateral treaty, the Universal Copyright Convention ("UCC"), which came into being in the 1950s, also has a substantial number of adherents. In the past decade, however, since the United States joined the Berne Convention, the UCC has been eclipsed in importance, due to Berne's more extensive protection and wider membership.

There is one major limitation on the coverage of both Conventions: They do not protect performers or producers of sound recordings. In many other countries of the world, the contributions of performers and producers are not considered to be copyrightable subject matter, but are protected instead by what are called "neighboring rights." The preeminent treaty dealing with neighboring rights is the Rome Convention for the Protection of Performers, Producers of Phonograms, and Broadcasting Organizations ("Rome Convention"). The Rome Convention operates on similar principles to Berne, setting out minimum rights and requiring national treatment (albeit in a more limited form). Its influence has been less pervasive, however, both because it permits countries to pick and choose among rights, and because it has a narrower membership, not including the United States.

Bilateral agreements have also played a major role in international copyright. Beginning in the nineteenth century, many countries took their first steps toward protecting foreign works on a country-by-country basis. Today, bilateral treaties are of primary importance in dealing with countries that are not yet party to the major multilateral conventions, or obtaining commitments in areas not covered by those conventions.

C. Trade Agreements

Another set of international links is created by trade agreements. In recent years, intellectual property has been recognized as an important component of trade between countries, and copyright provisions have been included in a number of their agreements on trade issues.

For the United States, the inclusion of intellectual property on the trade agenda led to copyright provisions in the North American Free Trade Agreement ("NAFTA"), which entered into force in 1994. NAFTA was shortly followed by the Agreement on Trade-Related Aspects of Intellectual Property Rights ("TRIPS"), which was concluded in the Uruguay Round of negotiations leading to the creation of the World Trade Organization ("WTO"), and entered into force in 1995. . . .

D. *Bilateral Trade Relations*

A critical element in the pattern of international copyright is the interaction between individual countries relating to trade. In the context of such interactions, including the establishment of watch lists under U.S. trade laws, the United States has convinced other countries to adopt treaty norms and generally increase their levels of protection and enforcement in several ongoing initiatives. . . .

Copyright is also becoming important in agreements dealing with the protection of investment. The United States is currently a party to a number of Bilateral Investment Treaties ("BITS") that define intellectual property as a form of investment, subject to significant national and MFN treatment obligations, requiring foreign investors to be treated as well as domestic investors. In the Organization for Economic Cooperation and Development ("OECD"), negotiations [were] underway for some time on a Multilateral Agreement on Investment ("MAI"), which would [have] extend[ed] this concept to a multilateral agreement among the world's most developed countries. . .

NOTES AND QUESTIONS

(1) **MAI Negotiations**. The MAI negotiations, which took place in the mid-to-late 1990s, were ultimately derailed by highly politicized disputes over the need for a cultural exemption, as well as other issues not related to intellectual property (primarily environmental and labor issues).

(2) **Bilateral Free Trade Agreements (FTAs)**. The United States is now negotiating a number of bilateral free trade agreements that have intellectual property components. In Chapter 2, we discussed the respective merits of multilateral and bilateral agreements generally. Are there advantages (or disadvantages) to addressing *copyright issues* on a bilateral, as opposed to multilateral, basis? Are there advantages or disadvantages to negotiating copyright issues in the context of trade negotiations?

SAM RICKETSON, THE BIRTH OF THE BERNE UNION[*]
11 COLUM.-VLA J. LAW & ARTS 9 (1986)

We are celebrating today the centenary of the first true multilateral convention on copyright, the Berne Convention for the Protection of Literary and Artistic Works. I use the adjective "true" advisedly, as prior to the Berne Convention there had been other multilateral conventions on copyright. However, these had been of limited territorial effect and had been entered into in order to overcome particular political problems, such as those that existed in

---

Germany and Italy prior to the unification of those countries. The Berne Convention, on the other hand, was open to all states without restriction, as long as they were prepared to comply with the obligations embodied therein. It is also important to see the convention in a broader context as it was only one of a series of impressive multilateral conventions that came into existence during this period. Of these, the International Telegraph Convention, the Universal Postal Convention, and, of course, the Paris Convention for the Protection of Industrial Property still remain in force today. The Berne Convention, then, can be seen as a manifestation of a period when human society was attempting, in a high-minded but practical spirit, to bring about change and development across a whole range of matters through international cooperation. . . . [M]y task here is to outline the circumstances and events that led to its formation.

In 1886, most national copyright laws were not much more than a few decades old. The United Kingdom was, of course, an exception as it had enacted the first modern copyright statute as far back as 1709 (the "Act of Anne"). The scope of this Act was quite limited, and it was restricted to books, but during the next hundred years protection was extended in piecemeal fashion to other kinds of works, including engravings, sculptures and dramatic works. In most other European countries, however, the situation as regarded the protection of authors was similar to that which had obtained in the United Kingdom prior to 1709: there was not express recognition of authors' rights, and the only protection available was that accorded through the grant of privileges or monopolies for the printing of particular books. These privileges were usually granted by governments to publishers and printers, rather than authors. . . . A similar situation prevailed for longer in most European countries, in particular France, the German and Italian states, and Spain. Even in this country, the members of the Stationers' Company strove long and hard throughout the eighteenth century to retain their traditional privileges with respect to the printing of books. Thus, it was not until the end of that century that it was firmly established that the rights accorded under the Act of Anne were authors' rights, rather than publishers' or printers' rights. In France, on the other hand, completely new ground was broken when the ancien régime was swept away by the revolution of 1789. The rights of man, now enshrined in the new revolutionary laws, were soon recognized to include the rights of authors in their works. A Law of 1791 therefore accorded an exclusive right of public performance to the authors of dramatic and musical works for a period lasting five years after their deaths. A second Law of 1793 granted, in respect of all works, what we would now call an "exclusive reproduction right," enduring for the life of the author. There was a conscious philosophical basis to these laws that was lacking in the Act of Anne, in that the former conceived of the rights of authors as being rooted in natural law, with the consequence that these laws were simply according formal recognition to rights that were already in existence. In the years following the French Revolution, this new conception of authors' rights spread to other continental European countries, in particular Belgium, the Netherlands and the Italian states. It also influenced the adoption of copyright laws in the various German states after the dissolution of the Holy Roman Empire brought an end to the system of imperial privileges that had formerly applied in those states. Other European countries followed suit, and by 1886 almost all the European states, including the newly unified states of Italy and Germany, had enacted their own copyright laws. Outside of Europe, the United States had had a copyright law since 1791, and laws on copyright were to be found in seven other states of Latin America. A number of other countries, such as Greece, Bulgaria and Turkey, protected authors' rights in a partial or incidental fashion through provisions in their general civil, criminal or press laws.

Many of these new laws drew on the models provided by the two French Laws of 1791 and 1793, although it should be noted that French copyright law continued to develop rapidly throughout the nineteenth century and to do so as much through the jurisprudence as through legislative enactments. Nevertheless, while the principal issues addressed by national laws were the same, the solutions adopted were often quite different. Most laws extended protection to a wide range of productions of a literary and artistic character, including works intended for public presentation, such as musical and dramatic works. But some categories of works, such as architectural, oral and choreographic works, were protected only in a few countries, and there were widely differing approaches to the protection of photographic works. Great diversity also existed in relation to the matter of duration of protection. In two Latin American countries, Guatemala and Mexico, this was perpetual, but in all other countries protection was limited in time. This was usually for a period comprising the life of the author together with a fixed period after his death. France had led the way here with a *post mortem auctoris* term of 50 years, but in 1879 Spain adopted a period of 80 years, and other nations had terms ranging between 5 and 50. A few other countries, such as the United States of America, had terms that were not fixed to the life of the author, and some, including the United Kingdom, accorded different terms of protection to different categories of works. Finally, in Italy there was a system of paying public domain, under which works were protected absolutely for a given period (the author's life or 40 years after publication), and this was followed by a further period of 40 years during which the work might be used by third parties subject to a payment of a compulsory royalty to the author.

The rights protected under these early national laws also varied considerably, although the principal ones recognized were those of reproduction and public performance. The right to make translations was recognized to differing degrees, and was often of far shorter duration than the other rights, particularly in the case of foreign authors. The scope of the reproduction right was also variously interpreted: some countries, for example, did not consider that artistic works in one dimension were infringed by the making of a reproduction in another dimension and the matter of adaptation of works was treated in widely differing ways. Again, the reproduction of musical works by mechanical devices, such as piano rolls and music boxes, was not considered as an infringement in certain countries. Most national laws recognized exceptions and limitations to the exercise of rights, for example, for educational or religious purposes, but, once again, there were great variations here. Finally, most laws required that the author comply with some kind of formality before protection would be accorded. The nature and effect of these formalities differed widely from country to country, but the chief ones were registration, the deposit of copies, and the making of declarations. In some cases, failure to comply with formalities was fatal, meaning that the work fell into the public domain; in other cases, it meant merely that the copyright owner was unable to enforce his rights until he rectified the omission. By 1886, only a few countries, including Belgium, Germany and Switzerland (but not France), had abolished formalities altogether.

The above sketch has concentrated on the contents of national copyright laws in the pre-1886 period. However, it will be clear that there is an equally important international dimension to the protection of authors' works. Literary and artistic works and musical compositions recognize no national boundaries, even where translation into another language is required for a work to be fully appreciated in a particular country. Thus it was that after the need for protection of authors by national laws had been recognized, the works of these authors still remained vulnerable to copying and exploitation abroad. These activities, commonly referred to as "piracy", had been a long established feature of European social and cultural life, and this continued to be the case for a considerable time after the enactment of national copyright laws. The attitudes of many countries to these practices were highly anomalous: whilst prepared to protect their own authors, they did not always regard the piracy of foreign authors' works as unfair or immoral. Some countries, in fact, openly countenanced piracy as contributing to their educational and social needs and as reducing the prices of books for their citizens. The particular victims of these practices were the United Kingdom and France. During the eighteenth century English authors suffered from the activities of Irish pirates who could flood both the English and other markets with cheap reprints; after the Act of Union with Ireland in 1800, the chief threat came from the publishing houses of the United States and this continued to be a major problem for the rest of the century. French authors, in turn, suffered from the activities of pirates located in Switzerland, Germany, Holland, and in particular, Belgium. By the early nineteenth century, Brussels was a major center for the piracy of French books, and this led to considerable strains in the relations between France and Belgium. Piracy was likewise rampant between the different German and Italian states.

This widespread piracy of foreign works was the principal reason for the development of international copyright relations in the mid-nineteenth century. The arguments that raged both for and against the protection of foreign authors at this time have a surprisingly modern ring to them. On the other hand, it could be said that the activities of the pirates resulted in cheaper copies and the greater availability of the work in question. In countries hungry for knowledge and enlightenment, this could only be to the advantage of the public interest; and this, indeed, was the reason for the persistent refusal of the United States to protect foreign works throughout the nineteenth century. On the other hand, the moral and practical arguments in the author's favor were obvious: not only was he being robbed of the fruits of his creativity, but this would discourage him from continuing to create, with resultant loss to his own, and other, countries.

It is hard to identify the point at which a country no longer sees advantage in the piracy of foreign works, and decides to extend protection to the authors of such works. It may be that the activities of its own authors have increased, and that the latter now desire protection for their own works abroad. It may also be that, after a while, a country wishes to obtain some kind of international respectability, and to avoid the opprobrium of being labelled as a nation of pirates. Another factor may be that countries with large literary and artistic outputs bring pressure to bear on their more recalcitrant neighbors, promising various forms of trade advantage in return for copyright protection for their authors. Finally, a pirate nation may come to recognize that the rights of authors in their works are of a proprietary nature, and that they should therefore be protected internationally in the same way as other property of foreigners. All these factors were certainly applicable in the case of Belgium, which, in the mid-nineteenth century, switched suddenly from being the chief center of piracy for French works to being one of the most zealous defenders of authors' rights. The same factors applied to many other countries as they began to enter into international copyright relations with each other. Indeed, agreements between states and the formal sanctions of copyright law are not always necessary to achieve protection for foreign authors, at least in a limited form, as systems of "courtesy" copyright operated with some effect during this time and sometimes predated formal international agreements. This was particularly so in the United States, where the major publishing houses observed an unwritten custom whereby each would refrain from publishing editions of foreign works in respect of which another had reached a publishing agreement with the author. This system of mutual self-restraint had several advantages for the parties concerned: it protected the first American publisher of a foreign work from the unfettered copying of his edition, and gave the author the opportunity of earning some remuneration, even if he were unable to prevent the American publication of his work in the first place. As a consequence, authors such as Dickens and Trollope received large sums in respect of the American sales of their works, although they did not enjoy protection under United States copyright law.

"Courtesy copyright," however, is only a partial substitute for full copyright protection, and, in any case, it was not really of great significance outside the American market. Many European countries therefore began to take more formal steps to secure the protection of their authors abroad. In a bold move in 1852, France passed a decree extending the protection of its laws to all works published abroad, irrespective of whether the law of the country in question accorded corresponding protection to the works of French authors. This measure was consistent with the philosophical basis of French copyright law, according to which authors' rights, being natural rights of property, should not be subject to artificial restraints such as nationality and political boundaries. Nevertheless, a practical motivation also lay behind the decree. Up to this time, France had found other nations reluctant to enter agreements for the protection of French works on a reciprocal basis. She therefore hoped that the unilateral grant of protection to authors from these countries in France would "shame" them into responding in like manner. Whether or not there is a causal connection is hard to say, but the fact remains that after 1852 the blockage cleared, and France entered agreements with a large number of their nations under which each agreed to accord protection to the works of the other.

Bilateral copyright agreements of this kind had, in fact, become quite common by the middle of the century. The first country to enter such agreements was the Kingdom of Prussia which made 32 of these with the other German states in the years 1827 to 1829. The basis of these agreements was simple or formal reciprocity, under which each state undertook to accord to the works of the other state the same treatment that it accorded to its own works (the principle of "national treatment"). These early German agreements, however, were of a special character, as their purpose was to fill the gap left by the failure of the legislature of the Germanic Confederation to enact a federal copyright law. Subsequent bilateral agreements between fully autonomous states tended to include more substantive provisions embodying common rules that each country undertook to apply to the works of the other, in addition to the basic principle of national treatment. The basis of these agreements thus came closer to what is called "material" or substantive reciprocity under which there is approximate parity between the level of protection accorded by each state to the works of the other. The first example of such a treaty was that between Austria and the Kingdom of Sardinia in May 1840, and France and the United Kingdom, the two leading literary countries of the period, were not far behind. By 1886, there was an intricate network of bilateral copyright conventions in force between the majority of European states, as well as with several Latin American countries. Of these, France was party to the most agreements (13), followed closely by Belgium (9), Italy and Spain (8 each), the United Kingdom (5) and Germany (5).

The basis of the majority of these conventions was national treatment, but, as stated above, they also contained a number of common rules which each country undertook to apply in its protection of works from the other country. There was usually a statement of the categories of works covered by the agreement, and specific provision was generally made for the protection of translation and performing rights. Restrictions in respect of particular kinds of use were also often allowed relating, for example, to education or the reproduction of newspaper articles. The scope and detail of these provisions differed considerably from one convention to another, but the most "advanced", in terms of protection of authors' interest, were to be found in the conventions made by France, Germany and Italy in the early 1880s. With regard to duration of protection, most of the pre-1886 conventions required material reciprocity, providing that country A was not obliged to protect the works of country B for any longer period than that accorded by state B to its own works, and in any event for no longer than country A protected its own nationals.

There were wider discrepancies with respect to formalities: under some conventions, compliance with the formalities of the country of origin of the work was sufficient to obtain protection in the other state; in other conventions, it was necessary for an author to comply with the formalities of both states. Matters were further complicated by the fact that the duration of many conventions was uncertain, in that they were linked to some wider treaty of trade or commerce between the countries in question and might suddenly fall to the ground if the latter was revoked or renegotiated. Another source of uncertainty arose from the insertion of "most favored nation" clauses in many copyright conventions. The effect of these was that the contracting parties agreed to admit each other to the benefits that might be accorded to a third state under another treaty that was made by one of them with that state. The effect of such clauses was that a copyright convention between countries A and B might be abrogated, in whole or in part, by the terms of another convention made by either country A or B with country C if this agreement contained additional measures for the protection of copyright. While these clauses did not mean any loss of protection for authors, they obviously made it difficult for an author from country A to know, at any one time, what level of protection he was entitled to in country B, and vice versa.

It will be clear that this network of bilateral agreements meant that there was little uniformity in the protection that an author might expect to receive in countries other than his own. As far as Europe was concerned, the threat posed by international piracy earlier in the century had largely disappeared by 1886, but quite a number of European states still remained reluctant to enter bilateral agreements on copyright. These included the Scandinavian countries, the Netherlands, Greece, the newly independent Balkan states, and, most importantly, the Russian and Austro-Hungarian empires. Outside Europe, much of the world's surface was then controlled by one of the chief European colonial powers. Of those states which were independent, very few had entered any international copyright agreements, and many, in fact, had no internal copyright laws. The most important of these countries was the United States, which throughout the nineteenth century continued to be a major center for pirated works and resisted efforts by other countries, in particular the United Kingdom, to draw it into bilateral agreements. Several such attempts were made, but the vested interests of publishers and printers, on the one hand, and the voracious appetite for cheap books from the rapidly growing American population, on the other, doomed them to failure.

In light of the above, it was not surprising that moves for a more widely based and uniform kind of international copyright protection began in the middle of the nineteenth century. Several schools of thought can be seen at work here. The first favored a universal codification of copyright law under which literary and artistic works would receive equal protection in every country. This was, of course, an idealist conception, which was based firmly on the natural law view of authors' rights according to which these rights should be protected universally without artificial constraints of time, nationality or territoriality. The precise mechanisms by which this state of affairs was to be brought about was never entirely clear, but presumably it would require some kind of international arrangement under which each nation would agree to adopt a common set of provisions guaranteeing protection to authors. In contrast to this was a more pragmatic approach that recognized the need for more uniform international protection of authors' rights, but advocated more limited means for achieving this, mainly through the replacement of the numerous existing bilateral agreements with a single multilateral instrument. At the start, it was the first of these views that predominated. . . .

. . . .

[I]n 1878, a major international literary congress was held in Paris at the time of the Universal Exhibition in that city. This was organized by the French Société des gens de lettres, and drew together some of the most distinguished authors, lawyers and public figures of the day from three continents. Presided over by no less a personage than Victor Hugo, the congress concerned itself with fundamental questions of principle concerning the protection of authors. After lengthy debates, a number of resolutions acknowledging the natural and perpetual rights of authors were passed, and a call was addressed to the French government to summon an international conference to formulate a "uniform convention for the regulation of the use of literary property." . . . [A] more practical development flowing from the 1878 literary congress was its decision to establish the *International Literary Association*. This was to be open to literary societies and to writers of all nations, and had the following objects:

1. The protection of the principles of literary property.

2. The organization of regular relations between the literary societies and writers of all nations.

3. The initiation of all enterprises possessing an international literary character.

The first president of the Association was Victor Hugo, and its initial membership was extremely wide, being drawn from nearly twenty countries. Since this time, it has played a significant and catalytic role in the majority of international copyright developments. Although it has always had a strong French orientation, its annual congresses have been held in many different cities, beginning with London in 1879. Five years after this, its membership was expanded to include artists, and its name was changed to its present title, the International Literary and Artistic Association (usually known as "ALAI" which is the abbreviation of its French title, "*l'Association littéraire et artistique internationale*"). To ALAI belongs the credit for being the initiator of the meetings and negotiations that led to the formation of the Berne Union. From the very start of its existence, it concerned itself with the legal questions relating to the international protection of authors. Strong universalist views were expressed at several of its early congresses, but at its congress in Rome in 1882 a more practical proposal for a limited multilateral convention was adopted. . . . [T]he motion charged the office of ALAI with the task of undertaking:

the necessary measures for initiating, in the press of all countries, as extensive and profound discussion as possible on the question of the formation of a Union of literary property, and for arranging at a date to be subsequently fixed, a conference composed of the organs and representatives of interested groups, to meet to discuss and settle a scheme for the creation of a Union of literary property.

The meeting place chosen for the conference was Berne, in neutral Switzerland. . . .

After three days of intensive discussions, the ALAI conference produced a compact convention of 10 articles. Its basic aim was stated to be the "constitution of a general Union for the protection of the rights of authors in their literary works and manuscripts." The fundamental principle of protection was national treatment, which was accorded on the criterion of place of publication or performance of the work rather than the nationality of the author claiming protection. This was subject to the condition that authors claiming protection had complied with the formalities required by the law of the country where such publication or performance had taken place. Protection was also extended to manuscripts and unpublished works . . . .

As for the rights protected under the Convention, these essentially remained a matter for national treatment. This was a long way removed from the universal codification of copyright principles which had been advocated by the earlier literary and artistic congresses. Nevertheless, it was clear that the ALAI draft was seen as a "progressive" text, which should be revised and augmented with time and the addition of new member states. . . .

[A] significant provision reserved to states of the proposed Union the right to enter separately between themselves particular arrangements for the protection of literary and artistic works, as long as these arrangements did not contravene the dispositions of the Convention. A similar provision had been included in the recently concluded Paris Convention on Industrial Property, and was an implicit acknowledgment that the draft convention was very far from representing a universal codification of the law of copyright. It was therefore clear that the convention only established a minimum level of protection which member states would be free to augment through other bilateral arrangements. Finally, provision was made for the establishment of an international office of the proposed Union which was to act as a kind of clearing house for the information relating to the copyright laws of member states.

The ALAI draft was a relatively limited document, by comparison with some of the bilateral conventions then in force. . . . Nevertheless, it is usually easier to include more detailed provisions in an agreement between two parties, and the ALAI draft was to form the basis of the final convention of 1886.

Events unfolded rapidly after the conclusion of the ALAI conference of 1883. The Swiss government now undertook formally the task of convening a diplomatic conference to settle the terms of a final agreement. . . .

. . . .

The 1884 Conference was a very small-scale affair: perhaps not more than twenty people meeting together in the same room. Nevertheless the document they produced went further than could reasonably have been predicted at the outset, in view of the number of nations represented and their different backgrounds and interests. . . .

. . . .

As for the so-called "principles recommended for an ulterior unification," these spoke in general terms of the difficulty at this point of time in achieving an international codification of copyright law, although it was boldly declared that this was in "the nature of things and would be effected sooner or later." . . . .

Although there was predictable disappointment among authors' and artists' societies that the 1884 draft convention had not gone further along the path to a universal codification, more progress had clearly been made than many, including the Swiss government, had thought possible at the commencement of the 1884 Conference. On the other hand, this had still only been a preliminary meeting, to explore the common ground between nations, and another conference would be necessary to settle the final terms of the new convention. . . .

. . . .

The new conference met in Berne in September 1885 with 26 delegates from 16 countries: Germany, Argentina, Belgium, Spain, France, the United Kingdom, Haiti, Honduras, Italy, Paraguay, the Netherlands, Norway and Sweden, Switzerland and Tunisia. Notable additions were, of course, Italy, Spain and the United States. The last-mentioned country, however, made it clear that it was attending only in the capacity of an observer and, that favorable as it was to the idea of the proposed Union in principle, there were strong domestic reasons why accession would prove very difficult, at least at this time. . . .

. . . . [T]he overall result of the conference was that the 1884 draft was not significantly extended, and in some respects was actually cut back. The choice before the conference was summed up in the opening paragraphs of the report of the general commission: whether to have a convention embodying a considerable degree of uniformity from which countries not so advanced in copyright would of necessity be excluded, or to have a less rigorous convention to which as many countries as possible would be able to adhere. The 1885 Conference chose the second of these approaches, although it must be noted that a significant minority of delegations, headed by France, preferred the first.

When the final conference met in Berne on 6 September 1886, 12 countries were represented: Germany, Belgium, Spain, the United States, France, the United Kingdom, Haiti, Italy, Japan, Liberia, Switzerland and Tunisia. Of these, only Japan and the United States were present as observers: the remainder all signed the final instrument. Japan, in fact, was to join only 12 years later, becoming the first Asian country to do so. As for the United States, . . . their delegate, Boyd Winchester, held out the promise of accession, if the circumstances should become appropriate . . . .

Of the 10 countries that signed the new Convention in Berne in September 1886, all but one (Liberia) ratified it, with the result that it came into force on 5 December 1887. Of the many other countries that had attended one or both of the two drafting conferences, several came close to signing, but were prevented from doing so because of the state of their internal laws. Examples of such countries were Sweden and Norway, both of which joined the Union within a decade. The Netherlands was a similar case, as was Austria-Hungary. As for the various Latin-American countries which had attended, it seemed that they did not see any advantage in membership of a Union which was so clearly Eurocentric: in any case, these states were shortly to establish their own multilateral convention.

Despite its relatively limited membership, the geographical sweep of the new Union was quite considerable when account is taken of the colonial possessions of its members. Nonetheless, it was far from universal and was also far from the universal codification of copyright that had been desired by the visionaries at Brussels in 1858 and at Paris in 1878. But the fact that such a Union had been achieved within 30 years of the meeting of the Brussels Congress was still a considerable achievement. Since this time, the Berne Convention has increased vastly in its membership and has made significant strides forward in the international protection of authors. . . .

BARBARA A. RINGER, THE ROLE OF THE UNITED STATES IN INTERNATIONAL COPYRIGHT—PAST, PRESENT, AND FUTURE
56 GEORGETOWN L.J. 1050 (1968)

If, as the familiar aphorism has it, copyright is the metaphysics of the law, then international copyright must be its cosmology. Though their true influence is dimly understood at best, a nation's copyright laws lie at the roots of its culture and intellectual climate. Copyright provides the inducement for creation and dissemination of the works that shape our society and, in an imperfect and almost accidental way, represents one of the foundations upon which freedom of expression rests. A country without personal liberty does not need a copyright law; where authorship and the communications media are controlled by the state, copyright becomes superfluous.

Copyrighted works represent intangible property that can cross national boundaries as easily and quickly as the communications techniques allow. Perhaps it is no accident that the emergence of the international copyright concept coincided historically with the development of steamships, locomotives, and telegraphy. The widespread use of foreign works in the education, entertainment, and communications of a country not only has significant economic and political consequences, but it can also bring about radical change in that country's culture and society.

Ideally, international copyright regulation should provide the fulcrum on which exchanges of intellectual materials between countries are carefully balanced. The existing multilateral copyright arrangements, however, have proved increasingly incapable of coping with the two main challenges of our half-century, the communications explosion and the demands of the developing nations. International copyright is facing a crisis, and the directions it takes will influence, if not determine the future intellectual climate and cultural achievements of the entire world.

Until the Second World War the United States had little reason to take pride in its international copyright relations; in fact, it had a great deal to be ashamed of. With few exceptions its role in international copyright was marked by intellectual shortsightedness, political isolationism, and narrow economic self-interest. The leadership of the United States in developing and implementing the Universal Copyright Convention[3] (U.C.C.) in the 1950's represented a sharp and admirable change in direction; but the U.C.C., successful in achieving its limited goals, was never contemplated as more than a temporary and partial

---

[3] *See generally* A. Bogsch, THE LAW OF COPYRIGHT UNDER THE UNIVERSAL COPYRIGHT CONVENTION (1964); UNIVERSAL COPYRIGHT CONVENTION ANALYZED (T. Kupferman & M. Foner ed. 1955).

solution to a fundamental world problem. The role of the United States in seeking a more permanent and effective solution to the crisis in international copyright is something policymakers both in and out of government must consider carefully and without delay.

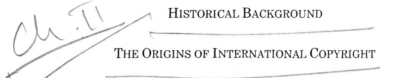

HISTORICAL BACKGROUND

THE ORIGINS OF INTERNATIONAL COPYRIGHT

Copyright as a legal concept originated in the form of direct sovereign grants of monopolies during the Renaissance as a response to the needs created by the invention of movable type. During the Age of Reason, copyright in the form of national statutory protection developed as part of the growth of organized publishing industries. Similarly, international copyright appears to have been a response to the Industrial Revolution; the expanding technology in communications necessitated reciprocal protection of works between countries.

At first, international copyright protection was the exception rather than the rule.[7] National copyright laws usually denied protection to works originating in other countries, and such exceptions as existed were derived from bilateral treaties negotiated between particular countries on the basis of strict reciprocity. Domestic printers and publishers were unwilling to give up their ready markets for unauthorized reprints but the local "piratical" copies were cheap in quality as well as price. Foreign authors had ample reason to complain of the mutilation of their works and the loss of royalties in other countries. National authors "found that their interests were prejudiced by the abundant publication and sale of unauthorized foreign works at cheap prices."[8]

European attitudes toward this situation first began to change around the middle of the 19th century. In 1852 France extended copyright protection to all works, foreign and domestic alike,[10] and while this generous gesture did not set a pattern, it accelerated the movements toward a multilateral copyright system. The Association Littéraire et Artistique Internationale (A.L.A.I.) was formed in Paris and took the lead in seeking ways to establish an international union of countries pledged to the protection of authors' rights.

DEVELOPMENT OF THE BERNE CONVENTION

A conference held under A.L.A.I. auspices in Berne in 1883 marked the end of the discussion phase and the beginning of actual work on what became the Berne Convention of 1886. The goals of the conference were: "(1) The study of the legislative enactments affecting literary property in all civilized countries; (2) the study of important points of these enactments with a view to unification

---

[7] Henn, *The Quest for International Copyright Protection*, 39 CORN. L.Q. 43, 44 (1953).
[8] 1 S. LADAS, THE INTERNATIONAL PROTECTION OF LITERARY AND ARTISTIC PROPERTY 24 (1938).
[10] Decree of Mar. 28, 1852. This remained a part of French law until the principle of reciprocity was introduced by Decree No. 67181 of Mar. 6, 1967.

and the foundation of a union for the protection of literary property; (3) the drawing up of certain articles, clear and concise, setting forth the principles that are most likely to be accepted by the various powers and which should constitute the text of a universal convention."[12]

. . . .

[T]he original Berne Convention of September 9, 1886, was a modest beginning; nevertheless, it was the first truly multilateral copyright treaty in history, and it established some important basic principles. Rather than reciprocity ("I'll protect your works, but only to the extent you protect my works"), the Berne Convention adopted the principle of national treatment ("I'll protect your works to the same extent I protect my own works, if you promise to do the same"). The convention set up a "Union for the protection of authors over their literary and artistic works" consisting of the contracting states,[15] and established a requirement that among Union members the right of translation had to be protected for a minimum of ten years. [art. V].

The original Berne Convention provided that rights enjoyed under it "shall be subject to the accomplishment of the conditions and formalities prescribed by law in the country of origin of the work, and must not exceed in the other countries the term of protection granted in the said country of origin." [art. II]. In the successive revisions of the Convention, the minimum requirements governing protection have been substantially expanded. A Berne Union member accepting the Brussels text of 1948, which is the latest revision now in effect, must, with some exceptions, accord protection to the works of other member countries without requiring compliance with any formalities, during the life of the author and fifty years after his death. [art. 7(1)]. The Convention provides specific minimum requirements with respect to the protection of certain exclusive rights,[21] most notably the so-called "moral rights" of the author. Any country that now wants to join the Berne Union must obligate itself to grant a very high level of copyright protection.

. . . .

INTERNATIONAL COPYRIGHT IN THE UNITED STATES BEFORE WORLD WAR II

For a century after enactment of the first United States copyright statute in 1790, only published works by citizens and residents of the United States could secure statutory copyright protection. For a century, the United States was exceptionally parochial in copyright matters, not only denying any protection to the published works of nonresident foreign authors, but actually appearing to encourage piracy.[30] Common law protection for unpublished works regardless of the nationality of their authors was cold comfort at a time when publication was the only profitable way to disseminate a work. "Under such circumstances,

---

[12]Solberg, *The International Copyright Union*, 36 YALE L.J. 68, 81 (1926).

[15]Berne Convention for the Protection of Literary and Artistic Works, Sept. 9, 1886 art. 1.

[21]These include, for example, the rights of translation, recording, broadcasting, performing, arranging, and adapting for motion pictures. Arts. 11-14.

[30]Henn, *supra* note 7, at 52.

other nations were understandably reluctant to protect American works."[32]

Literary piracy, particularly of British works, became common in the 19th century, and efforts began in the United States in the 1830's to secure an "international copyright law." In 1837 Henry Clay, as chairman of the Senate Select Committee, submitted a report strongly recommending enactment of international copyright legislation. "In principle," he said, "the committee perceives no objection to considering the republic of letters as one great community, and adopting a system of protection for literary property which should be common to all parts of it." The Clay bill was reintroduced several times between 1837 and 1842, but never reached a vote.

There followed more than a half-century of agitation for international copyright protection in the United States. Efforts to conclude a bilateral copyright treaty with Great Britain failed, and legislation to extend U.S. copyright protection to foreign authors attracted strong opposition, principally by American printing and publishing interests who believed that their livelihood depended upon cheap reprints of English books. They demanded that the extension of U.S. copyright to foreign works be conditioned on compliance with a requirement of manufacture in this country.[39]

The legislative phase of the international copyright movement in the United States began shortly after the Civil War and finally achieved success in the International Copyright Act of March 3, 1891. During much of this same period the Berne Convention of 1886 was under gestation, and its development was well known to those interested in international copyright in the United States. Yet U.S. government representatives refrained from participating directly in the development of the Convention, under circumstances that leave many questions unanswered.

The prevailing official attitude was summarized in a letter sent by Secretary of State Bayard on June 29, 1886, in response to a Swiss note inviting U.S. participation in the final diplomatic conference. Secretary Bayard stated that the question of international copyright pending before Congress had not advanced far enough in the legislative channel to enable the Executive to act with the assurance of congressional approval, and that the pendency of measures in Congress made it impracticable for the United States to appoint a plenipotentiary to attend the conference at Berne for the purpose of signing the proposed convention. The American government's attitude toward the project was "merely one of expectancy and reserve," favoring the plan in principle but without determinate views as to the shape it should assume. It was "unprepared to suggest modifications which might conform the convention to the legislation which Congress may hereafter deem appropriate." Secretary Bayard specifically held out the possibility of future accession to the convention "should it become expedient and practicable to do so," thus echoing President Cleveland's message to Congress on December 8, 1885. This possibility was also reflected in the language of the International Copyright Act of 1891:

---

[32] *Id.*

[39] *See* Sherman, *The Universal Copyright Convention: Its Effects on United States Law*, 55 COLUM. L. REV. 1137, 1161 (1955).

That this act shall apply to a citizen or subject of a foreign state or nation when such foreign state or nation permits to citizens of the United States of America the benefit of copyright on substantially the same basis as its own citizens; or when such foreign state or nation is a party to an international agreement which provides for reciprocity in the granting of copyright, by the terms of which agreement the United States may, at its pleasure, become a party to such agreement.

The compromise that made the Act of 1891 possible was the introduction of a requirement of domestic manufacture for "a book, phonograph, chromo, or lithograph." Under section 4956 of the Act, copyright could be secured only by making registration before publication and by depositing two copies of the work on or before the date of publication anywhere. Moreover, in the case of books and certain graphic works, the two copies had to be manufactured in the United States.

The requirements of the 1891 "manufacturing clause" were so rigid that they made the extension of copyright protection to foreigners illusory. Acts were passed in 1904 and 1905 in an effort to liberalize the clause by giving foreigners extra time to comply with the manufacturing requirement, and finally, in 1906, Congress undertook work on a general revision of the U.S. copyright laws. This revision effort was at its peak, when, on October 14, 1908, a major conference for revision of the Berne Convention was held in Berlin. The United States was invited to attend with "full freedom of action," but the delegate, Thorvald Solberg, the Register of Copyrights, was sent as an observer only. Mr. Solberg explained to the Conference that the United States found it impracticable to send a delegate authorized to commit it to actual adhesion to the Berne Convention since some of the questions to be discussed there were pending before the Congress and premature action at the Convention might embarrass the legislative branch of the Government.[50]

The original Berne Convention of 1886 had allowed member countries to impose certain formalities, such as notice, registration, and domestic manufacture, as conditions of copyright. This was changed by article 4 of the Berlin revision of 1908, which provided without qualification that "the enjoyment and exercise of these rights shall not be subject to the performance of any formality." This made it impossible for the United States to join the Berne Union without substantial changes in its domestic law.

In 1909, the year after the Berlin revision abolished formalities in international copyright, Congress passed a complete revision of the United States copyright law. The Act of March 3, 1909 . . . retained rather rigid notice formalities and, while further liberalizing the manufacturing provisions,[52]

---

[50]Solberg, *supra* note 12, at 98.

[52]The 1909 Act exempted foreign language works of foreign origin from the manufacturing requirements. It extended the privilege of securing an "ad interim" copyright, established by the 1905 statute, to English language works; if a copy was deposited in the Copyright Office within thirty days of the first publication abroad, and if an American edition was manufactured and published in the United States within thirty days from the date of deposit, then a full-term copyright could be secured.

retained the basic requirement of domestic manufacture as a condition of copyright in English-language books and periodicals. American adherence to the Berne Convention thus became impossible unless Congress could be persuaded to change the law again but this obviously was unfeasible in the immediate future. Active U.S. participation in the development and revision of the Berne Convention in its nascent stages might not have avoided this result, but it might have prevented the paths from diverging so sharply.

The 1909 Act continued the provision of the 1891 statute under which the President is empowered to proclaim the existence of bilateral copyright relations between the United States and particular foreign countries. This system has proved cumbersome and ineffective in comparison with the simplicity, certainty, and other advantages offered by multilateral arrangements. In fact, efforts to achieve adherence to the Berne Convention began less than 15 years after the enactment of the 1909 statute; following the First World War, the increasing use of American works in other countries brought with it a demand that the United States adhere to the Berne Convention. Beginning in 1922, a series of bills for this purpose was introduced in Congress.

The history during the 1920's and 1930's of the combined legislation programs to obtain general revision of the copyright law and U.S. adherence to the Berne Convention makes painful reading. One commentator attributed the total failure of both these programs to the effort to link them together, pointing out that "the development of radio and motion picture technology during the 1920's introduced new interest into the orbit of intellectual properties, and made more difficult the task of securing agreement on proposals to effect a general revision of the copyright law." On the other hand, a motion picture attorney felt that the United States never adhered to Berne "primarily because it contains concepts which are foreign to our concepts of copyright, such as copyright without formalities, protection of moral rights, retroactivity and also because of the requirement of our manufacturing clause."[59]

Whatever the reason for the failure of these legislative programs, the United States had become an exporter in the copyright trade, and something had to be done. It did not take American copyright owners long to discover an attractive loophole that has come to be known as the "backdoor to Berne." By the simple device of simultaneous publication of an American work in the United States and in a country which was a Berne Union member, such as Canada, a work became entitled to protection throughout the Berne Union without any corresponding obligations on the United States to protect Berne works. This practice of simultaneous publication became extremely widespread, and provoked resentment that is surprising only in its relative mildness. In 1914 the Berne Union adopted a retaliatory protocol[61] under which member countries could, if they chose, limit the protection of nonmember authors under certain conditions, and there were cases in which the existence of true simultaneous publication was decided on narrow grounds.

In 1928 the Berne Convention was revised at Rome, and the level of protection was again raised. In an effort to induce the United States to join the Union,

---

[59] Dubin, *The Universal Copyright Convention*, 42 CALIF. L. REV. 89, 98 (1954).
[61] Additional Protocol to the Revised Berne Convention of Nov. 13, 1908, Mar. 20, 1914.

however, the Rome Convention permitted nonmembers to adhere to the Berlin text of 1908 until August 1, 1931. Strenuous efforts in Congress to meet this deadline were unsuccessful; although Senate approval of the Rome version was prematurely obtained in 1935, it was immediately withdrawn. Another major effort sponsored by a committee formed under the auspices of an American organization related to the League of Nations resulted in the introduction of a bill in 1940, but it died in committee.

INTER-AMERICAN CONVENTIONS

Efforts to develop multilateral copyright arrangements in the Americas began in the 1880's at about the same time the Berne Convention and the United States International Copyright Act were being formed. These efforts produced a series of Pan-American copyright conventions, but for all practical purposes the United States is a member of only one of them, the Buenos Aires Convention of 1910.[68] It has failed to accept the later revisions adopted at Havana in 1928 and at Washington in 1946, which are more closely analogous to the principles of the Berne Convention.

Under the Buenos Aires Convention a work is protected in a member country if it has been copyrighted in another member country and bears a form of copyright notice. Since no legislation implementing it has ever been enacted, the conditions and extent of protection under this convention remain somewhat unclear in the United States. Furthermore, during the past twenty years there has been an unmistakable trend away from regional conventions and in favor of worldwide copyright arrangements, and the Universal Copyright Convention has superseded the Pan-American conventions in many cases.

THE UNIVERSAL COPYRIGHT CONVENTION

After the Second World War it became even more imperative for the Berne Union and the United States to reach an accommodation. The failure of the United States to offer foreign works the level of copyright protection generally available throughout the Berne Union gave rise to indignation, which was intensified by the practice of American copyright owners' taking full advantage of Berne protection in other countries. The situation grew worse with the emergence of the United States as the leading exporter of copyrighted works in the world. As one commentator has said, "Consideration was given to attracting the Americas into Berne, but member countries refused to tolerate their own retrogression for the simple expediency of attracting the American countries."[72] The postwar situation was urgent, but it seemed clear at that time that the Berne countries would refuse to lower protection sufficiently to attract

---

[68] 38 Stat. 1785 (1911), T.S. No. 593. The United States also adhered to the Mexico City Copyright Convention of 1902, but at present has relations only with El Salvador under that convention.

[72] Wells, *The Universal Copyright Convention and the United States: A Study of Conflict and Compromise*, in 8 Copyright Law Symposium 69, 86 (ASCAP 1957).

American adherence and that other efforts by the United States to join the Berne Union would be futile. The approach that was adopted represented a compromise: a new "common denominator" convention that was intended to establish, a minimum level of international copyright relations throughout the world, without weakening or supplanting the Berne Convention. The Universal Copyright Convention, as it came to be called, was sponsored by UNESCO,[74] and one of the leaders in its development was the United States.

Advocates of international copyright protection began once again to lay the groundwork for altering the domestic law in the United States while concomitantly devising universal agreement that would appeal to all countries committed to the promotion of cultural interchange. Furthermore, "vigorous leaders appeared in the United States among the champions of international copyright and organizations of creators, producers, and consumers of literary works became alerted to the[se] questions."[75]

The landmark Universal Copyright Convention was signed at Geneva on September 6, 1952, and, following the required 12 ratifications, took effect on September 16, 1955. The United States was one of the first signatories to ratify it. . . . [A]t least in comparison with the 1948 Brussels revision of the Berne Convention, the Universal Copyright Convention represents a rather low-level copyright arrangement, resembling in many ways the original 1886 Berne text.

The minimum requirements as to exclusive rights are extremely modest, being limited to providing "adequate and effective protection" and translation rights which can be subject to compulsory licensing. The requirements as to minimum duration of protection are also very permissive, and a system of copyright notice is actually sanctioned as a substitute for other formalities. It is therefore understandable that Berne Union members regarded the U.C.C. as a retrogressive step, and insisted on safeguarding the Berne Convention from the danger of being undermined by the defection of Berne members to the U.C.C. [through provisions that prohibit any Berne member from denouncing the Berne Convention and relying on the U.C.C. in its copyright relations with other Berne members].

DEVELOPMENTS, 1952-1967

U.S. RATIFICATION OF THE UNIVERSAL COPYRIGHT CONVENTION

Getting the United States to ratify the Universal Copyright Convention and to enact the statutory revisions necessary to implement it was more of an accomplishment than the development of the U.C.C. itself. That there was

[74]Article 27 of the United Nations Universal Declaration of Human Rights declares: "Everyone has the right freely to participate in the cultural life of the community, to enjoy the arts and to share in scientific advancement and its benefits . . . [and] the right to the protection of the moral and material interests resulting from any scientific, literary or artistic production of which he is the author."

[75]M. Janes, [The United States and the Movement for Universal Copyright, 1945-52 (Master's thesis, University of Southern California, 1953; photostat copy in Copyright Office Library)], at 21.

opposition goes without saying, but it was neutralized or overcome in a remarkably short time. On August 31, 1954, President Eisenhower signed Public Law 743 which conformed the indigenous copyright law to the Convention, and on November 5, 1954, he signed the instrument of ratification of the U.C.C. itself.

Since the Universal Copyright Convention was to a considerable extent tailored to meet the requirements of existing United States law, the changes necessary to implement it were, for the most part, technical. The most important alteration involved a complete waiver of all formalities as to deposit, registration, manufacture, and importation for foreign U.C.C. works, as long as the copies of the work bore the notice of copyright prescribed by the Convention. As a practical matter, this has removed the manufacturing requirement for the majority of English language works of foreign authorship and has induced a much greater use of copyright notices on foreign works.

CURRENT STATUS OF THE U.C.C.

In general, the Universal Copyright Convention has been a genuine success. It has been ratified or acceded to by 55 countries, nearly as many as belong to the Berne Union. It has vastly simplified the international copyright relations of the United States with other countries and of other countries with the United States, and it has brought some newly independent or developing countries into the international copyright community on terms that they found acceptable.

. . . .

CONCLUSION

The irony of the present American position in international copyright needs no elaboration. After a century as a virtual outlaw, a half century as an outsider, and 15 years as a stranger at the feast, the United States suddenly finds itself cast as a leading champion of literary property. . . [A]s the world's largest exporter of literary properties, we have an immediate stake in the future of international copyright. We can no longer afford to stand apart and content ourselves with sidelong glances. . . .

NOTES AND QUESTIONS

(1) **Developments since 1968.** This internationalist call to arms was issued by Barbara Ringer, who served as Register of Copyrights from 1973 until 1980. The article was written in the wake of the Stockholm revision of the Berne Convention, which occurred in 1967. At the time, as Register Ringer explains, the United States stood outside the premier international copyright union, the Berne Union. In the intervening thirty-one years, much has changed. As we

will see below, in 1989 the United States acceded to the Berne Convention. Indeed, the United States has become a leader (as has the EU) in the development of strong and effective copyright protection around the world. What do you think caused this change in U.S. attitudes toward international copyright law?

(2) **The "Hot Issues."** When Register Ringer wrote her article, the principal concern in international copyright law was the accommodation of developing countries within the international copyright family of nations. The Stockholm revision conference had centered on the treatment of developing countries. Today, the principal concern is the adaptation of copyright law to meet the demands of the digital environment.

BERNE CONVENTION IMPLEMENTATION ACT
H.R. Rep. No. 609, 100th Cong., 11-20 (1988)

A. THE BERNE CONVENTION IN INTERNATIONAL COPYRIGHT

. . . .

The Berne Convention is the oldest and most respected international copyright treaty.

In 1886, the Convention was concluded at Berne, Switzerland and the Berne Union came into being. Since then, the Convention has been successively completed and revised seven times: at Paris (1896), Berlin (1908), Berne (1914), Rome (1928), Brussels (1948), Stockholm (1967), and most recently, at Paris (1971). From an initial membership of eight [sic] states, the Union [in 1988] boast[ed] seventy-seven members, adhering to one or more of the principal Acts of the Union.

The Berne Union includes nations from all regions of the globe, at all levels of development. In the Western Hemisphere, Canada and 10 Latin American Republics adhere to Berne; in Europe, virtually every major state in Western and Eastern Europe adheres. Twenty-four states of Africa and 10 from Asia and the Pacific adhere. Membership includes highly industrialized nations such as Japan, Canada and France; industrializing countries such as India, Brazil and Mexico and developing countries such as Benin and Sri Lanka.

Major states not members of the Berne Union include the Soviet Union, China and the United States of America.

1. *History of the Convention*

. . . .

The original Convention was intended to promote five objectives: (1) the development of copyright laws in favor of authors in all civilized countries; (2) the elimination over time of basing rights upon reciprocity; (3) the end of discrimination in rights between domestic and foreign authors in all countries;

(4) the abolition of formalities for the recognition and protection of copyright in foreign works; and, (5) ultimately, the promotion of uniform international legislation for the protection of literary and artistic works.

The first Berne Convention was a simple document in which two cardinal principles were established, both of continuing vitality today:

a. The Union: the states adhering to the Convention organized themselves into a Union for the protection of the rights of authors in their literary and artistic works. In forming the Union, the original members contemplated an essentially political as well as legal undertaking: that adherents to the Convention would function as a cooperative unit which would continue in existence regardless of future accessions or withdrawals from the Convention itself.

b. The Rule of National Treatment: one of the cornerstones of international copyright is the rule, first recognized for copyright in the Berne Convention, that authors should enjoy in other countries the same protection for their works as those countries accord their own authors.

During the century of its existence, the Convention has been revised five times to meet changed conditions and technological development affecting authors' rights. Successive texts have generally improved and extended rights accorded authors and copyright proprietors; and, in 1967, the Berne Union confronted the special challenges to copyright policy posed by the emergence of numerous developing countries on the world scene.

2. *Successive Revisions of the Berne Convention*

a. 1908 Berlin Act. The principal achievement of the Berlin Revision Conference was the prohibition of formalities as a condition of the enjoyment and exercise of rights under the Convention. The minimum duration of protection was set at the life of the author and fifty years *post mortem*, but made subject to exceptions for each country so as to make it less than a mandatory rule. The Convention further expanded the minimum subject matter of copyright under the Convention, including photographs. Moreover, the Berlin Revision recognized the exclusive rights of composers of musical works to authorize the adaptation of these works and gave explicit protection to the authors of cinematographic works.

b. 1928 Rome Act. This revision was the first to recognize expressly the "moral rights" of authors: the right to claim authorship of a work and the right to object to modifications of the work which prejudiced the honor or reputation of the author. The Rome revision specifically recognized the right to authorize broadcasting of works, leaving details to be elaborated by national legislation.

c. 1948 Brussels Act. This revision established the term of protection of life of the author and fifty years *post mortem* as mandatory. It added improvements in copyright protection including recognition of the right of public recitation; rules governing mutual recognition of optional "resale royalty" laws (so called *droit de suite*); extension of the broadcasting article to secondary transmissions, including by wire; and, express recognition of cinematographic works and works produced by processes analogous to cinematography as distinct subjects of copyright protection.

d. 1967 Stockholm Act. For the first time, the implicit right of reproduction was expressly established in the Convention and special rules governing exceptions to that right were also included. Significant new rules relating to reconciling different national rules of authorship and ownership of motion pictures, defining the "nationality" of films for Convention purposes, were added at this revision. Protection was extended to include authors having habitual residence in a Union country, regardless of their citizenship. Finally, this revision established a "Protocol Regarding Developing Countries," which would have allowed developing countries broadly to limit rights of translation and reproduction. The 1967 Stockholm Act has not and will not come into force. It has effectively been superseded by the 1971 Paris Act.

e. 1971 Paris Act. The 1971 Paris Act of Berne—the only Act now open to accession—is essentially the 1967 Stockholm Act with significant revisions made to the Protocol Regarding Developing Countries. The thrust of these revisions will be discussed in the context of relations with developing countries.

. . . .

5. The Berne Convention and Developing Countries

The Berne Convention has played a constructive role in encouraging national creativity in developing countries through the enactment of national legislation based on the provisions of the Convention itself. Today, there is an augmented awareness of the importance of copyright in the developing world.

In 1900, of the twelve states members of the Berne Union only one (Tunisia) would today be considered a developing country. Indeed, with the exception of Japan, the Convention was totally European in membership.

On the eve of the Diplomatic Conference to draft the Universal Copyright Convention in 1952, the number of developing countries party to a text of the Berne Convention had reached eleven of a total of forty-two states. Today, developing countries constitute a slight majority of the 78 members of the Berne Union, the bulk having joined in the 1960's and early 1970's. Nine of the states joining in this period declared continuing adherence to the Convention following achievement of independence.

No understanding of the role of the Berne Convention in relation to developing countries is possible without coming to grips with the Stockholm revision conference, the challenge to the integrity of the global copyright system posed by the Protocol Regarding Developing Countries adopted at that Conference and the complex diplomacy which, in 1971 at Paris, resolved the Protocol crisis.

By the mid 1960's the growing number of developing countries in the United Nations system and in the Berne and Universal Copyright Conventions generated political pressures for the inclusion in the Berne Convention of special provisions designed to facilitate access to protected works by developing countries and, in other ways, to permit reservations on obligations deemed too onerous by developing countries. Through a series of preparatory meetings, a program for consideration of such special provisions was developed for the Stockholm Conference.

In a highly charged politicized atmosphere, the Stockholm Conference Protocol Regarding Developing Countries was adopted in a form which would have permitted deep cuts in the levels of copyright protection that developing countries would accord to protected works. The minimum term of protection could be reduced to life plus 25 years *post mortem*; exclusive rights with respect to broadcasting and retransmission of broadcasts could have been cut back to the level provided for in the 1928 Rome text, at least for non-commercial broadcast undertakings; translation and reproduction compulsory licensing systems would have been permitted; and, any use of a work (including performance, broadcasting and translation) for "teaching, study and research" would be allowed subject only to compensation at a level accorded national authors.

The struggle for control of the future of the Berne Convention was only one front in a conflict which also embroiled the Universal Copyright Convention. In 1966, efforts by developing countries were initiated in UNESCO to seek repeal of the "safeguard" provisions of the UCC. This effort was put on hold pending the outcome of the Stockholm revision conference.

The crisis which emerged out of Stockholm, though resting on technical matters and involving many different aspects of copyright, was essentially simple: no developed country was prepared to ratify the Stockholm Act because of its integral Protocol. Since a state cannot be bound by the terms of a treaty to which it has not adhered, the Stockholm Act could never serve as a basis to redefine the legal rights and privileges of the parties to this copyright dispute. The response of the developing countries was to threaten a revision conference for the Universal Copyright Convention, suspension of its safeguard clause, followed by wholesale withdrawals from the Berne Convention. The unraveling of the entire fabric of international copyright seemed possible.

In 1970, largely under the leadership of the United States through the Universal Copyright Convention, a compromise program was developed under which both Berne and the UCC would be revised to include less drastic concessions to developing countries, centered largely upon limited compulsory licensing options for translation and reprint rights in support of educational and developmental objectives. This program succeeded and in 1971 Berne and the UCC were jointly revised at Paris.

Since that time, relative stability in the Berne Convention has prevailed. Only two members of the Berne Convention and four members of the UCC have declared their intention, in accordance with the requirements of the two Conventions, to avail themselves of the compulsory licensing privileges of the Conventions. Indeed, as yet, no compulsory licenses have been issued in any of those countries.

The entire experience of the Stockholm Protocol had a material impact on the copyright related activities of the World Intellectual Property Organization. The establishment of a Permanent Committee on Development Cooperation in the Field of Copyright and Neighboring Rights to plan and coordinate the growing development assistance programs of the W.I.P.O. and the creation of the Joint International Copyright Information Service to assist users in developing countries in obtaining licenses from rightsholders in developed countries represent positive long-term institutional responses.

B. THE BERNE CONVENTION AND INTERNATIONAL TRADE

Recently, protection of intellectual property, including copyrights, has become an international trade issue. Improved technology and communications greatly facilitate the global dissemination of ideas, cultural views, and creative activity. Technological changes also facilitate the unauthorized copying of the creative work-product.

The United States, as a leader in the creation and global exploitation of copyrighted works, has a great interest in a strong and viable international copyright system. Under the U.S. Constitution, the primary objective of copyright law is not to reward the author, but rather to secure for the public the benefits derived from the authors' labors. By giving authors an incentive to create, the public benefits in two ways: when the original expression is created and second, when the limited term of protection expires and the creation is added to the public domain.

If framed properly, copyright protection fosters creative activity and innovation and encourages investment in commercialization of new ideas and technology. Trade in goods has expanded rapidly in the recent past. Domestic industries relying upon copyright protection to stimulate creative efforts represent a broad range of interests including all types of publishing, motion pictures, music and sound recordings and computer software. Goods and services produced by these industries consistently results in a trade surplus for the United States. A positive trade balance also sustains American jobs, thereby stimulating the domestic economy.

Recognizing the benefits of preserving rights of authors and providing incentives for future activities, our trade negotiators have engaged in a series of bilateral and multilateral efforts to persuade foreign countries to improve their protection of copyrightable works. The American negotiating position has been placed at a disadvantage with regard to improved copyright protection in foreign countries, however, because the United States neither belongs to the Berne Union nor has a copyright law that would allow us to join. Adherence of the United States to the Berne Convention will strongly encourage other countries to adopt and enforce high levels of protection.

In bilateral negotiations, foreign countries often point to the perceived deficiencies in U.S. protection, creating an excuse to avoid making improvements to their own laws. By way of illustration, in bilateral negotiations with Singapore and Korea, the American negotiators were repeatedly asked the difficult question of why the United States was pushing so hard for strong copyright protection in these countries while we did not adhere to the Berne Convention.

The absence of the United States in the Berne Union is also a significant consideration when our trading partners decide whether to adhere to the Berne

Convention or to the Universal Copyright Convention, which obligates signatories to provide less protection to copyrighted works. The Republic of Korea, for example, recently joined the UCC rather than Berne as part of that country's revision of its copyright laws undertaken in connection with the unfair trade investigation of Korea's protection of intellectual property. It is difficult for U.S. negotiators to argue that countries such as Korea should adhere to the Berne Convention when the United States has not taken the step itself.

Lack of U.S. membership in the Berne Convention makes it necessary to negotiate a series of bilateral copyright agreements with countries that are members of the Berne Union. Current negotiations with Thailand, a member of Berne, to confirm copyright protection of U.S. works provide an excellent example of the strain placed on U.S. relations resulting from non-adherence to Berne.

Following adherence to the Berne Convention, the United States will be able to establish copyright relations with twenty-four countries that are members of Berne. Two of these countries—Egypt and Turkey—are substantial trading partners. U.S. adherence to Berne will not only ensure protection of U.S. works but will promote trade in copyrighted works.

The United States successfully placed the topic of trade-related aspects of intellectual property on the agenda of the Uruguay Round Negotiations under the auspices of the General Agreement on Tariffs and Trade (GATT). The GATT meeting of Trade Ministers in Punte del Este recognized the relationship between trade and the protection and enforcement of intellectual property rights. Implicit in this recognition is the presumption that inadequate and ineffective protection of intellectual property rights can result in trade distortions.

U.S. membership in the Berne Union would contribute to the success of these multilateral negotiations.

First, adherence will manifest a firm and sustained commitment to achieving strong and uniform protection for intellectual property worldwide. Our trading partners will no longer be able to question the U.S. political will to gain that objective. Many participants in the Uruguay Round negotiations on intellectual property view increased participation in existing international conventions as the initial step in the protection of intellectual property rights. U.S. adherence to Berne could provide an incentive for other countries to reexamine their participation in international agreements.

Second, the substance of any multilateral agreement resulting from the Uruguay Round effort will undoubtedly reflect the international consensus embodied in the Berne Convention. U.S. membership in the Berne Union means that our trade negotiators can argue strongly for responsible standards without letting inconsistencies in U.S. copyright law change the focus of discussion as to why the U.S. currently does not—or cannot—belong to Berne. The United States should not be perceived as imposing a double standard on the rest of the world.

There is a potential danger of establishing international legal standards through trade agreements and GATT negotiations which, however desirable to particular private interests, are higher than those of our domestic law. Our trade negotiators obviously do not have the power to legislate. Only Congress can pass new or amend old laws.

The Berne Convention represents an international consensus on copyright protection. The United States should be in a position to take advantage of that consensus, to encourage other countries to join the common ground, and to use it to encourage expansion of legitimate trade. As to the latter, the relationship of Berne adherence to promotion of U.S. trade is clear. American popular culture and information products have become precious export commodities of immense economic value. That value is badly eroded by low international copyright standards. Berne standards are both high, reasonable and widely accepted internationally. Lending our prestige and power to the international credibility of those standards will promote development of acceptable copyright regimes in bilateral and multilateral contexts. Ultimately, a strong and viable international legal regime will develop to the benefit of the United States, not only to the advantage of proprietary interests but also to the public good.

NOTES AND QUESTIONS

(1) **Berne Membership.** In the twelve years since the United States joined Berne, the membership of the Berne Union has risen from 77 to 160 countries. Today, both Russia and China are also members. This increase has doubtless been due to in large part to a combination of U.S. accession to Berne and the conclusion of the TRIPS Agreement, which obligates WTO members to comply with almost all of Berne's obligations. *See* TRIPS art. 9(1). The impact has been to render the U.C.C. nearly irrelevant as a practical matter, since (as discussed below) the Berne obligations exceed those of the U.C.C., and its membership is now considerably greater.

(2) **Compulsory Licenses for Developing Countries.** Despite the turbulence that led to special treatment for developing countries in Berne and the U.C.C., the compulsory license privileges provided in the Conventions have to this day been little used. What do you think is the explanation for this?

WORLD INTELLECTUAL PROPERTY ORGANIZATION
INTELLECTUAL PROPERTY READING MATERIAL
¶¶ 5.446-449 (2d ed. 1998)

Neighboring rights are primarily an offshoot of technological development. At the national level, it was first the phonogram industry that looked for protection against unauthorized duplication of sound recordings of musical performances. At the international level, it was likewise the development of the phonogram industry that promoted the establishment of special protection for the so-called neighboring rights.

As in the case of some national laws, the first proposals aiming at the protection of producers of phonograms and performers at the international level were also based on copyright protection. The rights involved were discussed by the Berne Union for the Protection of Literary and Artistic Works at its Diplomatic Conference in Rome in 1928, where it was proposed that "when a musical work has been adapted to a mechanical instrument by the contribution of performing artists these latter should also benefit from the protection granted to that adaptation." Corresponding to this approach, a resolution was passed asking governments to consider the possibility of adopting measures to safeguard the interests of performers.

Later on, in 1934, CISAC, the International Confederation of Societies of Authors and Composers, signed an agreement in Stresa with the International Federation of the Gramophone Industry according to which during the forthcoming revision of the Berne Convention (i) the protection of phonograms against unauthorized duplication and (ii) the right of producers of phonograms to equitable remuneration for communication to the public of their phonograms by broadcasting or cinematography should be proposed by means of an annex to be added to the Berne Convention. On the other hand, the International Labour Organization (ILO) had maintained since 1926 a continuing interest in the protection of performers and the problem was considered at a meeting in Samaden, Switzerland, in 1939. Drafts were prepared in cooperation with the Bureau of the Berne Union but all progress was stopped for several years by the outbreak of World War II.

After the war, different committees of experts prepared drafts of conventions which also included protection of the interests of broadcasting organizations— the so-called Rome Draft (1951), a draft produced under the sponsorship of the International Labour Organization (1957) and the Monaco Draft (1957) prepared by experts convened by the International Bureau of the Berne Union and by UNESCO. Finally, in 1960, a Committee of Experts convened jointly by WIPO, UNESCO and the International Labour Organization, met at The Hague and drew up the draft convention. This served as a basis for the deliberations in Rome, where a Diplomatic Conference agreed upon the final text of the International Convention for the Protection of Performers, Producers of Phonograms and Broadcasting Organizations, the Rome Convention of October 26, 1961.

§ 4.02 International Treaty Obligations

[A]   Copyright

[1]   The Berne Convention

WORLD INTELLECTUAL PROPERTY ORGANIZATION
INTELLECTUAL PROPERTY READING MATERIAL
¶¶ 5.168-191, 5.199-204 (2d ed. 1998)

The aim of the Berne Convention, as indicated in its preamble, is "to protect, in as effective and uniform a manner as possible, the rights of authors in their literary and artistic works." Article 1 lays down that the countries to which the Convention applies constitute a Union for the protection of the rights of authors in their literary and artistic works.

Principal Provisions

(i) Basic Principles

The Convention rests on three basic principles. Firstly, there is the principle of "national treatment," according to which works originating in one of the member States are to be given the same protection in each of the member States as these granted to works of their own nationals. Secondly, there is automatic protection, according to which such national treatment is not dependent on any formality; in other words protection is granted automatically and is not subject to the formality of registration, deposit, or the like. Thirdly, there is independence of protection, according to which enjoyment and exercise of the rights granted is independent of the existence of protection in the country of origin of the work.

(ii) Works Protected

Article 2 contains a non-limitative (illustrative and not exhaustive) list of such works, which include any original production in the literary, scientific and artistic domain, whatever may be the mode or form of its expression. Derivative works, that is those based on other pre-existing works, such as translations, adaptations, arrangements of music and other alterations of a literary or artistic work, receive the same protection as original works (Article 2(3)). The protection of some categories of works is optional; thus every State party to the Berne Convention may decide to what extent it wishes to protect official texts of a legislative, administrative and legal nature (Article 2(4)), works of applied art (Article 2(7)), lectures, addresses and other oral works (Article 2*bis*(2)) and works of folklore (Article 15(4)). Furthermore, Article 2(2) provides for the possibility of making the protection of works or any specified categories thereof subject to their being fixed in some material form. For instance, protection of choreographic works may be dependent on their being fixed in some form.

One of the important provisions is the one that covers works or expressions of what is called "folklore." Without mentioning the word, the Convention provides that any member country may give protection to unpublished works where the identity of the author is unknown, but where there is every ground to presume that the author is a national of that country, by designating, through the national legislation, the competent authority which should represent the author of unknown identity and protect and enforce his rights in the countries party to the Convention. By providing for the bringing of actions by authorities designated by the State, the Berne Convention offers to countries whose folklore is a part of their heritage, a possibility of protecting it.

(iii) Owners of Rights

Article 2(6) lays down that protection under the Convention is to operate for the benefit of the author and his successors in title. For some categories of works, however, such as cinematographic works (Article 14*bis*), ownership of copyright is a matter for legislation in the country where protection is claimed.

(iv) Persons Protected

Authors of works are protected, in respect of both their unpublished or published works if, according to Article 3, they are nationals or residents of a member country; alternatively, if, not being nationals or residents of a member country, they first publish their works in a member country or simultaneously in a non-member and a member country.

(v)   Minimum Standards of Protection

Certain minimum standards of protection have been prescribed relating to the rights of authors and the duration of protection.

(vi) Rights Protected

The exclusive rights granted to authors under the Convention include the right of translation (Article 8), the right of reproduction in any manner or form, which includes any sound or visual recording (Article 9), the right to perform dramatic, dramatico-musical and musical works (Article 11), the right to broadcasting and communicating to the public by wire, by broadcasting or by loudspeaker or any other analogous instrument of the broadcast of the work (Article 11*bis*), the right of public recitation (Article 11*ter*), the right of making adaptations, arrangements or other alterations of a work (Article 12) and the right of making the cinematographic adaptation and reproduction of a work (Article 14). The so-called *"droit de suite"* provided for in Article 14*ter* (concerning original works of art and original manuscripts) is optional and applicable only if legislation in the country to which the author belongs so permits.

Independently of the author's economic rights, Article 6*bis* provides for "moral rights"—that is to say the right of the author to claim authorship of his work and to object to any distortion, mutilation or other modification of, or other derogatory action in relation to, the work which would be prejudicial to his honor or reputation.

(vii) Limitations

As a sort of counterbalance to the minimum standards of protection there are also other provisions in the Berne Convention limiting the strict application of the rules regarding exclusive rights. It provides for the possibility of using protected works in particular cases, without having to obtain the authorization of the owner of the copyright and without having to pay any remuneration for such use. Such exceptions, which are commonly referred to as free use of protected works, are included in Articles 9(2) (reproduction in certain special cases), 10 (quotations and use of works by way of illustration for teaching purposes), 10*bis* (reproduction of newspaper or similar articles and use of works for the purpose of reporting current events), and 11*bis*(3) (ephemeral recordings).

There are two cases where the Berne Convention provides the possibility of compulsory licenses—in Articles 11*bis*(2), for the right of broadcasting and communication to the public by wire by rebroadcasting or by loudspeaker or any other analogous instrument of the broadcast of the work, and 13(1) for the right of recording musical works.

In so far as the exclusive right of translation is concerned, the Berne Convention offers a choice, in that a developing country may, when acceding to the Convention, make a reservation under the so-called "ten-year rule" (Article 30(2)(b)). This provides for the possibility of reducing the term of protection in respect of the exclusive right of translation; this right, according to the said rule, ceases to exist if the author has not availed himself of it within 10 years from the date of first publication of the original work, by publishing or causing to be published, in one of the member countries, a translation in the language for which protection is claimed.

(viii)   Duration of Protection

The minimum standards of protection provided for in the Berne Convention also relate to the duration of protection. Article 7 lays down a minimum term of protection, which is the life of the author plus 50 years after his death.

There are, however, exceptions to this basic rule for certain categories of works. For cinematographic works, the term is 50 years after the work has been made available to the public, or, if not made available, then 50 years after the making of such a work. For photographic works and works of applied art, the minimum term of protection is 25 years from the making of the work (Article 7(4)).

A majority of countries in the world have legislated for life plus a 50-year term of protection since it is felt fair and right that the lifetime of the author and the lifetime of his children should be covered; this could also provide the incentive necessary to stimulate creativity, and constitute a fair balance between the interests of the authors and the needs of society.

The term of protection, insofar as moral rights are concerned, extends at least until the expiry of the economic rights.

The Latest (Paris) Act of the Convention

The Berne Convention was developed initially according to the standards and requirements of the industrialized countries in Europe. Particularly in the wake of the Second World War, when the political map of the world changed considerably, the Berne Convention also had to face new problems of development. Various newly independent countries had to consider the question of possible accession to the international system of copyright protection as contained in the Convention. They were free to join or not to join it or, where they were already members by virtue of a past colonial or similar status, to withdraw from the Convention.

While it was almost universally recognized that authors and other creators should be afforded the necessary protection for their intellectual creations, there was also a consciousness that the newly independent developing countries had genuine problems in gaining greater and easier access to works protected by copyright, particularly for their technological and educational needs, from the developed countries. Meanwhile, the advance of technology made more attractive the extension of the geographical scope of the international conventions and multilateral agreements to an increasingly larger number of countries.

Deliberations at the more recent revision conferences were, therefore, directed to adapting the systems of international protection of literary and artistic works to the needs of these newly independent countries. . . .

The Appendix to the Paris (1971) Act of the Berne Convention provides for special facilities open to developing countries concerning translation and reproduction of works of foreign origin. The Appendix augments the Convention's existing exceptions to the author's exclusive rights, including those of reproduction and translation (Articles 2*bis*, 9(2), 10(2), 10*bis*) and the ten-year rule (Article 30(2)(b)).

According to this Appendix, countries which are regarded as developing countries in conformity with the established practice of the General Assembly of the United Nations may, under certain conditions, depart from the minimum standards of protection provided for in the Convention. This exceptional regime concerns two rights, the right of translation and the right of reproduction. Details of such provisions in favor of developing countries appear . . . below.

Developing Countries and the Berne Convention

. . .The Appendix provides for the possibility of granting non-exclusive and non-transferable compulsory licenses in respect of (i) translation for the purpose of teaching, scholarship or research, and (ii) reproduction for use in connection with systematic instructional activities, of works protected under the Convention. These licenses may be granted, after the expiry of certain time limits and after compliance with certain procedural steps, by the competent authority of the developing country concerned. They must provide for just compensation in favor of the owner of the right. In other words the payment to be made by the compulsory licensee must be consistent with standards of royalties normally in vogue in respect of licenses freely negotiated between persons in the two countries concerned. Provision has also to be made to ensure a correct translation or an accurate reproduction of the work, as the case may be, and to indicate the name of the author on all copies of such translations or reproductions. Copies of translations and reproductions made and publication under licenses are not, however, allowed to be exported. Since the license is non-exclusive, the copyright owner is entitled to bring out and place on the market his own equivalent copies, upon which the power of the licensee to continue making copies under the license would cease. However, in that event, the compulsory licensee's stock can be exhausted.

Compulsory licenses for translations can be granted for languages generally spoken in the developing country concerned. There is a distinction between languages in general use also in one or more developed countries (English, French and Spanish, for example) and those not in general use there (largely local languages of developing countries). In the case of a language in general use in one or more developed countries, a period of three years, starting on the date of the first publication of the work has to elapse before a license can be applied for, whereas for other languages the period has been reduced to one year. To this has to be added a period of six to nine months, as the case may be, for obtaining licenses according to the formalities provided for in the Convention. It is also important here to point out that the system of translation licenses includes licenses for broadcasting, and this is important when we take into account the part played in today's context by the radio and television for educational purposes. These licenses, however, are not for authorizing the broadcasting of a translated work; they relate only to translations made for broadcasting purposes.

In respect of reproduction, the period after which licenses can be obtained varies according to the nature of the work to be reproduced. Generally it is five years from the first publication. For works connected with the natural and physical sciences and with technology (and this includes mathematical works) the period is three years; while for works of fiction, poetry and drama, the period is seven years.

The possibility that the Appendix provides for the grant of a compulsory license, if authorization is desired, may favorably influence negotiation and may lead to increased scope for voluntary licensing.

In so far as compulsory licenses for translation are concerned, instead of availing itself of the facility offered by the system mentioned earlier, the Berne Convention offers a choice in that a developing country may, when ratifying or acceding to the Paris Act, make a reservation under the so-called "ten-year rule" (Article 30(ii)(b)), which provides for the possibility of reducing the term of protection as far as the exclusive right of translation is concerned; this right, according to the said rule, ceases to exist if the author has not availed himself of it within ten years from the date of first publication of the original work, by publishing or causing to be published, in one of the countries of the Berne Union, a translation in the language for which protection is claimed. The Appendix to the Paris Act of the Berne Convention thus allows a choice between a compulsory license system and the possibility of limiting the right of translation to ten years as provided for in this Convention. Any developing country may choose between those possibilities but cannot combine them. In other words this "ten-year" system provides that for ten years from the publication of the work, the author's consent has to be sought before the right to translate is obtained; after this period the right of translation is in the public domain.

NOTES AND QUESTIONS

(1) **Retroactivity.** One important element of the Berne Convention not discussed in the preceding summary is the principle embodied in Article 18, usually referred to as "retroactivity." Article 18 requires Berne members to extend the Convention's protection to all otherwise eligible works that have not yet fallen into the public domain in their country of origin due to the expiration of their term of protection. What is the reason for this provision? In what sense is such protection "retroactive"? What problems might it cause? Note, in particular, paragraph 3 of Article 18, which allows countries to determine the "conditions of application of this principle." What types of conditions are intended?

(2) **European Origins.** What are the long-term consequences of the fact that "the Berne Convention was developed initially according to the standards and requirements of the industrialized countries in Europe"?

[2] The Universal Copyright Convention (UCC)

BARBARA A. RINGER, THE ROLE OF THE UNITED STATES IN INTERNATIONAL COPYRIGHT—PAST, PRESENT, AND FUTURE
56 GEORGETOWN L.J. 1050, 1061-62 (1968)

The most significant provisions of the [U.C.C.] can be summarized as follows:

1. *Adequate and effective protection.* Under article 1, the contracting states are obliged to "provide for the adequate and effective protection of the rights of authors and other copyright proprietors . . . ."

2. *National treatment.* Article II provides that the "published works of nationals of any Contracting State and works first published in the State shall enjoy in each other Contracting State the same protections that other State accords to works of its nationals first published in its own territory." There is a similar provision for unpublished works.

3. *Formalities.* Article III, which represents the great compromise of the U.C.C., provides that the formal requirements, such as notice, registration, and manufacture, of a contracting state's copyright law are satisfied with respect to foreign U.C.C. works "if from the time of first publication all of the copies of the

work . . . bear the symbol © accompanied by the name of the copyright proprietor and the year of first publication placed in such manner and location as to give reasonable notice of claim of copyright."

4. *Duration of protection.* Another major compromise is embodied in article IV of the U.C.C. The minimum term, subject to various detailed qualifications and exception, is to be either 25 years from the death of the author or from the date of first publication.

5. *Translation rights.* The U.C.C. in article V requires contracting states to give exclusive translation rights to foreign U.C.C. authors for at least seven years; thereafter a rather cumbersome compulsory licensing system can be established.

6. *Nonretroactivity.* Under article VII a contracting state is not obliged to protect works that are permanently in its public domain on the date the Convention becomes effective in that state.

7. *Berne safeguard clause.* An enormously important provision of the U.C.C. is found in article XVII and the "Appendix Declaration" attached to it. These provide, in effect, that no Berne country can denounce the Berne Convention and rely on the U.C.C. in its copyright relations with Berne Union members.

NOTES AND QUESTIONS

(1) **Status of the UCC.** The UCC is jointly administered by WIPO and UNESCO. It now has 97 members.

(2) **Comparison of the UCC and the Berne Convention.** What are the major differences between the substantive provisions of Berne and those of the U.C.C.? To what can they be attributed?

[B]   Rights of Performers, Record Producers and Broadcasters

[1] The Rome Convention

WORLD INTELLECTUAL PROPERTY ORGANIZATION
INTELLECTUAL PROPERTY READING MATERIAL
¶¶ 5.450-481 (2d ed. 1998)

Relation Between the Protection of Neighboring Rights and Copyright

Considering that the use of literary and artistic works was usually implied in the work of performers, recorders and broadcasters, the Diplomatic Conference at Rome established a link with copyright protection. The first article of the Rome Convention provides that the protection granted under the Convention shall leave intact and shall in no way affect the protection of copyright in literary and artistic works. Under the text of Article 1 it is clear that whenever, by virtue of the copyright law, the authorization of the author is necessary for the use of his work, the need for this authorization is not affected by the Rome Convention.

The majority of the Conference at Rome decided to go even further. They considered the possibility that the performers, producers of phonograms and broadcasting organizations of a country would enjoy international protection even when the literary and artistic works they used might be denied protection in that country, because it was not a party to at least one of the major international copyright conventions. The Rome Convention therefore provides that in order to become a party to the Convention a State must not only be a member of the United Nations, but also a member of the Berne Union or a party to the Universal Copyright Convention (Article 24(2)). Accordingly, a Contracting State shall cease to be a party to the Rome Convention as from that time when it is not party to either the Berne or the Universal Copyright Convention (Article 28(4)). Because of this link with the copyright conventions, the Rome Convention is sometimes referred to as a "closed" convention from the point of view of the circle of States which may adhere to it.

Principal Provisions

(i) National Treatment

As in the Berne Convention, the protection accorded by the Rome Convention consists basically of the national treatment that a State grants under its domestic law to domestic performances, phonograms and broadcasts (Article 2(1)). National treatment is, however, subject to the minimum of protection specifically guaranteed by the Convention, and also to the limitations specifically provided for in the Convention (Article 2(2)). This means that, apart from the rights guaranteed by the Convention itself as constituting that minimum of protection, and subject to specific exceptions or reservations allowed for by the Convention, performers, producers of phonograms and broadcasting organizations to which the Convention applies, enjoy in Contracting States the same rights as those countries grant to their nationals.

(ii) Eligibility for Protection

One of the most important questions to be answered unequivocally by each international convention is to whom and in what cases does it apply? The Rome Convention provides for its application by determining criteria of eligibility for national treatment.

National treatment should be granted to performers, if the performance takes place in another Contracting State (irrespective of the country to which the performer belongs) or if it is incorporated in a phonogram protected under the Convention (irrespective of the country to which the performer belongs or where the performance actually took place) or if it is transmitted "live" (not from a phonogram) in a broadcast protected by the Convention (irrespective again of the country to which the performer belongs) (Article 4). These alternative criteria of eligibility for protection allow for the application of the Rome Convention to the widest possible circle of performances.

National treatment should be granted to producers of phonograms if the producer is a national of another Contracting State (criterion of nationality) or the first fixation was made in another Contracting State (criterion of fixation) or the phonogram was first or simultaneously published in another Contracting State (criterion of publication) (Article 5).

The Convention allows reservations in respect of these alternative criteria. By means of a notification deposited with the Secretary-General of the United Nations, any Contracting State may at any time declare that it will not apply the criterion of publication or, alternatively, the criterion of fixation. Any State which, on the day the Convention was signed at Rome, granted protection to producers of phonograms solely on the basis of the criterion of fixation, can exclude both the criteria of nationality and publication. This possibility has been provided for mainly in view of the contemporary Nordic legislation, so that implementation of the Rome Convention could be adapted to conditions of protection already existing under different national laws.

National treatment has to be granted to broadcasting organizations if their headquarters is situated in another Contracting State (principle of nationality) or the broadcast was transmitted from a transmitter situated in another Contracting State, irrespective of whether the initiating broadcasting organization was situated in a Contracting State (principle of territoriality). Contracting States may declare that they will protect broadcasts only if both the conditions of nationality and of territoriality are met in respect of the same Contracting State (Article 6).

(iii) The Minimum Protection Required by the Convention

The minimum protection guaranteed by the Convention to performers is provided by "the possibility of preventing certain acts" done without their consent. Instead of enumerating the minimum rights of performers, this expression was used in order to allow countries like the United Kingdom to continue to protect performers by virtue of penal statutes, determining offenses and penal sanctions under public law. It was agreed, however, that the enumerated acts which may be prevented by the performer require his consent in advance. In fact, the possibility of preventing certain acts as defined in the Convention amounts to a distinct bundle of rights granted to performers.

The restricted acts comprise: broadcasting or communication to the public of a "live" performance; recording an unfixed performance; reproducing a fixation of the performance, provided that the original fixation was made without the consent of the performer or the reproduction is made for purposes not permitted by the Convention or the performer (Article 7).

Producers of phonograms have the right to authorize or prohibit the direct or indirect reproduction of their phonograms (Article 10). The Rome Convention does not provide for any right to authorize performances of the phonogram and does not explicitly prohibit distribution or importation of unauthorized duplicates of phonograms.

Broadcasting organizations have the right to authorize or prohibit: the simultaneous rebroadcasting of their broadcasts, the fixation of their broadcasts, the reproduction of unauthorized fixations of their broadcasts or reproduction of lawful fixations for illicit purposes, and the communication to the public of their television broadcasts by means of receivers in places accessible to the public against payment. It should be noted, however, that this last-mentioned right does not extend to communication to the public of merely sound broadcasts, and that it is a matter for domestic legislation to determine the conditions under which such a right may be exercised. It should also be observed that the Rome Convention does not protect against distribution by cable of broadcasts.

(iv) Provisions for Discretionary Regulation of the Exercise of Rights

The Rome Convention, over and above the minimum requirements of protection, also contains provisions allowing national laws to regulate certain aspects of protection at their discretion.

As regards the protection of performers, it is a matter for domestic legislation to regulate the protection against rebroadcasting of the performance and fixation thereof for broadcasting purposes, where the broadcasting of the performance was consented to by the performer. The principle of preeminence of contractual arrangements was embodied in a provision requiring that domestic laws shall not operate to deprive performers of the ability to control by contract their relations with broadcasting organizations (Article 7(2)) whereas it was understood that the meaning of contract in this context includes collective agreements and also decisions of an arbitration board, if involved.

If several performers participate in the same performance, the manner in which they should be represented in connection with the exercise of their rights may be specified by each Contracting State (Article 8).

Concerning both the protection of performers and producers of phonograms, Article 12 (perhaps the most controversial part of the Convention) provides that if a phonogram published for commercial purposes is used directly for broadcasting or any communication to the public, an equitable remuneration shall be paid by the user to the performers, or to the producers of the phonogram, or to both. This Article does not grant any right to either the performers or producers of phonograms to authorize or to prohibit the secondary use of a phonogram. By guaranteeing a single remuneration for the use of the phonogram it seems to establish a sort of non-voluntary license. It does not, however, obligatorily specify the beneficiary or beneficiaries of the remuneration for the secondary use of the performance and the phonogram embodying it. Article 12 only says that at least one of the interested parties should be paid for the use; nevertheless it provides that in the absence of agreement between these parties, domestic law may optionally lay down the conditions for the sharing of this remuneration.

The implementation of these provisions, however, can be excluded or restricted by the Contracting States at any time by an appropriate notification (Article 16(1)(a)). A State may declare that it will not apply the provisions of Article 12. A Contracting State may declare that it will not apply this Article in respect of certain uses, for instance as regards communications to the public other than broadcasting, or broadcasting of phonograms acquired before the date of the Convention, etc. It is also possible to apply this Article only as regards phonograms of which the producer is a national of another Contracting State. Furthermore, as regards phonograms of which the producer is a national of another Contracting State, the extent and term of protection can be limited so as to correspond to the protection granted by the other State concerned. The fact, however, that the protection in both countries concerned is not granted to the same beneficiary, cannot be considered as justifying the restriction of the protection provided for in Article 12.

(v)   Limitations

The Rome Convention allows for certain limitations of the rights granted and, as regards the performers, also imposes limitations on rights itself.

Any Contracting State may provide for exceptions as regards private use, use of short excerpts in connection with reporting current events, ephemeral fixation by a broadcasting organization by means of its own facilities and for its own broadcasts, and for all kinds of uses solely for the purpose of teaching or scientific research (Article 15(1)). This latter possibility of introducing exceptions may be of special benefit to developing countries.

Besides the exceptions specified by the Convention, any Contracting State may also provide for the same kind of limitations with regard to the protection of performers, producers of phonograms and broadcasting organizations as it provides for in connection with copyright protection. There is, however, an important difference: compulsory licenses may be provided for only to the extent to which they are compatible with the Rome Convention (Article 15(2)).

In view of the cinematographic industry's interest in exclusively exploiting the contributions made to their productions, Article 19 of the Rome Convention provides that once a performer has consented to the incorporation of his performance in a visual or audiovisual fixation, he shall have no further rights under the Rome Convention as regards the performance concerned.

(vi)   Duration of Protection

The minimum term of protection under the Rome Convention is a period of twenty years, to be computed from the end of the year in which the fixation was made, as far as phonograms and performances incorporated therein are concerned, or the performance took place, as regards performances not incorporated in phonograms, or the broadcast took place, for broadcasts (Article 14).

(vii) Restriction of Formalities

If a country requires compliance with formalities as a condition of protecting neighboring rights in relation to phonograms, these should be considered as fulfilled if all copies in commerce of the published phonogram or their containers bear a notice consisting of the symbol ℗, accompanied by the year of the first publication. If the copies or their containers do not identify the producer or his licensee, the notice shall also include the name of the owner of the rights of the producer and, if the copies or their containers do not identify the principal performers, the notice shall also include the name of the person who owns the rights of such performers (Article 11). It should be emphasized that this provision is not a formality requirement; it is a restriction of formalities, which may be required by some national laws.

The Implementation of the Rome Convention

The Rome Convention has been referred to as a "pioneer convention." Whereas the conventions concluded towards the end of the nineteenth century for the protection of copyright resulted from developments in national laws, this Convention defined standards of protection of neighboring rights at a time when very few countries had any rules enacted to protect performing artists, producers of phonograms and broadcasting organizations. Thus it was only natural that the impetus of the Convention in the field of the protection of neighboring rights during the first years following its adoption, could not be measured so much by the number of ratifications or accessions as by the impact the Convention had on national laws.

Since 1961, many countries have legislated on the protection of neighboring rights, thus greatly increasing the number of national laws protecting producers of phonograms or broadcasting organizations, and the majority of them as a result of the coming into existence of the Rome Convention. The disproportion between the number of national laws protecting performers' rights and those granting protection to producers of phonograms and broadcasting organizations is still unduly great. There are, however, further draft laws under preparation in several countries, which continue to demonstrate the tendency to pay more attention to the protection of performers' rights.

Since 1974, additional assistance is available to national laws in the form of a Model Law Concerning the Protection of Performers, Producers of Phonograms and Broadcasting Organizations, with a commentary on it, prepared by WIPO, UNESCO and the International Labour Organization, the international organizations which jointly administer the Rome Convention. This Model Law has proved an efficient aid, especially to developing countries.

The comparatively slow progress of national laws in the field of neighboring rights, and in particular the unequal development of protection as regards different beneficiaries of these rights, even today hinders accession to the Rome Convention, since it requires at the same time protection of performers, producers of phonograms and broadcasting organizations.

The Rome Convention and Developing Countries

A large number of the States party to the Rome Convention are developing countries. This is quite natural since most developing countries attach great importance to music, dance and other creations in their national heritage. The value of the Rome Convention to such countries stems from the fact that it affords the protection of those who contribute to the dissemination of that heritage abroad.

The Convention is particularly important to those countries whose civilization and tradition are oral and where the author is often the performer as well. In this context, the place occupied by expressions of folklore must be borne in mind and the interests of the artists constantly performing, and thus perpetuating them, must be safeguarded when use is made of their performances. Whilst the possibilities of protecting creations of folklore by copyright seem to be limited, and the establishment of a more adequate kind of protection *sui generis* appears to require more time, expressions of folklore can efficiently be protected indirectly by protecting performances, fixations, and broadcasts of them.

By also protecting the producers of phonograms, the Rome Convention promotes, particularly in developing countries, industry in a dynamic tertiary sector of the economy. Such an industry, while guaranteeing the dissemination of national culture, both within the country and throughout the world, can additionally constitute a substantial source of revenue for the country's economy and, in those cases where its activities extend beyond frontiers, can attract an inflow of foreign currency.

By giving performers and phonogram producers the possibility of benefiting from their performances and productions, the Rome Convention is instrumental in promoting the artistic heritage and represents an important incentive to creativity. It is also certain that, where the interests of performers and producers of phonograms are safeguarded by law, works will enjoy greater development and that those works will suffer less from the competition of unprotected performances of foreign works. Where performances and phonograms are exported, there is one reason more to protect them internationally, that is to say, by accepting the relevant international conventions.

Finally, the part played by the broadcasting organizations in the developing countries should not be forgotten either, since they also have an interest in the protection of their costly programs against rebroadcasting, reproduction and communication to the public of their broadcasts. The rebroadcasting or reception of television broadcasts in public places can be very profitable, especially when the subject of the original broadcast is an exceptional event. Frequently, the organizers of such events only allow broadcasting for certain territories or on the condition that no public reception close to the place of the event drains away potential spectators. The broadcasting organization must therefore be able to prohibit rebroadcasting and public reception. The same applies to broadcasting of performances or recordings of expressions of national folklore: the broadcasting organization should be entitled internationally to prevent rebroadcasting or fixation for reproduction of its own broadcast of works of the national heritage.

[2] The Geneva and Brussels Conventions

WORLD INTELLECTUAL PROPERTY ORGANIZATION
INTELLECTUAL PROPERTY READING MATERIAL
¶¶ 5.483-509 (2d ed. 1998)

The Other Special Conventions

Besides the Rome Convention of 1961 . . ., two other international instruments have been drawn up with regard to certain neighboring rights. These are the Convention for the Protection of Producers of Phonograms Against Unauthorized Duplication of their Phonograms, concluded in Geneva in October 1971 and generally referred to as "the Phonograms Convention," and the Convention Relating to the Distribution of Programme-Carrying Signals Transmitted by Satellite, concluded in Brussels in May 1974 and known briefly as "the Satellites Convention." These two Conventions are also within the area of neighboring rights, and their purpose is to protect producers of phonograms and broadcasting organizations, respectively, against certain prejudicial acts that have been widely recognized as infringements or acts of piracy.

With regard to the Rome Convention, the Phonograms Convention and the Satellites Convention may be regarded as special agreements, the conclusion of which is reserved for Contracting States insofar as the agreements grant to performers, producers of phonograms or broadcasting organizations more extensive rights than those granted by the Rome Convention, or contain other provisions not contrary to that Convention (Article 22 of the Rome Convention).

Reasons for and Purposes of the Special Conventions

The reason for the rapid acceptance . . . of the Phonograms Convention is due, on one hand, to the accelerating increase in international piracy during the last two decades, and, on the other hand, to the legal characteristics of the Convention itself.

While a number of countries were preparing new legislation in the field of neighboring rights in view of the standards set by the Rome Convention, international piracy of sound recordings was growing. The total value of pirated sound recordings sold worldwide has been increasing steadily. This made it necessary, even in the early seventies, to establish a special convention without delay. The subject was raised in May 1970 in the Preparatory Committee for the revision of the two major copyright conventions, and the new Convention was signed in less than 18 months in Geneva.

The Phonograms Convention takes into account all the measures that had already been adopted in various national laws, and allows for the application of all of them instead of requiring a uniform solution, as is the case under the

Rome Convention, which provides for the granting to producers of phonograms the right to authorize or prohibit the reproduction of their phonograms. Thus, amendments of existing national laws became largely unnecessary to States which already protected producers of phonograms by some other means and wanted to extend this kind of protection also at the international level.

The Satellites Convention was adopted because the use of satellites in international telecommunications has, since about 1965, been presenting a new problem for the protection of broadcasting organizations.

Nowadays the transmission of programs by satellite still takes place mainly indirectly. Electronic signals carrying broadcast programs pass through a satellite to reach remote parts of the globe that cannot be reached by traditional broadcasting; but the programme-carrying signals passed on by the satellite cannot be picked up directly by conventional receivers generally used by the public at large. They first have to be picked up by ground stations, which distribute them to the public.

In the case of direct broadcasting, which is in the process of becoming an everyday occurrence, the signals sent to the satellite are demodulated by the satellite itself; as a result, the signals transmitted down to earth can be received directly from space by ordinary receivers, without the intervention of ground receiving stations. However, the signals transmitted upwards to the satellite remain inaccessible to the public even with this mode of transmission.

The legal problem stems from the wording of Article 3 of the Rome Convention, under which broadcasting means the transmission by wireless means for public reception of sounds or of images and sounds. The difficulties with regard to satellite transmission are twofold: on one hand, the signals emitted by the originating organization are not suitable for public reception; on the other hand, the derived signals, generally obtained by means of ground stations, are frequently transmitted to the public by wire and not by wireless means.

The Satellites Convention provides a solution by requiring Contracting States to take adequate measures to prevent the distribution of any programme-carrying signals by any distributor for whom the signal emitted to or passing through the satellite is not intended. "Distribution" is defined by the Convention as the operation by which a distributor transmits derived signals to the public, and therefore also encompasses cable distribution.

Main Features of the Special Conventions

While it can be said that the Phonograms Convention and the Satellites Convention supplement the Rome Convention to a certain extent, it should nevertheless be mentioned that their approach is different, in three main respects.

First, the Rome Convention gives the beneficiaries of neighboring rights essentially a right to authorization or prohibition, without overlooking the safeguarding of the rights of authors. The Phonograms and Satellites Conventions, on the other hand, do not introduce private rights but rather leave the Contracting States free to choose the legal means of preventing or repressing acts of piracy in that area.

Second, the Rome Convention is based on the "national treatment" principle. That means that the protection prescribed by the Rome Convention is only minimum protection and that, apart from the rights guaranteed by that Convention itself as constituting that minimum of protection, and within the limits of reservations conceded by it, performers, producers of phonograms and broadcasting organizations enjoy the same rights in countries party to the Convention as those countries grant their nationals. The Phonograms Convention does not speak of the system of "national treatment," but defines expressly the unlawful acts against which Contracting States have to provide effective protection; consequently, the States are not bound to grant foreigners protection against all acts prohibited by their national legislation for the protection of their own nationals. For instance, countries whose national legislation provides protection against the public performance of phonograms are not obliged to make this form of protection available to the producers of phonograms of other Contracting States, because the Phonograms Convention does not itself guarantee any protection against the use in public of lawfully reproduced and distributed phonograms. It should be mentioned, however, that even the Phonograms Convention is in no way to be interpreted as limiting the protection available to foreigners under any domestic law or international agreement (Article 7(1)). The question of national treatment does not arise, as a general rule, in the Satellites Convention either. This Convention places Contracting States under the obligation to take the necessary steps to prevent just one type of activity, namely the distribution of programme-carrying signals by any distributor for whom the signals emitted to or passing through the satellite are not intended.

Third, in the interests of combating piracy over the widest possible area, the new international agreements were made open to all States members of the United Nations or any of the specialized organizations brought into relationship with the United Nations, or parties to the Statute of the International Court of Justice (virtually all States of the world). In contrast the Rome Convention is a "closed" Convention, its acceptance being reserved for States party to at least one of the two major international copyright conventions.

Substantive Provisions of the Phonograms Convention

As far as the substantive provisions are concerned, the Phonograms Convention differs from the Rome Convention mainly as regards (i) the criteria of eligibility for protection, (ii) the scope of protection, and (iii) the means of ensuring the protection provided for.

The Phonograms Convention requires only the criterion of nationality as a condition of granting protection. Any Contracting State, however, which on October 29, 1971, afforded protection solely on the basis of the place of first fixation may, by a declaration deposited with the Director General of WIPO, declare that it will apply this criterion.

Protection is granted not only against making duplicates of the phonogram, but also against the distribution of illicit duplicates and importation of such duplicates for distribution (Article 2). On the other hand, the scope of protection does not extend to claiming remuneration for secondary uses of the phonogram.

The means by which the Phonograms Convention is to be implemented are a matter for domestic legislation. They may include protection by granting copyright in the phonogram, by granting other specific (neighboring) rights, by the law relating to unfair competition, or by penal sanctions (Article 3).

The Phonograms Convention permits the same limitations as those accepted in relation to the protection of authors. The Convention also permits compulsory licenses if reproduction is intended exclusively for teaching or scientific research, limited to the territory of the State whose authorities give the license, and in return for equitable remuneration.

Regarding the term of protection, the same minimum duration is required by the Phonograms Convention as by the Rome Convention: if the domestic law prescribes a specific duration for the protection, that duration shall not be less than 20 years from the end either of the year in which the sounds embodied in the phonogram were first fixed or of the year in which the phonogram was first published.

It should be noted that the Phonograms Convention also contains a provision concerning performers. Under its Article 7, the national legislation of each Contracting State may lay down, where necessary, the scope of protection afforded to performers whose performance is fixed on a phonogram and the conditions of enjoying such protection.

Substantive Provisions of the Satellites Convention

The Satellites Convention enlarges the scope of the protection of broadcasting organizations, by suppressing the unlawful distribution of programme-carrying signals transmitted by satellite irrespective of the fact that such signals are not suited to reception by the public, and, consequently, irrespective of the fact that their emission does not constitute broadcasting according to the definition of this notion under the Rome Convention. Furthermore, the protection provided for by the Satellites Convention also applies when the derived signals are distributed by cable and not by wireless means, a kind of communication to the public of broadcasts not covered by the Rome Convention. Formally, however, the Convention gives no new right to the broadcasting organizations. It obliges the Contracting States to prevent the distribution of programme-carrying signals by any distributor for whom the signals passing through the satellite are not intended.

It should be noted that the Satellites Convention does not protect the transmitted program, since the subject of the protection is the signals emitted by the originating organization. As regards the rights related to the programs, the Convention simply lays down that it may not be interpreted in any way as limiting or prejudicing the protection afforded to authors, to performers, to phonogram producers and to broadcasting organizations.

The Satellites Convention permits the distribution of programme-carrying signals by non-authorized persons, if those signals carry short excerpts containing reports of current events or, as quotations, short excerpts of the program carried by the emitted signals, or, in the case of developing countries, if the program carried by the emitted signals is distributed solely for the purposes of teaching, including adult teaching or scientific research.

With regard to the duration of the protection, the Satellites Convention refers to national legislation in this special context. In any State in which the application of the above measures is limited in time, the duration is to be fixed by its domestic law.

The Satellites Convention is not to be applied when the signals emitted by the originating organization are intended for direct reception from a satellite by the public (Article 3). In such cases the signals emitted are not intended for any intervening distributor of derived signals; they are directly accessible to the public at large.

The Phonograms and Satellites Conventions and Developing Countries

It is particularly significant that the States that have joined the Phonograms and Satellites Conventions, as with the countries party to the Rome Convention, are not necessarily highly industrialized market economy States. This may be explained by the role that protection of neighboring rights is capable of playing in the development of those countries: the role of such protection in development, as explained under the Rome Convention . . . is similar where the Phonograms and Satellites Conventions are concerned.

———————

NOTES AND QUESTIONS

(1) **Membership of Neighboring Rights Conventions.** The three neighboring rights conventions described above have considerably smaller memberships than the Berne Convention or the TRIPS Agreement. As of June 1999, the Rome Convention had 61 members, the Geneva Phonograms Convention, 57, and the Brussels Satellite Convention, 23.

(2) **U.S. Accession to Neighboring Rights Conventions.** The United States has joined the Geneva and Brussels Conventions, but not the Rome Convention. What is the explanation for its failure to join Rome?

(3) **The Rights Granted.** How strong is the protection provided to performers by the Rome Convention? Note in particular Article 19, as well as the different formulation of protection for performers in Article 7 as compared to the rights of producers in Article 10 and the rights of broadcasters in Article 13 ("the possibility of preventing" versus "the right to authorise or prohibit"). As a practical matter, what economically significant rights do performers have under the current international treaties?

§ 4.03　Trade and Investment Treaties

[A]　The North American Free Trade Agreement (NAFTA)

**YSOLDE GENDREAU, COPYRIGHT HARMONIZATION IN THE
EUROPEAN UNION AND IN NORTH AMERICA**[*]
20 COLUM.-V.L.A. J.L. & ARTS 37, 42 & 46-48 (1995)

The parties to the NAFTA did not seek to establish a common market, but rather a free trade area. In terms of economic integration, such a structure provides the loosest form of integration . . . .

The NAFTA can best be described as a "mini-GATT." As such, it partakes in the current trend to include intellectual property rules in trade agreements and, unlike the Treaty of Rome, thus contains specific provisions on copyright. Indeed the preamble of the NAFTA declares that the parties have resolved "to promote creativity and innovation and to encourage the trade of goods and services that form the subject of intellectual property rights." Moreover, Article 102 of the agreement states as one of its objectives the effective protection and enforcement of intellectual property rights in the territory of each Party to the agreement. In light of such policy considerations, it is no surprise to see that a whole chapter of the NAFTA is devoted to intellectual property matters.

. . . .

Chapter 17 of the NAFTA comprises twenty-one articles, thirteen of which apply to copyright-related issues. Taken as a whole, they indicate that the goal of the agreement is to ensure compliance with the 1971 text of the Berne Convention and with the 1971 Geneva Convention on Phonograms, as well as to settle some other ad hoc issues that are not solved by these Conventions. In particular, the problem of the enforcement of the exclusive rights seems to have been of great importance.

The first four articles of chapter 17 cover topics of general interest in intellectual property, including fulfillment of the requirements of the international conventions, the possibility of greater protection than that prescribed by the NAFTA, a rule of national treatment, and a provision for control over the misuse of intellectual property rights. Articles 1714 to 1718 pertain to the enforcement of intellectual property rights. The last article of the chapter provides definitions. That leaves only three articles which clearly pertain to substantive copyright-related problems. Two of these address sound recordings and the unauthorized transmission of encrypted satellite signals. Thus, the sole article on copyright per se is article 1705, which contains all the material requirements for the protection of computer programs and databases, the minimal rights to be granted to copyright owners (importation, first distribution, communication to the public, and commercial rental of computer programs), a provision regarding the freedom of contract, term of protection, the exceptions to copyright, and the compulsory licenses that may be granted

---

[*]Copyright 1995, Ysolde Gendreau. Reprinted with permission.

pursuant to the Appendix of the Berne Convention. In all, the NAFTA copyright provisions appear to be a list of specific U.S. demands to its partners to bring their levels of protection in line with what is acceptable to U.S. interests.

There is nothing inherently wrong about a harmonization scheme that seeks to promote the higher standards of one country over less demanding criteria: lower thresholds necessarily breed greater discrepancy and are therefore not desirable if harmonization is indeed the goal. What is more disturbing, however, is the presence of rules that distort the professed intention to harmonize legislation. Three cases come to mind. First, while all three countries must give effect to the Berne Convention, the United States is exempt from Article 6bis on moral rights.[44] Thus, U.S. authors of, say, musical works can rely on the moral rights provisions of Canadian and Mexican legislation, but Canadian and Mexican authors have no clearly equivalent legal texts available to them under U.S. law.[45] Another example can be found in the article on national treatment: material reciprocity becomes the rule for performers' rights in sound recordings with regard to the secondary uses of these recordings because of the lack of such rights in the United States and Canada at the time of the drafting of the Agreement.[46] Lastly, the same article on national treatment, which applies to both the exclusive rights and the enforcement of these rights, is drafted in such a way as to allow for the U.S. registration requirement as a prerequisite for obtaining statutory damages and attorney's fees.[47]

In general, then, the NAFTA has not succeeded in establishing a true consensus on the issues of moral rights, neighboring rights as a whole, and formalities, three topics that are particularly sensitive in countries that belong to the copyright tradition.[48] Contrary to what seems to be taking shape in the European Union, the copyright tradition is clearly emerging as the dominant force in copyright harmonization in North America, a result which cannot come as a surprise.[49]

---

[44]NAFTA Agreement, art. 1701.3

[45]It is beyond the scope of this article to revive the long-standing debate on the existence or lack of substitutes for moral rights legislation in United States law. Suffice it to say that the existence of such a provision gives a rather strong indication that the touted substitutes do not seem to be considered as real equivalents to true moral rights legislation.

[46]NAFTA, art. 1703(1).

[47]See 17 U.S.C. §§ 504 (c), 505 (1994).

[48]In all fairness, however, one must mention that the United States has relented on the issue of copyright notices for films in the sense that the protection of Canadian and Mexican films that had fallen into the public domain in the United States because of a failure to comply with copyright notice requirements are now eligible to be revived. See NAFTA annex 1705.7. In the United States, this requirement of the NAFTA was implemented by Pub. L. No. 103-182, 107 Stat. 2057 (1993), and codified as 17 U.S.C. § 104A in 1993. However, Section 104A was subsequently repealed and replaced as required by the GATT. In Pub. L. No. 103-465, 108 Stat. 4814 (1994), the United States enacted a far broader provision making all Berne Convention works which fell into the public domain in the United States as a result of the failure to comply with United States formalities eligible for renewed copyright, with some restrictions. The new provision is also codified at 17 U.S.C. § 104A (1994).

[49]The most visible, if not the only, concession to the civilian tradition is the separation of the provisions on sound recordings, in article 1706, from those on copyright per se, in article 1705. NAFTA arts. 1705, 1706. Had the copyright position been fully pushed, one would have expected

. . . Th[e] absence of details can perhaps best be explained by the nature of the agreement. The NAFTA operates here like another international treaty: it leaves the bulk of the details to the national legislatures. Moreover, it is not per se a copyright convention like the Berne Convention where, because it is solely aimed at providing an array of copyright standards, it would be of its essence to arrive at as complete a set of rules as possible. The NAFTA is a general trade treaty that must make its niche without encroaching inappropriately upon the subject matter that comes within the domain of other international fora . . . .

. . . Another major difference [from the European approach] stems from the importance that is given in North America to the enforcement of intellectual property rights, including copyright. It can be explained by the fact that the NAFTA "is the first trade agreement of its kind which integrates the economies of developed and developing countries" and that Mexico "did not have a comprehensive enforcement mechanism for intellectual property."

NOTES AND QUESTIONS

(1) **Comparison of NAFTA and TRIPS.** The NAFTA intellectual property provisions were negotiated based on an early draft of the TRIPS Agreement, so the two agreements bear a striking resemblance to each other. Although all three NAFTA signatories are WTO members subject to the TRIPS Agreement, the NAFTA intellectual property provisions remain relevant for several reasons. NAFTA exceeds the protection required by the TRIPS Agreement in important respects: for example, NAFTA has a stronger national treatment obligation, and NAFTA contains shorter transition periods for implementation. (Moreover, NAFTA establishes its own distinct dispute settlement mechanism. *See infra* § 5.05.) What might explain the differences? Are you surprised by the extent of the similarity?

(2) **The Role of Parallel Fora.** What effect would you expect the NAFTA negotiations to have on the development of similar principles in the TRIPS Agreement? If you were responsible for negotiating international copyright agreements on behalf of the United States, how would your negotiating strategy in one forum be affected by developments in the other?

[B]   The TRIPS Agreement

As a broad-based multilateral agreement on intellectual property rights, the TRIPS Agreement was ground-breaking in many respects. Section 1 of Part II of the agreement covers copyright and related rights. It adopts and supplements the norms of the Berne and Rome Conventions in various respects.

First, TRIPS incorporates the substantive obligations of Berne, requiring WTO members to comply with Articles 1 through 21 of the Paris (1971) Act of

the rules pertaining to sound recordings to come under the copyright section.

Berne, as well as the Appendix. TRIPS Agreement art. 9(1). It explicitly excludes from coverage, however, moral rights under Berne article 6*bis*.

Resolving long-standing debates at the international level, the agreement also confirms that computer programs and compilations of data (those that "by reason of the selection or arrangement of their contents constitute intellectual creations") are copyrightable works, subject to protection under Berne. TRIPS Agreement art. 10. In a related provision, it articulates an international version of the idea/expression dichotomy, stating: "Copyright protection shall extend to expressions and not to ideas, procedures, methods of operation or mathematical concepts as such." *Id*. art. 9(2); *cf*. Berne Convention art. 2(8) ("The protection of this Convention shall not apply to news of the day or to miscellaneous facts having the character of mere items of press information").

The agreement adds one new exclusive right not found in the Berne or Rome Conventions: the right to authorize or to prohibit commercial rental to the public. The obligation to provide a rental right is limited, however, to three categories of works: computer programs, cinematographic works, and phonograms. *See* TRIPS Agreement arts. 11, 14(4). Even as to these three categories, the obligation is further limited in various respects. As to cinematographic works, it only applies if "such rental has led to widespread copying of such works which is materially impairing the exclusive right of reproduction in that Member [State]"; as to computer programs, it does not apply to rentals "where the program itself is not the essential object of the rental." *Id*. art. 11. As to phonograms, those member states that had systems of equitable remuneration in place for the rental of phonograms before the conclusion of the agreement may instead maintain such systems as long as the rental "is not giving rise to the material impairment of the exclusive rights of reproduction of right holders." *Id*. art. 14(4).

The agreement requires additional protection of neighboring rights, much along the lines of the Rome Convention. For performers, these rights consist of the possibility of preventing the following unauthorized acts: fixation of an unfixed performance, and the reproduction of such fixation, on a phonogram, as well as broadcasting by wireless means and communication to the public of a live performance. TRIPS Agreement art. 14(1). For producers of phonograms, there is a right to authorize or prohibit direct or indirect reproduction. *Id*. art. 14(2). Broadcasters have the right to prohibit the following unauthorized acts: fixation, reproduction of fixations, and rebroadcasting by wireless means of broadcasts, as well as communication to the public of television broadcasts of the same. *Id*. art. 14(3). Providing these rights to broadcasters, however, is not entirely obligatory; member states have the option instead to "provide owners of copyright in the subject matter of broadcasts with the possibility of preventing" these acts. *Id*.

No specific exceptions or limitations are provided. Rather, the agreement generalizes for all exclusive rights the three-step test applied to the reproduction right under article 9(2) of the Berne Convention. *See* TRIPS Agreement art. 13. In the case of related rights other than rental, it also explicitly permits member states to apply conditions, limitations, exceptions, and reservations to the extent permitted by the Rome Convention. *Id*. art. 14(6).

The agreement further provides a minimum term of protection for those works for which the term is calculated on a basis other than the life of a natural person: fifty years from the end of the calendar year of authorized publication, or, if not published within fifty years, fifty years from the end of the calendar year of their making. *See* TRIPS Agreement art. 12. For performers and producers of phonograms, the term is fifty years from the end of the calendar year of the fixation or performance; for broadcasters, twenty years from the end of the calendar year of the broadcast. *Id.* art. 14(5).

Finally, retroactive protection is required for related rights as well as copyright—that is, the treaty obligations apply to preexisting subject matter whose term of protection has not yet expired in the country of origin. *See* TRIPS Agreement arts. 9(1), 14(6).

NOTES AND QUESTIONS

(1) **General TRIPS Obligations**. Other elements of the TRIPS Agreement are also critical to the protection of copyright and related rights, but are not specific to those areas, applying to all forms of intellectual property. These include the requirement not only of national treatment but MFN treatment, *see supra* § 2.06, and the promotion of "transparency" through obligations to "notify" virtually every aspect of a country's relevant laws and regulations, and to respond to questions on those laws and regulations. The most important aspect of TRIPS, however, is that it supplies key elements lacking in Berne: mechanisms for enforcement of rights and for adjudication of disputes between member states over the adequacy of their implementation of treaty obligations. *See infra* § 5.03.

(2) **Grace Periods**. The TRIPS obligations in the area of copyright and related rights took effect for developed countries on January 1, 1996. Grace periods were provided for developing and least developed countries, which were not obligated fully to implement the copyright provisions of TRIPS until the years 2000 and 2006, respectively.

(3) **TRIPS Council Review**. In furtherance of the transparency goals of the TRIPS Agreement, a process was also established for countries to review each others' laws in the TRIPS Council. The first such review took place in July 1996, and covered the copyright and related rights laws of the developed countries. *See supra* § 2.03[B]. A description of the procedure followed and the substance of the questions posed by and to the United States can be found in Shira Perlmutter, *Copyright and International TRIPS Compliance*, 8 FORDHAM INT. PROP., MEDIA & ENT. L.J. 83 (1997). Two issues that were the subject of numerous questions on all sides were (1) how retroactive protection for existing works and subject matter of neighboring rights was implemented in national legislation, and (2) the scope of exceptions and limitations to rights. Both of these issues have since given rise to the first copyright disputes in the World Trade Organization; these disputes are discussed in the following section.

[1] Retroactive Protection for Pre-existing Works

MATTHIJS GEUZE AND HANNU WAGER, WTO DISPUTE SETTLEMENT PRACTICE RELATING TO THE TRIPS AGREEMENT*
2 J. Int'l Economic L. 347 (1999)

The first WTO dispute settlement case involving the TRIPS Agreement concerned the protection of phonograms (or sound recordings). The United States requested on 9 February 1996 consultations with Japan, claiming that Japan's legal regime for the protection of sound recordings appeared to be inconsistent with, *inter alia*, Articles 14 and 70 of the TRIPS Agreement. The European Communities and their member states joined these consultations.

By means of a communication dated 24 May 1996, the European Communities and their member states requested consultations with Japan on the same matter. In its complaint, the EC argued that by virtue of the TRIPS Agreement, particularly its Articles 14.6 and 70.2 in conjunction with Article 18 of the Berne Convention (1971), WTO Members were required to protect producers and performers of sound recordings for a period of 50 years from the end of the year in which the fixation was made or the performance took place and which had not yet fallen into the public domain. According to the complaint, this meant in practice that works which had come into existence since 1 January 1946 had to be given TRIPS level protection for the remainder of the 50-year period because the TRIPS Agreement became effective for the developed country Members of the WTO on 1 January 1996. The Japanese TRIPS legislation implementing the respective obligations (Law No. 112 of 1994) only provided for protection of those sound recordings produced after 1 January 1971. In the view of the EC, the Japanese legislation was therefore not compatible with Japan's obligations under the TRIPS Agreement, since it did not extend the protection of sound recordings produced in the time period between 1 January 1946 and 1 January 1971. The United States joined these consultations.

Both complaints appeared to deal with the interpretation of the provisions that determine how Member countries should protect the rights of performers and producers of phonograms in phonograms that existed at the date of application of the Agreement for the Member in question. Article 9.1 of the TRIPS Agreement obliges WTO Members to comply with Article 18 of the Berne Convention (1971). Article 14.6 of the Agreement provides that the provisions of Article 18 of the Berne Convention (1971) shall also apply, *mutatis mutandis*, to the rights of performers and producers of phonograms in existing phonograms. Article 70.2 of the Agreement further clarifies that in respect of paragraphs 2, 3 and 4 of Article 70 of the Agreement, copyright obligations with respect to existing works shall be solely determined under Article 18 of the Berne Convention (1971), and obligations with respect to the rights of producers of phonograms and performers in existing phonograms shall be determined solely under Article 18 of the Berne Convention (1971) as made applicable

---

under Article 14.6 of the Agreement.

Article 18 of the Berne Convention provides that the Convention shall apply to all works which, at the moment of its coming into force, have not yet fallen into the public domain in the country of origin through the expiry of the term of protection. If, however, through the expiry of the term of protection which was previously granted, a work has fallen into the public domain of the country where protection is claimed, that work shall not be protected anew. The application of this principle is subject to any provisions contained in special conventions to that effect existing or to be concluded between countries of the Union. In the absence of such provisions, the respective countries shall determine, each in so far as it is concerned, the conditions of application of this principle.

The United States and Japan informed the DSB on 24 January 1997 that they had reached a mutually agreed solution to the dispute. On 7 November 1997, the EC and Japan notified a mutually agreed solution. As regards the issues dealt with in these two notifications, we will quote only from the latter notification:

> The Community and its Member States requested consultations in the belief that the TRIPS Agreement requires Members of the World Trade Organization (WTO) to grant protection to performers first performing in a WTO Member and to producers of sound recordings first fixed in a WTO Member or fixed by a national of a WTO Member for a term of at least 50 years from the end of the calendar year in which the fixation was made or the performance took place and that this term of protection should extend to those existing recordings which have not yet fallen into the public domain in the country of origin or in the country where protection is sought.

> On 26 December 1996, the Government of Japan promulgated amendments to the Japanese Copyright Law, which entered into force on 25 March 1997 (Law No. 117). These amendments are intended to provide the above-described protection to performers and producers of sound recordings.

United States Department of Commerce
Patent and Trademark Office
Assistant Secretary and Commissioner
of Patents and Trademarks
Washington, DC 20231

Nov. 23, 1998

Dr. Kamil Idris
Director General
World Intellectual Property Organization
34, chemin des Colombettes
1211 Geneva 20
Switzerland

Dear Dr. Idris:

I am writing to you seeking the expertise of WIPO on a matter of great importance to the United States. In ongoing bilateral and multilateral consultations undertaken by the United States, the extent of the rights and obligations concerning the protection of existing works under Article 18 of the Berne Convention for the Protection of Literary and Artistic Works continue to surface. . . . To further our consideration of those issues, I would appreciate the further informal views of the International Bureau of WIPO. Of course, we are not requesting any "official interpretation" of the Berne Convention by the International Bureau; but, we are very interested in your informal views.

In particular, we are concerned about the treatment of certain works of U.S. origin in other Berne Union countries in light of the obligations of Article 18. Our concern is that U.S. works that may have fallen into the public domain in the United States solely as a result of noncompliance with our former formality-based copyright system may be denied a full term of protection in other Berne Union countries. At the core, it seems to us that the failure of an author to adhere to prior Berne-incompatible formalities such as notice, original registration or, in particular, renewal registration in the United States should not prevent that work from enjoying a full term of copyright protection in other Berne Union countries, even though such work may no longer enjoy protection in the U.S. At issue is the application of Articles 18, 5 and 7 of Berne to such works of U.S. origin.

The United States provides a very generous and Article 18-compatible form of full protection for all pre-existing, non-U.S. works from Berne Union and World Trade Organization (WTO) countries, including the restoration of protection for all such works which previously fell into the public domain in the United States because of failure to comply with formalities. We believe, therefore, that interpretations of Article 18 obligations by other countries that would cut short the term of protection for similarly situated U.S. works would be unfair and incompatible with their Berne obligations.

This restored protection in the U.S. is provided to works of origin other than the United States without any reciprocal or comparison of term obligations. Under 17 U.S.C. § 104A, effective January 1, 1996, all qualifying Berne and WTO works are granted the remainder of the U.S. term of protection they would have enjoyed had not they fallen into the U.S. public domain for failure to comply with U.S. formalities such as copyright notice, original registration or renewal. The term of protection for both foreign and domestic works has recently been extended to a minimum of the life of the author and 70 years or 95 years from publication for works made for hire. As a result the term of protection for subsisting foreign copyrights under section 104A would be 95 years for purposes of comparison of term.

In order to assist in framing the issues, we suggest as an example, a work of U.S. origin which was created in 1940 and first published in the United States in 1940. Given the time of its creation, such a work would have been subject to the 1909 U.S. Copyright Act. The 1909 Act conditioned copyright protection upon the observance of formalities, including, among other things, the use of a copyright notice upon publication and the timely filing of an original and a renewal registration, including proper filing of an application, deposit and fee. If a copyright owner failed to use a copyright notice upon publication, under certain conditions the work fell into the public domain. If a copyright owner did use proper notice but failed to file an original or a timely renewal registration application accompanied by the fee, copyright protection for that work was terminated, and could not be revived. Such a work created in 1940 thus would have fallen into the public domain in the U.S. at the end of the twenty-eighth year; in this example, in 1968 unless the formalities were observed. By contrast, if registration, renewal and all other formalities were properly followed, such a work from 1940 would be protected in the U.S. for a full term of 95 years from publication, that is, until 2035.

Our concern now, and our reason for writing you, is to seek your opinion on whether a work whose country of origin is the United States that may be in public domain in the United States for failure to comply with any of our old formalities, would be entitled to a "full term" of protection in other Berne Union countries. This "full term," we believe, should be provided so that where the comparison of terms rule is applicable, the U.S. term used for that comparison is not less than 95 years from the date of first publication.

The question is how application of Articles 5, 7 and especially 18, require other Berne Union countries to treat such a work in their territories. We believe that under the cited articles, other Berne Union countries are obligated to extend a "full term" of protection to such existing works, regardless of their public domain status in the United States. We would appreciate receiving your views on this important matter.

Sincerely,

Robert L. Stoll
Administrator, Office of Legislative and International Affairs

World Intellectual Property Organization

December 17, 1998

Mr. Robert L. Stoll
Administrator, Office of Legislative and International Affairs
United States Patent and Trademark Office
Department of Commerce
Washington, D.C. 20231
United States of America

Dear Mr. Stoll:

I have received your letter of November 23, 1998, addressed to the Director
General of the World Intellectual Property Organization (WIPO), in which you
have asked the International Bureau of WIPO to provide its informal view on
a specific issue of the application of Article 18 of the Berne Convention. The
International Bureau has the pleasure to be at the disposal of your office in
expressing its views on this issue, on the understanding—also indicated in your
letter—that the views expressed should not be considered an "official
interpretation" of the Convention. As I understand, you have referred to the
following legal situation under the legislation of the United States of America

(i) Under the Copyright Act of 1909, statutory copyright protection
was subject to the condition of certain formalities (copyright notice,
registration), and under its section 24, it endured for 28 years from
the date of first publication and for a further period of 28 years also
subject to a formality, namely to the registration of an application for
the renewal and extension of the term of protection at the Copyright
Office within one year prior to the expiration of the first 28 years.
The section provided that "in default of the registration of such
application for renewal and extension, the copyright in any work shall
determine at the expiration of twenty-eight years from first
publication."

(ii) In respect of works which were in the first 28 years of the term of
statutory protection on January 1, 1978, section 304 of the Copyright
Act of 1976 extended the second 28 year period to 47 years; the
conditions of renewal and extension of the duration of protection
remained the same.

(iii) When the United States adhered to the Berne Convention, the
Berne Implementation Act of 1988 divided pre-existing works into two
categories: those still protected by copyright and those in the public
domain in the United States of America. With regard to the first

category, the Act provided transitional provisions in harmony with the Convention, but, with regard to the other category, it did not resuscitate the works concerned from the public domain. It also eliminated formalities as conditions of protection.

(iv)   The Act to Implement the Results of the Uruguay Round of Multilateral Trade Negotiations of 1994, by its section 514 on "Restored Works" amended section 104A of the Copyright Law (Title 17 of the United States Code) as a result of which non-U.S. pre-existing works that had failed to comply with U.S. formalities, and therefore had fallen into the public domain in the United States, received retroactive protection. Under that legislation, effective January 1, 1996, all works enjoying protection through the Berne Convention and/or the TRIPS Agreement are granted retroactively the remaining term of protection of the 28+47=75 year term. This retroactive protection, however, does not extend to pre-existing U.S. works; they have remained in the public domain.

(v)   Recently, under the "Sonny Bono Copyright Term Extension Act" of 1998, the above-mentioned term was extended by 20 years to 95 years.

It is against this background that you have outlined the issue as [excerpted above] . . . .

I do agree with you that especially Article 18 of the Berne Convention is relevant in this context, the text of which is as follows:

> (1) This Convention shall apply to all works which, at the moment of its coming into force, have not yet fallen into the public domain in the country of origin through the expiry of the term of protection.
>
> (2) If, however, through the expiry of the term of protection which was previously granted, a work has fallen into the public domain of the country where protection is claimed, that work shall not be protected anew.
>
> (3) The application of this principle shall be subject to any provisions contained in special conventions to that effect existing or to be concluded between countries of the Union. In the absence of such provisions, the respective countries shall determine, each in so far as its is concerned, the conditions of application of this principle.
>
> (4) The preceding provisions shall also apply in the case of new accessions to the Union and to cases in which protection is extended by the application of Article 7 or by the abandonment of reservations.

. . . From the viewpoint of the issue raised by you, the interpretation of paragraph (1) of the above-quoted Article seems to be particularly important, since the fundamental question is whether or not the Convention is applicable for certain works whose country of origin is the United States of America and which are in the public domain there; that is, whether or not the other countries party to the Convention and/or Members of the World Trade Organization (WTO) (the latter, of course, subject to the transitional provisions) are obliged to protect such works.

As quoted above, under its paragraph (1) of Article 18, the Convention obliges the countries party to the Convention to protect all works which "at the moment of its coming into force, have not yet fallen into the public domain in the country of origin through the expiry of the term of protection." (Paragraph (4) makes it clear that this provision is also applicable in the case of new accessions to the Convention.)

In respect of those works which, due to the non-compliance with formalities (such as the requirement of publication with notice), have never been protected, it is clear that they "have not fallen into the public domain . . . *through the expiry of the term of protection*" (emphasis added) since there has been no term of protection applicable for them. Thus, . . . in such a case it is a clear obligation of the other countries party to the Convention and/or Members of WTO to protect such works.

This is also underlined by Article 5(2) which contains both the principle of formality-free protection and the principle of "independence of protection" and which reads as follows:

> (2) The enjoyment and the exercise of these rights shall not be subject to any formality; such enjoyment and such exercise shall be independent of the existence of protection in the country of origin of the work. Consequently, apart from the provisions of this Convention, the extent of protection, as well as the means of redress afforded to the author to protect his rights, shall be governed exclusively by the laws of the country where protection is claimed."

I believe that, if any questions may emerge concerning the application of Article 18(1) of the Convention in respect of works whose country of origin is the United States of America and which are in the public domain in the United States, then such a question may only concern those works which were protected for 28 years under the law referred to in point (i) but then fell into the public domain because no application was registered in due time for the renewal and extension of protection for the remaining 28 years, or later, for the remaining 47 (which became 67 years under the new U.S. law) years, of the duration of protection. In such a case also, the test which should be applied is the question of whether the works concerned have fallen into the public domain through the expiry of the term of protection or for some other reason, for example for non-compliance with a formality.

The provisions referred to in points (i) and (ii) are clear in this respect. Under the Copyright Act of 1909, the duration of protection was 28+28 years, and, under the Copyright Act of 1976, it was 29+47 (now 67). The second period, however, was subject to the fulfillment of a further formality, namely the registration of an application. It is obvious that the reason for the falling into the public domain of the works concerned was not that the cumulative term of protection was over; the only and exclusive reason was the non-compliance with a formality. Thus, the works did not fall into the public domain through the expiry of the term available under the law, but due to another reason. Therefore, subject to the provisions of the Convention concerning the term of protection and national treatment, the other countries party to the Convention and/or Members of WTO are obliged to apply the provisions of the Convention for such works.

The same interpretation of the phrase "expiry of the term of protection" is to be given also in the context of Article 18(2) of the Berne Convention. Accordingly, if a work of United States origin was previously not protected in a country due to the comparison of terms principle which was in effect prior to the adherence of the United States to the Berne Convention (such as that found in the Universal Copyright Convention) and the country's failure to protect such a work under such a principle was due to the work's falling into the public domain in the United States for failure to observe formalities, then such previous denial of protection under such circumstances does not exempt a country from being required to provide protection under Article 18(2). . . .

Turning now to the issue of the duration of protection of such works which the other countries party to the Convention and/or Members of WTO are obliged to grant, as you have rightly indicated in your letter, it is clear that Articles 5 and 7 of the Convention are applicable.

Article 5(1) of the Convention provides as follows:

> (1) Authors shall enjoy, in respect of works for which they are protected under this Convention, in countries of the Union other than the country of origin, the rights which their respective laws do now or may hereafter grant to their nationals, as well as the rights specially granted by this Convention.

Article 7(8) confirms this principle, but, at the same time, it also introduces a possible exception, as follows:

> (8) In any case, the term shall be governed by the legislation of the country where protection is claimed; however, unless the legislation of that country otherwise provides, the term shall not exceed the term fixed in the country of origin of the work.

The question is which term should be considered "the term fixed in the country of origin of the work" from the viewpoint of the above-quoted provision in the case of a work whose country of origin is the United States of America, and which, for the reasons of non-fulfillment of formalities, is in the public domain (either because it has never been protected due to the non-compliance with formalities at the time of its publication or because it has fallen into the public domain due to the non-compliance with a formality (registration) necessary for the continuation of the protection until the end of its cumulative duration).

I believe that the answer to this question is obvious, namely that that term should be considered to be "the term fixed in the country of origin of the work" which would be applicable provided that the formalities would have been complied with (or put in another way, provided that the formalities would not have existed). I do agree with you that the best way is through an example to present these issues and the solutions thereof. Let us use the example you refer to in your letter. [The Deputy Director General quoted the example from the Stoll letter.]

As I have indicated, in the cases where a work has fallen into the public domain through the non-compliance with formalities, the "term fixed in the country of origin of the work" should be considered that term which would be applicable provided that the formalities would have been fulfilled (or would not have existed). Therefore, in the case of the example outlined by you, the "term fixed in the country of origin of the work" is 95 years from publication, that is, it lasts until 2035. This is the term which should be taken into account by the other countries party to the Berne Convention and/or Members of the WTO when they apply the principle of "comparison of terms" provided for in Article 7(8) of the Berne Convention.

I hope that these informal views will be useful for you. We remain at your disposal for any further clarifications you may wish to have.

Sincerely yours,

Shozo Uemura
Deputy Director General

Notes and Questions

(1) **The Value of Old Works**. The works used in the example offered by the United States were fifty years old at the time. Why would the United States be concerned about such antique works?

(2) **U.S. Implementation of Article 18**. The United States restored copyright in foreign works that had fallen into the public domain as of January 1, 1996. *See* 17 U.S.C. § 104A. But the United States adhered to the Berne Convention in 1989; the Berne Convention Implementation Act of 1988 contained no such restoration provisions. What is the explanation for this delay in implementing Article 18 of Berne?

(3) **WIPO Views**. Both the United States and WIPO were careful to stress that WIPO was only giving its "informal views" on the issue of Article 18, and that it was not offering "an official interpretation" of the Berne Convention. Why? Given this caveat, what is likely to be the impact of the WIPO letter, and why did the United States seek such "informal views"? Should WIPO offer

authoritative interpretations? To do so, how would the organization have to change?

[2] Exceptions and Limitations

UNITED STATES—SECTION 110(5) OF THE U.S. COPYRIGHT ACT
Report of the Panel (WTO DSB, June 15, 2000), WT/DS160/R

II. Factual Aspects

The dispute concerns Section 110(5) of the US Copyright Act of 1976, as amended by the Fairness in Music Licensing Act of 1998 ("the 1998 Amendment"), which entered into force on 26 January 1999. The provisions of Section 110(5) place limitations on the exclusive rights provided to owners of copyright in Section 106 of the Copyright Act in respect of certain performances and displays.

. . . .

Subparagraph (A) of Section 110(5) essentially reproduces the text of the original "homestyle" exemption contained in Section 110(5) of the Copyright Act of 1976 [which exempted communication of a transmission embodying a performance of a work by the "public reception of the transmission on a single receiving apparatus of a kind commonly used in private homes" provided that no direct charge was made to see or hear the transmission and that the transmission was not further transmitted to the public.] When Section 110(5) was amended in 1998, the homestyle exemption was moved to a new subparagraph (A) and the words "except as provided in subparagraph (B)" were added to the beginning of the text.

A House Report (1976) accompanying the Copyright Act of 1976 explained that in its original form Section 110(5) "applies to performances and displays of all types of works, and its purpose is to exempt from copyright liability anyone who merely turns on, in a public place, an ordinary radio or television receiving apparatus of a kind commonly sold to members of the public for private use". "The basic rationale of this clause is that the secondary use of the transmission by turning on an ordinary receiver in public is so remote and minimal that no further liability should be imposed." "[The clause] would impose liability where the proprietor has a commercial 'sound system' installed or converts a standard home receiving apparatus (by augmenting it with sophisticated or extensive amplification equipment) into the equivalent of a commercial sound system."[10] A subsequent Conference Report (1976) elaborated on the rationale by noting that the intent was to exempt a small commercial establishment "which was not

---

[10]These quotations are from the Report of the House Committee on the Judiciary, H.R. Rep. No. 94-1476, 94th Cong., 2nd Sess. 87 (1976). The Report adds that "[f]actors to consider in particular cases would include the size, physical arrangement, and noise level of the areas within the establishment where the transmissions are made audible or visible, and the extent to which the receiving apparatus is altered or augmented for the purpose of improving the aural or visual quality of the performance".

of sufficient size to justify, as a practical matter, a subscription to a commercial background music service".

The factors to consider in applying the exemption are largely based on the facts of a case decided by the United States Supreme Court immediately prior to the passage of the 1976 Copyright Act. In *Aiken*,[12] the Court held that an owner of a small fast food restaurant was not liable for playing music by means of a radio with outlets to four speakers in the ceiling; the size of the shop was 1,055 square feet (98 m^2), of which 620 square feet (56 m^2) were open to the public. The House Report (1976) describes the factual situation in *Aiken* as representing the "outer limit of the exemption" contained in the original Section 110(5). This exemption became known as the "homestyle" exemption.

As indicated in the quotation [from the House Report above], the homestyle exemption was originally intended to apply to performances of all types of works. However, given that the present subparagraph (B) applies to "a performance or display of a nondramatic musical work", the parties agree, by way of an *a contrario* interpretation, that the effect of the introductory phrase "except as provided in subparagraph (B)", that was added to the text in subparagraph (A), is that it narrows down the application of subparagraph (A) to works other than "nondramatic musical works".

The Panel notes that it is the common understanding of the parties that the expression "nondramatic musical works" in subparagraph (B) excludes from its application the communication of music that is part of an opera, operetta, musical or other similar dramatic work when performed in a dramatic context. All other musical works are covered by that expression, including individual songs taken from dramatic works when performed outside of any dramatic context. Subparagraph (B) would, therefore, apply for example to an individual song taken from a musical and played on the radio. Consequently, the operation of subparagraph (A) is limited to such musical works as are not covered by subparagraph (B), for example a communication of a broadcast of a dramatic rendition of the music written for an opera.

The 1998 Amendment has added a new subparagraph (B) to Section 110(5), to which we, for the sake of brevity, hereinafter refer to as a "business" exemption. It exempts, under certain conditions, communication by an establishment of a transmission or retransmission embodying a performance or display of a nondramatic musical work intended to be received by the general public, originated by a radio or television broadcast station licensed as such by the Federal Communications Commission, or, if an audiovisual transmission, by a cable system or satellite carrier.

The beneficiaries of the business exemption are divided into two categories: establishments other than food service or drinking establishments ("retail establishments"), and food service and drinking establishments. In each category, establishments under a certain size limit are exempted, regardless of the type of equipment they use. The size limits are 2,000 gross square feet (186 m^2) for retail establishments and 3,750 gross square feet (348 m^2) for restaurants.

---

[12]Twentieth Century Music Corp. v. Aiken, 422 U.S. 151 (1975).

. . . .

If the size of an establishment is above the[se] limits . . . (there is no maximum size), the exemption applies provided that the establishment does not exceed the limits set for the equipment used. The limits on equipment [which relate to the number and location of loudspeakers and screen size] are different as regards, on the one hand, audio performances, and, on the other hand, audiovisual performances and displays. The rules concerning equipment limitations are the same for both retail establishments and restaurants above the respective size limits. [Regardless of the size or nature of the establishment, the exemption applies only if no direct charge was made to see or hear the transmission and if the transmission was not further transmitted to the public.]

The types of transmissions covered by both subparagraphs (A) and (B) of Section 110(5) include original broadcasts over the air or by satellite, rebroadcasts by terrestrial means or by satellite, cable retransmissions of original broadcasts, and original cable transmissions or other transmissions by wire. The provisions do not distinguish between analog and digital transmissions.

Section 110(5) does not apply to the use of recorded music, such as CDs or cassette tapes, or to live performances of music.

Holders of copyright in musical works (composers, lyricists and music publishers) normally entrust the licensing of nondramatic public performance of their works to collective management organizations ("CMOs" or performing rights organizations). The three main CMOs in the United States in this area are ASCAP, the Broadcast Music, Inc. (BMI) and SESAC, Inc. CMOs license the public performance of musical works to users of music, such as retail establishments and restaurants, on behalf of the individual right holders they represent, collect licence fees from such users, and distribute revenues as royalties to the respective right holders. They normally enter into reciprocal arrangements with the CMOs of other countries to license the works of the right holders represented by them. Revenues are distributed to individual right holders through the CMOs that represent the right holders in question. The above-mentioned three US CMOs license nondramatic public performances of musical works, including nondramatic renditions of "dramatic" musical works.

. . . .

VI. FINDINGS

. . . .

D. SUBSTANTIVE ASPECTS OF THE DISPUTE

1. General considerations about the exclusive rights concerned and limitations thereto

(a) *Exclusive rights implicated by the EC claims*

Articles 9–13 of Section 1 of Part II of the TRIPS Agreement entitled

"Copyright and Related Rights" deal with the substantive standards of copyright protection. Article 9.1 of the TRIPS Agreement obliges WTO Members to comply with Articles 1–21 of the Berne Convention (1971) (with the exception of Article 6*bis* on moral rights and the rights derived therefrom) and the Appendix thereto. The European Communities alleges that subparagraphs (A) and (B) of Section 110(5) are inconsistent primarily with Article 11*bis*(1)(iii) but also with Article 11(1)(ii) of the Berne Convention (1971) as incorporated into the TRIPS Agreement.

We note that through their incorporation, the substantive rules of the Berne Convention (1971), including the provisions of its Articles 11*bis*(1)(iii) and 11(1)(ii), have become part of the TRIPS Agreement and as provisions of that Agreement have to be read as applying to WTO Members.

  (i) Article 11*bis* of the Berne Convention (1971)

The provision of particular relevance for this dispute is Article 11*bis*(1)(iii). Article 11*bis*(1) provides:

> Authors of literary and artistic works shall enjoy the exclusive right of authorizing:
> (i) the broadcasting of their works or the communication thereof to the public by any other means of wireless diffusion of signs, sounds or images;
> (ii) any communication to the public by wire or by re-broadcasting of the broadcast of the work, when this communication is made by an organization other than the original one;
> (iii)   the public communication by loudspeaker or any other analogous instrument transmitting, by signs, sounds or images, the broadcast of the work.

In the light of Article 2 of the Berne Convention (1971), "artistic" works in the meaning of Article 11*bis*(1) include nondramatic and other musical works. Each of the subparagraphs of Article 11*bis*(1) confers a separate exclusive right; exploitation of a work in a manner covered by any of these subparagraphs requires an authorization by the right holder. For example, the communication to the public of a broadcast creates an additional audience and the right holder is given control over, and may expect remuneration from, this new public performance of his or her work.

The right provided under subparagraph (i) of Article 11*bis*(1) is to authorize the broadcasting of a work and the communication thereof to the public by any other means of wireless diffusion of signs, sounds or images. It applies to both radio and television broadcasts. Subparagraph (ii) concerns the subsequent use of this emission; the authors' exclusive right covers any communication to the public by wire or by rebroadcasting of the broadcast of the work, when the communication is made by an organization other than the original one.

Subparagraph (iii) provides an exclusive right to authorize the public communication of the broadcast of the work by loudspeaker, on a television screen, or by other similar means. Such communication involves a new public performance of a work contained in a broadcast, which requires a licence from the right holder.[33] For the purposes of this dispute, the claims raised by the European Communities under Article 11*bis*(1) are limited to subparagraph (iii).

(ii) Article 11 of the Berne Convention (1971)

Of relevance to this dispute are also the exclusive rights conferred by Article 11(1)(ii) of the Berne Convention (1971). Article 11(1) provides:

> Authors of dramatic, dramatico-musical and musical works shall enjoy the exclusive right of authorizing:
> (i) the public performance of their works, including such public performance by any means or process;
> (ii) any communication to the public of the performance of their works.

As in the case of Article 11*bis*(1) of the Berne Convention (1971), which concerns broadcasting to the public and communication of a broadcast to the public, the exclusive rights conferred by Article 11 cover *public* performance; private performance does not require authorization. Public performance includes performance by any means or process, such as performance by means of recordings (e.g., CDs, cassettes and videos).[35] It also includes communication to the public of a performance of the work. The claims raised by the European Communities under Article 11(1) of the Berne Convention (1971) are limited to its subparagraph (ii).

Regarding the relationship between Articles 11 and 11*bis*, we note that the rights conferred in Article 11(1)(ii) concern the communication to the public of performances of works in general. Article 11*bis*(1)(iii) is a specific rule

---

[33]The Guide to the Berne Convention, published by WIPO in 1978 ("Guide to the Berne Convention") gives the following explanation on the situation covered by Article 11*bis*(1)(iii): "This case is becoming more common. In places where people gather (cafés, restaurants, tea-rooms, hotels, large shops, trains, aircraft, etc.) the practice is growing of providing broadcast programmes. . . . The question is whether the licence given by the author to the broadcasting station covers, in addition, all the use made of the broadcast, which may or many not be for commercial ends. . . . The Convention's answer is 'no'. Just as, in the case of a relay of a broadcast by wire, an additional audience is created (paragraph (1)(ii)), so, in this case, too, the work is made perceptible to listeners (and perhaps to viewers) other than those contemplated by the author when his permission was given. Although, by definition, the number of people receiving a broadcast cannot be ascertained with any certainty, the author thinks of his licence to broadcast as covering only the direct audience receiving the signal within the family circle. Once this reception is done in order to entertain a wider circle, often for profit, an additional section of the public is enabled to enjoy the work and it ceases to be merely a matter of broadcasting. The author is given control over this new public performance of his work." *See* Guide to the Berne Convention, paragraphs 11*bis*.11 and 11*bis*.12, p. 68-69.

[35] However, public performance by means of cinematographic works is separately covered in Article 14(1)(ii) of the Berne Convention. Public performance of a literary work or communication to the public of the recitation is covered by Article 11*ter* of the Berne Convention.

conferring exclusive rights concerning the public communication by loudspeaker or any other analogous instrument transmitting, by signs, sounds or images, the broadcast of a work.

[T]he European Communities raises claims against Section 110(5) primarily under Article 11*bis*(1)(iii), which covers the communication to the public of a broadcast which has been transmitted at some point by hertzian waves. But the EC claims also relate to Article 11(1)(ii) to the extent that a communication to the public concerns situations where the entire transmission has been by wire.

We share the understanding of the parties that a communication to the public by loudspeaker of a performance of a work transmitted by means other than hertzian waves is covered by the exclusive rights conferred by Article 11(1) of the Berne Convention (1971).[36] Moreover, we note that both parties consider that it is the third exclusive right under Article 11*bis*(1)(iii)—i.e., the author's right to authorize the public communication of a broadcast of a work by loudspeaker or any other analogous instrument—which is primarily concerned in this dispute. But we also note that there is no disagreement between the parties that both subparagraphs (A) and (B) of Section 110(5) implicate both Articles 11*bis*(1)(iii) and 11(1)(ii)—albeit to a varying extent.

Both provisions, i.e., Articles 11*bis*(1)(iii) and 11(1)(ii) of the Berne Convention (1971) are implicated only if there is a *public* element to the broadcasting or communication operation. We note that it is undisputed between the parties that playing radio or television music by establishments covered by Section 110(5) involves a communication that is available to the *public* in the sense of Articles 11*bis*(1)(iii) and 11(1)(ii) of the Berne Convention (1971). We share this view of the parties.

As noted above, the United States acknowledges that subparagraphs (A) and (B) of Section 110(5) implicate Articles 11*bis*(1)(iii) and 11(1)(ii) of the Berne Convention (1971). Consequently, the core question before this Panel is which of the exceptions under the TRIPS Agreement invoked are relevant to this dispute and whether the conditions for their invocation are met so as to justify the exemptions under subparagraphs (A) and (B) of Section 110(5) of the US Copyright Act.

(b) *Limitations and exceptions*

(i) Introduction

. . . .

Article 13 of the TRIPS Agreement, entitled "Limitations and Exceptions", is

---

[36] In this respect we recall the explanation given in the Guide to the Berne Convention: "The communication to the public of a performance of the work . . . covers all public communication except broadcasting which is dealt with in Article 11*bis*. For example, a broadcasting organisation broadcasts a chamber concert—Article 11*bis* applies. But if it or some other body diffuses the music by landline to subscribers, this is a matter for Article 11." Guide to the Berne Convention, paragraph 11.5, p. 65.

the general exception clause applicable to exclusive rights of the holders of copyright. It provides:

> Members shall confine limitations or exceptions to exclusive rights to certain special cases which do not conflict with a normal exploitation of the work and do not unreasonably prejudice the legitimate interests of the right holder.

. . . .

(iii) The minor exceptions doctrine

. . . .

[T]he US view is that Article 13 of the TRIPS Agreement clarifies and articulates the scope of the minor exceptions doctrine, which is applicable under the TRIPS Agreement. Before considering the applicability of Article 13 to Articles 11*bis*(1)(iii) and 11(1)(ii) of the Berne Convention (1971) as incorporated into the TRIPS Agreement, we will first examine whether the minor exceptions doctrine applies under the TRIPS Agreement. This examination involves a two-step analysis. As the first step, we analyse to what extent this doctrine forms part of the Berne Convention *acquis*; in doing so, we will also consider the different views of the parties as to the scope of the doctrine. The second step is to analyse whether that doctrine, if we were to find that it applies under certain Articles of the Berne Convention (1971), has been incorporated into the TRIPS Agreement, by virtue of Article 9.1 of that Agreement, together with Articles 1–21 of the Berne Convention (1971).

. . . .

The legal status of the minor exceptions doctrine under the Berne Convention

. . . .

We note that, in addition to the explicit provisions on permissible limitations and exceptions to the exclusive rights embodied in the text of the Berne Convention (1971), the reports of successive revision conferences of that Convention refer to "implied exceptions" allowing member countries to provide limitations and exceptions to certain rights. The so-called "minor reservations" or "minor exceptions" doctrine is being referred to in respect of the right of public performance and certain other exclusive rights.[57] Under that doctrine, Berne Union members may provide minor exceptions to the rights provided, *inter alia*, under Articles 11*bis* and 11 of the Berne Convention (1971).

. . . .

---

[57]The other main category of implied exceptions are understood to apply to the use of translations of literary works.

With respect to public performance of works, until 1948 only a national treatment obligation was provided for under the Berne Convention. Subparagraphs (i) and (ii) of Article 11 of that Convention originated in the Brussels Act of 1948. Their wording remained essentially unchanged in the Stockholm Act of 1967 and the Paris Act of 1971. No specific exception clause applicable to this right was added to the text of the Convention. However, when the general right of public performance was embodied for the first time in Article 11 of the Brussels Act, a statement was included in the General Report of the Brussels Conference referring to the minor exceptions doctrine.

The provisions currently contained in Article 11*bis*(1)(i) and 11*bis*(2) were first introduced into the Berne Convention at the Rome Conference of 1928, but subsequently modified. Subparagraphs (ii) and (iii) of Article 11*bis*(1) were added to the Convention at the Brussels Conference of 1948. In discussing subparagraphs (ii) and (iii) of Article 11*bis*(1), the General Report of the Brussels Conference states that the minor exceptions doctrine applies also to the exclusive rights under Article 11*bis*.

More specifically, it was proposed at the Brussels Conference of 1948 that a general provision be inserted into the Berne Convention under which it would be permissible for States parties to the Convention to retain various minor exceptions that already existed in their national laws. However, the proposal was not adopted by the Conference due to a concern that such a general provision could encourage the widening of existing minor exceptions or the introduction of additional minor exceptions in national laws. But the Conference did not question the very existence and maintenance of minor exceptions in national laws as such. In the context of the discussions on Article 11, it was agreed that rather than dealing with this matter in the text of the Convention itself, a statement concerning the possibility to provide minor exceptions in national law would be included in the General Report.[61]

When ascertaining the legal status of the minor exceptions doctrine, it is important to note that the General Report states that the Rapporteur-General had been *"entrusted with making an express mention* of the possibility available to national legislation to make what is commonly called minor reservations."[62] We believe that the choice of these words reflects an agreement within the meaning of Article 31(2)(a) of the Vienna Convention [on the Law of Treaties ("the Vienna Convention")] between the Berne Union members at the Brussels Conference to retain the possibility of providing minor exceptions in national law. We arrive at this conclusion for the following reasons. First, the introduction of Articles 11*bis*(1)(iii) and 11(1)(ii) occurred simultaneously with

---

[61]The relevant part of the General Report of the Brussels Diplomatic Conference reads as follows:

"Your Rapporteur-General has been entrusted with making an express mention of the possibility available to national legislation to make what are commonly called minor reservations. The Delegates of Norway, Sweden, Denmark, and Finland, the Delegate of Switzerland and the Delegate of Hungary, have all mentioned these limited exceptions allowed for religious ceremonies, military bands and the needs of child and adult education. These exceptional measures apply to articles 11*bis*, 11*ter*, 13 and 14. You will understand that these references are just lightly pencilled in here, in order to avoid damaging the principles of the right." *See* Annex XII.1 to the letter from the Director General of WIPO to the Chair of the Panel.

[62]This is not merely a statement by a chair of a drafting group made in his/her personal capacity.

the adoption of the General Report expressly mentioning the minor exceptions doctrine. Second, this doctrine is closely related to the substance of the amendment of the Berne Convention in that it limits the scope of the exclusive rights introduced by Articles 11*bis*(1)(iii) and 11(1)(ii) of the Berne Convention. Third, an "agreement" between all the parties exists because, on the one hand, the Rapporteur-General is being "entrusted to expressly mention" minor exceptions and, on the other hand, the General Report of the Brussels Conference reflecting this express mentioning was formally adopted by the Berne Union members. We therefore conclude that an agreement within the meaning of Article 31(2)(a) of the Vienna Convention between all the parties on the possibility to provide minor exceptions was made in connection with the conclusion of a revision of the Convention introducing additional exclusive rights, including those contained in Articles 11*bis*(1)(iii) and 11(1)(ii), to which these limitations were to apply, and that this agreement is relevant as context for interpreting these Articles.[63]

As pointed out above, the wording of Articles 11*bis* and 11 remained essentially the same at the Diplomatic Conferences in Stockholm (1967) and Paris (1971) where the General Reports were also formally adopted by the Berne Union members. The reports of the Stockholm Conference reconfirm our conclusion concerning the existence of an agreement on minor exceptions. The report of the Main Committee I[64] refers to the existence of an agreement between the Berne Union members that minor exceptions are permitted, *inter alia*, in respect of Articles 11 and 11*bis* of the Berne Convention.

Furthermore, we recall that Article 31(3) of the Vienna Convention provides that together with the context (a) any subsequent agreement, (b) subsequent practice, or (c) any relevant rules of international law applicable between the parties, shall be taken into account for the purposes of interpretation. We note that the parties and third parties have brought to our attention several examples from various countries of limitations in national laws based on the minor exceptions doctrine.[67] In our view, state practice as reflected in the

---

[63]If there were no possibility for "minor exceptions" from Articles 11*bis* and 11, no *de minimis* exemptions in national law whatsoever, allowing the use of the rights conferred by these Articles without remuneration, could be justified under any provision of the Berne Convention.

[64]The relevant parts of the Report of the Work of Main Committee I (Substantive Provisions of the Berne Convention: Articles 1 to 20) read as follows:

"209. In the General Report of the Brussels Conference, the Rapporteur was instructed to refer explicitly, in connection with Article 11, to the possibility of what it had been agreed to call 'the minor reservations' of national legislation. Some delegates had referred to the exceptions permitted in respect of religious ceremonies, performances by military bands, and the requirements of education and popularization. The exceptions also apply to articles 11*bis*, 11*ter*, 13 and 14. The Rapporteur ended by saying that these allusions were given lightly without invalidating the principle in the right.

210. It seems that it was not the intention of the Committee to prevent States from maintaining in their national legislation provisions based on the declaration contained in the General Report of the Brussels Conference."

[67]For example, Australia exempts public performance by wireless apparatus at premises of, *inter alia*, hotels or guest houses. Belgium exempts a work's communication to the public in a place accessible to the public where the aim of the communication is not the work itself, and exempts the performance of a work during a public examination where the purpose is the assessment of the performer. Finland exempts public performance in connection with religious services and

national copyright laws of Berne Union members before and after 1948, 1967 and 1971, as well as of WTO Members before and after the date that the TRIPS Agreement became applicable to them, confirms our conclusion about the minor exceptions doctrine.

The scope of the minor exceptions doctrine

Apart from the legal status of the minor exceptions doctrine under the Berne Convention, the parties disagree also on the scope of the doctrine. . . .

The General Report of the Brussels Conference of 1948 refers to "religious ceremonies, military bands and the needs of the child and adult education" as examples of situations in respect of which minor exceptions may be provided. The Main Committee I Report of the Stockholm Conference of 1967 refers also to "popularization" as one example. When these references are read in their proper context, it is evident that the given examples are of an illustrative character.[71] We also note that the examples given in the reports of the Brussels and Stockholm Conferences are not identical. Furthermore, the examples are given in the context of Article 11(1) of the Berne Convention, but the reports clarify that minor exceptions can also be provided to the exclusive rights conferred under Articles 11*bis*, 11*ter*, 13 and 14, without giving any specific examples. It is also evident that existing minor exceptions vary between different countries. The information presented to us on state practice in respect of minor exceptions in different countries is illustrative of that fact. Furthermore, the academic literature supports the view that these examples of uses in respect of which minor exceptions could be provided are not intended to be exhaustive.[73]

We note that some of the above-mentioned examples (e.g., religious ceremonies, military bands) typically involve minimal uses which are not carried out for profit. With respect to other examples (e.g., adult and child education and popularization), however, an exclusively non-commercial nature of potentially exempted uses is less clear. On the basis of the information

---

education. Finland and Denmark provide for exceptions where a work's performance is not the main feature of the event, provided that no fee is charged and the event is not for profit. New Zealand exempts public performance of musical works at educational establishments. The Philippines exempts public performances for charitable and educational purposes. A similar exception applies in India, where also performances at amateur clubs or societies are exempted. Canadian law provides for exceptions with respect to different exclusive rights for educational, religious or charitable purposes, and also at conventions and fairs. South Africa exempts public performances in the context of demonstrations of radio or television receivers and recording equipment by dealers of or clients for such equipment. [cit.] Brazil allows free use of works in commercial establishments for the purpose of demonstration to customers in establishments that market equipment that makes such use possible. [cit.]

[71]For example, in their preparatory work for the Brussels Conference, the Belgian Government and BIRPI took the view that it would be impossible to list all of the pre-existing exceptions exhaustively in the Convention as they were too varied. Documents de la Conférence Réunie à Bruxelles du 5 au 26 juin 1948, published by BIRPI in 1951, p. 255.

[73]Ricketson notes that "[t]he examples of uses given in the records of the Brussels and Stockholm Conferences are in no way an exhaustive list or determinative of which particular exceptions will be justified." *See* SAM RICKETSON, BERNE CONVENTION 536 (1986).

provided to us, we are not in a position to determine that the minor exceptions doctrine justifies only exclusively non-commercial use of works and that it may under no circumstances justify exceptions to uses with a more than negligible economic impact on copyright holders. On the other hand, non-commercial uses of works, e.g., in adult and child education, may reach a level that has a major economic impact on the right holder. At any rate, in our view, a non-commercial character of the use in question is not determinative provided that the exception contained in national law is indeed *minor*.[74]

As regards the coverage of the minor exceptions doctrine in temporal respect, we cannot share the European Communities' view that the coverage was "frozen" in 1967.[75] In our view, the use of the term "*maintain*" in the Stockholm records[76] is not sufficient evidence to substantiate the interpretation that countries could justify under the minor exceptions doctrine only those limitations which were in force in their national legislation prior to the year when that Conference was held.

The legal status of the minor exceptions doctrine under the TRIPS Agreement

. . . Th[e] second step [of our analysis] deals with the question whether or not the minor exceptions doctrine has been incorporated into the TRIPS Agreement, by virtue of its Article 9.1, together with Articles 1-21 of the Berne Convention (1971) as part of the Berne *acquis*.

We note that the express wording of Article 9.1 of the TRIPS Agreement neither establishes nor excludes such incorporation into the Agreement of the minor exceptions doctrine as it applies to Articles 11, 11*bis*, 11*ter*, 13 and 14 of the Berne Convention (1971).[78]

We have shown above that the minor exceptions doctrine forms part of the context, within the meaning of Article 31(2)(a) of the Vienna Convention, of at least Articles 11 and 11*bis* of the Berne Convention (1971). There is no indication in the wording of the TRIPS Agreement that Articles 11 and 11*bis* have been incorporated into the TRIPS Agreement by its Article 9.1 without bringing with them the possibility of providing minor exceptions to the respective exclusive rights. If that incorporation should have covered only the text of Articles 1–21 of the Berne Convention (1971), but not the entire Berne

---

[74]In the literature, it has been argued that such exceptions to the rights protected under the relevant provisions of the Berne Convention must be concerned with minimal use, or use without significance to the author. *See* Ricketson, Berne Convention, op.cit., p. 532-535.

[75]As regards the year 1967 as a suggested cut-off date, we note that the substantive provisions of the Stockholm Act of 1967 have never entered into force. Its substantive provisions were later incorporated into the Paris Act of 1971, which entered into force on 10 October 1974.

[76]Paragraph 210 of the Main Committee I Report of the Stockholm Conference uses the term "maintain". However, the original statement in the General Report of the Brussels Conference of 1948, to which the Stockholm records refer, uses the expression "the possibility available to national legislation to make what are commonly called minor reservations".

[78]While Article 9.1 does not mention the minor exceptions doctrine, it does not exclude the possibility that this doctrine was incorporated into the TRIPS Agreement as part of the Berne *acquis* together with the above-mentioned provisions to which it applies under the Berne Convention (1971).

acquis relating to these articles, Article 9.1 of the TRIPS Agreement would have explicitly so provided.[79]

Thus we conclude that, in the absence of any express exclusion in Article 9.1 of the TRIPS Agreement, the incorporation of Articles 11 and 11*bis* of the Berne Convention (1971) into the Agreement includes the entire *acquis* of these provisions, including the possibility of providing minor exceptions to the respective exclusive rights.

We find confirmation of our interpretation in certain references to the minor exceptions doctrine in the documentation from the GATT Uruguay Round negotiations on the TRIPS Agreement.[80] A TRIPS Negotiating Group document reproduces a document that was prepared by the International Bureau of the WIPO following a decision taken by the Negotiating Group, on 3 March 1988, inviting the Bureau "to prepare a factual document to facilitate an understanding of the existence, scope and form of generally internationally accepted and applied standards/norms for the protection of intellectual property."[82] The Section on the "Scope of Rights" contains the following text on the minor exceptions doctrine:

> In addition to the limitations explicitly mentioned in the text of the Convention, there is one more possibility for certain exceptions about which there was express agreement at various revision conferences, namely the possibility of minor exceptions to the right of public performance (a concept which is close to the notion of 'fair use' or 'fair dealing'; see item (iii), below).

Another TRIPS Negotiating Group document[84] mentions the minor exceptions doctrine as forming part of existing international standards. We are not aware of any record in the Uruguay Round documentation of any country participating in the negotiations challenging or questioning the minor exceptions doctrine being part of the Berne *acquis* on which the TRIPS Agreement was to be built.[85]

---

[79]In this respect, we refer to the treatment of moral rights under the TRIPS Agreement. Article 9.1 explicitly excludes Members' rights and obligations in respect of the rights conferred under Article 6*bis* of the Berne Convention (1971) and of the rights derived therefrom.

[80]We recall that, according to Article 32 of the Vienna Convention, "recourse may be had to supplementary means of interpretation, including the preparatory works of the treaty and the circumstances of its conclusion, in order to confirm the meaning resulting from the application of Article 31 . . ." We see no need to determine whether the GATT Uruguay Round documentation constitutes "preparatory works" or relate to the "circumstances of . . . [the] conclusion" of the TRIPS Agreement as annexed to the Agreement Establishing the WTO.

[82]*See* GATT document MTN.GNG/NG11/6, paragraphs 39 and 40 and Annex

[84]MTN.GNG/NG11/W/32/Rev.2 of 2 February 1990 . . . sets out the provisions of the international treaties existing at that time corresponding to the proposals [made in the Group]. The Secretariat prepared the content [of the document] drawing on the above-mentioned document prepared by the International Bureau of WIPO. . . .

[85]We find a further confirmation of our interpretation in the negotiating history of Article 9.1 of the TRIPS Agreement. Earlier drafts of that Article referred merely to "the substantive provisions" of the Berne Convention (1971), indicating that the intention was to embody the overall Berne *acquis* rather than just the literal wording of the individual articles. During the negotiations a preference was expressed for identifying these substantive provisions. As a result, these provisions were identified in the final version of the Article as "Articles 1 through 21 of the Berne Convention

In the area of copyright, the Berne Convention and the TRIPS Agreement form the overall framework for multilateral protection. Most WTO Members are also parties to the Berne Convention. We recall that it is a general principle of interpretation to adopt the meaning that reconciles the texts of different treaties and avoids a conflict between them. Accordingly, one should avoid interpreting the TRIPS Agreement to mean something different than the Berne Convention except where this is explicitly provided for. This principle is in conformity with the public international law presumption against conflicts, which has been applied by WTO panels and the Appellate Body in a number of cases. [The Panel cited a number of cases not involving intellectual property rights.] We believe that our interpretation of the legal status of the minor exceptions doctrine under the TRIPS Agreement is consistent with these general principles.

. . . .

(iv) The scope of Article 13 of the TRIPS Agreement

. . . .

The language used in Article 13 of the TRIPS Agreement has its origins in the similar language used in Article 9(2) of the Berne Convention (1971),[94] although the latter only applies in the case of the reproduction right.

A general right of reproduction was not recognized under the Berne Convention until the Stockholm Act of 1967. The main difficulty in the preparation of this amendment was to find an appropriate formula which would allow exceptions to that right. In adopting the present text of Article 9(2) of the Berne Convention, the Main Committee I of the Stockholm Diplomatic Conference (1967) gave the following guidance on its interpretation:

> The Committee also adopted a proposal by the Drafting Committee that the second condition should be placed before the first, as this would afford a more logical order for the interpretation of the rule. If it is considered that reproduction conflicts with the normal exploitation of the work, reproduction is not permitted at all. If it is considered that reproduction does not conflict with the normal exploitation of the work, the next step would be to consider whether it does not unreasonably prejudice the legitimate interests of the author. Only if such is not the case would it be possible in certain special cases to introduce a compulsory license, or to provide for use without payment. A practical example may be photocopying for

---

(1971) and the Appendix thereto". It appears that this was done for the sake of clarity, and there is no indication in the records that there was an intention to change the aim of embodying the overall Berne *acquis*.

[94]Article 9(2) of the Berne Convention (1971) provides: "It shall be a matter for legislation in the countries of the Union to permit the reproduction of such works in certain special cases, provided that such reproduction does not conflict with a normal exploitation of the work and does not unreasonably prejudice the legitimate interests of the author."

various purposes. If it consists of producing a very large number of copies, it may not be permitted, as it conflicts with a normal exploitation of the work. If it implies a rather large number of copies for use in industrial undertakings, it may not unreasonably prejudice the legitimate interests of the author, provided that, according to national legislation, an equitable remuneration is paid. If a small number of copies is made, photocopying may be permitted without payment, particularly for individual or scientific use.[96]

Apart from the difference in the use of the terms "permit" and "confine", the main difference between Article 9(2) of the Berne Convention (1971) and Article 13 of the TRIPS Agreement is that the former applies only to the reproduction right. The wording of Article 13 does not contain an express limitation in terms of the categories of rights under copyright to which it may apply. . . .

[The panel rejected the arguments of the European Communities that (1) TRIPS Article 13 applies only to new rights added by the TRIPS Agreement, and not to preexisting provisions of the Berne Convention incorporated into TRIPS by reference, and (2) that Berne Article 11*bis*(2) requires that any exception to Article 11*bis*(1) provide equitable remuneration to the right holder. The panel concluded, first, that Article 13 is the applicable test for determining the scope of permissible minor exceptions to Berne rights, and, second, that Berne Article 11*bis*(2) was not relevant, as it covers different situations from TRIPS Article 13, involving conditions on the exercise of rights (such as compulsory licenses) rather than exceptions to rights.]

. . . .

2. The three criteria test under Article 13 of the TRIPS Agreement

(a) *General introduction*

Article 13 of the TRIPS Agreement requires that limitations and exceptions to exclusive rights (1) be confined to certain special cases, (2) do not conflict with a normal exploitation of the work, and (3) do not unreasonably prejudice the legitimate interests of the right holder.[105] The principle of effective treaty interpretation requires us to give a distinct meaning to each of the three conditions and to avoid a reading that could reduce any of the conditions to "redundancy or inutility."[106] The three conditions apply on a cumulative basis,

---

[96]Records of the Intellectual Property Conference of Stockholm, June 11 to July 14, 1967, Report on the Work of Main Committee I (Substantive Provisions of the Berne Convention: Articles 1 to 20) . . . .

[105][A]s we noted . . . above, the wording of Article 13 derives largely from Article 9(2) of the Berne Convention (1971) which applies, however, to reproduction rights only. Given the similarity of the wording, we consider that the preparatory works of Article 9(2) of the Berne Convention and its application in practice may be of contextual relevance in interpreting Article 13 of the TRIPS Agreement.

[106]Appellate Body Report on *United States—Standards for Reformulated and Conventional Gasoline*, adopted on 20 May 1996, WT/DS2/AB/R, p. 23.

each being a separate and independent requirement that must be satisfied. Failure to comply with any one of the three conditions results in the Article 13 exception being disallowed. Both parties agree on the cumulative nature of the three conditions. The Panel shares their view. It may be noted at the outset that Article 13 cannot have more than a narrow or limited operation. Its tenor, consistent as it is with the provisions of Article 9(2) of the Berne Convention (1971), discloses that it was not intended to provide for exceptions or limitations except for those of a limited nature. The narrow sphere of its operation will emerge from our discussion and application of its provisions in the paragraphs which follow.

In the following, we will first explore the interpretation of the first condition of Article 13 in general terms in the light of the arguments made by the parties. We will then examine, in turn, subparagraphs (B) and (A) of Section 110(5) of the US Copyright Act of 1976, as amended by the Fairness in Music Licensing Act of 1998, that contain, respectively, the business and homestyle exemptions. We will discuss the business exemption of subparagraph (B) first because most of the arguments raised by the parties focus on it. After that, we will similarly explore the interpretation of the second and third conditions and apply them to subparagraphs (B) and (A) of Section 110(5).

The parties have largely relied on similar factual information in substantiating their legal arguments under each of the three conditions of Article 13. We are called upon to evaluate this information from different angles under the three conditions, which call for different requirements for justifying exceptions or limitations. . . .

. . . .

(b) *"Certain special cases"*

(i) General interpretative analysis

. . . .

The United States submits that the fact that the TRIPS Agreement does not elaborate on the criteria for a case to be considered "special" provides Members flexibility to determine for themselves whether a particular case represents an appropriate basis for an exception. But it acknowledges that the essence of the first condition is that the exceptions be well-defined and of limited application.

In the view of the European Communities, an exception has to be well-defined and narrow in scope to meet the requirements under the first condition. . .

The European Communities argues that, in the light of the wording of the first condition in Article 9(2) of the Berne Convention (1971), which forms part of the context of Article 13, an exemption should serve a "special purpose". For the European Communities, in the case of Section 110(5), no such special public policy or other exceptional circumstance exists that would make it inappropriate or impossible to enforce the exclusive rights conferred by Articles 11 and 11*bis* of the Berne Convention (1971). In the EC view, the subparagraphs of Section 110(5) do not pursue legitimate public policy objectives.

In the US view, if the purpose of an exception is relevant at all, the TRIPS Agreement only requires that an exception has a specific policy objective. It does not impose any requirement as to the legitimacy of the policy objectives that a particular country might consider special in the light of its own history and national priorities.

We start our analysis of the first condition of Article 13 by referring to the ordinary meaning of the terms in their context and in the light of its object and purpose. It appears that the notions of "exceptions" and "limitations" in the introductory words of Article 13 overlap in part in the sense that an "exception" refers to a derogation from an exclusive right provided under national legislation in some respect, while a "limitation" refers to a reduction of such right to a certain extent.

The ordinary meaning of "certain" is "known and particularised, but not explicitly identified", "determined, fixed, not variable; definitive, precise, exact."[111] In other words, this term means that, under the first condition, an exception or limitation in national legislation must be clearly defined. However, there is no need to identify explicitly each and every possible situation to which the exception could apply, provided that the scope of the exception is known and particularised. This guarantees a sufficient degree of legal certainty.

We also have to give full effect to the ordinary meaning of the second word of the first condition. The term "special" connotes "having an individual or limited application or purpose", "containing details; precise, specific", "exceptional in quality or degree; unusual; out of the ordinary" or "distinctive in some way."[112] This term means that more is needed than a clear definition in order to meet the standard of the first condition. In addition, an exception or limitation must be limited in its field of application or exceptional in its scope. In other words, an exception or limitation should be narrow in a quantitative as well as a qualitative sense. This suggests a narrow scope as well as an exceptional or distinctive objective. To put this aspect of the first condition into the context of the second condition ("no conflict with a normal exploitation"), an exception or limitation should be the opposite of a non-special, i.e., a normal case.

The ordinary meaning of the term "case" refers to an "occurrence", "circumstance" or "event" or "fact."[113] For example, in the context of the dispute at hand, the "case" could be described in terms of beneficiaries of the exceptions, equipment used, types of works or by other factors.

As regards the parties' arguments on whether the public policy purpose of an exception is relevant, we believe that the term "certain special cases" should not lightly be equated with "special purpose."[114] It is difficult to reconcile the

---

[111]The New Shorter Oxford English Dictionary ("Oxford English Dictionary"), Oxford (1993), p. 364.

[112]Oxford English Dictionary, p. 2971.

[113]Oxford English Dictionary, p. 345.

[114]We note that the term "special purpose" has been referred to in interpreting the largely similarly worded Article 9(2) of the Berne Convention (1971). *See* Ricketson, The Berne Convention, op. cit., p. 482. We are ready to take into account "teachings of the most highly qualified publicists of the various nations" as a "subsidiary source for the determination of law". We refer to this phrase in the sense of Article 38(d) of the Statute of the International Court of Justice which refers to such "teachings" (or, in French "la doctrine") as "subsidiary means for the

wording of Article 13 with the proposition that an exception or limitation must be justified in terms of a legitimate public policy purpose in order to fulfill the first condition of the Article. We also recall in this respect that in interpreting other WTO rules, such as the national treatment clauses of the GATT and the GATS, the Appellate Body has rejected interpretative tests which were based on the subjective aim or objective pursued by national legislation. [cits.]

In our view, the first condition of Article 13 requires that a limitation or exception in national legislation should be clearly defined and should be narrow in its scope and reach. On the other hand, a limitation or exception may be compatible with the first condition even if it pursues a special purpose whose underlying legitimacy in a normative sense cannot be discerned. The wording of Article 13's first condition does not imply passing a judgment on the legitimacy of the exceptions in dispute. However, public policy purposes stated by law-makers when enacting a limitation or exception may be useful from a factual perspective for making inferences about the scope of a limitation or exception or the clarity of its definition.

In the case at hand, in order to determine whether subparagraphs (B) and (A) of Section 110(5) are confined to "certain special cases", we first examine whether the exceptions have been clearly defined. Second, we ascertain whether the exemptions are narrow in scope, *inter alia*, with respect to their reach. In that respect, we take into account what percentage of eating and drinking establishments and retail establishments may benefit from the business exemption under subparagraph (B), and in turn what percentage of establishments may take advantage of the homestyle exemption under subparagraph (A). On a subsidiary basis, we consider whether it is possible to draw inferences about the reach of the business and homestyle exemptions from the stated policy purposes underlying these exemptions according to the statements made during the US legislative process.

(ii) The business exemption of subparagraph (B)

As noted above, the United States argues that the essence of the first condition of Article 13 of the TRIPS Agreement is that exceptions be well-defined and of limited application. It claims that the business exemption of subparagraph (B) meets the requirements of the first condition of Article 13, because it is clearly defined in Section 110(5) of the US Copyright Act by square footage and equipment limitations.

. . . .

The European Communities contends that the business exemption is too broad in its scope to pass as a "certain special case", given the large number of establishments which potentially may benefit from it. For the European Communities, it is irrelevant that the size of establishments and the type of equipment are clearly defined, when the broad scope of the business exemption

---

determination of law." But we are cautious to use the interpretation of a term developed in the context of an exception for the reproduction right for interpreting the same terms in the context of a largely similarly worded exception for other exclusive rights conferred by copyrights.

turns an exception into the rule.

It appears that the European Communities does not dispute the fact that subparagraph (B) is clearly defined in respect of the size limits of establishments and the type of equipment that may be used by establishments above the applicable limits. The primary bone of contention between the parties is whether the business exemption, given its scope and reach, can be considered as a "special" case within the meaning of the first condition of Article 13.

The Congressional Research Service ("CRS") estimated in 1995 the percentage of the US eating and drinking establishments and retail establishments that would have fallen at that time below the size limits of 3,500 square feet and 1,500 square feet respectively. Its study found that:

(d) 65.2 per cent of all eating establishments;

(e) 71.8 per cent of all drinking establishments; and

(f) 27 per cent of all retail establishments would have fallen below these size limits.

The United States confirms these figures as far as eating and drinking establishments are concerned.

We note that this study was made in 1995 using the size limit of 3,500 square feet for eating and drinking establishments, and the size limit of 1,500 square feet for retail establishments, while the size limits under subparagraph (B) now are 3,750 square feet for eating and drinking establishments and 2,000 square feet for retail establishments. Therefore, in our view, it is safe to assume that the actual percentage of establishments which may fall within the finally enacted business exemption in the Fairness in Music Licensing Act of 1998 is higher than the above percentages.

The United States has also submitted estimates by the National Restaurant Association (NRA) concerning its membership. According to these estimates, 36 per cent of its table service restaurant members (i.e., those with sit-down waiter service) are of a size less than 3,750 square feet, and approximately 95 per cent of its fast-food restaurant members are of a size less than 3,750 square feet. . . [T]he NRA figures do not seem to contradict the estimates of the CRS study of 1995.

In 1999, Dun & Bradstreet, Inc. ("D&B") was requested by ASCAP to update the 1995 CRS study based on 1998 data and the criteria in the 1998 Amendment.[124] The European Communities explains that the methodology used by the D&B in 1998/1999 was identical to the methodology used in the analysis which the D&B prepared in 1995 for the CRS during the legislative process that eventually led to the adoption of the Fairness in Music Licensing

---

[124] . . . According to the European Communities, the 1998/1999 D&B's "Dun's Market Identifying Market Profile" is a database of more than 6.5 million US businesses, based on square footage. The European Communities explains that the figures of the D&B studies comprise bars, restaurants, tea-rooms, snackbars, etc. and retail stores. However, other sectors, e.g. hotels, financial service outlets, estate property brokers, and other types of service providers, in which a number of establishments are likely to be exempted as well, were not taken into account.

Act. The D&B study of 1999[125] concludes that approximately 73 per cent of all drinking, 70 per cent of all eating, and 45 per cent of all retail establishments in the United States are entitled under subparagraph (B), without any limitation regarding equipment, to play music from radio and television on their business premises without the consent of the right holders.[126]

. . . .

Referring to these studies, the European Communities points out that these 70 per cent of eating and drinking establishments and 45 per cent of retail establishments are all potential users of the business exemption, because they can at any time, without permission of the right holders, begin to play amplified music broadcasts.

The United States contends that even if 70 per cent of all eating and drinking establishments and 45 per cent of all retail establishments are implicated by the size limits under subparagraph (B) after the 1998 Amendment, many of these establishments would have to be subtracted for various reasons. These include (i) establishments that do not play music at all; (ii) those that would turn off the music if they became liable to pay fees; (iii) those that play music from sources other than the radio or television, such as tapes, CDs, jukeboxes or live performances; (iv) establishments that were not licensed prior to the enactment of the business exemption in 1998; (v) establishments that would take advantage of group licensing arrangements such as the one between the NLBA [National Licensed Beverage Association] and the CMOs.

We agree with the European Communities that it is the scope in respect of potential users that is relevant for determining whether the coverage of the exemption is sufficiently limited to qualify as a "certain *special* case". While it is true, as the United States argues, that some establishments might turn off the radio or television if they had to pay fees, other establishments which have

---

[125]According to the information submitted by the European Communities, the number of establishments contained in the D&B database in 1998 were as follows:

(a)　7,819 drinking establishments of a square footage below 3,750 square feet which amounts to 73 per cent of all US drinking establishments filed in the D&B database;

(b)　51,385 eating establishments of a square footage below 3,750 square feet which amounts to 70 per cent of all US eating establishments filed in the D&B database;

(c)　65,589 retail establishments of a square footage below 2,000 square feet or 45 per cent of all US retail establishments filed in the D&B database.

In addition, D&B estimated the total figures as follows:

(a)　49,061 drinking establishments of a square footage below 3,750 square feet which amounts to 85 per cent of all US drinking establishments filed in the D&B database;

(b)　192,692 eating establishments of a square footage below 3,750 square feet which amounts to 68 per cent of all US eating establishments filed in the D&B database;

(c)　281,406 retail establishments of a square footage below 2,000 square feet or 42 per cent of all US retail establishments filed in the D&B database.

[126]The European Communities calculates that the number of eating, drinking and retail establishments that fall below the size limits of subparagraph (B), compared to the number of establishments that fall below the size of the restaurant that was operated by Mr. Aiken, has increased by 437 per cent, 540 per cent, and 250 per cent, respectively. While we do not wish to accept or reject the particular percentage figures of these estimates, we note that there is a magnitude of difference in the coverage between the original homestyle exemption and the new business exemption.

not previously played music might do the opposite, because under the business exemption the use of music is free. Some establishments that have used recorded music may decide to switch to broadcast music in order to avoid paying licensing fees. It is clear that, in examining the exemption, we have to also consider its impact on the use of other substitutable sources of music. Consequently, we do not consider the US calculations of establishments to be deducted from the CRS or D&B estimates as relevant for ascertaining the potential scope of the business exemption in relation to the first condition of Article 13.

. . . .

The United States does not appear to make a distinction between, on the one hand, the eating and drinking or retail establishments whose size is within the applicable limits of subparagraph (B), and, on the other hand, larger establishments that may still use music for free if they comply with the applicable equipment limitations (e.g., concerning loudspeakers per room or screen size). We have not been provided with information concerning the absolute numbers or the proportion of these larger establishments qualifying under the business exemption. Suffice it to say that the percentage of all US eating, drinking and retail establishments that may fall within the coverage of subparagraph (B) could be even higher than the above figures or estimates suggest.

The United States further notes that the prohibitions against charging admission fees and retransmission in indent (iii) and (iv) of subparagraph (B) limit the field of application of the business exemption. The European Communities contends that these prohibitions have no potential whatsoever to limit the impact of the exemption. We have not been presented with information on whether these prohibitions significantly reduce the number of establishments that could otherwise qualify for the exemption. . .

We note that, according to its preparatory works, Article 11*bis*(1)(iii) of the Berne Convention (1971) was intended to provide right holders with a right to authorize the use of their works in the types of establishments covered by the exemption contained in Section 110(5)(B). Specifically, the preparatory works for the 1948 Brussels Conference indicate that the establishments that were intended to be covered were places "above all, where people meet: in the cinema, in restaurants, in tea rooms, railway carriages . . ." The preparatory works also refer to places such as factories, shops and offices.[133] We fail to see how a law that exempts a major part of the users that were specifically intended to be covered by the provisions of Article 11*bis*(1)(iii) could be considered as a *special* case in the sense of the first condition of Article 13 of the TRIPS Agreement.

We are aware that eating, drinking and retail establishments are not the only potential users of music covered by the exclusive rights conferred under Articles 11*bis*(1)(iii) and 11(1)(ii) of the Berne Convention (1971). The United States has mentioned, *inter alia*, conventions, fairs and sporting events as other potential users of performances of works in the meaning of the above Articles. However,

---

[133]Documents de la Conférence Réunie à Bruxelles du 5 au 26 juin 1948, published by BIRPI in 1951, p. 266. . . .

we believe that these examples of other potential users do not detract from the fact that eating, drinking and retail establishments are among the major groups of potential users of the works in the ways that are covered by the above-mentioned Articles.

The factual information presented to us indicates that a substantial majority of eating and drinking establishments and close to half of retail establishments are covered by the exemption contained in subparagraph (B) of Section 110(5) of the US Copyright Act. Therefore, we conclude that the exemption does not qualify as a "certain special case" in the meaning of the first condition of Article 13.

The European Communities warns that the potential coverage of both exemptions contained in Section 110(5) could become even larger because subparagraphs (A) and (B) could arguably exempt the transmission of musical works over the Internet. Given that we have found that the business exemption does not meet the first condition of Article 13 regardless of whether it potentially implicates transmission of works over the Internet, we see no need to address this question in the context of subparagraph (B). However, we will take up this question when we examine the homestyle exemption of subparagraph (A) in relation to the first condition of Article 13.

(iii) The homestyle exemption of subparagraph (A)

We examine now whether the homestyle exemption in subparagraph (A), in the form in which it is currently in force in the United States, is a "certain special case" in the meaning of the first condition of Article 13 of the TRIPS Agreement.

The United States submits that the exemption of subparagraph (A) is confined to "certain special cases", because its scope is limited to the use involving a "homestyle" receiving apparatus. In the US view, in the amended version of 1998 as well, this is a well-defined fact-specific standard. The essentially identical description of the homestyle exemption in the original Section 110(5) of 1976 was sufficiently clear and narrow for US courts to reasonably and consistently apply the exception—including square footage limitation since the *Aiken* case—in a number of individual decisions. For the United States, the fact that judges have weighed the various factors slightly differently in making their individual decisions is simply a typical feature of a common-law system.

The European Communities contends that the criteria of the homestyle exemption in subparagraph (A) are ambiguously worded because the expression "a single receiving apparatus of a kind commonly used in private homes" is in itself imprecise and a "moving target" due to technological development. Also the variety of approaches and factors used by US courts in applying the original version of the homestyle exemption are proof for the European Communities that the wording of subparagraph (A) of Section 110(5) is vague and open-ended.

Beneficiaries of the homestyle exemption

The wording of the amended version of Section 110(5)(A) is essentially identical to the wording of Section 110(5) in its previous version of 1976, apart from the introductory phrase "except as provided in subparagraph (B)". Therefore, we consider that the practice as reflected in the judgements rendered by US courts after 1976 concerning the original homestyle exemption may be regarded as factually indicative of the reach of the homestyle exemption even after the 1998 Amendment.

. . . In the evolution of case law, subsequent to the inclusion of the original homestyle exemption in the Copyright Act of 1976 in reaction to the *Aiken* judgement, US courts have considered a number of factors to determine whether a shop or restaurant could benefit from the exemption.[135] These factors have included: (i) physical size of an establishment in terms of square footage (in comparison to the size of the *Aiken* restaurant); (ii) extent to which the receiving apparatus was to be considered as one commonly used in private homes; (iii) distance between the receiver and the speakers; (iv) number of speakers; (v) whether the speakers were free-standing or built into the ceiling; (vi) whether, depending on its revenue, the establishment was of a type that would normally subscribe to a background music service; (vii) noise level of the areas within the establishment where the transmissions were made audible or visible; and (viii) configuration of the installation. In some federal circuits, US courts have focused primarily on the plain language of the homestyle exemption that refers to "a single receiving apparatus of a kind commonly used in private homes."

The European Communities emphasizes that in some US court cases large chain store corporations were found to be exempted provided that each branch shop met the criteria of the exemption, e.g., in respect of the size of the establishment and the equipment used by it, regardless of the ownership and the economic size or corporate structure of the chain store corporation.[136] It is our understanding that the European Communities does not argue that the ability of a corporate chain to pay or the number of individual stores in joint ownership or under the control of the chain store corporation should be a decisive factor for refusing to grant the exemption to a particular branch store. However, the European Communities cautions that these US court decisions are illustrative of a judicial trend towards broadening the homestyle exemption of 1976 in recent years.

The United States responds that, in applying Section 110(5) of the Copyright Act of 1976, only three US court judgements have found that a defendant was entitled to take advantage of the exemption. It also contends that only two US

---

[135]According to the European Communities, US courts have never favourably applied the homestyle exemption to an eating or drinking establishment of more than 1,500 square feet of total space nor to establishments using more than four loudspeakers.

[136]Broadcast Music, Inc. v. Claire's Boutiques Inc., US Court of Appeals for the Seventh Circuit, No. 91-1232, 11 December 1991.

court judgements (*Claire's Boutiques* and *Edison Bros.*[137]) dealt with the applicability of the exemption to particular branch shops of chain stores.

We note that the parties have submitted quantitative information on the coverage of subparagraph (A) with respect to eating, drinking and other establishments. [Here the Panel cites to the findings of the 1995 CRS study.]

We believe that from a quantitative perspective the reach of subparagraph (A) in respect of potential users is limited to a comparably small percentage of all eating, drinking and retail establishments in the United States.

We are mindful of the above-mentioned EC argument alleging a judicial trend towards broadening the homestyle exemption of 1976 in recent years. We cannot exclude the possibility that in the future US courts could establish precedents that would lead to the expansion of the scope of the currently applicable homestyle exemption as regards covered establishments. But we also note that since 1976 US courts have in the vast majority of cases applied the homestyle exemption in a sufficiently consistent and clearly delineated manner. Given the sufficiently consistent and narrow application practice of the homestyle exemption of 1976, we see no need to hypothesise whether at some point in the future US case law might lead to a *de facto* expansion of the homestyle exemption of 1998.

Homestyle equipment

We note that what is referred to as homestyle equipment (i.e., "a single receiving apparatus of a kind commonly used in private homes") might vary between different countries, is subject to changing consumer preferences in a given country, and may evolve as a result of technological development. We thus agree in principle with the European Communities that the homestyle equipment that was used in US households in 1976 (when the original homestyle exemption was enacted) is not necessarily identical to the equipment used in 1998 (when US copyright legislation was amended) or at a future point in time. However, we recall that the term "*certain* special cases" connotes "known and particularised, but not explicitly identified." In our view, the term "homestyle equipment" expresses the degree of clarity in definition required under Article 13's first condition. In our view, a Member is not required to identify homestyle equipment in terms of exceedingly detailed technical specifications in order to meet the standard of clarity set by the first condition. While we recognize that homestyle equipment may become technologically more sophisticated over time, we see no need to enter into speculations about potential future developments in the homestyle equipment market. At any rate, we recall that our factual determinations are invariably limited to what currently is being perceived as homestyle equipment in the US market.

---

[137]Broadcast Music, Inc. v. Edison Bros. Stores Inc., US Court of Appeals for the Eight Circuit, No. 91-2115, 13 January 1992.

Musical works covered by subparagraph (A)

We have noted the common view of the parties that the addition of the introductory phrase "except as provided in subparagraph (B)" to the homestyle exemption in the 1998 Amendment should be understood by way of an *a contrario* argument as limiting the coverage of the exemption to works other than "nondramatic" musical works. . . .

While taking this position on the interpretation of subparagraph (A), the European Communities has, however, cautioned that US courts might read a broader coverage into subparagraph (A) at a future point in time. In view of the common understanding of the parties in the current dispute, and given the EC responses to our questions about the scope of its claims, we see no need to speculate whether in the future subparagraph (A) could be interpreted by US courts to cover musical works other than those considered as "dramatic".

In practice, this means that most if not virtually all music played on the radio or television is covered by subparagraph (B). Subparagraph (A) covers, in accordance with the common understanding of the parties, dramatic renditions of operas, operettas, musicals and other similar dramatic works. We consider that limiting the application of subparagraph (A) to the public communication of transmissions embodying such works, gives its provisions a quite narrow scope of application in practice.

Internet transmissions

As we noted . . . above, the types of transmissions covered by both subparagraphs of Section 110(5) include original broadcasts over the air or by satellite, rebroadcasts by terrestrial means or by satellite, cable retransmissions of original broadcasts, and original cable transmissions or other transmissions by wire. The provisions do not distinguish between analog and digital transmissions.

The European Communities presumes that, given its open-ended wording, subparagraph (A) may apply to the public communication of musical works transmitted using new technologies such as computer networks (e.g., the Internet), the importance of which increases from day to day.[142]

The United States emphasizes that, in general, neither subparagraph of Section 110(5) exempts communication over a digital network. In its view, the transmission of works over a computer network involves numerous incidents of reproduction and could also implicate distribution rights. Therefore, Internet users would have to seek a licence for the reproduction and possibly for the distribution of works. The United States further developed its argumentation by adding that it was unclear whether the performance aspect of an Internet

---

[142]For example, an FCC-licensed radio (or TV) broadcaster parallels its over-the-air transmissions on the Internet (as an audio back-up to his web-site). These programmes are received by a PC connected with a number of loudspeakers in a bar or other establishment meeting all the conditions set out in Section 110(5) of the US Copyright Act.

transmission would be covered by either subparagraph of Section 110(5). It stated, however, that if an FCC-licensed broadcaster itself streams its signals over the Internet, the performance aspect of the broadcast might fall within the exemption.

Whether or not an establishment would need an authorization for the reproduction or distribution of musical works, in the situations envisaged under Section 110(5), does not in our view detract from the fact that an authorization is required for the exploitation of protected works in respect of the exclusive rights protected under Articles 11(1)(ii) or 11*bis*(1)(iii) of the Berne Convention (1971).

In the light of the parties' arguments, we cannot exclude the possibility that the homestyle exemption might apply to the communication to the public of works transmitted over the Internet. But we also note that, based on the information provided to us by the parties, there seems to be no experience to date of the application of the homestyle exemption in its original or amended form to the transmission of "dramatic" musical works over the Internet. In these circumstances, we cannot see how potential repercussions in the future could affect our conclusions concerning subparagraph (A) at this point in time in relation to the first condition of Article 13 of the TRIPS Agreement. But we also do not wish to exclude the possibility that in the future new technologies might create new ways of distributing dramatic renditions of "dramatic" musical works that might have implications for the assessment of subparagraph (A) as a "certain special case" in the meaning of the first condition of Article 13.

Other considerations

The European Communities contends that neither subparagraph of Section 110(5) discloses a "valid" public policy or other exceptional circumstance that makes it inappropriate or impossible to enforce the exclusive rights conferred.

[The panel cited the legislative history of the 1976 Act for the rationale of the original homestyle exemption.]

The United States further explains that the policy purpose justifying subparagraph (A) is the protection of small "mom and pop" businesses which "play an important role in the American social fabric" because they "offer economic opportunities for women, minorities, immigrants and welfare recipients for entering the economic and social mainstream."

We recall our considerations above that we reject the idea that the first condition of Article 13 requires us to pass a value judgement on the legitimacy of an exception or limitation. However, we also observed that stated public policy purposes could be of subsidiary relevance for drawing inferences about the scope of an exemption and the clarity of its definition. In our view, the statements from the legislative history indicate an intention of establishing an exception with a narrow scope.

Finally, we recall our conclusion that the context of Articles 11 and 11*bis* of the Berne Convention (1971) as incorporated into the TRIPS Agreement allows for the possibility of providing minor exceptions to the exclusive rights in question; i.e., the intention was to allow exceptions as long as they are *de minimis* in scope.

Taking into account the specific limits imposed in subparagraph (A) and its legislative history, as well as in its considerably narrow application in the subsequent court practice on the beneficiaries of the exemption, permissible equipment and categories of works, we are of the view that the homestyle exemption in subparagraph (A) of Section 110(5) as amended in 1998 is well-defined and limited in its scope and reach. We, therefore, conclude that the exemption is confined to certain special cases within the meaning of the first condition of Article 13 of the TRIPS Agreement.

[The panel concluded that it should examine the other two conditions as well, for purposes of judicial economy.]

(c) *"Not conflict with a normal exploitation of the work"*

(i) General interpretative analysis

. . . .

In interpreting the second condition of Article 13, we first need to define what "exploitation" of a "work" means. More importantly, we have to determine what constitutes a "normal" exploitation, with which a derogation is not supposed to "conflict".

The ordinary meaning of the term "exploit" connotes "making use of" or "utilising for one's own ends."[150] We believe that "exploitation" of musical works thus refers to the activity by which copyright owners employ the exclusive rights conferred on them to extract economic value from their rights to those works.

We note that the ordinary meaning of the term "normal" can be defined as "constituting or conforming to a type or standard; regular, usual, typical, ordinary, conventional. . . ."[151] In our opinion, these definitions appear to reflect two connotations: the first one appears to be of an empirical nature, i.e., what is regular, usual, typical or ordinary. The other one reflects a somewhat more normative, if not dynamic, approach, i.e., conforming to a type or standard. We do not feel compelled to pass a judgment on which one of these connotations could be more relevant. Based on Article 31 of the Vienna Convention, we will attempt to develop a harmonious interpretation which gives meaning and effect to both connotations of "normal".

If "normal" exploitation were equated with full use of all exclusive rights conferred by copyrights, the exception clause of Article 13 would be left devoid of meaning. Therefore, "normal" exploitation clearly means something less than

[150]Oxford English Dictionary, p. 888.
[151]Oxford English Dictionary, p. 1940.

full use of an exclusive right.[152]

In the US view, it is necessary to look to the ways in which an author might reasonably be expected to exploit his work in the normal course of events, when one determines what constitutes a normal exploitation. In this respect, it is relevant that Article 13 does not refer to particular specific rights but to "the work" as a whole. This implies that, in examining an exception under the second condition, consideration should be given to the scope of the exception *vis-à-vis* the panoply of all the rights holders' exclusive rights, as well as *vis-à-vis* the exclusive right to which it applies. In its view, the most important forms of exploitation of musical works, namely, "primary" performance and broadcasting, are not affected by either subparagraph of Section 110(5). The business and homestyle exemptions only affect what the United States considers "secondary" uses of broadcasts, and that too, subject to size and equipment limitations. In the US view, right holders normally obtain the main part of their remuneration from "primary" uses and only a minor part from "secondary" uses.

The European Communities rejects the idea that there could be a hierarchical order between "important" and "unimportant" rights under the TRIPS Agreement. For the European Communities, there are no "secondary" rights and the exclusive rights provided for in Articles 11*bis*(1)(iii) and 11(1)(ii) of the Berne Convention (1971) are all equally important separate rights.

The United States itself clarifies that it does not imply that a legal hierarchy exists between different exclusive rights conferred under Articles 11, 11*bis* or any other provision of the Berne Convention (1971) and that a country cannot completely eliminate an exclusive right even if that right be economically unimportant. But it takes the view that when a possible conflict with a normal exploitation of the work is analysed, it is relevant whether the exception applies to one or several exclusive rights. Similarly, the degree to which the exception affects a particular exclusive right is also relevant for the analysis of the second condition of Article 13.

---

[152]In the context of exceptions to reproduction rights under Article 9(2) of the Berne Convention (1971)—whose second condition is worded largely identically to the second condition of Article 13 of the TRIPS Agreement—the Main Committee I of the Stockholm Diplomatic Conference (1967) stated:

> "If it is considered that reproduction conflicts with the normal exploitation of the work, reproduction is not permitted at all. If it is considered that reproduction does not conflict with the normal exploitation of the work, the next step would be to consider whether it does not unreasonably prejudice the legitimate interests of the author. Only if such is not the case would it be possible in certain special cases to introduce a compulsory licence, or to provide for use without payment. A practical example may be photocopying for various purposes. If it consists of producing a very large number of copies, it may not be permitted, as it conflicts with a normal exploitation of the work. If it implies a rather large number of copies for use in industrial undertakings, it may not unreasonably prejudice the legitimate interests of the author, provided that, according to national legislation, an equitable remuneration is paid. If a small number of copies is made, photocopying may be permitted without payment, particularly for individual or scientific use."

See Records of the Intellectual Property Conference of Stockholm, 11 June–14 July 1967, Report on the Work of the Main Committee I (Substantive Provisions of the Berne Convention: Articles 1-20.)

It is true, as the United States points out, that Article 13 refers to a normal exploitation of "the work." However, the TRIPS Agreement and the Berne Convention provide exclusive rights in relation to the work. These exclusive rights are the legal means by which exploitation of the work, i.e., the commercial activity for extracting economic value from the rights to the work, can be carried out. The parties do not in principle question that the term "works" should be understood as referring to the "exclusive rights" in those works.[154] In our view, Article 13's second condition does not explicitly refer *pars pro toto* to exclusive rights concerning a "work" given that the TRIPS Agreement (or the Berne Convention (1971) as incorporated into it) confers a considerable number of exclusive rights to all of which the exception clause of Article 13 may apply. Therefore, we believe that the "work" in Article 13's second condition means all the exclusive rights relating to it.

While we agree with the United States that the degree to which an exception affects a particular right is relevant for our analysis under the second condition, we emphasize that a possible conflict with a normal exploitation of a particular exclusive right cannot be counter-balanced or justified by the mere fact of the absence of a conflict with a normal exploitation of another exclusive right (or the absence of any exception altogether with respect to that right), even if the exploitation of the latter right would generate more income.

We agree with the European Communities that whether a limitation or an exception conflicts with a normal exploitation of a work should be judged for each exclusive right individually. We recall that this dispute primarily concerns the exclusive right under Article 11*bis*(1)(iii) of the Berne Convention (1971) as incorporated into the TRIPS Agreement, but also the exclusive right under Article 11(1)(ii). In our view, normal exploitation would presuppose the possibility for right holders to exercise separately all three exclusive rights guaranteed under the three subparagraphs of Article 11*bis*(1), as well as the rights conferred by other provisions, such as Article 11, of the Berne Convention (1971). If it were permissible to limit by a statutory exemption the exploitation of the right conferred by the third subparagraph of Article 11*bis*(1) simply because, in practice, the exploitation of the rights conferred by the first and second subparagraphs of Article 11*bis*(1) would generate the lion's share of royalty revenue, the "normal exploitation" of each of the three rights conferred separately under Article 11*bis*(1) would be undermined.[155]

---

[154]These rights include, *inter alia*, the rights of public performance and broadcasting as well as the right of communication to the public in the meanings of Articles 11*bis*(1)(iii) and 11(1)(ii) of the Berne Convention (1971).

[155]Moreover, we need to keep in mind that the exclusive rights conferred by different subparagraphs of Articles 11*bis* and 11 need not necessarily be in the possession of one and the same right holder. An author or performer may choose not to license the use of a particular exclusive right but to sell and transfer it to another natural or juridical person. If it were permissible to justify the interference into one exclusive right with the fact that another exclusive right generates more revenue, certain right holders might be deprived of their right to obtain royalties simply because the exclusive right held by another right holder is more profitable.

Our view that exclusive rights need to be analysed separately for the purposes of the second condition is also corroborated by the licensing practices between CMOs and broadcasting organizations in the United States and the European Communities. These practices do not appear to take into account the potential additional audience created by means of a further communication

. . . .

We also note that the amplification of broadcast music will occur in establishments such as bars, restaurants and retail stores for the commercial benefit of the owner of the establishment. Both parties agree on the commercial nature of playing music even when customers are not directly charged for it. It may be that the amount yielded from any royalty payable as a consequence of this exploitation of the work will not be very great if one looks at the matter in the context of single establishments. But it is the accumulation of establishments which counts. It must be remembered that a copyright owner is entitled to exploit each of the rights for which a treaty, and the national legislation implementing that treaty, provides. If a copyright owner is entitled to a royalty for music broadcast over the radio, why should the copyright owner be deprived of remuneration which would otherwise be earned, when a significant number of radio broadcasts are amplified to customers of a variety of commercial establishments no doubt for the benefit of the businesses being conducted in those establishments. We also note that although, in a sense, the amplification which is involved is additional to and separate from the broadcast of a work, it is tied to the broadcast. The amplification cannot occur unless there is a broadcast. If an operator of an establishment plays recorded music, there is no legislative exception to the copyright owners' rights in that regard. But the amplification of a broadcast adds to the broadcast itself because it ensures that a wider audience will hear it. Clearly Article 11*bis*(iii) contemplates the use which is in question here by conferring rights on copyright owners in respect of the amplification of broadcasts.

That leaves us with the question of how to determine whether a particular use constitutes a normal exploitation of the exclusive rights provided under Articles 11*bis*(1)(iii) and 11(1)(ii) of the Berne Convention (1971). In academic literature, one approach that has been suggested would be to rely on "the ways in which an author might reasonably be expected to exploit his work in the normal course of events."[159]

The main thrust of the US argumentation is that, for judging "normal exploitation," Article 13's second condition implies an economic analysis of the degree of "market displacement" in terms of foregone collection of remuneration by right owners caused by the free use of works due to the exemption at issue. In the US view, the essential question to ask is whether there are areas of the market in which the copyright owner would ordinarily expect to exploit the work, but which are not available for exploitation because of this exemption. Under this test, uses from which an owner would not ordinarily expect to receive compensation are not part of the normal exploitation.

In our view, this test seems to reflect the empirical or quantitative aspect of the connotation of "normal", the meaning of "regular, usual, typical or ordinary." We can, therefore, accept this US approach, but only for the empirical or quantitative side of the connotation. We have to give meaning and effect also to the second aspect of the connotation, the meaning of "conforming to a type or

---

by loudspeaker of a broadcast of a work within the meaning of Article 11*bis*(1)(iii), i.e. no fees are collected from broadcasters for the additional audiences. . . .

[159]Ricketson, The Berne Convention, op. cit., p. 483.

standard". We described this aspect of normalcy as reflecting a more normative approach to defining normal exploitation, that includes, *inter alia*, a dynamic element capable of taking into account technological and market developments. The question then arises how this normative aspect of "normal" exploitation could be given meaning in relation to the exploitation of musical works.

In this respect, we find persuasive guidance in the suggestion by a study group, composed of representatives of the Swedish Government and the United International Bureaux for the Protection of Intellectual Property ("BIRPI"), which was set up to prepare for the Revision Conference at Stockholm in 1967 ("Swedish/BIRPI Study Group"). In relation to the reproduction right, this Group suggested to allow countries:

> [to] limit the recognition and the exercising of that right, for specified purposes and *on the condition that these purposes should not enter into economic competition with these works* in the sense that *all forms of exploiting a work, which have, or are likely to acquire, considerable economic or practical importance, must be reserved to the authors.*[161] (emphasis added).

Thus it appears that one way of measuring the normative connotation of normal exploitation is to consider, in addition to those forms of exploitation that currently generate significant or tangible revenue, those forms of exploitation which, with a certain degree of likelihood and plausibility, could acquire considerable economic or practical importance.

In contrast, exceptions or limitations would be presumed not to conflict with a normal exploitation of works if they are confined to a scope or degree that does not enter into economic competition with non-exempted uses. In this respect, the suggestions of the Swedish/BIRPI Study Group are useful:

> In this connection, the Study Group observed that, on the one hand, it was obvious that *all forms of exploiting a work which had, or were likely to acquire, considerable economic or practical importance must in principle be reserved to the authors*; exceptions that might restrict the possibilities open to the authors in these respects were unacceptable. On the other hand, it should not be forgotten that *domestic laws already contained a series of exceptions in favour of various public and cultural interests* and that it would be vain to suppose that countries would be ready at this stage to abolish these exceptions to any appreciable extent. (emphasis added).

We recall that the European Communities proposes to measure the impact of exceptions by using a benchmark according to which, at least, all those forms of use of works that create an economic benefit for the user should be considered

---

[161]Document S/1: Berne Convention; Proposals for Revising the Substantive Copyright Provisions (Articles 1-20). Prepared by the Government of Sweden with the assistance of BIRPI, p. 42.

as normal exploitation of works. We can accept that the assessment of normal exploitation of works, from an empirical or quantitative perspective, requires an economic analysis of the commercial use of the exclusive rights conferred by the copyrights in those works. However, in our view, not every use of a work, which in principle is covered by the scope of exclusive rights and involves commercial gain, necessarily conflicts with a normal exploitation of that work. If this were the case, hardly any exception or limitation could pass the test of the second condition and Article 13 might be left devoid of meaning, because normal exploitation would be equated with full use of exclusive rights.

We believe that an exception or limitation to an exclusive right in domestic legislation rises to the level of a conflict with a normal exploitation of the work (i.e., the copyright or rather the whole bundle of exclusive rights conferred by the ownership of the copyright), if uses, that in principle are covered by that right but exempted under the exception or limitation, enter into economic competition with the ways that right holders normally extract economic value from that right to the work (i.e., the copyright) and thereby deprive them of significant or tangible commercial gains.

In developing a benchmark for defining the normative connotation of normal exploitation, we recall the European Communities' emphasis on the potential impact of an exception rather than on its actual effect on the market at a given point in time, given that, in its view, it is the potential effect that determines the market conditions.

. . . .

Therefore, in respect of the exclusive rights related to musical works, we consider that normal exploitation of such works is not only affected by those who actually use them without an authorization by the right holders due to an exception or limitation, but also by those who may be induced by it to do so at any time without having to obtain a licence from the right holders or the CMOs representing them. Thus we need to take into account those whose use of musical works is free as a result of the exemptions, and also those who may choose to start using broadcast music once its use becomes free of charge.

We base our appraisal of the actual and potential effects on the commercial and technological conditions that prevail in the market currently or in the near future. What is a normal exploitation in the market-place may evolve as a result of technological developments or changing consumer preferences. Thus, while we do not wish to speculate on future developments, we need to consider the actual and potential effects of the exemption in question in the current market and technological environment.

We do acknowledge that the extent of exercise or non-exercise of exclusive rights by right holders at a given point in time is of great relevance for assessing what is the normal exploitation with respect to a particular exclusive right in a particular market. However, in certain circumstances, current licensing practices may not provide a sufficient guideline for assessing the potential impact of an exception or limitation on normal exploitation. For example, where a particular use of works is not covered by the exclusive rights conferred in the law of a jurisdiction, the fact that the right holders do not license such use in that jurisdiction cannot be considered indicative of what constitutes normal exploitation. The same would be true in a situation where, due to lack of effective or affordable means of enforcement, right holders may not find it worthwhile or practical to exercise their rights.

Both parties are of the view that the "normalcy" of a form of exploitation should be analysed primarily by reference to the market of the WTO Member whose measure is in dispute, i.e., the US market in this dispute. The European Communities is also of the view that comparative references to other countries with a similar level of socio-economic development could be relevant to corroborate or contradict data from the country primarily concerned. We note that while the WTO Members are free to choose the method of implementation, the minimum standards of protection are the same for all of them. In the present case it is enough for our purposes to take account of the specific conditions applying in the US market in assessing whether the measure in question conflicts with a normal exploitation in that market, or whether the measure meets the other conditions of Article 13.

(ii) The business exemption of subparagraph (B)

The United States contends that the business exemption does not conflict with a normal exploitation of works for a number of reasons. First, in view of the great number of small eating, drinking and retail establishments, individual right holders or their CMOs face considerable administrative difficulties in licensing all these establishments. Given that the market to which the business exemption applies was never significantly exploited by the CMOs, the US Congress merely codified the *status quo* of the CMOs' licensing practices. Second, a significant portion of the establishments exempted by the new business exemption had already been exempted under the old homestyle exemption. Thus owners of copyrights in nondramatic musical works had no expectation of receiving fees from the small eating, drinking or retail establishments covered by the latter exemption. Third, even if subparagraph (B) had not been enacted, many of the establishments eligible for that exemption would have been able to avail themselves of an almost identical exemption under the group licensing agreement between the NLBA and ASCAP, the BMI and SESAC ("US CMOs"). For these reasons, the United States assumes that, even before the 1998 Amendment, right holders would not have normally expected to obtain fees from these establishments. The United States believes that the number of establishments that would not have been entitled to take advantage of the original homestyle exemption of 1976 or the NLBA agreement and thus were newly exempted under subparagraph (B), is small. Viewed against the panoply of exploitative uses available to copyright owners under US copyright law, in the US view, the residual limitation on some secondary uses of broadcast works does not rise to the level of a conflict with normal exploitation.

The European Communities responds that administrative difficulties in licensing a great number of small establishments do not excuse the very absence of the right, because there can be enforcement of only such rights as are recognized by law. It also points out that the use of recorded music is not covered by the exemptions. Arguing that this differentiation is difficult to justify, it contends that, to the extent the licensing of a great number of establishments meets insurmountable difficulties, then such difficulties should occur independently of the medium used. It also notes that the EC CMOs are successfully licensing a great number of small businesses without encountering insurmountable obstacles, whereas the US CMOs due to the lack of legal protection have not developed the necessary administrative structure to licence small establishments.

In response to a question from the Panel, the United States clarifies that it does not argue that administrative difficulties in licensing small establishments are more severe with respect to broadcast music as opposed to CDs or live music. Part of the rationale for this distinction is rather an historical one.

In relation to its statement that the market to which the business exemption applies was never significantly exploited by the CMOs, the United States submitted information concerning the number and percentage of establishments that were licensed in the past by the CMOs. The United States explains that, in considering the original homestyle exemption of Section 110(5), the US Congress found that, prior to 1976, the majority of beneficiaries of the then contemplated exemption were not licensed. As regards the situation between the entry into force of the 1976 Copyright Act and the 1998 Amendment, the United States refers to the information provided by the NRA. Based on the US Census Bureau data for 1996 and a number of its own studies, the NRA estimates that 16 per cent of table service restaurants and 5 per cent of fast food restaurants were licensed by the CMOs at that time in the United States. According to the NRA estimates based on the Census Bureau data, there was approximately the same number of table service and fast food restaurants in the United States. Averaging these percentage figures, the United States concludes that approximately 10.5 per cent of restaurants were licensed by the CMOs.

In this context, the United States refers to the testimony of the President of ASCAP before the US Congress in 1997. Based on the total number of ASCAP restaurants licensees and the total number of restaurants estimated by the NRA on the basis of the Census Bureau data, the United States estimates that ASCAP did not license more than 19 per cent of restaurants at that time. This, in its view, also indicates a relatively low level of licensing of such establishments.

We recall that, in its study of November 1995, the CRS estimated that the size of 16 per cent of eating establishments, 13.5 per cent of drinking establishments and 18 per cent of retail establishments did not exceed at that time the size of the *Aiken* restaurant, i.e. 1,055 square feet. These establishments could benefit from the exemption under the original Section 110(5), subject to equipment limitations. The United States gives two estimates of the number of licensed restaurants at that time: on the one hand, 10.5 per cent of restaurants were licensed by the CMOs, and, on the other hand, 19 per cent of restaurants were licensed by ASCAP. The United States also estimates that 74 per cent of all restaurants play some kind of music.

Even when we deduct the share of the restaurants that were potentially exempted under the original homestyle exemption, we can agree with the

United States that these figures indicate a relatively low level of licensing of restaurants likely to play music. However, as we noted above, whether or not the CMOs fully exercise their right to authorize the use of particular exclusive rights, or choose to collect remuneration for particular uses, or from particular users can, in our view, not necessarily be fully indicative of "normal exploitation" of exclusive rights. In considering whether the 1998 Amendment conflicts with normal exploitation, the fact that it does not generally change the licensing practices in relation to those establishments that were already exempted under the old homestyle exemption is not relevant; it is evident that due to the pre-existing homestyle exemption such establishments could not be licensed. . . .

The restaurants that were licensed by the CMOs before the 1998 Amendment were presumably mostly restaurants which were above the *Aiken* size limits (or did not meet the equipment limits for smaller restaurants). The two US estimates of the share of licensed restaurants (10.5 and 19 per cent) read together with the US estimate of the share of restaurants that play some kind of music (74 per cent) imply that many restaurants, that were above the *Aiken* size limits and that were likely to play music, appear not to have been licensed. This tends to indicate that amongst similar users some paid licence fees while others did not. We have not been provided with any evidence that it would be considered normal to expect remuneration from some but not other similarly situated users.

We do not find the argument compelling, according to which an exception that codifies an existing practice by the CMOs of not licensing certain users should be presumed not to conflict with normal exploitation, as it would not affect right holders' current expectations to be remunerated. In our understanding, this would equate "normal exploitation" with "normal remuneration" practices existing at a certain point in time in a given market or jurisdiction. If such exceptions were permissible *per se*, any current state and degree of exercise of an exclusive right by right holders could effectively be "frozen". In our view, such argumentation could be abused as a justification of any exception or limitation since right holders could never reasonably expect remuneration for uses which are not covered by exclusive rights provided in national legislation. Logically, no conflict with normal exploitation could be construed. The same would apply where a low level of exercise of an exclusive right would be due to lack of effective or affordable means of enforcement of that right. In other words, the licensing practices of the CMOs in a given market at a given time do not define the minimum standards of protection under the TRIPS Agreement that have to be provided under national legislation.

[The panel rejected as irrelevant to the interpretation of Article 13 the United States' reliance on the terms of (1) a prior 1995 legislative proposal by the U.S. CMOs as a substitute for a then-pending bill to amend section 110(5), and (2) a 1995 private group licensing agreement between the U.S. CMOs and the NLBA.]

We recall that a substantial majority of eating and drinking establishments and close to half of retail establishments are eligible to benefit from the business exemption. This constitutes a major potential source of royalties for the exercise of the exclusive rights contained in Articles 11*bis*(1)(iii) and

11(1)(ii) of the Berne Convention (1971), as demonstrated by the figures of the D&B studies referred to under our analysis of the first condition of Article 13.

We recall that subparagraph (B) of Section 110(5) exempts communication to the public of radio and television broadcasts, while the playing of musical works from CDs and tapes (or live music) is not covered by it. Given that we have not been provided with reasons other than historical ones for this distinction, we see no logical reason to differentiate between broadcast and recorded music when assessing what is a normal use of musical works.

It is true, as the United States notes, that many of these establishments might not play music at all, or play recorded or live music. According to NLBA surveys, among its member establishments 26 per cent use CDs or tapes, 18 per cent rely on background music services, 37 per cent have live music performances, while 28 per cent play radio music. The United States estimates that overall approximately 74 per cent of US restaurants play music from various sources. The United States provided estimates also by the NRA concerning its membership on the percentage of restaurants that play the radio or use the television . . . . From this data, the United States assumes that no more than 44 per cent of licensing fees can be attributed to radio music.

We note that the parties agree that the administrative challenges for the CMOs related to the licensing of a great number of small eating, drinking and retail establishments do not differ depending on the medium used for playing music. We believe that the differentiation between different types of media may induce operators of establishments covered by subparagraph (B) to switch from recorded or live music, which is subject to the payment of a fee, to music played on the radio or television, which is free of charge. This may also create an incentive to reduce the licensing fees for recorded music so that users would not switch to broadcast music.

Right holders of musical works would expect to be in a position to authorize the use of broadcasts of radio and television music by many of the establishments covered by the exemption and, as appropriate, receive compensation for the use of their works. Consequently, we cannot but conclude that an exemption of such scope as subparagraph (B) conflicts with the "normal exploitation" of the work in relation to the exclusive rights conferred by Articles 11*bis*(1)(iii) and 11(1)(ii) of the Berne Convention (1971).

In the light of these considerations, we conclude that the business exemption embodied in subparagraph (B) conflicts with a normal exploitation of the work within the meaning of the second condition of Article 13.

(iii) The homestyle exemption of subparagraph (A)

[The panel did not state conclusions as regards the original pre-1998 homestyle exemption, but noted that according to the 1995 CRS study, the number of establishments that could benefit from the exemption was limited to a comparatively small percentage of all eating, drinking and retail establishments in the United States.]

. . . .

We recall that it is the common understanding of the parties that the operation of subparagraph (A) is limited [to dramatic musical works]. . . Consequently, performances of, e.g., individual songs from a dramatic musical work outside a dramatic context would constitute a rendition of a nondramatic work and fall within the purview of subparagraph (B).

It is our understanding that the parties agree that the right holders do not normally license or attempt to license the public communication of transmissions embodying dramatic renditions of "dramatic" musical works in the sense of Article 11bis(1)(iii) and/or 11(1)(ii). We have not been provided with information about any existing licensing practices concerning the communication to the public of broadcasts of performances of dramatic works (e.g., operas, operettas, musicals) by eating, drinking or retail establishments in the United States or any other country. In this respect, we fail to see how the homestyle exemption, as limited to works other than nondramatic musical works in its revised form, could acquire economic or practical importance of any considerable dimension for the right holders of musical works.

Therefore, we conclude that the homestyle exemption contained in subparagraph (A) of Section 110(5) does not conflict with a normal exploitation of works within the meaning of the second condition of Article 13.

(d) *"Not unreasonably prejudice the legitimate interests of the right holder"*

(i) General interpretative analysis

. . . .

We note that the analysis of the third condition of Article 13 of the TRIPS Agreement implies several steps. First, one has to define what are the "interests" of right holders at stake and which attributes make them "legitimate". Then, it is necessary to develop an interpretation of the term "prejudice" and what amount of it reaches a level that should be considered "unreasonable".

The ordinary meaning of the term "interests" may encompass a legal right or title to a property or to use or benefit of a property (including intellectual property). It may also refer to a concern about a potential detriment or advantage, and more generally to something that is of some importance to a natural or legal person. Accordingly, the notion of "interests" is not necessarily limited to actual or potential economic advantage or detriment.

The term "legitimate" has the meanings of

(a) conformable to, sanctioned or authorized by, law or principle; lawful; justifiable; proper;

(b) normal, regular, conformable to a recognized standard type.

Thus, the term relates to lawfulness from a legal positivist perspective, but it has also the connotation of legitimacy from a more normative perspective, in the context of calling for the protection of interests that are justifiable in the light of the objectives that underlie the protection of exclusive rights.

We note that the ordinary meaning of "prejudice" connotes damage, harm or injury. "Not unreasonable" connotes a slightly stricter threshold than "reasonable". The latter term means "proportionate", "within the limits of reason, not greatly less or more than might be thought likely or appropriate", or "of a fair, average or considerable amount or size."[201]

Given that the parties do not question the "legitimacy" of the interest of right holders to exercise their rights for economic gain, the crucial question becomes which degree or level of "prejudice" may be considered as "unreasonable". Before dealing with the question of what amount or which kind of prejudice reaches a level beyond reasonable, we need to find a way to measure or quantify legitimate interests.

In our view, one—albeit incomplete and thus conservative—way of looking at legitimate interests is the economic value of the exclusive rights conferred by copyright on their holders. It is possible to estimate in economic terms the value of exercising, e.g., by licensing, such rights. That is not to say that legitimate interests are necessarily limited to this economic value.[202]

In examining the second condition of Article 13, we have addressed the US argument that the prejudice to right holders caused by the exemptions at hand are minimal because they already receive royalties from broadcasting stations. We concluded that each exclusive right conferred by copyright, *inter alia*, under each subparagraph of Articles 11*bis* and 11 of the Berne Convention (1971), has to be considered separately for the purpose of examining whether a possible conflict with a "normal exploitation" exists.[203]

The crucial question is which degree or level of "prejudice" may be considered as "unreasonable", given that, under the third condition, a certain amount of "prejudice" has to be presumed justified as "not unreasonable."[205] In our view,

---

[201]Oxford English Dictionary, p. 2496.

[202]Panel Report on *Canada—Patent Protection of Pharmaceutical Products*, adopted on 7 April 2000, WT/DS114/R, ¶¶ 7.60ff. We note, however, the difference in wording between Articles 13 and 30 of the TRIPS Agreement. The latter also refers to "taking account of the legitimate interests of third parties."

[203]We also recall from our examination of Article 13's second condition that we were not presented with evidence of licensing arrangements between CMOs and broadcasting organizations, concerning mainly the exclusive rights of Article 11*bis*(1)(i) or (ii), that would make allowance for the additional communication to the public in the meaning of Article 11*bis*(1)(iii) by, e.g., the categories of establishments covered by the subparagraphs of Section 110(5). We believe that we have to analyse whether the exemptions in question cause unreasonable prejudice to the legitimate interests of right holders similarly in respect of each exclusive right. Our view is confirmed by the fact that, as we pointed out when examining the second condition of Article 13, particular exclusive rights conferred by the subparagraphs of Articles 11 and 11*bis* in relation to one and the same work may be held by different persons. . . .

[205]In respect of what could be the dividing line between "unreasonable" and "not unreasonable" prejudice, we consider the explanation of the Guide to the Berne Convention to be of persuasive value. It states in the context of the third condition of Article 9(2) of the Berne Convention, which is worded almost identically to Article 13 of the TRIPS Agreement but refers to exceptions to the reproduction right:

"Note that it is not a question of prejudice or no: all copying is damaging to some degree . . ." The paragraph goes on to discuss whether photocopying "prejudices the circulation of the review",

prejudice to the legitimate interests of right holders reaches an unreasonable level if an exception or limitation causes or has the potential to cause an unreasonable loss of income to the copyright owner.

. . . .

(ii) The business exemption of subparagraph (B)

The European Communities focuses on an analysis of the potential economic effects of subparagraph (B) on the legitimate interests of right holders. It argues that the unreasonableness of the prejudice caused to the right holder becomes fully apparent when 73 per cent of all drinking establishments, 70 per cent of all eating establishments and 45 per cent of all retail establishments are unconditionally covered by the business exemption, while the rest of the establishments may also be exempted under conditions which are easy to meet. In its view, the denial of protection has been turned into the rule and protection of the exclusive right has become the exception.

The United States does not focus on questioning the correctness of these figures that indicate the percentage of US eating, drinking and retail establishments that fall within the size limits of subparagraph (B). Taking these figures as a starting-point for alternative calculations, the United States, however, contends that they are not useful for estimating the economic impact or prejudice caused by subparagraph (B) to right holders, because they fail to account for many relevant factors that determine whether a right holder would be economically prejudiced at all by the business exemption. In order to obtain a reasonable estimate of the number of establishments from which copyright owners have truly lost revenue as a result of the business exemption, the United States subtracts from these figures those establishments that:

(i)   do not play music at all;

(ii)   rely on music from some source other than radio or TV (such as tapes, CDs, commercial background music services, jukeboxes, or live music);

(iii) were not licensed prior to the passage of the 1998 amendment and which the CMOs would not be able to license anyway;

(iv)   would take advantage of the NLBA agreement, whose terms are practically identical to subparagraph (B), if the statutory exemption were not available; and

(v)   would prefer to simply turn off the music rather than pay the fees demanded by the CMOs.

The United States concedes that it is impossible to estimate these figures, but assumes that there is ample reason to believe that they represent a substantial

---

whether it "might seriously cut in on its sales" and says that "[i]n cases where there would be serious loss of profit for the copyright owner, the law should provide him with some compensation (a system of compulsory licensing with equitable remuneration)." *See* Guide to the Berne Convention, ¶ 9.8, pp. 55-56. We do not believe that in this respect the benchmark has to be substantially different for reproduction rights, performance rights or broadcasting rights in the meanings of Articles 9, 11 or 11*bis* of the Berne Convention (1971).

number of establishments.

. . . .

No music or music from another source

In detailing its first, second and fifth reduction factor, the United States provides estimates on the percentages of restaurants that use various sources of music, which we have summarized . . . above. We agree that it is possible that some establishments that currently play broadcast music might decide to stop doing so, if they were required to pay fees to CMOs representing right holders in the absence of an exemption. But it is also evident that establishments that currently play recorded music may at any time decide to switch to music broadcast over the air or transmitted by cable in order to avoid paying licensing fees. Also, some establishments that do not play any music at all may start to use broadcast music, given that the only cost would be that of acquiring a sound system. Similarly, if amplified broadcast music would not be free of charge due to subparagraph (B) of Section 110(5), operators of establishments covered by that provision that currently use such broadcast music might switch to recorded music, to commercial background music services or to live music performances. Furthermore, an exemption that makes the use of music from one source free of charge is likely to affect, not only the number of establishments that opt for sources of music that require the payment of a licensing fee, but also the price for which the protected sources of music can be licensed.

It appears that the use of recorded music or commercial background music services can be easily replaced by the amplification of music transmitted over the air or by cable. Digital broadcasts and cable transmissions are increasing the supply of different types of music transmissions. The fact that one source of music is free of charge while another triggers copyright liability may have a significant impact on which source of music the operators of establishments choose, and on how much they are willing to pay for protected music. Therefore, in addition to the right holders' loss of revenue from the users that were newly exempted under subparagraph (B) of Section 110(5), the business exemption is also likely to reduce the amount of income that may be generated from restaurants and retail establishments for the use of recorded music or commercial background music services.

Although these considerations do not render irrelevant the statistics and estimations on the numbers and percentages of establishments that may play music from different sources or no music at all, it is clear that such statistics and estimations have to be considered with the *caveat* that, although they may reflect realities at a given point in time, they do not take into account the substitution between various sources of music that is likely to take place in the longer term.

Establishments not licensed before the 1998 Amendment and the NLBA Agreement

As to its third reduction factor, the United States submitted information concerning past licensing practices of establishments covered by Section 110(5). . . .

Based on these statistics about past licensing practices and ASCAP's revenue collection, the United States submits that the likely impact of the amended Section 110(5) on the revenues collected earlier by the CMOs from such establishments is likely to be minimal. . . .

The EC's main contention against the reduction factors applied by the United States to its estimates of potential prejudice is that actual distributions to right holders, past licensing practices and revenue collected or foregone by the CMOs in the past or at present are not representative of the potential economic effect of subparagraph (B), because collection practices of the CMOs are a function of the legal protection of the relevant exclusive rights.

More specifically, the European Communities points out that the long-standing exceptions to copyright protection (i.e., prior to 1976, the *Aiken* decision, the passage of the homestyle exemption of the 1976 Copyright Act, subsequent court decisions in *Claire's Boutique* and *Edison Bros.*) render the actual royalty collection practices of the CMOs in the past unrepresentative for measuring losses to right holders. . . .

We recall our conclusion that in the application of the three conditions of Article 13 to an exemption in national law, both actual and potential effects of that exception are relevant. As regards the third condition in particular, we note that if only actual losses were taken into account, it might be possible to justify the introduction of a new exception to an exclusive right irrespective of its scope in situations where the right in question was newly introduced, right holders did not previously have effective or affordable means of enforcing that right, or that right was not exercised because the right holders had not yet built the necessary collective management structure required for such exercise. While under such circumstances the introduction of a new exception might not cause immediate additional loss of income to the right holder, he or she could never build up expectations to earn income from the exercise of the right in question. We believe that such an interpretation, if it became the norm, could undermine the scope and binding effect of the minimum standards of intellectual property rights protection embodied in the TRIPS Agreement.[219]

We recall our consideration, in relation to the second condition of Article 13, of the relatively low level of licensing, before the 1998 Amendment, of restaurants above the *Aiken* size limits that were likely to play music. We concluded that, without further evidence, the fact that some similarly situated users were licensed, while others were not, could not be taken as an indication of normal exploitation. As regards the third condition of Article 13, we have not

---

[219]In comparison, we recall that in relation to the second condition, we noted that a low level of licensing cannot be determinative of normal exploitation to the extent that it results from lack of legal protection or of effective or affordable means of enforcement.

been provided with any persuasive arguments why the legitimate interests of the right holder would differ in respect of those similarly situated users that are currently licensed and those that are not; neither have we been given any persuasive explanation why some of these users were licensed and others not.

Therefore, in considering the prejudice to the legitimate interests of right holders caused by the business exemption, we have to take into account not only the actual loss of income from those restaurants that were licensed by the CMOs at the time that the exemption become effective, but also the loss of potential revenue from other restaurants of similar size likely to play music that were not licensed at that point.

As to the fourth US reduction factor, we note that we have already addressed the US argument about the similarity between the 1998 Amendment and the group licensing agreement reached between the CMOs and the NLBA in 1995 in our discussion of the second condition of Article 13. In that context, we noted that a private agreement constitutes a form of exercising exclusive rights and is by no means determinative for assessing the compliance of an exemption provided for in national law pursuant to international treaty obligations.

Summary of the relevance of the above factors

Consequently, we caution against attributing too much relevance to the factors proposed by the United States for reducing the EC figures intended to indicate the potential prejudice in relation to eating, drinking or retail establishments, and, accordingly, for the determination of the level of prejudice caused by the business exemption to the legitimate interests of right holders. At the same time, we recognize the difficulty of quantifying the economic value of potential prejudice. Most of the factual information on the current US licensing market provided by the parties relates to the immediate actual losses to the right holders; in particular, both parties have provided us with detailed calculations of the loss of income to the right holders resulting from the 1998 Amendment. Keeping in mind our conclusion that such figures cannot alone be determinative for the assessment of the level of prejudice suffered by right holders, we will now examine these calculations.

The alternative calculations by the parties of losses suffered by right holders

The United States estimates that the maximum annual loss to EC right holders of distributions from the largest US collecting society, ASCAP, as a result of the Section 110(5) exemption, is in the range of $294,113 to $586,332. Applying the same analysis, it estimates that the loss from the second largest society, BMI, is $122,000. In its calculation of ASCAP's distributions, the United States takes as a starting-point the total royalties paid to EC right holders by ASCAP. Second, it reduces the amount attributable to general licensing (i.e. licensing of commercial background music services, and a wide variety of licensees, including conventions and sports arenas, as well as restaurants, bars and retail establishments). Third, it makes a deduction to account for licensing revenue from general licensees that do not meet the statutory definition of an "establishment". Fourth, it deducts from the general licensing revenue the portion that is due to music from sources other than radio or television (e.g., tapes, CDs, commercial background music services, jukeboxes, live performances); and fifth, it reduces this amount to account for licensing revenue from general licensing of eating, drinking or retail establishments which play the radio but do not meet the size and equipment limitations of subparagraph (B) and thus do not qualify for the business exemption. . . .

The European Communities estimates that the annual loss to all right holders amounts to $53.65 million. The EC calculation takes as the starting-point the number of establishments that may qualify for the exception. Second, the European Communities makes a reduction from that number using the US hypotheses that 30.5 per cent of all eating and drinking establishments with a surface area below 3,750 square feet actually play music from the radio. Third, it applies to the remaining establishments the appropriate licensing fees selected from the licensing schedules of ASCAP and BMI. . . .

Overall, we consider that neither estimate is devoid of relevance for the purposes of estimating whether prejudice caused by subparagraph (B) to the legitimate interests of right holders amounts to a level that could be deemed unreasonable. The difference between the results of these two calculations can, to an extent, be explained by differences in the starting points and the parameters used for the calculations. The calculations use also a number of similar assumptions. We highlight below some of these differences and similarities.

The US estimate can be characterized as a "top-down" approach, which takes as its starting-point ASCAP's and the BMI's average total distributions of domestic income for the years 1996-1998. We recall that the United States estimates that only 10.5-19 per cent of restaurants were licensed at that time. Hence, this calculation based on the pre-existing collection does not take into account the potential income from establishments that were already covered at that time by the old homestyle exemption or from the larger restaurants that used music but were not licensed at that time.

The EC calculation can, in turn, be characterized as a "bottom-up" approach. It takes as its starting point the total number of restaurants and retail establishments that fall under the size limits of the exemption; then it applies to those establishments the lowest ASCAP and BMI licence fees, assuming a 100 per cent compliance rate among the establishments concerned.

The EC calculation covers all right holders, while the US calculation covers only the EC right holders' share. The United States estimates that this share is between 5 and 13.7 per cent of ASCAP's distributions of domestic income, and 8.15 per cent of the BMI's distributions.

Both calculations make a number of reductions from the above starting points based on estimations. In the absence of more detailed information from ASCAP, the United States estimates that 50 per cent of ASCAP's general licensing revenue is derived from the establishments covered by the business exemption. Based on the NRA and NLBA surveys, the United States estimates that 30.5

per cent of the establishments covered by the exemption play radio; the European Communities also uses this figure. Averaging the NRA estimations of the percentage of restaurants that meet the size limits, and the D&B study on the equivalent percentage of retail establishments, the United States estimates that 52.1 per cent of all establishments fall below the size limits of the business exemption.

Neither calculation takes into account the distributions of the third US CMO, SESAC, or music played on the television. The calculations do not attempt to estimate the losses from establishments above the size limits of subparagraph (B) of Section 110(5), which however comply with the respective equipment limitations. It appears that neither party assumes that these factors would essentially change the outcome of their estimations.

We note that both calculations include many estimations and assumptions. The fact that neither party was in a position to provide more direct information on the revenues collected from the establishments affected by the business exemption does not facilitate the estimation of the immediate effect of the exemption in terms of annual losses to the right holders.

One of the major differences between the calculations is that the US calculation takes into account the loss of income only from those establishments that were not already exempted under the old homestyle exemption and were actually paying licence fees. Given our considerations on the potential impact of the exemption, we are of the view that the loss of potential income from other users of music is also relevant.

. . . .

The United States also submits that its calculation does not take into account steps that ASCAP and the BMI might take to minimize any impact of the 1998 Amendment (e.g., focusing licensing resources exclusively on larger stores that generally pay larger fees, or by charging more for the playing of music from CDs and tapes). In the US view, the analysis should also take into account the limited resources of the CMOs and the small percentage of the market actually licensed by the CMOs. In the light of the certainty provided by the precise limitations of the business exemption contained in subparagraph (B), the CMOs can now efficiently redirect their licensing resources toward those establishments not eligible for the business exemption, and thus compensate for any minor prejudice they might suffer. The United States refers to an ASCAP statement of its intent to "reverse the effects" of the 1998 Amendment by redirecting its licensing resources toward establishments not covered by subparagraph (B) as well as by generating additional income by encouraging the use of live and recorded music, for which there is no exemption.

In our view, this line of argument is irrelevant for the issue before us, i.e., whether subparagraph (B) complies with Article 13's third condition. If we were to find that subparagraph (B) does not meet the conditions for invoking the exception of Article 13, there is no rule in WTO law compelling another Member or private parties affected by a Member's WTO-inconsistent measure to take steps to remedy any actual, or reduce the potential, nullification or impairment caused.

. . . In the light of our analysis of the prejudice caused by the exemption, including its actual and potential effects, we are of the view that the United States has not demonstrated that the business exemption does not unreasonably prejudice the legitimate interests of the right holder.

Accordingly, we conclude that the business exemption of subparagraph (B) of Section 110(5) does not meet the requirements of the third condition of Article 13 of the TRIPS Agreement.

(iii) The homestyle exemption of subparagraph (A)

. . . .

We recall our discussion concerning the legislative history of the original homestyle exemption in connection with the first and second conditions of Article 13. In particular, as regards the beneficiaries of the exemption, the Conference Report (1976) elaborated on the rationale of the exemption by noting that the intent was to exempt a small commercial establishment "which was not of sufficient size to justify, as a practical matter, a subscription to a commercial background music service". We also recall the estimations on the percentages of establishments covered by the exemption. Moreover, the exemption was applicable to such establishments only if they use homestyle equipment. . . .

Furthermore, we recall the common understanding of the parties that the operation of the homestyle exemption as contained in the 1998 Amendment has been limited, as regards musical works, to the public communication of transmissions embodying dramatic renditions of "dramatic" musical works (such as operas, operettas, musicals and other similar dramatic works). We have not been presented with evidence suggesting that right holders would have licensed or attempted to license the public communication, within the meaning of Article 11(1)(ii) or 11*bis*(1)(iii) of the Berne Convention (1971), of broadcasts of performances embodying dramatic renditions of "dramatic" musical works either before the enactment of the original homestyle exemption or after the 1998 Amendment. We also fail to see how communications to the public of renditions of entire dramatic works could acquire such economic or practical importance that it could cause unreasonable prejudice to the legitimate interests of right holders.

We note that playing music by the small establishments covered by the exemption by means of homestyle apparatus has never been a significant source of revenue collection for CMOs. We recall our view that, for the purposes of assessing unreasonable prejudice to the legitimate interests of right holders, potential losses of right holders, too, are relevant. However, we have not been presented with persuasive information suggesting that such potential effects of significant economic or practical importance could occur that they would give rise to an unreasonable level of prejudice to legitimate interests of right holders. In particular, as regards the exemption as amended in 1998 to exclude from its scope nondramatic musical works, the European Communities has not explicitly claimed that the exemption would currently cause any prejudice to right holders.

In the light of the considerations above, we conclude that the homestyle exemption contained in subparagraph (A) of Section 110(5) does not cause unreasonable prejudice to the legitimate interests of the right holders within the meaning of the third condition of Article 13.

VII. CONCLUSIONS AND RECOMMENDATIONS

In the light of the findings . . . above, the Panel concludes that:

(a) Subparagraph (A) of Section 110(5) of the US Copyright Act meets the requirements of Article 13 of the TRIPS Agreement and is thus consistent with Articles 11*bis*(1)(iii) and 11(1)(ii) of the Berne Convention (1971) as incorporated into the TRIPS Agreement by Article 9.1 of that Agreement.

(b) Subparagraph (B) of Section 110(5) of the US Copyright Act does not meet the requirements of Article 13 of the TRIPS Agreement and is thus inconsistent with Articles 11*bis*(1)(iii) and 11(1)(ii) of the Berne Convention (1971) as incorporated into the TRIPS Agreement by Article 9.1 of that Agreement.

The Panel *recommends* that the Dispute Settlement Body request the United States to bring subparagraph (B) of Section 110(5) into conformity with its obligations under the TRIPS Agreement.

NOTES AND QUESTIONS

(1) **Broader Significance of *Section 110(5)* Report.** This panel report is a groundbreaking development in international copyright law. It is the first binding interpretation of the meaning of language in a multilateral copyright treaty. The International Court of Justice has never ruled on the meaning of the Berne Convention, notwithstanding its jurisdiction to resolve disputes among member states. (No state has referred such a dispute.) And the *Section 110(5)* report was the first interpretation by a WTO dispute settlement panel of the relationship between the Berne Convention and the TRIPS Agreement, and of the meaning of a provision of the Berne Convention as incorporated into TRIPS. The panel report will be studied carefully not only for its implications for Section 110(5) of the U.S. Copyright Act, but also for what it means for the likely development of international copyright law by WTO panels. Indeed, because the language of Article 13 resembles that found in other parts of the TRIPS Agreement, the decision may be of import for international patent and trademark law also. *See Canada-Pharmaceutical Patents, supra* § 3.04[D][2]; *see also* TRIPS art. 30 (patent); TRIPS art. 17 (trademark).

(2) **"Certain Special Cases" and Fair Use.** The panel concluded that, in order to satisfy the first step of the three-step test, an exception must be (i)

clearly defined and (ii) sufficiently limited in its field of application that the cases to which it applied were not the rule. Some scholars have suggested that the fair use defense under U.S. law may fail to satisfy the three-step test. *See, e.g.,* Ruth Okediji, *Toward an International Fair Use Doctrine*, 39 COLUM. J. TRANS. L. 75, 114-36 (2000). Do you agree?

(3) **Panel Assessment of the Normative Basis of an Exception.** As part of its analysis of the first step of the three-step test, the panel declined the EU's invitation to engage in an intrusive assessment of the purposes of the exceptions at issue. The EU had argued that the exception must, to comply with the first step of the test, serve a "special purpose." Instead, the panel accepted the U.S. argument that it should "not impose any requirement as to the legitimacy of the policy objectives that a particular country might consider special in light of its own history and national priorities." All that the panel demanded was that the exception have some specific policy objective: in the case of the homestyle exemption, the United States identified the protection of small "mom and pop" businesses, which "play an important role in the American social fabric" because "they offer economic opportunities for women, minorities, immigrants and welfare recipients for entering the economic and social mainstream." Was the panel correct not to engage in an assessment of the appropriateness of that policy objective under international copyright law?

Even if the panel properly declined to evaluate the merits of that policy objective as such, should it have developed some standard for measuring the means by which that objective was pursued? For example, it might have considered whether the stated objective of the United States was in any way furthered by the means chosen (the homestyle exemption), or whether the exemption was a rational means, or a well-tailored means, or the least burdensome means, of pursuing that objective, to name but a few of the standards that a more intrusive analysis might have applied. *See* Graeme B. Dinwoodie, *The Development and Incorporation of International Norms in the Formation of Copyright Law*, 62 OHIO STATE L.J. 733, 751 n.73 (2001).

The panel noted that one connotation of the term "normal" in the second step of the three-step test required it to adopt a normative approach to defining "normal exploitation." To what extent did the panel engage in a normative analysis of the exception in considering the second step? In the third step?

(4) **Use of Statistics.** To what extent did the panel decision turn on quantitative analysis? How clear was the evidence in this regard? Is it appropriate to make a finding of a treaty violation based upon statistical analysis? At what point between the percentage of establishments found to be covered by the homestyle exemption and the percentage found to be covered by the business exemption would the panel draw the line between permissible and impermissible exceptions under international law?

(5) **Judicial Trends Before WTO Panels.** In its arguments to the panel, the EU made much of what it saw as a judicially developed trend toward broadening of the homestyle exemption. The panel noted that "since 1976 U.S. courts have in the vast majority of cases applied the homestyle exemption in a sufficiently consistent and clearly delineated manner" and that in light of that "it saw no need to hypothesise whether at some point in the future U.S. case law

might lead to a *de facto* expansion of the homestyle exemption of 1998." To what extent should the panel look at the terms of the statute as opposed to court decisions interpreting them? If a single district court applied an extremely generous interpretation of the scope of the homestyle exemption, permitting free use in circumstances well beyond those contemplated by Congress, would the United States be in violation of TRIPS? If not, at what stage does judicial expansion of the exemption beyond the limits defined by Article 13 become a violation of TRIPS? Might an assertive panel interpretation of developing case law in a member state such as the United States discriminate against the common law form of adjudication? *See infra* § 5.03 for more discussion of this issue.

(6) **The Relationship between National Legislative Debates and WTO Dispute Settlement Proceedings.** During Congress's consideration of the Fairness in Music Licensing Act that amended section 110(5), both the Administration and the Copyright Office opposed its enactment. They argued that the amendment was ill-advised as a matter of domestic policy, but also that it would cause international problems based on the obligations of the United States under the TRIPS Agreement. Most of their statements warned that other WTO members were likely to bring a dispute against the United States, rather than asserting that the then-pending version of the bill was inconsistent with TRIPS. If you were drafting the statements, how would you have characterized the international concerns? Why did Congress ignore these warnings, and would the result have been different if the statements were stronger? It is interesting to note that the EU repeatedly cited these statements by U.S. government officials, but that the panel never mentioned them in its report. Why, and why not?

(7) **Compliance Measures.** In July 2000, Deputy U.S. Trade Representative Rita Hayes informed the WTO Dispute Settlement Body that the United States would not appeal the finding that the Fairness in Music Licensing Act violated TRIPS. What is the United States required to do to bring itself into compliance with TRIPS? Would anything short of repeal of the business exemption be adequate? In particular, would a return to the pre-1998 version of section 110(5)—including a return to the older version of the homestyle exemption—be sufficient to ensure compliance? The European Union had complained about the TRIPS compatibility of the pre-1998 homestyle exemption, and was engaged in informal consultations with the United States regarding dispute settlement even prior to the enactment of the 1998 amendments.

To answer the compliance question, identify the basis for the panel's conclusion that the homestyle exemption was consistent with Article 13. Much of the panel's analysis in this regard rests on the premise that the homestyle exemption was (post-1998) limited to dramatic musical works. The European Union and the United States agreed with this interpretation of the new homestyle exemption. But the legislative history offers little support for the suggestion that Congress intended to limit the homestyle exemption in this way. *See* Laurence R. Helfer, *World Music on a U.S. Stage: A Berne/TRIPS and Economic Analysis of the Fairness in Music Licensing Act*, 80 B.U. L. Rev. 93, 97 n.7 (2000) (explaining why the agreed interpretation lacks support either in the statutory language or the legislative history). Would the homestyle exemption have been sustained absent this agreed interpretation? Why did the United States agree to this interpretation?

§ 4.04 Treatment of Foreigners

[A] National Treatment

S.M. STEWART, INTERNATIONAL COPYRIGHT AND NEIGHBOURING RIGHTS 37-43 (2d ed. 1989)[*]

(a) General

Seeking to apply the general principles of private international law to a multinational copyright treaty, theoretically two of the principles would appear to be suitable: the *lex loci* and the *lex fori*. The adaptation of the principle of *lex loci* (or *lex originis*) leads to the principle of country of origin of the work. This means treating a work like a person and saying that its nationality is either that of its father (the author) at the time of its birth, which would be the time of its creation if it remains unpublished or the time of its first publication, if published. Alternatively it would be the nationality of its birthplace, that is the country of its first publication. Like a person the work would then, so to speak, have a passport and take its nationality with it wherever it goes. For example, if Nigeria is a convention country, the work of a Nigerian author, first published in Nigeria, would have in the United Kingdom or France the same rights as it has in Nigeria.

The adaptation of the principle of *lex fori* to copyright leads (not necessarily but in practice) to the principle of national treatment, or as it is sometimes called, the principle of assimilation. This means that persons protected by the convention can claim in all contracting states the protection that the law of that state grants to its own nationals. Foreigners, if belonging to a convention country are "assimilated" to nationals.

The work of the same Nigerian author, published in Nigeria, would have in the United Kingdom the same rights as if it were created by a United Kingdom author and first published in the United Kingdom.

It will be seen that the advantage of adapting the first principle, would be that the same work will receive the same treatment in all member countries. The disadvantage is that lawyers and courts will continuously have to apply a large number of foreign laws, sometimes several laws in the same transaction or court case.

The advantage of the second principle, the *lex fori*, is that courts will always apply their own law. The disadvantage is that the same work will get varying levels of protection in convention countries according to the national law of the country where the protection is claimed.

(b) National treatment (assimilation)

In practice, the second principle, that of national treatment, has proved to be the only viable one. This is so mainly for two reasons, one psychological and the other political. The psychological reason is that courts prefer to apply their own law which they know, to having to apply foreign law which they do not know, and the quality of judgments will be better and the law therefore more certain under the principle of national treatment. The political reason is that right owners in countries of low level protection will realise that they get better treatment abroad in high level protection countries than they get at home and will bring pressure to bear on their governments to raise the level of protection at home. Thus, as the high level protection countries give a lead, the level of protection will gradually rise everywhere, thus getting nearer to the ideal of uniform treatment but on a high level.

National treatment is also in accord with the idea of international law that all men are equal before the law, regardless of whether they are nationals or foreigners, and in a period of history when more and more eminent authors and creators are expatriates or refugees, conventions have also assimilated these to nationals so that they enjoy the same privileges in the country of their choice. The principle of national treatment also means that both the question of whether the right exists and the question of the scope of the rights are to be answered in accordance with the law of the country where the protection is claimed . . . .

For these reasons the principle of national treatment was adopted as the basic principle of the Berne Convention in 1886 and of the copyright and neighbouring rights conventions which followed the Berne Convention. . . .

(c) Extensions of the principle of national treatment

(1) *Minimum rights*

The principle of national treatment is extended in the copyright conventions by providing minimum rights. . . . In a strictly conceptual sense, these minima are not rules relating to conflict of laws as they contain no reference to another legal system. They also do not compel a convention country to grant these conventional rights provided as minimum rights to its own nationals because the convention deals only with international situations and therefore, if nothing else is provided in the convention, only compel a state to grant these rights to foreigners who are nationals of member states. However, the principle of national treatment without minimum rights *jure conventionis* might produce a serious imbalance which states would find unacceptable. If countries A and B were members of a convention which provides only for national treatment and has no minimum rights and country A grants performance and broadcasting rights as well as a reproduction right, whereas country B grants only a reproduction right, the effect would be that the nationals of country B would enjoy performance and broadcasting rights in country A, but nationals of country A would not enjoy these rights in country B because the nationals of country B do not enjoy them either. This could produce a serious disequilibrium which would be unacceptable to country A.

The history of copyright and neighbouring rights conventions bears this out. The Berne Convention which was agreed at a time when the level of protection granted to authors still varied greatly from country to country started with only a minimum term and a translation right *jure conventionis*. The first task was to get as many countries as possible to accept these minimum rights in their legislation which they had to do before they could ratify the convention. Having thus created a common minimum level of protection in these respects the Revision Conferences added further minimum rights. The high level protection countries gave a lead to the lower level protection countries and it was hoped that the right owners of the lower level protection countries enjoying rights abroad which they did not have at home would bring pressure to bear on their governments to introduce them. These hopes proved amply justified.

When the Universal Copyright Convention was negotiated over 60 years later, the difference in the level of protection with regard to the rights covered by the convention had become less marked, and thus less stringent measures to insure against unacceptable differences in the level of protection were required. The term of 25 years *post mortem auctoris* and the translation right are minimum rights, whereas article I requiring contracting states "to adopt . . . such measures as are necessary to ensure the application of the convention" are only general guidelines. However this was considered enough to ensure that differences of levels of protection under the national treatment rule were not too great.

In the Rome Convention, the first neighbouring rights convention, the principle of national treatment is accompanied by minimum rights for each of the three beneficiaries: a right against unauthorised fixation for performers, a reproduction right for phonogram producers and broadcasters, a performance right in phonograms (subject to reservations) for producers and performers. If reservations are made the reciprocity rule can be applied to the states making a reservation. Thus, the principle of national treatment combined with minimum rights to assure a common denominator is moderated by the reciprocity rule to avoid injustices being caused by large divergences of levels of protection.

. . . .

(d) Limitations of the principle of national treatment

(1) *Reciprocity*

The principle of national treatment can be limited, sometimes severely limited, by the rule of reciprocity. The 'raison d'être' of reciprocity is: *"Manus lavat manum."* State A wants its citizens protected in State B and thus offers

to protect the citizens of State B in return. Reciprocity
be either "material" (or "substantive") reciprocity
reciprocity.

Material reciprocity means that country A will pr
B in the same manner as country B protects the
general rule the copyright conventions are opp
although there are exceptions.[2] This is made plai.
Material Reciprocity" which is included in the Report of the
Convention. One of the advantages of avoiding material reciprocity
conventions is that the courts of member states do not have to interpret ..
laws of other member states to see whether protection is given in respect of a
particular right. The rule of national treatment enables them instead to apply
their own law to foreigners. A disadvantage is that it permits sometimes great
disparities between the effective levels of protection so that the citizens of high
level protection countries get less rights in some convention countries than they
enjoy at home, whereas the citizens of low protection countries get better
protection in some convention countries than they get at home. However this
is balanced by the advantage that wide ranging copyright relations are
facilitated between countries of differing ideologies and differing stages of
economic development.

Formal reciprocity (or partial reciprocity) in copyright conventions means that
each member state will protect the works or citizens of other member states in
some manner but from such reciprocity nothing is to be implied with regard to
the nature of the protection. That is generally determined by the rule of
national treatment.

The "comparison of terms" under [Article 7(8) of] the Berne Convention is an
example. The term of protection is dealt with in the conventions by laying down
a minimum term: 50 years *post mortem auctoris*, but countries are free to grant
a longer term. Comparison of terms means that a country which grants a
longer term than 50 years to its nationals needs only grant that longer term to
foreigners if that term is also granted by their country of origin. For example
the Federal Republic of Germany gives 70 years pma, but Germany need only
give 50 years pma to United Kingdom right owners because that is the term of
their own national law. It does not have to give the full 70 years it gives to its
own nationals.

(2) *Reservations*

The rights granted by conventions can also be limited by reservations, which
give countries the opportunity to ratify the convention but to withhold the
giving of some rights wholly or partly. Some conventions, e.g. the Phonogram
Convention, permit no reservations, others, e.g. the Rome Convention, provide
for several. The reservations can relate to the scope of a right or to the
connecting factor, e.g. the reservations regarding the points of attachment in

---

[2]The *droit de suite* in the Berne Convention (art. 14*bis*) or the comparison of terms in the Berne
Convention (art. 7(8)).

Convention,[1] or to a whole right, e.g. the performance right in ...ms in the same convention.[2] The making of reservations is usually ...anied by the application of the rule of reciprocity so that the nationals ...ntry A which has made the reservation can be deprived of the exercise of ...se rights in country B because the nationals of country B are not granted ...ose rights in country A.

(e) Challenges to the principle of national treatment

Thus the principle of national treatment subject to extensions and limitations has proved itself as the fundamental principle of copyright and neighbouring rights conventions for nearly a century. It is however at present in danger of being undermined as governments try to cope with the rapid development of technology and communications. When a new right is being granted to copyright owners, governments have the option of granting it in the course of copyright revision and as a copyright, or of granting it as a new right in a separate law outside the copyright law. If the government decides to grant the new right as a copyright, the international conventions apply and the principle of national treatment may demand that foreigners who are nationals of convention countries which have not yet granted the new right have to be given the same right and thus become entitled to remuneration which flows from it. If on the other hand the government decides to create the new right outside the copyright law the conventions will not apply and foreigners will not be entitled to national treatment and therefore will not be entitled to participate in any remuneration for the use of the new right. Two practical examples will illustrate the position.

(1) *Public lending right*

This right has been introduced in several countries under which authors of literary works receive a royalty when their books are being borrowed from a library by members of the public. In the Federal Republic of Germany this right is granted in the Copyright Law and therefore, as Germany is a member of the Berne Convention and of the Universal Copyright Convention, foreigners who are nationals of convention countries are entitled to remuneration if their books are borrowed. On the other hand the Scandinavian countries[3] and the United Kingdom,[4] which also give a public lending right, have chosen to do so by separate legislation outside the copyright laws and are therefore not bound to grant the right to foreigners, although, like Germany, they are also members of both conventions and the remuneration paid for the lending right is therefore limited to works of national authors.

---

[1] Rome Convention, art. 5(1).
[2] Rome Convention, art. 16(1)(a)(i).
[3] *See e.g.,* Law on Public Libraries, 27 May 1969 (amended 26 June 1975), art. 19 in Denmark.
[4] Public Lending Right Act 1980.

(2) *Reprography*

This is the production of copies of printed matter by copying machines. One way of dealing with such copies produced for commercial purposes is to subject the reproduction right in respect of such copies to a compulsory license and give the author a right to equitable remuneration as in the Federal Republic of Germany.[5]

On the other hand France introduced a tax on the sale and importation of all machines producing reprographic copies in its Finance Act 1976. Part of the revenue of this tax is paid to the copyright owners of the material copied, but it is paid only to French copyright owners although France is a party to both copyright conventions. The principle of national treatment does not apply as the compensation does not arise from a copyright and foreigners are thus not compensated.

The distinction between the two examples is that the reproduction right is generally recognised in all copyright laws and is a fundamental right of both international conventions and unauthorised copying is only permissible as an exception (e.g. for private use), whereas a public lending right, far from being universally acknowledged, only exists in a few countries and does not form part of the *jus conventionis* of any of the international conventions. Thus, on grounds of natural justice and applying the principle of national treatment to a generally accepted right, the claim of foreigners who are convention nationals to compensation for reprographic use of their works is strong. In the case of the public lending right it is, so far, still weak whilst only few countries grant it.

Another distinction is that in the case of the reprographic right in the United States the royalty will be paid by the user, which is a characteristic of all copyrights, whereas the compensation (it is not termed a royalty) in the case of the public lending right in Scandinavia and in the United Kingdom is paid out of a public fund. That means that it comes from taxpayers' money as opposed to copyright users' money.

Thus by the simple device of calling the right to compensation something other than a copyright and introducing it by a separate piece of legislation[7] the application of the principle of national treatment can be avoided. Particularly in cases where the compensation is paid out of a government fund which can be called taxpayers' money, the temptation to restrict it to nationals is considerable. If that device is generally used by governments when dealing with the new uses of copyright material arising from new technology and new means of communication, the fundamental principle of national treatment and with it the copyright conventions based on it, could be seriously eroded in the near future.

---

[5]German Copyright Law, art. 54(2).
[7]A case where a "rose by any other name" does *not* "smell just as sweet."

GUNNAR W.G. KARNELL, THE BERNE CONVENTION BETWEEN AUTHORS' RIGHTS AND COPYRIGHT ECONOMICS—AN INTERNATIONAL DILEMMA[*]
26 I.I.C. 193, 211-13 (1995)

Whether Article 9 of the [Berne] Convention obliges members to institute systems for remuneration to authors for the private copying of authors' works on sound or audio-visual carriers (tapes, discs, etc.) and—eventually—also related to machinery for such copying, thereby making the principle of national treatment applicable to the distribution of considerable amounts of money internationally, is one of the main copyright issues internationally, and one of great economic importance to the Berne Union members.

Clearly, the text of the Convention does not mention any such obligation. Authors are given an exclusive right of authorising the reproduction of their works in any manner or form (Art. 9(1)); any sound or visual recording is to be considered as a reproduction (Art. 9(3)). Provided that such reproduction does not conflict with the normal exploitation of the work and does not unreasonably prejudice the legitimate interests of the author, it shall be a matter for legislation in Union member countries to "permit the reproduction of such works in certain special cases", *i.e.* to institute systems of legal licensing. But there is no obligation to do so, and, if done, it shall be a matter of permission to reproduce. Cassette levies have nothing to do with the users who reproduce—they cannot be accused of infringement if they use a cassette for which no levy has been paid; it is not even sure that the manufacturer, importer or seller of the thing which is used for reproduction lets the levy influence his pricing.

Nevertheless, in some countries, like France and Germany, rules about such remuneration have been introduced into the Copyright Acts and are there considered part of authors' rights, so as to make the Convention rule about national treatment applicable. In other countries, where rules about such remuneration have been introduced, they have not been seen to be covered by the national treatment provision. They can also be found clearly outside any legislation of copyright or authors' rights. In these latter cases, countries have instead shown willingness to apply a rule of material reciprocity, meaning that money collected under the respective national rules, called cassette levy rules or the like, will be distributed only to nationals, to the extent that similar rights are not given in the other country. The issue is . . . under study by the European Commission, and I see no reason to set out more elements of the debate about this very "hot" topic here in any detail.

There is, however, one factor that has considerable economic bearing on the authors' rights aspect of the Berne Convention, as compared to the one more directly related to copyright economics. All right holders suffer the effects of the abundant private copying by the use of sound and audio-visual carriers of protected works. Now, authors may sell their rights for any foreseeable uses,

---

[*]Reprinted with permission of Max Planck Institute for Foreign and International Patent, Copyright, and Competition Law, Wiley-VCH Publishers and Gunnar Karnell.

once and for all or in part, of each work of theirs, or else become deprived of sharing in the future revenues from uses of their works. However, under systems for cassette levies and similar arrangements related to reproduction machinery, authors typically remain entitled to money for trade in such goods, notwithstanding what rights may have been disposed of by agreements as mentioned. Money may not be distributed to them in full; there may be deductions for administrative costs of collecting societies and for national or regional cultural or even social purposes,[34] and they may have to share with others, but at least some part of what is being collected or paid out under the schemes becomes authors' money individually or collectively as the case may be. To a larger or lesser, but always to some, extent it will be protected as theirs against the market forces surrounding them as individuals.

Levies, as mentioned, provide *supporting measures to the notion of authors' rights*. They do not belong under the principle of national treatment, unless for one reason or another a country finds it opportune to choose that principle instead of the principle of material reciprocity or to let all money stay national. Regional objections may arise to the latest mentioned possibility, for instance within the EEA, and it is not in conformity with the philosophy of a literary or artistic world community to "go unconditionally national". Still, we may have noticed that high principles of cultural ethics play only a relatively discrete role in the world of copyright economics,[35] where the Berne Convention as it stands is quite insufficient for harbouring, by any reasonable interpretation of its text, even such solutions to present-day and future problems as the ones that most parties to the discussion agree upon . . . . In many respects . . . there appears to be reason for doubt whether the Berne Convention is a suitable foundation for balancing the conflicting interests in the market to be. In practice, probably, ever more commercial considerations, related to world trade, will take the upper hand in respects where earlier a traditional approach to the law as a law of authors' rights held out against the economics of copyright.

BERNE CONVENTION, ARTICLE 5

(1) Authors shall enjoy, in respect of works for which they are protected under this Convention, in countries of the Union other than the country of origin, the rights which their respective laws do now or may hereafter grant to their nationals, as well as the rights specially granted by this Convention.

---

[34]*See* F. Melichar, Deductions Made by Collecting Societies for Social and Cultural Purposes in the Light of International Copyright Law, 22 IIC 47 *et seq.* (1991).

[35]Countries may be excused for holding back on national treatment (in a case where there is no clear obligation binding it), towards a country which openly claims it, in member countries for a certain right, without making any perceivable efforts to institute itself the corresponding right, although it could economically well afford to provide for it in its laws. A slow process in legislative developments may explain the absence, over a long period of time, of what it might ultimately be willing to provide; but in the meantime money will roll just in one direction. Ethics or economics?

(2) The enjoyment and exercise of these rights . . . shall be independent of the existence of protection in the country of origin of the work. Consequently, apart from the provisions of this Convention, the extent of protection, as well as the means of redress afforded to the author to protect his rights, shall be governed exclusively by the laws of the country where protection is claimed.

ROME CONVENTION, ARTICLE 2

1. For the purposes of this Convention, national treatment shall mean the treatment accorded by the domestic law of the Contracting State in which protection is claimed:

> (a) to performers who are its nationals, as regards performances taking place, broadcast, or first fixed, on its territory;

> (b) to producers of phonograms who are its nationals, as regards phonograms first fixed or first published on its territory;

> (c) to broadcasting organisations which have their headquarters on its territory, as regards broadcasts transmitted from transmitters situated on its territory.

2. National treatment shall be subject to the protection specifically guaranteed, and the limitations specifically provided for, in this Convention.

TRIPS AGREEMENT, ARTICLE 3(1)

Each Member shall accord to the nationals of other Members treatment no less favourable than it accords to its own nationals with regard to the protection of intellectual property, subject to the exceptions already provided in, respectively, . . . the Berne Convention (1971) [and] the Rome Convention. . . . In respect of performers, producers of phonograms and broadcasting organizations, this obligation only applies in respect of the rights provided under this Agreement. . . .

NOTES AND QUESTIONS

(1) **Update**. Many of the differences in national laws that are identified in the examples given by Professor Stewart (for example, the different term of copyright in Germany and the United Kingdom) no longer exist, or at least not to the same extent. This is primarily the result of the harmonization efforts of the European Union. *See infra* § 4.05[C].

(2) **An Ongoing Point of Controversy.** National treatment is one of most controversial issues in international copyright law, and is one of the final items to be resolved in almost every treaty negotiation. It has been a particularly contentious point between the United States and the European Union. Why?

(3) **Exceptions to National Treatment in the Berne Convention.** The Berne Convention contains two major exceptions to national treatment. One is the so-called "rule of the shorter term" in Article 7(8), which allows countries to provide a shorter term of protection to a foreign work than to domestic works, matching the shorter term of protection provided by the foreign work's country of origin. The other relates to the *droit de suite* (or royalty on the resale of originals of works of art or manuscripts): Article 14*ter*(2) states that this form of protection "may be claimed in a country of the [Berne] Union only if legislation in the country to which the author belongs so permits . . ." What is the reason for these exceptions? What is the significance of the phrasing of Article 14*ter*(2)? Does it mean that a country cannot choose to provide the protection of *droit de suite* to works from another country that does not do so?

(4) **Different Approaches to National Treatment.** What is the substantive difference between the Berne and Rome approaches to national treatment? In what circumstances would national treatment be required under Berne, but not under Rome? What is the reason for this difference in approach?

(5) **"A Rose by Any Other Name . . ."** Because of the formulation of the national treatment provision in the Berne Convention, it can be important whether a particular legal benefit is called a copyright right (a "right" in a "work") or not. The excerpts from Professors Stewart and Karnell give a flavor of the debate. The issue of when national treatment is required with respect to funds that are connected to the use of copyrighted works remains controversial, and is likely to become even more so as more imaginative solutions are found to the enforcement difficulties posed by new technologies. Are you convinced by the above analyses by Karnell and Stewart? Do the schemes they describe violate Berne's national treatment obligation? What objective characteristics make a right a "copyright" subject to the national treatment obligations of the Berne Convention? To what extent has Article 3 of the TRIPS Agreement altered this debate? How would you rule as a member of a WTO dispute resolution panel faced with this issue?

In Ferdinand Melichar, *Deductions Made by Collecting Societies for Social and Cultural Purposes in the Light of International Copyright Law,* 22 I.I.C. 47 (1991), cited in the excerpt from Karnell, the author examines the practice of music collecting societies in many countries of deducting a portion of their revenues for use for social and cultural purposes, with the benefits of these portions shared with foreign authors only on the basis of reciprocity. He concludes that some of these practices are consistent with international treaty obligations and others are not. In particular, he writes that:

> * Deductions for social and cultural purposes from remuneration derived from "traditional rights" may be acceptable—almost as a kind of standard law—as long as these deductions do not exceed 10%.
>
> * To deal with the new types of exploitation, private copying and massive lending of books, arrangements outside the copyright rule of law are made which do not assign shares of the revenue to individual distribution. There can be no objection to this from a legal point of view under either the Berne Convention or the EC Treaty, though it

is open to question whether this solution is in keeping with the spirit of the international conventions.

* Schemes which assign individual shares to national authors only are in violation of both the Berne Convention and the EC Treaty (no matter how they are described).

* Schemes established by the copyright law which provide for statutory partial deductions for social purposes offer an acceptable compromise which does not contravene any relevant provisions of the Berne Convention; therefore they seem to present the best solution.

Id. at 60.

(6) **National Treatment and the Audiovisual Performances Treaty.** In connection with pending negotiations of a possible new WIPO treaty to protect audiovisual performances, *see infra* § 4.06[D][1], the United States proposed the following treaty language on national treatment:

(1) Each Contracting Party shall accord to nationals [eligible for protection under the treaty], in respect of the subject matter protected under this Treaty, the protection that it accords its own nationals with respect to:

   (i)   the exclusive rights provided in this Treaty;

   (ii) rights which derive from any exclusive right provided in this Treaty, including but not limited to rights of remuneration; and

   (iii) any other rights as to which another Contracting Party provides, under its domestic law, substantially the same level of protection for such subject matter.

(2) Any Contracting Party that, under its domestic law, provides for rights of remuneration or mandatory collective administration of exclusive rights with respect to a performance, fixed or unfixed, protected under this Treaty may provide in a Declaration to the Director General [of WIPO] that it will not provide the benefits of such rights to nationals of another Contracting Party. The Contracting Party making such declaration shall provide in its national law measures that preclude collection for such rights in respect of audiovisual performances by nationals of any other Contracting Party in respect of which such Declaration is made.

What are the reasons for the different clauses of this complex provision?

———————

JEAN-FRANÇOIS VERSTRYNGE, THE SPRING 1993 HORACE S. MANGES LECTURE: THE EUROPEAN COMMISSION'S DIRECTION ON COPYRIGHT AND NEIGHBORING RIGHTS: TOWARD THE REGIME OF THE TWENTY-FIRST CENTURY[*]
17 COLUM.-VLA J. L. & ARTS 187 (1993)

National treatment is a very important issue in these ongoing negotiations [of what became the TRIPS Agreement]. Indeed, it might prove to be the key that unlocks all or most other unresolved issues.

National treatment is the rule in the Berne and Rome Conventions. Reciprocity is the exception. One may ask why this is so, since in most international negotiations—and in particular in trade negotiations—reciprocity is the governing principle. In international trade, countries do indeed make concessions to one another only if they obtain some other trade concession in return.

International IPR Conventions such as the Paris Convention of 1883 and the Berne Convention of 1886 were conceived and negotiated more than one century ago when international relations were not always seen as primarily trade-related. Promotion of ideas, science and creativity around the world for their own sake was, rather, the objective at the end of last century. Transportation and telecommunications had not yet internationalized relations to the extent to which they now have. Nobody was talking about the world as a global village yet.

It is in this context that the national treatment rule was introduced in the Berne Convention, essentially to ensure that the effort at harmonization at the international level could not be demolished. This was against the background of a nineteenth-century largely dominated by nationalism and in which foreigners often had little or no rights.

The example of Victor Hugo was given. He did not enjoy protection of his writings in Germany the way he enjoyed them in France. Hence the national treatment rule of the Berne Convention.

The rule of national treatment has fulfilled its function for more than a century. It has largely operated to increase protection of copyright around the world and, combined with the unanimity rule for modifying the Berne Convention, has secured every country against a decrease in protection levels. Seen this way, it is the insurance policy of copyright. It has also been one of the features which has secured the geographic extension of the Berne Convention, which is well on the way to reach 100 parties. It was a very essential element in the decision of the United States to ratify the Berne Convention in 1989.

For all of these very good reasons, national treatment should remain the governing principle, be it in the Berne, the Rome or the Geneva Convention. It is, therefore, also to be applauded in my opinion that national treatment would be extended in the GATT/TRIPS context to cover all the new rights or features of increased protection which could be agreed upon in GATT.

---

634 COPYRIGHT AND RELATED RIGHTS CH. 4

Some exceptions do, however, exist from this rule of national treatment. For the Berne Convention, some rights such as *droit de suite*, some features of protection, such as the length of the term, and some aspects of geographic scope, such as protection for works published in non-Berne Party Countries, remain, under certain circumstances, subject to reciprocity. In the Rome Convention, a similar situation exists as regards Articles 12 and 16 for the remuneration right for the broadcasting of music, for example.

What is the common rationale behind these and similar exceptions? In my opinion, they all relate in one way or another to cases in which a higher level of protection could not be secured internationally, despite the fact that it was seen as desirable by a large number of countries participating in the relevant negotiations. *Droit de suite* was not generally accepted. A longer term than the minimum term of the Berne Convention could not be agreed upon (although it has in this century subsequently been increased to reach at present 50 years *post mortem auctoris*). Some countries had originally decided not to join the Berne Convention (even if many have since joined it). An agreement on the general rule of Article 12 of the Rome Convention proved impossible in 1961.

Countries were then unwilling to grant national treatment where other countries would be allowed to maintain a lower level of protection. This, however, did not matter as long as subsequent negotiations led to the adoption of revisions which included further agreement on a higher level of protection, which, once agreed upon by most countries, was then again covered by the national treatment rule. The several revisions of the Berne Convention since 1886 prove this point.

However, intensified international trade relations made revisions of this sort increasingly difficult. The Stockholm agreement of 1967 could only be solidified in 1971 in Paris. Some features such as Article 9(2) had to be left in very ambiguous language. Since 1971 no further progress has been made. In the GATT/TRIPS context the increase in levels of protection of copyright or neighboring rights will only be possible by concessions in other fields of the Uruguay Round such as agriculture, textiles, or basic products.

Soon national treatment started to have a perverse effect. Since it implied some automatic trade concessions to third countries which exported copyright works in large quantities, it started to prevent rather than enhance increased copyright protection.

For instance, the attempts to increase the protection against home copying are now plagued by this problem. Indeed, legislators around the world started to hesitate to increase the protection against home copying if the net result was to be large payments to third countries. They chose either not to increase protection at all (as did the United Kingdom), to fall back on reciprocity (as did Australia and Denmark), or to find some other legal limitation in order to avoid such payments, as is the case in several other countries.

Reciprocity can therefore be seen as an intermediate stage which allows for an increase in copyright protection in a situation in which general agreement on the increased level of protection cannot be obtained. It also can be an interim leverage for increasing protection in the long run. Once general agreement on an increased level of protection is possible, one can easily and securely return to the rule of national treatment. If *droit de suite* were more generally accepted—let's say by most OECD Countries—I am sure that it would quickly return to national treatment status. If 70 years of protection were more generally accepted, there would be little resistance to apply national treatment to it. The same applies to Article 12 of the Rome Convention. If international agreement could be reached on the increased protection of home copying, reciprocity might soon disappear. The obstacle is not so much resistance to national treatment, but refusal to increase protection.

The problem is indeed that no such agreement could be reached so far, neither in GATT/TRIPS, nor in WIPO. Hence, the issue of national treatment on such possible increases in the level of protection has also been disputed.

The problem is made worse when some countries which are large exporters of copyrighted works refuse at the same time to increase the level of protection domestically while maintaining that they should enjoy revenue from other countries which already have such a higher level of protection through the operation of the national treatment rule. By doing so they only increase the fears of other countries, which then start applying reciprocity and become suspicious against further increases in levels of protection. For the exporting country it soon becomes a self-defeating position. Quite logically and correctly, other countries claim that such a position from the exporting country is politically unacceptable.

Moreover, the interpretation of the national treatment rule of Berne, which is used to try to obtain these payments in foreign countries while maintaining a lower level of protection domestically, is legally quite incorrect. Indeed, the inclusion of the national treatment rule in the original Berne Convention was not and could not be intended to obtain higher levels of protection for foreigners. This would have gone against the predominant preoccupation of the end of the last century, which was focused on securing equal levels of protection for foreigners, not higher ones.

In my opinion, using the argument of national treatment to make claims for higher levels of protection, while maintaining domestically lower levels of protection, will fail. Such claims should, moreover, not be allowed to prevail if the benefit of a better long term overall protection of copyright is to be the international common objective. Indeed, once granted, they would eliminate any incentive for the exporting country to further increase its domestic level of protection.

In my opinion, reciprocity is the only intermediate answer as long as the exporting country does not increase its domestic level of protection.

In this context, reciprocity should not be considered a failure. Indeed, it will soon become evident that the exporting country will change its position by the very fact that revenues from a great number of third countries will outweigh the difficulty in increasing the level of protection domestically. Once this is realized, national treatment can again be considered.

Moreover, the effect of this issue of national treatment is different depending on whether one considers it bilaterally or in a multilateral context. Paradoxically, a multilateral agreement is easier to reach, due to the fact that concessions which have to be made to the exporting country can be balanced by gains from other countries engaged in the multilateral negotiation. Bilaterally, this does not happen.

Accordingly, the road to multilateral agreement for increased levels of protection of copyrighted works covered by national treatment (and what is true for copyright is also true for neighboring rights), has to be opened by an agreement on increased protection before national treatment can be considered and eventually secured. Domestic lobby groups, motivated by short-term interest—which may even be ill-conceived and self-defeating—should not be allowed to have their cake and eat it too. If the interests of these lobby groups are to prevail, the whole copyright community, including the exporting country, will lose out in the end.

NOTES AND QUESTIONS

(1) **A Case for Reciprocity?** Dr. Verstrynge was a primary official responsible for intellectual property policy at the European Commission when he delivered his lecture. What do you think of Dr. Verstrynge's arguments? What arguments could be made on the other side? What political or economic factors might determine a policy maker's approach on either side of the Atlantic?

(2) **The Language of International Copyright Policymaking**. Who are the "large exporters of copyrighted works [who] refuse at the same time to increase the level of protection domestically while maintaining that they should enjoy revenue from other countries which already have such a higher level of protection through the operation of the national treatment rule"? Who are the "domestic lobby groups, motivated by short term interest"? Why is Dr. Verstrynge using such vague references to advance his case?

[B]   Eligibility for Protection: Connecting Factors

S.M. STEWART, INTERNATIONAL COPYRIGHT AND NEIGHBOURING RIGHTS 43-47 (2d ed. 1989)*

On the national level the question whether copyright protection does exist or not is decided by asking first whether the subject matter attracts copyright protection or not. . . . If there is a copyright the second basic question to ask is whether the protection sought is covered by the scope of the right. . . . The third basic question to ask is what term the legislation grants to the work or subject matter in question. . . . On the international level a further question has to be answered: If the work is a foreign work or the author or right owner is a foreigner, what is the criterion for deciding whether the work or the right owner

---

*Copyright 1989, Butterworths & Co. Reprinted by permission of The Butterworths Division of Reed Elsevier (UK) Limited.

is protected? This is known as the connecting factor (*'point de rattachement'*, *'Anknupfungspunkt'*), the factor which connects the work or the author with a particular country. It is usually defined as the country with which there is 'the closest and most real connection'. When considering the possible connecting factors one has to bear in mind that copyright is an intellectual property right. It is a property right in the sense that it is a right *erga omnes*, thus resembling corporeal property rights, but the subject of that property is incorporeal. That means that although the work appears in the tangible form (*corpus mechnicum*) of a book, a film, a phonogram in one place, it can be reproduced or performed in lots of other places whilst still remaining the same work. Different criteria from those applied to corporeal property rights have to be found to serve as the relevant factors connecting the work or subject matter of the author or the right owner of the work with one particular country. These factors are:

(a) *Personal status connection of the author* (nationality, habitual residence etc)—referred to as 'the country to which the author (or the maker) of the work belong'. [Berne Convention art. 3(2)].

(b) *Geographical connection of the work*—referred to as 'the country of origin.' [Berne Convention art. 5(4))].

(c) *Geographical connection with the public*—referred to as 'the country of first publication,' [Berne Convention art. 3(1)(b)] the country where the work or subject matter of copyright was first made available to the public.

(d) *The lex fori*—referred to as the 'protecting country,' the country where protection is claimed, that is where the use of the work, be it legitimate exploitation or infringement, takes place.

(a) *The country to which the author belongs*

In accordance with the philosophy of the *droit d'auteur* that the quintessence of copyright is the progress of the work from the mind of the author to the general public, the personal status connection of the author and the geographical connection of first publication with the public were the essential points of attachment of the first international copyright convention, the Berne Convention. The nature of the personal status connection was defined as nationality, but those persons who have their 'habitual residence' in a country of the Berne Union are 'assimilated' to nationals[1] and the Universal Copyright Convention adopts the same structure using the common law concept of 'domicile' instead of the civil law concept of habitual residence.

In essence habitual residence is a question of fact for the court that tries the case to be judged by the length of time during which the author has lived in a country, whereas the concept of domicile differs from country to country and may depend on where the author ultimately intends to settle rather than where he resides, a matter sometimes more difficult to ascertain.

In more recent times where refugee and stateless authors have become more

---

[1] Berne Convention, art. 3(2).

frequent than they were in the nineteenth century, they too have been assimilated to nationals.[3]

Where the right owner is not a natural person but a legal entity like a corporation or company such as a film producer or a phonogram producer or a broadcasting organisation, the place of its seat or headquarters decides residence or domicile.

In the case of the personal connecting factor the question to which country the author or maker of the work belongs may have to be answered differently at different times as he may change his nationality and even more easily his habitual residence. The relevant date may be the date of the creation of the work in which case different works of the same author may have different connecting factors. It may be his nationality or residence at the time of publication in the case of a published work, or it may be the time when protection is claimed. The Berne Convention is silent on the point. It is, unless the national law provides a solution, a matter for the courts to decide. It is likely that the courts will choose the nationality or residence at the time when protection is claimed for the purely practical reason that it is probably the easiest to ascertain.

(b) *The country of origin*

At the earliest stages of drafting multilateral treaties the concept of the country of origin of the work was at the center of the scene. The underlying thought was that once a work is created or published it should have the same rights abroad as at home. The principle was tried in the Montevideo Convention 1889. It was not successful as a basic principle of a convention because it leads by definition to situations where different rights attach to similar works, because one originates in a country granting a high level of protection and the other in a country with a low level of protection. The creators of the Berne Convention did not make this mistake and based the convention on the principle of national treatment. However the convention contains a definition of the country of origin[4] to the effect that for a published work the country of origin shall be the country of first publication and for an unpublished work the country 'to which the author belongs'. Although the Paris Act 1971 still contains a more detailed definition,[5] to the same effect, the importance of this point of attachment seems to have declined with the years and neither the Universal Copyright Convention nor the neighbouring rights conventions contain the concept of country of origin.

It must be remembered that conventions deal only with international situations and therefore protection of nationals in the country of origin itself is regulated by the law of that country. Thus if a national author publishes at home no problem arises. If he publishes abroad the country of first publication

---

[3]*See* Berne Convention, art. 3(2) ("authors . . . who have their habitual residence" in a Union country).

[4]Berne Convention 1886, art. 2(3).

[5]Berne Convention 1971, art. 5(4).

takes the place of the country of origin. For unpublished works the country of origin becomes important if a subsequent publication, e.g. of a translation, takes place abroad.

The main importance of the country of origin today is for measuring the duration of protection. The rule of the comparison of terms[6] provides that although the term of protection is governed by the law of the country where protection is claimed, that term shall not exceed the term fixed in the country of origin of the work, unless the national law provides otherwise. When terms of protection varied widely the comparison of terms was often of crucial importance. It is less so now. However examples are to be found in the relation between countries which give the minimum term of 50 years after the death of the author and countries which give a longer term.

(c) *The country of first publication*

First publication is an important connecting factor.[1] If a writer writes a book in China (a state [at the time of this article] not a member of any international convention), it is unprotected anywhere else while it is unpublished. If he publishes it in China it is still unprotected anywhere else. If however he publishes it first in the United Kingdom it becomes protected by the Berne Convention or if he publishes it first in the United States it becomes protected by the Universal Copyright Convention. If the only publication within a convention country is an English translation published in the United Kingdom, or in the United States, that translation becomes protected as a separate work, but the original in Chinese still remains unprotected. The result is that anyone can make another English translation (or indeed a French or German one) and publish it in any convention country without the author's permission.[2] The concept of simultaneous publication is of vital importance as a connecting factor because it may considerably enlarge the protection of the work if the work is published in a non-convention country and would otherwise be unprotected. If it is 'simultaneously' published in a convention country this secures its protection.[3] The Berne Convention allows an interval of 30 days between the first and second publication to qualify the second one as a simultaneous publication. So does the Rome Convention for the publication of phonograms.[4] Simultaneous publication is particularly important in cases of works published in the same language (a translation is a new work) in several countries or in the

---

[6]Berne Convention, art. 7(8). Comparison of terms in the Universal Copyright Convention (art IV(a)), is made for published works by comparing with the country of first publication and for unpublished works by comparing with the country to which the author belongs. . . .

[1]For definitions of 'publication' see Berne Convention, art 3(3); . . . and Universal Copyright Convention, art VI. . . .

[2]If the work is valuable it may therefore be wise to publish a limited edition of the original in the U.K. or U.S. first to establish the connecting factor and secure protection by the conventions. [cit].

[3]Berne Convention, art. 3(4)

[4]Rome Convention, art. 3(d).

case of musical works or phonograms.[5]

(d) *The protecting country*

This is shorthand for the country where protection is claimed. As in practice an action is usually brought in the country where the infringement is committed, this usually means the *lex fori*. However there are exceptions where the infringement is committed in a country other than the one where protection is claimed. It is another question not settled by the convention whether in cases of infringements abroad legal protection based on foreign copyright can be claimed. In the past it has usually been accepted that the principle of territoriality applies and that legal protection before national courts can only be claimed in cases of infringements committed within the country concerned. However as Ulmer points out according to the general rules of private international law 'it seems consistent to expand the rule which may be derived from the conventions into a complete rule of conflict of laws whereby protection of intellectual property rights, irrespective of the country in which the action is brought, is to be governed by the law of the country in whose territory the act of infringement took place (the *lex loci delicti*)'[1]

The answer depends on the view taken by the national courts . . . .

BERNE CONVENTION
Article 3. Criteria of Eligibility for Protection

(1) The protection of this Convention shall apply to:

(a) authors who are nationals of one of the countries of the Union, for their work, whether published or not;

(b) authors who are not nationals of one of the countries of the Union, for their works first published in one of those countries, or simultaneously in a country outside the Union and in a country of the Union.

(2) Authors who are not nationals of one of the countries of the Union but who have their habitual residence in one of them shall, for the purposes of this Convention, be assimilated to nationals of that country

. . . .

(4) A work shall be considered as having been published simultaneously in

---

[5]Under the Rome Convention the criterion of first publication can be excluded as a point of attachment (art. 5(1) . . .); the result is that the sole points of attachment are the nationality of the producer or the fixation of the recording. If a country excludes the criterion of publication, as some Nordic countries do, it is for this very reason: to exclude simultaneous publication protecting a phonogram which is made in a non-convention country by a producer who is a national of a non-convention country.

[1]Ulmer, *Intellectual Property Rights and the Conflict of Laws* (1978) p. 10.

several countries if it has been published in two or more countries within thirty days of its first publication.

ROME CONVENTION
Article 4. Performances Protected

Each Contracting State shall grant national treatment to performers if any of the following conditions is met:

     (a) the performance takes place in another Contracting State;

     (b) the performance is incorporated in a phonogram which is protected under Article 5 of this Convention;

     (c) the performance, not being fixed on a phonogram, is carried by a broadcast which is protected by Article 6 of this Convention.

Article 5. Protected Phonograms

1. Each Contracting State shall grant national treatment to producers of phonograms if any of the following conditions is met:

     (a) the producer of the phonogram is a national of another Contracting State (criterion of nationality);

     (b) the first fixation of the sound was made in another Contracting State (criterion of fixation);

     (c) the phonogram was first published in another Contracting State (criterion of publication).

2. If a phonogram was first published in a non-contracting State but if it was also published, within thirty days of its first publication, in a Contracting State (simultaneous publication), it shall be considered as first published in the Contracting State. . . .

Article 6. Protected Broadcasts

1. Each Contracting State shall grant national treatment to broadcasting organizations if either of the following conditions is met:

     (a) the headquarters of the broadcasting organization is situated in another Contracting State;

     (b) the broadcast was transmitted from a transmitter situated in another Contracting State. . . . .

TRIPS AGREEMENT, ARTICLE 1(3)

Members shall accord the treatment provided for in this Agreement to the nationals of other Members. In respect of the relevant intellectual property right, the nationals of other Members shall be understood as those natural or legal persons that would meet the criteria for eligibility for protection provided for in . . . the Berne Convention (1971) [and] the Rome Convention . . . , were all Members of the WTO members of these Conventions.

NOTES AND QUESTIONS

(1) **Eligibility for Protection Under the Rome Convention.** Note the complex set of criteria in Article 4 of the Rome Convention for determining which performers are eligible for protection. Under what circumstances would a performer not be covered? Why the complexity? In the words of a German court:

> The purpose of this [provision] is to create a system in which a performance fixed on a phonogram is always protected if the producer of the phonogram enjoys protection, and in which a transmitted performance (except for that fixed on a phonogram) is always protected if the broadcasting organization arranging the transmission enjoys protection [citation omitted]. This [provision] means that the producers of phonograms or broadcasting organizations whose performance is protected by the Rome Convention are not placed in a better position than the performing artists whose performances are fixed on the protected phonograms or transmitted by the protected broadcast.

Bruce Springsteen and His Band, Case No. I/ZR 205/95 (Federal Supreme Court, 1998) (Ger.), reported at 31 IIC 107 (2000).

(2) **Permitted Reservations Under Rome.** As noted by Professor Stewart, for producers and broadcasters, the Rome Convention provides contracting states with an option to decline to apply certain of the specified points of attachment, if they deposit a notification to that effect with the Secretary General of the United Nations. *See* arts. 5(3) and 6(2). This is only one of several issues on which Rome permits countries to vary its standard terms, making implementation of this treaty inconsistent from country to country.

(3) **Update.** As more and more countries become members of Berne and TRIPS, some of the techniques described by Professor Stewart for obtaining treaty protection are less and less necessary. It should also be noted that the illustrations given reflect the state of international relations and treaty accessions as of 1989—before the intensive developments of the past decade.

(4) **Private International Law**. Toward the end of the excerpt, Professor Stewart mentions the relevance of private international law principles (such as choice of law) to these questions. We will discuss choice of law in greater detail *infra* § 7.05[A]. To what extent are rules of national treatment or conditions of eligibility that are found in treaties choice of law rules? Do they serve the same

function as choice of law rules?

U.S. COPYRIGHT ACT

Section 101. Definitions

An "international agreement" is–

(1) the Universal Copyright Convention;

(2) the Geneva Phonograms Convention;

(3) the Berne Convention;

(4) the WTO Agreement;

(5) the WIPO Copyright Treaty;

(6) the WIPO Performances and Phonograms Treaty; and

(7) any other copyright treaty to which the United States is a party.

A "treaty party" is a country or intergovernmental organization other than the United States that is a party to an international agreement.

Section 104. Subject matter of copyright: National origin

(a) UNPUBLISHED WORKS.–The works specified by sections 102 and 103, while unpublished, are subject to protection under this title without regard to the nationality or domicile of the author.

(b) PUBLISHED WORKS.–The works specified by sections 102 and 103, when published, are subject to protection under this title if–

(1) on the date of first publication, one or more of the authors is a national or domiciliary of the United States, or is a national, domiciliary, or sovereign authority of a treaty party, or is a stateless person, wherever that person may be domiciled; or

(2) the work is first published in the United States or in a foreign nation that, on the date of first publication, is a treaty party; or

(3) the work is a sound recording that was first fixed in a treaty party; or

(4) the work is a pictorial, graphic, or sculptural work that is incorporated in a building or other structure, or an architectural work that is embodied in a building and the building or structure is located in the United States or a treaty party; or

(5) the work is first published by the United Nations or any of its specialized agencies, or by the Organization of American States; or

(6) the work comes within the scope of a Presidential proclamation. Whenever the President finds that a particular foreign nation extends, to works by authors

who are nationals or domiciliaries of the United States or to works that are first published in the United States, copyright protection on substantially the same basis as that on which the foreign nation extends protection to works of its own nationals and domiciliaries and works first published in that nation, the President may by proclamation extend protection under this title to works of which one or more of the authors is, on the date of first publication, a national, domiciliary, or sovereign authority of that nation, or which was first published in that nation. The President may revise, suspend, or revoke any such proclamation or impose any conditions or limitations on protection under a proclamation.

. . .

(d) EFFECT OF PHONOGRAMS TREATIES.–Notwithstanding the provisions of subsection (b), no works other than sound recordings shall be eligible for protection under this title solely by virtue of the adherence of the United States to the Geneva Phonograms Convention or the WIPO Performances and Phonograms Treaty.

NOTES AND QUESTIONS

(1) **Implementation of Eligibility Conditions.** Other countries implement the treaties' eligibility requirements in varying ways, including: no limitations at all on the nationality or place of publication of the works that are protected under their laws; affirmative disqualification of works from countries which do not provide protection for their own works (*see* French Copyright Law Arts. L. 111-4 and 5, and Berne Convention art. 6, permitting such retaliation); or detailed tracking of the relevant provisions of each treaty to which they are members. What consequences, if any, attach to the means by which states implement eligibility conditions?

(2) **1998 Amendments.** Section 104 of the U.S. Copyright Act was amended (and the above definitions in section 101 added) in 1998 by the Digital Millennium Copyright Act, in order to implement the WIPO Copyright Treaty (WCT) and the WIPO Performances and Phonograms Treaty (WPPT), discussed *infra* § 4.06[B]. It is a valuable exercise to compare the pre-amendment version with the current text, and to analyze why the structure of section 104 was changed and the new definitions added. Note that paragraphs (5) and (6) of the definition of "international agreement" do not take effect until entry into force with respect to the United States of the WCT and the WPPT, respectively. WIPO Copyright and Performances and Phonograms Treaties Implementation Act of 1998, Pub. L. No. 105-304, tit. I, 112 Stat. 2860, 2877. The effective date of Section 104(d) is similarly delayed until entry into force of the WPPT with respect to the United States. *Id.* § 105. What is the purpose of paragraph (d)?

(3) **"Other Copyright Treaties."** How does the U.S. treatment of national eligibility compare to the requirements of Berne and other treaties? What qualifies as an "other copyright treaty to which the United States is a party" under the definition of "international agreement" in section 101? *See, e.g.*, New

York Chinese TV Programs, Inc. v. U.E. Enters., Inc., 954 F.2d 847 (2d Cir. 1992) (holding that 1946 Treaty of Friendship, Commerce & Navigation between U.S. and then-Republic of China constituted valid "copyright treaty" between U.S. and Taiwan for purposes of then-existing version of section 104).

§ 4.05 Copyright and Related Rights in the European Union

[A]   General Approach

JEAN-FRANÇOIS VERSTRYNGE, THE SPRING 1993 HORACE S. MANGES LECTURE: THE EUROPEAN COMMISSION'S DIRECTION ON COPYRIGHT AND NEIGHBORING RIGHTS: TOWARD THE REGIME OF THE TWENTY-FIRST CENTURY*
17 COLUM.-VLA J. L. & ARTS 187 (1993)

I. JURISDICTION

The European Community has entered the field of copyright and neighboring rights only very lately. These fields have been occupied by national and international law for more than a century. No specific provision of the EEC Treaty of 1957 gives it explicit jurisdiction over these fields. Copyright is not even mentioned in this Treaty. Only Article 36 refers to "the protection of industrial and commercial property" as one of the reasons to maintain derogations from the free circulation of goods rule of Article 30, even if there remains only a qualified possibility of derogation. Article 36 was clearly drafted in 1956/57 with the example of Article 20 of the GATT in mind, which also exempted intellectual property in principle from the GATT rules, except when discrimination could be established. It was not even clear whether the EEC Treaty and its Article 36 covered copyright under the expression "industrial and commercial property," but this was found to be the case early on in the case law of the Luxembourg Court. It was also rather quickly clarified that the derogation of Article 36 also applied as regards the rule in Article 59, which establishes the freedom to provide services in the Community.

However, as far as jurisdiction is concerned, these rules in the EEC Treaty do not transfer the essential power to deal with copyright or neighboring rights to the Community. On the contrary, the interpretation of the Court maintains the right of the Community to intervene in the realm of the "exercise" of these rights, meaning that some limitations to their full exercise under national law might flow from Article 30 or 59. A similar position was adopted by the Court under the antitrust rules, Articles 85 and 86 of the EEC Treaty. This is clearly the approach in the *Deutsche Grammophon* case of 1971 concerning neighboring rights, for instance.

In the *Deutsche Grammophon* case, no transfer of jurisdiction was involved so as to allow the Community to deal with the "essence" (or "existence") of copyright or neighboring rights. . . .

A change in Community law as regards jurisdiction was, however, made in 1987 with the entry into force of the Single European Act which modified the treaty by including, among other provisions, a new article, 100a, requiring only qualified majority voting to adopt measures aiming at the achievement of the objectives set out in the new Article 8a. This latter article provides that the Community shall adopt measures with the aim of progressively establishing the internal market over a period expiring on 31 December 1992, and, furthermore, that the internal market shall comprise an area without internal frontiers in which the free movement of goods, persons, services and capital is ensured.

Article 100a accordingly permits the Council to adopt the measures for the approximation of the provision laid down by law, regulation or administrative action in Member States which have as their object the establishment and functioning of the internal market. National rules for the protection of copyright or neighboring rights which under Article 36 legitimately derogated from either Article 30 or Article 59 and, therefore, prevented the establishment of the internal market, could thus from now on be harmonized by a qualified majority.

This is confirmed by the fourth section of Article 100a, which refers to "national provision on grounds of major needs referred to in Article 36" amongst the reasons to apply the particular procedure of Article 100a(4). If this special procedure might apply for the "major needs" referred to in Article 36, then it must also be true that Article 100a(1)—from which this special procedure derogates—covers harmonization of the major needs referred to in Article 36, and it has already been said that these include the "essence" of copyright and neighboring right protection.

The Community has thus clearly acquired the jurisdiction to deal with the "essence" of IPR protection whenever it conflicts with the objectives of Article 8a, and in particular with the achievement of the internal market by the end of 1992. This is specifically the case when a feature of copyright or neighboring right protection concerns the establishment and functioning of the internal market. Many aspects of these rights satisfy this latter test, as was already confirmed by the court in cases involving broadcasting, rental and duration, particularly in the Coditel, Niarner and Patricia cases.

The Council of Ministers also accepted this approach—if only by implication—for the first time in the copyright field by the adoption of the Software Directive of 14 May 1991. Indeed, this directive—adopted unanimously by the Council with the agreement of the European Parliament —harmonizes under Article 100a almost all aspects of the "essence" of software protection under copyright, including scope of protection, titularity, the nature of the protection, derogations, duration, etc.

The Rental Directive which was adopted on 19 November 1992 has confirmed this approach by its use of Articles 57, 66 and 100a [of the EEC Treaty] as its legal basis. . . .

The scope of jurisdiction for internal harmonization purposes in the European

Community is, furthermore, very important for the scope of external jurisdiction. Indeed, in the Community system, the Court of Justice established, under the ERTA (AETR) case, the rule that the Community possessed exclusive external jurisdiction whenever internal jurisdiction existed. Accordingly, whenever a new regulation or directive is adopted in Community law it therefore follows—now beyond doubt—that the Community is the only body entitled to deal with similar issues internationally.

There exists a controversy as to whether this also extends to the so-called area of "potential" jurisdiction. What, indeed, is the situation for an issue which would arise in an international negotiation, but which has not yet been harmonized by the Community, although the power to do so internally would clearly exist, for instance under Article 100a? In my opinion, these issues are also covered by the external jurisdiction of the Community. Any other conclusion would only lead to incoherent situations whereby Member States could use external measures to influence internal harmonization. This is clearly wrong since the reasoning in the *AETR* case implies the use of external jurisdiction in order to avoid conflicts with internal measures.

A last point regarding jurisdiction concerns the scope of Article 113, which establishes exclusive Community jurisdiction over commercial policy. Member States and the Council have so far avoided using Article 113 in the field of intellectual property. They have systematically deleted this additional legal basis whenever the Commission included it in its proposals. This was, for instance, the case in the semi-conductor directive, although it encompasses an elaborate external protection system based on reciprocity.

The scope of Article 113 is particularly relevant for the ongoing GATT/TRIPS negotiations (Trade Related Intellectual Property Rights). If it is indeed accepted that the protection of intellectual property—and hence of copyright and neighboring rights—is a trade-related matter, it would follow that the European Community possesses exclusive jurisdiction to deal with these issues under Article 113, regardless whether or not the same issues have been internally harmonized by the European Community.

Opponents of this position maintain sometimes that Article 113 does not concern services, but rather only products. This is nonsense. Services can indeed give rise to trade, as the intense negotiation in the GATT context abundantly demonstrates. Moreover, the Community has already concluded an agreement with Switzerland concerning some insurance services on the basis of Article 113.

Others maintain that IPR by its very nature could not give rise to trade. This is contradicted by the agreement during the mid-term review of the Uruguay Round in Montreal in 1988 to include IPR issues in the GATT negotiation. It is also contrary to measures already adopted under the new commercial policy instrument involving copyright and neighboring rights related issues. Indeed, Regulation 2641/84, which allows the Community to adopt such measures, is based on Article 113 and was, for instance, used against Indonesia for defaulting copyright protection. . . .

II. INTERNAL HARMONIZATION OBJECTIVES

Once jurisdiction has been established, the question of how this power should be used naturally arises.

From the Green Paper on copyright, published by the Commission in 1988, it could be concluded that the fundamental aim is the "establishment and functioning" of the internal market. This is also in line with the announcement of a Green Paper on copyright in the White Paper of 1985 concerning the internal market.

Since the establishment of the internal market is the essential basis upon which the Community grounds its jurisdiction, it can hardly be denied that the establishment of this market must be its essential objective.

But the question is more complicated than it appears. Indeed, if harmonization is to achieve the establishment and the functioning of the internal market, it remains to be decided whether to harmonize upwards (by increasing the protection to the highest level of any national regime) or downwards (by decreasing the protection to the lowest level of any national regime) or in between. Thus, even if harmonization can be neutral if it only pursues an internal market, the substance of the harmonization is never totally neutral.

That this is an important and relevant question is shown by the fact that the drafters of Article 100a(3) already found it necessary for some other fields to indicate that a high level of protection is required.

In other words, harmonization for the sake of creating the internal market cannot be divorced from the choice of the direction in which to harmonize. Since most areas of harmonization under Article 100a relate to the "grounds of major needs referred to in Article 36" or to essential requirements covered by the Cassis de Dijon case law, such as health, unfair competition, consumer protection, environment and possibly safety, political choices have to be made by the Institutions of the Community in this harmonization process related to these areas.

The approach adopted by the Commission's Green Paper, which was essentially oriented towards economic goals such as the fight against piracy and the problems created by the introduction of new technologies, was heavily criticized by several Member States and many interested parties. In 1989, the informal Council of Ministers of Culture in Blois asked the Commission to explain its choices. Similar criticisms were also made during the hearings which followed the publication of the Green Paper from 1988 to 1990.

As a response, the Commission adopted at the end of 1990 its working program for 1991/92 entitled "Follow-up to the Green Paper," and clarified its intentions by explaining that it wished, in principle, to reinforce the protection of copyright and neighboring rights. It stated:

> 1.3. Copyright provides a basis for intellectual creation. To protect copyright is to ensure that creativity is sustained and developed, in the interest of authors, the cultural industries, consumers, and

ultimately of society as a whole. Neighboring rights underpin these objectives in various ways, particularly by guaranteeing a proper return to performing artists and those who invest in the provision of these cultural goods and services.

1.4. The Commission will be guided by two principles here: firstly, the protection of copyright and neighboring rights must be strengthened; secondly, the approach taken must as far as possible be a comprehensive one.

1.5. The changes which technological advance has brought make it urgently necessary to strengthen the protection of copyright and neighboring rights, if an important economic and cultural asset in the Member States is not to be lost.

This new approach was then welcomed and endorsed by the Ministers for Culture in the framework of the Council in their conclusions of 7 June 1991.

. . . .

President Delors also endorsed this new approach by implication when he stated that culture could not be treated as any other product such as refrigerators or cars. In legal terms the question arises in the choice which has to be made essentially under Article 100a concerning the essence of copyright and neighboring right protection.

The Treaty of Maastricht on European Union, which was signed in February 1992, . . . permits a further legal argument to be found in Article 128(4). Indeed, it provides that: "The Community shall take cultural aspects into account in its action under other provisions of this Treaty."

It can therefore be argued that after the entry into force of the Maastricht Treaty, any harmonization initiative cannot remain neutral as far as cultural aspects are concerned. A legal requirement will exist. Presumably this point will then have to be [addressed] by the Commission and the Council respectively, in their proposals and final Regulations or Directives. A similar reasoning underlies the modification of Article 92(3) introduced by this Treaty in order to legalize "aid to promote culture and heritage conservation." Here, too, a new legal provision has explicitly and specifically been included to require a cultural dimension in Community action. In my opinion, these are mandatory requirements, which if they were violated could lead to the annulment of the involved measures.

It is therefore my opinion that any harmonization which would choose the lower level of protection of copyright or neighboring rights as its aim would risk to jeopardize this specific cultural requirement and, in particular, would endanger artistic and literary creation—especially in the audiovisual sector—in a way which would be contrary to the specific legal requirement of the new Article 128(4) of the Maastricht Treaty.

Internal harmonization of copyright and neighboring rights in the European Community will therefore have to aim in principle at increasing protection. The present harmonization program of the European Commission has already taken this approach. Such a result has already been achieved in the software directive. Further, the Commission proposed an exclusive rental right, giving better protection than a mere remuneration right for rental (as existed in Germany and must now be changed to implement the new Council directive of 1992 correctly). Another example lies in the proposal to harmonize duration upwards at 70 years *post mortem auctoris* for copyright, and 50 years after publication for neighboring rights. These, indeed, are the longer terms of protection which exist in the Community. . . .

It is, however, unclear whether the same approach will be chosen for issues for which the European Commission has not presented or announced proposals yet, such as home taping, reprography, *droit de suite* and moral rights, for instance. Since no proposals or positions have officially emerged after the hearings held during 1991-92, this question remains open.

Notes and Questions

(1) **Priorities.** Since Dr. Verstrynge delivered his lecture, several of the proposals referenced have been adopted by the European Union. Some, however, remain unenacted, or not even proposed, eight years later. As you review the following materials, consider why some proposals continue to languish—while others have been adopted and (arguably) have set the agenda for broader international developments.

(2) **Legislative Jurisdiction.** The jurisdictional analysis set out by Dr. Verstrynge (essentially a question regarding the allocation of competence in a quasi-federal system) has been of concrete consequence in several areas. For example, the European Court of Justice was faced with the question whether the final text of the TRIPS Agreement should be concluded (and signed) by the member states or by the European Commission on behalf of the EU. *See supra* § 2.03[C][8]. Similarly, the strength of the EU's claim to a separate vote in international intellectual property assemblies rests in part upon the scope of its competence in intellectual property matters. (It also rests in part upon the language of the intellectual property treaties in question. *See, e.g., infra* § 6.02[A] (Madrid Protocol dispute).)

(3) **EU Attitude Toward Copyright.** We noted above, *see supra* § 2.03[C][7], that the EU attitude toward intellectual property rights generally has evolved over the life of the union. As we discuss the EU legislative initiatives and judicial developments in the different sections that follow, consider whether they are consistent with Dr. Verstrynge's concern that "any harmonization which would choose the lower level of protection of copyright or neighboring rights . . . would . . . endanger artistic and literary creation." Why do you think he singles out the audiovisual sector in this regard?

[B]   The Interaction of Copyright and Common Market Policies

[1]   Free Movement of Goods

WARNER BROS. AND METRONOME VIDEO v. CHRISTIANSEN
Case 158/86, 1988 E.C.R. 2605 (E.C.J. 1988)

JUDGMENT:

By order dated 11 June 1986, the Oestre Landsret referred to the Court for a preliminary ruling under Article 177 of the EEC Treaty a question on the interpretation of Articles 30 and 36 of the EEC Treaty, with a view to establishing the extent to which national copyright legislation regarding the hiring-out of video-cassettes is compatible with the free movement of goods.

The question was raised in the context of proceedings brought by two companies, Warner Brothers Inc. ("Warner") and Metronome Video ApS ("Metronome"), against Mr Erik Viuff Christiansen.

Warner, the owner in the United Kingdom of the copyright of the film "Never Say Never Again," which it produced in that country, assigned the management of the video production rights in Denmark to Metronome.

The video-cassette of the film was on sale in the United Kingdom with Warner's consent. Mr Christiansen, who manages a video shop in Copenhagen, purchased a copy in London with a view to hiring it out in Denmark and imported it into that Member State for that purpose.

On the basis of Danish legislation, which enables the author or producer of a musical or cinematographic work to take action to restrain the hiring-out of videograms of that work until such time as he gives his consent, Warner and Metronome obtained an injunction from the Copenhagen City Court prohibiting the defendant from hiring out the video-cassette in Denmark.

In the context of the proceedings referred to it, the Oestre Landsret (Eastern Division of the High Court) decided to request the Court of Justice to give a preliminary ruling on the following question:

> Must the provisions of Chapter 2 in Title I of Part 2 of the EEC Treaty, on the elimination of quantitative restrictions between Member States, namely Articles 30 and 36, in conjunction with Article 222 of the Treaty, be interpreted as meaning that the owner of exclusive rights (copyright) in a video-recording which is lawfully put into circulation by the owner of the exclusive right or with his consent in a Member State under whose domestic copyright law it is not possible to prohibit the (resale and) hiring-out of the recordings is prevented from restraining the hiring-out of the video-recording in another Member State into which it has been lawfully imported, where the copyright law of that State allows such prohibition without

distinguishing between domestic and imported video-recordings and without impeding the actual importation of video-recordings?

. . . .

In submitting the question the national court seeks to ascertain, in essence, whether Articles 30 and 36 of the EEC Treaty preclude the application of national legislation which gives an author the right to make the hiring-out of video-cassettes conditional on his authorization, where those video-cassettes have already been put into circulation with his consent in another Member State whose legislation allows the author to control their initial sale without giving him the right to prohibit them from being hired out.

It should be noted that, unlike the national copyright legislation which gave rise to the judgment of 20 January 1981 in Musik Vertrieb Membran v GEMA (1981 ECR 147), the legislation which gives rise to the present preliminary question does not enable the author to collect an additional fee on the actual importation of recordings of protected works which are marketed with his consent in another Member State, or to set up any further obstacle whatsoever to importation or resale. The rights and powers conferred on the author by the national legislation in question comes into operation only after importation has been carried out.

Nonetheless, it must be observed that the commercial distribution of video-cassettes takes the form not only of sales but also, and increasingly, that of hiring-out to individuals who possess video-tape recorders. The right to prohibit such hiring-out in a Member State is therefore liable to influence trade in video-cassettes in that State and hence, indirectly, to affect intra-Community trade in those products. Legislation of the kind which gave rise to the main proceedings must therefore, in the light of established case-law, be regarded as a measure having an effect equivalent to a quantitative restriction on imports, which is prohibited by Article 30 of the Treaty.

Consideration should therefore be given to whether such legislation may be considered justified on grounds of the protection of industrial and commercial property within the meaning of Article 36—a term which was held by the Court, in its judgment of 6 October 1982 in Coditel v Cine-Vog (1982 ECR 3381) to include literary and artistic property.

In that connection it should first be noted that the Danish legislation applies without distinction to video-cassettes produced in situ and video-cassettes imported from another Member State. The determining factor for the purposes of its application is the type of transaction in video-cassettes which is in question, not the origin of those video-cassettes. Such legislation does not therefore, in itself, operate any arbitrary discrimination in trade between Member States.

It should further be pointed out that literary and artistic works may be the subject of commercial exploitation, whether by way of public performance or of the reproduction and marketing of the recordings made of them, and this is true in particular of cinematographic works. The two essential rights of the author, namely the exclusive right of performance and the exclusive right of reproduction, are not called in question by the rules of the Treaty.

Lastly, consideration must be given to the emergence, demonstrated by the

Commission, of a specific market for the hiring-out of such recordings, as distinct from their sale. The existence of that market was made possible by various factors such as the improvement of manufacturing methods for video-cassettes which increased their strength and life in use, the growing awareness amongst viewers that they watch only occasionally the video-cassettes which they have bought and, lastly, their relatively high purchase price. The market for the hiring-out of video-cassettes reaches a wider public than the market for their sale and, at present, offers great potential as a source of revenue for makers of films.

However, it is apparent that, by authorizing the collection of royalties only on sales to private individuals and to persons hiring out video-cassettes, it is impossible to guarantee to makers of films a remuneration which reflects the number of occasions on which the video-cassettes are actually hired out and which secures for them a satisfactory share of the rental market. That explains why, as the Commission points out in its observations, certain national laws have recently provided specific protection of the right to hire out video-cassettes.

Laws of that kind are therefore clearly justified on grounds of the protection of industrial and commercial property pursuant to Article 36 of the Treaty.

However, the defendant in the main proceedings, relying on the judgments of 22 January 1981 in Case 58/80 Dansk Supermarked v Imerco (1981 ECR 181) and of 20 January 1981 Musik Vertrieb Membran v GEMA, cited above, contends that the author is at liberty to choose the Member State in which he will market his work. The defendant in the main proceedings emphasizes that the author makes his choice according to his own interests and must, in particular, take into consideration the fact that the legislation of certain Member States, unlike that of certain others, confers on him an exclusive right enabling him to restrain the hiring-out of the recording of the work even when that work has been offered for sale with his consent. That being so, a maker of a film who has offered the video-cassette of that film for sale in a Member State whose legislation confers on him no exclusive right of hiring it out (as in the main proceedings) must accept the consequences of his choice and the exhaustion of his right to restrain the hiring-out of that video-cassette in any other Member State.

That objection cannot be upheld. It follows from the foregoing considerations that, where national legislation confers on authors a specific right to hire out video-cassettes, that right would be rendered worthless if its owner were not in a position to authorize the operations for doing so. It cannot therefore be accepted that the marketing by a film-maker of a video-cassette containing one of his works, in a Member State which does not provide specific protection for the right to hire it out, should have repercussions on the right conferred on that same film-maker by the legislation of another Member State to restrain, in that State, the hiring-out of that video-cassette.

In those circumstances, the answer to be given to the question submitted by the national court is that Articles 30 and 36 of the Treaty do not prohibit the application of national legislation which gives an author the right to make the hiring-out of video-cassettes subject to his permission, when the video-cassettes in question have already been put into circulation with his consent in another

Member State whose legislation enables the author to control the initial sale, without giving him the right to prohibit hiring-out.

———————

NOTES AND QUESTIONS

(1) **Rental Rights**. Subsequent to the *Warner Brothers* case, in 1992 the EU adopted Directive 92/100 on rental right and lending right and on certain rights relating to copyright in the field of intellectual property law, better known as the Rental Right Directive. This directive required member states to accord authors and certain neighboring rights holders, *see* art. 2(1), the right to authorize or prohibit the rental of copies of their works for direct or indirect economic or commercial advantage. *See infra* § 4.05[C]. The assertion of rights under the Rental Right directive was also challenged under ex-Article 30 of the EC Treaty, and again the exercise of rental rights in Denmark was upheld by the European Court of Justice (even though the right holder had authorized the rental of the copies of the work in another member state). *See* Foreingen AF Danske Videogramdistributorer v. Laserdisken, [1999] 1 C.M.L.R. 1297 (E.C.J. 1998).

(2) **Exhaustion**. The question whether placing copies of a work on the market in one country affects the ability of the right holder to exercise rights in another country with respect to those copies raises the question of so-called "exhaustion of rights." We address this topic *infra* § 7.06.

[2] Non-Discrimination

PHIL COLLINS v. IMTRAT HANDELSGESELLSCHAFT
CASE C-92/92, EMI V. PATRICIA, CASE C-326/92
[1993] 3 C.M.L.R. 773 (E.C.J. 1993)

OPINION OF ADVOCATE-GENERAL:

Two German courts have requested preliminary rulings on the questions whether copyright and related rights fall within the ambit of the EEC Treaty and whether a member-State which allows its own nationals to oppose the unauthorised reproduction of their musical performances must grant identical protection to nationals of other member-States, in accordance with the prohibition of discrimination on grounds of nationality laid down in Article 7 EEC.

Case C-92/92

The plaintiff in Case C-92/92 is Phil Collins, a singer and composer of British nationality.   The defendant Imtrat Handelsgesellschaft mbH ('Imtrat') is a producer of phonograms.   Collins gave a concert in California which was recorded without his consent.   Reproductions of the recording were sold in Germany by Imtrat on compact disc under the title 'Live and Alive.' Mr Collins applied to the [Regional Court, Munich 1] for an injunction restraining Imtrat from marketing such recordings in Germany and requiring it to deliver copies in its possession to a court bailiff.

It appears that if Mr Collins were a German national his application would undoubtedly have succeeded.   Section 75 of the [German Law on Copyright and related rights] (the "UrhG") provides that a performing artist's performance may not be recorded without his consent and recordings may not be reproduced without his consent.   Section 125(1) of the UrhG provides that German nationals enjoy the protection of section 75, amongst other provisions, for all their performances regardless of the place of performance.   However, foreign nationals have less extensive rights under the UrhG.   Under section 125(2) they enjoy protection in respect of performances which take place in Germany, and under section 125(5) they enjoy protection in accordance with international treaties.   The [Regional Court] refers to the Rome Convention of 26 October 1961 for the Protection of Performers, Producers of Phonograms and Broadcasting Organisations,[*] but deduces from its terms that Germany is required to grant foreign performing artists the same treatment as its own nationals only in respect of performances that take place within the territory of a Contracting State;[**] since the United States [where the performance was given] has not acceded to the Rome Convention, section 125(5) of the UrhG is of no avail to Mr Collins in the circumstances of the present case.[***]   Collins argued that he was entitled to the same treatment as a German national by virtue of Article 7 EEC.   The [Regional Court] therefore decided to refer the following questions to the Court:

1.   Is copyright law subject to the prohibition of discrimination laid down in Article 7(1) EEC?

2.   If so: does that have the (directly applicable) effect that a member-State which accords protection to its nationals for all their artistic performances, irrespective of the place of performance, also has to accord that protection to nationals of other member-States, or is it compatible with Article 7(1) to attach further conditions . . . to the grant of protection to nationals of other member-States?

---

[*][Ed. Note: Article 7(1) of the Rome Convention provides that "the protection provided for performers by this Convention shall include the possibility of preventing . . . (b) the fixation, without their consent, of their unfixed performance; (c) the reproduction, without their consent, of a fixation of the unfixed performance . . . if the original fixation itself was made without their consent].

[**][Ed. Note: Article 4 of the Rome Convention provides for the application of national treatment to artists who are nationals of the Contracting States, provided that the performance (a) takes place in one of those States or (b) that the phonogram has a connection with one of them.]

[***][Ed. Note: Eight member-States, including Germany and the United Kingdom, had acceded to the Rome Convention at the time of the dispute, but the United States had not.]

Case C-326/92

The plaintiff and respondent in Case C-326/92, EMI Electrola GmbH ('EMI Electrola'), produces and distributes phonograms. It owns the exclusive right to exploit in Germany recordings of certain works performed by Cliff Richard, a singer of British nationality. The defendants and appellants are Patricia Im- und Export Verwaltungsgesellshcaft ('Patricia'), a company which distributes phonograms, and Mr Kraul, its managing director. EMI Electrola applied for an injunction restraining Patricia and Mr Kraul (together with other persons) from infringing its exclusive rights in recordings of certain performances by Cliff Richard. The recordings were first published in the United Kingdom in 1958 and 1959, apparently by a British phonogram producer to which Cliff Richard had assigned his performer's rights in the recordings. That company subsequently assigned the rights to EMI Electrola.

The Landgericht granted EMI Electrola's application and that decision was confirmed on appeal. Patricia and Mr Kraul appealed on a point of law to the Bundesgerichtshof, which considers that, under German law, EMI Electrola would be entitled to an injunction if Cliff Richard were of German nationality but is not so entitled because he is British. It is not entirely clear from the order for reference how or why the Bundesgerichtshof arrived at the view that German law provides for such a difference of treatment. The reason appears to be that the performances in question took place before 21 October 1966, on which date the Rome Convention came into force in Germany, and that Germany is only required to grant 'national treatment' to foreign performers, under the Rome Convention, in respect of performances that take place after that date. [cit].

It is in any event common ground that a difference in treatment, depending on the nationality of the performer, exists in German law. The Bundesgerichtshof therefore referred the following questions to the Court:

1. Is the national copyright law of a member-State subject to the prohibition of discrimination laid down in Article 7(1) EEC?

2. If so, are the provisions operating in a member-State for the protection of artistic performances (section 125(2) to (6) of the UrhG) compatible with Article 7(1) EEC if they do not confer on nationals of another member-State the same standard of protection (national treatment) as they do on national performers?

The issues raised by the two cases

Both cases raise essentially the same issues: (a) whether it is compatible with Community law, in particular Article 7 EEC, for a member-State to grant more extensive protection in respect of performances by its own nationals than in respect of performances by nationals of other member-States and (b) if such a difference in treatment is not compatible with Community law, whether the relevant provisions of Community law produce direct effect, in the sense that a performer who has the nationality of another member-State is entitled to claim, in proceedings against a person who markets unauthorised recordings of his performances, the same rights as a national of the member-State in question.

I note in passing that, although both the national courts refer to copyright, the cases are in fact concerned not with copyright in the strict sense but with certain related rights known as performers' rights.

The prohibition of discrimination on grounds of nationality

The prohibition of discrimination on grounds of nationality is the single most important principle of Community law. It is the leitmotiv of the EEC Treaty. It is laid down in general terms in Article 7 of the Treaty, the first paragraph of which provides:

> Within the scope of application of this Treaty, and without prejudice to any special provisions contained therein, any discrimination on grounds of nationality shall be prohibited.

That general prohibition of discrimination is elaborated upon in other, more specific provisions of the Treaty. Thus Article 36 permits certain restrictions on the free movement of goods, provided that they do not constitute 'arbitrary discrimination' or a disguised restriction on trade. Article 48(2) requires the 'abolition of any discrimination based on nationality between workers of the member-States as regards employment, remuneration and other conditions of work.' Under Article 52(2), nationals of one member-State may work in a self-employed capacity in another member-State 'under the conditions laid down for its own nationals.' Under Article 60(3), a person providing a service may temporarily pursue his activity in the State where the service is provided 'under the same conditions as are imposed by that State on its own nationals.'

It is not difficult to see why the authors of the Treaty attached so much importance to the prohibition of discrimination. The fundamental purpose of the Treaty is to achieve an integrated economy in which the factors of production, as well as the fruits of production, may move freely and without distortion, thus bringing about a more efficient allocation of resources and a more perfect division of labour. The greatest obstacle to the realisation of that objective was the host of discriminatory rules and practices whereby the national governments traditionally protected their own producers and workers from foreign competition. Although the abolition of discriminatory rules and practices may not be sufficient in itself to achieve the high level of economic integration envisaged by the Treaty, it is clearly an essential prerequisite.

The prohibition of discrimination on grounds of nationality is also of great symbolic importance, inasmuch as it demonstrates that the Community is not just a commercial arrangement between the governments of the member-States but is a common enterprise in which all the citizens of Europe are able to participate as individuals. The nationals of each member-State are entitled to live, work and do business in other member-States on the same terms as the local population. They must not simply be tolerated as aliens, but welcomed by the authorities of the host State as Community nationals who are entitled, 'within the scope of application of the Treaty,' to all the privileges and advantages enjoyed by the nationals of the host State. No other aspect of Community law touches the individual more directly or does more to foster that sense of common identity and shared destiny without which the 'ever closer union among the peoples of Europe,' proclaimed by the preamble to the Treaty, would be an empty slogan.

Much has been written about the relationship between Article 7 and the other provisions of the Treaty which lay down more specific prohibitions of discrimination on grounds of nationality . . . . There is also a substantial body of case law on that relationship. The generally accepted position seems to be that recourse is to be had to Article 7 only when none of the more specific provisions prohibiting discrimination is applicable. [cit]. Thus one of the main functions of Article 7 is to close any gaps left by the more specific provisions of the Treaty.

It is sometimes said that, where rules are compatible with the specific Treaty Articles prohibiting discrimination, they are also compatible with Article 7. It would perhaps be more accurate to say that, if a national provision discriminates in a manner that is positively permitted by one of the more specific Treaty Articles, it cannot be contrary to Article 7. Thus, since Article 48(4) of the Treaty allows nationals of other member-States to be excluded from employment in the public service in certain circumstances, such a practice cannot be contrary to Article 7 notwithstanding its manifestly discriminatory nature. It would, however, be wrong to say that a rule discriminating against nationals of other member-States cannot be contrary to Article 7 simply because it is not caught by the specific provisions of Articles 48, 52, 59 and 60 of the Treaty. Otherwise Article 7 would cease to perform its gap-closing function.

In the circumstances of the present cases I do not think that it is necessary to explore more fully the relationship between the general prohibition of Article 7 and the more specific prohibitions laid down elsewhere. There cannot be any doubt that Article 7, either alone or in conjunction with other provisions of the Treaty, has the effect that nationals of a member-State are entitled to pursue any legitimate form of economic activity in another member-State on the same terms as the latter State's own nationals.

That simple observation is probably sufficient in itself to resolve the fundamental issues raised by the present cases. In so far as intellectual property rights assist the proprietor thereof to pursue the economic freedoms granted by the Treaty, in particular by Articles 30, 52 and 59, a member-State must accord the nationals of other member-States the same level of protection as it accords its own nationals. If, for example, a member-State granted patents only to its own nationals and refused to grant patents to the nationals of other member-States, it could not seriously be argued that such a practice was compatible with the Treaty.

Indeed, such discrimination was specifically identified by the Council in 1961 in the General Programme for the Abolition of Restrictions on Freedom to

Provide Services . . . and in the General Programme for the Abolition of Restrictions on Freedom of Establishment . . . . Both those programmes call for the abolition of 'provisions and practices which, in respect of foreign nationals only, exclude, limit or impose conditions on the power to exercise rights normally attaching to the provision of services [or to an activity as a self-employed person] and in particular the power . . . to acquire, use or dispose of intellectual property and all rights deriving therefrom.' It may be noted that the General Programmes provide 'useful guidance for the implementation of the relevant provisions of the Treaty.'

There are many ways in which the proprietor of intellectual property rights may seek to exercise those rights in pursuit of the economic freedoms guaranteed by the Treaty. A performer may for example have phonograms embodying his performance manufactured in his own country and export those goods to another member-State, in which case he is in a situation covered by Article 30. Or he may set up a company or branch in that other member-State and have phonograms manufactured there for sale in that country, in which case he is exercising his right of establishment under Article 52. Or again—and this is no doubt the commonest method of exploiting performers' rights and is the method used in the present cases—he may license another person to manufacture and sell phonograms embodying his performance in the other member-State; in that case he will doubtless receive a royalty for each sale and will be able to obtain further royalties by licensing a copyright management society (or, more accurately, a performers' rights management society) to authorise public performances of his recordings. Such licensing activities will constitute services which are provided across national frontiers and are as such covered by Article 59 EEC.

Whichever way a performing artist chooses to exploit his performances for commercial gain in another member-State, he will be in a situation covered by Community law. As such, he will be 'within the scope of application of the Treaty' and will be entitled to invoke the prohibition of discrimination on grounds of nationality laid down in Article 7 EEC. Indeed the Court has gone much further than that. It has held that a tourist who travels to another member-State may, as a recipient of services, benefit from a scheme for compensating the victims of violent crime on the same terms as nationals of that member-State [cit]; that a person who goes to another member-State for the purpose of receiving vocational training may not be required to pay a registration fee if no such fee is payable by nationals of that member-State [cit]; and that a migrant worker who is prosecuted in a criminal court is entitled to the same treatment, with regard to the use of languages in judicial proceedings, as a national of the host country. [cit]. It would be extraordinary if those who exercise the fundamental freedoms guaranteed by the Treaty were entitled to equality of treatment in relation to matters that are—while not without importance—peripheral and essentially non-economic in nature, but were to be denied equality of treatment in the field of intellectual property rights, the economic importance of which is considerable.

Certainly there can be no doubt about the economic importance of the performing artist's exclusive right to authorise the reproduction and distribution of recordings embodying his performance. The exercise of that right is essential to the commercial exploitation of a performance. The sale of unauthorised recordings damages the performing artist in two ways: first, because he earns no royalties on such recordings, the sale of which must inevitably reduce the demand for his authorised recordings, since the spending power of even the most avid record collector is finite; secondly, because he loses the power to control the quality of the recordings, which may, if technically inferior, adversely affect his reputation. . . .

Performers' rights also play a role in the field of consumer protection: the consumer doubtless assumes that recordings made by well-known, living performers are not released without the performer's authorisation and that such persons would not jeopardise their reputation by authorising the distribution of low-quality recordings; that limited guarantee of quality is lost entirely if recordings may be distributed without the performer's consent. It may thus be seen that performers' rights operate in much the same way as trade marks, the economic significance of which was recognised by the Court in the HAG II case (Case C-10/89, CNL SUCAL v. Hag GF [1990] I ECR 3711).

The defendants in both the present cases advance a number of arguments purporting to show that the contested German legislation is not contrary to the prohibition of discrimination on grounds of nationality. I shall briefly summarise the main arguments and state why, in my view, none of them is convincing.

Both defendants contend that the discrimination lies outside the scope of application of the Treaty. Imtrat reaches that conclusion on the grounds that the performance in question took place outside the territory of a member-State and that the existence of intellectual property rights is a matter for national law by virtue of Article 222 EEC. That cannot be correct. The place where the original performance took place is irrelevant; what matters is that Phil Collins and his licensees are denied protection, in an overtly discriminatory manner, when they attempt to exploit—or prevent others from exploiting—the performance in a member-State. The argument based on Article 222 EEC is equally untenable. That Article, which, it will be recalled, provides that the Treaty shall in no way prejudice the rules in member-States governing the system of property ownership, clearly does not authorise member-States to grant intellectual property rights on a discriminatory basis. It might just as well be argued that a member-State could prohibit the nationals of other member-States from buying land for business use.

It is contended on behalf of Patricia and Mr Kraul that the absence of Community legislation harmonising the laws of member-States on copyright and related rights removes such matters from the scope of the Treaty entirely. That argument is of course doomed to failure. The application of the principle of non-discrimination is not dependent on the harmonisation of national law; on the contrary, it is precisely in areas where harmonisation has not been achieved that the principle of national treatment assumes special importance.

It is true that the Court has several times held that in the absence of harmonisation it is for national law to determine the conditions governing the grant of intellectual property rights; see, for example, Thetford v. Fiamma (Case 35/87: [1988] ECR 3585]). But that does not mean that member-States are free to lay down discriminatory conditions for the grant of such rights. That much is clear from the *Thetford* judgment itself, in which the Court attached importance to the non-discriminatory nature of a provision of United Kingdom law relating to the grant of patents, there being 'no discrimination based on the nationality of applicants for patents'; the Court clearly implied that a patent granted on the basis of a discriminatory provision could not be relied on to justify a restriction on trade between member-States under Article 36 EEC. Moreover, the Council has also recognised, in the General Programmes referred to above, that the grant and exercise of intellectual property rights are matters falling within the scope of the Treaty and are therefore subject to the prohibition of discrimination.

Also relevant in this context is the Court's judgment in GVL v EC Commission (Case 7/82: [1983] ECR 483), in which the Court held that a performers' rights management society abused its dominant position, in breach of Article 86 EEC, by refusing to manage the rights of foreign performers not resident in Germany. The decision in issue in that case (Commission Decision 81/1030/EEC [1981] OJ 1370/49) was based partly on Article 7 EEC. As the Commission has pointed out, it would be very strange if undertakings were prohibited from discriminating on grounds of nationality, in the field of intellectual property, but member-States were allowed to maintain in force discriminatory legislation. The United Kingdom also cites GVL v EC Commission and submits, rightly in my view, that that judgment clearly shows that the management and enforcement of performers' rights are matters falling within the scope of the Treaty.

It is in any event not true to say that the Community legislature has been completely inactive in the field of copyright and related rights. Several measures have been adopted; notably, Council Directive 91/250 of 14 May 1991 on the legal protection of computer programs ([1991] OJ L122/42) and Council Directive 92/100 of 19 November 1992 on rental right and lending right and on certain rights related to copyright in the field of intellectual property ([1992] OJ L346/61). It is interesting to note that the 18th recital in the preamble to the latter directive states that measures based on Article 5 of the directive, which permits derogations from the exclusive lending right created by Article 1 of the directive, must comply with Article 7 of the Treaty. Mention may also be made of the Council Resolution of 14 May 1992 on increased protection for copyright and neighbouring rights ([1992] OJ C138/1). Article 1 of that resolution notes that the member-States undertake to become parties to the Berne Convention for the Protection of Literary and Artistic Works of 24 July 1971 (Paris Act) and to the 1961 Rome Convention. In the circumstances, the view that copyright and related rights lie outside the scope of the Treaty is clearly untenable.

The only argument advanced by either of the defendants that has some plausibility is the one based on the Rome Convention, on which great reliance is placed by Imtrat. According to that argument, all questions concerning the level of protection to be granted to foreign performers are to be resolved in the context of the Rome Convention, which has established a delicate balance based on considerations of reciprocity. The connecting factor, under the Rome Convention, is not nationality—which would be unworkable because many performances are given by groups of performers who may have different nationalities—but place of performance. Imtrat points out further that both Germany and the United Kingdom were bound by the Rome Convention before they became mutually bound by the EEC Treaty (presumably on 1 January 1973, when the United Kingdom acceded to the Communities) and argues that the Rome Convention should therefore take precedence over the EEC Treaty by virtue of Article 234 of the latter. Imtrat suggests that dire consequences would ensue if Article 7 of the Treaty were applied in the field of copyright and related rights: authors from other member-States would, for example, be able to claim in Germany the long term of protection (70 years after the author's death) provided for in German law, whereas under Article 7(8) of the Berne Convention Germany is not required to grant them a longer term of protection than the term fixed in the country of origin of the work.

In response to those arguments the following points may be made. First, even if the Rome Convention had been concluded before the EEC Treaty, Article 234 of the latter would not give precedence to the Convention as regards relations between member-States. Article 234 is concerned solely with relations between member-States and non-member-States. [cit].

Secondly, there is in any event no conflict between Community law and the Rome Convention. That Convention merely lays down a minimum standard of protection and does not prevent the Contracting States from granting more extensive protection to their own nationals or to nationals of other States. That much is clear from Articles 21 and 22 of the Convention. Article 21 provides:

> The protection provided for in this Convention shall not prejudice any protection otherwise secured to performers, producers of phonograms and broadcasting organisations.

Article 22 provides:

> Contracting States reserve the right to enter into special agreements among themselves in so far as such agreements grant to performers, producers of phonograms or broadcasting organisations more extensive rights than those granted by this Convention or contain other provisions not contrary to this Convention.

The Rome Convention does not prevent Germany from granting performers more extensive protection than the minimum provided for in the Convention. However, Article 7 of the Treaty requires that, if more extensive protection is granted to German performers, the same level of protection should be available to nationals of other member-States.

Thirdly, if nationality is unworkable as a connecting factor on account of the problem of multinational ensembles, it may well be asked why German law uses nationality as a connecting factor at all, as of course it clearly does since it grants differing levels of protection depending on whether the performer is German or of some other nationality. Moreover, even if only one member of an ensemble has German nationality, it seems that the performance is protected.

[cit]. That constitutes a very simple criterion for resolving the difficulties supposedly caused by multinational ensembles; it would be equally workable where one member of an ensemble had the nationality of another member-State.

Fourthly, as regards the consequences of applying the principle of non-discrimination to copyright law in general and to the question of the term of protection, it may well be the case that Article 7 of the Treaty requires each member-State to grant all Community nationals the same term of protection as its own nationals, even though the latter receive a shorter term of protection in other member-States. Clearly, the prohibition of discrimination will often have the effect, in the absence of complete harmonisation, that nationals of member-State A will be better protected in member-State B than vice versa. But the issue does not fall to be decided in these cases and it is clear that no serious consequence would ensue (except for the manufacturers of unauthorised recordings) if the protection granted to German performers, in respect of performances given in the territory of a State that is not a party to the Rome Convention or in respect of performances given before that Convention's entry into force, were extended to performers who are nationals of other member-States.

The direct effect of Article 7(1)

I turn now to the issue of direct effect. In my view, it is clear from the considerations set out above that the Treaty provisions which prohibit discrimination must be capable of being invoked by performers in the circumstances of the present cases. There is of course no doubt that the prohibition of discrimination laid down in Articles 52(2) and 60(3), produces direct effect [cit]. [These] cases show that the adoption of legislative measures was superfluous, as far as concerns the prohibition of discrimination on grounds of nationality, in view of the direct effect of the Treaty provisions. [cit].

The Court's case law also suggests that Article 7(1) has direct effect in so far as it prohibits discrimination within the scope of application of the Treaty. . . . [I]t is clear from a number of judgments [cit] that national courts are under a duty to disapply national provisions that are contrary to Article 7. It is equally clear that that duty arises not only in proceedings against the State but also in litigation between individuals. [cit].

A factual difference between Case C-92/92 and Case C-326/92

A final issue that remains to be explored is whether any significance attaches to an obvious factual difference between Case C-92/92 and Case C-326/92: in the former case the performer, Phil Collins, has remained the proprietor of the performer's rights and has granted an exclusive licence to a producer of phonograms to exploit those rights in Germany; in the latter case the performer, Cliff Richard, has assigned his rights to a British company, which has reassigned them to a German company. I am satisfied that that difference is not relevant to the issue of discrimination. Although in Case C-326/92 the direct victim of the discriminatory German legislation is a German company, the indirect victim will, on the assumption that royalties are paid to the performer by EMI Electrola, be Cliff Richard himself. Even in the case of an outright assignment without any provision for the payment of royalties, it would be wrong in principle to discriminate on the basis of the nationality of the performer and original right-holder. If such discrimination were permitted, it would mean that the exclusive right granted to a German performer would be an assignable asset, potentially of considerable value, while a British performer's exclusive right would have virtually no assignable value, since it would be extinguished on assignment. Thus the indirect victim of the discrimination would always be the performer himself. It would in any case be illogical, in the circumstances of the present cases, to distinguish between a performer's right which has been the subject of an exclusive licence and a performer's right which has been the subject of an assignment.

Conclusion

I am therefore of the opinion that the questions referred to the Court by the Landgericht Munchen I in Case C-92/92 and the Bundesgerichtshof in Case C-326/92 should be answered as follows:

By virtue of Article 7(l) of the Treaty, the courts of a member-State must allow performing artists who are nationals of other member-States to oppose the unauthorised reproduction of their performances on the same terms as the nationals of the first member-State.

JUDGMENT OF THE COURT OF JUSTICE:

. . . .

Subject-matter of references

The Court, when ruling in the framework of Article 177 EEC, cannot give decisions on the interpretation of national law or regulations or on their compatibility with Community law. Consequently it cannot interpret the UrhG or assess its compatibility with Community law. The Court can only give the national court guidance on interpretation under Community law which will enable it to resolve the legal problem before it. [cit].

The orders making the references mention the national rules applying to copyright and section 125 UrhG, which governs the rights of performing artists, the so-called 'neighbouring rights.' It is not for the Court to decide whether the main actions concern one or the other of these two types of rights. As the Commission proposes, the questions submitted should be regarded as relating to the rules applying to both.

The questions refer to Article 7(1) EEC, which lays down the general principle of non-discrimination on grounds of nationality. As the Article expressly states, such prohibition applies only within the scope of application of the Treaty. The questions must therefore be regarded as seeking in essence to establish whether:

— copyright and related rights are within the scope of application of the Treaty within the meaning of Article 7(1) and whether the general principle of non-discrimination laid down by that Article consequently applies to those rights;

— if so, whether Article 7(1) prevents the law of a member-State from refusing authors and performing artists of other member-States and their successors in title the right, which is granted by the same law to nationals, to prohibit the marketing in national territory of a phonogram made without their consent, if the performance in question was given outside national territory;

— whether Article 7(1) EEC can be relied upon directly before a national court by an author or artist of another member-State or his successor in title in order to obtain the protection given to nationals.

Application of the Treaty to copyright and related rights

The Commission, the German and British Governments, Phil Collins and EMI Electrola contend that copyright and related rights, in so far as they are economic rights determining the conditions under which works and performances by artists can be exploited commercially, fall within the scope of application of the Treaty, as shown by the Court's judgments applying Articles 30, 36, 59, 85 and 86 EEC to those rights and by the intense legislative activity concerning them in the Communities. In the rare cases where a specific provision of the Treaty does not apply, the general principle of non-discrimination laid down by Article 7(1) EEC must in any case be applied.

Imtrat contends, on the contrary, that the conditions for according copyright and related rights affect the existence, and not the exercise, of those rights and are not within the scope of application of the Treaty, as shown by Article 222 EEC and the Court's settled case law. Patricia and Mr Kraul, repeating on this point the findings of the Federal Supreme Court, argue in particular that copyright and related rights were not, in the absence of Community rules or harmonisation measures at the time of the acts with which the main action is concerned, governed by Community law. In the present state of Community law, and in the absence of Community measures or the harmonisation of national law, it is for the member-States to specify the conditions and rules for the protection of literary and artistic property, subject to complying with the relevant international agreements: Case 341/87, EMI Electrola ([1989] ECR 79).

The specific purpose of these rights, as governed by national law, is to protect the moral and economic rights of their owners. The protection of moral rights enables authors and artists to resist any distortion, mutilation or other alteration of the work which would be prejudicial to their honour or reputation.

Copyright and related rights also have economic characteristics in that they provide for the possibility of commercially exploiting the marketing of the protected work, particularly in the form of licences granted in return for the payment of royalties: Cases 55 & 57/80, Musik-vertrieb Membran ([1981] ECR 147).

As the Court observed in the last-mentioned judgment, while the commercial exploitation of copyright is a source of remuneration for the owner it also constitutes a form of control on marketing exercisable by the owner, the copyright management societies acting in his name and the grantees of licences. From this viewpoint the commercial exploitation of copyright raises the same problems as that of any other industrial or commercial property right.

Like other industrial and commercial property rights, the exclusive rights conferred by literary and artistic property are such as to affect trade in goods and services, as well as competition in the Community. For this reason, as the Court has consistently held, these rights, although governed by national law, are subject to the requirements of the Treaty and therefore fall within the scope of application.

Consequently they are subject to, for example, Articles 30 and 36 EEC on the freedom of movement of goods. As the Court has previously held, musical works are incorporated in phonograms which are goods, trade in which in the Community is governed by the abovementioned provisions: Cases 55 & 57/80, cited above.

In the same way the activities of copyright management societies are subject to Articles 59 and 66 EEC, relating to the freedom to provide services. As the Court observed in Case 7/82, GVL v EC Commission ([1983] ECR 483), these activities must not be conducted in such a way as to have the effect of impeding the free movement of services, particularly the exploitation of the rights of performers, to the extent of partitioning the Common Market.

Finally, the exclusive rights conferred by literary and artistic property are subject to the Treaty provisions concerning competition: Case 78/70, Deutsche Grammophon ([1971] ECR 487).

In addition, subsequently to the main actions, the Council adopted Directive 92/100 of 19 November 1992 on rental right and lending right and on certain rights related to copyright in the field of intellectual property ([1992] OJ L346/61) on the basis of Article 57(2), 66 and 100a EEC precisely in order to avoid the risk of obstacles to trade and distortions of competition.

It follows from what has been said that copyright and related rights, which fall within the scope of application of the Treaty particularly by reason of their effects on trade in goods and services in the Community, are necessarily subject to the general principle of non-discrimination laid down by Article 7(1) EEC, and there is no requirement to attach them to the specific provisions of Articles 30, 36, 59 and 66.

Therefore the reply to the question referred must be that copyright and related rights are within the scope of application of the Treaty within the meaning of Article 7(1); the general principle of non-discrimination laid down by that Article is consequently applicable to those rights.

Discrimination within the meaning of Article 7(1) EEC

Imtrat and Patricia contend that the distinction made in the cases referred to by the national courts between German nationals and nationals of other member-States is objectively justified by the differences in national laws and by the fact that not all the member-States have yet acceded to the Rome Convention. Under these circumstances, it is said, the distinction is not contrary to Article 7(1) EEC.

The Court has consistently held that Article 7 does not apply to differences in treatment and distortions which affect persons and enterprises under the jurisdiction of the Community and which may arise from differences in the laws of the member-States if such differences affect all persons to whom they apply, according to objective criteria and without regard to nationality: Case 14/68, Wilhelm ([1969] ECR 1).

Therefore, contrary to the arguments of Imtrat and Patricia, neither the differences in national laws relating to the protection of copyright and related rights nor the fact that not all the member-States have yet acceded to the Rome Convention can justify an infringement of the principle of non-discrimination laid down by Article 7(1) EEC.

By prohibiting 'any discrimination on grounds of nationality,' Article 7 EEC requires that persons in a situation governed by Community law be placed on a completely equal footing with nationals of the member-State. [cit]. Where this principle applies, it precludes a member-State from making the grant of an exclusive right subject to the condition of being a national of that State.

Consequently the reply to the question must be that Article 7(1) EEC must be interpreted as meaning that it prevents the law of a member-State from refusing, under certain circumstances, authors and performing artists of other member-States and their successors in title the right, which is granted by the same law to nationals, to prohibit the marketing in national territory of a phonogram made without their consent, if the performance in question was given outside national territory.

Effects of Article 7(1)

As the Court has consistently held, the right to equal treatment laid down by Article 7(1) EEC is conferred directly by Community law. [cit]. The right can therefore be relied upon before the national court when asking it to set aside the discriminatory provisions of a national law which refuses nationals of other member-States the protection accorded to nationals of the State in question.

Therefore the reply to the question is that Article 7(1) EEC must be interpreted as meaning that the principle of non-discrimination which it lays down can be relied upon directly before the national court by an author or artist of a member-State or his successor in title in order to seek the protection given to national authors and artists.

NOTES AND QUESTIONS

(1) **Member States' Adherence to the Berne and Rome Conventions.** As the advocate-general notes, the EU Council of Ministers in 1992 issued a Resolution requiring member states to adhere to the current texts of the Berne and Rome Conventions. Not all member states complied with that instruction in a timely fashion, causing the Commission to send reasoned opinions to recalcitrant national governments informing them of their non-compliance with Community law. Where this occurs, the Commission may bring an action before the Court of Justice against the member state for failure to fulfil an obligation under Community law. The remedy if such an action is sustained is to require compliance or, if that does not occur, to impose fines.

(2) **Effect of *Phil Collins* on Exceptions to National Treatment.** As hinted at by the advocate-general, the effect of the *Phil Collins* decision is far broader than performers' rights. The Berne Convention permits signatories to apply the rule of the shorter term, see art. 7(8), and thus condition the term of copyright protection upon reciprocity. *See supra* § 4.04[A]. (The United States does not take advantage of this provision, but the European Union did so when it enacted its Term Directive.) The effect of *Phil Collins* was to ensure that, as between member states of the EU, the rule of the shorter term was overriden by Article 7 of the EC Treaty, and thus EU states could not apply the rule to nationals of other EU states even if those other EU states offered less protection. The decision has also affected other EU initiatives where the applicable international conventions permitted discrimination among nationals depending upon reciprocal protection.

(3) **Effect of *Phil Collins* on the Legislative Process.** Should the decision in *Phil Collins* heighten or lessen the need for the Commission, Council and Parliament to agree on harmonization legislation? Does it have any significant effect?

[3] Competition Law

RADIO TELEFIS EIREANN v. EUROPEAN COMMISSION
JOINED CASES C-241-242/91 P ["MAGILL"]
[1995] All E.R. (EC) 416 (E.C.J. 1995)

OPINION OF THE ADVOCATE GENERAL (C GULMANN):

In these joined cases the Court of Justice of the European Communities is to rule on whether the European Commission, by a decision on the basis of art. 86 of the EC Treaty, can require undertakings to license their copyright works. The Court of Justice is thus asked to decide whether it is possible on the basis of the competition rules of the Treaty in special circumstances to interfere with the specific subject matter of copyright. The cases again raise the fundamental issue of the balancing of two conflicting interests, on the one hand the concern to protect industrial and commercial property rights based on national law, and on the other the concern for undistorted competition which it is one of the Community's tasks to ensure.

By Commission Decision (EEC) 89/205 of 21 December 1988 relating to a proceeding under art. 86 of the Treaty the Commission required three undertakings to license their television programme listings. That decision was upheld by judgments of the Court of First Instance of 10 July 1991 in *RTE v Commission* Case T-69/89 [1991] ECR II-485 and *ITP Ltd v EC Commission* Case T-76/89 [1991] ECR II-575. It is those judgments that are being challenged in these proceedings before the Court of Justice.

A. THE BACKGROUND TO THE CASES

Programme listings are lists of forthcoming television programmes which contain information as to the title, channel, date and time of broadcasts. They are produced by the television broadcasting organisations in connection with and for the purposes of their programme scheduling. Programme listings enjoy copyright protection as literary works and compilations under the United Kingdom Copyright Act . . . and the Irish Copyright Act 1963.

At the time of the Commission's decision three weekly television guides were marketed in Ireland and Northern Ireland, TV Times, Radio Times and RTE Guide, each containing programme listings for two of the six television channels that could be received by most households in Ireland and 30% to 40% of households in Northern Ireland. . . .

The TV Times contained the weekly programme listings for ITV and Channel 4 broadcast by television companies franchised by the Independent Broadcasting Authority . . . to broadcast independent television programmes. It was published by Independent Television Publications Ltd, London (ITP), which had been assigned the copyright in the programme listings by the producers of programmes for those two channels. Radio Times contained the weekly programme listings for BBC1 and BBC2 and was published by the wholly-owned subsidiary, the BBC Enterprises Ltd, which was assigned the copyright to the weekly programme listings by its parent organisation, the BBC. In the United Kingdom, the BBC and IBA had a duopoly for supplying national television services. The RTE Guide contained the weekly programme listings for RTE 1 and RTE 2 and was published by Radio Telefis Eireann (RTE) which has a statutory monopoly for radio and broadcasting services in Ireland.

Unlike in the other EC member states, on the market in Ireland and Northern Ireland there was no television guide containing all weekly programme listings for the channels which all or most television viewers could receive (the 'comprehensive weekly television guides'). The reason lay in the licensing practice of the three undertakings: daily and weekly newspapers and in some case magazines could receive free on request the weekly programme listings together with any programme summaries. [T]he newspapers could publish the daily listings or, at weekends and before public holidays, the listings for two days subject to certain conditions as to the format of the publication. . . .

In 1985 the Irish publisher Magill TV Guide Ltd (Magill) began to publish a weekly paper in Ireland and Northern Ireland containing information on forthcoming television programmes. At first the paper only contained information on the weekend programmes of RTE, the BBC, ITV and Channel 4 and highlights from the week's programmes. When in May 1986 an edition of Magill TV Guide appeared containing all the weekly listings for all television channels that could be received in the area, an Irish court, in response to an application from RTE, the BBC and ITV, issued an interim injunction restraining Magill from publishing the weekly programme listings of those undertakings on the grounds that such publication infringed their copyright. That decision was upheld by a judgment of the High Court of 26 July 1989. [cit].[4]

Before it published the comprehensive edition of Magill TV Guide, Magill had already lodged a complaint with the Commission under art 3 of Council Regulation (EEC) 17/62 implementing arts 85 and 86 of the Treaty. In art 1 of its decision of 21 December 1988 the Commission held:

> The policies and practices of ITP, BBC and RTE, respectively, in relation to their individual advance weekly programme listings, on programmes which may be received in Ireland and Northern Ireland, constitute infringements of Article 86 in so far as they prevent the publication and sale of comprehensive weekly TV guides in Ireland and Northern Ireland.

Accordingly, in art 2 of the decision the Commission required ITP, the BBC and RTE to bring the infringement of art. 86 to an end—

> by supplying each other and third parties on request and on a non-discriminatory basis with their individual advance weekly programme listings and by permitting reproduction of those listings by such parties. This requirement does not extend to information in addition to the listings themselves . . . If they choose to supply and permit reproduction of the listings by means of licences, any royalties . . . should be reasonable. Moreover, ITP, BBC and RTE may include in any licences granted to third parties such terms as are considered necessary to ensure comprehensive high-quality coverage of all their programmes, including those of minority and/or regional appeal, and those of cultural, historical and educational significance.

ITP, the BBC and RTE lodged applications for the annulment of the Commission's decision to the Court of Justice. [The cases were referred to the Court of First Instance, which, by judgments of 10 July 1991, found in favour of the Commission. RTE and ITP, but not the BBC, appealed against those

---

[4]In that judgment the court held that programme listings are copyright as literary works and compilations under Irish law. . . .

judgments to the Court of Justice. The Court of Justice gave Magill leave to intervene in support of the Commission and gave Intellectual Property Owners Inc ("IPO") leave to intervene in support of RTE and ITP.]

. . . .

For the sake of completeness it should be noted that new rules came into force in the United Kingdom on 1 March 1991, under which broadcasting organisations are obliged to license the reproduction of their programme listings (*see* section 176 of the UK Broadcasting Act 1990).

The BBC and ITP have each begun to market their own comprehensive weekly television guides. The Irish legislation has not been amended. However, RTE has obtained licences from the BBC and ITP with a view to marketing a comprehensive weekly television guide and has given licences for its own programme listings (RTE has stated that it gave public notice of its new licensing policy but that the BBC and ITP were the only parties to seek and obtain licences).

The three television guides RTE Guide, Radio Times and TV Times therefore now appear as comprehensive weekly television guides.

B. INTRODUCTORY REMARKS

Copyright is of fundamental importance both for the individual owner of the right and for society. The member states have entered into international commitments to give copyright owners sufficient protection in order to ensure an appropriate framework for their creative efforts and in their copyright legislation have given copyright owners the exclusive right to exploit the protected work. In other words copyright laws give copyright owners the right to restrict competition.

However those laws do not confer unrestricted exclusive rights on copyright owners. The [Berne] Convention envisages and accepts certain limits on the exclusive right and such limits are indeed contained in the copyright laws of the member states. The limits may consist of provisions conferring a limited right to free exploitation of the protected work or 'compulsory licences' which confer a right to make a certain use of the work on payment of a royalty. A characteristic feature of compulsory licences in the field of copyright is that permission to make certain use of the protected work stems from general legislative provisions, which may include provision for the question of royalties being submitted to a public authority.

. . . .

The copyright laws of the member states have thus duly balanced the various interests that must be protected by society—including on the one hand the protection of the interests of the copyright owner, and on the other undistorted competition.[10] The natural consequence of that is that compulsory licences under competition law, that is licences which undertakings are required to

---

[10]It must not be forgotten that to a certain extent copyright law—like other intellectual property right—also serves to promote competition. . . .

grant by competition authorities on the basis of competition rules, are practically without precedent in the member states in the field of copyright. In principle, where copyright law confers an exclusive right, that must be respected by competition law.[11]

The fact that the national rules have balanced the interests of the copyright owners against restrictions on competition resulting from copyright protection in the national ambit does not necessarily preclude further limitations on the copyright owners' exclusive right on the basis of the Treaty's competition rules, whose aim is to ensure undistorted competition in a single market. But the basic relationship between copyright law and competition law described above shows that it is natural to be cautious in dealing with issues concerning interference with copyright rights on the basis of the Community competition rules.

It seems to me that the Commission's decision and the judgments of the Court of First Instance produce a reasonable result in practice. There are strong reasons to suggest that it should not be possible for television broadcasting organisations to prevent, by means of their copyright in programme listings, publication of comprehensive weekly television guides. I do not consider that the copyright interests thus protected can be regarded as substantial and the Irish and United Kingdom consumers have a clear interest in being given access to a product which is common in the other member states and which offers a number of advantages by comparison with existing products.

But that does not necessarily mean that that result which is reasonable in this instance can be achieved by means of decisions adopted by the Commission under art. 86 of the Treaty. It is possible that that result can be achieved only by rules adopted by the national legislature, as happened in the United Kingdom, or by rules adopted by the Community legislature.

. . . .

---

[11]The legal position in the member states would appear to be that the competition authorities cannot impose compulsory licences in respect of copyright under French, Irish, Italian and Portuguese law while the issue has not been resolved under German, Belgian, Dutch, Luxembourg and Danish law. The Spanish competition authorities have relied on competition provisions to introduce a general obligation for TV broadcasting organisations which have exclusive rights to transmit certain sporting events to license retransmission. As mentioned above, the legal position in the United Kingdom following the adoption of the Broadcasting Act 1990, which amends the Copyright, Designs and Patents Act 1988, is that, taking account of competition factors and after a procedure involving the United Kingdom competition authorities, copyright may be endorsed by the competent minister with a licensing clause which signifies that the owner cannot refuse a licence to interested parties who satisfy any prescribed conditions. Apart from that, competition factors are not relevant for compulsory licences stemming from the copyright rules. By way of comparison, the position under patent law appears to be that in certain member states, such as Spain, Belgium and Germany, the competition authorities may in principle impose compulsory licences but there is no case law on the issue whereas no such possibility exists in other member states, such as France, Ireland, Italy and Portugal. Only in the UK have the competition authorities expressly been given a role, namely in connection with the above-mentioned licensing clause, while the final decision is still taken by the patent authorities. In certain other member states, such as Germany, Ireland and the Netherlands, the patent authorities may take account of competition factors in granting compulsory licences but that is not possible in other member states, such as France and Portugal.

D. The Question Whether The Court of First Instance Misconstrued the Concept of Abuse of a Dominant Position

In its decision the Commission found that the refusals by ITP and RTE to grant licences constituted an abuse of their dominant positions. That finding was upheld by the Court of First Instance. In its judgments the Court of First Instance took as its starting point the case law of the Court of Justice concerning the relationship between the Treaty rules on the free movement of goods and intellectual property rights based on national law and accordingly the concepts of the specific subject matter of copyright and its essential function formed an important part of its reasoning.

As I shall explain below, that approach is basically correct. The question does, however, arise, whether the conceptual structure relied on by the Court of First Instance was in every respect formulated and applied in an appropriate manner. The submissions in these appeals show that that conceptual structure gave rise to problems and it is on this point in particular that the judgments of the Court of First Instance drew criticism from academics. . . .

(a) *The question whether the concept of specific subject matter is relevant to an analysis under art. 86 of the Treaty*

In a number of judgments concerning arts 30 and 36 of the Treaty the Court of Justice has considered the balancing of the concern for free movement of goods on the one hand and that of protecting intellectual property rights on the other. The court weighs up those interests within the framework of its finding that art 36 only admits derogation from the fundamental principle of the free movement of goods within the common market to the extent to which they are justified for the purpose of safeguarding rights which constitute the specific subject matter of such property.[17]

The application of the concept of the specific subject matter is an expression of the reasoning that for each intellectual property right it is possible to identify a number of core rights which the owner of that right enjoys under national law and whose exercise is not affected by the Treaty rules.

The question is whether the starting point for the balancing, pursuant to art. 86 of the Treaty, of the concern for undistorted competition on the one hand and that of protecting intellectual property rights on the other may likewise be the determination of what constitutes the specific subject matter of that intellectual property right.

In its judgments the Court of First Instance answered that question in the affirmative . . . In the light of the case law of the Court of Justice that result is correct.

In its judgment in *Consten and Grundig v. EC Commission*, Cases 56 and

---

[17]*See eg* Deutsche Grammophon GmbH, Case 78/70 [1971] ECR 487, which concerned a right similar to copyright; Centrafarm BV v Sterling Drug Inc Case 15/74 [1974] ECR 1147 concerning patents; and Centrafarm BV v Winthrop BV Case 16/74 [1974] ECR 1183 concerning trade marks.

58/64 [1966] ECR 299 (Consten and Grundig) the Court of Justice ruled on the compatibility with art 85 of the Treaty, which prohibits anti-competitive agreements, of an exercise of national trade mark rights. The court took as its starting point art 222 of the Treaty, which provides: 'This Treaty shall in no way prejudice the rules in member states governing the system of property ownership'; it then drew a distinction between the existence of trade mark rights, which are not affected by art 85, and the exercise of those rights, which is limited to the extent necessary to give effect to the prohibition under art 85. The same reasoning in a slightly different formulation was put forward in the judgment in *Parke, Davis & Co v Probel, Reese, Beintema-Interpharm* Case 24/67 [1968] ECR 55, which related to both arts 85 and 86.

The distinction between the existence and the exercise of intellectual property rights is reiterated in a number of judgments relating to both the competition rules and the rules on the free movement of goods. It is apparent . . . that the concept of the specific subject matter was developed for the purposes of applying that distinction.[21] An exercise of rights that falls within the specific subject matter of an intellectual property right will relate to its existence. In other words, the distinction between the existence and the exercise of rights and the application of the concept of the specific subject matter are basically expressions of the same conceptual approach. . . .

In more recent judgments on the competition rules too, the Court of Justice has expressly taken as its starting point the determination of the rights which constitute the specific subject matter of the intellectual property right in question.[23] Thus in considering these cases the starting point must be a definition of the specific subject matter of copyright, which is used synonymously in the court's case law with the concepts of the actual substance of copyright and the essential rights of the copyright proprietor. . . .

(b) *The specific subject matter of copyright*

In determining the specific subject matter of copyright the Court of First Instance referred in particular to the judgment in *Warner Bros Inc v Christiansen*, Case 158/86 [1988] ECR 2605 at 2629, in which the Court of Justice pointed out that literary and artistic works may be the subject of commercial exploitation, whether by way of public performance or of the reproduction and marketing of the recordings made of them, and held that the 'essential rights of the author, namely the exclusive right of performance and the exclusive right of reproduction, are not called in question by the rules of the Treaty'. . . .

It is common ground that the exclusive right to reproduce the protected work forms part of the specific subject matter of copyright.

. . . .

---

[21]*See esp* Deutsche Grammophon GmbH, 78/70 [1971] ECR 487 at 499-450; [cit].

[23]*See* in particular its judgment in *Volvo (AB) v Veng (UK) Ltd* Case 238/87 [1988] ECR 6211 at 6235, which concerned art 86 of the Treaty . . . As regards art 85, *see* Windsurfing International Inc v EC Commission Case 193/83 [1986] ECR 611 at 655.

(c) *The question whether art 86 of the Treaty may be applied to the exercise of rights falling within the specific subject matter of copyright*

It is plain that a corollary of an exclusive right to reproduce the protected work is the right to refuse licences. Accordingly, the right to refuse licences forms part of the specific subject matter of copyright. That is borne out by the judgment of the court in *Volvo* [1988] ECR 6211 at 6260 (¶ 8), which concerned products protected by registered designs. The court held:

> ... an obligation imposed upon the proprietor of a protected design to grant to third parties, even in return for a reasonable royalty, a licence for the supply of products incorporating the design would lead to the proprietor thereof being deprived of the substance of his exclusive right, and ... a refusal to grant such a licence cannot *in itself* constitute an abuse of a dominant position. (My emphasis).

In these cases it is thus not disputed that the exercise of the exclusive right of reproduction by refusing to grant licences does not in itself constitute an abuse of a dominant position. The Commission has stressed that it agrees.

The central and fundamental issue in these cases is whether, and if so under what circumstances, a refusal to license—that is, the exercise of a right falling within the specific subject matter of copyright—notwithstanding the above-mentioned premise may constitute an abuse of a dominant position. The question is whether there may exist such special circumstances in connection with a refusal to license that it can no longer be regarded as a refusal to license in itself. . . .

RTE and ITP, supported by IPO, claim that they did no more than refuse to grant licences and that such an exercise of rights falling within the specific subject matter of copyright cannot be affected by art 86.

The Commission contends that an exercise of rights falling within the specific subject matter of copyright can be contrary to art 86 where that exercise takes place under special circumstances. The Commission stresses that the specific subject matter of copyright is not immune and that it cannot be precluded from taking action against abuse of a dominant position merely because the means for that abuse is an intellectual property right.

. . . .

It is important here, as the Commission pointed out, that the scope of art 30 and that of art 86 differ in so far as art 30 relates to all undertakings,[37] while art 86 only applies to undertakings in a dominant position. It is undoubtedly

---

[37]It is clear that arts 30 and 36 of the Treaty are addressed to the member states and lay down requirements regarding the content of their laws. But in fact judgments of the kind referred to above serve to prohibit the misuse by undertakings of the rights they have under national laws which are otherwise regarded as compatible with arts 30 and 36 of the Treaty. The national laws will be incompatible with arts 30 and 36 of the Treaty in so far as they afford a basis for rights which are in principle within the specific subject matter being exercised in the special circumstances in question.

true that in their commercial conduct undertakings in a dominant position must comply with higher standards than other undertakings. Many forms of commercial conduct will, in fact, only affect the proper functioning of the common market in so far as they are engaged in by undertakings in a dominant position. . . . In other words a number of circumstances may only be of significance if the right is being exercised by a dominant undertaking. That means that a specific exercise of rights which in principle are within the specific subject matter may be incompatible with art 86 even if the same conduct is acceptable with respect to arts 30 and 36.

For the same reason it is most appropriate to treat the restrictions imposed pursuant to art 86 on the exercise by undertakings of their rights under national intellectual property laws as exceptions from—interference with—the specific subject matter of the intellectual property right in question and not as specifying the scope of the specific subject matter, as in an arts 30 and 36 analysis. It should be affirmed that in principle the concept of the specific subject matter has the same content and function in relation to the Treaty rules on the free movement of goods and on undistorted competition. It will still be lawful under the Treaty for undertakings which are not in a dominant position to exercise the rights in question since they are within the specific subject matter of the intellectual property right concerned and since the special circumstances in question are significant for the proper functioning of the common market only if the rights are exercised by a dominant undertaking.[40]

The court's case law confirms that it is possible to interfere with the specific subject matter of an intellectual property right on the basis of art 86. . . .

It is common ground that art 86 may apply where a dominant undertaking demands unreasonable royalties or applies a discriminatory licensing policy. As the Commission pointed out in its judgments in *Basset v SACEM* Case 402/85 [1987] ECR 1747 and in *Ministre Public v Tournier,* Case 395/87 [1989] ECR 2521, the Court of Justice expressly held that the charging by a copyright management society of unreasonable royalties for the public performance of recorded musical works may constitute an abuse of a dominant position. The Commission contends that that shows that it is possible pursuant to art 86 to interfere with rights forming part of the specific subject matter.

. . . .

I consider that in fact, as the Commission has argued, unreasonable royalties and a discriminatory licensing policy are examples showing that it is possible pursuant to art 86 to interfere with rights within the specific subject matter where those rights are exercised in special circumstances. The dominant undertaking does not do anything more than exercise rights within the specific subject matter, namely impose royalties . . . and refuse to grant licences. But the exercise of those rights takes place under special circumstances since the undertaking demands royalties which are considerably higher than in other member states or refuses a licence at the same time as licences are in fact given

---

[40][T]he specific subject matter of copyright does unreservedly include a right to refuse to grant licences and the imposition of a compulsory licence pursuant to art 86 constitutes interference with the specific subject matter.

to others. Application of art 86 to the two situations would signify interference with rights falling within the specific subject matter since the possibility for the owner to freely determine his remuneration would be restricted and he would be required to grant a licence to the person against whom he had discriminated. There is no reason to define the charging of unreasonable royalties or operation of a discriminatory licensing policy as conduct which in general is outside the specific subject matter of copyright and thus as conduct which might potentially be incompatible with arts 30 and 36 since such conduct will not affect the proper functioning of the common market in so far as it is engaged in by undertakings which do not have a dominant position and which otherwise operate in accordance with usual market conditions (see art 85). . . .

It follows that both in an art 86 analysis and an arts 30 and 36 analysis the court must further specify whether rights which are in principle within the specific subject matter are exercised in such special circumstances that they create unacceptable hindrances to undistorted competition or the free movement of goods.

The key question in these cases is, of course, when there exist such special circumstances. I shall set out my position on this point in connection with my review of the judgments of the Court of First Instance.

(d) *The reasons given by the Court of First Instance for finding that it is possible to interfere with the specific subject matter of copyright: the essential function of copyright*

The Court of First Instance made the following remarks concerning the possibility of interfering with the specific subject matter of copyright:

> However, while it is plain that the exercise of the exclusive right to reproduce a protected work is not in itself an abuse, that does not apply when, in the light of the details of each individual case, it is apparent that right is exercised in such ways and circumstances as in fact to pursue an aim manifestly contrary to the objectives of Article 86. In that event, the copyright is no longer exercised in a manner which corresponds to its essential function, within the meaning of Article 36 of the Treaty, which is to protect the moral rights in the work and ensure a reward for the creative effort, while respecting the aims of, in particular, Article 86. In that case, the primacy of Community law, particularly as regards principles as fundamental as those of the free movement of goods and freedom of competition, prevails over any use of a rule of national intellectual property law in a manner contrary to those principles.

The Court of First Instance thus reaches the right result in principle but its formulation of the grounds for that result gives rise to problems in several respects.

(aa) *Conduct pursuing an aim manifestly contrary to the objectives of art 86*

. . . .

The Court of First Instance seems, wrongly in my view, to take as its premise that the exercise of copyright will constitute an abuse of a dominant position to the extent that it is found that that exercise pursues a manifestly anti-competitive aim. As ITP in particular has pointed out, the aim of copyright is precisely to give the proprietor the possibility of restricting competition and that possibility must also be afforded to a dominant undertaking. . . .

That does not of course mean that the question what aim is being pursued by the conduct in question is not relevant for the purposes of the application of art 86. . . .

(bb) *The definition of the essential function of copyright*

The Court of First Instance states that the essential function of copyright is to protect the moral rights in the work and ensure a reward for the creative effort while respecting the aims of, in particular, art 86.

The Court of First Instance here seems to be reading the aim pursued by art 86 into a definition of the essential function of copyright. That cannot be correct. The concept of the essential function is a concept of Community law but it is based on the national copyright laws. It is an expression of the Court of Justice's view of the essential aim pursued by the national copyright laws and is applied, as stated below, inter alia to determine where, pursuant to art 86, it is possible to interfere with rights within the specific subject matter of copyright. It does not make sense therefore to incorporate the aim of the competition rules in the determination of the essential function of copyright.

The Court of First Instance is right, on the other hand, in stating that the essential function of copyright is to protect the moral rights in the work and ensure a reward for creative effort. . . .

ITP has claimed that to define the essential function of copyright as including the protection of moral rights would signify that assignees of the creator, like ITP, could not avail themselves of such rights which are inalienable and thus could not exercise the right of exclusive reproduction. At the hearing, however, ITP clarified its view by stating that it can accept that the aim of copyright is to protect moral interests provided that the economic and commercial interests linked to copyright, which are the only ones that concern an assignee like ITP, are not forgotten.

Copyright does undeniably include economic and commercial rights. But that is of course not incompatible with the finding that copyright also includes moral rights and that the protection of those interests is so important a component of copyright that it must necessarily be taken into consideration in defining the essential function of copyright. National laws provide for the protection of moral rights even though the scope of the protection may vary from one country to another. It will, however, typically include protection of the author's right to claim authorship and protection of his right to oppose any prejudicial alterations of his work. Those components of copyright are normally inalienable. That characteristic of copyright law does not affect ITP's possibility of exercising the economic and commercial rights assigned to it. [cit].

[Although the parties agreed on the essential function of copyright, ITP, RTE and IPO criticised the use made by the Court of First Instance of the concept of essential function. They claimed that in applying that concept the Court of First Instance had reduced the rights of the copyright proprietor to the right to exploit the protected work through licences.]

(cc)   *The application of the concept of essential function*

The Court of First Instance states that where the copyright is no longer exercised in a manner which corresponds to its essential function the primacy of Community law prevails over any use of rules of national intellectual property law contrary to the principles of the free movement of goods and freedom of competition.

That result is correct in principle. But it is necessary to specify in what way the concept of essential function is relevant to an art 86 analysis.

I have already said that it may be assumed that art 86 as well as arts 30 and 36 may apply where rights within the specific subject matter are exercised in special circumstances. The key issue is, as mentioned above, how the Court of Justice is to determine whether such special circumstances exist. It is in this context that the concept of the essential function is relevant.

The determination of which rights fall under the specific subject matter depends on a balancing of, on the one hand, the concern of protecting the intellectual property right in question and, on the other, the concern for free movement of goods or undistorted competition. The question whether there exist special circumstances which signify that an exercise of rights which in principle fall within the specific subject matter may none the less be regarded as incompatible with the Treaty rules hinges on another balancing of those factors. The concept of the essential function is an auxiliary concept which enables the Court of Justice to carry out those assessments. The purpose of defining the essential function of the right is to determine the interests that must be balanced against contrasting interests of the free movement of goods or free competition.

The fact that there is a balance does not signify that both interests must be given equal weight. The balance must always be in favour of the intellectual property rights. The starting point set out in the Treaty is that intellectual property rights can be exercised even if that leads to obstacles to trade or restrictions on competition. Consequently if an exercise of a given intellectual property right is necessary in order for that right to be able to fulfil its essential function, that exercise is not affected by the Treaty rules. It is only where an exercise is not necessary in order to fulfil the essential function that the interest of free movement of goods or the interest of free competition must prevail over the interest of the owner of the right to engage in that exercise.

However, the question of what is necessary in order that the essential function of the intellectual property right is fulfilled is not an absolute concept but a relative one.

It is not true, as RTE, ITP and IPO seem to fear, that interference with the right to refuse licences is justified by the mere finding that the copyright owner will be able to demand royalties and in that way obtain a reward for his creative effort.

On the contrary, the starting point for the balance carried out by the court is precisely that rights within the specific subject matter are regarded as necessary for the intellectual property right in question to be able to fulfil its essential function. The right of exclusive reproduction and thus the right to refuse licences is, as a first principle, necessary in order to guarantee the copyright owner a sufficient reward for his creative effort.

However, the presence of specified circumstances may mean that the interests of the copyright owner carry less weight or that the interests of competition carry more weight than usual. In such a situation an analysis under art 86 may perhaps lead to the possibility of demanding royalties being regarded as sufficient to guarantee the owner a reward for his creative effort since the right to refuse licences cannot under those circumstances be regarded as necessary in order to fulfil the essential function.

At the same time it is clear that the concept of the essential function sets an absolute limit on what interference is possible pursuant to art 86 in rights falling within the specific subject matter. No such interference is possible if it would mean that the author cannot obtain a reward for his creative efforts or cannot be afforded the protection of moral rights that may be recognised by national law.

That limit would not be exceeded by a requirement to grant licences as it would be possible to demand royalties and because the author could not be precluded from taking steps against unlawful use or infringement of the protected work by the licensee and would also be able to obtain protection of his moral rights by laying down corresponding terms in the licensing agreement.[52]

The Court's case law concerning arts 30 and 36 confirms that that is the meaning to be attributed to the essential function... The court determines what rights are covered by the specific subject matter on the basis of an assessment of what is necessary in order to fulfil the essential function of the intellectual property right in question. [cit]. The presence of specified circumstances may, however, mean that the interests of the owner carry less weight and/or the interest of the free movement of goods carries more weight than usual and that the result of the balance is that an exercise in those circumstances is held to be incompatible with the Treaty rules. . . .

---

[52]It should be noted in this context that the protection of the special moral relationship between the author and his work must include a right for the owner to oppose completely the publication of his work. The fact that the essential function is said to include the protection of moral rights therefore signifies that it is not possible on the basis of art 86 to require an undertaking to grant licences in situations where the author does not wish the work to be made public. That issue is not relevant in these cases since RTE and ITP themselves publish the work and have also given a large number of licences for the partial publication of the work.

. . . .

There is an inherent risk here that the impression might be given that the concept of specific subject matter has been so relativised that it does not have any real meaning. Such a view would be wrong. Once the content of the specific subject matter of copyright has been laid down, it is always the starting point for the court's analysis and it is clear that substantial and weighty grounds must be put forward to show that rights covered by the specific subject matter of copyright can be exercised in a manner incompatible with the Treaty rules.

As regards in particular the right to refuse licences, it is clear that a requirement to grant licences constitutes a serious interference in copyright since it would be reduced merely to the right to receive an economic reward. There must therefore exist particularly substantial and weighty competition grounds for the right to refuse licences to be regarded as having been exercised in circumstances signifying that that exercise cannot be regarded as necessary for copyright to fulfil its essential function.

In the following sections I shall consider whether the circumstances cited by the Court of First Instance in its judgments as special circumstances that may justify application of art 86 meet that condition.

(e) *The emergence of a new product for which there exists a substantial potential demand from consumers*

. . . .

A clearly decisive factor for the application of art 86 in these cases was that by their conduct RTE and ITP were preventing the emergence of a new product. No one would doubt the fact that RTE and ITP were entitled to exercise their copyright in order to prevent the publication of television guides corresponding to their own respective guides. In its decision the Commission specified that art 86 had been infringed in so far as the practice and policy of the undertakings prevented the publication of a comprehensive television guide and its decision must therefore be interpreted as meaning that the requirement for the undertakings to license their programme listings only applies to the extent that the listings are to be used to produce comprehensive weekly television guides. . . .

The interest of consumers in the emergence of a new product is undoubtedly relevant when considering whether there exists conduct restricting competition within the meaning of art 86. . . .

At first sight, therefore, there might appear to be grounds for finding that special circumstances exist which signify that the exercise of rights included in the specific subject matter may be classified as an abuse where the exercise is carried out in order to prevent the emergence of a new product. Closer consideration shows, however, that such a conclusion is only right if the concept of a new product is qualified.

The first condition for there to be a new product is, of course, that the product does not exist on the relevant market.[59] But that cannot suffice in itself in order to require a copyright owner to grant licences. In the context of the circumstances of these cases, it is necessary to consider whether, in order for a product to be regarded as new, it suffices that it is furthermore a product that the copyright owner cannot produce himself, for example because such production presupposes a licence to use works protected by the copyright of other parties. Alternatively, is the relevant criterion whether the product in question competes with the product of the copyright owner?

The Commission contends that in classifying a product as new it is not relevant whether it will compete with the copyright owner's own products. . . .

I do not believe that the Commission's view is tenable.

I consider it appropriate to find that there is an abuse of a dominant position if a copyright owner by means of his copyright prevents the emergence of a product which does not compete with his product since it meets other consumer needs than those that are met by his product.

The contrary is true, in my view, if copyright is used in order to prevent the emergence of a product which is produced by means of the work protected by the copyright and which competes with the products produced by the copyright owner himself. Even if that product is new and better, the interests of consumers should not in such circumstances justify interference in the specific subject matter of the copyright. Where the product is one that largely meets the same needs of consumers as the protected product, the interests of the copyright owner carry great weight. Even if the market is limited to the prejudice of consumers, the right to refuse licences in that situation must be regarded as necessary in order to guarantee the copyright owner the reward for his creative effort.

RTE and ITP are not able themselves to produce a comprehensive weekly television guide. But a comprehensive weekly television guide would undoubtedly, as the Commission has stated, compete with their respective weekly television guides. A comprehensive weekly television guide would both be cheaper and give a better overview but it would basically meet the same consumer needs as may be met by buying weekly television guides for the individual television broadcasting organisations. In those circumstances the interests of the copyright proprietor should prevail over the interests of consumers. There is no new product in a sense that may be relevant for the application of art 86 and thus no special circumstance capable of justifying interference with the specific subject matter.

I also consider that the Court of First Instance was wrong to compare this situation with the situation described by the Court of Justice as the third

---

[59]If the undertakings had chosen jointly to produce a comprehensive television guide but had otherwise denied third parties that possibility, it would in any event not be possible to justify interference with the specific subject matter on the grounds that the undertakings' conduct prevented the emergence of a new product. However, such conduct might be indicative of discriminatory licensing policy and for that reason incompatible with art 86. That is in any event the view taken by the Commission . . . The UK legislation appears to have been amended in such a way that licences must be granted to all interested parties and similarly RTE has chosen to make licences for its programme listings generally available.

example of abusive conduct in its judgments in *Volvo* and *CICRA*. . . .

This example concerns products which the copyright owner is able to produce himself on the basis of his copyright but has for the time being chosen not to produce. The example shows that there may exist an abuse of a dominant position where the owner of a registered design refuses to grant licences and at the same time does not himself produce the products protected by the registered design. [For example, where a car manufacturer ceases production of spare parts notwithstanding a demand for such parts and refuses to license third party production.] As stated above, both those rights fall within the specific subject matter of a registered design.

However, . . . it cannot be true that a dominant undertaking is under a general obligation either to produce itself or to grant licences for its products protected by copyright. Such an obligation must be conditional on the existence of special circumstances in addition to the fact that consumers do not have access to the product.[61]

It seems clear to me that the court attached decisive importance to the fact that consumers are particularly dependent on the product where a car manufacturer refrains from producing spare parts for a particular car model even if there are still a large number of cars of that model and where the lack of access to spare parts for those cars may mean that consumers are obliged to buy a completely new car. The producer has himself created the need for spare parts and is thus abusing his registered design if by means thereof he prevents the need for spare parts from being met.

That example is thus different from the present situations and is not of decisive significance here since RTE and ITP have each provided consumers with the products which they were able to produce on the basis of their copyright, namely weekly television guides for their respective television channels.

(f) *Use of a dominant position on one market in order to retain for itself a derivative market*

The Court of First Instance attached significance in its judgments to the fact that "the applicant was thus using its copyright in the programme listings . . . . in order to secure a monopoly in the derivative market of weekly television guides."

[This] must be understood as meaning that the market for programme listings is regarded as the main market and the market for television guides as the derivative market. They must be read in conjunction with the Commission's decision in which it is stated that ITP and RTE each have a dominant position on one market, namely the market for their own programme listings, and use that position to retain for themselves a derivative market, namely the market

---

[61] In other words, the interest of consumers in having access to a product must basically be taken into account by national legislation on intellectual property rights which may afford a basis for granting compulsory licences in the public interest where the owner himself does not exploit the protected work to a reasonable extent . . .

for weekly television guides upon which competition could otherwise take place, particularly in relation to comprehensive weekly television guides. . . .

It is true that the fact that an undertaking makes use of its dominant position on one market in order to retain for itself a derivative market may constitute anti-competitive conduct which is incompatible with art 86. . . . The question is, however, whether such considerations are relevant in a case concerning the exercise of intellectual property rights.

RTE, ITP and IPO essentially argue that it is part of a normal exercise of copyright to make use of it in order to exclude competition on a derivative market. A copyright owner will often obtain remuneration for his creative effort by producing and selling products which incorporate the product created on the basis of the copyright, that is to say on a derivative market. ITP adds that it was precisely only on the market for television guides that ITP commercially exploited its copyright in its programme listings.

The Commission claims that the fact that the copyright is being exercised in order to keep out any competition on a derivative market constitutes a special circumstance which may justify application of art 86. . . .

The Commission has further claimed that the example from the judgments of the Court of Justice in *Volvo* and *CICRA* cited by the Court of First Instance is relevant to a decision in the present cases. According to the Commission the situation of Magill corresponds to that of an independent repairer in so far as both are dependent on the supply of products from an upstream market (in programme listings and car parts respectively) in order to carry on an activity on a derivative market (the market for television guides and the market for repairing Volvo and Renault cars respectively) where they compete with their suppliers (RTE's and ITP's own weekly television guides and Volvo's and Renault's authorised repairers respectively). The Commission concedes, however, that the analogy is not complete since Magill's situation differs in so far as the supply of a product was not sufficient for Magill to be able to carry out its activity as Magill needed to obtain a licence in order to produce copies of the protected work itself.

That difference is precisely crucial. As RTE and ITP point out, a distinction must be drawn between a refusal to supply a product to customers who wish to use that product on a derivative market and a refusal to grant a licence to a competitor who wishes to produce and sell products incorporating the protected work. In the first case the existence of any infringement of art 86 does not depend on whether the products concerned are protected by an intellectual property right. The analogy drawn by the Court of First Instance is therefore not apposite, nor are the judgments cited by the Commission relevant to a decision in these cases.

. . . .

There is therefore no basis for treating the exercise by a copyright owner of his copyright in order to prevent competitors from using the protected work differently according to the market on which such use takes place. As ITP points out, the possibility of exploiting the copyright on what is described as a derivative market must be regarded as necessary in order to obtain sufficient reward for creative effort.

(g) *The question of the existence of a discriminatory licensing policy or unreasonable licensing terms*

[The advocate-general rejected the argument that there was a discriminatory licensing policy since licences are granted to certain categories of publishers, namely those who wish to publish daily programme listings or highlights of the week's programmes, but not to other categories of publishers, namely those who wish to publish weekly programme listings, because discrimination presupposes the existence of comparable situations. That was not the case here. On the contrary, RTE and ITP granted licences to anybody who wished to have them and the same terms applied to all. The fact that the undertakings wished to reserve to themselves a certain use of the protected work could not be an indication of discrimination.]

(h) *The question whether programme listings are works meriting protection*

The Court of First Instance begins its discussion of the existence of an abuse by stating: 'In the absence of harmonisation of national rules or Community standardisation, the determination of the conditions and procedures under which copyright is protected is a matter for national rules'. [cit]. . . .

[However], the Commission submitted that 'the programme listings are not in themselves secret, innovative or related to research. On the contrary, they are mere factual information in which no copyright could therefore subsist'. It recognised that programme listings are protected under national law but claimed, on the basis of the factors mentioned, that 'the relevant policies and practices of the applicant are not covered by copyright protection as recognised in Community law' but on the contrary constitute an abuse of a dominant position. . . .

In the proceedings before the Court of Justice the Commission has stated that it is for the national authorities and courts to determine what works fall under copyright protection. At the same time, however, the Commission has stated that the Court of First Instance was right to take account of the unusual nature of the national right in deciding on the cases. . . .

RTE, ITP and IPO claim that [these statements] illustrate lack of respect for the principle that the scope of copyright protection is to be determined by national law. They claim that the decisions taken were in fact intended to censure the copyright protection of programme listings under Irish and UK law.

It follows from the foregoing review that I do not otherwise consider that the refusals to grant licences in these cases took place under such special circumstances as to justify application of art 86. I am therefore more inclined to endorse the undertakings' view that the actual grounds for applying art 86 in the present circumstances must in that case be that the programme listings were not regarded as meriting protection.

As indicated at the outset it may reasonably be claimed that the effort involved in drawing up programme listings is not so deserving of protection as to justify acceptance that the author may prevent the emergence of comprehensive weekly television guides. . . . If that factor is taken into consideration I see no difficulty in holding that the refusals to grant licences in these cases are indications of an improper exercise of copyright. The question is, however, whether the Court of Justice is able to attach significance to the nature of the work protected by copyright.

The Court of Justice has hitherto unreservedly held that it is for the national legislatures to determine what products may enjoy the protection of intellectual property rights. [cit]. In that respect national law is subject only to the limitations resulting from the second sentence of art 36 of the Treaty under which restrictions on trade must not constitute a means of arbitrary discrimination or a disguised restriction on trade between member states. Those limitations must be interpreted narrowly and there is nothing to suggest that they have been overstepped in these cases.[73]

In the present cases too the court should adhere to that principle which, in my view, reflects a fundamentally correct division of competence between national law and Community law. If there is a need under Community law to restrict the copyright protection of specific products, that must be done by rules adopted by the Community legislature. . . .

It may be considered whether it is possible to affirm that principle while at the same time opening the possibility of taking account of the nature of the protected work in deciding whether there is an abuse of a dominant position. However, I cannot propose that the court carry out such a balance even though it may be tempting and appear actually reasonable in the present cases. To accept that copyright owners must, in their commercial conduct, comply with different standards according to how deserving of protection their works are from the point of view of Community law would in any event signify that Community law is applied to censure rules in national intellectual property legislation on what products may obtain protection.

It must therefore be concluded that the fact that the programme listings are less deserving of protection is also not a circumstance that can justify interference with the exercise of copyright therein.

(i) *The question whether the refusals to grant licences were justified*

. . . .

It follows from what I have said above that I do not consider that there exists, in the present cases, anti-competitive conduct within the meaning of art 86 since the refusals to grant licences did not take place under such special circumstances that they may be classified as an abuse of a dominant position.

---

[73]Compare the judgment of the Court of Justice in *Deutsche Renault* [1993] ECR I-6227 at 6268 (¶ 27), where the court referred, as an example of a possible overstepping of the limitations resulting from the second sentence of art 36, to the situation where a producer from another member state could not enjoy, on the same terms, the protection afforded by German law to a trade mark, whether or not registered, or where such protection varied on the basis of the national or foreign origin of the products bearing the sign in question. . . .

There is accordingly no need to examine whether there is a valid justification for the undertakings' conduct. In those circumstances RTE and ITP, supported by IPO, are right to challenge the judgments of the Court of First Instance by pointing out that they cannot be required to justify their refusals to grant licences. . . .

It may . . . be assumed, in my view, that, as the Court of First Instance held, ITP and RTE did refuse to grant licences and thus excluded all competition from the market for comprehensive television guides solely in order to secure their monopoly on the market for weekly television guides. In other words, if the Court of Justice were to hold that the refusals to grant licences otherwise took place in special circumstances which are such as to render them liable to be classified as an abuse, they would be incompatible with art 86.

(j) *The further consequences of the judgment of the Court of Justice*

The Commission claims that a distinction must be drawn between literary and artistic works in the narrow sense and functional or utilitarian works, relating for example to telecommunications, computing, information technologies and databases. Whereas the former do not create dependence for competitors on derivative markets, copyright in the latter works is more likely to create economic dependence and thus dominant positions that may lead to anti-competitive conduct.

The Commission submits that the distinction is significant to a decision in these cases since it shows the need to confirm the principle that a refusal to grant licences may, in the context of the circumstances in which it took place, constitute an abuse of a dominant position. While the Commission's decision ordering the grant of licences will not be of appreciable significance for literary and artistic works in the narrow sense, it is essential in order to maintain effective competition, particularly in the computer and telecommunications industries.[76]

RTE and ITP have disputed the distinction drawn by the Commission, pointing out that the question of what products enjoy copyright protection is a matter for national law. But so far as I can see the Commission does not use the distinction as a basis for submitting that functional and utilitarian works are in general less deserving of protection than literary and artistic works and are therefore more susceptible to give rise to the application of art 86. The Commission in fact applies the distinction in order to illustrate the far-reaching

---

[76]In this connection the Commission referred to its conclusions decided on the occasion of the adoption of the Commission's proposal for a Council directive on the legal protection of computer programmes in which it states (OJ 1989 C 91, p 16): 'Companies in a dominant position must not abuse that position within the meaning of Article 86 of the Treaty. For example, under certain circumstances the exercise of copyright as to the aspects of a programme, which other companies need to see in order to write compatible programmes, could amount to an abuse. This could be the case if a dominant company tries to use its exclusive rights in one product to gain an unfair advantage in relation to one or more products not covered by these rights.' As is apparent from what has been said above, I consider that those examples are correct only in so far as concerns programmes or products which do not compete with the copyright product.

consequences it believes annulment of the judgments of the Court of First Instance would have for competition in a number of important areas where it perceives a greater risk that copyright protection may lead to or strengthen dominant positions.

As regards the Commission's fear that these cases may form a precedent in the field of computer software, ITP has claimed that the appropriate solution in that respect is legislation and that the Commission's concerns do not, moreover, appear to relate to the reproduction of protected works but to information concerning them which does not affect the copyright.

ITP, for its part, has claimed if the judgments of the Court of First Instance are confirmed, it would have very far-reaching consequences for copyright under national law. ITP submits that in that case the following would all be examples of abuses of a dominant position: a writer of short stories who opposes the publication of one of his stories in an anthology; a poster artist who opposes the use of a copyright drawing in a Christmas card; the owner of the copyright in Popeye who opposes the use of Popeye on a T-shirt; a playwright who opposes the use of one of his plays for the making of a film; the owners of Sunday newspapers who oppose the publication by ITP of their feature articles at the same time in TV Times; compilers of calendars of the movements of the moon and the tides, cooking recipes or lists of Norman churches in England who oppose the reproduction thereof. IPO has submitted similar examples.

The Commission retorts that ITP and IPO's fears of the consequences of confirmation of the judgments of the Court of First Instance are unfounded because it is highly unlikely that the copyright owners in the situations mentioned would hold dominant positions and their conduct cannot therefore be incompatible with art 86. It adds that in the four years since the judgment of the Court of Justice in *Volvo* art 86 has only once—that is, in these cases—formed the basis for a formal decision in order to remedy an abuse of intellectual property rights.

It is difficult to form a view on whether the parties' respective fears as to the further consequences of a judgment in one sense or the other are justified. Not least because of the disagreement on that point, it would not be appropriate on the present basis to attempt to assess the merits of the examples given.

But precisely because it is not possible to foresee the consequences of such a result I consider that the Court of Justice should not, in its judgment in these cases, rule out the possibility that in special circumstances a refusal to license may be incompatible with art 86. The Commission is right in my view in stating:

> . . . copyright law is unable to legislate explicitly for every single product-specific abuse that may arise. Countervailing policies, such as the competition rules, are essential to draw the correct balance between the interests of the right-holder and those dependent on the right-holder.

On the other hand the consequences of holding that refusals to license may be incompatible with art 86 when they take place in special circumstances are not unforeseeable. In that case it would be for the Court of Justice itself in deciding future cases to lay down progressively more specific guidelines as to the special circumstances under which refusals to licence may constitute an abuse of a dominant position. Moreover, the court, if it follows my opinion, will have held that such special circumstances do not exist in the present cases and that result will be an indication that very strict conditions apply to that way of applying art 86 to an exercise of rights falling within the specific subject matter of an intellectual property right.

. . . .

The foregoing does not however necessarily finally resolve the question whether art 86 constitutes a basis for requiring undertakings to grant licences for their copyright works. It has been contended in the course of these proceedings that such a result is incompatible with the Berne Convention.

E. THE QUESTION WHETHER THE COURT OF FIRST INSTANCE WRONGLY FAILED TO TAKE INTO CONSIDERATION THE BERNE CONVENTION

RTE and ITP claimed before the Court of First Instance that the Berne Convention must be regarded as forming part of Community law and that the Commission's decision is incompatible with art 9 of that convention on the right to reproduce the protected work.

The Court of First Instance prefaces its assessment of that plea by stating that . . . "the Community—to which, as Community law now stands, powers have not been transferred in the field of intellectual and commercial property—is not a party to the Berne Convention, which has been ratified by all the member states. . ."

The Court of First Instance goes on to consider the significance of the fact that the convention is binding on the member states. It refers first to art 234 of the Treaty, which provides:

> The rights and obligations arising from agreements concluded before the entry into force of this Treaty between one or more member states on the one hand, and one or more third countries on the other, shall not be affected by the provisions of this Treaty.

[Because Article 9 was ratified by the United Kingdom and Ireland before their accession to the Community on 1 January 1973 and, pursuant to the Court of Justice's interpretation of article 234 of the EC Treaty, provisions which were ratified before accession to the Community cannot, in intra-Community relations, affect the provisions of the Treaty, the plea that the decision was in conflict with Article 9 could be dismissed on that ground alone. However, the advocate-general thought it expedient to clarify and expand upon the reasons given by the Court of First Instance.]

The Court of First Instance examined the question of the legal situation applying if there is found to be an actual conflict between art 86 of the Treaty and the rules in the convention. I consider that that approach to the problem is too narrow. The rules in the Treaty on resolving conflicts between internationally binding rules and the Treaty's own rules only come into play if it is established that there is a conflict between the two sets of rules. That signifies that it is first necessary to determine whether the status of the convention is such that it must be taken into account as an element in the Court of Justice's interpretation of the Treaty rules and, if so, whether the provisions of the convention can be relied upon in support of a certain interpretation of the Treaty. The Court of First Instance should therefore have examined whether account must be taken of the provisions of the convention in interpreting art 86 of the Treaty and the implementing provisions, . . . in order, as far as possible, to avoid conflict between the two sets of rules.

I consider that it is appropriate to interpret art 86 in accordance with the convention. Many factors militate in favour of account being taken of the convention in interpreting the Treaty rules.[81]

. . . .

All member states have acceded to the convention and only Ireland and Belgium have not yet acceded to the Paris Act of 1971. On 14 May 1992 the Council adopted a resolution under which the member states of the Community, in so far as they have not already done so, undertake to become by 1 January 1995 parties to the Paris Act and to introduce national legislation to ensure effective compliance therewith. [cit]. In this connection see also the Commission's Proposal for a Council Decision concerning the accession of the member states to the Berne Convention (OJ 1991 C 24, p. 5), the fifth recital in the preamble to which states: "the accession of all the member states to the Berne Convention (Paris Act) . . . will provide a common basis for harmonisation on which to pursue more easily the construction of the Community edifice as regards copyright and neighbouring rights." See also art 1a in the Amended Proposal (OJ 1992 C 57, p. 13) according to which: 'In the exercise of its powers concerning copyright and neighbouring rights, the Community shall be guided by the principles and act in accordance with the provisions of the Berne Convention' as revised by the Paris Act. The resolution further states that it is in the interests of Community copyright holders that they should be ensured the minimum level of protection afforded by the convention in the maximum possible number of third countries and in that connection the Council invites the Commission, when negotiating agreements with third countries, to pay particular attention to the ratification of or accession to the convention by the third countries concerned and to the effective compliance of such countries with the convention.

There are several examples, as RTE has pointed out, of references in secondary legislation of the Community to the convention as an expression of

---

[81] . . . It should . . . be noted in this connection that in many instances the Court of Justice has held that the rules of the Treaty must be interpreted in the light of the Convention for the Protection of Human Rights and Fundamental Freedoms . . . .

a general and broadly accepted minimum standard. . . .[85]

Finally, I would point out that in its submissions in these cases the Commission itself has also stressed the desirability of Community law in the field of copyright being in accordance with international standards.

It is against that background that RTE's plea that art 2 of the Commission's decision is incompatible with art 86 of the Treaty and art 3 of Regulation 17/62, as those provisions must be interpreted in the light of the Berne Convention, is to be considered.

. . . .

RTE claims that a power for the Commission to require undertakings pursuant to art 86 and Regulation 17/62 to grant licences would be incompatible with art 9(2) of the convention, which provides:

> It shall be a matter for legislation in the countries of the Union to permit the reproduction of such works in certain special cases, provided that such reproduction does not conflict with a normal exploitation of the work and does not unreasonably prejudice the legitimate interests of the author.

RTE claims that art 9(2) entails the condition that compulsory licences can be granted only pursuant to specific legislation which clearly sets out how and when compulsory licences can be imposed. . . . Article 86 of the Treaty, on the other hand, according to RTE, does not meet that condition since it is not sufficiently clear in its terms to give copyright owners an adequate indication of when they may be required to grant licences but instead leaves such an obligation to be made precise and adapted from case to case at the Commission's discretion.

That view is not tenable.

[Quoting from the commentary on article 9 in the Guide to the Berne Convention, and the statement in particular that the language of Article 9(2) was intended to be "wide enough to cover all reasonable exceptions but not so wide as to make the right illusory," the advocate-general suggested that] there thus does not seem to be any autonomous and special significance attached to the fact that article 9 refers to restrictions on the right to reproduce the work being 'a matter for legislation'. It also seems to me to be going quite far to interpret such a neutral formulation, which was intended to 'cover all reasonable exceptions', as referring to legislation of a certain type and certain degree of detail. As the Commission has pointed out, it is hardly likely that all the countries which ratified the Paris Act of 1971 thereby intended to renounce the power to impose compulsory licences under competition rules.

I do not believe that anything more can be inferred from art 9(2) than that the convention does not preclude the possibility that in special cases the exclusive

---

[85]*See* Council Directive (EEC) 91/250 of 14 May 1991 on the legal protection of computer programs (See the twenty-fifth and twenty-ninth recitals in the preamble and art 1(1) and in particular art 6(3) whose wording corresponds in all material respects to art 9(2) of the Berne Convention.) . . . .

right to reproduce the work may be restricted and that it is left to the countries of the union in their legislation and in accordance with the conditions set out in that provision to determine how they wish to avail themselves of that possibility. It cannot be contrary to that provision to conclude that a general competition provision constitutes the necessary legislative basis.

Lastly, as regards the condition in art 9(2) that 'such reproduction does not conflict with a normal exploitation of the work and does not unreasonably prejudice the legitimate interests of the author', it seems clear that the power for the Commission, acting on the basis of the Treaty competition rules, to require undertakings to grant licences if the very restrictive conditions I have described above are met cannot in general be regarded as incompatible with that provision. As the Commission has pointed out, compliance with those conditions will ultimately be subject to review by the Court of Justice.

As regards the specific decision to require RTE and ITP to grant licences for their programme listings, I believe that the result set out above that that decision is incompatible with art 86 of the Treaty is borne out by art 9(2) of the convention, in particular because an obligation to grant licences for the production of products which basically meet the same consumer needs as the copyright owner's product, and which are therefore in competition with it, will in my view 'conflict with a normal exploitation of the work'.

On that basis the court can hold that the convention does not make it necessary to interpret art 86 of the Treaty as precluding undertakings from being required, on the basis of that provision and under special circumstances, to grant licences for their copyright works.

For the eventuality that the Court of Justice should agree that under special circumstances it may be incompatible with art 86 to refuse to grant licences and, contrary to the result I have proposed, find that such special circumstances do exist in these cases, I shall go on to consider the other pleas submitted to the Court of Justice.

. . . .

G. THE QUESTION WHETHER THE COURT OF FIRST INSTANCE DEFINED THE RELEVANT PRODUCT MARKET AND APPLIED THE CONCEPT OF A DOMINANT POSITION INCORRECTLY

[The advocate-general concluded that the Court of First Instance properly defined the relevant markets as weekly programme listings and the television guides in which those listings are published. On the question of whether RTE and ITP each has a dominant position on the market as so defined, the parties did not dispute the definition of a dominant position as "a position of economic strength enjoyed by an undertaking which enables it to hinder the maintenance of effective competition on the relevant market by allowing it to behave to an appreciable extent independently of its competitors and customers and ultimately of consumers." The advocate-general noted that an undertaking does not have a dominant position merely because it owns an intellectual property right, but supported the Commission's determination of a dominant position.]

H. THE QUESTION WHETHER THE COURT OF FIRST INSTANCE MISCONSTRUED THE CONCEPT OF EFFECTS ON TRADE BETWEEN MEMBER STATES

RTE claims that its licensing policy did not affect trade between member states and that the Community competition rules are not intended to remedy situations which are purely internal to a member state. If it is considered unsatisfactory that in Ireland and the United Kingdom, in contrast to the other member states, there does not exist a comprehensive weekly television guide, that problem must, according to RTE, be resolved by the member states concerned, as has now been done in the United Kingdom.

In its judgment the Court of First Instance finds that the condition in art 86 of an effect on trade between the member states is met . . . .

. . . .

In my view the requirement of an appreciable effect on trade must be held to be met in these cases simply because it can be seen that the conduct in question has led to the elimination of a competitor and excludes new competitors who might wish to produce a product for which there would undeniably exist a demand on the Irish market and on the part of the market in Northern Ireland where RTE's broadcasts can be received. . . I do not therefore consider that there are any grounds for criticising the judgment of the Court of First Instance in this respect. . . .

. . . .

JUDGMENT OF THE EUROPEAN COURT OF JUSTICE:

. . . .

THE EXISTENCE OF AN ABUSE OF A DOMINANT POSITION

. . . .

(a) *Existence of a dominant position*

So far as dominant position is concerned, it is to be remembered at the outset that mere ownership of an intellectual property right cannot confer such a position.

However, the basic information as to the channel, day, time and title of programmes is the necessary result of programming by television stations, which are thus the only source of such information for an undertaking, like Magill, which wishes to publish it together with commentaries or pictures. By force of circumstance, RTE and ITP, as the agent of ITV, enjoy, along with the BBC, a de facto monopoly over the information used to compile listings for the television programmes received in most households in Ireland and 30% to 40% of households in Northern Ireland. The appellants are thus in a position to prevent effective competition on the market in weekly television magazines.

The Court of First Instance was therefore right in confirming the Commission's assessment that the appellants occupied a dominant position.

(b) *Existence of abuse*

With regard to the issue of abuse, the arguments of the appellants and IPO wrongly presuppose that where the conduct of an undertaking in a dominant position consists of the exercise of a right classified by national law as 'copyright', such conduct can never be reviewed in relation to art 86 of the Treaty.

Admittedly, in the absence of Community standardisation or harmonisation of laws, determination of the conditions and procedures for granting protection of an intellectual property right is a matter for national rules. Further, the exclusive right of reproduction forms part of the author's rights, so that refusal to grant a licence, even if it is the act of an undertaking holding a dominant position, cannot in itself constitute abuse of a dominant position. *See Volvo,* 1988 E.C.R. 6211, at 6235.

However, it is also clear from that judgment that the exercise of an exclusive right by the proprietor may, in exceptional circumstances, involve abusive conduct.

In the present case, the conduct objected to is the appellants' reliance on copyright conferred by national legislation so as to prevent Magill—or any other undertaking having the same intention—from publishing on a weekly basis information (channel, day, time and title of programmes) together with commentaries and pictures obtained independently of the appellants.

Among the circumstances taken into account by the Court of First Instance in concluding that such conduct was abusive was, first, the fact that there was, according to the findings of the Court of First Instance, no actual or potential substitute for a weekly television guide offering information on the programmes for the week ahead. On this point, the Court of First Instance confirmed the Commission's finding that the complete lists of programmes for a 24-hour period and for a 48-hour period at weekends and before public holidays—published in certain daily and Sunday newspapers and the television sections of certain magazines covering, in addition, 'highlights' of the week's programmes, were only to a limited extent substitutable for advance information to viewers on all the week's programmes. Only weekly television guides containing comprehensive listings for the week ahead would enable users to decide in advance which programmes they wished to follow and arrange their leisure activities for the week accordingly. The Court of First Instance also established that there was a specific, constant and regular potential demand on the part of consumers.

Thus the appellants—who were, by force of circumstance, the only sources of the basic information on programme scheduling which is the indispensable raw material for compiling a weekly television guide—gave viewers wishing to obtain information on the choice of programmes for the week ahead no choice but to buy the weekly guides for each station and draw from each of them the information they needed to make comparisons.

The appellants' refusal to provide basic information by relying on national copyright provisions thus prevented the appearance of a new product, a comprehensive weekly guide to television programmes, which the appellants did not offer and for which there was a potential consumer demand. Such refusal constitutes an abuse under heading (b) of the second paragraph of art 86 of the Treaty.

Second, there was no justification for such refusal either in the activity of television broadcasting or in that of publishing television magazines . . . .

Third, and finally, as the Court of First Instance also held, the appellants, by their conduct, reserved to themselves the secondary market of weekly television guides by excluding all competition on that market, since they denied access to the basic information which is the raw material indispensable for the compilation of such a guide.

In the light of all those circumstances, the Court of First Instance did not err in law in holding that the appellants' conduct was an abuse of a dominant position within the meaning of art 86 of the Treaty.

It follows that the plea in law alleging misapplication by the Court of First Instance of the concept of abuse of a dominant position must be dismissed as unfounded. It is therefore unnecessary to examine the reasoning of the contested judgments in so far as it is based on art 36 of the Treaty.

EFFECTS ON TRADE BETWEEN MEMBER STATES

. . . .

In order to satisfy the condition that trade between member states must be affected, it is not necessary that the conduct in question should in fact have substantially affected that trade. It is sufficient to establish that the conduct is capable of having such an effect. [cit].

In this case, the Court of First Instance found that the applicant had excluded all potential competitors on the geographical market consisting of one member state (Ireland) and part of another member state (Northern Ireland) and had thus modified the structure of competition on that market, thereby affecting potential commercial exchanges between Ireland and the United Kingdom. From this the Court of First Instance drew the proper conclusion that the condition that trade between member states must be affected had been satisfied.

It follows that the plea in law alleging misapplication by the Court of First Instance of the concept of trade between member states being affected must be dismissed.

THE BERNE CONVENTION

So far as the Berne Convention is concerned, RTE had submitted before the

Court of First Instance that art 9(1) thereof conferred an exclusive right of reproduction and that art 9(2) allowed a signatory state to permit reproduction only in certain special cases, provided that such reproduction did not conflict with normal exploitation of the work and did not unreasonably prejudice the legitimate interests of the author. From this RTE deduced that art 2 of the contested decision was incompatible with the convention inasmuch as it conflicted with the normal exploitation of RTE's copyright in the programme listings and seriously prejudiced its legitimate interests.

. . . .

It is appropriate to observe at the outset, as the Court of First Instance did, that the Community is not a party to the Berne Convention.

Next, so far as the United Kingdom and Ireland are concerned, it is true that they were already parties to the convention when they acceded to the Community and that art 234 of the Treaty therefore applies to that convention, in accordance with art 5 of the Act of Accession. It is, however, settled case law that the provisions of an agreement concluded prior to entry into force of the Treaty or prior to a member state's accession cannot be relied on in intra-Community relations if, as in the present case, the rights of non-member countries are not involved. . .

Finally, the Paris Act, which amended art 9(1) and (2) of the convention (the provisions relied on by RTE), was ratified by the United Kingdom only after its accession to the Community and has still not been ratified by Ireland.

The Court of First Instance was therefore correct to hold that art 9 of the convention cannot be relied on to limit the powers of the Community, as provided for in the Treaty, since the Treaty can be amended only in accordance with the procedure laid down in art 236.

It follows that the plea that the Court of First Instance failed to have proper regard to the convention must be dismissed as unfounded.

. . . .

It follows that the appeals must be dismissed in their entirety. . . .

NOTES AND QUESTIONS

(1) **Originality and Compilations**. The standard of originality required to obtain copyright protection for databases in Ireland, discussed in the *Magill* case, was lower than in many other member states. But that low threshold is no longer the standard even in Ireland. The Database Directive, *see infra* § 4.05[C], harmonized the originality standard: databases will now be protected by copyright in the EU where, by reason of the selection or arrangement of their contents, they constitute the author's own intellectual creation. *See* Database Directive art. 3(1). Article 3(1) stresses that "no other criteria shall be applied to determine their eligibility for that protection." (But this does not mean that there is no longer any intellectual property protection for databases such as

those at issue in *Magill*. A different form of *sui generis* protection for databases was established in the same directive.)

(2) **Competition Law and Limits on Intellectual Property Rights.** The decision of the Court of First Instance in *Magill* was handed down while the Commission was formulating its proposed Database Directive. The decision caused the Commission to reconsider the need to include a compulsory license for circumstances where the database maker was the sole source of the data in question. Why would the *Magill* decision have that effect? Is it a good effect?

(3) **Cross-Currents in *Magill*.** The *Magill* case can best be understood as addressing a conflict between intellectual property rights and competition law. But other conflicts underlie the opinion. What are they and how do they affect the court's analysis? Why did the Court of Justice disagree with the advocate-general? Why might the court be somewhat unclear as to why it disagreed with the advocate-general?

(4) *Magill* **and TRIPS.** The advocate-general in *Magill* suggested that the imposition of compulsory licenses pursuant to Article 86 (now Article 82) of the EC Treaty would violate Article 9 of the Berne Convention. Do you agree? Are such licenses consistent with the standard announced and discussed in *United States—Section 110(5)*? If RTE wished to challenge the compulsory licenses, how would it do so? If the imposition of compulsory licenses by the Commission would violate Article 9 of the Berne Convention, and Article 13 of TRIPS, would the provision of the U.K. broadcasting statute discussed in *Magill* survive scrutiny? Is one measure—the Commission order or the statutory license— more likely to be found in violation of TRIPS than the other measure?

(5) **WIPO Guide to the Berne Convention.** In his analysis of Article 9(2) of the Berne Convention, the advocate-general referred to the WIPO Guide to the Berne Convention. That Guide states that

> This Guide is not, however, intended to be an authentic interpretation of the provisions of the Convention since such an interpretation is not within the competence of the International Bureau of WIPO, whose role is to be responsible for the administration of the Convention. The sole aim of this Guide is to present, as simply and clearly as possible, the contents of the Berne Convention and to provide a number of explanations as to its nature, aims and scope. It is for the authorities concerned, and interested circles, to form their own opinions.

To what extent and for what purposes should courts make reference to the WIPO Guide or to expressed WIPO opinions? *See supra* § 4.03[B][1].

(6) **Client Advice.** What is the practical impact of this decision? How would you advise a client who produced a database of factual information that could not be obtained elsewhere?

(7) **Comparison to U.S. Law**. Would the outcome of the dispute between Magill and RTE have been the same in the United States? On what grounds would a U.S. court have resolved the dispute?

[C]   Secondary Legislation (Harmonization)

YSOLDE GENDREAU, COPYRIGHT HARMONIZATION IN THE EUROPEAN UNION AND IN NORTH AMERICA[*]
20 COLUM.-VLA J. L. & ARTS 37, 39-57 (1995)

A. The Political Contexts

. . . .

[S]ince Community law is supranational and exists for the purpose of helping to secure a common market, while copyright law remains of national character, it did not take long before it was realized that there were limits to the power of Community law to override the national barriers that copyright laws were maintaining. The European Court of Justice became increasingly aware of the limits of its power to interpret the Treaty of Rome in such a way as to thwart the existence of legitimate national laws. For instance, Community law was of no avail to prevent a national from controlling the rental of video cassettes in his country when the country in which the video cassettes were first put on the market did not recognize such a right.[13] Similarly, the fact that a sound recording had fallen into the public domain in one country did not mean that it was no longer protected in countries that granted such objects a longer term of protection.[14] As it was stated in that case, "[I]n the present state of Community law, which is characterised by a lack of harmonization or approximation of legislation governing the protection of literary and artistic property, it is for the national legislatures to determine the conditions and detailed rules for such protection."

Talk of harmonization of copyright law was not misguided in 1989. In the previous year, the Commission of the European Communities had issued a Green Paper on Copyright and the Challenge of Technology in which it had identified several copyright issues that needed to be resolved in order to dismantle trade barriers and to prevent the distortion of competition. Since the Community is empowered, pursuant to Article 3(h) of the Treaty of Rome, to approximate the laws of Member States to the extent required for the proper functioning of the common market, work started on the harmonization of copyright law within the European Community with the issuance by the Council of directives that bind the Member States as to the result to be achieved, but leave them free as to the means to do so. The directives are thus an integral part of the drive towards a unified market for the European Union, even though no express power over copyright is granted to the Community authorities.

However, although they are its most important tools, the directives are not the only means to which the Council is resorting in order to harmonize copyright

---

[*]Copyright 1995, Ysolde Gendreau. Reprinted with permission.

[13]Case 158/86, *Warner Bros., Inc. v. Christiansen*, 1988 E.C.R. 2605 (1988).

[14]Case 341/87, *EMI Electrola GmbH v. Patricia Im-und Export Verwaltungsgesellschaft mbH*, 1989 E.C.R. 79

law within the European Union. In addition, the Council has issued a political Resolution in 1992 that requires the Member States to adhere to the 1971 Paris Act of the Berne Convention and to the Rome Convention of 1961 for the Protection of Performers, Producers of Phonograms and Broadcasting Organizations before January 1, 1995. A resolution does not have the same impact as a directive because it is merely a political commitment, not a legal instrument. As such, it can be regarded as a background to the various directives that are prepared.

B. The Textual Contexts

. . . .

That the thoroughness of the directives owes much to the context of their adoption leaves little doubt. Because the directives are a form of supranational legislation, the preparation of their texts is very similar to that of any piece of legislation. The Green Paper on Copyright and the Challenge of Technology had already identified several issues that deserved special attention, and these issues, as well as several others, are addressed according to the priorities set by the Commission. A directive will thus bear on one particular issue at a time, and its fate will depend on the speed with which a consensus is reached. For instance, given the pressing needs for a common approach to computer programs, it is not surprising that the first copyright directive bore on that topic.[27] On the other hand, the directive on cable and satellite broadcasting is actually an outgrowth of an earlier directive, Television Without Frontiers, in which the copyright dimension of the problem was originally included. The copyright provisions were however removed because further study was required before a satisfactory solution could be found.

The relative comprehensiveness of each directive is also a consequence of its being a form of legislation. Indeed, the four directives that have been adopted are each composed of between nine and fourteen sections, each one often comprising two or three subsections. The directive on computer programs is not a mere statement that Member States must protect computer programs as literary works nor does the directive on the rental and public lending of works simply declare that copyright legislation must provide for the rental and public lending of certain categories of works. Rather, several matters that must be addressed in order to ensure the full harmonization of the right at stake are included in each directive.

Examples here are quite numerous. The directive on computer programs provides a definition of the level of originality required to protect computer programs,[30] which was picked up again in the directive on the term of protection to determine the type of photographs that benefit from the standard term of

---

[27]Council Directive 91/250 of 14 May 1991 on the Legal Protection of Computer Programs, 1991 O.J. (L122) 42.

[30]Council Directive 91/250, *supra* note 27 art. 1(3). . . .

copyright protection.[31] In both cases, the originality of these works was giving rise to discrepancies in the determination of the copyright protection.[32]

Another example of such comprehensiveness is that the directive on the rental right and the public lending right includes rules of general application pertaining to neighboring rights,[33] as well as an authorship criterion for cinematographic works,[34] which is repeated in the directive on the term of protection.[35] Such precision was again necessary because some works to which these rights apply enjoy neighboring rights protection at varying levels in the different Member States. As for the authorship of cinematographic works, it is certainly one of the copyright issues on which the most divergent views are held, but for which a minimal common ground was necessary.

Finally, the directive on satellite diffusion and cable retransmission addresses the issue of neighboring rights and contains several provisions on the contractual aspects of the exercise of the rights.[37] While the same concerns for neighboring rights were in mind as in the case of the lending and rental directive, the preoccupation with the contractual elements of the question reflects the realities of the collective administration of these rights.

The list of the many details which the drafters of the directives have addressed could continue. Taken as a whole, they betray the meticulousness required by the need to deal with the general issue as completely as possible while reconciling at the same time various conceptions of copyright. The well-known opposition between copyright and *droit d'auteur* countries comes to mind, and one can perhaps discern through the various texts that the natural ascendancy of the civilian school in this context is being tempered to avoid ruffling copyright sensibilities. The opportunity to handle an issue in a comprehensive manner also enables the drafters of the directives to display some inventiveness in the solutions they are seeking. Nowhere is it more obvious than in the proposals for a directive on the protection for databases, in which the Commission advocates a *sui generis* right to prevent the unfair or unauthorized extraction of the contents of a database.

. . . .

---

[31]Council Directive 93/98 of 29 October 1993 on Harmonizing The Term of Protection of Copyright and Related Rights, art. 6, 1993 O.J. (L290) 9, 12.

[32]For instance, in Germany, the degree of originality that was required for computer programs to be entitled to copyright protection was so high as to prevent many programs from qualifying. *See* Thomas Hoeren, *Germany in* COPYRIGHT SOFTWARE PROTECTION IN THE EC 73, 76-77 (D.J. Jongen & Alfred P. Meijboom eds., 1993). Similarly, the standard for originality of a photograph depends upon its protection in several countries under either a copyright or a neighboring rights regime. *See* Ysolde Gendreau, *Aperçu comparatif de la protection des photographies*, 65 DIR. AUT. 337 (1994).

[33]Council Directive 92/100 of 19 November 1992 on Rental Right and Lending Right and on Certain Rights Related to Copyright in the Field of Intellectual Property, arts. 6-10, 1992 O.J. (L 346) 61, 64-65.

[34]*Id.* art. 2(2).

[35]Council Directive 93/98, *supra* note 31, art. 2(1) . . . .

[37]Council Directive 93/83, 1993 O.J. (L 248) 15.

THE IMPLEMENTATION OF THE COPYRIGHT POLICIES

It is beyond the scope of this article to analyze in detail how the supranational instruments have been implemented in the various countries that are subject to them. It could nevertheless be instructive to examine how some national legislatures have responded to the guidelines that have been set in order to determine if harmonization is indeed occurring. To this end, two aspects of the implementation process may prove to be telling: (A) the time it is taking for the states to comply formally with the requirements; and, more importantly, (B) their conformity to the instructions they must follow.

A. The Time Factor

A common feature of the European and North American harmonization processes is that deadlines are set for their implementation. . . . In the European Union, . . . since the directives are adopted one at a time, their implementation is staggered over the years: the required time varies between sixteen and twenty months.[54] The ideal, of course, is to have national legislations that resemble each other as much as possible within a reasonable period of time. Nevertheless, even if both the European directives and the NAFTA impose deadlines for their implementation, the coercive character of the European directives is the more pronounced of the two. A State that does not fulfill its obligations towards the Community and fails to implement a directive "jeopardises the attainment of the objectives"[55] of the Treaty and can be brought before the European Court of Justice by the Commission.[56] Moreover, the lack of action by the State can lead to its being sued by private parties for damages.[57]

One would therefore expect the Member States to be quite diligent. It appears, though, that few of them are actually successful in meeting the deadlines. For example, on January 1, 1993, the date set for the implementation of the software directive, eight Member States had not yet made the necessary amendments, and two had adopted measures that appeared unsatisfactory. Only two States, Denmark and the United Kingdom, seem to have acted in accordance with the dictates of the directive. Indeed, one country, Spain, has intimated that it will wait for the Council to have adopted all copyright-related directives before proceeding with their implementation. One reason for this lack of enthusiasm may be that the directives become directly

---

[54]The satellite and cable directive sets a time frame of about sixteen months, Council Directive 93/83, art. 14(1) . . . The computer program directive sets a date nearly eighteen months after its adoption, Council Directive 91/250, art. 10(1) . . . The deadline for the implementation of the term of protection directive is roughly nineteen months after its adoption. [cit]. A delay of almost twenty months has been allowed for the implementation of the lending and rental rights directive. [cit].

[55]EEC Treaty, art. 5(2).

[56]EEC Treaty, arts. 169, 171

[57]See, e.g., Joined Cases C-6 and C-9/90, Francovich v. Italy and Boniface v. Italy, 1991 E.C.R. 5357.

effective on the date set for their implementation,[61] and that the States leave it up to private parties to seek redress while the national legislations are being prepared.

. . . .

B. The Conformity to the Guidelines

It is difficult to properly assess the conformity of European national legislation to the directives when so few countries have succeeded in complying with the supranational requirements within the prescribed time limits. . . . However, the events to this point can form the basis of an informed preliminary opinion on the success of the harmonization programs.

By their very nature, the European directives allow national legislatures to decide how their objectives will be implemented. Member States have indeed adopted different approaches. Some have chosen to introduce amendments to existing copyright legislation that bear directly on the subject matter of the directive. This course of action was taken for the implementation of the computer program directive in Denmark and the United Kingdom. In France, a similar method was used, but the amending legislation also contained two sections unrelated to the protection of computer programs. In some other countries, punctual amendments were deliberately not introduced separately by the legislatures: because thorough revisions of copyright legislation were already taking place, the modifications that the directives required were included in the revision process. Such was the case in Greece and Belgium.

Yet another approach to the implementation of the directives was taken by two countries. Instead of integrating the changes into the copyright legislation itself, the legislatures in Italy and Belgium enacted a separate statute altogether with respect to the computer program directive. Although this may at first seem odd, it is not really surprising, since the status of computer programs within the categories of works protected by copyright, despite all that has occurred, remains controversial. . . .

. . . .

The method that is chosen to implement the supranational guidelines seems to have a direct impact on the extent to which the new national texts are in conformity with them. Actually, the national legislatures have two options: either they closely follow the guidelines or they choose a minimalist approach.

The texts of the directives take on a form very similar to that of national legislation and the possibility of transcribing them without further ado in national instruments is real. . . .The advantage, of course, is that the State cannot be accused of lack of compliance with the directive. However, this course of action also has negative implications. First, it brings grist to the mill of those who argue that the very detailed nature of the directives makes them too akin to regulations and thus creates a constitutional problem with the structure of

---

[61]*See* TREVOR C. HARTLEY, THE FOUNDATIONS OF EUROPEAN COMMUNITY LAW 200-211 (2nd ed. 1988).

the Treaty of Rome. Second, it constitutes an encroachment, albeit voluntary, upon the sovereignty of the Member States, which is intended to be preserved when the European authorities act through a directive rather than through a directly applicable regulation. Lastly, this process may tend to disturb the internal coherence of national legislation which already contains rules similar to those that are found in the directive.

The more prevalent method chosen by national legislatures . . . is the minimalist approach—the adoption of no more amendments than are strictly necessary to fulfil the international obligations. The idea, of course, is to preserve as much as possible the spirit of the basic legislation and to bring corrections to its working only when it is in conflict with new requirements. When modifications are made during the course of a general revision, the friction with the overall scheme of the law is muted, and only when one compares the new text with the old can one appreciate the impact of the new rules on the philosophy of the law.

The cumulative effect of this latter method can only be imperfect harmonization. One's opinion on the interpretation of any law will inevitably differ from that of someone else. Indeed, the comments that have been published on the implementation of the computer program directive and of the rental and public lending rights directive always display much caution in their assessment of the situation. For instance, it is widely believed that section 2(1) of the term of protection directive means that the British Copyright, Designs and Patents Act of 1988 needs to be modified because its current text does not contemplate the possibility of a film director as author of a cinematographic work.[77] Yet serious arguments have been put forward to intimate that the present Act already contains the seeds of this solution and needs only minimal clarification.[78]

Since the directives are fairly detailed, one would expect the chances of discrepancies among the national laws to be appreciably reduced. Such cannot be the case, however, when the directives are already drafted so as to give national legislatures some freedom of action. In the computer program directive, for example, it is provided [in Article 2(1)] that *"where collective works are recognized by the legislation of a Member State,* the person considered by the legislation of the Member State to have created the work shall be deemed to be its author." The rental and public lending rights directive and the cable and satellite directive, as well as the term of protection directive, allow the Member States to designate co-authors of cinematographic works in addition to the director.[80] The latter directive sets the term of protection for critical and scientific editions of works in the public domain—a publishers' neighboring right—for the Member States that recognize this form of protection.[81] The cable and satellite directive provides for the possibility that some States allow the

---

[77]*See* J.A.L. STERLING, INTELLECTUAL PROPERTY RIGHTS IN SOUND RECORDINGS, FILM & VIDEO 6 (1992); [cit].

[78]*See* Pascal Kamina, *Authorship of Films and Implementation of the Term Directive: The Dramatic Tale of Two Copyrights,* 16 E.I.P.R. 319 (1994).

[80]Council Directive 92/100, art. 2(2); Council Directive 93/83, art. 1(5); Council Directive 93/98, art. 2(1).

[81]Council Directive 93/98, art. 5.

contracts of the collecting societies to apply to copyright owners who are not members of those societies.[82] There are many other examples. One can only conclude that the end result of the European harmonization programme will not be perfect homogenization of national laws within the Union.[83] Such a goal would indeed be [elusive], with the exception of the more mathematical aspects of the term of protection directive.

. . . .

CONCLUSION

. . . [I]t is preferable to wait several years for an assessment of the European experience. Not only are the Member States taking longer to implement the directives than is required of them, but several others are in preparation. In addition to the legal protection of databases, other topics under the scrutiny of the European authorities include home copying of sound and audiovisual recordings, reprography, resale rights, collecting societies and moral rights. Moreover, the recent Green Paper on the Protection of Intellectual Property in the Information Society is bound to be followed by some measures bearing on copyright law.

NOTES AND QUESTIONS

(1) **Priorities . . . Again.** Some of the initiatives identified by Professor Gendreau as under the scrutiny of the European authorities, such as those dealing with home copying, reprography and moral rights, have not been pursued. Why? What forces have shaped the agenda since 1995?

(2) **Implementation Reports.** As Professor Gendreau notes, the Commission will pursue member states that fail to implement their obligations in a timely fashion. Issues may also arise as to whether the transposition effected by a member state is adequate to implement the terms of a directive. The Commission may bring an action if it believes that transposition was inadequate, but many such problems are forestalled by member states consulting closely with the Commission during the process of implementation. As the transposition date for different directives passes, the Commission is preparing reports summarizing the different national implementing laws. The first of these, on the implementation of the Software Directive, was published in April 2000. *See* Report from the Commission to the Council, the European Parliament and the Economic and Social Committee, on the Implementation and Effects of Directive 91/250/EC on the Legal Protection of Computer Programs, COM (2000) 199 final (April 10, 2000).

---

[82]Council Directive 93/83, art. 3(4), 1993 O.J. (L 248) 15, 19.

[83]Indeed these precedents should slacken the pressure on the drafters of the future directives, particularly for such a sensitive topic as moral rights.

**ALEXANDER A. CAVIEDES, INTERNATIONAL COPYRIGHT LAW:
SHOULD THE EUROPEAN UNION DICTATE ITS DEVELOPMENT?**[*]
16 B.U. INT'L L.J. 165, 210-22 (1998)

A. The Harmonization Drive within the European Union

In 1988, the European Commission issued its Green Paper on Copyright and the Challenge of Technology, in which it recognized the trend to develop copyright beyond its literary, musical and fine arts origins to new technologies. Though the Green Paper's harmonization measures were intended to facilitate the formation of the Internal Market, they failed to establish uniform protection within the EC. . . .

The Green Paper received significant criticism because most provisions attempted to protect entrepreneurs who exploit copyrighted works instead of the authors of the works. This situation improved upon issuance of the "Follow-up to the Green Paper: Working Programme of the Commission in the Field of Copyright and Neighbouring Rights" of January 17, 1991, in which the Commission announced that beyond a mere harmonization of copyright, efforts would be channeled towards raising the general level of protection in the Community. This goal was substantiated with the Software Directive of May 14, 1991, in which authors' rights were included and whose content was described as "state of the art." Moreover, inclusion of authors' rights has been continued in subsequent directives. What follows are brief discussions of the individual Community directives in the field of copyright.

B. Copyright Directives

1. Directive on the Legal Protection of Computer Programs

The European Commission's Software Directive of 1991 was issued to combat "certain differences in the legal protection of computer programs offered by the laws of the Member States" which "have direct and negative effects on the functioning of the common market as regards computer programs." The Directive addressed the three existing systems for the protection of software. The common law nations required that "skill, labour and investment" were expended with a degree of "originality," which merely meant that the work originated from the maker and had not been copied from another source. Italy, France, and most other nations required "originality" to the degree that the work must be an author's personal expression. Finally, in Germany, courts required that beyond the personal expression criteria, the work had to pass additional qualitative or aesthetic tests.

The Community chose to go with the middle position as article 1(3) of the Directive states: "A computer program shall be protected if it is original in the sense that it is the author's own intellectual creation. No other criteria shall be applied to determine its eligibility for protection." Article 1(1) obligates the Member States to protect computer programs by copyright as literary works within the meaning of the Berne Convention. Article 1(2) limits the protection to "the expression in any form of a computer program" but not to "ideas and principles which underlie an element of a computer program." As to questions of authorship, article 2(1) provides that natural persons or groups of natural persons creating the program shall be considered as the author, while those Member States which allow legal persons to be considered the rightholder may continue doing so.

Under article 2(3), employers exclusively are entitled to exercise the economic rights of programs created by employees in the execution of their duties. Article 4 lists acts that are subject to the author's authorization, and includes reproduction, translation or adaptation, and distribution and rental rights, the latter of which are still subject to the exhaustion principle. Article 5, on the other hand, provides exceptions to these restricted acts, such as creation of back-up copies or to correct errors. Article 6 was the subject of debate since it expressly allowed for decompilation in certain circumstances to "obtain the information necessary to achieve the interoperability of an independently created computer program with other programs."

Article 8 established a term of protection at fifty years added onto the end of the life of the author (or last surviving author), or fifty years after the program is made available to the public if it is an anonymous or pseudonymous work or where a legal person is designated as the author. Finally, article 9 clarified that the Directive shall be carried out without prejudice to other legal provisions that protect software through alternative legal schemes such as patent, trade-mark or unfair competition law. This is a far-sighted provision, in light of the several criticisms which have already been leveled against the use of copyright to protect computer programs.

2. Directive on Rental, Lending and Certain Neighbouring Rights

The Directive on Rental, Lending and Certain Neighbouring Rights ("Rental and Related Rights Directive") introduces rights which were new to most Member States. Specifically, articles 1 and 2 established exclusive rights to authorize or prohibit the rental and lending of originals or copies of copyright works for authors, of fixations of performances for performers, of phonograms for phonogram producers and of films for film producers. This reflects the Community's desire to ensure that authors and performers receive adequate compensation for their creative efforts, even absent the ownership of the economic rights to their works. Article 2(2) allows for persons other than the principal director (i.e. producers) also to be considered film authors, as is the case in the UK. Article 2(5) also [requires that member states provide that, subject to contractual clauses to the contrary, a performer shall be presumed to have transferred his rental rights] to the film producers who then own the exclusive rental rights. Nevertheless, article 4 provides that even after an author or performer has transferred his rental right concerning a phonogram or an original copy of a film to a producer, the creator retains the unwaivable right to obtain equitable remuneration for the rental, most likely through a collecting society. Authors may opt out of exclusive lending rights under article 5, if the Member States provide remuneration. In calculating such remuneration, Member States may take into account their own cultural promotion objectives, for example, the cultural and educational purposes of public libraries.

The Rental and Related Rights Directive repeats the main contents of the Rome Convention, yet several provisions extend beyond it. Articles 6-9 provide performers with exclusive rights with respect to the fixations of their performances, reproduction, broadcasting and communication to the public, and distribution. Phonogram producers, broadcasting organizations and film producers (who are not covered by the Rome Convention) also obtain reproduction and distribution rights. Article 6(2) also gives broadcasting organizations the right of prohibition in regard to the fixation of their broadcasts. Under article 8(2), Member States shall provide a right in order to ensure that a single equitable remuneration is paid if a commercial program is used for broadcasting or any communication to the public. This remuneration is to be shared between the relevant performers and phonogram producers. Under article 8(3), broadcasting organizations also have the prohibition right if a rebroadcast of their broadcast is made in a place accessible to the public against payment of an entrance fee. Finally, article 9(2) combats parallel imports by limiting exhaustion of the distribution right to the Community. Because Member States cannot allow the first sale in a non-EC country to result in the exhaustion of the distribution right within its territory, international exhaustion effectively is forbidden.

3. Directive on Satellite Broadcasting and Cable Retransmission

The Directive on the Coordination of Certain Rules concerning Copyright and Neighbouring Rights Applicable to Satellite Broadcasting and Cable Retransmission of 1993 ("Satellite Directive") was drafted in recognition of the tension between the territorial nature of copyright and the more transnational nature of satellite broadcasts. Under article 1(2)(b) of this Directive, communication to the public originates in the Member State from which the broadcasting organization introduces the program-carrying signals into an uninterrupted chain of communication from the satellite to earth. This is to avoid the cumulative application of several national laws to a single act of broadcasting. Article 2 states that "Member States shall provide an exclusive right for the author to authorize the communication to the public by satellite of copyright works." This clearly prohibits compulsory broadcasting license schemes, and means that broadcasters will only require copyright licenses in the Member State where communication to the public occurs. To prevent proliferation of "copyright havens" for countries with low levels of copyright protection to broadcast to countries with more protection and more difficult licensing procedures, article 4 of the Satellite Directive predicts harmonization of relevant EC copyright laws by aligning with those established under the Rental and Related Rights Directive.

Cable retransmissions of programs from other Member States may occur only if all applicable copyright and related rights are observed and then on the basis of individual or collective contractual agreements between right owners and cable operators. The Commission did not originally envision this contractual freedom, instead preferring the compulsory licensing route. The remaining constraint is in article 9(1) concerning the canalization of claims: "Member States shall ensure that the right of copyright owners and holders of related rights to grant or refuse authorization to a cable operator for a cable retransmission may be exercised only through a collecting society." This is merely the Community's recognition of the whole system of collective contractual agreements, supplemented by the obligatory intermediary of a collection society that was predominant in Europe. Beyond that, article 11 of the Satellite Directive provides for mediation where no authorization has been forthcoming for cable retransmission rights, but the mediation is far from binding, and thus has been labeled "soft."

4. Directive on the Term of Protection

The Directive Harmonizing the Term of Protection of Copyright and Certain Related Rights ("Duration Directive") harmonized copyright protection terms and certain related rights, increasing the traditional fifty years *post mortem auctoris* period to seventy years for copyright protection and raising the neighboring rights of performers, producers of phonograms and films and broadcasting organizations to fifty years after performance, fixation or broadcast, whichever is the case. Recital 9 of the Duration Directive explained that the increase to seventy years resulted from the desire to more fully realize the internal market, which would have been difficult under the existing disparity among Member States. While article 2 established that the principal director of a film shall be considered its author or one of its authors, it then hinged the seventy-year protection period upon the death of the last surviving of the quartet of principal director, screenplay author, author of the dialogue, and composer of the musical score, regardless of whether these persons are regarded as authors under relevant domestic law. Article 7(1) of the Directive follows the Berne Convention's rule of comparison of terms with respect to works originating in third countries, although the rule in the Directive is obligatory.

The Directive's most debated provision is contained in article 10(2): "The terms of protection provided for in this directive shall apply to all works and subject matter which are protected in a least one Member State" on July 1, 1995 "pursuant to national provisions on copyright or related rights." The sole beneficiary of this provision was Germany, with its seventy-year period being available since 1966. The interesting problem that emerged from this provision is that rights in works that had lapsed were entitled to be revived on July 1, 1995, if still protected anywhere in the Community. Although this would seem to profit only German works, the *Phil Collins* case and its interpretation of the obligation under article 6 of the EC Treaty raised further questions . . . .

One interpretation of this provision is that the European Commission decided in favor of the internal market even though it meant disappointing the public's legitimate expectations. Still, article 10(3) clarified that the Duration Directive shall be without prejudice to any acts of exploitation performed before July 1, 1995, so that acts undertaken during that period due to acquired rights are not punished. One commentator summarized that the Directive has increased the protection term to the German standard of seventy years. This occurred without a transition period, with the result that the copyright of German copyright holders who died between December 31, 1924 and January 1, 1945, no longer protected elsewhere in the EC due to national treatment, were revived Community-wide after July 1, 1995.

In closing, the Duration Directive also added photographs to the subject matter that may be protected through copyright in article 6 and included two new neighboring rights. Article 4 protects any person who publishes a previously unpublished work after its copyright has expired, for a term of twenty-five years. Article 5, on the other hand, provides Member States the option to protect critical and scientific publications of works that have become part of the public domain, for up to thirty years. While the presence of these rights within the Duration Directive may seem somewhat disorganized, that problem should be ironed out when the provisions are drafted into the various domestic legal systems.

5.   Directive on the Legal Protection of Databases

The protection scheme of the Directive on the Legal Protection of Databases ("Database Directive") is dual in nature as it aims to harmonize database protection by means of copyright, yet also to provide by means of a *sui generis* right, protection independent of copyright for aspects of databases that are not considered capable of copyright protection. Chapter II of the Directive deals with copyright. Article 3(1) requires originality in the sense that the database must be a collection of works or materials which, by reason of their selection or their arrangement, constitute an author's own intellectual creation. However, this protection does not extend to database contents. The *sui generis* right is contained in Chapter III. Article 7(1) provides a right for the database creator to prevent extraction or re-utilization if they have invested substantially in obtaining, verifying or presenting the contents. Article 10 establishes a term of protection for the *sui generis* right of fifteen years after January of the year following the date when the database was first made available to the public or when any substantial change is made to the database. Article 11 also includes a reciprocity provision to prod other states to adopt protection similar to the *sui generis* right.

One effect of the TRIPS Agreement was that the original database proposal was changed to include all databases, not merely electronic ones, which could have led to major confusion for databases published both electronically and through print. A deeper problem may be that the *sui generis* right is more limited when compared to copyright protection. While the *sui generis* right vests the right of first ownership in the database creator, who need not be a natural person, the copyright existing in the database itself would vest in the author, who could be a completely different individual. . . .

JANE C. GINSBURG, THE ROLE OF NATIONAL COPYRIGHT NORMS IN AN ERA OF INTERNATIONAL COPYRIGHT NORMS[*]
Paper Presented at the ALAI 1999 Congress, Berlin
THE ROLE OF NATIONAL LEGISLATION IN COPYRIGHT LAW 211, 216-18 (2000)

Beginning in 1991, the European Commission issued five Directives concerning copyright and neighboring rights; another is currently pending. Designed to lift impediments to the free movement of goods and services within the European Union, and to relieve the uncertainty caused by disparities in national laws, the Directives target subject matter or rights that member states have treated differently, for example, by imposing divergent standards of originality (computer programs; databases), or inconsistent levels of protection (duration, rental rights, cable and satellite retransmission). Significantly, unlike the Berne Convention and related multilateral accords, whose minimum standards apply only to member states' treatment of foreign works, the Directives require harmonization of E.U. members' substantive norms as a matter of internal domestic law, as well as a matter of treatment of foreigners.

The Directives do not purport to regulate all of copyright. Rather, pursuant to the rule of "subsidiarity," the Directives claim to address only those areas of copyright law in which national disparities threaten the smooth functioning of the internal market. As we shall see, however, particularly taking into account the pending Information Society Directive, the Directives in fact address many, if not most, issues in copyright law.

First, with respect to the subject matter of copyright, the Directives advertise only their coverage of software and databases, bringing them into the subject matter of copyright, and subjecting them to a uniform standard of originality: the work must be the "author's own intellectual creation."[32] But the Duration Directive, albeit a text concerning the regime of rights, also includes a subject matter provision: it imposes the same standard of originality on photographs, and further stresses that photographs are thereby brought within a uniform copyright fold, by cautioning: "No other criteria shall be applied to determine their eligibility for protection."[33] One might predict that the European Union-wide "author's own intellectual creation" standard of originality will eventually replace divergent national norms, such as the lower U.K. "skill and labour," or the higher French "imprint of the author's personality,"[35] thresholds.

---

[*]Copyright 2000, Jane C. Ginsburg. Reprinted with permission.

[32]Software Directive, art. 1.3; Database Directive, art. 3.1.

[33]Duration Directive, art. 6. The same cautionary note appeared in the Software Directive, art. 1.3, and the Database Directive, art. 3.1.

[35]*See, e.g.* ANDRÉ LUCAS & HENRI-JACQUES LUCAS, PROPRIÉTÉ LITTÉRAIRE ET ARTISTIQUE ¶¶ 80-86. *See also* W.R. CORNISH, INTELLECTUAL PROPERTY, at ¶¶ 10-09-10-10, comparing British, "authors rights" countries, and EU concepts of originality.

Second, with respect to copyright ownership, the Directives do not harmonize all ownership rules, but they do pose some significant uniform norms, for example, employer-ownership of computer programs,[37] and author-entitlement to equitable remuneration for exploitation of the rental right in films or phonograms.[38] Nonetheless, . . . the Directives do not harmonize ownership rules as intensively as they might.

Third, with respect to the regime of protection, the combination of the first five Directives and the pending Information Society Directive covers almost all of the rights and exceptions and limitations on copyright. Where the first five Directives detailed "restricted acts" and "exceptions to restricted acts" with respect to particular subject matter (software, databases) or rights (rental, lending, transmissions by cable and satellite), the Information Society Directive is based on the 1996 WIPO Copyright Treaty (WCT), and thus synthesizes most of the rights under copyright. The Directive therefore articulates a very broad scope for the reproduction right, specifically including temporary reproductions, in any manner or form.[39] The Directive also phrases the right of communication to the public in very broad terms, notably obliging member states to include making the work available to the public "in such a manner that members of the public may access the work from a place and at a time individually chosen by them."[40] As a result, the Directive requires member states to cover an extremely wide range of public performances and public displays of works of authorship, including all forms of transmissions, whether or not made by wire. The Directive also mandates a right of distribution of physical copies of works of authorship, and specifies that the right is not exhausted unless copies have been sold within the E.U. by or under the authority of the rightholder.[41] The Directive also implements the WCT's provisions on technological protections and copyright management information. It therefore requires member States to prohibit both the circumvention (direct or by means of dissemination of circumvention devices) of technological protection measures, and the removal or distortion of copyright management information.[42]

Equally, if not more importantly, in enumerating the limitations and exceptions to copyright for which member states may provide, the Information Society Directive appears to preclude Member States from introducing further exceptions or limitations. The Directive states, "Member States may provide for limitations to the exclusive right of reproduction provided for in Article 2 in the following cases: . . ." and "Member States may provide for limitations to the rights referred to in Articles 2 [reproduction] and 3 [communication to the public] in the following cases: . . ."[43] This suggests that, outside the listed cases, Member States may *not* provide for additional exceptions or limitations. Moreover, the proposed Directive, as amended by the European Parliament and

---

[37]Software Directive, art. 2.3.

[38]Rental Right Directive, art. 4.1.

[39][Amended Proposal for a European Parliament and Council Directive on the harmonisation of certain aspects of copyright and related rights in the Information Society (COM 1999 250 final 97/0359/COD) (May 21, 1999), hereinafter the "Draft Information Society Directive"], art. 2.

[40]*Id.* art. 3.1. The language comes from the WCT, art. 8.

[41]Draft Information Society Directive, art. 4.

[42]*Id.* arts. 6, 7.

[43]*Id.* arts. 5.2, 5.3.

revised by the Commission, further requires Member States to provide "equitable compensation" for many of the permitted acts, such as private copying (analog and digital), photocopying, and certain educational and research reproductions or transmissions.[44] Finally, even with respect to the listed cases, the Directive imposes the Berne Convention's "three-step test" the exceptions and limitations must be restricted to "certain specific cases, and may not be interpreted in such a way as to allow their application to be used in a manner which unreasonably prejudices the rightholders' legitimate interests or conflicts with a normal exploitation of their subject matter."[46]

There is another class of exceptions for which the Directives mandate even greater intra-Union uniformity. Unlike the exceptions reviewed above, which member States *may*, but need not, implement, the Directives require member States to provide for certain exceptions to or limitations on copyright. These EU-imposed restrictions on the scope of copyright concern the rights of lawful acquirers of copies to make backup copies of computer programs, to access the content of computer programs and databases,[47] and to decompile computer programs under certain circumstances.[48] The Draft Information Society Directive introduces an exemption from liability for "temporary reproductions which are an integral part of a technological process for the sole purpose of enabling use to be made of a work . . ." whether or not the initial communication of the work was lawfully made.[49]

NOTE: THE E-COMMERCE DIRECTIVE

The directive on certain legal aspects of Information Society services, in particular Electronic Commerce, in the Internal Market (the "Directive on electronic commerce") was adopted in June, 2000. Among other things, it provides limitations on the potential liability of online service providers when illegal content is stored or transmitted over their servers. The provisions on online service provider liability (articles 12-15) are reproduced below. The EU approach was to harmonize the laws of its member states on the issue of service provider liability generally, using a "horizontal approach" that covers all areas of the law, including but not limited to copyright.

---

[44]*Id.* arts. 5.2(a), 5.2(b), 5.2(b*bis*), 5.3(a).

[46]Draft Directive, art. 5.4; the language paraphrases Berne Convention art. 9.2 and WCT art. 10.

[47]Software Directive, art. 5; Database Directive, art. 6.1; *see also id.*, art. 8.1 (exception to *sui generis* right).

[48]Software Directive, art. 6.1.

[49]Information Society Directive, art. 5.1. The European Parliament amended this provision to require that the communication have been lawfully made (amendments 16 and 33), but the Commission rejected the amendment. [cit].

[Ed. Note: The Common Position adopted in September 2000, described *infra* § 4.06[C], separated the exception into two parts, one dealing with copies made to enable network transmission by an intermediary, and the other with copies made to enable lawful use.]

DIRECTIVE 2000/31/EC OF THE EUROPEAN PARLIAMENT AND COUNCIL OF 8 JUNE 2000 ON CERTAIN LEGAL ASPECTS OF INFORMATION SOCIETY SERVICES, IN PARTICULAR ELECTRONIC COMMERCE, IN THE INTERNAL MARKET

Section 4: Liability of intermediary service providers

Article 12: Mere conduit

1. Where an Information Society service is provided that consists of the transmission in a communication network of information provided by a recipient of the service, or the provision of access to a communication network, Member States shall ensure that the service provider shall not be liable for the information transmitted, on condition that the provider:

    (a) does not initiate the transmission;

    (b) does not select the receiver of the transmission; and

    (c) does not select or modify the information contained in the transmission.

2. The acts of transmission and of provision of access referred to in paragraph 1 include the automatic, intermediate and transient storage of the information transmitted in so far as this takes place for the sole purpose of carrying out the transmission in the communication network, and provided that the information is not stored for any period longer than is reasonably necessary for the transmission.

3. This article shall not affect the possibility for a court or administrative authority, in accordance with Member States' legal systems, to require the service provider to terminate or prevent an infringement.

Article 13: Caching

1. Where an Information Society service is provided that consists of the transmission in a communication network of information provided by a recipient of the service, Member States shall ensure that the service provider shall not be liable for the automatic, intermediate and temporary storage of that information, performed for the sole purpose of making more efficient the information's onward transmission to other recipients of the service upon their request, on condition that:

    (a) the provider does not modify the information;

    (b) the provider complies with conditions on access to the information;

    (c) the provider complies with rules regarding the updating of the information, specified in a manner widely recognised and used by industry;

    (d) the provider does not interfere with the lawful use of technology, widely recognised and used by industry, to obtain data on the use of the information; and

(e) the provider acts expeditiously to remove or to disable access to the information it has stored upon obtaining actual knowledge of the fact that the information at the initial source of the transmission has been removed from the network, or access to it has been disabled, or that a court or an administrative authority has ordered such removal or disablement.

2. This article shall not affect the possibility for a court or administrative authority, in accordance with Member States' legal systems, to require the service provider to terminate or prevent an infringement.

Article 14: Hosting

1. Where an Information Society service is provided that consists of the storage of information provided by a recipient of the service, Member States shall ensure that the service provider shall not be liable for the information stored at the request of a recipient of the service, on condition that:

(a) the provider does not have actual knowledge of the illegal activity or information and, as regards claims for damages, is not aware of facts or circumstances from which the illegal activity or information is apparent; or

(b) the provider, upon obtaining such knowledge or awareness, acts expeditiously to remove or to disable access to the information.

2. Paragraph 1 shall not apply when the recipient of the service is acting under the authority or the control of the provider.

3. This article shall not affect the possibility for a court of administrative authority, in accordance with Member States' legal systems, to require the service provider to terminate or prevent an infringement, nor does it affect the possibility for Member States to establish procedures governing the removal or disabling of access to information.

Article 15: No general obligation to monitor

1. Member States shall not impose a general obligation on providers, when providing the services covered by Articles 12 to 14, to monitor the information which they transmit or store, nor a general obligation actively to seek facts or circumstances indicating illegal activity. . . .

. . . .

2*bis*. Member States may establish obligations for Information Society service providers promptly to inform the competent public authorities of alleged illegal activities or information undertaken by recipients of their service or obligations to communicate to the competent authorities, at their request, information enabling the identification of recipients of their service with whom they have storage agreements.

NOTES AND QUESTIONS

(1) **Updates.** Since the articles excerpted above were written, harmonization efforts in the European Union have continued at a rapid pace. Three additional directives dealing with copyright issues have been or are on the point of being adopted: the directive on copyright and related rights in the information society mentioned in Professor Ginsburg's article was adopted in April 2001; the directive on electronic commerce, excerpted above, was adopted in 2000; and the Council and Parliament are in the midst of a legislative conciliation process regarding a directive on *droit de suite*.

(2) **Copyright Directive.** The directive on the harmonization of certain aspects of copyright and related rights in the Information Society (generally known as the "Copyright Directive" or the "Information Society Directive") is intended to implement the obligations of the two 1996 WIPO Internet treaties, the WIPO Copyright Treaty (the "WCT") and the WIPO Performances and Phonograms Treaty (the "WPPT"), both of which are discussed *infra* § 4.06[B], as well as to address other issues raised by digital technology. Thus, the directive also clarifies the scope of the reproduction right as including temporary copies (with a mandatory exception, as discussed above, for such copies in certain circumstances), and provides an exhaustive list of permissible exceptions and limitations to rights. The directive will become effective upon publication in the Official Journal; member states will then have eighteen months in which to implement the provisions. *See infra* § 4.06[C].

(3) **The E-Commerce Directive.** To what extent are the provisions of the E-Commerce Directive compatible with the limitations on service provider liability found in Section 512 of the U.S. copyright statute (enacted as Title II of the Digital Millennium Copyright Act of 1998 (the "DMCA"))? *See* 17 U.S.C. § 512 (addressing only copyright liability); *see generally* UNITED STATES COPYRIGHT OFFICE, SUMMARY OF THE DIGITAL MILLENNIUM COPYRIGHT ACT OF 1998 (Dec. 1998), available at http://www.loc.gov/copyright/legislation/dmca.pdf. What are the similarities and differences, and how can they be explained? It is also worth noting that the expressed intent was for the Copyright Directive and the E-Commerce Directive to come into force within a similar time period. *See* recital 12 to the Copyright Directive. What was the reason for this?

(4) *Droit de Suite* **Directive**. Adoption of the directive on *droit de suite* was delayed for several years by objections from the United Kingdom. The Council agreed on a Common Position in June 2000, after compromises were reached on several key provisions (primarily lowering the level of protection). One such compromise put into place an unprecedented implementation period of up to fifteen years. *See* Common Position (EC) No 42/2000 of 19 June 2000 adopted by the Council with a view to adopting a Directive of the European Parliament and of the Council on the resale right for the benefit of the author of an original work of art, O.J. C 300 (Oct. 20, 2000), p.1. The Commission rejected the Common Position, in large part because of the long implementation periods. After the Parliament agreed to various compromise amendments, the last phase of the codecision legislative procedure (called the conciliation procedure) is now under way.

(5) **Reciprocity.** In several of the EU directives adopted to date, the benefits of protection for subject matter from countries outside the European Union are conditioned on reciprocity, rather than provided on the basis of national treatment. This is particularly true of the directive on term, on *sui generis* database protection, and on *droit de suite*. As described in the excerpt by Dr. Verstrynge above, this pattern represents a deliberate strategic choice on the part of the EU.

So far, the strategy has been fairly successful in affecting policy makers across the Atlantic; the U.S. Congress has promptly responded by enacting or at least considering legislation to create comparable rights. The Sonny Bono Copyright Term Extension Act, Pub. L. No. 105-298, 112 Stat. 2827 (1998), added to the term of copyright partly to match the term available in the EU under the Term Directive. Database legislation, responding in part to the Database Directive, is still pending in the U.S. Congress after six years of deliberations. *See infra* § 4.06[D][2]. It remains to be seen whether the adoption of the EU *Droit de Suite* Directive, if it occurs, will prompt a legislative response in the United States. Bills introducing a resale royalty right were considered and rejected in the early 1990s, but at the time it was suggested that Congress might revisit the issue were the EU to adopt a harmonization directive on *droit de suite*. *See* DROIT DE SUITE: THE ARTIST'S RESALE ROYALTY, REPORT OF THE REGISTER OF COPYRIGHTS (1992).

(6) **A Review of the EU Copyright Reforms**. We have now discussed all the principal EU copyright reforms. Reconsider the question posed *supra* § 4.05[A]: to what extent has the EU effected the higher level of protection to which Dr. Verstrynge referred? Have you perceived any change in approach over time?

(7) **Future Agenda**. The European Commission is considering further initiatives on a number of topics. These include a harmonization directive intended to strengthen the enforcement mechanisms that are available to intellectual property right holders. The Commission expects to present a proposal for this directive, which would be the first "horizontal" directive addressing enforcement, in early 2002. The collective management of rights is also a current subject of attention at the Commission, and the Commission's conclusion on whether a harmonization directive on this topic is needed is also expected in early 2002.

§ 4.06 Current and Future Issues

[A] General Outlook

SHIRA PERLMUTTER, FUTURE DIRECTIONS IN INTERNATIONAL COPYRIGHT*
16 CARDOZO ARTS & ENT. L. J. 369, 376-82 (1998)

III. AROUND THE CORNER

[W]hat can be expected for international copyright in the short range? A number of issues are on the horizon, with work either completed or scheduled for the near future.

A. *Digital Issues*

Public attention has been devoted lately to the issue of adapting copyright to digital technologies. Individual countries and regions have begun to study this issue over the past few years. So far, the conclusion has been that existing copyright laws are generally adequate to the task, and need minor revisions rather than major overhauls.

On the international level, discussion has centered on the need to update the major international treaties. The current texts of Berne and Rome date back to more than a quarter century ago. The culmination of these discussions was the conclusion of two new World Intellectual Property Organization ("WIPO") treaties in Geneva in December 1996, dealing with copyright and neighboring rights. Among other things, these treaties and their interpretive statements require that rightholders enjoy exclusive control over on-demand electronic dissemination of their works, and confirm that the reproduction right is fully applicable in the digital environment. They also require member countries to provide legal protection for technologies used to prevent infringement, and for the rights management information that right-holders may choose to provide in digital form.

Perhaps equally notable is one subject the treaties do not address: the question of on-line service provider liability. Traditionally, the question of which parties in a chain of distribution of an infringing work are liable for the infringement has been left to the national laws of individual countries. Since the new treaties are silent on this question, for now national legislatures remain free to grapple with shaping the answer in the Internet context. As answers begin to emerge, there may be renewed calls for international harmonization.

The treaties are not yet in effect; they require ratification by thirty countries, which will not happen overnight. Once the treaties come into force, it is possible that they will be incorporated into the TRIPS Agreement.

B. *Future WIPO Work Schedule*

Four other copyright-related issues are currently on the WIPO agenda: (1) protection for audiovisual performers; (2) *sui generis* protection for databases; (3) protection for expressions of folklore; and (4) the rights and liabilities of broadcasters. The first two issues are holdovers from the December 1996 Diplomatic Conference. Negotiators were unable to agree on an appropriate form of protection for audiovisual performers, and agreed to continue discussions with an eye toward a possible protocol to the neighboring rights treaty. A draft treaty on *sui generis* protection for databases was never reached at the Conference. . . .

IV. LONGER TERM

What is the outlook for the longer term? Now I will venture to make a few predictions.

A. *Increased Level of Satisfactory Laws*

First, the trend toward satisfactory protection will continue. In the not-so-distant future, more and more countries will accept the emerging international consensus on basic copyright principles, with modern and balanced copyright laws becoming standard around the world.

This trend is rooted in a rational self-interest. Within their borders, countries may be persuaded that copyright protection will lead to more creation overall, and encourage foreign investment and technology transfer, advancing the domestic culture and economy. In the international arena, countries see the benefits they can obtain for their citizens by joining treaties on copyright and trade. Once they reach the stage of development where they perceive themselves as exporters of copyrighted works, not primarily users of works imported from abroad, the value of membership in a copyright treaty becomes clear. Even before that point, the trade-related benefits that may be obtained from joining a club like the WTO can outweigh any perceived drawbacks of adopting a new copyright law. Outside the parameters of the WTO, other countries like the United States may condition special trade treatment for developing countries on satisfactory protection of copyrighted works.

Major changes in copyright seem unlikely, however. The international norms embodied in legal systems around the world now reflect an accepted balance, ensuring that copyright owners can control economically significant uses of their works while allowing room for appropriate uses outside that control. The structure of the multilateral treaties permits and encourages this balance, by setting out only minimum rights and leaving considerable flexibility to national legislatures to determine what limitations on those rights are appropriate to their own conditions. This framework has stood the test of time and technological change; there is no reason why it should not continue to do so.

I do not believe that the list of copyright rights and subject matter will grow significantly. The future is likely to bring consolidation rather than expansion, with standards established on national levels being exported to more countries and eventually percolating upward into treaties. And of course, periodic adjustments will be required to adapt existing rights to new types of works and new forms of exploitation.

Now I will go out on a limb and make one truly long-term prediction. At some point, the pace of the adjustments required by the development of technologies may outstrip the ability of the law to keep up. After all, even today the state of the art in digital technology looks completely different every year, while the process of amending legal systems is slow and ungainly. Eventually a greater simplification of the system of rights may become desirable. Instead of specifically delineated rights tailored to particular techniques of exploitation, it might be preferable to provide authors with a general right to exploit the work in any manner, with an appropriate balance provided through exceptions relating to the purpose and economic effect of a use.

Some steps in this direction can already be seen in certain countries' laws that provide to copyright owners a general right to exploit a work or make it available. Similarly, the new WIPO Copyright Treaty pulls together a number of detailed and specific rights from the Berne Convention into a broad and general right of communication to the public.

B. *Issues of the Future*

Accordingly, the focal point of international copyright is likely to shift. Rather than conceptual questions of subject matter and scope of rights, more practical issues will take center stage. These issues are not new, but are already the subject of considerable discussion today. They arise from the nature of a global, digital marketplace, and relate to enforcement, the operation of the market, and choice of law. I will outline a series of questions:

1. Enforcement: How can rights be effectively enforced when works are made available electronically across national boundaries?

Customs agencies will no longer be able to assist in enforcement by seizing physical copies at borders. As in the analogue world, law enforcement agencies will need to work together to develop cooperative approaches in order to deal with pirates operating in more than one jurisdiction. Copyright owners must be able to take action against these pirates without the impossible burden of suing in every country. In this context, the issue of who is legally responsible in the chain of an unauthorized dissemination of a copyrighted work may take on heightened significance.

2. The Market: How can a market for the licensing and sale of copyrighted works operate safely and efficiently over the Internet?

The solution will involve a combination of many elements, including protection of the integrity of the information used to make the market function, as required by the new WIPO treaties; protection of the authenticity of the works communicated; adequate and internationally compatible information systems; and the technology to allow permissions to be given and payments to be made electronically.

One topic related to both enforcement and the operation of the market is the future role of collecting societies. On the one hand, the new technologies could increase the need for copyright owners to rely on collecting societies; on the other hand, they could make it easier for copyright owners to administer and enforce rights individually.

3. Choice of Law: Which country's law applies when a work is made available by a distributor in one country to users in several other countries simultaneously?

While it is often noted that the Internet creates tensions for the traditional territorial basis for copyright protection, I believe it is premature to predict its demise. The principle of territoriality is too deeply embedded in the copyright system, as part of the basic foundation. As long as copyright protection remains a function of each country's own law, it will be necessary to devise rules for choosing applicable laws in different settings. This problem has become a fashionable topic for examination at conferences, and a number of scholars have begun to develop possible solutions.

At the same time, the trend toward greater harmonization means that choice of law is less critical in determining outcome. Professor Jane Ginsburg, the leading U.S. commentator on this issue, has suggested an approach requiring courts to presume that a particular country's laws reflect the international consensus, placing the burden on the parties to prove otherwise. The international consensus could be established by the obligations of existing multilateral treaties, plus the contents of negotiated treaties reflecting widespread agreement, even if not yet in force. For example, the provisions of the two new WIPO treaties were adopted by consensus by the more than 100 countries participating in the 1996 Diplomatic Conference, and therefore can be seen as representing standards generally accepted as appropriate.

C. *Process and Players*

It is not only the substantive issues, but the process and the participants that are evolving.

One such direction is the intertwining of domestic and international concerns. In today's global market, it is no longer possible to evaluate changes to national law without considering the international implications. In weighing proposed legislation, Congress regularly considers questions of consistency with treaty obligations and the likely impact on other countries.

This is not simply an abstract exercise; questions posed to the United States at meetings of the TRIPS Council have made clear that every copyright bill introduced in Congress is under scrutiny by our trading partners. Nor is our interest purely defensive. U.S. legislation is inevitably part of an ongoing international mutual education process, and can serve as a starting point for discussion or a model for change. As countries grapple with issues posed for copyright by new technologies, they look to proposals developed elsewhere, particularly in the United States, for possible solutions. This is not a one-way street; debate on these issues at the Diplomatic Conference in Geneva was a valuable process, shedding further light on the problems and on the scope of evolving consensus.

Another path characterizing the process is the intertwining of intellectual property with other issues on the international agenda. For copyright, these include trade, protection of investment, and access to government data.

It has become increasingly clear in the past two years that the participants in the process have also changed. The days are over when international copyright was the province of a small club of copyright experts operating with a high degree of common language and mutual understanding. New players are involved in both the domestic and international debates, primarily as a result of the famed convergence in communications technologies in the digital age. Most notable is the involvement of the telecommunications industry, and providers of Internet services generally. At a relatively late date in the development of the WIPO treaties, these interests became quite active in the discussions, and were extensively represented at the Diplomatic Conference in Geneva.

Although these players are here to stay, their identities and interests, like those of the copyright industries, are metamorphosing over time. Their businesses are highly dynamic, marked by shifts in the nature of their activities and increasing consolidation. The lines between industries, and between content providers and service providers, may become increasingly blurred. The impact on copyright is hard to predict.

One final significant change is the role of the developing countries. The division between the developed and developing worlds is no longer as distinct as it once was. A number of shifts in attitudes and alignments have taken place since the 1960s and 70s. I believe these shifts can be attributed in substantial part to the impact of technology. Even though most developing countries may not yet be fully adapted to the latest digital technology, they see the future rapidly approaching. These technologies promise to level the playing field by making it possible to create and disseminate works around the world with a minimum of investment. All that is needed is creative minds with a basic level of training—not an expensive infrastructure of factories or physical distribution facilities.

Other influences include the increased and unavoidable globalization of markets, and the related rise of international conglomerates doing business around the world. Every country today is subject to both the lure and the pressure of potential investment from these businesses. The lobbying in Geneva was by no means limited to delegations from the developed world.

Finally, it is no longer possible to characterize developed countries as favoring a high level of rights across the board, with developing countries favoring a lower level. Positions today are more complex among particular regions of the developing world, which in WIPO has been organized into an Asian group, a Latin American and Caribbean group, and an African group. Even within those regions, there is little unanimity. It is clear, however, that in some areas, developing countries are seeking stronger rights than certain countries in the developed world, including the United States. This is particularly true in the areas of moral rights, protection for performers, and protection of folklore.

WIPO PRIMER ON INTELLECTUAL PROPERTY AND E-COMMERCE, ¶¶ 108-119 (2000)[*]

The protection of copyright and related rights covers a wide array of human creativity. Much of the creative content that fuels electronic commerce is subject to such protection. Under the most important international copyright convention, the Berne Convention, copyright protection covers all "literary and artistic works." This term encompasses diverse forms of creativity, such as writings, both fiction and non-fiction, including scientific and technical texts and computer programs; databases that are original due to the selection or arrangement of their contents; musical works; audiovisual works; works of fine art, including drawings and paintings; and photographs. Related rights protect the contributions of others who add value in the presentation of literary and artistic works to the public: performing artists, such as actors, dancers, singers and musicians; the producers of phonograms, including CDs; and broadcasting organizations.

Digital technology enables the transmission and use of all of these protected materials in digital form over interactive networks. While the transmission of text, sound, images and computer programs over the Internet is already commonplace, this will soon also be true for transmission of audiovisual works such as feature films, as the technical constraints of narrow bandwidth begin to disappear. Materials protected by copyright and related rights, spanning the range of information and entertainment products, will constitute much of the valuable subject matter of electronic commerce.

Given the capabilities and characteristics of digital network technologies, electronic commerce can have a tremendous impact on the system of copyright and related rights, and the scope of copyright and related rights in turn can have an effect on how electronic commerce will evolve. If legal rules are not set and applied appropriately, digital technology has the potential to undermine the basic tenets of copyright and related rights. The Internet has been described as "the world's biggest copy machine." The older technologies of photocopying and taping allow mechanical copying by individual consumers, but in limited quantities, requiring considerable time, and of a lower quality than the original.

---

[*]Reprinted with kind permission of the World Intellectual Property Organisation.

Moreover, the copies are physically located in the same place as the person making the copy. On the Internet, in contrast, one can make an unlimited number of copies, virtually instantaneously, without perceptible degradation in quality.[1] And these copies can be transmitted to locations around the world in a matter of minutes. The result could be the disruption of traditional markets for the sale of copies of programs, music, art, books and movies.[2]

It is therefore critical to adjust the legal system to respond to the new technological environment in an effective and appropriate way, and to do so quickly, because technologies and markets evolve increasingly rapidly. This will ensure the continued furtherance of the fundamental guiding principles of copyright and related rights, which remain constant whatever may be the technology of the day: giving incentives to creators to produce and disseminate new creative materials; recognizing the importance of their contributions, by giving them reasonable control over the exploitation of those materials and allowing them to profit from them; providing appropriate balance for the public interest, particularly education, research and access to information; and thereby ultimately benefiting society, by promoting the development of culture, science, and the economy.

Accordingly, the goal of policy makers has been to achieve an appropriate balance in the law, providing strong and effective rights, but within reasonable limits and with fair exceptions. If this effort is successful, the result should be a positive impact from all perspectives. Trade in copyrighted works, performances and phonograms will become a major element of global electronic commerce, which will grow and thrive along with the value of the material that is traded. If rights holders are secure in their ability to sell and license their property over the Internet, they will exploit this market fully and make more and more valuable works available through this medium. Appropriate limitations and exceptions will continue to safeguard public interest uses. The result will be a benefit to consumers, a benefit to rights holders, a benefit to service providers, and a benefit to national economies—a true "win-win" situation.

Overview of the Issues

The most fundamental issue raised for the fields of copyright and related rights is the determination of the scope of protection in the digital environment: how rights are defined, and what exceptions and limitations are permitted. Other important issues include how rights are enforced and administered in

---

[1] Indeed, in the earliest discussions concerning the Internet and its implications for copyright, some commentators argued that content subject to such rights could not be controlled on the Internet, and authors would have to find new ways to make money in cyberspace.... As the WIPO Internet Treaties of 1996 demonstrate, however, copyright continues to play an essential role in this new environment.

[2] Even without the effects that can result from copyright infringement, these markets will face considerable pressures generated by new business models and disintermediation in the networked environment. *See The Economic and Social Impacts of Electronic Commerce: Preliminary Findings and Research Agenda*, OECD, at ch.4 (1999) (URL) (in particular, the OECD highlights the effects of disintermediation).

this environment; who in the chain of dissemination of infringing material can be held legally responsible for the infringement; and questions of jurisdiction and applicable law.

The definition of rights is the key issue, as intellectual property is no more or less than the sum of the rights granted by law. Under existing treaties and national legislation, the owners of copyright and related rights are granted a range of different rights to control or be remunerated for various types of uses of their property. For both groups of rights holders, these rights include rights of reproduction and of certain acts of communication to the public, such as public performance and broadcasting. The development of digital technologies, permitting transmission of works over networks, has raised questions about how these rights apply in the new environment. In particular, when multiple copies are made as works traverse the networks, is the reproduction right implicated by each copy? Is there a communication to the public when a work is not broadcast, but simply made available to individual members of the public if and when they wish to see or hear it? Does a public performance take place when a work is viewed at different times by different individuals on the monitors of their personal computers or other digital devices?

Similar questions are raised about exceptions and limitations to rights. Are existing exceptions and limitations, written in language conceived for other circumstances, too broad or too narrow? Some exceptions, if applied literally in the digital environment, could eliminate large sectors of existing markets. Others may implement valid public policy goals, but be written too restrictively to apply to network transmissions. New circumstances may also call for new exceptions. These questions must be examined in light of the general standard established in treaties for the permissibility of exceptions and limitations to certain rights, known as the "three-step test"; exceptions are permitted "in certain special cases" that "do not conflict with a normal exploitation" of the work and "do not unreasonably prejudice the [owner's] legitimate interests."[3] How does this standard apply in the digital environment?

Issues of enforcement and licensing are not new, but take on added dimensions and urgency when works are exploited on digital networks. As noted above, the technologies pose substantial practical challenges. In order for legal protection to remain meaningful, rights holders must be able to detect and stop the dissemination of unauthorized digital copies, accomplished at levels of speed, accuracy, volume and distance that in the past were unimaginable. And for electronic commerce to develop to its full potential, workable systems of online licensing must evolve, in which consumers can have confidence. The answer to these challenges to a great extent will lie in the technology itself.

Another issue is raised by the very nature of digital networks. By definition, when a work is transmitted from one point to another, or made available for the public to access, numerous parties are involved in the transmission. These include entities that provide Internet access or online services. When such service providers participate in transmitting or making available materials provided by another which infringe copyright or related rights, are they liable for the infringement? Such liability could arise in one of two ways: if the

---

[3]Berne Convention, art. 9(2); TRIPS Agreement, art.13.

service provider itself is found to have engaged in unauthorized acts of reproduction or communication to the public, or if it is held responsible for contributing to or making possible the act of infringement by another.

Finally, electronic commerce in the subject matter of copyright and related rights raises important issues of private international law . . . .

Responses to Date

All of these issues have been examined for a number of years through various public and private processes, at WIPO and other international organizations, and at national and regional levels. Significant progress has been made, with international consensus having already emerged on some issues. In 1996, two treaties were concluded at WIPO: the WIPO Copyright Treaty (WCT) and the WIPO Performances and Phonograms Treaty (WPPT) (commonly referred to as the "Internet treaties"). These treaties, although not yet in force, address the issues of the definition and scope of rights in the digital environment, and some of the challenges of online enforcement and licensing.

[B]   The WIPO Internet Treaties

The WIPO Copyright Treaty ("WCT") and WIPO Performances and Phonograms Treaty ("WPPT") are the outgrowth of several years of debate and discussion at the international level, which culminated in a Diplomatic Conference in Geneva in December 1996. The WCT provides protection for literary and artistic works, the same subject matter as the Berne Convention. The WPPT protects certain neighboring or related rights, that is, rights of performers and producers of phonograms. Its coverage does not extend to all neighboring rights, however; it does not protect either broadcasters' rights or the rights of performers in audiovisual fixations.

The purpose of the 1996 WIPO treaties was to update and supplement the existing multilateral conventions, primarily in order to respond to developments in technologies and markets. Both the Berne and Rome Conventions were aging, the last revision of each dating back more than a quarter century, to a time before the existence of personal computers and the Internet. In addition, the Rome Convention had a relatively limited membership, and it was hoped that a more comprehensive and modern treaty would attract more countries from different legal traditions to join. Even the more recent TRIPS Agreement did not address many of the challenges posed by digital technologies, which are described in the excerpt above. Because the 1996 WIPO treaties do address these challenges, they are often referred to as the "Internet treaties."

It is important to understand, however, that the WCT and WPPT are not limited to dealing with digital issues. Other elements of the treaties, while they have received far less public attention, provide more complete and modern protection for authors, producers, and performers of creative works and phonograms, while providing leeway for reasonable limitations on their rights. The treaties' contents can be divided into three general categories: (1) the incorporation of several provisions of the TRIPS Agreement that had not previously been included in WIPO treaties; (2) certain updates that are not specific to digital technologies; and (3) the provisions that address the challenges of digital technologies. The following excerpt describes the third, and most well-known, category of treaty provisions.

WIPO PRIMER ON INTELLECTUAL PROPERTY AND E-COMMERCE, ¶¶ 120-25 (2000)[*]

Scope of rights

Perhaps the most basic right granted under both copyright and related rights is the right of reproduction, which under the Berne Convention covers reproduction "in any manner or form."[1] This right is at the core of electronic commerce, because any transmission of a work or an object of related rights presupposes the uploading of that work or object into the memory of a computer or other digital device. In addition, when the work or object is transmitted over networks, multiple copies are made in the memory of network computers at numerous points. It is therefore necessary to determine how the reproduction right applies to such copies. In 1982, at a meeting of government experts co-organized by WIPO and UNESCO, a broad-based understanding was reached that uploading into memory should be considered as an act of reproduction. This understanding was reconfirmed in 1996 in Agreed Statements to the WCT and WPPT, which state: "The reproduction right . . . and the exceptions permitted thereunder, fully apply in the digital environment, in particular to the use of works in digital form. It is understood that the storage of a protected work in digital form in an electronic medium constitutes a reproduction within the meaning of the [relevant treaty right]." The appropriate application of the reproduction right in the case of temporary copies in computer random access memory (RAM) continues to be a subject of debate at the national and international levels. The key question is whether such copies always require the consent of the rights holder in order to avoid infringement. Carefully tailored exceptions for such copies in certain circumstances have been enacted recently in the United States of America and proposed by the European Commission in a draft Directive.

The WCT and the WPPT also clarify the extent of rightholders' control when works, performances and phonograms are made available to the public for downloading or access on the Internet.[2] This type of transmission differs from

---

[*]Reprinted with kind permission of the World Intellectual Property Organisation.

[1]Berne Convention art. 9(1). *See also* Rome Convention art. 10 and TRIPS Agreement, art. 14 (providing to phonogram producers the right to authorize or prohibit the "direct or indirect" reproduction of their phonograms). The WPPT also provides to both phonogram performers and producers a broad right of reproduction, whether "direct or indirect," and "in any manner or form." WPPT arts. 7 and 11. . . .

[2]*See* WCT, art. 8; WPPT, art. 14.

broadcasting, in that the material is not selected and delivered by an active transmitter like a broadcaster to a group of passive recipients. Rather, it is transmitted interactively, that is, on demand from the individual users, at a time and place of their choosing. The treaties require that an exclusive right be granted to control such acts of "making available," while leaving it to individual countries to decide how to categorize this right under national law.

As to the scope of these exclusive rights, the new treaties continue to provide flexibility to individual countries to develop exceptions and limitations that are appropriate to their particular circumstances.[3] The general "three-step" test applied to the reproduction right in the Berne Convention and to all rights in the TRIPS Agreement is extended to apply to all rights in the Berne Convention and in the two treaties. An important Agreed Statement clarifies that this test permits countries to extend existing exceptions and limitations into the digital environment, or to add new ones, as appropriate.[4]

Technological Adjuncts to Rights

The WCT and the WPPT also break new ground in recognizing the emerging role to be played by technological protection measures, and by online management and licensing systems. They require member States to provide two types of technological adjuncts to the protection of copyright and related rights, in order to ensure that the Internet can become a safe place to disseminate and license protected material.

The first technological adjunct is generally referred to as an "anti-circumvention" provision.[5] It relates to the need of rightsholders to rely on technological measures to protect their works against infringement on the Internet. No matter how ingenious the technology used to protect works against unauthorized use, equally ingenious ways may be developed to circumvent it. The resulting level of insecurity could prevent rightholders from being willing to disseminate valuable materials on the Internet. Given the inability to achieve total security, a realistic goal is to make the technology sophisticated enough to deter the ordinary consumer from seeking to circumvent, while granting legal redress against those who represent a greater threat—hackers and those engaged in circumvention as a business. Toward this end, the treaties require member States to provide adequate legal protection and effective legal remedies against the circumvention of effective technological measures used by rightsholders to restrict unlawful and unauthorized acts. The treaty language is general enough to allow significant flexibility to national governments in determining the details of appropriate implementation.

As a second technological adjunct, the treaties protect "rights management information," providing legal support to network-based rights management

---

[3] *See* WCT, Article 10; WPPT, Article 16.
[4] *See* WCT, Agreed Statement Concerning Article 10; WPPT, Agreed Statement Concerning Article 16.
[5] *See* WCT, Article 11; WPPT, Article 18.

systems.[6] Such systems operate based on electronic data attached to the works and objects of related rights. The data may identify the author or performer, the rightsholder, and the work or object itself, and may further describe the terms and conditions for its use. Under the treaties, member States must provide adequate and effective legal remedies against the deliberate removal or alteration of such information, and against the dissemination of works, performances or phonograms from which such information has been removed or altered, where these acts are performed with at least reasonable grounds to know that they will induce, enable, facilitate or conceal infringement. This will enhance the ability of rightsholders to exploit their property on the Internet, and allow consumers to rely on the accuracy of the information they receive so they can feel secure transacting online.

As to the other two categories of treaty provisions referenced *supra* page 726, they can be summarized briefly.

TRIPS Provisions

The WCT incorporates, in almost identical language, several of the obligations in the TRIPS Agreement. First, it contains a separate article on the scope of copyright protection, stating that it "extends to expressions and not to ideas, procedures, methods of operation or mathematical concepts as such." WCT art. 2. Other articles require contracting parties to protect computer programs and original databases as literary works under copyright law. *Id.* arts. 4-5.

Both the WCT and the WPPT include rental rights for computer programs, cinematographic works, phonograms, and works embodied in and performances fixed in phonograms, subject to the same conditions as the TRIPS Agreement. WCT art. 7; WPPT arts. 9, 13.

Finally, the WPPT provides performers with a right to control the fixation of their performances, WPPT art 6, and establishes a similar 50-year term of protection for fixed performances and phonograms, *id.* art.17.

Other Nondigital Updates

The WCT includes a distribution right, explicitly applicable to tangible copies only. It is left to national legislation to determine the conditions under which the right is exhausted after the first sale of a particular copy. WCT art. 6. The WCT also generalizes the right of communication to the public scattered through various provisions of the Berne Convention, WCT art.8, and requires photographic works to be given the same term of protection as other works, WCT art. 9.

---

[6]*See* WCT, Article 12; WPPT, Article 19.

The WPPT provides a wider array of rights for performers and phonogram producers than those in the Rome Convention and the TRIPS Agreement. The rights in the WPPT include a broader reproduction right covering "direct or indirect reproduction . . . in any manner or form." WPPT arts. 7, 11. A distribution right is also provided, *id.* arts. 8, 12, as well as a right of remuneration for broadcasting and communication to the public (with an option for countries to choose to limit or not apply the remuneration right), *id.* art. 15. Unlike the rights provided to copyright owners by the WCT, this communication right is separate from the "making available" right in Article 14, which is exclusive in nature and covers on-demand interactive transmissions only. Finally, the WPPT provides moral rights for performers, similar to but somewhat more limited than the moral rights for authors under Berne. *Id.* art. 5.

Both treaties require contracting parties to make available to rightholders adequate and effective enforcement procedures, but without the specificity of the TRIPS enforcement procedures, discussed *infra* § 7.02. WCT art. 14; WPPT art. 23.

As noted above in connection with the digital issues, both treaties provide an overall standard for the acceptability of limitations and exceptions to rights, generalizing the test found in Berne Article 9(2) and TRIPS Article 13. Although the contentious issue with regard to this standard was its application to the digital environment (addressed in the Agreed Statement), the standard itself is technology-neutral.

Status

Each treaty must be adhered to by 30 countries before it enters into force. Each has already been signed by 50 or more countries, indicating their intent to ratify. As of May 2001, 24 countries had adhered to the WCT and 22 to the WPPT. These countries come from different regions of the world, and different levels of development. Many other countries have expressed the intent to ratify the treaties, and a number are already working on implementing legislation and/or the preparation of their instruments of ratification or accession for deposit with WIPO. When the EU joins, the requisite number would clearly be reached, but the EU is not likely to ratify the treaties until 2003, by which time the treaties may already be in effect. (The delay in EU ratification arises from the decision not to ratify the treaties until all member states have implemented the Copyright Directive).

PAMELA SAMUELSON, THE U.S. DIGITAL AGENDA AT WIPO[*]

37 Va. J. Int'l L. 369 (1997)

INTRODUCTION

In December 1996, the World Intellectual Property Organization (WIPO) hosted a diplomatic conference in Geneva to consider three proposals to update world intellectual property law. The conferees considered draft treaties to revise treatment of copyright issues, legal protection for sound recordings, and legal protection for the contents of databases. Each contained provisions intended to respond to challenges that global digital networks pose for intellectual property law. This Article will trace the fate of the U.S. digital agenda for these treaties. It will show that the treaties which were eventually concluded in Geneva, particularly the copyright treaty, are more compatible with traditional principles of U.S. copyright law than was the high-protectionist agenda that U.S. officials initially sought to promote in Geneva.

. . . .

. . . [T]he digital agenda negotiations warrant attention because they were a battle about the future of copyright in the global information society. To use that awful, shopworn metaphor just this once, the U.S. digital agenda at WIPO aimed to write the rules of the road for the emerging global information superhighway. . . .

. . . .

Insofar as the copyright treaty emanating from the diplomatic conference contains provisions addressing digital agenda issues, these provisions reflect an approach that strongly resembles the balancing-of-interests approach that has been traditional in U.S. copyright law. The WIPO Copyright Treaty even affirms "the need to maintain a balance between the interests of authors and the larger public interest, particularly education, research and access to information." This expression of renewed faith in the abiding value of a balanced public policy approach to copyright in the digital environment suggests that predictions of the end of copyright—that is, its displacement by trade policy in the aftermath of the Agreement on Trade-Related Aspects of Intellectual Property Rights (TRIPS)—may have been premature. . . .

. . . .

Not only was there support at the diplomatic conference for recognition of national authority to grant exceptions and limitations as a means of balancing the interests of copyright owners and the public, there was also support for making the principle of balance a fundamental purpose of the treaty by adding a new clause to the treaty's preamble. The preamble to the Chairman's original draft treaty had three parts:

Desiring to develop and maintain the protection of the rights of

---

authors in their literary and artistic works in a manner as effective and uniform as possible,

Recognizing the need to introduce new international rules and clarify the interpretation of certain existing rules in order to provide adequate solutions to the questions raised by new economic, social, cultural and technological developments,

Recognizing the profound impact of the development and convergence of information and communication technologies on the creation and use of literary and artistic works[.]

To these, the final treaty added another purpose:

Recognizing the need to maintain a balance between the rights of authors and the larger public interest, particularly education, research and access to information, as reflected in the Berne Convention[.]

This new preamble provision represents a major development in international copyright policy.

If copyright policy on an international scale had seemed to be veering away from traditional purposes such as the promotion of knowledge in the public interest and toward a solely trade-oriented set of purposes, this treaty can be seen as a timely correction in the course of international copyright policy. Though the Chairman's initial draft was consistent with a trade-based approach to copyright policy, the final treaty reaffirms faith in the concept of maintaining a balance between private and public interests in copyright policymaking and of recognizing that education, research, and access to information are among the important social values that a well-formed copyright law should serve.

. . . .

COMPONENTS OF THE U.S. DIGITAL AGENDA AND HOW THEY FARED AT WIPO

. . . .

D. Regulating Circumvention Technologies

An important part of the U.S. digital agenda at WIPO was establishment of a new international norm to regulate technologies and services likely to be used to circumvent technological protection for copyrighted works. The electronic future envisioned in the U.S. White Paper, as well as that for which many major content providers seem to be planning, contemplates broad use of technological measures, such as encryption, to protect content in digital form. As promising as such technologies are, they too pose a problem: what one technology can do, another can generally undo. Hence, the perceived need for law to regulate infringement-enabling technologies and services.

The impetus for this provision came largely from the U.S. motion picture industry, which has for many years been keen on the idea of regulating technologies that enable infringement. . . . As other content owners came to understand the desirability of technological solutions to the problem of protecting digital content, the motion picture industry gained new allies to support stronger regulation of circumvention technologies and services.

The ongoing WIPO treatymaking process offered an opportunity for an international accord on regulation of infringement-enabling technologies and services. This was important because without such an accord the effectiveness of any national regulation could not be assured. Even if the U.S. Congress could be persuaded to outlaw distribution of circumvention software in the United States, the availability of such software on servers in, for example, Finland or Indonesia would not stop U.S. nationals from gaining access to that software via the global Internet.

. . . .

E. Protecting Rights Management Information (RMI)

A fifth component of the U.S. digital agenda at WIPO was acceptance of a second unprecedented norm for an international copyright treaty, namely, an agreement to protect the integrity of copyright management information (CMI) that might be attached to digital copies of protected works. . . .

. . . .

The RMI provision of the draft treaty proved to be one of the least controversial parts of the digital agenda at WIPO. But even this limited version of the U.S. proposal was further trimmed in the course of diplomatic negotiations. Concerns had arisen that the U.S. proposal would inadvertently make illegal some alterations to RMI that presented no threat to the legitimate interests of rights holders. An alteration to RMI attached to licensed copies to correct RMI after a change in copyright ownership should not be illegal, but would have been under the Chairman's original draft. To overcome this problem, the RMI provision was amended so that alterations to RMI and distributions of copies with altered RMI would only be illegal insofar as they facilitated or concealed infringing activities.

As with the anti-circumvention provision in the WIPO Copyright Treaty, the U.S. delegation did not get exactly what it had originally sought. However, it was no small achievement to get as article 12 of the final treaty a provision that will significantly protect rights management information attached to digital copies of protected works transmitted via global networks.

. . . .

Reflections on the Outcome in Geneva

. . . Even though the U.S. delegation did not achieve all that it had hoped in Geneva, Commissioner Bruce Lehman was not just engaging in spin control when he announced a successful outcome for U.S. industries from the copyright treaty signed in Geneva.

. . . .

Whether one judges U.S. efforts to promote a digital agenda at WIPO as a success or a failure depends on what one decides to measure. By comparison with the high-protectionist agenda reflected in the White Paper and the U.S. submissions to WIPO, one would have to say that the U.S. efforts were largely unsuccessful. The conference rejected the temporary copying proposals that had initially had U.S. support. It decided to treat digital transmissions as communications to the public, rather than as distributions of copies (which may bring with it a widened possibility for some private transmissions of works). The treaty not only preserved existing user right privileges in national laws; it recognized that new exceptions might appropriately be created. The Chairman's variant on the U.S. White Paper's anti-circumvention provision garnered almost no support. Even though the treaty contains a rights management information provision, it is watered down by comparison with what the U.S. delegation had sought. . . .

Seen from another perspective, however, the U.S. digital agenda had considerable success. It is now clear that copyright law applies in the digital environment, and that storage of protected works is a reproduction that can be controlled by copyright owners. The treaty also protects copyright owners from digital transmissions insofar as they constitute communications to the public. The treaty reaffirms the three-step test that limits national authority to adopt exceptions or limitations to certain special cases that do not conflict with a normal exploitation of the work or unreasonably prejudice the legitimate interests of the author. It also requires states to have adequate protection and effective remedies against circumvention technologies and services, and to protect rights management information from alteration and removal insofar as these conceal or facilitate infringement. . . .

The copyright treaty that emerged from the diplomatic conference was a real success for the United States in part because that treaty is actually more consistent with the letter and spirit of U.S. copyright law than the digital agenda that Commissioner Lehman initially sought to promote in Geneva. For example, the conference decision not to overstretch the reproduction right of copyright law . . . is consistent with the general trend in U.S. caselaw.

. . . .

U.S. copyright law has long accorded copyright owners the right to transmit their works to the public. Hence, the treaty's endorsement of treating digital transmissions as communications to the public is consistent with U.S. copyright law. Now that the treaty has confirmed that copyright owners do have rights to control digital transmissions that communicate their works to the public, perhaps they will feel sufficiently protected and will begin digitally transmitting more of their commercially valuable works to the public.

The treaty's endorsement of balancing principles in copyright law, in particular, the importance of considering the impact of copyright rules on education, research, and access to information, is consistent with longstanding principles of U.S. copyright law. The treaty's confirmation of the viability of existing exceptions and limitations preserves the U.S. fair use defense, as well as other privileges embodied in the U.S. copyright statute. Also consistent with U.S. copyright principles is the treaty's stated expectation that new exceptions and limitations may emerge or evolve in digital networked environments.

Insofar as the U.S. copyright law already has a number of rules that regulate circumvention technologies, the treaty's provision on this subject is also consistent with U.S. law. . . . Even the RMI provision has some counterpart in existing U.S. copyright rules on removal and falsification of copyright notices. The more narrowly tailored treaty provision on RMI, as compared with the provision initially sought by the U.S. delegation, is also consistent with balancing principles of U.S. law.

. . . .

Although this Article has depicted the outcome of the digital agenda at WIPO in relatively rosy terms, this success should not be seen for more than it is. Just because balancing principles found their way into the recent copyright treaty does not mean that there will cease to be pressure to grant more extensive protection to copyright owners. . . . The Berne Convention, after all, only establishes minimum rules for national laws, not maximum rules. Moreover, other developments, such as widespread use of shrinkwrap licenses or electronic equivalents that substantially limit user rights, as well as emerging use of encryption and other technological protections may make the balancing principles of copyright law something of an historical anachronism.

However, there is still reason to cheer the digital agenda reflected in the copyright treaty signed in Geneva on December 20, 1996. Confidence in balancing principles, such as those reflected in the copyright treaty, may yet be carried over to other legal rules regulating digital information, such as those that will govern electronic commerce in digital information products and services. Moreover, consumer preference for unrestricted or more lightly restricted copies of digital works over the highly protected copies may cause many publishers to abandon the otherwise appealing mindset that would seek ever stronger technological protection for digital content. The right motto for the digital future may be: "protect revenues, not bits."

The phenomenal success of the software industry has, after all, occurred notwithstanding the unprotected nature of most copies sold in the mass-market. This should hearten traditional copyright industries which are now trying to retool their products and processes so they can commercially distribute works in digital networked environments. The market for copyrighted works in digital form is already very substantial, and it will continue to grow. Copyright owners cannot expect a digital future in which no unauthorized copies will be made. What they can expect, and what the digital agenda in the just-completed WIPO Copyright Treaty will bring, is enough protection so that the leakage that occurs does not become a hemorrhage.

NOTES AND QUESTIONS

(1) **The U.S. Strategy and the Negotiation Process.** Professor Samuelson's view is that of a prominent vocal critic of many of the U.S. government's policy goals on the digital issues, both in Congress and in the WIPO context. Her characterization of the U.S. delegation's strategy, positions, and objectives during the course of the negotiations leading up to and including the 1996 Diplomatic Conference has been vigorously contested by some of the participants. Her article also describes the intense lobbying efforts of opponents of the U.S. goals, both in Washington and with other government delegations in Geneva, giving a flavor of the passionate and polarized nature of this particular treaty process. Regardless of the disagreement and the sharply differing perspectives on the process, however, the ultimate outcome of the negotiations has been widely viewed as a reasonable compromise, with treaty provisions that are balanced and fair.

(2) **The U.S. Digital Agenda.** Compare the original U.S. treaty proposal with those made by the European Union and other countries. (The full proposals are available on the WIPO web page.) Which are "high-protectionist" and in what respects?

(3) **Areas of Controversy.** As reflected in Professor Samuelson's article, some of the most controversial provisions at the Diplomatic Conference related to digital issues. These included the treatment of temporary copies in computer RAM, online service provider liability, and the prohibition against the circumvention of technological protection measures. Other areas of significant controversy, however, were not digital issues. Much time was spent negotiating the issue of exhaustion of rights and the inclusion of performers' rights in audiovisual fixations. The outcome of both was essentially an agreement to disagree, although the techniques used were different. As to exhaustion, the second paragraph of the distribution right in each treaty leaves the question to be resolved by national law. How does this solution compare to the solution in Article 6 of the TRIPS Agreement? What is the purpose or effect of including such a provision rather than remaining silent on the issue? As to performers' rights, after strenuous attempts to overcome longstanding U.S. opposition to the inclusion of audiovisual performers in the WPPT through a last-minute compromise, in the end this subject matter was dropped from the treaty with a resolution to continue work toward a future protocol. *See infra* § 4.06[D][1]. Finally, the issue of national treatment was, as always, one of the final negotiating points. The United States pushed strongly for a broader Berne-style national treatment provision; the ultimate result, after a lopsided vote, was a narrower approach closer to Rome.

(4) **Scope of Rights in the WIPO Treaties.** Two aspects of the scope of rights required by the Internet Treaties are worthy of particular mention:

(a) *Distribution Right.* Why should a distribution right be limited to tangible copies? What is different about intangible copies of a work (whether to the copyright owner or the user of the work)? What is the best way to deal with distribution of intangible copies and how do the treaties do so? Which approach best reflects the social and economic realities of the twenty-first century?

(b) *Moral Rights for Performers*. In what ways are the moral rights provided for performers in the WPPT more limited than those provided for authors in the Berne Convention? In what circumstances would the outcome be different?

(5) **Compromise and Consensus.** It should be noted that the WCT and WPPT were adopted by consensus by more than 100 countries. All but one of the treaty provisions (national treatment in the WPPT) and all but one of the Agreed Statements (the scope of the reproduction right) were the product of such consensus and did not require any votes. The treaties therefore reflect a broad international agreement as to how copyright and related rights should be handled in today's environment, including the context of digital technologies. This is not surprising, as many compromises were made during the negotiation process between the demands of countries seeking stronger rights and those seeking greater protection for users and for intermediaries such as equipment manufacturers and communications infrastructure providers.

(6) **Exceptions in the Digital Environment.** The WIPO treaties may also affect the shaping of national laws on exceptions and limitations. As legislators begin the process of adapting existing exceptions and limitations to the digital environment, they must be mindful of not only the three-step test but the Agreed Statement, which approves such a process of adaptation, as well as the establishment of new exceptions and limitations, with the repeated proviso that the result must be "appropriate." So far, new and extended exceptions for the digital environment have involved primarily issues of temporary reproductions, and library preservation and loan activities. *See, e.g.*, DMCA § 404 (amending Section 108 of the Copyright Act); *see also* U.S. COPYRIGHT OFFICE REPORT ON COPYRIGHT & DIGITAL DISTANCE EDUCATION (1999) (recommending extension of Section 110(2) exemption for nonprofit instructional broadcasting to cover digital transmissions). Other discussions have focused on whether existing exemptions, such as for private copying, should be narrowed in the digital environment because their impact on rightholders' interests may be greater. *See* Jane C. Ginsburg and Yves Gaubiac, *Private Copying in the Digital Environment*, in INTELLECTUAL PROPERTY AND INFORMATION LAW: ESSAYS IN HONOR OF HERMAN COHEN JEHORAM (1998).

(7) **Internet Service Provider Liability**. One particular issue raised by the digital environment is the scope of potential liability of internet service providers. What is the legal responsibility of an online service or internet access provider for infringements initiated by a subscriber and taking place through its services? Although this issue was extensively discussed at the WIPO diplomatic conference in 1996, it was not addressed in the final treaties (other than in the Agreed Statement concerning Article 8 of the WCT); instead, the issue was left (at present) to national law. Case law and legislation is beginning to emerge in a number of countries. After service providers in the United States expressed strong concerns about the uncertainty of U.S. law and a need for clarification of how existing doctrines would apply to online activities, in 1998 Congress enacted Title II of the DMCA to limit the liability of online service providers in appropriate circumstances. *See* 17 U.S.C. § 512. (Earlier legislation had been enacted in the United States to limit service providers' liability for violations of other laws, such as defamation.) As discussed *supra* § 4.05[C], the European Union has harmonized the laws of its member states

on the issue of service provider liability generally, using a "horizontal approach" that covers all areas of the law, including but not limited to copyright. The issue of service provider liability is also under discussion in other countries and regions of the world. Singapore and Australia, for example, recently enacted legislation on the issue.

(8) **Developing Countries**. Included among the early ratifiers of the WIPO Internet Treaties are many developing countries. While developing countries have indicated dissatisfaction with the patent obligations undertaken in TRIPS, they appear much less resistant to copyright protection in the post-TRIPS era. Moreover, while critics charged that the accession of the developing world to the TRIPS Agreement was significantly influenced by reciprocal trade benefits of immense social and economic importance to those countries, ratifications of the WCT and WPPT have not been made upon pain of trade penalty. Can you explain these different attitudes?

(9) **Structural Change**. In the excerpt above, *see supra* § 4.06[A], Professor Perlmutter suggested that "the structure of the multilateral treaties permits and encourages a balance [between copyright owners' control of economically significant uses of their works and appropriate uses by others], by setting out only minimum rights and leaving considerable flexibility to national legislatures to determine what limitations on those rights are appropriate to their own conditions. This framework has stood the test of time and technological change; there is no reason why it should not continue to do so." Do you agree? Might there be a role for "substantive maxima" as well as "substantive minima" in intellectual property treaties? *See* Graeme B. Dinwoodie, *Federalized Functionalism: The Future of Design Protection in the European Union*, 24 AM. INTELL. PROP. L. ASS'N Q.J. 611, 715 n.274 (1996) (discussing EU design law). If "substantive maxima" were to parallel the notion of minimum rights of authors, what would be their parameters? *Cf.* Copyright Directive art. 5(1) (establishing a mandatory exception for certain temporary copies).

[C] Implementation of Treaty Provisions on the Prohibition of Circumvention

Most countries that have implemented the WIPO Internet Treaties have not found the process to be extremely burdensome. In general, the treaties do not require major changes to existing legal systems, especially for those countries already in compliance with Berne and TRIPS. The primary changes that have been necessary have been modifying the scope of rights to ensure that they cover the "making available" right for on-demand transmissions, adding moral rights for performers, and adding the technological adjuncts to rights (anti-circumvention and protection of rights management information). While moral rights for performers has been a stumbling block in some countries, the major area of difficulty, both technically and politically, has been in implementing the provision on anti-circumvention.

STATEMENT OF MARYBETH PETERS, REGISTER OF COPYRIGHTS

Before the House Subcommittee on Courts and Intellectual Property on
H.R. 2180 and H.R. 2281, 105th Cong., 1st Sess. (Sept. 16, 1997)

Technological Adjuncts to Copyright

Each of the WIPO treaties includes two provisions that require member
countries to provide technological adjuncts to copyright protection. These
technological adjuncts are intended to further the development of digital
networks by making them a safe environment for copyrighted works to be
disseminated and exploited. One provision protects against circumvention of
the technology that copyright owners may use to protect their works against
infringement. It is phrased in very general terms, leaving up to each country
precisely how to define the prohibited conduct. The other provision prohibits
the deliberate alteration or deletion of information that copyright owners may
choose to provide over the Internet to identify their works and the terms and
conditions of their use.

The bill would create a new Chapter 12 in Title 17 to implement these
obligations. The prohibitions themselves are contained in new sections 1201
and 1202; sections 1203 and 1204 set out civil remedies and criminal penalties,
respectively.

1. Anti-circumvention

a. Background and purpose

New section 1201 would implement Article 11 of the WIPO Copyright Treaty
and Article 18 of the WIPO Performances and Phonograms Treaty, which
require treaty members to "provide adequate legal protection and effective legal
remedies against the circumvention of effective technological measures that are
used by authors in connection with the exercise of their rights . . . and that
restrict acts, in respect of their works, which are not authorized by the authors
concerned or permitted by law."

This language was deliberately written to be broad and general, and to leave
to individual countries considerable flexibility in determining precisely how to
formulate the prohibition. There are likely to be different methods adopted in
different countries to satisfy this obligation. The ultimate test of treaty
compliance for any of them will be whether the language chosen "provide[s]
adequate legal protection and effective legal remedies."

After an extensive analysis, the Copyright Office has concluded that existing
protections under U.S. law are insufficient to satisfy the treaty obligation. . . .
We do not believe that the doctrine of contributory infringement provides
sufficient protection to fulfill the treaty obligation to provide "adequate legal
protection and effective legal remedies" against circumvention. As the Supreme
Court interpreted that doctrine in *Sony Corp. v. Universal City Studios, Inc.*,
464 U.S. 417 (1984), the manufacturer or distributor of a copying device is not

liable if the device is "merely capable of substantial noninfringing uses." *Id. at* 442. Most devices for circumventing technological measures, even those designed or entirely used for infringing purposes, will be capable of substantial noninfringing uses since they could potentially be employed in the course of a fair use, or in the use of a public domain work. It is therefore not surprising that the *Sony* standard, in practice, has been ineffective in addressing the circumvention problem. *See* Vault Corp. v. Quaid Software Ltd., 847 F.2d 255 (5th Cir. 1983). Copyright, moreover, may not afford any recourse against those who engage in acts of circumvention alone.

Some of the other laws we considered address particular aspects of circumvention of particular types of technological protection measures such as the scrambling of broadcast signals. In the aggregate, however, they fail to provide the general coverage required by the treaties.

The anti-circumvention issue is without doubt the most difficult of the issues presented in treaty implementation. The challenge is how to formulate a prohibition that provides meaningful protection to copyright owners, while avoiding chilling the development of legitimate consumer technology and lawful uses of copyrighted works and public domain materials. While a perfect solution may not be possible, we believe that an appropriate compromise can be found. Section 1201 of H.R. 2281 represents a reasonable attempt to reach such a compromise. It reflects the lengthy debate that took place in the United States and Geneva over the course of the past two years, and is narrower and more carefully tailored than prior proposals.

In the Copyright Office's November 1995 testimony on the NII Copyright Protection Act, we noted the importance of providing legal protection for technological measures used by copyright owners to protect their works against unauthorized use on the Internet. Unless copyright owners have confidence that their works can be secured against loss, they will not be willing to utilize this promising new means of exploitation to its full potential. As I stated then,

> One of the most serious challenges to effective enforcement of copyright in the digital environment is the ease, speed and accuracy of copying at multiple, anonymous locations. In order to meet this challenge, copyright owners must rely on technology to protect their works against widespread infringement. But every technological device that can be devised for this purpose can in turn be defeated by someone else's ingenuity. Meaningful protection for copyrighted works must therefore proceed on two fronts: the property rights themselves, supplemented by legal assurances that those rights can be technologically safeguarded.

It was for these reasons that the countries meeting in Geneva to negotiate the WIPO treaties agreed unanimously on the need for such a legal prohibition.

. . . .

c. Issues and concerns

Two main areas of concern have been identified with respect to section 1201: its coverage of products used to circumvent, such as consumer electronics and software, and its potential impact on fair use interests.[1]

Some have urged that the legislation not address the provision of products or services, but focus solely on acts of circumvention. They state that the treaties do not require such coverage, and argue that devices themselves are neutral, and can be used for either legitimate or illegitimate purposes.

It is true that the treaties do not specifically refer to the provision of products or services, but merely require adequate protection and effective remedies against circumvention. As discussed above, however, the treaty language gives leeway to member countries to determine what protection is appropriate, with the question being whether it is adequate and effective. Because of the difficulty involved in discovering and obtaining meaningful relief from individuals who engage in acts of circumvention, a broader prohibition extending to those in the business of providing the means for circumvention appears to be necessary to make the protection adequate and effective. It is the conduct of commercial suppliers that will enable and result in large-scale circumvention.

The bill's approach to manufacturing, importing and selling is essentially an application of the familiar concept that those who participate in or assist in a prohibited act may themselves be culpable. There is ample precedent for the approach. So-called "black boxes" for descrambling cable and satellite signals are banned under federal law, as are devices for thwarting serial copy management systems in digital audio recording devices. *See* 47 U.S.C. §§ 553(a)(2), 605(c)(4); 17 U.S.C. § 1002(c).

The challenge is how to limit the coverage of such activities sufficiently, so as not to chill legitimate development activities. There appears to be general agreement on two basic propositions: (1) People should not be able to engage in profit-making activities intentionally aimed at circumventing protection for copyrighted material; (2) the development and sale of multi-purpose products with substantial lawful uses should not be prevented. The difficulty lies in the grey area in between.

H.R. 2281 . . . imposes three limitations on circumstances where liability may be found. The provider would have to deliberately design the product to circumvent or advertise it as doing so, or the product would have to be essentially a circumvention device with only limited use for other purposes. In contrast, those items that have significant legitimate purposes or functions, such as general purpose computers, would not be covered despite the fact that they may also be used on occasion to circumvent.

The "only limited commercially significant purpose or use" test appears to

---

[1]These concerns relate not only to fair use, but to all permitted uses under the Copyright Act, including those made possible by the idea-expression dichotomy and the first sale doctrine. For purposes of our discussion here, we will refer to all of these user privileges collectively as fair use interests.

build on, but tighten, the *Sony* standard. It makes the standard more meaningful by referring to the extent to which the product is actually used for legitimate purposes, rather than its capability to be used for such purposes. At the same time, it is consistent with *Sony* in that it does not prohibit products with a substantial non-circumventing use, only those with merely limited commercially significant non-circumventing use.

These limitations improve on prior versions of anti-circumvention legislation, and aim more precisely at bad actors—those who deliberately facilitate unlawful activity. The limitations would rule out, for example, devices produced for a legitimate purpose that unexpectedly turn out to be used by consumers primarily to circumvent (as long as they were also used for their intended purpose to a commercially significant extent).

. . . .

The other major area of controversy relates to the impact of section 1201 on fair use and other user privileges under the Copyright Act. The Copyright Office firmly believes that the fair use doctrine is a fundamental element of the copyright law, and that its continued role in striking an appropriate balance of rights and exceptions should not be diminished. We also believe that it is possible to provide effective protection against circumvention without undermining this goal.

Section 1201 seeks to accomplish this result in several ways. First, it treats access-prevention technology separately from infringement-prevention technology, and does not contain a prohibition against individual acts of circumvention of the latter. As a result, an individual would not be able to circumvent in order to gain unauthorized access to a work, but would be able to do so in order to make fair use of a work which she has lawfully acquired. Second, it contains a savings clause that explicitly preserves fair use and other exceptions to rights in the Copyright Act.

Some argue, however, that these attempts do not go far enough and will not avoid damage to fair use interests. As a practical matter, they are concerned that access will not be made available for fair use purposes, and that there may be technological control over each occasion of use. They are also concerned that section 1201 will prevent the development of products that enable individuals to bypass such continued access controls, or infringement-prevention technology under paragraph (2), in order to make fair use. These are important issues that deserve careful consideration.

Some background may be helpful in considering the topic of access controls. It has long been accepted in U.S. law that the copyright owner has the right to control access to his work, and may choose not to make it available to others or to do so only on set terms. This means not only that a copyright owner may keep a work forever unpublished, but also that he can publish it while controlling the conditions under which others are allowed to see it—such as charging a fee or imposing restrictions on how the work may be used.[2] Users

---

[2]The extent to which restrictions can be imposed by contract on uses that would otherwise be permissible under copyright law has also become a controversial issue. *See, e.g.*, ProCD, Inc. v. Zeidenberg, 86 F.3d 1447 (7th Cir. 1996) (holding that the Copyright Act does not generally preempt contract claims).

generally pay for access and then, depending on the form in which the work is embodied, may accept the copyright owner's terms or negotiate for other terms. Libraries, for example, typically purchase a physical copy such as a book to make available on-site, or in obtaining access to works in electronic form, accept the terms presented or negotiate terms for use by their patrons.

The bill would continue this basic premise, allowing the copyright owner to keep a work under lock and key and to show it to others selectively. Section 1201 has therefore been analogized to the equivalent of a law against breaking and entering. Under existing law, it is not permissible to break into a locked room in order to make fair use of a manuscript kept inside.

In this area too, the treaties do not specifically require protection for access controls in themselves. Again, the determination to be made by Congress is how best to ensure adequate and effective protection for technological measures used by copyright owners to prevent infringement. It is our understanding that access controls such as encryption will be the primary and most effective measures that copyright owners are likely to use in the on-line environment.

One key issue is the type of access involved. Once a person has lawfully acquired access to a work, will he or she be able to make fair use? Or will such strong technological controls be imposed that each use will require additional authorization? If the former, users could be required to pay for access as they are today, and then subsequent uses might be permissible under Copyright Act exemptions. (Some have noted, however, that the existence of legal protection itself may change bargaining power in negotiating terms of use.) If the latter, it might not be possible ever to engage in such exempted conduct without payment of a new access fee.

Other critical questions are whether, as a practical matter, copyright owners will adopt reasonable terms for granting lawful access, including recognition of fair use interests; whether copyrighted works will remain available in formats other than electronic, encrypted form to be used for fair use purposes; and whether any technological means will be developed to allow individuals to circumvent for lawful purposes. The Copyright Office agrees that it would be extremely undesirable to end up with a world where fair use interests were not accommodated in an optimal manner. We share the concerns as to how these questions will be answered. If the fair use community's fears were realized, the risk would be high. If access for such purposes becomes unduly restricted, with fees charged for each use, unreasonable costs imposed, and copies not available in non-electronic form, a legislative solution would be called for.

NOTES AND QUESTIONS

(1) **U.S. Implementation**. The U.S. treaty implementation legislation was enacted in October 1998 as Title I of the Digital Millennium Copyright Act, after compromises were reached on the difficult issues described in the Register's testimony. The concerns as to the potential chilling effect on the development of devices and services were addressed by retaining the three-part test she

describes, and adding a provision that states explicitly that devices need not be designed to respond affirmatively to any particular technological measure (as a quid pro quo for this provision, a statutory exception requires that VCRs be manufactured to conform to certain specific technology for protecting audiovisual works against unauthorized copying, known as Macrovision). *See* 17 U.S.C. §§ 1201(c)(3) and (k).

The compromise on the fair use issue was more complex. As described in the Register's testimony, the bill as introduced included two elements intended to safeguard fair use interests: a savings clause stating that fair use and other limitations on copyright remained unaffected, and the division of technological protection measures into two categories—those measures that control unauthorized access, and those that prevent unauthorized copying or other use once access has been obtained. The act of circumvention is prohibited only as to the first category, the access-control measures; users remain free to circumvent measures that prevent copying. In the course of the debates, two major additional elements were added. First, there is a series of carefully-drawn exceptions to the prohibition, permitting certain acts of circumvention with a public interest purpose, such as circumvention by libraries to access a work to determine whether to acquire a copy for their collections, and circumvention for fair-use consistent reverse engineering of a computer program, or for encryption research or security testing.

Second, and most important, is the establishment of a mechanism for ongoing review by the government in order to avoid abuse of the system and the potential undermining of the balance of rights and exceptions built into existing copyright law. The Librarian of Congress, upon the recommendation of the Copyright Office, is to conduct a periodic rule-making to determine whether the prohibition on circumvention has caused or is likely to cause an adverse impact on the ability to make noninfringing uses of a particular class of works, and if so, the prohibition will not apply to users of that class of works during the period until the next rule-making. *See* 17 U.S.C. § 1201(a)(1)(B)-(C). The first such review was completed, and a report issued, in October 2000. It identified two narrow classes of work that qualified for the exception: compilations consisting of lists of websites blocked by filtering software applications; and literary works, including computer programs and databases, protected by access control mechanisms that fail to permit access because of malfunction, damage or obsolescence. *See* 65 Fed. Reg. 64555 (Oct. 27, 2000). For a summary of the legislation, and of the Register's first report under this mechanism, see the Copyright Office web site at www.loc.gov.

(2) **Legislative Approaches.** What do you think of these compromises? Do they adequately address the concerns raised? What are the pros and cons? Can you suggest a better approach, in terms of either effect or legislative drafting?

(3) **Other Implementing Legislation.** Other countries have begun to adopt their own differing solutions to similar concerns. In Japan, for example, the treaty implementation language applies to the provision of devices or services, but does not cover acts of circumvention in themselves; it applies to copy control technologies but not access control technologies (which, however, are apparently covered, at least to some extent, by unfair competition law); it also provides for liability for those who make copies for personal use (otherwise a permitted act

under Japanese law) knowing that the copying is made possible by the circumvention of technological protection measures. Compare the solution so far developed in the European Union in Article 6 of the Copyright Directive. (The Common Position is reproduced below.) Are these solutions compatible with the approach contained in the Digital Millennium Copyright Act? If not, will the incompatibility cause practical or legal problems? Which approach is preferable, and why?

COMMON POSITION (EC) NO. 48/2000 ADOPTED BY THE COUNCIL WITH A VIEW TO THE ADOPTION OF A DIRECTIVE ON THE HARMONISATION OF CERTAIN ASPECTS OF COPYRIGHT AND RELATED RIGHTS IN THE INFORMATION SOCIETY
O.J. C. 344 (Dec. 1, 2000) p. 1 (adopted Sept. 28, 2000)

Whereas:

. . . .

47. Technological development will allow rightholders to make use of technological measures designed to prevent or restrict acts not authorized by the rightholders of any copyright, rights related to copyright or the sui generis right in databases. The danger, however, exists that illegal activities might be carried out in order to enable or facilitate the circumvention of the technical protection provided by these measures. In order to avoid fragmented legal approaches that could potentially hinder the functioning of the Internal Market, there is a need to provide for harmonised legal protection against circumvention of effective technological measures and against provision of devices and products or services to this effect.

48. Such a legal protection should be provided to technological measures that effectively restrict acts not authorized by the rightholders of any copyright, rights related to copyright or the sui generis right in databases without, however, preventing the normal operation of electronic equipment and its technological development. Such legal protection implies no obligation to design devices, products, components or services to correspond to technological measures, so long as such device, product, component or service does not otherwise fall under the prohibition of Article 6. Such legal protection should respect proportionality and should not prohibit those devices or activities which have a commercially significant purpose or use other than to circumvent the technical protection. In particular, this protection should not hinder research into cryptography.

49. The legal protection of technological measures is without prejudice to the application of any national provisions which may prohibit the private possession of devices, products or components for the circumvention of technological measures.

50. Such a harmonised legal protection does not affect the specific provisions of protection provided for by [the Software Directive]. In particular, it should not apply to the protection of technological measures used in connection with computer programs, which is exclusively addressed in that Directive. It should not inhibit nor prevent the development or use of any means of circumventing

a technological measure that is necessary to enable acts undertaken in accordance with the terms of 5.3 or Article 6 of [the Software Directive]. Articles 5 and 6 of that Directive exclusively determine exceptions to the exclusive rights applicable to computer programs.

51. The legal protection of technological measures applies without prejudice to public policy, as reflected in Article 5, or public security. Member States should promote voluntary measures taken by rightholders, including the conclusion and implementation of agreements between rightholders and other parties concerned, to accommodate achieving the objectives of certain exceptions or limitations provided for in national law in accordance with this Directive. In the absence of such voluntary measures or agreements within a reasonable period of time, Member States should take appropriate measures to ensure that rightholders provide beneficiaries of such exceptions or limitations with appropriate means of benefiting from them, by modifying an implemented technological protection measure or by other means. However, in order to prevent abuse of such measures taken by rightholders, including within the framework of agreements, or taken by a Member State, any technological protection measures applied in implementation of such measures should enjoy legal protection.

52. When implementing an exception or limitation for private copying in accordance with Article 5(2)(b), Member States should likewise promote the use of voluntary measures to accommodate achieving the objectives of such exception or limitation. If, within a reasonable period of time, no such voluntary measures to make reproduction for private use possible have been taken, Member States may take measures to enable beneficiaries of the exception or limitation concerned to benefit from it. Voluntary measures taken by rightholders, including agreements between rightholders and other parties concerned, as well as measures taken by Member States, do not prevent rightholders from using technological measures, which are consistent with the exceptions or limitations on private copying in national law in accordance with Article 5(2)(b), taking account of the condition of fair compensation under that provision and the possible differentiation between various conditions of use in accordance with Article 5(5) [the three-step test for exceptions and limitations], such as controlling the number of reproductions. In order to prevent abuse of such measures, any technological measures applied in their implementation should enjoy legal protection.

. . . .

Chapter III
Protection of technological measures and rights-management information

Article 6
Obligations as to technological measures

(1) Member States shall provide adequate legal protection against the circumvention of any effective technological measures, which the person

concerned carries out in the knowledge, or with reasonable grounds to know, that he or she is pursuing that objective.

(2) Member States shall provide adequate legal protection against the manufacture, import, distribution, sale, rental, advertisement for sale or rental, or possession for commercial purposes of devices, products or components or the provision of services which:

(a) are promoted, advertised or marketed for the purpose of circumvention of, or

(b) have only a limited commercially significant purpose or use other than to circumvent, or

(c) are primarily designed, produced, adapted or performed for the purpose of enabling or facilitating the circumvention of,

any effective technological measures.

(3) For the purposes of this Directive, the expression "technological measures" means any technology, device or component that, in the normal course of its operation, is designed to prevent or restrict acts, in respect of works or other subject matter, which are not authorised by the rightholder of any copyright or any right related to copyright as provided for by law or the sui generis right provided for in [the Database Directive]. Technological measures shall be deemed "effective" where the use of a protected work or other subject matter is controlled by the rightholders through application of an access control or protection process, such as encryption, scrambling or other transformation of the work or other subject matter or a copy control mechanism, which achieves the protection objective.

(4) Notwithstanding the legal protection provided for in paragraph 1, in the absence of voluntary measures by rightholders, including agreements between rightholders and other parties concerned, Member States shall take appropriate measures to ensure that rightholders make available to the beneficiary of an exception or limitation provided for in national law in accordance with articles 5.2a, 2c, 2d, 2e, 3a, 3b or 3e [various exceptions not including private copying] the means of benefiting from that exception or limitation, to the extent necessary to benefit from that exception or limitation and where that beneficiary has legal access to the protected work or other subject matter concerned.

A Member State may also take such measures in respect of a beneficiary of an exception provided for in accordance with Article 5(2)(b) [exception for private copying], unless reproduction for private use has already been made possible by rightholders to the extent necessary to benefit from the exception or limitation concerned and in accordance with the provisions of Article 5(2)(b) and (5), without preventing rightholders from adopting adequate measures regarding the number of reproductions in accordance with these provisions.

The technological protection measures applied voluntarily by rightholders, including those applied in implementation of voluntary agreements, and technological measures applied in implementation of the measures taken by Member States, shall enjoy the legal protection provided for in paragraph 1.

The provisions of the first and second subparagraphs of [Article 6(4)] shall not apply to works or other subject matter made available to the public on agreed contractual terms in such a way that members of the public may access them from a place and at a time individually chosen by them.

When this Article is applied in the context of the [Rental Right Directive and the Database Directive], this paragraph shall apply *mutatis mutandis.*

NOTES AND QUESTIONS

(1) **Status Update.** The directive was finally adopted in April 2001 with minor changes. It is expected to be published in the Official Journal in June 2001, and member states will have eighteen months in which to implement.

(2) ***Mutatis Mutandis.*** The phrase *mutatis mutandis* appearing in the last sentence of Article 6(4) (literally, those things having been changed which should be changed) is used frequently by European policy makers. For example, the EU submissions to WIPO for the proposed new instrument on audiovisual performers' rights proposed an approach based on the WPPT *mutatis mutandis.* In essence, it means that an existing principle should be applied with only those changes made that are necessary for it to fit the current context. Why would a legislator choose to use this phrase rather than spelling out explicitly the changes he or she wished to make? What are the implications of this technique?

(3) **Article 6(4) of the Copyright Directive.** Under Article 6(4) of the Common Position, what voluntary measures must the rightholder undertake in order to avoid the member state taking its own measures to ensure that beneficiaries of an exception have a means of benefitting from that exception? What measures may the member state take? Notice that the first paragraph of Article 6(4) uses the term "shall" while the second paragraph uses the term "may." Why the difference? What is the meaning or effect of the fourth paragraph of Article 6(4)?

(4) **New Lawmaking Techniques.** As in the United States, European legislators have not been willing to rely solely on legislative language to resolve the policy issues involved in the prohibition of circumvention. Thus, the Copyright Directive also includes a requirement that the Commission prepare a report on the application of the directive, including in particular whether Article 6 confers a sufficient level of protection and whether acts permitted by law are being adversely affected by the use of technological measures. *See* art. 12(1).

[D] Issues on the International Agenda

[1] Audiovisual Performers' Rights

As noted above, audiovisual performers were omitted from the scope of the WPPT in 1996. Instead, a resolution was adopted calling for negotiation of a protocol to the WPPT by the end of 1998. Since that time, discussions have proceeded in the relevant Committee of Experts at WIPO, and a diplomatic conference took place in December of 2000 in Geneva.

Even before the conference, considerable agreement had been reached on many of the issues. First and most important was the fact that countries had agreed on the desirability of establishing a modern and effective international framework for audiovisual performers' rights—a breakthrough from past positions. As to the contents of the treaty, there was agreement on a number of the rights to be granted, including rights of fixation, reproduction, distribution, and the making available right (i.e., the right to control on-demand transmissions). There was even agreement that moral rights in some form should be included. As to the term of protection and the standards for exceptions and limitations, there was agreement that the WPPT rules should apply. Finally, the technological adjuncts contained in the WCT and WPPT (anti-circumvention and rights management information) would be included as well. The major substantive points of contention involved the inclusion and scope of broadcasting and communication rights, the scope of moral rights, how to deal with the contractual relationships and transfers of rights between producers and performers, retroactive application of rights to preexisting performances, and national treatment.

After two weeks of negotiations, provisional agreement was reached on nineteen of twenty articles. The delegates were unable to agree, however, on a provision regarding transfer of rights. The United States had proposed the following presumption of transfer: "Once a performer has consented to the incorporation of his performance in an audiovisual fixation, he shall be deemed to have transferred all exclusive rights of authorization provided for in this Treaty with respect to that particular fixation to its producer, subject to written contractual clauses to the contrary." The European Union sought to have the treaty remain silent on the question of transfer, leaving it to national law. The African regional group of countries proposed a compromise based upon a choice of law approach. Negotiations then centered on the African proposal, but the impasse on Article 12 could not be resolved.

DIPLOMATIC CONFERENCE ON THE PROTECTION OF AUDIOVISUAL PERFORMANCES GENEVA, DECEMBER 7-20, 2000 OUTCOME OF THE DISCUSSIONS IN THE WORKING GROUP PREPARED BY THE SECRETARIAT OF MAIN COMMITTEE I
WIPO Doc. No. IAVP/DC/34 (Dec. 19, 2000)

Article 4
National Treatment

(1) Each Contracting Party shall accord to nationals of other Contracting Parties the treatment it accords to its own nationals with regard to the exclusive rights specifically granted in this Treaty and the right to equitable remuneration provided for in Article 11 of this Treaty.

(2) A Contracting Party shall be entitled to limit the extent and term of the

protection accorded to nationals of another Contracting Party under paragraph (1), with respect to the rights granted in Article 11(1) and 11(2) of this Treaty, to those rights that its own nationals enjoy in that other Contracting Party.

(3) The obligation provided for in paragraph (1) does not apply to a Contracting Party to the extent that another Contracting Party makes use of the reservations permitted by Article 11(3) of this Treaty, nor does it apply to a Contracting Party, to the extent that it has made such reservation.

Article 5
Moral Right

(1) Independently of a performer's economic rights, and even after the transfer of those rights, the performer shall, as regards his live performances or performances fixed in audiovisual fixations, have the right

(i) to claim to be identified as the performer of his performances, except where omission is dictated by the manner of the use of the performance; and

(ii) to object to any distortion, mutilation or other modification of his performances that would be prejudicial to his reputation, taking due account of the nature of audiovisual fixations.

[(2) The rights granted to a performer in accordance with paragraph (1) shall, after his death, be maintained, at least until the expiry of the economic rights, and shall be exercisable by the persons or institutions authorized by the legislation of the Contracting Party where protection is claimed. However, those Contracting Parties whose legislation, at the moment of their ratification of or accession to this Treaty, does not provide for protection after the death of the performer of all rights set out in the preceding paragraph may provide that some of these rights will, after his death, cease to be maintained.

(3) The means of redress for safeguarding the rights granted under this Article shall be governed by the legislation of the Contracting Party where protection is claimed.]*

Agreed Statement Concerning Article 5

For the purposes of this Treaty and without prejudice to any other treaty, it is understood that, considering the nature of audiovisual fixations and their production and distribution, modifications of a performance that are made in the normal course of exploitation of the performance, such as editing, compression, dubbing, or formatting, in existing or new media or formats, and that are made in the course of a use authorized by the performer, would not in themselves amount to modifications within the meaning of Article 5(1)(ii). Rights under Article 5(1)(ii) are concerned only with changes that are

---

*[Ed. Note: Articles 5(2)-(3) are taken from the Understanding on Provisions of the Instrument (Doc. No. IAVP/DC/33) prepared by the Secretariat on December 16, 2000; we have added them to the document summarizing the Working Group Discussions. The Working Group Document addressed only those provisions regarding which there was any controversy.]

objectively prejudicial to the performer's reputation in a substantial way. It is also understood that the mere use of new or changed technology or media, as such, does not amount to modification within the meaning of Article 5(1)(ii).

Article 11
Right of Broadcasting and Communication to the Public

(1) Performers shall enjoy the exclusive right of authorizing the broadcasting and communication to the public of their performances fixed in audiovisual fixations.

(2) Contracting Parties may in a notification deposited with the Director General of the World Intellectual Property Organization (WIPO) declare that, instead of the right of authorization provided for in paragraph (1), they establish a right to equitable remuneration for the direct or indirect use of performances fixed in audiovisual fixations for broadcasting or for communication to the public. Contracting Parties may also declare that they set conditions in their legislation for the exercise of the right to equitable remuneration.

(3) Any Contracting Party may declare that it will apply the provisions of paragraphs (1) or (2) only in respect of certain uses, or that it will limit their application in some other way, or that it will not apply the provisions of paragraphs (1) and (2) at all.

Article 12
Transfer and Exercise of Exclusive Rights of Authorization

(1) Contracting Parties may provide that exclusive rights of authorization provided for in this Treaty are transferred from the performer to the producer of an audiovisual fixation, or may be exercised by the producer with the consent of the performer to the fixation.

(2) Without prejudice to international obligations and to public or private international law a transfer by agreement of exclusive rights of authorization granted under this Treaty, or [an agreement to exercise such rights] [an entitlement to exercise such rights based on the consent of the performer to the fixation], shall be governed by the law of the country chosen by the parties or, to the extent that the law applicable to the agreement between the performer and the producer has not been chosen, by the law of the country with which the agreement is most closely connected.

Agreed Statement Concerning Article 12

It is understood that Article 12 applies only to exclusive rights of authorization, consequently it does not apply to moral rights and rights of equitable remuneration.

Article 19
Application in Time

(1) Contracting Parties shall accord the protection granted under this Treaty to fixed performances that exist at the moment of the entry into force of this Treaty and to all performances that occur after the entry into force of this Treaty for each Contracting Party.

(2) Notwithstanding the provisions of paragraph (1), a Contracting Party may declare in a notification deposited with the Director General of WIPO that it will not apply the provisions of Articles 7 to 11 of this Treaty, or any one or more of those, to fixed performances that existed at the moment of the entry into force of this Treaty for each Contracting Party. In respect of such Contracting Party, other Contracting Parties may limit the application of the said Articles to performances that occurred after the entry into force of this Treaty for that Contracting Party.

(3) The protection provided for in this Treaty shall be without prejudice to any acts committed, agreements concluded or rights acquired before the entry into force of this Treaty for each Contracting Party.

(4) Contracting Parties may in their legislation establish transitional provisions under which any person who, prior to the entry into force of this Treaty, engaged in lawful acts with respect to a performance, may undertake with respect to the same performance acts within the scope of the rights provided for in Articles 5 and 7 to 11 after the entry into force of this Treaty for the respective Contracting Parties.

***

NOTES AND QUESTIONS

(1) **Comparing Performers.** Why was it so much more difficult to reach agreement on the rights of audiovisual performers at an international level than the rights of performers in phonograms? Why did it take more than three years from the conclusion of the WPPT to be able to agree to the convening of a diplomatic conference for this purpose?

(2) **Parallels With Other Treaties.** Throughout the discussions in the Committee of Experts, the EU advocated an approach as close as possible to that of the WPPT (*mutatis mutandis*, as noted above). In particular, it sought identical provisions on moral rights and national treatment, a similar silence on the issue of contractual provisions or transfer, and similar treatment of retroactivity (but omission of the rights of broadcasting and communication to the public). The United States, in contrast, proposed a number of provisions that were markedly different on these issues. Other governments supported one or the other approach, or made alternative proposals. Compare the provisions set out above to the corresponding provisions of the WPPT. What are the differences? What reasons underlie the varying approaches?

(3) **Article 12.** Compare the U.S. proposal on transfer of rights with Article 19 of the Rome Convention and Article 2(5) of the Rental Right Directive. What

are the differences? Why was the U.S. proposal controversial? Why was the choice of law approach not possible? What are the implications of the different bracketed options in Article 12?

(4) **Future Work.** The December 2000 diplomatic conference recommended that the diplomatic conference be reconvened to seek agreement on the outstanding issues. Any decision to do so will be taken at the September 2001 General Assemblies of the WIPO member states. In order to go forward with a diplomatic conference, however, WIPO will be looking for some indications of possible movement to resolve the impasse. No such indications have yet been forthcoming.

[2] *Sui Generis* Database Protection

The adoption of the European Database Directive in March 1996, *see supra* § 4.05[C], led to consideration at the international level of *sui generis* protection for databases outside of copyright. Within a few months of the directive's adoption, the EU submitted for discussion at WIPO a possible treaty on the subject. It pushed for prompt consideration on the same time line as the two treaties that became the WCT and WPPT, taking the view that databases constituted a critical component of the information society and their protection should therefore be an element of the international community's digital agenda.

The United States shortly thereafter submitted its own treaty proposal, similar in many respects to the EU's, but with some differences. This proposal became controversial in the United States as a matter of both substance and procedure, since such protection did not yet exist in U.S. domestic law. (Since that time, several bills have been introduced in the U.S. Congress, but none has yet passed.)

A basic proposal prepared by the chairman of the Committee of Experts from these two texts (the only ones to be submitted) was also on the table for negotiation at the diplomatic conference in December of 1996. This proposal was never reached, however, with the three weeks of the conference entirely consumed by negotiations of the WCT and WPPT. In addition, a number of countries had expressed the view that the issue was not ripe, as they had not yet been convinced of the need for this new form of protection in domestic or international law. The issue was moved to the ongoing agenda of the Standing Committee on Copyright and Related Rights ("SCCR"), where it has remained ever since. At present, the International Bureau of WIPO is in the process of commissioning a study on the economic impact of *sui generis* database protection in developing countries and countries in transition.

**BASIC PROPOSAL FOR THE SUBSTANTIVE PROVISIONS
OF THE TREATY ON INTELLECTUAL PROPERTY
IN RESPECT OF DATABASES TO BE
CONSIDERED BY THE DIPLOMATIC CONFERENCE**
Prepared by the Chairman of the Committees of Experts
on a Possible Protocol to the Berne Convention
and on a Possible Instrument for the Protection of the Rights
of Performers and Producers of Phonograms (Aug. 1996)

Article 1
Scope

(1) Contracting Parties shall protect any database that represents a substantial investment in the collection, assembly, verification, organization or presentation of the contents of the database.

(2) The legal protection set forth in this Treaty extends to a database regardless of the form or medium in which the database is embodied, and regardless of whether or not the database is made available to the public.

(3) The protection granted under this Treaty shall be provided irrespective of any protection provided for a database or its contents by copyright or by other rights granted by Contracting Parties in their national legislation.

(4) The protection under this Treaty shall not extend to any computer program as such, including without limitation any computer program used in the manufacture, operation or maintenance of a database.

Article 2
Definitions

For the purposes of this Treaty:

(i) "database" means a collection of independent works, data or other materials arranged in a systematic or methodical way and capable of being individually accessed by electronic or other means;

(ii) "extraction" means the permanent or temporary transfer of all or a substantial part of the contents of a database to another medium by any means or in any form;

(iii) "maker of the database" means the natural or legal person or persons with control and responsibility for the undertaking of a substantial investment in making a database;

(iv) "substantial investment" means any qualitatively or quantitatively significant investment of human, financial, technical or other resources in the collection, assembly, verification, organization or presentation of the contents of the database;

(v) "substantial part," in reference to the contents of a database, means any portion of the database, including an accumulation of small portions, that is of qualitative or quantitative significance to the value of the database;

(vi) "utilization" means the making available to the public of all or a substantial part of the contents of a database by any means, including by the distribution of copies, by renting, or by on-line or other forms of transmission, including making the same available to the public at a place and at a time individually chosen by each member of the public.

Article 3
Rights

(1) The maker of a database eligible for protection under this Treaty shall have the right to authorize or prohibit the extraction or utilization of its contents.

(2) Contracting Parties may, in their national legislation, provide that the right of utilization provided for in paragraph (1) does not apply to distribution of the original or any copy of any database that has been sold or the ownership of which has been otherwise transferred in that Contracting Party's territory by or pursuant to authorization.

Article 4
Rightholders

(1) The rights provided under this Treaty shall be owned by the maker of the database.

(2) The rights provided under this Treaty shall be freely transferable.

Article 5
Exceptions

(1) Contracting Parties may, in their national legislation, provide exceptions to or limitations of the rights provided in this Treaty in certain special cases that do not conflict with the normal exploitation of the database and do not unreasonably prejudice the legitimate interests of the rightholder.

(2) It shall be a matter for the national legislation of Contracting Parties to determine the protection that shall be granted to databases made by governmental entities or their agents or employees.

Article 6
Beneficiaries of Protection

(1) Each Contracting Party shall protect according to the terms of this Treaty makers of databases who are nationals of a Contracting Party.

(2) The provisions of paragraph (1) shall also apply to companies, firms and other legal entities formed in accordance with the laws of a Contracting Party or having their registered office, central administration or principal place of business within a Contracting Party; however, where such a company, firm or

other legal entity has only its registered office in the territory of a Contracting Party, its operations must be genuinely linked on an on-going basis with the economy of a Contracting Party.

Article 7
National Treatment and Independence of Protection

(1) The maker of a database shall enjoy in respect of the protection provided for in this Treaty, in Contracting Parties other than the Contracting Party of which he is a national, the rights which their respective laws do now or may hereafter grant to their nationals as well as the rights specially granted by this Treaty.

(2) Protection of a database in the Contracting Party of which the maker of the database is a national shall be governed by national legislation.

(3) The enjoyment and the exercise of rights under this Treaty shall be independent of the existence of protection in the Contracting Party of which the maker of a database is a national. Apart from the provisions of this Treaty, the extent of protection, as well as the means and extent of redress, shall be governed exclusively by the laws of the Contracting Party where protection is claimed.

(4) Makers of databases who are not nationals of a Contracting Party but who have their habitual residence in a Contracting Party shall, for the purposes of this Treaty, be assimilated to nationals of that Contracting Party.

Article 8
Term of Protection

(1) The rights provided for in this Treaty shall attach when a database meets the requirements of Article 1(1) and shall endure for at least

　　　Alternative A: 25

　　　Alternative B: 15

years from the first day of January in the year following the date when the database first met the requirements of Article 1(1).

(2) In the case of a database that is made available to the public, in whatever manner, before the expiry of the period provided for in paragraph (1), the term of protection shall endure for at least

　　　Alternative A: 25

　　　Alternative B: 15

years from the first day of January in the year following the date when the database was first made available to the public.

(3) Any substantial change to the database, evaluated qualitatively or quantitatively, including any substantial change resulting from the accumulation of successive additions, deletions, verifications, modifications in organization or presentation, or other alterations, which constitute a new substantial investment, shall qualify the database resulting from such

investment for its own term of protection.

Article 9
Formalities

The enjoyment and exercise of the rights provided for in this Treaty shall not be subject to any formality.

Article 11
Application in Time

(1) Contracting Parties shall also grant protection pursuant to this Treaty in respect of databases that met the requirements of Article 1(1) at the date of the entry into force of this Treaty for each Contracting Party. The duration of such protection shall be determined by the provisions of Article 8.

(2) The protection provided for in paragraph (1) shall be without prejudice to any acts concluded or rights acquired before the entry into force of this Treaty in each Contracting Party.

(3) A Contracting Party may provide for conditions under which copies of databases which were lawfully made before the date of the entry into force of this Treaty for that Contracting Party may be distributed to the public, provided that such provisions do not allow distribution for a period longer than two years from that date.

Article 12
Relation to Other Legal Provisions

The protection accorded under this Treaty shall be without prejudice to any other rights in, or obligations with respect to, a database or its contents, including laws in respect of copyright, rights related to copyright, patent, trademark, design rights, antitrust or competition, trade secrets, data protection and privacy, access to public documents and the law of contract.

NOTES AND QUESTIONS

(1) **U.S. Influence.** To a large extent, the international discussions can today be characterized as being on hold until the United States determines its own internal policy through adoption or clear rejection of national legislation on the subject. If legislation is enacted in the United States, it seems likely that it will be based on concepts of misappropriation and unfair competition rather than the exclusive property rights approach of the EU directive. In that case, the international community will be faced with a choice of different models, and the need to accommodate them both with flexible treaty provisions.

(2) **The Copyright Office Report.** Some of the U.S. concerns and objectives in this area are expressed in a Copyright Office report prepared in 1997. *See* U.S. COPYRIGHT OFFICE, REPORT ON LEGAL PROTECTION FOR DATABASES (Aug. 1997), available at http://www.loc.gov/copyright/docs/db4.pdf. Six topics were identified as of particular concern to participants in the Copyright Office consultations:

> (1) as a threshold question (determining whether it is necessary to reach the other issues), whether additional legal protection for databases is needed; (2) what form it should take, whether a new form of property right or a tort concept closer to unfair competition; (3) how critical concepts such as "database," "substantial investment," and "substantial" or "insubstantial" part should be defined; (4) how it can be ensured that public interest uses of information are not harmed by new protection; and (5) what should be the duration of any such protection; and (6) how "sole source" data should be handled.

See id. at 71-72. How are these topics addressed in the draft treaty provisions excerpted above? If the United States were to enact a misappropriation-based database protection law, would (from a U.S. perspective) these provisions need to be redrafted for further negotiation at the international level?

[3] Broadcasters' Rights

Another issue on the agenda in the WIPO SCCR is the subject of broadcasters' rights. Broadcasters have been urging the adoption of a new treaty, updating and supplementing the Rome Convention and TRIPS Agreement to take into account the impact of new technologies, ensuring the ability to exploit the results of their investments over the Internet and to guard against digital piracy and manipulation of broadcast signals. (Why is a new treaty necessary? How much protection is there for broadcasters under TRIPS? What is not covered by the Rome Convention?) Governments around the world have expressed general interest in such a treaty. Some of the difficult questions will relate to the definition of broadcasting in an era of media convergence and rapid technological change, as well as the interaction of protection for the broadcast signal and for the content being broadcast. A few governments have already submitted proposed treaty language and discussions are scheduled to continue.

[4] Electronic Copyright Management Systems

WIPO PRIMER ON INTELLECTUAL PROPERTY AND E-COMMERCE, ¶¶ 268-74 (2000)

Electronic Copyright Management Systems (ECMS)

. . . . The process of identifying works, determining which rights are associated with them, obtaining the necessary clearances from the corresponding rightsholders and monitoring the use that is made of such works to determine the royalties due (and eventually collect and distribute such royalties), is a complex, resource-intensive and costly affair, particularly in an international context and particularly when the work is intended for use on the Internet.

Four basic methods make up the process of rights management: (1) a method for accessing information concerning works, the rights associated with them and the corresponding rightholders (or agents acting on their behalf); (2) a method for securing permissions from these rightholders for the use of their works; (3) a method for tracking the use made of these works so as to measure the royalties due; and (4) a method for collecting such royalties and ensuring that they are ultimately received by the rightholders.

Any process for global rights management is complicated by a number of factors:

(a) Copyright and related rightholders do not own a single unitary right, but a bundle of different rights (such as the rights of reproduction, distribution, public performance, broadcasting and other communications to the public), which may exist independently from each other and which must all be taken into account.

(b) The creator of a work and the person who owns the rights in it are not necessarily the same person, as rights may be transferred either by statute or by contract, and it then becomes necessary to trace the chain of copyright transfers in order to deal with the current rightsholder.

(c) Copyright and related rights are territorial systems, and therefore the question of rights ownership must be considered for each country in which use of the work is intended.

The two WIPO Internet treaties, the WCT and WPPT, introduce obligations with respect to the integrity of rights management information systems, without specifying how these systems should be developed and operated. In this respect, information technology systems, which enable network-based rights management, hold great promise for addressing the complexities noted above, and for improving the efficiency of rights management in a global environment such as the Internet. With this in mind, a wide range of entities, including commercial technology enterprises, collecting societies and governments, are currently undertaking projects aimed at developing electronic copyright management systems (ECMS). Although the copyright community has not yet developed a universal set of standards for ECMS, significant progress has been made towards this goal.

An ECMS should consist of a database containing digital copyright works that will be accessible through the Internet. In its simplest form, such a database provides only information about the identity of rightsholders (or their agents), so that any interested person can more easily establish contact with the relevant parties in order to obtain the necessary authorizations. This information is provided by linking each digital work to a unique identifier, such as a number or code.[1] More sophisticated systems can permit the rights in question to be cleared online and, depending on the type of objects in question, allow them to be delivered through the Internet. These more sophisticated systems can incorporate elaborate computerized accounting modules that track and manage the financial aspects of the transactions in an automated manner. Attempts are also being made to formalize most stages of copyright transactions, in order to maximize automated processing.

On a national basis, for example, the Japan Copyright Office is developing the Japan Copyright Information Service (J-CIS), which is a comprehensive database system of copyright management information to cover almost all categories of works, performances and phonograms, in cooperation with relevant associations and organizations. Other governments are also considering the establishment of similar national systems.[2] In the private sector, there are several examples of joint national or regional organizations or projects which manage, or intend to manage, rights or rights information for a large range of different works and objects of related rights.[3]

While current developments in the area of ECMS offer exciting prospects for the future management and administration of rights in the course of electronic commerce, a number of fundamental issues will first need to be resolved. The most important of these issues are:

(a) *Interoperability.* The ECMS currently in development through various private and public sector initiatives are not centrally coordinated. As a result, the systems themselves are neither consistent nor interconnected, and therefore

---

[1]Such numbers or codes may be "intelligent," containing useful information about nationality, category of work or object, licensing conditions, etc., or they may be "dumb" or "mute," merely referring to a database from which the relevant information may be extracted. Projects are underway to develop network-based identification systems that build upon existing numbering systems, such as, for example, the International Standard Book Number (ISBN), the Publisher Item Identifier (PII), the International Standard Music Number (ISMN) and the *"Compositeur, Auteur, Editeur"* (CAE) code. One such project is the Digital Object Identifier (DOI) format, which is discussed in the presentation of Dr. N. Paskin, Director, International DOI Foundation, WIPO International Conference on Electronic Commerce and Intellectual Property (September 1999), *at* http://ecommerce.wipo.int/meetings/1999/index.html.

[2]For example, the Malaysian Multimedia Supercorridor, established by the Malaysian Government in 1994, will require a system of multimedia rights clearance.

[3]For example, the Media Image Resource Alliance (MIRA), the US-based Copyright Clearance Center (CCC), the UK Copyright Licensing Agency's Rapid Clearance Service (CLARCS), the Australian Copyright Agency Ltd.'s Copyright Xpress and the UK-based Authors' Licensing and Collecting Society's By-Line, discussed in the presentation of Dr. D. Gervais, Copyright Clearance Center, WIPO International Conference on Electronic Commerce and Intellectual Property (September 1999), *at* http://ecommerce.wipo.int/meetings/1999/index.html.

pose problems for interoperability. Interoperability would offer the significant benefit that users could simultaneously perform search and retrieval operations over multiple databases, instead of having to query each one separately to achieve the same result. Interconnectivity would also permit the systems to communicate and exchange information automatically, thus offering important efficiency gains. In order to attain this goal, the ECMS need to be developed on the basis of open "metadata" standards (which enable the network-based handling of different data attached to different categories of works and objects) that are themselves derived from generic models that enable the ECMS to communicate accurately and reliably. One of the leading projects in this connection is INDECS (Interoperability of Data in E-Commerce Systems), which is aimed at obtaining interoperability between different rights management systems in the intellectual property arena.[4]

(b) *Jurisdiction and applicable law.* Network-based rights management highlights the jurisdictional issue . . . of the tension between, on the one hand, global trade in intellectual property over the Internet and, on the other hand, the need to manage these transactions through a territorially-based legal system. In the course of international rights management, multiple questions arise: Which law applies, for example, to determine the owner of copyright in a particular work, the scope of the rights and the validity of any contractual transfer of rights? The answers to such questions vary from country to country, although a single rights transaction may have legal effect in multiple jurisdictions. This tension focuses attention on the need for harmonization of substantive legal norms, or the development of private international law rules that may adequately take into account intellectual property issues.

(c) *Privacy concerns.* Another issue . . . is the extent to which the tracking and control features that may be incorporated in ECMS can be made compatible with users' privacy concerns. Users may or may not tolerate information concerning their use being communicated to the relevant entities managing copyrights (for example, to ensure that payment based on actual use is received and distributed to the correct owners), and may oppose the same information being made available to others, including the right owners themselves. Certain technologies now offer information that is pertinent for rights management without disclosing the identity of the user.

---

[4]*See* INDECS Metadata Schema *at* http:/:www.indecs.org. Another project for development of a metadata system for use mainly with texts is the "Dublin Core" initiative, involving participants from Australia, Canada, Denmark, Finland, France, Germany, Japan, Norway, Sweden, Thailand, United Kingdom and the United States of America. *See* Presentation of D. Gervais, Copyright Clearance Center, WIPO International Conference on Electronic Commerce and Intellectual Property (September 1999), *at* http://ecommerce.wipo.int/meetings/1999/index.html.

[5] Impact of International Law on National Laws and Approaches

JANE C. GINSBURG, THE ROLE OF NATIONAL COPYRIGHT IN AN ERA OF INTERNATIONAL COPYRIGHT NORMS[*]
Paper Presented at the ALAI 1999 Congress, Berlin
THE ROLE OF NATIONAL LEGISLATION IN COPYRIGHT LAW 211 (2000)

INTRODUCTION

When Dr. Dietz asked me to address this topic, I inferred that the apparently declaratory title in fact concealed a question mark. (That is, that the title really should read: "*What* Role for National Copyright in an Era of International Copyright Norms?") At first blush, this inference might surprise. After all, it has long been said that there is no such thing as "international copyright." Rather, we have a system of interlocking national copyrights, woven together by the principle of national treatment. Admittedly, the Berne Convention has always imposed a minimum standard as to subject matter and rights protected, but this multilateral overlay scarcely detracted from the traditional image of international copyright as a bundle of national, territorially defined, rights. As a result, the title's suggestion that national copyright laws are an endangered species may seem jarring, if not provocative.

In fact, however, there is good reason to wonder what role national copyright laws do and should have in an era not only of international copyright norms, but of instantaneous transnational communication of copyrighted works. National copyright laws are a component of local cultural and information policies. As such, they express each sovereign nation's aspirations for its citizens' exposure to works of authorship, for their participation in their country's cultural patrimony. But works of authorship have an international vocation, now facilitated by digital communications. Perhaps that simply means that each country's local policies should prevail within its borders, whatever the national origin of the work locally received. On the other hand, the pervasive international dissemination of works of authorship also calls into question the extent to which authors and their works should be subject to different national standards. . . .

I. THE DISPLACEMENT OF DOMESTIC COPYRIGHT LAWS

A. By means of multilateral instruments

1. Berne Convention, the TRIPS Accord, and the Pending WIPO Copyright Treaty

    a. The genesis of the Berne Convention: roots of the debate between supranational norms and national treatment

From the outset of the movement for international copyright protection, two distinct principles have vied for primacy.   On the one hand, the non-discrimination principle of national treatment preserves the integrity of domestic legislation, but ensures that foreign authors will be assimilated to local authors. On the other hand, supranational norms guarantee international uniformity and predictability, and thus enhance the international dissemination of works of authorship. A compromise approach institutes national treatment, but avoids local underprotection by imposing minimum substantive standards that member countries must adopt. The development of the Berne Convention illustrates all three of these approaches.

   . . . .

    b. The 1886 Berne Convention and its successors: the growth of supranational norms

The basic structure of the Berne Convention has remained relatively unchanged throughout each of its revisions. It contains substantive minimum standards of protection, as well as a general directive to accord Unionist authors national treatment. Each subsequent revision of the Berne Convention, from 1896 through 1971, as well as the 1994 Trade Related Aspects of Intellectual Property [TRIPS] accord, and the 1996 WIPO Copyright Treaty [WCT], however, have adopted more substantive minimum standards to which Union members must adhere, while retaining a key "pragmatic" feature: the Berne minima apply to a Union member's protection of works from *other* Berne members; no Berne member is obliged to accord its *own* authors treaty-level protection. Thus domestic norms may continue to apply to purely domestic copyright controversies, although, as a practical matter, local legislators may have difficulty justifying better treatment of foreign than domestic authors.[14]

The original Berne Convention provided an explicit, but not exclusive, list of works to be protected. The Berne Convention also defined the conditions for protection, known as points of attachment, and also specified rules governing the term of protection.[16] Subsequent conferences have amended each of these

---

[14]*But see, e.g.,* 17 U.S.C. § 104A (restoring copyright in non-U.S. Berne and WTO works whose copyrights expired due to failure to comply with U.S. formalities).

[16]*See* Berne Convention, arts. 2 & 3.

provisions in order to increase the scope of authors' rights. Among the minimum standards that all member countries were required to recognize, the original Berne Convention first established the translation right;[17] more exclusive rights, as well as some optional exceptions, were added over the course of subsequent revisions.[18]

The actual impact of the Berne Convention on national norms also depends on whether or not the member State treats the Convention as self-executing. If it does not, but instead executes its treaty obligations by implementing the substantive dispositions through its national law, there is a risk that the national legislation will not fully conform to the Berne Convention's text.[19]

The adoption by members of the World Trade Organization of the TRIPS accord further extended the Berne Convention minimum standards to countries beyond the Berne Union who are members of the World Trade Organization.[20] The TRIPS accord also imposed new substantive minima, both with respect to subject matter (computer programs and original compilations of data),[21] and to rights protected (rental right).[22] TRIPS also generalizes the conditions for limitations and exceptions to protection.[23] In a significant enhancement to the Berne Convention's substantive minima, the TRIPS accord contains detailed provisions on enforcement of copyright.[24] Thus, while the TRIPS continues to leave to national legislation many details of copyright scope and enforcement, the outline of uniform mandatory measures has become increasingly explicit. The place of national policy thus shrinks accordingly.

Finally, the 1996 WCT, now open for ratification, not only continues the trend of increased specification of the minimum international content of copyright subject matter and rights, but creates new obligations to protect against the circumvention of technological protection measures, and against the removal or tampering with copyright management information.[25] While member states

---

[17]*See id.*, art. 5.

[18]For example the exclusive recording right of musical works and the right of authors to authorize the reproduction and public performance of their work by means of a cinematograph were introduced by the Berlin Revision of 1908 (art. 13 and art. 14), the moral right to claim paternity of a work and the right to "object to any deformation, mutilation or other modification" of the work as well as the broadcasting right were introduced at the Rome Revision Conference of 1928 (arts. 6*bis* and 11*bis*), and the *droit de suite* was added at the Brussels Revision of 1948 (art. 14*bis* para. 1). The 1971 revision set forth the reproduction right, but also posed general terms under which member states could provide for exceptions to that right (arts. 9.1, 9.2)

[19]For example, in 1989, when the U.S. adhered to the Berne Convention, it did not amend the 1976 Copyright Act to provide for the rights of attribution and integrity guaranteed by Berne Conv. Art. 6*bis*. Congress took the position that these rights already existed in the Copyright Act, or in other dispositions in the trademark law or at common law. *See* H.R. REP NO. 609, 100th Cong., 2d Sess. at 37 (stressing that then-Director-General of WIPO Arpad Bogsch endorsed the U.S. view that its pre-Berne adherence positive law satisfied art. 6*bis*). This assertion has prompted considerable skepticism, *see, e.g.*, Adolf Dietz, *The United States and Moral Rights: Idiosyncracy or Approximation? Observations on a Problematical Relationship Underlying United States Adherence to the Berne Convention*, 142 RIDA 222 (Oct. 1989).

[20]TRIPS does not, however, incorporate article 6*bis* of the Berne Convention (moral rights). *See* TRIPS art. 9.1.

[21]*Id.* art. 10.

[22]*Id.* art. 11.

[23]*Id.* art. 13.

[24]*Compare* TRIPS arts. 41-61 *with* Berne Convention art. 16.

[25]WCT arts. 11, 12.

may implement these new obligations in different ways, the terms of the new provisions may not leave substantial room for differing interpretations.[26]

2. Harmonization measures within the European Union

[Here Professor Ginsburg describes the European directives in the field of copyright and related rights, excerpted *supra* at page 710.]

The Directives thus set an overall, often quite detailed, framework guiding national legislators, considerably limiting the opportunities for national variance regarding the scope of copyright protection. I would further suggest that the uniform originality standard adopted in the Directives will come to constrain the freedom of national legislatures to vary the subject matter of copyright. In the case of copyright ownership, by contrast, the Directives do allow Member States a considerably freer hand to allocate rights among authors, employers, and transferees.

. . . .

II. WHAT PLACE REMAINS FOR NATIONAL COPYRIGHT NORMS?

Given the substantial muting of national norms by multilateral instruments, . . . it is now appropriate to inquire what place remains for national copyright norms.

A. Gaps left in the WIPO, WTO, and EU Multilateral Instruments

1. Berne Convention, TRIPS, and WCT

While the multilateral treaties are increasingly comprehensive with respect to the subject matter and scope of copyright, significant gaps remain, particularly with respect to authorship and ownership of copyright. Indeed, apart from the Berne Convention's much-criticized art. 14*bis*(2),[72] concerning ownership of rights in cinematographic works, none of the three principal treaties contain detailed provisions on copyright ownership.[73] The Berne

---

[26]With the following important exception: art. 11 requires member states to protect against "the circumvention" of technological measures; it is not completely clear whether this text requires prohibition not only of direct acts of circumvention, but also of the manufacture and dissemination of circumvention devices. The U.S. and the E.U. have interpreted art. 11 in the latter sense. See 17 U.S.C. § 1201(b); Amended Proposal for a European Parliament and Council Directive on the harmonisation of certain aspects of copyright and related rights in the Information Society (COM 1999 250 final 97/0359/COD) (May 21, 1999), art. 6.2.

[72]*See, e.g.,* HENRI DESBOIS, ANDRÉ FRANÇON, ANDRÉ KÉRÉVER, LES CONVENTIONS INTERNATIONALES DU DROIT D'AUTEUR ET DES DROITS VOISINS 216-21 (1976).

[73]*But see* Sam Ricketson, *People or Machines? The Berne Convention and the Changing Concept of Authorship,* 16 COLUM.-VLA J. L. & THE ARTS 1 (1991) (contending that the Berne Convention implicitly designates the human creator, rather than juridical persons, as the author and initial copyright owner).

Convention does, however, announce that authors are "entitled to institute infringement proceedings in the countries of the Union," and that authorship status shall be presumed if the author's name "appear[s] on the work in the usual manner."[74] If authors may enforce copyright, it follows that they are, at least initially, the owners of the rights they seek to enforce. On the other hand, the Berne Convention does not *require* that the actual creator's name appear on the work in the usual manner. As a result, its coverage of "authorship" and ownership is only partial. The TRIPS Agreement and the WCT do not supply further guidance.

With respect to the subject matter of copyright, the Berne Convention does not articulate a standard of originality, and thus may leave open the possibility of national variation.[75] TRIPS and the WCT, however, have closed that gap, at least in part, by imposing an "intellectual creation" standard for computer software and databases;[76] as with the E.U.'s "author's own intellectual creation" standard, this threshold for originality may be generalized across copyrighted works.[77] The TRIPS and WCT also specify that "Copyright protection extends to expressions, and not to ideas, procedures, methods of operation or mathematical concepts as such,"[78] but do not define the excluded elements. As domestic case law, at least in the U.S., reveals, courts may differ as to what constitutes an "idea" or "method of operation."[79] Perhaps countries party to the TRIPS and/or WCT will so diverge as well, leaving open the possibility that the same work may be copyrightable in one country, but not another.

With respect to the scope of rights and of exceptions, the 1971 Berne Convention text tended to address specific issues, rather than synthesizing rights and exceptions. The TRIPS and WCT, however, have undertaken the synthesis, and thus have largely filled gaps left by the Berne Convention's rather more pointillist approach.[80] Two significant gaps nonetheless remain. First, although art. 6*bis* of the Berne Convention requires Union members to protect authors' rights of attribution and of integrity, the TRIPS explicitly excludes art. 6*bis* from its incorporation of Berne Convention norms.[81] As a practical matter, this leaves a gap because failure to implement unincorporated Berne Convention norms carries no meaningful sanction, while non-compliance with TRIPS obligations can lead to trade sanctions against the recalcitrant country.[82] Second, while the Berne Convention does not specify a right to

---

[74]Berne Conv., art. 15.1.

[75]*See* Jane C. Ginsburg, *Surveying the Borders of Copyright*, 41J. COPYR. SOC. 322, 327 (1994).

[76]TRIPS, art. 10; WCT, art. 5 (databases).

[77]. . . Query whether the EU's "*author's own* intellectual creation" standard (emphasis supplied) is higher than the TRIPS-WCT "intellectual creation" standard.

[78]TRIPS, art. 9.2; WCT art. 2.

[79]*Compare* Lotus v. Borland, 49 F.3d 807 (1st Cir. 1995), *aff'd. by an equally divided court*, 116 S.Ct. 804 (1996) (spreadsheet program's menu commands held a "method of operation") with American Dental Association v. Delta Dental Plans Ass'n., 126 F.3d 977 (7th Cir. 1997) ("taxonomy," system of classifying dental procedures, held not a "method of operation").

[80]*Compare* Berne Conv. Arts. 10 (certain exceptions), 10*bis* (certain exceptions), 11 (certain public performance rights), 11*bis* (broadcasting rights), 11*ter* (certain public performance rights) *with* TRIPS art. 13 (exceptions); WCT arts. 8 (right of communication to the public); 10 (exceptions and limitations).

[81]*See* TRIPS, art. 9.1.

[82]*See* TRIPS, art. 64 (dispute settlement). . . .

distribute copies, both the TRIPS and WCT do; both treaties, however, explicitly leave it to member countries to determine under what circumstances, if any, that right will be deemed exhausted.[83]

Finally, it is important to note that the rights concerned are minimum rights: signatory countries may provide for greater rights than those required, so long as they accord national treatment.[84] Similarly, the treaties set forth maximum exceptions: signatory countries *may* restrict the scope of protection, to the extent permitted by the treaties, but signatories are not obliged to impose all (or any) of the limitations that the treaties authorize. This means that multilateral instruments set a floor, but no ceiling, for the scope of copyright protection. National copyright laws thus retain a role to set the upper limits of copyright, by affording greater rights, or by selecting which permitted exceptions to impose.

2. EU Directives

The European Union, however, by imposing certain restrictions on the scope of copyright, and by giving greater detail to permitted exceptions, has constricted the role of national law to vary the height of the ceiling, as we have already seen. On the other hand, if the mandatory exceptions ensure that member States must impose a ceiling on copyright, member States nonetheless may further drop the ceiling by adopting some or all of the various Directives' authorized (as opposed to obligatory) exceptions. For example, one E.U. member State may exempt certain uses of works on behalf of the visually-or hearing-impaired (subject to "equitable compensation"), as authorized by art. 5.3(b) of the Draft Information Society Directive, while another may choose not to limit copyright in that way. Thus, exceptions to copyright remain an area of potential, albeit tempered, disparity within the E.U.

Regarding the rights protected, the Duration Directive specifies that it does not purport to harmonize moral rights; none of the other Directives touches moral rights either.[86] Thus, the content, as well as the duration, of rights of attribution, and particularly of integrity, may vary considerably among the fifteen member States.

But the principal gaps in the E.U. regime concern authorship and ownership. The Directives continue to tolerate divergent national laws governing authorship status, initial rights ownership, and presumptions of transfer. With respect to authorship status, for example, the Software Directive and the Database Directive leave to national law the determination of whether the "author" may be a juridical, as well as a natural, person.[87] Those Directives, as well as the Duration Directive, refer to joint works and to collective works, but do not define these terms.[88] Indeed, the Rental Right Directive and the Satellite Directive explicitly permit member States to designate whom, in addition to the

---

[83] *See* TRIPS, art. 6; WCT, art. 6.2.

[84] *See* TRIPS, art. 3; Berne Conv., art. 19.

[86] *See* Duration Directive, art. 9; Recital 21.

[87] *See* Software Directive, art. 2.1; Database Directive, art. 4.1.

[88] *See* Software Directive, art. 2.1; Database Directive, art. 4.2; Duration Directive, arts. 1.2, 1 4.

principal director, shall be considered a co-author of an audiovisual work.[89] Different national laws may supply differing definitions, not only of who is a co-author, but of the category of joint works. For example, are "joint works" only those in which the contributions are inseparable, or may they also be discrete, but interdependent, as are the music and lyrics comprising a song?[90] It seems that the Directives deliberately avoid more precise definition of joint works. Indeed, the Duration Directive appears to want it both ways: art. 1.4 provides that either the duration for a single authored work, *or* the duration for a work of joint authorship shall apply to "identified authors whose *identified contributions* are included in [collective] works." (Emphasis supplied.)[91] To be "identified," the "contributions" would be interdependent, rather than inseparable; the Directive thus leaves it to national law to determine whether such contributions should be considered individual or joint works.

With respect to initial rights ownership, the Software, Duration, and Database Directives allow those member countries that vest initial ownership in collective works (a term the Directives do not define) in juridical persons, to continue to do so.[92]

With respect to presumptions of transfer, the Rental Right Directive permits member States to provide for presumptions of transfer of rental rights from authors to the film producer.[93] The Directives do not require revision of national laws setting forth other presumptions of transfer from authors to film producers, producers of collective works, or other employers or commissioning parties.

. . . .

III. WHAT ROLE *SHOULD* REMAIN FOR NATIONAL COPYRIGHT LAW IN AN ERA OF INTERNATIONAL NORMS?

International uniformity of substantive norms favors the international dissemination of works of authorship. If the goal is to foster the world-widest possible audience for authors in the digital age, then one might conclude that national copyright norms are vestiges of the soon-to-be-bygone analog world. But not all copyright exploitations occur over digital networks, and, more importantly, national laws remain relevant, even for the Internet.

Two principal areas for national preservation are copyright ownership and exceptions. But the interplay of these national norms with choice of law rules should differ. In the case of allocation of ownership rights, the multilateral

---

[89]*See* Rental Right Directive, art. 2.2; Satellite Directive, art. 1.5.

[90]*Compare* Federal Republic of Germany, Copyright Law of 1965 (as amended), art. 8.1 (joint works are those whose "respective contributions cannot be separately identified"); U.K., 1988 Copyright Designs and Patents Act, art. 10(1) ("contribution of each author is not distinct from that of the other author or authors") *with* Belgium, Copyright Law of June 30, 1994, art. 5.1 (joint works contributions may be "individualized"); France, Code of Intellectual Property, art. L-113-2.1 (joint work is "a work in the creation of which more than one natural person has participated").

[91]*See* Duration Directive, art. 1.1 (single authored work's duration), 1.2 (joint work's duration), 1.4 (collective work's duration).

[92]*See* Software Directive, art. 1.2, Duration Directive, art. 1.4; Database Directive, art. 4.1.

[93]*See* Rental Right Directive, art. 1.6.

treaties' and E.U. Directives' deference to national law in matters of copyright ownership indicates that national norms regarding employment or commissioned work relations should prevail. Not only should these norms govern within the territory of the State from which the work originates, but also in other countries in which the work is exploited. Choice of law rules should designate a single applicable law, that of the country with the most significant relationship to the work's creation.[110] Other countries rarely have an interest in contravening employer-employee (or commissioned work) relationships among foreign parties. (To the extent they do, they may assert that interest by way of the *ordre public* exception.) Hence, with respect to copyright ownership, national norms continue to play an important role, but only one national norm per controversy, rather than all national norms simultaneously.

Regarding exceptions to copyright, by contrast, a stronger case may be made for application of each country's laws on its own territory. While international instruments impose a general framework, they preserve some national autonomy regarding the content (and, outside the E.U., the form) of copyright exceptions. Thus, the flexible (perhaps unpredictable) U.S. fair use exception may co-exist with a more rigid continental-style closed list of specific exemptions and limitations.[117] Arguably, the multilateral instruments' tolerance of substantive diversity says nothing about whether a single national norm limiting copyright should apply (for example, the law of the country from which the work is made available to the public, particularly via digital communications), or whether each country of receipt should apply its own norms regarding exceptions and limitations. Several considerations nonetheless point toward discrete territorial application of local norms limiting copyright, even for digital transmissions.

National legislatures establish copyright exceptions for the benefit of local users. This is particularly true of the "pork barrel" and "subsidy" kinds of limitations.[118] For example, the U.S. may wish (perhaps in contravention of its TRIPS obligations) to exempt small businesses and restaurants from paying performance rights royalties for radio and television performances;[119] there is no reason that this solicitude should benefit restaurants outside the U.S. Or the German federal legislature may compel authors to subsidize German schools by subjecting works used in school anthologies to compulsory licensing;[120] there is no reason this subsidy should extend to schools outside Germany, in countries that lack similar provisions.

Even with respect to free speech-motivated exceptions, such as criticism, commentary and parody, in the absence of greater international harmonization, local norms should determine how much free or price-controlled use the exception permits. For example, the Draft Information Society Directive

---

[110]This is usually the country of origin, but it could also be the one whose law is designated in the employment or commissioned work contract.

[117]*Compare* 17 U.S.C. § 107 (fair use) *with* Draft Information Society Directive, art. 5.2-3 (list of authorized exceptions).

[118]*See* Jane C. Ginsburg, *Copyright or "Infograb"? Comment on General Report on Limitations Found Outside Copyright* (forthcoming in the proceedings of ALAI Study Days, Cambridge, U.K. 1998).

[119]*See* 17 U.S.C. § 110(5)(B) . . . .

[120]German copyright law, art. 46.

permits quotation for purposes of criticism or review, if the use is "in accordance with fair practice, and to the extent required by the specific purpose."[121] Fair practice according to each member State's norms? According to a harmonized E.U. norm? National norms of fairness may differ: for example, the *revue de presse* may be a tradition in some countries, but not in others.[122] It is not obvious that an extensive *revue de presse* exception in the country from which the work is made available to the public should apply in countries of receipt that lack such an exception.

If the country of a digital communication's origin should not extrude its copyright exceptions to countries of receipt, what about the reverse proposition? Should countries of receipt apply their own exceptions, regardless of the law of the country of departure? Suppose for example, that a U.S. party made available over a digital network (and U.S.-based server) a parody whose copying exceeded U.S. fair use bounds, but was consonant with French practice. Should France apply its exception to parodies received in France? Outside the context of digital communications, for example, were the parody of a U.S. work created or exploited by analog media in France, principles of national treatment would subject the U.S. work to the same copyright limitations as French works incur. While simplicity, and ease of international commerce, counsel against the same result when a work is simultaneously made available in innumerable countries via the Internet, logical consistency would retain the application of the national norm. Moreover, the norm is an expression of the receiving country's cultural and information policy, manifested here by a choice to enhance its residents' exposure to certain kinds of works based on or incorporating portions of copyrighted works (e.g., parody). To the extent that the receiving country can apply its norm, without foisting that norm on other countries, it should be able to do so.

Conclusion

"International copyright" can no longer accurately be described as a "bundle" consisting of many separate sticks, each representing a distinct national law, tied together by a thin ribbon of Berne Convention supranational norms. Today's international copyright more closely resembles a giant squid, whose many national law tentacles emanate from but depend on a large common body of international norms. (At the risk of excessively pursuing this mollusk-ular metaphor, I would further note that the squid's body houses its ink; since we all know what happens when a squid releases its ink, we shall hope that this does not foretell an obscure future for international norms.) In the meantime, while international norms continue to constrain, if not supercede, national copyright laws, some national norms remain significant. Sometimes national norms persist by designed deference to local labor and cultural policies, as seems to be the case with copyright ownership, and may be the case with exceptions and

---

[121]Draft Information Society Directive, art. 5.3(d).

[122]*Compare*, German copyright law, art. 49.1; France CPI, art. L-122-5, 3o(b) (both specifying *revue de presse* exceptions) *with* U.K. CDPA, art. 30; Belgian copyright law, arts. 21-22 (neither specifying a *revue de presse* exception).

limitations on copyright. Sometimes, however, national norms endure from a failure of the political will of the drafters of multilateral instruments, as may also be the case with exceptions and limitations on copyright.

GILLIAN DAVIES, THE CONVERGENCE OF COPYRIGHT AND AUTHORS' RIGHTS—REALITY OR CHIMERA?*
26 I.I.C. 964 (1995)

Introduction

The distinctions between the principles governing copyright protection in common law countries and those governing authors' rights *(droit d'auteur, derecho de autor, Urheberrecht)* in countries of civil law tradition, have been thrown into sharp relief since 1988 in various contexts. Perhaps the most important development in the international copyright/authors' rights world of this period was the adherence of the United States of America to the Berne Convention for the Protection of Literary and Artistic Works (the Berne Convention) in 1989. The US copyright tradition has thereafter had a considerably greater impact than hitherto on international developments in this area and the policy differences between the USA and other Berne Union members have been highlighted.

In the 1990s, that development was followed by the negotiations leading to the adoption in April 1994 of the Agreement on Trade-Related Aspects of Intellectual Property, Including Trade in Counterfeit Goods (the TRIPS Agreement), as part of the GATT Uruguay Round of trade negotiations and the simultaneous discussions under the auspices of WIPO on a possible Protocol to the Berne Convention and a New Instrument for the Protection of Producers of Phonograms and Performers, which are still continuing.** The harmonisation programme of the European Commission has also drawn attention to the difficulties of reconciling different approaches to the protection of the various categories of right owners protected by copyright and authors' rights respectively.

. . . .

Are the Copyright and *Droit d'Auteur* Systems Converging?

Having considered the nature of the principal divergences between the systems, the question now to be answered is whether the gap between the two systems has been or is being bridged within the contexts of both the Berne Union and the Rome Convention and as a result of increased intergovermental cooperation on the subject, in connection with the TRIPS negotiations, the

---

*Reprinted with permission of Max Planck Institute for Foreign and International Patent, Copyright, and Competition Law, Wiley-VCH Publishers and Gillian Davies.

**[Ed. Note: These discussions led to the December 1996 adoption of the WCT and WPPT, discussed above.]

current WIPO legislative programme and, finally, under the harmonisation programme of the European Union. And, if so, to what extent?

Converging Influence of the Berne Convention

Historically, since its adoption in 1886, the Berne Convention and its successive revision conferences served as a forum in which the differences of approach of the civil law and common law systems could generally be accommodated, and the successive Acts of the Convention were framed in such a way as to obtain the adherence of countries of both civil law and common law traditions. The Convention was influenced by national law developments, adding new subject-matter of protection as time went by (e.g. cinematographic works were added to the list of works in Art. 2(l) of the Berne Convention at Brussels in 1948)[33] and became a harmonising influence on national laws. For example, in the case of the term of protection, increased at Berlin in 1908 to 50 years *post mortem auctoris* (pma), many countries including Britain and Germany had to amend their laws so as to conform with the Convention. As regards the authorship of films, the Berne Convention provided a compromise according to which the determination of the ownership of copyright in a film was left to national legislation in the country where protection is claimed, thus embracing both the civil law approach of considering the individual creators to be co-authors and the common law approach whereby the producer was recognised as the author.[34]

Moral rights were not dealt with by the Convention until 1928, when Art. 6*bis* was introduced in the Rome Act of the Convention. As Dworkin has pointed out, this was a compromise draft that was acceptable to the common law countries since it refrained from requiring national copyright laws to contain express moral rights provisions, but also tacitly acknowledged that the protection then offered at common law and equity by the common law countries was adequate for the purposes of the new provision.

The influence of the moral rights provision of the Berne Convention has gradually had an impact on the major common law jurisdictions. The United Kingdom introduced specific protection for moral rights in the 1988 Copyright Act. The United States of America on joining the Berne Union declared that the existing protection afforded authors under a great many common law precedents, state statutes and federal laws satisfied its obligations under Berne, and the moral rights doctrine was not incorporated expressly in US law. Moreover, in 1990, Congress enacted the Visual Artists Rights Act, which affords limited rights of attribution and integrity to a narrowly defined class of visual artists with respect to certain artistic works and photographs.

The United States also brought its legislation into line with the Berne Convention by abolishing the formalities previously required for the subsistence of copyright and by providing for a term of protection based on the life of the

---

[33]The Berne Convention had in fact accorded protection to certain kinds of cinematographic production since the Berlin Act 1908 (Art. 14(2) and (3)).

[34]*Cf.* Berne Convention, art. 14*bis*(2)(a).

author and 50 years thereafter.

There is one area, however, where no consensus has been reached to date in the Berne Union and which remains controversial. When, at successive Berne Convention revision Conferences (Berlin, Rome and Brussels), the British delegation proposed adding sound recordings, protected by copyright in the UK and other common law countries, to the list of works to be protected under Art. 2 of the Convention, the suggestion was rejected.[37] Throughout that period, the need for specific protection of sound recordings in civil law countries was barely recognised and at the Brussels Conference a resolution was passed suggesting instead that the matter be dealt with separately and considered together with two other candidates for protection, broadcasts and performances. This proposal led, after many years of negotiation, to the adoption of the Rome Convention in 1961 and formalised the basic divergence between the common law and civil law traditions on this issue, creating the new category of rights, rights neighbouring on authors' rights, already referred to.

Diverging Influence of the Rome Convention

Following the adoption of the Rome Convention in 1961, many civil law countries revised their legislation to conform to the categorisation example of the Convention. Thus, countries which had previously incorporated the protection of sound recordings in their authors' rights legislation, often by extension of the existing law to the new category of works by legislation or case law (see, e.g., the cases of Spain[39] and Germany[40]), when revising their legislation distinguished clearly between literary and artistic works on the one hand and neighbouring or related rights on the other. Meanwhile, the common law countries continued to protect sound recordings under their copyright laws.[41] This difference of approach remains a thorny issue, particularly as concerns sound recordings, and has been the subject of dispute during the negotiations on the TRIPS Agreement and concerning a possible Protocol to the

---

[37]See RICKETSON, THE BERNE CONVENTION, at 6.78 *et seq*. Ricketson points out (at 6.76) that the exclusion of sound recordings is anomalous in view of the protection of cinematographic and photographic works under the Berne Convention and suggests this is better explained in terms of history than any argument based on the relative merits of the skills and originality required for each kind of production. The exclusion appears even more anomalous now that computer programs and databases are accepted as meeting the requirements of the Berne Convention. The originality in the selection, coordination or arrangement of the recorded performance is as much a creation as the selection, coordination or arrangement of data.

[39]Decree of 10 July 1942 conferring on phonographic works the character of works protected by the Law of Intellectual Property, 1879.

[40]Prior to the 1965 Act, the protection of performers and producers of phonograms was governed by the Act Concerning Copyright in Literary and Musical Works, of 19 June 1901, as amended in 1910, and the Act extending the term of copyright protection of 13 December 1934. Section 2(2) of the Act, as amended in 1910, assimilated recordings of literary and musical works to adaptations of those works. The performer was the beneficiary of the right, the producer acquiring rights of his own by contract. According to ULMER, 1961 *Le Droit d'auteur* 14, the intention of the legislature was to protect the record producer against unauthorised reproduction.

[41]The major exception to this rule was the United States of America, which did not introduce specific federal protection under the copyright law for sound recordings until 1971 (Public Law 92-140 (92d Congress S. 646) of 15 October 1971).

Berne Convention (see below).

There has therefore developed a so-called international classification of rights as reflected in the international conventions—particularly the Berne Convention and the Rome Convention. As WIPO noted in connection with the preparation of a Model Law on Copyright in 1990:

> According to that classification, only the protection of literary and artistic works can be regarded as copyright protection; the protection of any productions not qualifying as literary and artistic works can either be called by their own name, e.g. the protection of performances, phonograms or broadcasts, or be referred to by the said general term—used for the sake of brevity—that is, the protection of neighbouring rights.

This classification argument overlooks the fact that it is for national legislation to determine what may or may not be considered to be a literary or artistic work under the Berne Convention. The definition of such works in Art. 2(1) is non-limitative and by merely listing examples allows member countries to go further and treat other productions in the literary, scientific and artistic domains as protected works. Moreover, the Rome Convention came into existence as a bridge-building exercise so as to provide a link for national treatment between those countries which protected certain subject-matter by means of copyright and, in many cases, under the Berne Convention, and those who were only prepared to do so under a related right and a separate Convention. It is not therefore a valid argument to suggest that countries are precluded by the existence of the Rome Convention from protecting this subject matter by copyright.

It is also often argued that the safeguard of copyright proper contained in Art. 1 of the Rome Convention establishes a hierarchy of rights and that the rights of beneficiaries of the Convention must be subordinated to the exercise of the rights of authors. It is clear from the General Report of the Diplomatic Conference for the adoption of the Rome Convention that this interpretation is incorrect. Article 1 is limited to making clear that the legal situation of the copyright owner is unaffected. Thus, as the WIPO Guide to the Convention states:

> Whenever, by virtue of the copyright law, the authorisation of the author is necessary for the reproduction or other use of his work, the need for this authorisation is not affected by the Convention. Conversely, when, by virtue of this Convention, the consent of the performer, recorder [sic] or broadcaster is necessary, the need for his consent does not disappear because authorisation by the author is also necessary.

However, on the positive side, although the Rome Convention owes its origins to differences in the civil law and common law traditions, in the long run it has exercised a profound influence on the development of national legislation in the field of copyright/authors' rights and related rights. Since at the time the Convention was adopted, there were very few countries whose legislation was in conformity with it in respect of all three of its beneficiaries, it has often been referred to as a pioneering Convention. Yet today there is hardly a new law passed in this area of law which does not provide protection for the beneficiaries of the Convention, whether by copyright or related rights. The scope of the protection given has tended also in recent years towards a standard similar to that afforded to copyright works proper and is substantially higher than the minimum standards laid down over 30 years ago in the Convention.

Impact of the TRIPS Agreement

The Agreement on Trade-Related Aspects of Intellectual Property Rights, Including Trade in Counterfeit Goods (the TRIPS Agreement), adopted in April 1994 in Marrakesh, as part of the successful outcome of the Uruguay Round of the GATT trade negotiations, contains in Section 1 of Part II, entitled "Standards Concerning the Availability, Scope and Use of Intellectual Property Rights," new international rules for the protection of "copyright and related rights." This is the most recent conventional text adopted in the area of copyright and related rights and its impact on the convergence between the common law and civil law approaches to these rights is therefore of particular interest.

. . . .

There is little in the TRIPS Agreement to illustrate a narrowing of the gap between the copyright and authors' rights approaches. As Correa has pointed out, "the negotiations in the copyright area were characterised by a North-North confrontation on a number of issues"[47] including the concept of the author as applied to various works and on the scope of protection accorded to them. The negotiations drew attention, in particular, to copyright policy differences between the United States of America on the one hand and other Berne Union members, including those of the European Union, on the other. The USA proposed a "Berne-Plus" package, including eight issues not covered by the Berne Convention:

(1) the right to control public distribution of copies of works, including parallel imports;

(2) rental rights for computer programs and sound recordings;

(3) a definition of the term "public", in relation to public performance rights;

(4) affirmation of the entitlement of a Member State of the Berne Convention to treat legal entities as authors in domestic legislation;

(5) copyright protection for sound recordings;

(6) an international "fair use" standard;

---

[47]CARLOS M. CORREA, *TRIPS Agreement: Copyright and Related Rights*, 25 I.I.C. 543 (1994).

(7) express incorporation into the Berne Convention of computer programs (as literary works) and databases (as works that would qualify under the Convention as collections or compilations);

(8) detailed enforcement obligations for the suppression of piracy.

Of these, only items (2), (6), (7) and (8) were expressly achieved. The right to control parallel importation, corporate authorship and copyright for sound recordings were rejected, although related rights to authorise or prohibit reproduction and commercial rental of sound recordings were recognised. In relation to corporate authorship, the US position was accommodated to the extent that Art. 12 of the TRIPS Agreement provides that, where the term of copyright protection of a work is calculated on a basis other than the life of a natural person, the term should be not less than 50 years. The USA succeeded, however, in its aim of excluding the moral rights provisions of the Berne Convention from the Agreement, so that to this extent it may be described as a "Berne-Minus" text. The proponents of the authors' rights approach ensured that databases would only merit protection as copyright works if they constituted intellectual creations and that sound recordings remained protected by means of related rights and not as works.

The rights of performers and producers of sound recordings have undoubtedly been strengthened as a result of the TRIPS Agreement in that it will be applicable to a very considerably larger number of States than the Rome Convention, which to date has less than 50 Member States. They will also benefit from a fifty-year term of protection.

The TRIPS Agreement would appear to have achieved the extremely important objective of establishing minimum international standards for the protection of intellectual property, including copyright and authors' rights and certain related rights. It has not, however, established a bridge between the different legal approaches to these latter rights. On the contrary, the negotiations would appear to have provided yet another forum for dogmatic defence of doctrinal differences. Indeed, the negotiations were characterised by what seems to have become a regular feature of intergovernmental discussions on these issues in recent years, namely what Cornish has described as "mutual incomprehension and . . . much sterile argument . . . over the comparative virtues of different national approaches" and the increasing entrenchment of the proponents of the various approaches in their divergent views.

WIPO Legislative Programme

Model Law on Copyright

The difficulties of reaching agreement on bridging the gap between the copyright and authors' rights approaches have been thrown into sharp relief in the context of the work of WIPO in this area over the past ten years or so. During the 1980s, WIPO held a series of meetings to discuss the copyright problems affecting various categories of works in the light of new technology.

These meetings were followed in 1989 and 1990 by three meetings of a Committee of Experts for the purpose of drafting a Model Law on Copyright. Difficulties arose from the outset. As the preparatory document for the last meeting noted: "The main dividing line seemed to be between delegations from countries with 'continental' (or 'Roman') legal traditions and delegations from countries with 'common law' (or 'Anglo-Saxon') traditions." On a number of issues, the advocates of the "continental" approach insisted that the Model Law should be based exclusively on that approach, arguing that only such provisions corresponded to the spirit and letter of the Berne Convention.

An important issue in this respect was sound recordings. As already discussed, many common law countries protect these as copyright works and indeed there are also countries which protect them specifically as literary and artistic works. There were, therefore, calls for sound recordings to be covered by the model law. WIPO considered them to fall within the category of related or so-called neighbouring rights, however, and described the problem thus:

> The protection of the so-called neighbouring rights is one of the points where the "common law" and the "continental" copyright approaches differ from each other, although the difference seems, in general, more of a terminological nature than of a really substantive one. The notion of "copyright" is used in a wider meaning in countries with "common law" traditions than the one in which this word is used in respect of the Berne Convention . . . In the face of the differing meanings of the notions of "copyright" and "neighbouring rights", the draft model law followed the international classification of the various productions involved as reflected in the international conventions—particularly the Berne Convention and the Rome Convention—administered by WIPO. According to that classification, only the protection of literary and artistic works can be regarded as copyright protection; . . . [T]he Model Law . . . therefore . . . should only cover the protection of literary and artistic works and should not extend to the so-called neighbouring rights.

This approach was endorsed by the continental law countries, while the common law countries argued forcefully but in vain for sound recordings to be included, the United States stressing "that the future of the Berne Convention depended, to a large extent, on the constructive coexistence and cooperation between the 'continental' and 'common law' approaches."

Possible New Protocol to the Berne Convention

The work on the Model Law set the scene for continuing disagreement on these issues in WIPO's subsequent work. Positions had become polarised by the time work began on the proposed new Protocol to the Berne Convention in 1991. It had become apparent by 1990 that there was a need for a new international instrument to update the Berne Convention in order to deal with the technical developments which had emerged since the adoption of the Paris Act 1971 and to remedy shortcomings in the standards of protection set thereby. Thus, the purpose of the Protocol, according to WIPO's programme, was to clarify the existing or establish new international standards where, under the present text of the Berne Convention, doubts existed as to the extent to which the Convention applied to certain subject-matters of protection and certain rights. The desirability of covering the rights of producers of sound recordings in the protocol was also to be examined.

. . . After the first two meetings [of the Committee of Experts responsible for the Protocol], its terms of reference were modified, mainly because it had not been possible to reach agreement on the inclusion of the protection of producers of sound recordings in the possible Protocol. The outcome of the discussion on this issue was described in the following terms by a US representative.

> To the United States, the Protocol was not only an instrument that would advance the norms of the Berne Convention. It would also act as a "bridge" convention between countries that favour neighbouring rights protection for sound recordings, and those that favour copyright. . . .We wanted to reconcile differences between how Europe protects record producers and performers and how we protect authors of sound recordings—in short, a bridge between the principles of authorship, subject matter and ownership which the US brings to Berne and others have brought to the Rome Convention. It went down in flames. . . .

. . . A separate Committee of Experts on a Possible Instrument for the Protection of the Rights of Performers and Producers of Phonograms (sound recordings) was established to discuss all questions concerning the effective international protection of the rights of performers and producers of sound recordings. . . .

All this has served only to emphasise and deepen differences of approach and to confirm the international classification of rights according to the continental law system, with a sharp divide between authors' rights and related rights.

Harmonisation Within the European Union

The past twenty years have seen astonishing progress in the harmonisation of the national laws of the present Member States of the European Union in the field of copyright/authors' rights and related rights. . . .

Quite apart from any measures taken by the Commission, the individual Member States of the Community have been faced with the need to modernise their laws in the area of copyright/authors' rights and related rights in the light of technical developments and of the new categories, and new uses, of works requiring protection. Thus, since 1974, all twelve of the [then] current Member States of the European Union have legislated in this area. Within the present Union, there are of course representatives of both the common law and continental law approaches to copyright/ authors' rights and the influence of the

Commission's harmonisation programme on bridging the gap between the two is discussed below. What is noticeable, however, is the extent to which in the last twenty years the differences in approach to the protection of related rights have narrowed, both under the influence of the Rome Convention and as a result of the phenomenon of piracy of sound recordings which first became a serious problem in the 1970s and drew attention to the need for adequate protection for producers of sound recordings and performers in this context. In 1974, of the then twelve Member States of the European Union, only six provided any specific protection for one or more of the beneficiaries of the Rome Convention, namely Denmark, the Federal Republic of Germany, Ireland, Italy, Spain and the United Kingdom. Of these, only Ireland and the United Kingdom provided any such protection for a period of 50 years. In the meantime, all the present fifteen EU Member States have legislated to provide a level of protection for the beneficiaries of the Rome Convention which is generally higher than the minimum provided for therein. Of the former twelve Member States, only Luxembourg and Spain still have to bring their legislation into line by extending the period of protection afforded to these categories of right owners to 50 years, this already having been achieved in the other ten. Of the three new Member States, Austria needs to prolong the period of protection for broadcasting organisations from 30 to 50 years.

In this respect, therefore, there has been a considerable bridging of the gap between the countries of common and civil law traditions within the European Union, even though producers of sound recordings and broadcasters benefit from copyright protection and are recognised as authors in Ireland and the UK, while in the other Member States they are protected by virtue of related rights. Thus while a difference of philosophy remains, in practice, the level of protection, in terms of rights, duration and remedies, afforded to authors and related rights owners is already similar and this process will be carried further once all Member States have brought their laws into line with the provisions of the various Directives referred to above insofar as they deal with related rights.

In recent years, however, as a result both of decisions of the European Court and of the various Directives referred to above adopted as a result of the copyright harmonisation programme of the European Commission, a bridging of the gap is beginning to be perceived in relation to copyright/authors' rights proper. The first area in which an approximation of the common law and civil law systems can be observed is in the treatment of the issue of originality in Community legislation. Within the Member States, there were as many as three approaches: (i) the common law approach of the UK and Ireland requiring the expenditure of skill, labour and judgement and that the work must originate from the author; (ii) the generally recognised civil law approach according to which the work must be an expression of the personality of the author; (iii) finally, the very high standard set in Germany where a personal intellectual creation is required. There, in interpreting this requirement, the courts have applied qualitative tests concerning the level of skill used, in relation in particular to computer programs.[63]

---

[63]Copyright Act 1965, Sec. 2(2); and *see* Federal Supreme Court. Case No. IZR 52/83, *Inkasso-Programm*, 17 IIC 681 (1986).

In reconciling these standards the computer program Directive defines original as "original in the sense that it is the authors' own intellectual creation" and making it clear that no other criteria are to be applied to determine the eligibility of a computer program for protection. This steers a middle course, ruling out the high standards set by Germany but requiring a higher standard than that of the common law test for originality in that the creation has to be *intellectual*. The same definition of originality has also been used by the Commission in other Directives, in relation to photographs in Art. 6 of the Directive on Duration and to databases in Art. 2(3) of the draft Directive on Databases.

The issue of the authorship of legal entities (corporate authorship) has also arisen in relation to the authorship of films. In the UK and Ireland, the film producer is to date considered the author of the film, whereas in the civil law countries of the Community various creative contributors to the making of the film are considered to be co-authors, subject to presumptions of assignments of their economic rights to the producers. The Community compromised by providing that "the principal director of a cinematographic or audiovisual work shall be considered as its author or one of its authors. Member States may provide for others to be considered as its co-authors" (Rental Directive, Art. 2(2)). This definition has been repeated in the Satellite Directive (Art. 1(5)) and in the Directive on Duration (Art. 2(1)). This compromise will enable the UK and Ireland to continue to treat the producer as the author of a film but will force them to change their laws in order to provide that the principal director of a film is to be considered a co-author.

Finally, compromise has also been reached in relation to works made in the course of employment. In the UK and Ireland (in this case joined by the Netherlands), where a work is made in the course of employment, the employer is deemed to be the copyright owner in the absence of any agreement to the contrary; whereas, in the continental countries copyright vests in the author of the work in the first place. The Computer Program Directive follows the common law approach so far as economic rights are concerned. Article 2(3) reads: "Where a computer program is created by an employee in the execution of his duties or following the instructions given by his employer, the employer exclusively shall be entitled to exercise all economic rights in the program so created unless otherwise provided by contract."

Here the compromise lies in the fact that the moral rights remain with the employee author; although in the case of computer programs this seems a questionable proposition, especially in the light of protection for a duration of 70 years *post mortem auctoris*.

The same solution has been applied in the draft Database Directive for databases made in the course of employment (Art. 3(4)).

However, the dividing line between authors' rights and related rights has been emphasised in the Directive on Duration. The Directive provides for a uniform period of protection of 70 years *p.m.a.* for authors, while as regards related rights, the period of protection is set at 50 years from publication or communication to the public. This poses a problem for Ireland and the United Kingdom, which both protect producers of sound recordings and broadcasters as authors of copyright works. It would seem that the Directive precludes them from granting these right owners protection for 70 years as that would defeat the object of harmonisation. The result will be to introduce a new distinction between various categories of authors under the national laws of these countries.

While the various compromises on matters of principle referred to may not appear very daring, they nevertheless will lead to harmonisation on topics of great importance where the common law and civil law approaches were previously opposed. Standards of originality, corporate authorship and employed authorship are key issues in copyright law. They also go further than any other international harmonisation initiatives to date in bridging the gap between the two approaches. The impact of these developments on the international copyright scene is likely to be important. As Loewenheim has observed: "Even if this process may have direct effects only in the Member States, one should not forget that meanwhile the European Union represents a powerful economic and political factor which is likely to have considerable influence on the future development of copyright in the world." The dominant role of the European Union in this respect has also been noted by Oman, who commented in 1993 on the "forceful emergence of the Commission of the European Communities as the copyright arbiter of western Europe and the shaper of every copyright law from Dublin to Vladivostok." [cit].

NOTES AND QUESTIONS

(1) **The Role for National Law**. What should be the role, if any, for national copyright law in the twenty-first century? If Professor Ginsburg is correct that exceptions and limitations reflect local cultural policies and priorities, to what extent should international harmonization intrude? What does this mean for the concept of "substantive maxima" raised *supra* § 4.06[B]? Is your answer different in the digital environment? To what extent is the use of choice of law rules an appropriate alternative to harmonization? *See infra* § 7.05[A].

(2) **Copyright and *Droit d'Auteur***. What is *your* perception of how much influence the difference between copyright and *droit d'auteur* systems has had on the development of international copyright law and policy? Would the differences that remain in national copyright laws (for example, as to the work for hire doctrine) exist were it not for the divergent philosophies underlying the copyright and *droit d'auteur* systems? If the gap between national laws based on these different systems is narrowing, what does this augur for the long-term development of international copyright law?

(3) **Universal Copyright Code?** Would the best solution to the issues discussed in this Chapter be the development of a universal copyright code applicable in all countries? *See* J.A.L. STERLING, WORLD COPYRIGHT LAW 709-11 (1998) (suggesting that policymakers move toward a "unified global system of copyright"); J.A.L. Sterling, *International Codification of Copyright Law: Possibilities and Imperatives*, 6 INTERNATIONAL INTELLECTUAL PROPERTY LAW AND POLICY § 37-1 (Hansen ed. 2001).

Chapter 5

DISPUTES BETWEEN STATES

In this Chapter, we discuss the different means by which state to state disputes regarding international intellectual property law may be resolved. The conclusion of the TRIPS Agreement, and the incorporation of TRIPS within the WTO dispute settlement system, has revolutionized this subject. There were, however, disputes between states regarding appropriate levels of international intellectual property protection prior to the TRIPS Agreement. We start this Chapter with a brief consideration of how disputes were handled before TRIPS, and continue with discussion of the unilateral trade measures (adopted primarily by the United States) that might be seen as a transitional stage on the road to TRIPS. These materials not only place the TRIPS Agreement in historical perspective, but remain relevant because resort to these alternative means of resolving disputes provides the backdrop against which any rejection or revision of TRIPS and/or WTO dispute settlement will take place. The materials also raise in stark relief issues concerning the relationship between developed and developing countries that the conclusion of the TRIPS Agreement may temporarily obscure, but which we fully expect to occupy much of the post-TRIPS debate.

§ 5.01   Dispute Resolution in WIPO-Administered Treaties

Both of the leading pre-TRIPS multilateral intellectual property conventions, the Paris Convention and the Berne Convention, made provision for the submission of disputes to the International Court of Justice. *See* Berne Convention art. 33(1); Paris Convention art. 28(1). This mechanism was never used. Moreover, no state invoked the doctrine of retaliation and retorsion under public international law, as a state could have done if it believed another country was in violation of its treaty obligations. *See* J.H. Reichman, *Enforcing the Enforcement Procedures of the TRIPS Agreement*, 37 VA. J. INT'L L. 335, 339 n.17 (1997). Why do you think that neither the express mechanism of the International Court of Justice referral nor the general remedies of public international intellectual property law were used?

WIPO has also sought to create intellectual property-specific dispute resolution mechanisms. In particular, prior to the conclusion of TRIPS it convened a Committee of Experts to consider a proposed Dispute Resolution Treaty. Although the Committee of Experts continued to meet post-TRIPS, the accommodation of the Paris and Berne Conventions within the TRIPS/WTO dispute settlement mechanism has made this proposed treaty a lesser priority and it is barely an active issue at WIPO. What relevance might it still have? If you were in charge of setting priorities at WIPO, where would the conclusion of such a treaty fit on your list? Reconsider this question after reading the materials on WTO Dispute Resolution.

§ 5.02   Unilateral Trade Measures

[A]   The United States: Special 301

KIM NEWBY, THE EFFECTIVENESS OF SPECIAL 301 IN CREATING LONG TERM COPYRIGHT PROTECTION FOR U.S. COMPANIES OVERSEAS[*]
21 SYRACUSE J. INT'L L. & COM. 29, 32-62 (1995)

III. THE DEVELOPMENT OF SPECIAL 301

In 1974, the United States enacted the Trade Act of 1974 which provides for action to be taken against those trading partners of the U.S. that engage in "unfair competition."[25]   Title III of the Act, "Relief From Unfair Trade Practices," expands the ability of the United States to counter offensive trade practices by including, among other sections, Chapter 1, § 301, "Responses to certain trade practices of foreign governments."

Section 301 provided the President with broad authority to retaliate against both unreasonable as well as unjustifiable import restrictions that affect U.S. commerce. . . .   Retaliatory measures could include the suspension of trade benefits or the imposition of duties or other import restrictions on the products of the offending foreign country. [§ 301(a)].

The enacting of § 301 was seen as a direct result of Congressional dissatisfaction with the manner in which U.S. trade was being protected under GATT. Trade deficits in the United States were growing and the U.S. economy appeared to be suffering at the expense of the growth of other nations. The Legislative History is instructive in this regard. The History states that:

> The President ought to be able to act or threaten to act under section 301, whether or not such action would be entirely consistent with the General Agreement on Tariffs and Trade.   Many GATT

---

[*]Copyright 1995, Kim Newby; Syracuse Journal of International Law and Commerce. Reprinted with kind permission. Ms. Newby practices technology law in Boston, Massachusetts.

[25]Trade Act of 1974, Pub. L. No. 93-618 § 2, 88 Stat. 1978 (1975), Statement of General Purposes sets out that: The purposes of this Act are, through trade agreements affording mutual benefits–(1) to foster the economic growth of and full employment in the United States and to strengthen economic relations between the United States and foreign countries through open and nondiscriminatory world trade; (2) to harmonize, reduce, and eliminate barriers to trade on a basis which assures substantially equivalent competitive opportunities for the commerce of the United States; (3) to establish fairness and equity in international trading relations, including reform of the General Agreement on Tariffs and Trade; (4) to provide adequate procedures to safeguard American industry and labor against unfair or injurious import competition, and to assist industries, firms, workers, and communities to adjust to changes in international trade flows; (5) to open up market opportunities for United States commerce in nonmarket economies; and (6) to provide fair and reasonable access to products of less developed countries in the United States markets.

articles . . . are either inappropriate in today's economic world or are being observed more often in the breach, to the detriment of the United States. . . Congress is not urging that the United States undertake wanton or reckless retaliatory action under section 301 in total disdain of applicable international agreements. However, the Committee felt it was necessary to make it clear that the President could act to protect U.S. economic interests whether or not such action was consistent with the articles of an outmoded international agreement initiated by the Executive 25 years ago and never approved by Congress.[30]

Still unhappy with the growing budget deficits, Congress in 1988 enacted the Omnibus Trade and Competitiveness Act. Among the measures taken in this comprehensive trade legislation was an expansion of section 301 powers. The new § 301 takes the power of determining which countries to investigate and retaliate against out of the hands of the President and puts it into the hands of the United States Trade Representative ("USTR").[33] The revised § 301 also imposes strict time limits within which the USTR must act once an offending country is cited; previously no strict time limits were imposed. The corollary to this is that the USTR has no discretion to act once a country is cited; such action is mandatory. [O]ther amendments to § 301 caused significant controversy among U.S. trading partners. . . . [including] "Special 301."[36]

. . . .

Special 301 . . . addresses only the protection of U.S. intellectual property . . . . [It] requires that the USTR prepare an annual list of countries that allow the most flagrant violations of protection for U.S. intellectual property. The process of determining and naming these countries, along with a credible threat of retaliation against them, is the heart of Special 301 . . . .

IV. HOW SPECIAL 301 WORKS

A. Determination of Problem Countries

Each year by a specified time,[37] the USTR must identify countries that deny effective protection of intellectual property or equitable market access to United States persons who rely upon intellectual property protection. In addition, those countries that the USTR determines to be "Priority Foreign Countries" must be identified and reported in the Federal Register.

A Priority Foreign Country is a country: (1) that has the most "onerous or

---

[30]S. REP. NO. 1298, 93d Cong., 2d Sess. (1974), *reprinted in* 1974 U.S.C.C.A.N. 7186, 7304.

[33]The Office of the United States Trade Representative (USTR) was established in 1982 under 19 U.S.C. § 2171. The USTR is an office within the Executive Office of the President. The USTR is responsible for conducting international trade negotiations. [cit].

[36]19 U.S.C. §§ 2411-2420 (1988).

[37]Generally, by April 30 of each year.

egregious" practices that deny protection or equitable market access; (2) whose practices have the "greatest adverse impact," either actual or potential, on the relevant U.S. products; or (3) that is not engaging in good faith negotiations to provide effective protection of intellectual property rights. [19 U.S.C. § 2242 (b)(1).]

In order to make the determination of which countries' practices cause that country to rise to the level of Priority Foreign Country status, the USTR has a number of sources upon which to rely. The statute explicitly provides that the USTR shall confer with the Register of Copyrights, the Commissioner of Patents and Trademarks, and other "appropriate officers of the Federal government," in identifying Priority Foreign Countries. [19 U.S.C. § 2242 (b)(2)(A).] The USTR also must consider any sources that may be available to the USTR and such information as may be submitted to the USTR by interested persons.[41] Congressional hearings to discuss Special 301 are a good source of this information. During these hearings, Congress discusses the successes of Special 301 with the USTR and industry representatives. In addition, testimony is given as to which countries are the most problematic for certain industries with regard to intellectual property protection.[43]

The USTR determines that a country is denying adequate and effective protection of intellectual property rights if non-citizens of that country are denied adequate and effective means under the law to "secure, exercise, and enforce rights" related to intellectual property. [19 U.S.C. § 2242(d)(2).] A foreign country is deemed to deny fair and equitable market access if that country denies domestic market access to a product protected by copyright, patent or trademark and such denial is through laws or practices that violate provisions of international law or international agreements, or that constitute discriminatory non-tariff trade barriers. [19 U.S.C. § 2242(d)(3).]

Each year the USTR also identifies and publishes "priority watch list" and "watch list" countries. These lists are not required by statute, but the publishing of these lower level watch lists alerts countries that their practices are being monitored by the USTR. As such, these lists provide a significant deterrent on their own.

B. The Investigation

Once identified as a Priority Foreign Country, within thirty days the USTR must initiate an "investigation" against that country and its offending practices. [19 U.S.C. § 2412(b)(2)(A).] The only time that an investigation is not required in such situations is when the USTR determines that initiation of the

[41]The definition of an interested person "includes, but is not limited to, domestic firms and workers, representatives of consumer interests, United States product exporters, and any industrial user of any goods or services that may be affected" by actions taken under section 301. 19 U.S.C. § 2411(d)(9).

[43]In the 1993 Congressional hearings, for example, Nintendo of America and Cone Mills Corp. (textile manufacturer) as well as the U.S. Trademark Association, the Recording Industry of America, the International Intellectual Property Alliance, the Business Software Alliance, and the Pharmaceutical Manufacturers Association, all submitted testimony, among others.

investigation "would be detrimental to United States economic interests." [19 U.S.C. § 2412(b)(2)(A).] Any decision not to initiate an investigation, however, must be fully documented in a report to Congress. Such report must include the reasons for this decision and the U.S. interests that would be adversely affected by the investigation. [19 U.S.C. § 2412(b)(2)(C).]

[I]t is important to remember that even without the mandatory listing of Priority Foreign Countries under Special 301, Section 301 requires that an investigation be commenced against any country whenever the USTR determines that (1) the rights of the U.S. under trade agreements are being denied; or (2) any policy or practice of a foreign country denies U.S. benefits that it is entitled to under trade agreements, or is unjustifiable and burdens or restricts U.S. commerce. [19 U.S.C. § 2411(a)(1).] Unjustifiable or unreasonable policies or practices explicitly include any act, policy or practice that denies national or most-favored-nation treatment, denies the rights of establishment, or denies adequate and effective protection of intellectual property rights. [19 U.S.C. § 2411(d)(3)(B), (d)(4)(B).]

Under Section 301, an investigation shall be commenced either upon the independent decision of the USTR or upon the receipt of a petition by an interested party that the USTR decides to act upon. The decision to act upon any submitted petition must be made within forty-five days after the date of the USTR's receipt of such petition. [19 U.S.C. § 2412(a)(2).]

In either 301 action, however, once an investigation has been initiated, the USTR is required to request consultations with the foreign country to discuss the offending practices and a resolution of the situation. [19 U.S.C. § 2413(a)(1).] For matters involving the violation of a bilateral or multilateral trade agreement, the USTR must request that the formal dispute mechanism of the agreement involved be invoked if the two countries are not able to come to an agreement acceptable to the U.S. within a specified period of time. [19 U.S.C. § 2413(a)(2).] If no formal bilateral or multilateral agreement is involved, the USTR must conduct its investigation, consultations, and negotiations within a period of six months in most cases. This deadline may be extended to nine months if the USTR sees "substantial progress" in the Priority Foreign Country's drafting or implementing of measures that will provide effective protection of intellectual property rights. [19 U.S.C. § 2414(a)(3)(B).] On the basis of the consultations and negotiations conducted within the statutory deadlines, the USTR must make a final determination. The determination made by the USTR must be published in the Federal Register together with a description of the facts upon which the determination, either to proceed further or drop the matter, was made. [19 U.S.C. § 2414(c).] If the USTR finds that the violations that spawned the investigation do in fact exist and if no substantial progress has been taken by the Priority Foreign Country within the period of investigation, then the USTR must take action. [19 U.S.C. § 2411(a)(1).] This action generally must be taken within thirty days of the date of determination. [19 U.S.C. § 2415(a)(1).]

C. Taking Responsive Action

The Trade Representative has broad discretionary authority in deciding what actions to take against a Priority Foreign Country. The three main tools that the USTR may invoke are the suspension of trade benefits, the imposition of duties or other import restrictions, and the entering into of binding agreements committing the country either to stop the offending practices or provide the U.S. with compensatory trade benefits. [19 U.S.C. § 2411(c)(1).] The office of the USTR may choose to focus its actions on the entire Priority Foreign Country, or on particular goods or economic sectors of that country. The fact that not all of that country's goods or sectors of its economy are involved in the particular offending practice complained of does not preclude the USTR from targeting the entire country. [19 U.S.C. § 2411(c).] The USTR must, however, ensure that any action taken to eliminate a practice is imposed to affect the Priority Foreign Country in an amount that is "equivalent in value to the burden or restriction imposed by that country on United States commerce." [19 U.S.C. § 2411(a)(3).]

Once a measure is chosen, the USTR must monitor the implementation of the measure and any progress the country takes to change its practices to conform to U.S. requests. During monitoring, if the USTR determines that the Priority Foreign Country is not implementing a 301-imposed measure or agreement, the USTR may take further action as authorized in the act. [19 U.S.C. § 2416(b).] Conversely, if during the monitoring process the Priority Foreign Country removes the offending practices or if the burden on U.S. commerce begins to outweigh the benefits of the measures taken against the Priority Foreign Country, then the USTR may modify or terminate any action taken under 301. [19 U.S.C. § 2417.]

Although once the USTR identifies a Priority Foreign Country mandatory action against that country generally is required, action need not be taken in two situations. The first is when an arbitration committee (under GATT or bilateral agreement dispute resolution committees) determines that the practices complained of do not impair benefits to the U.S. under any trade agreement or do not violate rights of the United States. [19 U.S.C. § 2411(a)(2)(A).] The second situation is when the USTR finds one of the following: (1) that the country has taken or has agreed to take measures to eliminate the offending practices; (2) it is not possible for the country to take such measures, but compensatory trade benefits will be provided to the U.S.; (3) action against the country would have an adverse effect on the U.S. economy out of proportion to the benefits that would be achieved; or (4) action against the country would cause serious harm to the national security of the United States. [19 U.S.C. § 2411(a)(2)(B).] In these two situations, the USTR has the discretion to decide whether to take action or not.

V. SPECIAL 301 IN ACTION

. . . .

B. China

China began its Special 301 journey in 1991 when it was one of the first three countries to be named a Priority Foreign Country.[80] Failure to provide adequate patent protection and a marked lack of copyright protection for U.S. works, especially computer software programs, were the driving reasons behind putting China on this list.

Lengthy negotiations between the United States and China resulted in a comprehensive Memorandum of Understanding ("MOU"). This MOU was signed on January 17, 1992, just hours before U.S. retaliatory measures were to be implemented. Articles 1 and 2 of the MOU relate to patent rights. Article 3 sets out the steps China will take to implement an effective, world-standard copyright protection regime. These steps include acceding to the Berne Convention, acceding to the Geneva Convention (protection of phonograms), updating the Chinese copyright law to meet requirements of these two conventions, and, particularly, clarifying the rights of distribution that [apply] to all works and sound recordings, including rental rights and the rights of first sale. In addition, China agreed that by the time that China accede[d] to the Berne Convention, China [would] protect computer programs as literary works under the Berne Convention. Article 4 protects trade secrets as provided for under the Paris Convention for Protection of Industrial Property. Article 5 states that both Governments will provide effective measures to prevent infringement of intellectual property rights within their borders and yet in doing so "shall avoid creating obstacles to legitimate trade." Article 6 relates to consultations between the parties, and Article 7 states that as of the date that the MOU is signed, the U.S. will revoke China's designation as a Priority Foreign Country under the Special 301 provisions.

During the 1992 Senate hearings on Special 301, Senator Max Baucus (Mont.) called this result with China "the most important Special 301 victory to date." He stated of the process: "[U.S. trade negotiators] combined hard negotiations, solid deadlines and the credible threat of retaliation to reach this agreement. . . In the end, they were able to convince China to agree to a regime of intellectual property protection that is in some ways superior to what we were able to win in the draft GATT agreement." In 1992, China was one of eighteen Watch List countries, the lowest level of priority named by the USTR. The signing of an agreement with a country, however, is usually not enough. As stated in the 1993 Senate hearings by the General Counsel of the office of the USTR:

> The 1992 Memorandum of Understanding on intellectual property that was entered into with China, represented an enormous amount of progress with respect to the intellectual property regime of China.

---

[80] Up until this time, Special 301 had been used to name countries on the two Watch Lists only. In 1991 the Bush administration identified China, India and Thailand as the first Special 301 Priority Foreign Countries. [cit].

Now it will not be self- executing. What I tried to do in my testimony is to say that once other countries have adopted laws, we have to make sure that these laws are real.[87]

During those same hearings, there were calls to put China on the Priority Watch List because of non-transparent rules and regulations.

China was upgraded from the Watch List to a Priority Watch List on November 30, 1993, and was designated as a Priority Foreign Country in 1994. The reasons for this stem from continued lack of enforcement of the measures that Beijing has implemented absent satisfactory progress in enforcement measures. The Chinese were upset at this turn of events and viewed it as a betrayal after they had worked to comply with unilateral U.S. demands.

The USTR's actions towards China in late 1994 and early 1995 showed a marked increase in the level of aggressiveness in pursuit of Special 301 goals. The United States threatened 301-allowed trade sanctions on more than one billion dollars worth of Chinese products as punishment for Chinese lack of enforcement of their intellectual property laws.[91] After the U.S. announced its intention, the Chinese threatened retaliatory measures as a response to such trade sanctions.[92] The result was a threatened trade war which ended with a last-minute (actually, past dead-line) agreement. In the agreement, the Chinese continue pledges to crack down on piracy and improve enforcement of existing laws. Although this may be seen as at least a short-term victory for U.S. industry, it remains to be seen if substantive changes will result. One clear consequence, however, is the sharpening of Chinese attitudes towards the United States. Chinese anger and frustration is not just aimed at what they perceive as U.S. meddling in internal Chinese affairs, but also at the lack of [patience] the U.S. trade negotiators have shown. Li Changxu, head of the China United Intellectual Property Investigation Center stated "It's like building a house. You can have the house structure all set up, very beautiful. But then, you need electricity and water pipes. That takes more time."[93]

---

[87]Special 301 and the Fight Against Trade Piracy: Hearing Before the Subcomm. on International Trade of the Comm. on Finance, 103d Cong., 1st Sess. 19 (1993) . . .

[91] . . . The Chinese, however, have not only beefed up their intellectual property regulatory regime, but also have increased penalties for violators. As of July of 1994, it is a criminal offense to violate a copyright in China (although punishment is only for those who have knowledge that they are violating another's copyright). [cit]. Even before that, however, the Chinese would occasionally come down hard on serious violators of intellectual property rights. In January of 1994, for example, an approximately $25,000 fine was levied on a Chinese computer copyright infringer, [cit], and in 1993 one man was sentenced to death for charges related to the selling of counterfeit brand-name cigarettes. [cit].

Even with all this, however, the Business Software Alliance estimates that software piracy in China costs U.S. industry $322 million each year and states that there is a 94% software piracy rate in that country. [cit].

[92]Threats to block imports of U.S. records, cigarettes, alcoholic beverages, televisions shows, and movies were made by Chinese officials and the Chinese Ministry of Foreign Economic Trade and Economic Cooperation stated that it would refuse to consider requests from U.S. companies to establish subsidiaries in China. *U.S. & China Spar Over Piracy*, NEWSBYTES NEWS NETWORK, Jan. 3, 1995.

[93]Marcus W. Brauchli & Joseph Kahn, *China Moves Against Piracy As U.S. Trade Battle Looms*, ASIAN WALL ST. J., Jan. 6-7, 1995, at 1.

Similar sentiments came from Gao Linghan, Deputy Director of the National Copyright Administration of China: "Give us five years to end this problem. If we can solve these problems in five years, then I think we will have done a good job."

. . . .

VI. HOW SPECIAL 301 IS EFFECTIVE IN DEVELOPING COPYRIGHT PROTECTION OVERSEAS

It is obvious from the above that Special 301 actions grab the targeted country's attention. Being cited on one of the USTR lists and the credible threat of retaliation behind the Special 301 process compel countries to work with the USTR to arrive at a position sufficient, at least, to ward off retaliatory actions. Without the pressure of Special 301 actions against them, Taiwan, China, and Thailand most likely would not have taken steps to strengthen their copyright regimes in the manner that they did from 1989 to the present.

One indication of success is that in 1993 it was reported that from the start of the anti-piracy drive in Thailand as a result of U.S. pressure, there has been a 30% increase in sales of legal cassettes there. Likewise, a statement last Spring by the head of the WIPO commended China on the swift progress that country has made in the realm of developing a copyright protection system. As WIPO director-general Arpad Bogsch stated, China has gone from no system just fifteen years ago to one of the most advanced countries in the developing world in this regard. Many of the measures cited as evidence of this progress were measures implemented as a result of U.S. Special 301 pressure.

Another example of Special 301 successes includes the Indonesian government involvement in a Business Software Alliance[107] raid on printers in Indonesia. The raids resulted in the confiscation of more than 17,000 illegally printed computer software manuals. As described by one who was involved in the raid: "It was an extraordinarily difficult operation—we had been working for a long time gathering enough information and evidence to persuade the authorities to help and get search warrants, . . . This time the Indonesian Government was involved in helping us to break the ring and we're confident we'll achieve a favourable result." The reason for the cooperation was that the USTR was hinting at upgrading Indonesia on the Special 301 lists.

In order to justify the unilateral action that Special 301 imposes, the actions may simply be seen as "damages" for breach of an implied trade contract. Trading with the United States on favorable, most-favored-nation terms is a privilege, not a right.[111] If . . . U.S. copyright owners are not being adequately

---

[107] The Business Software Alliance ("BSA") is a U.S. industry group dedicated to protecting the property and rights of member industries. Member companies account for over 70% of the U.S. prepackaged software market. Members include Aldus Corp., Apple Computer, Autodesk, Borland International, GO Corp., Lotus Development, Microsoft, Novell, and WordPerfect. BSA has been very active and visible in countries that BSA feels do not adequately protect its members' products.

[111] This may not be as obvious as it sounds. The base tariff rate for goods imported into the United States was developed under the Tariff Act of 1930 and is commonly called the Smoot-Hawley tariff rate. These rates are very high and, in fact, are considered to be one of the triggering events to the self-interested policies that led to the collapse of the world economy in the 1930s. The great

protected in foreign markets, it is only right to rectify the situation, so the justification may go. As one music industry member put it, "[Special 301] has a very simple predicate, that nations who want to trade with us on favorable terms have an obligation to grant us access to their markets and further, to ensure that the products of American ingenuity and creativity are not pirated or counterfeited."

The USTR and supporters of 301 actions further justify this unilateral bullying by insisting that the United States is not the only party that benefits from these actions. One BSA official recognized the role that Special 301 played in Taiwan's recent copyright regime developments, but he also stated that "[the Taiwanese] are developing their own software industry and, while it's fledgling, they're beginning to understand the frustrations of being ripped off." Further, General Counsel at the office of the USTR had this to say about developing countries in general and developments in Mexico in particular:

> If you look around the world, there are some developing nations that have been quite forthcoming in terms of intellectual property protection. Sometimes, as in the example of Mexico, this is in part because their leadership recognizes the advantages to them as a country. They will advance more rapidly if they create a climate where intellectual property is protected. This is a point you made earlier with respect to Thailand. We are obviously pursuing our intellectual property interests because they matter a great deal to our companies and our jobs here and to our industrial and technological strength, but frankly, it is in the interest of these other countries to upgrade their intellectual property as well. It will strengthen their economy.

It may be more likely, however, that Mexico was trying desperately to meet the demands of the United States in order to have the [NAFTA] passed through the U.S. Congress. In general, it may be said that each country will eventually find it in its best interest to adopt an effective copyright protection scheme; the United States is making sure that targeted countries find adopting such a scheme in their best interests sooner than might otherwise occur.

There are theoretical bases for this justifying that both the U.S. and the targeted countries benefit. In a 1990 law review article funded by the Pharmaceutical Manufacturers Association, two researchers used regression analysis and other statistical models to show how the level of economic development of a nation corresponds with the level of patent protection afforded by that country.[116] The theory postulates that with effective intellectual

---

majority of products imported into the U.S., however, are imported under the Most Favored Nation rates. These rates are considerably lower and are amended to reflect latest trade agreement rates. As for the General System of Preferences ("GSP") benefits, at present over 100 countries receive these preferential tariff rates. Other preferential status rates that the United States has employed include Caribbean Basin Initiative, NAFTA, and Israeli Free Trade Agreements. Therefore, the "privilege" is extended to most countries.

[116]Richard T. Rapp & Richard P. Rozer, *Benefits and Costs of Intellectual Property Protection in Developing Countries*, 24 J. WORLD TRADE 75 (1990).

property protection a country is able to attract technology into its own economy. The new technology will spread through the country and eventually, through the incentives intellectual property protection provides, local industries will develop. If there is no protection, there is no incentive to develop new technologies or products and "technological backwardness will result."

Although the statistical correlation shown by the analysis in this article may be compelling and . . . may be accurate with regard to some of the countries cited in the article, for example Bulgaria or Poland, . . . it cannot be extended too broadly and certainly cannot be analogized outside the field of patent protection. For example, Germany, with some of the highest rates of computer software piracy is simultaneously one of the world's most developed economies. In addition Taiwan and Thailand, with annual growth rates of 9% and 8% respectively, are consistently cited among the world's worst pirates of intellectual property and appear to be outside the scope of the analysis. Finally, the article cannot explain how the United States' high level of piracy fits in. As General Counsel of the office of the USTR stated in 1992, " . . . In dollar volume, there may be as much intellectual property piracy here in the United States as there is around the world, largely because we have such a large market." The type of analysis found in this law review article may be used in statements by the USTR and President when discussing the possibility of sanctions, and also used by the Congress to justify supporting such actions. One significant problem with such analysis is that it ignores development patterns that may differ from that followed by the United States and other Western, industrialized countries.

In general, it may be true that the long-term benefits of a strong intellectual property regime in a developing country will help stimulate innovation in research and development and production processes. Such developments may lead to a more highly skilled labor force and encourage other nations to invest in and transfer technology to that country. In addition, the benefits in quality to consumers of protected, genuine products may in some instances outweigh the benefits of accessibility to poor quality, inexpensive pirated products. These determinations of the scope, pace, and direction of development, however, are for the governments of each individual country to make.

VII. HOW SPECIAL 301 IS INAPPROPRIATE FOR DEVELOPING COPYRIGHT PROTECTION OVERSEAS

[S]pecial 301 has been evolving with the "Priority Watch Lists" and "Watch Lists" in addition to the "Priority Foreign Country" listing, and with "out-of-cycle" reviews that may now take place so that the USTR need not wait until one specified date each year to cite the most egregious violators of U.S. intellectual property rights. In enacting this unilateral trade tool, however, the United States ignores the situation and society behind the violations.

Once a country is entered onto a Special 301 list, that country's government enters into negotiations with the United States for the sole purpose of removing the threat of retaliatory sanctions against that country. It is unlikely that within a developing country itself there is a strong lobby to demand or even support increased protection of copyrightable property. Until the government of a country has the political power and will to strengthen its copyright regimes, little will change; until a country itself decides that it is worth the scarce resources of the government to make a stand on increased copyright protection, changes will be incremental and mainly formalistic. Changes in targeted countries often will be just sufficient to prevent the United States from retaliating. And after the threat of retaliation has passed, it is possible that little will be done in the way of follow up—that is until the U.S. returns the next year to complain. This can be seen in the examples of Taiwan, China and Thailand noted above. Each year these countries work to provide the U.S. with indications of progress, but progress has been incremental and even where it has taken place enforcement measures are not commensurate with the improved legislation.

A. The Response of the Developing Countries

Developing countries in particular resent the United States determining what statutory regimes are in that country's best interest. Such countries see the forcing of U.S. copyright regimes upon them as a new form of colonialism. In addition, it is often simply not practical for a developing country to adopt a developed country's standards in such areas. Developing countries generally understand that a strong, western-style copyright regime will eat up resources in the instituting, monitoring and enforcing of such a system. Without access to copied products and processes, both private and public resources must be garnered to finance the research and development necessary to license or replicate expensive methods already developed in other nations. This problem may be particularly acute in the area of education, where access to books, software, and computers is crucial to raise living standards, yet prohibitively expensive within developing countries. The added restrictions on access to technology and products that strong copyright protection regimes impose are considered an unnecessary constraint to development. It is a struggle for a developing country's government to balance imposing such a regime to cater to U.S. demands (and avoid the threat of retaliation) and providing necessary resources to the population.

B. The Response of the Rest of the World

The developing countries are not alone in expressing anger with Special 301 measures. Most of the United States trading partners, both developing countries and industrialized countries, have protested against the unilateral nature of Special 301. The main complaint raised against the United States with regard to Special 301 is that such unilateral measures destroy attempts to maintain a balanced world trading system developed through multilateral negotiations. By adding parties with various positions, multilateral negotiations provide countries in a less strong position support for their views. On the other hand, the United States, with its strong bargaining position, has a perceived unfair advantage when pursuing bilateral negotiations with less developed nations, as it does when it commences a Special 301 action.[126]

India, Japan, France, and Brazil are among the most consistent and vocal opponents of Special 301. Brazil has been adamant in pursuing international condemnation against the United States for perceived violations of GATT agreements by using Special 301. Brazil has filed complaints with GATT authorities stating that Special 301 actions violate U.S. responsibilities under GATT.

On the other hand, the French have been pressing for a European equivalent of Section 301. . . .

It is, in fact, precisely to guard against such escalation of self-interested actions by nations that the multilateral GATT with its "most favored nation" concept was initiated. When the United States pursues unilateral measures and coerces bilateral negotiations under the threat of sanctions, GATT is undermined. The U.S. has consistently been a supporter of GATT and by ignoring GATT most favored nation treatment and dispute resolution mechanisms, the U.S. sends a message that GATT need not be adhered to. It will be difficult for the United States to persuade other nations to enter into further GATT negotiations and abide by GATT provisions if the U.S. is viewed as a flagrant violator of GATT. As one commentator put it, the United States must recognize that its actions are "norm creating" and that the U.S. should encourage behavior that all nations will find acceptable for years to come.[129] The United States may not always be among the world's top trading powers, and it would be in the long-term interest of the U.S. to strive (while it is still on top) to develop an international trade regime that takes more into consideration than the current cries of big business lobbyists. This strategy will benefit the U.S. not only today by developing better relations with our trade partners, but also in the future when the U.S. may require the benefits of a more understanding world trade regime.

. . . .

D. An Undermining of U.S. Long-Term Interests

. . . It would be more wise, for the interest of the United States in the future and the harmony of the international trading order now, if the U.S. would consider working with, instead of against, its trading partners to come to mutually acceptable resolutions to trade disagreements.

A world where each country is looking out only for its best interests, even if to the detriment of its allies (a return to the pre-World War II "beggar-thy-neighbor policies" which led in large part to the disintegration of the world economies in the early part of this century) would lead to any particular individual country being worse off. Such activity may further encourage the development of regional trade blocs, where countries could again work to reduce

[126] George Y. Gonzalez, *An Analysis of the Legal Implications of the Intellectual Property Provisions of the North American Free Trade Agreement*, 34 HARV. INT'L L.J. 305, 314 (1993).

[129] Jonathan C. Carlson, *Law and Leadership in the Global Schoolyard*, 75 IOWA L. REV. 877, 886 (1990).

trade barriers among themselves.

Worries of retaliation, or at least a backlash, for Special 301 actions are now a reality in U.S.-China trade relations. Even with the Special 301 tool at its disposal, the U.S. record industry had been hesitant to request action in China. With the assistance of overseas (primarily Hong Kong and Taiwan) equipment and capital, piracy of cassettes, and now CDs, is rampant in China. With the rise of disposable income in China, the demand for music has become enormous (the record market estimate for 1994 is $1 billion). The potential market for U.S. industry is great, both for the marketing of Chinese artists (there are more than 200 record companies in China) and the ever-popular American singers. For this reason, record industry officials had been trying to work with the Chinese both to gain market access and reduce piracy. Now that 301 threats have been made, however, the Chinese may be a long time in welcoming U.S. inroads into this booming consumer market.

[Moreover, Senator Hatch has explained], Chinese retaliation would most likely cost U.S. industries and consumers money in higher tariffs imposed by China, and while U.S. companies would be shut out of the Chinese market due to high costs, tariffs, or outright restrictions, companies from other nations would take their place in China. Finally, he estimated that if the U.S. enters into such a trade war with China, there would be little incentive for the Chinese to protect the American technology and intellectual property that would remain in China.

One final interesting argument against Special 301 actions is that they will hurt the United States by actually causing targeted countries to become more competitive. As one Columbia University economist stated, such countries "will be a little more original and a little more creative" and, thus, end up beating the U.S. at our own game. Such an argument is short-sighted, at best, but raises the type of concern that argues against forcing change where change is not yet primed to occur.

. . . .

VIII. ALTERNATIVE SOLUTIONS TO U.S. COPYRIGHT CONCERNS

. . . .

B. Resolving Problems in Non GATT-Member Countries

[Newby argued that, with respect to nations that are not members of GATT, mostly developing or non-market economies, the United States should strive for a more long-term, mutually acceptable solution than Special 301.] There are two main ways in which to do this. One is through government and government-sponsored measures. The other is through private business measures, with businesses either acting individually or through alliances of companies and industries.

Government activities could involve the governments of the industrially and technologically developed nations contributing to programs that assist nations that want to strengthen their domestic protection of copyrights. Such programs might discuss developing or strengthening copyright legislation and the development of effective enforcement measures. . . Tight economies in developed countries, however, undoubtedly will limit the time and resources that those countries will be willing to devote to other nations' development.

Private measures involve nothing more basic than U.S. companies working within the countries in which they are having problems. To achieve the most effective and long-term protection in these countries, U.S. owners of copyrights should increase efforts to create the proper climate for protection.

For the time that Levi Strauss was there, it was very successful in China by working directly with the entities involved, both infringers and local authorities.[151] By cultivating relationships and addressing the problem directly, Levi Strauss created a long-term framework in which to resolve infringement problems. Such a strategy, however, requires devotion to a market and insights beyond a short-term gain. In addition, this strategy can only be practicable with a company and a product strong enough to withstand potential infringement when first entering the market.

Likewise, in Thailand, U.S. companies that experience copying of videos and software could work with the major distributors of such goods to ensure that genuine, quality goods are available at a reasonable price. By working directly with corporate purchasers and distributors, U.S. companies can be sure to understand local needs while creating a support network to report and help counter piracy activities. . .

Although there are examples of companies being willing to engage in such activities, it is more realistic to expect such action to be taken by a consortium or alliance of interested companies. The Business Software Alliance provides an example of the core interested companies in the U.S. computer software industry pouring money and time into engaging investigators and attorneys to police the world. Resources may be more beneficially allocated to working with governments to meet their local needs as well as targeting U.S. alliance member concerns. Although this may sound altruistic, it is actually good business sense that considers long-term development and benefits over short-term gains.

One model may be the Taiwanese Information Product Anti-Piracy Union. The union is aimed at intensifying crackdowns on counterfeit computer products and will be patterned after the Business Software Alliance. At present, more than thirty Taiwanese computer software manufacturers have joined the new union. BSA has even agreed to sponsor seminars on software management and other activities promoting protection over piracy. In addition, BSA has offered incentives to encourage Taiwan residents to inform the Alliance of instances of software piracy.

What happens when non-GATT countries still do not cooperate? . . . In deciding what action to take against the country in response to repeated infringing activities, public (global) policy would suggest that the U.S. look at what property is being infringed. Property protected by copyright is as valuable as that protected by trademark or patents, but it may be useful to distinguish

---

[151]Levi Strauss decided to leave the China market in late 1993, stating that it was opposed to the use of prison and other "slave" labor in China.

between these properties for reasons of public safety and the advancement of a developing country's education and general welfare.

Although many developing countries do not extend patent protection to pharmaceuticals, by enforcing its patent rights on these and other products abroad, the United States ensures that safe, quality products are being distributed to consumers. The strong protection of trademarks abroad likewise ensures the distribution of genuine products to consumers. The false marking of auto parts, electrical appliances, sports equipment, and a range of other products leads consumers to a false sense of safety. Often shoddy, knock-off goods can result in serious health and safety concerns for end-users. In addition, a country cannot claim that the selling of knock-off goods (for example, leather goods, clothing, and jewelry) is economic activity that develops the country. Although such sales may generate enormous profits for pirates and may even increase tourism to a particular country, these industries do little to advance the economy technologically. The United States would be justified in taking unilateral retaliatory actions against such dangerous and predatory practices in non-GATT member countries.

Copyright infringement may be viewed differently. The goods copied may certainly be used to generate profits for pirates, but the ready accessibility of low cost books and software in the economy is of great importance to a nation's overall development. By denying such access with strict copyright protection laws, U.S. companies may be gaining some otherwise "lost" sales, but the harm and retardation on economic advancement may outweigh such speculative, pecuniary gains. By enforcing copyright laws for U.S. companies with trade sanctions and loss of trade privileges, this will further slow the process of development.

More importantly for U.S. businesses, however, copyrighted software and books that are prohibitively costly will not be used by the general population and so a market demand for these items will be slow in developing. The quickest way for a U.S. company to create a long-term demand is to work with the local government and education officials to develop a program of cheap access immediately that will lead to greater profits later on. One example of this would involve a company, or group of companies, working with local educational facilities to develop a program that will use donated or reduced-cost computers and software, but that [commits] that facility to continue using that company's products, to be paid for after the initial period, for a contracted period of time.

Even with copyright infringement, however, the United States should distinguish between goods used for domestic consumption and those exported for profit. There is no reason to allow countries to export goods based upon U.S. products. Not only does such export activity more clearly reduce potential U.S. sales, it also does little to assist the country in its independent development. The United States should make clear, ideally through multilateral cooperation, that such exporting of pirated goods is not acceptable.

IX. Conclusion

. . . .

At the point when the U.S. desires to pursue a retaliatory action against offending nations, the U.S. should pursue measures sanctioned by the world community, such as a WTO-imposed TRIPS remedy. This way the U.S. can pursue remedies fully without violating trade agreements, and the targeted country will have the spotlight of the world trading community upon it if it does not comply with WTO-imposed measures.

On the private side, U.S. companies must take responsibility for their entrance into a country because their actions in a country, particularly a developing country, often affect the economy of that country and also the way in which the citizens of that country view the United States. . .

By developing a coherent policy that is consistent and based upon both demands at home and understanding of the situation in many countries abroad, the U.S. can implement its policies with more respect and effectiveness in the world community. In a time of growing trade tensions and increasing regionalism, the United States can best insure its long-term competitiveness in the world economy by pursuing less bullying tactics and working within, not against, other nations to create an integrated world economy.

WILLIAM P. ALFORD, HOW THEORY DOES—AND DOES NOT—MATTER: AMERICAN APPROACHES TO INTELLECTUAL PROPERTY LAW IN EAST ASIA[*]
13 UCLA Pac. Basin L.J. 8, 12-24 (1994)

II. Neglect and Discovery

. . . .

[I]ntellectual property issues came to prominence in our public life [in part] because of the link forged between them and the growth of our trade deficit during the mid-1980s. To be sure, the United States had begun to experience trade problems from the days of the Vietnam War. They continued to grow, especially vis-à-vis Japan, irrespective of steps we took. What was to change in the 1980s, however, was the assertion by intellectual property producing industries—later picked up by the government—that the unlawful appropriation by others of our intellectual property could in important measure explain our burgeoning trade deficit. If only those making unauthorized use of our intellectual property would instead pay retail price for it, so this thinking went, the revenues so generated would in effect wipe out much of our deficit.

[T]his thinking had a certain allure. Yet, attractive though it may have been, it was premised on a somewhat faulty assumption: namely, that if precluded from making unauthorized copies, alleged infringers would certainly purchase the item at its full retail price, rather than, for example, negotiating a discount, purchasing cheaper alternatives, developing their own surrogates, or simply forgoing it altogether. Proponents of the notion that intellectual property leakage is a central factor in explaining our trade deficit seemed not to understand how unlikely a citizen of the People's Republic of China (P.R.C.) earning fifty dollars a month would be to fork out more than a month's salary to buy even such an outstanding work as Melville Nimmer and Paul Geller's treatise on worldwide copyright. And they slighted the fact that any responsible effort to balance the books would need to take account of the foreign intellectual property that we Americans historically have used without authorization.[20]

Despite its many limitations, however, this vision of reality had a great deal of appeal in government and media circles. For one thing, it was most seemingly cogent in the very parts of the world—East Asia and especially Japan—where we were experiencing many of our largest deficits. For another, it spoke to some of our less attractive, subconscious fears, offering a possible explanation of why people with traditions different from our own—who some here considered less creative and capable than ourselves—were besting us at our own game. And, neatly enough, it did all this by turning one of our greatest vulnerabilities, our seemingly unquenchable thirst for imported goods, into a weapon—namely access to our market—that we could then use against the very people who had purloined our intellectual property, all of whom needed to sell their wares here.

This link between intellectual property and trade, especially concerning East Asia, soon became more than just rhetorical. Indeed, by the mid- to late 1980s, it had become an important element of our public policy. [So the United States created Special 301 and] on the multilateral front . . . the United States demanded that the Uruguay Round of the GATT produce a code authorizing trade sanctions in response to intellectual property violations. The United States championed this cause even though many of our trading partners argued that such a step both diminished the authority of existing international bodies in this area—such as the World Intellectual Property Organization and the United Nations Economic, Social and Cultural Organization—and took GATT off in wholly new directions that were not necessarily consistent with its basic purposes and premises.

If anything, this attention to intellectual property in our public arena has become even more conspicuous in recent years. First the Bush administration and now the Clinton administration elevated it into one of the central objectives of American foreign policy generally, and particularly concerning East Asia. . . . [W]hile he was Secretary of State, James Baker informed the leadership of the P.R.C. that there were three issues of equal importance that would determine the fate of U.S.-P.R.C. relations: the spread of weapons of mass destruction, human rights, and trade—of which protection for American intellectual property headed the list. Much the same message has been since reaffirmed by the Clinton administration.

I like Mickey Mouse as much as the next red-blooded American—indeed, I hope that I can convince the Stanford University Press to have him adorn the

---

[20]American piracy is discussed in ALBERT J. CLARK, THE MOVEMENT FOR INTERNATIONAL COPYRIGHT IN NINETEENTH CENTURY AMERICA (1960).

cover of my book. However, there is something somehow out of whack about putting the little rodent up there with nuclear war and torture. . . .

III. WHAT THEORY DOES—AND DOES NOT—TELL US

Interestingly, the link forged in the public arena between intellectual property and East Asia by and large has not found a counterpart in academe in this country or elsewhere in the West. With very few exceptions—of whom Dennis Karjala[27] and Charles McManis[28] are among the most notable—American scholars, whether in law or other fields, have simply not paid much heed to this topic.

This notwithstanding, I believe that the principal schools of [intellectual property] thought . . . can be of help in our effort to understand more about intellectual property in East Asia and about U.S. interaction therewith, even if it is in most instances more in a heuristic, rather than definitive, fashion. . . . Let me turn first to economic analysis. . . One is hard put to look at intellectual property in East Asia without recognizing the importance of economic considerations. To put it in its starkest terms, for example, those nations in East Asia that are the least developed economically are generally those that accord the least protection to intellectual property, while those that are highly developed economically are, for the most part, the most faithful adherents to something approaching international standards of protection.

Having guided us to this level of insight, however, there are many more particular, but highly significant, questions that economic analysis leaves unanswered, at least to the extent it has been applied to this field of inquiry. Let me pose one or two, perhaps in overly simplistic form, to make my point. I begin with perhaps one of the starkest: is respect for intellectual property rights the result of economic development, a principal cause thereof, or both? If it is the result of economic development, how, for example, does one explain the virtually total absence of any concept of such rights in Tang Dynasty (618–906) and Song Dynasty (960–1279) China—for a goodly portion of which China was the world's most economically developed and technologically advanced nation? Our examples need not be only historical. How, for instance, does one explain the ongoing problems that many foreign firms and even some small and middle-sized Japanese enterprises claim to experience in securing their rights in Japan, although it has one of the world's most developed economies?

If, on the other hand, respect for intellectual property rights is most noteworthy as a stimulus,[31] what are we to make of the possibility that Japan,

---

[27]See, e.g., Dennis S. Karjala, *Copyright, Computer Software and the New Protectionism*, 28 JURIMETRICS J. 33 (1987).

[28]See, e.g., Charles McManis, *International Protection for Semiconductor Chip Designs and the Standard of Judicial Review of Presidential Proclamations Issued Pursuant to the Semiconductor Chip Protection Act of 1984*, 22 GEO. WASH. J. INT'L L. & ECON. 331 (1988).

[31]This view is suggested by the work of Richard Adelstein and Steven Peretz–whose work might be seen as an elaboration of North and Thomas on the indispensability of clear property rights to economic development. *See* Richard P. Adelstein and Steven I. Peretz, *The Competition of*

and now China, are flourishing economically because at particular stages of their economic development they liberally made unauthorized use of foreign technology? Indeed, much the same point might be made regarding the United States a century ago. And what are we to make of the fact that Hong Kong, Korea, and Taiwan are far more vibrant economically than Great Britain, Portugal, and Ireland even though ideas of intellectual property rights are far more deeply entrenched, and means of protecting them are far better established, in the latter rather than the former group of nations? Nor need our data in this regard all be modern. We should not forget that it was East Asia—first Korea and then China—that gave the world the printing press and yet neither has done much with copyright until quite recently.

But as interesting as these matters may be, there are even more fundamental issues raised as we think of applying tools of economic analysis. In casting economic considerations—and at their heart, property rights—in a central role, are we not assuming that the definitions and attributes of property rights are uniform world-wide? Is that a wholly warranted assumption? Research on Chinese legal history and recent developments in the P.R.C. suggest that we not rush to judgment here. This is so particularly if we break property into its constituent elements, rather than treat it as an undifferentiated whole that one either has or lacks. And it is even more so if we pause to consider how the availability of remedies and the willingness to invoke them—which are two different things—shape rights in very real and important ways. Indeed, scholars of such different orientations as Critical Legal Studies theorist James Boyle and the historian of Chinese science Nathan Sivin at least implicitly raise the suggestion that far from being universal, it is the ideas of ownership embedded in modern Western intellectual property that are the historical aberrations, and that these ideas have achieved the currency they now enjoy internationally as much because they are backed by great economic might as because of their appeal to our common sense or their innate conceptual force.

Although holding very different views than proponents of economic analysis as to what motivates behavior, scholars who seek to understand intellectual property in more philosophical terms also, at least implicitly, share a basic belief not only in universals—as opposed to more culturally specific factors—but in universals comprised principally of rights. Their ideas are certainly useful in helping us appreciate the link between intellectual property and other rights—and particularly political rights. Copyright in the Anglo-American world originated with the granting of a royal monopoly by the British Throne to the London Stationers Company in return for the latter's suppression of controversial texts. Nonetheless, it appears that, as was the case with the correlation between economic development and respect for intellectual property rights, so too, one finds that the greater a nation's commitment to the overall rights of its populace, the more likely it is to have serious protection for intellectual property. In a way, it would be hard for this to be otherwise—for societies that sharply constrain their citizens' rights are likely to tolerate far less in the way of private expressive activity, and, in any event, the value of whatever property rights these societies may provide is likely to diminish

---

Technologies and the Market for Ideas: Copyright and Fair Use–An Evolutionary Perspective, 5 INT'L REV. L. & ECON. 209 (1985).

sharply in the absence of mechanisms for their vindication.

But as with connections between economic development and intellectual property rights, scholarly approaches to intellectual property rights grounded in rights theory leave many questions unanswered, especially as we look to East Asia. If there is a link between political and intellectual property rights, why, for example, is it that problems of piracy have become greater in the P.R.C. as the country has become freer politically and economically? And why is it that today there are probably more instances of infringement in South Korea than in the North? There may well be answers to such questions consistent with a rights-oriented approach, but those working in this field have yet to address such questions. And, as was the case with economic analysis, there are the more basic—and I think more difficult to answer—questions as to how proponents of a vision of society grounded in notions of inalienable rights account for countries in which this type of thinking has only lately taken hold, and then not necessarily in precisely the same ways it has in the West.

At first blush, the deconstructionists would seem to have escaped some of the problems of a universalist posture that arguably afflict both economic- and rights-focused approaches. In seeking to show ways in which ideas of copyright are not absolute or preordained, but contingent upon particular historical circumstances, they too make a valuable contribution. Their work makes less inexplicable the fact that Tang China could reach and stay at the pinnacle of the world economically, politically, technologically, and militarily for more than a century without anything resembling intellectual property rights. And although not focused on contemporary U.S.-East Asian relations as such, the abiding lessons of the Critical Legal Studies movement about the linkage of power and legality are instructive as to why intellectual property issues are so prominent on the American diplomatic agenda and why so many East Asian jurisdictions now are adopting such law.

Caution is, however, no less warranted with regard to the deconstructionists than any of the other schools I have been examining. For one thing, notwithstanding their attacks upon Eurocentrism, their work is almost exclusively grounded in the historical experience of Western Europe and the United States. This foundation is then treated, essentially without qualification, as if it were common for all humankind.[39] But if our modern Western conception of authorship is, as Woodmansee, Rose, and others suggest, so clearly a product of Romantic conceptions of individual genius, what are we to make of authorship in East Asian societies which did not experience the Enlightenment, at least directly? How does one account for images of the author, whether in historical times or at present? Are such scholars being sufficiently careful not to project themselves—or an idealized statement of their hopes for their own society—on East Asia? In short, until deconstructionists move beyond a rhetoric of inclusiveness and begin to take other societies more seriously, it may not be unfair to ask whether their vision of the contingent nature of authorship and its concomitant critique of copyright tells us as much

---

[39] The implications of this problem are treated at greater length in William P. Alford, *The Inscrutable Occidental: Roberto Unger's Uses and Abuses of the Chinese Past*, 64 TEX. L. REV. 915 (1986) and William P. Alford, *On the Limits of "Grand Theory" in Comparative Law*, 61 WASH. L. REV. 945 (1986).

about the historical circumstances of a part of today's professorate as it does about the birth of notions of intellectual property rights.

. . . .

IV. OF MICKEY (MOUSE AND KANTOR) AND GOOFY

If each of the schools of thought I have briefly sketched above has shortcomings, each, nonetheless, gets us much further than the thinking embodied in U.S. governmental policy toward these issues. . . .

American policy has proceeded on the underlying assumption that a society's commitment to intellectual property protection is not contingent on its level of economic development, commitment to basic rights, or even particular historical circumstances. Rather, it is essentially a question of will. That is, if governments are so inclined or can be sufficiently pressured if they are not so inclined, adherence to something approximating an international standard of intellectual property protection will be relatively forthcoming.

As flawed as this vision is, it seems to me that one cannot dismiss it out of hand as one seeks to understand intellectual property in East Asia. The history of the West's relations with East Asia over the past century and a half is replete with examples of the impact of might, even when it has not made right. And one would be disingenuous when assessing intellectual property developments in the ROC and Korea—and even in Japan and the P.R.C.—to ignore the impact of threats to limit access to the American market.

Once again, however, caution is warranted. [Both the USTR and their counterparts in the P.R.C.] display an extraordinary faith in formal legality and a corresponding inattention to what motivates behavior. Each, in their own way, even if only for political effect, vests enormous significance in the mere articulation of new rules—as if promulgating new intellectual property laws and exhortations to follow them from Beijing were tantamount to changing the way in which people in the provinces conduct themselves on a daily basis.[42] Indeed, in my more perverse moments, I am tempted to write an article entitled "Why China Has Too Much Law—And Too Little Legality."

The folly in believing that the rapid-fire issuance of an elaborate web of formal new rules on intellectual property, brought about chiefly through external pressure, will swiftly transform long-standing attitudes and practices comes into sharper focus if we consider recent Chinese trends. A good case can be made that since the United States began to apply considerable pressure to the P.R.C. on this front, infringement of American copyrighted and trademarked items has at least held steady, if not increased significantly. However, in fairness, it should be noted that the reasons for this may have as much to do with the P.R.C.'s liberalization—which has been substantial with respect to markets and more modest politically—as with U.S. policy as such. . . .

---

[42]Of late, in its dealings with the P.R.C., the USTR has begun to emphasize enforcement–but again with the assumption that Beijing has the capacity readily to control economic activity in Guangdong and other distant areas. The fallacy of that assumption is discussed in William P. Alford, *Underestimating a Complex China*, CHI. TRIB., May 24, 1994, at 23.

But the real deficiencies of vision in U.S. policy are not those of . . . the policy's inability to deliver promised results. They are even more fundamental, lying in this policy's utter failure honestly and carefully to think through what might engender a genuine and sustained respect for intellectual property or any other type of rights in China—or, for that matter, anywhere else. The effort to foster serious, widespread, long-term adherence to something approximating an international level of protection for intellectual property, after all, entails significant transformations in a people's attitudes toward intellectual creation, toward property, toward rights, toward the vindication of such rights through formal legal action, toward government, and so forth. Without apologizing for indifference or deception on the Chinese side, how can we realistically expect that such attitudes will change overnight or that the institutions needed to nurture and support them will suddenly emerge, particularly if there is any truth to suggestions that adherence to intellectual property is correlated either to economic development or political openness or is shaped by culture. Even in our own society, which is economically mature, politically open, and born of the very culture that gave the concept of intellectual property to the world, respect for such rights was a long time in coming and is still far from being universal. Indeed, as Dennis Karjala suggests, there remain very real and legitimate disagreements amongst us as to how to balance protection for intellectual property with the access to data needed to spur further innovation and ensure the citizenry's full participation in our democratic polity.

These, however, are not the only costs to an American policy that consists of little more than crude threats and to the psychology that underlies it. Our policy on intellectual property toward China, or other parts of East Asia, does not occur in a vacuum. The tactics we have been using—and even celebrating—resonate all too much of a past in which the United States and other foreign powers undertook many an act having a great impact on the nations of East Asia in the name of making the world safe for our concerns, including intellectual property. Some such measures were no doubt of value to all involved, but others were of questionable morality and limited efficacy. Without suggesting history will necessarily repeat itself, it might not be a bad idea for our policy makers to look at why earlier foreign efforts at the turn of the century and again in the 1920s and the 1940s through the 1980s to press Chinese society to adopt an idealized version of intellectual property law were failures.

If our policy makers had a better appreciation of the historical context of their actions, they might not only be more tactically adept, but they might also more fully comprehend the depth of bitterness that recent U.S. measures evoke and therefore better understand the impact of our intellectual property policy on broader relations between our nation and those of East Asia. To make this point is not to subscribe to a victimization theory that seeks to excuse any and all Chinese actions today because of what may have happened a century ago. Instead, it is to urge that we take full heed of the impact of what we are doing. To give but one example, when I spoke on U.S.-ROC intellectual property negotiations at National Taiwan University in 1991, the topic prompted an extraordinary reaction: senior government officials cried publicly in frustration at the humiliation they believed they had experienced at the hands of U.S.

negotiators, and serious lawyers and scholars castigated prominent Chinese attorneys who assisted U.S. interests as traitors to Taiwan (*Taijian*).[45]

Clearly, our government's determination to place so much emphasis on intellectual property issues and so readily to resort to pressure to achieve objectives in this area limits what it can expect to achieve in other crucial dimensions of our relations—particularly when dealing with a nation as powerful as the P.R.C. It was saddening to see the Bush administration—which staunchly resisted efforts to address strongly human rights problems in China on the grounds that we should not be interfering in their sovereign affairs—threatening the Chinese with almost one billion dollars of punitive tariffs, opposition to the P.R.C.'s GATT bid, and an end to most favored nation (MFN) status if they did not agree to revise their intellectual property law to our satisfaction and on a schedule essentially of our liking. Much the same point can be made regarding the present administration . . . .

V. CONCLUSION

. . . .

[In applying the major scholarly approaches toward intellectual property to the East Asian situation,] I do hope . . . that we will remain vigilant as to the basic terms we use and take nothing for granted. . . . When we mention property, we should be mindful of which of its many attributes or constituent elements we are speaking. When we endeavor to explain a phenomenon by reference to culture, let us not take it as a static monolith throughout East Asia, but instead realize its immense variety over time, across national boundaries, and among different people within any country. When we speak of interests, whose interests are we concerned with and at what cost to those of others? And when we refer to intellectual property law, do we mean formal doctrine or the manner in which the law plays itself out in society—and if the latter, how are we to measure it?

. . . .

NOTES AND QUESTIONS

(1) **The Purposes of Special 301.** Review the purposes of the Trade Act of 1974 set out in footnote 25 of the Newby article. To what extent do you think those stated purposes accurately reflect what Congress was seeking to achieve in 1988? *See* Robert Burrell, *A Case Study in Cultural Imperialism: The Imposition of Copyright on China by the West*, 3 PERSP. IN INTELL. PROP. 195, 213 (1998) (discussing broader political concerns). Have the steps taken under Special 301 furthered those purposes? To what extent are the purposes of the Trade Act consistent with the stated purposes of TRIPS? *See* United

[45]The standard Chinese phrase for traitor, *hanjian*, literally means "traitor to the Chinese." The cited adaptation suggests the deep fissures that course through the ROC and its legal profession.

States—Sections 301–310 of the Trade Act of 1974, WT/DS152/R (WTO Panel Report, Dec. 22, 1999). To what extent are they consistent with the purposes of intellectual property law?

(2) **Assessing the Success of Special 301.** Special 301 was in part a response to the inadequacies of the GATT pre-1994. It may therefore have accelerated the conceptual shift to enforceable minimum standards found in the TRIPS Agreement. Viewed in that light, can Special 301 be hailed as an unqualified success? Newby complains that progress in developing countries acting under pressure from the United States has been "incremental." Is this a fair criticism?

(3) **The Demands Made of China.** Review the demands made of China in 1991. To what extent can these demands be characterized as demands to comply with applicable international intellectual property standards at the time? In what ways did they go beyond that? If the United States was not asking China to adhere to extant standards of international intellectual property law, what was it asking? Was that appropriate or justified?

(4) **Cultural Imperialism.** Some scholars have described aggressive unilateral trade measures such as Special 301 as "cultural imperialism" when applied to countries such as China. *See* Burrell, *supra*, at 195. What is it about Special 301 that arguably permits its characterization as "imperialistic"? Is cultural domination of developing countries by the developed countries of the West more likely with or without intellectual property protection? Does the answer vary as between different forms of intellectual property? Is the dynamic of cultural subordination, which makes some European countries fear international laws that facilitate the expansion of American pop culture, different as between two developed countries?

(5) **Commonality of Values?** China had a vibrant commercial publishing industry for popular works of fiction, drama, and religious tracts at least from the end of the ninth century. This industry regularly received official patronage and commissions, and suffered the attendant injuries from economic competitors. Consider the following:

> In the work Fangyu Shenglan (A [Grand Tour] of the Territories) compiled by Zhu Mu of the Song Dynasty (960–1279), there [is] placed after the compiler's preface a "Notice Issued by the Viceroy of Zhejiang [province]" which says that the book is the result of the compiler's "assiduous labour of a lifetime and cannot be compared with the plagiarisms by others," [and] whereas "there are recently people in the book market hankering after gains, who are incapable of compiling works based on their own views but devote their efforts to reprinting," [therefore] "a public notice is hereby issued jointly by the viceroy of Zhejiang and the governor of East Zhejiang prohibiting reprinting activities; and if anyone reprints the work for profit, Zhu has the right to "report the act, track down the offender, destroy the plates and enforce the ban, so as to stop acts of piracy."

Zheng Chengsi, *Further on Copyright Protection in Ancient China*, CHINA PATENTS & TRADEMARKS Q. 62, 63 (Oct. 1996). Note particularly the references to "plagiarism" (*piaoqie*) and "piracy" (*fankan zhihuan*—literally "harmful reprints"). Might stopping others from reprinting books for profit or other forms of "free riding" be more universal than cultural critics suggest? *See also* Graziella M. Sarno, Comment, *Viet Nam or Bust: Why Trademark Pirates Are Leaving China for Better Opportunities in Viet Nam*, 14 DICK. J. INT'L L. 291 (1996).

(6) **Arguments on Both Sides.** Was the Chinese Government justifiably irked with the impatience of the United States negotiators in 1995? If you had been negotiating on behalf of the Chinese Government, how might you have best conveyed the sentiment that it takes time to bring an intellectual property system into compliance with international standards? *Cf.* Burrell, *supra*, at 207-08 (discussing development of the Universal Copyright Convention). If you had been negotiating on behalf of the U.S. Trade Representative, how might you have approached the task of persuading the Chinese negotiators that providing the intellectual property protection sought by the United States was in China's best interests? Does the instrumentalist nature of U.S. intellectual property protection make it harder to assert the inherent propriety of enhanced intellectual property protection? Are there other explanations of intellectual property that might offer more persuasive justifications? (And are those other explanations of intellectual property persuasive?)

(7) **Expediting Change.** Newby writes that "[i]n general, it may be said that each country will eventually find it in its best interest to adopt an effective copyright protection scheme; the United States is making sure that targeted countries find adopting such a scheme in their best interests sooner than might otherwise occur." Newby, *supra*, at 49. What are the costs and benefits of ensuring that "targeted countries find adopting such a scheme in their best interests sooner than might otherwise occur"? If the date at which it would have been in a country's best interests to reach a mature system of copyright protection was twenty years hence, what is the effect of altering "incentives" such that it implements that system immediately? Does this ensure (or at least assist) that country in capturing the benefits of copyright protection twenty years earlier than would otherwise have been the case?

(8) **Cause and Effect.** How does one answer Professor Alford's question: is respect for intellectual property rights the result of economic development, a principal cause thereof, or both? To what extent can intellectual property laws dictate cultural attitudes? Professor Alford cites examples of economically and technologically advanced societies operating without intellectual property rights. Are those examples compelling ? Can one explain those examples? Do we have to be able to explain those examples before acting as the USTR has acted?

(9) **Later Developments in U.S.-China Relations**. The debate between the United States and China regarding the latter's protection of intellectual property did not end with the February 25, 1995, agreement. On May 15, 1996, based on monitoring of the agreement's implementation carried out under section 306(a) of the Trade Act, the USTR expressed dissatisfaction with implementation of the agreement and proposed yet again to impose prohibitive

tariffs on imports of certain products from China. This crisis was resolved with another agreement on June 17, 1996. In its 1999 Annual Report, the USTR concluded that:

> China now has a functioning system capable of protecting intellectual property rights. China has made progress on software end-user piracy including the recent issuance of a State Council directive to all government ministries mandating that only legitimate software be used in government and quasi-government agencies. Enforcement of intellectual property rights has become part of China's nationwide anti-crime campaign; the Chinese police and court system have become involved in combating IPR piracy. The production of pirated copyrighted works has dropped dramatically.

OFFICE OF THE UNITED STATES TRADE REPRESENTATIVE, RESULTS OF SPECIAL 301 ANNUAL REVIEW (Apr. 30, 1999). The report also noted, however, that "retail piracy and counterfeit goods remain widespread in China. And that the structure of IPR administration and enforcement in China remains opaque. Enforcement at the provincial level is sporadic. Corruption remains a problem and convictions only occasionally result in jail time." *Id.* For a recent discussion of American foreign intellectual property policy toward China, see Peter K. Yu, *From Pirates to Partners: Protecting Intellectual Property in China in the Twenty-First Century*, 50 AM. U. L. REV. __ (2001) (forthcoming).

(10) **Imposition of Law**. To what extent can the use by the United States of Special 301 powers be described as "imposing foreign law" on other countries? In what circumstances might such "imposition" be justified? In what circumstances might it be wise as a matter of U.S. policy? Might there be circumstances where use of Special 301 might be justified but not wise?

(11) **Respect for Difference.** To what extent should the United States take into account "development patterns that may differ from that followed by the United States and other Western, industrialized countries" in requiring the enactment of intellectual property protection? How should those differences be balanced against the claims of U.S. industries that they are suffering huge losses as a result of piracy? How do you balance respect for the sovereignty of other nations with the protection of domestic industries? Can that analysis be performed in the abstract? What do you think of Newby's alternative suggestions for addressing perceived inadequacies in intellectual property protection? *Cf.* Burrell, *supra*, at 201 (arguing that "there would seem to be little point in trying to force China to adopt a system of property relations which will inevitably emerge with the development of China's economic base"). Would these be more effective than use of Special 301? Would they be more appropriate? Is Newby correct that certain inadequacies in intellectual property protection warrant greater immediate attention than others? What should those priorities be?

(12) **Individual Rights and Intellectual Property**. If there is, as Alford suggests, a connection between respect for intellectual property and respect for individual rights generally, should that affect the policy of the United States

toward countries that are perceived as offering inadequate intellectual property protection? If so, how should that affect the conduct of international intellectual property relations? How should the United States respond to news that Chinese citizens have been executed for counterfeiting? In what ways, and by emphasizing which priorities, could U.S. international intellectual property policy accommodate both goals? Can Special 301 measures against China be justified as supportive of human rights? Will greater respect for human rights bring greater protection of intellectual property, or will enhanced protection for intellectual property lead to greater respect for human rights? What is the connection between the two?

(13) **Changes in Chinese Intellectual Property Laws.** What is the significance of the statement by former WIPO director-general Arpad Bogsch that "China has gone from no system just fifteen years ago to one of the most advanced countries in the developing world"? What does Dr. Bogsch mean by "no system" and "one of the most advanced"? What does that change portend for the long-term health of intellectual property protection in China?

(14) **Culturally Contingent Discussions.** How does one avoid infusing this discussion with a culturally-contingent set of values regarding individual ownership, the roots of creativity, or the relevance of free information? Can one? If not, should we abandon the endeavor?

(15) **China and the WTO.** In November 1999, the United States and China reached a trade agreement designed to facilitate China's entry into the WTO. China agreed to a wide-ranging set of market access reforms in return for the establishment of permanent normal trade relations ("PNTR"). But, under U.S. law, PNTR, formerly called most favored nation status, is dependent upon congressional approval of the agreement. Congress passed the necessary legislation in 2000. Several other WTO members are also negotiating agreements relating to terms of entry with China, and these various bilateral agreements will in turn be encompassed within a multinational agreement. China's entry will ultimately be determined by a vote of current WTO members; a two-thirds majority is required for membership. *See* WTO Agreement art. XII(2).

The U.S.-China agreement was welcomed by free traders not only for the liberalization of Chinese markets that it mandates, but also for its potential to effect significant political change in China. In what ways might membership of the WTO cause political liberalization? Does this suggest a broader basis upon which to ground support for enhanced intellectual property protection? Will WTO obligations drive the creation of the legal infrastructure and cultural mindset necessary not only to comply with the WTO Agreement but also to accord greater respect for human rights, as the Clinton administration argued? Which aspects of Chinese society will be most challenged by the involvement of the WTO in China's national affairs? Which aspects will provide the greatest challenge for the WTO?

NOTE: SPECIAL 301 AFTER TRIPS

As will be discussed in greater detail below, failure to comply with obligations of international intellectual property law may now be pursued (post-TRIPS) by complaining countries before the WTO dispute settlement body. This did not, however, result in the termination of the Special 301 process. Indeed, section 314(c) of the Uruguay Round Agreements Act, which implemented the GATT Agreement, amended the Trade Act to provide expressly that a failure to provide adequate and effective protection of intellectual property could still trigger Special 301 measures "notwithstanding the fact the foreign country may be in compliance with the specific obligations of the TRIPS Agreement." Trade Act, § 301(d)(3). Thus, the U.S. Trade Representative continues to exercise Special 301 powers, and continues to publish a report on April 30 of each year identifying countries that deny adequate and effective enforcement of intellectual property rights. *See, e.g.*, Notice of Office of the United States Trade Representative, 65 Fed. Reg. 26652 (May 8, 2000). The Special 301 Report builds upon the National Trade Estimate Report on Foreign Trade Barriers, which is published annually by the USTR on March 30 and which produces frenetic activity in Washington.

A short excerpt from the 2000 Special 301 Report follows. A full copy of the report, as well as a summary of all cases initiated under Section 301, and their outcome can be found on the homepage of the USTR at http://www.ustr.gov/reports/301report/act301.htm. Since the conclusion of TRIPS, the Special 301 process has become one of the means by which the USTR identifies issues that it might ultimately pursue before the WTO Dispute Settlement Body. We will return to a discussion of the interaction between Special 301 and the TRIPS dispute settlement process after a more detailed analysis of the latter.

OFFICE OF THE UNITED STATES TRADE REPRESENTATIVE
RESULTS OF SPECIAL 301 ANNUAL REVIEW (April 28, 2000)

United States Trade Representative Charlene Barshefsky today announced the results of the 2000 "Special 301" annual review which examined in detail the adequacy and effectiveness of intellectual property protection in over 70 countries. . .

2000 SPECIAL 301 DECISIONS

Under the Special 301 provisions of the Trade Act of 1974, as amended, Ambassador Barshefsky today identified 59 trading partners that deny adequate and effective protection of intellectual property or deny fair and equitable market access to United States artists and industries that rely upon intellectual property protection.

In today's action, the United States Trade Representative identified Ukraine for potential Priority Foreign Country designation on August 1, 2000. Ambassador Barshefsky stated that the United States has worked with Ukrainian officials over the past several years in an effort to reduce alarming levels of copyright piracy and to improve Ukraine's overall intellectual property regime. Regrettably, according to estimates from our copyright industry, Ukraine is the single largest source of pirate CDs in the Central and East European region. The U.S. Government currently is engaged with the Government of Ukraine in an intense effort to resolve this problem. At this juncture, the United States considers its interests to be best served by continuing these efforts over the next few months. However, Ukraine will be identified as a Priority Foreign Country if it fails to make substantial progress toward eliminating pirate optical media production prior to August 1, 2000.

Copyright piracy in Ukraine is extensive and enforcement is severely lacking, resulting in increasing unauthorized production and export of CDs and CD-ROMs. . . . In addition, a number of Ukraine's intellectual property laws . . . fall short of compliance with the minimum standards set out in the TRIPS Agreement and the 1992 U.S.-Ukraine bilateral trade agreement. . .

Ambassador Barshefsky again designated Paraguay and China for "Section 306 monitoring" to ensure both countries comply with the commitments made to the United States under bilateral intellectual property agreements. Special concern was expressed that Paraguay's efforts have not been sufficient in recent months, and further consultations will be scheduled.

Ambassador Barshefsky also announced placement of 16 trading partners on the "Priority Watch List": Argentina, the Dominican Republic, Egypt, the European Union, Greece, Guatemala, India, Israel, Italy, Korea, Malaysia, Peru, Poland, Russia, Turkey, and Ukraine. She also placed 39 trading partners on the "Watch List." . . .

Finally, Ambassador Barshefsky noted that while she was not listing El Salvador or the West Bank and Gaza, USTR will conduct out-of-cycle reviews of each in September and December 2000, respectively. The review of El Salvador will assess the government's efforts to improve enforcement procedures and to promote the use of authorized software in all government ministries. The review of the West Bank and Gaza will assess its progress toward implementation of promised enforcement actions against pirate CD manufacturers.

INTELLECTUAL PROPERTY AND HEALTH POLICY

On December 1, 1999, President Clinton announced that the United States is committed to helping developing countries gain access to essential medicines, including those for HIV/AIDS. . . .

. . . When a foreign government expresses concern that U.S. trade law related to intellectual property protection significantly impedes its ability to address a health crisis in that country, USTR will seek and give full weight to the advice of the Department of Health and Human Services (HHS) regarding the health considerations involved. This process will permit the application of U.S.

trade-related intellectual property law to remain sufficiently flexible to react to public health crises brought to the attention of USTR. It will also ensure that the minimum standards of the TRIPS Agreement are respected. [For the first time, HHS participated actively as a member of the Special 301 Trade Policy Staff Sub-Committee that is charged with developing the Special 301 recommendations.]

. . . .

IMPLEMENTATION OF THE WTO TRIPS AGREEMENT

. . . .

While developed countries are already required to fully implement TRIPS, developing countries were given a five year transition period—until January 1, 2000—to implement most of the Agreement's provisions. Ensuring that developing countries are in full compliance with the Agreement now that this transition period has come to an end is one of this Administration's highest priorities with respect to intellectual property rights. With respect to least developed developing countries, and with respect to the protection of pharmaceuticals and agriculture chemicals in certain developing countries, an even longer transition was provided.

Substantial progress has been made over the past year by developing countries toward full implementation of their TRIPS obligations. The United States has worked diligently to assist countries in meeting this goal through consultations and bilateral technical assistance.

. . . .

Progress continues by many countries toward more effective enforcement against piracy and counterfeiting, though there are notable exceptions highlighted in this report. This is an ongoing effort which USTR is addressing in a number of ways, including pressing for government software legalization decrees and controls on optical media production.

. . . .

GOVERNMENT USE OF SOFTWARE

In October 1998, Vice President Gore announced a new Executive Order directing U.S. Government agencies to maintain appropriate, effective procedures to ensure legitimate use of software. . .

[L]ast year, China, Colombia, Jordan, Paraguay, and the Philippines issued decrees mandating the use of only authorized software by government ministries. This year Colombia, Macau, Lebanon, and Taiwan have each issued similar decrees. Ambassador Barshefsky noted her pleasure that these governments have recognized the importance of setting an example in this area. . . .

WTO DISPUTE SETTLEMENT

As in previous years, Ambassador Barshefsky is using the annual Special 301 announcement as a vehicle to announce the launch of WTO dispute settlement proceedings against countries that have not met their TRIPS obligations. A priority of this year's Special 301 review is the proper and timely implementation of the WTO TRIPS Agreement, particularly developing country implementation which was required as of January 1, 2000 for most obligations.

In December 1999, USTR initiated an out-of-cycle review of developing countries' progress toward implementing their TRIPS obligations. This review was conducted in tandem with this year's Special 301 review. In conducting the review, it was determined that the vast majority of developing countries have made a serious effort to comply with their TRIPS obligations, though further progress in the area of enforcement is particularly needed. The United States will continue to work with developing countries that are in the process of finalizing their implementation of the Agreement and expects further progress in the very near future to complete this process. However, in those instances where additional progress is not likely in the near term, or where we have been unable to resolve concerns through bilateral consultation, USTR is pursuing U.S. rights through WTO dispute settlement proceedings.

Specifically, Ambassador Barshefsky today announced the initiation of WTO dispute settlement proceedings against Argentina and Brazil, and that we will take the next step in our dispute with Denmark and request the establishment of a WTO panel unless progress is made imminently.

Argentina

Argentina has failed to grant exclusive marketing rights for pharmaceuticals, despite being obliged to do so under the TRIPS Agreement, since Argentina does not provide patent protection for such products. In addition, Argentina fails to protect confidential test data submitted to government regulatory authorities for pharmaceuticals and agricultural chemicals. Other deficiencies in Argentina's patent law include the denial of certain exclusive rights for patents, such as the protection of products produced by patented processes and the right of importation; the failure to provide prompt and effective provisional measures to address patent infringement; and the exclusion of micro-organisms from patentability. Many of these deficiencies relate to concerns regarding Argentina's compliance with the TRIPS Agreement obligations that applied to Argentina as of January 1, 2000. As such, these claims are being added to the already on-going dispute settlement case against Argentina announced in last year's Special 301 report.

Brazil

Brazil's patent law imposes a "local working" requirement as a condition for enjoyment of exclusive patent rights. This requirement can only be satisfied by local production, and not importation, of the patented product. This appears inconsistent with Brazil's obligations under Article 27 of the WTO TRIPS Agreement . . . Brazil has stated repeatedly that it disagrees with this interpretation of the TRIPS Agreement. In order to resolve this longstanding difference in views over this issue, as well as to address the concern that other countries may cite the Brazilian "local working" requirement as a justification for proposing similar legislation, the United States is now requesting WTO consultations with Brazil to pursue this single-issue case.

. . . .

Potential Dispute Settlement Cases

In addition to the above, there are a number of other WTO Members that likewise appear not to be in compliance with their TRIPS obligations, and which we are still considering as possible future dispute settlement cases. . . We will continue to consult in the coming months with all these countries in an effort to encourage them to resolve outstanding TRIPS compliance concerns as soon as possible. We will also gather data on these countries' enforcement of their TRIPS obligations and assess the best cases for further action if consultations prove unsuccessful.

COUNTRY BY COUNTRY DESCRIPTION

Section 306 Monitoring

China: China is currently engaged in completing the first major revision to its overall [intellectual property rights (IPR)] regime since our bilateral IPR agreements were concluded in 1992 and 1995. China has agreed in the context of the negotiations on accession to the World Trade Organization to implement the TRIPS Agreement without recourse to any transition period. In the meantime, ensuring effective implementation of our bilateral agreements remains an important effort. While the production of pirated copyrighted works has dropped dramatically since 1996, imports of pirated products remain a concern. U.S. companies report that retail piracy and counterfeit goods remain widespread in China, in part because of the inadequacy of deterrent sanctions, including lack of criminal penalties. The structure of IPR administration and enforcement in China still remains too opaque. Enforcement at the provincial level is sporadic, but steps in Guangdong province to increase sanctions against piracy and counterfeiting were a positive development. In addition, four Chinese enforcement authorities have joined together to act against optical media, including DVD, pirates. Most recently, in March 2000, the State Press and Publication Administration, the National Copyright Administration of China, the Ministry of Public Security, and the State Administration of Industry and Commerce issued an urgent joint circular to urge every provincial, regional and municipal government authority to launch a special campaign against DVD piracy in China. End-user piracy of business software (particularly in companies), trademark infringement, and problems in obtaining administrative protection for pharmaceuticals are persistent problems. . . .

Paraguay: On January 16, 1998, Paraguay was identified as a Priority Foreign Country (PFC) . . . In November 1998, the U.S. Government and the Government of Paraguay signed a Memorandum of Understanding (MOU) on the Protection of Intellectual Property. While Paraguay initially made progress toward fulfilment of its obligations under the MOU, more recently progress has stalled. Last year, the Government of Paraguay, in coordination with industry, seized and destroyed two multi-million dollar pirate CD factories and made several important reforms to its legal regime for the protection of intellectual property. However, Paraguay continues to be a regional center for piracy, especially of optical media, as well as for counterfeiting, and continues to serve as a transshipment point for an alarming volume of infringing products from Asia to the larger markets bordering Paraguay, particularly Brazil. In addition, Paraguay has failed to implement its obligation under the WTO TRIPS Agreement and the bilateral MOU to enact a modern patent law, among other reforms . . . Failure to aggressively prosecute known pirates, such as one high-profile case in which a pirate was twice released on bail despite substantial evidence, is a worrisome sign that further progress toward correcting Paraguay's role as a haven for piracy and counterfeiting is threatened. Therefore, the United States has requested consultations under the MOU which will be held in the coming months. If further results are not forthcoming, the United States may consider other options for resolving concerns regarding protection for intellectual property in Paraguay.

Priority Watch List

Argentina: . . . In contrast to the lack of protection in other areas, Argentina's copyright regime has continued to improve over the past two years with Argentina's enactment of legislation in 1999 to ratify the WIPO Copyright Treaty and Performance and Phonograms Treaty. Regrettably, enforcement against copyright piracy and trademark counterfeiting remains significantly below TRIPS standards.

Dominican Republic: The Dominican Republic has failed to correct deficiencies in its legal framework to meet its obligations under the TRIPS Agreement. Draft copyright legislation would be a major improvement over current law. However, draft patent legislation does not appear to meet TRIPS Agreement standards. The U.S. looks to the Government of the Dominican Republic to pass TRIPS-consistent legislation in both areas in conformance with its international commitments. We will continue to consult informally with the Government of the Dominican Republic in an effort to encourage it to resolve outstanding TRIPS compliance concerns as soon as possible in the coming months. Lax enforcement also remains a problem. . . In response to a petition from the copyright industry, USTR is reviewing the eligibility status of the Dominican Republic under the Generalized System of Preferences (GSP) program.

Egypt: Egypt's intellectual property laws do not comply fully with the TRIPS Agreement. The copyright law remains deficient in the area of protection for pre-existing sound recordings. Egypt's patent law does not provide protection for pharmaceutical and agricultural chemical products and contains other provisions that do not comply with TRIPS Agreement obligations. The government has drafted a new patent law, but had announced previously that it intends to avail itself of the full transition period for product patent protection, i.e., until January 1, 2005. Although the Government of Egypt recently adopted a decree nominally designed to comply with the TRIPS Agreement obligation to provide exclusive marketing rights for pharmaceutical and agricultural products, the adequacy of the decree remains untested. Egypt is considering a revision of its trademark law to meet TRIPS Agreement standards, but the existing trademark law is not enforced strenuously and the courts have only limited experience in adjudicating infringement cases. Although raids have increased, enforcement on the whole remains lax and therefore copyright piracy and trademark infringement remain unchecked. We will continue to consult informally with the Government of Egypt in an effort to encourage it to resolve outstanding TRIPS compliance concerns as soon as possible in the coming months.

The European Union: In 1999, the United States initiated WTO dispute settlement proceedings against the European Union regarding its regulation concerning geographical indications for foodstuffs and agricultural products. Concerns have been expressed that this regulation denies national treatment and does not adequately protect pre-existing trademarks. The EU continues to deny national treatment to U.S. intellectual property right holders in other areas as well. For example, the reciprocity requirement in the data base directive continues to be of concern. Restrictions in certain member states also deny market access opportunities for U.S. right holders. The Administration has made several efforts to address other intellectual property issues of concern to the United States in the context of the U.S.-EU TransAtlantic Economic Partnership—those efforts have produced little result to date, though the United States remains hopeful of progress in these areas.

Greece: In 1998, USTR announced the initiation of WTO dispute settlement consultations with Greece and the European Union regarding the high rates of television piracy in Greece. During the course of these consultations, the Government of Greece has taken steps toward addressing this problem, including the passage of additional legislation and the closure of a number of television stations which continued to broadcast programing without authorization. However, Greece has yet to provide assurances that it would implement its new enforcement procedure in a strong and consistent manner, and to take steps to improve the handling of intellectual property cases in the court system for the purposes of resolving this dispute. . . .

Guatemala: Guatemala's Criminal Procedures Code requires that all criminal enforcement be brought as "private actions", making criminal penalties difficult to obtain in cases of copyright infringement. Piracy, including by government agencies, is widespread, and the Government of Guatemala has failed to take effective enforcement action. . . .

India: India continues to lack adequate and effective patent protection, failing to comply with the obligations of the TRIPS Agreement in a number of areas, especially with regard to local working requirements, patentable subject matter and exclusive patent rights, term of protection, and protection for test data. Although not required to do so under the TRIPS Agreement until 2005, India has yet to provide patent protection for pharmaceutical and agricultural chemical products. Patent legislation has been drafted but not yet passed. While India's copyright law is generally compliant with the TRIPS Agreement, amendments passed in 1999 undermine TRIPS requirements concerning protection for computer programs. In addition, enforcement against piracy, especially cable piracy, remains a growing concern for U.S. copyright industries, as well as enforcement against imports of pirated products coming from Southeast Asia, for the most part Malaysia. . . .

Israel: The Knesset enacted TRIPS omnibus legislation in December 1999 covering a number of areas, including patents, trademarks and copyright. In the last six months, the Government of Israel has allocated additional resources, including hiring new policemen for intellectual property enforcement and funding new prosecutors, to combat widespread copyright infringement. However, we remain very concerned about the unacceptably high rate of piracy of all forms of optical media in Israel. Israel remains a key distribution hub in a multi-country network (including Eastern Europe and Russia) for pirated optical media product, much of which is still manufactured in Israel. We urge the Government of Israel to expedite its ongoing review of CD plant controls, including mandatory use of source identification codes, and to implement quickly effective controls. Other concerns with Israel's intellectual property regime include possible TRIPS deficiencies such as failure to protect adequately confidential test data and to provide criminal penalties for unauthorized end-user copying of computer software . . . .

Italy: Despite five years of effort, the Government of Italy has failed to enact anti-piracy legislation that includes TRIPS-consistent penalties sufficient to provide an effective deterrent to piracy and counterfeiting . . . Italy's failure to pass this important legislation is of particular concern because it has some of the lowest criminal penalties in Europe and one of the highest rates of piracy. Piracy and counterfeiting of American intellectual property in Italy continue to be relatively widespread practices, particularly with regard to piracy of video, sound recordings, computer software, books, and video games. As a result of Italy's continued failure to enact this anti-piracy legislation, USTR will conduct an out-of-cycle review of Italy in September of this year. . . .

Korea: Korea is being elevated to the Priority Watch List this year because of a number of longstanding issues, concerns about enforcement, and new issues relating to recent amendments to Korean copyright laws. Despite numerous U.S. attempts, including at the highest levels, and in a variety of fora, several longstanding issues remain unresolved. . . The United States . . . has ongoing concerns about the consistency, transparency, and effectiveness of Korean enforcement efforts, particularly with regard to piracy of U.S. computer software and books. . . .

Malaysia: Over the past year, Malaysia has focused its efforts on legislation intended to strengthen IPR enforcement against piracy. These priority measures include . . . enactment of a law necessary to implement a comprehensive regime regulating the production of optical disks. . . Malaysia also continues to work closely with U.S. companies to deter unlicenced use of software by end-users. However, there is a substantial backlog of IPR cases in the Malaysia courts, and when penalties are imposed they are often insufficient to deter future or repeat offenses. While the number of raids initiated by government authorities increased during 1999, more needs to be done to address general nationwide enforcement. . . .

Peru: The Government of Peru has put in place an ambitious plan to strengthen IPR enforcement during 2000. We are encouraged by the initial steps already taken by the government to implement the plan by bolstering its inter-agency coordination and by collaborating more actively with key private sector interests. . . U.S. industry continues to express concern about decisions by the [courts] that are not adequate to deter piracy. We look forward to seeing more complete results from these efforts by late 2000. With respect to patents, the provisions of the revised Andean Community Decision 344 have not yet been brought into conformity with the TRIPS Agreement. We will continue to consult informally with Andean Community governments in an effort to encourage them to resolve the outstanding TRIPS compliance concerns as soon as possible in the coming months.

Poland: Poland has not yet brought its copyright regime into line with its obligations under the TRIPS Agreement. . . The parliament has made significant progress in preparing amendments to the Copyright Law that would provide for the TRIPS-mandated 50-year retroactive protection of sound recordings and would clarify the point of attachment for sound recordings. We urge the Government of Poland to pass these amendments quickly. The amendments would significantly strengthen Poland's regime for the protection of intellectual property, and passage would trigger a review of Poland's Special 301 status. With respect to enforcement, prosecutors and judicial authorities have not vigorously protected intellectual property rights. . .

Russia: A number of the intellectual property laws, especially the patent, copyright and data protection laws, and the enforcement regime of the Russian Federation do not comply with the TRIPS Agreement or the intellectual property provisions of the U.S.-Russian Federation bilateral trade agreement signed in 1991. Despite a significant number of police raids, and commendable official efforts to improve the enforcement climate, criminal enforcement of intellectual property rights remains minimal in Russia. . . Russia's ineffective criminal enforcement system and the lack of any border control not only have allowed the domestic market to become saturated by Ukrainian and Asian-origin pirate products, but have also resulted in the development of Russia into a major transit country for counterfeit products destined for European markets.

Turkey: To date, Turkey has not yet addressed all of the benchmarks set out in the 1997 review. Remaining work needs to be done to enhance Turkey's copyright regime to include copyright protection for pre-existing works and sound recordings and ex parte and injunctive relief, and to include deterrent penalties and jail terms. Passage of amendments to the copyright law to address these concerns is anticipated in the near future, and we urge expeditious legislative action. . . .

. . . .

Watch List

Armenia: Armenia has several remaining steps to take to fulfill its intellectual property commitments under the 1992 U.S.-Armenia Trade Agreement and to make its intellectual property regime consistent with the TRIPS Agreement. . . . In addition, we are concerned about weak enforcement of intellectual property rights in Armenia. Although new criminal penalties for intellectual property violations have been adopted, there have been no convictions under the new law and police authority to commence criminal copyright cases is unclear. Further, Armenia's Customs Code does not provide the proper authority to seize material at the border as required by the TRIPS Agreement. If not addressed, ineffective border enforcement could cause Armenia to become a target for illegal optical media producers, a problem that other countries of the region have faced.

. . . .

Bolivia: Bolivia has made some progress this past year with the long-awaited appointment of a director to the National Intellectual Property Service (SENAPI), created by President Banzer in 1997. SENAPI officials appear to be making a good faith effort to train personnel and acquire the resources needed to strengthen the institution. However, SENAPI continues to be seriously underfunded, lacks trained technical personnel, and has no mechanism to enforce intellectual property protections. Overall, enforcement of intellectual property protection in Bolivia remains weak. Software piracy continues to flourish unabated and counterfeit products are produced in Bolivia and imported into the country with impunity, despite efforts by a new national customs service to control contraband at Bolivia's borders and ports of entry. . . .

Brazil: Brazil made substantial progress on an April 1998 commitment to process pipeline applications in an expedited manner, and it has significantly increased the rate at which it processes regular patent applications. . . . Progress has not been sufficient on Brazil's commitment to increase effective enforcement actions, from raids through judicial decisions, against intellectual property infringement; the rate of CD piracy in Brazil continues to worsen. . . .

Canada: A WTO dispute settlement panel recently confirmed that Canada's patent law fails to grant a full twenty-year patent term to certain patents as required by the TRIPS Agreement. In 1999, Ambassador Barshefsky announced initiation of WTO dispute settlement proceedings to address this situation. The United States looks to the Government of Canada to comply swiftly with the panel's ruling and bring its patent regime into compliance with Canada's international obligations before further losses are suffered by patent owners in Canada. In 1997, the Government of Canada adopted amendments to its copyright law that discriminate against the interests of some U.S. copyright holders. Canada has established a right of remuneration for the public performance of sound recordings and performances. It also has established a levy on blank audio recording media, the revenues from which are intended to compensate performers and producers for the performance and unauthorized home-taping of their works in Canada. The United States remains extremely concerned that U.S. performers and record producers are denied national treatment with respect to both these provisions and also that the remuneration right for public performances does not give producers and performers exclusive rights over on-demand and interactive uses. We will closely monitor their implementation and any future reform of Canada's copyright laws. More recently, U.S. industry has expressed concern over specific deficiencies in Canada's enforcement against piracy and counterfeiting, particularly at the border. . . .

Chile: While generally strong, Chile's intellectual property laws are not yet consistent with its obligations under the WTO TRIPS Agreement which came into force on January 1, 2000. . . Inadequate enforcement against piracy and counterfeiting remains a serious concern, as does the large backlog of pending patent applications. We look to the Government of Chile to eliminate the backlog of patent applications and to bring its legal regime into compliance with TRIPS without further delay.

. . . .

Costa Rica: Costa Rica has made significant efforts to improve its legal framework for the protection of intellectual property. The Government of Costa Rica passed seven laws at the end of 1999 in an effort to bring its regime into compliance with its obligations under the TRIPS Agreement, including a provision to extend patent protection terms to TRIPS levels. However, a number of problems remain on the enforcement side, particularly with respect to criminal prosecutions, as evidenced by continued high levels of piracy. The U.S. looks to the Government of Costa Rica to build on its recent progress by taking adequate and effective enforcement actions.

Czech Republic: The Czech Republic has enacted patent, trademark, customs, and criminal and civil code amendments to bring its intellectual property rights regime in line with TRIPS Agreement obligations. . . However, the Czech Republic still does not explicitly provide for ex parte search and seizure authority in civil proceedings, and alternative measures in the Civil Procedure Code do not appear to be adequate. In addition, despite relatively good cooperation with police and customs officials, enforcement problems with prosecutors and courts remain pervasive throughout all sectors of the copyright industry. As a result, piracy of audiovisual, software, sound recording, book and optical media products continues to be a serious problem in the Czech Republic. We will continue to consult informally with the Czech Republic in the coming months in an effort to encourage it to resolve outstanding TRIPS compliance concerns, including enforcement, as soon as possible.

Denmark: The United States initiated WTO dispute settlement proceedings against Denmark in 1997 as a result of Denmark's failure to implement its obligations under the TRIPS Agreement requiring provisional remedies, including ex parte procedures in civil enforcement proceedings. Courts must be granted the ability to order unannounced raids in appropriate cases to determine whether infringement is taking place and to preserve evidence of infringements, as well as the ability to order that allegedly infringing activities be stopped pending the outcome of a civil infringement case. This type of enforcement remedy is particularly important to the enforcement efforts of the software industry. After numerous consultations with the United States, the

Government of Denmark established a Special Legislative Committee to consider the issue and determine the need for amendments to Danish law. The Committee is currently in the process of drafting the necessary legislation, but this process is significantly behind schedule. Therefore, USTR will take the next step in our dispute with Denmark and request the establishment of a WTO panel unless progress is made imminently.

. . . .

Hungary: Hungary has enacted copyright, patent, trademark, and criminal and civil code amendments to brings its intellectual property rights regime in line with its obligations under the TRIPS Agreement and its obligations to the United States and the European Union. However, questions remain whether sufficient legal authority exists as required by the TRIPS Agreement for civil ex parte search procedures. . . . With respect to enforcement, despite good cooperation with the police, video and cable television piracy is widespread, and local television and cable companies regularly transmit programs without authorization. Prosecutors and judicial authorities have generally not dealt with piracy cases in an expeditious manner or imposed deterrent level fines and jail sentences . . . .

Indonesia: . . . Draft legislation in the areas of trade secrets, industrial design and integrated circuits, as well as amendments to existing patent, trademark and copyright laws, was prepared to meet the January 1, 2000 deadline for compliance with the TRIPS Agreement. While the Indonesian Parliament did not act on these proposals prior to that deadline, the legislation was resubmitted to Parliament in February 2000. Police raids were stepped up, but optical media piracy remains rampant and effective enforcement continues to be hindered by corruption and a non-transparent legal and judicial system. . . .

Ireland: It has been over five years since the WTO TRIPS Agreement came into force and the Government of Ireland has yet to implement a fully TRIPS-consistent copyright law. Three years ago, the United States initiated dispute settlement proceedings to address our concern over this situation. After numerous consultations with the United States, Ireland committed to enact comprehensive copyright reform legislation by December 1, 1998, and agreed to pass a separate bill, on an expedited basis, to address two particularly pressing enforcement issues. Consistent with this agreement, Ireland enacted legislation in June 1998 raising criminal penalties for copyright infringement and addressing other enforcement issues. However, Ireland's commitment to enact comprehensive copyright legislation has not been met. We understand recent progress has been made toward finalizing this legislation and expect it will be enacted by parliament before its summer recess. The U.S. Government remains hopeful that Ireland will take the steps necessary to complete the legislative process in the very near future, but will feel compelled to consider other options in the face of any further delay.

. . . .

Latvia: Although Latvia has made progress in improving its intellectual property rights regime since it became a member of the WTO in February 1999, there is still much room for improvement. Latvian law does not allow for civil ex parte searches. . . Although pirate optical media production currently is not a problem, there exists a pervasive transshipment problem in Latvia, not only in optical media but in other copyrighted products as well, with much of Latvia's pirated business software flowing over the border from Russia.

Lebanon: The new copyright law provides a firm basis for copyright protection for U.S. works and sound recordings. However, the law contains exemptions that are not consistent with international standards, and there has been little enforcement against piracy. End-user piracy of computer software is pervasive among large companies, banks, trading companies, and most government ministries. In addition, optical media production facilities are reportedly being set up, with the potential for Lebanon to become an exporter of pirated product. . . . Concerns also remain that health authorities are registering unauthorized copies of patented pharmaceuticals. We look to Lebanon to take swift action to address these concerns.

. . . .

Macau: Over the past six months, Macau has made reasonable progress in attacking the piracy problems that led to its placement on the Special 301 Priority Watch List. . . . Over the next several months, we look to Macau to organize a new customs department, incorporating elements of both the Macau Economic Services Department and the Marine Police. . . . Macau's courts have implemented a special expedited prosecution system that allows a suspect to be brought immediately to trial. We now look to Macau to vigorously prosecute those responsible for piracy. . . .

. . . .

Oman: As part of its efforts to accede to the WTO, Oman is currently working with WTO Members to amend its current copyright law to comply with the provisions of the TRIPS Agreement. Although Oman has started to take steps to combat software piracy, no action has been taken to date against end-users of unauthorized computer software. . . .

Pakistan: Pakistan's regime for protection of intellectual property does not yet comply with the obligations of the TRIPS Agreement. The Government of Pakistan has undertaken the task of rewriting legislation in the areas of copyrights, patents, and trademarks, but this work appears to have been hampered by lack of a central coordinating authority. . . .

The Philippines: The Philippines has been inconsistent in its nationwide enforcement efforts which rarely result in the imposition of deterrent penalties. . . .It is . . .unclear whether existing law provides right holders an ex parte search and seizure remedy as required by TRIPS Article 50, which is a major priority for the United States. . . .We are also concerned about ineffective enforcement against cable television piracy, and about the persistence of unacceptably high levels of piracy of U.S. textbooks and other publications. In reaction to increased reports about the proliferation of infringing optical disc production in the Philippines, the United States strongly urges the Philippine Government to adopt an effective regulatory system to combat this problem. . . .

Qatar: Despite isolated enforcement actions, Qatar has not yet pursued sustained and deterrent enforcement against end-users of unauthorized computer software, including government entities and against retail shops selling pirated software. . . .

Romania: Although Romania has joined the Berne Convention and the Geneva Phonograms Convention, and is a signatory of the WIPO treaties, it has yet to ratify the treaties or pass legislation necessary to implement them. Criminal enforcement against copyright piracy and trademark counterfeiting (especially of U.S. distilled spirits) continues to be lax, resulting in troubling levels of infringements against imported products and growing domestic production of pirated goods. . . .

Saudi Arabia: As part of its effort to accede to the WTO, Saudi Arabia is currently working with WTO Members to revise its intellectual property laws, including patent and copyright laws, to bring them into conformity with the TRIPS Agreement. . . While the government has been working with the U.S. copyright-based industries to conduct some raids, overall enforcement is not carried out with sufficient regularity and is not accompanied by the appropriate level of publicity and sentences to reduce the level of piracy. . . .

Singapore: Overall piracy rates in Singapore decreased slightly during 1999, while the number of police-organized raids increased. . . . The United States urges Singapore to continue its anti-piracy consumer education campaign and to reassess the existing "self-help" approach to intellectual property enforcement which shifts to right owners the primary burden and expense of investigating and prosecuting infringement. . . . Further, we remain concerned about insufficient efforts at the border to stop the in-flow and transshipment of infringing articles through Singapore.

Spain: . . . Government enforcement activities have increased substantially in recent years with exemplary cooperation from Spanish police. However, recent court decisions have called into question the adequacy of protection for well-known trademarks. . . .The slow pace of both civil and criminal court proceedings and lack of sufficient criminal penalties is thought to have diluted the impact of the increased raids in certain areas.

. . . .

Taiwan: Taiwan has had mixed results on intellectual property during the last year. On the positive side, top level support within the Ministry of Economic Affairs has finally resulted in the establishment of an effective Intellectual Property Office. This office has been well staffed with energetic people. . . . On the negative side, responsibility for intellectual property matters is still badly fragmented among different agencies. Repeated U.S. Government requests for action to improve access to the judicial system in infringements cases, to enforce existing source identification code regulations, and to adopt an effective chip marking system have been rebuffed. Taiwan is now among the world's largest producers of optical media. Toleration of extremely lax procedures in enforcing intellectual property rights in this area is out of step with Taiwan's increasing role as an originator of intellectual property.

. . . .

Thailand: Thailand's . . . intellectual property courts are imposing criminal penalties; however, these are often not sufficient to deter infringement and are often suspended pending appeal. Thai prosecutors remain unwilling to charge infringers for violations of customs and revenue laws, in addition to intellectual property infringement. Moreover, the periodic disappearance from police custody of critical evidence of copyright and trademark infringement continues to hamper prosecution. . . .The government . . needs to do more to address increasing levels of optical media piracy in Thailand. In this regard, the United States will monitor closely ongoing efforts to enact legislation necessary to implement a comprehensive regulatory regime to control optical media production. We also urge Thailand to address the inability of enforcement authorities to conduct raids outside business hours; this deficiency has become a significant liability to the effectiveness of the government's efforts to strengthen intellectual property enforcement.

. . . .

Uruguay: Reform of outdated patent and copyright legislation has been underway in Uruguay for a number of years. The Uruguayan Congress enacted the patent bill in September 1999, but the new law contains several problematic areas, including omission of protection for confidential test data, overly broad compulsory licensing provisions, failure to address exclusive marketing rights, and international exhaustion of patent rights. We urge the Government of Uruguay to enact TRIPS-consistent copyright legislation and to amend the new patent law to bring it into full compliance with TRIPS Agreement obligations. . .

. . . .

Vietnam: The Government is still in the formative stages of drafting, enacting and enforcing intellectual property laws. . . . On December 27, 1998, the bilateral copyright agreement between the United States and Vietnam entered into force, following the issuance of implementing regulations by Vietnam. The agreement grants U.S. works copyright protection in Vietnam for the first time. We look to the Government of Vietnam to enforce its new copyright regime vigorously to reduce piracy levels measurably, and to take steps to ensure that all government offices use only legitimate software. We also expect the Government of Vietnam to address intellectual property rights issues in the contexts of negotiations on a bilateral trade agreement and its accession to the WTO.

QUESTIONS

This edited version of the April 28, 2000 announcement by the USTR provides a representative sample of the comments included by the trade representative with respect to different countries. From the report's summary of areas of concern, can you detect the current priorities of the USTR (in addition to those explicitly acknowledged)? Do you agree with these priorities? To some extent, these annual reports reflect concerns expressed by intellectual property trade associations. *See, e.g.*, Letter from Eric Smith, President, International Intellectual Property Alliance, to Joseph Papovich, Assistant USTR for Intellectual Property, in Response to Request For Submissions Regarding Identification of Countries Under Section 182 of the Trade Act (Special 301), February 16, 1999 (reporting views of coalition of seven trade associations representing segments of U.S. copyright industries and suggesting specific

Special 301 categorization of 58 countries), *reprinted in* 46 J. COPR. SOC'Y 99 (1999). Is any apparent area of concern an inappropriate subject of comment by the United States? To what standards does the USTR appear to be holding other countries? Are these standards appropriate? Identify the different means by which and the different fora in which the USTR is seeking to achieve its objectives? Do the responses being sought by the United States from other countries appear consistent with the nature of international intellectual property relations?

[B]   European Union Trade Barrier Regulation

As suggested in the Newby article *supra*, the EU has responded somewhat in kind to the review aspects of the Special 301 device by enacting a Trade Barrier Regulation. *See* Council Regulation (EC) No. 3286/94 laying down community procedures in the field of the common commercial policy in order to ensure the exercise of the community's right under international trade rules, in particular those established under the auspices of the World Trade Organization, O.J. 1994 L 349/71 of 31 December 1994, as amended by Council Regulation (EC) No. 356/95, O.J. 1995 L 41/3 of 23 February 1995. Under this regulation, individual companies may file a complaint with the European Commission if their trade opportunities in third-country markets are restricted by foreign trade barriers (such as inadequate intellectual property protection). The Trade Barrier Regulation replaces the similar, but weaker and thus little used, mechanism established in 1984 by the New Commercial Policy Instrument ("NCPI"). *See* David Rose, *The EU Trade Barrier Regulation: An Effective Instrument for Promoting Global Harmonisation of Intellectual Property Rights*, 21 EUR. INTELL. PROP. REV. 313 (1999). The NCPI had not specifically addressed inadequacies in intellectual property (although it was used in matters of intellectual property), and had given the Commission very limited powers to deal with third countries. The Trade Barrier Regulation remedies those weaknesses. Complaints alleging third country obstacles to trade may be filed with the Commission either by a community industry or a community enterprise. After consultation with member states (by the vehicle of an advisory committee), the Commission decides whether there is evidence of a basis upon which to conduct an examination of the third country practices. The examination procedure includes an information gathering process that is not unlike that used by the USTR, involving broad solicitation of input from interested parties. The examination procedure takes between five to seven months, and results in the submission of a report by the Commission to the advisory committee of member states' representatives. The Commission may terminate the proceedings if further action is not in the community's interest, may suspend proceedings pending resolution of the matter with the country concerned, or may take retaliatory trade measures. Article 12(2) of the Trade Barrier Regulation requires that where international obligations require the Commission to address the dispute through a particular dispute settlement process, that process must be followed prior to the imposition of retaliatory measures. For a thorough explanation of the Trade Barrier Regulation and its use thus far, see *id.*

In its first four years, the Commission ruled on eight complaints. Several of the referrals have led to the initiation of the WTO dispute settlement mechanism by the EU. For example, the EU challenge to the Fairness in Music Licensing Act, *see supra* § 4.03[B][2], flowed from a complaint filed by the Irish collecting society, the Irish Music Rights Organization ("IMRO"), supported by the Members of the Groupement Européen des Sociétés d'Auteurs et Compositeurs ("GESAC"), a grouping of twenty-four of the largest licensing and collecting societies in Europe. *See* Notice of initiation of an examination procedure concerning an obstacle to trade, within the Meaning of Council Regulation (EC) No. 3286/94, consisting of trade practices maintained by the United States in relation to cross-border music licensing, O.J. 1997 C177/5 of 11 June 1997. The use of the Trade Barrier Regulation mechanism is likely to increase as the WTO dispute settlement process develops further.

§ 5.03　Multilateral Trade Measures: WTO Dispute Settlement

[A]　An Introduction to the System

The conclusion of TRIPS in 1994 dramatically altered the nature of international intellectual property law. Most significantly, international obligations imposed upon countries are now backed up by real, effective enforcement mechanisms. But the newness of this enforcement system raises many first-impression issues for international intellectual property law (and, indeed, for the GATT system). In a groundbreaking article published before any complaints alleging violations of TRIPS were filed, Professors Rochelle Dreyfuss and Andreas Lowenfeld of New York University School of Law provided an insightful combined trade/intellectual property perspective on these issues. The Dreyfuss/Lowenfeld analysis is built around five hypothetical cases, which serve superbly to highlight many of these first impression issues. Excerpts from the article follow. After each of the hypothetical cases analyzed by Dreyfuss and Lowenfeld, we have inserted notes and questions. These notes and questions not only probe the analysis offered by Dreyfuss and Lowenfeld, but also reflect observations based upon cases actually filed or decided and scholarly commentary authored since the article's publication. It is perhaps a testament to the value of this article that we use the Dreyfuss/Lowenfeld article discussing hypothetical cases as the basis for our discussion of actual cases. (As of April 30, 2001, six panel reports and two Appellate Body reports have been issued on complaints regarding TRIPS compliance, and two cases are pending before panels.)

First, however, David Palmeter has succinctly described the basic dispute resolution procedure and the background to the 1994 GATT Agreement, which gave rise to the World Trade Organization on January 1, 1995. An excerpt from that description precedes our case discussion.

DAVID PALMETER, NATIONAL SOVEREIGNTY AND
THE WORLD TRADE ORGANIZATION[*]
2 J. WORLD INTELL. PROP. 77, 78-81 (1999)

III. Background

GATT was a multilateral trade agreement that grew out of the aftermath of World War II. In its 47 years of existence, GATT served as the forum for eight rounds of tariff-cutting negotiations . . . GATT was a complex agreement, but it was based on three core 'constitutional' Articles, which remain fundamental in the WTO. In fact, the 1947 GATT has been brought into the WTO word for word, where it is now part of 'GATT 1994.' . . .

The first core constitutional provision of GATT, set out in Article I, is 'most favoured-nation' treatment, which is an unusual way of saying 'normal' treatment. It means that each GATT party, and now each WTO member, receives the same tariff treatment as the 'most favoured' Party or Member—in other words, they are treated the same. Any favour granted to one is granted to all. The second principle, set out in Article II, is tariff-binding. This is simply a promise not to raise tariffs above agreed levels. The third principle, set out in Article III, is 'national treatment'. It means that once foreign goods have entered the national market of another Member, once the bound tariff is paid and import formalities are completed, foreign goods will be treated the same as domestic goods for tax and all other regulatory purposes.

[GATT] was less than a year old when its first dispute arose . . .The Chairman of the meeting at which the complaint was made ruled that the [tax on imports levied by one state were a violation of GATT]. . . This is how dispute settlement began, with a simple ruling from the Chair in 1948. . . . Over time, the complexity of the questions increased, and the chair began to refer them to working parties comprised of the disputants and any others interested in the issue. Eventually, this evolved into a system of panels composed of delegates from parties not involved in the dispute who heard arguments from the disputants. Still later, non-delegates, usually academics and retired government officials, began serving as panelists from time to time.

. . . .

One characteristic of this system reflected its origin as a multi-party agreement: the requirement that concurrence of the entire membership was necessary for any action, including the adoption of dispute settlement reports. Nothing in GATT gave the Chair the authority to decide that question in 1948. Canada's Dana Wilgress simply was in the chair when the question was raised and he ruled. Any party, most particularly the party he ruled against, could have objected. But no-one did, and that was the key to the GATT dispute settlement.

Reports of working parties and, later of panels were brought before the entire membership. Objection—usually by the losing party—was enough to prevent

---

[*]This article was originally published in the January 1999 issue of the Journal of World Intellectual Property (Vol. 2 No. 1) and is reproduced by permission of the publisher.

their adoption. Dissatisfaction with the system, primarily by the United States, led to the adoption of the WTO's Understanding on Rules and Procedures Governing the Settlement of Disputes—the DSU.

IV. WTO Dispute Settlement

The move from GATT to the WTO very much reflects a move away from a diplomatic approach to solving problems toward a juridical approach. Brazil's ambassador to the WTO, Celso Lafer, has used the term "thickening of legality" to describe the change. Vestiges of the diplomatic remain in dispute settlement . . . and at times these have provided ammunition for critics of the WTO.

Formal dispute settlement begins with a request for consultations from the complaining party to a potential defendant. . . [I]n many instances extensive discussions between the governments concerned will already have occurred well before a request for formal consultations is made. Frequently, a decision to request consultations in reality is a decision to start the formal process.

If consultations do not produce a solution, the complaining party may request the Dispute Settlement Body—the DSB—to establish a panel. The WTO Secretariat presents the names of possible panelists to the parties. These names are drawn from a list of qualified individuals maintained by the Secretariat, [which] includes names provided by [WTO] Members. If the parties cannot agree on three names, either party eventually may ask the Director-General to name the panel. This has happened on occasion, although Members generally prefer to avoid it as too unpredictable.

After panelists are agreed upon or are named by the Director-General, the process begins. The parties submit written briefs and meet with the panel, and then repeat the process with rebuttal briefs and a second meeting. The panel subsequently presents an interim report to the parties on which they may comment and point out errors. . .

The panel gives whatever consideration it deems appropriate to the comments of the parties on the interim report, and then issues its final report first to the parties and, about two weeks later, to the entire membership. In theory, the interim report is confidential; it is intended to give the parties the chance to settle the case before the report is made public. But leaks to the press of the results of interim reports are notorious . . . On at least one occasion, however, the [process] has worked [as hoped]. In a dispute between Canada and the European Communities, the parties settled after they received the final report but before it was made public.

. . . .

Once a panel report has been issued—by being circulated to all the Members of the WTO, at which time it is also released to the public—it will be adopted unless it is appealed or unless there is a consensus not to adopt. Since it is highly unlikely that the winning party would join a consensus not to adopt a decision in a case it just won, adoption is all but automatic.

This is just the opposite of the GATT system where decisions were not adopted unless there was a consensus to do so, consensus [requiring] agreement of the losing party. While the losing party agreed to adopt GATT reports in about 90% of the cases, a number of reports in important cases were blocked and others were adopted only after several years. Change in this system of blockage and delay was an important negotiating goal of the United States in the Uruguay Round. . .

The right to appeal from a panel decision is another extremely important innovation of the Uruguay Round. There was no appeal in the GATT. The Uruguay Round negotiators believed, however, that with the new system of near automatic adoption of reports, appellate review was necessary. The Appellate Body, a semi-permanent group of seven members, three of whom serve on a particular case, was the result. . . .

NOTES AND QUESTIONS

(1) **Adjudication versus Negotiation**. Which aspects of the system described by David Palmeter reflect the shift toward adjudication rather than diplomatic negotiation? Which aspects retain the "vestiges of the diplomatic"? As you read the excerpt from Dreyfuss and Lowenfeld that follows, consider which approaches or analyses suggested by the authors reflect the different models. In the context of private dispute resolution, we have witnessed over the last few years a trend from adjudication of disputes to mediation of disputes. Why did countries agree to move in the other direction—from negotiated resolutions to adjudicated decisions—in the Uruguay Round in 1994? Why does the WTO dispute settlement process retain *any* aspects of the diplomatic model?

(2) **Transparency**. The United States and the EU have expressed concerns about the transparency of the WTO dispute settlement process. Parties' submissions to the panel are kept confidential by states, *see* DSU art. 18(2), and the meetings between the parties and the panel members are closed to the public. The United States and the EU have argued that documents should be available to the public and that hearings should be open to the public. Would this be advisable? What benefits would it provide? Why do you think that some countries, particularly developing countries, have been more leery of opening up the process? *See The Review of the WTO's Dispute Settlement Understanding: Which Way?*, 1 J. WORLD INTELL. PROP. 447, 459 (1998) (comments of John Kingery); Kim Van der Borght, *The Review of the WTO Understanding on Dispute Settlement: Some Reflections on the Current Debate*, 14 AM. U. INT'L L. REV. 1223, 1228 (1999).

THE WTO DISPUTE SETTLEMENT PROCESS: A FLOWCHART

http://www.wto.org/wto/about/dispute2.html

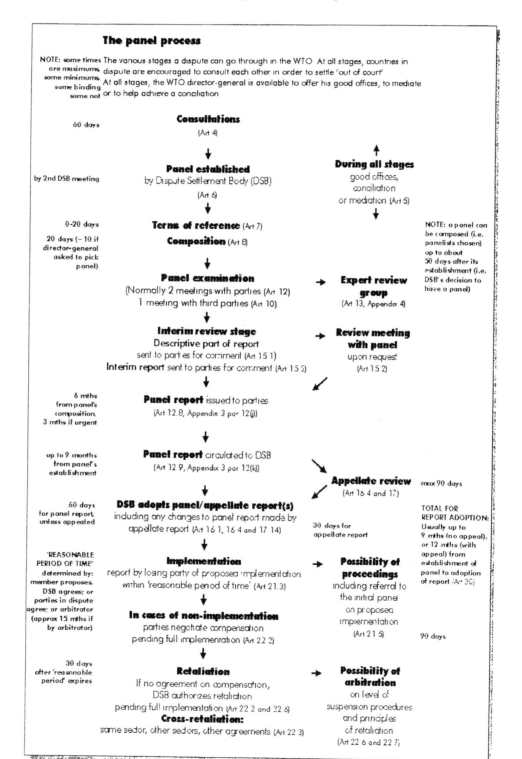

ROCHELLE COOPER DREYFUSS AND ANDREAS F. LOWENFELD
TWO ACHIEVEMENTS OF THE URUGUAY ROUND:
PUTTING TRIPS AND DISPUTE SETTLEMENT TOGETHER[*]
37 VA. J. INT'L L. 275-97 (1997)

Introduction

In many ways, completion of the Uruguay Round was a miracle, a package deal with so large an agenda that no state or group of states, and no professional community, could fully grasp the significance of everything that was finally subsumed within the new General Agreement on Tariffs and Trade (GATT). The United States, for instance, was allied with the larger developing countries on agriculture, with the European Community on the other side; but on intellectual property, the United States was, roughly speaking, allied with the European Community, and it was the developing countries that were on the other—or perhaps, better, on another—side. Add in investment issues, services, government procurement, and the traditional trade issues—subsidies, dumping, and safeguards—and the shifting conditions and interests were something like a kaleidoscope.

There were two major breakthroughs in the Uruguay Round. The one that seems to have been the most surprising to the participants was agreement on a strict and binding system of dispute settlement and enforcement. . .

The second significant achievement concerned intellectual property, previously the province of bilateral and multilateral agreements that generally lacked enforcement provisions. The incorporation of an Agreement on Trade-Related Aspects of Intellectual Property Rights (TRIPS) into the GATT means that member states will, for the first time, have a place to resolve disputes concerning the recognition of copyright, patent, trademark, and related rights. Moreover, because every member must now accept all the agreements negotiated during the Uruguay Round, TRIPS signals the entry of many new states into the intellectual property community.

As salutary as these developments are, they raise important questions. While the enforcement system of the new WTO was probably one of the most attractive features of the GATT to the intellectual property community, the architects of the Understanding on Dispute Settlement[2] were thinking more about curing the perceived shortcomings of the prior GATT dispute settlement mechanism–about how to handle disputes concerning measures enforced by states on imports or exports of goods–than they were about the TRIPS Agreement. They apparently gave little thought to such issues as the differences between rights in intellectual property and other forms of property,

---

[2]Understanding on Rules and Procedures Governing the Settlement of Disputes, art. 3.8, Apr. 15, 1994, Marrakesh Agreement Establishing the World Trade Organization [hereinafter WTO Agreement], Annex 2, Legal Instruments–Results of the Uruguay Round vol. 31, 33 I.L.M. 112 (1994) [hereinafter DSU].

between tangible and intangible goods, between disputes that arise among countries and among firms, and between disputes that arise as a result of judicial, as contrasted with legislative, decision-making.

. . . .

Under prior GATT practice, the parties' duties were often clarified through diplomatic negotiations or dispute resolution that avoided legalistic interpretation of the terms of the Agreement. But the GATT/WTO system is now clearly more adjudicatory than in the past, as well as richer than ever before in the subjects on which member states have come together. To cope with the new and expanded law of international trade, the GATT/WTO system has created an elaborate Understanding on Dispute Settlement (DSU). The DSU provides for a Dispute Settlement Board (DSB), made up of representatives of all the member states but with a separate chairman and secretariat, a standing Appellate Body, to be discussed hereafter, and dispute panels to be established ad hoc on the basis of carefully drafted criteria.

The obligations contained in the TRIPS Agreement are somewhat different than those in the GATT. Of the TRIPS Agreement's three core commitments—national treatment, most-favored-nation treatment, and minimum standards—only the first two are obligations derived from pre-Uruguay Round versions of the General Agreement. Indeed, since they are the only provisions that address conditions that make it more difficult for foreigners, relative to domestic producers, to extract profits, they are the only ones that deal with direct obstacles to trade. In contrast to the traditional GATT provisions, the minimum standards propounded by the TRIPS Agreement are based on the Berne and Paris Conventions, treaties that are principally aimed at promoting innovation by curbing practices deemed to constitute free riding. Free riding is always a problem to those who invest in innovation. However, because a country's refusal to protect against copyists leaves all innovators operating within that country on something of an equal footing, the absence of intellectual property protection is not a direct barrier to international trade.[10]

This difference in focus between TRIPS and the remainder of the GATT means that participants in disputes involving intellectual property will be moving in largely uncharted waters. They will probably not receive much guidance from the case law that developed during the resolution of prior GATT disputes. Article 3.1 of the Understanding on Dispute Settlement acknowledges formal adherence to rules and procedures followed under GATT 1947; the issues that arise under the TRIPS Agreement, however, may be too novel to make former practices helpful to dispute resolution.

Moreover, the vocabulary of intellectual property and the vocabulary of the GATT sit in uneasy contrast. For instance, consider the terms "competitive" and "protective." For the intellectual property community, pro-competitive

---

[10] In one scenario, innovations could flow more readily across state lines in the absence of intellectual property protection: competitive markets produce more goods at cheaper prices, making works available in markets that could not afford to pay the monopoly rents associated with exclusive rights. In the opposite scenario, innovations flow through investment and licensing, which is made more likely by the existence of intellectual property protection in the receiving country.

measures are those that promote innovation by maximizing the public's ability to utilize intellectual products already a part of the storehouse of knowledge.

Patents, copyrights, trademarks, and trade secrets limit public access. They are, therefore, considered anti-competitive. Within the GATT/WTO system as it has emerged from the Uruguay Round, the thinking is reversed. The TRIPS Agreement, intended mainly to promote global competition, treats patents, copyrights, trademarks, and trade secrets as pro-competitive. Similarly, the GATT disfavors protectionism—a word the intellectual property community has long used to describe precisely the copyright, patent, trademark, and trade secret policies that the TRIPS Agreement mandates.[12]

These differences may turn out to be mere semantics. But in both the world of diplomacy and the world of reasoned decision making, words have persuasive power. More important, these words represent issues that for the intellectual property community are, in many cases, acutely controversial. Intellectual property regimes were initially to be integrated by the World Intellectual Property Organization (WIPO). For many years, that effort was stalled in part because its members could not agree on issues such as whether (and when) consumer welfare is enhanced by sacrificing competition to protect profits in creative efforts. The Uruguay Round succeeded where WIPO failed for a variety of reasons. One of the reasons, it seems, was that the architects of the TRIPS Agreement used words—and a concept of minimum standards—that allowed each state to read into the Agreement what it wished to see.[14]

One may hope that the persons who administer the Understanding on Dispute Settlement will have both the authority and the expertise to clarify the meaning of the many agreements making up the WTO system. But neither the DSU, nor the TRIPS Agreement, nor the Berne or Paris Conventions, provide guidance on how minimum standards—rather than actual or optimal standards—will work in conjunction with an adjudicatory dispute resolution system that is backed with enforcement procedures. Success will depend on how well the GATT/WTO system addresses the differences between intellectual property and other trade matters. With these perspectives in mind, we examine the

---

[12]It is not insignificant that one of the places where negotiations over the TRIPS Agreement in the Uruguay Round broke down was over the issue of parallel imports. Doctrines that deem authorized sales in one trading region to exhaust intellectual property interests in other regions have the advantage of facilitating the movement of goods. Thus, an exhaustion doctrine would be in the spirit of the remainder of the free trade provisions of the GATT. At the same time, however, these doctrines limit rights holders' ability to extract maximum profits from their intellectual products by granting distinct territorial licenses to different users. Thus, exhaustion doctrines discourage innovation and are somewhat contrary to the spirit of TRIPS. Exhaustion, then, is one issue that could have forced the drafters of TRIPS to consider the inconsistency between free trade and intellectual property protection. Instead, they provided in article 6 that "nothing in this Agreement shall be used to address the issue of the exhaustion of intellectual property rights." TRIPS Agreement art. 6; [cit].

[Ed. Note: Exhaustion is addressed *infra* Chapter 7.]

[14]For example, [Gail] Evans [has] note[d] that the Punta del Este Declaration described the TRIPS negotiating group's mandate as aimed at reducing "distortions and impediments to international trade," quoting Ministerial Declaration on the Uruguay Round, Sept. 20, 1986, GATT B.I.S.D. (33d Supp.) at 25-26 (1986). "Trade distortion" was interpreted by the United States as loss of comparative advantage through failure to enforce intellectual property rights. The same term was interpreted by India as foreign government intervention in the market place in the name of protecting intellectual property rights. . .

jurisprudential issues that the decision makers operating under the DSU will encounter—questions concerning the source of the law to be applied; the scope of Appellate Body review; and the deference that should be paid to the decisions of other rulemaking authorities, including national courts and administrative agencies. Because our focus is on actual dispute resolution, we have framed our discussion of these matters around a series of hypothetical cases, built upon the substantive issues of major concern to the intellectual property community.

I. Threshold and Subject Matter Issues

It is impossible to predict exactly how complaints involving the TRIPS minimum standards will evolve. Formally, disputes will always be between member states—not between intellectual property producers and consumers. There will be continuing issues on how states will choose which practices to challenge, which cases to use as vehicles for these challenges, and which states to sue. However, because the thrust of the TRIPS initiative was to induce developing countries to move toward effective protection of intellectual property, one may expect that much of the WTO litigation in this area will be between developed countries as complainants and developing countries as respondents.

Moreover, although some of the complaints will surely concern clear breaches—such as failure to sufficiently prevent trademark and copyright piracy, or refusals to protect particular technologies, such as health-related inventions—we expect that many complaints will not be so straightforward. Our expectation stems from the nuanced nature of intellectual property laws. Because these laws are structured so that a country can, at any given point in its intellectual history, achieve what it regards as an appropriate balance between the proprietary interests of producers and the access needs of consumers, they are difficult to draft. Clear cases are unlikely because newcomers to the intellectual property community have little choice but to base their laws on those of developed countries. But literal conformity to the TRIPS Agreement does not tell the entire story: a state intent on preserving access can use the flexibility of the law to strip intellectual property holders of any meaningful protection. These are the cases that we envision, and we expect that they will be difficult to decide.

For example, intellectual property law creates an important distinction between the utilization of ideas and the ideas themselves. Utilizations (expressions for copyright law, applications for patent law) are protectable subject matter, but the ideas themselves cannot be protected. A parallel line is drawn at the enforcement stage, where only certain uses are considered to be infringements. These distinctions are important and generally observed because they assure that the storehouse of knowledge can grow. End-uses are protected, but the building blocks of knowledge are released to all potential innovators. By providing assurance that information essential to progress remains available to all users, these distinctions make it less risky for states not previously party to the international intellectual property conventions to take the step of joining and conforming to the TRIPS Agreement. At the same time, however, the distinctions between ideas and applications may provide a way to avoid complying with the obligations of the TRIPS Agreement. Legislation can appear to be conforming, but lack all bite. Thus, it is almost inevitable that disputes will arise over the question whether a state that has adopted conforming legislation has nonetheless failed to provide meaningful protection to innovators.

One other important, though little understood, aspect of GATT dispute settlement needs to be mentioned here before we consider the first of our cases. The Understanding on Dispute Settlement contemplates several different types of disputes. Under article XXIII(1) of the GATT, retained without change from the 1947 version, the dispute resolution process can be utilized both when a member state asserts that a benefit accruing to it under the Agreement is nullified or impaired by a measure taken by another member state (a violation complaint), or when a member state asserts that any objective of the Agreement is being impeded as the result of any measure applied by another member state, whether or not it conflicts with the Agreement (a nonviolation complaint). Complaints involving failure to carry out obligations—violation complaints—are relatively easy to bring, because such breaches are presumed to cause harm. [DSU art. 3.8]. Indeed, in the half-century history of the GATT, violation complaints have been by far the most common complaints filed. Complaints alleging that countries have undertaken activities or experienced events that have resulted in frustrating the objectives of the Agreement even when not in breach of it (that is, nonviolation complaints) have been rare, in substantial part because in such cases the burden of proving a causal relation between the challenged measure and the alleged injury rests on the complaining party. Moreover, the complaining party must demonstrate not only that it suffered a trade injury as a result of the challenged measure but that it was justified in relying on the nonoccurrence of that measure or event. . . Because the burdens of persuasion and proof are different in violation and nonviolation complaints, a threshold issue for a dispute panel may well be how to characterize a particular complaint.

Perhaps because of the difficulty in resolving nonviolation complaints in respect of an agreement in which all the premises are new, or perhaps out of concern that vulnerability to nonviolation complaints would put too much pressure on developing countries faced with the political problem of passing conforming legislation, the TRIPS Agreement provides a five-year moratorium for nonviolation complaints.[19] Nevertheless, we begin our series of cases with this fundamental question, to illustrate the complexity of fitting together the GATT, the DSU, and the TRIPS Agreement.

---

[19] Article 64(2) of the TRIPS Agreement provides that subparagraphs 1(b) and 1(c) of article XXIII of the GATT 1994, the non-violation provisions, "shall not apply to the settlement of disputes under this Agreement for a period of five years from the date of entry into force of the WTO Agreement." This special moratorium is applicable to all member states, and is independent of the grace periods available to developing countries or countries in transition to market economies.

Case I

Macrohard is the creator of a computer program that is protected in Xandia, its home country, and elsewhere. It discovers that this program is being sold without authorization in Patria. Macrohard sues the sellers for infringement in Patria, but loses. Patria has not enacted patent protection for programs. Although Patria has enacted copyright protection, the Patrian court holds that Macrohard's program is no more than a principle, system, or method of operation, and so is excluded from protection. Macrohard contends that Patria is engaging in a pattern of nonenforcement; that what it is actually doing is refusing to provide any intellectual property protection for programs, in violation of the TRIPS Agreement. It prevails upon Xandia to bring a complaint to the WTO. After consultation fails to result in a resolution of Xandia's complaint, a panel is formed to consider the allegations.

A. Violation or Nonviolation Complaint

If Patria had failed to enact any protection for computer programs, the assertion by Xandia that Patria had violated article 10 of the TRIPS Agreement would be easily established. Patria has, however, met the literal requirement of article 10, by providing in its legislation that computer programs may be subject to copyright; its court has simply found Macrohard's program to be nonprotectable subject matter. Thus, Patria argues to the dispute panel that it has carried out its obligations; court decisions such as Macrohard are, at most, measures that impede the attainment of an objective of the Agreement. Is this, then, a violation or a nonviolation complaint? . . .

How should the characterization question be resolved? The preliminary question, choice of law, is easily answered: since characterizing the complaint is an issue only because of the terms of the TRIPS Agreement and the GATT, GATT law applies. But what should this law be? If it is necessary to characterize the complaint in order to determine whether the moratorium applies, the issue should be determined by investigating the reasons for the moratorium. Apparently its purpose was to give the Council for TRIPS, which was provided for in the Agreement establishing the World Trade Organization, time to "examine the scope and modalities for nonviolation complaints;" accordingly, then, doubts on characterization should be resolved in favor of Patria. Subject matter issues are among the most difficult of all intellectual property issues. Allowing the parties' understanding of TRIPS to mature before these questions are answered makes considerable sense. But if such a first case is decided as we suggest, it will be important to explain the reasoning with care—not always possible in a collegial body—so that it does not become a precedent for later cases, where, as we discuss below, the priorities and values will be different.

The other reason for characterizing this complaint as a violation or nonviolation complaint is to determine whether Xandia must, as a threshold issue, demonstrate reliance and injury. In this context, one might conclude that doubts should be resolved in favor of Xandia, the complaining party.

Threshold requirements determine the availability of relief. Given that dispute resolution is a primary way in which the TRIPS Agreement will be enforced, the threshold for bringing an action should not be so high as to imperil the success of the enterprise. If we are right in predicting that many complaints will be based on allegations that the flexible features of intellectual property law are systematically misinterpreted to avoid the commitments embodied in the TRIPS Agreement, it is important that the decision makers are able to reach these interpretive questions. And if the experience of countries with well-developed intellectual property law is any indication, DSU panels will need to reach the issue many times before parties achieve a genuine understanding of all its parameters. Thus, at least after the moratorium, it seems that such complaints should be characterized as violation-type complaints.

Characterizing this complaint as a violation complaint would have the additional advantage of avoiding serious questions as to what constitutes an adequate demonstration of reliance and injury. In other parts of the WTO system, treating violation and nonviolation complaints differently makes considerable sense. Breach of a GATT obligation is itself a serious matter; thus, it is efficient for panels to presume that a nullification or impairment has occurred when a party has breached. The effect of other actions or situations is not so clear, and so it is reasonable to require the complainant to establish that harm of the sort that GATT is meant to prevent has occurred. But while prior custom and practice should certainly act as precedent for deciding issues such as the burden of proof in TRIPS disputes,[26] attention also needs to be paid to the differences between intellectual property and the other sorts of goods (and services) encompassed by the WTO system. In Case I, for example, it is the firm, rather than the complaining state, that would have the task of showing reliance. A firm such as Macrohard may have made its decision to invest in producing a major new computer program in small increments, over time, long before the dispute in Patria arose, and in response to other technological changes, as well as to various factors in the economy and in its own industry. Thus, it would probably be very difficult for Macrohard (or any other member of the computer industry) to establish that any specific decision was made in express reliance on protection in Patria. Accordingly, if the TRIPS Agreement is to be successful in encouraging investment in innovation, it would be wise not to impose a severe burden of showing reliance in TRIPS cases. Indeed, given that intellectual property law is based on the premise that innovation is spurred by the promise of protection, a strong argument could be made that reliance should be presumed. To fit such a standard into the GATT/WTO system, however, would require receptiveness to treating borderline cases as violation, not nonviolation, complaints.

Much the same can be said about demonstrating injury. As with reliance, this issue should be determined under the law of the GATT. But, as with reliance, the GATT precedents may not fit intellectual property disputes. Traditional GATT disputes have focused on loss of trading opportunities by the claimant

---

[26] *See* DSU arts. 3.1, 26.1

exporting country by reason of restraints imposed by the respondent importing country; in contrast, the failure by a respondent state to enact or enforce intellectual property protection will never directly interfere with trade. In our Case I, Patria is not preventing Macrohard from selling its products in Patria. Macrohard can fully participate in the market so long as it is willing to sell its program at the competitive price. And if, as seems likely, Macrohard earned back its investment in countries where computer programs are more fully protected, Xandia might well not even be able to demonstrate that Macrohard's incentives to be innovative were harmed.

To be sure, Xandia might be able to show that Macrohard earned less from sales in Patria, both in volume and in price markup, than it would have earned had Patria been in full compliance with Xandia's vision of the TRIPS Agreement, and less than it earned in other states with similar markets. Should such a showing be required before Xandia would be allowed to prevail in its complaint? Or is such a standard too high to achieve the objectives of the Agreement? In domestic copyright cases in the United States, for example, where a showing of injury is required, it often is presumed. The thinking is that the lack of promised exclusivity distorts the market. Once the market is distorted, it is difficult to reconstruct the effect of copying or to evaluate the extent to which the creator was harmed. The law establishes a presumption of injury in order to make sure that infringement is adequately deterred. By the same reasoning, adequate enforcement of the TRIPS Agreement may require either relaxing the standard for demonstrating injury in nonviolation complaints, or treating cases such as Case I as involving a violation complaint.

B. Compliance with TRIPS Article 10

The above analysis leads inevitably to the next question: Is Patria meeting its international obligations, as set out in the TRIPS Agreement? Since it has enacted a copyright law covering computer programs, Patria's obligation under article 10 of the TRIPS Agreement seems to be met, at least prima facie. Patria's patent law does not cover programs. That omission may be inconsistent with article 27(1), which states that, subject to stated exceptions (not including computer programs), patents shall be available "in all fields of technology." If a panel is asked to resolve this inconsistency, it should construe the TRIPS Agreement in accordance with the guidance given by the DSU.

Article 3.2 of the DSU refers to "customary rules of interpretation of public international law," a vague guidepost that may or may not include the negotiating history of the TRIPS Agreement and scrutiny of the domestic laws of the members as they existed when the TRIPS Agreement entered into force.[29] We would urge that both the negotiating history and the concerns and practices of the proponents of the TRIPS Agreement be taken into account in answering

---

[29]*Compare* Vienna Convention on the Law of Treaties, opened for signature May 23, 1969, arts. 31-32, 1155 U.N.T.S. 331, 8 I.L.M. 679 (1969) [hereinafter Vienna Convention] which lists the preparatory work of a treaty and the circumstances of its conclusion as "supplementary means of interpretation," *with* RESTATEMENT (THIRD) OF THE FOREIGN RELATIONS LAW OF THE UNITED STATES § 325 cmt. e (1986), which, reflecting the American practice, is more receptive to using negotiating history and other surrounding circumstances as aids to interpretation of international agreements.

the question, along with the less controversial resort to the "ordinary meaning" of the terms of a treaty in the light of the treaty's object and purpose.[30]

Thus, the question whether article 27 of the TRIPS Agreement requires protection for programs should be addressed, first, by noting that it is a general provision. Article 10, on the other hand, is specifically addressed to computer programs and should take priority as the lex specialis. Second, the negotiating history of the TRIPS Agreement indicates that the developed countries were concerned about the inadequacy of the then-extant international intellectual property treaties on the issue of computer programs.[31] The dispute over the extent to which programs should be protected persisted throughout the early years of the Uruguay Round. The record shows that the discussion was limited to the question of considering computer programs as "literary works" for the purpose of extending copyright protection,[32] and that the outcome was a provision expressly requiring only copyright protection. The inference would seem to be clear that the TRIPS Agreement should not be interpreted to require patent protection as well.

As to the domestic practices of member states, we submit that these are relevant not because they apply of their own force, but because they shed light on two significant issues: the understanding of the parties when the Agreement was signed, and the practicalities of requiring compliance with the interpretation put forth by Xandia. Here, experience supports the conclusion that Patria is not required to enact patent protection for programs. The parties were not thinking along the lines of protecting programs with patents. Although patents on programs have been issued in the United States, the experience during the time of the Uruguay Round was that the sophistication required to examine patents and determine whether they have been infringed outstripped the abilities of both the Patent Office and the courts. Given that the United States has long enjoyed more technological resources than are available to many of the other parties, it seems sound to conclude that article 10 in the copyright chapter of the TRIPS Agreement was intended to be the sole source of protection for computer programs, and that it should be understood as implicitly rejecting a requirement that parties provide patent protection to computer programs.[36]

If, then, the focus is on copyright, and not on patent, the next question is whether Patria's decision in the Macrohard case is inconsistent with the requirement of article 10 that "[c]omputer programs, whether in source or object

---

[30]Vienna Convention, *supra* note 29, art. 31(1).

[31][*Cf.*] 1 THE GATT URUGUAY ROUND: A NEGOTIATING HISTORY (1986-1992) 2246 (Terence P. Stewart ed., 1993) [hereinafter NEGOTIATING HISTORY], noting that several contracting parties were dissatisfied with various aspects of then-extant international intellectual property treaties. . . .

[32]*See* 1 NEGOTIATING HISTORY, *supra* note 31, at 2290-91.

[36]*See generally* J.H. Reichman, *The Know-How Gap in the TRIPS Agreement: Why Software Fared Badly, and What Are the Solutions*, 17 HASTINGS COMM. & ENT. L.J. 763, 768 (1995) [hereinafter Reichman, Know-How Gap], noting that there was general reluctance to grant patents on programs in all the developed countries. The United States relented first. After that, patents on software were issued in Japan and European Union countries, but considerable ambivalence on the question remains. Professor Reichman would regard it as incompatible with the TRIPS Agreement for a member state to refuse to permit an inventor to even argue that a particular program met the standards for patent protection. *Id.* at 769.

code, shall be protected as literary works under the Berne Convention." This is likely to be the most difficult issue in the case. Countries that have already provided copyright protection for programs have had a hard time differentiating between unprotectable programming ideas and protectable expression. . . .

C. Lawmaking at the Frontier

One might think that the WTO dispute resolution mechanism, with access to the advice of experts from around the world, would be the ideal way to resolve difficult, high-stakes open questions such as this one. Moreover, the existence of a standing Appellate Body provides a capacity for finding the "best" rules of law for the global economy. If the DSU works as many hope, then these "best" rules might be accepted into the domestic laws of the parties (or at least, into the laws of those parties where the question has not yet been fully answered), leading ultimately to genuine global harmonization.

However, lawmaking in the process of adjudication, a familiar concept to those raised in the common law, is formally circumscribed by the admonition, stated twice in the Understanding on Dispute Settlement, that rulings of the DSB "cannot add to or diminish the rights and obligations provided in the covered agreements."[40] While this statement will surely acquire considerable gloss if the intent to make dispute resolution more adjudicative becomes a reality, the GATT's history of conciliation and diplomacy is likely to exert some influence on how disputes are resolved. Thus, at least in its early stages, dispute resolution in the WTO may not be characterized by the sort of give-and-take likely to produce the "best" rule of law.

Furthermore, the limited role permitted to third parties, which requires the third party to have an existing trade interest in the controversy in question, may well distort the decision making process viewed at long range.[41] It is well recognized that creating intellectual property requires a considerable level of sophistication. It is somewhat less recognized—but nonetheless true—that in many areas, even copying requires a measure of technical capacity. Thus, it is likely that all the early disputes in areas such as computer copyright infringement will be among states that have some degree of technological expertise; states with less capability will not be respondents or complainants; nor will they be able to show the "substantial trade interest" necessary to support intervention. The members that participate in dispute resolution will

---

[40]DSU arts. 3.2, 19.2. The concern about lawmaking by WTO panels is not confined to states in the civil law tradition. *See, e.g.,* U.S. Uruguay Round Agreements Act § 102 (a)(1), 19 U.S.C. § 3512 (a)(1), which provides:

> No provision of any of the Uruguay Round Agreements, *nor the application of any such provision to any person or circumstance,* that is inconsistent with any law of the United States shall have effect. (emphasis added).

[41]Third parties are entitled to participate both in the consultation process that precedes formal adjudication, DSU art. 4.11, and in the actual proceedings before panels, *id.* art. 10. They may also participate in a limited way in appeal proceedings. *Id.* art. 17.4. In each context, however, it is understood that third parties must have an actual and current trade interest in the dispute, and participation in the appeal proceeding appears to be limited to members that have participated in the proceeding before the panel.

not, therefore, be representative of the entire membership of the WTO. Since disputants will surely argue for the rules that work best for them, the early years of the Agreement are not likely to produce "best" rules when judged from the point of view of the WTO membership as a whole or from the perspective of the global economy. And, unlike adjudication within many of the parties' national courts, there is no legislative check or balance on dispute resolution in the WTO.

To be sure, the TRIPS Agreement also creates a Council for TRIPS, which is charged with the duty to "monitor the operation of this Agreement." Though the intent of the drafters does not appear to have been to create the Council as a rule-enunciating body, it is possible that the system will evolve in a way that will allow the Council to use the occasion of disputes to consider and articulate "best" rules.[43] But, until some body in the WTO—the panels, the Appellate Body, or the Council—develops a capacity to give generally applicable interpretations of the law, disputes will need to be resolved under some other source of law.

One obvious source is the World Intellectual Property Organization. As the administrator of the Madrid Arrangement, and especially the Berne and Paris Conventions, WIPO has a special claim to a role in articulating international intellectual property norms. Its practice of appointing informal groups of experts to consider disputes under the treaties it administers provides, at least in theory, a mechanism for finding best rules. Besides, drawing on WIPO resonates well with the negotiating history of the TRIPS Agreement: the Uruguay Round would not have produced TRIPS had not the administrators of WIPO participated in the identification of generally accepted international norms. The TRIPS Agreement itself contemplates (in article 68) that the Council will consult with WIPO and "shall seek to establish . . . appropriate arrangements for cooperation with bodies of that Organization." We view this provision as a mandate to the TRIPS Council—and to the GATT/WTO system as a whole—to keep up with developments in intellectual property law. Thus, drawing on developments within WIPO seems to be an attractive solution, at least in the early period of the WTO when both the DSU and the TRIPS Agreement are still to some extent in experimental stages, and probably in the long run as well.

The problem with this suggestion is that while it is in harmony with WIPO's aspirations, it fails to take into account WIPO's past performance. WIPO has tended to operate through coordinated group voting rather than through genuine consensus building. For at least the last fifteen years, politicization of deliberations in WIPO has interfered with its lawmaking efforts. Indeed, one principal reason that intellectual property wound up in the WTO was that WIPO had become unable to keep its treaties responsive to the needs of the innovation community. Another reason for the embrace of intellectual property by the WTO is, of course, that only the WTO, as it emerged from the Uruguay Round, has an effective enforcement mechanism. If this mechanism produces a substantial body of decisions at the frontier of intellectual property law, it will

---

[43] *See also* Reichman, *Know-How Gap, supra* note 36, at 773, who suggests that as consensus emerges on particular issues among member states, the topics should be set down for review pursuant to the terms of article 71 of the Agreement.

inevitably exert an influence over developments within WIPO. . .

It may seem attractive, at least until the transition period is over, or until an arrangement for coordination with WIPO develops, for panels working on a difficult question to consult the laws of developed countries. If a good solution to the problem of, say, drawing the line between ideas and expressions in computer program cases has been found, a panel could adopt such a solution in an international context. The member states would, under this approach, function as laboratories—much as states or provinces do in a federal system. Once one jurisdiction finds a position that appears to work over time, the GATT/WTO system would provide a mechanism for internationalizing that rule.[54] As attractive as this option may seem, however, we would urge the same caution that we suggested with respect to case-by-case adjudication. The risk of looking to early solutions of national authorities is that predominant attention would be given to the states with the most-developed and sophisticated technology, whose priorities may not be the same as for all members of the WTO.

More fundamentally, we are skeptical that there will always be a "best" rule for every problem that will arise under the TRIPS Agreement. Promoting innovation requires that care be taken not to raise the cost of knowledge to so high a level that it impedes further inventiveness. How that problem is best solved can depend on a country's intellectual and industrial development, its culture, and the types of creative work in which its citizens are engaged. Thus, the nature (and advantage) of a minimum standards regime is that where there is no "best" rule that will work in every economy, each country can tailor the law to its own needs. In short, in areas such as those presented by Case I, where the issue involves that balance between users and producers, drawing the rules from solutions worked out elsewhere—particularly in highly developed economies—may be inappropriate.

D. Deciding Case I

Coming back to Case I, the preceding discussion leads us to urge that a panel begin by according a degree of deference to Patria's own decision in the Macrohard case. Assuming the courts of Patria have made a careful evaluation of the controversy free from improper influences or discrimination by nationality, a WTO panel ought to be reluctant to condemn the result reached by those courts. The panel might inquire whether the Macrohard case was an exception or reflected a pattern of decisions by Patrian authorities that ought to be judged by the TRIPS/WTO dispute settlement mechanism. If a policy concerning protection of computer programs emerged, the panel should inquire (1) whether Patria was furthering a goal shared by countries that protect computer programs (in this case, releasing ideas, as contrasted with applications, into the public domain); and (2) whether Patria's announced law or policy (here, its law differentiating between ideas and copyrightable expression) is recognized elsewhere. If both these inquiries result in affirmative

---

[54]For a somewhat different approach, see Reichman, *Know-How Gap, supra* note 36, at 773, who suggests that a panel could take judicial notice of an emerging consensus among member states.

answers, the panel should operate on a presumption that Patria's law and announced policy conform to its treaty obligations. The burden would then shift to Xandia to show the practice is inconsistent with its announced policy by failing to protect the innovations it purports to protect. Xandia might seek to demonstrate that Patria's programming cases lack justification, or that the relevant officials of Patria had disclosed an intent either to avoid the provisions of article 10 of the TRIPS Agreement or to discriminate against foreign holders of programming copyrights.

In the final analysis, a combined approach may be the best way to effectuate the concept of minimum standards. Deference to WIPO when there is an international norm on which member states have agreed would allow the WTO to assume the enforcement role long missing from the Berne and Paris Conventions. In the absence of such a norm, deference to each state's own law is appropriate, on the theory that lack of consensus is an indication that there is no "best rule" and that different economies and cultures require different rules.[57]

NOTES AND QUESTIONS

(1) **Early TRIPS Litigation**. Dreyfuss and Lowenfeld predicted that much WTO TRIPS litigation would involve complaints by developed countries against developing countries. This prediction has been borne out in part. In the first six years, twenty-four TRIPS dispute resolution proceedings were initiated (concerning eighteen discrete matters), comprising almost ten per cent of all cases initiated before the WTO to this point. *See* Dara Williams, *Developing TRIPS Jurisprudence: The First Six Years and Beyond*, 4 J. WORLD INTELL. PROP. 177, 179 (2001) (providing a chart of all twenty-four proceedings and their nature and disposition). A continually updated summary of the status of WTO proceedings generally (not limited to TRIPS matters) can be found at http://www.wto.org/english/tratop_e/dispu_e/stplay_e.doc. The position as of February 2001, can be summarized as follows:

> Resolutions have been reached in 11 of the 24 disputes; five have been the subject of mutually agreed solutions following bilateral consultations under Article 4 [of the DSU], and in six cases panels have been established and panel reports subsequently adopted by the DSB. Two of the panel reports were appealed. Panels have been established in two more cases . . . The other 11 disputes are the subject of bilateral consultations. . . . The complainants in all but one

---

[57]This approach is in agreement with the views of Steven P. Croley & John H. Jackson, *WTO Dispute Procedures, Standard of Review, and Deference to National Governments*, 90 AM. J. INT'L L. 193 (1996). Croley and Jackson urge deference to national outcomes on the theory that this will best promote voluntary compliance and multilateral consensus. They also suggest that the variety in cultural values of the parties, the lack of fact-finding resources by panels, and other shortcomings in international procedure argue against panel activism. *Id.* at 211-13.

dispute to date have been developed countries, with the United States initiating two thirds (16), the EC one quarter (6) and Canada one dispute. In February 2001, Brazil became the first developing country to initiate a TRIPS dispute with its request for consultations with the United States. [*See supra* § 3.04[D][2].] Developed countries have also been the respondent in a majority of cases, with only seven of the 24 disputes (29%) involving complaints against developing countries.

Williams, *supra,* at 177-78. Why does this record from 1995–2001 depart in part from the developed/developing country alignment that Dreyfuss and Lowenfeld predicted? Are there any reasons why this alignment is likely to change? In what ways might the alignment of complaining and defending members affect either the success of TRIPS or the content of international intellectual property law?

(2) **Initiation of Complaints.** How would Macrohard have successfully "prevailed upon" Xandia to bring an action against Patria? In what ways will the need of private firms to "prevail upon" their governments to bring actions shape the content of international intellectual property law? Can Xandia (or Macrohard) really complain that Patria is engaging in a pattern of nonenforcement based upon this single adverse judicial decision? This is an aspect of trade relations that TRIPS brings to the fore. Should Macrohard be obliged to exhaust its remedies (or at least its judicial remedies) in Patria before bringing the action before the WTO? To what extent should WTO complaints be built upon single judicial decisions? Or should a failure by the Xandian legislature to address unsatisfactory judicial decisions be the triggering event?

(3) **Interpretive Approaches**. What does the obligation in Article 10 of TRIPS to protect computer programs "as literary works" mean? No country has applied its traditional copyright law to computer programs without some adjustment for the particularities of software; so it would appear unlikely that the drafters intended for there to be no form of special tailoring for software. How do we interpret its meaning in international law?

(a) *Relevance of Minimum Standards.* As Dreyfuss and Lowenfeld note, the TRIPS Agreement embodies minimum standards, not optimal standards. How should that affect interpretive devices and considerations that domestic courts might employ in resolving cutting-edge issues? Should Xandia and Patria be able to argue over whether treating the Macrohard program as nothing more than a "method of operation" results systemically in the most efficient and pro-competitive balance between producers and second comer innovators? Can and should WTO panels reach the issue of what is an appropriate exclusion of "methods of operation"? *Cf.* Lotus Dev. Corp. v. Borland Int'l Inc., 49 F.3d 807 (1st Cir. 1995) (denying protection to menu command hierarchy of spreadsheet program), *aff'd by an equally div. court,* 516 U.S. 233 (1996). Can this answer be resolved as a question of textual interpretation, rather than as a question of optimal competitive balance? *See id.* (Boudin J., concurring).

(b) *Relevance of Article 3(2) DSU.* Article 3(2) provides that rulings of the DSB "cannot add to or diminish the rights and obligations provided in the covered agreements." How should this affect the way in which we interpret the TRIPS Agreement? (Article 9(2) of TRIPS provides simply that copyright protection shall not extend to methods of operation, without further elaboration.) Are there any domestic approaches to statutory interpretation that Article 3(2) would appear to embody? Is it possible for panels to heed this instruction? *See* Neil W. Netanel, *The Next Round: The Impact of the WIPO Copyright Treaty on TRIPS Dispute Settlement*, 37 VA. J. INT'L L. 441, 445 (1997) (suggesting that "many of TRIPS's copyright provisions are highly indeterminate, leaving considerable room for varying interpretation and application"). Can panels engage in "gap-filling" consistent with the above-quoted language from Article 3(2) of the DSU? Can panels "provide security and predictability to the multilateral trading system," DSU art. 3(2), without gap-filling? Petro Mavroidis has argued that "when you discuss a multilateral agreement between one hundred and thirty-two members of different development, different culture, different everything, the end product can only be at a level of generality that it invites interpretation by definition." *The WTO Appellate Body: The First Four Years*, 1 J. WORLD INTELL. PROP. 425, 434 (1999). Do you agree? How should the interpretation of the TRIPS Agreement by WTO panels be affected by the fact that language was intentionally used in TRIPS "that allowed each state to read into the Agreement what it wished to see"?

(c) *Customary Rules of Interpretation.* Article 3(2) of the DSU also affirms that dispute settlement is intended to "preserve the rights and obligations of members under the covered agreements, and to clarify the existing provisions of those agreements in accordance with customary rules of interpretation of public international law." These rules of interpretation are found in the Vienna Convention on the Law of Treaties, *see supra* § 2.01, and thus permit reference in much of the copyright context to the Berne Convention and state practice thereunder, in addition to the negotiating history of TRIPS referenced by Dreyfuss and Lowenfeld. *Cf.* Laurence R. Helfer, *Adjudicating Copyright Claims under the TRIPS Agreement: The Case for a European Human Rights Analogy*, 39 HARV. INT'L L.J. 357, 431 (1998) (suggesting that panels should rely on emergent state practice where there is concordant state practice in all four developmental categories). What relevance and role did the panel in *United States-Section 110(5) of the U.S. Copyright Act, supra* § 4.03[B][2], assign to the different exemptions granted under national copyright laws? Does this fit with the use that Dreyfuss and Lowenfeld suggest panels make of national approaches to the copyright protection of computer programs in deciding Case I? To what extent did the panel in *Canada-Pharmaceutical Patents, supra* § 3.04[D][2], use national patents laws to support its construction of Article 30? Is that consistent with the Dreyfuss and Lowenfeld analysis?

(d) *"Berne in TRIPS".* Reference to "the Berne Convention" and state practice thereunder is not, however, as simple it sounds. Neil Netanel has helpfully phrased the dilemma as whether there is a difference between "Berne qua Berne" and "Berne in TRIPS". He concludes that "state practice under Berne should indeed be the fundamental starting point for interpreting Berne in TRIPS, although the Berne provisions that are incorporated into TRIPS will necessarily be colored by TRIPS's state practice and overall object and purpose as well." Netanel, *supra*, at 447. Did the panel's report in *United States-Section*

110(5) of the U.S. Copyright Act, supra § 4.03[B][2], reflect this distinction? In what ways is the broader context of TRIPS different from the context and content of Berne such that the embedding of Berne in TRIPS might tilt the balance of interpretation in favor of the rights holder? *See id.* at 455-63; *see also* TRIPS arts. 7-8. Is that what the architects of incorporating Berne within TRIPS sought to achieve? In what ways other than "tincturing" the provisions of Berne with a "trade hue," as Netanel puts it, might the provisions of TRIPS affect the interpretation of the Berne Convention? *See* Vienna Convention art. 31(3). The decision to bring the Berne Convention within the GATT framework could have been achieved in a number of ways, including: repeating the text of the Berne Convention verbatim in the text of TRIPS, requiring all WTO members to adhere to the Berne Convention, or incorporating the terms of the convention (absent Article 6*bis*) by reference. What is the significance of the parties choosing the last of these three options? How would WTO panel interpretation of Berne provisions be affected by the choice made by the drafters? *See* Netanel, *supra*, at 452-53.

(e) *Other Sources.* Netanel has also argued that

> the international law of freedom of expression should require a WTO dispute panel to balance the TRIPS objective of rigorous intellectual property protection with the need for breathing space for public access to and creative reformulations of existing cultural expression. In particular, the dispute panel should accord considerable deference to an allegedly noncompliant member state's own interpretation of TRIPS where that interpretation reflects such free speech concerns.

Id. at 448; *see also* Helfer, *supra*, at 433. Which provision of the Vienna Convention authorizes resort to this source? Netanel argues that an international standard of free expression *permits* member countries to provide certain free expression-based exceptions to copyright, and is relatively less assertive as to whether it requires member countries to create such exceptions. If an "international law of freedom of expression" is relevant to interpreting the scope of TRIPS, why does it not *mandate* free expression-based exceptions? What is the content of the "international law of freedom of expression"? *See* Universal Declaration of Human Rights art. 19. Are WTO panels competent to consider questions of the appropriate international norms of free expression? Is it possible to address questions of copyright without some regard for free expression values?

(f) *Interpretive Focus.* Do you agree with the different sources—TRIPS negotiating history, domestic laws, developments in WIPO—to which Dreyfuss and Lowenfeld turned for guidance? What should be the focus of the interpretive process required to decide Case I between Xandia and Patria? That is, what precisely is a WTO panel trying to decide when confronted with Case I? Does the reasoning behind Dreyfuss and Lowenfeld's suggested resolution of Case I reflect that focus? If there are other considerations or criteria underlying their conclusion, what are they? Are they appropriate or necessary? Is the focus of the Dreyfuss/Lowenfeld interpretive process the same as that exhibited by the panels in *United States-Section 110(5), supra* § 4.03[B][2], and *Canada-Patent Pharmaceutical Patents, supra* § 3.04[D][2]?

Scholars in the United States have noted the parallel between domestic judicial interpretation of statutes and treaties. Which devices of statutory interpretation do you think should have, and should not have, application in interpreting treaties? Does this vary whether the interpretation is by courts construing their effect in domestic law or international panels construing their meaning as part of international law? What other jurisprudential tools would be appropriate in this context? In what ways might an activist DSB be of greater concern than an activist domestic court? *See The Review of the WTO's Dispute Settlement Understanding: Which Way?*, 1 J. WORLD INTELL. PROP. 447, 464-65 (1998) (comments of Thomas Cottier); Graeme B. Dinwoodie, *A New Copyright Order: Why National Courts Should Create Global Norms*, 149 U. PA. L. REV. 469, 570-71 (2000) (discussing the different status of national and international law).

Larry Helfer has argued that in developing a methodological approach to TRIPS disputes, WTO panels could learn from and build upon the experiences of the European Court of Human Rights. *See* Helfer, *supra.* He bases this suggestion upon systemic or structural similarities between the two bodies: (1) interpretation of minimum standards of international obligation; (2) national discretion as to the means of implementing international obligations in national law; (3) historical divergence in national approaches to the subject matter; and (4) risks of non-compliance with rulings of the relevant tribunal. Helfer concludes that these structural characteristics make an analogy to the European Court of Human Rights (which is not part of the EU system) more persuasive than seeking to learn from the European Court of Justice. The European Court of Human Rights adjudicates claims brought by citizens of thirty European countries against their governments under the European Convention on Human Rights. In light of your reading of EU materials, which aspects of the EU system and the role of the ECJ support Helfer's conclusion? (In what ways is the WTO system different from the EU system? In what ways is it similar?) Helfer's argument would suggest that WTO panels refrain from the teleological mode of interpretation adopted by the ECJ, and instead rely on far less dynamic forms of interpretation.

(4) **Third Party Involvement.** Dreyfuss and Lownfeld note that the limited role permitted to third parties "may well distort the decision making process viewed at long range." In what ways might this occur? The panel's report in *United States-Section 110(5) of the U.S. Copyright Act, supra* § 4.03[B][2], made frequent reference to submissions made by Australia. On what basis was Australia allowed to make submissions to the panel? In what ways did it help the panel?

If the International Organization for Open Source Code, a non-profit group committed to open source code, were able to participate in the process, how might this affect the development of international intellectual property law? In *United States-Import Prohibition of Certain Shrimp and Shrimp Products*, the Appellate Body interpreted DSU article 13 as permitting panels to accept amicus briefs and other submissions by interested persons other than governments. *See* Report of Appellate Body, WT/DS58/AB/R, ¶ 110 (Oct. 12,

1998). Is this appropriate? Is it meaningful or appropriate absent other moves toward a more open and inclusive process? Would it assist panels in making the determinations that they are instructed to make? What more would you need to know about the International Organization for Open Source Code in order to answer this question?

(5) **Nonviolation Complaints.** Because Xandia's claim was filed before January 1, 2000, Patria sought to take advantage of the five year moratorium on nonviolation proceedings. *See* TRIPS art. 64. What are the arguments for and against the use of nonviolation complaints? *See* ERNST-ULRICH PETERSMANN, THE GATT/WTO DISPUTE SETTLEMENT SYSTEM: INTERNATIONAL LAW, INTERNATIONAL ORGANIZATIONS AND DISPUTE SETTLEMENT 173 (1997) (arguing against the use of nonviolation complaints in TRIPS cases). If Patria, because it grants copyright protection to computer programs, has not violated a defined obligation of TRIPS, does that not mean that the countries have retained sovereignty beyond that issue?

(a) *Moratorium.* Even if the arguments in favor of nonviolation complaints are persuasive, are there arguments for extending the moratorium? Several countries have argued for the temporary extension of this moratorium; others have suggested eliminating the possibility of nonviolation actions. The status of the moratorium is currently being debated in the TRIPS Council. At the March 2000 TRIPS Council meeting, several countries suggested that the moratorium should remain in effect until new provisions on the "scope and modalities" of nonviolation complaints are agreed upon as contemplated by the TRIPS Agreement. The United States favored ending the moratorium, and took the position that the moratorium had automatically expired on January 1, 2000. (But the United States indicated that it is not preparing non-violation cases for the near future, and would for the moment restrict TRIPS complaints to violation cases.)

(b) *Characterization of the Complaint.* Dreyfuss and Lowenfeld suggest that characterization of a complaint as a violation or nonviolation complaint should depend upon whether the reason for the characterization is the application of the moratorium (which would favor classification as nonviolation) or the requirements in nonviolation cases of demonstrating reliance and injury (which would favor classification as a violation complaint). Accepting the persuasiveness of that distinction, if the moratorium on nonviolation complaints is extended, and the action by Xandia was brought after January 1, 2000, which approach to characterization should a panel adopt? Is there an alternative approach to characterization that should be used in that context?

(c) *Elements of a Nonviolation Complaint.* Dreyfuss and Lowenfeld suggest that if the Xandian action were classified as a nonviolation complaint, then it should be the firm rather than the complaining state that would have the task of showing reliance. Why? What is different about nonviolation complaints that might be reflected in and effectuated by a "reliance" requirement? In light of that, how might you frame a reliance requirement other than requiring Macrohard to establish that a specific decision to invest was made in express reliance on protection in Patria?

(d) *Interpretive Approaches in a Nonviolation Case.* If the panel in Case I had classified the Xandian complaint as a nonviolation complaint, would the panel be required to adopt a different interpretive approach than that developed in deciding the matter as a violation complaint? *See* Joel P. Trachtman, *The Domain of WTO Dispute Resolution*, 40 HARV. INT'L L.J. 333, 370 (1999) (arguing that the nonviolation concept "serves as an invitation to construction, or a catch all, to limit defection by WTO members through the use of avenues of defection with respect to which they have accepted no positive commitment"). Trachtman characterizes nonviolation decisions as involving "construction" rather than "interpretation" of the treaty. In what ways are those two processes different? *See id.* at 339. Is dynamic interpretation and gap-filling more or less appropriate in adjudicating nonviolation complaints?

The panel in a non-TRIPS case, Japan—Measures Affecting Consumer Photographic Film and Paper, WT/DS44/R (98-0886) (WTO Panel, Mar. 31, 1998), has interpreted the scope of nonviolation complaints narrowly to require that the challenged measures could not have been reasonably anticipated at the time of the treaty negotiation. What effect would a similarly strict interpretation of the scope of nonviolation actions under TRIPS have on the future conduct of intellectual property treaty negotiation?

INDIA—PATENT PROTECTION FOR PHARMACEUTICAL AND AGRICULTURAL CHEMICAL PRODUCTS
WT/DS50/AB/R (WTO App. Body, Dec. 19, 1997)

. . . .

. . .The dispute that gives rise to this case represents the first time the TRIPS Agreement has been submitted to the scrutiny of the WTO Dispute Settlement system. . . .

IV. The *TRIPS Agreement*

. . . .

. . .With respect to patent protection for pharmaceutical and agricultural chemical products, certain specific obligations are found in Articles 70.8 and 70.9 of the TRIPS Agreement. The interpretation of these specific obligations is the subject of this dispute. Our task is to address the legal issues arising from this dispute that are raised in this appeal.

. . . .

V. Interpretation of the *TRIPS Agreement*

[In seeking to identify the principles of international law to apply, the panel had first referred to the "disciplines formed under GATT 1947 (the so-called GATT *acquis*)" for the principle that the legitimate expectations of the members regarding the conditions of competition must be protected, including, as adapted for the context of the TRIPS Agreement, "the competitive relationship between a Member's own nationals and those of other Members." Although the Appellate Body affirmed the relevance of the GATT *acquis* to the WTO system, the Appellate Body declared that the panel had erred in its interpretation of the GATT *acquis*. In particular, the Appellate Body found that the doctrine of protecting reasonable expectations had developed in the context of nonviolation complaints under the GATT. But this case involved a violation complaint, and thus the panel erred in concluding that the principle of legitimate expectations must be taken into account in interpreting the provisions of TRIPS. The Appellate Body noted that, under Article 64, whether nonviolation complaints should be available for disputes under the TRIPS Agreement remained to be determined by the TRIPS Council pursuant to Article 64(3) of the TRIPS Agreement, and was not a matter to be resolved through interpretation by panels or the Appellate Body.]

In addition to relying on the GATT *acquis*, the Panel relies also on the customary rules of interpretation of public international law as a basis for the interpretative principle it offers for the TRIPS Agreement. Specifically, the Panel relies on Article 31 of the Vienna Convention, which provides in part:

> 1. A treaty shall be interpreted in good faith in accordance with the ordinary meaning to be given to the terms of the treaty in their context and in the light of its object and purpose.

With this customary rule of interpretation in mind, the Panel stated that:

> In our view, good faith interpretation requires the protection of legitimate expectations derived from the protection of intellectual property rights provided for in the Agreement.

The Panel misunderstands the concept of legitimate expectations in the context of customary rules of interpretation of public international law. The legitimate expectations of the parties to a treaty are reflected in the language of the treaty itself. The duty of a treaty interpreter is to examine the words of the treaty to determine the intentions of the parties. This should be done in accordance with the principles of treaty interpretation set out in Article 31 of the Vienna Convention. But these principles of interpretation neither require nor condone the imputation into a treaty of words that are not there or the importation into a treaty of concepts that were not intended.

In *United States—Standards for Reformulated and Conventional Gasoline*, we set out the proper approach to be applied in interpreting the *WTO Agreement* in accordance with the rules in Article 31 of the *Vienna Convention*. These rules must be respected and applied in interpreting the *TRIPS Agreement* or any other covered agreement. The panel in this case has created its own interpretative principle, which is consistent with neither the customary rules of interpretation of public international law nor established GATT/WTO practice. Both panels and the Appellate Body must be guided by the rules of treaty interpretation set out in the *Vienna Convention*, and must not add to or diminish rights and obligations provided in the *WTO Agreement*.

This conclusion is dictated by two separate and very specific provisions of the

DSU. Article 3.2 of the DSU provides that the dispute settlement system of the WTO:

> . . . serves to preserve the rights and obligations of the Members under the covered agreements, and to clarify the existing provisions of those agreements in accordance with customary rules of interpretation of public international law. Recommendations and rulings of the DSB cannot add to or diminish the rights and obligations provided in the covered agreements.

Furthermore, Article 19.2 of the DSU provides:

> In accordance with paragraph 2 of Article 3, in their findings and recommendations, the panel and Appellate Body cannot add to or diminish the rights and obligations provided in the covered agreements.

These provisions speak for themselves. Unquestionably, both panels and the Appellate Body are bound by them.

For these reasons, we do not agree with the Panel that the legitimate expectations of Members and private rights holders concerning conditions of competition must always be taken into account in interpreting the TRIPS Agreement.

VI. *Article 70.8*

Article 70.8 states:

> Where a Member [as permitted under the grace periods afforded developing countries by Article 65] does not make available as of the date of entry into force of the WTO Agreement patent protection for pharmaceutical and agricultural chemical products commensurate with its obligations under Article 27, that Member shall:
>
> (a) notwithstanding the provisions of Part VI, provide as from the date of entry into force of the WTO Agreement a means by which applications for patents for such inventions can be filed;
>
> (b) apply to these applications, as of the date of application of this Agreement, the criteria for patentability as laid down in this Agreement as if those criteria were being applied on the date of filing in that Member or, where priority is available and claimed, the priority date of the application; and
>
> (c) provide patent protection in accordance with this Agreement as from the grant of the patent and for the remainder of the patent term, counted from the filing date in accordance with Article 33

of this Agreement, for those of these applications that meet the criteria for protection referred to in subparagraph (b).

With respect to Article 70.8(a), the Panel found that:

> . . . Article 70.8(a) requires the Members in question to establish a means that not only appropriately allows for the entitlement to file mailbox applications and the allocation of filing and priority dates to them, but also provides a sound legal basis to preserve novelty and priority as of those dates, so as to eliminate any reasonable doubts regarding whether mailbox applications and eventual patents based on them could be rejected or invalidated because, at the filing or priority date, the matter for which protection was sought was unpatentable in the country in question.

In India's view, the obligations in Article 70.8(a) are met by a developing country Member where it establishes a mailbox for receiving, dating and storing patent applications for pharmaceutical and agricultural chemical products in a manner that properly allots filing and priority dates to those applications in accordance with paragraphs (b) and (c) of Article 70.8. India asserts that the Panel established an additional obligation "to create legal certainty that the patent applications and the eventual patents based on them will not be rejected or invalidated in the future". This, India argues, is a legal error by the Panel.

The introductory clause to Article 70.8 provides that it applies "[w]here a Member does not make available as of the date of entry into force of the WTO Agreement patent protection for pharmaceutical and agricultural chemical products commensurate with its obligations under Article 27 . . ." of the *TRIPS Agreement*. Article 27 requires that patents be made available "for any inventions, whether products or processes, in all fields of technology", subject to certain exceptions. However, pursuant to paragraphs 1, 2 and 4 of Article 65, a developing country Member may delay providing product patent protection in areas of technology not protectable in its territory on the general date of application of the *TRIPS Agreement* for that Member until 1 January 2005. Article 70.8 relates specifically and exclusively to situations where a Member does not provide, as of 1 January 1995, patent protection for pharmaceutical and agricultural chemical products.

By its terms, Article 70.8(a) applies "notwithstanding the provisions of Part VI" of the *TRIPS Agreement*. Part VI of the *TRIPS Agreement*, consisting of Articles 65, 66 and 67, allows for certain "transitional arrangements" in the application of certain provisions of the *TRIPS Agreement*. These "transitional arrangements," which allow a Member to delay the application of some of the obligations in the *TRIPS Agreement* for certain specified periods, do not apply to Article 70.8. Thus, although there are "transitional arrangements" which allow developing country Members, in particular, more time to implement certain of their obligations under the *TRIPS Agreement*, no such "transitional arrangements" exist for the obligations in Article 70.8.

Article 70.8(a) imposes an obligation on Members to provide "a means" by which mailbox applications can be filed "from the date of entry into force of the WTO Agreement." Thus, this obligation has been in force since 1 January 1995. The issue before us in this appeal is not whether this obligation exists or whether this obligation is now in force. Clearly, it exists, and, equally clearly, it is in force now. The issue before us in this appeal is: what precisely is the "means" for filing mailbox applications that is contemplated and required by Article 70.8(a)? To answer this question, we must interpret the terms of Article 70.8(a).

We agree with the Panel that "[t]he analysis of the ordinary meaning of these terms alone does not lead to a definitive interpretation as to what sort of 'means' is required by this subparagraph." Therefore, in accordance with the general rules of treaty interpretation set out in Article 31 of the *Vienna Convention*, to discern the meaning of the terms in Article 70.8(a), we must also read this provision in its context, and in light of the object and purpose of the *TRIPS Agreement*.

Paragraphs (b) and (c) of Article 70.8 constitute part of the context for interpreting Article 70.8(a). Paragraphs (b) and (c) of Article 70.8 require that the "means" provided by a Member under Article 70.8(a) must allow the filing of applications for patents for pharmaceutical and agricultural chemical products from 1 January 1995 and preserve the dates of filing and priority of those applications, so that the criteria for patentability may be applied as of those dates, and so that the patent protection eventually granted is dated back to the filing date. In this respect, we agree with the Panel that,

> . . . in order to prevent the loss of the novelty of an invention . . . filing and priority dates need to have a sound legal basis if the provisions of Article 70.8 are to fulfil their purpose. Moreover, if available, a filing must entitle the applicant to claim priority on the basis of an earlier filing in respect of the claimed invention over applications with subsequent filing or priority dates. Without legally sound filing and priority dates, the mechanism to be established on the basis of Article 70.8 will be rendered inoperational.

On this, the Panel is clearly correct. The Panel's interpretation here is consistent also with the object and purpose of the *TRIPS Agreement*. The Agreement takes into account, *inter alia*, "the need to promote effective and adequate protection of intellectual property rights." We believe the Panel was correct in finding that the "means" that the Member concerned is obliged to provide under Article 70.8(a) must allow for "the entitlement to file mailbox applications and the allocation of filing and priority dates to them." Furthermore, the Panel was correct in finding that the "means" established under Article 70.8(a) must also provide "a sound legal basis to preserve novelty and priority as of those dates." These findings flow inescapably from the necessary operation of paragraphs (b) and (c) of Article 70.8.

However, we do *not* agree with the Panel that Article 70.8(a) requires a Member to establish a means "so as to eliminate any reasonable doubts regarding whether mailbox applications and eventual patents based on them could be rejected or invalidated because, at the filing or priority date, the matter for which protection was sought was unpatentable in the country in question." India is *entitled*, by the "transitional arrangements" in paragraphs 1, 2 and 4 of Article 65, to delay application of Article 27 for patents for pharmaceutical and agricultural chemical products until 1 January 2005. In our view, India is obliged, by Article 70.8(a), to provide a legal mechanism for the filing of mailbox applications that provides a sound legal basis to preserve both the novelty of the inventions and the priority of the applications as of the relevant filing and priority dates. No more.

But what constitutes such a sound legal basis in Indian law? To answer this question, we must recall first an important general rule in the *TRIPS Agreement*. Article 1.1 of the *TRIPS Agreement* states, in pertinent part:

> . . . members shall be free to determine the appropriate method of implementing the provisions of this Agreement within their own legal system and practice.

Members, therefore, are free to determine how best to meet their obligations under the *TRIPS Agreement* within the context of their own legal systems. And, as a Member, India is "free to determine the appropriate method of implementing" its obligations under the *TRIPS Agreement* within the context of its own legal system.

India insists that it has done that. India contends that it has established, through "administrative instructions," a "means" consistent with Article 70.8(a) of the *TRIPS Agreement*. According to India, these "administrative instructions" establish a mechanism that provides a sound legal basis to preserve the novelty of the inventions and the priority of the applications as of the relevant filing and priority dates consistent with Article 70.8(a) of the *TRIPS Agreement*. According to India, pursuant to these "administrative instructions," the Patent Office has been directed to store applications for patents for pharmaceutical and agricultural chemical products separately for future action pursuant to Article 70.8, and the Controller General of Patents Designs and Trademarks ("the Controller") has been instructed not to refer them to an examiner until 1 January 2005. According to India, these "administrative instructions "are legally valid in Indian law, as they are reflected in the Minister's Statement to Parliament of 2 August 1996. And, according to India:

> There is . . . *absolute certainty* that India can, when patents are due in accordance with subparagraphs (b) and (c) of Article 70.8, decide to grant such patents on the basis of the applications currently submitted and determine the novelty and priority of the inventions in accordance with the date of these applications. (emphasis added)

India has not provided any text of these "administrative instructions" either to the Panel or to us.

Whatever their substance or their import, these "administrative instructions" were not the initial "means" chosen by the Government of India to meet India's obligations under Article 70.8(a) of the *TRIPS Agreement*. The Government of India's initial preference for establishing a "means" for filing mailbox applications under Article 70.8(a) was the Patents (Amendment) Ordinance (the "Ordinance"), promulgated by the President of India on 31 December 1994 pursuant to Article 123 of India's Constitution. Article 123 enables the President to promulgate an ordinance when Parliament is not in session, and when the President is satisfied "that circumstances exist which render it necessary for him to take immediate action." India notified the Ordinance to the Council for TRIPS, pursuant to Article 63.2 of the *TRIPS Agreement*, on 6 March 1995. In accordance with the terms of Article 123 of India's Constitution, the Ordinance expired on 26 March 1995, six weeks after the reassembly of Parliament. This was followed by an unsuccessful effort to enact the Patents (Amendment) Bill 1995 to implement the contents of the Ordinance on a permanent basis. This Bill was introduced in the Lok Sabha (Lower House) in March 1995. After being passed by the Lok Sabha, it was referred to a Select Committee of the Rajya Sabha (Upper House) for examination and report. However, the Bill was subsequently not enacted due to the dissolution of Parliament on 10 May 1996. From these actions, it is apparent that the Government of India initially considered the enactment of amending legislation to be necessary in order to implement its obligations under Article 70.8(a). However, India maintains that the "administrative instructions" issued in April 1995 effectively continued the mailbox system established by the Ordinance, thus obviating the need for a formal amendment to the Patents Act or for a new notification to the Council for TRIPS.

With respect to India's "administrative instructions," the Panel found that "the current administrative practice creates a certain degree of legal insecurity in that it requires Indian officials to ignore certain mandatory provisions of the Patents Act"; and that "even if Patent Office officials do not examine and reject mailbox applications, a competitor might seek a judicial order to do so in order to obtain rejection of a patent claim."

India asserts that the Panel erred in its treatment of India's municipal law because municipal law is a fact that must be established before an international tribunal by the party relying on it. In India's view, the Panel did not assess the Indian law as a fact to be established by the United States, but rather as a law to be interpreted by the Panel. India argues that the Panel should have given India the benefit of the doubt as to the status of its mailbox system under Indian domestic law. India claims, furthermore, that the Panel should have sought guidance from India on matters relating to the interpretation of Indian law.

In public international law, an international tribunal may treat municipal law in several ways.[52] Municipal law may serve as evidence of facts and may provide evidence of state practice. However, municipal law may also constitute evidence of compliance or non-compliance with international obligations. For

---

[52] *See*, for example, I. Brownlie, Principles of Public International Law, 4th ed. (Clarendon Press, 1990), pp. 40-42.

example, in *Certain German Interests in Polish Upper Silesia*, the Permanent Court of International Justice observed:

> It might be asked whether a difficulty does not arise from the fact that the Court would have to deal with the Polish law of July 14th, 1920. This, however, does not appear to be the case. From the standpoint of International Law and of the Court which is its organ, municipal laws are merely facts which express the will and constitute the activities of States, in the same manner as do legal decisions and administrative measures. *The Court is certainly not called upon to interpret the Polish law as such; but there is nothing to prevent the Court's giving judgment on the question whether or not, in applying that law, Poland is acting in conformity with its obligations towards Germany under the Geneva Convention.*[53] (emphasis added)

In this case, the Panel was simply performing its task in determining whether India's "administrative instructions" for receiving mailbox applications were in conformity with India's obligations under Article 70.8(a) of the *TRIPS Agreement*. It is clear that an examination of the relevant aspects of Indian municipal law and, in particular, the relevant provisions of the Patents Act as they relate to the "administrative instructions," is essential to determining whether India has complied with its obligations under Article 70.8(a). There was simply no way for the Panel to make this determination without engaging in an examination of Indian law. But, as in the case cited above before the Permanent Court of International Justice, in this case the Panel was not interpreting Indian law "as such;" rather, the Panel was examining Indian law solely for the purpose of determining whether India had met its obligations under the *TRIPS Agreement*. To say that the Panel should have done otherwise would be to say that only India can assess whether Indian law is consistent with India's obligations under the *WTO Agreement*. This, clearly, cannot be so.

Previous GATT/WTO panels also have conducted a detailed examination of the domestic law of a Member in assessing the conformity of that domestic law with the relevant GATT/WTO obligations. For example, in *United States—Section 337 of the Tariff Act of 1930*, the panel conducted a detailed examination of the relevant United States legislation and practice, including the remedies available under Section 337 as well as the differences between patent-based Section 337 proceedings and federal district court proceedings, in order to determine whether Section 337 was inconsistent with Article III:4 of the GATT 1947. This seems to us to be a comparable case.

And, just as it was necessary for the Panel in this case to seek a detailed understanding of the operation of the Patents Act as it relates to the "administrative instructions" in order to assess whether India had complied with Article 70.8(a), so, too, is it necessary for us in this appeal to review the Panel's examination of the same Indian domestic law.

---

[53] [1926], PCIJ Rep., Series A, No. 7, p. 19.

To do so, we must look at the specific provisions of the Patents Act. Section 5(a) of the Patents Act provides that substances "intended for use, or capable of being used, as food or as medicine or drug"are not patentable. "When the complete specification has been led in respect of an application for a patent", section 12(1) *requires* the Controller to refer that application and that specification to an examiner. Moreover, section 15(2) of the Patents Act states that the Controller "shall refuse" an application in respect of a substance that is not patentable. We agree with the Panel that these provisions of the Patents Act are mandatory. And, like the Panel, we are not persuaded that India's "administrative instructions" would prevail over the contradictory mandatory provisions of the Patents Act. We note also that, in issuing these "administrative instructions," the Government of India did not avail itself of the provisions of section 159 of the Patents Act, which allows the Central Government "to make rules for carrying out the provisions of [the] Act" or section 160 of the Patents Act, which requires that such rules be laid before each House of the Indian Parliament. We are told by India that such rule-making was not required for the "administrative instructions" at issue here. But this, too, seems to be inconsistent with the mandatory provisions of the Patents Act.

We are not persuaded by India's explanation of these seeming contradictions. Accordingly, we are not persuaded that India's "administrative instructions" would survive a legal challenge under the Patents Act. And, consequently, we are not persuaded that India's "administrative instructions" provide a sound legal basis to preserve novelty of inventions and priority of applications as of the relevant filing and priority dates.

For these reasons, we agree with the Panel's conclusion that India's "administrative instructions" for receiving mailbox applications are inconsistent with Article 70.8(a) of the *TRIPS Agreement.* . . .

NOTES AND QUESTIONS

(1) **The Role of Legitimate Expectations**. Why did the Appellate Body find that the panel had misapplied Article 31 of the Vienna Convention? In what way, according to the Appellate Body, are "legitimate expectations" relevant to interpretation of the TRIPS Agreement? For a detailed discussion of the panel and Appellate Body reports, see Matthijs Geuze & Hannu Wager, *WTO Dispute Settlement Practice Relating to the TRIPS Agreement*, J. INT'L ECON. L. 347, 365-67 (1999) (summarizing arguments); J.H. Reichman, *Securing Compliance with the TRIPS Agreement after U.S. v. India*, J. INT'L ECON. L. 585, 592 (1998).

(2) **The Argument for Circumspection.** The Appellate Body report notes, circumspectly, that "principles of interpretation neither require nor condone the imputation into a treaty of words that are not there or the importation into a treaty of concepts that were not intended." Does this answer the dilemmas posed above regarding interpretive approaches? Indian commentators viewed

the Appellate Body decision in *United States-India* as preferable to the panel decision because they believe it adhered more closely to the TRIPS Agreement that was negotiated. Jayashree Watal went so far as to say that the Appellate Body decision "restores some of the faith that we had lost in the WTO." *The WTO Appellate Body: The First Four Years*, 1 J. WORLD INTELL. PROP. 425, 432 (1999) (comments of Jayashree Watal). Does this observation affect how you think the TRIPS Agreement should be interpreted? Did the panels in *United States-Section 110(5), supra* § 4.03[B][2], and *Canada-Pharmaceutical Patents, supra* § 3.04[D][2], display the circumspection demanded by the Appellate Body in *United States-India?*

In order to fulfil the objectives of the dispute settlement process, to which values must the Appellate Body adhere most faithfully? Are these values different from those that should motivate the TRIPS Council? If so, why? Joel Trachtman has noted that in the *Shrimp-Turtle* case, the WTO Appellate Body "refined its interpretive tools by rejecting a strict 'original intent' interpretation . . . in favor of a more dynamic interpretation to fit modern circumstances. In doing so, it aggregated substantial power to itself, both to engage in balancing and to 'modernize' the interpretation of Article XX [of the GATT]." Joel P. Trachtman, *The Domain of WTO Dispute Resolution*, 40 HARV. INT'L L.J. 333, 364 (1999). How would the extension of that interpretive philosophy to TRIPS disputes affect the development of international intellectual property law? In what ways would the decision by WTO panels to adopt a dynamic gap-filling methodology or a minimalist textualist methodology affect the future conduct of international intellectual property relations? *See* Paul Edward Geller, *Intellectual Property in the Global Marketplace: Impact of TRIPS Dispute Settlement*, 29 INT. LAW. 99, 113 (1995).

(3) **Stare Decisis.** The panel in *EU v. India* indicated that it did not feel bound by the reports of the panel or the Appellate Body in *United States v. India*. *See* EU v. India, Panel Report, WT/DS79/R (Aug. 24, 1998). Why not? Should it have? *See* Adrian T. Chua, *Precedent and Principles of WTO Panel Jurisprudence*, 2 BERK. J. INT'L L. 171, 172-74 (1998). Does failure to apply principles of stare decisis undermine the purposes of the WTO adjudicative system? *Cf.* DSU art. 3.2. Would the adoption of a system of binding precedent have generated other unfavorable consequences? What lesser presumptions might the panel in *EU v. India* have considered even if it did not feel formally bound by the precedent of *United States v. India? See* EU v. India, Panel Report, WT/DS79/R (discussing EU's prima facie case). In large part, the position adopted by the *EU-India* panel merely reflected the practice of pre-WTO GATT panels. In what way does the nature of the new WTO proceedings (as opposed to the prior GATT practice described in the Dreyfuss and Lowenfeld article) support, or undermine, the development of a system of binding precedent? Could it be argued that earlier panel reports adopted by the DSB are part of "subsequent practice in the application of the treaty" under Article 31(3)(b) of the Vienna Convention on the Law of Treaties and thus part of the "customary rules of interpretation of public international law" under Article 3.2 of the DSU? *See* Japan—Taxes on Alcoholic Beverages, Appellate Body Report, Nov. 1, 1996, WT/DS8/AB/R, WT/DS10/AB/R, WT/DS11/AB/R (discussing whether the adoption of a panel report should be treated as subsequent practice,

defined by the Appellate Body as "a 'concordant, common and consistent' sequence of acts or pronouncements sufficient to establish a discernible intent implying the parties' agreement regarding its interpretation"); *see also* Chua, *supra* at 183-85 (arguing that panel reports might constitute binding precedent in certain circumstances notwithstanding *Japan-Alcoholic Beverages*). In what ways are the considerations supporting characterization as subsequent practice under international law inconsistent with those considerations that would support treating panel reports as "binding precedent" in the sense that that term is used in common law jurisdictions adjudicating disputes between private parties? What does this tell you about the nature of public international law?

(4) **The GATT** *acquis*. The term "GATT acquis" has been adopted by the Appellate Body as a useful term by which to describe the pre-existing body of GATT practices and understandings. The term *acquis communautaire* is commonly found in the case law of the European Court of Justice. There, it means the "whole body of rules, principles, agreements, declarations, resolutions, opinions, objectives and practices concerning the European Communities . . . whether or not binding in law, which has developed since their establishment and which has been accepted by the Community . . . as governing their activities." Mary Footer, *The Role of Consensus in GATT/WTO Decision-Making*, 17 Nw. J. Int'l L. Bus. 653 (1996–1997).

[B] The Scope of Intellectual Property Protection in the WTO

DREYFUSS AND LOWENFELD, CASE II:
THE SCOPE OF PROTECTION[*]
37 Va. J. Int'l L. 275, 297-307

In many ways, limitations on the subject matter entitled to protection provide rather coarse control over the balance between public access and private incentives. By fencing off entire fields from protection, such limitations make intellectual property law unavailable as a source of encouragement for whole industries. Moreover, they skew the decisions that individual innovators make about where to invest their resources. Ironically, industries devoted to subject matter that is considered too socially important to protect can wind up being underfunded. For this reason, it makes sense for states to be generous on the question of subject matter protectability, and then to safeguard the public's interest in access in more finely tuned ways. For example, a state may tighten the scope of what it considers infringement—adjusting the degree of similarity for finding infringement of copyrights, and the degree of equivalence needed for finding infringement of patents.[54]

For the TRIPS Agreement, the ability to fine tune raises the danger that a member state could use these measures in the way we previously discussed for

---

[*]Copyright 1997, Rochelle Cooper Dreyfuss and Andreas F. Lowenfeld.

[54]For simplicity, the text considers only these alternatives. What is said here, however, applies to other fine-tuning provisions, such as the fair use defense in copyright law or the experimental use defense in patent law.

coarse tuning: to appear to comply with the Agreement while really sidestepping its obligations. As to that issue, what we have said previously applies here as well. In this section, we discuss the role of the GATT/WTO system in considering the more subtle question of whether the particular balance that a state strikes is permissible under the TRIPS Agreement.

Case II

Monastery Labs developed a new pharmaceutical for treating Sallyheimer disease. The drug, a complex organic compound bound to magnesium, is patented both in Monastery's home country, Xandia, and in Patria, a developing country that has adopted patent legislation conforming to the TRIPS Agreement. A Patrian pharmaceutical company sells the same complex compound, except that its product substitutes manganese for magnesium. Monastery Labs sued the Patrian company in Patria, but lost. The court found (1) that before Monastery Labs invented this compound, it was common knowledge that Sallyheimer sufferers had a problem with metals, so this compound was not inventive enough to qualify for protection; and (2) that Monastery's patent described "alkaline earth metal bonds" and manganese is not an alkaline earth metal, with the result that the Patrian company's product does not infringe Monastery's patent. Monastery prevailed upon the government of Xandia to bring a complaint to the WTO. Again, after consultation, the dispute was referred to a panel for resolution.

The complaint alleges that Patria violated article 27(1) of the TRIPS Agreement by requiring an inventive leap rather than an "inventive step." Further, the complaint asserts that Patria permitted infringement of Monastery's valid patent, thereby violating article 28(1)(a) by failing to prevent others from using Monastery's insight without its authorization. Patria, in its answering papers, contends that its courts applied settled principles of Patrian patent law, without discriminating by nationality, on the basis that an applicant for monopoly protection has a heavy burden of establishing both nonobviousness[55] and infringement.

A. Alternative Approaches

It is not clear, at the outset, how a WTO panel should resolve this controversy. Case II demonstrates how differently two countries could administer intellectual property laws that ostensibly comply with the TRIPS Agreement. At one time, a court in the United States, for instance, might have handled this case as follows: if it found that the identification of a metals problem was part

---

[55]A footnote to article 27(1) of the TRIPS Agreement states: "For the purposes of this Article, the term[ ] 'inventive step' . . . may be deemed by a Member to be synonymous with the term[ ] 'nonobvious'."

of the art existing prior to Monastery's invention, it might consider using magnesium compounds "obvious to try." It would then ascertain how many metal-delivery systems there are. If there are many, it could hold Monastery's discovery patentable on the theory that the ordinary artisan would not have found this one easily. The inquiry on infringement would be, in a sense, the reverse: the court would inquire whether it would be obvious to the ordinary artisan to substitute manganese for magnesium—a question that in another context the U.S. Supreme Court has already answered in the affirmative. Accordingly, under the doctrine of equivalents as applied in the United States, Monastery's patent would be considered to be infringed.

One could easily imagine that Patria could take a very different approach. If it is a developing or least-developed country, the transition provisions in the TRIPS Agreement give it a grace period before it is required to extend patent protection to such products.[63] A decision to enact legislation concerning pharmaceuticals without such delay could well indicate that Patria is trying to promote indigenous research and development. A research and development industry, however, requires a technologically trained labor force. One way to encourage the creation of such a resource might be by teaching unskilled labor to work in laboratories. That strategy, in turn, would require that there be meaningful work for this labor force to do. Finding alternatives to expensive foreign medicines certainly seems like an attractive objective. Thus, it might make sense for Patria to reject the "obvious to try" doctrine and argue that in developed countries patent protection is needed in this context to motivate someone to engage in the labor-intensive effort of finding the right choice among many, but that in Patria, where a cheap labor force is looking for work, trudging through obvious alternatives requires no particular encouragement. In other words, supracompetitive profits should be reserved to those who confer genuinely unique and major social benefits by denying a separate patent to the sort of advance over prior art that Monastery's invention represents. Alternatively, Patria could allow its work force to train on Monastery's invention by deciding that any rights that Monastery wishes to assert must be expressly claimed in the patent document. That would release variations for domestic researchers to find. In short, whether these arguments are after-the-fact rationalizations or actually describe Patria's motivation, the challenged failure to grant Monastery the same protection it receives in the home country is not an obvious or clear violation of the TRIPS Agreement.[65]

---

[63]For developing countries, there is a four-year grace period. TRIPS Agreement art. 65(2). For countries that had not previously enacted legislation to protect pharmaceuticals, there is an additional five-year grace period. *Id.* art. 65(4). Least-developed countries may have ten years from the date of application of the substantive provisions of the Agreement to fully comply with these provisions. *Id.* art. 66(1).

[65]The basic Paris Convention does not guarantee to patent holders in one state patent protection in other member states, but leaves the issues of patentability and infringement to each member state's laws. Paris Convention, art. 2(1). The question here raised is how far this deference to lex fori is changed by the WTO system—the TRIPS Agreement in combination with the DSU.

B. Special Treatment for Developing Countries

If this dispute were brought during the transition period allowed to developing and least-developed countries, Patria might argue that since it was not yet required to offer patent protection to Monastery, Xandia should not be heard to complain that Patria offers less protection than Xandia finds ideal. To evaluate this position, two issues must be decided: first, whether Patria is a country that can avail itself of the special benefits offered to developing economies, and second, the exact scope of these special benefits.

. . . .

Assuming that Patria qualifies as a developing country, the next question is how much leeway it should be given on that account. One might conclude that the transition provisions are exclusive and that once a country moves out of the transition period (voluntarily or under the pressure of time limits), it is expected to conform its laws in every respect to the norms of the developed world. There are, however, significant reasons to refrain from taking so hard a line. It is important to remember that the impact of the TRIPS Agreement on the developing world was not comprehensively considered at the time the Agreement was drafted. The principal negotiators were almost uniformly interested in strengthening the international intellectual property regime. And because the GATT/WTO system requires its members to accept all the principal agreements negotiated in the Uruguay Round, there was no practical way for any country, including Patria, to stay outside the TRIPS Agreement.

Now that there is time to be more reflective, we should recognize that as far as developing countries are concerned, the TRIPS Agreement could have a substantially different impact from the remainder of the WTO agreements. One effect is obvious: the cost to member states of enforcing intellectual property rights is formidable. Monitoring is expensive, the obligation to destroy infringing materials entails high social costs, and countries with weak civil justice systems must spend the money to create them. All of this is in addition to the cost of setting up copyright, trademark, and patent offices and staffing them with trained personnel.

Even after these costs are borne, the TRIPS Agreement may present a significant problem to developing countries. Experience shows that in other economic sectors, comparative advantage tends to shift over time. As each party has (more or less) an equal opportunity to acquire an advantage in any economic sector, each trade barrier that is lowered is either a current benefit or a potential benefit. In contrast, it can be argued that a technologically undeveloped country that agrees to the TRIPS Agreement is handicapping itself. Instead of following the strategy (which many developed countries once pursued) of absorbing the world's knowledge base and coming up to technological speed before protecting foreign intellectual property, a country that enters into the TRIPS Agreement at this stage, before it has a creative community in place, may well raise the costs of acquiring the knowledge it needs. The TRIPS Agreement might, therefore, improve the *incentives* for a developing country's citizens to become innovative, but put the *cost* of becoming innovative out of reach. The opposite argument, which prevailed in the

Uruguay Round (though one can debate how much choice the developing countries had at the end) is that by providing secure protection for intellectual property, a member state can remain in the mainstream of technological progress, while denying protection might leave it on the sidelines of innovation[69]. . . [T]hese considerations suggest that unless the TRIPS Agreement is sympathetically interpreted to safeguard public access, it could wind up preventing certain member states from ever becoming players in the intellectual property sector.[76]

C. Deferring to Patria

All of this goes to argue that on the substantive side, Patria's decision ought to be given considerable deference. Allowing Patrians to make variations on Monastery's drug without incurring the costs of infringement is one way to develop the skills Patria needs if it is ever to see advantages from joining the TRIPS Agreement. Accordingly, whereas in Case I we suggested that deference to Patria's own decisions may properly depend on whether Patria was taking positions consistent with policies of states with demonstrated commitments to intellectual property, in Case II it would probably be wise for a WTO panel—at least with respect to developing countries—to defer even in circumstances where Patria's decisions look quite atypical.

Even if Patria were not a developing country, the better course might well be to make it nearly impossible to prevail before the WTO on a complaint involving fine-tuning, except on an additional showing of violation of the non-discrimination provisions—national treatment and most-favored-nation treatment. Although the TRIPS Agreement is drafted as a set of standards for the protection of innovators, there are two sides to every innovation coin: the greater the protection granted to the innovator, the less is the public's access to the products of intellectual activity. To the extent that DSU panels are instructed not to "diminish rights or obligations," they should be equally careful not to diminish the rights that users of innovative efforts have in particular countries.[80] Again, this is the core difference between a minimum standard and

---

[69]An interesting illustration of this debate was recently provided by Martin J. Adelman & Sonia Baldia, *Prospects and Limits of the Patent Provision in the TRIPS Agreement: The Case of India*, 29 Vand. J. Transnat'l L. 507, 525-33 (1996). The authors draw the conclusion from India's large infrastructure in pharmaceutical production, coupled with its past failure to contribute innovations in the pharmaceutical field, that strong intellectual property protection has always been in India's interest. In contrast, J.H. Reichman uses the same data to argue that free-riding is a way for a developing economy to accumulate the skills and capital necessary to become innovative. J.H. Reichman, *Compliance with the TRIPS Agreement: Introduction to a Scholarly Debate*, 29 Vand. J. Transnat'l L. 363, 381 (1996).

[76]*See also* article 8.10 of the DSU, which calls for at least one member of a panel to be chosen from a developing state if the controversy concerns such a state; *id.* art. 21.7, which requires that the impact on the economy of developing countries be taken into account in the panel's recommendations. Article 24 calls for additional consideration and restraint on the part of complaining parties in disputes with least-developed member states.

[80][S]ee also article 7 of the TRIPS Agreement, which states that the Agreement's objective is to:

contribute to the promotion of technological innovation and to the transfer and dissemination of technology, to *the mutual advantage of producers and users* of

an optimum or harmonized rule: a minimum standard allows each member state to create a law that is suited to the needs of its own creative community; an "optimum" rule would, in contrast, require each state to adopt a single law, whether it was right for its economy or not. The drafters of the TRIPS Agreement chose minimum standards, just as the drafters of the Berne and Paris Convention did. We agree with that choice because we believe that it best promotes innovation.[81]

Further, disputes involving fine-tuning can be quite different from cases where the respondent is charged with a clear failure to protect innovative works.   The failure to protect intellectual products often results in counterfeiting. In Case I, for example, Patria was countenancing sales of pirated programs. The campaign against counterfeiting was the original incentive for the Uruguay Round to become engaged in the field of intellectual property, and so it makes sense to entertain claims that a country is systematically failing to protect subject matter. Of course, to the extent that Case II was decided on the ground of no infringement, there was no counterfeiting. Patria's laws permitted a product very similar to the protected product to go on the market.   However, creating that product required considerable investment. Since the Patrian defendants did not get a free ride, it is unlikely that they could price Monastery out of the Patria (or world) market. Indeed, Monastery's product remains attractive to any Sallyheimer sufferer intent on purchasing the "real thing."[84]

Other issues of fine-tuning—for instance the scope of the fair use defense in copyright—call, in our judgment, for a similar approach in the WTO. The United States, for example, permits certain unauthorized uses of copyrighted materials for socially worthy purposes, so long as the "potential market for or value" of the work is not unduly sacrificed.   The TRIPS Agreement countenances exceptions to protection, but only for "special cases which do not conflict with a normal exploitation of the work and do not unreasonably prejudice the legitimate interests of the right holder."[86]   Whether these provisions are consistent with one another is not at all clear. Yet, it seems to us that panels ought to tread lightly in this area. Indeed, member states ought to resist pressures from their constituents to bring complaints involving such issues to the WTO. The extent to which fair use is considered necessary

---

technological knowledge and in a manner conducive to social and economic welfare, and to a *balance* of rights and obligations. (emphasis added).

[81]We note that Judith Bello, *Some Practical Observations About WTO Settlement of Intellectual Property Disputes*, 37 VA. J. INT'L L., suggests that in taking this view, we are "fabricating" rights or "usurp[ing]" the role of negotiators. However, it is evident to us that any definition of an intellectual property right implies some right for users, and that the TRIPS Agreement, like the Berne and Paris Conventions, reflects this perspective.

[84]If the case were decided by the Patrian court on the ground that Monastery's invention was obvious, then counterfeiting is a possibility. If Xandia can show a persistent unwillingness to recognize any pharmaceutical inventions as inventive enough to merit protection, the case would resemble Case I. If there is no element of persistence, then Patria's decision represents a determination that not much of an investment was needed to create the invention. That determination is some indication that this is not a case where countenancing competitive sales would significantly reduce the incentive to innovate.

[86]TRIPS Agreement art. 13 (with respect to copyright); *id.* art. 30 (with respect to patents).

depends on fundamental national values such as the importance and extent of free speech, on artistic traditions, and on aesthetic sensibilities.[88] Setting a worldwide standard on this issue would, therefore, reduce flexibility and produce a kind of cultural homogenization that might either induce noncompliance or turn the world into a much less stimulating environment.

In the final analysis, the way to handle complaints about fine-tuning may be the same in all cases. There ought to be a presumption that these issues are for individual member states, with intervention by the international community only on the basis of a showing of a pattern of discrimination or failure to grant protection without defensible reasons.

<hr/>

NOTES AND QUESTIONS

(1) **Developing Countries.** Developing countries such as Patria in Case II have been given some preferential treatment by way of transitional provisions delaying the application of the TRIPS Agreement. Moreover, Article 67 of the TRIPS Agreement calls on developed country members, on request and on mutually agreed terms, to lend assistance (meaning both financial and technical) to developing country members. Professor Reichman has argued that "by shifting international intellectual property protection to the framework of multilateral trade negotiations, developed countries have implicitly acknowledged that compensation has become the new master principle." J.H. Reichman, *Universal Minimum Standards of Intellectual Property Protection under the TRIPS Component of the WTO Agreement*, 29 INT. LAW. 345, 384-85 (1995). In particular, Professor Reichman suggests that developing countries under pressure to enact higher standards of protection may present "counterclaims for the higher social costs that such standards would entail." *Id.* What are the costs to which Professor Reichman refers and to what extent would the measures included in TRIPS to assist developing countries affect the viability of such claims?

(2) **Articles 7-8 of TRIPS.** If Patria sought to support its argument of compliance by reference to the purpose of the agreement, in what way could it make use of Article 7 of TRIPS, which provides that the

> protection and enforcement of intellectual property rights should contribute to the promotion of technological innovation and to the transfer and dissemination of technology, to the mutual advantage

<hr/>

[88] *See, e.g.,* Marci A. Hamilton, *Art Speech,* 49 VAND. L. REV. 73, 86-96 (1996). Many of these same points can be made with respect to cultural questions raised in the GATT system for the first time by the TRIPS Agreement. For example, may a member state erect a barrier to services when the services in question are performances and the country is concerned that the importing country's culture will drown out its own? May a member state permit unauthorized utilization of trademarks if it believes that trademarks are among the few symbols that many of its citizens can read? May a member give adapters greater leeway with copyrighted works when adaptation is needed to make the works effectively available to the domestic audience? One wonders how these questions would be addressed in the context of membership by China in the WTO, . . .

of producers and users of technological knowledge and in a manner conducive to social and economic welfare, and to a balance of rights and obligations?

Do the arguments for Patria advanced by Dreyfuss and Lowenfeld find support in Article 7? Article 8(1) permits countries to adopt measures to "promote the public interest in sectors of vital importance to their socio-economic and technological development, provided that such measures are consistent with the provisions of this Agreement." To what extent could Patria rely on this provision to support its case? What are the limits of Article 8(1)? If a panel were to adopt a purposive interpretation of the agreement, would the purpose of the GATT/WTO be the relevant purpose? The purpose of TRIPS? *Cf.* United States—Import Prohibition of Certain Shrimp and Shrimp Products, AB-1998-4, WT/DS58/AB/R (98-3899) (Appellate Body, Oct. 12, 1998) (using "purposes" in manner different from panel). To what extent did the panel in *Canada-Pharmaceutical Patents, supra* § 3.04[D][2], make use of Articles 7-8 in assessing the Canadian law in question?

(3) **Deference to Member Countries.** Dreyfuss and Lowenfeld conclude that in Case II a panel should display some deference to the ways in which Patria has implemented its TRIPS obligations, but base deference on a different rationale than Case I. What is the range of arguments for a WTO panel to exhibit deference to member countries? Why and in what circumstances do U.S. domestic courts accord deference to actions of administrative or legislative bodies? Are these reasons the same? *See The Review of the WTO's Dispute Settlement Understanding: Which Way?*, 1 J. WORLD INTELL. PROP. 447, 456 (1998) (comments of David Palmeter).

(4) **Fine-Tuning: Exceptions and Limitations.** Dreyfuss and Lowenfeld characterize Case II as a case involving "fine-tuning." They are surely correct that such cases are particularly apt cases for deference to national determinations. Intellectual property law contains a series of fine-tuning devices. Is there a danger in articulating a rule of deference in all instances of "fine-tuning"? In copyright law, one could argue that fine-tuning is performed not only through the idea/expression distinction, but in the test for infringement, and in the range of exemptions and privileges found in the statute. Should exceptions in national law be afforded the same degree of deference by WTO panels? *See* Jane C. Ginsburg, *The Role of National Copyright in an Era of International Copyright Norms*, in THE ROLE OF NATIONAL LEGISLATION IN COPYRIGHT LAW 211, 212 (2000) (commenting that "exceptions to copyright present a more difficult, but potentially persuasive, case" for reservation to national norms).

Certain fine-tuning devices may be subject to more explicit provisions of TRIPS. For example, Article 13 of TRIPS imposes specific constraints on the types of limitations and exceptions that can be imposed upon a copyright owner's rights. The law of almost every country contains exceptions that might be vulnerable if this provision is strictly interpreted. (What interpretive lesson should one draw from that observation?) To what extent might the arguments of deference advanced by Dreyfuss and Lowenfeld in discussing Case II between Xandia and Patria (and in discussing the general defense of fair use in U.S. law) have been of assistance to the United States in defending the Fairness in Music Licensing Act? *See supra* § 4.03[B][2]; *see* Neil Netanel, *The Next Round: The Impact of the WIPO Copyright Treaty on TRIPS Dispute Settlement*, 37 VA. J. INT'L L. 441 (1997); Geert A. Zonnekeyn, *The Protection of Intellectual Property Rights under the EC Trade Barriers Regulation: An Analysis of The IMRO Case*, J. WORLD INTELL. PROP. 357 (1999); Laurence R. Helfer, *World Music on a US Stage: A Berne/TRIPS and Economic Analysis of the Fairness in Music Licensing Act*, 80 B.U. L. REV. 93 (2000). Did the WTO panel in *United States-Section 110(5) of the U.S. Copyright Act* show deference to the United States consistent with the approach suggested by Dreyfuss and Lowenfeld? *See* Graeme B. Dinwoodie, *The Development and Incorporation of International Norms in the Formation of Copyright Law*, 62 OHIO STATE L.J. 733 (2001). What about the panel in *Canada-Pharmaceutical Patents, supra* § 3.04[D][2]?

DREYFUSS AND LOWENFELD, CASE III: VIOLATION OF ANTITRUST LAWS, PATENT MISUSE, AND COMPULSORY LICENSING[*]
37 VA. J INT'L L. 275, 307-16

Cases I and II were concerned with the problem of insuring that intellectual property protection does not undermine its own goals by interfering with or unduly raising the costs of innovation. Intellectual property law holds another risk—abuse of the market power created by exclusivity. For example, intellectual property licenses have been used to disguise cartel arrangements, to use power in one market as leverage for dominating another market, and to inhibit the incentive to innovate. Such effects are generally sought to be controlled through the concept of intellectual property misuse and through invocation of competition or antitrust laws. The negotiators of the Uruguay Round did not place competition law on their agenda ... The TRIPS Agreement does, however, explicitly permit members to adopt appropriate measures to control abuse of intellectual property rights,[95] and provides certain guidelines as to the form that these measures might take.[96] Article 40(3) seeks to facilitate the effort to prevent the abuse of intellectual property rights by requiring each member state to consult on request with other members concerning alleged violations of the requesting member's competition law by intellectual property owners domiciled in the requested member state. As in other areas, the TRIPS Agreement lays down a floor; how far states can circumscribe intellectual property rights in the name of furthering competition is not fully delineated.

---

[*]Copyright 1997, Rochelle Cooper Dreyfuss and Andreas F. Lowenfeld.

[95]*See* TRIPS Agreement arts. 8(2), 40(2).

[96]*See, e.g., id.* arts. 31, 40.

Case III

Bilker Metals, a Xandian company, is the world's largest producer of molten metals. It holds many important patents on molten metal technology. In 1996, the government of Patria filed a complaint in a Patrian court against Bilker, alleging that certain of its licensing practices limited the worldwide competitive opportunities of Patrian molten metal producers and chilled their incentives to innovate. Specifically, the complaint alleged that Bilker committed a per se violation of Patria's antitrust laws by requiring its licensees to accept licenses of both patents and know-how (a package license) for a period extending beyond the terms of the patents, and to undertake to assign to Bilker rights in any improvements made by the licensee (a grant back-provision). Further, the government of Patria alleged that Bilker was refusing to license the copyrights in its computerized servicing protocols. Because these protocols were the only cost-effective way to service the equipment needed to practice Bilker's inventions, the refusal amounted to a tie-in of equipment, patents, and servicing. If not an antitrust violation, Patria charged, the tie-in was a misuse of Bilker's copyrights that would render them unenforceable in litigation.

Following extensive litigation, the Patrian court entered a decree enjoining Bilker from enforcing its grant-back and package-licensing provisions, and from utilizing its copyrights as servicing restrictions, anywhere in the world. Moreover, Bilker was ordered to grant worldwide licenses to Patrian firms for certain of its patented technologies at a reasonable royalty. After the Patrian court entered its decree, Xandia filed a complaint with the WTO. Under Xandian law, package licensing and grant backs are considered competition problems only when the technology being licensed has no reasonable substitutes and the patentee has substantial market power. Moreover, Xandia does not recognize the concept of copyright misuse; copyright holders are allowed absolute discretion over licensing decisions. Xandia's complaint asserts that the judgment of the Patrian court amounted to a compulsory license that violates article 31 of the TRIPS Agreement concerning the conditions of compulsory licenses, frustrates the objectives of the TRIPS Agreement set out in article 7, and undermines the principles of article 8(2), which permit only "appropriate measures" to prevent abuse of intellectual property rights.

A. Tensions Between TRIPS, Trade Law, and Antitrust

Case III illustrates the problems we noted in the Introduction concerning the differing goals of trade law and intellectual property law. When competition law is included, the problems become even harder to sort out. On the one hand, the Patrian judgment in Case III could be said to encourage innovation: freed of grant-back obligations, Patrian molten metal producers have the incentive to improve on Bilker's technology. The judgment could also be said to promote trade in that it allows Bilker's competitors to sell molten metals and related technology on a worldwide basis. Moreover, the prohibition against tie-ins and package licensing could further the objective of the TRIPS Agreement to employ technological innovation "in a manner conducive to social and economic welfare," in that it may lower the worldwide cost of using Bilker's technology both during the term that the intellectual property rights are in force and after they expire.

On the other hand, the judgment also might have significant anti-innovation, competition, and welfare consequences. Patria's position on licensing could substantially restrict the manner in which innovators can capture the social benefits bestowed by their innovations, and reduce their capacity to coordinate developments in their fields. To the extent these restraints are imposed as per se rules—with no investigation of their competitive effect and no opportunity for Bilker to justify its practices—they diminish the incentive to innovate without evidence that they enhance competition.

Nor is it necessarily true that the Patrian approach will improve the conditions of trade. Although the judgment frees all Patrian producers to do business all over the world, not every market is large enough and stable enough to attract investors. In less-developed countries, the efficiencies produced by cooperative and coordinated decision making are sometimes needed to pool all the capital and technical capacity that is available. Without violating some of the competition norms of developed nations, these economies may have considerable difficulty in modernizing. Similarly, underdeveloped economies sometimes use the promise of exclusivity to encourage technology transfers; under the Bilker decree, exclusive rights are not available because Bilker is apparently required by the Patrian judgment to license any Patrian firm that asks.[100] Finally, package licenses can be good for poor economies. Sometimes, extending royalty payments beyond the terms of the relevant intellectual property rights functions as a loan: the initial cost of licensing is lowered because part of the payment is deferred to later years (when the licensee is better able to afford them). As long as there are suitable substitutes for the licensed technology, package licensing can both promote trade and enhance welfare.

Tensions such as these help to explain why the architects of the Uruguay Round did not wade too deeply into the muddy waters of competition law. Appreciating these tensions does not, however, make dispute resolution easier. In this case, developing countries may seek to intervene; consultations among participants might then enable the DSB to find a method for dealing with Bilker's business practices in a manner that optimizes world trade and research in molten metals. Should the parties fail to reach an agreement, however, it is very difficult to see how a panel would go about resolving this dispute.

The only specific guidelines provided by TRIPS are the fourteen conditions

---

[100]We say "apparently" because there is doubt that a Patrian court could order Bilker to give a license for activity in Tertia contrary to the laws of that country. *See, e.g.*, RESTATEMENT (THIRD) OF THE FOREIGN RELATIONS LAW OF THE UNITED STATES § 403(2)(g) and Reporter's Note 3 (1986).

that article 31 places on compulsory licensing. Certain of these conditions were met by Patria: the case was considered on an individualized basis, the rights holder was involved, and the disposition was subject to judicial review. [TRIPS, arts. 31(a), (b), (i) and (j)]. However, the scope and duration of the judgment is quite broad and includes conditions that affect rights outside of Patria. Such a disposition is permissible, [TRIPS arts. 31(c), (k)], and the Agreement states that grant-back conditions and coercive package licensing are practices that members may by legislation specify as abusive. [TRIPS art. 40(2)]. It is not clear, however, whether measures to control such practices may be implemented by Patria in the absence of "judicial or administrative process" [TRIPS art. 31(k)] evaluating evidence that the challenged practices actually produced abusive effects.[107] A WTO panel might here look for precedents from GATT dispute settlement practice; but that practice was not uniform, and in any event might not be regarded as applicable.

B. Resolving the Tensions: Some Suggestions

That the intellectual property/competition interface would raise difficult questions was not lost on those who commented on the TRIPS Agreement at the time it went into force. In an early article, our colleague, Professor Eleanor Fox, suggested a way to deal with at least some of the problems that will arise. She noted that, at the time that the TRIPS Agreement came into force, the European Community and the United States took widely divergent positions on this issue. In effect, their laws staked out two ends of a spectrum, with the United States taking the pro-intellectual property side, and the European Community more oriented towards competition.[109] She then suggested a principle of preference whereby any antitrust enforcement action by a member state that fell within this spectrum should be considered presumptively valid under the TRIPS Agreement.

It seems to us that such an approach could run counter to the consensus that emerged from the Uruguay Round, where member states agreed to uphold minimum standards of intellectual property law, but did not make substantive decisions regarding competition law: such disparate treatment could be interpreted to mean that in close cases, innovation policy must trump competition policy in all member states. Thus, we do not believe that a principle of deference to U.S. or European Community competition law (or something in between) should be read into the TRIPS Agreement. We do, however, think that

---

[107]Article 40(2), for example, speaks of "practices or conditions that may *in particular cases constitute* an abuse of intellectual property rights" (emphasis added). *See also id.* art. 31(a), which specifies that compulsory licenses cannot be authorized without considering the individual merits of the situation; *cf.* Ernst-Ulrich Petersmann, *International Competition Rules for the GATT-MTO World Trade and Legal System*, J. WORLD TRADE, Dec. 1993, at 35, 59 (1993), who interprets this clause to require case-by-case analysis.

[109]See [Eleanor M. Fox, *Trade, Competition and Intellectual Property—TRIPS and its Antitrust Counterparts*, 29 VAND. J. TRANS. L. 481, 487-88 (1996)], who cites as examples the questions whether patentees may charge excessive prices, refuse all licensees, divide territories, or require grantbacks from licensees—all issues that had arisen in both the United States and the European Community at the time the TRIPS Agreement entered into force. All the cited practices appear to be valid under U.S. law, but to violate EC law.

Professor Fox offers an attractive approach for interpreting what the minimum standards of the TRIPS Agreement mean by abuse. Thus we would accept her suggestion to compare Patria's law and implementing decree with the laws of the European Community and the United States: if Patria's measures are consistent with those laws (particularly if the practice challenged by Bilker would violate the law of both jurisdictions and the remedy imposed by Patria would be consistent with both their laws), they should be upheld by a WTO panel unless expressly prohibited by the TRIPS Agreement. However, if, for instance, Patria required Bilker to issue a compulsory royalty-free license for its patented products, such an order would be inconsistent with article 31(h) of the TRIPS Agreement, regardless of U.S. or European Community law, and a challenge to the order by Xandia should be upheld by the DSU panel.[111]

Nor does Professor Fox purport to address all of the problems raised by cases such as Case III. She does not provide a method for considering measures that fall outside the EC/U.S. competition-law spectrum. Such situations are easy to imagine. The competition law of the United States and the European Community may well not be appropriate for developing countries and member states in transition to market economies. States that, prior to TRIPS, lacked intellectual property protection did not have rights that could be abused, nonmarket economies had no need for antitrust laws, and many developing countries still have not reached a stage where competition policy is of major concern. Once such countries begin to implement their obligations under the TRIPS Agreement by enacting intellectual property law, antitrust rules are likely to follow. However, it is not necessarily the case that any of the antitrust regimes extant at the time of the Uruguay Round will meet their needs. As we have noted, some countries may consider themselves better off sacrificing a little competition in order to attract investment in infrastructure. Conversely, a country that is trying to find technological opportunities for an emerging work force may be justified in being less tolerant of tie-ins that limit the growth of niche industries such as servicing. Even if competition law does not become a major item on the agenda of the WTO, we conclude that the relation between competition law and intellectual property law merits further study, possibly in connection with the review of the TRIPS Agreement that is due in five years' time. We would not expect this rethinking to take place in the course of a dispute settlement proceeding.

---

[111]Article 31 of the TRIPS Agreement provides:

> Where the law of a Member allows for other use of the subject matter of a patent without the authorization of the right holder, . . . the following provisions shall be respected:
>
> . . . .
>
> (h) the right holder shall be paid adequate remuneration in the circumstances of each case, taking into account the economic value of the authorization[.]

Under paragraph (k), some other conditions are not obligatory when a compulsory license is imposed to remedy a practice determined after judicial or administrative process to be anti-competitive. Paragraph (h) is not among the conditions that may be avoided in such case.

C. Deciding Case III

How, then, after this lengthy excursion, should a dispute panel decide whether the disposition by the Patrian court in the Bilker case is consistent with the TRIPS Agreement? Given the lack of consensus on the correct balance between antitrust and intellectual property law, and given what we said in connection with Case II about not second-guessing domestic decisions regarding fine-tuning, it is tempting to start with a presumption that Patria's decision in Bilker should be sustained. Indeed, the approach of article 31 of the TRIPS Agreement is to defer to the decisions of competent national authorities. There are problems with a presumption of deference, however. Competition cases are likely to have more of an impact on rights holders than the sorts of questions raised in connection with Case II. In contrast to fine-tuning mechanisms, the decision to hold an intellectual property right unenforceable permits wholesale copying. In Case III, for example, the judgment of the Patrian court would permit anyone wishing to enter the service business to copy Bilker's servicing protocol programs; in other cases, the decision to hold a patent right unenforceable would allow anyone to enter into competition with the patentee. Indeed, such a decision may allow a product to be sold in any country that has a worldwide exhaustion doctrine.[113] Deciding the issue simply on the basis of deference to national law therefore seems inappropriate.

One approach to evaluating the validity of the decree would be for the dispute panel to examine the extent to which the Patrian court inquired into the facts of the case and then to examine whether the court analyzed these facts in a manner that would plausibly identify practices abusive to its economy. If the court has acted on the sort of facts that, say, the U.S. Justice Department uses when it proposes a consent decree, then, subject to two caveats, its actions should be considered valid. The first caveat concerns the impact of a decree on countries of very different economic development from the one that issued the decree... [T]he panel should supplement Patria's fact-finding with information about the effect of the decree on different economies. Deference would be accorded to Patria's decision only to the extent that its decree affects the economies of states similarly situated to Patria.

The second caveat concerns Patria's per se rules regarding package licensing and tie-ins. It is not clear that the TRIPS Agreement tolerates broad orders based on per se views of particular licensing practices, that is, practices regarded as so bad (such as price-fixing, for instance) that inquiry into the reason for the practice is neither required nor permitted. Per se judgments are not necessarily alien to WTO dispute settlement: Article 3.8 of the Understanding on Dispute Settlement states that when there is an infringement by a member state of the obligations assumed under a covered agreement, the action is considered prima facie to constitute nullification or

---

[113]As pointed out in note 12, article 6 of the TRIPS Agreement specifically provides that the Agreement should not be interpreted to address the issue of exhaustion. Usually, exhaustion is found when the product is sold under the authority of the intellectual property holder. Thus, whether the statement in the text is true in a given country will depend on whether the sale of a product in a country that refuses to enforce the intellectual property right is deemed to be a sale under the rights holder's 'authority.'

impairment. But Case III involves only a charge of violation by a Xandian company of the law of Patria, and a response that the challenged conduct is protected by the TRIPS Agreement or that the remedy imposed by Patria exceeds what is permissible under that Agreement.

It seems to us that before pronouncing on Case III, the panel should afford both sides the opportunity to present facts and economic analysis. If this is sound, Bilker ought to have the opportunity to defend its practices in the Patrian court, and to contend to that court that the TRIPS Agreement protects its practices or limits the remedies that may be imposed by Patria. If Bilker has not previously been given such opportunity, the panel should rule that Patria has not complied with the TRIPS Agreement, and should recommend that the case be reopened in that country.

NOTES AND QUESTIONS

(1) **Judicial Analysis of Competition Law**. Dreyfuss and Lowenfeld conclude that "the relation between competition law and intellectual property law merits further study, [but we] would not expect this rethinking to take place in the course of a dispute settlement proceeding." Why not? Patent and copyright misuse doctrines were developed by U.S. courts to mediate the abuse of intellectual property rights. Aside from the language of Article 3(2) of the DSU (and is that more of a constraint here than elsewhere?) are there institutional considerations that might make it inappropriate for WTO panels to engage in "lawmaking" in the way that we might expect of domestic courts?

(2) **(Non-Intellectual Property) Sources of Guidance.** Where should a panel look when the topic before them has only rarely (if ever) been addressed by the sources that we considered in our analysis of Case I? Is the extent of reference to national competition approaches suggested by Professor Fox appropriate? Should panels be able to look to broader international law principles (for example, in bilateral or multilateral competition law agreements)? By doing so, are panels exceeding their jurisdiction? Remember that competition law is not covered by the GATT. If the panel could apply only "WTO law," what does that say about the value of the panels as a mechanism of international relations? Is it possible for them to decide intellectual property disputes under TRIPS without looking beyond TRIPS? What are the consequences of broadening the perspective of panel members? What are the consequences of confining their perspective? How would you respond to an argument by Patria that it was complying with provisions of a multinational or bilateral competition law agreement? What would be the appropriate forum to litigate an issue if provisions of other agreements were raised by the parties? The International Court of Justice? Could those fora address WTO-related issues? *See* DSU art. 23. *Compare* Joel P. Trachtman, *The Domain of WTO Dispute Resolution*, 40 HARV. INT'L L.J. 333, 342-44 (1999)(discussing scope of reference to non-WTO international law), *with* David Palmeter & Petros C. Mavroidis, *The WTO Legal System: Sources of Law*, 92 AM. J. INT'L L. 398, 399

(1998) and Thomas J. Schoenbaum, *WTO Dispute Settlement: Praise and Suggestions for Reform*, 47 INT'L & COMP. L.Q. 647, 653 (1998). What if two or more countries established a supranational panel to adjudicate competition law issues? *Cf.* BRIAN F. HAVEL, IN SEARCH OF OPEN SKIES: LAW AND POLICY FOR A NEW ERA IN INTERNATIONAL AVIATION (1997) (proposing such a body for international airline competition relations). Should the WTO panel stay the case before it?

(3) **Revisiting Deference.** Why are Dreyfuss and Lowenfeld apparently less reluctant to show deference to Patria here? Can their reasoning be reconciled with the approach to deference shown in Cases I and II? Does a less deferential attitude to Patria's activity trouble you where the issue before the panel was one on which there was minimal guidance in TRIPS?

(4) *Magill.* Could the order of the European Commission in *Magill, supra* § 4.05[B][3], be challenged by Ireland (assuming that it wished to do so) before the WTO? How would the Commission's order, and the decision of the European Court of Justice upholding it, fare under the test proposed by Professor Fox? Under the approach proposed by Dreyfuss and Lowenfeld? (What additional information would you need to know?). How would the legislation enacted by the U.K. parliament (section 176 of the U.K. Broadcasting Act 1990) to create the compulsory licence of copyrighted television listings fare under the same analysis? Should it matter whether the remedial measure is found in broadcasting legislation, administrative competition law sanctions, or a judicial decree?

[C]　The Appellate Body

DREYFUSS AND LOWENFELD, CASE IV:
THE APPELLATE PROCESS[*]
37 VA. J. INT'L L. 275, 316-24

One of the major innovations in the Uruguay Round was agreement that decisions of dispute panels were to be treated like judgments—that is, that they could not be blocked by the losing party or even by a majority vote of the membership of the WTO. Once that decision had been taken, it became necessary to provide for some type of review, both to correct errors that might be made by an ad hoc panel and to give participants dissatisfied with the outcome a second chance to be heard. The solution, in keeping with the preference for the judicial over the diplomatic model for dispute settlement, was creation of a standing Appellate Body, made up of seven persons drawn from different constituencies included in the WTO.[114] The Appellate Body is supposed to complete its work in sixty days from the date of the appeal (ninety

---

[*]Copyright 1997, Rochelle Cooper Dreyfuss and Andreas F. Lowenfeld.

[114]*See* DSU arts. 17 & 18. . . Members of the Appellate Body are elected for four-year terms and may be reelected once, except that three of the members first appointed, selected by lot, will have an initial term of two years, so that the entire membership will never be changed over at once. Any given appeal is heard by three of the seven members of the Appellate Body serving in rotation, without reference to their nationality.

days for exceptionally difficult cases), and appeals are to be "limited to issues of law covered in the panel report and legal interpretations developed by the panel." [DSU arts. 17.7, 17.6.]

Distinguishing legal from factual questions for purposes of jurisdiction is, of course, a common problem in all legal systems. The fact/law distinction is particularly troublesome in the context of patent controversies, where resolution of issues of novelty, prior art, and scope of inventions is dependent both on determinations of fact and on interpretation of imprecise legal standards. For our purposes, however, we illustrate the problem in an apparently easier context—concerning the right to register a trademark.

Case IV

Koka Kola, Ltd., a Xandian company, has registered its mark, KOKA KOLA, for carbonated beverages (soda pop) in Xandia and in most of the world. As a result of Koka Kola's sponsorship of every Olympic Games since World War II, it had every reason to believe that the mark was familiar everywhere. Nonetheless, when it sought registration in Patria, its application was denied, on the ground that the same mark had recently been registered by a Patrian who was in the process of starting a company to manufacture and distribute his version of Koka Kola soda pop. When Koka Kola was unsuccessful in having the other registration canceled, it persuaded the government of Xandia to bring a complaint in the WTO.

According to Xandia's complaint, Koka Kola is a well-known mark for soda pop and Patria's refusal to register it violated article 16(2) of the TRIPS Agreement. A dispute panel was convened. Xandia submitted consumer surveys showing that substantial numbers of Patrian soda pop consumers recognized the mark and that an even higher percentage of consumers in larger markets recognized it. Upon consideration of these surveys and after seeing evidence that since 1980, all telecasts of the Olympic Games could be received on television sets in Patria, the panel determined that the mark was well-enough-known within the meaning of the TRIPS Agreement to qualify for the special protection offered by TRIPS article 16(2). Patria appeals to the Appellate Body, pursuant to article 16 of the DSU.

A. Jurisdiction to Hear the Appeal: The Fact/Law Distinction

Xandia might well contend that there is only one issue in this case—whether the Koka Kola mark for soda pop is well-known—and that any lay person would say that this is a question of fact. Thus, Xandia could argue that there is no basis for reviewing the panel report in the Appellate Body. Or, more subtly, Xandia might argue that given the relationship between the resolution of the appeal and the application of article 16(2) of the TRIPS Agreement, the issue sought to be put before the Appellate Body is a mixed question of law and fact, and that resolution of mixed questions is also beyond the mandate of the Appellate Body.

It is important to recognize in this context that the fact/law distinction is jurisdictional. Whether the Appellate Body may hear the appeal depends on an interpretation of the Understanding on Dispute Settlement and the covered Agreement in question, and cannot be decided according to the law of any particular member state. Given the reasons for creation of the Appellate Body and the limited time available for completion of its assignment, our view is that respondent parties in the appeal process—typically (as in Case IV) the party that prevailed before the panel—should be discouraged from raising challenges to the jurisdiction of the Appellate Body; further, if such a challenge is raised, the Appellate Body should be very reluctant to dismiss an appeal over an issue of jurisdiction. Findings of particular facts made by the panel can be accepted. For instance, in Case IV the Appellate Body need not make an independent inquiry into the broadcast history of the Olympic Games or their reception in Patria. It can satisfy itself that the information submitted to the Panel was reliable, or, if differing information was submitted, that the panel made a rational choice as to which version to accept. But as to the ultimate issue—whether Patria complied with the criterion in the TRIPS Agreement regarding knowledge of the mark in the relevant sector of the public—the Appellate Body should make its own decision, free, we would urge, from any debate about whether the decision is based on "fact" or on "law."

[In Case IV] . . . , if the Appellate Body declined to take jurisdiction of the appeal, it would, in effect, exclude itself from participating in the elucidation of one of the most important provisions in the TRIPS Agreement—the provision that enables producers to develop and maintain a worldwide marketing strategy without fear of "trademark pirates" to hold them up. If a panel can address the issue, it must be that the Appellate Body can and should do so as well.

It is instructive in this context to contrast the TRIPS Agreement with the Agreement on Dumping and Antidumping Measures,[119] also concluded as an obligatory part of the Uruguay Round package [and subject to WTO dispute settlement review. Under article 17.6 of the Antidumping Agreement, however, if the panel finds that (i) the establishment of the facts by the national authority of the importing country that has imposed antidumping duties on the product of another country was proper, and the evaluation was unbiased and objective, then that evaluation shall not be overturned by the panel even if it would have reached a different conclusion, and (ii) a relevant provision of the Agreement admits of more than one permissible interpretation, the panel shall find the authorities' measure to be in conformity with the Agreement if it rests upon one of those permissible interpretations.]

This provision was inserted upon the insistence of the United States, which feared that international panels unsympathetic to the provisions on dumping generally and in particular to the hard-to-confirm findings on causation of injury might hold antidumping measures ordered by the U.S. Department of

---

[119]The formal name of this Agreement . . . is the Agreement on Implementation of Article VI of the General Agreement on Tariffs and Trade 1994, Apr. 15, 1994, WTO Agreement, Annex 1A.

Commerce and the U.S. International Trade Commission to be inconsistent with the international understanding.[120] The last-minute solution, for what the United States delegates said was a "deal breaker," was to accord an extra degree of deference to national authorities—for dumping cases only. If Patria considers that a panel convened to review its antidumping measure has exceeded the limitations of article 17.6, such a contention could, it seems clear, be made the subject of an appeal to the Appellate Body. The Appellate Body would not be authorized to examine the underlying issues of price comparison and causation of injury (the "fact issues"), but would be limited to determining whether or not the panel had exceeded the limitations imposed by article 17.6.

No provision comparable to article 17.6 of the Antidumping Agreement appears in the TRIPS Agreement,[121] and we believe that none should be read into it either by panels or by the Appellate Body, in the guise of making rulings on "jurisdiction" or distinguishing "fact" from "law." The ultimate issue—whether denominated "fact," "law," or "mixed,"—should be considered (if a party so desires) at two levels, first by the ad hoc panel that assembles the record, hears the parties, and makes an initial determination, and second by the standing Appellate Body, that considers, for instance, how the Koka Kola case fits in with other intellectual property cases and with the jurisprudence of the GATT/WTO system generally.

B. The Role of the Appellate Body

The problems in Case IV—which seemed to be the easy case—do not quite disappear even after the decision is made to consider the ultimate issue one of law. TRIPS article 16(2) calls for inquiry into "the knowledge of the trademark in the relevant sector of the public, including knowledge in the Member concerned which has been obtained as a result of the promotion of the trademark." Here, then, are several sub-issues: How much knowledge is necessary for the mark to be considered well known: must a majority of the relevant public recognize it, or is a substantial minority enough? What is the relevant sector: soda pop drinkers or all beverage consumers? What is considered promotion of the trademark in the member state: is Koka Kola considered to have promoted the mark in Patria by reason of buying air time on an event that could be picked up on television receivers in Patria, or must it have advertised on actual local broadcasts? Even after it is determined that the ultimate issue—the strength of the mark—is a question of law, the issue of

---

[120]A pattern along these lines had developed in cases brought under chapter 19 of the Canada-United States Free Trade Agreement, cheered by some but condemned by others. For an early account, see Andreas F. Lowenfeld, *Binational Dispute Settlement Under Chapter 19 of the Canada-United States Free Trade Agreement: An Interim Appraisal*, 24 N.Y.U. J. INT'L L. & POL. 269 (1991).

[121]Indeed, it is reported that when the suggestion was made that a single (deferential) standard should be made applicable to all WTO panels reviewing national administrative decisions, the proposal was "greeted with fury" by U.S. intellectual property interests, which did not wish to give to other countries' patent and copyright authorities the deference which the U.S. Trade Representative sought for American antidumping decisions. See Gary N. Horlick & Eleanor C. Shea, *The World Trade Organization Antidumping Agreement*, J. WORLD TRADE, Feb. 1995, at 5, 31.

characterizing these penultimate questions remains.

Once again, the line between fact and law can only be drawn by reference to the underlying principles to which the adjudicatory system is dedicated, that is, by considering why line drawing is needed under the circumstances. For example, in domestic intellectual property cases in the United States, controversies, such as over the strength of a trademark, that require resolution of a series of penultimate questions are often handled by considering those questions to be ones of fact and the ultimate question one of law. In this way, the opportunity to appeal the outcome of the controversy is preserved, yet the litigants' respect for the trial court as the primary forum for dispute resolution is maintained.[122]

Such allocation of authority may, however, not be generally suitable to disputes under the TRIPS Agreement, where the policy interests can be very different. Dispute panels are chosen in a manner designed to promote considerable respect from the parties. Panel members are selected by the Director General of the WTO, in consultation with the Chairman and counsel of the DSB, from a roster of persons who have served in their own governments, often as judges, or in other capacities in the GATT. [DSU art. 8]. Some are academic experts in the issues raised by the dispute. However, because the panels are chosen for a particular case, there is no assurance that members of a panel will have the same commitment to long-term consistency that is expected from the members of the Appellate Body.[124] Accordingly, one might conclude that less deference is owed to panel decisions than is accorded to court decisions in the United States.

On the other hand, at least one, and possibly all members of a panel in a dispute focused on the TRIPS Agreement may be expected to be experts in intellectual property, whereas it is highly unlikely that any member of the Appellate Body possesses comparable knowledge or experience.[125] Thus, it may well be desirable for the Appellate Body to give greater deference to legal decisions of a panel in intellectual property disputes than it would in disputes about, say, export subsidies or import safeguards—and also more deference than a national appellate court would give to a trial court. Indeed, the role of the Appellate Body, as we see it, is not primarily to articulate intellectual property norms in the international economy, but to oversee the work of dispute panels with an eye to the general principles of open markets and nondiscrimination embodied in the GATT/WTO system. In fact, as noted earlier, it is the Council for TRIPS that is charged with monitoring the operation of the Agreement and cooperating with WIPO in setting international

---

[122]See, e.g., Graham v. John Deere Co., 383 U.S. 1 (1966), where the Court held that in a patent case the ultimate issue of nonobviousness consists of four questions: What is in the prior art?; What is the difference between the applicant's invention and the prior art?; What does a person with ordinary skill in the art know?; Could such a person fill the gap? The first three are issues of fact, the last is deemed to be an issue of law.

[124]In the past, the Secretariat has endeavored to fill the role of supplying the sense of continuity, and it may be expected to continue to do so in the future.

[125]Of the first seven members of the Appellate Body, two are (or were) professors of law (but not intellectual property law), one was a justice of his country's Supreme Court, two were career diplomats, one was a professor of economics, and one (the U.S. member) is a practicing attorney and former member of Congress.

norms. The Appellate Body, then, is not the only, or even necessarily the best, source of authoritative articulation of intellectual property norms.

We do suggest, however, that where system-wide rules are desirable, the provision in the DSU concerning "issues of law" should receive broad scope when applied to the TRIPS Agreement; where it is permissible for members to maintain legal regimes that differ from one another, the need for uniform interpretation of the TRIPS Agreement by the Appellate Body is less compelling, and it is "questions of fact" that should be interpreted generously.

As the TRIPS Agreement is written, members have considerable discretion to maintain their own intellectual property regimes. Article 1(1) provides:

> ... Members *may, but shall not be obliged to,* implement in their law more extensive protection than is required by this Agreement, provided that such protection does not contravene the provisions of this Agreement. *Members shall be free to determine the appropriate method* of implementing the provisions of this Agreement within their own legal system and practice. (emphasis added)

Thus, where the panel has deferred to the respondent state's national authorities, the inclination (not to say presumption) of the Appellate Body ought to be to defer as well. In contrast, a contention by Patria that a panel has acted inconsistently with article 1 in ruling against a practice that does not clearly violate the TRIPS Agreement should be heard and determined by the Appellate Body. In such cases, the proper role for the Appellate Body is to monitor whether panels have been too interventionist, a question of judgment that does not fit easily into the "law" or "fact" classification.

One might be tempted to conclude from this discussion that the Appellate Body needs wide authority only in disputes such as those illustrated by Case I, where the question was what the minimum standards require. A review of our other cases demonstrates that this is only sometimes true. It may be true for cases in the category of Case II, where the differing circumstances of member states require that they be allowed to make differing adjustments between the rights of innovation producers and innovation users. The application of the doctrine of equivalents in patent law, for example, should probably be left to interpretation by each member state, subject to intervention by the WTO only upon a showing of discrimination. But the fact that member states have discretion under the TRIPS Agreement to implement their own legal regimes is not necessarily conclusive of the proper role of the WTO panel or the Appellate Body. For instance, Case III, the antitrust case, raised the question of the permissible extraterritorial effect of decisions of a national authority. On that issue, as in Case IV, neither the panel nor the Appellate Authority should defer to the national authority. It is up to the international authority to step in, to declare, for example, whether it is permissible for member states to order worldwide relief for antitrust violations or intellectual property misuse, and if so, whether they may do so on the basis of per se rules, without permitting justification through market-by-market analysis. Furthermore, if the Appellate Body determines that per se rules are objectionable, it will need to have a role in deciding such fact-sounding issues as when an entity occupies a "dominant position," when a technology has suitable substitutes, and how to define separate markets.

In the end, we can offer only discussion of the problem, not hard rules. The Appellate Body is not a Supreme Court, but part of a process not yet tested, which will include the evolution of norm-setting in WIPO, the activity of the Council on TRIPS, and the progress made among the parties in developing a shared understanding of the not always consistent values of intellectual property and competition.

NOTES AND QUESTIONS

(1) **Composition of Panels and the Appellate Body.** The creation of the Appellate Body was intended not only as a check on panel decisions but also, by virtue of its standing nature, to bring some consistency and uniformity to the development of WTO law. At present, the three members of the Appellate Body who hear a case have been chosen without regard for whether a member is from a country appearing before the body. Thus, American nationals on the Appellate Body have sat on cases involving the United States. This contrasts with the panel stage of the proceedings, where nationals of participating countries generally do not sit. *See* DSU art. 8(3) (nationals of parties should not be appointed to a panel unless the parties agree); *cf. id.* art. 8(10) (allowing developing countries litigating against a developed country to request that at least one of the panelists before whom they appear will be from a developing country). What effect might the recusal of nationals on panels have on the development of WTO law? The EU has proposed that the panel composition be determined like the Appellate Body. Would you support such a change? *See The WTO Appellate Body: The First Four Years*, 1 J. WORLD INTELL. PROP. 425, 428 (1998) (comments of Edwin Vermulst). Or should the practices of the Appellate Body composition be conformed to those used in composing the members of the panel? *See id.* at 431 (comments of Guiguo Wang). One commentator has suggested that the question of balance transcends nationality, and that the panels evince a distinctly Western cultural approach to law. *See id.* (comments of Jacques Bourgeois). How might that be avoided? Can it be avoided?

The EU has also proposed that the ad hoc panels be replaced by a standing body, not unlike the Appellate Body, comprised of between 15–24 members. On the basis of a rotation mechanism, the Panel Body would itself form a chamber of three to deal with each new case as it arose. *See* Kim Van der Borght, *The Review of the WTO Understanding on Dispute Settlement: Some Reflections on the Current Debate*, 14 AM. U. INT'L L. REV. 1223, 1240 (1999) (quoting EU proposal). What are the advantages of each approach? *See The Review of the WTO's Dispute Settlement Understanding: Which Way?*, 1 J. WORLD INTELL. PROP. 447, 449 (1998) (comments of Prof. Brigitte Stern); *id.* at 460 (comments of John Kingery) (describing such a change as a "major step" that would "change the nature of dispute settlement quite a bit"); *id.* at 468-69 (comments of Geoffrey Hartwell). Jayashree Watal has commented that "the WTO is so political that it is not possible for the Appellate Body . . . to be really too activist . . . without facing criticism from the members. In this sense, the WTO is very different from any other international organization in the field of public international law." *The WTO Appellate Body: The First Four Years, supra,* at 436. In what way is the WTO "so political"? Would a change to a standing body of panelists reduce or increase the political nature of the process?

(2) **Remand Authority.** Dreyfuss and Lowenfeld suggested above that in order to decide Case III, the panel might have to supplement Patria's fact-finding with information about the effect of the decree on different economies. If the panel failed to engage in that fact-finding, and the Appellate Body finds those facts necessary as a matter of law to decide whether the Patrian court's order complies with TRIPS, what should the Appellate Body do? The DSU failed to provide the Appellate Body with the right to remand the case to the panel. *See* David Palmeter, *National Sovereignty and the World Trade Organization,* 2 J. WORLD INTELL. PROP. 77, 85 (1999). Absent such a right, what options does the Appellate Body have? *See* United States—Import Prohibition of Certain Shrimp and Shrimp Products, AB-1998-4, WT/DS58/AB/R (98-3899) ¶ 123 (Appellate Body, Oct. 12, 1998). Can the Appellate Body simply declare that it is remanding a case even absent express authority in the DSU? If you were a member of the Appellate Body would you vote to create a remand power judicially? What other procedural or institutional changes would be required for a remand procedure to work? *See The Review of the WTO's Dispute Settlement Understanding: Which Way?, supra,* at 454 (comments of Thomas Cottier).

(3) **The Fact/Law Distinction.** Does the Dreyfuss-Lowenfeld suggestion on how to interpret the law/fact distinction—with an eye to the proper role of the Appellate Body—contain a substantive bias? Is it one that is appropriate? In what way (if any) are the circumstances in which, or reasons for which, Dreyfuss and Lowenfeld might encourage the Appellate Body to defer to the panel the same as those that they invoked in support of panel deference to member countries?

In *India—Patent Protection for Pharmaceutical and Agricultural Chemical Products,* Panel Report, WT/DS50/R (WTO Panel, Sept. 5, 1997), *aff'd,* WT/DS50/AB/R (WTO App. Body, Dec. 19, 1997) [hereinafter *United States-India*], India sought to make use of the fact/law distinction before the panel (and the Appellate Body) but in a much more traditional manner, quite different from the use of that distinction envisaged by Dreyfuss and Lowenfeld. India sought to classify Indian law as a question of fact in order to oblige the United States to prove Indian law as part of its case. *Cf.* Walton v. Arabian Am. Oil Co., 233 F.2d 541 (2d Cir. 1956) (traditional approach to proving foreign law in private litigation in U.S. courts). Are India's arguments persuasive? In what ways could the panel have "sought guidance from India on matters relating to the interpretation of Indian law" as India alternatively suggested? *See United States-India,* Appellate Body Report, ¶ 64.

(4) **Deciding Case IV.** If the Appellate Body were to decide Case IV, how would it determine the meaning of "well-known mark" in Article 16 of TRIPS?

To what extent should a panel determining Patria's compliance with Article 16 look to the resolution on the protection of well known marks adopted by the joint meeting of the General Assembly of WIPO and the Assembly of the Paris Union in September 1999? (At the September 1999 Assembly, Asian and African nations insisted on the removal of references in the preamble to TRIPS, arguing that such a reference may cause WTO dispute panels to interpret the recommendation as binding.)

(5) **Trademark Complaints before the WTO.** Only three trademark cases have thus far been pursued through the WTO dispute settlement system, and only one of those has resulted in a panel report. In that case, the complaint by the United States against Indonesia was largely obscured by other non-TRIPS claims under other GATT agreements. *See* United States v. Indonesia, WT/DS59, IP/D/6 (98-2505) (Panel Report, July 2, 1998). The United States claimed that the Indonesian National Car Programme (the "INCP") violated Articles 3, 65(5), and 20 of TRIPS because it allegedly discriminated against nationals of other WTO countries with regard to the acquisition and maintenance of trademarks. The INCP grants various tax and other benefits to cars that are part of the program. To qualify for the program, however, the trademark used with the car must be owned by an Indonesian company (or an Indonesian joint venture including foreign companies as partners). What would be the strongest arguments in support of the United States' claims? *See* Matthijs Geuze & Hannu Wager, *WTO Dispute Settlement Practice Relating to the TRIPS Agreement*, J. INT'L ECON. L. 347, 370-74 (1999) (summarizing the extremely lengthy arguments and panel report). Why did the United States include a claim based upon Article 3 of TRIPS?

The other two trademark cases remain pending. Consultations continue regarding the complaint filed by the United States against the EU challenging the EU system of geographical designations of origin. *See supra* § 3.02[B]. And a panel report is expected soon in the case brought by the EU against the United States in the wake of the *Havana Club* litigation. *See supra* § 3.01[J].

[D] Enforcement

DREYFUSS AND LOWENFELD, CASE V: ENFORCEMENT*
37 VA. J. INT'L L. 275, 324-32 (1997)

Two key enforcement issues are likely to confront the WTO in the intellectual property area. The first concerns enforcement by member states of the intellectual property rights that they have recognized, at least on paper. The second issue, not limited to intellectual property controversies, concerns enforcement of member states' obligations, once these have been determined by the dispute settlement process. Our last case directly raises the first issue, and could well raise the second one also.

Case V

This case is a continuation of Case IV. Xandia, having taken up the case of Koka Kola, has prevailed before a panel established under the DSU. The panel's decision has been upheld by the Appellate Body, and the Report of the Appellate Body has been adopted by the DSB. According to article 21 of the Understanding on Dispute Settlement, Patria is supposed to inform a meeting of the DSB within thirty days of its intention in respect of implementation of the recommendations and rulings of the DSB. In this case, the ruling was that Koka Kola's trademark was widely recognized in Patria, and the recommendation was that the relevant Patrian authority cancel the registration of the local rival and approve the registration of the mark by the multinational company based in Xandia. If necessary, the Patrian authority was to seek an injunction or comparable remedy against infringement. The ruling was upheld by the Appellate Body.

Patria, however, states that it is not in a position to comply with the recommendation and ruling, because its domestic law does not permit the measures recommended by the panel. Alternatively, Patria contends that its prosecutors have considerable discretion in allocating their resources, and putting a stop to trademark infringement is not a high priority.

A. Competing Priorities

In addressing Patria's defense of lack of resources or competing priorities, a WTO panel or the Appellate Body will need to come to grips with an interesting ambivalence reflected in article 41, the General Obligations article of the TRIPS Agreement. Paragraph 1 of article 41 states that "[m]embers *shall ensure* that enforcement procedures . . . are available under their law so as to permit effective action against any act of infringement of intellectual property rights . . . including expeditious remedies . . . and remedies which constitute a deterrent to further infringements." Paragraph 5 of the same article, however, states that "[n]othing in this Part creates any obligation with respect to the distribution of resources as between enforcement of intellectual property rights and the enforcement of law in general."

If Patria's concern is really the allocation of limited resources, the problem may be addressed by a recommendation of the Panel that the period of compliance be stretched out—for instance until completion of the next session of the legislature—and (if Patria is a developing country) that financial and technical resources be made available to Patria under article 67 of the TRIPS Agreement.

B. Patterns of Nonenforcement

A pattern of nonenforcement by Patria, coupled with an allegation by Xandia that Patria had the resources to carry out its obligations, would be difficult to establish, and certainly could not be established in the first case. Possibly, Xandia could show that repeated efforts to bring infringement proceedings in Patria had led to no effective results. An assertion by Xandia that bringing such proceedings would be fruitless would, we expect, not be sufficient to lead to a determination that Patria was in violation of article 41(1). But if a pattern of non-enforcement by Patria of its laws were established, we believe that a panel could find a violation, and if no improvement were apparent, the controversy could be moved into the compliance stage, as discussed below.[133]

We think that the government of Xandia should hesitate before bringing Case V before the WTO dispute system. A better way to encourage enforcement of intellectual property rights—whether before or after litigation, as illustrated by the preceding cases—may be outside of the dispute resolution system. In many instances, we expect, intellectual property holders could serve their own cause by helping infringers find ways to utilize the investment they have sunk into infringing activities. In Case V, for example, Koka Kola may gain more by licensing to the so-called Patrian "trademark pirate" than by fighting him through to the end under the WTO system. With licensing, his plant would be utilized and Patrian workers would be employed; yet, Koka Kola could protect its marks by regulating the output for quality and quantity. If the relationship became valuable enough to the licensee, the impulse to cheat—for instance by exporting outside the territory covered by the license—might be reduced more than it could ever be controlled by a Patrian police force.[134]

C. Enforcing the Decisions of the Panel or Appellate Body

In the past, that is, under the GATT prior to completion of the Uruguay Round, Patria might have been able to block adoption of the panel report; even if it did not do so, it might have been able to fend off "suspension of equivalent concessions" by Xandia, because such a step required approval of a majority of the Contracting Parties, and retaliation was generally disfavored. The architects of the [DSU] sought to put teeth into the system, with an elaborate (but as yet untried) set of steps applicable if the preferred dispute settlement process breaks down.

First, if Patria cannot comply immediately, it will have a reasonable period of time to do so. Determination of what is a "reasonable period" is subject to approval by the DSB or to an agreement with Xandia within forty-five days of

---

[133]The problem of nonenforcement of laws supposed to protect internationally recognized rights is not limited to intellectual property. It became a major issue, for instance, in the negotiation of the North American Free Trade Agreement, and particularly of the so-called side agreements on environmental cooperation and labor cooperation forced through by the Clinton administration after the principal agreement had been completed during President Bush's term. Those side agreements address a concern that a treaty partner (read Mexico) would place acceptable standards on its books but not enforce them; the solution, if it can be called that, was to establish a joint commission, to which nongovernmental as well as governmental organizations could make submissions, which could lead to a process of consultation, arbitration, reports, monetary penalties, and ultimately suspension of benefits under the Free Trade Agreement.

[134]On the other hand, it is worth pointing out that disputes about the enforcement of intellectual property rights have been major impediments to admission into the World Trade Organization for states that have persistently failed to enforce such rights, notably China and Taiwan.

adoption of the Report, or—if no agreement is reached—to binding arbitration. The arbitration is to be held within ninety days of issuance of the Report and is limited to the issue of the "reasonable period" for compliance.[135]

Next, the DSU makes provision for disagreement between the parties over whether a corrective measure proposed by the respondent party is consistent with the GATT or the covered agreement. That question is also to be referred to impartial decision making—not by the arbitrator but by a panel, if possible the panel that heard the original dispute. [DSU art. 21.5] It is hard to imagine how there could be disagreement over implementing the ruling in the Koka Kola case, but in other cases, including other intellectual property cases, a proposed corrective measure might well give rise to continuing controversy.[137]

Third, if all else fails, two more possibilities are set out in the DSU. If Patria fails within the "reasonable period" to carry out the recommendation to terminate or modify the practice found to be inconsistent with the Agreement, it may negotiate with Xandia for mutually acceptable compensation. The term is not defined in the DSU, but it seems to mean some offer by Patria of trade interest to Xandia.[138] If no agreement on compensation is reached within twenty days of the expiration of the "reasonable period," Xandia, the prevailing party, may, upon authorization of the DSB, retaliate against Patria by suspending the application to Patria (this time on a discriminatory basis) of concessions or other obligations. [DSU art. 22.2]. Suspension of a concession or other obligation is subject to authorization by the DSB, but article 22.6 of the Understanding on Dispute Settlement provides that the DSB shall grant the authorization within thirty days of the expiry of the "reasonable period," unless it decides by consensus to reject the request.[140]

What kind of suspension might be authorized? Considering that retaliation is generally disfavored in the GATT/WTO system—because it means that not one but two distortions to normal trade will prevail—the Understanding on Dispute Settlement contains surprisingly detailed provisions in answer to this question. [DSU arts. 22.3-6, 22.8] The general principle is that the complaining party should first seek to suspend concessions or other obligations with respect to the same sector(s) as that in which the panel or Appellate Body has found a

---

[135]All of the above is set out in article 21 of the DSU. Article 21.4 indicates that the "reasonable period" shall not exceed 15 months from the date of establishment of the panel, which would leave 90 days from completion of the appellate process in normal cases, with more time to be added on if either the panel or the Appellate Body asked for additional time.

[137]For instance, in the case about protection for computer programs, Patria might issue a regulation or adopt legislation that went part way, but not completely, to protecting the innovative aspects of computer programs, or that seemed to grant adequate protection but provided such slight punishment for infringement as to lead Xandia to complain that no real deterrence was involved. Of course, even in Koka Kola, if the panel recommendation included legislative reform or revised resource allocation, renewed controversy might arise about the adequacy of implementation by Patria.

[138]Though the DSU does not say so, it seems clear that any offer by Patria in this context must be granted on a most-favored-nation basis, because it would not fit into any of the permitted exceptions to that most fundamental principle of the GATT/WTO system.

[140]If the respondent party, Patria in our example, objects to the level of the suspension proposed or claims that the suspension is not consistent with the principles discussed hereafter, the DSU makes provision for still another arbitration, to be completed within 60 days of the expiry of the 'reasonable period.'

violation. If that is not practicable, the complaining party may seek to suspend concessions or other obligations in other sectors under the same agreement—in our case the TRIPS Agreement. If that is still not practicable, the complaining party may suspend concessions or other obligations under another covered agreement. Retaliation is not punishment. Article 22.4 of the DSU states clearly what has been understood in the GATT since its origins: "The level of the suspension of concessions or other obligations authorized by the DSB shall be equivalent to the level of nullification or impairment."

Should Xandia now propose to refuse to recognize trademarks owned by nationals and companies of Patria? Or trademarks on soft drinks? On all food products, or all products sold in grocery stores? We worry about all proposals of this kind. Any form of trade retaliation brings with it a substantial measure of injustice, because it nearly always affects persons that have had no prior involvement in the controversy. We suspect that the adverse effects of retaliation—trade distortion and injustice—could be more severe if implemented in a tit-for-tat last act in an intellectual property dispute than in the traditional fields of exchange of goods.

For example, consider a Xandian factory tooled to manufacture high-quality merchandise under license from a Patrian company. The factory may have been very expensive to build, and it may well employ a large and expensive workforce. If Xandia retaliates by refusing to recognize the Patrian company's trademark, it may be that the price of the output will have to be lowered because of confusing use of the mark in Xandia. At that point, it may no longer be profitable to keep the factory in operation. Retaliation will, in short, have idled an expensive assembly line, hurting both Xandian enterprises and Xandian workers, with some loss also to the Patrian firm whose royalty income is reduced, but with no gain for the original injured party, Koka Kola.

Perhaps more significant, retaliation of this kind could have an adverse effect on consumers and on the market place. Trademark law, after all, is partly geared to consumer protection. Unambiguous signals denoting particular goods allow consumers to make informed purchasing choices. Without effective signals, search costs increase. When they do, the unseen hand of the marketplace begins to allocate resources inefficiently. Even after the retaliation is withdrawn, these effects could persist. Having lost the ability to control their marks and send clear messages to their customers, producers will have difficulty notifying consumers that the meaning of the mark has been restored.

An alternative might be for Xandia to announce that its retaliation would take the form of a refusal to register new trademarks originating in Patria. Continuing to enforce old marks would preserve the reliance interests of those who owned or licensed marks in Xandia at the time the retaliation took effect. However, the refusal to register new marks might also lead to confusion among consumers and distortions of the market. Xandian consumers traveling abroad or receiving signals on television or the internet would be exposed to the way that marks are used outside Xandia, and consumers outside Xandia might well be exposed to the unauthorized usages permitted inside Xandia. Indeed, the whole problem of Case IV arose because of the significance of trans-border exposure, recognized in article 16(2) of the TRIPS Agreement. Allowing Xandia to refuse to recognize marks that are new to Xandia will not, therefore, contain the possibility of confusion in a meaningful way. On the one hand, this means that despite the apparently limited nature of the retaliation, it could have a large enough impact on Patrian business to inspire Patria to conform its behavior to the requirements of the TRIPS Agreement. On the other hand, however, the impact of even this narrow action could be unacceptably high, for there is no way to prevent dislocations in other markets. As in Case III, administration of the TRIPS Agreement needs to be sensitive to extraterritorial effects of intraterritorial actions.

Given that any retaliation focusing on trademarks is unattractive, the next-favored retaliatory measure would be cross-agreement, that is, still within the field of intellectual property governed by the TRIPS Agreement, but addressed to patents or copyrights, rather than to trademarks. Refusal to enforce or register patents and copyrights originating in Patria, however, would raise many of the same issues of expropriation that are raised by canceling or refusing to register trademarks. Although the danger of confusing consumers would not be present, the problem of frustrating the reliance interests of rights holders and licensees would exist at least equally. Moreover, there might well be an extraterritorial effect if products could be exported from Xandia into countries that recognize a doctrine of worldwide exhaustion of copyright and patent rights.

It may be that cross-sectoral retaliation would be the most attractive alternative for Xandia, as in the action taken in 1988 by the United States against Brazil under the famous Section 301, when the Reagan administration imposed 100% tariffs on imports of microwave ovens, quality writing paper, and a number of other products from Brazil, in retaliation for that country's refusal to grant patent protection for pharmaceutical products.[144]

The difficulty in fashioning an appropriate form of retaliation is not a reason to disparage either the TRIPS Agreement or the Understanding on Dispute Settlement. The whole thrust of the WTO dispute settlement regime is that retaliation should never take place. Retaliation should be considered a pain to Patria and Xandia so severe that both member states would be induced to reach agreement before it came to this last of the seven steps provided in the DSU. That the reciprocal pain comes more quickly in the intellectual property area may be attributable to the fact that in contrast to goods, which can be only in one place at one time, intellectual property, being intangible, travels in many directions and can come to rest in many places at once. The moral we draw is that the initial steps in the dispute settlement process, that is the work of the panels and the Appellate Body, should be carried on with great care in the intellectual property area—*terra incognita* for the GATT/WTO system—with attention not only to the outcome of a given case but to the persuasiveness of the reasoning and explanations, for the parties and for the wider interests at stake.

---

[144]*See* Proclamation No. 5885, 53 Fed. Reg. 41,551 (1988). Brazil called for creation of a GATT panel to rule on whether the U.S. action was legal under GATT, and a panel was in fact convened, but the President of Brazil announced that he would seek legislation to provide patent protection for pharmaceuticals, and the U.S. sanctions were withdrawn before the panel could issue a ruling.

NOTES AND QUESTIONS

(1) **The Nature of TRIPS's Effective Enforcement Provisions.** Most of the early complaints focused on violations of substantive, relatively delineated TRIPS obligations, but as the system matures one might expect an increasing number of complaints to focus on measures for the enforcement of intellectual property rights. This would reflect a parallel progression in the focus of the United States Trade Representative's efforts under Special 301 against, for example, the People's Republic of China. And it would exploit one of the TRIPS Agreement's other novel contributions to international intellectual property law, namely, attention to measures provided by states to ensure the effective enforcement of intellectual property rights. *See generally* J.H. Reichman, *Enforcing the Enforcement Procedures of the TRIPS Agreement*, 37 VA. J. INT'L L. 335 (1997). But the language used by the TRIPS Agreement to define members' obligations relating to enforcement is that of broad principles or standards rather than carefully delineated rules. One would therefore expect these standards to prove less fertile ground for complainants in a system where the text of the DSU admonishes against panel activism and explicitly allows member states discretion as to how to implement international obligations in national law. Yet, complaints addressing enforcement measures have already been filed and resolved. *See* Matthijs Geuze & Hannu Wager, *WTO Dispute Settlement Practice Relating to the TRIPS Agreement*, J. INT'L ECON. L. 347, 381 (1999) (discussing proceedings brought against Sweden by the United States for failure to make provisional measures available in civil actions involving intellectual property rights); *see also id.* at 381 (discussing pending consultations between the United States and Denmark regarding the latter's compliance with Article 50). Why might the drafters have used broader, more indeterminate language in the agreement (especially when addressing enforcement of rights)? What advantages might accrue from the use of more vague language? How might that affect the way that dispute settlement panels should interpret such language? *See* Joel P. Trachtman, *The Domain of WTO Dispute Resolution*, 40 HARV. INT'L L. J. 333, 346-47 (1999). Trachtman suggests that the "decision between rules and standards is not a decision between more international law and less international law. While rules may be developed by tribunals, the decision is often an institutional choice between adjudicators and legislators. This observation depends upon the perception that tribunals applying standards legislate, even when they purport not to do so." *Id.* Are you persuaded by this argument? What does it mean for who controls the future direction of international intellectual property law? Why might you prefer adjudicators over legislators, or vice versa?

(2) **Article 41(5).** In Case V, the DSB recommendation was that the relevant "Patrian authority cancel the registration of the local rival and approve the registration of the mark by the multinational company based in Xandia. If necessary, the Patrian authority was to seek an injunction or comparable remedy against infringement." Which of Patria's responses—inconsistent domestic law, or prosecutorial discretion—is most persuasive, and why? Which, if either, implicates the allocation of limited resources such as to trigger reliance upon Article 41(5)?

(3) **Responsibility for Devising Remedial Measures.** In the *United States-India* case, the United States tendered to the panel a suggested form by which India should comply with its obligations. But the panel declined to set out in any great detail the means by which India should bring itself into compliance with TRIPS. In what ways is a detailed recommendation of remedies inconsistent with the philosophy underlying the TRIPS Agreement? *See* TRIPS Agreement art. 1(1); *cf.* DSU art. 19.

(4) **Effect of Settlement.** What would have been the effect of a settlement between Xandia and Patria regarding the allocation of a more limited enforcement than Xandia would regard as ideal? *See* DSU art. 3(6) (requiring notification). Are settlements to be encouraged? Do settlements have any disadvantages? *See The Review of the WTO's Dispute Settlement Understanding: Which Way?*, 1 J. WORLD INTELL. PROP. 447, 462-67 (1998) (discussing different arguments).

(5) **Scope of Remedy.** After the panel report had been issued in *United States-India* (but before the Appellate Body upheld the panel's report) the EU filed an identical complaint to that filed (and successfully prosecuted) by the United States. *See* India—Patent Protection for Pharmaceutical and Agricultural Chemical Products—Request for Consultations by the European Communities, WT/DS79/1 (WTO Dispute Settlement Body, May 6, 1997). The EU made that filing because remedies under the DSU are available only to WTO members acting with the authorization of the Dispute Settlement Body (which in turn requires panel and Appellate Body reports to act). Does this make sense? Should such apparently duplicative filings be encouraged? Should they be barred? (India had argued that the EU had lost the right to submit its own case to the WTO.) More fundamentally, are these filings duplicative? What procedural devices that you have seen in other adjudicative models might be considered to eliminate or reduce duplication? *See* DSU arts. 9-10. To what extent are these devices inappropriate because of the different character and purpose of WTO proceedings? *See* Geuze & Wager, *supra* at 357-58 (discussing conduct of EU-India proceeding).

(6) **Private Party Losses.** The panel in *United States–India* suggested that, although India had discretion under Article 1(1) of TRIPS as to the means of implementing its obligations, it should take into account the interests of persons who would have filed patent applications since 1994 had India offered an appropriate (TRIPS-compliant) mechanism for doing so. *See United States–India*, Panel Report, WT/DS50/R, ¶¶ 8.2, 7.66. *Compare* Notification by Pakistan to the Dispute Settlement Body, IP/N/1/PAK1 (WTO Dispute Settlement Body, Mar. 5, 1997) (providing details of ordinance issued by Pakistan to settle the same dispute with the United States). But an intellectual property owner cannot bring an action against a member state for losses sustained as a result of the failure of that member state to implement its TRIPS obligations. In contrast, under EU law, private citizens are entitled to damages from member states that fail timely to implement EU directives. *See* Francovich v. Italy, [1993] 2 CMLR 66 (E.C.J. 1991); *see also* R v. Secretary of State for Transport, ex parte Factortame, [1990] 3 CMLR 1 (E.C.J. 1990) (granting injunction against enforcement of U.K. statute that was in violation of EU law). Why the difference?

(7) **Monitoring Compliance.** In *United States-India,* the parties agreed that India would have fifteen months in which to implement the DSB recommendations. The EU and India then agreed to a shorter implementation time frame, resulting in an implementation date that matched that required by the *United States-India* agreement. India has since promulgated ordinances amending its law. The United States has, however, followed up with a request for consultation with India regarding whether the ordinance established a system of exclusive marketing rights that complied with the requirements of Article 70. How should the United States proceed if it remains unsatisfied with the content of the ordinance? *See* DSU art. 21(5); *see also The Review of the WTO's Dispute Settlement Understanding: Which Way?, supra,* at 461 (comments of John Kingery) (noting that the EU and the United States are in disagreement over the meaning of Articles 21(5) and 22).

(8) **Cross-Sectoral Retaliation.** Dreyfuss and Lowenfeld illustrate the dilemma faced by Xandia in Case V in trying to fashion effective retaliatory measures within the intellectual property sector that did not cause more harm than good. It is perhaps unsurprising, therefore, that cross-sectoral retaliation was frequently touted by U.S. representatives as one of the primary advantages of addressing inadequate intellectual property protection within trade law mechanisms and institutions (whether through Special 301 or the WTO). In which circumstances does cross-sectoral retaliation provide the most significant advantage over traditional intra-intellectual property law measures? Can it be argued that non-intellectual property based retaliation is not only more effective in certain circumstances, but may also be most appropriate? Is retaliation in the form of refusal to recognize the intellectual property rights of parties from the violating country a permissible form of retaliation? Even if it is permissible, what limits on its use would you recommend? Are there some types of intellectual property disputes where it would be particularly inadvisable to recommend this form of suspension? Developing countries have argued that retaliation is not an effective enforcement mechanism for them and wish to develop alternative enforcement vehicles (such as the award of monetary damages). *See* Kim Van der Borght, *The Review of the WTO Understanding on Dispute Settlement: Some Reflections on the Current Debate,* 14 AM. U. INT'L L. REV. 1223, 1232 (1999). Why might a prevailing developing country be unhappy with retaliation as its only form of relief?

The possibility of cross-sectoral retaliation theoretically works in both directions. But the following arbitrators' opinion suggests that some of the difficulties that might persuade Xandia to look outside the TRIPS Agreement for relief in Case V might also caution against authorizing suspension of TRIPS obligations as retaliation for non-TRIPS GATT violations.

EUROPEAN COMMUNITIES—REGIME FOR THE IMPORTATION, SALE AND DISTRIBUTION OF BANANAS–RECOURSE TO ARBITRATION BY THE EUROPEAN COMMUNITIES UNDER ARTICLE 22.6 OF THE DSU
(Decision by the Arbitrators, March 24, 2000)

[The EC banana regime was found to be inconsistent with Articles I and XIII of GATT and Articles II and XVII of the General Agreement on Trade In Services (GATS). The original panel was reconvened, pursuant to Article 21.5 of the DSU, upon request by Ecuador, and its report was adopted by the DSB. There were no findings of violations under the TRIPS Agreement in the report of the reconvened panel. On 8 November 1999, Ecuador requested authorization by the DSB to suspend concessions or other obligations under the TRIPS Agreement, the GATS and GATT 1994 in an amount of US$450 million. Ecuador submitted that withdrawal of concessions in the goods sector was not practicable or effective. The EU requested arbitration pursuant to Article 22.6 of the DSU, arguing (i) that the amount of suspension of concessions or other obligations requested by Ecuador was excessive since it has suffered far less nullification or impairment than alleged; and (ii) that Ecuador had not followed the principles and procedures set forth in Article 22.3 of the DSU in suspending concessions or other obligations across sectors and agreements. The DSB referred the matters to arbitration in accordance with Article 22.6 of the DSU. The arbitrators were the members of the original panel. After resolving various procedural issues and stressing the "basic rationale" that "the suspension of concessions or other obligations across sectors or across agreements (beyond those sectors or agreements under which a panel or the Appellate Body has found violations) remains the exception," the Arbitrators considered Ecuador's request for suspension of other obligations under the TRIPS Agreement, pursuant to subparagraph (c) of Article 22.3, as obligations which it intends to suspend across sectors and agreements.]

I. REMARKS ON THE SUSPENSION OF TRIPS OBLIGATIONS

A. The Scope of the Suspension to Be Authorized under the TRIPS Agreement

We recall that Article 19 of the DSU provides that "the panel or the Appellate Body may suggest ways in which the Member concerned could implement the recommendations". While Article 19 does not explicitly mention arbitration proceedings under Article 22, in our view, there is nothing in the DSU that would preclude Arbitrators, acting pursuant to Article 22.6, from making suggestions on how to implement their decision. Given that this case is the first one involving subparagraphs (b)-(e) of Article 22.3 and the first one concerning the suspension of TRIPS obligations, we believe that it is particularly appropriate to set out our views on the suspension of TRIPS obligations. We also note that Ecuador has expressed its interest in hearing our views on these issues.

We first note that Article 1.3 of the TRIPS Agreement defines in general the reach of the TRIPS Agreement:

> Members shall accord the treatment provided for in this Agreement to the nationals of other Members. In respect of the *relevant intellectual property right*, the nationals of other Members shall be understood as those *natural or legal persons* that would meet the criteria for eligibility for protection provided for in the Paris Convention (1967), the Berne Convention (1971), the Rome Convention and the Treaty on Intellectual Property in Respect of Integrated Circuits, were all Members of the WTO members of those conventions. . . (emphasis added, footnotes omitted).

Thus, an authorization by the DSB of the request for suspension vis-à-vis the European Communities would permit Ecuador to suspend the treatment provided for in the TRIPS provisions in question with respect to nationals within the meaning of Article 1.3 of those 13 EC member States[41] which the request for suspension by Ecuador refers to.

. . . .

[E]cuador's request for the suspension of TRIPS obligations refers to Article 14 of Section 1 of the TRIPS Agreement on "Copyright and related rights" as well as Section 3 on "Geographical indications" and Section 4 on "Industrial designs".

In respect of the protection of *performers, producers of phonograms* (sound recordings) and *broadcasting organisations* within the meaning of Article 14 of the TRIPS Agreement, criteria for eligibility for protection of persons are defined in the Rome Convention. In this respect, it is important to point out that, in the case of suspension of obligations under Article 14, as requested by Ecuador, there may be different right holders of the different rights related to phonograms and that these right holders do not necessarily all have the nationality, within the meaning of Article 1.3 of the TRIPS Agreement, of one of those 13 member States in question, even if the phonogram concerned has been produced in one of those member States. The performer having rights to a phonogram under Article 14 may be a non-national of these 13 member States, but the producer of the phonogram may be a national of those member States. Such complicated situations will have to be carefully considered by Ecuador in implementing the suspension of TRIPS obligations, if authorized by the DSB, so as not to adversely affect right holders who cannot be regarded as nationals of those 13 EC member States.

In respect of the criteria for eligibility for the protection of *industrial designs*, the Paris Convention is relevant.

The legal protection of *geographical indications* is enjoyed by "interested parties" within the meaning of Articles 22.2 and 23.1 of the TRIPS Agreement. Article 22.1 of the TRIPS Agreement creates a clear link between a region, locality or territory and a protectable geographical indication. This implies that

---

[41] Ecuador's request for suspension under Article 22.2 excludes Denmark and the Netherlands.

the suspension of protection of geographical indications would concern parties interested in geographical indications which identify a good as originating in the territory of one of the respective 13 EC member States, or a region or locality in that territory.

It should be emphasized that in its relation to all other WTO Members and the natural or legal persons that are their nationals, Ecuador continues to be bound by its obligations under the TRIPS Agreement and that all these WTO Members continue to be entitled to exercise their rights under the DSU with respect to Ecuador.

B. The Suspension of TRIPS Obligations and the Relation with the Conventions Administered by World Intellectual Property Organisation (WIPO)

The parties disagree on whether Article 2.2 of the TRIPS Agreement prevents or permits the suspension of TRIPS obligations which have a relation to the Paris Convention, Berne Convention, the Rome Convention or the IPIC Treaty. Article 2.2 provides:

> Nothing in Parts I to IV of this Agreement shall derogate from existing obligations that Members have to each other under the Paris Convention, the Berne Convention, the Rome Convention and the Treaty on Intellectual Property Rights in Respect of Integrated Circuits.

This provision can be understood to refer to the obligations that the contracting parties of the Paris, Berne and Rome Conventions and the IPIC Treaty, who are also WTO Members, have between themselves under these four treaties. This would mean that, by virtue of the conclusion of the WTO Agreement, e.g. Berne Union members cannot derogate from existing obligations between each other under the Berne Convention. For example, the fact that Article 9.1 of the TRIPS Agreement incorporates into that Agreement Articles 1-21 of the Berne Convention with the exception of Article 6*bis* does not mean that Berne Union members would henceforth be exonerated from this obligation to guarantee moral rights under the Berne Convention.

In any event, Article 2.2 only refers to Parts I to IV of the TRIPS Agreement, while the provisions on "Dispute Prevention and Settlement" are embodied in Part V. This Part of the TRIPS Agreement contains, inter alia, Article 64.1 which provides that the DSU applies to disputes under the TRIPS Agreement unless otherwise specifically provided therein. . . However, nothing in Article 64 or other Articles of the TRIPS Agreement provides specifically that Article 22 of the DSU does not apply to the TRIPS Agreement.

We further note that subparagraphs (f)(iii) and (g)(iii) of Article 22.3 of the DSU[46] explicitly define that Sections of the TRIPS Agreement are "sectors", and that the TRIPS Agreement is an "agreement", in respect of which the suspension of TRIPS obligations may be sought, pursuant to subparagraphs (b-c) of Article 22.3, by a complaining party and authorized by the DSB. Provided that Ecuador's request for the suspension of certain TRIPS obligations is consistent with all the requirements of Article 22 of the DSU, including paragraphs 3 and 4 thereof, neither Article 2.2 read in context with Article 64 of the TRIPS Agreement, nor any other provision of the WTO agreements indicate that an authorization by the DSB of that request would in theory be prohibited under WTO law.

It is not within our jurisdiction as Arbitrators, acting pursuant to Article 22.6 of the DSU, to pass judgment on whether Ecuador, by suspending, once authorized by the DSB, certain TRIPS obligations, would act inconsistently with its international obligations arising from treaties other than the agreements covered by the WTO (e.g. the Paris, Berne and Rome Conventions which Ecuador has ratified). It is, if at all, entirely for Ecuador and the other parties to such treaties to consider whether a specific form chosen by Ecuador for implementing such suspension of certain TRIPS obligations gives rise to difficulties in legal or practical terms under such treaties.

C. The Effect on Third-country WTO Members of the Suspension of Certain TRIPS Obligations by Ecuador with Respect to the European Communities

It is evident that an authorization by the DSB for Ecuador to suspend certain TRIPS obligations would concern Ecuador only. Such authorization does not exonerate any other WTO Member from abiding by its WTO obligations, including those under the TRIPS Agreement.

The obligations of other WTO Members include those in respect of action against imports of goods which involve other infringements of intellectual property rights. In this context, Article 51 in Section 4 on "Special Requirements Related to Border Measures", contained in Part III of the TRIPS Agreement, provides that "Members shall . . . adopt procedures to enable a right holder who has valid grounds for suspecting that the importation of counterfeit trade or pirated copyright goods may take place", to request customs authorities to suspend release into free circulation of such goods. According to footnote 14 to Article 51, "pirated copyright goods" include copies made without the consent of the right holder or person duly authorized by the right holder in the country of production, where the making of that copy would have constituted an infringement of a copyright or a related right under the law of the country of importation.

---

[46] Article 22.3(f) of the DSU: "for purposes of this paragraph, 'sector' means:

(iii) with respect to trade-related intellectual property rights, each of the categories of intellectual property rights covered in Section 1, or Section 2, or Section 3, or Section 4, or Section 5, or Section 6, or Section 7 of Part II, or the obligations under Part III, or Part IV of the Agreement on TRIPS;"

Article 22.3(g) of the DSU: "for purposes of this paragraph, 'agreement' means:

(iii) with respect to intellectual property rights, the Agreement on TRIPS."

We note that, as a result of an authorization by the DSB of Ecuador's request to suspend Article 14 of the TRIPS Agreement, phonograms would be produced in Ecuador consistent with WTO law. However, such phonograms would still be copies made without the consent of the right holder or a person duly authorized by the right holder in the country of production. Pursuant to footnote 13 to Article 51, WTO Members are under no obligation to apply procedures concerning "special requirements related to border measures" to imports of goods put on the market in another country by or with the consent of the right holder. However, with respect to phonograms produced in Ecuador without the consent of the right holder, but consistent with an authorization by the DSB under Article 22.7 of the DSU, the obligations of Article 51 of the TRIPS Agreement to apply such procedures would remain in force for all WTO Members.

Distortions in third-country markets could be avoided if Ecuador would suspend the intellectual property rights in question only for the purposes of supply destined for the domestic market. An authorization of a suspension requested by Ecuador does of course not entitle other WTO Members to derogate from any of their obligations under the TRIPS Agreement. Consequently, such DSB authorization to Ecuador cannot be construed by other WTO Members to reduce their obligations under Part III of the TRIPS Agreement in regard to imports entering their customs territories.

D. The Suspension of TRIPS Obligations and Interference with Private Rights

We are conscious that the requested suspension of certain TRIPS obligations ultimately interferes with private rights owned by natural or legal persons. These persons are highly unlikely to have any connection with the ongoing failure of the European Communities to fully comply with the DSB rulings in the proceeding under Article 21.5 of the DSU in Bananas III between Ecuador and the European Communities. The same logic holds true for the suspension of concessions or other obligations under the GATT (or other agreements in Annex 1A) and the GATS as well. However, the interference with private property rights of individuals or companies may be perceived as more far-reaching under the TRIPS Agreement, given the potentially unlimited possibility to copy phonograms or use other intellectual property rights. In contrast, producers of goods and service suppliers which are affected by the suspension of concessions or other obligations under the GATT or the GATS may stop exporting to the Member imposing such suspension.

We are aware that the implementation of the suspension of certain TRIPS obligations may give rise to legal difficulties or conflicts within the domestic legal system of the Member so authorized (and perhaps even of the Member(s) affected by such suspension). The resolution of such difficulties is of course a matter entirely within the prerogatives of the Member requesting authorization. Obviously, the degree of such difficulties is likely to depend on the means chosen by Ecuador for implementing the suspension of certain TRIPS obligations in relation to the 13 EC member States.

E. Concluding Observations on the Suspension of TRIPS Obligations

[The Arbitrators read their mandate under Article 22(6)-(7) of the DSU with respect to comparing the level of impairment suffered with the level of suspension of concessions proposed, as limited to estimating Ecuador's losses (in actual and potential trade and trade opportunities) in Ecuadorean bananas and distribution services by suppliers of Ecuadorean origin.] However, in the light of the provisions of Article 19.1 of the DSU referred to above, we wish to make some remarks on Ecuador's intentions on how to implement the suspension of certain TRIPS obligations, if authorized by the DSB.

We note with approval that, in implementing the suspension of certain TRIPS obligations at a level not exceeding the level authorized by the DSB, Ecuador intends to account not only for the actual impact of the suspension of intellectual property rights currently used subject to the authorization by the right holder and subject to the payment of remuneration. The mechanisms described in detail below reflect Ecuador's intention to consider also the potential impact of such suspension in terms of the additional use of the intellectual property rights in question. Such use may be expected to increase as a result of the fact that the DSB's authorization would allow using such intellectual property rights without payment of remuneration to EC right holders and without their authorization, provided that prices for the products incorporating the intellectual property rights concerned decrease.

More specifically, we note that in its response to questions by the Arbitrators, Ecuador submits that it never had the intention to simply abolish all rules on "related rights" and to put all EC produced phonograms in the public domain which it could arguably do only if it had requested suspension of Article 9 of the TRIPS Agreement, too. If Ecuador were authorized by the DSB to suspend the application of "related rights" under Article 14 vis-à-vis the European Communities, it would consider installing a system whereby companies or individuals established in Ecuador could obtain an authorization from the Ecuadorean government to apply the suspension of concessions derived from Article 14 of the TRIPS Agreement within the Ecuadorean territory. This authorization would be granted through a licensing system which limits the suspension of concessions in terms of quantity, value and time. The Ecuadorian government would reserve its right to revoke these licences at any time. Each reproduction of a sound recording under this licensing scheme would correspond to a "suspension value" equivalent to the "related right value" of a new, commercially most interesting sound recording. For that purpose, Ecuador would use the average "related right value" of sound recordings in Europe as estimated by the International Federation of the Phonographic Industry (IFPI). A certain proportion of this value would represent the performer's share and another, larger part would represent the producer's share. If the level of suspension thus calculated were to risk reaching (together with authorized suspension in other sectors and/or under other agreements, if any) the level of nullification and impairment suffered by Ecuador, the authorization scheme would be stopped. Ecuador believes that the chances that this would happen are very close to nil.

Regarding geographical indications, Ecuador notes that the analysis should be different from the analysis with regard to Article 14 of the TRIPS Agreement. The non-respect of "related rights" on a sound recording results in a product that is identical in all respects to the product that is put on the market with the authorization of the "related rights" holder. The CD that would be produced under Ecuador's licensing scheme would be cheaper than a CD produced with the authorization and remuneration of the "related rights" holder, and the former would become a substitute for the latter. For products identified by a geographical indication that would be clearly different. For these products it is only possible to make use of the geographical indication, which is different from reproducing the original product. However, the use of geographical indications could be licensed in similar terms as explained for sound recordings above. Licences could be granted for a determined product and a determined value, quantity and time. The licences would be granted for the exclusive use of the holder of the licence and the Ecuadorean government would reserve its rights to revoke these licences at any time. The test for determining the level of suspension would be the extent to which protected EC products would be replaced by non-protected products from other sources.

With respect to industrial designs, Ecuador envisages a similar licensing system as described above even though it considers that the economic effect of suspending the protection of industrial designs would be limited.

In our view, the mechanisms envisaged by Ecuador for implementing the suspension of certain sections of the TRIPS Agreement, if authorized by the DSB, would take account of many of our remarks made in the preceding sections.

Finally, we recall that, according to Article 22.8 of the DSU, an authorization by the DSB of a request for the suspension of concessions or other obligations is in principle a temporary action, pending the removal of the WTO-inconsistent measure at issue, a solution remedying the nullification or impairment of benefits, or a mutually satisfactory solution. Given this temporary nature of the suspension of concessions or other obligations, economic actors in Ecuador should be fully aware of the temporary nature of the suspension of certain TRIPS obligations so as to minimise the risk of them entering into investments and activities which might not prove viable in the longer term.

. . . .

[The Arbitrators concluded that (i) Ecuador's request had not followed, albeit to a limited extent, the principles and procedures set forth in Article 22.3, especially regarding the suspension of concessions under the GATT with respect to goods destined for final consumption, and that (ii) the level of suspension requested by Ecuador exceeded the level of nullification and impairment suffered by it as a result of the EC's failure to bring the EC banana import regime into compliance with WTO law within the reasonable period of time foreseen for that purpose. Accordingly, the Arbitrators suggested to Ecuador that it submit another request to the DSB for authorization of suspension of concessions or other obligations consistent with the panel's conclusions. The panel then set out its calculations from which Ecuador could determine an appropriate suggestion. In particular, it suggested that Ecuador may request, pursuant to paragraph 7 of Article 22, and obtain authorization by the DSB to suspend concessions or other obligations of a level not exceeding US$201.6 million per year which the Arbitrators estimated to be equivalent within the meaning of Article 22.4 to the level of nullification and impairment suffered by Ecuador as a result of the WTO-inconsistent aspects of the EC import regime for bananas. The arbitrators commented that Ecuador may request, pursuant to subparagraph (a) of Article 22.3, and obtain authorization by the DSB to suspend concessions or other obligations under the GATT concerning certain categories of goods in respect of which suspension of concessions is effective and practicable, and to suspend commitments under the GATS with respect to "wholesale trade services" in the principal sector of distribution services.]

To the extent that suspension requested under the GATT and the GATS . . . is insufficient to reach the level of nullification and impairment indicated [above], Ecuador may request, pursuant to subparagraph (c) of Article 22.3, and obtain authorization by the DSB to suspend its obligations under the TRIPS Agreement with respect to the . . . sectors of that Agreement [listed in its request] . . . .

We recall the general principle set forth in subparagraph (a) of Article 22.3 that the complaining party should first seek to suspend concessions or other obligations with respect to the same sectors as those in which the panel or Appellate Body has found a violation or other nullification or impairment. In this respect, we recall that, according to the report in the proceeding between Ecuador and the European Communities under Article 21.5, the GATT and the sector of distribution services under the GATS are those sectors within the meaning of subparagraph (f) of Article 22.3 in which violations were found by the reconvened panel. More specifically, we recall that the reconvened panel in the above-mentioned proceeding under Article 21.5 found the revised EC banana regime, inter alia, to be inconsistent with Articles I and XIII of GATT.

. . . .

We have made extensive remarks above on the suspension of obligations under the TRIPS Agreement and in particular concerning the legal and practical difficulties arising in this context. Given the difficulties and the specific circumstances of this case which involves a developing country Member, it could be that Ecuador may find itself in a situation where it is not realistic or possible for it to implement the suspension authorized by the DSB for the full amount of the level of nullification and impairment estimated by us in all of the sectors and/or under all agreements mentioned above combined. The present text of the DSU does not offer a solution for such an eventuality. Article 22.8 of the DSU merely provides that the suspension of concessions or other obligations is temporary and shall only be applied until the WTO-inconsistent measure in question has been removed, or the Member that must implement recommendations or rulings provides a solution to the nullification or impairment of benefits, or a mutually satisfactory solution is reached. We trust that in this eventuality the parties to this dispute will find a mutually satisfactory solution.

NOTES AND QUESTIONS

(1) **Suspension of TRIPS Obligations and Other Treaties.** The arbitrators suggest that they do not have jurisdiction to determine whether the suspension of certain TRIPS obligations by Ecuador, even if authorized by the DSB, might violate obligations arising from other treaties not covered by the WTO. If the EU sought to pursue the argument that Ecuador's actions in such circumstances violated other international obligations, where would the EU initiate proceedings? If you were counsel for Ecuador, how would you respond? If this did give rise to a violation of those other treaties, what does this suggest about the incorporation of intellectual property within the multilateral trade dispute settlement system?

(2) **Enforceable Standards and National Sovereignty.** Some U.S. critics of the WTO system have complained that the possibility of retaliation against the United States upon receipt of adverse DSB determinations represents a loss of U.S. sovereignty. Is that true? If the WTO system, and the TRIPS Agreement, were not in place, how might other countries respond to perceived inadequacies in U.S. intellectual property protection? To what extent has national sovereignty been surrendered and by whom? *See* David Palmeter, *National Sovereignty and the World Trade Organization*, 2 J. WORLD INTELL. PROP. 77, 89-91 (1999).

(3) **Effect of Binding Dispute Settlement**. What are the different ways in which national authorities might react to an adverse decision of the WTO Dispute Settlement Body? In what ways might the binding, legalistic nature of such decisions help or hurt domestic national debates about intellectual property? *See* Daniel A. Farber & Robert E. Hudec, *Free Trade and the Regulatory State: A GATT's Eye View of the Dormant Commerce Clause*, 47 VAND. L. REV. 1401, 1405-06, 1445 (1994) (suggesting helpful effects). In what ways might the possibility of binding WTO dispute settlement affect national authorities addressing issues with potential TRIPS implications?

Would it have been better to strengthen the jurisdiction and enforcement powers of the International Court of Justice rather than to assign international intellectual property law to WTO panels? *See* Joel P. Trachtman, *The Domain of WTO Dispute Resolution*, 40 HARV. INT'L L.J. 333, 376 (1999) ("How can a WTO dispute resolution decision ignore other international law? On the other hand, how can the WTO dispute resolution process purport to interpret and apply non-WTO international law?"). To what extent has the fate of international intellectual property law been assigned to WTO panels?

(4) **The Importance of the DSU.** Throughout Chapters 3-4, we raised questions regarding whether various national laws (real and supposed) would be in compliance with TRIPS. Review those questions, and consider whether your answers would have been different had you taken into account the detailed provisions of the DSU? If so, what does this tell you about the DSU and the purpose of the WTO dispute settlement process? Might it be appropriate for your analysis of the national law in the abstract to be different from your analysis in the context of the WTO dispute settlement process? If so, why?

[E]   Ministerial Review of the Dispute Settlement Understanding

Members have submitted comments and suggested reforms of the system as part of a planned review of the DSU. The review was scheduled to be completed within four years of the establishment of the WTO, *see Decision on the Application and Review of the Understanding on Rules and Procedures Governing the Settlement of Disputes*, 33 I.L.M. 1125, 1159 (1994), but has been extended because of the volume of proposals. As noted above, both the United States and the European Union have urged greater transparency (principally, open hearings and removal of restrictions on publication of the parties' submission) and the EU has proposed reforming the panel composition in the image of the Appellate Body. *See* Kim Van der Borght, *The Review of the WTO Understanding on Dispute Settlement: Some Reflections on the Current Debate*, 14 AM. U. INT'L L. REV. 1223, 1238-41 (1999). For a general discussion of some possible reforms, see Robert E. Hudec, *The New WTO Dispute Settlement Procedure: An Overview of the First Three Years*, 8 MINN. J. GLOBAL TRADE 1 (1999). The cloak of secrecy is pervasive at present. Indeed, the panel in *United States-Section 110(5) of the U.S. Copyright Act, supra* § 4.03[B][2], commented adversely on the confidentiality of information that "did not assist" the panel in discharging its duty to make findings that would best enable the DSB to perform its dispute settlement functions. *See id.* at nn.194, 211.

The European Commission has also suggested that the DSU be amended to include clearer statements about the role of pre-complaint consultations. Before a dispute panel is constituted, the party alleging a violation must request consultations with the putative defendant. Only upon the expiry of sixty days without the conclusion of an agreement between the parties can a complaint be filed with the WTO. *See* DSU art. 4.7. What should be the role of consultations? *See* DSU arts. 3-4. Do they fit in the WTO process? *See* David Palmeter, *National Sovereignty and the World Trade Organization*, 2 J. WORLD INTELL. PROP. 77, 80 (1999). Many disputes concerning TRIPS compliance have been resolved by bilateral consultations between the members concerned without recourse to formal dispute settlement proceedings. And, indeed, even where formal dispute settlement proceedings are initiated, discussions between the parties are encouraged throughout the process with a view to reaching a mutually acceptable solution. *Cf.* DSU art. 3(7) (reciting the philosophy of mutually acceptable solutions). If a member country displayed a derisory attitude toward its obligation to consult with another country, would you support that conduct being raised before a WTO panel? What would be the basis upon which the issue could be raised, and what would be the relief that a panel could grant? The European Commission's proposals would amend the DSU to (1) require that the request for consultations outline the complainant's case unambiguously; (2) confirm that the legal claims made before the panel must have been raised during consultations; (3) make clear that statements made during consultations cannot be used before the panel; and (4) permit the parties to seek written answers from each other. *See The Review of the WTO's Dispute Settlement Understanding: Which Way?*, 1 J. WORLD INTELL. PROP. 447, 448 (1998) (comments of Prof. Brigitte Stern); Van der Borght, *supra*, at 1235-

38). Would you support these changes, and why? *Cf.* DSU art. 6(2). In what ways is the current role of consultations different from private court-based litigation?

In what other ways is the model of state to state litigation before the WTO different from other adjudicatory models? Consider in particular the differences between the WTO process and: (1) other state to state forms of dispute resolution, and (2) private litigation models. Can you explain those differences? How do they affect the ability of the WTO dispute resolution process to achieve its objectives? Should the shift be taken further toward juridicization of the process, and in what ways? What would be the costs and benefits of furthering this shift? *See The Review of the WTO's Dispute Settlement Understanding: Which Way?*, 1 J. WORLD INTELL. PROP. 447, 462 (1998) (comments of John Kingery); *id.* at 472 (comments of Thomas Cottier). That is, how would a highly adjudicatory system change the nature of international intellectual property dispute resolution (and possibly international intellectual property law)? Would the costs and benefits fall disproportionately on one group or another?

In addition to a desire for enforcement mechanisms other than retaliation, developing countries have sought increased funding for and access to legal expertise necessary to prosecute and defend actions. The DSU currently provides developing countries with legal assistance from the WTO Secretariat, *see* DSU art. 27(2), and proposals from developing countries focus on enlarging the Secretariat to increase that assistance. One such proposal suggests creating a Permanent Defense Counsel to assist developing countries in proceedings brought against them. *See* Van der Borght, *supra*, at 1230-32.

[F]   The Relationship Between WTO Dispute Settlement And Special 301

The Special 301 mechanisms were introduced by Congress in 1988 largely as a result of the ineffectiveness of the pre-1994 GATT system. Does the WTO system, between periodic TRIPS Council review and binding dispute settlement with effective enforcement, make the Special 301 mechanism unnecessary? Congress did not appear to think so. Section 314(c) of the Uruguay Round Agreements Act, which implemented the GATT Agreement, amended the Trade Act to provide that a failure to provide adequate and effective protection of intellectual property could still trigger Special 301 measures "notwithstanding the fact the foreign country may be in compliance with the specific obligations of the TRIPS Agreement." Trade Act § 301(d)(3).

OFFICE OF THE UNITED STATES TRADE REPRESENTATIVE RESULTS OF SPECIAL 301 ANNUAL REVIEW (April 30, 1999)

PREVIOUSLY-FILED WTO TRIPS CASES

Over the past year, significant results have been achieved in several of the dispute settlement cases previously announced by Ambassador Barshefsky. In

1997, Ambassador Barshefsky announced initiation of WTO dispute settlement proceedings against Sweden, Ireland and Denmark. In 1998, Ambassador Barshefsky initiated dispute settlement proceedings against Greece and the European Union concerning rampant television piracy in Greece and their failure to comply with the enforcement provisions of the TRIPS Agreement.

On November 25, 1999, Sweden passed legislation amending its intellectual property laws to provide provisional remedies in civil enforcement proceedings. This type of remedy is particularly important for enforcement efforts in the software industry. On December 2, 1998, the United States and Sweden formally notified the WTO that they had reached a mutually satisfactory resolution to the U.S. complaint.

The cases against Ireland, Denmark, Greece and the EU are still pending, although progress has been achieved over the past year. In February 1998, Ireland committed to accelerate its work on a new comprehensive copyright law, and in July 1998 passed expedited legislation addressing two pressing enforcement issues. Denmark is presently considering options for amending its law to strengthen provisional remedies available to intellectual property right holders. In Greece, the rate of television piracy declined in 1998, and in September, Greece enacted legislation that provides an additional administrative enforcement procedure against copyright infringement by television stations. Ambassador Barshefsky stated, "We urge the Government of Greece to implement its new enforcement procedure in a strong and consistent manner, and to take steps to improve the handling of intellectual property cases in the court system in order to resolve this dispute."

Ambassador Barshefsky also expressed satisfaction today with the recent conclusion of the United States' dispute settlement proceedings against India. In December 1997, the WTO Appellate Body upheld a panel ruling in favor of the United States in this case involving patent protection for pharmaceuticals and agricultural chemicals. India's deadline for compliance was April 19, 1999. Earlier this year, the Government of India promulgated a temporary ordinance to meet its obligations, and then last month, it enacted permanent legislation entitled the Patents (Amendment) Act 1999. Through these mechanisms, the Government of India has established a mechanism for the filing of so-called "mailbox" patent applications, and a system for granting exclusive marketing rights for pharmaceutical and agricultural chemical products. The United States has expressed serious concerns regarding certain features of the new Indian law regarding exclusive marketing rights; however, in light of the discretionary nature of some of the problematic provisions of the new law, as well as the significant steps that India has taken or pledged to take to mitigate the impact of others, the USTR has concluded that no further action is appropriate at this time. Should any of the problematic provisions in the Indian law be invoked to the detriment of U.S. right holders in the future, the United States retains its rights to take further action.

United States—Sections 301-310 of The Trade Act of 1974, WT/DS152/R (WTO DSB Panel Report, Dec. 22, 1999). The EU requested consultations with the United States under Article XXII:1 of GATT and subsequently requested the establishment of a panel concerning the effect of the Section 301 process instituted by the Trade Act of 1974 (not Special 301). In its panel request, the EU claimed that a number of the procedures followed by the United States under the Trade Act (such as certain time limits and obligations upon the USTR to act) violated several provisions of the DSU and GATT, including *inter alia* the obligation of the United States under Article 23.2 DSU not to make determinations concerning the acts of other member states "except through recourse to dispute settlement in accordance with the rules and procedures of [the DSU]" and to "obtain DSB authorization" prior to suspending concessions or other obligations. The EU argued that Section 301 created an unacceptable "sword of Damocles effect" and jeopardized the security and predictability of international trade. The United States responded that "the U.S. Administration has carved out WTO covered situations from the general application of the Trade Act, . . . inter alia, through a Statement of Administrative Action ("SAA") submitted by the President to, and approved by, Congress." Under the SAA so approved "it is the expectation of the Congress that future administrations would observe and apply the [undertakings given in the SAA]". One of these undertakings was to "base any section 301 determination that there has been a violation or denial of US rights on the panel or Appellate Body findings adopted by the DSB."

In a report issued on December 22, 1999, the Panel agreed with the United States, finding that the language of the Trade Act, especially when taken along with the SAA, allows the existence of multilateral dispute resolution proceedings to be taken into account under the Section 301 procedure, and allows for determinations by the USTR to be postponed until after the exhaustion of DSU proceedings. The panel found that:

> [T]he statutory language of Section 304 constitutes a serious threat that [Section 304] determinations contrary to Article 23.2(a) may be taken and, in the circumstances of this case, is *prima facie* inconsistent with Article 23.2(a) read in the light of Article 23.1. We then found, however, that this threat had been removed by the aggregate effect of SAA and the U.S. statements before this Panel in a way that also removes the *prima facie* inconsistency and fulfils the guarantees incumbent on the US under Article 23. In the analogy . . ., the sign 'No Trespassing—Trespassers may be shot on sight' was construed by us as going against the mutual promise made among the neighbors always and exclusively to have recourse to the police and the courts of law in any case of alleged trespassing. Continuing with that analogy, we would find in this case that the farmer has added to the original sign which was erected for all to read another line stating: 'In case of trespass by neighbours, however, immediate recourse to the police and the courts of law will be made.'

We would hold—as we did in this case—that with this addition the agreement has been respected..

Id. ¶ 7.131.

NOTES AND QUESTIONS

(1) **Special 301 and "TRIPS-Plus."** What is the purpose of retaining Special 301? Is it appropriate? Is it prudent policy? Is it hurting or helping the appropriate development of international intellectual property law? Is it hurting or helping U.S. interests? What would be the consequences of the United States pursuing measures under Special 301 where a panel has held the other country in question to be in compliance with TRIPS? Could this be used by the United States to circumvent the moratorium on nonviolation complaints? Could it be used to require other countries to implement standards that the United States was unable to include in the agreement during negotiations? Are there any circumstances where this may be more appropriate?

(2) **Special 301 in a Multilateral Context.** To what extent do the procedures pursued through Special 301 mesh with or interfere with the mechanisms established by the TRIPS Agreement? To what extent would the USTR's unilateral actions against China in 1994–95 be available if China joined the WTO and the United States now pursued its claims through the WTO mechanisms? To what extent were the priorities of the United States with respect to China reflected in the priorities of the TRIPS Agreement? (Compare the summary of U.S.-China agreements in the Newby article with the important provisions of TRIPS.) Compare the suggestions made earlier in this Chapter by Newby regarding alternative means of dealing with inadequate intellectual property protection with the forms of assistance to developing countries contemplated by TRIPS. To what extent have the views of Newby been reflected in the TRIPS system, whether in the dispute resolution procedure or other aspects of the WTO or TRIPS system?

(3) **Special 301 and WTO Obligations.** The ability of member states to enforce international intellectual property obligations of other states through the WTO process is hailed as one of the most significant achievements of TRIPS. But countries are also obliged "not to make a determination that a violation [of TRIPS] has occurred except in accordance with [the DSU] procedures and not to retaliate except in accordance with authorization from the WTO's Dispute Settlement Body." Matthijs Geuze & Hannu Wager, *WTO Dispute Settlement Practice Relating to the TRIPS Agreement*, J. INT'L ECON. L. 347 (1999). Does current U.S. practice under Special 301 comply with the letter or spirit of this concomitant obligation regarding the exclusivity of the WTO system? Does current EU practice comply with the same obligation?

(4) **The U.S. Record in the WTO.** The United States has pursued several complaints before the WTO in addition to those referenced in the excerpt from the 1999 USTR Annual Report; the United States has now initiated sixteen

proceedings. Several of these have been referenced throughout this book, most notably the successful proceedings brought against India and the recent successful complaint against Canada regarding patent term. The United States has been the respondent in four cases, including the challenge brought by the EU to section 110(5) of the U.S. Copyright Act.

§ 5.04   WIPO/WTO Relations in the Era of WTO Dispute Settlement

[A]   The WIPO-WTO Agreement

The incorporation of international intellectual property law within the GATT/WTO system threatened (perhaps destroyed) the primacy of the WIPO in international intellectual property relations.   Yet, although the TRIPS exercise was in part motivated by dissatisfaction with the ability of the WIPO-based system to develop and enforce international standards of intellectual property protection, the expertise of the WIPO was important in concluding the TRIPS Agreement.   And the TRIPS Agreement expressly contemplates a continuing role for WIPO, both in the context of WTO dispute settlement, *see* TRIPS art. 68, and in the periodic reviews of TRIPS implementation for which the TRIPS Council is responsible under Article 71.   Although WIPO is not permitted to provide interpretations of the conventions that it administers, WIPO may (upon the request of a WTO panel) be able to supply information regarding such matters as the negotiating history of a WIPO-administered convention.   And WIPO offers significant assistance to countries involved in drafting, revising, or implementing their intellectual property laws in such a way as to be TRIPS-compliant.   For a discussion of the institutional relationship between WIPO and the WTO going forward, see Frederick M. Abbott, *The Future of the Multilateral Trading System in the Context of TRIPS*, 20 HAST. INT'L & COMP. L. REV. 661 (1997).

In December 1995, the two institutions signed a cooperation agreement formalizing their relations on an ongoing basis. *See Agreement Between World Intellectual Property Organization and the World Trade Organization*, Dec. 22, 1995, 35 I.L.M. 754.   Under this agreement, WTO members and nationals of WTO members are entitled to copies of laws and regulations, and copies of translations thereof, that exist in WIPO's collection, and access to any computerized database of such laws, on the same terms as apply to the member states of WIPO and to nationals of the member states of WIPO. *See* art. 2. Similar benefits are accorded the WTO Secretariat and the Council for TRIPS in order that they can carry out their responsibilities under the TRIPS Agreement. *See, e.g.*, TRIPS art. 68.   In return, the WTO Secretariat undertook to transmit to the International Bureau of WIPO, free of charge, a copy of the laws and regulations received by the WTO Secretariat from WTO members under Article 63.2 of the TRIPS Agreement.

WIPO also agreed to make available to developing country WTO members which are not member states of WIPO the same assistance for translation of laws and regulations for the purposes of Article 63.2 of the TRIPS Agreement, the same legal-technical assistance relating to the TRIPS Agreement, and the same technical cooperation, as it makes available to members of WIPO which are developing countries. The Agreements also affirmed more generally that the International Bureau of the WIPO and the WTO Secretariat will enhance cooperation in their legal-technical assistance and technical cooperation activities relating to the TRIPS Agreement for developing countries.

[B]   The Use of Post-TRIPS WIPO Treaties and TRIPS Council Developments in WTO Dispute Settlement Proceedings

Despite the conclusion of the TRIPS Agreement, WIPO has continued in its role as a primary vehicle for drafting, revision and conclusion of international intellectual property treaties. As suggested by Dreyfuss and Lowenfeld, WTO panels will almost certainly refer to developments in WIPO to assist in the interpretation of TRIPS. But what is the basis upon which they can do so, and what influence will such developments have? The issue was touched upon briefly by the panel in *United States—Section 110(5) of the U.S. Copyright Act*, where the United States had invoked the language of the WIPO Copyright Treaty to support its interpretation of the Berne Convention minor exceptions doctrine.

At first glance, the WIPO Copyright Treaty would not appear to have any application in the TRIPS environment, or with respect to interpretation of the Berne Convention. *See* WIPO Copyright Treaty art. 1 ("This Treaty shall not have any connection with treaties other than the Berne Convention, nor shall it prejudice any rights and obligations under any other treaties.") The panel was apparently not distracted by that provision and clearly took notice of the provisions in the WIPO Copyright Treaty. A short excerpt from the opinion follows.

UNITED STATES—SECTION 110(5) OF THE US COPYRIGHT ACT
Report of the Panel (WTO DSB, June 15, 2000), WT/DS160/R

[In support of its interpretation of the legal status of the minor exceptions doctrine under the TRIPS Agreement, the panel discussed subsequent developments, and in particular, the WIPO Copyright Treaty, which contains provisions similar to the three-step test found in the Berne Convention and TRIPS.]

Subsequent developments

The United States argues that Article 10 of the WIPO Copyright Treaty ("WCT"), adopted at a Diplomatic Conference on 20 December 1996 organized under the auspices of WIPO, reflects the standard set forth in Article 13 of the TRIPS Agreement. Paragraph (1) of that Article provides a standard for permissible limitations and exceptions to the rights granted to authors under the WCT, while paragraph (2) extends this standard to the application of the provisions of the Berne Convention (1971). In the view of the United States, it becomes clear from the Agreed Statement concerning Article 10 of the WCT that the signatories of the WCT, which include the European Communities and its member States and the United States, commonly recognized the minor exceptions doctrine. In support of its view, the United States also points out that Article 10 of the WCT is based on Article 12 of the Basic Proposal for the 1996 Diplomatic Conference. The commentary in the Basic Proposal explains that the TRIPS Agreement already enunciates the standard of that Article for limitations and exceptions in Article 13 of the TRIPS Agreement, and further states that "[n]o limitation, not even those that belong in the category of minor reservations, may exceed the limits set by the three-steps test".

The European Communities argues that the WCT has to date been ratified by only a small number of contracting parties and has not yet reached the threshold of thirty ratifications necessary for its entry into force.

We note that the subsequent developments just mentioned do not constitute a subsequent treaty on the same subject-matter within the meaning of Article 30, or subsequent agreements on the interpretation of a treaty, or subsequent practice within the meaning of Article 31(3). Thus such subsequent developments may be of rather limited relevance in the light of the general rules of interpretation as embodied in the Vienna Convention. However, in our view, the wording of the WCT, and in particular of the Agreed Statement thereto, nonetheless supports, as far as the Berne Convention is concerned, that the Berne Union members are permitted to provide minor exceptions to the rights provided under Articles 11 and 11bis of the Paris Act of 1971, and certain other rights. It appears that the objective was not to disallow the provision of such minor exceptions by WCT parties, but rather to make their application subject to the "three step test" contained in Article 10(2) of the WCT.

[W]e discussed [above] the need to interpret the Berne Convention and the TRIPS Agreement in a way that reconciles the texts of these two treaties and avoids a conflict between them, given that they form the overall framework for multilateral copyright protection. The same principle should also apply to the relationship between the TRIPS Agreement and the WCT. The WCT is designed to be compatible with this framework, incorporating or using much of the language of the Berne Convention and the TRIPS Agreement. The WCT was unanimously concluded at a diplomatic conference organized under the auspices of WIPO in December 1996, one year after the WTO Agreement entered into force, in which 127 countries participated. Most of these countries were also participants in the TRIPS negotiations and are Members of the WTO. For these reasons, it is relevant to seek contextual guidance also in the WCT when developing interpretations that avoid conflicts within this overall framework, except where these treaties explicitly contain different obligations.

NOTES AND QUESTIONS

(1) **The Current Relevance of the WCT**. The panel accepted that the WCT constituted neither a subsequent agreement nor practice within the meaning of Article 31(3) of the Vienna Convention. How is the WCT relevant and what weight was it afforded by the panel? Was this appropriate? *See* Graeme B. Dinwoodie, *The Development and Incorporation of International Norms in the Formation of Copyright Law*, 62 OHIO STATE L.J. 733, 773-75 (2001) (noting the relationship between the panel's use of the WCT and the dynamic development of international copyright law)

(2) **WCT as Subsequent Agreement and State Practice.** Neil Netanel has offered a thoughtful analysis of how the WTO dispute settlement process might be infused by consideration of recent international copyright law developments, and in particular the WIPO Copyright Treaty. *See* Neil W. Netanel, *The Next Round: The Impact of the WIPO Copyright Treaty on TRIPS Dispute Settlement*, 37 VA. J. INT'L L. 441, 464-75 (1997). Netanel suggests that the WCT and the accompanying Agreed Statements may constitute subsequent agreement and state practice under both Berne and TRIPS, and thus be relevant to a WTO panel's interpretation of TRIPS. (This will, Netanel concedes, depend upon a variety of considerations such as how many WTO members adhere to the WCT and the practice of WCT parties in implementing those obligations.) Netanel's resort to the WCT in interpreting TRIPS is in large part filtered through the WCT's relevance to the interpretation of the Berne Convention. Under which interpretive provision of the Vienna Convention would the WCT be relevant to an interpretation of a *Berne* provision? What about the Agreed Statements? The WCT is declared to be a "special agreement" under Berne. *See* WCT art. 1(1). How does that affect the use of the WCT in interpreting the Berne Convention before a WTO panel? *See* Berne Convention art. 20.

Even if the WCT is relevant to the meaning of the Berne Convention *qua* Berne, is it relevant to what Netanel calls the "Berne Convention in TRIPS"? It is not obvious that it must be because, although the Berne Convention *qua* Berne is clearly relevant to the Berne Convention in TRIPS, the WCT was concluded after the TRIPS Agreement was finalized. TRIPS imposed an obligation to comply with Berne as it was understood at the time of TRIPS; as yet, TRIPS does not require member countries to comply with the WCT. Netanel acknowledges this argument but suggests that because of the closeness in time between the conclusion of TRIPS and the WCT, the WCT and Agreed Statements retain probative value as indications of the parties' understanding of Berne at the time of TRIPS. *See* Netanel, *supra* at 471. Are you persuaded by the logic of Netanel's argument? *See also* TRIPS art. 68. If it is correct, does it support his further conclusion that panels could temper what he describes as the "maximalist" purpose of TRIPS with consideration of the "more balanced" WCT and Agreed Statements? That is, are there any limits on the ways in which the WCT can affect panel interpretation of TRIPS?

If the WCT and Agreed Statements were relevant to TRIPS interpretation only indirectly through the Berne Convention, this would limit their relevance to Berne-derived provisions, and thus (Netanel argues) prevents their consideration in construing independent provisions such as Article 13 of TRIPS. Does Netanel give too little force to his "indirect effect" argument in reaching this conclusion? How might the WCT and Agreed Statements still be relevant to an interpretation of Article 13 of TRIPS (other than as used by the panel in *Section 110(5))*? If Netanel is correct about the limits of his "indirect effect" argument, might the WCT and Agreed Statements be directly relevant to the interpretation of TRIPS? Despite Article 1(1) of the WCT, which disclaims any connection to any treaty other than Berne, Netanel argues that the Agreed Statements (which include no corresponding disclaimer but include references to their concordance with TRIPS) may be relevant as subsequent agreements under Article 31 of the Vienna Convention. Does this mean that the Agreed Statements will be accorded more weight in interpretation than the WCT itself? (Netanel ultimately argues that the WCT and Agreed Statements would both be directly relevant as indications of subsequent state practice.)

Netanel highlights the significance of permitting resort to the WCT by considering whether a hypothetical application of the U.S. fair use doctrine permissible under the Berne Convention would also be permissible under Article 13 of TRIPS.[*] Can the meaning of Article 13 be textually determined? If not, one has to ask where else panels would look for guidance. *See* Paul Edward Geller, *Intellectual Property in the Global Marketplace: Impact of TRIPS Dispute Settlement*, 29 INT. LAW. 99, 112-13 (1995). Netanel suggests that a WTO panel should make reference not only to the negotiating history of Article 13—which suggests that Article 13 is a compromise between the repetition of the Berne Convention and the United States' efforts to implement a market failure based notion of fair use—and the trade context of the TRIPS Agreement, but also on the WCT (Article 10(2), which repeats Article 13 of TRIPS) and its accompanying Agreed Statements. He concludes that "seen in light of the Agreed Statements and the Copyright Treaty's 'public interest' preamble, Copyright Treaty article 10(2) and TRIPS Article 13 are meant simply as short-hand descriptions of the multivalent limitations and exceptions to copyright owner rights that are permissible under the Berne Convention...."

Thus, under this argument, post-TRIPS international agreements, both regional and global (and both true minimum standards instruments and optimal harmonization instruments), might be subsumed within the TRIPS/WTO system, and thus made enforceable as the highest statements of public international intellectual property law, in a variety of ways. They may be accommodated in part through the dispute settlement mechanism. For example, as higher standards become international norms through these other agreements, failure by some countries to implement those standards might be seen as distortions of trade in the same manner as were inadequacies in protection in 1994. Nonviolation complaints may provide a vehicle for the expansion of the literal text to accommodate new (probably higher) standards. Or, as Netanel suggests, those multinational agreements might be used to affect the interpretation of state practice relevant (under the Vienna Convention) to the interpretation of TRIPS.

---

[*]Netanel based his particular hypothetical upon a set of facts that fell within the "quotation" exemption provided by Article 10(1) of the Berne Convention.

(3) **Relevance of TRIPS Council Developments.** The TRIPS Council (established by Article 69) is authorized by Article 71 to "undertake reviews in the light of any new developments which might warrant modification or amendment of the Agreement." How should the availability of Article 71 reviews affect a WTO dispute settlement panel's use of post-TRIPS developments in either of these two manners? In other areas, commentators have noted the complementary roles of the dispute settlement process and "the more political legislative process." *See, e.g.,* Trachtman, *supra* at 365 (discussing interaction between Committee on Trade and the Environment and panel decision in *Shrimp-Turtle* case). How might the TRIPS Council discussion of geographical indications, *see supra* § 3.02[D], interact with the pending complaint on a similar topic by the United States against the EU? How might a decision by a panel affect the discussions in the TRIPS Council? Should it affect those discussions? How should the TRIPS Council respond to a decision?

In *United States-India*, India sought to rely on the fact that notifications relating to the implementation of Article 70.9 had been made to the TRIPS Council and no laws implementing the obligation in the manner sought by the United States had been enacted by the countries concerned (i.e., those that could avail themselves of the benefits of the transitional provisions). *See* United States v. India, Panel Report WT/DS50/R, ¶ 4.27; *see also* Matthijs Geuze & Hannu Wager, *WTO Dispute Settlement Practice Relating to the TRIPS Agreement*, J. INT'L ECON. L. 347, 375 (1999) (discussing issues raised in the TRIPS Council prior to filing of an action in *EC v. Canada*, WT/DS/114). What weight should have been given to this fact? (Six months before the United States initiated proceedings against India for failure to comply with Articles 70(8) and 70(9) it also requested consultations with Pakistan on the same issue and followed up with a request to establish a dispute settlement panel. The parties reached a mutually acceptable solution, which obviated the need for formal dispute resolution proceedings.)

[C]   The Future of a WIPO Dispute Resolution Treaty?

Does the continued negotiation and revision of treaties within WIPO frustrate the objectives of the TRIPS Agreement? Why did countries decide to negotiate the WCT within the confines of WIPO rather than seek to amend TRIPS through the TRIPS amendment processes? *See* Frederick M. Abbott, *The Future of the Multilateral Trading System in the Context of TRIPS*, 20 HAST. INT'L & COMP. L. REV. 661, 667-70 (1997) (describing the amendment process). Should we encourage countries to act only within a single forum? If a concurrent process of treaty negotiation is to occur within WIPO, is it important to conclude a dispute resolution treaty for disputes concerning such treaties, or are WIPO treaties intended to serve merely as adjuncts to the TRIPS/WTO process? Thus, reconsider the question we asked at the beginning of this Chapter: What relevance might a WIPO Dispute Resolution Treaty have? Professor Fred Abbott has suggested several reasons for pursuing such a treaty, including that the creation of a dispute settlement forum outside the WTO may permit states to resolve IPR-related disputes in an environment that is less politically charged than the WTO . . . States may find it useful to be able to submit IPR-related disputes to neutral dispute settlement without the threat of trade sanctions looming against losing parties.

Id. at 672. If Abbott is correct, what does this say about the WTO dispute settlement process? Do you agree with his assessment? What issues would the existence of concurrent dispute settlement processes raise? *Cf.* DSU art. 23.

Where would the greatest support for a WIPO-based dispute settlement process come? The developing countries, who perceive more favorable treatment within WIPO, might be expected to support a shift in focus from the WTO to WIPO. But Abbott notes that "a striking aspect [of the WIPO Dispute Resolution Treaty] negotiations . . . is that they are being pursued with considerable vigor by many of the same OECD governments that moved the international IPRs center of gravity from WIPO into the WTO." *Id.* at 672. Why might such countries be interested in a WIPO dispute resolution process? (The United States is a notable exception, having displayed no enthusiasm for the WIPO Dispute Settlement Treaty.)

From what you have read, what roles in the international intellectual property process should be allocated to the WTO and which should be assigned to the WIPO? (Ask yourself what are the strengths and weaknesses of each institution?) Are there any that should be assigned to both institutions (or to neither)? *See* Abbott, *supra* at 678-82 (suggesting an allocation of institutional responsibilities). Bearing that in mind, how would you assign judicial competence between WTO dispute settlement and any WIPO dispute settlement process? Abbott has proposed the creation of an Inter-Institutional IPRs and Trade Governing Council, comprised of members from the WTO TRIPS Council and the WIPO governing bodies, which would, among other things, propose a "proper dispute settlement forum of first instance if a conflict between the parties arises." *Id.* at 679-80.

§ 5.05   NAFTA Dispute Resolution

The NAFTA Agreement, signed one year before the TRIPS Agreement, contemplates that disputes be submitted to NAFTA dispute settlement panels. Chapter 20 of the NAFTA provides a means for resolving disputes among the NAFTA governments over the application and interpretation of the NAFTA. The process involves consultation (typically for thirty days) between the parties, an attempt at mediation and conciliation (also typically thirty days) before the "Free Trade Commission," submission of the dispute to an arbitral panel, and implementation of the panel report (with failure to do so giving rise to a right to suspend equivalent benefits). The "Free Trade Commission," which consists of the trade ministers from the three NAFTA governments, oversees the implementation of the agreement and the resolution of disputes. The agreement also creates a NAFTA secretariat to provide assistance to the

NAFTA Free Trade Commission and to the panels established under chapter 20. Once a party has taken dispute settlement under chapter 20 to the stage of placing the matter before the Commission, the member country is precluded from seeking parallel action under the WTO. *See* NAFTA art. 2005(6). The process is no more transparent than the WTO process. One scholar has noted that:

> the Chapter 20 panel process is intended to remain confidential between the parties, reflecting an almost obsessive concern for secrecy on the part of the governments. Thus, the Rules of Procedure must and do provide that 'the panel's hearings, deliberations, and initial report, and all written submissions to and communications with the panel shall be confidential'.

David Gantz, *Dispute Settlement under the NAFTA and the WTO: Choice of Forum Opportunities and Risks for the NAFTA Parties*, 14 AM. UNIV. J. INT'L L. 1025, 1043 (1999). Unlike the WTO, there is no appeal from panel reports.

As of yet, there have been no intellectual property disputes decided by a NAFTA panel. In what circumstances might a NAFTA panel be the appropriate forum for settlement of an intellectual property dispute? Consider the following. Articles 11(1)(ii), 11*bis*(1), 11*ter*(1), 14(1) and 14*bis*(1) of the Berne Convention require (for different types of work) that authors be granted the exclusive right to authorize the "communication" of their works to the public. Universal Pictures, Inc., owners of copyrighted motion pictures, communicates some of its works to the public in the United States by encoded (i.e., scrambled) broadcast. It discovers that unauthorized "decoders" are being manufactured and sold to the public in Canada and then later being used in the United States to enable unauthorized (and hence uncompensated) viewing of the Universal motion pictures. If Canada provides no rights for copyright owners to restrain the manufacture and sale of this equipment, could the United States bring an action against Canada under the TRIPS Agreement? *See* Paul Edward Geller, *Intellectual Property in the Global Marketplace: Impact of TRIPS Dispute Settlement*, 29 INT. LAW. 99, 111-12 (1995); *cf.* BBC Enters. Ltd. v. Hi-tech Xtravision Ltd., [1992] R.P.C. 167, 202 (House of Lords, U.K.) (finding liability under U.K. decoding prohibition for extraterritorial sales because otherwise the protections of the law could easily be "bypassed" by devices being made abroad). If, alternatively, decoding devices were being manufactured, sold and used in Canada to decode Universal's motion pictures broadcast by satellite into Canada from the United States, could the United States bring an action against Canada under the TRIPS Agreement? How would your conclusion be affected by the existence of Article 1707 of NAFTA, which expressly requires contracting parties to criminalize and create civil liability for the manufacture, import, sale or lease of devices or systems that are primarily of assistance in decoding an encrypted program-carrying satellite signal without the authorization of the lawful distributor of such signal? *See* NAFTA art. 1707. To what extent is your analysis affected by Article 8 or Article 11 of the WIPO Copyright Treaty (if it goes into effect)? Article 8 of the WCT expressly recognizes a broad right of communication in authors of literary and artistic works; Article 11 imposes obligations to provide adequate protection against the unauthorized circumvention of technological measures used by authors in connection with the exercise of their rights. In which fora could (and should) the United States raise any complaint? *See* NAFTA art.2005(2) (disputes regarding NAFTA "normally shall be settled under" the agreement); DSU art. 23; Berne Convention art. 33(1). Would this affect the determination of pertinent international intellectual property law?

The U.S. government has interpreted Article 11 of the WCT as obligating signatory countries to render actionable the manufacture and sale of certain devices designed to circumvent technological measures used by authors to protect their rights (e.g., to prevent copying) under the Copyright Act. *See* Pamela Samuelson, *Intellectual Property and the Digital Economy: Why the Anticircumvention Regulations Need to Be Revised*, 14 BERKELEY TECH. L.J. 519, 531 (1999) (criticizing this interpretation); Digital Millennium Copyright Act § 1201 (implementing legislation based upon this interpretation). The WCT has not, however, been signed by all WTO member countries. In what ways might the United States bring an action against another WTO country for failure to permit copyright owners to enjoin the manufacture and sale of such devices? *Cf.* Netanel, *supra* at 493-94 (analyzing similar hypothetical claim *against* the United States based upon pre-Digital Millennium Copyright Act U.S. law). The original draft of Article 11 (Article 13 of the Basic Proposal) would have explicitly required member countries to prohibit the manufacture, importation or distribution of devices undertaken with the "primary purpose or primary effect" of circumventing anti-copying measures when the manufacturer had reasonable grounds for knowing such devices would be used for unauthorized and nonpermitted uses. The final version of Article 11 uses more general language and provides instead that "Contracting Parties shall provide adequate legal protection and effective legal remedies" against circumvention of anti-copying measures. What effect would this change in language have on your interpretation of Article 11? *See* Netanel, *supra* at 495 (describing final language as a compromise designed to ensure flexibility). The EU has proposed a directive that implements Article 11 in a somewhat similar (but not identical) manner. *See supra* Chapter 4. If repeated by several states other than the EU and the United States, what effect would these national forms of implementation have on the interpretation of Article 11? What would you wish to know about the national legislation before answering that question? What does this tell you about the process of making international copyright law?

PART III

ACQUISITION AND ENFORCEMENT OF RIGHTS INTERNATIONALLY

Chapter 6

MECHANISMS FOR THE ACQUISITION OF INDUSTRIAL PROPERTY RIGHTS

As economic globalization quickens, the need for producers to obtain industrial property rights (primarily, patent, trademark and design rights) on a multinational basis becomes more pressing. The Paris Convention offers only limited assistance to U.S. applicants in this regard. It provides post-application grace periods in which a U.S. applicant can file an application in a Paris Union country and receive the priority of its U.S. application date. However, to secure registered rights in those other countries, the U.S. applicant must file and pursue a separate application in each country in which a registration is sought. In this Chapter, we consider mechanisms that provide greater assistance in securing rights on a multinational basis. At the global level, these mechanisms have primarily involved the centralized filing of an application in pursuit of several national registrations. At the regional level, however, there have been more ambitious efforts to facilitate multinational protection. These efforts, which are being most fully tested in the EU, involve systems that begin to move industrial property law—in differing ways, and to a differing extent—beyond purely national rights.

§ 6.01 Global Patent Registration Agreements

[A] Introduction: Early Visions of a Global Patent

A consistent distinguishing feature of the national patent laws of European countries from the very beginnings of the industrial revolution has been the international thrust of the policies behind them. In Chapter 3, for example, we examined the English Statute of Monopolies, the goal of which was to provide incentives to introduce foreign technology into that country. In high contrast to this, the American patent system from its earliest days to the present has placed its emphasis on creating incentives for inventors within the United States, although foreigners were (almost!) always welcome to participate. Earlier in the twentieth century, developing and some developed countries resisted pressures to give up their compulsory licensing regimes in the belief that such systems created incentives for the substitution of cheaper domestic products for expensive imported technology. (As we saw in Chapter 3, Article 31 of the TRIPS Agreement has since placed significant limits on the discretion of states to impose compulsory licensing.) While no nation or culture holds a monopoly on creativity or innovative initiative, real differences in national character and culture drive the engines of technological and economic development policy, including patent policy, in various countries. These differences have had a chilling effect on the development of a world patent system in the past and continue to do so today.

The ideal of a world patent system is not new. Efforts to create an international patent system, begun in Vienna in 1874, were renewed in earnest after World War I. But as we have seen, variations in the patent systems and the philosophies which underpin them, both between the industrialized and the developing countries and among the industrialized countries themselves, have not yet been reduced beyond the minimalist standardization of the TRIPS Agreement, much less eradicated. Because of the current uniqueness of the American first-to-invent system and the stubborn unwillingness of the United States to change it aside, serious questions remain as to whether conditions for the grant of patents in the various jurisdictions or standards for their enforceability are likely to be harmonized. One authority, observing the British patent law and its harmonization with the European Patent System over the last twenty years, notes that "the resulting edifice is byzantine in complexity." Real difficulties and seemingly insurmountable obstacles have been encountered in attempts at harmonizing substantive patent law internationally, as seen, for example, with the 1991 Patent Law Treaty negotiations mentioned in Chapter 3. The continuing disarray among national courts interpreting the supposedly harmonized patent law of the regional European Patent Convention is discussed in Chapter 7.

But camouflaged by this apparent disharmony and disarray, international patent lawyers and patent office officials in both national offices and international organizations continue to work diligently to simplify and rationalize the complexity and attendant expense entailed in filing patent applications internationally. The pressures to reduce patent costs are felt most by the biggest users of the international patent system—primarily multinational corporations—but in the global economy of the twenty-first century, innovators great and small will likely be affected.

Yet, notwithstanding the fact that states have not been able to come to agreement about substantive harmonization of patent laws, they continue to be spurred to move toward agreement about procedure. The more limited PLT, concluded in June, 2000 is a testament to this. In this section, we examine early ideas about how to create a world patent in the period between the two World Wars. Next, we observe the major efforts to bring the vision of a worldwide patent granting process to fruition, from the establishment of the Patent Cooperation Treaty [PCT] regime in the 1960s to the twenty-first Century. As we proceed, we may reflect on the extent to which, if at all, procedural simplification and unification have paved the way to substantive harmonization and how the vision of a global system for the protection of patents has evolved over the course of the twentieth century—if at all.

SCOTT H. LILLY, INTERNATIONAL USE OF PATENT SEARCHES
1 J. PAT. OFF. SOC'Y 268-69 (1919)

The Director of the Canadian Patent Office, in an address before the employees of the United States Patent Office, expressed the wish that his office might have the benefit of searches as to novelty made in the United States. He stated that the great majority of applications filed in Canada are filed in substantially the same form in the United States, and in these cases one search as to novelty should be sufficient, and that the one search could be more efficiently made in the United States, where the facilities for search are better.

That wish might be realized if the Canadian office would forward to the United States each application filed, for a report on its novelty. Where a corresponding application had been filed in the United States the report would require little but the copying of the citations made as a result of the previous search, and in other cases the report could be kept available for a subsequently filed application, so that in the majority of cases little extra work would be entailed in preparing such reports. It should be easy to set a price for such reports, which would be much less than the cost to Canada of making searches as to novelty and still would more than cover the cost of the extra work of preparing the reports, so that the arrangement would be mutually advantageous.

Making searches in two offices where they could be confined to one, not only duplicates the work of searching such applications as are presented in duplicate, but it duplicates the cost of providing facilities for searching and lessens the efficient division of labor amongst searchers. Probably a greater proportion of the applications in the Canadian Patent Office than in any other are duplicated in the United States; but it seems worthy of investigation whether, considering both work and plant, it could not be made profitable for the United States to report as to novelty not only to Canada but to England and her other colonies having patent systems.

Now, when the full efficiency of every man is needed and cooperation in other lines between Great Britain and the United States is being extended, should be an auspicious time for inaugurating cooperative searches as to novelty.

After returning from South America, former Commissioner Moore related that a number of representatives of South American countries had expressed their appreciation of the advantages of a patent system, indicating that their countries appreciated the difficulties arising from the grant of patents without search as to novelty and the great cost of a plant in which such searches could be made with any reliability. If the opportunity were properly presented, South American countries might gladly avail themselves of reports as to novelty made by the United States.

The more countries use one office for novelty reports the cheaper can [such reports] be made. With many countries using the reports of one office a report as to one invention may be used not only twice but many times, so that the cost for each use of the report is reduced.

Our facilities for searching are far from perfect. Making greater use of the facilities we have would make increased expenditures in perfecting them more reasonable to everyone, not excepting Congress, so that increased use should make it possible for the work to be done with less cost for each application and with greater reliability.

The logical first step seems to be to learn as nearly as possible the proportion of Canadian applications duplicated in the United States and in what respects, if any, the information as to novelty desired by Canada differs from that required in our system. Then an estimate of cost could be made and a definite offer presented to Canada. The logical ultimate goal would seem to be, not only a pan-English speaking and pan-American office, but a highly perfected plant and force justly maintaining itself as the authority on novelty for the whole world.

LE BREVET INTERNATIONAL

Chimie et Industrie, Dec. 1922, at 1332-36
Abstracted in 5 J. PAT. OFF. SOC'Y 342-344 (1923)

Since the question of an international patent seems not to admit of salutation at present, it has been suggested that efforts be made to take a first step which will bring nearer the goal which it is desired to reach. A proceeding is proposed, which would permit attainment of a single registration by limiting to three the number of patents which the inventor would need to take out for protection in all the countries.

In examining the different legislation, the countries could be divided into three general classes:

1. Those which grant patents without any preliminary examination; language of Latin origin,
2. Those which grant patents after a perfunctory examination; English language (with the exception of the United States).
3. Those which grant patents only after thorough examination; language of Germanic origin.

Considering these facts, it is thought that three groups of nations might be formed, each of which could grant a patent valid in all the nations belonging to that group.

Perhaps the objection will be made that in the various participating countries diminution of receipts will result. Since the multiplicity of formalities to be fulfilled now [in order] to get protection in several countries and the [accompanying] great expense prevent the great majority of inventors from protecting their inventions in foreign countries, is it not logical to predict that by simplifying the formalities and reducing the expenses, a very large number of inventors will be led to apply for patents in one or the other of the three groups, if not in all? We believe that, far from diminishing receipts, on the contrary a surplus will be recorded in which the various countries will share in a proportion to be determined for each of them. Perhaps this proportion will not be as difficult to determine as could be supposed. Why not ask each country to contribute to expenses as has been done for the International Bureau at Berne, afterwards sharing the receipts under the same conditions?

The unification of legislation would, it appears, not be difficult, even though limited to the principal nations, but it seems that a concentration for the creation of three patents as above suggested might be achieved without too much difficulty. Most of the countries by making only slight modifications to their own legislation could be classed in one or the other of the three groups.

. . . .

ENRICO LUZZATO, ABOUT INTERNATIONAL PROTECTION OF INVENTIONS
4 REVISTA 583-588 (1931)

The present system of international protection of inventions is far from being perfect, so much the more when compared with the system of protection of other branches of industrial property, notwithstanding that inventions are really the most important branch of industrial property.

Indeed inventions do not enjoy the wide protection granted to copyright and cannot even be protected by means of a single international registration as is possible for trade marks since the creation of the international office of Bern for the protection of industrial property. On the contrary, for inventions it is necessary to file a separate application for patent in every country and to submit to all the formalities and provisions demanded by domestic laws.

If we examine what are the advantages granted by international conventions to inventors, we notice that these are: the right of priority (that is to say the term of 12 months for filing the patent in foreign countries), the right of independence of patents, [and] the limitation of the obligation of working in comparison with the provisions of national laws.

Therefore, an inventor who wishes to have his invention protected in all countries adhering to the international convention is obliged to file a separate application translated into the language of each country, [including] drawings etc., in every country in which the protection is desired, and this altho[ugh] there is an international union. Of course this entails heavy expense and trouble for the inventor.

Is it possible to improve this position and to obtain . . . better international protection of the rights of the inventor?

Three different ways can be taken into consideration.

1. By making national laws uniform,

2. By the creation of an international patent,

3. By admitting an international filing of applications for patents.

The first system appears to be impossible not so much on account of the differences among the various legislations as on other grounds.

I am of the opinion that there is no essential difference among the various national laws; on the contrary they are on the whole similar and those who hold a different opinion are mistaken.

I believe that if it were possible to ascertain how many patents granted in an important country (for example Great Britain) have been refused in another country (for example Germany) it would come to light that the patents not granted are few.

And if it were possible to know how many of these patents have remained in force after being granted, it would appear that [there are] very few . . . cases in which an invention has been granted protection in a country adhering to the union and has been refused protection in another. These cases are really exceptional and depend on special circumstances rather than on essential differences among the principles of the various laws.

This shows that the real invention is generally protected in the whole world altho[ugh] in different forms and ways, while what cannot be patented is generally no invention in the true sense.

However, altho[ugh] the substance of national laws is on the whole the same, this is not sufficient to achieve uniformity, however relative, in the necessary formalities for the granting of a patent. This happens because the laws on patents and the provisions relating thereto are not isolated and independent but are connected with the fundamental laws of the states and are influenced by them; they are subject to the systems adopted in the various states for the practical application of laws, and these systems vary according to the mentality and traditions of every country.

It has often been said . . . that these different manners of applying the law are only the consequence of different social and economic conditions and of different interests on the part of every country. But this is not [the whole story.]

At first sight it appears to be so, but it is more appearance than reality. [There are] very few . . . provisions of the law which have been enacted only on account of special national interests; [moreover, such] provisions are merely the result of a temporary situation. The difference among the laws depends really on the fact that some theoretical and old conceptions had survived [from] when the law was enacted, that there are some provisions which are bound up with the traditional procedure and are still applied only by custom; and it is very difficult to change all these legal traditions and customs.

I will give the following instance regarding Italy. This country, together with Hungary, has been the last to oppose the abolition *of the reservation of the right of third parties*, in connection with priority right. This attitude of Italy, in whatever way it is interpreted, ought to correspond to an interest, and an important one, of the country, considering that Italy not only wants to keep in force this right of third parties but maintains this attitude; notwithstanding the contrary opinion of nearly all the countries adhering to the union. Now, the opposition has really no practical grounds and depends only on . . . theoretical prejudices. The evident demonstration of this consists in the fact that we do not know what interest Italy has, to maintain this provision. There has never been in the past 20 years a law suit regarding the right of third parties and this provision has never been applied outside of the courts.

I have mentioned this only in order to show one of the aspects of the difficult problem of the unification of laws and I am obliged to conclude that unfortunately there are apparent and real reasons (which may be only of form but cannot be eliminated owing to the different mentality of nations and the different formation of the laws) that make it impossible to unify the laws on patents today and in [the] future for a period which cannot be fixed; this holds true even tho[ugh] the differences may be merely formal, but cannot be eliminated owing to [the] different mentality of nations and [the] different formation of laws.

The second possible system would be the creation of an international patent but such a creation is still more difficult than the unification of the laws. Indeed creating an international patent is equivalent to the unification of laws, at least regarding the issuance of patents, because all countries that would admit an international patent would be also obliged to have the same system for issuing it.

Indeed . . . litigations following the granting of the patent might be decided by the courts of the different countries and according to national laws, but it would be absolutely necessary in order to make an international patent possible that in granting a patent all countries follow a uniform system and uniform criteria, however different from the system and criteria adopted in other countries. Which could be this system?

Would it be necessary to have a preliminary examination of patents? And should an examination be established and accepted by all countries? Of what country would be the examiners and which form would be chosen among the many different forms adopted today in the various countries?

I think that no great substantial difference exists in the different countries regarding the granting of patents, but there is on the contrary a great difference in the procedure, that is to say in the form of the application, in the way the rights of the inventor must be identified and established in connection with the rights of others etc. Therefore [while] it is perhaps possible to accept one of the systems now applied, it is certainly impossible to follow many systems at the same time, and mix together various criteria which are too different.

If a board of persons of different countries [were to] judge on the validity of patents, it would be a tower of Babel; the same would happen if we should adopt for one industrial branch the criteria adopted in one country and different criteria for another. Therefore an international patent is impossible at present.

Another possible system would be the international registration of patents. In this case we should apply to inventions a system which is already applied for trade marks with good results. The Madrid arrangement for the international registration of trade marks does not invalidate the laws of the different countries. It only makes it possible to register the trade mark at the international office in Bern through the patent office of the country of origin, and the registration at the international office is valid for all contracting countries.

It would be necessary to have at the international office a special branch for filing the patent applications, and this filing would have an international validity. The international office, on [its] part, should inform (as [it does] for trade marks) the different countries of the filing, and these countries then ought to inform the office whether they accept this filing or not. This would be sufficient to free the inventor from the very numerous formalities which are now necessary for filing a patent in all countries. I think that an accord could be reached on this system if there were not the difficult[ies] arising from the examination of the patent.

Of course, if the filing of the application is refused in the countries where there is the examination of patents, the same procedure would begin which now takes place after the direct filing in the country and in this case the inventor would be obliged to appoint a representative, etc. as he is obliged to do now.

This trouble cannot be at present avoided, but it would be a great advantage to be able to get rid of many formalities and several separate applications by means of a unique application in the country of origin, together with the application for transmission to the international office.

In this manner the inventor could obtain a patent in a short time in all countries, and only alterations of form would perhaps be required in the countries where there is no examination of the patent, and after the examination in the others.

The only real difficulty is caused by the differen[t] . . . manner of establishing in the various countries what is the invention and its contents, with the consequence of making the patent applications and the claims quite different in the various countries.

This is today a very serious question; indeed, the drafting of applications and claims in order to have the greatest possible protection . . .has become a true profession with an artistic touch in it and is followed by eminent specialists. However, I think that this difficulty could be overcome. It would perhaps be possible to establish by means of an international conference some rules for rendering the patent applications suitable to the laws of the different countries so as to have an application generally acceptable everywhere.

Indeed it would be sufficient to establish some basis which would render the application acceptable to the mentality of the different patent office officials so that the procedure of examination would follow in the ordinary course.

This may seem to be a minor result, but in reality it would be a great forward step for the inventor who has so many difficulties to contend with; moreover we cannot hope to obtain at present more than this and it is useless to lose time inventing unworkable theories.

[B]   Realizing the Vision of a Global Patent: The Strasbourg Agreement Concerning the International Patent Classification [IPC] (1971), the Budapest Deposit Treaty of 1977, and the Patent Cooperation Treaty [PCT] (1970)

THE STRASBOURG CONVENTION AND PATENT CLASSIFICATION

The two pillars of the existing international mechanism for protection of patents are the Strasbourg Agreement Concerning the International Patent Classification [IPC] and the Patent Cooperation Treaty [PCT]. (The IPC should not be confused with the Strasbourg Convention of 1963 harmonizing certain points of patent law of 1963, which was the foundation of the European Patent Convention.)

The IPC was signed in 1971 and establishes the international patent classification system of approximately 67,000 alphanumeric categories. (It is found at Number 51 of the "Internationally Agreed Upon Numbers for Identification of Data" [INID Numbers] on the first page of the patent document.) There are currently 41 member states including all the EPC countries, the U.S., Canada, Australia, China and Japan. According to Article 3 of the IPC Agreement, the purpose of the Agreement is solely administrative. Classification is important both for searching prior art and for assigning applications to examiners examining patents. The United States continues to use the U.S. Patent Classification System (*see* MPEP 902.01) as its principal system of classification and the IPC as a subsidiary system, as is allowed under Article 4(2) of the IPC. The U.S. system is primarily a classification by structure while the IPC system is based primarily on function. Until such time as the U.S. adopts the IPC as its principal classification system, disparities between the search results of a U.S. search and an IPC search are likely to continue. More recently, the IPC as a search tool is gradually being superceded by electronic online search tools. The EPO uses the EPOQUE system, the Japanese Patent Office [JPO] uses what is called the F-term system, and the United States uses the Automated Patent System [APS]. (Efforts toward the development of common ground rules [CGRS] for searching patents between the USPTO, EPO, and JPO are discussed further below.)

THE BUDAPEST TREATY

The Budapest Treaty on the International Recognition of the Deposit of Microorganisms for the Purposes of Patent Procedure was signed in 1977. The Budapest Union member states must allow or require the deposit of microorganisms in order to meet the enablement requirement of the patent specification for inventions involving cell lines; and Budapest member states which meet certain standards may be designated as international depositories. There are 35 member states as of January 1, 1998, including the United States.

THE PATENT COOPERATION TREATY

The PCT was signed in Washington in December 1970 and entered into force on January 1, 1978 for the United States. It provides for a system of coordinated international search, possibility of a preliminary (and advisory) patentability examination, and a single international application designating the PCT countries selected by the applicant. The PCT application is transmitted to national offices of the elected contracting states for further processing in what is known as the "national phase." In states that have acceded to Chapter II of the PCT (including the U.S.) a non-binding Preliminary Examination may be conducted based upon very general criteria set forth in PCT Article 33 and Rule 64. The PCT leads to a bundle of patents which may differ in scope. A significant advantage of the PCT process is that translations on parallel applications may be postponed until after at least a prior art search has been carried out and the results made available, and in some cases for as long as 30 months. The PCT is merely a filing procedure and does not create an international patent. In 1979, 2,625 international applications were received by the International Bureau. The corresponding numbers were 38,906 in 1995 and 47,291 in 1996. The average number of designations per application was 6.66 in 1979 and 56.18 in 1996.

The PCT, its Rules of Procedure, and implementing legislation in the United States are discussed in the reading below, which also discusses the PCT's unique vocabulary as well as some of the advantages (and pitfalls!) which may be encountered in its use.

JAMES R. CARTIGLIA, THE PATENT COOPERATION TREATY: A RATIONAL APPROACH TO INTERNATIONAL PATENT FILING[*]
76 J. PAT. & TRADEMARK OFF. SOC'Y 261 (1994)

Most successful businesses have come to understand that competing in today's marketplace requires expansion onto the international stage. A strong competitive position in the United States is no longer enough, when one's competitors are global in scope. The truly successful business must also be strong in foreign markets. It follows just as clearly that a strong patent position in the United States cannot help protect a company's position overseas. Consequently, acquiring patents internationally can be as important as securing effective patents in the United States.

Unfortunately, the cost of filing patent applications around the world, even if limited to highly industrialized nations, such as the European countries, Japan, Korea, etc., can be prohibitive.[1] More importantly, since international filing must take place within one year of the U.S. filing date of an application in order to claim priority from the U.S. filing, patentability or commercial viability may remain uncertain. It is not uncommon for a broad international filing program to be effected, only to find that the invention was not patentable or commercially practical and the foreign filing costs wasted.

International filing via the Patent Corporation Treaty (the PCT) can alleviate some of these problems. Under the PCT, a single application is filed within the convention year,[4] and any or all of the PCT member countries or regions

---

[1]It is not uncommon for the cost of filing a patent application with the European Patent Office or with the patent offices of oriental countries such as Japan and the Republic of Korea (South Korea) to be several thousand dollars. A patent application of moderate length may cost over six thousand dollars to file. A broad program of international patent filing, therefore, may cost tens of thousands of dollars.

[4]That is, the twelve month period provided by Article 4 of the Paris Convention during which priority from an earlier filing can be claimed. There is no requirement that an application filed pursuant to the PCT claim priority from an earlier application. However, since a claim for priority is most often made when filing a PCT application, this article will focus on that situation. The principal difference between filing a claim for priority and not filing one relates to the dates when certain actions (either by the PCT or by the applicant) take place. These differences will be pointed out where appropriate.

designated.[6] Although use of the PCT adds costs to a foreign filing program, it spreads the costs out over an additional eight months (or until twenty months after the U.S. filing date) and can spread the costs out over an additional eighteen months (or until thirty months after the U.S. filing date) depending upon how the PCT is employed.

More importantly, the additional time provided by the PCT can save much of the cost of international filing if the invention proves to be unpatentable or commercially unimportant. If, during the additional eight or eighteen months provided by the PCT, it is discovered that the claimed invention is either not patentable or not commercially viable in any or all of the designated countries or regions, the application can be withdrawn in those countries or regions prior to payment of the national or regional filing fees. The savings which result from the withdrawal of unpatentable or unimportant applications can be substantial.[12]

Furthermore, the PCT provides another advantage[:] if ten countries or regions are designated, there is no further charge for designating the remaining countries or regions. This permits the designation of all countries and regions if ten are originally desired. In this way, if a jurisdiction for which designation was not originally intended ultimately proves to be commercially or otherwise meaningful, its designation means patent protection is still available.

I. FILING VIA THE PATENT COOPERATION TREATY

A PCT filing begins what is referred to as the "international stage" of foreign filing, which continues through "national stage" entry—that is, the formal commencement of prosecution in the individual countries or regions, when translations and national and regional filing fees come due. The PCT consists of two distinct phases: Chapter I, which involves the initial filing of the application and designation of the countries or regions in which it is to be effective; and Chapter II, which is optional and is initiated seven months later. Chapter II formally involves a preliminary, albeit non-binding, examination of the invention. However, the real advantage of Chapter II is in delaying the "national stage" costs an additional ten months (from twenty months after the priority date to thirty months after the priority date). Although using the PCT

---

[6]When an applicant pursuant to the PCT is filed, it is accompanied by a Request containing a petition to process the application according to the provisions of the PCT. The Request also includes a designation of the member countries or regions for which protection of the invention is desired on the basis of the application. Article 4, PCT.

[12]This aspect of PCT use is specifically endorsed by the International Bureau. In describing the usefulness of the PCT, one of [the] points raised is that "Before the applicant goes to the effort and expense of having translations prepared, paying the national or regional fees and appointing agents in the various countries, his views are able to mature to a greater extent than would be possible without the PCT, . . . because of the longer time he has for making decisions, he is better placed to assess the technical value and economic interest of patent protection and to select the particular countries in which he desires to continue seeking protection for his invention. As a result, substantial savings can be made in both translation and filing costs for those countries which are no longer of interest to the applicant." PCT Applicant's Guide, Vol. I, Paragraph 27, July 1992, page 5.

for international filing increases the cost of international filing, . . . the advantages in delaying international filing costs until thirty months after the priority date can often be more significant than the increased costs. Moreover, the savings realized when national stage costs are avoided by abandoning an invention found to be unpatentable or commercially unfeasible prior to national stage entry can justify using the PCT for all international filings.

a. Chapter I Procedures

The filing of an international application pursuant to the PCT involves the filing of a Request, a description, at least one claim, drawings (where appropriate) and an abstract. The application can be filed with the PCT branch of the U.S. Patent and Trademark Office (PTO),[28] which is referred to as the Receiving Office. Although the PCT is commonly used for filing a U.S. application in a variety of foreign countries or regions, the United States can also be designated when the application being filed is a continuing application, especially a continuation-in-part (CIP) application, with respect to the priority application. In this way, the CIP application can be filed as the PCT application, when it is the CIP application for which international filing is desired. . .

Once the application is filed, the Receiving Office checks to ensure that a filing date should be granted, checks for formal defects in the application and if any drawings referenced are submitted, ensures that the proper fees have been paid, and conducts a review for a foreign filing license.[37]

Once the PCT application is filed, a search is conducted by the designated International Searching Authority. When the U.S. is selected as International Searching Authority, it can be expected that the search will be conducted by the same examiner who is examining the priority application in the PTO. It is likely that the search results will coincide with the art of record in the PTO.[39] The search report is issued by the PTO, acting as International Searching Authority, approximately sixteen months after the priority date. The search report can be important because it provides an indication of the significance of

---

[28]The international application can be filed with the PCT branch in any of the designated countries or regions, provided that at least one of the applicants is a resident or national, pursuant to Rule 19, PCT. *See also* 37 C.F.R. § 1.421. In the United States, since the inventors are applicants, at least one of the inventors must be a U.S. resident or national in order to file an international application with the PCT branch of the PTO. 37 C.F.R. § 1.421(b). . . .

[37]37 C.F.R. § 1.412(c)(5). If any correctable defects are noted during the review conducted by the PTO acting as Receiving Office, the applicant will be given time to correct them, usually one month. Typical correctable defects pursuant to Article 14, PCT include lack of signature by the applicant or a designated agent (provided a Power of Attorney is received or on file), the applicants are not correctly identified, there is no title or abstract, or the physical requirements of the application are not complied with. These physical requirements include paper size, margins, drawing clarity, etc.

[39]Since the standards defining prior art differ somewhat from those of the PTO, it is possible that some prior art cited in the U.S. prosecution of the priority application will not be cited in the international search. However, since the differences in the definition of prior art are minor, it is unusual for the prior art cited in the international search to differ from that before the PTO. The international definition of relevant prior art is set out in Rule 33, PCT.

the art cited.[41] This can be valuable if the significance of the cited art to the examiner had not yet become apparent during the prosecution of the priority application, or if there is no priority application.

Once the search report is established, the applicant has the opportunity to amend the claims in response to the report. The amendment may be accompanied by explanatory comments. Amendment at this stage will not result in any official indication of patentability; nevertheless, it will serve to amend the application in all designated countries. Where it is expected that the amendments would have to be made in any case, amendment at this point eliminates the need to specifically amend the application in each designated jurisdiction after national stage is initiated (and avoids the costs associated therewith). Any amendment of the claims pursuant to Article 19 must be filed within two months of establishment of the search report.

Once the period for amendment of the claims under Article 19 of the PCT expires, the application, along with its search report and any Article 19 amendments, is "communicated" to each of the designated Patent Offices, i.e., a copy of the application and related documents is provided to each of the designated countries or regions.

At approximately eighteen months after the priority date, the PCT application is published by the International Bureau.[46] If the search report is available when the application is published, it is appended to the application, as are any amendments made pursuant to Article 19 of the PCT. However, it is not uncommon for the search report to be issued after publication of the application, in which case the cover page of the published application is re-published with the search report.

At twenty months after the priority date (or eight months after the expiration of the convention year), national stage entry is effected (unless Chapter II treatment had been demanded one month earlier) by formally initiating prosecution in each of the designated countries and regions, filing any translations which may be required and paying the required fees. Any national requirements for patent applications have to be met at this point. For instance, where the United States is a designated country, a declaration pursuant to 37 C.F.R. § 1.63 and/or 1.68 executed by the inventors must be submitted when national stage processing is begun.

The applicant is also afforded the opportunity to amend the application once

---

[41]Each piece of prior art cited in the search report has associated with it a letter code, which corresponds to a "rating" applied to the art by the International Searching Authority. The most significant of these are "X", which indicates that one or more of the claims of the application are not patentable in light of the reference (that is, the claims are not novel, or are anticipated by, the "X" references); "Y", which indicates that one or more of the claims are not patentable in light of the reference when combined with other like categorized references (that is, the claims do not show inventive step, or are obvious, in light of the "Y" references); and "A," which indicates that the cited reference merely defines the general state of the art and is not of particular relevance.

[46]Article 21 and Rule 48, PCT. However, if the United States is the only country or region designated in the international application, publication does not occur. This is a result of a reservation included by the United States pursuant to Article 64(3)(b), PCT. In addition, the application is not published if it is withdrawn or considered to be withdrawn prior to completion of the technical preparations for publication. Article 21(5), PCT.

more, this time before the individual designated offices, within one month after the twenty month limit for national stage entry provided by Article 22 of the PCT. The designated offices are not permitted to either grant or refuse to grant a patent on the application prior to expiration of the month provided.

With the initiation of the national stage, the international stage of prosecution is over, and national (or regional) prosecution begins in each jurisdiction. The role of the PCT essentially ends once national stage is initiated.

b. Chapter II Procedures

If Chapter II preliminary examination is desired, with its concomitant ten month extension of the time for entry into the national stage, a Demand Under Chapter II must be filed within nineteen months after the priority date. When a Demand is filed, national stage entry is no longer required by twenty months after the priority date. Rather, national stage entry need only take place within thirty months of the priority date. In this way, the costs of international filing are delayed until eighteen months after the expiration of the convention year.

A Chapter II Demand identifies the application, and indicates which of the designated countries or regions become elected countries or regions become elected countries or regions—that is for which countries or regions Chapter II will be effective. In addition, the International Preliminary Examining Authority (IPEA) must be selected in the Demand.[61] It is with the IPEA that the Demand is filed. National stage entry must be effected by twenty months after the priority date in jurisdictions for which Chapter II is not elected, else the application is considered withdrawn or abandoned in those jurisdictions.

The filing of a Demand Under Chapter II formally begins preliminary examination of the subject application. However, as noted above, the actual advantage of Chapter II is in delaying national stage entry an additional ten months. This is especially true where the U.S.P.T.O. is selected as the IPEA. Since the Examiner for international preliminary examination is prone to be the same Examiner who examined the priority application, it should be clear how successful preliminary examination is liable to be, since U.S. prosecution has been ongoing for over twenty months by the time International Preliminary Examination begins.

More particularly, if examination in the U.S. led to an indication of allowability, then making the same arguments and/or amendments will most probably lead to a positive preliminary examination report. If examination in the U.S. has not yet led to an indication of allowability, then it is unlikely that the Examiner would be convinced to change his/her position, unless dramatically new arguments or amendments were to be put forward.

However, since the preliminary examination report is merely advisory and not binding on any of the elected countries or regions, it serves no real purpose to

---

[61]Article 31(6) and Rule 53.7, PCT. The PTO can act as IPEA for international applications filed with it. 37 C.F.R. § 1.416. U.S. applicants have the option of having the European Patent Office act as IPEA, provided the European Patent Office was also the International Searching Authority. PCT Applicant's Guide, Vol. 1, Annex C, July, 1992.

struggle for a positive international preliminary examination report. If a positive report could be obtained relatively easily, such as by making the same amendments or arguments which were successful in the U.S., it is probably worthwhile doing. Where a positive report is not easily obtainable, then the non-binding nature of the report counsels against expending a great deal of effort to obtain a positive report.

A positive preliminary examination report is undeniably better than a negative preliminary examination report, even if non-binding. Nevertheless, the advantages of the ten month delay in national stage entry are clear, whereas the advantages of a positive preliminary examination report are nebulous at best.[65]

Chapter II preliminary examination of the invention of the international application begins with the transmittal of a first Written Opinion from the IPEA. The first Written Opinion corresponds generally to a first Official Action in U.S. prosecution of a patent application, and indicates whether the claimed invention meets the international standards of novelty, inventive step and industrial applicability. Unity of invention is also considered, regardless of any determination made during Chapter I.

The applicant is then given a set period within which to respond to the Written Opinion, usually two months. The response can include arguments and amendments, and an interview with the Examiner in international examination can be held. If a response to the first Written Opinion is received early enough, a second Written Opinion may be issued, allowing the applicant a second opportunity to file a response. However, this is unusual, because the first Written Opinion generally comes late enough that even the immediate filing of a response does not provide enough time for a second Written Opinion, since adequate time has to be provided to the applicant to respond to the second Written Opinion.

Whether or not a response has been filed, the IPEA establishes an international preliminary examination report, which indicates whether the international application and the invention claimed therein appear to meet the international standards, including novelty, inventive step and industrial applicability.[76] The report is due 28 months from the priority date.[77] This provides two months for the applicant to decide whether to proceed with entry into the national stage for the elected countries or regions.

---

[65]For instance, it is questionable how much a Japanese patent examiner will rely on a positive examination report issued by a U.S. examiner. There still remains a great deal of national or regional bias with respect to the quality of examination of other patent offices. When recognition of the quality of other patent offices becomes more widespread, a positive preliminary examination report will carry more weight.

[76]Article 35(2) specifically states that the international preliminary examination report shall not include any statements concerning whether the claimed invention is patentable according to any national law. Rather, the report states "whether [each] claim appears to satisfy the criteria of novelty, inventive step (non-obviousness), and industrial applicability, as defined for the purposes of the international preliminary examination in Article 33(1) to (4)."

[77]According to Rule 69.2 of the PCT Rules, the international preliminary examination report is established by 28 months from the priority date "if the demand was filed prior to the expiration of 19 months from the priority date."

Although, as noted above, the international preliminary examination report is not binding on any of the elected countries or regions, a positive report can be useful. If national processing is to be held in the country or region which issued the report, such as when the international application comprises a CIP application and the United States is an elected country, the Examiner would have to justify disagreeing with a positive report established by his/her own office before rejecting the claims. Indeed, since the examiner in preliminary examination is generally the same examiner before whom the priority application is prosecuted, and before whom the CIP application is likely to be prosecuted, rejecting the claims during national stage prosecution after establishing a positive international preliminary examination report would be inconsistent.

Moreover, other jurisdictions can be requested to explain why they disagree with the positive preliminary examination report when rejecting the claims. The report acts as an opinion of a neutral party of patentability, and may pressure another jurisdiction to find patentable subject matter if a sound basis for disagreeing with the report cannot be presented.

II. NATIONAL STAGE ENTRY

After receipt of the international preliminary examination report, the international stage of the application is essentially over. The applicant has until thirty months after the priority date to enter the national stage in any or all elected countries or regions. Once again, amendment of the application prior to initiation of prosecution is permitted.

Entry into the national stage in even one of the elected jurisdictions is not mandatory. If changing conditions or an indication of unpatentability convince the applicant that national stage entry is not justified, then the application can be abandoned simply by not entering the national stage in any of the countries or regions which had been elected. Likewise, if commercially practicality or patentability only appears to be present in some of the elected jurisdictions, then national stage entry can be effected for those jurisdictions only.

In this way, maximum return from investment in an international filing program can be ensured, by "weeding out" those inventions for which international filing becomes undesirable, for whatever reason. Because this decision is made thirty months following the filing of the initial U.S. application, the decision is made with significantly better information.

CONCLUSION

Use of the Patent Cooperation Treaty has notable advantages for business wishing to project themselves internationally. The PCT provides a vehicle for broad international filing of a patent application, while maintaining the ability to curtail expenses up to thirty months after the priority date should those expenses no longer be justified. Moreover, the PCT can provide a means by which the ability to file an application in countries or regions which may not initially appear to be candidates for international filing is preserved without any additional expenditure. It can also furnish an early indication of patentability.

Although use of the Patent Cooperation Treaty involves incurring some expenses which would not be required if filing directly to the individual countries or regions was performed, those expenses are justified when broad international patent protection is being pursued, and commercial opportunities and patentability are not certain.

. . . .

MANUAL OF PATENT EXAMINING PROCEDURE, § 1840
Matters to be Considered When Choosing an International Searching Authority

Choosing the European Patent Office (EPO) as an International Searching Authority could be advantageous to United States applicants who designate countries for European Regional patent protection in the PCT International applications for the following reasons:

(A) Claims may be amended according to EPO search results before entering the European Office as a designated Office.

(B) The EPO search fee need not be paid upon entering the European Office as a designated Office.

(C) The EPO search results may be available for use in a U.S. priority application.

(D) The EPO international search may be obtained without the need for a European professional representative.

(E) The European Patent Office search could provide the U.S. applicant with the benefit of a European art search (which may be different from the applicant's own or the USPTO's search) before it is necessary to enter the European Patent Office or other designated Offices.

[C]   Quasi-Substantive Harmonization

PATENT COOPERATION TREATY, ARTICLE 27

Nothing in this Treaty and the Regulations is intended to be construed as prescribing anything that would limit the freedom of each Contracting State to prescribe such substantive conditions of patentability as it desires.

UNITY OF INVENTION
PCT APPLICANT'S GUIDE, ¶¶ 113-122 (WIPO 1998)

What is meant by the requirement of "unity of invention"? An international application should be drafted so that the claims relate to only one invention or to a group of inventions so linked as to form a single general inventive concept. This principle is laid down in Rule 13. Observance of this requirement is checked by neither the receiving Office nor the International Bureau, but it is checked by, and is important to the procedure before, the International Searching Authority [cit] and the International Preliminary Examining Authority [cit], and may be relevant in the national phase before the designated and elected Offices. Since separate searches and examinations are required for distinctly different inventions, additional fees are required if the international search or international preliminary examination is to cover two or more inventions (or groups of inventions linked as just described).

How is the requirement of unity of invention satisfied? Unity of invention is present only when there is a "technical relationship" among the claimed inventions involving one or more of the same or corresponding "special technical features." The expression "special technical features" means those technical features that define a contribution which each of the claimed inventions, considered as a whole, makes over the prior art. The determination whether a group of inventions is so linked as to form a single inventive concept is made without regard to whether the inventions are claimed in separate claims or as alternatives within on the assumption that the claims avoid the prior art will be made before the prior art search but may be reconsidered on the basis of the results of the search. Annex B of the Administrative Instructions contains detailed criteria governing the determination whether an international application complies with the requirement of unity of invention under Rule 13. The following paragraphs set out a summary of some of the more important criteria discussed in that Annex. Illustrations of three particular situations are explained in detail below:

(i) combinations of different categories of claims (for example—product, process, use, and apparatus or means),

(ii) so-called "Markush practice," and

(iii) the case of intermediate and final products.

May different categories of claims be combined in an international application? The method for determining unity of invention contained in Rule 13 is construed as permitting, in particular, the inclusion of any one of the following combinations of claims of different categories in the same international application:

(i) in addition to an independent claim for a given product, an independent claim for a process specially adapted for the manufacture of the said product, and an independent claim for a use of the said product, or

(ii) in addition to an independent claim for a given process, an independent claim for an apparatus or means specifically designed for carrying out the said process, or

(iii) in addition to an independent claim for a given product, an independent claim for a process specially adapted for the manufacture of the said product and an independent claim for an apparatus or means specifically designed for carrying out the said process, it being understood that a process is specially adapted for the manufacture of a product if it inherently results in the product and that an apparatus or means is specifically designed for carrying out a process if the contribution over the prior art of the apparatus or means corresponds to the contribution the process makes over the prior art.

An apparatus or means shall be considered to be "specifically designed for carrying out" a claimed process if the contribution over the prior art of the apparatus or means corresponds to the contribution the process makes over the prior art. Consequently, it would not be sufficient that the apparatus or means is merely capable of being used in carrying out the claimed process.

What is permitted under the "Markush Practice"? Rule 13.2 also governs the "Markush practice" wherein a single claim defines alternatives of an invention—a common drafting practice for inventions in the chemical field. In this special situation, the requirement of a technical interrelationship and the same or corresponding special technical features as defined in Rule 13.2, is considered to be met when the alternatives are of a similar nature.

When the Markush grouping is for alternatives of chemical compounds, they are regarded as being of a similar nature where the following criteria are fulfilled:

(i) all alternatives have a common property or activity, and

(ii)(a) a common structure is present—that is, a significant structural element is shared by all of the alternatives, or

(b) in cases where the common structure cannot be the unifying criteria, all alternatives belong to a recognized class of chemical compounds in the art to which the invention pertains.

When dealing with alternatives, if it can be shown that at least one Markush alternative is not novel over the prior art, the question of unity of invention will be reconsidered by the examiner. Reconsideration does not necessarily imply that an objection of lack of unity will be raised.

Can both intermediate and final products be claimed? The situation involving intermediate and final products is also governed by Rule 13.2. The term "intermediate" is intended to mean intermediate or starting products. Such products have the ability to be used to produce final products through a physical or chemical change in which the intermediate loses its identity. Unity of invention should be considered to be present in the context of intermediate and final products where the following two conditions are fulfilled:

(i) the intermediate and final products have the same essential structural element, in that:

(a) the basic chemical structures of the intermediate and the final products are the same, or

(b) the chemical structures of the two products are technically closely interrelated, the intermediate incorporating an essential structural element into the final product, and

(ii) the intermediate and final products are technically interrelated, this meaning that the final product is manufactured directly from the intermediate or is separated from it by a small number of intermediates all containing the same essential structural element.

Unity of invention may also be considered to be present between intermediate and final products of which the structures are not known—for example, as between an intermediate having a known structure and a final product the structure of which is not known, or as between an intermediate of unknown structure and a final product of unknown structure. In order to satisfy unity in such cases, there must be sufficient evidence to lead one to conclude that the intermediate and final products are technically closely interrelated as, for example, when the intermediate contains the same essential element as the final product or incorporates an essential element into the final product.

An international application which complies with the unity of invention requirements laid down in Rule 13 must be accepted by all the designated and elected Offices, since Article 27(1) does not allow any national law (as defined in Article 2(x)) to require compliance with requirements relating to the contents of the international application different from or additional to those provided for in the PCT.

CATERPILLAR TRACTOR CO. v. COMM'R OF PATENTS AND TRADEMARKS
231 U.S.P.Q. 590 (E.D. Va.1986)

BRYAN, CHIEF JUDGE.

In this action involving an international patent application the plaintiff attacks, as contrary to a treaty provision, a rule of the Patent and Trademark Office (PTO). The provision and rule relate to "unity of invention," and the practical effect of the PTO's ruling on the plaintiff's application is that the plaintiff will have to file two applications instead of one. The treaty provisions involved are in the Patent Cooperation Treaty (PCT). The matter is before the court on cross motions for summary judgment, both parties agreeing that it is appropriate to resolve the issue presented by such motions.

Rule 13 of the PCT provides, in part:

Rule 13, Unity of Invention

13.1 Requirement

The international application shall relate to one invention only or to a group of inventions so linked as to form a single general inventive concept ("requirement of unity of invention").

13.2 Claims of Different Categories

Rule 13.1 shall be construed as permitting, in particular, either of the following two possibilities:

(i) . . .

(ii) in addition to an independent claim for a given process, the inclusion in the same international application of one independent claim for one apparatus or means specifically designed for carrying out the said process.

The words "specifically designed" are what give rise to the present controversy. The PTO rule, which allegedly is in conflict with the PCT rule, reads as follows:

In addition to a claim for a given process, a claim for one apparatus or means specifically designed for carrying out of the said process, *that is, it cannot be used to practice another materially different process.* 37 CFR § 1.141(b)(2) (emphasis added).

The PTO interprets this regulation to mean: Process and apparatus for its practice can be shown to be distinct inventions, if either or both of the following can be shown: (1) that the process *as claimed* can be practiced by another materially different apparatus or by hand, or (2) that the apparatus *as claimed* can be used to practice another and materially different process. MPEP 806.05(e).

If the rule and interpretation of the PTO conflicts with the PCT, it runs afoul of Article 27 of the PCT which provides in part:

(1) No national law shall require compliance with requirements relating to the form or contents of the international application different from or additional to those which are provided for in this Treaty and the Regulations.

An example, while not completely analogous, may help to illustrate the issue. If the process was the removal of a man's beard from his face, and a safety razor was the apparatus, the PTO rule and interpretation would hold that, because the razor could also be used to scrape paint from a pane of glass it was not "specifically designed" for removal of the beard. It would also hold that because the process could be performed with the use of a straight razor the safety razor was not "specifically designed" for the removal of the beard.[1]

The court finds the added [emphasized] portion of the PTO rule, quoted above, and its interpretation to be contrary to the PCT and thus contrary to law.

Only a lawyer would have a problem with what appears to the court to be the plain language of the PCT. And that plain language refutes the interpretation which the PTO gives the language and which it says is no different from that language. The PTO's position is that its interpretation is the only one which accords the word "specifically" any meaning; and that the interpretation urged by the plaintiff could be accomplished by use only of the word "designed" without the preceding adverb. Perhaps, but it does not follow that the PTO's interpretation of the word "specifically" is the correct one. The PTO's interpretation, as expressed in its opinion, is that "specifically designed" means " . . . that the process and apparatus can only be used with each other." In re Caterpillar Tractor Co., 226 U.S.P.Q. (BNA) 625, 639 (Comm'r. Pat. 1985). In the court's view this is an unreasonable interpretation. . . . The court will therefore grant summary judgment to the plaintiff. The rejection by the PTO of the plaintiff's application is contrary to law.

NOTES AND QUESTIONS

(1) **Substance or Procedure**. Is a single standard for unity of invention a substantive or a procedural harmonization?

(2) **National Stage Procedures**. For a detailed review of PCT national stage procedures in the United States, see Brian W. Brown, *Patent Cooperation Treaty (PCT) National Stage Commencement and Entry in the United States Of America*, 79 J. PAT. & TM OFF. SOC'Y 296 (1997).

---

[1]The specific application here was much more complicated than the example. Here, the plaintiff sought to apply for an international patent for a process or method of making a toothed segment used in the drive sprocket of the final drive assembly of Caterpillar crawler tractors. The drive sprocket receives the power of the diesel engine. The toothed segments engage the chain of the track that propels the tractor. Plaintiff's application claimed the invention of a forging process, which included use of a three-part forging die. This process obtained the close tolerances needed on three crucial surfaces of the toothed segment so that no machining of those surfaces was required before mounting on the final drive assembly. Claims 1 to 4 of the application relate to the method of forging a sprocket segment for a track-type vehicle undercarriage; claims 5 through 9 are directed to an apparatus, including the three-part die, for forging the track-type undercarriage sprocket segment to the desired, finished dimension. The PTO here initially ruled that the plaintiff's application did not comply with the requirements of unity of invention under the PCT because the method in claims 1 to 4 could be performed by a two-segment die, in addition to the three-segment die contemplated in the application. PTO's acting group director later found Caterpillar's protest to be unjustified, and upheld the patent examiner's findings. The acting group director also ruled that the apparatus as claimed (i.e., the three-segment die) could be used in a materially different process: a process of making a corrugated member. The Assistant Commissioner upheld the prior PTO decisions, In re Caterpillar Tractor Co., 226 U.S.P.Q. (BNA) 625 (July 22, 1985), and reiterated his position on reconsideration, 228 U.S.P.Q. (BNA) 77 (November 26, 1985).

(3) **Markush Practice**. The term "Markush practice" refers to a claim to a genus by enumeration of species, which has been allowed in the United States since the decision in *Ex parte Markush*, 1925 Dec. Comm'r Pat. 126. Intermediates which have unity of invention with regard to their function are allowable under U.S. practice. *See In re Jones*, 74 U.S.P.Q. 149 (1947). Reference to "Markush practice" in the PCT Guide reflects U.S. usage. The rules in the European Patent Office and the Japanese Patent Office are similar to the PCT Rules as well.

(4) **Prior Art Effect of a PCT Application**. A U.S. Provisional Application was filed on November 15, 1996. On November 15, 1997, a PCT application filed claiming priority to the November 15, 1996 application designating the United States was filed. On May 15, 1999, a PCT application enters the U.S. National stage under section 371. The effective date of the application for the purpose of prior art effect under section 102(e) is May 15, 1999. A U.S. provisional application was filed on November 15, 1996. On November 15, 1997, a PCT application filed claiming priority to the November 15, 1996 application designating the United States is filed. On May 15, 1999, a continuation of the PCT application is filed under section 365(c). The effective date of the application for the purpose of prior art effect under section 102(e) is November 15, 1996. Why the difference? *See* Allen E. Hoover, *Further Comments on PCT/USA National Phase Applications and Section 102(e)*, 79 J. PAT. & TM. OFF. SOC'Y 643 (1997); *International Patent Applications and the Section 102(e): Dates of Patents Issuing Therefrom*, 80 J. PAT. & TM. OFF. SOC'Y 289 (1998); *see also* Edward P. Heller, *Letter to the Editor*, 79 J. PAT. & TM. OFF. SOC'Y 883 (1997); Richard A. Neifeld & Edward P. Heller III, *The 35 U.S.C. 102(e) Date of a Continuation of an International Application*, 80 J. PAT. & TM. OFF. SOC'Y 71 (1998). Section 102(e) was amended effective November 29, 2000. Under the amended provision, and international application published in the English language will be effective as of its filing date. *See* 35 U.S.C. § 102(e) (Supp. 2001).

(5) **Cooperation Between Patent Offices**. Cartiglia, in footnote 65 above, questions the extent to which a Japanese patent examiner will rely on a positive examination report issued by a U.S. examiner, and the value of a PCT examination itself before the national patent offices. He notes that there still remains a great deal of national or regional bias with respect to the quality of examination of other patent offices, and ventures that when recognition of the quality of other patent offices becomes more widespread, a positive preliminary examination report will carry more weight. Efforts to promote mutual recognition of patent examiners are discussed in the next reading.

(6) **Legal Representation in PCT Procedures**. An American attorney can represent a PCT applicant in proceedings before the European Patent Office when it is acting as ISA and/or IPEA. A European patent attorney need only be retained when the PCT international stage is completed and the application enters the national stage in the EPO. The likelihood that an EPO examining panel will give deference to a favorable search and preliminary examination report by another European examiner is very high, and the EPO frequently grants the patent on the PCT application without further substantive examination. Corporate attorneys employed in U.S. companies may represent

the corporation in European patent proceedings even further in the process—all the way to the point where the European patent is submitted to the national patent offices for validation, at which time a local attorney must be engaged. For practical advice, see Joahim Weber, *How to Draft a European Patent Application Based on a US-Style Application*, 23 AIPPI J. (Jan. 1998).

[D]   Trilateral And Multilateral Initiatives For The Future

[1]   The USPTO/JPO/EPO Trilateral Conference

JOINT PRESS RELEASE: TRILATERAL CONFERENCE
NOV. 14, 1997

The European Patent Office (EPO), the United States Patent and Trademark Office (USPTO) and the Japanese Patent Office (JPO), at the Fifteenth Trilateral Conference held in Kyoto on November 13-14, 1997, agreed on the following conclusions:

Kyoto Action Plan

The three offices recognize that the globalization of industry and trade creates the need for a world-wide system for the grant of patents. The advantage of such a system for the users of the patent system would be:

* reduction of costs

* improved quality of granted patents

* improved dissemination of patent information

* reduced processing time in the patent granting procedure

With these objectives in mind, the three offices identify the following lines of action:

1. Trilateral Patent Network. The three offices will develop between them a trilateral network for data exchange concerning administrative and technical patent data. . . .

2. Trilateral Concurrent Search and Examination. The three offices agreed to undertake further steps through collaboration on concurrent searches concerning applications filed in each of the three offices and improving search effectiveness by increased reliance on each others search result for examination purposes. . . .

3. Trilateral Web Site. The three offices will promote the use of the internet to disseminate patent information. They agree to study and prepare the concrete implementation of a trilateral web site concept accessible free of charge. . . [The web site is now established at http://www.european-patent-office.org/tws/twsindex.htm].

NOTES AND QUESTIONS

(1) **Advantages of the Trilateral Approach**. The USPTO has been working with the EPO and JPO to cooperate in search and examination of PCT applications ("task-sharing") to reduce workloads, eliminate duplication of efforts, and reduce the costs of the system to the offices themselves and to the users. What are the advantages of a trilateral approach among the European, Japanese, and U.S. Patent Offices over a "multilateral approach" within the PCT system? Given that over eighty percent of all patents filed throughout the world ultimately originate from applicants within the trilateral region, would a trilateral approach lead to the formation of an exclusive club of patent administrators and examiners (and patent attorneys) from these countries?

(2) **Work Reduction Through Task Sharing**. The USPTO internally has a policy of "full faith and credit" providing for mutual recognition of the results of patent searches and examinations between U.S. patent examiners. *See* MPEP § 706.04. What would prevent U.S. examiners from extending its full faith and credit policy to EPO and JPO examiners and vice versa? Are the benefits which would be achieved by mutual recognition of search and examination results worth the risks? What *are* the risks?

(3) **"Insourcing" Legal Representation**. A major stumbling block on the road to a global patent system is the question of legal representation of patent applicants and the extent to which patent attorneys in developing countries would continue to find enough incoming work if patent attorneys in developed countries could represent inventors to acquire patent protection abroad—say, in China or India. Would such a trend lead to improvement or thwart the ultimate goals of a truly international patent system?

(4) **Outsourcing Legal Representation**. PCT Rule 83.1*bis* states that

> Where the International Bureau is the Receiving Office . . . [a]ny person who has the right to practice before the national Office of, or acting for, a Contracting State of which the applicant . . . is a resident or national shall be entitled to practice in respect of the international application before the International Bureau in its capacity as receiving Office.

If a PCT Patent becomes a reality, should the common nationality requirement be dropped? If so, might the "competitive advantage" flow to the private patent bar in less expensive jurisdictions? Would some cost-conscious U.S. patent applicants conceivably choose outsource their business, i.e., choose to be represented by, say, an Indian or Chinese patent attorney before the WIPO "World Patent Office" if the cost of the representation was lower and the resultant quality was at least the same?

(5) **"The More Things Change . . ."** To what extent do the issues addressed by the IPC, PCT, and Trilateral Conference mirror the challenges contemplated by the early visionaries such as Lilly and Luzzato? Have changes in information technology and international cooperation paved the way toward the

development of a global patent or have they no effect?

(6) **Future Developments**.   Notwithstanding the collapse of efforts to achieve substantive international harmonization of patent law in the early 1990s, do procedural simplification and unification increase the likelihood of an global patent to any great extent? Or are the differences in ideology between the goals of the patent systems in different countries make the attainment of a unitary world patent unlikely in the near or distant future? This question will be explored in the next reading.

[2] The Multilateral Approach

REPORT OF THE COMMITTEE OF EXPERTS
ON THE PATENT LAW TREATY
WIPO Doc. PLT/CE/IV/4, Fourth Session, Geneva, June 23 to 27, 1997

I. INTRODUCTION

The Committee of Experts on the Patent Law Treaty . . . held its fourth session in Geneva from June 23 to 27, 1997. [In addition to states that are members of WIPO and/or the Paris Union], representatives of the World Trade Organization (WTO), the European Communities (EC), the European Patent Office (EPO) and the Organization of African Unity (OAU) took part in the session in an observer capacity.

Representatives of the following non-governmental organizations took part in the session in an observer capacity: American Bar Association (ABA), American Intellectual Property Law Association (AIPLA), Asian Patent Attorneys Association (APAA), Brazilian Association of Industrial Property (ABPI), Chartered Institute of Patent Agents (CIPA), Committee of National Institutes of Patent Agents (CNIPA), Compagnie nationale des conseils en propriété industrielle (CNCPI), Confederation of Indian Industry (CII), Federal Chamber of Patent Attorneys (Germany) (FCPA), Federation of German Industry (BDI), Institute of Professional Representatives before the European Patent Office (EPI), International Association for the Protection of Industrial Property (AIPPI), International Federation of Industrial Property Attorneys (FICPI), International League of Competition Law (LIDC), Japan Intellectual Property Association (JIPA), Japan Patent Attorneys Association (JPAA), Korea Patent Attorneys Association (KPAA), Max Planck Institute for Foreign and International Patent, Copyright and Competition Law (MPI), Trade Marks, Patents and Designs Federation (TMPDF), Union of European Practitioners in Industrial Property (UEPIP) and Union of Industrial and Employersí Confederations of Europe (UNICE) (21). . . .

II. GENERAL DECLARATIONS

The Delegation of Germany was in favor of most of the provisions in the draft

Treaty, but had the intention of raising a number of matters during the discussions. It further expressed the wish that the preparatory work should be completed at the earliest possible time in order to prepare for a diplomatic conference.

(a) The Delegation of the United States of America declared that, as it had already stated at the first, second and third sessions of the Committee of Experts, it was still not in a position to discuss substantive patent law harmonization. Accordingly, the Delegation considered that the distinction to be made between formal and substantive matters continued to be critically important for the ongoing discussions.

(b) The Delegation said that its concern that the current draft Treaty did not impinge upon substantive matters remained. For example, while the issue of unity of invention was not explicitly included in any of the Articles to be discussed during that week, its alleged implicit inclusion in the form or contents reference in Article 5 raised some concerns for the United States of America and might create an impediment to that country's full participation in the effort to harmonize formal matters. The Delegation recalled that it had consistently raised this concern in preceding sessions of the Committee of Experts and that it had not really heard a reason why unity of invention could not be excepted from the draft Treaty.

(c) The Delegation noted further that, in the course of the last three meetings of the Committee of Experts, there had been an additional shift towards substantive matters. In addition to Article 5, Article 6 dealing with validity of patents and revocation, Article 12 dealing with corrections of mistakes and Article 15 dealing with belated claiming of priority could, in the view of the Delegation, be regarded as moving towards a discussion of substantive matters.

(d) Furthermore, the Delegation continued to question the intent and expected results of the entire work of the Committee of Experts. It appeared that many of the provisions had been drafted in a manner to accommodate all currently existing systems. However, the Delegation was pleased to see that some of the Articles were moving away from that approach, tending to be simpler and not an accommodation for all systems, thereby actually making a harmonization effort. Unfortunately, the remaining Articles which attempted to accommodate all systems were not to promote uniformity, simplification or cost reduction, although those considerations were currently of paramount importance to those seeking patent protection throughout the world.

(e) Additionally, many of the proposed Articles and Rules were unduly complex, difficult and costly for national offices to administer. In addition, the Delegation was still not convinced that the subject matter dealt with by the Committee of Experts was treaty level material. Much of what was addressed in many of the Articles of the draft Treaty dealt with matters that did not rise to a level above regulatory status. The Delegation believed that it would not be prudent to elevate the status of those matters to the level of treaty articles, as the practices involved in those articles would be subject to more frequent changes than it would be possible to accommodate if they were dealt with in the Treaty. . . .

(f) Notwithstanding those comments, however, the Delegation continued to view the harmonization of formalities to be a very laudable goal. The resultant ability to prepare an application in a single format, preferably in electronic form that would be accepted by all offices, a universal acceptance policy in other words, was eagerly sought by the users of its country and would be widely applauded.

(g) A first step on the road to achieving the goal of offering to its users a system in which they could prepare an application in a single format that would be accepted by all offices could simply be the mandated acceptance of a [PCT] compliant filing as a national filing. In that regard the PCT could serve as a model for a system which would enable users to prepare an application in one format that would be acceptable to all offices. A second step would be to recognize the limitations of the current paper-based PCT and to seek improvements in that Treaty and associated rules in order to, among other things, accommodate electronic filing. The Delegation noted that there had been some effort in that direction in meetings that were held as recently as in the week preceding the meeting of the Committee of Experts. The Patent Law Treaty could then be subsumed in the modernization of the PCT in that a provision for mandating universal application acceptance for national filings, such as Articles 4 and 5, could be added to such a rejuvenated PCT.

(h) A key motivating factor for the Patent Law Treaty was the recognition that no office, when undergoing the complex and costly process of automation, desired to create two electronic systems, one for national and another for international applications. To that end, the Patent Law Treaty and the PCT needed to converge to the greatest extent practicable, so that offices intending to automate would be able to develop a system capable of handling both national and international applications. The Treaty would provide the same benefit to inventors, applicants and owners interacting with the offices through the world, for those customers likewise would greatly prefer to purchase or develop a single automated system for preparing applications suitable for filing as international applications and as national applications throughout the world.

(i) The Delegation of the United States of America then went on to propose a list of Patent Law Treaty principles that it thought were underlying the work of the Committee of Experts. The proposed Articles and Rules should be measured against those principles in order to reduce the number of necessary Articles and Rules. Examples of such principles could include simplicity in procedures since procedures in some of the Articles were becoming extremely complicated; avoidance of costly requirements that may not always be necessary such as, for example, in regard to translations and certifications; avoidance of the loss of patent rights by allowing late submissions; late revivals and reinstatements; provisions for electronic record management, including legally admissible documents for enforceability and the promotion of standards for electronic prosecution history; mutual recognition of the processing results by different offices; lastly, the creation of a single application, preferably in electronic form, that could be used multiple times by applicants filing in more than one national office.

. . . .

The Delegation of Japan said that, in the information age where documents or money were flowing in an electronic form, electronic processing of patent-related information tended to be more and more adopted. In particular, a flow of patent related documents usually consisted of filing an application with the office, clerical processing within the office, substantive examination, registration and dissemination. Dealing with the information by electronic means, from the input through the output, made processing more easily enhanced, efficiency and improved quality. In this regard, the Delegation considered it to be a step in the right direction that the draft Patent Law Treaty contained positive provisions relating to electronic means of communication. With regard to developments in the near future, due to which modern information technologies would be applied around the world, it hoped that those provisions would be more refined. The Delegation announced its readiness to make a contribution in rule-making in this area and to try, as a pioneer country, to undertake electronic processing from the input to the output. Furthermore, the Delegation said that it supported the idea to introduce user-friendliness into the interfaces between users and the office. It noted, however, that this concept did not work well without a sense of responsibility of the individual users, as well as well-functioning dispute settlement procedures between the parties. Furthermore, the Delegation supported the approach that the Patent Law Treaty provisions be in conformity with PCT provisions where appropriate. It supported this idea in the light of the growing importance of PCT and future harmonization of formalities. While recognizing the importance that harmonization of formalities be successfully concluded, the Delegation said that it continued to stress the significance of harmonizing substantive matters.

The Delegation of Chile expressed its support of the draft Treaty. . . . The Delegation stressed the importance of concluding a Treaty which would provide applicants with simple, flexible procedures at a low processing cost. It welcomed that the draft Treaty referred to the PCT provisions. It also favored the flexibility introduced in the draft Treaty with regard to the possibility of electronic filing in the future. Finally, it expressed its gratitude for WIPO's efforts to harmonize patent law and hoped that this would lead to a simple and user-friendly Treaty.

The Delegation of the Republic of Korea expressed its hope that the efforts to harmonize the patent law requirements at the international level would result in an efficient harmonized treaty. . . . However, the Delegation expressed some concern about the contents of the draft Treaty. First, there seemed to be a provision in the draft Treaty obliging Contracting Parties to accept the electronic filing of applications. The Delegation said that this provision needed further discussions because currently only few countries had the capacity to comply with it. Secondly, some provisions in the draft Treaty seemed to make a single request sufficient even where the changes related to more than one application or patent. In the view of the Delegation, these provisions would make it difficult for the Office of its country to determine the contents of a request with respect to an application or patent for which a separate request had not been furnished. In this connection, the Delegation announced that it would intervene during the discussion and that it would do its best to reach a consensus.

The Delegation of Canada expressed its continued support for the work of the Committee of Experts on the Patent Law Treaty. It said that it would very much prefer to be able to include in the discussions matters of greater substance such as, for example, providing a grace period. It further expressed its hope that it would be possible to resume discussions of substantive patent law harmonization in the not too distant future. In the meantime, however, the Delegation supported the work of the Committee of Experts on the more limited issues that were currently being dealt with since it felt that harmonization, even if only in respect of formalities issues, would still be of significant benefit for patent offices and users of the system. In general, the Delegation of Canada viewed favorably the proposals put forward by the International Bureau for this meeting; however, it was concerned that in some areas the approach taken was becoming overly complex. For example, although it supported the principle of aligning the formal requirements under the Patent Law Treaty and under the PCT, it found the currently proposed link between the Patent Law Treaty and the PCT to be less than completely transparent; admittedly this was due in a large measure to the tremendous complexity of the PCT and the Regulations under the PCT. As another example, although Canada had in the past and continued to strongly favor the inclusion of provisions allowing missed time limits to be remedied under certain conditions, the proposals in Articles 13 and 14 for this purpose appeared to be far too detailed and complex. Referring to the continued development of the Patent Law Treaty, the Delegation of Canada encouraged the International Bureau and the Committee of Experts to try to find approaches to harmonization that, as much as possible, were simple, straightforward and easily understandable.

The Delegation of China expressed its appreciation of contributions which the Japanese Patent Office (JPO), United States Patent and Trademark Office (USPTO) and European Patent Office (EPO) had made within the framework of a meeting of consultants held in February 1997 in Geneva in respect of questions relating to electronic filing and transmission of documents. Furthermore, the Delegation expressed its satisfaction about the fact that the revised documents reflected the results of the last session of the Committee of Experts. It considered Articles 1 to 5 to be much simpler than the former drafts and appreciated the fact that they aimed at being consistent with the PCT. The Delegation believed that all these efforts would guarantee the success of the present meeting, thereby facilitating the early conclusion of the Patent Law Treaty. It expressed its hope for further discussions in the meeting over issues of common concern and, especially, on how to facilitate the operations of the offices while at the same time being user-friendly, as, in the final analysis, the offices and the applicants shared a common interest.

The Delegation of Portugal stressed the importance of concluding a Patent Law Treaty that would contribute to harmonization at the worldwide level. However, it would have preferred a treaty with more substantive provisions. Being aware of the difficulties in that respect, it nevertheless expressed its support for the draft Treaty. It intended to submit observations on various Articles during the deliberations of the Committee of Experts and pointed to the importance of achieving an international treaty that was clear, unambiguous and thus would avoid problems of interpretation after conclusion of the Treaty.

The Delegation of France welcomed the fact that the draft Treaty had been aligned wherever possible with the PCT as had been agreed at the third session of the Committee of Experts. It regretted that it had not always been possible to deal with the harmonization of substantive matters and noted that the issue would be discussed at the forthcoming meeting of the Governing Bodies. It noted that certain provisions, such as Article 15, had an effect on matters of substance and held that clarification as to the scope and field of application of the Treaty would be desirable. Although welcoming the increased flexibility of the rules for the benefit of applicants and of an increased conviviality between applicants and offices, it nevertheless wished that the simplification would be carried out with due account taken of third party rights and that it would not be to the detriment of comprehension of the Treaty provisions.

The Delegation of Switzerland stated that the draft Treaty as submitted contained numerous provisions of considerable usefulness for users and emphasized that as its main objective. It considered that the great majority of the proposed provisions should be included within the Treaty itself and repeated its wish to see the Treaty adopted as rapidly as possible. While acknowledging that the draft Treaty constituted an excellent basis for discussion, it stated its intention to make various observations during the detailed discussions, particularly as regards Articles 13 and 14, which could be simplified.

The Delegation of the United Kingdom declared that the working documents prepared by the International Bureau offered a very effective summary of the position the Committee of Experts had reached in its discussions so far, and noted with satisfaction that a number of the issues which had been raised in previous meetings of the Committee of Experts were dealt with in the documents. The Delegation commended progress so far and felt the present documents would contribute in a very effective manner. In the view of the Delegation, the Committee of Experts was concerned with, on the one hand, deregulation in favor of removing burdens on applicants and, on the other hand, with obviating problems of legal certainty relating to rights obtained when the patent was granted. The Delegation further noted that the International Bureau had made a strong attempt to relate the issues before the Committee of Experts to the changes and the discussions currently being undertaken within the framework of the PCT. However, the relationship between the provisions of the draft Patent Law Treaty and the Patent Cooperation Treaty would need to be investigated with some care and caution. Furthermore, the Delegation noted with satisfaction that the issue of electronic filing had been placed within the Regulations rather than in an Article in the Treaty. The Delegation announced that it would make further comments at the appropriate time during the discussions and concluded by reiterating that it was seeking effective harmonization on as many issues as it was possible to obtain agreement.

The Delegation of Belgium was favorable on the whole of the draft Treaty and welcomed the efforts undertaken to establish an electronic filing system. It stressed the importance of the link between the draft Treaty and the PCT. As for Article 7(2)(i) relating to mandatory representation for filing translations in the case of regional patents, it considered it useful to link that matter to the question of the certification of translations which was sometimes required. It further wished for various clarifications on the matter of evidence referred to in Articles 5, 8, 9, 10, 11, 12 and 13. The Delegation would like to see a transfer of various provisions in the Treaty to the Regulations. Finally, it stressed the importance of maintaining the one year priority period, which could involve a reservation with regard to Article 15 of the draft Treaty.

The Delegation of Australia stated that it supported the draft Treaty since it avoided unnecessary costs for applicants and reduced the risks for applicants in the various States to loose their rights. The Delegation said that it preferred simple provisions over complex provisions and that it supported any suggestion that went in that direction. Furthermore, it expressed its wish that substantive provisions would be contained in the draft Treaty under consideration.

The Delegation of Indonesia referred to the recommendations made at the third session of the Committee of Experts, in which the need that the format of a national or regional patent application should be in line with the PCT requirements had been clearly stated. In that context, the Delegation informed the meeting that Indonesia had recently ratified the PCT. Its national legislation was currently amended in order to apply the PCT as of September 1997. The Delegation stated that, as a result of the meeting of the Committee of Experts, it would be able to anticipate the features of the regulations and administrative matters to be dealt with by a national office under the PCT.

The Representative of the EPO stated that his organization was more or less content with the present draft of the Patent Law Treaty. He said that aligning the application requirements of the draft Patent Law Treaty with the PCT was an important step forward. This would largely avoid the introduction of additional formality standards, thus facilitating the acceptance of the draft Treaty. Although the EPO would like to see the Treaty to contain more provisions on substance, the Representative said that he believed that the draft before the Committee of Experts was a balanced package and a compromise on which the Committee should go forward.

The Representative of the Japan Intellectual Property Association (JIPA) expressed the support of his Organization for the draft Treaty prepared by the International Bureau. As a user of the patent systems, JIPA welcomed to newly introduced Articles relating to electronic filing because an electronic filing system would reduce a regional disparity between applicants. The Representative declared that the new draft Treaty had become more user friendly since the requirements for an application in the new draft Treaty were fewer than the requirements under the PCT. The Representative of JIPA said that his organization believed that the new draft Treaty covering formalities had a great significance and that it hoped that the Patent Law Treaty covering formalities would be entered into at an early stage. Finally, he said that it was JIPA's position that the discussion of substantive issues of patent law harmonization should be continued.

(a) The Representative of the Japan Patent Attorneys Association (JPAA) identified three aspects of the Patent Law Treaty: first, particular provisions on the Patent Law Treaty; second, provisions on improvement of the PCT; and third, provisions on electronic applications.

(b) As regards the first category, the Representative said that it covered the provisions relating to representation and address for service, extension of a time limit and the belated claiming of priority. The JPAA supported the new Articles providing for an extension of time limits and the belated claiming of priority, since those provisions were minimum requirements. The more flexible approach represented in those provisions was seen to be in favor of the basic principle of sufficient patent protection. As regards representation, the Representative of JPAA referred to the second and third sessions of the Committee of Experts, where JPAA had already stressed the importance of a high quality of a first application. Due to the barrier of language, professional knowledge of practice was considered to be essential in order to obtain sufficient patent protection when an application was filed abroad. The effective cooperation between the national patent offices and the qualified representatives served the maintenance of high quality of application and examination prosecution. From this point of view, Article 7 was acceptable for JPAA.

(c) Concerning the second category of provisions, the Representative said that the PCT had an important function. He expressed JPAA's belief that the PCT was a model of a system which would enable users to prepare an application in a single format. Therefore, maximum improvements in the PCT were considered to be acceptable.

(d) Thirdly, referring to the provisions on electronic applications, the Representative said that his organization had about seven years of experience in filing electronic applications. He considered electronic applications to be very effective for communications between the patent office and patent attorneys. . . .

NOTE: THE "NEW" WIPO PATENT LAW TREATY [PLT]

Years of diligent work by the experts from national patent offices, WIPO, and interested non-governmental organizations culminated in the signing of the "new" Patent Law Treaty on June 2, 2000 by forty-three states and regional intellectual property offices, including the United States, the EPO, EAPO, and ARIPO. The purposes of the treaty are to streamline national patent filing procedures along the lines of the PCT application, reduce requirements for local representation in routine patent application procedures, and to bring the patent systems of the world into the electronic age.

The treaty is characterized as providing no limitations on states with regard to requirements of substantive patent law. Article 2 PLT. (Recall the position of the United States in the previous reading.) The treaty and its rules apply to national, regional, and PCT applications. Article 3 PLT. An applicant may only be required to submit three items in order to receive a filing date: (1) an indication to the effect that the filing is a patent application, (2) identity of the applicant and means of contact, and (3) what appears facially to be a description. The first two items may be required to be in an official language but the description can be in any language. Article 5 PLT. No patent office may make requirements for the form or contents of an application which exceed the requirements of a PCT application, nor may it require formalities in connection with translations or evidence unless it provides a reason for doing so. Article 6 PLT. A patent office may not require the applicant to appoint a local representative for the purpose of filing the application, mere payment of a fee (including a maintenance fee), or where the regulations otherwise prescribe; nor may it require a separate power of attorney document for more than one application by the same applicant. Article 7 PLT. Any member office may exclude paper filings and require electronic filing of patent applications after June 2, 2005, and if it does so, it must make the requirements for the filing of national applications identical to those for PCT applications. Article 8 PLT. A patent may not be revoked for a non-fraudulent failure to comply with specified formalities, Article 10 PLT, and rights of an applicant or patentee may be reinstated after a finding of due care or unintentionality. Article 12 PLT. Under the Agreed Understandings which accompany the treaty, the International Bureau is tasked to create and build an electronic database ("digital library system") of all priority documents. Finally, the PLT Assembly will meet regularly with the PCT Assembly, and it is contemplated that participation in one or the other of the treaties will facilitate participation in both.

NOTES AND QUESTIONS

(1) **Divergent Priorities**. What are the main concerns of the various delegations? Which states are most supportive of the International Bureau's draft and why? How does the position of the United States delegation differ on issues of substance and why? What kinds of issues does the U.S. delegation view as substantive in this supposedly "procedural" treaty?

(2) **Difficult Issues**. From the standpoint of the July, 1997 report, which kinds of issues are likely to be most easy to resolve, and which are likely to be the most difficult?

(3) **A World Patent?** For an idealized vision of how a "world patent" might look, see Michael A. Meller, *Planning For a Global Patent System* 12 WORLD INT. PROP. REP. 210 (1998). Consider the possibility of a world patent in ten, twenty, or thirty years. Given the expertise of the International Bureau of WIPO, the fact that it administers the PCT and has become one of the best-funded and best-equipped U.N. agencies thereby, and the fact that it will be the repository of a digital library system of priority documents, how likely is it that the patent part of the WIPO will transmogrify into a "World Patent Office" [WPO] over time? Or should the United States, Europe, and Japan pursue a trilateral office? Would it be in the best interests of patent applicants in the new millennium to have a one stop address for all their patent filing needs? If so, are there any downsides? If not, why stop there? If the United States adopts electronic filing of all patent applications in five years and refuses to accept paper filings anymore, is there any reason not to have all U.S. applications (including PCT and national applications) filed with the International Bureau and close down the USPTO mail room entirely? What about examination? Who will examine a world patent application? Who will represent the applicant for a world patent?

§ 6.02   Global Trademark Registration Agreements

[A]   The Madrid System

At the global level, there exist two primary agreements facilitating international trademark registration—but the United States has not yet adhered to either such agreement. These agreements are: (1) The Madrid Agreement Concerning the International Registration of Marks, which dates back to 1891 (the "Madrid Agreement"); and (2) the Protocol Relating to the Madrid Agreement Concerning the International Registration of Marks (the "Madrid Protocol"), adopted in 1989. Each of these agreements—which, although related, are separate agreements—establishes a system under which trademark owners in member countries may secure trademark rights in other member countries by a single filing with their home country's trademark office.

JEFFREY M. SAMUELS AND LINDA B. SAMUELS, THE CHANGING LANDSCAPE OF INTERNATIONAL TRADEMARK LAW*
27 GEO. WASH. J. INT'L. L & ECON. 433, 441-454 (1994)

A.   *The Madrid Agreement*

While the United States is a member of the Paris Convention for the Protection of Industrial Property and of several regional and bilateral trademark treaties,[68] the United States is not currently a party to any international trademark registration system. However, an international registration system has existed for over 100 years. Its terms are set forth in the Madrid Agreement Concerning the International Registration of Marks [adopted Apr. 14, 1891] [hereinafter Madrid Agreement]. Almost forty countries, including the Russian Federation, China, and most of Europe are currently members. Under the Madrid Agreement, an international registration by itself confers no substantive rights. [Art. 3(1).] Rather, substantive rights flow from the extensions of protection emanating from the international registration. . . . On average, each international registration is extended to ten countries.

The Madrid Agreement affords member country trademark owners the opportunity to obtain trademark rights in other member countries through a single filing with their home country's trademark office. [Art 1(2).] Under the

---

*Copyright 1994, Jeffrey M. Samuels and Linda B. Samuels; The George Washington University. Reprinted with permission.

[68] *See, e.g.,* Treaty of Friendship, Commerce and Navigation, Apr. 2, 1953, U.S.-Japan, art. X, 4 U.S.T. 2063, 2071; Treaty of Friendship, Commerce and Navigation, Aug. 23, 1951, U.S.-Isr., art. X, 5 U.S.T. 550, 561; Treaty of Friendship, Commerce end Navigation, Aug. 3, 1951, U.S.-Greece, art. X, 5 U.S.T. 1829, 1853; Treaty of Friendship, Commerce, and Navigation, Feb. 2, 1948, U.S.-Italy, art. VIII, 63 Stat. 2255, 2268; Treaty of Friendship, Commerce and Navigation, Nov. 4, 1946, U.S.-P.R.C., art. IX, 63 Stat. 1299, 1308; General Inter-American Convention for Trade Mark and Commercial Protection, Feb. 20, 1929, 46 Stat. 2907, 124 L.N.T.S. 357.

Agreement, the owner of a home country trademark registration, commonly referred to as the "basic registration," may file an international application with its national trademark office designating those other member countries in which extension of protection is desired. [Arts. 3(1), 3*ter*(1).] The international application is then forwarded to the WIPO, which issues an international registration for the mark, publishes the mark in the international trademark gazette (Les Marques Internationales), and forwards the application to the designated countries for examination pursuant to national law. [Arts. 3(4), (5).] Unless a designated country acts within one year to refuse protection, the mark is deemed protected. [Arts. 5(1), (2), (5).] An international trademark applicant may assert a claim of priority under the Paris Convention as long as the international application is filed within six months of the first-filed application. [Art. 4(2).] While the United States is not a party to the Madrid Agreement, a U.S. corporation may obtain multi-national registrations under the Agreement in the name of a subsidiary corporation domiciled in one of the Madrid Agreement countries. [Arts. 1(2), (3).]

B. *Reasons Why the United States Is Not a Member of the Madrid Agreement*

The United States has not joined the Madrid Agreement for a number of good reasons. First, the fact that a trademark owner may not file an international application until after obtaining a home country or basic registration operates to disadvantage U.S. trademark owners because it takes longer to obtain a registration in the United States than in most other countries.[*] Thus, if a U.S. trademark owner and a French trademark owner, for example, were seeking international protection for the same mark, the French owner would almost always win the race for protection.

Second, given the relatively lengthy examination processes followed in the United States, the twelve-month period available to refuse protection to a mark that is the subject of an international registration is considered too short. To meet its obligation under the Agreement, the U.S. PTO would have to give priority to the examination of Madrid Agreement applications. This would result in increased pendency for domestic applications.

Third, the Madrid Agreement includes a provision known as "central attack," which provides that if the home country registration is successfully attacked during the first five years of the term of the international registration, all extensions of protection in the designated countries also fall. [Art. 6(3).] This would have a particularly unfair impact on U.S. trademark owners because many of the possible grounds for attacking U.S. registrations are not available in other countries.[82]

---

[*][Ed. Note: At year end 1996, the average pendency was between fifteen and seventeen months. *See* U.S. DEP'T. OF COM. PAT. AND TRADEMARK OFF., 1996 ANNUAL REVIEW, Tbl. 16, *available at* http://www.uspto.gov/web/offices/com/annual/1996/addinf.html.]

[82]For example, while a prior user of a mark may successfully attack a U.S. registration, prior user rights are not generally recognized in other countries.

Fourth, the only official language under the Agreement is French.[83] As a practical matter, this means that if the United States joins the Agreement, all documents submitted under the Agreement would require translation into French by the U.S. PTO.

Finally, the Agreement provides for a relatively inexpensive fee schedule. Users of the Madrid system would pay substantially lower fees than applicants for U.S. registration. Because the federal registration system in the United States is entirely funded through user fees, U.S. adherence to the Agreement would effectively require U.S. trademark owners to subsidize the examination of applications filed by foreigners under the Agreement.

C. *The Madrid Protocol*

In the early 1980s, the Madrid Union Assembly, the governing body of the Madrid Agreement, requested that the WIPO investigate ways in which a link could be established between the proposed European Community Trade Mark and the Madrid Agreement. The Assembly also requested that the WIPO consider changes to the Agreement that would make it possible for the four non-Agreement E.C. members (Great Britain, Ireland, Denmark, and Greece) to become part of the Madrid Union. These efforts resulted in the "Protocol Relating to the Madrid Agreement Concerning the International Registration of Marks," referred to as the "Madrid Protocol." A diplomatic conference adopted the Protocol in Madrid on June 27, 1989. Though similar in many respects to the Madrid Agreement, the Protocol includes a number of innovations designed to make it possible for the United States and other countries to join the Madrid system.

. . . .

D. *How the Protocol Differs From the Agreement*

. . . .

The Protocol differs from the Agreement in a number of significant respects. First, it provides that an international application may be filed based upon a home country "basic application," or alternatively upon a home country "basic registration." [Art. 2(1).] Given the existence of intent-to-use filing in the United States, U.S. companies would be able to file international applications at a much earlier point in time under the Protocol than under the Agreement and would not be disadvantaged in this regard as against foreign competitors.

Second, under the Protocol, the United States could elect to take eighteen months, rather than twelve months, to enter refusals on international applications. [Art. 5(2)(b).] A country may also apply national law in

---

[83]Regulations under the Madrid Agreement Concerning the International Registration of Marks 78, Rule 7, WIPO Pub. No. 240(E) (entered into force Oct. 1, 1992) [hereinafter Madrid Agreement Regulations].

determining whether a mark is registrable.[105] The Protocol further provides that, for those countries with opposition systems, refusals may be entered after the eighteen-month period provided that the notification of this refusal is made within seven months of the opposition period commencement or within one month of the opposition period expiration, whichever is sooner. [Art. 5(2)(c)(ii).]

Third, while an international registration under the Protocol is still subject to "central attack," [arts. 6(3), (4)], the Protocol provides that if the basic registration or application is successfully attacked during the first five years of the international registration term, trademark owners may transform their extensions of protection in the designated countries into national filings and retain the effective filing date of the international registration. [Art. 9*quinquies*.] Thus, the effect of "central attack" under the Protocol is substantially ameliorated.

The Protocol also provides that member countries may elect to charge their national fees for the examination of applications. [Art. 8(7)(a).] In addition, both English and French are official languages under the treaty.[111]

E. *Proposed Madrid Protocol-Implementing Regulations*

The Protocol contains a number of innovations making it possible for the United States to join an international trademark registration system. Indeed, following the adoption of the Protocol, the Board of Directors of the former U.S. Trademark Association (now the International Trademark Association) adopted a resolution supporting "in principle" U.S. adherence to the Madrid Protocol, "subject to the successful conclusion of efforts to promulgate Implementing Regulations." In sessions held by the WIPO Committee of Experts on the Harmonization of Laws for the Protection of Marks, representatives of the International Trademark Association stressed that the regulations implementing the Madrid Agreement and Madrid Protocol would be acceptable only if they did not unduly disrupt current U.S. trademark law and practice and did not have an adverse impact on national applicants. The U.S. government similarly emphasized that the simplification of administrative procedures was its ultimate goal. The Protocol-implementing regulations largely meet these standards.

Most significantly, the current text of the regulations allows the United States to require any foreign trademark owner seeking extension of protection of its international registration into the United States to allege a bona fide intent to use the mark in U.S. commerce. [Draft Regulations, Rule 9(6)(d).] This feature of the regulations is extremely important to the U.S. trademark community. Absent its presence in the regulations, U.S. adherence to the Protocol would not be possible.

Why is this requirement so crucial to the United States? As part of the Trademark Law Revision Act of 1988, Congress amended section 44 of the U.S.

---

[105]*Id.* art. 5(1), at 21; Paris Convention, art. 2

[111]Draft Regulations Under the Madrid Agreement and the Madrid Protocol 16, Rule 6(2)(i), WIPO Doc. GT/PM/VI/2 (Mar. 18, 1994) [hereinafter Madrid Draft Regulations].

Trademark Act to require foreign trademark owners who seek protection in the United States based on their foreign application or registration to allege a bona fide intent to use the mark in U.S. commerce. The decision of the Trademark Trial and Appeal Board in *Crocker National Bank v. Canadian Imperial Bank of Commerce* [223 U.S.P.Q. (BNA) 909 (T.T.A.B. 1984)] prompted this amendment. The *Crocker* court held that Canadian Imperial Bank, a Toronto-based institution, had filed a valid application for trademark registration in the United States even though it did not allege use of its mark anywhere in the world. Prior to November 16, 1989, a U.S. company could not even file for trademark registration in the United States until it had actually used the mark in commerce. Thus, the amendment to §44 of the Act made the playing field between U.S. and foreign trademark owners more level. U.S. trademark owners now must allege either "use in commerce" or a "bona fide intention" to use the mark in commerce as the basis for filing an application for a U.S. registration. Some inequality remains, however, because only U.S. trademark owners must use their marks in commerce prior to issuance of a U.S. registration. Any change to U.S. trademark law that would result in a return to pre-1988 amendment days is not politically feasible.

The proposed Protocol regulations would not only require foreign trademark owners seeking protection in the United States under the Madrid Protocol to allege a bona fide intent to use the mark in the United States, but would also require Madrid applicants, like applicants for U.S. registrations, to allege under oath or declaration that they believe they are entitled to use the mark in the United States and that no one else has the right to use the mark or a confusingly similar one. [Draft Regulations, Rule 9(6)(d).]

In another important provision of the regulations, the WIPO committed to maintain an electronic database of all international applications and registrations and to make the database available, for a fee, to the general public. This is important to U.S. trademark owners because, under the Protocol, requests for extension of protection may not reach the national offices until nine months after the application's effective filing date.[126] During this period of time, a U.S. business may decide to file a national application covering the same mark which is the subject of the international application, reasonably believing that the mark is free for use. Access to the WIPO database should minimize the number of times that a U.S. business will be ambushed by an international request for extension of protection to the United States that carries an earlier effective filing date.

. . . .

G. *Advantages of the Madrid Protocol*

Although adherence is uncertain at this time, the Protocol is generally viewed favorably in the United States by the business and legal communities.

---

[126]Madrid Agreement Protocol, arts. 4(2), 7(4) (providing a six-month grace period for international registration renewals); Madrid Draft Regulations, Rules 11-13 (allowing a three-month period of time for applicants to correct any deficiencies in their international applications).

Adherence will facilitate U.S. business in its efforts to sell registered products and services in overseas markets. No longer would U.S. business suffer the expense and trouble of filing separate trademark applications in each country in which protection is sought.[148] The Protocol provides a centralized and much-simplified means for securing trademark protection abroad. Under the Protocol, a U.S. business could conceivably obtain protection for its mark in scores of countries through the filing of a single application with the U.S. PTO in a single language [Draft Regulations, Rule 6(2)(i)], with the payment of a single set of fees in a single currency. [Protocol art. 8(1).]

Whether U.S. trademark owners will save money in obtaining protection through use of the Protocol is dependent upon whether the Trademark Office in the designated country enters a preliminary refusal of the application. If it does, little, if any, savings would be realized because the trademark owner would need to retain local counsel to help prosecute the application. However, if no preliminary refusal were entered (a common occurrence in many countries), local counsel would not be needed and savings would be achieved.

While the Protocol does not guarantee savings to the trademark owner in obtaining protection abroad, significant economies of scale would be realized in maintaining protection and assigning rights. As mentioned earlier, the Protocol provides that renewal of an international registration is secured upon mere payment of a fee with the WIPO. For those U.S. companies that protect their marks in a number of countries and that must now file separate renewal applications with each country, practice under the Protocol will greatly simplify the maintenance of their trademark rights and reduce costs.

The same is true of trademark assignments. Under the Protocol, the assignment of an international registration is accomplished through a single request with the WIPO, which will then record the change in the owner's name in the International Register. [Art. 9.] This will significantly improve the current, incredibly complicated, time-consuming, and costly process of assigning trademark rights. Documents are often required to be executed, notarized, and legalized in accordance with each country's law.*

Further, under current practice, an international registration may not be assigned to a U.S. business because under the Agreement (and the Protocol as well), an international registration may not be assigned to one who is not eligible to file an international application. [Agreement art. 9(2); Protocol art. 2(1).] This restriction has an adverse impact on the ability of U.S. firms to transact international business and provides another important reason for joining the Protocol.

Use of the Protocol is not mandatory when seeking trademark protection abroad. Trademark owners in a signatory country may still file directly in each country in which protection is sought [art. 2(1)]; indeed, under certain circumstances, they may find it advantageous to do so.

---

[148]See Madrid Agreement Protocol, art. 2(1). The current need to file applications in each country in which protection is sought requires an applicant to retain local counsel in each jurisdiction and to prepare separate applications for each country.

*[Ed. Note: For recent improvements, see Trademark Law Treaty, discussed supra § 3.01[K].]

ALLAN ZELNICK, THE MADRID PROTOCOL—SOME REFLECTIONS[*]
82 TRADEMARK REPORTER 651 (1992)

It seems quite clear that United States adherence to the Madrid Protocol would likely achieve two results. The first should be a significant cost saving to domestic trademark owners who elect to utilize its provisions in place of separate filings in individual countries, as is the present practice. . . .These savings would, of course, be proportional to the number of adhering countries, but presumably would likely be significant over time. Adherence would also undoubtedly be accompanied by a substantial influx of applications for registrations in the United States on the part of trademark owners from other adhering countries, who likewise would wish to avail themselves of the potential reduction in costs which they are likely to achieve in filing here.

Unfortunately, while the United States Patent and Trademark Office will almost assuredly be burdened with the added examination obligation involved (and trademark owners with significant added clutter of the register) it seems likely that, on the whole, most American trademark owners who file abroad today are unlikely to make use of the Madrid Protocol. The reason for this conclusion is that under our practice the specification of goods or services that will appear in the domestic application, on which the international application will be based, must be narrowly drawn to the specific goods or services in respect of which the mark shall have been used in interstate or foreign commerce of the United States (in the case of applications based on use) or restricted to the particular items or services identified by their common trade names in respect of which the applicant shall have a bona fide intention to use the mark.[2] Since the international application under the Madrid Protocol will have the same specification of goods or services as the United States application upon which it is based, we will have, in effect, transferred our domestic practice in this regard to United States trademark owners' international filings.

It is believed that few if any American companies presently filing applications in foreign countries restrict the specification of goods or services in their applications to the precise articles or services in respect of which they have actually made use or have an intention to use and indeed to do so would be foolhardy in light of the practice in most other countries. In the United Kingdom and some other jurisdictions with British law roots, for example, the concept of what constitutes trademark infringement is limited to uses of similar marks on the precise goods or services specified in a registration. Nevertheless, fairly broad specifications are generally permitted and, as often, employed. In others, where that problem does not exist, there are nevertheless substantial advantages to broad coverage. Accordingly, and since notions of use are largely irrelevant, applications are routinely filed for descriptions of goods or services so broadly drawn as to be wholly unacceptable under our practice. Frequently

---

[*]Copyright 1992, Allan Zelnick.

[2]An additional minor impediment may arise on occasion in that a United States application may not cover all of the goods or servıces of interest because Trademark Rule 2.33(d) provides that one may not include in a single application both goods or services for which there is an intention to use and goods or services based on actual use.

they incorporate not only the goods or services of actual use, if any, but also the goods of prospective use or any goods related to the line of business in which the applicant engages or, indeed, to the entire class heading in some countries. To the extent then that an international application under the Madrid Protocol might be based on an application filed in a country which permits such a broad specification, the applications of United States companies' foreign competitors would give them far broader protection in all other countries adhering to the Madrid Protocol than would the applications of United States filers based upon their home filings.

Under the present system, United States applicants filing in foreign countries most often tailor the specifications of their applications to what is permissible, appropriate and desirable under the practice of each country, thus placing their trademark protection on a par with their competitors in every other country. Indeed, for these reasons, it is not uncommon to forgo the advantages available in claiming the right of priority of their United States applications, which claim would limit applicant to the coverage of the home application. Under the Madrid Protocol system, however, American applicants extending their applications to foreign countries would in many cases be at a distinct disadvantage vis-à-vis their foreign competitors.

. . . .

The . . . Trademark Law Revision Act of 1988—which added the right to file based on a bona fide intention to use the mark here—was intended in large measure to level the domestic playing field as between United States domiciled applicants, who otherwise had to base their applications in their home country on actual use, and foreign applicants who under the Paris Convention had the right to file here not only without use but based on the specification of their home country filings and who also received the benefit of the "constructive" use flowing from the right of priority established under that Convention. While intention to use has not totally leveled that playing field, it has at least substantially eliminated the domestic owner's disadvantage in its own country. The Madrid Protocol, as presently constituted, however, would appear to open a different gap on the international scene, in favor of foreign trademark owners, in the manner described.

What then ought to be the response of the United States to this situation? There appear to be two obvious choices. One is not to adhere to the Madrid Protocol, thus contenting ourselves with the status quo while denying American companies the obvious benefits of international protection at probably considerably reduced cost. The second and clearly more desirable course, is to modify the practice in the Patent and Trademark Office to permit applications to be filed with broader specifications of goods or services than are presently permitted.

The problem here grows from a familiar root. The reasons underlying our present practice with regard to specifications, of course, are exactly the same notions which generated the inequalities flowing from our adherence to the Paris Convention and which were attempted to be rectified by the Trademark Law Revision Act of 1988. That is to say, almost uniquely among countries of the world, we required of domestic applicants actual use prior to filing as a predicate to registration, while Convention applicants were not so constrained.

The reason for that position was the common law concept that without a trade identified by a mark there was not trademark. By continuing our present practice of requiring narrow specifications tailored to the goods or services of actual use or, in the case of intention to use, [that are] intended to be used, we once again, based on the same outmoded concept of what constitutes a trademark, would place domestic applicants under the Madrid Protocol at a disadvantage vis-à-vis their competitors around the world. . . . The result of the *Lemon Tree* decision construing the Paris Convention right of priority made it imperative that we establish a basis for filing which would eliminate the advantages bestowed upon non-United States filers by modifying our notions of what constituted a registrable trademark to include marks intended to be used. So too, it is submitted, we must once again alter our practice with regard to specifications in applications and registrations so as to accommodate our practice to international standards in order to secure for domestic trademark owners the undoubted benefits of the international filing mechanism presented by the Madrid Protocol. While the problems inherent in such a change are not to be underestimated they must be weighed against the benefits of this treaty and, ultimately of conforming our practices and law more closely to that of the international community of industrialized nations.

One must conclude, therefore, that if the United States adheres to the Madrid Protocol such adherence must be accompanied by a contemporaneous modification of our requirements for filing by domestic trademark owners so that nationals of all adhering countries will be playing by the same rules in all countries. In the absence of such a change, adherence to this treaty would seem not only pointless but more than likely, counter-productive.

NOTE: U.S. ACCESSION TO THE MADRID PROTOCOL

On March 14, 2001, the U.S. House of Representatives passed H.R. 741, 107th Cong. 1st Sess., the Madrid Protocol Implementation Act, which would amend the Lanham Act to permit U.S. accession to the Madrid Protocol. (The House had passed identical legislation, H.R. 769 and H.R. 567, in the previous two congressional sessions, but the parallel Senate bills did not make it out of Committee.) A counterpart bill, S. 407, has been introduced in the Senate and referred to the Judiciary Committee. (An identical counterpart was approved by the Senate Judiciary Committee in the last session of Congress.) The legislation, if adopted, would come into effect on the date upon which the Protocol enters into force with respect to the United States. For seven years, the Clinton Administration declined to send the Protocol to the Senate for ratification because of a dispute with the EU regarding voting rights in the governing assembly of the Madrid Union; the EU would receive a separate vote in the Assembly in addition to the votes of its constituent member states. Various compromise proposals were considered. For example, the Secretary of State transmitted a démarche to the European Commission requesting that the EU agree to a compromise voting rights structure based upon the WIPO Copyright Treaty negotiated in Geneva in December 1996; this would permit the EU to participate in the Assembly, but not to cast a vote in addition to votes cast by individual EU member states. *See* H.R. Rep. No. 81, 106th Cong. 1st

Sess. 3 (1999); *see also Madrid Protocol To Enter Into Force Dec. 1, As China Accedes To Treaty*, 50 P.T.C.J. (BNA) 678 (Oct. 12, 1995) (noting possible compromise permitting U.S. applicants access to the benefits of the Protocol based upon surcharge mechanism similar to that available under Patent Cooperation Treaty). While discussion of this and similar compromise proposals continued, congressional action on the legislation was intended to send a signal to the international community that Congress was committed to the United States participating in the Madrid system. Finally, in February 2000, the EU indicated its intent to proceed by consensus in matters before the Madrid Assembly and agreed that, should any vote be required, the EU would first consult with the United States and other like-minded parties in order to develop a common position. The EU also committed that, if a common position cannot be reached after such consultations, it would not cast a block of votes in excess of the number of EU member states. *See* S. Rep. No. 249, 106th Cong. 2d Sess. 3 (2000). This proposal met with the approval of the United States, and the Protocol was sent by President Clinton to the Senate for ratification on September 5, 2000. It was expected that the United States would deposit its instrument of accession with WIPO some time in 2001. But Senate action (either on ratification or on implementing legislation) has now been delayed by the ongoing *Havana Club* rum dispute. *See supra* § 3.01[J]. *See* H.R. Rep. No. 107-19, 107th Cong. 1st Sess. 34-35 (2001).

NOTE: THE MADRID PROTOCOL IMPLEMENTATION ACT

The implementation legislation, H.R. 741, 107th Cong. (2001), would add a new title to the Lanham Act establishing procedures by which the U.S. would become part of the Madrid system. Most importantly for U.S. trademark owners, the owner of a trademark application or registration filed with the U.S. Patent & Trademark Office (termed a "basic application" or "basic registration") would be able to file an "international application" with the PTO requesting rights pursuant to the Madrid Protocol mechanism. The PTO would review the international application for the purpose only of certifying that the information on the international application corresponded to the information on the basic application or registration; after that review, the PTO would forward the international application to WIPO, which would issue an international registration for the mark and transmit the application to all countries in which the applicant requested an "extension of protection" of its international registration. An applicant may seek an extension of protection to any or all of the Contracting Parties to the Protocol. Likewise, of course, applicants in other Contracting Parties to the Protocol would be able to file an international application with their trademark office and request an extension of protection of their international registration to the U.S. In such a case, the International Bureau of WIPO would forward the request for extension of protection to the PTO.

Neither the Madrid Agreement nor the Madrid Protocol harmonizes the national laws of signatory states. Rather, the Madrid system acts as a bridge between different national trademark laws; it is a procedural vehicle by which a trademark applicant may efficiently obtain and maintain rights in as many participating countries as the applicant chooses. A request for extension of protection under the Madrid system is therefore evaluated under the laws of each country in which protection is sought, and substantive rights flow only from the grant of national extensions of protection, not from the international registration as such. Thus, if a U.S. applicant files an international application with the PTO requesting an extension of protection in France and Russia, that request (when forwarded to the respective national authorities by WIPO) will be examined separately under French law by the French Trademark Office and under Russian law by the Russian Trademark Office. If each request is granted, the applicant will hold separate French and Russian registrations.

Similarly, a request for extension of protection in the U.S. will be examined for compliance with the provisions of the Lanham Act. *See* section 68(a). Although registration could not be refused on the grounds that the mark has not been used in commerce, *see id.*, section 66(a) of the proposed legislation would require that any request for extension of protection to the U.S. include a declaration of the applicant's bona fide intent to use the mark in commerce. This requirement comports with the obligations imposed upon applicants under section 44 of the Lanham Act. The legislation would also establish rules for determining the international applicant's priority in the United States; these rules permit reliance upon the six-month priority right accorded by Article 4 of the Paris Convention. *See* sections 66-67. If the request for extension of protection is granted, the extension of protection in the United States will have the same effect and validity as a registration on the Principal Register.

The concept of "dependency" is central to the Madrid system. That is to say, any national extension of protection is dependent upon the continued validity of the international registration, which is itself dependent upon the continuation of the basic registration upon which the international application was first based. The consequence of cancellation of the basic application or registration is, however, less severe under the Protocol than under the Agreement, and this is reflected in the implementing legislation. In the event that an applicant's basic registration or international registration is canceled, Section 70(c) of the proposed legislation would permit transformation and retention of priority to occur provided that the national application is filed within three months after the date on which the international registration was canceled.

The implementing legislation also reflects the limited procedural nature of the Madrid mechanism. For example, the Protocol requires that a renewal filing be made with WIPO every ten years in order to maintain the international registration. Domestic U.S. law imposes more stringent maintenance obligations, and requires the owner of a registration to file an affidavit of continued use between the five and six year anniversary of the registration, as well as upon every ten year anniversary. *See* 15 U.S.C. §§ 1058-1059. The implementing legislation would ensure that, in addition to the maintenance obligations imposed by the Protocol with respect to the international registration, the maintenance obligations under U.S. law continue to apply to those who obtain U.S. rights under the Madrid system. *See* Section 71. Similarly, although the Madrid Protocol permits the assignment of the international registration without reference to any accompanying goodwill, *see*

Protocol art. 9, under proposed section 72 the assignment of any U.S. extension of protection must (like the assignment of any U.S. trademark) be accompanied by the goodwill associated with the mark in order to be valid.

NOTES AND QUESTIONS

(1) **Inter-Treaty Arrangements.** The Madrid Agreement is a "special arrangement" under Article 19 of the Paris Convention, such that states adhering to the Madrid Agreement "constitute a Special Union for the international registration of marks," known as the "Madrid Union." Madrid Agreement art. 1. What are the consequences of such a status? *Cf.* Madrid Protocol art. 14(1)(a). States adhering to the Madrid Protocol are also members of the Madrid Union, Madrid Protocol art. 1, notwithstanding that the Madrid Protocol is an international agreement separate from the Madrid Agreement. Moreover, common regulations governing the operation of the two systems have been promulgated, and it is expected that most (if not all) of the countries that are parties to the Madrid Agreement will become parties to the Madrid Protocol. Three different groupings of states will thus arise: states party only to the Madrid Agreement; states party only to the Madrid Protocol; and, states party to both treaties. Determination of the particular treaty applicable to an extension request is governed by a Safeguard Clause contained in the Protocol. *See* Madrid Protocol art. 9*sexies*.

(2) **Underlying Philosophies.** The structure of the Madrid Agreement can be traced in part to the political fragility of the then just-concluded Paris Union:

> We must remember [the Madrid Agreement] was concluded in 1891, and that the first draft was prepared in 1886. It is curious to note that the primary motive for the adoption of the Agreement then was to consolidate the Union for the Protection of Industrial Property created by the Paris Convention of 1883. After the creation of this Union, a reactionary spirit had developed, especially in France, and there was a serious danger of that country's withdrawal from the Union. France felt that it made too many concessions in becoming a party to the Convention, and it was desired to give to French nationals an advantage which they would not be willing to give up, and therefore would not quit the Convention. French nationals under their own law obtained automatic registration in France by mere filing of an application for registration, and the Madrid Agreement was therefore in effect an extension of the French system giving to French nationals automatic registration in a number of countries.

Stephen P. Ladas, *The Position against Adherence: The Madrid Agreement for the International Registration of Trademarks and the United States*, 56 TRADEMARK REP. 346, 349-50 (1966). To what extent can the Madrid Protocol be characterized as an "extension" of the French (or, now, the EU) system? To what extent, and in what ways, does the Protocol replicate the Agreement's adherence to the philosophy of "dependency," namely, that "an international trademark registration be strictly co-existive and co-extensive with the applicant's home registration." Daniel C. Schulte, *The Madrid Agreement's Basis in Registration-Based Systems: Does the Protocol Overcome Past Biases (Part II)?*, 77 J.P.T.O.S. 729, 731-32 (1995).

(3) **Maintenance Obligations.** Proposed section 71 of the implementing legislation imposes maintenance obligations on applicants seeking extended protection in the United States. What is the purpose of insisting on these additional maintenance obligations? Are they consistent with the letter or spirit of the Protocol? *Cf.* Ladas, *supra*, at 358 (questioning relationship between Madrid Agreement and section 8 of the Lanham Act); *Samuels and Samuels, supra*, at 452 (noting that one Madrid Agreement country, Portugal, requires "the recipient of an extension of protection in that country to file a document every five years attesting to its continued interest in using the mark"). Should the provisions of the Protocol be regarded merely as limited facilitation mechanisms leaving countries free to mold variations that mesh with their existing domestic law? Or should the spirit of the Madrid Protocol precipitate broader and more fundamental reforms of U.S. law? If you were a member of Congress, would you support joining the Madrid system without proposed section 71 in the implementing legislation?

(4) **Effects on the U.S. Trademark System.** Do you agree with former Acting Commissioner of Patents & Trademarks Michael K. Kirk, who testified that the "Protocol will have no effect on the integrity of the U.S. trademark system"? *House Panel Airs Bill to Implement U.S. Accession to Madrid Trademark Pact*, 46 P.T.C.J. (BNA) 94, 95 (May 27, 1993). Some U.S. commentators have argued that clearing marks for trademark applicants will be substantially complicated if the United States were to join the Madrid system. Why might that be the case? What, if any, provisions of the implementing U.S. legislation or Protocol regulations address concerns regarding increased searching costs and difficulties?

(5) **U.S. Accession.** Should the United States adhere to the Madrid Protocol? At the same hearing before the U.S. House Subcommittee referenced above, the former director-general of WIPO, Arpad Bogsch, urged accession, commenting that "the U.S. should be among the first because other countries don't need it as much as you do." *Id.* Other commentators have suggested that "the more sagacious approach would be careful observation of the implications in other member countries of the Protocol." Ian Jay Kaufman, *Draft Regulations, Like Protocol, Lack Answers*, N.Y. LAW JOURNAL, Nov. 13, 1992, at 5. Do some countries gain more than others from the Madrid system? If so, why, and which countries? Would the United States suffer any long-term harms from not joining the Protocol, which was drafted in large part with the previously-expressed concerns of the United States in mind? (Consider the objections of the U.S. State Department to the extra vote of the European Union after re-reading Articles 1 and 10(3)(a) of the Protocol.) What other international initiatives might the United States have considered to remedy what the State Department saw as the inequity of the initial voting rights provision?

(6) **Filing Strategies.** Professor Samuels suggests that in certain

circumstances direct national filing will be more advantageous than using the Protocol mechanism. Would you advise U.S. companies to make use of the Madrid machinery when available, or would you advise continuation of the practice of pursuing separate applications in each country in which a registration is sought? What factors or considerations might affect your advice? Are you persuaded by Zelnick's arguments about the disadvantages to U.S. applicants that flow from U.S. practice regarding the specification of goods in connection with which the registration is sought? *See* Jeffrey M. Samuels, *Letter to the Editor*, 82 TRADEMARK REP. 810, 811-12 (1992) (challenging suggestion that U.S. companies would not use Protocol because of comparatively strict U.S. practice regarding identification of goods on registrations). This problem, if real, would be particularly acute with companies such as those owning entertainment properties, where the company typically would want to reserve a claim to a broad range of goods. Should U.S. practice be modified as suggested by Zelnick?

(7) **Central Attack**. The "central attack" feature of the Madrid Agreement would have been particularly problematic for U.S. companies that sought to exploit foreign markets through licensing arrangements:

> The [Madrid Agreement] contemplates that when an international registration is transferred without a simultaneous transfer of the home country registration, the assignee's rights continue to be dependent on the validity of the assignor's home country registration. Many U.S. firms prefer to exploit foreign markets through licensing arrangements. Such arrangements frequently involve assignment of the right to use the trademark of the U.S. firm. If a French or German licensee of the U.S. firm knows that the right to exclusive use of the U.S. trademark is dependent—for at least five years—on the mark surviving any potential challenge in the U.S. courts, that naturally tends to complicate negotiations. At a minimum, it implies that the prospective licensee would not be willing to pay as large a royalty as when the right to use the mark was less precarious. Under these circumstances, many U.S. firms prefer to obtain separate national registrations in those nations where they plan to do business, despite the accompanying administrative inconvenience.

Roger E. Schechter, *Facilitating Trademark Registrations Abroad: The Implications of U.S. Ratification of the Madrid Protocol*, 25 GEO. WASH. J. INT'L. L. & ECON. 419, 427 (1991).

Do the changes made to the central attack provision in the Madrid Protocol solve these problems, or would you continue to advise U.S. companies that use foreign licensing arrangements to file separate national applications? *See* Madrid Protocol art. 9*quinquies*. *See also* James T. Walsh, *The Madrid Protocol: United States Participation*, 1 INT'L INTELL. PROP. L. & POL. 289, 294 (1996) (describing "transformation" procedure as applied to U.S. extensions).

(8) **Extensions of Protection in the United States**. Would you advise non-U.S. companies to designate the United States as an extension country under

the Protocol, or alternatively would you recommend pursuing a separate U.S. registration application under section 1 or section 44 of the Lanham Act? Although an extension request will be examined according to U.S. law, registration cannot be refused on the grounds of non-use. Does this offer advantages to foreign applicants seeking protection under the Madrid system over those applicants filing a section 44 application based upon a foreign trademark registration? What problems might the asymmetry between U.S. and foreign practice in the specification of goods cause the foreign Madrid applicant seeking extension of protection in the United States? *Cf. In re* Société Générale des Eaux Minérales de Vittel, 1 U.S.P.Q.2d 1296, 1298-99 (T.T.A.B. 1986) (addressing section 44 application), *rev'd on other grounds*, 3 U.S.P.Q.2d 1450 (Fed. Cir. 1987).

(9) **U.S. Participation in Madrid Without U.S. Accession.**   U.S. multinational corporations have access to the mechanisms of the Madrid Agreement or the Madrid Protocol if they have a branch or subsidiary in a signatory state, or if they have a "real and effective industrial establishment" in a signatory state. *See* George F. Souter, *The Right of Nationals of Non-Madrid Union Countries to Own International Registrations*, 17 EUR. INTELL. PROP. REV. 333 (1995).   Relying on the foreign subsidiary to pursue the international registration raises other issues (including ownership of the registration), however, which may complicate later enforcement efforts by the U.S. company in the foreign country. Consequently, many U.S. multinational corporations have adopted a corporate policy specifying that the proprietorship of all intellectual property, including trademarks, shall reside with the parent company. *See* Michelle Michel, *Comparison between the Community Trademark System and the National Registration System—A Multinational Perspective*, Paper Presented at Annual Meeting of International Trademark Association (May 1997) (describing policy of 3M, and explaining why 3M does not use the Madrid systems through its subsidiaries).

(10) **The Pressure to Join Madrid.**   The pressure to join the Madrid Protocol has only increased as more countries of commercial significance have joined the system.   Opponents of U.S. adherence to the Madrid Agreement frequently cited both the absence of many significant commercial nations and the lack of interest shown by U.S. manufacturers in marketing their products in nations that were members. *See, e.g,* Ladas, *supra,* at 353 (noting disinterest of American companies in registering their marks in countries of small commercial significance and in "Iron Curtain Countries"); Eric D. Offner, *The Madrid Agreement and Trends in International Trademark Protection,* 56 TRADEMARK REP. 368, 374 (1966) (making similar claim). The conclusion of the more flexible Madrid Protocol in 1989 not only encouraged additional countries to join the Madrid system; it also coincided with the political and commercial liberalization of the countries of Eastern Europe, broader international efforts to reduce barriers to trade, and huge technological advances that have facilitated international marketing.

(11) **Priorities.**   Is a centralized filing system the priority to which negotiators should devote their primary attention in developing international trademark law? *Cf.* Offner, *supra,* at 378 (suggesting alternatives). Is the most important concern currently facing international trademark owners the need

to obtain easier and cheaper rights in a greater number of countries? Is this objective given too much primacy in assessing the value of the Madrid system in international trademark law? What other concerns might be given too little weight by the structure of that system? *See* Ladas, *supra*, at 350. How have the priorities for trademark owners changed over the last three decades, and why? *Cf. id.* at 358.

(12) **Madrid and Consumers**. Much of the analysis of the merits of the Madrid system has focused on the interests of trademark owners seeking to market products in an increasingly global economy. Yet, trademark law should also take account of the interests of increasingly mobile consumers living in an increasingly global society. In what ways does the Madrid system protect or further consumer interests, and how should that affect whether the United States should join? *See* Schechter, *supra*, at 445-46.

(13) **The Reach of the Madrid System**. The adoption of the Protocol, which entered into force on December 1, 1995, and took effect on April 1, 1996, was motivated by a desire to encourage the United States and other commercially significant nations to join the international fold, and in this regard the Protocol has been a qualified success. Fifty-one countries (including China, Germany, the United Kingdom and Japan) are now parties to it, and the EU is planning to become a party as a separate trademark-registering intergovernmental organization. *See* Protocol art. 14 (any intergovernmental organization may become party to the Protocol if it has a regional office for the registration of trademarks in the territory of the organization or at least one of the members states of that organization is a party to the Paris Convention). Upon EU accession, an applicant will be able to use a Community Trademark Registration, *see infra* § 6.05[A], or application as the basis for an international application, or may designate the EU as a jurisdiction in which extended protection is sought. It was initially thought that EU accession would be relatively routine, but the amendment of the Community Trademark Regulation necessary to accommodate Protocol-related applications and permit accession has been stalled by internal EU disagreements, including objections by Spain to the language regime under the Protocol (English or French). *See Proposal for Council Regulation Modifying Regulation 40/94 on Community Trade Mark*, 1996 O.J. C300/11. Is a system of regional trademarks, connected through the Madrid mechanisms, the optimal apparatus for international trademark registration? What advantages might flow from such a system over a Madrid-based linking of purely national registrations or (on the other extreme) the development of a supranational "global" mark (even if such an utopian ideal were achievable)?

(14) **Language**. As is perhaps reflected in Spain's objections to EU accession to the Protocol, the official languages of the Protocol disadvantage many countries where the first language is neither English nor French. For example:

> out of ten countries in South America, nine speak Spanish and one Portugese. All Central American countries speak Spanish and one of the North American countries, Mexico, also speaks Spanish. Only

three countries in Continental America—Brazil, Canada and the United States—speak a language different from Spanish. In addition, other languages are used in small countries in the Carribean Basin.

José Barreda, *The Madrid Protocol: Does it Require a Revision?*, 118 TRADEMARK WORLD 29, 30 (June 1999). Should Spanish (or any other languages) be added to the official list of Protocol languages?

[B]   The Trademark Registration Treaty

DANIEL C. SCHULTE, THE TRADEMARK REGISTRATION TREATY*

. . . .

After the most recent revision of the Madrid Agreement (the MTA), [and before the conclusion of the Madrid Protocol], many interested parties realized that no modification of the MTA would be sufficient to entice U.S. membership. The World Intellectual Property Organization, at the prompting of the United States, began drafting a new treaty independent of the Madrid Trademark Agreement. The result was the Trademark Registration Treaty (the TRT), concluded on June 12, 1973, and entered into effect on August 7, 1980.

The drafters of the TRT understood how provisions of the MTA unequally affected nationals of different potential member countries. They made a concerted effort to account for the interests of both registration-based and use-based trademark systems, by creating a new agreement, independent of the Madrid system. Still, the TRT and the MTA are to some unavoidable degree, similar. Debates over the TRT involved several of the same issues debated in considering the MTA, including dependency, use requirements, and proliferation of deadwood on national registers.

As a substantial improvement over the MTA, the TRT eliminated dependency of an international registration upon a home registration. Under the TRT, an international trademark applicant files an original international trademark application directly with WIPO in Geneva. This original registration is independent of a home registration. With this improvement, the drafters of the TRT overcame the MTA's favorable treatment of countries like France, which posed the least hurdles to a home registration.

Also eliminated by the TRT was the possibility of central attack. Because of the profound complications involved with this issue, the TRT simply includes no central attack provision. . . .

Unfortunately, what the TRT achieved by eliminating dependency and central attack, it lost with the Non-Use Proviso. The TRT's Non-Use Proviso dictates

---

*Excerpted from Daniel C. Schulte, *The Madrid Trademark Agreement's Basis in Registration-based Systems: Does the Protocol Overcome Past Biases? (Part II)*, 77 J. PAT. & TRADEMARK OFF. SOC'Y 729, 748-51 (1995). Copyright 1995, Daniel C. Schulte. Reprinted with permission.

INDUSTRIAL PROPERTY ACQUISITION MECHANISMS   CH. 6

that once a mark has been registered, it cannot be refused or canceled for nonuse for at least three years. In other words, member states are not allowed to enforce a use requirement, but can require at most that trademark applicants declare an intention to use a mark. As a consolation to use-based systems, member states were given the option to prohibit infringement suits until after a mark was used. Still, a restriction on use requirements contradicted the basic American use-based philosophy. To accept the TRT the U.S. would have had to simultaneously abandon its long-standing prior use requirement. Many U.S. trademark interests were not amenable to such a "drastic change in United States Trademark Law."

Considered in a more positive light, proponents of the TRT saw the Non-Use Proviso as an opportunity to modernize American trademark law. The time had come, they argued, for the U.S. to finally adopt an intent to use standard.

In the end, the United States never ratified the Trademark Registration Treaty. Despite its positive accomplishments of eliminating central attack and dependency, and allowing efficiency through centralized filing, the overall provisions of the TRT were not sufficiently improved over the MTA to entice U.S. ratification. The elimination of dependency and central attack were major steps forward in the evolution of international trademark agreements. But from the viewpoint of the United States, the critical substantive difficulty was the Non-Use Proviso. For the above reasons the TRT, although signed by the U.S., was never ratified. Today, the TRT is of little practical value.

QUESTIONS

(1) **Historical Lessons.** In what ways was the Trademark Registration Treaty different from the Madrid Protocol? With hindsight, which agreement would have been better as the premier international trademark registration agreement from the United States' standpoint? What do you take from the reasons offered for the United States' failure to adhere to the TRT? *Cf.* TRIPS art. 19; 15 U.S.C. § 1127.

(2) **Adherence to Madrid?** Reconsider the question posed above regarding the effect of U.S. non-adherence to the Madrid Protocol—drafted in large part to accommodate the United States, and with U.S. observers involved—after reading the discussion of the motives behind the Trademark Registration Treaty.

§ 6.03 Global Design Deposit Agreements: The Hague Agreement

The Hague Agreement Concerning the International Deposit of Industrial Designs has been in place for 75 years. It establishes a mechanism, not unlike that of the Madrid Agreement and Protocol for trademarks, by which an applicant may make a single deposit of a design with its country of origin or with WIPO and request protection in any number of countries that are members of the Hague Agreement. The United States is not currently a member of the Hague Union; existing texts of the Hague Agreement, the most recent of which is the 1960 Act (the "Hague Act"), were crafted to cater to countries that do not carry out substantial examination of design registration applications and thus rely essentially on a deposit system. For the last several years, WIPO has been supervising efforts to conclude a revised version (a new "act") of the agreement. This new act has been drafted with a view to persuading other countries (such as the United States, Japan, and the United Kingdom) to join the system, and it was concluded at a diplomatic conference in July, 1999 in Geneva (the "Geneva Act"). In this Section, we consider the basic features of the existing Hague system, and the issues raised by the most recent revision process.

PIERRE MAUGUÉ, THE INTERNATIONAL PROTECTION OF INDUSTRIAL DESIGNS UNDER THE INTERNATIONAL CONVENTIONS[*]
19 U. BALT. L. REV. 393, 397-400 (1989)

The institution of an international registration of industrial designs was the subject of a wish expressed by the Washington Diplomatic Conference in 1911. It was not until November 6, 1925, however, that the Hague Agreement was adopted. That Agreement, which constitutes a "special agreement" within the meaning of article 19 of the Paris Convention, took force on June 1, 1928, and has been revised several times. Depending on the contracting state, the provisions of substance that currently apply are those of the 1934 and 1960 Acts. This Article focuses on the provisions of the 1960 Act which were finalized by the 1967 Act.

The principle of international deposit of industrial designs arose from the need for simplicity and economy. Its main purpose was to enable protection to be obtained for one or more industrial designs in a number of countries through a single deposit filed with the International Bureau of [WIPO].

Under . . . the Hague Agreement, any person entitled to effect an international deposit may obtain, by means of a single deposit, protection for his industrial designs in a number of countries involving a minimum of formalities and expense. Consequently, the applicant is relieved of the need to make a separate national deposit in each of the countries in which the design requires protection, and avoids the inherent complication of procedures that vary from one country to another. The applicant does not have to submit the required documents in various languages or keep watch on the deadlines for renewal of a whole series of national deposits. Also avoided is the need to pay a series of national fees and agents' fees in varying currencies.

Under the Hague Agreement, the same results can be obtained through a single deposit made with a single office, in one language, on payment of a single set of fees, and in one currency. Presently, there are twenty-one member countries of the Hague Union established by the Hague Agreement.[**]

[**][Ed. Note: As of April 15, 2001, there were twenty-nine members of the Hague Union.]

Any national of a contracting country can make an international deposit, and an international deposit does not require any prior national deposit.[23] One makes an international deposit directly with the International Bureau of WIPO, through the depositor or his representative on a form provided . . . by the International Bureau. [Alternatively, the international] deposit may be effectuated . . . through the national office of a contracting country, if the law of the country so permits.

The law of a contracting country also may require, in cases where that country is the state of origin, that the international deposit be made through the national office of that country.[25] Noncompliance with this requirement, however, does not prejudice the effects of the international deposit in the other countries. The international deposit has the same effect in each of the countries for which protection is requested, as if the designs included in the deposit had been deposited directly in that state on the date of the international deposit, subject to the special rules established under the Hague Agreement. This is true particularly in regard to the term of protection.

. . . Any contracting country whose domestic legislation offers the possibility of refusing protection as the result of an *ex officio* administrative examination, or of opposition by a third party, may refuse protection for any industrial design, if it fails to meet the requirements of its domestic law.

Refusal of protection may not, however, extend to the formalities and other administrative acts that are to be considered by each contracting country as having been accomplished at the time the international deposit is recorded at the International Bureau. . . .

The national office of a contracting country must notify the International Bureau and . . . the depositor on the refusal to publish the deposit within six months of the date on which the national office received the periodical bulletin in which the international deposit was published. The depositor has the same remedies against the decision to refuse protection that he would have had if he had deposited the refused design at the national level with the office of the country that refused protection. If the refusal is not noted within the applicable six-month period, the international deposit then achieves the same status as a deposit entered in the national register of each of the countries for which protection has been requested.

International deposits are published by the International Bureau in a monthly periodical called the *International Designs Bulletin*. This publication includes a reproduction of the article or articles in which the deposited designs are to be incorporated. . . .

---

[23]A "national" is any natural or legal person having the nationality of one of those countries included in the Union or any individual having his domicile, headquarters, or a real and effective industrial or commercial establishment, in one of those countries.

[25]The state of origin is to be understood as the state party to The Hague Agreement in which the depositor has a real and effective industrial or commercial establishment, or where the depositor has such establishments in more than one state party to the Agreement, the state he has designated in the application or, failing this, the state party to the Agreement in which he has his residence (or headquarters), or failing this, the state party to the Agreement of which he has the nationality.

The depositor may request that publication be deferred for a period not to exceed twelve months from the date of the international deposit or, where appropriate, from the date priority is claimed. The owner of an international deposit enjoys the priority right afforded under article 4 of the Paris Convention, if he claims this right and if the international deposit is made within six months of the first national, regional, or international deposit made in one of the countries party to the Paris Convention, or if he makes a deposit having effect in one of those countries.

An international deposit is made for an initial term of five years, and can be renewed at least once for an additional period of five years for all or part of the designs included in the deposit, or for all or only some of the countries in which it has effect. For those contracting countries whose domestic legislation allows a term of protection greater than ten years for national deposits, an international deposit may be renewed more than once.

In each case, a renewal may be made for an additional period of five years, with effect in each country up to the expiration of the total allowable term of protection for national deposits under that country's domestic legislation. . . .

The working languages for the implementation of the Hague Agreement are English and French. International deposits and any amendment affecting the deposits are entered in the international register and published in English or French. Correspondence between the International Bureau and the depositor is drafted in English or French, depending on the language used in completing the application for the international deposit. . . .

The offices of the contracting countries have no specific tasks in the implementation of the Hague Agreement except in those cases where the domestic or regional legislation of the country permits or requires the international deposit to be effected through them or calls for a novelty examination for deposited designs.

WILLIAM T. FRYER, SEEKING A BENEFITS BALANCE IN THE INDUSTRIAL DESIGN TREATY REVISION (HAGUE AGREEMENT): FIFTH MEETING OF EXPERTS, HELD JUNE 13-16, 1995[*]
77 J. PAT. & TRAD. OFF. SOC'Y 931, 941-942 (1995)

EU members [participating in the Hague revision process] recognized that the [existing text of the] Hague Agreement was based on design protection systems that did not examine for novelty (non-examination systems). These national systems were characterized by relatively prompt formalities review and publication of the design. Rights were established from the filing date, usually. If there was a novelty question, it was raised by a third party after registration.

The Hague Agreement members have received prompt design protection with only a formality view by WIPO, using a system modeled after their non-examination systems. The first Hague Agreement Act (1934) did not allow for refusal by a member country after WIPO formality review. The 1960 Act attempted to accommodate novelty examination countries by allowing a six months refusal period.

Examination countries, in sharp contrast, do not award a design right until completion of an extensive examination, including novelty and adequacy of the design reproduction. This examination process is the reason for the extended time . . . now in the draft treaty for refusal of IDR effect. Even after the first office action which reports the results of a novelty search, the concern for issuing only valid design protection requires that new issues can be raised in subsequent stages before the right is granted. Design protection in examination countries will occur only after two or more years from filing, usually . . . Even with the current U.S. effort to reduce the time it takes to obtain a design patent, it will never be as short a period as the time to obtain a registration in non-examination countries.

. . .

In summary, there are two basic types of design protection systems in the world. The current Hague Agreement members are trying to accommodate examination systems while retaining the benefits of the current Hague Agreement which was set up primarily for non-examination systems. If there is significant flexibility allowed in this integration, the two systems can be interfaced to achieve benefits currently received by Hague Agreement members.

FRANÇOIS CURCHOD, THE REVISION OF THE HAGUE AGREEMENT CONCERNING THE INTERNATIONAL DEPOSIT OF INDUSTRIAL DESIGNS[*]
24 AM. INTELL. PROP. L. ASS'N Q.J. 599 (1996)

I. INTRODUCTION

The Program of [WIPO] for the 1996-97 biennium provides that "the International Bureau will prepare, convene and service in 1996 a session of a committee of experts on the preparation of a new treaty on the international registration, with WIPO, of industrial designs." . . .

. . . .

II. THE TWO OBJECTIVES OF THE REVISION

The draft new Act ("the new draft"), which will be discussed by the Committee of Experts in November 1996, has been prepared with two main objectives in mind: first, expanding the geographical scope of the Hague system for the international registration of industrial designs; and, second, making the Hague system a more efficient instrument for obtaining protection for industrial designs in more than one country, especially for the design-intensive industries, and in particular the textile and fashion industries. These two objectives are not always immediately compatible. Expanding the geographical scope requires the accommodation of at least the basic requirements of States whose law requires the examination of applications as to substance. Such an accommodation, in turn, requires, for example, the extension of the time period allowed for the refusal of the effect of an international registration. This extension, in turn, runs contrary to the desire of various industries, particularly those in which product cycles are short, to obtain protection as quickly as possible.

In addressing the first objective of expanded geographical scope, the approach adopted in the drafts considered by the Committee of Experts to date has involved the addition of a further layer to the procedure under the 1960 Act of the Hague Agreement. This further layer would apply only where an applicant seeks protection in a Contracting Party whose law requires the examination of applications as to substance. The adoption of this approach is based on an understanding that the purpose of an international registration treaty, such as the Hague Agreement, is to facilitate, through one centralized procedure, the procurement of protection in all the Contracting Parties rather than to harmonize the legislation of those Contracting Parties. It is to be noted that this approach was contested in previous sessions of the Committee of Experts on the ground that it allows nationals of countries having relatively complicated national systems easy access to design protection in countries having simpler systems (based upon a mere deposit), without any reciprocal concession on the part of the former countries.

III. THE TWO-CHAPTER SYSTEM

The new draft maintains this approach but, in accordance with the discussions that took place during the fifth session of the Committee of Experts, it consists, apart from two introductory provisions, of two Chapters. Chapter I provides for a simple and quick system of protection of industrial designs desired by future Contracting Parties that do not have, or do not intend to maintain, a substantive examination system. Chapter II contains additional requirements, some or all of which would have to be complied with by applicants designating Contracting Parties that have, and intend to maintain, a substantive examination system.

There would be limits, however, placed on the registration requirements for "Chapter II Contracting Parties." . . .

. . . .

IV. OTHER MAIN FEATURES OF THE REVISION

The other main features of the revised system for the international registration of industrial designs under the Hague Agreement envisaged by the new draft are as follows:

. . . .

(3) Subject to any requirements concerning security clearance in the applicable national or regional law, applicants may file an international application, at their option, either directly with the International Bureau or indirectly through the intermediary of the Office of a Contracting Party. The international application would be accorded a filing date, which would be the date of its receipt by the International Bureau, when the international application is filed with the International Bureau. When the international application is filed indirectly, the filing date would be that of its receipt by the intermediary filing Office, provided that the Office transmits the international application to the International Bureau within one month of its receipt by the Office. The revised system does not envisage any role on the part of an intermediary filing Office in checking the formalities of the international application. Rather, the formal examination would be undertaken by the International Bureau in the case of applications filed either directly or indirectly. However, if at the time a Contracting Party becomes bound by the new Act its law requires the review of applications for the purpose of granting security clearance, the Office of such a Contracting Party, when serving as an intermediary filing Office for an international application, would not transmit applications to the International Bureau before the application has first been reviewed for this purpose. In such cases, the period of one month allowed for the transmission of an international application from the intermediary filing Office to the International Bureau may be extended to three months without affecting the filing date. At the request of the Delegation of the United States at the Committee of Experts, a provision was made to allow for an extension of this period up to six months without affecting the filing date, provided that the Office concerned (for all practical purposes, the United States Patent and Trademark Office) notifies both the International Bureau and the applicant that, due to the security clearance, the three-month time limit cannot be respected. If the applicable time limit—one month, three months, or six months, as the case may be—for the transmission of the international application to the International Bureau is not observed, the filing date will be the date on which the International Bureau receives the international application.

(4) In order to accommodate some of the varying requirements of the different national and regional systems for the registration of industrial designs, the revised system envisages three different categories of requirements in an international application:

(a) The first category covers the requirements that all international applications, regardless of which Contracting Parties are designated, must satisfy in order to register in the International Register the industrial design that is the subject of the international application. The requirements in the first category correspond to those requirements which would need to be satisfied in all Contracting Parties in a national (or regional) application for a filing date to be accorded to the national (or regional) application under the law of each of those Contracting Parties.

(b) The second category covers certain additional requirements specified in Chapter II that must be satisfied in an international application when Contracting Parties having those requirements are designated. These additional requirements are limited to those imposed by the Contracting Party, in addition to the requirements in the first category, for the grant of a filing date in a national (or regional) application received by that Party's Office. In addition, these requirements are only applicable with respect to Contracting Parties whose Offices examine applications as to substance and who impose them at the time that they enter into the treaty. In the interest of keeping the international system as simple as possible, the list of those additional requirements is limited in the new Act itself.

(c) The third category covers certain additional requirements that must be satisfied in certain Contracting Party States in order to ensure that the international registration is given the effect of a national (or regional) registration. They are not, however, mandatory requirements for the purposes of the international application. An international registration may be obtained with respect to all Contracting Parties on the basis of an international application that does not satisfy these requirements (assuming, of course, that the requirements of the first and, where appropriate, second categories are satisfied). Rather, the requirements in the third category correspond to requirements under the national (or regional) law of the designated Contracting Parties that must be satisfied, not for the purpose of obtaining a filing date, but for the purpose of the grant of protection. Failure to satisfy any such requirements in the international application may form the basis for a refusal, on the part of the concerned designated Contracting Party, to recognize the effect of the international registration. These additional requirements will be specified in the Regulations under the new Act as optional requirements that the applicant may wish to fulfill in the international application in order to avoid unnecessary refusals from the Offices of Contracting Parties having such requirements.

(5) The date of an international registration would be the filing date of the international application, subject to provisions requiring the postponement of the date of international registration in the case of certain irregularities.

(6) The international application may contain a request for deferment of publication. A flexible system is provided with respect to deferment of publication in order to accommodate differing national (or regional) approaches to deferment. Essentially, where an international application contains a request to defer publication, publication would be deferred for the shortest period of deferment recognized under the applicable laws of all of the designated Contracting Parties. Thus, for example, if two Contracting Parties were designated, and they recognized under their applicable laws deferment of publication for periods of twelve and twenty-four months, respectively, publication of the international application would be deferred for a period of twelve months. In any case, the maximum period of deferment of publication is thirty months. It is also possible that a Contracting Party refuses to recognize deferment of publication under its laws. If an international application containing a request for deferment of publication designated such a Contracting Party, the applicant would be notified by the International Bureau that deferment of publication would not be possible with respect to that designated Contracting Party. If the applicant did not withdraw the designation of that Contracting Party within a certain time limit, the request

for deferment of publication in the international application would be disregarded by the International Bureau.

(7) Designated Contracting Parties may refuse to recognize an international registration. The normal period allowed to communicate a refusal is six months, but may be extended up to thirty months[*] by a Contracting Party whose Office examines applications as to substance. However, the possible grounds for refusal are limited.

(8) In order to accommodate differing national (or regional) approaches to the stage at which protection commences, Contracting Parties must recognize an international registration as having two different effects, which may commence at different times. First, from the date of international registration, each designated Contracting Party must recognize an international registration as having the same effect, including prior art effect, as a regularly-filed application for the grant of protection. Second, the international registration must be recognized by each designated Contracting Party as having the same effect as a grant of protection under its applicable law as of a date no later than the expiration of the period allowed to communicate a refusal (assuming that a refusal has not been communicated by the concerned Contracting Party).

(9) The provisions on fees contain two features designed to attract wider participation in the revised system:

(a) The first feature is designed to ensure that Contracting Parties whose Offices examine applications as to substance are adequately compensated for the work involved in the examination of an international registration. It allows Contracting Parties to replace the standard designation fee payable to each Contracting Party by an individual designation fee, the amount of which is determined, subject to certain limits, by the Contracting Party.

(b) The second feature is designed to make the revised system attractive to applicants seeking deferment of publication in order, inter alia, to determine whether or not to proceed with the international registration upon the expiration of the deferment period. Only a prescribed portion of the international registration fee must be paid at the time of filing the international application, the balance being payable two months before the expiration of the deferment period.

(10) Each designated Contracting Party must recognize a minimum period of fifteen years, subject to renewal, from the date of international registration to the expiration of the period of protection obtained through international registration. Any designated Contracting Party whose applicable law allows for a longer period of protection must recognize the equivalent, longer period of protection.

(11) A saving provision is included to confirm that the new Act would not affect any other equivalent or greater form of protection accorded by the applicable law of a Contracting Party, any protection accorded to works of art

---

[*][Ed. Note: In the final version of the Geneva Act, this extended period for refusal was set at twelve months after receipt of the IDR from WIPO. *See* Geneva Regulations, Rule 18].

or works of applied art by international copyright treaties and conventions, or any protection accorded to industrial designs under [TRIPS].

. . . .

WILLIAM T. FRYER, SEEKING A BENEFITS BALANCE IN THE INDUSTRIAL DESIGN TREATY REVISION (HAGUE AGREEMENT): FIFTH MEETING OF EXPERTS, HELD JUNE 13-16, 1995[*]
77 J. PAT. & TRADE. OFF. SOC'Y. 931, 944-946 (1995)

The draft text [considered by the Fifth Meeting of the Committee of Experts in 1995 allowed] a reservation for a member to retain the prior art effect of an IDR as other than from its Paris Convention (Convention) date. [1995 Draft Act art. X.] U.S. law, under the *In re Hilmer* [359 F.2d 859 (C.C.P.A. 1966)] decision, gives a Convention application prior art effect from the U.S. filing date.

It is hard to draw a line between substantive and procedural provisions, but prior art effect is primarily substantive. Since the Hague Agreement revision has the purpose of procedural uniformity, prior art effect should not be a topic for discussion. Each country should have its national law apply. In most of the current Hague Agreement countries prior art effect is from the Convention filing date. Consequently, current members desire to harmonize this important feature.

Prior art effect has been a hotly contested issue in connection with harmonization of utility patent law. It has carried forward to the Hague Agreement revision. Since this issue could not be resolved during the more extensive utility patent negotiations, it is unlikely that Hague Agreement discussions can make any greater progress. The fact that U.S. law on prior art effect applies to utility and design patents makes it even more unlikely that a change can be made only for designs, without resolving beforehand all the utility patent law harmonization issues.

The U.S. has consistently stated at the Hague Agreement meetings that the principle of prior art effective date for U.S. design patents could not be changed. Draft text article X was prepared by WIPO for consideration, to make it clear that the U.S. could retain its current law under *Hilmer* by reservation. In fact article X is not needed, as the revised treaty states that national law will apply and, therefore, prior art effect under current U.S. law would be retained. [1995 Draft Act art. 10.] Article X merely restates this fact and highlights it as a disputed topic. . . .

The concern over U.S. law on prior art effect may not be as serious as some may think. A review of U.S case law suggests that prior art effect of a IDR will be from the WIPO publication date, under 35 U.S.C. § 102(a) for most registrations.[36] For deferred registrations, the question of prior art effect will need to be analyzed further. It appears that when the IDR is sent to the PTO, the date it is received would complete the file and establish the effective U.S. filing date under 35 U.S.C. § 102(e) and the *Hilmer* decision.

While the *Hilmer* law will remain in force, the prior art effective date for an IDR will be earlier. It is not as early as the Convention filing date for prior art effect, but it is closer to a harmonization approach. There is a possible six months gap for the Convention based IDR, but in most situations design filings take place quickly and the practical loss of time for prior art purposes should not be of significance. Non-deferred applications filed directly with WIPO will have about a three months gap until prior art effect under U.S. patent law, the time between filing and IDR publication.

Foreign practitioners have a valid point when they state it is better sometimes to file a national design application directly to receive prior art effect at the earliest time. This step avoids the use of a Convention application and the *Hilmer* restriction, but it does not utilize the convenient centralized filing under the Hague Agreement.

The Patent Cooperation Treaty (PCT) incorporates the *Hilmer* law, and in spite of this fact it has been very successful. An application filed under PCT receives prior art effect on receipt in the PTO of the international application.[37] The fact that PCT use has grown suggests that filing in a centralized design system, like the Hague Agreement, will have sufficient benefit to attract members, even if the *Hilmer* barrier exists.

NOTES AND QUESTIONS

(1) **Structure of the Geneva Act.** The system established by the Final Act signed on July 2, 1999, in Geneva is in substance largely as described by François Curchod three years earlier. (The most significant substantive change was the reduction, from thirty months to twelve months, of the extended period for countries with Examining Offices to notify any refusal to register a design.) The act was not, however, neatly divided into two chapters. *Compare* Basic Proposal For The New Act of the Hague Agreement Concerning the International Registration of Industrial Designs (Submitted by Director General, WIPO, Dec. 15, 1998) with Geneva Act of the Hague Agreement Concerning the International Registration of Industrial Designs (July 2, 1999). Although a separate set of provisions was included to address the role of

---

[36]The Federal Circuit settled, in *In re Carlson*, 983 F.2d 1032 (Fed. Cir. 1992), the issue of whether a third party unpublished foreign design registration was patented prior art under 35 U.S.C. § 102(a). The Federal Circuit followed the holding of In re Ekenstam, 256 F.2d 321 (C.C.P.A. 1958). The Federal Circuit held that Section 102(a) required public access to the patent document. Another case taking the same position was Ex parte Winter, 144 U.S.P.Q 124 (Pat. and Trademark Off. Bd. of App.). An IDR publication is prior art from its publication date under 35 U.S.C. § 102(a), if prior to the invention date.

[37]35 U.S.C.A. § 363 (West Supp. 1995); M.P.E.P. § 1895.01(1).

Examining Offices, these are interwoven through the final Agreement. *See, e.g.,* Geneva Act art. 5(2) (setting out additional mandatory content requirements for application designating country with Examining Office); Geneva Regulations, Rule 18 (providing countries with Examining Office longer time in which to notify refusal of registration).

(2) **Place of Deposit.** Article 4(2) of the 1960 Act allowed contracting states to require their nationals seeking to use the Hague Agreement to make an international deposit through their national office rather than directly. The Geneva Act does not allow states to deny use of the direct deposit with WIPO, *see* Notes on the Basic Proposal for the New Act of the Hague Agreement Concerning the International Registration of Industrial Designs (WIPO, Dec. 15, 1998) at 7, although a state may still decline to offer use of its office as an intermediary for indirect deposit. *See* Geneva Act art. 4(1)(b). Why might this change have been made?

(3) **Multiple Design Registration and the Locarno Agreement.** One of the most significant aspects of the Hague Agreement is that, like most of the non-examination countries that comprise the Hague Union, it permits registration of multiple designs in the same classification class under the Locarno Agreement in a single registration. *See* Geneva Act art. 5(4); Geneva Regulations, Rule 7(6) (all products to which the designs in the same international application are to be applied must be in the same class under the Locarno Agreement). In an examination country, such as the United States, multiple design registrations have traditionally not been allowed; under the new Act, such countries may not refuse protection on the ground that the international application includes several designs, except if the designs that are the subject of the same application do not conform to a requirement of "unity of design." *See* Geneva Act art. 13. Why is the possibility of a multiple design registration important? And why have examination systems generally not permitted such registrations? *See* Fryer, *Seeking a Benefits Balance, supra,* at 947.

The Locarno Agreement, signed in 1968, established a classification system for industrial designs. The United States was a party to this treaty at its inception, but later withdrew, and thus U.S. design patents for several years included both the international classification and the U.S. classification. Although a state may adhere to the Hague Agreement without being a member of the Locarno Union, *see* Notes on the Basic Proposal for the New Act of the Hague Agreement Concerning the International Registration of Industrial Designs (WIPO, Dec. 15, 1998) at 5, the multiple design registration provision relies upon the Locarno system, in that only designs that fall within a single International Classification subclass can be included in the application. Geneva Regulations, Rule 7(6). If the United States joins the Hague system, this mandatory reference to the Locarno system might prompt reconsideration of whether to participate in the Locarno Agreement.

(4) **Contents of Hague Application.** In order to obtain a filing date, a Hague application must comply with a series of mandatory content requirements as well as with the specific requirements of the contracting states (so-called "additional mandatory" content requirements) designated as countries in which protection is sought. These additional requirements come from states

with an administrative examination of novelty (termed "Examination Offices"). The United States had indicated in negotiations that the only additional requirements from Article 5(2)(b) of the Geneva Act that it will impose are a claim and the name of the creator of the design. Determinations that the application satisfies the requirements of the Hague Agreement as to form and content are to be made by WIPO. Once the IDR is received by the designated countries, it will be examined as would any domestic application. Thus, the United States PTO would subject the IDR to the same examination process as it would a domestic design patent applicant. The grounds for refusal will be determined by U.S. law, with the exception that refusal cannot be based on noncompliance with a requirement relating to the form or content of the international application. *See* Geneva Act art. 12(1). For example, a designated state cannot require applicants to provide a translation of the application into a language that is not required by the agreement. Any notification of refusal to register must be communicated to WIPO within six months, or twelve months in the case of countries (such as the United States) with Examining Offices. *See* Geneva Regulations, Rule 18. What developments in the U.S. design patent application process might cause the PTO to issue a refusal to register? *See* Notes on the Basic Proposal for the New Act of the Hague Agreement Concerning the International Registration of Industrial Designs (WIPO, Dec. 15, 1998) at 16-17.

(5) **Deferred Publication**. One of the most significant issues over the course of the negotiation has been how to handle international design registrations for which the applicant has requested deferral of publication (as the Hague Agreement permits, *see* Geneva Act art. 5(5)). In particular, these registrations impede a proper analysis of prior art in those countries undertaking a full novelty examination. Under the Geneva Act, a copy of a deferred registration will be forwarded to each office designated in the IDR application, but the receiving office will be required to treat it as confidential. Which other parties or interests are threatened by the existence of deferred publication IDRs? *See* Geneva Act art. 10(5)(b) (identifying persons to whom and circumstances in which, subject to confidentiality obligations, the Office may divulge the contents of an IDR requesting deferred publication).

(6) *Hilmer*. The Geneva Act did not expressly address the issue of the *Hilmer* doctrine. Are you persuaded by Professor Fryer's arguments both that the express provision (1995 Draft Article X) was not needed to permit U.S. application of the doctrine, and that the *Hilmer* doctrine has very little effect on parties' rights? *See* Geneva Act art. 14; PTO Notice Inviting Public Comment on Hague Agreement on Industrial Designs, 64 Fed. Reg. 19135, 19138 (Apr. 19, 1999) (suggesting that identically-phrased antecedent of Article 14 conflicted with *Hilmer*); Letter from Margaret Boulware, President, American Intellectual Property Law Association, to PTO, (May 6, 1999) (rejecting PTO interpretation).

(7) **Entry Into Effect**. The Geneva Act will enter into effect three months after six states, including at least three "active design" states (i.e., states that received a prescribed number of design filings in the last set of annual statistics), deposit instruments of ratification. *See* Geneva Act art. 28(2). This provision is based upon Article 63(1) of the Patent Cooperation Treaty. What objectives does it serve: why not simply condition effectiveness upon any six

states adhering to the new act? *Cf.* Notes on the Basic Proposal for the New Act of the Hague Agreement Concerning the International Registration of Industrial Designs (WIPO, Dec. 15, 1998) at 34 (listing states that would satisfy conditions for "active design states"). Article 31 makes the standard provision for relations between states party to different acts of the Hague Agreement, essentially mandating the application of the most recent text (1999, 1960 or 1934) to which both states are party. Examine the different variations referenced in Article 31: is there any relationship that is not addressed? *See id.* at 35.

(8) **The Status of the EU.** Both states and certain intergovernmental organizations may become party to the agreement. *See* Geneva Act art. 27(1)(ii). The principal organization that might take advantage of this provision are the EU, when the Community Design Regulation is in place, and the African Intellectual Property Organization ("OAPI"). It is also possible that the African Regional Industrial Property Organization ("ARIPO") might become a party. *See* Notes on the Basic Proposal for the New Act of the Hague Agreement Concerning the International Registration of Industrial Designs (WIPO, Dec. 15, 1998) at 31 (noting possible argument that the 1982 Harare Protocol establishes a system of registration of industrial designs that meets Article 27 standards). As with several recent treaty negotiations, the issue of separate intergovernmental organization (largely, EU) voting rights was a sticking point in concluding the Geneva Act. Eventually, a compromise was agreed. Although the EU may participate in the assembly of the Hague Union in addition to its constituent states, Article 21(4)(b)(ii) provides that

> any Contracting Party that is an intergovernmental organization may vote, in place of its Member States, with a number of votes equal to the number of its Member States which are party to the Act, and that no such intergovernmental organization shall participate in the vote if any one of its Member States exercises its right to vote, and vice-versa.

(9) **Term.** One of the areas where the Hague Agreement has attempted substantive harmonization has been the term of protection. Early versions of the agreement contained minimum and maximum terms; the 1960 text contained a minimum term of ten years. Article 17(3) of the Geneva Act adopts a fifteen-year minimum IDR term, which will be measured from the date of the international registration? Does the U.S. design patent term satisfy this obligation? *See* 35 U.S.C. § 173; Geneva Act art. 10(2) (date of international registration).

(10) **Textile Designs.** Design patents are the primary means for protection of clothing shape (as opposed to two-dimensional patterns) in the United States, and thus the ease of design patent protection impacts TRIPS compliance by the United States regarding special attention to the needs of the textile industry. *See* TRIPS art. 25(2). If you were arguing for U.S. adherence to the Geneva text based upon its capacity to enhance protection for textile designs, which features of the system would you identify as particularly important? *See* Geneva

Regulations, Rules 12(2), 16(3), Geneva Act arts. 5(1)(iii), 5(4).

(11) **U.S. Adherence**. The United States has participated vigorously in the negotiation of the Geneva Act (although WIPO officials have noted that the United States also participated in the diplomatic conference leading to the 1960 act). Industry and the intellectual property bar in the United States have been generally supportive of U.S. adherence. Would you support adherence to the new act?

§ 6.04 Regional Patent Registration Agreements

[A] Europe

[1] Historical Perspective

Sixty years ago, an observer noted that substantive patent examination tended to be strict in Germany, medium in the United States, liberal in Britain and free and easy in Latin countries. *See* EMERSON STRINGHAM, PATENTS AND GEBRAUCHMUSTER IN INTERNATIONAL LAW 142 (1934). "Britain occupied a midway position between Germany, the Netherlands, and Switzerland, on the one hand, vis-à-vis France, Belgium, and Italy on the other. It provided for a limited search and examination together with the possibility of third party opposition on somewhat wider grounds." WILLIAM CORNISH, INTELLECTUAL PROPERTY: PATENTS, COPYRIGHT, TRADE MARKS AND ALLIED RIGHTS 76 (2d ed. 1989). Was there ever to be a common ground? The first den of activity for substantive harmonization of patent law has been on the European continent.

LEONARD J. ROBBINS, THE PROPOSED NEW EUROPEAN PATENT[*]
5 PAT., TRADE., & COPR. J. OF RESEARCH AND EDUC., 217-232 (1961)

2. PRIOR PROPOSALS FOR COMMON PATENTS

In 1909, Du Bois-Raymond of Germany first suggested a single world-wide patent. During the First World War, uncompleted steps were taken for common patents in Germany and Austria. In 1919, proposals for a single patent covering the British Commonwealth died in the discussion and conference stage. On November 15, 1920, an Arrangement for an international patent was actually concluded in Paris and was signed by eleven countries. However it never went into practical effect. During the height of the Second World War, from 1941 to 1943, a number of detailed proposals for a single European patent were published in the German periodical *Gewerblicher Rechtsschutz und Urheberrecht* [GRUR]. In 1946, Kucera of Czechoslovakia and in 1949, Longchambon of France offered proposals for the creation of a single European

---

[*]Copyright 1961, by PTC Research Foundation and Franklin Pierce Law Center. Reprinted with permission.

Patent Office. Since 1952, the governments of the Scandinavian countries [considered] the possibilities of a common patent while retaining the national laws and patent offices. . . .

3. Prior Proposals For Harmonization of Patent Laws

The Treaty of Rome emphasizes the desirability of harmonization of the national laws of the member states in all fields. It is well known that Article 85 of the Treaty is exceedingly vague as regards patents, but it is generally agreed that the general principle of harmonization does apply to patent laws. However, harmonization ha[d] been under consideration long before the Common Market came into being. In fact, the broad idea actually goes back to 1883 when the International Convention for the Protection of Industrial Property was established. Among the numerous countries adhering to the International Convention much conformity has been achieved since then by voluntary amendments of national patent laws, but basic differences still remain.

[In] 1947, the governments of the Benelux countries—Belgium, Holland and Luxembourg—[began] studying the possibility for uniformity of their three patent laws. . . . Also, in 1947, the Benelux countries and France established the Institut International des Brevets (International Patent Institute) at the Hague as a central agency for the novelty examination of patents. The purpose [was] to relieve the burden from national patent offices and avoid duplication of effort. . . . In 1951, Dr. Reimer, the then President of the German Patent Office, proposed a single filing system using national patent offices, with extension to other countries, a centralized novelty examination, and various modifications of national procedures to take place over a period of years in successive steps. In 1954, three other comparable proposals along generally similar lines were made by Dr. Reimer himself, by Mr. de Haan, President of the Dutch Patent Office, and by Dr. Was, a Dutch patent attorney.

In 1958, the heads of various European patent offices, at a meeting in Vienna produced the "Vienna Plan" for a so-called joint application. In the same year, CNIPA, a committee of European national patent associations, submitted a slightly different but comparable plan.

There [were] still other proposals, all of them, like those previously mentioned, of a non-official or at best semi-official origin, and none of them under the aegis of an official international organization having the political power of action. . . .

The basis of harmonization is the preservation of national patent laws. But in the six countries of the Common Market (and in fact throughout Europe) there are two systems. In the civil law countries, France, Belgium, Luxembourg and Italy, patents are granted on the basis of simple registration by payment of a government fee ("*Sans guarantie du Gouvernement*" as explicitly printed on a French patent). In some of them there is an examination of certain formalities, but this is not of basic interest. The scope of patents in these non-examination countries can only be determined by the courts if the patents are litigated. On the other hand, in Germany and Holland, patent applications are submitted to a rigorous patent office examination for novelty, inventive height and advance in the art, followed by availability for opposition by third parties.

In the German and Dutch Patent Offices, the sheep are separated from the goats before grant. There is an inference even if not a presumption of the validity of such patents and they are difficult to upset.

As a result, during the last 100 years or so, separate bodies of case law leave been built up involving widely different attitudes towards interpretation, validity and infringement. . . .

4. THE ORIGIN OF THE NEW PROPOSAL FOR EUROPEAN PATENTS

The management of big technological industry in Europe—that is, industry involved in mass production (so rapidly acquiring U.S. techniques) and particularly the steel and non-ferrous metals industries, the electrical industry and the chemical industry, led or at any rate urged on primarily by German interests—has become impatient with the basic problems, and the complexities of possible compromises involved in harmonization. It considers that some form of political and legal federation of European countries is not too far over the horizon, and when this comes it wants a strong autonomous patent system already in existence. . . . What has happened appears to be as follows.

Starting some time during 1959, the powerful and tightly organized inner group applied pressure at the governmental level and used the already established machinery of the Common Market to introduce a concept which is actually outside the provisions of the Rome Treaty—namely, an autonomous European patent to be established by a new Treaty or Convention and to extend throughout the territories of adhering states.

It is true that the powers of the governing and executive bodies of the Common Market are exceedingly broad. However, it is difficult to find a mandate in the Rome Treaty for creating a new supranational industrial property right. What is to be the status or fate of national patents? Numerous legal commentators have interpreted Article 85 of the Rome Treaty to mean that legitimate uses of national patents are excluded from the rules applying to restrictive business practices. Article 36 has been interpreted as sustaining national sovereignty over patents. Seemingly there is no authority whatever to suppress national patents. In any event, for obvious practical reasons, national patents could not suddenly be abolished. Therefore the new proposal includes the reservation that national patents should remain and coexist indefinitely with European patents. Presumably if and when political federation is achieved many national laws will be superseded by unitary laws. Thus, on this distant day, the proposed Convention for European patents may in fact become the single patent law of the new superstate.

At the end of 1959, the Commission of the Common Market started its machinery moving to put this plan into effect. The Commission is the executive body charged with ensuring the functioning and development of the Common Market.

The Commission controls a Committee of Coordination, which, as a first step in February, 1960, appointed Dr. Haertel, an official of the German Ministry of Justice, to prepare a report on the feasibility of the plan and to make proposals for its implementation.

5. THE HAERTEL REPORT

The lengthy Haertel Report was finished by the fall of 1960. It [was] rumored that much preliminary work had already been done, and that representatives of German industry were consulted. . . .

He first considered three possibilities–

(a) A European patent obtained by extending a patent granted in one country to the others;

(b) A European patent granted by any of the national patent offices having full examination;

(c) A European patent granted by a new European authority under more severe conditions than any national patent.

In view of serious practical objections to the first two possibilities, Haertel considered his mission to be confined to the third possibility of creating an autonomous European patent, which would not be just the sum of national patents, but which would co-exist with the national patents. He emphasized that his task was not harmonization but the creation of a new right.

A.

1. *Extent of Inventions to Be Protected*

(a) Inventions against public order and good morals not patentable,

(b) Inventions the exploitation of which would be contrary to specific domestic laws permissible (with reservations),

(c) Pharmaceutical process patents permissible,

(d) Independent product protection for chemical and pharmaceutical products questionable, but generally approved,

(e) Independent protection for food products approved,

(f) Plant patents—possibly.

2. *Concept Of Novelty*

After a long discussion of limited novelty and absolute novelty, more strict or less strict than existing national concepts, Haertel conclude[d] that the standard of novelty for the European patent should correspond to the most severe national laws.

3. *Technical Progress*

After discussing whether this should lie a requirement at all and analyzing existing national viewpoints, Haertel's conclusion [was] that technical progress—*i.e.* advance in the art—should be a requirement for the European patent but considers that a new European judicial authority rather than the European Patent Office may be necessary for examination of this criterion.

4. *Inventive Height*

Haertel . . . propose[d] that inventive height should be essential for patentability—at the German level or even stricter.

5. *Territorial Coverage*

The European patent must cover all the territory of the countries involved and not be divisible in effect.

6. *Scope of Patent*

This is a long section reviewing problems of deferred examination after grant, full preliminary examination before grant, claims as defining the scope of the patent, nullity and infringement. His conclusion is that these problems should be resolved to provide a strong European patent, else scope of which should not be subject to the uncertainties of litigation in the courts throughout its life. His proposals are given in the following sections.

B. GRANT WITH OR WITHOUT PRELIMINARY EXAMINATION

Haertel consider[d] novelty the most important feature for the European patent. In view of the uncertainty in scope of simple registration patents, an official novelty examination [was] recommended, which industry also agree[d was] the ideal procedure. . . .

C. NULLITY

Since the European patent w[ould] be an autonomous right, it c[ould] not be nullified in any one country only. Nullity requirements are different in the various countries—*erga omnes* in some, *inter partes* in others. Therefore for uniformity a separate European authority will be necessary for nullity proceedings.

D. INFRINGEMENT

At first sight a separate European authority for infringement proceedings appear[ed] the ideal solution for uniformity of decision. But this would [have been] impractical in view of the volume of litigation for a single court. Therefore Haertel propose[d] that proceedings in the first instance should be in the national courts, with appeal to a European authority. . . .

. . . .

F. CREATION OF EUROPEAN PATENT OFFICE

The problems of administration, permissible languages, and location.

G. USE OF THE HAGUE INSTITUTE

According to its constitution, as established by the treaty setting it up, the Hague Institute would not be suitable as an office for granting patents. However it could be used for making novelty searches, if search and novelty examination are divided, which would then be used by a separate novelty examination organization having the power to grant or validate patents.

H. EUROPEAN JURISDICTION

This discusse[d] the establishment of a new European judicial patent tribunal (as distinguished from a European Patent Office).

I. PERSONAS HAVING THE RIGHT TO BE GRANTED EUROPEAN PATENTS

Proper applicants would be both nationals and *ressortissants* of the adhering States.

. . . .

K. ACCESSION OF THIRD PARTY COUNTRIES

This section merely discusses possibilities. What are to be the limits and requirements? Any country? Countries of the International Convention? Countries in the Council of Europe?

L. VIS-A-VIS THE INTERNATIONAL CONVENTION

Haertel argues that the establishment of a new European patent system would not be in conflict with the provisions of the International Convention.

M. OTHER TREATIES

Haertel assert[ed] that a new independent treaty creating the European patent would merely take its place alongside various other independent treaties such as the Benelux and Euratom Treaties.

He regard[ed] the European patent as a base patent with possibilities of extension to "*associated countries.*" He discusses the meaning of true accession to the new European Patent Convention and "*association*" by virtue of Art. 238 of the Rome Treaty.

N. CONCLUSION

The European patent w[ould] definitely require a separate European Patent Office to be created in steps. The new treaty establishing the European patent can be regarded as a *particular arrangement—see* Art. 15 of the [Paris] Convention.

. . . .

7. PROTOCOL OF THE SECRETARIES OF STATES OF THE COMMON MARKET COUNTRIES

At Brussels, in December, 1960, the Secretaries of State of the six Common Market countries placed their stamp of approval on the project in a protocol of which the following is a summary with trademark and design references deleted.

The Secretaries of State have studied the conclusions of the Coordination Committee, and have noted two fundamental principles—

(a) The contemplated simplification and unification in the field of patent rights can only be realized by a new Convention.

(b) The restricted extent of the dispositions in the Rome Treaty concerning industrial property, and the possibility of adhesion by third party countries, implies that this new Convention must exceed the scope of the Rome Treaty and must therefore be submitted to the governments of the individual countries for ratification.

They have also noted that the Coordination Committee proposes on the one hand to harmonize national legislation (notably for chemical, pharmaceutical and food processes and products) and on the other hand to study a Convention for patents. It will prepare common rules and define the functions of the organizations granting these rights.

Concerning general principles, they recognize:

1. The European rights should coexist with national legislation, which will be retained with the reservation of eventual necessary harmonization.

2. The European rights will be autonomous and not a juxtaposition of national rights.

3. The preliminary draft of the Convention will propose independent administrations and jurisdictions.

4. Existing obligations (e.g. the [Paris] Convention) will not be contravened.

5. The new Convention will be open to adherence of third party countries with unanimous approval of member countries.

6. Third party countries could adhere to a part only of the Convention—by association established with each of them.

7. The European patent will be autonomous and granted lay an independent international organization working on else basis of searches made by the Hague Institute. Infringement will lie handled in the national courts and nullity in an international court.

8. Ultimately to facilitate adhesion of third party states to the new European Convention, the President of the Coordination Committee should inform representatives of interested countries concerning tile orientation and advancement of the work of the Committee.

8. THE PRELIMINARY DRAFT OF THE EUROPEAN PATENT CONVENTION [EPC]

A Working Group was then immediately formed comprising representatives of the six Common Market countries. It is significant that the President of this Working Group is Dr. Haertel. It is also significant that the majority of the representatives are officials of the Ministries of Justice or Ministries of Economic Affairs of their respective countries, and that Patent Office officials are a small minority.

The drafting has proceeded very rapidly and very secretly. Several unofficial international groups have endeavoured to secure an entree to the Working Group as consultants or as observers at the sessions of the Group, but without success. There is some purely informal or semi-official contact between the national representatives in the Working Group and "outsiders" in their own countries, and possibly some proposals and criticisms thus filtered in may have some effect on the internal deliberations of the whole Group.

A preliminary draft of the Patent Convention was ready early in 1961. This was complete in broad outline, with some articles fully prepared and others very tentative, including remarks concerning the differences of opinion within the Group. As can well be imagined, the principal bones of contention involved–

(a) The nature of the examination—*i.e.* full preliminary examination before grant or some form of deferred examination. The national representatives in the Group split several ways on this question; there is some indication that the final proposal *may* provide for an initial novelty search for record, and a deferred examination for patentability.

(b) The admission of third party states by so-called "partial adherence" or "association." Apparently only a small minority of the national representatives supported full adherence only. The others favored some form of compromise participation in view of the interpretation of the obligations of the International Convention. . . .

As regards the draft Convention as a whole, many European lawyers privately consider it is basically very impressive and sound—a distillation of the best European concepts and experience. It naturally contains many provisions which are more or less fundamental and standard in the patent laws of all major countries: it contains others which to some extent go beyond or modify the provisions of existing national laws. . . .

9. General Comments and Speculations

. . . .

Ultimately the Convention in final form will be submitted to each of the six countries of the Common Market for ratification; possibly several years from the present time. Thereafter there may be very long delays before regulations are prepared, personnel recruited and the new system is actually operative. The year 1970 is being mentioned among European sources as a target date—though they all say it may be sooner in view of the extraordinary and unexpected vitality of the Common Market generally.

Present predictions are that European patents will be difficult and expensive to obtain if the contemplated high standards for patentability are initiated and maintained. Therefore, they are likely to be confined to inventions of major importance. Furthermore both large and small industry may continue to take out national patents as a form of insurance in the event that they are unable to secure grant of a European patent.

As distinguished from the United States, European countries have always objected to non-use of patents and have employed compulsory licensing and possible revocation as a remedy. A new situation may arise with the European patent, since working in any one of the adhering states may be sufficient to render it free from attack. If in the future most of the other European states should adhere to the new Patent Convention in addition to the original six, then the European patent will indeed become massive and invulnerable.

However, it may still be hedged around with antitrust provisions. In recent years there has been a rapid growth in Europe of anticartel and antimonopoly legislation and control of restrictive business practices. The regulations under Articles 85-89 of the Rome Treaty are now being formulated and are likely to include wide powers to prevent uses of patents for restrictive purposes, which may have correspondingly greater effect on broad European patents than national patents.

10. The Position of the United States

Any state which adheres to the new European patent convention obviously cedes a small amount of sovereignty. It seems unlikely that the U.S. Senate would agree to ratify a Treaty whereby an industrial property right obtained abroad by foreign nationals would extend over U.S. territory, and be subject to litigation in a supra-national court. However it is not at all certain that even the possibility of full adherence would ever be offered to countries outside continental Europe, and in any event unanimous consent of the original six countries of the Common Market would be necessary.

The possibilities of simple association as referred to above are clearly highly interesting. There may be political reasons in Europe for desiring both full adherence and also simple association by third party states, but there may also be very strong opposition from European business, particularly medium and small business, to granting such powerful rights to third party countries on a non-reciprocal basis.

If it is impossible for the United States to become a full adhering member of the European Patent Convention, it would of course still be permissible, as at the present time, for U.S. applicants to obtain national patents. However there might be some disadvantages, particularly when negotiating with European interests if the latter were the only ones able to hold broad European patents. At the same time, operating European subsidiaries of U.S. corporations would apparently be in the position of legitimate *ressortissants* and would be able to obtain European patents. But the ownership would presumably have to remain with such subsidiary, since assignment to the U.S. parent corporation could be regarded as a subterfuge: this would raise numerous policy problems.

If actually the United States could join the European Patent Convention on a simple associate basis, then clearly U.S. applicants would be in substantially the same position as European applicants; there would be strong inducements for obtaining European patents on important inventions, but national patents would still be of interest. . . . It will be interesting to find out if any broad U.S. viewpoint will develop and whether this in turn can have any influence on the future course of events in Europe.

. . . .

NOTE: CONVENTION ON THE UNIFICATION OF CERTAIN POINTS OF SUBSTANTIVE PATENT LAW ON PATENTS FOR INVENTIONS ("STRASBOURG UNIFICATION CONVENTION")

The 'Haertal Draft' of 1962 was followed by the proposal of the Council of Europe in 1963 for a Convention on the Unification of Certain Points of Substantive Patent Law on Patents for Inventions (hereinafter called the "Strasbourg Unification Convention" to distinguish from the "Strasbourg

Classification Convention" of 1971). *See* Ind. Prop. 13 (1964). "Patentable inventions" had been defined in the Haertal proposal as follows: "European patents will be granted for new inventions capable of industrial use and resulting from inventive activity." The definitions of patentable invention of Article 1 of the Strasbourg Unification Convention, for exceptions from patentability of Article 2, for "novelty" under Article 4, and for "industrial application" under Article 3 were subsequently incorporated directly into corresponding articles 52, 53, 54, and 57 respectively of the EPC. The definition of "inventive step" of Article 5 of the Strasbourg Convention did not make reference to "a person skilled in the art" (as does Article 54 EPC), nor did it make mandatory the EPC Article 54's provision that the contents of a previously filed European application may be considered part of the state of the art only for purposes of determining the existence of novelty—not for the purposes of determining the existence of an inventive step. Nor was there a requirement that there be an "advance" in the art (what Robbins refers to above as "technical progress") in order for there to be found an inventive step. *See generally* HANS ULLRICH, STANDARDS OF PATENTABILITY FOR EUROPEAN INVENTIONS: SHOULD AN INVENTIVE STEP ADVANCE THE ART? (1977). Ullrich observes that the Strasbourg Convention became the "least common denominator" which influenced the formulation of the law of validity in the EPC and Community Patent Convention [CPC] (see below). But it did not itself enter into force until 1980. Nor did it evoke much comment or opposition at the time of its drafting "due to the necessity of strong departure from law of Switzerland and Germany, where advance in the art has been cherished as an indispensable standard of patentability." *See id.*, at 2. The U.K. set up the Banks Committee in 1967 to study the implications of ratification of the Strasbourg Convention. Subsequent to the proposal of the Strasbourg Convention but prior to its enactment, France abandoned its registration system for patents in favor of a search with examiner commentary in the French Patent Law of 1968. Ullrich also noted that the French "*activité inventive*" in articles 6(2) and 9 of the French Patent Law of 1968 is the non-obviousness standard. The draft of the European Patent Convention appeared in 1965. A flurry of new patent legislation appeared throughout Europe in the decade following the Strasbourg Convention and the first EPC draft, including the Uniform Scandinavian Patents Act of 1968 and the U.K. Patents Act of 1977.

[2] The European Patent Convention (EPC)

The European Patent Convention ("EPC") was signed on 5 October 1973 in Munich. It created a single granting system under the administration of a new organization, the European Patent Organization ("EPO"), supervised by an Administrative Council consisting of representatives of the member States (usually national patent office officials.). The EPC is a special agreement under the Paris Convention (EPC Preamble) which provides free accessibility and national treatment and right of priority (EPC Articles 87-89) in compliance with Article 4 of the Paris Convention. The EPC qualifies as a regional patent treaty under Article 45 of the Patent Cooperation. An applicant may file a PCT application to obtain a European patent in all the contracting parties, all of whom are also contracting parties of the PCT. (*See* Part X of the EPC for special rules on the PCT). The EPC has been amended only once (Article 63) since it entered into force; and the difficulties in amending the convention have had an impact on further developments.

The EPO is an autonomous and self-supporting intergovernmental organization which is completely independent of the EU. It is recognized as an intergovernmental organization under Article 9 of the Budapest Treaty on the International Recognition of the Deposit of Microorganisms for the Purposes of Patent Procedure. The TRIPS Agreement is not directly binding on the EPO, although the standards of the EPC are in compliance with the patent provisions of TRIPS. The relationship of the EPC to the laws of member States (the "legal framework"), the TRIPS Agreement, and the European Union is explored in the following case.

LENZING AG'S EUROPEAN PATENT (UK)
[1997] R.P.C. 245 (Ch. D. 1996) (UK)

JACOB, J.

INTRODUCTION

An Austrian company, Lenzing AG, apply for a variety of forms of relief arising out of allegations that a European Patent Office Board of Appeal (BoA) mishandled an opposition to their patent and wrongly ordered or, as Lenzing say, purported to order, that it be revoked. They seek judicial review of the BoA's decision and judicial review of the decision of the Comptroller-General of the British Patent Office to mark the U.K. Register of Patents with an entry to the effect that their patent has been revoked. Those are proceedings in the Crown Office of the High Court. By way of alternative attack Lenzing invoke the jurisdiction of the Patents Court to order rectification of the entry in the Register of Patents. Also in the Patents Court Lenzing's principal (but not only) commercial adversaries, Courtaulds Fibres (Holdings) Ltd. and other Courtaulds companies seek an order dismissing Lenzing's claim for infringement . . . on the ground that the patent has been revoked. Lenzing resist that, contending that the revocation of their patent is a nullity. . . .

It is first necessary to explain the legal framework of the problem. Until 1978, a patent for an invention in the U.K. could only be obtained by application to the U.K. Patent Office. The procedures for this were laid down in the Patents Act 1949 and the Rules made pursuant to the rule-making power conferred by the Act. Ultimately any decision adverse to an applicant could be the subject of appeal to the Patents Court. Patents in other countries had to be obtained by applications to the national patent office of each country concerned. This was widely regarded as wasteful. . . .

Accordingly in 1973 a number of European countries entered into the European Patent Convention (EPC). This set up the European Patent Office (EPO) in Munich. The 1977 [U.K.] Patents Act was passed, as its recital says, "to give effect to certain international conventions" of which the EPC was one. I described the broad effect of the position prevailing after the 1977 Act came into force (mid-1978) in Aumac Limited's Patent ([1995] F.S.R. 501) as follows:

> One can obtain a patent in this country by one of two routes. One can simply apply to the British Patent Office who will process the application and if all goes well grant the patent. One can also or alternatively apply to the EPO. This operates as a central processing patent office for the states parties to the EPC. In making one's application there, one must "designate" the states in which one wants a patent. Once the EPO grants a patent it takes effect in each designated state in the same way as a patent from the national office of that state. A patent granted by the EPO which takes effect here is called a "European patent (UK)." There is provision that one cannot at the same time have a patent granted by a national office and the EPO for the same invention. The EPO patent prevails and the corresponding national patent must be revoked. But this happens only when the EPO grants the patent. Until then one can process an application through the two systems simultaneously. Once the EPO has granted a patent, there is a system of "opposition" (really revocation) which is operated by the EPO whereby it is possible to apply within 9 months of grant to have the EPO patent revoked. If it is, the revocation works for all designated states—a central "knock-out" system.

Lenzing's patent has been knocked out centrally. Can they challenge that . . . at least so far as the U.K. patent is concerned? That is what I have to decide.

The patent concerned is (or was) No 0,356,419. . . .Opposition was entered in the EPO . . . within the 9 month period from grant provided for by Article 89(1) of the EPC. On 6 May 1994 the Opposition Division orally announced its decision, refusing the opposition. It gave its reasons on 4 July 1994. The opponents appealed to the BoA, to which appeals lie pursuant to the provisions of Articles 106-111. . . . The BoA received written submissions. It held an oral hearing. . . . In accordance with its usual practice (. . . often criticized), following an adjournment of an hour or so, it announced its decision. The patent was revoked. . . .

The fact of revocation was recorded. . . . There is no attempt to attack that entry in these proceedings. The decision was duly communicated to the Comptroller-General of Patents who caused an entry to be made in the U.K. register. . . . The communication took the form of the supply of the information on a tape or disc which the Comptroller simply ran to alter the electronically kept Register. He did not purport to exercise his discretion.

Meanwhile proceedings had started in the Patents Court. . . . The revocation of the patent intervened. Courtaulds now apply for the action to be dismissed and for their costs of the action and petition.

Lenzing say that the written reasons for the decision show that there was a serious procedural injustice. In particular they say that the reasons were never put to them, either at the hearing or before, and were not argued by the opponents...

Lenzing further say that the decision was irrational or perverse, misunderstanding and misconstruing both the cited prior art and their patent. And they say that the BoA made up its mind in advance of the hearing and that such was admitted by the Chairman of the Board in a conversation with their patent agent. This makes the procedural misfeasance allegations all the more serious: The claim is that the Board knew in advance of the grounds of their proposed decision, yet deliberately kept it back. Lenzing say that if they had known of the point, they could have answered it or offered suitable amendments to their patent to deal with it.

Lenzing say the result of the events which they allege is that the decision of the BoA should be regarded as a nullity. They accept that judicial review will not lie against the impugned decision itself (because of the immunity of the EPO from process) but, they say, that does not prevent a collateral attack. They make that attack in three ways....

THE MAIN ARGUMENT

. . . .

[Lenzing] say that Parliament only requires a European patent (UK) to be treated as revoked if that revocation is in accordance with the EPC.... Or, put slightly differently, if a party here ... seeks to rely upon an order of revocation in the EPO it is open to the patentee to rebut the prima facie conclusion that the patent has been revoked by showing that the tribunal ordering revocation ... did not act in accordance with the Convention.

. . . .

[So] anyone who consulted the EPO register and said "The patent is gone for all Europe: I need not bother to look at national registers" would be misled. And even more seriously, anyone who in reliance on the revocation as being final has made an investment accordingly (either by way of direct investment in plant or R&D or on the stock market) would be adversely affected.

Lenzing accept that all [of] that follows from their argument. Nonetheless they boldly submit that Parliament did intend that there could be inquiry by way of collateral attack here.... Further, they say, it would require very strong language indeed for Parliament to exclude an inquiry into the lawfulness of what was done to deprive a party of a U.K. property right. They say no such language is used here....

It is, I think clear . . . that the "opposition" procedure was and is really regarded so far as the Convention is concerned as part of the grant process. It is somewhat Pickwickian to described a post-grant attack on a patent as "opposition" but the word does convey the notion that one is concerned with the early life of the patent. Hence the fact that the attack must be within 9 months of grant. The founding fathers of the Convention had to choose between an opposition proper . . . and this form of "belated opposition." They chose the latter. We had a similar system.... Be that as it may, I think it is indisputable that . . . the contracting States intended that the opposition procedure and result should apply to the European patent as a whole. That is so as a matter of public international law. And that is what the U.K. signed up to in joining the EPC.

Next, say Courtaulds, the activities of the EPO are not . . . justiciable in English courts. It is not open to the English courts to consider whether or not the decision was "in excess" of the powers of the BoA. They say that is so even if the BoA had taken a bribe. . . . Thus, say Courtaulds and the Comptroller, all that Parliament has required . . . is proof that the EPO has . . . revoked a European patent. Once that is shown, then our law automatically treats the European patent . . . as revoked. The Comptroller in making the entry in the register is acting in a purely administrative capacity, just recording what has been done.

I have no doubt that Courtaulds and the Comptroller are right. . . . This country has agreed with . . . the EPC that the final arbiter of revocation under the new legal system is to be the Board of Appeal of the EPO. Other States would be justly entitled to complain if we in this country were to ignore such a final decision. If Lenzing are right, for example, the commercial freedom of action of Akzo-Nobel, a Dutch company, is impeded in this country. That might well concern Holland, the State. Likewise an attack in Germany (and I am told one has been mounted before the constitutional court), if successful, would or might well have the effect of putting Germany in breach of its international obligations. . . .

One can put the matter another way: The EPO has an internal legal system of its own. . . . The position is described succinctly in International Institutional Law (Schermers & Blokker) (3rd rev. ed. 1995 ¶ 1141):

> Unlike private international organisations, public international organisations are not subject to any national law. Thus, they must create their own internal law. The resulting law is an exclusive part of a separate legal order... independent of any other legal order. . .

Perhaps recognising the full destructive power . . . of a jurisdiction to permit a collateral attack on all the grounds. . ., Mr. Prescott devised a more limited class of attack. . . . This is the principle that the English court will not recognise and enforce a judgment of a foreign court where the proceedings in that court were in breach of the principles of "natural justice" (. . . "due process" as the Americans call it).

This, I felt, was Mr. Prescott's most attractive argument. Why should the English court . . . have to accept a decision of a BoA reached by unfair means? The answer, which I think is clear, is that it would be contrary to the international treaty even to inquire into the question. . . . The U.K. and the other Member States have agreed . . . that the BoA is the final arbiter of oppositions. It is the agreed EPO equivalent of the House of Lords, Cour de Cassation, or Bundesgerichthof. It is not for national courts to query its doings, whether in a direct or collateral attack.

Mr. Prescott's final main submission was this: that the EPO was different from other international organisations. Unlike, say the Tin Council, it is a body whose decisions take effect in national law. He said (correctly) that those decisions only take effect by virtue of an Act of Parliament. So the EPO should be regarded as a public body constituted by Act of Parliament, rather like any other U.K. decision making tribunal. This is fallacious. The EPO is clearly recognised on the plane of international law. The Patents Act causes its decisions to be recognised here as a matter of national law. But its decisions remain decisions at the international level so it is no business of our courts to go into them. . . .

So the main argument fails. Those who apply for patents in the EPO must accept the results of its findings and its methods of procedure. Whether they can or should be strengthened is a matter for the Administrative Council. . . .

THE TRIPS AGREEMENT

Article 32 [of TRIPS] is commendably short:

Revocation/Forfeiture

An opportunity for judicial review of any decision to revoke or forfeit a patent shall be available.

. . . Does a Board of Appeal provide a means of judicial review?

Lenzing . . . boldly submit that the Boards of Appeal of the EPO do not provide a means of "judicial review". A reader may well have been wondering why I set out so many provisions of the EPC earlier. . . . They are relevant to this point. But . . . it is, I think, telling how our Act and our House of Lords have considered the matter. Both call the Boards of Appeal "a court". The Act does so in its definition section . . . And in *Merrell Dow Pharmaceuticals Inc v. H.N. Norton & Co., Ltd.* ([1996] R.P.C. 76, at 82) Lord Hoffmann said of decisions of the EPO:

> These decisions are not strictly binding upon courts in the U.K. but they are of great persuasive authority; first, because they are decisions of expert courts (the Boards of Appeal and Enlarged Board of Appeal of the EPO) involved daily in the administration of the EPC.

I have emphasized Lord Hoffmann's use of the word "court". He could hardly have used that word if he did not think that what the Boards were doing was acting as a court—providing a means of judicial review in any ordinary sense.

Next I turn to the provisions of the EPC. . . . I conclude that the Boards of Appeal do provide judicial review within Article 32 of TRIPS. Although strictly this is a matter purely of international law, I also conclude that there is no doubt whatsoever that the ECJ [European Court of Justice] (which has competence to consider the point) would also so find. . . . That is not to say that the judicial structure and procedures of the EPO could not be strengthened. Some hold the view it needs to be in view of the increasing success and importance of the EPO and of the current delays in opposition procedure. But that is a matter for the Administrative Council and not a matter for national courts to consider.

———

NOTES AND QUESTIONS

(1) **Determining the Validity of a European Patent.** The EPC as conceived and elaborated in the Haertel Report ended up without any kind of centralized nullity proceeding. This has proved very controversial, since opposition proceedings must be initiated within nine months and revocation proceedings for national patents take place in national courts. The EPC creates a centralized procedure for the filing, prosecution, and grant of a European patent. The opposition applies to the European patent in all the contracting states in which that patent has effect. *See* EPC art. 99(2). Once granted, the European patent becomes a bundle of national patents in the selected countries and European grounds for revocation of a European patent are binding on national authorities. *See* EPC art. 138. The inspiration for the post-grant opposition procedure of the EPC was the "belated oppositions" procedure of the former British Patents Act of 1949. *See* WILLIAM CORNISH, INTELLECTUAL PROPERTY: PATENTS, COPYRIGHT, TRADE MARKS AND ALLIED RIGHTS 135 (3d ed. 1996). Does that fact color the court's attitude as to the wisdom of getting to the merits of the case? (Note the judge's concern as to the practical impact of reviving patent rights which had been revoked, and assessment that the European Court of Justice would have reached the same decision.) The disparities between revocation proceedings in European national courts has been described as a "harlequin's suit." Vito Mangini, *The Legal Framework for Infringement and Revocation Proceedings in Patent Matters in the Contracting States of the European Patent Convention*, 14 IIC 776, 791 (1983). Calls for a unified forum for determining the validity of a European patent are discussed below in connection with proposals for a Community Patent for the European Union, discussed below. Until such time as a Community Patent Appellate Court ("COPAC") is established, is there any likelihood that national court judges could agree to defer to a leading role of the EPO on questions of validity? *See* Jan J. Brinkhof & Marie-Helene D.B. Schutjens, *Revocation of European Patents—A Study of the Statutory Provisions and Legal Practice in the Netherlands and Germany*, 27 IIC 1, 25 (1996). European patent judges now meet regularly to exchange views on patent law interpretation. *See, e.g.*, Fabienne Gauye Wolhändler et al., *Seventh Symposium of European Patent Judges*, 27 IIC 266 (1996).

(2) **Patents as Property.** What does the court make of the petitioner's "natural justice" argument? Do states who become party to the EPC abdicate their rights to protect their nationals from due process violations? (Note the judge's concern as to the practical impact of reviving patent rights which had been revoked.) Compare the treatment of nationals and corporations seeking restoration of real and moveable property expropriated in former Communist nations such as East Germany and the Soviet Union.

(3) **National Tactics.** The purpose of the EPC was to rationalize procedures for the grant of patents in Europe including substantial examination. According to one observer:

> when the U.S. took the lead in promoting the [PCT] in 1967, France sought refuge in a revival of the EEC plan [of the Haertal Draft of 1962 and the Strasbourg Unification Convention of 1963.] With only the beginnings of an examination system, she found reason to fear the advent of international applications for France which would carry the impress of a PCT search and preliminary examination.

Cornish, *supra*, at 76.

(4) **Translation and The Scope of Protection.** A European patent can sometimes differ from a national patent in a European country where an applicant chooses also to obtain a national patent. The text of a European patent is used in infringement cases except where a national translated version has a narrower scope of protection. A narrower scope of interpretation of a national patent prevails over the official text of a European patent in infringement proceedings.

(5) **EPO Membership.** The European Patent Organization has twenty members as of this book's printing. Of these, fifteen are the current members of the EU; non-EU members are Switzerland, Liechtenstein, Monaco, Turkey and Cyprus. In addition, there are six "extension states" recognizing European patents: Albania, Lithuania, Latvia, former Yugoslav Republic of Macedonia, Slovenia, and Romania. In extension states, only a translation of the claims of a European patent is required to obtain national patent protection. States associated with the EU and committed to applying for accession to membership in the EPO are Bulgaria, Czech Republic, Hungary, Poland, Romania, and Slovakia. The two additional states entitled to join under the accession provisions of Article 166 of the EPC without invitation are Iceland and Norway. Robbins's speculation that the U.S. might be invited to become a member of the EPC never materialized.

(6) **Official Language.** The official languages of the European Patent Organization are English, French, and German. *See* EPC art. 14. Natural or legal persons in contracting states where an official language other than the three official languages of the EPO is used may submit an application in that language, but must submit a translation into one of the EPO official languages for prosecution of the application. EPC Art. 14(2).

(7) **Legal Status of the EPO.** In a 1996 case, *Plants/NOVARTIS*, T 1054/96, the Technical Board stated:

Not all member states of the European Patent Convention are members of the EU, and the EPO is not an organ of the EU. Nor is the EPO a signatory to TRIPS. To meet their obligations under the EU or under TRIPS it would be sufficient for Contracting States to modify their national patent laws. The Board does not see the possibility of giving the EPC any interpretation different from that it had on signing, merely because of the existence of TRIPs or EU directives. To change the EPC a conference of the Contracting States is necessary pursuant to Article 172 EPC. For the Boards of Appeal to take any other view would be to set up as legislators.

Is the EPO a "rogue institution" under international law? *See* Hans-Rainer Jaenichen, *Recent Developments in the Patenting of Plants at the EPO*, 17 BIOTECH. L. REP. 242 (1998).

(8) **Revisions to the EPC.** The EPC was revised at a diplomatic conference held in November, 2000. The Conference authorized the Administrative Council to adapt the EPC to reflect international treaties and developments in the EU. The conference also streamlined EPO procedures and rearranged some provisions, but refused to make substantive changes in the law regarding biotechnology or computer software. The approved revisions will not come into effect until ratified by all of the parties, which will take several years. *See* http://www.european-patent-office.org/news/pressrel/2000_11_29_e.htm.

NOTE: ORGANS OF THE EUROPEAN PATENT ORGANIZATION

The organs of the EPO include the European Patent Office ("EPO"). EPC arts. 6, 10. The EPO has its headquarters in Munich, a branch at the Hague, and sub-offices in Berlin and Vienna. EPC Articles 15-20 establish the departments of the EPO, including the Receiving Section and Search Divisions (DG1 in the Hague and Berlin), and the Examining and Opposition Divisions (DG2 in Munich), and the Legal Division (DG5 in Munich), and the Patent Information Center ("EPIDOS") in Vienna. Jurisdiction over the granting of European patents is under the supervision of the Boards of Appeal and Enlarged Board of Appeal (DG3 in Munich). EPC arts. 21-24. An Administrative Council (EPC Articles 26-36) provides overall supervision of the operation of the EPO. EPC art. 4(3). Each contracting state provides one representative to the Council under the direction of the President. EPC art. 10.

The EPC provides for common substantive law for the contracting parties with respect to requirements for patentability, EPC arts. 52-57, and disclosure, EPC art. 83. Each application is examined by three examiners. Granted European patents are subject to national law of the contracting states. EPC art. 2(2). However, European patents are to be treated by the contracting states in accordance with uniform principles or interpretation. Among the uniform principles is a common set of grounds for opposition, EPC arts. 99, following the grant of a European patent and a common term of the patent (twenty years from the date of filing, EPC art. 63. The rights conferred by the patent are also (at least theoretically) unified, including the extension of the protection for a patented process to products directly obtained by the process, EPC art. 64(2), common scope of protection, EPC art. 69, and that the claims should be interpreted on the basis of the description and the drawings and should be understood neither according to their strict literal meaning only nor should they serve only as a guideline (the protocol to EPC Article 69). According to reliable German and British authority, "[t]he aim has been to achieve a standard mid-way between the severity of the Dutch and the lenience of the Austrian and British approaches: the German standard was thought to be 'about right.'" WILLIAM CORNISH, INTELLECTUAL PROPERTY: PATENTS, COPYRIGHT, TRADE MARKS AND ALLIED RIGHTS 90 n.7 (2d ed. 1989); *see also* J. B. van Bentham & Norman Wallace, *The Problem of Assessing Inventive Step in the European Patent Procedure*, 9 I.I.C. 297, 298 (1978).

Applications may be filed in Munich, the Hague, Berlin, or in the national offices. EPC art. 75. Examination on filing as to formalities, the search report, and publication of the application, including the description, the claims and any drawings as filed, the European search report, and the abstract eighteen months from the date of filing or, if priority has been claimed, as from the date of priority, are all conducted by DG1. EPC arts. 90-93. Substantive examination and opposition procedures, if any, are conducted by DG2. EPC arts. 96, 97, 99ff. Appeal from the Examining Division or the Opposition Division is made to the Boards of Appeal. EPC arts. 21, 106. Validation and revocation are up to the national authorities.

NOTE: FILING A EUROPEAN PATENT APPLICATION

There are four elements required for a filing date: an indication that a European patent is sought; the designation of at least one contracting state; information identifying the applicant; and a description of the invention and at least one claim in an allowable language. EPC art. 80. Applicants having their residence or principal place of business within the contracting states may act themselves or through an employee who need not be a professional representative. EPC art. 133(3). Other applicants must be represented by a professional representative appearing on the EPO roster or a legal practitioner of a contracting state to the extent allowed in the respective state. EPC arts. 133(2), 134. Other formal requirements (which can be remedied later, EPO Rules 26-36) are the request for grant, abstract, EPC art. 85, physical requirements for the specification, EPO Rule 40, and designation of the inventor, EPO Rule 17.

NOTE: THE DECISION TO FILE A EUROPEAN PATENT APPLICATION

There are several oft-stated advantages in filing directly with the EPO. An applicant has to file and prosecute only one application, and potentially undergo but a single opposition and appeal proceeding. The whole procedure, including oppositions and appeals, can be conducted in one language, e.g. English. The European Patent Office conducts reliable searches and responsive examination.

There are also disadvantages. The major one is the high cost. One half of all the annuities (maintenance fees) collected by the European Patent Office are channeled directly to the national patent offices, which have a conflict of interest in that they are the constituents of the Administrative Council. National patent offices are not accountable for how they spend maintenance fees paid to the European system. Fees have been reduced considerably since July 1997 but remain high—particularly with translation costs of activation in member states. A recent estimate is that a "modest" patent application might cost $15,000 to grant and an additional $15,000 in activation costs, national fees, translation, and local agent's charges for only a few countries. Filing in all member countries requires translation of the entire specification into nine foreign languages. A second considerable disadvantage is the central attack provision illustrated by *Lenzing's* case—that the applicant is putting all her eggs in one basket. If the Board of Appeals finally decides not to grant a patent then the applicant may have lost patent protection in a few European countries where a national patent (for what it is worth) would have been granted. There have been some difficulties for applicants resulting from the operation of the system as well. EPO search reports are sometimes not available for several years, and some applications are still pending for up to ten years.

Applications for European patents continue to grow in number notwithstanding the expense, and now number approximately 120,000 per year. But associations of users, such as the Union of Industrial and Employers' Confederation of Europe ("UNICE") and the American Intellectual Property Law Association have been vocal in their complaints over costs. Approximately fifty percent of EPO applications in 1996 were of European origin, while thirty percent were from the United States. Euro-PCT applications (that is, PCT applications designating the EPO) accounted for fifty-two percent of all EPO applications in 1996.

[3] The Luxembourg ("Community Patent") Convention

The Community Patent Convention ("CPC" or "Luxembourg Convention") was signed in Luxembourg in 1973. Yet to enter into force, it contemplates a unitary patent covering the entire territory of the European Community. It was originally conceived to be the natural outcome of the European patent system. It adopts the same standards of patentability as the EPC but also includes a uniform code for the substantive law of patent infringement. The grant of a Community Patent would require a translation of the entire document into the official language of each of the member states. Six of the twelve states which were members of the European Community at the time of signature of the CPC have ratified it: Denmark, France, Germany, Greece, Luxembourg, and the United Kingdom.

The CPC is distinct from the EU and is not subject to the jurisdiction of such community organs as the Council of Ministers, the European Parliament, or the European Court of Justice. The primary reason it has not yet come into force is that much of European industry is opposed to it, primarily due to the cost of translating patents into all of the languages of the member states, and misgivings over its proposed system for dealing with patent disputes. Unlike the European Patent applicant, who can designate selected European countries in which to activate the patent the Community Patent applicant must seek protection throughout the member states. A proposed Community Patent Appellate Court ("COPAC") would hear appeals from national court proceedings on infringement or revocation of Community Patents; however, it would not hear appeals from decisions to grant or not to grant a patent by the EPO. The 1989 Agreement relating to the Community Patent (the "Luxembourg Agreement"), which solidified the language requirement, has only been ratified by seven of the twelve signatories (Denmark, Germany, France, U.K., Greece, Luxembourg, and the Netherlands). The following reading by a former president of the European Patent Office discusses some of the controversies surrounding the CPC.

J. B. VAN BENTHEM, THE EUROPEAN PATENT SYSTEM AND EUROPEAN INTEGRATION[*]
24 I.I.C. 435 (1993)

[T]he preparatory work which ultimately led to the two European patent conventions was begun in 1960 by the then six contracting parties to the Treaty of Rome in response to a proposal from the Commission of the European Economic Community. There was nothing surprising about this, as Art. 2 of the Treaty of Rome stipulates that the aim of the Community is to establish a Common Market and to gradually bring about the harmonization of economic policy in the member states. And as you know, industrial property rights are instruments of economic policy in that they promote the use and spread of new technology in the economy. Furthermore, overcoming the problems posed by the fact that each Common Market country has its own national industrial property laws is an important step towards the establishment of a Common Market. This "European Economic Community phase", as Haertel called it in his Commentary, came to an end in 1965 with the production of a complete draft of an EEC patent law, which not only provided for a centralized grant procedure for unitary European patents, but also a system of law governing them.

Following a break of four years due to political reasons, work on the European patent law was resumed on a new basis in 1969, which caused Haertel to refer to it as "the great European phase." The original draft was divided up into two separate conventions. The first convention was intended to create a centralized European procedure for granting European patents which would have the legal value of a bundle of national patents having the same content. Any European country would be able to participate in this convention, whether or not it was a member of the EEC. It was thus no longer a part of European integration within the EEC, and instead became an autonomous agreement between countries of the Paris Convention, just like the PCT, for example. It led to the Munich Patent Convention of 1973.

The second convention was to remain within the EEC's sphere of economic integration. where it would combine the granted European bundle of patents for the EEC countries into a unitary Community patent, setting out the laws governing Community patents. This became the Luxembourg Community Patent Convention of 1975.

I would now like to turn to two questions. The *first* question is whether, in the light of what we now know, 22 years after the decision was made to split the original convention into two, the development of the European patent system has shown that this decision was right. The second question is whether, in view of subsequent developments, it is still right to have two conventions today. I can only touch upon these questions in the course of this paper, but I feel that it is important for them to be raised.

III.

Starting with the *first* question, which was whether developments have vindicated the decision to create two conventions, I would say that, as far as the Munich Convention is concerned, the answer must be a resounding yes. It should not be forgotten that back in 1969 both the concept of European integration and economic necessity were forces pressing for the creation of a centralized European patent grant procedure. The patent offices of the European states were overloaded, and industry desperately wished to be relieved of the time-consuming business of filing numerous national patent applications for one invention in Europe. It therefore made political and economic sense to agree to allow the EFTA countries of Great Britain, Sweden, Austria and Switzerland to participate in the preparatory work. In this way, in addition to the six EEC states, other European countries which had close economic ties with the six and innovative, patent-oriented industries could be included in this centralized European grant system.

Furthermore, the autonomy of the Munich Convention meant that its coming into force could be made dependent not on unanimous ratification by all EEC states, but on ratification by a minimum of six states, regardless of membership of the EEC. The way in which the Munich Convention has developed, the fact that it came into force only a few years after it was signed, and the steady increase in the number of member states, which reflects the success of the centralized grant procedure, all go to prove that the decision to split the original convention into two was clearly right. Just imagine what would have happened had the convention remained within the EEC and, for example, if Ireland, with its constitutional problems which until recently prevented ratification of the Luxembourg Convention, had been able to delay the coming into force of a centralized European patent grant procedure by many years.

What would the answer to my first question be as far as the Luxembourg Community Patent Convention of 1975 is concerned? Have developments since the Luxembourg Conference shown that the decision to divide the original convention into two was the right one for the Community patent as well? Everyone in our field is familiar with the sad and shameful story of this Convention. After three successive diplomatic conferences to improve it—two in Luxembourg in 1975 and 1989, and another in 1992 (which, incidentally, failed to achieve its aims)—the Convention has yet to be ratified by some of the EEC states 17 years after the first Luxembourg Conference. And there is no telling whether it will ever come into force at all.

The difficulties could be ascribed to internal problems between the member states. First there was the British Government's problem with the settlement of disputes about infringements of the Community patent and about its legal validity. This, it must be said, led to an improved system which for the sake of simplicity I will refer to as COPAC. Then there were constitutional and political problems in Ireland and Denmark which prevented ratification by these two countries. However, that is only one side of the coin.

The other side is that European industry, in a number of EEC countries at least, now has little or no interest in the Community patent. It originally asked for the two conventions not to be introduced at the same time, as it wanted to try out the European patent grant procedure first. However, it has since become so used to the European bundle of patents that it manages very well with it, even within the EC. In addition, the European Court of Justice has in its case law now settled the question of the exhaustion of the rights conferred by national or European patents in such a way that the Common Market cannot be divided up again as a result. There is thus no longer any pressure from this direction either for the introduction of a unitary Community patent. As far as my first question is concerned, I would therefore conclude that the decision to divide the original convention into two was not the right decision for the Community patent. As part of an overall solution to the problem of the European patent system in the EEC, the unitary Community patent could have been established using economic pressure and in the wake of the impetus towards the establishment of a centralized European patent grant procedure. The split took the wind out of the sails of the Community patent and left it in the doldrums, where it remains to this day.

IV.

I would now like to turn to my second and much more difficult question: in the light of the situation today, is it still right to have two separate conventions?

Let us first of all look at the situation with regard to the Munich Convention. I think it can safely be said that it has been very successful since coming into force in 1977, for not only has the number of European or Euro-PCT applications increased to +/- 60,000 per year, but the number of member states has also gone up from 7 to 17.

From an examination of the expansion of the European Patent Organisation, three facts stand out. Firstly, following Ireland's accession, all the EC states are members of the EPO. Secondly, apart from Liechtenstein and Monaco, the remaining three member states of the EPO, namely Sweden, Switzerland and Austria, have applied to join the European Community and it is unanimously assumed in Community circles that their political and economic situation will allow accession to be negotiated very quickly. The member states of the EC would then be identical to those of the EPO. Thirdly, the countries which acceded to the Munich Patent Convention later, that is Denmark Spain, Portugal, Greece and Ireland, did not do so spontaneously, but rather under the constraints of the so-called *"acquis communautaire,"* in other words as a result of their obligation on entering the European Community to accept the Community's existing laws, including the Community Patent Convention and, consequently, the Munich Patent Convention. These later accessions were therefore primarily motivated by European integration within the Community.

Drawing these three strands together, one is forced to ask if the time has come to give serious consideration to the question of whether the European patent grant procedure should be brought back into the sphere of European integration in the EC, where the preparatory work was begun, and if so, how this should be done. One argument in favor of such a step would be that it is no longer necessary to have two separate conventions because the industrialized countries of Europe which were interested in a centralized European patent grant system and which were previously divided into two blocks will soon all be members of the EC. There are other important arguments, too.

Look at the economic situation in the world today. In addition to the EC, there are two other large economic blocks, the United States and Japan. In view of the striking economic growth rate in Central Asia, we should expect the formation in the future of further large economic blocks such as China and India, which will play an increasing role in technological innovation and the patent business this will produce. The patent system as an economic tool is firmly integrated in the political and economic systems of all these large economic blocks except Europe. In the EC, the European patent grant system is governed by an autonomous, independent convention between what will soon be 15 EC countries. The organs of the EC, that is the Commission, the Council and the Parliament, which are determining European integration to an increasing extent, are not responsible for the Convention in any way. In view of the progress of European integration within the EC—and I am thinking in particular of the completion of the single market on 1 January 1993 and the Maastricht Treaty—I feel that this situation is no longer appropriate and indeed is actually rather dangerous.

In a purely co-operative association of European contracting states with no higher, joint structure of political and economic integration, it is all too easy for national interests to override the interests of integration. I would like to illustrate this point with a few examples.

Firstly, let us look at the language problem. As you know, the Munich Convention sensibly stipulates that the European Patent Office should have only three official languages, English, French and German. European patent applications may be submitted and processed in one of these three official languages only. When a patent is granted, the patent specification itself is published in the language of the proceedings only, either English. French or German, together with a translation of the claims in the other two official languages. This regulation not only aids the process of integration and co-operation between the contracting states, but is also very practical. It simplifies the work of the Office and is sufficient for the purposes of what I like to call the patent community, by which I mean anyone involved in patents. Taking its lead from a patent-oriented economy, this patent community has long since adopted an international outlook and has become correspondingly conversant with foreign languages. Patent experts can search patent documentation in the above-mentioned three languages (published European patent applications constitute an essential part of the documentation and are in any case published only in the language of proceedings. That is in one of the three official languages) and can usually manage quite well with a translation of the claims. Moreover, in any assessment of the scope of protection of a patent, the version of the patent specification in the language of the proceedings is used. In the early years of the European patent system, the patent community in a number of the contracting states was quite happy with a system in which European patent specifications did not have to be translated into the language of the country concerned. There were few problems or protests.

Unfortunately, we added Art. 65 to the Munich Convention. This article states that if a European patent specification is not drawn up in one of the official languages of a particular contracting state, then that state may prescribe that the proprietor of the patent shall supply a translation. This provision was politically unavoidable, although there was at the time justifiable hope that the contracting states would, for the reasons I have already mentioned, make sparing use of it. And that is what happened at first, although since then almost all the contracting states have made it a requirement to submit a translation. The reasons for this have less to do with the needs of those using the European patent system than with national political interests and the like.

Let me illustrate the result of this development with reference to the Netherlands. Assuming that 60,000 European and Euro-PCT applications are filed per year, one can expect 70%, or 42,000, granted European patents. Around 60% of these patents are granted for the Netherlands, that is about 25,000 European patents per year. This means that 25,000 translations into Dutch are filed each year with the Dutch Patent Office, where they quietly gather dust and, as can be proved, are rarely consulted. If, as we know from experience. the cost of a translation can be assumed to be around DM 4,000, then we are talking about a figure of +/- DM 100 million per year which is added unnecessarily to the cost of European patents in the Netherlands. I suspect that the situation is pretty much the same in other contracting states. It would be interesting to investigate further.

I cannot produce any exact figures for translations in the other 16 member states. but I would estimate the total cost of translations of European patents to be around +/- DM 1 billion per year. Because this figure is about the same as the total costs of the European Patent Office, it can be said that national translation requirements double the cost of obtaining a European patent. The European Patent Office came to the same conclusion when it calculated the cost of a European patent with seven designations.

The national interests of the contracting states have thus overridden the interests of the European patent system to such an extent that the system is now in jeopardy. It has gradually become too expensive for a large proportion of small and medium-sized firms, which thus no longer have access to the centralized European patent grant procedure, and all for the sake of interests which, although they may be justifiable culturally, and perhaps even politically, are no longer justifiable in economic terms, because the practical needs of the economy are paramount. In moving the political and cultural problem of language into the sphere of the European patent system, the contracting states have moved it into the economic sphere, where it does not belong. By doing so they have overshot the mark in the matter of retaining their national cultural heritages. The fact that the European patent system is at risk because of this directly affects the subject of European integration within the Community. A further example of the danger of national interests overriding the interests of European integration is provided by the financing of the European Patent Office. Like every other patent office, it earns its income on the one hand from procedural fees and on the other hand from renewal fees for granted patents. The renewal fees for European patents are, however, a bundle of national renewal fees, which has two disadvantages for the European patent system.

The first of these is that the contracting states have a completely free hand in fixing the amount of the renewal fees applying to European and national patents equally. The second disadvantage is that the Administrative Council of the EPO, which consists of delegations from the contracting states, is entitled under Art. 39 EPC to fix the proportion of the renewal fees for the granted European bundle of patents to be remitted to the Office. A minimum percentage is specified in favour of the contracting states, but no minimum is fixed for the Office. This was quite clearly a mistake on our part. Although there is as a result scope for balancing national interests with European interests, in practice a considerable degree of risk is involved, as the present situation shows. Many years ago, the Administrative Council fixed the proportion of the renewal fees to be remitted to the Office at 50%—an understandable decision at a time when both the Office's running costs and the income generated by the renewal fees were quite low. Since then, however, the Office's costs have gone up following an increase in staff resulting from the growth in the number of patent applications, and, with almost 200,000 patents granted, income from renewal fees has also risen.

A review of the financial requirements of the European Patent Office on the one hand and of the contracting states and their national patent offices on the other would appear to be called for. However, the contracting states are apparently not willing to do this because of national financial interests. But if the situation stays as it is, it will have a dual negative effect on the European patent system. Firstly, with regard to the financing of the European Patent Office, the proportion of the Office's costs covered by renewal fees is too small compared with other patent offices, which results in relatively high procedural fees. Secondly, the proportion of the renewal fees for granted European patents received by the contracting states is so high that it far exceeds the amount spent by the national patent offices on administering European patents, and consequently substantial surplus amounts are available for use elsewhere in the national patent system, or even end up in the treasury. The proprietors of European patents thus have not only to pay the costs of the European patent grant system, but also to contribute towards national patent systems or the treasuries of some of the contracting states.

My third example relates to co-operation between the European Patent Office and the national patent offices. The European patent system was not set up to replace the national patent systems, but to operate alongside them, giving applicants the choice between a European and a national patent. This structure was intended both to accommodate the interests of applicants and to bring about a sensible division of work between the European Patent Office and the national patent offices. It was assumed that applicants wishing to obtain protection for their inventions in three or more contracting states would use the European patent system, while the others would continue to use the national patent offices. This has proven to be the case.

However, the number of patent applications filed with some national patent offices has dropped to a level which has gradually prompted the question, nurtured by purely national interests, as to the extent to which the Munich Convention permits searches or examinations relating to European patent applications to be transferred to the national offices of the contracting states. The transfer of such work was possible on a restricted scale under the terms of the Protocol on Centralization. Following the expiry on 31 May 1993 of the limited period within which such work could be transferred under the Protocol, the question now touches the basic substance of the Munich Convention, which centralizes the granting of European patents at the European Patent Office. Such centralization was intended to ensure a uniform standard in European searches and examination, and to promote European integration, because in the EPO, as in other European authorities, men and women of different nationalities are working together with a common responsibility towards Europe. The possible decentralization of the European patent grant procedure is thus not just a question of law or a problem of quality, but a basic question of the shaping of European integration. I believe that under a purely co-operative agreement between contracting states without support from higher political structures for European integration, national interests could once again gain the upper hand.

The three examples I have mentioned reinforce my view, as far as the Munich Convention is concerned, regarding the answer to my second question, namely that—in the light of developments so far—the splitting of the original convention into two is no longer useful.

V.

Let me now ask the same question for the Luxembourg Community Patent Convention. As I have already mentioned, this Convention has a sad history. Seventeen years after the Luxembourg Conference in 1975, it still has not been ratified by some of the EC states. It is doubtful whether it will ever come into force at all. Splitting the original convention into two took the wind out of the sails of the Community patent and left it in the doldrums forever. Indeed, many people probably now quite rightly believe that the disadvantages of the Convention outweigh its advantages. Some of these advantages have been anticipated by developments, for example the case law of the European Court of Justice on the exhaustion of patent rights in the Common Market, and the voluntary harmonization of provisions on the rights conferred by patents undertaken by the contracting states on the basis of the Luxembourg Convention. However, the Convention still has some indisputable advantages, including the fact that it is much simpler to administer a Community patent having uniform renewal fees, and the new provisions dating from 1985 for settling disputes about infringements of Community patents and about their legal validity. These advantages are, however, offset by one significant disadvantage of the new 1989 version of the Convention, and that is the provision on languages in Art. 30 CPC.

According to the 1975 version of the CPC, applicants had to provide a translation of the claims only in all the languages of the Community. However, the transitional regulations allowed any contracting state to require that a translation of the whole specification be submitted in its official language. I wish to make three observations about this. Firstly, the Council of the European Communities was authorized to delete this reservation at a later date. Secondly, the translation could be submitted at any time following the grant of the patent because it was only a condition for the enforceability and not the validity of the patent. Thirdly, it was hoped at the time that, in view of the circumstances, not all the contracting states would make use of this reservation.

Surprisingly, the 1989 Luxembourg Conference then tightened up Art. 30 CPC considerably to make the filing of a translation of the full specification in all the languages of the Community within a specified time limit a prerequisite for the validity of a Community patent. Under these circumstances, applicants have understandably been given the opportunity to obtain a normal European bundle of patents for the designated contracting states instead of a Community patent.

This new ruling on translations dealt the fatal blow to the Community patent. How many applicants would still be interested in a Community patent if they had to pay for a translation of the specification into eight languages, that is into two of the three official languages (English, French and German), plus Spanish, Italian, Danish, Dutch, Portuguese and Greek? That would amount to 8 x 4,000 = DM 32,000 per Community patent. And as new countries join the EC, further languages and costs will be added. It therefore looks as though this provision will make the Community patent so expensive that all potential applicants will avoid it because they can save a considerable amount of money by obtaining European bundles of patents for only those states of economic interest to them.

Ratification of the 1989 Luxembourg Agreement relating to Community Patents would therefore be equivalent to "putting a dead man on the throne." It would be both pointless and dangerous, for once Art. 30 CPC comes into force, it can only be changed unanimously and with the approval of the parliaments of all the member states. It would therefore be better, in my opinion, if ratification of the Luxembourg Agreement continued to be blocked so that the language problem could be reconsidered.

VI.

It would then also be possible to consider whether the two separate conventions should be dispensed with in favor of transferring the entire European patent system to the Community in the form of a new convention or a European Council Regulation. In any case, I think it would be appropriate to raise these ideas at the negotiations for entry into the EC of Switzerland,

Austria and Sweden. Combining the two conventions would be good for both. As I have already explained, I feel that the future of the entire European patent system is only safe if it is part of the process of European economic and political integration within the European Community, which is where its real basis is to be found. The efforts of the President of the European Patent Office to bring about closer co-operation with the EC Commission are commendable, but I do not think they are enough in the long term.

Let me illustrate this with reference to the difficulties arising from the language problem. Combining the two conventions would enable a common solution to this problem to be found for both conventions. In view of the difficult political situation regarding languages in the Community, some may doubt that the problem could be solved more easily in the Community itself rather than within the framework of an autonomous European patent convention. In reply, I would say that as far as the Community is concerned, with the pressure towards European integration, we have no choice but to ask whether we want a unitary Community patent for the Common Market with a sensible solution to the language problem which is advantageous to the applicant, or no Community patent at all. As far as an autonomous European Patent Convention is concerned, the question is somewhat different. Will the language problem be solved in such a way as to promote the European patent grant procedure or to promote the endangered national patent grant procedures or other related national interests? In the long term, any solution to the language problem undertaken outside the Community would in my opinion have an uncertain outcome. The same applies to the other problems which have been addressed in this paper.

NOTES AND QUESTIONS

(1) **Decline of National Patents in Europe**. National patent applications in Europe have fallen precipitously with the upsurge in European patent applications. In some states (such as the Netherlands), there is no examination of activated European patents whatsoever and the national office has been reduced to ministerial functions. The president of the EPO, Dr. Kober, recently questioned whether anyone could have foreseen the continued existence of national offices at the turn of the century. What purposes do national patent offices serve in a modern Europe? Are there better reasons for maintaining national patent offices in a state such as Ireland (population 3.5 million) or Denmark (population 5.1 million) when a single patent in the United States covers a market of 250 million? One writer has recently proposed that the European Union issue a directive *forbidding* member states of the EPC from granting national patents! *See* Clifford Lees, *European Patents: What Is Going On?*, 103 PATENT WORLD 19-24 (July 1998).

(2) **Higher Costs**. The costs of a European patent are much higher than a U.S. counterpart. According to an EPO *Report on the Cost of Patenting in Europe*, the procedural fees of the EPO (9,900 German marks) are more than three times higher than those of the U.S. Patent and Trademark Office (3,000

German marks) and more than four times higher than those of the Japanese Patent Office (2,200 German marks). Then there are the validation costs of a European patent, i.e. expenditures necessary to validate a patent granted by the EPO in each designated state, including the cost for mandatory translations of the complete patent specification into the official language of each of the designated contracting states and official validation fees of the national patent offices of those states. According to one eminent critic:

> Taking into account that in a European patent on average eight Contracting States are designated, *i.e.* a market volume more or less comparable to that of the United States of America or Japan, the successful European applicant has to spend an average of 36,000 German marks as compared with the 3,000 German marks mentioned in the case of the United States of America or with 2,200 German marks in the case of Japan, but his patent still does not cover the entire Community area. . . . Worse and in terms of Community perspectives difficult to explain and justify are the figures if the annual renewal fees are included in the comparison of the official fees between the USA and the EPC: wherever eight Contracting States are designated, which means that nearly half of the EU Member States are not, the total cost for obtaining and maintaining a patent for its full term is about US $ 120,000 under the EPC, whereas in the US the respective amount is only US $13,000. As it has been pointed out, one must note that the principle of the exhaustion of the patent right applies in the Member States of the Community, thus in order to secure the same market volume in Europe as in the United States—with its national exhaustion—not only an American and Japanese but equally a European patent owner has to spend over ten times more.

Joseph Straus, *The Present State of the Patent System in the European Union As Compared with the Situation in the United States of America and Japan,* 1997 EUR 170.14 EN (1997) (Document of the European Commission).

(3) **Replacing the CPC.** Should the EPC be replaced by a patent law for the EU instead of the CPC? If so, what happens to states such as Switzerland which is not a member of the EU? A Green Paper issued by the European Commission in 1997 and a Judges' Proposal put forward by Judge Jacob of the U.K. Patents Court in July of the same year both press for change. The Green Paper pointed to the high costs of translations for all the member states (ten languages) and uncertainties over consistency of interpretation of patents. *See* Green Paper, *at* http://europa.eu.int/comm/dg15/en/intprop/indprop/558.htm; *see also* Richard Tyler, *Combating Europe's Innovation Deficit,* MANAGING INTELL. PROP. 23 (July/Aug. 1997). A recent study of the European situation conducted under the auspices of the European Commission Directorate-General for Telecommunications, Information Market and Exploitation of Research is highly critical of the status quo, and urges that the European patent law be made subject of a community regulation like the European Trademark System. *See generally* Strauss, *supra.*

[4] A European Union Patent?

Apace with increasing criticism of the European Patent Convention's bundle of national rights approach and the failure of the Community Patent Convention to garner the slightest interest among European states, the organs of the EU have moved ahead on several fronts. One has been the proposal of an EU-wide patent.

COMMISSION OF THE EUROPEAN UNION, PROPOSAL FOR A COUNCIL REGULATION ON THE COMMUNITY PATENT
Explanatory Memorandum, COM(2000) 412 final (Aug. 1, 2000)

Context

In the European Union, patent protection is currently provided by two systems, neither of which is based on a Community legal instrument: the national patent systems and the European patent system.

The national patent appeared first. In the Member States of the European Community, the national patent has undergone de facto harmonisation. First of all, all the Member States are parties to both the Paris Convention for the Protection of Industrial Property of 20 March 1883 (as last amended on 14 July 1967) and the Agreement of 15 April 1994 on Trade Related Aspects of Intellectual Property Rights (referred to hereinafter as the TRIPS Agreement). Several Member States are also party to the Council of Europe's Convention of 27 November 1963 on the unification of certain elements of patent law.

The idea of the Community patent dates back to the 1960s. At that time, initial thought was given to the creation of a patent system applicable to the nascent European Community in its entirety. However, it quickly became apparent that this approach could not take on more tangible form in a purely Community context. Thus it was that the initiative finally led to the signature on 5 October 1973 of the Convention on the Grant of European Patents(referred to hereinafter as the "Munich Convention"), to which all the Member States gradually acceded.

The Munich Convention is governed by conventional international law and does not form part of the Community legal order. The Munich Convention established a European Patent Organisation, the constituent bodies of which are the European Patent Office (referred to hereinafter as the "Office") and the Administrative Council. It lays down a single procedure for the granting of patents. This task has been assigned to the Office. However, once the European patent has been granted, it becomes a national patent and is subject to the national rules of the contracting States designated in the application. At present, nineteen countries are members of the European Patent Organisation. Apart from the Member States of the European Community, these are Switzerland, Liechtenstein, Monaco, Cyprus and, in the near future, Turkey. What is more, several Central and Eastern European countries [Bulgaria, the

Czech Republic, Estonia, Hungary, Poland, Romania, Slovakia and Slovenia] have been invited to accede to the Munich Convention from 1 July 2002 at the earliest.

A second attempt by the EC Member States to create a Community patent led in 1975 to the signing of the Luxembourg Convention on the Community patent (referred to hereinafter as the "Luxembourg Convention"). This Convention was amended by an Agreement concluded in Luxembourg on 15 December 1989 concerning Community patents and including, amongst other things, the Protocol on the Settlement of Litigation concerning the Infringement and Validity of Community Patents.

The Luxembourg Convention is a Community convention. In essence, the Convention would have transformed the national stages in the granting of European patents into a single stage common to the Member States. The Luxembourg Convention never entered into force because the only MemberStates to ratify it were France, Germany, Greece, Denmark, Luxembourg, the United Kingdom and the Netherlands.

The failure of the Luxembourg Convention has generally been attributed to the costs of the Community patent, chiefly that of translation, and to the judicial system. Under the Convention, a patent had to be translated into every Community language. Interested parties felt that this requirement was excessive. Under the highly complex judicial system, national judges would have been able to declare a Community patent invalid with effect for the entire territory of the Community. This aspect aroused the distrust of interested parties, who considered it to be a major element of legal uncertainty.

Recent work

Following the failure of the Luxembourg Convention, the Commission's Green Paper on the Community patent and the European patent system, which was part of the follow-up to the First Action Plan for Innovation in Europe, launched a broad discussion on the need to take new initiatives in relation to patents. The Green Paper elicited a large number of opinions from interested parties, the European Parliament and the Economic and Social Committee. In addition, the Commission, together with the Luxembourg Presidency of the Council, held a hearing on 25 and 26 November 1997 open to all users of the patent system. The Commission also staged a meeting of experts from Member States on 26 January 1998.

After this extensive consultation process, the Commission adopted, on 5 February 1999, a Communication on the follow-up to the Green Paper on the Community patent and the patent system in Europe. The aim of this Communication was to announce the various measures and new initiatives which the Commission was planning to take or propose in order to make the patent system attractive for promoting innovation in Europe..The initiative concerning the Community patent was announced and sketched out in broad outline in the Communication dated 5 February 1999. This proposal incorporates most of that broad outline. At the European Council in Lisbon on 23 and 24 March 2000, the Heads of State or Government of the Member States underlined the importance of introducing a Community patent without delay.

Proposal For A Council Regulation

. . . .

This proposal for a Regulation is aimed at creating a new unitary industrial property right, the Community patent. It is essential for eliminating the distortion of competition which may result from the territorial nature of national protection rights; it is also one of the most suitable means of ensuringthe free movement of goods protected by patents.

The creation of a Community patent will also enable undertakings to adapt their production and distribution activities to the European dimension. It is considered to be an essential tool if we are to succeed in transforming research results and the new technological and scientific know-how into industrial and commercial success stories—and thereby put an end to the "European paradox" in innovation—while at the same time stimulating private R&D investment, which is currently at a very low level in the European Union compared with the United States and Japan.

The Community patent system will coexist with the national and European patent systems. Inventors will remain free to choose the type of patent protection best suited to their needs.

Legal basis

. . .[T]he legal basis of the proposal for a Regulation is Article 308 [ex-Article 235] of the EC Treaty. Use of this legal bas[is] is in accordance with what has been done in relation to the Community trade mark and Community designs.

The form chosen for the instrument—a Regulation—is warranted by a number of considerations. The Member States cannot be left with any discretion either to determine the Community law applicable to the Community patent or to decide on the effects and administration of the patent once it has been granted. The unity of the patent could not be guaranteed by less "binding" measures.

Link between the Regulation on the Community Patent and the European Patent Organisation

The main thrust of this proposal is the creation of a "symbiosis" between two systems: that of the Regulation on the Community patent, a European Community instrument, and that of the Munich Convention, a classic international instrument. This means not only that the Regulation on the Community patent will have to be adopted, but also that the Munich Convention and the status of the Office will have to be taken properly into account, that the Community will have to accede to the Munich Convention, and that account must be taken of the scope for ensuring consistency in the future development of the Regulation and the Convention.

The Regulation on the Community patent

By virtue of the Community's accession to the Munich Convention and the designation of the Community as the territory for which the Community patent can be granted, the provisions of that Convention applying to European patent applications will, in principle, be applicable to applications for Community patents. Even though this text refers to an application for the Community patent, in legal terms such an application will, under the Munich Convention, be an application for a European patent designating the territory of the Community. Only when the patent has been granted by the Office will it become a Community patent under the Regulation. In the light of Community accession to the Munich Convention, it is not necessary for the Regulation to refer to the substantive rules of the Munich Convention and its Implementing Regulations in force on a specific date. In essence, the Regulation is limited to governing the Community patent once granted. The Regulation will also contain specific rules which will depart from the Convention. The Regulation will, for instance, introduce some improvements compared with the European patent as regards the cost of the patent, translations and the system of appeals to courts of law.

The Office and the Munich Convention

As already mentioned, the authority responsible for examining patent applications and granting Community patents will be the Office. However, the Office is not a Community body. It is nevertheless intended that it will grant Community patents by virtue of the Community's accession to the Munich Convention and of a revision of that Convention. The current Munich Convention does not allow the Office to perform these functions. To achieve that, the Convention would have to be amended. Now is an opportune time to act, as the Munich Convention is currently undergoing revision. In accordance with the mandate adopted by the intergovernmental conference of the member states of the European Patent Organisation in Paris on 24 and 25 June 1999, two working parties were set up to carry out the preparatory work for a reform of the patent system in Europe, particularly with a view to reducing the cost and lead time involved in the granting of a patent, and for the harmonisation of litigation relating to the Community patent. It should be borne in mind that the envisaged revision of the Munich Convention will require the Contracting States, including four non-EU countries, to agree to the Convention being amended in such a way as to enable the Office to assume these new functions and make accession by the Community possible. The objective of the proposed Regulation is not to amend the present structure of the European patent system. The Regulation does not provide for the setting-up of new special departments within the Office. Rather, the Office would be charged with specific tasks relating to the Community patent. What is more, it will continue its activities concerning the European patent as an international body independent of the Community. Similarly, the Office will apply to the Community patent the case law which it has developed for the European patent, to the extent that the rules in the Regulation and the Convention are identical.

Community accession to the Munich Convention

Community accession to the Munich Convention is the essential instrument for achieving the objectives of the Regulation. To this end, the Commission will present to the Council a recommendation for a negotiating mandate. The accession of the Community to the Munich Convention should make it possible to achieve the best possible symbiosis between the European Patent Organisation and the Community. The EC Member States, which already have an obligation to ensure compliance with Community law in matters relating to the legal protection of biotechnological inventions in the international arena, will be required under the proposal concerning the Community patent to coordinate to an even greater extent the opinions which they express within the bodies of the European Patent Organisation, pursuant to Article 10 (ex Article 5) of the EC Treaty.

Consistent and simultaneous development of the Regulation on the Community patent and of the Munich Convention

The Munich Convention is currently undergoing revision, and further amendments may follow. Independently of this work, it is possible that the Regulation will have to be amended in line with future developments in society. In order to guarantee, as far as possible, the consistent and simultaneous development of the Regulation and the Munich Convention, the following factors will have to be taken into account:

– first, amendments to the Munich Convention made prior to the adoption of the Regulation on the Community patent will automatically apply to the Community patent;

– secondly, in order to guarantee that the revision of the Munich Convention moves in the right direction, under Article 10 of the EC Treaty Member States should, after the proposal for a Regulation has been adopted by the Commission, cooperate loyally in the negotiations with the European Patent Organisation with a view to facilitating the realisation of the objectives of the proposal. After the adoption of the Regulation, external jurisdiction over the Community patent shall fall within the exclusive remit of the Community.

– Thirdly, as regards subsequent developments in the framework of the Munich Convention, it will be possible to lay down corresponding rules according to the nature of the changes made, either in the form of an amendment to the Regulation or within the Implementing Regulations which will be adopted via a comitology procedure.

– fourthly, given that Member States currently form a large majority among the Contracting States of the European Patent Organisation, they should be in a position effectively to ensure that revisions made to the Munich Convention do not jeopardise either the integrity of Community law or the desired consistency between the Regulation and the Munich Convention.

The main features of the Community patent

The Community patent must be of a unitary and autonomous nature. It must stem from a body of Community patent law, be affordable, have appropriate language arrangements and meet information requirements, guarantee legal certainty and coexist with existing patent systems. . . .

The Community patent must be unitary in nature. It will produce the same effect throughout the territory of the Community and may be granted, transferred, declared invalid or allowed to lapse only in respect of the whole of the Community. The Community patent must be of an autonomous nature. It shall be subject only to the provisions of the proposed Regulation and to the general principles of Community law. . . . The proposed Regulation introduces specific provisions applicable to Community patents. It is important to note that the Regulation does not set out to depart substantially from the principles embodied in national patent law already in force in the Member States; these have all acceded to the Munich Convention and have, moreover, largely harmonised substantive patent law in accordance with the Luxembourg Convention, even though the latter Convention has never entered into force. The same applies concerning the specific rules of the TRIPS Agreement, which links the Community and the Member States. On this basis, the provisions of the Munich Convention concerning such subjects as conditions of patentability, for example, will be applicable to the Community patent. Thus, in accordance with the provisions of the Munich Convention, Community patents will be granted in respect of inventions, whether products or processes, provided that they are new, involve an inventive step and are capable of industrial application. Similarly, exceptions to patentability will be covered by the Munich Convention. Amendments made to the Convention in the course of the intergovernmental conference currently under way for the revision of the Convention will of course be applicable to the Community patent. By contrast, the effects of the Community patent, once granted, will be governed by the provisions of this Regulation. This applies, for instance, to the limitations of the effects of the Community patent. As regards the use of a patented invention without the patent proprietor's authorisation, the proposed Regulation would incorporate the best practice in force in the Member States: the granting of compulsory licences would thus be possible. Although the Regulation makes no such specific provision, Member States would remain free to take any action necessary for the protection of their essential security interests, in accordance with Article 73 of the TRIPS Agreement.

Affordable cost of the Community patent

At present, an average European patent (designating eight Contracting States) costs approximately EUR 30 000. The fees due to the Office for such an average European patent account for approximately 14% of the total cost of the patent. The cost of representation before the Office represents 18% of the total cost. The translations required by the Contracting States account for approximately 39% of the total cost. The renewal fees currently paid to Member States represent something in the order of 29% of the cost of an average European patent (between the fifth and the tenth years). Of this income, 50% accrues to the Office and 50% to the Contracting State concerned. This proposal is aimed at making the Community patent more affordable and more attractive than the present European patent. These aspects depend to a very large extent on the costs associated with translations, procedures, and litigation.

Translation costs

As far as translation costs are concerned, the comparative table below gives a fairly accurate idea of the probable effect of the recommended solution. The three scenarios are based on the following assumptions: applications comprising an average volume of 20 pages, three pages for the claims, 15 claims. As the texts concerned are of a highly complex and technical nature and relate to new matters and processes, the average output of a translator will probably be in the region of three pages per day. Translation costs are therefore estimated at EUR 250 per day.

Translation costs in three scenarios:

Scenario No. 1: Luxembourg Convention

Complete translation of the patent documents into the ten working languages.

Translation costs: EUR 17,000

Scenario No. 2:

Translation of the patent documents into the three working languages of the Office.

Translation costs: EUR 5,100

Scenario No. 3: Proposed solution

Translation of the patent documents into one of the Office's three working languages and of the claims into the other two.

Translation costs: EUR 2,200

Overall, this comparative assessment shows a significant differential in favour of the solution put forward in this proposal for a Regulation. In terms of translation costs, the planned Community patent will be both more affordable than the patent proposed in the first Luxembourg Convention and more attractive than the European patent.

Fees and other procedural costs

Apart from translation costs, the different fees and costs associated with the granting and renewal of a Community patent should also be taken into account. It is essential that the overall cost of a Community patent should be in the same order of magnitude as that associated with patents granted by the Community's main trading partners, or even be more attractive.

. . . .

The cost of the current European patent is . . . three to five times higher than that of Japanese and US patents.

There is thus an urgent need to remedy this situation, which does not provide any incentive for inventors to apply for a patent in Europe.

Under the proposed Regulation, the Office will examine Community patent applications and grant and administer Community patents. The fees charged by the Office during the examination of a patent application are laid down in the Munich Convention. By contrast, it is planned that the annual renewal fees for patents granted, as well as their amount, will be determined in a Commission Regulation on fees which will be adopted according to the comitology procedure. The Regulation provides that the annual renewal fees must also be paid to the Office.

Language arrangements—access to information

The arrangements concerning translations of the patent are a particularly important aspect in terms of the cost of the Community patent (*see* Table above). The cost of translating the patent into all the official languages of the Community would entail a risk of the entire Community patent project foundering, placing as it would too heavy a burden on inventors, above all small and medium-sized enterprises. Such a burden would discourage them from using the Community patent and give them an incentive to seek protection only in certain European countries. With the enlargement of the Union, compulsory translation into all the official languages would have even more negative effects in terms of cost.

To remedy this problem, the proposed Regulation provides that the Community patent, once it is has been granted in one of the procedural languages of the Office and published in that language, with a translation of the claims into the two other procedural languages, will be valid without any other translation. A translation could become necessary in legal proceedings against a suspected infringer. In such a situation, a suspected infringer who has been unable to consult the text of the patent in the official language of the Member State in which he is domiciled, is presumed, until proven otherwise, not to have knowingly infringed the patent. In order to protect a suspected infringer who, in such a situation, has not acted in a deliberate manner, it is provided that the proprietor of the patent will not be able to obtain damages in respect of the period prior to the translation of the patent being notified to the infringer. This system will make for a considerable reduction in translation costs.

The proposed system is regarded as appropriate, primarily because the universal language in the field of patents is, in reality, English. Translations are very rarely consulted. For example, at the Institut National de la Propriété Industrielle, the French national institute of industrial property rights, translations are consulted in only 2% of cases. Moreover, any obligation to translate the patent into all the Community languages would not necessarily guarantee easy access to this information for all economic operators established in the Community.

Incidentally, separate information and assistance systems can be put in place or upgraded in order to help small and medium-sized enterprises, in particular, in searching for information on patent applications and patents published.

Secondly, the proposed system is regarded as providing sufficient protection with respect to a suspected infringer, given that the Regulation's provisions on damages will enable the Community intellectual property court, which will be established to deal with Community patent matter, to take into account all the relevant factors in each individual case.

Moreover, this provision is in line with the work begun in the IGC on the revision of the Munich Convention, particularly that undertaken by the working party on cost reduction, whose remit from the member states of the European Patent Organisation is to put forward proposals for lowering the cost of the European patent. Accordingly, it is also provided that translations of the patent—which will, moreover, be optional for the proprietor—must be filed with the Office rather than with national patent offices in several Member States. This should yield a considerable cost reduction compared with the total cost of an average European patent.

Legal certainty of the Community patent: the judicial system

European undertakings and inventors expect a judicial system that provides maximum legal certainty for the European patent. Only if this is the case can the often considerable research and development costs incurred upstream of the patent be offset. Only a centralised Community court can guarantee without fail unity of law and consistent case law. This relates exclusively to litigation between private parties. Appeals against administrative decisions relating to the Community patent will be governed by the procedures provided for by the Munich Convention. Finally, the link between the proposal for a Regulation and the Intergovernmental Conference on Institutional Reform and the division of responsibilities within the centralised Community court must be pointed out.

The judicial system in relation to litigation between private parties

The system adopted in the Luxembourg Convention has not been followed in this proposal. It would have enabled a national court hearing a counterclaim for a declaration of invalidity to declare the Community patent invalid throughout the Community. The solution adopted in this proposal is ambitious: it provides for the creation of a centralised judicial system specialising in patent matters, particularly for the examination of questions concerning validity and infringement of the Community patent. To this end, a "Community Intellectual Property Court" will be established. This court will comprise chambers of first instance and appeal. These two instances, whose jurisdiction will cover the entire Community territory, may deal with questions relating to the actual facts of a case as well as to points of law. They will apply their own rules of procedure, grant provisional measures, determine penalties and award damages. The judgments of the court will be enforceable. Enforcement will be governed by the rules of civil procedure in force in the State in the territory of which it is carried out. The national authorities shall automatically issue an enforcement order in respect of an authentic judgment. It is planned to establish this court by way of an amendment to the EC Treaty currently under discussion in the Intergovernmental Conference on Institutional Reform. The Commission regards the creation of a centralised Community judicial system as being necessary for several reasons: first of all, less ambitious solutions which have been negotiated or sketched out in the past have failed. Inventors would not use the future Community patent without "Community-level" legal certainty. A non-centralised judicial system such as that for European patents, under which, for example, legal actions relating to the validity of a patent have to be instituted separately in all the Contracting States for which the patent has been granted, would be unacceptable for the Community patent. Not only would the management of patent rights under such a system be very costly for the proprietor, but—above all—a non-centralised system would not give proprietors of the Community patent the necessary legal certainty as regards the validity of the patent throughout the territory for which it was granted. Only a centralised judicial system can guarantee unity of law and consistent case law. Moreover, it is necessary to avoid from the outset a situation where a national court with no experience of industrial property matters could decide on the validity or infringement of the Community patent. Due account has also been taken of the need for the centralised court to have all the requisite qualifications in patent matters. The composition of the court should be such as to guarantee that the judges have the necessary qualifications in the field of patents, which can involve the examination of highly technical questions. This is not currently the case at the Court of First Instance of the Court of Justice, which has not had the opportunity to gain experience in patent matters.

The creation of a new centralised judicial system is also necessary in order to address the problem of excessive workload which is affecting both the Court of Justice and the Court of First Instance. For the Community patent, it is essential that questions relating to the validity and infringement of the patent be answered definitively within a period of two years. This time limit takes into account the relatively short duration of the protection offered by the patent, which in principle is 20 years but in reality is much shorter on account of the progressive nature of the annual renewal fees which the proprietor of the patent has to pay and the rapid advance of technology. For these reasons, the interesting alternative of assigning to the Court of First Instance the role of a court of appeal against national court decisions which would have decided on the validity of the patent throughout the Community territory was dropped. The jurisdiction of the centralised court would cover only certain categories of actions. It is essential that it be able to deal at the same time with disputes relating to the infringement and the validity of the patent (for example, actions for a declaration of non-infringement, invalidity proceedings, or counterclaims for invalidity). The reason for this is that defendants in infringement actions almost always make a claim of patent invalidity as a means of defence. Separating the jurisdictions for these two types of action would be conducive neither to the sound administration of justice nor to the efficiency aimed for in this Regulation, given that the factors which the judge has to examine in the two cases are essentially the same. The centralised court should also handle litigation relating to use of the patent in the period between publication of the application and the actual granting of the patent. The same applies to actions relating to the limitation or lapse of the patent. It is essential that the jurisdiction of the centralised court be exclusive. This jurisdiction is based on the validity of the patent in the territory of the Community, as well as on the location of the facts and activities concerned taking place in the Community. The Regulation will have to provide that all other disputes between private parties which do not specifically come under the jurisdiction of the centralised court are to be dealt with by the national courts of the Member States. Such disputes might concern, for example, the right to the patent, the transfer of the patent or contractual licences. For situations where jurisdiction resides with national courts, the Regulation provides that the rules set out in the 1968 Brussels Convention on Jurisdiction and Enforcement of Judgments in Civil and Commercial Matters (the "Brussels Convention") shall, in principle, be applicable. The Regulation will specify the necessary exceptions and adaptations. This Convention will be transformed into a Regulation. It is understood that, for the Member States concerned, the reference to the Brussels Convention is to be deemed a reference to the Implementing Regulations once these have been definitively adopted by the Council. However, whenever an action relates to the validity or infringement of the Community patent, the national court before which the case has been brought will be obliged to decline jurisdiction and declare the action inadmissible. If the validity of the patent is a preliminary issue in a case relating to another subject, e.g. unfair competition, the national court hearing the case will stay the proceedings to enable the parties to resolve the issue of a preliminary nature in an action brought before the centralised court. The national courts remain free to submit a request to the Court of Justice for preliminary rulings on matters falling within their jurisdiction, for example concerning interpretation of Directive 98/44/EC on the legal protection of biotechnological inventions. However, national courts will not, in principle, be authorised to request preliminary rulings concerning the validity of the Community patent on the basis of the Regulation, since they will not have jurisdiction in the matter.

Appeals against decisions of the Office and of the Commission

The Office's internal opposition and appeal procedures will be applicable to the Community patent. Decisions by the Office will not be subject to appeal before the centralised Community court. This solution has been adopted with a view to retaining for as long as possible the unified treatment of simultaneous application for a Community patent and a European patent. It also avoids burdening the centralised Community court with a proliferation of appeals lodged during the examination procedure and before the Community patent has been granted. The solution is also appropriate from the point of view of the legal status of the Office's Boards of Appeal. A board of appeal has been regarded, in the United Kingdom for example, as being entirely equivalent to a court, to the extent that its decisions were final and based on objective criteria, and the independence of its members was guaranteed by the Munich Convention. Account will also have to be taken of the fact that the validity of a patent granted by the Office may subsequently be the subject of litigation between private parties before the Community intellectual property court under the conditions laid down by the Regulation. At present, however, the solution has the disadvantage of considerably delaying the adoption of a final decision on the validity of the Community patent. This delay is due to the sometimes very long examination periods of the Office's Opposition Division and Boards of Appeal. It would appear, however, that a revision of the Munich Convention on this point could resolve the problem. Moreover, it is clear that judicial review of decisions taken by the Commission falls within the jurisdiction of a Community court. Such jurisdiction is vested in the Court of Justice (Court of First Instance) under Article 230 of the EC Treaty. Examination of appeals relating to decisions taken pursuant to the Regulation on the Community patent will in future often require knowledge in the field of competition law. In particular, these will be appeals against decisions by the Commission concerning compulsory licences and licences of right. The Court of First Instance remains best placed to examine the last-named type of appeal, concerning which it has already gained experience. It is, therefore, not proposed to change the attribution of areas of jurisdiction which reside with the Court of First Instance. This solution is an appropriate means of guaranteeing the consistency of Community case law in this field.

Link between the proposal for a Regulation and the Intergovernmental Conference on Institutional Reform

It is understood that the Community intellectual property court will be established by way of an amendment to the EC Treaty. Discussions to this effect are currently under way in the Intergovernmental Conference on Institutional Reform. The EC Treaty would then also provide that this court, like the Court of First Instance (Articles 225 and 243 to 245 of the EC Treaty), would adopt its own rules of procedure and order provisional measures, and that its judgments would be enforceable in the Member States in the same way as decisions of the Court of Justice. Relations between the Community courts, including the mechanism for referral in the interest of the law referred to below would also be laid down in the EC Treaty. The Commission has already suggested, in its opinions of 26 January and 1 March 2000, that the Intergovernmental Conference discuss an amendment to the Treaty designed to provide adequate legal certainty in matters of Community intellectual property. Thus, in its Additional Contribution to the Intergovernmental Conference on Institutional Reform, the Commission took the view that, "regarding intellectual property rights under Community law, particularly with the prospect of the Community patent, consideration should be given to establishing a specialised tribunal with jurisdiction in cases concerning patent validity and infringements, in order to secure legal certainty regarding unitary documents having effect throughout the Community and to relieving the Court of Justice and the CFI of all this highly specialised litigation."

Pending the outcome of the negotiations under way in the Intergovernmental Conference, the Commission has therefore introduced, in this proposal for a Regulation, fundamental provisions corresponding to its Contribution. It goes without saying that more detailed provisions will have to be adopted, concerning in particular the rules of procedure applicable by the new Community court. These provisions, as well as the status of the court, will be laid down in subsequent instruments.

Division of responsibilities within the centralised Community court

As already mentioned above, the new court would have jurisdiction in certain situations where jurisdiction would normally have been vested in the Court of First Instance. As already mentioned. . . ., the Court of First Instance will nevertheless continue to have jurisdiction in respect of decisions taken by the Commission. Appeals against the Court's decisions will be governed by the current provisions of the EC Treaty. As far as the new court is concerned, the planned provisions would not include the possibility of lodging a direct appeal before the Court of Justice against decisions of the chamber of appeal of the Community intellectual property court. Nor is it planned to introduce into the relationship between the new Community court and the Court of Justice a mechanism for requesting preliminary rulings like the one that is a feature of relations between the national courts and the Court of Justice. In spite of this, the proposed system would not affect the role of the Court of Justice as the supreme court of Community law. If the Community intellectual property court had to interpret more general aspects of Community law in the cases it dealt with, the amended EC Treaty would provide scope for the matter subsequently to be brought before the Court of Justice in the interest of the law. This mechanism would make it possible to verify whether or not the interpretation of Community law made by the Community intellectual property court was in conflict with the interpretation handed down by the Court of Justice. The principle and the mechanism for requesting preliminary rulings are similar to those adopted in the 1971 Protocol annexed to the Brussels Convention (Article 4). Accordingly, such a referral can only be made in respect of judgments by the chamber of first instance or the chamber of appeal which have become res judicata. The Registrar of the Court of Justice shall give notice of the request to the Member States and Institutions of the Community; they shall then be entitled, within two months of the notification, to submit statements of case or written observations to the Court. What is more, the interpretation given by the Court of Justice in response to such a request shall not affect the decision which gave rise to the request for interpretation. No fees shall be levied or any costs or expenses awarded in respect of the proceedings. In contrast to the provisions of the said Protocol, the Commission can, as guardian of the EC Treaty, bring an action before the Court of Justice. It goes without saying that, as a Community court, the new court would be subject to the case law of the Court of Justice, whether this related to interpretations in appeals made in the interest of the law or to preliminary rulings issued at the request of national courts in cases coming under their jurisdiction.

Links with other patent systems

The Community patent system will coexist with the national and European patent systems. Inventors will remain free to choose the patent system best suited to their needs. For a Community patent to be granted, the territory of the Community will have to be designated in the application for a European patent. It will not be possible to designate, in an application for a European patent, both the territory of the Community and one or more Member States. However, an applicant will be able to request at the same time a patent for the territory of the Community and a European patent for Switzerland, Cyprus, Monaco or Liechtenstein. It is also provided that, at any time up to the grant of the European patent, a European patent application designating all the Member States of the Community can be converted into a European patent application designating the entire territory of the Community. Similarly, a European patent application which designates the entire territory of the Community may be converted into a European patent designating one or more

Member States of the Community. The principle of conversion and the procedures for its application should be the subject of negotiations in the context of the Community's accession to the Munich Convention. Once granted, a Community patent may not be converted into a European patent. Nor will it be possible to convert national patents or a European patent into a Community patent. It will not be possible for one and the same invention belonging to one and the same person to be simultaneously protected by a Community patent and by a European patent designating one or more Member States, or by a national patent granted by a Member State.

Justification For Proposal In Terms Of Proportionality And Subsidiarity Principles

What are the objectives of the proposed measure in relation to the obligations incumbent on the Community? The proposal is aimed at improving the operation of the internal market and, in particular, at adapting the manufacture and distribution of patented products to the Community dimension. The proposal is also part of the drive to promote innovation and growth in the European Community. Does the measure satisfy the criteria of subsidiarity? These objectives cannot be attained by the Member States acting alone or collectively and must therefore, by reason of the cross-border impact, be attained at Community level. Are the means deployed at Community level proportional to the objectives? The Court of Justice has ruled that Community intellectual property rights cannot be created by harmonising national legislation. Having regard to the unity of the right, Member States cannot be left with any discretion concerning its implementation. The proposed instrument, a Regulation, is thus confined to the minimum needed for the attainment of these objectives and does not exceed what is necessary for that purpose.

[B]   Eurasian Patent Convention

JOHN RICHARDS, RECENT PATENT LAW DEVELOPMENTS IN ASIA[*]
7 FORDHAM INTELL. PROP. MEDIA & ENT. L.J. 599 (1997)

Marco Polo's silk route proceeds to the countries that are parties to the Eurasian Convention. The Eurasian Convention became operative on January 1, 1996, and could be designated in PCT applications under code EA since that date. Its present members are: Armenia, Azerbaijan, Belarus, Kazakstan, Kyrgyzstan, the Republic of Moldova, the Russian Federation, Tajikistan, and Turkmenistan. This means that, aside from the Baltic republics, which have oriented themselves towards the European Patent Office, the only former Soviet republics not to have joined the Eurasian Patent Convention are Georgia, Ukraine, and Uzbekistan, although Georgia and Ukraine were both signatories to the original treaty.

The standard for patentability under the Eurasian Convention is the now-standard one of novelty, inventive step, and industrial applicability. However, the treaty establishing the Convention left to the Convention's Administrative Council—which consists of the heads of the national patent offices of the member states—the definitions to be adopted for these features. In fact, it appears that the Russian Patent Office will carry out the search and that worldwide publication, use, or disclosure are as destructive of novelty as is a previously-filed Eurasian patent application. Disclosures by, or deriving from, an applicant or inventor are, however, subject to a six-month grace period from the date of disclosure if an application is filed in the Eurasian Patent Office or, apparently, in another patent office if priority is claimed from it.

Under the Eurasian Convention, a single patent application designating all of the Contracting States is filed in Russian in the central Eurasian Patent Office in Moscow, where the application procedure is similar to that of the European Patent Office. There will, therefore, be an early publication of the application eighteen months from either the Eurasian filing date or the national filing date from which priority is claimed. The applicant must request substantive examination within six months of that publication. Unlike the European Patent Office, however, the Eurasian Convention does not require "completion" of the patent in the various designated countries or filing of a translation of the patent in the languages of the designated non-Russian-speaking countries at the end of the prosecution. Renewal fees for a Eurasian patent will depend on the number of countries in which the patentee wishes to keep the patent in force.

The term of a patent under the Eurasian Convention is twenty years. As with the new Russian law, there will be publication of the application before grant, and a right to compensation for use of the invention during the pendency of the actual patent grant.

An interesting side effect of the use of the European Patent Convention as a model for the Eurasian Convention is the Eurasian Convention's attempt to incorporate a counterpart to the infamous Article 69 of the European Patent Convention and its protocol on the interpretation of claims. Rule 12 of the regulations promulgated under the Eurasian Convention provides that the scope of protection shall be determined by the claims, taking into account each feature, and possibly an equivalent of each feature, of the claims, interpreted in light of the description. Such an interpretation, however, will be not only to elucidate what is unclear or indefinite, but also to determine the true meaning of the claim, which is to be neither its literal meaning nor its general inventive idea.

. . . .

NOTES AND QUESTIONS

(1) **Russian Patent Law**. The break-up of the Soviet Union created complications in the effect of patents granted prior to 1991. A new patent law was adopted by the Russian Federation in 1992. These developments are discussed in John M. Romary & Howard A. Kwon, *Adapting to the Modern World*, 76 MANAGING INTELL. PROP. 27 (1998).

(2) **Eurasian Patent Law as a Model.** What attributes of the Eurasian patent system, if any, might serve as models for an improved European patent? The Eurasian system was the product of the rapid disintegration of the Soviet system and rapid reintegration of the same countries, unlike the European system which has grown steadily in tandem with European integration.

[C] African Intellectual Property Organization [OAPI] and the African Regional Industrial Property Organization [ARIPO]

TSHIMANGA KONGOLO, THE AFRICAN INTELLECTUAL PROPERTY ORGANIZATIONS: THE NECESSITY OF ADOPTING ONE UNIFORM SYSTEM FOR ALL AFRICA[*]
3 J. WORLD INT. PROP. 265 (2000)

I. Introduction

. . . [A]t present in Africa, two major regional organizations dealing with intellectual property matters exist: the African Regional Industrial Property Organization (hereinafter the ARIPO) and the Organisation Africaine de la Propriete Intellectuelle (OAPI). The two Organizations were established after the independence of most African countries. However, it is unfortunate to notice that only a few African countries are members of the ARIPO and the OAPI. It should be mentioned at the outset that the systems of protection provided under these Organizations do not reflect, in a strict sense, the African realities. They are, to some extent, simply the transposition of the so-called international protection system to the regional level, almost without adjustment. In other words, the ARIPO and the OAPI systems are modeled after the Western style of intellectual property protection which does not always correspond and fit to the African realities and environment. Notwithstanding that the Organizations have played a significant role in the harmonization of the intellectual property laws of their Members, it should be pointed out that these Organizations are not without shortcomings. Their systems would be more effective if they would take into consideration African needs, priorities and realities. They should guide African countries for the setting up of a unique African system of protection of intellectual property which would enable the international community to acknowledge the African vision. . . .

II. Overview Of The ARIPO And The OAPI

A. The ARIPO

1. The Background of the ARIPO

The ARIPO was previously known as the Industrial Property Organization for English-Speaking Africa (ESARIPO). The idea of developing a regional patent system arose as early as 1972 when representatives of English-speaking African countries attending a seminar on copyrights called on the World Intellectual Property Organization and the United Nations Organization to assist in the establishment of a regional industrial property office for English-speaking Africa. The change in name became necessary when it became open to all Member countries of the Organization of African Unity (OAU). Its headquarters is based in Harare, Zimbabwe. The ARIPO Agreement was adopted at Lusaka, Zambia, in 1976 and supplemented by two Protocols, namely the Protocol on Patents and Industrial Designs within the Framework of the ARIPO, adopted at Harare on 10 December 1982, and the Banjul Protocol on Marks, adopted at Banjul, The Gambia, on 19 November 1993.

2. The Objectives of the ARIPO and its Membership

Article III of the Agreement on the Creation of the ARIPO lays down the objectives of the ARIPO as follows:

(a) to promote the harmonisation and development of the industrial property laws, and matters related thereto, appropriate to the needs of its Members and of the region as a whole;

(b) to foster the establishment of a close relationship between its Members in matters relating to industrial property;

(c) to establish such common services or organs as may be necessary or desirable for the co-ordination, harmonization and development of the industrial property activities affecting its Members;

(d) to establish schemes for the training of staff in the administration of industrial property laws;

(e) to organize conferences, seminars and other meetings on industrial property matters; to promote the exchange of ideas and experience, research and studies relating to industrial property matters;

(f) to promote and evolve a common view and approach of its Members on industrial property matters;

(g) to assist its Members, as appropriate, in the acquisition and development of technology relating to industrial property matters; and

(h) to do all such other things as may be necessary or desirable for the achievement of the objectives.

It is not the purpose of this study to examine whether these objectives have been achieved. What can be said is that this Agreement does not contain any objective which would safeguard, foster or promote African values, traditional knowledge and folklore, or facilitate the recognition, under the international framework, of African traditional components and the African vision as regards the protection Of intellectual property in general, and industrial property in particular. This is unfortunate.

Regarding membership, according to Article IV of the Agreement of the Creation of the ARIPO, membership of the Organization shall be open to the State members of the UN Economic Commission for Africa or the Organization of African Unity. At present, the ARIPO is made up off fourteen members. The number of Members is very small. Several reasons restrain countries from adhering to this Organization. One of the barriers is the language. The official language being only English, it is quite obvious that French-speaking countries would not adhere.

3. The ARIPO Agreement and Protocols

The ARIPO is principally governed by the Agreement on the Creation of the ARIPO and by two Protocols, namely, the Protocol on Patents and Industrial Designs within the Framework of the ARIPO, and the Banjul Protocol on Marks.

Besides the Agreement on the Creation, the two Protocols are accompanied by two Regulations; the main features of the Agreement and Protocols will be highlighted below.

(a) Agreement on the Creation of the ARIPO

This Agreement encompasses sixteen Articles that include objectives, organs and functions, membership status, privileges and immunities, obligations of Members of the Organization, settlement of disputes, amendment, etc. The Organization is composed of three main organs, namely, the Council of Ministers, the Administrative Council and the Secretariat. The Agreement has established a special relationship with the UN Economic Commission for Africa, the Organization of African Unity and the WIPO. The ARIPO may co-operate with Governments of States not members of the Organization and with other organizations, institutions and bodies.

(b) Protocol on Patents and Industrial Designs within the Framework of the ARIPO

This Protocol comprises provisions regarding patents and industrial designs. As regards both patents and industrial designs, the ARIPO is empowered to grant, register and administer such patents and industrial designs on behalf of the Contracting States. According to the ARIPO Regulations for Implementing the Protocol on Patents and Industrial Designs, the ARIPO Office shall maintain a Patents Register and an Industrial Designs Register in which shall be recorded, respectively, all patents granted and all industrial designs registered under the Protocol. Applications for the grant of patents or the registration of industrial designs by the ARIPO Office shall be filed by the authorized representative of the applicant or by the applicant with the industrial property office of a Contracting State. The industrial property office with which the application is filed shall, without delay, transmit that application to the Office of the ARIPO. The application may contain a declaration claiming, in respect of one or several designated States, the priority, as provided for in the Paris Convention, of one or more earlier national, regional or international applications filed by the applicant or his predecessor in title in or for any State party to the Paris Convention. Pursuant to the Regulations, the ARIPO has acknowledged the first-to-file principle.

(i) Patents

Under the ARIPO [agreement], the patentee files a single application and designates any Member country of the Contracting States in which the patent will have validity, unless any Member country makes prior renunciation of the same. The ARIPO Office examines the compliance with formal requirements by the applicant and notifies each designated State when the prescribed requirements are met. Before the expiration of six months from the date of the notification, a designated State may declare that the patent shall have no effect in its territory for the reason that the invention is not patentable in accordance with the provisions of the Protocol, or that the nature of the invention is out of the protected subject-matter as stipulated under the national law of that State.

The ARIPO is designated to be an additional system of protection coexisting with the national patent systems of the member States. Its main purpose is the grant of regional patents having effect in all designated Member countries through a common granting authority, under its own rules and standards of patentability. Under the Protocol of the ARIPO various provisions of substantive patent law are set out, such as conditions for patentability, patent granting procedure, and establishment of an independent patent system. In addition, the ARIPO recommends its Members to adhere to the PCT.

It is set out that on each anniversary of the filing of the application, the ARIPO office shall collect the prescribed annual maintenance fee, part of which shall be distributed among the designated States concerned. The amount of the fee shall depend on the number of States in respect of which the application or patent is maintained. Moreover, a patent granted by the ARIPO Office shall, in each designated State, have the same effect as a patent registered, granted or otherwise having effect under the applicable national law but not beyond the maximum duration provided for under the said law. Under paragraph 11 of Section 3, a patent granted by the ARIPO Office shall, in each designated State, be subject to the provisions of the applicable national law on compulsory licences, forfeiture, or the use of patented inventions in the public interest.

The ARIPO, under its Protocol and Regulations, has provided special norms and rules in respect of patents relating to micro-organisms. . . .

4. The Relationship between the ARIPO and the PCT

The ARIPO recommends that its Members adhere to the Patent Co-operation Treaty. The ARIPO operates almost in the same way as the PCT. It is stipulated in Article 3bis(3) of the Protocol on Patents and Industrial Designs, pertaining to international applications, that the ARIPO Office may act as receiving Office under Article 2(XV) of the PCT in relation to an international application filed by an applicant who is a resident or national of a Contracting State which is also bound by the PCT. From the same perspective, an international application in which a Contracting State which is also bound by the PCT is designated for the purposes of obtaining a patent under the provisions of the Protocol shall be considered to be an application for the grant of a patent under this Protocol. In addition, the provisions of the PCT shall apply to such international application in addition to the provisions of this Protocol and the Regulations under this Protocol; in case of conflict, the provisions of the PCT shall prevail.

B. The Organisation Africaine De La Propriete Intellectuelle

"OAPI" is the commonly used acronym for the African Intellectual Property Organization. The acronym OAPI is derived from the French name of the Organization which is Organisation Africaine de la Propriete Intellectuelle. The OAPI is constituted of French-speaking African countries. It has its headquarters in Yaounde, Cameroon.

This section endeavours to scrutinize the main provisions embodied in the OAPI. Attention will be principally drawn to the following matters:

1. The background of the OAPI
2. The objectives of the OAPI and its Membership
3. OAPI Annexes.

1. The Background of the OAPI

After some of the French colonies gained their independence, they joined hands and created the OAPI. The first Agreement, signed at Libreville on 13 September 1962, was known as the Agreement Relating to the Creation of an African and Malagasy Office of Industrial Property. This Agreement was revised at Bangui on 2 March 1977, and called the Agreement Relating to the Creation of an African Intellectual Property Organization which replaced the African and Malagasy Office of Industrial Property. This revised Agreement is called and known as the Bangui Agreement, and it entered into force on 8 February 1982.

It is meaningful to point out that the Bangui Agreement has been under revision since February 1999 so that it will meet the requirements of the TRIPs Agreement. Substantial amendments to the Agreement, which will enter into force after ten Contracting States ratify it, are attached as an Annex to this article. It should be noted that the Bangui Agreement encompasses nine Annexes which cover, respectively: patents; utility models; trademarks and service marks; industrial designs; trade names and protection against unfair competition; appellations of origin; copyright and the cultural heritage; central body for patent documentation and information Documentation Center); and Annex IX (untitled). This will change when the Amended Agreement comes into force (see the Annex to this article).

2. The Objectives of the OAPI and its Membership

The main aim of the OAPI is to have a uniform system of protection of intellectual property rights within the national framework of its Members. The OAPI countries have adopted a uniform system of protection whereby intellectual property rights are granted on their behalf by the Organization. In the same context, the OAPI aims at contributing to the promotion of the protection of literary and artistic property and to the recognition of the cultural and social values of artistic and literary property. For each of the Member States, the OAPI serves both as the national industrial property service within the meaning of Article 12 of the Paris Convention and as the central patent documentation and information body. In other words, the OAPI Office serves as the National Office of its Member States.

According to Article 2 of the Agreement, nationals may claim application for their benefit of the provisions of the Paris Convention for the Protection of Industrial Property, the Berne Convention for the Protection of Literary and Artistic Works and/or the Universal Copyright Convention, as well as the Agreements, additional Acts and closing Protocols which have amended or will amend these Conventions, in cases where such provisions are more favourable than those of the present Agreements and its Annexes in protecting intellectual property rights. Furthermore, under Article 14, in the case of discrepancies between the provisions of the present Agreement and its Annexes and those of the international conventions to which the Member states are party and which are administered by the International Bureau of the WIPO, the latter shall prevail.

Regarding membership, the Bangui Agreement provides that any African State which is not a signatory to the present Agreement but which is party to the Convention Establishing the WIPO, to the Paris Convention and to the Berne Convention and/or the Universal Copyright Convention may apply to accede to the present Agreement. In addition, any State may become an associated Member. The OAPI is constituted of fifteen Member countries. . . .

3. The OAPI Annexes

As mentioned above, each Annex deals with a specific intellectual property category:

Annex I: Patents

. . . .

Under this paragraph, attention will be drawn to the conditions for eligibility and scope of protection, rights conferred, the working of patents and compulsory licences, and enforcement of rights.

(i) Conditions for eligibility and scope of protection

Article 1 (1) of Annex I lays down the conditions of eligibility for patents: the invention shall be new, involve an inventive step and be industrially applicable. Articles 2, 3 and 4 define and specify the extent of each condition for patentability. It should be pointed out that patents are not available for inventions which are contrary to public order or morality. In addition, patents are not available in respect of scientific and mathematical theories, inventions having as their object plant varieties, animal species, essentially biological processes for the breeding of plants or animals, other than microbiological processes and the products of such processes, schemes, rules or methods for doing business, performing purely mental acts or playing games, methods for treatment of the human or animal body by surgery or therapy, as well as diagnostic methods, straightforward presentation of information, computer programs, and works of an exclusively ornamental nature.

Under this Annex, plant varieties and computer programs are out of the ambit of patent protection. Regarding the former a specific law or sui generis regime would be preferable. As to the latter, the copyright regime would be suitable.

(ii) Rights conferred

Under this Annex, the patentee is entitled to preclude any person from exploiting the patented invention without his consent. He has the exclusive rights, in respect of a product or a process, of making, importing, offering for sale, selling and utilizing the product or process. Further, the patentee may preclude any person from stocking such product for the purposes of offering for sale, selling or utilizing it.

It should be mentioned that the patentee is entitled to assign or license his exclusive rights to another person.

The exclusive rights of the patentee are protected for a period of ten years following the date of the filing of the application. This period can be extended for five years if the patentee proves that his invention is being worked on the territory of one of the Member States at the date of request, or that there are legitimate reasons for failing to so work it. TRIPS, however, requires Members to grant patent protection for twenty years from the filing date of the application.

(iii) Working of patents and compulsory licences

According to Article 6(3), working of patents means the manufacture of a patented article, the application of a patented process or the use, in manufacture, of a patented machine, by effective and serious establishment and on a scale which is adequate and reasonable in the circumstances. In the same line of reasoning, the import of a patented product is not deemed to be the working. It is necessary to state this under this Annex, the prior-use regime has been acknowledged. The date of the filing of an application for a patent, or three years from the date of the grant of a patent, a compulsory licence may be granted on the request of any interested person, principally if the patented invention is not worked in the territory of a Member State at the time the request is made. As stated above, the importation of patented products is not deemed to be a working of a patent. The request for the grant of a compulsory licence shall be made to the civil court of the domicile of the patentee. Further, the Annex has provided the regime of licences of right and ex offico licences.

(iv) Enforcement of rights

Under Annex 1, both civil and criminal remedies are provided in the case of infringement of the patentee's exclusive rights. Nevertheless, no action for infringement of a patented invention is accepted if the patented invention had not been worked five years after the grant of patent. It should be mentioned that what constitutes infringement is the fact of knowingly received, sold, exhibited for sale or introduced on the national territory of one of the Member States one or several infringing objects by any person....

QUESTIONS

Assess the extent to which the OAPI and ARIPO (and Eurasian, *see* above) systems serve the interests of the developing or transition economy countries of their member states. How do the mechanisms established in the Libreville and Lusaka Agreements compare to the European patent system? The number of patent applications filed in the OAPI office in Yaounde has been falling consistently. Can you attribute that to any of the characteristics of the "Libreville system"? National applications filed in the ARIPO office have dwindled as well. Some reasons for this may be due to the economic conditions in these countries. But others may be systemic. Does it make sense to "preserve the activity of [local] practitioners" in fashioning a multilateral system? On the other hand, for example, do you think that proximity of Yaounde practitioners to the OAPI office (or for that matter, the proximity of Munich law firms to the EPO) provides a competitive advantage not enjoyed by law firms, say, in Lome or Ouagadougou (or Helsinki and Copenhagen)? To what extent do the interests of patent practitioners *in fact* affect the way an international patent system is structured? To what extent *should* they?

[D] Latin America

Patent law reform and regional cooperation between Latin American states is taking place at a rapid pace. Two Central American countries, Guatemala and El Salvador, were among the eleven founding countries of the Paris Convention in 1883, but both denounced the convention shortly thereafter. Of all the countries of Latin America, only ten were members of the Paris Convention in 1994 (Argentina, Barbados, Brazil, Chile, Cuba, Dominican Republic, Haiti, Mexico, Trinidad and Tobago, and Uruguay).

Mexico modernized its patent law in 1991 and became a member of the North American Free Trade Agreement in 1994. The patent provisions of the NAFTA generally parallel those of the TRIPS Agreement, with the addition of "pipeline protection" for pharmaceutical and agricultural chemicals. NAFTA art. 1709.4.

("Pipeline protection" offers the holder of an unexpired patent on such products in another NAFTA member state patent protection in Mexico for the unexpired term of the patent in the United States or Canada, as long as the product has not been marketed in Mexico.) Enforcement and validity of Mexican patents are determined in the first instance by the Mexican Institute of Industrial Property ("IMPI").

The five Central American countries (Guatemala, El Salvador, Honduras, Nicaragua, and Costa Rica) signed the Central American Convention for the Protection of Industrial Property in 1968; however, this agreement did not cover patents. It did establish the Central American Permanent Secretariat on Economic Integration ("SEICA"), which began work on a regional covenant for patents in February 1997. That work is ongoing.

On October 21, 1993, the four countries of the Andean Pact (Columbia, Ecuador, Peru, and Venezuela) which are parties to the Cartagena Agreement adopted Decision No. 344, entitled *Common Provisions on Industrial Property*. *See* INDUS. PROP. (March 1994) Text 1-012. This decision established uniform standards of patentability throughout the Andean Pact countries (now called the "Andean Union"). Among the items still excluded from patentability by Decision No. 344 are inventions relating to pharmaceutical products appearing on the List of Essential Drugs of the World Health Organization. Art. 7(e). Decision No. 344 also established that working requirements for an Andean patent could be met by importation. Art. 38.

The countries of the South American Common Market, MERCOSUR (Brazil, Argentina, Uruguay and Paraguay) recently established an intellectual property commission to study and propose harmonized treatment of intellectual property. The focus of these discussions is not on patents, however, but on trademarks.

Broader discussions have taken place within the framework of the Latin American and Caribbean Forum on Intellectual Property Policies of the Latin American Economic System ("SELA"), which has its permanent secretariat in Caracas, and which has focused its studies on the impact of the TRIPS Agreement on the member countries. UNESCO has been a source of support for the activities of SELA.

[E] Proposed Free Trade Area of the Americas ("FTAA")

Following acceptance of the NAFTA by Canada, Mexico, and the United States in late 1993, and the Andean Pact and MERCOSUR developments mentioned above, focus of attention among trade officials shifted to expanding the depth and scope of international economic relations between a greater number of the countries of the Western Hemisphere, consistent with the obligations of these countries under Article XXIV of the GATT Agreement and Article V of the GATS Agreement. Intellectual property became one of the central issues in negotiating broader multilateral trade cooperation between the United States and a greater number of countries in the South and Central American region. This culminated in negotiations between the United States and a number of other countries in the Western Hemisphere toward closer economic integration through the Free Trade Area of the Americas at a ministerial level meeting in 1995 in Miami. Intellectual property rights were originally one of the key areas for negotiation of the FTAA. One purpose of the FTAA negotiations was to maximize the openness of markets through high levels of compliance with the existing agreements (such as the TRIPS Agreement) regarding intellectual property rights and their creation, maintenance, and protection and eventual adoption of "TRIPS-plus" or even "NAFTA-level-plus" protection of IPRs throughout the Western Hemisphere.

The Miami ministerial meeting also requested progress reports from the Working Group on Smaller Economies to recommend measures, including technical assistance, to facilitate the integration of smaller economies into the FTAA. The Inter-American Development Bank ("IDB") was slated to set up a multilateral investment fund as a principal way of stimulating the development of intellectual property rights in Latin American countries. In December 1995, the Office of the USTR promulgated proposed terms of reference for action by the Working Group on Intellectual Property including the following recommendations:

> • [to] create an inventory of intellectual property agreements, treaties, and arrangements that exist in the region, including all international conventions (*e.g.*, Berne, Paris, Geneva Phonograms, WIPO, etc.) to which countries are parties;
>
> • compile in the most efficient manner possible an inventory of intellectual property protection laws, practices, and remedies in the region and, on the basis of this information, identify areas of commonality and make specific recommendations in accordance with the goal of establishing a high and effective level of protection throughout the Hemisphere and of ensuring that standards of protection are not eroded by advances in technology;
>
> • recommend methods to promote understanding of the TRIPS Agreement and recommend measures for the effective and prompt implementation of that Agreement;
>
> • identify measures to eliminate possible restrictions on the market access of intellectual property-related products and services throughout the Hemisphere, including through electronic transmission;
>
> • identify measures to improve the administration of intellectual property rights, such as by facilitating the application for and grant of intellectual property rights;
>
> • identify needs for training and technical assistance, involving both the substantive levels of intellectual property protection and the effective enforcement of intellectual property rights; and
>
> • recommend methods to promote greater public understanding of the nature and importance of intellectual property protection throughout the Hemisphere.

The above proposed terms of reference were presented to the March 1996 Second Ministerial Trade Meeting at Cartagena, Columbia. There, they were revised, under the chairmanship of Honduras, to eliminate the emphasis on market restrictions and administrative improvements which had been central to the U.S. position.

A ministerial meeting was held in Belo Horizonte, Minas Gerais, Brazil in May 1997, where one of the areas under consideration was expanded coordination of intellectual property protection standards within the FTAA. At the Belo Horizonte meeting, in the face of continued inability of the U.S. to obtain Congressional approval for fast-track authority for U.S. negotiators, Brazil's support for the concept of FTAA as a merger of smaller regional trade agreements, with NAFTA and MERCOSUR as co-equal anchors, grew in popularity. Thus, there appears to be considerable and continued resistance to a pan-American intellectual property system spearheaded by and dominated by the United States—particularly in the area of patent law, and support for Latin American integration in patent matters as a counterbalance to the United States. At the Sixth Ministerial Meeting in April 2001, the headquarters of the FTAA Secretariat was moved to Panama. *See* www.ftaa-alca.org.

§ 6.05 Regional Trademark Registration Agreements

[A]   The European Union: The Community Trademark

[1] An Introduction to the CTM System

In Chapter 3, we discussed the EU Trademark Directive, which sought to harmonize significant aspects of the national trademark laws of the EU member states.   The EU has also adopted an even more ambitious trademark instrument, the Community Trademark Regulation. *See* Council Regulation 40/94 of 20 December 1993 on the Community Trademark, 1994 O.J. (L 11) [hereinafter Trademark Regulation]. The Trademark Regulation put in place a system under which an applicant may, by filing a single application, obtain a Community Trade Mark registration ("CTM") according rights throughout the entire territory of the EU. The cost of a CTM application is approximately that of separate applications in between three and four member states of the EU.

The Trademark Directive focused on harmonizing the substantive national trademark laws of the member states. The Trademark Regulation, because it establishes an administrative machinery, additionally makes detailed provision regarding the processes of application, examination, opposition, cancellation, and enforcement. Details regarding the working of the Community Trademark Office, which is based in Alicante, Spain, and formally operates under the title of the Office for Harmonization in the Internal Market, Trade Marks and Designs ("the OHIM"), can also be found in subsequent regulations. *See, e.g.*, Commission Regulation No. 2868/95 of 13 December 1995 implementing Council Regulation 40/94, 1995 O.J. (L303/1) [hereinafter Implementing Regulation]; Commission Regulation No. 216/96 of 5 February 1996 (laying down the rules of procedure of the Boards of Appeal of the Office for Harmonization in Internal Market (Trade Marks and Designs), O.J. L28/11 (Feb. 6, 1996); Notice of Opposition and Explanatory Notes (March 1997). (References herein to '"the regulation" are, however, references to the Trademark Regulation unless otherwise stated.) The OHIM started accepting applications in 1996 and publishing marks for opposition in March 1997. It maintains an extremely helpful web site, http://oami.eu.int, where decisions of the OHIM Boards of Appeal are posted (as are opposition decisions and a list of marks refused registration). The site also contains a bi-monthly newsletter—OAMI News—that includes the latest statistics on the CTM system. The Community Trade Mark Bulletin, which is where CTM applications are published for opposition, is not as of yet online. Several helpful commentaries on the Trademark Regulation are now available. *See, e.g.,* EUROPEAN COMMUNITY TRADEMARK: COMMENTARY TO THE EUROPEAN COMMUNITY REGULATION (Mario Franzosi ed., 1997); RUTH ANNAND & HELEN NORMAN, BLACKSTONE'S GUIDE TO THE COMMUNITY TRADEMARK (1998).

Standing to Apply

The CTM system is an open system, meaning that it is available not only to applicants domiciled or with their principal place of business in the EU, but also to persons from a member country of the Paris Union or the WTO (and to nationals of other countries with whom the EU has made reciprocity-based arrangements, such as Taiwan). *See* Trademark Regulation art. 5. In this regard, the CTM is significantly more accommodating than the Madrid system. In order to secure the benefits of either the Madrid Agreement or the Madrid Protocol, an applicant must file an international application with its "office of origin," and thus only applicants who are nationals of, domiciled in, or who have a "real and effective industrial or commercial establishment" in, a member state of the Madrid Union can make use of the respective mechanisms established by the Agreement and Protocol. U.S. applicants thus remain deprived of direct participation in the premier systems facilitating international trademark registration. But U.S. applicants have made significant use of the CTM system. Since the OHIM opened, U.S. companies have filed a greater number of applications than persons from any other single country. *See Statistics of Community Trade Marks (Application Statistics)* (Mar. 31, 2001), *available at* http://oami.eu.int/pdf/diff/stat.2001.pdf (showing, as of March 31, 2001, that 27% of applications filed since opening of office were filed by U.S. applicants, almost double the number filed by applicants from any other country). If the applicant is domiciled or has its principal place of business in the EU, it may deal with the OHIM directly. Other applicants, such as U.S. companies, must be represented by an agent in the EU (who must be a legal practitioner or professional representative in one of the EU member states qualified, in either case, to act as a representative in trademark matters).

A Unitary Trademark System

Article 1(2) of the Trademark Regulation provides that "a Community Trademark shall have a unitary character. It shall have equal effect throughout the Community." The CTM system is unitary in all respects: with a single application an applicant can obtain rights throughout the EU rather than having to file separately in several national trademark offices; a CTM registration can be renewed with a single filing in the OHIM; and an assignment of a CTM need be recorded only with the OHIM rather than with all the national offices. The unification of these different processes offers significant cost savings over filing separate applications, renewals, and assignments for the mark in each country of the EU. The unitary character of the CTM cuts both ways, however. If the CTM is declared invalid, the registration is invalidated for the entire EU (subject to a conversion procedure, *see infra*), and a CTM can only be assigned for the EU in its entirety. Moreover, the unitary nature of the system means that an application will be defeated if it would be unregistrable in just one EU country. Thus, the prize for a successful applicant may be larger, but it may be a more difficult prize to obtain.

The Contents of the Application

An application for a CTM may be filed either directly with the OHIM or through the intermediary of a national trademark office in the EU (including the Benelux Trademark Office). In order to receive a filing date, the application must comply with certain formalities. It must identify the mark, the applicant, and the goods or services for which protection is sought. No allegation of use or intent to use is required; the CTM is a first to file system. The application must also include a graphic or photographic representation of the mark. The OHIM Boards of Appeal, which hear appeals from decisions of the OHIM Examiners, have (with one exception) strictly interpreted the graphic representation requirement, holding that a verbal description does not suffice. *See In re* Antoni & Alison, Case R-4/97-2, 1998 E.T.M.R. 460 (Bd. of App. 1998) (description of packaging inadequate); QlickSmart Pty. Ltd.'s Application, Case R 1/98-2, 1999 E.T.M.R. 190 (Bd. of App. 1998) (description of sound mark as "click" inadequate). *But see* Vennootschap Onder Firma Senta Aromatic Marketing's Application, Case R 156/98-2, 1999 E.T.M.R. 429, 433 (Bd. of App. 1999) (holding that a verbal description of olfactory mark—"the Smell of Fresh Cut Grass"—complied with requirement of graphic representation because "it gives clear enough information to those reading [it] to walk away with an immediate and unambiguous idea of what the mark is when used in connection with tennis balls"). Any claim for priority based upon a foreign trademark must also be made in the application. The CTM system incorporates the Paris Convention's six month priority period, *see supra* § 3.01[F][4], granting that benefit to persons whose prior registration or application is in a member state that is party to the Paris Convention or is a member state of the WTO. *See* Trademark Regulation arts. 29-31.

An application for CTM registration may be filed in any official EU language (of which there now are eleven). The applicant must also, however, designate a second language, which must be one of the five "office languages" (namely, English, French, German, Italian, and Spanish) and must be different from the language of the application. *See* Trademark Regulation art. 115. The languages chosen affect the language in which any post-registration proceedings (such as opposition, revocation, or invalidity) will be conducted. If the language of the application was not one of the five official office languages, then the post-registration proceeding will be conducted in the designated second language. If the application was in an official office language, the party seeking to oppose or revoke may choose to proceed in either the language of the application or the designated second language.[*] As of January 1999, 43% of the applications used English as their first language, 19% used German, and 11% used Dutch. English was chosen as the second language 52% of the time and French 29% of

---

[*]Parties may also agree to conduct the opposition in any official language of the Community. *See* Trademark Regulation, art. 115(7).

the time.** These provisions represent a complex compromise, but a crucial one, because the adoption of the regulation was delayed for several years in part because of disagreements over the language to be used in proceedings before the OHIM.*** The provisions are also being strictly enforced by the OHIM. *See* Hubert Schur GmbH's Application: Opposition of Salomon, Case B 2784, (Opp. Div., Dec. 17, 1997), *noted at* 1998 E.T.M.R. 627 (dismissing opposition where notice of opposition filed in language other than those designated and without translation into either of the two possible languages of opposition).

Substantive Law of the CTM System

The substantive provisions of trademark law (e.g., definition of trademark, requirements for protection, grounds for denial of protection, and scope of protection) found in the regulation are intended to mirror those found in the Trademark Directive discussed in Chapter 3. Thus, for example, a mark must be "capable of being represented graphically," "it must be capable of distinguishing the goods and services of one party from those of another party," and it must not "consist exclusively of an indication of quality of the goods." *See* Trademark Regulation art. 7. The definition of "mark" in the regulation repeats the liberal definition found in the directive, *see* Trademark Regulation art. 4, and it has been construed broadly by the OHIM. In addition to the registration of product designs and colors, *see* Wm. Wrigley's Application/Light Green, Case R 122/98-3 (Bd. of App., Dec. 18, 1998) (recognizing that color per se could be registered but suggesting that such registrations will be rare), the Board of Appeal recently held that an olfactory mark (the "smell of fresh cut grass" for tennis balls) could be registered. *See* Vennootschap Onder Firma Senta Aromatic Marketing's Application, Case R 156/98-2, 1999 E.T.M.R. 429 (Bd. of App. 1999); *cf. In re* Clarke, 17 U.S.P.Q.2d 1238 (T.T.A.B. 1990).

The Examination Process

The OHIM examines applications only for compliance with the formalities discussed above (such as graphic representation) and absolute grounds for denial (e.g., lack of distinctiveness, functionality). *See* Trademark Regulation art. 38 (requiring examination for absolute grounds). No CTM application will be refused publication in the Community Trade Mark Bulletin because of a prior conflicting mark. *See id.* art. 7 (listing absolute grounds for denial of application). Instead, the OHIM relies on third parties to raise prior conflicting

---

**As of August 2, 1999, this resulted in 77% of the opposition proceedings having been conducted in English, followed by German (11%), French (6%), Spanish (5%), and Italian (1%). In order to control the language of any potential opposition, applicants frequently file the application in a language other than an Office language (i.e., Danish, Dutch, Finnish, Greek, Portugese, or Swedish) regardless of whether it is the language spoken in the applicant's country of origin, thus ensuring that any opposition proceedings will be in the designated second language. *See* Florent Gevers & David Tatham, *The Opposition Procedure in the Community Trade Mark System*, 20 Eur. Intell. Prop. Rev. 22, 25 (1998). This also ensures that if there are multiple oppositions, they will be in the same language.

***The site of the office, which was also a sticking point, was resolved through a political compromise involving the establishment of other (unrelated) EU offices in other countries of the union.

rights by way of opposition proceedings. *See infra.* Because of the unitary nature of the CTM system, a mark will be denied registration if it is unregistrable in a single country of the EU. *See* Trademark Regulation art. 7(2). Thus word marks will be examined for descriptiveness in several languages. *See* USA Detergent's Application, Case R 20/97-1, 1998 E.T.M.R. 562, 566 (Bd. of App. 1998) (rejecting application of XTRA for laundry detergent under Article 7(1)(b)-(c) after considering the meaning of the aurally equivalent term "extra" in English, French, Spanish, Italian, and Dutch dictionaries and concluding that "in at least five of the official languages of the EU the word 'extra' may be used to denote products of superior quality"); *see also* REALTONE, Case R 149/98-1 (Bd. of App., Jan. 26, 1998) (mark descriptive in a single country should be denied CTM protection even if it has no meaning in other parts or languages of the EU); Ford Motor Co. v. OHIM, Case T-91/99, 2000 E.T.M.R. 554 (C.F.I. 2000) (holding that even if applicant could show that mark OPTIONS for financial services had acquired distinctiveness in the United Kingdom, lack of distinctiveness in France was an insuperable obstacle to CTM registration).

Although the OHIM does not examine for relative grounds upon which to deny registration, before publishing the application for opposition the Office does conduct a search of prior marks for informational purposes. *See* Trademark Regulation art. 39. The OHIM conducts its own search of prior CTM registrations and relies on reports from national offices to detect conflicting national registrations. At present, however, some national offices (Germany, France, and Italy) are not performing national searches, and not all national offices search with the same thoroughness (Spain and the United Kingdom are known for their thoroughness). The national offices conducting searches have three months in which to provide reports to the OHIM. *See id.* art. 39(3). The information produced by this search is provided to the applicant and to any CTM owner (but not to a national mark owner) whose prior conflicting mark is revealed by the search. If the applicant does not withdraw its application within one month of receipt of this information, the application is published in the Community Trade Mark Bulletin in all the official languages of the EU, *see* Trademark Regulation art. 40, and any conflict between the marks in question will be resolved in opposition proceedings. This informational search process was intended to encourage the voluntary withdrawal or modification of clearly problematic applications, but the inadequacies in national search reports, coupled with the failure of national offices to inform national mark owners whose marks are identified in search reports, has meant that very few of the early applications were withdrawn or modified based upon the "informational" search. *See* Florent Gevers & David Tatham, *The Opposition Procedure in the Community Trade Mark System*, 20 EUR. INTELL. PROP. REV. 22, 23 (1998).

Oppositions and Observations

Notices of opposition must be filed directly with the OHIM within three months of the publication of the contested application. *See* Trademark Regulation arts. 42-43. They may be filed by the owner of an earlier conflicting right, but the assignee of such an earlier mark may only oppose if the assignment is recorded or if the request for recording the assignment is on file. *See id.* art. 17(7). As of August 2, 1999, 18.6% of published applications have been opposed. 60% of the oppositions decided on matters of substance were rejected, and of the remaining 40% that were successful, just over half led to the rejection of the application in its entirety. *See* OAMI News 1999, Issue 4, available at http://oami.eu.int/oaminews/oami4-99.pdf. Copies of any Notices of Opposition that are filed are forwarded to the applicant and, after taking evidence, the opposition decision will be made by a three-member OHIM Opposition Division. *See* Trademark Regulation art. 127. When an opposition is filed, the parties are given a two-month "cooling-off period" (which can be extended) in which they are encouraged to resolve their differences and reach an amicable settlement. *See* Implementing Regulation, R. 19. If that settlement involved a partial or full withdrawal of the CTM application, the opponent is refunded the opposition fee. As of August 2, 1999, about 40% of oppositions have been successfully resolved during the cooling-off period. *See* OAMI News 1999, Issue 4, *supra*. If the applicant withdraws the application in whole or part, the withdrawn CTM application can be converted into national applications.

Oppositions must be based on relative, rather than absolute, grounds for denial of the application. Indeed, the opposition stage of the proceedings may prove to be the most difficult part of the CTM system for applicants because it is here that relative grounds for denial will first be raised. Moreover, in order to acquire rights in this enlarged territory, an applicant must "clear rights" in a larger number of countries. That is to say, a prior conflicting right in a single EU country might defeat a CTM registration. An opposition can be based upon on a number of different kinds of earlier rights: applications or registrations for CTMs; applications or registrations in a member state of the EU or the Benelux; international registrations having effect in an EU member state; marks that are well-known in an EU member state; and even unregistered marks or other signs that are of more than mere local significance (provided that the law of the member state governing such mark or sign grants its proprietor the right to prohibit the use of a subsequent mark). *See* Trademark Regulation arts. 8, 42. The earlier right will be a basis for opposition if registration of the mark as a CTM would result either in confusing similarity or, in the case of prior marks other than unregistered marks, in dilution of the earlier mark. *See id.* arts. 8(1), 8(5).

Decisions of the Opposition Division (like those of OHIM Examiners and the Cancellation Division) may be appealed within two months to a three-person Board of Appeal (of which there are three at present), and thereafter to the Court of First Instance and the European Court of Justice. *See id.* art. 63. Thus far, the Court of First Instance has issued over a dozen opinions under the Trademark Regulation. The Court of Justice has not yet decided any cases under the regulation, although the advocate-general recently issued his opinion in Procter & Gamble v. Office for Harmonization in the Internal Market, Case C-383/99P (April 5, 2001), *see infra* § 6.05[A][2], and thus the first decision from the Court of Justice under the regulation should occur in the near future. Interestingly, all of the decisions issued by the Court of First Instance to date have involved appeals from a refusal of the OHIM to register a mark on the basis of an absolute ground set forth in Article 7 of the Trademark Regulation; none have involved *inter partes* proceedings where a conflict with a prior mark has been alleged.

Although oppositions are the means by which third parties object to an application on relative grounds, the regulation provides for the filing of written "observations" by third parties arguing that an application should be refused on absolute grounds. *See* Trademark Regulation art. 41. Such third parties do not become party to the application, and the OHIM has discretion either to re-examine the application before issuing a registration or ignoring the observation without explanation. To be considered by the OHIM, observations must be filed between publication of the application for opposition and one month after the expiration of the three month opposition period. *See* Circular Letter from Vice-President (OHIM) to International Non-Governmental Organisations 2 (Nov. 3, 1999), *available at* http://oami.eu.int/pdf/301art41.pdf. Observations can be filed in any official language of the EU because the OHIM does not treat such filings as falling within the language provisions of the Regulation. *See id.*

Conversion to National Applications

If a CTM application is refused or restricted, either by the examiner or after an opposition, the CTM applicant can, by making the appropriate filing with the OHIM within three months, convert its CTM application into separate national applications and (if successful in those applications) receive the priority filing date of its CTM application. The converted applications will also receive the benefit of any claimed seniority in that member state. *See* Trademark Regulation art. 108(3). Conversion will ordinarily not be available if the ground for refusal or revocation of the CTM was non-use, because such a finding will necessarily be premised upon lack of any genuine use in the EU. *See id.* art 108(2)(a) (noting exception where the member state in question would accept the sufficiency of "use" not accepted by the OHIM or court adjudicating the CTM). Similarly, if the grounds for refusal of registration of the CTM, or grounds for revocation or invalidity of the CTM registration identified by the OHIM or court, include a basis for refusal of registration in a member state, conversion is not available in that member state. *See id.* art. 108(2)(b). For example, if the OHIM refused an application because a prior confusingly similar mark was registered in Greece, conversion could occur only in member states other than Greece. If the application is converted into national applications, the applicant will lose its original CTM filing fees, pay a conversion fee to OHIM, and pay the national application fees in each country of conversion. Moreover, it will have to comply with the procedural requirements that a member state may impose upon a conversion applicant. *See id.* art. 110(2)-(3) (listing requirements that national authority can impose). For example, if an applicant seeks to convert a CTM application that was filed with the OHIM in English into an Italian national application, the Italian PTO will require an Italian translation of the request for conversion originally addressed to the OHIM as well as of the CTM application and all documents pertaining to the application. *See IPTO Issues Rules for Conversion of CTM into National Trademark*, 13 WORLD INTELL. PROP. REP. 153 (May 1999).

Canceling Registrations: Revocation and Invalidity

Registrations are canceled through one of two related proceedings. A Declaration of Invalidity of the registration may be sought by making the appropriate filing with the OHIM (Cancellation Division) on any ground that could have been the basis for denial of the registration (i.e., absolute or relative grounds) as well as on the ground that the application was filed in bad faith. *See* Trademark Regulation arts. 51-52. The CTM registration never becomes incontestable. But owners of prior national or CTM rights may not seek a declaration of invalidity based upon such rights if they have knowingly acquiesced in the use of the later CTM for a period of five years. *See id.* art. 53. Revocation is the appropriate procedure where the ground for cancellation is one that has arisen since issuance of the registration, such as abandonment through non-use (for a period of five years) or the mark having become generic. *See id.* art. 50. A claim for revocation or invalidity can also be raised as a counterclaim in infringement proceedings. If the CTM is canceled, the former registrant may within three months seek to convert the CTM into national registrations as described above.

Post-Registration Dealings with the CTM

Although use is not required to obtain a registration, genuine use within five years is required to maintain the registration. *See* Trademark Regulation art. 15. Genuine use of the mark anywhere within the EU is sufficient to meet this requirement. This latter rule is found only in a series of statements approved by the Council in adopting the Trademark Regulation. *See* Statements for Entry in the Minutes of the Council Meeting at Which the Regulation on the Community Trade Mark Is Adopted, Statement 10, *reprinted as* Appendix 2 to Charles Gielen, *European Trade Mark Legislation: The Statements*, 18 EUR. INTELL. PROP. REV. 83, 88 (1996). Regardless of the debate regarding the use of these statements to construe the Regulation, *see generally* Gielen, *supra*, this rule is in any event consistent with the unitary nature of the CTM. The CTM registration lasts for ten years and is renewable for further ten year periods. *See* Trademark Regulation arts. 45-47. Assignments of the CTM can be made only for the entire EU. *See id.* art. 17. Geographically limited licensing is, however, permitted. *See id.* art. 22. Assignments and licenses must be entered upon the CTM Register in order to be effective as against third parties. *See id.* art. 23.

Enforcement

While the filing date of a CTM determines the priority of the mark over competing marks, the full rights granted by a CTM registration are available against infringers only when the registration is published. *See* Trademark Regulation art. 9(3). The scope of rights that attach to a CTM registration mirrors the full scope of rights found in the Trademark Directive. *See id.* art. 9; Trademark Directive art. 5. Each member state is required to designate as "CTM Courts" one or more national courts (at the trial and appellate level) that will hear trademark disputes within the member state. CTM courts have exclusive jurisdiction in all actions for infringement, declaration of non-infringement, or counterclaim for revocation or declaration of invalidity of, the CTM. *See* Trademark Regulation arts. 91-92. When such national courts are sitting as CTM courts they will be applying the substantive law of the regulation rather than the national, directive-consistent trademark law of the state in which they sit. Certain matters are, however, left to national law, such as rules of procedure, remedies for infringement other than injunctions, interim measures, and appeals. *See id.* arts. 97-99, 101.

Article 93 determines the jurisdictions in which the CTM registrant may bring enforcement proceedings. Actions may be brought in the state where the defendant is domiciled or, if the defendant is not an EU domiciliary, in the state in which the defendant has an establishment. If the defendant lacks either such connection, then the action can be filed in the state where the plaintiff is domiciled or, if the plaintiff is not an EU domiciliary, in the state in which the plaintiff has an establishment. If the plaintiff also lacks either such connection, the action may be brought in Alicante, Spain. It is also possible to pursue an action for infringement in the member state in which that has occurred or is threatened, but in such cases jurisdiction exist only over those acts of infringement and thus relief may extend only to the borders of the member state involved. See Trademark Regulation art. 94(2). If the jurisdiction of the court is based upon domicile or establishment, the CTM owner may obtain injunctive relief across the EU. *See id.* art. 94(1). At present, subject to some exceptions being developed primarily by the Dutch courts, *see infra* § 7.05[B][2], injunctive relief based upon national registrations will only be granted on a national (or Benelux) basis. While trademark owners have significant experience, and courts have developed expertise, in enforcing national registrations, it is not clear to what extent the enforcement of the CTM will raise new or different issues (either doctrinally or in terms of judicial mindset).

Relationship Between CTM and National Rights

It remains possible to file separate applications in the national trademark offices of the EU member states; national trademark laws will continue to co-exist with the Community-level system. An applicant may use the national systems for some marks and the CTM system for others. Indeed, it is also possible to apply for a national and CTM registration for the same mark. Indeed, in the early months of the CTM system, this was a common practice.

Many of the applications being filed with the CTM are for new marks; a prior national trademark registration within the EU is not a prerequisite to a CTM filing. But the EU wishes to encourage a transition from national rights to community-wide rights even with respect to existing national registrations, and thus owners of existing national trademark registrations in the EU member states who apply for a CTM registration for the identical mark may claim "seniority" of their national registrations in respect of the member state for which it is currently registered. *See* Trademark Regulation arts. 34-35; *see also* VICEROY, Case R 5/97-1 (Bd. of App., May 15, 1998) (noting purpose of seniority provision). Seniority is one of the most complicated, but also one of the most important, aspects of the CTM system. To obtain seniority, the marks and the goods in question must be identical, as must be the owner of the prior national mark and the CTM. *See* THINKPAD, Case R 10/98-2 (Bd. of App., July

15, 1998) (comparing marks side by side and holding that prior registration in Greece of THINK PAD was substantially identical to THINKPAD for which applicant sought seniority in its CTM application); VICEROY, Case R 5/97-1 (Bd. of App., May 15, 1998) (addressing identity of owner requirement where CTM applicant had been assigned the senior national marks but those assignments had not been recorded). Seniority may be claimed in a CTM application, *see* Trademark Regulation art. 34, or at any time after registration, *see id.* art. 35. In either case, "seniority shall have the sole effect . . . that where the proprietor of the CTM surrenders the earlier [national] trade mark or allows it to lapse, he shall be deemed to continue to have the same rights as he would have had if the earlier trade mark had continued to be registered." *Id.* art. 34(2). Claiming seniority, which involves the payment of no extra fees, is thus effectively a means of maintaining the national trademark registration(s) without having to file a series of national renewals. One commentator has helpfully described the effect of seniority as being that the national registration remains as a "shadow" mark behind the CTM. *See* Florent Gevers, *The Continung Story of the Examination of Seniority Claims by the OHIM in Alicante*, 21 EUR. INTELL. PROP. REV. 228 (1999). The non-renewed national mark for which seniority is claimed may provide the separate basis for infringement proceedings and thus offer the mark holder greater choice as to where to bring an infringement proceeding than does Article 93 of the Trademark Regulation. *See id.* And it provides the national mark holder some guarantee that the transition from a national registration to a CTM registration (with a necessarily later priority date) will not result in the loss of existing national rights.

The Trademark Regulation itself did not impose any obligation upon the OHIM to examine and pass on the validity of seniority claims. But the office indicated in its Examination Guidelines that it would do so. *See* Decision Ex-96-2 of the President's Office of Mar. 26, 1996, § 6 (Sept. 1996) (OHIM Examination Guidelines). The OHIM suspended substantive examination of seniority claims in November 1998, however, because of the volume of these claims and now only conducts what is unofficially called an "examination for plausibility." But before that suspension, the OHIM would make known its acceptance of any seniority claims by notifying the relevant national trademark office (but not the applicant) and indicating the seniorities claimed and accepted on the registration certificate and in the Community Trade Marks Bulletin. *See* Examination Guidelines § 6.7. Since the suspension, the OHIM is now publishing the fact that seniorities had been claimed but not indicating any acceptance of their validity. *See* Florent Gevers and David Tatham, *The Continuing Story of the Examination of Seniority Claims by the OHIM in Alicante*, 21 EUR. INTELL. PROP. REV. 228, 231 (1999).

NOTES AND QUESTIONS

(1) **The Advantages of the CTM.** In what ways is the CTM system conceptually different from the Madrid system? Is it a better system of regulating trademark rights in a global market? Is it better for (all) trademark

owners? Is it better for consumers? Are there any ways in which it may be harmful?

(2) **Comparison to Federal Rights in the United States**. In some respects, the ability to obtain rights throughout the EU with a single application and maintain those rights with use in a single EU state, parallels the right to base federal registration in the United States upon use in interstate commerce even where the mark is only being used in one part of the United States. To what extent does the parallel exist? What differences exist? What issues are relevant in the EU, but not in the United States, and vice-versa?

(3) **Filing Strategies.** Why did the EU decide to retain national trademark systems? What are the different strategies that an applicant may now adopt to secure trademark rights in the EU? In which circumstances will the different strategies be available to the applicant? What are the advantages and disadvantages of these different trademark prosecution strategies? It may be that the best approach will vary depending upon the type of product or the type of mark involved. In which circumstances (and for which products or marks) will one strategy be more advisable than others? If you were trademark counsel presented with the following cases, how would you advise a client to proceed with its application(s)? If you need more information from the client in order to offer advice, what information would you need? If more than one strategy seems possible, which considerations would you highlight for the client?

• Emerald, Inc. is a small New York-based corporation that markets specialty vacation packages (called SHAMROCK vacations) to parts of New York state that would be of particular interest to persons of Irish ancestry. At present, Emerald markets its vacation packages to Irish-Americans in the United States, but would like to tap into the market in Ireland and the United Kingdom for vacation travel to the United States. To that end, it wishes to obtain Irish and U.K. registrations for SHAMROCK. Based upon very preliminary marketing surveys, Emerald does not presently anticipate marketing its packages elsewhere in Europe (although the degree of interest that the surveys revealed in Finland, Denmark, and Sweden was higher than Emerald had expected). Emerald does not own any registrations for the SHAMROCK mark in the United States, although it has recently filed a use-based application with the U.S. PTO.

• Joseph O'Leary is an entrepreneur based in Dublin, Ireland. He has developed a new brand of a traditional Irish product (potato-based whiskey called poitín, or potcheen in English). Although potcheen is common in Ireland, it is unknown in other countries of the EU. O'Leary believes that it would be very popular with the well-heeled élites of Scandinavian and German society (particularly in the long northern winters). He would like to market his product under the mark THAR BARR; "thar barr" translates in Irish Gaelic as "superior" or "excellent." O'Leary has no interest in marketing the product in Ireland, where for many years potcheen was illegal and has acquired a reputation as a cheap downmarket drink. Although Irish Gaelic is the official language of Ireland and a "semi-official" EU language, it is the native language of only a very small percentage of the Irish population based primarily in the west of Ireland. Otherwise, English is the language spoken by most Irish people, and Irish Gaelic is largely understood only by a small educated elite.

• ABC Inc. is a large French corporation that has developed a wholly new software product that enables users to split their computer screen between several different functions in ways not currently possible. The software will be sold in CD-ROM format, and will also (upon development of proper security technology) be made available online for downloading by purchasers. The software market is extremely dynamic and ABC wishes to launch its product as soon as possible throughout the EU. As you requested, the marketing department of ABC has narrowed its choice of preferred brand names for the new product to two: FLIP-FLOP, and ESPLIT. The marketing department would strongly prefer to use ESPLIT. You commission full search reports on each of these proposed marks in all countries of the EU. The search results reveal very few insurmountable problems for FLIP-FLOP. But a Finnish company has, for ten years, owned a Finnish registration in ESPLIT for software-related products. The report on ESPLIT reveals no other problems.

• Peter Bledsoe owns a small business based in Manchester, England. For eight years, he has held a U.K. trademark registration for the mark GLACIER for ice cube trays that are designed to facilitate the extraction of the formed ice cubes from the trays. Bledsoe would like to expand his market (in the short-term) to include France, Italy, Spain, and Portugal, and (in the long-term, finances permitting) as much of the rest of the EU as possible, as well as several countries outside the EU (including Norway, Poland, and the Czech Republic). Before moving forward, he would like to obtain trademark registrations for GLACIER in all the additional countries in which the product will be marketed. As a small businessman, Bledsoe is extremely concerned about keeping the costs of this exercise to a minimum.

• Quick-Print, Inc. is a Delaware corporation that since 1989 has owned the U.S. registered mark ZOOMM for cameras. The application to register the mark had initially been rejected by the U.S. PTO, but was accepted upon proof of secondary meaning. In the United States, the ZOOMM camera has also been marketed under the slogan "THE CAMERA THAT SHOOTS STRAIGHT." Registration of that slogan as a trademark was also initially rejected by the PTO, but likewise was registered based upon secondary meaning after several years of use by Quick-Print. Quick-Print decides that it would like to expand sales of its ZOOMM cameras to the EU, and to that end has just established a subsidiary in Barcelona, Spain. Quick-Print would like to market the ZOOMM cameras under that mark in all member countries of the EU and possibly some countries of Central Europe. It would also like to use the slogan that has been successful in the United States, namely THE CAMERA THAT SHOOTS STRAIGHT, but recognizes that it might need to translate the slogan for use in several non-English speaking countries. (Quick-Print provides you with the translation of the slogan into several European languages; these translations had been performed by a clerk in the New York office of Quick-Print with the aid of several dictionaries from the New York public library.)

• Franco Rossi is an Italian carpenter based in a small town outside Milan. He designs and commences production of a new line of bedroom furniture that is well-received in Milan. He markets the furniture in Italy under the coined term ABARRASTI, which has no meaning in Italian, and wishes to expand into France, Spain, and Portugal. He is concerned about the costs involved in searching national registers and wishes to proceed without commissioning search reports (if possible).

• Farbenschaft is a German company that manufactures baby food. It sells the baby food under the mark ESSENGRITT, and has obtained registrations for that mark in Germany, Finland, Denmark, Sweden, the Benelux, and Austria. It wishes to obtain rights throughout the EU.

The European Communities Trade Mark Association ("ECTA") is the premier professional association of trademark counsel who practice before the OHIM. *See* http://www.ecta.org/. ECTA is in frequent consultation with the OHIM regarding ways in which the CTM system could be improved. Armed with the experience of your seven clients, if you were a representative of ECTA speaking with the OHIM how would you suggest that the system be improved? To what extent would the reforms that your clients would like to see be consistent with the interests of consumers throughout the EU?

(4) **Clearing Marks Under the CTM.** What effect might the need to clear rights in all countries have on the nature of marks adopted by producers marketing in the EU? Is the approach adopted by the OHIM in *USA Detergent's Application* the same as would be followed by a court applying the doctrine of foreign equivalents in U.S. law? *See supra* § 3.01[C]. If so, is there anything that the OHIM could learn from the case law applying the doctrine in the United States? Is an examination for registerability in the several countries of the EU, the same as an examination of registerability in the many official languages of the EU?

The OHIM currently asks whether the mark would be descriptive and thus fail to be distinctive in any single country of the EU. In Ford Motor Co. v. OHIM, Case T-91/99, 2000 E.T.M.R. 554 (C.F.I. 2000), the office refused to register the mark OPTIONS for financing and lease-purchase services on the grounds that the term OPTIONS was devoid of distinctive character in English and French. The applicant adduced evidence showing that the mark had been used and become distinctive in Belgium, Denmark, the Netherlands, Portugal, Sweden, and the United Kingdom (but not France). The applicant argued that registration should be granted where "distinctiveness acquired through use can be demonstrated in a substantial part of the European Community, including one major country such as, in this case, the United Kingdom." *Id*. at 557. The OHIM argued that Article 7(3) of the Trademark Regulation, which authorizes registration based upon acquired distinctiveness, "requires that acquisition of distinctiveness through use be demonstrated with regard to the part of the Community where distinctiveness was denied. If the ground for refusal exists everywhere in the Community, acquired distinctiveness must be demonstrated everywhere in the Community." *Id*. at 558. The Court of First Instance affirmed the refusal to register, holding that in order to rely on Article 7(3) an applicant must show distinctiveness had been acquired through use in "the substantial part of the Community where it was devoid of any such character under Article 7(1)(b), (c), or (d)." *Id*. at 560. Because the mark had not been used in such a way as to acquire distinctiveness in France, the application was properly refused. The court's reasoning rested largely on the unitary character of the CTM. Does the unitary character mandate that secondary meaning be required in all EU countries? In a unitary system, should the question not simply be whether the mark is "descriptive, or has acquired distinctiveness, in the EU"? In what ways is this a different question? Why does the EU regulation appear to ask the former, rather than the latter, question?

(5) **The Single Mark Rule and Medicines.** To gain regulatory approval to market a medicinal product in the EU the product must obtain regulatory approval. The EU has sought to harmonize regulatory procedures and requirements, and has created the option of a centralized procedure. The

centralized procedure involves obtaining regulatory approval from the European Commission after analysis by the European Medicines Evaluation Agency ("EMEA"), and this procedure (rather than serial national regulatory approvals) is mandatory for certain products. As part of the Commission/EMEA approval process, the applicant is required to identify the name of the proprietary product. The Commission has taken the position that, under the centralized procedure, which gives authorization for a unitary territory, only one proprietary name for the product can be authorized. Thus a single mark throughout the EU is required. When pharmaceutical manufacturers noted the difficulties of obtaining rights in the same mark in every country of the EU, the Commission suggested that applicants obtain a CTM registration (rather than separate national registrations). This "single trademark rule" has been heavily criticized by U.S. pharmaceutical industries and has resulted in only minor accommodation by the Commission. *See* Richard Binns & Anna Brackenbury, *A Single Mark for a Single EU Pharmaceutical Marketing Authorization*, TRADEMARK WORLD, July 1998, at 20. Why do you think the Commission is pursuing the single trademark rule for certain medicinal products? Is it justified?

(6) **EURONICE Project**. The Nice Classification system has greatly standardized trademark application formats. The EU is seeking to refine this process further. The OHIM recently launched its EURONICE project, which will involve constructing a database of the translation of expressions used most frequently by CTM applicants to describe the goods and services covered by their marks. *See* http://oami.eu.int/en/marque/euronice.htm. This project should, especially when fully available to applicants, greatly reduce translation costs and ensure consistency between applications.

[2] The Relationship Between National and EU Authorities: Deference, Opposition, Seniority and Conversion

One commentator has suggested that "the CTM offers the possibility of a registration standard that differs from those of some of the Member States of the EU. Thus, it may be possible to obtain protection under the CTM for marks in which it would be difficult to obtain protection in some of the Member States using the national registration system." Michelle Michel, *Comparison Between the Community Trademark System and the National Registration System—A Multinational Perspective*, Paper Presented to 1997 Annual Meeting of INTA (San Antonio, May 1997). In what respects might the standards be different, and why might the application of the standards differ? The OHIM is sufficiently concerned about the need for consistency between the interpretation of national law under the directive and CTM law under the regulation that it would like to have input into the Commission pleadings in cases involving the directive before the ECJ. The OHIM has indicated, however, that because it is an autonomous examining office, it does not regard itself as bound by registerability decisions made by national trademark offices (even though the directive and the regulation establish similar grounds for refusal of an application). *See* ULTRA MOIST, R 84/98-1, 1999 E.T.M.R. 896 (Bd. of App. 1998) (refusing CTM registration to mark on ground of non-distinctiveness notwithstanding that the mark had been registered in Benelux, France, Ireland, and Spain). Why? Is this merely an institutional power gambit, or are there substantive reasons for the OHIM to make wholly independent decisions? To what extent is it (or should it) be bound by the determinations of national offices? Are national offices ever bound by determinations of the OHIM? *Cf.* Trademark Regulation art. 108(2). Should they be? Are there certain circumstances where, although not formally be bound by each other, the OHIM should give deference to national offices and vice-versa? *See* Jochen Pagenberg, *Opposition Proceedings for the Community Trademark—New Strategies in Trademark Law*, 29 I.I.C. 406, 418 (1998) (noting scholarly criticism of failure to consider decisions of other countries on harmonized trademark law); *see also In re* Antoni & Alison, R-4/97-2 (Bd. of App., Jan. 21, 1998) (declining to consider member state interpretation of Directive on question of compliance with formalities of application), *reported at* 30 I.I.C. 98, 100 (1999). As seen in the following two cases, the relationship between national and OHIM determinations has already raised itself in the context of OHIM registrability decisions, but it may also be relevant in other contexts (including oppositions based on conflicting national rights, in adjudicating seniority claims, and in conversion proceedings). In considering the Notes and Questions that follow these cases, please review the summary of opposition, seniority, and conversion issues discussed above in the *Introduction to the CTM System*. *See supra* § 6.05[A][1]. Also carefully review the relevant provisions of the Trademark Regulation, principally: Articles 7-8, 42-43 (opposition), Articles 34-35 (seniority), and Articles 108-110 (conversion).

Procter & Gamble's Application, Case T-163/98, [1999] E.T.M.R. 240 (Bd. of App.1998), *aff'd in part, rev'd in part*, [1999] E.T.M.R. 767 (C.F.I. 1999), *Advocate-General's opinion issued sub. nom* Procter & Gamble v. Office for Harmonization in the Internal Market, Case C-383/99P (April 5, 2001), *appeal pending*. Procter & Gamble sought a CTM registration for the mark BABY-DRY for "disposable diapers made out of paper or cellulose" and "diapers made out of textile," in classes 16 and 25, respectively, of the Nice Agreement. The examiner refused the application on the ground that under Article 7(1)(c) of the Trademark Regulation "trade marks which consist exclusively of signs or indications which may serve, in trade, to designate the kind, quality, quantity, intended purpose, value, geographical origin or the time of production of the goods or of rendering of the service, or other characteristics of the goods or service" are not to be registered. Procter & Gamble appealed noting that the trademark had been registered in Denmark, Finland and France and that "both Denmark and Finland, operate examination systems. The Community Office should not be more demanding than the national offices; otherwise trade mark owners would find it preferable to continue to seek national protection." Procter & Gamble also offered to submit evidence of "acquired distinctiveness, since Baby-Dry diapers had been on sale throughout Europe since 1993 and were heavily advertised." The Board of Appeal affirmed the examiner's conclusion under Article 7(1)(c) of the Trademark Regulation. The board commented that

> the existence of registrations in Member States may be taken into account by the examiner in view of the harmonisation of the provisions on absolute grounds of refusal effected by the [Trademark Regulation and the Trademark Directive]. However, where the competent

authorities in one or more Member States have held a mark to be eligible for registration, the same finding does not necessarily have to be reached by the examiner of the [OHIM], who must in each case make his own assessment as to the existence of absolute grounds of refusal. It may also be noted that the objection to the registerability of BABY-DRY for diapers applies in particular to countries in which English is an official language. On account of the linguistic differences in Europe, it is by no means unusual if certain trademarks are regarded as descriptive in some member states but not in others. In view of the terms of Article 7(2) of the [Trademark Regulation], a trade mark cannot be registered as a CTM if it is descriptive in only part of the Community. In that event a possible solution might be to obtain national registrations in those member states in which the obstacle to registration does not arise.

The board also concluded that the applicant's arguments of secondary meaning under Article 7(3) of the Trademark Regulation were inadmissible because they were not raised before the examiner, and commented that this "does not affect the [applicant's] right to make a further application for a CTM and to adduce evidence of acquired distinctiveness at the examination stage in the context of that application." Procter & Gamble appealed both conclusions of the board to the Court of First Instance, seeking an order requiring the OHIM to assign a filing date to the CTM application or, in the alternative, a remand of the case to the Board of Appeal to determine the question of whether the mark had become distinctive through use (i.e., secondary meaning). During the proceedings, Procter & Gamble amended its request for relief (under its first argument) to seek an order requiring the office to publish the CTM application pursuant to Article 40 of the regulation. The Court of First Instance affirmed the board on its interpretation of Article 7(1)(c), finding that "the term Baby-Dry, read as a whole, immediately informs consumers of the intended purpose of the goods." However, the Court concluded that, because Procter & Gamble had indicated at the end of the written statement setting out its grounds of appeal to the board that it intended to rely on Article 7(3), it was not open to the Board of Appeal simply to reject the applicant's arguments based on Article 7(3) solely on the ground that they were not raised before the examiner. Having considered the appeal, it should have either ruled on the substance of that issue or remitted the matter to the examiner, and thus the board had violated Article 62 of the regulation.

Procter & Gamble appealed to the European Court of Justice and the advocate-general recently issued his opinion. (The Court's judgment, which will be the first interpreting the regulation, is expected soon.) The advocate-general disagreed with the analysis of descriptiveness found in the board and Court of First Instance opinions. The advocate-general concluded that the board should have taken into account elliptical nature of the phrase, its unusual and opaque grammatical structure, and its incompleteness as a description. If it had done so, he reasoned, it may have reached a different conclusion. Accordingly, he proposed that the Court of Justice annul the Court of First Instance ruling.

WM. WRIGLEY/LIGHT GREEN, CASE R/122/98-3
[1999] E.T.M.R. 214 (Bd. of App. 1998)

[Wm. Wrigley Jr. Co. applied to register the color "light green" for chewing gum. The examiner denied protection on the ground that the mark was devoid of all distinctive character under Article 7(1)(b) of the Trademark Regulation ("CTMR") because it consisted exclusively of one color. The Board of Appeal dismissed the appeal.]

Reasons for the Decision

. . . .

As the Board has already stated, in general, a colour per se may be protectable as a Community trade mark under Article 4 of the Trademark Regulation (*see* Decision of 12 February 1998 in Case R 7/1997-3 ORANGE, OJ OHIM No 5/98, p. 641, paragraph 16). . . .

On the one hand, it is true that the CTMR, unlike the harmonised trade mark laws of certain Member states, does not expressly include a colour per se, without a delimitation in extent or by shape, amongst the possible forms of trade marks. In this respect, in France, Article L 711-1(2)(c) of the Intellectual Property Code includes "*combinaison ou nuances de couleurs*" ("combinations or shades of colours"). Similarly, in Italy, Article 16 of Decree No 929 of 21 June 1942 includes "*le combinazioni o le tonalità cromatiche*" ("colour combinations or tonalities"). Likewise, in Germany, Section 3(1) of the Trade Mark Act includes "*sonstige Aufmachungen einschließlich Farben und Farbzusammenstellungen*" ("other forms including colours and combination of colours"). It is to be noted further, in this respect, that in Hungary Section 1 of the Protection of Trade Marks and Geographical Merchandise Marks Act of 11 March 1997 includes "a colour, a combination of colours", and the second sentence of Article 15(1) of [TRIPS] includes "combinations of colours."

On the other hand, it is also true that the wording of the CTMR, unlike as in Spain and Portugal, does not expressly exclude a colour per se from being conferred protection. In Spain, Article 11(1) of Trade Mark Law No 32/88 provides in material part: "*No podrán registrarse como marcas . . . los siguientes: . . . (g) El color por sí solo. Sin embargo, podrá registrarse siempre que esté delimitado por una forma determinada*" ("The following may not be registered: . . . (g) colour in itself. It may, however, be registered provided it is delimited by a given form"). Similarly, in Portugal, Article 166(1)(d) of the Industrial Property Code (Decree Law No 16/95) provides that a trade mark may not consist of "colours, except when they are combined together or with graphics, wording or other elements in a particular and distinctive manner." That the list of examples in Article 4 CTMR is not exhaustive is evident from the use of the word "particularly" in that article.

Furthermore, the Council and the Commission, in their Joint Statements entered in the minutes of the Council Meeting at which the [Regulation] was adopted, consider that Article 4 does not rule out the possibility of registering as a Community trade mark a combination of colours or a single colour, provided they are capable of distinguishing the goods and services of one undertaking from those of other undertakings. [cit]. The same statement is included, concerning Article 2 [of the Trademark Directive], in the Joint statements by the Council and the Commission entered in the minutes of the Council Meeting at which that Directive was adopted. [cit].

Whilst it is acknowledged that those statements are not part of the Community legal texts and are without prejudice to the interpretation of those texts by the Court of Justice, they are, nonetheless, of importance since they document the intention of the legislature.

Finally, on this point, it follows from a systematic and teleological interpretation that Article 4 CTMR must be construed such that a colour per se, without an associated shape, as in the present case, is protectable as a trade mark since it falls within the meaning of the wording "any signs" in that article. That wording must be interpreted as a very broad, "open" and general term encompassing all conceivable types of marks (including, for example, sound marks and three-dimensional marks). To restrict the protection of colour marks to a specific presentation would be contrary to the spirit of Community trade mark law.

. . . .

NOTES AND QUESTIONS

(1) **The Role of Member State Institutions.** What different methodologies does the board use in *Wrigley* to determine whether color per se can be registered as a mark under the Trademark Regulation? In what way is the weight being attached to national determinations different in *Wrigley* than in *Procter & Gamble*? Why? In Penny Makinson's Application, Case R68/98-3, 1999 E.T.M.R. 234 (Bd. of App. 1998) the Third Board of Appeal held that the mark POLY PADS for equine back protectors and pads for saddles was unregisterable as a CTM because it would be regarded as descriptive in Ireland and the United Kingdom. *See id.* at 238. The applicant produced evidence that the mark had been registered in the United Kingdom (under what the applicant described as "the substantially more difficult" standards of the pre-Directive law, but with the term PADS disclaimed, which it was not in the CTM application), Germany, and the United States. Indeed, the applicant sought to claim seniority for the German and U.K. marks. To what extent should each of these registrations be relevant? *See id.* at 238-39 (discussing relevance of each registration); *see also* REALTONE, R 149/98-1 (Bd. of App., Jan. 26, 1998) (discussing relevance of non-EU registrations). If the U.S. and U.K. registrations had been based upon secondary meaning, would they have been entitled to more or less weight? Should it matter that the registrations predate the Harmonization Directive? Should the antiquity of the relevant national registrations help or hurt the CTM applicant? *See* British Petroleum's Application, Case R 55/98-2, 1999 E.T.M.R. 282, 286 (Bd. of App. 1998). Should it be relevant that a mark claimed as a CTM, although registered in several member states, was not registered in the member state in which the applicant was based? *See id.* at 286-87 (noting no registration for three dimensional container mark in the United Kingdom). If it is relevant at all, to what extent would this depend upon the member state in question? Which other information might be relevant to the question?

(2) **Dangers of Deference.** What are the dangers with the OHIM registering a CTM largely on the basis of determinations by national offices? *Cf. Ergopanel Trade Mark Application, supra* § 3.01[C] (discussing dangers of one national court deferring to registrability decision of other national courts). Although the board's approach to descriptiveness in *Procter and Gamble* was criticized by the advocate-general, its analysis of the level of deference to be given to national registrations is consistent with the approach adopted by other courts. *See, e.g.,* Procter & Gamble Co. v. Office for Harmonisation in the Internal Market, 2000 E.T.M.R. 580, 589 (C.F.I. 2000) (noting that, in assessing an application to register the shape of a bar of soap, existing national registrations were a factor to be taken into consideration without being given decisive weight).

(3) **Preserving Arguments.** In *British Petroleum's Application, supra,* a decision handed down between the decision of the Board of Appeal and the opinion of the Court of First Instance in *Procter & Gamble,* the Second Board of Appeal adopted a strict approach to the question of whether an applicant can raise the question of secondary meaning before the board without having raised it in its application. The board concluded that the Trademark Regulation

> does not permit the applicant to introduce for the first time the issue of factual distinctiveness under Article 7(3) before the examiner after his final decision without making a fresh application. . . .If such a situation were to be permitted, applicants would simply be disposed to make submissions on inherent distinctiveness at the examination stage of the process and, only if unsuccessful, undertake the more burdensome task of trying to demonstrate factual distinctiveness under Article 7(3).

Is this too harsh? Can it be reconciled with *Procter & Gamble?* Why does BP not wish to simply file a new application? Should claims of seniority in the application serve as per se evidence of use thus permitting an applicant to say that it has raised the question of acquired distinctiveness? *See British Petroleum's Application,* 1999 E.T.M.R. at 289.

(4) **Council Minutes**. When the Council adopted the Trademark Regulation, it approved a series of statements that provide some guidance not found in the text of the document. *See* Statements for Entry in the Minutes of the Council Meeting at Which the Regulation on the Community Trade Mark Is Adopted, reprinted as Appendix 2 to Charles Gielen, *European Trade Mark Legislation: The Statements,* 18 EUR. INTELL. PROP. REV. 83, 88 (1996). As we saw in Chapter 3, some courts have been reluctant to place weight upon these statements, *see Wagamama, supra* § 3.01[I][3], but reference to them continues to appear in opinions. *See, e.g.,* Wm. Wrigley/Light Green, Case R/122/98-3 (Bd. of App., Dec. 18, 1998) ("Whilst it is acknowledged that those statements are not part of the Community legal texts and are without prejudice to the interpretation of those texts by the Court of Justice, they are, nonetheless, of importance since they document the intention of the legislature."). For consideration of this question, see Charles Gielen, *European Trade Mark Legislation: The Statements,* 18 EUR. INTELL. PROP. REV. 83 (1996).

(5) **Case Law on Descriptiveness under the Regulation**. The advocate-general's opinion in BABY DRY seeks to resolve a split in opinion regarding the descriptiveness standard (particularly in assessing combined terms) that has

developed among the two chambers of the Court of First Instance assigned to hear trademark cases. In a series of cases, the second chamber has taken the position that the descriptiveness exclusion in Article 7(1)(c) of the regulation will apply only where the combined term immediately informs the customer of the intended purpose of the goods. *See, e.g.,* Case T-324/00, The Sun Rider Corp. v. Office for Harmonisation in the Internal Market (C.F.I. Jan. 31, 2001). This approach allows a court to consider the different factors (such as grammatical structure etc.) referred to by the advocate-general in the BABY DRY case. In contrast, the fourth chamber has rejected a number of applications because there was no element in the combined term that cannot be used to indicate the intended purpose of the goods. *See, e.g.,* Case T-331/99, Mitsubishi v. Office for Harmonisation in the Internal Market (C.F.I. Jan. 31, 2001). The advocate-general appears to prefer the more liberal approach of the second chamber.

(6) **Nature of Opposition in the CTM.** The opposition procedure is a blend of features from several different national systems within the EU. *See* Florent Gevers & David Tatham, *The Opposition Procedure in the Community Trade Mark System,* 20 EUR. INTELL. PROP. REV. 22, 31 (1998) (suggesting that the CTM opposition procedure is probably most similar to those which operate in France and Germany). By precluding the OHIM from considering relative grounds for denial of an application and leaving that issue to be resolved through inter partes proceedings, the Trademark Regulation essentially privatizes some of the work of the office. In light of that, it is perhaps surprising that the costs and expenses of opposition proceedings are subject to a "loser pays" structure, subject to some limitations. *See* Trademark Regulation art. 81(1).

(7) **Opposition Practices.** In light of the national examination and reporting practices referenced above, are there any patterns that you would expect to see in oppositions filed? Based on an analysis of the opponents' representatives, the OHIM concludes that 76% of the oppositions come from three countries: Germany (34%), Spain (29%), and the United Kingdom (13%). *See Statistics (Situation at the Beginning of August, 1999): Community Trade Mark Applications,* OAMI NEWS Issue, 4, 1999, *at* http://oami.eu.int/oaminews/Oami4-99.pdf. To what extent are these figures surprising? Might the OHIM's method of analyzing "where the oppositions come from" be a bad indicator of the nationality of the rights being asserted in opposition? Very few observations have been filed with the OHIM, in contrast to the thousands of oppositions that have been filed. What might explain this disparity?

(8) **Applying the Regulation Provisions.** On January 1, 1999, Westlink Co. filed an application with the OHIM seeking a CTM registration for the mark BLOCKER for sports fitness equipment. The mark BLOCKER was published for opposition. A Notice of Opposition was filed by Kermiso, a Spanish company, based upon its ownership of a Spanish trademark registration dated March 15, 1992 for BLOCKED for sports apparel. Westlink owns a Spanish trademark registration dated February 11, 1990 for BLOCKER for sports fitness equipment.

(a) Should the opposition succeed? If you are counsel to Westlink, how would you advise that it proceed?

(b) Would the answer or advice change if Westlink had claimed seniority based upon its 1990 Spanish registration?

(c) If Westlink and Kermiso had previously entered into a consent to use agreement under which they agreed to tolerate each other's use of their respective marks, would your analysis be affected? *See* Gevers & Tatham, *The Opposition Procedure, supra,* at 29-30; Jochen Pagenberg, *Opposition Proceedings for the Community Trademark—New Strategies in Trademark Law,* 29 I.I.C. 406, 415 (1998).

(d) If Kermiso had made exclusive, extensive, continuous, and trademark use of the term BLOCKED in Spain since 1992 but had not registered the mark with the Spanish trademark office, would that change your analysis? Is there any additional information that would you need to know?

(e) If Kermiso owned a French registration for BLOCKED dated March 15, 1992, instead of a Spanish registration, would your answer change? If the Westlink Spanish mark was well known in France at the time that Kermiso registered its own mark, would your analysis or advice change? Is there any additional information that would you need to know?

(9) **Consent to Use Agreements.** In the United States, the assertion of prior conflicting rights is frequently resolved by consent to use agreements between the parties regulating (among other things) the geographic extent to which they will each tolerate concurrent use by the other of the mark in question. These consent to use agreements may raise difficult issues under both EU competition law and the Trademark Regulation. Article 85(1) of the EC Treaty prohibits agreements between undertakings that restrict competition within the EU and affect trade between member states; consent to use agreements based upon territorial division of rights may come within this prohibition. *See* Simon Topping & Sean-Paul Brankin, *Trademark Delimitation Agreements Under EC Competition Law,* WORLD LICENSING L. REP., Apr. 1999, at 20. Restrictions in agreements contrary to Article 85(1) are void under EU law and may subject undertakings involved to fines of up to 10% of turnover imposed by the European Commission (and to private actions for damages under national laws). These consequences can be obviated by seeking an exemption from the Commission under Article 85(3), although the circumstances under which consent to use agreements may receive an exemption are not yet clear. *See id.* at 24. Moreover, the Trademark Regulation does not permit the division of the EU territory by the issuance of concurrent registrations for different countries in the EU. This might make oppositions more difficult to resolve. How might you structure a settlement of a CTM opposition under which the parties agree to geographically remote concurrent use?

(10) **Seniority Requirements.** Since the inception of its examination of seniority claims, the OHIM has become less stringent in its interpretation of the substantive requirements for seniority. *See* Florent Gevers and David Tatham, *The Continuing Story of the Examination of Seniority Claims by the OHIM in Alicante,* 21 EUR. INTELL. PROP. REV. 228, 230-32 (1999). In particular, the Boards of Appeal issued decisions allowing applicants some room for deviation in demonstrating "triple identity" of goods, mark and owner, *see* THINKPAD, R 10/98-2 (Bd. of App., July 15, 1998), and the office began, under time pressure, to make only a very cursory analysis of similarity of goods. Gevers and Tatham have criticized these developments, arguing that seniority is essentially a "free" renewal and should thus be governed by the strict "no

change" requirements that countries impose at the renewal stage. *See* Gevers & Tatham, *The Continuing Story, supra,* at 231.

(11) **The Operation of the Seniority Provisions.** For owners of a bundle of existing national registrations within the EU, the attractiveness of making a transition to a single CTM registration would be enhanced if the effect of securing a CTM was to give such a mark owner the same rights throughout the EU that it already had nationally. But this may be difficult to achieve where the registrations are slightly different in different countries, especially regarding identification of goods. Although the seniority provisions play an important part in fostering the transition to EU level registrations, they are not intended to ensure the automatic extension of national rights to the EU level. Instead, they seek to provide a more limited assurance that making the transition to a CTM registration will not jeopardize existing national rights.

Moreover, the holder of a prior national registration is not obliged to claim seniority when it applies for the corresponding CTM. And, even if seniority is claimed, the cautious registrant may continue also to renew the national registration. Although the goal of seniority is to encourage the transition to CTM rights *rather than* separate national registrations, it is not clear that the current legislation achieves this goal as fully as it might. Gevers and Tatham have stressed that "just because a seniority claim has been accepted by the Office, it is not necessarily valid." Gevers & Tatham, *The Continuing Story, supra,* at 229. What do Gevers and Tatham mean by this statement? Could a national court, presented with an infringement suit brought on the basis of a seniority claim, find that the seniority claim was invalid? If it did, and in the meantime the registrant had not renewed its national registration upon which seniority had been claimed, does this mean that the registrant has forfeited its earlier national registration in obtaining a CTM registration? *See* Trademark Regulation art. 34(2). National authorities have not thus far indicated how they will deal with registrations for which seniority has been claimed and which have not been renewed nationally. *See id.* What weight should such a national court give to an OHIM determination of seniority?

Another dilemma arises if the CTM in connection with which seniority was claimed is declared invalid. Seniority will be lost if the corresponding CTM registration is canceled. But the registrant may at that time convert the CTM into national applications. How should a national trademark office deal with any such conversion request? The regulation makes no express provision for how the national authorities must deal with the lapsed seniority right. The conversion applicant must of course re-endure any examination process that the national trademark law imposes. But must the national trademark office accord any special protections to such an applicant? For example, is the office obliged to recognize a priority date based upon the earlier national registration? The philosophy of encouraging registrants to make the transition to CTM registrations surely requires that the national trademark authorities grant the registrant seeking to convert back to national registrations the benefit of its earlier national priority date. Is the argument for this interpretation of the effect of lapsed seniority upon CTM cancellation any stronger (or weaker) than an argument that national courts should recognize OHIM determinations of seniority? Do the provisions on seniority provide sufficient protection to the national registrant seeking to make the transition to a single CTM registration? If not, what changes need to be made? Absent such changes, would you advise a client holding national registrations in all states of the EU (and claiming seniority for each) to let national registrations lapse?

---

[3] Enforcement

Before considering the Notes and Questions that follow, please review the section on enforcement in the *Introduction to the CTM System, supra* § 6.05[A][1]. Also review Articles 91-101 of the Trademark Regulation. The Regulation is reproduced in the Documentary Supplement.

NOTES AND QUESTIONS

(1) **The EU Court System.** The creation of the CTM system in many ways contributes to the further development of a set of federal (EU-level) governmental institutions. Thus far in the growth of the EU, the dictates of EU law have largely been enforced by the national courts of the member states. The traditional role of the European Court of Justice has been to ensure the supremacy of EU law and to avoid national courts from engaging in inconsistent interpretation of EU law. *See supra* § 2.03[C]. But there is no "federal" court system akin to that of the United States. In some respects, the Trademark Regulation is consistent with this philosophy in that it commandeers the national courts of the member states as CTM courts to enforce the rights of CTM holders. In CTM infringement proceedings, there is no direct appeal from CTM courts to the ECJ (although the Court may be called upon to provide guidance by way of its preliminary reference jurisdiction). Yet in other respects the regulation moves beyond the existing model by establishing a direct EU level judicial hierarchy: decisions of the Boards of Appeal of the OHIM may be appealed under Article 63 of the regulation to the Court of First Instance and hence onwards to the European Court of Justice. The Court of First Instance and the European Court of Justice will necessarily become more directly involved in the day-to-day evolution of EU trademark law as a quasi-federal law. The OHIM has estimated that 400 cases will be brought before the Court of First Instance annually under Article 63. *See* Stathis Koutsochinas, *Jurisdiction and Procedure in Legal Actions Relating to Community Trademarks*, 115 TRADEMARK WORLD 31, 32 (1999). The Council recognized that the extent of the involvement of the Court of First Instance and the ECJ in the appeals process would need to be monitored in order to ensure that these two sole courts of the EU were not overwhelmed by the demands of trademark law. *See* Statements for Entry in the Minutes of the Council Meeting at Which the Regulation on the Community Trade Mark Is Adopted, Statement by the Council No. 1, *reprinted as Appendix 2* to Charles Gielen, *European Trade Mark Legislation: The Statements*, 18 EUR. INTELL. PROP. REV. 83, 88 (1996).

This heightened role for the Court of Justice in appeals from the OHIM will also bring into sharp focus the continuing relationship between the national laws based upon the directive and the EU law embodied in the regulation. In addition to its existing role in the interpretation of the directive in national laws, the Court's rulings on parallel provisions in the regulation will no doubt affect the development of the directive-based national laws. Might the need to reconcile national and EU trademark law, and national and EU office and court determinations, cause the Court to develop principles of constitutional federalism and administrative deference with broader import for the system of law in the EU? What would those principles be?

(2) **National Courts Sitting as CTM Courts**. Are there advantages to be gained from commandeering the national courts to sit as CTM courts rather than deciding CTM infringement questions centrally through a EU court in Alicante or though a system of separate CTM courts sitting throughout the EU? When national courts are sitting as CTM courts they will be applying the substantive law of the regulation rather than the national directive-consistent trademark law of the state in which they sit. What case law, if any, should guide CTM courts in such cases? Should the U.K. courts be bound by principles of stare decisis when sitting as a CTM court? To what extent should national trademark courts designated as CTM courts look to case law on the CTM from CTM courts in other EU jurisdictions? Is that possible? Wise? Likely? At present, there is no significant case law on the enforcement of CTMs in national courts. But some commentators have expressed doubts as to whether national courts will enforce CTMs with as much vigor as they would national registrations. Why might this be so? What considerations might affect the way that a national judge would enforce a CTM registration?

(3) **Enforcement Strategy**. Jenkins, Inc. is a small U.K. company, with a place of business (or establishment) in both London, England, and Paris, France. Jenkins manufactures and sells an electronic personal organizer under the mark WIZARD. In 1996, Jenkins applied for the CTM registration for WIZARD. Jenkins's application was in Swedish, and English was designated as the second language. Jenkins included in its CTM application an ultimately successful claim for seniority based upon a prior (1992) French registration. A Notice of Opposition was filed by an Austrian company alleging that its earlier Austrian registration of the mark WHIZZZ for a calculator should preclude the grant of a CTM registration for WIZARD. The opposition proceedings were conducted in English. The opposition was rejected by the Opposition Division on the ground that the marks and goods were not identical and the dissimilarities between the respective marks and the respective goods were sufficient to avoid confusion. Jenkins thus owns the CTM registration on the mark WIZARD for electronic personal organizers and is using the mark in both the United Kingdom and France, its primary markets. It also sells the product in Germany under the same mark. Jenkins discovers that Kurt Dunger & Co., a Delaware company with a place of business in New York, New York; Frankfurt, Germany; and Vienna, Austria, is selling electronic pagers of questionable quality under the mark WIZARD. Dunger & Co. is selling the products in the United Kingdom, France, Germany, Austria, and the Netherlands. This has been going on for some time. Jenkins wishes to stop the sale of WIZARD electronic pagers and to secure damages from Dunger. Review Articles 91-100 of the Trademark Regulation.

(a) If Jenkins wishes to bring an action against Dunger for infringement of its CTM, where may it file the action? If you were advising Jenkins, where would you suggest that it file the action? What considerations would motivate your choice?

(b) Assume that you decide to file your infringement action in Germany. Dunger files a counterclaim seeking a declaration that Jenkins's CTM registration is invalid on the ground that the term WIZARD consists exclusively of an indication of the quality of the goods. *See* Trademark Regulation art. 7(1)(c). In what ways might Jenkins respond? *See id.* arts. 96, 100.

(c) Assume instead that prior to Jenkins filing a claim, it sent a cease and desist letter to Dunger, which served only to provoke Dunger into filing an action seeking a Declaration of Invalidity of Jenkins's CTM registration with the OHIM (and a declaration of non-infringement). *Cf.* Trademark Regulation art. 93(5). Would this affect your decision as to where Jenkins should file, and what other steps would you advise Jenkins to take? *See id.* arts. 99-100. If Dunger's action for invalidity is also based upon its ownership of a 1994 German registration for WIZARD for electronic pagers, would this change your analysis?

[4] The Future and Significance of The CTM

The creation of the CTM was motivated in part by the difficulties that national rights presented to an institution such as the EU that was based upon the free movement of goods. The European Court of Justice has struggled to address those difficulties through different exhaustion doctrines, *see infra* § 7.06, but the CTM represents a different means of confronting that problem. *See* Thomas Ardell Larkin, *Harmony in Disarray: The European Community Trademark System*, 82 TRADEMARK REP. 634, 649 (1992). As similar issues of the conflict between free trade principles and national intellectual property rights are addressed elsewhere, the CTM system might come to have much broader significance as a model for ameliorating the difficulties that arise. But for the CTM to reach its full potential, whether as a functioning supranational trademark registration system or as an experiment to be replicated elsewhere, a variety of tough issues must be addressed by the European Union.

NOTES AND QUESTIONS

(1) **Connection to the Madrid System.** The intent of the EU was to adhere to the Madrid Protocol as an intergovernmental organization that grants trademark rights and thus permit Madrid applications to be based upon a CTM home application. Conversely, Madrid applicants basing their international application on an application from elsewhere could designate the EU as a jurisdiction in which to seek an extension of protection. As discussed above, this development has encountered some political obstacles. *See supra* § 6.02[A].

(2) **EU Enlargement**. New difficulties may present themselves when the EU is enlarged to include new countries (mostly from central Europe). In particular, it is by no means clear how the unitary nature of existing CTM registrations—registration with the same effect throughout the EU—will mesh with the national systems of new EU states. If there is no conflicting national registration in a new EU state at the time of accession, the CTM could be extended to that territory without any derogation from existing rights. Similarly, if the CTM owner owns the mark in a new EU state, the CTM can

without significant problem be extended (with the added benefit of seniority). But if there is a conflicting mark in a new EU state that is owned by another party, how should the conflict be reconciled? If the terms of the current regulation were applied without modification to new states, what would happen? If the conflicting mark predated the CTM registration, what would be the result? *See* Bojan Pretnar, *Is the Future Enlargement of the European Union an Immediate Issue for the Community Trademark System*, 19 EUR. INTELL. PROP. REV. 185 (1997).

(3) **As a Model for Regional (or Global) Trademark Systems.** Do you think that the CTM system is one that could be replicated in other regions of the world? How would you define those regions? Could it be replicated on a broader global scale? What additional issues might other regions of the world present? What additional issues would a broader "global" system present? *Cf.* Florent Gevers & David Tatham, *The Opposition Procedure in the Community Trade Mark System*, 20 EUR. INTELL. PROP. REV. 22, 24 (1998) (noting the difficulty of establishing a constant meaning of "confusing similarity" across the EU, given differences in pronunciation and meaning that exist in language and customs of the 15 EU member states). Even if the CTM system could be replicated (regionally or globally), would it be wise to do so? Would you support the creation of a North American Trademark along the lines of the CTM? Does the negotiation of the FTAA provide a realistic vehicle for such an endeavor? The Inter-American Convention, which resulted in the setting up—but not the functioning—of an Inter-American Trademark Office, was to some extent a response to the European establishment of the Madrid Agreement in 1891. Does the FTAA provide a similar vehicle for a response to the Madrid Protocol? What are the difficult issues that the expansion of the geographic scope of a trademark regime encounters? What social costs arise from such an expansion? What advantages accrue?

[B]   Other Regional Groupings

Reforms of EU trademark law have been heavily influenced by Benelux law not only because (to use the language of Professor Gielen) Benelux trademark law is more "modern," but also because the Benelux exercise was in many respects a smaller version of the EU's drive toward the free movement of goods. The Benelux system thus provided a useful institutional model through which to make the transition to unitary rights, as well as a model for substantive trademark law provisions. The concept of seniority, for example, is one developed by Benelux law. The Benelux also established a Benelux court system to interpret and apply the uniform law.

Other regional groupings in Latin America, Asia, and Africa have developed systems that are not unitary in nature—the instruments in question can fairly be described as harmonization measures—but these systems also adopt certain rules that facilitate multinational acquisition of rights and perhaps presage the creation of a unitary system. In 1993, ARIPO concluded the Banjul Protocol, which established a central registry for trademark applications. *See generally* Brenda M. Wood-Kahari, ARIPO Trademarks: A New Regional System for Trademarks in African States, Paper Presented to INTA Annual Meeting (San Antonio, 1997). The workings of the registry were set out in implementing regulations in November 1995. The regulations put in place a system that resembles the Madrid Protocol system and that has accepted registration applications since 1997. Applicants may make a filing with ARIPO seeking registration in any number of ARIPO states that have adhered to the protocol—which presently means only Malawi, Swaziland, and Zimbabwe of the fourteen member states of ARIPO. The ARIPO office forwards the application to the national offices of the various countries in which protection is sought, for examination under those national laws. Examining countries must notify the ARIPO office of any objection to registration within twelve months. If one of the countries designated refuses to register the mark, the applicant may convert its ARIPO-filed applications into national applications. Although the national offices apply their own law to an ARIPO application, the Banjul Protocol did contain some substantive provisions which, in the event of conflict with national law, will be applied to ARIPO applications. In particular, use in one state would constitute use sufficient to maintain registration in all states designated in the ARIPO application. In what ways is the ARIPO system different from the Madrid system? In what ways is it different from the CTM system? Do these changes improve the system as a means of securing multinational protection of trademarks?

The member countries of the Association of South-East Asian nations ("ASEAN"), meaning Brunei, Indonesia, Laos, Malaysia, Myanmar, the Philippines, Thailand, Singapore, and Vietnam, have adopted the ASEAN Framework Agreement on Intellectual Property, which includes the establishment of a regional trademark office. No timetable for implementation of the framework has been agreed to, and it is not clear whether the creation of a regional office would involve the development of centralized filing or a unitary registration. *See* Assafa Endeshaw, *Harmonization of Intellectual Property Laws in ASEAN*, 2 J. WORLD INTELL. PROP. L. 3 (1999).

In 1995 the Mercosur countries adopted the Protocol of Harmonization of Intellectual Property Provisions in Mercosur concerning Trademarks, Indications of Source and Denominations of Origin. *See* Decision No. 8/95 of the Council of the Mercosur Common Market (Argentina, Brazil, Paraguay, and Uruguay). The main thrust of the decision is the harmonization of the trademark laws of the Mercosur countries along the lines of the Paris Convention and TRIPS. *See* Protocol art. 2. In addition, however, the protocol addresses issues particular to the Mercosur grouping. Thus, Article 4 obliges states to move toward the elimination of translation requirements for filings that are in Spanish or Portugese, Article 13 establishes Mercosur-wide exhaustion of rights, and Article 16 provides that use of a trademark in any member country should be sufficient to avoid cancellation. For an update on the Protocol, which still awaits ratification by Brazil and Argentina, see Santiago R. O'Conor, *Update: Protocol of Harmonization in Mercosur*, 118 TRADEMARK WORLD 23 (June 1999). The Andean Pact, whose Decision No. 344 on Industrial Property is also primarily a harmonization measure, is also considering a revision of the decision to require protection of marks that have acquired distinctiveness based upon use in any Andean Community country. *See* 13 WORLD INTELL. PROP. REP. 277, 278 (1999). If adopted, this would minimally modify the basic proposition of the Andean Pact Decision 344, namely that the protection in the Andean pact countries remains purely national in nature.

§ 6.06 Regional Design Rights

[A]   The European Union: Proposed Design Regulation*

In 1991, the European Commission undertook a review of existing design protection within the countries of the EU. This revealed a wide divergence in the means by which individual countries protected designs, generating significant costs for EU producers and erecting barriers to the free movement of goods. Thus, two years later, in order to reduce territorial obstacles to the efficient working of the internal market and to ease the burden on producers seeking separate national design registrations in order to secure Community-wide protection, the Commission proposed a regulation that would create unitary EU-wide *sui generis* design rights. *See* Proposal for a European Parliament and Council Regulation on the Community Design, COM(93)342 final (Dec. 1993). The alternative of harmonizing member states' laws (which had been used in minimizing differences in national protection accorded computer software, databases, and semiconductor topographies) would be inadequate in this context. Harmonization in itself would not preclude the partitioning of markets that territorial protection creates; in contrast, the introduction of a single, autonomous law obviates the problems wrought by territorial protection. And where registered rights are involved, unlike the rights by which databases or software was protected, harmonization would not substantially reduce the costs involved in applying for rights separately in each country. Strategically, the Commission found exclusive reliance on a harmonization directive unappealing because approximation of the many different national systems of copyright and unfair competition under which designs are protected looked infeasible, and the Commission believed that the negotiation of a new instrument "could be developed with greater freedom than change to be introduced in existing legislation . . . . One could hope that member states would look for the most appropriate and advanced solutions when starting from scratch." Accordingly, the cornerstone of the proposals was the creation of federal design rights, to be implemented by the enactment of a regulation.

The proposed regulation would provide a producer with two separate, but related, EU-wide rights with which to protect its design: a Registered Community Design, obtained by application to the Community Design Office, with an initial term of five years (renewable up to twenty-five years); and an Unregistered Community Design right that endures for a period of three years after the design is made available to the public. Most member states have some form of registered design protection at present—and those that do not (Greece) will be required by the parallel Design Harmonization Directive adopted in 1998 to establish such protection, *see supra* § 3.03[B]—but the introduction of the unregistered right is an innovation, if one that is based largely on a similar right first introduced in the United Kingdom in 1988. The purpose of providing protection without registration is to accommodate industries that develop large numbers of designs, only a few of which are commercially exploited, and whose

---

*This analysis is based upon a more lengthy (and earlier) consideration of the proposals in Graeme B. Dinwoodie, *Federalized Functionalism: The Future of Design Protection in the European Union*, 24 AM. INTELL. PROP. L. ASS'N Q.J. 611 (1996).

products are short-lived. For these industries, such as fashion and textiles, almost any registration process will remain an overly expensive, unduly time-consuming and not particularly helpful proposition. The registration *process*, particularly if it involves a substantive examination, ordinarily extends beyond the commercial life of the design. For these industries, some form of automatic short-term protection against unauthorized reproduction is necessary (and, largely, sufficient).

Assertion of rights under the unregistered community design system will not prevent application for a community registered design. The two forms of protection are granted on the same conditions and are subject to the same exclusions; any design that could be registered will be entitled to unregistered design protection. Indeed, one of the benefits that the Commission foresees from this structure is the ability of the producer to test the design in the marketplace with the protection offered by the unregistered design right and, if the design proves successful, within one year (the applicable grace period) to seek registration of that design. The substantive provisions governing eligibility for protection under the regulation—in either unregistered or registered form—are intended to mirror those found in the recently-enacted Harmonization Directive. *See supra* § 3.03[B]. Consequently, a revised version of the initial proposal, incorporating changes made to the directive during its progress through the legislative process, was published for consideration on June 21, 1999. *See* Amended Proposal for a Council Regulation on Community Design, COM(1999)310 final (June 21, 1999). After receiving opinions and proposed amendments from the European Parliament and the Economic and Social Committee, the Commission published a further revised proposal in November 2000. *See* Amended Proposal for a Council Regulation on Community Design, COM(2000)660 final/2 (Nov. 23, 2000) (the "Further Amended Proposed Regulation"). The proposed regulation, even its further amended form, does not seek to resolve the contentious repair clause debate and, pending the expected Commission proposal to amend the directive after analyzing its effect on the spare parts market, so-called must-match parts will be excluded from EU registration. *See* Further Amended Proposed Regulation art. 10a. Instead, the last sticking point, to be discussed with a view to compromise at the June 2001 Internal Market Council meeting, is likely to relate to languages to be used in the Community Design system.

The primary differences between the registered and unregistered rights relate to the date of commencement of protection, and the term and scope of protection obtained. The unregistered protection subsists upon the design being made available to the public within the EU, while registered protection runs from the date of the filing of an application for registration. *See id.* arts. 12-13. While the rights conferred by a design registration are in the nature of monopoly rights, the owner of the unregistered community design obtains only the right to prevent unauthorized reproduction. *See id.* art. 20. That is to say, independent creation is a defense in an action for infringement of an unregistered, but not a registered, design. *See* Explanatory Memorandum Accompanying the Amended Proposal for a Council Regulation on Community Design, COM(2000)660 final/2 (Nov. 23, 2000) at 4. The Commission settled on a term of three years for unregistered protection; however, because the conditions for protection do not vary as between registered and unregistered designs, each design protected for three years can, by timely application, receive protection of a patent-like nature for up to twenty-five years. *See* Further Amended Proposed Regulation arts. 12-13.

To accommodate the concerns of industry regarding the costs and delay of design registration, the Commission's proposals suggested two changes to a full-blown registration system. First, the unregistered design right has been included as an integral part of the solution. Second, the registration system will be a "passive" registration (or deposit) system.* The Community Design Office will check applications only for obviously inappropriate subject matter and formal deficiencies. *See* Official Commentary on Proposed Article 48, in Explanatory Memorandum Accompanying the Proposal for a European Parliament and Council Regulation on the Community Design, COM(93) 342 final-COD 463 (Brussels, 3 Dec. 1993). The Community Design Office will be the same institution established to deal with trademark applications under the Trademark Regulation, and the procedural mechanisms thus bear strong similarity to those under which the Trademark Office in Alicante has been working since January 1, 1996. For example, an application for design registration may be filed at the Community Design Office or at the central industrial property office of a member state. *See* Amended Proposed Regulation art. 37. In most countries of the EU, the registration of the design leads to its publication, and that will generally be the case under the design proposals. Provision is made, however, for the possibility of deferred publication in order to maintain the secrecy of the design.

Over the course of the evolution of these proposals, the abolition of substantive examinations appears to have become a priority in the thinking of the Commission. Ironically, however, although the 1960 text of the Hague Agreement was not tailored to accommodate systems that perform extensive substantive examinations, *see* Hague Agreement Concerning the Deposit of Industrial Designs (Hague text, 1960) art. 8(1) (requiring member countries to issue rejection within six months), the recent revision of that agreement is largely intended to permit the involvement of countries that subject design registration applications to substantive examination. *See supra* § 6.03.

Notes and Questions

(1) **Scope of Protection**. One of the few distinctions between the registered community design and the unregistered community design right is the scope of protection. In practice, how big a difference does this make, especially if courts assessing infringement of unregistered rights follow copyright jurisprudence and are willing to presume copying from access and probative similarity? Should courts indulge that presumption? Should it be modified when dealing with functional designs, and if so, in what ways? *Cf.* Computer Assocs. v. Altai, Inc., 982 F.2d 693, 708 (2d Cir. 1992) ("Under [the circumstance that programmers are trying to create the most efficient programs possible], the fact

---

*The use of passive registration mirrors the nature of the examination under design laws currently in place in several countries of the European Union. (For example, the registration proceedings in the Benelux countries do not involve substantive examination, nor do those in France, Italy and Spain. The U.K. authorities do examine for substantive compliance with the requirements of their act.)

that two programs contain the same efficient structure may as likely lead to an inference of independent creation as it does to one of copying.")

Why did the Commission wish to offer designers patent-like rights upon registration? Would producers' legitimate concerns have been addressed by a lesser scope of rights? *See* Dinwoodie, *supra*, at 701-02. What justifies the broader scope of protection for registered rights? Do those justifications extend to the type of registration envisaged by the proposed regulation? *See id.* at 722 (criticizing the grant of "drive-through monopoly rights"). Should variables other than registration affect the scope of protection granted by intellectual property rights? *See id.* at 655-57 n.123-25 (discussing other linkages); Uma Suthersanen, *Breaking Down the Intellectual Property Barriers*, 2 INTELL. PROP. Q. 267, 289-90 (1998) (linking scope of protection to constraints on the creative process). For example, why does copyright offer a lesser scope of protection than patent? Is the registered nature of patent rights the sole reason?

(2) **Unregistered Rights**. If the Commission wished to create an automatic, short-term protection against unauthorized copying, what options were available to it? Why do you think it chose to introduce the (relatively new) concept of an unregistered design right? What dangers flow from granting industrial property rights without registration? Do these justify insisting upon registration before protection? What are the problems of using a novelty standard for unregistered rights? *See* Lionel Bently & Alan Coulthard, *From the Commonplace to the Interface: Five Cases on Unregistered Design Right*, 19 EUR. INTELL. PROP. REV. 401, 407 (1997) (discussing dangers of novelty standard).

(3) **Institutional Issues**. Authoritative interpretations by the European Court of Justice will, to some extent, assist in establishing a common understanding of the new design protection thresholds. That standardizing influence will, however, only be felt periodically, and in a non-examining system there will be fewer *administrative* determinations from which to forge a collective sense of these concepts. The primary administrative proceeding in which such a sense could be developed would be actions for declarations of invalidity of the registered community design, for which the Community Design Office will have primary, but not exclusive, jurisdiction. *See* Further Amended Proposed Regulation art. 56 (conferring jurisdiction on Community Office), arts. 26(2), 85(c) (conferring jurisdiction on national courts designated as community design courts to adjudicate counterclaims seeking declaration of invalidity of registered community design, and to adjudicate direct actions for declaration of invalidity of unregistered community design). Should the central institutions—the European Court or the Community Design Office—have exclusive jurisdiction in such matters? What benefits would such a change produce? Would it have any costs?

The initial proposal expressly reserved the right of the Commission to challenge a registered community design before the Community Design Office and the European Court of Justice if it believed that the design did not meet the standards of protectability, *see* Proposed Regulation art. 56, and an advisory committee on designs would have been established to assist the Commission in determining whether such action needed to be taken. In the amended proposal, however, the standing of the Commission (and member states) to bring or appear in invalidity proceedings before the office has been removed. *See* Further Amended Proposed Regulation art. 56. The explanatory memorandum accompanying the 1999 proposals suggested that such office standing would be neither "appropriate nor opportune," but notes the inherent right of the Commission and member states (under Court of Justice case law) to bring an action before the Court of Justice against any decision by the office, or (under the statute of the Court of Justice) to intervene in any appeal before the Court. *See* Explanatory Memorandum Accompanying Amended Proposal for a Council Regulation on Community Design, COM(1999)310 final (June 21, 1999) at 10.

(4) **Passive Examination.** What is the value of a registration system that foregoes substantive examination and instead triggers the formalities-only search envisaged by the EU proposals? *See* Report of the Departmental Committee on Industrial Designs (Johnston Committee), Cmnd. 1808 (1962) (U.K.) ¶ 12 (noting that the textile industry relied on the "limited" searches conducted by the Manchester Registry as a "rough and ready test of infringement" that would influence whether the manufacturer exploited the design commercially).

(5) **The Relationship Between National and Community Design Rights.** The continued existence of the varied national forms of design protection might be expected to precipitate the need to referee inevitable conflicts that will occur between community and national rights. The Commission appears to have relied upon the fact that (in most cases) the universal, time-unlimited nature of the novelty and individual character determinations will ensure that protection under the national law of a member state will prevent protection as a Community design, or as a registered design under the newly-harmonized national laws. One express provision on "conflict resolution" is included in the regulation. Several member states provide the option of maintaining the secrecy of a design registration in various circumstances. Such "unpublished" designs will not destroy the novelty or individual character of any later design seeking protection as a community design because they are not "made available to the public." Yet, the secrecy provisions of national laws would be rendered meaningless if these earlier national registrations were superseded by the community rights. Accordingly, the community rights will be invalid as against the holder of the national registration in the country of that registration, but not as against third parties or in other countries of the union. *See* Further Amended Proposed Regulation arts. 27(1)(d), 27(3).

(6) **Treatment of Third Country Designers.** The U.K. government took the position that it could condition *its* unregistered design right on reciprocal protection without violating its obligations under either the Paris or Berne Conventions. *See* CHRISTINE FELLNER, INDUSTRIAL DESIGN LAW 125-26 (1995) (explaining reasoning of the U.K. government). While the TRIPS Agreement retained the exceptions to national treatment found in the Paris and Berne Conventions, *see* art. 3, commentators have suggested that the MFN obligations contained in Article 4 should void such conditions of material reciprocity. *See* J. H. Reichman, *Universal Minimum Standards of Intellectual Property Protection under the TRIPS Component of the WTO Agreement*, 29 INT. LAW. 345, 349 n.27 (1995). Although the spirit of the TRIPS Agreement (and the Paris Convention) would suggest that design rights should be available on a national treatment basis, the Commission's intentions with respect to the conditions under which the proposed unregistered community design right would be available to non-EU producers are not evident from any of its formal communications.

(7) **Legislative Basis of the EU Legislation.** Initially, the Commission grounded the submission of both the directive and the proposed regulation on Article 100a of the EC Treaty, under which enactment requires adoption by a majority of the European Parliament and a qualified majority of the Council of Ministers. After the Commission submitted its design proposals, however, the member states suggested (and the Commission agreed) that the proper legal basis for adoption of the regulation was Article 235 of the E.C. Treaty. Article 235 (the "necessary and appropriate" clause of the EC Treaty) provides for the consideration of legislation pursuant to the more straightforward "consultation" procedure, which requires unanimous approval by the member states (as represented in Council) but envisages a lesser role for the European Parliament. In particular, legislation can be enacted under Article 235 over the objections of the Parliament. In the amended versions of the proposal, the stated legal basis for the regulation has been altered, confirming the indications that had already been given by the Commission. It has now been proposed under Article 235 (new Article 308) rather than Article 100a (new Article 95). *See* Explanatory Memorandum Accompanying Amended Proposal for a Council Regulation on Community Design, COM(1999)310 final (June 21, 1999) at 2-3.

(8) **Link to the Hague Agreement.** The Commission has indicated an intent to link the community design to the Hague Agreement in much the same way that the community trademark has been linked to the Madrid Protocol. *See* Geneva Act of the Hague Agreement Concerning the International Registration of Industrial Designs art. 27(1)(ii) (July 2, 1999).

[B] Other Regional Groupings

Like developments in the trademark area, the EU exercise is not the sole example of regional groupings that have moved toward unitary supranational design rights. The EU regulation, if adopted, would frame current debate, but other regions already have unitary design rights. Again, the Benelux has been a leader, introducing the unitary Benelux design right in 1975. Design has, however, always been the poor cousin of international intellectual property laws, and thus there has been less international pressure to develop effective design laws. Accordingly, many of the regional groupings discussed above that have given detailed consideration to regional patents and trademarks, have only tentatively addressed the question of unitary design rights. Whether the revised Hague Agreement gives international design protection new impetus remains to be seen.

EPILOGUE

The different international agreements discussed in this Chapter all move from national to international forms of protection in slightly different ways: they represent, in short, different degrees of internationalization. Can you place each of the systems instituted on a spectrum from national to international models? What are the elements common to each system; in what ways are they different? Would a single model work for all of the different intellectual property rights? Would the same model work for both regional and global agreements? If not, why not?

Chapter 7

INTERNATIONAL ENFORCEMENT OF INTELLECTUAL PROPERTY RIGHTS BY RIGHT HOLDERS

§ 7.01 Remedies Under National Laws

A range of remedies are available for the infringement of intellectual property rights under national laws, including criminal penalties as well as various forms of monetary and equitable or injunctive relief. The nature and extent of these remedies varies from country to country, depending in large part on variations in legal systems. They share common goals, however: to put a stop to the infringement; to make the right holder whole; and to punish infringers and provide meaningful deterrence. The relative mix and effectiveness of civil and criminal actions is different in different countries, depending on such factors as the efficiency and cost of the judicial system and the willingness of the government to initiate prosecutions.

The legislation of most countries typically makes available a combination of some or all of the following civil remedies: actual damages suffered by the right holder; some form of statutory, exemplary or punitive damages; recovery of the infringer's profits; injunctions against continued infringement (both as part of the ultimate judgment in the lawsuit and provisionally, to prevent the infringement from continuing pending the resolution of the lawsuit); seizure of infringing materials and/or the equipment used to make them; and a mechanism for customs agencies to prevent entry into the country of infringing materials.

Virtually all countries provide for the recovery of actual damages in cases of copyright infringement. It is also common for the copyright owner to be able to recover the defendant's profits (in the United States, to the extent that they are attributable to the infringement and are not duplicative of elements of damages). Because it is often difficult to prove actual damages in copyright cases (where the damage may essentially be the loss of exclusivity and control), many countries provide for statutory damages as well. In the United States, a court may award such damages within its discretion within a range set by statute, with lower awards authorized in cases of innocent infringement and higher awards in cases of willful infringement. Some countries provide for the possibility of punitive damages.

As to equitable remedies, final injunctions are virtually always available to require the defendant to cease the infringing acts. Most countries also provide some form of provisional relief during the pendency of the lawsuit, with the purpose of preserving the status quo, preventing the accumulation of damage from ongoing infringement, and ensuring that evidence is not destroyed. Typical of these remedies are the temporary restraining order in the United States and the Anton Piller order in the United Kingdom. Courts may also be authorized to order the seizure or destruction of infringing copies and/or the equipment used to make them. Finally, customs agencies often have authority to seize infringing materials at the border to prevent their importation into the country. The standards and requirements of proof to trigger such government action differ from country to country. In the United States, for example, it is necessary to record a certificate of registration with customs.

Criminal penalties are available in cases brought by the government, and in some countries, in private actions as well. They are generally limited to the more egregious cases of infringement, involving wrongful intent and often some degree of commerciality. The penalties include fines as well as prison terms. There is a tremendous range from country to country in the level of both fines and prison terms, reflecting perceptions of what is sufficient deterrence for such a crime in the conditions prevailing in that particular country.

The protection of intellectual property in the United States is supported by several provisions imposing criminal sanctions for certain infringements. Section 2319 of title 18 sets out the applicable criminal fines and imprisonment for criminal infringement of copyright under section 506 of the Copyright Act, and trademark counterfeiting may also attract criminal penalties. The legislative tendency in recent years has been to strengthen criminal copyright penalties and to impose criminal sanctions as an early response to new technological challenges to the integrity of copyright works. *See, e.g.,* No Electronic Theft Act, Pub. L. No. 105-147; 17 U.S.C. § 1204(a) (West Supp. 1998). Why has criminal liability assumed a more prominent role in the furtherance of copyright policy objectives? Which advantages does criminal enforcement bring? Are there any dangers with using the criminal law as a tool of intellectual property rights? Might it be more appropriate to use the criminal law in some areas of intellectual property enforcement than in others? What strategic advantages might the United States be pursuing through the enactment of criminal liability for violation of intellectual property rights?

§ 7.02 National Enforcement Under International Law

It is frequently remarked that the achievement of the TRIPS Agreement was its "enforcement" provisions. This term is, however, often used in two different senses. First, as seen in Chapter 5, the TRIPS Agreement addressed the enforcement of states' international obligations by making compliance an issue that could be subject to the WTO Dispute Settlement procedures. Second, the substantive provisions of the TRIPS Agreement went beyond existing intellectual property conventions by delineating standards to which procedures for private enforcement of domestic intellectual property rights would be measured. This second set of "enforcement" provisions are covered in this section of Chapter 7.

ADRIAN OTTEN, THE FUNDAMENTAL IMPORTANCE OF THE TRIPS AGREEMENT FOR A BETTER ENFORCEMENT OF COPYRIGHT*

Paper Presented to ALAI Congress (Berlin, June 1999)

One of the major features and innovations of the TRIPS Agreement is that it gives as much attention to the enforcement of intellectual property rights through domestic legal procedures as it does to the substantive standards which should be provided for their protection. A weakness of the pre-existing international law in the area of intellectual property was that it was very largely silent on the issue of enforcement. . . . I will discuss the requirements in the TRIPS Agreement on Members to provide domestic procedures and remedies so that right holders can secure the effective enforcement of their rights.

. . . .

Procedures and Remedies for the Enforcement of Intellectual Property Rights

Part III of the TRIPS Agreement concerns procedures and remedies to be provided at the national level for the enforcement of intellectual property rights. These provisions have two main objectives:

> * First, to permit effective action against any act of infringement, including expeditious remedies to prevent infringements and remedies which constitute a deterrent to further infringements.
>
> * Second, they aim to avoid the creation of barriers to legitimate trade and to provide for safeguards against the abuse of procedures. This second aspect reflects the underlying concern in the TRIPS Agreement to provide for a balance between the interests of producers and those of users of intellectual property. Provisions which reflect this concern can be found notably in the safeguards that have to be provided in relation to the use of measures of a provisional nature, including border measures, such as in regard to time-limits, the possibility that applicants may be required to lodge a security, etc.

[T]he TRIPS enforcement rules . . . constitute the first international disciplines ever negotiated on domestic enforcement procedures and remedies. Thus, to some extent, we are still in the testing phase. Notably, it remains to be seen how successful were the negotiators in producing a set of rules that is precise enough to be meaningful and, if necessary, justiciable through the WTO dispute settlement mechanism, but yet on the other hand sufficiently general to take into account differences in national legal systems, as was required by

---

the mandate given to the negotiators, as well as to respect judicial discretion.

The rules in the TRIPS Agreement on enforcement are not intended to be revolutionary, nor are they intended to lead to a harmonization of national enforcement systems. Rather, they are a compilation of the basic features of good enforcement procedures and remedies that can be found in the main national legal systems. Moreover, it should be recalled that, like the rest of the TRIPS Agreement, they are minimum standards, in the sense that Members are free to, but not obliged to, implement in their law more extensive protection than that required by the Agreement, provided that, in doing so, they do not contravene the provisions of the Agreement. Most persons who read them will find little that is new or surprising in them. However, many countries have had or will have to make some changes to be fully in conformity, especially, but not only, in the area of special border measures.

Also by way of a general observation concerning the TRIPS enforcement rules, I think it is useful to distinguish within them two types of obligation:

> * The first are those which prescribe procedures and remedies that must be provided by each Member in its national legal system. Much of this is set out in terms of the authority that must be available to judges and courts or other competent authorities, such as the customs administration.
>
> * The second type of obligation is what might be described as "performance standards" in relation to the workings of these procedures and practice. For example, they must be such as to permit effective action against infringing activity, expeditious and deterrent remedies and applied in a manner that will avoid the creation of barriers to legitimate trade.

The enforcement provisions of the TRIPS Agreement are divided into five sections. The first of these entitled "General Obligations" relates to all enforcement procedures and remedies. The next two, regarding civil and administrative procedures and remedies and provisional measures, concern the infringement of any intellectual property right covered by the TRIPS Agreement, that is to say the seven categories of intellectual property with which the TRIPS Agreement deals. The last two sections, those relating to border measures and criminal procedures, must apply at least to trademark counterfeiting and copyright piracy, but Members are, of course, free to apply such procedures to other infringing acts as well.

Section 1: General Obligations

This section contains the basic objectives and performance standards to which I have already referred. It also contains some basic rules of due process—that procedures should be fair and equitable, and that decisions should, as a rule, be in writing and reasoned, made available without undue delay and based only on the evidence in respect of which parties are offered the opportunity to be heard. It also provides for rights of review. In addition, it requires that procedures shall not be unnecessarily complicated or costly, or entail unreasonable time limits or unwarranted delays.

A further part of the general obligations section addresses concerns that were raised during the negotiations, particularly by developing countries, about the problems that they would have if they were required to devote disproportionate resources to the enforcement of intellectual property rights. The formulation that was reached after negotiation reads as follows:

> It is understood that this Part does not create any obligation to put in place a judicial system for the enforcement of intellectual property rights distinct from that for the enforcement of law in general, nor does it affect the capacity of Members to enforce their law in general. Nothing in this Part creates any obligation with respect to the distribution of resources as between enforcement of intellectual property rights and the enforcement of law in general.

Section 2: Civil Administrative Procedures and Remedies

This section is essentially concerned with civil judicial procedures but also requires that if civil remedies can be ordered as a result of administrative procedures, such procedures shall conform to principles equivalent in substance to those set forth in the section.

The section firstly fleshes out the concept of fair and equitable procedures in regard to such matters as rights to written notice, rights of representation, rights to present evidence and the protection of confidential information. It also addresses the authority that judges must have to order that evidence be produced by a party, against its will, in appropriate situations. This is, of course, an area where there is a wide difference between the practices of WTO Members, for example the discovery system in the United States and the civil law practices in Continental Europe. Nonetheless, a formulation acceptable to all Members was reached.

Most of the rest of the section specifies the remedies that judges and courts must have the authority to order, including injunctions, damages and, in appropriate situations, forfeiture and disposal outside the channels of commerce of infringing goods as well as materials and implements predominantly used in their production. There is also a provision requiring judicial authorities to be able to order the indemnification of defendants who have been wrongfully enjoined or restrained as a result of abuse of enforcement procedures by a plaintiff.

Section 3: Provisional Measures

Under the TRIPS Agreement, WTO Members must ensure that their judicial authorities have the power to order prompt and effective provisional measures both to prevent an infringement and to preserve relevant evidence in regard to an alleged infringement. In appropriate cases, they must have the authority to do this without prior notice being given to the respondent, in particular where any delay is likely to cause irreparable harm to the right holder or where there is a demonstrable risk of evidence being destroyed.

The question of the availability of provisional measures on an ex parte basis under civil judicial procedures has been the subject of two dispute settlement complaints, both by the United States; one against Denmark and the other against Sweden. This issue appears to be one of particular concern to the computer software industry, given the apparent ease with which evidence of the use of infringing programs can be eradicated if prior notice of search and seizure measures is given. One of these disputes, that concerning Sweden, has led to a bilateral mutually agreed solution. The WTO was informed that, to fulfil its TRIPS obligations, Sweden had amended its intellectual property laws so as to give judicial authorities in Sweden the authority to order provisional measures in the context of civil proceedings involving [intellectual property rights] (IPRs). The legislation provides that if there is reason to believe that a person has taken or is about to take action to infringe IPRs, the court may order a search for infringing materials, documents or other relevant evidence and that this might be done *inaudita altera parte* if there is a risk that materials or documents could be moved, destroyed or altered. The other complaint is still the subject of consultations under the dispute settlement process.

The remaining provisions of the section on provisional measures concern various forms of safeguards to ensure that such measures are not abused or used as barriers to legitimate trade.

Section 4: Special Requirements Related to Border Measures

The basic obligation under this section is that Members must provide a means, whether through administrative or judicial bodies, by which right holders can obtain the assistance of the customs administration to prevent the importation of at least counterfeit trademark goods and pirated copyright goods. For this purpose, counterfeit trademark goods are, in essence, defined as goods involving more flagrant types of copying of trademarks and pirated goods as goods which violate a reproduction right in the area of copyright or related rights. Members are free to apply these procedures to other types of infringing activity, provided they respect the safeguards required, but not obliged to do so. Goods in transit, parallel imports and small quantities of a non-commercial nature do not have to be covered by these procedures.

The requirement in the TRIPS Agreement is to put in place a mechanism which can be initiated by the right holder lodging an application to the competent national authorities. Ex officio action by national authorities is not a requirement, but is envisaged provided the appropriate safeguards are respected.

Section 5: Criminal Procedures

The TRIPS Agreement requires Members to provide criminal procedures and penalties to be applied at least in cases of wilful trademark counterfeiting or copyright piracy on a commercial scale. Remedies must be sufficient to provide a deterrent consistent with the level of penalties applied for crimes of a corresponding gravity. Once again, although it is not a requirement, the Agreement envisages that Members may provide for criminal procedures and penalties to be applied in other cases of infringement of IPRs, in particular where they are committed wilfully and on a commercial scale.

Compliance with the requirements of this section, read in conjunction with the general enforcement obligations of the TRIPS Agreement that I referred to earlier, is the subject of a dispute between the United States on the one hand and Greece and the European Communities on the other. This concerns the availability of effective remedies against copyright infringement in Greece with respect to unauthorized broadcasts of motion pictures and television programmes. This matter is at the consultation phase of the dispute settlement system.

HERMES INT'L v. FHT MARKETING CHOICE BV
1998 E.T.M.R. 425 (E.C.J. 1998)

By order of 1 February 1996, received at the Court on 22 February 1996, the Arrondissementsrechtbank (District Court) Amsterdam referred to the Court for a preliminary ruling under Article 177 of the EC Treaty a question on the interpretation of Article 50(6) of the [TRIPS Agreement], as set out in Annex 1C to the Agreement establishing the World Trade Organisation (hereinafter the WTO Agreement), approved on behalf of the Community, as regards matters within its competence, in Council Decision 94/800/EC of 22 December 1994 (OJ 1994 L 336, p. 1).

That question was raised in proceedings between Hermes International (hereinafter Hermes), a partnership limited by shares governed by French law, and FHT Marketing Choice BV (hereinafter FHT), a company incorporated under Netherlands law, concerning trade mark rights owned by Hermes.

Legal Background

Article 99(1) of Regulation 40/94 [the Community Trade Mark Regulation] states, under the heading Provisional and Protective measures, as follows:

> Application may be made to the courts of a Member State, including Community trade mark courts, for such provisional, including protective, measures in respect of a Community trade mark or Community trade mark application as may be available under the law of that State in respect of a national trade mark, even if, under

this Regulation, a Community trade mark court of another Member State has jurisdiction as to the substance of the matter.

. . . Article 1 of Decision 94/800 provides as follows:

The following multilateral agreements and acts are hereby approved on behalf of the European Community with regard to that portion of them which falls within the competence of the European Community:

–the Agreement establishing the World Trade Organisation, and also the Agreements in Annexes 1, 2 and 3 to that Agreement. . . .

Article 50 of the TRIPS Agreement provides:

1. The judicial authorities shall have the authority to order prompt and effective provisional measures:

(a) to prevent an infringement of any intellectual property right from occurring, and in particular to prevent the entry into the channels of commerce in their jurisdiction of goods, including imported goods immediately after customs clearance;

(b) to preserve relevant evidence in regard to the alleged infringement.

2. The judicial authorities shall have the authority to adopt provisional measures *inaudita altera parte* where appropriate, in particular where any delay is likely to cause irreparable harm to the right holder, or where there is a demonstrable risk of evidence being destroyed.

3. The judicial authorities shall have the authority to require the applicant to provide any reasonably available evidence in order to satisfy themselves with a sufficient degree of certainty that the applicant is the right holder and that the applicant's right is being infringed or that such infringement is imminent, and to order the applicant to provide a security or equivalent assurance sufficient to protect the defendant and to prevent abuse.

4. Where provisional measures have been adopted *inaudita altera parte,* the parties affected shall be given notice without delay after the execution of the measures at the latest. A review, including a right to be heard, shall take place upon request of the defendant with a view to deciding, within a reasonable period after the notification of the measures, whether these measures shall be modified, revoked or confirmed.

. . . .

6. Without prejudice to paragraph 4, provisional measures taken on the basis of paragraphs 1 and 2 shall, upon request by the defendant, be revoked or otherwise cease to have effect, if proceedings leading to a decision on the merits of the case are not initiated within

a reasonable period, to be determined by the judicial authority ordering the measures where a Member's law so permits or, in the absence of such a determination, not to exceed 20 working days or 31 calendar days, whichever is the longer. . . .

The Final Act embodying the results of the Uruguay Round of multilateral trade negotiations (hereinafter the "Final Act") and, subject to conclusion, the WTO Agreement were signed in Marrakesh on 15 April 1994 by the representatives of the Community and of the Member States.

Article 289(1) of the Netherlands Code of Civil Procedure (hereinafter the "Code") provides as follows:

> In all cases in which, having regard to the interests of the parties, an immediate provisional measure is necessary on grounds of urgency, the application may be made at a hearing which the President shall hold for that purpose on working days which he shall fix.

In such a case, Article 290(2) of the Code provides that the parties may appear before the President under his voluntary jurisdiction to grant interim measures, in which case the applicant must be represented at the hearing by counsel, whereas the defendant may appear in person or be represented by counsel.

According to Article 292 of the Code, an interim measure adopted by the President does not prejudge the examination of the merits of the main proceedings.

Lastly, under Article 295 of the Code, an appeal against the provisional order may be lodged before the Gerechtshof (Court of Appeal) within two weeks of the delivery of that decision.

The facts in the main proceedings

By virtue of international registrations R196756 and R199735 designating the Benelux, Hermes is proprietor of the name HERMES and the name and device HERMES as trade marks.

Hermes applies those trade marks to inter alia neckties which it markets through a selective distribution system. . . . On 21 December 1995, Hermes, believing that FHT was marketing copies of its ties, seized, with leave of the President of the Arrondissementsrechtbank at Amsterdam, 10 ties in the possession of FHT itself and attached 453 ties held by PTT Post BV to the order of FHT.

On 2 January 1996, Hermes then applied to the President of the same court for an interim order requiring FHT to cease infringement of its copyright and trade mark. Hermes also requested the adoption of all measures necessary to bring the infringement definitively to an end.

In the order for reference, the President . . . found that Hermes' claim that the ties seized at its request were counterfeit was plausible and that FHT could not reasonably argue that it had acted in good faith. He therefore granted Hermes' application and ordered FHT to cease any present or future infringement of Hermes' exclusive copyright and trade mark rights.

In the same proceedings Hermes also requested the President . . . to fix a period of three months from the date of service of the interim decision as the period within which FHT could, under Article 50(6), request revocation of those provisional measures and a period of 14 days as the period within which Hermes could initiate proceedings on the merits of the case, that period to run from the date on which FHT requested revocation.

The President of the Arrondissementsrechtbank considers that this last request of Hermes cannot be granted because Article 50(6) of the TRIPS Agreement does not place any time-limit on the defendant's right to request revocation of provisional measures. He considers that the intention of that provision is, on the contrary, to allow the defendant to request revocation of a provisional measure at any time prior to delivery of judgment in the main proceedings. The period envisaged in that provision for initiation of proceedings on the merits cannot therefore be determined by reference to a period within which the defendant must request revocation of the provisional measures.

Nevertheless, the President . . . is uncertain whether a period should be fixed within which Hermes must initiate proceedings on the merits. Such an obligation would be required if the measure ordered in the interim proceedings in question constituted a "provisional measure" within the meaning of Article 50 of the TRIPS Agreement.

The President . . . observes that in interim proceedings under Netherlands law the defendant is summoned to appear, the parties have the right to be heard, and the judge hearing the application for interim measures makes an assessment of the substance of the case, which he also sets out in a reasoned written decision, against which an appeal may be lodged. Moreover, although the parties then have the right to initiate proceedings on the merits, in matters falling within the scope of the TRIPS Agreement they normally abide by the interim decision.

In those circumstances, the national court decided to stay proceedings and to refer the following question to the Court for a preliminary ruling:

> Does an interim measure, as, for example, provided for in Article 289 et seq. of the Code of Civil Procedure, whereby an immediate, enforceable measure may be sought, fall within the scope of the expression "provisional measures" within the meaning of Article 50 of the Agreement on Trade-Related Aspects of Intellectual Property Rights?

Jurisdiction of the Court of Justice

The Netherlands, French and United Kingdom Governments have submitted that the Court of Justice has no jurisdiction to answer the question.

They refer in that regard to paragraph 104 of Opinion 1/94 of 15 November

1994 [cit], in which the Court held that "the provisions of the TRIPS Agreement relating to measures . . . to secure the effective protection of intellectual property rights," such as Article 50, essentially fall within the competence of the Member States and not that of the Community, on the ground that at the date when that Opinion was delivered, the Community had not exercised its internal competence in this area apart from in Council Regulation (EEC) No 3842/86 of 1 December 1986 laying down measures to prohibit the release for free circulation of counterfeit goods. [cit]. According to the Netherlands, French and United Kingdom Governments, since the Community has still not adopted any further harmonising measures in the area in question, Article 50 of the TRIPS Agreement does not fall within the scope of application of Community law and the Court of Justice therefore has no jurisdiction to interpret that provision.

It should be pointed out, however, that the WTO Agreement was concluded by the Community and ratified by its Member States without any allocation between them of their respective obligations towards the other contracting parties.

Equally, without there being any need to determine the extent of the obligations assumed by the Community in concluding the agreement, it should be noted that when the Final Act and the WTO Agreement were signed by the Community and its Member States on 15 April 1994, Regulation No 40/94 had been in force for one month.

Article 50(1) of the TRIPS Agreement requires that judicial authorities of the contracting parties be authorised to order provisional measures to protect the interests of proprietors of trade mark rights conferred under the laws of those parties. To that end, Article 50 lays down various procedural rules applicable to applications for the adoption of such measures.

Under Article 99 of Regulation No 40/94, rights arising from a Community trade mark may be safeguarded by the adoption of provisional, including protective, measures.

It is true that the measures envisaged by Article 99 and the relevant procedural rules are those provided for by the domestic law of the Member State concerned for the purposes of the national trade mark. However, since the Community is a party to the TRIPS Agreement and since that agreement applies to the Community trade mark, the courts referred to in Article 99 of Regulation No 40/94, when called upon to apply national rules with a view to ordering provisional measures for the protection of rights arising under a Community trade mark, are required to do so, as far as possible, in the light of the wording and purpose of Article 50 of the TRIPS Agreement (*see*, by analogy, Case C-286/90 Poulsen and Diva Navigation 1992 ECR I-6019, paragraph 9, and Case C-61/94 Commission v. Germany 1996 ECR I-3989, paragraph 52).

It follows that the Court has, in any event, jurisdiction to interpret Article 50 of the TRIPS Agreement.

It is immaterial that the dispute in the main proceedings concerns trade marks whose international registrations designate the Benelux.

First, it is solely for the national court hearing the dispute, which must assume responsibility for the order to be made, to assess the need for a preliminary ruling so as to enable it to give its judgment. Consequently, where the question referred to it concerns a provision which it has jurisdiction to interpret, the Court of Justice is, in principle, bound to give a ruling [cit].

Second, where a provision can apply both to situations falling within the scope of national law and to situations falling within the scope of Community law, it is clearly in the Community interest that, in order to forestall future differences of interpretation, that provision should be interpreted uniformly, whatever the circumstances in which it is to apply. [cit]. In the present case, as has been pointed out . . . above, Article 50 of the TRIPS Agreement applies to Community trade marks as well as to national trade marks.

The Court therefore has jurisdiction to rule on the question submitted by the national court.

The question referred for a preliminary ruling

The national court asks whether a measure whose purpose is to put an end to alleged infringements of a trade mark right and which is adopted in the course of a procedure distinguished by [several features referenced and discussed below] is to be regarded as a provisional measure within the meaning of Article 50 of the TRIPS Agreement.

It should be stressed at the outset that, although the issue of the direct effect of Article 50 of the TRIPS Agreement has been argued, the Court is not required to give a ruling on that question, but only to answer the question of interpretation submitted to it by the national court so as to enable that court to interpret Netherlands procedural rules in the light of that article.

According to Article 50(1) of the TRIPS Agreement, that article applies to "prompt and effective" measures, whose purpose is "to prevent an infringement of any intellectual property right from occurring."

A measure such as the order made by the national court in the main proceedings meets that definition. Its purpose is to put an end to an infringement of trade mark rights; it is expressly characterised in national law as an "immediate provisional measure"; and it is adopted "on grounds of urgency."

Furthermore, it is common ground that the parties have the right, whether or not they make use of it, to initiate, following the adoption of the measure in question, proceedings on the merits of the case. Thus, in law, the measure is not regarded as definitive.

The conclusion that a measure such as the order made by the national court is a provisional measure within the meaning of Article 50 of the TRIPS Agreement is not affected by the other characteristics of that order.

First, as to the fact that the other party is summoned and is entitled to be heard, it should be observed that Article 50(2) of the TRIPS Agreement provides that where "appropriate" provisional measures may be ordered *inaudita altera parte* and that Article 50(4) lays down specific procedures in that regard. Although those provisions allow for the adoption, where appropriate, of provisional measures *inaudita altera parte* that cannot mean that only measures adopted in that way are to be characterised as provisional for the purposes of Article 50 of the TRIPS Agreement. It is, on the contrary, clear from those provisions that in all other cases provisional measures are to be adopted in accordance with the principle *audi alteram partem*.

Second, the fact that the judge hearing the application for interim measures gives a reasoned decision in writing does not preclude that decision being characterised as a provisional measure within the meaning of Article 50 of the TRIPS Agreement, since that provision lays down no rule as to the form of the decision ordering such a measure.

Third, there is nothing in the wording of Article 50 of the TRIPS Agreement to indicate that the measures to which that article refers must be adopted without an assessment by the judge of the substantive aspects of the case. On the contrary, Article 50(3), in terms of which the judicial authorities are to have authority to require the applicant to provide any reasonably available evidence in order to satisfy themselves with a sufficient degree of certainty that his right is being infringed or that such infringement is imminent, implies that the provisional measures are based, at least to a certain extent, upon such an assessment.

Fourth, as regards the fact that an appeal may be brought against a measure such as that in question in the main proceedings in this case, it should be observed that, although Article 50(4) of the TRIPS Agreement expressly provides for the possibility of requesting a review where the provisional measure has been adopted *inaudita altera parte*, no provision of that article precludes that provisional measures should in general be open to appeal.

Lastly, any possible willingness of the parties to accept the interim judgment as a final resolution of their dispute cannot alter the legal nature of a measure characterised as "provisional" for the purposes of Article 50 of the TRIPS Agreement.

The answer to the question submitted must therefore be that a measure [of the type described in the question] is to be regarded as a "provisional measure" within the meaning of Article 50 of the TRIPS Agreement. . . .

NOTES AND QUESTIONS

(1) **Direct Effect of TRIPS Article 50.** The Court of Justice in *Hermes* stressed that it was not ruling on the direct effect of Article 50 of the TRIPS Agreement but rather was "answer[ing] the question of interpretation submitted to it by the national court so as to enable that court to interpret Netherlands procedural rules in the light of that article." Is this a distinction of significance? Did the court effectively give direct effect to Article 50? Does this decision of the European Court of Justice require a change in Dutch practice?

The Court of Justice did address the question of the direct effect of TRIPS in Case C-149/96, Portugal v. Council, 1999 E.C.R. I-8395, where it held that the provisions of TRIPS do not, as a matter of EU law, create rights upon which individuals may rely directly before national courts. *See id.* at ¶¶ 42-46. And in a recent case, Case C-300/98, Parfums Christian Dior v. Tuk Consultancy, 2001 E.T.M.R. 276 (E.C.J. 2000), the Court was asked to confront directly whether Article 50(6) has direct effect such that it could be invoked by litigants in the absence of a corresponding provision in Dutch law. The Court affirmed its holding in *Portugal v. Council,* but emphasized that, under *Hermes*:

> in a field to which TRIPS applies and in respect of which the Community has already legislated, [national courts] are required by virtue of Community law, when called upon to apply national rules [regarding] provisional measures for the protection of rights falling within such a field, to do so as far as possible in light of the wording and purpose of Article 50 of TRIPS.

Id. at 289. If the field is one in which the Community has not legislated, EU law "neither requires nor forbids" member states from giving direct effect to Article 50(6) and permitting individuals from relying on its terms. *See id.*

(2) **Jurisdiction**. On what basis did the European Court of Justice assume jurisdiction over the question before it? On what basis had the plaintiff sought provisional relief from the Dutch courts? To what extent was the Community Trade Mark scheme relevant to the Court's analysis? The Court notes "where a provision can apply both to situations falling within the scope of national law and to situations falling within the scope of Community law, it is clearly in the Community interest that, in order to forestall future differences of interpretation, that provision should be interpreted uniformly, whatever the circumstances in which it is to apply." Is the Court hinting at the development of new structural constitutional principles in this opinion? In its recent *Parfums Christian Dior* opinion, the Court based its jurisdiction on similar grounds, but took pains to emphasize that the procedural nature of Article 50 made its assumption of jurisdiction particularly appropriate. *See Parfums Christian Dior,* 2001 E.T.M.R. at 287. Why should this affect the Court's analysis? Is uniformity of procedural rules more important to the Community order than uniformity of substantive rules?

(3) **Scope of the Decision**. To what extent does this decision affect national courts other than those designated as Community Trade Mark courts in the application of national trademark law under the EU Trademark Directive?

(4) **WTO Proceedings With Respect to Enforcement Obligations**. As Adrian Otten notes in his paper, the United States is engaged in consultations with Greece regarding compliance with obligations found in Part III of the TRIPS Agreement. Indeed, of the twenty-four TRIPS complaints initiated thus far, nine have involved (at least in part) compliance with obligations found in Part III of TRIPS.

§ 7.03 Customs and Counterfeits

Although issues surrounding the sale of counterfeit good arise in contexts other than customs seizures, we treat the role of customs and the increasingly important range of provisions addressing counterfeit goods together in the following section. This is an extremely important part of the customs' role in the intellectual property infrastructure.

[A]   The United States

ROSS COSMETICS DISTRIB. CENTERS, INC. v. U.S.
34 U.S.P.Q.2d 1758 (U.S. Ct. Int'l Trade 1994)

DICARLO, CHIEF JUDGE: Before the court is the remand determination of the United States Customs Service . . . issued pursuant to the court's decision in Ross Cosmetics Distrib. Centers, Inc. v. United States [cit]. Customs' remand determination ruled that certain labels and packages of cosmetic products proposed by plaintiff for importation constitute counterfeit use of United States trademarks and, if imported, would be subject to seizure and forfeiture. Plaintiff renews its Rule 56.1 motion for judgment upon the agency record, challenging Customs decision as arbitrary, capricious, an abuse of discretion, and otherwise not in accordance with law. The court's jurisdiction in this case is provided by 28 U.S.C. § 1581(h) (1988).

Background

Plaintiff, an importer of cosmetics, toiletries, and related products, requested Customs to issue a pre-importation ruling pursuant to 19 C.F.R. § 177.2 (1993), regarding whether its packaging for certain bath oils and fragrance oils proposed for importation conformed with Customs-administered laws and regulations relating to trademarks, trade names, and similar intellectual property rights. Specifically, plaintiff's packages for its bath oil products GORGEOUS, LOVE BIRDS, WHISPER, OBLIVION, OSCENT, and MORNING DREAM bear language inviting customers to compare these products to the well-known products of GIORGIO, L'AIR DU TEMPS, OMBRE ROSE, OPIUM, OSCAR, and YOUTH DEW respectively. Plaintiff's products are sold at a fraction of the price of the well-known products.

Customs issued its initial ruling on June 27, 1991. [cit]. The Agency held that, because GIORGIO, OPIUM, and YOUTH DEW are trademarks registered with the United States PTO and recorded with Customs for protection against infringing importation, plaintiff's use of these marks on its packaging constituted a counterfeit use of these marks. Accordingly, plaintiff's products, if imported, would be subject to seizure and forfeiture for violation of 19 U.S.C. § 1526 (1988). Customs also held in its Ruling that it was unable to issue a binding ruling regarding plaintiff's use of other marks not recorded with Customs. The Ruling stated, however, that if these marks were registered with the PTO, articles bearing such marks would be subject to seizure under 19 U.S.C. § 1595a(c) (1988) for violation of 18 U.S.C. § 2320 (1988). Plaintiff filed this action challenging Customs' initial ruling and seeking a judgment upon the agency record. The court issued a decision on August 10, 1993, holding that the Ruling was arbitrary, capricious, an abuse of discretion, or otherwise not in accordance with law. . . . The court held that before Customs could conclude plaintiff's products were counterfeits, Customs must first make a finding that plaintiff's packages were "identical with or substantially indistinguishable from" the registered marks, and that Customs had failed to do so. . . . The court also held that the Ruling was arbitrary, because in finding that plaintiff's packages were likely to cause customer confusion, Customs simply compared plaintiff's packages to the facsimile copies of the recorded marks, rather than to the actual packages of the products, or a reasonable reproduction representing the design and color of the trademarks. . . . The court further held that, with respect to the unrecorded marks, Customs should investigate whether these marks are registered with the PTO. . . . The court remanded the Ruling to Customs for redetermination.

On November 10, 1993, Customs issued its remand determination. The remand determination ruled: (1) plaintiff's products using the trademarks OMBRE ROSE, OPIUM, and OSCAR are admissible as non-infringing goods; and (2) plaintiff's products using the trademarks GIORGIO, YOUTH DEW, and L'AIR DU TEMPS are considered to infringe the rights of the respective trademark owners, and constitute a counterfeit use of these trademarks. Because GIORGIO and YOUTH DEW are recorded with Customs and L'AIR DU TEMPS is not, products using the trademarks GIORGIO and YOUTH DEW, if imported, would be subject to seizure and forfeiture under 19 U.S.C. § 1526(e), and products using the trademark L'AIR DU TEMPS, if imported, would be subject to seizure and forfeiture under 19 U.S.C. § 1595a(c) for violation of 18 U.S.C. § 2320. . . .

Plaintiff now contests Customs' remand determination concerning plaintiff's use of the trademarks GIORGIO and L'AIR DU TEMPS. . . .

. . . .

Discussion

This court's review will be limited to that part of the remand determination challenged by plaintiff; that is, Customs' decision concerning plaintiff's use of the trademarks GIORGIO and L'AIR DU TEMPS on the proposed packaging of its products GORGEOUS and LOVE BIRDS, respectively.

1. The Products

a. GIORGIO v. GORGEOUS

The trademark GIORGIO is owned by Giorgio Beverly Hills, Inc., which has three valid trademark registrations with both the PTO and Customs for GIORGIO perfume and toiletry products: (1) the word mark GIORGIO; (2) a GIORGIO crest design; and (3) a design of alternating yellow and white vertical stripes. . . . The GIORGIO packages use the stripe design as background, and bears the GIORGIO crest and the word mark GIORGIO in various styles and sizes. . . .

The proposed package of plaintiff's product GORGEOUS invites the consumer to compare GORGEOUS to GIORGIO. The package of GORGEOUS uses diagonal yellow and white stripes as the background. a crest design appears above the name GORGEOUS. At the top of the front panel is the language "COMPARE TO GIORGIO YOU WILL SWITCH TO . . .," in which the word mark GIORGIO is followed by the registered trademark symbol and appears in a bold and larger size print than the rest of the words. At the bottom of the front panel is a disclaimer: "OUR PRODUCT IS IN NO MANNER ASSOCIATED WITH, OR LICENSED BY, THE MAKERS OF GIORGIO." The word mark GIORGIO is again followed by the registered trademark symbol. All words in the disclaimer appear to be in the same size print. . . .

b. L'AIR DU TEMPS v. LOVE BIRDS

The trademark L'AIR DU TEMPS is owned by Nina Ricci, S.A.R.L., and is registered with the PTO . . . but is not recorded with Customs. In addition to the word mark L'AIR DU TEMPS, Nina Ricci has two valid trademark registrations with the PTO, each with a design mark of a swirled glass bottle with a closure, with one topped by one three-dimensional dove, and the second topped by two three-dimensional doves. The sample box of L'AIR DU TEMPS shows a yellow background, a golden oval containing two white doves in flight in a prominent position on the front panel, a golden band across the bottom of the front panel, and the word mark L'AIR DU TEMPS in gold print between the oval and the band.

The proposed packaging for plaintiff's product LOVE BIRDS has a primarily yellow background with thin white stripes. The front panel of the box shows an orange oval in a prominent position and an orange band across the bottom. The orange oval contains four birds in flight and the words LOVE BIRDS, all in gold color. At the top of the front panel is the language "COMPARE TO L'AIR DU TEMPS YOU WILL SWITCH TO . . .," in which the word mark L'AIR DU TEMPS is followed by the registered trademark symbol and appears in a bold and larger size print than the rest of the words. At the bottom of the front panel and within the orange band is a disclaimer: "OUR PRODUCT IS IN NO MANNER ASSOCIATED WITH, OR LICENSED BY, THE MAKERS OF L'AIR DU TEMPS." The word mark L'AIR DU TEMPS in the disclaimer is also followed by the registered trademark symbol. All words in the disclaimer appear to be in the same size print . . . .

2. Statutory and Regulatory Scheme; Customs Policy

The applicable statutes in this case are the Trademark Act of 1946 (the Lanham Act), 15 U.S.C. § 1051 et seq., and sections under title 19 of the United States Code concerning the protection of trademark rights by the Customs Service. In general, goods that infringe the rights of United States trademark owners are not permitted importation; infringing goods are subject to seizure and forfeiture by the Customs Service. *See* 15 U.S.C. §§ 1124, 1125 (1988); 19 U.S.C. §§ 1526(e), 1595a(c).

a. Applicable Statutory Violations

Section 42 of the Lanham Act, 15 U.S.C. § 1124, forbids importation of any goods that "copy or simulate" a trademark registered with the PTO. "A 'copying or simulating' mark" is either "an actual counterfeit of the recorded mark or name[,] or is one which so resembles it as to be likely to cause the public to associate the copying or simulating mark with the recorded mark or name." 19 C.F.R. § 133.21(a) (1993).

Section 43(b) of the Lanham Act, 15 U.S.C. § 1125(b), forbids importation of any goods "marked or labeled in contravention of" section 43(a). . . . By virtue of this broad coverage of section 43, Customs' protection of trademark rights extends to all trademarks and trade dresses, regardless of whether they are registered with the PTO or recorded with Customs.

b. Penalties

Under 19 U.S.C. § 1526(e), any merchandise "bearing a counterfeit mark" imported into the United States in violation of 15 U.S.C. § 1124 "shall be seized and, in the absence of the written consent of the trademark owner, forfeited for violations of the customs laws." A "counterfeit" is defined as "a spurious mark which is identical with, or substantially indistinguishable from, a registered mark." 15 U.S.C. § 1127 (1988).

Under 19 U.S.C. § 1595(c), any merchandise imported into the United States "may be seized and forfeited" if the merchandise or its packaging violates section 1124, 1125, or 1127 of title 15 of the United States Code, or § 2320 of title 18 of the United States Code, which imposes criminal liability on any person who intentionally traffics in counterfeit goods.   19 U.S.C. § 1595a(c)(2)(C).

c. Counterfeit v. Confusingly Similar

In order to facilitate the enforcement of trademark protection at the border, Customs currently divides trademark infringement cases into two categories: those which bear a "counterfeit" mark, and those which bear a "confusingly similar" mark. . . . A "counterfeit" mark is defined in accordance with 15 U.S.C.§ 1127. A "confusingly similar" mark is defined by Customs as one "that is likely to cause confusion, or to cause mistake, or to deceive the consumer as to the origin, affiliation, or sponsorship of the goods in question." . . . This definition appears to track the language contained in section 43(a) of the Lanham Act. In addition, Customs draws a distinction between trademarks that are registered and recorded with Customs, and trademarks that are registered but not recorded with Customs. . . .

Thus, imported articles bearing "counterfeit" versions of marks recorded with Customs are subject to seizure and forfeiture under 19 U.S.C. § 1526(e). Imported articles bearing "counterfeit" versions of marks not recorded with Customs are subject to seizure and forfeiture under 19 U.S.C. § l595a(c) for violation of 18 U.S.C. § 2320. . . .

Imported articles bearing "confusingly similar" versions of marks recorded with Customs are ultimately subject to seizure and forfeiture under 19 U.S.C. § l595a(c) for violation of 15 U.S.C. § 1124. Imported articles bearing "confusingly similar" versions of marks not recorded with Customs are currently not prohibited for importation. [cit].

3. Counterfeit v. Mere Infringement

Under Customs' laws and regulations, goods that infringe upon rights of trademark owners are classified into two categories. The first category consists of counterfeit merchandise which bears "a spurious mark which is identical with, or substantially indistinguishable from, a registered mark." 15 U.S.C. § 1127. Usually, "counterfeit merchandise is made so as to imitate a well-known product in all details of construction and appearance so as to deceive customers into thinking that they are getting genuine merchandise." 3 J. Thomas McCarthy, McCarthy on Trademarks and Unfair Competition section 25.01 [5][a] (3d ed. 1992).

The second category consists of "merely infringing" goods which are not counterfeits but bear marks likely to cause public confusion. This category includes merchandise which bears a mark that "copies or simulates" a registered mark so as to be likely to cause the public to associate the copying or simulating mark with the registered mark. *See* 15 U.S.C. § 1124; 19 C.F.R. § 133.21; *see also* Montres Rolex, S.A. v. Snyder, 718 F.2d 524, 527-28 (2d Cir. 1983), *cert. denied,* 465 U.S. 1100 (1984) (distinguishing copying or simulating mark that is counterfeit mark from copying or simulating mark that is a merely infringing mark). Also included in this category is merchandise which uses any word, name, symbol, or any combination thereof, in such a manner that is likely to cause public confusion as to the origin, sponsorship, or approval of the merchandise by another person. *See* 15 U.S.C. § 1125(a)(2).

The significance of the distinction between counterfeits and merely infringing goods lies in the consequences attached to the two categories. Counterfeits must be seized, and in the absence of the written consent of the trademark owner, forfeited. *See* 19 U.S.C. § 1526(e); 19 C.F.R. § 133.23a(b) (1993). Merely infringing goods, on the other hand, may be seized and forfeited for violating 15 U.S.C. §§ 1124 or 1125. *See* 19 U.S.C. § 1595a(c)(2)(C). Under Customs regulations, merely infringing goods may be imported if the "objectionable mark is removed or obliterated prior to importation in such a manner as to be illegible and incapable of being reconstituted." 19 C.F.R. § 133.211(a), (c)(4).

4. Whether Plaintiff's Use of Registered Trademarks Constitutes Counterfeit
Use

Customs determined that plaintiff's use of the word marks GIORGIO and
L'AIR DU TEMPS on the packaging of its own products constituted a
counterfeit use of these marks, because plaintiff applied marks "identical to the
registered trademarks" to its goods without the authorization of the trademark
owners. . . . The court disagrees.

It is clear that plaintiff's products are not counterfeits. Plaintiff's products
GORGEOUS and LOVE BIRDS do not imitate the well-known products
GIORGIO and L'AIR DU TEMPS in all details of construction and appearance.
Rather, plaintiff uses the marks GIORGIO and L'AIR DU TEMPS to market its
products GORGEOUS and LOVE BIRDS.

The use of another person's trademark in the context of marketing one's own
product is not prohibited by law unless it creates a reasonable likelihood of
confusion as to the source, identity, or sponsorship of the product. *See*
Saxlehner v. Wagner, 216 U.S. 375, 380-81 (1910) (permitting seller of mineral
water to use competitor's trademark denoting geographical source to truthfully
state he was selling water identical in content to that of trademarked water);
. . .Saxony Prods., Inc. v. Guerlain, Inc., 513 F.2d 716, 722 (9th Cir. 1975)
(holding Saxony may use Guerlain's trademark SHALIMAR to apprise
consumers that its fragrance product is "like" or "similar" to SHALIMAR,
provided such representation is truthful and that consumer confusion is not
likely to result); [cit]. Customs' practice shows its acceptance of this principle.
See, e.g., C.S.D. 89-172, 3 Cust. B. & Dec. 547, 549 (1988) (holding that
reference to trademarks NINTENDO and NINTENDO ENTERTAINMENT
SYSTEM on packages for video game joystick to indicate its compatibility with
NINTENDO system is permissible); [cit].

Thus, at issue is not whether plaintiff may use the marks GIORGIO and
L'AIR DU TEMPS on the packaging of its own products, but whether such use
is likely to cause consumer confusion. If a likelihood of confusion exists,
plaintiff's use of the marks would constitute trademark infringement, but not
a counterfeit use of the marks.

In reaching the conclusion that plaintiff's use of the marks constitutes a
counterfeit use, Customs misapplied 15 U.S.C. § 1127, which defines a
counterfeit as a spurious mark "identical with, or substantially
indistinguishable from, a registered mark." According to Customs, any
reference to another person's mark in the context of marketing one's own goods
(whether a parallel use or comparative advertising) would constitute counterfeit
use if a likelihood of confusion is found. This is because, under Customs'
reasoning, the mark used in such a context would be necessarily "identical" to
the registered mark. Customs' application of the statutory definition of
counterfeit ignores the distinction between counterfeit and mere infringement,
and therefore is not in accordance with law.

5. Whether Plaintiff's Use of Registered Trademarks Constitutes Infringement

Having held that plaintiff's use of the marks GIORGIO and L'AIR DU TEMPS does not constitute a counterfeit use, the court must now address whether such use nevertheless infringes the rights of the trademark owners.

The basic test for statutory trademark infringement is "likelihood of confusion," which has been construed by courts to mean a probability of confusion rather than a possibility of corrosion. [cit]. In order to determine whether a likelihood of confusion exists, courts apply and balance multiple factors. [cit].

Although courts may also consider an alleged infringer's use of a disclaimer stating that it is not connected with the trademark owner, the mere presence of a disclaimer does not necessarily prevent consumer confusion. [cit]. In fact, under certain circumstances, use of a disclaimer may even aggravate brand confusion. [cit]. Generally, the relative location and size of the disclaimer within the overall context of the advertisement is an important consideration in evaluating the effectiveness of a disclaimer. For instance, in Charles of the Ritz Group v. Quality King Distributors., 832 F.2d 1317 (2d Cir. 1987), where the packaging of the fragrance "Omni" used the trademark "Opium" in its comparative advertising slogan, while simultaneously mimicking Opium's trade dress and scent, the court held that the disclaimer, which was in a smaller type size and located in a less prominent position than the words "Omni" and "Opium," was inadequate to obviate consumer confusion. [cit].

In this case, Customs applied commonly accepted factors, and determined that the use of the marks GIORGIO and L'AIR DU TEMPS on the packaging of GORGEOUS and LOVE BIRDS is likely to cause confusion, and that the disclaimers on the packaging are insufficient to dispel the likelihood of confusion. . . . Plaintiff agrees that the factors Customs used to determine the likelihood of confusion are appropriate. Plaintiff asserts, however, that Customs incorrectly applied these factors to the two packages, and that Customs was arbitrary in finding the disclaimers ineffective.

Upon examining the record, which contains photocopies and samples of GIORGIO and L'AIR DU TEMPS products as well as plaintiff's proposed packaging, the court sustains Customs' finding of likelihood of confusion.

a. GIORGIO v. GORGEOUS

. . . .

The court holds that Customs properly applied the relevant factors in determining a likelihood of confusion, and that Customs' examination of the adequacy of the disclaimer was consistent with the applicable law. Although the court may not necessarily come to the same conclusion if reviewing the case de novo,[3] it finds there is a rational connection between the facts found and the determination made by Customs.

The court sustains Customs' finding of a likelihood of confusion with respect to plaintiff's packaging for GORGEOUS. Accordingly, packages identical to that of GORGEOUS shall be denied entry and, if imported, are subject to seizure and forfeiture under 19 U.S.C. § 1595a(c).

b. L'AIR DU TEMPS v. LOVE BIRDS

[The court sustained Customs' determination with respect to LOVE BIRDS for the same reasons]. The court holds that plaintiff's packaging for LOVE BIRDS infringes upon the rights of the trademark owner of L'AIR DU TEMPS under 15 U.S.C. § 1125(a). Importation of packages identical to that of LOVE BIRDS may therefore be subject to seizure and forfeiture in accordance with 19 U.S.C. § 1595a(c).

Conclusion

For the reasons stated above, the court holds that Customs' determination that plaintiff's proposed packages of GORGEOUS and LOVE BIRDS infringe the rights of the trademark owners of GIORGIO and L'AIR DU TEMPS is not arbitrary, capricious, or an abuse of discretion, and is otherwise in accordance with law.

Further, the court holds Customs' conclusion that plaintiffs use of the trademarks GIORGIO and L'AIR DU TEMPS is a counterfeit use is not in accordance with law.

NOTES AND QUESTIONS

(1) **Scope of Importation Ban.** At one point in its opinion, the *Ross* court suggests that "imported articles bearing 'confusingly similar' versions of marks not recorded with customs are currently not prohibited for importation." L'AIR DU TEMPS was not recorded with customs. On what basis, therefore, did the court sustain the seizure of the LOVE BIRDS product? Is the court's statement an accurate statement of the law? Section 1595a(c)(2)(C) of Title 19 of the U.S. Code provides that merchandise introduced into the United States may be seized and forfeited by customs if it is "merchandise or packaging in which copyright, trademark, or trade name protection violations are involved (including but not limited to violations of sections 1124, 1125, or 1127 of Title

---

[3]Because plaintiff filed a Rule 56.1 motion seeking judicial review upon the agency record, the issue of whether the court has de novo review in this action was not raised. Depending upon the particular circumstances of the case, the court may have de novo review in an action brought under 19 U.S.C. §1581(h). *See* 28 U.S.C.A. §2640(e), 5 U.S.C. §706(a)(F).

15, sections 506 or 509 of Title 17, or sections 2318 or 2320 of Title 18)." Given that in *Ross* customs seized both recorded and unrecorded (non-counterfeit) products, why might you advise a client to record its mark with customs? Notice that section 1595a(c) does not reference patent infringements. Patent owners seeking the assistance of the customs service in stopping infringing imports may instead use procedures set out in section 337 of the Tariff Act 1930. Why might patent infringements be treated differently from copyright and trademark violations?

(2) **Destruction of Seized Merchandise.** Section 603(c) of the Copyright Act authorizes government seizure and forfeiture of imported works that constitute copyright infringements. The Anti-Counterfeiting Consumer Protection Act 1996 amended section 603(c) to eliminate the provision allowing the customs service to return seized counterfeit merchandise to its source. Similarly, Section 526(e) of the Tariff Act of 1930, which allows automatic customs service seizure of imported goods bearing a counterfeit mark, was amended by the 1996 Act to provide that customs is required to destroy all counterfeit merchandise that it seizes, unless the trademark owner consents to some other disposition of the merchandise and the merchandise is not a health or safety threat. What was the purpose of these changes?

(3) **Ex Parte Seizure by Intellectual Property Owners**. Section 34(d) of the Lanham Act enables the owner of a registered trademark, upon ex parte application, with notice to the local U.S. Attorney and upon deposit of a security, to obtain an order seizing goods bearing a counterfeit mark (as that term is defined in 15 U.S.C. § 1127) as well as the means of making the goods and any records related thereto. The seized goods are taken into custody of the court. The Anti-Counterfeiting Consumer Protection Act 1996 made it easier to execute such seizures by allowing them to be conducted by any federal, state, or local law enforcement officer, not just by federal marshals. *See* Lanham Act §34(d)(9). Why are ex parte seizure orders important with respect to counterfeit goods? *See id.* § 34(d)(4) (setting out conditions necessary for court to grant such an order).

(4) **Monetary Relief.** Section 35 of the Lanham Act, which authorizes monetary relief generally for trademark infringements, provides that treble damages shall be awarded in the case of intentional use of counterfeit marks "absent extenuating circumstances." 15 U.S.C. § 1117(b). The court is given greater discretion, and is less likely to make an enhanced award of damages, in trademark infringement cases. *See* 15 U.S.C. § 1117(a). Section 35(c) permits the trademark owner to elect to recover, in lieu of actual damages and profits, statutory damages ranging from $500 to $100,000 per counterfeit trademark for each type of merchandise involved; if the violation is wilful, damages of up to $1 million per mark per type of goods may be available.

(5) **Criminal Penalties**. The Trademark Counterfeiting Act, § 18 U.S.C. § 2320, makes intentional trafficking in counterfeit goods a criminal offense. Penalties under the act were significantly increased in 1995. The maximum penalty is a fine of $2 million ($5 million for repeat offenders and non-individuals) and/or imprisonment for a term of ten years (twenty years for repeat offenders). Repeat offenders that are persons other than individuals may be fined up to $15 million.

(6) **The Harms of Counterfeiting.** Why is counterfeiting dealt with more severely than other acts of intellectual property infringement? Are the rationales for acting against counterfeits different from those used to support the grant of intellectual property protection generally? Products commonly the focus of counterfeit activities are: perfumes, machine parts, medicines, children's toys, video games, compact disks. *See* Cong. Rec., June 4, 1996, H5776; *see also id.* (remarks of Mr. Hyde) (arguing that "we must consider who is selling these goods: the Chinese communist government, the Mob, and common criminals. These are not people that Americans want to finance."); *id.* (remarks of Mr. Goodlatte) (noting that "an estimated five per cent of products sold worldwide are phony" and commenting that "counterfeiting is a highly lucrative, but relatively low-risk crime").

(7) **TRIPS Compliance.** Does U.S. law regulating customs' authority in relation to infringing and counterfeit goods, and as regards remedies against counterfeiting generally, comply with the obligations of the TRIPS Agreement?

[B]   The European Union

Measures designed to regulate the movement of goods at the border present philosophical challenges for the European Union. The European Union is founded on the principle of the free movement of goods; measures that impede that movement, whether physically or through the imposition of financial costs, are looked upon with suspicion. Yet, the objective of preventing trade in counterfeit and pirated goods is also of concern to the EU. These dueling concerns underlie the EU's legislation in this area.

The current system came into effect in July 1995, replacing a prior system that had been established by Council Regulation No. 3842/86 of December 1, 1986 laying down measures to prohibit the release for free circulation of counterfeit goods. The 1986 system contained a variety of ambiguities that resulted in continuing variation among national approaches. *See* Andrew Clark, *The Use of Border Measures to Prevent International Trade in Counterfeit Goods: Implementation and Proposed Reform of Council Regulation 3295/94,* 20 EUR. INTELL. PROP. REV. 414 (1998) (providing a thorough analysis of the problems of the 1986 system). This was problematic because the 1986 system was designed to regulate only the *external* borders of the EU—free movement being a very strong norm *within* the union—and thus the ineffectiveness of a single system in stopping counterfeit and pirated goods affected the entire territory of the EU. (This relaxation of border controls within a customs union such as the EU is expressly sanctioned by footnote 12 to the TRIPS Agreement.)

The 1994 regulation attempted to remedy these weaknesses. The existing system, and some of the points at which tension with yet further values might arise, are well described in the following case.

IN RE ADIDAS AG

[1999] 3 C.M.L.R. 895 (E.C.J. 1999)

By decision of 16 June 1998, the Kammarrätten i Stockholm (Administrative Court of Appeal, Stockholm) referred to the Court for a preliminary ruling under Article 177 of the EC Treaty (now Article 234 EC) a question on the interpretation of Council Regulation (EC) No 3295/94 of 22 December 1994 laying down measures to prohibit the release for free circulation, export, re-export or entry for a suspensive procedure of counterfeit and pirated goods (OJ 1994 L 341, p. 8; hereinafter 'the Regulation').

The question has been raised in proceedings brought by Adidas AG, the holder in Sweden of a trade mark for various sports articles, sports wear and leisure wear, against the refusal of the Arlanda customs office to disclose to it the identity of the consignee of goods suspected of being counterfeits of Adidas branded goods which it had intercepted.

THE REGULATION

According to the second recital in its preamble, the aim of the Regulation is to prevent, as far as possible, counterfeit goods and pirated goods from being placed on the market and, to that end, to adopt measures to deal effectively with unlawful trade in such goods.

For that purpose, the Regulation lays down, first, the conditions under which the customs authorities are to take action where goods suspected of being counterfeit or pirated are entered for free circulation, export or re-export, or found when checks are made on goods placed under a suspensive procedure (Article 1(1)(a) thereof) and, second, the measures to be taken by the competent authorities with regard to those goods where it has been established that they are indeed counterfeit or pirated (Article 1(1)(b) thereof).

Under Article 3 of the Regulation, the holder of a trade mark, copyright or neighbouring rights, or a design right ('the holder of the right') may lodge an application in writing with the competent service of the customs authority for action by the customs authorities in respect of goods which he suspects of being counterfeit or pirated. That application is to be accompanied by a description of the goods and proof of his right. It must also specify the length of the period during which the customs authorities are requested to take action. The holder of the right must, in addition, provide all other pertinent information to enable the customs authorities to take a decision in full knowledge of the facts without, however, that information being a condition of admissibility of the application. That application is then dealt with by the competent service which is forthwith to notify the applicant in writing of its decision.

According to Article 4 of the Regulation, the customs authority may also detain goods of its own accord where, in the course of checks made under one of the customs procedures referred to in Article 1(1)(a) of the Regulation and before an application by the holder of the right has been lodged or approved, it is clear to the customs office that goods are counterfeit or pirated. In accordance with the rules in force in the Member State concerned, the same authority may notify the holder of the right, where known, of a possible infringement thereof. The customs authority is authorised to suspend release of the goods or detain them for a period of three working days to enable the holder of the right to lodge an application for action in accordance with Article 3 of the Regulation.

Article 5 of the Regulation provides that the decision granting the application by the holder of the right is to be forwarded immediately to the customs offices of the Member State which are liable to be concerned with the counterfeit or pirated goods referred to in the application.

According to the first subparagraph of Article 6(1), where a customs office to which the decision granting an application by the holder of the right has been forwarded pursuant to Article 5 of the Regulation is satisfied, after consulting the applicant where necessary, that particular goods correspond to the description of the counterfeit or pirated goods contained in that decision, it is to suspend release of the goods or detain them.

The second subparagraph of Article 6(1) of the Regulation, the provision at the heart of the present case, provides:

> The customs office shall immediately inform the service which dealt with the application in accordance with Article 3. That service or the customs office shall forthwith inform the declarant and the person who applied for action to be taken. In accordance with national provisions on the protection of personal data, commercial and industrial secrecy and professional and administrative confidentiality, the customs office or the service which dealt with the application shall notify the holder of the right, at his request, of the name and address of the declarant and, if known, of those of the consignee so as to enable the holder of the right to ask the competent authorities to take a substantive decision. The customs office shall afford the applicant and the persons involved in any of the operations referred to in Article 1(1)(a) the opportunity to inspect the goods whose release has been suspended or which have been detained. Suspension of release or detention of the goods is temporary. In accordance with Article 7(1) of the Regulation, if, within 10 working days of notification of suspension of release or of detention, the customs office which took action has not been informed that the matter has been referred to the authority competent to take a substantive decision on the case or that the duly empowered authority has adopted interim measures, the goods are to be released, provided that all the customs formalities have been complied with and the detention order has been revoked. This period may be extended by a maximum of 10 working days in appropriate cases.

In addition, the Regulation provides for a number of securities in favour of the declarant and the consignee of the goods checked. [For example,] Article 3(6) of the Regulation states that:

Member States may require the holder of a right, where his application has been granted, or where action as referred to in Article 1(1)(a) has been taken pursuant to Article 6(1), to provide a security:

– to cover any liability on his part vis-à-vis the persons involved in one of the operations referred to in Article 1(1)(a) where the procedure initiated pursuant to Article 6(1) is discontinued owing to an act or omission by the holder of the right or where the goods in question are subsequently found not [to] be counterfeit or pirated,

– to ensure payment of the costs incurred in accordance with this Regulation, in keeping the goods under customs control pursuant to Article 6.

. . . .

[In addition], Article 9(3) of the Regulation provides:

The civil liability of the holder of a right shall be governed by the law of the Member State in which the goods in question were placed in one of the situations referred to in Article 1(1)(a).

THE SWEDISH LEGISLATION

It follows from the first subparagraph of Paragraph 2 of Chapter 9 of the Sekretesslagen (1980:100) (Swedish Law on Protection of Confidential Information) that, subject to exceptions not relevant in the present case, the principle of protection of confidentiality applies to information concerning an individual's personal or financial circumstances obtained in the course of customs control. The second subparagraph of Paragraph 2 of the Sekretesslagen, in which reference is made to Paragraph 1 thereof, provides, however, that information obtained in the course of customs control may be disclosed if it is shown that this will not result in any damage to the individual concerned.

THE MAIN PROCEEDINGS

On 16 February 1998, the Arlanda Customs Office (Stockholm) decided, pursuant to Article 4 of the Regulation, to suspend the release for free circulation of certain goods and informed Adidas AG that they might be counterfeits bearing the registered mark Adidas.

A representative of Adidas Sverige AB, a subsidiary of Adidas AG, inspected the goods and found that they were counterfeit. Adidas AG lodged an application pursuant to Article 3 of the Regulation. On 17 February 1998, the Customs and Excise Authority decided to grant the application.

Under the Regulation, the goods could be detained until 17 March 1998 inclusive. After that date, the customs authorities considered that they could no longer lawfully detain the goods since Adidas AG had not referred the case to an ordinary court.

Since it did not know either the declarant or the person indicated as the consignee of the goods, Adidas AG had requested information about the identity of the consignee with a view to bringing an action against him. That application had been rejected by the Arlanda Customs Office pursuant to Paragraph 2 of Chapter 9 of the Sekretesslagen.

Adidas AG appealed to the Kammarrätten i Stockholm against that refusal. It claimed that, in order to refer the case to an ordinary court, it had first of all to obtain information about the consignee of the goods.

The Kammarrätten found that, since disclosure of the information requested by Adidas AG was likely to cause damage to the consignee of the goods, the Sekretesslagen prohibited the Arlanda Customs Office from disclosing the information in its possession.

The Kammarrätten in Stockholm therefore decided to stay proceedings and to refer the following question to the Court for a preliminary ruling: "Does Council Regulation (EC) No 3295/94 constitute a bar to application of rules of national law under which the identity of declarants or consignees of imported goods, which the trade-mark owner has found to be counterfeit, may not be disclosed to the trade-mark owner?"

THE NATIONAL COURT'S QUESTION

It should be recalled, at the outset, that according to the settled case-law of the Court, in interpreting a provision of Community law it is necessary to consider not only its wording but also the context in which it occurs and the objects of the rules of which it is part. [cit].

Next, where a provision of Community law is open to several interpretations, only one of which can ensure that the provision retains its effectiveness, preference must be given to that interpretation. [cit].

Further, where the implementation of a Community regulation is a matter for the national authorities, as in the case of Regulation No 3295/94, recourse to rules of national law is possible only in so far as it is necessary for the correct application of that regulation and in so far as it does not jeopardise either the scope or the effectiveness thereof. [cit]. Under the obligations laid down in Article 5 of the EC Treaty (now Article 10 EC), those national measures must, in general, facilitate the application of the Community regulation and not hinder its implementation. [cit].

In that respect, it is to be noted, first, that, with a view to preventing, as far as possible, counterfeit and pirated goods from being placed on the market, the Regulation gives an essential role to the holder of the right. It is clear from Articles 3 and 4 of the Regulation that the detention of goods by the customs authorities is, in principle, subject to an application on his part. Second, in order for a final judgment to be given against such practices by the national authority competent to rule on the substance of the case, the case must first be referred to it by the holder of the right. If the case is not so referred by the holder of the right, the measure of suspension of release or of detention of the goods promptly ceases to have effect, pursuant to Article 7(1) of the Regulation.

Consequently, effective application of the Regulation is directly dependent on the information supplied to the holder of the intellectual property right. So if the identity of the declarant and/or the consignee of the goods cannot be disclosed to him, it is in practice impossible for him to refer the case to the competent national authority.

The reference in the second subparagraph of Article 6(1) of the Regulation to national provisions on the protection of personal data, commercial and industrial secrecy and professional and administrative confidentiality cannot, in those circumstances, be understood as precluding disclosure to the holder of the right of the information which he needs in order to safeguard his interests.

Furthermore, a number of provisions of the Regulation are designed to protect the declarant and the consignee of goods that are subject to control, in order to prevent the disclosure of their names and addresses to the holder of the right from causing them damage.

First, where a customs office finds on checking goods that they fit the description of counterfeit or pirated goods, it is immediately to inform the declarant pursuant to the second subparagraph of Article 6(1) of the Regulation. Under Article 7(2) of the Regulation, the owner, the importer or the consignee of the goods is entitled to have the goods in question released or their detention revoked against provision of a security.

Next, it is clear from the second subparagraph of Article 6(1) of the Regulation that the holder of the right may use the information disclosed by the customs office only with a view to asking the competent national authority to take a substantive decision. If that information is used for other purposes, the holder of the right may incur liability under the civil law of the Member State in which the goods in question are to be found, pursuant to Article 9(3) of the Regulation.

Finally, reparation of damage resulting from unlawful use of the information or any other damage suffered by the declarant or the consignee of the goods is facilitated by the fact that the Member States may require the holder of the right to provide a security under Article 3(6) of the Regulation.

In view of the foregoing considerations, the answer to be given to the national court must be that, on a proper construction, the Regulation precludes a rule of national law under which the identity of declarants or consignees of imported goods which the trade-mark owner has found to be counterfeit may not be disclosed to him.

___

NOTES AND QUESTIONS

(1) **The 1994 Regulation**. The regulation applies both to "counterfeit goods," which are defined as "goods . . . bearing without authorisation a trade mark which is identical to the trade mark validly registered in respect of the same type of goods, or which cannot be distinguished in its essential aspects from such trade mark, and which thereby infringes the rights of the holder of the trademark," and to "pirated goods," which are defined as "goods which are or embody copies made without the consent of the holder of the copyright or

neighbouring right, or of the holder of a design right, whether registered . . . or not . . . where the making of those copies infringes the rights in question." Regulation No. 3295/94, art. 1(2). Although the extension of the system to cover "pirated goods" protected by copyright or design right was considered a significant reform of the 1986 system, a 1998 report by the Commission showed that over 90% of customs' interventions still involve infringement of trademark rights.

(2) **The Role of Right Holders and the National Courts**. Right holders play an important role in the 1994 regulation, which gives the intellectual property owner the right to ask the customs administrations directly to seize goods rather than having to apply first to the courts (as was required in many member states under the 1986 regulation). But once the seizure takes place, the right holder has ten days within which to seek judicial sanction for continuing customs' possession of the goods or to authorize their destruction.

(3) **Reform of the 1994 Regulation**. In 1998, the Commission published a report on the 1994 regulation suggesting various reforms. These reforms included the extension of the system to patented products, and permitting Community Trademark holders to register with all national customs authorities through a single filing. (At present, intellectual property owners seeking EU-wide customs protection must file separate customs forms with each national authority.) The European Parliament later adopted its own report, which was largely supportive of the Commission's proposals. *See* Report on the proposal for a Council Regulation amending Regulation 3295/94 laying down measures to prohibit the release for free circulation, export, re-export or entry for a suspensive procedure of counterfeit and pirated goods, June 4, 1998, European Parliament Working Document A4-0223/98. After a further Green Paper, *The Fight Against Counterfeiting and Piracy in the Internal Market*, and several recent hearings to gauge public attitudes to the question of counterfeiting, on November 30, 2000 the Commission adopted a Communication announcing a series of new anti-counterfeiting measures. These included examining the establishment of a mechanism to facilitate cooperation between national authorities and the drafting of a proposal to harmonise national laws.

(4) **Informational Obligations under TRIPS**. TRIPS requires the adoption of procedures to enable copyright and trademark owners to prevent the entry into circulation of counterfeit trademarked or pirated copyright goods when such merchandise is detained at the border for suspected infringement. Article 57 requires signatory countries "without prejudice to the protection of confidential information" to "provide the competent authorities the authority to give the right holder sufficient opportunity to have any product detained by the customs authorities inspected in order to substantiate his claims." It also permits member states, where a positive determination has been made on the merits of a case, to "provide the competent authorities the authority to inform the right holder of the names and addresses of the consignor, the importer and the consignee and of the quantity of the goods in question." Why do you think that this particular provision is couched in permissive rather than mandatory language?

Provisions paralleling Article 57 are found in Article 1718(10) of the NAFTA. In light of these provisions, changes were made in 1995 to U.S. customs regulations in order to permit the disclosure of more information to intellectual property rights owners when potentially infringing goods are seized. *See Proposals on Notice of Infringing Imports are Revised and Reissued*, 50 PAT., TRAD. & COPYRIGHT. J. 289 (July 20, 1995). These changes were well-received by right holders: the additional information both facilitates private enforcement actions and improves the lines of communication between intellectual property rights owners and customs' officers seeking to determine whether an imported article is genuine.

§ 7.04   Extraterritorial Protection of Intellectual Property Rights

[A]   Copyright Law

[1] Extraterritorial Application of National Copyright Law

SUBAFILMS, LTD. v. MGM-PATHE COMMS. CO.
24 F.3d 1088 (9th Cir. 1994) (en banc)

D.W. NELSON, CIRCUIT JUDGE:

In this case, we consider the "vexing question" of whether a claim for infringement can be brought under the Copyright Act when the assertedly infringing conduct consists solely of the authorization within the territorial boundaries of the United States of acts that occur entirely abroad. We hold that such allegations do not state a claim for relief under the copyright laws of the United States.

FACTUAL AND PROCEDURAL BACKGROUND

In 1966, the musical group The Beatles, through Subafilms, Ltd., entered into a joint venture with the Hearst Corporation to produce the animated motion picture entitled "Yellow Submarine" (the "Picture"). Over the next year, Hearst, acting on behalf of the joint venture (the "Producer"), negotiated an agreement with United Artists Corporation ("UA") to distribute and finance the film. Separate distribution and financing agreements were entered into in May, 1967. Pursuant to these agreements, UA distributed the Picture in theaters beginning in 1968 and later on television.

In the early 1980s, with the advent of the home video market, UA entered into several licensing agreements to distribute a number of its films on videocassette. Although one company expressed interest in the Picture, UA refused to license "Yellow Submarine" because of uncertainty over whether home video rights had been granted by the 1967 agreements. Subsequently, in 1987, UA's successor company, MGM/UA Communications Co. ("MGM/UA"), over the Producer's objections, authorized its subsidiary MGM/IJA Home Video,

Inc. to distribute the Picture for the domestic home video market, and, pursuant to an earlier licensing agreement, notified Warner Bros., Inc. ("Warner") that the Picture had been cleared for international videocassette distribution. Warner, through its wholly owned subsidiary, Warner Home Video, Inc., in turn entered into agreements with third parties for distribution of the Picture on videocassette around the world.

In 1988, Subafilms and Hearst ("Appellees") brought suit against MGM/UA, Warner, and their respective subsidiaries (collectively the "Distributors" or "Appellants"), contending that the videocassette distribution of the Picture, both foreign and domestic, constituted copyright infringement and a breach of the 1967 agreements. The case was tried before a retired California Superior Court Judge acting as a special master. The special master found for Appellees on both claims. . . [T]he district court adopted all of the special master's factual findings and legal conclusions. Appellees were awarded $2,228,000.00 in compensatory damages, split evenly between the foreign and domestic home video distributions. In addition, Appellees received attorneys' fees and a permanent injunction that prohibited the Distributors from engaging in, or authorizing, any home video use of the Picture.

A panel of this circuit, in an unpublished disposition, affirmed the district court's judgment on the ground that both the domestic and foreign distribution of the Picture constituted infringement under the Copyright Act. With respect to the foreign distribution of the Picture, the panel concluded that it was bound by this court's prior decision in Peter Starr Prod Co. v. Twin Continental Films, Inc., 783 F.2d 1440 (9th Cir. 1986), which it held to stand for the proposition that, although "'infringing actions that take place entirely outside the United States are not actionable'[under the Copyright Act, an] 'act of infringement within the United States' [properly is] alleged where the illegal *authorization* of international exhibitions *t[akes] place in the United States*," Subafilms, slip op. at 4917-18 (quoting *Peter Starr*, 783 F.2d at 1442, 1443 (emphasis in original). Because the Distributors had admitted that the initial authorization to distribute the Picture internationally occurred within the United States, the panel affirmed the district court's holding with respect to liability for extraterritorial home video distribution of the Picture.[3]

We granted Appellants' petition for rehearing *en banc* to consider whether the panel's interpretation of *Peter Starr* conflicted with our subsequent decision in Lewis Galoob Toys, Inc. v. Nintendo of Am., Inc., 964 F.2d 965 (9th Cir. 1992), *cert. denied*, 113 S.Ct. 1582 (1993), which held that there could be no liability for authorizing a party to engage in an infringing act when the authorized "party's use of the work would not violate the Copyright Act." *See also* Columbia Pictures Indus., Inc. v. Professional Real Estate Investors, Inc., 866

---

[3]At oral argument before this court Appellants' counsel conceded that the relevant authorization occurred within the United States. Counsel for Appellees, accepting this concession, additionally insisted that the authorization necessarily included the making of a copy of the negative of the Picture within the United States. Appellants' counsel responded that this contention was made before neither the special master nor the panel, and was not supported by the record. For the purposes of this decision, we assume, as apparently the panel did, that each of the defendants made a relevant "authorization" within the United States, and that the acts of authorization consisted solely of entering into licensing agreements.

F.2d 278, 279-81 (9th Cir. 1989) (holding that a hotel was not liable under the Copyright Act for making available videodisc players for in-room viewing), *rev'd on other grounds,* U.S. 113 S.Ct. 1920 (1993). Because we conclude that there can be no liability under the United States copyright laws for authorizing an act that itself could not constitute infringement of rights secured by those laws, and that wholly extraterritorial acts of infringement are not cognizable under the Copyright Act, we overrule *Peter Starr* insofar as it held that allegations of an authorization within the United States of infringing acts that take place entirely abroad state a claim for infringement under the Act. Accordingly, we vacate the panel's decision in part and return the case to the panel for further proceedings.

DISCUSSION

I. The Mere Authorization of Extraterritorial Acts of Infringement
Does not State a Claim under the Copyright Act

As the panel in this case correctly concluded, *Peter Starr* held that the authorization within the United States of entirely extraterritorial acts stated a cause of action under the "plain language" of the Copyright Act. Observing that the Copyright Act grants a copyright owner "the *exclusive rights* to do and *to authorize*" any of the activities listed in 17 U.S.C. § 106(l)-(5), and that a violation of the "authorization" right constitutes infringement under section 501 of the Act, the *Peter Starr* court reasoned that allegations of an authorization within the United States of extraterritorial conduct that corresponded to the activities listed in section 106 "allege[d] an act of infringement within the United States." Accordingly, the court determined that the district court erred "in concluding that 'Plaintiff allege[d] only infringing acts which took place outside of the United States,'" and reversed the district court's dismissal for lack of subject matter jurisdiction.[5]

---

[5]Appellants insist that *Peter Starr* should be limited to its holding relating to subject matter jurisdiction and that any intimation by the court that the plaintiff stated a valid cause of action should be disregarded as dicta. *See also* Danjaq, S.A. v. MGM/UA Communications, *Co.,* 773 F. Supp. 194, 203 (C.D. Cal. 1991) (so interpreting *Peter Starr*), *aff'd on other grounds,* 979 F.2d 772 (9th Cir. 1992). We do not read *Peter Starr* in this manner. Appellants undoubtedly are correct that the existence of subject matter jurisdiction under 28 U.S.C. § 1338(a) is distinct as a general matter from the question of whether a valid cause of action is stated. [cit]. However, the *Peter Starr* court treated the jurisdictional inquiry as dependent on whether "[t]he complaint ... allege[d] an act of infringement within the United States," and expressly concluded that allegations of an invalid "authorization" "state[] a cause of action [for infringement] under the plain language" of the Copyright Act. Even if the *Peter Starr* court erred in framing the subject matter jurisdiction inquiry as coextensive with the question of whether the allegations in the complaint stated a good cause of action, a question we do not decide, it undoubtedly held that a claim had been stated. Indeed, most courts have read *Peter Starr* in precisely this manner. *See, e.g.,* Update Art, Inc. v. Modiin Publishing, Ltd., 843 F. 2d 67, 72-73 (2d Cir. 1988) (concluding that subject matter jurisdiction existed because the plaintiffs "stated a claim fully cognizable under the copyright laws" by alleging a predicate act of infringement within the United States); ITSI T.V. Prods., Inc. v. California Auth. of Racing Fairs, 785 F. Supp. 854, 863-64 (E.D. Cal. 1992) (explaining that the *Peter Starr* court "was required to address both jurisdiction and [the sufficiency of the claim] in the course of disposition" because "the jurisdictional question and the merits [were] intertwined"), *rev'd on other*

The *Peter Starr* court accepted, as does this court, that the acts authorized from within the United States themselves could not have constituted infringement under the Copyright Act because "[i]n general, United States copyright laws do not have extraterritorial effect," and therefore, "infringing actions that take place entirely outside the United States are not actionable." *Peter Starr*, 783 F.2d at 1442 [citation omitted]. The central premise of the *Peter Starr* court, then, was that a party could be held liable as an "infringer" under section 501 of the Act merely for authorizing a third party to engage in acts that, had they been committed within the United States, would have violated the exclusive rights granted to a copyright holder by section 106.

Since *Peter Starr*, however, we have recognized that, when a party authorizes an activity not proscribed by one of the five section 106 clauses, the authorizing party cannot be held liable as an infringer. In *Lewis Galoob*, we rejected the argument that "a party can unlawfully authorize another party to use a copyrighted work even if that party's use of the work would not violate the Copyright Act," *Lewis Galoob*, 964 F.2d at 970, and approved of Professor Nimmer's statement that "'to the extent that an activity does not violate one of th[e] five enumerated rights [found in 17 U.S.C. § 106], authorizing such activity does not constitute copyright infringement,'" *id.* (quoting 3 DAVID NIMMER & MELVILLE B. NIMMER, NIMMER ON COPYRIGHT §12.04[A][3][a], at 12-80 n. 82 (1991)). Similarly, in *Columbia Pictures,* we held that no liability attached under the Copyright Act for providing videodisc players to hotel guests when the use of that equipment did not constitute a "public" performance within the meaning of section 106 of the Act. *See Columbia Pictures,* 866 F.2d at 279-81.

The apparent premise of *Lewis Galoob* was that the addition of the words "to authorize" in the Copyright Act was not meant to create a new form of liability for "authorization" that was divorced completely from the legal consequences of authorized conduct, but was intended to invoke the preexisting doctrine of contributory infringement. [cit]. We agree.

Contributory infringement under the 1909 Act developed as a form of third party liability. Accordingly, there could be no liability for contributory infringement unless the authorized or otherwise encouraged activity itself could amount to infringement. *See, e.g.,* Gershwin Pub. Corp. v. Columbia Artists Management, Inc., 443 F.2d 1159, 1162 (2d Cir. 1971) ("[O]ne who, with knowledge of the infringing activity, induces, causes or materially contributes to the *infringing conduct of another,* may be held liable as a 'contributory' infringer." (emphasis added)). . . .

As the Supreme Court noted in *Sony,* and this circuit acknowledged in *Peter Starr,* under the 1909 Act courts differed over the degree of involvement required to render a party liable as a contributory infringer. Viewed with this background in mind, the addition of the words "to authorize" in the 1976 Act appears best understood as merely clarifying that the Act contemplates liability for contributory infringement, and that the bare act of "authorization" can suffice. This view is supported by the legislative history of the Act. . . .

---

grounds, 3 F. 3d 1289 (9th Cir. 1993).

Consequently, we believe that "'to authorize' [wa]s simply a convenient peg on which Congress chose to hang the antecedent jurisprudence of third party liability." 3 Nimmer, *supra*, § 12.04[A][3][a], at 12-84 n.81.

Although the *Peter Starr* court recognized that the addition of the authorization right in the 1976 Act "was intended to remove the confusion surrounding contributory . . . infringement," *Peter Starr*, 783 F.2d at 1443, it did not consider the applicability of an essential attribute of the doctrine identified above: that contributory infringement, even when triggered solely by an "authorization," is a form of third party liability that requires the authorized acts to constitute infringing ones. We believe that the *Peter Starr* court erred in not applying this principle to the authorization of acts that cannot themselves be infringing because they take place entirely abroad. As Professor Nimmer has observed:

> Accepting the proposition that a direct infringement is a prerequisite to third party liability, the further question arises whether the direct infringement on which liability is premised must take place within the United States. Given the undisputed axiom that United States copyright law has no extraterritorial application, it would seem to follow necessarily that a primary activity outside the boundaries of the United States, not constituting an infringement cognizable under the Copyright Act, cannot serve as the basis for holding liable under the Copyright Act one who is merely related to that activity within the United States.

3 NIMMER, *supra*, § 12.04[A][3][b], at 12-86 (footnotes omitted).

Appellees resist the force of this logic, and argue that liability in this case is appropriate because, unlike in *Lewis Galoob and Columbia Pictures,* in which the alleged primary infringement consisted of acts that were entirely outside the purview of 17 U.S.C. § 106(1)-(5) (and presumably lawful), the conduct authorized in this case was precisely that prohibited by section 106, and is only uncognizable because it occurred outside the United States. Moreover, they contend that the conduct authorized in this case would have been prohibited under the copyright laws of virtually every nation. *See also* 1 PAUL GOLDSTEIN, COPYRIGHT: PRINCIPLES, LAW AND PRACTICE, § 6.1, at 706 n.4 (suggesting that *"Peter Starr's* interpretation of section 106's authorization right would appear to be at least literally correct since the statute nowhere requires that the direct infringement occur within the United States."); ITSI T.V. Prods., Inc. v. California Auth. of Racing Fairs, 785 F. Supp. 854, 863 (E.D.Cal. 1992) (asserting that "because 'authorization' is itself actionable as a 'direct' act of copyright infringement, the fact that the act 'authorized' occurs abroad is irrelevant"), *rev'd on other grounds,* 3 F.3d 1289 (9th Cir. 1993).

Even assuming *arguendo* that the acts authorized in this case would have been illegal abroad, we do not believe the distinction offered by Appellees is a relevant one. Because the copyright laws do not apply extraterritorially, each of the rights conferred under the five section 106 categories must be read as extending "no farther than the [United States'] borders." 2 GOLDSTEIN, *supra,*

§ 16.10, at 675. *See, e.g.,* Robert Stigwood Group v. O'Reilly, 530 F.2d 1096, 1101 (2d Cir. 1976) (holding that no damages could be obtained under the Copyright Act for public performances in Canada when preliminary steps were taken within the United States and stating that "[t]he Canadian performances, while they may have been torts in Canada, were not torts here"); *see also* Filmvideo Releasing Corp. v. Hastings, 668 F.2d 91, 93 (2d Cir. 1981) (reversing an order of the district court that required the defendant to surrender prints of a film because the prints could be used to further conduct abroad that was not proscribed by United States copyright laws). In light of our above conclusion that the "authorization" right refers to the doctrine of contributory infringement, which requires that the authorized act itself could violate one of the exclusive rights listed in section 106(1)-(5), we believe that "[i]t is simply not possible to draw a principled distinction" between an act that does not violate a copyright because it is not the type of conduct proscribed by section 106, and one that does not violate section 106 because the illicit act occurs overseas. Danjaq, S.A. v. MGM/UA Comms., Co., 773 F. Supp. 194, 203 (C.D. Cal. 1991), *aff'd on other grounds,* 979 F.2d 772 (9th Cir. 1992). In both cases, the authorized conduct could not violate the exclusive rights guaranteed by section 106. In both cases, therefore, there can be no liability for "authorizing" such conduct.

To hold otherwise would produce the untenable anomaly, inconsistent with the general principles of third party liability, that a party could be held liable as an infringer for violating the "authorization" right when the party that it authorized could not be considered an infringer under the Copyright Act. Put otherwise, we do not think Congress intended to hold a party liable for *merely* "authorizing" conduct that, had the *authorizing* party chosen to engage in itself, would have resulted in no liability under the Act. *Cf. Robert Stigwood,* 530 F.2d at 1101.[8]

Appellees rely heavily on the Second Circuit's doctrine that extraterritorial application of the copyright laws is permissible "when the type of infringement permits further reproduction abroad." Update Art, Inc. v. Modiin Publishing, Ltd., 843 F.2d 67, 73 (2d Cir. 1988). Whatever the merits of the Second Circuit's rule, and we express no opinion on its validity in this circuit, it is premised on the theory that the copyright holder may recover damages that stem from a direct infringement of its exclusive rights that occurs *within* the United States. *See Robert Stigwood,* 530 F.2d at 1101; Sheldon v. Metro-Goldwyn Pictures Corp., 106 F.2d 45, 52 (2d Cir. 1939) (L. Hand, J.) ("The negatives were 'records' from which the work could be 'reproduced', and it was a tort to make them in this country. The plaintiffs acquired an equitable interest in them as soon as they were made, which attached to any profits from their exploitation."), *aff'd,* 309 U.S. 390 (1940).[9] In these cases, liability is not based on contributory

---

[8]We express no opinion on whether liability might attach when a party authorizes an act that could constitute copyright infringement, but the "attempted" infringement fails.

[9]Professor Nimmer formulates the doctrine in the following terms: "[I]f and to the extent part of an 'act' of infringement occurs within the United States, then, although such act is completed in a foreign jurisdiction, those parties who contributed to the act within the United States may be rendered liable under American copyright law." 3 Nimmer, *supra,* § 17.02, at 17-19 (footnotes omitted).

infringement, but on the theory that the infringing use would have been actionable *even if* the subsequent foreign distribution that stemmed from that use never took place. *See, e.g., Famous Music,* 201 F. Supp. at 569 ("[T]hat a copyright has no extra-territorial effect . . . does not solve th[e] problem of [whether liability should attach for preparing within the United States tapes that were part of a] manufacture [completed abroad] since plaintiffs seek to hold defendant liable for what it did *here* rather than what it did abroad." (emphasis in original)). These cases, therefore, simply are inapplicable to a theory of liability based merely on the authorization of noninfringing acts.

Accordingly, accepting that wholly extraterritorial acts of infringement cannot support a claim under the Copyright Act, we believe that the *Peter Starr* court, and thus the panel in this case, erred in concluding that the mere authorization of such acts supports a claim for infringement under the Act.

II. The Extraterritoriality of the Copyright Act

Appellees additionally contend that, if liability for "authorizing" acts of infringement depends on finding that the authorized acts themselves are cognizable under the Copyright Act, this court should find that the United States copyright laws *do extend* to extraterritorial acts of infringement when such acts "result in adverse effects within the United States." Appellees buttress this argument with the contention that failure to apply the copyright laws extraterritorially in this case will have a disastrous effect on the American film industry, and that other remedies, such as suits in foreign jurisdictions or the application of foreign copyright laws by American courts, are not realistic alternatives.

We are not persuaded by Appellees' parade of horribles.[10] More fundamentally, however, we are unwilling to overturn over eighty years of consistent jurisprudence on the extraterritorial reach of the copyright laws without further guidance from Congress.

The Supreme Court recently reminded us that "[i]t is a long-standing principle of American law 'that legislation of Congress, unless a contrary intent appears, is meant to apply only within the territorial jurisdiction of the United States.'" EEOC v. Arabian American Oil Co., ("Aramco"), 499 U.S. 244, 248 (1991).

---

[10]As Appellants note, breach of contract remedies (such as those pursued in this case) remain available. Moreover, at least one court has recognized that actions under the copyright laws of other nations may be brought in United States courts. *See* London Film Prods. Ltd. v. Intercontinental Communications, Inc., 580 F. Supp. 47, 48-50 (S.D.N.Y.1984). *See generally* 2 Goldstein, *supra,* § 16.3, at 683 ("Subject to jurisdictional requirements, a copyright owner may sue an infringer in United States courts even though the only alleged infringement occurred in another country."). *But see ITSI,* 785 F. Supp. at 866 (discerning, despite *London Film,* "no clear authority for exercising such jurisdiction" . . and stating that "American courts should be reluctant to enter the bramble bush of ascertaining and applying foreign law without an urgent reason to do so"). Finally, although we note that the difficulty of protecting American films abroad is a significant international trade problem, . . . the United States Congress, in acceding to the Berne Convention, has expressed the view that it is through increasing the protection afforded by foreign copyright laws that domestic industries that depend on copyright can best secure adequate protection. *See* H.R.Rep. No. 609, 100th Cong., 2d Sess. 18-20; S.Rep. 352. 100th Cong., 2d Sess. 2-5, *reprinted in* 1988 U.S.C.C.A.N., 3706, 3707-10.

Because courts must "assume that Congress legislates against the backdrop of the presumption against extraterritoriality," unless "there is 'the affirmative intention of the Congress clearly expressed'" congressional enactments must be presumed to be "'primarily concerned with domestic conditions.'" *Id.* at 248.

The "undisputed axiom," [cit], that the United States' copyright laws have no application to extraterritorial infringement predates the 1909 Act, and, as discussed above, the principle of territoriality consistently has been reaffirmed. [cit]. There is no clear expression of congressional intent in either the 1976 Act or other relevant enactments to alter the preexisting extraterritoriality doctrine. Indeed, the *Peter Starr* court itself recognized the continuing application of the principle that "infringing actions that take place entirely outside the United States are not actionable in United States federal courts." [cit].

Furthermore, we note that Congress chose in 1976 to expand one specific "extraterritorial" application of the Act by declaring that the unauthorized importation of copyrighted works constitutes infringement even when the copies lawfully were made abroad. *See* 17 U.S.C.A. § 602(a) (West Supp. 1992). Had Congress been inclined to overturn the preexisting doctrine that infringing acts that take place wholly outside the United States are not actionable under the Copyright Act, it knew how to do so. [cit]. Accordingly, the presumption against extraterritoriality, "far from being overcome here, is doubly fortified by the language of [the] statute," [cit], as set against its consistent historical interpretation.

Appellees, however, rely on dicta in a recent decision of the District of Columbia Circuit for the proposition that the presumption against extraterritorial application of U.S. laws may be "overcome" when denying such application would "result in adverse effects within the United States." Environmental Defense Fund, Inc. v. Massey, 986 F.2d 528, 531 (D.C. Cir. 1993) (noting that the Sherman Act, Lanham Act, and securities laws have been applied to extraterritorial conduct). However, the *Massey* court did not state that extraterritoriality would be *demanded* in such circumstances, but that "the *presumption* is *generally* not *applied* where the failure to extend the scope of the statute to a foreign setting will result in adverse [domestic] effects." *Id.* at 531 (emphasis added). In each of the statutory schemes discussed by the *Massey* court, the ultimate touchstone of extraterritoriality consisted of an ascertainment of congressional intent; courts did not rest solely on the consequences of a failure to give a statutory scheme extraterritorial application. More importantly, as the *Massey* court conceded, [cit], application of the presumption is particularly appropriate when "[i]t serves to protect against unintended clashes between our laws and those of other nations which could result in international discord." *Aramco,* 499 U.S. at 248 . . .

We believe this latter factor is decisive in the case of the Copyright Act, and fully justifies application of the *Aramco* presumption even assuming *arguendo* that "adverse effects" within the United States "generally" would require a plenary inquiry into congressional intent. At the time that the international distribution of the videocassettes in this case took place, the United States was a member of the Universal Copyright Convention ("UCC"), and, in 1988, the United States acceded to the Berne Convention for the Protection of Literary and Artistic Works ("Berne Conv."). The central thrust of these multilateral treaties is the principle of "national treatment." A work of an American national first generated in America will receive the same protection in a foreign nation as that country accords to the works of its own nationals. *See* UCC Art. II: Berne Convention Art V. Although the treaties do not expressly discuss choice-of-law rules,[15] . . . it is commonly acknowledged that the national treatment principle implicates a rule of territoriality. *See* [cit]; 3 Nimmer, *supra*, § 17.05, at 17-39 ("The applicable law is the copyright law of the state in which the infringement occurred, not that of the state of which the author is a national or in which the work was first published."). Indeed, a recognition of this principle appears implicit in Congress's statements in acceding to Berne that "[t]he primary mechanism for discouraging discriminatory treatment of foreign copyright claimants is the principle of national treatment," H.R. Rep. No. 609, 100th Cong., 2d Sess. 43 [hereinafter House Report], and that adherence to Berne will require "careful due regard for the[ ] values" of other member nations, *id.* at 20.

In light of the *Aramco* Court's concern with preventing international discord, we think it inappropriate for the courts to act in a manner that might disrupt Congress's efforts to secure a more stable international intellectual property regime unless Congress otherwise clearly has expressed its intent. The application of American copyright law to acts of infringement that occur entirely overseas clearly could have this effect. Extraterritorial application of American law would be contrary to the spirit of the Berne Convention, and might offend other member nations by effectively displacing their law in circumstances in which previously it was assumed to govern. Consequently, an extension of extraterritoriality might undermine Congress's objective of achieving "'effective and harmonious' copyright laws among all nations." House Report, *supra*, at 20. Indeed, it might well send the signal that the United States does not believe that the protection accorded by the laws of other member nations is adequate, which would undermine two other objectives of Congress in joining the convention: "strengthen[ing] the credibility of the U.S. position in trade negotiations with countries where piracy is not uncommon" and "rais[ing] the like[li]hood that other nations will enter the Convention." S. Rep. 352, 100th Cong., 2d Sess. 4-5.[16]

Moreover, although Appellees contend otherwise, we note that their theory might permit the application of American law to the distribution of protected materials in a foreign country conducted exclusively by citizens of that nation. A similar possibility was deemed sufficient in *Aramco* to find a provision that, on its face, appeared to contemplate that Title VII would be applied overseas, insufficient to rebut the presumption against extraterritoriality. [cit]. Of course,

---

[15]The Berne Convention specifies that domestic law governs a work's protection in its country of origin. *See* Berne Conv. Art. V(3). For acts of infringement that occur in other nations, however, the treaty uses the ambiguous concept of the "law of the country where protection is claimed." *Id.* Art. V(2); [cit].

[16]Indeed, the concern that action by the courts could interfere with Congress's efforts to secure a multilateral regime of intellectual property protection has been heightened by the use of the Berne Convention as the model for the "TRIPS" agreement on intellectual property protection that emerged as part of the recently-completed GATT negotiations. . . . One of Congress's stated objectives in adhering to Berne was to provide a firm foundation for the enactment of a more comprehensive agreement on intellectual property protection through GATT. [cit].

under the Berne Convention, all states must guarantee minimum rights, *see* Berne Conv. Art. IV, and it is plausible that the application of American law would yield outcomes roughly equivalent to those called for by the application of foreign law in a number of instances. Nonetheless, extending the reach of American copyright law likely would produce difficult choice-of-law problems, *cf.* House Report, *supra,* at 43 ("[Berne] does not, however, require all countries to have identical legal systems and procedural norms."), dilemmas that the federal courts' general adherence to the territoriality principle largely has obviated. *See* 3 NIMMER, *supra,* § 17.05, at 17-39 (noting that the "national treatment" principle has resulted in the absence of "[c]onflicts of law problems . . . in the law of copyright"); *see also* 2 GOLDSTEIN, *supra,* § 16.2, at 681-82, § 16.3, at 683. Even if courts, as a matter of comity, would assert extraterritorial jurisdiction only when the effects in the United States and the contacts of the offending party with this country are particularly strong, that the assertion of such jurisdiction would engender new and troublesome choice-of-law questions provides a compelling reason for applying the *Aramco* presumption. *Cf. Massey,* 986 F.2d at 533 (noting that the absence of "'choice of law' dilemmas" in applying the National Environmental Policy Act to projects in Antarctica provided a reason for not applying the presumption).

Accordingly, because an extension of the extraterritorial reach of the Copyright Act by the courts would in all likelihood disrupt the international regime for protecting intellectual property that Congress so recently described as essential to furthering the goal of protecting the works of American authors abroad, we conclude that the *Aramco* presumption must be applied. Cf. Benz v. Compania Naviera Hidalgo, 353 U.S. 138, 147 (1957) ("For us to run interference in such a delicate field of international relations there must be present the affirmative intention of the Congress clearly expressed."). Because the presumption has not been overcome, we reaffirm that the United States copyright laws do not reach acts of infringement that take place entirely abroad. It is for Congress, and not the courts, to take the initiative in this field.

III. Other Arguments

Appellees raise a number of additional arguments for why the district court's judgment should be affirmed. Relying upon the Second Circuit's doctrine described above, Appellees maintain that they may recover damages for international distribution of the Picture based on the theory that an act of direct infringement, in the form of a reproduction of the negatives for the Picture, took place in the United States. Appellees also suggest that they may recover, under United States law, damages stemming from the international distribution on the theory that the distribution was part of a larger conspiracy to violate their copyright that included actionable infringement within the United States. In addition, they maintain that Appellants are liable for the international distribution under foreign copyright laws. Finally, Appellees argue that the district court's damage award can be sustained under the breach of contract theory not reached by the panel.

We resolve none of these questions, but leave them for the panel, in its best judgment, to consider. . . .

Conclusion

We hold that the mere authorization of acts of infringement that are not cognizable under the United States copyright laws because they occur entirely outside of the United States does not state a claim for infringement under the Copyright Act. *Peter Starr* is overruled insofar as it held to the contrary. Accordingly, we vacate Part III of the panel's disposition, in which it concluded that the international distribution of the film constituted a violation of the United States copyright laws. We also vacate that portion of the disposition that affirmed the damage award based on foreign distribution of the film and the panel's affirmance of the award of attorneys' fees. Finally, we vacate the district court's grant of injunctive relief insofar as it was based on the premise that the Distributors had violated the United States copyright laws through authorization of the foreign distribution of the Picture on videocassettes. *Cf. Filmvideo*, 668 F.2d at 93-94.

The cause is remanded to the panel for further proceedings consistent with the mandate of this court.

CURB v. MCA RECORDS, INC.
898 F. Supp. 586 (M.D. Tenn. 1995)

JUDGE WISEMAN:

. . . .

MCA agreed in 1990 to license some of its master recordings ("the Licensing Agreement") by a variety of artists to Curb for distribution in the United States, Canada and the United Kingdom ("the Territory"). The licensing agreement, including a variety of older recordings by such diverse artists as Bing Crosby (including "White Christmas"), Gladys Knight, Debbie Reynolds, and Conway Twitty, permitted Curb to release the recordings in the Territory. The License Agreement, however, did not provide Curb authority to release the recordings in any other country, except by permission of UA (Warner/Elektra/Asylum) (WEA), MCA's worldwide licensee.

In February 1991, Curb asked WEA for permission to sub-license some of the MCA recordings outside the Territory. A February 14, 1991, response from WEA indicated that its agreement with MCA expired in March 1991 and that any approval it might give would be irrelevant; the response referred Curb to MCA for approval. Subsequently, Curb entered into contracts to license recordings to sublicensees around the world, including Japan, Finland, Malaysia, Austria, South Africa, and Hong Kong.

MCA claims that some of the recordings included in the 1990 Licensing Agreement made its way onto tapes and albums overseas via Curb's contracts with its foreign sublicensees. Curb does not appear to challenge this assertion.

The only fact apparently in dispute is whether the Licensing Agreement required Curb to get *anyone's* approval for worldwide release of the recordings once WEA's agency with MCA expired in March 1991. Curb claims it needed no further authority. MCA claims that WEA put Curb on notice that a change was in the works in MCA's licensing agreements and that, in fact, BMG replaced WEA as MCA's worldwide licensee in 1991. MCA claims Curb needed BMG's approval to release the recordings outside the Territory.

In its amended counter-claim, MCA has sued Curb under the Licensing Agreement alleging copyright infringement, unfair competition, conversion and intentional interference with present and prospective economic advantage.

Curb now moves for a judgment on the pleadings pursuant to Fed.R.Civ.P. 12(c) or, in the alternative, summary judgment.

Relying on a recent holding by the Ninth Circuit Court of Appeals, Curb argues that he is entitled to judgment on the pleadings because, he asserts, U.S. law does not apply to overseas acts that, if done in this country, would constitute infringement of a copyright owner's exclusive rights under 17 U.S.C. § 106.

. . . .

Curb argues that it did nothing more than sign contracts with entities abroad to distribute copies of sound recordings in which Curb held a license to reproduce. Curb's argument at law is this: Even assuming that such an action violated U.S. copyright law, such illegality is beyond the reach of this Court. There is recent precedent [Subafilms, Ltd. v. MGM-Pathe Communications Co., 24 F.3d 1088 (9th Cir. 1994)] outside the Sixth Circuit that bears examination.

. . . .

Early commentators suggest that *Subafilms* opens the door to massive foreign infringement of American cultural works, a devastating blow considering the worldwide popularity of U.S. films, books, videos and music. [cit]. The key, however, to understanding *Subafilms'* applicability to this case is to break down what it stands for and what it does not.

First, *Subafilms* relies upon a peculiar interpretation of the scope and nature of the authorization right in 17 U.S.C. § 106. This interpretation, tying the authorization right solely to a claim of justiciable contributory infringement appears contrary both to well-reasoned precedent, statutory text, and legislative history.

Even if the Court accepted *Subafilms'* interpretation lashing the section 106 authorization right solely to claims of contributory infringement, however, a critical question remains: Is there any primary infringement? MCA argues there is. *Subafilms* emphasizes at several points that its holding goes only to the application of the Copyright Act against defendants who have committed no primary acts of infringement in the United States. *See, e.g., Subafilms,* 24 F.3d at 1099 (expressing no opinion on copyright holder's argument that an act of domestic infringement—reproducing the film—made damages for foreign infringement appropriate). Therefore, in order for Curb to obtain summary judgment on this issue, it must show there is no issue as to this most material fact.

This threshold question may be called "localizing infringement." PAUL E.

GELLER & MELVILLE B. NIMMER, I INTERNATIONAL COPYRIGHT LAW AND PRACTICE, Intr. Section 3[b][i] (6th ed. 1994) ("Geller & Nimmer"). "More generally, in dealing with transborder conduct, it is advisable to analyze it down into discrete component acts country by country, before asking which law or laws should apply to which acts." *Id.* at INT-46. Simply put, the Court must determine whether an act of copyright infringement occurred within the boundaries of the United States. For if it did, even *Subafilms* concedes that further extraterritorial acts will not thwart a U.S. court's jurisdiction. *Subafilms,* 24 F.3d at 1094.

The Copyright Act defines infringement in two sections. "Anyone who violates any of the exclusive rights of the copyright owner as provided by sections 106 through 118 . . . is an infringer of the copyright. . . ." 17 U.S.C. § 501(a). Section 106 provides a copyright holder the exclusive rights *to do and to authorize* any of the following:

> (1) to reproduce the copyrighted work in copies or phonorecords;
>
> . . . .
>
> (3) to distribute copies or phonorecords of the copyrighted work to the public by sale or other transfer of ownership, or by rental, lease, or lending;

17 U.S.C. § 106 (emphasis added).

In this case, MCA indisputably held copyrights in the sound recordings at issue, [cit]. By the Licensing Agreement, MCA authorized Curb to reproduce and distribute copies of the recordings in the United States, Canada, and the United Kingdom.

MCA argues that when Curb expanded the market for these recordings to other countries, it infringed upon at least three of MCA's exclusive rights: reproduction, distribution, and authorization. If MCA can "present affirmative evidence" showing that genuine issues of material fact exist as to any of these allegations, it defeats Curb's motion. [cit].

The first question—one of reproduction—is precisely the question the *Subafilms* court avoided. [cit]. A famous illustrative answer is found in Sheldon v. Metro-Goldwyn Pictures Corp., 106 F.2d 45 (2d Cir. 1939), in which Judge Learned Hand wrote that an illicit lifting of copyright owner's play in this country gave rise to damages for distribution of the derivative film work overseas. *Id.* at 52.

MCA has produced copies of Curb's sublicensing agreements with entities in Hong Kong, Japan, and Australia. Each agreement required Curb to deliver duplicate master recordings to facilitate their reproduction. . . . Curb's unauthorized creation of duplicate master tapes for release into these countries would appear to amount to an infringement of MCA's reproduction right.

Curb responds that the Licensing Agreement permitted Curb to reproduce the recordings anyway. However, the Licensing Agreement clearly restricts Curb's rights to the United States, Canada, and the United Kingdom. If Curb's argument were valid, it could make as many copies of MCA's recordings as it wished, so long as the copies were not used for infringing purposes. While this argument sounds fine at first blush, it is undercut by its own faulty premise: Why would any copyright holder authorize reproduction for the domestic market when such a transfer could lead to unsanctionable reproduction for wholesale distribution in foreign markets?

Curb's reproduction of the masters, if it occurred (and it did unless Curb shipped its only copy in a circuit from foreign distributor to distributor), for distribution into unauthorized territory, therefore amounts to a primary. infringement of MCA's exclusive rights. 17 U. S.C. §§ 106(l), 501. Curb has not shown that no genuine issue of material fact exists as to its reproduction; indeed, [in its briefs to the court,] it appears even to concede it.

. . . .

Subafilms does, however, speak to the scope and extent of MCA's authorization right. *Subafilms* holds that section 106's authorization right is implicated only in cases of contributory infringement. [cit]. When no primary infringer is reachable by U.S. copyright law, either because the conduct falls short of infringement or because infringing conduct occurs outside the United States, the Ninth Circuit will not find the person who authorized the conduct liable. "In both cases, the authorized conduct could not violate the exclusive rights guaranteed by section 106. In both cases, therefore, there can be no liability for 'authorizing' such conduct." [*Subafilms*, 24 F.3d at 1094.]

The Ninth Circuit rejected the argument that the 1978 addition of the words "to authorize" in section 106 created an independent right, just as the words "to do" do. Instead, *Subafilms* holds that "to authorize" merely codifies the doctrine of contributory infringement. [cit]. *Subafilms*, thus, reads the authorization right out of the Act in cases of foreign infringement.

But piracy has changed since the Barbary days. Today, the raider need not grab the bounty with his own hands; he need only transmit his go-ahead by wire or telefax to start the presses in a distant land. *Subafilms* ignores this economic reality, and the economic incentives underpinning the Copyright Clause designed to encourage creation of new works, and transforms infringement of the authorization right into a requirement of domestic presence by a primary infringer. Under this view, a phone call to Nebraska results in liability; the same phone call to France results in riches. In a global marketplace, it is literally a distinction without a difference.

A better view, one supported by the text, the precedents, and, ironically enough, the legislative history to which the *Subafilms* court cited, would be to hold that domestic violation of the authorization right is an infringement, sanctionable under the Copyright Act, whenever the authorizee has committed an act that would violate the copyright owner's section 106 rights.

This was the approach taken by the court in ITSI T.V. Productions v. California Authority of Racing Fairs, 785 F. Supp. 854 (E.D. Cal. 1992). Faced with domestic authorization of infringing closed-circuit TV broadcasts in Mexico, the court found that sections 106 and 501 establish a direct cause of action for illegal authorizations under the Copyright Act. [cit]. The court held that the location of the authorized act is irrelevant, so long as it is the sort of activity that infringes upon a copyright owner's exclusive 106 rights. [cit].

Other courts agree. "There may be many reasons why a party may not be held accountable for its conduct in court. What is important is that contributory infringement be hinged upon an act of primary infringement, even if the primary infringer for some reason escapes judicial scrutiny." Danjaq, S.A. v. MGM/UA Comms. Co., 773 F. Supp. 194 (C.D. Cal. 1991).

The legislative history, though brief, is also illustrative:

> Use of the phrase "to authorize" is intended to avoid any questions as to the liability of contributory infringers. For example, a person who lawfully acquires an authorized copy of a motion picture would be an infringer if he or she engages in the business of renting it to others for purposes of unauthorized public performance.

H.R. Rep. No. 1476, 94th Cong., 2d Sess. 61, *reprinted in* 1976 U.S.C.C.A.N. 5659, 5674. *See Subafilms*, 24 F.3d at 1093 (citing this language).

In this case, even taking Curb's argument that it lawfully acquired and reproduced copies of MCA's sound recordings as true, the act of authorizing the distribution of the recordings for sale to a worldwide public seems equally sanctionable under sections 106 and 501. That Curb authorized these sales does not appear to be in dispute. MCA's production of letters raising the overseas sales as issues with Curb executives are unchallenged by Curb's insistence upon *Subafilms* as its sole shield.

The Court is sensitive to the sovereignty and rule of law in other countries. Such sensitivity is only enhanced by the recognition of the United States' obligation under multilateral treaties such as the 1971 Geneva Phonograms Convention and the recently adopted TRIPS component of the General Agreement on Tariffs and Trade. However, a careful exercise of domestic jurisdiction is consistent with the approach of the leading treatise in the field of international copyright law:

> A U.S. court, for example, could grant injunctive remedies under U.S. law for acts that commence a course of infringing conduct in the United States, for example, acts of authorizing or copying, without regard for whether eventual exploitation is to take place at home or abroad. Such an injunction would be justifiable if it forestalled piracy, whether at home or abroad, but did not risk interfering with such relief as might be granted under foreign laws for exploitation abroad.

GELLER & NIMMER, *supra*, section 3[b][ii] at INT-51-52.

Because, therefore, issues of fact remain with regard to domestic infringement and authorization, the Court need not reach the question of whether domestic or foreign law may be applied to ultimately resolve the question of infringement. Curb's motion is disposed of simply by reference to [the] summary judgment standard . . . . Given the facts at hand and the law as it exists, *Subafilms* notwithstanding, the Court must DENY Curb's motion for summary judgment.

NOTES AND QUESTIONS

(1) **The Presumption Against Extraterritoriality.** In many areas, Congress has legislated for, and the courts have recognized that U.S. laws may have, certain extraterritorial effects. *See, e.g.,* Hartford Fire Ins. Co. v. California, 509 U.S. 764, 796 (1993) (antitrust laws); Itoba Ltd. v. Lep Group PLC, 54 F.3d 118, 121-22 (2d Cir. 1995) (antifraud provisions of federal securities laws). Why should copyright, as a general rule, not operate extraterritorially? A strict approach to territoriality is consistent with approaches in jurisdictions other than the United States. *See, e.g.,* Def Lepp Music v. Stuart-Brown [1986] RPC 273 (Eng.) (U.K. copyright law not infringed by conduct abroad). What constitutional limits exist on the extraterritorial application of federal statutes? *Cf.* Lauritzen v. Larsen, 345 U.S. 571 (1953). What limits are required by international intellectual property law? What limits are prudentially warranted? To what extent should these limits be aligned?

(2) **The *Charming Betsy* Canon.** Assume that Congress legislated for the extraterritorial application of U.S. copyright law. Justice Scalia has suggested that even if the presumption against extraterritoriality is overcome or otherwise inapplicable, courts should also be guided by a second (and independent) canon of interpretation, namely that "an act of congress ought never be construed to violate the law of nations if any other possible construction remains." Hartford Fire Ins., 509 U.S. at 814-15 (Scalia, J., dissenting) (quoting The Charming Betsy, 2 Cranch 64, 118 (1804)). Even if Congress sought to apply the Copyright Act extraterritorially, what limits does the "law of nations" impose (which the U.S. Congress should be presumed not to have exceeded in enacting copyright protection)? In *Hartford Fire*, Justice Scalia looked to the Restatement (Third) of Foreign Relations to determine the relevant principles of customary international law that would, through this canon of construction, guide his understanding of the scope of U.S. antitrust legislation. *See id.* at 815-21. Is that where a court performing the same analysis in a copyright case should look?

(3) **Globalization.** Does the presumption against extraterritoriality make sense in our current economic context? Does globalization require us to adhere more faithfully to the presumption, or does globalization require us to modify its effect? How would proponents of the different versions of isolationism referenced *supra* § 1.02 regard the extraterritorial application of U.S. copyright law? What about the *Charming Betsy* canon? Does globalization suggest a greater or lesser value to that canon?

(4) **The Extraterritorial Application of U.S. Copyright Law**. In what circumstances is the extraterritorial application of U.S. law most warranted? Does current copyright case law capture those factual circumstances? If not, what approaches or analytical devices would you suggest courts develop to ensure its application to those circumstances? Consider the facts of a pre-

Subafilms case, *GB Mktg. USA Inc. v. Gerolsteiner Brunnen GmbH & Co.*, 782 F. Supp. 763 (W.D.N.Y. 1991). A German bottler sold bottled water, bearing labels allegedly infringing plaintiff's copyright, to a German exporter. The labels were put on the bottles by the bottler in Germany and the sale to the exporter took place in Germany. Is the bottler's conduct in Germany actionable under the U.S. Copyright Act? Would it matter that the bottler specifically prepared the bottles for the American market in various ways, such as the manner in which they were packed for shipment? *Cf. Hartford Fire Ins.*, *supra* (justifying extraterritorial application of Sherman Act where "foreign conduct was meant to produce and did produce some substantial effect in the United States"); *see also* Metzke v. May Dep. Stores Co., 878 F. Supp. 756 (W.D. Pa. 1995) (defendant can be liable where it supplied copy of design to copier in Taiwan if it knew or should have known that unauthorized copies made in Taiwan would be distributed in the United States).

(5) **Mere Authorization.** The courts remain split on whether "mere authorization" is sufficient to ground U.S. copyright liability. The *Curb* court has its supporters, *see, e.g.,* Expediters Int'l, Inc. v. Direct Line Cargo Mgt. Servs., Inc., 995 F. Supp. 468, 477 (D.N.J.1998), as does the Ninth Circuit, *see, e.g.,* Fun-Damental Too v. Gemmy, 41 U.S.P.Q.2d 1427 (S.D.N.Y. 1996). In what way does "*Subafilms* open . . . the door to massive foreign infringement of American cultural works," *Curb*, 898 F. Supp. at 593, as the *Curb* court appears to suggest? Which approach to the authorization issue is most supportive of the protection of U.S. copyright works? Is the *Curb* court correct that, under the *Subafilms* approach, "a phone call to Nebraska results in liability; the same phone call to France results in riches"?

The *Subafilms* court suggested that its conclusion on the authorization question would not be altered by whether the acts authorized abroad were illegal abroad. Should that make a difference? The *Curb* court held that because factual issues remained, it "need not reach the question of whether domestic or foreign law may be applied to ultimately resolve the question of infringement." Which law should apply? *See infra* § 7.05[A].

Los Angeles News Serv. v. Reuters T.V. Int'l Limited, 149 F.3d 987 (9th Cir. 1998). Los Angeles News (LANS) produced video tape recordings of newsworthy events and licensed them for profit. During the April 1992 riots following the Rodney King verdict, LANS covered the events in Los Angeles from its helicopter, producing two videotapes: "The Beating of Reginald Denny" and "Beating of Man in White Panel Truck" (the works). LANS licensed these works to National Broadcasting Company, Inc. (NBC), which used them on the *Today* show with the logo of KCOP, a Los Angeles station not affiliated with NBC, superimposed (known in the trade as the downstream). Under the agreement, LANS retained ownership of the works and the right to license them. Reuters Television International, Ltd., Reuters America Holdings, Inc., and Reuters America, Inc. (collectively Reuters) are television news agencies that gather and provide audiovisual and other news material to their subscribers throughout the world for an annual fee. Visnews International

(USA), Ltd. (Visnews), a joint venture of Reuters Television Limited, NBC and the British Broadcasting Company, had a news supply agreement with NBC News Overseas. When NBC broadcast the *Today* show featuring the LANS footage to its affiliates, it simultaneously transmitted the show via fiber link to Visnews in New York. Visnews made a videotape copy of the works as broadcast and transmitted it to subscribers in Europe and Africa. It also transmitted copies of the videotape to the New York office of the European Broadcasting Union (EBU), which in turn made a videotape copy and transmitted it via satellite to Reuters' London branch, which provided copies to its subscribers. LANS brought an action for copyright infringement against the Reuters defendants and Visnews. Defendants moved for summary judgment on several grounds. The district court granted defendants' motion with respect to the extraterritorial acts of infringement, relying on *Subafilms*. After a bench trial on the remaining issues, the district court found that Visnews had infringed by making one copy of each videotape and contributing to the making by EBU of one copy of each tape, and entered judgment for LANS for $60,000 in statutory damages based on the four domestic infringements by Visnews. LANS appealed the ruling barring extraterritorial damages. The Ninth Circuit reversed, finding the case different from *Subafilms* because Visnews completed acts of infringement in the United States when it copied the works in New York and then transmitted them to EBU which also copied them in New York.

> Each act of copying constituted a completed act of infringement. It was only after these domestic acts of infringement had been completed that Visnews and EBU transmitted the works abroad.
>
> In *Subafilms*, the allegedly infringing conduct consisted solely of authorization given within the United States for foreign distribution of infringing videocassettes. Similarly, in *Allarcom* [*see infra* page 1117] the alleged infringement consisted either of authorization given in the United States for infringement in Canada or broadcasts of copyright material from the United States into Canada, with the infringement not completed until the signals were received in Canada. [cit].
>
> The issue before us—which the *Subafilms* court did not resolve—is whether LANS "may recover damages for international distribution of the [works] based on the theory that an act of direct infringement, in the form of a reproduction of the . . . [works], took place in the United States." [cit]. While this circuit has not heretofore addressed the issue, the Second Circuit has done so in a line of cases beginning with Sheldon v. Metro-Goldwyn Pictures Corp., 106 F.2d 45, 52 (2d Cir.1939), *aff'd*, 309 U.S. 390 (1940). In *Sheldon* the court held, in an opinion by Judge Learned Hand, that plaintiff could recover the profits from exhibiting a motion picture abroad where the infringing copy had been made in the United States. . . . *Subafilms* described these cases as being "based . . . on the theory that the infringing use would have been actionable even if the subsequent foreign distribution that stemmed from that use never took place." [cit]. Recovery of damages arising from overseas infringing uses was

allowed because the predicate act of infringement occurring within the United States enabled further reproduction abroad.

LANS urges us to adopt the Second Circuit's rule because the unauthorized copying of its works in the United States enabled further exploitation abroad. While the extraterritorial damages resulted from Reuters' overseas dissemination of the works received by satellite transmissions from Visnews and EBU, those transmissions were made possible by the infringing acts of copying in New York. The satellite transmissions, thus, were merely a means of shipping the unlicensed footage abroad for further dissemination.

The *Subafilms* court's concerns are inapplicable to the present case. The Second Circuit rule would not permit application of American law to "acts of infringement that take place entirely abroad." *Subafilms*, 24 F.3d at 1098. Nor would a copyright holder be entitled to recover extraterritorial damages unless the damages flowed from extraterritorial exploitation of an infringing act that occurred in the United States. In *Subafilms*, the court reasoned that liability based solely on the authorization of infringing acts "would produce the untenable anomaly, inconsistent with the general principles of third party liability, that a party could be held liable as an infringer for violating the 'authorization' right when the party that it authorized could not be considered an infringer under the Copyright Act." [cit]. Under the Second Circuit's rule, by contrast, a party becomes liable for extraterritorial damages only when an act of infringement occurs within the United States, subjecting it to liability as an infringer (or a contributory infringer) under the Copyright Act. . . .

The Court therefore held that LANS was entitled to recover damages flowing from exploitation abroad of the domestic acts of infringement committed by defendants, affirmed the district court's finding that the fair use defense did not apply, and remanded the case for a new trial on the question of actual damages.

NOTES AND QUESTIONS

(1) **Predicate Act Theory.** As the *LANS* court notes, the predicate act theory was first developed in the Second Circuit, and that court continues to apply the theory. For example, in *Update Art, Inc. v. Modiin Pub., Ltd.*, 843 F.2d 67 (2d Cir. 1988), the defendants reproduced a copyrighted poster in the United States and then published it abroad in Israeli editions of the same newspaper. The Second Circuit affirmed the award of damages that included those for the extraterritorial acts of copyright infringement occurring in Israel, recognizing that a copyright holder may recover damages from extraterritorial acts of infringement flowing from a predicate act of infringement (the copying of the poster) occurring within the United States. *Cf.* Fantasy v. Fogerty, 664 F. Supp. 1345, 1351 (N.D. Cal.1987) ("[W]here some infringing acts do take

place in the United States, a plaintiff may recover through a constructive trust the extraterritorial profits derived from those infringing acts.").

(2) **Applying the Predicate Act Theory.** Should the theory give rise to actionability in the United States where the defendants, prior to making an unauthorized public performance in Canada, rehearsed the work in private in the United States? *See* Robert Stigwood Group v. O'Reilly, 530 F.2d 1096 (2d Cir. 1976). If the defendant made an unauthorized recording of a musical work in the United States and later made an unauthorized performance of the work in France, which of these unauthorized acts should give rise to liability in the United States? *See* Gaste v. Kaiserman, 863 F.2d 1061 (2d Cir.1988).

Plaintiff develops and sells novelty gifts, toys and houseware items to a wide variety of retail outlets. After it began shipping a new product to retail stores internationally, a large toy manufacturer requested a sample of the new product and expressed interest in purchasing it for sale in its retail toy stores. However, instead, the defendant delivered a sample copy of the product that the plaintiff gave to it to a factory in China for copying, where knock-offs were made for the defendant and then sold internationally, including in Canada. The defendant generally supervised the activities of the factory, knew of the copies, and authorized their sale. Plaintiff brings a copyright infringement action in the Southern District of New York, and the defendant moves to dismiss the claim because the plaintiff has alleged only acts of infringement which took place outside the United States. Plaintiff's allegations presented two domestic acts: transport of a sample of the product from the United States to the Chinese factory; and, authorization and approval of the Chinese factory's activities from within the United States. If you were the judge in the Southern District of New York, how would you rule? *See* Fun-damental Too, Ltd. v. Gemmy Industries Corp., 41 U.S.P.Q.2d 1427 (S.D.N.Y. 1996).

(3) **Satellite Transmission.** In *National Football League v. Primetime 24 Joint Venture,* 211 F.3d 10 (2d Cir. 2000), the defendant satellite carrier captured transmissions of broadcasts of copyrighted television broadcasts (of National Football League games) and retransmitted them to owners of satellite dishes in the United States, as permitted by the statutory license found in section 119 of the U.S. copyright statute. However, the defendant also (without securing permission from the copyright owners) made those retransmissions available to subscribers in Canada. The copyright owner, the National Football League, brought suit for copyright infringement in the United States. The defendant argued that it was not making a public performance or display of the broadcast in the United States because such performance or display occurs during the downlink from the satellite to the subscriber in Canada (where U.S. copyright law does not apply). The Court of Appeals for the Second Circuit rejected that argument, holding that "a public performance or display includes 'each step in the process by which a protected work wends its way to its audience,'" *id.* at 13 (citing David v. Showtime/The Movie Channel, Inc., 697 F. Supp. 752, 759 (S.D.N.Y. 1988)), and thus the defendant's "uplink transmission of signals captured in the United States is a step in the process by which a protected work wends its way to a public audience." *Id.* Accordingly, the defendant was liable for unauthorized public performance of the work in violation of U.S. copyright law.

The Ninth Circuit has taken a different view on whether satellite retransmission from the United States to a foreign country gives rise to U.S. performance. In *Allarcom Pay T.V. Ltd., v. General Instrument Corp.*, 69 F.3d 381 (9th Cir. 1995), Allarcom owned the Canadian performance rights for certain motion pictures; Showtime had the right to exhibit many of the same pictures on its service in the United States. Showtime transmitted its programming by means of satellite to authorized receivers, but the "footprint" of that satellite signal allowed it to be received in Allarcom's territory. The Ninth Circuit had to consider whether federal copyright law preempted various state law claims brought by Allarcom against Showtime for transmission of the motion pictures in Canada. Because U.S. federal copyright law does not apply to extraterritorial acts of infringement, it does not preempt causes of action premised upon extraterritorial conduct. The Ninth Circuit found that public performance and hence any potential infringement occurred in Canada once the signal was received and viewed. Accordingly, U.S. copyright law did not apply, and therefore did not preempt Allarcom's state law claims against Showtime.

Which approach best promotes effective and appropriate international copyright protection? How is your analysis affected by Section 119 of the U.S. copyright statute, which creates a compulsory license for satellite carriers to retransmit certain broadcasts—but only to households in the United States? *See* 17 U.S.C. § 119(a)(7). Compare the facts of *Primetime 24* and *Robert Stigwood*, note 2, *supra*. Should the same result be reached in these cases? If not, why not?

(4) **EU Cable and Satellite Directive.** The EU recently adopted a legislative solution to the problems posed by satellite communication. In the Cable and Satellite Directive, the Union adopted a rule that the copyright law of the country of uplink would apply to satellite transmissions within the EU, reversing the previous rule of some countries (known as the "Bogsch theory" after the former head of WIPO) whereby all countries in the "footprint" of the satellite signal might apply their copyright law. *See* Council Directive 93/83 of 27 September 1993 on the Coordination of Certain Rules Concerning Copyright and Rights Related to Copyright Applicable to Satellite Broadcasting and Cable Retransmission art. 1(2)(b), 1993 O.J. (L 248) 15. Hence, under the Bogsch theory, rights for any copyrighted work transmitted by satellite had to be acquired in all "footprint" countries; under the directive, rights need be cleared only in the country of uplink. This approach has the advantage of certainty and efficiency. What are the dangers of such an approach? (Hint: the EU directive also harmonized the copyright rules governing satellite communications in EU states. Why was this important?).

[2] Adjudication of Foreign Copyright Infringement Claims

LONDON FILM PRODS. v. INTERCONTINENTAL COMMS.
580 F. Supp. 47 (S.D.N.Y. 1984)

ROBERT L. CARTER, DISTRICT JUDGE.

This case presents a novel question of law. Plaintiff, London Film Productions, Ltd. ("London"), a British corporation, has sued Intercontinental Communications, Inc. ("ICI"), a New York corporation based in New York City, for infringements of plaintiff's British copyright. The alleged infringements occurred in Chile and other South American countries. In bringing the case before this Court, plaintiff has invoked the Court's diversity jurisdiction. [cit]. Defendant has moved to dismiss plaintiff's complaint, arguing that the Court should abstain from exercising jurisdiction over this action.

BACKGROUND

London produces feature motion pictures in Great Britain, which it then distributes throughout the world. ICI specializes in the licensing of motion pictures, produced by others, that it believes are in the public domain. London's copyright infringement claim is based mainly on license agreements between ICI and Dilatsa S.A., a buying agent for Chilean television stations. The agreements apparently granted the latter the right to distribute and exhibit certain of plaintiff's motion pictures on television in Chile. London also alleges that ICI has marketed several of its motion pictures in Venezuela, Peru, Ecuador, Costa Rica and Panama, as well as in Chile.

Plaintiff alleges that the films that are the subjects of the arrangements between Dilatsa S.A. and defendant are protected by copyright in Great Britain as well as in Chile and most other countries (but not in the United States) by virtue of the terms and provisions of the Berne Convention.[2] The license agreements, it maintains, have unjustly enriched defendants and deprived plaintiff of the opportunity to market its motion pictures for television use.

Defendant questions this Court's jurisdiction because plaintiff has not alleged any acts of wrongdoing on defendant's part that constitute violations of United States law,[3] and, therefore, defendant claims that this Court lacks a vital interest in the suit. In addition, assuming jurisdiction, defendant argues that because the Court would have to construe "alien treaty rights," with which it has no familiarity, the suit would violate, in principle, the doctrine of *forum non conveniens*. In further support of this contention, defendant maintains that the law would not only be foreign, but complex, since plaintiff's claims would have

---

[2] . . . Chile adhered to the Convention on June 5, 1970, but the United States [at the time of the decision is not yet] a party thereto.

[3] The films named, although formerly subject to United States copyrights, are no longer so subject.

to be determined with reference to each of the South American states in which the alleged copyright infringements occurred.

DETERMINATION

There seems to be no dispute that plaintiff has stated a valid cause of action under the copyright laws of a foreign country. Also clear is the fact that this Court has personal jurisdiction over defendant; in fact, there is no showing that defendant may be subject to personal jurisdiction in another forum. Under these circumstances, one authority on copyright law has presented an argument pursuant to which this Court has jurisdiction to hear the matter before it. M. Nimmer, 3 NIMMER ON COPYRIGHT (1982). It is based on the theory that copyright infringement constitutes a transitory cause of action,[4] and hence may be adjudicated in the courts of a sovereign other than the one in which the cause of action arose. *Id.* at § 1703. That theory appears sound in the absence of convincing objections by defendant to the contrary.

Although plaintiff has not alleged the violation of any laws of this country by defendant, this Court is not bereft of interest in this case. The Court has an obvious interest in securing compliance with this nation's laws by citizens of foreign nations who have dealings within this jurisdiction. A concern with the conduct of American citizens in foreign countries is merely the reciprocal of that interest. An unwillingness by this Court to hear a complaint against its own citizens with regard to a violation of foreign law will engender, it would seem, a similar unwillingness on the part of a foreign jurisdiction when the question arises concerning a violation of our laws by one of its citizens who has since left our jurisdiction. This Court's interest in adjudicating the controversy in this case may be indirect, but its importance is not thereby diminished.

Of course, not every violation of foreign law by a citizen of this country must be afforded a local tribunal, and defendants cite several cases in which, basically under general principles of comity, it would be inappropriate for this Court to exercise its jurisdiction. [cit]. This is not one of those. The line of cases on which defendants rely can be distinguished on significant points. The Court in Vanity Fair Mills, Inc. v. T. Eaton, Ltd., 234 F.2d 633 (2d Cir.) *cert. denied*, 352 U.S. 871 (1956), the principal case of those cited, found that the district court had not abused its discretion in declining to assume jurisdiction over a claim for acts of alleged trademark infringement and unfair competition arising in Canada under Canadian law. As defendant here has acknowledged, the complaint raised a "crucial issue" as to the validity of Canadian trademark law. This factor weighed heavily in the Court's decision.

> We do not think it the province of United States district courts to determine the validity of trademarks which officials of foreign countries have seen fit to grant. To do so would be to welcome conflicts with the administrative and judicial officers of the Dominion

---

[4]*See* 3 Nimmer, *supra* at § 12.01[C] (copyright is intangible incorporeal right; it has no situs apart from domicile of proprietor).

of Canada.

Id. at 647. But as Nimmer has noted, "[i]n adjudicating an infringement action under a foreign copyright law there is . . . no need to pass upon the validity of acts of foreign government officials," [cit], since foreign copyright laws, by and large, do not incorporate administrative formalities which must be satisfied to create or perfect a copyright. *Id.*

The facts in this case confirm the logic of Nimmer's observation. The British films at issue here received copyright protection in Great Britain simply by virtue of publication there. Copinger, Law of Copyright (9th ed. 1958), 21 et seq. Chile's adherence to the Berne Convention in 1970 automatically conferred copyright protection on these films in Chile. Therefore, no "act of state" is called into question here. Moreover, there is no danger that foreign courts will be forced to accept the inexpert determination of this Court, nor that this Court will create "an unseemly conflict with the judgment of another country." [cit]. The litigation will determine only whether an American corporation has acted in violation of a foreign copyright, not whether such copyright exists, nor whether such copyright is valid.

With respect to defendant's *forum non conveniens* argument, it is true that this case will likely involve the construction of at least one, if not several foreign laws.[5] However, the need to apply foreign law is not in itself reason to dismiss or transfer the case. [cit]. Moreover, there is no foreign forum in which defendant is the subject of personal jurisdiction, and an available forum is necessary to validate dismissal of an action on the ground of *forum non conveniens*, for if there is no alternative forum "the plaintiff might find himself with a valid claim but nowhere to assert it." Farmanfarmaian v. Gulf Oil Corp., 437 F. Supp. 910, 915 (S.D.N.Y. 1977) (Carter, J.), *aff'd*, 588 F.2d 880 (2d Cir. 1978).

While this Court might dismiss this action subject to conditions that would assure the plaintiff of a fair hearing, [cit], neither plaintiff nor defendant has demonstrated the relative advantage in convenience that another forum, compared to this one, would provide. [cit]. The selection of a South American country as an alternative forum, although it would afford greater expertise in applying relevant legal principles, would seem to involve considerable hardship and inconvenience for both parties. A British forum might similarly provide some advantages in the construction of relevant law, however, it would impose additional hardships upon defendant, and would raise questions, as would the South American forum, regarding enforceability of a resulting judgment. *See* American Rice, Inc. v. Arkansas Rice Growers Co-op. Assn., 701 F.2d 408, 417 (5th Cir. 1983). Where the balance does not tip strongly in favor of an alternative forum it is well-established that the plaintiff's choice of forum should not be disturbed.

---

[5]Plaintiff has alleged infringements in Chile, Venezuela, Peru, Ecuador, Costa Rica and Panama. Since, under the Berne Convention, the applicable law is the copyright law of the state in which the infringement occurred, defendant seems correct in its assumption that the laws of several countries will be involved in the case. 3 NIMMER, *supra* at §17.05.

For all of the above reasons, the Court finds it has jurisdiction over the instant case and defendant's motion to dismiss is denied, as is its motion to have the Court abstain from exercising its jurisdiction here. . . .

Boosey & Hawkes Music Pubs. v. The Walt Disney Co., 145 F.3d 481 (2d Cir. 1998). In 1940, Disney released the animated motion picture Fantasia, starring Mickey Mouse. The soundtrack to the film included a performance of The Rite of Spring by Igor Stravinsky, performed by the Philadelphia Orchestra under the direction of Leopold Stokowski. Because under U.S. law the work (the Rite of Spring) was in the public domain, Disney needed no authorization to record or distribute it in the United States, but permission was required for distribution in countries where Stravinsky enjoyed copyright protection. In 1939 the parties executed an agreement giving Disney rights to use the work in a motion picture in consideration of a fee to Stravinsky of $6000. For more than five decades Disney exhibited The Rite of Spring in Fantasia under the 1939 license; the film was re-released for theatrical distribution at least seven times since 1940, and although Fantasia has never appeared on television in its entirety, excerpts including portions of The Rite of Spring have been televised occasionally over the years. In 1991 Disney released Fantasia in video cassette and laser disc format. The video has been sold in foreign countries, as well as in the United States. By 1998, the Fantasia video release had generated more than $360 million in gross revenue for Disney. Boosey & Hawkes Music Publishers Ltd., the assignee of Igor Stravinsky's copyright for The Rite of Spring, sued Disney in federal district court in New York, contending that the 1939 license did not authorize distribution in video format. Boosey sought damages for copyright infringement deriving from Disney's sales of videocassettes of Fantasia in at least eighteen foreign countries. The district court summarily held that video distribution was not covered by the license, but granted partial summary judgment to Boosey, under the doctrine of *forum non conveniens,* in so far as it sought relief for foreign copyright claims. The court concluded that these claims should be tried in each of the nations whose copyright laws are invoked. Although the Second Circuit vacated the summary grant of declaratory judgment in Boosey's favor on whether the license covered video distribution, the court reversed the order dismissing the foreign copyright claims on *forum non conveniens* grounds and remanded to the district court for trial. The Second Circuit criticized the district court for failing to consider whether there were alternative fora capable of adjudicating Boosey's copyright claims, as is required prior to making a *forum non conveniens* dismissal. For example, it made no determination whether Disney was subject to jurisdiction in the various countries where the court anticipated that trial would occur and did not condition dismissal on Disney's consent to jurisdiction in those nations. In a footnote, the Second Circuit noted that it did need not decide whether *forum non conveniens* dismissal requires the dismissing court to ascertain a single alternative court with jurisdiction over the claims. *See* 145 F.3d 481 at n.8. The appeals courts also rejected the district court's analysis of the so-called "public interests" that are part of *forum non conveniens* analysis. The district court had reasoned that the trial would require extensive application of foreign copyright and antitrust jurisprudence, bodies of law involving strong national interests best litigated "in their respective countries," and that these necessary inquiries into foreign law would place "an undue burden on our judicial system." The Second Circuit stressed that "while reluctance to apply foreign law is a valid factor favoring dismissal under *Gilbert*, standing alone it does not justify dismissal" and noted that "numerous countervailing considerations suggest that New York venue is proper: defendant is a U.S. corporation, the 1939 agreement was substantially negotiated and signed in New York, and the agreement is governed by New York law. The plaintiff has chosen New York and the trial is ready to proceed here. Everything before us suggests that trial would be more easy, expeditious and inexpensive in the district court than dispersed to 18 foreign nations."

NOTES AND QUESTIONS

(1) **Applying Foreign Law.** The theory approved by the *London Films* court has not been without its critics. In *ITSI T.V. Prods, Inc. v. California Authority of Racing Fairs*, 785 F. Supp. 854 (N.D. Cal. 1992), *rev'd on other grounds*, 3 F.3d 1289 (9th Cir. 1993), the federal district court for the Northern District of California, after noting that it did not have jurisdiction over acts committed in Mexico, refused plaintiff permission to amend its complaint to state a cause of action against the defendant (Caliente) under Mexican copyright laws for those acts (broadcast of copyrighted works) in Mexico. The Court commented that:

> Although one district court has accepted jurisdiction over an action for foreign copyright infringement, *see London Films*, I discern no clear authority for exercising such jurisdiction. Moreover, it appears to me that American courts should be reluctant to enter the bramble bush of ascertaining and applying foreign law without an urgent reason to do so. No such reason has been tendered in this case and, as a matter of common sense and judicial self-restraint, I think it appropriate to decline plaintiff's invitation.

In a footnote, the court addressed Nimmer's observation (quoted favorably in *London Films*) that jurisdiction over foreign claims was more acceptable in copyright rather than trademark cases because "under virtually all foreign copyright laws there are no administrative formalities, which must be satisfied in order to create or to perfect a copyright" and thus there was no need to pass on the validity of administrative acts of foreign officials. The Court responded that "assuming that Professor Nimmer is right, that generalization does not answer the question whether in any given case the particular foreign law does have administrative formalities which must be satisfied." *See id.* at n.19. Is this a persuasive response to Professor Nimmer's observation?

In the last few years, several courts have entertained the possibility of adjudicating foreign copyright infringement claims. *See, e.g.,* Carell v. Shubert Org., 104 F. Supp. 2d 236, 257-59 (S.D.N.Y. 2000) (permitting claims based on foreign copyright laws to proceed notwithstanding the plaintiff's failure to specify in her complaint the particular countries under whose laws the claims were made); Armstrong v. Virgin Records, 91 F. Supp.2d 628, 637-38 (S.D.N.Y. 2000) (entertaining claims based on unspecified foreign copyright laws on the basis of diversity jurisdiction and pendent jurisdiction). The *ITSI* court mentions the difficulty of applying foreign law as a reason for moving more cautiously in this area. Is the application of foreign copyright law any more difficult than the application of foreign contract or tort law (which courts do routinely)? What difficulties might trial of the claims in *London Films* encounter? Are these difficulties any greater than would exist with the trial of foreign causes of action other than copyright?

(2) **Proving Foreign Law.** Historically, foreign law was treated as a question of fact that had to be pleaded and proved before a U.S. court. The modern approach in federal court, sanctioned by Rule 44.1 of the Federal Rules of Civil Procedure, is to ascertain the content of foreign law from any source available, meaning that the court may seek oral or affidavit testimony from experts or may conduct independent research into the foreign law. *See* Universe Sales Co., Ltd. v. Silver Castle, Ltd., 182 F.3d 1036 (9th Cir. 1999).

(3) **Parallel Developments in the United Kingdom**. English courts have typically not entertained claims under foreign copyright laws. The same was true in other commonwealth countries. The British courts have, however, recently recognized that certain foreign copyright claims might be adjudicated before the U.K. courts. *See* Pearce v. Ove Arup Partnership, [1999] 1 All E.R. 769 (Ct. Appeal, 1999) (Eng.). The *Pearce* court permitted a claim for copyright infringement based upon conduct in Holland to proceed in the English courts. Mr. Pearce, an architect, produced drawings for a town hall while completing his diploma in architecture in London. Several years later he noticed a town hall in Rotterdam, Holland, that he alleged was copied from his drawings. He brought an infringement action in the U.K. against the City of Rotterdam and the architects and civil engineers responsible for the construction of the building. The court acknowledged that because the acts of copying took place in Holland, they could not constitute infringements of the plaintiff's U.K. copyright. The civil engineer was domiciled in the U.K., while the other defendants were domiciled in the Netherlands. Under section 2(1) of the Civil Jurisdiction and Judgments Act 1982, the provisions of the Brussels Convention governed the resolution of disputes in civil and commercial matters between persons domiciled in the parties to the Brussels Convention. The U.K. defendant could clearly be sued in the United Kingdom. The court accepted that the English courts had jurisdiction in relation to the claims against the non-U.K. defendants under article 6(1) of the Brussels Convention, which provides that a person domiciled in a contracting state may be sued, where he is one of a number of defendants, in the courts for the place where any one of them is domiciled. The court concluded that rules of U.K. law that previously restricted the adjudication of foreign intellectual property claims had been overridden by the Brussels Convention (and other legislative developments) where the parties

were from contracting states, and that the case could therefore proceed.

The *Pearce* court noted that it was not

> necessary to decide whether . . .an action for alleged infringement of
> a foreign copyright by acts done outside the United Kingdom in a
> state not party to the Brussels Convention, in a case where no
> question as to the validity or registration of the right was in issue,
> was . . . justiciable in an English court.

The court, discussing *Tyburn Productions Ltd. v. Conan Doyle,* [1990] 1 All ER
909, where an English court rejected plaintiff's request to declare that the
defendant had no rights under U.S. copyright and trademark laws, noted that

> it is important to keep in mind that the question [there] was
> whether . . . the defendant had . . . rights under the copyright, unfair
> competition or trademark laws of the United States which would be
> infringed by what the plaintiff was proposing to do. [The court there]
> was invited to investigate the existence and validity of the rights
> claimed; not to decide whether there had been an infringement of
> rights the existence and validity of which were not in issue.

The court thus recognized some distinction between questions of validity and
infringement, which is a distinction to which we will return *infra* § 7.05[B][2],
when we consider the operation of the Brussels Convention in the industrial
property context.

[B]   Trademark Law

STEELE v. BULOVA WATCH CO.
344 U.S. 280 (1952)

Mr. Justice Clark delivered the opinion of the Court.

The issue is whether a United States District Court has jurisdiction to award
relief to an American corporation against acts of trade-mark infringement and
unfair competition consummated in a foreign country by a citizen and resident
of the United States. Bulova Watch Company, Inc., a New York corporation.
sued Steele, petitioner here, in the United States District Court for the Western
District of Texas. The gist of its complaint charged that BULOVA, a
trade-mark properly registered under the laws of the United States, had long
designated the watches produced and nationally advertised and sold by the
Bulova Watch Company; and that petitioner, a United States citizen residing
in San Antonio, Texas, conducted a watch business in Mexico City where,
without Bulova's authorization and with the purpose of deceiving the buying

public, he stamped the name BULOVA on watches there assembled and sold. Basing its prayer on these asserted violations of the trade-mark laws of the United States, Bulova requested injunctive and monetary relief. Personally served with process in San Antonio, petitioner answered by challenging the court's jurisdiction over the subject matter of the suit and by interposing several defenses, including his due registration in Mexico of the mark BULOVA and the pendency of Mexican legal proceedings thereon, to the merits of Bulova's claim. The trial judge, having initially reserved disposition of the jurisdictional issue until a hearing on the merits, interrupted the presentation of evidence and dismissed the complaint "with prejudice," on the ground that the court lacked jurisdiction over the cause. This decision rested on the court's findings that petitioner had committed no illegal acts within the United States. With one judge dissenting, the Court of Appeals reversed; it held that the pleadings and evidence disclosed a cause of action within the reach of the Lanham Trade-Mark Act of 1946. The dissenting judge thought that "since the conduct complained of substantially related solely to acts done and trade carried on under full authority of Mexican law, and were confined to and affected only that Nation's internal commerce, (the District Court) was without jurisdiction to enjoin such conduct." We granted certiorari.

Petitioner concedes, as he must, that Congress in prescribing standards of conduct for American citizens may project the impact of its laws beyond the territorial boundaries of the United States. Resolution of the jurisdictional issue in this case therefore depends on construction of exercised congressional power, not the limitations upon that power itself. And since we do not pass on the merits of Bulova's claim, we need not now explore every facet of this complex and controversial Act.

The Lanham Act, on which Bulova posited its claims to relief, confers broad jurisdictional powers upon the courts of the United States. The statute's expressed intent is [inter alia] "to regulate commerce within the control of Congress by making actionable the deceptive and misleading use of marks in such commerce; . . . and to provide rights and remedies stipulated by treaties and conventions respecting trade-marks, trade names, and unfair competition entered into between the United States and foreign nations." To that end, section 32(1) holds liable in a civil action by a trade-mark registrant "(a)ny person who shall, in commerce," infringe a registered trade-mark in a manner there detailed. "Commerce" is defined as "all commerce which may lawfully be regulated by Congress." Section 45. The district courts of the United States are granted jurisdiction over all actions 'arising under' the Act, and can award relief which may include injunctions, 'according to the principles of equity,' to prevent the violation of any registrant's rights.

The record reveals the following significant facts which for purposes of a dismissal must be taken as true: Bulova Watch Company, one of the largest watch manufacturers in the world, advertised and distributed BULOVA watches in the United States and foreign countries. Since 1929, its aural and visual advertising, in Spanish and English, has penetrated Mexico. Petitioner, long a resident of San Antonio, first entered the watch business there in 1922, and in 1926 learned of the trade-mark BULOVA. He subsequently transferred his business to Mexico City and, discovering that BULOVA had not been registered in Mexico, in 1933 procured the Mexican registration of that mark. Assembling Swiss watch movements and dials and cases imported from that country and the United States, petitioner in Mexico City stamped his watches with BULOVA and sold them as such. As a result of the distribution of spurious "Bulovas," Bulova Watch Company's Texas sales representative received numerous complaints from retail jewelers in the Mexican border area whose customers brought in for repair defective "Bulovas" which upon inspection often turned out not to be products of that company. Moreover, subsequent to our grant of certiorari in this case the prolonged litigation in the courts of Mexico has come to an end. On October 6, 1952, the Supreme Court of Mexico rendered a judgment upholding an administrative ruling which had nullified petitioner's Mexican registration of BULOVA.

On the facts in the record we agree with the Court of Appeals that petitioner's activities, when viewed as a whole, fall within the jurisdictional scope of the Lanham Act. This Court has often stated that the legislation of Congress will not extend beyond the boundaries of the United States unless a contrary legislative intent appears. The question thus is "whether Congress intended to make the law applicable" to the facts of this case. For "the United States is not debarred by any rule of international law from governing the conduct of its own citizens upon the high seas or even in foreign countries when the rights of other nations or their nationals are not infringed. With respect to such an exercise of authority there is no question of international law, but solely of the purport of the municipal law which establishes the duty of the citizen in relation to his own government." As Mr. Justice Minton, then sitting on the Court of Appeals, applied the principle in a case involving unfair methods of competition: "Congress has the power to prevent unfair trade practices in foreign commerce by citizens of the United States, although some of the acts are done outside the territorial limits of the United States." Nor has this Court in tracing the commerce scope of statutes differentiated between enforcement of legislative policy by the Government itself or by private litigants proceeding under a statutory right. The public policy served is the same in each case. In the light of the broad jurisdictional grant in the Lanham Act, we deem its scope to encompass petitioner's activities here. His operations and their effects were not confined within the territorial limits of a foreign nation. He bought component parts of his wares in the United States, and spurious "Bulovas" filtered through the Mexican border into this country; his competing goods could well reflect adversely on Bulova Watch Company's trade reputation in markets cultivated by advertising here as well as abroad. Under similar factual circumstances, courts of the United States have awarded relief to registered trade-mark owners, even prior to the advent of the broadened commerce provisions of the Lanham Act. Even when most jealously read, that Act's sweeping reach into "all commerce which may lawfully be regulated by Congress" does not constrict prior law or deprive courts of jurisdiction previously exercised. We do not deem material that petitioner affixed the mark BULOVA in Mexico City rather than here, or that his purchases in the United States when viewed in isolation do not violate any of our laws. They were essential steps in the course of business consummated abroad; acts in themselves legal lose that character when they become part of an unlawful scheme. "(I)n such a case it is not material that the source of the forbidden effects upon . . . commerce arises in one phase or another of that program." In sum, we do not think that petitioner by so simple a device can evade the thrust of the laws of the United States in a privileged sanctuary beyond our borders.

. . . .

Nor do we doubt the District Court's jurisdiction to award appropriate injunctive relief if warranted by the facts after trial. Mexico's courts have nullified the Mexican registration of BULOVA; there is thus no conflict which might afford petitioner a pretext that such relief would impugn foreign law. The question, therefore, whether a valid foreign registration would affect either the power to enjoin or the propriety of its exercise is not before us. Where, as here, there can be no interference with the sovereignty of another nation, the District Court in exercising its equity powers may command persons properly before it to cease or perform acts outside its territorial jurisdiction.

Affirmed.

MR. JUSTICE BLACK took no part in the decision of this case

MR. JUSTICE REED, with whom MR. JUSTICE DOUGLAS joins, dissenting.

VANITY FAIR MILLS, INC. v. T. EATON CO., LTD.
234 F.2d 633 (2d Cir. 1956)

WATERMAN, CIRCUIT JUDGE:

This case presents interesting and novel questions concerning the extraterritorial application of the Lanham Act and the International Convention for the Protection of Industrial Property (Paris Union). Plaintiff's complaint . . . alleged trade-mark infringement and unfair competition both in the United States and Canada. Defendants moved to dismiss . . . on the grounds that [inter alia] . . . the district court lacked jurisdiction over the subject matter of the complaint insofar as it related to defendants' alleged trade-mark infringement and unfair competition in the Dominion of Canada; and that the district court was an inconvenient forum for the trial of those issues. The district court found that . . . it lacked subject matter jurisdiction over that portion of the complaint raising Canadian trade-mark issues, and, alternatively, that it was an inconvenient forum for the trial of such issues. That portion of the complaint asserting claims based upon violation of United States trade-marks and unfair competition in this country was recognized by the district court as within its jurisdiction, but because the complaint was thought to inextricably combine the Canadian and American issues, the court dismissed the complaint in its entirety, with leave to file an amended complaint stating separately the American issues. Plaintiff chose to stand on its original complaint, and appealed from the judgment dismissing the complaint.

. . . .

Plaintiff, Vanity Fair Mills, Inc., is a Pennsylvania corporation, having its principal place of business at Reading, Pennsylvania. It has been engaged in the manufacture and sale of women's underwear under the trade-mark VANITY FAIR since about the year 1914 in the United States, and has been continuously offering its branded merchandise for sale in Canada since at least 1917. . . .

. . . .

Beginning in 1914 plaintiff has protected its trade-mark rights by registrations with the United States Patent Office of the trade-mark VANITY FAIR as applying to various types of underwear. . . .

Defendant, The T. Eaton Company, Limited, is a Canadian corporation engaged in the retail merchandising business throughout Canada, with its principal office in Toronto, Ontario. It has a regular and established place of business within the Southern District of New York. On November 3, 1915, defendant filed with the proper Canadian official an application for the registration in Canada of the trade-mark VANITY FAIR, claiming use in connection with [various items of women's clothing]. On November 10, 1915, the proper Canadian official granted defendant's application for the registration of that mark. . . In 1919 plaintiff sought to register the trade-mark Vanity Fair in Canada for ready made underwear, but its application was rejected as a matter of course because of the prior registration of defendant . . . .

During the years 1945-1953 the defendant ceased to use its own 'Vanity-Fair' trade-mark, purchased branded merchandise from the plaintiff, and sold this merchandise under advertisements indicating that it was of United States origin and of plaintiff's manufacture. These purchases by defendant from plaintiff were made through defendant's New York office. In 1953 defendant resumed the use of its own trade-mark Vanity Fair and, simultaneously, under the same trade-mark, sold plaintiff's branded merchandise and cheaper merchandise of Canadian manufacture. Defendant at this time objected to plaintiff's sales of its branded merchandise to one of defendant's principal competitors in Canada, the Robert Simpson Company. The Simpson Company discontinued purchases of plaintiff's branded merchandise after being threatened with infringement suits by defendant.

. . . .

. . . [P]laintiff asserts that defendant has advertised feminine underwear in the United States under the trade-mark 'Vanity Fair,' and that it has sold such underwear by mail to customers residing in the United States.

The complaint seeks injunctive relief against the use by defendant of the trade-mark VANITY FAIR in connection with women's underwear both in Canada and the United States, a declaration of the superior rights of the plaintiff in such trade-mark, and an accounting for damages and profits.

The initial question is whether the district court had jurisdiction over all, or only part, of the action. . . .

Plaintiff, however, does not rely other than incidentally on diversity as the basis for federal jurisdiction, but asserts that its claims arise under the laws of the United States and should be governed by those laws. The result sought —extraterritorial application of American law—is contrary to usual conflict-of-laws principles. *First*, the legal status of foreign nationals in the

United States is determined solely by our domestic law—foreign law confers no privilege in this country that our courts are bound to recognize. And when trade-mark rights within the United States are being litigated in an American court, the decisions of foreign courts concerning the respective trade-mark rights of the parties are irrelevant and inadmissible. George W. Luft Co. v. Zande Cosmetic Co., 2 Cir., 1944, 142 F.2d 536, 539. Similarly, the rights and liabilities of United States citizens who compete with foreign nationals in their home countries are ordinarily to be determined by the appropriate foreign law. This fundamental principle, although not without exceptions, is the usual rule, and is based upon practical considerations such as the difficulty of obtaining extraterritorial enforcement of domestic law, as well as on considerations of international comity and respect for national integrity. *Second*, the creation and extent of tort liability is governed, according to the usual rule, by the law of the place where the alleged tort was committed (*lex loci delicti*). The place of the wrong (*locus delicti*) is where the last event necessary to make an actor liable takes place. If the conduct complained of is fraudulent misrepresentation, the place of the wrong is not where the fraudulent statement was made, but where the plaintiff, as a result thereof, suffered a loss. Thus in cases of trade-mark infringement and unfair competition, the wrong takes place not where the deceptive labels are affixed to the goods or where the goods are wrapped in the misleading packages, but where the passing off occurs, *i.e.*, where the deceived customer buys the defendant's product in the belief that he is buying the plaintiff's. In this case, with the exception of defendant's few mail order sales into the United States, the passing-off occurred in Canada, and hence under the usual rule would be governed by Canadian law.

Conflict-of-laws principles, however, are not determinative of the question whether the International Convention and/or the Lanham Act provide relief in American courts and under American law against acts of trade-mark infringement and unfair competition committed in foreign countries by foreign nationals. If the International Convention or the Lanham Act provide such relief, and if the provisions are within constitutional powers, American courts would be required to enforce these provisions. [*See* Steele v. Bulova Watch Co., 1952, 344 U.S. 280]. It is therefore necessary to determine whether the International Convention or the Lanham Act provide such relief. Only if it is determined that they do not provide such extensive relief, and hence that the only jurisdictional basis for the suit is diversity of citizenship, do we reach the question whether the district court abused its discretion in dismissing the complaint because of *forum non conveniens*.

I. The International Convention

Plaintiff asserts that the International Convention for the Protection of Industrial Property (Paris Union), to which both the United States and Canada are parties, is self-executing; that by virtue of Article VI of the Constitution it is a part of the law of this country which is to be enforced by its courts; and that the Convention has created rights available to plaintiff which protect it against trade-mark infringement and unfair competition in foreign countries. Plaintiff would appear to be correct in arguing that no special legislation in the United

States was necessary to make the International Convention effective here, but it erroneously maintains that the Convention created private rights *under American law* for acts of unfair competition occurring in foreign countries.

The International Convention is essentially a compact between the various member countries to accord in their own countries to citizens of the other contracting parties trade-mark and other rights comparable to those accorded their own citizens by their domestic law. The underlying principle is that foreign nationals should be given the same treatment in each of the member countries as that country makes available to its own citizens. In addition, the Convention sought to create uniformity in certain respects by obligating each member nation "to assure to nationals of countries of the Union an effective protection against unfair competition."

The Convention is not premised upon the idea that the trade-mark and related laws of each member nation shall be given extraterritorial application, but on exactly the converse principle that each nation's law shall have only territorial application. Thus a foreign national of a member nation using his trade-mark in commerce in the United States is accorded extensive protection here against infringement and other types of unfair competition by virtue of United States membership in the Convention. But that protection has its source in, and is subject to the limitations of, American law, not the law of the foreign national's own country. Likewise, the International Convention provides protection to a United States trade-mark owner such as plaintiff against unfair competition and trade-mark infringement in Canada—but only to the extent that Canadian law recognizes the treaty obligation as creating private rights or has made the Convention operative by implementing legislation. Under Canadian law, unlike United States law, the International Convention was not effective to create any private rights in Canada without legislative implementation. However, the obligations undertaken by the Dominion of Canada under this treaty have been implemented by legislation. If plaintiff has any rights under the International Convention (other than through section 44 of the Lanham Act), they are derived from this Canadian law, and not from the fact that the International Convention may be a self-executing treaty which is a part of the law of this country.

II. The Lanham Act

Plaintiff's primary reliance is on the Lanham Act. Plaintiff advances two alternative arguments, the first one based on the decision of the Supreme Court in *Steele v. Bulova Watch Co.*, giving the provisions of the Lanham Act an extraterritorial application against acts committed in Mexico by an American citizen, and the second based specifically on section 44 of the Act, which was intended to carry out our obligations under the International Conventions.

A. *General Extraterritorial Application of the Lanham Act—Bulova*

Section 32(1)(a) of the Lanham Act, one of the more important substantive provisions of the Act, protects the owner of a registered mark from use 'in commerce' by another that is 'likely to cause confusion or mistake or to deceive purchasers as to the source of origin' of the other's good or services. 'Commerce' is defined by the Act as 'all commerce which may lawfully be regulated by Congress.' Section 45. Plaintiff, relying on *Steele v. Bulova Watch Co.*, argues that section 32(1)(a) should be given an extraterritorial application, and that this case falls within the literal wording of the section since the defendant's use of the mark VANITY FAIR in Canada had a substantial effect on 'commerce which may be lawfully be regulated by Congress.'

While Congress has no power to regulate commerce in the Dominion of Canada, it does have power to regulate commerce 'with foreign Nations, and among the several States.' Const. Art. 1, § 8, cl. 3. This power is now generally interpreted to extend to all commerce, even intrastate and entirely foreign commerce, which has a substantial effect on commerce between the states or between the United States and foreign countries. . . . Thus it may well be that Congress could constitutionally provide infringement remedies so long as the defendant's use of the mark has a substantial effect on the foreign or interstate commerce of the United States. But we do not reach this constitutional question because we do not think that Congress intended that the infringement remedies provided in section 32(1)(a) and elsewhere should be applied to acts committed by a foreign national in his home country under a presumably valid trademark registration in that country.

The Lanham Act itself gives almost no indication of the extent to which Congress intended to exercise its power in this area. While section 45 states a broad definition of the "commerce" subject to the Act, both the statement of Congressional intent in the same section and the provisions of section 44 indicate Congressional regard for the basic principle of the International Conventions, *i.e.*, equal application to citizens and foreign nationals alike of the territorial law of the place where the acts occurred. And the Supreme Court, in *Steele v. Bulova Watch Co.*, the only other extraterritorial case since the Lanham Act, did not intimate that the Act should be given the extreme interpretation urged upon us here.

In the *Bulova* case, the Fifth Circuit, assuming that the defendant had a valid registration under Mexican law, found that the district court had jurisdiction to prevent the defendant's use of the mark in Mexico, on the ground that there was a sufficient effect on United States commerce. Subsequently, the defendant's registration was canceled in Mexican proceedings, and on review of the Fifth Circuit's decision, the Supreme Court noted that the question of the effect of a valid registration in the foreign country was not before it. The Court affirmed the Fifth Circuit, holding that the federal district court had jurisdiction to prevent unfair use of the plaintiff's mark in Mexico. In doing so the Court stressed three factors: (1) the defendant's conduct had a substantial effect on United States commerce; (2) the defendant was a United States citizen and the United States has a broad power to regulate the conduct of its citizens in foreign countries; and (3) there was no conflict with trade-mark rights established under the foreign law, since the defendant's Mexican registration had been canceled by proceedings in Mexico. Only the first factor is present in this case.

We do not think that the *Bulova* case lends support to plaintiff; to the contrary, we think that the rationale of the Court was so thoroughly based on the power of the United States to govern 'the conduct of *its own citizens* upon the high seas or even in foreign countries *when the rights of other nations or their nationals are not infringed*', that the absence of one of the above factors might well be determinative and that the absence of both is certainly fatal.[14] . . . . [T]he action has only been brought against Canadian citizens. We conclude that the remedies provided by the Lanham Act, other than in section 44, should not be given an extraterritorial application against foreign citizens acting under presumably valid trade-marks in a foreign country.

B. *Section 44 of the Lanham Act.*

Plaintiff's alternative contention is that section 44 of the Lanham Act, which is entitled 'International Conventions,' affords to United States citizens all possible remedies against unfair competition by foreigners who are nationals of convention countries, including the relief requested in this case.

. . . .

Since United States citizens are given by subsection (i) of section 44 only the same benefits which the Act extends to eligible foreign nationals, and since the benefits conferred on those foreign nationals have no extraterritorial application, the benefits accorded to citizens by this section can likewise have no extraterritorial application.

III. Forum Non Conveniens

With respect to the trade-mark infringement and unfair competition alleged to have occurred within Canada, the complaint, as we have seen, does not state a claim arising under the laws of the United States. Therefore, the jurisdiction of the district court over this part of the action rests solely on diversity of citizenship.[17]   Plaintiff contends that actions for unfair competition are transitory, and that the district court was required to exercise its jurisdiction over the action, even though the passing off occurred outside of the United States, because plaintiff is an American citizen and personal jurisdiction over defendant can be obtained within the United States only in the Southern District of New York. We think, however, that the district court did not abuse its discretion in declining to exercise its jurisdiction over that portion of the case arising in Canada and governed by Canadian trade-mark law.

---

[14]At the time the Fifth Circuit decided the *Bulova* case, the defendant's Mexican registration had not been canceled. Since the Fifth Circuit assumed that the defendant had a valid Mexican registration, it thought the presence or absence of a foreign trade mark was not a determinative factor. We need not decide that question because of the additional fact that the defendant here is not an American citizen.

[17]In a diversity action brought to enforce state-created rights, we must apply the law of New York, including its conflict-of-laws rules. Klaxon Co. v. Stentor Electric Mfg. Co., 313 U.S. 487 (1941). New York follows the almost universal rule that the law governing a tort is the law of the place where the alleged wrong occurred. Consequently, Canadian law governs the unfair competition occurring in Canada.

The doctrine of *forum non conveniens* is now firmly established in federal law. . . . Whether jurisdiction should be declined is determined by balancing conveniences, but the plaintiff's choice of forum will not be disturbed unless the balance is strongly in favor of the defendant. *See Gulf Oil Corporation v. Gilbert*, 330 U.S. 501 (1947). Finally, in the determination of a motion to dismiss for *forum non conveniens*, the court may consider affidavits submitted by the moving and opposing parties.

An American citizen does not have an absolute right under all circumstances to sue in an American court. However, where, as here, application of the doctrine of *forum non conveniens* would force an American citizen to seek redress in a foreign court, courts of the United States are reluctant to apply the doctrine. . . .

We are convinced that the balance of convenience is strongly in favor of defendant, but it is unnecessary for the following reasons for us to rely solely on that ground.

The crucial issue in this case is the validity of defendant's Canadian trade-mark registration under Canadian trade-mark law. The Canadian Registrar of Trade-Marks has registered the mark VANITY FAIR in defendant's name and has refused registration of plaintiff's VANITY FAIR mark on the ground that it interfered with defendant's prior registration. . . . [T]he Canadian Trade-Mark Act of 1952 give[s] the Canadian registrant of a trade-mark the statutory right to prevent the use in Canada of a confusing mark, unless the Canadian registration is shown to be invalid. Such a showing could be made in any Canadian court of competent jurisdiction as a defense to an infringement action brought by defendant, or plaintiff could initiate proceedings in . . . Canada to expunge or amend defendant's registration. . . . Under these circumstances, we do not think a United States district court should take jurisdiction over that portion of this action turning on the validity or invalidity of defendant's Canadian trade-mark.

In the first place, courts of one state are reluctant to impose liability upon a person who acts pursuant to a privilege conferred by the law of the place where the acts occurred. In the second place, it is well-established that the courts of one state will not determine the validity of the acts of a foreign sovereign done within its borders. These precedents have not involved the acts of trade-mark officials of foreign countries, but their rationale would appear to extend to that situation. Moreover, in *George W. Luft*, we assumed the validity of foreign trade-mark registrations in holding that the lower court could not enjoin an American manufacturer from labeling his product with an infringing mark in the United States for shipment to foreign countries in which he had a presumably valid registered trade-mark. "We do not see upon what 'principles of equity' a court can enjoin the initiation of acts in the United States which constitute no wrong to the plaintiff in the country where they are to be consummated. Nor can we perceive upon what theory a plaintiff can recover damages for acts in the United States resulting in a sale of merchandise in a foreign country under a mark to which the defendant has established, over the plaintiff's opposition, a legal right of use in that country. Consequently neither the injunction nor the accounting should cover activities of the defendants, either here or abroad, concerned with sales in countries where the defendants have established rights superior to the plaintiffs in the name Zande." 142 F.2d at 540.

Were this merely a transitory tort action in which disputed facts could be litigated as conveniently here as in Canada, we would think the jurisdiction of the district court should be exercised. But we do not think it the province of United States district courts to determine the validity of trade-marks which officials of foreign countries have seen fit to grant. To do so would be to welcome conflicts with the administrative and judicial officers of the Dominion of Canada. We realize that a court of equity having personal jurisdiction over a party has power to enjoin him from committing acts elsewhere. But this power should be exercised with great reluctance when it will be difficult to secure compliance with any resulting decree or when the exercise of such power is fraught with possibilities of discord and conflict with the authorities of another country.

The district court, therefore, did not abuse its discretion in refusing to entertain the claims of trade-mark infringement and unfair competition occurring in Canada. Were it not for the fact that plaintiff did not press its American claims, and they appear to be of somewhat minor significance, we would think it improper to dismiss the entire complaint, since we think that the claims of trade-mark infringement and unfair competition occurring in the United States can be clearly ascertained from the complaint. However, under the circumstances, we will affirm the dismissal, but allow plaintiff, if it so desires, to file an amended complaint within thirty days from date of our mandate herein, stating separately the American issues.

Affirmed as modified.

OCEAN GARDEN, INC. v. MARKTRADE COMPANY, INC.
953 F.2d 500 (9th Cir. 1991)

TROTT, CIRCUIT JUDGE.

Ocean Garden Products ("OGP") was awarded a preliminary injunction preventing Marktrade, Inc. and Alberto Soler (collectively, "Marktrade") from imitating, copying, or making unauthorized use of OGP's trademarks or trade dress. Marktrade appeals the preliminary injunction. We affirm.

I.

OGP markets canned fish and seafood products including Mexican abalone under the "Calmex" brand name. Marktrade markets similar products under the brand names "Sardimex" and "Seamex," and distributes "Rey Del Mar" canned abalone for export to the Far East. Marktrade uses trade dress similar to OGP's "Wheel Brand" abalone.

. . . .

III.

Marktrade argues that the district court lacked jurisdiction because the canned abalone OGP complains of "is exclusively harvested, processed, and canned in Mexico by the Cooperatives, which is a Mexican association of Mexican abalone fisherman." This abalone is sold exclusively in the Far East. OGP contends there is jurisdiction on two grounds. First, OGP alleges that Marktrade's trademark and trade dress infringement affects United States foreign commerce. Marktrade orchestrates and manages its business from the United States and both OGP and Marktrade are California corporations. Secondly, it claims there is jurisdiction because the goods pass through a United States foreign trade zone in Los Angeles.

In the instant case, we find both extraterritorial jurisdiction, and jurisdiction resulting from shipment through a United States foreign trade zone.

A.

. . . .

In interpreting the jurisdictional scope of the Lanham Act, the Supreme Court has stated that the Lanham Act provides a "broad jurisdictional grant" that extends to "all commerce which may lawfully be regulated by Congress." Steele v. Bulova Watch Co., 344 U.S. 280, 283, 286 (1952). "Various circuits have recognized the Supreme Court's view of the 'sweeping jurisdictional language' of the Lanham Act." [cit]. Moreover, "Congress has the power to prevent unfair trade practices in foreign commerce by citizens of the United States, although some of the acts are done outside the territorial limits of the United States." *Bulova*, 344 U.S. at 286.

"[T]he Lanham Act's coverage of foreign activities may be analyzed under the test for extraterritorial application of the federal anti-trust laws set forth in Timberlane Lumber Co. v. Bank of America National Trust & Savings Ass'n., 549 F.2d 597 (9th Cir. 1976) (Timberlane 1)." Star-Kist Foods v. P.J. Rhodes & Co., 769 F.2d 1393, 1395 (9th Cir. 1985). Under *Timberlane I*, there are three criteria that must be considered: (1) there must be some effect on American foreign commerce; (2) the effect must be sufficiently great to present a cognizable injury to plaintiffs under the federal statute; (3) the interest of and links to American foreign commerce must be sufficiently strong in relation to those of other nations. *Star-Kist*, 769 F.2d at 1395.

With respect to the first criterion, OGP argues that it is losing millions of dollars in revenues through trademark infringement. We find that "the sales of infringing goods in a foreign country may have a sufficient effect on commerce to invoke Lanham Act jurisdiction." . . .

As for the second criterion, OGP claims that Marktrade dilutes OGP's trademark in the United States. This is not at all clear from the facts of this case. The injury would seem to be limited to the deception of consumers in the Far East. However, both OGP and Marktrade are U.S. corporations, and there is monetary injury in the United States to OGP, which is cognizable under the Lanham Act. 15 U.S.C. §§ 1116, 1117 (1988).

OGP's claim is also very strong with respect to the third criterion. The third Timberlane factor is divided into seven components—these weigh heavily in granting extraterritorial jurisdiction in this case. *See Star-Kist*, 769 F.2d at 1395.

(1) *Degree of conflict with foreign law*: In the case before us, there are no pending proceedings in Hong Kong or Taiwan. Therefore this case is distinguishable from *Star-Kist*, where there was an ongoing petition pending in the Philippine Patent Office. As in American Rice, Inc. v. Arkansas Rice Growers, 701 F.2d 408 (5th Cir.1983):

> Absent a determination by the [foreign] court that [the defendant] has a legal right to use the marks, and that those marks do not infringe [the plaintiff's] mark, we are unable to conclude that it would be an affront to [the foreign country's] sovereignty or law if we affirm the district court's injunction prohibiting the defendant from injuring the plaintiff's [foreign] commerce conducted from the United States.

American Rice, 701 F.2d at 415-16; [cit].

(2) *Nationality of the parties*: Marktrade and OGP are both California corporations.

(3) *Extent to which enforcement is expected to achieve compliance*: The injunction would be effective against Marktrade because it is a U.S. corporation which "orchestrated [its] infringing activities," *Reebok*, 737 F. Supp. at 1520, from the United States. Marktrade, in response, argues that the Mexican cooperative could continue infringement activities on its own. However, the facts in the record indicate extensive involvement by Soler and Marktrade in these activities.

(4) *Relative significance of effects on U.S. as compared to elsewhere*: Here OGP is also a United States corporation, and therefore the losses involved affect a domestic corporation.

(5) *Explicit purpose is to harm U.S. commerce*: There is evidence that Marktrade's infringing acts were intentional. Therefore, Marktrade's actions may be said to have the explicit purpose of harming a U.S. corporation.

(6) *Foreseeability of such effect*: Because the above five factors weigh in OGP's favor, such effect was foreseeable.

(7) *Relative importance of violations within the U.S.*: Again, OGP is a U.S. corporation and is hurt by the infringement. Moreover, the goods were exported through a United States foreign trade zone and therefore the violation may be said to have importance in U.S. commerce.

We find that we can exercise extraterritorial jurisdiction in this case. As in one lower court case, "[e]ven though no [counterfeit items] entered the United States, the defendants . . . were residents of California, [were] subject to the state's jurisdiction[,] and orchestrated their . . . counterfeiting activities from California." [cit].

B.

We also find that the court has jurisdiction without having to exercise extraterritorial jurisdiction because the infringing goods passed through a United States foreign trade zone. Foreign trade zones are areas within the United States where Congress "established Government-supervised bonded warehouses where imports are stored duty free for prescribed periods." Goods that are in these zones may be stored, sold, exhibited, broken-up, repacked, assembled, distributed, sorted, and mixed with foreign or domestic merchandise without being subject to customs laws. 19 U.S.C. § 81c (1988). Through these zones, "United States citizens could be involved in and, consequently financially profit from the breaking down, repacking and relabeling of the goods." "The Act stimulated foreign commerce by allowing goods in transit in foreign commerce to retain in secure storage, duty free, until they resumed their journey in export."

The scope of subject matter jurisdiction under the Lanham Act is quite broad. It makes actionable the deceptive use in "commerce which may be lawfully regulated by Congress," marks that are protected by having been registered in the United States Patent and Trademark Office. 15 U.S.C. § 1127. The jurisdictional question this presents is whether Congress has the power to regulate commerce within United States foreign trade zones, or whether it has precluded the reach of the Lanham Act into such zones by withdrawing from them Congress' relevant regulatory powers.

We hold that instead of withdrawing its power to regulate commerce in these zones, it is apparent that Congress has retained that authority, and delegated its use to a board consisting of the Secretary of Commerce, the Secretary of the Treasury, and the Secretary of the Army. 19 U.S.C. § 81a. Section 81c of the same act states that "[F]oreign and domestic merchandise of every description, *except such as is prohibited by law*, may, without being subject to the customs law of the United States . . . be brought into [such zones]." 19 U.S.C. § 81c (emphasis added).

. . . .

Thus, Congress has and does exercise the power to regulate commerce—including "merchandise that infringes trademarks"—inside foreign trade zones. Given this fact, entry of infringing goods into a foreign trade zone is a sufficient act in commerce to trigger subject matter jurisdiction in federal courts under the Lanham Act . . . .

. . . .

Our rule does *not* create plenary federal court jurisdiction over every item that touches a foreign trade zone. Take, for example, a Swiss company selling French goods in Hong Kong, with a trademark not protected in the United States. Should it turn out that the French goods are infringing on an English company's mark, the fact that the goods stopped in a United States foreign trade zone would be insufficient to establish jurisdiction in a suit brought in our courts by the English company against the Swiss company. The United States has no interest in such a case.

If the above cause of action were based, however, on a mark protected by the

Lanham Act, then jurisdiction in our federal courts would attach. Section 44 of the Lanham Act allows a foreign national to register a mark even though the mark has never been used in U.S. commerce. [cit]. It is necessary, however, for the foreign registrant to use the mark in U.S. commerce within a reasonable time or it is deemed abandoned. [cit]. Moreover,

> if such a foreign registrant does not use the registered mark in United States trade within a reasonable time, the registration is subject to cancellation for abandonment. Under the Lanham Act, non-use for two consecutive years is prima facie evidence of abandonment and is an evidentiary basis for the required use within a "reasonable time" after registration by a foreign resident.

[Cit]. Even if there is no abandonment challenge, it is necessary to file a section 8 affidavit—showing that a mark has been used in commerce during the fifth year of U.S. registration—before the end of the sixth year. [cit]. Without filing this affidavit, the U.S. registration is automatically canceled. Given the requirement of a U.S. use for all registered trademarks, a Lanham Act claim, even involving foreign parties, will involve U.S. interests. If the goods that violate the Lanham Act are also shipped through a U.S. foreign trade zone, that is a sufficient act in commerce for subject matter jurisdiction. Therefore, jurisdiction was proper in the district court in the present case. . . .

. . . .

We find that the district court had jurisdiction to order the preliminary injunction. We find both that the court had extra-territorial jurisdiction and that the court had jurisdiction because the goods were shipped through a foreign trade zone.

––––––––

Totalplan Corp. of America v. Colborne, 14 F.3d 824 (2d Cir. 1994). The plaintiff, Totalplan, a domestic corporation, alleged that the sale of cameras in Japan by Lure, a Canadian corporation with which it had previously had contractual relations, violated its U.S. trademark and was thus actionable under the Lanham Act. (Plaintiff also claimed that defendants packaged the cameras in the United States for eventual sale in Japan.) The Second Circuit affirmed the conclusion of the district court that the Lanham Act did not reach appellees' Japanese distribution of cameras. The court explained as follows:

> First, none of the [defendants] is a United States citizen. Thus, unlike *Bulova*, this case does not implicate the United States "broad power to regulate the conduct of its citizens in foreign countries." *Vanity Fair*, 234 F.2d at 642. Although [defendant's] Canadian citizenship alone may not be sufficient to defeat Totalplan's claim of Japanese infringement, it is a factor weighing against extraterritorial application of the Lanham Act. *Cf.* Calvin Klein Industries v. BFK Hong Kong, Ltd., 714 F. Supp. 78, 80

(S.D.N.Y. 1989) (finding jurisdiction under Lanham Act where defendant not a United Sates citizen but resided in the United States and controlled co-defendant New York corporation). Second, the district judge did not err in finding that Totalplan failed to demonstrate that Lure's shipment of Love cameras abroad had a substantial effect on United States commerce. Unlike *Bulova*, there is no evidence that infringing goods have affected United States commerce by re-entering the country and causing confusion. Furthermore, although Totalplan relies on the Fifth Circuit's decision in American Rice, Inc. v. Arkansas Rice Growers, 701 F.2d 408 (5th Cir.1983), for the proposition that the packaging and shipment of goods from the United States constitutes a "substantial effect" on United States commerce, *American Rice* merely established that such activities, when combined with diversion of foreign sales from a plaintiff, constitute "more than an insignificant effect on United States commerce." *Id.* at 414-15. *American Rice* is in conflict with *Vanity Fair*, because it specifically rejected the "substantial effect" requirement in favor of a more lenient "some effect" standard. *Id.* at 414 n.8.

Totalplan has not shown that any foreign sales of Love cameras have been diverted from it by Lure's shipment to Japan. . . .

Two of the three conditions necessary to bring appellees' conduct within the Lanham Act, United States citizenship and a substantial effect on United States commerce, have thus not been established by Totalplan. As was the case in *Vanity Fair*, the absence of two of the three *Bulova* factors in this case is fatal to an argument that the conduct is governed by the Lanham Act. [cit]. Therefore, we need not reach the third factor, the existence of a conflict with foreign trademark law. . .

. . . .

Totalplan also relies upon George W. Luft Co. v. Zande Cosmetic Co., 142 F.2d 536 (2d Cir.), *cert. denied*, 323 U.S. 756 (1944), to bring appellees' conduct within the reach of the Lanham Act. *Luft* was decided prior to *Bulova* and the passage of the Lanham Act. However, the Court in *Bulova*, citing *Luft*, indicated that the Lanham Act did not constrict jurisdiction of the 1905 Trade-Mark Act as construed by courts, [cit], and therefore, we also consider whether *Luft* calls for application of the Lanham Act in the instant case. In *Luft*, the plaintiff, who owned the registered trademark "Tangee" for cosmetics, sought to enjoin the defendant from selling cosmetics in the United States and abroad under the label "Zande." The district court granted a broad injunction prohibiting the defendant from using the name "Zande" in connection with the sale of cosmetics anywhere.

On appeal, we concluded that the injunction had to be modified to differentiate between three categories of foreign countries: (1) countries where both parties marketed their goods and where defendant had established by local law the right to use its trade name, (2) countries where both parties marketed their goods and where the defendant had not established a right to use its trade name, and (3) countries where the defendant was doing business and "the plaintiff has not proved that it has ever done business or is likely to do it." [cit]. We held that the district court had no jurisdiction to enjoin the defendant from manufacturing products in the United States for sale in countries encompassed in the first and third categories. With respect to countries where both parties were marketing their goods and the defendant had not established a superior right to use its mark, we held that the district judge should enjoin the defendant's United States production. In the instant case, the district judge was not clearly erroneous in concluding that Totalplan had not proved that it marketed or was likely to market Love cameras in Japan and therefore this case falls within the third category. Consequently, *Luft* does not compel the extraterritorial application of the Lanham Act to appellees' conduct.

NOTES AND QUESTIONS

(1) **The *Vanity Fair* Factors.** Courts applying the *Vanity Fair* factors typically recite that "none of these three criteria is dispositive of the analysis concerning the Lanham Act's extraterritorial effect, and a court must employ a balancing test of all three factors to determine whether the statute is properly implicated." Warnaco Inc. v. VF Corp., 844 F. Supp. 940, 950 (S.D.N.Y. 1994); *see also* Nintendo of Am., Inc. v. Aeropower Co., Ltd., 34 F.3d 246, 251 (4th Cir. 1994) (vacating injunction for failure to consider all factors). However, the Court of Appeals in *Vanity Fair* itself and later courts have suggested some brighter line applications of the factors. Which "bright lines" can you detect?

(2) **Citizenship.** Although courts reject a mechanical application of the *Vanity Fair* factors, several courts have noted pointedly that the citizenship of the parties has had a significant effect on whether courts assert jurisdiction over extraterritorial conduct under the Lanham Act. *See* Aerogroup Int'l, Inc. v. Marlboro Footworks, Ltd., 955 F. Supp. 220 n.12 (S.D.N.Y. 1997), *aff'd*, 152 F.3d 948 (Fed. Cir. 1998); Nintendo of Am., Inc. v. Aeropower Co., Ltd., 34 F.3d 246, 251 (4th Cir. 1994) (vacating injunction against foreign defendant's conduct abroad that had a significant impact on United States commerce for failure to consider, inter alia, the defendant's citizenship). In *Aerogroup Int'l, Inc. v. Marlboro Footworks, Ltd.*, 955 F. Supp. 220 (S.D.N.Y. 1997), *aff'd*, 152 F.3d 948 (Fed. Cir. 1998), Aerogroup, an American shoe manufacturer, brought an action alleging that the sale of knock-offs of its shoes in Canada violated its trade dress and trademark rights under the Lanham Act. The action was pursued against an American buying agent (who arranged for the production of shoes overseas with a design that knocked off Aerogroup's trade dress) and a Canadian shoe retailer that was a customer of the buying agent. Although there was evidence of effects on the U.S. plaintiff's sales in Canada, the court dismissed the action against the Canadian retailer, but found that the claim against the U.S. buying agent could be brought under the Lanham Act. In part, this distinction reflected greater U.S. conduct on the part of the American buying agent. But

the court also interpreted case law as indicating that "the citizenship of the defendant is the most significant factor in determining whether to apply the Lanham Act extraterritorially to a defendant's foreign activities. Consequently, courts have been reluctant to extend the reach of the Lanham Act to actions of foreign defendants taken abroad." The court suggested that "when a plaintiff has sought to extend the Lanham Act to the foreign activities of foreign defendants, courts have scrutinized with care the nexus between the foreign defendant's activities within the United States and the conduct giving rise to the Lanham Act claims." Did the *Bulova* court suggest that the defendant's citizenship should be as significant as these dicta suggest? Is it appropriate for the plaintiff's citizenship to be as significant in the extraterritoriality analysis as the *Ocean Garden* court suggests? Is either approach, considering the plaintiff's or defendant's citizenship, consistent with the obligation of national treatment under the Paris Convention?

In dismissing the claim against the Canadian retailer, the *Aerogroup* court noted only three cases within the Second Circuit "in which subject matter jurisdiction was found over a foreign defendant, and in each of these cases the foreign defendant's activities in this country strongly supported the exercise of jurisdiction." Is analysis of contacts insufficiently distinct from the test for personal jurisdiction? Is a convergence of those tests appropriate? What would be the "lenses" through which the contacts in question should be viewed in analyzing whether personal jurisdiction or subject matter jurisdiction under the Lanham Act, respectively, exists?

(3) **Conflict with Foreign Trademark Rights.** The *Vanity Fair* factors require a court to consider whether the assumption of jurisdiction under the Lanham Act would conflict with foreign trademark rights. What is required to make out the argument that such a conflict exists? In some cases, a pending application has been treated as giving rise to the potential for conflicts. *See, e.g.* American White Cross Labs., Inc. v. H.M. Cote, Inc., 556 F. Supp. 753 (S.D.N.Y. 1983). But if the evidence suggests that the foreign application is unlikely to succeed, courts have given less weight to the potential for conflict. *See* Les Ballets Trockadero De Monte Carlo, Inc. v. Trevino, 945 F. Supp. 563, 567-68 (S.D.N.Y. 1996) (noting uncontradicted testimony of plaintiff's expert on Japanese trademark law to the effect that defendant's application would fail because the plaintiff's mark was well known in Japan). Does the consideration of the question of the likely outcome of a foreign proceeding by a U.S. court of itself amount to interference with the administrative procedures of a foreign sovereign? Should the mere existence of a foreign proceeding be sufficient to reject extraterritorial jurisdiction in the United States? *See* Reebok Int'l, Ltd. v. Marnatech Enters., Inc., 970 F.2d 552, 554-55 nn. 2&5 (9th Cir. 1992).

ATLANTIC RICHFIELD CO. v. ARCO GLOBUS INT'L CO.
150 F.3d 189 (2d Cir. 1998)

WINTER, CHIEF JUDGE:

This case concerns the extent to which the Lanham Act applies to allegedly infringing conduct that occurs outside the United States. The Atlantic Richfield Company ("Arco") appeals from Judge Keenan's dismissal, after a three-day bench trial, of Arco's claims against two related companies using the name Arco Globus International Company (collectively "AGI"). Arco's claims concern AGI's use of "Arco Globus International" to identify AGI's oil and gas operations, particularly in the former Soviet Union. Arco alleges that AGI's use of the word "Arco" infringes Arco's registered "ARCO" mark under 15 U.S.C. § 1114(1), violates the Lanham Act's prohibition against false designation of origin, 15 U.S.C. § 1125(a), and amounts to unfair competition and dilution. Judge Keenan held that the Lanham Act does not reach AGI's present use of the "ARCO" mark in the former Soviet Union. [cit]. We agree and affirm.

BACKGROUND

Arco is a well-known company in the domestic and foreign oil and gas industry. In the United States, Arco sells gasoline to retail customers in five western states, operates various oil refineries and two chemical companies, and distributes aviation and diesel fuels, petrochemicals, and plastics. In addition, Arco produces, markets, and trades bulk crude oil and is a member of the New York Mercantile Exchange where it trades oil futures. Arco, through a subsidiary, Arco International Oil and Gas Company, also has extensive operations throughout the world.

The trademark "ARCO" was first used in 1909 by the Atlantic Refining Company in connection with the sale of lubricants. After Atlantic Refining merged with the Richfield Oil Company in 1966, the merged companies began operating extensively under the name "ARCO." Beginning in 1987, the "ARCO" mark was used in all its petroleum and petrochemical businesses. Currently, more than 50 of Arco's 250 United States registrations are for ARCO and ARCO-prefix trademarks, for use on products such as lubricating oils, diesel fuel, petroleum products, motor oils, and greases.

AGI is a "small beginning company," that was formed in 1990. AGI's principal activity is identifying products to be traded by its *de facto* parent, Arco Globus Company Ltd., a Channel Islands corporation engaged in the financing, processing, and sale of crude oil, the trading of oil and gas derivatives, and the provision of refinery engineering services. AGI's involvement in the Soviet Union began in 1990 when it opened a Moscow office. It began trading oil in Russia in 1991.

AGI also engages in activity in the United States. It is a New York company with a New York office and has two American employees. However, Judge Keenan found that it has never offered products for sale in the United States. AGI has no plans to expand its petroleum operations here, but is looking into domestic timber processing. Arco does not dispute these findings, but asserts that AGI's domestic business activities are much more extensive than that which is reflected in Judge Keenan's opinion. For example, according to Arco, AGI escorted the management of Soviet oil-refinery managers on tours of United States refineries, attempted unsuccessfully to establish a Texas-based petroleum joint venture, and deposited money from foreign sales in a New York bank.

After a three-day bench trial, Judge Keenan concluded that the Lanham Act did not reach AGI's allegedly infringing activities abroad because they did not have a substantial effect on United States commerce. Judge Keenan concluded further that, even if the Lanham Act were to apply, Arco did not prove a violation of it. Judge Keenan also dismissed Arco's unfair competition and dilution claims. This appeal followed.

DISCUSSION

The Lanham Act may reach allegedly infringing conduct that occurs outside the United States when necessary to prevent harm to commerce in the United States. *See, e.g.,* Fun-Damental Too, Ltd. v. Gemmy Indus. Corp., 111 F.3d 993, 1006 (2d Cir. 1997). The Supreme Court first addressed the extraterritorial reach of the Lanham Act in Steele v. Bulova Watch Co., 344 U.S. 280 (1952). . . .

From *Bulova,* we have concluded that three factors—the so-called *"Vanity Fair* factors"—are relevant to whether the Lanham Act is to be applied extraterritorially. . . . Judge Keenan found, and the parties agree, that two of these three factors are present here: AGI is a United States citizen and there exists no conflict with foreign law. The question on appeal, therefore, is whether AGI's activity has a substantial effect on United States commerce.[4]

Significantly, Arco conceded in oral argument, as it had to, that AGI's allegedly infringing activities—all of which took place in foreign nations—do not themselves have a substantial effect on United States commerce. Certainly, there is no evidence that domestic consumers have been misled or have come to view the ARCO mark less favorably as a result of those foreign activities. Arco claims, rather, that AGI's activities in the United States bring AGI's foreign activities within the scope of the Lanham Act, at least insofar as those domestic activities "were designed to further and support [AGI's] foreign conduct." In support of this proposition, Arco relies primarily on language in *Bulova* in which the Court described the defendant's purchases of components in the United States as an "essential step[ ]" in the course of "an unlawful scheme." 344 U.S. at 287.

However, *Bulova* is distinguishable in two ways. First, *Bulova* does not hold that a defendant's domestic activity, even if "essential" to infringing activity abroad, is alone sufficient to cause a substantial effect on United States commerce. In *Bulova,* the infringing product, although manufactured and sold abroad, was coming into the United States for sale, resulting in consumer

---

[4]Arco reads *Vanity Fair* to suggest that, where the first two factors are present, extraterritorial application of the Lanham Act may be appropriate even in the absence of a substantial effect on United States commerce. *Vanity Fair* stated only that "the absence of one of the [first two] factors might well be determinative and that the absence of both is certainly fatal." 234 F.2d at 643; *see also Totalplan,* 14 F.3d at 831 (absence of any two factors is fatal). . . .This language from *Vanity Fair* indicates, at most, that the presence of one and perhaps both of the first two factors is generally necessary; it says nothing about whether the presence of the first two factors is sufficient. Indeed, we have never applied the Lanham Act to extraterritorial conduct absent a substantial effect on United States commerce.

confusion and harm to the plaintiff's goodwill in the United States. *See Totalplan*, 14 F.3d at 830 (interpreting *Bulova*); [cit]. Here, AGI's allegedly infringing activities did not confuse Arco's customers in the United States or lessen the value of its mark in this country.

Second, even if *Bulova* is read to indicate that a defendant's infringing extraterritorial conduct has a substantial effect on United States commerce whenever some non-infringing domestic activity is "essential" to that extraterritorial conduct, none of AGI's domestic activities can be deemed essential to its foreign conduct. AGI has only two employees in the United States, no American customers, and no plans to expand its petroleum operations into the United States. To be sure, there is evidence of other domestic activities in which AGI has engaged: escorting oil-refinery managers on tours of United States refineries, attempting to participate in a joint venture, and depositing money from foreign sales in a New York bank. However, these activities are in no sense essential to AGI's allegedly infringing activities abroad. Unlike *Bulova*, where parts of the infringing product were manufactured in the United States, or other cases where the product traveled in United States commerce, *see* Levi Strauss & Co. v. Sunrise Int'l Trading Inc., 51 F.3d 982, 985 (11th Cir. 1995) (Lanham Act applies to foreign sales of counterfeit jeans where some pairs of jeans were found at defendants' premises in United States and were shipped through United States); Babbit Elecs., Inc. v. Dynascan Corp., 38 F.3d 1161, 1179 (11th Cir.1994) (Lanham Act applies to sales of cordless telephones abroad because telephones were shipped through United States free-trade zone); American Rice, Inc. v. Arkansas Rice Growers Coop. Ass'n, 701 F.2d 408, 414-15 (5th Cir.1983) (domestic processing, packaging, transporting, and distributing rice products deemed "essential steps" under *Bulova* where ultimate sale occurred abroad), Arco has shown only that AGI had some contact with United States commerce. It has not shown that, without such contact, AGI's foreign activities would be impeded or rendered more costly. The tours of refineries, failed attempt at a joint venture, and use of American banks for deposits are either irrelevant to, or of *de minimis* support for, the allegedly infringing activities.

At best, Arco has shown that AGI has a geographic presence in the United States and, by inference from that fact, that some decision-making regarding AGI's foreign activities has taken place on American soil. We do not think that such a presence suffices to trigger an extraterritorial application of the Lanham Act. The ultimate purpose of the Lanham Act pertinent to this appeal is to encourage domestic sellers to develop trademarks to assist domestic buyers in their purchasing decisions. *See* Mishawaka Rubber & Woolen Mfg. Co. v. S.S. Kresge Co., 316 U.S. 203, 205 (1942). Where (i) an alleged infringer's foreign use of a mark does not mislead American consumers in their purchases or cause them to look less favorably upon the mark; (ii) the alleged infringer does not physically use the stream of American commerce to compete with the trademark owner by, for example, manufacturing, processing, or transporting the competing product in United States commerce; and (iii) none of the alleged infringer's American activities materially support the foreign use of the mark, the mere presence of the alleged infringer in the United States will not support extraterritorial application of the Lanham Act. The presence of a foreign infringer, without more, simply does not call into play any purpose of that Act. That being the case, Arco has failed to meet *Vanity Fair's* substantial-effect requirement.

We therefore affirm.

NOTES AND QUESTIONS

(1) **Substantial Effect on U.S. Commerce.** What amounts to a "substantial effect on United States commerce"? We have seen assertions of jurisdiction based upon consumer confusion in the United States, diversion of foreign sales from an American plaintiff, or harm to the plaintiff's goodwill in the United States. *See also* Warnaco Inc. v. VF Corp., 844 F. Supp. 940, 951 (S.D.N.Y. 1994) (substantial effect based upon diversion of sales); Calvin Klein Indus., Inc. v. BFK Hong Kong, Ltd., 714 F. Supp. 78, 80 (S.D.N.Y. 1989) (substantial effect based upon threatened sale of inferior goods bearing mark); American Rice, Inc. v. Arkansas Rice Growers Coop. Ass'n, 701 F.2d 408, 414-15 (5th Cir. 1983) (diversion of sales); *see generally Warnaco*, 844 F. Supp. at 951-52. The standard, and the effect of the *ARCO* decision on the standard, was considered recently in *Piccoli A/S v. Calvin Klein Jeanswear Co.*, 19 F. Supp.2d 157 (S.D.N.Y. 1998). This case involved a battle between two distributors of Calvin Klein jeans in different territories. Piccoli A/S ("Piccoli"), a former exclusive distributor of Calvin Klein jeans in Scandinavia, brought an action under, inter alia, section 43(a) of the Lanham Act against its North American counterpart Calvin Klein Jeanswear Co. ("Jeanswear"), alleging that Jeanswear conspired with others to export Jeanswear's surplus jeans from the United States to Scandinavia and thus to destroy Piccoli's market. Piccoli had established a distribution network of upscale retailers in Scandinavia; the surplus jeans exported by Jeanswear ended up on the shelves of Scandinavian discount stores, and Piccoli began to receive letters from its upscale customers complaining of the imported jeans and canceling orders. Piccoli asserted that the defendant's export of Calvin Klein jeans to Scandinavia deceived Scandinavian retailers and consumers as to the quality and origin of the jeans. The agreement under which Jeanswear had been appointed exclusive North American distributor of Calvin Klein jeans prohibited Jeanswear from selling Calvin Klein products outside North America and also from selling to third parties whom it knew or should have known would sell the products outside North America. There was thus no argument that the defendant's alleged conduct was legitimate under its contract with Calvin Klein Inc. (the beneficial owner of the Calvin Klein trademarks) licensing the distribution of Calvin Klein jeans. Although Piccoli's false designation of origin claim sought to apply the Lanham Act to conduct, any deceptive effect of which occurred in Scandinavia, the federal district court declined to dismiss the Lanham Act claim.

The court noted that, although the first two *Vanity Fair* factors were present, there was considerable dispute concerning whether the substantial effect factor was met, and that under *ARCO*, "the absence of a substantial effect on domestic commerce would be fatal to a plaintiff's attempt to apply the Lanham Act to extraterritorial conduct regardless of whether the first two factors are satisfied." The court acknowledged that "some courts have concluded that a substantial effect on United States commerce exists also where 'the defendant's activities are supported by or related to conduct in United States commerce.'" *See, e.g.,* Levi Strauss & Co. v. Sunrise International Trading, Inc., 51 F.3d 982 (11th Cir. 1995) (granting injunction under Lanham Act barring shipment of counterfeit jeans to foreign countries based on negotiation and arrangement of shipment being made in the United States); *see also* Calvin Klein Industries, Inc. v. BFK Hong Kong, Ltd., 714 F. Supp. 78, 80 (S.D.N.Y. 1989) (noting that in *Bulova*, the Supreme Court relied in part upon defendant's purchase of component parts in the United States). However, the court expressed the view that it was not clear from the *ARCO* decision whether the line of cases finding a substantial effect on United States commerce on the basis of domestic conduct related to or supportive of deceptive actions abroad would be followed in the Second Circuit. The court read the statement by the *ARCO* court that "*Bulova* does not hold that a defendant's domestic activity, even if 'essential' to infringing activity abroad, is alone sufficient to cause a substantial effect on United States commerce" to suggest strongly that the Lanham Act does not reach conduct abroad unless it deceives U.S. consumers. But the court also noted other language in the *ARCO* opinion pointing in the other direction. In particular, the court focused upon the following passage from late in the *ARCO* opinion:

> Where (i) an alleged infringer's foreign use of a mark does not mislead American consumers in their purchases or cause them to look less favorably upon the mark; (ii) the alleged infringer does not physically use the stream of American commerce to compete with the trademark owner by, for example, manufacturing, processing, or transporting the competing product in United States commerce; and (iii) none of the alleged infringer's American activities materially support the foreign use of the mark, the mere presence of the alleged infringer in the United States will not support extraterritorial application of the Lanham Act.

The *Piccoli* court suggested that this "passage thus arguably suggests that the Lanham Act is inapplicable only where *none* of the three enumerated circumstances exists and thus that it applies where *any* is present." Because "Piccoli alleges that the defendant engaged in an organized scheme pursuant to which Jeanswear sent promotional materials to prospective purchasers which invited them to come to its U.S. showrooms to view, negotiate for and purchase Calvin Klein jeans for unrestricted international distribution" the court saw an allegation of "use of the physical stream of American commerce that was essential to the alleged infringement" and thus declined to dismiss the Lanham Act claim. Which is the better reading of the position adopted by the Second Circuit in *ARCO*? Should Piccoli be able to bring a claim under the Lanham Act? Which reading of *ARCO* fits with the other Second Circuit case law you have read?

Les Ballets Trockadero de Monte Carlo, Inc. ("the Trocks") is an all male satirical ballet troupe that sought to enjoin a competing troupe that was using a similar name to promote its alternative performances in Japan. The Trocks are based in New York, but have performed for more than twenty years in the United States and abroad. The Trocks stage approximately forty performances every summer in Japan, and Japan represents the Trocks' largest market. The competing troupe was also a New York corporation, formed by communications with dancers across the United States. The recruitment of the defendant's dancers, negotiation of their contracts, organization of music for their performances, rehearsals, and a variety of other administrative arrangements were made in the United States. Do these facts suggest that a substantial effect on U.S. commerce has been made out such as to warrant an injunction against use in Japan? *See* Les Ballets Trockadero De Monte Carlo, Inc. v. Victor Trevino, 945 F. Supp. 563 (S.D.N.Y. 1996).

(2) **Alternative "Effect" Requirements**. The Second Circuit has repeatedly affirmed its substantial effect test. *See, e.g., Totalplan Corp.*, 14 F.3d at 830; Sterling Drug Inc. v. Bayer AG, 14 F.3d 733, 746 (2d Cir. 1994). The Ninth Circuit has regularly applied the test used in *Ocean Garden. See, e.g.,* Wells Fargo & Co. v. Wells Fargo Express Co., 556 F.2d 406 (9th Cir. 1977) (rejecting the "substantial" effect test adopted by the Second Circuit, and approving the "some" effect test previously rejected by the Second Circuit as part of the comparable test used to determine extraterritorial reach of the federal antitrust laws); Reebok Int'l, Ltd. v. Marnatech Enters., Inc., 970 F.2d 552, 554 (9th Cir. 1992). As the *Totalplan* court acknowledged, the Fifth Circuit has (like the Ninth Circuit) also taken a more assertive attitude toward the assertion of jurisdiction over extraterritorial activities and required only "some effect" on U.S. commerce. *See* American Rice, Inc. v. Arkansas Rice Growers, 701 F.2d 408 (5th Cir. 1983); *see also* Nintendo of Am., Inc. v. Aeropower Co., 34 F.3d 246, 250-51 (4th Cir. 1994) (requiring "significant effect" on U.S. commerce).

(3) **The Relevance of Consumers.** In *Modus Vivendi plc v. Keen (World Marketing)* (High Court) (UK), reported at 18 EUR. INTELL. PROP. REV. N-82 (1996), the U.K. courts found a defendant liable for passing off manufacturing products bearing an infringing trade dress (packaging for butane gas cans) in England notwithstanding that the products were sold only in China under an export contract. In determining whether consumers would be confused such as to provide relief under the English law of passing off, the Court focused on the consumers in China. This was relevant because the addition of a different house mark on the defendant's products was of no assistance when very few of the purchasers read English; in such circumstances, the visual similarity of the packaging (trade dress, or "get-up" in English law terminology) was far more important. Should the location of consumers who are alleged to be confused be taken into account in deciding whether relief should be granted? Is this question relevant to the issue of adjudicatory jurisdiction?

(4) **The Relevance of Intent.** Should the conscious efforts of the defendant to affect the U.S. market affect the assertion of extraterritorial jurisdiction? *See* Reebok Int'l, Ltd. v. Marnatech Enters., Inc., 970 F.2d 552 (9th Cir. 1992). In *Aerogroup Int'l, supra*, the court based its conclusion of substantial effect upon U.S. commerce not only upon diverted sales in Canada but also on the fact that

the defendant's activities

> [were] conducted almost exclusively in the United States and that it engaged in the same infringing activities in the United States regardless of whether its customers were American or Canadian. It solicited these customers at shoe shows in the United States, used the same factories for the manufacturing of the shoes, offered its American and Canadian customers the same shoe styles, and was paid by both American and Canadian customers on a commission basis. . . [I]t was blind to national borders, and used the same methods and the same systems of operation to sell shoes and infringe [the plaintiff's] trademark rights in both Canada and the United States. . . Marlboro conducted its business almost exclusively within the United States and used the instrumentalities of American commerce to profit at [plaintiff's] expense without regard to where the sales of shoes ultimately occurred . . . .

Does such wilful failure to avoid the U.S. market give rise to the same arguments for extraterritorial jurisdiction?

Sterling Drug, Inc. v. Bayer AG, 14 F.3d 733 (2d Cir. 1994). The defendant, Bayer AG, was a German company that owned rights to the BAYER mark in most countries of the world (including Germany), but not the United States. The U.S. rights were owned by the plaintiff, Sterling Drug. Sterling brought an action to restrain certain uses of the mark BAYER by the defendant, alleging both trademark infringement and violation of agreements between the parties regarding the use of the mark in the United States. The district court found that Bayer violated both Sterling's contract and trademark rights, and enjoined Bayer AG and its subsidiaries from using the BAYER mark in the United States, or abroad if such foreign use might make its way to the American public (for example, in press releases likely to be reported on in the United States, or in advertisements in newspapers with significant U.S. distribution). Bayer appealed, arguing that the injunction's extraterritorial provisions interfered impermissibly with its rights under foreign laws, and impaired "the ability of one of Europe's largest corporations to conduct its everyday business in its home country and around the world." The government of Germany appeared as amicus curiae and contended that the extraterritorial prohibitions of the injunction failed to respect its sovereign rights. The Court of Appeals for the Second Circuit vacated the injunction's extraterritorial provisions because the district court had not considered whether the *Vanity Fair* factors supported the extraterritorial aspects of the injunction. The court, however, remanded the case to the district court rather than simply revise the injunction to eliminate its extraterritorial provisions. In so doing, the court indicated some flexibility toward the application of the *Vanity Fair* factors:

[I]f we applied the *Vanity Fair* test mechanically to the instant case, we would forbid the application of the Lanham Act abroad against a foreign corporation that holds superior rights to the mark under foreign law. But such an unrefined application of that case might mean that we fail to preserve the Lanham Act's goals of protecting American consumers against confusion, and protecting holders of American trademarks against misappropriation of their marks. A more careful application of *Vanity Fair* is necessary because the instant case is not on all fours with *Vanity Fair*. In *Vanity Fair*, the plaintiff sought a *blanket prohibition* against the Canadian retailer's use of "Vanity Fair" in connection with the sale of defendant's products in Canada. Sterling, on the other hand, seeks to enjoin only those uses of the "Bayer" mark abroad that are likely to make their way to American consumers.[7] Sterling is not concerned with Bayer AG's use of the mark abroad so long as that use does not enter the channels of international communication that lead to the United States. While the stringent *Vanity Fair* test is appropriate when the plaintiff seeks an absolute bar against a corporation's use of its mark outside our borders, that test is unnecessarily demanding when the plaintiff seeks the more modest goal of limiting foreign uses that reach the United States. Though Congress did not intend the Lanham Act to be used as a sword to eviscerate completely a foreign corporation's foreign trademark, it did intend the Act to be used as a shield against foreign uses that have significant trademark-impairing effects upon American commerce.

The court also offered some guidance to the district court:

In establishing the parameters of injunctive relief in the case of lawful concurrent users, a court must take account of the realities of the marketplace." [cit]. In today's global economy, where a foreign TV advertisement might be available by satellite to U.S. households, not every activity of a foreign corporation with any tendency to create some confusion among American consumers can be prohibited by the extraterritorial reach of a District Court's injunction. . . . Upon remand, the District Court may grant an extraterritorial injunction carefully crafted to prohibit only those foreign uses of the mark by Bayer AG that are likely to have significant trademark-impairing effects on United States commerce. If the Court finds that Bayer AG's use of the mark abroad carries such significant effects in the United States, the District Court may require Bayer AG to take

---

[7]Sterling seizes upon this distinction to argue that the instant injunction is therefore not an "extraterritorial" application of the Lanham Act at all. Sterling conflates the effect of the challenged conduct with the effect of the challenged injunction. While it is true that the injunction seeks to reach only the domestic effects of Bayer's conduct, it does so through the mechanism of an extraterritorial injunction, i.e., one that prohibits Bayer AG from undertaking certain actions outside U.S. borders. The injunction has provisions that are clearly extraterritorial, including, for example, one that prohibits Bayer AG from advertising in foreign magazines such as Der Spiegel because their American circulations exceed 5,000 copies.

appropriate precautions against using the mark in international media in ways that might create confusion among United States consumers as to the source of "Bayer" pharmaceutical products in the United States. It might be appropriate, to take examples offered by appellee, to prevent Bayer AG from placing a full-page "Bayer" advertisement in the U.S. edition of a foreign magazine or newspaper, or inviting representatives of the U.S. press to an offshore briefing in which Bayer AG distributed materials describing "Bayer's" analgesics products for publication in the U.S. On the other hand, it might be inappropriate, to take examples offered by the *amicus curiae*, to leave the injunction so broad as to ban the announcement of new medical research in *Lancet*, or an employment notice in *Handelsblatt*, or a press conference in England to publicize a new over-the-counter remedy developed in the United States, or sponsorship of a German soccer team if that team might appear, wearing "Bayer" jerseys, on a television broadcast carried by an American sports cable channel.

In fashioning the injunction, the Court should "balanc[e] . . . the equities to reach an appropriate result protective of the interests of both parties." [cit.] Where, as in the instant case, both parties have legitimate interests, consideration of those interests must receive especially sensitive accommodation in the international context. While Bayer AG suggests that we must accept these conflicts as the unavoidable result of an international community of nations in which each nation exercises the power to grant trademark rights, we prefer to allow the District Court to fashion an appropriately limited injunction with only those extraterritorial provisions reasonably necessary to protect against significant trademark-impairing effects on American commerce.

NOTES AND QUESTIONS

(1) **Liberalizing the *Vanity Fair* Analysis?** To what extent do the social and economic circumstances described by the *Sterling Drug* court warrant a change in the courts' attitude to the extraterritorial application of the Lanham Act? Why should the reach of the Lanham Act be extended at a time when the reach of the Copyright Act has arguably been restricted by such developments as the overruling of *Peter Starr* by the Ninth Circuit in *Subafilms*? Why might courts be more willing to apply the Lanham Act extraterritorially than the Copyright Act? *See* 15 U.S.C. § 1127. One writer has suggested that the difference can be explained by the fact that extraterritorial application of copyright laws would effectively deprive the marketplace of something that local law has provided shall be available, whereas extraterritorial application of trademark laws would deprive the local marketplace only of the symbol used to market the product, not the product itself. *See* David R. Toraya, Note, *Federal*

Jurisdiction over Foreign Copyright Infringement Action—An Unsolicited Reply to Professor Nimmer, 70 CORNELL L. REV. 1165, 1171-72 n.41 (1985). Is this explanation sufficient (or indeed accurate in light of modern trademark law)? Is there a difference, as the court suggests, between the "blanket" relief granted in *Vanity Fair* and the relief sought by the plaintiff in *Sterling Drug*? If you were the district court judge on remand, what relief would you consider appropriate?

(2) **Truly an Effects Test?** Does *Sterling Drug* suggest that the Second Circuit is moving towards a test based upon effects rather than conduct in the United States? Might that be appropriate? What dangers (or advantages) might such a test bring?

PLAYBOY ENTERS, INC. v. CHUCKLEBERRY PUB., INC.

939 F. Supp. 1032 (S.D.N.Y. 1996)

SHIRA SCHIENDLIN, DISTRICT JUDGE:

Plaintiff, Playboy Enterprises, Inc. ("PEI"), has moved for a finding of contempt against Defendant, Tattilo Editrice, S.p.A. ("Tattilo"). PEI alleges that by operating an Internet site from Italy under the PLAYMEN label, Tattilo has violated a judgment dated June 26, 1981, enjoining it from publishing, printing, distributing or selling in the United States an English language male sophisticate magazine under the name "PLAYMEN" ("Injunction").

For the reasons enunciated below, the motion is granted. . . .

I. Facts

In 1967, Tattilo began publishing a male sophisticate magazine in Italy under the name PLAYMEN. Although the magazine carried an English title, it was written entirely in Italian. In July 1979, Tattilo announced plans to publish an English language version of PLAYMEN in the United States. Shortly thereafter, PEI brought suit against Tattilo to enjoin Tattilo's use of the name PLAYMEN in connection with a male sophisticate magazine and related products. PEI has published the well-known male entertainment magazine "PLAYBOY" since 1953, which is sold throughout the world in a multitude of foreign languages. Plaintiff's suit for injunctive relief alleged trademark infringement, false designation of origin, unfair competition based on infringement of plaintiff's common law trademark rights, and violations of the New York Anti-Dilution Statute.

A permanent injunction was awarded on April 1, 1981, and a judgment subsequently entered on June 26, 1981, permanently enjoining Tattilo from:

. . . .

c. using "PLAYBOY", "PLAYMEN" or any other word confusingly similar with either such word in or as part of any trademark, service mark, brand name, trade name or other business or commercial designation, in connection with the sale, offering for sale or distributing in the United States, importing into or exporting from the United States, English language publications and related products.

PEI was similarly successful in enjoining the use of the PLAYMEN name in the courts of England, France and West Germany. However, the Italian courts ruled that "lexically" PLAYBOY was a weak mark and not entitled to protection in that country. The publication of PLAYMEN in Italy continues to the present day.

On approximately January 22, 1996, PEI discovered that Tattilo had created an Internet site featuring the PLAYMEN name. This Internet site makes available images of the cover of the Italian magazine, as well as its "Women of the Month" feature and several other sexually explicit photographic images. Users of the Internet site also receive "special discounts" on other Tattilo products, such as CD ROMs and Photo CDs. Tattilo created this site by uploading these images onto a World Wide Web server located in Italy. These images can be accessed at the Internet address http://www.playmen.it.[3]

Two distinct services are available on the PLAYMEN Internet site. "PLAYMEN Lite" is available without a paid subscription, allowing users of the Internet to view moderately explicit images via computer. It appears that the main (if not sole) purpose of the PLAYMEN Lite service is to allow prospective users to experience a less explicit version of the PLAYMEN product before committing to purchasing a subscription. In addition, the PLAYMEN Internet site offers the more sexually explicit service called "PLAYMEN Pro." PLAYMEN Pro is available only to users who have paid the subscription price.

In order to access the Lite version of the PLAYMEN Internet service, the prospective user must first contact Tattilo. The user will then receive a temporary user name and password via e-mail. To subscribe to PLAYMEN Pro, the prospective user must fill out a form and send it via fax to Tattilo. Within 24 hours, the user receives by e-mail a unique password and login name that enable the user to browse the PLAYMEN Pro service.

The PLAYMEN Internet site is widely available to patrons living in the United States. More to the point, anyone in the United States with access to the Internet has the capacity to browse the PLAYMEN Internet site, review, and obtain print and electronic copies of sexually explicit pages of PLAYMEN magazine. All that is required to establish the account is the brief contact with Tattilo outlined above.

. . . .

III. Discussion

The primary issue before the Court is whether the Defendant distributed or

---

[3] . . . it"—such as appears in the PLAYMEN Internet site address—indicates that the accessed computer is located in Italy.

sold the PLAYMEN magazine in the United States when it established an Internet site containing pictorial images under the PLAYMEN name.[4]

A. Whether the Injunction Could Have Been Violated

As an initial matter, the question arises whether a fifteen-year-old injunction prohibiting certain traditional publishing activities should be applied to the recent development of cyberspace and the Internet. If the dissemination of information over the Internet, in any form, cannot constitute a violation of the Injunction, then the inquiry is over.

[The court rejected the argument that because the case involved new technology that did not exist when the Injunction was issued the complained of activities cannot be "clearly and unambiguously" barred.]

[T]hat this use of the images could not have been contemplated by the parties does not prevent the Injunction from applying to the modern technology of the Internet and the World Wide Web. The purpose behind the Injunction was to restrict the ability of Defendant to distribute its product in the United States, where it has been found to infringe upon the copyright of Playboy. Allowing the Defendant to contravene the clear intent of the Injunction by permitting it to distribute its pictorial images over the Internet would emasculate the Injunction. The Injunction's failure to refer to the Internet by name does not limit its applicability to this new medium. Injunctions entered before the recent explosion of computer technology must continue to have meaning.

. . . .

B. Whether the Injunction Was Violated

[The court noted that three conditions must be met to support a finding of a violation of subsection 1 (c) of the Injunction. The first two clearly were: the word PLAYMEN had been used as a trade name or business or commercial designation of the Internet site, both in the URL and on the site's home page; and the name had been used in connection with an English language publication or related product (although a portion of the text was written in Italian, enough sections appeared in English to allow an English-speaking user to navigate the site with ease). The court acknowledged that the third condition—a distribution or sale to have taken place within the United States—was analytically more difficult. However, applying an interpretation of "distribution" developed in two cases interpreting the meaning of that term in the Copyright Act, the court held that there was a distribution.]

Here, Defendant does more than simply provide access to the Internet. It also provides its own services, PLAYMEN Lite and PLAYMEN Pro, and supplies the

---

[4]Defendant first argues that this Court has neither personal nor subject matter jurisdiction to determine the issues raised herein. Tattilo is an Italian corporation with no agent or office within the United States; it does not sell, distribute, publish or advertise for its text-based Italian PLAYMEN magazine in this country. However, this Court retained jurisdiction over Defendant for the purposes of enforcing the 1981 Injunction.

content for these services. Moreover, as in *Frena* [the copyright case], these pictorial images can be downloaded to and stored upon the computers of subscribers to the service. In fact, Defendant actively invites such use: the Internet site allows the user to decide between viewing and downloading the images. Thus this use of Defendant's Internet site constitutes a distribution.

In order to violate the Injunction, however, Defendant must distribute the pictorial images within the United States. Defendant argues that it is merely posting pictorial images on a computer server in Italy, rather than distributing those images to anyone within the United States. A computer operator wishing to view these images must, in effect, transport himself to Italy to view Tattilo's pictorial displays. The use of the Internet is akin to boarding a plane, landing in Italy, and purchasing a copy of PLAYMEN magazine, an activity permitted under Italian law. Thus Defendant argues that its publication of pictorial images over the Internet cannot be barred by the Injunction despite the fact that computer operators can view these pictorial images in the United States.

Once more, I disagree. Defendant has actively solicited United States customers to its Internet site, and in doing so has distributed its product within the United States. When a potential subscriber faxes the required form to Tattilo, he receives back via e-mail a password and user name. By this process, Tattilo distributes its product within the United States.

Defendant's analogy of "flying to Italy" to purchase a copy of the PLAYMEN magazine is inapposite. Tattilo may of course maintain its Italian Internet site. The Internet is a world-wide phenomenon, accessible from every corner of the globe. Tattilo cannot be prohibited from operating its Internet site merely because the site is accessible from within one country in which its product is banned. To hold otherwise "would be tantamount to a declaration that this Court, and every other court throughout the world, may assert jurisdiction over all information providers on the global World Wide Web." Such a holding would have a devastating impact on those who use this global service. The Internet deserves special protection as a place where public discourse may be conducted without regard to nationality, religion, sex, age, or to monitors of community standards of decency. *See generally* American Civil Liberties Union v. Reno, 1996 U.S. Dist. LEXIS 7919, Civ. A. 96-963, 1996 WL 311865 (E.D. Pa. June 11, 1996).

However, this special protection does not extend to ignoring court orders and injunctions. If it did, injunctions would cease to have meaning and intellectual property would no longer be adequately protected. In the absence of enforcement, intellectual property laws could be easily circumvented through the creation of Internet sites that permit the very distribution that has been enjoined. Our long-standing system of intellectual property protections has encouraged creative minds to be productive. Diluting those protections may discourage that creativity.

While this Court has neither the jurisdiction nor the desire to prohibit the creation of Internet sites around the globe, it may prohibit access to those sites in this country. Therefore, while Tattilo may continue to operate its Internet site, it must refrain from accepting subscriptions from customers living in the United States. In accord with this holding, an Italian customer who subsequently moves to the United States may maintain his or her subscription to the Internet site.

I therefore conclude that Tattilo has violated subsection 1(c) of the Injunction by using its PLAYMEN Internet site to distribute its products in the United States. The clear intent of the Injunction was to prohibit Tattilo from selling its PLAYMEN magazine and related products to United States customers. Tattilo has knowingly attempted to circumvent the Injunction by selling its products over the Internet. Cyberspace is not a "safe haven" from which Tattilo may flout the Court's Injunction.

. . . .

Tattilo is required, within two weeks of the date of this Order, to: (1) either shut down its Internet site completely or refrain from accepting any new subscriptions from customers residing in the United States; (2) invalidate the user names and passwords to the Internet site previously purchased by United States customers; (3) refund to its United States customers the remaining unused portions of their subscriptions; (4) remit to PEI all gross profits earned from subscriptions to its Internet service by customers in the United States; (5) remit to PEI all gross profits earned from the sale of goods and services advertised on its PLAYMEN Internet service to customers in the United States; (6) revise its Internet site to indicate that all subscription requests from potential United States customers will be denied; and (7) remit to PEI its costs and attorney's fees incurred in making this application. If these conditions have not been met within the stated two-week period, Tattilo shall pay to PEI a fine of $ 1,000 each day thereafter until it fully complies with this Order.

NOTES AND QUESTIONS

(1) **Motion for Reconsideration.** On July 12, 1996, Judge Schiendlin denied defendants' request to amend her order. Defendant argued that "the Court misconstrued the process by which a user of the Internet site accesses PLAYMEN Lite, resulting in the incorrect determination that the PLAYMEN Lite service violated the Injunction." Tattilo claimed that "not only is a password not necessary to peruse the PLAYMEN Lite service, but in reality no contact with Tattilo is required for a potential user to access PLAYMEN Lite." The Court reaffirmed its original order, concluding that:

> while the Opinion held that deliberate and intentional contact with the United States was established based on the requirement that prospective customers fax subscription forms to Italy, and that user names and IDs are sent to United States customers from Italy, this is not the only basis for finding that a distribution occurred within the United States. The PLAYMEN Lite service allows (indeed invites) a user to download Tattilo's pictorial images onto his or her home computer. PLAYMEN Lite can thus be viewed as an 'advertisement' by which Tattilo distributes its pictorial images throughout the United States. That the

local user 'pulls' these images from Tattilo's computer in Italy, as opposed to Tattilo 'sending' them to this country, is irrelevant. By inviting United States users to download these images, Tattilo is causing and contributing to their distribution within the United States.

Judge Schiendlin held that "PLAYMEN Lite represents a free distribution of Tattilo's product, a product which has been banned in this country since the 1981 Injunction. I decline to hold that Tattilo may maintain some portion of its service but shut down other portions of its Internet site." Thus, she ordered that:

> Tattilo must either shut down PLAYMEN Lite completely or prohibit United States users from accessing the site in the future. The simplest method of prohibiting access by United States users is to adopt a method of access similar to the one which I had believed was already in place: require users of the PLAYMEN Lite service to acquire free passwords and user IDs in order to access the site. In this way, users residing in the United States can be filtered out and refused access.[4]

PEI also asked Judge Schiendlin to amend her judgment and order Tattilo to refrain from "publishing, promoting and selling in the English language PLAYMEN publications and related products." The court also denied this motion to amend, noting that the court had "no power to restrict Tattilo from providing its PLAYMEN Internet service outside the United States. There are many English speaking countries throughout the world. This court has no jurisdiction to control Tattilo's activities in those countries. As a result, PEI's motion for an order prohibiting Tattilo from using English on its Internet site is denied."

(2) **Conflicts with Non-Exclusive Foreign Rights.** If the defendant has (as in *Playboy*) no foreign trademark rights in the term but does have the right to use the term in a foreign country (e.g., because the courts or trademark office in the foreign country have determined that a term is generic, descriptive or otherwise unprotectable, and thus can be used by any trader) should this affect the *Vanity Fair* analysis? Are *exclusive* rights to use a mark required for this factor to favor the defendant? *Cf.* Libbey Glass, Inc. v. Oneida, Inc., 61 F. Supp.2d 720, 723 (N.D. Ohio 1999) ("because [the Turkish defendant] has not shown a registration under Turkish law, there is no evidence to support the proposition that Turkey has an interest in this litigation that conflicts with the application of the Lanham Act"). The *Vanity Fair* court articulated the third *Bulova* factor as whether there was a "conflict with trademark rights established by foreign law." 234 F.2d at 642. Is there a difference between a conflict with foreign trademark *law* and foreign trademark *rights*?

---

[4]If technology cannot identify the country of origin of e-mail addresses, these passwords and user IDs should be sent by mail. Only in this way can the Court be assured that United States users are not accidentally permitted access to PLAYMEN Lite.

GRAEME B. DINWOODIE, PRIVATE INTERNATIONAL ASPECTS OF THE PROTECTION OF TRADEMARKS (2001)
WIPO Doc. No. WIPO/PIL/01/4

Cyberspace might be regarded as akin to any new territory that one, and only one, of several existing mark owners may add to their existing territories. But the scenario presented by cyberspace is different in at least one important way: the ownership of the exclusive right to use the mark in this new territory—cyberspace—may impinge upon the ability of the respective mark owners to exercise fully the rights that they already own in existing territories. If Producer X owns the mark ORANGE for computers in Country A and Producer Y owns that same mark in Country B, acquisition of the rights in Country C determines only which of the two producers can now market their goods in that new country. But if the new territory for which exclusive rights are granted is not Country C, but cyberspace, the exclusive right to use the mark online will affect the ability of the respective producers to use the marks that each owns in Country A or Country B.

. . . .

Courts in several countries have adopted expansive interpretations of the reach of domestic trademark rights in the online context. For example, some courts have reasoned that the accessibility in their country of a foreign web site that contains trademarks involves use of those marks in their country. If there were widespread adoption of the principle that prescriptive jurisdiction of a particular country can be premised upon the mere accessibility of a web site in that country, then a producer would require to clear its trademark use in every country of the world. With respect to future marks, this would significantly increase the cost of trademarks, and hence of goods to consumers. It would convert truly local uses into global uses, giving rise to innumerable conflicts, causing the depletion of available marks, and eviscerating the concept of local use through which trademark law has facilitated co-existence of marks in the past.

With respect to existing marks, this might cause producers currently operating offline with legitimately acquired trademark rights from expanding into the online environment lest they interfere with competing rights in other countries. As suggested above, one might view this merely as akin to the inability to expand globally into other geographic markets where competing mark ownership exists. But in this context, the inability to expand online effectively regulates domestic conduct (where the producer owns the trademark) as well as the foreign market (where some other party owns the mark). The foreign mark ownership thus effectively regulates the producer's use in the domestic market where the producer has rights, highlighting the extraterritorial effects that will flow from broad trademark rights, and broad assertions of adjudicative and prescriptive jurisdiction, in this context. All that the domestic producer acquires through ownership of the domestic rights is the corresponding capacity (assuming that the courts where the domestic producer owns rights are similarly intrusive) to prevent the foreign producer from using its legitimate foreign rights online for its own domestic purposes. Trademark rights are thus reduced to their most destructive form, namely, a mutual ability to undermine the sales efforts of competitors in other countries by blocking certain commercially significant uses. This "mutual blocking" capacity is neither efficient nor a positive contribution to the globalization of markets or the development of ecommerce.

. . . .

The problems that the internet has caused private international trademark law have recently been addressed by the WIPO Standing Committee on the Law of Trademarks, Industrial Designs and Geographical Indications (the "SCT"). In particular, over the past two years the Committee has sought to harmonize national approaches to the question of "use" of marks on the internet, and has therefore developed a draft set of provisions on the concept of "use." In use-based systems, such as the United States, the concept is obviously central to the acquisition of rights. But even in registration-based systems, the maintenance and enforcement of rights may require use of the mark by the producer, and infringement depends upon use of the mark by the defendant. Use is central to trademark law, whether in a use-based or registration-based system.

The SCT proposal consists of two primary components. Under the first component, use of the sign on the internet would only be treated as use in any particular state for the various purposes identified above if the use of the sign has a "commercial effect" in that state. The proposal further details the factors relevant to a determination whether a sign has a commercial effect in a state. The factors are non-exhaustive and include whether the user is doing or planning to do business in a particular state (although use of the sign can have a commercial effect in a country without the user doing business there). The language and currency used on the web site where the mark is used, as well as any explicit disclaimer of the ability to delivery goods in a particular state, would be relevant. Actual restraints on the ability of the producer to deliver goods (for example, regulatory hurdles) would also provide guidance, as would whether the web site had actually been visited by persons from a particular state. The interactivity of the web site might also be an important factor.

. . . .

The second component of the SCT proposal limits the liability of the owner of trademark rights (or a good faith user entitled to use a mark) in one country who uses the mark online in a way that *has* a commercial effect in another state. In particular, such a mark owner will not be liable to the mark owner in that other state prior to receiving a "notification of infringement" provided that its rights were not acquired in bad faith and that contact details are provided on the web site where the sign is displayed. Even upon receiving a notification, the user could avoid liability by expeditiously taking "reasonable measures which are effective to avoid commercial effect in the Member State" in question and to avoid confusion with the mark owner in that country. If those steps include the use of a disclaimer in accordance with the terms of Section 12 of the draft provisions, the user is conclusively presumed to have satisfied the standard. Such disclaimers should, *inter alia,* make clear that the user of the sign does not intend to deliver goods to the particular member state where a conflicting right exists and that he has no relationship with the owner of the conflicting right.

———————

NOTES AND QUESTIONS

(1) **U.S. Law and the SCT Resolution.** The SCT resolution on "use" on the Internet was finalized in March 2001, and will be voted on by the WIPO General Assemblies in September 2001. As with other recent initiatives of the committee, it will be a non-binding resolution. Does U.S. law comport with the standards set forth in the proposal? How would *Playboy* be decided under the standards set out in the proposal? If U.S. law is inconsistent with those standards, how would U.S. law have to be changed? Would you support such a change? Should the currency used to price products on the site be relevant? Does a pricing in U.S. dollars indicate an intent to target and have a commercial effect in the United States? *See* Euromarket Designs, Inc. v. Crate & Barrel Ltd., 96 F. Supp.2d 824, 837 (N.D. Ill. 2000). What does the use of the English language on a web site suggest?

(2) **Limits on Injunctive Relief.** The SCT proposal also contains provisions regarding relief to be granted in the context of online infringement involving competing marks. The proposals would instruct national courts granting a remedy against internet use to consider the effect that any injunction would have in other states. Any remedy must be proportionate to the commercial effect of the use in the member state in question. In particular, the remedies should not force a good faith user who has rights to use a mark in one country with which it has a connection to wholly abandon use of the mark on the internet if it has acted in good faith. Such global injunctions are expressly prohibited by section 15. The draft provisions contain examples of alternative remedial options (such as gateway web pages), which have grown out of practice and experience over the past few years. When might global injunctions be appropriate? Would use of technology (such as software that restricted access according to geographical origin) to "reterritorialize" the internet be an appropriate means of resolving these problems of national marks in an inherently non-national setting? Are there any costs associated with relying on such technological fixes?

(3) **Beneficiaries of the SCT Limitations on Liability**. A significant point of debate during the March 2001 SCT meeting was whether the benefit of both the "notice and avoidance of conflict" provision and the limitations on injunctive relief should be available to users "with rights in a mark" in one country or users "entitled to use a mark" in one country. What is the significance of this distinction? Who benefits from the latter formulation but not the former? Article 9 of the draft resolution makes the benefits of the provisions available to good faith users "permitted to use the sign, in the manner in which it is being used on the internet, under the law of [a country] to which the user has a close connection." What does this phrase mean? Who does it cover?

[C]   Patent Law

A basic premise of the patent right has always been the principle of territoriality. In the United States, for example, 35 U.S.C. § 261 establishes that patents have the attributes of personal property and that "[t]he applicant, patentee, or his assigns or legal representatives may. . . convey an exclusive right under his application for patent, or patents, *to the whole or any specified part of the United States*." Likewise, § 271(a) establishes that "whoever without authority makes, uses, offers to sell, or sells any patented invention, *within the United States* or imports *into the United States* any patented invention during the term of the patent therefor, infringes the patent." Section 154(a)(1) of the Patent Act mandates that the contents of the patent must make the territorial provisions of the patent grant explicit:

> (a)(1) Contents. Every patent shall contain a short title of the invention and a grant to the patentee, his heirs or assigns, of the right to exclude others from making, using, offering for sale, or selling the invention *throughout the United States* or importing the invention *into the United States*, and, if the invention is a process, of the right to exclude others from using, offering for sale or selling *throughout the United States, or importing into the United States*, products made by that process, referring to the specification for the particulars thereof.

One authority has recently observed that "of the three principal forms of intellectual property, patent rights are the most explicitly territorial." Donald S. Chisum, *Normative and Empirical Territoriality in Intellectual Property: Lessons from Patent Law*, 37 VA. J. INT'L L. 603, 605 (1997). "Patents are considered territorial, having legal effect only in the territory of the issuing state. Accordingly, the United States has no jurisdiction to apply its law to validate or invalidate a foreign patent, regardless of the origin of the invention, or the nationality, residence, or principal place of business of the holder of the patent or of any licensee." RESTATEMENT (THIRD) OF THE FOREIGN RELATIONS LAW OF THE UNITED STATES, § 415, cmt i. Americans are sensitive to imposition of foreign standards on U.S. patent law, stressing the uniqueness and long history of U.S. patent traditions. Along with national treatment and minimum standards, territoriality is a core governing principle of patent protection, and (as we have seen in Chapters 3 and 6) the concept of international patent rights is still incipient if not inchoate.

But inchoate concepts can take or be given more concrete form with great rapidity under the proper historical circumstances. Technological advances do not recognize national boundaries. The following case discusses term and territorial limits on a U.S. patent owner's right to exclude a competitor from activities within the bounds of a claimed invention covered by a U.S. patent.

JOHNS HOPKINS UNIVERSITY, et al. v. CELLPRO, INC.
152 F.3d 1342 (Fed. Cir. 1998)

LOURIE, CIRCUIT JUDGE:

. . . .

E. The Repatriation Order

CellPro's final argument is that the court exceeded the scope of its power when it ordered the repatriation and destruction of the six vials that it exported to its business partner, Biomira, in Canada, as well as cloned vials and antibodies produced therefrom. CellPro contends that it has not committed an infringing act with respect to the exported vials. CellPro summarizes its activities as follows: it produced approximately 100 vials of 12.8 hybridoma to create a United States master cell bank prior to the issuance of the '204 patent, it exported six of those vials to Canada after issuance, and it used those vials in Canada to supply markets outside of the United States. CellPro asserts that none of these acts—pre-issuance manufacture, export, or use outside of the United States—constitutes infringement under 35 U.S.C. § 271, and accordingly that such acts are beyond the scope of the court's equitable powers.

Hopkins responds that the district court's order was properly predicated on the determination that CellPro used (i.e., by cloning or testing) other vials from its United States cell bank in the United States after the issuance of the patent and thereby infringed with respect to the United States cell bank "as a whole." Hopkins asserts that the injunctive power of the district courts is not limited to the prohibition of those activities that constitute patent infringement, but also extends to prohibitions necessary in order to fashion a meaningful remedy for past infringement. Hopkins argues that repatriation in this case is such a meaningful remedy and will prevent CellPro from unfairly capitalizing upon its infringement.

Section 283 of the Patent Code empowers the courts to "grant injunctions in accordance with the principles of equity to prevent the violation of any right secured by patent, on such terms as the court deems reasonable." 35 U.S.C. § 283 (1994). In accordance with the clear wording of this section, "an injunction is only proper to the extent it is 'to prevent the violation of any right secured by patent.'" A "necessary predicate" for the issuance of a permanent injunction is therefore a determination of infringement. *Id.* When deciding whether a district court abused the discretion provided by Section 283, we are mindful of the fact that the district courts are in the best position to fashion an injunction. *See* Joy Techs., Inc. v. Flakt, Inc., 6 F.3d 770, 777 (Fed. Cir. 1993) (citation omitted). However, judicial restraint of lawful noninfringing activities must be avoided. *See id.* (citing Deepsouth Packing Co. v. Laitram Corp., 406 U.S. 518, 529-31 (1972)).

We agree with CellPro that the district court abused its discretion in ordering the repatriation and destruction of the exported vials. The repatriation aspect of the order does not enjoin activities that either have infringed the '204 patent or are likely to do so and thus does not prevent infringement—the proper purpose of an injunction under Section 283. It is clear that the six vials standing alone have not infringed the '204 patent. Mere possession of a product which becomes covered by a subsequently issued patent does not constitute an infringement of that patent until the product is used, sold, or offered for sale in the United States during the term of the patent. *See* Cohen v. United States, 487 F.2d 525 (1973); Columbia & N.R.R. Co. v. Chandler, 241 F. 261 (9th Cir. 1917) (holding that, while the patentee could not recover damages for the manufacture of infringing trucks prior to the issuance of the patent, it did not follow "that the trucks were set free from the monopoly of the patent, and could thereafter be used, without liability to the inventor"); *see also* Hoover Group, Inc. v. Custom Metalcraft, Inc., 66 F.3d 299, 304 (Fed. Cir. 1995) ("[The patentee] may of course obtain damages only for acts of infringement after the issuance of the patent."). Likewise, neither export from the United States nor use in a foreign country of a product covered by a United States patent constitutes infringement. *See* 35 U.S.C. § 271(a) (1994) ("[W]hoever without authority makes, uses, offers to sell, or sells any patented invention, within the United States or imports into the United States any patented invention during the term of the patent therefor, infringes the patent."); *see also* Paper Converting Mach. Co. v. Magna-Graphics Corp., 745 F.2d 11, 16 (Fed. Cir. 1984) ("[B]y the terms of the patent grant, no activity other than the unauthorized making, using, or selling of the claimed invention can constitute direct infringement of a patent, *no matter* how great the adverse impact of that activity on the economic value of a patent.") (emphasis in original).

That CellPro used other vials from the cell bank in an infringing manner in the United States does not taint the six exported vials with infringement.[31] The exported vials were not "guilty by association." One may consider the pre-issuance manufacture of two machines, one of which is used after the patent is issued and the other of which is exported. An injunction requiring return of the exported machine, which was never made, used, or sold during the term of the patent in the United States, is beyond the scope of Section 283 and hence an abuse of discretion. The same principle applies here to the vials exported to Canada. Accordingly, the court's conclusion that use of some of the vials of the cell bank constituted a use of the cell bank "as a whole" as a means of justifying its repatriation order was an abuse of discretion.

Moreover, there is also no evidentiary basis for concluding that the district court's order was necessary to prevent CellPro from committing further infringing activities. An injunction under Section 283 can reach extraterritorial activities such as those at issue here, even if these activities do not themselves constitute infringement. It is necessary however that the injunction prevent

---

[31]We do not suggest, and neither party argues, that the court had no injunctive power with respect to those vials which were not exported but which were also not used in the United States. That these vials, like the exported vials, did not infringe does not free them from the court's equitable power under Section 283. Because CellPro had used some of its vials in the United States, a clear act of infringement, its propensity to infringe has been sufficiently established such that the court could conclude that enjoining the use of United States-based vials was necessary to prevent infringement.

infringement of a United States patent. For example, in Spindelfabrik Suessen-Schurr v. Schubert & Salzer, 903 F.2d 1568 (Fed. Cir. 1990), the infringer argued that the district court's injunction "impermissibly extend[ed] the reach of American patent law beyond the boundaries of the United States" because it prohibited the infringer from making, in Germany, machines "for use in the United States" and machines "destined for delivery to the United States." This court held that the injunction was "a reasonable and permissible endeavor to prevent infringement in the United States and not a prohibited extra-territorial application of American patent law. They were well within the district court's authority." *Id.* at 1578.

The record in this case does not, as in *Spindelfabrik*, suggest that the exported vials will be used in a manner which will infringe the patent. CellPro has stipulated, and Hopkins does not refute, that Biomira intended to produce antibodies for CellPro in Canada "for use in products to be sold outside of the United States." CellPro's Opening Brief at 40 ("At no time has CellPro imported back into the United States the 12.8 monoclonal antibodies manufactured by Biomira in Canada or the cell suspension derived from using the 12.8 monoclonal antibodies."). Because the record is devoid of evidence upon which the district court could have concluded that its order would prevent further infringement, there was no basis for the court to order the exported hybridomas and its byproducts to be shipped to the United States.

We also do not find persuasive Hopkins' argument that the scope of the district court's order can be justified because it is necessary to fashion a meaningful remedy for CellPro's past infringement. Section 283 does not provide remedies for past infringement; it only provides for injunctive relief to prevent future infringement. The section under which a litigant must seek compensation for past infringement is Section 284. *See* 35 U.S.C. § 284, para. 1 (1994) ("Upon finding for the claimant the court shall award the claimant damages adequate to compensate for the infringement."). We do not understand Hopkins to seriously dispute that it has not received adequate compensation for CellPro's infringement. However, to the extent that Hopkins complains that CellPro's infringement has damaged its ability to service foreign markets, Hopkins must rely on foreign patent protection. *See Deepsouth*, 406 U.S. at 531 ("Our patent system makes no claim to extraterritorial effect. . . . To the degree that the inventor needs protection in markets other than those of this country, the wording of 35 U.S.C. §§ 154 and 271 reveals a congressional intent to have him seek it abroad through patents secured in countries where his goods are being used.") (citations and quotation omitted). Such a complaint cannot be remedied by the imposition of an injunction under Section 283.

Hopkins further argues, mimicking the district court's "as a whole" rationale, that it would be fair under the circumstances to order repatriation and destruction because CellPro has committed other clear acts of infringement with respect to other vials in the United States cell bank. We do not agree. As we have already stated, we disagree that this rationale provides a sufficient premise for the court's order given the facts of this case. Moreover, premising the order on this rationale amounts to punishment of CellPro for its infringement. This is not the proper purpose of injunctive relief under Section 283. [cit]. Those portions of the district court's permanent injunction order that ordered repatriation and destruction of vials exported by CellPro to Biomira and byproducts produced thereby are not consistent with the stated purpose of Section 283—to prevent infringement. Thus, the court abused its discretion, and those portions of the order are vacated.

NOTES AND QUESTIONS

(1) **Section 271(f).** The *CellPro* court referred to *Deepsouth Packing Co. v. Laitram Corp.*, 406 U.S. 518, 529-31 (1972) for the proposition that "judicial restraint of lawful noninfringing activities must be avoided." In that case, export of unassembled components of a patented shrimp-deveining machine (to be easily assembled abroad) was held not to be an infringement of a U.S. patent because the machine itself was not "made" under the U.S. patent law. Subsequently, Congress took the hint and in 1984 added section 271(f) to the patent law, subsection 1 of which states that

> [w]hoever without authority supplies or causes to be supplied in or from the United States all or a substantial portion of the components of a patented invention, where such components are uncombined in whole or in part, in such manner as to actively induce the combination of such components outside the United States in a manner that would infringe the patent if such combination occurred within the United States, shall be liable as an infringer.

Can Congress similarly close the loophole that allows CellPro to use outside the United States the vials which were exported from the United States prior to issuance of the patent? Assume you are a Congressional staff member and have been asked to draft such a provision. What would it look like? Would any such provision be an extraterritorial application of U.S. law? *Compare* RESTATEMENT (THIRD) OF THE FOREIGN RELATIONS LAW OF THE UNITED STATES § 415(3) cmt. i & Reporters' note 6. Does the *Cellpro* court's reference to the "intent of Congress" in its interpretation of section 154 bear upon your answer?

(2) **Offers to Sell.** In *Rotec Industries Inc. v. Mitsubishi Corp.*, 215 F.3d 1246 (Fed. Cir. 2000), the Federal Circuit affirmed a summary judgment that Mitsubishi did not infringe Rotec's patent for a conveyor system for carrying concrete over long distances. Mitsubishi sold a system for the Three Gorges Dam project on the Yangtze River in China. The central issue was whether Mitsubishi's "offer to sell," as that term is used in the 1994 patent code amendment, occurred in the United States or in China. The Federal Circuit decided that the phrase "offer to sell" should be interpreted according to its ordinary meaning in contract law, and the evidence did not show that an offer to sell within that meaning occurred in the United States. Judge Newman concurred on the ground that because no components of the equipment were made in the United States, and thus the sale did not infringe, the offer to sell

could not infringe.

§ 7.05 Other Multinational Enforcement Issues

[A] Choice of Law

In the case law in the previous section on the extraterritorial application of intellectual property laws, the assumption by a U.S. court of jurisdiction under the U.S. Copyright Act or Lanham Act (or indeed by a foreign court under its own intellectual property statute) ordinarily resolved the question of the law applicable to the claims before the court. Where jurisdiction is based on the case arising under the U.S. copyright or trademark statute, the decision to hear a case generally results in the unquestioned application of U.S. law. Cases such as *London Films* and *Boosey & Hawkes* represent exceptions to that rule. The premise of territoriality typically precluded any detailed analysis of choice of law; that premise, backed up by an expansive (and arguably incorrect) interpretation of the principle of national treatment, resulted in U.S. courts almost inflexibly applying U.S. law to copyright claims brought before them. In recent years, however, courts have given greater attention to choice of law questions in intellectual property disputes, particularly in copyright cases. The advent of widespread digital communication has cast further light on choice of law questions in intellectual property law.

ITAR-TASS RUSSIAN NEWS AGENCY v. RUSSIAN KURIER, INC.,
153 F.3d 82 (2d Cir. 1998)

Jon O. Newman, Circuit Judge:

This appeal primarily presents issues concerning the choice of law in international copyright cases and the substantive meaning of Russian copyright law as to the respective rights of newspaper reporters and newspaper publishers. The conflicts issue is which country's law applies to issues of copyright ownership and to issues of infringement. The primary substantive issue under Russian copyright law is whether a newspaper publishing company has an interest sufficient to give it standing to sue for copying the text of individual articles appearing in its newspapers, or whether complaint about such copying may be made only by the reporters who authored the articles. Defendants-appellants Russian Kurier, Inc. ("Kurier") and Oleg Pogrebnoy (collectively "the Kurier defendants") appeal from the March 25, 1997, judgment of the District Court for the Southern District of New York (John G. Koeltl, Judge) enjoining them from copying articles that have appeared or will appear in publications of the plaintiffs-appellees, mainly Russian newspapers and a Russian news agency, and awarding the appellees substantial damages for copyright infringement.

. . . .

BACKGROUND

The lawsuit concerns *Kurier*, a Russian language weekly newspaper with a circulation in the New York area of about 20,000. It is published in New York City by defendant Kurier. Defendant Pogrebnoy is president and sole shareholder of Kurier and editor-in-chief of *Kurier*. The plaintiffs include corporations that publish, daily or weekly, major Russian language newspapers in Russia and Russian language magazines in Russia or Israel; Itar-Tass Russian News Agency ("Itar-Tass"), formerly known as the Telegraph Agency of the Soviet Union (TASS), a wire service and news gathering company centered in Moscow, functioning similarly to the Associated Press; and the Union of Journalists of Russia ("UJR"), the professional writers union of accredited print and broadcast journalists of the Russian Federation.

The Kurier defendants do not dispute that [without authority from the plaintiffs] *Kurier* has copied about 500 articles that first appeared in the plaintiffs' publications or were distributed by Itar-Tass.

. . . .

Preliminary injunction ruling. After a hearing in May 1995, the District Court issued a preliminary injunction, prohibiting the Kurier defendants from copying the "works" of four plaintiff news organizations. . . .

Preliminarily, the Court ruled that the request for a preliminary injunction concerned articles published after March 13, 1995, the date that Russia acceded to the Berne Convention. The Court then ruled that the copied works were "Berne Convention work[s]," 17 U.S.C. § 101, and that the plaintiffs' rights were to be determined according to Russian copyright law. [Article 14(2) of the Russian copyright law, paralleling the U.S. work for hire doctrine, gives employers the exclusive right to "exploit" the "service-related work" produced by employees in the scope of their employment, absent some contractual arrangement. However, Article 14(4) specifies that subsection 2 does not apply to various categories of works, including newspapers. After hearing from expert witnesses on both sides regarding the meaning of Russian law, the district court judge ruled that Article 14(2), though exempting newspapers, applies to press agencies, like Itar-Tass. Moreover, the district court found that the newspapers also had rights to sue for infringement of copyright in the articles in question by virtue of Article 11(2) of the Russian copyright law. That provision gave publishers of compilations rights in "the [compiled] work as a whole." Considerable scholarly debate existed in Russia as to the nature of a publisher's right "in a work as a whole." But the district court accepted the view of the plaintiff's expert witness that the newspaper could prevent infringing activity "sufficient to interfere with the publisher's interest in the integrity of the work," and thus that a preliminary injunction was warranted because what *Kurier* had copied was "the creative effort of the newspapers in the compilation of articles including numerous articles for the same issues, together with headlines and photographs." The Court's preliminary injunction opinion left it unclear whether at trial the plaintiffs could obtain damages only for copying the newspapers creative efforts as a compiler, such as the selection and arrangement of articles, the creation of headlines, and the layout of text and graphics, or also for copying the text of individual articles.]

Trial ruling. [At trial, the district court judge heard from several expert witnesses regarding the meaning of the provisions of Russian law. He affirmed the view of Russian law that he had taken at the preliminary injunction stage, relying on a textual revision of the Russian copyright law in 1993 and an opinion of the Judicial Chamber for Informational Disputes of the President of the Russian Federation ("Informational Disputes Chamber"), issued on June 8, 1995. That opinion had been sought by the editor-in-chief of one of the plaintiffs in the litigation, who specifically called the tribunal's attention to the pending litigation between Russian media organizations and the publisher of *Kurier*. The Informational Disputes Chamber stated, in response to one of the questions put to it: "In the event of a violation of its rights, including the improper printing of one or two articles, the publisher [of a newspaper] has the right to petition a court for defense of its rights." The district court judge also reasoned that publishers have "the real economic incentive to prevent wholesale unauthorized copying," and that, in the absence of assignments of rights to individual articles, widespread copying would occur if publishers could not prevent *Kurier* 's infringements.]

DISCUSSION

I.   Choice of Law

The threshold issue concerns the choice of law for resolution of this dispute. That issue was not initially considered by the parties, all of whom turned directly to Russian law for resolution of the case. Believing that the conflicts issue merited consideration, we requested supplemental briefs from the parties and appointed Professor William F. Patry as Amicus Curiae. Prof. Patry has submitted an extremely helpful brief on the choice of law issue.

Choice of law issues in international copyright cases have been largely ignored in the reported decisions and dealt with rather cursorily by most commentators. Examples pertinent to the pending appeal are those decisions involving a work created by the employee of a foreign corporation. Several courts have applied the United States work-for-hire doctrine, *see* 17 U.S.C. § 201(b), without explicit consideration of the conflicts issue. *See, e.g.,* Aldon Accessories Ltd. v. Spiegel, Inc., 738 F.2d 548, 551-53 (2d Cir. 1984) (U.S. law applied to determine if statuettes crafted abroad were works for hire); . . .Other courts have applied foreign law. *See* Frink America, Inc. v. Champion Road Machinery Ltd., 961 F. Supp. 398 (N.D.N.Y. 1997) (Canadian copyright law applied on issue of ownership); Greenwich Film Productions v. DRG Drugs Inc., 1992 WL 279357 (S.D.N.Y. Sept. 25, 1992) (French law applied to determine ownership of right to musical work commissioned in France for French film); Dae Han Video Production Inc. v. Doug San Chun, 17 U.S.P.Q.2d 1306, 1310 n. 6 (E.D. Va. 1990) (foreign law relied on to determine that alleged licensor lacks rights); . . . In none of these cases, however, was the issue of choice of law explicitly adjudicated. The conflicts issue was identified but ruled not necessary to be resolved in Greenwich Film Productions S.A. v. D.R.G. Drugs, Inc., 25

U.S.P.Q.2d 1435, 1437-38 (S.D.N.Y.1992).

The Nimmer treatise briefly (and perhaps optimistically) suggests that conflicts issues "have rarely proved troublesome in the law of copyright." Nimmer on Copyright § 17.05 (1998) ("Nimmer") (footnote omitted). Relying on the "national treatment" principle of the Berne Convention and the Universal Copyright Convention ("U.C.C."), Nimmer asserts, correctly in our view, that "an author who is a national of one of the member states of either Berne or the U.C.C., or one who first publishes his work in any such member state, is entitled to the same copyright protection in each other member state as such other state accords to its own nationals." *Id.* (footnotes omitted). Nimmer then somewhat overstates the national treatment principle: "The applicable law is the copyright law of the state in which the infringement occurred, not that of the state of which the author is a national, or in which the work is first published." *Id.* (footnote omitted). The difficulty with this broad statement is that it subsumes under the phrase "applicable law" the law concerning two distinct issues—ownership and substantive rights, *i.e.*, scope of protection.[8] Another commentator has also broadly stated the principle of national treatment, but described its application in a way that does not necessarily cover issues of ownership. "The principle of national treatment also means that both the question of whether the right exists and the question of the scope of the right are to be answered in accordance with the law of the country where the protection is claimed." S.M. Stewart, International Copyright and Neighboring Rights § 3.17 (2d ed. 1989). We agree with the view of the Amicus that the Convention's principle of national treatment simply assures that if the law of the country of infringement applies to the scope of substantive copyright protection, that law will be applied uniformly to foreign and domestic authors. *See* Murray v. British Broadcasting Corp., 906 F. Supp. 858 (S.D.N.Y.1995), *aff'd*, 81 F.3d 287 (1996).

Source of conflicts rules. Our analysis of the conflicts issue begins with consideration of the source of law for selecting a conflicts rule. Though *Nimmer* turns directly to the Berne Convention and the U.C.C., we think that step moves too quickly past the Berne Convention Implementation Act of 1988 . . . Section 4(a)(3) of the Act amends Title 17 to provide: "No right or interest in a work eligible for protection under this title may be claimed by virtue of . . . the provisions of the Berne Convention. . . . Any rights in a work eligible for protection under this title that derive from this title . . . shall not be expanded or reduced by virtue of . . . the provisions of the Berne Convention."[9] 17 U.S.C.

---

[8]Prof. Patry's brief, as Amicus Curiae, helpfully points out that the principle of national treatment is really not a conflicts rule at all; it does not direct application of the law of any country. It simply requires that the country in which protection is claimed must treat foreign and domestic authors alike. Whether U.S. copyright law directs U.S. courts to look to foreign or domestic law as to certain issues is irrelevant to national treatment, so long as the scope of protection would be extended equally to foreign and domestic authors.

[9]Other pertinent provisions are:

Section 2(2), which provides: "The obligations of the United States under the Berne Convention may be performed only pursuant to appropriate domestic law."

Section 3(a)(2), which provides: "The provisions of the Berne Convention . . . shall not be enforceable in any action brought pursuant to the provisions of the Berne Convention

§ 104(c).

We start our analysis with the Copyright Act itself, which contains no provision relevant to the pending case concerning conflicts issues.[10] We therefore fill the interstices of the Act by developing federal common law on the conflicts issue. *See* D'Oench, Duhme & Co. v. FDIC, 315 U.S. 447, 472 (1942) (Jackson, J., concurring) ("The law which we apply to this case consists of principles of established credit in jurisprudence, selected by us because they are appropriate to effectuate the policy of the governing Act."). In doing so, we are entitled to consider and apply principles of private international law, which are "'part of our law.'" Maxwell Communication Corp. v. Société Generale, 93 F.3d 1036, 1047 (2d Cir.1996) (quoting *Hilton v. Guyot*, 159 U.S. 113, 143 (1895)). The choice of law applicable to the pending case is not necessarily the same for all issues. *See* Restatement (Second) of Conflict of Laws § 222 . . .We consider first the law applicable to the issue of copyright ownership.

Conflicts rule for issues of ownership. Copyright is a form of property, and the usual rule is that the interests of the parties in property are determined by the law of the state with "the most significant relationship" to the property and the parties. *See id.* The Restatement recognizes the applicability of this principle to intangibles such as "a literary idea." *Id.* Since the works at issue were created by Russian nationals and first published in Russia, Russian law is the appropriate source of law to determine issues of ownership of rights. That is the well-reasoned conclusion of the Amicus Curiae, Prof. Patry, and the parties in their supplemental briefs are in agreement on this point. In terms of the United States Copyright Act and its reference to the Berne Convention, Russia is the "country of origin" of these works, *see* 17 U.S.C. § 101 (definition of "country of origin" of Berne Convention work); Berne Convention, Art. 5(4), although "country of origin" might not always be the appropriate country for purposes of choice of law concerning ownership.[11]

To whatever extent we look to the Berne Convention itself as guidance in the development of federal common law on the conflicts issue, we find nothing to alter our conclusion. The Convention does not purport to settle issues of

---

itself."

    Section 3(b)(1), which provides: "The provisions of the Berne Convention . . . do not expand or reduce the right of any author of a work, whether claimed under Federal, State, or the common law . . . to claim authorship of the work."

[10]The recently added provision concerning copyright in "restored works," those that are in the public domain because of noncompliance with formalities of United States copyright law, contains an explicit subsection vesting ownership of a restored work "in the author or initial right holder of the work *as determined by the law of the source country of the work.*" 17 U.S.C. § 104A(b) (emphasis added); *see id.* § 104A(h)(8) (defining "source country").

    This provision could be interpreted to be an example of the general conflicts approach we take in this opinion to copyright ownership issues, or an exception to some different approach. *See* Jane C. Ginsburg, *Ownership of Electronic Rights and the Private International Law of Copyright,* 22 Colum.-VLA J.L. & Arts 165, 171 (1998). We agree with Prof. Ginsburg and with the amicus, Prof. Patry, that section 104A(b) should not be understood to state an exception to any otherwise applicable conflicts rule. *See* Ginsburg, *id.*; [cit].

[11]In deciding that the law of the country of origin determines the ownership of copyright, we consider only initial ownership, and have no occasion to consider choice of law issues concerning assignments of rights.

ownership, with one exception not relevant to this case. *See* Jane C. Ginsburg, *Ownership of Electronic Rights and the Private International Law of Copyright*, 22 Colum.-VLA J.L. & Arts 165, 167-68 (1998) . . . .

Selection of Russian law to determine copyright ownership is, however, subject to one procedural qualification. Under United States law, an owner (including one determined according to foreign law) may sue for infringement in a United States court only if it meets the standing test of 17 U.S.C. § 501(b), which accords standing only to the legal or beneficial owner of an "exclusive right."

Conflicts rule for infringement issues. On infringement issues, the governing conflicts principle is usually *lex loci delicti*, the doctrine generally applicable to torts. *See* Lauritzen v. Larsen, 345 U.S. 571, 583 (1953). We have implicitly adopted that approach to infringement claims, applying United States copyright law to a work that was unprotected in its country of origin. *See* Hasbro Bradley, Inc. v. Sparkle Toys, Inc., 780 F.2d 189, 192-93 (2d Cir.1985). In the pending case, the place of the tort is plainly the United States. To whatever extent *lex loci delicti* is to be considered only one part of a broader "interest" approach, [cit], United States law would still apply to infringement issues, since not only is this country the place of the tort, but also the defendant is a United States corporation.

The division of issues, for conflicts purposes, between ownership and infringement issues will not always be as easily made as the above discussion implies. If the issue is the relatively straightforward one of which of two contending parties owns a copyright, the issue is unquestionably an ownership issue, and the law of the country with the closest relationship to the work will apply to settle the ownership dispute. But in some cases, including the pending one, the issue is not simply who owns the copyright but also what is the nature of the ownership interest. Yet as a court considers the nature of an ownership interest, there is some risk that it will too readily shift the inquiry over to the issue of whether an alleged copy has infringed the asserted copyright. Whether a copy infringes depends in part on the scope of the interest of the copyright owner. Nevertheless, though the issues are related, the nature of a copyright interest is an issue distinct from the issue of whether the copyright has been infringed. [cit]. The pending case is one that requires consideration not simply of who owns an interest, but, as to the newspapers, the nature of the interest that is owned.

II. Determination of Ownership Rights Under Russian Law

Since United States law permits suit only by owners of "an exclusive right under a copyright," 17 U.S.C. § 501(b), we must first determine whether any of the plaintiffs own an exclusive right. That issue of ownership, as we have indicated, is to be determined by Russian law.

Determination of a foreign country's law is an issue of law. *See* Fed.R.Civ.P. 44.1; [cit]. Even though the District Court heard live testimony from experts from both sides, that Court's opportunity to assess the witnesses' demeanor provides no basis for a reviewing court to defer to the trier's ruling on the content of foreign law. In cases of this sort, it is not the credibility of the experts that is at issue, it is the persuasive force of the opinions they expressed. [cit].

Under Article 14 of the Russian Copyright Law, Itar-Tass is the owner of the copyright interests in the articles written by its employees. However, Article 14(4) excludes newspapers from the Russian version of the work-for-hire doctrine. The newspaper plaintiffs, therefore, must locate their ownership rights, if any, in some other source of law. They rely on Article 11. The District Court upheld their position, apparently recognizing in the newspaper publishers "exclusive" rights *to the articles*, even though, by virtue of Article 11(2), the reporters also retained "exclusive" rights to these articles.

Having considered all of the views presented by the expert witnesses, we conclude that the defendants' experts are far more persuasive as to the meaning of Article 11. In the first place, once Article 14 of the Russian Copyright Law explicitly denies newspapers the benefit of a work-for-hire doctrine, which, if available, would accord them rights to individual articles written by their employees, it is highly unlikely that Article 11 would confer on newspapers the very right that Article 14 has denied them. Moreover, Article 11 has an entirely reasonable scope if confined, as its caption suggests, to defining the "Copyright of Compilers of Collections and Other Works." That article accords compilers copyright "in the selection and arrangement of subject matter that he has made insofar as that selection or arrangement is the result of a creative effort of compilation." Russian Copyright Law, Art. 11(1). Article 11(2) accords a publisher of compilations the right to exploit such works, including the right to insist on having their names mentioned, while expressly reserving to "authors of the works included" in compilations the "exclusive rights to exploit their works independently of the publication of the whole work." *Id.* Art. 11(2). As the defendants' experts testified, Article 11 lets *authors* of newspaper articles sue for infringement of their rights in the text of their articles, and lets *newspaper publishers* sue for wholesale copying of all of the newspaper or for copying any portions of the newspaper that embody their selection, arrangement, and presentation of articles (including headlines)—copying that infringes their ownership interest in the compilation.

[The] contrary interpretation [by plaintiff's expert, Mr. Newcity], according publishers (and reporters) exclusive rights to the text of articles, draws entirely unwarranted significance from the shift of the phrase "as a whole" from the first to the second paragraph of Article 11(2) [which occurred during the 1993 revision of the copyright law]. One would not expect drafters of the revised Article 11(2) to accomplish a major broadening of the rights of newspaper publishers simply by shifting the placement of this phrase. Moreover, the drafter of the revision testified that the shift was a matter of grammar, and not of any substance. Furthermore, Newcity's interpretation rests on the untenable premise that both the publisher of a newspaper and the author of an article have exclusive rights to the same article. Under his interpretation, as he acknowledged, the publisher could grant a license to a third party to publish an article, the "exclusive" rights to which are held by the author. That unlikely result cannot be accepted in the absence of clear statutory language authorizing it.

The opinion of the Informational Disputes Chamber is not a sufficient basis for upholding the plaintiffs' interpretation. As the defendants' experts pointed out, the bylaws of that body confine its authority to matters affecting free press issues, and explicitly preclude it from adjudicating issues arising under copyright law. Moreover, the opinion that the Chamber rendered does not necessarily support the plaintiffs' position. In asserting that a newspaper may petition for redress "in defense of its rights," the Chamber might have meant only that a newspaper can protect its limited compilation rights in the selection and arrangement of articles even when only a small number of articles are copied. The opinion of the Chamber does not state that the newspaper has a protectable copyright interest in the text of each article.[14]

Nor can the District Court's conclusion be supported by its observation that extensive copying of newspapers will ensue unless newspapers are permitted to secure redress for the copying of individual articles. In the first place, copying of articles may always be prevented at the behest of the authors of the articles or their assignees. Second, the newspapers may well be entitled to prevent copying of the protectable elements of their compilations. Lastly, even if authors lack sufficient economic incentive to bring individual suits, as the District Court apprehended, Russian copyright law authorizes the creation of organizations "for the collective administration of the economic rights of authors . . . in cases where the individual exercise thereof is hampered by difficulties of a practical nature." Russian Copyright Law, Art. 44(1). Indeed, UJR, the reporters' organization, may well be able in this litigation to protect the rights of the reporters whose articles were copied by *Kurier*. [The court ruled that UJR had standing to sue on behalf of its members.]

Relief. Our disagreement with the District Court's interpretation of Article 11 does not mean, however, that the defendants may continue copying with impunity. In the first place, Itar-Tass, as a press agency, is within the scope of Article 14, and, unlike the excluded newspapers, enjoys the benefit of the Russian version of the work-for-hire doctrine. Itar-Tass is therefore entitled to injunctive relief to prevent unauthorized copying of its articles and to damages for such copying, and the judgment is affirmed as to this plaintiff.

Furthermore, the newspaper plaintiffs, though not entitled to relief for the copying of the text of the articles they published, may well be entitled to injunctive relief and damages if they can show that Kurier infringed the publishers' ownership interests in the newspaper compilations.[15]

. . . .

In view of the reckless conduct of the defendants in the flagrant copying that infringed the rights of Itar-Tass, the rights of the authors, and very likely some

---

[14]Also unpersuasive is the opinion of an arbitration court of the Altai Region of Russia, *Closed Stock Company Komsomolskaya Pravda v. Limited Liability Company RIA Nasha Pressa*, Case # 235/98-10 (City of Barnaul, Russian Federation, Feb. 25, 1998), which awarded damages to a newspaper for another publication's reprinting of two articles from the newspaper. The opinion of the arbitration court (furnished to us by the appellees) deems exclusive rights in the articles to be owned by the newspaper by virtue of Article 14(2) of the Russian Copyright Law, ignoring the provision of Article 14(4), which renders Article 14(2) inapplicable to newspapers.

[15] . . .Moreover, though the parties do not raise the issue, we may assume that the authors of the articles, by submitting them to their newspaper publishers, gave the publishers an implied license to use the articles in the newspaper compilations. That non-exclusive license, of course, does not entitle the publishers to sue in the United States for infringement of the articles as such.

aspects of the limited protectable rights of the newspapers, we will leave the injunction in force until such time as the District Court has had an opportunity, on remand, to modify the injunction consistent with this opinion and with such further rulings as the District Court may make in light of this opinion.[16]

CONCLUSION

Accordingly, we affirm the judgment to the extent that it granted relief to Itar-Tass, we reverse to the extent that the judgment granted relief to the other plaintiffs, and we remand for further proceedings.

NOTES AND QUESTIONS

(1) **National Treatment and Choice of Law**. Do you agree with the *Itar-Tass* court that Professor Nimmer overstated the principle of national treatment? Is Professor Patry correct that the principle of national treatment is "not really a conflicts rule at all"? *See* Berne Convention art. 5. If it is not a conflicts rule, does it restrain national courts in any way in their choice of law determinations? Review Article 5(2) of the Berne Convention: what precisely does it mean? If Article 5(2) does establish a choice of law rule, what is it? What is meant by "the laws of the country where protection is claimed"? Which laws? Which country?

(2) **Developing a Choice of Law Rule**. The *Itar-Tass* court concluded that it was free to develop a choice of law rule for international copyright as a matter of federal law. Given that, would you have selected the same rule as the court? What are the advantages and disadvantages of applying the "law of the place with the most significant relationship" to the parties and the transaction? Are there any bright line alternatives that would be feasible? Is it appropriate to have different choice of law rules for different forms of intellectual property? For different issues in a single copyright litigation? Which values should we seek to further in developing conflicts rules for copyright law? Should these be values deduced from conflicts law or from substantive copyright law?

Why must a court apply a single national law to resolve a multinational dispute? Would you support courts crafting a rule for international copyright litigation drawn from an amalgam of different national laws (and incorporating consideration of international treaty provisions)? What are the advantages and disadvantages of such an approach? *See* Graeme B. Dinwoodie, *A New Copyright Order: Why National Courts Should Create Global Norms*, 149 U. PA. L. REV. 469 (2000).

---

[16]Upon remand, the District Court will also have to consider, if the claim is pursued, what relief might be accorded to plaintiff-appellee Heslin Trading Ltd., the publisher of *Balagan*, a Russian language comic magazine published monthly in Israel. What ownership interests Heslin might have, under Israeli law, that have been infringed, under United States law, by *Kurier's* copying was not explicitly considered by the District Court.

(3) **The Law of the State with the Most Significant Relationship.** How should a court determine which state has the most significant relationship with a particular dispute (or issue)? *See* RESTATEMENT (SECOND) OF CONFLICTS § 6. In applying this test in non-copyright cases, two considerations are crucial: first, which "connecting factors" provide a state with a plausible claim to have its law apply; and, second, according to what principles are competing claims to be weighed? Which "connecting factors" should be relevant in a copyright case? Which were determinative in *Itar-Tass*? Are there others that you think relevant? What values or policy objectives underlie provisions relating to ownership of copyright? Does that help determine which connecting factors are relevant to the question of ownership?

(4) **Applying *Itar-Tass* (I).** In *Bridgeman Art Library Ltd. v. Corel Corp.*, 25 F. Supp.2d 421 (S.D.N.Y. 1998), *aff'd on reconsideration*, 36 F. Supp.2d 191 (S.D.N.Y. 1999), an English company, the Bridgeman Art Library, Ltd. ("Bridgeman"), claimed that it owned copyright in photographic transparencies of a substantial number of well-known works of art located in museums around the world (as well as in digital images that it made from the transparencies). Bridgeman alleged that the defendant Corel Corporation ("Corel"), a Canadian corporation, was marketing in the United States and abroad compact disks containing digital images copied from its transparencies, and that (inter alia) this amounted to copyright infringement under U.S. and foreign law. Corel moved for summary judgment. The district court initially applied U.K. law to the question of whether the transparencies were sufficiently original to warrant copyright protection, and found that they were insufficiently original to receive protection under U.K. law. In determining to apply U.K. law, the court purported to follow *Itar-Tass* and apply the "law of the state with 'the most significant relationship' to the property and the parties." The Court concluded that the United Kingdom had the most significant relationship to the issue of copyrightability because the transparencies were produced either by the museums owning the original works of art (mostly in the United Kingdom, with some in Italy and France) or by freelance photographers employed by Bridgeman, which was based in the United Kingdom. In addition, many of the underlying works were still in Britain, and the transparencies were first published there. After receiving an unsolicited letter from Professor William Patry, amicus curiae in *Itar-Tass*, the court applied U.S. law to the question of copyrightability (but reached the same result). Under *Itar-Tass*, which law should determine the copyrightability of the transparencies?

(5) **Applying *Itar-Tass* (II).** Graveney Fabric is a New York corporation that manufactures and sells fabric, including fabric bearing an original design called "Chic" in the United States. Graveney had purchased the rights in the artwork on which the Chic design was based from an Italian company called "Lui 2," whose employee allegedly created it. The agreement between Graveney and Lui 2, which was negotiated and executed in Milan, Italy, warranted that the artwork had never been "copyrighted, reproduced, published, or used in any manner prior to this sale." The fabric design created and sold by Graveney was made in and for the United States by its in-house design team. Graveney brings an infringement action against a company selling low-price copies of the Chic fabric. The defendants resisted plaintiff's motion for summary judgment by

arguing that the ownership of the copyright in the fabric design should be determined by Italian law, which it claimed was the state with the most significant relationship to the work and to the parties. The alleged absence of a work for hire doctrine in Italian law would mean that Lui 2's anonymous employee, and not Lui 2 itself, owned the copyright in the artwork and thus there would remain a disputed issue of fact as to whether Graveney could have received any valid rights to the design from Lui 2. Should summary judgment be denied? Which state has the most significant relationship to the parties and the work? *Cf.* Cranston Print Works Co. v. J. Mason Products, 49 U.S.P.Q.2d 1669 (S.D.N.Y. 1999).

(6) **Applying *Itar-Tass* (III).** In 1995 and 1996, Rizzoli distributed in Italy and in the United States a catalog of an exhibition of Marilyn Monroe photographs and memorabilia entitled *Marilyn Monroe: The Life: The Myth* that had been staged in Rome. The catalogs were compiled and printed in Italy. The photographers and artists whose works were included, without authorization, in the catalog sued Rizzoli for copyright infringement. The plaintiffs included citizens of both the United States and foreign countries. The defendant sought summary judgment with respect to 105 photographs on the ground, inter alia, that the photographs were in the public domain. The plaintiffs responded that although the photographs were in the public domain in the United States by virtue of failure to comply with renewal formalities, Italy did not have a renewal requirement and thus the photographs were still protected in Italy. The plaintiffs suggested that Italian law applied because "under the Berne Convention, the applicable law is the copyright law of the state in which the infringement occurred," which the plaintiffs argued was Italy. A majority of the 105 photographs were first published outside the United States; but some were first published in the United States. Which state had the most significant relationship to the works and the parties? *See* Shaw v. Rizzoli Int'l Pubs., Inc., 51 U.S.P.Q.2d 1097 (S.D.N.Y. 1999). Does *Itar-Tass* answer that question? *See id.* at n.10 To what extent will the nationality of the different plaintiffs affect this question? *See id.* On what other grounds might the defendants seek to dismiss the complaint?

The *Shaw* court noted that even if Italian law applied to the question of ownership, the infringement claims by U.S. plaintiffs would still be barred because under the rule of the shorter term contained in Article 7(8) of the Berne Convention, any American work "which has not been renewed under U.S. law will at the end of the first U.S. term enter the public domain in Italy." *See id.* at n.11 (quoting NIMMER ON COPYRIGHT). Is that analysis correct? Are there any additional facts that you would need to know to determine whether it is correct?

(7) **Applying Foreign Law.** What were the reasons that persuaded the *Itar-Tass* court as to the proper interpretation of Russian law? Were these appropriate considerations in interpreting Russian law? Should the court have deferred to the interpretations of Russian courts that had addressed the issue? If the court had found that Russian law was the law applicable to the question of infringement (for example, if most of the acts of copying had occurred in Russia), how would the court have resolved the case? Would it have dismissed the case?

(8) **Standing to Sue.** The *Itar-Tass* court noted that even if a foreign law determines ownership, U.S. law would apply to determine whether a particular plaintiff has standing to sue. *See Itar-Tass*, 153 F.3d at 91. Why should this be so?

(9) **Section 104A.** The U.S. copyright statute contains no explicit generally-applicable choice of law rule, but the provisions on the restoration of foreign copyrights introduced in section 104A identify the law of the "source country" to determine who is the copyright owner. The owner is the person entitled to claim the restored rights.

(10) **Article 14*bis*(2)(a) of the Berne Convention**. The Berne Convention expressly provides that "[o]wnership of copyright in a cinematographic work shall be a matter for legislation in the country where protection is claimed." Berne Convention art. 14*bis* (2)(a). Does this suggest anything about whether a general choice of law rule is implied by the Berne Convention?

HUSTON v. SOCIÉTÉ D'EXPLOITATION DE LA CINQUIÈME CHAINE

Decision of the Cour de cassation, May 28, 1991 (France)

Citing clause 2 of article 1 of law No. 64-689 of July 8, 1964 [the law concerning international reciprocity in copyright protection], together with article 6 of the law of March 11, 1957 [the copyright law];

Whereas, according to the first of these texts, in France, no violation may be made of the integrity of a literary or artistic work, whatever the territory on which the work was first disclosed; whereas the person who is the author of the work from the sole fact of the work's creation is invested with moral rights which are established for his benefit by the second of the texts cited above; whereas these rules are laws of imperative application;

Whereas the Huston plaintiffs are the heirs of John Huston, the co-director of the film "Asphalt Jungle," created in black and white, but of which the Turner Company, grantee of the producer, established a colored version; whereas, invoking their right to compel the respect of the integrity of John Huston's work, the Huston plaintiffs, joined by various entities [authors' rights societies], have requested the judges below to prohibit the television station "La Cinq" from broadcasting, this new version; whereas the Court of Appeals dismissed their claim on the ground that the elements of fact and law found by the appellate court "prohibited the eviction of the American [copyright] law and the setting aside of the contracts" that had been concluded between the producer and the directors, contracts that denied the latter persons the status of authors of the film "Asphalt Jungle";

Whereas in so holding, the Court of Appeals has violated the above-cited texts by refusal to apply them;

For these reasons, and without need to hold on the other objections raised in the petition for this Court's review:

Reverse and annul, in all respects, the decision rendered by the Court of Appeals of Paris, July 6, 1989, reinstate therefore the case and the parties in the state in which they were before said decision and, for resolution of the case, send the parties before the Court of Appeals of Versailles.

NOTES AND QUESTIONS

(1) **Laws of Imperative Application.** In *Huston*, the defendant had contractually obtained all rights in the motion picture, which had been created in the United States, and all transactions with respect to the rights purported to be governed by U.S. state and federal law. Yet, the *Huston* court suggested that French rights of integrity will be available to the heirs of John Huston regardless of where the work was first disclosed and regardless of contractual provisions to the contrary because the French law in question is a "law of imperative application." Does U.S. copyright law contain any such rules that would apply regardless of the law otherwise determined to be applicable through choice of law analysis? What is it about a rule of copyright law that would make it one of "imperative application"?

(2) *Huston* **in the United States.** Does the decision of the French court comply with international treaty obligations? If the plaintiff had sued in the U.S. courts, which law would a U.S. court have applied under *Itar-Tass*? Would *Itar-Tass* govern? If the U.S. court applied a law other than French law, would the U.S. court have complied with international treaty obligations.

DIGITAL PROBLEMS

The choice of law question has become even more complex in the digital environment. There have been very few cases discussing the implications of choice of law in internet copyright cases, but several scholars have begun to address the topic in detail. *See* Graeme W. Austin, *Domestic Laws and Foreign Rights: Choice of Law in Transnational Copyright Infringement Litigation*, 23 COLUM.-V.L.A. J. L. & ARTS 1, 6 n.15 (1999) (listing scholarship). Consider the following hypothetical, drawn from Graeme B. Dinwoodie, *A New Copyright Order: Why National Courts Should Create Global Norms*, 149 U. PA. L. REV. 469 (2000).

> Sam Appletart is an American artist, and the owner of the copyright in a series of four paintings entitled "Liberty." Appletart has licensed the U.S. publication of the Liberty series in various formats, including in coffee table books of modern American art, and in textbooks on American art. She discovers that a reproduction of the Liberty series has been posted, without her permission, on a web site hosted by a university in the European country of Caledonia (which, like the United States, is a signatory to the Berne Convention, TRIPS and the WIPO Copyright Treaty). The paintings had been scanned into digital format by the university. The paintings are posted on a

web page established for a university course on contemporary North American art. The university imposes no restrictions on access to the web page; it adheres to the view that education is the right of all citizens, and that free access to course materials is consistent with this philosophy. It also does not wish to use precious university resources on technological restraints to restrict access to class members; it has discovered from experience that students are remarkably adept at circumventing such measures, and that the cost of ensuring effective protection is prohibitive. The Caledonian university has a sister-university relationship with New York University, which involves student and faculty exchanges and the administration of a summer program in New York City. The web site is accessible from the United States. Let us assume that the unauthorized posting of the paintings would constitute infringement under U.S. law (if applicable). Let us also assume that Caledonian law offers broad exceptions to educational institutions to reproduce copyrighted material for instructional purposes. In an effort to encourage distance learning—Caledonia is a large country with students in far flung locales—it has extended its broad exemptions into the digital environment. Thus, if U.S. law applied to the university's activities, the web site would be held to be infringing. An injunction would ordinarily issue to restrain infringement. If Caledonian law applies, the university would get off scot-free.

Which law should apply? The law of the place where the allegedly infringing work was uploaded? *See* EU Cable and Satellite Directive art. 1(2)(b). The law of any place from where the allegedly infringing work can be accessed? What are the arguments for and against the different options? How would the *Itar-Tass* court resolve the issue? *See* National Football League v. TVRadio Now Corp., 53 U.S.P.Q.2d 1831, 1834-35 (W.D. Pa. 2000) (locating infringing acts in the United States where web site in Canada accessible from the United States and clearly targeted at U.S. audience). Would you regard that as a satisfactory outcome? Does your consideration of this problem cause you to revise any of your conclusions regarding an appropriate choice of law rule in copyright cases? If so, do we need a separate choice of law rule for the internet?

Professor Jane Ginsburg has written extensively on this subject. She proposes the following approach to choice of law in the internet context:

1. The law applicable to the entirety of a defendant's alleged Internet infringement is:

a. If the allegedly infringing content is found on a website, the law of the country in which the operator of the website has its residence or principal place of business, so long as this country's domestic copyright law is consistent with Berne Convention, WTO [and WCT] norms; or

b. If the allegedly infringing content is not found on a website, the law of the country of the residence or principal place of business of the person or entity that initiated the communication, so long as this country's domestic copyright law is consistent with Berne Convention, WTO [and WCT] norms;

2. If the law of the country identified in # 1 does not conform to Berne Convention, WTO [and WTC] norms, then the law applicable to the entirety of the defendant's alleged Internet infringement is the law of the country in which the server that hosts the alleged infringing content is located, so long as this country's domestic copyright law is consistent with Berne Convention, WTO [and WCT] norms;

3. Notwithstanding #1 and #2, if a third country is shown to have a more significant relationship with the controversy—for example, if a third country is shown to have been the principal target of the infringing communication, then the law applicable to the entirety of the defendant's alleged Internet infringement is the law of that third country, so long as this country's domestic copyright law is consistent with Berne Convention, WTO [and WCT] norms;

4. In the absence of a Berne, WTO, [and WCT]-compliant country having a significant relationship with the controversy, then the law applicable to the entirety of the defendant's alleged Internet infringement is the law of the forum, so long as the forum is a member of the Berne Union or WTO [or WCT];

5. In fashioning any remedies, the court may take into account the extent to which, for particular countries in which acts alleged to be infringements occurred, the domestic law is substantially either more or less protective than the copyright or related rights law of the law chosen in accordance with ## 1-4

Jane C. Ginsburg, *Private International Law Aspects of the Protection of Works and Objects of Related Rights Transmitted Through Digital Networks, 2000 Update*, WIPO Doc. No. PIL/01/02 (2000). What is the purpose of this complex cascade of rules? (Which problems do you think Professor Ginsburg is seeking to address?) Would this approach resolve the hypothetical problem above to your satisfaction? What are the advantages and disadvantages of this approach? In what ways is it consistent with the approach taken by the *Itar-Tass* court? In what ways does it depart from *Itar-Tass?*

[B]   Multinational Litigation

[1] National Enforcement of a European Patent

EDWARD ARMITAGE, INTERPRETATION OF EUROPEAN PATENTS (ART. 69 EPC AND THE PROTOCOL ON THE INTERPRETATION)*
14 I.I.C. 811-817 (1983)

1. Introduction

In any patent action the essential questions for the court are: is the patent valid and is it infringed? These questions may be taken separately, by different courts, as in Germany, but they may also be taken by the same court and have commonly to be considered together in the same action. For both questions, the interpretation of the patent, and more particularly of the patent claims, is of crucial importance.

The role of the claims in a European patent, and the principles governing their interpretation, are set out in Arts. 69 and 84 of the [European Patent Convention] ("EPC") and the Protocol on Interpretation of Art. 69. Before looking more closely at the significance of these provisions, perhaps we should ask: to what extent are they binding on national courts in an action on a European patent in what one might call "the national phase?"

2. The European Patent in the National Phase

Article 2(2) EPC states that the European patent shall, in each of the Contracting States for which it is granted, have the effect of and be subject to the same conditions as a national patent granted by the State, unless otherwise provided in the Convention. Does the Convention provide that Arts. 69 and 84 shall override the corresponding provisions of national law which would otherwise be applied to a European patent as to a national patent? Admittedly there is nothing in the Convention which says so directly and one has to turn to the implications of the main exception to the application of national law, *viz.* Art. 138.

Article 138(1) says, in effect, that the validity of a European patent can be attacked in the national phase (*i.e.* after grant) only on the basis of what one might call "European" grounds, *i.e.* the same grounds on which it was granted. Two of these grounds are particularly relevant:

Ground (a)—that the patent is not patentable under the terms of the substantive law in EPC Arts. 52 to 57.

Ground (d)—that the protection conferred by the European patent has been

---

extended.

In granting the patent, the European Patent Office applies Arts. 52-57 and Art. 123(3) (which corresponds to ground (d) just mentioned) in the context of the other Articles of the Convention. In particular, the effect of the patent claims, in applying Arts. 52-57 and 123(3), is determined by Arts. 69 and 84. Similarly, grounds (a) and (d) in Art. 138 cannot operate in a vacuum but carry with them the provisions of Arts. 69 and 84.

It seems inescapable, therefore, that a court will be bound by Arts. 69 and 84 as regards the validity of a patent. But is it equally bound to interpret claims in accordance with those Articles as regards infringement? Surely this must be so. It would be absurd—some might say a recipe for disaster—to interpret claims on one basis in determining their validity and on a different basis in then deciding whether they are infringed. This argument is particularly telling as regards validity ground (d); this ground is concerned with the extent of protection conferred by the patent which is, of course, exactly what the court is concerned with as regards infringement.

It is assumed, therefore, in what follows that the EPC provisions on interpretation are binding on national courts in European patent actions. What, then, do those provisions amount to?

Effect of Arts. 69(1) and 84 and the Protocol

The first point to note is that Art. 84 states that the claims define the matter for which protection is sought. Thus in deciding what it is that is to be protected against infringement, the court cannot look beyond the claims. But what, then, is to be the extent of that protection? (Here we are talking of technical features of a potential infringement, not the acts—making, using, selling etc.,—which constitute infringement, for which one has to look to national law.) This is where Art. 69(1) comes in. This states that the claims, in addition to defining the protected invention, also determine the extent of that protection. But a court, in applying Art. 69(1), is not forced to adopt the strict literal meaning of the claims. It can do so, of course, taking the claim to mean exactly what it says. But the court has some freedom to depart from the strict wording by virtue of the following:

(a) According to Art. 69(1), it is the "terms" of the claims ("teneur" in French and "Inhalt" in German), not the strict wording, which determines the extent of protection.

(b) Again, according to Art. 69(1), the description and drawings can be used to interpret the claims, so that the words in the claim may have to be given, for consistency with the description, a meaning different from that which they have in common usage.

(c) The flexibility thus afforded by Art. 69 is to be applied in accordance with the Protocol on its interpretation.

To appreciate the significance of all this, it may be useful to have a brief look at the history of those provisions in the Convention.

3. History

It is well known that Art. 69(1) derives from the corresponding provision (Art. 8) of the Strasbourg Convention on the harmonization of substantive patent law. This Article defining the function of the claims was one of the most difficult to agree [upon.] At the time, not all member countries of the Council of Europe had patent claims, properly speaking. In those that had, they were taken to define the invention but only in some (*e.g.* UK, Sweden and Switzerland) were they also stated to define the scope of the protection afforded by the patent. This reflected two different traditions of claim drafting and interpretation, exemplified by the Federal Republic of Germany and the Netherlands on the one hand and Switzerland and the UK on the other hand.

In German practice, the claims concentrated on defining the inventive step; a claim commonly generalized the invention only slightly; and the court had wide powers of generalizing from the claims in considering potential infringements. In UK practice, the generalization took place almost entirely in the wording of the claims as drafted, the court being prepared to generalize further to only a very limited extent. It was necessary to choose between these systems or to adopt some definable intermediate position.

The drafters of the Convention took a big step by stating that the claims should define "the protection applied for" rather than the "invention." At the same time it was accepted all round that courts should be free to depart from the literal meaning of the claims in the interests of justice either (a) where the claim was at variance with the description or (b) where the literal meaning would involve a quite unreasonable or pointless restriction. To deal with (a), the Swiss law was followed, requiring the description to be used to interpret the claims. To deal with (b) the Convention adopted the by-now familiar formula "the extent of the protection conferred by the patent shall be determined by the terms of the claims." It is important to know that "terms of the claims" and "teneur des revendications" in the French version were adopted deliberately as being somewhat broader than "words".

It was recognized that this still left the danger of this formula being applied either over-restrictively or over-liberally. To avoid this, the Council of Europe Committee recorded of the formula that "it seeks to lay down a principle for interpreting claims which is somewhere between the system in which claims may be interpreted strictly according to the letter and that in which they do not play a decisive part in defining the limits of protection."

So much for the Strasbourg history, which is highly relevant because the Strasbourg formula was adopted unchanged in Art. 69(1) of the EPC. But here a new problem arose over the German language term "Inhalt" corresponding to "terms" and "teneur" (the Strasbourg Convention was in English and French only). It was recognized as decidedly wider in significance than the English and French terms but there was no agreement to narrow the German term to match the English and French or to widen the English and French to match the German. This failure to agree highlighted the danger of subsequent divergent interpretations of the Convention. Eventually, the (admittedly varying) language texts were adopted unchanged on the basis that no one language was dominant and that all three versions have to be recognized as influencing the interpretation, and hence the application, of Art. 69. This was reinforced by the Protocol on Interpretation of Art. 69 which aimed to guard against an extreme interpretation of any one text. The Protocol follows very much the lines of the statement by the Council of Europe Committee, adding the desideratum of combining "a fair protection for the patentee with a reasonable degree of certainty for third parties."

4. Problems for Courts

This, then, is the background against which national courts will have to interpret the claims of European patents. The history shows the fears of the legislators that courts might diverge seriously by continuing to follow the long-standing traditions developed under earlier national laws. And, indeed, it is here that courts are likely to find most difficulty in harmonizing their attitudes.

However, this question of claim interpretation is the one where the courts have the biggest role to play in developing the system of European patent law. The Convention has been able to express only the broad lines and it remains now for court jurisprudence to fill in the details.

Two things are clear: that claims should be interpreted in the light of the patent specification as a whole and that courts are not bound by the literal meaning of the words of the claim. The crucial question is: how far should a court be prepared to stretch a claim beyond that literal meaning in the interests of fairness to the patentee? There seem to be two constraints at least:

> 1. In view of Art. 69(1), it seems that the claims must be assumed to have been broadly drafted in the first place, which perhaps suggests caution in any further broadening.
>
> 2. The requirement of "a reasonable degree of certainty for third parties" (Protocol) suggests that any stretching of the claim to cover an infringement should be reasonably predictable by a third party.

Could it be said of these constraints that they indicate that a stretched interpretation of a claim should not "do violence" to the language of that claim as read, in the light of a description, by an instructed person of the kind to whom the patent specification is addressed?

Within such constraints, however, "a fair protection for the patentee" (Protocol) suggests that claims may be stretched in interpretation so as to correct forgivable drafting oversight (no draftsman of claims is perfect) or failure to foresee possible variants of the claimed invention (no draftsman is omniscient).

I have concentrated almost entirely on the interpretation of claims in connection with infringement because it is there that the influences of Art. 69 and the Protocol are of supreme importance. I mentioned interpretation of claims in determining their validity only to say that the same principles apply. I should like to add something.

Professor Cornish has also referred to claim interpretation in considering novelty and inventive step and he made the same point when he said of the "invention" to which tests of novelty and inventive step are to be applied:

> I shall assume that the invention consists of anything . . . within the scope of protection sought by the claims of the specification.

I quite agree, but does this mean that in considering novelty and inventive step the EPO and national courts have to speculate as to the full range of manufactures which constitute potential infringement?

I would say most definitely "no." For one thing, it is not a practical proposition. It is one thing to decide that a claim can be stretched to cover an actual case of manufacture by a third party; it is quite another thing to decide what imaginary cases of manufacture the claim might be stretched to cover. More importantly, though, such speculation is unnecessary.

In considering whether a claim is valid in the face of a particular disclosure in the prior art, the Patent Office or court does not need to find that the disclosed manufacture falls within the terms of the claim. It has at its disposal EPC Art. 56. It suffices if it can be seen that what is claimed is an obvious variant of the prior art manufacture.

In practice, therefore, I think that claims can be taken at their face value as regards validity, although even then Art. 69 applies. The Patent Office or court must decide what the face value is, interpreting the "terms", "teneur" or "Inhalt" of the claims in the light of the specification as a whole, including the descriptions and drawings.

5. Recognition of Decisions in Different Countries

Just one more point. What influence does a decision on interpretation of a European patent, made by one national court, have on the courts of other member countries and on the EPO itself? Professor Mangini has rightly said that, strictly speaking, decisions of national courts on infringement or validity are effective only in the country concerned. Dr. Bruchhausen has amplified this, saying that although legal precedents in one Contracting State are not binding on interpretation in another, interpretation in one country should take account of precedents from other countries. I would respectfully agree. It is very much to be hoped that the courts of all member countries will contrive to develop a consistent common jurisprudence, much as the courts of Commonwealth countries have done in the past in applying similar provisions of their respective patent statutes. Decisions, while not binding, have been persuasive.

Consider an example. Identical infringing articles are marketed in France and Italy. The scope of protection of the European patent is the same in France and Italy, being determined by Art. 69. The validity is the same in both countries, being governed by Art. 138. A French court finds that the European patent is valid and infringed by the marketing in France. What influence will that have on the Italian court? Is the Brussels Convention on recognition of judgements applicable? Possibly not, but at least the French decision must be highly persuasive in Italy.

Consistent and harmonious jurisprudence is necessary not only to satisfy the aims of the Convention. It is essential if the EPO is to function smoothly. Dr. Bruchhausen has pointed out that decisions of the EPO on interpretation of the Convention are not paramount, *i.e.* binding on national courts. Indeed, surely the reverse applies? Every national Patent Office has to respect and apply interpretations of the law laid down by the national courts. Similarly the EPO has to be guided by interpretations laid down by the courts of Member States, but it can only be so guided to the extent that there is a consensus among the states. Where there is consensus on a particular point of law, the EPO can apply it firmly and confidently during the patent granting procedure. But if the jurisprudence is inconsistent and divergent, the EPO will be forced into a very cautious attitude, since it ought not to be refusing patents which national courts would find valid.

Of course, for full harmonization in litigation of the European patent in the EEC, and for central guidance for the EPO, we need—as referred to by Professor Mangini—the Community patent plus COPAC. But that is another story.

6. Conclusions

a. Article 69(1) and the Protocol do govern interpretation of European patents in national courts. We may hope that the same will apply to national patents.

b. Article 69(1) and the Protocol will tend to induce applicants to draft broad claims.

c. In deciding how much further to stretch the interpretation of claims, courts will have to bear in mind the presumption of broad drafting by the applicant.

d. It is to be hoped that national courts will treat decisions of other courts on European patents as highly persuasive. To that end, publication of important decisions in translation is most important.

e. Uniformity would be greatly assisted if COPAC were to be created. In the meantime, periodical meetings of judges should be of great value.

f. The European patent system is working well at the patent granting stage. Finally, however, the success of the system is in the hands of the courts.

IMPROVER CORP. AND SICOMMERCE v. REMINGTON PRODS.
CASE NO. 2 U 27/89
Dusseldorf Court of Appeals (Oberlandesgericht) (1991) (Germany)
excerpted at 24 I.I.C. 838-845 (1993)

From the Facts:

The plaintiffs accuse the defendant of infringement of European Patent 0101656 (patent in suit, Enclosure 1 or 1a, respectively). This patent is based on an application of July 29, 1983 and was published on November 5, 1986. By decision of the Technical Board of Appeal of the European Patent Office of April 24, 1991, the English language patent was maintained in the granted version, claim 1 of which reads as follows:

An electrically powered depilatory device comprising: a hand held portable housing (2); motor means (4, 4') disposed in said housing; and a helical spring (24) comprising a plurality of adjacent windings arranged to be driven by said motor means in rotational sliding motion relative to skin bearing hair to be removed, said helical spring (24) including an arcuate hair engaging portion arranged to define a convex side whereat the windings are spread apart, and a concave side corresponding thereto whereat the windings are pressed together, the rotational motion of the helical spring (24) producing continuous motion of the windings from a spread apart orientation at the convex side to a pressed together orientation at the concave side and for engagement and plucking of hair from the skin of the subject, whereby the surface velocities of the windings relative to the skin greatly exceeds the surface velocity of the housing relative thereto. . . .

In June 1988, the defendant started distributing an electrically driven depilatory device, placing it into circulation in the Federal Republic of Germany under the designation, "Lady Remington Liberty". This device operates by means of an arcuate roll of rubber-like plastics, the smooth outer surface of which features a plurality of radial, spaced apart cuts which are distributed over the circumference of the roll and penetrate the plastics element partially only. By means of the motor, this roll is driven in a rotational motion about its longitudinal axis, so that the cuts open to form gaps at the convex side, and so that the side walls thereof are firmly pressed together when the cuts rotate to the concave side of the arcuate roll.

The plaintiffs asserted that the rubber roll provided with radial slits and used as hair-engaging element in the disputed depilatory device constitutes an equivalent to the helical spring provided by the invention. . . .

With judgment of December 30, 1988, the district court found against the defendant. . . . Against this judgment, the defendant lodged appeal. . . .

From the Opinion:

The defendant's admissible appeal is not successful on the merits. . . . [T]he district court rightfully found that the disputed embodiment makes use of the teaching of patent claim 1 of the patent in suit, so that, taking into account the following statements, reference may be made to the reasons for decision of the appealed judgment. . . .

[I]t is the object of the teaching of the patent in suit to suggest a motor-driven depilatory device with the described operation, so that efficient hair removal is ensured. In addition, however, the device according to its size, complexity, production costs and convenience of use should be suited for home use in such a way as is already the case for the electrical razor.

The solution according to the patent in suit (claim 1) makes use of the finding which is already revealed by Swiss Patent 268696, *i.e.* that a coil spring is an elastic element which opens gaps on bending at the convex side and closes at the concave side, in a device which operates by motor-driven rotational motion of the windings of the spring, namely by a rotational motion which is quicker than the velocity at which the depilatory device is moved by the user's hand over the areas of the skin to be depilated. The coil spring, therefore, operates in such a way that the gaps of the windings are spread apart in the area provided for admission of the hairs, and that the windings are pressed together by the rotation, so that, relative to any hair introduced, the place taken by it between the adjacent windings is continuously narrowed, the hair is clamped by the walls of the winding facing the hair, and the hair is plucked due to the rotational motion which is quick in relation to the forward movement of the device.

Patent claim 1 describes this solution of the problem of the patent by the following features:

The electrically powered depilatory device comprises

1. a hand held portable housing,

2. motor means positioned in said housing,

3. a helical spring comprising a plurality of adjacent windings,

4. the windings are arranged to be driven by said motor means in rotational sliding motion relative to skin bearing hair to be removed,

5. said spring includes a hair engaging portion which

    a) is arcuate,

    b) defines a convex side whereat the windings are spread apart and

    c) defines a concave side corresponding to said convex side whereat the windings are pressed together,

6. the rotational motion of the spring produces a continuous motion of the windings from a spread apart orientation at the convex side to a pressed together orientation at the concave side and for engagement with the hair and for plucking of hair from the skin of the subject,

7. the surface velocity of the windings relative to the skin greatly exceeds the surface velocity of the housing relative thereto.

The depilatory device, "Lady Remington Liberty," introduced in the German market by the defendant makes use of the teaching of the patent in suit as just explained.

The depilatory device distributed by the defendant fulfills features 1 and 2 literally. Features 3 to 7, however, are not given literally since the disputed embodiment uncontestedly does not feature a helical spring. The disputed embodiment instead has a massive roll-shaped body of a flexible and elastic rubber-like plastic material, featuring radial spaced apart cuts on its circumferential surface. This arcuate and motor-driven rubber roll is, however, a replacement means equivalent to the coil spring of the patent, so that features 3 to 7 of patent claim 1 are given in equivalent form.

First of all, the court . . . has no doubts that the disputed embodiment is identical in effect to a device making use of the wording of claim 1 of the patent in suit. The roll of the disputed embodiment unites a plurality of adjacent elements, namely the areas separated by the cuts (cf. feature 3); these areas are arranged to be driven by the motor means in rotational motion relative to skin-bearing hair to be removed (cf. feature 4). The roll comprises a hair-engaging portion which is arcuate, defines a convex side whereat the elements are spread apart and a concave side corresponding to the convex side whereat the elements are pressed together (cf. feature 5). The rotational motion of the roll produces a continuous motion of the elements from a spread apart orientation at the convex side to a pressed together orientation at the concave side for engagement with the hair and for plucking of hair from the skin of the subject (cf. feature 6). The surface velocity of the roll relative to the skin greatly exceeds the surface velocity of the housing relative to the skin (cf. feature 7). The disputed embodiment thus achieves that a hair that has reached the spaced apart areas of the roll is approached ever more closely by the walls of these areas as a consequence of the rotational movement, which walls then clamp the hair and pluck it out. With respect to the principle and success of the desired hair removal, which is efficient and suited for home use, the hair undergoes the same treatment as with a device using the wording of the patent in suit. In conjunction with this, reference can also be made to the description of the patent in suit, according to which wedge-shaped slits (gaps) are instrumental for the depilatory effect of the device. For wedge-shaped gaps are also featured by the roll of the disputed embodiment. The fact that these—due to the different orientation and depth of their gaps in comparison with the inclined windings of a common coil spring—may move the hair differently before plucking it, namely bend it first, as to be seen from the private expert opinion, is therefore irrelevant for the question of identical effect. . . .

A difference, however, is constituted by the fact that with a roll comprising cuts, part of the hair to be removed may first reach an area of the roll which does not comprise a cut yet (but only when the roll continues to rotate), while with a "helical spring" there will always be an entry gap for those hairs which do not hit upon the front sides of the windings themselves. Also according to the expert opinion this is, however, not a question of identical effects, but only refers to the efficiency, or, in other words, only to the question of the quantity of hair removed. This has to be left to the decision of the person skilled in the art who designs constructions according to the patent in suit. As to be seen therefrom, patent claim 1 does not give any indication of how thick or thin the windings of the spring and how wide the area of the gaps in the arcuate state has to be, considered individually or as a whole.

Therefore, the efficiency of the device, according to the patent as required, according to the object of the invention, cannot consist in removing a certain number of hairs during one revolution or on the whole, but only in overcoming the drawbacks of the state of the art. In this context, the expert correctly drew attention to the fact that "much" would increase the user's pain, while "fast" would reduce it, thereby characterizing the different efficiencies of, for example, the manually operated device according to the Swiss patent specification already mentioned and the device to be evaluated here.

It is furthermore irrelevant for determining the identical effect that, with the accused embodiment, each cut (be it closed or in the form of a gap that opens or closes to a higher or lower extent) travels around the circumference of the roll on rotation, whereas the cut is stationary when a "helical spring" is used. According to its object, the patent in suit does not deal with introducing hairs into a constantly opened gap. The desired efficient depilatory device which is relatively simple and convenient to use rather results from the fact that with a "helical spring" the gaps automatically close in the process of rotation, and hairs which have entered them are clamped and plucked. Accordingly, it is also irrelevant what else the individual hair will undergo when entering the gap and when being in the gap, and how this will happen, so that it is not a shortcoming of the expert opinion that only schematic drawings were attached and that the details were not examined with a high-speed camera. A peculiar configuration of the disputed embodiment concerning the treatment of a hair in the gap before being clamped and plucked may at best constitute a surplus of a device which otherwise operates in the same way. In this respect, too, the expert correctly only spoke of a secondary question and referred to the fact that this question would not change the fact that the disputed embodiment makes use of an elastic body with slits or gaps in the same way as the teaching according to the patent in suit, and that the hair—as taught—is taken along via the gap walls by means of friction and is finally plucked.

When evaluating the scope of protection of claim 1 of the patent in suit, however, the argument cannot be limited to the identity of effect only. . . . For the purpose of fairly delimiting the actual improvement of the field of technical knowledge achieved by an inventor on the basis of Art. 69(1) EPC and the Protocol on Interpretation, the protected invention will only be considered to be used if a person skilled in the art, on the basis of reflections progressing from the meaning of the patent claims, *i.e.* the invention described therein, could find out, with the help of his professional knowledge at the priority date, the modified means used with the disputed embodiment as a means being identical in effect for solving the problem underlying the invention. . . .

After the expert opinion, the court is convinced that a person skilled in the art—owing to the content of the claims of the patent in suit—was capable of arriving at the disputed embodiment in this sense.

The starting point for this conclusion is that a person skilled in the art will recognize by virtue of his professional knowledge that in the patent—in any case as far as the basic teaching of claim 1 is concerned—it is not a matter of the use of a "helical spring" as such. For, it is—as has already been mentioned initially here and in the prior art by the device according to the Swiss patent—used contrary to its common application . . . or, as the expert also expressed, atypically. . . . The knowledge that, in the patent, the coil spring does not act as a power unit as usual, automatically results in the fact that those criteria of a helical spring are sought in order to determine why it is proposed in the patent. With this, however, a person skilled in the art in the field of interest here, and with the education mentioned by the expert and the skills resulting therefrom, will easily recognize that the coil spring is only proposed for the reason that it is an elastic cylindrical body which may be quickly rotated in the arcuate state and, above all, for the reason that it features—by virtue of its windings and their sides (walls) facing each other and separating the windings—means that stretch the surface of the body to form gaps at the convex side, while at the concave side they result in clamping areas with the help of which the hairs that entered the gaps may be clamped and plucked. In this way, to a person skilled in the art, the instruction of claim 1 of the patent in suit reads in a functional respect: Take a cylinder-shaped elastic element comprising separated walls of areas of material, to the effect that gaps will form on the convex side and clamping areas will form of the concave side if it is bent, and select—according to material and quality—an element that may be rotated at high speed when bent. If evaluated as a whole, the expert based his written opinion on this understanding. In view of the undisputed technical knowledge of the expert, both with respect to the technical field of interest here and with respect to his experience in patent litigation matters, the court does not see any reason not to follow the logic of the expert in that a person skilled in the art will actually understand the teaching of the patent in suit in this way. Moreover, the court's expert also confirmed this on inquiry of the defendant and the court. The basic thesis that a person skilled in the art will not interpret the coil spring as a spring, but as an elastic body with gaps is convincing, as it is obvious that the helical spring is not used as a spring per se, and as its use in accordance with the teaching of the patent in suit—and also, however, with the state of the art to be seen from the Swiss patent specification, for example—requires the abstraction by a person skilled in the art that this spring is an elastic element which opens at the convex side and closes at the concave side when bent, and which is furthermore so stable that it may be driven at relatively high speed. This abstraction therefore was professional knowledge in view of the state of the art, and it was rendered obvious by the claims of the patent in suit, respectively, if seen in the light of the description.

However, if the patent in suit conveyed this knowledge, it was also obvious to use a roll with cuts as in the accused embodiment as a hair-plucking element. It could be recognized with the help of professional knowledge that cuts in a cylindrical body would be sufficient, as, according to the above, the only thing that is essential is that the hair must be able to enter between adjacent areas of the body (walls), and that the walls must approach it up to clamping it. As opposed thereto, however, it is recognizably unimportant whether the body be completely hollow, feature a core or be massive, which is why a person skilled in the art could easily think of applying a massive roll with cuts. To produce the arcuate cut hair-plucking element of rubber or rubber-like plastic material could already be considered possible by a person skilled in the art for the reason that the wording of the patent in suit (claim 1) does not stipulate a certain material, but the question of the material is left open to the expert choice of a designing engineer proceeding on the basis of the patent in suit. Rubber-like plastic material is known to be a preferred material in conjunction with the use of an elastic, bendable element. Moreover, it can easily be provided with separating cuts, for which reason there was the possibility of having an element with which—like with a coil spring—areas of material and separations (windings and gaps, which may vary in width depending on the degree of bending or spreading) alternate and with which the requirement of having gaps at the convex side and clamping areas at the concave side could easily be met, not only by means of circumferential cuts of 360 [degrees,] but also by means of cuts of smaller circumference, as in the case of the disputed embodiment. A person skilled in the art would even prefer those shorter cuts since questions of durability and stability of the hair-plucking element had to be taken into consideration, too, in particular in view of its high rotational speed.

. . . From the response of the court's expert to question 11, the court moreover concludes that, in case of the variation forming the disputed embodiment, the problems to be faced with regard to drive and stability would not have been so large as to prevent a person skilled in the art from taking a cut roll made of rubber-like plastic material into consideration and testing it. In view of the fact that questions as to the drive and stability of the hair-plucking element could have resulted above all from the selected material, as is also confirmed by the oral statements made by the court's expert, it has to be pointed out once again that the patent in suit does not exclude rubber-like plastic material, but leaves this choice open. Accordingly, this cannot, at any rate, have been an obstacle to putting the teaching of patent claim 1 into practice, even for a person skilled in the art, and the fact is irrelevant that all the looped shapes which are depicted on the patent specification should not be possible with the roll of the disputed embodiment. On the contrary, equivalence has to be determined with regard to features 3 to 7 of the patent.

At best it could be said that the disputed embodiment, by the selection of the length, depth and number of cuts, or possibly also by the selection of a particularly suited material for the cylinder-shaped, elastic and arcuate hair-plucking element, gains additional advantages, such as, for example, a maximum decrease in pain for the user, since with each rotation fewer hairs are plucked at a time than would be the case with a steel spring with thin windings and—in the arcuate state—wide gaps in relation thereto. This, however, would not change anything about the fact that the disputed embodiment, at any rate according to its genus, is identical in effect to a device according to the patent, and could also, according to its genus, be found as an alternative to a device making use of the teaching of claim 1 of the patent in suit by a person skilled in the art orientating himself to the meaning of the patent claims, with the help of findings available to him due to his professional knowledge. The court also considers, as an indication of this finding, the history of the origin of the disputed embodiment as it is described in the British court decision which has been mentioned several times. The starting point was a device according to the patent with a metal coil spring. It was found that the use of this device was annoying because it plucked too many hairs at a time, but the principle of depilation according to the patent was not criticized. This points to the fact that the designing engineer of the disputed embodiment, having proceeded from the starting point assumed above, must have actually thought about what the "helical spring" really meant in the device presented to him. It further suggests that even though only metal coil springs had been used in the prior art, except for the so-called disk solutions, that fact did not actually represent an obstacle to a deviation therefrom.

Finally, it is also undisputed that it cannot be claimed that the disputed embodiment results in an obvious way from prior art . . . .

IMPROVER CORPORATION AND OTHERS v. REMINGTON CONSUMER PRODS. LTD.
1990 F.S.R. 181(Ch. D. 1989) (UK)

HOFFMANN J: This is an action for infringement of a European patent for an electrically powered cosmetic device for removing hair. The commercial embodiment of the plaintiff's invention is called "Epilady" and the defendant's device is called "Smooth & Silky." The defences are, first, that Smooth & Silky does not infringe the claims of the patent and secondly, that the patent is invalid for obviousness and insufficiency. In my judgment the patent in suit is valid but the defendant's device does not infringe. The action is therefore dismissed. (A point taken on the title of some of the plaintiffs to sue therefore does not arise.)

The Invention

Depilation means the removal of hair by the root, as opposed to shaving which leaves the root behind. The advantage of depilation is that the hair takes much longer to regenerate. Various methods have been used in the past for cosmetic depilation, but none was completely satisfactory. An article published in an American marketing journal in 1976 ("Where to look for good product ideas" by Joseph J Montesano in Product Management, August 1976) began as follows:

> If you were seeking a truly new product that meets a genuine consumer need you might start with the women's depilatory market. After many years of looking—ever since ancient Egypt—women still say they have not found the ideal product to remove hair from legs and face.
>
> Pull it off with a hardened wax? It hurts. Use a chemical that dissolves hair? It has an offensive odour. Electrolysis? You need an expert and it's expensive. Use a razor—even a new idea like the disposables? There are still nicks and scratches—at least some women still think so.
>
> It's a huge, waiting market, and the company that comes up with a safe, effective product will hit the jackpot . . . Everyone knows the market is there and some in the field have been searching for the key

to unlock the treasure . . . .

Epilady was invented by two Israelis in 1982. It consists of a small electric motor in a hand-held plastic housing to which is attached a helical steel spring held by its ends and stiffened by a guide wire to form a loop. The arcuate form of the spring causes the gaps between the windings to open on its convex side but to be pressed together on the concave side. When the spring is held close to the skin and rotated by the motor at about 6,000 revolutions per minute, hairs enter the gaps on its convex side and are gripped between the windings as the rotational movement brings them round to the concave side. The effect is to pluck them out of the skin.

Marketing of Epilady began in June 1986. It was an enormous commercial success. In the first two years over 5.8 million devices were made, generating a gross retail turnover in excess of US $340,000,000.

The Patent in Suit

The patent in suit is European Patent (UK) No. 0101656. It refers by way of prior art to six patents. Four involve manually operated helical springs. In Schubiger (US Patent 2,486,616), Binz (US Patent 1,743,590) and Kerr (US Patent 2,458,911) the windings of the coils are used as multi-jawed tweezers and are either pressed together or allowed to come together to engage the hairs, which are then pulled out by a jerking movement with the device. Fischer (Swiss Patent 268,696) consists of two small helical coils each held in arcuate form by a stiff guide wire. The patent requires the coils to be rolled over the surface of the skin so that the hairs are engaged and gripped by the rotation of the spring in the same way as in the patent in suit. Extraction is performed by a jerky movement but the specification is not clear as to whether this is the same movement over the skin by which the hairs are engaged or a movement away from the skin after the hairs have been gripped. The power-operated inventions are Schnell (US Patent 2,900,661), a device for plucking feathers or hair, which uses a power-driven row of rotating discs on an axle with cams to push the edges of the discs together and grip the feathers or hair, and Daar (US Patent 4,079,741), an earlier patent by one of the inventors of the patent in suit. This is a complicated device—a motorized Schubiger by which a helical spring is reciprocatingly compressed and extended by a cam driven by an electric motor to engage and grip the hairs and at the same time intermittently rotated to extract them.

The basic description of the patent in suit declares that–

> There is thus provided in accordance with an embodiment of the present invention an electrically powered depilatory device including a hand held portable housing, motor apparatus disposed in the housing, and a helical spring composed of a plurality of adjacent windings arranged to be driven by the motor apparatus in rotational sliding motion relative to skin bearing hair to be removed, the helical

spring including an arcuate hair engaging portion arranged to define a convex side whereat the windings are spread apart, and a concave side corresponding thereto whereat the windings are pressed together, the rotational motion of the helical spring producing continuous motion of the windings from a spread apart orientation at the convex side to a pressed together orientation at the concave side and for the engagement and plucking of hair from the skin, whereby the surface velocities of the windings relative to the skin greatly exceed the surface velocity of the housing relative thereto.

A preferred embodiment of the invention is said to be one in which the helical spring arcuate hair engaging portion–

extends along an arc subtending more than 90 degrees and preferably more than 180 degrees, whereby the surface velocities of windings of the helical spring simultaneously include components extending in mutually perpendicular directions, for significantly enhanced hair removal efficiency.

The looped configuration to which this description refers can be seen illustrated in figures 1 and 2 of the patent drawings (see next page). Its advantages are further explained as follows:

The looped spring configuration of the present invention is a particular feature thereof in that there are simultaneously present at all times windings of the helical spring whose component of velocity relative to the hair extends in mutually perpendicular directions. The apparatus thus is operative to remove hair oriented in various directions without requiring movement of the housing against the skin in all of these directions.

The description ends, however, with the following general statement, which I shall later refer to as the "equivalents clause:"

It will be evident to those skilled in the art that the invention is not limited to the details of the foregoing illustrative embodiments, and that the present invention may be embodied in other specific forms without departing from the essential attributes thereof, and it is therefore desired that the present embodiments be considered in all respects as illustrative and not restrictive, reference being made to the appended claims, rather than to the foregoing description, *and all variations which come within the meaning and range of equivalency of the claims are therefore intended to be embraced therein.* (Emphasis supplied.)

Claim 1 reads as follows: . . . [same as in the decision of the German court above] . . . .

Smooth & Silky

Smooth & Silky also consists of a small electric motor in a hand held housing but the element attached to the motor and used to extract the hair is not a helical metal spring. Instead it is a cylindrical rod of elastomerised synthetic rubber held by its ends to form an arc subtending about 60 degrees. I shall for convenience call it "the rubber rod." A number of parallel radial slits have been cut into the rubber. The arcuate form of the rod causes the slits to open on its convex side but to be pressed together on the concave side. When the rod is held close to the skin and rapidly rotated by the motor, hairs enter the gaps on its convex side and are gripped between the walls of the slits as the rotational movement brings them round to the concave side. The effect is to pluck them out of the skin.

. . . .

Mr. Gross [the inventor] has been granted a patent in the United States (US 4,726,375). . . .

. . . .

Dr. Laming, a distinguished design engineer called as an expert witness by the defendants, said that Mr. Gross's specification contained nothing which distinguished Smooth & Silky from Epilady by function. The difference lay in their respective forms (Evidence Day 6, p 16A).

Infringement

The question of infringement turns upon a short but undoubtedly difficult point of construction, namely whether the rubber rod is a "helical spring" as that expression is used in the claims of the patent in suit. In the Court of Appeal at the interlocutory injunction stage of this action Dillon LJ said that a more attractive way of putting the question, from the plaintiff's point of view, was to ask whether the rod was a "mechanical equivalent" for a helical spring. But I think with respect, for reasons which I shall explain, that these are different ways of saying the same thing.

The proper approach to the interpretation of patents registered under the Patents Act 1949 was explained by Lord Diplock in Catnic Components Ltd. v. Hill & Smith Ltd., 1982 RPC 183, 242. The language should be given a "purposive" and not necessarily a literal construction. If the issue was whether a feature embodied in an alleged infringement which fell outside the primary, literal or acontextual meaning of a descriptive word or phrase in the claim ("a variant") was nevertheless within its language as properly interpreted, the court should ask itself the following three questions:

(1) Does the variant have a material effect upon the way the invention works? If yes, the variant is outside the claim. If no—

(2) Would this (*i.e.* that the variant had no material effect) have been obvious at the date of publication of the patent to a reader skilled in the art. If no, the variant is outside the claim. If yes—

(3) Would the reader skilled in the art nevertheless have understood from the language of the claim that the patentee intended that strict compliance with the primary meaning was an essential requirement of the invention. If yes, the variant is outside the claim.

On the other hand, a negative answer to the last question would lead to the conclusion that the patentee was intending the word or phrase to have not a literal but a figurative meaning (the figure being a form of synecdoche or metonymy) denoting a class of things which included the variant and the literal meaning, the latter being perhaps the most perfect, best-known or striking example of the class. . . .

In the end, therefore, the question is always whether the alleged infringement is covered by the language of the claim. This, I think, is what Lord Diplock meant in *Catnic* when he said that there was no dichotomy between "textual infringement" and infringement of the "pith and marrow" of the patent and why I respectfully think that Fox LJ put the question with great precision in Anchor Building Products Ltd. v. Redland Roof Tiles Ltd. ((CA), unreported, 23 Nov. 1988) when he said the question was whether the absence of a feature mentioned in the claim was "an immaterial variant which a person skilled in the trade would have regarded as being *within the ambit of the language*" (My emphasis). It is worth noticing that Lord Diplock's first two questions, although they cannot sensibly be answered without reference to the patent, do not primarily involve questions of construction: whether the variant would make a material difference to the way the invention worked and whether this would have been obvious to the skilled reader are questions of fact. The answers are used to provide the factual background against which the specification must be construed. It is the third question which raises the question of construction and Lord Diplock's formulation makes it clear that on this question the answers to the first two questions are not conclusive. Even a purposive construction of the language of the patent may lead to the conclusion that although the variant made no material difference and this would have been obvious at the time, the patentee for some reason was confining his claim to the primary meaning and excluding the variant. If this were not the case, there would be no point in asking the third question at all.

Catnic was a decision on the Patents Act 1949. Section 125 of the Patents Act 1977, which is declared by section 139(7) to be framed to have as nearly as practicable the same effect as Article 69 of the European Patent Convention, says that the invention shall be taken to be that specified in a claim, as interpreted by the description and drawings. Section 125(3) applies to English patents the Protocol on the Interpretation of Article 69 which, if I may paraphrase, says that Article 69 and section 125(1) mean what they say: the scope of the invention must be found in the language of the claims. Extrinsic material such as the description can be used to interpret those claims but cannot provide independent support for a cause of action which the language of the claim, literally or figuratively construed, simply cannot bear. On the other hand, the claims should not be interpreted literally but in a way which "combines a fair protection for the patentee with a reasonable degree of certainty for third parties."

Dillon LJ said in his judgment at the interlocutory stage of this action that Lord Diplock's speech in Catnic indicated the same approach to construction as that laid down by the Protocol. This view has been adopted by the Court of Appeal. . . .I regard it as binding upon me. I must therefore ask Lord Diplock's three questions to ascertain whether "helical spring" should be interpreted to mean a class of bendy, slitty rods of which a close-coiled helical spring in its primary sense is a striking and elegant example but which includes the defendant's rubber rod.

(1) Does the variant have a material effect on the way the invention works?

The answer to this question depends upon the level of generality at which one describes the way the invention works. At one extreme, if one says that the invention works by gripping and pulling hair, there is obviously no difference; the same would be true of a pair of tweezers. At the other extreme, if one says that it works by gripping hairs between metal windings of circular cross-section wound in a continuous spiral around a hollow core, there obviously is a difference. . . . .

. . . .

It seems to me that the right approach is to describe the working of the invention at the level of generality with which it is described in the claim of the patent. As I have said, Dr. Laming agreed that there was no difference between the descriptions in Mr. Gross's patent and the patent in suit of the way the inventions worked. The differences lay entirely in the descriptions of the hardware. In my judgment, at the appropriate level of description, the rubber rod works in the same way as the helical spring and the differences I have mentioned, so far as they exist, are not material.

(2) Would it have been obvious to a man skilled in the art that the variant would work in the same way?

. . . .

Dr. Laming and Dr. Sharp, the eminent engineer called as an expert by the plaintiff, agreed that it would have been obvious to the skilled man that the attributes which enabled the helical spring to function in the way described in the specification were that it was capable of rotating, capable of transmitting torque along its length to resist the forces involved in plucking hairs, bendy (to form an arc) and slitty (to entrap hairs by the opening and closing effect of rotation). They also agreed that it would have been obvious that any rod which had these qualities in sufficient degree and did not have other defects such as overheating or falling to bits would in principle work in the same way and that the rubber rod plainly belonged to that class. On this evidence the second question must in my judgment be answered yes. I express no view on whether the rubber rod was also an inventive step.

On the other hand, the evidence shows that although the rubber rod could be used in a device which would function in the way described in claim 1 of the patent in suit, it would work only in a limited number of embodiments. In particular, it could not be used in the loop formation described as the preferred embodiment.

(3) Would the skilled reader nevertheless have understood that the patentee intended to confine his claim to the primary meaning of a helical spring?

This brings one to the question of construction. Since the question is what the skilled reader would have understood, I set out the views of the rival experts.

Dr. Sharpe placed considerable emphasis on what I have called the equivalents clause. He said in his report (Report, page 14):

> it would have been obvious to me that all the inventor wanted a helical spring for was as a convenient rotating bent beam in which slits formed by the adjacent windings would open and close as it rotated. It would then have been equally obvious to me that he could not have intended to exclude equivalents like the [rubber] rod . . . in thinking of equivalents I feel driven by the last paragraph of the specification before the claims [the equivalents clause] to think that the inventor was trying to make me think of equivalents for the helical spring . . . some other element that would do the same job.

Dr. Sharpe said that in the course of his own work he had used a slitted rod instead of a helical spring to serve as a coupling (Report, page 9):

> In my experience it is common practice to replace a close coiled helical spring by a rod with slits in a situation where the rod/spring forms an arc. For example, similar circular cross-section beam/spring forms are commonly used for coupling rotating shafts where the axis of the shafts have angular misalignment. These couplings are commonly "close wound" helical springs or in the form of a rod with saw cut slits arranged in a regular staggered pattern as used in the [Smooth & Silky]. I have used a rod with such saw cut slits as part of a mechanism for positioning micro-electrodes.

He concluded (Report, page 14):

> It would have been quite natural for me to have thought of my recent experience and use of a slitted bendy rod [either] with the slits being discontinuous—the only alternative to their being continuous.

In cross-examination Dr. Sharpe was questioned about the process of reasoning which would have taken him from the helical spring to the rubber rod. He said:

> One would look for equivalence and as an engineer I would know that
> there are many equivalents for providing torque in a bent condition
> and one of those is obviously a solid rod of a more flexible material.
> This is the way couplings are made. That is a common way—a
> common alternative. I see the step as one which the competent
> engineer or man in his working shop would, sort of, look through the
> files in his mind, and out would pop a number of alternatives.

> Q. You are viewing this just as a coupling. You are viewing the
> Epilady spring as a form of coupling.
> A. In the sense that one of its primary functions is to transmit torque
> and that is an important one, then obviously methods for
> transmitting torque in an arc situation would be the obvious thing to
> come to mind. The fact that you can then put slits in it is something
> that we have done readily. I mean, I have done it in my own
> experience for various reasons and I have also known of hair being
> caught in these slits.

Later he was asked about the disadvantages of the rubber rod (Transcript,
Day 3, p 73).

> Q. And the change from a hollow helical spring with those windings
> to a solid rubber rod would involve the sort of problems we have been
> talking about: heat build up, length of the roller and the rest of them,
> is that not correct?
> A. Once you had made the mental step of choosing an alternative that
> was a rubber rod, then obviously your mind is directed, as a designer,
> to the problems that ensue from that, which are indeed [that] the
> internal damping material is higher, the heat build up etc.

> Q. And, thirdly, having decided on your solid rubber rod, you change
> from some helical slit along the circumference to an array of pairs of
> slits perpendicular to the axis; is that correct?
> A. I think you would put the slits in. It is much easier to put them in
> at right angles to the axis, it is easier to manufacture it that way, and
> therefore you just put them in . . . .

Dr. Laming, on the other hand, said that a helical spring was a very specific
engineering concept. It meant a bar or wire of uniform cross-section wound into
a helix. This definition was also accepted by Dr. Sharpe, although he suggested
that the rubber rod could also be regarded as a helical spring in a more literal
sense because it was springy and had torque stresses running through it in a
helical pattern. I do not think it would occur to the ordinary skilled man to

think of the rubber rod as a helical spring. Dr. Laming thought that in the context of the specification the skilled man would also not understand a helical spring to mean a genus of bendy, slitty rods. The references to prior art did not suggest that the function of a helical spring was simply to be a bendy slitty rod. In the patents in which they had been used, they were plainly essential features. Dr. Laming said (Report, paragraphs 7.2, 7.3, 4.2, 7.6):

> My opinion is that there is no way of interpreting the [plaintiff's] specification such that anything other than a helical spring (as defined above) is intended. The simple reason for this is, in my view, that the inventor had in mind what he regarded as a novel use of a familiar and readily available engineering component and saw the nub and center of the invention as that use.

> I have now read the European Patent several times and it is clear that nothing other than a helical spring is referred to. If there were alternatives to a helical spring which the inventor or draftsman of the patent had in mind he did not indicate anywhere that such alternative might be used. This stands in contrast to suggested alternatives with regard to e.g. alternative drive arrangements suggested in Column 6 . . .

> The flexibility conferred on the helical spring by its essential features is obtained for the elastomeric rod by quite other means—by its being made of a material of very low elastic modulus, a material about 30,000 times more flexible than the steel of the spring. The difference of material is inherent in the difference between the two devices: the helical spring, if made of the elastomeric material, would be useless spaghetti; and the arcuate rod made of steel would be an undriveably rigid bar . . .

> If the [plaintiff's] specification contained anywhere such words as "or any other configuration of an elastic member or members whereby rotation of the member or members causes a spread apart orientation at one position and a pressed together orientation at another position or point in the cycle" then at least one might be led to think about alternatives to the helical spring. Whether I would have thought of an elastomeric rod in such a case is hard to say in hindsight but the likelihood is made less by consideration of the Figures 9-14 which show possible configurations which the patentee had in mind. Except possibly for the first (Fig 9) these configurations could not be adopted by an elastomeric rod without some internal wire guide, and in that case, the friction developed between elastomer and guide would in my opinion be prohibitive.

On this last point Dr. Sharpe agreed.

Dealing with the equivalents clause, Dr. Laming said:

> It is true that [in the equivalents clause] reference is made to

embodiment 'in other specific forms' and it asks there for reference to be made 'to the appended claims rather than the foregoing description.' But what follows is a series of claims in which the variations are all on such matters as the angle subtended by the arcuate portion (claims 2, 3 and 18), the degree of opening of the windings (claims 5 to 8), various mechanical drive options (claims 13 and 14) and different surface speeds (claims 19 and 20). A constant feature of all the claims is the specification of a helical spring which itself is the only type of element mentioned in the text of the specification and shown in the figures.

In my judgment the difference between the experts depends upon how one construes the equivalents clause. The first part of the clause merely says that the description should not be used to restrict the meaning of the language used in the claims. That is not the question here. What matters is the final words: "and all variations which come within the meaning and range of equivalency of the claims are therefore intended to be embraced therein." If this means: "whatever contrary impression the skilled man may be given by the language of the claims read in the context of the rest of the description, all references in the claims to hardware are deemed to include any other hardware which would in any circumstances function in the same way" then I think Dr. Sharpe must be right. In my judgment, however, the clause does not have so wide an effect. The words I have quoted say that the variation must still come within the meaning of the claims and the reference to "range of equivalency" means in my judgment no more than "don't forget that the claims must be interpreted in accordance with *Catnic* and the Protocol."

Thus interpreted, I do not think that "helical spring" can reasonably be given a wide generic construction and I accept Dr. Laming's reasons for thinking that a skilled man would not understand it in this sense. . . . . The rubber rod is not an approximation to a helical spring. It is a different thing which can in limited circumstances work in the same way. Nor can the spring be regarded as an "inessential" or the change from metal spring to rubber rod as a minor variant. . . . . It would be obvious that the rubber had problems of hysteresis which might be very difficult to overcome. The plaintiff's inventors had done no work on rubber rods. Certainly the rubber rod cannot be used in the loop configuration which is the plaintiff's preferred embodiment. On the other hand, drafting the claim in wide generic terms to cover alternatives like the rubber rod might be unacceptable to the patent office. I do not think that the hypothetical skilled man is also assumed to be skilled in patent law and he would in my judgment be entitled to think that patentee had good reasons for limiting himself, as he obviously appeared to have done, to a helical coil. To derive a different meaning solely from the equivalents clause would in my view be denying third parties that reasonable degree of certainty to which they are entitled under the Protocol.

The German decisions

The patent in suit is being litigated in a number of countries but the only one in which the action has come to trial is in Germany, where the Landgericht of Dusseldorf found in favor of the plaintiff [affirmed by the Oberlandesgericht above.] This naturally causes me concern because the Landgericht was interpreting the same patent according to the same Protocol and came to a different conclusion. It seems to me that the reason for the difference between me and my colleagues in Dusseldorf is that, having answered what I have labeled as Lord Diplock's first two questions in the same way as I have, they treated those answers as concluding the matter in favor of the plaintiff and did not find it necessary to ask the third question at all. The specification, they said, conveyed to the expert "the understanding that the configuration of the hair engaging portion as helical spring has to be understood functionally" (Translation, p. 15) and that the expert to whom the patent was directed would have "no difficulties in perceiving and understanding this meaning of the teaching of the invention." This does seem to me with respect to be an interpretation closer to treating the language of the claims as a "guideline" than the median course required by the Protocol. I also detect some difference in approach between the Landgericht and the Oberlandesgericht (Court of Appeal) which had previously discharged an interlocutory injunction granted by the Landgericht. The Court of Appeal placed much more emphasis upon the language of the specification. Its view on the primary meaning of a helical spring was as follows:

> A spiral or helical shape is characterized by curved lines such as those showing on the level a spiral and, three-dimensionally, more or less the rising turns of a screw. Nothing else is meant by the theory of the [plaintiff's] patent and this is made clear to a person skilled in the art by the state of the art to which the patent refers and on which its proposition is undoubtedly based. A solid roller-shaped hair-engaging part with vertical incisions at a distance from each other can therefore at the most constitute an equivalent means of replacement for the helical spring.

The court went on to say that the rubber rod undoubtedly worked in the same way as the helical spring (*i.e.* it answered Lord Diplock's first question in the same way as I have). Although it does not specifically say so, I think it may be assumed that it would have regarded this as equally obvious to anyone skilled in the art. But when dealing with the question whether this would affect the question of construction, *i.e.* whether the skilled man would have regarded the rubber rod as included in the claims of the patent, the Court of Appeal expressed considerable doubt. He could have done so if he had analyzed the function of the spring in the invention and then set about thinking of equivalents to perform the same function. But the court doubted whether—

the average person skilled in the art thinks in such a theoretical way.

This applies particularly to the present case because there appeared to be no need for theorizing in view of the fact that a normal helical spring was known as a perfectly suitable means for plucking.

It may be said that the expert evidence before the Landgericht at the trial was different, but I doubt whether this could have been so. There was no real difference between the views of Dr. Sharpe and Dr. Laming on questions of engineering: the difference lay in the approach to construction, which is really a question of law.

[The court went on to find that the invention was not invalid for obviousness and insufficiency.]

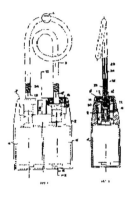

NOTES AND QUESTIONS

(1) **Inter-National Influence?** Armitage says:

> Consider an example. Identical infringing articles are marketed in France and Italy. The scope of protection of the European patent is the same in France and Italy, being determined by Art. 69. The validity is the same in both countries, being governed by Art. 138. A French court finds that the European patent is valid and infringed by the marketing in France. What influence will that have on the Italian court? . . . [A]t least the French decision must be highly persuasive in Italy.

Section 130 of the U.K. Patents Act says that the act is "framed as to have, as nearly as practicable, the same effects in the U.K. as do the corresponding provisions" of the European Patent Convention, the Community Patent Convention, and the Patent Cooperation Treaty, in the territories to which they apply. *See* WILLIAM CORNISH, INTELLECTUAL PROPERTY: PATENTS, COPYRIGHT, TRADE MARKS AND ALLIED RIGHTS 87 (2d ed. 1989). In *Smith Kline v. Harbottle*, Whitford J said

> it is of the greatest importance that in this jurisdiction we should take note of the decisions of the [European Patent Office] and that, so far as may be possible in all those countries which are now bound by the common interest created by the Convention, an attempt should be made to give the same meaning to relevant provisions, whichever the jurisdiction which is being invoked.

(2) **Divining the Meaning and Scope of the Claims of a European Patent**. A commentator recently observed that:

> Courts in the United Kingdom and Germany have led Europe in analyzing infringement, and the Dutch, Austrians, and Swiss have traditionally followed the direction of German courts. Courts in the United Kingdom have emphasized the actual language of the patent claims, which has resulted in careful, wide-as-possible draftsmanship by counsel[] for the inventors. Courts in Germany, by contrast, have looked for the essence of the claim, going beyond the literal language.

MICHAEL P. RYAN, KNOWLEDGE DIPLOMACY 42 (1998).

Indeed, in a parallel *Improver* decision mentioned in the facts of the German decision above, the Hague Court of Appeals (Gerechtshof) in 1992 generally followed the "genus" approach of the Oberlandesgericht, stating, "this court is of the opinion that third parties should realize that the concept of a helical spring contained in the patent claims warrants such a measure of abstraction that a device such as the one manufactured by Remington falls within the patent's scope of protection." Improver Corp. v. Beska B.V. and Remington Prods. Inc. 24 I.I.C. 832-36 (1992). The Gerechtshof also opined, "[w]hether or not such protection is unfair towards third parties must be determined on the basis of what scope of protection an expert in the Netherlands should expect, on the understanding that this expectation is also based on earlier decisions by Dutch courts. This inevitable 'circle' renders it more difficult to arrive at a uniform 'European' scope of protection, but it does not violate the Protocol to Art. 69 of the [EPC]." Is there a lesson in claim draftsmanship to be learned from these cases or not? The November 2000 diplomatic conference revising the EPC expressly approved the adoption of the doctrine of equivalents in Europe, although the revisions agreed at the 2000 conference will not come into effect until all the member countries have ratified the revised convention.

(3) **Establishing a European Patent Judiciary**. The European Commission, responding to a 1996 request of the European Council, issued its Green Paper on the Community Patent System in June 1997. *See supra* § 6.04[A][4]. A June 1998 report of the Select Committee on European Communities of the U.K. House of Lords predicts that the Community Patent

Convention is a "failure" and is highly unlikely ever to come into force. An important reason for the failure according to the Confederation of British Industries is the "absence of adequate judicial arrangements." Negotiations are ongoing in Europe with a view to establishing an Optional Protocol on the Settlement of Litigation Concerning European Patents within the EPC system. *See* http://www.european-patent-office.org/news/headlns/2000_08_03_e.htm. Whether there would be a central court, a "roving court" or regional courts, who would serve on a European Patent Judiciary, and whether the new system would replace the national courts or run parallel for an extended period of time, are questions as yet unanswered.

[2] Multinational Enforcement of Industrial Property Rights: The Brussels Convention

Historically, U.K. courts (and courts from other British Commonwealth countries) were reluctant to adjudicate claims of foreign intellectual property infringement. Doctrinally, this policy was given effect in both jurisdictional and choice of law rules. As a jurisdictional matter, intellectual property actions were treated as local (rather than transitory) causes of action, to be litigated only where fictionally situated. *See supra* § 7.04 (discussing U.S. approach). As a matter of choice of law, foreign intellectual property claims inevitably failed the so-called "double actionability rule." This rule permitted relief for conduct occurring abroad only if it would be actionable under both the law of the forum and the law of the place where the conduct occurred. *See* G.W. Austin, *The Infringement of Foreign Intellectual Property Rights*, 113 LAW QUART. REV. 321 (1997).

Within Europe, the Brussels Convention on Jurisdiction and Enforcement of Judgments in Civil and Commercial Matters (1968) has caused a shift in this position. This Convention now governs civil litigation among EU citizens in EU courts. The Schlosser Report, one of the two reports (along with the Jenard Report) that represents the authoritative history of the purpose and meaning of the Convention's provisions, emphasized that "in accordance with the general spirit of the 1968 Convention, the fact that foreign law has to be applied, either generally or in a particular case, should not constitute a sufficient reason for a court to decline jurisdiction. Where the courts of several States have jurisdiction, the plaintiff has deliberately been given a right of choice . . ." Thus, as noted *supra* § 7.04[A][2], the U.K. courts have in recent years, for example, entertained causes of action for infringement of a Dutch copyright in light of the liberal jurisdictional rules found in the Convention. And several European courts (most notably, but not exclusively) the Dutch courts began to use the liberal jurisdictional rules in the Convention to offer cross-border injunctive relief (especially in patent cases). This led in the 1990s to a spate of decisions from the U.K. and Dutch courts seeking to establish the parameters of this form of relief. Before reading two recent cases from the English and Dutch courts, however, consider again whether (and why) we should permit courts to adjudicate foreign intellectual property claims. What is the value of cross-border litigation (and relief)? Are there any costs associated with it?

BRUSSELS CONVENTION ON JURISDICTION AND ENFORCEMENT OF JUDGMENTS IN CIVIL AND COMMERCIAL MATTERS (1968)

Article 2

Subject to the provisions of this Convention, persons domiciled in a Contracting State shall, whatever their nationality, be sued in the courts of that State. . . .

Article 5

A person domiciled in a Contracting State may, in another Contracting State, be sued

. . . .

(3) In matters relating to tort . . . in the courts for the place where the harmful event occurred.

Article 6

A person domiciled in a Contracting State may also be sued—

(1) Where he is one of a number of defendants, in the courts for the place where any one of them is domiciled

Article 16

The following courts shall have exclusive jurisdiction, regardless of domicile

. . . .

(4) In proceedings concerned with the registration or validity of patents, trade marks, designs, or other similar rights required to be deposited or registered, the courts of the Contracting State in which the deposit or registration has been applied for, has taken place or is under the terms of an international convention deemed to have taken place

Article 19

Where a court of a Contracting State is seised of a claim which is principally concerned with a matter over which the courts of another Contracting State have exclusive jurisdiction by virtue of Article 16, it shall declare of its own motion that it has no jurisdiction.

Article 24

Application may be made to the courts of a Contracting State for such provisional, including protective, measures as may be available under the law of that State, even if, under this Convention, the courts of another Contracting State have jurisdiction as to the substance of the matter.

FORT DODGE ANIMAL HEALTH LTD v. AKZO NOBEL NV
1998 F.S.R. 222 (Court of Appeal, 1997) (Eng.)

LORD WOOLF M.R.:

. . . The Appellants have petitioned in the English Patents Court to revoke EP (UK) No 0189958 which is owned by the first Respondent, Akzo Nobel NV. The other Respondent, Intervet International BV, is a wholly owned subsidiary of Akzo and claims to have an exclusive licence under the patent.

The Appellants seek to reverse the order of Laddie J of 16 October 1997 which refused to grant relief which, in essence, would have prevented the Respondents from maintaining legal proceedings in the Netherlands for infringement of the United Kingdom patent in respect of acts committed in England. The Appellants contend that such relief is appropriate because the U.K. courts have sole jurisdiction to determine the dispute. They say that is urgent as the proceedings which the Respondents have commenced in the Netherlands, seeking relief both in respect of acts committed in the Netherlands and acts committed in the United Kingdom, are about to be heard. For this reason and to enable the Netherlands courts to know our views we have expedited this appeal.

The Facts

Akzo are a large multinational company domiciled in the Netherlands. They are the owners of the United Kingdom patent and a corresponding Dutch patent. Both patents stem from an application filed at the European Patent Office on 21 January 1986. . . .

There are five Appellants, [all of whom are defendants in the Dutch infringement proceedings and all of whom are part of the American Home Products Group of Companies.] [O]ne of the Appellants is domiciled in the Netherlands. One is domiciled in Australia and the rest in the United Kingdom. [The Dutch domiciliary carried out acts in the Netherlands which are alleged to infringe the Dutch patent; the Australian domiciliary was alleged to have delivered infringing vaccines to other defendants for sale in the United Kingdom and Holland]. It is not alleged that any of the United Kingdom domiciled companies have actively participated in the acts of any company which are alleged to infringe the Dutch patent. What is alleged is that they have carried out acts which are alleged to infringe the United Kingdom patent.

. . . .

On 28 April 1997, Akzo and Intervet commenced proceedings in the Netherlands seeking both preliminary and final relief in respect of alleged acts of infringement of both the Dutch patent and the United Kingdom patent. It is contemplated that, subject to appeal, a decision, at least on interim relief, will be reached after a hearing due to take place on 7 November 1997.

On 22 September 1997 the Appellants petitioned the English Patents Court for revocation of the Akzo United Kingdom patent [on grounds inter alia of lack of novelty and obviousness]. The answer to that petition was due within 21 days. It is likely that if the proceedings are prosecuted by the parties with diligence, it can be determined at first instance in about a year to 18 months time.

The dispute

The Appellants' case on the application before Laddie J and before us is that in the circumstances of this case the only court which has jurisdiction to determine whether the Appellants have infringed the United Kingdom patent is the English Patents Court. That being so, it is said that prosecution of that claim in the Dutch Courts against Appellants domiciled in the United Kingdom is vexatious and should be restrained by injunction. Alternatively, if there be doubt on the question of jurisdiction, guidance should be sought from the European Court of Justice as to the true construction of the relevant Conventions and in the meantime there should be an injunction to protect the Appellants' position. Alternatively, if the Patents Court does not have exclusive jurisdiction by reason of the relevant Conventions, it is nevertheless the appropriate court to decide all issues relating to the United Kingdom patent and therefore the relief sought should be granted.

The Respondents contend that the Dutch courts do have jurisdiction to determine the matters raised in their pleaded case in the Dutch proceedings and in particular to determine whether the Appellants who are domiciled in the United Kingdom are infringing the United Kingdom patent. In any case, the United Kingdom courts have no jurisdiction to grant the relief sought on the present application and should not do so. The correct course is to leave it to the Dutch court to decide whether it has the appropriate jurisdiction.

At the outset we make it clear that we do not believe that consideration of the procedures adopted by the Dutch courts to resolve patent disputes is material to the issue before us nor is it appropriate for the courts of the United Kingdom to voice any opinion upon them. At the heart of the dispute between the parties is whether the English Patents Court has exclusive jurisdiction in respect of the issues concerning the United Kingdom patent. That does not depend upon whether the Respondents are seeking to litigate in the Netherlands as opposed to another State which is a signatory to the Brussels Convention.

One of the purposes of the Brussels and Lugano Conventions was to eliminate disputes as to where actions should be decided and to avoid the need to consider whether one jurisdiction was more appropriate than another. It is therefore necessary to look to those Conventions for a solution.

The Brussels Convention

The Brussels Convention, by section 2 of the Civil Jurisdiction and Judgments Act 1982, has the force of law in the United Kingdom. . . .

We believe that articles 2 and 5(3), subject to the exclusion contained in Article 16, apply to actions in respect of intellectual property rights. Thus an owner of an appropriate right can take proceedings in respect of that right either in the country of domicile of the Defendant or where the infringement takes place. . . .

Mr. Silverleaf QC who appeared for the Appellants submitted that such a conclusion was contrary to the Paris Convention of 1883 as revised, the [TRIPS Agreement], the European Patent Convention and article 222 of the Treaty of Rome. We do not believe that these Conventions or the Treaty are directly concerned with jurisdiction. No doubt it was contemplated, prior to the Brussels Convention, that intellectual property rights, being national rights, would be litigated in the State where the right was registered. Indeed there are cases in this country which so held. Even so, those Conventions and the Treaty are not inconsistent with the provisions of the Brussels Convention which apply to intellectual property rights just as much as to other rights. That we believe to be *acte clair*.

Article 6(1) provides another special jurisdiction in that a Defendant, who is one of a number of Defendants, may be sued in the State where one of them is domiciled. The Article has been interpreted as being an exception to the general rule and is to be treated in such a way as to avoid the principle set out in articles 1 to 5 being called into question. In Kalfelis v. Schroder, Case 189/87 [1988] ECR 5565, the European Court said that there must be a connection between the claim made against the person not domiciled in the State where the litigation is pending and the claim made against the party domiciled in that State. The connection must be of "such a kind that it is expedient to determine those actions together in order to avoid the risk of irreconcilable judgments resulting from separate proceedings."

In the present case there has been no examination of the facts and therefore no concluded view can be reached as to whether there is the necessary connection in respect of some of the Appellants. However, a number of Appellants are only alleged to have infringed the United Kingdom patent and it would appear tenuous to suggest that it was expedient to determine together an action for infringement of a Dutch patent, with which they are not concerned, and a United Kingdom patent with which they are, so as to avoid irreconcilable judgments. They are actions relating to two different national rights. True they stem from the same patent application and similar rules of construction will be applicable, but the rights given by those patents are national rights limited in territory to the State in which they are registered and the ambit of the monopolies will not necessarily be the same as amendment is possible. There is no risk of irreconcilable judgments because a judgment on infringement in the United Kingdom will depend upon a national right having effect only in the United Kingdom. The same applies to a judgment on the Dutch patent.

[Under Article 16(4)] there can be no doubt that all proceedings for revocation of a patent have to be decided by the court of the State where the patent is registered. In this case proceedings for revocation of the United Kingdom patent have to be decided by the English Patents Court. That also applies to proceedings "concerned with the registration or validity of patents." [Based upon language in the Jenard report, the court concluded that Article 16(4) "should be construed as differentiating between actions for infringement and proceedings concerned with validity."]

In the United Kingdom it is possible to have both an action for infringement by a patentee and the equivalent action for a declaration of non-infringement by a person threatened by a patent. Where questions of infringement and validity both arise it is invariably not possible to conclude there is infringement without validity being determined. An extreme example, known as a *Gillette* defence, is where the alleged infringer's case is that the patent is invalid if the alleged infringing acts fall within the ambit of the claims. That appears to be part of the Appellants' contentions in this case. It follows that the split contemplated in the Jenard Report between actions for infringement and proceedings concerned with validity cannot always be made.

Article 64 of the European Patent Convention states that a European Patent confers on its proprietor the same rights as those of a national patent and that infringement shall be dealt with by national law. In the United Kingdom those rights are defined in section 60 of the Patents Act 1977. They are rights which apply only so long as the patent is in force. In proceedings for infringement, validity of the patent is often disputed and, if the attack on the patent is successful, it will be revoked pursuant to section 72 of the 1977 Act. Such revocation has the effect of revoking the grant of the patent and therefore its registration as a patent, and is the reason for the view held in the United Kingdom that it is not possible to infringe an invalid patent. In many cases the attack on the patent prompts the patentee to seek amendment so as to limit the ambit of his monopoly. In the United Kingdom that is possible under section 75 of the 1977 Act. Any amendment has effect and is deemed always to have had effect from the grant of the patent. [cit].

As article 64 of the European Patent Convention requires the national law to be determinative of what will and what will not amount to infringement, it follows that when there is a bona fide challenge to the validity of a United Kingdom patent, any proceedings for infringement must in English eyes be "concerned with" the validity of the patent. Often, perhaps normally, the issue of validity will be the principal element of the dispute. No conclusion as to the chances of a claim of infringement succeeding can be made until a decision has been reached as to the strength of the allegations of invalidity. No concluded view on infringement can be reached until a decision has been reached as to whether any amendment should be made and the attack on the patent has been rejected.

In the present case the Appellants have raised a substantial attack on the validity of the United Kingdom patent and also intend to rely upon a Gillette defence. This is a case therefore in which no conclusion on the infringement can be reached without consideration of the validity of the patent. We believe that for the purposes of Article 19 the claim by the Respondents in respect of acts carried out in the United Kingdom are principally concerned with validity of the United Kingdom patent and therefore by reason of that Article and Article 16 the claim falls within the exclusive jurisdiction of the United Kingdom court.

In our view Laddie J was correct in Coin Controls Ltd. v. Suzo International (UK) Ltd. [1997] 3 All ER 45 when he [noted that although "where there are multiple discrete issues before a court it may be possible to sever one or more claims from another and to decline to accept jurisdiction only over those covered by Article 16, that approach does not apply where infringement and validity of an intellectual property right are concerned because they are so closely interrelated."]

Article 24 relates to provisional, including protective, measures. As explained in the Jenard Report, application may be made to the courts of a Contracting State for such provisional measures as may be available under the internal law of that State. However, the measures must be provisional and, in our view, granted in aid of or as an adjunct to some final determination then in contemplation.

Upon the evidence before this court, provisional relief by way of injunction would not be granted in the United Kingdom to restrain continuance by the Appellants of the acts complained of as infringement because of the delay by the Respondents in taking action. However that delay may or may not be determinative in the eyes of a Dutch court. But that is the court in which Akzo seek provisional relief in respect of acts taking place in the United Kingdom, and it is for that court to determine the effect of the delay.

Mr. Silverleaf accepts that a Dutch court has to apply Dutch law when deciding whether to grant provisional relief pursuant to the jurisdiction conferred by article 24. He submits that the United Kingdom Patents courts has by reason of articles 2, 5 and 16(4) exclusive jurisdiction over the dispute between Akzo and the English domiciled Appellants relating to the United Kingdom patent. It follows, he submits, that provisional relief could only be granted in aid of or as an adjunct to a final determination in the United Kingdom courts. Akzo have not initiated any proceedings in the United Kingdom and have not stated any intention of doing so. It followed that there was no jurisdiction under article 24 to grant provisional relief as sought by Akzo.

Mr. Prescott QC, who appeared for the Respondents, submits that the Dutch court can order provisional relief as an adjunct to Akzo's claim for final relief in the Dutch proceedings. That provisional relief would do justice between the parties pending resolution of the question of validity by the United Kingdom Patents court.

The crucial difference between the submissions of the parties is the effect of Article 16(4). If the United Kingdom courts have exclusive jurisdiction over the dispute concerning the United Kingdom patent, then there is no justification for the Respondents attempting to obtain from the Dutch court even provisional relief as an aid to or an adjunct of the claim for final relief in respect of the United Kingdom patent. It would be vexatious to seek such relief. If our conclusion as to the proper application of Article 16(4) is correct, it follows that article 24 does not provide jurisdiction to grant provisional relief restraining infringement within the United Kingdom as an adjunct to the claim for full relief pleaded in the Dutch proceedings.

The question of relief

We have expressed definite views as to the construction of Articles 16(4) and 24 and their application to the facts. We have also expressed views as to the ambit of article 6. However we accept that a contrary opinion is tenable. The matter is accordingly not "acte clair". The question which view is right is one of considerable importance to the enforcement of intellectual property rights in jurisdictions subject to the Brussels Convention. We believe that it is necessary for the European Court of Justice to consider the construction of those Articles and their application to the facts and therefore it would be right to refer appropriate questions to that Court. That we believe to be the correct course, despite the submission of Mr. Prescott that we did not have jurisdiction to grant any relief and that in any case no reference should be made because it was not necessary. We turn to give our reasons why those submissions should not be accepted.

Mr. Prescott submitted that this court has no jurisdiction to grant an injunction in favour of the United Kingdom domiciled Appellants which would restrain Akzo from maintaining proceedings before the Dutch court in respect of the United Kingdom patent. [We believe that submission is wrong.] The United Kingdom courts have jurisdiction to prevent vexation and oppression by persons subject to their jurisdiction. In particular, the courts are entitled to prevent persons domiciled in this country from being submitted to vexatious or oppressive litigation whether started or to be started in this country or another country. As was stated in the advice of the Privy Council in Société National Industrielle Aerospatiale v. Lee Kui Jak [1987] 1 AC 871 a court can restrain a person from pursuing proceedings in a foreign Court where a remedy is available both in that foreign court and this country, but will only do so if pursuit by the person "would be vexatious or oppressive." Further, since such an order indirectly affects the foreign court, the jurisdiction must be exercised with caution and only if the ends of justice so require. We emphasise that injunctions granted for such purposes are directed against the vexatious party and not the courts of the other jurisdiction.

In the present case we have concluded that the dispute relating to the United Kingdom patent comes, by reason of Article 16(4), within the exclusive jurisdiction of the United Kingdom Patents Court. We have also concluded that the matter is not "acte clair". In those circumstances we do not consider we would be justified in reaching a final conclusion that the pursuit, by Akzo, of the claim in the Dutch courts in respect of the United Kingdom patent would be vexatious. It follows that we are not prepared to grant a final injunction at this time. The reference is necessary in order to decide whether final relief by way of injunction or declaration would be appropriate. We now therefore proceed to consider whether interim relief by way of injunction or otherwise would be appropriate pending the determination of the reference to the European Court.

Despite the fact that the relief would be directed against the Respondents, we have in mind that it would indirectly affect the Dutch court which has not yet considered what action, if any, would be appropriate. We have every confidence that the Dutch court will, when deciding what to do, take into account that this court will be referring to the European Court of Justice questions to elucidate how articles 6, 16(4), 19 and 24 should be applied to the dispute. It will give proper weight to our conclusion that it would be wrong for this court to anticipate the decision of the European Court. It will, we believe, also consider carefully the other views expressed in this judgment and, of course, the submissions of the parties and the facts. That being so we have come to the conclusion that justice does not require that this court should grant any relief at this stage. The nature of the parties' businesses means that it is most unlikely that they will suffer any significant harm pending the decision of the European Court which will not be compensated by the award of damages.

We shall therefore adjourn this appeal pending a judgment of the European Court upon questions to be referred to them. When the views of the European Court are known we shall decide what further relief, if any, is appropriate.

EXPANDABLE GRAFTS P'SHIP v. BOSTON SCIENTIFIC BV

[1999] F.S.R. 352 (Court of Appeal, The Hague) (Neth.)

. . . .

In the originating summons [plaintiffs] EGP claimed interim injunctions "prohibiting each of the defendants individually from infringing European Patent 0335 341 either directly or indirectly, in particular by offering, selling, delivering or at any rate marketing the [allegedly infringing] NIR stents, not only for the Netherlands but also with respect to any direct or indirect infringements in other countries in which the patent applies, with the exception of Germany."

The wording of the summary of claims gives rise to misapprehensions. It makes it appear as if the case concerns one single European Patent which is valid in a number of countries. But this is not the case.

The European Patent in question has been granted for: Austria, Belgium, Switzerland, Germany, Spain, France, Great Britain, Greece, Italy, Liechtenstein, Luxembourg, the Netherlands and Sweden. But there is not one European Patent, one common patent, which is valid in the aggregate territory of all countries for which the patent has been granted. The fact is that according to general and common terminology a European Patent consists of a bundle of national patents, in the present case of national patents which are valid in each of the countries just mentioned. These separate national patents have in common that they have been granted in accordance with the rules of the European Patent Convention (EPC) following one single grant procedure by the European Patent Office at Munich and that after being granted they are governed not only by the national patent laws, which have been harmonised to a considerable extent but are not yet quite identical, but also by a number of provisions of the EPC. *See* EPC, Article 2, paragraph 2, which provides:

> The European Patent shall, in each of the Contracting States for which it is granted, have the effect of and be subject to the same conditions as a national patent granted by that State, unless otherwise provided in this Convention.

and EPC, Article 64, paragraph 1, which provides:

> A European Patent shall subject to the provisions of paragraph 2, confer on its proprietor from the date of publication of the mention of its grant in each Contracting State in respect of which it is granted the same rights as would be conferred by a national patent granted in that State.

EGP are claiming . . . injunctions prohibiting each of the defendants not only from infringing the respective national patents originating from the European Patent granted by the European Patent Office and applicable in the respective countries in which the individual defendant corporations have their respective seats, but also from infringing all other national patents belonging to the bundle of patents in the designated countries.

The Court of Appeal further understands the claims thus, that EGP have not wished to raise the issue of possible infringements of the German patent which belongs to the European bundle. EGP have not maintained the part of their action concerning the infringement of the British patent.

The [defendant] BS corporations which have their seats abroad entered an appearance exclusively for the purpose of taking issue with the jurisdiction of the Dutch courts.

EGP have taken the position that the Dutch courts do have jurisdiction over the actions against the defendants which have their seats in the Netherlands by virtue of Article 2 of the Brussels Convention on Jurisdiction and the Enforcement of Judgements in Civil and Commercial Matters (the Brussels Convention) and that the Dutch courts also have jurisdiction over the actions against the other defendants, "by virtue of the provision with respect to the right to summon foreigners into a Dutch court of Article 6(1) Brussels/Lugano Convention, or at any rate of section 126, subsection 7, Dutch Code of Civil Procedure, and (as far as the interim injunctions are concerned) in conjunction with Art 24 Brussels/Lugano Convention."

International jurisdiction in patent cases is an issue that is under discussion in various countries. In its judgment of October 27, 1997 the London Court of Appeal has referred questions on this issue to the [European] Court of Justice for a preliminary ruling. *See* Fort Dodge Ltd. v. Akzo Nobel NV [1998] F.S.R. 222.

In view of the claims and the countries in which the defendants have their seats, the jurisdiction must be decided according to the Brussels Convention and the Lugano Convention, respectively, on Jurisdiction and the Enforcement of Judgements in Civil and Commercial Matters. The Court of Appeal will first examine whether the jurisdiction of the Dutch courts can be based on Article 6(1) of the Brussels/Lugano Convention . . . .

The Court of Appeal states first of all that in accordance with the principal rule of both Conventions as embodied in Article 2 in conjunction with Article 53, companies and corporations must be sued in the courts for the state in which they have their seats. Article 6(1) contains a special jurisdiction rule.

The literal text of Article 6(1) does not seem to impose any restrictions on the possibilities available to a plaintiff to choose the courts for the desired country by suing defendants from different countries. Thus it would seem as if the plaintiff has as many options as the number of different countries in which the defendants have their seats. This is not the case.

[The court quoted at length from the opinion of the Court of Justice in *Kalfelis* and concluded that] the rule laid down in Article 6(1) therefore applies where the actions brought against the various defendants are related when the proceedings are instituted, that is to say where it is expedient to hear and determine them together in order to avoid the risk of irreconcilable judgments resulting from separate proceedings. It is for the national court to verify in each individual case whether that condition is satisfied.

As appears from paragraph 11 of the judgment of the Court of Justice, the problems under consideration here show a strong affinity to those of Article 22 of the Brussels Convention, which Article deals with connection between actions. In the *Tatry* case, [1994] ECR I-5439, the Court of Justice said at page 5478:

> In order to achieve proper administration of justice, that interpretation must be broad and cover all cases where there is a risk of conflicting decisions even if the judgments can be separately enforced and their legal consequences are not mutually exclusive.

It appears from the above that although this is not expressed in the text of Article 6(1) itself, yet the possibilities of applying this paragraph are certainly subject to restrictions.

Having regard to the reasons stated by the [lower court] for its decision, the question arises whether there is question of related actions as mentioned by the Court of Justice in the *Kalfelis / Schroder* case when in one procedure the proprietor of a European Patent brings an action for, for instance, an injunction prohibiting a defendant domiciled in the Netherlands from infringing the Dutch patent of the European bundle of patents by marketing a certain product in the Netherlands and for an injunction prohibiting a defendant domiciled in France from infringing the French patent of the same European bundle of patents by marketing an identical product in France.

[We are] of the opinion that this question must be answered in the negative. Even if the outcome of the judgments in the Netherlands and in France would differ—which is possible in spite of the application of the same rules of substantive patent law—it cannot be said that the judgments are irreconcilable. The fact is that the national patents out of the European bundle exist independently of each other. It is therefore quite possible for one national patent out of the European bundle to be declared wholly or partially null and void while another is held to be valid. It is moreover not impossible that the scope of protection of one patent turns out to be different from that of the other one. One might say that what the patents originating from a European Patent have in common is, in particular, the past and that, after being granted, each of them lives its own life. It is undeniably true that in a case like the present it is onerous for a patent proprietor who wishes to put a stop to the infringements in the Netherlands and in France, that he is forced to start proceedings in both countries and runs the risk, moreover, that different judgments will be issued regarding the same infringements in the two countries. However, having regard to the pivotal meaning of Article 2 of the Brussels/Lugano Convention and the fact that Article 6(1) forms an exception, the interest of the defendant in being sued in the courts for the country in which he is resident or domiciled must outweigh the inconvenience to the patent proprietor, taking account of the fact that the possibility of different judgments is inherent in the European Patent. [We] comment in this respect that the countries that concluded the EPC must have foreseen this inconvenience to patent proprietors and did not remove it.

If, however, in the example discussed above the Dutch and the French defendants belong to the same group of companies, a different approach may be called for. Where several companies belonging to one group of companies are selling identical products in different national markets, this will have to be considered as one joint action based on a joint business plan. In such case the proper administration of justice calls for the simultaneous hearing and settlement of cases, which is made possible by Article 6(1) of the Brussels/Lugano Convention. This does not mean to say, however, that the plaintiff must have the option of suing all the parties belonging to the group in the courts for the domicile of any one of the companies belonging to the group, at his own choice. In the opinion of the Court of Appeal this would be contrary to the predictableness of the competent court contemplated by the Conventions [cit]. The best way of harmonising the interests which Article 2 and Article 6(1) of the Brussels/Lugano Convention purport to serve is to take the view that in such case, by analogy with the case law concerning the applicability of Article 5(3) of the Brussels Convention [cit], all the actions may only be brought in their entirety in the courts for the domicile of the head office in question which is in charge of the business operations in question and/or from which the business plan originated. The relation between the actions and these courts will be the closest. This solution has the advantage of avoiding jurisdiction being conferred on more than one forum and consequently of reducing the possibilities of forum shopping, which according to Advocate-General Darmon in his advisory opinion in the *Shevill / Presse Alliance* case (paragraphs 57 and 67) is precisely what is contemplated by the Brussels Convention.

The above has the following consequences for the case now before the Court of Appeal.

In the written summary of the argument by Mr. Ebbink in the first instance the following can be read:

> BSC is an American enterprise having offices all over the world. As far as relevant to the present case, the corporate structure of BSC in Europe is as follows.

> The European headquarters are located in Paris under the name of BS International BV. BS Paris is charged with the central management of the European offices of BSC. Its duties include the European management, marketing, staff services, communications with and reporting to BSC America etc. The Dutch branch of BS International BV is a small office. The 'centre of activities of the BSC Group outside America', . . . is not in the Netherlands but in Paris. The fact that BS Paris has chosen to be incorporated in the legal form of a Dutch private company (BV) has a fiscal background. The Dutch office of BS International BV serves as a warehouse for the continental European market. In the Netherlands, (Beek, Limburg) the stents are awaiting further distribution.

The activities of the local BS companies among the defendants . . . only include the local marketing and sale of the NIR stents, controlled, as stated before, by BS Paris. The local companies have a high degree of autonomy. They promote the stents in their respective countries or regions, they approach (potential) customers, subsequently order the NIR stents directly from the distributor (the Dutch office of BS International BV) and invoice directly to their customers.

It can be inferred from the above that BS International BV is, as the parties have called it, the spider in the web. All other defendant BS corporations in Europe are controlled from this corporation. All these corporations are acting jointly under the management of BS International BV. In this case the actions for injunctions against infringement may all be brought in their entirety in the courts for the place where BS International BV has its seat.

The parties differ in opinion on the question where BS International has its seat. According to EGP it is the Netherlands, according to BS, France.

The Court of Appeal takes the following position regarding this issue. The second sentence of Article 53 of the Brussels Convention reads as follows:

> In order to determine that seat, the court shall apply its rules of private international law.

Under Dutch private international law a company is held to have its seat at its registered seat . . . . It appears from the extract from the commercial register that the registered seat of BS International is at Maastricht. So BS International BV has its seat in the Netherlands.

Consequently the Dutch courts have jurisdiction over the infringement actions.

The present proceedings are not main proceedings on the merits but interim injunction proceedings. All the grounds stated above relate to the court's jurisdiction in main proceedings on the merits. In the opinion of the Court of Appeal it is the position that in a case in which the Dutch courts have jurisdiction over actions in main proceedings on the merits, the Dutch courts also have jurisdiction over actions brought in interim injunction proceedings.

Yet another complication presents itself in the present case. BS has taken the position that the European Patent at issue in these proceedings was granted wrongfully. Though it is true that BS has not filed an opposition with the Opposition Department of the European Patent Office, it has instituted nullity proceedings in a great number of countries.

According to BS this must result in the Dutch courts no longer having jurisdiction over the infringement actions relating to the foreign patents. BS is relying on Article 16(4) in conjunction with Article 19 of the Brussels/Lugano Convention.

By virtue of Article 16(4) of the Brussels/Lugano Convention, exclusive jurisdiction over actions for the nullification of foreign patents does not vest in the Dutch courts but in the courts for the countries in which the patents in question apply. If a Dutch court should be seised of an action for the nullification of a foreign patent, then by virtue of Article 19, the Dutch court would have to declare of its own motion that it has no jurisdiction.

The actions brought by EGP are infringement actions. With respect to these actions the jurisdiction of the courts does not cease to exist by operation of the law as soon as nullity actions are instituted. For it is the opinion of the Court of Appeal that the jurisdiction issue must be decided on the basis of the claim stated in the summons.

Consequences of the institution of nullity actions for the jurisdiction issue

The institution of nullity actions may have consequences, though, for the hearing of the infringement actions. It is a fact that infringement and nullity are indissolubly linked with each other, since it is impossible to infringe a patent that is null and void. Unless it is immediately clear that a nullity action cannot be deemed to be meant seriously, in the case of main proceedings on the merits the court which is asked to pronounce judgment on the infringement issue will have to adopt a cautious attitude towards the infringement action and in principle will have to stay the infringement proceedings until the foreign court has pronounced judgment on the nullity issue.

Obviously the separate hearing and settlement of the infringement issue and the nullity issue by two different national courts is far from ideal. It would be desirable for the infringement and nullity issues to be decided by the same court. It would also be desirable if the hearing and settlement of actions for infringement and nullity of several patents originating from one European bundle of patents could be concentrated in one court. But this solution is barred by Article 16(4) of the Brussels/Lugano Convention. National courts cannot make the said wishes come true. Amendment of the Conventions seems to be inevitable.

In the opinion of the Court of Appeal the assessment of the interim infringement injunctions claimed in the present proceedings is in fact affected by the nullity actions. This situation calls for at least the same degree of caution.

As will appear in the following, it is not in the least clear right away that the arguments put forward by BS in support of the allegation that the national patents originating from the European Bundle of patents should be declared null and void, must be considered inadequate. The result must be that the Dutch courts will have to refuse the interim injunctions prohibiting infringement of the foreign patents.

Jurisdiction by virtue of Article 24 of the Brussels / Lugano Convention

To the extent that EGP have taken the position that Article 24 of the Brussels/Lugano Convention will avail them, the Court of Appeal cannot subscribe to this view. This Article offers the possibility of imposing provisional or protective measures even in those cases in which the courts of another Contracting State have jurisdiction as to the substance of the matter. The Court of Appeal holds the opinion that in such a case the measures to be imposed can be operative only within the territory of the state of the court. . . . [T]he justification for the said additional jurisdiction lies in the fact that the local courts are in the best position to judge the circumstances on the ground of which the requested measures are to be allowed or refused. It is irreconcilable with this ruling that a Dutch court which has jurisdiction exclusively by virtue of Article 24, should issue regulatory measures having effect abroad.

Jurisdiction by virtue of Dutch Code of Civil Procedure, section 126(7)

Section 126, subsection 7 of the Dutch Code of Civil Procedure cannot apply since the defendants have their seats in countries which are signatories of either the Brussels Convention or the Lugano Convention. The provisions of these Conventions prevail.

Conclusion with regard to the claims for cross-border prohibitive injunctions

The conclusion to be drawn from the above is that though the Dutch courts have jurisdiction over the infringement actions instituted against all the BS corporations that have been summoned, yet the actions for interim injunctions against infringement of the foreign patents must be refused because the likelihood is that the foreign patents will be declared null and void.

Jurisdiction over the claim for an injunction against infringement of the Dutch patent

On the same grounds as are stated above with respect to the jurisdiction over the actions for cross-border prohibitory injunctions, the court has jurisdiction over the action for an injunction against infringement of the Dutch patent.

Consequences of the action for nullity of the Dutch patent

[The Court of Appeals concluded that there was a likelihood that the patent would be declared null and void in the designated countries, and thus the interim injunction against infringement of the Dutch patent was also denied].

NOTES AND QUESTIONS

(1) **Dutch Case Law**. Dutch cross-border injunctions had been the topic of much comment up until April 23, 1998. Indeed, the literature addressing these developments is voluminous. For a good background discussion of the pertinent provisions and case law, see Ian Karet, *Intellectual Property Litigation—Jurisdiction in Europe*, 3 INTELL. PROP. Q. 317 (1998); Jan J. Brinkhof, *Summary Proceedings and Other Provisional Measures in Connection with Patent Infringement*, 26 I.I.C. 762 (1993). The *Expandable Grafts* court restricted the availability of pan-EU relief by interpreting the requirement of relatedness of claims more strictly and rejecting the argument that sufficient connection may be grounded on the infringement of national patents derived from a common European patent application. For commentary on this more recent case law and the so-called "spider in the web" doctrine developed by the Dutch courts to set the parameters of this jurisdiction, see Charles Gielen, *District Court Refines Case Law on 'Spider in the Web' Doctrine*, 14 WORLD INTELL. PROP. REP. 186 (June 2000).

(2) **Trademark Cases**. Most of the leading cases involving cross-border relief under the Brussels Convention have involved patent rights (typically national patent rights stemming from a common European patent); but some cases have involved trademark claims. *See, e.g.*, Yakult v. Danone, 1998 E.T.M.R. 465, 472 & 479 (Hague Dist. Ct. 1998) (Neth.) ("The system under the Brussels Convention requires that . . . a court must apply foreign trade mark law in the appropriate cases," but declining to extend the injunction to France "although competent to do so" because of a lack of urgency).

(3) **Exclusive Jurisdiction**. The exclusive jurisdiction provision in Article 16(4) of the Brussels Convention applies only to registered rights. The registration variable is said to be significant for several reasons, including respect for foreign administrative officials and concerns of institutional competence. First, it is argued that registered rights are more likely directly to implicate decisions of the administrative organs of a state. Courts are generally

reluctant to pass on the correctness of the governmental acts of a foreign state. Second, according exclusive jurisdiction to the conferring state on matters implicating validity or nullity of registered rights reflects concern regarding the ability of foreign judges to make judgments regarding the validity of registered rights, which are normally granted only after detailed administrative examination by specially trained national officials. Consider also the following dictum from Mr. Justice Aldous in *Plastus Kreativ AB v. Minnesota Mining and Manufacturing Co.* [1995] RPC 438 (Eng.), where he explained some of the reasons why he was reluctant to adjudicate foreign patent rights:

> For myself I would not welcome the task of having to decide whether a person had infringed a foreign patent. Although patent actions appear on their face to be disputes between two parties, in reality they also concern the public. A finding of infringement is a finding that a monopoly granted by the state is to be enforced. The result is invariably that the public have to pay higher prices than if the monopoly did not exist. If that be the proper result, then that result should, I believe, come about from a decision of a court situated in the state where the public have to pay the higher prices. One only has to imagine a decision of this court that the German public should pay to a British company substantial sums of money to realise the difficulties that might arise. I believe that, if the local courts are responsible for enforcing and deciding questions of validity and infringement, the conclusions reached are likely to command the respect of the public.

Are any of these arguments persuasive? Are they more persuasive for some forms of intellectual property than others? Are they more persuasive as regards registered rights than unregistered rights (such as copyright)? Could the concerns underlying the exclusive jurisdiction provision be addressed in a manner that permits the full use of the liberal jurisdictional provisions in Articles 2, 5 and 6? For example, could the court hearing the request for cross-border relief refer the question of validity to the national court of the state that granted the registered right?

(4) **The Scope of the Conventions**. The Brussels Convention governs jurisdiction in the courts of EU states in actions involving European citizens. The parallel Lugano Convention, referenced in *Fort Dodge*, extends the same principles to states in the European Free Trade Association (EFTA). *See* Convention on Jurisdiction and Enforcement of Judgments in Civil and Commercial Matters, Sept. 16, 1988, 1988 O.J. (L 319) 1. The Brussels and Lugano Conventions are in the process of being revised and incorporated directly into EU law. *See* Amended Proposal for a Council Regulation on Jurisdiction and the Recognition and Enforcement of Judgments in Civil and Commercial Matters, COM(2000) 689 final (October 26, 2000).

(5) **The Role of the European Court of Justice**. The European Court of Justice is accorded jurisdiction to interpret the meaning of the Brussels Convention. *See* Protocol on the Interpretation by the Court of Justice of the

Convention of 27 September 1968 on Jurisdiction and Enforcement of Judgments in Civil and Commercial Matters, 1990 O.J. (C189) at 25. (The parties in *Fort Dodge* settled prior to the European Court handing down a decision.) The Court has developed a substantial body of case law on the meaning of the Convention. Notice, however, that the U.K. court decided that certain matters of treaty interpretation were *acte claire* and thus did not require the involvement of the European Court. This doctrine enables national courts to apply allegedly unambiguous interpretations of the Convention and thus to function on a day-to-day basis without the involvement of the European Court.

(6) **Proposed Hague Convention.** A draft convention on jurisdiction and enforcement of foreign judgments has been prepared by the Hague Conference on Private International Law and it is closely modeled upon the Brussels Convention. A two-stage diplomatic conference has been scheduled to discuss the draft; the first session in mid-2001, with the concluding session in early 2002. The draft convention is controversial for a number of reasons not restricted to intellectual property. But the intellectual property provisions have attracted significant attention, both internationally (from WIPO and the WTO) and in the United States (where the State Department, the Copyright Office and the Patent & Trademark Office are each debating what position the United States should adopt). Article 12(4) of the proposed Hague Convention would mirror Article 16(4) of the Brussels Convention, but the precise scope of the provision remains a matter for negotiation. At its narrowest, the exclusion may be limited to challenges to the validity of registered rights. But some countries have suggested that the exclusive jurisdiction provision should be extended to infringement questions on the theory that the scope of rights (and hence determinations of infringement) is linked to validity; a restrictive approach to one might justify an expansive approach to the other, and vice versa. Would you support such an extended exclusion from the general rules of jurisdiction? What advantages might accrue from applying more liberal jurisdictional rules in multinational patent infringement disputes?

The European Court of Justice has jurisdiction to interpret the meaning of the Brussels Convention. No such court will have a similar role with the Hague Convention. Uniformity will instead be pursued by requiring national courts to interpret the Convention in light of its international character, the need for uniformity, and the case law of other contracting states. *See* Draft Convention art. 38. How will this affect the development of international rules on consolidation of international intellectual property litigation?

§ 7.06 Parallel Imports/Gray Goods

Most intellectual property laws have developed the concept of exhaustion of rights (sometimes called the first sale doctrine in copyright law) that in some form is essential to ensure the free alienability of goods. Rights may be exhausted with respect to a particular good when that good is placed on the market by or with the consent of the rights owner. That is to say, the right owner may not assert its intellectual property rights to restrain the free transfer of those goods. Several questions are raised by the exhaustion doctrine, most significantly: (1) what is the geographic scope of exhaustion, i.e., does it matter where the rights owner marketed the goods? (2) are rights exhausted where the goods are placed on the market not by the rights owner but by a company in a form of an economic relationship with the rights owner? and (3) are trademark (or other) rights revived, and capable of being asserted, with respect to goods that are placed on the market by the mark owner but then modified or repackaged without the mark owner's consent?

These issues are not new. But in the context of global trade they have assumed heightened significance. The free trade philosophy underpinning our present economic environment, the inclusion of intellectual property law within free trade agreements such as GATT, and the ongoing development of intellectual property laws by a supranational institution (such as the EU) committed to eradicating barriers to the free movement of goods within a multinational territory, has each brought the exhaustion issue to the forefront of current debate. The territorial nature of intellectual property rights clashes with an absolutist vision of free international trade in goods. The exhaustion doctrine mediates to some extent that clash, by determining whether and to what extent a right holder in country A can assert its rights and thus prevent the entry into country A of legitimate goods put on the market in country B. (These goods imported from country B are called "parallel imports" or "gray goods.") In this area, international agreements remain relatively sparse. Thus, after setting out briefly those provisions that exist, we review the approaches to exhaustion adopted in different national and regional jurisdictions, primarily in the United States and the European Union.

[A]   International Treaty Provisions

TRIPS AGREEMENT, ARTICLE 6

For purposes of dispute settlement under this Agreement, subject to the provisions of Articles 3 and 4 above [national treatment and most-favored nation treatment] nothing in this Agreement shall be used to address the issue of exhaustion of intellectual property rights.

WIPO COPYRIGHT TREATY, ARTICLE 6(2)

Nothing in this Treaty shall affect the freedom of Contracting Parties to determine the conditions, if any, under which the exhaustion of the [right of distribution] applies after the first sale or other transfer of ownership of the original or a copy of the work with the authorization of the author.

PAUL J. HEALD, TRADEMARKS AND GEOGRAPHICAL INDICATIONS: EXPLORING THE CONTOURS OF THE TRIPS AGREEMENT*
29 VAND. J. TRANSNAT'L L. 638, 656-658 (1996)

. . . Presumably, the TRIPS Agreement does not require a member to reject or accept the importation of legitimately trademarked goods that are intended to be sold without the permission of the trademark's local owner. Whether this stance is consistent with the agreement's stated goal to advance "the transfer and dissemination of technology, to the mutual advantage of producers and users . . . in a manner conducive to social and economic welfare" is highly debatable. . . .

. . . .

The TRIPS Agreement [thus] specifically sidesteps the issue of the propriety of importing gray market goods. In most circumstances, gray market goods are legitimately trademarked genuine goods bought in nation A and transported for sale to nation B without the consent of the trademark owner in nation B. For example, large U.S. merchandisers frequently buy consumer goods in Asia and import them for resale in their domestic stores without the permission of the trademark's U.S. owner. This generally creates price competition with limited or exclusive dealerships in the United States supported by the U.S. trademark owner. In the United States, the legality of such imports depends on the nature of the relationship between the domestic trademark owner and the foreign manufacturer. Although the extent to which a gray market should be fostered is debated in many nations, the negotiators of the GATT Uruguay Round should have been able to find common ground regarding genuine gray market goods.[150]

Within any particular nation, one can understand why a debate over the legitimacy of gray market goods may rage. In the United States, for example, consumers benefit from the downward pressure on prices caused by an active gray market. Some individuals worry, however, that U.S. corporate trademark owners, and therefore their employees and stockholders, will suffer when they are unable to control the local availability and prices of goods manufactured for them overseas.[152] Within a nation, the empirical question of whether wealth is

---

*Copyright 1996, Paul Heald; Vanderbilt Journal of Transnational Law. Reprinted with permission.

[150]The author's argument in favor of gray market goods does not encompass those goods that are not identical to those sold with permission of the local trademark owners. Depending on the country of manufacture or intended sale, goods sometimes have different ingredients or formulas. When these goods find their way outside their intended market, a potential for confusion exists. Consumers may need protection from legitimately trademarked products that have the potential to cause confusion. *See, e.g.*, Ferrero U.S.A., Inc. v. Ozak Trading, Inc., 753 F. Supp. 1240, 1545-47 (D. N.J. 1991) (imported "Tic Tacs" contained more calories than U.S. "Tic Tacs", causing confusion actionable under the Lanham Act.).

[152]Some individuals also worry that importers will "free ride" on advertising conducted by the local trademark owner. This argument, however, goes too far. Virtually all sellers benefit from the tastes created by the advertising of their competitors. When Chrysler's advertising convinced U.S. car buyers that the mini-van was a superior product, Ford and Chevrolet quickly took advantage of the new market created by Chrysler's advertising and marketed their own competing versions of the same product. Free riding is a time-honored, and probably efficient, business activity. . . .

increased or decreased by the gray market may be difficult to answer. From a global perspective, however, a strong argument can be made that the free movement of legitimately trademarked goods is supported by GATT principles. The philosophy of the GATT is premised on the notion that global wealth and prosperity is tied to the free movement of goods. Tariffs, the quintessential impediment to free trade, are suspect because they slow the flow of goods and generally result in diminished competition, higher prices, and lower quality goods. Particular tariffs may benefit a particular country but, in theory, the global community as a whole is better off without them.

A legal rule that prohibits the importation of legitimately trademarked goods looks much like a tariff; it creates a barrier at the border that certain sorts of goods cannot cross. Given the nature of gray market goods, the barrier is difficult to justify. By definition, the goods are not counterfeit; the trademarks they bear are affixed with the authorization of the trademark owner. If for some reason the goods are defective, noxious, dangerous, or likely to cause confusion in the market, a ban on importation is easy to justify. The vast majority of such goods, however, pose no threat to consumers. Gray market Nikon cameras sold by New York City mail order houses are real Nikons, identical to Nikons sold by authorized Nikon dealerships. No consumer protection rationale can justify a ban on these sorts of legitimately trademarked goods.

One can understand why Nikon management, employees, and stockholders might be upset by the price competition created by New York mail order houses, but they are hard-pressed to offer a rationale for banning imports that is consistent with GATT principles. Their essential claim is that they will lose profits if the government does not stop certain goods at the border. That may be true, but General Motors and Ford can make exactly the same claim: "We will lose profits if the government does not stop Hondas at the border, or impose a high tariff on Hondas." Protecting the profit margin of certain producers by stopping goods at the border is precisely the sort of activity that the GATT was meant to discourage. One can only hope that future negotiations will consider mandating the free movement of all legitimately trademarked goods.

PRELIMINARY QUESTION

Before we consider the case law in different jurisdictions, ask yourself whether we should permit intellectual property owners to restrain parallel imports? What legitimate interests of the intellectual property owner are being protected? Do consumers benefit from parallel imports? In all circumstances? If not, what considerations should determine whether parallel imports should be permitted? What changes in global marketing, whether those now occurring or those that might soon occur, might alter the importance of the gray market? How does this affect your analysis of the appropriate approach to parallel importing?

[B]   Treatment Under U.S. Law

[1]   The Lanham Act

A. BOURJOIS & CO., INC. v. KATZEL
260 U.S. 689 (1923)

MR. JUSTICE HOLMES delivered the opinion of the Court.

This is a bill to restrain the infringement of the trade marks "Java" and "Bourjois" registered in the Patent Office of the United States. A preliminary injunction was granted by the District Court, but the order was reversed by the Circuit Court of Appeals, one Judge dissenting. A writ of certiorari was granted by this Court. In 1913 A. Bourjois & Cie., E. Wertheimer & Cie., Successeurs, doing business in France and also in the United States, sold to the plaintiff for a large sum their business in the United States, with their good will and their trade marks registered in the Patent Office. The latter related particularly to face powder, and included the above words. The plaintiff since its purchase has registered them again and goes on with the business that it bought, using substantially the same form of box and label as its predecessors and importing its face powder from France. It uses care in selecting colors suitable for the American market, in packing and in keeping up the standard, and has spent much money in advertising, etc., so that the business has grown very great and the labels have come to be understood by the public here as meaning goods coming from the plaintiff. The boxes have upon their backs: "Trade Marks Reg. U.S. Pat. Off. Made in France–Packed in the U.S.A. by A. Bourjois & Co., Inc., of New York, Succ'rs. in the U.S. to A. Bourjois & Cie., and E. Wertheimer & Cie."

The defendant, finding that the rate of exchange enabled her to do so at a profit, bought a large quantity of the same powder in France and is selling it here in the French boxes which closely resemble those used by the plaintiff except that they have not the last quoted statement on the backs, and that the label reads "Poudre de Riz de Java," whereas the plaintiff has found it advisable to strike out the suggestion of rice powder and has "Poudre Java" instead. There is no question that the defendant infringes the plaintiff's rights unless the fact that her boxes and powder are the genuine product of the French concern gives her a right to sell them in the present form.

We are of opinion that the plaintiff's rights are infringed. After the sale the French manufacturers could not have come to the United States and have used their old marks in competition with the plaintiff. That plainly follows from the statute authorizing assignments. Act of February 20, 1905, § 10. If for the purpose of evading the effect of the transfer, it had arranged with the defendant that she should sell with the old label, we suppose that no one would doubt that the contrivance must fail. There is no such conspiracy here, but, apart from the opening of a door to one, the vendors could not convey their goods free from the restriction to which the vendors were subject. Ownership of the goods does not carry the right to sell them with a specific mark. It does not necessarily carry the right to sell them at all in a given place. If the goods were patented in the United States a dealer who lawfully bought similar goods abroad from one who had a right to make and sell them there could not sell them in the United States. Boesch v. Graff, 133 U.S. 697. The monopoly in that case is more extensive, but we see no sufficient reason for holding that the monopoly of a trade mark, so far as it goes, is less complete. It deals with a delicate matter that may be of great value but that easily is destroyed, and therefore should be protected with corresponding care. It is said that the trade mark here is that of the French house and truly indicates the origin of the goods. But that is not accurate. It is the trade mark of the plaintiff only in the United States and indicates in law, and, it is found, by public understanding, that the goods come from the plaintiff although not made by it. It was sold and could only be sold with the good will of the business that the plaintiff bought. [cit]. It stakes the reputation of the plaintiff upon the character of the goods. [cit]. The injunction granted by the District Court was proper under sections 17 and 19 of the Trade Mark Act.

Decree of Circuit Court of Appeals reversed.

LEVER BROTHERS CO. v. UNITED STATES OF AMERICA
877 F.2d 101 (D.C. Cir. 1989)

WILLIAMS, CIRCUIT JUDGE:

Two affiliated corporations, one operating in the United States and one in the United Kingdom, use the same words, Shield and Sunlight, as trademarks for products that differ materially in the two countries. The products differ because the manufacturers have adjusted them to the countries' differing tastes and conditions. Third parties have directly or indirectly acquired the UK Shield and Sunlight products and imported them to the United States over the objection of the US affiliate, the domestic markholder. Two principles of trademark law—acceptance of manufacturers' interest in signalling the character of their products and consumers' interest in trusting those signals, and the recognition that trademarks may be regional—point toward prohibiting these importations. Deference to the views of the agency entrusted with enforcement of the statute points the other way. The matter ultimately turns, however, on the interpretation of section 42 of the Lanham Act of 1946, and we remand to the district court for it to complete that interpretation with the benefit of any further light that section 42's legislative history and any related administrative practice may disclose.

Lever Brothers Company is a domestic corporation which we shall refer to as either Lever or Lever US. Lever Brothers Ltd. is an English corporation, affiliated with Lever US through the latter's corporate grandparent,[1] and here referred to as Lever UK. Both Lever US and Lever UK manufacture a deodorant soap under a Shield trademark and a liquid dishwashing detergent under a Sunlight trademark.

The Shield logo on the wrapper of the two different products is virtually identical and the only difference in the appearance of each wrapper lies in fine print revealing the country of origin and, on the US version, the ingredients. But US Shield contains a higher concentration of coconut soap and fatty acids, and thus more readily generates lather. The manufacturing choice evidently arises in part out of the British preference for baths, which permit time for lather to develop, as opposed to a US preference for showers. Moreover, Britons interested in a soap's lathering properties turn to "beauty and cosmetic" soaps rather than to deodorant soaps. Further, US Shield contains an agent that inhibits growth of bacteria; Lever accounts for this difference in terms of some mix of "differing consumer preferences, climatic conditions and regulatory standards." Finally, the two bars contain differing perfume formulas and colorants.

The two versions of Sunlight use the same word in similar lettering. Their external appearances differ more than the two Shields, however. The UK product comes in a cylindrical drum rather than the flattened hourglass shape employed by the US version. The UK version carries the designation, "washing up liquid" rather than the US's "dishwashing liquid," and it displays at the top a royal emblem, along with the legend "By Appointment to Her Majesty the Queen." The contents of the packages differ materially. UK Sunlight is designed for water with a higher mineral content than is generally found in the United States, and therefore does not perform as well as US Sunlight in the "soft water" typical of US metropolitan areas.

Consumers are apparently capable of detecting the differences between the contents of the UK and US products—once they start using them. In support of its request for a preliminary injunction, Lever US submitted letters it received from consumers expressing their rage or disappointment with what they had believed, at the time of purchase, to be a discounted version of the familiar US product. Lever argues that these letters evidence consumer confusion, imperiling its reputation for quality.

Third parties import UK Shield and UK Sunlight without authorization by Lever US or, so far as appears, by Lever UK.[3] Despite requests by Lever US,

---

[1] . . . At oral argument, counsel for Lever US stated that Unilever PLC and Unilever N.V. were subject to common control. Thus there appears to be no dispute over the application of 19 C.F.R. § 133.21(c)(2) (1988), especially in light of 19 C.F.R. § 133.2(d), defining common control as "effective control in policy and operations and. . . . is not necessarily synonymous with common ownership.". . .

In general we rely on Lever US's account of the facts; the Customs Service does not contradict it, but disclaims ability to assess its truth.

[3] The customs forms evidently are not designed to elicit any statement by a domestic trademark owner as to whether foreign affiliates have consented to importation into the US of products purchased from the foreign affiliate. Although we have found no explicit assertion of non-consent by Lever UK in the record, Lever US's theory would seem to collapse if such consent had been given.

the Customs Service will not halt the importation. It declines to do so only because the trademarks are used abroad by an affiliate of Lever US.

Lever rests its claim that Customs is bound to seize such imports on section 42 of the Lanham Act of 1946, which provides that:

> no article of imported merchandise which shall *copy or simulate the name* of the [sic] any domestic manufacture, or manufacturer, or trader, . . . or which *shall copy or simulate a trademark* registered in accordance with the provisions of this chapter or shall bear a name or mark calculated to induce the public to believe that the article is manufactured in the United States, or that is manufactured in any foreign country or locality other than the country or locality in which it is in fact manufactured, shall be admitted to entry at any customhouse of the United States. . . .

15 U.S.C. § 1124 (1982) (emphasis added). At its core, Lever's contention is that where affiliated domestic and foreign firms produce goods bearing the same trademark, but different in physical content, the foreign products "copy or simulate" the domestic trademark, so that section 42 forbids their importation, notwithstanding the fact of affiliation.

The Customs Service rests on a regulation whose substance evidently dates back to 1936. While its regulations call as a general matter for seizure of foreign-made articles bearing a trademark identical with one owned and recorded by a US corporation, *see* 19 C.F.R. § 133.21(b) (1988), they make a number of exceptions:

> (c) Restrictions not applicable. The restrictions set forth in paragraphs (a) and (b) of this section do not apply to imported articles when:
>
> (1) Both the foreign and the U.S. trademark or trade name are owned by the same person or business entity;
>
> (2) The foreign and domestic trademark or trade name owners are parent and subsidiary companies or are otherwise subject to common ownership or control (*see* sections 133.2(d) and 133.12(d));
>
> (3) The articles of foreign manufacture bear a recorded trademark or trade name applied under authorization of the U.S. owner.[4]
>
> . . . .

19 C.F.R. § 133.21 (c) (1988). The critical clause for our purposes is subsection (c)(2), the affiliate exception.[5]

---

[4] In K Mart Corp. v. Cartier, Inc., 486 U.S. 281 (1988), the Supreme Court struck down 19 C.F.R. § 133.21(c)(3) as inconsistent with § 526 of the Tariff Act of 1930, 19 U.S.C. § 1526 (1982).

[5] Another regulation, 19 C.F.R. § 133.12(d), evidently adopted to facilitate implementation of § 133.21(c)(2), requires that applications to record a trade name with Customs list affiliates using it abroad, and Lever US's 1986 applications did so.

In the Customs Service's view, as embodied in the affiliate exception, goods are genuine—and thus neither copy nor simulate a domestic trademarked good—when they bear trademarks valid in their country of origin and the foreign manufacturer is affiliated with the domestic trademark holder. Where the affiliation between producers exists, Customs regards as irrelevant both physical differences in the products and the domestic markholder's non-consent to importation.

Lever sought a preliminary injunction against the Customs Service's continued application of the affiliate exception on the ground that it violated section 42 of the Lanham Act. The district court essentially agreed with the Customs Service's interpretation of section 42. Regarding the law as clear, the court denied the request without reaching the other issues that govern an application for a preliminary injunction—the balance of hardships among the parties and the public interest. [cit]. . . .

Review of the Customs Service's regulation comes to us in an unusual posture. The Service is charged with implementation of section 42 of the Lanham Act, and accordingly we owe its interpretation deference. If we find, using "traditional tools of statutory construction," that Congress clearly expressed an intent on the matter, of course we give that intent effect; otherwise we must accept the Customs Service's interpretation if reasonable. *See* Chevron U.S.A., Inc. v. NRDC, 467 U.S. 837, 842-43 (1984); [cit]. But as the substance of the disputed regulation considerably antedates the Administrative Procedure Act, 5 U.S.C. §§ 551 et seq., the Service appears not to have supported it with the "concise general statement of [the rule's] basis and purpose" required by section 553(c). Thus, despite the stricture of SEC v. Chenery Corp., 318 U.S. 80, 94 (1943), that "courts cannot exercise their duty of review unless they are advised of the considerations underlying the action under review," a precept developed in the context of adjudication but later extended to rulemaking, [cit], we have no choice but to review without the benefit of any rulemaking record disclosing the agency's train of thought. [cit]. On the basis of the briefs before us, however, we can tentatively reach the view that the Service's construction of section 42 defeats its purpose and is therefore contrary to its intent. Our conclusion here is tentative, however, as the parties have not joined issue in any detail on the legislative history or on Customs' administrative practice, and we remand to the district court for further development of the record.

. . . .

The plain language and general sweep of the Lanham Act undeniably bespeak an intention to protect domestic trademark holders from foreign competitors who seek a free ride on the goodwill of domestic trademarks. But neither section 42 nor the Lanham Act as a whole draws an explicit line between goods that "copy or simulate" a trademark and ones that do not—known as "genuine" goods. We will address first the origins of the exception and a Customs claim of ratification, then the relevant judicial authority, and finally turn to factors bearing upon the correct construction but not addressed earlier.

History of the Exception

The Service promulgated the substance of the affiliate exception in 1936 as an implementation of both the Tariff Act of 1930 and section 27 of the Trademark Act of 1905, the predecessor of section 42 of the Lanham Act. [cit]. The 1936 version was narrower than today's, as it allowed the importation of trademarked goods only if the domestic and foreign maker were "owned by the same person, partnership, association, or corporation." . . . The Service broadened the exception in 1953 to introduce a concept of affiliation and has evidently hewed to it in substance ever since. [cit].

In 1946 Congress enacted section 42 of the Lanham Act, substantially reenacting section 27 of the 1905 Act. At oral argument, counsel for the Customs Service appeared to argue that the reenactment ratified the affiliate exception. Such history as we have uncovered lends no support to that view. . . .

Case Authority

We turn first to the trio of Supreme Court cases, all revolving around face-powder, which bear upon section 42's predecessor, the almost identical section 27 of the Trademark Law of 1905: A. Bourjois & Co. v. Katzel, 260 U.S. 689 (1923); A. Bourjois & Co. v. Aldridge, 263 U.S. 675 (1923) (per curiam); and Prestonettes, Inc. v. Coty, 264 U.S. 359 (1924). Although the cases do not control the present one, they demonstrate the Court's understanding of trademark law as intended to protect a manufacturer's reputation and goodwill and to prevent confusion among consumers. They also reflect and enforce trademark territoriality.

[The Court discussed Justice Holmes' opinion in *Katzel*.] Holmes' failure to mention section 27 of the 1905 Act at all, and his reliance in the last quoted sentence on the infeasibility of the French firm's both selling and retaining the US goodwill, leave the case's bearing on section 27 uncertain. But the second case of the trilogy, [*Aldridge*], forges a link to section 27, albeit a vulnerable one. *Aldridge* appears to involve the same business transfer as lay at the root of *Katzel*. The Second Circuit described the US firm A. Bourjois & Co. as having acquired the "exclusive right to manufacture and sell in the United States any and all toilet preparations now made by [Wertheimer & Cie.]." [cit]. The sale included the trademark "Manon Lescaut," used in selling a face-powder. As in *Katzel*, an unaffiliated importer bought Manon Lescaut face-powder from the French firm and resold it in the United States under that label. The only noticeable difference between the products' packaging was small print identifying the seller. (The ingredients of plaintiff's own Manon Lescaut powder, though chemically the same as the French version, were not always bought from the French firm.) The action was brought against the Collector of Customs, however, seeking to force him to exclude the third party's product. The Second Circuit certified two questions to the Supreme Court:

(1) Is the sale in the United States of Wertheimer's Manon Lescaut powder an infringement of plaintiff's registered trade-marks?

(2) Is the collector, by section 27 of the Trade-Mark Law, required to exclude from entry genuine Manon Lescaut powder so as aforesaid made in France?

The government's three-page brief conceded that *Katzel* controlled. The Court replied that "the two questions certified by the Circuit Court of Appeals for Second Circuit are answered in the affirmative, upon the authority of *Bourjois & Co. v. Katzel*, the defendant not objecting."

While *Aldridge* reads section 27 to protect a domestic trademark holder from imports of trademarked merchandise that are "genuine" abroad, its precedential force is obviously weakened by the defendant's lack of opposition. Cases dealing with "parallel importation" or "gray goods" have relied on this weakness in discounting *Aldridge*. In such cases, both the holder of a domestic trademark and another party import goods manufactured at the same plant abroad and physically identical. But we think the case for exclusion far stronger here than in that context: here the goods imported are not physically identical to the goods sold by the US trademark holder, and the misrepresentation implicit in the use of the US trademark is far stronger than any present in the sale of gray goods.

The defendant further stresses that in *Aldridge* there was no affiliation between the French manufacturer and the US trademark holder. It persuaded the district court that the presence of affiliation here undercut equities that it viewed as having been determinative there. We shall return to the significance of this point in addressing Customs' policy arguments for its interpretation.

The third of the trilogy, Prestonettes, Inc. v. Coty, 264 U.S. 359 (1924), emphasizes truthfulness. The defendant purchased genuine "Coty" products, including facepowder, repackaged them with its own binder, and sold them with clearly distinguishable labels. The Court assumed defendant's conduct to be that which was permitted by a district court decree secured by plaintiff and acquiesced in by defendant. The decree permitted defendant to use the trademarked name in the sale of its products, but only in an explanatory 18-word message, with all words in equal size, color, type and general distinctiveness, stating truthfully that the primary ingredient was Coty's and that the packer and seller, Prestonettes, was "not connected with Coty." [cit]. Justice Holmes, again writing for the Court, said that this did not amount to actionable infringement:

> The plaintiff could not prevent or complain of [defendant's] stating the nature of the component parts and the source from which they were derived if it did not use the trade mark in doing so. . . . If the compound was worse than the constituent, it might be a misfortune to the plaintiff, but the plaintiff would have no cause of action, as the defendant was exercising the rights of ownership and only telling the truth. . . . A trademark only gives the right to prohibit the use of it so far as to protect the owner's good will against the sale of another's product as his. [cit]. There is nothing to the contrary in [*Katzel*].

When the mark is used in a way that does not deceive the public we see no such sanctity in the word as to prevent its being used to tell the truth. It is not taboo. [cit]

Prestonettes would aid the defendant only if one denied the fact that language is a social artifact, the meaning of words determined by their use in a particular social context. In Britain a request for "beer" will yield "bitter," a sort of ale with no exact equivalent here; an American seeking our "beer" over there must ask for "lager." Because of the differing conditions in the United States and United Kingdom, and the Lever affiliates' response to these conditions in the design of their products, Shield and Sunlight likewise have different meanings in the two countries. Thus the use of the trademarks for the UK versions in the United States is simply not truthful. The reasons that persuaded Holmes to deny relief in *Prestonettes* point toward granting it here.

We do not essay any grand resolution of the face-powder trilogy's legal message. None of the cases addresses the problem of affiliates generally, nor the special problem of affiliates using identical trademarks to sell products tailored for specific national conditions and tastes. On the other hand, the cases clearly view trademarks as having specific territorial scope, and are at least consistent with the view that section 27 of the 1905 Act protects a domestic trademark holder from goods genuinely trademarked abroad but imported here by parties hoping to exploit consumer confusion between the domestic and foreign products.

The Customs Service relies heavily on a variety of "parallel importation" or "gray market" cases, where a US trademark holder and a third party import goods that are not only identical in physical characteristics but are manufactured by the same firm abroad. All of the cases except K Mart Corp. v. Cartier, Inc., 486 U.S. 281 (1988) are from courts of appeal or district courts. In *K Mart*, as noted above [note 4], the Supreme Court held that in the gray goods context the affiliate exception of section 133.21(c)(2) did not violate section 526 of Tariff Act of 1930; it did not reach the question of the exception's validity under section 42 of the Lanham Act. But in Olympus Corp. v. United States, 792 F.2d 315, 321 (2d Cir. 1986), and Weil Ceramics & Glass, Inc. v. Dash, 878 F.2d 659 (3rd Cir. 1989), the Second and Third Circuits considered section 42 and found it no bar to the admission of gray goods. . . .

Where the goods bearing a foreign trademark valid abroad are physically different from the US trademarked goods, however, courts have indicated a readiness to find infringement. In Original Appalachian Artworks, Inc. v. Granada Electronics, Inc., 816 F.2d 68 (2d Cir. 1987), the American trademark holder licensed a Spanish firm to make Cabbage Patch dolls and to sell them in Spain, the Canary Islands, Andorra and Ceuta Mellila. While the dolls of the US trademark owner contained English-language "adoption papers," which could be filled in and would lead to receipt of a birthday card from the US firm on the doll's "birthday," those of the Spanish licensee had Spanish-language "adoption papers" and seemingly lacked any equivalent of the birthday card system. A third-party imported and sold the Spanish version at about half the price of the US doll. The court found a violation of section 32 (1)(a) of Lanham Act, . . . which prohibits use of a trademark where it "is likely to cause confusion, or to cause mistake, or to deceive." [cit]. *Compare* Weil Ceramics & Glass, Inc. v. Dash, 878 F.2d 659, 689 n.11 (3rd Cir. 1989) (holding importation of identical gray market goods did not constitute infringement under section 42, but expressly resting on absence of finding that goods were materially different).

. . . .

One may distinguish *Original Appalachian Artworks . . .*on several grounds, but only one seems of much weight here. First, there the goods were produced by a foreign licensee rather than by an affiliate. But this distinction shows only that while in *Artworks . . .* the foreign production was with the explicit consent of the US trademark holder, here it was with a consent inferred from the affiliation. The absence of consent to importation is the same. Second, *Artworks . . .* rests on section 32 rather than section 42 of the Lanham Act. But the deceit that the Second Circuit found controlling in *Artworks. . .* seems, under the face-powder trilogy, equally relevant under section 42. Third, the Second Circuit in part distinguished *Olympus* on the ground that there plaintiff had sought judicial relief against the Customs Service, to propel it into action, whereas in *Artworks* the suit ran against the importer. We have already noted the deference due Customs as the agency entrusted with enforcement of section 42 and of course we must accept its view unless it is precluded by Congress or otherwise unreasonable; we will consider below Customs' additional contention that enforcement of plaintiff's reading of section 42 would entail unmanageable administrative difficulties.

Remaining Interpretative Concerns

Customs' central thesis, that affiliation between the foreign producer and domestic markholder automatically defines the foreign goods as genuine, draws on an important truth that a trademark holder cannot infringe its own mark. Thus, if a US markholder itself imports goods (or licenses another to do so), the markholder's conduct of or authorization of the importation makes the goods authentic, whether they are better, worse, or the same as the US markholder's domestic products. To the extent that the affiliate exception extends this principle to goods imported into the US by companies affiliated with the US markholder, it does nothing more than treat the two companies as being constructively one for infringement purposes. As such it seems unobjectionable.

But the exception contained in 19 C.F.R. § 133.21(c)(2) does more. Merely on the basis of affiliation between the US markholder and the foreign *producer*, it extends the non-violation that is implicit in importation by the markholder or with its consent to a radically different matter, imports *by third parties.* Inferring non-violation from that relation seems no more plausible than an inference of consent to import from the US markholder's licensing production abroad, which the *Artworks . . .* court . . . obviously rejected.

Apart from its attempted reliance on authority and the impossibility of self-infringement, the Customs Service asserts some policy arguments. First, it contends that because of the affiliation, the dispute is better suited for resolution "in the boardroom" than the court room. As often proves true of pleasing rhetorical phrases, this seems largely irrelevant to the issue. Even if all the Lever affiliates were collapsed into a single corporate entity, its board could not single-handedly implement a decision to limit sales of UK Shield and UK Sunlight to the United Kingdom. So long as it uses third-party middlemen and retailers, it must launch those products into the stream of commerce, with the risk that some purchasers may seek to exploit the opportunity to ride on the US trademarks' value. Indeed, at some exchange rates an arbitrageur could buy Shield and Sunlight at retail from a completely vertically integrated Lever UK and profitably resell them here. We are not told how either the US markholder or the foreign affiliate is to prevent this without invoking governmental authority, either in the form of Customs Service action or trademark-based injunctions against the importer.

Of course the "boardroom" that evidently controls both Lever US and Lever UK could solve the problem by abandoning use of the Shield and Sunlight trademarks in the United Kingdom, or at least by abandoning their use for physically distinct products. But this solution is obviously costly. The Lever affiliates have succeeded in attaching to products designed for their respective markets ordinary words that have both a favorable "spin" and a natural link to those products. Customs has offered us no shadow of a reason why it would serve any public interest implicit in section 42 to compel Lever to abandon the resulting goodwill, or (looking ahead) to refrain in the first place from establishing such goodwill by use of identical words. The resources of English are finite and the quest for an apt word costly.

Second, Customs suggests there is a consumer interest in access to the lower-priced UK products. But trademark law inherently denies consumers access to cheap goods sailing under false colors. Further, even if we were to accept Customs' dubious premise, it points to nothing supporting the idea that the mere fact of affiliation makes it more likely than in the general case that this potential consumer loss would exceed the gain from accurate signalling of quality by means of trademarks.

Third, Customs suggests that its interpretation of the Lanham Act is an administrative necessity. The alternative to the exception, it claims, is that "Customs Service agents [would be] required to assess at the border the amount of consumer confusion and/or loss of goodwill likely to result from the importation of goods bearing genuine foreign trademarks." We think this greatly overstates the problem. No one is suggesting that Customs assess the degree of consumer confusion or loss of goodwill, only that it distinguish between identical and non-identical goods. If Lever US's submissions here are correct, that would not be difficult in a case such as this. It is hard to see why Customs' arguments calls for more than allowing it room to choose inactivity in marginal cases. [cit].

Lever argues that the administrative problem is completely non-existent: that US markholders will seek to block the imports of goods produced by affiliates only when in fact they are different and therefore likely to erode the US holder's goodwill. We think this somewhat oversimplifies. *K Mart* upheld the affiliate exception as applied to parallel imports (but only in reference to plaintiffs' Tariff Act challenge), approving (for example) Customs' decision to permit third-party purchasers to buy goods produced abroad by a foreign subsidiary of a US firm and import them over the US firm's opposition. If we were to hold that Customs must bar goods produced by a US firm's affiliate when the US and foreign goods differ, and *K Mart* is extended to permit Customs to apply the affiliate exception where a US firm's *domestically* manufactured goods are identical to the imports, then US firms would have an incentive to raise false claims of non-identity.

Nonetheless, we find that the specter of false claims that possible future extensions of *K Mart* might generate is not enough to validate Customs' administrative inconvenience theory. First, *K Mart* did not evaluate the affiliate exception as against an attack under section 42. Second, the *K Mart* Court never addressed the issue of foreign surrogates competing with *domestically* produced trademarked goods. We hesitate here to evaluate the probabilities of these two extensions of *K Mart*, neither of which is before us or has been briefed. We do note, however, that if the two extensions occur and if Customs' administrative practicality argument is controlling, section 42 will have become a dead letter for a surprisingly wide range of cases, the gray-goods tail wagging the dog of flat-out deception. We hesitate to impute such broad effects to *K Mart*, even in the face of the Service's disclaimer of ability to identify what is genuine.

. . . .

We think the natural, virtually inevitable reading of section 42 is that it bars foreign goods bearing a trademark identical to a valid US trademark but physically different, regardless of the trademarks' genuine character abroad or affiliation between the producing firms. On its face the section appears to aim at deceit and consumer confusion; when identical trademarks have acquired different meanings in different countries, one who imports the foreign version to sell it under that trademark will (in the absence of some specially differentiating feature) cause the confusion Congress sought to avoid. The fact of affiliation between the producers in no way reduces the probability of that confusion; it is certainly not a constructive consent to the importation. The cases are entirely congruent with this view. Customs' assertion of administrative difficulties appears overdrawn, and in any event would seem to justify no more than inaction in those cases that are close on the factual issue of product identity. Thus, despite the deference we owe Customs under *Chevron*, we believe that the affiliate exception does not square with section 42.

For now, however, our conclusion must remain provisional. Neither party has briefed the legislative history nor administrative practice in any detail. . . . [W]e adopt a reading of the statute tentatively, and reverse and remand to the district court so that the parties may join issue on those points. Subject to some persuasive evidence running against our tentative conclusion, we must say that Lever's probability of success on its legal argument is quite high; at this preliminary stage we go no further. We of course express no opinion on the weights to be accorded to the various equitable elements that the district court may have to balance if, on further submissions, that probability is established..

NOTES AND QUESTIONS

(1) **Remand and Response.** On remand in *Lever Brothers*, the district court accepted the suggestions of the court of appeals and found the affiliate exception inconsistent with section 42. *See* 796 F. Supp. 1 (D.D.C. 1989). The court of appeals later affirmed that decision. *See* 981 F.2d 1330 (D.C. Cir. 1993). In a notice published in the *Federal Register* on February 24, 1999, the Customs Service made final rules it had proposed in 1998 (*see* 63 Fed. Reg. 14662 (1998)) to implement changes to the customs regulations required by the *Lever Brothers* ruling. *See* 64 Fed. Reg. 9058 (1999). The new rules adopt an extremely narrow reading of *Lever Brothers* and appear still to adhere to the traditional customs' view that "enforcement of the distribution rights of a gray market article produced abroad by a party related to the U.S. trademark holder was a matter to be addressed through private remedies." *See id.* at 9058. The Customs Service interpreted *Lever Brothers* as drawing a distinction "between identical goods produced abroad under the affiliate exception and goods produced abroad under the affiliate exception that were physically and materially different from the goods authorized by the U.S. trademark owner," and as concluding that "section 42 of the Lanham Act precluded customs' application of the affiliate exception with respect to physically, materially different goods." *Id.* Does *Lever Brothers* invalidate the affiliate exception only for goods that are "physically and materially different"? What about goods that are physically similar, but different in other material respects? Under *Lever Brothers*, can they be freely imported if covered by the affiliate exception?

Based upon this restricted reading of *Lever Brothers*, the new rules provide that gray goods covered by the affiliate exception will not be restricted from importation if they bear a prescribed label informing the ultimate retail purchaser that they were not authorized by the U.S. trademark owner and were physically and materially different from the goods that were so authorized (New Regulation § 133.23(b)). Is the labeling provision consistent with the rationale, holding or spirit of *Lever Brothers*? Is the label proposed by the Customs Service adequate to protect the rights of trademark owners upheld in *Lever Brothers*? *See Comments on Proposed Rule and Responses of Customs Service*, summarized at 64 Fed. Reg. 9058, 9059.

(2) **Impermissible Differences.** What are "material, physical" differences within the meaning of *Lever Brothers*? A difference in price? A difference in product composition? A difference in packaging? *See* Société Des Produits Nestlé v. Casa Helvetia, Inc., 982 F.2d 633 (1st Cir. 1992) (considering these factors as applied to chocolates). What more would you need to know to determine whether these were differences covered by the *Lever* opinion? What if the imported product came only with a non-English language owner's manual ands was covered by different warranties? *See* Fender Musical Instruments Corp. v. Unlimited Music Center Inc., 35 U.S.P.Q.2d 1053 (D. Conn. 1995) (finding such differences to be material when imported guitars bearing the identical mark also differed, inter alia, in the shape of their neck).

[2] Copyright Law

QUALITY KING DISTRIBS. v. L'ANZA RESEARCH INT'L, INC.
523 U.S. 135 (1998)

JUSTICE STEVENS delivered the opinion of the Court.

Section 106(3) of the Copyright Act of 1976 (the Act), gives the owner of a copyright the exclusive right to distribute copies of a copyrighted work. That exclusive right is expressly limited, however, by the provisions of §§ 107 through 120. Section 602(a) gives the copyright owner the right to prohibit the unauthorized importation of copies. The question presented by this case is whether the right granted by § 602(a) is also limited by §§ 107 through 120. More narrowly, the question is whether the "first sale" doctrine endorsed in § 109(a) is applicable to imported copies.

I

Respondent, L'anza Research International, Inc. (L'anza), is a California corporation engaged in the business of manufacturing and selling shampoos, conditioners, and other hair care products. L'anza has copyrighted the labels that are affixed to those products. In the United States, L'anza sells exclusively to domestic distributors who have agreed to resell within limited geographic areas and then only to authorized retailers such as barber shops, beauty salons, and professional hair care colleges. L'anza has found that the American "public is generally unwilling to pay the price charged for high quality products, such as L'anza's products, when they are sold along with the less expensive lower quality products that are generally carried by supermarkets and drug stores." [cit]. L'anza promotes the domestic sales of its products with extensive advertising in various trade magazines and at point of sale, and by providing special training to authorized retailers.

L'anza also sells its products in foreign markets. In those markets, however, it does not engage in comparable advertising or promotion; its prices to foreign distributors are 35% to 40% lower than the prices charged to domestic distributors. In 1992 and 1993, L'anza's distributor in the United Kingdom arranged the sale of three shipments to a distributor in Malta; each shipment contained several tons of L'anza products with copyrighted labels affixed. The record does not establish whether the initial purchaser was the distributor in the United Kingdom or the distributor in Malta, or whether title passed when the goods were delivered to the carrier or when they arrived at their destination, but it is undisputed that the goods were manufactured by L'anza and first sold by L'anza to a foreign purchaser.

It is also undisputed that the goods found their way back to the United States without the permission of L'anza and were sold in California by unauthorized retailers who had purchased them at discounted prices from Quality King

Distributors, Inc. (petitioner). There is some uncertainty about the identity of the actual importer, but for the purpose of our decision we assume that petitioner bought all three shipments from the Malta distributor, imported them, and then resold them to retailers who were not in L'anza's authorized chain of distribution.

After determining the source of the unauthorized sales, L'anza brought suit against petitioner and several other defendants.[3] The complaint alleged that the importation and subsequent distribution of those products bearing copyrighted labels violated L'anza's "exclusive rights under 17 U.S.C. §§ 106, 501 and 602 to reproduce and distribute the copyrighted material in the United States." The District Court rejected petitioner's defense based on the "first sale" doctrine recognized by § 109 and entered summary judgment in favor of L'anza. Based largely on its conclusion that §602 would be "meaningless" if § 109 provided a defense in a case of this kind, the Court of Appeals affirmed. Because its decision created a conflict with the Third Circuit, see Sebastian Int'l, Inc. v. Consumer Contacts (PTY) Ltd., 847 F.2d 1093 (3d Cir. 1988), we granted the petition for certiorari. [cit].

II

This is an unusual copyright case because L'anza does not claim that anyone has made unauthorized copies of its copyrighted labels. Instead, L'anza is primarily interested in protecting the integrity of its method of marketing the products to which the labels are affixed. Although the labels themselves have only a limited creative component, our interpretation of the relevant statutory provisions would apply equally to a case involving more familiar copyrighted materials such as sound recordings or books. Indeed, we first endorsed the first sale doctrine in a case involving a claim by a publisher that the resale of its books at discounted prices infringed its copyright on the books. Bobbs-Merrill Co. v. Straus, 210 U.S. 339 (1908).

In that case, the publisher, Bobbs-Merrill, had inserted a notice in its books that any retail sale at a price under $1.00 would constitute an infringement of its copyright. The defendants, who owned Macy's department store, disregarded the notice and sold the books at a lower price without Bobbs-Merrill's consent. We held that the exclusive statutory right to "vend" applied only to the first sale of the copyrighted work:

> What does the statute mean in granting 'the sole right of vending the same'? Was it intended to create a right which would permit the holder of the copyright to fasten, by notice in a book or upon one of the articles mentioned within the statute, a restriction upon the subsequent alienation of the subject-matter of copyright after the owner had parted with the title to one who had acquired full dominion over it and had given a satisfactory price for it? It is not

---

[3]L'anza's claims against the retailer defendants were settled. The Malta distributor apparently never appeared in this action and a default judgment was entered against it.

denied that one who has sold a copyrighted article, without restriction, has parted with all right to control the sale of it. The purchaser of a book, once sold by authority of the owner of the copyright, may sell it again, although he could not publish a new edition of it.

In this case the stipulated facts show that the books sold by the appellant were sold at wholesale, and purchased by those who made no agreement as to the control of future sales of the book, and took upon themselves no obligation to enforce the notice printed in the book, undertaking to restrict retail sales to a price of one dollar per copy.

Id. at 349-50. The statute in force when *Bobbs-Merrill* was decided provided that the copyright owner had the exclusive right to "vend" the copyrighted work. Congress subsequently codified our holding in *Bobbs-Merrill* that the exclusive right to "vend" was limited to first sales of the work. Under the 1976 Act, the comparable exclusive right granted in 17 U.S.C. § 106(3) is the right "to distribute copies . . . by sale or other transfer of ownership." The comparable limitation on that right is provided not by judicial interpretation, but by an express statutory provision. Section 109(a) provides:

Notwithstanding the provisions of section 106(3), the owner of a particular copy or phonorecord lawfully made under this title, or any person authorized by such owner, is entitled, without the authority of the copyright owner, to sell or otherwise dispose of the possession of that copy or phonorecord. . . ."[9]

The *Bobbs-Merrill* opinion emphasized the critical distinction between statutory rights and contract rights.[10] In this case, L'anza relies on the terms of its contracts with its domestic distributors to limit their sales to authorized retail outlets. Because the basic holding in *Bobbs-Merrill* is now codified in § 109(a) of the Act, and because those domestic distributors are owners of the products that they purchased from L'anza (the labels of which were "lawfully made under this title"), L'anza does not, and could not, claim that the statute would enable L'anza to treat unauthorized resales by its domestic distributors as an infringement of its exclusive right to distribute copies of its labels. L'anza does claim, however, that contractual provisions are inadequate to protect it from the actions of foreign distributors who may resell L'anza's products to

[9]The comparable section in the 1909 and 1947 Acts provided that "nothing in this Act shall be deemed to forbid, prevent, or restrict the transfer of any copy of a copyrighted work the possession of which has been lawfully obtained." Copyright Act of 1909, ch. 320, § 41, 35 Stat. 1084; *see also* Copyright Act of 1947, ch. 391, § 27, 61 Stat. 660. It is noteworthy that § 109(a) of the 1978 Act does not apply to "any copy"; it applies only to a copy that was "lawfully made under this title."

[10]"We do not think the statute can be given such a construction, and it is to be remembered that this is purely a question of statutory construction. There is no claim in this case of contract limitation, nor license agreement controlling the subsequent sales of the book." Bobbs-Merrill Co. v. Straus, 210 U.S. 339, 350 (1908).

American vendors unable to buy from L'anza's domestic distributors, and that § 602(a) of the Act, properly construed, prohibits such unauthorized competition. To evaluate that submission, we must, of course, consider the text of § 602(a).

III

The most relevant portion of § 602(a) provides:

> Importation into the United States, without the authority of the owner of copyright under this title, of copies or phonorecords of a work that have been acquired outside the United States is an infringement of the exclusive right to distribute copies or phonorecords under section 106, actionable under section 501. . . ."[11]

It is significant that this provision does not categorically prohibit the unauthorized importation of copyrighted materials. Instead, it provides that such importation is an infringement of the exclusive right to distribute copies "under section 106." Like the exclusive right to "vend" that was construed in *Bobbs-Merrill*, the exclusive right to distribute is a limited right. The introductory language in § 106 expressly states that all of the exclusive rights granted by that section—including, of course, the distribution right granted by subsection (3)—are limited by the provisions of §§ 107 through 120. One of those limitations, as we have noted, is provided by the terms of § 109(a), which expressly permit the owner of a lawfully made copy to sell that copy "[n]otwithstanding the provisions of section 106(3)."

After the first sale of a copyrighted item "lawfully made under this title," any subsequent purchaser, whether from a domestic or from a foreign reseller, is obviously an "owner" of that item. Read literally, § 109(a) unambiguously states that such an owner "is entitled, without the authority of the copyright owner, to sell" that item. Moreover, since § 602(a) merely provides that unauthorized importation is an infringement of an exclusive right "under section 106," and

---

[11]The remainder of § 602(a) reads as follows: "This subsection does not apply to–

"(1) importation of copies or phonorecords under the authority or for the use of the Government of the United States or of any State or political subdivision of a State, but not including copies or phonorecords for use in schools, or copies of any audiovisual work imported for purposes other than archival use;

"(2) importation, for the private use of the importer and not for distribution, by any person with respect to no more than one copy or phonorecord of any one work at any one time, or by any person arriving from outside the United States with respect to copies or phonorecords forming part of such person's personal baggage; or

"(3) importation by or for an organization operated for scholarly, educational, or religious purposes and not for private gain, with respect to no more than one copy of an audiovisual work solely for its archival purposes, and no more than five copies or phonorecords of any other work for its library lending or archival purposes, unless the importation of such copies or phonorecords is part of an activity consisting of systematic reproduction or distribution, engaged in by such organization in violation of the provisions of section 108(g)(2)."

since that limited right does not encompass resales by lawful owners, the literal text of § 602(a) is simply inapplicable to both domestic and foreign owners of L'anza's products who decide to import them and resell them in the United States.[14]

Notwithstanding the clarity of the text of §§ 106(3), 109(a), and 602(a), L'anza argues that the language of the Act supports a construction of the right granted by § 602(a) as "distinct from the right under Section 106(3) standing alone," and thus not subject to § 109(a). Otherwise, L'anza argues, both the § 602(a) right itself and its exceptions[15] would be superfluous. Moreover, supported by various *amici curiae*, including the Solicitor General of the United States, L'anza contends that its construction is supported by important policy considerations. We consider these arguments separately.

IV

L'anza advances two primary arguments based on the text of the Act: (1) that § 602(a), and particularly its three exceptions, are superfluous if limited by the first sale doctrine; and (2) that the text of § 501 defining an "infringer" refers separately to violations of § 106, on the one hand, and to imports in violation of § 602. The short answer to both of these arguments is that neither adequately explains why the words "under section 106" appear in § 602(a). The Solicitor General makes an additional textual argument: he contends that the word "importation" in § 602(a) describes an act that is not protected by the language in § 109(a) authorizing a subsequent owner "to sell or otherwise dispose of the possession of" a copy. Each of these arguments merits separate comment.

The Coverage of § 602(a)

Prior to the enactment of § 602(a), the Act already prohibited the importation of "piratical," or unauthorized, copies.[16] Moreover, that earlier prohibition is retained in § 602(b) of the present Act.[17] L'anza therefore argues (as do the Solicitor General and other *amici curiae*) that § 602(a) is superfluous unless it covers non-piratical ("lawfully made") copies sold by the copyright owner, because importation nearly always implies a first sale. There are several flaws in this argument.

First, even if § 602(a) did apply only to piratical copies, it at least would

---

[14]Despite L'anza's contention to the contrary, the owner of goods lawfully made under the Act is entitled to the protection of the first sale doctrine in an action in a United States court even if the first sale occurred abroad. Such protection does not require the extraterritorial application of the Act any more than § 602(a)'s "acquired abroad" language does.

[15]*See* note 11, *supra.*

[16]*See* 17 U.S.C. §§ 106, 107 (1970).

[17]Section 602(b) provides in relevant part: "In a case where the making of the copies or phonorecords would have constituted an infringement of copyright if this title had been applicable, their importation is prohibited. . . ." The first sale doctrine of § 109(a) does not protect owners of piratical copies, of course, because such copies were not "lawfully made."

provide the copyright holder with a private remedy against the importer, whereas the enforcement of § 602(b) is vested in the Customs Service. Second, because the protection afforded by § 109(a) is available only to the "owner" of a lawfully made copy (or someone authorized by the owner), the first sale doctrine would not provide a defense to a § 602(a) action against any non-owner such as a bailee, a licensee, a consignee, or one whose possession of the copy was unlawful.[19] Third, § 602(a) applies to a category of copies that are neither piratical nor "lawfully made under this title." That category encompasses copies that were "lawfully made" not under the United States Copyright Act, but instead, under the law of some other country.

The category of copies produced lawfully under a foreign copyright was expressly identified in the deliberations that led to the enactment of the 1976 Act. We mention one example of such a comment in 1961 simply to demonstrate that the category is not a merely hypothetical one. In a report to Congress, the Register of Copyrights stated, in part:

> When arrangements are made for both a U.S. edition and a foreign edition of the same work, the publishers frequently agree to divide the international markets. The foreign publisher agrees not to sell his edition in the United States, and the U.S. publisher agrees not to sell his edition in certain foreign countries. It has been suggested that the import ban on piratical copies should be extended to bar the importation of the foreign edition in contravention of such an agreement." Copyright Law Revision: Report of the Register of Copyrights on the General Revision of the U.S. Copyright Law, 87th Cong., 1st Sess., 125-126 (H.R. Judiciary Comm. Print 1961).

Even in the absence of a market allocation agreement between, for example, a publisher of the U.S. edition and a publisher of the British edition of the same work, each such publisher could make lawful copies. If the author of the work gave the exclusive U.S. distribution rights—enforceable under the Act—to the publisher of the U.S. edition and the exclusive British distribution rights to the publisher of the British edition,[20] however, presumably only those made by the

---

[19]In its opinion in this case, the Court of Appeals quoted a statement by a representative of the music industry expressing the need for protection against the importation of stolen motion picture prints: "We've had a similar situation with respect to motion picture prints, which are sent all over the world—legitimate prints made from the authentic negative. These prints get into illicit hands. They're stolen, and there's no contractual relationship. . . . Now those are not piratical copies." Copyright Law Revision Part 2: Discussion and Comments on Report of the Register of Copyrights on General Revision of the U.S. Copyright Law, 88th Cong., 1st Sess., 213 (H.R. Judiciary Comm. Print 1963) (statement of Mr. Sargoy), [cit].

[20]A participant in a 1964 panel discussion expressed concern about this particular situation. Copyright Law Revision Part 4: Further Discussion and Comments on Preliminary Draft for Revised U.S. Copyright Law, 88th Cong., 2d Sess., 119 (H.R. Judiciary Comm. Print 1964) (statement of Mrs. Pilpel) ("For example, if someone were to import a copy of the British edition of an American book and the author had transferred exclusive United States and Canadian rights to an American publisher, would that British edition be in violation so that this would constitute an infringement under this section?"); *see also id.*, at 209 (statement of Mr. Manges) (describing similar situation as "a troublesome problem that confronts U.S. book publishers frequently").

publisher of the U.S. edition would be "lawfully made under this title" within the meaning of § 109(a). The first sale doctrine would not provide the publisher of the British edition who decided to sell in the American market with a defense to an action under § 602(a) (or, for that matter, to an action under § 106(3), if there was a distribution of the copies).

The argument that the statutory exceptions to § 602(a) are superfluous if the first sale doctrine is applicable rests on the assumption that the coverage of that section is co-extensive with the coverage of § 109(a). But since it is, in fact, broader because it encompasses copies that are not subject to the first sale doctrine—*e.g.*, copies that are lawfully made under the law of another country—the exceptions do protect the traveler who may have made an isolated purchase of a copy of a work that could not be imported in bulk for purposes of resale. As we read the Act, although both the first sale doctrine embodied in § 109(a) and the exceptions in § 602(a) may be applicable in some situations, the former does not subsume the latter; those provisions retain significant independent meaning.

Section 501's Separate References to §§ 106 and 602

The text of § 501 does lend support to L'anza's submission. In relevant part, it provides:

> (a) Anyone who violates any of the exclusive rights of the copyright owner as provided by sections 106 through 118 or of the author as provided in section 106A(a), or who imports copies or phonorecords into the United States in violation of section 602, is an infringer of the copyright or right of the author, as the case may be . . . .

The use of the words "*or* who imports," rather than words such as "*including* one who imports," is more consistent with an interpretation that a violation of § 602 is distinct from a violation of § 106 (and thus not subject to the first sale doctrine set out in § 109(a)) than with the view that it is a species of such a violation. Nevertheless, the force of that inference is outweighed by other provisions in the statutory text.

Most directly relevant is the fact that the text of § 602(a) itself unambiguously states that the prohibited importation is an infringement of the exclusive distribution right "under section 106, actionable under section 501." Unlike that phrase, which identifies § 602 violations as a species of § 106 violations, the text of § 106A, which is also cross-referenced in § 501, uses starkly different language. It states that the author's right protected by § 106A is "independent of the exclusive rights provided in Section 106." The contrast between the relevant language in § 602 and that in § 106A strongly implies that only the latter describes an independent right.[21]

Of even greater importance is the fact that the § 106 rights are subject not only to the first sale defense in § 109(a), but also to all of the other provisions of "sections 107 through 120." If § 602(a) functioned independently, none of those sections would limit its coverage. For example, the "fair use" defense embodied in § 107 would be unavailable to importers if § 602(a) created a separate right not subject to the limitations on the § 106(3) distribution right. Under L'anza's interpretation of the Act, it presumably would be unlawful for a distributor to import copies of a British newspaper that contained a book review quoting excerpts from an American novel protected by a United States copyright.[23] Given the importance of the fair use defense to publishers of scholarly works, as well as to publishers of periodicals, it is difficult to believe that Congress intended to impose an absolute ban on the importation of all such works containing any copying of material protected by a United States copyright.

In the context of this case, involving copyrighted labels, it seems unlikely that an importer could defend an infringement as a "fair use" of the label. In construing the statute, however, we must remember that its principal purpose was to promote the progress of the "useful Arts," . . . by rewarding creativity, and its principal function is the protection of original works, rather than ordinary commercial products that use copyrighted material as a marketing aid. It is therefore appropriate to take into account the impact of the denial of the fair use defense for the importer of foreign publications. As applied to such publications, L'anza's construction of § 602 "would merely inhibit access to ideas without any countervailing benefit." [cit].[24]

Does an importer "sell or otherwise dispose" of copies as those words are used in § 109(a)?

Whether viewed from the standpoint of the importer or from that of the copyright holder, the textual argument advanced by the Solicitor General—that the act of "importation" is neither a sale nor a disposal of a copy under § 109 (a)—is unpersuasive. Strictly speaking, an importer could, of course, carry merchandise from one country to another without surrendering custody of it. In a typical commercial transaction, however, the shipper transfers "possession,

---

[21]The strength of the implication created by the relevant language in § 106A is not diminished by the fact that Congress enacted § 106A more recently than § 602(a), which is part of the Copyright Act of 1976. Section 106A was passed as part of the Visual Artists Rights Act of 1990 in order to protect the moral rights of certain visual artists. Section 106A is analogous to Article 6bis of the Berne Convention for the Protection of Literary and Artistic Works, but its coverage is more limited. *See* 2 P. Goldstein, *Copyright* § 5.12, p. 5:225 (2d ed. 1996) (§ 106A encompasses aspects of the moral rights guaranteed by Article 6*bis* of the Berne Convention, "but effectively gives these rights a narrow subject matter and scope").

[23]The § 602(a) exceptions, which are substantially narrower than § 107, would not permit such importation. *See* note 11 *supra*.

[24]L'anza's reliance on § 602(a)(3)'s reference to § 108(g)(2), *see* note 11, *supra*, to demonstrate that all of the other limitations set out in §§ 107 through 120—including the first sale and fair use doctrines—do not apply to imported copies is unavailing for the same reasons.

custody, control and title to the products" to a different person, and L'anza assumes that petitioner's importation of the L'anza shipments included such a transfer. An ordinary interpretation of the statement that a person is entitled "to sell or otherwise dispose of the possession" of an item surely includes the right to ship it to another person in another country.

More important, the Solicitor General's cramped reading of the text of the statutes is at odds not only with § 602(a)'s more flexible treatment of unauthorized importation as an infringement of the distribution right (even when there is no literal "distribution"), but also with the necessarily broad reach of § 109(a). The whole point of the first sale doctrine is that once the copyright owner places a copyrighted item in the stream of commerce by selling it, he has exhausted his exclusive statutory right to control its distribution. As we have recognized, the codification of that doctrine in § 109(a) makes it clear that the doctrine applies only to copies that are "lawfully made under this title," but that was also true of the copies involved in the *Bobbs-Merrill* case, as well as those involved in the earlier cases applying the doctrine. There is no reason to assume that Congress intended either § 109(a) or the earlier codifications of the doctrine to limit its broad scope.[27]

In sum, we are not persuaded by either L'anza's or the Solicitor General's textual arguments.

V

The parties and their *amici* have debated at length the wisdom or unwisdom of governmental restraints on what is sometimes described as either the "gray market" or the practice of "parallel importation." In K Mart Corp. v. Cartier, Inc., 486 U.S. 281(1988), we used those terms to refer to the importation of foreign-manufactured goods bearing a valid United States trademark without the consent of the trademark holder. [cit]. We are not at all sure that those terms appropriately describe the consequences of an American manufacturer's decision to limit its promotional efforts to the domestic market and to sell its products abroad at discounted prices that are so low that its foreign distributors can compete in the domestic market.[29] But even if they do, whether or not we think it would be wise policy to provide statutory protection for such price discrimination is not a matter that is relevant to our duty to interpret the text of the Copyright Act.

Equally irrelevant is the fact that the Executive Branch of the Government has entered into at least five international trade agreements that are apparently intended to protect domestic copyright owners from the

---

[27]*See, e.g.,* H.R. Rep. No. 1476, 94th Cong., 2d Sess., 79 (1979) ("Section 109(a) restates and confirms" the first sale doctrine established by prior case law); S.Rep. No. 473, 94th Cong., 1st Sess., 71 (1975) (same).

[29]Presumably L'anza, for example, could have avoided the consequences of that competition either (1) by providing advertising support abroad and charging higher prices, or (2) if it was satisfied to leave the promotion of the product in foreign markets to its foreign distributors, to sell its products abroad under a different name.

unauthorized importation of copies of their works sold in those five countries.[30] The earliest of those agreements was made in 1991; none has been ratified by the Senate. Even though they are of course consistent with the position taken by the Solicitor General in this litigation, they shed no light on the proper interpretation of a statute that was enacted in 1976.[31]

The judgment of the Court of Appeals is reversed.

JUSTICE GINSBURG, concurring.

This case involves a "round trip" journey, travel of the copies in question from the United States to places abroad, then back again. I join the Court's opinion recognizing that we do not today resolve cases in which the allegedly infringing imports were manufactured abroad. *See* W. Patry, *Copyright Law and Practice* 166-170 (1997 Supp.) (commenting that provisions of Title 17 do not apply extraterritorially unless expressly so stated, hence the words "lawfully made under this title" in the "first sale" provision, 17 U.S.C. § 109(a), must mean "lawfully made in the United States"); *see generally* P. Goldstein, *Copyright* § 16.0, pp. 16:1-16:2 (2d ed. 1998) ("Copyright protection is territorial. The rights granted by the United States Copyright Act extend no farther than the nation's borders.").

NOTES AND QUESTIONS

(1) **Gray Goods.** Why is the Supreme Court unsure whether to describe the *Quality King* scenario as involving gray goods? In *Sebastian Int'l, Inc. v. Consumer Contacts (PTY) Ltd.*, 847 F.2d 1093 (1988), where the Third Circuit adopted the approach later endorsed by the Supreme Court in *Quality King*, the court noted that, although a copyright case, the case (also involving labels on hair care products) really raised issues of "parallel importing." What is unusual about these cases? What is different from the gray goods cases litigated under the Lanham Act? Do these differences mandate a different approach to the question of exhaustion? *See* Parfums Givenchy v. Drug Emporium, 38 F.3d 477, 483-485 (9th Cir. 1994). What are the differences between the rules now governing claims asserted under the Lanham Act and the Copyright Act?

(2) **Geographic Licensing.** As the *Quality King* court suggests, *see* note 20, books written in English are often published in the United States and Britain at different times, for different prices, and in different form (for example, environmentally friendly paper is more common in the United States, but less popular in Britain). Under *Quality King*, can properly authorized copies of a

---

[30]The Solicitor General advises us that such agreements have been made with Cambodia, Trinidad and Tobago, Jamaica, Ecuador, and Sri Lanka.

[31]We also note that in 1991, when the first of the five agreements was signed, the Third Circuit had already issued its opinion in Sebastian Int'l, Inc. v. Consumer Contacts (PTY) Ltd., 847 F.2d 1093 (1988), adopting a position contrary to that subsequently endorsed by the Executive Branch.

novel released first in Britain be imported into the United States prior to publication in the United States? If not, why not? What interests are being served by preventing the British edition being available immediately in the United States? How has the advent of online selling (and perhaps online distribution) changed the analysis of whether a copyright owner should be able to prevent the importation of copies lawfully made in another country? For example, the *Harry Potter* series of children's books, although released in Britain several months before publication in the United States, was available to U.S. purchasers through amazon.co.uk or another online bookseller and had become a leading seller in the United States before its U.S. publication. If you were the licensee of the U.S. publication rights, how would you have responded?

———————

Parfums Givenchy, Inc. v. Drug Emporium, Inc., 38 F.3d 477 (9th Cir. 1994). In this case, decided four years before *Quality King*, Parfums Givenchy USA ("Givenchy USA") sought and obtained an injunction against the importation and sale of Amarige, a perfume that was produced in France by Givenchy USA's parent company, Parfums Givenchy, S.A. ("Givenchy France"). Amarige was marketed in distinctively decorated individual boxes designed by employees of Givenchy France. Givenchy France began importing Amarige to the United States in early 1992, and shortly thereafter sold its United States copyright interests in the Amarige box design to Givenchy USA. Givenchy USA then registered the box design with the Copyright Office and began a multi-million dollar national advertising campaign to promote the perfume. A third party purchased large quantities of Amarige abroad and imported the Amarige into the United States without the authorization of either Givenchy France or Givenchy USA. The Amarige was packaged in the distinctive box. Drug Emporium, a nationwide retail chain, purchased the Amarige from the importing third parties in the United States, and began marketing the perfume in the United States in its original copyrighted packaging.

Drug Emporium argued that a lawful sale abroad of U.S. copyrighted foreign goods terminates the exclusive right of the U.S. copyright holder to import and distribute those goods in the United States, in the same way that a lawful domestic sale terminates the exclusive distribution rights of domestically manufactured materials. The Ninth Circuit rejected that argument in 1994. How would this case, where the copies of the work (the box design) were made abroad, be decided after the Supreme Court decision (reversing the Ninth Circuit) in *Quality King*? Should it matter that Givenchy USA was a wholly-owned subsidiary of Givenchy France? If Section 109(a) does not extend to copies made abroad by related companies, how might multinational enterprises structure their production and marketing to maximize their intellectual property rights? How would your answer be altered if other countries also interpreted their copyright statutes in such a fashion? Should it matter that Drug Emporium was not the importer of Amarige but rather purchased its Amarige from a wholesaler in the United States? Does the Supreme Court's emphasis upon where the copies were made mean that foreign manufactured goods are not subject to the first sale doctrine, even after a sale in the United

States? *See* Denbicare USA Inc. v. Toys "R" Us, Inc., 84 F.3d 1143, 1149-1150 (9th Cir. 1996).

[3] Patent Law

PATENTS AS A "NEGATIVE RIGHT" TO EXCLUDE

As noted above, territoriality is the most basic premise of patent law. A second basic tenet of patent law is the fact that while the patent contains within its terms the right to exclude competitors from engaging in economic activity, this right is fundamentally different from a monopoly right. As stated by the U.S. Supreme Court,

> monopolists have the sole right to buy, sell, or make and others are deprived of a preexisting right to buy, sell, or make. The patent grant gives the patentee only the right to exclude others; his own right to practice the invention may be subservient to another patent. Moreover, since novelty is a requisite of patentability, the grant does not exclude the public from a pre-existing right.

Standard Oil v. United States, 221 US (1911).

Likewise, in United States v. Dubilier, 289 U.S. 178 (1933), the Court stated:

> [t]hough often so characterized, a patent is not, accurately speaking, a monopoly. . . . [t]he term monopoly connotes the giving of an exclusive privilege for buying, selling, working or using a thing which the public freely enjoyed prior to the grant. Thus a monopoly takes something from the people. An inventor deprives the public of nothing which it enjoyed before his discovery, but gives something of value to the community by adding to the sum of human knowledge. . . . He may keep his invention secret and reap its fruits indefinitely.

Patents may be implicated in anti-competitive behavior, such as in an arrangement to fix prices or to control availability of a product. But competition laws and patent laws go hand-in-hand, and rarely collide with one another within a single jurisdiction. As the Federal Circuit said in Atari Games Corp. v. Nintendo of Am., Inc., 897 F.2d 1572, 1576 (Fed. Cir. 1990):

> [T]he two bodies of law are actually complementary, as both are aimed at encouraging innovation, industry and competition . . . There may on occasion exist . . . a fine line between actions protecting the legitimate interests of a patent owner and antitrust law violations.

On the one hand, the patent owner must be allowed to protect the property right given to him under the patent laws. On the other hand, a patent owner may not take the property right granted by a patent and use it to extend his power in the marketplace improperly, *i.e.* beyond the limits of what Congress intended to give in the patent laws. The fact that a patent is obtained does not wholly insulate the patent owner from the antitrust laws. . . .

"The patent is a shield to protect an invention," the court went on to say, "not a sword to eviscerate competition unfairly." *Id.*

Inevitably, the "territorial" and the "negative right" principles of patent law become intertwined in the international patent environment. As trade becomes more open between nations and the free movement of goods (including those protected by patents) becomes an increasingly important economic policy objective, the tensions between the two principles can escalate. The "limits of what Congress intended to give in the patent laws" have an international as well as a domestic policy-choice perspective. Defining the "international patent environment" may require reflection on what is the correct "international patent public policy" and not just the interests of any one country or group of countries. While the economic inefficiencies that may result from differences between national patent laws may not justify the extravagant rhetoric indulged in by some critics of the entire international patent environment, policy-makers must be vigilant to assure that the international exploitation of patents encourages competition without increasing the cost of innovation, including both competition between the young, rapidly growing economies of the developing countries and economies of countries which achieved developed status in the past, as well as competition between small and medium enterprises and multinational corporations. The international patent environment is not a disguise crafted to preserve (and mask) a privileged position for those national economies and large enterprises which are already technologically developed and economically mature. Proper patent policy, in the international no less than in the national arena, lies in striking a balance between underprotection which steals the rewards of the early innovator and overprotection which stifles the later one. The following materials explore the scope of the territorial and negative right principles in the context of parallel importation of patented goods legally made and sold in a different country.

CURTISS AEROPLANE & MOTOR CORP. v. UNITED AIRCRAFT ENGINEERING CORP.
266 F. 71 (2d Cir. 1920)

ROGERS, CIRCUIT JUDGE. This suit is brought under the Patent Laws of the United States for the alleged infringement by defendant of thirteen patents issued by the United States. . . . The defendant is charged with selling and offering for sale in the United States aeroplanes manufactured in Canada pursuant to certain agreements between plaintiff and the British government; the Canadian manufacture having been conducted by a corporation created by that government for that purpose. The total number of claims involved is 80. All the patents involved are for improvements in aeroplanes, and are capable of conjoint use, and are so used by plaintiff and defendant.

The bill of complaint alleges that all of the patents referred to were, by instruments in writing duly executed and recorded in the United States Patent Office, assigned to the plaintiff, and that plaintiff is the sole and exclusive owner of each and all of them. It also alleges that defendant has infringed each and all of said patents by offering for sale, selling, and using within the Southern District of New York, as well as elsewhere within the United States, aeroplanes, each of which embodies the improvements claimed in each and all of said patents. It contains the following statement:

> That the plaintiff, Curtiss Aeroplane & Motor Corporation, has developed at large expense, and produced in large quantities, aeroplanes of a distinctive type known throughout the aeroplane industry and among aviators as the Curtiss JN-4 machine; that such machine and the various parts thereof are embodiments of the several inventions of the letters patent heretofore set forth; that the defendant is now selling in the United States aeroplanes known as Canadian Curtiss or Canadian JN-4 machines, which are copies, in form, appearance, and mechanical details, of plaintiff's JN-4 machine, all in violation of plaintiff's rights under such patents and in an unfair and unlawful manner.

The bill prays an injunction and asks for an account of profits and damages resulting from the infringement which it alleges, and that any damages assessed may be tripled. The court below dismissed the bill for lack of merit, with costs to defendant.

The plaintiff, prior to the beginning of the [First] World War, was engaged in the manufacture of aeroplanes, and as a result of the war its business was greatly extended. In 1916 the plaintiff entered into certain contracts with the British government from which it received some $4,000,000. The contract into which the plaintiff entered with the British government is found in two separate documents: First, the agreement of November 20, 1916, with the annexed schedule, which is a contract of sales; second, the simultaneous agreement of the same date, which is an agreement on the plaintiff's (the seller's) part to promote the manufacture by the British government (the buyer) of the aeroplanes and engines of the type sold. The record contains a third document, dated December 6, 1916. The parties to this document are the Curtiss Aeroplane & Motors, Limited, of the first part, and the Canadian Aeroplanes, Limited, of the second part. The Curtiss Aeroplane & Motors, Limited, is a subsidiary company organized in Canada, in which the plaintiff owned 83 per cent of the outstanding capital stock; and the Canadian Aeroplane, Limited, is a company which the Imperial Munitions Board had caused to be incorporated to take over the plant of the Curtiss Aeroplanes & Motors, Limited.

The document above referred to as a contract of sales was executed on behalf of his Britannic Majesty's Government by J. P. Morgan & Co., agents. That document contains the statement that the British government has contracted to purchase from the plaintiff, and the seller has contracted to manufacture and sell to the buyer, at the price, and subject to the terms and conditions specified, the "seller's JN-4A type aeroplane, each equipped with one seller's OX5 type 90 H.P. engine, spare parts for such aeroplanes, blueprints and such aeroplanes, seller's OX5 type 90 H.P. engine, and spare parts for such engines." It also provides for the sale of a specified number of additional engines and of sets of spare parts of such engines.

The second document of those referred to was executed by his Britannic Majesty's Government, acting by the Imperial Munitions Board of Canada, and it provides in its first clause as follows:

> The seller agrees to cause to be sold and delivered to the buyer within ten (10) days of the date of the fixing of the purchase price therefor, as hereinafter provided, and the buyer agrees to accept and pay for, all of the tools, machinery, drawings, patterns, jigs, etc., of the Canadian company for use in the manufacture of seller's JN-4 aeroplanes, including raw materials and material manufactured and in process of manufacture at said Toronto plants for use in the manufacture of such aeroplanes, the buyer to pay therefor to the Canadian company. . . .

It provides in its third clause as follows:

> The seller agrees that at the option of the buyer it will grant or cause to be granted to the buyer, as part of the consideration moving from the seller to the buyer for this agreement, the exclusive right and license under any and all Canadian patents and applications for Canadian patents now or at any time hereafter owned by the seller or the Canadian company, and any further inventions now or hereafter owned and controlled by them or either of them embodying changes in or improvements of seller's JN-4 type aeroplanes and of seller's type engines, to manufacture such aeroplanes and/or engines within the Dominion of Canada, for sale to or use by the British government or the government of any of its possessions, but not for manufacture, use, or sale otherwise.

The plaintiff alleges that it was not within the contemplation of the parties to the agreements made between plaintiff and the British government, or within plaintiff's intention or by its permission, that the aeroplanes were to be sold or used by the public, or for other than war purposes, or in the United States. These allegations are denied absolutely in an affidavit presented by one who was connected with the Imperial Munitions Board of Canada, which made the contracts, and who was the superintendent of aeronautical supplies; this department being a branch of the Air Ministry in Great Britain and responsible only to the government of Great Britain. His affidavit states that in entering into the contracts made with the plaintiff it was understood that the property manufactured or otherwise acquired by the munitions board should become the absolute property of the board, to be disposed of as it should see fit. This was purely a war organization, and as soon as hostilities ceased the board proceeded to sell off everything controlled by it, including lands, buildings, aeroplanes, motor transports, motorboats, and thousands of patented articles of all kinds, including those complained of by the plaintiff.

It is admitted that the JN-4 aeroplanes which are said to infringe were made in Canada for the British government under the agreements to which reference has been made, and that after the war defendant purchased them from the British government, and, as it appears, is now proceeding to sell them in the United States. It is also admitted that the defendant has announced its intention of establishing warehouses at various parts of the United States, and such warehouses have been established already by it in New York and Chicago, in order that it may supply individuals and companies with the spare parts of air planes of all kinds and descriptions and all standard parts which may be used in their manufacture and development, including the supplying of standard air plane parts for the particular Canadian planes herein involved.

The defendant corporation has a capital of $500,000, and as the record shows, it is in the management of men of character and of excellent business standing. The chief engineer of the Curtiss Aeroplane & Motors Limited, of Canada, states in his affidavit that "their staff of engineers is composed of the leading aeronautical engineers of this country." It was organized on November 22, 1918, which was prior to the signing of the armistice, and was established, it is said, with the idea of organizing an aeronautical engineering and consulting corporation of the highest type. At the time of its incorporation there was no intention of purchasing any of the property of the Imperial Munitions Board of Canada. It appears that after the armistice, and when defendant was first approached on the subject of the purchase of some part of the aeroplane equipment of the British government, which was located in Canada, it declared through its president that it was not interested in any extent whatsoever. In January, 1919, the Imperial Munitions Board sold a number of its machines to the Canadian government, and the remainder of its equipment was sold to F. G. Ericson, a citizen of the United States, at the time a resident of Toronto, Canada. They were purchased by Ericson in his own name, but as a matter of fact he was acting for defendant. He is a member of the Society of Automotive Engineers and a Fellow of the Aeronautical Society of Great Britain, and had been for nine years engaged in the development of aeronautics. In 1915 he was appointed chief engineer of the Curtiss Aeroplane & Motors, Limited, of Canada, and when that concern was taken over by the Canadian Aeroplanes, Limited, he became its chief engineer. Before the sale to Ericson was made he informed the director of aviation of the Imperial Munitions Board what disposition he intended to make of the property upon acquiring it, and that he expected to sell a few of the planes in Canada, but that most of them would be sold for commercial purposes in the United States, and that he expected to establish a depot for such sales in or near Baltimore. With this information in its possession the Imperial Munitions Board made the sale, and made it entirely without restriction of condition, and gave Ericson full right to sell and dispose of the property whenever and wherever he might see fit. It may be remarked in passing that the counsel of the munitions board, who is referred to in one of the affidavits "as one of the most prominent attorneys in Canada," furnished that board with an opinion in which he denied the claims set up by the plaintiff as to the rights which the British government had under the agreements already referred to.

The bill charges no infringement by manufacture, nor does it raise the question when assembling ends and manufacturing begins. It deals with nothing but the right to bring into the United States certain JN-4's which the plaintiff gave permission to make, and in the making of which it aided, and for every one of which it has been compensated. The right to bring these machines into the country is the sole question with which the bill deals.

An aeroplane has been said to be the most mobile article manufactured, and it is not confined by geographical boundaries. It is susceptible of use anywhere in the world. As was said at the argument, aeroplanes were used by the British government, not only in England and Canada, but over the battle fields of Belgium and France, in Egypt, Palestine, Mesopotamia, Northern Russia, South Africa, and indeed wherever hostilities existed. In the very nature of things, and from the language used in the agreements, it is evident that the contracting parties contemplated such widespread use. After this country entered the war, the aviation fields in Texas and in other states were placed at the disposal of the British authorities and were actually used by them as training fields for Canadian aviators. It does not appear in this record whether any of these Canadian JN-4 planes were then brought into the United States for use by Canadian aviators on our aviation fields, who were there undergoing training. If, however, such planes were then brought into the United States, and if they contained the plaintiff's manufactured engines, it would be difficult to believe that any one would seriously contend that their introduction involved any violation of the plaintiff's patents.

The plaintiff and the British government alike understood and intended that the aeroplanes to be manufactured by that government as well as those to be supplied to it by the plaintiff were to become the absolute property of the government, and were to be disposed of as the latter should see fit. The express language of the contract is that the aeroplanes and other articles should "become and be the absolute property of the British government."

The plaintiff, in becoming the owner of the patents in suit, acquired the exclusive privilege of making, using, and vending, and of authorizing others to make, use, and vend the subject-matter of the respective inventions without its permission. Bloomer v. McQuewan, 14 How. 539. The exclusive right of an inventor in his invention was not recognized by the common law, which conferred no such monopoly upon him. The right in the United States rests upon article 1, section 8, of the Constitution, which gives to Congress the power to promote the progress of science and the useful arts by securing for limited times to authors and inventors the exclusive right to their respective writings and discoveries. While a patent is undoubtedly a monopoly it belongs to a class made legal by the constitutional provision referred to.

It is important to determine what right or rights passed to the British government under the agreements which it entered into with the plaintiff. As we have seen, the owner of a patent has three distinct rights, which he can dispose of either together or singly: (1) The right to make the article. (2) The right to use it. (3) The right to sell it. Waterman v. Mackensie, 138 U.S. 252. A grant which does not transfer all these rights is a license. So, also, is the right to make, use, and sell the article for specified purposes only. Gamewell Fire-Alarm Telephone Co. v. Brooklyn (C.C.) 14 Fed. 255; Bogart v. Hinds (C.C.) 25 Fed. 484. *See* 22 Am. & Eng. Encyc. of Law, 430.

That the British government secured the right to manufacture the aeroplanes, and the engines as well, is not open to doubt. In the fourth clause of the agreement of sale the plaintiff bound itself from time to time to furnish the British government all information useful to it "in the building of such aeroplanes and engines, including engineering data, blueprints in detail of such aeroplanes and engines," etc. The sixth clause of that agreement reads as follows:

> The seller agrees that at the request of the buyer from time to time it will send to the plant to be established by the buyer in the Dominion of Canada a competent engineer, familiar with the design, construction, and methods of manufacture of such aeroplanes and/or engines, to assist and advise the buyer in the manufacture thereof. Such engineer shall report his observations and recommendations to the general manager of the plant so to be established by the buyer, or any other person designated by it for that purpose, and shall continue in the exclusive employment of the buyer during its pleasure, receiving compensation from the buyer at a rate not to exceed fifty dollars ($50) per week during the time of such continuous and exclusive employment.

And the seventh clause provides that the British government shall pay "on each such engine manufactured" by it a specified sum, adding:

> "And such exclusive right and license shall be granted only upon the further condition that the buyer shall pay to the seller," etc.

There is much more in the agreements which proves what the plaintiff's intention was respecting the right of the British government to manufacture, but it is not necessary to set it forth herein. It does not in any way restrict or qualify the right of the British government.

That government plainly acquired the right under its license to make. Did it also have the right to use and to vend? The answer to this question depends upon whether the authorization to make was general and unrestricted or subject to qualification and conditions, as to the disposition of the planes by the British government. The agreements will be searched in vain for any restriction of condition as to the right to use or to vend; and in the absence of such restriction we understand the law to be that the British government obtained a full and unqualified right to use and sell the planes and engines, and that this right passed to all subsequent purchasers, and therefore to this defendant. No American or British decision asserting a contrary doctrine is known to us.

The plaintiff relies on certain cases, but an examination shows that they are plainly distinguishable, and do not support the plaintiff's contention. The cases upon which it relies belong to one or the other of two classes: (1) Those in which there has been a sale of a patented article, or a license to manufacture, but accompanied by explicit and unequivocal restrictions as to the time, or place, or manner of using the article so sold or licensed, or as to the ultimate disposal thereof. Dickerson v. Matheson, 57 Fed. 524; Dickerson v. Tinling, 84 Fed. 192; Dickerson v. Sheldon, 98 Fed. 621. (2) Those in which there has been no participation whatever by the owner of the patent, either as a party or as a privy, in the putting out of the article which is alleged to infringe. Boesch v. Graff, 133 U.S. 697; Featherstone v. Ormonde Cycle Co. (C.C.) 53 Fed. 110; Daimler v. Conklin, 170 Fed. 70. And if a patentee retains title to the patented machine, which was not done in this case, he may restrict its manner of use, in the lease or other contract. United States v. United Shoe Machinery Co., 247 U.S. 32, 58. In Chaffee v. Boston Belting Co., 22 How. 217, 223, the Supreme Court said:

> When the patented machine rightfully passes to the hands of the purchaser from the patentee, or from any other person by him authorized to convey it, the machine is no longer within the limits of the monopoly. . . . By a valid sale and purchase, the patented machine becomes the private individual property of the purchaser, and is no longer protected by the laws of the United States. . . .

In Bloomer v. Millinger, 1 Wall. 340, 350, the court said:

> Patentees acquire the exclusive right to make and use, and vend to others to be used, their patented inventions for the period of time specified in the patent; but when they have made and vended to others to be used one or more of the things patented, to that extent they have parted with their exclusive right. They are entitled to but one royalty for a patented machine. and consequently, when a patentee has himself constructed the machine and sold it, or authorized another to construct and sell it, or to construct and use and operate it, and the consideration has been paid to him for the right, he has then to that extent parted with his monopoly, and ceased to have any interest whatever in the machine so sold or so authorized to be constructed and operated.

The purchaser of a patented article from a territorial licensee (one whose rights are limited to a restricted territory) may, unless there is a specific agreement to the contrary, use the article so purchased outside of the territory without interference from the patentee. The article is no longer within the monopoly of the patentee, and the purchaser can use it anywhere. This principle was announced in Adams v. Burke, 17 Wall. 453, 456, where it was said:

> It seems to us that, although the right of Lockhart & Seelye to manufacture, to sell and to use these coffin lids was limited to the circle of 10 miles around Boston, that a purchaser from them of a single coffin acquired the right to use that coffin for the purpose for which all coffins are used; that, so far as the use of it was concerned, the patentee had received his consideration, and it was no longer within the monopoly of the patent. It would be to ingraft a limitation upon the right of use not contemplated by the statute, nor within the reason of the contract to say that it could only be used within the 10-mile circle.

And see, to the same effect, Hobbie v. Jennison, 149 U.S. 355; Keeler v. Standard Folding Bed, 157 U.S. In the case last cited the court said:

> Upon the doctrine of these cases we think it follows that one who buys patented articles of manufacture from one authorized to sell them becomes possessed of an absolute property in such articles, unrestricted in time or place. . . . The conclusion reached does not deprive a patentee of his just rights, because no article can be unfettered from the claim of his monopoly without paying its tribute. The inconvenience and annoyance to the public that an opposite conclusion would occasion are too obvious to require illustration.

If a patentee or his assignee sells a patented article, that article is freed from the monopoly of any patents which the vendor may possess. If the thing sold contains inventions of several United States patents owned by the vendor, the article is freed from each and all of them; and if the vendor has divided his monopoly into different territorial monopolies, his sale frees the article from them all. If the vendor's patent monopoly consists of foreign and domestic patents, the sale frees the article from the monopoly of both his foreign and his domestic patents, and where there is no restriction in the contract of sale the purchaser acquires the complete title and full right to use and sell the article in any and every country. This doctrine was recognized by Judge Wallace in the Circuit Court for the Southern District of New York in 1885, in Holiday v. Mattheson, 24 Fed. 185. That case raised the question whether the owner of a patent in the United States for an invention, and who had sold the patented article in England without restrictions or conditions, could treat as an infringer one who had purchased the article in England of a vendee of the patentee, and could restrain him from using or selling the article in the United States. In deciding the question adversely Judge Wallace said:

> When the owner sells an article without any reservation respecting

its use, or the title which is to pass, the purchaser acquires the whole right of the vendor in the thing sold, the right to use it, to repair it, and to sell it to others; and second purchasers acquire the rights of the seller, and may do with the article whatever the first purchaser could have lawfully done if he had not parted with it. The presumption arising from such a sale is that the vendor intends to part with all his rights in the thing sold, and that the purchaser is to acquire an unqualified property in it; and it would be inconsistent with the presumed understanding of the parties to permit the vendor to retain the power of restricting the purchaser to using the thing bought in a particular way, or in a particular place, for a limited period of time, or from selling his rights to others. It is quite immaterial whether the thing sold is a patented article or not, or whether the vendor is the owner of a patent which gives him a monopoly of its use and sale. If these circumstances happen to concur, the legal effect of the transaction is not changed, unless by the conditions of the bargain the monopoly right is impressed upon the thing purchased; and if the vendor sells without reservation or restriction, he parts with his monopoly so far as it can in any way qualify the rights of the purchaser.

And *see* Morgan Envelope Co. v. Albany Perforated Wrapping Paper Co. (C.C.) 40 Fed. 580.

Counsel for plaintiff relies strongly upon Société Anonyme des Manufactures de Glaces v. Tilgman's Patent Sand Blast Co., L.R. 25 Ch. Div. 7. That case, however, is readily distinguishable in its facts. There were two patents for the same invention, one Belgian and one British. The two patents were owned by the same concern. A third party had purchased the patented article in Belgium, and had then undertaken to import his purchase into England. The owner of the British patent had not manufactured the article, nor sold it, nor in any way authorized the purchaser to bring it into England, and therefore was not estopped from enforcing his rights against the purchaser. The owner of the patent had granted to the Belgian Société Anonyme a mere ordinary license to operate under the Belgian patent, and the court held that, inasmuch as the relationship was that of ordinary licensor and licensee, the Belgian product was not immune from infringement within Great Britain. In the course of his opinion in that case Cotton, L.J., however, said:

When an article is sold without any restriction on the buyer, whether it is manufactured under either one or the other patent, that, in my opinion, as against the vendor gives the purchaser an absolute right to deal with that which he so buys in any way he thinks fit, and of course that includes selling in any country where there is a patent in the possession of and owned by the vendor.

The extract quoted fits the facts of this case. The plaintiff herein as the original vendor gave to the British government, as purchaser, an absolute right to deal with that which it purchased in any way it thought fit, and defendant herein derives its right from that government to bring the aeroplanes into the United States in the manner it did, and the plaintiff is without ground of complaint. As the plaintiff has already been paid for these aeroplanes the full price it asked, it is no longer concerned about the price at which the article is sold, or whether the article is kept in Canada, or in Great Britain, or in the United States. We may summarize our conclusions:

It is admitted that, if the aeroplanes which are alleged to infringe had been built in Canada under a limited license, or under a Canadian patent, and then brought into the United States, infringement would have been made out. But that is not this case.

It appears that the aeroplanes complained of were manufactured under a license from the plaintiff and with the latter's active assistance, and that they contain engines furnished by the plaintiff with the intent that they should be so used.

It appears that the plaintiff has been paid a sum in excess of $4,000,000 for the aeroplanes and engines, which plaintiff sold or agreed might be manufactured.

It appears that the license under which the aeroplanes were manufactured contained no restriction or limitation as to time, or place, or manner of use of the aeroplanes, nor as to the ultimate disposition which might be made of them, and that they were therefore freed from the monopoly of the plaintiff's patents.

The decree appealed from is in all respects affirmed, with the costs of both courts.

AN INTERVIEW WITH JUDGE GILES S. RICH
U.S. COURT OF APPEALS FOR THE FEDERAL CIRCUIT
15 ABA-IPL Newsletter 1, 6 (1999)

Q: While we're on the subject of misnomers, I've heard that you disagree with the reasoning of the so-called "first sale doctrine." What's wrong with the idea that the first authorized sale of a patented product "exhausts" the patentee's right to control the subsequent disposition of that particular item?

Judge Rich: My position is simple: No patent right is involved, and nothing is exhausted. Talking about exhaustion of the patent right is nonsense, and it's about time to stop talking nonsense. To explain, I have to discuss two things: (1) what the patent right is; and (2) what is the meaning of "exhaustion." It is no longer debatable what the patent right is. . . . [T]he Supreme Court told the country in 1852 in Bloomer v. McQuewan that it consists altogether in the right to exclude others—and that is all it is. It is not an ambiguous "exclusive right"; it is a simple right to exclude others. Period.

Now, the premise is that the patentee made and sold the patented invention. That was the so-called "first sale." What did his right to exclude others have to do with those acts? Absolutely nothing. In manufacturing, was he excluding anyone? No. In selling, was he excluding anyone? No. Then he wasn't exercising his patent right, was he? The trouble stems from the old ambiguous statutory definition of the patent right as the "exclusive right to make, use and sell."

Turning to the meaning of "exhaustion," it means the state of being drained or used up completely. It assumes that there is something to be used up. Well, since the patent right is not involved, how could it be used up? It couldn't have been used, even a teeny bit, and it certainly was not exhausted.

But that's not all there is to the analysis. What is this so-called "first sale" of an article on which the seller happens to have a patent? It is a simple transfer of ownership—a chattel or personal property—from one person to another. The rights of the buyer are governed by the laws of property or the law of sales or both. And the law of patents has nothing whatever to do with those rights. Any restraints on the new owner have to be made under the law of contracts, and any contractual restrictions are subject to the antitrust laws. So there is neither use nor exhaustion of patent rights.

Conclusion: The term "exhaustion doctrine" is meaningless nonsense. The legal result is OK, but the reasoning is all wrong. The simple fact is that no patent right is involved in the sale of merchandise by the patentee, nothing is exhausted, and the adjective "first" in "first sale" is also without significance. Let's clear up the thinking about this law.

***

NOTES AND QUESTIONS

(1) **Exhaustion and First Sale.** The *Curtiss* court, in dictum, says that "if the vendor's patent monopoly consists of foreign and domestic patents, the sale frees the article from the monopoly of both his foreign and his domestic patents, and where there is no restriction in the contract of sale the purchaser acquired the complete title and full right to use and sell the article in any and every country." Can the effect of exhaustion be limited by contractual provision? Even with respect to a bona fide third party purchaser without notice?

(2) *Bloomer.* Is the *Curtiss* court in agreement with Judge Rich on the significance of *Bloomer v. McQuewan*? Does 35 U.S.C. § 261, which states that "subject to the provisions of this title, patents shall have the attributes of personal property," clarify whether a patent is a monopoly? To what extent do divisions of international markets by patent owners by grant of territorial licenses create non-competitive effects, justifying legal limitations on the freedom of the patentee to contract?

(3) **Statutory Language.** Is there any significance to the fact that there is an explicit limitation on the rights of a copyright owner upon transfer of a particular copy in the Copyright Act of 1976 and no such limitation on the patentee's right in the Patent Act of 1952? Should the decisions in *Lever Brothers* and *Quality King* affect the interpretation of the patent statute?

[C] The European Union

TREATY ESTABLISHING THE EUROPEAN COMMUNITY

Article 28 (ex-Article 30)

Quantitative restrictions on imports and all measures having equivalent effect shall, without prejudice to the following provisions, be prohibited between Member States.

Article 30 (ex-Article 36)

The provisions of Articles 30-34 shall not preclude prohibitions or restrictions on imports . . . justified on grounds of . . . the protection of industrial and commercial property. Such prohibitions or restrictions shall not, however, constitute a means of arbitrary discrimination or a disguised restriction on trade between Member States.

[1] Geographic Scope of Exhaustion

The contours of the exhaustion doctrine under EU law were first developed by the European Court of Justice in interpreting the relationship between ex-Articles 30 and 36 of the EC Treaty (quoted above). But the issue has now been addressed in EU legislation, namely the Trademark Harmonization Directive and the Community Trade Mark Regulation. Prior to that legislation, many countries within Europe adhered in their national law to a principle of "worldwide exhaustion," namely that placing particular goods on the market anywhere exhausted the trademark owner's rights with respect to those goods. The EU Trademark Directive provides that the owner of the mark will be unable to assert its rights in relation to goods which it has placed on the market within the community, but does not make clear whether this is a minimum scope of exhaustion only; if it were, member states could continue to apply the broader principle of worldwide exhaustion. The European Court of Justice recently addressed this issue.

SILHOUETTE INTERNATIONAL SCHMIED GMBH & CO. v. HARTLAUER HANDELSGESELLSCHAFT
[1998] 2 CMLR 953 (E.C.J.)

Mr. Francis Jacobs (Advocate-General)

The Court's case law on Articles 30 and 36 EC established for trade marks, as well as for other forms of intellectual property, a principle of Community-wide exhaustion:[1] thus the sale in the Community of trade marked goods, by or with the consent of the trade mark owner, exhausts the trade mark rights throughout the Community, and he cannot, other than in exceptional circumstances, oppose the use of the mark by others in subsequent transactions anywhere in the Community.

Article 7(1) of the Trade Marks Directive gives effect to the principle of Community exhaustion as developed by the Court's case law. It provides that "a trade mark does not entitle the proprietor to prohibit its use in relation to goods which have been put on the market in the Community under that trade mark by the proprietor or with his consent." Subsequently the principle was extended, by virtue of the Agreement on the European Economic Area (the "EEA"), to the territory of the EEA, now consisting of the Community on the one hand and Iceland, Liechtenstein and Norway on the other hand. But can the trade mark owner prevent a third party from using the mark in the Community or in the EEA, for goods which have been put on the market under that mark, by or with the consent of the owner, outside the EEA? The question comes by way of a request for a preliminary ruling from the Oberster Gerichtshof (Supreme Court), Austria.

The issue therefore is whether Community law requires Member States to provide for exhaustion only when the goods have been marketed in the EEA, or whether Member States may (or perhaps even must) provide for exhaustion when the goods have been marketed in a third country—a principle of international (*i.e.*, worldwide) exhaustion.

The Trade Marks Directive

The Trade Marks Directive was adopted under Article 100a EC. Its aim was not "to undertake full-scale approximation of the trade mark laws of the Member States" but simply to approximate "those national provisions of law which most directly affect the functioning of the internal market" (third recital of the preamble to the Directive).

The first, third, and ninth recitals of the preamble to the Directive state, respectively:

> Whereas the trade mark laws at present applicable in the Member States contain disparities which may impede the free movement of goods and freedom to provide services and may distort competition within the Common Market; whereas it is therefore necessary, in view of the establishment and functioning of the internal market, to approximate the laws of Member States;
>
> . . . .
>
> Whereas it does not appear to be necessary at present to undertake full-scale approximation of the trade mark laws of the Member States

---

[1]The principle was established, in relation to trade marks, by Case 16/74, *Centrafarm v. Winthrop*, [1974] 2 CMLR 480.

and it will be sufficient if approximation is limited to those national provisions of law which most directly affect the functioning of the internal market;

. . . .

Whereas it is fundamental, in order to facilitate the free circulation of goods and services, to ensure that henceforth registered trade marks enjoy the same protection under the legal systems of all the Member States; whereas this should however not prevent the Member States from granting at their option extensive protection to those trade marks which have a reputation.

[The advocate-general noted that the directive harmonized many central aspects of national trademark law, but that, with respect to certain other issues, member states were given discretion to decide whether to adopt the rules provided for in the directive. Finally, the directive left certain matters (such as the procedure concerning the registration of marks and provisions relating to unfair competition) to member states. *See supra* § 3.01[I][1].]

The most important provisions in relation to the present case are Articles 5 and 7, entitled, respectively, "Rights conferred by a trade mark" and "Exhaustion of the rights conferred by a trade mark".

Article 5 provides that:

1. The registered trade mark shall confer on the proprietor exclusive rights therein. The proprietor shall be entitled to prevent all third parties not having his consent from using in the course of trade:

(a) any sign which is identical with the trade mark in relation to goods or services which are identical with those for which the trade mark is registered;

(b) any sign where, because of its identity with, or similarity to, the trade mark and the identity or similarity of the goods or services covered by the trade mark and the sign, there exists a likelihood of confusion on the part of the public, which includes the likelihood of association between the sign and the trade mark.

. . . .

3. The following, inter alia, may be prohibited under paragraphs 1 and 2:

(a) affixing the sign to the goods or to the packaging thereof:

(b) offering the goods, or putting them on the market or stocking them for these purposes under that sign, or offering or supplying services thereunder;

(c) importing or exporting the goods under the sign;

(d) using the sign on business papers and in advertising.

Article 7 provides as follows:

> 1. The trade mark shall not entitle the proprietor to prohibit its use in relation to goods which have been put on the market in the Community under that trade mark by the proprietor or with his consent.
>
> 2. Paragraph 1 shall not apply where there exist legitimate reasons for the proprietor to oppose further commercialization of the goods, especially where the condition of the goods is changed or impaired after they have been put on the market.

Provisions on exhaustion of similar effect to those contained in Article 7 have been included in other Community instruments on intellectual property rights.[4] The most relevant in that respect is the Community Trade Mark Regulation, which I consider below.

The EEA Agreement

Although Article 7(1) of the Trade Marks Directive refers to marketing in the Community, the principle of the exhaustion of rights, as previously mentioned, was extended for certain purposes to the EEA. The Directive was one of the legislative acts incorporated into EEA law by the Agreement establishing the EEA, which entered into force on 1 January 1994. . . . Annex XVII to the Agreement amends Article 7(1) of the Directive "for the purposes of the Agreement" so as to refer to marketing within the EEA rather than the Community: it replaces the words "in the Community" with the words "in a Contracting Party." Moreover, a protocol to the Agreement, Protocol 28 on intellectual property, contains an article, Article 2, headed "Exhaustion of rights." Article 2(1) provides:

> To the extent that exhaustion is dealt with in Community measures or jurisprudence, the Contracting Parties shall provide for such exhaustion of intellectual property rights as laid down in Community law. Without prejudice to future developments of case law, this provision shall be interpreted in accordance with the meaning established in the relevant rulings of the Court of Justice of the European Communities given prior to the signature of the Agreement.

No issue under that Protocol arises in the present case, the facts of which occurred after Austria (previously an EEA Member State) acceded to the

---

[4]*See*, for example, Article 9(2) of Council Directive 92/100 on rental right and lending right and on certain rights related to copyright in the field of intellectual property, [1992] OJ L346/61. The Commission considers that those provisions also have the effect of excluding international exhaustion: see its answer to a Written Question in the European Parliament, [1994] OJ C340/37.

Community on 1 January 1995.

The facts

The plaintiff, Silhouette International Schmied Gesellschaft mbH & Co. KG ("Silhouette"), is an Austrian company which produces fashion spectacles in the higher price ranges. It distributes the spectacles worldwide under the word and picture trade mark "Silhouette", which is registered in Austria and in most countries of the world, as well as internationally. In Austria, Silhouette supplies the spectacles to specialist opticians; in other countries it has subsidiary companies or distributors.

The defendant, Hartlauer Handelsgesellschaft mbH ("Hartlauer"), sells spectacles in numerous branches in Austria and solicits customers mainly by its low prices. It is not supplied by Silhouette because Silhouette considers sales by Hartlauer to be harmful to the image which Silhouette has created for its products as fashionable spectacles of special quality.

In October 1995 Silhouette sold 21,000 spectacle frames of an out-dated model which had expired to a firm called Union Trading for US$261,450. The transaction was arranged by Silhouette's sales representative for the Middle East. Silhouette directed him to instruct the purchaser to sell the frames in Bulgaria or the States of the former Soviet Union only and not to export them to other countries. The sales representative informed Silhouette that he had instructed the purchaser accordingly. The Oberster Gerichtshof observes that it has not been possible to ascertain whether that actually happened.

Silhouette delivered the goods to Union Trading in Sofia in November 1995. Hartlauer subsequently acquired the goods (according to the Oberster Gerichtshof, it has not been possible to ascertain from whom) and offered them for sale in Austria from December 1995. It announced in a press campaign that, although it had not been supplied by Silhouette, it had succeeded in purchasing 21,000 Silhouette frames from abroad. In its observations, Hartlauer maintains that when it acquired the products it was assured that there would be no obstacle to importing them into Austria.

Silhouette objects to the sale of its frames by Hartlauer in Austria and seeks an order prohibiting Hartlauer from marketing under its trade mark spectacles or spectacle frames which were not put on the market in the EEA by it or with its consent. It argues that it has not exhausted its trade mark rights because the Directive provides that such rights can be exhausted only by reason of marketing within the EEA by the trade mark owner or with his consent. . . .

Hartlauer contends that Silhouette did not sell the frames subject to the instruction that any import into the Community was excluded and that Silhouette's application should be dismissed.

Silhouette's action failed before the Landgericht Steyr (Steyr Regional Court) and on appeal to the Oberlandesgericht Linz (Linz Higher Regional Court). The current reference is made [under Article 234EC] in the context of an appeal by Silhouette to the Oberster Gerichtshof against the decision of the Oberlandesgericht Linz.

Article 7 of the Trade Marks Directive was implemented into Austrian law, almost word for word, by the 1992 amendments to the Markenschutzgesetz. Paragraph 10a of the Markenschutzgesetz provides that the trade mark does not entitle the owner of the trade mark to prohibit a third party from using the mark for goods which have been put on the market in the EEA under that mark by the owner or with his consent.

The Oberster Gerichtshof explains that, prior to the implementation of the Trade Marks Directive, the principle of international exhaustion had been applied by the Austrian courts. [cit]. The position subsequent to implementation of the Directive, however, is unclear. According to the explanatory memorandum, it was intended that the question of the validity of the principle of international exhaustion should be settled by legal practice.

The Oberster Gerichtshof accordingly wishes to ascertain whether the Directive allows Member States to apply a rule of international exhaustion.

The Oberster Gerichtshof has submitted [two questions, including this first question, reproduced below] to this Court:

> Is Article 7(1) of the First Council Directive 89/104 to approximate the laws of the Member States relating to trade marks . . . to be interpreted as meaning that the trade mark entitles its proprietor to prohibit a third party from using the mark for goods which have been put on the market under that mark in a State which is not a Contracting State?
>
> . . . .

The reference to a Contracting State is to be understood as referring to a Contracting Party to the EEA Agreement, *i.e.*, on the EFTA side, those EFTA States which are parties to the Agreement (currently Iceland, Liechtenstein and Norway), and on the Community side, the Community and/or the EC Member States. [cit]. Hence the questions are concerned with goods put on the market outside the EEA. It is unnecessary to consider what the position would be in relation to goods marketed within the EEA and subsequently imported into the Community. For convenience I shall refer in what follows to importing into the Community goods marketed outside the EEA.

. . . .

Question 1

[T]he Oberster Gerichtshof asks whether Article 7(1) of the Trade Marks Directive is to be interpreted as meaning that the proprietor of a trade mark is entitled to prohibit a third party from using the mark for goods which have been put on the market under that mark in a State which is not a member of the EEA. It is not specified in the question whether the trade mark owner consented to such marketing in the non-EEA State. However, it is clear from the order for reference that Silhouette did consent to marketing in Bulgaria since it is stated that Silhouette gave directions for the sale of the goods there and delivered them to the purchaser in Sofia. The question should accordingly be addressed on the assumption that the trade mark owner consented to the marketing of his products outside the EEA.

It should also be assumed for present purposes that Silhouette did not consent to its products being resold within the EEA. That is so even though the national court expresses some doubt as to whether the restrictions upon resale were passed on to the purchaser. If Silhouette had consented to marketing in the EEA, the answer to the first question referred would clearly be that Silhouette could not oppose the import of its products into Austria.

The Oberster Gerichtshof has not suggested that there are any "legitimate reasons" within the meaning of Article 7(2) of the Directive for Silhouette to oppose the resale of its spectacles in Austria.

Thus, in the present case, the Court is faced squarely with the question whether the Trade Marks Directive, in referring to the exhaustion of trade mark rights following marketing in the Community, requires Member States to allow a trade mark owner to oppose the import into the Community of products placed on the market outside the EEA by him or with his consent simply because he has not consented to the marketing of those products within the Community: *i.e.*, whether it precludes Member States from adopting the principle of international exhaustion.

The terms of the Directive

Article 7(1) of the Directive provides for exhaustion only where the goods have been put on the market in the Community: it provides therefore only for Community-wide, not for international exhaustion.

It is accepted on all sides, and with good reason in my view, that the Directive does not require Member States to provide for international exhaustion: at most, it leaves that open as an option for Member States. If the Directive had sought to impose international exhaustion, Article 7(1) would not have referred only to marketing in the Community.

That the Directive did not intend to impose international exhaustion is confirmed by the legislative history of the Directive. The Commission's original proposal would have imposed international exhaustion. [cit]. The Commission subsequently changed its view, and its amended proposal [cit.] explicitly limited the exhaustion principle to goods which had been put on the market "in the Community".

As to whether the Directive precludes international exhaustion, or leaves that open, the language of Article 7(1) inclines me to the former view. Article 7(1) spells out the circumstances in which the trade mark rights are exhausted: it is naturally read as doing so exhaustively. In providing that the rights are exhausted when the goods are marketed in the Community, Article 7(1) is naturally understood as meaning that the rights are not exhausted when the goods are marketed in a third country. It is true that the Directive does not specifically preclude international exhaustion, but that effect can reasonably be inferred from the language. I accept that there are arguments which go the other way, but those arguments derive little support from the language of the Directive.

My view of the effect of the language of Article 7(1) is supported by the structure of the Directive. Article 7(1) is a derogation from the rights conferred on the trade mark owner by Article 5(1). In general derogations should not be construed broadly. Here Article 7(1) cannot be construed more broadly than as providing for Community exhaustion. It would be necessary to read into the Directive a further, implied derogation leaving open the possibility of provision for international exhaustion, which seems contrary to the structure of the Directive.

The aims and scope of the Directive

Since the terms of the Directive are not conclusive, the aims and scope of the Directive are of crucial significance in interpreting its provisions. The indications in the preamble, however, do not all point in the same direction. On the one hand, it will be recalled that the Directive does not purport to "undertake full-scale approximation of the trade mark laws of the Member States" but aims to approximate "those national provisions of law which most directly affect the functioning of the Common Market." On the other hand, the Directive seeks to ensure, with certain limited exceptions, that trade marks "enjoy the same protection under the legal systems of all the Member States."

Those who favour international exhaustion point to the limited nature of the harmonization attempted by the Directive and contend that the reference to Community exhaustion in Article 7(1) should be regarded only as a minimum standard.

Moreover, they argue that the intention of Article 7 was simply to codify the Court's existing case law on the exhaustion of rights since the Court has stressed that Article 7 is to be interpreted in the same way as the Court's case law on Articles 30 and 36. They contend that, prior to implementation of the Directive, Member States had a discretion as to whether or not to adopt the principle of international exhaustion; and that, in the absence of express language to the contrary, that should remain the position under the Directive.

The opponents of international exhaustion, relying on the wording of the third recital of the preamble to the Directive, argue that, whilst it is true that the Directive is not a measure of total harmonization, the application by a Member State of the principle of international exhaustion is one of the provisions which "most directly affect the functioning of the internal market" and is accordingly the type of issue which the Directive sought to harmonize. Moreover, the purpose of the Directive was to ensure that trade marks "enjoy the same protection under the legal systems of all the Member States." Although the protection afforded by the Directive does not impose a totally uniform system since certain areas are left to the discretion of the Member States, those areas are very limited and the choice carefully specified.

As regards the scope and effects of the Directive, it can, in my view, be argued that the Directive has transformed the impact of Community law on trade mark protection. Previously the only issue under Community law was that of the impact of Articles 30 to 36 of the Treaty on national trade mark law. The Directive harmonizes the essential conditions and consequences of trade mark protection. Although in an internal Community context the Court has treated Article 7 of the Directive as codifying the previous case law, it cannot be assumed that that is the sole function of Article 7. The Directive regulates the substance of trade mark rights, and its provisions are designed to be substituted for the diverse national laws across the whole range of its provisions.

If the Directive is seen as establishing the essential terms and effects of trade mark protection, it is difficult to argue that it leaves Member States free to opt for international exhaustion. The scope of the exhaustion principle is after all central to the content of trade mark rights.

But even if one takes a narrower view of the character of the Directive, it seems clear that international exhaustion is one of the matters which "most directly affect the functioning of the internal market" and which the Directive therefore seeks to harmonize. If some Member States practice international exhaustion while others do not, there will be barriers to trade within the internal market which it is precisely the object of the Directive to remove.

It is above all on that ground that the Austrian, French, German, Italian and United Kingdom Governments and the Commission all submit that the Directive should be interpreted as precluding the principle of international exhaustion. Essentially they argue that, if the Member States were free to determine whether trade mark owners could prevent imports from third countries, then the same products could be the subject of parallel imports into one Member State but not into another, a result incompatible with the internal market. It is of course no answer to that submission to suggest that once goods were imported into one Member State which did provide for international exhaustion they could then benefit from free movement throughout the Community, since that suggestion would have the effect of imposing international exhaustion on all Member States which, as has been seen above, would be contrary to the Directive. The submission of the five Member States and of the Commission has in my view much force.

A similar argument was advanced by some Member States (France, Germany and the United Kingdom) and by the Commission before the EFTA Court in Mag Instrument Inc v. California Trading Company Norway, Ulsteen (Case E-2/97, advisory opinion of 3 December 1997). That case concerned the interpretation of Article 7(1) of the Directive and in particular the issue of international exhaustion in relation to the EFTA States. As mentioned above, Article 7(1) was extended, for the purposes of the EEA Agreement, to goods marketed throughout the EEA. The EFTA Court responded as follows:

> This argumentation has to be rejected in so far as it concerns the EFTA States. Unlike the EC Treaty, the EEA Agreement does not establish a customs union. The purpose and the scope of the EC Treaty and the EEA Agreement are different. [cit]. Thus, the EEA

Agreement does not establish a customs union, but a free trade area.

The abovementioned differences between the Community and the EEA will have to be reflected in the application of the principle of exhaustion of trade mark rights. According to Article 8 EEA, the principle of free movement of goods as laid down in Articles 11 to 13 EEA applies only to goods originating in the EEA, while in the Community a product is in free circulation once it has been lawfully placed on the market in a Member State. In general, the latter applies in the context of the EEA only in respect of products originating in the EEA. In the case at hand, the product was manufactured in the United States and imported into Norway. Accordingly, it is not subject to the principle of the free movement of goods within the EEA.

The EFTA Court concluded that it was for the EFTA States, *i.e.*, their legislators or courts, to decide whether to introduce or maintain the principle of international exhaustion with regard to goods originating outside the EEA. However the EFTA Court did not consider the question of goods originating within the EEA.

Article 100a of the Treaty

In the present case the Swedish Government, in contrast to the other Governments, contends that the Directive leaves the issue of international exhaustion to be resolved by national law. It argues that a directive based solely on Article 100a of the Treaty could not regulate the question of international exhaustion. The Swedish Government contends that that question concerns the relations between the Member States and third countries; moreover according to Opinion 1/94 on the WTO Agreement, the external competence in matters of intellectual property is not exclusive to the Community.

It seems to me however that a distinction has to be made between measures of commercial policy on the one hand and provisions governing the effects of trade mark rights within the Community on the other. Although to preclude international exhaustion clearly has an effect on external trade, it is less clear that it actually regulates such trade: contrary to the suggestion of the Swedish Government, the Directive, if interpreted as precluding international exhaustion, would not "regulate relations between Member States and third States." Rather, the Directive lays down the rights of trade mark owners in the Community. It provides for the conditions under which the trade mark owner can take action against the marketing of certain goods, which may or may not be imported from third countries. Moreover it is inevitable that internal market measures will affect imports from third countries. Thus measures harmonizing technical standards will affect goods from third countries, but can properly be based on Article 100a of the Treaty.

With regard to Opinion 1/94 and the external competence of the Community, that issue would arise only if negotiations were to be undertaken with third countries to deal with international exhaustion. No doubt considerations of commercial policy and concern about the possible lack of reciprocity were among the reasons why the provision for international exhaustion which featured in the Commission's original proposal was not maintained. But the existence of such underlying policy considerations does not limit the material scope of a measure based on Article 100a. It does not lead to the conclusion that a measure based on Article 100a cannot be construed as having dealt with the subject of international exhaustion. It seems to me that the Community can regulate under Article 100a the rights of trade mark owners within the Community in respect of goods bearing their mark whether they have been marketed inside or outside the Community.

The origin function of trade marks

The Swedish Government also relies on the Court's case law on the function of trade marks. That function is essentially to guarantee the consumer the possibility of identifying the origin of the product. It is no part of the function of a trade mark to enable the owner to divide up the market and to exploit price differentials. The adoption of international exhaustion would bring substantial advantages to consumers, and would promote price competition.

I confess to finding those arguments extremely attractive. However it must be remembered that the Court's case law on the function of trade marks was developed in the context of the Community, not the world market. Indeed in EMI v. CBS, [1976] 2 CMLR 235, the Court held that its case law under Articles 30 to 36 could not be transposed to imports from third countries. Circumscribing the protection of trade mark rights by defining their essential function was considered necessary to prevent restrictions on trade between Member States.

Such compelling considerations do not apply to imports from third countries. On the contrary, to allow Member States to opt for international exhaustion would itself, as has been seen, result in barriers between Member States.

There is of course a powerful argument based on the concern for free trade at the international level. To some commentators the exclusion of international exhaustion will appear protectionist and therefore harmful. [cit]. Commercial policy considerations may however be more complex than they allow for. I have already alluded to concern about the possible lack of reciprocity if the Community were unilaterally to provide for international exhaustion. In any event it is no part of the Court's function to seek to evaluate such policy considerations.

As regards price competition and the benefit to consumers, such benefits again have to be set against the threat to the integrity of the internal market. That integrity would be severely prejudiced if one Member State provided for international exhaustion while another did not. Only consumers in the first State would benefit from the lower prices of imports from third countries. Price competition within the internal market would be distorted.

As regards the Community's competition policy, the ruling to be given by the Court on international exhaustion will in no way limit the possible application of the competition rules of the Treaty. It will not exclude the possibility that Articles 85 and 86 of the Treaty may apply to agreements between undertakings, or to unilateral behaviour by a dominant undertaking, seeking to divide up the markets.

Finally, it should be recalled that some Member States, and some third countries, do not practice international exhaustion, and that that has not been held to be contrary to the General Agreement on Tariffs and Trade (the GATT). The situation is not changed in that respect by the WTO Agreement. [TRIPS] provides by Article 6 that, for the purposes of dispute settlement under that Agreement, nothing in the Agreement (subject to certain provisions) shall be used to address the issue of the exhaustion of intellectual property rights.

The Community Trade Mark Regulation

Further guidance on the interpretation of the Directive is provided by the Community Trade Mark Regulation. [cit]. The Regulation, which provides for a single Community mark valid throughout the Community, was drafted concurrently with the Directive and it contains a virtually identical provision on exhaustion.

Article 11(2) provides that a Community trade mark has "a unitary character" and that:

> It shall have equal effect throughout the Community: it shall not be registered, transferred or surrendered or be the subject of a decision revoking the rights of the proprietor or declaring it invalid, nor shall its use be prohibited, save in respect of the whole Community. This principle shall apply unless otherwise provided in this Regulation.

Article 13, entitled "Exhaustion of the rights conferred by a Community trade mark", provides as follows:

> 1. A Community trade mark shall not entitle the proprietor to prohibit its use in relation to goods which have been put on the market in the Community under that trade mark by the proprietor or with his consent.
>
> 2. Paragraph 1 shall not apply where there exist legitimate reasons for the proprietor to oppose further commercialization of the goods, especially where the condition of the goods is changed or impaired after they have been put on the market.

Thus, except for the reference to the "Community trade mark", Article 13 of the Regulation is in identical terms to Article 7 of the Directive.

As in the case of the Directive, the Commission's original proposal for the

Regulation would have provided for international exhaustion, but again the proposal was amended and the Regulation provides for exhaustion only for goods which have been put on the market "in the Community." Once again, therefore, it is impossible to read the Regulation as imposing international exhaustion. The choice would then be between precluding international exhaustion or leaving the issue to the Member States.

In the case of the Regulation, however, it seems scarcely possible to contend that the Member States have a discretion. Whereas the Directive, as has been seen, in a partial measure of harmonization of national laws, the Regulation governs comprehensively the incidents and effects of a Community trade mark. Moreover Article 14(1) provides that: "The effects of Community trade marks shall be governed solely by the provisions of this Regulation," leaving only infringement actions to be governed by national law in accordance with Title X of the Regulation, which is concerned only with jurisdiction and procedure in legal actions relating to Community trade marks.

It therefore seems impossible to contend that the Trade Mark Regulation confers a discretion on Member States to opt for international exhaustion. The question then is whether the provisions on exhaustion in the Regulation and Directive, notwithstanding their common origin and their identical wording, can be construed differently. There are of course well-known examples of identical provisions being construed differently in different contexts, notably in the context of the EC Treaty on the one hand and in the context of a Free Trade Agreement on the other, as in Polydor v. Harlequin Record Shops (Case 270/80, [1982] 1 CMLR 677). The advisory opinion of the EFTA Court cited above provides a further illustration of the reasons for adopting a different approach, justified by the different context, to the very provision in issue in the present case. In the present case however the context is, both for the Regulation and for the Directive, the Community's internal market. Although an argument can be advanced that the objectives of the two instruments are different, since the Directive only aims to achieve a limited measure of harmonisation, it must be accepted that the Regulation provides at least some further support for the view that the Directive precludes international exhaustion.

I accordingly conclude, having regard to the wording and purpose of the Directive, its legal history, the identical wording in the Trade Mark Regulation, and the undesirable effects of leaving the question to the discretion of the Member States, that Article 7(1) of the Directive precludes Member States from adopting the principle of international exhaustion.

Thus, in answer to the first question, Article 7(1) of the Directive is to be interpreted as meaning that the proprietor of a trade mark is entitled to prevent a third party from using the mark for goods which have been put on the market under that mark outside the territory of the EEA. Member States are accordingly precluded from adopting the principle of international exhaustion.

. . . .

DECISION OF THE COURT:

. . . .

Question 1

By its first question the Oberster Gerichtshof is in substance asking whether national rules providing for exhaustion of trade mark rights in respect of products put on the market outside the EEA under that mark by the proprietor or with his consent are contrary to Article 7(1) of the Directive.

. . . .

In the light of [recitals 1, 3 and 9], Articles 5 to 7 of the Directive must be construed as embodying a complete harmonization of the rules relating to the rights conferred by a trade mark. That interpretation, it may be added, is borne out by the fact that Article 5 expressly leaves it open to the Member States to maintain or introduce certain rules specifically defined by the Community legislature. Thus, in accordance with Article 5(2), to which the ninth recital refers, the Member States have the option to grant more extensive protection to trade marks with a reputation.

Accordingly, the Directive cannot be interpreted as leaving it open to the Member States to provide in their domestic law for exhaustion of the rights conferred by a trade mark in respect of products put on the market in non-member countries.

This, moreover, is the only interpretation which is fully capable of ensuring that the purpose of the Directive is achieved, namely to safeguard the functioning of the internal market. A situation in which some Member States could provide for international exhaustion while others provided for Community exhaustion only, would inevitably give rise to barriers to the free movement of goods and the freedom to provide services.

Contrary to the arguments of the Swedish Government, it is no objection to that interpretation that since the Directive was adopted on the basis of Article 100a EC, which governs the approximation of the laws of the Member States concerning the functioning of the internal market, it cannot regulate relations between the Member States and non-member countries, with the result that Article 7 is to be interpreted as meaning that the Directive applies only to intra-Community relations.

Even if Article 100a of the Treaty were to be construed in the sense argued for by the Swedish Government, the fact remains that Article 7, as has been pointed out in this judgment, is not intended to regulate relations between Member States and non-member countries but to define the rights of proprietors of trade marks in the Community.

Finally, the Community authorities could always extend the exhaustion provided for by Article 7 to products put on the market in non-member countries by entering into international agreements in that sphere, as was done in the context of the EEA Agreement.

In the light of the foregoing, the answer to be given to the first question must be that national rules providing for exhaustion of trade mark rights in respect of products put on the market outside the EEA under that mark by the proprietor or with his consent, are contrary to Article 7(1) of the Directive, as amended by the EEA Agreement.

. . . .

NOTES AND QUESTIONS

(1) **Implementing Legislation.** The French trademark statute (Article 16) implementing Article 7 of the directive adopted a rule of community exhaustion. *See* Marie Danielle Poisson-Schodermeier, *Changes in French Trade Mark Law: The 1991 Act*, 14 EUR. INTELL. PROP. REV. 104, 105 (1992). Many member states, however, had (like Austria) expressly avoided the question in their implementing legislation. *See* Annette Kur, *Harmonization of Trademark Laws in Europe*, 28 I.I.C. 1, 16 (1997) (explaining different responses).

(2) **EFTA States.** In *Mag Instrument Inc. v. California Trading Co. Norway* (Case E-2/97), [1998] 1 CMLR 331 (EFTA Court 1997), mentioned by the advocate-general in *Silhouette*, the Fredrikstad City Court in Norway requested an advisory opinion under Article 34 of the agreement between the EFTA states on the establishment of a Surveillance Authority and a Court of Justice. Mag, the owner of the Norwegian registration for the mark "Maglite" for lights, produced Maglite lights in the United States and sold them in Norway through an authorized sole distributor. The defendant, CTC, parallel-imported Maglites bearing the trade marks from the United States into Norway for sale there without Mag's consent. When Mag sought an injunction under the Norwegian Trade Mark Act, CTC argued that Mag's trademark rights had been exhausted when Mag had originally marketed the products in the United States. Mag argued that Article 7(1) of the Trademark Directive, applied to Norway by the EEA, provided for only EEA and not international exhaustion. Article 2(1) of Protocol 28 on Intellectual Property of the EEA deals with "exhaustion of rights." It reads as follows:

> To the extent that exhaustion is dealt with in Community measures or jurisprudence, the Contracting Parties shall provide for such exhaustion of intellectual property rights as laid down in Community law. Without prejudice to future developments of case law, this provision shall be interpreted in accordance with the meaning established in the relevant rulings of the Court of Justice of the European Communities given prior to the signature of the Agreement.

Norwegian law applied a rule of international exhaustion; the Norwegian government argued that to restrict exhaustion to products placed on the market in the EEA would allow for price discrimination, stronger segmentation of the markets and reduced price competition, thereby lessening the efficiency of the economy. The EFTA Court concluded that the issue had not been decided by the European Court of Justice (the case preceded *Silhouette*), and that therefore nothing in the Court of Justice's case law required member states of the community to abandon the principle of international exhaustion. The Court concluded that the principle of international exhaustion was in the interest of free trade and of consumers and was fully in line with the main function of a trade mark, which was to allow consumers to identify with certainty the origin of goods.

(3) **Pressure for International Exhaustion.** What reasons exist for the EU to mandate community-wide exhaustion only, and to prohibit national laws from following a principle of international exhaustion? In *Silhouette*, Advocate-General Jacob hints at some sympathy for the substantive economic argument in favor of international exhaustion but notes that such policy decisions are not for the Court of Justice. At the request of certain member states, the Commission published a study on the economic issues surrounding exhaustion in order to examine whether the question of international exhaustion should be reconsidered. *See Trade Mark Exhaustion—Study on the Economic Consequences of Alternative Regimes* (National Economic Research Associates, Feb. 1999). On May 25, 2000, at the Internal Market Council, the commissioner responsible informed member states that the Commission had decided, *at this stage*, not to propose a change to the approach of community-wide exhaustion. Four member states supported the Commission's decision, while eight indicated regret and emphasized the need for change (the other member states took no position). What are the arguments for international exhaustion? If you were a member of the European Commission, would you recommend a change to international exhaustion? Should that principle be mandated by EU law, or should the question be left up to individual member states? Should a principle of international exhaustion be adopted by the EU absent international agreement? If a member state were free to adopt international exhaustion as its standard, should it?

[2] The Nature of a Mark Holder's Consent

In its case law predating the directive, the European Court had been faced with the question of what constituted the placing of the goods on the market in the community with the mark owner's "consent." For example, goods placed on the market by a company affiliated with the mark holder (e.g., a subsidiary) will be treated as having been placed on the market "by or with the consent of the mark holder." *See* Phytheron Int'l SA v. Jean Bourdon, [1997] 3 C.M.L.R. 199, 203-04; IHT Internationale v. Ideal Standard, [1994] 3 C.M.L.R. 857. After the *Silhouette* decision prevented parallel importers in the EU from arguing exhaustion of rights based solely upon the marketing of goods by the mark holder outside the EEA, those importers have argued for an expansive interpretation of when goods are placed on the market in the community with the "consent" of the mark holder.

SEBAGO INC. v. GB-UNIC SA

1999 E.T.M.R. 681 (E.C.J. 1999)

ADVOCATE-GENERAL JACOBS:

In its recent judgment in the case of *Silhouette*, the Court held that national rules providing for the exhaustion of trade-mark rights in respect of products placed on the market outside the European Economic Area ('the EEA') under the mark by the proprietor or with his consent are contrary to Article 7(1) of the Trade Marks Directive. Thus it is only the placing of products on the market within the EEA by the trade-mark proprietor or with his consent which prima facie exhausts trade-mark rights: placing products on the market outside the EEA by the trade-mark proprietor or with his consent does not exhaust such rights. Community trade-mark law accordingly recognizes a principle of EEA exhaustion but not international exhaustion.

The main question raised by the Cour d'Appel, Brussels, in its request for a preliminary ruling is whether the proprietor of a trade mark can be said to have consented to the marketing within the EEA of a batch of his products imported from outside the EEA on the grounds that he has consented to the marketing within the EEA of other batches of identical or similar articles.

The facts

The first appellant, Sebago Inc., is a company incorporated in the United States of America. It is the proprietor of two Benelux trade marks in the name 'Docksides' and three Benelux trade marks in the name 'Sebago.' All five trade marks are registered, inter alia, for shoes.

The second appellant, Ancienne Maison Dubois et Fils SA, is the exclusive distributor in Benelux of Sebago's shoes and other footwear articles. I shall refer to the appellants collectively as 'Sebago.'

Sebago claims that the respondent, GB-Unic, infringed its trade marks by marketing goods within the Community without its consent. GB-Unic has explained that it purchased 2,561 pairs of shoes 'made in El Salvador' from a company incorporated under Belgian law which specialises in parallel importation (and which had thus presumably imported the shoes in question from outside the EEA). In the tenth issue of its 1996 brochure entitled 'La quinzaine Maxi-GB', announcing prices valid from 29 May until 11 June 1996, GB-Unic advertised Docksides Sebago shoes for sale in its Maxi-GB hypermarkets. It sold its entire stock during the summer of 1996.

Sebago does not dispute that the shoes sold by GB-Unic were genuine goods. It contends, however, that since it had not consented to sale of those shoes in the Community GB-Unic had no right to sell them there. . . .

. . . The Cour d'Appel observes that the parties' interpretation of Article 13A(8) [of the Uniform Benelux Law on Trade Marks, which is in similar terms to Article 7(1) of the Trade Marks Directive (the Directive)] differs . . . as to the conditions under which the trade-mark proprietor's consent may be deemed to have been given.

Concerning [that] question, GB-Unic argues that in order to satisfy the requirement of consent in Article 13A(8) it is sufficient that similar goods bearing the same trade mark have been lawfully marketed in the EEA with the consent of the proprietor of the trade mark. . . . Sebago, on the other hand, argues that its consent must be obtained in relation to each defined parcel of goods, *i.e.* each consignment imported at a particular time by a particular importer. Thus it considers that it can be deemed to have given its consent only if GB-Unic can prove, which it has not, that it obtained the shoes in question from a seller who was part of the distribution network established by Sebago in the Community, or from a reseller who, although not part of the network, had obtained those shoes lawfully within the Community.

GB-Unic also argued before the national court that Sebago did not prohibit its licensee in El Salvador from exporting its goods to the Community and that Sebago should accordingly be deemed to have given its implied consent to the marketing of those goods in the Community. However, the Cour d'Appel expressly dismisses the relevance of that argument on the ground that it has not been proven that Sebago granted a licence to use its trade mark in El Salvador (indeed Sebago disputes the allegation that it did grant such a licence).

. . . .

Appraisal

. . . .

[Under *Silhouette*] even if the shoes were put into circulation outside the EEA with Sebago's consent, that would not suffice to prevent Sebago from exercising its trade-mark rights in relation to those shoes within the EEA.

The key issue in the present case is accordingly . . .: does the consent of a trade-mark proprietor to the marketing of one batch of a certain type of goods within the EEA bearing his trade mark mean that he has exhausted his right to object to the marketing within the EEA of other batches of his identical (or similar) goods bearing the same trade mark? In other words, can the reference in Article 7(1) of the Directive to 'consent' to the placing on the market in the Community of 'goods' be read as meaning consent to the marketing of a certain type of product (*i.e.* product line), rather than to each batch of a certain type of product?

. . . .

It is useful first to consider the nature of the exhaustion principle when applied in a purely intra-Community context. Under Community law, the exercise of intellectual property rights may hinder the free movement of goods within the Community but may be justified under Article 36 of the EC Treaty. Since the 'use' of a trade mark is a very wide concept, many different dealings with goods may constitute trade-mark infringement. Thus, if no limitation were imposed upon the exercise of trade-mark rights, resellers wishing to sell trade-marked goods which they have lawfully acquired could in theory be obliged to obtain the consent of the trade-mark proprietor to such re-sale and any further dealings concerning the goods.

It is clear that the exhaustion principle in Community law is concerned with subsequent dealings with trade-marked goods once they have been put 'into circulation' within the EEA by the trade-mark proprietor or with his consent. If a trade-mark proprietor places on the market one particular batch of goods it is only that batch of goods which he puts into circulation: obviously he does not thereby put into circulation all other batches of identical (or similar) goods remaining in his warehouse, and so he retains, in respect of those remaining batches, all such rights as he may enjoy to impose conditions of retail sale.

It is true that the exhaustion principle has usually been expressed rather loosely by reference simply to exhaustion of intellectual property rights in relation to the 'goods' placed on the market by the trade-mark proprietor or with his consent. That wording is reflected in Article 7(1) of the Directive. However, Article 7(1) should be read in conjunction with Article 7(2) concerning exceptions to the exhaustion principle, which refers to the 'further commercialisation' of the goods. In French the term used is *commercialisation ultérieure,*' which to my mind makes it even clearer than the English text that the exhaustion principle concerns not other sales of the same type of goods but rather subsequent dealings with individual products following first sale.

. . . .

It is accordingly abundantly clear, at least as regards the purely intra-EEA context, that the Community law principle of the exhaustion of trade-mark rights relates to individual goods or batches of goods, not whole product lines.

I turn now to the question whether the trade-mark owner has the right to prevent the import of a particular batch of goods which has been marketed, by him or with his consent, outside the EEA. GB-Unic accepts that, under the terms of Article 7(1), the trade-mark owner will only have exhausted his rights to prevent the import of that batch if he has consented to its marketing within the EEA. However, it argues that there has been such consent within the meaning of Article 7(1) when the trade-mark owner has consented to the marketing in the EEA of other individual batches of the product in question since he has thereby impliedly consented to the marketing within the EEA of the whole of that product line.

GB-Unic seeks to justify its view by arguing that, in cases concerning the marketing of genuine products outside the EEA, the import of such products into the EEA does not prejudice the functions of a mark as an indication of the origin and quality of the product. As I observed in my Opinion in *Silhouette,* such arguments are extremely attractive. However, they were insufficient to defeat the conclusion in that case that the Directive prohibits Member States from practising international exhaustion. They can accordingly not be invoked now in order effectively to overturn that judgment, which, as I shall show, would be the practical effect of accepting GB-Unic's interpretation of Article 7(1).

According to GB-Unic's view, Article 7(1) allows the trade-mark proprietor to keep out parallel imports from third countries unless and until he has himself commenced marketing an identical (or similar) product within the EEA, but not thereafter. There may, it is true, be some cases in which that limited right confers a real advantage on the trade-mark proprietor, since there may be an advantage in being able to select appropriate markets and time the launching of a product on to a particular market. However, in the vast majority of cases where the trade-mark proprietor is not already marketing the product in the EEA it is likely either that he will have no objection to the products being marketed there since they are not competing against his own marketing or that he has a 'legitimate reason', within the meaning of Article 7(2), for objecting to their import, for example because, for some justifiable reason, the product in question is unsuitable for the EEA market. Thus the question of international exhaustion is unlikely to become an issue unless the trade-mark proprietor is already marketing identical (or similar) goods within the EEA: it is then that he becomes sensitive to 'parallel' imports.

To say that once a trade-mark proprietor has consented to the marketing of one particular batch of products within the EEA he must be deemed to have consented to the marketing of other identical (or similar) batches would accordingly deprive the Court's limitation of the exhaustion principle to EEA-wide exhaustion of much of its practical effect. It would for most practical purposes effectively impose a rule of international exhaustion since, in the absence of a legitimate reason, all parallel imports would necessarily have to be admitted into the EEA.

Such a limitation upon the effect of the Directive as interpreted in the Court's judgment in *Silhouette* may seem desirable and would no doubt be welcomed in many circles. However, as the Court observed in *Silhouette*, no argument has been presented to the Court that the Directive could be interpreted as imposing a rule of international exhaustion. The dispute centered only on whether the Directive left the matter to the discretion of the Member States. The imposition of international exhaustion in the way suggested by GB-Unic does not follow easily from the wording of Article 7(1). Nor does it appear to have been the intention of the Community legislature.

The Court cannot in my view be expected to stand legislation on its head in order to achieve an objective, even were it to be considered desirable. If the Directive is found to have effects which are unacceptable, the correct remedy is to amend the Directive or, as the Court observed in paragraph 30 of its judgment in Silhouette, to enter into international agreements in order to extend the principle of exhaustion to products put on the market in non-member countries, as was done in the EEA Agreement.

I conclude, therefore, that Sebago cannot be deemed to have consented to the placing on the market in the EEA of the particular batch of products in question by virtue of having consented to the marketing within the EEA of other batches of identical or similar goods. Article 7(1) of the Directive must accordingly be interpreted as meaning that where goods have been marketed by the trade-mark owner or with his consent within the EEA, he is not thereby precluded from exercising his trade-mark rights to oppose the importation into the EEA of other identical or similar goods bearing his mark.

JUDGMENT OF THE COURT:

. . . .

The text of Article 7(1) of the Directive does not give a direct answer to [this] question. Nevertheless, the rights conferred by the trade mark are exhausted only in respect of the individual items of the product which have been put on the market with the proprietor's consent in the territory there defined. The proprietor may continue to prohibit the use of the mark in pursuance of the right conferred on him by the Directive in regard to individual items of that product which have been put on the market in that territory without his consent.

That is the interpretation of Article 7(1) that the Court has already adopted. Thus, the Court has already held that the purpose of that provision is to make possible the further marketing of an individual item of a product bearing a trade mark that has been put on the market with the consent of the trade-mark proprietor and to prevent him from opposing such marketing (Parfums Christian Dior v. Evora, [1997] ECR I-6013, ¶¶ 37-38, and BMW v. Deenik, [1999] ECR I-0000, ¶ 57). That interpretation is, moreover, confirmed by Article 7(2) of the Directive which, in its reference to the 'further commercialisation' of goods, shows that the principle of exhaustion concerns only specific goods which have first been put on the market with the consent of the trade-mark proprietor.

Furthermore, in adopting Article 7 of the Directive, which limits exhaustion of the right conferred by the trade mark to cases where the goods bearing the mark have been put on the market in the Community (in the EEA since the EEA Agreement entered into force), the Community legislature has made it clear that putting such goods on the market outside that territory does not exhaust the proprietor's right to oppose the importation of those goods without his consent and thereby to control the initial marketing in the Community (in the EEA since the EEA Agreement entered into force) of goods bearing the mark. That protection would be devoid of substance if, for there to be exhaustion within the meaning of Article 7, it were sufficient for the trade-mark proprietor to have consented to the putting on the market in that territory of goods which were identical or similar to those in respect of which exhaustion is claimed.

. . . .

NOTES AND QUESTIONS

(1) **Individual Consent**. Why did the court hold that consent to the particular goods is the only consent relevant to Article 7(1)? Was this a purely textual analysis? Was it because any other holding would have undermined *Silhouette*? If *Sebago* had been decided in favor of the defendant, how would producers seeking to control their market in the EU have to restructure their

global product distribution? Would that interfere with the objectives of the EU or of the Trademark Directive?

(2) **Contractual Provisions.** Although the *Sebago* court declined to address the defendant's argument of implied consent based upon its transactions with its El Salvadoran licensee, the issue has since been taken up by the U.K. courts. In Davidoff v. A & G Imports Ltd., [1999] 2 C.M.L.R. 1056 (Ch. D. 1999) (Eng.), the plaintiff sold perfume under the mark COOL WATER for half the price at which it sold the same goods in the EU. The plaintiff's Singapore distributor agreed not to sell products outside South East Asia and also to impose similar conditions upon its sub-distributors. The defendant imported goods from Asia into the United Kingdom. Mr. Justice Laddie held that a trade mark owner cannot enjoin parallel importation into the EU (or EEA) of products that were put on the market outside the EEA if either: (i) he has agreed expressly or impliedly to their entry into the EEA; or (ii) he has placed the goods, directly or otherwise in the hands of a third party without restrictions as to onward distribution. This latter question was to be determined by all relevant circumstances, including the terms of any contracts of sale and the provisions of any applicable law governing the transaction. Effectively, Mr. Justice Laddie thus imposed an obligation upon the trademark owner seeking to prevent parallel imports affirmatively to prohibit the goods from entry into the EEA. Mr. Justice Laddie denied the plaintiff's motion for summary judgment because he concluded that the goods were placed on the market in circumstances where the plaintiff could have placed, but did not in fact, place an effective restraint on their further sale. This conclusion was based in part upon an analysis of the law applicable to the contracts of sale, which was assumed to be English law. The advocate-general has recently issued her opinion suggesting that the Court of Justice develop a community notion of consent rather than relying on applicable national laws (and, in turn, national rules of choice of law). *See* Case C-414/99, Davidoff v. A & G Imports Ltd. (Opinion of Advocate-General Stix Hackl, April 5, 2001) at ¶ 65. The Court's decision is awaited.

How workable is the approach suggested by Mr. Justice Laddie? Is it consistent with *Silhouette*? How would trademark owners alter their operations to maximize their rights under his approach and would those changes generate costs or efficiencies (to be passed on, favorably or unfavorably, to consumers)? What would be the effect of allowing the rights of third parties under Article 7 to be determined by the "law of the contract of supply" or the "law of the non-EEA country in which the sale to the third party takes place"?

[3] Legitimate Reasons to Oppose Further Commercialization

BRISTOL-MYERS SQUIBB v. PARANOVA
[1997] 1 C.M.L.R 1151 (E.C.J. 1996)

JUDGE GULMANN:

. . . .

Bristol-Myers Squibb markets in various Member States pharmaceutical products manufactured by itself or an associated company, and holds the rights in relation to the registration in Denmark of the trade marks "Capoten," "Mycostatin," "Vepesid," "Vumon" and "Diclocil." Capoten is used for lowering blood pressure and is marketed as tablets in blister packs. Mycostatin is a mixture for the treatment of mycotic infections of the mouth marketed in flasks. Vepesid is an anti-cancer drug sold in phials or as tablets in blister packs. Vumon is also an anti-cancer drug packaged in ampoules. Diclocil is an anitbiotic for treating infections, marketed as capsules in blister packs.

Boehringer manufactures pharmaceutical products in Germany and markets them throughout the Community. It registered in Denmark the trade mark "Boehringer Ingelheim," which is used generally on its pharmaceuticals. and the trade marks "Atrovent" "Berodual," "Berotec" and "Catapresan," which are used to designate specific pharmaceutical products. Atrovent, Berodual and Berotec are used for the treatment of bronchial asthma and sold in aerosols. They are marketed throughout all Member States in aerosol inhalers, but with differing quantities of the active ingredient. Catapresan is used to treat high blood pressure and marketed as tablets in blister packs.

Bayer manufactures and markets in various Member States a pharmaceutical product under the name "Adalat," which it had registered as a trade mark in Denmark along with its company name Bayer. Adalat is used to treat heart and circulatory diseases. For a number of years, it was marketed in Denmark in packages of 30 or 100 tablets, in blister packs containing 10 tablets each. Since 1990, only packages of 100 tablets have been sold in Denmark. In other Member States, Adalat is sold in packages of varying sizes, containing 20, 30, 50, 60 or 100 tablets.

Paranova is a company which distributes pharmaceutical products imported in parallel. It has purchased the abovementioned products in batches in Member States where prices are relatively low (Greece, the United Kingdom, Spain and Portugal) and imported them into Denmark, where it sells them below the manufacturers' official prices while still making a profit.

For the purposes of sale in Denmark, Paranova repackaged all the medicines in new external packaging with a uniform appearance and its own style, namely white with coloured stripes corresponding to the colours of the manufacturers' original packaging. That packaging displayed, inter alia, the respective trade marks of the manufacturers and the statement that the product had been manufactured respectively by "Bristol-Myers Squibb", "Boehringer Ingelheim" and "Bayer," together with the indication "imported and repackaged by Paranova."

In the case of Capoten, Diclocil, Catapresan and Adalat, the repackaging by Paranova involved a change in packet size.

Regarding Adalat in particular, the Danish packaging used by Bayer bore the words "Adalat 20 mg." Paranova imported Adalat from Greece, where the product was sold in a packet of three blister packs of 10 tablets each, and repackaged it in packets with the description "Adalat retard" containing 10 blister packs of 10 tablets.

In addition to replacing the external packaging, Paranova carried out the following operations.

In the case of Vepesid and Vumon, it removed the phials and ampoules from their surrounding padding and attached to each phial or ampoule a new self-stick label covering that of the manufacturer. The new label bore the trade mark of Bristol-Myers Squibb together with the indications "manufactured by Bristol-Myers Squibb" and "imported and repackaged by Paranova." The phials and ampoules were then replaced in the original padding and put in the new external packaging. In the case of Mycostatin, Atrovent, Berodual and Berotec, Paranova also covered the original labels of the flasks or inhalers with its own label showing, inter alia, the manufacturers' trade marks.

In the case of Vepesid, Vumon, Berodual and Berotec, Paranova included with the new packaging user information in Danish.

In the packaging of Mycostatin, Paranova replaced the spray in the original packaging with a spray from a source other than Bristol-Myers Squibb.

In addition, and in accordance with the relevant Danish rules, Paranova registered the products as pharmaceutical specialities in the Danish register of such specialities, using the same names as the manufacturers.

Bristol-Myers Squibb and Boehringer brought proceedings against Paranova before the Sø-og Handelsret, claiming, inter alia, that the defendant should be obliged to recognise that it had infringed the plaintiffs' trade marks by affixing them without the plaintiffs' consent to products it offered for sale, and that the defendant should be ordered to desist from affixing those trade marks to the products it repackaged and marketed.

The national court decided to stay the proceedings and referred the following questions to the Court for a preliminary ruling:

1. Is Article 7(1) of Council Directive 89/104 to approximate the laws of the Member States relating to trade marks to be interpreted as meaning that unless Article 7(2) applies the proprietor of a trade mark who has put goods into circulation in a Member State under a trade mark cannot prevent a third party from importing the goods into another Member State in order to market the goods there under the same trade mark even if that third party has attached to the inner packaging of the goods labels on which the trade mark is affixed and substituted for the original outer packaging a new packaging on which the trade mark is affixed?

It is stressed that the question does not seek a ruling on cases in which the second sentence of Article 36 of the Treaty might justify repackaging and reaffixing a mark in accordance with the principles set out in Case 102/77 [*Hoffman La-Roche v. Centrafarm*, [1978] 3 C.M.L.R. 217] but only on whether Article 7(1) is to be construed as meaning that apart from laying down the general principle of the exhaustion of trade mark rights within the European Community it also entails a general limitation on the rights otherwise conferred on trade mark proprietors regarding use of the trade mark for which the trade mark proprietor has not given his consent.

2. If the answer to Question 1 is affirmative, does Article 7(2) of Directive 89/104, after implementation, entail that the case law of the Court of Justice as set out in Case 102/77 and developed subsequently comes to be of subsidiary importance since the right to repackage will primarily fall to be determined in application of national provisions corresponding to Article 7(2) of the said Directive?

In Case C-427/93, the Sø-og Handelsret also referred the two following questions:

3. On the premise that Article 7(1) of the said Directive is intended to permit parallel importers to reaffix trade marks, must the fact that goods are repackaged be regarded as "legitimate reasons" for the purposes of Article 7(2)?

In particular, does it make any difference that it is only the outer packaging that has been repackaged and remarked but not the inner packaging?

4. With regard to the derogating provision in the second sentence of Article 36 of the Treaty and in the light of the judgment of the Court of Justice in Case 102/77, what may be described as a partitioning of the market for a specific product and, in particular, what distinguishing factors are to be taken into account in assessing whether an artificial partitioning of markets between the Member States can be said to exist for a specific product in connection with the sales system applied by the trade mark proprietor?

. . . .

Bayer brought proceedings against Paranova before the Sø-og Handelsret, which dismissed the action. It then appealed to the Højesteret, which referred the following questions to the Court:

1. Must the possibility for a trade mark proprietor to oppose a parallel importer's action in replacing wholly or in part the original packaging of his goods by new packaging on which the parallel importer reaffixes the trade mark be determined under national trade mark law only in conjunction with Article 7(1) and (2) of the First Council Directive (89/104) to approximate the laws of the Member States relating to trade marks or also in conjunction with the first and second sentences of Article 36 EC?

2. In assessing the legal steps that may be taken by the trade mark proprietor, is it significant whether there may be said to exist an "artificial partitioning of the markets" for trade in the goods in question? If so, the Court is asked to specify what is the significance as regards such steps.

3. If Question 2 is answered in the affirmative, is it significant for the rights of the trade mark proprietor whether he had the intention to create or exploit such an artificial partitioning of the markets? If so, the Court is asked to specify what is the significance as regards those rights.

4. In connection with Question 3, must the parallel importer show or else establish a probability that there was intent or must the trade mark proprietor show or establish a probability that there was not intent?

5. Is the reaffixing of the trade mark, as described in Question 1, in itself sufficient "legitimate reason" within the meaning of Article 7 of the Directive or must the trade mark proprietor in addition show further circumstances, for example that the condition of the goods is changed or impaired when they are put on the market by the parallel importer?

. . . .

By order of the President of the Court of 18 November 1993, those cases were joined for the purposes of the written procedure, the oral procedure and the judgment.

. . . .

The application of Article 7 of the Directive

. . . .

Where Community directives provide for the harmonisation of measures necessary to ensure the protection of the interests referred to in Article 36 of the Treaty, any national measure relating thereto must be assessed in relation to the provisions of that directive and not Articles 30 to 36 of the Treaty. [cit].

Article 7 of the Directive is worded in general terms and comprehensively regulates the question of the exhaustion of trade mark rights for products traded in the Community. Therefore, national rules on the subject must be assessed in the light of that article.

Like any secondary legislation, however, the directive must be interpreted in the light of the Treaty rules on the free movement of goods and in particular Article 36.

The answer to the first question in Case C-436/93 must therefore be that the reliance by a trade mark owner on his rights as owner in order to prevent an importer from marketing a product which was put on the market in another Member State by the owner or with his consent where that importer has repackaged the product and reaffixed the trade mark without the owner's authorisation, is to be assessed on the basis of the combined provisions of national trade mark law and Article 7 of the Directive, interpreted in the light of Article 36 of the Treaty.

The interpretation of Article 7(1) of the Directive

. . . .

Article 7(1) of the Directive provides that the rights conferred by a trade mark do not entitle the proprietor to prohibit its use in relation to goods which have been put on the market in the Community under that trade mark by the proprietor or with his consent.

That provision is framed in terms corresponding to those used by the Court in judgments which, in interpreting Articles 30 and 36 of the Treaty, have recognised in Community law the principle of the exhaustion of the rights conferred by a trade mark. It reiterates the case law of the Court to the effect that the owner of a trade mark protected by the legislation of a Member State cannot rely on that legislation to prevent the importation or marketing of a product which was put in the market in another Member State by him or with his consent"; [cit].

It has nevertheless been argued by the plaintiffs in the main actions and by the German Government that Article 7(1) of the Directive does not confer on the parallel importer any right other than to resell the products in the form in which the trade mark owner put them on the market in another Member State. In their view, the owner's exclusive right under Article 5 of the Directive to affix the trade mark to a product is not exhausted, so that, even apart from the exceptions set out in Article 7(2), the owner may prohibit the affixing of the trade mark to repackaged products.

That argument cannot be accepted.

The Court's case law on Article 36 of the Treaty shows that the owner's exclusive right to affix a trade mark to a product must in certain circumstances be regarded as exhausted in order to allow an importer to market under that trade mark products which were put on the market in another Member State by the owner or with his consent. [cit].

To accept the argument that the principle of exhaustion under Article 7(1) cannot apply if the importer has repackaged the product and reaffixed the trade mark would therefore imply a major alteration to the principles flowing from Articles 30 and 36 of the Treaty.

There is nothing to suggest that Article 7 of the Directive is intended to restrict the scope of that case law. Nor would such an effect be permissible, since a directive cannot justify obstacles in intra-Community trade save within the bounds set by the Treaty rules. The Court's case law shows that the prohibition on quantitative restrictions and measures having equivalent effect applies not only to national measures but also to those emanating from Community institutions. [cit].

The answer to the first question in Cases C-427/93 and C-429/93 must therefore be that, save in the circumstances defined in Article 7(2), Article 7(1) of the Directive precludes the owner of a trade mark from relying on his rights as owner to prevent an importer from marketing a product which was put on the market in another Member State by the owner or with his consent, even if that importer repackaged the product and reaffixed the trade mark to it without the owner's authorisation.

The interpretation of Article 7(2) of the Directive

. . . The national courts are essentially asking for a definition of the circumstances in which a trade mark owner may, under Article 7(2) of the Directive, oppose the further marketing of a pharmaceutical product which has been repackaged by the importer and to which the owner's trade mark has been reaffixed. In particular, they ask whether the case law under Article 36 of the Treaty is relevant when applying Article 7(2) of the Directive, and, if it is, what is the significance and content of the concepts established by that case law regarding the "artificial partitioning of the markets" and adverse effect on "the original condition of the product."

Article 7(2) of the Directive provides that the owner of a trade mark may oppose the further commercialisation of products where there is a legitimate reason for doing so, especially where the condition of the products has been changed or impaired since they were put on the market. The use of the word "especially" shows that the case envisaged is given only as an example.

Article 7 of the Directive, like Article 36 of the Treaty, is intended to reconcile the fundamental interest in protecting trade mark rights with the fundamental interest in the free movement of goods within the Common Market, so that those two provisions, which pursue the same result, must be interpreted in the same way.

The Court's case law under Article 36 must therefore be taken as the basis for determining whether, under Article 7(2) of the Directive, a trade mark owner may oppose the marketing of repackaged products to which the trade mark has been reaffixed.

The Court's case law shows that Article 36 allows derogations from the fundamental principle of the free movement of goods within the Common Market only in so far as such derogations are justified in order to safeguard the rights which constitute the specific subject-matter of the industrial and commercial property in question.

Trade mark rights, the Court has held, constitute an essential element in the system of undistorted competition which the Treaty is intended to establish. In such a system, undertakings must be able to attract and retain customers by the quality of their products or services, which is possible only thanks to the existence of distinctive signs allowing them to be identified. For the trade mark to be able to fulfil that function, it must constitute a guarantee that all products which bear it have been manufactured under the control of a single undertaking to which responsibility for their quality may be attributed; [cit].

Thus, as the Court has recognised on many occasions, the specific subject-matter of a trade mark is in particular to guarantee to the owner that he has the exclusive right to use that trade mark for the purpose of putting a product on the market for the first time and therefore to protect him against competitors wishing to take advantage of the status and reputation of the trade mark by selling products bearing it illegally. . . .

It follows that, as mentioned above, the owner of a trade mark protected by the legislation of a Member State cannot rely on that legislation in order to oppose the importation or marketing of a product which was put on the market in another Member State by him or with his consent (*see*, in particular, *Winthrop*; *HAG II*; and *IHT Internationale Heiztechnik*).

Trade mark rights are not intended to allow their owners to partition national markets and thus promote the retention of price differences which may exist between Member States. Whilst, in the pharmaceutical market especially, such price differences may result from factors over which trade mark owners have no control, such as divergent rules between the Member States on the fixing of maximum prices, the profit margins of pharmaceutical wholesalers and pharmacies, or the maximum amount of medical expenses which may be reimbursed under sickness insurance schemes, distortions caused by divergent pricing rules in one Member State must be remedied by measures of the Community authorities and not by another Member State introducing measures which are incompatible with the rules on the free movement of goods. . . .

In answering the question whether a trade mark owner's exclusive rights include the power to oppose the use of the trade mark by a third party after the product has been repackaged, account must be taken of the essential function of the trade mark, which is to guarantee to the consumer or end user the identity of the trade-marked product's origin by enabling him to distinguish it without any risk of confusion from products of different origin. That guarantee of origin means that the consumer or end user can be certain that a trademarked product offered to him has not been subject at a previous stage of marketing to interference by a third person, without the authorisation of the trade mark owner, in such a way as to affect the original condition of the product. . . .

Therefore, the right conferred upon the trade mark owner to oppose any use of the trade mark which is liable to impair the guarantee of origin so understood forms part of the specific subject-matter of the trade mark right, the protection of which may justify derogation from the fundamental principle of the free movement of goods. [cit].

In *Hoffmann-La Roche*, the Court held, applying those principles, that Article 36 of the Treaty must be interpreted as meaning that a trade mark owner may rely on his rights as owner to prevent an importer from marketing a product put on the market in another Member State by the owner or with his consent, where that importer has repackaged the product in new packaging to which the trade mark has been reaffixed, unless:

- it is established that the use of the trade-mark right by the owner, having regard to the marketing system which he has adopted, will contribute to the artificial partitioning of the markets between Member States;
- it is shown that the repackaging cannot adversely affect the original condition of the product;
- the owner of the mark receives prior notice before the repackaged product is put on sale; and
- it is stated on the new packaging by whom the product has been repackaged.

In accordance with that case law, Article 7(2) of the Directive must therefore be interpreted as meaning that a trade mark owner may legitimately oppose the further marketing of a pharmaceutical product where the importer has repackaged it and reaffixed the trade mark, unless the four conditions set out in the *Hoffmann-La Roche* judgment have been met.

That case law must, however, be clarified further in the light of the arguments raised in these cases, and in the cases of Eurim-Pharm v. Beiersdorf C71-73/94) and MPA Pharma v. Rhone-Poulenc (C-232/94), in which the Court has also given judgment today.

Artificial partitioning of the markets between Member States

Reliance on trade mark rights by their owner in order to oppose marketing under that trade mark of products repackaged by a third party would contribute to the partitioning of markets between Member States in particular where the owner has placed an identical pharmaceutical product on the market in several Member States in various forms of packaging, and the product may not, in the condition in which it has been marketed by the trade mark owner in one Member State, be imported and put on the market in another Member State by a parallel importer.

The trade mark owner cannot therefore oppose the repackaging of the product in new external packaging when the size of packet used by the owner in the Member State where the importer purchased the product cannot be marketed in the Member State of importation by reason, in particular, of a rule authorising packaging only of a certain size or a national practice to the same effect, sickness insurance rules making the reimbursement of medical expenses depend on the size of the packaging, or well-established medical prescription practices based, *inter alia*, on standard sizes recommended by professional groups and sickness insurance institutions.

Where, in accordance with the rules and practices in force in the Member State of importation, the trade mark owner uses many different sizes of packaging in that State, the finding that one of those sizes is also marketed in the Member State of exportation is not enough to justify the conclusion that repackaging is unnecessary. Partitioning of the markets would exist if the importer were able to sell the product in only part of his market.

The owner may, on the other hand, oppose the repackaging of the product in new external packaging where the importer is able to achieve packaging which may be marketed in the Member State of importation by, for example, affixing to the original external or inner packaging new labels in the language of the Member State of importation, or by adding new user instructions or information in the language of the Member State of importation, or by replacing an additional article not capable of gaining approval in the Member State of importation with a similar article that has obtained such approval.

The power of the owner of trade mark rights protected in a Member State to oppose the marketing of repackaged products under the trade mark should be limited only in so far as the repackaging undertaken by the importer is necessary in order to market the product in the Member State of importation.

Finally, contrary to the argument of the plaintiffs in the main actions, the Court's use of the words "artificial partitioning of the markets" does not imply that the importer must demonstrate that, by putting an identical product on the market in varying forms of packaging in different Member States, the trade mark owner deliberately sought to partition the markets between Member States. By stating that the partitioning in question must be artificial, the Court's intention was to stress that the owner of a trade mark may always rely on his rights as owner to oppose the marketing of repackaged products when such action is justified by the need to safeguard the essential function of the trade mark, in which case the resultant partitioning could not be regarded as artificial.

Whether the original condition of the product is adversely affected

In the light of the arguments of the plaintiffs in the main actions, it should be clarified at the outset that the concept of adverse effects on the original condition of the product refers to the condition of the product inside the packaging.

The trade mark owner may therefore oppose any repackaging involving a risk of the product inside the package being exposed to tampering or to influences affecting its original condition. To determine whether that applies, account must be taken, as the Court held in paragraph [10] of the *Hoffmann-La Roche* judgment, of the nature of the product and the method of repackaging.

As regards pharmaceutical products, it follows from the same paragraph in *Hoffmann-La Roche* that repackaging must be regarded as having been carried out in circumstances not capable of affecting the original condition of the product where, for example, the trade mark owner has placed the product on the market in double packaging and the repackaging affects only the external layer, leaving the inner packaging intact, or where the repackaging is carried out under the supervision of a public authority in order to ensure that the product remains intact.

It follows from that case law that the mere removal of blister packs, flasks, phials, ampoules or inhalers from their original external packaging and their replacement in new external packaging cannot affect the original condition of the product inside the packaging.

The plaintiffs in the main actions have argued nevertheless that even operations of that kind entail the risk of adversely affecting the original condition of the product. Thus, blister packs coming originally from different packets and grouped together in single external packaging might have come from different production batches with different use-by dates, products might have been stored for too long, and light-sensitive products might have been damaged by light during repackaging.

Those arguments cannot be accepted. It is not possible for each hypothetical risk of isolated error to suffice to confer on the trade mark owner the right to oppose any repackaging of pharmaceutical products in new external packaging.

As for operations consisting in the fixing of self-stick labels to flasks, phials, ampoules or inhalers, the addition to the packaging of new user instructions or information in the language of the Member State of importation, or the insertion of an extra article, such as a spray, from a source other than the trade mark owner, there is nothing to suggest that the original condition of the product inside the packaging is directly affected thereby.

It should be recognised, however, that the original condition of the product inside the packaging might be indirectly affected where, for example:

- the external or inner packaging of the repackaged product, or a new set of user instructions or information, omits certain important information or gives inaccurate information concerning the nature, composition, effect, use or storage of the product, or
- an extra article inserted into the packaging by the importer and designed for the ingestion and dosage of the product does not comply with the method of use and the doses envisaged by the manufacturer.

It is for the national court to assess whether that is so, in particular by making a comparison with the product marketed by the trade mark owner in the Member State of importation. The possibility of the importer providing certain additional information should not be excluded, however, provided that information does not contradict the information provided by the trade mark owner in the Member State of importation, that condition being met in particular in the case of different information resulting from the packaging used by the owner in the Member State of exportation.

The other requirements to be met by the parallel importer

If the repackaging is carried out in conditions which cannot affect the original condition of the product inside the packaging, the essential function of the trade mark as a guarantee of origin is safeguarded. Thus, the consumer or end user is not misled as to the origin of the products, and does in fact receive products manufactured under the sole supervision of the trade mark owner.

Whilst, in these circumstances, the conclusion that the trade mark owner may not rely on his rights as owner in order to oppose the marketing under his trade mark of products repackaged by an importer is essential in order to ensure the free movement of goods, it does nevertheless confer on the importer certain rights which, in normal circumstances, are reserved for the trade mark owner himself.

In the interests of the owner as proprietor of the trade mark, and to protect him against any misuse, those rights must therefore, as the Court held in *Hoffmann-La Roche*, be recognised only in so far as the importer complies with a number of other requirements.

Since it is in the trade mark owner's interest that the consumer or end user should not be led to believe that the owner is responsible for the repackaging, an indication must be given on the packaging of who repackaged the product.

As the Court has already stated, that indication must be clearly shown on the external packaging of the repackaged product. . . . That implies, as the Advocate General pointed out in paragraph 128 of his Opinion, that the national court must assess whether it is printed in such a way as to be understood by a person with normal eyesight, exercising a normal degree of attentiveness.

It is, however, not necessary to require that the further express statement be made on the packaging that the repackaging was carried out without the authorisation of the trade mark owner, since such a statement could be taken to imply, as the Advocate General pointed out, that the repackaged product is not entirely legitimate.

However, where the parallel importer has added to the packaging an extra article from a source other than the trade mark owner, he must ensure that the origin of the extra article is indicated in such a way as to dispel any impression that the trade mark owner is responsible for it.

Similarly, as paragraph [11] of the *Pfizer* judgment [Pfizer v. Euri-Pharm, Case 1/81, [1982] 1 C.M.L.R. 406] shows, a clear indication may be required on the external packaging as to who manufactured the product, since it may indeed be in the manufacturer's interest that the consumer or end user should not be led to believe that the importer is the owner of the trade mark, and that the product was manufactured under his supervision.

Even if the person who carried out the repackaging is indicated on the packaging of the product, there remains the possibility that the reputation of the trade mark, and thus of its owner, may nevertheless suffer from an inappropriate presentation of the repackaged product. In such a case, the trade mark owner has a legitimate interest, related to the specific subject-matter of the trade mark right, in being able to oppose the marketing of the product. In assessing whether the presentation of the repackaged product is liable to damage the reputation of the trade mark, account must be taken of the nature of the product and the market for which it is intended.

In the case of pharmaceutical products, that is certainly a sensitive area in which the public is particularly demanding as to the quality and integrity of the product, and the presentation of the product may indeed be capable of inspiring public confidence in that regard. It follows that defective, poor quality or untidy packaging could damage the trade mark's reputation.

However, the requirements to be met by the presentation of a repackaged pharmaceutical product vary according to whether the product is sold to hospitals or, through pharmacies, to consumers. In the former case, the products are administered to patients by professionals, for whom the presentation of the products is of little importance. In the latter case, the presentation of the product is of greater importance for the consumer, even if the fact that the products in question are subject to prescription by a doctor may in itself give consumers some degree of confidence in the quality of the product.

Finally, as the Court pointed out in *Hoffmann-La Roche*, the trade mark owner must be given advance notice of the repackaged product being put on sale. The owner may also require the importer to supply him with a specimen of the repackaged product before it goes on sale, to enable him to check that the repackaging is not carried out in such a way as directly or indirectly to affect the original condition of the product and that the presentation after repackaging is not likely to damage the reputation of the trade mark. Similarly, such a requirement affords the trade mark owner a better possibility of protecting himself against counterfeiting.

NOTES AND QUESTIONS

(1) **Article 7 and the EC Treaty.** The *Paranova* court would appear to regard Article 7 of the Directive—or, at least, Article 7(2)—as a consolidation of the principles it had previously developed on the basis of ex-Articles 30 and 36 of the EC Treaty. *Cf.* Fernando Castillo De La Torre, *Trade Marks and Free Movement of Pharmaceuticals in the European Community: To Partition or Not to Partition the Market*, 19 EUR. INTELL. PROP. REV. 304, 310-11 (1997) (noting the "mixing" by *Paranova* court of exhaustion doctrine with earlier "subject-matter of the right" case law under Article 36, and criticizing that development for failing to recognize that a right may not be exhausted but still be incapable of enforcement under Article 36). Given that ex-Articles 30 and 36 are fundamental principles of the constitutive document of the European Community, in what circumstances should a directive potentially alter or influence the operative principles developed by the Court of Justice as a matter of treaty interpretation? That is to say, what does Article 7(2) add to the jurisprudence of the European Court? *See* Berend-Jan Drijber, *Recent and Pending Cases Before the Court of Justice*, 5 INT'L INTELL. PROP. L. & POL. (2001) (forthcoming) (suggesting that in assessing whether a national measure is immunized by Article 36 the Court may "where appropriate, take account of standards of protection defined in (draft) secondary legislation").

(2) **Repackaging Principles.** What are the essential principles governing the repackaging of parallel imports articulated by the *Paranova* court? Which, if any, of the conditions laid down by the Court might be regarded as specific to the pharmaceutical industry? Should different approaches be followed depending upon the nature of the product being repackaged? For example, if the product in question were mass-market computer software, how would you implement the essential principles of *Paranova*? Does a notice and specimen requirement (*Paranova* condition 3) place an undue burden (and cost) on the parallel importer? Could (slow but strict) enforcement of this condition not be used by producers to restrain parallel importing even where the products should be permitted to move freely under Article 7?

(3) **Prestige Preservation.** Christian Dior France owns the exclusive rights in the Benelux countries in the trademarks EAU SAVAGE, POISON, FAHRENHEIT and DUNE and the picture marks associated therewith for various luxury cosmetic products, including perfumes. Dior Netherlands is the sole representative of Dior France in the Netherlands. In common with Dior France's sole representatives elsewhere in Europe, Dior Netherlands makes use of a selective distribution system for the distribution of Dior products. The products may be sold only by selected retailers and on condition that those retailers supply only to ultimate consumers or other selected retailers. Evora operates a chain of chemist shops (drugstores). Evora shops have not been appointed as selected distributors of Dior products. However, they sell Dior

products (at lower prices than the authorized distributors) obtained by means of parallel imports. As part of a Christmas promotion, Evora advertised for sale various Dior products that it was selling. The advertising, which was of a type customary to mass-market cosmetic retailers, depicted the Dior products and thus reproduced the marks in which Dior owns the rights. Dior was not pleased with the nature of the advertisements (a Christmas sale catalogue) and brought an action against Evora alleging, inter alia, trademark infringement. Dior argued (1) that the exhaustion of rights, which permitted Evora to sell Dior trademarked goods, did not grant Evora the right to use the mark collaterally in advertising the goods and bringing them to the attention of the public, and (2) that the "condition of the goods" as used in Article 7(2) of the Directive encompassed the "mental condition of the goods . . . mean[ing] the allure, prestigious image and aura of luxury surrounding the goods, resulting from the manner in which the trademark proprietor has chosen to present and advertise the goods using his trade mark rights." *See* Parfums Christian Dior v. Evora, 1998 R.P.C. 166 (E.C.J. 1997). Are either of these arguments persuasive?

If trademark law allows the mark owner to assert rights in order to preserve the prestige of luxury goods, what does that enable the mark owner to prohibit? (What is it that contributes to "prestige" or "luxury" status?) Is the maintenance of a selective distribution system a legitimate interest that EU trademark law should seek to protect over the free movement of goods? If a trademark owner can control the means by which its goods are presented to the public, does that mean that a trademark owner could object to the sale of shop-soiled goods? *See* Davidoff v. A & G Imports Ltd., [1999] 2 C.M.L.R. 1056 (Ch. D. 1999) (Eng.). Does that amount to "poor quality or untidy packaging [that] could damage the trademark's reputation?"

If "condition" in Article 7(2) cannot be read to include "mental condition" as argued by Christian Dior, what other arguments might be made to limit the right of the parallel importer to advertise its goods? Should there be *any* limits on Evora's advertising of its parallel imports? If so, what might they be, and against what standard or test should they be measured? *See* Parfums Christian Dior v. Evora, 1998 R.P.C. 166 (E.C.J. 1997). Is the "legitimate interest" in preserving reputation absolute, or what encroachment to enable the free movement of goods are we willing to allow? (In constructing a test, bear in mind the competing concerns that the *Paranova* court thought legitimate.) Should Evora's conduct have to be such that consumers would likely be confused as to any association between Evora and Dior? *Cf. Sabel, supra* § 3.01[I][3]. Does the defendant's conduct in *Evora* meet the test and why? Would your answer change if Evora were a store in a red light district rather than a drugstore? What if the advertisement depicted the Dior perfumes heaped in a "sale bin" along with rolls of toilet paper and toothbrushes? If authorized distributors advertised in a similar fashion, how would that affect your analysis? How might Dior reframe its claim in such circumstances? *See* BMW v. Deenik, [1999] 1 C.M.L.R. 1099, ¶¶ 39-41 (Advocate-General Jacobs).

(4) **Identifying Codes.** George Ballantine & Sons is a producer of various brands of Scotch whisky, all of which enjoy a high reputation throughout the world. Ballantine places "identification numbers" on its products, allegedly to facilitate both the recall of defective products and the fight against

counterfeiters.   Loendersloot is a Dutch parallel importer who purchases Ballantine products in low-price countries and, before reselling the whisky at higher prices to traders in various European countries and the United States, removes the identification labels from the whisky bottles and replaces the labels with new labels.   The new labels are copies of the old labels with the name of the importer (and sometimes the word "pure") removed and replaced by the name of an importer with no contractual relationship with Ballantine. Ballantine sued Loendersloot in the Netherlands for trademark infringement and sought injunctive relief to prevent Loendersloot engaging in these acts of "repackaging."   Loendersloot argued that its conduct was necessary to effect parallel imports, and that Ballantine was attempting to partition the markets within the EU and elsewhere in order to maintain artificial differences in prices. More particularly, Loendesloot claimed that the identification numbers and the names of the importers are removed to preserve the anonymity of dealers engaging in parallel trade and thus prevent Ballantine from exerting pressure on those dealers. (It also alleges that the word "pure" may not be lawfully used under the laws of some of the countries to which it exports the whisky.) What relief should the trademark owner receive? *See* Loendersloot v. George Ballantine & Sons, 1997 E.T.M.R. 306 (A.G. Jacobs 1997), 1998 F.S.R. 544 (E.C.J. 1997); *Davidoff, supra*, [1999] 2 C.M.L.R. 1056 (Ch. D. 1999) (Eng.).

If the obligation to number products in order to facilitate product recall were imposed by law, would that change your analysis? What if that obligation were instead contractually imposed upon the manufacturer?   Even if these obligations—legal or contractual—are legitimate concerns, what weight is to be given to the consequential effect of impeding or effectively preventing parallel imports (if that consequential effect is proven)?   How are these dueling legitimate concerns to be reconciled?   What relief might a court grant to accommodate both concerns?

Loendersloot was also exporting the Scotch whisky in question to the United States. Could a mark owner prevent the importation of goods altered in this manner under U.S. law? *See* Proposed Antitampering Act of 1999, HR 2100, 106th Cong., 1st Sess (1999) (proposing civil and criminal remedies for unauthorized changes to product identification codes). For discussion of similar conduct by a parallel importer outside the EU, see Chanel S.A. Genève v. EPA AG, 1997 E.T.M.R. 352 (Federal Court Oct. 23, 1996) (Switz.) (sale of parallel imports after rendering "tracking" code illegible by superimposition of punched pinhole pattern did not constitute an infringement of the provisions of Swiss trademark law or of unfair competition law).

(5) **Reconditioned Goods.** In *Levi Strauss*, Case No. I/ZR 210/93 (Federal Supreme 1995) (Germany), reported at 28 I.I.C. 132 (1997), the plaintiff owned several registered trademarks in Germany, including LEVI'S and LEVI STRAUSS, for clothing. The defendant, a German retailer, sold the plaintiff's jeans bearing the plaintiff's trademark on pockets and buttons. However, although the jeans had been manufactured in the United States by the plaintiff, they had, without the plaintiff's consent, been bleached and dyed (and some cut down to shorts) and then imported by a third person into Germany. The quality of the jeans material is reduced by the chlorine substances used during bleaching. Plaintiff sought to enjoin the defendant from selling jeans under the

LEVI'S mark if the jeans had been dyed by another manufacturer. The Court held that, even under the principles of worldwide exhaustion followed under the previous German law, the plaintiff could prohibit the sale in Germany of jeans bearing its trademark but which have been dyed by another party without its consent because such conduct changed the characteristics of the goods.

(6) **Authorized Dealers.** Bayerische Motorenwerke ("BMW") owns the rights in the mark BMW for cars and related accessories. BMW markets its vehicles through a network of dealers, who are authorized to use the BMW mark for the purpose of their businesses. Ronald Deenik owns and manages a garage; he specializes both in the sale of second-hand ("previously-owned") BMW cars and in the repair of BMW cars. Mr. Deenik promotes both aspects of his business by advertising that he "specializes in BMWs." Can Deenik rely on Article 7 to justify his advertising? *See* BMW v. Deenik [1999] 1 C.M.L.R. 1099 (E.C.J. 1999). What arguments might BMW have that it can restrain Deenik's use of its mark under Article 7(2)? *See also* Trademark Directive art. 6(1).

(7) **Unfair Competition Protection.** If a mark is declared invalid on the grounds of deceptiveness in Italy but not in France, and under Italian law the trademark owner is thus enjoined from using the mark, can an Italian court grant to an Italian distributor (who previously purchased the goods in Italy from the mark owner) an injunction under unfair competition law against the parallel importation from France of goods bearing the same mark? *Cf.* Fratelli Graffione SNC v. Fransa, [1997] 1 C.M.L.R. 925 (E.C.J. 1996). Against what type of competitive injury might the distributor claim the need for relief? On what grounds might the parallel importer resist the action? Do the provisions of the Trademark Directive affect the answer? *See* art. 12; *see also* Recitals 5-6. How does the legal effect of invalidation of a trademark registration affect the relief that might be granted? What variables might cause a mark to be misleading in one European country but not another and thus lead to the situation addressed in *Fransa? See* Fratelli Graffione SNC v. Fransa, [1997] 1 C.M.L.R. 925, 931 (E.C.J.).

(8) **Relationship With Copyright Rules.** If the labels in *Loendersloot* were copyrighted and contain copyright management information, might the WIPO Copyright Treaty be implicated? *See* WIPO Copyright Treaty art. 12; *cf.* 17 U.S.C. § 1201 et seq. Is it problematic that parallel importers are permitted to conduct business in a particular fashion by trademark law, but different obligations are imposed by copyright law? In *Parfums Christian Dior v. Evora,* 1998 R.P.C. 166 (E.C.J. 1997), discussed above, Dior rested its claim for injunctive relief both on its trademarks and on its copyright in the labels. Copyright legislation of the EU has not addressed exhaustion of rights, but the assertion of copyright to restrain the free movement of goods remains subject to Article 28 (ex-Article 30) of the Treaty of Rome. The *Evora* court reasoned as follows on the copyright claim:

> [W]hile the commercial exploitation of copyright is a source of remuneration for the copyright owner, it also constitutes a form of control on marketing exercisable by the owner and that, from this point of view, commercial exploitation of copyright raises the same

issues as that of any other industrial or commercial property. [cit]. The Court has thus held that the exclusive right of exploitation conferred by copyright cannot be relied on by its owner to prevent or restrict the importation of sound recordings of protected works which have been lawfully marketed in another Member State by the owner himself or with his consent. [cit].

Having regard to that case-law—there being no need to consider the question whether copyright and trade mark rights may be relied on simultaneously in respect of the same product—it is sufficient to hold that, in circumstances such as those in point in the main proceedings, the protection conferred by copyright as regards the reproduction of protected works in a reseller's advertising may not, in any event, be broader than that which is conferred on a trade mark owner in the same circumstances.

The court then formulated an answer as to the circumstances in which copyright could be relied upon to prevent the sale of "decoded" products in precisely the same language as it used in the trademark context, thus assimilating the assertion of trademark and copyrights for the purpose of controlling marketing of goods. Compare the approach to exhaustion in the United States. Should all intellectual property rights be subject to the same scope of exhaustion, or are there arguments for treating different intellectual property rights differently?

[4] Exhaustion of Patent Rights in Europe

In *Merck & Co. Inc. and Others v. Primecrown Limited and Others* (ECJ Joined Cases C 267-268/95) [1997] 1 CLMR 93, Merck brought an action in the Patents Court in the United Kingdom to restrain parallel imports of pharmaceutical products from states where such products were not patentable, claiming that Primecrown had infringed the patents Merck held in the United Kingdom for certain pharmaceutical products by importing those products from Spain and Portugal and selling them in the United Kingdom. (At the relevant time, Spain and Portugal had joined the community, but had not yet made patent protection available for the products in question and the transitional provisions gave patent holders such as Merck the right to prevent parallel imports until the end of the third year after which Spain and Portugal had made the products patentable.) The Patents Court referred the case to the ECJ under ex-Article 177 EC. The European Court of Justice, striking a balance "between the principle of free movement of goods in the Community and the principle of protection of patent rights," followed the holding in its decision in *Merck v. Stephar* (Case 197/80, [1981] ECR 2063) that where the holder of a patent for a pharmaceutical product sold the product in one member state where patent protection existed, and then marketed the product himself in another member state where there was no patent protection, "he had to accept the consequences of his choice as regards the possibility of parallel imports" and could not rely on his patent rights in the first member state in order to prevent others from importing the product from the second member state and marketing it in the first member state. The patent holder could prevent imports if it had a legal obligation to market the product in a state with no patent protection, but not if it were merely ethical considerations which induced the patentee to continue its marketing. While there are no decisions in the EC or EFTA addressing the question of parallel importation of patented goods into a state from outside, decisions in trademark and copyright cases may shed some light on the question.

NOTES AND QUESTIONS

(1) **Pharmaceuticals.** In the area of pharmaceuticals, are patent holders "free" to cease marketing a product if they wish to stem the flow of such products to another country? Should they be? Can a company decide not to market a drug in one country to protect its market in another? *See* Maarten Meulenbelt, *Parallel Imports of Medicinal Products: A New Balance?*, 1 J. WORLD INTELL. PROP. 525 (1998).

(2) **. . . And the Purpose of TRIPS.** Recall the Preamble of the TRIPS Agreement. Do high-technology manufacturers (including multinational pharmaceutical companies) enhance global welfare more by intra-brand and inter-brand price competition or by competition in drug research and development? Do expansive policies on patent exhaustion lead to increased global welfare, or do they merely maximize global trade? *See* Alexander J. Stack, *TRIPS, Patent Exhaustion and Parallel Imports*, 1 J. WORLD INTELL. PROP. 657, 684 (1998).

[D] Other Jurisdictions

BBS KRAFTFAHRZEUG TECHNIK AG v. KABUSHIKI KAISHA RACIMEX
Case No. Heisei 7(wo)1988 (Supreme Court of Japan, 1997)

I

This case was brought by Petitioner against Respondents who engaged in a so-called parallel importation by way of importing and reselling in Japan products manufactured and sold in the Federal Republic of Germany by Petitioner. In this case, Petitioner sought an injunction on importation and sale of products, and damages based on a patent right which Petitioner owns in Japan. The following facts were duly found final by the High Court.

(1) Petitioner owns, in Japan, a patent right entitled "Wheel for Automobile" (filed on October 29, 1983 claiming a priority based on a patent application filed before the European Patent Office on May 27, 1983), published for opposition

on January 12, 1990, and granted Patent 1629869 on December 20, 1991. (The patent is hereinafter referred to as the "subject patent" and the invention as the "subject patented invention.")

(2) Petitioner owns a patent right in Germany to cover an invention similar to the subject patented invention. (It was filed on May 27, 1983 before the European Patent Office with Germany and other countries as designated countries. It was given an application number of 83105259.2 and was granted a patent on April 22, 1987.) (This patent is hereinafter referred to as "the corresponding German patent.")

(3) Up until August 1992, Respondent, Jap-Auto Products imported aluminum wheels for automobiles, "BBS/RS," as described in Appendix 1 which was attached to the Decision of the District Court, and aluminum wheels for automobiles, "ROLINZER RSK," as described in Appendix II and sold them to another Respondent, Racimex Japan. Pacimex Japan engaged in the sale of these aluminum wheels at least up until August 1992. It is likely that Respondents would continue their importation and sale. (Hereinafter, the aluminum wheels mentioned here are collectively referred to as the "subject goods" including both products already sold and those to be sold in the future.)

(4) The subject goods fall within the technical scope of the subject patented invention.

(5) The subject goods were manufactured as the product under the corresponding German patent, and sold by Petitioner in Germany after the German patent became effective.

II.

In the petition to this Court, Respondents argue for what is called international exhaustion. Namely, the effect of the subject patent applicable to subject goods has exhausted because of legitimate distribution by Petitioner of the subject goods in Germany. Therefore, Respondents' importation and sale of the subject goods in Japan does not constitute infringement of the subject patent.

The High Court dismissed the claim filed by Petitioner against Respondents for injunction and damages under the subject patent. The High Court reasoned that Petitioner manufactured and sold the subject goods as products under the corresponding patent in Germany. It was clear that Petitioner was provided an opportunity to secure remuneration for disclosing its invention. There were no admissible facts showing that such opportunity to secure remuneration was legally restricted when the subject goods were distributed. Legitimate distribution in Germany should be deemed to have caused the subject patent to be exhausted with respect to the subject goods.

III.

The High Court decided that Petitioner's claims against Respondents for injunction and damages under the subject patent have no grounds. This Court is agreeable to the conclusion of the High Court decision. Reasons for this

Court's agreement are as follows.

1. The Paris Convention . . . as amended in 1979 (hereinafter referred to as the "Paris Convention") provides in Article 4*bis* that:

(1) Patents applied for in the various countries of the Union by nationals of countries of the Union shall be independent of patents obtained for the same invention in other countries, whether members of the Union or not.

(2) The foregoing provision is to be understood in an unrestricted sense, in particular, in the sense that patents applied for during the period of priority are independent, both as regards the grounds for nullity and forfeiture, and as regards their normal duration.

This provision denies the interdependence of patent rights and stipulates that a patent right of each country is independent from others with respect to its grant, changes and surrender. In other words, the existence of a patent right is not affected by the invalidation, forfeiture, expiration, etc. of a patent right in a different country. The question of whether a patentee is allowed to enforce its patent right under certain circumstances is not a matter stipulated in that provision.

Also, the principle of territoriality denotes, in the context of a patent right, that the grant, assignment, validity or the like of a patent right in each country is governed by the law of that country and that the patent right is effective only in the territory of that country.

When a patentee enforces its patent right in Japan, would such fact that a product subject to that patent right was already sold outside Japan by the patentee or the like, affect enforceability of the Japanese patent right? This question is a matter of interpretation of the Japanese Patent Law and is irrelevant to the Paris Convention and the principle of territoriality. It is clear from the foregoing that any interpretation in this respect, whatever interpretation it might be, is not in breach of the provision of Article 4*bis* and the principle of territoriality.

2. A patentee has an exclusive right to commercially exploit its patented invention (*see*, Patent Law, Section 68). In the case of invention of a product, acts of using, assigning or leasing constitute the exploitation of the invention (*see*, Patent Law, Section 2(3)(iii)). If so, acts of a commercial use or resale to a third party by the buyer who obtained products covered by the patent (hereinafter referred to as "patented product") from the patentee or its licensee, or acts of a commercial use or further sale or lease to others by the third party who obtained the patented products from the buyer would appear, on the surface, to constitute the exploitation of a patented invention to cause infringement of the relevant patent. However, in the case of the sale of patented products in Japan by the patentee or its licensee, a relevant patent in Japan should be deemed to have its right exhausted with respect to the product. In that case, the effect of the patent should no longer extend to the acts of use, assignment or lease of the patented product.

This Court bases this interpretation on the following.

(i) The protection of an invention under the patent law has to be achieved in harmony with public interest;

(ii) In general, through the act of a sale, all rights adherent to the goods are transferred to the buyer. The buyer receives all rights which the seller has owned. When a patented product is placed on the market, the buyer enters into a deal with a prerequisite that he would obtain rights to freely use and resell the product as a business. If the sale of a patented product requires approval from the patentee for each transaction, the free flow of products on the market would be interrupted and the smooth distribution of patented products would be disturbed. This would result in adverse affects on the patentee's interests and would be contrary to the purpose of the patent law which aims at encouraging inventions by promoting their protection and utilization so as to contribute to the development of industry. (*See*, Patent Law, Section 1);

(iii) On the other hand, a patentee receives proceeds including reward for disclosing its patented invention when the patentee sells its patented product. When it licenses the patent, it receives royalty payments. It can be said that an opportunity to secure a reward for disclosing its patented invention is guaranteed. Thus, once the patentee or its licensee sells patented products, there is no need to allow the patentee to obtain double profits through the process of distribution.

3. However, this rationale cannot be automatically applicable to the case where a patentee of a Japanese patent has sold its patented products outside Japan, because, in that case, the patentee may not have a patent for the same invention as covered by the Japanese patent (hereinafter referred to as "the counterpart patent"). Even if the patentee owns the counterpart patent, it should be noted that its patent in Japan is separate from its counterpart patent in the country where the sale took place. In light of this fact, the patentee shall be free from any claim about double profits even if the patentee enforces its Japanese patent against the product which is a subject matter of the counterpart patent.

4. Now, the adjustment between the flow of products in international trade and the patentee's right is discussed below. In light of the fact that international trade is being conducted on a tremendously broad and sophisticated basis, it is necessary that freedom of trade including freedom to import should be paid utmost respect when a dealer in Japan imports a patented product marketed in a foreign country to put it in a distribution channel in Japan. Through economic transactions outside Japan, a seller transfers his rights to the product to a buyer. The buyer enters into a deal with the prerequisite recognition that he receives all rights which the seller has owned with respect to the product. In light of the status-quo of international trade in modern society, it is naturally anticipated that the buyer or a third party who purchased a patented product from the buyer can commercially import it into Japan, and commercially use it or resell it to others in Japan, even if the product is sold by the patentee outside Japan. Thus, in the case where the owner of a patent in Japan or a person who can be recognized as an entity identical to the patent owner, sells its patented products outside Japan, a reasonable interpretation is that the patentee should not be allowed to enforce its patent in Japan against the buyer unless the buyer explicitly agrees to exclude Japan from the place of sale or use, and against a third party or subsequent buyers who purchased patented products from the buyer unless a

notice of such agreement is clearly placed on the patented products. To be more specific:

(i) As was discussed earlier, it can be naturally anticipated that a patented product sold outside Japan might be imported into Japan. If the product was sold outside Japan without a reservation, it should be construed that the right to control the purchased product was implicitly given to the buyer and its subsequent purchasers without any restriction under the patent in Japan;

(ii) With respect to the right of the patentee, it is permissible for the patentee to reserve the right to enforce its patent in Japan when the patentee sells the product outside Japan. In the case where the buyer explicitly agrees with the patentee to an exclusion of Japan from the place of sale and use of the purchased product, and such exclusion is clearly indicated on the product, the subsequent purchasers will be in a position to learn the product is subject to certain restrictions irrespective of the involvement of other persons in the distribution process. They can fully decide whether or not to buy the patented product, taking into account the presence of such restriction; and

(iii) When the product is sold outside Japan by a subsidiary or an affiliated company which can be regarded as an entity identical to the patentee, such transactions should be deemed as the sale of the patented product by the patentee itself; or

(iv)The buyer of the patented product usually trusts in the free flow of the purchased product. That trust should be well protected. It should not matter whether or not the patentee has a counterpart patent in the country of first sale.

QUESTION

The *BBS* court states that the question of enforcement of a patent right under Japanese law is solely a question of municipal law—not international law of the Paris Convention, at least. Do any international standards apply? Do Article 6 of TRIPS or the prior GATT place any limitations on a patentee's ability to limit the international distribution of patented goods through license restrictions? Should it, given the fact that all WTO countries are equal parties at the TRIPS table?

§ 7.07 International Domain Name Litigation

The digital revolution has forced intellectual property law to confront many new issues. This section focuses on the registration and use of domain names where those domain names are similar to existing trademarks. Conflicts between trademark rights and domain name registrants occur in a number of settings. Most publicity has centered on what is called "cybersquatting," very loosely defined as the abusive registration of a domain name that is similar to a trademark owned by another person (often with a view to selling that registration to the trademark owner for a substantial fee). The materials that follow are not restricted to the problem of cybersquatting; the potential conflict between domain names and trademarks is far broader. But other aspects of the conflict have already been addressed periodically throughout the casebook, and studying the development of the rules pertinent to cybersquatting offers several insights into current international intellectual property lawmaking. Thus, we have given cybersquatting disputes particular prominence in this section.

[A] The Conflict Between Domain Names and Trademark Law

GRAEME B. DINWOODIE, (NATIONAL) TRADEMARK LAWS AND THE (NON-NATIONAL) DOMAIN NAME SYSTEM
21 U. PA. J. INT'L ECON. L. 495 (2000)

The Conflict Between Trademark and Domain Name Regimes

What precisely is the conflict between trademarks and domain names? Before examining the conflict in detail and the different ways in which it might be addressed, I should identify the characteristics of the [domain name system]. Domain names are the unique addresses assigned to particular computers that are connected to the Internet. Without such unique addresses, computers would not be able to send packets of information to the correct location.[4] The naming system, and the history of its development, are well-explained elsewhere.[5] For our current purposes, four aspects of the system are pertinent. First, domain names currently say very little about the nature or location of the domain name registrant. Every domain name has a top-level domain name (the suffix at the end of the domain name) that will consist of either a generic top-level domain name (such as .edu or .com)[6] or a country code (such as .uk, for the United Kingdom, or .it, for Italy).[7] But, as presently constituted, even the top-level domain name is not determinative of the nature or location of the registrant in question. Although the registrars responsible for country code registers may impose residency requirements, domain names are available in the generic top-level domains regardless of physical location and many country code

---

[4] The actual Internet addresses (Internet Protocol addresses) are unique numbers, each with an assigned corresponding unique name in order to deal with the frailty of human memory. Thus, the Internet address of the University of Pennsylvania is actually 128.91.2.28, but it is easier to remember the name that corresponds to that number, namely, www.upenn.edu.

[5] See generally Joseph P. Liu, Legitimacy and Authority in Internet Coordination: A Domain Name Case Study, 74 IND. L.J. 587 (1999) (discussing the history of domain name system and proposals for reform).

[6] The present generic top-level domain names include .edu, .com, . gov, .org, .net, .int, and .mil. [T]he Internet Corporation for Assigned Names and Numbers ("ICANN") has proposed the creation of a variety of new top-level domain names.

[7] The administration of country code top-level domains is delegated by ICANN (performing the functions formerly performed by the Internet Assigned Numbers Authority to authorities ("managers") in the relevant country. . .

registrars are not insistent on residency requirements.[10] And, while the four principal generic top-level domains were once indicative of the nature of the domain name's owner (.edu signified educational institutions, .gov was found at the end of government agency addresses, .com was used by commercial enterprises, and .mil was restricted to military users), the expansion of users and an open registration system have reduced the value of the suffix as an indicium of the nature of the user (except for .edu, .gov, and .mil).

Second, and related to the lack of connection between address and location, because the accreditation of registrars is performed by a single body, ICANN,[13] there is close to (but not complete)[14] uniformity of registration practices among registrars, at least with respect to the generic top-level domains. Third, within each top-level domain, there cannot be two identical names, or computers would not know where to send information. Thus, while there may be separate domain name registrations of apple.com and apple.net, there cannot be two domain name registrations of apple.com. Finally, domain names are registered on a first-come, first-served basis. There can only be one apple.com, and it goes to the first person to register it. The only check, on initial application, is whether an identical name is already registered in that domain.

In some ways, the allocation of domain names may appear to evade the dilemmas presented by cyberspace in other areas of regulation . . . (such as tax or securities law) . . . . In particular, because the domain name system is an element of the architecture of the Internet, domain names would appear inevitably linked to the non-national vehicle of the Internet; registration can be made in top-level domains without regard to national status or location. And, names are not allocated by national governments.[15] Finally, unlike other activities (such as the issuance or trading of securities), no differing national regulatory domain name regimes have previously been established. The domain

---

[10]Some country code domains have become attractive for reasons unrelated to geography. For example, doctors in the United States are purchasing names in the Moldova country code domain, namely, .md. . . .

[13]ICANN is a not-for-profit corporation that was created by the U.S. government to operate the domain name system, among other things, in accordance with parameters set by the Commerce Department. *See* Management of Internet Names and Addresses, 63 Fed. Reg. 31,741 (proposed June 10, 1998).

[14]The flexibility that causes slightly different practices among registrars reflects the notion that the system of registering generic top-level domain names would benefit from competition in the registration process. This was an important part of the shift from administration of the system by Network Solutions, Inc. [Before the U.S. government established ICANN, responsibility for registering .com domain names—the most valuable names—lay with Network Solutions, Inc. (to whom the government had outsourced the job).]

[15]National governments are more likely to be involved in the management of country code domains. But the manager of a country code domain need not be a national governmental organization. The appropriate managers of the country code domains are determined in accordance with principles set out in a document (referred to as ICP-1) entitled "Internet Domain Name System Structure and Delegation" at http://www.icann.org/icp/icp-1.htm. This was issued in May 1999 to reflect then current policies of the Internet Assigned Numbers Authority in the administration of delegations to manage country code domains. And many managers are wholly unrelated to the national government. *Cf. id.* at 2 (noting that "the desires of the government of a country with regard to delegation of a [country code top-level domain] are taken very seriously . . . . Significantly interested parties in the domain should agree that the proposed [top-level domain] manager is the appropriate party.").

name system thus appears to be a ripe candidate for an approach transcending national regulation.

This impression changes, however, when trademarks are used as domain names. Intellectual property rights traditionally have been national in nature, and there are only a few derogations from this territorialist philosophy. . . .

[T]he use of nationally delimited trademarks in the non-nationally delimited domain name system thus compels consideration of which boundaries (if any) are pertinent. So when trademarks are used as (or as part of) domain names, the domain name system can no longer avoid the question of whether national, international, or supranational law should determine rights where two or more parties have competing claims. The domain name system must confront the dilemma facing other areas of regulation, and I will discuss below the different ways in which it is doing that

[But]domain names also challenge the conceptual boundaries of trademark law. To see the ways in which this is so, let's briefly explore the conceptual boundaries of trademark law. . . . The scope of U.S. trademark rights was limited both by reference to the products on which the mark was used and by reference to the geographic area in which the mark was used. . . . [E]ach of these limits . . . reflected a desire to restrain the activities of legitimate traders only to the extent necessary to further the two primary purposes of trademark law. If the products upon which the mark was used were wholly different from those of the first mark owner, the public would not purchase the goods of the second producer believing them to be those of the first producer. Thus, although Apple owns the mark APPLE for personal computers, a manufacturer of shoes could use the mark APPLE on shoes without affecting the goodwill established by the Apple company or deceiving consumers in their purchasing decisions. DOMINO's is used for both pizzas and sugar without harm to either company (despite efforts to suggest otherwise). To use an example on the services side, United Airlines and United Van Lines each own trademark rights in the mark UNITED, for airline services and moving services, respectively.

Limits on the geographic scope of rights were similarly motivated: if Apple computer did not use its mark in State A, then consumers in State A would not come to associate the mark APPLE with the products made by the Apple company, and thus the use of the term—even by another computer producer—would not confuse consumers or endanger any consumer perceptions of the quality of the product of the Apple company (because there are no such perceptions). . . .

The domain name system presents a series of conflicts with these basic principles of U.S. trademark law. There can only be one united.com;[29] should that domain name be granted to the airline or the moving company, or should prior trademark ownership be irrelevant? What is the geographic scope of use

---

[29]The extent to which this remains a problem may depend on the maintenance of the current architecture of the Internet. For example, where more than one trademark holder (or other person) has a legitimate claim to united.com, that address may take the user to a registrar-administered site listing (and linking to the sites of) all claimants to the UNITED name, relegating those users to concurrent use of united.com and exclusive use only of some other configuration including "united".

where a trademark is used as a domain name: has the user now made use of the mark globally, potentially causing the acquisition of rights in all use-based systems and infringement of rights in all countries where the mark is owned by another?[*] . . . .

The domain name system, and its operation apart from the trademark system, will also require the courts to develop new responses to old questions. For example, how does one assess confusion in cyberspace? The courts must construct a cyberconsumer, whose purchasing and browsing habits clearly encompass the use of domain names as well as trademarks in the searching process.[32] And, if use retains any importance in the system of trademark protection, then how does one assess whether a trademark is being "used" in cyberspace: is registration of a domain name the "use of a mark in commerce" sufficient either to acquire trademark rights or (if that mark is owned by another) to infringe trademark rights? Again, this will require courts to apply classical principles with an eye to new consumer practices. Whether and to what extent domain names will serve as trademarks is not a question of abstract philosophy, but a matter of how consumer practices and comprehension develop in cyberspace. Even in the last few years, consumer attitudes about what a domain name signifies have changed; trademark law must reflect those changes.

. . . .

Addressing the Conflict

Spatial Boundaries

In the context of domain name/trademark disputes, principles have developed at the national, international, and supranational levels. Many different national courts have addressed the registration of domain names including trademarks by persons other than the mark owner. But while national courts throughout the world have consistently offered relief against blatant cybersquatting,[43] differences in the precise contours of national protection are likely to develop as courts confront more contentious issues in disputes between competing mark owners or mark owners and other legitimate users. The issue has been tackled at the international level by the World Intellectual Property Organization. In September 1999, WIPO member states agreed to a nonbinding resolution calling for the per se protection of well-known marks against bad

---

[*][Ed. Note: The proposals of the WIPO Standing Committee on the Law of Trademarks, Industrial Designs and Geographical Indications on this issue are discussed *supra* page 1157].

[32]These habits may, however, change as technological options for cybersearching grow. The use of keywords, available with different browsers, for example, altered the reliance of consumers on domain names. *See* Andy Johnson-Laird, *Looking Forward, Legislating Backward?*, 4 J. SMALL & EMERGING BUS. L. 95 (2000).

[43]*See, e.g.*, Sporty's Farm L.L.C. v. Sportsman's Market, Inc., 202 F.3d 489, 495 (2d Cir. 2000), cert. denied, 120 S. Ct. 2719 (2000); Panavision Int'l, L.P., v. Toeppen, 141 F.3d 1316, 1322 (9th Cir. 1998); Landgericht Dusseldorf, GRUR 34 O 191/96 (Apr. 4, 1997), 158 (Germany), reported at 1998 Eur. C.L.Y.B. 963, 963 (May 1998) . . .

faith registration as part of the domain names of someone other than the mark owner. But, even if this form of "soft law" has the long-term effect that WIPO hopes, it will simply ensure that most countries offer basic protection against infringement of famous marks. Implementation of that protection will remain a matter for national law, and (as the number of reservations noted in the resolution suggests) there exists wide disagreement over the appropriate scope of protection for marks beyond very basic notions.

If this were all, national law would remain paramount, as it still does in almost all other areas of intellectual property law. This would cause reliance on traditional private law techniques of jurisdiction, choice of law, and recognition of judgments, to localize and adjudicate non-national disputes before national courts according to national laws. . . . [But traditional approaches to choice of law have significant problems of application and provide little guidance to courts in the digital environment.]

On the other hand, the isolated application of autonomous, universal cybernorms causes other problems. Just as cyberspace creates spillover effects from one country to another, it also causes spillover from online to offline contexts, implicating more than merely cyberinterests. Online activities have offline consequences, legitimating online (national) regulation. National interests have a role to play in the development of international solutions. Passing over them too quickly disserves a truly international solution by ignoring helpful laboratories of laws, failing to take advantage of developed democratic political structures that nation states (on the whole) provide,[50] and ignoring the legitimate claims of nation states to (partial) legislative competence.

The domain name system does, however, include a form of supranational adjudication in addition to the national and international mechanisms discussed above. When the U.S. Government established ICANN, it required that ICANN devise a mandatory uniform dispute resolution policy. Thus, when ICANN accredited additional registrars to administer the generic top-level domains, it required each registrar to adopt the Uniform Dispute Resolution Policy ("UDRP"). The UDRP establishes an arbitration process by requiring domain name registrants to submit to arbitration before one of the ICANN-approved dispute resolution providers as a condition of registration. And it contains a set of principles (both substantive and procedural) according to which disputes between registrants and mark owners are to be resolved.

. . . .

---

[50]It is not clear that the different constituencies comprising the fledgling political structure of ICANN serve as any better proxy than nations for the different interests that are implicated in this context. And the structure of ICANN raises many other concerns regarding the body's legitimacy and representativeness. *See* Common Cause & Ctr. for Democracy & Tech., ICANN's Global Elections: On the Internet, for the Internet (March 2000), at http://www.cdt.org/dns/icann/study/icannstudy.pdf.

Conceptual Boundaries

Trademark law, especially in use-based systems such as the United States, is generally cautious about the dispensation of rights. Trademark rights are granted only when the term in question assumes certain affirmative characteristics (if they act as source-identifiers); absent such characteristics, the mark is insufficiently important to protect, because protecting it would restrain the use by others for no gain in terms of informational shortcuts. Similarly, some marks or devices are too important to protect by trademark, either because their allocation to a single market participant would be anticompetitive or would collide with other important values such as the First Amendment or the integrity of the patent system. The domain name, as we saw above, is not nearly as cautious. It dispenses rights with abandon.

The clash between these two systems could be dealt with simply by assimilating one system to the other. . . Alternatively, . . .one may recognize that the domain name system and the trademark system can operate in tandem: first, by assigning domain names on a basis designed to facilitate Internet development; and second, by applying trademark principles to acts of domain name registration that impact trademark rights. The initial response of courts in the United States to the clash between domain name owners and mark owners has mirrored this approach. Courts have used not only classical principles of trademark law but also trademark dilution protection. With respect to the latter, the courts have interpreted the federal dilution statute in ways that have had the effect of protecting trademark rights broadly in the digital environment. It was only later that Congress, through specific federal legislation, enacted separate rights specifically designed to protect mark owners against cybersquatting.

A claim for trademark infringement or dilution requires that the defendant has used the mark within the meaning of the Lanham Act. Although registration of a domain name does not of itself constitute use in commerce, early U.S. courts addressing domain name/trade-mark conflicts stretched the notion of use in commerce to cover egregious cybersquatting activities.[67] The lack of any real use made it difficult to fashion a claim of consumer confusion (although clearly such a claim is possible where the domain name registrant uses the name). And, early on, courts seized on a single line of the legislative history of the federal dilution statute[68] to support the notion that the dilution law enacted in 1995 was aimed in part at abusive domain name registration--without any real consideration of whether the particular mark in question was famous, or whether the use in question diluted the distinctiveness of the mark, both of which (along with use in commerce) are prerequisites for a dilution claim. Indeed, this trend was so pervasive that some commentators started to reconceptualize dilution case law as covering three cases:

---

[67]See, e.g., Panavision Int'l, L.P. v. Toeppen, 141 F.3d 1316, 1325 (9th Cir. 1998) (holding that the offer to sell domain names to trademark owners whose marks were incorporated in the domain names was use in commerce).

[68]See 141 Cong. Rec. S19312 (daily ed. Dec. 29, 1995) (statement of Sen. Leahy) ("[I]t is my hope that this antidilution statute can help stem the use of deceptive Internet addresses taken by those who are choosing marks that are associated with the products and reputations of others.").

tarnishment, blurring, and cybersquatting. Despite these largely pro-mark owner developments—and perhaps to avoid this level of creativity in adjudication—the new legislation (the Anticybersquatting Consumer Protection Act) creates a cause of action based on bad faith registration of a domain name that is identical or confusingly similar to the plaintiff's trademark (without any requirement of famousness, consumer confusion, dilution, or use in commerce).[71] It also introduced an action *in rem* against the domain name, which is intended to address (and is limited to) the situation where the defendant is not subject to the personal jurisdiction of the U.S. courts.

NOTES AND QUESTIONS

(1) **Assimilation of Systems.** What would be involved in assimilating the U.S. trademark system to the domain name registration system? What advantages would that realize? Would it generate any costs? Alternatively, how would one change the domain name registration system to make it more like U.S. trademark law? Would you support such changes? Is assimilation of the two systems a solution to the difficulties discussed in the excerpt? What policy objectives should one consider in making that decision?

(2) **Cyber-Consumers.** Professor Dinwoodie suggests that the use of trademarks as part of domain names means that "the courts must construct a cyberconsumer, whose purchasing and browsing habits clearly encompass the use of domain names as well as trademarks in the searching process." In what ways is a "cyberconsumer" different from an offline consumer? How do domain names figure in consumer behavior? What role do domain names play in producer behavior? Should trademark law seek to shape these behaviors and, if so, how? Reconsider your answers after reading the next excerpt.

[B] Treatment of the Conflict Under General Principles of Trademark Law

Brookfield Comms., Inc. v. West Coast Ent. Corp., 174 F.3d 1036 (9th Cir. 1999).

[The plaintiff (Brookfield) owned a federal trademark registration on the mark "Moviebuff" for software featuring a searchable database of entertainment-industry related information. It first used the mark in 1993. In 1996, the plaintiff sought to register "moviebuff.com" as a domain name with Network Solutions, Inc. (NSI), but the requested domain name had already been registered by West Coast Entertainment Corp. West Coast claimed that it chose the domain name because the term "Movie Buff" is part of its service

----

[71]In the case of famous marks, protection extends against acts of bad faith registration of a domain name that is dilutive of the famous mark. *See* 15 U.S.C.A. § 1125(d) (West Supp. 2000).

mark, "The Movie Buff's Movie Store," on which a federal registration issued in 1991 covering "retail store services featuring video cassettes and video game cartridges" and "rental of video cassettes and video game cartridges." West Coast has since 1986 also used various other phrases including the term "Movie Buff" to promote goods and services available at its video stores in Massachusetts, including "The Movie Buff's Gift Guide"; "The Movie Buff's Gift Store"; "Calling All Movie Buffs!"; "Good News Movie Buffs!". Brookfield subsequently registered "moviebuffonline.com" with NSI. In October 1998, Brookfield learned that West Coast intended to launch a web site at "moviebuff.com" containing, inter alia, a searchable entertainment database similar to MovieBuff. Brookfield filed suit alleging that West Coast's proposed offering of online services at "moviebuff.com" would constitute trademark infringement and unfair competition in violation of sections 32 and 43(a) of the Lanham Act. The Court outlined the traditional eight factors used for guidance in determining likelihood of confusion, in the Ninth Circuit these being known as the *Sleekcraft* factors. The Court began its analysis by issuing a word of caution: "this eight-factor test for likelihood of confusion is pliant. Some factors are much more important than others, and the relative importance of each individual factor will be case-specific. . . . Moreover, the foregoing list does not purport to be exhaustive, and non-listed variables may often be quite important. We must be acutely aware of excessive rigidity when applying the law in the Internet context; emerging technologies require a flexible approach." An excerpt from the court's analysis of the question of likely confusion follows.]

In the present case, the district court found West Coast's domain name "moviebuff.com" to be quite different than Brookfield's domain name "moviebuffonline.com." Comparison of domain names, however, is irrelevant as a matter of law, since the Lanham Act requires that the allegedly infringing mark be compared with the claimant's trademark, which here is "MovieBuff," not "moviebuffonline.com." Properly framed, it is readily apparent that West Coast's allegedly infringing mark is essentially identical to Brookfield's mark "MovieBuff."" In terms of appearance, there are differences in capitalization and the addition of .com in West Coast's complete domain name, but these differences are inconsequential in light of the fact that Web addresses are not caps-sensitive and that the .com top-level domain signifies the site's commercial nature.

Looks aren't everything, so we consider the similarity of sound and meaning. The two marks are pronounced the same way, except that one would say "dot com" at the end of West Coast's mark. Because many companies use domain names comprised of .com as the top-level domain with their corporate name or trademark as the second-level domain, [cit], the addition of .com is of diminished importance in distinguishing the mark. The irrelevance of the .com becomes further apparent once we consider similarity in meaning. The domain name is more than a mere address: like trademarks, second-level domain names communicate information as to source. [M]any Web users are likely to associate "moviebuff.com" with the trademark "MovieBuff," thinking that it is operated by the company that makes "MovieBuff" products and services.[4] Courts, in fact, have routinely concluded that marks were essentially identical in similar contexts. *See, e.g.,* Public Serv. Co. v. Nexus Energy Software, Inc., 36 F. Supp.2d 436 (D.Mass.1999) (finding "energyplace.com" and "Energy Place" to be virtually identical); Minnesota Mining & Mfg. Co. v. Taylor, 21 F. Supp.2d 1003, 1005 (D. Minn.1998) (finding "post-it.com" and "Post-It" to be the same); [cit]. As "MovieBuff" and "moviebuff.com" are, for all intents and purposes, identical in terms of sight, sound, and meaning, we conclude that the similarity factor weighs heavily in favor of Brookfield.[5]

The similarity of marks alone, . . .does not necessarily lead to consumer confusion. Accordingly, we must proceed to consider the relatedness of the products and services offered. . . . A Web surfer who accessed "moviebuff.com" and reached a web site advertising the services of Schlumberger Ltd. (a large oil drilling company) would be unlikely to think that Brookfield had entered the oil drilling business or was sponsoring the oil driller. [cit]. At the least, Brookfield would bear the heavy burden of demonstrating (through other relevant factors) that consumers were likely to be confused as to source or affiliation in such a circumstance.

The district court classified West Coast and Brookfield as non-competitors largely on the basis that Brookfield is primarily an information provider while West Coast primarily rents and sells videotapes. . . [But here] both companies offer products and services relating to the entertainment industry generally, and their principal lines of business both relate to movies specifically . . . .Thus, Brookfield and West Coast are not properly characterized as non-competitors.

Not only are they not non-competitors, the competitive proximity of their products is actually quite high. Just as Brookfield's "MovieBuff" is a searchable database with detailed information on films, West Coast's web site features a similar searchable database, which Brookfield points out is licensed from a direct competitor of Brookfield. Undeniably then, the products are used for similar purposes. . . . The relatedness is further evidenced by the fact that the two companies compete for the patronage of an overlapping audience. . . .

In addition to the relatedness of products, West Coast and Brookfield both utilize the Web as a marketing and advertising facility, a factor that courts have consistently recognized as exacerbating the likelihood of confusion. [cit]. Both companies, apparently recognizing the rapidly growing importance of Web commerce, are maneuvering to attract customers via the Web. Not only do they compete for the patronage of an overlapping audience on the Web, both "MovieBuff" and "moviebuff.com" are utilized in conjunction with Web-based products.

Given the virtual identity of "moviebuff.com" and "MovieBuff," the relatedness

---

[4]In an analogous context, courts have granted trademark protection to phone numbers that spell out a corporation's name, trademark, or slogan. *See* Dial-A-Mattress Franchise Corp. v. Page, 880 F.2d 675, 677-78 (2d Cir.1989) (granting trademark protection to "(area code)-MATTRES"); [cit].

[5]The fact that West Coast's second-level domain is exactly the same as Brookfield's mark is particularly important since potential customers of "MovieBuff" will go to "moviebuff.com," and not, for example, "moviebuffs.com." Had West Coast used the latter mark, the similarity factor would have favored Brookfield to a lesser extent.

of the products and services accompanied by those marks, and the companies' simultaneous use of the Web as a marketing and advertising tool, many forms of consumer confusion are likely to result. People surfing the Web for information on "MovieBuff" may confuse "MovieBuff" with the searchable entertainment database at "moviebuff.com" and simply assume that they have reached Brookfield's web site. [cit]. In the Internet context, in particular, entering a web site takes little effort—usually one click from a linked site or a search engine's list; thus, Web surfers are more likely to be confused as to the ownership of a web site than traditional patrons of a brick-and-mortar store would be of a store's ownership. Alternatively, they may incorrectly believe that West Coast licensed "MovieBuff" from Brookfield, [cit], or that Brookfield otherwise sponsored West Coast's database. [cit]. Other consumers may simply believe that West Coast bought out Brookfield or that they are related companies.

Yet other forms of confusion are likely to ensue. Consumers may wrongly assume that the "MovieBuff" database they were searching for is no longer offered, having been replaced by West Coast's entertainment database, and thus simply use the services at West Coast's web site. [cit]. And even where people realize, immediately upon accessing "moviebuff.com," that they have reached a site operated by West Coast and wholly unrelated to Brookfield, West Coast will still have gained a customer by appropriating the goodwill that Brookfield has developed in its "MovieBuff" mark. A consumer who was originally looking for Brookfield's products or services may be perfectly content with West Coast's database (especially as it is offered free of charge); but he reached West Coast's site because of its use of Brookfield's mark as its second-level domain name, which is a misappropriation of Brookfield's goodwill by West Coast.

[The Court also considered the remaining factors, and concluded that they supported a finding of likely confusion.]

We thus turn to intent. . . . The district court found that the intent factor favored West Coast because it did not adopt the "moviebuff.com" mark with the specific purpose of infringing Brookfield's trademark. The intent prong, however, is not so narrowly confined.

This factor favors the plaintiff where the alleged infringer adopted his mark with knowledge, actual or constructive, that it was another's trademark. [cit]. In the Internet context, in particular, courts have appropriately recognized that the intentional registration of a domain name knowing that the second-level domain is another company's valuable trademark weighs in favor of likelihood of confusion. [cit]. There is, however, no evidence in the record that West Coast registered "moviebuff.com" with the principal intent of confusing consumers. Brookfield correctly points out that, by the time West Coast launched its web site, it did know of Brookfield's claim to rights in the trademark "MovieBuff." But when it registered the domain name with Network Solutions, West Coast did not know of Brookfield's rights in "MovieBuff" (at least Brookfield has not established that it did). Although Brookfield asserts that West Coast could easily have launched its web site at its alternate domain address, "westcoastvideo.com," thereby avoiding the infringement problem, West Coast claims that it had already invested considerable sums in developing its "moviebuff.com" web site by the time that Brookfield informed it of its rights in the trademark. Considered as a whole, this factor appears indeterminate.

[The Court concluded that the final three *Sleekcraft* factors—evidence of actual confusion, likelihood of expansion in product lines, and purchaser care—did not affect the ultimate conclusion regarding the likelihood of confusion, namely that Brookfield has demonstrated a likelihood of success on its claim that West Coast's use of "moviebuff.com" violates the Lanham Act.]

NOTES AND QUESTIONS

(1) **Actionable Confusion.** Did the *Brookfield* court accurately describe the habits of a cyberconsumer? How should those habits be determined? Do you agree that West Coast's use of the domain name moviebuff.com would likely result in each of the different types of confusion envisaged by the court? Should each of these types of confusion be actionable under the Lanham Act? One form of confusion that, if treated as actionable, enhances the rights of the trademark owner is "initial interest confusion." This occurs where a consumer's attraction to the good is induced by confusing similarity even though upon closer inspection the consumer will not be confused as to the source of the respective goods. The Ninth Circuit has recognized that the use of another's trademark in a manner calculated "to capture initial consumer attention, even though no actual sale is finally completed as a result of the confusion, may be still an infringement." Might there be a need to limit the application of this doctrine in the domain name context?

(2) **Tacking.** The court rejected West Coast's claims that it was the senior user by virtue of its service mark registration "The Movie Buff's Movie Store". The court acknowledged "the ability of a trademark owner to claim priority in a mark based on the first use date of a similar, but technically distinct, mark—but only in the exceptionally narrow instance where the previously used mark is 'the legal equivalent of the mark in question or indistinguishable therefrom' such that consumers consider both as the same mark." But the court held that the standard for "tacking" (which this is called) is exceedingly strict: "The marks must create the same, continuing commercial impression, and the later mark should not materially differ from or alter the character of the mark attempted to be tacked." Here, the court concluded that "'The Movie Buff's Movie Store' and 'moviebuff.com' are very different, in that the latter contains three fewer words, drops the possessive, omits a space, and adds .com to the end," and because there was no showing that consumers view the terms as identical, West Coast could not tack its priority in "The Movie Buff's Movie Store" onto "moviebuff.com." What is the purpose of tacking? Should the standard for its application be modified in the domain name context?

(3) **Different Top Level Domains.** If West Coast had registered the domain name moviebuff.net, would that alter your analysis of whether a trademark infringement had occurred? *See* Avery Dennison Corp. v. Sumpton, 189 F.3d 868 (9th Cir. 1999). What about moviebuff.co.uk? Would your answer to this last question depend upon the ownership of the U.K. trademark registration?

YAHOO! INC. v. AKASH ARORA

[1999] F.S.R. 931 (High Court of Delhi 1999) (India)

The present suit has been instituted by the plaintiff against the defendants seeking a decree of [interim and] permanent injunction restraining the defendants . . . from operating any business and/or selling, offering for sale, advertising and in any manner dealing in any services or goods on the Internet or otherwise under the trademark/domain name "Yahooindia.Com" or any other mark/domain name which is identical with or deceptively similar to the plaintiff's trademark "Yahoo!" and also for rendition of accounts and damages.

[T]he plaintiff submitted that [it] is the owner of the trademark "Yahoo!" and domain name "Yahoo.com", which are very well-known and have acquired distinctive reputation and goodwill and the defendants by adopting the name "Yahooindia" for similar services have been passing off the services and goods of the defendants [because that name is] identical to, or deceptively similar to, the plaintiff's trademark. It was submitted that a domain name/trademark adopted by the plaintiff is entitled to equal protection against passing off as in the case of a trademark. . . . It was submitted that the trademarks and domain names are not mutually exclusive and there is an overlap between the trademarks and services rendered under domain names and thus by adopting a deceptively similar trademark "Yahooindia", the defendants have verbatim copied the format, contents, lay out, colour scheme, source code of the plaintiff's prior created regional section on India at Yahoo.com.sg and thus passing off the services of the defendants as that of the plaintiff. [Counsel for plaintiff] submitted that Internet users are familiar with the practice of companies to select domain names that incorporate their company name, well-known trademark, and/or product/service name and generally attempt to locate a particular company's Web site by simply typing in www.(company name).com or www.(product name).com when they are unsure of the Internet address of the Company. According to him, thus, it would not be unusual for someone looking for an authorised "Yahoo!" site with India-specific content to type in "Yahooindia.com" i.e., the defendants' domain name and thereby instead of reaching the Internet site of the plaintiff, the said person would reach the Internet site of the defendants. He further submitted that the plaintiff in fact provides extensive content on India, both on its Yahoo! Asia site and at its main Yahoo.com site, under the categories "Regional:Countries:India". It was submitted that the defendants being in the same line of activity as that of the plaintiff, the defendants have tried to be cybersquatters and, thus, dishonesty is writ large as the defendants have adopted a trademark similar to that of the plaintiff which is "Yahoo.com" which has acquired a distinctive name, goodwill and reputation.

. . . .

The domain name "Yahoo.com" is registered in the plaintiff's favour with Network Solution Inc since 18th January, 1995. The trademark "Yahoo!" and its variance are registered or pending registration in 69 countries of the world. As is disclosed from the records, an application for registration of the trademark of the plaintiff "Yahoo!" is also pending in India. The plaintiff is a global

Internet media rendering services under the domain name/trade name "Yahoo!".... The plaintiff, it is stated, was amongst the first in the field to have a domain name "Yahoo" and also to start a web directory and provide search services....

....

The services of the plaintiff under the trademark/domain name "Yahoo!" have been widely publicised and written about globally. In an Internet service, a particular Internet site could be reached by anyone anywhere in the world who proposes to visit the said Internet site. With the advancement and progress in technology, services rendered in the Internet have also come to be recognised and accepted and are being given protection so as to protect such provider of services from passing off the services rendered by others as that of the plaintiff. As a matter of fact in a matter where services are rendered through the domain name in the Internet, a very alert vigil is necessary and a strict view is to be taken for its easy access and reach by anyone from any corner of the globe. There can be no two opinions that the two marks/domain names "Yahoo!" of the plaintiff and "Yahooindia" of the defendant are almost similar except for use of the suffix "India" in the latter. The degree of the similarity of the marks usually is vitally important and significant in an action for passing off for in such a case there is every possibility and likelihood of confusion and deception being caused. When both the domain names are considered, it is crystal clear that the two names being almost identical or similar in nature, there is every possibility of an Internet user being confused and deceived in believing that both the domain names belong to one common source and connection, although the two belong to two different concerns.

Counsel for the defendant also argued that the Internet users are sophisticated users and only literate people who are able to ascertain can approach the actual Internet site that they intend to visit. The said submission does not appear to have force for even if an individual is a sophisticated user of the Internet, he may be an unsophisticated consumer of information and such a person may find his/her way to the defendant Internet site which provides almost similar type of information as that of the plaintiff and thereby confusion could be created in the mind of the said person who intends to visit the Internet site of the plaintiff, but, in fact reaches the Internet site of the defendant.

....

... Besides, the plaintiff itself is using regional names after Yahoo! like Yahoo.ca (for Canada) and Yahoo.fr (for France). Thus, there is every possibility of the Internet users to believe that "Yahooindia" is another one in the series of Yahoo marks/names and thereby there is every possibility of confusion being created and thereby preventing these users from reaching the Internet site of the plaintiff.

....

The defence as raised in the present suit by the defendants is, therefore, prima facie found to be without any merit.... In my considered opinion and as discussed above, the plaintiff has been able to make out a prima facie case for grant of ad interim injunction in its favour and, therefore, an ad interim injunction is passed in favour of the plaintiff....

NOTE: DOMAIN NAME LITIGATION IN CHINA

The courts in China have recently begun to provide quite strong protection against cybersquatting. On June 20, 2000, Beijing No. 2 Intermediate People's Court IP Chamber upheld a complaint by the Swedish furniture retailer IKEA and ruled that the domain name registration www.ikea.com.cn was null and void, and ordered the defendant (CINET) to withdraw the registration. This was the first domain name dispute in China involving a foreign party, and the first court judgment in favor of a trademark owner against a cybersquatter. The court found the mark IKEA to be well-known by virtue of the Swedish company's sales in 29 countries, worldwide advertising and trademark registrations in many countries, and that the registration of the domain name by CINET would be misleading. The court also found the registration by CINET to be in bad faith, largely as a result of their registration of a number of domain names without having used them. As a result, although the court noted no specific law in China governing disputes between trademarks and domain names, it applied the "spirit and principles" of the law, and found that the defendant had violated the spirit of the Paris Convention and the basic principles of the unfair competition law. *See China IP Express*, No. 24 (June 22, 2000) (Rouse & Co.). Cinet also lost another case four days later when Procter & Gamble (owner of the mark WHISPER) persuaded the same court to issue an injunction against that company's registration of www.whisper.com.cn. In addition to the injunction, the court awarded damages of $2,5000 and court fees. (The damages covered attorneys' fees and translation costs). Both the injunction and the damages award were issued from the bench during the first hearing in the case. The court's reasoning tracked that of the court in the *IKEA* case, but additionally noted that the defendant had violated the Interim Rules for the Registration and Administration of Chinese Domain Names. *See China IP Express*, No. 26 (July 7, 2000) (Rouse & Co.).

[C] Proceedings Before ICANN Panels

[1] The Internet Corporation for Assigned Names and Numbers (ICANN)

The Internet Corporation for Assigned Names and Numbers (ICANN) is now the de facto manager of the most commercially important internet domain names. ICANN is a not-for-profit corporation that was created by the U.S. government to operate the domain name system, among other things, in accordance with parameters set by the Commerce Department in a memorandum of understanding with ICANN. *See* Management of Internet Names and Addresses, 63 Fed. Reg. 31,741 (June 10, 1998). An important aspect of the Commerce Department strategy was the creation of competition among registrars in the principal generic top level domains. ICANN authorizes individual registrars to issue domain names in the principal generic top level domain names, and the administration of country code top level domains is delegated by ICANN to authorities ("managers") in the relevant country. Based upon this very brief description of ICANN, what problems or concerns might you expect ICANN and ICANN-based lawmaking to encounter, and how might these be addressed?

[2] The First WIPO Domain Name Process

FINAL REPORT OF THE WIPO INTERNET DOMAIN NAME PROCESS (EXECUTIVE SUMMARY, APRIL 30, 1999)
http://ecommerce.wipo.int/domains/process/eng/final_report.html

Background

On the proposal of the Government of the United States of America, and with the approval of its Member States, WIPO has since July 1998 undertaken an extensive international process of consultations ("the WIPO Process"). The purpose of the WIPO Process was to make recommendations to the corporation established to manage the domain name system, the Internet Corporation for Assigned Names and Numbers (ICANN), on certain questions arising out of the interface between domain names and intellectual property rights. Seventeen consultation meetings were held in 15 different cities throughout the world in the course of the WIPO Process, and written submissions were received from 334 governments, intergovernmental organizations, professional associations, corporation and individuals.

An Interim Report containing draft recommendations was issued in December 1998 as part of the WIPO Process. The present document constitutes the Final Report. It is being submitted to ICANN and to the Member States of WIPO. The main recommendations in the Final Report are summarized below.

. . . .

Administrative Procedure Concerning Abusive Domain Name Registrations

(v) ICANN should adopt a dispute-resolution policy under which a uniform administrative dispute-resolution procedure is made available for domain name disputes in all generic top level domains (gTLDs). In the Interim Report, it was recommended that domain name applicants should be required to submit to the procedure in respect of any intellectual property dispute arising out of a domain name registration. The Final Report recommends that the scope of the administrative procedure be limited to cases of bad faith, abusive registration of domain names that violate trademark rights ("cybersquatting," in popular terminology). Domain name holders would thus be required to submit to the administrative procedure only in respect of allegations that they are involved in cybersquatting, which was universally condemned throughout the WIPO Process as an indefensible activity that should be suppressed.

(vi) The administrative procedure would be quick, efficient, cost-effective and conducted to a large extent on-line. Determinations under it would be limited to orders for the cancellation or transfer of domain name registrations . . . Determinations would be enforced by registration authorities under the dispute-resolution policy.

Exclusions for Famous and Well-known Marks

(vii) Famous and well-known marks have been the special target of predatory and parasitical practices on the part of a small, but active, minority of domain name registrants. A mechanism should be introduced whereby the owner of a famous or well-known mark can obtain an exclusion in some or all gTLDs for the name of the mark where the mark is famous or well-known on a widespread geographical basis and across different classes of goods or services. The effect of the exclusion would be to prohibit any person other than the owner of the famous or well-known mark from registering the mark as a domain name.

(viii) The exclusion mechanism gives expression in cyberspace to the special protection that is established for famous and well-known marks in the Paris Convention for the Protection of Industrial Property and the TRIPS Agreement.

(ix) Since an exclusion would cover only the exact name of the famous or well-known mark, and since experience shows that cybersquatters typically register many close variations of famous or well-known marks, an exclusion, once granted, should give rise to an evidentiary presumption in the administrative procedure. The effect of the evidentiary presumption would [be] to place the burden of proving justification for the use of a domain name on the domain name holder where the domain name is identical or misleadingly similar to the famous or well-known mark and the domain name is being used in a way that is likely to damage the interests of the owner of the mark.

New gTLDs

(x) The evidence shows that the experience of the last five years in gTLDs has led to numerous instances of abusive domain name registrations and, consequently, to consumer confusion and an undermining of public trust in the Internet. It has also led to the necessity for intellectual property owners to invest substantial human and financial resources in defending their interests. This arguably wasteful diversion of economic resources can be averted by the adoption of the improved registration practices, administrative dispute-resolution procedure and exclusion mechanism recommended in the Final Report of the WIPO Process.

(xi) In view of past experience, intellectual property owners are very apprehensive about the introduction of new gTLDs and the possible repetition in the new gTLDs of that experience.

(xii) Many issues other than intellectual property protection are involved in the formulation of a policy on the introduction of new gTLDs. Insofar as intellectual property is concerned, it is believed that the introduction of new gTLDs may be envisaged on the condition that the recommendations of the WIPO Final Report with respect to improved registration practices, dispute resolution and an exclusion mechanism for famous and well-known marks are adopted, and on the further condition that any new gTLDs are introduced in a slow and controlled manner that allows for experience with the new gTLDs to be monitored and evaluated.

First Steps and Outstanding Issues

The recommendations of the Final Report of the WIPO Process have been directed at the most egregious problems between intellectual property and domain names and at obtaining effective solutions to those problems. Other issues remain outstanding and require further reflection and consultation.

[3] The Uniform Domain Name Dispute Resolution Policy (the "UDRP")

ICANN adopted a Uniform Domain Name Dispute Resolution Policy on August 26, 1999. The policy went into effect on December 1, 1999 for all then-accredited registrars, with the exception of America On-line, the N@me IT Corp. and Network Solutions, Inc., which had to comply as of January 3, 2000. All later-accredited registrars are required to adopt the policy. The policy essentially adopts the recommendations made in the Final Report of the WIPO Internet Domain Name Process, although the Report's proposal with respect to an exclusionary form of protection for famous marks was not adopted.

UNIFORM DOMAIN NAME DISPUTE RESOLUTION POLICY
(Approved by ICANN on October 24, 1999)

1. Purpose. This Uniform Domain Name Dispute Resolution Policy (the "Policy") has been adopted by the Internet Corporation for Assigned Names and Numbers ("ICANN"), is incorporated by reference into your Registration Agreement, and sets forth the terms and conditions in connection with a dispute between you and any party other than us (the registrar) over the registration and use of an Internet domain name registered by you. Proceedings under Paragraph 4 of this Policy will be conducted according to the Rules for Uniform Domain Name Dispute Resolution Policy (the "Rules of Procedure"), available at www.icann.org/udrp/udrp-rules-24oct99.htm, and the selected administrative-dispute-resolution service provider's supplemental rules.

2. Your Representations. By applying to register a domain name, or by asking us to maintain or renew a domain name registration, you hereby represent and warrant to us that (a) the statements that you made in your Registration Agreement are complete and accurate; (b) to your knowledge, the registration of the domain name will not infringe upon or otherwise violate the rights of any third party; (c) you are not registering the domain name for an unlawful purpose; and (d) you will not knowingly use the domain name in violation of any

applicable laws or regulations. It is your responsibility to determine whether your domain name registration infringes or violates someone else's rights.

3. Cancellations, Transfers, and Changes. We will cancel, transfer or otherwise make changes to domain name registrations under the following circumstances:

a. subject to the provisions of Paragraph 8, our receipt of written or appropriate electronic instructions from you or your authorized agent to take such action;

b. our receipt of an order from a court or arbitral tribunal, in each case of competent jurisdiction, requiring such action; and/or

c. our receipt of a decision of an Administrative Panel requiring such action in any administrative proceeding to which you were a party and which was conducted under this Policy or a later version of this Policy adopted by ICANN. (See Paragraph 4(i) and (k) below.)

We may also cancel, transfer or otherwise make changes to a domain name registration in accordance with the terms of your Registration Agreement or other legal requirements.

4. Mandatory Administrative Proceeding. This Paragraph sets forth the type of disputes for which you are required to submit to a mandatory administrative proceeding. These proceedings will be conducted before one of the administrative-dispute-resolution service providers listed at www.icann.org/udrp/approved-providers.htm (each a "Provider").

a. Applicable Disputes. You are required to submit to a mandatory administrative proceeding in the event that a third party (a "complainant") asserts to the applicable Provider, in compliance with the Rules of Procedure, that

(i) your domain name is identical or confusingly similar to a trademark or service mark in which the complainant has rights; and

(ii) you have no rights or legitimate interests in respect of the domain name; and

(iii) your domain name has been registered and is being used in bad faith.

In the administrative proceeding, the complainant must prove that each of these three elements are present.

b. Evidence of Registration and Use in Bad Faith. For the purposes of Paragraph 4(a)(iii), the following circumstances, in particular but without limitation, if found by the Panel to be present, shall be evidence of the registration and use of a domain name in bad faith:

(i) circumstances indicating that you have registered or you have acquired the domain name primarily for the purpose of selling, renting, or otherwise transferring the domain name registration to the complainant who is the owner of the trademark or service mark or to a competitor of that complainant, for valuable consideration in excess of your documented out-of-pocket costs directly related to the domain name; or

(ii) you have registered the domain name in order to prevent the owner of the trademark or service mark from reflecting the mark in a corresponding domain name, provided that you have engaged in a pattern of such conduct; or

(iii) you have registered the domain name primarily for the purpose of disrupting the business of a competitor; or

(iv) by using the domain name, you have intentionally attempted to attract, for commercial gain, Internet users to your web site or other on-line location, by creating a likelihood of confusion with the complainant's mark as to the source, sponsorship, affiliation, or endorsement of your web site or location or of a product or service on your web site or location.

c. How to Demonstrate Your Rights to and Legitimate Interests in the Domain Name in Responding to a Complaint. When you receive a complaint, you should refer to Paragraph 5 of the Rules of Procedure in determining how your response should be prepared. Any of the following circumstances, in particular but without limitation, if found by the Panel to be proved based on its evaluation of all evidence presented, shall demonstrate your rights or legitimate interests to the domain name for purposes of Paragraph 4(a)(ii):

(i) before any notice to you of the dispute, your use of, or demonstrable preparations to use, the domain name or a name corresponding to the domain name in connection with a bona fide offering of goods or services; or

(ii) you (as an individual, business, or other organization) have been commonly known by the domain name, even if you have acquired no trademark or service mark rights; or

(iii) you are making a legitimate noncommercial or fair use of the domain name, without intent for commercial gain to misleadingly divert consumers or to tarnish the trademark or service mark at issue.

d. Selection of Provider. The complainant shall select the Provider from among those approved by ICANN by submitting the complaint to that Provider. The selected Provider will administer the proceeding, except in cases of consolidation as described in Paragraph 4(f).

e. Initiation of Proceeding and Process and Appointment of Administrative Panel. The Rules of Procedure state the process for initiating and conducting a proceeding and for appointing the panel that will decide the dispute (the "Administrative Panel").

f. Consolidation. In the event of multiple disputes between you and a complainant, either you or the complainant may petition to consolidate the disputes before a single Administrative Panel. This petition shall be made to the first Administrative Panel appointed to hear a pending dispute between the parties. This Administrative Panel may consolidate before it any or all such disputes in its sole discretion, provided that the disputes being consolidated are governed by this Policy or a later version of this Policy adopted by ICANN.

g. Fees. All fees charged by a Provider in connection with any dispute before an Administrative Panel pursuant to this Policy shall be paid by the complainant, except in cases where you elect to expand the Administrative Panel from one to three panelists as provided in Paragraph 5(b)(iv) of the Rules of Procedure, in which case all fees will be split evenly by you and the complainant.

h. <u>Our Involvement in Administrative Proceedings</u>. We do not, and will not, participate in the administration or conduct of any proceeding before an Administrative Panel. In addition, we will not be liable as a result of any decisions rendered by the Administrative Panel.

i. <u>Remedies</u>. The remedies available to a complainant pursuant to any proceeding before an Administrative Panel shall be limited to requiring the cancellation of your domain name or the transfer of your domain name registration to the complainant.

j. <u>Notification and Publication</u>. The Provider shall notify us of any decision made by an Administrative Panel with respect to a domain name you have registered with us. All decisions under this Policy will be published in full over the Internet, except when an Administrative Panel determines in an exceptional case to redact portions of its decision.

k. <u>Availability of Court Proceedings</u>. The mandatory administrative proceeding requirements set forth in Paragraph 4 shall not prevent either you or the complainant from submitting the dispute to a court of competent jurisdiction for independent resolution before such mandatory administrative proceeding is commenced or after such proceeding is concluded. If an Administrative Panel decides that your domain name registration should be canceled or transferred, we will wait ten (10) business days (as observed in the location of our principal office) after we are informed by the applicable Provider of the Administrative Panel's decision before implementing that decision. We will then implement the decision unless we have received from you during that ten (10) business day period official documentation (such as a copy of a complaint, file-stamped by the clerk of the court) that you have commenced a lawsuit against the complainant in a jurisdiction to which the complainant has submitted under Paragraph 3(b)(xiii) of the Rules of Procedure. (In general, that jurisdiction is either the location of our principal office or of your address as shown in our Whois database. See Paragraphs 1 and 3(b)(xiii) of the Rules of Procedure for details.) If we receive such documentation within the ten (10) business day period, we will not implement the Administrative Panel's decision, and we will take no further action, until we receive (i) evidence satisfactory to us of a resolution between the parties; (ii) evidence satisfactory to us that your lawsuit has been dismissed or withdrawn; or (iii) a copy of an order from such court dismissing your lawsuit or ordering that you do not have the right to continue to use your domain name.

5. <u>All Other Disputes and Litigation</u>. All other disputes between you and any party other than us regarding your domain name registration that are not brought pursuant to the mandatory administrative proceeding provisions of Paragraph 4 shall be resolved between you and such other party through any court, arbitration or other proceeding that may be available.

6. <u>Our Involvement in Disputes</u>. We will not participate in any way in any dispute between you and any party other than us regarding the registration and

use of your domain name. You shall not name us as a party or otherwise include us in any such proceeding. In the event that we are named as a party in any such proceeding, we reserve the right to raise any and all defenses deemed appropriate, and to take any other action necessary to defend ourselves.

7. Maintaining the Status Quo. We will not cancel, transfer, activate, deactivate, or otherwise change the status of any domain name registration under this Policy except as provided in Paragraph 3 above.

8. Transfers During a Dispute.

    a. Transfers of a Domain Name to a New Holder. You may not transfer your domain name registration to another holder (i) during a pending administrative proceeding brought pursuant to Paragraph 4 or for a period of fifteen (15) business days (as observed in the location of our principal place of business) after such proceeding is concluded; or (ii) during a pending court proceeding or arbitration commenced regarding your domain name unless the party to whom the domain name registration is being transferred agrees, in writing, to be bound by the decision of the court or arbitrator. We reserve the right to cancel any transfer of a domain name registration to another holder that is made in violation of this subparagraph.

    b. Changing Registrars. You may not transfer your domain name registration to another registrar during a pending administrative proceeding brought pursuant to Paragraph 4 or for a period of fifteen (15) business days (as observed in the location of our principal place of business) after such proceeding is concluded. You may transfer administration of your domain name registration to another registrar during a pending court action or arbitration, provided that the domain name you have registered with us shall continue to be subject to the proceedings commenced against you in accordance with the terms of this Policy. In the event that you transfer a domain name registration to us during the pendency of a court action or arbitration, such dispute shall remain subject to the domain name dispute policy of the registrar from which the domain name registration was transferred.

9. Policy Modifications. We reserve the right to modify this Policy at any time with the permission of ICANN. We will post our revised Policy at <URL> at least thirty (30) calendar days before it becomes effective. Unless this Policy has already been invoked by the submission of a complaint to a Provider, in which event the version of the Policy in effect at the time it was invoked will apply to you until the dispute is over, all such changes will be binding upon you with respect to any domain name registration dispute, whether the dispute arose before, on or after the effective date of our change. In the event that you object to a change in this Policy, your sole remedy is to cancel your domain name registration with us, provided that you will not be entitled to a refund of any fees you paid to us. The revised Policy will apply to you until you cancel your domain name registration.

The first proceeding under the UDRP was brought on December 9, 1999 and involved the domain name worldwrestlingfederation.com. The panel opinion, issued on January 14, 2000, is excerpted below. ICANN has accredited four dispute-resolution service providers: the WIPO Arbitration and Mediation Center (based in Geneva, Switzerland), the eResolution Consortium (based in Montreal, Canada), the National Arbitration Forum (based in Minneapolis, Minnesota), and the CPR Institute for Dispute Resolution (based in New York, New York). These providers operate under the UDRP, the Rules for Uniform Domain Name Dispute Resolution Policy (promulgated by ICANN and applicable to all dispute resolution service providers) and the separate supplemental rules promulgated by and applicable to each separate provider. During the first fifteen months of the UDRP's operation, over 3400 proceedings, involving over 6000 domain names, have been initiated. Over 2500 decisions have been issued. Every decision is accessible online at the ICANN web site, http://www.icann.org/udrp/udrp.htm, as well as on the web sites of the respective dispute settlement providers. The ICANN web site offers a function to search the panel opinions, and similar searching capacity is offered by the Domain Name Law Reporter at http://dnlr.com/searchindex.html.

WORLD WRESTLING FEDERATION ENTERTAINMENT INC. v. BOSMAN
Case No. D-99-0001 (WIPO Arb. and Mediation Center, 2000)

M. Scott Donahey, Panelist:

1. The Parties

The complainant is World Wrestling Federation Entertainment, Inc., f/k/a Titan Sports, Inc., a corporation organized under the laws of the State of Delaware, United States of America, having its principal place of business at Stamford, Connecticut, United States of America. The respondent is Michael Bosman, an individual resident in Redlands, California, United States of America.

2. The Domain Name(s) and Registrar(s)

The domain name at issue is worldwrestlingfederation.com, which domain name is registered with MelbourneIT, based in Australia.

3. Procedural History

A Complaint was submitted electronically to the World Intellectual Property Organization Arbitration and Mediation Center (the "WIPO Center") on December 2, 1999, and the signed original together with four copies forwarded by express courier under cover of a letter of the same date. . . .

On December 3, 1999 a Request for Registrar Verification was transmitted to the registrar, Melbourne IT requesting it to [confirm the current registrant of the domain name, and the email address(es) available in the registrar's Whois database for the registrant of the disputed domain name, the technical contact, the administrative contact and the billing contact].

On December 8, 1999, MelbourneIT confirmed by reply e-mail that the domain name worldwrestlingfederation.com is registered with MelbourneIT and that the respondent, Michael Bosman, was the current registrant of the name. The registrar also forwarded the requested Whois details, as well as copies of the registration agreement and applicable dispute resolution policy.

The policy in effect at the time of the original registration of the domain name at issue provided that "Registrant agrees to be bound by the terms and conditions of this Registration Agreement" [which] provides in pertinent part:

> Registrant agrees, as a condition to submitting this Registration Agreement, and if the Registration Agreement is accepted by MelbourneIT, that the Registrant is bound by MelbourneIT's current Dispute Policy ("Dispute Policy"). Registrant agrees that MelbourneIT, in its sole discretion, may change or modify the Dispute Policy, incorporated by reference herein, at any time. Registrant agrees that Registrant's maintaining the registration of a domain name after changes or modifications to the Dispute Policy become effective constitutes Registrant's continued acceptance of these changes or modifications. Registrant agrees that if Registrant considers any such changes or modifications to be unacceptable, Registrant may request that the domain name be deleted from the domain name database. Registrant agrees that any dispute relating to the registration or use of its domain name will be subject to the provisions specified in the Dispute Policy.

Effective December 1, 1999, MelbourneIT adopted the [UDRP]. There is no evidence that respondent ever requested that the domain name at issue be deleted from the domain name database. Accordingly, respondent is bound by the provisions of the Policy.

. . . .

A Formal Requirements Compliance Checklist was completed by the assigned WIPO Center Case Administrator on December 8, 1999. The Panel has independently determined and agrees with the assessment of the WIPO Center that the Complaint is in formal compliance with the requirements of the Policy, the Rules for Uniform Domain Name Dispute Resolution Policy, as approved by

ICANN on October 24, 1999 (the "Uniform Rules"), and the WIPO Supplemental Rules for Uniform Domain Dispute Resolution Policy, in effect as of December 1, 1999 (the "WIPO Supplemental Rules"). . . .

No formal deficiencies having been recorded, on December 9, 1999, a Notification of Complaint and Commencement of Administrative Proceeding (the "Commencement Notification") was transmitted to the respondent (with copies to the complainant, MelbourneIT and ICANN), setting a deadline of December 28, 1999, by which the respondent could file a Response to the Complaint. The Commencement Notification was transmitted to the respondent by e-mail to the e-mail addresses indicated in the Complaint and specified in MelbourneIT's Whois confirmation, as well as to postmster@worldwrestlingfederation.com; no e-mail addresses were found at any web page relating to the disputed domain name. In addition, the complaint was sent by express courier to all available postal addresses. Having reviewed the communications records in the case file, the Administrative Panel finds that the WIPO Center has discharged its responsibility under Paragraph 2(a) of the Uniform Rules "to employ reasonably available means calculated to achieve actual notice to Respondent." In any event, evidence of proper notice is provided by the evidence in the record of the respondent's participation in the settlement negotiations with the complainant.

On December 14, 1999, in view of the complainant's designation of a single panelist (but without prejudice to any election to be made by the respondent) the WIPO Center invited M. Scott Donahey to serve as a panelist in Case No. D99-0001, and transmitted to him a Statement of Acceptance and Request for Declaration of Impartiality and Independence.

On December 29, 1999, having received no Response from the designated respondent, using the same contact details and methods as were used for the Commencement Notification, the WIPO Center transmitted to the parties a Notification of Respondent Default.

Having received on December 14, 1999, M. Scott Donahey's Statement of Acceptance and Declaration of Impartiality and Independence, also on December 29, 1999, the WIPO Center transmitted to the parties a Notification of Appointment of Administrative Panel and Projected Decision Date, in which M. Scott Donahey was formally appointed as the Sole Panelist. The Projected Decision Date was January 11, 2000. The Sole Panelist finds that the Administrative Panel was properly constituted and appointed in accordance with the Uniform Rules and WIPO Supplemental Rules.

Following these transmittals, the WIPO Center received a series of emails from the respondent and the complainant's representative, indicating that the parties intended to settle and had reached a settlement in principle. On January 6, 2000, the WIPO Center received a copy of an unsigned settlement agreement, with assurances that a signed copy would be transmitted by facsimile. On January 6, 2000, in view of the settlement negotiations between the parties, the Case Administrator notified the parties that the time in which the Panel was to issue a decision on the merits had been extended to January 15, 2000.

Following repeated requests from the WIPO Center for a copy of the fully executed final settlement agreement, on January 12, 2000, a copy of an agreement, signed only by respondent, was received. While the Panel is aware that the parties are close to completing their settlement, the Panel is also mindful of its responsibility to issue a timely decision, and one in compliance with the deadlines established by the Uniform Rules, the WIPO Supplemental Rules, and those established by the WIPO Center in accordance with those rules. *See, e.g.,* Uniform Rules, paras. 10(c) and 15(b). Accordingly, this decision is issued prior to having received completely executed settlement documents, and, as such, does not rely on any purported settlement agreement.

The Administrative Panel shall issue its Decision based on the Complaint, the e-mails exchanged, the Policy, the Uniform Rules, the WIPO Supplemental Rules, and without the benefit of any Response from respondent.

4. Factual Background

The complainant has provided evidence of the registration of the following marks:

1. Service Mark: WORLD WRESTLING FEDERATION, registered for a term of 20 years from January 29, 1985, with the United States Patent and Trademark Office;

2. Trademark: WORLD WRESTLING FEDERATION, registered for a term of 20 years from November 7, 1989, with the United States Patent and Trademark Office.

The respondent registered the domain name worldwrestlingfederation.com for a term of two years from October 7, 1999. [cit]. The respondent is not a licensee of complainant, nor is he otherwise authorized to use complainant's marks.

. . . .

On October 10, 1999, three days after registering the domain name at issue, respondent contacted complainant by e-mail and notified complainant of the registration and stated that his primary purpose in registering the domain name was to sell, rent or otherwise transfer it to complainant for a valuable consideration in excess of respondent's out-of-pocket expenses. By e-mail dated December 3, 1999, respondent contacted complainant's representative and offered to sell the complainant the domain name at issue for the sum of US$1,000.00. In his e-mail, respondent stated that cybersquatting cases "typically accomplish very little and end up costing the companies thousands of dollars in legal fees, wasted time and energy." The payment of US$1,000 would represent more than payment for respondent's time and money, but also and "most important" [sic] would serve as consideration for "the right of current ownership of the domain name 'worldwrestlingfederation.com.'"

Respondent has not developed a Web site using the domain name at issue or made any other good faith use of the domain name. The domain name at issue is not, nor could it be contended to be, a nickname of respondent or other member of his family, the name of a household pet, or in any other way identified with or related to a legitimate interest of respondent. [The Respondent did not contest the allegations of the Complaint.]

. . . .

6. Discussion and Findings

Paragraph 15(a) of the Rules instructs the Panel as to the principles the Panel is to use in determining the dispute: "A Panel shall decide a complaint on the basis of the statements and documents submitted in accordance with the Policy, these Rules and any rules and principles of law that it deems applicable." Since both the complainant and respondent are domiciled in the United States, and since United States' courts have recent experience with similar disputes, to the extent that it would assist the Panel in determining whether the complainant has met its burden as established by Paragraph 4(a) of the Policy, the Panel shall look to rules and principles of law set out in decisions of the courts of the United States.

Paragraph 4(a) of the Policy directs that the complainant must prove *each* of the following:

1) that the domain name registered by the respondent is identical or confusingly similar to a trademark or service mark in which the complainant has rights; *and,*

2) that the respondent has no legitimate interests in respect of the domain name; *and,*

3) the domain name has been registered and used in bad faith.

It is clear beyond cavil that the domain name <worldwrestlingfederation.com> is identical or confusingly similar to the trademark and service mark registered and used by complainant, WORLD WRESTLING FEDERATION. It is also apparent that the respondent has no rights or legitimate interests in respect of the domain name. Since the domain name was registered on October 7, 1999, and since respondent offered to sell it to complainant three days later, the Panel believes that the name was registered in bad faith.

However, the name must not only be registered in bad faith, but it must also be *used* in bad faith. The issue to be determined is whether the respondent used the domain name in bad faith. It is not disputed that the respondent did not establish a Web site corresponding to the registered domain name. Accordingly, can it be said that the respondent "used" the domain name?

It is clear from the legislative history that ICANN intended that the complainant must establish not only bad faith registration, but also bad faith use. "These comments point out that cybersquatters often register names in bulk, but do not use them, yet without use the streamlined dispute-resolution procedure is not available. While that argument appears to have merit on initial impression, it would involve a change in the policy adopted by the Board. The WIPO report, the DNSO recommendation, and the registrars-group recommendation all required both registration *and* use in bad faith before the streamlined procedure would be invoked. Staff recommends that this requirement not be changed without study and recommendation by the DNSO." Second Staff Report on Implementation Documents for the Uniform Dispute Resolution Policy, submitted for Board meeting of October 24, 1999, para. 4.5,a.

Paragraph 4,b,i of the Policy, provides that "the following circumstances . . . shall be evidence of the registration and *use* of a domain name in bad faith: . . . circumstances indicating that you have registered or you have acquired the domain name primarily for the purpose of selling, renting or otherwise transferring the domain name registration to the complainant who is the owner of the trademark or service mark . . . for valuable consideration in excess of the documented out-of-pocket costs directly related to the domain name." (Emphasis added.)

Because respondent offered to sell the domain name to complainant "for valuable consideration in excess of" any out-of-pocket costs directly related to the domain name, respondent has "used" the domain name in bad faith as defined in the Policy.

Although it is therefore unnecessary to consult decisions of United States' courts, the panel notes that decisions of those courts in cases which determine what constitutes "use" where the right to a domain name is contested by a mark owner support the panel's conclusion. For example, in the case of Panavision International, L.P. v. Dennis Toeppen, et al., 141 F. 3d 1316 (9th Cir. 1998), the Court of Appeals held that the defendant's intention to sell the domain name to the plaintiff constituted "use" of the plaintiff's mark . . . .

. . . .

The Panel notes with approval that the Policy and Rules set out by ICANN encourage settlement and that the parties in this case have engaged in extensive settlement negotiations. It was noted by the complainant in an email to the respondent regarding possible settlement that, while it was not the complainant's policy to pay individuals to stop infringing its intellectual property, it was also complainant's policy not to litigate against its fans. Complainant acknowledged that it could have proceeded to litigation under the United States "Anticybersquatting Consumer Protection Act," but that it elected not to. By engaging in this proceeding, complainant has sought to protect complainant's intellectual property interests while preserving the relationship between complainant and its fans at a minimal cost to all concerned.

7. Decision

For all of the foregoing reasons, the Panel decides that the domain name registered by respondent is identical or confusingly similar to the trademark and service mark in which the complainant has rights, and that the respondent has no rights or legitimate interests in respect of the domain name, and that the respondent's domain name has been registered and is being used in bad faith. Accordingly, pursuant to Paragraph 4,i of the Policy, the Panel requires that the registration of the domain name <worldwrestlingfederation.com> be transferred to the complainant.

TELSTRA CORP. LTD v. NUCLEAR MARSHMALLOWS
Case No. D2000-0003 (WIPO Arb. and Mediation Center Feb. 18, 2000)

ANDREW F. CHRISTIE, PANELIST:

The Complainant is Telstra Corporation Limited, a company incorporated in Australia, with its registered office in Melbourne, Australia. The Respondent is Nuclear Marshmallows. Nuclear Marshmallows is an unregistered business name of an unidentifiable business entity. The address of the Respondent as contained in the domain name registration is a post office box in Gosford, NSW, Australia. . . .

[The Complainant is the largest company on the Australian Stock Exchange, is the proprietor of more than 50 registrations in Australia of trademarks consisting of or containing the word TELSTRA, and is the registrant of the following domain names containing the word TELSTRA: telstra.com, telstra.net, telstra.com.au, telstra-inc.com, and telstrainc.com. The Respondent is the registrant of the domain name <telstra.org>, the Registrar of which is Network Solutions, Inc. of Herndon, Virginia, USA.]

Paragraph 4(b) of the Uniform Policy identifies, in particular but without limitation, four circumstances which, if found by the Administrative Panel to be present, shall be evidence of the registration and use of a domain name in bad faith. The precise wording of this paragraph is as follows:

> b. *Evidence of Registration and Use in Bad Faith.* For the purposes of Paragraph 4(a)(iii), the following circumstances, in particular but without limitation, if found by the Panel to be present, shall be evidence of the registration and use of a domain name in bad faith:
>
> (i) circumstances indicating that you have registered or you have acquired the domain name primarily for the purpose of selling, renting, or otherwise transferring the domain name registration to the complainant who is the owner of the trademark or service mark or to a competitor of that complainant, for valuable consideration in excess of your documented out-of-pocket costs directly related to the domain name; or
>
> (ii) you have registered the domain name in order to prevent the owner of the trademark or service mark from reflecting the mark in a corresponding domain name, provided that you have engaged in a pattern of such conduct; or
>
> (iii) you have registered the domain name primarily for the purpose of disrupting the business of a competitor; or
>
> (iv) by using the domain name, you have intentionally attempted to attract, for commercial gain, Internet users to your web site or other on-line location, by creating a likelihood of confusion with the complainant's mark as to the source, sponsorship, affiliation, or endorsement of your web site or location or of a product or service on your web site or location.

It is worthy of note that *each* of the four circumstances in paragraph 4(b), if found, is an instance of "registration and use of a domain name in bad faith", notwithstanding the fact that circumstances (i), (ii), and (iii) are concerned with the primary intention or purpose of the registration of the domain name, whilst circumstance (iv) is concerned with an act of use of the domain name. The significance of this point is discussed . . . below.

. . . .

[Although the first two elements of Paragraph 4(a) are clearly made out,] it is less clear cut whether the Complainant has proved the third element in paragraph 4(a) of the Uniform Policy, namely that the domain name "has been registered and is being used in bad faith" by Respondent. The Administrative Panel notes two things about this provision. First, the provision contains the conjunction "and" rather than "or". Secondly, the provision refers to both the past tense ("has been registered") and the present tense ("is being used").

The significance of the use of the conjunction "and" is that paragraph 4(a)(iii) requires the Complainant to prove use in bad faith as well as registration in bad faith. That is to say, bad faith registration alone is an insufficient ground for obtaining a remedy under the Uniform Policy. This point is acknowledged in [World Wrestling Federation v. Bosman], the first case decided under the Uniform Policy. In paragraph 6 of that Decision, the Administrative Panel refers to the legislative history of the Uniform Policy, and in particular to the Second Staff Report on Implementation Documents for the Uniform Dispute Resolution Policy submitted to the ICANN Board at its meeting on October 24, 1999. . . .

From the fact that the ICANN Board accepted the approach recommended in the Second Staff Report, and thus adopted the Uniform Policy in the form originally proposed, it is clear that ICANN intended that bad faith registration alone not give rise to a remedy under the Uniform Policy. For a remedy to be available, the Complainant must prove both that the domain was registered in bad faith and that it is being used in bad faith.

This interpretation is confirmed, and clarified, by the use of both the past and present tenses in paragraph 4 (a)(iii) of the Uniform Policy. The use of both tenses draws attention to the fact that, in determining whether there is bad faith on the part of the Respondent, consideration must be given to the circumstances applying both at the time of registration and thereafter. So understood, it can be seen that the requirement in paragraph 4(a)(iii) that the domain name "has been registered and is being used in bad faith" will be satisfied only if the Complainant proves that the registration was undertaken in bad faith *and* that the circumstances of the case are such that Respondent is continuing to act in bad faith.

Has the Complainant proved that the domain name "has been registered in bad faith" by the Respondent? [T]he Administrative Panel finds that the Respondent does not conduct any legitimate commercial or non-commercial business activity in Australia. [T]he Administrative Panel further finds that the Respondent has taken deliberate steps to ensure that its true identity cannot be determined and communication with it cannot be made. Given the Complainant's numerous trademark registrations for, and its wide reputation in, the word TELSTRA, . . . it is not possible to conceive of a plausible circumstance in which the Respondent could legitimately use the domain name telstra.org. It is also not possible to conceive of a plausible situation in which the Respondent would have been unaware of this fact at the time of registration. These findings, together with the finding . . .that the Respondent has no rights or interests in the domain name, lead the Administrative Panel to conclude that the domain name <telstra.org> has been registered by the Respondent in bad faith.

Has the Complainant proved the additional requirement that the domain name "is being used in bad faith" by the Respondent? The domain name <telstra.org> does not resolve to a web site or other on-line presence. There is no evidence that a web site or other on-line presence is in the process of being established which will use the domain name. There is no evidence of advertising, promotion or display to the public of the domain name. Finally, there is no evidence that the Respondent has offered to sell, rent or otherwise transfer the domain name to the Complainant, a competitor of the Complainant, or any other person. In short, there is no positive action being undertaken by the Respondent in relation to the domain name.

This fact does not, however, resolve the question. [T]he relevant issue is not whether the Respondent is undertaking a positive action in bad faith in relation to the domain name, but instead whether, in all the circumstances of the case, it can be said that the Respondent is acting in bad faith. The distinction between undertaking a positive action in bad faith and acting in bad faith may seem a rather fine distinction, but it is an important one. The significance of the distinction is that the concept of a domain name "being used in bad faith" is not limited to positive action; inaction is within the concept. That is to say, it is possible, in certain circumstances, for inactivity by the Respondent to amount to the domain name being used in bad faith.

This understanding of paragraph 4(a)(iii) is supported by the actual provisions of the Uniform Policy. Paragraph 4(b) of the Uniform Policy identifies, without limitation, circumstances that "shall be evidence of the registration and use of a domain name in bad faith", for the purposes of paragraph 4(a)(iii). Only one of these circumstances (paragraph 4(b)(iv)), by necessity, involves a positive action post-registration undertaken in relation to the domain name (using the name to attract custom to a web site or other on-line location). The other three circumstances contemplate either a positive action or inaction in relation to the domain name. That is to say, the circumstances identified in paragraphs 4(b)(i), (ii) and (iii) can be found in a situation involving a passive holding of the domain name registration. Of course, these three paragraphs require additional facts (an intention to sell, rent or transfer the registration, for paragraph 4(b)(i); a pattern of conduct preventing a trade mark owner's use of the registration, for paragraph 4(b)(ii); the primary purpose of disrupting the business of a competitor, for paragraph 4(b)(iii)). Nevertheless, the point is that paragraph 4(b) recognises that inaction (eg. passive holding) in relation to a domain name registration can, in certain circumstances, constitute a domain name being used in bad faith. Furthermore, it must be recalled that the circumstances identified in paragraph 4(b) are "without limitation"—that is, paragraph 4(b) expressly recognises that *other* circumstances can be evidence that a domain name was registered and is being used in bad faith.

The question that then arises is what circumstances of inaction (passive holding) other than those identified in paragraphs 4(b)(i), (ii) and (iii) can constitute a domain name being used in bad faith? This question cannot be answered in the abstract; the question can only be answered in respect of the particular facts of a specific case. That is to say, in considering whether the passive holding of a domain name, following a bad faith registration of it, satisfies the requirements of paragraph 4(a)(iii), the Administrative Panel must give close attention to all the circumstances of the Respondent's behaviour. A remedy can be obtained under the Uniform Policy only if those circumstances show that the Respondent's passive holding amounts to acting in bad faith.

The Administrative Panel has considered whether, in the circumstances of this particular Complaint, the passive holding of the domain name by the Respondent amounts to the Respondent acting in bad faith. It concludes that it does. The particular circumstances of this case which lead to this conclusion are:

(i) the Complainant's trademark has a strong reputation and is widely known, as evidenced by its substantial use in Australia and in other countries,

(ii) the Respondent has provided no evidence whatsoever of any actual or contemplated good faith use by it of the domain name,

(iii) the Respondent has taken active steps to conceal its true identity, by operating under a name that is not a registered business name,

(iv) the Respondent has actively provided, and failed to correct, false contact details, in breach of its registration agreement, and

(v) taking into account all of the above, it is not possible to conceive of any plausible actual or contemplated active use of the domain name by the Respondent that would not be illegitimate, such as by being a passing off, an infringement of consumer protection legislation, or an infringement of the Complainant's rights under trademark law.

In light of these particular circumstances, the Administrative Panel concludes that the Respondent's passive holding of the domain name in this particular case satisfies the requirement of paragraph 4(a)(iii) that the domain name "is being used in bad faith" by Respondent.

The Administrative Panel decides that the Complainant has proven each of the three elements in paragraph 4(a) of the Uniform Policy. Accordingly, the Administrative Panel requires that the domain name <telstra.org> be transferred to the Complainant.

NOTES AND QUESTIONS

(1) **Advantages of the UDRP.** The *World Wrestling Federation* panel noted that the complainant could have filed a complaint in the U.S. courts under the Anticybersquatting Consumer Protection Act 1999 (ACPA), which entered into force almost simultaneously with the UDRP. *See infra* § 7.07[D]. Why might

the Federation have used the UDRP instead? What advantages does the UDRP offer a trademark owner?

(2) **The Basis for Panel Jurisdiction.** It is a basic principle of most national systems of private law that the submission of a dispute to arbitration depends upon the consent of the parties. The term "mandatory arbitration" is, at least formally, a misnomer. Did Bosman consent to the UDRP proceedings? (Recall that he registered his domain name on October 7, 1999; the UDRP was approved by ICANN on October 24, 1999). Notice that the ICANN proceedings are denominated in the UDRP as "administrative proceedings," notwithstanding that they are conducted by arbitration centers and look very much like arbitrations. Why was the term "administrative proceeding" chosen?

(3) **The Role of Panel Opinions.** Paragraph 4(j) of the UDRP provides that "all decisions under this Policy will be published in full over the Internet, except when an Administrative Panel determines in an exceptional case to redact portions of its decision." Why is this important? The parties appeared on the verge of settlement on January 14, 2000; the panelist had received a draft settlement signed by the respondent. Yet the panelist issued an opinion. Why? Would a national court have acted similarly? When the respondent in *World Wrestling Federation* did not respond in a timely fashion, a Notice of Default was issued. And the panel noted in its opinion that it would issue its decision "without the benefit of any Response from respondent." In fact, many respondents default and many panels have issued opinions without respondent involvement. Is this appropriate? How might it affect the nature of ICANN jurisprudence, if such a thing exists?

(4) **Sources of Law.** According to what rules of law are panels to decide disputes? To which sources did these two panels look for guidance in interpreting the UDRP? Why? What weight did they give the different sources? Were these sources appropriate?

(5) **The Role of Traditional Choice of Law Variables.** In *World Wrestling Federation*, both parties were American, the trademarks in question were registered in the United States, and the registrar of the domain name was based in Australia. In *Telstra*, both parties were Australian, the trademarks were registered both in Australia and worldwide, and the registrar was based in the United States. Should these variables affect the panel's determination, or at least its means of analysis? (The panelist in *World Wrestling Federation* was American, and the panelist in *Telstra* was Australian). If Mr. Bosman had, like the registrar, been based in Australia and the World Wrestling Federation had no trademark registration in Australia, should the *World Wrestling Federation* panel's determination have been different? *See infra Ty Productions, Maddona Ciccone.*

(6) **Bad Faith Registration *and* Use.** ICANN intended that a claim for cybersquatting under the UDRP require bad faith registration and use. Are the interpretations of paragraph 4 of the UDRP found in *World Wrestling Federation* and *Telstra* consistent with that objective? If an animal rights activist concerned with the well-being of penguins registered the domain name penguin.com with the intent of developing a web site highlighting the plight of penguins, but later decided to use the domain name in connection with a web

site selling books, could Penguin Books, Inc. (which holds trademark registrations for PENGUIN for books in several countries) bring a successful action under the UDRP?

(7) **Bad Faith and Settlement Offers**. Assume that the respondent in *World Wrestling Federation*, Michael Bosman, had registered the domain name with the intent of hosting a site for wrestling fans "but decided to offer it to the federation after realizing that he had neither the capital nor technical expertise" necessary to do that. *See* Jeri Clausing, *Wrestling Group Wins Back Use of Its Name on the Internet*, N.Y. TIMES, Jan. 17, 2000 at C4. If Bosman had registered the domain name, but made no use of it before receiving a cease and desist letter from the World Wrestling Federation, how might he propose a settlement involving the transfer to the federation of the domain name without appearing to engage in cybersquatting? If you were counsel to a registrant in such a situation, how would you suggest proceeding? Reconsider this question, and the advice that you might offer, after reading the Anticybersquatting Consumer Protection Act enacted by the U.S. Congress. *See infra* § 7.07[D].

(8) **The Role of WIPO**. The WIPO Arbitration Center was the administrator in over 1800 of the 2500 panel opinions issued thus far. Before the UDRP was established, the WIPO Arbitration Center was almost unused. Does this broadening of the services offered by WIPO blur any lines of responsibility that you think need to be maintained? Or, is this the perfect use of the different aspects of expertise available at WIPO?

J. CREW INT'L, INC. v. CREW.COM

Case No. D2000-0054 (WIPO Arb. and Med. Center April 20, 2000)

RICHARD W. PAGE, PRESIDING PANELIST, MARK V.B. PARTRIDGE, PANELIST:

Complainant, [a Delaware corporation with its corporate headquarters in New York], is a leading retailer of women's and men's apparel, shoes and accessories and is the owner of two United States trademarks (1) J. CREW for bags, clothing and catalog services, Reg. No. 1308888, issued December 11, 1984, and (2) CREW for clothing, Reg. No. 1348064, issued July 19, 1985. Complainant has been using its principal trademark J. CREW since 1982. It has used in a more limited manner its secondary trademark CREW for in-store signs, but not in its primary advertising. . . .

Respondent, [an entity located in Washington D.C.], registered the domain name <crew.com> [with NSI] on July 12, 1998, then later registered the domain name <j.crew.com> as a sub-account. Respondent's alter ego is Telepathy, Inc., which . . . has registered or acquired more than 50 domain names consisting of words that may be trademarks of others or are generic words that others may wish to use. . . .

None of Telepathy's domain names (other than its own domain name telepathy.com) is being used for an active website. Telepathy is clearly in the business of offering its domain names for sale. Its purpose in registering or acquiring these domain names has been expressly stated on its website, www.telepathy.com:

> Telepathy has acquired attractive domains both for use in its own
> development efforts and for its development partners and clients.
> Telepathy registered or acquired these domain names primarily for
> the purpose of selling, renting, or otherwise transferring the domain
> name registrations to its "clients."

The same appears to be true of Respondent's domain name crew.com.

Complainant registered the trademarks J. CREW and CREW before
Respondent registered the domain name <crew.com> or the variation domain
name <j.crew.com>.

Respondent has used its domain name <crew.com> only for a website linked
to Complainant's web site, and for no other purpose.

After Respondent had registered the domain name <crew.com>, an employee
of Complainant invited Respondent to join Complainant's affiliate network.
Pursuant to this affiliate program, Respondent was permitted to place a banner
ad on Respondent's website which was linked to Complainant's website.
Complainant promised Respondent a commission for sales made to customers
using that link, but has apparently defaulted on its obligation. The only
material on Respondent's website was the banner ad linked to Complainant's
website.

When Complainant's attorney asked Respondent's attorney whether
Respondent might be willing to sell its domain name <crew.com> to
Complainant, Respondent's attorney said that Respondent had "spent over 6
figures for domain names" and "would not be interested in a nominal sum."
Complainant then revoked Respondent's participation in the affiliate network.
Respondent is not a licensee of Complainant, nor has Respondent ever been
authorized by Complainant to use Respondent's domain name <crew.com> or
the variation domain name <j.crew.com>.

In response to a request by Complainant to Network Solutions, Inc. ("NSI"),
Respondent's domain name <crew.com> was placed on "Hold" on September 3,
1999 in accordance with NSI's Domain Name Dispute Policy. However, under
the new ICANN Uniform Domain Name Dispute Resolution Policy, NSI has
informed Complainant that Respondent's domain name <crew.com> will be
reactivated on February 11, 2000 unless it receives a copy of the Complaint in
this matter.

. . . .

Respondent contends that it has rights and legitimate interest in <crew.com>
because of Respondent's legitimate business of developing domain names for its
own use and for sale to its clients.

Respondent contends that its registration and use of <crew.com> is in good
faith because it had no actual knowledge of the CREW or J. CREW trademarks
when it registered the domain name and because it was asked to join
Complainant's affiliates group.

Discussion and Findings

Identity or Confusing Similarity

The domain name presently at issue is <crew.com>. The "crew" portion of this domain name is identical to Complainant's trademark CREW. Therefore, a majority of the Panel finds that the requirement of the Policy paragraph 4(a)(i) is satisfied.

The Complainant has not offered sufficient proof to warrant a finding that the domain name <crew.com> is confusingly similar to Complainant's trademark J. CREW or to its domain name <jcrew.com>.

Rights or Legitimate Interest

Respondent is a speculator who registers domain names in the hopes that others will seek to buy or license the domain names from it. Speculation means the practice of registering or acquiring domain names without any demonstrable plan for a specific use of that domain name. The speculator hopes to license or sell the domain name in the future for profit, but has no specific use in mind at the time of registration or acquisition. Such conduct does not fall within any of the circumstances listed under Paragraph 4 of the Policy as evidence of rights or legitimate interest in the domain name. Such conduct precludes others who have a legitimate desire to use the name from doing so. Persons precluded by such conduct may be those who have no prior right or interest in the name, as well as those who have a demonstrable prior interest in the name. Speculation is not recognized by the Policy as a legitimate interest in a name, and the Policy should not be interpreted to hold that mere speculation in domain names is a legitimate interest. To hold otherwise would be contrary to well-established principles that preclude mere speculation in names and trademarks and would encourage speculators to appropriate domain names that others desire to put to legitimate use. Ultimately, speculation in domain names increases costs to the operators of websites and limits the availability of domain names.

The Complainant and the Respondent are both domiciled in the United States of America. Therefore, the case law on United States trademarks gives the most persuasive point of reference for resolution of the legitimacy of speculation in domain names and provides authority that speculation in the registration and use of domain names corresponding to another's trademark is an abusive registration.

Respondent asserts that its activities are no different than what other entrepreneurs do in developing intent to use trademarks. However, Respondent is in error in its suggestion that speculation in trademarks is permissible. Under United States trademark law, an applicant must have a demonstrable bona fide intent to use a trademark before filing an intent to use application. 15 U.S.C. § 1051(b). Failure to present evidence of a demonstrable plan to use the mark can result in a finding that the application is invalid. *See* Commodore

Electronics Ltd. v. CBM Kabushiki Kaisha, 26 U.S. P.Q.2d 1503, 1507 (T.T.A.B. 1993) . . . .

Further, the applicant may not obtain a registration before it has made actual use of the mark. 15 U.S.C. § 1051(d). While the application is pending, the application may not be sold to any other party except in connection with a sale of the underlying business. 15 U.S.C. § 1060. Otherwise, the application becomes void and any subsequent registration is subject to cancellation. Clorox Co. v. Chemical Bank, 40 U.S.P.Q.2d 1098, 1104-1106 (T.T.A.B. 1996)(holding that the assignment of an intent to use application and resulting registration were void). These statutory rules were carefully considered and serve a valuable purpose of preventing mere speculation in the registration of trademarks. As discussed in Clorox, the provisions of United States law preventing the assignment of intent to use applications without the sale of the underlying business is part of a strong public policy recognized by the United States Congress to prevent trafficking or speculation in trademarks. *Id.* at 1104. The policy against trafficking in trademarks has also been adopted in other countries besides the United States.

The ICANN Policy is based on the principle of "abusive registration" set forth in the Report of the WIPO Internet Domain Name Process, April 30, 1999 (the "WIPO Report"). Paragraph 172 of the WIPO report identifies situations not considered to fall within the definition of an abusive registration [such as where a small business that had registered a domain name could show, through business plans, correspondence, reports, or other forms of evidence, that it had a bona fide intention to use the name in good faith.]

Here, Respondent has failed to show demonstrable evidence of plans to use the domain name in good faith. Indeed, its response concedes that it had no definite plan for use of the <crew.com> domain name when it obtained the registration and made no bona fide use of the domain name prior to being contacted by Complainant to participate in Complainant's affiliate program.

Respondent has given various justifications for its registration of <crew.com>, claiming that the domain name could be used for rowing or for construction teams. Shifting justifications for the selection of a domain name has been deemed to support a finding of bad faith. *See* Northern Light Technology, Inc. v. Northern Lights Club, 2000 U.S. Dist. LEXIS 4732 (D. Mass. Mar. 31, 2000) (finding the defendant's various explanations to be mere pretext).

Mere speculation in domain names is distinguishable from the conduct allowed in other cases where the domain name registrant has prevailed over the objections of a trademark owner. For example, in Avery Dennison Corp. v. Sumpton, 189 F.3d 868 (9th Cir. 1999), on which Respondent relies, the defendant was making bona fide use of the domain names at issue. That is not the case here. Further, the Court decisions have not yet interpreted the meaning of "abusive registration" within the context of the ICANN policy.

This also is not a case of reverse domain name "hijacking." The typical case of reverse domain name hijacking arose where a trademark owner would use the old NSI policy to place a domain name on "Hold" status even though the domain name holder was using the name in connection with unrelated goods or services or was already known by the name. Here, Respondent has not presented any evidence of demonstrable plans to use the domain name in connection with a bona fide offering of goods or services or actual use of the domain name. Rather, it has registered the domain name for purely speculative purposes despite the fact that it had constructive notice as a matter of law that the name was a registered trademark of another.

Therefore, a majority of the Panel finds that Respondent has no rights or legitimate interest in the domain name <crew.com> and that the requirement of the Policy paragraph 4(a)(ii) is satisfied.

Bad Faith

Paragraph 4[(b)] of the Policy provides that evidence of bad faith registration and use includes circumstances showing:

> (ii) you have registered the domain name in order to prevent the owner of the trademark or service mark from reflecting the mark in a corresponding domain name, provided that you have engaged in a pattern of such conduct.

a. Preclusion

Respondent's registration prevents Complainant from using the <crew.com> or <j.crew.com> domain names corresponding to Complainant's registered trademarks. We recognize that Complainant has registered the domain name <jcrew.com>. However, the ability of the Complainant to obtain alternate domain names should not make this provision inapplicable. Otherwise, the provision would always be inapplicable for it would nearly always be possible for the Complainant to obtain an alternative domain name or even to register the same name as its trademark in another gTLD or ccTLD.

b. Constructive Notice

Although Respondent claims it acquired the domain name without knowledge of Complainant's trademark registration, Respondent had constructive notice of that registration as a matter of United States trademark law pursuant to 17 U.S.C. § 1072. As a result, Respondent cannot rely on lack of knowledge as a defense to its conduct. It knew or should have known that its registration of <crew.com> prevented Complainant from reflecting its CREW trademark in a corresponding .com domain name. Because of the constructive notice provisions of United States trademark law, lack of actual knowledge is not a defense and it is not necessary to find actual knowledge to conclude that the use or registration of a mark is in bad faith.

c. Pattern of Conduct

Respondent admits it is engaged in a pattern of conduct involving the speculative registration of domain names for profit. While Respondent owns a long list of registrations, it has given only one example where it has made bona fide use of a domain name. This pattern of conduct prevents others from making bona fide use of desirable domain names that may correspond to their trademarks.

Therefore, a majority of the Panel finds that Respondent has registered and used the domain name <crew.com> in bad faith and that the requirement of the Policy paragraph 4(a)(iii) is satisfied.

Prior Decisions Regarding Speculation

A majority of the Panel has considered the decision in General Machine Products Company, Inc. v. Prime Domains, ICANN Case No. FA0001000092531, finding that registration of the domain name <craftwork.com> was not an abusive registration. In *General Machine*, Respondent's alter ego Telepathy, Inc. (then known as Prime Domains) was in the business of selling generic and descriptive domain names. Respondent demonstrated that the phrase "craftwork" was commonly used as a descriptive term, and claimed that it registered the domain name without actual knowledge of the complainant's trademark because it had widespread use as a descriptive or generic term.

Although *General Machine* appears to be directly applicable to the present case, the panel in that case did not discuss the fact that Respondent had constructive notice as a matter of law of the complainant's mark and the decision does not disclose whether the Respondent had a demonstrable plan to use the domain name when it was registered. A majority of the present Panel could only agree with the result in *General Machine* if there were evidence of a demonstrable plan at the time of registration. If it is the holding of the panel in General Machine that the Policy permits speculative registration of names that happen to be the trademarks of others without a demonstrable plan for bona fide use of the domain name, then a majority of the present Panel must respectfully disagree with the decision.

In reaching our opinion we are well aware that trademarks are not "rights in gross" and we do not think our opinion grants trademark owners rights beyond those recognized under applicable law, particularly in the United States where Congress has enacted the Anti-Cybersquatting Consumer Protection Act ("ACPA"), in part, to prevent trafficking in domain names that are the same as the trademarks of another. [The panel cited U.S. case law holding that bad faith intent to profit from registration of a domain name that matched the plaintiff's CELLO mark could be inferred because the defendant had no proprietary rights to the 'Cello' mark when he registered 'cello.com,' he had not previously used it, and he had engaged in a pattern of registering domain names that could be of interest to others and then trying to sell them.] Thus, our conclusion—that the Respondent's registration of <crew.com> was an abusive registration—is consistent with the scope of protection afforded consumers and trademark owners under U.S. law.

The majority of the Panel does not decide that all speculation in domain names is prevented by the Policy. Rather, for the purpose of this case, we merely hold that registration of domain names for speculative purposes constitutes an abusive registration when (1) the respondent has no demonstrable plan to use the domain name for a bona fide purpose prior to registration or acquisition of the domain name; (2) the respondent had constructive or actual notice of another's rights in a trademark corresponding to the domain name prior to registration or acquisition of the domain name; (3) the respondent engages in a pattern of conduct involving speculative registration of domain names; and (4) the domain name registration prevents the trademark holder from having a domain name that corresponds to its registered mark. This definition is consistent with the considerations stated in the WIPO Report and allows speculation in domain names that do not correspond to registered marks or where the registrant has a demonstrable plan to use the domain name for a bona fide purpose prior to registration or acquisition.

A majority of the Panel concludes (a) that the domain name <crew.com> is identical to the trademark CREW, (b) that Respondent has no rights or legitimate interest in the domain name and (c) that Respondent registered and used the domain name in bad faith. Therefore, pursuant to paragraphs 4(i) of the Policy and 15 of the Rules, a majority of the Panel orders that the domain name <crew.com> be transferred to Complainant J. Crew International, Inc.

G. GERVAISE DAVIS III, PANELIST (dissenting):

I respectfully dissent from the decision of the majority of this panel because their decision creates and applies a test for "abusive domain name registrations" which is not, in my opinion, part of the ICANN Uniform Dispute Resolution Policy nor consonant with the stated and very limited purpose of this Policy. It does so in what I deem a mistaken view that it is up to the panel to enforce a non-existent policy of ICANN to prevent people from registering domain names for resale to others than the trademark owner. Whether such activity is proper or improper is not before us under the ICANN Policy and we do not, in any event, have the authority to so decide under the ICANN rules. Even if the decision were correct under the Anti-Cybersquatting Consumer Protection Act, which I do not think is the case, we are not here authorized to apply that Act which differs significantly from the ICANN Policy and Rules. The majority decision goes far beyond the scope of the present ICANN Policy.

The panel holds "that the registration of domain names for speculative purposes constitutes a abusive registration when (1) the Respondent has no demonstrable plan to use the domain name for a bona fide purpose prior to registration or acquisition of the domain name; (2) the Respondent had constructive or actual notice of another's rights in a trademark corresponding to the domain prior to registration or acquisition of the domain name; (3) the respondent engages in a pattern of conduct involving speculative registration of domain names; and (4) the domain name registration prevents the trademark holder from having a domain name that corresponds to its registered trademark."

Unfortunately, the biased test the panel has used here automatically creates a situation, in every case, where there is only one element left to test, if the Complainant has a registered trademark and the domain registered by the Respondent is similar to the Complainant's registered trademark. Since every ICANN case, by definition, has to have these two other elements the decision obviates two thirds of the tests set up under the ICANN Policy. The majority view boils each case down to the single question, "Did the Respondent have a specific bona fide purpose or use in mind prior to acquisition of the domain name?" It rejects the idea that someone might not know exactly how he or she intends to use the domain name, and makes such uncertainty bad faith registration. That is not what the Policy we, as rule bound arbitrators, are directed to apply by the Rules.

The majority has identified the second element as "knowledge." This test, however, is always satisfied *per se* by what the majority identifies as automatic "constructive" notice of another's trademark rights. This is not a test, since this element would be satisfied for all registered trademarks by virtue of the simple fact of registration under the majority's logic.

Similarly, the third element of the majority's test is also satisfied *per se* any time the second level domain name and the registered trademark are similar or identical. Thus, the only test left, in each case, is whether the Respondent had a demonstrable plan to use the domain name for a bona fide purpose prior to registration or acquisition of the domain name. This is a gross over-simplification of the issues involved in preventing abusive domain name registrations. It ignores the planned limits of the ICANN Policy and adds wholly new purposes to what is presently a fairly clear set of rules. These rules were worked out as a compromise between the one view of assuming all registrations of domains that are the same as or similar to a trademark were abusive, and the other that recognizes that it is not against the trademark laws of the world to register a domain with an intent to use it that is not fully developed at the time of the registration. The majority decision would create a world where Intent to Use Registrations could be destroyed by simply showing that the ITU registrant has changed his mind after the fact, or was not entirely certain how the mark would finally be used or on what type of product or service. I do not believe this was the intent of the ICANN Directors or the many people who participated in developing these rules. To do so, would be tantamount to repeal of some of the very sound reasons the US and other nations permit ITU registrations.

Factual Background

. . . .

The parties to this dispute are not unfamiliar with each other. Long prior to this dispute, Respondent was solicited *by Complainant* to become part of Complainant's affiliate network advertising its goods. Respondent agreed to permit Complainant to place banner ads on Respondent's Web site that were linked to Complainant's web site. Complainant promised Respondent to pay a commission on sales made to customers using that link, but defaulted on its obligation to pay the commission. At one time Complainant's attorney apparently unilaterally offered to purchase the <crew.com> domain name from Respondent. When it became clear that Respondent would not sell the domain name for a nominal sum, Complainant revoked Respondent's participation in the affiliate network and instituted this action. One might question whether this does not suggest that, in fact, this is a case of reverse domain name hijacking in which the Complainant has unilaterally decided this is a domain it would now like to have, after encouraging its use by another, and that it is now trying to use the ICANN rules to achieve what it cannot do by negotiations for the purchase of the name.

Nature of the word and trademark "CREW"

It is not disputed that the Complainant's trademark CREW and the Respondent's domain name are essentially the same. Paragraph 4 (a) (i) of the ICANN Policy requires that the domain name be identical or confusingly similar to the Complainant's trademark. The Complainant clearly meets this test. In this case, however, that fact cuts both ways because the word CREW is so generic. [The dissenting panelist quoted the American Heritage Dictionary definition of CREW].

As discussed below, the fact that CREW is a generic term permeates any analysis for trademark purposes. The majority's contention that any trademark registration by Complainant means that Respondent should automatically be imbued with constructive knowledge of the existence of the registration for purposes of the ICANN Policy, while incorrect in and of itself, is particularly inappropriate for a generic term. Additionally, as numerous courts have stated, a trademark owner is not by definition entitled to all domain names incorporating their trademark or even those identical to their trademark. [cit]. This is especially so where the mark is generic and a common term. . . This is exactly the situation here, and the same logic should apply.

Furthermore, the majority seems to assume that a trademark owner has some sort of God given right to use the trademark to the exclusion of others. [But] the Complainant does not own all rights to the generic word CREW by virtue of its trademark registration.

Registrant Rights or Legitimate Interests

Paragraph 4 (a)(ii) of the ICANN Policy asks whether the Respondent has any rights or legitimate interests in respect of the domain name. Where the domain name and trademark in question are generic, and in particular where they comprise no more than a single, short, common word, the rights and interests inquiry is more likely to favor the domain name owner. As the court held in Hasbro, Inc. v. Clue Computing, Inc., 66 F.Supp.2d 117 (D. Mass., 1999), holders of a famous mark are not automatically entitled to use that mark as their domain name; trademark law does not support such a monopoly. If another Internet user has an innocent and legitimate reason for using the famous mark as a domain name and is the first to register it, that user should be able to use the domain name, provided that it has not otherwise infringed upon or diluted the trademark.

The ICANN policy is very narrow in scope; covers only clear cases of "cybersquatting" and "cyber piracy," and does not cover every dispute that might rise over domain names. See, for example, Second Staff Report on Implementation Documents for the Uniform Dispute Resolution Policy (October 24th, 1999), http://www.icann.org/udrp/udrp-second-staff-report-24oct99.htm 4.1(c) which states:

> Except in cases involving "abusive registrations" made with bad-faith intent to profit commercially from others' trademarks (e.g., cybersquatting and cyberpiracy), the adopted policy leaves the resolution of disputes to the courts (or arbitrators where agreed by the parties) and calls for registrars not to disturb a registration until those courts decide. The adopted policy establishes a streamlined, inexpensive administrative dispute-resolution procedure intended only for the relatively narrow class of cases of "abusive registrations." Thus, the fact that the policy's administrative dispute-resolution procedure does not extend to cases where a registered domain name is subject to a legitimate dispute (and may ultimately be found to violate the challenger's trademark) is a feature of the policy, not a flaw.

The majority decision spends substantial effort attempting to demonstrate that what it terms "speculation in domain names" is sufficient *per se* to be an "abusive registration." However, carefully reviewing the tests provided in the ICANN policy indicates otherwise.

Bad Faith Registration and Use

The third element of the ICANN policy requires that Complainant prove that the domain name was registered and is being used in bad faith. . . The Complainant in the instant case has not and cannot meet any of the four alternative elements of a bad faith registration and use. [The dissenting panelist concluded that "while it is possible that the Respondent acquired the domain name for the purpose of selling renting or otherwise transferring the domain name, because CREW is a common word, it cannot merely be assumed that Respondent's intent was to sell and transfer the domain name to the Complainant. Similarly, he concluded that, without additional evidence, one cannot impute that when one registers a generic name he or she by definition does so to prevent the owner of the trademark on a generic word from having or using that domain name. He noted that "while a court of law might come, after having taken proper evidence, listened to testimony, and properly weighed the evidence, to a determination that this was the intent of the domain name registrant, it is not place of this panel to do so, based on unsupported assumptions of intent." Finally, because he viewed the term CREW as generic, he concluded that the respondent's use could not have an immediate relationship to the Complainant any more than it does to thousands of CREW teams around world or any of a number of its other meanings. Indeed, the dissenting panelist suggested that any confusion which may have occurred was at least, in part, due to the conduct of the Complainant whose own solicitation of the link on the web site of www.crew.com caused an implied relationship. It is, the dissenting panelist argued, "highly illogical to find that by placing the banner ad, solicited and sanctioned by the Complainant, that directing traffic to the Complainant's business should be considered an intentional attempt to create confusion as to the source of the domain. To the contrary, it seems an admission by Complainant that there is no confusion likely."]

Conclusion

We are not legislators, but arbitrators. The majority, in an effort to stop a practice that it seems to take upon itself to believe is an unstated purpose of the ICANN Policy, has completely over-stepped its mandate as arbitrators. The decision creates a new and unauthorized test out of whole cloth, based on assumptions of fact by arbitrators without evidence on the subject, instead of using the appropriate and carefully crafted three step test for required evidence set out by the ICANN' Policy and Rules. In my judgment, the majority's decision prohibits conduct which was not intended to be regulated by the ICANN policy. This creates a dangerous and unauthorized situation whereby the registration and use of common generic words as domains can be prevented by trademark owners wishing to own their generic trademarks in gross. I cannot and will not agree to any such decision, which is fundamentally wrong. I respectfully dissent from the majority decision of my fellow professional panelists.

NOTES AND QUESTIONS

(1) **NSI Policy.** The complainant in *J. Crew* brought its UDRP proceeding after NSI indicated that it would reactivate the domain name which it had placed on hold under its pre-UDRP policy. Given NSI's role prior to the creation of ICANN and the development of competition among registrars, what effect would you expect NSI's reactivation policy to have on early UDRP jurisprudence?

(2) **Gap-filling**. The dissenting panelist in *J. Crew* complains that the majority are formulating principles that had not been articulated by ICANN. And, to be sure, the UDRP does not expressly address the question of domain name speculation. To what extent is "gap-filling" more or less appropriate by ICANN panels interpreting the UDRP than gap-filling by national courts stretching to provide relief against cybersquatting? To whom would the

dissenting panelist assign the gap-filling function?

TY INC. v. JOSEPH PARVIN d/b/a DOMAINS FOR SALE

Case No. D2000-0688 (WIPO Arb. and Mediation Center, Nov. 9, 2000)

M. Scott Donahey, Presiding Panelist, Jeffrey M. Samuels,
G. Gervaise Davis III, Panelists:

1. The Parties

The Complainant is Ty Inc., a corporation organized under the laws of the State of Delaware, United States of America, having its principal place of business in Oak Brook, Illinois, United States of America.

The Respondent is Joseph Parvin, an individual giving an address at For Sale Domains, FirstDomains.com, 9 Brendan Place, Lawrenceville, New Jersey, United States of America.

2. The Domain Name(s) and Registrar(s)

The domain names at issue are <ebeanies.com>, <e-beanies.com>, <ebeaniebabies.com>, and <ebeaniebaby.com>, the first two of which domain names are registered with Network Solutions, Inc., based in Herndon, Virginia, United States of America, and the third and fourth of which are registered with the CORE Internet Council of Registrars.

. . . .

4. Factual Background

Complainant registered the trademark "Beanie Babies" in connection with plush toys with the United States Patent and Trademark Office ("USPTO"). The registration issued on April 1, 1997, [and date of first use of the mark was November 1993.]

Complainant registered the trademark "beanies" in connection with plush toys with the Benelux Trademark Office on February 20, 1998.

Complainant registered the trademark "beanies" in connection with stuffed toys and other toy related fields with the German Patent Office. The application was filed on February 19, 1996, and issued on March 27, 1998.

Complainant registered the trademark "beanies" in connection with stuffed animals and other toys with the Japanese Patent Office. The registration issued on October 15, 1999. The application was made on August 21, 1997.

Complainant registered the trademark "beanies" in connection with plush toys with the Korean Industrial Property Office. The registration issued on November 11, 1998.

Complainant created the successful "beanie babies" plush toys and has marketed these and related products throughout the world. Complainant has sales in excess of one billion dollars, and has spent millions of dollars marketing its plush toys under the marks "beanies," "beanie babies," "beanie buddies," "teenie beanie babies," "beanie buddies collection," and "beanie babies collection."

Complainant markets its products not only through traditional retail outlets, but also on the world wide web via its web site at <beaniebabies.com>.

Respondent is not a licensee of Complainant nor otherwise authorized to use Complainant's marks for any purpose.

Respondent registered the domain names at issue between August 3 and 15, 1998.

On June 27, 1997, the Complainant applied for the registration of the mark "beanie" with the USPTO. That action is currently under suspension. On February 12, 1999, Complainant filed four applications with the United States Patent and Trademark Office to register the marks "e beanie" and "e beanies." Two of those applications are currently pending, and two are currently under suspension.

Complainant did not mention in its Complaint the facts set out in [the preceding paragraph, numbered 4.10]. In his Response, Respondent asserted that the Complainant had filed three such applications and that "its attempts to register [the above-described marks] have been rebuffed by the USPTO. These failed registration attempts occurred *after* the registration of EBEANIES.COM AND E-BEANIES.COM."

The Panel has consulted the United States Patent and Trademark Office web site to determine the facts set out in this paragraph 4.10, above. Such reference to publicly available information is tantamount to the taking of judicial notice by a United States Federal Court. *See* Federal Rules of Evidence, Rule 201. Prior Panel decisions have sanctioned consideration of such evidence. *See, e.g.,* Chernow Communications, Inc. v. Jonathan D. Kimball, ICANN Case No. D2000-0119; America Networks Inc. v. Tariq Masood and Solo Signs, ICANN Case No. D2000-0131.

Respondent has not used the domain names at issue to resolve to active web sites.

Complainant has alleged and Respondent has effectively conceded that <ebeanies.com> and <e-beanies.com> were registered under the name "Domains For Sale" and that this is tantamount to offering the names for sale.

Complainant alleges that Respondent has offered the domain names at issue for sale on the web site <domains.com> and has attached as Annex 14 to the Complaint screen print outs which demonstrate that <ebeanies.com> and <e-beanies.com> were posted on the <domains.com> web site and bids therefor were invited. Although Respondent dismisses this allegation as "another misrepresentation," he denies the allegation only as to <ebeaniebabies.com> and <ebeaniebaby.com>.

Complainant alleged that Respondent registered the domain names at issue with knowledge of Complainant's ownership and widespread use of the marks.

Respondent replied that "[t]he mark of which the Respondent reasonably might be assumed to have been aware is the BEANIE BABIES mark." Moreover, while Respondent contends that "beanies" is a generic term, Respondent makes no such contention as to "beanie babies."

Complainant alleges that Respondent has registered 633 other domain names and has warehoused those names for future sale. Complainant fails to identify the names allegedly registered. In a rambling statement, Respondent apparently denies this allegation.

. . . .

6. Discussion and Findings

. . . .

At the outset, it is important to discuss the Panel's view of its role in these proceedings. We view our role as a limited one, circumscribed by the terms of the [Uniform Domain Name Dispute Resolution Policy] and the [Supplemental Rules for Uniform Domain Name Dispute Resolution Policy], supplemented by the Supplemental Rules established by the providers and by such other principles of law that the Panel might find of assistance in applying the Rules and the Policies to a given set of facts. We do not view our role to be limited by the unavailability of United States style discovery procedures; rather our role is limited by the agreement of the parties to a jurisdiction whose boundaries are the Policy and the Uniform Rules.

The Panel is an international body, not an American centric one. Civil law jurisdictions, which are predominant internationally, do not provide for American type discovery, yet those systems function quite well. In civil law jurisdictions, documentary evidence is given great weight, while oral testimony is given relatively little. The practice of the Panels, then, is much closer to civil law, than to common law.

As an international body, it is not for the Panel to elevate one country's laws over those of another or to second guess the rulings of national trademark bodies, at least absent compelling evidence of changed circumstances. EAuto L.L.C. v. Triple S. Auto Parts d/b/a Kung Fu yea Enterprises, Inc., ICANN Case No. D2000-0047.

The parties have agreed that we are to apply to the facts that they have submitted or which are publicly known, the Policy, the Uniform Rules, and such principles of law as may assist us. "A Panel shall decide a complaint on the basis of the statements and documents submitted in accordance with the Policy, these Rules, and any rules and principles of law that it deems applicable." Uniform Rules, Rule 15(a). In this process, we should look to prior panel decisions to offer guidance, and, to the extent reasonable, we should attempt to harmonize our decisions with those of prior panels. The decision we reach should naturally flow from that process. It is not our role to moralize or to decide areas of law which are not part of our mandate.

In following this procedure, we look to the [three] questions that [Paragraph 4(a) of] the Policy requires us to determine. . . .

The Complainant has a valid trademark issued by the United States Patent and Trademark Office in the mark "beanie babies." Since the addition of an "e" has been found not to distinguish a domain name from a registered mark (Busy Body, Inc. v. Fitness Outlet, Inc., ICANN Case No. D2000-0127; International Data Group, Inc. v. Maruyama & Co., Ltd., ICANN Case No. D2000-0420), nor does a change from singular to plural form or the reverse (MatchNet plc. v. MAC Trading, ICANN Case No. D2000-0205; PlayNetwork, Inc. v. Play Industries, ICANN Case No. FA 0003000094232), the Panel finds that the domain names <ebeaniebaby.com> and <ebeaniebabies.com> are identical or confusingly similar to the mark in which Complainant has rights.

The Complainant has valid trademarks issued by the Benelux Trademark Office, the German Patent Office, the Japanese Patent Office, and the Korean Industrial Property Office in the mark "beanies." For the same reasons set out above . . . the Panel finds that the domain names <e-beanies.com> and <ebeanies.com> are identical or confusingly similar to the marks in which Complainant has rights.

Nor does the majority believe that Respondent has any rights or legitimate interest in respect of the domain names at issue. All of the trademarks discussed, *supra*, were applied for and three issued before Respondent registered any of the domain names at issue. Before any notice of this dispute, Respondent had not used, or demonstratively prepared to use, the domain names at issue in connection with a bona fide offering of goods or services. Policy, ¶4(c)(i). Respondent has not been commonly known by the domain names at issue. Policy, ¶4(c)(ii). Respondent is not making legitimate or noncommercial use of the domain names at issue. Policy, ¶ 4(c)(iii). A majority of the Panel believes that the Complainant has carried his burden in establishing that Respondent has no right or legitimate interest in respect of any of the four domain names at issue. Do the Hustle, LLC v. Tropic Web, ICANN Case No. D2000-0624. The dissenting panelist expresses in his dissent some concern about this conclusion as to the "e-beanies domains," but fully agrees with the Majority as to the two "beanie baby" domains.

The Panel finds that Respondent registered the domain names <ebeanies.com> and <e-beanies.com> under the name "Domains For Sale." The Panel also finds that the same domain names were offered for sale on the <domains.com> web site. This constitutes an offer for sale. A majority of the Panel concludes that such an offer for sale constitutes bad faith registration and use. Policy, ¶4(b)(i); The Avenue, Inc. and United Retail Incorporated v. Chris Guirguis d/b/a Lighthouse Web Design and/or Cannibal, and Sam Guirguis, ICANN Case No. D2000-0013.

The Panel finds and Respondent admits that Respondent reasonably should have been aware of the "beanie babies" mark at the time it registered the domain name in question. Moreover, the full Panel believes that it is clear beyond cavil that the mark "beanie babies" is, at this point, a famous mark. Registration in such circumstances is done in bad faith. Christian Dior Couture SA v. Liage International Inc., ICANN Case No. D2000-0098; Chi-Chi's, Inc. v. Restauran Commentary (Restaurant Commentary), ICANN Case No. D2000-0321. In light of all of the circumstances of this case, including the offer for sale of the domain names identical or confusingly similar to Complainant's famous related marks, the Panel finds that the bad faith registration of the domain names incorporating the famous marks is evidence of bad faith registration and use. *Kabushiki Kaisha Toshiba v. Shan Computers*, ICANN Case No. D2000-0325.

The dissent indicates that it believes that Respondent has legitimate rights and interests in respect of the domain names <e-beanies.com> and <ebeanies.com> and that the Respondent did not register and use these domain names in bad faith.

The dissent accuses the complainant of "Foreign Trademark Shopping," which it defines as going to a non-English speaking country "to register a mark that would have been generic in an English speaking country, and register(ing) the generic mark there four years before attempting to register it in an English speaking country." Even if the majority agreed that there was something improper in such a practice, which it does not, that is not the situation we have before us. Complainant applied for the registration of the mark "beanie" with the U.S.P.T.O. on June 17, 1997. This appears to be earlier than all but one of the applications made in foreign countries for this mark.

If the dissent intends to suggest that the Complainant sought registration abroad because the Complainant was unsuccessful in attempting to register the marks in the United States, that, too, is erroneous. All of Complainant's applications for marks are currently pending before the USPTO. Some are currently in suspension status. The majority refuses to speculate as to what the USPTO might ultimately determine with respect to the applications.

The majority declined to ask the Complainant to supplement its presentation by providing information as to the status of the proceedings before the USPTO for a number of reasons. Most importantly, in the majority's view, the outcome of the USPTO proceedings will not detract from the fact that the Complainant has "rights" in the "beanies" mark, within the meaning of the Policy. The Policy does not require this Complainant, or any Complainant, to possess U.S. rights in order to meet the requirements of the Policy. Second, the majority believes that any representations by the Complainant would likely be self-serving and not subject to contradiction by the Respondent, who is not a party to those proceedings.

Does the dissent intend to suggest that English language marks should only be registered in English speaking countries, or that for purposes of the UDRP panelists should only give effect to trademarks that are registered in a country whose language is the same as the language of the mark? If so, the majority strongly disagrees.

The dissent suggests that our decision will enable the owner of a foreign trademark to "take away from another party domain names . . . which the registrant has a perfect legal right to register for use *or sale* in his own country under his own trademark laws." (Emphasis in the dissent.). The majority not only disagrees with this assertion, but is troubled by its implications. Does the dissent propose that the panel undertake to determine whether a trademark registered under the law of a sovereign country may be a generic term in some country in which the language of the mark is spoken, and, if so, deny recognition to such a mark in performing the panel's duties under the UDRP? The majority finds such a proposal beyond both the panel's abilities and the scope of the panel's charge.

The dissent even invokes the United States Constitution to suggest that a U.S. citizen has a Constitutional right to have United States law apply to his activities in the United States. While the majority believes that its limited task of attempting to regulate "cybersquatting" in the area of Internet domain names is of some small importance, we do not believe that the steps we are taking rise to the level of invading Constitutional areas. Moreover, we are dealing not with the sovereign territory of the United States and its laws, but with cyberspace, which is the "territory" in which domain names exist.

The dissent suggests that the majority is "mak[ing] law that could only be done by treaties, approved by the President and Congress under U.S. law. This has the effect of permitting informal arbitration rules, adopted by ICANN and imposed on all the domain name registrars of the world, to modify U.S., and for that matter the trademark laws of every nation in the world, without any of the legislative bodies of those nations passing on this important policy decision." With all due respect, we fail to see how a decision ordering the transfer of the registration of the domain names <e-beanies.com> and <ebeanies.com> can be said to rise to such grandiose levels. In fact, by respecting the registered trademarks of each sovereign nation and giving the registrations of each equal weight, the majority believes that it is acting responsibly and within the limited powers which have been conferred on it.

In the end, the majority simply believes that the role of ICANN panels is limited to applying the applicable Policy as currently adopted, not as a panel believes it should have been adopted or may be adopted in the future.

7. Decision

For all of the foregoing reasons, the full Panel decides that the domain names registered by Respondent are confusingly similar to the trademarks in which the Complainant has rights, that the Respondent has no rights or legitimate interests in respect of the BEANIE BABY domain names at issue, and that the Respondent's BEANIE BABY domain names have been registered and are being used in bad faith. One panelist disagrees with the last two conclusions as to the e-beanie marks. Accordingly, pursuant to Paragraph 4(i) of the Policy, the full Panel requires that the registration of the domain names <ebeaniebaby.com>, and <ebeaniebabies.com> be transferred to the Complainant. A majority of the Panel also directs that the <e-beanies.com>, <ebeanies.com> domains be transferred to Complainant, while the dissenting Panelist disagrees as to those two domain names for the reasons expressed in detail in the Partial Dissent set forth below.

PANELIST G. GERVAISE DAVIS III (dissenting in part):

I am in full agreement with the Majority as to the requirement of transfer of the ebeaniebaby.com and ebeaniebabies.com domains for the reasons we all agreed upon in the above decision. Furthermore, even Respondent made only a half-hearted attempt to defend those two domains. I must confess that I am also not entirely convinced of the good faith of the Respondent in his registration of any of the four domains, due to his public offer of sale of them, and other aspects of his apparent business; however, as to the e-beanies domains I think this possible defect is over-ridden by the unresolved public policy issues I comment on below. Therefore, I do not, by this dissent, however, wish to be considered as condoning bad faith registration of valid trademarks as domain names. I have previously, and will continue to when presented with the proper facts, ruled against such activities in proceedings under the ICANN Rules, as I have here as to two of the domains.

However, I am disturbed by the peculiar facts and circumstance of this case, as presented by the Complainant and Respondent, which indicate existence of what might be termed "Foreign Trademark Shopping," and the effect this decision may have in the future on U.S. and other nationally-based trademark laws vis a vis international use of domain names, when considering the effect of the Majority's decision to transfer the ebeanies.com and e-beanies.com domains, in dispute here, to Complainant. By the phrase "Foreign Trademark Shopping," I mean the fact that Complainant deliberately went to four non-English speaking countries to register a mark that would have been generic in an English speaking country, and registered the generic mark there four years before attempting to register it in an English speaking country (the U.S.) suggests to me that Complainant was attempting to gain an advantage over a U.S. citizen that it would not have had under U.S. trademark law. Encouraging this subterfuge is poor public policy and was not, I think, intended by the ICANN Board when it adopted the dispute resolution rules.

I am concerned that by ruling for Complainant on these facts, as to two domains that may well be . . . generic terms in the English language, we are creating a situation in which a U.S. or other English speaking origin business can forum shop for a place where common generic English words can be easily registered as trademarks, while they could not be registered in an English speaking country. Then, using the ICANN rules and ICANN proceedings, that trademark owner can, later, take away from another party domain names based on the generic English words, which the registrant has a perfect legal right to register for use *or sale* in his own country under his own trademark laws. To permit this kind of foreign trademark shopping is to make a fundamental change in nationally-based trademark laws. I deem this a highly undesirable situation that we ought not encourage. We are not a national court, but merely arbitrators trying to follow hastily developed rules to stop a pernicious activity of abusive registration of legitimate trademarks as domain names. We ought not make international policy decisions concerning national-based trademark laws. This is not just a U.S. centric view, since the same situation could occur under the Majority's decision if the domains were generic French words, and the trademark owner took advantage of that fact and registered them in an Arabic speaking country.

I do not think that we are so bound by the ICANN rules in our review of the facts that we have no right to consider the significant international policy implications of our decisions. The ICANN rules were adopted as a compromise, with the intent that they be reviewed after use for a short period, and they are by design intended only to apply in obvious abusive registration cases. I feel that if there is a serious unresolved international policy decision involved, as here, we ought to leave such matters to the Courts, and not to make such a ruling in a summary proceeding like this. By denying the transfer of these two disputed domains, we would leave this momentous significant international policy decision to the U.S. Courts who have the procedural tools and authority to ascertain the full facts of this case that we do not. Deferring this decision and permitting the Courts to resolve it will not seriously harm Complainant, and by doing so, we do not set precedents in a case that I seriously doubt anyone who agreed to the establishment of the ICANN rules ever thought would occur. I would prefer that approach, which is why I dissent, in part, to this decision. I do not disagree with the Majority, that if we ignore the fact this decision will have the effect of creating a super-national trademark law for the Internet, that one might reach the decision they did. I simply disagree that we have the authority to change national trademark laws in an international arbitration proceeding, or that we should do so.

I am also concerned that, on the peculiar facts of this specific case, the ICANN rules are being applied here, *retroactively*, in a manner that elevates the ICANN rules to the point they actually overrule existing U.S. trademark law in a case between two U.S. citizens. That does not seem appropriate to me for us to do in an arbitration proceeding, and I do not think that any reasonable U.S. citizen registering a domain name with a U.S. based registrar would have ever considered this possible. By ruling as the Majority does, that a U.S. citizen has to consider if his registration of a generic English domain name might violate a pending foreign trademark registration in every other non-English speaking country, we are in effect charging every domain name registrant with constructive notice of every pending and existing trademark registration in the world. This is not reasonable, and certainly not reasonable when applying such a rule retroactively to facts and events—*all of which occurred before the existence of the ICANN rules.*

Furthermore, while Constitutional law is not my forte, I have a strong feeling that, as between two U.S. domiciliaries and citizens, this is an un-Constitutional derogation of a U.S. citizen's right to have U.S. law applied to his activities in the U.S. This is not, after all, a decision involving a German company and a U.S. resident—it is a complaint between two U.S. citizens. What the Majority is doing, when it applies the ICANN rules in this manner is creating a super-national rule to transactions between U.S. citizens in a manner never adopted nor formally authorized by the U.S. Congress. This decision makes law that could only be done by treaties, approved by the President and Congress, under U.S. law. This has the effect of permitting informal arbitration rules, adopted by ICANN and imposed on all the domain name registrars of the world, to modify U.S., and for that matter the trademark laws of every nation in the world, without any of the legislative bodies of those nations passing on this monumental important policy decision. For this reason, alone, I would dissent from that aspect of the decision.

Finally, factually, I am deeply troubled by Complainant's failure to tell the Panel, candidly, that it has apparently been unsuccessful in obtaining a trademark registration in the country of origin of the Beanie Baby products and the situs of Complainant's business, the United States, and that the only place it has been successful in obtaining such registrations is in non-English speaking countries like Germany and Japan, where the word "beanies" is presumably not recognized as being a generic English term. I am disappointed in Complainant's concealment of this material fact, which I believe it had an obligation to disclose, as a U.S. based Complainant.

Respondent suggests, although because of lack of discovery and the lack of candor of the Complainant we have no way of knowing for certain, that the reason for the lack of U.S. registration is because the word "beanies" is so generic that registration is being denied in the U.S., at least until the mark can be established as having achieved secondary meaning after five years. As an experienced trademark attorney in the U.S. I suspect that that is exactly why the U.S. registrations have been held up, since that would be an obvious conclusion to anyone that spoke English as his or her native language. However, none of the Panelists have any way of knowing this for sure, so I suggested to the Panel that we ask the Complainant to supplement its presentation by providing that information. The Majority declined to do so on the basis that whatever the reason, it would not make any difference in their final decision. While I respect their considerable experience and judgment in the area of trademark law, I respectfully disagree with this conclusion, as well.

Conclusion

In short, I believe, under these disputed facts and because of the timing of the events here, there is a reasonable basis to believe that the registration of the ebeanies.com and e-beanies.com domains was not made in bad faith. Since the word "beanies" was likely a generic English word in 1998 when Respondent registered the e-beanies domain names, I cannot hold that Complainant has proven bad faith registration, given the national based status of U.S. and international trademark law at the time of registration of the domains in 1998. The ICANN rules did not exist at the time, and at that time no trademark lawyer in the world would, I believe, have advised a U.S. client that registration of a generic English word as a domain name by a U.S. citizen was prohibited because someone had registered it as a trademark in Germany or Japan, for example. The burden of proof on the law and the facts on this issue is upon the Complainant, and not the Respondent. It is not up to us to provide this critical evidence, nor can we ignore the state of the law at the time of registration of the domains.

Since the ICANN rules in 4(a)(iii) require such a bad faith finding, I would not order the transfer of these two domains, but would leave the issues discussed above to a national Court to decide. I, therefore, respectfully dissent in part from the decision of the Majority as to transferring these two domains, while acknowledging the good faith differences of opinion in this matter between the Majority and myself, as the dissenting Minority Panelist.

MADONNA CICCONE, P/K/A MADONNA v. DAN PARISI

Case No. D2000-0847 (WIPO Arb. and Mediation Center Oct. 12, 200)

MARK V.B. PARTRIDGE, PRESIDING PANELIST, JAMES W. DABNEY AND DAVID E. SORKIN, PANELISTS

Factual Background

Complainant is the well-known entertainer Madonna. She is the owner of U.S. Trademark Registrations for the mark MADONNA for entertainment services and related goods (Reg. No. 1,473,554 and 1,463,601). She has used her name and mark MADONNA professionally for entertainment services since 1979. Complainant's music and other entertainment endeavors have often been controversial for featuring explicit sexual content. In addition, nude photographs of Madonna have appeared in Penthouse magazine, and Complainant has published a coffee-table book entitled "Sex" featuring sexually explicit photographs and text.

Respondent is in the business of developing web sites. On or about May 29, 1998, Respondent, through its business Whitehouse.com, Inc., purchased the registration for the disputed domain name from Pro Domains for $20,000. On June 4, 1998, Respondent registered MADONNA as a trademark in Tunisia. On or about June 8, 1998, Respondent began operating an "adult entertainment portal web site." The web site featured sexually explicit photographs and text, and contained a notice stating "Madonna.com is not affiliated or endorsed by the Catholic Church, Madonna College, Madonna Hospital or Madonna the singer." By March 4, 1999, it appears that Respondent removed the explicit sexual content from the web site. By May 31, 1999, it appears that the site merely contained the above notice, the disputed domain name and the statement "Coming soon Madonna Gaming and Sportsbook."

. . . .

The word "Madonna," which has the current dictionary definition as the Virgin Mary or an artistic depiction of the Virgin Mary, is used by others as a trademark, trade name and personal name. After Respondent's receipt of Complainant's objection, it appears that Respondent had communication with Madonna Rehabilitation Hospital regarding the transfer of the domain name to the Hospital. It further appears that Respondent has not identified all of its communications on this matter. Nevertheless, the transfer had not taken place at the time this proceeding was commenced.

By his own admission, Respondent has registered a large number of other domain names, including names that matched the trademarks of others. . .

Parties' Contentions

. . . .

Respondent does not dispute that the disputed domain name is identical or confusingly similar to Complainant's trademark. Respondent, however, claims that Complainant cannot show a lack of legitimate interest in the domain name because Respondent (a) made demonstrable preparation to use the domain name for a bona fide business purpose; (b) holds a bona fide trademark in the word MADONNA; and (c) has attempted to make bona fide noncommercial use of the name by donating it to the Madonna Rehabilitation Hospital.

Respondent also contends that it has not registered and used the domain name in bad faith because (a) there is no evidence that its primary motivation was to sell the disputed domain name; (b) the domain name was not registered with an intent to prevent Complainant from using her mark as a domain name; (c) respondent is not engaged in a pattern of registering domain names to prevent others from doing so; (d) the use of a disclaimer on the web site precludes a finding that Respondent intentionally seeks to attract users for commercial gain based on confusion with Complainant's mark; and (e) the use of a generic term to attract business is not bad faith as a matter of law. Finally, Respondent claims that Complainant cannot legitimately claim tarnishment because she has already associated herself with sexually explicit creative work.

Discussion and Findings

A. The Evidentiary Standard For Decision

Paragraph 4(a) of the Policy [states the three matters that] the complainant must prove. . . .A threshold question in proceedings under the Policy is to identify the proper standard for reaching a decision on each of these issues. The limited submissions allowed under the Policy makes these proceedings somewhat akin to a summary judgment motion under the United States Federal Rules of Civil Procedure. On a summary judgment motion, the movant has the burden of showing that there are no disputes of material facts. All doubts are to be resolved in favor of the non-moving party. If there are material disputes of fact, the motion must be denied and the case will advance to a hearing before a trier of fact, either judge or jury.

Although the nature of the record is similar to that found on a summary judgment motion, our role is different than that of the Court on a summary judgment motion. Paragraph 15 of the Rules states that the "Panel shall decide a complaint on the basis of the statements and documents submitted and in accordance with the Policy. . ." Paragraph 10 of the Rules provides that the "Panel shall determine the admissibility, relevance, materiality and weight of the evidence." Paragraph 4 of the Policy makes repeated reference to the Panel's role in making findings of fact based on the evidence.

Based on the Policy and the Rules, we disagree with the view that disputes over material facts should not be decided in these proceedings. Rather, it is clear to us that our role is to make findings of fact as best we can based on the evidence presented provided the matters at issue are within the scope of the Policy. There may be circumstances due to the inherent limitations of the dispute resolution process or for other reasons where it would be appropriate for a panel to decline to decide a factual dispute. However, the mere existence of a genuine dispute of material fact should not preclude a panel from weighing the evidence before it and reaching a decision.

Since these proceedings are civil, rather than criminal, in nature, we believe the appropriate standard for fact finding is the civil standard of a preponderance of the evidence (and not the higher standard of "clear and convincing evidence" or "evidence beyond a reasonable doubt"). Under the "preponderance of the evidence" standard a fact is proved for the purpose of reaching a decision when it appears more likely than not to be true based on the evidence. We recognize that other standards may be employed in other jurisdictions. However, the standard of proof employed in the United States seems appropriate for these proceedings generally, and in particular for this proceeding which involves citizens of the United States, actions occurring in the United States and a domain name registered in the United States.

In this case, there are factual disputes over Respondent's intent in obtaining and using the disputed domain name. For the reasons just stated, these disputes do not preclude a decision. Instead, we reach a decision based on the preponderance of the evidence submitted by the parties on the basic issues under the Policy.

B. Similarity of the Disputed Domain Name and Complainant's Mark

As noted above, Respondent does not dispute that its domain name is identical or confusingly similar to a trademark in which the Complainant has rights. Accordingly, we find that Complainant has satisfied the requirements of Paragraph 4(c)(i) of the Policy.

C. Lack of Rights or Legitimate Interests In Domain Name

Complainant has presented evidence tending to show that Respondent lacks any rights or legitimate interest in the domain name. Respondent's claim of rights or legitimate interests is not persuasive.

First, Respondent contends that its use of the domain name for an adult entertainment web site involved prior use of the domain name in connection with a bona fide offering of goods or services. The record supports Respondent's claim that it used the domain name in connection with commercial services prior to notice of the dispute. However, Respondent has failed to provide a reasonable explanation for the selection of Madonna as a domain name. Although the word "Madonna" has an ordinary dictionary meaning not associated with Complainant, nothing in the record supports a conclusion that Respondent adopted and used the term "Madonna" in good faith based on its ordinary dictionary meaning. We find instead that name was selected and used by Respondent with the intent to attract for commercial gain Internet users to Respondent's web site by trading on the fame of Complainant's mark. We see no other plausible explanation for Respondent's conduct and conclude that use which intentionally trades on the fame of another can not constitute a "bona fide" offering of goods or services. To conclude otherwise would mean that a

Respondent could rely on intentional infringement to demonstrate a legitimate interest, an interpretation that is obviously contrary to the intent of the Policy.

Second, Respondent contends that it has rights in the domain name because it registered MADONNA as a trademark in Tunisia prior to notice of this dispute. Certainly, it is possible for a Respondent to rely on a valid trademark registration to show prior rights under the Policy. However, it would be a mistake to conclude that mere registration of a trademark creates a legitimate interest under the Policy. If an American-based Respondent could establish "rights" vis a vis an American Complainant through the expedient of securing a trademark registration in Tunisia, then the ICANN procedure would be rendered virtually useless. To establish cognizable rights, the overall circumstances should demonstrate that the registration was obtained in good faith for the purpose of making bona fide use of the mark in the jurisdiction where the mark is registered, and not obtained merely to circumvent the application of the Policy.

Here, Respondent admits that the Tunisia registration was obtained merely to protect his interests in the domain name. Respondent is not located in Tunisia and the registration was not obtained for the purpose of making bona fide use of the mark in commerce in Tunisia. A Tunisian trademark registration is issued upon application without any substantive examination. Although recognized by certain treaties, registration in Tunisia does not prevent a finding of infringement in jurisdictions outside Tunisia. Under the circumstances, some might view Respondent's Tunisian registration itself as evidence of bad faith because it appears to be a pretense to justify an abusive domain name registration. We find at a minimum that it does not evidence a legitimate interest in the disputed name under the circumstances of this case.

Third, Respondent claims that its offer to transfer the domain name to the Madonna Hospital in Lincoln, Nebraska, is a legitimate noncommercial use under Paragraph 4(c)(iii) of the Policy. We disagree. The record is incomplete on these negotiations. Respondent has failed to disclose the specifics of its proposed arrangement with Madonna Hospital. Complainant asserts that the terms of the transfer include a condition that Madonna Hospital not transfer the domain name registration to Complainant. It also appears that the negotiations started after Complainant objected to Respondent's registration and use of the domain name. These circumstances do not demonstrate a legitimate interest or right in the domain name, and instead suggest that Respondent lacks any real interest in the domain name apart from its association with Complainant. Further, we do not believe these circumstances satisfy the provisions of Paragraph 4(c)(iii), which applies to situations where the Respondent is actually making noncommercial or fair use of the domain name. That certainly was not the situation at the time this dispute arose and is not the situation now.

Respondent cites examples of other parties besides Complainant who also have rights in the mark MADONNA, but that does not aid its cause. The fact that others could demonstrate a legitimate right or interest in the domain name does nothing to demonstrate that Respondent has such right or interest.

Based on the record before us, we find that Complainant has satisfied the requirements of Paragraph 4(a)(ii) of the Policy.

D. Bad Faith Registration and Use

. . . .

The pleadings in this case are consistent with Respondent's having adopted <madonna.com> for the specific purpose of trading off the name and reputation of the Complainant, and Respondent has offered no alternative explanation for his adoption of the name despite his otherwise detailed and complete submissions. Respondent has not explained why <madonna.com> was worth $20,000 to him or why that name was thought to be valuable as an attraction for a sexually explicit web site. Respondent notes that the complainant, identifying herself as Madonna, has appeared in Penthouse and has published a "Sex" book. The statement that "madonna" is a word in the English language, by itself, is no more of a defense than would be the similar statement made in reference to the word "coke". Respondent has not even attempted to tie in his web site to any dictionary definition of madonna. The only plausible explanation for Respondent's actions appears to be an intentional effort to trade upon the fame of Complainant's name and mark for commercial gain [and thus falling within Paragraph 4(b)(iv)]. That purpose is a violation of the Policy, as well as U.S. Trademark Law.

Respondent's use of a disclaimer on its web site is insufficient to avoid a finding of bad faith. First, the disclaimer may be ignored or misunderstood by Internet users. Second, a disclaimer does nothing to dispel initial interest confusion that is inevitable from Respondent's actions. Such confusion is a basis for finding a violation of Complainant's rights. See Brookfield Communications Inc. v. West Coast Entertainment Corp., 174 F.3d 1036 (9th Cir. 1999).

The Policy requires a showing of bad faith registration and use. Here, although Respondent was not the original registrant, the record shows he acquired the registration in bad faith. The result is the equivalent of registration and is sufficient to fall within the Policy. Indeed, Paragraph 4(b)(i) of the Policy treats acquisition as the same as registration for the purposes of supporting a finding of bad faith registration. We therefore conclude that bad faith acquisition satisfies the requirement of bad faith registration under the Policy.

Respondent's reliance on a previous ICANN decision involving the domain name <sting.com> is misplaced. See Gordon Sumner p/k/a/ Sting v. Michael Urvan, Case No. 2000-0596 (WIPO July 24, 2000). In the Sting decision there was evidence that the Respondent had made bona fide use of the name Sting prior to obtaining the domain name registration and there was no indication that he was seeking to trade on the good will of the well-known singer. Here, there is no similar evidence of prior use by Respondent and the evidence demonstrates a deliberate intent to trade on the good will of complainant. Where no plausible explanation has been provided for adopting a domain name that corresponds to the name of a famous entertainer, other Panels have found a violation of the Policy. See Julia Fiona Roberts v. Russell Boyd, Case No. D2000-0210 (WIPO May 29, 2000); Helen Folsade Adu p/k/a Sade v. Quantum Computer Services Inc., Case No. D2000-0794 (WIPO September 26, 2000).

There is also evidence in the record which tends to support Complainant's claim that Respondent's registration of the domain name prevents Complainant from reflecting her mark in the corresponding .com domain name and that Respondent has engaged in a pattern of such conduct. It is admitted that Respondent registers a large number of domain names and that some happen to correspond to the names or marks of others. We find, however, that the record is inconclusive on this basis for finding bad faith and do not rely on this evidence for our conclusion.

Respondent asserts that we should reject Complainant's claims because she has been disingenuous in claiming that her reputation could be tarnished by Respondent's actions. Respondent suggests that her reputation cannot be tarnished because she has already associated herself with sexually explicit creative work. That argument misses the point. Even though Complainant has produced sexually explicit content of her own, Respondent's actions may nevertheless tarnish her reputation because they resulted in association with sexually explicit content which Complainant did not control and which may be contrary to her creative intent and standards of quality. In any event, we do not rely on tarnishment as a basis for our decision.

Because the evidence shows a deliberate attempt by Respondent to trade on Complainant's fame for commercial purposes, we find that Complainant has satisfied the requirements of Paragraph 4(a)(iii) of the Policy.

Decision

Under Paragraph 4(i) of the Policy, we find in favor of the Complainant. The disputed domain name is identical or confusingly similar to a trademark in which Complainant has rights; Respondent lacks rights or legitimate interests in the domain name; and the domain name has been registered and used in bad faith. Therefore, we decide that the disputed domain name <madonna.com> should be transferred to the Complainant.

NOTES AND QUESTIONS

(1) **Evidentiary Difficulties.** The lack of evidentiary hearings can clearly affect a panel's ability to award relief. In Reuters Limited v. Ghee Khaan Tan, WIPO Case No. D2000-0670 (Aug. 4, 2000), the panelist made findings of confusing similarity and a lack of legitimate respondent interest, but declined to find bad faith given the respondent's denials and a lack of objective contradictory evidence placing the defendant within any of the scenarios set out in paragraph 4(b). The domain name ereuters.com had been registered by the proprietor of a maid service in Singapore. The panelist concluded that "for the panel to hold that the respondent registered the domain name in bad faith and is now using it in bad faith, the panel has to reject the respondent's denial and find that he has not told the truth. That is a very serious finding to have to

come to in circumstances such as these where there is next to no information on the respondent and his business in the papers before the panel and where the panel has no opportunity of examining the demeanor of the respondent. For the panel to hold that the respondent is a liar, the circumstantial evidence has to be overwhelmingly in favor of the complainant. While . . . the panel understands why the complainant is suspicious, the Panel finds that the evidence is insufficient for that purpose." Is such deference appropriate? If so, should the UDRP procedures be revised? (Panelists have been willing to reject pleas of good faith or legitimate interests that are implausible or which are belied by objective indicia.).

(2) **Foreign Trademark Shopping?** In what ways is the trademark registration owned by the complainant in *Ty* different from the Tunisian registration owned by the respondent in *Madonna*?

BRUCE SPRINGSTEEN v. JEFF BURGAR AND BRUCE SPRINGSTEEN CLUB
Case No. D2000-1532 (WIPO Arbit. and Mediation Center, Jan. 25, 2001)

Gordon D. Harris, Presiding Panelist, A. Michael Froomkin, Panelist:

Factual Background

. . . The Complainant is the famous, almost legendary, recording artist and composer, Bruce Springsteen. Since the release of his first album in 1972 he has been at the top of his profession, selling millions of recordings throughout the world. As a result, his name is instantly recognisable in almost every part of the globe. There is no assertion made on behalf of Bruce Springsteen that his name has been registered as a trade mark but he rather relies upon common law rights acquired as a result of his fame and success. [The respondent, of Alberta, Canada, registered <brucespringsteen.com> with Network Solutions Inc. on 26 November 1996].

The Parties' Contentions

Representatives of Bruce Springsteen have succinctly addressed the requirements under the UDRP . . .[and] rely heavily on authorities, and produce copies of a number of previous decisions and court cases which they believe to be relevant.

Mr Burgar, on his own behalf, has produced a substantial response, far in excess of the guideline size for such responses set out in the WIPO rules. It is easy to understand his desire to make a point, but it does substantially increase the workload of the Panelists who have to wade through a large volume of material. For the purposes of this section, the Panel will refer only to that part of Mr Burgar's submission which relates specifically to the three requirements under the UDRP. . . .

Panel's Findings

Under paragraph 4 of the UDRP, . . the first question to be considered is whether the domain name at issue is identical or confusingly similar to trade marks or service marks in which the Complainant has rights.

It is common ground that there is no registered trade mark in the name "Bruce Springsteen". In most jurisdictions where trade marks are filed it would be impossible to obtain a registration of a name of that nature. Accordingly, Mr Springsteen must rely on common law rights to satisfy this element of the three part test.

It appears to be an established principle from cases such as *Jeanette Winterson*, *Julia Roberts*, and *Sade* that in the case of very well known celebrities, their names can acquire a distinctive secondary meaning giving rise to rights equating to unregistered trade marks, notwithstanding the non-registerability of the name itself. It should be noted that no evidence has been given of the name "Bruce Springsteen" having acquired a secondary meaning; in other words a recognition that the name should be associated with activities beyond the primary activities of Mr. Springsteen as a composer, performer and recorder of popular music.

In the view of this Panel, it is by no means clear from the UDRP that it was intended to protect proper names of this nature. As it is possible to decide the case on other grounds, however, the Panel will proceed on the assumption that the name Bruce Springsteen is protected under the policy; it then follows that the domain name at issue is identical to that name.

It is a clearly established principle that the suffix ".com" does not carry the domain name away from identicality or substantial similarity.

The second limb of the test requires the Complainant to show that the domain name owner has no rights or legitimate interests in respect of the domain name. The way in which the UDRP is written clearly requires the Complainant to demonstrate this, and the mere assertion that the Respondent has no such rights does not constitute proof, although the panel is free to make reasonable inferences. That said, a Respondent would be well advised to proffer some evidence to the contrary in the face of such an allegation. Paragraph 4(c) of the UDRP sets out specific circumstances to assist the Respondent in demonstrating that he or she has legitimate rights or legitimate interests in the domain name. The circumstances are stated to be non-exclusive, but are helpful in considering this issue.

Dealing with each in turn as follows:

(i) The first circumstance is that, before any notice of the dispute to the Respondent, the Respondent had shown demonstrable preparations to use the domain name in connection with a bona fide offering of goods or services. In this case, there is no suggestion that the domain name <brucespringsteen.com> had in fact been used in this way prior to notification of the complaint. Instead, the domain name resolved to another website belonging to Mr Burgar, namely "celebrity1000.com".

(ii) The second circumstance is that the Respondent has "been commonly known by the domain name, even if he has acquired no trade mark or service mark rights". This is much more problematic. Mr Burgar would say that the domain name at issue was registered in the name of "Bruce Springsteen Club" and consequently that the proprietor of the domain name has "been commonly known by the domain name" as required in the UDRP. The question in this case involves the meaning of the words "commonly" and "known by".

(iii) It is hard to say that the mere use of the name "Bruce Springsteen Club" can give rise to an impression in the minds of internet users that the proprietor was effectively "known as" Bruce Springsteen. It is even more remote that it could be said that the proprietor was "commonly" recognised in that fashion. Accordingly the Panel finds that this circumstance in paragraph 4(c) is not met.

The third circumstance is that the Respondent is "making a legitimate non-commercial or fair use of the domain name, without intent for commercial gain to misleadingly divert customers or to tarnish the trade mark or service mark at issue".

There are a number of concepts contained within this "circumstance" which make it a complex issue to resolve. For example, at what point does use of a domain name become "commercial" or alternatively what amounts to "fair use" since those concepts appear to be in the alternative.

An internet search using the words "Bruce Springsteen" gives rise to literally thousands of hits. It is perfectly apparent to any internet user that not all of those hits are "official" or "authorised" sites. The user will browse from one search result to another to find the information and material which he or she is looking for in relation to a search item, in this case the celebrity singer Bruce Springsteen. It is therefore hard to see how it can be said that the registration of the domain name at issue can be "misleading" in its diversion of consumers to the "celebrity1000.com" website.

There have been examples in other cases of blatant attempts, for example, by the use of minor spelling discrepancies to entrap internet users onto sites which have absolutely no connection whatsoever with the name which is being used in its original or slightly altered form. In this case, the internet user, coming upon the "celebrity1000.com" website would perhaps be unsurprised to have arrived there via a search under the name "Bruce Springsteen". If the internet user wished to stay longer at the site he or she could do so, or otherwise they could clearly return to their search results to find more instructed material concerning Bruce Springsteen himself.

Accordingly, it is hard to infer from the conduct of the Respondent in this case an intent, for commercial gain, to misleadingly divert consumers. There is certainly no question of the common law rights of Mr Springsteen being "tarnished" by association with the "celebrity1000.com" website. The Panelists' own search of that site indicates no links which would have that effect, for example connections to sites containing pornographic or other regrettable material.

Accordingly the Panel finds that Bruce Springsteen has not satisfied the second limb of the three part test in the UDRP.

Moving on to the question of bad faith, once again the UDRP contains helpful guidance as to how the Complainant may seek to demonstrate bad faith on the part of the Registrant. The four, non-exclusive, circumstances are set out in paragraph 4(b) of the UDRP, and can be dealt with as follows:

(i) The first circumstance is that there is evidence that the Registrant obtained the domain name primarily for the purpose of selling, renting or otherwise transferring it to the Complainant or to a competitor. This can be dealt with swiftly. There is simply no evidence put forward by the Complainant that there has been any attempt by Mr Burgar to sell the domain name, either directly or indirectly.

(ii) The second circumstance is that the Registrant obtained the domain name in order to prevent the owner of the trade mark or service mark from reflecting that mark in a corresponding domain name, provided that there has been a pattern of such conduct. In this case, Bruce Springsteen's representatives point to the many other celebrity domain names registered by Mr Burgar as evidence that he has indulged in a pattern of this conduct.

However, Mr Burgar is clearly experienced in the ways of the internet. When he registered the domain name at issue in 1996, he would have been well aware that if he had wanted to block the activities of Bruce Springsteen or his record company in order to extract a large payment, or for whatever other reason there may be in creating such a blockage, he could, at nominal cost, have also registered the domain names <brucespringsteen.net> and <brucespringsteen.org>. He did not do so, and indeed subsequently in 1998 Mr Springsteen's record company registered the name <brucespringsteen.net> which has been used as the host site for the official Bruce Springsteen website since that time. It appears in the top five items in a search on the internet under the name "Bruce Springsteen".

It is trite to say that, by registering the domain name at issue, the Registrant has clearly prevented Bruce Springsteen from owning that name himself. However, that does not have the effect required in paragraph 4(b)(ii) of the UDRP. That paragraph indicates that the registration should have the effect of preventing the owner of a trade mark or service mark from reflecting the mark "in a corresponding domain name". In these circumstances what is meant by the word "corresponding"? Nothing that has been done by Mr Burgar has prevented Bruce Springsteen's official website at <brucespringsteen.net> being registered and used in his direct interests. That is surely a "corresponding domain name" for these purposes, as the expression "corresponding domain name" clearly refers back to the words "trade mark or service mark" rather than the domain name at issue referred to in the first line of paragraph 4(b)(ii).

It is perhaps pertinent to observe that the so-called "official" site at <brucespringsteen.net> was registered in 1998. It seems unlikely that, at that time, the existence of the domain name at issue did not become apparent. Whilst this is pure surmise, and consequently in no way relevant to the findings of the Panel, it might be thought that the alleged "blocking" effect of the domain name at issue might have given rise to a complaint at that time, if only in correspondence.

This Panel believes that previous Panels have all too readily concluded that the mere registration of the mark, and indeed other marks of a similar nature, is evidence of an attempt to prevent the legitimate owner of registered or common law trade mark rights from obtaining a "corresponding domain name". This is an issue which should be looked at more closely, and for the purposes of this complaint, the Panel finds that the "circumstance" in paragraph 4(b)(ii) does not arise for the purpose of demonstrating bad faith on the part of the Registrant.

(iii) The third circumstance is that the Registrant has obtained the domain name "primarily for the purpose of disrupting the business of a competitor". This can be dealt with very swiftly as there is no suggestion that that is the case in the present complaint.

(iv) The fourth circumstance is that, by using the domain name, the Registrant has "intentionally attempted to attract, for commercial gain, internet users to his website or other online location, by creating a likelihood of confusion with the Complainant's mark as to the source, sponsorship, affiliation or endorsement of the website or location or of a product or a service on the website or location".

Once again, this sub-paragraph contains a number of concepts which render it complex to analyse and apply. However, the key issue appears to be the requirement that the use of the domain name must "create a likelihood of confusion with the Complainant's mark". As indicated above, a simple search under the name "Bruce Springsteen" on the internet gives rise to many thousands of hits. As also indicated above, even a relatively unsophisticated user would be clearly aware that not all of those hits would be directly associated in an official and authorised capacity with Bruce Springsteen himself, or his agents or record company. The nature of an internet search does not reveal the exact notation of the domain name. Accordingly, the search result may read "Bruce Springsteen—discography", but will not give the user the exact address. That only arises on a screen once the user has gone to that address. The relevance of this is that it is relatively unlikely that any user would seek to go straight to the internet and open the site <brucespringsteen.com> in the optimistic hope of reaching the official Bruce Springsteen website. If anyone sufficiently sophisticated in the use of the internet were to do that, they would very soon realise that the site they reached was not the official site, and consequently would move on, probably to conduct a fuller search.

Accordingly, it is hard to see that there is any likelihood of confusion can arise in these circumstances.

The name of the Registrant is not shown in an internet search, accordingly the fact that the Registrant in this case is "Bruce Springsteen Club" would not have the effect of giving rise to the sort of confusion which might satisfy the test under paragraph 4(b)(iv).

The Panel therefore finds that none of the circumstances in paragraph 4(b) of the UDRP are met in this case.

Paragraph 4(b) makes it quite clear that the four "circumstances" are non-exclusive. In this case, the Complainant has urged the Panel to find bad faith on the grounds of the use of the "fictitious" name "Bruce Springsteen Club" as the Registrant. It may be that there is some element of bad faith in the conduct of Mr. Burgar in registering in the name of "Bruce Springsteen Club". However, on reflection, the Panel does not believe that it is sufficient to satisfy the necessary burden under the UDRP.

Before moving onto the final decision, it is perhaps appropriate in a case of this complexity and profile, that the Panel should briefly consider the authorities which have been referred to, in particular by the Complainant.

Bruce Springsteen's representatives referred to the court decision in the "Northern Lights case" as evidence of the conduct and consequently the bad faith of Mr Burgar. The written decision appended to the complaint is inconclusive, and contains no valid decisions on contested items of evidence such as the allegations that certain conversations took place which are denied by either party to the case in different circumstances. Accordingly, the Panel cannot read anything of significance into that decision.

There have been a number of cases concerning celebrity names, some of which were referred to in this case. Many of those decisions are flawed in some way or another.

The case of Jeannete Winterson v Mark Hogarth (WIPO case number D2000-0235) has been credited with establishing the principle that common law rights can arise in a proper name. The case is also notable for an erroneous interpretation of the third requirement, namely the demonstration of bad faith. There is an indication in the case that the burden falls on the Registrant to demonstrate that the domain name at issue has been used in good faith. That is clearly not the case, and that confusion appears to have knocked on into other cases, for example the Julia Roberts case. The burden is clearly with the Complainant to demonstrate that bad faith has been shown.

In the case of Julia Fiona Roberts v. Russell Boyd (WIPO case number D2000-0210) the question of "permission" arises. In relation to the question of "rights or legitimate interests" it is stated that "Respondent has no relationship with or permission from Complainant for the use of her name or mark". As indicated above, that is simply irrelevant. It is perfectly clear from general principles protecting registered and unregistered trade marks the world over, and indeed from the UDRP, that whilst permission might be conclusive against an allegation of infringement if it can be shown to have been granted, the absence of permission is not conclusive that an infringement has occurred, nor is it conclusive proof that the alleged infringer has no rights of his or her own.

Further, in the Julia Roberts case, there is a suggestion that the registration of the domain name <juliaroberts.com> "necessarily prevented the Complainant from using the disputed domain name". As indicated above, that is not sufficient to meet the criteria required under the URDP for the relevant circumstance in paragraph 4(b).

The case of Daniel C. Marino Jnr v. Video Images Productions (WIPO case number D2000-0598) contains a passage highlighted when annexed to the complaint in this case in the following terms:

> in fact, in light of the uniqueness of the name danmarino.com, which is virtually identical to the Complainant's personal name and

common law trade mark, it would be extremely difficult to foresee any justifiable use that the Respondent could claim. On the contrary, selecting this name gives rise to the impression of an association with the Complainant which is not based in fact.

This Panel contends that that assertion is erroneous. For all the reasons set out above, the users of the internet do not expect all sites bearing the name of celebrities or famous historical figures or politicians, to be authorised or in some way connected with the figures themselves. The internet is an instrument for purveying information, comment, and opinion on a wide range of issues and topics. It is a valuable source of information in many fields, and any attempt to curtail its use should be strongly discouraged. Users fully expect domain names incorporating the names of well known figures in any walk of life to exist independently of any connection with the figures themselves, but having been placed there by admirers or critics as the case may be.

Accordingly, in all the circumstances the Panel does not believe that Bruce Springsteen has met the necessary criteria to sustain a complaint under the URRP.

Decision

In light of the foregoing, the Panel decides that although the domain name at issue is identical to the un-registered trade mark of the Complainant, the Registrant has demonstrated that he has some rights or legitimate interests in respect of the domain name, and the Complainant has failed to demonstrate that the domain name was registered and has been used in bad faith.

Accordingly, the Panel orders that the registration of the domain name be left as it stands.

RICHARD W. PAGE, PANELIST (dissenting):

Paragraph 4(a)(i) of the UDRP requires a Complainant to show the existence of "a trade mark or service mark in which Complainant has rights." The majority has presumed (and should have concluded) that the personal name "Bruce Springsteen" has acquired distinctive secondary meaning giving rise to common law trademark rights in the "famous, almost legendary, recording artist and composer, Bruce Springsteen."

The majority notes that no evidence was presented to establish secondary meaning but the complaint includes allegations of secondary meaning and common law rights [based upon Springsteen's reputation and record sales]. In addition, the majority later notes that "an internet search using the words 'Bruce Springsteen' gives rise to literally thousands of hits." Therefore, secondary meaning has been adequately shown.

Regardless of commentary that personal names (presumably without secondary meaning) are not protected, the language of paragraph 4(a)(i) does not exclude any specific type of common law trademarks from protection. The majority further concludes that the disputed domain name is identical with the common law mark. Therefore, Complainant has met the requirements of paragraph 4(a)(i).

Paragraph 4(a)(ii) requires a Complainant to show Respondent has no rights or legitimate interest in the disputed domain name. Although the way in which the UDRP is written requires the Complainant to demonstrate this, the logic of this burden of proof is questionable in that it requires the Complainant to prove the nonexistence of certain facts. In effect the assertion by Complainant that Respondent has no rights in the mark, through permission or consent of the Complainant or otherwise, is sufficient to shift the burden to Respondent.

Paragraphs 4(c)(i)-(iii) describe the nonexclusive circumstances which may be used to prove that Respondent has rights or legitimate interest in the disputed domain name. The majority bases its decision on a finding that Complainant has failed to disprove 4(c)(iii). This circumstance allows Respondent rights or legitimate interest upon a showing of noncommercial or fair use without misleading diversion of customers. Specifically, the majority finds that Respondent has not misleadingly diverted customers to Respondent's website www.celebrity1000.com. The majority assumes that the internet user will search literally thousands of hits on "Bruce Springsteen" without going directly to brucespringsteen.com and without concluding that "brucespringsteen.com" resolves to a website sanctioned by Complainant. Apparently the Presiding Panelist conducted his independent search in this manner and concludes that a hypothetical internet user would search in the same manner. This is an insufficient basis to conclude that resolution of the domain name brucespringsteen.com into Respondent's website www.celebrity1000.com is not misleading.

The Dissenting Panelist concludes that the average internet user would not sift through thousands of hits searching for information on Bruce Springsteen. Instead, the internet user would devise shortcuts. One obvious shortcut is to go directly to brucespringsteen.com with the expectation that it would lead to the official website. Respondent alludes to the phenomenon that "postponing the creation of other tlds until the '.com' name space dominated the world just sort of happened." The dominance of the ".com" name space is reflected in the common usage of the phrase ".com" as being synonymous with commercial activity on the Internet. Given a vast array of information on the performer Bruce Springsteen, the internet user is more likely than not to associate <brucespringsteen.com> with commercial activity and with an official domain name, resolving to an official website. Therefore, the Dissenting Panelist concludes that that resolution of the domain name <brucespringsteen.com> into Respondent's website www.celebrity1000.com is misleading.

Complainant has alleged that Respondent has no rights or legitimate interest in the disputed domain name, through permission, consent or otherwise. Respondent has not presented sufficient evidence that any of the circumstances in paragraph 4(c)(i)-(iii) is present. Therefore, Complainant has made the necessary showing under paragraph 4(a)(ii).

Paragraphs 4(b)(i)-(iv) describe the nonexclusive circumstances which may be used to prove that Respondent has registered and used the disputed domain name in bad faith. Complainant relies on paragraphs 4(b)(ii) and (iv) to demonstrate Respondent's bad faith. Proving either of these two circumstances is sufficient. Paragraph 4(b)(iv) requires Complainant to prove that Respondent has intentionally attracted internet users to Respondent's website for commercial gain by creating a likelihood of confusion as to the source of the website.

The majority reiterates its analysis that internet users will not be confused by resolution of the <brucespringsteen.com> domain name to Respondent's website and have no expectation of finding an official website. The Dissenting Panelist has already concluded to the contrary.

The remaining element under paragraph 4(b)(iv) is to show that Respondent is engaged in a commercial undertaking. Respondent states in his Response that: " . . . given the hundreds of millions of dollars presently lost by companies such as Amazon and Infospace on the Internet, we are not ashamed to say, we do not have any commercial gain. We lose money." The test of a commercial undertaking is not that the enterprise turns a profit. From Respondent's statements, the Dissenting Panelist infers that the activities of respondent are commercial. Therefore, the circumstances of paragraph 4(b)(iv) are met.

The Dissenting Panelist would rule that Complainant has met his burden and that the disputed domain name should be transferred.

NOTES AND QUESTIONS

(1) **Protection for Personal Names**. As the *Bruce Springsteen.com* panel noted, various other celebrities have successfully invoked the ICANN UDRP procedure based upon common law trademark rights in their names (notwithstanding lack of registration). Indeed, Mr. Burgar has been the losing party in other similar cases. *See, e.g.,* Celine Dion v. Jeff Burgar operating as Celine Dion Club, WIPO Case No. D2000-1838 (Feb. 13, 2001). In the *Julia Roberts* case (where both parties were from the United States), the panel decided that Julia Roberts had common law rights under U.S. law; in the *Jeanette Winterson* case, referenced in the *Springsteen* opinion, both parties were domiciled in the United Kingdom, the panel decided that common law rights existed under English law. If the parties were from different countries, only one of which offered common law protection to personal names, which law should a panel apply? Are panels qualified to determine whether valid common law rights exist under national law? If so, should panelists also be able to make determinations regarding the invalidity of a national registration upon which a UDRP claim is premised? Would these two evaluations implicate different considerations? *Compare supra* § 7.04[B] (cases discussing the attitude of *U.S. courts* to the review of foreign trademark registrations).

WIPO has, at the request of various member states, agreed to study whether the scope of the UDRP should be broadened to address cases such as those involving personal names of celebrities even absent common law trademark status. (The Anticybersquatting Consumer Protection Act already contains provisions in this regard. *See infra* § 7.07[D].) WIPO published the interim report as part of this so-called "Second WIPO Domain Name Process" on April 12, 2001. *See* The Registration of Rights and the Use of Names in the Internet Domain Name System, Interim Report of the Second WIPO Domain Name Process (April 12, 2001), at http://wipo2.wipo.int/process2/rfc/rfc3/pdf/report.pdf.

(2) **Paragraph 4(b)(ii)**. Do you agree with the *Springsteen* majority's interpretation of paragraph 4(b)(ii) to the effect that the registration of brucespringsteen.com did not preclude the registration by the trademark owner?

(3) **Protection for Geographical Names**. The Second WIPO Domain Name Process is also currently considering whether the UDRP should make explicit provision for the protection of geographical terms. Again, however, ICANN panels have addressed the protection of geographical terms under the existing policy. In *Excelentisimo Ayuntamiento de Barcelona v. Barcelona.com*, WIPO Case No. D2000-0505 (Aug. 4, 2000), the domain name barcelona.com was ordered transferred to the City of Barcelona. The city owned numerous Spanish trademark registrations dating back to 1984 incorporating the name BARCELONA, and its application for a Spanish trademark registration for barcelona.com was pending at the time at which the ICANN proceedings were initiated. The respondent had owned the domain name registration in question since 1996, and claimed that the main purpose of the registration had been to develop links between the different cities having the name Barcelona (and to provide information relating thereto). The panel concluded that "anybody requiring information about the city of Barcelona . . . will naturally start the search by attempting to locate it through the expression Barcelona. Hence, respondent is definitely taking advantage of the normal confusion of the public," who, the panel suggested, would expect to reach some official representative of the city of Barcelona at that site. Is this reasoning persuasive? In *Port of Helsinki v. Paragon International Projects Ltd.*, WIPO Case No. D2001-0002 (Feb. 12, 2001), the Port Authority of the City of Helsinki, Finland, sought the transfer of the domain name registration for portofhelsinki.com. Although the city owned no trademark registration for the term PORTOFHELSINKI, it asserted unregistered rights (such rights being available under Finnish trademark law) in the term and noted that it owned the Finnish country code registration portofhelsinki.fi, and registrations in the .fi country code top level domain are granted by the relevant Finnish authority not on a first-come-first-served basic but only to parties "entitled to the name." Because port business is international, the complainant argued, portofhelsinki.com is where the public would first look for information concerning the port. The panelist rejected the complaint and noted that the UDRP does not presently apply to conflicts between domain names and geographical indications or signs or symbols that are not supported by a trademark or service mark. The panel found that the complainant had no unregistered trademark rights under Finnish law. Is the panelist in *Port of Helsinki* correct in his interpretation of the Policy? If so, should the Policy be amended to enable the domain name registration consisting of a geographical name to belong to the legal authority of the area in question? If it should, to which domains should this rule extend?

(4) **National Court "Appeals" of ICANN decisions**. When filing a UDRP

complaint, a trademark owner must agree to submit itself to the jurisdiction of one of two national "courts of mutual jurisdiction" for purposes of reviewing a UDRP panel decision. The trademark owner may select either the courts of the country where the registrar in question is located or the country where the domain name registrant is located (as shown in the registrar's Whois data). Under the UDRP, if a losing respondent files a court action in a national court of mutual jurisdiction within ten days of the panel decision, and transmits a copy of such a complaint to the relevant registrar, the registrar will stay implementation of the transfer or cancellation of the domain name registration ordered by the panelist. *See* UDRP Rules, ¶¶ 1, 3(b)(xiii). The respondent in the *Julia Roberts* case immediately filed a suit in federal district court in the Eastern District of Virginia claiming that, as a site containing news, satire and parody related to Ms. Roberts, the transfer of the domain name implicated issues of free expression that outweighed intellectual property considerations. *See* Web Site Operator sues Julia Roberts in Domain Dispute, Bloomberg News, CNET News.com, June 19 (2000) (quoting statement in the complaint that "the provision of Internet domain names is fundamentally a human rights issue, not an intellectual property issue"). This caused the suspension of the panel order. A similar fate befell Ian Anderson, member of the musical band Jethro Tull. *See* The Ian Anderson Group of Companies Ltd. v. Denny Hammerton, WIPO Case No. D2000-0475 (July 12, 2000) (ordering transfer of jethrotull.com); Chase Squires, *Land O'Lakes Man Fights to Keep Web Site's Name,* ST. PETERSBURG TIMES, Wed. Aug. 9, 2000 at 1 (reporting lawsuit by respondent in the jethrotull.com ICANN proceeding also alleging that "the provision of Internet domain names is fundamentally a human rights issue, not an intellectual property issue" and seeking injunctive and monetary relief). And the City of Barcelona also saw its ICANN victory challenged in U.S. court. *See infra* note 5. What is the purpose of the provision enabling national court proceedings to cause the suspension of a panel decision? What weight should be given panel determinations in the national proceedings? Despite these examples, only a very few losing registrants have filed national court proceedings. What might explain this small number of national "appeals"?

5. **Section 32(2)(D)(v).** The ACPA, discussed in more detail below, permits domain name registrants whose domain name has been canceled or transferred pursuant to the UDRP (or any similar policy) to file a civil action in U.S. federal court against the prevailing party to establish that the registration and use of the domain name was lawful (under the Lanham Act). *See* 15 U.S.C. § 1114(2)(D)(v) (West Supp. 1999). If the domain name registrant is successful, the court may "grant injunctive relief to the domain name registrant, including the reactivation of the domain name or transfer of the domain name to the domain name registrant." *Id.* Although complaints have been filed in a U.S. district court invoking this provision, *see, e.g.,* Barcelona.com Inc. v. Excelentisimo Ayuntamiento de Barcelona (filed Aug. 17, 2000), http://www.domainbattles.com/lawsuit3.htm, there have been no reported decisions involving this provision. What purpose does this provision serve?

(6) **Trademarksucks Cases.** Several cases have been brought by trademark owners against the owners of domain names that consist of the complainant's trademark plus the suffix "sucks". Early cases were favorable to the trademark

owners.   In *Wal-Mart Stores, Inc. v. Wallmartcanadasucks.com,* Case No.
D2000-1104 (WIPO Arb. & Med. Center Nov. 23, 2000), however, the panelist
declined to transfer the registration for Wallmartcanadasucks.com to Wal-Mart
Stores, the trademark owner.   A later panel, over a dissent, concluded that
there should be a per se privilege for use of "sucks." *See* Lockheed Martin Corp.
v. Dan Parisi, Case No. D2000-1015 (WIPO Arbitration and Mediation Center,
Jan. 26, 2001).   What are the arguments for and against transfer of a
"trademarksucks" registration? Even if the use of a "trademark.sucks" domain
name were confusingly similar to a trademark registration of "trademark," how
else might a domain name registrant defend its registration under the UDRP?
Are there advantages to developing a "cybergriping" jurisprudence under the
rubric of confusingly similarity or elsewhere in a panel's analysis? Do you agree
with the development of a *per se* rule that treats domain names consisting of a
trademark with the "sucks" suffix or prefix as not confusingly similar to the
trademark in question? Is the case-by-case approach of the panelist in
wallmartcanadasucks.com preferable? How would your analysis of these two
cases be affected by the introduction of a new .sucks generic top level domain?
In light of that, do you support the introduction of such a generic top level
domain?   What restrictions, if any, would you impose on ownership of
registrations in the .sucks domain, and how might *those restrictions* affect your
analysis of alleged violations of the UDRP in the .com domain?

(7) **New Generic Top Level Domains.** ICANN recently announced that it
would create several new generic top level domain names. How will this change
the nature of consumer use of domain names? (Does that depend upon the new
names?) How will it change domain name registration practices? To what
extent can the domain name allocation process affect the shape of trademark
law in this area? Should it?

[D]   Cybersquatting Specific National Legislation: the ACPA

THE ANTICYBERSQUATTING CONSUMER PROTECTION ACT
Pub. L. 106-113, Tit. III

In addition to judicial efforts, in many countries, to protect trademark holders
against cybersquatting under existing trademark and unfair competition laws,
the United States Congress in late 1999 enacted additional legislation aimed at
the problem. Section 3002(a) of the Anticybersquatting Consumer Protection
Act creates a new Section 43(d) of the Lanham Act, which provides as follows:

Section 43(d)

(1)(A) A person shall be liable in a civil action by the owner of a mark,
including a personal name which is protected as a mark under this section, if,
without regard to the goods or services of the parties, that person–

(i) has a bad faith intent to profit from that mark, including a personal name which is protected as a mark under this section; and

(ii) registers, traffics in, or uses a domain name that—

(I) in the case of a mark that is distinctive at the time of registration of the domain name, is identical or confusingly similar to that mark; [or]

(II) in the case of a famous mark that is famous at the time of registration of the domain name, is identical or confusingly similar to or dilutive of that mark; . . .

(B) (i) In determining whether a person has a bad faith intent described under subparagraph (A), a court may consider factors such as, but not limited to—

(I) the trademark or other intellectual property rights of the person, if any, in the domain name;

(II) the extent to which the domain name consists of the legal name of the person or a name that is otherwise commonly used to identify that person;

(III) the person's prior use, if any, of the domain name in connection with the bona fide offering of any goods or services;

(IV) the person's bona fide noncommercial or fair use of the mark in a site accessible under the domain name;

(V) the person's intent to divert consumers from the mark owner's online location to a site accessible under the domain name that could harm the goodwill represented by the mark, either for commercial gain or with the intent to tarnish or disparage the mark, by creating a likelihood of confusion as to the source, sponsorship, affiliation, or endorsement of the site;

(VI) the person's offer to transfer, sell, or otherwise assign the domain name to the mark owner or any third party for financial gain without having used, or having an intent to use, the domain name in the bona fide offering of any goods or services, or the person's prior conduct indicating a pattern of such conduct;

(VII) the person's provision of material and misleading false contact information when applying for the registration of the domain name, the person's intentional failure to maintain accurate contact information, or the person's prior conduct indicating a pattern of such conduct;

(VIII) the person's registration or acquisition of multiple domain names which the person knows are identical or confusingly similar to marks of others that are distinctive at the time of registration of such domain names, or dilutive of famous marks of others that are famous at the time of registration of such domain names, without regard to the goods or services of the parties; and

(IX) the extent to which the mark incorporated in the person's domain name registration is or is not distinctive and famous within the meaning of subsection (c)(1) of section 43.

(ii) Bad faith intent described under subparagraph (A) shall not be found in any case in which the court determines that the person believed and had reasonable grounds to believe that the use of the domain name was a fair use or otherwise lawful.

(C) In any civil action involving the registration, trafficking, or use of a domain name under this paragraph, a court may order the forfeiture or cancellation of the domain name or the transfer of the domain name to the owner of the mark.

(D) A person shall be liable for using a domain name under subparagraph (A) only if that person is the domain name registrant or that registrant's authorized licensee.

(E) As used in this paragraph, the term `traffics in' refers to transactions that include, but are not limited to, sales, purchases, loans, pledges, licenses, exchanges of currency, and any other transfer for consideration or receipt in exchange for consideration.

(2) (A) The owner of a mark may file an in rem civil action against a domain name in the judicial district in which the domain name registrar, domain name registry, or other domain name authority that registered or assigned the domain name is located if--

(i) the domain name violates any right of the owner of a mark registered in the Patent and Trademark Office, or protected under subsection (a) or (c); and

(ii) the court finds that the owner–

(I) is not able to obtain in personam jurisdiction over a person who would have been a defendant in a civil action under paragraph (1); or

(II) through due diligence was not able to find a person who would have been a defendant in a civil action under paragraph (1) by--

(aa) sending a notice of the alleged violation and intent to proceed under this paragraph to the registrant of the domain name at the postal and e-mail address provided by the registrant to the registrar; and

(bb) publishing notice of the action as the court may direct promptly after filing the action.

(B) The actions under subparagraph (A)(ii) shall constitute service of process.

(C) In an in rem action under this paragraph, a domain name shall be deemed to have its situs in the judicial district in which–

(i) the domain name registrar, registry, or other domain name authority that registered or assigned the domain name is located; or

(ii) documents sufficient to establish control and authority regarding the disposition of the registration and use of the domain name are deposited with the court.

(D) (i) The remedies in an in rem action under this paragraph shall be limited to a court order for the forfeiture or cancellation of the domain name or the transfer of the domain name to the owner of the mark. Upon receipt of written notification of a filed, stamped copy of a complaint filed by the owner of a mark in a United States district court under this paragraph, the domain name registrar, domain name registry, or other domain name authority shall--

(I) expeditiously deposit with the court documents sufficient to establish the court's control and authority regarding the disposition of the registration and use of the domain name to the court; and

(II) not transfer, suspend, or otherwise modify the domain name during the pendency of the action, except upon order of the court.

(ii) The domain name registrar or registry or other domain name authority shall not be liable for injunctive or monetary relief under this paragraph except in the case of bad faith or reckless disregard, which includes a willful failure to comply with any such court order.

NOTES AND QUESTIONS

(1) **Remedies**. The civil action established under paragraph (1) and the *in rem* action established under paragraph (2) of the new Section 43(d) are in addition to any other civil action or remedy otherwise applicable. Section 3003 provides that damages and injunctive relief will be available under the statute, as will statutory damages under a new Section 35(d) of the Lanham Act, which provides that "in a case involving a violation of section 43(d)(1), the plaintiff may elect, at any time before final judgment is rendered by the trial court, to recover, instead of actual damages and profits, an award of statutory damages in the amount of not less than $1,000 and not more than $100,000 per domain name, as the court considers just."

Section 3004 limits the monetary liability of any domain name registrar, registry, or other registration authority that takes action affecting a domain name in accordance with the procedures set out in the legislation: they shall not be liable for monetary relief or, with limited exceptions, for injunctive relief, to any person for such action, regardless of whether the domain name is finally determined to infringe or dilute the mark. Section 43(d) applies to all domain names registered before, on, or after the date of the enactment of the Act, except that damages shall not be available with respect to the registration, trafficking, or use of a domain name that occurs before the date of the enactment of the ACPA. *See* Section 3010.

(2) **Protection for Personal Names.** The statute also creates a cause of action in Section 3002(b) intended to offer additional protections for individuals. This provides that "any person who registers a domain name [on or after December 2, 1999] that consists of the name of another living person, or a name

Salmons, has no connection with the Eastern District of Virginia—other than registering the domain names with a registry located in Herndon, Virginia—and he is not subject to this Court's in personam jurisdiction. However, Congress has determined that where an internet domain name infringes a U. S. trademark, a suit to enforce the U.S. intellectual property rights may proceed *in rem* in the District where the registry is located. NSI, the company that registered the Defendant domain names, is located in the Eastern District of Virginia. As such, the Court finds that jurisdiction in this district exists, 15 U.S.C. § 1125(d)(2)(A), and that the statute allows a properly narrow and constitutional exercise of that jurisdiction.

2. Defendants' 28 U.S.C. § 1655 Argument

Defendants contend that the exercise of *in rem* jurisdiction in this case is improper under the statute providing for in rem proceedings in federal court, 28 U.S.C. § 1655. [Before Section 1655 may be successfully invoked by a litigant, the suit must, inter alia, be one to enforce a legal or equitable lien upon, or claim to, the title to real or personal property, or to remove some encumbrance, lien or cloud upon the title of such property].

Plaintiff has no legal claim to the domain names at issue. It did not register the names nor pay the registration fee for them. Plaintiff's legal right to bring this suit instead stems from its interest in the U.S. *trademarks* infringed by the name. These are fundamentally different interests. The ACPA gives Plaintiff the right to challenge the infringement of its intellectual property rights engendered by the registration of Defendant domain names, but it does not give Plaintiff the sort of legal or equitable lien on the domain names [that is required by case law interpreting Section 1655]. Section 1655 does not provide the Court with jurisdiction over Plaintiff's action in this case.

3. Defendants' *Forum Non Conveniens* and International Comity Arguments

Defendants next argue that dismissal is proper for reasons of forum non conveniens and international comity, which militate against a Virginia court's deciding the issues presented here. A district court faced with an issue with repercussions beyond U.S. borders should consider issues of comity in deciding whether to retain jurisdiction over a case before it. "Comity, in the legal sense, is neither a matter of absolute obligation, on the one hand, nor of mere courtesy and good will, upon the other." Hilton v. Guyot, 113 U.S. 159, 163-64 (1895). The doctrine of forum non conveniens allows a district court for the convenience of parties and witnesses and in the interest of justice, to transfer any civil action to any other district or division where it might have been brought.[7]

. . . .

Defendants describe the inconvenience to Registrant Salmons of litigating the

---

[7]The Court finds that its discussion of forum non conveniens embraces any issues of comity that might arise concerning forum selection.

matter in the Eastern District of Virginia, including the location in Canada of all witnesses and documents and the financial burden the litigation would impose on him. These factors [are] to be weighed by the Court in its exercise of discretion.

The Fourth Circuit has explained that "[a] forum non conveniens dismissal must be based on the finding that, when weighed against plaintiff's choice of forum, the relevant public and private interests strongly favor a specific, adequate, and available alternative forum. [cit]. The Supreme Court laid out specific factors to guide a forum non conveniens assessment in Gulf Oil Corp. v. Gilbert, 30 U.S. 501 (1947).

> An interest to be considered, and the one likely to be most pressed, is the private interest of the litigant. Important considerations are the relative ease of access to sources of proof; availability of compulsory process for attendance of unwilling, and the cost of obtaining attendance of willing, witnesses;... and all other practical problems that make trial of a case easy, expeditious and inexpensive. There may also be questions as to the enforcibility [sic] of a judgement if one is obtained...[U]nless the balance is strongly in favor of the defendant, the plaintiff's choice of forum should rarely be disturbed. . .
>
> Factors of public interest also have place in applying the doctrine . . . There is an appropriateness, too, in having the trial of a diversity case in a forum that is at home with the state law that must govern the case, rather than having a court in some other forum untangle problems in conflict of laws, and in law foreign to itself.

330 U.S. at 508-09. *See* Rankine v. Rankine, 166 F.3d 333 (4th Cir. 1998).

Applying these factors to the issue here, it is clear that if he chooses to defend his interest in the domain names in the Eastern District of Virginia, Registrant Salmons will face a financial burden. Litigating the matter in this District may also create problems of access to proof. The parties, relevant witnesses and documents are in Canada. The Court cannot compel unwilling witnesses in Canada to appear before it, and even willing witnesses will face financial burdens if they participate in the litigation. However, the Fourth Circuit has indicated that the balance of factors should "strongly" weigh in favor of transfer, [cit], echoing the Supreme Court's suggestion in *Gulf Oil* that the plaintiff's choice of forum should be respected, as far as possible. As a general proposition, litigation is expensive and burdensome. Registrant may face more hardship than most in that regard, but he has not shown that it will literally be financially impossible to litigate in this District, not that witnesses and documents will be entirely unavailable here.

Moreover, public factors bearing on the question lean toward retaining the matter in this District. A Canadian court would be less familiar with the provisions of the ACPA than is this Court. Even if it prevailed, Plaintiff might face difficulties enforcing the Canadian court's judgement in the United States, which would arguably undercut its U.S. trademark rights in its "technodome" mark.[8] A trademark holder seeking to enforce its U.S. registered marks against infringing domain name registrants should not be penalized in the exercise of those rights merely because the parties involved are not United States citizens.

On a more basic level, Plaintiff may not be able to assert the same rights in Canada, which lacks a body of law equivalent to the ACPA and whose enforcement of its trademark laws cannot extend into the United States. Defendants suggest Canadian intellectual property law, drawing upon recent English case law, might view the registration of a trademark-infringing domain name as an actionable trademark violation. This outcome is particularly likely, Defendants argue, in a case like the one at the bar, involving both registration and use of the mark. However, Defendants' prediction of what the Canadian courts will do when presented with this issue is necessarily speculative and provides little support for the argument that Canada is a satisfactory alternative forum for this lawsuit.[9]

Defendants also contend that another forum provides the same remedies for a victorious suitor as those sought here, namely forfeiture of transfer of [a] domain name that was registered in bad faith: the Internet Corporation for Assigned Names and Numbers ("ICANN").[10] Plaintiff initiated proceedings before ICANN in March 2000 but withdrew from those proceedings upon receiving a preliminary ruling that the court selected to review the outcome of the arbitration should be in Canada.[11] This ruling was contrary to Plaintiff's preference for review by the Eastern District of Virginia, which was a permissible alternative under the ICANN rules. Plaintiff then filed the instant lawsuit.

Plainly, ICANN's dispute resolution proceedings are not equivalent to the formal consideration of a cause by a court record. ICANN lacks the enforcement power of the court system. For these reasons, ICANN is not an adequate substitute for this court's consideration of the issues presented here.

In sum, Defendants have not overcome the presumption that favors the

---

[8]Plaintiff's ability to enforce its trademark rights in the United States is of particular importance given its use of the mark in connection with a theme park in Queens, New York.

[9]The Court does not give this factor conclusive weight in the analysis, *see* Piper Aircraft Co. v. Reyno, 454 U.S. 235, 247 (1981), but considers it as one factor among several in the forum non conveniens assessment.

[10]According to ICANN's web site:

All registrants in the .com, .net, and .org top-level domains follow the Uniform

Domain-Name Dispute-Resolution Policy (often referred to as the "UDRP"). Under the policy, most types of trademark-based domain-name disputes must be resolved by agreement, court action, or arbitration before a registrar will cancel, suspend, or transfer a domain name. Disputes alleged to arise from abusive registrations of domain names (for example, cybersquatting) may be addressed by expedited administrative proceedings that the holder of trademark rights initiates by filing a complaint with an approved dispute-resolution service provider.

To invoke the policy, a trademark owner should either (a) file a complaint in a court of proper jurisdiction against the domain-name holder (or where appropriate an in rem action concerning the domain name) or (b) in cases of abusive registration submit a complaint to an approved dispute-resolution service provider..." <http://www.icann.org/udrp/udrp.hem> (October 20, 2000).

[11]The procedural history discussed here does not affect the Court's reasoning in this case.

plaintiff's choice of forum. *See* Piper Aircraft v. Reyno, 454 U.S. 236, 255 (1981). Accordingly, the Court finds that dismissal on the grounds of comity and forum non conveniens is not proper.

IV. Conclusion

For the above-stated reasons, Defendants' Motion to Dismiss is DENIED.

NOTES AND QUESTIONS

(1) **Choice of Law and *In Rem* Jurisdiction.** The *Heathmount* court did not attempt any analysis of whether Canadian or U.S. law should be applied to the dispute between two Canadian citizens? What does this tell you about the ACPA? If Canada had enacted a statute identical to the ACPA, which law should the court have applied and why? (Should the court hear such a case?)

(2) **Adequate Alternative Fora.** What must Canadian law provide in order for Canada to be adjudged an adequate forum in which to resolve a domain name dispute between two Canadians? Does the lack of an exact replica of the ACPA mean that Canada can never be an adequate alternative forum in a domain name/trademark dispute? If substantive Canadian law contained a cause of action based upon the same elements as the ACPA, but provided for more limited relief would that be adequate? In what ways will the *Heathmount* court's analysis affect the development of both national and international rules on the conflict between domain names and trademarks?

(3) **National Court Treatment of ICANN.** Why does the *Heathmount* court not regard ICANN as an adequate alternative? U.S. courts have thus far indicated that they will not treat ICANN panel opinions as binding on them. *See, e.,g.* Weber-Stephen Prods. v. Armitage Hardware & Bldg. Supply, 54 U.S.P.Q.2d (BNA) 1766, 1768 (N.D. Ill. 2000). This would appear to have been the intent of the drafters of the UDRP. Rule 4(k) makes clear that a proceeding under the UDRP does not preclude either party from pursuing an action in a court of competent jurisdiction. *See* BroadBridge Media, L.L.C. v. Hypercd.com, 55 U.S.P.Q.2d (BNA) 1426, 1428-29 (S.D.N.Y. 2000) (holding that the pendency of an arbitration under the UDRP does not foreclose a concurrent court action under the ACPA).

In *Referee Enters., Inc. v. Planet Ref, Inc.*, a federal district court in Wisconsin issued a preliminary injunction prohibiting the defendants from using the term ereferee.com as part of its domain name under both confusion-based and dilution theories of trademark infringement. *See* Referee Enters., Inc. v. Planet Ref, Inc., Case No. 00-C-1391 (E.D. Wis. Jan. 24, 2001), Order for Preliminary Injunction, http://www.loundy.com/Cases/Referee_Ent_v_Planet_Ref.html. Yet the plaintiff had previously failed to persuade an ICANN panel that the defendant's conduct violated the UDRP. *See* Referee Enters., Inc. v. Planet Ref, Inc., NAF Case No. FA4000094707 (June 26, 2000) (finding that the respondent had a legitimate interest in the domain name given the "sports background" of the respondent business and the generic meaning of the term "referee," and noting that while the complainant had registered trademark rights in the term REFEREE with respect to magazines concerning sports officiating, this cannot preempt all uses of the term). Should national courts give any weight to panel opinions? Might it be appropriate to give weight to panel opinions for some purposes but not others? If so, for which purposes might they be considered? How might the attitude of national courts affect the success or role of the ICANN panels, and how might that attitude contribute to the appropriate development of international intellectual property law.

(4) **Scope of Relief in National Courts.** One advantage that might persuade a plaintiff to proceed under the cybersquatting legislation (other than having already failed before ICANN) is the scope of relief available. The district court order in *Ereferee* prohibited the defendant, *inter alia*, from "using the mark REFEREE or any other mark confusingly similar to [plaintiff's] REFEREE trademark, either alone or in combination with other words, specifically including, but not limited to *eReferee, ereferee.com, ereferee.net, ereferee.org, refereecamp.com, refereecamps.com*, as a mark, domain name or highlighted term, or in any way other than in common textual reference, any other mark or second-level domain name including the term "referee" in any form." Should this breadth of relief be available under national law?

PART IV

ISSUES IN INTERNATIONAL INTELLECTUAL PROPERTY LAW AND POLICY LOOKING FORWARD

Chapter 8

ISSUES IN INTERNATIONAL INTELLECTUAL PROPERTY LAW AND POLICY LOOKING FORWARD

§ 8.01   Institutional Agendas and Challenges Post-TRIPS

PAUL VANDOREN, THE IMPLEMENTATION OF THE TRIPS AGREEMENT[*]
2 J. WORLD INTELL. PROP. L. 25 (1999)

I. SOME CONSIDERATIONS RELATING TO THE TRIPS AGREEMENT

. . . .

C. Transitional Periods

Given that the TRIPS Agreement provides a significant number of new obligations, transitional periods were agreed upon to enable WTO members to review and amend their legislation.

Developed country members had a transition period of one year after the date of entry into force of the WTO Agreement, i.e. up until 1 January 1996. Developing country members [had], in general, five years (up until 1 January 2000) and least-developed country members have eleven years (up until 1 January 2006). A member in transition [was] given the possibility of a transition period until the year 2000 if [certain] criteria [were] met.

. . . .

However, all WTO members had to meet the national treatment and most-favoured-nation requirements as of 1 January 1996. In addition, there is the standstill clause, providing that during a transition period, member countries shall not make changes in their legislation or practices which would result in a lesser degree of consistency with the provisions of the TRIPS Agreement.

Experience has shown that, in practice, some . . . members do not wait until the end of the transitional period of which they can avail themselves, to amend their legislation. The world's major trading nations have encouraged . . . members to advance the implementation of their obligations on a voluntary basis, without much success however. . . . In this respect, the Directors-General of the [WIPO] and the [WTO] recently took a joint initiative on technical co-operation.

---

[*]This article was originally published in the January 1999 issue of the Journal of World Intellectual Property (Vol. 2 No. 1) and is reproduced by permission of the publisher.

In order to facilitate the implementation of the TRIPS Agreement, in particular by developing and least-developed country members, developed country members shall provide technical and financial co-operation. Such co-operation shall include assistance in the preparation of laws and regulations on the protection and enforcement of intellectual property rights and the prevention of their abuse. It shall also include support for the establishment or reinforcement of domestic offices and agencies, including the training of personnel. The European Community is one of the major providers of technical assistance in this area . . . .

As far as future new WTO members are concerned, the European Community and its major trading partners have requested [that] such countries implement their TRIPS obligations as of the day of their accession, i.e. without a transitional period. This is not unreasonable, given that by then these countries will have known for several years the contents of the TRIPS Agreement and will have had several years to amend their legislation. To this end, the European Community co-operates with countries such as Russia and China.

II. The TRIPS Council

A. Review of The Implementing Legislation

An important feature of the WTO is that the monitoring of the operation of the Agreements and, in particular, of members' compliance with their obligations, is done in a systematic way. This is also true for the TRIPS Agreement, which is monitored by the TRIPS Council, to which members are obliged to submit their implementing legislation for examination.

In 1996 and 1997, the implementing legislation of all developed country members was reviewed in four meetings of the TRIPS Council which each lasted for about a week. [*See supra* § 2.03[B].] In addition, the TRIPS Council reviewed the legislation of the following Eastern and Central European countries: Bulgaria, Hungary, the Czech Republic, Romania, Slovakia, Slovenia and Poland. As far as the developing country members are concerned, Korea, Singapore and Hong Kong indicated that they would be open to participate in an advance review. Cyprus also took a similar position. Unfortunately, no agreement on "ground rules" for such a review could be reached in the TRIPS Council.

Overall, the review of the implementing legislation of the above-mentioned countries was clearly interesting, [albeit] time-consuming . . . [T]he exercise was well worth the effort, mainly for the following reasons:

* it raised in a significant way the awareness and understanding of WTO members of the TRIPS obligations;

* it helped to identify shortcomings, and in many cases to remove them (others might be dealt with in the WTO dispute settlement procedure); and

   * an important precedent has been set which is likely to serve as the standard for the upcoming review of the legislation of the developing country members as of the year 2000, although some changes concerning the procedures might be necessary.

B. The Built-in Agenda

1. *Geographical Indications*

On the basis of TRIPS, Article 24(2), work in this area has started with the preparation by the WTO Secretariat, with the input of WTO members, of a checklist of questions in relation to the national regimes for the protection and enforcement of geographical indications, to which WTO members have been asked to respond.

Article 23(4) of the TRIPS provides that, in order to facilitate the protection of geographical indications for wines (and spirits), negotiations shall be undertaken in the TRIPS Council on the establishment of a multilateral system of notification and registration. Preliminary work has been undertaken by the WTO Secretariat and preliminary discussions have taken place amongst WTO members. [*See supra* § 3.02[D].]

2. *Patentability*

Article 27(3)(b) of the TRIPS Agreement provides for the review of the provisions of patentability of plants and animals other than micro-organisms, and the protection of plant varieties as of 1999. [*See supra* § 3.04[F].] With respect to the question of patentability of plants and animals, the Community pharmaceutical and chemical industry generally has a vested interest in this matter. However, progress is likely to depend on more general and politically sensitive considerations such as the question of life forms or traditional knowledge. The [OECD] is also working on this matter. Account also needs to be taken of the fact that the Community recently, and after lengthy debates, adopted the Directive on the legal protection of biotechnological inventions. It is uncertain whether the Community will be in a position to go further than what is provided in this Directive. With respect to the question of the protection of plant varieties, account needs to be taken of developments in the International Union for the Protection of New Varieties of Plants (UPOV).

3. *Review of the Implementation of the TRIPS Agreement*

Article 71(1) provides that the TRIPS Council shall review implementation of the TRIPS Agreement as of 1 January 2000 [and subsequently, every two years]. . . .

4. *Non-Violation Complaints*

Under Article 64(3) of the TRIPS Agreement the TRIPS Council is required to examine, during the period from 1 January 1995 to 1 January 2000, the scope and modalities for "non-violation" complaints, and to submit its recommendations to the Ministerial Conference for approval. Any decision of the Ministerial Conference to approve such recommendations or to extend the five-year period has to be made by consensus. During that five-year period, the rules on "non-violation" do not apply. The Community supports this automatic "re-inclusion" of such complaints into the dispute settlement procedures.

III. DISPUTE SETTLEMENT

The WTO Dispute Settlement system is gradually becoming a major instrument for providing further clarification of the TRIPS Agreement. . . .

. . . .

IV. NEED FOR A TRIPS II?

The Community favours the launching of a comprehensive [new] WTO Round . . . If such a launch takes place, consensus will also be required concerning the subject-matter to be included. The question, therefore, arises: should TRIPS be included?

The TRIPS Agreement was not, of course, intended to be a static instrument but one capable of development. It is obvious that it does not solve all problems in the area of international rules on intellectual property matters and that new problems have emerged, e.g. as a result of new technologies or new ways of communication.

[T]he TRIPS Council will hold a review of the TRIPS Agreement after five years, i.e. as of the year 2000, but is also empowered to review it at any time in the light of any relevant new developments which might warrant modification and amendment (Article 71, paragraph 1). However, the TRIPS Council has no competence to take decisions on these amendments. Generally, amendments to the TRIPS Agreement have to be adopted through a formal acceptance process by all WTO members. In special cases, the TRIPS Agreement provides for a simplified procedure where amendments merely serve the purpose of adjusting higher levels of protection of intellectual property rights (Article 71, paragraph 2).

Apart from the items covered by the built-in agenda mentioned above, the TRIPS Agreement does not address the issues:

> * which were left out of the negotiations in the Uruguay Round, such as the resale right for artists and the question of moral rights in the copyright area; the definition of the "inventive moment" ("first-to-file" or "first-to-invent"), the inclusion of UPOV, improved

protection for textile designs and appellations of origin in the industrial rights area;

* where multilateral consensus building, notably in WIPO, made progress only recently, such as protection of copyright and related rights in the Information Society or the introduction of a *sui generis* protection for databases;

* which would further increase the level of protection by expanding beyond what has been agreed upon in the TRIPS Agreement or facilitate the processes of obtaining existing rights, such as the introduction of world-wide patents and trademarks, the extension of the term of patent protection or rules clarifying the protection of trademarks in relation to Internet domain names. In addition, strengthened enforcement mechanisms could add to improving intellectual property right protection.

Consultations with representatives of different categories of right-holders are still ongoing. It is clear, however, that transitional periods already agreed upon during the Uruguay Round negotiations are not negotiable in any new Round.

NOTES AND QUESTIONS

(1) **Speed of Review**. Since the Vandoren article was written, the review by the TRIPS Council of developing countries' legislation has been slow but steady. Delays may cause a short de facto extension of the transitional periods for developing countries. In advance of the Seattle ministerial conference in December 1999, proposals were made to extend the transitional periods, but no agreement on extension was reached. You should now have a keen sense of the role of WIPO in international intellectual property lawmaking. In order to expedite the review process, would it be appropriate for WIPO to offer developing countries assistance in responding to TRIPS Council questions? Would your answer change if WIPO had helped in the drafting of the developing country's legislation?

(2) **Technical Cooperation**. Should there be any limits to the nature and extent of the "technical cooperation" provided by developed countries to the developing countries? What dangers attend this process? What gains does it generate?

(3) **The "Built-in" Agenda**. The TRIPS Council continues to discuss the scope and modalities of nonviolation complaints, but no great progress has been made. In the meantime, countries appear reluctant to test the limits of the concept, and no country has indicated an intent to file a nonviolation complaint in the near future. The nonviolation complaint has the potential, however, depending upon how the concept is applied, to affect the future shape of international intellectual property law. *See supra* § 5.03[A].

(4) **The TRIPS II Agenda.** Would you support a "TRIPS II"? If so, based upon your study of international intellectual property law and policy, which items should be on the agenda? Do you agree with the suggestions made by Paul Vandoren? Other frequently mentioned topics include the protection of traditional knowledge, *see infra* § 8.02, the relationship between intellectual property and biodiversity, *see infra* § 8.03, issues raised by e-commerce, the incorporation of post-TRIPS conventions (such as the TLT, the WCT and the WPPT), as well as the relationship between intellectual property rights and access to health care. *See supra* § 3.04[D][2]. Why should a TRIPS II Agreement not have transitional periods? *Cf.* Proposed EU *Droit de Suite* Directive, *supra* § 4.05[C].

(5) **WIPO and the TRIPS Council: Parallel or Competing Tracks?** An example of the delicate interplay between the WIPO-based mechanisms and those of the WTO was seen at the first session of the newly formed WIPO Standing Committee on the Law of Trademarks, Industrial Designs and Geographical Indications in Geneva in July 1998. The question arose whether the committee should give priority to work on the protection of geographical indications. Several delegations suggested that because such work was taking place within the framework of the TRIPS Council, and "in order to avoid unnecessary duplication, the Standing Committee should not deal with the question." Other delegations were of the opinion that the Standing Committee should "give a high priority to work on geographical indications in parallel with the work of WTO in that field." Yet others said that "although WTO's work did not preclude the Standing Committee from dealing with that issue, the two Organizations should draw from each other's experience, and that cooperation between the two Organizations should be pursued." Standing Committee on the Law of Trademarks, Industrial Designs and Geographical Indications, First Session (July 13-17, 1998), Report prepared by the International Bureau ¶¶ 28-29, WIPO Doc. SCT/1/6 (Nov. 5, 1998).

(6) **Other Horizontal Issues.** Are there any other issues that appear to pervade international intellectual property lawmaking, and the resolution of which would facilitate progress on a variety of fronts? Several scholars have bemoaned the poor quality of "harmonized" law. What do they mean by "poor quality"? Do you agree that the process of harmonization is affecting the quality of intellectual property law? In the industrial property context, as registration systems expand their geographic reach, how are we to confront the sensitive issue of the languages used in such systems?

§ 8.02   Genetic Resources, Traditional Knowledge and Folklore

The development of principles relating to genetic resources, traditional knowledge, and folklore is on the agenda of a variety of international intellectual property policymaking institutions. From 1998, WIPO engaged in intensive fact finding regarding traditional knowledge (or "TK"), a process which included dispatching fact-finding missions to different parts of the globe and convening a roundtable on intellectual property rights and traditional knowledge. *See* Report on the Protection of Traditional Knowledge: A Global Intellectual Property Issue, WIPO/IPTK/RT/99/2 (WIPO Oct. 22, 1999); *see also* Michael Blakeney, *What Is Traditional Knowledge? Why Should it Be Protected? Who Should Protect It? For Whom?: Understanding the Value Chain,* WIPO/IPTK/RT/99/3 (Oct. 6, 1999). In September 1999, the WIPO Standing Committee on Patents placed the protection of genetic resources on its agenda. And, although WIPO's work on the protection of folklore goes back to cooperative efforts with UNESCO in 1978, its interest in the topic has intensified in the last few years.

In September 2000, WIPO established the Intergovernmental Committee on Intellectual Property and Genetic Resources, Traditional Knowledge and Folklore (WIPO IGC) to deal with each of these issues. The WIPO IGC met for the first time in April 2001. These issues have also been raised in the TRIPS Council, particularly by the developing countries. For example, in the context of the TRIPS Council's Article 27(3)(b) review, *see supra* § 8.01, developing countries sought to discuss the interaction between TRIPS obligations and biological diversity, as promoted by the Convention on Biological Diversity (CBD). The CBD provides that states have sovereign rights over their genetic resources, which includes the right to regulate access to and sharing the benefits of those genetic resources. A number of developing countries suggested that there was conflict between TRIPS obligations and the provisions of the CBD, to which many WTO countries are signatories. (We deal separately with this issue *infra* § 8.03.)

The greatest momentum on these issues, however, would appear to be within WIPO. The remit of the WIPO IGC covers a broad range of subject matter, as the formal title of the IGC suggests. (The phrase "traditional knowledge" is often used as shorthand for the entire subject matter, however, and we do so also in the following discussion unless otherwise stated.) Developments in the field of traditional knowledge affect a variety of policy areas in addition to intellectual property, such as food and agriculture, human rights (particularly of indigenous peoples), cultural heritage, health, and the environment. Two quite distinct, but related, issues are at the interface between intellectual property law and traditional knowledge. First, to what extent should traditional knowledge be protected as intellectual property and, if so, who should own those rights? Second, to what extent must the rules of intellectual property law be tailored to reflect the sometimes competing demands of traditional knowledge policy? To use a trademark example, should a native tribe that has for centuries used a symbol to assert its distinctive identity as a people be able to claim exclusive (trademark-like) rights to use the symbol? Conversely, and independent of the first question, should the tribe be able to enjoin the adoption of the symbol as a trademark by a third party commercial entity? Similar concerns regarding (i) assertions of ownership and (ii) protection against appropriation by others, are raised with respect to patent-like subject matter (traditional medicines based upon local plants, for example) and copyright-like subject matters (such as traditional music or dances).

In July 2000, WIPO published a draft report for public comment entitled Fact-Finding Missions on Intellectual Property and Traditional Knowledge (1998-1999). A revised report is being prepared presently; an excerpt from the executive summary of the draft report follows below.

FACT-FINDING MISSIONS ON INTELLECTUAL PROPERTY
AND TRADITIONAL KNOWLEDGE (1998-1999)
WIPO Draft (For Comment, July 3, 2000)
wipo.int/traditionalknowledge/report/contents.html

. . . .

[IP] is not limited to existing categories such as patents, copyright and trademarks. Indeed, the definition of IP in the Convention Establishing [WIPO] makes it clear that "intellectual property" is a broad concept and can include productions and matter not forming part of the existing categories of intellectual property, provided they result, as the definition states, "from intellectual activity in the industrial, scientific, literary or artistic fields." . . . IP is evolutionary and adaptive. New advances in technology—information technology and biotechnology particularly—and changes in economic, social and cultural conditions require continuous appraisal of the system and at times adjustment and expansion, accompanied often by controversy. For example, the last few decades have seen the recognition of new forms of IP, such as a *sui generis* form of protection for plant varieties (in the 1950s and 1960s), patent protection for biological material, plants and animals (in the 1970s and 1980s), a *sui generis* form of protection for layout designs (topographies) of integrated circuits (1980s), copyright protection for computer software (1980s) and protection for databases and compilations of data (1980s and 1990s). The possible protection of tradition-based innovations and creations by the IP system . . . is a more recently articulated question.

. . . .

The Report seeks to summarize, reflect upon and draw broad conclusions on what may be considered to be the main and most prevalent IP-related needs and expectations expressed to WIPO . . . by TK holders and others with whom WIPO consulted. The main needs and expectations may be summarized as follows:

* The selection of an appropriate term or terms to describe the subject matter for which protection is sought.

* A clear definition or description of what is meant (and not meant) for IP purposes by the term or terms selected.

. . . .

* The prevention of the unauthorized acquisition of IPRs (particularly patents) over TK by documenting and publishing TK as searchable prior art, where so desired by the relevant TK holders.

* An analysis of how prior art is established for purposes of patent examinations in the context of TK.

* Greater awareness-raising of the IP system, particularly among sectors of society and communities unfamiliar with it, such as indigenous and local communities and Governmental offices not directly involved in IP law and administration.

* Greater understanding by the IP community of the perspectives, expectations and needs of TK holders.

* Facilitation of dialogue and contact between TK holders, the private sector, governments, NGOs and other stakeholders to assist in development of modalities for cooperation between them, at community, national, regional and international levels.

* Enhanced participation by the national and regional IP offices and the IP community at large in TK-related processes in which IP issues are raised.

* Study of the relationship between collectivity of TK and IPRs, more particularly testing of options for the collective acquisition, management and enforcement of IPRs by TK holders' associations, including the applicability of collective management of IPRs to TK.

* Study of customary law and informal IP regimes in local and traditional communities, including conclusions relevant for the formal IP system.

* In the shorter term, testing the applicability and use of existing IP tools for TK protection, through practical and technical community-level pilot projects and case studies; and, provision of technical information and training to TK holders and Government officials on possible options under the existing categories of IP for TK protection.

* In the longer term, the possible development of new IP tools to protect TK not protected by existing IP tools, the elaboration of an international framework for TK protection, using *inter alia* the WIPO-UNESCO Model Provisions for National Laws on the Protection of Expressions of Folklore Against Illicit Exploitation and Other Prejudicial Actions, 1982, as a possible foundation, and the development of a *sui generis* system of "community" or "collective" rights to protect TK.

* Facilitating access to the IP system, to enable TK holders to use and enforce rights under the IP system.

* The provision of information, assistance and advice with respect to the enforcement of TK protection.

* The provision of legal/technical assistance with TK documentation, including information and advice on the IP implications of TK documentation.

* The provision of IP advice and assistance in respect of legislation, regulations, guidelines, protocols, agreements (including model terms), policies and processes on access to and benefit-sharing in genetic resources.

* Assistance and training for TK holders in the negotiation, drafting, implementation, and enforcement of contracts.

* The development and testing, with the close involvement of indigenous peoples and local communities, of "best contractual practices," guidelines and model clauses for contracts.

* Awareness-raising on the potential commercial value of TK and the development of tools for the economic valuation of TK.

It is evident that some of the needs and expectations conflict, or reflect competing policy objectives. WIPO has not attempted to mediate the needs or "resolve" conflicts, but rather to report as fully as possible on the information received from [fact-finding mission] informants. WIPO recognises that it cannot address all these needs and a collaborative effort by other relevant organizations and processes would be desirable. The needs as identified pose challenges for the entire IP community—national and regional IP offices, collective management societies, the private sector, NGOs, civil society, consumers, and the international community, including WIPO and its Member States. . . .

. . . .

An efficient IP system that protects TK will promote continued creation and innovation based on that knowledge. IP is not only about conferring property rights. It is also about recognition of and respect for the contributions of human creators. From this perspective, IP has a very important role to play in protecting the dignity of holders of TK and, by recognizing property rights in relation to such knowledge, giving those holders a degree of control of its use by others. The protection of TK also benefits third parties, who are able to enjoy access to protected tradition-based innovation and creation that may not be collected, captured in some media, or find channels of distribution without IP protection.

The [fact-finding missions] have shown the richness and diversity of TK on a global scale, both in terms of its inherent creativity and as potential subject matter for IP protection. . . . There are nevertheless certain conceptual difficulties. However, the fact that existing standards of IP may not be in perfect harmony with elements of TK worthy of protection, should not be seen as an insuperable obstacle. IP has consistently evolved to protect new subject matter, such as software and layout-designs, the emergence of which was unforeseeable even twenty years earlier. Copyright protection has been extended to the digital environment. IP is now moving forward to protect databases. Given its evolutionary and adaptive nature, it is not inconceivable that the IP system might provide effective protection for traditional knowledge.

NOTES AND QUESTIONS

(1) **Needs of Traditional Knowledge Holders**. The draft WIPO report acknowledged difficulties defining "traditional knowledge," and identified the selection of appropriate terminology as a pressing need. As a working definition, WIPO used the term "traditional knowledge" to refer to:

> Tradition-based literary, artistic, or scientific works; performances; inventions; scientific discoveries; designs; marks, names and symbols; undisclosed information; and, all other tradition-based innovations and creations resulting from intellectual activity in the industrial, scientific, literary or artistic fields. The notion "tradition-based" refers to knowledge systems, creations, innovations and cultural expressions which: have generally been transmitted from generation to generation; are generally regarded as pertaining to a particular

people or its territory; have generally been developed in a non-systematic way; and, are constantly evolving in response to a changing environment. Categories of traditional knowledge include: agricultural knowledge; scientific knowledge; technical knowledge; ecological knowledge; medicinal knowledge, including related medicines and remedies; biodiversity-related knowledge; "expressions of folklore" in the form of music, dance, song, handicrafts, designs, stories and artwork; elements of languages, such as names, geographical indications, and symbols; and, movable cultural properties. Excluded from this description of traditional knowledge would be items not resulting from intellectual activity in the industrial, scientific, literary or artistic fields, such as human remains, languages in general, and "heritage" in the broad sense.

Draft WIPO Report, *supra,* at 4. What concerns underlie the "needs" listed by the draft WIPO report? In what ways do some of the needs and expectations of holders of traditional knowledge "conflict or reflect competing policy objectives," as the draft WIPO report suggests? What weight should we give these objectives? Is intellectual property law the appropriate vehicle for pursuit of these objectives?

(2) **Traditional Knowledge as Intellectual Property**. Recall the definition of "intellectual property" tendered by Professor Koumantos in the first excerpt in this book. *See supra* § 1.02. Does traditional knowledge, or some parts of traditional knowledge, fall within his definition? If not, what would that tell us about our notion of "intellectual property" and should we broaden that notion? Is protection of traditional knowledge justified by some theories of intellectual property but not others? Which intellectual property regimes appear most able to accommodate the protection of traditional knowledge?

(3) **Maori Words and Symbols**. In 1994, as part of broader trademark law reform, the New Zealand Ministry of Commerce established a Maori Focus Group to consider the trade marking of Maori words and symbols. In New Zealand, until then, Maori words and symbols were found in many trademarks. For example, in 1996, Air New Zealand applied to register the Koru symbol. These issues came to the fore both as a result of growing Maori consciousness in New Zealand, but also through the consultations with Maori that are an inherent part of the New Zealand legislative process (in recognition of Treaty of Waitangi obligations). The Maori Focus Group concluded that New Zealand's intellectual property laws did not provide sufficient protection for Maori words and symbols. These symbols have often been developed over several generations and are regarded as property of the community. In what ways do Maori claims to ownership of Maori words and symbols conflict with or challenge premises of our existing intellectual property law? The focus group advanced several proposals designed to enhance protection for traditional Maori symbols. Thus an applicant could register a Maori word or symbol as a trademark only upon proof of the cultural origin of the mark and with permission of the relevant tribe. What problems does this raise? *See* Andrew Brown, *Maori Trademarks—Cultural Sensitivity Revisited,* 29 INTELL. PROP. FORUM 40 (May 1997). It was also proposed that the Commissioner of Trade

Marks be given power to refuse registration of trademarks that would be culturally inappropriate to a section of the community, including an extended Maori family. Indeed, standing to oppose such a registration would be available to any person who is "culturally aggrieved." What difficulties would you foresee from this provision? Are these difficulties worth bearing to achieve broader policy objectives? How would you propose dealing with trade marks that comprise Maori words and symbols and which have been registered and used for many years? Have you seen any models for addressing this issue in the different intellectual property systems discussed throughout the course?

(4) **Native American Symbols.** On what basis might the trademark registration of symbols invoking Native American culture be challenged in the United States? In *Harjo v. Pro-Football, Inc.*, 50 U.S.P.Q.2d 1705 (T.T.A.B. 1999), the Trademark Trial and Appeal Board ordered the cancellation of the registration of the mark REDSKINS for the Washington Redskins football team on the ground that the mark was disparaging under section 2(a) of the Lanham Act. The case is presently on appeal. *See* Jack Achiezer Guggenheim, *The Indians' Chief Problem: Chief Wahoo as State Sponsored Discrimination and a Disparaging Mark*, 46 CLEV. ST. L. REV. 211 (1998) (suggesting arguments by which the federal trademark registration of the mascot of the Cleveland Indians baseball team, which is seen by many in the Native American community as an emblem that denigrates Native American culture, may be challenged). Should the question of registrability depend upon whether the symbol in question is offensive to Native Americans? The 850-member Zia pueblo, in New Mexico, has used as a sacred symbol for 800 years, the Zia sun sign, as a "symbol of collective identity." In 1997, a tour company obtained federal registration of a mark that included the Zia sun sign. *See* Phil Patton, *Trademark Battle over Pueblo Sign*, N.Y. TIMES, Jan. 13, 2000, at F1. On what basis might it be argued that *any* trademark that uses traditional Native American symbols should be denied federal registration? If current U.S. law permits such registration, should it? What changes to the Lanham Act might be appropriate? In a recent report, the PTO proposed no amendment of the Lanham Act to address the concerns of Native American tribes, but rather suggested that the PTO compile a database of official tribal insignia in order to assist the office in better applying existing statutory rules. Is this an adequate response? *See* UNITED STATES PATENT AND TRADEMARK OFFICE, REPORT ON OFFICIAL INSIGNIA OF NATIVE AMERICAN TRIBES (Nov. 1999).

(5) **International Solutions**. Why might it be important to address such issues internationally? Are these concerns inherently local or national in nature? If not, what has caused them to become international concerns? What prompted the developing countries in particular to raise the question of protection for traditional knowledge in the TRIPS Council? If an international agreement is the solution, what measures might the international intellectual property community adopt?

§ 8.03   Intellectual Property and Biological Diversity

COMMITTEE ON TRADE AND THE ENVIRONMENT, THE ENVIRONMENT AND TRIPS
WTO Doc. No. WT/CTE/W/8 (June 8, 1995)

The April 1994 Marrakesh Ministerial Decision on Trade and Environment states that "the Committee on Trade and Environment will consider the work programme envisaged in the Decision on Trade and Services and the Environment and the relevant provisions of the Agreement on Trade-Related Aspects of Intellectual Property Rights as an integral part of its work." This paper has been prepared in response to the request to the Secretariat by the Committee for a background document to assist its work in the latter area.

. . . .

I. PROVISIONS OF THE TRIPS AGREEMENT THAT EXPLICITLY REFER TO THE ENVIRONMENT

Article 27.2 is the only provision in the TRIPS Agreement that makes an explicit reference to the environment. It states that "Members may exclude from patentability inventions, the prevention within their territory of the commercial exploitation of which is necessary to protect ordre public or morality, including to protect human, animal or plant life or health or to avoid serious prejudice to the environment, provided that such exclusion is not made merely because the exploitation is prohibited by their law." Thus, if it is necessary to ban the commercial exploitation of an invention in order to avoid serious prejudice to the environment, a WTO Member is free to refuse a patent for the invention concerned.

II. THE CONVENTION ON BIOLOGICAL DIVERSITY: MAIN ASPECTS AND A BRIEF NEGOTIATING HISTORY

An important concern in the area of environment has been that global biodiversity (including genetic resources) is being depleted over time and hence a need to conserve and use it in a sustainable manner has been emphasized. Biodiversity is valued for maintaining the possibility of responding to new situations that may arise, for instance, in the area of agriculture and medicine, and because of its links to the sustainability of certain ecosystems. The initial response of the international community to the threat of genetic erosion was to build a network of "gene banks" where genetic materials, for example, seeds of abandoned varieties, could be stored and conserved *ex situ*. "*Ex situ* conservation" is defined as the conservation of components of biological diversity outside their natural habitats. However, this method of conservation led to some loss of viability and of characteristics and, over time, the focus has changed towards *in situ*. "*In situ* conservation" is defined as the conservation of ecosystems and natural habitats and the maintenance and recovery of viable populations of species in their natural surroundings and, in the case of domesticated or cultivated species, in the surroundings where they developed their distinctive properties. Therefore, incentives for conserving and sustaining animal and plant biodiversity in the natural habitats have been increasingly emphasized. For example, farmers and local communities are now being encouraged to conserve traditional plant varieties on-farm or *in situ*. *In situ* agro-biodiversity was seen by many to be a result of informal innovations, knowledge and practices of farmers, local communities and indigenous populations, and it was argued that they should get a return on these efforts. Such returns were also seen as important because they would provide incentives to continue to perform the task of preserving biodiversity.

The Convention on Biological Diversity (the Biodiversity Convention) was negotiated under the auspices of the United Nations Environment Programme ("UNEP") and was opened for signature at the United Nations Conference on Environment and Development in 1992. The Convention came into force on 29 December 1993. . . .

The Biodiversity Convention operates at three levels, *i.e.* genes, species, and ecosystems, and extends to all genetic resources, namely, plant, animal and microbial. It affirms that the conservation of biodiversity is "a common concern of humankind," and that States have sovereign rights over the biological resources in their territories. Article 15 recognizes the sovereign rights of States over their natural resources and the preamble reaffirms that "States have sovereign rights over their own biological resources". Article 15.1 states that "[r]ecognizing the sovereign rights of States over their natural resources, the authority to determine access to genetic resources rests with the national governments and is subject to national legislation." The question of ownership (or property rights) is not addressed by the Convention, and is subject to national law. Under the Biodiversity Convention, States are responsible for conserving their biological diversity and for using it in a sustainable manner. Access to a Party's genetic resources must be on mutually agreed terms and on the basis of prior informed consent of the Party providing the resources. Prior informed consent under Article 15 is not an obligation, but an option to be exercised by the Contracting Party providing genetic resources. Article 15.5 states that "[a]ccess to genetic resources shall be subject to prior informed consent of the Contracting Party providing such resources, unless otherwise determined by that Party." The objectives of the Biodiversity Convention are "the conservation of biological diversity, the sustainable use of its components and the fair and equitable sharing of the benefits arising from the use of genetic resources, including by appropriate access to genetic resources and by appropriate transfer of relevant technologies, taking into account all rights over those resources and to technologies, and by appropriate funding." Article 1 of the Biodiversity Convention. This also reflects a view that such sharing of benefits would provide incentives for conservation of biodiversity in the regions where it exists (*i.e.* incentives for *in situ* conservation).

The Biodiversity Convention provides for sharing research and development activities, benefits from the results of research and development, and commercial use of these results on mutually agreed terms. Access to or transfer of technology has to be provided in line with the provisions mentioned below, and as far as possible and as appropriate, incentives have to be provided to preserve genetic diversity. Similarly, in order to preserve and make sustainable use of biodiversity, the Convention provides for increased encouragement and interaction with regard to information, research, training, public education and awareness, and technical and scientific cooperation. With regard to several aspects including, inter alia, sharing in research and development, in the benefits of the results of research and development and of the commercial application of these results, such sharing has to be on mutually agreed terms. *See*, for example, Articles 15.4, 15.7, 16.2, 16.3, 18.5 and 19.2.

In the negotiation of the Biodiversity Convention, issues related to intellectual property rights (IPRs) were important in the context of provisions dealing with access to and transfer of technology (Article 16 of the Convention); in the Biodiversity Convention, the term "technology" includes biotechnology, and covers technologies that assist further conservation and sustainable use of genetic resources as well as technologies that do not cause significant damage to the environment and result from the use of genetic resources to which access is provided by Contracting Parties.

Relevant features of the Biodiversity Convention

The principles of the Convention are that "States have, in accordance with the Charter of the United Nations and the principles of international law, the sovereign right to exploit their own resources pursuant to their own environmental policies, and the responsibility to ensure that activities within their jurisdiction or control do not cause damage to the environment of other States or of areas beyond the limits of national jurisdiction" (Article 3). The role of indigenous and local communities in conserving biodiversity is recognized in the preamble; the importance of maintaining their knowledge and practices relevant to the conservation of biodiversity and the sustainable use of its components is also recognized, as is the need to encourage equitable sharing of benefits derived from the use of their knowledge, innovations and practices (Articles 8(j) and 10(c)). Identification and monitoring of biodiversity is viewed as an ongoing process involving development of the capacity of the Parties to fulfil the objectives on a long term and sustainable basis (Article 7). The Biodiversity Convention provides that, as far as possible and as appropriate, incentives have to be provided for the conservation and sustainable use of components of biodiversity (Article 11). In order to preserve and make sustainable use of biodiversity, the Convention provides for increasing encouragement and interaction with regard to information, research, training, public education and awareness, and technical and scientific cooperation (Articles 12, 13, 14, 17 and 18). Article 18.3 provides that the Contracting Parties have to determine at their first meeting how to establish a clearing-house mechanism to promote and facilitate technical and scientific cooperation.

The Biodiversity Convention applies to *in situ* and *ex situ* genetic resources acquired in accordance with the Convention, but not those taken and deposited in gene-banks prior to the Convention's entry into force. It emphasizes *in situ* conservation (Article 8). Article 8 of the Biodiversity Convention calls for measures ranging from the establishment of a system of protected areas to the rehabilitation of degraded ecosystems and recovery of threatened species, the protection of natural habitats and the maintenance of viable populations of species in natural surroundings. *Ex situ* conservation measures are called for principally to complement *in situ* conservation (Article 9). Recognizing the sovereign rights of States over their natural resources, the authority to determine access to genetic resources rests with national governments and is subject to national legislation (Article 15.1). However, each Party to the Biodiversity Convention must endeavour to create conditions to facilitate access to genetic resources for environmentally sound uses by other Parties and must not impose restrictions that run counter to the objectives of the Biodiversity Convention (Article 15.2). Where access to genetic resources is granted, it has to be on mutually agreed terms and be subject to prior informed consent of the Party providing the resources, unless otherwise determined by that Party (Articles 15.4 and 15.5). Genetic resources provided by any Party to the Biodiversity Convention are only those resources that are provided by Parties which are countries of origin of those resources or by Parties that have acquired the genetic resources in accordance with the Convention (Article 15.3). For those Parties providing access to genetic resources, the benefits include possibility of participation in scientific research based on the genetic resource supplied (Articles 15.6). Article 15.6 states that "[e]ach Contracting Party shall endeavor to develop and carry out scientific research based on genetic resources provided by other Contracting Parties with the full participation of, and where possible in, such Contracting Parties," of sharing results of research and development and benefits arising from commercial and other utilization of genetic resources on mutually agreed terms (Article 15.7). Article 15.7 states that "[e]ach Contracting Party shall take legislative, administrative or policy measures, as appropriate, and in accordance with Articles 16 and 19 and, where necessary, through the financial mechanism established by Articles 20 and 21 with the aim of sharing in a fair and equitable way the results of research and development and the benefits arising from the commercial and other utilization of genetic resources with the Contracting Party providing such resources. . . . Article 19.2 states that "[e]ach Contracting Party shall take all practicable measures to promote and advance priority access on a fair and equitable basis by Contracting Parties, especially developing countries, to the results and benefits arising from biotechnologies based upon genetic resources provided by those Contracting Parties. Such access shall be on mutually agreed terms." *See also* Article 8(j), which states that "[e]ach Contracting Party shall, as far as possible, and as appropriate, subject to its national legislation, respect, preserve and maintain knowledge, innovations and practices of indigenous and local communities embodying traditional lifestyles relevant for the conservation and sustainable use of biological diversity and promote their wider application with the approval and involvement of the holders of such knowledge, innovations and practices and encourage the equitable sharing of benefits arising from the utilization of such knowledge, innovations and practices."

Access to and transfer of technology is addressed by Article 16. In order to get an overall perspective on different aspects related to transfer of technology under Articles 16, it is important to also bear in mind certain other provisions in the Biodiversity Convention, for example, Article 12 (research and training), Article 17 (exchange of information), Article 18 (technical and scientific cooperation), and Article 19 (handling of biotechnology and distribution of its benefits). These provisions emphasise both the soft component of technology (such as skills, know-how and design) and the hard component (machinery and equipment, and other tangible inputs). Experience with operation of technology has shown that the soft and hard components have to work in a complementary manner to result in successful transfer of technology. Intellectual property rights are explicitly mentioned in the second, third and fifth paragraphs of Article 16. . . .

Article 19 addresses handling of biotechnology (including biosafety aspects), access to information and research and distribution of benefits of biotechnology. Under Article 20, new and additional financial resources are to be provided to developing countries to enable them to meet the agreed full incremental costs to them of the measures needed to implement the Biodiversity Convention's obligations. The agreement on the composition of these costs is to be bilaterally reached between each developing country Party and the institution chosen to handle the financial mechanism. The mechanism for providing financial resources to developing country Parties is set out in Article 21. The mechanism will operate under the authority of the Conference of the Parties (established under Article 23) to which it will be directly accountable, and funds will be provided on a grant or concessional basis. Article 25 establishes a subsidiary body on scientific, technical and technological advice for timely advice relating to the implementation of the Biodiversity Convention. . . .

Resolution Three of the Nairobi Final Act of the Conference for the Adoption of the Agreed Text of the Convention on Biological Diversity (22 May 1992) identified the need to seek solutions to some unresolved issues, *e.g.* farmers' rights. . . .

III. RELEVANT ONGOING WORK IN OTHER INTERNATIONAL ORGANIZATIONS

This section reports on certain ongoing work at United Nations Environment Programme, Biodiversity Convention, Consultative Group on International Agricultural Research, Food and Agriculture Organization, World Intellectual Property Organization and UPOV that is relevant for a discussion of environment and TRIPS.

United Nations Environment Programme (UNEP)

In 1993, UNEP's Governing Council approved the creation of two Centres, both based in Japan. The purpose of the Centres is to promote the development and transfer of environmentally-sound technologies, with a particular emphasis on sustainable freshwater management technologies, as well as other environmentally-related technologies. At the Session of UNEP's Governing Council in 1995, governments requested that such Centres include work on developing "modalities for financing endogenous capacity-building of scientific and technology centres, in particular in developing countries and countries with economies in transition."

Consultative Group on International Agricultural Research (CGIAR)

The CGIAR is a consortium of donor and development agencies that supports autonomous research Centres which aim to develop technologies and information relevant to improving the productivity and sustainability of agricultural, forestry and aquatic systems in developing countries. One of the activities of the CGIAR is *ex situ* conservation and use of plant genetic resources. The CGIAR Centres have collected and stored seeds or other reproductive parts of their mandate crops. Each year, more than 120,000 germplasm accessions from the in-trust collections and 500,000 samples of improved material are distributed by the Centres, the large majority to developing countries. The Centres are also involved in research to improve technologies for *in situ* conservation.

Under agreements signed in October 1994, the Centres of the CGIAR that maintain germplasm collections have placed these collections under the auspices of FAO. The agreements contain obligations that the material will be made available to all users, and that the Centres will not claim any property rights on these materials. These conditions will apply also to the material with the users to which it is made available, except for "the repatriation of the germplasm to the country that provided such germplasm."

Food and Agriculture Organization (FAO)

In 1983, the FAO established a Global System for the Conservation and Utilization of Plant Genetic Resources for food and agriculture. The Global System is being developed and monitored by the intergovernmental Commission on Plant Genetic Resources (CPGR) within the context of the International Undertaking on Plant Genetic Resources, a non-binding agreement that was adopted by the FAO Conference in 1983. The Undertaking recognizes a principle of free access to genetic resources. It includes a provision for an international fund for the conservation and utilization of plant genetic resources. However, compensation was not necessarily to be provided directly to farmers. The fund has not yet become operational. The CPGR is an intergovernmental forum of donors and users of plant genetic resources, technology and funds. Currently 144 countries are formally part of the system. It has negotiated a Code of Conduct for Plant Germplasm Collecting and Transfer which provides guidelines for collecting and transferring plant genetic resources to facilitate access and promote their use and development on an equitable basis. This code of conduct was adopted by the FAO Conference in 1993; a draft Code of Conduct on Biotechnology which includes provisions on IPRs is under development.

The CPGR has also provided a framework for agreements negotiated between various States and institutions, such as the International Agricultural Centres of the Consultative Group on International Agricultural Research. Moreover, in 1989 and 1991, the FAO Conference adopted resolutions on farmers' rights. The role of the farmers in developing plant varieties was recognized at the FAO Conference in 1989, which endorsed a concept of farmers' rights. It was stated that farmers have "rights arising from the past, present and future contributions of farmers in conserving, improving, and making available plant genetic resources [which] allow farmers, their communities, and countries in all regions, to participate fully in the benefits derived, at present and in the future, from the improved use of plant genetic resources, through plant breeding and other scientific methods," (FAO Resolution 5/89) and plant breeders' rights. Plant breeder's right or plant variety protection is an exclusive right granted to the breeder of a new plant variety to exploit his new variety. The nature of these rights can vary depending on the system of protection adopted in this context. See for example the note in Annex 1 to this paper. For more details on plant breeder's rights, *see* International Union for the Protection of New Plant Varieties of Plants (1994), *UPOV National Seminar on the Nature of and Rationale for the Protection of Plant Varieties under the UPOV Convention,* UPOV/ISB/94/1, 10 November 1994.

One of the CPGR's areas of interest relates to IPR over plant varieties, related technologies and farmers' germplasm. During the sessions of the Commission, discussions on these matters have been conducted among member countries since 1983, and following [the 1992 Rio Earth Summit], further discussions are being held on access to plant genetic resources for food and agriculture, access to related technologies, and the realization of farmers' rights. Other matters being discussed by the Commission include the impact of IPRs on the environment, (especially the distinctiveness, uniformity and stability criteria for plant breeders' rights), and a revision of the International Undertaking on Plant Genetic Resources to harmonize it with the Biodiversity Convention (including negotiations on access to plant genetic resources and the realization of farmers' rights). . . .

World Intellectual Property Organization (WIPO)

WIPO offers a range of assistance and services to developing countries. In respect of intellectual property and the environment, two types of assistance are of special interest to developing countries:

(i)   the provision of advice and training to governments and public and private sector organizations, and their staff, on negotiations and arrangements relating to the licensing of intellectual property and the management of such property, where such arrangements have an impact on the environment;

(ii)   the provision, with the cooperation of some industrialized countries, of technological state-of-the-art search reports covering various categories of technology, including technology relevant to the environment. Those reports, which are provided free, are prepared on the basis of information available from patent documents, of which some 30 million are in existence, held by those industrialized countries. Since the search service started, some 8,000 such search reports have been provided.

International Union for the Protection of New Varieties of Plants (UPOV)

UPOV administers the International Convention for the Protection of New Varieties of Plants, notably the 1978 Act which is presently in force, and the 1991 Act which is yet to enter into force. . . .

UPOV develops test guidelines for the conduct of tests for "distinctness, homogeneity and stability" of plant varieties. This is an ongoing task involving four Technical Working Parties, responsible respectively for test guidelines for individual species for agricultural crops, for fruit crops, for ornamental crops and forest trees, and for vegetables. In addition, there are two special Working Parties.

One studies the application and harmonization of biochemical and molecular techniques in the field of plant variety protection, and the other focuses on the possibility of automation and the harmonization of computer programmes within UPOV with a view to promote the harmonization of the method used by member states in distinguishing between plant varieties.

In order to avoid duplication of tests of varieties for which applications for protection are filed with more than one member State, cooperation in technical examination has been achieved on the basis of agreements between the competent authorities of member States, under which the testing of a given species is effected for a group of member States by one member State, and the purchase by a member State on an ad hoc basis of the result of a test carried out by another member State. The office of UPOV maintains and updates a list of species for which offers for cooperation in examination have been made.

The Office of the UPOV collects national laws on plant breeders' rights and prepares translations of them into English. It also provides assistance in the development of the legal systems in different countries to take account of the criteria mentioned in the UPOV Convention. . . .

. . . .

V. PROVISIONS OF THE TRIPS AGREEMENT RELEVANT TO MATTERS RAISED IN DISCUSSIONS IN ENVIRONMENTAL FORA

While the TRIPS Agreement covers all the main areas of intellectual property . . . , the intellectual property related issues that have been raised in the environmental fora concern essentially those IPRs relevant to technology, in particular patents. . . .

[Several] issues are considered in turn [below]. . . . These points are addressed without prejudice to whether they are all intellectual property related or indeed environment related but because they have been raised in environmental fora by at least some as having an IPR dimension.

(a) Promotion of environmentally-sound technologies

The importance of promoting environmentally-sound technology has been referred to in many discussions in environmental fora; for example, it is reflected in Agenda 21 [of the 1992 Rio Earth Summit]. . . . The IPR system provides protection to the results of investment in the development of new environmentally-friendly technology, thus giving the incentive and the means to finance such research and development. A combination of a well-functioning IPR system and appropriate price signals in the market, which direct research and development effort to environmentally-sound technologies, can play a major role in developing the technologies that will respond to environmental problems. The TRIPS Agreement will help reinforce this in a wider range of countries.

The objective of promoting the development of new technology is referred to in Article 7 of the TRIPS Agreement which says that "the protection and enforcement of intellectual property rights should contribute to the promotion of technological innovation and to the transfer and dissemination of technology, to the mutual advantage of producers and users of technological knowledge and in a manner conducive to social and economic welfare, and to a balance of rights and obligations."

With this objective in mind, the TRIPS Agreement (Article 27.1) requires that patents be available for any invention, in all fields of technology, subject to certain limited exceptions (mainly for inventions in the area of plants and animals. . . . [M]inimum rights that a patent must confer on its owner are set out in Article 28. These are subject to a number of exceptions, some of which are discussed . . . below . . . .

A number of other provisions of the TRIPS Agreement are also of relevance to the promotion of technological innovation. One is Article 39 on the protection of undisclosed information. . . .

(b) Access to and transfer of technology

This issue is addressed in the Biodiversity Convention, in Agenda 21 [of the 1992 Rio Earth Summit] and in a number of other agreements on environmental matters. As indicated above, it is an objective of the TRIPS Agreement to promote not only technological innovation, but also the transfer and dissemination of technology . . . [Article 7].

The objectives of promoting technological innovation and the transfer of technology are usually mutually consistent since right holders are generally more willing to transfer technology voluntarily where a country's IPR system provides effective protection. In addition, the disclosure requirements of the patent system and exceptions to patent rights for experimental use are designed to maximize the degree to which knowledge of new technology becomes publicly available and can be the basis for further technological development. Moreover, the TRIPS Agreement contains some specific requirements on developed country Members to provide incentives for technology transfer to least-developed country Members. . . .

In the event that there is tension between the objectives of promoting technological innovation and the transfer of technology, and with the aim of securing the objectives of Article 7, the TRIPS Agreement contains a number of provisions, in particular on compulsory licensing and control of anti-competitive practices, to establish an appropriate balance between these two objectives, and thus between the interests of producers and users of technological knowledge, conducive to social and economic welfare. . . .

Most technology is in the public domain . . . because protection was never sought in the first place. In order to benefit from patent protection, it is necessary to obtain a separate patent in each jurisdiction and that patent is only valid in that jurisdiction. The extent to which patents are taken out varies greatly from country to country. . . .

When technology, whether patented or not, is in the control of a government, that government is of course free to transfer it on concessional terms if it so wishes.

There is nothing in the TRIPS Agreement that would prevent a government or an international financial mechanism from providing financial assistance to enable the voluntary transfer of privately-held proprietary technology on concessional terms.

. . . [W]here a developing country does not presently give product patent protection in a particular area of technology, the introduction of such protection can be delayed for up to ten years. In respect of pharmaceutical and agricultural chemical products, there are special additional transition provisions that take account of the regulatory delay before such products are approved for marketing (Articles 70.8 and 70.9).

(i) Disclosure

One of the purposes of the patent system is to encourage inventors to disclose new technology rather than attempt to keep it secret, so that new technology can become part of the common pool of knowledge of mankind. Article 29 establishes an obligation on Members to require that patent applicants disclose the invention.

The obligation to disclose has a number of important consequences for the transfer of and access to technology. For the duration of the term of protection, information is readily available about from whom the technology can be obtained; [a]t the end of the patent term, the disclosed invention falls into the public domain and is freely available to all; [and f]urther research and development is facilitated—see next heading.

(ii) Experimental use

Article 30 allows Members to make "limited exceptions" to the rights conferred by a patent, subject to certain conditions.

(iii) Incentives to transfer of technology

As mentioned earlier, the TRIPS Agreement does not stand in the way of governments providing incentives for the transfer of technology. Indeed, Article 66.2 of the TRIPS Agreement requires developed country Members to "provide incentives to enterprises and institutions in their territories for the purpose of promoting and encouraging technology transfer to least-developed country Members in order to enable them to create a sound and viable technological base."

(iv)   Compulsory licences, also sometimes referred to as "non-voluntary licences"

The TRIPS Agreement contains a provision allowing a compulsory licence (*i.e.* a licence granted without the agreement of the patent owner) to be granted to an applicant to use a patented invention where the right holder has not been willing to grant a voluntary licence on reasonable commercial terms and conditions within a reasonable period of time, subject to a number of conditions aimed at protecting the legitimate interest of the patent owner. In cases of national emergency or other circumstances of extreme urgency and in cases of public non-commercial use, a Member may waive the requirement to first seek a voluntary licence. The relevant provisions of the TRIPS Agreement are [in] Article 31.

. . . .

(c) Technology that may adversely affect the environment

A concern highlighted in various discussions on environmental matters is the need to curb the adverse effect of certain technology on the environment. In the work on the Biodiversity Convention, in FAO and elsewhere, the issue of control of the release of new biotechnological products into the environment has been prominent. In discussions on plant variety protection and "farmer's rights", concern about the possible effect of uniform new varieties displacing the biodiversity provided by traditional varieties has been expressed by some. Similarly, a long-standing subject of attention in most countries has been the environmental effects of agricultural chemicals, which are generally subject to a testing and approval procedure before being authorized for marketing.

As far as the TRIPS Agreement is concerned, the main point is that it does not affect the right of governments to restrict research or development or the use of technology on the grounds of protecting the environment. A patent gives the right to the patent owner to prevent others from using the protected invention (subject to certain exceptions), but does not guarantee the patent owner the right to exploit the technology in question. . . . In this regard, the provisions of Article 8.1 of the TRIPS Agreement should be noted. . . .

Although . . . the possibility for a government to restrict the use of technology on environmental grounds is not affected by the grant of a patent, it should also be noted that Article 27.2 of the TRIPS Agreement enables a Member to exclude from patentability inventions whose use would seriously prejudice the environment. . . .

Also of relevance to controls on the use of environmentally-prejudicial technology are the provisions of Article 39.3 on the protection of undisclosed test or other data submitted in order to obtain marketing approval for pharmaceutical and agricultural chemical products which utilize new chemical entities. These provisions provide protection to the very considerable investment that frequently has to be made in testing such products to ensure their usefulness and safety, notably for the environment in the case of agricultural chemicals. While one of the forms of protection that should be granted is against disclosure of the information, this does not apply where disclosure is necessary to protect the public or where steps are taken to ensure that the data is protected against unfair commercial use.

(d) Patentability of genetic material/life forms

The extent to which genetic material and life forms should be patentable is an active issue in many contexts—in the judicial, legislative and executive branches of many governments, in commercial circles, and in public opinion. Environmental groups have participated actively in this debate. Concerns that they have raised include the issue of the environmental safety of biotechnological inventions and the possible effect on biodiversity of the uniformization of productive varieties/races. . . . Ethical questions about the patenting of life forms have also been raised as well as economic questions about the effects on users and the distribution of benefits with the suppliers of the underlying genetic material.

The first point to note is that Article 1.1 of the TRIPS Agreement makes it clear that there is no expectation that countries will have identical patent laws: the obligation is to meet the minimum standards of the TRIPS Agreement while being free to grant more extensive protection than is required by the Agreement. The implication of this is that the fact that patents may be granted in response to certain applications in some countries does not necessarily mean that this would be an obligation under the TRIPS Agreement.

Article 27.1 of the TRIPS Agreement establishes the basic criteria for patentability. . . . Thus, the TRIPS Agreement allows each Member to refuse to grant a patent for any claimed invention which does not meet any one of the following criteria: it must be new; it must involve an inventive step or be non-obvious; it must be capable of industrial application or useful (and it must have been adequately disclosed). A country would remain free to refuse a patent for biological or genetic material which has been merely discovered or where the use of it claimed as the subject of the invention was already known.

Even if an application meets the basic tests of patentability, Article 27.3(b) of the TRIPS Agreement allows Members to exclude from patentability certain plant and animal inventions. . . . Even if an invention meets the basic criteria for patentability of Article 27.1 and does not fall within the exceptions allowed under Article 27.3(b), a patent may still be refused under Article 27.2 if the invention is offensive to ordre public or morality, including to human, animal or plant life or health or to avoid serious prejudice to the environment. . . . [T]he main condition attached to the use of this exception to patentability is that the prevention of the commercial exploitation of the invention is necessary to protect ordre public or morality, including to avoid serious prejudice to the environment.

(e) Contribution of countries/communities sources of genetic material

In discussions in fora concerned with environmental matters, such as in the negotiation of the Biodiversity Convention and in the FAO Commission on Plant Genetic Resources, the issue of recognizing the contribution of indigenous peoples and local communities through the provision of traditional knowledge and informal innovation practices has been raised. In the FAO, the concept of "farmer's rights" has been defined as "rights arising from the past, present and future contribution of farmers in conserving, improving and making available plant genetic resources, particularly those in the centres of origin/diversity" (FAO Resolution 5/89). Attention is also given in the Biodiversity Convention to the question of the participation of countries [that are] sources of genetic resources in research activities using such resources and, on mutually agreed terms, in the results and benefits arising from biotechnologies using such genetic resources.

This matter has two aspects. One is the question of the recognition of the intellectual contribution made by indigenous peoples/local communities. The strengthened protection of IPRs worldwide that should flow from the TRIPS Agreement will help indigenous and local communities benefit from their contributions where the conditions for protection [for existing IPRs] . . . are met. The question of new forms of protection adapted to the particular circumstances of such peoples/local communities was not raised during the TRIPS negotiations.

The second aspect concerns the contribution of countries/communities through the conservation and provision of genetic resources in their natural state. The TRIPS Agreement is silent on the question of the participation of countries/communities in the benefits from the use of technology based on genetic resources originating in their territories. There is also nothing in the TRIPS Agreement that stands in the way of contractual arrangements between countries and companies seeking to use genetic resources from those countries, public transfers of funds or any other mechanism compatible with its provisions.

. . . .

VII. ARTICLE XX OF GATT 1994 AND THE TRIPS AGREEMENT

Article XX of GATT 1994 specifies certain conditions under which a Member is exempted from obligations under other provisions of GATT 1994. Similarly, the TRIPS Agreement has provisions which exempt Members from certain obligations imposed by other provisions of the TRIPS Agreement. For example,

Articles 27.2 and 27.3 permit exemption from patenting in specified circumstances or for specified inventions. Article 30 permits certain exemptions to the rights conferred by patents, and Article 31 permits the use of patented technology without authorization of the right holder provided certain conditions are met. . . .

In the Marrakesh Agreement Establishing the World Trade Organization ("WTO Agreement"), there are provisions that regulate conflict between the WTO Agreement and the multilateral trade agreements in its Annexes. *See* Article XVI.3 of the WTO Agreement, between GATT 1994 and other Agreements in Annex 1A See, for example, the general interpretative note to Annex 1A., and between certain Agreements in Annex 1A (such as Agreement on Technical Barriers to Trade and Agreement on the Application of Sanitary and Phytosanitary Measures. *See* Article 1.5 of the Agreement on Technical Barriers to Trade.). There is no provision regulating conflict between Agreements in Annex 1A and Agreements in Annexes 1B or 1C to the WTO Agreement.

THE CONVENTION ON BIOLOGICAL DIVERSITY AND THE AGREEMENT ON TRADE-RELATED ASPECTS OF INTELLECTUAL PROPERTY RIGHTS (TRIPS): RELATIONSHIPS AND SYNERGIES

Conference of the Parties to the Convention on Biological Diversity
Third meeting, Buenos Aires, Argentina, November 4-15 1996
UNEP/CBD/COP/3/23

1. INTRODUCTION

In response to a request by the second meeting of the Conference of the Parties (COP), this paper reviews synergies and relationships between the Convention on Biological Diversity and the TRIPS Agreement . . . This paper also includes options for the third meeting of the COP to consider in preparing a possible input to the Committee on Trade and Environment (CTE) of the WTO.

The relationships between the TRIPS Agreement and the Convention on Biological Diversity are multifaceted and complex, as are the links between intellectual property rights (IPR) and the Convention. . . . The COP may wish to identify specific topics within this issue area for further work. The CTE of the WTO is discussing the relationship between the TRIPS Agreement and the sustainable development and protection of the environment, which creates a specific opportunity for exploring the relationship between the TRIPS Agreement and the Convention's objectives.

. . . .

2. BACKGROUND

In Decision II/12 on intellectual property rights, the COP asked the Executive Secretary to, inter alia, "[l]iaise with the Secretariat of the World Trade

Organization to inform it of the goals and the ongoing work of the Convention on Biological Diversity and to invite the Secretariat of the World Trade Organization to assist in the preparation of a paper for the Conference of the Parties that identifies the synergies and relationship between the objectives of the Convention on Biological Diversity and the TRIPS Agreement".

The COP noted that "[t]his paper could be the basis for consideration by the third meeting of the Conference of the Parties in preparing a possible input for negotiations that are taking place in the Committee on Trade and Environment of the World Trade Organization."

A number of other items on the provisional agenda of the third meeting of the COP are relevant to the relationship between the Convention and the TRIPS Agreement.   Most important is Item 14.1, a discussion of the impact of intellectual property rights systems (IPR systems) on the objectives of the Convention. . . . Also relevant is Item 11.1, regarding the implementation of Article 8(j) concerning the knowledge, innovations and practices of indigenous and local communities . . . .

. . . .

4. RELATIONSHIP BETWEEN THE CONVENTION ON BIOLOGICAL DIVERSITY AND THE TRIPS AGREEMENT

Intellectual property rights are important under both the Convention on Biological Diversity and the TRIPS Agreement, but the two agreements approach them from very different perspectives. A large and growing number of countries are both Parties to the Convention and members of the WTO (156 Parties to the Convention on Biological Diversity as of 4 November 1996; 125 members of the WTO as of 23 October 1996).   This creates a powerful motivation to develop a mutually supportive relationship and to avoid conflicts. Both the COP and the WTO are beginning to explore the complex interrelationships between IPR and biological diversity. At this stage, the most critical issue for the relationship between the Convention on Biological Diversity and the TRIPS Agreement appears to be whether and how to establish procedures for consultation and cooperation between the bodies associated with the two agreements.

Both the Convention on Biological Diversity and the TRIPS Agreement allow a significant degree of flexibility in national implementation. This suggests that there is potential for complementary and perhaps synergistic implementation. Because both agreements entered into force recently and discussions of the relationships between IPR and biological diversity are preliminary, specific legal or policy mechanisms that would create synergies between the two agreements or their implementing measures have yet to be identified. Nevertheless, some general areas for complementarity have been noted.

For example, mutually agreed-upon terms for access to genetic resources could allocate IPR as part of the benefits to be shared among parties to an agreement on genetic resources . . . Such IPR could be defined under TRIPS-compatible IPR systems.

Another possibility is for the Convention and the TRIPS Agreement to develop procedures for exchanging relevant information. Article 16 of the Convention on Biological Diversity, and possibly others as well, prescribes IPR obligations for the Parties. The implementation of these obligations would likely fall within the scope of the notification requirement found in Article 63 of the TRIPS Agreement. . . . Countries implementing measures that implicate both agreements such as rules requiring patent applications to disclose the country of origin of biological material might report them to the TRIPS Council while at the same time disclosing the same information to the clearing-house mechanism for scientific and technical cooperation established under Article 18(3) of the Convention, or including information regarding the measures in the national reports required under Article 26 of the Convention. It may be useful to note that the WTO and the World Intellectual Property Organization (WIPO) recently concluded an agreement formalizing arrangements for the exchange of information, in particular copies of IPR laws and regulations received by the two organizations.

Other policy and legal proposals involving interrelated implementation of both the Convention on Biological Diversity and the TRIPS Agreement may warrant further examination. One proposal, for example, is to require or encourage disclosure in patent applications of the country and community of origin for genetic resources and informal knowledge used to develop the invention. This has been proposed by a number of commentators (*e.g.*, Gadgil and Devasia 1995; Hendrickx et al. 1994; Gollin 1993). Some evidence suggests that such disclosures are already common practice in filing patent applications. Possible elements of such a requirement, which could help to encourage the implementation of both Article 15 and Article 8(j), are outlined in the Executive Secretary's background paper on Article 8(j). . . .

In spite of the flexibility of the Convention and the TRIPS Agreement, and the potential for synergies, there is still a possibility that conflicts could arise (Downes 1995). For example, national measures to promote technology transfer under Article 16 might raise most-favored nation issues if Convention Parties and non-Parties were treated differently, might raise national-treatment issues if foreign nationals received less favorable treatment, and might raise TRIPS issues if owners of proprietary technology were compelled to license technologies on grounds other than those prescribed in the TRIPS Agreement.

Looking to the provisions of the agreements regarding conflicts, Article 22(1) of the Convention provides that its provisions "shall not affect [a Party's] rights and obligations . . . deriving from any existing international agreement, except where the exercise of those rights and obligations would cause a serious damage or threat to biological diversity." It is not clear how this Article would apply in the case of conflicts with the TRIPS Agreement. The TRIPS Agreement contains no explicit reference to its relationship to the Convention on Biological Diversity or any other environmental agreement.

If WTO members cannot resolve disagreements regarding the implementation of the TRIPS Agreement through consultations, one member may bring a complaint against another for failure to meet its obligations, using the dispute resolution procedures generally applicable for WTO members (Article 64). . . .

If Parties to the Convention have a dispute about its interpretation or application, they may seek solution by negotiation, by the mediation of a third party, by conciliation, or (if they agree to be bound by such a means of dispute settlement) by arbitration or submission of the dispute to the International Court of Justice (Article 27). These procedures have not yet been invoked by a Convention Party. Like the WTO procedures, dispute-resolution procedures for the Convention emphasize avoidance of direct conflict by requiring other steps, such as negotiation.

There are several possible scenarios for conflict. A dispute might arise between countries that are both Convention Parties and WTO members; or between a country that is a Convention Party and a WTO member, and a country that is either a WTO member or a Convention Party. A conflict concerning the two agreements would presumably involve a claim, in a forum associated with one of the instruments, that a country had violated its obligations, countered by a defense that the alleged violation constituted implementation of the other instrument, and was obligated or authorized by it. In such disputes, it is likely that a forum associated with one instrument would need an interpretation of the other agreement. In such a case, it is unclear how a dispute-resolution proceeding would reach such a determination; neither instrument provides for such an eventuality. The absence of a clear mechanism for reconciling perceived differences further emphasizes the value of cooperation to avoid such differences.

. . . .

The CTE's agenda includes ten items. Of these, several are particularly relevant to the subject of this paper. Most important is item 8, "[r]elevant provisions of the Agreement on Trade-Related Aspects of Intellectual Property Rights." Also significant is item 1, "[t]he relationship between provisions of the multilateral trading system and trade measures for environmental purposes, including those pursuant to multilateral environmental agreements". Potentially relevant is item 2, "[t]he relationship between environmental policies relevant to trade and environmental measures with significant trade effects and the provisions of the multilateral trading system." . . . Discussions to date have been preliminary in nature, and have focused on ideas put forward by some delegations on the following issue areas:

(a) the protection of rights to biological resources and measures to ensure the equitable sharing of benefits from patentable products derived from these resources. This has included considerable discussion of protecting the interests of indigenous peoples and enhancing their ability to protect and preserve biological diversity;

(b) methods (such as patent restrictions) for discouraging the development and exploitation of environmentally harmful products. One area of concern has been IPR as to genetically modified organisms, as an ethical as well as an environmental issue; and

(c) the appropriate level of IPR protection, in light of the impact of such protection, on the development of environmentally sound technology (EST), and on access to it and transfer of it. On the one hand, some developing country delegates have called for reforms to TRIPS to facilitate the transfer of EST, while some developed country representatives have argued that IPR are in fact essential to the development of EST and, therefore, to environmental protection. There has also been discussion of the impact of IPR on both developing countries and the environment as applied to technologies that are restricted or otherwise affected by measures pursuant to multilateral environmental agreements.

. . . .

In these discussions, a number of WTO members have highlighted the importance of reconciling TRIPS and its IPR objectives with the CBD objectives of equitable sharing and sustainability. Other delegations do not see any irreconcilability between the two agreements. Some delegations would prefer to limit discussion of the second issue, relating to environmentally harmful products, anticipating that the negotiation of a biosafety protocol to the Convention on Biological Diversity may address many relevant concerns.

. . . .

As discussed above, the TRIPS Council will review Article 27.3(b) of the TRIPS which addresses the exclusion from patentability of plants and animals, the protection of plant varieties, and the right of countries to develop their own system to protect plant varieties in 1999. It is possible that the CTE might study this issue in preparation for the 1999 review.

. . . .

6. OPTIONS FOR FUTURE WORK

In light of the synergies and relationships discussed above, the COP might wish to consider the following options relating to a possible input to the CTE:

(a) Forwarding to the CTE relevant decisions and discussions of the COP contained in the chair's report, as well as this and other relevant papers prepared by the Executive Secretary. Relevant papers might include this study, as well as The Impact of Intellectual Property Rights Systems on the Conservation and Sustainable Use of Biological Diversity and on the Equitable Sharing of Benefits From Its Use: A Preliminary Study, and/or Knowledge, Innovations and Practices of Indigenous and Local Communities: Implementation of Article 8(j).

(b) Commending the CTE and WTO Secretariat for de-restricting and transmitting documents relating to the work of the CTE, inviting the WTO to continue to transmit future relevant documents as they are produced, and requesting the Convention Secretariat to reciprocate by transmitting similar documents to the CTE in the future.

(c) Seeking a role in the deliberations of the CTE, possibly by applying to participate in the CTE as an observer.

(d) Suggesting that Parties that are also WTO members notify the TRIPS Council (pursuant to the notification requirement of Article 63 of the TRIPS Agreement) of those laws and regulations implementing the provisions relating to IPR of Article 16 of the Convention on Biological Diversity. The COP might also wish to suggest that those Parties simultaneously notify the Secretariat of the Convention so that such measures can be communicated through the clearing-house mechanism.

(e) Exploring additional ways to cooperate with the WTO on exchanging information.

(f) Continuing its exploration of issues relating to IPR by developing informational inputs for the CTE regarding the impact of patenting of genetically modified organisms, including animals and plants and essentially biological processes, in preparation for the 1999 review by the TRIPS Council of Article 27.3(b) of the TRIPS Agreement.

(g) Sending a statement to the WTO CTE. The statement might refer to one or more of the following points:

(i)   the large number of countries that are both Parties to the Convention on Biological Diversity and members of the WTO;

(ii)   the important interrelationships between the CBD and the WTO agreements, including the TRIPS Agreement; noting that the interrelationships extend beyond TRIPS, although TRIPS is the focus of this statement;

(iii)   the international and national processes of implementation now underway for both agreements;

(iv)   the significant potential for complementarities in implementing the two agreements, as reflected in the Executive Secretary's report;

(v)   the important roles of both institutions in the area of IPR and biological diversity, in cooperation with other relevant international institutions and instruments;

(vi)   an invitation to the CTE to present questions to the COP regarding the relationship of IPR and the obligations of the TRIPS Agreement and the Convention's objectives.

(h) The COP might wish to continue exploring the relationships between trade and trade law and policy and the achievement of the objectives of the Convention, possibly with particular attention to Articles of the Convention that appear most closely linked to these relationships, such as articles 5, 7(c), 8(l), or 11. The COP might wish to draw the attention of the CTE to any plans for such work.

NOTES AND QUESTIONS

(1) **Technology and the Environment.** Is there a fundamental clash between technological development and environmental protection in the twenty-first century? *See* Charles R. McManis, *The Interface between International Intellectual Property and Environmental Protection: Biodiversity and*

Biotechnology, 76 WASH. U. L. Q. 255 (1998). Are there hopeful signs in the juxtaposition of biotechnology and biodiversity? For an interesting example of how post-modern authors view the issues of conservation and human development and the juxtaposition of modern and traditional civilizations, see, e.g., VIRGINIA D. NAZAREA, CULTURAL MEMORY AND BIODIVERSITY (1998).

(2) **Section 102(f).** Section 102(f) of the U.S. patent act precludes the award of a patent when the applicant did not invent the subject matter sought to be patented. It has been suggested that patent applications whose claims merely duplicate processes known to indigenous and local communities fail the statutory bar of subsection 102(f) and should be rejected. Section 102(f), which literally says an applicant is entitled to a patent unless "he did not himself invent the subject matter sought to be patented," is sometimes called the "derivation" provision. Section 102(f) has invariably been applied by the courts in situations where the applicant is shown to have acquired the invention from another person, and the party challenging the patent must demonstrate that there was "communication of a complete conception . . . sufficient to enable one of ordinary skill in the art to construct and successfully operate the invention." Hedgewick v. Akers, 497 F.2d 905, 908 (C.C.P.A. 1974). But the statute nowhere uses the word "derivation." Should a patent application fail for lack of novelty under 102(f) merely because an indigenous people are shown to have known of the invention and the precise derivation is unknown?

(3) **The Ayahuasca Patent**. On November 3, 1999, the ayahuasca patent granted by the U.S. PTO on a plant considered sacred by some Amazon indigenous peoples was ruled invalid in a reexamination proceeding on the basis that plant specimen sheets in herbarium collections are prior publications because they are publicly available and catalogued. *See Plant Patent's Rejection Highlights Conflict Between Tradition and IP Law*, 1 INTELL. PROP. L. WEEKLY 741 (Nov. 17, 1999).

(4) **Search Obligations**. An applicant for a patent is under no current obligation to conduct a search prior to filing an application. *See* American Hoist & Derrick Co. v. Sowa & Sons, 725 F.2 1350, 1362 (Fed. Cir. 1984). Some scholars have proposed requiring patent applicants to conduct a prior art search of traditional knowledge before filing. Most patent applicants do a search prior to filing an application in any event, given the significant costs of drafting an application and the Section 112 prohibition against adding "new matter" to a disclosure after the filing date. What purposes are served by the present state of the law relieving the applicant of any obligation to search? Wouldn't interests of economy suggest that some sort of search be required of the applicant prior to filing a patent application, particularly given that the applicant is or should be in a better position than the examiner to know where prior art lies?

(5) **The Cord Blood Controversy**. Article 27(2) of TRIPS allows a state to "exclude from patentability inventions, the prevention within their territory of the commercial exploitation of which is necessary to protect ordre public or morality." In early 1999, the European Patent Office revoked a patent covering the use of human blood cells (cord blood) for medical purposes. The patent application, filed in 1989 by the U.S. Company Biocyte, related to the isolation and preservation of fetal and neonatal hematopoietic stem and progenitor cells of the blood. The EPO justified its decision arguing that human blood cannot

be placed within the realm of invention. Similarly, the U.S. Patent and Trademark Office has rejected a patent application claiming a part-human "chimera." Is the "appropriation and commodification of a widely held religious system" less offensive to the public policies supposedly upheld by the patent law than patents relating to human beings? Should Congress add explicit exceptions to patentability in the patent law concerning scandalous subject matter, similar to those found in section 2(a) of the Lanham Act?

(6) **UPOV and *Sui Generis* Protection of Plant Varieties**. Recall that under TRIPS Article 27(3)(b), members may also exclude from patentability "plants and animals other than microorganisms, and essentially biological processes for the production of plants or animals other than non-biological and microbiological processes." But it goes on to say, "however, Members shall provide for the protection of plant varieties either by patents or by an effective *sui generis* system or by any combination thereof. The provisions of this sub-paragraph shall be reviewed four years after the entry into force of the Agreement Establishing the WTO." In January 1999, a foreign ministry-level meeting of the sixty-two member Organization of African Unity ("OAU") in Lusaka called for a hold on intellectual property protection of plant varieties until an Africa-wide alternative system to patents has been developed. The proposed system would aim to divide the intellectual property rights of new plant forms between plant breeders and indigenous communities that might have contributed to early varieties in accordance with the "equitable sharing" provisions of the CBD. Two weeks later in Bangui, a meeting of patent office officials from member states of the OAPI countries reached a decision to recommend that the sixteen states collectively adopt the 1991 version of the UPOV convention. Subsequently (according to news reports), Johnson Ekpere, secretary-general of the Scientific, Technical and Research Commission of the OAU, said, "This is a case of the right hand not knowing what the left hand is doing" and described as "unlikely" any attempts to ratify the UPOV convention in an African parliament. Mzondi Haviland Chirambo, director-general of ARIPO, agreed, stating that he believes that ARIPO member states are unlikely to follow the lead set by OAPI countries. Does the language of the final sentence of Article 27(3)(b) quoted above suggest that the entire subsection is subject to renegotiation? *See* GENETIC RESOURCES ACTION INT'L [GRAIN], TRIPS VERSUS BIODIVERSITY: WHAT TO DO WITH THE 1999 REVIEW OF ARTICLE 27.3(B), available at http://www.grain.org/publications/reports/tripsmay99.htm; Philippe Cullet, *Revision of the TRIPS Agreement Concerning the Protection of Plant Varieties: Lessons from India concerning the Development of a* Sui Generis *System,* 2 J. WORLD INTELL. PROP. 617 (1999). If so, are the developing country member states of the WTO still obliged to enact a system for protection of plants now that the TRIPS Agreement has taken effect in those countries?

(7) **Patent Protection and "Biopiracy."** The protection of indigenous knowledge is a key concept of the CBD. *See* CBD art. 8(j). The Coordinating Body for Indigenous Organizations of the Amazon Basin ("COICA"), in its fifth Congress in May of 1997, decided to declare a citizen of the United States, Loren Miller, the *Banisteriopsis* patentee, an "enemy of indigenous people." After that time COICA prohibited his entry into any indigenous territory. In an Open Letter to the U.S. Congress, in April 1998, COICA alleged that as a result:

the Inter-American Foundation (IAF)—a body of the U.S. government—has decided to break relations with our organization. In doing so, they have denied any type of collaboration (*sic*) with more than one and a half million indigenous peoples of the Amazon Basin, while we are making an effort to maintain our cultures, as well as, trying to avoid the destruction of the largest rainforest on the planet. . . . COICA will not renounce its legitimate right to defend and preserve the knowledge, practices, innovations and natural resources of the peoples whom we represent. This right has been explicitly recognized in the Treaty of Biological Diversity that was ratified by more than 170 countries. . . . We believe that you the Congressmen/women, should know the fundamental reason which allows your fellow citizens to patent our plants and appropriate our knowledge. There is a lack of ratification by the U.S. Congress of the Treaty of Biological Diversity, and a lack of approval for accurate laws that impede this known worldwide practice of "biopiracy."

Communication from coica@uio.satnet.net. The United States signed the CBD on June 4, 1993, but has not ratified it. Assuming that the COICA allegations regarding the IAF are correct, once having signed on (even if not acceding) to the CBD, is the United States obliged under international law not to work against the CBD's objects and purposes by applying such political pressure on indigenous groups? As a rhetorical gesture, is the use of the term "biopiracy" by NGOs against the uncompensated use of indigenous knowledge in developing countries any different in impact or validity from the use of the term "piracy" by developed countries for counterfeit goods?

(8) **Access to Biodiversity**. For a frank discussion of the issues involving access to biodiversity and intellectual property, see The Greening of Technology Transfer: The Protection of the Environment and of Intellectual Property (William O. Hennessey ed.) (1994), at http://www.fplc.edu/green/contents.htm. *See also* William O. Hennessey, *Sustainable Development Is Win-Win*, 31 LES NOUVELLES 15-19 (Mar. 1996).

TABLE OF CASES

Principal excerpted cases are listed in upper case format and the page number at which the excerpt appears is italicized

Page

Page

Page

Page

Page

Page

Page

Page

INDEX

[References are to pages.]

[References are to pages.]

(Rel 1—2001 Pub 3068)

[References are to pages.]

[References are to pages.]

[References are to pages.]

[References are to pages.]

(Rel 1—2001 Pub 3068)

[References are to pages.]

[References are to pages.]

(Matthew Bender & Co , Inc)   (Rel 1—2001 Pub 3068)

[References are to pages.]

[References are to pages.]

[References are to pages.]

(Matthew Bender & Co., Inc.)

[References are to pages.]

[References are to pages.]

[References are to pages.]